THE GOOD SCHOOLS GUIDE

Boarding Schools

www.goodschoolsguide.co.uk

The Good Schools Guide is a registered trademark

"These ALL-ROUNDERS *are* ACADEMIC HEAVYWEIGHTS *to boot..."*

Tatler Schools Guide 2021

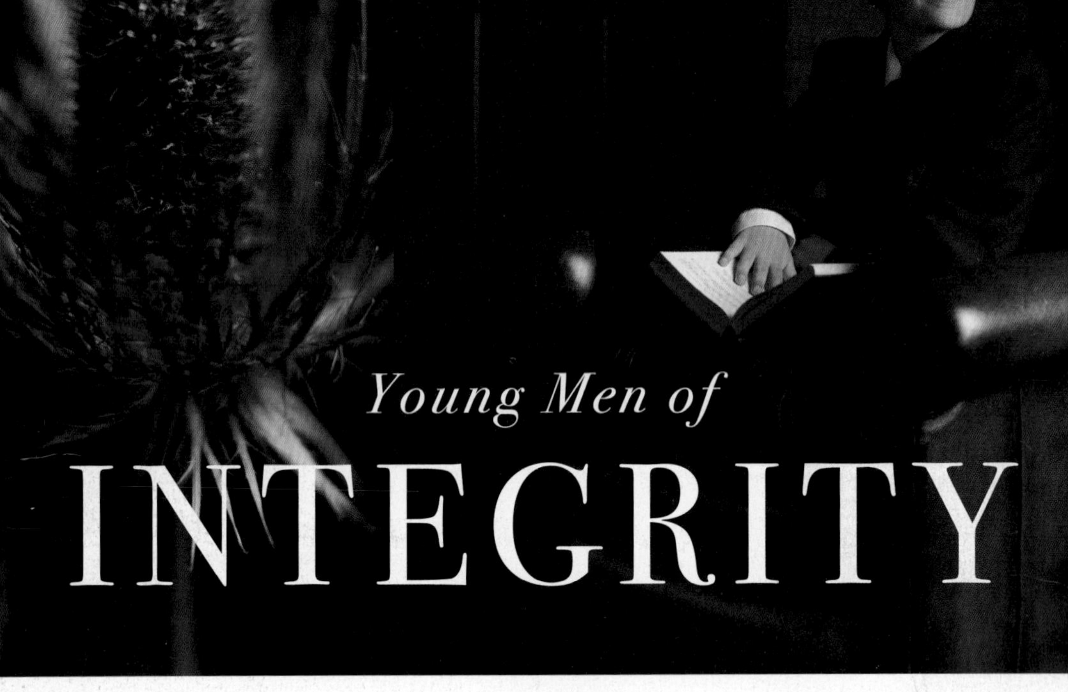

READY AY READY

MERCHISTON
EDINBURGH

Tel: +44 (0) 131 312 2201 Email: admissions@merchiston.co.uk
MERCHISTON.CO.UK

A BOARDING AND DAY SCHOOL FOR BOYS AGED 7-18
A member of the World Leading Schools Association, the only school in Scotland.

Learn to **#ADifferentBeat**

Outstanding girls' day and boarding school in the heart of Oxford

Flexible boarding options from age 11

Book your visit at www.headington.org/visit

The King's School
Canterbury

www.kings-school.co.uk

CO-EDUCATIONAL | 13-18 YEARS | DAY & BOARDING

Under one hour from London via HS1 (St Pancras International)

A 21st Century education within the historic City of Canterbury

Junior King's
Canterbury

www.junior-kings.co.uk

CO-EDUCATIONAL | 3-13 YEARS | DAY & BOARDING

Fourth Edition published 2022 by Lucas Publishing Ltd
The Good Schools Guide, 4/4a Bloomsbury Square, London WC1A 2RP
www.goodschoolsguide.co.uk
ISBN 978-1-909963-27-6

A CIP catalogue record for this book is available from the British Library
Copyright © 2022, Lucas Publications Ltd
Printed by Cambrian Printers Ltd

All rights reserved. No part of this publication may be reproduced, stored in or introduced into a retrieval system, or transmitted in any form, or by any means (electronic, mechanical, photocopying, recording, or otherwise) without the prior written permission of the publisher. Any person who does any unauthorised act in relation to this publication may be liable to criminal prosecution and civil claims for damages.

Every care has been taken to ensure that all information was correct at the time of going to press. The publishers accept no responsibility for any error in detail, inaccuracy or judgement whatsoever.

Acknowledgements

Writers

Alison Cooper
Anne Hadley
Bernadette John
Beth Noakes
Camilla Smiley
Carolyn Murphy
Catherine Goldwater
Catriona Prest
Charles Cowling
Charlotte Obolensky
Charlotte Phillips
Claire Bore
Claire Kingston
David Hargreaves
Debbie Reed
Eli Gillen
Elizabeth Coatman
Elizabeth Moody Stuart
Elsa Booth
Emma Lee Potter
Fenella Douglas Miller
Grace Moody-Stuart
Guy Canning
Jane Thomas
Janette Wallis
Janita Clamp
Jo Russell
Judith French
Juliet Austin
Karen Fitzpatrick
Kate Hilpern
Katie Mclean
Lisa Freedman
Lucinda Wallis
Lucy Heywood
Lucy Higginson
Lucy Marsh
Mary Ann Smillie
Mary Bremner
Mary Pegler
Melanie Bloxham
Melanie O'Shea
Melanie Sanderson
Nicky Adams
Patrea More Nesbitt
Phoebe Bentinck
Rosemary Taylor
Sarah Evans
William Bancroft
Zoe Bing

Design: David Preston

Cover illustration: Tam Preston, tampreston.co.uk

Typesetting: Theresa Hare, Optima Information Design

Editorial review by Janita Clamp and team: Kathryn Berger, Simon Coury, Marijke Doldersum, Victoria Edwards, Sophie Irwin, Katie Mclean, Keith Morgan, Amanda Perkins, Melanie O'Shea

Advertising sales: Charlotte Hollingshead, assisted by Jo Dodds, Publishing Matters

Project management: Skye O'Neill

Everything held together by: Shari Lord and Amanda Perkins

Photography: Thanks to all the schools who supplied photographs.

Can you spot the good schools?

We can.

From planning your child's education to last minute places; from expert special needs support to family relocations. Let our Education Consultants do the hard work for you.

www.goodschoolsguide.co.uk | 0203 286 6824 | office@goodschoolsguide.co.uk

THE GOOD SCHOOLS GUIDE

Happy girls
are successful girls

- Flexi, weekly and full boarding
- Excellent academic achievement
  — *72% A*–B at A-Level (five-year average)*
- 120-acre campus
- Just 20 minutes by train from King's Cross
- 'Pastoral care uniformly "phenomenal"'
  — *Good Schools Guide*

queenswood.org/open-events

A LEADING INDEPENDENT BOARDING AND DAY SCHOOL FOR GIRLS AGED 11-18

Charity number 311060

Brookmans Park, Hertfordshire AL9 6NS | 01707 602500

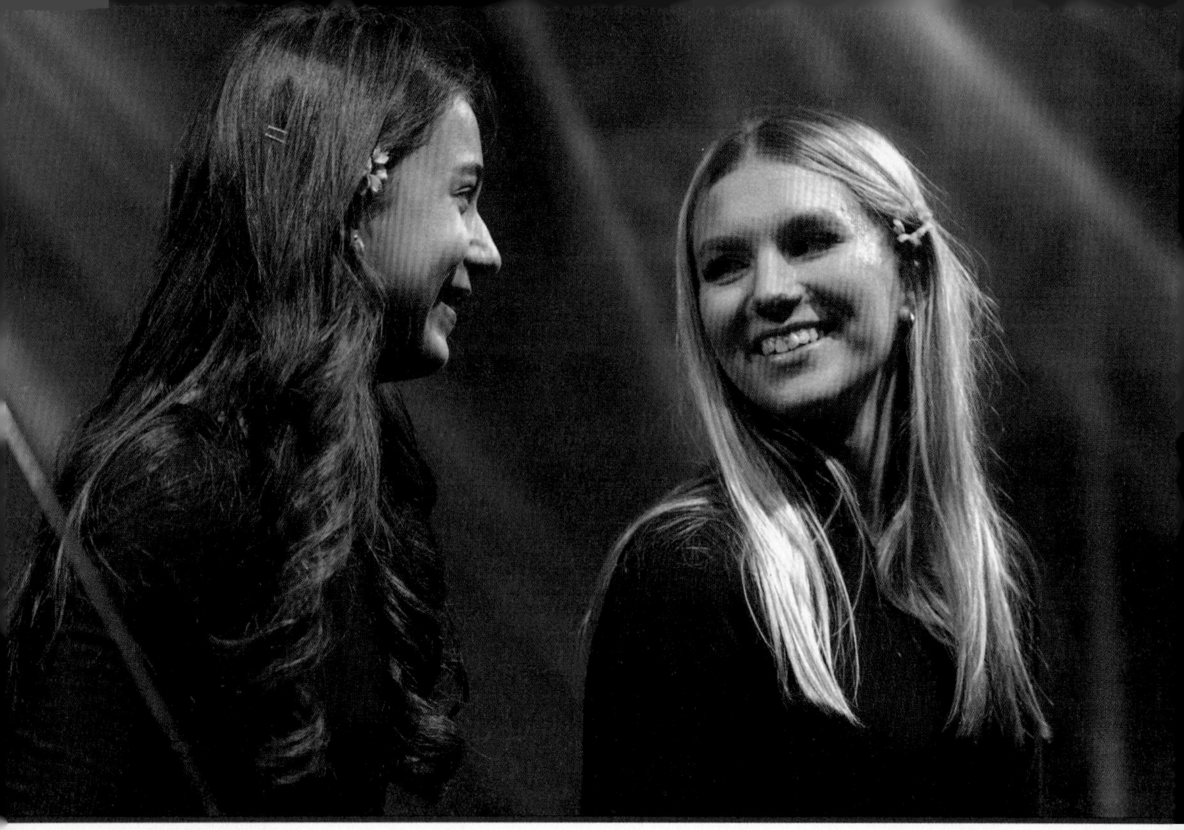

Thrive

as a boarder at Bishop's Stortford College

Our boarders enjoy a total living and learning experience that prepares them for life in the wider world. The dedicated care and support of our House Staff and the first-class accommodation of our boys' and girls' boarding houses fully supports the academic and extra-curricular opportunities pupils find here. Pupils join our busy, purposeful and exciting campus and gain the confidence to fulfil their aspirations and reach their true potential.

FACEBOOK/BishopsStortfordCollege
INSTAGRAM@TheBishopsStortfordCollege
TWITTER@BSCollege

find out more at:
www.BishopsStortfordCollege.org

Welcome

Welcome to the fourth edition of The Good Schools Guide, Boarding Schools. Choosing a school for your child can be an overwhelming and time-consuming experience – never more so when that school is also going to be their home from home. Our aim in publishing this book is to furnish parents with as much information as possible and to provide insights that they won't find in prospectuses, websites or on slick school open days. Our focus is not on lists of facilities or league table positions (although these, and exam results, are always covered in our reviews); we bring you the real inside scoop on what it's actually like to be a pupil at one of our schools; its ethos, culture and unique personality. It goes without saying that the schools we write about are good, but no school is perfect; a school that would suit one type of child might not be the right choice for another. In a world where marketing seems to make every school look similarly flawless, our reviews help parents cut through the gloss and answer the question: would my child be happy here?

How do we do this? Our writers – all parents themselves – travel the length and breadth of the country to visit the best boarding schools in the UK. The process is rigorous, with unfettered one-to-one interviews with head teachers, senior leadership teams and house parents. We are privileged to be allowed unsupervised conversations with current pupils as well as their parents who we find through our own networks – schools know we speak with their parent body, but not to whom – so we can be sure of getting the 'warts and all' truth. We go out of our way to avoid talking exclusively to prefects, scholars and sports captains (although we do like their opinions too!). As a result, the portrait we paint for our readers is accurate and insightful. No parental dissatisfaction is left unquestioned, no school lunch (always in the school dining room alongside pupils) left untasted. During the Covid-19 pandemic of 2020

PRIOR'S FIELD

The place to achieve

GSA Girls' Boarding and Day School 11-18, Godalming Surrey

Achievement in all its forms is alive and kicking in every part of their school day.
- Tatler Schools Guide 2021

BELIEVE * ACHIEVE * SUCCEED

Full, weekly and flexi boarding options - 11+, 13+ and 16+ entry
Visit our website to book your place at our next Open Event
01483 810551 www.priorsfieldschool.com

Registered Charity

A Catholic co-educational day and boarding school for pupils aged 11 -18

St Edmund's College

Old Hall Green, Ware,
Hertfordshire SG11 1DS

Discover boarding at St Edmund's College

Our friendly boarding community is at the heart of St Edmund's.
To book a tour please visit our website, or call: 01920 824 247

We offer an education for the whole person through academic, spiritual and co-curricular development.

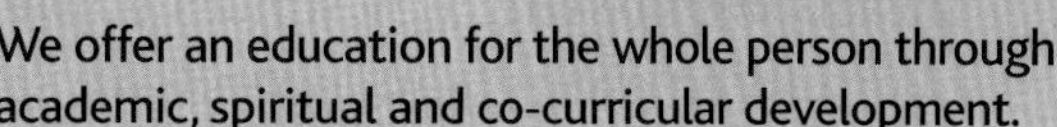

- Full, weekly and flexi boarding options available
- Modern facilities and excellent academic support
- Exciting timetable with no exeat weekends
- Located 20 minutes from Stansted Airport and within easy reach of London and Cambridge

Telephone: 01920 824 247 www.stedmundscollege.org

and 2021, we continued to update our reviews virtually, incorporating as many of the components of a real visit as was possible at the time. Now that schools are able to welcome us back in person once again, we're clocking up the miles to keep our reviews totally up to date.

Parents already familiar with our reviews may notice that we have made some improvements to their structure since the last edition. For secondary schools, latest academic results now have their own section and the all-important entrance and exit sections have been moved to the top so readers can easily identify, for example, feeder preps or popular university destinations before reading on. We have bolstered the information relating to provision for pupils with SEND and, in the wake of Everyone's Invited, Me Too and Black Lives Matter, our writers are briefed to zoom in closer on how schools are tackling toxic or sexist culture, inclusivity and diversity and report back in our pastoral care section.

Our absolute commitment to critical distance remains intact. We are the only school guide that can truthfully claim to be entirely independent; separation of our editorial and commercial concerns is absolute. No school can pay or choose to be included in – or indeed excluded from – The Guide. We cover our costs by selling advertising space, exclusively to reviewed schools, in our books and on our website, as well as licenses to allow schools to use their reviews in their own marketing. Whether a school chooses to take advertising or buy a license has no bearing on its inclusion in The Guide, nor the content of its review.

Our mission is to inform, enlighten and entertain our readers. We hope you enjoy reading our school reviews as much as we, collectively, enjoy writing them. We love receiving feedback from our readers, so if you have any comments on our reviews or questions

Rossall
INSPIRING EXCELLENCE

More THAN JUST A School

about our commercial policy, please contact editor@goodschoolsguide.co.uk. If you need further help with your school search or decision making, our team of expert consultants are on hand to help. All Good Schools Guide writers, they know the schools, admissions processes and pitfalls inside out and love solving your educational dilemmas. Email consultants@goodschoolsguide.co.uk for more information.

An Excellent rated (ISI) school welcoming children aged 3 months to 19 years.

Find out how we can help support your child to achieve their aspirations in our unique prep, middle and senior four-school model.

Call to arrange a private tour or join us for one of our open days.

Visit www.qe.org for more information

"To be the best that I can, with the gifts that I have."

www.qe.org | admissions@qe.org | 01423 333330 | York YO26 9SS

"With excellent leadership and now girls on board, too, The Oratory seems to be thriving."

The Good Schools Guide - November 2021

Only 1 hour's drive from London, 45 mins from Heathrow

- High academic standards
- Outstanding sporting tradition
- Day, weekly, flexi and full boarding
- Entry points at 11+, 13+ and 16+
- Private tours and meetings with the Head Master available

"An active choice for families looking for a small, nurturing environment."

The Good Schools Guide - November 2021

HMC CO-EDUCATIONAL 11 - 18 CATHOLIC BOARDING & DAY SCHOOL

Near Reading • 01491 683522 • registrar@oratory.co.uk • oratory.co.uk

Contents

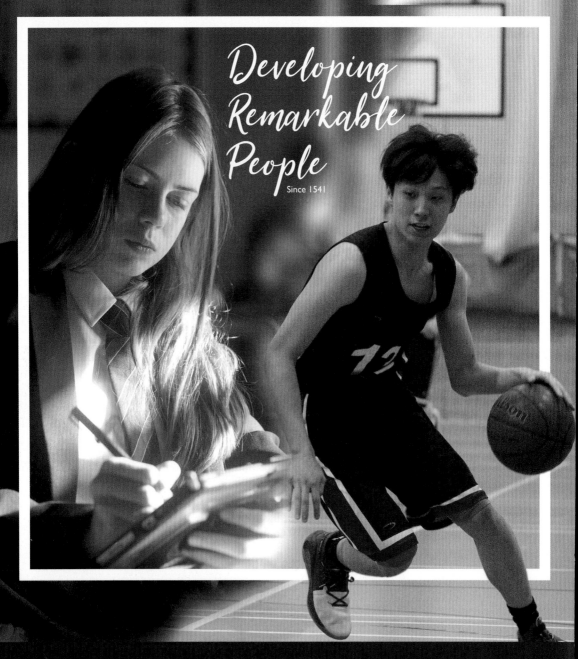

Developing Remarkable People
Since 1541

Girls • Boys • Sixth

International boarding from 14 -18 years

World Ready

A Preparation for Life

REGISTER FOR A FORTHCOMING
OPEN DAY ON OUR WEBSITE
WWW.ARDINGLY.COM

Today at school...

'I made a firework'

#TALESOFHXP

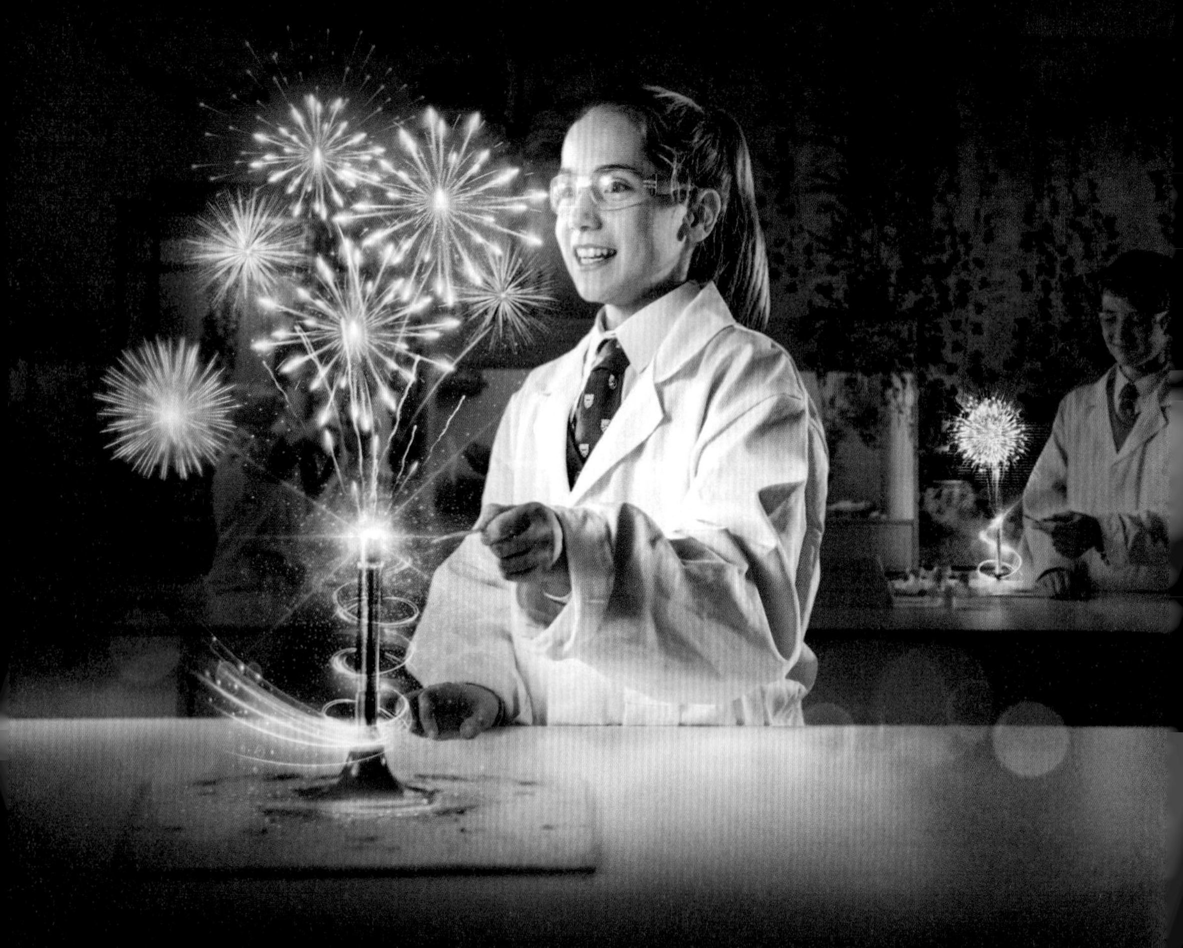

Day & Boarding • Girls and Boys aged 2 to 13
Bus Services from Sussex, Surrey and London

Handcross, Haywards Heath, West Sussex, RH17 6HF

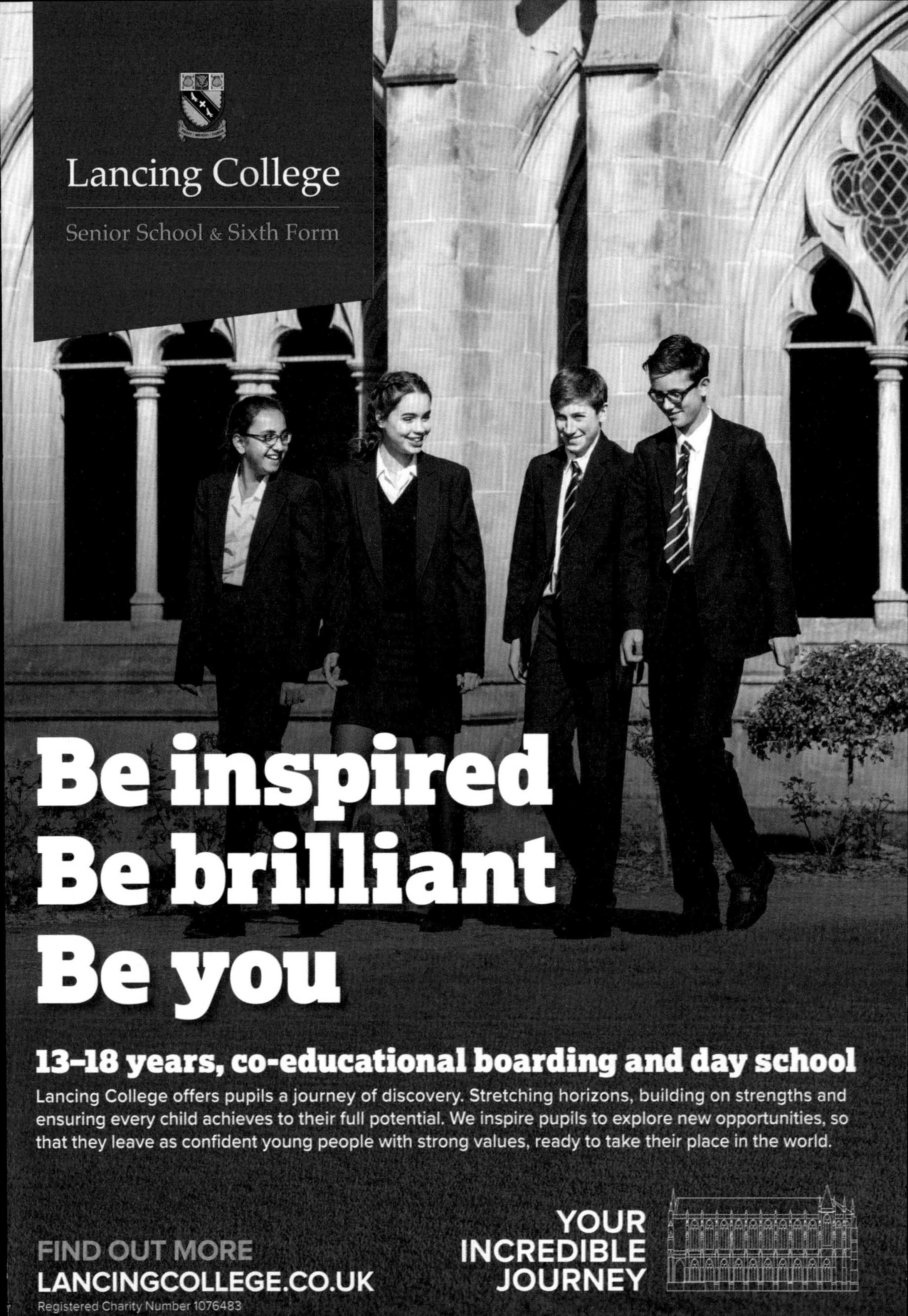

Lancing College

Senior School & Sixth Form

Be inspired Be brilliant Be you

13–18 years, co-educational boarding and day school

Lancing College offers pupils a journey of discovery. Stretching horizons, building on strengths and ensuring every child achieves to their full potential. We inspire pupils to explore new opportunities, so that they leave as confident young people with strong values, ready to take their place in the world.

FIND OUT MORE
LANCINGCOLLEGE.CO.UK
Registered Charity Number 1076483

YOUR INCREDIBLE JOURNEY

Key to symbols

The age range of a school is shown by the colour of the title bar.

Junior School

Senior School

 Girls' school

 Quaker school

 Boys' school

 Roman Catholic school

 Co-ed school

 Boys' school with co-ed sixth form

 Girls' school with co-ed sixth form

 Co-ed pre-prep, then boys only

 Co-ed pre-prep, then girls only

REPTON

A perfectly balanced education in the heart of England for girls and boys aged 3-18.

"WE WANT OUR CHILDREN TO STAY CHILDREN FOR LONGER."

reptonprep.org.uk

To arrange your personal tour call Ellie Jones on **01283 707112** or email **admissions@repton.org.uk**

SEVENOAKS SCHOOL

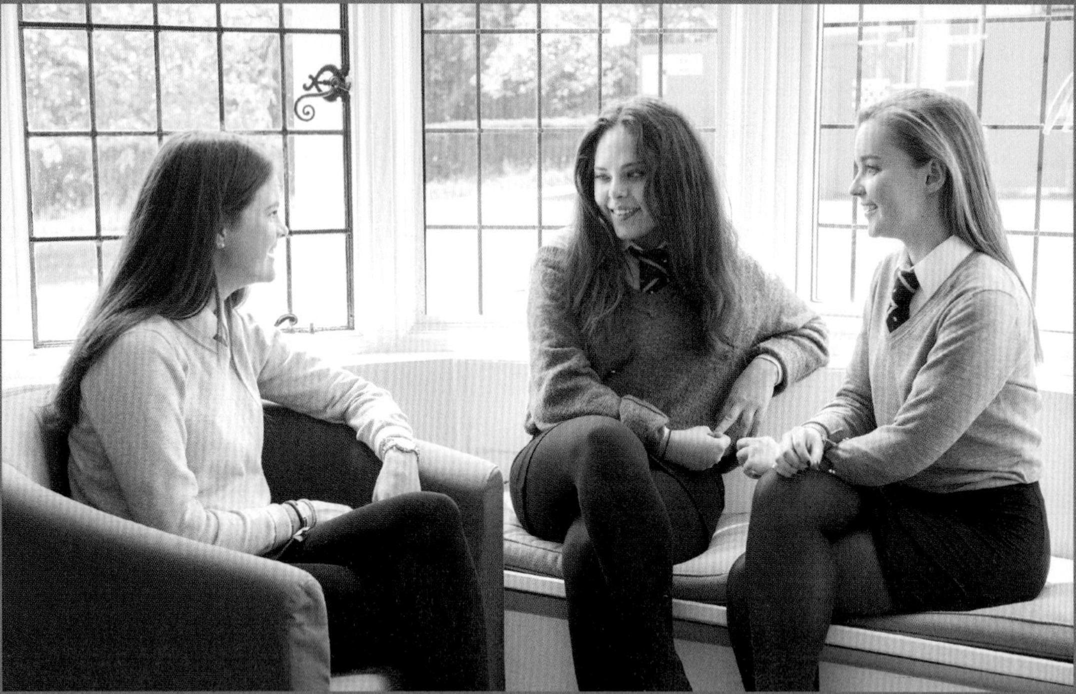

"It's hard to find a more liberal, progressive and culturally diverse boarding school in the UK. At Sevenoaks, you feel respected and admired for who you are."

Sixth Form student

www.sevenoaksschool.org

Registered charity 1101358

2021-2024

GENUINE. INSPIRING. HAPPY.

At Frensham, there is an energy, a feeling of happiness and calmness. It comes from everyone being comfortable in their own skins. Teachers don't need to spend time telling students to pull up their socks. Instead, they have conversations and build relationships, really special relationships, based on genuine, mutual respect and interest. Relationships that spark learning.

Get in touch at hello@frensham.org to find out more.

www.frensham.org

A progressive day and boarding school in Surrey for children from 3 to 18 | refreshingly different since 1925

Boarding schools overview map

For UK-wide map of state boarding schools see p.1288

BROMSGROVE SCHOOL

Founded 1553

A strong House and tutor system to look after your child's pastoral and academic wellbeing

An outstanding range of extra-curricular activities

Day and Boarding, weekly boarding available from age 7

990 pupils aged 13 - 18

720 pupils aged 2 - 13

A FLOURISHING BOARDING COMMUNITY

100 prep boarders aged 7 -13
and 480 senior boarders

OUTSTANDING EDUCATION

A LEVEL

62%
A*/A GRADES

89%
A*/B GRADES

40.2
AVE IB SCORE
IN 2021

BTEC
Approved Centre from Pearson

42%
DISTINCTION*

Contact Admissions to organise an individual visit

admissions@bromsgrove-school.co.uk 01527 579679

bromsgrove-school.co.uk

FLAIR • DISCIPLINE • ACADEMIC RIGOUR

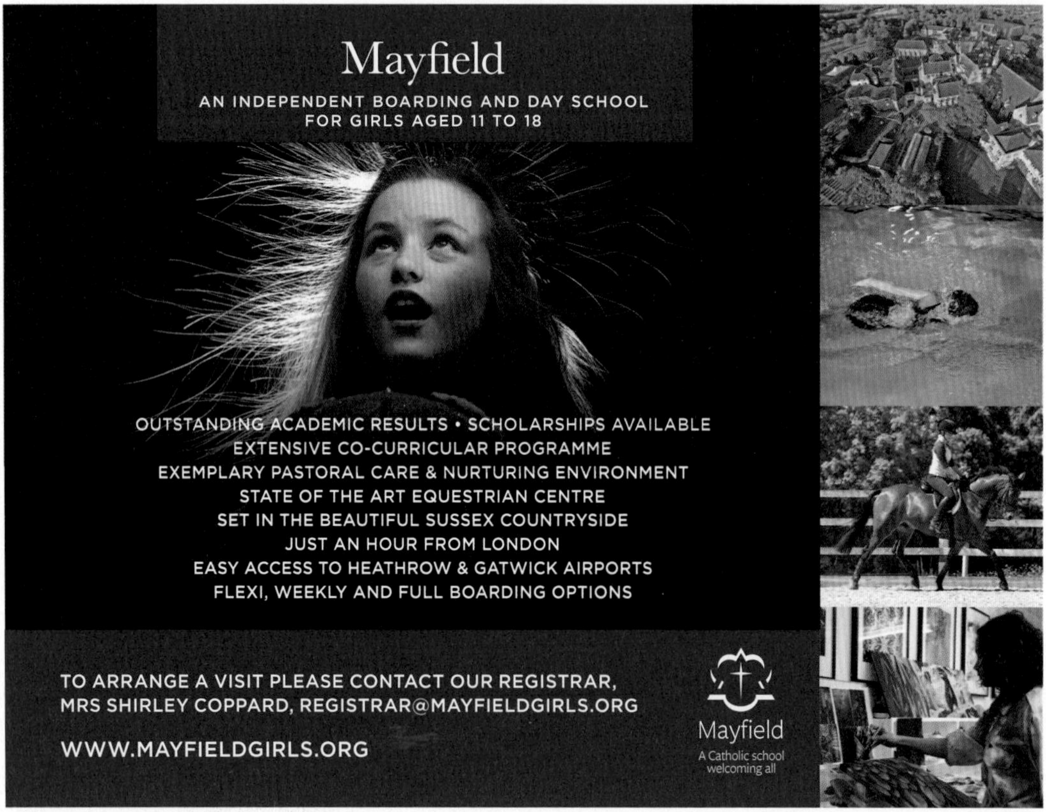

Mayfield

AN INDEPENDENT BOARDING AND DAY SCHOOL
FOR GIRLS AGED 11 TO 18

OUTSTANDING ACADEMIC RESULTS • SCHOLARSHIPS AVAILABLE
EXTENSIVE CO-CURRICULAR PROGRAMME
EXEMPLARY PASTORAL CARE & NURTURING ENVIRONMENT
STATE OF THE ART EQUESTRIAN CENTRE
SET IN THE BEAUTIFUL SUSSEX COUNTRYSIDE
JUST AN HOUR FROM LONDON
EASY ACCESS TO HEATHROW & GATWICK AIRPORTS
FLEXI, WEEKLY AND FULL BOARDING OPTIONS

TO ARRANGE A VISIT PLEASE CONTACT OUR REGISTRAR,
MRS SHIRLEY COPPARD, REGISTRAR@MAYFIELDGIRLS.ORG

WWW.MAYFIELDGIRLS.ORG

Mayfield
A Catholic school
welcoming all

Find your inspiration

Find your Downe House

Open Days and individual tours available

registrar@downehouse.net | 01635 204701

www.downehouse.net

An outstanding independent boarding school for girls aged 11 to 18 years

89% Grades 9-7 GCSE	*98% Grades A*-B A Level*	*94% First-Choice University*	*26% STEM at University*

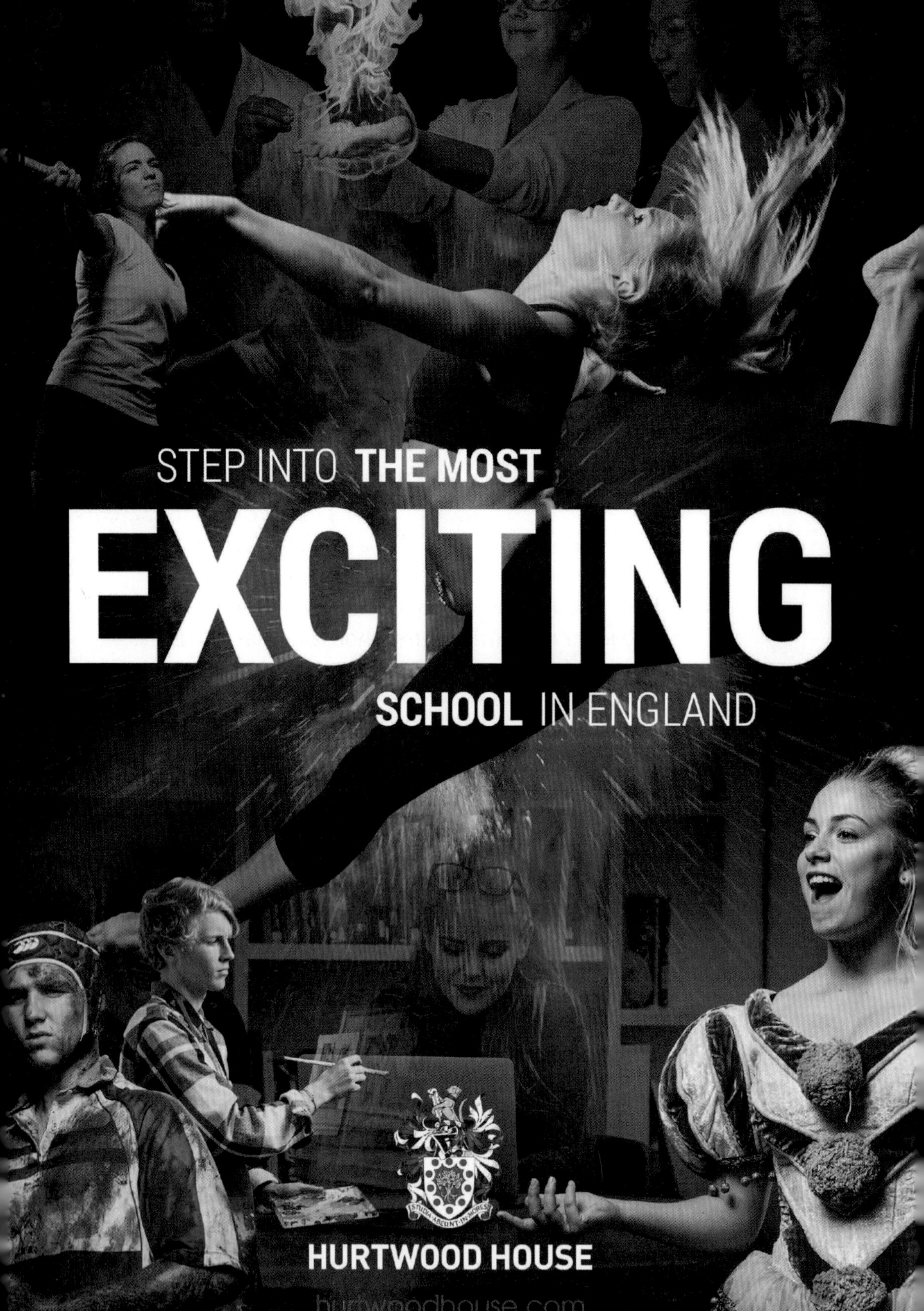
STEP INTO THE MOST
EXCITING
SCHOOL IN ENGLAND
STUDIA ABEUNT IN MORES
HURTWOOD HOUSE
hurtwoodhouse.com

Introduction

Why boarding? Why indeed. Almost no other educational topic provokes such vehement and polarised opinions. Popular cliches about boarding schools – good and bad – endure, but over the last few decades a quiet revolution has taken place and today's boarding schools look nothing like they did 40 or 50 years ago. Traditional full boarding schools remain, albeit in much reduced numbers, but for many children 'boarding' now means staying at school a couple of nights a week.

Heads tell us that the boarding family profile is much more varied than it used to be. It's likely that both parents are working – sometimes abroad or a long commute away. Boarding is still a tradition for some, we have visited schools where two or three generations have been members of the same house (though not under the same house master or mistress!), but more families are coming to it for the first time.

The decision to board is undoubtedly a big one that will involve children as much as parents, and the reasons that lead up to each family's choice will be different. For instance, if a child has a particular aptitude, then there are boarding schools with the facilities and specialist staff on hand to develop sporting or musical talents. Families with several children may opt for flexi or weekly boarding because it's preferable to hours in the car on multiple school runs. Sixth-form boarding is particularly popular and a great preparation for university – although some may find the accommodation at university a little less salubrious than school. Sometimes a small, nurturing boarding school can provide stability and a haven for a child with an unhappy home life.

Forces personnel posted abroad have always been a core group for whom boarding schools are essential. The allowances have become considerably less generous in the

Game-changing education...

Discover where Strathallan could take you at www.strathallan.co.uk

Strathallan School, Forgandenny, Perthshire, PH2 9EG | www.strathallan.co.uk | +44(0)1738 812 546 | admissions@strathallan.co.uk

Co-Educational Day and Boarding School for ages 3-18
Set in a beautiful, 230 acre Cotswold estate

Visit us: - www.rendcombcollege.org.uk/visit
Admissions Tel: - 01285 832 306
email: admissions@rendcombcollege.org.uk

RENDCOMB COLLEGE
NURSERY • JUNIOR • SENIOR

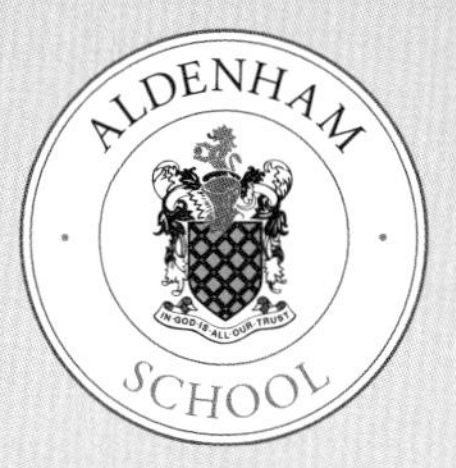

Come and visit...

ALDENHAM SCHOOL

A quintessentially British coeducational boarding school set in 110 acres of glorious Hertfordshire countryside, yet only 11 miles from central London and under an hour to 4 international airports.

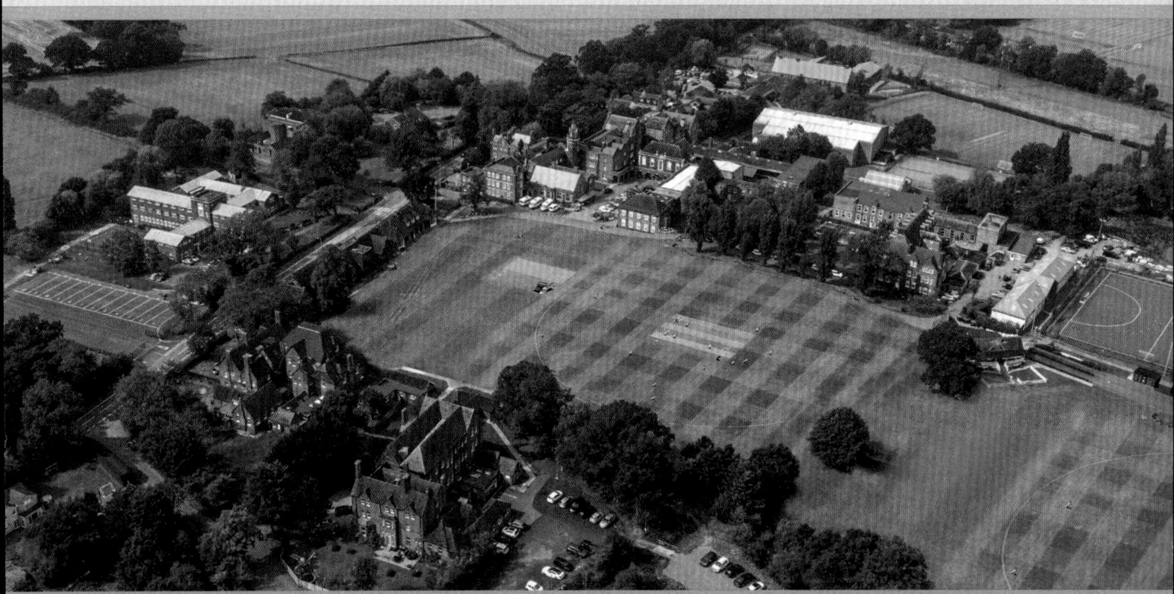

01923 858122 · enquiries@aldenham.com

www.aldenham.com

Aldenham School, Elstree, Hertfordshire, WD6 3AJ

last few years but many state and independent boarding schools give priority and some financial assistance to children from these families.

One thing that hasn't changed for the better is the cost of sending a child to boarding school, now often comfortably above £40,000 a year for full boarding. This hasn't discouraged applications from wealthy international families, but there are real concerns that the middle-class British parents, who for years have just managed to afford private education by scrimping, saving and re-mortgaging, are being priced out of the market. Places at state boarding schools, where parents only pay for the boarding element (usually around £13,000-£16,000 a year) and tuition is free, are consequently more sought after than ever.

Some years ago, possibly as a result of the economic downturn, the boarding demographic in some schools was not well managed. While this may have secured short-term benefits, bursars quickly realised that parents – whether they come from Beijing or Bognor – want their children to be part of a diverse and well-integrated boarding community. These days you will find that schools take great care to ensure that this is the case and for most it seems that around 15 – 20 per cent international pupils achieves the right balance. Those who want a 'traditional' English education without their sending children half way round the world can do so courtesy of the many international incarnations of some of the UK's most famous schools.

This book contains over 300 of the Good Schools Guide's highly informative and famously frank reviews. Every school has been visited by our writers, who check out everything from dorms to food and weekend activities. We also speak to heads, parents and, most important of all, pupils.

Boarding, 21st-century style continues to flourish, holding strong even through the recent global pandemic.

LVS Ascot

A Co-educational Day & Boarding School
for young people aged 4 - 18

Our students are **supported** at **every stage** of their journey through school

For information on upcoming open days and to book your place please visit **www.lvs.ascot.sch.uk/admissions** or call **01344 882770**

Families from all over the world tell us how impressed they have been by the quality of boarding schools' online provision – not just lessons, but sport, music, pastoral care and even things like sponsored walks, concerts and plays. Boarding is now a positive and popular option and the decision to board is, as often as not, made by children themselves.

Whether you're interested in full or flexi boarding, big names, local treasures, state boarding schools or country preps where your child can board along with their pony, this book is your unbiased and invaluable guide to all that's best in British boarding.

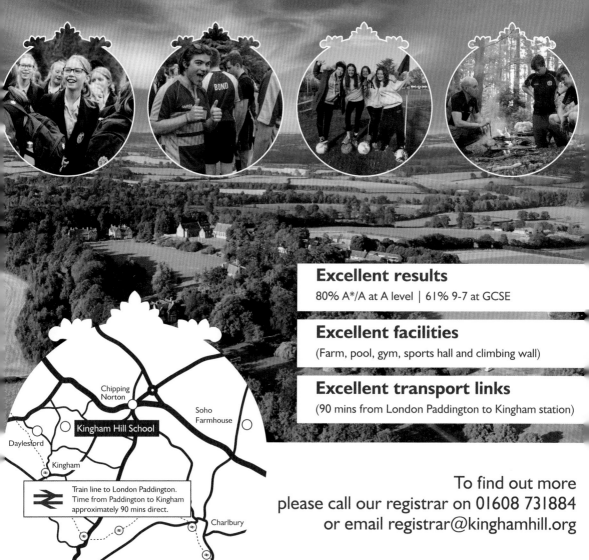

Kingham Hill School

A small, independent, co-educational day and boarding school for pupils aged 11-18 set in 100 acres of the Oxfordshire Cotswolds

A clearer view towards your child's future

Excellent results

80% A*/A at A level | 61% 9-7 at GCSE

Excellent facilities

(Farm, pool, gym, sports hall and climbing wall)

Excellent transport links

(90 mins from London Paddington to Kingham station)

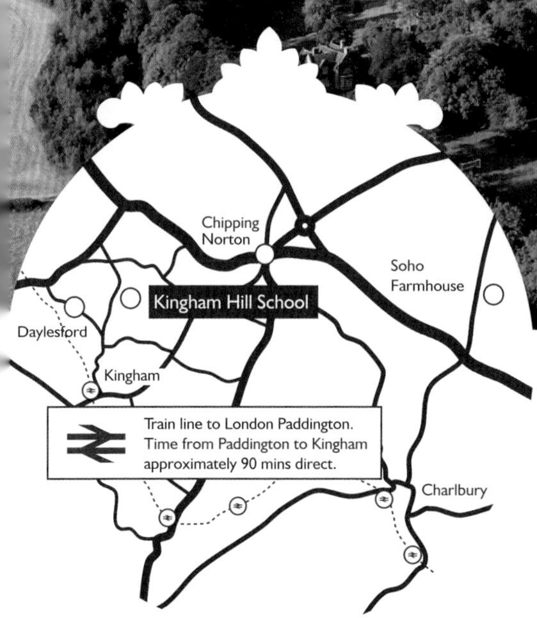

Chipping Norton
Soho Farmhouse
Kingham Hill School
Daylesford
Kingham
Charlbury

Train line to London Paddington. Time from Paddington to Kingham approximately 90 mins direct.

To find out more
please call our registrar on 01608 731884
or email registrar@kinghamhill.org

www.kinghamhill.org.uk

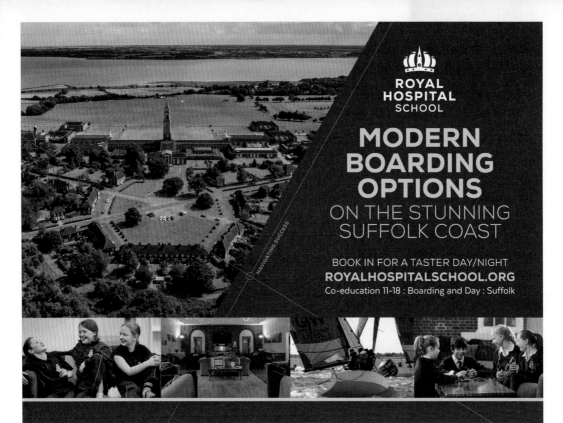

ROYAL HOSPITAL SCHOOL

NAVIGATING SUCCESS

MODERN BOARDING OPTIONS

ON THE STUNNING SUFFOLK COAST

BOOK IN FOR A TASTER DAY/NIGHT

ROYALHOSPITALSCHOOL.ORG

Co-education 11-18 : Boarding and Day : Suffolk

Felsted for *me*

Leading all-round education with pupil wellbeing at its heart. Give your child the space to thrive with our variety of modern boarding & day options. Based on a safe rural campus just one hour from London.

Developing character, making a difference.

Co-educational, ages 4-18, boarding & day.

Book your visit and find out more at felsted.org

 #FelstedForMe

Felsted

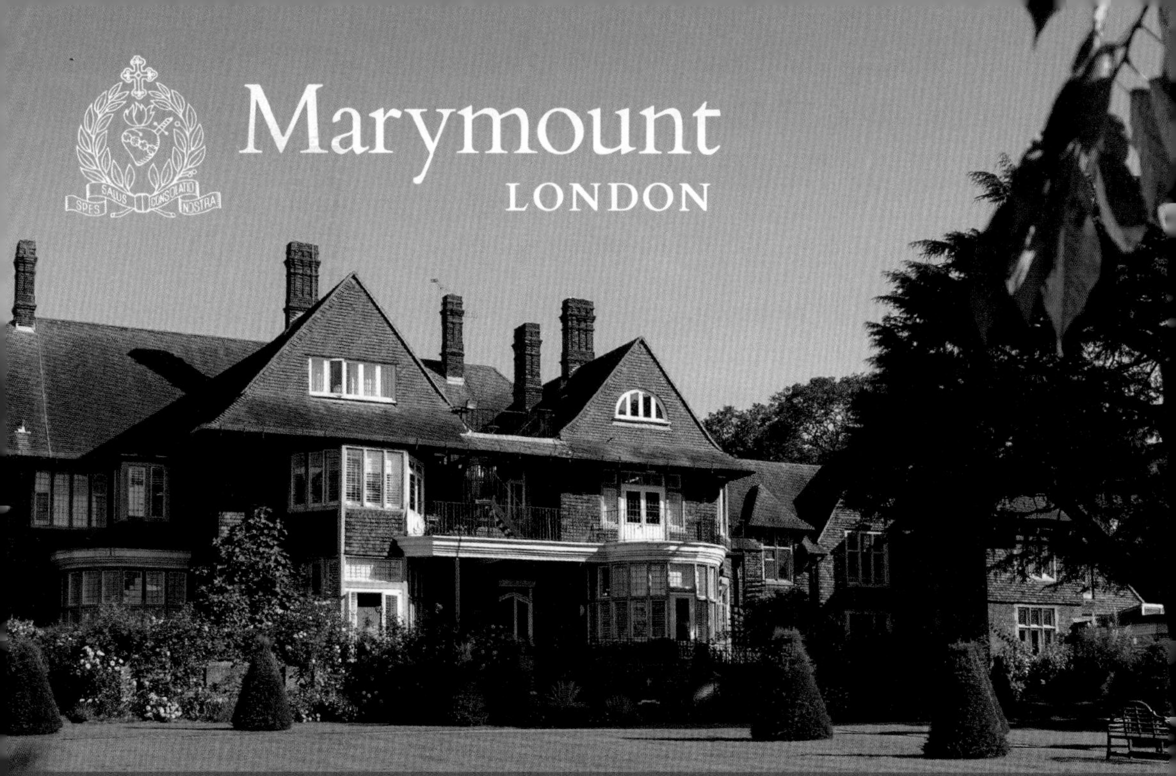

Marymount
LONDON

SPES SALUS CONSOLATIO NOSTRA

A boarding experience like no other

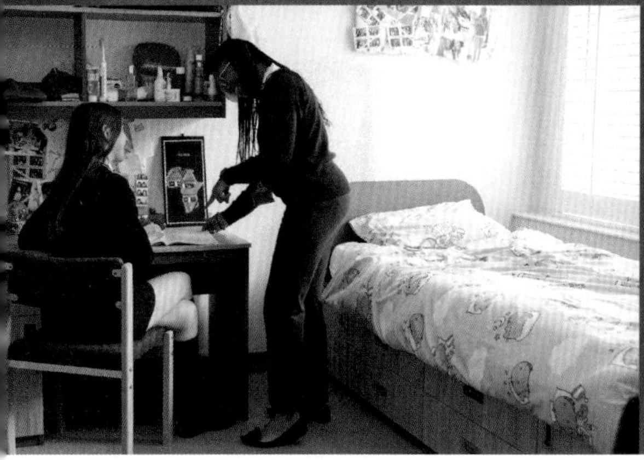

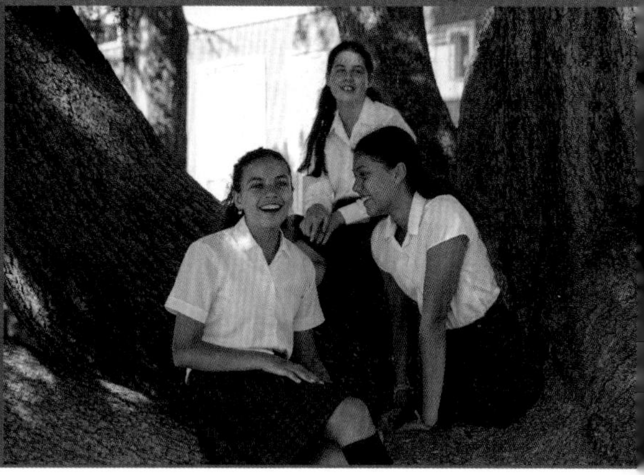

Set in 7 acres of beautiful parkland, yet only 12 miles from Central London. Marymount London has all the benefits of a traditional boarding experience, on the doorstep of one of the greatest cities in the world. Our rigorous and challenging IB programme prepares your daughter for a successful future, in an environment that provides structure, support, and plenty of fun!

www.marymountlondon.com

What type of boarding – full, weekly or flexi?

If you're reading this you've probably already decided that boarding might suit your son or daughter. If so, the next step is to consider the arrangement that best fits in with your family – and your pocket. Unlike the old days, when youngsters were packed off to school at the age of 7 or 8 and didn't see home again until the end of term, many of today's boarding schools offer parents a range of options – anything from the occasional night to weekly or full-time. Not all schools are equally flexible and whatever package you choose must usually be agreed upon from term to term, but schools have adapted to parents' needs and there's certainly more choice than ever before. For instance, a child who starts off boarding for one or two days a week may decide to weekly board during exam times or become a full boarder in the sixth form

Whichever option you choose, there's no doubt that boarding schools are more skilled than ever at helping their charges settle in and feel at home. They may run taster weekends, get new pupils to start before the rest of the school arrives and appoint buddies and mentors to guide them through the first few weeks and beyond. Pupils are encouraged to keep in regular touch with their parents – and it's not just a handwritten letter hastily scribbled before chapel on Sunday mornings either. Children can email, Skype, Zoom and – if mobile phones are allowed – text or phone home whenever they wish. And if your child's too busy to get in touch (it does happen) you can always contact house staff for an update.

Full boarding

'Proper' full boarding schools have diminished in number, many that were once full boarding only have adapted to meet parents' preference for weekly or flexi options. But,

FROM CONGESTION ZONE

TO SPACE TO BREATHE

For example, it takes only 40 minutes by train to get from the traffic and pollution of London's Charing Cross Station to the open air of Tonbridge. Our beautiful and historic campus has some of the finest facilities of any school in the country, from award-winning academic buildings to 150 acres of superbly-maintained playing fields. Here there is space to think, to grow, to thrive, to breathe.

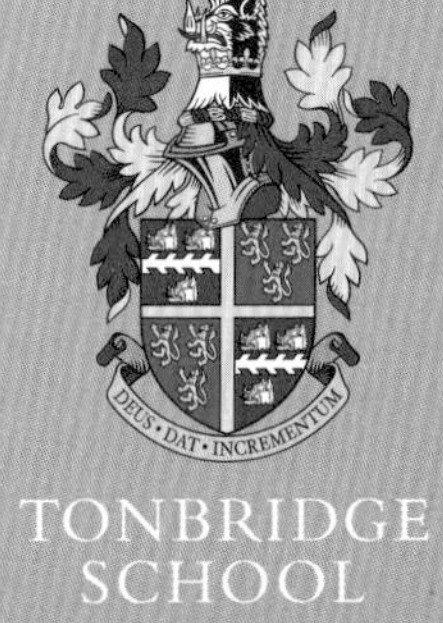

TONBRIDGE SCHOOL

Arrange a visit:
admissions@tonbridge-school.org
tonbridge-school.co.uk

if you're looking for a school where everyone or nearly everyone boards full time and there isn't a mass exodus at weekends, you still have quite a few options. The shape of the school day at full boarding schools can be different because there is theoretically more space in the timetable, but from what we see this tends to mean pupils just do even more. If your child likes to have plenty of down time then full boarding may not suit!.

Boys' full boarding schools

These include some of the most famous names in British education such as Eton, Radley and Harrow. Winchester College broke ranks in 2021, announcing not only that it would take day boys in the sixth form from 2022, but also offer day and, from 2024, boarding places to girls. We see no signs of the other three following suit, so far.

Historically, boys from the English upper classes were sent to these schools to be educated as future leaders, statesmen, bishops and military commanders. Nowadays, boys from all over the world and many different backgrounds compete for places. Nor do you necessarily have to come from a wealthy family. The former head of Eton, Anthony Little, believes schools like Eton should be 'needs blind'. He told The Good Schools Guide, 'We do not want to be a finishing school for the titled and rich.' Noble sentiments and ones that schools such as Eton and many others are trying to live up to with scholarships and 100 per cent bursaries. At many schools a significant number of pupils will be in receipt of some financial support, but the reality is that with fees heading past £40,000 pa, the average pupil at a full boarding school is not going to come from a family of modest means.

The shape of the day at full boarding schools is different because there is more space in the timetable

BRAMBLETYE

PRE-PREP | PREP | BOYS & GIRLS
DAY & BOARDING | AGED 2 - 13 YEARS
IN THE HEART OF THE SUSSEX COUNTRYSIDE

Brambletye, Lewes Road, Sussex
www.brambletye.co.uk | +44 (0) 1342 321004 | registrar@brambletye.com

At these schools all the boys board and may go home only for exeats, usually two or three long weekends per term ; sometimes sixth formers have extra leave days as privileges. However, parents are more involved with school life than formerly; those who live near enough can attend matches, concerts and plays, and technology enables much closer contact over long distances too with many events live streamed. Boys at these senior schools will often have attended full boarding boys' preps such as Cothill House and Horris Hill or preps where boarding is compulsory for all in the last two years (7 and 8) such as Caldicott and Papplewick.

Girls' full boarding schools

There are now very few exclusively full boarding schools for girls, Benenden was the latest to announce that it will start admitting a small number of day pupils. Downe House, Wycombe Abbey, Sherborne Girls and Tudor Hall only offer full boarding (no flexi/weekly) but also take a few local day pupils. Hanford School in Dorset and Sunny Hill in Somerset are two of a tiny handful of girls-only boarding preps.

The best-known girls' boarding schools such as Roedean, Badminton and Cheltenham Ladies' College were established in the mid- to late-19th century by formidable pioneers of women's education. This makes them relative newcomers compared to the likes of boys' schools such as Abingdon School, founded in the 11th century or Winchester College, founded in 1382. For this reason most girls' schools lack the extensive property portfolios and endowments held by their brothers, making resources for bursaries etc much more limited.

Co-ed full boarding schools

If you want your sons and daughters to attend a full boarding school together there are quite a few co-ed

An Independent Catholic School in Leicestershire

Boys and Girls • Boarding and Day • 3-18 Years

Encouraging Big Ideas

Catholic School, inclusive of all with a real sense of community

Full, weekly, flexi and casual boarding available

First-class teaching and outstanding pastoral care

In the Top 10% for students' progress at A Level in England

Specialist music and sports tuition available

Broad co-curricular activities offer

Visit us at one of our **Open Mornings** to find out more

www.ratcliffecollege.com/visit

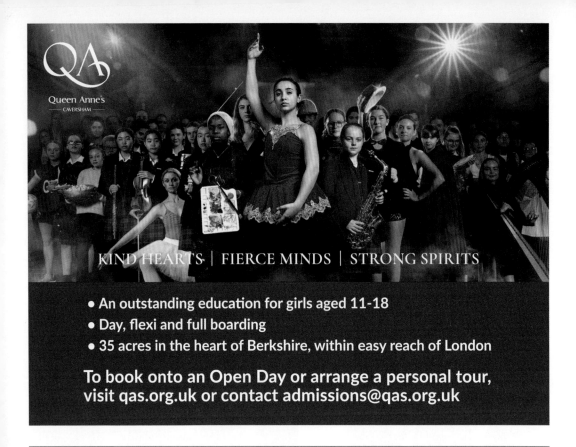

QA
Queen Anne's
CAVERSHAM

KIND HEARTS | FIERCE MINDS | STRONG SPIRITS

- An outstanding education for girls aged 11-18
- Day, flexi and full boarding
- 35 acres in the heart of Berkshire, within easy reach of London

To book onto an Open Day or arrange a personal tour, visit qas.org.uk or contact admissions@qas.org.uk

LEIGHTON PARK
FOUNDED 1890

Awarded Best Co-Ed School South East England

Find out more www.leightonpark.com/visit-leighton-park

independent • co-educational • day/boarding • 11-18 years

Education & Training Awards

choices, including Oundle, Uppingham and Marlborough College. Rugby School, Shrewsbury School and Malvern College are also majority full boarding only but have more day pupils. Because of its proximity to London, Wellington College is de facto weekly boarding since so many pupils go home for Saturday night. All these schools take a small number of day pupils but don't offer weekly or flexi boarding options. Girls and boys live in separate boarding accommodation with clear rules about what is out of bounds to visitors of the opposite sex. Some schools have co-ed sixth-form boarding houses, but boundaries are in place. See 'Sex, drugs and homesickness', page 58, for more information on this.

Weekly boarding

Weekly boarding is growing in popularity, particularly for children who live too far away to be day pupils or whose parents work long hours and/or frequently travel abroad. Weekly boarders go home either on Friday evenings or Saturday afternoons and return to school on Sunday evenings or Monday mornings. For many children, this offers the best of both worlds: they have all the benefits of a full boarding school during the week, work hard and spend lots of time with their friends, then relax at home with their parents on Saturdays and Sundays. Parents are keen on weekly boarding too. They like the fact that they don't have to nag about homework or getting up on time in the morning and feel that home time is 'quality time'. Many opt for boarding schools within an hour's drive so they can still turn up for sports matches, concerts and drama productions during the term.

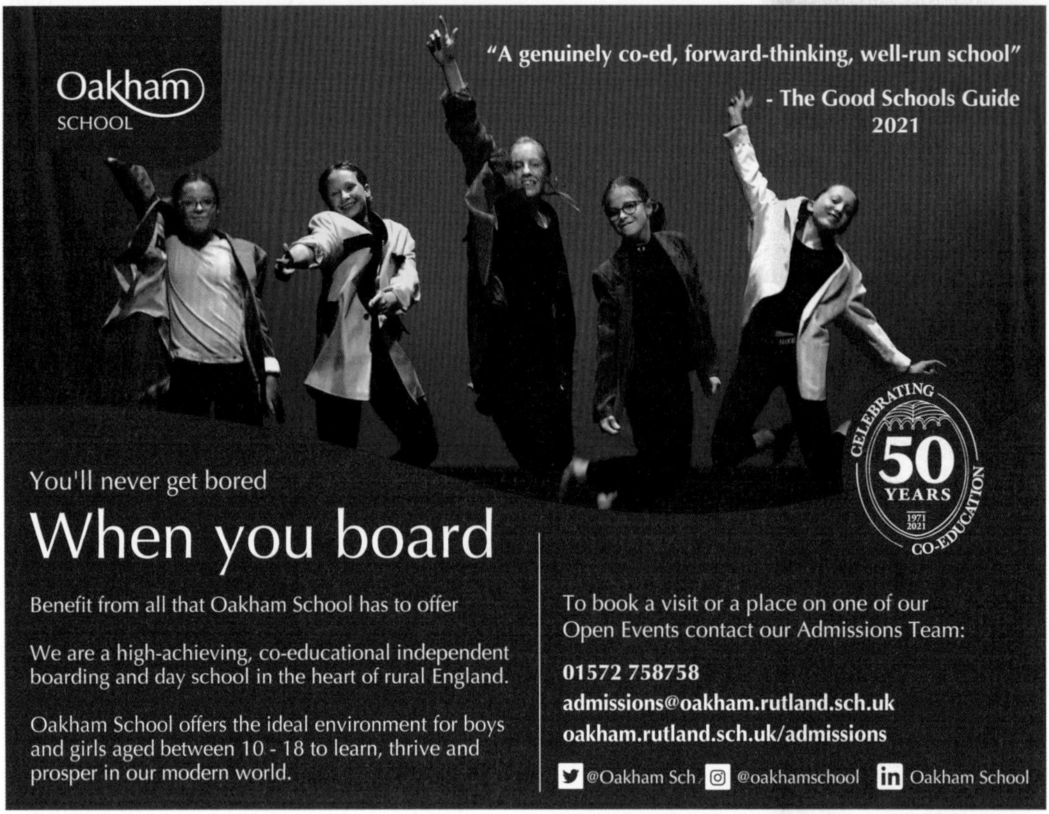

"A genuinely co-ed, forward-thinking, well-run school"

- The Good Schools Guide 2021

Oakham SCHOOL

CELEBRATING 50 YEARS 1971 2021 CO-EDUCATION

You'll never get bored

When you board

Benefit from all that Oakham School has to offer

We are a high-achieving, co-educational independent boarding and day school in the heart of rural England.

Oakham School offers the ideal environment for boys and girls aged between 10 - 18 to learn, thrive and prosper in our modern world.

To book a visit or a place on one of our Open Events contact our Admissions Team:

01572 758758
admissions@oakham.rutland.sch.uk
oakham.rutland.sch.uk/admissions

@Oakham Sch @oakhamschool Oakham School

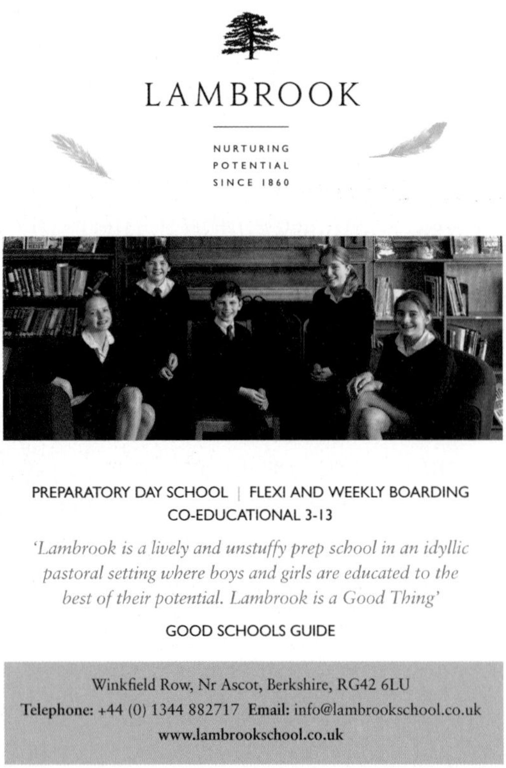

LAMBROOK

NURTURING POTENTIAL SINCE 1860

PREPARATORY DAY SCHOOL | FLEXI AND WEEKLY BOARDING
CO-EDUCATIONAL 3-13

'Lambrook is a lively and unstuffy prep school in an idyllic pastoral setting where boys and girls are educated to the best of their potential. Lambrook is a Good Thing'

GOOD SCHOOLS GUIDE

Winkfield Row, Nr Ascot, Berkshire, RG42 6LU
Telephone: +44 (0) 1344 882717 **Email:** info@lambrookschool.co.uk
www.lambrookschool.co.uk

Great minds...

The National
Mathematics and Science
College

natmatsci.ac.uk

Top performing UK school in national and international science and mathematics olympiads

93% A*/A at A-level

Almost 1 in 5 into Oxbridge

An independent Sixth Form College specialising in A-level STEM subjects

For students aged 15 - 19, aiming to study at the world's leading universities

GO FURTHER...

COME RUN WITH THE SWIFT

> Academic Excellence
> Boarding

Flexi boarding

Flexi boarding gets a mixed press; parents are generally in favour but for some schools it's a step too far. One prep headmaster describes it as 'a bit of a nightmare, like glorified hotel management'. Unlike full and weekly boarding, one school's definition of 'flexi' may not be the same as another's. It's very rarely bed and breakfast at the drop of a hat. Most schools require parents to book boarding nights at the beginning of each term, with Thursdays and Fridays being the most popular. Not surprising if it means parents can enjoy a night out without having to find a babysitter (and not have to get up for the Saturday morning school run). Many tell us that they will always do their best to accommodate a pupil at short notice if there's a family emergency.

While it can be complicated for schools to manage, flexi boarding could be just the ticket if your child has to stay at school late for sport, music or drama one or two nights a week, or if you want to dip your toe in the water and see if boarding suits your family. Schools that offer flexi boarding will inevitably have some spare beds, but your child may not get the same bed or even the same room. Some schools have (comfortable) camp beds for occasional boarders. Arrangements differ quite widely so it's worth asking exactly what is provided for flexi or occasional boarders.

ROYAL HIGH SCHOOL
BATH
GDST
Nursery | Prep | Senior | Sixth Form
Day | Boarding

Making friends family

Contact Admissions:
01225 313877

Girls making their mark

Day, weekly & full boarding HMC co-educational school.
Caterham School is easily accessed from Surrey, Kent, Sussex and London

01883 335058 | admissions@caterhamschool.co.uk | | caterhamschool.co.uk

State boarding schools

If you think your child would benefit from a boarding school education, but are put off by the high fees and consequent limited social mix of a typical independent boarding school, you may find that a state boarding school is the answer. These have seen a surge of popularity in recent years, partly due to increasing numbers of families with both parents working long hours. 'We all work hard during the week, and get together at weekends,' said one father. 'It's much less stressful than trying to oversee homework and music practice after a long day at work and travelling, and my daughter is happy to spend week nights at school with her friends.' Those schools offering full boarding are popular with families working abroad, in the Forces, the diplomatic service or with international companies.

What do they cost?

State boarding schools are comparatively cheap – mostly somewhere between £15,000 and £20,000 a year in boarding fees – because the government foots the bill for tuition. The majority of pupils in most state boarding schools are day pupils, but many stay for after-school activities alongside the boarders – 'a boarding experience minus the bed,' as one school put it. Some of the schools, such as Gordon's in Surrey, levy a 'day boarding' fee of several thousand pounds to all day pupils to cover after-school activities (though bursaries are available for low-income families). Others, such as Hockerill Anglo-European, have free day places for normal school hours attendance, but charge a day boarding fee to those who wish to arrive for breakfast and stay for activities, supper and homework.

There are 34 state boarding schools in Britain with 5,000 places. Some offer full boarding, others only weekly or sixth form

Making history, creating the future

Register Now

for flexi / weekly / full boarding and day places for year 7 (aged 11) and Sixth Form.

For all open events please **view our video** now at **www.oshsch.com** and ch the open day page for the latest update

You are welcome to visit us on any day, simply contact us to organise.

discover

who you can be

admissions@oshsch.com | 01384 817325 | oshsch.com

Heath Lane, Stourbridge, West Midlands, UK DY8 1QX

Who can apply?

As with other state schools, these are open to British citizens, EU passport holders and anyone with a right of residence in the UK. Some are academically selective, some are single sex, and they are permitted to interview pupils (which other state schools are not) in order to ensure they are suitable candidates for boarding. Detailed information regarding admissions criteria for applicants from the UK and other countries can be found on schools' websites.

How many are there?

There are 34 in Britain, including one in the Scilly Isles and one in Scotland – the latter for children from Forces families – with a total of some 5000+ places. Some offer full boarding, others only weekly boarding and some have boarding for sixth formers only.

What to consider

As with any other school, read prospectuses, school magazines and newsletters, inspection reports and reviews such as those in this book. We review about half of British state boarding schools, and have extensive data for all of them on our website. See page 1287 for our reviews of state boarding schools.

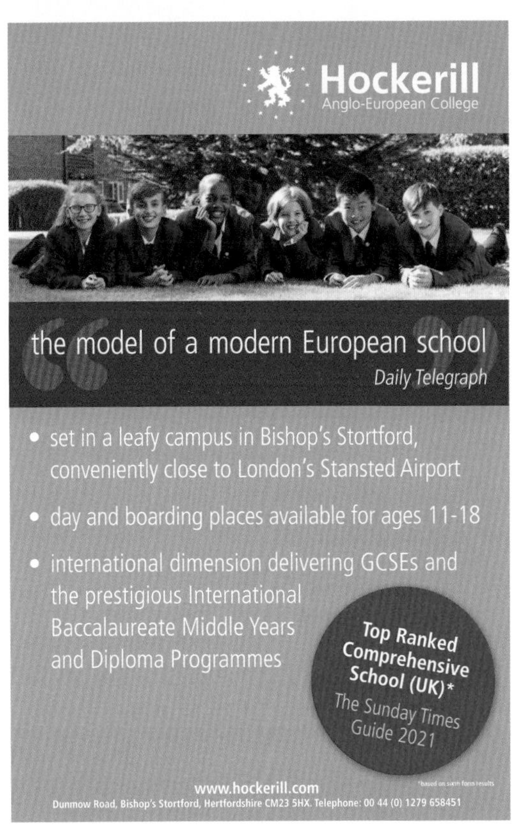

The missing piece since 1614

Day & Boarding | No Tuition Fees | Full & Weekly Options

Admissions for our **Ofsted Outstanding** state boarding are open for **September 2022**, with entry at **Year 9** and **Sixth Form.**

www.sgs.uk.net | 01903 817601

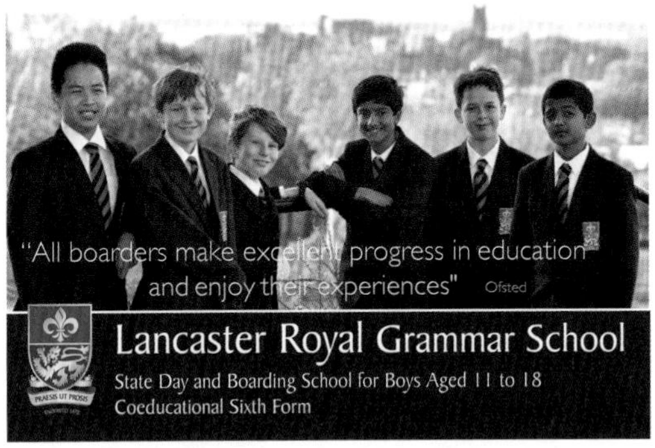

Founded in 1472 we are one of the UK's top grammar schools for boys with a coeducational Sixth Form.

Exceptional value for money with free tuition. Fees for boarding are only one third of the fees of independent schools.

Our commitment to achieving excellence at an educational and extracurricular level makes LRGS an exceptional place to learn and grow as an individual.

Welcoming girls and boys for Sixth Form boarding.

Ofsted Boarding Inspection 2019: "outstanding in all areas"

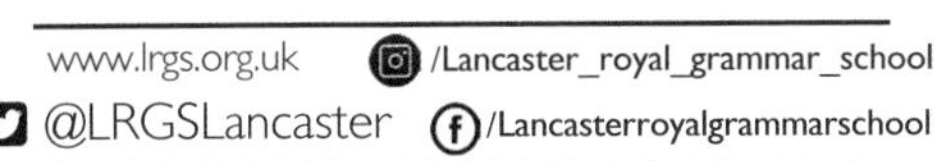

Praesis ut Prosis
'Lead in order to Serve'

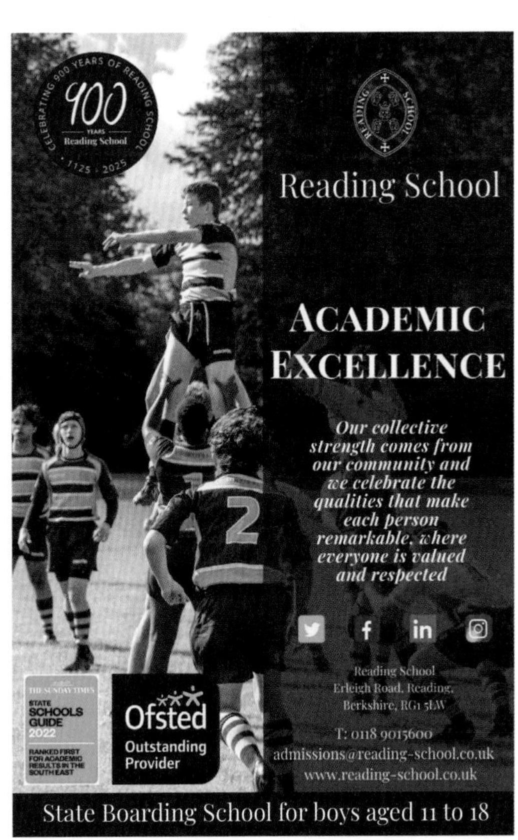

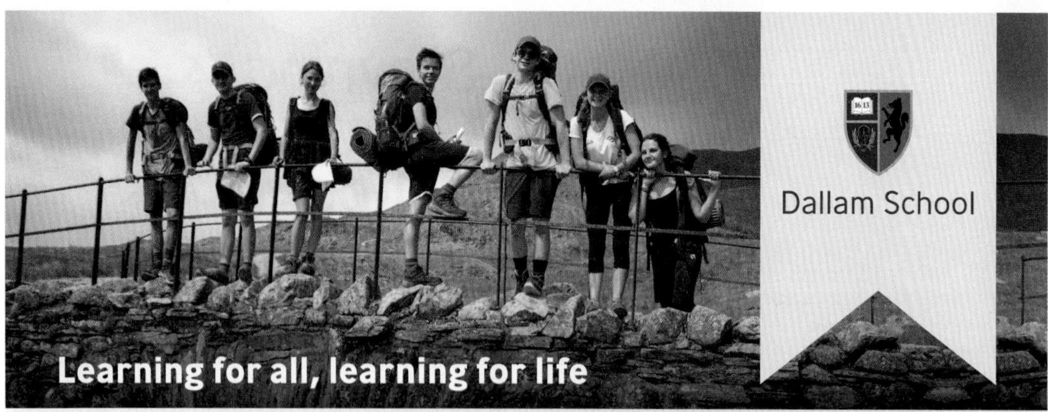

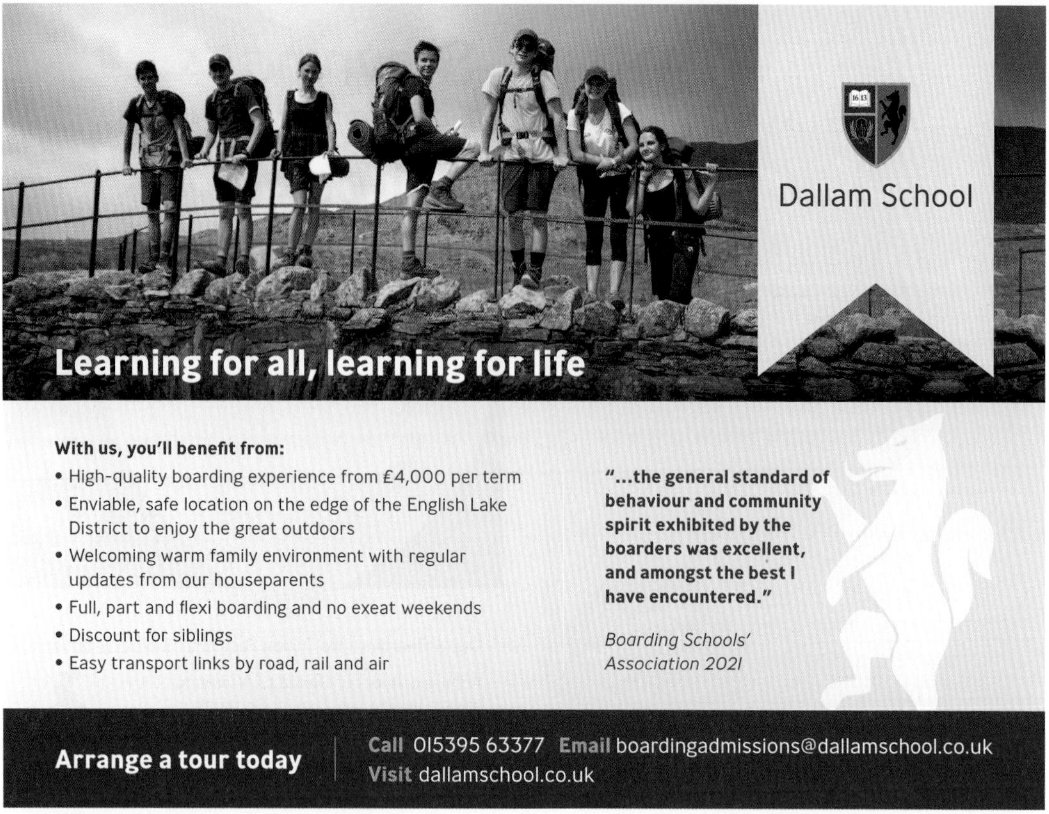

Dallam School
Learning for all, learning for life
With us, you'll benefit from:
• High-quality boarding experience from £4,000 per term
• Enviable, safe location on the edge of the English Lake District to enjoy the great outdoors
• Welcoming warm family environment with regular updates from our houseparents
• Full, part and flexi boarding and no exeat weekends
• Discount for siblings
• Easy transport links by road, rail and air
"...the general standard of behaviour and community spirit exhibited by the boarders was excellent, and amongst the best I have encountered."
Boarding Schools' Association 2021
Arrange a tour today
Call 015395 63377 Email boardingadmissions@dallamschool.co.uk
Visit dallamschool.co.uk

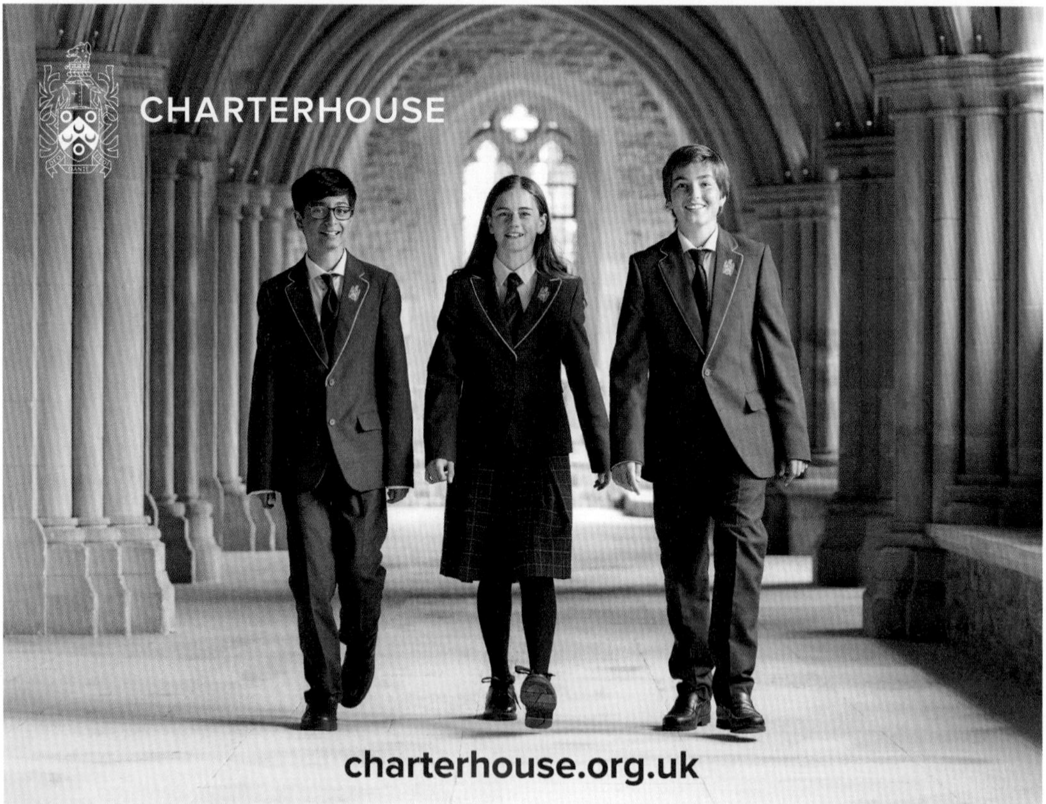

CHARTERHOUSE
charterhouse.org.uk

What age to start boarding?

Most children start boarding at the age of 11 or 13. At this age children themselves tend to have a say in the matter. Indeed, Good Schools Guide writers report that children often ask their parents to let them board – rather than the other way around. Some prep schools admit boarders under the age of 10 and make special provision for them with bedrooms that look much closer to how things are at home (rather than dorms) and, because numbers will be small, an evening regime that is flexible. At Horris Hill, for example, where they have a few boarders under the age of 10, 'if it's hot they can have a swim, if everyone's exhausted they go to bed early.'

The sixth form is another entry point for first-time boarders. We visit many schools where there are more boarders in the sixth form than lower down the school – largely because 16- to 18-year-olds are keen to concentrate on their studies, socialise with their friends in their spare time and get a taste of living away from home prior to university. Sixth-form boarders will generally have their own study bedrooms in separate accommodation with well-equipped kitchens (Ocado will deliver to boarding schools!), washing machines, even yoga studios. At Westonbirt School, where over three-quarters of sixth formers board, one girl told us, 'There aren't so many distractions, it helps us stay focused on our studies.'

Most children start boarding at the age of 11 or 13. At this age they tend to have a say in the matter

Today's boarding schools pride themselves on helping students become more independent before university. At Heathfield, an all-girls' boarding school in Ascot, Berkshire, girls in the upper sixth live in their own bungalow on site, while Burford School, a co-ed state boarding school in Oxfordshire, has created a flat within the boarding house for a group of sixth-form girls to get them ready for the university years. At Rendcomb School in Gloucestershire,

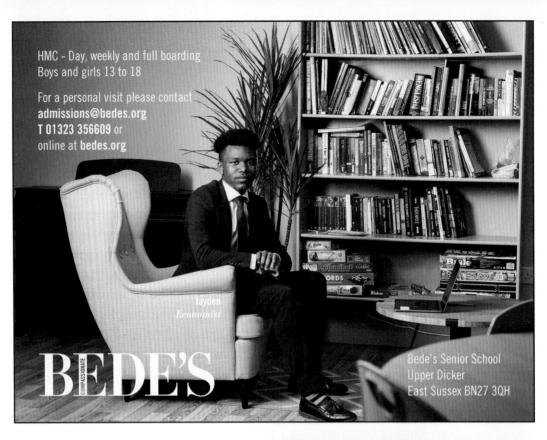

HMC - Day, weekly and full boarding
Boys and girls 13 to 18

For a personal visit please contact
admissions@bedes.org
T 01323 356609 or
online at **bedes.org**

Jayden
Economist

COMPASSIONATE
BEDE'S

Bede's Senior School
Upper Dicker
East Sussex BN27 3QH

MOWDEN HALL SCHOOL

Leading Co-educational
Prep School

Day, Flexi and Full Boarding
for 3-13 Years

PERSONAL
VISITS
AND TOURS
All Year Round

Newton, Stocksfield, Northumberland NE43 7TP
Tel: 01661 842147 www.mowdenhallpst.org
info@mowdenhallpst.org

"You would struggle to find better in the North."
THE GOOD SCHOOLS GUIDE

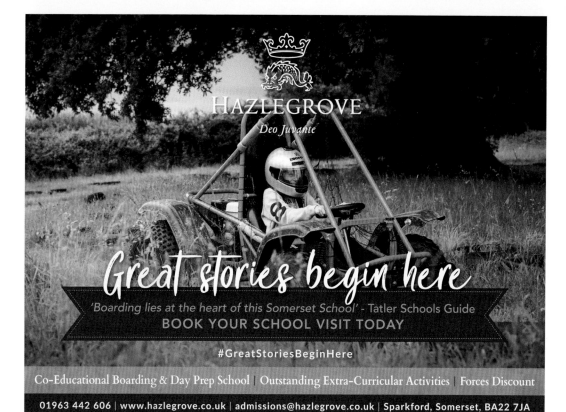

HAZLEGROVE
Deo Juvante

Great stories begin here

'Boarding lies at the heart of this Somerset School' - Tatler Schools Guide
BOOK YOUR SCHOOL VISIT TODAY

#GreatStoriesBeginHere

Co-Educational Boarding & Day Prep School | Outstanding Extra-Curricular Activities | Forces Discount

01963 442 606 | www.hazlegrove.co.uk | admissions@hazlegrove.co.uk | Sparkford, Somerset, BA22 7JA

Futures Found

Independent day and boarding school for girls aged 11 - 18
wychwoodschool.org

groups of sixth formers take turns to stay for five days in the school flat in the nearby village. They are given housekeeping money and (apart from lunch at school) must manage this and the chores. Apparently sometimes it runs like clockwork, sometimes 'mummies deliver food parcels and help clean up at the end'.

Which house?

Parents often ask us how to get their child into a particular house – maybe they've heard on the grapevine that 'x' is the 'sporty' house or 'y' is the 'best' house. While it's true that the character of the house parents or housemaster/mistress is inevitably going to have an influence, schools tell us that they work hard to ensure every house has a good mix of types. It's also worth bearing in mind that during your child's years at the school house staff may leave, so it's best not to pin all your hopes on someone you happen to particularly like. Families are encouraged to look round several, if not all, boarding houses and apply in order of preference – but school has the final say. In the end it probably doesn't matter, house identity and loyalty is so strong that whichever house your child goes into will very soon be the best in their eyes.

Houseparents

House parents, as the name suggests, will be most closely involved in your child's day-to-day life at school. They are your first point of contact and you should feel able to ask them anything and expect to get prompt answers to your questions. This is a highly professional and responsible job and to a great extent your child's happiness will depend on their (and your) relationship with these people.

Many, but not all, house parents are married couples, often with children – and pets – of their own. One (or very often both) is likely to teach at the school. They live in

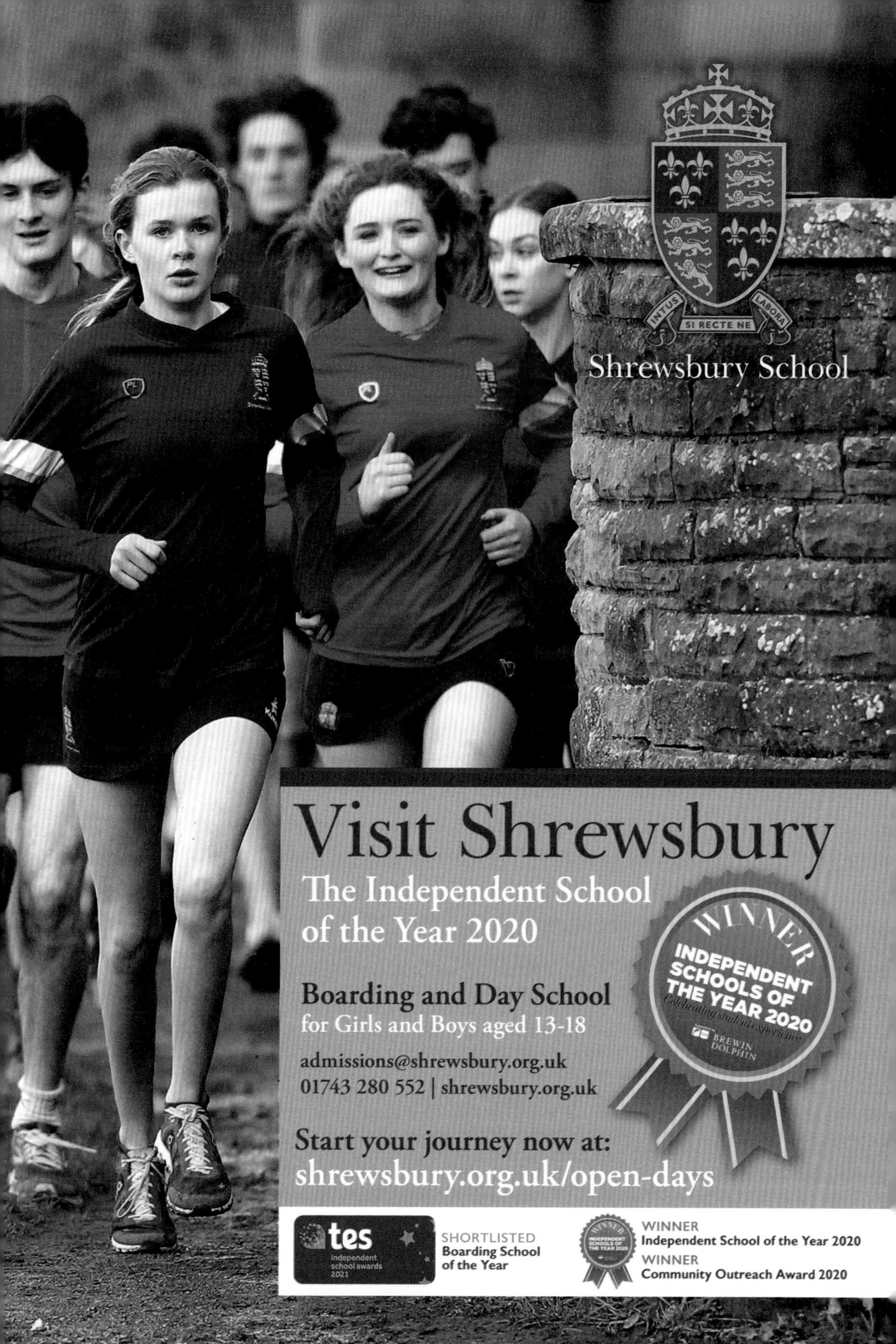

INTUS SI RECTE NE LABORA
Shrewsbury School
Visit Shrewsbury
The Independent School of the Year 2020
WINNER
INDEPENDENT SCHOOLS OF THE YEAR 2020
Celebrating student experience
BREWIN DOLPHIN
Boarding and Day School
for Girls and Boys aged 13-18
admissions@shrewsbury.org.uk
01743 280 552 | shrewsbury.org.uk
Start your journey now at:
shrewsbury.org.uk/open-days
tes
independent school awards 2021
SHORTLISTED
Boarding School of the Year
WINNER
Independent School of the Year 2020
WINNER
Community Outreach Award 2020

the boarding house along with several other adults such as 'gappies' (young people, often from Australia or South Africa), matrons and/or tutors. The nomenclature and precise arrangement will depend on the school and the number/age of boarders, but there's generally at least one resident adult per corridor/floor.

Most schools have 'vertical' (mixed age) boarding from 13-18 although in some cases sixth formers are accommodated separately. Any year 7 and 8 boarders may also be in a separate house. A few smaller schools have 'horizontal' (year group) boarding houses. In either case, there will be separate bedtimes, rules and other arrangements that are appropriate to the age of the children.

House or home?

While people are always more important to the ethos of a school than buildings, architecture can have an influence. Pupils at Westonbirt School sleep under the high ceilings of grade 1 listed staterooms and our reviewer found 'priceless silk wallpaper, preserved under Perspex, rubbing shoulders with One Direction posters'. Boarders at Cheltenham College live in elegant town houses – one advantage of this is that it puts a little distance between school and 'home'. Modern, purpose-built boarding houses, while less characterful, are likely to have better plumbing. All in all, boarding accommodation seems to be improving year on year, no doubt keeping local building trades very busy over the summer holidays. In most schools pupils sleep in dormitories (usually about three to five beds in a room) until years 10 or 11 when they move into single or double study bedrooms. Sixth formers almost always have individual

House parents will be most closely involved in your child's day-to-day life at school

Windlesham House School

An independent day and boarding school
for boys and girls aged 4 to 13.

• Occasional, Flexible, Weekly & Full Boarding
• Uniquely designed Windlesham House Challenge & Diploma
• Extensive Activities Programme • Weekly Bus to London • Incredible Facilities

Contact us 01903 874701 | admissions@windlesham.com
windlesham.com | 10 Minutes from Worthing & Horsham | RH20 4AY

BELIEVE.
ACHIEVE.
SUCCEED.

By the time they leave School, they are able to think critically, have high aspirations and a self-belief that there are few things they cannot achieve. *Independent School Inspectorate*

You want your daughter to achieve academically but you want her to be intelligent in other ways too – to be confident socially, to have a strong moral compass, to shape the world around her, to believe in herself.

At St Catherine's we support your daughter in building the intellect and character that will help her develop as a bright, confident, compassionate and vibrant individual. At the heart of this is developing her sense of self-belief, that she can achieve whatever she is driven to do in life.

St Catherine's, Bramley
GSA Day & Boarding School since 1885 | 4 - 18 years
Guildford GU5 0DF | admissions@stcatherines.info

www.stcatherines.info

study bedrooms. House captains or senior prefects sometimes have the privilege of getting the 'best' rooms.

Food glorious food

You will be relieved to hear that our reviewers, who always try and have lunch in the schools they visit, have never been faced with the grim fare endured by the likes of Oliver Twist and Jane Eyre. Nor, we hope, will today's boarders find themselves afflicted in adult life with 'boarding school eating'. This not entirely polite style of consumption, which stems from parsimonious portion control at schools in the 1960s and 70s, is characterised by rapid scoffing of everything in sight before someone else snaffles it. Food is always a hot topic when we speak to pupils and never more so than at boarding school. Schools increasingly outsource provision to some extent, rather than cook everything from scratch in house, and quality, quantity and variety of what's provided can come in for some trenchant criticism both from pupils and parents. While you can't please everyone, schools do their best to be responsive to criticism – some are even trialling limited menu options for pupils to select what they want to eat in advance.

Wonderful cooked breakfasts (almost always the favourite meal of the day, according to pupils), vegetarian and vegan options, salad bars, in-house coffee shops and cafes are almost standard these days. Most schools have a central dining hall, but at some, such as Winchester College, Rugby, Oundle and Malvern College, boarders eat all meals in their houses. This may be a practical arrangement if houses are a little distance from the main school building, but it also has a beneficial influence on table manners as well as making it easier for staff to spot a child who isn't eating. Boarders will also have access to house kitchens with toasters, microwaves etc, and fresh fruit is always available. Nor have tuck boxes been

WANT TO PROTECT OUR PLANET?

YOU HAVE ENDLESS OPPORTUNITIES

We give you the strength to make a difference

11+ / 13+ /16+
SCHOLARSHIPS
AVAILABLE

'THE FRIENDLY AND OPEN CULTURE COMBINED WITH A GENUINE RESPECT FOR KNOWLEDGE CREATES A SOLID GROUND ENABLING CHILDREN TO THRIVE ACADEMICALLY, SOCIALLY AND SPIRITUALLY.'
CURRENT PARENT

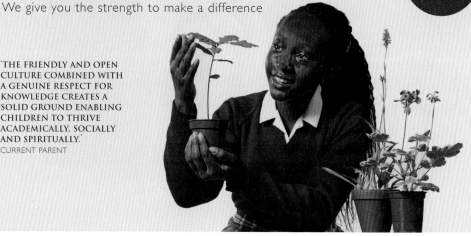

ARRANGE YOUR VISIT: +44 (0)1761 235103 ADMISSIONS@DOWNSIDE.CO.UK
WWW.DOWNSIDE.CO.UK

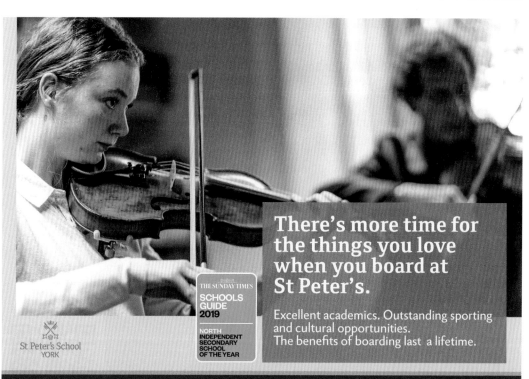

THE SUNDAY TIMES
SCHOOLS GUIDE 2019
NORTH INDEPENDENT SECONDARY SCHOOL OF THE YEAR

St Peter's School
YORK

There's more time for the things you love when you board at St Peter's.

Excellent academics. Outstanding sporting and cultural opportunities.
The benefits of boarding last a lifetime.

Visit our website:
www.stpetersyork.org.uk

tes independent school awards 2021

Winner
Independent school of the year
St Peter's School, York

Shortlisted
Prep school of the year
St Peter's School, York

Winner
Pre-prep school of the year
St Peter's School, York

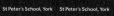

Brentwood School
Boarding
We are one of the UK's leading independent schools for boys and girls aged 3 to 18 with a history spanning almost 500 years.
Book your visit online
www.brentwoodschool.co.uk
01277 243 314

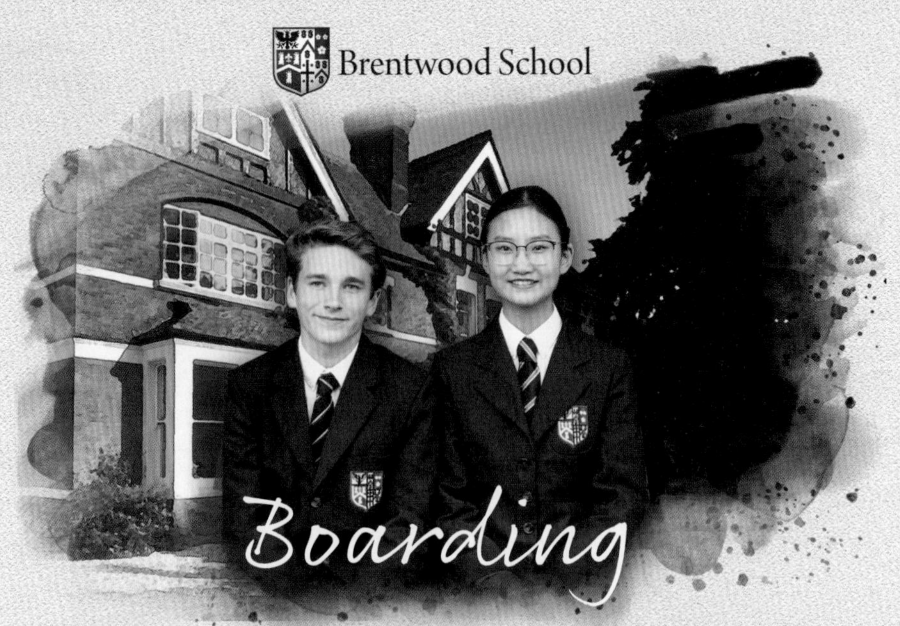

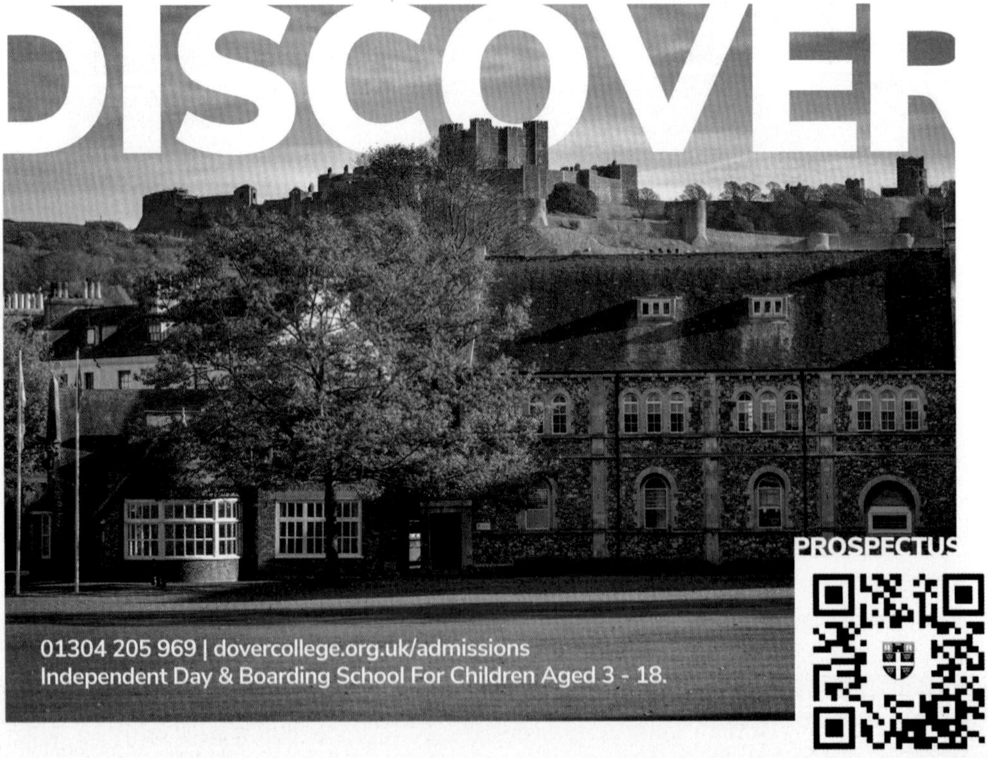

DISCOVER
PROSPECTUS
01304 205 969 | dovercollege.org.uk/admissions
Independent Day & Boarding School For Children Aged 3 - 18.

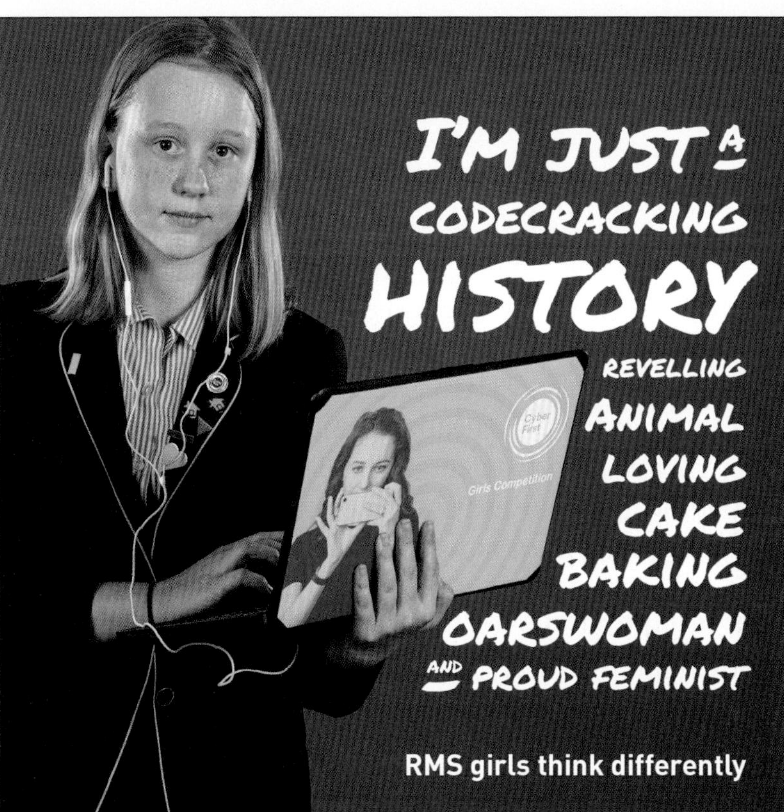

Ages 2-18
Boarding from age 8
(full, weekly and flexi)

Learn more at
RMSforgirls.com

The Royal Masonic School
for Girls, Rickmansworth,
Hertfordshire, WD3 4HF
01923 773168
rmsforgirls.com

DISCOVER YOUR TALENT AT CRANLEIGH

WEEKLY BOARDING WITH EXCELLENT ACADEMICS SUPPORTED BY A FULL PROGRAMME OF MUSIC, SPORT, ART, DESIGN AND DRAMA.

REGISTERING NOW FOR 2023 AND 2024.

ADMISSIONS@CRANLEIGH.ORG OR
WWW.CRANLEIGH.ORG | 01438 276377

consigned to history; they're still used to keep favourite treats under lock and key.

At Tudor Hall School sixth formers told us they like to buy bacon and eggs from the nearby farm shop and make their own breakfasts at the weekend. Boarders at town schools will find that the local takeaways are more than happy to deliver – most do a roaring trade at weekends.

Pupils with physical disabilities

Historic buildings rarely make for easy disabled access and if your child needs special arrangements you must to discuss these with the school well in advance. This won't just apply to boarding houses; classrooms may be up several flights of stairs and there can often be a fair way to walk between lessons. That being said, we know of many schools who have done all they can to accommodate pupils in wheelchairs or with visual or hearing impairments.

TAUNTON SCHOOL

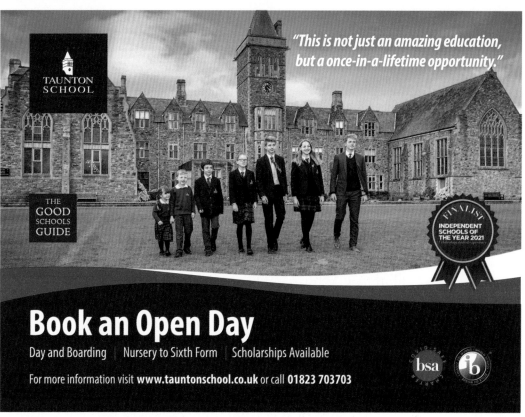

"This is not just an amazing education, but a once-in-a-lifetime opportunity."

THE GOOD SCHOOLS GUIDE

FINALIST INDEPENDENT SCHOOLS OF THE YEAR 2021

Book an Open Day

Day and Boarding | Nursery to Sixth Form | Scholarships Available

For more information visit **www.tauntonschool.co.uk** or call **01823 703703**

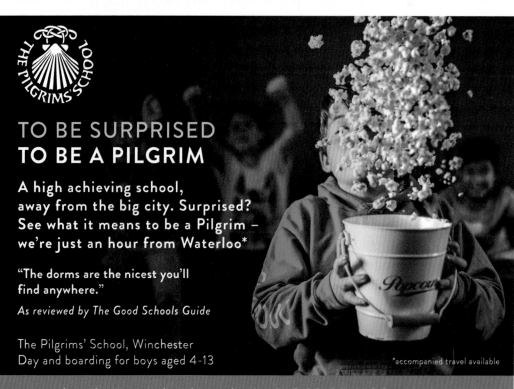

COVID-SAFE CHARTER bsa

THE PILGRIMS' SCHOOL

TO BE SURPRISED
TO BE A PILGRIM

A high achieving school, away from the big city. Surprised? See what it means to be a Pilgrim – we're just an hour from Waterloo*

"The dorms are the nicest you'll find anywhere."

As reviewed by The Good Schools Guide

The Pilgrims' School, Winchester
Day and boarding for boys aged 4-13

*accompanied travel available

www.thepilgrims-school.co.uk | 01962 854189

Scholarships and bursaries

Boarding schools, like all schools, want clever children. Children who will shine in arts and sports, children who will be excellent all-rounders and who will contribute generously to the academic, cultural and social life of the school. To this end they will offer considerable financial help to families with children who meet this description but who would not otherwise be able to attend because of high fees. Many good boarding schools offer scholarships and bursaries in order to attract able and talented pupils. Scholarships are now usually worth more in glory than in fee reduction but bursaries can be worth up to 100 per cent of fees plus supplementary help for trips and equipment, if needed.

But how do you find out what financial assistance could be out there for you? Often, the information on schools' websites is hazy and unhelpful and you have no option but to call up and, perhaps, tell more about yourselves than you feel ready to with so little information.

The GSGEC Scholarships and Bursaries Service

The Good Schools Guide Education Consultants has created a unique central resource for parents. We now hold information on the fee assistance available at more than 500 schools in The Good Schools Guide and, increasingly, at other good schools.

We won't be able to tell you exactly what – in raw financial terms – a school might offer you in terms of bursarial help, as this will depend on many things, such as your income, your financial commitments and the number of children you have – but we will be able to tell you about the school's criteria for scholarships and bursaries. We also know of odd and unusual awards eg for the children of clergy or sailors or children whose parent has died. We

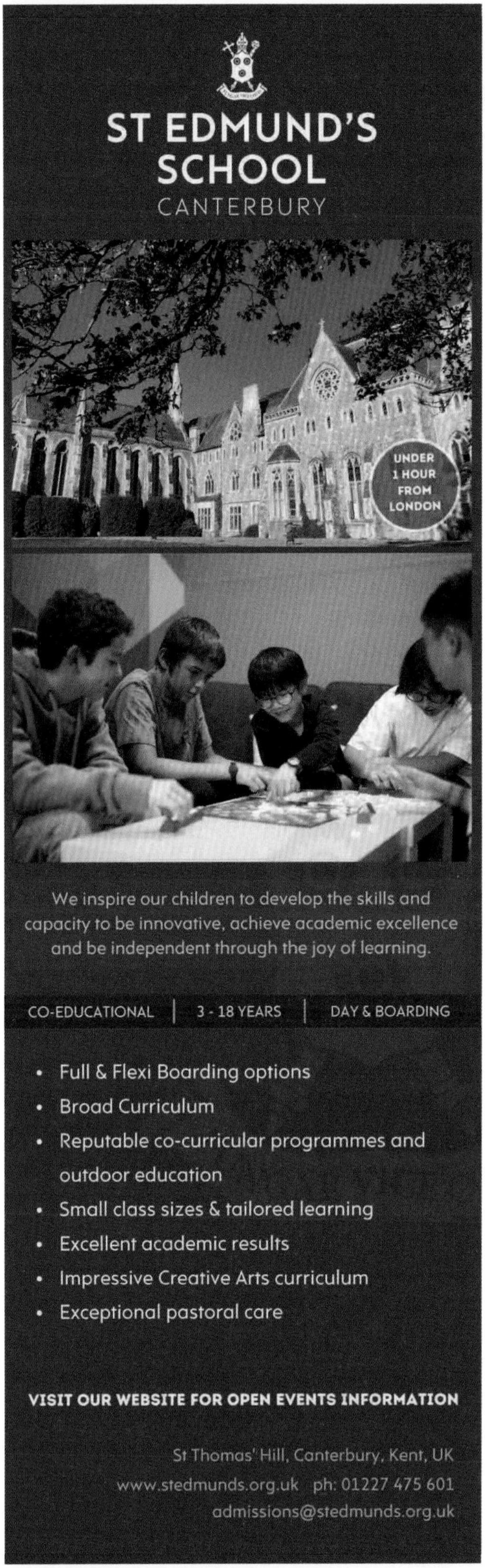

We inspire our children to develop the skills and capacity to be innovative, achieve academic excellence and be independent through the joy of learning.

CO-EDUCATIONAL | 3 - 18 YEARS | DAY & BOARDING

- Full & Flexi Boarding options
- Broad Curriculum
- Reputable co-curricular programmes and outdoor education
- Small class sizes & tailored learning
- Excellent academic results
- Impressive Creative Arts curriculum
- Exceptional pastoral care

VISIT OUR WEBSITE FOR OPEN EVENTS INFORMATION

St Thomas' Hill, Canterbury, Kent, UK
www.stedmunds.org.uk ph: 01227 475 601
admissions@stedmunds.org.uk

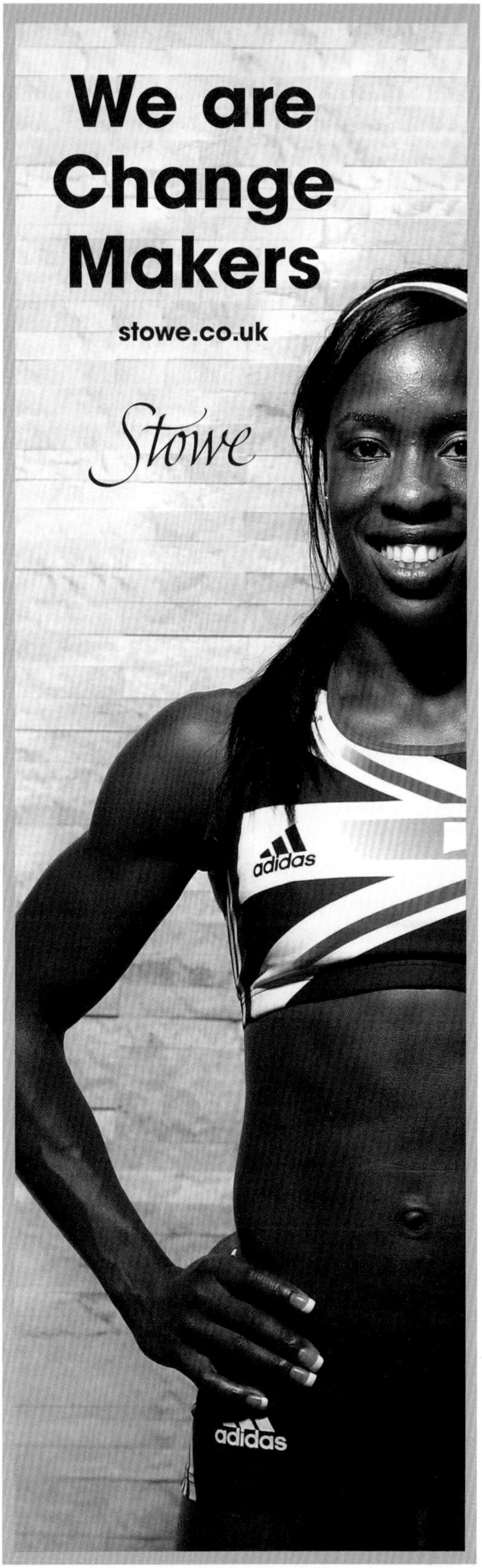

We are Change Makers

stowe.co.uk

Stowe

adidas

adidas

www.christcollegebrecon.com

01874 615440 | admissions@christcollegebrecon.com

Godstowe

"As a boarder, I have met people from countries I've never visited and learned about their cultures. The boarding community feels like a big family." - Naysa, Art Scholar

A happy and thriving day and boarding preparatory school, for girls aged 3 to 13 and boys aged 3 to 7.

To arrange a visit, please contact our admissions team on 01494 429006 or register online at www.godstowe.org/admissions

will be able to explain to you how a scholarship might be topped up by a bursary and answer any other questions you may have.

The Good Schools Guide Scholarships and Bursaries Service is a fee-paying service but we keep those fees as low as possible. Our charges depend on the number of schools or the breadth of the area you would like us to research.

Far more parents apply for fee assistance than get it. Schools' resources – even the rich ones – are limited and they disburse money with great care. Your child may be top of everything at his primary school and your family income may be low, but this does not entitle you to a place or help with fees at any school. Informing yourself, getting the timing right and applying realistically is the best approach and – as around one third of all children at fee-paying schools now have some fee remission – it has to be worth a try.

Sex, drugs and homesickness

Given that the majority of boarding school pupils are aged from 13 upwards, some parents might think school fees a small price to pay for letting trained professionals steer their hormonal offspring over the turbulent waters of adolescence. Even so, we all know that risk-taking, underage drinking, drugs, sex, cyber-bullying, self-harm, anorexia and the other ills that teenage flesh is heir to, can occur right under parents' noses. What then should you expect boarding schools to do to keep young people safe?

Pastoral care and well-being are now up there with academic results as key measures of any school's success and as closely monitored as exam performance. In addition to the normal school inspection visits (Ofsted for state schools, ISI for independent schools), government inspectors visit all boarding schools to check every aspect of provision from fire escapes to mattresses, and they also talk to staff, pupils and parents. All schools should have a link to the latest boarding inspection report (and their response to any issues raised) on their website. But knowing the number of locks on a dormitory window won't tell you if someone will notice your child staring miserably out of it.

Googling a school may lead you to press reports about historic sexual abuse, expulsions for drug use and other stories guaranteed to make a parent's blood run cold. The measure of a school is not so much that these things happened (they do, though thankfully very infrequently), but how such serious and unfortunate incidents are handled. If a school declares, for instance, that possession of drugs will lead to immediate expulsion but fails to expel those who break this rule, you should make your own judgement. (Some schools will allow pupils to return to sit public exams.)

Remember, too, that although occurrences like this are surprisingly rare, just because a school has a squeaky-clean record is no guarantee that something won't happen in the future. You will have to take much on trust, just as the school will trust your child not to break the rules.

All schools provide copious information on how they ensure pupils' safety, usually termed 'safeguarding', and well-being (if they don't, make your excuses and leave). They also organise seminars and advice sessions, usually run by external professionals, on all aspects of teenage health and wellbeing exclusively for parents. It's up to you to attend the open days, go to the talks, read the literature, and then weigh up whether the regime will suit your child. See page 76 for more details about Safeguarding.

Playing by the rules

Even in the sixth form it's unlikely that your son or daughter will enjoy the freedoms they have at home. Parents and children will be expected to agree to and abide by the school's policies on everything from uniform, energy drinks, alcohol to PDAs (public displays of affection – kissing, holding hands, etc) and random drugs testing. These policies (all of which will be on the school's website) have been drawn up to ensure not just your child but the whole boarding community is safe.

Some schools allow 18-year-olds to visit 'approved' pubs or restaurants in the nearest town, but such freedoms are a privilege instantly rescinded if abused. Others – perhaps in more rural areas – have a sixth-form bar where alcohol is dispensed under supervision and always with parents' consent. At some full boarding schools older pupils may apply for permission to host parties in designated areas. What happens under the radar is, inevitably, another matter – as it often is at home.

Relationships between pupils at boarding schools are a concern for parents and, we imagine, a chronic headache for staff – especially at co-ed full-boarding establishments. At most schools 'intimate or explicit sexual relations' are classed as 'misconduct' that can lead to suspension or expulsion. Some schools ban any public display of affection; some don't. However, as with drink and drugs, banning sex doesn't mean it won't happen.

Some schools allow 18-year-olds to visit 'approved' pubs or restaurants in the nearest town

Parents of girls in particular may want to get a feeling for the state of gender relations in the school. The barrage of publicity generated by the testimonies on the 'Everyone's Invited' website has led to schools reviewing and sharpening up their PHSE offering, widening debate and actively listening and if necessary, acting upon pupils' concerns. We also now give more coverage specifically to what schools are doing around equality and diversity in our reviews.

Rules about what happens on school premises are fair enough, but it's a much greyer area when full boarders attend private parties at, for instance, a day pupil's house. Parental permission must be obtained to attend this kind of event, but responsibility for policing pupils' behaviour under these circumstances cannot be the school's.

You should feel able to raise questions and discuss concerns about this or any other matter with the school. Talking to parents with older children at the school is also a good idea if you want to find out just how intimate the relationship is between policy and reality. The 'Pastoral care, well-being and discipline' section of our reviews covers these issues.

If your own domestic regime is more Liberty Hall than Dotheboys Hall you will need to discuss potential schools' disciplinary policies with your child and be realistic if you think the worlds are too far apart.

Homesickness

Homesickness is almost always a short-term problem that the school, the parents and the child can weather by working together. It's not a universal affliction, but many children away from home and family for the first time are likely to have a bout. Schools manage this by keeping their charges busy, busy, busy during the first few weeks and being ultra-vigilant. Several have told us that managing parents during this time is equally challenging and that, depending on circumstances, it can be more settling if children aren't chatting to anxious mummy every night. Some children sail through their first term but come down with a nasty case when they return to school after the Christmas holidays. No school will want to keep a child boarding if they are profoundly and persistently unhappy, and in these relatively rare circumstances parents are advised accordingly. Sometimes it's a case of trying again after a few terms, but sometimes a different type of school is the only answer.

Advice for international applicants

British boarding schools have never enjoyed a higher standing abroad and each year thousands of pupils from all over the world pile in for a taste of the boarding experience. In fact, roughly five per cent of the UK's boarding school pupils are from abroad – that's 20,000 children from around 100 different countries.

Pastoral care is now given as much prominence as academic standards. Newly refurbished accommodation is bordering on luxurious (but don't expect many en suite bathrooms) and the transformation of school food is nothing short of miraculous, though fish and chips and custard – separately, of course – remain culinary fixtures. But before completing your registration form and paying the deposit, it's worth checking that you know what you are buying and whether it will suit your family.

English language support

The vast majority of international pupils follow a mainstream curriculum and work towards standard 16- and 18-plus qualifications. For those whose English isn't yet quite good enough or whose previous education puts them behind others of the same age, extra support from teachers who specialise in EAL (English as an Additional Language) may be needed.

Schools may run separate classes in key subjects, structured to allow more time for the language component so that maths and science students, for example, have sufficient understanding to decode word-based problems. A growing number of boarding senior schools also run international study centres that offer a range of specially structured courses in what is effectively a school within a school. Some run a 'pre-sixth form' year that enables overseas students to get their English up to scratch before joining the sixth form. Pupils may board or play sport with

Moreton Hall
Girls 3-18 | Boys 3-13

tes
independent school awards
WINNER
Boarding School of the Year

www.moretonhall.com

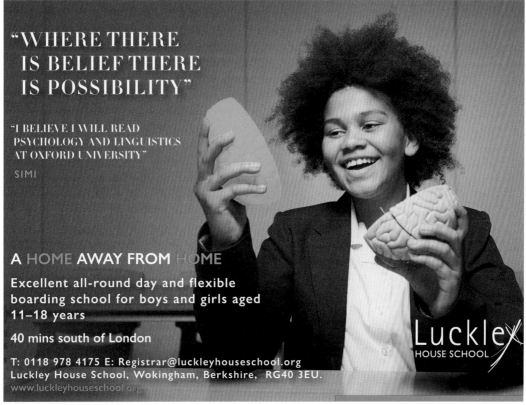

"WHERE THERE IS BELIEF THERE IS POSSIBILITY"

"I BELIEVE I WILL READ PSYCHOLOGY AND LINGUISTICS AT OXFORD UNIVERSITY"

SIMI

A HOME AWAY FROM HOME

Excellent all-round day and flexible boarding school for boys and girls aged 11–18 years

40 mins south of London

T: 0118 978 4175 E: Registrar@luckleyhouseschool.org
Luckley House School, Wokingham, Berkshire, RG40 3EU.
www.luckleyhouseschool.org

Luckley
HOUSE SCHOOL

Helping boys to become the very best version of themselves.

An independent day and boarding school in the centre of Loughborough. Educating boys from 10 – 18 years.

A school which achieves academic excellence, supported by a strong pastoral system and a busy and varied extra-curricular programme.

www.lsf.org/grammar

THE LOUGHBOROUGH SCHOOLS FOUNDATION

Wycliffe

Based in the Cotswolds

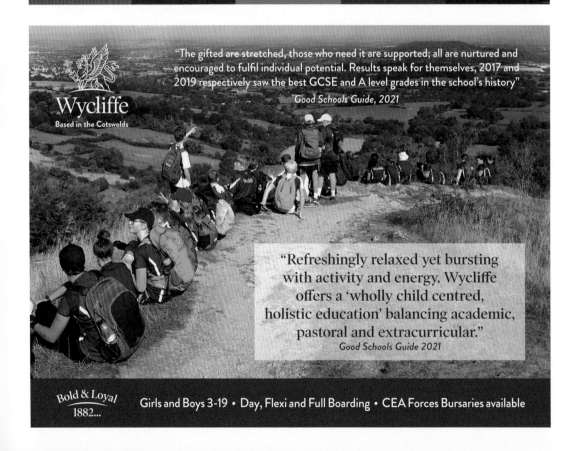

"The gifted are stretched, those who need it are supported; all are nurtured and encouraged to fulfil individual potential. Results speak for themselves, 2017 and 2019 respectively saw the best GCSE and A level grades in the school's history"

Good Schools Guide, 2021

"Refreshingly relaxed yet bursting with activity and energy, Wycliffe offers a 'wholly child centred, holistic education' balancing academic, pastoral and extracurricular."

Good Schools Guide 2021

Bold & Loyal
1882...

Girls and Boys 3-19 • Day, Flexi and Full Boarding • CEA Forces Bursaries available their 'mainstream' peers but will follow a largely separate and slimmed-down academic programme, working towards a smaller number of GCSEs with a big emphasis on learning English. These are covered in more detail on page 74.

Social life

While the academic side of boarding is undoubtedly important, the social dimension is just as vital. Good Schools Guide reviewers regularly hear of enduring friendships that span religious or cultural divides, or of lessons enriched by pupils on opposite sides of wars, sanctions or economic policy.

Things work less well if a school operates a monoculture policy. A large number of pupils from one nation in a single year group may help fend off homesickness, but can reduce the motivation for pupils to speak English socially or immerse themselves in their host country's way of life – an opportunity lost rather than gained. It's okay to ask admissions staff for numbers if you're at all concerned.

Similarly, a school where the number of overseas pupils is so small that they are swamped by the prevailing culture can also lead to a miserable experience – particularly if they are the only full boarders in the place at weekends while everyone else goes home. It's essential to find out just how many pupils of your child's age are actually around over the weekend; many schools start off with a packed house for Saturday morning lessons or matches but empty out seconds after the final whistle (or bell) sounds.

Over the past few years, some of the most famous names in education have opened offshoots overseas

Exporting education – big names abroad

Finally, for those happy to ditch some of the trimmings and all of the British weather, it's increasingly possible to get the

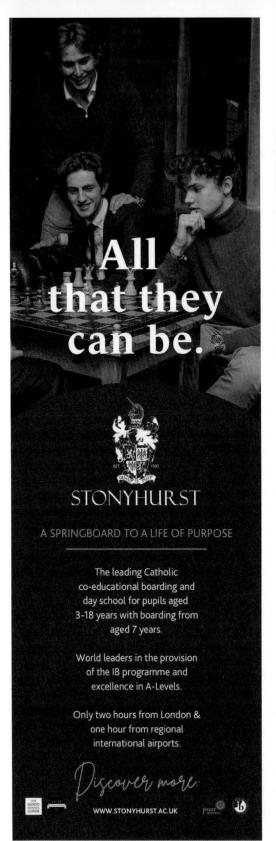

All that they can be.

STONYHURST

EST. 1593

QUANT JE PUIS

A SPRINGBOARD TO A LIFE OF PURPOSE

The leading Catholic co-educational boarding and day school for pupils aged 3-18 years with boarding from aged 7 years.

World leaders in the provision of the IB programme and excellence in A-Levels.

Only two hours from London & one hour from regional international airports.

Discover more:

WWW.STONYHURST.AC.UK

ethos, results and teaching quality of a traditional British education without travelling anywhere near the UK. Over the past few years, some of the most famous names in education have opened offshoots overseas. You can get a Harrow education in Bangkok, Beijing or Hong Kong, become a Rugby pupil in Thailand or sign up for Brighton College in Abu Dhabi. Westminster School has set up no fewer than six schools in China (teaching the Chinese curriculum the Westminster way). Ethos and teaching standards are recognisably the same even if the facilities (sport is often air-conditioned and inside, for example) aren't.

Some important points:

- Distrust any educational firms offering to find your child a place in a UK school. If free to you, they may well be getting a commission. Similarly, a bill for securing you a 'guaranteed' school place should also sound alarm bells. Speak to the school yourself.
- The key entry points into UK schools are at age 11, 13 or 16. Many schools will consider potential applicants outside these times, but bear in mind that it's often on a one in, one out basis – places become available only if another pupil leaves.
- Look past fabulous exam results. Top schools do well because they select top pupils. What it proves is that parents of the brightest children send them there. It doesn't necessarily tell you how well it teaches them.
- Check how EAL provision (if required) is organised. Ideally, ask to sit in on some lessons to give you an idea of the standards/commitment and enthusiasm you'll be getting – and try to talk to similar pupils.
- Consider applying for scholarships if your child is outstanding (academic, musical and sporting excellence

are the norms) and ensure that your idea of excellence is the same as the school's, but…

- Don't be won over by worthless scholarships, sometimes offered as an incentive by schools to seal the deal.
- Check how often a child won't be boarding. Half terms, bank holidays and occasional weekend exeats all add up to a considerable chunk of time when pupils aren't in school and will need somewhere else to stay. Most schools require parents who live abroad to appoint a guardian for their child (see page 70), but you may also want to ensure family visits coincide with these dates.

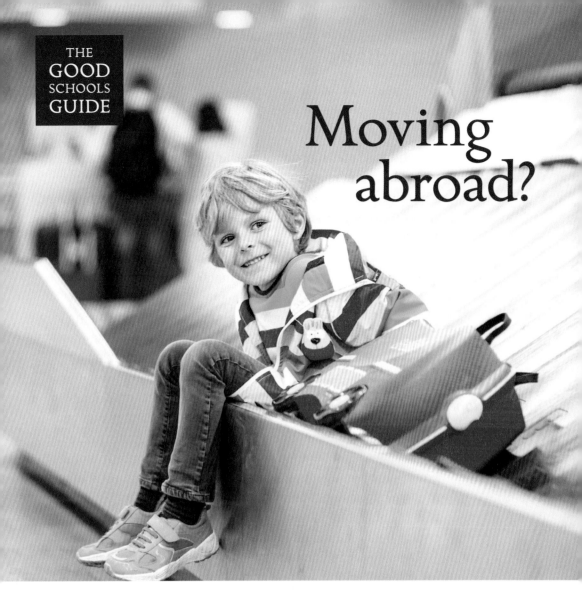

THE GOOD SCHOOLS GUIDE

Moving abroad?

 Tickets

 Passports

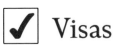

 Visas

 Schools

Still need to sort your schooling?

Go straight to The Good Schools Guide International.

The first class guide to world class schools.

goodschoolsguide.co.uk/international

Guardians

If a child is starting school in the UK and their parents live abroad, it makes sense to have another adult in the frame, someone who can act as a stand-in parent and become a trusted presence in their lives when they need someone to turn to. This person is known as a guardian (or education guardian). Sometimes the role is taken by a relative, but if the family has no relatives in the UK a professional guardian can be appointed.

Guardians meet and greet their charges from the airport at the start of term and do the reverse when it ends. In addition, they may sign forms, attend parent teacher meetings or sort out things such as mobile phone contracts and dentists' appointments. Guardians may also need to step in at very short notice at times of crisis, for instance if a child hits a problem and is excluded, suspended, or needs urgent medical treatment. The importance of the guardian's role was highlighted during the global pandemic when some pupils became 'stranded' in the UK, unable to fly home.

The importance of the guardian's role was highlighted during the global pandemic

Despite what you may read online, there is in fact no legal requirement to appoint a guardian and education guardians have no formal status. Aegis (the Association for the Education and Guardianship of International Students), which is the closest the industry comes to a trade body, confirmed that it is not a legal requirement for an international student to have an education guardian when studying in the UK. However, while failure to appoint an education guardian isn't against the law, it may tax your relationship with a school and severely impede the chances of your child being offered a place (it's often made a condition of acceptance).

3 WAYS GUARDIANSHIP CAN BENEFIT CHINESE PARENTS

1

Why is it important for guardians to speak the same language?

We work with Chinese parents and students because we know how important it is to communicate efficiently and have your needs understood when you start a new life in the UK. To assist with cultural differences, a guardian is a bridge to connect you and your children with the schools, and help express your concerns clearly for the best solutions.

Eve Leung,
Founder of Elite Anglo-Chinese Services

2

What are the advantages offered by a guardian?

Schooling is only one-third of your child's life and career development. Throughout your children's whole study journey abroad, a guardian will accompany them starting from school to social activities, and assist with such matters as school subjects, host family, cultural adaptation, and career planning.

We also commit to respond to emergencies 24/7 and can be reached on WhatsApp and WeChat. Additionally, premium clients can arrange a guardian to visit their child at the schools.

3

How do you choose a trusted guardian?

Trust is founded on long-term relationships. Having stayed in London for two decades, I have built an extensive network of local schools and communities in the UK, and achieved a high rate of successful school admission.

I founded the agency in 2012 and I am delighted to have on our team Mr Gwyn Philips, a devoted educator with 40 years of experience and close ties to the Far East. A former Deputy Head and Director of Admissions in boarding school, Gwyn moved into guardianship following his retirement and he thoroughly understands the UK education system and the challenges it presents for overseas pupils. His extensive knowledge of schools brings valuable insight to provide the best study and life skill advice for your child in the UK.

Gwyn Philips,
Host Family Co-ordinator

Tel: +44 020 8144 2145 **WhatsApp/ Signal:** +852 6810 8836
UK Office: The Fold Space, 20 Clyde Terrace, London, SE23 3BA
HK Office: Unit 66, 16/F, Lee Garden Two, 28 Yun Ping Road, Causeway Bay, Hong Kong

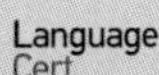

TRINITY LISTED EDUCATION AGENT

Certified British Council Agent
GAL/ 24295

www.eliteacs.com

BARNARD CASTLE SCHOOL

A leading independent day and boarding school for girls and boys aged 4-18, set amid stunning countryside in Northern England

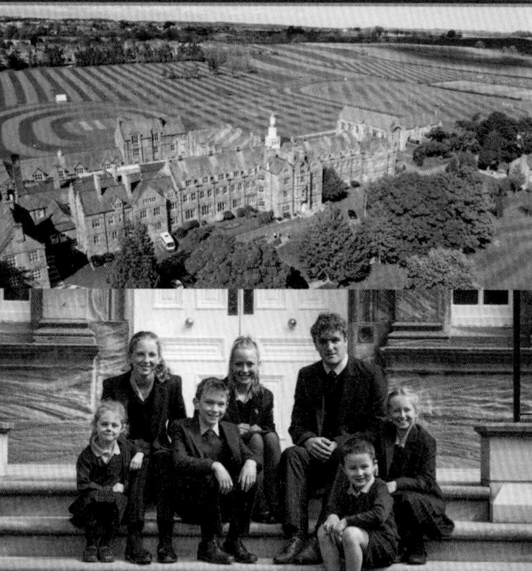

Home away from home full-time and flexi boarding in a happy, stable environment

Situated in a stunning rural environment that is well served by a range of excellent transport links

Scan to learn more about our School and what makes a 'Barney' education so special

Alternatively, contact 01833 696030 or email admissions@barneyschool.org.uk

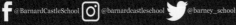

@barnardcastleschool @barney_school

Barnard Castle School | Co Durham DL12 8UN | www.barnardcastleschool.org.uk

THE KEY TO YOUR FUTURE

An outstanding independent school for boys and girls aged 0-18

- Exceptional academic results at A Level and IB
- Scholarships availiable in Year 9 and 12
- Gifted and Talented development programme
- Garden Cottage Nursery from age 0-3
- Idyllic 80 acre site with our own farm

Kent College
Canterbury

Book your place online at **kentcollege.com** or **Call 01227 763231**

Guardianship firms

These are businesses that charge fees of up to £1,000 a term for basic support that includes round-the-clock emergency help, at least in term time. Many firms also give families the option of paying more for a 'premium' service.

Some guardianship firms specialise in one particular nationality, others are cannily expanding into new areas such as day school packages, where children board with a host family in term time. All guardianship firms should recruit and vet host families, ensuring they lead blameless lives, have squeaky clean records and, importantly, live within easy travelling distance of your child's school.

Unfortunately, membership of Aegis, which runs its own inspections, remains optional. The organisation is campaigning for safeguarding to be tightened and inspections made mandatory, but with only 10 per cent of schools currently working with Aegis members, it still has a lot of convincing to do. In the meantime, there are other ways of finding a guardian. Schools sometimes recruit – very sensibly – through their own parents. Other families prefer to make their own arrangements, turning to friends or relations as stand-in, and stand-by, mums and dads. This will only work, however, if they live in easy reach of the school.

For overseas pupils, a compatible guardian who cares about your child's well-being and happiness almost as much as you do can be an essential part of the educational experience.

International study centres

International study centres are found all over the UK. They serve as a means of teaching young people (usually from age 11-16) academic English and introducing them to English culture and English education. The aim of most of these schools is to provide a gentle transition for foreign (non-English-speaking) adolescents into life in an English school, often as boarders, and to prepare them for either A levels or, in some cases, the IB diploma, which then leads to university entry. In some cases GCSEs or IGSCEs are offered alongside intensive English-language programmes to facilitate this preparation.

A growing number of independent boarding and day schools have seen the income potential of attracting foreign-national pupils and some have opened international study centres as what might be described as adjunct 'feeder schools' within the main school.

If you are thinking of sending your child to an international study centre, here's a checklist of the things you should consider:

- What are the admissions criteria? How does the school assess the pupil's level of English language and other learning?
- Are the teachers trained in EAL teaching, and used to working with children from all over the world?
- How does the school welcome new pupils, make them feel at home and integrate them?
- Is there a good mix of pupils? Too many from one country may tend to talk amongst themselves rather than learning English and mixing with others.
- Are pupils encouraged to celebrate and share their culture?
- Are diverse diets and religious practices catered for?
- Can pupils keep up their own language to a high academic level?

- How much interaction do international study centre pupils have with those at the mainstream school? Do they mix for sport, clubs, evening and weekend activities?
- What percentage of international pupils move into the mainstream school? What happens to those who are not admitted, and how much help do they get with finding a place elsewhere?
- Does the centre have the authority to issue CAS letters for those who need a visa?
- If you are working with a third-party agent, make sure that all financial agreements are transparent and reasonable.

Safeguarding

Any parent preparing to entrust their child to a school – whether day or boarding – will rightly expect that child's safety and well-being to be a priority at all times. Such expectations are nearly always fulfilled but in a sad minority of cases that is not what happens.

We have all read news reports of bullying and abuse and shuddered to imagine the horror felt by the children and families involved. A flood of historical allegations against schools and subsequent court cases, not to mention mobile phones, flexi-boarding, more parental involvement and heightened awareness have together helped usher in some sunlight and fresh air.

Safeguarding policies, found on every school website, now make explicit reference to the possibility of abuse at schools – something rarely contemplated a generation ago.

Boarding schools in particular can be very closed worlds but abuse can occur at any school, anywhere. Fame is no protection, and nor is obscurity. Some kinds of school, though, need to take particular care – and how they do this should be obvious to you when you visit. International schools have transient pupil populations, and teachers whose histories may be overseas and hard to research. Specialist music teaching necessarily involves a good deal of physical contact with the teacher and the pupil alone in a closed room. Religious schools may have a system of authority that serves to keep abuse concealed. Special schools may have to deal with a large range of communication and emotional difficulties.

What can you do?

Parents should talk to their children – gently but seriously – about the dangers, however remote these may be. It is worth pointing out that abuse can come from anyone – including a teacher or an adult they know well, or from another child at the school. Having this discussion will make it easier for a child to come to you with anything they're worried about.

When visiting a school, inquire about the steps taken to safeguard children in the same way you might ask about bullying or learning support. As always, much can be gleaned from the head's attitude when questions about child protection are asked. Is he or she ill at ease or happy to engage and proud of the steps their school has taken? Openness is what you're looking for.

You could also ask about how a child or parent would go about reporting an incident. Schools make this possible in a variety of ways; what matters is that passing on concerns is a routine thing (children and parents do it about lots of things all the time), and is welcomed by the school. Doing this should be low-stakes, in other words the person registering the concern knows that they are not putting their relationships within the school at risk, let alone threatening someone's place in the school. That may seem an odd thing to say, but if you fear to report, say, careless management of a museum trip because it could harm an otherwise much-loved teacher, you might choose to keep quiet. An environment that seems hostile to raising such concerns may mean you never pass on those troubling observations that may be the outward indication of serious problems. To be safe, schools need to hear the little voices, not just the shouting.

And finally, do not think less of a school because a case of abuse has been brought to light there. Tabloid coverage can be the price the school has to pay for handling a case of abuse or bullying openly. It is inevitable that abuse will occur somewhere. What matters is how well the school deals with it, how well it performs in bringing the abuse to light and how open it is on the subject with current and future parents.

The Good Schools Guide Education Consultants

The Good Schools Guide has been trusted by generations of parents to provide expert, honest and unbiased information about schools. Our education consultancy provides the same high standards of expertise, independence and professional integrity to individual families. Every day our highly experienced consultants successfully help clients from all over the world find the right schools for their children. However urgent the deadline, however complex the circumstances, call 0203 286 6824 (UK) or +44 203 286 6824 (international) or email consultants@goodschoolsguide.co.uk to find out how we can solve your educational dilemmas.

Our consultants

All our consultants have personally visited and reviewed countless schools for our website and publications; many also have professional backgrounds or specialist qualifications in education. Between them they have direct experience of every aspect of both the British and international education systems, not to mention invaluable local knowledge about schools in London and all areas of the UK. Our team includes experts in SEN, school appeals, scholarships and bursaries, grammar schools and relocation to the UK from abroad.

Consultancy built around your needs

Our consultancy packages range from a 30-minute telephone consultation to a fully bespoke service tailored to meet complex, urgent or other specific circumstances. Additional services include accompanied school visits, providing translators and educational assessments and arranging specialist tuition. We can also provide detailed information on scholarships and bursaries. For full details please visit www.goodschoolsguide.co.uk

Full, weekly and flexi boarding options available
Excellent GCSE, A Level and IB results
Exciting extra-curricular programme including competitive sailing
Two new award-winning boarding houses in the school grounds in Ryde

OPEN MORNINGS:
www.rydeschool.org.uk/open-days-visits

FOR MORE INFORMATION
Call **+44 (0)1983 617970** or
visit **www.rydeschool.org.uk**

Queen's Road, Ryde, Isle of Wight, PO33 3BE

RYDE SCHOOL
WITH UPPER CHINE

An Island School with a Global Outlook

– More than just a school...
...a true community in the widest sense

A co-educational country prep school in a beautiful setting, combining outstanding academic and extra-curricular success, with a culture of kindness founded on Catholic principles.

Moor Park - Ludlow - Shropshire - SY8 4DZ
www.moorpark.org.uk head@moorpark.org.uk

The British student's guide to great universities in the USA from Harvard to Yale

Tells you how to choose, how to apply and how to pay

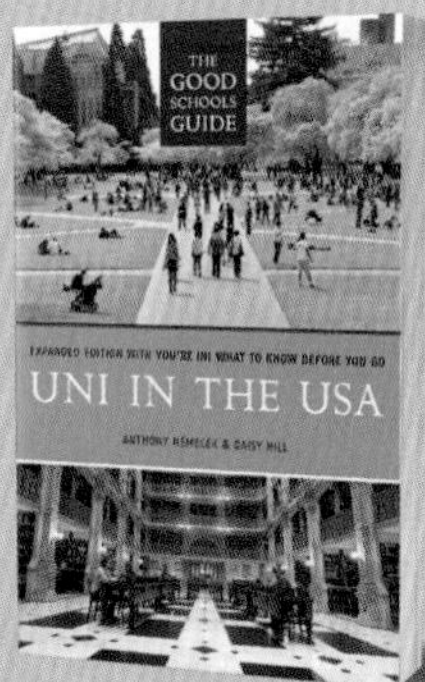

UNI IN THE USA
THE GOOD SCHOOLS GUIDE

£25 for the book or 12-month subscription
goodschoolsguide.co.uk/university

BEESTON HALL SCHOOL
CO-EDUCATIONAL PREPARATORY SCHOOL, AGED 4-13

Outstanding education on
the North Norfolk coast

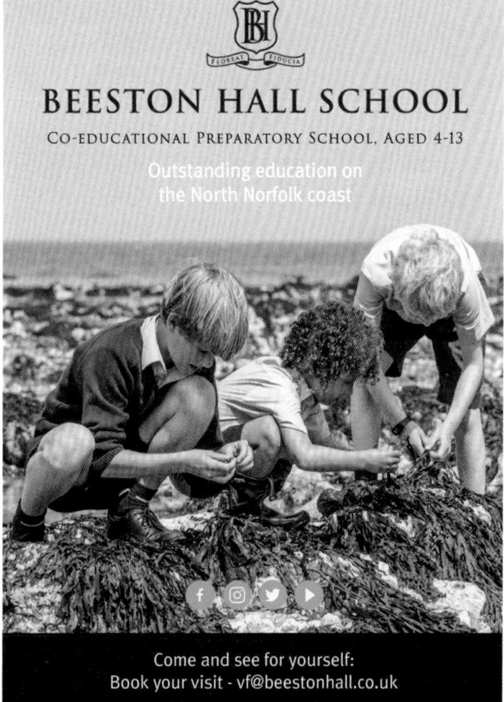

Come and see for yourself:
Book your visit - vf@beestonhall.co.uk

WWW.BEESTONHALL.CO.UK

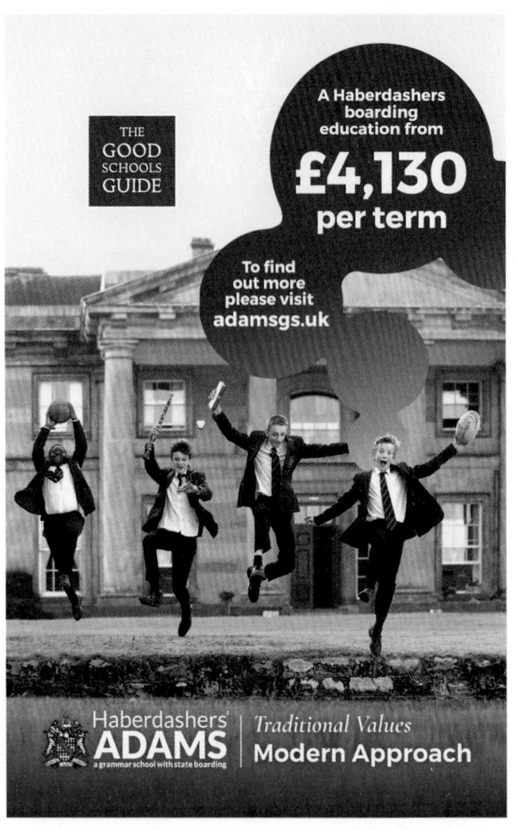
THE GOOD SCHOOLS GUIDE
A Haberdashers boarding education from
£4,130
per term
To find out more please visit
adamsgs.uk
Haberdashers' ADAMS
a grammar school with state boarding
Traditional Values
Modern Approach

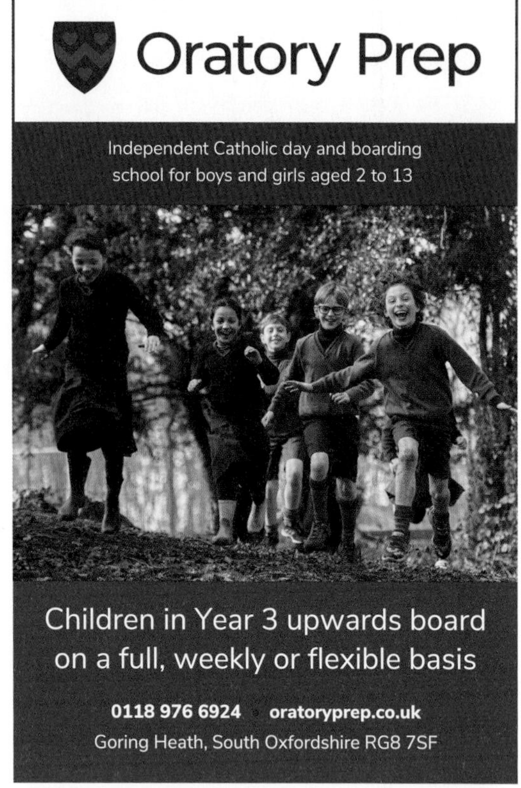
Oratory Prep
Independent Catholic day and boarding school for boys and girls aged 2 to 13
Children in Year 3 upwards board on a full, weekly or flexible basis
0118 976 6924 · oratoryprep.co.uk
Goring Heath, South Oxfordshire RG8 7SF

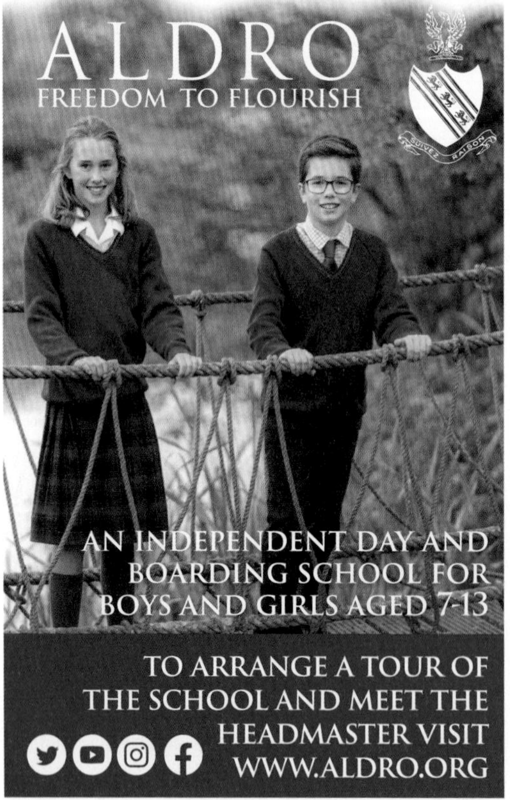
ALDRO
FREEDOM TO FLOURISH
AN INDEPENDENT DAY AND BOARDING SCHOOL FOR BOYS AND GIRLS AGED 7-13
TO ARRANGE A TOUR OF THE SCHOOL AND MEET THE HEADMASTER VISIT
WWW.ALDRO.ORG

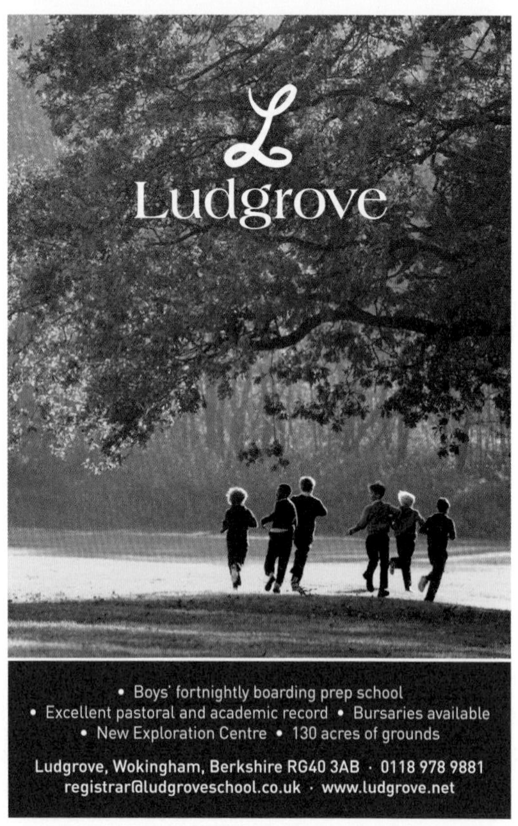
Ludgrove
• Boys' fortnightly boarding prep school
• Excellent pastoral and academic record • Bursaries available
• New Exploration Centre • 130 acres of grounds
Ludgrove, Wokingham, Berkshire RG40 3AB · 0118 978 9881
registrar@ludgroveschool.co.uk · www.ludgrove.net

Contact us

Phone us on +44 (0)203 286 6824 or send a brief email to consultants@goodschoolsguide.co.uk outlining what you need. Tell us the age of your child and where you live plus your contact details. We will contact you within 48 hours, discuss how best to help you and ensure we match you with the right consultant. Consultations can be by phone, email or face to face, and we can find a consultant to speak to you within an hour if necessary.

How much?

Ours is one of the most competitively priced tailor-made education consultancy services in the UK. Check our website for current fees.

Our guarantee

The Good Schools Guide has an international reputation for providing unbiased, independent advice on educational matters. We have no commercial links whatsoever with any school. This gives our educational consultants the freedom to consider a huge range of schools in order to find the best one for you. You can have complete confidence that if our consultants recommend a school it is because, and only because, they consider it to be suitable for your child. You can also be assured that we maintain the highest possible standards of privacy and all dealings with clients are completely confidential.

Because no-one said you have to do it alone.

Our consultants know the best schools for every type of special need.

The Good Schools Guide Education Consultants

0203 286 6824 | goodschoolsguide.co.uk/SEN | consultants@goodschoolsguide.co.uk

South West

City of Bristol
Cornwall
Devon
Dorset
Gloucestershire
Somerset
Wiltshire

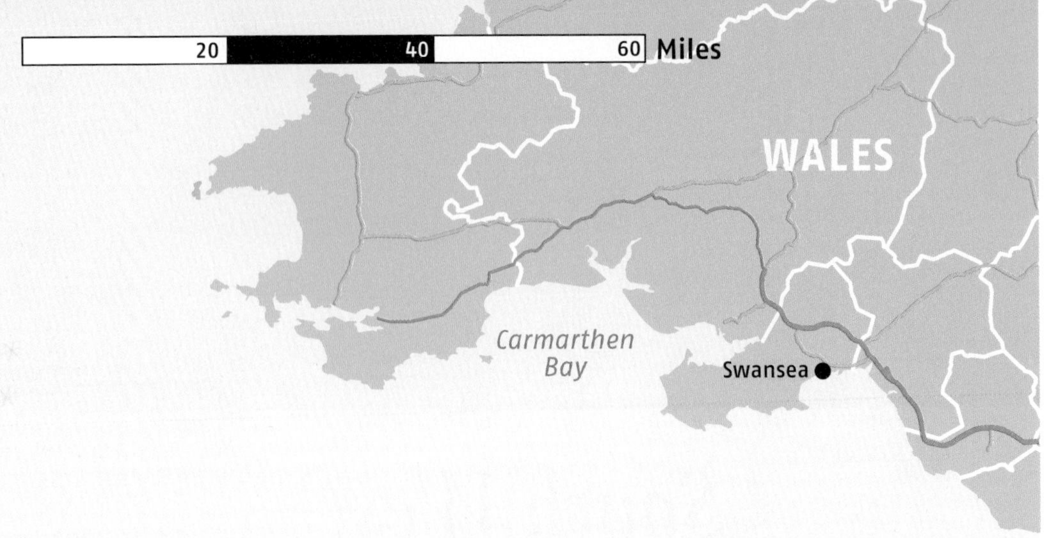
20
40
60 Miles
WALES
Carmarthen Bay
Swansea
Bristol Channel
Minehead
68
Barnstaple Bay
Barnstaple
29
53
Bude
DEVON
21
Exeter
59
41
40
Tavistock
63
Torquay
44
Newquay
CORNWALL &
ISLES OF SCILLY
Plymouth
64
65
Truro
Penzance

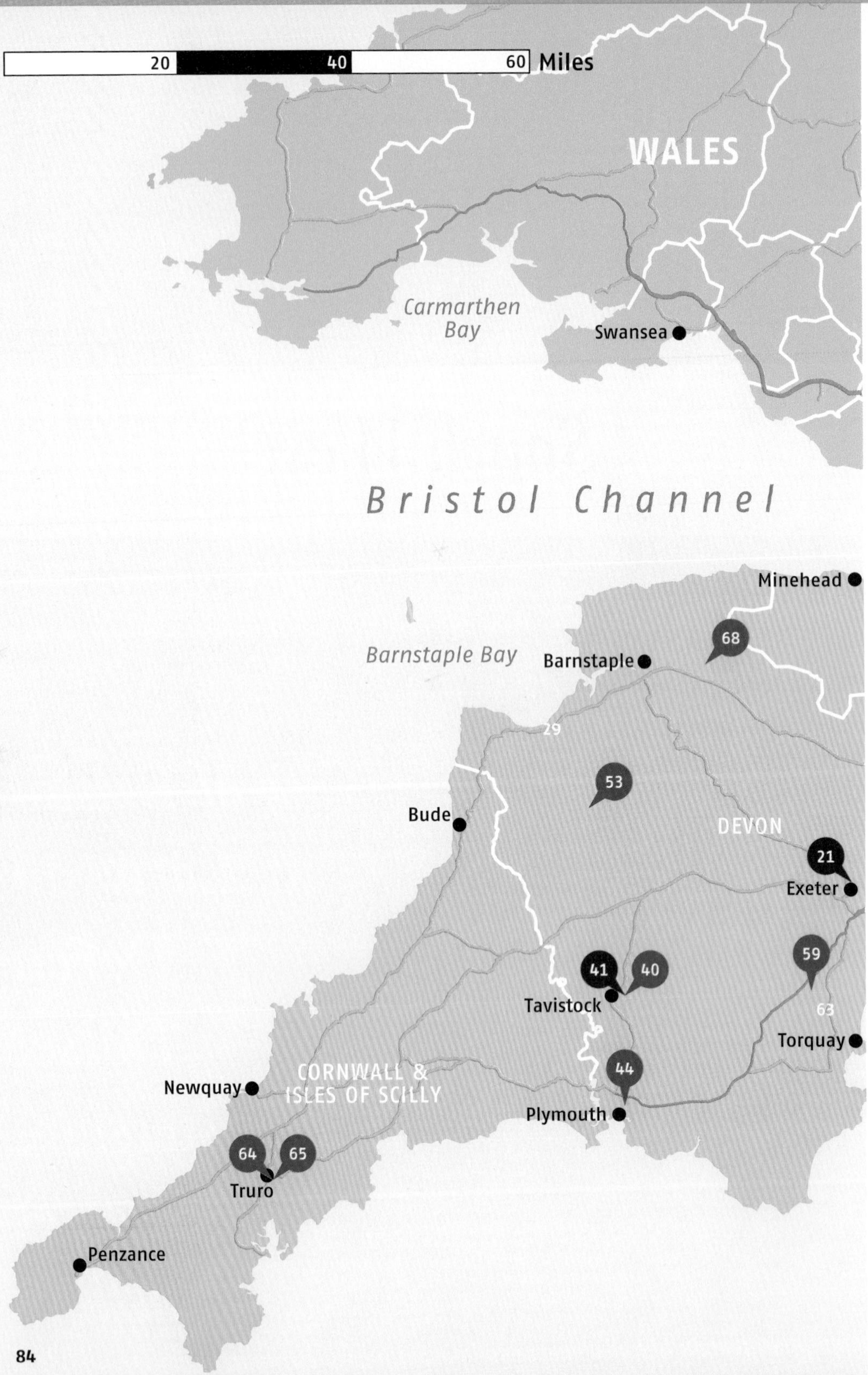

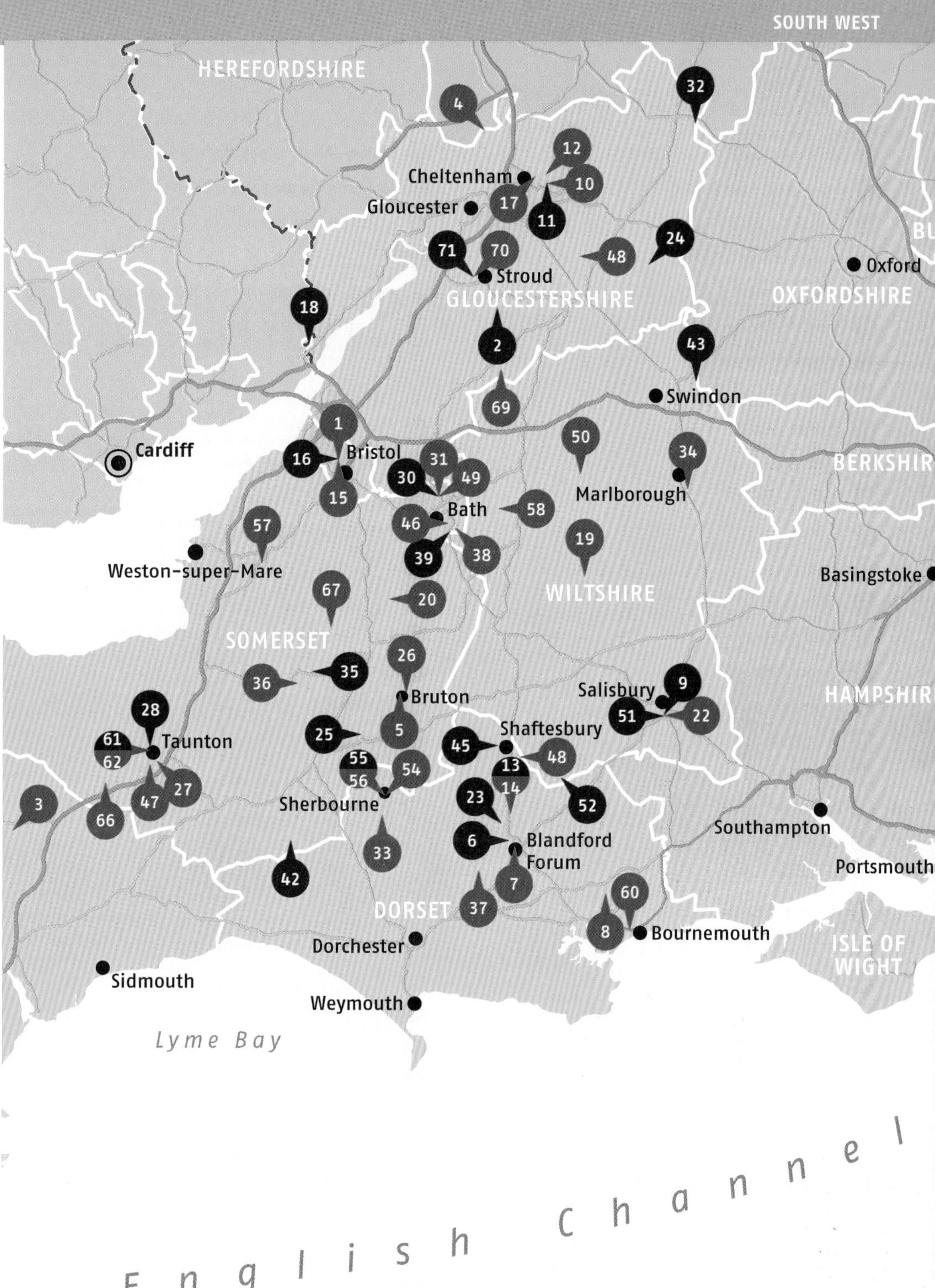
HEREFORDSHIRE
GLOUCESTERSHIRE
OXFORDSHIRE
BERKSHIRE
WILTSHIRE
SOMERSET
HAMPSHIRE
DORSET
ISLE OF WIGHT
Cheltenham
Gloucester
Stroud
Oxford
Swindon
Cardiff
Bristol
Bath
Marlborough
Weston-super-Mare
Basingstoke
Bruton
Salisbury
Shaftesbury
Taunton
Sherbourne
Blandford Forum
Southampton
Portsmouth
Bournemouth
Dorchester
Sidmouth
Weymouth
Lyme Bay
English Channel

SOUTH WEST

Badminton School

Westbury Road, Westbury-on-Trym, Bristol BS9 3BA

01179 055271 | admissions@badmintonschool.co.uk | www.badmintonschool.co.uk

Ages: 11-18

Pupils: 550; sixth form: 105; Boarders: 180 full

Fees: Day £10,395- 17,430; Boarding £23,700 – £40,500 pa

Headmistress: Since 2012, Rebecca Tear (40s) BSc MA PGCE. Her degree in chemistry from Exeter preceded a career in teaching science almost exclusively to girls, and which included other significant responsibilities, eg head of sixth form and deputy head at Wycombe Abbey, taking in a master's in leadership in education along the way. An unequivocal believer in single sex education from her early teaching practice, where she saw how the less confident girls needed bringing out in lessons, she says, 'Teaching girls by themselves breaks down any preconceptions, barriers or stereotyping; when subjects don't acquire masculine or feminine connotations, girls tend to make more realistic personal choices.'

Somewhat jolly hockey sticks in manner – she strode across the drawing room, extending a hand and introducing herself as 'Bex' – we warmed to her no-nonsense and open personality; staff describe her as a real hit with the girls. For her part, Mrs Tear has made strenuous efforts to bring parents and guardians into school more: new ventures like the summer fair and fireworks night have been welcomed. 'I don't want the first time I meet a parent to be in a bad news situation,' she says.

Married to another chemistry teacher, she has two sons who doubtless counterbalance all those girls. Passions include outdoorsy things like running, ski-ing and cycling with her family, and she is a keen cook – though at home she regrets the lack of a lab technician to wash up for her.

Entrance: Most arrive in year 7, but everyone below sixth form is required to sit papers in English (English as a foreign language for those who have been at school in the UK for less than two years) and maths and to do an online reasoning test. The transition from the junior school is not automatic and girls do exactly the same assessments as those coming from elsewhere (in practice, the vast majority are accepted). Sixth form hopefuls must sit papers in two of the subjects they intend studying at A level, plus a general paper. All applicants are interviewed, via Skype when necessary. School prefers overseas girls to do UKiset.

Exit: Some fall-out after GCSEs (around a quarter) from day girls wanting pastures new, and perhaps boys in particular. Those who stay go to prestigious universities, including two overseas in 2021 – to NYU and Boston College. London is the most popular destination, also Durham, Edinburgh and Bristol, and a good handful to Oxbridge most years (four in 2021). Wide choice of degree courses, more sciences than arts. Six medics in 2021.

Latest results: In 2021, 77 per cent 9-7 at GCSE; at A level 80 per cent A*/A (92 per cent A*-B). In 2019 (the last year when exams took place), 78 per cent 9-7 at GCSE: 56 per cent A*/A (85 per cent A*-B).

Teaching and learning: Selective entry, rigorous exam preparation and small classes (averaging 14 until GCSE) all the way through the school make for stunning results, and a reputation as Bristol's most academic school. Majority of girls take four A levels (newest subject offered is dance). GCSE options are (unusually) not blocked, so virtually any subject combination is possible (newest subject offered is business). SAT training also provided for those hoping to go to American universities.

Girls greatly encouraged to take on all manner of academic challenges outside school; one recently came in the top 50 of the intermediate maths Olympiad, and a few presented by invitation of CERN and the Institute of Physics at WOMAD in 2018. Everyone does English Speaking Board exams, which, for the year 8 class we visited, involved learning, reciting and discussing chunks of poetry – a Shakespeare sonnet in one case. Years 8 and 9 are also offered a 10-week STEM experience with engineering or manufacturing companies with Go4SET. Global Thinking Skills course for year 9 'which combines enhancing the girls' knowledge of the world they live in alongside developing their ability to think critically'. 'They push them, but not in any way too much,' said one mother, who also appreciated the way teachers go over work with individuals when they find it difficult.

Learning support and SEN: SEN provision is modest – not much call for it here – and all now delivered by 'flexible in-house support'. More emphasis is given to extending the gifted and talented – a term the school avoids. EAL is also offered in school to support overseas girls.

The arts and extracurricular: Artistic life flourishes, with top notch music, drama and art. Much is rightly made of high-calibre musicians (one to the Royal College on Saturdays, two to the National Children's Orchestra, several playing in city orchestras, a recent leaver in training for The Sixteen) and school is fortunate to perform in St George's Bristol, a national concert venue. Most girls learn one instrument if not two, and school is proud of the number and scope of ensembles it lays on for musicians of all standards and persuasions. New music building has enabled school to bring all of its music teaching and practice activities to a single location and created a new focus for the department. The building includes teaching and practice rooms, a new music library and a generous classroom for curricular music lessons. Drama reasonably prominent too, with six productions a year plus a staff pantomime, as well as collaborations with outside initiatives at local innovative theatre the Tobacco Factory and Garden Opera, recently as a chorus of urchins in Carmen. Several notable actresses are OBs: Clare Bloom, Phyllida Law and Rosamund Pike.

Achievement of all kinds is recognised, but interestingly there is no honours board; the only prize awarded is the Iris Murdoch (an OB) prize for creative writing

Art is housed in a most appealing setting, where mannequins dressed in creations fit for a Milan catwalk grace the entrance. Textiles, ceramics, painting, digital media (aka photography) and all types of artistic endeavour go on here. Badminton girls gain places at prestigious colleges such as Central St Martins.

Sport: Games and sports are now exceedingly well catered for (Astro, tennis courts, netball courts, 25m pool, and since 2018 an eye-catching new sports hall incorporating cricket nets and climbing wall) on the school's site, unlike so many of Bristol's schools, whose playing fields are a bus ride away across the suspension bridge. Hockey, netball, tennis and swimming are the main sports, but an innovative range of activities including kickboxing and water polo means that no-one has an excuse to be idle. Badminton's riders have enjoyed success too. Hockey and netball players are regularly selected for the county. One parent was unhappy that only top players were ever picked for teams, and that mediocre participants barely got a game (school says they now have a C team and offer wider variety of sports). Swimming pool used by local state schools for a few hours a week.

Boarding: From age 9, although there's only a handful of junior boarders. Boarders accommodated in three houses grouped by age – Bartlett houses girls from years 5-8, spanning both junior and senior schools. Sanderson is the newest build for the middle girls; sixth formers are separate. One parent reported a tendency to cliques among the girls, which she felt the school did little to address, and that it 'feels like a boarding school which day girls attend'; another felt that integration was fine.

Weekends fairly relaxed for those who stay in school: girls might be involved in sports or drama, off on a surfing trip, going out for a meal or to the theatre. As elsewhere boarders from abroad are required to have a guardian, but here they do so much more than that rather dry word suggests and are more like surrogate mums – we applaud this.

Ethos and heritage: Founded over 160 years ago, Badminton is older than most girls' schools of its type and was set up to provide the same educational opportunities for girls as their brothers enjoyed. That sense of academic seriousness, courage, confidence and an international outlook still prevail – girls here tackle any academic challenge head-on. Originally sited in Badminton House in nearby Clifton, it moved to its present premises on the edge of the downs in Bristol, arguably the greenest and most desirable part of the city. Main building is Georgian and gracious (we were ushered in to a warm and luxuriously carpeted drawing room, where Classic FM played discreetly); over the years the site has been filled in with all sorts of additions of varying degrees of beauty, making the school compact, rather than crowded. Nestling on the edge of the Badminton site, the junior school is certainly the senior school's little sister and firmly under its wing.

Groups of girls scurry purposefully about the place in their practical uniform of blue shirts, sweaters and checked skirts. 'Why no trousers?' asked one mum. Sixth form dress is much less restricted than in some schools: torn jeans and strappy tops are out, otherwise more or less anything goes.

Male company is provided mostly by QEH, Bristol's only remaining boys' school (which now

Main building is Georgian and gracious. We were ushered into a luxuriously carpeted drawing room where Classic FM played discreetly

admits sixth form girls) – academic and social interactions, we gather, which include a shared minibus from Chepstow.

Old Badmintonians include Indira Ghandi and Princess Haya bint Hussein of Jordan.

Pastoral care, inclusivity and discipline: Discipline, inasmuch as it is needed in this high-achieving environment, works on girls' general desire to please, and dislike of letting people down, so the head might well say, 'I am rather disappointed that I have to speak to you, Jemima' on the rare occasions that girls come before her. Smoking, alcohol and drugs will lead sinners straight to her study. Achievement of all kinds is recognised, but interestingly there is no honours board, and school's annual open day is more about displays, demonstrations, music, drama and food than interminable speechifying; the only prize awarded is the Iris Murdoch (another OB) prize for creative writing.

Pastoral care reads as well as one would expect for a school like this, with a tutor assigned to each girl, a vertical house system and peer mentoring, but one mother told us her daughter's confidence had been undermined by too great an emphasis on academics, and too little on making supportive friendships.

Pupils and parents: Quite mixed socially and ethnically, but united by high academic expectations and aspirations. We found the girls friendly, unpretentious and open-minded – and were pleased to see some tucking into the sponge pudding we are probably no longer allowed to call spotted dick. 'The school does not turn out a mass product,' said one mother with several years' knowledge.

Overseas girls are welcome here and come in droves, mostly from Hong Kong but a good few from Russia and Nigeria; a sprinkling from the rest of the world. Bristol's own ethnic and religious mix well represented and catered for too: any dish containing pork was firmly labelled at lunch.

Money matters: Fees are much in line with comparable schools, though boarders from outside the EU pay over £2,000 more per year to cover the cost of escorted journeys to UK international airports – and of the boarding travel co-ordinator. Scholarships are awarded to a maximum of 20 per cent of fees; bursaries are means tested. Newish regional award for girls 'who will bring something special to Badminton'; the school intends this as a way to recognise wider achievement and potential than the range of scholarships currently on offer.

The last word: Undoubtedly a distinguished Bristol institution, yet its size, compact site, high proportion of boarders and fearsome academic reputation (which frightens some off) mean it enjoys a lower profile than it should in the city. The head describes it as a hidden gem, so her mission, should she choose to accept it, is perhaps to polish up all its facets so it shines a brighter local light.

Beaudesert Park School

2

Minchinhampton, Gloucestershire GL6 9AF

01453 832072 | office@bps.school | www.beaudesert.gloucs.sch.uk

Ages: 3-13

Pupils: 400; Boarders: 160 flexi

Fees: Day £10,050 – £13,830; Boarding £23,790 pa Flexi-boarding £40 per night

Headmaster: Since 2018, Chris Searson BA (40s). An English degree from Warwick preceded spells at several prep schools in the south of England and several roles including head of drama, houseparent and SENCO, all of which were doubtless useful for this, his first headship. He came most recently from Highfield, a special place in his heart as he met his delightful wife Harriet there and somewhere he thought he would find hard to leave. 'The Beaudesert job was the only one my previous boss had ever pushed my way – and I didn't think I'd get it!' he admitted disarmingly.

'But when I visited, I realised Beaudesert was somewhere I could fall in love with. Those first impressions are still with me.'

Very different from the previous ebullient, eccentric and longstanding head, Mr Searson countered our question about making Beaudesert his own with what we learnt was typical modesty: 'I won't – the school is so much bigger than the head.' Changes have not come too thick and fast: lessons are now 50 minutes instead of 35, and Saturday school, though still compulsory from year 5, has been revamped so that everyone goes home at lunchtime. And how has he gone down? Very well, according to the parents and children we spoke to. 'Energetic, cheerful and always smiling,' our charming chatty lunching companions told us. 'Visible and receptive,' say parents – and keen to encourage links with the local community and its schools. 'This will be a very different school in six to seven years' time reflecting today's more diverse society, once Chris has brought it into the modern age,' one perceptive mother remarked and we doubt he will ever acquire the complacency or cockiness of some heads we meet.

Much takes place on the school's own 30 acres, but it's a tradition to run like mad across the common to its extramural windswept pitches. No minibus molly-coddling here!

Enjoys family time with his two children (both in the school), riding his bike (with small daughter on the back), walking his dog and spending time outside. 'I couldn't live in a city,' he smiled with a shudder.

Entrance: Completely non-selective and remarkably straightforward. Two open days per year and/or a tour with the head precede an invitation to spend half a day or a day at the school to those who intend joining it.

Exit: To a range of state and independent schools, both at 11 and 13 (Beaudesert has no senior school exerting a pull). These include Marlborough College, Eton, Cheltenham Ladies' College, Cheltenham College, St Edward's Oxford, Malvern College. 'The children's faces pop into my head as I walk round senior schools,' the head revealed. The Gloucestershire grammar schools' formidable reputation and absence of fees make them an attractive proposition for the brightest and egalitarian sparks at 11; the majority, however, go on to some of the UK's most prestigious independent schools at 13, many collecting awards en route. Head does not shrink from discouraging parents set on the wrong choice of senior school; equally, some parents feel detailed advice on matters such as Eton housemasters needs sharpening up.

Our view: Founded as a boys' prep school in Henley-in-Arden in 1908 and named after a long-defunct Norman castle nearby, the school spent only 10 years there before moving to Gloucestershire, and to a mock-Tudor Victorian country house high on Minchinhampton Common with its roaming bovines and stunning views across the steep valley to Nailsworth. Stylish modern timber-clad additions such as the performing arts complex and Qube teaching block, whose windows look straight out into the trees, only enhance the setting. Wide curriculum which includes two modern languages and one ancient one. We liked the look of the range of lessons we popped into: the youngest children were designing wellies for a welly walk topic, year 5 discussing the difference between carnivores and omnivores, while older children were head down in English comprehension and algebra. Mixed-ability teaching for all until year 4 when children are set for maths; English and French follow in year 5. Although the teaching looks traditional, there is plenty of IT gadgetry – it just isn't allowed to dominate the teaching. Parents like the mix of 'old school' and 'lightning rods' among the staff and the head is proud of the 'perfect balance between youth and experience'. English, history, geography and the sciences get a particular thumbs-up from the pupils. Form tutors oversee academic progress and general well-being, but some parents think academic work has not been taken sufficiently seriously, and that CE preparation has been patchy. Initiatives such as interview practice have been welcomed.

SEND provision has been thought inadequate in the past, resulting in a posse of mothers demanding improvements. One-to-one sessions are paid for separately and take place in what at least one parent considers rather a cramped space; other support happens in class. Usual specific difficulties catered for by specialists. No mention on the school website of autism spectrum disorders, let alone neurodiversity, but the school is turning a spotlight on this increasingly common incidence, and devising support packages to ease the passage of those children through school. Parents with SEN provision at the top of their agenda might like to compare the offering with other nearby schools.

If fresh air and fun were the cure to all ills, then nothing would be amiss at Beaudesert. Young lungs are oxygenated between lessons as pupils scurry between buildings, and there is simply masses of sport. Usual offer of rugby/hockey/netball enlivened by the addition of football for the boys and cricket for the girls, plus tennis and athletics in the summer. Much takes place on the school's own 30 acres, but it's a tradition to run like mad across the common to its extramural windswept pitches. No minibus molly-coddling here! This being Gloucestershire, there are strong equestrian teams across all disciplines – but only for those who have their own ponies. Otherwise, riding can be done as an activity at local stables. Indoor and outdoor swimming pools complete a fantastic array of sport appreciated by all we spoke to, though 'extreme measures need to be taken to water down the alpha rugby threat,' in the words of one mother, who reckoned there was too little choice apart from organised team games and gender-typical sports. 'We're addressing that and introducing a greater range of individual and non-ball sports,' the head assured us. 'We're a "sport-for-all school" with as much importance placed on enjoyment and participation as winning.' Like it or loathe it, the emphasis on rugby pays off: at the time of writing, the first team were unbeaten through the whole season.

Activities take place on four weekday afternoons all year round – and there's a lot of choice, from the cerebral (ancient Greek) to the creative (super doodling) to the strenuous (mountain biking). In an effort to introduce a bit of urban grit to the rural idyll which is Beaudesert, trips to the local skate park are laid on and privilege checked by means of community service. The sensational performing arts centre hosts too many dramatic and musical ensembles to list, but 'Oliver with a Twist' was a recent year 8 production. Informal concerts encourage débutant players and singers. The art department is fortunate enough to boast a fully equipped pottery studio, laser cutter and 3D printer. Much of the (very impressive) work is the pupils' response to and interpretation of existing artists.

Houses are not a particular feature of Beaudesert life, but the head has plans to develop them, not in terms of a physical base, more as a place of allegiance and cohesion of a vertical grouping of children. 'However, I don't want to encourage overt competition between them,' he assured us.

Kindness and respect for oneself and everyone else are the watchwords at Beaudesert, and we were assured by the children we spoke to that there were plenty of adults to go to with worries, unhappiness or confusion. A system of credits records good work, behaviour and deeds; any debits are 'worked off by doing helpful jobs', unless they stack up to a point where a detention is imposed. Rules and discipline do not seem to loom large: in fact, the freedom to roam the entirety of the grounds, get muddy and climb trees (conditional on getting your tree licence!) just add to the charm of the place. We saw only one child with his arm in plaster...

One view which we heard over and over was that the best thing about the school is the emphasis placed on the innocence of childhood, and prolonging it as long as possible

Beaudesert's reputation in certain affluent circles as 'the only prep school in Gloucestershire' still attracts that kind of socially influential family, with a side order of 'flashy showbiz types', according to one mother. Beloved of and known to those making the big move out of London, the school reinforces its overwhelmingly white middle class image by bottle green uniform (Tattersall checked shirts for the boys, tartan pinnies for the littler girls), lots of snazzy monogrammed sports kit and a car park crammed with 4x4s. We picked up some unease about a lack of diversity, not just in the pupil profile, but in the views of more than one parent about the importance of exposing children to the notion of other families very different to their own in terms of income, comfort and societal norms. The head was at pains to tell us about the existence of tricky family circumstances of a few children and of his previous experience of supporting children questioning or experiencing alternative sexuality, if not family life, but the impression is one of endemic homogeneity and conformity. 'We need to get better at sharing with parents what we do in school on different life experiences and stories in the PHSE curriculum and through external speakers,' he concedes. Sensitive ground here of course: one aspect of Beaudesert which we heard over and over was the best thing about the school is the emphasis placed on the innocence of childhood, and prolonging it as long as possible by keeping children away from life's grittier realities by, inter alia, banning all mobile technology. Innocent and unselfconscious children yes, but not blind to difference or inhibited from expressing it.

Boarding: Boarding, which takes place only during the week (max five nights), occupies the upper storeys of the main house, girls and boys housed on separate creaky floors. The boys sleep in a series of interconnected rooms without doors, the girls in rooms of up to six beds, and the set-up is clean and homely, not to say scruffy round the edges. But they (mostly) love it, hot-bunking and all, with its snappy system of rolling up bedding and remaking the bed for the next occupant. Parents must make a firm and regular booking for their offspring, bearing in mind that different year groups are allocated different nights. No drop-in boarding.

The last word: A charming, slightly bonkers place to work, rest and play, Beaudesert lets kids be kids for as long as they can – 'Don't grow up too fast!' as the wooden height measure in the head's office exhorts. But Mr Searson's mark on the school could and should be to rub a few of the magic sprinkles off the windswept windows of Beaudesert and let in a view of a more complex contemporary world.

Blundell's School

Blundell's Road, Tiverton, Devon EX16 4DN

01884 252543 | registrars@blundells.org | www.blundells.org

Ages: 3-18

Pupils: 615; sixth form: 203; Boarders: 127 full, 152 weekly/flexi

Fees: Day £15,135 – £24,015; Boarding £17,520 – £38,985 pa

Head: Since 2018, Bart Wielenga BCom BEd (40s), former deputy. Born in Holland but brought up and educated in South Africa with degrees in economics and HR, Mr Wielenga was all set for a career in management consulting until, as he laughingly admits, he was 'conned into teaching' during his postgrad gap year. Spells at Michaelhouse in Kwa Zulu Natal and at Wellington College as head of economics and housemaster preceded his arrival at Blundell's in 2012 – 'I have never minded the idea of a doing a long apprenticeship,' he muses – where he has turned his unflinching gaze on process in the school. 'Results are the product of good process, especially as we are not particularly academically selective,' he states firmly, adding that academic and pastoral aims must be coherent. His near miss as a management consultant became evident as we delved further, with the culling of some sacred cows and much emphasis placed on how Blundell's can 'do things better – it's not enough just to be normal. I want it to be distinctive.' Initiatives to startle Blundell's out of any Devon torpor include efforts to take on teachers with overseas experience (from Singapore, Malaysia and Abu Dhabi for example) and to 'recruit well, but recruit young'. The pandemic saw the school as well prepared as it could be to tackle the many challenges it necessitated: 'I am thankful that we installed a whole new communication platform just before it started,' said Mr Wielenga, still visibly relieved, 'and we have learnt a lot about how and when children work, as well as giving them an incredible opportunity to try out new things and take ownership of their own learning.' He has gone down well with parents, who like his calmness (not least during the pandemic), his down-to-earth approach coupled with, in the words of one father, 'his inspired vision for education'. Time away from work entails a lot of time outdoors with his beach-loving sporty family (two sons both at the school); longer trips back to South Africa and its game reserves when time permits. Holiday reading? Classy historical fiction such as CJ Sansom, Robert Harris and Bernard Cornwell.

The prep school has been headed by Andy Southgate BA Ed (40s) since 2011. Raised in Maidstone, but ventured westwards for his degree in physical education and history at St Luke's Exeter, after which he spent the first 13 years of his career at Moulsford Prep, ending up as deputy head. Our last review described him as 'impossibly youthful' and despite now having two teenage children in the senior school, this description is still fair; his live performances (antics on occasion!) during lockdown became legendary. His aim has been to 'build a culture of aspiration tempered with warmth and kindness' and parents have been fulsome in their praise of the latter. Both he and Laura Clifford, head of pre-prep are approachable and visible – popular too, judging by the enthusiastic greeting they received from children during our tour.

Entrance: The prep school will take all comers, only turning away children 'who would not thrive in this environment'. Transition to the senior school is generally seamless (existing pupils do entrance exams only for scholarship purposes, to the dismay of at least one dad), with any doubtful runners being identified by about year 4 to give parents the chance to look for alternatives. Children from elsewhere sit the school's own entrance tests for entry to year 7; Common Entrance at 13+ or entry tests in maths and English for those whose previous schools don't cater for it. At sixth form, the minimum requirement is five GCSEs at a grade 5 or above, though in practice this tends to be much higher for external candidates especially, plus interview. For most A level choices, 6s are required, 7s for sciences and maths.

Exit: Very few leave the prep school for other senior destinations, although a handful depart to do CE for traditional public schools elsewhere. Senior school leavers pursue a variety of courses up and down the land, with over 90 per cent gaining a place 'at the university of their choice'. Half to Russell Group. Durham, Newcastle, Cardiff, Exeter, Reading, Edinburgh, UCL, Bath and Bristol popular.

Latest results: In 2021, 76 per cent 9-7 at GCSE; 68 per cent A*/A at A level (87 per cent A*-B). In 2019 (the last year exams took place), 56 per cent 9-7 at GCSE; 40 per cent A*/A at A level (68 per cent A*-B).

Teaching and learning: A Blundell's education is about so much more than exams and results, which are very much regarded as a passport to the next stage, rather than an end in themselves. As such, pastoral care and the development of character (taught as a discrete lesson by the head) go hand in hand with academic life. Nine GCSEs are now the norm, with school feeling that students could be doing something more profitable or interesting than that 10th GCSE. Twenty-one subjects on offer with Mandarin, Italian and Greek by arrangement; at A level, the choice expands to 27 which includes ethics and philosophy, and film studies. While online learning seemed to employ huge amounts of technical wizardry, the teaching we witnessed in school looked traditional, with some studious younger pupils head down in a junior maths challenge and others being taught the subtleties of French phonetics, listening to the difference between 'poisson' and 'poison' – crucial. Academic scholars are stretched with a specifically designed programme, but anyone can sign up for the phoenix society 'for the intellectually curious'. One parent described the teaching as 'rigorous, lively and consistent' – high quality across the board. Lockdown has provided an unexpected opportunity to see how young people learn and the notion of periods of deep and intense work carrying on until a task is done is gaining momentum. Another forthright parent also reckoned the school had benefitted from a 'good shake-up' from Covid, but that academic focus still needs about 10 per cent more input. Worth noting though that even the younger children are taught not just the three Rs, fact and figure, but – just as importantly – how to learn. In the pre-prep, learning is thematic – the topic of minibeasts looked at obvious things like habitat but also shapes and indeed butterfly cakes. Much use is made of the generous outdoor space, including the school's version of forest school, Wild Wonders – not just for fun, but as a genuine adjunct to learning in the classroom, eg reading tepees. The outdoorsiness for which Blundell's is famed starts early! Specialist teachers from the prep school complete the offering with French, music and games.

Learning support and SEN: At entry to the pre-prep, any difficulties in speech are language are identified straightaway often by class teachers and according to the SENCo, dyscalculia is on the rise. Interventions are put in place early, but the staff are conscious of developmental variations. Although most special needs are well catered for (school enjoys good relationships with the county SENCo), accommodating profound difficulties such as severe autism are beyond the school's capability. We heard praise for the way the pre-prep school handles a child who is 'not easy' in the words of his mother; another said they had 'worked miracles' on her son. About 10 per cent of senior school students receive support in English, maths, study skills or executive function. Any potential access needs for public exams are looked at in year 10.

The arts and extracurricular: The Ondaatje Hall, named for the generous OB and philanthropist who endowed it, is the jewel in the crown of performing arts facilities – used mostly for drama, and on the day we visited, the scene of an A level devised piece on the rituals of going out, something close to sixth formers' hearts post-pandemic, we imagine. The range of speech and drama exams taken, plus the opportunity to take part in three whole-school plays per year (one musical), several house plays and a play reading group all place drama centre stage at Blundell's. Three students have been offered places at competitive drama schools in the past year.

Music does not enjoy such good premises (plans are afoot to extend the space thanks to a generous bequest), but there is plenty of it with two full orchestras, six choirs and numerous ensembles for all of the 21 instruments taught. A handful of Blundell's musicians head off to conservatoires and choral scholarships most years. A collaboration with the London Chamber Orchestra since 2016 resulted in interval music played by a Blundell's quartet as part of an online concert being streamed around the world. In the prep and pre-prep, children are encouraged to perform informally as well as more formal plays and concerts.

The art school is a beautiful space, where our eye was particularly drawn by the exciting textile work and imaginative use made of ancient bath tubs by senior artists. At A level, art is split into fine art and photography – very strong here, perhaps because students are routinely taught how to use cameras, rather than ever-present smartphones. Senior school students lay on activities such as gargoyle-making in the art school for prep school children – much enjoyed by all. DT has its own spacious premises (Popham Centre), whose excellent provision includes computer-aided graphic design and manufacturing capability and whose shelves bear impeccable wooden labels hand carved by the head of department.

Lockdown provided an unexpected opportunity to see how young people learn; the notion of deep and intense work carrying on until a task is done is gaining momentum

Simply masses on offer; the school takes full advantage of its superb position on the edge of Dartmoor for DofE, CCF and all manner of roughy-toughy character-building stuff. There may be an unfair advantage having the setting for Ten Tors on the doorstep, but that's no help for the Devizes to Westminster canoe race. Senior clubs range from the strenuous (canoeing, sailing) to the gentle (knitting for charity) via the offbeat: a Doctor Who appreciation society. In the prep school, some clubs extend timetabled learning, such as art and drama, others like yoga are unrelated; take-up is high. They run until 5.30pm and the prep and pre-prep is proud of its wraparound care. In past years, trips have gone as far as Morocco and Peru; younger children start closer to home with Exmoor Zoo and Plymouth Aquarium.

Sport: A resolutely sporty school with acres of pitches, both grass and Astro, equally at the disposal of the prep and pre-prep, who have four games sessions a week. Conventional offering for everyone below year 10, which takes in tennis, athletics and swimming in the just-about-heated outdoor pool in the summer term. Some plucky swimmers were braving it on the changeable day of our visit. Year-round swimming for the whole school takes place in the public pool in Tiverton; an indoor pool has been on the wish list for some years and planning permission has been submitted. Girls' cricket is on the up. Sports philosophy is one of making the experience enjoyable for all – but winning also matters, with plenty of success at county level and some at national, such as girls' hockey and boys' rugby sevens. It is no surprise that the school can boast quite a roll call of notable cricketers (Dom Bess, Hugh Morris) and rugby players (Matt Kvesic, Jack Maunder). Less mainstream sports also feature and enjoy success – at the time of writing, the equestrian team had just qualified for the area eventing at Hickstead.

What Blundell's is truly famous for though is the Russell, a gruelling, muddy cross-country race of about seven miles over neighbouring farmlands and the aptly named Heartbreak Hill (access granted for the occasion by local landowners). Serious training precedes this keenly anticipated, hotly contested feat of endurance (everyone runs it for their house) bearing the name of the celebrated parson who first bred the even more famous terrier. If that doesn't build character, we don't know what does.

Boarding: About two-thirds of the senior school board, a mix of full, weekly and flexi – no boarding before that. Some parents lament that, at just 22 per cent, there are not more full boarders; we sense that the proportion increases at sixth form. The school's seven houses scattered across the grounds comprise both day students and boarders and are grouped according to age. School House accommodates both girls and boys in their first two years; the middle houses are single sex, then sixth formers move into co-ed Westlake for their final year to prepare them for mixed halls or university colleges.

Accommodation is comfortable rather than plush, except for Westlake which is probably better than much first-year university provision. Houses vary in style and character but all were clean, light and homely, with well-equipped kitchens for after hours snacks. 'My daughter would rather board,' sighed one mother.

Ethos and heritage: A rare example of a school which still bears the name of its founder, Peter Blundell, a wealthy cloth merchant whose will provided for the endowment of 'schooling for 150 protestant grammar scholars' in the early 1600s. Over 200 years later, the school moved to its present handsome Victorian buildings of warm reddish stone arranged round an immaculate green, complete with a beautiful chapel which inevitably can no longer house the whole school, either side of Blundell's Road (now crossed safely with a light-controlled crossing). Some supposedly temporary PE buildings are still there and some parts could definitely use a lick of paint. The prep, pre-prep and nursery sited just a few hundred yards down the road in light airy red-brick buildings designed for the purpose have their own outdoor space – and masses of it, including a mud kitchen and den area for 'feral play'. Each classroom has an external door with tiny pairs of wellies lined up in readiness. Inevitably, Blundell's started life as a boys' school and even today the balance of the sexes is still slightly skewed in their favour.

Certain rather wonderful traditions persist, such as Latin Prayer – what other schools might call assembly, where news, notices and the occasional pep talk from the head are given out. 'I don't like Latin and I don't like praying, but I do like this!' one mother declared. 'It's an old school adapting to modern times very well.'

Day-to-day uniform in the senior school is one hangover from a past age: rather charming with its brown tweed jackets for lower years (dubbed something far too rude for the pages of this review) and outrageously striped blazers for those sixth formers who have gained their colours, awarded for achievements way beyond the sports field. Students we spoke to (from the tiniest up) were proud to wear uniform – no obvious longing for torn jeans and hoodies permissible in some sixth forms. Uniform from the nursery onwards is purple, the best item being the all-over waterproof suits for outdoor play for the littlest ones.

Mr Wielenga is very keen that Blundell's looks out to the wider world from its small Devon town and its student body is diverse for a school of its size and location. We heard praise for how well the school accepts students arriving from overseas and judging by the tears we saw from a sixth former from south Asia who was about to move on to Westlake, we have to agree.

Pastoral care, inclusivity and discipline: Right at the top of the school's priorities, pastoral care extends to the whole family, with one father telling us movingly of the support not just his young children had received during an exceptionally difficult time, but also himself. A couple more expressed gratitude for the warm and thoughtful welcome their children – refugees from other schools – had received. Students reckon there is always someone to talk to when things go wrong, and we were impressed by the obvious kindliness and professionalism of the full-time medical centre. Relations between girls and boys seem genuinely respectful and although many of the challenges of teenage life seemed outside the experience of the youngsters we met, the prevailing climate seems very much one of openness and acceptance. As the head thoughtfully remarked, 'We look at the things that unite us, not divide us and see each other as people first. I'm not keen on identity politics here.' International students have their own hub, where they can drop in for a friendly chat and advice.

What Blundell's is truly famous for is the Russell, a gruelling, muddy cross-country race of about seven miles over neighbouring farms and the aptly named Heartbreak Hill

The need for discipline does not seem to rear its head too often and is based on the principle of natural justice – 'consensus', as one father put it. 'I have complete confidence in the school to deal with misdemeanours without glossing over them or blowing them out of proportion.' another prep school dad told us. The school appears to impose boundaries consistently and does not shrink from expulsion in rare cases.

Pupils and parents: Crisply categorised by the school into types, comprising local families 'who have lived around the area for ever' (some Blundell's dynasties), those seeking the good life from London or the south east and a diverse overseas contingent. A range of parental occupations support a Blundell's education, but a marked lack of pretension and bling unite a genuine community – 'an absolute lifesaver', as one mother told us. Students we met were thoughtful, polite and well aware of their good fortune at being there. Equally that they are in a bubble, which must surely burst once they leave.

Money matters: Usual array of scholarships awarded, and in case of exceptional need, foundation bursaries can be given up to 100 per cent of fees. Lower rates for families living within 10 miles of the school, plus special terms for boarders whose parents are in the armed forces. Minor gripes about the cost of all that monogrammed uniform, but there is a second-hand shop.

The last word: No longer 'the school for people who will never leave Devon', Blundell's is fast becoming the school of choice for parents who consider that the way it turns their children into thoughtful (and fit!) young people is as important as straight As. A place where they get outside and get on with it with a lack of pretension which is great to see.

Bredon School

Pull Court, Bushley, Tewkesbury, Gloucestershire GL20 6AH

01684 293156 | admissions@bredonschool.co.uk | www.bredonschool.org

Ages: 7-18

Pupils: 234 (30 per cent girls); sixth form: 45; Boarders: 88

Fees: Day £12,000 – £23,850; Boarding + £14,355 pa

Head teacher: Since September 2019, Nick Oldham. Previously deputy principal of West Heath School in Sevenoaks, an independent special school founded by Al-Fayed. Grew up on a farm in East Sussex, boarding from age 7, first at Holmwood House, then Eastbourne College. BA QTS in PE from Southampton, after which he toyed with the idea of the military or professional rugby (he played for England) but settled on teaching PE and sports science at Trinity, which 'I loved'. Six years later he moved to the Skinners' School, where his eight-year stint saw him promoted to director of sport, then made 'management move' to West Heath School, based in the premises of Princess Diana's old school, again staying for eight years. Feels his current role completes the circle by drawing on all these experiences though makes it crystal clear that he's here to steer the school away from SEN, except for dyslexia.

'Very inspiring,' reckoned a parent – 'he walks the talk and sets a clear direction.' Another described him as 'a breath of fresh air – we were just ticking over before but he has a vision.' Also praised for 'pushing the extracurricular', 'getting parents more involved' and 'bringing in an amazing new management team and great new teaching staff' (all are now QTS and are coming in from the likes of Sedburgh, Malvern College, Dean Close, Sherborne, Forest School and Ampleforth). An advocate of learning outside the classroom, he is also appreciated for making good use of the school's farm and forest school, not to mention its rugby pitches. Some (inevitable, perhaps) frustration from parents who who feel a once inclusive school now cherry-picks only milder SEN: 'I'm flummoxed, we fought so hard for Bredon,' one told us.

Treads that fine line of affability with instinctively commanding respect – 'Is that you, Mr Oldham?' said one junior pupil excitedly on our tour, promptly sitting up straighter. Lives five minutes away with his wife, who teaches art at the school, and his three children (the oldest here, the others at King's School Gloucester). Fresh air beckons in any spare time he has, and he especially enjoys farming, fishing and 'although I know it's not very politically correct, shooting'.

Entrance: The first step is to send in your child's school reports and professional assessments (if applicable). If the school feels it is suitable for your child, you will be invited for an interview, followed by a guest stay of three days for a day pupil, or a week for a boarder. During this time, the school undertakes its own assessments, and monitors how well the child is interacting with the other children. 'The process can be quicker if necessary – we recently took three children on from a local school and they started the next day,' says head. Children are able to join all through the year, and at any stage of the school up until year 10 – there tends to be a swell in numbers when parents realise CE will not be the best route for a child. Monthly open days, with current parents on hand to quiz.

Around half the pupils have a primary diagnosis of either dyslexia or dyscalculia but all pupils have at least average cognitive ability; nobody is admitted if they are deemed unlikely to be able to gain at least maths and English GCSEs (though there is the opportunity to re-take in sixth form). Sticks ever closer to this than ever – won't admit children with social, emotional or behavioural difficulties. So while the school currently has 84 EHCPs, head expects this to dwindle to around 10 per cent of the school roll by 2026 as EHCPs may become harder to gain for primary dyslexia. School is 'very much a school on a journey back to our original roots in this sense,' he says.

Exit: Up to 30 per cent leave post GCSEs, mainly to Hartpury College. They study courses such as engineering, catering and farming. Around a third of sixth formers to university including Loughborough, Westminster, Oxford Brookes, Kent, Southampton, Bournemouth and Plymouth. Rest into apprenticeships or work. School can help with this through its work experience programme, careers advice and links with employers.

Mock interview practice also arranged with external companies to hone interview skills.

Latest results: In 2021, 57 per cent of students taking GCSE qualifications achieved grades 9-4 in five subjects or more; 82 per cent achieved 9-4 in both English and maths. At A level, 89 per cent A*-B; 100 per cent Dist*-Dist at BTEC.

Teaching and learning: Bredon stands out for its support for children with dyslexia although it also caters for non-dyslexic pupils, with over half the pupils taking up to eight GCSEs. The more able children are often siblings of children who have been placed here for the additional support or from families who want to swap exam factories for a more rounded, outdoorsy education – 'a greenhouse, not hothouse, education,' as the head says. Classes max at 12, many much smaller.

The junior school is small, with under 25 pupils – just two in year 4 when we visited, although numbers rise in juniors throughout the year (11 in the year before we visited). It is set in cosy wooden huts, with a jumble of scooters and wellies outside, a clue to how often pupils learn outside in eg forest school, building shelters, making hot chocolate over camp fires, weaving, and studying natural habitats (daddy long legs when we visited).

The school is set on a full working farm, with pupils learning animal and crop husbandry, horticulture, livestock production and animal welfare

In seniors, there are three pathways. First, the academic route – GCSEs and up to four A levels from a choice of 29 courses (art and photography are popular); AS level over two years is also available. Second is the vocational route – with options of BTECs (including business studies, catering and engineering options) and other vocational courses. Third is the onsite Cisco Academy – run in partnership with technology giant Cisco Systems; this offers students who enjoy programming and taking apart computers the training for technical jobs, and qualifications for higher education courses in engineering and computer science. Pupils can compete for places on a Cisco apprenticeship – one recent ex-pupil is now working in the US. In a classroom which will have teenage techies salivating, pupils study eg cabling and safety issues around static electricity; others build their own computers.

Self-esteem has often taken a battering before children arrive here so school works extra hard at (a) finding subjects they enjoy and (b) pitching at the right educational level: the aim is that children only take exams they'll pass, or – if the mere thought of exams freaks them out – they take coursework-based assessments where possible. In some cases, students will need to repeat GCSE maths and English but this doesn't stop them getting into sixth form and continuing with other studies – we heard of one pupil who took his maths six times (entry qualifications are required for those who don't succeed to meet government requirement). Sixth formers have the option of a day a week work experience relating to their course, eg in a hotel if they are studying hospitality.

School stands out for DT, agricultural options and catering options, all of which are timetabled. In a dedicated engineering building, year 7s make metal wind chimes as an introduction to manipulating materials, practising health and safety and measuring, marking out and linking to other subjects. Year 8s make a hammer to get used to the larger machines – 'can be very daunting at age 12' – then year 9s get more artistic by making a metal person before deciding whether DT is something they want to pursue. The school is set on a full working farm, with pupils learning animal and crop husbandry, horticulture, livestock production and animal welfare, and workshop-based skills such as welding, and vehicle and machinery maintenance. Lots of rare breeds. Pupils prepare the animals to show at major agricultural events and make, market and sell sausages from the pork produced on the farm, among other things. Again, lots of linking to other subjects – working out the feeding schedule of the ewes can be a far more effective way of learning maths than sitting in the classroom for some pupils. In catering lessons we watched pupils perfecting pizzas (which we tried – delicious), iced buns, bread, calamari and cheesecakes.

No modern foreign language provision except via visiting teachers on a one-to-one basis (costs extra).

Learning support and SEN: Dyslexia is treated as a gift and the creative and communicative side, that dyslexics often excel in, is celebrated, while the kind of support that helps them is deemed to help all pupils. All makes for varied, active classes – we saw geography pupils miming places they pass on the way to school (cemetery, pub etc) as part of a lesson on mapping. A recent STEM day focused on how to avoid a zombie apocalypse – involved morse code, designing a zombie detection system and shoes that don't make a noise. An English lesson on the novel, Holes, involved the teacher borrowing the lizard from science, and a history lesson had pupils trying out a medieval cup and ball game. If an approach doesn't work – as we saw in a maths class where a girl said, 'I just don't understand!' – they try something else, true to their ethos of 'making the glove fit the hand'. 'Whereas in my child's last school, he had to be taken out of class for extra support, here it is embedded in everything they do – it means nobody feels different and his confidence has flourished,' said a parent. Chromebooks with assisted technology are readily available, and nobody is expected to copy off the board.

The arts and extracurricular: More outdoor pursuits than you could shake a stick at, and then some, all within stunning 84-acre grounds: 'the main uniform requirement is an overall and wellies'. Everyone gets stuck in, with mornings dedicated to classroom learning (might also include learning outdoors) and afternoons activity based. Lots of clubs – swimming, cookery, yoga, dancing, computing, chess and film club etc. Full bushcraft area, where pupils make fish traps out of willow. Ray Mears, eat your heart out. DofE attracts good numbers for bronze, silver and gold. CCF a huge growth area and has its own contingent – almost half of eligible pupils take part. 'We go on loads of trips,' a pupil told us, pointing to a noticeboard jam packed with photos – a pupil holding a neanderthal skull at Oxford University through to group photos in the wilds of Wales.

There's a huge cabinet of silverware in the entrance hall, but true to form, the trophies recognise all kind of talents, including farmer of the year, and gardener of the year

Parents praise the new head of art and facilities overhaul, now boasting three spacious, well-decorated areas including a collaborative space solely for sixth formers where a large table was filled with 3D work and books on eg Banksy and Mondrian when we visited. Drama and music disappointingly lacking – head promises he's on the case, with LAMDA now available and the first whole-school production planned for Christmas.

Sport: The school has a purpose-built shooting ground, and its clay pigeon team regularly wins the Schools Challenge competition. One former pupil is tipped to be an Olympic competitor in the sport and currently shoots for GB. There's also archery, marathon kayaking, paddleboarding and fishing (on their stretch of the River Severn), climbing (they have their own wall), mountain biking and BMX-ing (they have their own track) and swimming (in their own outside pool), among others. All juniors get to muck out and ride horses (included in fees). New director of sport and head of girls' sport have been tasked with upping the ante on team sports ('it really needs it,' said a parent), with Saturday morning sport recently introduced for all with a revised full fixtures list during the afternoons. Rugby, hockey and cricket for boys; hockey, netball and cricket for girls. Plus athletics and tennis. Great sports hall, new Astro, feature among the well-kept facilities.

Boarding: Head is a major fan of boarding, with full, weekly and flexi on offer from year 5. Boys' boarding is on three landings in Pull Court. Younger children share a room with four to six beds, while years 8 and 9 have two-bedded rooms and sixth formers sometimes get singles. The house's grand proportions make for spacious rooms (including common rooms, one of which overlooks the pool) and the upper corridor benefited from a £70K refurbishment project during Covid. Bedrooms neat but little or no personal touches ('We do try,' said director of boarding), which cannot be said for the girls' boarding based over in converted stables. Girls mainly have single rooms though some get bunk beds if they prefer to share – again, lovely and tidy. All have shared bathrooms. Allow a good few minutes if you decide to ask, as we did, who the dog beds belong to – there's a long list including Goose, Wilf, Ronnie, Sheba and even a cat that's walked on a lead ('That's Bredon for you!' laughed director of boarding).

Evening activities include rugby, horse riding, badminton, art club, biking, gym and basketball. All students get two sessions with 45 minutes of access to electronics in between. Pool was still open in October when we visited 'just because the children wanted it'. Weekends – when around half of boarders go home – include optional shopping trips, paintballing etc. Boarders can stay for exeat weekends, but the school closes completely half terms and holidays.

'My child started flexi boarding but loves it so much that he's now full-time – that's a common story here,' said one parent.

Ethos and heritage: Founded in 1962 by Lt Col Tony Sharp OBE for affluent farmers' sons who couldn't get into the likes of Cheltenham College and the larger HMC schools in the area due to CE pass criteria, but whose families wanted them to have the full works by way of independent education. They loved the splendour of the

Dyslexia is treated as a gift and the creative and communicative side, that dyslexics often excel in, is celebrated

house and grounds and the fact that they regularly won against the big-hitting schools on the sports pitches, but mostly they loved the school's inventive and stress-reducing approach to educating their sons who were almost certainly (though undiagnosed back then) dyslexic and dyscalculic. A Spanish company bought it in the 1990s when it fell on hard times, changing the goal posts of SEN to – as the head says – 'get bums on seats, an approach also favoured by local authorities as it was cheaper than special schools.' In 2014, Cavendish Education, specialists in neurodiverse education, bought Bredon (its owner proudly dyslexic), aiming to grow numbers, develop the school and bring it back to a mainstream school with a dyslexia specialism.

Parents describe Bredon as 'transformational' and 'life changing' and it's not unusual for them to first consider it for a child who is experiencing difficulties but then decide its style will suit all of their children. 'I'm thinking of giving up my hot ticket for Cheltenham Ladies' College because the style of teaching suits my daughter so much,' said one.

Arrival is impressive – it takes several minutes to drive through the grounds, past grazing sheep, cattle and pigs and extensive views of rolling hills, to reach the main school building, the glorious Pull Court 16th-century mansion in Cotswold stone. A roaring fire greeted us in the grand hall with its oak panelling and imposing staircase. Outside, a new full-time gardener is bringing the formal gardens back to their former glory. It's not all grandeur, mind – many of the main teaching blocks are as ordinary as in any school, some in need of a lick of paint, and some (though fewer than in the past) are portacabins. 'But they're good at investing in facilities – nothing gets too left behind,' said a parent. Most recently, sixth formers got their own independent study area and common room. Uniform – 'historically shabby', now sharpened up – features blazer, house ties and badges with outdoor wear where relevant.

There's a huge cabinet of silverware in the entrance hall, but true to form, the trophies recognise all kind of talents, including farmer of the year, and gardener of the year. There's an alumni association, and former pupils are invited back to inspire the children.

Pastoral care, inclusivity and discipline: Has always been a strength, now stronger still thanks to eg new house system, mindfulness sessions, full-time counsellor and a mental health nurse. Pastoral office is a busy hub where pupils pop in to discuss anything from academic concerns to just saying hi. 'All staff have an easy-going often humour-filled way with these kids and know them so well – it's a joy to watch,' said a parent.

Rewards include house points, mentions in assemblies, wall charts etc and there's a new five-tiered sanction system, starting with warnings and ending with permanent exclusions (none in recently years, though head admits he comes 'to an agreement with some that it's not the right school'). Around five temporary exclusions a term – one pupil recently brought in tobacco and another bunked off lessons. School is hot on bullying, we heard – 'There was a case recently that was dealt with straightaway – they are very much on point.' Pupils hand in mobiles on arrival and don't get them back until they leave at the end of the day. Lots of pupil committees – on food, on boarding, a prefects' group, and a weekly pupil welfare meeting with the deputy head – where children can voice opinions and air any disgruntlement.

Pupils and parents: Pupils are confident and talk easily to adults. They travel quite some distance, reaching as far as the other side of Cirencester up to just shy of Birmingham, and down to the Forest of Dean and the Cotswolds. A fleet of nine-seater buses help bring some in, though more than ever are opting to board. The school is popular among Forces families, and overseas pupils (mainly expats, so no EAL needed) make up around seven per cent of the school population, currently from eg Europe, Africa, UAE and Australia. The school is 45 minutes from Birmingham airport. Socio-economic mix is changing as more families fund themselves, but there's not much ethnic diversity. Seventy per cent are boys. Newish Friends of Bredon welcomed by parents, but we heard some grumbles about communications from the school – 'could be clearer and more consistent'; 'sometimes they forget about the juniors' etc.

Money matters: Around a third of pupils are funded by (mainly Worcester and Gloucestershire) local authorities but school is looking to dramatically reduce these numbers. Withdrawal lessons, therapy, dedicated TA support, and EAL courses are charged as extras. Ten per cent discount for siblings and Forces families. Sport scholarships available from September 2022.

The last word: For children who don't sit easily in large or high-pressure mainstream schools, or special schools, Bredon can feel like a breath of fresh air – and the emphasis on being outdoors means children get this in the literal sense too. Great for dyslexics, but – increasingly so – for any child from the anxious and timid to the hale and hearty who prefer learning with tools in hand and mud on feet. Either way, expect quirkiness with classmates and be warned it might mean a house move or considering boarding. Three word summary? Gordonstoun with dyslexia.

Bruton School for Girls

Sunny Hill, Bruton, Somerset BA10 0NT

01749 814400 | admissions@brutonschool.co.uk | www.brutonschool.co.uk

Ages: 11-18

Pupils: 198; sixth form: 41; Boarders: 55 full, 23 weekly/flexi

Fees: Day £18,696 ; Boarding £31,848 pa

Headmistress: Since 2021, Jane Evans, previously director of outreach and partnerships (and before that assistant head and sixth form head) at Queen's College, Taunton. Educated at Bath High School for Girls and King Edwards, Totnes. Degree and PGCE, both from Surrey and both in English and dance. First post was teaching at Guildford High School for Girls, after which she went on to become an examiner and ran departments in both independent and state schools.

Entrance: Via online verbal and non-verbal reasoning tests to assess potential, plus interview. At sixth form the bar is higher, at five GCSEs at grade 5 or above, with 6s at subjects to be taken at A level. Termly open days and visits by arrangement. Main feeders at year 7 are the prep and local primary schools, at year 9 local preps. Several buses serve surrounding area within 20 mile radius.

Exit: Around 15 per cent leave after GCSEs. Sixth formers to a wide range of universities and an equal variety of courses. Edinburgh, Exeter, York, Warwick, Southampton, Bath, Durham, King's College London, Plymouth, Loughborough, UCL and Manchester all popular. Courses range from astrophysics to creative events management. Two to Oxbridge in 2021, and three medics. One overseas in 2021 – to Poznan University of Technology to study logistics.

Latest results: In 2021, 67 per cent 9-7 at GSCE; 79 per cent A*/A at A level (94 per cent A*-B). In 2019 (the last year when exams took place), 60 per cent 9-7 at GCSE; 50 per cent A*/A at A level.

Teaching and learning: School scores highly on value-added. Before GCSE, the curriculum includes compulsory classics (including Greek and Latin), DT and 'home technology'. In sixth form, Leiths certificate in food and wine is popular – we would happily have stayed in any ski chalet catered by BSG students, judging by what was being made in the kitchen. Typically, girls take nine or 10 subjects at GCSE, to include separate sciences, but no language, ancient or modern, is compulsory; a choice of French, German, Spanish or Latin is offered. Flexible and enlightened enough to allow girls to take certain GCSEs (eg French and maths) two or three years early, in exceptional cases. Twenty-one subjects to choose from in sixth form.

Small class sizes, averaging under 10, hard work and the 'enthusiastic, effective teachers – the kind you get in a grammar school,' according to one parent, contribute to the school's academic success. The wide ability range 'has meant my girls have learnt to tolerate all levels of ability, which is much more like real life,' commented one thoughtful mother of clearly bright girls. Stand-out subjects are English, drama, art and biology; some report that maths is currently in flux. Our impression was of interesting subject matter (West Side Story being used to demonstrate the realities of immigration for Hispanics, capital punishment v the safety and protection of prisoners) being delivered with IT as support rather than as a substitute for honest-to-goodness teaching, to a very compliant, quiescent flock – just for our benefit?

Learning support and SEN: High praise is given to SEN diagnosis and support: 'My daughter's in-house plan is tailored to her,' said one, whose daughter had fled the local comprehensive.

The arts and extracurricular: Music comes in for high praise – deservedly so, judging by the singing practice for the director of music's own composition that we heard, the recital at assembly and admissions to national and county youth choir and orchestra. A school orchestra, smaller ensembles for brass and strings inter alia, a baroque group, theory classes for those taking grades and plenty of opportunities to play beyond the school gates make for a rich musical offering: we enjoyed the CD (and cookies) we were given on departure very much.

Drama takes place in the Hobhouse theatre: although it is a popular option, outside the devised and scripted requirements of public exams – when we witnessed genuine belly laughs and dramatic talent in the GCSE piece we saw – the scope seems limited to one musical per year, but 'Please please don't make us play boys again,' beg the girls. The art department is truly vibrant – a crammed creative space where girls seem to be able to pursue any artistic fancy: the series of photographs resulting from one girl persuading an obliging friend to immerse herself in milk in a variety of poses was memorable. Good links with the arty town of Bruton enrich the life of the school – the installation by a local artist of felt poppies suspended on threads to commemorate the First World War was innovative and moving. Plenty of trips to local and not so local theatre, concerts and galleries complement the lively arts scene within school.

Sport: Hockey and netball the main games here, with no fewer than 17 netball teams. An impressive fixture list where BSG looks more like David up against local Goliaths Sherborne Girls and King Edward's Bath. Several netball courts doubling up for tennis, a delightfully sunny Astro where strenuous hockey practice was taking place when we visited, plus an athletics track behind the main group of buildings. At present the swimming pool is an outdoor, solar-heated, summer-only affair; the five swimming teams use opponents' indoor facilities for matches at less clement times of year. An indoor pool is top of the parental wish list. Although there is a riding team, this is not the kind of place where girls bring their own steeds, and the ability to pilot a horsebox is not a requirement for entry. Sporty activities include quidditch and tchoukball (truly – we wished we'd seen either).

Boarding: Boarding (officially from year 3 in Sunny Hill Prep, but occasionally younger in the case of one small girl we met whose elder sisters all board and who was determined not to miss out) takes place in the cosy old vicarage where all junior boarders (just a handful from the prep) up to year 9 are housed. Day girls are free to join in with weekend activities and intermittent sleepovers. Two other boarding houses for senior school boarders. Accommodation is homely and not obsessively tidy: a couple of sixth form girls had transformed their room into a Christmas grotto, complete with glitter and a snow scene, without attracting the wrath of the domestic staff. Intra-school allegiance, which might attach to houses with full vertical boarding in a bigger school, is created by assigning each girl (day and boarding) to one of four halls named for local stately homes.

Ethos and heritage: One of a disproportionate number of schools in Bruton (owing to the beneficence of Hugh Sexey, an auditor of the exchequer in the early 1600s), a small charming Somerset market town of golden stone, BSG sits on Sunny Hill, certainly so the day we visited, with distant hazy views of Glastonbury Tor. Established in 1900 and known originally as Sunny Hill School (the name retained by the prep), it has mostly been independent but spent 30 years in the maintained sector early in the last century. It is possibly this which gives the school a delightful lack of pretension and snobbery, 'a place where the teachers don't parade like cockerels, but where they get a remarkable amount out of the girls,' in the words of one mother. 'It's slightly Enid Blyton with cocoa and biscuits at break,' said another. We liked the fresh air and heartiness about the place – the gaps between buildings necessarily mean a breather between lessons, through the beautifully tended grounds and eccentric pop-up garden, with its giant chessmen.

'Friendly' kept popping up as the most common adjective used to describe the school: 'My daughter took all of two days to settle in,' reported one happy mother

Proud and unapologetic to be a girls' school, where both the girls and their parents choose to be: 'My daughter was offered the chance to move at sixth form and declined,' one parent told us, another recounted a story of her daughter taking refuge from the local state offering and finding sanctuary at BSG. 'We landed on our feet here', said yet another satisfied customer. The school's size means that girls form friendships across year groups, and we felt a genuine sense of community over a delicious lunch of steak pie and fresh veg. 'Friendly' kept popping up as the most common adjective used to describe the school:

'My daughter took all of two days to settle in,' reported one happy mother.

Famous old girls include Clarissa Farr, ex-high mistress of St Paul's Girls' School and journalists Viv Groskop, Imogen Sellars and Catherine Davies.

Pastoral care, inclusivity and discipline: The pastoral side and the immense care the school takes over every girl in it are hugely appreciated by parents. Hot on friendship issues, a perennial subtext in girls' schools. 'Bruton stood out over other local schools,' in one parent's view, 'and the school is not afraid to tackle issues head on, yet sensitively.' Tutor groups are mixed age until sixth form (these meet daily), and between tutors and heads of halls, no-one appears to fall through the net. Relationships between staff and students and among the students themselves are sound and supportive, 'but we do teach them resilience and that things going wrong isn't necessarily a problem,' adds the school. 'Honourables' are awarded for exceptional work, 'hallmarks' for acts of courtesy and community-mindedness, colours for sporting prowess. Discipline is not a matter which seems to rear its ugly head very often: rudeness, lateness and wilder interpretations of uniform do not go unremarked; smokers and drinkers can expect a sliding scale of punishment, whilst druggies and persistent offenders face exclusion. 'Fluffy and lenient we are not,' states school.

Pupils and parents: 'Confident without being arrogant' – that overworked phrase to which every school aspires – is echoed by parents. We found the girls, who arrive in anything from helicopters to old bangers, cheerful, unpretentious and very happy to be at this school. 'This isn't the place for hair-flicking city types, but for well-grounded families, wanting the best for their girls. Our parents aren't flashy but aren't without aspiration either.' A welcoming parent community helps to reassure first-time buyers that they have made a wise choice. About one fifth of girls from overseas.

Money matters: As independent education goes, good value for money, at about 25 per cent cheaper than its most expensive competitors. 'Bruton offers everything academic and holistic a parent could ask from a 21st century girls' school, without charging the ridiculous fees that most other schools charge,' said one mother. Scholarships, awarded for the usual range of talents, are nominal, but governors' exhibitions are awarded in cases of means-tested need to a maximum value of 40 per cent of fees.

The last word: 'It's just not very BSG to promote itself,' one father remarked, but if we were expecting an apologetic little school lurking in rural Somerset, we did not find it. Hidden gem is more like it – a place of unpretentious endeavour where girls can be girls and achieve as much as they are capable of. 'Follow the gleam' may be the school motto, but in our view it could be time for a spotlight.

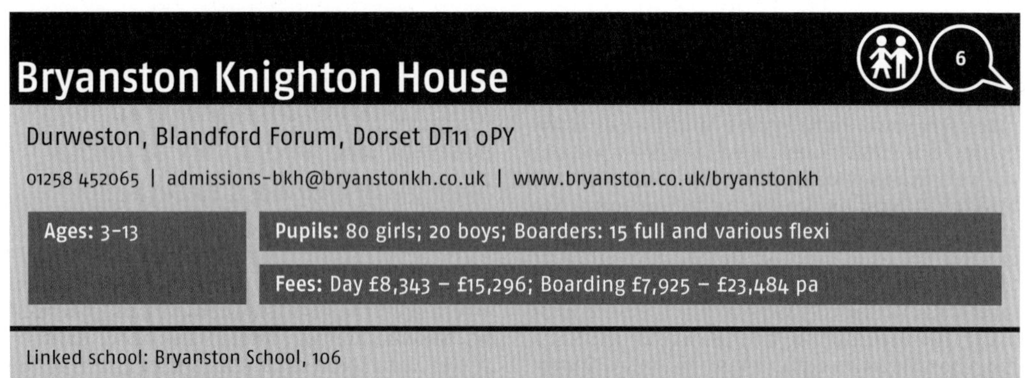

Bryanston Knighton House

6

Durweston, Blandford Forum, Dorset DT11 0PY

01258 452065 | admissions-bkh@bryanstonkh.co.uk | www.bryanston.co.uk/bryanstonkh

Ages: 3-13

Pupils: 80 girls; 20 boys; **Boarders:** 15 full and various flexi

Fees: Day £8,343 – £15,296; Boarding £7,925 – £23,484 pa

Linked school: Bryanston School, 106

Head: Since September 2021, Will Lockett, previously head of Abberley Hall in Worcestershire and before that housemaster at Bryanston school, so knows this part of the world and the landscape for independent schools well. A classicist, he was educated at Winchester and Manchester University and then worked in engineering before finding his vocation as a teacher. 'The strength of the merger between Bryanston and Knighton House is a clear vision – to guide pupils as they develop into confident, curious, open-minded and kind members of society,' he told us. 'We do this by enabling creative and rigorous thinking. What they will have learned here matters, but how they learned it matters more.'

Entrance: Non-selective. Come any time so long as there's room. Invariably an ongoing swelling of numbers by children unhappy at their present school. Taster days. Parents local, Forces and expats. Not much of an ethnic mix, this being Dorset, but it wouldn't be an issue in the slightest. Always a horizon-broadening contingent from Spain, France, Italy, Belgium.

Now fully co-ed, so school is accepting boys up to and including year 8 as day pupils. Since September 2021, school has merged with Bryanston, hence recent name change.

Exit: Most to independent seniors, some to state schools. Experts at matching children to the right one. Dorset offers a full range of choice from highly academic to those offering learning support. Lots to Canford, Sherborne and Leweston. Also Bryanston, Clayesmore, Milton Abbey, Sherborne, St Mary's Calne and the Thomas Hardye School. Eleven scholarships in 2021, including to Bryanston, Clayesmore, Wells Cathedral and Leweston.

Our view: Standing on rising ground above the floodplain of the river Stour in the hushed and tiny village of Durweston (very pretty church), the school (now merged with Bryanston) stands apart from busy world yet is well connected by road to all parts Dorset – and beyond. Once a dower house on the estate of the viscounts Portman, the building is domestic in scale, not a bit stately, a wisteria-clad hodge-podge. The toffs (back in the day) lived a mile away up in the Norman Shaw château that is now Bryanston school.

A still-young school founded in 1950 by Peggy and John Booker (parents of controversialist Christopher) as an antidote to their own character-building schooldays which had been defined by all the miseries, chilblains, iron bedsteads, splintery floors and random acts of discipline reckoned indispensable to the raising of young persons in those days. School was instead to be a home from home where girls could be girls, play in the fresh air to their hearts' content, learn kindness, love learning and develop what a present parent identifies as 'bedrock confidence'. Romantic and gently revolutionary in its time, this is mainstream stuff nowadays; everyone else has played catch-up. There's quite a lot of retro-country boarding around just now, done somewhat self-consciously via artful marketing – prospectuses read like fashion shoots for Boden, and look, there's the head in the just the right country casuals, accessorised by a dog. The school, a governor told us, is forward-looking, 'we're not seeking to return to the 1960s'. At the same time, it remains recognisably the school everyone remembers. A parent who was a pupil there in the 80s told us the school 'remains exactly what it's always been'. Not a lot of schools could have pulled that off.

The Bookers' greatest legacy was that, unlike so many schools created by reformers in their own image, it never developed the sort of captivating idiosyncrasy (cultishness, if you like) that makes the job of successors so difficult. Captivating yes, idiosyncratic no; progressive yes, offbeat never. So the school has enjoyed a remarkably steady and howl-free evolution. This played to its advantage in 2013 when some of the school's governors almost made a strategic misstep of existential proportions. A proposal to merge with a nearby school was swiftly strangled by a coalition of parents and there have been no aftershocks, but it was a crisis that wasn't allowed to go to waste – indeed, one parent described it as 'the best thing that ever happened to us'. The episode focused minds on the intrinsic qualities that make the school so distinctive and precious. It awakened awareness of the school's uniqueness and value and reinvigorated the parent body. Other happy outcomes include the purchase of the school's freehold and the appointment of a very bright, eclectic board of governors.

Riding is huge. School is one of Horse & Hound's 'Six dream schools for horsey children' and ponies have been at the centre of school life forever

Parent power is one of those things that can go either way. Parents have not by any means taken to throwing their weight around; on the contrary, they're a supportive lot. Notably unpretentious and dressed down, they range from what one parent described as 'heavy duty aristocracy' to members of the armed forces, expats, local professionals and farmers, businesspeople, creatives and other members of the digital diaspora. In the words of one parent, 'They're not remotely flashy, they're cheery, low-key and I have no idea who's rich and who isn't.' They find the school 'brilliantly supportive of working parents', 'wonderfully accommodating of late-to-collect crises'. Significantly, the school is very much the school of choice for teachers (who know a thing or two about schools) at local independents. Nice touch: grandparents' days.

Academically hearty. Until the merger-most-foul episode the school had been falling off the pace. Now, gaps have been plugged, below-par staff eased out and there's a continuing focus on the quality of teaching. Rising numbers of scholarships testify to this, and they'll let you know about it. It's not all about getting the best out of just the brightest, though, and non-schol girls don't feel at all like also-rans. Small classes play their part, and teachers who really know the children. No danger of Gradgrind values; the mother of a very bright 8-year-old told us, 'They are definitely stretching her, but not in ways she's really aware of.' The overall philosophy remains 'in your own way, in your own time' – but definitely not 'when you feel like it', or as one mum put it another way, they're 'challenged and encouraged'. A parent who moved down from London reckons his daughter got to the same place academically that she would have reached in her mirthless pressure-cooker; another said, 'People are once again sending their bright girls to Knighton.' Senior schools confirm this.

The school is forward-looking, but remains recognisably the school everyone remembers. A parent who was a pupil there in the 80s told us the school 'remains exactly what it's always been'. Not a lot of schools could have pulled that off

Conventional curriculum, maths 'brilliant', Latin from year 6, art superb and there's a fine personal enrichment programme that goes off-piste into history of art, public speaking, you name it. In common with many other preps, there is now no CE at Knighton – instead they have introduced their own KED (knowledge enlightenment discovery) curriculum which school says allows a balance between curriculum content and skills such as being resilient, optimistic and self-motivated.

Surprisingly well-resourced across the board, classrooms in converted farm buildings. Careers talks for years 7 and 8 because 'there are no limits to what girls can achieve'. Special needs a strength as you've every right to expect of a non-selective school. Learning support spans short-term interventions – everything from reinforcement to gifted and talented – to long term SENDs. No wheelchairs when we called but, says the school, 'We'd do what we needed to do.' Something you don't notice till it's pointed out: no ungainly school bags being lugged, swinging, from class to class. They're banned. Take just what you need from your locker. Amazingly civilising.

The girls are mostly outdoorsy types so it's no surprise they're a sporty lot. There's been a focus on quality of coaching in the last few years and the best go on to county and national levels. If you're bookish or not sporty that's fine but you'll be expected to join in. Riding is huge and maybe why you're reading this. School is one of Horse & Hound's 'Six dream schools for horsey children' and ponies have been at the centre of school life forever. Around half the children ride. They're good, too, up there with the best.

A lot happens in fresh air. They play outside in their dens, make up games with bits of sticks, climb trees and converse with ponies, goats, hamsters etc. We watched them at it. A delight. What they (arguably) do best indoors is sing. The music-making tradition here is as old as the ponies. Instrumental practice begins before breakfast (yes, seriously) and most girls play something. Lots of ensembles and an orchestra. Singing compulsory for years 3-5 and if you're top-drawer you can audition for the super-elite chapel choir which sings at, no less, professional standard in some really nice venues. Music is a big part of the school's identity; it's a bigger deal to be head chorister than head girl.

Universal praise for pastoral care. Teachers are 'very accessible and always give you time'; 'they really understand the children'. School has long been noted for this; in the words of a former pupil it's 'deeply ingrained'. Wherever we questioned we got the same responses: 'nurturing', 'loving', 'home from home'.

Unanimous and, dare we say, fervent praise for the pre-prep, the Orchard – 'exceptional,' in the words of a mother you wouldn't want to get on the wrong side of. Girls and boys 3-7 plus babies and toddlers every Thursday.

School judiciously makes sure its pupils outgrow the school by setting them slightly above and apart in their final year in the Alpha flat. Children get some more independence and turn their eyes to what comes next. It's well done.

By their bright red dungarees ye shall know them, for this is the school uniform. They're not about aah-factor, though they are certainly not deficient in that; they're just the job for playing out and doing horses. They can be spotted by teachers if the occupant strays too far or climbs too high. Above all, they're democratising. Red dungarees are just one of the elements that create the rare social atmosphere, with the unaffected friendliness, the way the pupils look out for each other, older ones for tiny ones among others. The school's small size is a factor: children feel they belong here, this isn't just a school they go to. Another factor is the example set by the staff, because nothing good happens in a school that does not derive from role modelling by adults who care deeply about their work.

Clifton College

While we were in the (former) head's office we scanned the books on the coffee table. One was by Christine Pullein-Thompson, author of wildly popular pony books for girls. For us it provided the vital clue to what the school is all about. The PTs (there were three of them) created a world whose values are wholeheartedness, pluck, resourcefulness and good humour. They invented a genre which has been described as 'feminist way before its time': in their own words, 'We convinced girls they were as good as chaps.' Their spirit lives on here not as creed nor affectation but in an internalised way – eg in the annual award for Gumption. Triers are rewarded, exemplifying a culture of 'you can do anything' which is borne out by the estimation of senior schools, one of which told us that their children 'are amongst the most rounded academically and socially'.

Boarding: Currently around 15 full-time boarders plus all the flexi options. Overnighting and weekending joyously popular because the boarding staff are lovely and make it such fun, and the head of boarding is a force of nature who lives and breathes her job and is amazing, and has to be marched off the premises on her days off otherwise she'd never have one. It took the school a while to find her and on the way it parted company with a few who didn't make the grade – a reminder that extraordinary kindness in any regime is achieved only by rigour and, yes, steel. Facilities all being updated to allow for change to co-ed.

Money matters: Scholarships. Bursaries (Greenwood Awards) for families who wouldn't otherwise be able to afford it.

The last word: The school has never blown its own trumpet other than understatedly and is free of the sort of marketing machine that blights so many other schools. Hurrah. The school is clad in values and practices that make it very current, unencumbered by trad baggage, financially strong and blessed by a once-and-future ethos which makes it, in the words of a parent, 'very happy in its own skin'. Is there magic in the air? Yes.

Bryanston School

7

Bryanston, Blandford Forum, Dorset DT11 0PX

01258 452411 | admissions@bryanston.co.uk | www.bryanston.co.uk

Ages: 13–18

Pupils: 849; sixth form: 284; Boarders: 706 full

Fees: Day £33,525; Boarding £40,890 pa

Linked school: Bryanston Knighton House, 102

Acting head: Since November 2021, Richard Jones MA (educational leadership), formerly second master and business and economics teacher. Has experience as housemaster and previously taught at Canford and St John's, Leatherhead. Lives on site with his wife, Emily, and their two sons.

Entrance: Now merged with Knighton House Prep School, making this a 3-18 school from September 2021. Online ISEB pre-test in year 7 to determine if your child is in the zone academically. Common Entrance used as a 'profiling tool', pass mark 50 per cent – not a high bar – though the average score is 60-70 per cent. Parents really like the way the school suits brothers and sisters of differing personalities and talents. Sixth form takes on 25-30 new students per year, 40 points needed at GCSE – as for current students – plus tests and interview.

Exit: Up to 15 per cent leave after GCSEs. University applications guidance recently beefed up by adoption of the BridgeU platform. Almost half apply after A level. Terrific after-sales service, no problem if you don't make up your mind for even a year or two, just get in touch for, as they say, 'Bryanston is not just a five-year experience.' Most to university in the UK or abroad and most do conventional courses. Some join the forces. Army liaison officer visits. One to Oxbridge in 2021, plus three medics. Popular destinations: Oxford Brookes, Bristol, Exeter and Cardiff. Fifteen overseas in 2021 including Berklee College of Music, UCLA, Georgetown, Boston and McGill; some also to Netherlands and Spain. 'But we like the fact that it's not all about university,' one mother told us – 'different destinations are celebrated.'

Latest results: In 2021, 52 per cent 9-7 at GCSE; 50 per cent A*/A at A level (78 per cent A*-B). IB average point score 38. In 2019 (the last year when exams took place), 48 per cent 9-7 at GCSE; 23 per cent A*/A at A level (54 per cent A*-B).

Teaching and learning: Academically they do things differently at Bryanston. It's a DNA thing. It derives from an educational theory adopted by the school's founders favouring self-reliance – the Dalton system, still referred to today. Assignments aren't bite-size, set to be tested tomorrow, they're bigger and they're completed over a week. Instead of a central library there are departmental ones with specialist teachers on hand to help out. You get more 'free' periods than you would at most schools. To support you there's your tutor, whom you meet at least once a week to review how things are going. This enables you learn from what's going well and what isn't, and incrementally apply the lessons of experience. From year 12 you also have one-to-one meetings with your subject teacher to iron out bugs. Keeping on top of the workload requires rigorous time management. Progress is assessed weekly by grade and comment, recorded electronically and shared with students and teachers. The eChart, they call it. The objective is to develop a spirit of self-motivation and independent enquiry, and any independent-minded child is going to love it. Parents can see weekly attitude scores and more detailed marks and comments every month.

If you're a fired-up self-starter, great. But if the classroom doesn't play to your best strengths and your appetite for intellectual enquiry isn't your defining characteristic, there's a danger of daydreaming and dawdling. Which is why, over the years, the system has become more interventionist. A parent told us admiringly that if you start goofing off 'they're on your case immediately'. Another savoured the irony that though the school is often mistakenly perceived as progressive and a bit laissez faire, 'I can't imagine a school more tightly controlled.' Is it nevertheless the case that a child who is not especially self-reliant and/or academic could find this tough, and may therefore be better suited to smaller assignments with a faster turnaround? The school is aware of this lingering anxiety and any apprehensive parent would do well to take it up with them.

As for the eChart, a parent advises, 'Read it, but my advice: don't discuss it with your child, it works best as an internal document.' Which goes to show how much faith parents (rightly) place in Bryanston's teachers and testifies to the amount of time teachers give to their students. It is exceptionally rare for a student to spend as much structured time on their own with a teacher as they do here. As one teacher expressed it, 'It's all about relationships – we're all in it together.'

Stats matter, though, and for better or worse exam stats matter most, here as anywhere. They are entirely respectable bearing in mind that the students' academic range here is pretty broad. Noteworthy that a quarter do Latin GCSE.

The new music school is a thing of great loveliness – it even has a professional-standard recording studio and masses of scope for aspiring techies, too

At A level, students opt for the full range and there's something for all abilities. As many do Eng lit as maths. Sciences are strong, design and tech very much so. Art is a longstanding strength. Most popular of all? Economics. Value added score places the school in the top 15 per cent nationally.

Learning support and SEN: Likely to enjoy a much higher profile under impressive new head of department. Any need for learning support will probably be picked up at the pre-test in year 7; commendably, Bryanston works with individual prep schools to facilitate a child's journey to Common Entrance. All new arrivals are screened on entry. Highest demand is for maths support, we were told, but the most common identified needs are slow processing speed and working memory. Fortunately the Dalton plan, which underpins the school's philosophy, has the building in of extra time for the reinforcement of learning at its core, so there are few if any conflicting demands on a student's time. One-to-one lessons (chargeable) where needed. Students on the autism spectrum might have a reduced timetable but any student needing a differentiated curriculum is likely to get one. The department also has an important pastoral role and students can refer themselves for any difficulties they might be experiencing; tutors coordinate all learning support provision and are the first port of call. As to attitudes, any unhelpful and persistent negative views are addressed by the head of learning support.

The arts and extracurricular: To know anything about Bryanston is to know that it is famously creative. It's one reason why it is often mistakenly typecast as progressive. It remains as creative as ever in art, design, drama and music. Standards in all three remain outstanding. But you don't have to be arty to get in – 'People respect all achievements' is a sentiment fervently echoed by the students, who are adamant that there is no hierarchy of achievement here. Having said which, a creative, artistic child can only soar. Facilities are first class. The new music school is a thing of great loveliness – it even has a professional-standard recording studio and masses of scope for aspiring techies, too. Much of the music and drama here is student devised and directed. One parent whose daughter wanted to do design technology at university found that 'the facilities are just as good, if not better, at school'.

Best testament of all, perhaps, is the number of outstanding arty alumni the school has produced, many of whom remain committed to the place. Very few schools can boast quite so many. In art: Lucian Freud and Howard Hodgkin. In music: Sir John Eliot Gardiner, Sir Mark Elder and Mark Wigglesworth. In TV and film: Ben Fogle and Emilia Fox. In architecture and design: Quinlan Terry, Terence, Jasper and Sebastian Conran. These are just the eminent creatives; there are heaps more in other fields.

There are masses of after-school activities to choose from and they're not just for fun. The schools sets great store by its co-curriculum, regarding it as a vital part of a student's voyage of self-discovery. The students we spoke to buy in to this. Extracurricular activities abound plus charity outreach – visits to care homes, working with SEN pupils in local schools, hosting riding for the disabled and fortnightly meetings of senior citizens. Lots of outdoor ed, no CCF. No excuse ever for time hanging heavy.

The founders embedded the school's genetic code in the deceptively simple motto: 'Et nova et vetera' – 'both new and old', the best of both. This was a stroke of genius

Sport: In keeping with the definition of Bryanston as a place where you can 'discover who you are and what you want to be', there's high-level coaching for those who love their sport and, they claim, healthy fun for those averse to being buried alive under a scrum. We met the head of sport, who expresses his philosophy in a strikingly humane, even poetic, way. He wants, he says, Bryanston boys and girls to develop 'an affectionate connection with sport'. Everyone can have a go at everything, see how they get on and settle for their level. He adds, 'If we get the process right, the results will follow.' And they do. All the usual sports on offer and there's a full fixture programme featuring up to three teams per year group, so anyone wanting to play for the school gets a good shot at it. The sports centre is an amazing resource, shared with the local community. Highlight for those who like to let off steam after prep is the new climbing wall with super-cushioned base.

Boarding: Full-time boarding being, now, not so much normative as a matter of circumstance (eg parents abroad), many families like to get together of a weekend. Roughly every other weekend they can and you can leave for Salisbury station at 12.30pm on a Saturday, commitments permitting, and be at Clapham Junction by 2.30pm. On other weekends everyone stays in school and works towards a community event. Students who mostly board full time told us they feel anything but left behind and the school always lays on something fun and different, though none of this is compulsory. One parent who lives abroad told us, 'The children are kept very busy. Many times we had to encourage them to go and visit their grandparents!' Early homesickness is well handled, one mother told us.

Ethos and heritage: The school was founded in 1928, a time when you could buy a second-hand country house for a song, start a school in your own image and do things differently from the sclerotic Victorian public schools with their fagging, flogging and character-building subordination of individuality. The Bryanston estate is a whopping 400 acres and the school is centred on a handsome 'château' designed by Norman Shaw.

The founders' manifesto centred on 'putting right everything that was wrong with their own [school]'. Out went fagging and flogging, in came 'freedom, self-development and self-discipline'. And short trousers and bags of fresh air. The founders weren't revolutionaries, mind, they were pragmatists; they embedded the school's genetic code in, of all places, the deceptively simple motto: 'Et nova et vetera' – 'both new and old', the best of both. This was a stroke of genius because it has informed the continuous evolution of the school.

To this day Bryanston remains, in the words of one of the teachers, 'a school that thinks about itself differently'. 'Bryanston likes change, new ideas, we like to challenge convention,' while at the same time remaining, in this Guide's view, in many ways thoroughly conventional. It's the near-paradox of 'et nova et vetera' that explains why the school eludes lazy stereotyping. Progressive? Sure, there's no school uniform but there are also no first names for teachers. Creative? Yes – in the broadest sense. Liberal? Absolutely. Easygoing? This conjures up another paradox. One parent told us, 'I've never seen anything so monitored

The academic objective is to develop a spirit of self-motivation and enquiry, and any independent-minded child is going to love it

– yet they feel so free.' No ambiguity whatever attaches to what everyone agrees is the salient characteristic of the school: its happiness. 'My children adore the school,' one parent told us, speaking for all. 'Twas ever thus. Of the school's 18 governors, 10 are former pupils. They have 'a fierce focus on who we are'.

Pastoral care, inclusivity and discipline: Given the highly personal nature of the school, the emotional health of pupils is the responsibility of everyone. For teachers this is indeed a lifestyle job. We were struck by the warmth, humanity, commitment and sheer calibre of every teacher we met. The school depends on 'lunatic enthusiasts' as much as ever and the head is determined to counter the common narrative of a generation of young people 'lost to Covid'. It is typical of the values of the school that it acknowledges also the pastoral importance of non-teaching staff, indicative of the 'we're all in it together' mindset here. One example was supplied by a student who told us, 'Everyone turns up to school events' and illustrated it by telling us of the student who was giving an after-prep piano recital. He didn't expect more than a handful – he was playing Schubert. As he connected with his mum on Skype so she could watch him, his whole year group rocked up to support. One parent told us, 'All of the key people who surrounded all of my [three] children had their fingers on all pulses at all times. In a short time they figured out my children's various characteristics and embraced them.'

Formal responsibility for wellbeing lies with the houseparent together with the academic tutor, handpicked for compatibility. Such is the bond that, if a pupil gets into hot water, their tutor will act as advocate of last resort and defend them to the death. Rigorous vigilance is the best way to nip bad stuff in the bud, but even so, it occasionally happens, and if it's something like drugs you're likely to find yourself packing; school deploys sniffer dogs on occasion. The school used to be reckoned absorbent of a little bit of offbeat recreational malarkey. If it ever was, that's history.

Teachers are trained in mental health and all staff have received training in LGBTQ+ issues; school has Stonewall gold school champion status. The chaplain has an integral role in the school's pastoral care system and aims to offer pupils the experience of genuine committed Christian worship – 'Christian values blend well with Bryanston values.' On Sundays pupils must either go to a lecture in the theatre or walk a mile to the little estate church. An impressive number opt for the latter and around 20 are confirmed every year.

There are houses, three of them in the big house, which helps to reduce tribalism, which is further diluted not just by the emphasis the school places on being yourself but also by the fact that the big house is big enough to be the school's social hub. Top tip: if you want to plug in to the vibe, spend some time on the basement corridor. Boys go into a junior house for their first year to acclimatise; girls don't because older girls are reckoned better at looking after little ones. There are prefects, whose role is more pastoral than disciplinary. They support the younger boys and girls, for which they get minor rewards but no privileges – the job is its own reward.

The dress code – polo shirt, black trousers/skirt – is, they say, 'hard to subvert', and enables students to 'blend in with the local community'. The sixth form code is more relaxed. We saw no evidence of competitiveness or self-consciousness. Everyone looks natural and businesslike – unremarkable. The look is deceptively tightly regulated. Food is exceptional, the best we've eaten anywhere, and the dining hall was designed by former pupil Terence Conran.

Pupils and parents: Most from up to an hour or so away but a good chunk from west London and further afield. Coaches from London, Oxford, Exeter and Lewes. Especially popular with the arty/liberal elite. Small international contingent. Around 12 per cent day students; their day ends at 9pm.

Money matters: Fees nudging the upper end of the scale. Scholarships up to 10 per cent. Top-up or standalone bursaries from five to 100 per cent; around 100 beneficiaries and 20+ students in receipt of 90+ per cent support. Two significant measures of value: the amount of personal attention here and the excellent use made of the educational opportunity offered by the long boarding school day.

The last word: Secure in its identity, superbly staffed, safe, kind, rigorous and highly likeable, a school in buoyant form that celebrates all sorts and all achievements and which strikes the balance between freedom and structure. In the words of one mother, exhilarating.

Canford School

Wimborne, Dorset BH21 3AD

01202 847207 | admissions@canford.com | www.canford.com

Ages: 13-18

Pupils: 643; sixth form: 282; Boarders: 404 full

Fees: Day £29,985; Boarding £39,390 pa

Headmaster: Since 2013, Ben Vessey BA MA MBA (50s). Educated at Magdalen College School, Oxford, then read history at Southampton. Intended to join the army but after tearing both knee ligaments playing rugby worked as an oil and gas broker for five years in the City and on placement in Texas. 'But when I came back from the US I realised that it wasn't what I wanted to do,' he says. Dauntsey's, Millfield and six years as senior deputy head at Christ's Hospital (plus an MA in history, a PGCE and an MBA in education management along the way) led him to Canford, where he was seduced by the staff and student buzz and vibrant school community. Loves teaching and teaches five periods a fortnight to a year 9 history set. 'I write reports and do parents' meetings and it keeps me in touch with the rhythms of teachers' busy routines,' he says. Much in evidence around the school and makes a point of dropping in on lessons to see colleagues in action in the classroom. Has lunch with pupils and staff as often as possible and supper with them twice a week, plus, on one occasion, helping some retrieve a shoe which had inexplicably ended up in a tree. 'I leave them alone at breakfast,' he jokes.

Energetic, enthusiastic and looking impossibly youthful for a head of his seniority and experience, he lives and breathes the school. He loves Sounds of Canford (the school's informal concert series), watches as many concerts, plays and sports matches as he can and catches up with the latest episode of the pupil-led podcast 'This Canford Life' as he cycles on his spin bike. Lives in a house on site with his wife Harriet, their three sons (the eldest at Durham, the others still at school) and three dogs. In his spare time he plays golf (lockdown would find him hitting golf balls out of the school long jump pit), cycles and reads (he's a fan of Bernard Cornwell's Sharpe novels and other historical fiction). Just in case he runs out of things to do, he also chairs the HMC professional development sub-committee. 'I'm not good at unstructured time,' he admits... Winston Churchill is his hero and a bronze miniature of the legendary PM left to the school by old boy Terrence Cobden Pike has pride of place in his sumptuous study with its gilded ceiling and elegant olive green walls.

Entrance: For years 6 and 7, ISEB common pre-test is the first sift, followed by a day of assessment at the school. Offers are made to more than 60 per cent of those applying for 13+ places. Director of admissions says school is looking to identify 'attitude and a have a go mentality as much as raw ability'. If you don't register in time for pre-assessment, 'the door isn't closed'; a few places usually come up in year 8. CE benchmark is 55 per cent, although vast majority achieve higher. Candidates who haven't attended prep schools take entrance exam in year 8 (this aims to spot academic potential rather than test knowledge). Around 125 places for year 9 cohort (known as Shells), including 30 to 35 scholarships. Pupils come from around 100 prep schools. Large numbers of boarders from Twyford, Port Regis, Highfield, Chafyn Grove, Walhampton, Westbourne House and Forres Sandle Manor. Day pupils often from nearby Castle Court and Dumpton.

Between 25 and 30 join in the sixth form – assessment test in November the year before plus minimum of 42 points on students' best seven GCSEs. Grade 7s required in subjects to be studied at A level and at least 6s in English and maths. Highly competitive at this stage – around four applicants (slightly more girls than boys) for every place.

Exit: Up to 10 per cent leave after GCSE – for academic or personal reasons or for a change of scene. After A level, more than 95 per cent to university. Exeter, Durham, Bristol, Bath and Edinburgh perennially popular, and usually good numbers to Oxbridge. Courses range from biochemical sciences and medicine to history and business. Twenty medics in 2021. Interest in US universities is growing and school has its own international university adviser and is an official SAT testing centre. Three overseas in 2021

– Colgate University, NY and State University of Montana in the US, plus Nagoya in Japan. Degree apprenticeships also on the up.

Latest results: School won't release 2021 or 2020 results, believing it is not right to publish them in a year when exams were not sat (we were though assured that this strong cohort went on to the next stage of their education successfully). In 2019 (the last year when exams took place), 70 per cent 9-7 at GCSE; 48 per cent A*/A grades and 77 per cent per cent A*-B at A level (figures include Pre-U for art and languages).

Teaching and learning: Results are easily as good as other co-ed schools with illustrious names. Considering the breadth of intake this speaks volumes for the first-rate teaching. Maths, chemistry and biology are the most popular A level subjects but many pupils do a mix of sciences, arts and humanities subjects. EPQ on offer too. Sixth formers we spoke to were full of praise for the support in the run-up to A levels and the study skills workshops on offer. Study leave is awarded on an individual basis but most sixth formers opt to stay in school, keen to make the most of timetabled lessons, past papers and one-to-one help. 'Everyone works hard here,' a sixth former told us while another said, 'The teachers want you to do well and they really support you.'

Canford pupils achieved the highest Pre-U grades for art for two years running and up to eight students a year go on to do art foundation courses. Music is terrific too

Year 9s choose between French, Spanish, German and Latin. Most take 10 subjects at GCSE, including at least one language and two sciences. Pupils are set for maths and languages from the word go. Computer science has been introduced throughout the school and is increasingly popular – 16 taking it at GCSE when we visited, 11 at AS and three at A2. 'Prep schools should be trying to embed computer science in the curriculum, rather than just IT,' we were told. Year 9's curriculum focuses on developing 'habits, skills and literacy' with plenty of cross-curricular projects. Average class size is 15 in years 9 to 11, nine in the lower sixth and eight in the upper sixth. Numerous opportunities for intellectual enrichment such as an annual festival of ideas and internal and external essay competitions.

Lockdown provision highly highly praised by parents and – crucially – students. 'Obviously I would rather be back at school, but it really has been super and such a collaborative experience,' one reflected.

Facilities throughout the school are second to none. New library under construction, with current facility offering 18,000 books, DVDs and audio CDs, plus thousands of virtual resources. Excellent science labs. We liked the fact that every classroom and office has an inspiring and appropriate moniker – Roddick (after Body Shop founder Anita Roddick) for economics and business and Olympus for classics are just two examples. Even the book cupboard in the classics department gets its own name – Hades, of course.

Proactive careers department organises advice on GCSE and A level subjects, annual careers symposium and interview experience. Work experience isn't compulsory but a growing number of students are applying for internships and work placements.

Learning support and SEN: Known as SFL (Support for Learning) here and headed by an absolutely lovely SENCo. Good provision for those with learning difficulties – mostly dyslexia, mild dyspraxia and attention difficulties, some ASD – all happens in the centrally placed Lovell Building, which also houses humanities subjects. Year 9 pupils who need additional support can take extra English instead of Latin, while in years 10 and 11 learning skills are offered for a number of pupils instead of one GCSE subject, with focus on developing study skills. The approach is a practical one, where issues of self-esteem are placed centre stage and the ambience warm and welcoming – the department even has its own well-being dog, Lola. Open to all and runs drop-in sessions for anyone feeling overwhelmed. One-to-one tuition available when the need arises at no extra charge. EAL offered too, of course. Several staff members have been trained as emotional literacy support assistants.

The arts and extracurricular: Art is stunning – and in many cases highly original and ambitious. We were particularly taken with a vast oil painting (3.5m x 1.5m) of a turtle family. Canford pupils achieved the highest Pre-U grades for art for two years running and up to eight students a year go on to do art foundation courses. Music is terrific, with a large number of choirs, orchestras, strings groups and jazz band. Around half of pupils take individual music lessons. Two major concerts a year, one at Canford, the other at the Lighthouse in Poole, home of the Bournemouth Symphony Orchestra. Lots of drama, with opportunities on stage, backstage and in technical roles. Several pupils have won National Youth Theatre places in recent years. Productions, house plays and an annual school musical take place in the Layard Theatre, opened by film and theatre director Sir Richard Eyre in 1999. Theatre used by professional companies too.

CCF isn't compulsory but is very popular – voted best in the country by The Week in 2020. Others opt for DofE or adventure training and all will doubtless enjoy testing out the new outdoor education centre opened in 2020. Seniors work in local primary schools and with disabled groups, run drama workshops and coach sport while juniors work as conservation volunteers as part of the community service programme. School is the lead sponsor of the Bourne Academy, a secondary school in Bournemouth. Canford pupils act as teaching assistants for languages, computing and science and sign up for book clubs and quizzes.

School is full of bright ideas – everything from student newspaper The Blue Bubble to Connections, a general studies programme that challenges pupils to think beyond the curriculum and links different academic disciplines. Another innovation that caught our eye was Yellow Hour, an hour set aside twice a term for pupils and staff to perform in front of an informal audience. Recent highlights included the director of studies performing a maths equation and the head reading a short story he'd written. Year 9s do a carousel of activities every Wednesday – sculling, mixed lacrosse, bell ringing, even etiquette. A plethora of academic, sporting and cultural trips abroad as well as community projects in Argentina, Ghana and India. The Canford Partnership was set up following the discovery (and sale) of a £7 million Assyrian frieze in the school tuck shop in 1994 and supports worthwhile community projects in the UK and Third World. Links with a school in the US and another in India mean students can be involved in joint academic and cultural projects – this Global Connections programme ranks among the achievements the head is most proud of.

Sport: Sport is a big deal here and Canford teams score notable successes at every level. Main sports are rugby, hockey and cricket for boys, hockey, netball and tennis for girls and athletics and rowing for both. Rowing VIII were Henley finalists recently. Acres of pitches, floodlit Astroturf, real tennis court (there aren't many of those around), fitness suite and a 25-metre indoor swimming pool. In years 9 to 11, four teams regularly fielded per year group so everyone gets the chance to represent the school. Other options include cross-country, sailing, dance, basketball, golf, squash, badminton, canoeing and fitness. Sports facilities and pool are used by local community at allotted times. When we visited a keep fit class for the elderly was in full swing in the sports hall.

One of the most beautiful schools in the country, it even has its own Victorian arboretum, complete with 350 tree species

Boarding: Full boarding only, no weekly boarding. Flexible exeat system means pupils can spend several Saturday nights a term at home if they want but some 70 per cent of boarders stay in school at weekends. Seven boarding houses – four for boys and three for girls (plus three mixed day houses). Each house has a married houseparent, three tutors and at least one matron (described by one teacher as 'the heart and soul of the boarding house'). Houses are modern and well equipped. In Beaufort, one of the girls' houses, youngest girls are in dorms of four, year 10s and 11s in twos and sixth formers get singles. When pupils arrive at 13 they are assigned a mentor from the year above and are kept so busy that they settle in quickly – weekend activities programme includes an assault course, pizza nights and trips to the beach. Beaufort housemistress has two cats and two dogs – 'They're brilliant therapy for anyone who feels homesick,' she says.

By 2022 all four boys' boarding houses should be located at the top end of the school grounds. Boys in the existing further flung houses told us they enjoy the stroll; some bike or skateboard back and forth. Youngest pupils hand their mobile phones in at night but a housemaster we spoke to says pupils are so busy that electronic devices aren't generally a problem. Boys in his house prefer to play Connect Four and chess than stare at screens in their spare time. Very refreshing to hear.

Ethos and heritage: Canford is one of the most beautiful schools in the country. Located in 250 acres of parkland beside the River Stour, it even has its own Victorian arboretum, complete with 350 tree species and one of the largest sweet chestnut trees in the UK. A building of some sort has stood on the Canford site since the Domesday Book. The oldest parts are a pretty Norman church, used for services but too small to take the whole school, and the early 15th-century John O'Gaunt's kitchen, used for debates, meetings and receptions. The stunning 19th-century main building, originally known as Canford Manor and designed by Edward Blore and later Sir Charles Barry (architect of the Houses of Parliament), is Grade I listed and can boast Winston Churchill as a guest when it was in private hands. Lord Wimborne sold the manor in 1923 and the school was founded the same year. It first admitted girls into the sixth form in 1969, went fully co-ed in 1995 and is now 60 per cent boys, 40 per cent girls.

School is a mix of grand, historic buildings and ultra-modern, but stylish additions (new library up next, due in 2021). Dining hall, known as the Great Hall, where Edward, Prince of Wales danced in 1890 following a ritual slaughter of birds at a shooting party, is particularly magnificent. These days a modern cafeteria system is in place. Food is cooked in-house and gets the firm thumbs-up from pupils. All meals eaten in the Great Hall but there are kitchens with tea and toast-making facilities in every house, plus a new café-style coffee shop. The new assembly hall opened in 2020 now means the whole school can get together in one place. New library from autumn 2021.

In Yellow Hour, pupils and staff perform in front of an informal audience. Recent highlights included the director of studies performing a maths equation

The whole place fizzes with activity from dawn till dusk. Youngsters we spoke to said there's so much going on that it can be 'a bit overwhelming' at first but they quickly learn time management skills. Day pupils must be in school by 8.15am and leave at 6pm, although many stay on later. All look smart – blue jumpers and tartan skirts for girls up to year 11, tweed jackets and ties for boys, sixth form girls in navy. Everyone has to be presentable, we were told. No heavy eyeliner for girls – the look is 'healthy and glowing'.

Pastoral care, inclusivity and discipline: Wellbeing is taken very seriously. At the time of writing, a sleep programme was in the planning stages: in the opinion of learning support staff, sleep disruption due in part to digital device overload is one of the greatest difficulties facing today's young people. Parents told us that there's plenty of support via the tutor system. Doctors' surgeries held every weekday and confidential counselling services available on site. Before and during lockdown, the close attention paid to emotional well-being has not gone unnoticed and efforts to ensure that this time has not just been 'not lost, but is as positive it can be' have been remarked upon by parents. Pupils describe the chaplain, known as Rev Jack, as 'really charismatic' and praise him for the way 'he involves everyone'. Midweek chapel for all, plus compulsory service for boarders on Sundays.

The sharp focus on racial inequality brought about by the killing of George Floyd in 2020 has led to a greater coherence and recognition across the curriculum, driven by the equality and diversity pupil leaders. Each subject and extra-curricular offering has its own pupil leader(s) – this is a school where the pupil voice is loud, strong and listened to. An equality, diversity and inclusion research project has been running at the school. Other kinds of diversity are welcomed: 'Intolerance of any kind is not acceptable at Canford,' as the pupil code of conduct baldly states. Students are free to explore gender expression.

School aims to educate pupils about 'sensible, social drinking under controlled conditions' and sixth formers are allowed to have maximum of two drinks (wine and beer) with food at Saturday evening socials in the sixth form centre. 'It is very closely monitored,' we were told by a group of upper sixths. Zero tolerance on drugs, however, and if pupils are caught smoking outdoors they get detention (parents are informed). Indoor smoking results in suspension.

Pupils and parents: Most pupils live within a 90-minute drive of the school. A sizeable chunk come from Dorset, Hampshire, Sussex, Surrey and Wiltshire and a smattering from London and further afield. Around three per cent of boarders are international students – from places like Hong Kong, Poland and Bulgaria. Quite a few sons and daughters of Old Canfordians and lots of siblings and cousins. Day pupils come from all directions. School puts on 50-seater coach from Bournemouth and Poole, plus minibuses from Dorchester, Blandford and Wool to the west and Christchurch, Ringwood and Fordingbridge to the east.

The pupils we met said personalities of all types thrive at Canford. 'If you are a quiet sort of person the teachers will help you gain confidence,' one girl told us. Those we met were enthusiastic, full of appreciation for the quality of teaching and delightfully unpretentious. Parents (who include lots of medics) praised the place for its academic results, good communication and down-to-earth atmosphere ('It's not stuffy at all,' one said), plus – emphatically – its ability to embrace everyone from academic front runners to those who find school harder.

Money matters: A range of 13+ and 16+ scholarships, plus means-tested bursaries worth up to 100 per cent of fees.

The last word: A very special school and one that can easily hold its own with the most popular in the country. With its first-rate teaching, stunning setting and innovative ideas, Canford is definitely at the top of its game and set for a glittering centenary in 2023.

Chafyn Grove School

Bourne Avenue, Salisbury, Wiltshire SP1 1LR

01722 333423 | office@chafyngrove.co.uk | www.chafyngrove.co.uk

Ages: 3-13

Pupils: 220 (90 boys; 130 girls); Boarders: 25 full, 10 weekly, 50 flexi (from 8 years)

Fees: Day £7,857 – £18,597; Boarding + £6,258 – £8,070 pa

Headmaster: Since 2016, Simon Head, previously headmaster of Moreton Hall School in Suffolk. Educated at Stonyhurst, he held a short service limited commission with the Royal Green Jackets ('good fun and a great leveller') before studying classics, followed by a PGCE at Cambridge. Taught at Dulwich College Prep and Pembroke House in Kenya and then became deputy head at St John's Beaumont in Windsor where he met his wife. First headship was Moreton Hall (Suffolk). Married to Sarah, also a teacher, they have two sons.

As a child he wanted to be a vet so maybe there is something in nominative determinism (his surname either raises a smile or causes confusion) because his mother was a headmistress and his twin is also a teacher. At first he resisted following suit and on his father's advice took a little longer to decide on his profession. He says, 'I wanted to do something rewarding and I've no regrets; I love it', adding, 'it does help when you have grown up in the system.' Takes year 8 for Latin and under-9 games and describes teaching as 'the most important job after farming … it is a vocation, it matters to do something meaningful.'

At the time of our conversation around two-thirds of children were in school (lots of parents in the army or work for the NHS), but it was clear how much he missed having all Chafyn's pupils together: 'They need to see us and we miss them.' While he is proud of how staff and parents have rallied together to make online learning work, he says, 'Something is lost, it's not the same.' Recalling his time in Kenya he adds, 'That experience was formative, it made me understand that teaching is all about relationships.'

We found Mr Head both thoughtful and insightful on what it is that schools do, a perennial topic thrown into sharper relief by the pandemic. 'It's the things that can't be measured that are more interesting than those which can,' he mused. 'There's so much in a school which is ineffable.' Ineffable. Now that's a great word we don't hear very often from heads. Less focus on data and a bit more appreciation of mystery – Mr Gradgrind would be horrified!

Parents describe him as 'personable', 'professional' and 'approachable' and marvel at his ability to put names not just to pupils' faces but parents' as well. All appreciate his presence, along with dog, Peggy, at pick-up. And it's walks with Peggy, running, football in the garden with his children and reading (favourite authors are John Buchan and Graham Greene) that have been welcome distractions during lockdown. He also tries to get in the odd bit of fly fishing: 'It's a time to tune in to what nature's doing, to unhook the mind.'

Entrance: Children join at all ages and stages and from all over the area. Entry is non-selective. Applicants are invited to spend a day at the school the term before they begin.

Exit: Bryanston, Godolphin, Canford, Warminster, Marlborough College, Clayesmore, Winchester, Rugby, Radley, Sherborne and Clifton College top the list of 'next schools'. Around ten leave at age 11 each year for the Salisbury grammar schools and independents.

Our view: Founded in 1876 as Salisbury School and changed its name in 1916 following an endowment by Lady Chafyn Grove. A 1914 school photograph shows just 17 boys and three members of staff sitting in the grounds of a large Victorian building. Today, that handful of solemn Edwardian scholars would be very surprised to find 200 boys and girls at Chafyn Grove.

Along with many prep schools Chafyn Grove has moved away from teaching Common Entrance. 'It's good to have a finishing post, but by year 8 pupils are essentially running laps,' says Mr Head. 'Exams are important, but the change has been invigorating. Senior schools want interested and interesting pupils.' Language teaching in particular has benefitted from this change with less emphasis on writing and more on developing skills. Spanish and French are on offer throughout the school and Latin enters the mix in year 6. Science is taught in dedicated labs by specialists from year 3 and maths is also streamed from this age. Scholarship success is strong, particularly in sport, but academic, art, music, drama and DT awards are also gained to the full range of senior schools.

From year 3, after-school clubs are embedded into the timetable rather than given a twilight slot. These activities range from parkour and bushcraft to sign language, coding and sailing. All in all, over 60 pursuits are covered over the course of the year as part of the school's commitment to breadth, balance and 'finding something for every child to hang their hat on'. Reading passports, where children complete routes around the world, encourage a love of books.

Because many parents are in the Forces or key workers, a relatively high proportion of pupils has been in school for lessons during lockdown. At first teachers filmed lessons for those learning from home but after parent feedback quickly switched from pre-recorded to live lessons so that pupils could learn with their peers. 'It gives a proper structure to the day,' said one parent. Praise too for the weekly newsletter and social media posts keeping home schooling and in-school families updated together.

A great treat is to be chosen as head's lunch guest, although whether the attraction is him or the 'special ice-cream' wasn't clear

Learning support takes place in The Link where a team of specialists provide one-to-one support for children with particular learning needs, as well as in the classroom. This teaching is included in the general fees until year 4. Parents impressed by how quickly staff readjusted to provide continuity of SEN provision for pupils during lockdown.

Chafyn Grove has long been known for its winning ways on the sports field and while there has been no dilution in standards there has been a change in ethos. The head would rather 'lose by one than win by ten' as part of an approach which emphasises teamwork rather than winning at all costs. 'If we beat everyone then we're picking the wrong fixtures,' he says. Cricket in the summer is not divided into boys/girls but has open selection throughout and increasingly equal representation in senior teams. Outdoor swimming pool used in summer and up to October! Regular attendance at National Athletics finals and recently the school won the ISA national hockey championships at the Olympic stadium. On-site facilities include two Astros, a sports hall, squash and tennis courts, a bouldering wall and low-ropes course.

Art studio is roomy and light, with plenty of high-quality work (standard is 'incredible', say parents) on display throughout the school and also in Salisbury. A dedicated workspace for scholars, as well as a ceramics room and DT lab make this a well-resourced and used department. Drama is on the timetable and there is a range of plays for everyone wishing to be involved, whether on or behind the stage. Stronger drama provision was on parents' wish list and head has appointed a new head of music and drama. Singing is very popular and there are three choirs, as well as a school orchestra, training orchestra and jazz band. Large performance hall has good acoustics, a grand piano and an organ. Practice rooms are small but masses of space for storing instruments and music.

Regular trips for every year group. Ski trip takes parents too 'with memorable consequences'. Choir recently toured to Barcelona and Montserrat (the monastery). Chafyn Challenges run alongside the main curriculum, ranging from delivering a match report to a lamb, as well as cooking the Sunday roast (no links with the former). The tenet of 'Enjoyable Challenge' informs as much as possible, from giving new things a go to helping others. The Chafyn Champs mentor scheme of older children looking after younger finds many expressions, from listening to reading to getting in the pool with pre-prep.

The original Victorian building is still home for the boarders, but most of the teaching takes place in modern buildings which seem to flow into one another on school's well-proportioned site. Children are happy, grounded and energetic. Head sets great store by staff sitting with children at lunch and simply chatting. We hear that a great treat is to be chosen as head's lunch guest, although whether the attraction is him or the 'special ice-cream' wasn't clear (both, we're sure). Food is prepared in-house by the chef and served cafeteria style; meal times are informal and children sit where they like. Wraparound care runs from 8am till 6pm and can be extended further to take in breakfast or dinner.

Emphasis on accessibility of staff extends to parents. As well as encouraging a daily liaison as much as possible between teachers and parents, the Friends (parents' association) and class reps meet regularly with the headmaster to discuss provision in detail. Every pupil belongs to an Eight (house) with appealing names – Wasps, Frogs, Birds and Knights. Some year groups are 'a bit boy heavy', inevitable with a girls' prep just down the road, but aspiration is to reach equal numbers all through.

Lovely modern pre-prep with bright, spacious classrooms, own hall and play area. Nursery starts small, after which numbers gradually increase into two classes of around a dozen children in each. Children in pre-prep can stay until 6pm and have their own after-school clubs and activities including ballet, (Lego) engineering and drama. Transition to prep managed very well by all accounts.

Parents tend to come from Salisbury and surrounding villages; roughly a quarter of the children are from military families. Army contingent can be somewhat transient but parents describe the whole school community as welcoming and sociable, something that has been a great help during lockdown, 'It's been hard for everyone but Chafyn parents have been so supportive of each other.' Year group WhatsApp keeps everybody in touch.

Boarding: Boarding accommodation is comfortable and recently refurbished. The houseparents also teach in the school, supported by residential staff, gappers and matrons. Boarders have a sitting room and green room where they can Skype parents. Mobiles are not allowed. As well as weekly and full boarding, there are flexi and occasional options. There are usually around 15 full boarders – mostly British plus a few Spanish – and the same number again boarding most nights during the week. Boarders can walk into town (accompanied) on Saturday and there are a variety of excursions on Sunday, covering the beach, New Forest and usual attractions. Parents of boarders really appreciate the fact that staff take footage of matches so that they can watch their children in action on the pitch.

Money matters: Forces discounts (normally 10 per cent day and 15 per cent full boarding) and sibling discounts from five to 15 per cent available. Means-tested bursaries typically range between 10 and 40 per cent of the fees.

The last word: A happy, busy school where children are individually understood. A recently retired long-serving member of staff says, 'Chafyn is a kinder school than ever.'

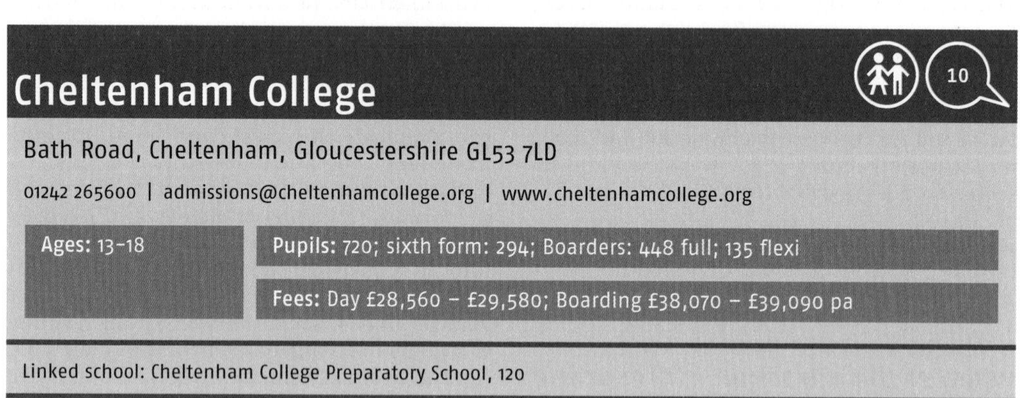

Cheltenham College

10

Bath Road, Cheltenham, Gloucestershire GL53 7LD

01242 265600 | admissions@cheltenhamcollege.org | www.cheltenhamcollege.org

Ages: 13-18

Pupils: 720; sixth form: 294; Boarders: 448 full; 135 flexi

Fees: Day £28,560 – £29,580; Boarding £38,070 – £39,090 pa

Linked school: Cheltenham College Preparatory School, 120

Head: Since 2018, Nicola Huggett MA PGCE (40s), previously head of Blundell's in Devon. Educated at St Gabriel's, Newbury and Marlborough, she read PPE at St Hugh's, Oxford (she was captain of her college boat club and president of the university riding club). After university she spent three years at J. Walter Thompson but decided that advertising wasn't for her. She shadowed a history teacher at a state school in Newbury for a week and loved it from the moment she set foot in the classroom. 'I couldn't believe no one had ever suggested teaching to me before,' she says. 'I've put that right now. I often talk to pupils about teaching as a career.' Following a PGCE at Oxford, she taught history part-time at Downe House while pursuing an eventing career but later decided to become a full-time teacher. She taught at Woodford County High School in Essex, then moved to Haileybury, where she became a housemistress and head of boarding. Spent six years as deputy head of Downe House, before a six-year stint as head of Blundell's.

Warm and engaging (a group of sixth formers told us: 'We love Mrs Huggett' – praise indeed for a head), she is very visible around the school. 'I try to go to everything,' she says. 'You often have the best conversations on the touchline or walking along.' Despite her busy schedule, she still teaches a year 9 history set. 'I like being in the classroom with pupils,' she says. 'I write reports, do parents' evenings and experience all the things as a teacher that everyone else does.' Parents and pupils are impressed. 'She's tightened up the academics and really commands respect,' one told us. Another said: 'She's such an asset to the school. She's a bit like the queen; she does her utmost for the school without taking any of the credit.'

She lives in a house on the school site with husband Spencer, who works for an automotive software consultancy. They have four children – the eldest is about to start a law conversion course, the second is reading medicine at St Andrews and the youngest two are pupils at Cheltenham College. In her spare time she enjoys riding, cycling and walking the family cocker spaniel.

Entrance: The school is academically selective (55 per cent at CE required). Up to a third of year 9s come from Cheltenham College Prep while others arrive from a host of preps, including Pinewood, St Hugh's, Beaudesert Park, Moor Park, The Elms, Abberley Hall, Farleigh and the Dragon. In 2019 pupils came from 18 new preps and interest seems to be growing from London preps like Thomas's and Fulham Prep. Entrants from schools that don't prepare pupils for CE take the school's own papers in English and maths. A small number of places are available at 14+.

All pupils going into the sixth form need at least five grade 6s and must have grade 5s or above in English and maths. External candidates, often from girls' schools and the state sector, also take entrance papers in subjects to be studied at A level.

Exit: A few leave after GCSEs, sometimes for grammar schools and occasionally because they haven't got the grades for the sixth form. At 18 almost all head to university, with Durham, Exeter, King's College London, Manchester, Bristol and Edinburgh the top choices. Five to Oxbridge in 2021, and four medics. Popular subjects include economics and finance, natural science, engineering and history. Growing interest in apprenticeships and last year a girl chose to do a global business apprenticeship.

Latest results: In 2021, 71 per cent 9-7 at I/GCSE; 75 per cent A*/A at A level. In 2019 (the last year when exams took place), 65 per cent 9-7 at I/GCSE; 'over a third' A*/A at A level.

Teaching and learning: The head has focused on making learning 'exciting' – and the impact is evident in the exam results. Most pupils take ten GCSEs and IGCSEs, including maths, English, English literature, at least two sciences and at least one language.

Teaching staff are determined that 'no one slips through the net' and any academic issues are tackled speedily via a range of interventions. 'The college is brilliant at identifying children's needs, desires, wants and abilities,' a parent told us. 'We never thought our son would be able to do a highly competitive science degree at university because he didn't like maths. But not once did the college say "you aren't going to be able to do that". They supported him and gave him the confidence to succeed and he's had five offers from five universities. His maths teacher took him under her wing and incentivised and motivated him and now he's one of the top scientists.'

The head is very visible around the school. 'I try to go to everything,' she says. 'You often have the best conversations on the touchline or walking along'

The school has a 'thriving society culture' – societies for every academic subject, all pupil led and encouraging pupils to research and deliver talks themselves. French, Spanish and German taught, although school can also arrange languages like Russian, Italian and Chinese on request. Sixth formers take three or four subjects. New A levels on offer at 16+ include art history, business studies, psychology, economics and government and politics) and everyone does the EPQ.

Teaching staff are enthusiastic and engaging. Amazingly, they include three intrepid individuals who have climbed Mount Everest. Can this feat be matched by any other school? One of them, the educational visits coordinator, even wrote a book about it called The Longest Climb.

Despite its traditional exterior, the school prides itself on being innovative and forward-thinking. We liked the idea of pupil-led learning lunches, where students deliver a talk to staff on everything from social media and the dangers of vaping to dyslexia and learning styles. There's also the lower sixth electives programme, designed to allow pupils to develop new skills. Current options include ancient history, life drawing, cyber discovery, a global mini MBA, leadership and Italian. 'We are big enough to have lots of different niches so pupils can develop their passions,' says the head. 'We see ourselves as a school where all children can thrive.'

Learning support and SEN: EAL pupils have an induction programme before the start of their first term to help them find their feet as fast as possible. Learning support staff give one-to-one or small group teaching, mentoring, revision or study skills support for students with difficulties such as mild dyslexia, dyspraxia and ADHD. The learning support team includes a learning mentor who visits boarding houses in rotation to help pupils with revision and offer support. All pupils' literacy skills are screened on arrival at the school and in year 12.

The arts and extracurricular: Around half the pupils learn a musical instrument and there are choirs (from Schola Cantorum to pop), orchestras, bands and ensembles galore. Most days start with a half-hour service in the glorious chapel – generally a hymn and a sermon or talk. The chapel was designed by former pupil Henry Prothero to celebrate the college's 50th anniversary and was dedicated in 1896. The college is famous for its singing and the director of music leads hymn practice for all once a week. 'We make it fun, getting different sections to stand up or sit down,' he says. The school puts on at least six drama productions a year, including two house plays, with students performing onstage or doing the lighting, sound, stage management and directing. Art takes place in a wing of an inspiring Grade I listed building with high ceilings, chandeliers, ornate cornices and massive windows.

Two afternoons a week are spent on activities of pupils' choice, such as CCF, DofE, photography, pottery and water polo. An impressive community action programme enables 150 pupils to volunteer in local schools, care centres, community groups and the local hospital every week. The school has also formed a range of partnerships with primary and secondary schools at home and abroad. For example, college science teachers run regular science workshops for local primary pupils and college students have raised thousands of pounds over the years for a school for children with special needs in Romania.

Sport: Cheltenham College is undoubtedly a sporty school, with scores of county and national triumphs in rugby, hockey, cricket, tennis, rowing and polo. Two years ago pupils won gold and silver at the British Alpine Skiing Championships, a year 11 was selected to play for England Hockey's under-18 team, two students signed contracts with Gloucester Rugby, two played rugby for England's under-18 team and the school recently won national polo and rugby championships. The talented athlete programme is run by specialist sports professionals and provides structured training and mentoring for outstanding young athletes in their chosen sports. Facilities are first-rate, including a vast sports centre, a 25-metre swimming pool, eight rugby pitches, five cricket squares and a historic cricket pavilion, all on the school site. There is plenty of choice for pupils who prefer other sports, such as equestrian pursuits, shooting and rackets (a forerunner of squash that the school excels at).

Teaching staff are enthusiastic and engaging. Amazingly, they include three intrepid individuals who have climbed Mount Everest

Boarding: Very much a boarding school, with 80 per cent boarding. Most are full boarders but there are also day boarders who can board for up to 35 days each term. Eleven houses (six boys' and five girls' houses), including two day houses, all dotted around the perimeter of the school. Even the furthest is only a ten-minute walk away from the main school.

Each house is led by a resident housemaster or housemistress, supported by a team of tutors (their duties include running academic clinics outside lessons) and matrons. Queen's, the day girls' house, is a gorgeous Georgian building, with views over the college field and the chapel and boasting one of the most stylish common rooms we've visited in a long time, a pretty garden and a dorm with four beds (girls are allowed to stay six nights a year for free if they have school commitments; otherwise it's £45 a night). The houses seem genuinely plugged into the local community. Each house adopts its own local charity. When we visited Boyne, one of the boys' houses, the housemaster had left a box by the door for parents and pupils to contribute food – 'because local food bank levels are getting low'.

Ethos and heritage: The front-facing school buildings are a vision to behold, a row of beautiful mellow Victorian gothic buildings stretching along Cheltenham's Bath Road. Founded in 1841, the school moved to its present site two years later and accepted day boys as well as boarders. It went fully co-ed in 1998.

Much of the school has undergone a major revamp in recent years, but pupils told us that their favourite bits are the ancient chapel, historic library and wood-panelled dining hall, where students often sit for up to an hour in the evenings and chat. The redeveloped science centre, with 15 university-standard labs, inspires many pupils to study science at A level. We were very taken with a 'funky' (a pupil's description) interactive periodic table in the foyer – a display of boxes explaining the chemical elements. Items include an oxygen meter from a military aircraft, aluminium bike brakes and a piece of iron barbed wire from Second World War trenches. As the head says, 'We are historic and traditional on the outside but on the inside we are modern, forward-thinking and grounded.'

Old Cheltonians include polar explorer Edward Wilson, broadcaster Rageh Omaar, actors Nigel and Jack Davenport, film producer Tim Bevan and female racing driver Jamie Chadwick.

Pastoral care, inclusivity and discipline: Parents say the pastoral care is exemplary. 'I judge a school on how happy the children are and both my kids are thriving and reaching their full potential,' one told us. 'They have made lifelong friendships with their peer groups and their housemaster and housemistress will be important to them for ever. There is a real generosity from the staff in terms of their time.' As well as their housemaster or housemistress, pupils have a tutor who is responsible for their academic, pastoral and social welfare. The deputy head (pastoral) heads the welfare management team, which meets regularly and includes the school's chief doctor, lead nurse and two full-time counsellors. Trained peer mentors often pick up on fellow pupils' worries before they can escalate. PSHE is delivered weekly via the Floreat programme, which promotes health, wellbeing and life skills. There are firm rules on mobile phones. For instance, year 9s are only allowed their phones for an hour a day (and not at all on tech-free Tuesdays). Staff see year 9 as a time for pupils to get to know each other and to learn about sensible phone use. If they use social media they are encouraged to add a prefect as a friend – so older ones can alert staff to anything worrying. The school takes a firm line on drugs, drink and smoking but these aren't generally a problem.

A housemaster told us there's an 'educated, graduated approach' to going into Cheltenham. Pupils can walk into the town centre on Sundays – and to nearby Bath Road (lots of cafés and supermarkets) four afternoons a week as long as they get permission. 'I wouldn't like to go to a school in the middle of nowhere,' one girl told us. 'It's nice to be able to go to a coffee shop with your friends.'

Pupils told us the school is 'quite strict' – but not in an excessive way. Sixth formers are allowed to go out for a meal at an approved restaurant at 17 and to an endorsed pub at 18. Their only grumble was that they'd like a bit more freedom. A raft of prefects, including head boy and head girl and deputies, plus a school council with reps from every year group.

Pupils and parents: Unlike many co-ed schools Cheltenham College is 50:50 boys and girls. The pupils we met were charming and enthusiastic, with a can-do attitude. 'They create such decent, caring people,' a mother told us. Our visit was at the start of the coronavirus crisis and when staff decided they had to hold the GCSE French, Spanish and German oral exams early sixth formers and staff dropped everything on a Sunday morning to help year 11s prepare. 'It was a head's dream to walk in at 9am on a Sunday and find how everyone had stepped up,' smiles the head. Similarly, many local families offered to have international pupils to stay for the holidays when they heard they couldn't get home. Sixth formers say that the school 'isn't cliquey or snobby' and that they can walk into the dining room and sit with anyone. 'The culture here is to be yourself,' they said.

Most boarders live within a 90-mile radius, while day pupils tend to live within a 20 to 30-minute drive. Many travel in by school bus from as far afield as Stow-on-the-Wold, Gloucester and Tewkesbury. Parents include Old Cheltonians, forces families and many new to the school. Around 18 per cent of pupils are international, from places like Kenya, Thailand, Hong Kong, China, the Middle East, Russia, Ukraine, Japan and Barbados.

We were very taken with a display explaining the chemical elements: an oxygen meter from a military aircraft, aluminium bike brakes and a piece of iron barbed wire

Pupils generally give the thumbs-up to their navy and cerise uniform and like wearing their own choice of pastel shirts. In the sixth form girls wear elegant navy midi skirts and prefects are allowed to don a jumper of their choice. 'My favourite is an electric blue one,' a trendsetting boy told us.

Money matters: Scholarships and exhibitions are offered at 13+ and 16+ for academic performance, art, drama, music, choral and sport. Award holders are easily identifiable by their distinctive bright pink ties. The college offers discounts for parents serving in the UK armed forces and means-tested bursaries are available for parents or guardians who are unable to afford the fees.

The last word: A happy, successful school that inspires huge affection and loyalty in its pupils and staff. It may look traditional and grand on the outside but it's a forward-thinking place that offers a top-notch 21st-century education.

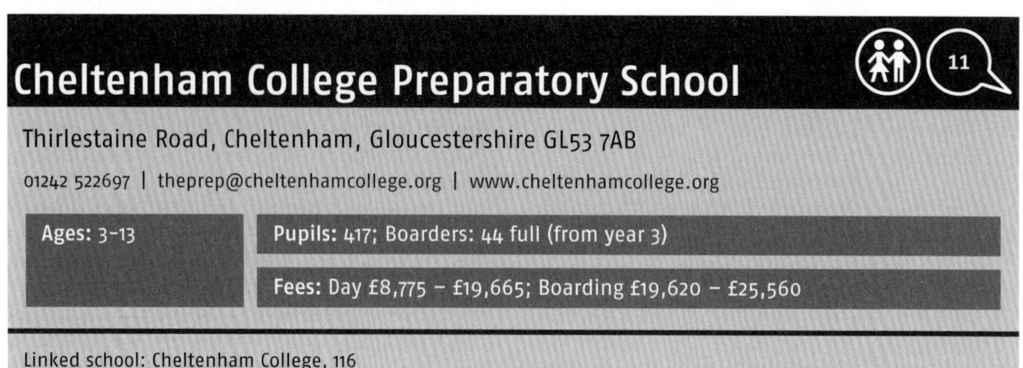

Cheltenham College Preparatory School

Thirlestaine Road, Cheltenham, Gloucestershire GL53 7AB

01242 522697 | theprep@cheltenhamcollege.org | www.cheltenhamcollege.org

Ages: 3–13

Pupils: 417; Boarders: 44 full (from year 3)

Fees: Day £8,775 – £19,665; Boarding £19,620 – £25,560

Linked school: Cheltenham College, 116

Head: Since 2018, Tom O'Sullivan LLB PGCE (40s), previously head of Old Buckenham Hall in Suffolk. Educated at Pate's Grammar School in Cheltenham and Durham University, where he read law. Most of his family are teachers but he resisted the idea for a while, first working as a graduate trainee for WH Smith and then as a headhunter in investment banking. 'I had a flat overlooking Singapore Harbour at the age of 23 but I hated my job,' he says. He followed his destiny and at 26 did a PGCE at Cambridge. 'It was the easiest decision in the world,' he says. 'It was so obvious to everybody except me that I should become a teacher and ten seconds into my first lesson I knew I wouldn't do anything else.'

First teaching job was at Beaudesert Park, where he worked as a science teacher, put on plays and coached sport, followed by six years at Mowden Hall as deputy head and then four years at Old Buckenham Hall as head. 'They have all been schools I've been able to put my heart and soul into,' he says. He still teaches science to years 7 and 8, as well as Thrive, the prep's PSHE programme. 'I knew I wanted to teach the 10 to 13 age group because they still laugh at my jokes,' he says. He wants lessons to be exciting and inspiring and prefers the word 'prep' to 'preparatory'. 'It's not enough that schools simply prepare the children for the challenges that lie ahead,' he says. 'Their schooldays should be the most magical time of their life.'

He sets great store by keeping in close touch with parents, standing outside the front of school most mornings and insisting that all tutors speak to every parent either face to face or on the phone during the first week of every term. 'I bore the staff by saying they should use email as little as possible,' he says. 'If it's positive news then an email is fine but if there is a concern then we must speak to parents. I want us to be accessible and to listen.' Parents say he has done a great job 'in moving the school forward'. The prep was a flourishing school before his arrival but he has made a few 'tweaks', such as simplifying the timetable and changing lunch arrangements, enabling 'all the staff to sit and talk with the children for an extra two and a half hours a week'. He works closely with the senior school head. They started in their respective posts at the same time and he appreciates talking to someone 'who is doing the same job'.

In his spare time he enjoys sport ('I've spent my whole life charging after a ball,' he jokes), theatre and walking Scooby, his gentle Great Dane. Therapy dog Scooby comes to school every day and is a huge hit with the children. The head has even launched Scooby awards for children who have excelled in some way. They each get a prized sketch of Scooby, drawn by the head's dad, and a small reward.

Entrance: Pupils start in all years, especially as Cheltenham is 'quite a transient place', with GCHQ and the ARRC (NATO Allied Rapid Reaction Corps) headquarters close by. Entry into the pre-prep (known as Kingfishers) is on a first come, first served basis while children entering in years 3 to 6 take part in a taster day and sit age-appropriate assessments. Entrance at 11 is selective – children attend an assessment day, doing verbal and non-verbal reasoning tests that can't be revised for. They also have an experience day, joining peers for fun activities, workshops and taster lessons. Being offered a place at the prep in year 7 or year 8 usually guarantees entry to Cheltenham College at 13+. Children still take CE in year 8 (the head has reviewed this and believes it's key to have 'an end point so children can feel they have accomplished something important') but it's only used for setting.

Exit: A tiny number leave at the age of 11 for local grammars or girls' schools. The majority stay till 13, when around 90 per cent move across the road to the senior school (in 2021, over 30 awards). A handful head elsewhere, mainly to Marlborough, Radley and Rugby.

Our view: Founded in 1863 as the college's junior department, the prep moved to its present site – a friendly mix of Edwardian red brick and newer additions over the road from the senior school – in 1908. The pre-prep is housed in a separate low-rise building, with plenty of outdoor play and learning, including forest school.

Therapy dog Scooby comes to school every day and is a huge hit with the children. The head has launched Scooby awards for those who have excelled in some way

The prep is 55 per cent boys and 45 per cent girls so genuinely co-ed. The year groups grow in size as children progress up the school, with two classes in reception but three or four classes per year from year 6. High-ceilinged classrooms, old wooden desks and iPads so teaching and learning are a creative blend of traditional and modern. Small classes, subject specialist teaching and lots of individual attention means that pupils can progress at their own rate. School uses 'learning power' ethos for learning, teaching skills like creative thinking, planning, learning from others and trying again when things are tough. A parent whose children joined in year 7 told us: 'My children came from a state primary and they were miles behind everybody else but the school nurtured and handheld them and it was divine. They quickly caught up.'

Lovely revamped library, with an inspiring display of teachers' favourite books, including The Chronicles of Narnia, The Naughtiest Girl in the School and The BFG. The school runs the Accelerated Reader programme, with children taking short quizzes after reading a book to check they've understood it. We saw some exciting teaching – from year 7s learning about the use of the semi-colon to a year 3 class confidently preparing presentations to chart the flow of a river. French taught from nursery and Latin currently taught from year 5. All pupils get a weekly computing lesson, incorporating internet safety, Python, coding, Raspberry Pi and Scratch. School caters for mild specific learning difficulties – dyslexia, maths learning difficulties, APD, dyspraxia, ADHD/ADD. Three full-time and two part-time learning support staff help children in small groups, pairs or one to one. No charge for this in pre-prep but parents pay for prep children's learning support.

Like its senior counterpart, the prep does masses of sport. Chief sports are rugby, hockey, cricket and athletics for boys and hockey, netball, tennis, athletics and cricket for the girls – all very inclusive. 'Everybody gets put in a team,' our spirited year 8 guides told us. 'You are never left out.' Pupils benefit from using the school facilities, including its 25-metre swimming pool, vast sports hall and impressive science and technology centre. Music department is based in the rather grand Lake House. Most pupils play at least one instrument and there are countless opportunities to perform – 20 musical ensembles, ranging from jazz bands to choral groups. Children throw themselves into drama with gusto, especially the upper school production in the spring term. 'The school nurtures this intangible quality of boundlessness – the idea that anything is possible,' said a parent. When we visited one of our guides came hotfoot from a dress rehearsal for The Three Musketeers. The school also runs more than 30 clubs and activities at lunchtime and after school, including karate, chess, street dance, baking, Lego and Scouts.

Parents praise the prep's pastoral care. Up to years 3 and 4 children have a form teacher but by year 5 they have a tutor. 'The tutor is base camp,' says the deputy head (pastoral), who meets weekly with section heads for the lower school, middle school and upper school, head of wellbeing, head of boarding and two school counsellors. Older children act as peer mentors to younger ones and every child belongs to one of six houses – Athens, Troy, Sparta, Persia, Rome and Corinth. Pupils are hugely proud of their school – the duo who showed us round couldn't stop talking about the myriad opportunities they'd had, from eating snails on a trip to France to watching newly-hatched chicks in science.

Boarding: Full and flexi boarding from the age of 7. Boarders live in a central boarding house on two floors of the main school building (girls below, boys above, plus several shared common rooms). Boarding team consists of head of boarding and his wife, tutors, matrons and gap students. Homely dorms range from fours and fives to the ever-popular long dorms for year 8s. Each long dorm houses 16 children and is divided into charming curtained cubicles with cabin beds.

The head wondered about getting rid of the long dorms but the children love them and wouldn't hear of it. Boarders from 10 different countries but never more than two or three from the same place. After activities in the evening year 7 and 8 boarders have supervised prep while the younger ones prepare for the next day. A host of weekend activities, including swimming, climbing, skateboarding and launching model boats on the prep's own lake. S

The last word: A lovely school, with dedicated teachers and sparky children who tackle everything with vim and vigour. They achieve great academic results and clearly have a lot of fun along the way.

Cheltenham Ladies' College
12
Bayshill Road, Cheltenham, Gloucestershire GL50 3EP
01242 520691 | enquiries@cheltladiescollege.org | www.cheltladiescollege.org
Ages: 11-18
Pupils: 873; sixth form: 330; Boarders: 682
Fees: Day £26,700 – £30,390; Boarding £39,780 – £44,790 pa

Principal: Since 2011, Eve Jardine-Young (late 40s), an old girl herself, she won a scholarship to the sixth form here from her school in Malawi where she grew up. Previously director of studies at Blundell's, she was also housemistress and head of sixth form development at Epsom College. She started her professional life as a structural engineer after studying engineering at Cambridge before changing tack to teach economics at Radley.

Parents remark on the strength of her relationship with the girls, who hold her in high esteem. She thinks hard about behaviour management and prefers, she says, to avoid 'thou shalt not' which contradicts the power of 'thou shalt'. Choosing to govern through trust, she sets out to win the hearts and minds of her pupils. Ms Jardine-Young, with typical humility, attributes her success to the fact that despite being a 'poster girl for achievement' with six A levels, and a degree in engineering from Cambridge, she is no stranger to disaster and has been through dark periods of questioning her own self-worth. 'How we feel about ourselves affects our behaviour,' she says. 'Students need to know that it's not all plain sailing – they may well get rejected from a number of jobs, it's not about letting anyone down.'

A woman who combines an endearing vulnerability with determined resilience, she still occasionally stumbles in her speech, a stutter that dogged her teenage years but which she keeps tightly tethered now.

She 'found her voice', she says, when she moved from engineering into teaching. She is a commanding presence despite or perhaps because of her broad toothy grin, heart on sleeve manner and most importantly of all, a deep commitment to her vocation. Parents notice how the girls listen carefully to her speeches. No fidgeting and sidelong whispers but instead a curious, attentive focus.

Still an academic at heart she spends a lot of time thinking and thinking more. Foremost in these thoughts is how to bring out the best in the young people (which is how she prefers to describe the girls) in her care. 'It's not about grades, qualifications and outcomes,' she says passionately, 'but the building of the person for the long term and for life. We need to enable them to become life-long learners, ready for the next step.' This is particularly important for women, she concedes.

Having experienced all-boys boarding schools she is determined that her young students will not be fodder for the social circuit (at least during term time). She eschews 'socials' that involve bus loads of girls being shipped to boys' schools to dance, and instead prefers to concentrate on building relationships with local state secondaries: 'What's important is that the pupils learn to mix with lots of different kinds of people. I see my role as encouraging them to become more thoughtful, and more grounded. Included in this is the work the school embraces with other local schools, state and independent, as well as with key industries in the town and its environs, including the Cheltenham Festival and GCHQ. My concern is to give to each student things they cannot get at home, from engineering to Greek as well as social interaction. I would like to create children who can challenge hierarchy,' she avers, an ambition we suspect is a far cry from that of the college's principal when Ms Jardine-Young was a pupil here. Fearless – 'My husband's the only person who has called me brave,' she confides – and yet brave is a much more apt adjective, as it's in countering the fear that she excels and she is astute in encouraging her pupils to do the same. A memorable head and woman, she is far from finished with rolling back boundaries and chipping away at glass ceilings. We think her ten predecessors in the role would approve.

Entrance: Girls apply for boarding places from over 500 preps and senior schools all over the UK – one of the most diverse intakes of any of the senior independent schools we visit. Around a third are non UK nationals (girls come from 47 different countries); a small proportion (about 20 per cent) of very local families apply for day places.

A memorable head and inspiring woman, Ms Jardine-Young is far from finished with rolling back boundaries and chipping away at glass ceilings

Main entries are at 11+ into year 7 and 13+ into year 9 and both years are heavily oversubscribed. Indeed, the number of applicants has risen during the pandemic as word spread about the success of the online provision here. At 11+ 45 boarding places and 25 day places available and about 45 places available at 13+. Applicants for an 'occasional place' in year 8 or year 10 will also be considered.

About 45 places available each year in the sixth form. Candidates are accepted on the basis of success in exams (up to four subjects for A level students, up to six for IB) and interview. For existing pupils there is no academic bar from continuing into the sixth form – as long as you've done your best, you stay. A few leave each year, to eg co-ed sixth forms and day schools.

Parents should note that for the 11 and 13 plus (maths, English and reasoning assessments) there is a high bar for the English assessment. If your daughter excels in maths, but struggles with English, you can forget it. Much weight is put on the interview as well as on spoken and written English. Nor is selection based solely on academics. Ask yourself what your daughter will contribute. Will she thrive here, taking advantage of all the opportunities?

Exit: For the daunting prospect of life beyond CLC each student is supported and advised by the Professional Guidance Centre. Staff support girls in choosing future pathways, not just which university, but also with a view to the longer term such as higher degrees and career options. There are talks too, by representatives from a huge range of colleges and universities in the UK and the USA, Canada and Asia.

Ms Jardine-Young takes a typically careful and modest approach to the success stories of her pupils. 'I could be plastering exits all over the website but some girls don't get in and I don't want to create that pressure,' she says. Unlike many academically successful schools, CLC are not afraid to support marginal candidates for Oxbridge at the potential expense of data. As long as they embody excellence – independence, inspiration and empowerment – the school will back them.

Ninety per cent to Russell Group in 2021, with Imperial, LSE, UCL, King's College London, Durham and Edinburgh all popular. In 2021, 13 to Oxbridge, and 23 medics. Lots to US too, including Yale, Brown, Berkeley, Columbia, Georgetown, Johns Hopkins, Berklee College of Music, Swarthmore, Chicago, Southern California, Northeastern and Vanderbilt. Others across the rest of the globe, including to Bocconi (Italy), Hong Kong, Navarra (Spain) and New South Wales (Australia). A wide range of courses, from aeronautical engineering and geography to costume design and music.

Latest results: In 2021, 96 per cent 9-7 at GCSE; 85 per cent A*/A at A level (96 per cent A*-B). IB average score 42. In 2019 (the last year exams took place), 90 per cent 9-7 at GCSE; 72 per cent A*/A at A level. IB average score 40.

Teaching and learning: Still proudly retains its place as one of the leading academic schools in the country (IB results are among the best in the UK). However, they themselves acknowledge that they lag behind schools with a similar history and profile. The spin is a positive one. They are firmly not results-driven; they set out to educate the whole child for the long run and that goes far beyond GCSE and A levels.

Among the outstanding provision that grabbed our interest was EET (engineering, enterprise and technology). Launched as part of the curriculum in 2015, girls can take it up as early as 11. 'Breaking the rules and learning from mistakes,' James Dyson's wise pronouncement on learning design technology, perfectly encapsulates the culture that is the face of the modern CLC. Students have fun; they enjoy taking risks. They laugh, they experiment, and they innovate and this results in some impressive products from rockets to bridges, robots to vehicles. Textiles, another strong and well-established subject, is part of the course and students are given the option to incorporate an HPQ (higher product qualification) into their GCSEs. Motivation and ambition run high with several prizes won in national competitions – a sign language translator, one of their most acclaimed innovations. The momentum and strength of this course is evident from the high uptake and the impressive number of girls who win Arkwright engineering scholarships.

Traditional 'feminine' subjects still taught – food and nutrition GCSE is popular and in textiles we saw a light-up pillow, a fairy tutu and a mosquito-proof jumpsuit.

Each house has its own dedicated 'prep room' where the younger girls can do timetabled, supervised study each evening. It lays the groundwork for organised self-disciplined study, which they are ready for by year 10, from when they have their own desks in their dormitory where they do most of their work.

Students regard the stronger subjects to be science, particularly biology and chemistry. Languages GCSEs are taken early – as soon as they are ready. Parents like the fact that there is no spoon-feeding. Pupils are guided and supported to think independently from the start.

Around two hundred visiting speakers each year deliver talks, which form a natural part of the enrichment programme. Leaders in their field talk on an impressively wide range of subjects, from ethnomusicology to body image. Professor Grayling has visited, as have notable old girls including artists Kate Daudy and Clare Marx.

Academic provision during lockdown was regarded universally as exceptional. 'We constantly had to pivot at speed,' says Ms Jardine-Young, slightly breathlessly, 'but nimbleness paid off,' with constant tweaking, listening to feedback from parents and pupils, and an awareness of all the different pressures pupils were under – some in separate time zones, some doing the IB, others GCSE or A level and others needing to feel the safe structure of a school day routine. The swift introduction of new devices for all pupils, recording all lessons to facilitate joining lessons in different time zones as well as constant availability of staff are just some measures that have been adopted. National exam results themselves were testament to this commitment. Another battle fought hard by all the academic staff, determined to place the school beyond criticism, while ensuring their students won the results they deserved.

Learning support and SEN: For a school with a high academic profile, there is a surprisingly broad mix of ability. As well as girls with mild learning difficulties, the school can accommodate pupils with moderate hearing and visual impairments. The main campus is fully accessible for pupils with mobility issues and one boarding house offers wheelchair access. Parents are encouraged to communicate any specific needs to the admissions department.

One of the country's leading academic schools but not results driven; they set out to educate the whole child for the long run

The arts and extracurricular: The arts take centre stage here. More than 1,000 pupils are involved in music lessons (timetabled so that no one ever misses an academic lesson). Each boarding house has its own practice rooms and some have a fine grand piano in the main sitting room where girls can practise or perform. A wealth of orchestras, ensembles and bands from a full symphony orchestra to Hellacappella, with lots of chances to perform at various concerts throughout the year. An advantage of a large school is that in addition to whole-school events, there are the house competitions and concerts which are a particular highlight for the girls, full of ribaldry and in-jokes. Music scholars mentor younger students. A recording studio is a relatively recent addition; the Princess Hall is a jewel of the history of the school, with capacity of over a thousand, where a number of the formal concerts take place.

The impressive Parabola Arts Centre is a 325-seat auditorium that is also used by Cheltenham Festival and incorporates a full orchestra pit and extendable stage. Girls not only play in the orchestra and perform on stage but also get involved with theatre management, lighting and stage design. Nor do they confine themselves to the excellent inside areas made for performance, creative use is made of the gardens, and open air productions include Love's Labours Lost and Othello.

The Cheltenham Performing Arts Festival is a highlight in the calendar, a chance for the whole college to participate actively in an internationally renowned event on their doorstep, to contribute and to learn from the experience. Students compete in drama and art as well as contributing to the logistics of the event, with musical classes ranging from solo, duet and trio to world folk music and songs from the shows.

Five drama productions each year, for which all girls in each year group can audition. Senior girls also direct younger ones in smaller productions. We hear a lot from schools about pupils getting involved with every detail of a production but it is refreshing when we see that actually happening. 'Beware of being swept under the carpet if you are not talented enough,' muttered a couple of 15 -year-olds into their soup.

A treasure cave of a library with thousands of delicious-smelling old books and lots of sixth formers beavering away. If a book isn't there it will be produced in a whisper, by the next day if not immediately. Academic journals and papers can be accessed and students can borrow music and films for the week end. The lower school library by contrast is modern, light and colourful, a welcoming environment to develop and enhance a love of learning.

These girls were not born articulate (although you would be forgiven for thinking they were). A classical liberal education would be hollow without a good dose of oratory and you will find it in spades here. Debating takes place in all corners of the school but young female Ciceros can flex their skills particularly powerfully under the watchful eye of works by illustrious artists, Edward Burne-Jones and William Morris, in the magnificent Council room with its stained-glass rose window and high vaulted wooden ceiling.

Sport: Sport has long been the Achilles' heel of CLC. It's certainly not for want of facilities, these are as tip-top as the rest. An all whistles and bells health and fitness centre that the public are lucky enough to be able to book, a 25-metre pool with such up-to-date hygiene provision that it boasts 'no chlorine!' And who needs one, when you could have three sports halls, the most recent of which can be divided to make a fourth hall or a venue for cream teas or Pimm's in the rain. Astro hockey pitches galore, a share of Cheltenham rowing club, squash courts, aerobics and yoga studios, mirrors, large windows and shiny floors all brought together with a tidy purple colour scheme. Inspiration is also shipped in in the form of university students running athletics programmes for junior girls.

There are 21 sports on offer, from trampolining and badminton to the more traditional hockey, tennis, lacrosse and netball. So, what's the problem? Parents suggest it's giving the girls choice early on between 'team sports' and 'multi sports'; those who choose the latter (dance, badminton etc) apparently become demotivated and lose their competitive edge. Girls tell a slightly different story: too much emphasis placed on talent and winning, not enough 'joining in'. Some responsibility may lie with the timetable which has space for only two hours of sport in the week and an hour and a half on Saturday. The swimming pool, for all its eco cleanliness, is very rarely used, we were told. The girls 'generally hate swimming and won't get in the pool unless we're forced to.' Even the house sports competitions fail to match their music rivals in enthusiasm and humorous tales to recount after lights out.

The school is aware that more needs to be done and swanky facilities are never enough. Effort has already been made – appointments into the sports department as well as restructuring how sport is organised. Covid has played some part in delaying the fruition of these efforts, but the seeds have been sown.

Boarding: Eleven houses (six junior, five for sixth form only) are dotted around the town, Girls here need flat comfortable shoes and are still in danger of 'September heels' they cover so much ground during the day. A rolling programme of refurbishment means that while the houses are very different, with distinct characters, they all have a similar blueprint. Sophisticated security systems for entrance and exit. Polished parquet floors, huge comfy sofas and similarly large scale televisions, with the odd grand piano downstairs. Studies for the younger years to do prep at their individual desks and cubicles and study bedrooms for the older girls. Two to four girls in a room in the junior houses, sixth formers have their own bedroom. Not quite to five-star hotel standard but not far off and certainly a far cry from the draughty Victorian bedrooms and crowded dormitories of the last century.

Traditional 'feminine' subjects still taught – food and nutrition GCSE is popular and in textiles we saw a light-up pillow, a fairy tutu and a mosquito-proof jumpsuit

All girls eat in their houses, canteen style but at round tables in small numbers, an atmosphere of civilised café rather than school dining room. House entertainment/celebrations/competitions and church foster a family feel which inspires a sense of belonging, security and being able to escape the bustle of the school day. 'A sanctuary,' says the school website. We would agree, and if you are lucky enough to have an excellent housemistress (who tend to be recruited specially for the job rather than from the teaching staff) then you have a winning formula.

The choice, until the academic year 21/22 has always been between day and full boarding. Weekends are busy, with Saturday morning school and matches in the afternoon. Numbers of boarders low below year 9 but increase further up the school as day girls choose to board. This is partly a reflection of the success of boarding here but also 'because school is so much easier if you board,' confided one girl. Encouraged by parents in response to a questionnaire, a flexi boarding option is being trialled offering day pupils the chance to stay overnight during the week (but not on Saturday). Full boarders will also be able to go out each weekend rather than only at fixed exeats.

Ethos and heritage: Retiring the universally loathed dowdy green uniform was one of the first changes introduced by Eve Jardine-Young, 'essential for their confidence'. Battalions of girls in stylish tailored cyan wool jackets complete with suede collars and indigo skirts at a flattering length (trousers also an option) march across the road and just when you think there can't be any more, another regiment appears.

Girls' confidence and leadership qualities develop naturally as part of girls' fulfilment rather than being pursued separately as ends in themselves

Founded in 1853, Cheltenham Ladies' was always one of the more (if not the most) serious of the all-girls boarding schools. It was school of choice for parents who wanted their daughters to have a thorough academic education and to be taken seriously in the outside world for their brains as well as their feminine charm. Serious they still may be but bluestockings they are not. Tradition and history emanate from every stained-glass window and marble-tiled corridor and the nine former headmistresses stare down from their portraits in the Lower Hall, but there is a fresh, modern breeze running through the school. It's not just about new facilities and uniform, but rather the diversity of the pupil body, the attitudes of the staff and the innovation that you see in all parts of the curriculum.

A strong sense of giving back has always been part of the ethos here. The school has now developed 26 partner organisations across town – including special schools and state primaries – where pupils can contribute through voluntary work or collaboration. Girls spend 1,000 hours per week working with these community projects and often ask to continue when they are on study leave, anxious to fulfil their commitment.

CLC's glittering array of alumni reflects a pioneering ethos that has survived and evolved through the centuries. Girls are educated to be who they are and follow their passions, they are not pigeon-holed and funnelled into particular professions. The list is long and spans actresses and fashion designers (Kristin Scott Thomas and Katharine Hamnett) to politicians and journalists (Amber Rudd and Rosie Boycott). Those who have recently left are showing similar flair and can-do attitude, many of them working to make the world a better place whether it be the environment, education, creative arts or the UN as well as AI, tech and PR. One recently completed a challenge with her brother rowing across the Atlantic in 43 days.

Pastoral care, inclusivity and discipline: 'Cheltenham has always been diverse,' Eve Jardine-Young tells me firmly – 'Queen Victoria's god-daughter was the first black student here in the early 1880s.' Nor was the school ever exclusively or specifically Christian. The circular prayer room was designed to be inclusive and hosts different religious groups throughout the week.

The demographic now is certainly diverse, with pupils from all over the world as well as all parts of the UK. Greater cultural awareness and understanding of different experiences is carefully nurtured by the school. International ambassadors help other girls from a particular country and pupils are encouraged to give mutual support while retaining a sense of identity.

Aware that cliques can form along national lines, much is done to ensure there is integration but not at the expense of happiness and security. The school will say their endeavours are successful, reports from pupils paint a slightly less rosy picture, but it's a difficult balance to strike.

Heightened awareness of mental wellbeing applies here as much as anywhere. There is a deep understanding of the challenges girls face in today's society, whether it be eating disorders, LGBTQ+ or Everyone's Invited, where the issue of consent is so central. The focus has been on enabling peer support and encouraging close working with staff. The Black Lives Matter movement following the death of George Floyd has led to senior pupils leading house-based workshops with younger pupils; staff have also had training to develop best practice and deepen intercultural understanding. One of the school's founding objectives was the provision of a 'sound and broad education' based on Christian principles. Tolerance is a big part of this and an attribute that is key to addressing LGBTQ+ issues, says Eve Jardine-Young.

Essentially, we are told, these things are dealt with in the course of the day, the week, the term

Hatherop Castle School

– 'The issues are not regarded as main events – but a natural and seamless part of everyday life and discussion.' 'The girls are not nervous about how they come across and lead the charge in breaking down residual taboos.' A year 10 pupil who identified as transgender was supported by the school and they chose to continue through the sixth form.

On a practical level, significant steps have been taken to address mental health across the board. These include halving the number of lessons from 12 to six longer periods of 55 minutes in order to slow the pace of the day and increase a sense of calm. In addition, for one hour a week the whole school is off timetable to allow for a wellbeing programme to bring different year groups together. Sacrosanct hours which can be devoted to peer mentoring in whole school year groups and small masterclasses (girls remarked that they enjoy being able to participate and give input, and now that the focus has moved away from bullying they feel more engaged). Two confidential counsellors are permanently available in the medical centre (pupils can self-refer).

Giving back has always been part of the ethos here. School has now developed 26 partner organisations across town – including special schools and state primaries – where pupils contribute through voluntary work or collaboration

Equality, diversity and inclusion (EDI) are given prominence in school's documents and the acronym rolls off the tongue of members of staff we spoke to. There is some self-consciousness about the antiquated nature of 'Ladies' in the school name. They choose to keep it, as they choose to preserve other historic features that might appear anachronistic to today's eyes, but Eve Jardine-Young prefers to address the school as 'everyone' in whole school assembly, and avoids the collective 'ladies' or 'girls'.

Pupils and parents: However diverse the College may (or may not) have been in Queen Victoria's time there are now more different cultures and nationalities forming part of the school community than ever before, with 30 different languages spoken and over 40 nationalities. What they all share is a refreshingly unselfconscious, purposeful attitude. They value the important friendships that are made in these precious formative years and learn that they belong to something greater than themselves while at the same time developing a strong sense of self, and what they are capable of. Confidence and leadership qualities develop naturally as part of their fulfilment rather than being pursued as ends in themselves and girls emerge at 18 with a strong sense of empowerment.

The English families tend to be fairly conservative, observed one parent, but that doesn't prevent their daughters from boldly carving out their own course in life and the school gives them the grounding and confidence to do this. There is a lot of money, particularly among international families, and another parent suggested that children of 'just about managing' families, or those joining from the state sector can struggle to settle.

The pupils have very little school-arranged contact with boys – the odd Calsoc ball with their obvious all-boys counterparts in the junior years, and some more intellectual pursuits such as science symposiums with eg Winchester College in the sixth form. More than one 15-year-old pined for more: 'The Cheltenham College boys don't want us – they have their own girls.' But Eve Jardine-Young will not be swayed, whether by the pupils or their parents, from her conviction that it is in her pupils' best interests to learn, develop and grow in the secure environs of the school, where they can get used to having their voices heard, and where the notion that they wouldn't be considered for a leadership role would never enter their heads.

Money matters: Nine per cent of pupils on means-tested bursaries, four per cent have 100 per cent fee remission, and three per cent have a remission of 50 per cent or more. Families can apply for assistance with fees (from one to 100 per cent, depending on their circumstances).

Around 20 per cent of pupils are scholars – no fee remission but the scholarship programme has a wealth of opportunities aimed at stretching and developing individual talent for the benefit of the whole community. This is a highly honoured position at CLC and those who earn the title play a key role in the life of the school and enjoy the chance to lead and inspire others while fulfilling their own potential.

The last word: An education for young women with purpose (as well as brains). Ideal for the all-rounder who wants to get on in life and take advantage of every opportunity – but primarily with the end game of giving something back rather than self- aggrandisement. If your daughter is bright, open-minded and bursting with energy and enthusiasm, look no further.

Clayesmore Preparatory School

Iwerne Minster, Blandford Forum, Dorset DT11 8PH

01747 812122 | admissions@clayesmore.com | www.clayesmore.com

Ages: 2-13

Pupils: 170; Boarders: 52 full (from year 3)

Fees: Day £8,025 – £17,250; Boarding £26,124 pa

Linked school: Clayesmore School, 131

Head: Since 2019, Jonathon Anderson, previously deputy head at Westbourne House Prep. Degree in business economics from Exeter; spent two years working in financial services before teacher training course. After five years at Swanbourne House School, he joined Exeter Junior School as head of maths, moving to Westbourne House with his wife Hester as houseparents. They have two children and the essential prep head's labrador.

Entrance: Pre-prep numbers now growing again after slight fall, helped by free come-and-play toddler and parent sessions. Plenty of well-connected locals, but don't expect huge amounts of socialising as many work full time. 'Some parents… think they'll get into a niche little coffee club but it doesn't happen,' said mother.

Further up, healthy levels of prep applications in top years, but not a school for all comers. While they take from a wider ability range than the competition, pupils must be able to access curriculum. Numeracy and literacy assessments for applicants into years 6-8. Ask for reports and may observe child at current school (avoids shattering expectations if they attend taster day here and aren't offered a place). Will only accept in top junior years if child will make transition to senior school and 'at least get some GCSEs'.

Best to recover equilibrium by reciting routes of the school buses – who wouldn't be drawn to Compton Acres, Sturminster Marshall and Spetisbury.

Exit: Currently, 85 per cent plus move up to senior school but not prescribed. Happily accommodate those preparing for entrance exams elsewhere, including grammars and other independents (Canford inevitably takes a few) though more stay to join the senior school as 'our reputation for bringing the best out of individuals grows,' says school.

Once here, families tend to stay on, decision reinforced during compare and contrast open day visits elsewhere. 'I suddenly thought, "I love it but need to look around," so did all the local ones and came back,' says mother. 'Has just got the most amazing feel to it.'

Only time pupils have been asked to leave (single figures, says school) is down to bullying. 'We do everything we possibly can but there comes a point where it's not acceptable.'

Our view: Set in a generous corner of school's 62 acres with a comfortable, home-like feel. Operationally run as a separate school with own uniform including much loved long tartan skirt. 'It keeps your legs warm and the stains don't show – had food all over mine,' said nostalgic senior pupil.

While resources are shared with senior school, they're clearly delineated. Path from main building to music block divides the play areas: 'Like Mexican wall though more porous.' Pupils go to main hall for lunch and use eg swimming pool and forest school. Memories of original prep school site, in nearby Charlton Marshall, are summoned by impressive cedar of Lebanon which towers over the turning circle – a decision sentiment rather than species-led.

Tales of year 8 pupils still enjoying school's adventure playground, the perk of ringing large, wall-mounted bell at supper time and links with the community – Brownie pack, run by staff, is the only one 'in the valley' and includes local children and pupils – reinforce sense of a compact and reassuring world.

Low-rise buildings house the youngest pupils – nursery and reception/year 1 – in big, bright and open plan classrooms, amid plentiful greenery and the odd unexpected touch (sixth former's 'spaceman' sculpture.)

Focus is on encouragement and thoughtful planning, from visual timetables in boarding houses – sun for wake up, 'good for reluctant readers' – to description of mini adventure playground as 'confidence equipment'. Seems to work (two boys tearing around on crutches during our visit).

Plenty to enjoy including path that winds round the back, taking in glasshouse (once used to grow melons, now used for ceramics). Out front there's the Everett Building (2008) – very attractive – and 70s teaching and boarding block building that isn't, though disguised by greenery. 'A well-functioning machine if not a beautiful one.'

Emphasis on creativity: Macbeth-inspired poems were enjoyably big on yuck factor – 'sprinkle in fly vomit so grim...'; 'an autumn dragon with 'hurricane breath'

Keep work pressure to a minimum (no prep until year 5, for example) – sensible given range of activities done by some pupils and timetable recently rejigged so tutor time happens at end of day ('more effective learning time'). A recent prospectus may state firmly that 'every child achieves academic success', but is more specifically about recognising individual potential.

Specialist teaching in all subjects from year 5, and in art, music and DT from year 2. Latin added in year 7. Much setting and streaming (English and maths from year 3, most other subjects by year 6) so can cater for broad ability range.

Emphasis throughout on sensible learning habits. Youngest 'plan, do and review' while new Clayesmore Compass emphasises collaboration (contribution award has replaced man or woman of the match), plus risk taking, challenge and (from year 6) creativity.

Not that pupils need much telling. Macbeth-inspired poems were enjoyably big on yuck factor – 'sprinkle in fly vomit so grim...'; an autumn dragon with 'hurricane breath'. Librarian encourages ambitious reading with initiatives like book spine poetry (pile up the titles and see how they sound): 'The railway children/bowl like the devil/into battle/a wrinkle in time.'

Plenty of high tech resources as well, courtesy of Google Classroom – now in use across the school – 'helps children become responsible for own learning'. While not everyone was convinced ('I don't like reading, it's boring – have to sound out the letters and do it at home,' thought one little lad in reception) we couldn't see much in the way of deprivation, judging by universal enthusiasm for recent task – delights of windmills they'd just created. 'Had to make the sails turn.'

Learning support praised by all and accredited by CReSTeD (specific learning difficulties) and NACE (gifted children) though felt to be poorly understood in wider world. 'There is a misconception that school specialises in SEN. It doesn't specialise, it just does it amazingly well,' said mother.

Currently around 90 pupils with SEN – most SpLD but also ASD and ADHD, support courtesy of learning resource centre in middle of school, staff able to do just about anything, one working with pupil to pick out describing words for teeth – 'mysterious, tiny, heavy...' In class, gap year students are not-so-hidden weapon – one looks gangling next to the pupil he's supporting (though doesn't look so very much older) – a particular asset with behaviour management.

Upwards pressure on ambition translates into other areas – such as sports – though not excessively so. School reckons that rival teams who used to be drawn primarily by the location and the quality of match teas now come because 'they'll get a good game as well as all the trimmings'.

Main sports rugby, hockey plus soupcon of football though most successful tend to be cricket (U13 county champions) and cross-country – school organises major inter-school event for 20 schools or so. Most pitches grass plus Astro shared with senior school.

Bar desire for slight pepping up of sports generally (less rounders, more football), few mega grumbles from parents who feel that there's a decent number of matches. 'There is an A, B and C team and they do ensure that they have fixtures,' said parent. 'Quite a variety – and can do horse riding,' agreed another.

Arts generally very highly rated. Music team housed in what was once the trophy room with must-have zebra heads would be all the better for purpose built performance spaces – chapel, currently main venue, just too small. Otherwise, impressively successful, with over 130 pupils learning at least one instrument, numerous ensembles and assorted competitions across the school.

Boarding: Boarders mainly year 4 upwards, though one pupil in year 3 having a great time courtesy of year 6 mentor – 'very kind and does French plaits for me'. All happens above the shop, in large, generally bright and very clean rooms, if a tad low on ambience. Loads of clothes storage (often empty thanks to almost non-stop, highly efficient laundry system).

Gentle approach to rewards and sanctions keeps things home-like. Spickest, spannest dorm gets surprise 'muck' (jargon for afternoon break treat). Individual winners get slap-up meal at head of boarding's house. For older boarders, perks include moving closer to the bathroom. Saturday school keeping bustle going well into the weekend.

Money matters: Wide range of scholarships awarded to year 7 pupils, though fee reduction – between 2.5 and 10 per cent – doesn't shave much off that chunky termly invoice.

The last word: A buzzy, ambitious school with a homely vibe that's encouraging, nurturing and innovative in its teaching – including for SEN.

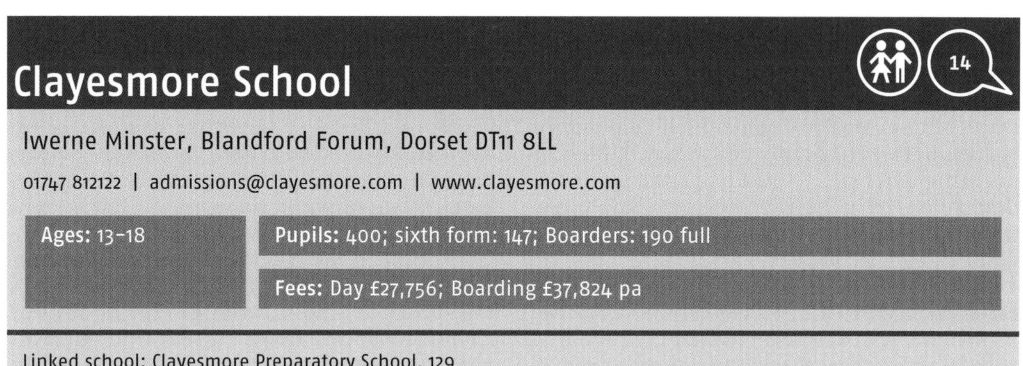

Clayesmore School

Iwerne Minster, Blandford Forum, Dorset DT11 8LL

01747 812122 | admissions@clayesmore.com | www.clayesmore.com

Ages: 13–18

Pupils: 400; sixth form: 147; Boarders: 190 full

Fees: Day £27,756; Boarding £37,824 pa

Linked school: Clayesmore Preparatory School, 129

Head: Since 2016, Joanne Thomson BA MBA (40s). First headship. Previously joint deputy head for eight years at Christ's Hospital School, preceded by 13 years at Aiglon College. First post was at Repton Prep as English teacher, assistant houseparent and sports coach.

Model of modern marriage offers cheering example of give and take. Husband Frank, another senior teacher, is head of PSHE here, has worked at most of same schools and is happy to let Mrs T take the lead. 'There's never a power struggle,' she stresses. Two children, both at young adult stage.

Parents at Christ's praised her 'industriousness and conviviality'. We were struck by her calm, understated kindness (the only head this reviewer has ever met who physically booked us a cab back to the station – though possibly to ensure we actually left…).

Never envisaged being a head and, 'It's not about the power but making a difference.' She's succeeding, said a parent, by effective delegation. 'Doesn't have a finger in every pie but lets the school get on with it which is better for the staff.' Senior pupil praised her 'interaction' with pupils. 'Clear to see philosophy,' said year 10 guide. Particular strength is 'thought for the day' speeches. 'I was like "How is she able to be so relatable?"' How, indeed?

Spent first year desk-bound, sorting systems and structures that were under pressure from rise in pupil numbers. Time-consuming but necessary which meant that some parents felt they didn't see enough of her. That's now being rectified. Also – somehow – completed an MBA over the school holidays. Sent out questionnaire and is implementing suggestions – including extending autumn half term to two weeks.

This school (like others she's worked in) is notable for exceptional pastoral care – it's a must-have, she says. Isn't planning drastic change but sensible rethinking so school can do its best by all pupils throughout the ability spectrum. Inclusiveness will be helped along with greater focus on tailored learning and monitoring, supported by extensive, joined-up digital technology. Small but beautifully designed booklet serves up changes with strong dose of reassurance.

Her younger (state-educated) self would baulk at independent school career – hence desire to share resources as widely as possible. Community-related activity includes pupils working at local special school, local elderly regularly invited in for events, while pipe band – goes with school's name, rather than location – 'is out and about' (not as threatening as it sounds).

Best part of the job? No surprises that it's the pupils. 'They keep you grounded, especially ours, they're very open and tell it like it is, they're great.'

Entrance: The normal battle over semantics. School says 'non-selective' when what it means is 'as non-selective as you can be,' says head. Bottom line is that all prospective pupils must be able to access the curriculum and be capable of achieving 'some' GCSEs (numbers will vary fairly widely but will include core subjects).

Around half of senior entry comes from junior school plus local preps (Forres Sandle

Manor, Castle Court, Dumpton, Walhampton, Durlston Court, Salisbury Cathedral). Increasingly fed by families from London and the south east. Boy heavy – 100 or so more than girls. Evenly split day and boarding.

Take around 90 in year 9; handful in year 10 and around 20 into the sixth form (with at least five grade 4 passes at GCSE).

Exit: The 20 per cent fall-out after GCSEs includes several short-stay Germans returning home. Others relocate or move to state sector and some leave (after extensive discussion) if demands of curriculum would simply be too much. Most to uni or apprenticeships – vast range of courses and destinations including Exeter, Bristol, Edinburgh, Oxford Brookes, Bath and York. A few on gap years. One medic in 2021.

Latest results: In 2021, 40 per cent 9-7 at GCSE; 33 per cent A*/A at A level (64 per cent A*-B). In 2019 (the last year when exams took place), 27 per cent 9-7 at GCSE; 20 per cent A*/A at A level (48 per cent A*-B).

Teaching and learning: Everyone – not just teachers and pupils but their parents and our taxi driver (a past parent, daughter now on the way to being something massive in the City) – stresses that families don't need to divide and rule, sending most academically able child elsewhere. School will do wonders with them all.

Former head of drama, heavy Twitter user, is clearly loving new role as digital learning supremo and runs regular insets on the wonders of podcasting

'Still marked as being a school where they do a fabulous job with learning support but they're brilliant with everybody else as well,' said parent. Not everyone will get A*s and As but 'what you will see is people who nobody ever expected it doing well.' Even inspectors could only pick on the consistency of marking as needing improvement.

Teachers hold frequent meetings about pupils – 'Try to get beyond the label,' agrees deputy head – and are equally good at winkling out hidden staff talent. One, outed as successful novelist, now runs creative writing workshops.

Class sizes drop steadily down the years, average 16 in year 9 (maximum 17), 11 in years 10 and 11 (max 19) and just eight in sixth form (13) with a pupil/teacher ratio of eight to one. Teachers 'young and dynamic', says school – average age is 41, so perhaps young-ish, but definitely committed (16 at the school for more than a decade).

Does the range, from facilitating A levels plus others – economics to psychology, photography to textiles as well as (very unusually) six BTECs (IT – most popular – plus sport, music technology, hospitality, travel and tourism and performing and production arts). Were sniffed at by Russell Group unis but things are changing, says school – though pupils are encouraged to mix with A levels.

Mega A level subjects are business (most popular) followed by geography, maths and photography – an eclectic mix that reflects the diverse enthusiasms of pupils though a fair few D and E grades in tough subjects at GCSE and A level.

Not much that's outré, unless offer of computer science and ICT IGCSE counts. Large take-up for DT, no surprise given rave reviews from teacher and range of goodies produced – papaya chess board a highlight mentioned by parents. Surprisingly low numbers for drama – single figures, just ahead of Latin.

Teaching is fun and animated. We watched year 10 maths where teams worked on probability problems, chains of different coloured arrows climbing up the whiteboards. Maths teacher is 'best I've ever had,' testified pupil. 'Understands how to have the class gripped as well as learning.'

Sensible use of technology, so joined up it must have created a virtuous circle, is now a feature of all subjects. Former head of drama, heavy Twitter user who's 'really into pedagogy,' says head, is clearly loving new role as digital learning supremo – runs regular insets on the wonders of podcasting (many staff do their own).

Other fresh ideas include the new Clayesmore Courses, covering areas like history of art. No assessment pressure. Instead, 'we're starting to show kids that school can be quite fun.'

For those in need of reassurance, you'll hear (lots) about school's most successful pupils. The bottom line is that this is learning without tears – an exceptionally happy and successful school that does well by all its pupils.

Learning support and SEN: Particular strength is whole-school commitment to SEN. Around 130 pupils have needs such as SpLD, mild ASD and ADHD/ADD and school ensures that training and regular insets extend to all staff, including rugby coaches. Differentiation is 'staggering', says head. 'I've never been in a place where teachers are so united and committed to the cause.'

All pupils have CAT test in year 9 designed as 'stress free screening' to establish 'range of possibilities'. Those needing extra support can attend informal drop-in maths sessions or may swap languages for extra classes in teaching and learning centre (TLC, geddit?) which is located slap bang in middle of school – 'no wooden hut in the grounds,' says head – and universally rated as phenomenal. Separate classrooms for those needing EAL support.

Particular strength is whole-school commitment to SEN. 'I've never been in a place where teachers are so united and committed to the cause,' says head

Specialist staff, some full, some part time, many with teaching responsibilities, all with post-grad qualifications, are regularly consulted by other teachers wanting to know eg how to support the very able. Accreditation from NACE (gifted children) and CReSTeD (specific learning difficulties) reflects school's strengths in both areas.

The arts and extracurricular: 'Don't have to be good at activities to have fun,' said pupil. 'I'm not specially good – I just like to get involved.'

If the grounds and activities weren't enticement enough (CCF so popular that one year 11 pupil joined them for major chunk of summer holidays), school also invites pupils to complete 100 activities in 10 categories including sport and arts – as well as academics. Must demonstrate leadership, participation and passive involvement (watching stuff – our favourite). One year 10 winner of – external – debating competition even watched the inauguration of President Trump.

Award for completion (including chunky cash prize) currently being rethought. 'I want pupils to participate for intrinsic reasons rather than monetary reward,' says head.

School's small size leads to variable results (not necessarily ideal for families fixated on winning at all cost) – but has benefits, too, when younger and older pupils work in same space in art and drama, for example. 'Gives positive role models,' says art teacher.

Bar school-wide desire for bigger and better performance space (delightful but bijou chapel with electric – though not, sadly, solar-powered – organ is currently a major venue for whole school), music and drama both highly praised and on everyone's radar, including parents whose children aren't performers. Dedicated head of music felt to be upping standards across the board – particularly for choral music, though range of opportunities for instrumentalists (to grade 8, a few at diploma level) – concert band, jazz and brass ensembles, for example – also highly rated.

'Might not have the sportiest or the most academic reputation but it does all of them to a very good level and includes everyone in that,' said parent.

Sport: Strongest sports tennis, athletics and, especially, cricket (school makes Wisden's top 100), played three times a week, with year 10s upwards adding individual favourites including dressage (Jemima and Buttons the stars here). The head, sporty herself, is keen to boost excitement levels for girls with more staff and own cricket team (if worthy opponents can be found) – girls' rugby and football already offered.

Parents positive but realistic. 'We go to win but it's a numbers game. It's a very different culture.' Consolation provided by exceptional match teas, renowned in the area – scones, cheese straws, sandwiches and 'massive cakes', said pupil.

Boarding: Five boarding houses – three for boys, two for girls, each housing up to 50 pupils and strictly segregated (sight of boy boarder briefly wandering, shirtless, down corridor, reduces female tour guide to helpless giggles).

Appearance ranges from the grand (Wolverton – girls – approached up impressive staircase in the main house) to the homely (Gate – boys – prettily set around former stable yard). Devine, the most distant, village-based house, has been revamped and pupils given day room at school.

Varying dorm sizes, some sleeping six or more in junior years, though a couple of spares kept unoccupied for emergencies. Otherwise boarding full with waiting lists in most year groups. Nicest (girls' rooms) are elevated with wardrobes at the end. 'We lean up on the wardrobes and chat,' said girl. Single rooms for some lower and all upper sixth, who also get more advanced cooking privileges and own meeting areas. Only downside can be lack of space for day pupils.

No official weekly boarding but locals are allowed to go home after Saturday school. Some overseas Brits – FO, MoD, expats – though fewer than you might think (currently less than 20) given substantial presence of army bases in the area. Others from all over including Germany, China and Russia, with a few others from USA, Italy, Japan and Sweden.

Strong sense of community. Boarders and day pupils 'all mix and match,' said a parent. 'School is really lovely if you want to have a boarder for the weekend.' Pain of staying in eased by dogs (owned by staff in three out of five boarding houses), hot chocolate and plenty of talking therapy for homesickness, plus luxurious lie in to 10.45am on Sunday morning with potato cubes (baby chips) and bacon and egg sandwiches the star attractions on the brunch menu.

'Suits people who like to be busy,' said pupil. 'You'll be joining in without realising it.' What with regular off-site outings – shopping bus, cinema, spectacular coastline – and onside delights of, among others, squash, archery and kayaking, pupils reckon 'there's just not enough time to fit everything in' (no doubt the reason for untouched copy of The Times in boarding house reception).

Ethos and heritage: Founded in 1896 in Enfield, school led peripatetic existence, settling in Pangbourne, then Winchester, before final landing here in 1933. House, Iwerne Manor, was rebuilt in peak Victorian perpendicular Gothic style by local squires (whose goodness to villagers extended to equipping each house with red blinds).

Main house floats like an island in a sea of grass in the centre of 62 acres, commanding splendid views of land and sky, represented in the blue and green crescents on girls' blazer crests. (Traditionalists may prefer double headed dragon – still sported by boys – over corporate minimalism.)

Nicest dorms (girls' rooms) are elevated with wardrobes at the end. 'We lean up on the wardrobes and chat,' said girl

Many attractive original buildings survive, though with substantial additions and rebuilds, ranging from striking new DT extension to three classroom blocks. Large sports hall, swimming pool, multi-surface pitch don't detract from lake, fountain and scenery and with exception of grimly functional 70s prep block, new builds generally fit into place rather than attempting to dominate it, a tribute to good architect ego management.

Doing bit for the environment, too, with biomass boiler plus big solar panels on three of the roofs (now produce almost 10 per cent of energy – as well as pepping up temperature and pressure to delightful levels in boarding house showers).

Pupils – some here with considerable sacrifice from parents – do count their blessings. 'Everyone feels very lucky to be here – it says something that you realise it now,' said thoughtful guide.

Pastoral care, inclusivity and discipline: Fabulous and A-Z. Starting point is (relatively) small size of school – 'can spot quickly if things aren't quite right and get in early,' says head.

Strong tutor system, supplemented with pupil mentoring and low levels of cynicism – house loyalty, we were told, stays at fever pitch levels even at the top of the school. Lots of house competitions – organised by upper sixth who 'choreograph dances, pick song, arrange music, lower key if pitch too high.'

Occasional departure for drugs but more humane than most: instant expulsion for dealing and hard drugs, potential for discussion at least for cannabis, though 'only if it's a first offence and then followed up with regular testing to ensure no repeat,' says school.

Fully aware of how issues (such as eating disorders) can escalate and potentially shattering consequences if not spotted in time. 'So far, no transgender pupils but would go all out to make sure needs met,' says school. Approach geared to individual needs – haven created for one pupil, for example, who found classroom environment overwhelming and went on to achieve top exam grades.

Currently developing digital journal where pupils record, in images or writing, their emotional journey through school. 'Will help them think about times in their lives where they've made real leaps forward or had setbacks... could be so powerful when they look back,' says Mrs Thomson. Aim is to help them see social media as tool for future reflection – not just for mass transmission of selfies.

Pupils and parents: When it comes to socialising, spirit is willing but, with both parents working in many families, flesh and timetables are weak and coffee morning slots often elusive. When they do meet up, mood is correspondingly jolly. 'Gifted chaps' and 'all-round splendid fellows' pop up at intervals in annals of Clayesmore Society (open to all), and retiring nurse is a 'vision in waterproofs and wellies'. Translates into mixed bag of alumni from artist Edward Ardizzone to Beatles manager Brian Epstein and top surgeon Sir Rodney Sweetnam.

Locals and neighbouring counties (Dorset, Hants and Wiltshire) dominate – inevitable army contingent, though London is also on its patch (have had some families fleeing terrorism as well as its hothouse atmosphere). Low sterling value has upped interest from overseas, though long-term Brexit impact yet to be seen.

Though a fair few parents arrive from state sector, there's plenty of dosh about, with school events ranging from clay shoot (a tenner a head) to a reunion with lavish canapés and fizz (free, but you have to get yourself to Guernsey).

Money matters: Generous sibling discounts – ask, as not easily discoverable online. About a quarter of senior school pupils receive means-tested bursaries (some substantial) and though generous, head would like to extend 'for talented but needy'.

Scholarship are available (10 per cent off fees) but head isn't a big fan. Feels labelling the talented can impose unnecessary pressure at an early age and ignores late developers, who very often go on to scoop the glittering prizes. Children 'should just be enjoying time at school for the right reasons'.

The last word: Lovely location; warm, inclusive ethos. Ignore dinner party chit chat about SEN focus and do all your children a favour by seeing it for yourself.

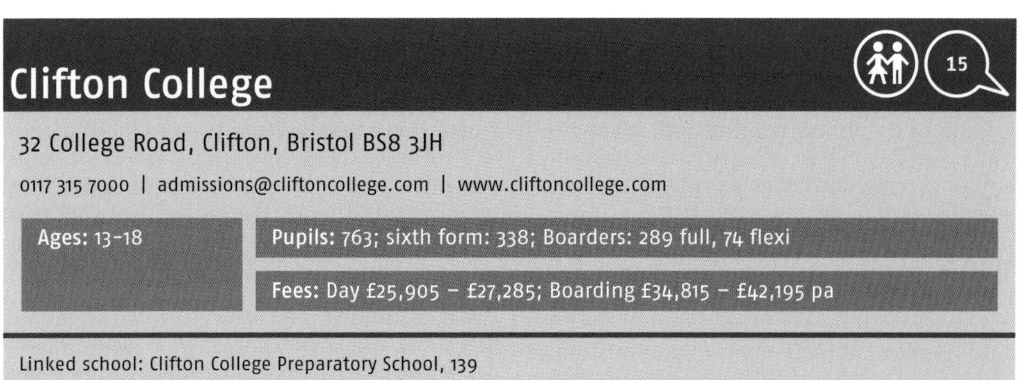

Clifton College

32 College Road, Clifton, Bristol BS8 3JH

0117 315 7000 | admissions@cliftoncollege.com | www.cliftoncollege.com

Ages: 13-18

Pupils: 763; sixth form: 338; Boarders: 289 full, 74 flexi

Fees: Day £25,905 – £27,285; Boarding £34,815 – £42,195 pa

Linked school: Clifton College Preparatory School, 139

Head of College: Since 2016, Dr Tim Greene MA DPhil (early 50s), an inorganic chemist by academic discipline and indeed by occupation in his earlier life, as a senior research fellow at Oxford (his alma mater), before moving on to Exeter. During his time there he involved himself in outreach to schools, widening access to higher education in particular, and grabbed an opportunity to fill in for a member of Queen's Taunton's chemistry department on a year's sabbatical – 'And that was that,' as he put it. Teaching seemed upbeat and positive, and Dr Greene still loves to do it, putting A level chemists through their paces and wanting to extend his reach to lower years, time permitting. 'It's a huge mistake for heads not to teach,' he avers. He also does duties in boarding houses, as it connects him to students, and 'gives them a hotline to the top,' he added with a wink. Judging by the jolly but purposeful meeting with the senior prefects ('praeps' in the school's vernacular) we sat in on, he enjoys excellent relations with the students, boundaries into excessive familiarity never seemingly crossed either way.

Raised and educated in Northern Ireland – still discernible if you listen carefully. He came to Clifton in 2006, rising to the post of deputy head before being appointed to head it in 2016, after a difficult chapter in the school's history. We are told that a three-minute standing ovation greeted news of his appointment when it was announced in the school's (magnificent) chapel. 'Friendly, welcoming, approachable and very visible: he makes an effort to come and watch things, and he knows people's names,' students said of him, approvingly. Parents we spoke to are also fans: 'He knows who I am, and I know I could knock on his door,' said one mother, while another liked the fact that he 'doesn't waste time with fancy sales speeches'. 'A very good thing' and 'doing a good job', we also heard.

Married to Lydia, whom he met at Oxford; they have three sons, the youngest still at the college. Holidays are likely to be spent walking with the family, but term time has become too busy for him to pursue any singing: 'I miss it,' he said regretfully. 'It would be good really to exercise the diaphragm occasionally.'

Entrance: At 13+, the 130 students arrive not only from Clifton's own prep school but several others. The process starts early, with visiting suggested at least three years before (regular open days) and a pre-assessment in year 7 by means of interviews and references. Academic testing – either Common Entrance, scholarships or the school's own tests in English, maths and science – does not take place until year 8. Application dates vary: beware. At sixth form, three GCSEs at grade 7 or above and three at grade 6 are expected, as well as tests and interviews in two subjects to be taken at A level for the 45 or so external candidates.

Exit: Between 15 and 20 per cent decamp after GCSEs. The vast majority of sixth form leavers go on to university – fewer than a fifth take a gap year. Popular choices include Edinburgh, Exeter, Birmingham, UCL, Reading, King's College London and Cardiff. A sprinkling of art foundation and overseas universities – including to Sorbonne (France), Groningen (Netherlands) and Fordham (USA) in 2021. Often a few medics and students to Oxbridge. The sixth formers we encountered were full of praise for the help and guidance received, from the careers fair and the weekly bulletin to the outside speakers and the nitty gritty of the personal statement. And it doesn't stop there: 'Clifton's not just for when you're there,' the head told us. 'There's support at university and the whole of the OC network.' Judging by the list of reunions both around the country and across the Atlantic, it's thriving and has some pretty distinguished members such as Simon Russell Beale and John Cleese.

Latest results: In 2021, 77 per cent 9-7 at GCSE; 70 per cent A*/A at A level (88 per cent A*-B). In 2019 (the last year when exams took place), 62 per cent 9-7 at GCSE; 71 per cent A*-B.

Teaching and learning: Right up there with the other Bristol independents (but not top) in terms of results. Ancient and modern languages results at GCSE and A level particularly impressive, probably related to their early emphasis (two is normal, one for weaker linguists or non-native speakers); Latin and/or Greek available as a third language.

Two of the most sumptuous school libraries we have ever seen: the Percival, with a splendidly ornate wooden ceiling, and the Stone, a dedicated science library

In the sixth form, 39 subjects, including history of art, and some BTEC options are on offer; no IB though. Sixth formers are expected to embark on four subjects, usually dropping one half way through lower sixth. They are also encouraged to lift their eyes from the purely academic and allow them to fall on the interesting possibilities in soi-disant Sector E: BTECs in IT and teamwork and personal development, a performance certificate from LAMDA and a non-examined photography course, inter alia. Favourite subjects? 'Maths, biology – in fact science in general, and humanities,' replied our delightful lunching companions when asked.

Parents note the calibre and collective intellect of the teaching staff, one describing the academic offering as 'fantastic' and expressing her appreciation that her son got to try out 'a load of different stuff' intellectually, even though for him, the point of going to school is to play with a ball. Plenty of opportunity for that too. Teaching spaces, light and functional rather than fancy for the most part, eclipsed by two of the most sumptuous school libraries we have ever seen: the Percival, with a splendidly ornate wooden ceiling, and the Stone, a dedicated science library boasting some 5,000 volumes, including a first edition of Isaac Newton's Principia Mathematica. Book learning is brought to life by a range of trips of which classics, most recently to Crete, garners particular praise. Clifton has produced a good crop of academic heavyweights, such as Sir Henry Newbolt, pioneering computer designer John Pinkerton, LP Hartley, three scientific Nobel prize winners, mathematicians, philosophers and engineers, of whom WO Bentley is the most eminent.

Learning support and SEN: Learning support is housed in a small building down a side street, but is not sidelined in importance. The department and in-house educational psychologist look at issues lying behind barriers to learning, such as ADHD or high levels of anxiety. 'You can lay on all the reading programmes you like, but if that child is unhappy, they probably won't be very effective,' staff told us. The holistic approach involves pastoral staff as well as academic, and includes the management of poor behaviour – 'It's less punitive,' the ed psych (on maternity leave at the time of writing but who phoned in to speak to us) affirmed. Students with more complex needs get longer term interventions and the department works closely with parents. We did not pick up any sense of stigma or discrimination towards those who get extra help. EAL shares the building: it's a busy place as 38 per cent of Clifton students use a language other than English at home. These may take EAL as a language option, with IGCSE English as a second language.

The arts and extracurricular: The trackless expanses of Wales and surprisingly wild Mendip and Quantock hills provide an easily accessible setting for DofE practice, CCF and an eight-week survival course, where participants learn to make string and rope from animal sinew, amongst other life-skills. Post-Brexit, this could be handy. Clifton in the Community caters for those of more pacifist ideals, who do good altruistic stuff locally.

Terrific music. At the top end, the school produces a commendable crop of Oxbridge choral, instrumental and organ scholars (six in the last eight years) and at least one recent musician of the calibre to play with the Royal Philharmonic while still at school, Julia Hwang, who attributed part of her success to the fact that the school tweaked her timetable to accommodate all that practice. Joseph Cooper, an Old Cliftonian, gave his name to the music school which boasts a gorgeous recital hall and high tech recording and mixing facilities alongside normal practice rooms. Truly some sort of music for everyone (orchestra and chamber groups to blues and swing), and it was touching to hear the enthusiasm, nay love, expressed by our guides for congers, the compulsory hymn practice in chapel each Saturday morning for Sunday services, to which day students are encouraged to go about twice a term. Sir David Willcocks, another notable OC, would be proud.

Despite a highly traditional setting and undoubted Anglican principles preached every day in chapel, an atmosphere of acceptance prevails: it seems a safe place to be different

Clifton was one of the first schools to have a theatre, named for Sir Michael Redgrave (yet another OC) which opens to the public, both audience and players, and hosts 40 productions a year; recent shows include School of Rock, the technical challenges of The Railway Children and Miss Saigon and plenty of Shakespeare. A junior play and hotly contested house drama also: last year's winner staged Posh, where characterisation ranged from 'arrogance to unease' – qualities we absolutely did not find in any of the students we met. Dance also strong, and enjoying a revamped studio.

Art, strangely, gets less exposure in the school's glossy literature, but the provision is wide: we like the fact that the compulsory course in the first year moves away from Europe to study Islamic, Asian and Aboriginal art, inter alia. A sculpture specialist and ceramicist on site. At A level, students choose either drawing/painting or sculpture/ceramics. Plenty of other artistic pursuits available as activities. Museum and gallery trips for all. Bloomsbury art critic and artist Roger Fry, Peter Lanyon of the St Ives school and impossibly romantic painter Robbie Duff-Scott are distinguished OCs.

Sport: No entry would be complete without the celebrated lines of Sir Henry Newbolt: 'There's a breathless hush in the Close tonight, Ten to make and the match to win', and the later exhortation to 'Play up! play up! and play the game!' Cricket in summer and rugby in winter are played by girls and boys on this hallowed turf, overlooked by the school's fine Victorian buildings, but most ball sport takes places on the expanse of pitches at Beggar's Bush, a short minibus ride away across Brunel's iconic suspension bridge. Here, 90 acres encompass several all-weather and grass pitches, indoor tennis courts housed in a bubble, plus facilities to welcome visiting teams and host other events. A swimming pool and indoor sports complex, including courts for the rarefied games of rackets, fives and real tennis, are within the school site.

Sport is massive at Clifton, but we did not detect a jock culture – thankfully. Rugby has long been a success story, but recently girls' hockey has burst through the tape, producing several international players in the last 10 years and the super-talented Lily Owsley, who captained the England team while still at the school and nabbed an Olympic gold at Rio in 2016. The head told us he is keen that the school should 'take the top sportspeople through, as we do the top academics', but that he believes sport is for all and that everyone will find something which will suit them, as well as being given the chance to play for the school. There is certainly plenty on offer for those not mad about ball games, some provided on site (eg aerobics, fencing), others in the surprisingly dramatic environs of Bristol, such as climbing in nearby gorges – Avon or Cheddar – and water sports, eg water polo, sailing and kayaking.

Boarding: School runs on a boarding model, but manages the integration of and equality of the experience for day students better than many. Boarders are allocated to one of seven single-sex houses scattered about the gracious roads surrounding the main school. Staffing is generous and ensures plenty of support with matters academic and pastoral, including a cuddle with the resident dog or cat, where necessary. We found the girls' houses notably cheerier than the boys', some of whose bathrooms could definitely do with a facelift. Communal space divided by age: some of the spaces for younger boys struck us as subterranean and drear. Leather sofas, a huge TV and a dartboard surrounded by holes in the wall from near misses seem to be the only décor deemed necessary for the boys; the girls tend towards cosier sofas, colourful rugs and bean bags. Younger ones housed in small dorms, some with study facilities, integrating a bed and desk. Modern purpose-built furniture in pale wood makes the best of available space. Some houses could use an upgrade, in the view of students. Parents we spoke to had varying views. 'My daughter's housemistress really listens to the kids and gives them mummy-love. She is easy to contact and quick to respond,' one parent told us. Another, though, expressed his son's view that the boarding experience is not so good for a full British boarder whose parents live abroad and who therefore doesn't go home at weekends. The majority do after Saturday commitments; overseas students tend to stick together and relax into their native tongues after a week of speaking English, and apparently there isn't always enough to do at weekends, eg when matches are cancelled.

Ethos and heritage: Founded by local businessman Sir John Percival in the 1860s and, at his insistence, placing an equal emphasis on science and humanities. This progressive thinking extended to racial and religious tolerance, influenced by having a close friend who happened to be a practising Jew, and a belief in the education of women, though it took well over 100 years for the school to admit girls, who did not arrive until 1987. There is no longer a Jewish boarding house, but the synagogue is still there, still used and now presided over by the school's first ever rabbi on the chaplaincy team. One parent told us that the reason his father had chosen the school for him was so that he could maintain his Jewish heritage; this holds true today.

The impression given by outstanding high Victorian Gothic buildings, built of warm red stone and surrounding the manicured green velvet of the close, is of a very traditional public school, but we were amused to find out that the head was put straight by a young hopeful at interview, who informed him that the school was not covered by the original Public Schools Act. Whatever – one would be hard put to spot the difference: glossary, different ties for everything etc. Eleven day and boarding houses are dotted about the surrounding roads – all quiet and residential – and all within earshot, if not sight, of Bristol Zoo in the smartest part of the city next to the glorious expanse of the downs. Students seem genuinely appreciative of their privileged setting, and abide by the rule of silence when walking through the memorial arch, where the names of the school's war dead are inscribed.

House identity and friendly rivalry flourish: masses of ways in which to compete such as house matches and music, and to bond over trips, dinners and so on, but this does not descend into tribalism, perhaps helped by the fact that most meals are taken in the fabulous lofty two-storey dining hall (Big School), adroitly serving the entire school, upper and lower. Extra rations can be bought from Grubber (tuck shop) and each house has a kitchen for each age group for the preparation of that vital school fuel: toast.

Despite the highly traditional setting and undoubted Anglican principles preached every day in chapel, an atmosphere of acceptance prevails towards those of different faiths, races and sexuality: it seems a safe place to be different. 'Pupils are permitted to wear the uniform which best corresponds to their gender identity, with permission from the headmaster' according to the policy, but it is only recently that girls have been allowed to wear trousers in school routinely. The LGBTQ+ group meets on a Tuesday like any other club.

There are rewards for all kinds of endeavour. A 'good egg' prize is awarded in each house for – well, being a good egg

Pastoral care, inclusivity and discipline: Pastoral care appears to be wraparound. First point of contact for any concerns or questions is the housemaster/mistress (HoMs) both for students and parents, but all teachers are members of the pastoral team in individual houses, and all do duties there. The well-staffed medical department keeps its eyes and ears out for problems which extend beyond the physical. Mental health is prominent on the school's agenda: the chaplain is an accredited mental health first aid trainer, each house has its own mental health first aider and some sixth formers act as voluntary mental health peer mentors. Students told us there was no taboo surrounding it, and that they could 'tell my houseparent anything. There are loads of people to go to when things go wrong and someone would notice, anyway.' The emphasis the school places on the growing problem of our youngsters' mental health may or may not be one response to the horrific discovery in 2014 of a housemaster spying on and videoing students without their knowledge, which knocked the school community sideways and shattered confidence in it in some quarters. Since then, the school has tightened up its practices and a climate of unobtrusive vigilance prevails. It is the only school where this editor was asked to read and sign a leaflet outlining the school's safeguarding guide before proceeding beyond reception.

Rewards for all kinds of endeavour and contributions to the school community are abundant, and the climate is undoubtedly one of positive reinforcement. A 'good egg' prize is awarded in each house for – well, being a good egg. Punishments on a sliding scale are meted out for all the misdemeanours one might expect. Poor work might attract detention to improve or finish it, frequent poor behaviour or the breaking of rules 'gating' – ie being confined to the house or school grounds. Suspension is reserved for the most serious (such as drugs) or persistent breaches of school rules; the purpose is to give the student a chance for 'reflection and [doubtless full and frank] discussions with parents and guardians'. We were most disappointed not to meet the Marshal, the distributor of lighter sanctions and upholder and recorder of weightier ones; students try not to catch his beady eye as he looks for uniform infringements. On balance, the students we spoke to reckoned punishments were fair, though one described some as petty.

Pupils and parents: Hearteningly down to earth and aware of how very fortunate they are – and not, we hope, just because they are instructed to 'check their privilege' in PHSE lessons. They appreciate the importance the school places on the whole person, the care they receive in all aspects of their school lives, and the fact that they can get everything done at school. This is certainly Bristol's smartest school, but those we met did not behave like that. Students arriving from state schools speak well of welcome and integration.

Parents seem extremely happy with the school, and enjoy an active social scene on the touchline or at house events. 'The least judgmental set of parents I have ever met,' in the opinion of one mother. Like all but a tiny minority of boarding schools, Clifton families tend not to live more than an hour or so away, apart from the 25 per cent overseas students, most of whom come either from Russia or China, including Hong Kong.

Money matters: Fees much in line with comparable schools both for boarding and day students; it's the most expensive day provision in Bristol, however. 'I want to ensure we offer more bangs for the parental buck,' the head told us in justification. Scholarships for art, music, sport and drama as well as academics at 13+, to a maximum of 25 per cent of fees. Sixth form scholarships available as above, but include an organ scholarship – good fodder for collegiate universities. Bursary provision subject to normal means-testing, including one worth 20 per cent for a Forces child and some for Jewish applicants who 'demonstrate an interest in Judaism and take part in Jewish activities in the school'.

The last word: Clifton, with its fancy buildings, gorgeous situation, sparkling alumni and own vernacular, is arguably the city's poshest school and the subject of dinner party gossip; the one the Daily Mail might most like to take a pop at. But that would be to ignore or skate over its other, less visible achievements. These include some significant advances in and resources directed towards child protection, mental health and ironing out the differences between the haves and the have-nots, albeit in a privileged environment. 'We've made considerable sacrifices to send our daughter here,' one mother told us, 'but it's worth every working moment and every night of worry.'

Clifton College Preparatory School

The Avenue, Bristol BS8 3HE

0117 315 7160 | prepadmissions@cliftoncollege.com | www.cliftoncollege.com/prep

Ages: 3-13

Pupils: 464; Boarders: 23 full, 11 flexi (from year 6)

Fees: Day £10,725- £18,600; Boarding £17,460 – £30,690 pa

Linked school: Clifton College, 135

Headmaster: Since 2018, Jim Walton BA PGCE (late 40s). Brought up in Warwickshire and an old boy of Warwick school, Mr Walton went north for his university studies, with a first degree (business studies) from Sheffield and a PGCE from Manchester Met. A couple of years as education officer at the Lost Gardens of Heligan on graduation lit his path into primary teaching, then he spent several years at Cheltenham College Junior School, latterly as a housemaster, thence to Elizabeth College Guernsey as deputy head before his first appointment to headship there. 'I wasn't really looking for a change,' he said of the Clifton job, 'but I liked the fact that it was properly co-ed and had a mix of boarding and day.' Integration (of the prep, pre-prep and nursery) and streamlining (of staff and management roles) could sum up his achievements since he arrived, but those dry words do not do justice to the fizz and bubble Mr Walton brings to the job. 'Maybe the staff think I'm too informal,' he conceded with a knowing grin, before telling us how he demonstrated a perfect headstand at a recent gym showcase.

Our first encounter was through the car window at the busy pedestrian crossing outside the prep, where Mr Walton was on lollipop duty in a hi-viz jacket, greeting everyone by name at the start of the day. Once inside in his modest office, Mr Walton expanded on his priorities for Clifton Prep, namely to enable the children to gain the most from their co-education: the girls to learn greater resilience, the boys greater emotional intelligence. 'Kindness and empathy are our watchwords,' he told us, and it was indeed heartening to hear the many achievements picked out for awards at the celebration assembly we were invited to. Pupils find him likeable and funny, enjoying his cheesy jokes and willingness to receive a full face custard pie, yet value his involvement in their school lives and his visibility. And parents? Ditto, really – they like the fact that the children like him (and that it is mutual), and that they can get hold of him when they want to. In the words of one mum: 'a great guy'.

Fabulous facilities and activities are the reason many families choose the school, plus the length of the day, designed to suit boarders (and working parents)

Mr Walton is married to Melanie, whom he met in the role of his mentor when he was an NQT at Clifton High. They have two sons, one in the upper school and one in the prep. Family holidays – of the more active variety; they all surf – tend to happen on islands: Anglesey, the Isles of Scilly (roughing it on the uninhabited ones a particular favourite) and Sri Lanka. 'Must be a legacy of our time in Guernsey,' muses Mr Walton.

Jo Newman (40s) heads the pre-prep and nursery. A master's in geography and sports science from Brunel University (impressively while raising two children) and a PGCE from UEA preceded a teaching career, latterly as head of the pre-prep of Yateley Manor School before her move to Clifton in 2015. 'I'm a caver, so I was delighted to move nearer the Mendips,' she told us. This love of the outdoors has led to the development of and passion for the forest school (complete with mud kitchen and fire pit), all beautifully sited in a comparative wilderness next to the extensive pitches at Beggar's Bush across the suspension bridge; Mrs Newman takes the reception class there herself on Fridays, and it would be hard to say who loves it more. Warm and energetic, Mrs Newman knows all her charges by name, even the tiniest tots. Parents reckon she is 'great with the kids'. 'I want excited staff and children,' she told us, going on to explain her plans for the pre-prep, such as a new library and revamped cookery room.

Entrance: First come, first served to the nursery (from age 3 months) and reception plus informal assessment during a half-day visit, but from years 1-3, literacy and maths are assessed against the 'average standard level of attainment for the age group'. From year 4 onwards, children are assessed in English, maths and general ability and expected to reach the average national Sats level for the age group, plus a decent reference from the previous school.

Exit: The vast majority (95 per cent) to the upper school by means of 'transfer exams' and scholarship papers for the brightest sparks. Very few leave for anything other than relocation reasons, such as returning to Europe after a parental stint at British Aerospace, Airbus or similar. Doubtful runners for the upper school are given the nod in year 5 or 6.

Our view: Founded in 1908 and still fondly known as Butcombe (pre-prep) and the Pre (prep), the school occupies some fine Victorian buildings in the fine Victorian roads surrounding the college proper; not that easy to find your way about, but the blue tennis court at the centre of it all is a useful constant. The nursery and pre-prep are separate from the prep with age-appropriate play areas and dining facilities. We caught the youngest members of the Clifton community seated at tiny tables eating healthy snacks of fruit with the utmost decorum and apparent enjoyment.

EYFS and an emphasis on the development through play of physical and social skills alongside language, rather than structured formal learning, goes on for the first four years. A thematic and values-based curriculum with classrooms decked out in ever more imaginative ways (space, dinosaur habitat) make learning truly fun: even the so-called 'grammar hammer' work sheet was engaging the kids. At the end of year 3, children move up to the prep. Here, the learning is more formal and they are set for maths and English. We were much taken by the incitement to rebellion encouraged by the study of Animal Farm, even if the head looked somewhat uneasy. IT is considered an aid to teaching, rather than an end in itself, though IT skills are taught discretely. One science class was doing an online test when we visited; a maths class was being shown different ways of calculating ratios. The younger prep pupils start French, with Mandarin as an option; later on German and Spanish are added, along with Latin. Foreign language trips run every other year. Both the pre-prep and the prep have a library; the prep school librarian is a Carnegie Medal judge. Academic life seems stimulating and enjoyable but not unduly pressured.

Younger pupils were fresh from and flushed with success after a production of Jack and the Giant, given no fewer than five stars in the Bristol Post

Pupils are not routinely screened on entry, only if baseline assessments flag up any concerns. The new academic deputy is tightening up the criteria for extra help for SEN, placing the responsibility for allocating resources with teaching staff, rather than granting parental requests for extra maths etc; instead, they are given strategies for use at home in cases where a little extra help is needed. SEN happens in a dedicated unit – the coach house – and sessions take place within normal lesson times so that children do not miss out on break or other activities. Dyslexia, dyscalculia and dyspraxia are the main areas addressed in the coach house, along with EAL for children from overseas, but mild ASD also accommodated in emergent cases. We were heartened by the sensitive treatment of one such boy who proudly showed us his work in the pre-prep, but 'It's not necessarily the school for everyone,' we were told.

Fabulous facilities and activities are the reason many families choose the school, plus the length of the day, designed to suit the boarders (and working parents) and giving time to fit it all in. And fabulous they are: from the sports pitches – both on site and at Beggar's Bush – to the 25m swimming pool, the gorgeous chapel and proper theatre, the Redgrave (named for OC Sir Michael), quite young children benefit from first-class amenities and the staff to use them effectively. Masses of opportunities to take part, perform and compete if that's your thing: a talented young pianist wowed everyone at the celebration assembly the day we visited, and that evening the senior netball players were off to Epsom College to play in the national finals the next day – the head was to be up at 6am to go and support them in person. Younger pupils were fresh from and flushed with success after a production of Jack and the Giant, given no fewer than five stars in the Bristol Post. Pupils love the range of things on offer, particularly the sport and team games. Sensibly, school lays on a parents' evening for non-examined subjects, ie the arts. We especially liked the art showcased, with visiting abstract artist Feona Ness live in the studio, and the racing kit car being built in DT, complete with cradle for an iphone to which real time information from the engine could be transmitted to the cab via Bluetooth. Equally impressive was a rendition Pachelbel's Canon, given a garage overlay… (a musical genre, not a mechanical one, note).

House spirit, even among the day pupils, is one of the best things about Clifton Prep, according to pupils: rivalry, rather than tribalism, expressed in house sports and the ubiquitous house song. In year 3, pupils are given their first taste of the house system by being given their own common room. House allocation and boarding start at year 4, as does compulsory Saturday school which, it is fair to say, enjoys a mixed press.

'Busy' was the word pupils used to describe school life, but we were assured there were plenty of people to go to if it all got too much, or with other troubles: resident gap students lend a listening ear. The balance between reward and sanction also good, with the former promoted over the latter. Parents (mostly) happy with the way their offspring's transgressions are handled.

Despite being Bristol's smartest prep school, there is diversity among Clifton families in terms of nationalities: it tends to attract overseas families working in the city's aerospace industry, plus armed forces families needing boarding and those elsewhere in the UK for whom the school is a tradition. Parents really like the global feel of the school, and though one overseas mother felt the intricacies of the British education system could be have been better explained, another gave the support her children received in mastering English top marks; they are now bilingual.

Boarding: Four co-ed day and boarding houses, one girls' and one boys' day and boarding house. We greatly liked the combined kitchen and living rooms, with a table large enough for all the boarders to sit round of an evening. The girls' dorm (bright, cheery and not preternaturally tidy) overlooks the penguins and seals at Bristol zoo; the boys can hear the lions roar from theirs, eye-catchingly themed with huge stencils of extreme sports, superheroes etc. The sole bone of contention we picked up was the limited use of mobile phones, which boarders think should be available to them in their free time. Other than that, pupils struck us as exceedingly happy with their lot.

The last word: Once children are signed up to the nursery, it is hard to see any reason, barring financial or academic disaster, not to leave them at Clifton until the age of 18 – a truly fulfilling, seductive offering for almost every child.

Dauntsey's School

17

West Lavington, Devizes, Wiltshire SN10 4HE

01380 814500 | info@dauntseys.org | www.dauntseys.org

Ages: 11–18

Pupils: 829; sixth form: 250; Boarders: 316 full

Fees: Day £20,295; Boarding £33,600 pa

Head master: Since 2012, Mark Lascelles BA (Hons) PGCE (50s). Joined Dauntsey's from the more formal King's School, Canterbury where he was lower master and acting head during a particularly turbulent time. Educated at Shrewsbury School and Durham (geography) prior to completing teaching practice in the state sector in Gateshead and at Boldon Colliery School in South Shields. Thence returned to Shrewsbury to teach geography, becoming master-in-charge of football, cricket and fives before moving on to be housemaster at The Grove in 2003.

Very much the sportsman, reaching county level and beyond, he always strives to be out and about around the school, saying of his wood-panelled office: 'Time in here kills me!' Living on site, he is out of the door at 7am, at his desk by five past. Married to Amber, a teacher and Loughborough graduate, who was a national level canoeist. They have three young daughters from eight to 13 years, either at the school or heading this way.

Under his tenure the fabric of the school has had a £15m refresh, academics have strengthened, results up and down a little with the ebb and flow of individual cohorts but generally strong, and excellent word of mouth has ensured that numbers are up. He sees his remit as happy children and satisfied parents and is most pleased with the culture and climate of the school.

Parents tell us he's 'very professional, approachable and a real family man. He is fair and exercises his duty with a certain level of humour.' 'He doesn't miss a game and is always so supportive of the children.' 'He seems keen to promote strong moral values and manners… as well as academic excellence.'

He tells us, 'If I went under a bus, I'd like people to think he really cared.' Thankfully, few buses in this locale and with students marvelling at how he remembers them all ('I don't know how he does it – spreadsheets?'; 'He only met my grandmother once, but he always asks after her'), his legacy seems secure.

Entrance: Not overly selective. The most competitive entry point is 11+ where the ratio is just under 2:1. Every child is interviewed, sometimes giving the school the opportunity to say yes to a child who fails the exam but who has something about them.

Pupils arrive from over 80 schools. At 11+ (day and boarding places) half arrive from state primaries and half from independent preps including St Margaret's Prep Calne, St Francis, Pewsey and Heywood Prep, Corsham. Exams and interviews take place in mid-January of the year of entry. Papers in English, maths and verbal reasoning.

At 13+ (boarding places only) pupils join from local prep schools as well as schools in Dubai, Oman and Europe. Selection is based on the ISEB common pre-test and interview, or Dauntsey's exams. A formal interview and taster day follow in March of year 7. The ISEB Common Entrance papers taken at prep schools in the summer of year 8 are marked by Dauntsey's staff and used for initial setting purposes. For those not at a prep school, entry is via interview and examination papers (English, maths and science) taken in the autumn term of a pupil's year 8.

At 16+ (day and boarding places), pupils join from local state schools and independent schools such as West Lavington, Devizes, Salisbury Grammar Schools and St Mary's Calne. Selection is based on predicted grades, school reference and an interview. Candidates need a minimum of three level 7s and three level 6s at I/GCSE.

Appropriate access arrangements for pupils with SEN. See the school's website for separate arrangements for overseas candidates.

Exit: At 16+ around 10 per cent leave. At 18+ almost all then head to university. Around three-quarters go to Russell Group and usually a few to Oxbridge. Cardiff is the most popular university destination followed by Exeter, Newcastle, Manchester, Bath, UCL, Oxford Brookes, KCL, Birmingham and Reading. Some head off for a year in industry. A huge variety of subjects, eg motorsport engineering and games design, modern and medieval languages, computer science and AI. Many also study art at prestigious destinations including the Ruskin School of Fine Art, Central St Martins and Kingston University. Three medics in 2021.

Latest results: In 2021, 77 per cent 9-7 at GCSE; 64 per cent A*/A at A level (88 per cent A*-B). In 2019 (the last year when exams took place), 42 per cent A*/A at A level.

Teaching and learning: Mathematicians and scientists are no slouches here. Half of the sixth form take maths; half of mathematicians and a third of scientists turned in top grades this year and maths and STEM subjects are the most popular university subject choices. Strong performances from the linguists (especially in German and Spanish) and literature students too.

Speakers visit to inspire sixth formers, recently including an expert on the Arab world, a war photographer and someone living with a brain tumour

Everyone takes three A levels (out of 25 on offer) plus either an additional A level, the EPQ, the school's own sport and leadership qualification or its maths for science course. Politics is the latest addition and freedom of choice means sciences can be combined with humanities or languages with ease.

The head has shaken up staff turnover somewhat to bring in new faces, while appointing a head of professional development and putting teachers under greater pressure to raise their game. Parents are full of praise: 'We've seen our daughter really blossom since she joined – confidence in the classroom and also with her peers. The learning approach is fun – but coupled with a responsibility to manage your own time and put in the hard work.' A mother: 'It all seems to be thorough and rigorous and I never feel that my children are "cruising".' And following parents evening: 'Teachers very quickly know and understand each child and this is clearly demonstrated through their canny observations and advice.' From first formers to upper sixths, pupils all tell us that they are actively encouraged to seek out teachers for extra help. Independent and curious creative thinkers much in evidence.

Class sizes average 18 or 19 on entry to nine at A level.

Sixth formers taking the EPQ have investigated subjects as diverse as Genghis Khan and Chaos Theory. Efforts to close the gender gap in STEM subjects include appointing a second female physics specialist as role model. A sixth former recently won a prestigious degree apprenticeship in engineering.

There is one full-time head of careers ('but he's like a whole department,' enthuses a sixth former) with two part-time staff. The head stresses that his remit is to ensure pupils don't just get to uni but succeed there. Speakers visit to inspire sixth formers, recently including an expert on the Arab world, a war photographer and someone living with a brain tumour. Themed careers events, such as one recently on agri-business, introduce pupils to industry sectors.

Learning support and SEN: A busy SEN team of four provides support within the timetable but at an additional cost. One hundred and fifteen pupils receive some form of learning support, up to two individual lessons a week – although most have one and others visit the department when needed. A typical SEN profile would be a pupil with mild dyslexia, dyspraxia or slow processing. A parent of a dyslexic boy told us, 'Learning support has been fantastic.' There is also a dedicated EAL department.

The arts and extracurricular: Sedentary children may be on the rise, but not here. The superlative sport is often a reason for joining the school. We could tell you about the rugby, the athletics, the hockey, but why start here when Dauntsey's is the only school in the country to have its own tall ship, the Jolie Brise, based on the south coast, on which pupils have won hundreds of races across the world – extraordinary life-changing experiences for many. Adventure education is a fundamental part of the school.

There's a resident Bear Grylls (actual job title is head of adventure), building confidence with night hikes, canoeing and camping, just part of specific programmes for each year group. There are options to take part in challenges and expeditions far and wide from the Brecon Beacons to Iceland, Arctic Sweden, Bhutan and Tanzania. Some of them truly stunning for pupils of their age. Second formers stay in a cabin on the edge of the Arctic circle in sub-zero temperatures and get to try their hands at dog sledding, ice fishing and snow shoeing. Clearly inspired, four hundred pupils have completed the infamous Devizes to Westminster canoe race, paddling 125 miles over the Easter weekend – the equivalent of a marathon a day.

Pupils will only be limited by what they can cram into their time. 'Performing arts is particularly strong,' says a parent. Just over half take a musical instrument, then there are 19 ensembles, ranging from jazz and folk to choirs, a dance band and orchestras. Every year pupils form bands for Rock Fest: 'So cool. Each band has professional lighting design.' Much praise for the vibrant and inclusive dance programme – and 150 pupils, including 31 first-timers, recently took their production of Billy Elliott to the West End for one night only.

Artists consistently dazzle. Creative skills are valued as likely to future-proof careers. Wonderful original art is on display throughout the school and the art block, with dedicated photographic suite, is top class.

Second formers stay in a cabin on the edge of the Arctic circle in subzero temperatures and get to try their hands at dog sledding, ice fishing and snow shoeing

More than 80 different clubs from archery to model railway, ballet to concert band, climbing to Lego mind storms. Post GCSEs, fifth formers steer clear of the classrooms with 'lessons for life'. As you'd expect, more adventurous than button-sewing – abseiling, lifeguarding, emergency first aid and wild camping. The outreach and charities programme is huge, with pupils raising a quarter of a million pounds for their chosen charities in the past ten years. The Mercers' Lecture series, regularly attracting audiences of over 800, brings speakers to the school such as Dr Lucy Worsley, Frank Gardner OBE and Alison Weir.

Sport: Pupils in years 7 to 9 have two games lessons and one PE lesson per week, plus sporting clubs and societies. Younger pupils seem thrilled with their opportunities to try new things. Pupils in GCSE and A level years have two lessons per week and options outside the main sports such as football, badminton, Pilates, yoga, dance, kayaking, swimming, cross country and basketball. Girls' sports have strengthened over the past few years: the girls' athletics team has been unbeaten for six years.

Everywhere facilities are extremely smart – the shiny new sports pavilion, with deck for sunny days and raised viewing lounge for supporting in comfort; the brand new athletics track (athletics is valued as counterbalance to summer exam stress); even the standard-issue sports hall appears freshly painted on the day of our visit. The rugby pitch seems to be the heart of the school community: a match is in progress, everyone is following the score in and out of every building, lots of parents on the sidelines despite the week day and pupils hang out on benches showing support at teatime.

Boarding: There are five boarding houses, staffed by houseparents who live on site with their families. Pupils aged 11 to 14 years stay at the coeducational Manor, a gentle introduction to life away from home, before graduating to the single-sex senior boarding houses.

Girls' and boys' houses for years 10 upwards are pretty similar. Pupils are two to a room or have their own as they get older. Some are ensuite. There are TV rooms with rows of sofas, even some elevated so that everyone gets a good view. Computer rooms for printing out homework. A kitchen or snacking area for lashings of toast. In the boys' house, a pool table and proudly contested pool competition. Extremely clean and modern, plenty of open windows – nothing to love or loathe décor-wise, but a lovely family atmosphere between pupils and house staff much in evidence. The housemaster we meet is on site 24/7 with his family and support staff and clearly knows the 50 or so boys in his care well.

Saturday morning lessons and lunch for all are followed by team sports. Around two-thirds of boarders are in school for the whole weekend. Junior years are kept busy with a programme of activities while there are options for seniors such as the cinema at Salisbury, the trampoline park, ice-skating, baking and Bath Christmas markets.

Meals are included in the fees. The school's catering seems to divide opinion, receiving either rave reviews, particularly the 'live cook' or disappointing reports from the pupils and parents we speak to. The school assures us that overall feedback is excellent. Evenings are structured with prep and downtime scheduled. For sixth formers, the '17 Club' gives them a mini taste of a students' union with two alcoholic drinks allowed per week.

Ethos and heritage: Founded in West Lavington in 1542 on the deathbed largesse of William Dauntsey, master of the worshipful company of Mercers, the school opened on its present site in 1895 as Dauntsey's Agricultural School. The Mercers' company still provides six governors, occasional generous financial help and an annual get-together for its associated schools from St Paul's in London to Peter Symonds College, two new academies and the Royal Ballet School.

Set in the middle of farming country, encircled by views of Salisbury Plain, the school feels serene. Smart newer red-brick buildings of various styles complement the original one. Pupils feel the school really comes into its own during good weather with everyone enjoying the outdoor space.

The housemaster we met is on site 24/7 with his family and support staff and clearly knows the 50 or so boys in his care very well

The head feels it's a traditional school with a fairly conservative parent body. No 'year 7' nomenclature here. We were struck, however, by how unstuffy it feels: a school with both eyes open to the challenges of modern life for today's teenagers. A sixth former told us, 'The support here is crazy: they're really up for you doing what you want to do.'

Pastoral care, inclusivity and discipline: The head feels that 'looking after children is what we do better than anything else' and there is a careful structure for the delivery of pastoral care starting with the deputy head pastoral.

Thirty of the staff have safeguarding responsibilities. Sixth formers mentioned the newly introduced CCTV and fingerprint entrance technology for boarding houses making them feel safer as the campus is quite open. Pupils we spoke to feel there is little bullying or unkindness in general and a new father told us, 'We couldn't get over how kind all the children are to each other.' Staff feel that discipline is not a huge issue.

Uniform lower down the school is standard issue (girls rather belatedly may soon be able to choose trousers) but sixth formers show off their style and character – whether in a slim-cut tweed jacket with skinny chinos (boys) or floral trousers and a cropped jacket (girls) – while still looking businesslike.

Naturally, students are sometimes in relationships by the time they reach the sixth form and we walk into two pupils enjoying a prolonged hug. Our guides tell us the school is pretty relaxed about such things, although the school's rules state no PDAs. Boys and girls are allowed to hang out together at certain times in the common rooms, but in the words of a housemaster, 'nothing horizontal'.

Pupils and parents: Many boarders live within an hour's commute of the school, others come from London, Yorkshire, Scotland as well as Europe, the US and Asia Pacific. There's been a rebalancing of the number of international pupils in the school, now effectively capped. Currently, 70 overseas nationals from countries including Nigeria, Portugal, Spain, Russia and China. Day pupils head in from a distance of 30 miles with multiple bus routes. Mostly 'down to earth' with 'pockets' of competitiveness, says a father of fellow parents. 'Unpretentious and family-oriented,' says another.

Money matters: A good proportion of pupils are in receipt of scholarships and bursaries: 247 currently. The school also operates a 100 per cent bursary scheme for three pupils each year, publicised among local schools.

The last word: Country boarding at its best. Outdoor education to rival any we've seen, tip-top sporting facilities, dedicated teaching getting increasingly fab results and a lovely family atmosphere make Dauntsey's definitively one for the list.

Dean Close St John's

18

Castleford Hill, Tutshill, Chepstow, Monmouthshire NP16 7LE

01291 622045 | admissions@deanclosestjohns.org.uk | www.deanclosestjohns.org.uk

Ages: 1–13

Pupils: 162; **Boarders:** 7 full, 15 flexi

Fees: Day £9,900 – £15,600; Boarding £20,100 – £21,450 pa

Linked school: Dean Close School, 148

Head: Since January 2021, Nick Thrower. Previously assistant head and chaplain at Lambrook and before that director of sport and houseparent at St Andrew's in Turi, Kenya. He lives at the school with his wife Jo and their teenage son and daughter. Walking and photography are his two big passions.

Kingswood School

Entrance: Entry is by gentle taster day assessment. Children come from Newport, the Wye Valley, Cardiff, Monmouth and Forest of Dean, both sides of the border. Lots of minibuses make this work. St John's runs two nurseries off site in Newport and Chepstow as well as the onsite Hedgehogs, which provide about half the reception intake.

Exit: Around a third head off to Dean Close Senior School. Clifton College, Monmouth School, Monmouth Girls, Wycliffe School and King's Gloucester are also popular.

School says it doesn't believe in cramming for secondary school entrance because the senior schools know and value the results of a St John's education. A few leave at 11 but school firmly believes that most schools value the extra confidence the last two years at St John's give their 13+ intake.

Our view: Perched on an idyllic site above the River Wye, St John's is jumbled into a pretty little Georgian manor with a scatter of other houses and purpose-built school facilities. The overall impression fluctuates from the gracious Embassy Room and black and white flagged passage through a few darkish corners brightened with child-created murals to some really up-to-date buildings like the pre-prep. School has been in situ since 1923, under a number of guises, and as a co-ed educational trust since the 60s. The Dean Close Foundation took over when the school got into financial difficulties in 2015. The school is still recovering from a stormy interlude of acute money shortages and anxious parents, leaving a few year groups with uneven numbers of boys and girls. Bustling and friendly with confident children, there's masses going on. A full court hearing with real judge and magistrate advising the pupil barristers and officials was in progress on the day of our visit.

Lovely pre-prep department with private gardens for each class, delightfully muddy and enjoyable forest school and exceptionally attractive and well-planned modern buildings. Classes were quietly enjoying reading time in our visit but there was evidence of academic progress all around, with joined up writing from the very beginning. Oodles of work on display and really up-to-date IT.

Prep years are in less luxurious but cheerful classrooms with small classes (16 maximum) with good science areas and recently updated IT. One parent said staff had been a little slow to 'get behind' a reluctant learner but everything is now tightening up. The curriculum, currently offering French, Spanish and Latin, is being overhauled for 'modern needs' which may include another language in future replacing Latin. After pre-prep there is a gradual transition to specialist teaching in all subjects and gifted children get the chance, for instance, to tackle GCSE maths. Learning support is for high flyers as well as strugglers. PSB (pre-senior baccalaureate) has replaced Common Entrance. The non-selective intake means some need quite a lot of help, mainly in class but occasionally one-to-one. All pupils are tested with a battery of CATs etc. Regular reports are now electronic. Plenty of inspiring trips and in-school one-offs to enhance learning like the visit to St Fagan's iron age farm, or entering the competitive maths challenge, with some pretty impressive results. A particularly enjoyable English department inspired bout of typoglycemia (being able to read a word with the letters wrongly ordered) spawned some cunningly misspelt notices around school – which believe it or not is a great way to reinforce spelling and reading because pupils have to think.

An English department inspired bout of typoglycemia (being able to read a word with the letters wrongly ordered) spawned some cunningly misspelt notices around school

Plenty of sport, in keeping with school's distinguished past record, and they had already notched up several rugby wins in September when we visited. Enthusiastic girls were practising hockey. One mother was thrilled that children were getting extra coaching and games skills from Dean Close specialists. Good sports hall and lovely covered pool with doors opening in summer to outside viewing areas which also give a view of Astroturf. Acres of grassy grounds with a lovely treehouse project under way for year 8s to learn practical skills on. The music department has some ambitious musical projects: audition processes and organisation being licked into shape by head of music. All children are encouraged to take up instruments (at the time of our visit, 97 pupils were learning an instrument). Choirs are beginning to take off. Year 7s have and love a three-week trip to South Africa including time on safari and a day in a township school, and there is an annual sports trip. Those we spoke to really appreciated the opportunities they get here and the kindness of the staff.

No charge for any activity run by the school though some – such as dance – requiring outside tuition have to cover their costs. Parents can drop off children early for breakfast though few do. Staff are exceptionally dedicated and all take on after-school or weekend duties and activities.

Parents say that the smallness of the school means that it has a truly family atmosphere and that staff know children exceptionally well, though the downside of this is that one or two year groups are have very small groups of either boys or girls. Friendliness and a happy atmosphere seem to extend to all parents and visitors as well. Poor behaviour is sensibly dealt with and bullying picked up quickly and effectively, though it seems to be rare. Food is pretty good and children like it. The house system is largely social, since the main pastoral care for all pupils is via the form. Lots of responsibility for year 8 pupils with head boy and girl as well as house and sports captains, who speak confidently of their duties and ambitions.

Supportive parents' association provides activities like fireworks parties for school and raises funds. Parents from all backgrounds, mostly within the large catchment both sides of the border, and they hope for more from Bristol now the toll on the Severn Bridge has been removed. A few military families. Past pupils include Richard Mead, Olympic showjumper, and Welsh rugby player Marc Batten.

Boarding: Boarding accommodation, in a rambling town house on site, has been freshened up and is spruce and welcoming. Currently it is very flexi, though some children with distant, military or expat parents stay for weekends with matron or go to guardians. Separate boys' and girls' dorms but everyone mixes in together, and like everywhere at St John's a family feel is the key. Regular influxes of groups from China and Spain each year bring an international flavour as well as taking up current spare places, though boarding has already expanded a little. Wraparound care possible for day pupils with supervised afterschool homework and masses of activities and sport, sustained by biscuits and fruit.

Money matters: Bursaries for services, police, clergy and staff children. 'School really helped to ensure we could afford to educate all our five children at St John's and had something left to live on,' said one grateful parent.

The last word: Much loved by parents, pupils and staff for its exceptionally friendly and supportive atmosphere, and for the sporting and academic traditions it strives to maintain. The school is part of the Dean Close Foundation and plans to increase numbers to about 250, which should mean it is financially viable in the future. Certainly a school well into recovery and worth watching for the future.

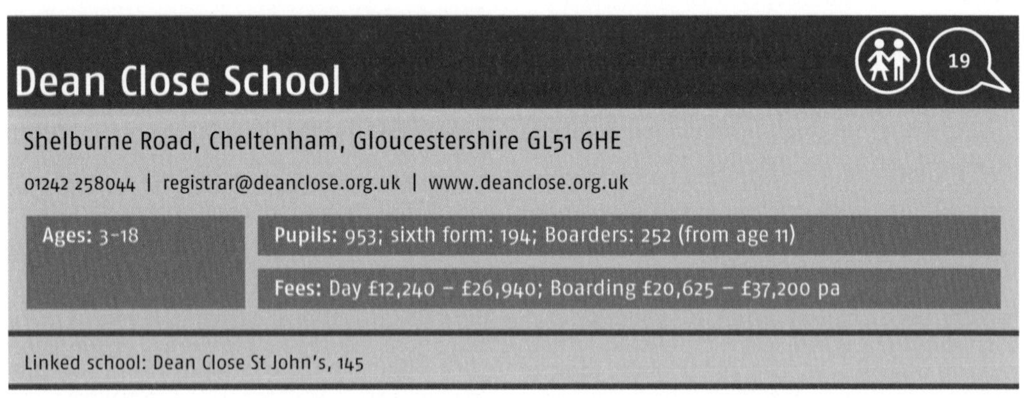

Dean Close School

19

Shelburne Road, Cheltenham, Gloucestershire GL51 6HE

01242 258044 | registrar@deanclose.org.uk | www.deanclose.org.uk

Ages: 3-18

Pupils: 953; sixth form: 194; Boarders: 252 (from age 11)

Fees: Day £12,240 – £26,940; Boarding £20,625 – £37,200 pa

Linked school: Dean Close St John's, 145

Headmaster: Since 2015, Bradley Salisbury MEd PGCE (40s), previously deputy head since 2009. Son of a vicar, he was educated at Monkton Combe School. First degree (theology) from Leeds, and then on to Bristol where he completed his PGCE and later a master's in educational leadership. It was while training for his PGCE that he met his wife, Claire. Taught religious studies at Gordano School before moving to Bristol Cathedral School as head of RS and head of years 10 and 11; thence to Wells Cathedral School where he was head of RS and a housemaster.

Friendly, full of energy and clearly enjoying his headship. Parents approve: 'Holistic, open-minded, very approachable', 'definitely listening'. Pupils lost for sufficiently eulogistic words when asked to describe him and settled for, 'Just so, so good.' His assemblies are 'amazing', and he 'gives everyone targets for the year ahead and writes pupils personal letters if they do well'. Oh, and, 'He's always walking round the school and he knows everyone's names.'

Mr Salisbury acknowledges that boarding has changed hugely since he was at school but believes that one of its enduring strengths is that it teaches young people how 'to work through relationships. You can't just go home at the end of the day and sweep problems aside, you have to figure out ways of getting on with everybody… it's great for social agility.'

A fair bit has changed since The Good Schools Guide last visited Dean Close, not least its acquisition of Monmouthshire prep, St John's-on-the-Hill (now known as Dean Close St John's), plus five nurseries. It's a rather canny way of 'growing the brand' by ensuring a good flow of pupils into the onsite prep as well as the senior school, but Mr S has no plans for significant expansion. 'Our size is just right for us to be a real community – we have lots of events where the whole school can come together in one place, and that's really important.' Ambitious five-year building and refurbishment programme well underway – yes there will be new stuff, but emphasis seems to be on 'ergonomics', improving classrooms and streamlining departments to form academic 'hubs' (eg maths/science; business).

Head believes that one of boarding's enduring strengths is that it teaches young people how 'to work through relationships. You can't just go home at the endof the day and sweep problems aside'

Unlike many schools, Dean Close has not consigned the robust Christianity of its founders to history and an obscure corner of its website, nor is this likely to happen on theologian Mr Salisbury's watch. He sees it as central to the school's educational ethos. 'We value each pupil and will always put an individual's best interests first, even if they may be at odds with those of the school. For instance, we don't just push everyone to go to Russell Group universities, even though that would be advantageous for our profile.'

Mr Salisbury's wife works in the prep as head of religious studies and the couple have three daughters at the school. Relaxation takes the form of kite flying – he used to be in a kite team – and cooking, 'I don't have a signature dish, I never cook the same thing twice!' Favourite read? True Blue (captain facing down a mutiny and sticking to his guns in the heat of competition in the Oxford and Cambridge boat race).

Head of prep since 2015, Paddy Moss, BA in geography and economics from SOAS (40s). Joined after nine years teaching in a prep school in Kenya and has 'lived all over the world'. Though Cheltenham may be less exotic, he describes the move as 'a wonderful fit'. That's pretty much exactly what parents say about him and Mr Salisbury too. Thinks the prep's size (around 300) 'ensures close pupil, parent and staff relationships'. Families must agree, there's now a waiting list for places.

Mr Moss is a big fan of the year 7-9 curriculum (all 13+ prep school heads are…) and says school is developing its own syllabus, 'uniquely designed to promote love of learning' and a 'seamless transition' to senior school across the way.

Has brought his love of the outdoors with him from Africa and enjoys bushcraft, camping and walking the Cotswold Way. Like Mr Salisbury, he also has three daughters at the school. A good fit indeed.

Entrance: Admission to pre-prep by taster day. For year 3 upwards it's cognitive ability and English papers, interview and school report. Around a third more pupils enter prep at year 7 and all are 'guaranteed' a place in the senior school. External candidates for senior school need 50 per cent or more in CE; entrants from state schools sit verbal reasoning, English and maths tests. Six I/GCSEs minimum grade 4-5 (grade 7-9 for subjects to be studied at A level) required for entry to sixth form, plus verbal reasoning test and papers on three A level subjects.

Exit: A few leave prep at 11 or 13 for grammars or single-sex boarding schools. Loses some (around 25 per cent) post-GCSE to FE colleges and also apprenticeships. Over 60 per cent to Russell Group. Birmingham, Royal Holloway, Sheffield Hallam, Durham and Cardiff Met all popular. Three to Oxbridge in 2021, plus one medic (in Toronto). Engineering and business courses particularly popular. One or two to degree apprenticeships.

Latest results: In 2021, 59 per cent 9-7 at GCSE; 63 per cent A*/A at A level (83 per cent A*-B). In 2019 (the last year when exams took place), 60 per cent 9-7 at GCSE; 28 per cent A*/A at A level (70 per cent A*-B).

Teaching and learning: Twenty-two subjects offered at I/GCSE. Most take 10 or 11, smallish numbers for classics, Latin and Greek. Maths, separate sciences, English and religious studies fare particularly well. Maths, further maths, art and design, history and modern foreign languages lead the A* pack at A level, but there's a healthy spread of marks in all subjects.

In addition to three A levels, sixth formers take timetabled 'enrichment courses', each of which leads to a qualification. One-year options include an EPQ plus a music diploma, computer software or sports leader qualifications. Two-year options include GCSE German, AS philosophy, maths or ancient history. Sounds pretty full-on so it's no surprise that even some local sixth formers opt to board.

Parents praised the school's community action programme – 'All pupils do voluntary work every week, they don't make a big thing of it, it's just expected'

Parents incredibly positive about how teachers bring out the very best in each child, whatever their ability. 'They are so generous with their time, nobody minds asking for help.' Praise too for careers guidance – school has good links with local businesses and supports pupils applying for apprenticeships and degree apprenticeships.

Teaching in the prep school was described to us as 'progressive, but with old-fashioned values'. Half the teachers are male and school thinks this 'makes a positive difference'. Latin introduced in year 6 (some drop this in year 7); Spanish starts at age 3 in the pre-prep. 'Moving away from Common Entrance.' Big focus on making year 9 transition as smooth as possible.

Learning support and SEN: Learning support came in for much praise. Short or long-term specialist tuition offered for literacy, numeracy or 'curriculum' (for pupils who need help with organisation/study skills). The most able are stretched via extension societies and participation in school and national competitions (maths and physics Olympiads; Latin and Greek reading; European Youth Parliament). Top set mathematicians take IGCSE maths a year early and then do IGCSE additional maths in year 11; triple science and the charmingly named 'Gratin' (Greek and Latin) can be taken as accelerated double and single GCSE options respectively.

The arts and extracurricular: All of the above pursued with gusto and considerable success. Year 9 do a carousel of 'creatives' (product design and manufacture, art, music, drama and cookery). Product design is one of the school's particular strengths and we saw some very impressive work – fabulous wooden standard lamps that wouldn't have looked out of place in an interior design showroom. Product design teacher says she's 'in heaven' and couldn't stop smiling proudly as she showed us her domain – full of traditional and high-tech kit. 'Our focus is on teaching skills, but we don't spoon feed, they have to work things out independently – it's what the industry is looking for.'

Lots of excitement about new cookery school – home to GCSE food and nutrition, cookery clubs and (fanfare) the Leiths Introductory Food and Wine Certificate. Sixth formers can do this either as part of their timetabled extension programme, or off-timetable in the evening. In return, not only will they get UCAS points, they also join the 'Leiths List', passport to a gap year cooking in ski chalets and private dining rooms.

Long tradition of choral excellence starts in the prep with the exquisitely trained voices of the Tewkesbury Abbey Schola Cantorum choristers (boys only). Both prep and senior school attract serious musical talents (regular choral/organ scholarships to Oxford and Cambridge). Prep has two orchestras and four choirs of its own.

Members of the school's quartet in residence, the Carducci Quartet, teach string players of all ages alongside their professional commitments. They also give performance classes, coach chamber music groups and run orchestra sectionals. All this excellence doesn't mean exclusivity, each pupil is encouraged to find their own voice/instrument. One of our guides said, 'I came to Dean Close on a sports scholarship, but now I'm singing.' Parents agree: 'Music is incredible, but it's really inclusive – everyone's encouraged.' Drama comes in for similar praise but some felt that it could take a leaf out of music's book: 'It can be a bit cliquey', said one. Another said, 'Anyone can have a part, but not everyone gets to speak and that puts some off.' Twas ever thus.

Bacon Theatre (named after former pupil, Francis Bacon) seats 550 and apparently has 'the largest stage in Gloucestershire'. More than 50 concerts and 10 major drama productions (including regular sell-out slot at Edinburgh Fringe) a year, plus lots of ad-hoc performance opportunities. School sponsors events and takes an active part in Cheltenham's literary, science and music festivals.

In addition to wide range of extracurricular options including CCF and DofE, parents praised the school's community action programme – 'All pupils do voluntary work every week, they don't make a big thing of it, it's just expected.' Energetic fundraising supports school for poor and orphaned children in Uganda.

Sport: School says that 'participation and team spirit are the real values of sport' and it used to be that in rugby at least Dean Close were plucky underdogs, rather than top dogs. That's no longer true: school has partnered with Gloucester Rugby Club and pupils told us proudly about how 'our rugby's so much better, we got through to the last 16 of the Nat West Cup.' Hockey is excellent and boys' and girls' teams have played in 19 national finals in the last five years. Riders are galloping ahead and it's rosettes all the way in team and individual showjumping, eventing and dressage. No on-site equestrian facilities, lessons take place at nearby stables; polo training is offered at Birdlip and school regularly fields tournament teams.

Boarding: Just over half of pupils are full boarders and school has also rather smartly addressed local demand for something a little less full: 'day boarders' are attached to a boarding house and have the option of staying two nights a week. Shelburne, a senior girls' house, is school's flagship boarding accommodation and very nice it is too. Year group to a floor, three or four to a dorm, sixth formers have single rooms with connecting bathrooms. Apparently boys' accommodation is somewhat plainer fare – as is often the case. Meals are eaten together in the dining hall; boarding and day houses also provide fruit, tea and toast. Saturday morning lessons, followed by afternoon matches, mean a six-day school week for most pupils whether they're boarders or not.

Dean Close has not consigned the robust Christianity of its founders to history and an obscure corner of its website, nor is this likely to happen on theologian Mr Salisbury's watch

Around a third of prep school pupils board and nearly all are full boarders. Accommodation is in three Regency houses with live-in houseparents who run things on an 'extended family' model. Up to three nights a week flexi boarding option also proving popular. Being on the same site as the senior school means access to facilities such as the swimming pool and cricket nets on summer evenings and there's a full programme of weekend activities.

Ethos and heritage: Founded in 1886 as a memorial to the Very Reverend Francis Close, Dean of Carlisle Cathedral and well known for his robust sermons decrying the evils of tobacco, alcohol, horseracing and the theatre. What would he make of Cheltenham today now that racing and the creative arts are two of its biggest attractions?

In 2015 the school became a foundation when it acquired St John's-on-the-Hill, a prep school in Monmouthshire, and five nearby nurseries. Another addition to the DC stable has been Mrs Emma Taylor, the warden. She's hugely experienced and delightful company and it's her job to ensure that the foundation is run in a 'businesslike way' but that the individual schools themselves remain 'personal'.

Site and buildings are familiar mix of old, newish and very new – the latter thoughtfully designed. Nothing grand or ostentatious, that's not the Dean Close vernacular. Currently under construction are a sixth form common room, a 'village' of four new day houses and a separate 'hub' for socialising between houses.

Former pupils (Old Decanians) include lots of eminent members of the clergy and military, plus rugby players, cricketers, artist Francis Bacon, actors Will Merrick and Hugh Quarshie, and writers George Adamson (Born Free), George Wilson Knight (Shakespeare scholar) and Jon Foster (TV comedy).

Pastoral care, inclusivity and discipline: 'Safe, happy, comfortable' was how one parent summed up the Dean Close experience. Others said it was a school where pupils are 'expected to be kind', that it was 'good for square pegs' and there was 'no one type, no cool crowd'. Parents say tutors, houseparents and teachers all respond promptly to calls and emails – 'They're on the case and really get to know the pupils.' Head puts big emphasis on school as a 'community' and says, 'Our size means we can have whole school dining and come together for chapel or theatrical performances.' He's also directing attention to things like pupil induction, improvements to changing room facilities (more privacy) and mobile phone use. Parents are positively encouraged to get involved if they can and there's now a parent society that hosts social events as well as talks on issues such as drugs and mental health (pupils get these too).

Pupils and parents: Mostly local. 'It's not a posh school,' thought one parent, 'pupils aren't spoilt or precious, they're aware how fortunate they are.' Longstanding links with Forces, diplomatic and clergy families. Smallish international contingent, includes Spanish and German children who come over for one year ('can make it hard to develop friendships,' thought one parent). Nearby GCHQ and Hitachi add Americans and Japanese to the mix.

Money matters: Comparatively good value for money. Scholarships and exhibitions at 13+ and sixth form. Some full bursaries available, including some specifically for children from Forces or church families.

The last word: We sensed renewed verve and confidence when we visited Dean Close. Energetic and forward-thinking leadership has resulted in nimble moves to accommodate changing work and family patterns. Yes, the school is looking to the future, but its founding moral and social values are as secure as ever.

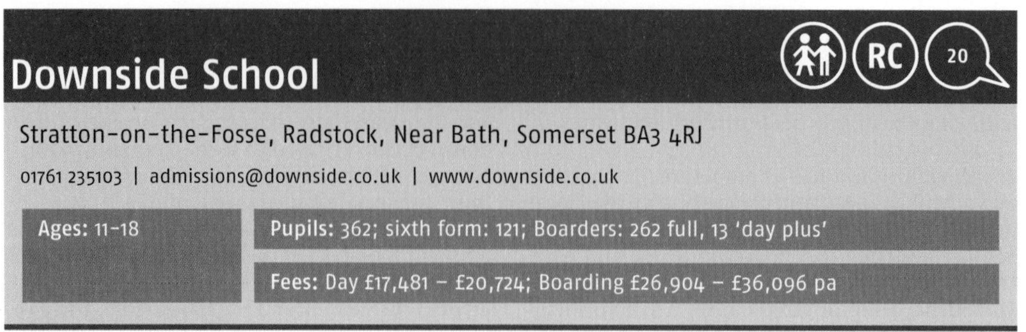

Downside School

Stratton-on-the-Fosse, Radstock, Near Bath, Somerset BA3 4RJ

01761 235103 | admissions@downside.co.uk | www.downside.co.uk

Ages: 11-18

Pupils: 362; sixth form: 121; Boarders: 262 full, 13 'day plus'

Fees: Day £17,481 – £20,724; Boarding £26,904 – £36,096 pa

Head: Since 2018, Andrew Hobbs BA (mid 50s), previously deputy head. A product of Worth Abbey, not unlike the school he now heads, Mr Hobbs read classics at Cambridge before a couple of years teaching at Hurstpierpoint, 16 at Canford, where he was also in charge of cricket and rugby (he is a rugby blue), before arriving at Downside in 2008 as deputy. He took the helm as acting head after a difficult period for the school but went through a rigorous selection process to get the top job. 'I always wanted a school with a purpose at its core,' he told us – 'and at this point, Downside needed continuity.' That purpose is to educate children 'for eternal life, not just till the age of 18,' as he puts it – and 'our results are the by-product of everything else, particularly acting in accordance with our Benedictine values'. Of these more anon, but while of course rooted firmly in the Christian faith, there are very contemporary references to community, concern for the individual and service to others. Only the second lay head of Downside, Mr Hobbs is married to Damaris, an NHS physio, and a father of four grown-up children, two working (one in teaching) and two still at university. It is possibly his palpable pride in his family or perhaps his appealingly wide smile, generous guffaw, little round glasses and shiny pate – or maybe just the cut and thrust of his sparkling conversation – which makes him so well liked by students and parents alike – the usual plaudits like 'approachable, visible and knows everyone' don't really do him justice. Our session with him overran massively, so engaging was the chat and full of references to books we had not got round to reading, such as Thinking Fast and Slow (Daniel Kahneman) and Rebel Ideas (Matthew Syed), but he clearly had. Cerebral yet warm, full of spirituality yet down to earth, Mr Hobbs is an ideal role model and seems the right helmsman to steer the school into calmer but uncharted waters as it severs its links with the monks who plan to leave Downside Abbey for a new home.

Entrance: A few into year 7 but mainly into year 9 and about 25 into sixth form. Year 7 entry is by online CAT tests plus an assessment day and interviews held in January each year. For year 9, the process is more formal and starts earlier, with ISEB pre-tests or CAT tests and an assessment day in February of year 6 or 7. At sixth form, unconditional offers are made on the basis of sufficiently good entrance papers in chosen A level subjects; conditional offers are dependent on predicted grades and school reference. Surprisingly high numbers also join in other years, including year 11 – some of these will be short-term overseas students.

Exit: About 10 after GCSE. After A levels, Downside students depart for a range, not just of British universities, but overseas also. At the time of writing, two Polish students were accepted onto the prestigious Our Future Foundation programme, which helps young Poles access the world's top universities. Most popular university destination in 2021 was Exeter, followed by Bristol and Durham; a variety of courses including four medics and English literature with gender.

Latest results: In 2021, 56 per cent 9-7 at GCSE; at A level 56 per cent A*/A. In 2019 (the last year in which exams took place), 36 per cent A*/A at A level (63 per cent A*-B). School has not provided 9-7 grades at GCSE.

Teaching and learning: The academic life (and it is academic) of the school is bound up with the Benedictine idea of transformation, so the journey is as important as the destination. The curriculum is broad from the start. A modern language is encouraged rather than enforced – French from the off but keen linguists can take up Spanish or German (or indeed Latin or ancient Greek) in year 9 and keener ones still can avail themselves of private lessons in Russian, Chinese or Italian. Ten or 11 GCSEs are the norm (12 on request) from a range of 20 subjects. Religious studies is compulsory alongside core subjects of maths, English and sciences. Weaker scientists can opt for combined science rather than the rigours of biology, chemistry and physics. Students for whom English is not their native tongue take IGCSE in English as a second language and there's an intensive one-year GCSE course for international students. At A level, 24 subjects are on offer including history of art, psychology, Latin and Greek, plus a BTEC in sport. A level sets are run with tiny numbers (we met students who were the sole takers of physics and Latin) but we picked up a little parental dissatisfaction with GCSE option blocks. Student satisfaction, however, is generally high and their experience enhanced by the academic clubs – many of which are open to all ages – which enrich each subject, such as the Oolite Society (geography), Bede Society (history) and Aelfric Society (linguistics).

Downside is a school which delivers 21st-century education not through technical wizardry or fabulous facilities but through rigorous and intellectual teaching

Downside is not a school which delivers 21st-century education through technical wizardry or fabulous facilities but through rigorous and intellectual teaching. We liked the translation of prayers into Spanish and students seemed happily immersed in a French listening exercise through headphones, but the biology lab we saw could well use an update. The main library is handsome and run by a chartered librarian but small for the size of the school – well-stocked departmental libraries compensate for this and history lucks out with the Sligger library. Reading is undoubtedly part of the culture of the school.

Parents we spoke to endorse the high academic standards and expectations the school sets and appreciate the intellectual work-out their children get. 'Downside is able to fulfil the high expectations I have of schools,' one mother told us; another that her son had been admonished* for laziness (*not the word she used!). Equally, it is generally reckoned that any sense of a student being academically overwhelmed will be picked up by his/her tutor.

Learning support and SEN: The department comprises five members of staff whose expertise seems to be concentrated on literacy. All new junior arrivals are screened on entry and the school clearly states that learning support is open to all. Students with specific learning difficulties receive targeted help, sometimes on an individual basis. The department definitely gets the thumbs up and there is no stigma about attending it. More information on the website would be helpful.

The arts and extracurricular: First out of fabulous facilities must be the Grade I listed abbey church, not only the physical centre of the religious life of the school, but also a visually and acoustically stunning venue, particularly for music. Very strong here, with four auditioned choirs including the prestigious Schola Cantorum (invitation only) which provides choral music for school services in the abbey church. Organists are lucky enough to practise on its renowned Compton organ. In no way does secular music fall behind, with plenty of opportunity for instrumentalists to play in orchestras, chamber ensembles and bands, the newest of which is the function band comprised of students and staff, but still room for charming traditions such as the singing of madrigals on May morning from the top of the abbey church tower. Downside has long had a reputation for its brass and jazz, which shows no sign of diminishing, but masses of opportunity for aspiring rock stars, rappers and beatboxers too – there is even a staff band called The Educators with the head on drums... The CCF marches to the stirring strains of its own band. Distinguished Old Gregorian (as past students are called) musicians include classical pianist Philip Fowke, blues guitarist Todd Sharpville and former drummer of Echo and the Bunnymen Pete de Freitas.

The 400-seat theatre has recently benefitted from a refurbishment and has welcoming social space upstairs and down. Close collaboration between music and drama departments over productions such as Little Shop of Horrors, whose rehearsals started in lockdown. A 'serious' senior play and a couple of junior ones, plus house drama and the chance for committed thespians to take LAMDA qualifications, mean there is probably something for everyone. Those who have a backstage contribution to make are equally welcomed, plus anyone nifty enough to put on a production of Singing in the Rain in three days flat at the end of the summer term! Jared Harris (award-winning performances in The Crown and Chernobyl), Peter Morgan (screenwriter for The

Crown) and Eugene Simon (My Family and Other Animals, Game of Thrones) are all OGs.

Visual arts and DT have their own adjoining dedicated space, open in the evening and at weekends also. Facilities include a Mac studio for digital design and a print screen room – creativity across different media is encouraged. Some younger students gave this part of the curriculum top marks. We loved the crinoline under construction for a GCSE art project we saw, but were sorry to miss the A level ballgown – sewing club and knit'n'natter for those who would rather keep their efforts outside the exam system. Lockdown inspired one fitness fanatic to design and make his own weights bench for home use – that was after he had designed a motorised stretcher for military use as his DT practical. In normal times, there is an artist-in-residence and plenty of trips to museums and galleries.

Downside has long had a reputation for its brass and jazz, which shows no sign of diminishing, but masses of opportunity for aspiring rock stars, rappers and beatboxers too

Downside has long had close and proud links with the Irish Guards and an active CCF, generally enjoyed by those who take part: the army section has recently adopted the headdress of the household division. We saw them marching to the beat of their own band on the school's immaculate turf; elsewhere students were loading improbably large rucksacks for their DofE gold expedition.

Sport: Known for its sport and easily spotted on any pitch or Astro with its distinctive – not to say garish – maroon and mustard kit. Beautiful green spaces seem to run in all directions with Astros discreetly sited away from the main buildings. 'But please could they build loos there?!' begged some students. The most glorious asset is the immaculate cricket pitch, surrounded by mature trees and adorned by a handsome pavilion which looks down on the school. A touching memorial to a Second World War pilot killed in training and buried in the abbey churchyard, a tragic accident taking the lives of nine boys also, is set into one wall.

Usual sporting offer of rugby, cricket, hockey, netball and tennis, depending on the season; less usual is the promotion of the values of discipline, honesty and stewardship underpinning it all and emblazoned on the gym wall ('could use updating,' some parents reckon). Personal best is placed above winning at all costs, though wins are celebrated too. Girls' sport beyond school enjoying particular success with girls trying out for league hockey, Somerset county cricket (one also winning a written commentary competition) and one being accepted onto the netball futures pathway at Bath University. Despite this, some parents think girls' sport 'could be polished up and paid more attention to by the head'. Closer links with the performance pathway at Bath Rugby have been forged in recent years, culminating in an academic scholarship for one talented and delightful young man to study for a degree in maths at Bath while continuing his rugby development. Plenty for those less inclined to team games and ball sports too, such as sailing (school has its own boats), weight-training and bootcamp. A full-time physio is there to get students back on the pitch when it all goes wrong. Somehow typical of Downside is the inclusion of sports outreach and sports leadership in its list of activities – it certainly isn't all about winning. Legendary match teas too, we're told.

Boarding: Eighty per cent full boarders (no weekly) housed in one of six houses: one for junior boys up until the end of year 9, three senior boys' and two for girls of all ages. The latter are purpose-built and fit modern expectations of boarding accommodation more closely than the boys', who mostly 'live above the shop' in the main building. All jolly quaint but rather dark and old-fashioned in places with beds for junior boys lined up in long dorms with low ceilings to keep the heat in and divided into cubicles for privacy. They don't seem to mind one jot, however, and parents are happy that 'my daughter does not live in a five star hotel' and 'it's not too expensive to play in – we'd rather have shabby and homely!' said one. Verging on scruffy, we'd say.

We heard of one youngster who started as a boarder during Covid and has chosen to stay on, of another girl whose mother told us she would rather board, and from another parent who said her boarding children never have a problem going back to school. 'Fun' was the most common description from the students we spoke to, plus praise for house spirit and loyalty and the welcoming family feel of all boarding houses, where all year groups can mix. The calm wisdom of house staff goes down well too – 'They are firm when needed but always caring and not swayed by teenage moods,' parents told us. Day students are part of boarding houses, there is some flexi-boarding but at least every student has the same bed – not always the case at other schools.

A 9pm finish for almost everyone who wants to take part in the extensive activity programme means day students just about lay their heads on their pillows at home during the week in term time. Whatever the boarding lacks in luxury is made up for by the food, which is now outstanding and vastly improved from past visits. Contracted out to a catering firm, the menu reads very well, with healthy dishes and those good for the planet's future given their own icons. Word had got out the day of our visit and the kitchen tried out its test menu for following week on us – restaurant standard it was too. Tempura battered seaweed and feta banana blossom, anyone?!

Ethos and heritage: Proudly and unequivocally Catholic, but equally firm on the idea of Benedictine community through the eight values which the school espouses. First among these is welcome, which means that non-Catholics are indeed welcome, although they are expected to respect and take part in the religious and spiritual life of the school. 'Not the place for a dyed-in-the-wool atheist,' in the view of one parent, but we were struck by the number of times students and their parents brought up the Benedictine values of listening, reverence and concern for the individual as being pretty good cornerstones of a school community – 'a framework to function in,' according to one mother. It's perfectly okay to discuss questions about faith, dogma or to express doubts – 'There's a difference between a debate and a dialogue,' the head mused, 'and we are definitely pro free speech.' 'God is interested in individual gifts and talents and whether people are kind to each other – and not particularly in their sexuality,' he went on, in response to our question about how the school resolves conflict between the teachings of the Catholic church on homosexuality and modern attitudes. The notion of personal best pervades school life in general, with academic excellence propelled by yet another Benedictine value, that of personal discipline. Students work hard here and a seriousness of purpose underscores academic life – 'The kids are bloody well there to learn!' said one father in no uncertain terms. The best EPQ submissions are now published in a journal named Tessera, 'capturing the depth and breadth of academic endeavour in our community'.

Downside's ethos and heritage are hard to separate. Although the school was founded in France in 1617, it did not arrive at its present magnificent home in the slightly down-at-heel village of Stratton-on-the-Fosse for another 200 years, after a history of persecution in France in the 18th century and a few years taking refuge in Shropshire. The school houses are all named for people who helped the school along its turbulent journey to the present day, Isabella (a Spanish/Portuguese infanta who protected the community) being the most recent girls' house. Its (mostly!) impressive buildings hark back to an era when high Victorian Gothic architecture was popular and a lot of wide yet slightly gloomy corridors with acres of wonky parquet persist. Somehow that, and the somewhat old-fashioned uniform – particularly for boys with pin-striped trousers and black jackets and a hierarchy of waistcoats in sixth form (the apogee for head boy and girl is dove grey, double-breasted with a watch chain) – contribute to the strong sense of a 400-year-old school. Girls have been around only for just over 15 years, so their uniform is less distinctive – curious midi-length grey kilts, maroon jumpers for those below sixth form, black for sixth form, plus jacket.

Whatever the boarding lacks in luxury is made up for by the food, which is now outstanding. Tempura battered seaweed and feta banana blossom, anyone?!

Any mention of Downside is, regrettably, likely to stir recollections of historic child abuse, widely reported in recent years and resulting in an IICSA investigation and report in 2018. The resultant publicity has been very difficult for the school; on that point, the head expressed his relief that the allegations were now known and that there has been greater transparency. He regularly reiterates that the school can never be complacent and all staff members remain vigilant. One key requirement of the IICSA is the separation of the school from the abbey, which is now complete.

Pastoral care, inclusivity and discipline: Highly thought of by students and parents alike, and plenty of people to turn to when the going gets tough. As well as tutors, housemasters/mistresses (HsMs) and house mothers (matrons), there's an independent listener and a strong chaplaincy team, who look after the spiritual welfare of students. The health centre is staffed 24 hours a day and houses a counselling room and quiet space for students to retreat to when it all gets a bit much. A room with sensory resources is planned. We heard that the school is good at sorting out friendship issues and that bullies are fairly dealt with. Perhaps it is the Benedictine values of welcome and respect which make Downside as inclusive as it seems to be, plus the space for discussion in SMSC (the school's PHSE programme) and the voluntary Lectio Divina, where a Bible passage is read and reflected upon by groups of students.

We picked up a slight sense of inequality between boys and girls (inferior sports kit and everyday uniform now being tweaked so girls can wear trousers – not sure if that will extend to boys wearing kilts) and the emotive publicity of Everyone's Invited and the murder of Sarah Everard produced some tensions, now largely resolved.

Discipline does not seem to be a major part of life at Downside – skiving lessons and sports sessions will land you in trouble, smoking or drinking will get you suspended. The withdrawal of 'Co-op privileges', ie permission to walk to nearby Chilcompton and stock up on crisps and Mars bars, seems to be a huge deterrent. Punishments are generally reckoned to be a fair cop and students appreciate recognition for all sorts of achievement, not just academic or sporting.

Pupils and parents: About 70 per cent Catholic, many local, some seeking a more spiritual education if not actually Catholic; 26 nationalities (majority from Hong Kong and Poland) and 14 languages spoken. Not particularly affluent, as independent school families go – 'The cars in the car park at Speech Day aren't too flashy,' one dad remarked. 'People here are unpretentious – and very Somerset!' another (from the home counties and very happy he stumbled upon Downside) told us. We found the young people we met to be articulate, thoughtful, positive and grateful for all they have with very few grumbles about anything.

Money matters: Fees broadly in line with comparable schools, although years 7 and 8 are notably cheaper. Usual array of scholarships at usual entry points although more options for year 9 admissions. Choral exhibitions and product design awards also. Bursaries can also be granted from the start in exceptional circumstances and in cases of unexpected hardship.

The last word: It would be hard to leave Downside without a sense of the 'poetry of life', whether that comes from the setting, the imposing buildings, the music or the ancient scholarship which the walls seem to exhale. A singular education, with its focus on the spiritual, but one which seems to equip its young people to look beyond the transience and insistent clamour of 21st-century life. 'My daughter will come out a better person than if she had gone to the local competition,' in the words of one father. Downside – a contradictory name, as we could find very few.

Exeter Cathedral School

21

The Chantry, Palace Gate, Exeter EX1 1HX

01392 255298 | admissions@exetercs.org | www.exetercathedralschool.co.uk

Ages: 3–13

Pupils: 278; Boarders: 40 full (from 8 years)

Fees: Day £8,469 – £13,869; Boarding + £8,166

Headmaster: Since 2016, James Featherstone (40s). Previously head of lower school at Perse School, Cambridge. Studied French and Spanish at Durham, followed by a PGCE. The son of a headmaster growing up on site in schools, most formatively Radley, he has an intuitive understanding of how they work.

Exuberant, enthusiastic and driven. Since taking over the headship, he has devoted himself to a campaign of reinventing, reconfiguring and reigniting this school and he's nowhere near finished, sharing exciting plans structurally, pastorally and for co-curricular development. One parent said he 'has brought in progressive thinking to an old choral prep, bringing it absolutely up to speed without losing its charm.' He comes in for particular praise for having restructured the senior leadership team and elevated academic expectations with demonstrable results right through to reaffirming sporting prowess, refuelling the catering and increasing pupil voice.

Lives and breathes music. He was a choral scholar at Durham Cathedral and later joined the choir of Jesus College, Cambridge as well as becoming part of a professional quintet at St-John-at-Hampstead, London. He still sings both with groups out of the school and in the cathedral – 'I have just had the magical moment of singing alongside my son, who is a chorister, for the first time – a real hairs on the back of the neck experience.'

Married to Julia, interim director of music at ECS; they live on site with their two young children who are both at the school. Together, they form a strong musical canopy with an appreciation of the rigours of a chorister's life and the benefit of a supportive pastoral network. 'Julia is a vicar's daughter and I grew up in school boarding houses so we are both used to an open-door life at the centre of our community.' Family time away from school is always 'mental health boosting – big skies and big scenery'.

Entrance: Non-selective entry to nursery and pre-prep, with 80 per cent of nursery children moving into the school, forming half of the reception intake. Additional places available throughout prep, with a bulge at year 4 to accommodate choristers. 'The way a school assesses for entrance says a lot about its culture – here we like to teach rather than test our applicants,' claims head. Accordingly, prep entrance focuses on gentle taster day with potential pupils attending a class lesson in maths and English and staff feeding back their views on attitude, behaviour, team playing and problem solving skills in advance of an informal interview with the head. Voice trials for choristers held annually and selection is based on attitude and enthusiasm as much as vocal skill.

Exit: A handful head off to local grammar schools at 11+. Rest leave at 13+ to a broad spectrum of independent schools with strong support and advice on choice. Destinations include the local day options of Exeter School and Maynards and the boarding powerhouses of King's Taunton, Queen's Taunton, Blundell's, Wellington, Marlborough, Sherborne, Eton, Charterhouse or Clifton College. Around 85 per cent of 13+ leavers are awarded scholarships in everything from music to academic, art, drama or sport.

Our view: This is a 12th-century school with 21st-century vision. Proud of its choir school heritage, its soul is surrounded by music but its sights are focused on a modern, inclusive and dynamic approach. One of only 44 choral schools in the UK, it is the only independent boarding school in Exeter.

Housed in several buildings encircling the cathedral, it oozes historical importance and offers stunning backdrop views across this ancient site. Pupils walk the cobbled paths between the buildings with accompanying members of staff for all but the eldest year groups.

Hall House is a former canonry that houses reception to year 2. Securely enclosed by ancient Roman walls (and keypads), it is welcoming, bright and playful. A new spongy all-weather playground separates the main building from the purpose-built nursery. Little ones can play outside under awning in an area that leads to the shared playground at one end and the woodland garden at the other. Centred around a large oak tree, there's a mud kitchen, bug hotel and the hide – a shed to birdwatch, play games or make dens. Beyond this there are allotments for each class and the gardening club.

Reception to year 2 classrooms are bright and imaginative, with plenty of scope for immersive learning. Pupils proudly showed off their posters about sun safety in reception, while others practised copying words and sounds from the wall displays. We loved the gentle teaching of respect for others through 'work in progress' signs that pupils propped against Lego creations and train track set-ups. Lots of happily engaged faces, calm productive teaching and staff on hand to offer help, cuddles and inspiration. In year 1, children were learning about travelling the world, stopping off in various countries to explore culture, climate and biodiversity. An interactive wall display has a push-button rainforest soundtrack and recording of the children talking about their discoveries. 'The teaching staff are utterly fantastic and the children feel safe, cared for and nurtured whilst in the pre-prep,' said a parent. These pupils walk to the Chantry for lunch, where meals are eaten in a wood panelled dining room. The catering has recently been completely overhauled after poor feedback from parents.

Microsoft nominated ECS as an independent school leader for its online provision during the recent pandemic

From years 3 to 8, pupils are taught in classrooms scattered between the Chantry and other buildings around the Palace Gate area of the cathedral close, with the omnipresent cathedral forming the physical, spiritual and musical hub of life here. Core curriculum subjects are taught in the mornings with extended curriculum in the afternoons – many by specialist teaching staff. 'The teachers have a wonderful gauge of each child, pushing those that need a nudge and offering great support to those that are flying,' said a parent.

The school provides excellent preparation for senior school, according to parents. 'The level of thought development as they move up the school is astounding,' said one. Small class sizes mean children receive personalised learning and detailed feedback and parents told us they know the 'young and dynamic' staff well, enjoying easy access to them with any concerns or queries, either in person at the school gate or via email and phone.

The online provision during the recent pandemic was 'absolutely incredible, well communicated and indicative of how flexible and adaptable they are as a school,' said a parent. This was supported by Microsoft, who nominated ECS as an independent school leader for its online provision.

Pupils are calm and attentive, responding confidently to class tasks and questions. The older year groups show a warm familiarity with staff that's full of fun without overstepping the mark. Parents laughed that the pupils tend to be on 'the right side of cheeky', confirming that 'they are not overly disciplined but absolutely know what behaviour is appropriate or expected and very much live up to this.' Head, in particular, is praised for his 'sensitive and spot-on resolution of issues and his wonderfully warm, open door policy for those pupils needing some ongoing emotional support.' 'It's usually simply a question of bumping people back on track and ensuring that we are setting the right habits for life,' he told us.

One small chorister staggered into rehearsals swamped by a huge cricket bag and even bigger cello on his back, his school books held to his chest and a huge grin on his face

The school was recruiting a SENCo lead when we visited, but even without one they handled learning support well, catering for all needs where reasonable adjustments can be made, typically for dyslexia, dyscalculia, ADHD, ADD and ASD at extra cost. Small classes are beneficial and a big draw for these parents. Some pupils have an EHCP.

As an ancient chorister school, music is at the heart of everything. We started our visit sitting in on the early morning chorister rehearsals in the cathedral and the goosebump-triggering beauty of their voices echoed way beyond the cathedral to greet other pupils as they arrived at school. Choristers are well catered for and the ability to nurture, rehearse and perform their talent without them missing out on other school activities is impressive. One small chorister staggered into rehearsals swamped by a huge cricket bag and even bigger cello on his back, his school books held to his chest, a huge grin on his face as he excitedly chatted about the afternoon's cricket practice to the cathedral's head of music – a testament to the varied experiences this school offers. 'It is an unbelievable privilege to be a part of the chorister community yet it is by no means elitist, they are very much a normal part of the wider school community,' said a parent.

Whether you are a chorister or not, 'there is an excellent musical education' at the school, said a parent. Over 200 music lessons take place every week, every child is in a choir and opportunities to perform either with the multitude of orchestras or bands at the termly musical performances or solo via the half-termly Performance Platforms are inspiring. 'This is definitely not a school that churns out painful school music recitals – the level of each performance is extraordinary and of a staggeringly professional level,' said a parent.

Art takes place in a small but high-ceilinged, light-filled room overlooking the beautiful walled Dean's Garden. A veritable Aladdin's cave including boxes of treasures, salvaged goodies and examples of past work. During our visit, pupils were busy making seascapes from recycled blackboard scrolls found in the depths of a school cupboard, listening to music and chatting quietly about their work underneath stunning examples of vast Gaudi-inspired masks, which had been produced for scholarship entries. Every inch of wall and ceiling space dedicated to works of art, a room full of colour and fun that was mirrored in the art teacher herself.

'Dramatic opportunities, development and training are all absolutely fantastic here,' gushed one parent. The annual year group performances are said to be 'incredible' and are supported by smaller investigative productions of English classics such as Shakespearean Macbeth cameos. The drama teacher was praised for their ability to 'enrich drama way beyond the prep school realm' with 'extremely advanced characterisation studies' that left the children enthused.

Children (and parents for that matter) settle in quickly and easily, with parents praising the 'kindness and helpfulness of the older children to those in the younger years' and vouching for the family feel that 'made it very easy to find your feet both as a new pupil and parent'.

Outside space is limited. The main prep playground at Chantry House is half taken over by a vast wooden climbing frame that had been nominated for replacement until the student council unanimously voted to keep it and spend the budget allocated to its replacement instead on a meditative, wooden outside seating area where children can sit and chat or hold meetings. 'It was a wonderful idea and has proved absolutely invaluable as a school space, I'm so impressed by their choice,' remarked the head. The Dean's Garden is a much-favoured, walled, cottage garden space, home to relaxed breaktime gatherings and, when we visited, outdoor lessons – taking advantage of it as a haven of dappled shade and a small lawn.

This is a city centre school with the disadvantage that it lacks onsite green playing fields. 'But the facilities that the children use daily are of county and international standard, way beyond what one would expect from a prep school of this size,' said one parent. Bussed from year 2 upwards to either the Exeter University pitches or county cricket fields, pupils see the minibus trips as a highlight of the games lessons rather than a bore and the sporting tuition is widely praised. 'The new head of games is brilliant, gently coaching every pupil to view sport as something fun, inclusive and healthily for all,' said a parent. There's some 60+ fixtures per term plus an under-7s festival for netball, soccer and athletics. Other sports include judo, squash, swimming, cross-country and athletics plus outdoor pursuits like climbing, kayaking and Dartmoor walks.

Trips make the most of the local area including Roman walks. Years 5-7 go to France every other year, year 8 goes camping on Dartmoor, plus there's a Buckfast Abbey choir camp.

Former pupils include 14th-century theologian Boniface; more recently, bass player Orlando le Fleming; Chris Martin, lead singer of Coldplay (who apparently once said, 'ECS is where it all began'); Hampshire CCC manager Giles White and Dave Webb, ENO.

Boarding: Accommodation is made up of three Georgian houses with 22 boys' beds and 18 girls' beds for 7-13-year-olds. All boarders are from the UK, most from within an hour's drive, and around half are choristers, facilitating their busy rehearsal and performance schedules. The large dorms have three bunk beds each and a piano, or in some cases a harp. Older pupils can have a double room with two single beds. There's a comfy common room, a TV room, a prep room, and the Cosy Club in the basement with sofas, DVDs, a games table and a crafts area.

The young French head of boarding is warm and calmly on top of everything and everyone. At weekends, there can be anything from a handful of pupils to 25, and activities include trips to Haven Banks, Dartmoor or beaches. Spanish tapas evenings, Irish evenings and making sushi are popular.

Money matters: Choristerships are worth 25 per cent off tuition fees.

The last word: A warm, enveloping family of a school where pupils are, in the words of one parent but echoed by many, 'allowed to be individuals, encouraged to be true to themselves and helped to flourish in whatever they find a passion for'.

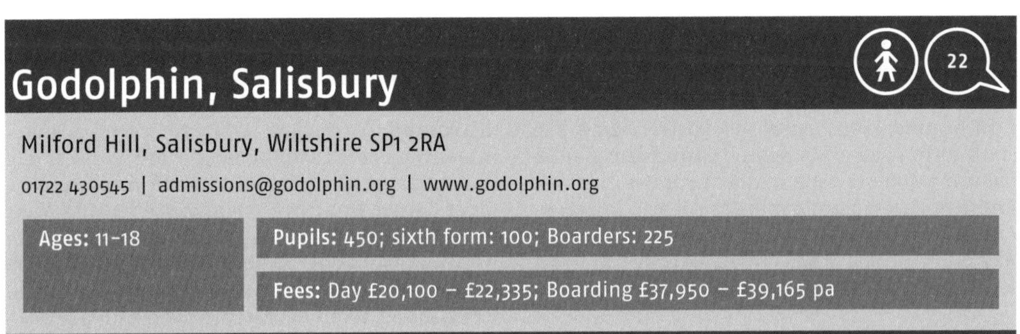

Godolphin, Salisbury

22

Milford Hill, Salisbury, Wiltshire SP1 2RA

01722 430545 | admissions@godolphin.org | www.godolphin.org

Ages: 11-18

Pupils: 450; sixth form: 100; Boarders: 225

Fees: Day £20,100 – £22,335; Boarding £37,950 – £39,165 pa

Headmistress: Since 2014, Emma Hattersley. Studied music at Durham before continuing on to the Royal Academy of Music. Was housemistress at Canford, moving to become deputy head of Sherborne Girls for four years before taking up her current post. Interests outside school include her two dogs, spending time with her husband, three adult children and grandchildren, and camping, with the recent acquisition of a camper van. Music remains a passion as does gardening, and she enjoys comparing notes – horticultural, not musical – with the school's head gardener. A stroll around the immaculate school grounds would suggest that he doesn't needs any tips.

As head of a historic all-girls school Mrs Hattersley sees her role as a juggling act. She's conscious of treasuring the school ethos and values, while keeping pace with today's social and educational demands. Acknowledges the need to look at education in the round, attaching importance to both academic and personal skills, creative and STEM subjects. 'If we're preparing girls for the real world and want more women to go into scientific subjects, having that creative element will bring something slightly different to the table. You want imaginative scientists, who can contribute to a team.' It's a lot of balls to have in the air, but her calm and thoughtful manner reassures that she's more than able to cope.

She lists greater collaboration with local schools, moving forward on digital engagement, and mental health and wellness of students as the priorities on the strategic plan. On this latter point she is a firm believer that 'if the emotional support is right, success will follow'. Has a strong rapport with students, with a self-professed soft spot for the underdog. She is committed to building strength of character and resilience through engendering a happy atmosphere, in which girls feel safe to stretch themselves and build their confidence. All evidence suggests she's getting it right. Parents enthuse about her 'super impressive' and 'forward thinking' approach, and the school is often chosen by families because of her performance and this focus. She is approachable and has breakfast, lunch and tea in small groups to get to know girls better. Her door is open, even, one struggling parent reports, her front door during the summer holidays.

Entrance: Described as 'softly selective'. Majority of girls transition from Godolphin prep, but for new candidates at 11+ and 13+ entry there is an assessment day in which papers in English and maths are taken plus interview with head or senior member of staff and reference taken from existing school. Sixth form entrants are expected to gain at least five GCSEs at grade 5 with a minimum of 7 in proposed A level subjects, plus interview and exams.

Exit: Around 15 per cent leave post-GCSE. Half of sixth form head off to Russell Group universities choosing courses ranging from engineering and international relations to history of art. University of Arts London, Bath, Bristol, Durham, Edinburgh, Exeter, Manchester and Oxford Brookes all popular. Some to art college and foundation courses.

Latest results: In 2021, 64 per cent 9-7 at GCSE; 60 per cent A*/A at A level (85 per cent A*-B). In 2019 (the last year exams took place), 50 per cent 9-7 at GCSE; 29 per cent A*/A at A level (58 per cent A*-B)

Teaching and learning: Not that this was explicitly said, but we suspect the mantra should be that Godolphin aims for girls to be the best that they can be, rather than hothoused to be the best. While academic results have fluctuated from year to year, head says she's 'never too fussed' by league tables and results and points instead to the fact that the school is in the top seven per cent for value added.

Girls across the academic spectrum, both in terms of ability and interest, are catered for. In the sixth form, performing arts BTEC and level 3 food technology are offered alongside core STEM subjects, further maths and classics, and the increasingly popular psychology and geology. French, German and Spanish are available, with Mandarin as an optional GCSE. Take-up of STEM subjects is healthy, beating the national average for girls taking science subjects at A level by 20 per cent.

Years 7–10 use Microsoft Surface Pros in the classroom, dispensing with the need for exercise books, and meaning that girls no longer need their phones in school

One parent reported the school's willingness to accommodate different courses, 'no matter how small the class'. No one area outshines the others (although art seems extremely popular and roughly half take art GCSE). The school science quiz is as big an event as the performing arts competition.

There is a scholars' programme for able students, centred around additional lectures designed to stimulate intellectual curiosity. These take place on Friday afternoons which must be a pretty tough sell, but hard to find space in a packed extracurricular timetable.

The Bright Futures career programme is ably supported by a thriving alumnae network. Recent leavers are more than happy to come back and share their stories of the great wide world, while parents and alumnae with more years' experience under their belt contribute to Find Your Future Friday, discussing their career paths. We were struck by the number of former pupils who are now parents, teachers or support staff. It all contributes to an overarching sense of a happy, enduring family.

As part of the digital drive, years 7-10 use Microsoft Surface Pros in the classroom, dispensing with the need for exercise books. A happy (presumably less so for students) consequence of this shift is that girls no longer need their phones in school.

Learning support and SEN: Just under a fifth of girls receive SENCo support and the school is well equipped to cope. 'Any girl who comes under learning support is literally just scooped up,' says one grateful parent. Housed in a separate building, the department offers a safe haven. Head of learning support also gets five-star reviews, with one parent commenting that their daughter 'is on an upward trajectory', despite on occasion the department's positive input not being matched by all subject teachers (an issue that was resolved). Specialist maths teacher offers one-to-one support. Girls are steered towards the most appropriate GCSEs and personal support extends to finding the most suitable exam board, this level of attention leaving another parent 'with absolutely zero worries'.

The arts and extracurricular: This is where the school comes into its own. The impressive arts block is a magnet for a wealth of creative talent. Hugely impressive artwork adorns the walls and most available spaces. The breadth and depth of areas covered – ceramics, fashion and textiles, painting drawing and printmaking, 3D design – must help retain interest and could account for the large take-up to GCSE and A level. Exposure to visiting artists from an early age means that girls are confident to approach practising artists for advice when compiling their portfolios. And confident they are. Former pupils are on hand to talk through their success at gaining places at Central St Martins, City & Guilds and the like.

A smart performing arts centre hosts performances, including student-led and whole-school musicals such as Made in Dagenham. Music department offers a range of options, from the highly regarded vocal ensemble to the open to all-comers choir. Instrumentalists can join orchestra, concert band and a strong (award-winning) chamber music section. Numerous opportunities to perform throughout the year, including at Salisbury Cathedral with which the school has a close connection.

School doesn't take itself too seriously. Ents, an annual play in which pupils parody the staff, has the potential to go horribly wrong, but so far as we know hasn't – yet

For those who prefer the great outdoors, CCF beckons and Godolphin has the largest all-girls CCF contingent in the country. Alongside the novelty of muddy faces, khaki kit, and activities such as canoeing and raft-building there is also the highly demanding Ten Tors challenge, to which the school regularly sends teams.

Unique to the school is the Elizabeth Godolphin award, a compulsory sixth form programme conceived by Mrs Hattersley. It combines academic enrichment with practical skills such as car maintenance, presentation and interview skills, digital competence and cultural appreciation. She believes that the sixth form programme develops girls into great role models for the younger years. Having seen the friendly but authoritative way in which our guide (who was not a prefect) moved girls blocking the stairs, we tend to agree.

Sport: Lacrosse and netball take centre stage through winter, moving over for athletics, cricket and tennis in the summer. After-school clubs ensure that there is a multitude of other options available, anything from handball and fencing to basketball and touch rugby. Other sports that don't fit easily into the programme are supported through financial assistance and flexible timetabling – something the equestrian team and international standard hammer thrower are taking full advantage of.

Competitive sport took a hit during the Covid pandemic – an unfortunate time for the new sports director to have arrived – but matches are generally played midweek for netball and Saturdays for lacrosse (means talented girls can play both). Sports staff have to fight hard against competing interests in the timetable and are pushing a 'commitment culture'. Regular opponents include Sherborne Girls, St Mary's Calne, Guildford High and Cheltenham Ladies. Facilities include a 25-metre swimming pool and a small gym, packed with exercise equipment. There's also a sports hall, three lacrosse pitches that double up as athletics track and grass tennis courts in the summer, and four hard court netball courts. Not bad at all for a school this size.

Boarding: Just over a third board. Split into three houses, Walters for lower school (8-13), Cooper for senior school (13-16) and School House for sixth form. Weekly boarding is a popular option for local parents, with full boarders in the minority (around 15-20 out of 90 in Cooper), and no plans to try and increase this number – that would 'not be Godolphin'. House staff live on site and accommodation for girls ranges from bunk beds in Walters to a mix of single and shared rooms for sixth formers. All are clean and at teenager standards of tidy. Large communal areas (known as the Sit) allow the house to gather together for activities.

Positions of responsibility include an international rep to act as a link for new international girls when they arrive. Prefects can run some evening activities, attend house council meetings and, touchingly, are also in charge of birthday cards and flowers for cleaning and residential staff.

Activities, somewhat curtailed during the pandemic, include yoga, karaoke, movies. For full boarders, weekend activities can include ice skating, and trips to theme parks, although some parents think that a few more interesting activities might encourage more to stay.

In senior school, electronic devices are taken in an hour before bed. Staff are wise to attempts to flout the rule and have a drawer full of confiscated alternative devices.

Ethos and heritage: Founded in 1726 by Elizabeth Godolphin, the school moved to its current 16-acre site in 1891. It benefits from being on the edge of Salisbury, allowing easy access to town for girls and yet providing stunning views over the downs. The original main hall and two classrooms remain but have been joined by modern accoutrements – everything from the performing arts centre to the sixth form café. The Gothic hall, now a little too small to accommodate the whole school, is adorned by portraits of fearsome-looking former heads. We wondered what those heads would think of today's more welcoming, less tight-lipped Godolphin.

Many are attracted by the lack of glitz and glamour and its traditional values: 'I like the fact that it's old fashioned and girls stay girls for longer,' said one parent

The emphasis is on community. One of head's first tasks was to refurbish the lower school locker area and transform it from 'a horrible spot with metal lockers' to a bright and airy social space with tables and chairs to encourage group chatting. There are currently 400 students on the roll, with no plans to increase that number and risk losing the family feel. The school can still gather together three times a week, for example. However, there are murmurings that widening the community to include more interactions with boys' schools would be a good thing. Social events are limited and, in one parent's view, more debates with boys might add perspective to some of the more strident views held.

School doesn't take itself too seriously. Annual 'Muckup' day, when the departing upper sixth have a licence to run amok, is tolerated with a smile – even when head finds herself barred from her office by string covering the door. Similarly, Ents, an annual play in which pupils parody the staff, has the potential to go horribly wrong, but so far as we know hasn't – yet.

Pinnies are another tradition. Blue pinafores (or special pink ones for birthdays) are worn by all girls below sixth form over the top of their uniforms, a quirky feature that contributes to the feeling of togetherness and perhaps a slightly old-fashioned vibe that appeals to some parents – 'There's no sassiness, it's more idyllic St Trinian's,' commented one.

Pastoral care, inclusivity and discipline: Parents universally agree that pastoral care is a core strength. Care meetings at which every girl is discussed occur fortnightly with deputy head, house staff, heads of year, and SENCo. The pastoral team, which includes pastoral lead, school nurse and chaplain, is on hand to support girls and is highly rated by parents. Girls talk freely about the level of support on offer, both from staff and each other. A new equality, diversity, and inclusion officer will further strengthen the team. Mealtimes are monitored with staff eating with the girls, and the school catering team provide additional nutritional guidance.

Mental health and wellness taken extremely seriously and led from the top. School organises the well-received GoParent, a day conference for parents and extended to the whole of Salisbury, at which visiting speakers give advice on issues such as self-harm, eating disorders and confidence building. Upper sixth are trained in mental health first aid, and available to offer help to local primary schools.

Girls understand and respect the boundaries and tend to self-regulate, even down to the rare smokers who, says one sixth former, 'we told to stop'. One expulsion in the last four years (social media incident).

Pupils and parents: Parents mainly local, even boarding parents who enjoy the flexibility of weekly boarding to fit around work commitments. Many are attracted by the lack of glitz and glamour – absence of long sweeping drives and rows of Range Rovers in car park is seen as a bonus. So too are its traditional values: 'I like the fact that it's old fashioned and girls stay girls for longer,' said one parent. 'Not a very worldly school,' said another, swiftly followed by, 'It's a bit of a gem and we're lucky to have it close by.' Unworldly does not mean shy and retiring; girls struck us as confident (without being pushy) and unpretentious.

Alumnae include Minette Walters and author Jilly Cooper, whose continuing involvement – she still writes to the girls – has led to a boarding house being named after her. TV personalities include Dragon's Den businesswoman Deborah Meaden, Katie Knapman of Countryfile, presenters Helen Bishop and Louise Beale. Plus sportswoman Ruby

Smith, yachtswomen Hannah White and Nicola Rodriguez and actress Charlotte Longfield.

Money matters: Means-tested bursaries available plus HM forces and sibling discounts. Scholarships confer prestige but no fee reduction.

The last word: This is a lovely, happy school. Small enough for every girl to be known as an individual but large enough for challenge and diverse opportunities. With solid academics and excellent extracurricular options, girls can grow in confidence and strength of character in a supportive environment. During our late summer visit departing sixth formers confessed to bittersweet feelings – sad to be leaving but 'completely prepared for whatever comes next'. For a head watching keenly as their students leave the nest there can surely be no better affirmation of a job well done.

Hanford School

23

Child Okeford, Blandford Forum, Dorset DT11 8HN

01258 860219 | office@hanfordschool.co.uk | www.hanfordschool.co.uk

Ages: 7–13

Pupils: 100; Boarders: 60 full, 10 weekly/flexi

Fees: Day £18,750; Boarding £23,550 pa

Headmaster: Since 2014, Rory Johnston BA (Cantab). Mr J, to the girls, has used his past life in the City to good effect ensuring that Hanford's future is healthy and secure. After many years in finance he followed the hunch of a friend who reckoned he'd make a good teacher and landed the top job at Hanford after a stint as head of classics and boarding housemaster at Horris Hill. 'A brilliant headmaster – he likes running it his own way but he's completely saved the school,' said one mother. 'Extremely clever, he's been very good for the academic side,' remarked another.

'I'd only been teaching for four years when I joined here and my views have changed quite a lot over time,' he told us. 'Teaching has made me happier, more thoughtful and kinder. I'm much more focused on what matters.' He uses his classics degree to teach 'the gospel according to Latin' and has realised through lockdown how much time he spends – and missed – 'just wandering the school, checking on everybody and having quick chats'.

This is a prep where the head's spouse contributes almost as much as the head. Georgina – Mrs J to the girls, George to parents – is head of pastoral and 'an undiluted joy', according to one mother. Ever aware of the dynamics between the girls, she is also 'brilliant with parents, very reassuring and very sweet and maternal with the girls'. The Johnstons have two teenage children.

That one parent describes arriving at Hanford as 'a bit like time travelling to the 1950s' is alright with Mr J. He works hard to protect girlhood, putting pony riding, tree climbing and parlour games above screen time and make up (mobiles are banned – though girls may call home whenever they wish). Much emphasis on 'letting girls be children and develop in their own time'.

Clearly passionate about Hanford's gorgeous if slightly shabby-chic house and stables (his home and workplace), he relaxes by fly-fishing and cycling ('safer and quicker than horses').

Sarah Canning, daughter of the founders, head and owner since 1959, handed over to a charitable trust in 2003. She died in 2017 but her legacy lives on: Hanford remains very much the school she made.

Entrance: Informal, non-selective, girls can come at any time if there's room. Some at 7, but more commonly as 8 or 9-year-olds. Year 7 has been popular lately too, so the senior years are the fullest. Growing numbers of locals, plus Wessex girls, Londoners desperate to give their girls a rural childhood (regular coach to Battersea) and numerous families posted or working abroad (especially popular with Forces and FCO families). A few from overseas including Spain, China etc. Parents as ever unshowy and unsnobby; new money prefers anywhere blingier.

Exit: Many continue with all-girl boarding. Sherborne Girls, with St Mary's Calne, Downe House and St Mary's Ascot are regular destinations. But some do go mixed, mainly to Bedales, Bryanston, Downside, King's Bruton, Milton Abbey and Marlborough.

Our view: Ask any former parent or pupil about Hanford and you'll be bombarded by passionate paeans in celebration of its glories: its quirkiness, its changelessness, its quintessential Englishness. Evocations of Malory Towers and Hogwarts will ensue, together with a reverent inventory of the school's more bonkers traditions – the manners system which grades girls from Piglet to Royal Guest and the nutty names of the branches on a cedar tree that girls are encouraged to climb. (When girls – and staff – became nervous about scaling it, an old girl was invited back to show how it's done.)

You'll get the sense of a school that (with the exception of the new purpose-built junior building) has somehow lain undisturbed for aeons, a time capsule, a girly Neverland; a place of butter-coloured sunlight, blissful children, long shadows, honey for tea, the whole timeless-idyll schtick. And to be sure, all of this grabs you when you go and see for yourself. The school's location is paradisal, the manor house beyond beguiling. Stand and be captivated by the genius loci. Blandings Castle must surely be on the other side of the hill.

Some of the school's more endearingly quirky traditions include the manners system which grades girls from Piglet to Royal Guest and the nutty names of the branches on a tree that girls climb

The cold reality, back in the days before overarching regulatory frameworks, didn't fall far short of this arcadia. This was the school where the late Tara Palmer-Tompkinson remembered, 'After swimming we used to run naked round the gardens because it saved the bother of tumble-drying the towels.'

Mr Johnston saw that some people thought the girls a little free-spirited and has addressed this: 'It's about close contact and making it clear that we have very high expectations about behaviour.' He is otherwise proud of how little has changed at Hanford, though there is the Rotunda, a new timber-built building with 360 windows for years 3, 4 and 5. They have also Astro-carpeted the netball court, and made plans for a new art barn.

Hanford has always had a free-radical feel to it. When the Rev Clifford Canning, newly retired headmaster of Canford, founded it with his wife in 1947, they decreed no uniforms and no prefects – which raised eyebrows back then. And though it is famously, let's say, retro – 'My mother-in-law couldn't believe how little had changed since the 70s,' says one parent – what makes the school brilliantly different is the spirit in which it's done things, with idealism, creativity and joy, wholly unselfconsciously. It's a marmite eccentricity that either thrills or alienates parents. 'The two 13-year-olds who showed us round looked absolutely dreadful,' one mother recounts. 'Hairy legs, unkempt hair and nothing matched. And I thought, Fantastic! I don't want my daughter to give a stuff about what she looks like at that age.'

The lack of uniform fits well with the outdoor pursuits at Hanford, tending the chickens, climbing trees, horse riding, looking after gardens (each girl gets around a square yard each). They like the way this builds self-reliance and develops friendships; the way it instils, as one parent put it, 'gumption' – these are decidedly not snowflake children. Hanford parents like the adventurousness and muddy knees. In horsey circles the school is legendary – everyone can ride, and nothing sets you up for the day like a pre-breakfast canter from the lovely stables, Grade II listed – 'more listed than the manor,' a groom tells us.

For a school that is determinedly low-tech – they weren't exactly in the first flush to add computing to the timetable – they blew everyone away with their online provision through Covid. 'It was phenomenal,' says one parent, 'and this is not a high-tech school.' 'Perception wise, people would have had us low on the list to nail it,' chuckles Mr J, but nail it they did, their website awash with glowing testimony. One family received a laptop from school the moment they realised they were one short. Live lessons, chapel, plus regular tutor meetings, and art and handwork sessions (Hanford's name for textiles/ needlework) were delivered, balanced with independent learning packs posted to those who struggle with screen time – 'We also wanted to continue handwriting through virtual learning.'

If the idea of handwork makes you pause, consider how the nation turned back to baking, puzzles and sewing in lockdown, and embraces very similar projects labelled as 'mindfulness'. 'I won't be scrapping it,' confirms Mr J, adding with pride that two girls recently went for interview at Sherborne in dresses they'd made themselves. 'There is a huge link between creativity and confidence. I'd rather urge boys' schools to do handwork too.'

Beyond the ponies and the outdoor pool, sports facilities might otherwise be described as serviceable. An Astro hockey pitch would be nice but 'These things cost a fortune… our job now is to make better use of our friends at Bryanston and Clayesmore,' says Mr Johnston. 'We have what we need here and nothing else.'

King's Hall School

Parents prefer to have fees invested in good teaching staff, and there are (almost) no complaints on this score, with many staff mentioned in dispatches. 'People travel quite a long way to work at Hanford because it has this reputation for being creative and a bit different, besides academic,' says one teacher. 'I have such a lot of freedom about how I teach my subject – I might struggle to go to another school now.' Being small, with an all-hands-on-deck attitude, teaching staff get to know the girls extremely well. There are three forms in year 7 and two in year 8, typically with just 12 to a form. The girls usually win eight to 10 scholarships a year, their names added to an honours board in the main corridor.

In horsey circles the school is legendary – everyone can ride, and nothing sets you up for the day like a pre-breakfast canter from the Grade II listed stables

One family said they'd prefer to have their hand held a little more through the secondary school application process, and don't expect your child to be drilled in the latest VR and NVR questions ahead of this. 'I'm resolutely against that, though don't mind if you want to do that in your own time,' says Mr Johnston. 'We genuinely do not see our girls being held back as a result – and I prefer a girl who's going to knock your socks off in interview.' Parents confirm that everyone seems to go to their first-choice school – 'possibly because they are judiciously advised'.

Masses of music, instrumental and choral – especially choral. Almost everyone plays an instrument. Dedicated music block. Drama very strong as you'd expect of a school which sets such store by play and imagination, but art, in a range of media, is considered a particular strength, seriously good, very well taught and produces a lot of successful art scholars. 'Lucy Tabberer [head of art] is a well-regarded artist in her own right,' one mother tells us.

Around 10 per cent of the girls receive some degree of learning support and are attended to by specialists, though this is charged for. 'We work quite hard to keep our fees reasonable,' explains Mr J, and this is one way of doing so. Interventionist support given to anyone needing it as and when but this is not the right school for 'substantial' educational needs.

A lot of people think that Hanford is an alternative sort of school. Couldn't be wider of the mark. Kindness matters most here. Close on its heels comes old-fashioned courtesy, hence the quaint manners league where you begin as a Boa Constrictor and earn your way up through Squirrel, Primrose etc, but risk plummeting to Piglet. It's aspirational, so there's very little Piglet-shaming. By all accounts it works. The same goes for the committee system, which takes the place of prefects. It's designed to bring out the helpfulness in girls, not the bossiness.

Both systems contribute to what one parent described as the school's climate of 'support, positivity and warmth' – a place where 'no one thinks they're better than anybody else'.

Boarding: Boarding doesn't suit everyone, nor the fees, so some don't. Everyone has a bed all the same and can stay overnight more or less at the drop of a hat for free up to 20 days a year. 'It's always made up ready for you – my daughter loves that,' says a mother.

Day girls go home after prep at 6.35pm. Dormitories are upstairs in the manor house, hugger-mugger, in rooms that adapt remarkably congenially to the purpose. Though once famous for their super-spartan furnishings, they have recently been made more comfortable and '21st century', as one mother put it, by Mrs J, with some murals added courtesy of the gappies.

The school accommodates just about any request for a weekend at home, while ensuring no one rattles around who stays in: Mr J considers anything under 40 in for the weekend 'a little light'. Weekend activities are usually on site, home-spun and lots of fun; barbecues, after-dinner games and one or two ideas Mr J has shamelessly stolen from his Horris Hill days, like big prize bingo.

Money matters: Some bursaries and a good deal for Forces families.

The last word: 'Old fashioned but liberal,' says one parent, an oxymoron that hits the mark. 'We haven't changed hugely, we're just a little bit less shabby,' says the head. The numbers of second and third generation girls here (some even come back to be married in the chapel) tells you just how much this marvellous school is treasured by those who get what it's all about; delivering a fine schooling around a brilliant country childhood. 'It's been a lovely place to be a little girl, grow up and learn to be brave and kind,' says one mother. And what could be less shabby than that?

Hatherop Castle School

Hatherop, Cirencester, Gloucestershire GL7 3NB

01285 750206 | admissions@hatheropcastle.co.uk | www.hatheropcastle.co.uk

Ages: 3–13

Pupils: 243; Boarders: 12 full, 21 weekly/flexi (from 7 years)

Fees: Day £8,985 – £15,510; Boarding + £7,800 pa

Headmaster: Since September 2017, Nigel Reed MEd BSc PGCE (30s). Formerly deputy head of Wallhampton School, Hampshire. Educated at Trinity School and Kelly College, both in Devon, and boarded from the age of 10 ('I loved it'). His father and grandfather were both in the navy and so, nearly, was he, but a taste of sports coaching while studying for his degree precipitated a sharp about turn into teaching. He started at Dulwich Prep in Kent where he taught PE and was a boarding house tutor, thence to Wallhampton where he was director of sport and, ultimately, deputy head.

Mr Reed met his wife, Jo, at Wallhampton – she's a forest school leader and a qualified teacher of mindfulness and meditation to children. She is also trained as an emotional literacy support teacher and has introduced emotional literacy to the school's pastoral care team: 'We already do a huge amount to promote physical well-being so we're keen to give the same attention to emotional literacy – offering support to parents, as well as children.' The couple have two boys at the school; 'It's a great adventure for us all.' We think they make a great team – relaxed, cheerful and full of energy.

Mr Reed is only the second head since the school started in its present guise as a prep in 1992 (before that it was a girls' school). We imagine that stepping into the shoes of Mr Easterbrook, who ran the show for 26 years, must have been a little daunting, but all seems to have gone very smoothly. Mr Easterbrook himself continues to work for the Wishford Group, who have owned Hatherop since 2014. Parents seem to agree: 'The transition was managed really well; we saw him (Mr Reed) quite a few times before he started and knew he was just the right fit.' The rapport was mutual; Mr R told us, 'I loved the feel of the place at once.'

He favours a collaborative style of headship and has appointed two new deputies, one academic, one pastoral. Of course, he has other plans – what new head doesn't – but parents who adore Hatherop because, not in spite of, its faded grandeur and old-fashioned courtesies have nothing to worry about on that score. 'Good manners are so important. We sit together at meals and all pupils from reception to year 8 shake a member of staff's hand at the end of the day.' Building up the boarding has been one of the school's priorities and London parents keen to 'educate their children out of the rat race' are catching on.

Mr Reed teaches computing and coaches rugby and girls' hockey. Since knee problems forced him to give up football, golf and cycling have become his recreational sports. He likes the fact that golf 'turns frustration into a positive' and that you can 'have a game at any age'. When he's not outside, Mr R enjoys reading crime novels and autobiographies – Douglas Bader's Reach for the Skies 'inspired him as a child'. And if all this sounds a bit hearty, he's also a huge fan of musical theatre and loves a good, old fashioned panto. He says he 'always wanted run his own school' and now finds himself doing just that – and king of a castle to boot. 'It's fabulous, I'm loving every minute.'

Entrance: No formal entrance tests; prospective pupils are assessed during the course of a taster day and on the basis of reports from previous schools. Exams and assessments for academic, art and music scholarships take place during the lent term.

Little Owls nursery takes from age 2 and there's a toddler group on Friday mornings where parents can bring their children (6 months upwards) to familiarise them with nursery life. Be warned – children who enter at nursery but do not continue through to reception forfeit their deposit.

Exit: At 11+ to Gloucestershire state schools and grammars. At 13+ mainly to local-ish day and boarding schools. Cheltenham College, Dean Close, Abingdon School all popular. Others to eg Marlborough College, Rendcomb, Cheltenham Ladies'.

Our view: Hatherop is recorded in the Domesday Book as 'Etherope', which means 'high outlying farmstead', and 900 years have not diminished the name's descriptive accuracy. To reach village and school requires a delightful meander through the lush meadows of the River Coln, followed by a steep ascent of its eponymous valley. At the height of summer this is a vision of quintessential English pastoral; what it's like on a dark winter's evening may be another story (imagine less romantic, more slippery); we hope it's on the council's gritting lorry route. The approach through classic estate parkland is hardly likely to disappoint, but the building that rises to meet you is definitely more stately home than fortified residence. If you happen to have any back-seat passengers who demand crenellations and a moat of their castles you may need to manage expectations (but only until you get inside).

Hatherop is recorded in the Domesday Book as 'Etherope', meaning 'high outlying farmstead', and 900 years have not diminished the name's descriptive accuracy

For the youngest pupils at Little Owls nursery, the emphasis is on creativity, outdoor learning and imaginative play, embodied by the delightfully sticky 'mud kitchen' and wooden pirate ship outside. Pirates and mud chefs were having 40 winks when we crept round but we spied nothing amiss. Like much at Hatherop, nursery facilities are spick and span, if somewhat make-do and mend. Friendly, dedicated staff and nurturing atmosphere more than make up any lack of superficial glitz and parents we spoke to were verging on evangelical; 'It was the nursery that sold the school to us,' said one. Several said that for them, the fact that the nursery is run along 'traditional' lines was a deciding factor. 'There's a caring, family ethos and they're brilliant at slow, but sure, nurturing.' Specialist teaching from 'transition' (age 3-and-a-half) onwards in French, music, and gym. Little Owls is open for 50 weeks a year. From the nursery buildings in their walled garden just off the yew walk, pupils move to the stable yard for reception and pre-prep. A serious game of Castle Vet was under way when we dropped in here (we very much hope the blue snake has recovered). Reception pupils may not yet be 5, but it's never too early to have a taste of work experience and they enjoy the chance to 'help' school maintenance or kitchen staff.

This is a small, inclusive school and parents love the fact that every child is known as an individual: 'Teachers work with parents on developing each child's strengths – each child finds their place and all progress is celebrated.' The learning support department says school can accommodate children with 'mild to moderate SEN'. Staff will work with pupils who may just need a 'couple of terms' catch-up' and longer term one-to-one help is also available at extra cost. Study skills sessions are provided for pupils in years 7-8 to help them prepare for entrance exams. Our pupil guides took us in and out of lots of lessons and we saw quiet individual study, energetic teamwork, eager questions and answers, role play and great pupil-teacher rapport. One parent told us, 'I've yet to meet a teacher here who regards their work as "just a job"; they all give so much time and energy.' School has won the Lego robotics regional finals for the past two years and last year came eighth nationally.

An Astro was high on everyone's wish list and one is now destined for the newly acquired market garden site. It will make a huge difference to the sports fixture programme, enabling school to host home matches. Head wants to build up girls' sport – not just hockey but also football, with girls' rugby 'a possibility'. Other sporting ambitions include developing school's own equestrian team – riders currently put through their paces at the local riding stables – and introducing golf. Fencing is one of Hatherop's strengths – the high-ceilinged ground floor reception rooms must make excellent salles. Also on offer as clubs are judo, gymnastics, cross-country, ballet, Scottish dancing and yoga. The new performing arts centre is a well-designed modern venue that sits comfortably in the grounds. Drama and music programme is busy and ambitious, pupils of all ages and abilities are encouraged to take part in plays and concerts.

Girls who studied here in the 1940s had the use of the house's original grand ground floor library. Today Hatherop's pupils make do with a fairly dreary kind of box-room cum book store – let's hope that new library comes after new Astro Mr R's to-do list. New treehouse classroom is a huge boon though – used by all year groups.

Parents told us it was the pupils who made the biggest impact when they visited: 'I saw the year 8s and just thought how much I wanted my own child to turn out like that.' Another said how impressed she'd been with pupils' good manners and confidence: 'That's what sold the school to me.' Our guides were charming, thoughtful and very proud of their school, telling us with some nostalgia about 'cross-country runs through the woods', 'wonderful' Christmas activities and the disco in the front hall; 'Pupils from all the Wishford schools come here for that.' The tradition of year 8 leavers jumping into the outdoor pool in uniform on their last day was being eagerly anticipated.

Food got the thumbs up, particularly fish and chips, roast chicken and brownies. Parents say it's much improved over the last few years with increased use of local produce and sensible efforts to reduce sugar. We certainly enjoyed a delicious roast when we visited.

Parents told us about their first visit: 'I saw the year 8s and just thought how much I wanted my own child to turn out like that'

Like many stately homes, Hatherop (and its charming adjacent church) has been owned, sold, built and rebuilt over the centuries. In the 1860s it was leased by a maharajah – there are tales of elephants on the lawn – but he didn't stay long because the railway authorities refused to give the estate its own station. It first became a school (of sorts) in the 1920s when the owner's wife, Mrs Francis Cadogan, offered to educate a handful of her friends' daughters alongside her own. One of those girls was Nancy Mitford, who recalls enjoying her time at Hatherop apart from the cold – morning wash with an icy sponge, anyone? When Mrs Cadogan's children had all flown the nest the school was moved to Cambridge where it became known as Owlstone Croft (hence Little Owls nursery and school owl mascot), under the governance of a Mrs Theodora Fyfe. By 1946 the school had outgrown its Cambridge premises and returned to Hatherop where Mrs Fyfe was known for producing girls who 'finished very well and debbed beautifully'. Mrs Fyfe and her successor, Dr Pandora Moorhead, sound like redoubtable characters; apparently Dr Moorhead installed a carousel on the lawn to provide relaxation for the girls. Her idea of discipline was, 'Come to the drawing room for a sherry darling and we'll talk about it.' Those were the days.

Boarding: School offers full, weekly and flexi boarding; numbers aren't huge, but they're growing as parents from further afield 'discover' Hatherop. There are currently about 30 beds but scope for expansion in this area if necessary. Small regular contingent of short-term boarders from Spain and other, mainly European countries, dilute the Anglo-Saxon mix just a little. No Saturday school means everyone gets a proper weekend and weekly boarders from London can return home by train, accompanied all the way to Paddington on the Friday Cotswold Flyer (Kemble/Swindon stations are both close by), homework done and with a packed supper provided. A member of staff will meet them at Paddington on Sunday evening for the return journey. There's a programme of castle fun and excursions for boarders who stay at school for the weekend and weekly boarders can join in at no extra cost. Things are flexible enough that pupils can be scooped up in a crisis and one-off bed and breakfast option is very reasonable £35 per night – better value and more convenient than a babysitter. Working parents love the 8am-6.30pm wraparound care option too.

Head describes the Hatherop boarding vibe as 'homely' and we'd agree. Boarders sleep in large, comfortable rooms up in the eaves – apparently the children 'prefer to be together in a big dorm' together rather than smaller rooms. We were impressed by the decoration of both boys' and girls' rooms – there was a competition to redesign them and parents judged the entries. Home duvets and lots of quirky touches, not to mention stunning views over trees and honey-coloured Cotswold stone cottages more than make up for paintwork and carpets in the corridors that are showing inevitable wear and tear. A recent ISI inspection declared the boarding provision (and pretty much everything else at Hatherop) to be 'excellent' and we concur.

Money matters: Hatherop was acquired by Wishford Schools in 2014, joining a group of seven preps located in Kent and along the M4 corridor. Prior to this the school was suffering as a result of changes to Forces school subsidies (RAF Fairford and Brize Norton are nearby), not to mention the financial burden of upkeep to a historic building. Let's be frank, if it's flash you're after then Hatherop isn't the place for you, but parents say that investment from Wishford has made a real difference, citing improvements to everything from food to communications. Some means-tested bursarial support available.

The last word: Venerable trees, an Italian garden, rumours of secret passages, mullion windows and acres of green space – Hatherop feels like the setting for the kind of storybook childhood most parents, above all urban parents, want their children to have. It's an idea the school has taken and run with – their interactive prospectus is even called 'The adventure of childhood' and references Narnia, Enid Blyton and, of course, Harry Potter. Cynics may scoff, but if your school happens to be a castle in glorious rural surroundings, conjuring such visions is hardly a liberty. Any resident dragons and fairies must have made themselves invisible when they heard The Good Schools Guide was visiting, but we still caught a whiff of magic in the air.

Hazlegrove School

Hazlegrove, Sparkford, Yeovil, Somerset BA22 7JA

01963 442606 | admissions@hazlegrove.co.uk | www.hazlegrove.co.uk

Ages: 2–13

Pupils: 365; **Boarders:** 100

Fees: Day £9,228 – £18,711; Boarding £21,705 – £27,696 pa

Linked school: King's Bruton, 173

Headmaster: Since 2017, Mark White MA (Edinburgh) PGCE (early 50s), previously academic deputy head at the Dragon for 13 years. As urbane and considered as one would expect of an Old Etonian, Mr White has nonetheless seen the rougher end of education, having done his teaching practice in one of Bristol's most deprived suburbs before moving on to the more genteel setting of a Cheltenham comprehensive. The celebration and prolonging of childhood and the absence of hothousing initially attracted him to Hazlegrove, its beautiful rural surroundings an added bonus. When we asked him about his priorities as a head, his reply was unequivocal – 'the children's wellbeing and the school's core values of kindness, integrity, courage, grace and generosity,' said he without missing a beat. Not endless scholarships then, although they also turn up year after year.

Mr White has not introduced any startling changes since he arrived and has kept virtually all the staff but there is a sense that things have been tightened up, presentations about senior schools earlier on and fewer dogs at matches being two examples. Parents like his visibility ('It's not all about him though,' one mother told us) and his approachability; the children too, judging by the enthusiasm with which even the tiniest hailed him during our tour. Older ones rate his teaching of history. Suited and booted like all the male members of staff, Mr White came across as somewhat straight-laced… until he let slip that he had once played the dame in a Dragon pantomime, after which we saw him in a whole new light.

Married to Serena, who supports pupils in class, with three grown-up children, Mr White's interests include political literature, theatre, cricket and tennis.

Entrance: From year 1 through informal assessment and observation on a taster day, following a look at the school either on an open day or private tour. Age-appropriate tests in English and maths are designed to give 'a snap shot of current academic ability,' states the policy. Rather less formal for reception and earlier, with these younger children meeting a member of pre-prep staff and/or attending a Squirrels parent/toddler group. A handful join at year 7 for the final run-up to CE or scholarships to senior schools.

Exit: About 40 per cent on to King's Bruton, which, as part of the same eponymous Tudor foundation, is effectively its senior school. Others to a wide range of up to 40 independent senior schools including some of the UK's finest – Marlborough, Winchester, Cheltenham Ladies', Sherborne, Millfield etc. In 2021, 18 scholarships (majority for sport) to a spread of 11 schools.

Our view: The sometimes unpredictable journey (there are longhorn cattle and oncoming 4x4s to dodge on a single-track road) up the long winding drive through the greenest of pastures to Hazlegrove leaves the busy A303 behind in favour of a more gracious world. The stunning four-square 18th-century house of golden stone looks out on immaculate lawns and topiary; more utilitarian buildings are tucked away so as not to spoil knockout first impressions (nursery and pre-prep in what was the walled kitchen garden). The school only moved to the house and acquired its current name and identity in 1947; its adopted crest of bearded dolphin and crown reflects the fortunes and history of the house. The school's exact location before that is not entirely clear but it can trace its origins back to the 16th century.

These days, it's a place where children work and play hard, but where they also as importantly have bucketloads of fun and stay children (lanky boys literally in short trousers) until they leave at 13. Learning starts in the nursery, much of it child-initiated, and even the tiniest children enjoy forest school and have the run of the considerable prep school facilities – closely supervised of course! Specialist teachers too – we were charmed by the lively rendition of Wheels on the Bus to guitar accompaniment (teacher) and enthusiastic shaking of maracas (children) we saw on our tour. The EYFS is followed until the end of reception, thereafter learning becomes more formal with the building blocks of English – phonics are taught daily – and maths every morning when young brains are at their sharpest; practical hands-on subjects take place in the afternoons and children routinely go home in their PE/outdoor kit with their uniform in their rucksack.

In the prep school, day-to-day communication (prep etc) between parents and school is via each child's journal, where the days of the week are printed in no fewer than three languages – two modern, one ancient – and where the owner is reminded of common courtesies (listen carefully when people are speaking to you; look interested etc) and invited to reflect on his/her own learning and activities. Reading tops the list of academic priorities and the Accelerated Reading Scheme is embraced with enthusiasm; the beautiful well-stocked senior library painted a pleasing shade of oxblood red and staffed by an exceptional librarian can only help.

Humanities take place in the Fitzjames building, a fantastic, flexible and innovative addition to the teaching space whose light, bright classrooms open on to first floor gallery and full height atrium where a huge globe hangs from the ceiling; broad steps double as informal seating. Beautifully white, light well-used food technology space too. Two fancy new science labs.

Teaching is usually mixed ability, with some setting in French and maths. Mandarin timetabled from year 5 and Latin from year 6. For the final two years, however, children are sorted into scholarship and CE classes. Teaching is generally thought to be rigorous and thorough – perhaps short on fun at times. We were jolly nearly caught out by a rogue question from a Latin vocab test during our tour (readers, our rusty recall did not fail us) but reassuringly reminded of the consequences of moving the decimal point left or right, beautifully explained to one child needing one-to-one support (from the head's wife, no less).

The use of educational IT is not excessive but from year 6 onwards, pupils are required to have their own iPad, supplied but not paid for by the school. According to the children, best subjects are maths, geography and English. Saturday morning school from year 4.

Learning support, housed in the beautiful Fitzjames building, has a staff of four who offer emotional as well as academic bolstering. About 20 per cent of children in the prep school have dedicated (payable) lessons to address their specific needs; one-to-one support is offered in class only in the pre-prep. 'My husband thinks it's all a bit fluffy,' one mother confided, 'but it's given my dyslexic kids confidence.' Help for all moderate learning difficulties is available, including a busy happy EAL department, catering for the Chinese, Spanish and children of any other nationality who come for a term, a year or for the whole of their prep school career.

We were struck by the attention paid to the emotional wellbeing of all the children, commented on by parents and indeed pupils: 'There isn't a teacher you couldn't go to for help,' one boy told us. Any of the younger children, including those on the autism spectrum, might be invited to join a 'treasure group' to help them navigate social situations with support from staff trained in emotional literacy support (ELSA). Girls on Board is an initiative the school has recently signed up to to help their girls through the choppy waters of female friendships.

Humanities take place in the Fitzjames building, whose bright classrooms open on to first floor gallery and full height atrium where a huge globe hangs from the ceiling

Beyond the classroom, there is simply masses going on. Deservedly known for its sport and lucky enough to have acres of space (not just an array of pitches and courts, but also areas to run about and get lost in), Hazlegrove is a sporting force to be reckoned with on the local circuit. One mother told us she thought the school worked hard for its reputation, and that 'the sporting cream is very quickly skimmed off the top. There is real currency being a member of the A teams.' Games include the usual offer of rugby, hockey and cricket for boys and hockey, netball and cricket – hurrah – for girls. Tremendous facilities for a prep school include a 25m pool, three all-weather pitches (one floodlit), plus long jump, squash courts and a six-hole golf course. PE sessions take up chunks of the timetable and team players are expected to turn out on Saturday afternoons.

Music has always been good but it seems particularly vibrant under a newish head of music. Groups include a girls' and boys' vocal group, percussion group, swing band and new rock band for older pupils. Children are encouraged to learn an instrument, to sit their grades and aspiring music scholars grade five theory. 'I have loved learning the marimba and the bagpipes,' one leaver reminisced. But not enough enforcement of individual music practice, in the view of one mother. Annual carol service takes place in Wells Cathedral.

Drama very strong too and benefits hugely from close collaboration with the music department – at the time of our visit, casting for the year 8 play, shoehorned into the few brief weeks after CE, was eagerly anticipated. All year groups put on their own production each year and those pupils who do not want to appear on stage (or at their own request to read or perform in assembly) are encouraged to get stuck in to set design and backstage help in the school's own theatre, not enormous but with raked seating and a lighting rig. Speech and drama are provided as an optional chargeable extra, leading to LAMDA exams and a special showcase evening. The fact that the drama department is headed by a West End trained dance teacher only burnishes the offering. 'The plays are some of my best memories,' another misty-eyed leaver told us.

One sight you will not see is children clustered round screens: apart from the classroom and limited evening use of approved devices, Hazlegrove is a mobile-free zone

Other hands-on extracurricular stuff includes go-karting around the track in the grounds, building 'impact buggies' in the well-equipped DT workshop to attempt the notorious ramp of doom and trips to local stables and Pony Club centre to ride; anyone with their own pony wanting to compete can represent the school by arrangement. Trips and jaunts abound: little ones might go to Bristol Zoo, older ones to nearby Montacute House, year 7 have a week at a River Dart activity centre (a particular highlight) and leavers to Cornwall. A valiant effort to recreate Wales in the grounds for year 5 before Covid restrictions were lifted looked pretty authentic, with a sea of tents, field kitchen, piles of bulging rucksacks and most importantly, grinning muddy children. 'They are forever outside!' exclaimed one delighted mother. The prevailing vibe is very much of getting children to try things out such as pistol shooting (or recently laser shooting where Hazlegrove has done very well) or 'everyone doing everything,' as one parent put it. 'I have three very different children and the school has played to all their strengths,' another told us; yet another that the school had 'found something in my daughter – that was DT and she now has a scholarship to her next school'.

The school has 'quite a punchy environment and likes kids who crack on and get involved, but it could be trickier for less confident children who have less belief in their own abilities,' in the opinion of one mother. The pupils we met were very positive and grateful for all they have – not angels either: they reckon punishments are fair and not dished out until both sides of the story have been heard. In their view, there is not much bullying and it is fairly dealt with. All kinds of achievements are recognised, sometimes publicly in assembly. Rainbow awards are handed out for kindness, effort and hard work. 'Arrogant children are not liked,' one mother told us.

One sight you will not see at Hazlegrove is children clustered round screens: apart from the classroom and limited evening use of approved devices, this is a mobile-free zone. Some parents love this part of keeping children young and outside for as long as possible, others wonder if the school should be helping its young people chart a sensible course through the Scylla and Charybdis of TikTok and Instagram, rather than stop their ears to the siren song of social media.

Boarding: From year 4 and divided into 3 houses: all girls, junior and senior boys in separate buildings on the site. About 100 board altogether, with about 30 flexi-boarders. Each house is generously staffed, run by a married couple, kids, pets etc, plus three residential staff and gap students to help out and inject fun.

The exceptionally thoughtful and committed head of boarding showed us round the light, bright dorms and living spaces. Several younger pupils to a dorm, fewer as they get towards the top of the school which makes at least one mother wonder if year 8 girls get quite enough privacy. You could probably swing a modest sized cat between sets of bunkbeds. It was all fresh air and a strong whiff of bleach when we visited, and immaculately clean; comfortable rather than luxurious.

The head's highest priority for the boarding is that it should be fun – fun enough to keep full boarders in at weekends (there are two compulsory weekend exeats per term and two closed weekends, the first and last of each term). It certainly sounded fun to us, with boarders raving about Total Wipeout, an inflatable war zone on the school playing fields, and the termly boarders' feast. You can't bring your own device but you are welcome to bring rollerblades or a ripstick.

Boarding numbers are concentrated in the upper years, so perhaps not such a fulfilling experience for younger children. One mother told us Hazlegrove feels more like a day school with boarders tacked on, partly due to the comparatively early finish of 4pm for day pupils. Very much a family feel though – we liked the sound of 'family service', where siblings sit together at supper and children serve each other; food gets a thumbs up and there is always cereal and toast available in boarding house kitchens for any evening munchies. Grace before breakfast and supper, prayers before bedtime, a weekly informal Sunday service taken by a member of staff (if not the chaplain), a weekly hand-written letter home and shoe-cleaning – 'a Hazlegrove tradition,' said the head of boarding with a wink – hark back to a largely bygone age of boarding.

Money matters: Limited range of scholarships and bursary help. Discount of 25 per cent for the third child educated in the King's Foundation (older siblings could be at King's Bruton) and help with CEA, the complicated fees allowance system for Forces children.

The last word: Notable west country prep school keeping children young as long as possible before sending them on to a range of mostly west of England schools after a great deal of traditional outdoors fun, tempered by hard work.

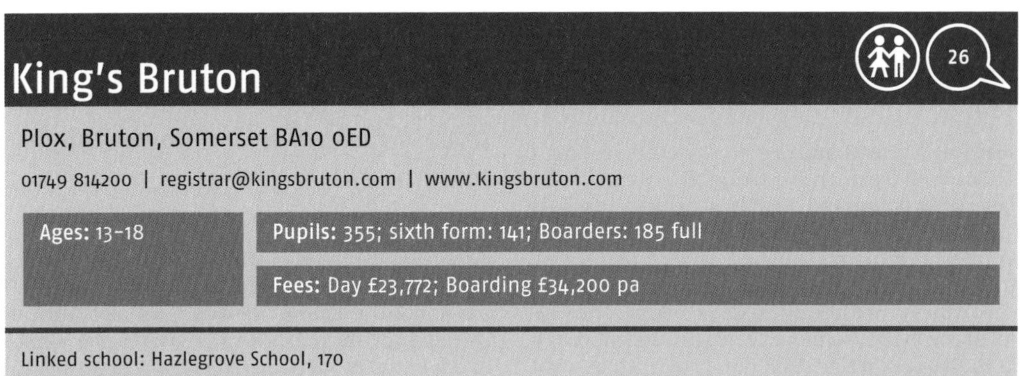

King's Bruton

26

Plox, Bruton, Somerset BA10 0ED

01749 814200 | registrar@kingsbruton.com | www.kingsbruton.com

Ages: 13–18

Pupils: 355; sixth form: 141; Boarders: 185 full

Fees: Day £23,772; Boarding £34,200 pa

Linked school: Hazlegrove School, 170

Headmaster: Since 2009, Ian Wilmshurst MA PGCE (50s). A Scotsman by birth. After reading geography at Cambridge and the briefest of flirtations with the army, he spent two terms sampling teaching at the Dragon School before returning to his old college for his PGCE. The roll-call of schools where he has taught since then include Highgate, Merchiston Castle and Royal Hospital where, as the sole deputy head, he had terrific exposure to the top job.

Attracted to King's by its location and the prospect of being able to make a discernible mark on an important school, he moved to Somerset with his wife and two daughters, both of whom went through King's. His eldest daughter is now studying international relations at York and the younger one planning to head to Durham to study psychology. Parents say he is 'approachable, down-to-earth and caring'; easy to see in action if you walk the school with him, a font of anecdotes about every pupil, demonstrating an innate understanding of what makes each tick. Communication between pupils and head was a genuine mixture of jovial familiarity and courteous mutual respect. 'He is a really lovely head, super enthusiastic and easy to talk to about anything and everything,' enthused one pupil. Determined to see the school further expand and 'punch above its weight' in every avenue, he leads with focused enthusiasm and drive.

Hobbies revolve around sport – a sometime rugby player and cricketer, he also enjoys cycling and golf, having been known to treat pupils to a game at his local club. Downtime is fuelled by an interest in military history and escaping with the family to their house in Charmouth.

Entrance: For 13+, places offered in year 7 based on standardised test scores, school reports and interview with head. Sets in year 9 allocated from this and from CE results. Scholarships are awarded based on papers in six subjects, plus a cognitive ability test. About 30 per cent come from Hazlegrove, the linked prep school; others from anything up to 15 other prep schools.

At sixth form, the bar is five GCSEs with a 7 at subjects to be taken at A level, plus interview and references. They have a good supply (17–20) of new starters at this stage, attracted from local and London day schools as well as international students. German pupils frequently join in year 11 and 12 for either two terms or a year; pupils from China and Hong Kong often join for the two-year A level programme.

Places in other year groups occasionally come up. 'The head, teachers and pupils have all been incredibly warm and inclusive, making the school move so easy that I wish we'd come to King's years ago,' said one parent.

Exit: About 10 students leave post GCSEs, some to seek the comparative economic or pastoral freedom and wider BTEC options at local sixth form colleges (school has addressed the latter by expanding its own BTEC offering). Post A level, to a wide range of universities and courses, with around half to Russell Group. Cardiff is a perennial favourite, along with Swansea and York. A handful head overseas. Sometimes a sprinkling to Oxbridge, but none in 2021. One medic in 2021.

Latest results: In 2021, 43 per cent 9-7 at GCSE; 44 per cent A*/A at A level (72 per cent A*-B). In 2019 (the last year when exams took place), 40 per cent 9-7 at GCSE; 34 per cent A*/A at A level (60 per cent A*-B).

Teaching and learning: Not overly selective, King's prides itself on accommodating all academic abilities via 'dynamic and nimble' teaching. Teachers are, in the main, young and vibrant including several Old Brutonians, newly qualified and raring to teach. Head has no qualms about shaking up departments not hitting laudable heights, recruitment revolving around 'exuberance and ambition as much as experience'. A pupil told us that what unites all the teachers 'is approachability and endless enthusiasm about their subject'.

There's an emphasis on the individual student here – no room for drifting. 'One of my priorities is to keep the balance between SEN and Oxbridge,' says head. Everyone is expected to achieve their personal best: 'We reckon our top 30 per cent is comparable academically to more selective schools.' Setting from the off in maths and, interestingly, French.

Two things set King's teaching apart in the mind of one parent: 'Firstly, the level of one-on-one or small group support is incredible – the staff run drop-in clinics in every subject to help all pupils feel secure. In addition, the plethora of tests mean that exam phobia is not a thing here – they are very used to being examined, it doesn't faze them at all.' Pupils concur: 'The subject clinics are brilliant, it's really helpful to get extra help every week if I need it, without that being a big deal,' said one.

At I/GCSE, 24 subjects on offer with a core of compulsory maths, English, sciences and a modern language plus a solid range of options in humanities, the arts, technology and sport. Year 11 pupils are given early assistance to start thinking about A level choices, which includes a taster programme for 'new' subjects such as psychology, where they sit in on lessons to get a feel for the topic. No allocated blocks and almost all get their first preferences.

At A level, maths, geography, business studies and history are consistently good performers and the introduction of psychology has proved hugely popular and successful. Timetable allows for the odd maths and English GCSE retake – it's almost unheard of for pupils to be thrown out for poor grades, not unknown in other schools. Pupils take four subjects in year 12 making their final selection of three on entry to year 13. Class sizes range from two or three (eg music tech) to 17 in the most popular.

'The plethora of tests mean that exam phobia is not a thing here,' said one parent. 'They are very used to being examined, it doesn't faze them at all'

BTECs are offered in performing arts, enterprise and entrepreneurship, sport and hospitality (school has a commercial kitchen). The latter had the honour of helping to cater and serve for the Queen and 100 guests on her visit to the school to celebrate its 500th anniversary, an enviable CV inclusion.

Pupils feel the mix of subjects on offer is broad and comprehensive. A few said they'd like politics and law to be available – 'although I am sure if we officially asked for them, the head would find a way,' said one. (Spoiler alert: politics is being introduced from September 2022.)

Careers support is spot on, say parents, with three dedicated members of staff focusing on everything from apprenticeships (notably hospitality management at the nearby, highly acclaimed The Newt) to Oxbridge or medical pathways and everything in between.

Learning support and SEN: Assessment for all on arrival. The staff of two, plus other prominent teaching staff with SEN qualifications, address a range of SEN, mainly dyslexia and dyspraxia but also processing difficulties. Speech therapist and ed psych visit routinely. Two dedicated EAL staff support around 40 students. School confident that they can support all except those who need a full-time personal classroom assistant.

The arts and extracurricular: The Queen herself opened the Queen Elizabeth Music School on site in 2019. Music is of a scope and standard befitting a much bigger school. From the military band and numerous choirs to fully functioning recording studios and soundproofed percussion rooms, there truly is something for everyone. We witnessed bespoke DJ coaching for an A level pupil who had landed herself a gig in Amsterdam.

Music tech offered at A level – a handful of students have gone on to study the highly specialised Tonmeister degree course at Surrey. Forty concerts a year in the impressive concert hall give beginners upwards a chance to conquer performance nerves.

Drama well provided for in Fitzjames theatre, where everyone – not just those studying GCSE or BTEC performing arts – is encouraged to get involved, whether treading the boards or backstage in lighting, sound or set design. Two house plays per year on rotation, alongside whole school, sixth form and junior productions, in close collaboration with the music dept. Recent shows include Little Shop of Horrors with rehearsals just beginning for The Crucible. 'It is going to be intense, dark and amazing,' expounded one student. The theatre manager writes some of the material. Annual trip to London takes in workshops as well as several shows.

'Not everyone is going to be a painter,' says the head of art, whose department offers an impressive range of media (3D design, sculpture and digital media, for example) to students who might go on to take a GCSE in art, craft and design. History of art available at A level, with outstanding results and a trip to Florence. Of course, it does no harm to have the internationally renowned Hauser and Wirth gallery just down the road, with its education director keen to be involved and the gallery already responsible for funding a new exhibition space in the school.

Strong Christian ethos includes celebrations of major festivals. Parents praised a 'young, dynamic chaplain who enthuses on the values of kindness and compassion'

Monday afternoon enrichment programme for sixth formers focuses on employability, CV and interview skills and key life skills for the next step of independence. This is backed up with an inspired list of Old Brutonian talks on everything from how to survive the first year at university to apprenticeship opportunities.

Trips (historians to Poland, linguists and musicians all over Europe, geographers to Iceland, hockey to South Africa) and all manner of physical and artistic exploration abound, with strong showings at CCF, DofE and that perennial west country ordeal, Ten Tors. 'The options for extracurricular adventures are fantastic,' enthused a parent. 'I feel as though the school goes out of its way to introduce us to everything possible, to try to light a spark in something we may never have heard of,' said a pupil. From astro-photography to trampolining, there didn't seem much that wasn't on offer.

Sport: Taken seriously. Extensive facilities include ubiquitous sports hall, grass pitches, two Astroturfs (one floodlit), eight tennis/netball courts. The fitness suite boasts a full-time head of strength and conditioning offering a bespoke 'athlete development programme'. Hockey scales heights that would be remarkable for a much bigger school. The U16 girls have qualified for seven national finals in the last 10 years. Numerous pupils (girls and boys) represent their county or region and five have gone on to play for junior international teams since 2019, with one of these currently in the USA on a hockey scholarship, having been awarded her first full GB senior cap aged 19. Importantly, everyone gets the chance to represent the school, with pupils coached from the start by the hockey pro and director of sport to identify burgeoning talent. But it's not just those competing at top level who are cheered on enthusiastically by their peers. When the head innocently asked if a hockey team had won their match he was chided, 'We don't always have to win, sir, sometimes it is just as beneficial to have fun, keep fit and make friends!' Rugby, netball, tennis, cricket and athletics prominent and successful. King's teams regularly compete at county and regional netball finals and individual pupils are involved in the Somerset County Academy. Rugby stars have access to the Bath Rugby Academy programmes through the school. King's athletes complete well and various pupils are involved in county cricket set ups, while the school's winter nets programme is extensive and popular in preparation for matches over the summer. No onsite pool, but school makes use of the 25m pool at Hazlegrove. Broader sport enthusiasts accommodated with a range of options including volleyball, cycling and yoga with King's horse riders supported in their individual British eventing commitments.

Boarding: Over half (13 per cent from overseas) board in six single-sex houses where day students are fully integrated; there is no separate day house. The houses are scattered throughout the grounds or within five minutes' walk through the beautiful town. Dorms of up to four to start with; most have single rooms at sixth form.

Day pupils are allocated a room share so they can flexi board (at additional cost) as and when required, as well as having full access to the facilities of the boarding house. 'The inclusion through this approach has been amazing,' reported a parent.

Houseparents are praised for getting to know pupils very quickly and facilitating caring environments with strong intermixing between year groups. 'Boarding at King's is absolutely brilliant,' vouched a boarder, whilst day pupils agreed. 'We do feel as though we miss some of the fun not staying the night here – supper and hanging out together afterwards is a really sociable time and we all try to stay for that as often as we are able,' said one.

Ethos and heritage: Ancient (sits on the site of a Benedictine monastery dissolved in 1537 – one wall survives). Three generous Bruton-born benefactors decided to found the first school here. Varying (mis)fortunes meant it was down to just one boy in 1812, but the first half of the 20th century saw it increase to numbers approximating the ones it has today, and it has taken over buildings the other side of the busy road to Castle Cary and elsewhere in Bruton. The school works with its venerable buildings, not against them, using the parish church for whole-school services, but its own movingly beautiful memorial hall for assemblies.

The sixth form centre houses a mix of social and study space, half of which is a supervised silent working area. 'They will talk if left totally unsupervised,' smiled the head, whilst the other is a university styled, collaborative work space. Comfortable sofas abound, chess games sit tantalisingly primed and tea and coffee facilities are on tap. Parents and students love the school's size and the fact that 'it has soul, has its feet on the ground and is not a grand or overly entitled setting'.

Strong Christian ethos includes celebrations of major festivals and rites such as confirmation. Parents praised a 'young, dynamic chaplain who enthuses on the values of kindness and compassion'. His online (inspired by the pandemic) 'chats about spirituality and general moral guidance for the soul' have, according to parents, led to a surprisingly enthralled response from hitherto nonchalant teenage pupils. A handful of Catholics and Muslims fit in comfortably and lend diversity.

Famous alumni include some heroes (Hugh Sexey, auditor to Elizabeth I, RS Blackmore, author of Lorna Doone), a villain (William Dampier, 17th century buccaneer), an Air Chief Marshal and decorated Falklands War fighter pilot (Sir Peter Squire) and an historian (James Holland).

Pastoral care, inclusivity and discipline: The tutor system ensures a close understanding and overview of each child, which parents can easily feed into with any emotional or academic concerns. Supported by a diligent and 'hugely approachable' matron and houseparent network, with parents feeling that many problems are nipped in the bud before having the chance to develop.

Though King's students might seem a biddable lot, 'The headmaster can do Scottish strict when required,' reckoned a parent. Indeed, transgressions are treated seriously and publicly – drinkers can expect to wear uniform at the weekend, for example.

Anxiety levels and eating disorders sadly on the rise since Covid, mirroring the national trend, but staff are accustomed to and accomplished at dealing with both. 'Our counselling staff are incredible,' said one pupil 'There are so many people here that you can turn to, you honestly feel that you have someone constantly ensuring you're okay.' Others agreed, speaking freely and refreshingly openly about the school's Whisper website that allows you to voice concerns for your own or others' mental or physical wellbeing, thereby alerting the head of welfare to any problems anonymously and safely. Everyone's Invited has led to school covering gender politics more openly than ever.

Pupils and parents: Pupils we met were an engaging bunch – enthusiastic, modest and considerate. 'There is no one mould fits all – they are unique individuals who are compassionate, kind and full of friendship,' said a parent. Boarders from southern England, Europe, SE Asia and Kenya. Saturday school compulsory for all with half a day of lessons and half of sport. Parents include those with strong family connections to the school and newcomers drawn to Bruton's skyrocketing appeal as a west country cultural and culinary hotspot. One parent summed up, 'Bruton's burgeoning "coolness" has brought with it a wonderfully eclectic mix of new school parents from the trendy worlds of media, art and film, mixing remarkably seamlessly with the existing farmers, military families and local business owners. It's definitely not a silver spoon, snobby school.'

Money matters: Impressively strong financial performance at the end of a tricky global pandemic period speaks volumes about the successful management of this school. Scholarships available to a maximum value of 20 per cent of fees. Bursarial help available on application.

The last word: A small historical bastion of a school that is absolutely booming in the 21st century. The icing on the cake for parents heading for the artistically inspired and gastronomically fuelled escapism of Bruton's rolling countryside. As one parent put it, 'King's is not grand so does not attract those seeking this. We are wonderfully under the radar and all the better for it.'

King's College (Taunton)

South Road, Taunton, Somerset TA1 3LA

01823 328204 | admissions@kings-taunton.co.uk | www.kings-taunton.co.uk

Ages: 13-18

Pupils: 470; sixth form: 200; Boarders: 319 full

Fees: Day £23,880; Boarding £35,370 pa

Linked school: King's Hall School, 181

Headmaster: Since 2007, Richard Biggs BSC MA (50s), previously deputy head at Lancing. A South African, he studied for his first degree (physics) at University of Cape Town before coming to the UK to study for a master's (maths and philosophy) at Oxford as a Rhodes scholar. Intending to head home afterwards, a job offer changed his course leading to 13 years teaching at Magdalen College School as teacher of maths and physics then director of studies, before being promoted to deputy head at Lancing, where he stayed for six years.

His 14 years at the helm of King's College have been a resounding success story with academic results, sporting reputation, co-curricular offering and admissions booming. Recently they have reached capacity in most year groups and have opened a waiting list for the first time in the school's history. There are no big plans afoot to change their winning strategy – 'We do extremely well with all aspects of our offering being in balance and have no wish to specialise or become pigeonholed away from this stance.'

Parents unequivocally support his approach, with one describing him as 'a quiet, very effective leader'. A calm, twinkly eyed academic, he earns respect with his approachable, empathetic manner and ensures a good relationship with the pupils in every year group. He fenced to county level and was president of the fencing society at Oxford and, while he sadly admits those days are over, he coaches hockey at the school, cycles, walks and is an avid reader – 'I always have several books on the go at the same time and constantly ask for recommendations from every member of my academic staff' (leading him to expound on everything from the travel writer Eric Newby to theoretical biology texts).

Married with two sons, both of whom went through King's. The eldest graduated from Durham last year and is now at the Royal Military Academy Sandhurst while the younger one is taking a gap year before heading to either Durham or St Andrews to study classics.

Entrance: Aims to take 90 into year 9 via a meeting with the head and sitting the school's own tests in maths, English and verbal reasoning. Places are usually offered before the CE results come out so these are used for setting rather than as entry criteria.

Most come from their associated prep, King's Hall, with others joining from prep schools across the south west (most notably Hazlegrove), Bristol or London day schools and overseas. They look for 'passionate all-rounders, rather than being restrictively academically selective' and are not afraid to say if they feel it is not the right choice for a child. Of the current cohort, 17 per cent are from military families and they have a cap of 25 per cent on international students.

Another '10 or so' in for year 10 GCSEs and an additional 15 into year 11, usually international students, 'predominantly Germans', to take advantage of the school's reputation in delivering a one-year intensive GCSE core subject course. Around 25 to 30 new starters in the sixth form, at which point they offer a 16+ scholarship programme and attract very good people from local state and independent schools. The school looks for 'quality not quantity' in GCSE results, ideally predictions of 8s and 9s with a couple of 7s and entrance is determined pre-GCSE via papers in two exam subjects of the applicant's choice.

Exit: They lose a quarter after GCSEs. Most of those are the international students on the one-year placement, the others (usually around 10) head across the road to the highly regarded state sixth form college, Richard Huish.

Just under half head to Russell Group universities. Exeter, Durham, Leeds, Bath, Bristol, Birmingham, UCL and Liverpool all popular, and a steady stream to other destinations, most notably Oxford Brookes. One to Oxbridge in 2021, and three medics. Some follow their hearts and skills into further education in music, drama or professional sport (they are justifiably proud of the

England cricketers Jos Buttler and Tom Banton, who started his professional contract from here).

Latest results: In 2021, 63 per cent 9-7 at GCSE; 96 per cent 9-4 in maths and English. At A level, 57 per cent A*/A (84 per cent A*-B). In 2019 (the last year when exams took place), 50 per cent 9-7 at GCSE; 45 per cent A*/A at A level (77 per cent A*-B).

Teaching and learning: This is a school that gradually – and with 'a deliberate strategy' – has lifted its academic game. While still standing by its inclusivity banner and celebrating the not (overly) selective image that it fosters, it is quietly achieving great results. The erudite deputy head lauded the teaching team for galvanising this turnaround, encouraging a culture among pupils to work hard in a happy, collaborative environment without the need for divisive competition. Teachers work by the same approach, mentoring each other with a focus on sharing ideas (there is a weekly staff breaktime forum to do just this) and developing pedagogy to ensure that pupils want to learn. Parents welcomed the fact that 'it is cool to be clever here'. The 'long boarding day' gives teachers ample time to enhance this ethos.

Extremely proud of being what the head described as 'the best cricket school in the world' – top notch training facilities and close links to Somerset County Cricket Club

Refreshingly, teaching is decisively not constrained by the criteria required to pass the exams but rather designed to 'inspire thought, provoke questions and foster deep enjoyment of each subject'. The effect of this has not been missed by parents – 'The children are really enthused and inspired by their teachers who all seem to have an incredible passion for their subjects and are able to creatively connect each child to their topic,' said one. Exemplary provision throughout the global pandemic, they told us; if anything, they strengthened the academic offering – 'My son felt as though he had a personalised experience in every subject,' said one parent.

Year groups are streamed from the start into five groups based on English and science performance. There is some additional setting for maths. Only the top three sets sit single GCSE science exams, with the others following the combined science curriculum. Taking one language is highly recommended for most students, with a broad range on offer and multiple options available for good linguists.

Pupils are encouraged across all subjects to 'give it their best shot and know that they can make mistakes in a positive environment'. They are also actively involved in their teachers' appraisals, completing anonymous questionnaires on each teacher's performance, a modern approach that is praised by parents as 'encouraging excellence'.

At A level they aim for 70 per cent A*-B and have hit this for the last two years, primarily through better steering and advice for pupils on subject selection – 'Obviously we want them to follow their dreams but they need their results to open doors for them as well.' The head has set a high bar here – 'We would like to be the top A level school in Somerset.' They offer 24 subjects at A level – biology and maths are the most popular together with a sprinkling of the other sciences; good results in arts, humanities and psychology. The offer of an extended BTEC diploma in sport has been revolutionary for those wanting a different path, taken at differing levels from the highest (worth three A levels) to a two A level equivalent – it is drawing in around four new students to the sixth form a year as its reputation grows. Students completing this route have gone on to study sports management and social sciences at Newcastle and Exeter.

Learning support and SEN: An SEN team that parents describe as 'phenomenal', accessed through a 'learning strategies' programme and adept at identifying and assisting those with additional needs. Around 20 per cent have entitlement to additional exam access arrangements and, of these, 10–15 per cent have additional lessons with personalised support. School is small enough to tailor support to the needs of the child and can handle most minor educational needs from dyslexia to mild autism and ADHD. They draw the line where 'with the best will in the world' they cannot facilitate the required help – they are unable, for example, to supply constant one-on-one care or a permanent teaching assistant.

The arts and extracurricular: With a head who believes that 'the creative is equally as important as the analytical,' it comes as no surprise that the arts are strong. All students are immersed in music, music tech, performing arts, drama and DT, in line with the 'have a go' encouragement fostered in all – and there are some discernible results.

The new art building provides four floors of light, bright studio space, leaving parents singing the praises of its 'design brilliance' – the investment has left the subject thriving with pupils gaining access to prestigious art colleges post A level. Fine art, film, photography, DT and textiles all on offer. The DT department is self-professed as 'one of the best in the country' and has won Arkwright scholarships and GSG awards on several occasions.

The roots of the school go back to an ancient boys' grammar, founded in the ninth century, allegedly by Alfred the Great, and relocated to its current site in the 1860s

Peripatetic lessons available in 17 musical instruments, including singing. About half the school learn one, with brass especially popular and a notable jazz band. Some grade 8 and diploma-level players among senior students. Singers abound, their repertoire from the popular to the highbrow, from rock bands to the chapel and chamber choirs, via the barbershop quartet.

Performing arts are big news here with dance classes in urban, tap, ballet and musical theatre, LAMDA training and lots of on-stage happenings: from termly showcases of dance, music and drama to impressive annual whole-school productions where everyone including the band and the backstage crew are pupils. Recent spectacles include A Christmas Carol, Grease and Twelfth Night with students currently rehearsing for Chicago, all performed in the school's own theatre. Junior plays offer performances such as Fantastic Mr Fox or Lady in the Van in the school amphitheatre. Performing arts scholars take it one step further with unique showcase performances accompanying a black-tie sit-down meal and audience interaction – shy parents be warned.

The house system provides a myriad interhouse activities and competitions in everything from debating to general knowledge quizzes and the opportunities to get involved and do your best are endlessly encouraged.

'Super curriculum' sixth form options include a scholar programme that has seen them crowned as south west champions in debating 'three times in the last five years' and university-style academic societies in most core subjects. Academic and career next steps are facilitated by a school networking website, giving pupils access to coaching and work experience from alumni and parents plus an impressive timetable of external speakers that – during the Covid summer term – managed to host virtual sessions with speakers including the director general of the BBC and the president of AstraZeneca UK.

Outdoor activities abound, overseen by a full-time head of outdoor education – primarily through the ever-popular CCF but also via DofE, Ten Tors and countless domestic and international expeditions. This school is endlessly on the go, from climbing up mountains and canoeing down rivers to mountain biking and surfing trips.

Sport: While they have upped the ante academically, this remains a sporty school and – in line with the exuberance for everything on offer here – the sports menu is muscle tingling; there is literally something for everyone. Extremely proud of being what the head described as 'the best cricket school in the world' – top notch training facilities and close links to Somerset County Cricket Club. They also excel at girls' football (winning the nationals numerous times), hockey (top eight nationally), squash and swimming – the head describes the coach as 'messianic, an absolute force of nature!'

Year-round impressive facilities and beautiful pitches in the heart of the school, although parents moaned that 'the gym needs some updating'. They punch well above their weight for a small school and pupils are encouraged to be sporting all-rounders, not simply a master of one, to ensure full teams and great results.

Traditional offerings of rugby, football, hockey and netball covered with strong coaching and excellent results in a full programme of fixtures against other titans of the west country, Millfield always being the one to beat. Parents say what sets King's apart from others is the resounding encouragement, whether their team wins or loses – 'It blows me away every time we go to a match to see the heartfelt warmth with which the older ones support the younger teams.'

The latest addition to the sport menu is a fully updated equine offering, teaming up with Taunton Polo Club to give glossy stabling, a sand school and professional instructors as well as (in the not-too-distant future) polo coaching. Pupils can keep their own horses at the school or ride the school's own mounts, with an enviable option to do so every afternoon.

Boarding: While this is predominantly a boarding school (over 65 per cent fully board) King's prides itself on its inclusion of day pupils. There is no day house but every boarding house has a percentage of day pupils and each of these can stay – at no extra charge – for one night a week, with flexi boarding options impressively bendy. 'Whilst both of our sons are day pupils, they choose to stay at school for all their meals, to do prep, sports clubs etc. It is so inclusive that they almost seem boarders in everything but name,' said one local parent.

Boarders come from all over the UK and there is a good peppering of international students with children of 21 different nationalities. Aside from China and Hong Kong, they have a good pool of European students and strong links with Kenya, South Africa and the Emirates.

Boarding houses are tight knit across year groups – 'They are literally her other family,' felt one parent. Inter-house competition is healthy and fun with no one house coming out consistently as top dog. There are seven different boarding houses (three for girls and four for boys) where boarders sleep predominantly in rooms of four, although sixth formers have privilege of single rooms or sharing with one friend. Houseparents and an army of live-in assistants run the house, senior pupils hold vital mentoring roles in looking after younger members of the house.

Inter-house competition is healthy and fun with no one house coming out consistently as top dog. There are seven boarding houses (three for girls and four for boys)

Food is served in the central dining hall so pupils can all eat together. As with most schools, there were mumblings amongst parents and pupils about quantity and stories of lugging cases full of top-up snacks back to school with them; no surprise for growing teenagers doing this amount of sport and strongly rebuffed by the head. Sadly, the pandemic restrictions made it impossible to us to form our own opinions this time.

Ethos and heritage: A Woodard School, one of about 30 founded by a visionary Victorian cleric. Today 'religious literacy', in the words of the resident chaplain, is inculcated without a whiff of evangelism. Collective worship is a big part of school life; all faiths and none are made welcome. The roots of the school go back to an ancient boys' grammar, founded in the ninth century (allegedly by Alfred the Great) and relocated to its current site in the 1860s.

It's fair to say that it still feels and looks quite traditional, from the impressive gothic façade to the conventional uniform of designer tweed jackets and blue shirts. Parents describe the buildings as 'characterful', with 'a bit of an obvious update needed in some areas'. There are plans afoot for a brand new sixth form building which it is unanimously agreed will be 'a hugely welcome bonus'. 'It's not the glitziest or the most stunningly slick but there is something really special about this place,' sums up one parent.

Pastoral care, inclusivity and discipline: Inclusivity is a given here – friendship and integration are key selling points of the school and oft-repeated buzzwords among staff and parents. Both are done remarkably well, with the arms of friendship wrapping around the world in every year group.

There is a clear, strong pastoral network including tutors and house staff, overseen by deputy head pastoral and consistent across the school. Sixth formers choose their tutor from the academic staff to ensure strong relationships. Parents feel in touch with their child's emotional as well as academic progress and questions are answered swiftly. Punishments are rare, with the head claiming that they are 'a pretty biddable lot' with 'very seldom any major disciplinary issues'. Parents concur – 'Through a zero-tolerance approach, the historical laddish culture has disappeared and there is a lot more respect,' said one. Parents value the encouragement of distinction – 'There is no shaping or moulding into a King's College clone here, they celebrate and applaud individuality.'

Pupils and parents: This is a school where children thrive. In the words of one parent, 'Everyone seems to leave here with impressive life skills: they are grounded, hard-working, great to have around, confident at communicating with adults, full of beans, diligent and ambitious.'

Parents are an upbeat bunch including the Somerset county set with historic links to the school to those working every hour to send their children here. Pupils and parents alike seemed unpretentious, happy to be there and grateful for all the opportunities the school offers.

Alumni, known as Aluredians (spotlighting the tenuous link to Alfred the Great), include Laura Bates (writer), Jos Buttler MBA (England cricketer), Geoffrey Cox QC MP (Attorney General 2018-20), Maddie Hinch MBA (GB hockey player) and Ted Nash (mobile media entrepreneur).

Money matters: Scholarships for academic, sporting and artistic prowess – to a maximum value of 20 per cent of the day fee – are awarded at 13+ and sixth form. Academic scholars are expected to contribute to the intellectual life of the school, not just pulling in stonking exam results.

The last word: This school is flying, brimming with enthusiasm and passion for learning, smashing it on the sports field and bounding with extracurricular opportunities. Children here are not babysat but encouraged and celebrated in achievements across the board and respond with a genuine happiness to be at the school. 'This is a brilliant choice,' summed up one parent.

King's Hall School

Kingston Road, Taunton, Somerset TA2 8AA

01823 285920 | schoolOffice@kingshalltaunton.co.uk | www.kings-taunton.co.uk

Ages: 2-13

Pupils: 308; Boarders: 45 full, 15 flexi

Fees: Day £8,580 – £17,670 Boarding £19,770 – £25,695 pa

Linked school: King's College (Taunton), 177

Headmaster: Since 2009, Justin Chippendale BSc (late 40s). His education and subsequent career have caused him to shuttle between Oxford and Taunton, starting at the Dragon, thence to King's Taunton, back to Oxford Brookes for a degree in biology, exercise and health, a stint as housemaster at the Dragon, a detour to Chafyn Grove as deputy head, then back to Taunton. Affectionately and inevitably known as Mr Chips, he works hard to put the child's experience (of personal development, academic stimulus, physical challenge, artistic exploration and so on) as top priority at King's Hall, closely followed by the quality of relationships: between staff and pupils/parents/each other. 'I work on the invisibles and immeasurables,' says he. But that's not to endanger academic expectations: 'It has to be cool to work, and okay to talk about work here,' he adds, and makes it his business to ensure that his charges (and their parents) make well-informed suitable choices for their next schools, even when the majority go on to King's Taunton.

Mr Chips is a keen sportsman and retains the physique of a rugby player, still occasionally coaching. Married with three children at the school, he enjoys entertaining parents 'in order to understand each family's own context' (though a few grumble about not being on the head's dinner list), and he is generally well-liked by both pupils and parents. 'He knows everyone, takes a real interest in us, and we love the Chips Challenge,' opined pupils, who might be asked to research an arcane matter, solve a puzzle or achieve a physical feat.

Entrance: Many join the pre-prep (school also comprises a nursery from 2), but some come from local primary schools and London at 7+. From years 1-4, new children are informally assessed during a welcome day; from years 5-8 they are tested in maths, English and verbal reasoning for which special preparation is not required, says school. Quite an intake also welcomed into year 7 for the final two years before moving on at 13+.

Exit: The majority (85 per cent) to King's College at 13+. Others to Wellington School, Taunton School, Queen's College, Sherborne School, Canford, Eton, Millfield, Sherborne School for Girls, Loughborough and Concord College. Every child gets into the school of his/her first choice, apparently; 'We didn't get the hard sell for King's,' said one mother with a sigh of relief. Famous ex-pupils include actress Juno Temple, founder of Everyday Sexism project Laura Bates, and mad adventurers Ross and Hugo Turner.

Our view: Sited in the mellow golden former home of the Yea baronetcy Pyrland Hall, dating from 1760, and surrounded by 50 acres of parkland and woods, this is an idyllic setting just minutes from Taunton. But it's not precious – pupils here make the most of the space, freedom and mud to pursue a terrific range of activities and outdoor pursuits beyond the school day which finishes at 4.30pm, mountain biking and archery being just two. Some 15 acres of pitches, an Astroturf and a sports hall mean all major sports are well catered for and fulfil all expectations, but an indoor pool is undoubtedly on the parental wish list; as it is, swimming is an extracurricular activity until the school's outdoor pool is opened in the summer term. But it all amounts to a slice of gracious enough living for the young.

King's Hall is reckoned to be Taunton's smartest and most academic prep school, partly because it's the only place which prepares children for Common Entrance (and scholarships) at 13+, still the measure and starting point for the most prestigious public schools. From year 3, children are taught in classes of about 15 by specialist teachers. All begin French in year 1 but there's the opportunity to pick up Spanish from year 5 or Latin from year 6. Science and geography get thumbs-up from pupils, but 'We don't go to any lessons and think "Oh no!",' said one. Prep amounts to two half-hour subjects per night for the oldest: 'It's OK to make mistakes and they will be explained to you again,' said another. One mother observed that some children are held back until they have learnt some basics by rote, and wondered if there should be more 'aspiration and challenge before they have everything right'. Both prep and pre-prep have own library. Some 49 children are currently on the learning support register; school has policy of not withdrawing children from vital lessons to have their two half-hour individual sessions per week.

Pastoral care for the children highly rated; class teachers assume pastoral responsibilities in year 3, tutors with mixed horizontal tutor groups thereafter. The newly formed Friends of King's Hall provides purely social events for parents, and is working on extending its reach to everyone. We liked the enshrining of the school rules into six positive exhortations, such as 'do work hard, and do be honest'.

The arts are well catered for. Pupils' art was displayed everywhere we went and the design side has facilities for 2D and 3D design. Three major productions a year for years 4, 6 and 8 put on in the school's theatre or outside in the rose garden are complemented by prizes for acting and poetry recital at local festivals. About half the children learn a musical instrument, achieving grade 6 or 7 in rare cases, and the newish director of music has gone down well.

Boarding: About 50 children board (four per cent of boarders from overseas) in a variety of arrangements; school entices children with regular year group boarding nights and film nights for the whole prep school. One busy mum told us her youngest had boarded just for a night at the age of 5 – and loved it. The sole boarding house has separate areas for senior boys, junior boys and girls, each with its own common room and quiet areas. 'It's fun and as homely as possible – I board to relax!' one boy told us, and all reckoned that boarders of all persuasions are well integrated. Parents tell us that facilities have improved, but the school 'doesn't have that horrible bling-tastic feel that the other Taunton schools have'. Well, thank goodness! Day pupils are welcome to join in the weekend activities with boarders, which might include dry skiing or making the most of the beautiful Quantock Hills nearby for a 16-mile orienteering exercise; facilities at King's College are also on offer at weekends.

Day pupils join in weekend activities with boarders, which might include dry skiing or making the most of the beautiful Quantock Hills

Money matters: Generous arrangements are available for Forces families and scholarships, open to all, are awarded at 11+. They continue through the college, subject to annual review.

The last word: So what's it really like? A question probably best answered by the pupils: 'I look forward to going back.' 'The weeks pass really quickly.' And to sum up? 'I don't instantly feel like the walking dead when I arrive.' Job done, Mr Chips.

Kingsley School

29

Northdown Road, Bideford, Devon EX39 3LY

01237 426200 | admissions@kingsleyschoolbideford.co.uk | www.kingsleyschoolbideford.co.uk

Ages: 11–18

Pupils: 204; sixth form: 42; Boarders: 78 full, 2 weekly/flexi

Fees: Day £13,080 – £13,860; Boarding £21,735 – £32,280 pa

Head: Since September 2021, Alastair Ramsay (interim head).

To be replaced in July 2022 by Robert Pavis, currently deputy head (pastoral) at Gordon's School, Surrey. Attended Lawrence Sherriff Grammar in Rugby; degree from Durham. Taught English in Japan, returning to the UK in 1995 to teach English at Grittleton House School for a short stint before moving to Wycliffe College in Gloucestershire where he worked for 15 years, initially as assistant housemaster and head of Japanese and German, and then for 12 years as housemaster and head of MFL. In 2011 he moved to Steyning Grammar School in Sussex as assistant head and director of boarding before moving to Gordon's three years later. Married to Heather, currently head of a girls' day boarding house at Gordon's, with whom he has three children – George, a post-doctorate researcher at Exeter University; Harry, who lives and works in Spain as a website and social media consultant; and Edith, in her third year at Bath. He is a keen sportsman and environmentalist – and loves getting stuck in to outdoor activities and adventurous pursuits around his home in Cornwall.

Entrance: Vast majority come from the onsite prep school with newbies drawn by open days, taster sessions and word of mouth. 'It has a fantastic reputation locally as a happy, family friendly school,' agreed parents. Often chosen by those that have found it difficult to find their feet academically or socially elsewhere. 'We have a reputation for attracting and succeeding with the quirkier children and are immensely proud of that, it highlights the bespoke nature of our offering.' Recent events have seen a burgeoning of numbers due to parents seeking to redress poor pandemic provision elsewhere. Boarding pupils come from across the UK, Asia, Europe and the Middle East.

Entry by informal test and interview, screening is carried out for any discrepancies. Sixth form new starters need a decent set of GCSE results, school reports and the right attitude. No problems with settling in: 'From day one he absolutely loved it! We have never heard him say he doesn't want to attend.'

Exit: Between 20 and 30 per cent leave after GSCEs, many heading for apprenticeships at local colleges or to experience A levels in a bigger pond at larger independent schools. Post sixth form nearly all go to university with half heading to Russell Group. Degree choices range from biochemistry to commercial music.

Latest results: In 2021, 33 per cent 9-7 at GCSE; 59 per cent A*/A at A level (80 per cent A*-B). In 2019 (the last year when exams took place), 13 per cent 9-7 at GCSE; 51 per cent A*/A at A level (67 per cent A*-B). (GCSE figures include those from the Grenville Centre.)

Teaching and learning: A unique school, proud of its flexible, bespoke approach to the curriculum. 'There is absolutely not a one size fits all approach to our teaching,' the deputy head told us. 'Quirky' children can find a welcoming, accepting and supportive environment in which to flourish and the most capable student is also given wings to fly, eg via the 'top universities programme'.

Core subjects aside, pupils are consulted on what subjects they would like to learn at GCSE and teaching is then arranged accordingly – puts pupil at the forefront of their own learning. A language is compulsory up to year 9. BTEC in engineering is available at GCSE level, replacing traditional DT. Sixteen A levels on the menu, plus five BTECs including business, outdoor education and performing arts, a Cambridge Technical in sport or applied science and the EPQ. Maths is strong, with around 60 per cent take up at A level. Other top performers include biology, chemistry, English and geography.

The school is proud of its flexible, bespoke approach to the curriculum. 'Quirky' children can find a welcoming and supportive environment in which to flourish

'Exemplary' is how one parent summed up online pandemic provision – school says the process has taught them immeasurable lessons in recognising and harnessing the independent learning abilities of their pupils. 'We are actively looking at how we can continue to foster this independence and ensure that the passion and dedication of our teaching staff doesn't lead to an overreliance on them as pupils progress up the school.'

Children are not 'boxed in' to their year group, with opportunities for those needing more time or more challenge to learn with other year groups as appropriate. Admirable new Earth Centre initiative has seen the school instil 'a project-based sustainable edge to the full curriculum' – pupils have environmental issues and solutions 'imprinted on them when they leave'. Offers everything from seed planting sessions for the smallest members of the school through to EPQ opportunities in eg food production, animal husbandry and soil biology – all facilitated by a newly recruited, full-time member of staff.

Learning support and SEN: Inclusivity and acceptance are key. Kingsley attracts a lot of families who have one child with SEN and siblings without, but who want their children to be educated in the same school. One such parent told us, 'While not being a specific special needs school, they cater for those who have this requirement incredibly impressively alongside offering an

Monkton Prep School

outstanding education for their mainstream siblings. We have one child with dyslexia-related educational needs and one very sporty one who is also on an all-rounder scholarship – both love Kingsley and are absolutely thriving.'

The school has two strands of SEN offering, firstly the dedicated onsite Grenville Centre that specialises in ASD. Strict limit on numbers here (24 for senior pupils), with places offered to those with anxiety-based issues rather than severe behavioural problems, which they are not set up to accommodate. The children are taught predominantly in the centre, although can join in with the mainstream classes for creative/outdoor/sport options if able. Secondly, Kingsley is a CReSTeD school: accredited in its teaching of dyslexic pupils, who make up 25 per cent of the school.

Other SENs are catered for, mainly behavioural issues associated with dyslexia but, again, nothing too complex. For those requiring it, pupils are taught English and maths in small (five to10) dyslexia-only classes by qualified SEN teachers. One-to-one tuition and support in after-school prep sessions also available. One parent commented, 'In a very short time my son who had been labelled and dismissed as unregisterable and underperforming in his previous school is actively engaged, happy and positively flying at Kingsley.'

There are regular formal meetings where mainstream and Grenville staff exchange information on individual pupils and discuss how best to teach them. Teachers use visual aids for all lessons and reminders of current topic or homework tasks are clearly displayed on the wall. One teacher told us this is all done in a subtle, unobtrusive way 'without anyone blinking an eye'.

The value added is impressive – SEN pupils are given good support in class and in exams and do well. One recent leaver with A level grades A*, A and B had been told by his previous school he would never amount to anything. With hard work and the specialist support of the dyslexia centre he has more than proved them wrong. Some take fewer subjects, often dropping a language if it helps them to focus. One parent said, 'Kingsley School has positively changed our profoundly dyslexic son. He was very passive and feared failure, he felt that he was not an achiever and his contribution was of little value, but in the six years that he has attended Kingsley School, we have seen him grow into a very confident and happy young man.'

The arts and extracurricular: There is a senior school orchestra, but numbers are limited so quartets and ensembles are more common. Plus a highly regarded choir which recently won South West School Choir of the Year, affording them the prize performance in Exeter Cathedral and a UK tour. Peripatetic teaching in 12 different instruments, singing and speech and drama.

In line with the school's 'quirkiness' and its proximity to the north Devon coast, the main sports are judo, handball and surfing

Termly productions feed the love of drama – one such performance won the National Theatre Connections finals. The prize was performing it at the Plymouth's Theatre Royal to an audience that included the playwright himself who, in turn, was so bowled over by the strength of their production that he invited them up to perform it at the National Theatre in London. No mean feat for a small school from Devon. Other performances include an annual whole-school talent show 'open mic' event known as 'Kingsley Entertains', featuring everything from 4-year-olds showing off their ballet to a grade 8 LAMDA student recital. 'Kingsley Rocks' is the more edgy production in the summer term where students and teachers alike let their hair down.

The art department commands the whole of the top floor of the main building, School House. Two huge studios, plus photographic facilities. Some great, and very large, pieces on display, with plenty more space to fill. Annual exhibition at the local Burton Art Gallery.

After-school activities include choirs, Mandarin Chinese, judo, trampolining, debating, surfing, yoga, gardening and DofE. Trips locally to places like the Eden Project, Cheddar Gorge and Exmoor and further afield to London, Paris and Iceland.

Sport: In line with the school's 'quirkiness' and its proximity to the north Devon coast, the main sports are judo, handball and surfing. Judo is up to Olympic standard, surfers and windsurfers do well in local, regional and national competitions with one of the TA team being a qualified surf instructor. Pupils regularly win national titles in gymnastics, netball, judo and biathlon. Peripatetic coaching is available across most sports and trampolining. There are regular weekend fixtures for rugby, cricket, hockey, athletics, table tennis, swimming and cross-country. However, several parents warned, 'This may not be the ideal choice for a super sporty high flyer.' Anecdotally we were told that any children who leave during their time at the school tend to do so for smarter and larger sporting facilities and opportunities. Due to its size, the school cannot always raise a rugby XV, for example, which has been addressed by recruiting the local 'Mr Rugby' as head of PE and establishing close links to the local Bideford Rugby Club. For most pupils the inclusive, enthusiastic element compensates for the numbers issues and, as one parent put it, 'It's a bit like a scene from the film Nativity, we're the small apparent underdog with boundless excitement and enthusiasm but with the secret weapon of incredibly inspirational and talented teaching staff – we do surprisingly well.'

Boarding: Currently a 70/30 boy/girl split among boarders, 80 per cent from overseas (over three-quarters Asian). Majority board full time, but some short-term boarders from Europe, usually to brush up on their language skills for a term or two. Three large, well looked-after boarding houses on the school campus – Belvoir for girls, Carisbrooke for junior (years 7-9) boys and Longfield for senior boys. During the pandemic they used one house with separate wings for girls and boys – the effect of both genders living together in the boarding house communal areas has proved so positive that they are considering rolling this approach out.

'Boarders' voice' meetings allow suggestions for any improvements to boarding life to be expressed and largely acted on, 'apart from the endless request to change bedtimes'

Brilliant pastoral care with houseparents and assistants all living in and ensuring that the house runs 'like the home of a large extended second family'. Gap students and house prefects add big brother or sister role models to the mix. One parent said, 'He felt immediately at home and appreciates the warm-hearted atmosphere of the school and the boarding complex.' Another praised the communication home: 'We get detailed and regular updates on how they are doing.'

The boarding houses have homely kitchens where pupils congregate to do their prep, chat or cook incredible meals for friends, with everyone eating communally. The atmosphere is friendly and there's an emphasis on celebrating the different cultures represented, eg Chinese New Year.

One four-bedded room and a couple of three-beds, but majority of the sharing rooms are for two. Prefects and sixth formers get the option of singles but many choose to share with friends. 'Boarders' voice' meetings allow pupil suggestions for any improvements to boarding life to be expressed and largely acted on, 'apart from the endless request to change bedtimes'.

Devices for all up to year 10 are handed in at set times. Plenty of activities, but pupils are also given downtime, just like home. No Saturday lessons but there are sports fixtures or shopping trips in the afternoons, and activities like quad biking, combat zone, cinema, bowling, climbing, theatre, zoo, theme parks and local city trips on Sundays. As soon as the weather brightens up, surf's up and as much time as possible is spent making the most of north Devon's beach life. Awesome.

Ethos and heritage: Formed in 2009 by the amalgamation of Edgehill College and Grenville College. Formerly a part of the Methodist school group, purchased in 2019 by China First Capital Group's KSI Schools.

School House is the main building – inviting, large and very white. The sixth form centre is in a separate, spacious building, well equipped with a modern café, social area with pool table, table football, piano and large dining table. Several study rooms for small groups. The school is fondly described by parents as 'well-loved and a little bit tatty', with one expressing that 'it was tired in comparison to the flashy marketing videos but compensated with the wonderful sense of family, warmth and inclusivity'. This was countered by others celebrating that 'lots of positive renovations seem to be underway since the new (2019) ownership'.

Pastoral care, inclusivity and discipline: 'Altruism and inclusivity are the beating heart of this school,' summed up a parent – echoed by others, plus staff members too. All enthused over the happy and family style approach to pastoral care. The school prides itself on its warmth and success, particularly with those who might be socially or academically excluded elsewhere. 'My son knows he can fly here as he has the backing of every single member of the school to do so,' was one parent's view.

Discipline is structured and clear but not overly rigid. The mutual respect shown between staff and children means that disruption is not the norm and often all that is needed to reset is 'a quiet conversation to share problems that might be leading to difficult behaviour'.

Pupils and parents: Day pupils come from a wide local area and school buses go as far as Croyde, North Molton, Torrington and Holsworthy. Termly airport buses for overseas boarders. A real social mix of a school: 'Some parents own half of Devon whilst for others both parents work every hour possible to send their children here.' GPs, teachers, gardeners and builders, the children represent a whole raft of society and in the words of one parent, 'Thankfully it is not a posh, high-end ivory tower just a natural extension of our community and our family.'

The school communicates well with parents with the usual channels of emails, letters and reports. Queries or concerns are responded to quickly, 'usually within a matter of a couple of hours,' one parent told us. 'We also have phone calls from the form tutors to make sure that there are no concerns.' Another said, 'Any teacher is readily available either personally or via email.'

Money matters: Academic, performing arts and sports scholarships available at 11 and 13. Sixth form scholarships based on GCSE performance or excellence in music, drama, art and sport. Means-tested bursaries offered, plus bursaries to Forces families and sibling discounts. In the senior school, fees for the dyslexia department and EAL are additional.

The last word: What teenager wouldn't want to combine school life with beaches, surfing and friends from around the world? That may all sound too much like fun rather than education, but Kingsley has got the balance right – a great campus, a nurturing and inclusive atmosphere, a bespoke approach to the curriculum and academically inspiring teachers. The SEN children at Kingsley progress further than anyone's expectations and bright children celebrate strong successes academically so it's not surprising that one parent told us, 'We can honestly say it was and will remain the best decision we have made for his education.'

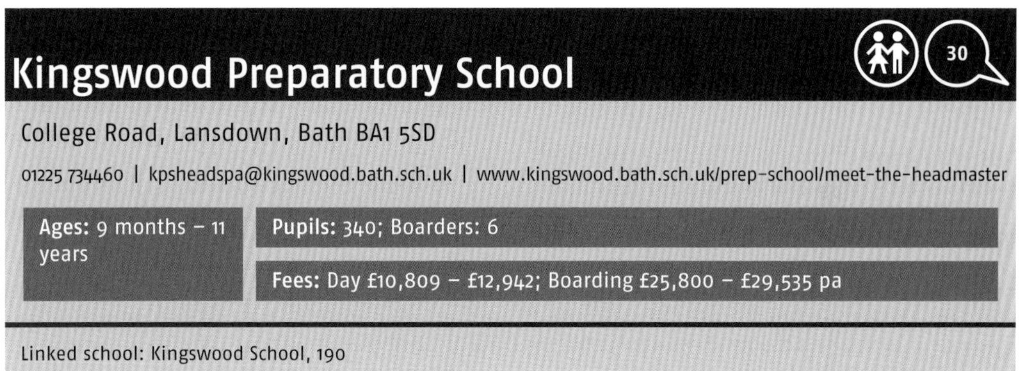

Kingswood Preparatory School

30

College Road, Lansdown, Bath BA1 5SD

01225 734460 | kpsheadspa@kingswood.bath.sch.uk | www.kingswood.bath.sch.uk/prep-school/meet-the-headmaster

Ages: 9 months – 11 years

Pupils: 340; Boarders: 6

Fees: Day £10,809 – £12,942; Boarding £25,800 – £29,535 pa

Linked school: Kingswood School, 190

Head of Prep: Since September 2011, Mark Brearey (50s). Having self-professedly 'limped through school', his mission is to ensure that no-one follows in his footsteps. He wants his school to offer 'both an inspiring scaffolding and structure for academic strugglers whilst ensuring that the brightest never get bored', achieved via an absolute balance across music, art, sport and academia.

Having studied history and sports at Leicester, he went on to run adventure holidays for young people in Devon which resulted in him being offered a teaching post at St Peter's Lympstone. Three years at an international school in Kenya followed, where the wildness, space and focus on outdoor education influenced the head he was to become. Returning to the UK, married with three children – all then under the age of five – he was housemaster at Millfield for three years before taking on an eight-year deputy headship at Forres Sandle Manor, heading from there to his current headship at Kingswood.

A restless soul, he exudes a relentless quest for perfection and loves nothing more than new challenges. Easy to talk to, as well as caring and funny, his office is a sanctuary for many of the children, benefiting from the calming presence of his golden retriever. 'The balance is spot on – a respectful but friendly relationship,' said one parent. Pupils describe him as 'a brilliant head, we love him', while parents say he is 'really jolly', especially praising his 'lovely manner with the children, demonstrating a positivity that they really respond to'.

Entrance: Nursery from nine months, places based on availability with automatic continuation from end of pre-school into the prep. Three-quarters of the reception cohort come from the pre-school. School entrance prioritised for those with sibling or family connections. Admissions start with a meeting with the head and tour of the school, followed by age-appropriate assessments. For reception to year 2, a morning spent in class, including an informal assessment of learning behaviour. For years 3-6, places awarded after a successful session of reading, spelling, maths and non-verbal assessments with the head of learning support, together with current school reports.

Muddy, outdoor education is key – every class has a welly rack at its doorway. A yurt provides a covered classroom for those days it is 'absolutely impossible to stay out in', with composting toilets handily to one side

Usually 10 new starters in year 3, when number of classes increases from two to three. Year 6 places restricted to entry at the start of the school year.

Exit: Most go on to the senior school via the standard entrance exam, unless the school feels that the child will not benefit from its academic rigours, in which case careful conversations begin early with full support given to finding an alternative. Applies at most to two families per year – 'It's never easy, but has to have the child's best interests at heart,' says the head, who tours potential alternatives with parents.

Our view: The clever few who discovered this 'secret' prep before the waiting lists set in have every right to feel smug. Tucked away on the edge of Bath, it offers a brilliant outdoorsy, country education just minutes from the historical city centre and makes full use of its setting on the hill below the linked senior school. The driveway boasts sweeping country views on one side and equally impressive new prep buildings on the other. Turn the corner and at the end of an immaculate lawn is a Georgian stone façade that would rival any in central Bath. 'Oh that's just the dining room,' a pupil shrugged. 'I think it's been here even longer than we have and we're in year 6!'

Not simply residing in past glories, this is a school that has used and improved on every part of its 100 acres of land and buildings, thanks in no small part to the drive of the current head. 'When I arrived here it was drab, dark and underutilised in so many areas.' Having experienced education in the wilds of Africa, where children had space and light in which to play, he swiftly got to work on a 10-year plan to redesign and redefine the school.

Today, every class has a welly rack at its doorway and muddy, giggle-inducing outdoor education is key. 'The wildness makes it,' enthused one parent. 'They come home from school filthy, running through the grounds with the hugest of smiles, it is a brilliantly happy school.' A deserted woodland to the side of the site has been transformed into a forest school to rival any we have seen. A yurt provides a covered classroom for those days it is 'absolutely impossible to stay out in', with composting toilets handily to one side. A hanging tepee blows in the wind over the top of a teaching area of log seats whilst rope swings, fire pits – and above all gently guided teaching – make this treasure trove an inspiration. One hour a week is spent here from nursery (once they can walk) to the end of year 2; pupils in years 3-6, who have a plethora of outdoor adventures through sports and trips, can also access sessions on site via eco club after school. The rest of the school echoes this focus. There are numerous outdoor play areas, adventure climbing frames and a spongy all-weather playground full of equipment from a football goal zone to a covered pergola seating area and a wooden train.

Inside, every classroom has had a makeover or sits in a new building – airy and compelling. The architectural team behind the site's overhaul won a RIBA national award for the design and the red-cedar and golden brick design blends beautifully with its natural setting and offers light-filled rooms with the calming scent of wood all pervading.

Beyond the core of English and maths – and French (taught from the off) – learning is topic based, exploring set themes from every angle. 'My absolute favourite topic was chocolate,' said our year 6 guide, 'because we went to Cadbury World in Birmingham, where we learned everything about chocolate and ate loads of it!' Turns out the project included everything from reading and performing Charlie and the Chocolate Factory, geographically and historically looking at where chocolate comes from, creating new chocolate recipes with the science team and designing new packaging and branding – 'a real life project combining every aspect of their education,' explained a teacher. Other projects include eg outer space. Specialist teaching in science, humanities, music, drama, art and DT, with all teachers praised by parents for their insight into each pupil and what makes them tick. Parents praise the 'brilliant diagnostics' offered by the head of learning support, who ensures that no child is left behind in terms of SEN – and adds on bespoke intervention as and when required. Experienced LAs then work with children in small groups.

The immaculate science block is an inspirational space for curious minds – packed with tantalising equipment, lab coats and bright display. One pupil told us how the new young head of science 'has turned around our approach to science'. We felt giddy just watching the year 4s working in teams to try and spin as many times as the earth rotates in one year while discussing how each rotation would move them around the sun. In the bespoke computer science lab year 6 pupils were busy filming interviews against a green screen, promoting apps they had created in a previous lesson.

The art room boasts ever-present natural light and a stunning array of work. 'Wonderfully inclusive,' is how one parent described the teaching, making this a highly sought-after space. 'I could stay in here all day,' mused our tour guides – thankfully there are plenty of art clubs by which they can get their fix. From fiery dragons to huge parrots and personalised knights in armour, art is on display throughout the school and the introduction of a kiln has meant that designing in clay has become a firm new favourite. The design studio is a hive of activity and equipment too – STEM is taught as a key skill here and the class was about to start work on its Green Cars, hoping to design, build then race these eco kit cars in the near future.

Learning is topic based, exploring set themes from every angle. 'My favourite topic was chocolate,' said our year 6 guide, 'because we went to Cadbury World in Birmingham, where we learned everything about chocolate and ate loads of it!'

Drama and music lessons from reception up. School has its own small wood-panelled drama studio although the year 5 and 6 productions take place in the senior school's theatre. Inclusivity is key, with every pupil taking part in an annual production, starting with the nursery nativity. 'The productions are phenomenal here,' said one parent. LAMDA and ESB exams prepared for and there are chances for budding young actors to compete in countless regional dramatic events and star in visiting performances. Music is also prioritised, with several choirs and orchestral ensembles offering pupils the chance to perform. Most learn at least one instrument, with a good peripatetic range on offer.

'This is a very sporty school but with the "everyone's a winner" mentality,' reckoned one parent. Sport is designed to ensure that everyone has fun, with every child having the chance to represent the school in a team or individual competition. From cross-country running around the 'cow field' to fencing, swimming (school has its own pool) and dance, there's little not on offer. Traditional mix of hockey, rugby, football, netball, cricket and tennis all well catered for with competitive options reaching out into the likes of orienteering and triathlon.

The purpose-built nursery, The Garden at Kingswood, opened its doors in 2018 with a five-year plan to reach capacity but did so well before that. Each wooden, age-stage room has its own outdoor space. Pre-school aged children are in the re-modelled old prep boarding house with its own garden areas and increasing access to the broader facilities of the pre-prep, including lessons with teachers of PE, art, swimming, music, technology, IT and French.

Pastorally, pupils feel safe and 'know who they can talk to'. Rapport between teachers and pupils is strong, with worry boxes enabling children to quietly post notes about any concerns. A team of counsellors, pupil wellbeing mentors and AS tracking all help flag children needing 'talking time'.

Parents, usually dual income, are 'tight knit, wonderfully welcoming and casual, a very nice crowd,' according to one parent, although there is some anxiety that 'numbers are growing and we are slightly concerned that we may lose the intimate family feel we have always loved about this place.' As more London escapees swell the pupil numbers, there is definitely a sense of slight change in the air, although the head is keen to calm nerves. 'People buy into this school because of its down to earth, personalised and outdoorsy approach to education – that is not going to change and will always attract the same sort of people.'

Boarding: Boarding (both full and flexi) available for years 5 and 6. Co-ed and set in the grounds of the senior school for a maximum of 20 pupils (currently six), it has a family home feel, complete with dog. From helping with homework to trips to local trampolining parks, boarders are well cared for and entertained.

The last word: A happy school where children are given the education and facilities to find the foundations of lifelong passions while revelling in the freedom of endless outdoor adventures.

Kingswood School

Lansdown Road, Bath BA1 5RG

01225 734200 | admissions@kingswood.bath.sch.uk | www.kingswood.bath.sch.uk

Ages: 11–18

Pupils: 843; sixth form: 238; Boarders: 165 full, 24 weekly

Fees: Day £16,413; Boarding £25,800 – £35,376 pa

Linked school: Kingswood Preparatory School, 187

Headmaster: Since September 2020, Andrew Gordon-Brown (50s), formerly headmaster at Truro School for seven years. A warm, considered and visionary South African. Educated at Hyde Park High School in Johannesburg, studied commerce at University of Cape Town and then qualified as a chartered accountant. Spent 12 years in financial services both in South Africa and the UK for the likes of Deloitte, UBS and JPMorgan Chase. A rowing fanatic, he competed for South Africa in the 1992 Olympics (coming a commendable eighth) then set his heart on Oxbridge rowing. Taking a study break from his thriving finance career, he completed an MSc in agricultural economics and a diploma in social studies at Keble College, Oxford; met his now wife, Harriet, and earned a rowing blue in the 1994 Boat Race. In 2003, he made a benevolent midlife career change, swapping the City for schools, starting with four years at Radley College teaching economics and history alongside coaching rowing and rugby. He completed a QTS simultaneously through the University of Gloucester. Five years followed as deputy head at Stonyhurst in Lancashire before moving to Truro.

Being a successful head is, he believes, down to having 'an optimism, energy and vision that you can communicate clearly – asking governors, staff, parents and pupils to "come with you" on the journey'. One year in and the feedback is unwaveringly positive: 'He very quickly got to grips with the school, increasing the warm community feel and giving very consistent, clear messages to the children,' said one parent, while a staff member told us, 'He has clearly pinpointed some fantastic next steps for the school and is focused on achieving them.'

He has three children – the eldest is reading English at Edinburgh, his son is at Radley (wanting a sixth form experience without his father as head) and his younger daughter is currently at Kingswood. Aside from the ubiquitous rowing he loves walking, music and trips to the family holiday home in Falmouth.

Entrance: On average 50-55 per cent from the linked prep school, all of whom sit the competitive entrance papers. For entry to years 7 and 8, papers in maths, English and non-verbal reasoning. For years 9 (additional 10-20 places) and 10, science and a foreign language as well. Places offered based on entrance exam results, interviews and scholarship assessment; existing school links through siblings or alumni also a factor.

Around 25 join at sixth form – criteria is 6s at GCSE in humanities subjects selected for A level and 7s for maths and sciences. All are interviewed by the head and need a current school report.

Exit: About 19 per cent leave post GCSEs, mostly to local sixth form colleges. Post A level, almost all to university with a strong Russell Group leaning. Favourites include Cardiff, Edinburgh, Newcastle, Warwick and UCL. Two to Oxbridge in 2021, and seven medics at destinations including Manchester and Queen Mary's.

Latest results: In 2021, 77 per cent 9-7 at GCSE; 63 per cent A*/A at A level (90 per cent A*-B). In 2019 (the last year when exams took place), 62 per cent 9-7 at GCSE; 34 per cent A*/A at A level (67 per cent A*-B).

Teaching and learning: Locally viewed as 'the caring, pastoral and holistic choice', the school's modesty belies the fact that it does rather well academically. While definitely not an academic hothouse, parents are resolutely 'delighted with the approach and results, with pupils not overly pushed but given the incentive and internal drive to succeed. They are happy and willing to learn and that leads to impressive results.'

The deputy head academic has his sights set on realigning the reputation with the aim to 'get academics on the same high level as the pastoral profile of the school'. In his view it's all about increasing the 'breadth of experience', which translates into a strong range of subjects on offer, over 20 at GCSE, with subjects such as Latin, Mandarin and computer science boosting the choices. 'We are really lucky that we don't have option blocks so can usually choose any combination of subjects,' enthused one pupil. Most take up to nine or 10 GCSEs with English, maths, at least one language and the sciences all compulsory.

Classes are capped at 22 in years 7-8 and 20 in years 9-11. No aggressive setting but pupils are grouped on ability and style or speed of learning from the start in year 7 for maths and for science and English from year 9. 'Pupils can get a 9 at GCSE from any of the bands,' assured the academic head. Parents concur, with one telling us, 'Pupils seem unconcerned about which set they have been put in – there is no competitive slurring, it's handled perfectly.' All three sciences studied until the end of year 10 when the lowest band pupils can opt to take combined science instead.

A parent told us the new head has 'made an encouraging start' by recruiting 'new blood to replace some incongruous old wood in certain teaching positions'. Others remarked that teaching is on the up, with it now being 'good across the board with pockets of excellence'.

Locally viewed as 'the caring, pastoral and holistic choice', the school's modesty belies the fact that it does rather well academically. While definitely not an academic hothouse, parents are 'delighted with the approach and results'

The teaching we witnessed was delivered by enthusiastic staff in classes of engaged pupils. Year 9 physics had the teacher running a quick-fire quiz on electrical circuits with pupils willing to raise their hands to answer or question the points before they were let loose on a mind-boggling circuit-building exercise – which he simultaneously delivered to several students who had dialled in via Microsoft Teams. 'The online provision is very effective, with staff quickly adapting to the needs of the children,' praised a parent.

Teacher communication said to be excellent, with tutors the primary port of call for all concerns – parents say their responses are 'amazingly proactive'. Termly parent evenings, while online reports score pupils on attainment (class median score given to assist in comparative comprehension) and organisation – an 'arbitrary' score, according to both pupils and parents.

Over 24 subjects offered at A level. Most take three and a few, particularly mathematicians, four. Refreshingly, it's all about breadth so not unusual to find a scientist adding art to their choices. Economics, psychology and politics are the latest subject additions. Social sciences, geography and history most popular, with biology the highest performing. Most pupils start the EPQ, though not all complete it. Disappointing lack of BTec options on offer, though sport a recent addition.

Learning support and SEN: Staffed by three full-timers, all praised by parents for 'making Kingswood work for everyone' and their 'recognition that children learn in different ways'. That said, there was a united feeling among parents we spoke to that learning support was not the strongest area of the wider school. 'Kingswood enabled me to keep all my children together in their education, from the brightest to one with SEN, however I would not recommend it for a SEN child alone,' said one. Others said that while the support and individual management provided by the learning support team were 'excellent', the translation of this into the actual classroom was the missing link. 'The teaching staff need far greater confidence in, awareness and understanding of SEN to ensure that early identification is improved and that the resultant ideas coming out of the learning support team are followed up in an implementable and supportive manner in the classroom,' said one. We were impressed to hear of LS team taking more anxious new starters around the school quietly and personally in the holiday period, as well as their easy access to an ed psych and other specialist external support where necessary.

The arts and extracurricular: Music is quite literally the heart of the school, sitting proudly in the middle of the school site. Around 240 individual music lessons each week and choirs, orchestras and ensembles galore. A vast range of performance opportunities from charity concerts to whole-school events and key stage recitals held in school, Bath Abbey and at regional music festivals. We sat in on a small informal showcase of what a handful of pupils are currently working on, performed (among much applause and heartfelt whooping) to parents, peers and staff. From an A level pianist to a tiny trumpeter and goose-bump inducing solo singers, the standard was striking. Pupils can excel in music here and speak fondly of the department as 'a sanctuary where you can switch off from everything else'. Around 14-18 take GCSE music per year, three at A level.

Housed in an aptly Arts and Crafts style, three-storey, light-filled building, the art department is a hive of activity and exhibition. Courses are open church, with pupils from the start taught to experiment widely with every medium to find what they love – drawing, painting, printmaking, sculpture, ceramics and photography all on offer. We watched A level pupils answering the same fine art brief with a myriad responses, ranging from pencil studies of hands to stunning origami cranes in flight, computer simulated eco-car designs, short film compilations and a photographic study of the 'scaffolding of self as seen through tattoo art'. Fabulous.

Strong emphasis placed on vertical inter-year 'buddying' from the start. Mentoring taken seriously with peer schemes at key transition points for every pupil

Drama is 'excellent', according to both parents and pupils. There is a drama studio and an impressive 366-seat theatre housing two major productions per year – one senior and one junior. Rehearsals currently underway for Antigone, with recent productions including A Christmas Carol and Our Country's Good as well as plays written by staff and students. Pupils are encouraged to get involved onstage or backstage and can take over the technical reins. 'We have some seriously expert kit here,' said the theatre's technical director, 'giving an obvious pathway into a role in professional theatre.'

The extracurricular activities programme is mandatory and extensive. Pupils are encouraged to stay on until 5.30pm and take advantage; we were tempted to dive into the compelling menu ourselves, from kayaking, orienteering, frisbee and climbing to jewellery, calligraphy, Greek and crochet. Each option we popped our head into seemed well supported and fun.

In hushed tones, we were let in on the news that the school is currently negotiating a deal with Leiths School of Food and Wine to become their flagship academy. Watch this space for a September 2022 launch of a course and venue.

Sport: Sport is taken very seriously and is the highlight and focus of many pupils' experiences: 'It literally made my time here when I was asked to be in the A team for rugby,' glowed one pupil. Others spoke of the 'exciting and enthusiastic atmosphere around sport, particularly the big matches'. Strong referral links to the Bath city and university teams in rugby and hockey for those at the top of their game. Impressive facilities include eight rugby pitches, three cricket squares, two Astroturfs and a sports hall, some encircling the school and others half a mile up the hill. Sports on offer via the curriculum lessons are 'heritage sports... very private school,' according to the head; parents hope his sporting background will inspire 'greater sports options on offer and boost team inclusivity and opportunity'. Sports staff praised for their support and encouragement of all players, irrespective of their skill, but criticised for the elitist investment on training and match opportunities for the A and B teams despite the school fielding over 20 teams in key sports like hockey. 'Not all children have had the same experience in these sports at prep age so it seems unfair to pick a team from those that have and then be unwilling to allow others the chance to develop alongside them. Mixing up the teams and offering greater match access would make an enormous difference,' reckoned one parent.

Boarding: Every pupil, whether day or boarding, is assigned to a boarding house and the house structure is at the centre of school life and resolutely praised. 'Kingswood comes out on top with its fantastic boarding provision, akin to a close family experience; children are safe and given great pastoral care with strong bonds between year groups and day and boarding pupils,' lauds one parent.

The seven boarding houses are all slowly being updated with the best featuring wet rooms, outdoor decking, ensuite bathrooms and state-of-the-art technology whilst the worst, according to pupils, 'still have nasty bathrooms and horrible carpets'. We didn't get shown those parts, strangely.

Houseparents resolutely acclaimed by all and boarders' highlights are 'the weekend lie-ins, in-house breakfasts, walking into town with friends, great trips and pizza nights'.

Pupils in years 7 and 8 have a gentle start with the bespoke, co-ed Westwood house enabling them to slowly grow up in their own time and space, the much-loved house dog cementing the homely feel and giving wonderful greetings to all who come through the door.

Ethos and heritage: Founded by John Wesley as the first Methodist school, it opened in 1748 for the sons and daughters of Wesley's friends but was soon restricted to the sons of Methodist preachers and leaders. Went co-ed again in 1974 and moved to its current site in 1852 – an imposing collection of purpose-built Victorian Gothic buildings on the steep northern slopes above Bath (a 20-minute walk away). Surrounded by 214 acres of manicured grounds (the views are magnificent), it is dotted with other buildings of varying age and beauty including the delightful chapel. The head wants to protect and enhance these venerable buildings with a target to get the site 'pristine'. Sixth form centre, the Dixon – an eyesore of a postwar building – is next in the firing line, and we were shown impressive architectural plans which school hopes are realised by September 2022. Pupils seem immune to any visual horrors, however, and love the building's studies, kitchen and relaxation areas, all of which will be enhanced and improved in the new design. Still a Methodist school, but now pupils from all denominations and none, with chapel 'woven into the week'. 'We offer a gentle, personally developed life philosophy, which is something Methodists do quite well.'

Music is the heart of the school. We sat in on a small informal showcase of what a handful of pupils are currently working on, performed (among much applause and heartfelt whooping) to parents, peers and staff. From an A level pianist to a tiny trumpeter and goose-bump inducing solo singers, the standard was striking

Food, served from a new refectory-style counter, then carried into the stunning, Hogwarts-like central dining room, is delicious. Uniform is tidy and businesslike, with girls in black blazers, white blouses and tartan skirts and boys in black blazers, charcoal trousers and school ties. Sixth formers wear dark suits. Parents speak of the Kingswood ethos being the decision maker on their initial selection and the reason behind their unwavering support of the school. Friendly, down-to-earth, inclusive and kind, we heard.

Famous alumni include actor Tim Curry, director and writer Jonathan Lynn, the historian and writer EP Thompson and Reggie Tsiboe, one of the lead singers of pop band Boney M.

Pastoral care, inclusivity and discipline: Pastoral care is 'exemplary', say parents, who enthuse about the quality of pupil and staff relationships and the overall sense of 'being part of a community that cares about each other'. One described it as 'the perfect blend of warmth and respect. There is a sense of trust here – if something goes wrong pupils will talk about it.' Parents considered too, with over 100 attending online pastoral evenings during the recent lockdown.

Tutors are central to pastoral, social and academic care with pupils assigned to specialist tutors for each stage of their education, changing from their initial tutor in year 9 and again in year 12. AS tracking offers staff a tool to identify vulnerable pupils and help is on hand to pick these up via on-site counsellors, the medical centre and the chaplain. Strong emphasis placed on vertical inter-year 'buddying' from the start. Mentoring taken seriously with peer schemes at key transition points for every pupil (year 12s meet year 9s for weekly one-on-one GCSE selection advice, for example). Community mentoring options for all senior pupils, reaching out into the local state school network to support local children.

Pupils told us they see themselves as 'altogether on a journey to eradicate inequalities, harassment and bullying' and are 'unafraid to call it out'. The school is peppered with downloadable QR codes offering pupils a quick and anonymous way to report anything untoward. Pupils are 'educated to make the right choices' and school has strictly enforced rules on drinking, drugs and smoking. Parents spoke of 'problems being sorted before they were even aware'.

Pupils and parents: Aside from a few flash cars in the car park, parents are mainly dual incomers who work hard to send their children here. Lots of medics, lawyers, business people and an increasing number of London re-locators. Around 15 per cent are international, from 23 countries. Pupils are enthusiastic about their school, eloquent and modest.

Money matters: Scholarships at years 7, 9 and 12, together with the John Wesley Boarding Awards – recognising potential in all-round contribution to school life. Currently eight per cent on bursaries – head is keen to make the process more transparent.

The last word: A superb school, offering a fantastic education with the emphasis firmly on kindness and community. 'What we love most is that there is no pomp and circumstance here – the children are valued and look out for each other,' said a parent, who echoed the view of many others. 'It is an extremely happy, friendly school, where children do well and are celebrated for being themselves.'

Kitebrook Preparatory School

Little Compton, Moreton-in-Marsh, Gloucestershire GL56 0RP

01608 674350 | admissions@kitebrookpst.org | www.kitebrookpst.org

Ages: 3-13

Pupils: 304; Boarders: 50

Fees: Day £7,545 – £15,300 pa; Boarding + £55 per night

Head: Since 2013, Susan McLean BSc, MA (50s). Born and educated in Michigan, USA. Awarded sports scholarship to Central Michigan University for BSc in special education. Father English, mother Canadian, piquing a lifelong interest in travel. Keen to discover British heritage, she crossed the Atlantic for a teaching exchange programme in Winchester. Further academia followed with degrees in elementary education and psychology, plus a master's in administrative leadership. Taught at the American International School in Riyadh, Saudi Arabia, staying on in Saudi to establish the early years and pre-prep British International School. A desire to return to the UK saw her take proprietorial headship of the Old Vicarage, Derby, from 2002 to 2007.

Perpetually seeking new challenges, Mrs McLean decided to leave education for the world of business but at the eleventh hour her gambit was halted when the CEO of the Cothill Trust asked her to become headmistress of Kitebrook. She seized the opportunity to take on and turn around this small 'tired' school in urgent need of renovation and restructure. Coming across as much the CEO of a dynamic business as headmistress, she has done just that. Clearly both the head and the heart of Kitebrook. One parent captured it perfectly, 'She leads from the front with a no-nonsense approach and always a smile.'

Mrs McLean welcomed us warmly into her office which, with its high ceilings, sumptuous sofas and floor-to-ceiling windows, felt more like a drawing room. Over coffee and cake we enjoyed an animated conversation after which we were left in no doubt as to her determination to communicate the burgeoning success of Kitebrook.

Described by parents as 'a force of nature, professional, a stickler for good manners, an enormous heart for the children and a smile no matter what'. Children say she's 'quite friendly' and 'likes to talk a lot'. Both, however, would like to see more of her. According to pupils, 'She doesn't come to see us much' and parents comment, 'We don't see her around the school.' As the non-teaching headmistress of a school undergoing significant restructuring, this is something of which Mrs McLean is very aware. 'I know I need to get out and about more. The demands of growing and regenerating our school make it difficult but we are reaching the point when I can, once again.' This doesn't stop the children seeking out the approachable headmistress. A parent relayed that her son had no compunction in making an appointment when he found himself in a conundrum. Mrs McLean guided him to a propitious resolution, demonstrating her resolve that children should be 'independent, confident to ask for help, and use resources to achieve their ends'.

Married with two adult children, her go-getting, globe-trotting approach to life seems to have rubbed off on her offspring who, in 2019, rowed the Atlantic together to promote gender equality, achieving two world records.

Entrance: Non-selective. Headmistress meets parents informally. Children attend taster day or visit school to confirm 'readiness' of child.

Exit: Early conversations and guidance given for ongoing education. Recent destinations include Kingham Hill, Cheltenham College, Cheltenham Ladies' College, Bloxham, St Edward's Oxford, Radley, Oundle, Tudor Hall, Downe House and Warwick. Five scholarships in 2021.

Our view: Stately and welcoming, Kitebrook's Cotswold stone residence surveys a generous sweep of formal lawn, canopied woodlands, meadows and hills that stretch as far as the eye can see. Established in 1959 by Anne McDermott, the school has stayed true to its founder's aim of providing academic rigour in a familial setting with individual holistic care. During our interview Mrs McLean eschewed any notion that this style of education is outdated, insisting McDermott was progessive, visionary even, and that her core principles remain fundamental to learning and personal development, 'never more so than now'. Adding, 'Children only have one childhood, they should be nurtured whilst being gently pushed out of their comfort zone to seek their own limits and take risks.'

Kitebrook has flourished in size and stature under this headmistress who clearly knows her market. Public speaking, tree climbing, manners and prayers are tabs under the 'Tradition' heading on its polished website. Numbers are healthy at 300 pupils and the boy/girl ratio is all but equal in this historically all-girls institution. Once considered a pre-prep for other establishments, it is now a serious contender up to 13+.

Chatting to parents, Kitebrook is overwhelmingly seen as 'such a happy school', 'fun and full of energy', with 'space and freedom to play and be a child'. Describing their preliminary tour on a scorching hot day, a parent recalled coming across a 'whole school water fight on the front lawn to cool the children off. It was very Enid Blyton.'

Head described by parents as 'a force of nature, a stickler for good manners, and a smile no matter what'. Children say she's 'quite friendly' and 'likes to talk a lot'

Kitebrook's acres are a playground come wellies or sunscreen where children are encouraged to climb trees, take risks, test resolve and hone independence. Outside learning across all subjects is undertaken wherever possible. For many parents this is 'part of the draw'.

Our visit was seamlessly coordinated with the same businesslike efficiency that propels this school forward. A relay of enthusiastic, immaculate and engaging pupils dotted the route awaiting handover, prompt cards at the ready. First stop, a wintry Wake and Shake on the front lawn. Wellies and raincoats donned for a quick work-out to music with teachers and pupils alike enthusiastically flinging themselves in all directions, smiles aplenty.

Mrs McLean declares one of Kitebrook's greatest strengths is its teachers, whose style is described by parents as 'creative, practical, interactive and fun', a sentiment echoed by children who enthusiastically told us of 'amazing teachers', 'exciting' lessons and 'awesome' classrooms. Classes of around 14 are shuffled termly to propagate new friendships and encourage personal development.

On our tour we were swept along in a re-enactment by pupils and teacher, at the ready in steel helmets, gas masks round necks. An air raid siren was enthusiastically (and ear-splittingly) cranked into action and all descended to an underground cellar turned WW2 air raid shelter. Lights extinguished, utterly inspired pupils spoke animatedly of hearing recordings of overhead bombings and wartime singalongs. One pupil, totally immersed, endearingly pointed to an area of damaged bricks suggesting that could have been caused by a bomb blast! Cross-discipline learning included 'dig for victory' in outdoor education and wartime literature in English.

Our next guide was bursting to show us the Harry Potter themed classroom. We were charmed when, with total awe, a 'real' snitch was proffered for viewing in her outstretched hands. On through passageways peppered with artwork and projects to more creative handiwork – the magnificent castle ramparts of the history room. We were impressed by a 'collaboration' room with rolling tables to facilitate flexible groupings and a 'white' room where pupils can write up maths problems on the walls. IT suite furnished with computers for each class member.

At lesson changeover the corridors were bustling with happy, smiling faces and chirpy hellos. This merry confidence continued undiminished during our chat with pupils, all of whom were exceptionally well mannered and utterly charming. A little too steadfastly loyal and positive about their school? We were amused as gasps rang out when any of their number suggested even the most mildly negative viewpoint. Well prepped or not, they certainly seemed genuine.

We noted throughout the day that pupils are actively encouraged to innovate; whether ideas for new badges, masterminding engineering projects or initiating social events. 'It is what we are all about,' a member of staff commented. Badges to fill the uniform blazer's moss tweed lapel are keenly sought, but pupils must earn their stripes. Each candidate stands before school assembly to be challenged in their endeavours. When asked if that presented a pressure to some, Mrs McLean declared that 'failing is merely an opportunity to try again'. Inquiring whether one pupil felt nervous at impending test we were met with a smiling, confident response: 'Not really, I know it off by heart.' Later, said pupil was proud to seek out this reviewer to communicate fresh victory, delightedly displaying a shiny new badge on a blazer already festooned with awards.

Kitebrook runs a 'baccalaureate' programme alongside Common Entrance and assessed growth mindset skills. Mrs McLean believes this is a unique and holistic approach. In her opinion, while the baccalaureate model suits many children, Common Entrance can be a better indicator of academic ability while growth mindset allows for continued individual assessment.

Following 'excellent' academic provision during first lockdown, school canvassed parental opinion, increasing remote provision to include after-school clubs and social links for pupils. A parent complimented the school's 'outstanding achievement to deliver as much of the whole school experience as possible'.

Staff are experienced in assisting children with additional needs: audio processing, visual impairment, dyslexia. While wheelchair access is limited to ground floor in upper school, if necessary timetables are swiftly adjusted to move whole classes downstairs to accommodate.

Dedicated SEN department is located at the centre of the school. Approximately 50 pupils have some learning support, meeting with staff before and after school or at breaktimes. Approximately 35 attend an enrichment scheme for more able pupils in English and STEM. One parent commented on the school's provision in this area, 'It's all wholly positive, there's no difference in the way catch up or extension is presented. Everyone's special and everyone's individual.'

Kitebrook's acres are a playground come wellies or sunscreen where children are encouraged to climb trees, take risks, test resolve and hone independence

'We hold no boundaries in any age group,' head stressed during our interview. 'If a child needs stretching it is made available to them.' Although not official until higher in upper school, children streamed in maths and English from year three with scholarship sets for those demonstrating particular ability.

Art and performing arts seen by head as two of Kitebrook's strongest areas. In the art department, bursting with eclectic and accomplished creations, large picture windows revealed breathtaking patchwork pastures of Gloucestershire countryside. What inspiration!

'Drama is amazing!' a parent enthused. Each child treads the boards in at least one production a year. 'It offers such important life skills,' headmistress attested. Pupils build sets, help backstage, organise costumes and make-up. Year 5s devise own pieces and pen scripts. LAMDA exams garner stellar results and school was among the first to take up the English Speaking Board exams (oral English).

Sport is flourishing under Kitebrook's renovation plan. Parents bemoan the 'slightly shabby' facilities; school assures us upgrades are in pipeline. Keen to challenge every child to represent school, Kitebrook now fields A and B teams in rugby, hockey, football, tennis and cricket. Opponent schools selected to challenge and build confidence. Handful of county players in cricket and tennis. Represented in IAPS. Sporting pathway with individual coaching for those keen to excel.

Suitably bucolic house names: Ash, Beech, Cedar and Oak. Rewards for personal development and traditional competition. We loved the innovation of the 'welly tally', four primary-coloured wellies representing each house – boots move up and down a staggered podium, to the delight of pupils.

Educational trip to Iceland, tour of Pompeii and Herculaneum, and visit to battlefields in recent years. More locally, team-building residential trips – notably one for potential prefects who undergo stringent interview process, having first proposed themselves in writing to headmistress. A plethora of after-school clubs: ecology, languages, music, jewellery making, debating, sport, drama, kit car making. All well attended.

Mixed year upper school tutor groups meet twice a day. We saw benefit as younger children gain insight from senior cohort's experience and older children encourage those yet to tread their path. Tutors constantly monitor the development and wellbeing of pupils and any issues are dealt with 'swiftly'. One child quipped, 'If you have a problem you know the tutor will help you.' Parents talk of raising concerns with headmistress, who is 'amazingly reassuring and helps to put things right'.

Academically, Kitebrook 'push to do well but aren't pushy,' said one parent. Head says results speak for themselves and that a full school, healthy waiting list and exit pupil achievement demonstrate that scholastic rigour and a nurturing approach go 'hand in hand'.

School's location in Moreton-in-Marsh puts it well within range of well-heeled London escapees in Oxfordshire's nearby Chippings (Norton and Campden). Parents describe themselves as 'a real mix' of London commuters, farming and local families. An active parents' committee 'PECK' stages events and fundraisers. Socials organised via year WhatsApp groups. For some, the comment was that parents can be 'a little cliquey'. Culturally school mix is, as a parent carefully put it, 'one-dimensional', reflecting local demographic.

Boarding: A mix of weekly and flexi from year 3 upwards, who are housed in main school. Cosy dorm-style bedrooms, a common room and kitchenette offer homely experience. Short-notice flexi boarding option is popular with parents and enjoyed as a 'fun sleepover' by children. One parent commented that boarding is seen by many as an opportunity for older pupils to have taster experience before senior boarding. Boarders have popcorn and film nights and occasional camp outs.

Money matters: Fees set to be retained currently. No formal bursary or scholarship programmes.

The last word: Over the last eight years Kitebrook's profile and reputation have blossomed under the determined leadership of its dynamic headmistress. This 'extremely friendly, supportive school' promises a challenging, nurturing and creative education, imbued with 'fundamental' life skills. Parents love its traditional values and evocation of a healthy, old-fashioned, tree-climbing childhood in an idyllic setting.

Leweston School

Sherborne, Dorset DT9 6EN

01963 211015 | admissions@leweston.dorset.sch.uk | www.leweston.co.uk

Ages: 0-18

Pupils: 556; sixth form: 49; Boarders: 80, 32 full, 48 weekly/flexi

Fees: Day £6,285 – £16,356; Boarding £18,315 – £29,469

Headmaster: Since January 2020, John Paget-Tomlinson (40s), previously deputy head (academic) at Portsmouth High School GDST. Educated at Wells Cathedral School, where he modestly says he played the trombone 'very badly'. Read history and philosophy at Reading, followed by a master's in war studies at King's College London, a research master's at King's, PGCE at the University of Chichester and an MSc in education leadership at Portsmouth. 'I'm an eternal student,' he laughs. He's fascinated by military history and after a spell in the navy he joined the Royal Naval Volunteer Reserve in intelligence. First teaching job was at Churcher's College, where he was rapidly promoted to head of history and then deputy head of sixth form, before moving to Portsmouth High for eight years.

When he first visited Leweston he was struck by the atmosphere and the pupils' enthusiasm for the school. 'It was beyond anything I had come across before,' he says. The school has grown since his arrival – from 197 in the senior school, including 22 boys, to 273, including 76 boys. 'It's been quite a year for pupil growth,' he told us. The increase in numbers is partly due to the closure of two local schools but there are other factors too. 'The school's reputation has grown and parents are impressed by our location, our emphasis on community values, the opportunities we offer and our expertise,' says the head. Parents like his approach. 'He is very pragmatic, calm, capable and reassuring,' said one. Another told us, 'He's fab – very down-to-earth, accessible and has a great sense of humour.'

He teaches history and Latin to year 7s and at GCSE and A level. 'I think it's really important for heads to teach.' Has two daughters and in his spare time enjoys reading (he has nearly 7,000 books, mostly about international relations, history and philosophy), walking, camping and riding. We spoke to him via Zoom on the day pupils returned to school after a lockdown and admired two pictures on his study wall – one of the bombardment of Sebastopol in 1854 and the other of his adorable spaniel Arthur, who was snoozing underneath his desk and boasts his own Instagram account.

Head of preparatory school is Alanda Phillips BA PGCE MEd, formerly head of the school's Early Years Foundation Stage. She also teaches French, Spanish and PSHE across the prep.

Entrance: Non-selective. Pupils start at multiple points so it's always worth contacting the school. They join the senior school from state primaries and preps like Castle Court, Hanford, Knighton House, Sandroyd, Sherborne Prep, Perrott Hill and Sunninghill in Dorchester. Prospective pupils take part in a taster day – juniors have an informal assessment while seniors take academic, numerical and perceptual reasoning tests. New sixth formers require six good GCSE passes.

Exit: Forty per cent leave after GCSEs. Some head to local state schools like the Gryphon School in Sherborne and the Thomas Hardye School in Dorchester while others go to independents. A few miss Leweston so much they 'boomerang back' after a few weeks.

Ninety-five per cent progress to university. A vast array of destinations, including Exeter, UCL, Cardiff and Manchester, with one or two to Oxbridge some years (but none in 2020 or 2021). Up to a third chooses STEM subjects, medicine or veterinary science (three medics in 2021). Students sometimes won places to study music at King's College London as well as creative courses at the University of the Arts London and the Royal Central School of Speech and Drama. 'There's no one version of a Leweston pupil,' says the head.

Latest results: In 2021, 67 per cent 9-7 grades at GCSE; 69 per cent A*/A grades at A level or Pre-U equivalent (83 per cent A*-B). In 2019 (the last year when exams took place), 51 per cent 9-7 grades at GCSE; 38 per cent A*/A at A level or Pre-U equivalent.

Teaching and learning: Results are good, particulary for a non-selective school. Most pupils take 10 subjects at GCSE, including English, English lit, at least one language (French or Spanish), maths, RS and either combined science or three separate sciences. In 2019 the school switched to the diamond model in years 9 to 11, with single-sex classes for maths, physics, chemistry and biology. 'Pedagogical evidence shows that it's the best of both worlds,' says the head. Pupils regularly excel in STEM Olympiads.

The diamond model means single-sex classes for maths, physics, chemistry and biology in years 9 to 11. 'Evidence shows that it's the best of both worlds,' says the head

When it comes to value added, performance at GCSE consistently ranks Leweston in the top 10 per cent of schools nationally. Pupils are able to choose almost any combination of 21 A level subjects and can also do BTECs in health and social care, business and sport and exercise science. Small A level classes (often three or four for less popular subjects so lots of individual attention) appreciated by the pupils, who have the option to do the EPQ too. The sixth form is fairly small but a parent said she's confident it will grow in size. The head brings a wealth of sixth form experience to the school and is about to launch the LEaD (Leweston Enrichment Diploma), a mix of core modules that includes community service, leadership skills and enrichment activities like cookery and car maintenance. Year groups lower down the school range from 36 to 60, with average class sizes of 16.

Prep school (with 160 pupils and another 90 in the nursery) is housed in a separate building and fizzes with activity. Single-form entry in the prep, with class sizes capped at 20, and two forms per year from year 3. Almost 50:50 boys and girls. Parents choose the prep because of the breadth of its curriculum and its superb outdoor provision. When we visited, a year 6 teacher was showing the first edit of a 20-minute film of A Midsummer Night's Dream made by his pupils. Most move seamlessly from the prep to the senior school (the occasional one or two head elsewhere). When we visited the prep our sixth form guide told us nostalgically, 'It still has the same familiar smell.' Separate nursery takes children aged 3 months to 4 years.

When children returned after the 2021 lockdown parents were impressed by the prep's approach. Staff took time to settle children socially, focusing on the NHS's five steps to mental wellbeing, extending playtimes and lunch breaks and running playground activities like skipping, finger knitting and making daisy chains.

Learning support and SEN: Leweston's 'individual needs' department is led by a dyslexia expert and supports pupils with dyslexia and those who need help with cognitive processing skills, either in class, in small groups or one-to-one. Support also available for literacy, numeracy and study skills, revision strategies and exam planning. A sixth former praised the support she'd received when struggling to memorise poetry for her English lit GCSE. EAL lessons are provided as part of the curriculum as an alternative to studying a language.

The arts and extracurricular: Around a third of pupils play a musical instrument and there are choirs, orchestras and bands to join. New music school opened in 2019. Seniors take part in the Sherborne Schools' Sinfonia and Symphony Orchestra. Up to four pupils take GCSE and A level music each year. Art is very popular, giving pupils the chance to try their hand at everything from portraiture to graphic design. The school offers A level textile design (including a fashion component), photography and fine art. Lots of drama, from James and the Giant Peach at the prep to Sister Act at the senior school.

Everyone does practical cookery and many opt to take home economics (cookery and nutrition) GCSE. A group was busy making sweet potato and shallot quesadillas and Viennese tartlets when we visited. One young pupil, completely unprompted, kindly gave us one to take home. The school offers the Leiths basic certificate in food and wine.

DofE on offer and plenty of opportunities for community work, including mentoring younger pupils and visiting the elderly. One of our sixth form guides was off to teach Spanish in a local primary school, a voluntary activity she'd fixed up off her own bat.

The pupils were enthusiastic, unpretentious and charming. A parent told us, 'When we drive through the gates every morning I think how lucky our kids are'

A plethora of clubs and activities on offer in the prep, such as chess, fencing, public speaking, mindfulness, pottery and yoga and all prep pupils have forest school (four acres designated for this).

Sport: Leweston is a very sporty school, with a 25-metre covered pool, eight netball courts, 15 tennis courts, sports hall, fitness suite and Astroturf. Besides the conventional hockey, netball, football, rugby and tennis, the school is an official Pentathlon GB Training Hub, offering opportunities in the triathlon, biathlon, tetrathlon and modern pentathlon. Pupils regularly qualify to represent Team GB at the European and World Championships and those with sporting ambitions are supported by specialist teachers and coaches. 'We have got some gutsy pupils,' says the director of sport. 'Despite our size, we really punch above our weight.' Boys' sport is thriving. A parent whose son excels at swimming, running and shooting specifically chose Leweston because of its sports provision.

Ballet, zumba, kickboxing, fencing, shooting and sailing (at nearby Portland Olympic Sailing Academy) on offer too. The school has a growing reputation for equestrian competition and has won the NSEA Regional Points League for the past four years, taking the title with the most points of any team in the country in 2019.

Boarding: Pupils can board from year 4 although boarding numbers increase as pupils progress up the school. By the sixth form many board on a weekly or full basis. Flexi-boarding and occasional B&B nights available too. There are currently 67 boarders – 49 girls and 18 boys.

Four boarding houses, all within the main school – three for girls of different age groups and a new one for boys of all ages. Attractive dorms with views across the lush green countryside – eight in the youngest dorms, four in year 9 dorms and single rooms for older girls. Boys have double or single rooms.

Head of boarding is an experienced houseparent with a background in both prep and senior boarding so is well equipped to deal with any problems. 'It's a very close knit community and the students really look out for each other,' she says. No Saturday school but around 80 pupils in school at weekends. Day pupils are welcome to join the weekend programme too. Boarders have a Saturday prep session followed by cultural and shopping trips, expeditions to nearby Lyme Regis, Burton Bradstock and Studland beach, art and crafts, board games, quiz sessions and movie nights.

Ethos and heritage: The school is set in 48 acres of beautiful parkland, at the end of a long drive and three miles outside Sherborne. Founded in Sherborne in 1891 by the Religious of Christian Instruction, a group of nuns from Ghent. Moved to its present site, a Palladian manor house, in 1948. Lots of later additions to the sprawling site, some visually pleasing, others less so. No nuns these days but the school chapel is central to school life. Daily prayers, masses and other school services are held there and pupils, staff and parents can visit when they wish. The tiny 17th-century Trinity Chapel, one of the first post-Reformation Catholic churches in the country, seats 50 and is used for smaller services.

The school went fully co-ed in 2018 but parents say this was 'very smooth' and hasn't changed the ethos, although some years have more boys than others. The day starts at 8.15am and ends at 4.20pm, followed by clubs, activities and after-school care for the youngest. Uniform is distinctive – tartan skirts and blazers for girls up to year 11, plus sailor dresses for juniors in the summer. Boys wear grey trousers, navy jumpers and blazers. No uniform for sixth formers but they are encouraged to look smart – definitely no denim. We didn't spot anyone flouting the rules although a pupil once turned up in slippers as a joke. Older pupils are allowed to go into Sherborne several afternoons a week to meet friends and have coffee. There are socials with other schools too. Sixth formers have their own sixth form area, complete with comfy Chesterfield sofas, outdoor courtyard and dedicated study centre as well as privileged access to the school's café.

Atmosphere everywhere is friendly, yet purposeful. As one parent put it, 'We wanted somewhere that would stretch our children, whilst giving them the confidence to be themselves. We didn't want a product.' Another told us, 'The kids are really happy – very polite and friendly, not arrogant. My girls were incredibly shy before they started here and they have really come out of their shells.' Pupils eat all their meals in the dining room but spill out onto the outside picnic tables in good weather. Plenty of choice, with vegetarian and gluten-free options.

Former pupils are known as Old Antonians and include Dame Kristin Scott Thomas, Erin Pizzey, founder of the UK's first women's refuge, former NHS Test and Trace head Dido Harding, entrepreneur Sarah McVittie and sculptor Serena de la Hey.

Pastoral care, inclusivity and discipline: Pupils say the school is warm and welcoming and like the fact that they are encouraged to achieve their potential. 'Everyone is kind to you here,' a year 6 girl told us. When pupils arrive they are assigned a peer mentor to help them settle in and everyone knows everyone.

Head prefect, two deputies, heads of the four houses and other prefects in place. They all keep a weather eye out for each other and for the younger students. Pupils can turn to tutors, houseparents, chaplain, counsellor and the two health centre nurses for help if they need it. The head of boarding, mindful of the pressures on today's young people, says: 'One of the things that Leweston does very well is helping the pupils to develop a sense of balance.' PSHRE covers everything from e-safety to tolerance.

Pupils and parents: Day pupils come from up to an hour away. School minibuses ferry pupils in from as far afield as Wincanton, Beaminster, Shaftesbury and Dorchester. Boarders mostly from the south west but a sprinkling from London. Around 17 per cent of pupils are from overseas – mainly Europe and Asia. A third of students are Catholic but pupils of any faith and none are welcomed. Everyone is expected to attend whole school mass on Wednesdays, whatever their faith.

The pupils we met were enthusiastic, unpretentious and charming, with a sense of fun. 'They're comfortable in their own skin,' agreed the head of boarding while a parent told us. 'When we drive through the gates every morning I think how lucky our kids are.'

Money matters: Mindful of the tough economic climate, the school aims to keep its fees 'competitively priced'. 'Our parents are very down-to-earth and come from a wide range of backgrounds,' says the head.

Senior school offers scholarships for academic attainment, art and design, drama, music and sports, including equestrian and pentathlon. Bursary awards are typically worth between 10 to 20 per cent of day fees.

The last word: With its stunning setting, friendly atmosphere and nurturing ethos, Leweston is a school that achieves very good results. The pupils work hard, make lifelong friends and clearly love the place.

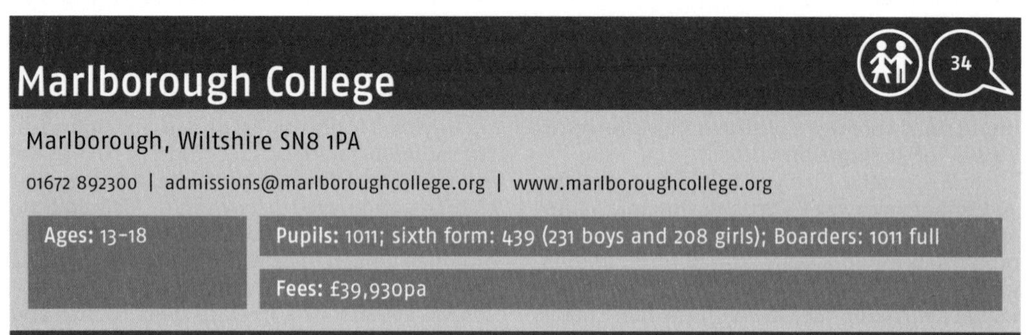

Marlborough College
34
Marlborough, Wiltshire SN8 1PA
01672 892300 | admissions@marlboroughcollege.org | www.marlboroughcollege.org
Ages: 13–18
Pupils: 1011; sixth form: 439 (231 boys and 208 girls); Boarders: 1011 full
Fees: £39,930pa

Master: Since 2018, Louise Moelwyn-Hughes MA (40s), previously head of St Edmund's School in Canterbury. She grew up on a council estate in Northern Ireland and at 11 was awarded a place at Methodist College in Belfast, known to locals as Methody, one of Northern Ireland's leading grammar schools. 'My parents couldn't afford the bus fare but my county stepped in and gave me a bus pass,' she recalls. She began studying ancient Greek at 12 and loved reading and translating so much that in the sixth form her teacher stopped her in the corridor and said she should apply to Cambridge. 'How do I do that?' she asked. He wrote three colleges on a scrap of paper and she chose Magdalene College because she liked the name. Her father drove her to Cambridge for her interview – 'my first time on the mainland'. It started snowing as they walked along the Backs and they both shed a tear of emotion. 'My education has enabled everything in my life,' she says.

In her last year at Cambridge she applied to join the diplomatic service but then spotted three job ads in an education magazine. Marlborough snapped her up before anyone else ('the only boarding schools I'd come across before were St Trinian's and Malory Towers') and she spent 13 happy years there, teaching classics and Arabic, getting involved in sport and music and becoming a housemistress (Princess Eugenie was in her house). She then headed to The Perse School, Cambridge to become their first female senior deputy head and six years later moved to the top job at St Edmund's.

She hadn't been looking to move again but leapt at the chance to take the reins at Marlborough (she received a handwritten letter asking her to apply). Right from the start her two main aims have been to put academics at 'the absolute core' of the school and to expand access. 'These two things are so important to me,' she says. Marlborough is launching an ambitious plan to raise £50 million over 10 years, enabling the college to offer 100 110 per cent bursary places – 'for children and families who couldn't afford an education like ours, for those who would thrive here and relish the opportunity.'

On the academic side she says that Marlborough has been reticent about calling itself an academic school in the past – but she's determined to change all that, especially as pupils' average grades at A level are already an impressive AAB. Everyone is encouraged to be 'academically ambitious' (70 or 80 now apply to Oxbridge each year rather than 30 in the past), academic successes are celebrated in assemblies along with sports triumphs and there are more academic prizes on prize day. She visibly brightened when we told her about a group of year 11 pupils we'd met who were fizzing with enthusiasm about their A level choices. 'That's music to my ears,' she says.

Popular with parents and pupils alike. A recent sixth former described her as 'lovely' and told us that 'pupils really like her', while a mother said: 'She's wonderful – a very level-headed leader.' Another described her as 'the most amazing, inspirational woman. She's softly spoken but no-nonsense and she's steering the ship on a very steady path.'

She is enjoying 'every minute' of her Marlborough role, particularly the extensive bursary project. 'We have ten years to raise the money so there is a huge job to be done here,' she says. Her teacher husband used to be head of politics at King's School, Canterbury but has been looking after their three young children during the pandemic. They live in a house on site and she laughingly says that her hobbies outside work 'used to be squash, walking and reading'. She's 'quite big on languages' – during her first stint at Marlborough she learned Arabic in a year and ended up teaching it herself. She doesn't teach these days but hopes to get back to it in the future.

Entrance: Parents can register children up to five years prior to entry (from September of year 4). The school advises registering in good time. Selection for 13+ entry is based on a reference from a child's current school, interview and ISEB pre-test results. Most applicants are assessed in year 6, when around 70 per cent of places are allocated. 'The move to year 6 assessments has cast the net a lot wider,' says the director of admissions. Approximately 25 per cent of places are awarded in year 7 and five per cent in year 8. Most applicants take CE and their results are used for setting when children start at the school. Those with confirmed places are expected to achieve an average of 60 per cent at CE. 'The intellectual side is important but we are also looking for character, energy, creativity and spark,' says the deputy head (academic).

On the academic side the master says that Marlborough has been reticent about calling itself an academic school in the past – but she's determined to change all that

The school does its best to accommodate siblings but it isn't automatic. Pupils come from around 260 prep schools (100 preps represented in each year group alone). A fifth from London but the majority from the south (from Devon across to Kent), plus a few from Scotland. Around 12 per cent are international pupils, from the US, Japan, Singapore, Malaysia, Hong Kong and India among others. 'We're really global,' says the school.

Entry into the sixth form is very competitive, with one in four applicants getting in. 'They have to be academically ambitious, willing to get involved in co-curricular activities and contribute to the boarding community,' says the director of admissions. At this stage selection is based on references from a pupil's current school, VRQ test, exams in proposed A level subjects and an interview.

Exit: Very few, if any, leave after GCSEs. 'Everyone stays because it's so nice in the sixth form,' a year 11 told us. At 18 pupils head off in all directions. Up to 15 per cent opt for overseas universities – most recently to Brown, Michigan State University, NYU, UCLA, Georgetown, CU

Boulder, McGill, British Columbia, Parsons, Boston and Miami, with pupils also receiving offers not taken up to RISD, Duke, Middlebury, Vassar and Toronto. Most popular UK destinations are Durham, Newcastle, Edinburgh, Exeter and Bristol (90 per cent of university offers are from 'high tariff universities'). There's a new head of Oxbridge admissions and six went to Oxbridge in 2021. Wide range of degree subjects.

Latest results: In 2021, 79 per cent 9-7 at GCSE; 75 per cent A*/A at A level (94 per cent A*-B). In 2019 (the last year that exams took place), 68 per cent 9-7 at GCSE; 45 per cent A*/A at A level (79 per cent A*-B).

Teaching and learning: Marlborough has always performed well academically but the master is determined to shift up a gear. Most pupils now take three A levels as standard rather than four (they can do more if they wish but the thinking is that with three they will have more time to devote to other things too, like the EPQ, short courses and learning a new language).

All the usual A level subjects on offer, plus business, classical civilisation, economics, exercise and sports sciences, history of art, music technology and psychology. No block system – the school does its best to accommodate subject combinations. Definitely a school for keen linguists. The deputy head (academic) describes languages as 'our Rolls-Royce department' and pupils can choose French, German, Greek, Italian, Latin, Mandarin Chinese, Russian and Spanish, Arabic, Hebrew and Japanese. Maths and politics are the most popular A level subjects and along with art and biology achieve stand-out results. Around two-thirds of sixth formers take the EPQ – recent endeavours include a research-based report on the social impact of the ska music movement in the Midlands and a practical project that involved designing a BMX race track. Plans are underway to introduce a level 2 EPQ for year 11s.

Most pupils take 11 GCSEs, including English lang and lit, maths, a modern foreign language (some take two or three), RS and double or triple science. Bright linguists can take a language GCSE early – at the end of year 10. Class sizes of between five and 13 at A level and between 10 and 20 in years 9 to 11.

The school offers an exciting approach to learning from the start. Shell pupils (year 9s) do something called Form, a multidisciplinary enquiry into the origins of human civilisation. These lessons take the place of separate English, history and RS and aim to develop intellectual curiosity. Lots of interest in entrepreneurship – 'we aren't just educating people for dusty libraries,' says the deputy head (academic) – and the

Definitely a school for keen linguists. The deputy head (academic) describes languages as 'our Rolls-Royce department'

school is introducing an entrepreneurship programme for the youngest pupils. Setting in maths and sciences.

Innovation Centre opened in 2021 – a hub for social enterprise, engineering and technology. 'We plan to equip pupils with the skills, confidence and creativity to face the challenges of the fourth Industrial Revolution – from advanced robotics to artificial intelligence,' says the master. The library is a hive of activity. Open seven days a week, it sends out weekly newsletters, hosts visiting speakers and helps sixth formers with research for their EPQs. We liked the Everest Reading Challenge, which encourages younger pupils to read ten books for pleasure.

Learning support and SEN: Approximately 100 pupils have learning difficulties, such as moderate dyslexia, dyspraxia and ADHD, and receive one-to-one support from the five-strong learning support team.

The arts and extracurricular: There's so much on offer beyond the academic timetable that it's hard to know where to start. 'This is a very busy place,' says the deputy head (co-curriculum and outreach). Superb facilities and inspirational specialist teaching mean that every pupil, no matter what their prowess, gets involved in sport and the arts. Wise advice from year 11 pupils – known as 'the Hundred' – is to 'get stuck into as much as you can while you're here'.

Drama productions staged at the Bradleian, a 135-seat studio theatre, and the Ellis Theatre, which seats up to 450. They include lower school plays, main school productions, Penny Readings (staged by Shell) and Tiny Bites, short independent plays produced by pupils. In 2020 17 took the GCSE in theatre studies, six took A level and many more opt to do LAMDA public speaking qualifications. Nearly half have individual music lessons and house music competitions get everyone doing something tuneful. There's a plethora of music groups to join – symphony orchestra, chamber orchestra, chapel choir and big band among others.

Art is huge, with 61 taking the subject at GCSE in 2020 and 34 doing art A level. The art school is open seven days a week and comprises six studio spaces, plus specialist areas for painting, printmaking, ceramics, photography, engraving and drawing. The school's own art gallery, the Mount House, is next door.

The school is a founder member of CCF, with 300 cadets and a 25-metre indoor range. Those who choose not to join the CCF do outreach activities – hearing children read at local primary schools, mentoring maths students at a Slough secondary school, working with Riding for the Disabled, volunteering in charity shops and doing conservation work on the River Kennet. Countless outdoor activities on offer, including climbing, canoeing, kayaking, mountain biking, sub-aqua diving, an annual week-long year 9 trip to the Brecon Beacons and the arduous 125-mile Devizes to Westminster canoe race.

Sport: Marlborough is an ultra-sporty school. 'We expect all pupils to be physically active in some way,' says the deputy head (co-curriculum and outreach) – and they take him at his word. Rugby is massive – Marlborough played its first inter-schools rugby match in 1864 and since then the school has produced four England captains and 38 internationals – but so are hockey, netball, cricket, tennis, athletics and swimming.

There's an abundance of sports pitches, including two all-weather, floodlit pitches, plus a sports hall complex, fitness room, two studios and a fencing salle, a 25-metre indoor swimming pool, an outdoor activities centre (with a climbing wall) and squash, rackets and fives courts. The former town gaol is now the college gym.

Many pupils represent the school (and their county and country) but there are lots of house competitions too, from cross-country to water polo. 'They are very ambitious on the sports front,' said a parent. 'There is a very high standard at the top but there are enough teams for everyone who wants to play.'

Boarding: 'Marlborough is a genuine seven-day-a-week boarding school,' says the master. Ninety-eight per cent boarding (only a handful of day pupils, mostly children of teaching staff). Sixteen boarding houses: six girls', six boys' and four mixed (boys plus sixth form girls, each with their own designated areas). Vertical (mixed age) boarding encourages cohesion between the year groups and house loyalty is fierce.

At the time of our tour visitors weren't allowed into the boarding houses due to the pandemic (parents weren't either) but a group of year 11s gave us the lowdown. First year pupils sleep in dorms of four or five but as they get older they get their own rooms, some with ensuites. Every house has its own distinct character. A mother described Dancy, the newest girls' boarding house, as 'like a hotel' while a recent sixth former said Ivy, a girls' house on the High Street, is highly sought-after. In the sixth form the mixed houses are very popular, especially as pupils eat breakfast and dinner in-house. Parents say housemasters and housemistresses are 'very present' and 'very encouraging' and that every house is different in design and character.

When we asked year 11 pupils for their advice on choosing a house we were told: 'Each house is different so go with your gut. I walked into Ivy and I knew it was the one I liked the best.' A boy said he chose his house because the housemaster was 'so great'. Lots to do at weekends – from rock climbing to pottery – but there's downtime too, whether it's a coffee in town with friends or a rummage through vintage clothes in local charity shops.

Ethos and heritage: Marlborough was established in 1843, when a group of Church of England clergy, with the backing of the Archbishop of Canterbury, decided to found a boarding school to provide an affordable education for clergymen's sons. They leased the Castle Inn and admitted 199 boys. The college grew rapidly and now comprises 250 glorious acres and more than 1,000 pupils.

The college site is impressive, and the eclectic mix of ancient and modern architecture across it embodies the breadth and quality of a Marlborough education

The college site is bordered by water meadows, trout lakes, downs, the River Kennet and the town itself and is one of the most impressive we've seen in two decades of visiting schools. It's full of architectural gems – there can't be another school in the country where you can walk out of a glorious Victorian gothic revival chapel (with stained glass by Burne Jones and former Marlburian William Morris and sculpture by Eric Gill) and come face-to-face with a neolithic mound. Known as Merlin's Mound, it's the second largest manmade mound in Europe and boasts a 17th-century grotto at its base (often used for poetry readings). Floodlit at night, it has been restored in recent years and a path winds its way round and round to the top.

For budding young archaeologists, architects and art historians the Marlborough campus is a fascinating treasure trove. Edward Blore, who designed Buckingham Palace, built two boarding houses and the master's lodge while William Newton created the Memorial Hall in memory of the 749 Marlburians who lost their lives in the First World War. The acoustics at this neoclassical theatre and assembly hall are world-class (Julian Lloyd Webber, Tasmin Little, Emma Kirkby and the BBC Big Band have all played there).

Peeping out from behind the Memorial Hall is another William Newton creation – a white-painted 1930s concrete science block with Crittall windows (very chic these days) and wittily topped with a golden gourd (the senior science master at the time was called Arthur Gourd). We could wax lyrical about these architectural delights all day but as we said in a previous review, the eclectic mix of ancient and modern across the school site embodies the breadth and quality of a Marlborough education. We were shown round by the director of international admissions, an architectural historian who knows the provenance of every wall and window and can't believe his luck at working in such an extraordinary place. At the time of our visit he was working on a project called Marlborough in a Hundred Objects, a collection of artefacts belonging to the college.

Marlborough is an ultra-sporty school. Rugby is massive – Marlborough played its first inter-schools rugby match in 1864 and since then the school has produced four England captains and 38 internationals

Marlborough has always been a trailblazer and in 1968 became one of the first schools to admit girls in the sixth form. It went fully co-ed in 1989 (there are still slightly more boys than girls but it isn't far off 50:50).

The view of the teens we met is that Marlborough is traditional but definitely not snooty and that it's easy to make friends. We heard a couple of grumbles that more could be done to integrate new sixth formers but they were in the minority. Pupils like their uniform – sixth form girls are particularly keen on their ankle-length black skirts. 'It's great in winter because you can chuck them on over your pyjamas or trackie bottoms,' one told us. Sixth form boys wear suits – 'occasionally you'll see a wild one,' we were told. Lower down the school, girls wear tartan kilts and striped blouses while boys sport grey trousers, white or striped shirts and house ties. Lots of distinctive Marlborough jargon – teachers are beaks, a weekend out is a priv and a disco is a bar.

Pastoral care, inclusivity and discipline: Marlborough describes itself as 'a talking school' and stresses the importance of pupils seeking advice if they are concerned about their own or someone else's mental wellbeing. The school is keen on 'informal conversations' where pupils can chat to housemasters and housemistresses, personal tutors, dames, prefects, the school counsellor and staff at the medical centre (known to all as the 'sani'). Youngsters told us they were clear about who to go to if problems arise. There's also a new safeguarding pastoral hub where pupils can drop in and talk about issues that are bothering them. When the Everyone's Invited website hit the headlines the school invited Wiltshire County Council to advise and work with them. 'It's about giving pupils the tools to make the right decisions,' say staff. Marlborough has also created a health and wellbeing council and is about to be part of a forum with other schools, receiving training from the police and social services.

The word 'happy' cropped up a lot in our conversations with parents. 'It has been a very happy place for our daughters,' one said. Others told us it is a 'very caring' school. 'It produces well-rounded, happy, polite young people and is big on kindness and community,' we were told. Another parent said that 'everyone supports each other' and makes lifelong friends while a former pupil described it as 'really great and really social'. Current pupils' view is that there are so many different characters at Marlborough that 'everyone fits in'.

Pupils told us there are 'a fair amount of rules', particularly about punctuality, looking smart and being polite. 'It's good preparation for later life,' they said cheerfully. Clear policies on smoking, alcohol and drugs – all spelled out to pupils and parents. Lesser sanctions for misdemeanours like turning up late, back-chatting or handing in work late. The school is very keen on pupil voice and all ages get plenty of opportunities to air their views (pupils even run Marlborough's Instagram account).

Pupils and parents: Marlborough pupils are a great advert for coeducation – charming, friendly and sparky, the sort who can fit in anywhere. Parents get to know their children's friends at weekends and during the holidays and pupils make friends for life.

Old Marlburians are an impressive bunch. In addition to ranks of clerical and military worthies, notable former pupils include William Morris, John Betjeman, Louis MacNeice, Siegfried Sassoon, Bruce Chatwin, Sir Francis Chichester, Wilfrid Hyde-White, James Robertson Justice, Michael Pennington, Jack Whitehall, Lauren Child, Cressida Cowell, Frances Osborne, Sally

Bercow, Samantha Cameron, journalists Frank Gardner, Tom Newton Dunn and Hugh Pym and Oscar-winning screenwriter, actress and director Emerald Fennell – plus, of course, the Duchess of Cambridge and Princess Eugenie.

Money matters: A raft of scholarships (more honour than hard cash) but also directors' scholarships, which recognise outstanding excellence in music and sport and carry a fee reduction of 20 per cent. The master and the College Council are committed to expanding the bursary scheme and have launched an ambitious fundraising campaign (see above). At the moment around 100 pupils (nearly 10 per cent of the school) receive some form of means-tested bursarial support.

The last word: The college defines its values as 'respect, responsibility and rigour', an ethos that is at once modern and ambitious, yet in keeping with its Anglican traditions. A Marlborough education is 21st-century co-ed boarding at its very best. As one parent puts it: 'Getting a place here is like winning a golden ticket.'

Millfield Prep School

35

Edgarley Hall, Glastonbury, Somerset BA6 8LD

01458 832446 | admissions@millfieldprep.com | www.millfieldschool.com

Ages: 2–13

Pupils: 460 (217 girls; 243 boys); Boarders: 133

Fees: Day £9,030 – £19,845; Boarding £30,255 pa

Linked school: Millfield School, 208

Headmaster: From January 2022, Dan Thornburn, previously head at Edgeborough School, Surrey since 2017, where he oversaw a merger and helped grow the school by over 20 per cent, as well as leading a transformation of the curriculum, introducing the Pre-Senior Baccalaureate and expanding co-curricular. Before that, he was head of St Petroc's, north Cornwall, and his earlier teaching career included spells at Lockers Park and Chafyn Grove. Will be joined by his wife Emi, currently a maths teacher and head of marketing at Edgeborough, and their two children – Molly (year 7) and Walter (year 5), who will both attend the school – along with their golden retrievers Humphrey and Parsnip. Is an advocate of boarding, having boarded from a young age himself at Packwood Haugh.

Entrance: Essentially non-selective, though 'we do have an academic and behavioural benchmark,' the school points out. The school professes to be looking for 'well-motivated boys and girls with… interests that stretch beyond the academic curriculum'. Hopefuls are interviewed and assessed – the latter a computer-based verbal and non-verbal reasoning test. Children needing or likely to need extra help meet the head of learning support for their assessment. Admissions into the pre-prep from 2 and the prep from 7, but the largest intake is into year 7; applications are considered into any year group at any time, space permitting. One mother was full of praise for the welcome her son had received in year 6.

Exit: Mostly to the senior school (over 95 per cent), where transfer is automatic barring the blotting of any copybooks, but quite open to children going elsewhere at year 9 – four to Sherborne in 2021 (two scholarships).

Our view: This a school that has pretty well everything for pretty well everybody with the means to pay for it. Academically, the range is very broad indeed: we loved the Latin class for better linguists who were busy bringing a dead language back to life by speaking it, but the sensitive and encouraging teaching in the tiny physics class of just five – to whom this subject evidently didn't come easily – was inspiring too. From the off, pupils are set for maths and English; languages follow in year 7. Most subjects are taught by a group tutor until year 6, then all by specialists. Classes are small, and the curriculum extensive, enquiry-based and global in outlook. Parents feel that the 'lingering reputation of the school as being not very academic,' as one put it, and so not suitable for a very bright child, is misconceived.

Chess lessons with the resident grandmaster are compulsory in years 3 and 4, and students are encouraged to take part in national competitions, such as Salters Festival of Chemistry (winners in 2017). Thoughtful Learner programme aims to set its adherents up for life. Technology is not quite as embedded as in the senior school, but students are expected to have their own iPad from year 7. Millfield generally is known for its SEN provision, notably specialist dyslexia support, and is the reason why some parents choose the school. A busy learning development centre staffed by one part-time and five full-time members of staff delivers multi-sensory programmes to address many, if not all, aspects of dyslexia, such as processing and organisational difficulties. The centre is so integral to the school that students attend extra lessons with no stigma attached to it whatsoever. 'He just goes – he doesn't care,' said one mother of her son.

Chess lessons with the resident grandmaster are compulsory in years 3 and 4, and students are encouraged to take part in national competitions

Outside the classroom, there's everything a young person could possibly want to do – and then some. The facilities, coaching and degree to which timetables can be tweaked for the sporting elite are exceptional for a prep school and some choose it for that reason. All are, however, encouraged to try a variety, and all represent the school at some point in something. Particular recent successes include girls' hockey (at the time of writing, the girls U13 were IAPS champions), golf, fencing and triathle, in which the school boasts a junior world champion. Pitches, courts, nets abound, plus a 25m pool, nine-hole golf course, stables and an outdoor arena, where a solitary rider on a palomino cantered circles in the dusk as we concluded our visit. The school's wonderful setting, nestled under Glastonbury Tor, means a limit on artificial lighting.

Artistic achievement limited only by talent: from the artist in residence, to the 3D laser cutter, to the area dedicated to the sculpting of stone – it's all here for the taking. Clubs thrive alongside timetabled art, plenty of space to show it all off and a prominent place for Picture of the Week in the dining room. Imaginative collaborations take place with the music department on occasion, such as Painting Sound and Woven Sound.

No shortage of ambition on the drama front, either. Everyone is encouraged to get involved and there are productions for individual year groups; recent shows include Beauty and the Beast (where three of the principle male roles were played by girls) and The Highwayman. Music is outstanding. The number and scope of ensembles would not disgrace a senior school, with opportunities in school (we liked the sound of brunch masterclasses in piano and strings) and out (eg workshops with eminent vocal performers such as the Gesualdo Six). Every child is encouraged to perform, producing a varied crop of confident and accomplished singers, fiddlers, trumpeters and so on, plus those who just do it for fun. The highlight of our visit was the tea and music concert, in which children of all ages played and sang short pieces. From breathy flutes to hesitant pianists to a talented young singer who could make Adele look to her laurels – all were brave enough to strut their stuff in front of parents and staff and receive warm applause. And we haven't even mentioned the array of cakes...

We found more than satisfied customers and very few gripes. 'Unlike the senior school, everyone knows each other at the prep,' one mother told us. 'My son's friends are lovely, grounded, thoroughly good people,' added another. The global friendships formed and the school's skill in dealing with friendships gone wrong get the thumbs up. The nurturing environment – not so cosy that children are not gently pushed beyond familiar pastimes – also meets with parental approval: 'He's tried cookery and public speaking, and has grown in confidence so much that now he volunteers for things at school,' one happy parent reported.

The group tutor is the go-to person for day students and has the overview of their lives at school; for boarders, it's houseparents.

It would be hard to find a child who would not enjoy Millfield Prep, though the head did concede that they have to be organised – it's a huge site with a lot on. 'Might not suit an agoraphobic either,' she added wryly. At the request of students, the uniform has recently been rejigged to include culottes for anyone who wishes to wear them. Checked shirts for every day, white for best, ties for all; sports kit in Millfield colours of navy, scarlet and green branded within in an inch of its life.

Boarding: Very little boarding until year 6, then numbers pick up in years 7 and 8, until about 60 per cent finish their prep school careers as boarders. High praise for boarding, including some rather rueful in tone: 'You don't need to board – we live five miles away!' one mother told her children, but board they do, 'because they love

Marlborough College

it'. Another told us that her child was hard to get hold of, as he was so busy and 'within five minutes, he's saying Bye!'. International parents kept fully in the picture; in fact everyone we encountered spoke highly of communication in general, and the full-page email from each subject teacher for those parents unable to make parents' evenings is much appreciated.

Boys' houses tend to be older and more scattered; recently one girls' house was relocated to be next to the other, both purpose built. We found them warm, homely and welcoming, with cosy dorms and kitchens for those all-important snacks. All mobile devices have to be handed in at night.

Money matters: Scholarships to 15 per cent of fees (but often honorary) for academic, sporting and musical prowess and, unusually, in chess, plus all rounders, and headmistress's scholarships to a generous 50 per cent for outstanding ability or talent.

The last word: Millfield Prep is less daunting and more nurturing than its size might suggest, and previous (mis)conceptions of it being somewhere for sporty, rich children with a bit of schooling thrown in are inaccurate. But there's no ducking the immensely privileged environment – it's all there for the taking.

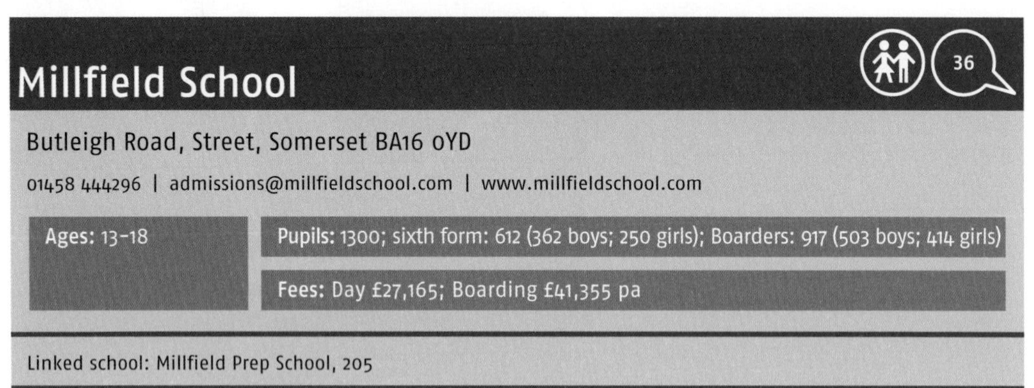

Millfield School

Butleigh Road, Street, Somerset BA16 0YD

01458 444296 | admissions@millfieldschool.com | www.millfieldschool.com

Ages: 13-18

Pupils: 1300; sixth form: 612 (362 boys; 250 girls); Boarders: 917 (503 boys; 414 girls)

Fees: Day £27,165; Boarding £41,355 pa

Linked school: Millfield Prep School, 205

Headmaster: Since 2018, Gavin Horgan MA (Oxon) (40s). Previously head of Worksop College. Educated at Stonyhurst College, where he was awarded an assisted place and bursary, and Oxford, where he read classics. 'My father was a postmaster and my mother was a special needs teacher and they lived in an ex-mining village in Dumfriesshire so it's very clear to me that without the bursary or the assisted place my fortunes in life would have been very different,' he says.

After university he worked for the Red Cross and then taught in Sri Lanka. On his return to the UK he taught English at Calthorpe Park School in Hampshire and Archbishop Tenison's School (overlooking the Oval), qualifying as a teacher through the Graduate Teacher Programme. Spent two years at deputy head of St George's College in Buenos Aires before being appointed as deputy rector of Glasgow Academy. He spent six years as head of Worksop College – 'a small mixed-ability boarding and day school' – where he organised a school trip to scale previously unclimbed mountains in Greenland, believing that risk is essential to children's development. The pupils spent a year preparing for the harsh conditions in the Arctic Circle, flew there in a Catalina seaplane and carried out scientific research. He'd like to organise something similar at Millfield.

He believes that his diverse experience has been invaluable to his Millfield role. 'I've been like a magpie in my career, trying to put myself in different educational settings so I can bring the best of all of them to the role I'm in,' he says. He admits that when he first visited Millfield he was stunned by its scale. 'Like so many people I was guilty of thinking that a school this big must be daunting or intimidating when actually the reality is that a school this big provides a place for everybody in a way that smaller schools can't.'

He's hugely proud of Millfield's sporting achievements but highlights its myriad academic and musical successes too. 'Millfield has always been determinedly diverse and hasn't cared a fig about tradition in a way that other independent schools thrive off their traditions,' he says. 'It's very refreshing in this day and age.'

Parents like his dynamic approach. One told us, 'He is a nice, personable guy who makes a point of knowing all the kids.' Another said, 'He is very impressive – both as an individual and as a head. He has innate leadership qualities and is thoroughly likeable too. His heart is all about the students, the staff and the school.' We also heard that when the lunch queue was moving slowly one day he joined the kitchen staff to help serve food. On another occasion a student's post was mistakenly delivered to his office and instead of sending it via the internal mail he walked round to the boarding house and delivered it in person.

The head is proud of the fact that Millfield isn't overly selective. 'You achieve the best academic results by treating every child as an individual and that's what Millfield has always done,' he says. He believes that everyone has brilliance in them and that 'we can help them to discover it', citing the example of a sixth former who was highly commended in a national entrepreneur competition for his sustainable cycling business and is now being mentored by Dragon's Den star Peter Jones.

Despite his claim that he isn't sporty – 'I'm a dyspraxic classicist, I can't even do a star jump' – he's a keen mountaineer, winter mountain leader, runner and cyclist in his spare time. He's involved with a number of charitable organisations and education charities and although he doesn't teach these days he observes lessons every week. Married to Alison, an academic who works in the museums sector, with two children, both at Millfield Prep.

Says Millfield is 'the most exciting independent school in the UK to run because of its determined modernity, the fact that it isn't shackled by tradition, has the resource to do things and also because we care about public benefit. We give away £6.5 million every year in bursaries.'

Entrance: Two hundred pupils join in year 9, half from Millfield Prep and half from 120 other prep schools all over the world. Between 30 and 50 places are available in year 10. Places are offered on the basis of an interview with a senior member of staff, an online verbal and non-verbal reasoning assessment ('which can't be prepared for') and a reference from current school. Around 100 to 130 join in the sixth form. Those doing A levels require a minimum of 30 points from their best six subjects at GCSE, including English and maths, while those doing BTECs need at least 20 points from their best five subjects. At the moment there are waiting lists for year 9 day pupils and for year 12 boarding.

Exit: Up to a quarter leave after GCSEs (usually because they're going abroad or don't have the required points for the sixth form). University support praised. Ten per cent go to US universities, some with sports scholarships – recently Parsons School of Design in New York; Ivy League Dartmouth College; and Massachusetts University. Rest to eg Bath, Edinburgh, Exeter, Newcastle, Nottingham, Bristol and University of Arts in London. Few gap years these days. Three to Oxbridge in 2021, and three medics.

Latest results: School not releasing 2021 results. In 2019 (the last year when exams took place), 46 per cent 9-7 at GCSE; 30 per cent A*/A at A level (59 per cent A*-B).

Teaching and learning: Millfield is an exciting place to learn and teachers are full of innovation. A previous review said 'academics will never be the point of Millfield' but today's parents disagree with this – and so does the head. 'We have 300 children in a year at A level and 15 per cent get straight As,' he says. He points out that a year 13 Millfield girl was the highest placed female competitor in the world at the International Mathematical Olympiad for the last two years – 'and there are others who challenge her here as well'.

The head is proud of the fact that Millfield isn't overly selective. 'You achieve the best academic results by treating every child as an individual,' he says

The school recently launched its Brilliance Curriculum, which links subjects in an inspiring way. Following a 'big curriculum think' the programme has been rolled out across year 9 but the plan is to introduce it for older students too. For example, history schemes of work have been rewritten so year 9s take modules like Conflict and Cooperation Through Time, where they learn about topics like the Holocaust, the Cold War and 9/11 and the War on Terror, or Disruptors, where they study everything from the suffragettes to Black civil rights in the US. Teachers are keen to show pupils how subjects overlap so they don't study ocean warming in geography until they have learned about specific heat capacity in physics and they don't study The Great Gatsby in English until they have looked at the Great Depression in history. 'We want to make sure the jigsaw fits together,' says the deputy head (academic). 'It's about giving students a bedrock of really good understanding.'

Other initiatives include the Millfield Certificate and the Millfield Diploma, both of which are voluntary but are on offer after summer term exams. Year 11s can take a certificate in a new subject they are considering for A level while year 13s can opt to do a subject they'd like to revisit. The diplomas are designed to bridge the gap between upper sixth and undergraduate level.

During the 2021 lockdown the school came up with the idea of The Ultimate School Trip, a series of live virtual visits to Australia, Japan, Italy and Iceland hosted by the head, deputy head (academic) and assistant head (academic) and culminating in a concert performed by Millfield students around the world (including a year 13 student playing a piece she composed for the guzheng, a traditional Chinese instrument). The event was so successful that 300 other schools signed up too.

The school runs an academic enrichment programme for years 9 to 11, including maths, science, enterprise, languages and debating. Sixth form enrichment programme features lectures and events hosted by academic departments and is designed to inspire curiosity and a spirit of enquiry. Students are invited to join Eureka!, where mixed aged groups meet fortnightly to follow an informal critical thinking programme. There's also a regular biology breakfast, where pupils of all ages give presentations on themes that interest them.

This is unquestionably the place for your budding Olympian. Whatever Millfield does – and it does almost everything – it does exceptionally well

Depending on ability and aptitude, most students take nine GCSEs, including a foreign language and either single sciences or combined science. A plethora of choice – everything from computer science to dance. Sixth formers either take A levels, BTECs or a mix of both. BTECs include art and design, business, enterprise and entrepreneurship, music production and sport. EPQ available. Other qualifications range from Leiths introductory certificate in food and wine to the British Horse Society's complete horsemanship certificate. Small class sizes (maximum of 14), with students setted for maths, English and languages.

When it comes to university and careers, there's a weekly Oxbridge programme overseen by the head of academic extension (a former academic herself), a full-time SAT coordinator, a US universities counsellor, a universities counsellor and a vocational specialist. The school is also an SAT centre, so very geared up for applications to US universities.

High praise for the school's digital learning offer during the pandemic – and for the teaching staff. 'They are engaging and enthusiastic and know the kids,' said a parent. 'I'm very tough on people but I couldn't speak more highly of the school in every sense. I like the fact that it isn't an exam factory. They are teaching my daughter to think and she is developing a very good critical mindset.' Another told us, 'The teachers who are responsible for my son know him really well.'

Learning support and SEN: SEN provision underpins much of Millfield's successes and appeal. Just over a third of students have an identified need, addressed and supported by a team of learning support experts (six full-time staff, three part-time staff, a speech and language therapist, eight peripatetic staff and two visiting educational psychologists). Support is based on literacy, the key to the entire curriculum, but help is available for all manners of barriers to learning including dyscalculia, dyspraxia and organisation skills. The sheer numbers receiving support means a total lack of stigma. Our delightful young guide came straight to the point: 'I am very dyslexic and here I get all the help I need.' Close liaison between teachers, house staff, tutors and learning support staff provides continuity and reassurance.

The arts and extracurricular: Millfield is a busy place and students often discover new talents whilst at the school. A girl who arrived at Millfield in year 9 with a music and art scholarship was swimming for Kenya by the time she left. 'She hadn't realised that she was a particularly good swimmer until she came here but that's what Millfield enables you to do,' says the head. 'Our best musician is a concert standard vocalist and she hadn't sung before she came to us.'

Art and DT happen in a gorgeous spacious block – needless to say, all equipment is bang up to the mark. The nationally known Atkinson Gallery hosts four major exhibitions a year and new work for the sculpture trail is regularly commissioned or purchased. Music is 'astonishingly good'. A parent told us, 'The sport is terrific but music is out of this world.' Exposure to music is part of every Millfieldian's first year, when learning an orchestral instrument is compulsory. Major concerts often take place in Wells Cathedral, where the choir sings regular services.

Drama is popular and well resourced, with several studios as well as the Meyer Theatre. Just one whole-school production a year but a ton of other things, such as a sketch show, a Spanish play, and opportunities to get involved in all goings-on backstage. Applications to drama school are well supported and success rates high. During the pandemic an enterprising sixth former used

Everyone eats together in the magnificent cafeteria – the range of choice is almost bewildering. Menus embrace all sporting diets

his school stage management experience to illuminate Glastonbury Tor in blue after the national clap for health workers and carers every week.

The Millfield Activities Programme (MAP to its friends) offers 100 different pursuits for all students up until year 12 and is intended to offer breadth. French cinema, German card games, skiing race training, silversmithing – it's all there for the taking. Local volunteering opportunities with a range of charities.

Sport: It's difficult to know where to start. This is unquestionably the place for your budding Olympian and the fact that it has produced so many top-flight athletes and sportspeople is no accident. During the 2021 Guinness Six Nations rugby championships the school had a representative in every home nation squad – Mako Vunipola (England), Huw Jones (Scotland), Callum Sheedy (Wales) and Rhys Ruddock (Ireland).

Both provision and facilities abound, from the famous 50-metre Olympic swimming pool with all the wizardry and coaches associated with training future national champions to the acquisition of a Swingulator that enables rowers to train all year round. It is typical of the Millfield seriousness of purpose that, having only introduced rowing a few years ago, investment in a year-round programme including nutrition, video analysis and diverse training has resulted in the school beating many established rowing schools and even universities.

Whatever Millfield does – and it does almost everything – it does exceptionally well, devoting considerable sums, land and care in recruiting top coaches to its unequalled sporting offer. We could wax lyrical about the provision for riders, comprising a polo ground, cross-country course and gallops, or about the fencing salle, but the more usual school sports are outstandingly provided for too. The school's level of commitment is matched by that of the students – for example, a daily 5.40am reveille is quite common for elite swimmers.

Boarding: Three-quarters of students board. Nineteen boarding houses scattered across the 240-acre campus (there are five separate houses for day pupils). Year 9s have their own houses for that vital first year to ensure solid friendships across the year group. After that students have a say in their final house but staff are careful to try to avoid the forming of cliques. Most rooms are twins, singles further up the school, some with ensuite shower rooms; all were clean and functional rather than luxurious and we noted the congenial common room space with pool tables and ping pong, rather than more screens. Pleasant outside space specially designed for barbecues and summer socialising. House staff come in for praise. Parents like the high staff:student ratio, the 15-bed medical centre, complete with physio clinic, and the fact that there's plenty to keep pupils occupied at weekends.

During the week, day students can stay at school till 8.30pm if they want and parents told us there are plenty of opportunities for day and boarding pupils to mix in and out of lessons. Everyone eats together in the magnificent cafeteria, where the range of choice is almost bewildering. Menus embrace all sporting diets. Further flung boarding houses have the occasional dinner in their own dining rooms on special occasions.

Ethos and heritage: For one of the UK's most successful boarding schools, Millfield is really quite a new kid on the block. It was founded in 1935 by Jack Meyer, a former civil servant and accomplished cricketer, following his return to the UK with seven Indian boys, six of them princes. It was originally based in Millfield House (now a boarding house), which was rented from the nearby Clark family of shoe fame. Innovation was the name of the game from then on. Co-ed from 1939, the school put as much emphasis on excellence and opportunity in sport and the arts as on academic success. In 1942, Martin Attlee, son of deputy prime minister Clem Attlee, joined the school in the hope of overcoming 'word-blindness'. The Millfield method proved so successful that Martin Attlee progressed to university and the school gained fame as the first in the country to deal successfully with dyslexic students.

The feel and look of the place is fresh and contemporary – no hallowed portals here. Instead, buildings of all materials, types and function are scattered across the huge site. It's more akin to a small university campus. A culture of entrepreneurship still prevails – a new sixth former received encouragement and plaudits for setting up his own charity club to raise funds for less fortunate youngsters. No overwhelming sense of entitlement, privilege or history among the students either. Those we spoke to expressed in forthright terms their good fortune at being there.

Famous alumni, especially sporting ones, are too numerous to list, but stand-outs are Gareth

Edwards and Chris Robshaw (rugby), Duncan Goodhew, Joanne Atkinson and James Guy (swimming), singer/songwriter Ella Eyre, rower Helen Glover, writer Sophie Dahl and defence secretary Ben Wallace. Thirteen Old Millfieldians competed at Tokyo 2020, including six swimmers; James Guy alone won three medals (two gold).

Pastoral care, inclusivity and discipline: Concerned that nobody gets lost, overlooked or away with too much in this big school, house staffing levels have increased considerably to ensure no one slips through the net. The school hit the headlines during the head's first week in post when two pupils were suspended amid initiation ritual claims. The head went into 'rapid culture change mode' and says nothing like that has happened since. The parents we spoke to concurred. The school has introduced anonymous reporting (via a QR code that children can scan), there's a network of student counsellors and students 'can and do' email the head directly. There's also an equality and inclusion group made up of staff and students.

The general levels of affluence and huge geographical catchment might cause some to suspect illicit contraband like drink and drugs but this passed unmentioned by those we spoke to. Parents seem to be happy with the way in which their concerns are dealt with and students feel that punishments are fair and appropriate. The fact that academic work is commended both for achievement and effort goes down well also. Positive Education and PSHEE (personal, social, health and economic education) programme is designed to equip students with the skills and knowledge to deal with life after school. A dedicated email address exists to report any incidents of bullying.

Pupils and parents: Everyone we spoke to talked of the diversity of families – the much-vaunted Millfield mix. Parents told us the school is 'down to earth', 'isn't snobby' and that the pupils 'aren't all walking round in designer clothes – nothing like that'. There's an extensive outreach programme and parents say the school is firmly rooted in the community. 'They did a fantastic job of supporting the local community during the pandemic,' said one parent. 'We live nearby and they are very engaged and well thought of locally.' The boy:girl ratio is 55:45 and the head is confident it will be 50:50 within five years.

Money matters: In the past Millfield was the most expensive school in the UK but current fees, while substantial, are less than those of Eton. Some activities are chargeable where outside staff are brought in, such as polo, specialist therapy, EAL and individual learning support.

Scholarships (including academic, all-rounder, art, chess, design and innovation, music and sport) awarded to a maximum of 10 per cent of fees. Extensive bursary provision (up to 100 per cent in exceptional circumstances).

The last word: A big, refreshingly innovative school welcoming all talents, Millfield excels at educating talented young sportsmen and women, musicians and artists while achieving admirable academic results. The school's facilities are second to none and the staff are brilliant at helping youngsters to discover their talents, wherever they may lie.

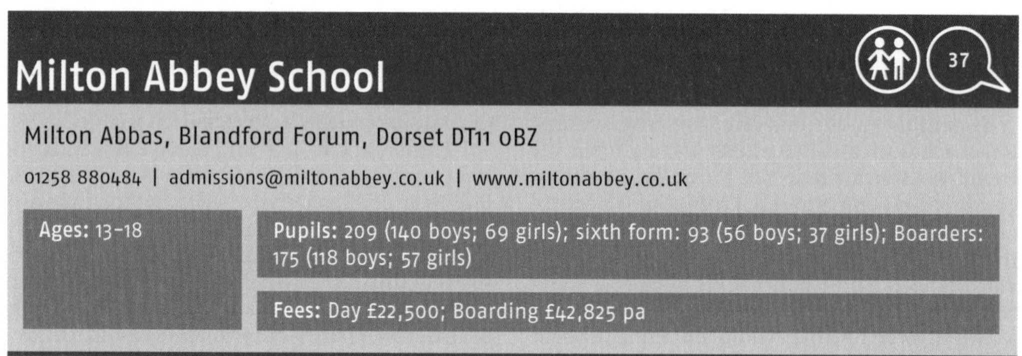

Milton Abbey School

37

Milton Abbas, Blandford Forum, Dorset DT11 0BZ

01258 880484 | admissions@miltonabbey.co.uk | www.miltonabbey.co.uk

Ages: 13–18

Pupils: 209 (140 boys; 69 girls); sixth form: 93 (56 boys; 37 girls); Boarders: 175 (118 boys; 57 girls)

Fees: Day £22,500; Boarding £42,825 pa

Head: Since 2018, Judith Fremont-Barnes MA MEd (early 50s), previously head of Duke of Kent School in Surrey. Her first teaching post at JAGS ('just while I decided what to do with my life') after her English degree at Oxford was the start of a love affair with teaching and a massive span of a career which has included Radley, King Edward VI Southampton and More House, a boys' SpLD school in the home counties – oh and five years in Japan as a university lecturer plus her own master's studies. 'I'm an educational magpie!' she told us from her sumptuous book-lined study, adding that Milton Abbey felt like everything she had ever done, rolled into one. Such 'a patchwork career', as she disparagingly describes it, would seem ideal preparation for heading up Milton Abbey, where there is a tightrope to be trodden between inclusion and excellence, her avowed priorities. Since her arrival, she has overhauled the third form (year 9) curriculum to give students more say over subject choices, and 'challenged lurking', ensuring that boarders have more purposeful things to do in the evenings – and actually do them. Then there's the small matter of Covid… This first female head of Milton Abbey has gone down well with parents and students: her visibility and warmth, her interest in the whole family, her sense of fun ('She fizzes!' one father remarked), the fact that she has not altered the 'feeling and heart of the school' and her ability to give speeches without notes. Mrs Fremont-Barnes (Ma'am to the students) is just the sort of jolly conversationalist you would want to sit next to at dinner – as she says of the youngsters she hopes Milton Abbey turns out.

Milton Abbey has long been ahead of the curve when it comes to vocational learning, having pioneered the offer of BTECs in the independent sector

Married to Gregory, a transplanted American and military historian lecturing at that most British of institutions RMA Sandhurst, she has two grown-up sons, one at university, the other working. The lack of live arts during lockdown has been felt keenly by Mrs Fremont-Barnes, theatre and gallery enthusiast as she is, but it has all meant more time for books (the last Duchess of Devonshire's autobiography, E Lockhart's We were Liars and Nigel Slater's Kitchen Diaries are on her bedside table) and her gorgeous border terrier Ruby whom we were delighted to meet on Zoom.

Entrance: Usual entry points are 13 and 16 but a handful of students start in year 10, often because they didn't settle at their original choice of school. CE requirements have been lifted, but the school describes itself as 'inclusive but selective' and interviews students and their parents in detail to make sure their goals align with the school's and that prospective entrants have the desire to thrive and contribute at the school – head says there is 'no room for passengers'. A positive attitude, willingness to work hard and a good reference from a previous school (plus an ed psych report if applicable) are more valuable than past academic results. At sixth form, hopefuls are judged on individual merit but a GCSE grade 6 is usually required for any subject taken at A level; greater latitude for BTEC courses.

Exit: School loses around 10 per cent of students after GCSEs sometimes for financial reasons – and not because it chucks anyone out if they don't make their GCSE grades: head believes that when a school accepts a youngster at 13 it should stick with them for the duration wherever possible. Courses and destinations post sixth form are wide ranging, with lots of land management and creative courses at institutions old and new. Recently includes students heading off to study modern languages and culture at Durham, architecture at Cardiff, drama at Exeter, product design technology at UWE, fashion marketing at UAL London College of Fashion, event management at Oxford Brookes, computer game design at Staffordshire and football coaching and talent development at UCFB Wembley. Occasional students to Oxbridge, a few to Russell Group universities. School also has strong links with international catering colleges, such as Glion and Les Roches in Switzerland, and several students have headed to these in the past. Others off to take up apprenticeships, military training or set up their own companies.

Latest results: School not releasing results for 2021 – all they will tell us is that both their GCSE pass rate of 92 per cent and their BTEC pass rate of 100 per cent are the same as the previous year. For A levels, there was a 98 per cent pass rate and 86 per cent A*-C.

Teaching and learning: Milton Abbey's strengths lie in its value-added and it has long been ahead of the curve when it comes to vocational learning too, having pioneered the offer of BTECs in the independent sector some 15 years ago – school is proud to have been awarded BTEC school of the year in 2019. Students range from a boy who got three A*s at A level and headed to Oxford to read archaeology and anthropology to those who find formal academic learning 'really difficult' and opt for a more vocational route. The school's strapline is Learn Differently; it prides itself on tailoring an academic programme to suit individual students. Students can and do take level 2 BTECs (latest in digital content production) alongside GCSEs – between seven and nine is the norm with everyone doing English, maths and a science. At sixth form, about a third of students take A levels, a third take a combination of A levels and BTECs and a third take BTECs – students' GCSE profiles are taken into account and subject combinations are based on advice from tutors and teachers, plus subjects which ignite individual passion. Milton Abbey's offer of 12 BTECs is one of the broadest in the independent sector and it's one of the few schools to offer BTECs at extended diploma level – equivalent to three A levels. BTECs aren't an easy option, though – work is continually assessed with a small percentage of the course examined at the end of two years. The school's most recent ISI report commended its approach, saying that 'students, who come with widely different educational backgrounds and needs, often suffering a negative experience of education elsewhere, are enabled to rebuild the foundation of their knowledge and skills, as well as the self-confidence needed to progress.'

Hymn practice is held in the abbey every Friday, when the whole school gathers to sing at the tops of their voices. 'The volume creeps up bit by bit and it sounds wonderful'

Class sizes are small – a huge attraction for the parents we spoke to – and sets are drawn up flexibly, taking pace of learning into account. School library is well stocked and students are encouraged to read or listen to books for pleasure as well as for study. Online provision during the pandemic has been widely praised, not least for its full timetable.

Learning support and SEN: Milton Abbey is resolutely mainstream although about 70 per cent of its students have some kind of identified learning challenge, we were told. Its famed learning development department really is at the heart of the school and its philosophy of 'for every student, in every classroom, for every subject' is not, according to the students we spoke to, mere empty words. A wide range of what the school calls learning differences with associated degrees of severity are skilfully supported, mostly in class. Issues of self-esteem and social skills (curiously, no mention at all of ASD, autism or Asperger's on the website) also sensitively dealt with. Each student is treated as an individual and given personalised strategies and a toolkit – support might include dictation technology, a scribe or visualisation techniques for assignments, but bucketloads of encouragement and emotional support come as standard. 'I don't know what I'd do without it,' one boy said simply. The department is open to all including after hours and the provision so integral to academic life that there were blank faces when we asked about stigma.

The arts and extracurricular: Art is a popular subject and a year 12 boy showed us an astonishing oil painting inspired by renaissance art that he'd worked on over the summer. School puts on a big drama production in its theatre every year and there's a vast array of music. Congregational hymn practice (Congo) is held in the abbey every Friday, when the whole school gathers to sing at the tops of their voices. 'The volume creeps up bit by bit and it sounds wonderful,' a sixth form boy told us.

Entrepreneurship in Residence competition aims to inspire students with ambitions to launch their own business. Top-notch designers like Anya Hindmarch, Johnnie Boden, Cath Kidston and purveyor of delicious oven-ready fish pie Charlie Bigham have all fronted the scheme. Unlike some boarding schools, students do work experience – usually with school alumni (an Inner Temple barrister and a Coutts banker were among those who volunteered recently). Other activities include DofE, farm club and the Ten Tors expedition across Dartmoor. School is a member of Round Square, a worldwide organisation that encourages young people to broaden their horizons and gain greater understanding of the wider world through exchange trips, community work and themed activities within school. All this carried on pretty seamlessly if virtually through lockdown.

Sport: Sport taken seriously but the emphasis is on enjoyment and building a lifelong love of it. Loads on offer therefore – all the usual team games (interestingly, not compulsory for anyone) plus golf on the school's own course (plus indoor simulator), but room for individual sports not necessarily involving a ball too – 'My son lives for his sailing,' one mother told us. Elite scholarship programmes for cycling, golf and football. The fixtures list and results show the school punches above its weight on the sports field. Relatively small number of girls means they all get the chance to represent the school at hockey, netball, lacrosse, tennis and rounders. Mountain biking and road cycling increasingly important (two teams regularly entered for road racing events). Facilities include a 25-metre swimming pool, a squash court, all-weather pitch, sports hall and outdoor pitches galore. Everyone does games on Tuesdays, Thursdays and Saturdays but the sportiest do far more. During lockdown families were included, one father causing hilarity when he joined in a HIIT class from home.

'Round Square Wednesdays' (afternoons) are given over to CCF or community service (including visiting the elderly, taking dogs for walks and cleaning the local church). There are of course all manner of country pursuits, like fishing and a student-run shoot.

It's possible to combine a burgeoning equestrian career with school life. Students can bring their own steeds – many of the keenest riders take a BTEC in equine management and keep their horses at the school stables. They manage the day-to-day care of their horses and can choose to ride instead of playing other sports.

Boarding: Offers full boarding or day places – the school is committed to busy and fulfilling weekends for its boarders (with little or no lurking). Two three-day exeats a term to allow for longer journeys home and international students can stay in school should they wish to. Five boarding houses – three for boys and two for girls. We visited the two newest houses, both wholesome and welcoming, with disabled access and underfloor heating. Students are helped to prepare for life beyond school. One matron told us she'd just taught a boy how to iron his shirt – 'it was important he learned how to do it himself'. Quite so!

Common rooms in the boarding houses are equipped with TVs, out of bounds during the day. There's no mobile phone signal on much of the site but reliable WiFi throughout means students easily can stay in touch with family and friends, social media and so on.

Ethos and heritage: With 76 acres of rolling countryside, it is one of the prettiest schools in the country. You can't fail to be enchanted by the ancient abbey nestling in a wooded Dorset valley, one of the finest Capability Brown landscapes, 15 minutes' drive from Blandford. 'It's deeply rural, but not remote.' We visited on a sunny day but were assured that it looks lovely in the rain and mist too. Founded in 1954, it occupies the converted monastery buildings. The vast abbey belongs to the diocese of Salisbury but the school has full use of it, with services four times a week. It also has its own farm (with pigs, sheep, goats, turkeys and chickens), makes its own honey and grows flowers, fruit and vegetables.

Students eat all their meals in the Abbot's Hall, a grand dining room complete with stags' heads and a huge mural of the school painted by a parent to commemorate the school's 50th anniversary. Pasta, salads, wraps and paninis on offer at lunchtime, as well as hot meals, plus snacks at break, fresh fruit and cake in the afternoons. 'No one goes hungry,' grinned one boy.

Younger girls wear tartan skirts or trousers and blazers, boys tweed jackets, grey trousers and ties. Uniform persists into sixth form, where it's a question of tweed jackets for all, plus grey trousers or skirts; smart dark suits for formal occasions. 'More tweed than Berwick,' as a previous head quipped.

Parents told us they love the fact that their children aren't glued to their phones, tablets and laptops – 'you don't have to have the latest trainers, just a Barbour and wellies!'

Former students include Professor Jonathan Freeman-Attwood, the principal of the Royal Academy of Music, photographer, screenwriter and TV director Harry Hook, restaurateur Oliver Gladwin, sculptor Robert Rattray, documentary maker Anthony Geffen, actor Rupert Evans and Professor Alastair Bruce, royal, religious and constitutional affairs commentator for Sky News.

Pastoral care, inclusivity and discipline: Pastoral care highly praised by students and parents alike. 'The school is small enough to make sure no-one gets lost,' and, according to students, there is always someone to talk to if things go wrong. Tutors see tutees at least twice a week and around the boarding house. The diversity of student population and approach stemming from the Round Square ideal enhances this small country school where, say students, differences are ignored and similarities unite. School's system of rewards and sanctions also takes in behaviour (the policy was rewritten in 2020 with input from the prefects – called 'pilots' here), so acts of kindness and contributions to school life are also recognised. The consequences of wrongdoing are explained and good decisions v bad decisions unpicked, rather than simply punishing the wrongdoer. Good communication with parents – a portal where parents have access to weekly notes on everything from a missed prep to an academic triumph is supplemented by webinars on all manner of subjects, useful for far-flung parents of boarders.

Pupils and parents: Quite a few from London and from as far afield as Northumberland – fair to say that Milton Abbey has a niche national profile. International students make up 30 per cent and come from 23 different countries. Day students tend to live within a 30-minute drive – their day ends at 6pm but there's the option to stay on for supper, activities and prep. School minibus service covers local area but changes depending on demand.

Despite such privileged surroundings, the students we met were delightfully unsnobby and profoundly thankful to be where they were. Sixth formers summed the school's appeal up in a nutshell. 'For the people it's right for, this is the best school in the country,' one boy declared. 'I love it. My sister's at Millfield and her year group is as big as this whole school. Here, everybody knows everybody and the support you get is second to none.' A girl said she liked being 'a big fish in a small pond', while parents told us they love the family atmosphere, plus the fact that their children get loads of country air and aren't glued to their phones, tablets and laptops – plus 'you don't have to have the latest trainers – just a Barbour and wellies!' one London mum told us with a sigh of relief. In fact, parental feedback has been nothing short of gushing – despite our efforts to tease it out, not one had anything critical to say of the school.

Money matters: A range of scholarships at 13+ and 16+ – academic, all-rounder, art, DT, drama, music and increasing numbers for sport. All worth 10 per cent of the fees, although these may be increased 'where financial need is demonstrated'. School also offers means-tested bursaries, plus scholarships for day pupils living in Dorset.

The last word: Milton Abbey's spectacular setting, innovative mix of qualifications and countryside expertise gives students, some of whom may not have thrived elsewhere, a host of opportunities to shine – both inside and outside the classroom. Let us give the last word to the students: an 'exciting, unique, adventurous, proactive' school.

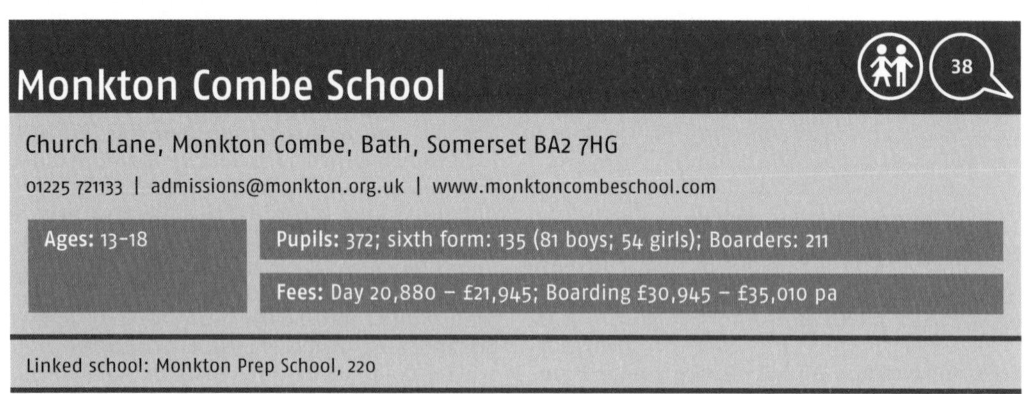

Monkton Combe School

38

Church Lane, Monkton Combe, Bath, Somerset BA2 7HG

01225 721133 | admissions@monkton.org.uk | www.monktoncombeschool.com

Ages: 13–18

Pupils: 372; sixth form: 135 (81 boys; 54 girls); Boarders: 211

Fees: Day 20,880 – £21,945; Boarding £30,945 – £35,010 pa

Linked school: Monkton Prep School, 220

Principal: Since 2016, Christopher Wheeler BA PGCE (40s). The son of a general and educated at the thoroughly pukka institutions of Winchester, Durham (where he read English and philosophy) and Bristol (PGCE), Mr Wheeler started his teaching career at St John's Leatherhead, where he left as head of English to take up several roles (head of English and drama, registrar, deputy head – where did he find the time??) at Peponi School in Kenya. Since then, his working life has ping-ponged between the UK and Kenya, never staying anywhere very long and combining teaching with the usual climb up the managerial ladder with spells as a housemaster at Brighton College, head of its prep St Christopher's Hove and, latterly, principal and CEO of Hillcrest International School in Nairobi. 'Africa gets under your skin,' he says – something he discovered during his gap year in Zimbabwe – but now as a father of three young children, he is conscious of security concerns in Kenya, prompting a move back to the UK.

Very different from his cerebral predecessor, Mr Wheeler has something of the showman about him: one might even say show-off, with the remarkable breaking into a rendition of One Day More (that stirring number from Les Mis) in the middle of his address at Speech Day 2017. (It went viral and the school was shortlisted for a social media award.) But he has taken the place by the horns since his arrival with the introduction of the notion that Emotional Quotient (EQ) is a more helpful measure than IQ, and of the growth mindset, developed by Carol Dweck, where students are encouraged to believe that intelligence is not fixed but malleable, and that improvement and achievement are therefore very much in their own hands. More controversially, he has brought in peer review of staff; several key members of long standing have left.

Improbably boyish for such a senior role, he bowled us over with a flood of exuberant verbiage: future plans include repositioning the entrance to befit 'a proper public school' and creating an equestrian centre on site in a redundant part of the extensive grounds. 'After all, riding, rowing and reeling are life skills, aren't they?' says he (reely??). Students find him approachable and charismatic: he has made a point of weekly lunches with different groups and take-up of his morning dog walks was so popular that he was begged to reinstate them after discontinuing them in the winter. He reckons they provide a brilliant opportunity to chat to teenagers without discomforting eye contact. Parents broadly positive, staff possibly less so. Married to Georgie, who teaches sport and is a keen horsewoman, Mr Wheeler doubles as action man during the holidays, enjoying paragliding and snowboarding in the Alps.

Entrance: At year 9, half come from the prep school by means of Common Entrance, provided hopefuls have come through broad assessment, taken in year 6 and 7. Overseas students are required to sit UKiset and, if English is not their first language, an English placement test. A few students come straight into year 10 by means of the CAT 4 test. For sixth form entry, at least five GCSEs above a C (new grade 4/5) with an average of a B/6 across them all is required from the 30 or so new students who come. Maths and sciences require an A and languages a B. Monkton reserves the right to restrict entry to year 13 if AS results are not up to what the school considers snuff.

Exit: About a quarter leave after GCSEs, possibly for greater freedom and post-16 choices, possibly for financial reasons. After A levels, the vast majority go to university – a range of degree courses at institutions old and new up and down the land: Birmingham, Bristol, Durham, Exeter, Manchester and Southampton all popular. We picked up some dissatisfaction about guidance on university choices from one parent, however. Sometimes a few to Oxbridge (none in 2021) and the odd medic too (two in 2021).

Latest results: In 2021, 70 per cent 9-7 at GCSE; 63 per cent A*/A at A level (83 per cent A*-B). In 2019 (the last year when exams took place), 59 per cent 9-7 at GCSE; 60 per cent A*/A at A level (72 per cent A*-B).

Teaching and learning: Not particularly selective, though the previous principal upped the academic ante. Results more than respectable, especially at sixth form. Two languages taken in year 9, which can include Mandarin and Latin – why no German? – and pupils are strongly encouraged to take a modern language but not obligatory at GCSE. Extra English or maths takes the place of languages for those needing it. Twenty-seven subjects on offer at A level, of which maths is the most popular and DT (3D Design) and Latin the least – but good that the choices of the minority are still honoured. Monkton sixth formers are expected to start and complete three A levels and an EPQ. No IB nor plans to offer it.

Our visit fell during exam season, so much of what we saw was rigorous preparation and revision classes; of the teachers' commitment and dedication including at weekends there can be no doubt whatsoever: 'My daughter's ambition to get to Oxbridge was fully supported by her teachers,' one mother told us, adding that the school had also suited her dyslexic sibling. Small class sizes averaging 15 or so below sixth form and around nine at A level must help. 'Inspiring academic ambition is a key priority,' intones the website, an aspiration underpinned by the importance placed on growth mindset (see above) and the instilling of a good work ethic by one-to-one tutoring; students have some discretion to change if the allocated tutor does not work out. Well-stocked library for all ages with limited computer facilities: the vast majority of students doubtless have their own laptops. Though the bright and modernised classrooms and labs we saw were all suitably equipped with interactive whiteboards etc, we did not sense that this was a school where technology was, refreshingly, the be-all and end-all.

The head of music is widely lauded for his 'desperate enthusiasm', and his innovations like the choir who can't sing (mostly boys) and the choir who won't sing (mostly girls)

Learning support and SEN: Monkton used to be something of a refuge for SEN students, but it no longer has CReSTed status, catering only for minor difficulties these days. The learning support department is right at the centre of the school and staffed by two SpLD teachers. Difficulties in organisation and processing as well as exam technique are also addressed, and all students are assessed on entry. Most of the site has been made accessible for wheelchairs.

The arts and extracurricular: The upgrade to the arts facilities is astonishing. Both art/DT and music have had sensational new (or hugely enhanced) buildings, adding pleasing contemporary touches to quite a traditional campus. Visitors to the art school go straight into the gallery, filled when we saw it with enormous textile print hangings using beetroot juice. Textiles a particular strength and the specialism of the current artist in residence. The art dept is proud of the numbers getting places at Central St Martins.

Huge dark room and industrial printing facilities (busy with a school promotional banner when we were there) complete a superb set-up. As for music – it's just 'Wow!' Jewel in the crown must be the concert hall, quite an intimate space with acoustic design and its requisite mosaic (non-technical term for technical necessity) ceiling, but the more hi-tech musicians are thrilled with the recording facilities all linked to a central studio. It's not just the surroundings though: the head of music is widely lauded for his 'desperate enthusiasm', and his innovations like the choir who can't sing (mostly boys) and the choir who won't sing (mostly girls). The vast majority who can and do play and sing, however, gain merits and distinctions in their music exams; accomplishment a rigorous counterpoint to enjoyment. Monkton has had a long tradition of jazz and the Longmead jazz festival attracts the general public, who can enjoy a smart picnic in a spectacular setting. Drama facilities fall behind those for art and music (on the list for improvement), but commendably less usual fare produced, such as Arabian Nights, Swallows and Amazons and After Mrs Rochester recently. Informal drama evenings give aspiring writers as well as actors a chance to participate. CCF, DofE and Ten Tors of course. More sedate extracurricular choices include baking, knitting and chess. After 35 years of dormancy, their observatory is being refurbished – watch this space for new astronomical society.

Situated in the lusciously green Midford Valley just outside Bath. School has acres of pitches including, according to Wisden, one of the most beautiful cricket grounds in the country

New Wild Monkton programme is based around four areas of development – wellbeing (through exposure to the outdoor environment), learning (increasing knowledge and understanding of the school's natural setting and improving life skills), conservation (stewarding the estate to enhance the landscape, habitats and biodiversity) and sharing (allowing others to benefit from their setting – includes working with a community charity). Activities include clearing the streams, lining a natural path in the woods, tree planting, making bird feeders – and there are more outdoor learning spaces than ever. Every house now has an allotment patch.

Sport: Surely something for everyone here, with acres of pitches including, according to Wisden, one of the most beautiful cricket grounds in the country, with its views of the perfect honey-coloured viaduct carrying the busy A36 out of Bath. Rugby, hockey, netball and tennis (hard and grass courts, plus Astro) all on site, though swimming takes place in the delightful indoor pool at the prep school just up the hill, since Mr Wheeler had the old outdoor pool filled in. Rowing is a big deal here: with a good stretch of river just yards from school and Olympian oarsmen Steve Williams and Rowley Douglas, plus GB single sculler Olivia Caesar among former pupils. Senior rowers benefit from a splendid new boathouse and a (better) stretch of the Avon at Saltford (about 20 minutes away), used also by the university crews of Bath and Bristol. Lots else to do too, though, such as fencing, dance (now available as GCSE) and riding.

Boarding: First and foremost a boarding school, with the late evenings (10pm pick-ups not uncommon for day students and their long-suffering parents) and the only compulsory Saturday morning school in Bath. All-age single-sex houses are presided over by married houseparents, who go out of their way to create a homely and welcoming feel, with their own families and pets. Just as well really, as the boys' accommodation we saw was, shall we say, functional rather than luxurious (but since improved). Girls are reckoned to need more 'talking time' – to house staff, rather than each other – so school has policy of making girls' houses smaller by around 10 students. A new girls' house opened in 2017. Each year group has a kitchen for making snacks, toast and hot drinks; pizza, curry and Chinese food can be ordered in no more than three times a week. What with a good supply of fruit and tuck, no-one appeared to miss nipping into Bath for comestibles. School food okay (not the most inspiring menu we've seen), but 'definitely improved and breakfast is the best meal of the day,' say students. Everyone eats in the beautiful light dining hall, with its huge windows and high ceilings. Five and four-night boarding options exist alongside full boarding, and day students get 10 nights' free boarding thrown in each year.

Ethos and heritage: In the lusciously green Midford Valley just outside the golden city of Bath snakes a narrow lane lined with the honey-coloured buildings of Monkton Combe. The school, founded by the evangelical Revd Pocock in the 1860s, takes up much of this idyllic village, and still attracts many families wanting an overtly Christian setting for their children's education. Although it's definitely not a faith school, the Christian underpinnings exert a palpable influence: 'It's a very kind place,' we kept hearing. 'Even if you're not a fervent Christian, you're not made to feel bad for that, and it teaches you a way to behave,' one mother told us. Mutual respect for personal faith (of whatever kind – a few Muslims also attend Monkton) or a lack of it seems to be the (commendable) watchword. 'There is rigorous questioning in RE lessons, and we're taught all about comparative religions,' students told us, alongside a very active student-led Christian Union.

First and foremost a boarding school, with the late evenings (10pm pick-ups not uncommon for day students and their long-suffering parents) and the only compulsory Saturday morning school in Bath. Everyone eats in the beautiful light dining hall

It struck us as a tolerant place – tolerant of difference and celebrating all kinds of achievement, not just academic. Its relative isolation outside Bath and general feel suggest somewhere where children don't have to conform quite as rigidly, or grow up quite as fast – fondly referred to as the Monkton bubble at the school, disparagingly so by other Bath institutions. School held in great affection by students and parents alike, and much made of the Monkton family, something that persists long beyond schooldays with a very strong alumni network: the school was way ahead of the game in developing links with former students (and doubtless tapping them up for funds).

Notable alumni include Antarctic explorer Eric Marshall (school has his sledge from Shackleton's expedition of 1909), author Bernard Cornwell, musical funny man Richard Stilgoe, former head of MI6 Sir Richard Dearlove and Olympic oarsmen Stephen Williams and Rowley Douglas.

Pastoral care, inclusivity and discipline: Traditionally a great strength and the reason many families choose the school – and an aspect much touted by the principal and registrar. Transition arrangements and welcome praised by parents, and the efforts houseparents and academic staff go to to get acquainted with each new student. 'Pastoral care is integral to creating academic success stories,' we were told; parents describe it as 'stand-out' and 'unparalleled'. This school goes one step further with its recent introduction of Affective Social Tracking: a twice-yearly online questionnaire taken by all students as a gauge of their emotional wellbeing and 'areas for development'. No outright opposition to this from the biddable flock of Monkton students; we heard some cynical mutterings about it being a ridiculous waste of time, but none about what struck us as the slightly sinister intrusion into the adolescent mind with its growing need for independence and privacy. Discipline is not a concept that looms large here: the emphasis is much more on celebrating achievement and intrinsic rewards. Bullying is tackled through the lens of restorative justice, where appropriate. 'The kids feel safe here,' we kept hearing, one mother adding that 'as the students have no fear of cruel ridicule, they are not afraid to make fools of themselves'. Our last review talked of 'unfailing support for the troubled' – and we see no change. But we sense that the principal would not hesitate to get tough with miscreants if required, even if he thought very hard before throwing them out.

Pupils and parents: Kind, thoughtful and nice to each other (we liked the easy way in which students from different year groups interacted over our shared lunch). Some might say unworldly, but that would be to undersell the extent to which these kids think about the profound problems of the world such as hunger and poverty, albeit from a largely Christian perspective. Parents 'do all they can to send their children here,' according to the principal, 'and the car park is full of Land Rovers and Audis, not Maseratis.' Many drive considerable distances to get to school; boarders, unless from overseas, tend to be no more than an hour and a half away. Monkton family dynasties still exist.

Money matters: Fees are comparable with similar schools and the full boarding makes this arguably better value than those schools with a shorter week. Scholarships amount to a maximum of 25 per cent of fees but bursaries go as far as full fees in exceptional cases; special consideration is given to the offspring of clergy or missionaries. For many years the school has cultivated a highly effective development office, so its financial health is, we are sure, rude.

The last word: An appealing option in an idyllic location for those wanting a truly Christian education for their children, or at least one that embraces its values and where they do not have to grow up too fast. Atheists, agnostics, humanists with inquisitive and open minds also welcome. New principal pushing the exceptional pastoral care, while buffing up its boarding houses, social cachet and media profile too.

Monkton Prep School

Combe Down, Bath, Somerset BA2 7ET

01225 831202 | admissions@monktonprep.org.uk | www.monktonprep.com

Ages: 2–13

Pupils: 269 (122 girls; 147 boys); Boarders: 44 full, 5 weekly

Fees: Day £10,221- £17,985; Boarding £22,950 – £25,920 pa

Linked school: Monkton Combe School, 216

Head: Since 2020, after the departure of the previous head following a management restructure, Mrs Catherine Winchcombe (40s), previously head of the pre-prep. A first degree from Cambridge and a master's in educational leadership from Nottingham kick-started a career which has encompassed the state sector and posts in the Middle East. Dynamic, stylish and warm, she fizzes with enthusiasm for all things Monkton. 'Exciting!' was the word she uttered most often during our visit. A consummate professional, whose way of leading the school is tacitly underpinned by her Christian faith, Catherine is married to Simon and has two grown-up daughters.

Entrance: For those entering the prep from age 2 to 7, admission is by visit, informal interview and reference from a current school if there is one. For entry aged 7, 8, 9 and 10, there is a series of short standardised tests in reading, spelling and maths plus a reference from the candidate's current school and, where possible, feedback from the staff involved in the taster day. For those entering aged 11 to 13, standardised assessment involving reasoning, maths and English, a reference from the candidate's current school and an interview where possible.

To enter the senior school, children are invited to take part in a 'fun' assessment day, assessing pupils in seven areas: creativity, collaboration, confidence, craftsmanship, communication, commitment and curiosity.

Exit: Was, until recently, the only prep school in the area to prepare children for Common Entrance at 13+. But even this school has ditched it now, offering the Pre-Senior Baccalaureate instead. A few leave at 11 to join local day schools, state and independent; a significant majority of the rest (82 per cent of all students in 2021) to Monkton senior school, others mostly to day and boarding schools in Bath and the south west, including Millfield, Canford and the Sherborne schools. Generally a good clutch of various scholarships, especially to Monkton.

Our view: Founded in 1888 and beautifully positioned on top of a hill in Combe Down (a desirable villagey part of Bath) with stunning views over rolling countryside from the back of the site, Monkton's buildings range from handsome to utilitarian – but the acres of green space surrounding them (mostly turned over to rugby or cricket pitches or an athletics track in the summer, plus Astro) make up for any aesthetic failings. The lower prep school building was purpose-built in 2016, with safe enclosed play areas and delightful light classrooms where lots of phonics are dinned into happy children by means of Read, Write, Inc, and where they are praised for what they can do, and encouraged to adopt the growth mindset philosophy of 'I can't do this – yet'. Cross-curricular learning here too, and a healthy attitude to risk: tiny children were chopping up apples with sharp knives and close supervision when we visited in late summer. Average class size 16, and children benefit from specialist teachers from the prep school for sport, French and music.

For the first years in the prep, children are taught mostly in their own classrooms, but subject teachers feature from year 6; a mixture of streaming and setting is used for differentiation. Common Entrance (scholarship for the most academic) syllabus proper starts in year 6: those exams are set in English, maths, the sciences and languages (French and Latin; Greek for the brightest sparks) with extended projects in the humanities. Parents generally reckon that just enough pressure – 'but not to the point of freaking them out,' as one mother put it – is applied to ensure entry to the senior school of choice, but some felt children could be stretched more, with greater focus on getting them into better known public schools outside the south west. Monkton is the only Bath school to retain Saturday school from year 5; this time is now used for the study of themes beyond the narrow CE syllabus, such as migration and the concept of a just war. Masterclass Saturdays laid on three times a year: the principal of the senior school might teach Chaucer, or kids might learn to play the ukulele in a morning.

Children with SEN are looked after by the learning support team, and four categories of need are clearly set out in the school's policy, including social and emotional aspects alongside mild to moderate SpLD. The behaviour management policy acknowledges that 'some pupils on our SEN register find [shouting out, fiddling, making silly noises for example] very difficult not to do' and offers ideas to help manage them in the classroom. Some children arrive with identified needs, others are diagnosed while at the school. Parents greatly value the inclusive approach taken by the school as a result of its overt Christian ethos: 'We believe each individual is uniquely created by God and has a distinct contribution to make to our community.' One mother told us how the family had moved 200 miles to go to Monkton and that the school had been 'unequivocally welcoming' to her child with a complex chronic long term health condition. A few children are turned away at the enquiry stage if the school genuinely feels it cannot meet their needs.

Cross-country running a Monkton perennial and it was wonderful to see stumbling stragglers cheered home as warmly as the loping long-distance runners

Masses on offer outside the classroom too, for 'the guiding principle of a Monkton education – the development of character'. Extensive outdoor space – not just for sport, but also for play – is complemented by a super indoor pool, dance studio and rather tired sports hall, in line for a facelift. Usual sports on offer but these days, boys can (and do) opt out of rugby. Sports teaching widely praised and even the tiniest in the pre-prep benefit. Minor grumbles from competitive parents about small schools having to field the sporting talent available to them – and being (on occasion) thrashed by bigger ones. Cross-country running a Monkton perennial, and it was wonderful to see any stumbling stragglers cheered home as warmly as the loping long-distance runners. Monkton runners is open to anyone, and enthusiastically led by the joint head of boarding. Drama traditionally a strength too, with several productions grouped by age in a year: recent offerings include A Midsummer Night's Dream – not watered down, either – and Joseph and the Amazing Technicolor Dreamcoat. Much enjoyment and silverware gained at LAMDA and the Mid-Somerset Festival. Music has had a shot in the arm with the arrival of a new head of music, teaching 'Oats and beans and barley grow' to the youngest children to the accompaniment of her guitar when we saw her in the pre-prep's charming assembly hall with its glass lantern. Over a third of pupils learn an instrument individually, but class music and singing are timetabled. Musical highpoints of the year include hotly contested house music, a joint concert with the senior school and the carol service in Bath Abbey. Art has a proper messy room, where work of considerable talent is produced, and then hung around the walls of the school. DT is taught by an infectious dynamo, whose projects include a Greenpower car – which has been round the famed racetrack at nearby Castle Combe.

Unapologetically Christian in its foundation and prevailing ethos with all chapel Bible-led, Monkton's faith is a living one, according to the head, who explained it in terms of 'doing what we talk about in chapel. You can't inflict faith on people.' Whether believers, churchgoers or not, everyone we spoke to profoundly appreciated the school's values, and often chose the school for them. 'Christian values are not just a strapline,' said one mother. 'Every child really is a unique blessing.' And looked after as such: two parents told us how their child 'walked taller since coming to Monkton and was the best version of [him/herself]'. Had they been primed? We suspect not. Even when things go wrong, the school seems to handle it well, with the emphasis on remedy and explanation rather than punishment, though detentions are given for repeat offences.

Boarding: Although boarders are in a minority, Monkton is run as a boarding community with its long days, Saturday school and spare beds. Hatton House occupies the two upper floors (one for girls, the other for boys) of the main building, all presided over by the delightful and flamboyantly clad houseparents and team, not forgetting Spotto the whippet. Light dorms with homely touches and plenty of space to pin up photos and posters alongside clean, functional bathrooms and cosy communal spaces make it comfortable rather than luxurious, but there's a tangible warmth coming from all the staff: it's a very happy and united ship. Children are kept busy with activities in the evening and a weekly pancake night in the houseparents' kitchen. Mobile phone use kept to a minimum and as a means of keeping in touch rather than mindless YouTubing or Instagram; all devices are handed in to charge overnight.

The last word: Monkton has particular appeal in Bath and beyond to those seeking an education based as much on Christian values and opportunities as on academics, but also to those wanting an 'old school' prep school, to take their offspring through Common Entrance to the public school of their choice, likely as not Monkton senior. Many families make great sacrifices to send their children, and fortunately find little to complain about. 'If I had beef, I'd tell you,' affirmed one mother; we didn't doubt it.

Mount Kelly

Parkwood Road, Tavistock, Devon PL19 0HZ

01822 813193 | admissions@mountkelly.com | www.mountkelly.com

Ages: 13–18

Pupils: 350; sixth form: 141 (56 girls); Boarders: 195 full, 18 weekly

Fees: Day £18,540, Boarding £32,970 pa

Linked school: Mount Kelly Prep, 227

Head master and principal of Mount Kelly Foundation: Since April 2019, Guy Ayling MA (late 40s). A historian (master's in medieval history from St Andrews), he was previously head of Llandovery College in Wales and before that spent 15 years at Sedbergh, where he was housemaster and deputy head. A keen rugby, cricket and hockey player, he captained the St Andrews 1st XV and played for Scottish Universities.

Upbeat, easygoing and emotionally intelligent – just the kind of chap about whom you'd think, 'Thank goodness for that' if seated next to him at dinner party full of strangers. Reflective, but also candid (was educated at Rugby during the Thatcherite 80s – 'I loved school but it took me 10 years to get over some of the views we were taught') and takes constructive criticism on the chin (why oh why, we asked, didn't he have any of the students' artwork on his walls when it's so bloomin' good – 'very good point,' he responded, making mental note). 'Hilarious', 'engaging' and 'down to earth – just what we wanted for our unpretentious school', say parents, while students told us he 'singles us out when we do well – makes you feel really valued'. Managed, in true Harry Potter style (or perhaps he just has a very fast car), to get to three different matches many miles apart on the Saturday afternoon before we visited – genuinely appreciated by students. Very much a teacher at heart (still takes history classes) yet also known for shrewd delegating skills, it's apparent that he still gets a real kick out of seeing students blossom, reeling off plenty of (non-identifying) examples, all accompanied by a beaming smile. In short, doesn't take himself too seriously, but couldn't take what he does more seriously – a winning combo for a head, if ever we saw one.

Lives on site with wife Heather, who works as TA at the prep, and their three sons, all at the school. Spends spare time 'dragging them around places of historical interest' – from WWII bunkers to castles and abbeys in Brittany, where they regularly holiday ('maybe they'll appreciate it in the long run, maybe they won't!') and either watching them play, or taking them to watch, sport (had just taken his youngest to his first football match when we visited – 'absolutely loved it, reckon that's going to be our new thing'). Shares office with his black lab, Elvis.

Entrance: Between 80 and 85 per cent of the prep move up to Mount Kelly at 13+, which makes up three-quarters of the year 9 intake, with the rest coming from all over including local day, and UK and international boarders. School looks for the bright-eyed and bushy-tailed with a have-a-go approach – that goes as much for the rugby players as potential Nobel Prize winners. Around 20 newbies enter sixth form – requirement is five grade 6s or above at GCSE with some subject specific criteria for subjects including maths and biology.

Exit: Vast majority go on to the sixth form, the rest tend to head off to local colleges. Nearly all sixth form leavers to university, around a third to Russell Group. Edinburgh, Durham, Bristol, Exeter, Cardiff, Plymouth and Southampton all popular. One to Oxbridge in 2021, and three overseas (USA, Lithuania and Netherlands). Courses wide ranging, from medics (one in 2021) and law to sports science and humanities.

Latest results: In 2021, 47 per cent 9-7 at GCSE; 52 per cent A*/A at A level (73 per cent A*-B). In 2019 (the last year when exams took place), 41 per cent 9-7 at GCSE; 31 per cent A*/A (54 per cent A*-B).

Teaching and learning: A level results commendable, especially for a school which is not academically selective, with maths impressive at all levels. While in the past parents may have felt the urge to go further afield for 'a real academic education', school is now seeing growing numbers swayed by these improving outcomes and growing evidence that teaching and learning are taking centre stage. Interestingly, there's an increasingly strong top end among the otherwise broad church – perhaps precisely because word is spreading. 'Of course we offer a holistic education, but let's face it, no parent ever said, "It's a shame Jonny failed his A levels but hey, at least he played in the 1st XV," because ultimately priorities are always the other way round,' says head.

'Of course we offer a holistic education, but let's face it, no parent ever said, "It's a shame Jonny failed his A levels but hey, at least he played in the 1st XV,"' says head

'There's no doubt they've upped the ante academically – you feel it at every turn,' was a typical parent comment. School attributes improvement to recruitment of increasingly high calibre staff, sharing of good practice, unity of expectation with prep and recent timetable changes to get 'as much juice out of the lemon when it comes to contact time'. Parents credit small class sizes (sometimes two or even one at A level) and 'lots of rigorous monitoring, with great half termly reports' – no stock phrases here. Definitely not a frenetic school, though (with the possible exception of exam time), with students describing it as 'generally pretty relaxed' but with a 'give it a go attitude – failure is seen as part of learning'. 'My children are pushed but not overly so – you never feel there's undue pressure or that students are working themselves into the ground,' said a parent. But one parent felt there should be 'more advice on how to support your child's learning'.

Setting in maths, English and science from year 9. French or Spanish from year 9, with around three quarters taking a modern language at GCSE. Most take nine GCSEs – geography and DT currently popular, with science, maths, DT and art the shining stars on results day. At A level (22 on offer), three is the norm and a dozen or so do EPQ – PE, art, DT, geography, French get best results, with economics and business studies currently popular (watch this space for a BTEC in business studies, set to join the existing BTEC in sport – head is a big fan of them as 'they broaden accessibility to tertiary education'). In the lessons we observed there was full-on engagement from every student, from a debate on 'what is hierarchy?' in business studies to studying rivers in geography.

Learning support and SEN: Does excellent job of walking the tightrope of being inclusive of mild to moderate SEN and knowing its limits. Lovely warm approach, report families, and lots of willingness to work with parents to find funding for additional support. We heard how there is a personalised approach, plus well thought-of SENCo, but common sense and honesty prevail if they think they'll be out of their depth or disrupt other learners. 'They helped us get all the assessments we needed, as well as bringing in all the right staff from tutor to mentor, and assistance like language modification – they're absolutely on it, with all the most up to date evidence-based support and they communicate with you well,' raved one parent.

The arts and extracurricular: Since the college snuggles into a valley on the edge of Dartmoor, outdoorsiness is in these kids' DNA with wide take-up for the myriad of extracurricular activity on offer including DofE, CCF, the 125-mile canoe marathon from Devizes to Westminster and the Ten Tors expedition, as well as training in shooting and mountaineering, among others. The Shackleton Programme offers more than glorified field trips – youngsters are simply plonked in the middle of nowhere and stay in bunkhouses to learn resilience, teamwork etc (supervised, of course). Overseas trips also plentiful, while for those preferring to stay closer to home, there are clubs in everything from gardening to astronomy, as well as some great opportunities for older pupils to volunteer down at the prep.

School is old-fashioned enough to insist on blazers with ribbons and badges festooned all over athletic gods and goddesses, but we noticed musicians, artists, thespians and prefects are equally decorated. Four choirs and a 20-piece (not bad for a school this size) orchestra regularly perform and compete (from weekly assemblies to BBC level) and there are all the usual ensembles. One student told of how she decided she wanted to learn the baritone saxophone and the school

Monkton Combe School

found her an instrument and a teacher, both in record time.

Two annual whole-school drama productions – one foot-tapping, clap-along-to musical and something a little more highbrow or at least all-talking. Plenty of lighting and costume opportunities and we met one student who was proud to be co-directing a play.

Shackleton Programme offers more than glorified field trips – youngsters are plonked in the middle of nowhere and stay in bunkhouses to learn resilience, teamwork etc

Head of art widely recognised for drawing out artistic talent among those who least expect it and the department is reported as being a particular haven for some who find academic subjects more challenging. We loved it – jazz playing softly in the background with a labyrinth of rooms including special sixth form hideaway attic complete with graffitied beams and a richness of textures across every piece of work. You could while away hours admiring the creative painting (especially portraits), installations, pottery and more. DT department also well-equipped with adjoining ICT room to encourage more digitised endeavours. Regular trips to eg St Ives.

Sport: Swimming is definitely a Mount Kelly superpower. Results are pretty much neck and neck with mighty Millfield and on current trajectory Mount Kelly is well on its way to becoming the leading school in the country, with its swimmers, who train in the school's 50-metre Olympic-standard pool, regularly representing the UK either nationally or internationally. Whereas once the keenest swimmers could use training as an excuse to get out of the likes of chapel, the school now bills itself as a school that does swimming rather than a swimming school with a few lessons attached – great if your ambitious water-obsessed child wants a more academic plan B. Parents say the comprehensive training programme is run by 'second to none' coaches and is considerably less stressful and a lot cheaper than the constant travel, early mornings and compromises with school that many young swimmers have to make. But one parent warned how the swimming families 'feel like quite a separate entity'.

Good news for non-swimmers is that all this ambition seems to be seeping sideways, with the rest of the sports department also on the up. Students spoke excitedly about hockey (boys and girls do well, with U16 girls currently regional finalists), netball ('We were just one goal away from reaching the London finals,' said a student) and cricket (the core sports), plus rugby (does well on regional basis), netball, triathlon and more. Struck us as all quite gendered, but we were assured girls' rugby and cricket are soon to be introduced, plus the school has recently introduced a girls' football academy with the Chelsea Foundation. No shortage of pitches and grounds – superbly managed in both prep and college areas, including two Astros smack in the middle of both; school also uses the prep's vast sports hall. Sailing now popular, thanks to school's recent acquisition of Olga the boat.

Boarding: Two-thirds board. Around a quarter are international and around a third are swimmers from England and abroad. Flexi boarding is very flexi. Each house is managed by housemasters and housemistresses with a team of tutors drawn from academic staff as well as non-teaching matrons. Full medical service on hand.

Brace yourself for the accommodation – it is home to some of the scruffiest sofas and the messiest bedrooms we've seen, not to mention the spit and sawdust games rooms (chipped paintwork, cupboards falling off etc) and the dirty plates piled high in the hallway during our visit. But students don't seem to notice or care and ditto for parents – why bother yourself with décor when most of the fun is to be had outside anyway?

One parent describes 'a big culture shock from the prep, with reins suddenly released and lots of independence – all for the good, but just takes a bit of getting used to'. Activities range from basketball to beach surfing and from shopping in Exeter to paintballing (a favourite). Students commented on the usefulness of having teachers among the boarding staff – 'meant I got to run through some chemistry homework I was stuck on with a one to one session,' said one.

School is planning to change current boarding system (of mixed-gender houses for younger years and mix of day and boarders in each house) in favour of two boys' and two girls' boarding houses and a boys' day house and a girls' day house. Head feels that staying in the same house from year 9 all the way up will instil more house loyalty and means youngsters have the same house staff all the way through. It's also hoped that this will lead to more integration between different year groups – some students feel there currently isn't enough.

Ethos and heritage: In the back of beyond. At least, that's how it feels when you drive for mile upon mile across the magnificent moors, though in fact it is on the edge of Dartmoor and not too far from the pretty town of Tavistock. The buildings have historical connections with the Duke of Bedford who donated the land for the college, founded in 1877 by an Admiral Kelly. In 2014, it joined forces with Kelly Prep (now used to home teachers) and Mount House (now home to the joint prep) to become the Mount Kelly Foundation – a merger that older students occasionally refer to but which for the younger ones must seem like ancient history as the school cultivates its own identity. Very naturally co-ed, such has been the case for 40+ years, and although we wondered how the girls felt about their impossibly long tartan skirts (which actually require lifting to walk up stairs), you'll hear no complaints, not least because as one girl confided, 'Some of us wear leggings or even PJ bottoms under them – so comfy and warm.'

Swimming is definitely a Mount Kelly superpower. Swimmers train in the school's 50-metre Olympic standard pool, and regularly represent the UK in national and international competitions

Despite gentle lawns and lush green pitches, it's quite a craggy looking place, all Gothic arches, dark wood and stone staircases, echoing corridors and lots of pointy bits. Academic mustiness, however, is banished by skilfully placed features of interest, pictures, honours and information about the school's past and the pupils' futures. The handsome library is presided over by enthusiastic librarian; the dusty looking (actually it isn't) chapel still exudes an odour of past sanctity and is used on Mondays and Fridays. All in all, you get the feeling the current programme of refurbishment may never end, such is the need for a lick of paint (or more) in at least some part of every building – and yet the children and staff have a really contagious affection for it all and the sense of space is hard to beat. Science block, gymnasium and boarding next on head's refurb wish list – but a plea from us: keep all the pet snakes, scorpions, frogs and geckos that surround the biology lab (a student told of how the perfectly formed shed skin of a tarantula was left on the desk of one teacher by another – 'you should have seen her face, but she took it in good humour in the end!').

Plenty of outside speakers. Food popular – head chef jumped ship from a local chi-chi hotel (and is so well thought of that he gets a whole page all to himself in the prospectus). We enjoyed a delicious chickpea curry on a 'meat free Monday' (though were puzzled to find ham and chicken on the salad bar). Overall Mount Kelly vibe is friendly and relaxed – this is a place where youngsters don't have to grow up before their time, yet it doesn't feel like a bubble.

Alumni include Dawn Airey, CEO at Getty Images (former Yahoo executive and chairman of Channel 5); Lord Owen, former Foreign Secretary and Leader of the SDP; novelist and former ITN correspondent Gerald Seymour; author Peter Hitchens and his journalist brother Christopher; actor Adrian Lukis; former England rugby captain Philip de Glanville.

Pastoral care, inclusivity and discipline: Not strict exactly, but all the usual common sense school rules prevail. Around 12 temporary suspensions a year; head had just given them to six boys for 'being a pain in lessons' – he doubts he'll have any trouble from the rest of the year group, currently identifiable by their rabbit in headlight expressions. Bullying always a possibility, report students, parents and staff (quite right too – always naïve to think otherwise), but all feel school is both proactive and protecting so it's rare and nipped in the bud when it does rear its ugly head. There's a good rapport between staff and students – comfortable enough for a little friendly banter here and there and students said they feel they can talk to most of them about any concerns, including the head.

Pupils and parents: Parents range from the occasional landed gentry to local farmers; majority from the professional classes, many dual income. A friendly and (mainly) grounded lot, from what we could gather – all see the school an aspirational option that bridges the gap between being a good local option for the west country and a more traditional public school. Students we met were on the shy side – not a whiff of arrogance (and we searched high and low).

Money matters: Scholarships and bursaries are available, including for incoming sixth formers. Forces families may receive 10 per cent discount – don't be afraid to ask.

The last word: Mount Kelly offers some of the best aspects of traditional private schooling but is not weighed down by history or excessive grandeur. A nimble school that's heading towards the premier league unhampered (thank goodness) by snobbery and over-sophistication. Just what the west country needs.

Mount Kelly Prep

Mount Tavy Road, Tavistock, Devon PL19 9JL

01822 813193 | admissions@mountkelly.com | www.mountkelly.com/prep

Ages: 3-13

Pupils: 250; **Boarders:** 21 full, 11 weekly

Fees: Day £7,620 to £14,880. Boarding £20,460 to £25,860 pa

Linked school: Mount Kelly, 222

Head of prep: Since 2016, Dominic Floyd BA PGCE (40s). Previously assistant head at Hazlegrove. Geography degree and PGCE from London University; taught geography at Cothill House and Westminster Under School; director of studies and deputy head at Polwhele House; head of Ashdown House. As with so many heads with teaching in the blood (his father and brother became heads), he did his utmost to find a different career – 'but still it was the calling'.

We first encountered him discussing the pros and cons of HS2 with a bunch of year 8s in the assembly hall, part of his popular ethics classes which he teaches in addition to English 'and a tiny bit of geography'. Pre-prep gets a slice of the pie too since he loves to attend their show and tell sessions (last time he brought a Star Wars figurine of Yoda). Though how he tears himself away from his large oak-panelled study, we are not sure – its view is among the finest we've seen: picture postcard rolling hills with the attractive buildings of Tavistock on the right in the distance. Tall, dapper and oozing merriment, he is – according to parents – 'excellent at getting down to the children's level', 'knows them all by name' and 'has a genuinely open door policy'. 'He's awesome,' lauded one – 'a very gregarious, substantive individual with good vision, good ethics and a great speaker.' 'His lessons lead to some great discussions and that ethos of curiosity, inspiration and enthusiasm really spills down,' voiced another. Thumbs up from kids too, who say 'he plays football with us' and 'can be really fun and silly'.

Lives on site with wife Maria (an artist and illustrator who teaches EAL, among other school duties) and their three young children (two at the school; other one wanted to stay at Bryanston). Six other staff families also live here which adds to the family atmosphere. Wide range of interests includes hiking, tennis, squash, skiing and gardening. Micro-adventures also beckon – these short snappy bursts of travel 'get me sleeping out under the stars and relying on nothing more than the bivvy bag on my back'.

Entrance: Wide ability range – tests in English and maths more for benchmarking than selection. Most entrants attend a taster day in February prior to admission. After nursery the largest intake is at year 7, growing from a trickle in years 4 and 5 and then a few more in year 8 who see it is a good preparation for the college. No waiting lists. Boarding from year 3. A few means-tested bursaries available.

Exit: Few leave at 11+, despite the two excellent grammars in Plymouth. Rest are prepared for 13+ transfer to the college at Mount Kelly (where 80-85 per cent head off) or elsewhere (mainly Sherborne, Bryanston, Sherborne Girls and Marlborough).

Our view: On the glorious winter's day we visited, we were greeted at the front door of the elegantly proportioned, stone-built Georgian manor house by chickens – orange feathers vibrant against the bright blue sky and squawking excitedly, perhaps in appreciation of their gorgeous surroundings. Bordering Dartmoor National Park, the location of this school could hardly be more idyllic with grounds including a beautiful lake (great for science), rolling hills (ideal for playing) and even a river (handy for fishing).

The result of a 2014 merger between Kelly Prep and Mount House, now firmly established with its own identity, the school's original foundations date back to 1877. The manor house has, as you'd expect, had a number of additions since then – some historic; others more purpose-built. The hall, accessed rather curiously through an office rather than its lovely glass doors, is huge, with the head's study on one side and school dining hall complete with Cath Kidston spotty tablecloths on the other. This leads to a large conservatory with comfy sofas, in use even in colder months (we don't envy those heating bills). Upstairs, things get even cosier with sink-into carpets and homely boys' and girls' dorms in separate areas dotted along the wide corridors, plus sick bay.

Most of the classrooms are an extension of the main building – all well-equipped with attractive displays. Other buildings cluster behind the main house – highlights include the original stables cleverly converted into, among other facilities, a lovely art studio; vast sports hall is shared with the seniors (includes two squash courts) and there are two large science labs; and a roomy music centre – impressive for a school this size. For pre-prep, there's purpose built, low level accommodation where, if future career aspirations are realised, we'll have no shortage of vets, cricket players, motorbike riders or tooth fairies. Outdoor play area could perhaps be more inspiring, as could the library which is spacious but rather messy (and smelt damp).

Bordering Dartmoor National Park, the location of this school could hardly be more idyllic with grounds including a beautiful lake, rolling hills and even a river

Academically on the up, say parents – 'It needs to be to keep up with the college, which has also become more academic,' said one. A varied curriculum is taught in average class sizes of 14-16 with plenty of opportunity for teachers (whom parents describe as 'endlessly kind') to go off piste and generate individual enthusiasm. Classes we sat in on ranged from interactive (year 5s learning about metres squared with carpet shop role play) to heads down (ambitious spelling test for year 4 with beautifully neat handwriting wherever we looked). French from nursery and Spanish from year 7, although one parent felt, 'Languages are not as robust and broad as they could be – maybe an opportunity for greater links with the college?' Setting in maths and science from year 6. Fewer specialist teachers than other preps, but school's philosophy is that 'the more children see teachers do different things the better'. SEN is downplayed – the help is there, but it's mainly classroom based and propped up by booster classes which some non-SEN children also attend. 'We don't make a big fuss and we don't take, for example, dyslexic children out of English classes as it can double up the stress,' says head. New AI-based report system a hit with parents. All teachers are expected to run at least two clubs – what luck there are so many (not so hidden) talents with, for example a science teacher who doubles as a great pudding chef and an English teacher with a flair for interior design.

School signs up to the Learning Outside the Classroom programme, with every year group doing something residential, beginning with year 3s camping out at night right up to a week away in the Brecons for year 8s (school owns a remote bunkhouse). From bog runs to jumping off cliffs, it's all about getting these already outdoorsy kids out of their comfort zones – no wonder that even teachers get terrified by some of the activities. Climate change is a biggie here (and a personal passion of the head's) so school now has meat-free Mondays, a ban on single-use plastic and a plethora of strategies such as Tidy Tavy, Beach Guardian scheme and a weekly BAFTA-type award for anyone making a difference (most recent winners were three year 3 girls who did an unprompted litter-picking session). Astrosmurf deserves a mention – the children are very proud of creating and launching this latex balloon with camera into space and there are some fabulous photos as a result.

All pupils get out to do something physical every day, whether it's PE, swimming in the Olympic-size 50m pool in the college or playing a fixture. Every substitute plays, say parents – 'they're not there just to make up the numbers on the timesheet'. School had just had good rugby and netball seasons when we visited, all helped by the new blood in the sports department. Individual successes include the children who represent Devon in cricket and hockey. Plus, of course, those on the elite swimming programme, which attracts top-level swimmers from around the world who buy into the ambitious and comprehensive coaching programme. 'The package is kept deliberately broad so they don't burn out by specialising too young,' claims school, although one parent said some of these families have 'huge aspirations, and I mean huge' – indeed, for many, it fulfils their Olympic dreams.

Twice-weekly art and from year 8, DT at the college. We sneaked a peek in the attic above the art room – a treasure chest of everything from woodwork to ceramics to paintings that boarders haven't yet had a chance to take home. In the art room itself, year 6s were having a whale of a time cutting out pizza and doughnut-shaped textiles ready to make food-themed cushions for a pop art display. Falmouth Art School grads often help out.

Music teacher, say children, is 'best in world' – and with a dedicated band practice room where 100 children belong to a whopping 15 bands (which all perform together annually), she could not be accused of failing to keep things modern (although no need for the traditionalists to panic as there's a 'proper' church choir which contributes to festivals and a full orchestra, both popular). 'Music is not something I thought my son would be good at, but it turns out he is,' said a parent, not untypically. Around half learn an instrument – harp, oboe and French horn in addition to more trad options. 'Drama could do with a bit of work – they don't even have a dedicated staff member to drive it,' grumbled one parent. Every year group puts on a performance of some kind or another, but nothing across the whole school.

High expectations rather than strict discipline. No detention system, but pupils are clear about the big no-nos and reprimands are mainly restorative. Social graces including a firm handshake and looking adults in the eye are consciously driven, although one parent felt 'they are not as hot on manners as they once were'. Tutor system considered important for what parents say is 'an excellent pastoral system'. The new bridge across the Tavy has (quite literally) improved links with the senior school but while pupils told us of seniors regularly coming over to the prep site, we'd like to have heard of more little footsteps heading the other way. Food popular and tasty.

Parents are as unpretentious as the school – clientele being an eclectic mix of farmers, hoteliers, medics from Derriford Hospital and other professionals.

Boarding: Homely dorms catering for between four and 11 are clean, fresh, tidy-ish (one parent quite liked that there were clothes on the floor when she first visited – 'shows it really is like at home') and nicely personalised with teddies, pictures and own duvet sets.

Around 40 board (though it feels more), a quarter of whom are international – currently Chinese and Spanish dominate, plus a few Forces families. The swimmers come from both UK and overseas. Half are full boarders, the rest weekly or flexi. No cliques, with even the youngest getting scooped up by the older ones into the family-like atmosphere. Prep finishes at 7pm for older pupils (younger ones have clubs) when these pupils use every inch of the lovely hidey-holes around the main school, including the bright red multilingual telephone box, although most spill out into grounds if weather and daylight permit. The six couples/families living on site rotate weekend duties, when pupils eat at the main school – 'great as makes the transition easier,' reckons parent – and Sundays are usually spent out and about, eg sailing from Plymouth, surfing at Polzeath, Eden Project, along with lower-key activities such as pizza making and bowling. Parents praise the 'size of the boarding house' and say it's 'home from home'. 'They are given very little free time – fabulous as it keeps them out of mischief,' says one, while another was pleased 'they take parents' comments on board'. One told us, 'Sometimes I've come down to take my children out on a non-exeat weekend and they don't want to leave – difficult to swallow as a parent but living proof of how much they enjoy it.'

Money matters: Bursaries advertised locally when available (two available for whole school). Individual music and learning support incur an additional cost, likewise some activities.

The last word: We found pupils slightly on the reserved side in adult company but their joie de vivre was apparent when watching from more of a distance. 'In the summer term, after school, you see them running around the grounds and jumping in the pool and when they come home they've always got something to tell you about the exciting stuff they've learned – what more can you ask for?' said a parent.

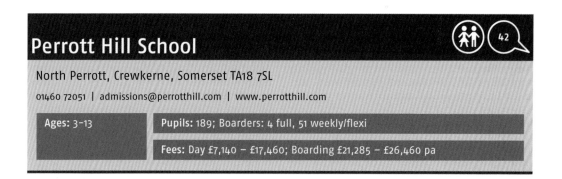

Perrott Hill School

42

North Perrott, Crewkerne, Somerset TA18 7SL

01460 72051 | admissions@perrotthill.com | www.perrotthill.com

Ages: 3-13

Pupils: 189; Boarders: 4 full, 51 weekly/flexi

Fees: Day £7,140 – £17,460; Boarding £21,285 – £26,460 pa

Headmaster: Since 2018, Alex McCullough BA (40s), previously head of Polwhele House, a prep school near Truro. Educated at St Wilfrid's Church of England High School in Blackburn (he was also a chorister at Blackburn Cathedral) and Durham University, where he read music. After his PGCE at Aberystwyth he taught at an Accrington primary school for four years and became deputy head of a primary in Lytham St Anne's at the tender age of 27. Moved to Foremarke Hall (now Repton Prep) as academic director and also taught maths, music and sport, before spending nine years at Polwhele House.

When he visited Perrott Hill for the first time his overwhelming impressions were of the school's 'sense of warmth and all-embracing welcome' – and parents say he has preserved that. He sees his role as 'galvanising the team and moving the school forward successfully', adding that one of the many reasons he loves Perrott Hill is because 'it's a traditional prep school with a broad offering'. He loves his job and considers it to be a 'privilege'. 'I really believe in what I'm doing,' he says. 'I view it as acting on behalf of the children in my care and giving them all the opportunities and life chances we can.' Parents are clearly impressed by his levelheadedness and ability to listen. 'He's fabulous,' said one. 'He exudes calm confidence. He's exactly the sort of head you want – the safest pair of hands you could wish for.'

He still finds time to teach PSHE – 'which is great because I get to know all the children really well'. He and his wife Helen, a reception class teacher and head of early years, live in a house on the school site. They have two children, both pupils at the school. In his spare time he enjoys singing, playing the piano, cooking and baking ('I'm very proud of my lemon meringue pie'), long-distance walking (Alfred Wainwright's 182-mile Coast to Coast walk was the 'pinnacle') and playing golf.

Entrance: Via an interview with the parents, consideration of previous school reports and short academic assessment on test day. The experience is 'homely, smiley, personal and fun', a parent told us.

Exit: Nearly all stay until 13 and the majority head to a wide range of boarding schools, with Blundell's, Bryanston, Canford, King's Bruton, King's Taunton, Sherborne and Sherborne Girls popular. Around 20 scholarships most years, plus several exhibitions and awards.

Our view: Founded in 1946, Perrott Hill is situated in 28 acres of beautiful grounds and woodland close to the Somerset-Dorset border. 'The children have got so much outdoor space,' says an ultra-appreciative parent. The school became part of Stirling Education in 2020, a group that includes schools and universities across Europe, India and the Middle East. But apart from having new owners, nothing else has changed. 'The school retains its character and identity and it's business as usual,' says the head.

Parents wax lyrical about the school's stunning location, academic achievements, family feel and 'nurturing' ethos. A family that recently relocated from the south-east told us: 'We were originally looking at some of the big-name schools but then we visited Perrott Hill and were utterly enchanted. My two children are very different but they really celebrate the character and strength of each child.' This is a traditional prep that embraces its surroundings and promotes good country living, a big selling point for many parents. One said, 'Our children love the outdoor opportunities – double woods sessions, golf before lunch, farming in the afternoon; they didn't get to do that in London.'

'We are committed to being a full boarding school,' says the head. 'It's how the school started back in 1946 and that strand has run all the way through the school ever since'

It's a small school, with an average of 12 in a class. Where class sizes allow, years 6, 7 and 8 are streamed in preparation for Common Entrance. Excellent learning support department, highly praised by parents. One told us, 'My child, having received learning support for a few years, is now leaving with scholarships. He has been made a prefect, his confidence has increased and his academic ability has improved enormously.' Another said, 'With the individualised teaching and fantastic learning support it is like Pandora's box has been opened. It is so wonderful to see.' A third said, 'My eldest was very shy and within a year was in the final of the school poetry recital performing in front of the whole school and parents. With confidence and self-belief you can go far.'

The head of SEN is a literary specialist and there is an in-house team of five assistants, plus an external team that provides speech and language therapy and educational psychology. The school provides good support for dyslexia and dyscalculia and extra tuition can take place instead of Latin or French (at an extra cost). Overseas students with at least basic English can come for a term or more – the EAL specialist offers two weeks of intensive tuition to bring them up to speed.

The long school day (8.20am-5.45pm for year 5 pupils and above) includes a variety of activities – ballet, karate, fencing, riding and gymnastics at extra cost and free activities such as art, beekeeping, ceramics, sports, eco-club or playing in the woods. We particularly liked the sound of the Perrott Parrot, the school newspaper. 'Everything is incorporated into the school day,' says the head. 'Parents can pick up at 5.45pm knowing their children have had a busy day doing lessons, activities and sport – and that their prep is done.' Year 5s and up have Saturday school until 4pm, with lessons, sports fixtures and – the highlight of the day – French lunch. Not all pupils and parents are enthusiastic about the extra day but they all agreed that 'you soon get used to it'.

Everyone enthuses about the 'exceptional' art department and we saw plenty of projects in the small but very productive art studio. A year 3 pupil recently created a 3D scarab beetle collection as part of a cross-curricular project with history and art scholars' work on chiaroscuro (the treatment of light and shade in drawing and painting) was particularly impressive. The school has its own kiln and ceramics is now part of the curriculum. 'The art department is fantastic and with the resources it has bats way above other schools,' we were told. 'But we would love there to be a bigger art room and facilities as it is such an amazing department.' We would definitely second that.

The science department has a similarly creative environment in the old changing rooms, with movable benches and storage to allow room for experiments and flexible teaching. There is also a Tinker Lab full of Lego, Meccano, BBC micro:bits and anything else that can be taken apart and rebuilt, plus the chance to try out new technology such as drones and 3D printing.

The music centre sits in the natural slope of the hill, clad in cedar. Concertina doors open out onto the decking looking across the Somerset hills. Fantastically inspirational. The department is run by an 'excellent' teacher who promotes music for all. Anyone can join the orchestra and all year 2s learn the violin for a year. Music is so popular the choirs have increased by 15 per cent over the past two years. Plenty of drama productions in the well-equipped theatre. Year 6 recently performed Goodnight Mister Tom while the leavers' production was Willy Russell's Our Day Out.

The library opens out onto a terrace, a rose garden, the monkey woods (a maze) and fields as far as the eye can see. Alongside playing fields and courts, including an Astro, there's a sports hall, swimming pool, climbing wall and pitch and putt course. Nestled under the trees is the forest school, with a newly built roundhouse and large fire-pit. When we visited, it was alive with activity – one group was rubbing flints to make fire, another was learning to saw and a third group was making doughnuts (normal and gluten-free, of course). Other culinary delights have included wild garlic bread and nettle soup, all foraged and picked by the children.

Pupils and parents clearly love the school. 'Perrott Hill produces good eggs, children who are real all-rounders,' said one. 'I'm constantly astounded by the work my 7-year-old produces.' Several praised the school's response to the pandemic and their 'excellent' communication with parents. 'The lessons they provided were fantastic,' a mother told us. 'They created engaging content and my son's teacher did a live story-time that lasted for a blessed hour every day.' Others were bowled over by the teachers' creativity, including launching the school's first radio show and a Strava challenge where families totted up the miles they ran and cycled in a week.

The school runs a fleet of five minibuses, with day pupils arriving from as far afield as Axminster, Bridport, Chard, Dorchester and Lyme Regis. Quite a few families have relocated from London and the south-east (there's a direct train from nearby Crewkerne to London so some parents commute to the capital once or twice a week).

Boarding: Full (from year 5), weekly and flexi-boarding (from year 3). A few pupils from Spain and France, but most from the UK, a large number fairly local. 'We are committed to being a full boarding school,' says the head. 'It's how the school started back in 1946 and that strand has run all the way through the school ever since.' Flexi boarders must book regular days but Friday night boarding is popular with parents. 'The boarding house is very family orientated and they have a lovely time in the evenings,' a parent told us.

Activities include a variety of games as well as more sedentary pursuits. There are 'family weekends' spent with the houseparents and 'activity weekends' when day pupils can join in too. Themes include Inspector Gadget, Indiana Jones (with an assault course), Harry Potter and Making a Musical. 'The boarding staff are fantastic – my children have always been very happy to board, although we tend to build it up over a few years as they get older and have more stamina,' a parent told us. Another said, 'They love it. We live 15 minutes away and the older boys choose to weekly board and flexi board. They have a lot of fun.'

Money matters: Means-tested bursaries available, and scholarships are awarded for academic, sport, music, drama and art excellence.

The last word: A delightful school in a beautiful setting. Academic results are undeniably impressive but it's nurturing, engaging and fun too. As a parent told us, 'It's brilliant at helping children to find what they are good at and encouraging them all the way.'

Pinewood

43

Bourton, Shrivenham, Wiltshire SN6 8HZ

01793 782205 | office@pinewoodschool.co.uk | www.pinewoodschool.co.uk

Ages: 3–13

Pupils: 400; **Boarders:** 139 weekly/flexi

Fees: Day £10,230 – £19,695; weekly boarding + £4,800 pa

Head: Since September 2020, Neal Bailey (40s). International Business Management at Newcastle and then eight years as an investment manager before going into teaching, first at Cothill House (his alma mater, and where brother Duncan is now head), then as head to Château de Sauveterre and Mowden Hall. An unbelievable rise to the top, really – if he wasn't so nice, we'd be suspicious. Married to Nici, also a teacher and his inspiration for going into education; they have two sons, both now at Pinewood.

Joined the school between lockdowns. Spent every morning of his first year getting to know parents through their windscreens at drop-off – 'By Easter I could recognize a Pinewood car in the Sainsbury's car park.' Prep school through and through – a natural sports coach, according to parents, in his element running around on a Saturday morning with a whistle. In fact, a total sports nut – give him a racket, a ball or a surfboard and Mr Bailey's a happy man. Calm, confident and, we imagine, unflappable. How does he do it? 'A twenty-minute run seems to do the job', he says, 'and I don't lose sleep over anything.'

Objective is to move the school gently forwards, but nothing dramatic on the cards – 'modernising tradition', he calls it. Wants to raise aspiration and broaden leavers' destinations, encouraging parents and pupils to aim high. Facilities also on the hit list, including a second Astro, enclosing the outdoor pool and perhaps an enhanced focus on design, 'to encourage practical skills, everything from frying an egg to building a robot'. Excited to build his team – has already made some popular new recruits – and get word out there about the school. Big on kindness ('Pupils probably think, "Here he goes again, telling us to be nice to each other",' he laughs). Glass is half full – 'Someone described me recently as "nauseatingly positive" – I wasn't sure whether that was a compliment or not' – but he'll take it.

Parents like what they've seen so far, but it's relatively early days and it's been difficult to get to know the Baileys during Covid. School playing catch-up – a zillon come-and-have-coffee-with-the-head events since the world started opening up again.

Entrance: Non-selective ('hoorah!' cry London exiles), so get in quick. Taster day for year 3 upwards includes 'low key' assessments in English, maths and reading 'for setting purposes'. References sought from current school 'to assist a smooth transition to Pinewood'. Ensures school can fully meet child's needs.

A tilt towards boys in almost every year group, though parents of girls aren't concerned and head says this is the 'most coeducational environment I've been in'. Boys and girls seem to mix very naturally.

Exit: Around 85 per cent stay until the end of year 8, enjoying all the responsibility and fun that comes with being top of the pack. Those that leave after year 6 head off to independent day schools, grammars or comprehensives. Cheltenham College and Marlborough College vie for most popular every year; St Edward's Oxford and Bradfield growing in popularity; ones and twos to the other usual suspects. Quite an old-school approach from parents – 'I want to go to Eton because all of my ancestors went there,' one little boy told us proudly at lunch (though overwhelmingly they go co-ed, with Radley and the Sherbornes being the only single-sexers that feature regularly). Twenty scholarships in 2021 including five academic and art awards and six in sport.

Our view: Founded in 1875 but rather nomadic until 1946, when it settled in a very pretty house in the middle of the charming village of Bourton. Since then, stable blocks converted and more modern developments added – pupils particularly excited to tell us about when Charles and Camilla opened super new teaching block, the Hoyland, in 2021. 'We had to stand in a very straight line,' they told us, declaring the visitors 'really nice' (good to know). Classrooms throughout the school feel loved – photos, pupil work, bunting.

One interactive whiteboard had a huge photo of the teacher's wet-nosed terrier as its screensaver. Library central to school life. School uses Accelerated Reader scheme – 'word millionaires' leaderboard in pride of place outside head's study.

A big school, but effectively divided into units to maintain the family feel, with head of school at each level. Between 14 and 18 in each class. No plans to ditch the CE – 'as an exit exam in the core subjects it works well' – though year 7 and 8 humanities curriculum is now thematic with lots of cross-curricular links. 'We can be reactive to what's going on,' says academic deputy. Lots of discussion of COP 26 when we visited.

Outdoor learning for all in the woods or, for the little ones, the 'squirrel classroom'. Treetops adventure playground with stunning views over the countryside, mountain bike track and mud kitchen – so outdoor-learning-but-really-just-loads-of-fun. Come breaktime, you'll find most of the school on the pitches, either running around with a ball or just hanging out.

Early years arranged around their own outside space – lots of flow between nursery and reception. 'What they really like is splashing in puddles,' staff tell us – wellies and boiler suits essential. Tinies walk all the way to the woods to explore – 'we make the walk itself into an adventure, we stop and look at the clouds' – and come home completely exhausted. We met one, very proud of a self-portrait that she'd just produced – 'Look, I have arms and legs and shoes!' Ballet every week for boys and girls.

Classrooms throughout the school feel loved – photos, pupil work, bunting. One interactive whiteboard had a huge photo of the teacher's wet-nosed terrier as its screensaver

Head of wellbeing position created a few years ago and department has blossomed, moving from its original spot in the eaves to a bright, welcoming room in the centre of the school. Children and staff come in for regular sessions, drop-ins or just for a quiet moment. 'This morning I've had tearful year 8 girls in here' – and occasionally 'tearful mummies' too. Indoor break sessions an option to those finding things tricky who aren't 'enjoying the frantic ball throwing'. Staff praise the Baileys' support of wellbeing and willingness to invest in it. School linked with a school outside Mombasa, where their fundraising covers the annual salary of a teacher as well as basic infrastructure projects.

Long tables for lunch, teachers mingling with pupils. Dining room decorated with pupil art – today's menu (curry – hooray) written on the blackboard. Our year 8 guides were sad about the prospect of senior school – 'We've heard the food isn't nearly as good as it is here.' Cooking club – Taste Appreciation Society – encourages children to 'get their fingers in the bowl' and consider a healthy lifestyle and waste. Recent delicacies include banana boats for bonfire night. Pre-preppers grow veg – annual potato challenge involves, we assume, growing and eating lots of potatoes ('so much better homegrown,' we are advised by one wise year 8) and 'enjoy pulling up their turnips' each year.

Almost 200 play an instrument. Every year 3 learns a string instrument – no doubt a bracing experience when they all come together – and lots of opportunities to perform. House music competition from year 5 is a raucous affair. We sat in on angelic year 5 choir rehearsal, pupils (mainly girls) crowded around the piano, all plaits and pigtails. 'Make your eyes twinkle!' head of music trilled, 'eyebrows up!' as they rehearsed Away in a Manger for the upcoming carol concert. Art department lively, every wall crammed with pupil work. We popped our nose into a lesson on Magritte which looked set to be fun; one year 5 recently had a portrait chosen for a Royal Academy competition (presumably the face was not obscured by an apple).

With 84 acres of proper Wiltshire countryside – including woods for den-building and a nine-hole golf course – there's no excuse not to be out getting fresh air into the lungs, and sport is a big draw for parents. Team sport really big here in a traditional, country-prep way – oodles of fixtures and splendid match teas laid on afterwards, including for the dogs ('I really know my match teas,' one mum tells us, 'and these are the best around'). Beautiful pitches stretching away from the school for rugby, football, cricket. Astroturf for hockey, netball, tennis and planning permission for a second. Overall cross-country champions at Shrewsbury School recently; school's own track finishes with a mad dash through an enormous puddle on the grass in front of the school. Tough mudder-style event – 'the rubber legs' – involves 1.5km of tyres, tackle bags and a water jump ('They jump over the water?' we asked naively – no, they run through it). Objective is to sow the seeds for a lifetime of cardio fitness and enjoyment of a good runaround.

Outdoor swimming pool is only slight downer on this front, though head told us that this is being looked at – parents felt that swimming programme not much more than 'splashing around'. Annual 'ice breaking', when head jumps into the pool followed by the children, is charming but not a substitute for year-round swimming. Girls' sport also flagged as an area for investment – 'It could do with a boost,' said one mum. School has recognised that and a new sports coordinator has recently been appointed to focus in part on competitive girls' sport.

Four specialists look after learning skills department; school 'advocates a graduated approach' – ie can provide whatever level of support is appropriate, from differentiation within lessons to group support or one-to-ones (which are charged as extras). Dedicated space in the Hoyland with meeting rooms, classroom and chill-out zone complete with beanbags and Lego. Thoughtful advice on suitable senior schools for those with SEND, including Milton Abbey and Shiplake.

Families from a circle around the school that stretches from Burford to Pewsey, Oxford to Chippenham. A big gang down towards Marlborough, we hear (lots of Marlborough staff have their children here), but otherwise spread out. Sociable: dinners and dog walks mainly, as far as we could tell. Parents thrilled by recent fireworks display (apparently two years' budget rolled into one after Covid scuppered 2020), organised by Friends of Pinewood, who are generally busy and active. Demographic modernising slowly – more ethnically and socially diverse than previously, particularly in pre-prep. No longer have lessons on a Saturday, just fixtures every other weekend.

Boarding: School offers flexi boarding from year 5 – just over half take them up on it regularly. Rooms are cosy and chaotic (in a good way) – bunk beds, posters, artwork, teddies. Bathrooms clean and modern. Common rooms cleverly positioned between girls' zone and boys' zone to give them somewhere to hang out together. 'Amazing' matron. Varied breakfast menu (pastries today; full English tomorrow; Belgian waffles coming up on Friday) and treaty suppers including a 'Chinese banquet' on Thursday night. Pupils seem very happy boarding – as Mr Bailey says, 'There's not a single child upstairs who hasn't gone home and said, "Mummy, it's basketball tonight and chicken nuggets for tea, I want to board!".' Post-Covid, children need to stay for two consecutive nights – not as 'flexi' as some parents had hoped.

Money matters: No scholarships. Means-tested bursarial support available with four per cent of annual fee income put aside for this purpose. Try to support temporary hardship where they can.

The last word: If Richard Curtis made prep schools, we think they'd be a bit like Pinewood. Honey-coloured Cotswold stone, wellies neatly lined up outside classrooms, a roaring fire and a soundtrack of children singing their little hearts out in hymn practice, just missing the high notes. We were surprised not to find Andie MacDowell curled up on the sofa with a hot chocolate. Parents agree that there's a sparkle about the place – 'It's got a magical feel,' they gushed, 'just divine!' A traditional, muddy, rosy-cheeked prep school with an unusual warmth. Stick the dog in the boot and pop your Barbour on – this gem is absolutely worth a visit.

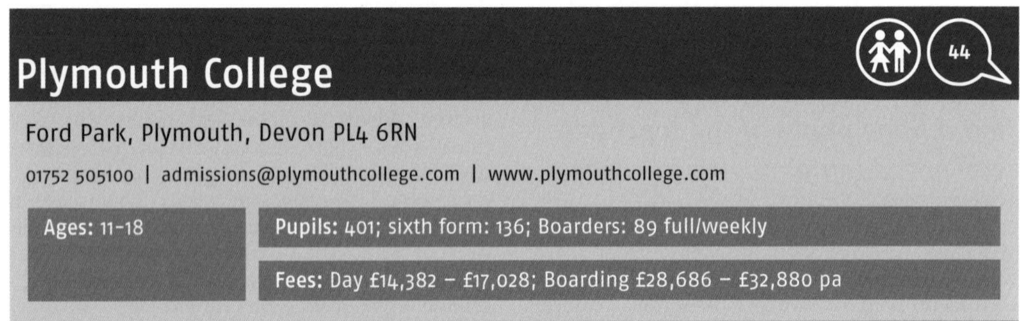

Plymouth College

44

Ford Park, Plymouth, Devon PL4 6RN

01752 505100 | admissions@plymouthcollege.com | www.plymouthcollege.com

Ages: 11–18

Pupils: 401; sixth form: 136; Boarders: 89 full/weekly

Fees: Day £14,382 – £17,028; Boarding £28,686 – £32,880 pa

Head: Since August 2020, Jo Hayward (40s), previously interim head and before that deputy head since 2016. Geography degree from Downing College, Cambridge; PGCE from Leeds. A lively, engaging and positive leader, she is revelling in having the prep and senior schools newly on the same site and is full of plans for their future. Pupils like that she is encouraging them to get stuck in too: 'Easy to talk to and really open to experimenting with our ideas for the school,' said one. Parents agree that listening to pupils is a forte.

Educated at Ashville College in Harrogate, she spent a gap year working at a boarding school in Zimbabwe before university. Her first job as a transport consultant saw her as part of the creative team behind the London congestion charge after which she had a career 'epiphany', changing tack to become a teacher and studying for a PGCE at the Leeds. Taught geography and games (plus boarding house responsibilities) at Pocklington School for four years, thence to Trent College as head of geography for three years before heading off to the Mount School in York as a head of sixth form, then deputy principal. It was this last role that opened her eyes to a different type of leadership, founded on the Quaker principles of building a supportive and trustworthy community together.

Lives on site with her husband, a Zimbabwean; their daughter is at the school.

Entrance: Academically non-selective, but entrance exams in maths and English and for scholarships. Around 50 per cent of intake come from the prep. Others mainly from local primaries, with parents who want to avoid the testing for local grammars. For sixth form entry, a minimum of six 5s at GCSE including English and maths, with 6s in the subjects to be studied at A level.

Exit: Around 20 per cent leave after GCSEs to local grammars and sixth form colleges, though a 'solid handful' bounce back in again when they realise the grass isn't greener. Others swiftly replaced with external applicants. Post A levels, 50 per cent to Russell Group; many of the elite sportspeople head to international universities on scholarship programmes, over half of these to the top 10 US universities. Back home, favoured university destinations include Exeter, Cardiff, Bath, Nottingham, Surrey and Plymouth. In 2021, one to Oxbridge, one medic and three overseas – to Miami, Berkeley and Tampa.

Latest results: In 2021, 51 per cent 9-7 at GCSE: 51 per cent A*/A at A level (77 per cent A*-B). In 2019 (the last year when exams took place), 38 per cent 9-7 at GCSE; 33 per cent A*/A at A level (56 per cent A*-B).

Teaching and learning: In a city boasting three single-sex, academically rigorous grammars, parents say this school is the hidden gem because, 'instead of pressure, they offer a sense of belonging where pupils are accepted whatever their ability and talent, making them happy enough to fly academically.' The school certainly demonstrates universal appeal, from nurturing Oxbridge students and educating the world's sporting elite to gently teaching those who shy away from academic pressures: 'We're small enough to make a difference and big enough to accommodate all.'

Flexibility is a buzzword, and this is no better demonstrated than by the large number of elite swimmers whose rounded yet pared-down academic experience is squeezed alongside 24+ hours a week of swim training. But it's not just the elite that benefit – every pupil is taken seriously here, with both GCSE and A level options annually tailored to accommodate that year group's subject choices.

The most striking thing about this school is its all-action, adventurous heart, with three full-time outdoor education experts and its own outdoor centre on Dartmoor

While every school claims to put 'each individual child first', this one puts its money where its mouth is, with a detailed 'flightpath' system created by the director of studies – tracking, projecting and delivering against pupils' every academic move. Anomalies in progress are discussed at weekly staff meetings, enabling quick intervention. Parents, while not seeing their child's whole flightpath, are kept closely updated. 'The reporting we get is fantastic, the staff really know where the children are at and ensure that we do too,' expressed one. Reports are issued every half term with grades and comments; ad hoc emails to parents praising or encouraging pupils are also frequent.

Class sizes max at 20 up to year 9, dropping to 10 by A levels. Lessons range between quiet concentration and exuberant participation, according to the teacher's requirements. In a Blankety Blank style A level revision class for classical civilisation date recall, we joined the hilarity as one pupil hotly contested the marking of her test paper before demonstrating her knowledge and competency with the correct answer. In a German class, we watched a German teacher coach his year 11s through the heart-stopping nerves of spoken exams – despite their fears, we were impressed by their fluency. In a biology class, the teacher laughed, 'I try to enthuse about plants but I am a zoologist at heart.' There is a sense of warm familiarity between pupils and staff, supported by a polite respect.

From year 7, setting in humanities based on the pupils' English ability, and in sciences based on their maths. Most take 10 GCSEs, but school will flex if sporting commitments or academic ability make this tricky. Options include Latin, classics and business. At A level, psychology, economics and philosophy all on offer, although there were some grumblings among parents that 'a broader choice could be offered'. Sport baccalaureate a popular alternative – 15 per cent opt to take this instead of A levels, gaining a level 3 BTEC in sport and outdoor education, one of only a handful of schools in the country offering this speciality which has enabled many students to gain top triple distinction star marks and places at Russell Group universities. EPQ offered, together with a 'life skills' sixth form enrichment programme.

Learning support and SEN: 'Exceptional,' say parents. Around 15 per cent of pupils have some form of mild educational need, with the learning support team (led by head of learning support SENCo plus two peripatetic teachers) offering tailored programmes that focus on numerical and literacy skills, on a one-to-one basis in the 'hub'. The team was praised by parents for their speed in referring pupils to diagnostic experts, as well as managing alternative exam arrangements and overseeing pastoral wellbeing of pupils in their care. The head of learning support regularly leads staff training for all teaching staff to join the dots. Bespoke arrangements are in place to accommodate the handful with more severe needs.

The arts and extracurricular: The most striking thing about this school is its all-action, adventurous heart. Not content to simply offer DofE and Ten Tors (both of which it excels at), the school has three full-time outdoor education experts who ensure that every pupil has after-school club access to an adrenalin-fuelled menu of activities. Options range from whitewater rafting trips down the River Dart to sea kayaking, sailing, mountain biking, scuba diving, hillwalking, caving and climbing. School owns an outdoor centre on Dartmoor, with visits beginning with year 7 camps – 'a great bonding experience to kick off senior school,' say parents. Other UK adventure trips abound, including the Three Peaks challenge – the ultimate annual goal for lower sixths. International volunteering trips are a biennial highlight to destinations such as Malawi and Tanzania.

CCF offered in all three services, with RAF numbers kept small to ensure maximum flying time and army cadets heading excitedly off to fire guns on the moor when we visited. Naval numbers are soaring due to the solid number of US and Dutch navy marine families at the school.

Trying not to play second fiddle to the activities offered is the impressive programme of art, drama and music, which are offered both on – and in addition to – the curriculum. All three are compulsory until year 9 and small but enthusiastic groups take each at GCSE and A level. The art block houses two light-filled studios and a photographic darkroom. Students can choose to specialise in fine art, graphic design or photography at GCSE and A level. Striking portraits line the walls and portfolios lie open for inspiration, demonstrating some eye-catching images from paranormal photographic illusions to abstract self-portraiture. The DT studio was buzzing with year 9 students building miniature wooden Artek stools on our visit.

Flexibility is a buzzword, as demonstrated by the large number of elite swimmers whose rounded yet pared-down academic experience is squeezed alongside 24+ hours a week of swim training

The small but recently renovated music department has a new head of music who is working hard to raise the school's music profile. Four choirs, 14 peripatetic teachers, three bands and a string plus guitar ensemble give a flavour of what's on offer. Performance opportunities are a focal point, with regular open-mic sessions. Thirty students were performing at the City of Plymouth Music Festival when we visited, and there are goals to perform in Devon county music festivals and the National Concert Band Festival in the next year.

Over in drama, annual productions range from the Addams Family to The Great British Bump Off – an interactive murder mystery, which one sixth former cited as the 'absolute highlight of his time at the school'. No formal theatre but two large halls on hand, together with a small drama studio.

Sport: This has always been a sporty school, competing with Millfield and Mount Kelly as the top south west school for elite swimming. It excels at taking the trauma of raising top athletes out of the hands of exhausted parents, delivering rigorous, internationally acclaimed training programmes, and wraparound pastoral care. Programmes include onsite nutritionists, physiotherapists and counsellors, plus all the top-end facilities you could wish for. Parents of elite swimmers spoke of the 'unrivalled warm and personal support from peers, teachers, trainers and boarding house staff' that set it apart from its competitors and had enabled their children to find the rigorous training manageable. The elite swimmers and divers train at the city's Life Centre 50-metre pool under the college; swim coaches produce national, international and Olympic competitors in a close relationship with the Plymouth Leander team, which they compete for.

School's large sports centre is aptly located smack, bang in the centre of the site, where cardio gym and weights room with personal trainers are on hand. Other notable facilities include two squash courts, Astroturf, playing fields, and cricket nets, plus a 25-metre indoor swimming pool. Swimming is on curriculum from the off, alongside a traditional mix of sports. Small nod towards football, with fencing, badminton, gymnastics and golf broadening also in the offering. International rugby players, GB fencers and county cricket players are all trained and schooled here but you don't have to be at that level to play for the school – 'We're a relatively small school so we will always field enough teams to give everyone a chance to represent us and rotate players in the top teams to ensure all those that are keen get the chance to experience playing at a high level.' Parents confirmed this, with plenty of stories of team inclusions for those still mastering the skills. Those who find team sports unappealing will be relieved to hear there are no expectations beyond the basic curriculum – they can even opt out of the Friday afternoon sessions to try their hand at anything from cycling proficiency to 'crate stacking' – think human Jenga involving crates and climbing equipment!

Boarding: Two onsite single-sex boarding houses are located in a terraced row of large cream stucco 19th-century villas, with the head of boarding and his family in the middle property. Befitting their age, the houses have high embossed ceilings and large windows. The feeling is of a calm, rather grand family home. Both house parents have young children, the 1-year-old in the girls' house being a regular on the waking up rounds in the morning. Various sitting rooms, some with and some without technology, vast pool table for the boys, piano for the girls. Co-ed mixing in communal areas actively encouraged in both houses, although there are evenings when they opt for single-sex sessions 'if we just need some girls' time'. Sixth formers have their own well-stocked kitchen and can opt to self-cater at weekends. Single bedrooms available for sixth formers if requested; others share rooms of two to three with identical university-style furniture kits, all very new and welcoming. Daily room checks through 'five o'clock club' and penalties including collecting laundry for a week for those not complying. Smart and immaculate bathrooms. Laundry done by staff – parents, beware of impossibly high laundering expectations on holiday returns.

Boarding staff we met were a welcoming and compassionate bunch. 'We are parents and understand how important it is not to miss out on every little thing, from first day photos to a little message if the child has had a bad day.' 'I have never had a day's worry since she started,' remarked one parent. 'Nothing happens without you knowing,' said another.

High levels of care taken of the elite swimmers and divers, who form 60 per cent of the boarding cohort. Great team camaraderie around morning wake ups – 4.30am for swim training from 5am. 'It makes such a difference that there are a group of us doing this intense training and competing together rather than being at home and the only one in the house getting up in the middle of the night!' said one pupil.

Half of the boarders are from the UK, the rest from an international mix of 38 different countries. Very few younger year boarders; five to 10 weekly boarders. No formal exeats as swim training is consistent, but boarders free to spend the weekend with a day friend or family throughout the year. Evening and weekend options are wide and adventurous with trips and expeditions aplenty, taking full advantage of the coastal setting and moorland proximity.

Ethos and heritage: Founded in 1877 as Plymouth High School for Boys, the school moved to its current site at Ford Park in 1880, changing its name to Plymouth College three years later. Several mergers with girls' schools followed, becoming fully co-ed in 1995. The fenced school site is a sprawling mix of grand old 19th-century villas, the Gothic 'old school building' and charmless post-war additions. Boasting everything from 'the oldest parquet floor in the UK' to a re-designed larch-clad prep building. This is not an immaculately presented school – 'shabby but extremely well loved,' as one member of staff described it. But then again, everyone is far too busy having fun to worry about what things look like.

Co-ed mixing in communal areas actively encouraged in boarding houses, although there are evenings when they opt for single-sex sessions 'if we just need some girls' time'

Past pupils include Tom Daley, Olympic diver, and Cassie Patten, Olympic swimmer, plus Henry Slade and Paul Ackford, both England rugby internationals.

Pastoral care, inclusivity and discipline: 'Fantastic pastoral care, I utterly trust the school to spot if something is amiss and to be able to deliver incredible support when needed,' said a parent. Nobody could slip under the radar here, we heard, which was demonstrated on our visit. Staff-pupil relationships are warm, personal and informed – and every member of staff seems to know every pupil well, with lots of moments seized to stop and catch up, initiated by pupils as much as staff.

Mental wellbeing is seen as the responsibility of all staff, with early detection of any subtle changes in behaviour being key. Eating disorders are sadly commonplace among school-age swimmers nationally so this issue is hotly on the radar, with an experienced team ready to jump if needed. 'I was emailed immediately when teachers noticed a weight change in my child and, thanks to the school's involvement, we were given an instant referral from our GP. The proactive, early action from staff was absolutely pivotal,' praised one parent.

There is 'absolutely no tolerance' of bulling or harassment, we heard, and pupils are not afraid to call it out. A former head of year 11 was sacked from his role several years ago after pupils went to other members staff with concerns over his conduct. 'We try not to be simply reactive,' said the deputy head, who insists they are 'constantly introducing the pupils to a broad range of speakers and having age-appropriate discussions on every aspect of sex and relationship concerns, drug and alcohol abuse'. Random drug testing is the norm but drug issues are, says school, exceptionally low – 'most likely due to the elite sports programme,' says head. Alcohol issues also rare, with the most common abuses of trust being inappropriate online behaviour; they have strict firewalls to pick this up and a robust 'safer internet programme'. Sanctions range from handing in phones to internal or external suspensions. There have been no expulsions in the last two years.

The school welcomes and celebrates the cultural diversity of its international boarders and the candid openness of its several gay members of staff all helps to create an atmosphere of 'fundamental acceptance'.

Pupils and parents: Pupils we met were lively, enthusiastic, modest and up for adventure. The 'whole school' ethic is a key focus, all helped by vertical inter-year relationships, peer mentors and sixth formers actively helping out at the prep. 'Definitely not an ivory tower,' according to parents, who cite a 'real life mix of families, from those who can easily afford it to those sacrificing everything to send their children here'. It gives the children 'a wonderfully real and rounded outlook,' reckoned one.

Money matters: Scholarships include all-round, academic, art, drama, music, performing arts and sport. Means-tested bursaries also available, as well as discounts for siblings and military families.

The last word: Muddy-faced, huge smile, boundless enthusiasm – that's what this school would look like as a person. Oh, and did we mention they'd be dedicated to their passions and with intelligent opinions? There's not much wrong with that!

Port Regis

Motcombe Park, Shaftesbury, Dorset SP7 9QA

01747 857914 | admissions@portregis.com | www.portregis.com

Ages: 2–13

Pupils: 304; **Boarders:** 80 full, 30 weekly/flexi

Fees: Day £9,990 – £21,750 pa; Boarding £17,385 – £29,280 pa

Headmaster: Since January 2021, Titus Mills, previously head of Walhampton since 2012. Before that spent six years as head at the Paragon School in Bath and was head of George's International School in Rome. Has also been deputy head in a state primary school in Lambeth and spent two years teaching in Uganda. An Old Etonian, he read history of art at university before his PGCE (Oxford). He and his wife Jemima have three children; one attends Eton, another Canford and the youngest is currently at Walhampton.

Entrance: Main entry points are nursery and year 3 but children join all the way through the school. Pre-prep is first come, first served, while entry to the prep is via an interview with the head, assessment (verbal and non-verbal reasoning) and report from previous school. Children join from a raft of preps and from local state primaries. Virtually all pre-prep children move up to the main school (no assessment required).

Exit: Port Regians go on to a wide range of co-ed, single-sex, boarding and day schools. Most popular destinations are Eton, Marlborough, Bryanston, Canford, Sherborne, King's Canterbury and King's Bruton.

Senior schools tell Port Regis that Port Regians are children who are 'resilient, self-reliant and know how to get on with things'. Most pupils stay until 13 (one or two girls leave at 11 for schools like Wycombe Abbey but school doesn't encourage this). In 2021, 39 scholarships and prizes – a new record (covering nearly half of pupils).

Our view: Located in 150 acres of sweeping Dorset parkland, yet only a couple of miles from the hilltop town of Shaftesbury. Visitors gasp at the setting – it could easily be mistaken for a senior school, with its long drive, stunning architecture, modern classrooms, central lake, huge treehouse and extensive playing fields and grounds – plus, most recently, a new rose garden and open air theatre. Main school building is a Victorian mansion built in 1894 by Baron Stalbridge but it is surrounded by a collection of stylish, purpose-built additions. School was founded in London in 1881. It moved to Motcombe House in 1947 (via stints at Folkestone, Broadstairs, Bryanston and St Albans). First admitted girls in 1972.

Mildly selective – school claims to be 'a broad church' – but academic results are very good. Setting from year 5, with scholarship sets introduced in the last two years. Maximum class size of 15 throughout. French taught from the start and Latin from year 6. Spanish on offer from year 6 and there are opportunities to study Italian, Russian and Mandarin outside the main curriculum. Ancient Greek is taught as an after-lunch club in years 6-8. Staff give it a try too; when we visited the director of studies had just signed up. History and geography recently removed from CE in favour of in-house syllabus.

Pupils have a form teacher till the end of year 6, then get the chance to choose their own tutor for years 7 and 8. Excellent learning support department in new centre and under new SENDCo. A fifth of pupils access support, mainly for dyslexia, dyspraxia, ASD, mild ADD and speech and language therapy. School has produced a senior school guide to help parents choose the next schools for their children and head meets parents to discuss choices when children are in year 5.

Well-known far and wide for its sporting prowess, school offers a plethora of sport. Boys play rugby, football, hockey and cricket while girls do hockey, netball, rounders and tennis. As well as acres of playing fields there's an Astroturf, new Astro just for hockey, nine-hole golf course, rifle range, heated swimming pool and impressive indoor sports complex that serves as a national centre for junior gymnastics. School does particularly well at hockey, rugby and athletics (11 pupils qualified for 15 different events at a recent IAPS national athletics championships). Big on outdoor learning too, with pupils enjoying their own camp on site; old Port Regians come back to help out with eg team building, bushcraft and life skills.

The girls' boarding house is stunning, complete with disco lights on the hall ceiling, a double tier sofa to snuggle up on and breakfast bar stools made from riding saddles

Art, DT and pottery (there can't be many prep schools with a whole room devoted to ceramics) are amazing. We were particularly taken with a vast sculpture of a pear core created by a 13-year-old. The year 8 guide who showed us round the DT department told us: 'This is a place where ideas can be formed.' Many senior schools would give their eyeteeth for facilities like these – everything from a 3D printer to a laser-cutting machine (great for making stickers). The children really let their imaginations run riot here. We saw an iPod speaker inspired by an old-fashioned toaster, a hanging chair and a lamp that projected a bat-shaped shadow on the wall. 'They surprise me all the time with their designs,' beams the head of DT. Annual summer exhibition gives pupils a chance to show off their creative flair.

Music is top notch too. Every 7-year-old learns the recorder and how to read music and every 8-year-old learns the violin. Music is taught in the striking Farrington Music School, an octagonal building overlooking a small lake known as Bob's Pond. It boasts a 132-seat recital hall, music technology room and 17 teaching rooms. Wind, brass and string ensembles, school orchestra, senior and junior choirs, samba band, swing band and lots of other groups, all of which put on regular concerts. Plenty of drama. Each year group puts on a play and there's a leavers' show at the end of the summer term. More than 70 activities and hobbies (we'd love to do them all), including aerobics, backgammon, beekeeping, film animation, computer coding, friendship bracelets and trampolining. Debating, or 'persuasive talks', are very popular, with children encouraged to discuss the issues of the day.

Year 8s given responsibility – there's a head boy and head girl, plus dorm captains for boarders. No prefects. 'We don't think it's good to single out children at this age,' says school. Children encouraged to be children for as long as possible. No electronic devices or mobile phones (apart from pupils whose parents live abroad). Boarders can Skype their parents on the boarding house computers. Pastoral care is very much at the forefront, with form tutors and houseparents the first port of call when problems arise. Very few behaviour issues here. Indeed, Port Regis is hot on manners, pleases and thank yous and holding doors open for visitors. School is also planning a kindness day – 'We want children to understand that it's cool to be kind,' says school. 'It's not to be derided. It's a real strength.' Slightly more boys than girls but school has appointed a head of girls' games and a senior tutor, who is effectively head of girls (she is also head of classics, has a PhD from Cambridge and has written two critically acclaimed books).

School food is among the very best we've tasted. Head chef (whose family runs a local restaurant) and his five-strong team cook up to 1,000 meals a day – breakfast, lunch and supper, using fresh locally sourced ingredients as much as possible. We happily tucked into a lunch of fillet of sea bass (freshly caught off the coast of Brixham) topped with caper and lemon sauce, spinach and roasted new potatoes. Salads and vegetarian options always on offer – avocado and chargrilled peppers, quorn wraps and lentil soup when we visited.

We happily tucked into a lunch of fillet of sea bass (freshly caught off the coast of Brixham) topped with caper and lemon sauce

Pre-prep (with 52 pupils) is housed in a stable block, just a few minutes walk from the main school. Idyllic setting, complete with forest school, enclosed playground, rose garden for imaginary play, loads of outdoor space and plenty of scooters and helmets. When we visited children had been picking apples and were about to cook their own apple crumble. Head of pre-prep is a former Team GB underwater hockey player and is passionate about outdoor learning.

Pupils are chirpy, enthusiastic and refreshingly down-to-earth. We saw a group of year 4s, all dressed up as chimney sweeps, street children and lords and ladies of the manor, throw themselves with relish into a Victorian Day workshop led by a guest speaker. Parents say there's 'a buzz about the school' and like the way it treats every child as an individual. A mix of local families and those who have moved to the country in search of a healthier, less pressurised lifestyle. Some from London – school is only two hours from the capital and Heathrow by train. Day pupils come from as far afield as Sherborne, Salisbury, Bruton and Warminster, mostly places within a 40-minute drive. School is building up a network of minibuses for day pupils. Parents are very involved in the school, attending quiz nights, balls, the Christmas fair, debates and lectures.

Illustrious alumni include the abstract painter Adrian Heath, former Press Council chairman Sir Louis Blom-Cooper, fashion designer Jasper Conran, singer/songwriter Bo Brudenell-Bruce, Olympic medallist horsewoman Zara Phillips and historian Jonathan Gathorne-Hardy.

Boarding: School is firmly committed to boarding. 'It feels like a second home really,' one boy told us. Around 60 per cent of children board in some way, whether it's full boarding, flexi-boarding or the odd night here and there (via an efficient online booking system). 'We have tried to listen to what our parents want,' says school. Apart from half term and holidays, the school never shuts. While some boarders go home at weekends, 70 to 80 children (around a third of the main school) stay at school. Around 35 per cent of boarders are from overseas (17 per cent of the school community) but many closer to home too, especially since 2021 when all children in year 3 have been able to board up to two nights a week as part of their day fee. Lots on offer for the boarders – staff and 12 gap students put on activities like face painting, cooking, weekend walks and trips galore. Most staff live on site.

Boarding facilities are top notch – way better than some senior schools we've seen. Junior boarders (years 3 to 6) are housed in the main school building – girls on one side, boys on another. Recently upgraded dorms of four or six, each with a dorm captain. Older boys and girls have separate boarding houses in the grounds. The girls' boarding house is stunning, complete with disco lights on the hall ceiling, a double tier sofa to snuggle up and watch movies at weekends and breakfast bar stools made from riding saddles. Each girl has her own 'cubie', with a bed, desk and wash basin – separated with a stylish bead curtain at the door. There's even a retro caravan in the garden (the enterprising bursar snapped it up on eBay). The senior boys' house is pretty nifty too – the games room ceiling is decorated with real surfboards. A lot of thought has been given to helping new children settle in. New pupils get a shadow to guide them through the early weeks. Boarders write letters home every Tuesday.

The last word: As we've said before, it's difficult to find fault with Port Regis. It has sometimes been seen as the preserve of the very rich but in reality children come from a wide variety of backgrounds. Scholarships and means-tested bursaries on offer too. The pupils we met clearly love the place and, as a parent told us, 'If anyone is going to bring out what your child is good at, Port Regis will.'

Prior Park College

Ralph Allen Drive, Bath, Somerset BA2 5AH

01225 831000 | admissions@priorparkschools.com | www.priorparkcollege.com

Ages: 11–18

Pupils: 624; sixth form: 203; Boarders: 120 full, 24 weekly/flexi

Fees: Day £15,942 – £17,595 Boarding £23,058 – £35,001 pa

Head master: Since 2019, Ben Horan (late 30s). Brought up on a council estate in south east London and encouraged to apply to Oxford to read history by an inspirational teacher, he went straight into teaching, taking in some prestigious schools: St Benedict's in Ealing, Eton and finally senior deputy head academic at Merchant Taylors'. He has done the lot: head of department, pastoral tutor, cricket and rugby coach; all excellent preparation for his first headship. Of Prior Park he says, 'I was swayed by the sixth form guides – I felt the community was so full of love.' It is heartwarming to hear this big burly 'cricket-crazy' historian talk so disarmingly of love: 'It's a verb, not a noun, and it's central to all we do here,' he told us, adding that he never saw himself as a 'systems and structures guy', so has overhauled the SLT better to deliver what students need and deserve. Getting the school through the Covid crisis ('exhausting, gruelling but definitely worth [the effort] for the students') just six months into his headship meant Mr Horan has not met as many parents as he would have liked; one parent described him as personable and relatable, another felt that he could cut down on the verbiage in his emails on occasion – 'and in assembly!' said one young lady with feeling. We would disagree, finding him thoughtful and candid, particularly on the knotty question of keeping Prior true to its Catholic foundations when 70 per cent of its students are not Catholic: 'Too much focus on hierarchy and dogma does not have traction for parents,' he reflected, 'but the true values of Catholicism and the gospel do.'

He is proud of his blended family of four sons, three of whom are at Prior; his partner Jane teaches at Eton. Any spare time will find him watching or listening to sport (this is a 5am Test Match Special man), cooking, walking Chlöe the dog or compiling/solving themed cryptic crosswords.

Entrance: Selective. Don't miss the application deadline – details on the website. School's own tests for 11+ entrants; CE and scholarship at 13. At any other time, report, interview and assessments. Year 7 entrants from, equally, local state schools and Paragon Junior. At year 9 a wodge from other preps and international schools. Around 20 join post-GCSE from other schools, telling you something about the strength of the sixth form, whose entrants need a minimum six GCSEs with As in A level subjects preferred.

Exit: Small exodus of around 15 per cent post-GCSE, most to vocational courses. Over half the sixth form leavers are Russell groupies; Exeter is top of the pops and Durham and Nottingham are also popular destinations. Good and varied balance of arts and sciences. In 2021, one to Oxbridge and two medics. The odd few head overseas.

Latest results: In 2021, 63 per cent 9-7 at GCSE; 68 per cent A*/A at A level (89 per cent A*-B). In 2019 (the last year when exams took place), 44 per cent 9-7; 33 per cent A*/A at A level (64 per cent A*-B).

Teaching and learning: No point in looking at government performance tables for raw data and comparison because this school, along with others, doesn't enter them. Why? Because school feels there's more to education than exam results and performance tables take no account of 'creativity and inspiration', the only true measure is how far a school raises its students.

Headline figures vary little from year to year and school does consistently well by its fairly broad intake. This is not an exam factory because there is no relenting in the commitment to all-round personal development. Neither is roundedness achieved at the expense of best-possible exam results – a neat trick which the school pulls off adroitly. There's pressure all right, but it's judiciously applied and it works because – this is the culture of the place – teachers know their students very well as people, they pick up on stress, lethargy and waywardness just like that and make time to give support. One student said, 'They always help when you're finding it difficult and get you back for a bit of tuition to help you through.' Another said, 'No teacher here would ever turn down a request for help.' The PHSCE programme is substantial and delivered with purpose. All students are now equipped with a personal learning device (a laptop by any other name) as part of the school's digital strategy. Online teaching provision has mostly been live and generally okay: 'Some teachers are not cut out to be movie stars,' as one mother observed wryly, but their kindness and commitment is in no doubt. A little more clarity and rigour around the use of cameras in lessons would be helpful.

Prep (homework) is supervised up to sixth form and the relatively long day (no Saturday school) means that you can break the back of it before you get home. Parents like this: 'There's usually not all that much to do at home so we can relax together as a family.' As you age it increasingly spills over, of course. There's currently a curriculum review in progress which aims to fine tune already estimable value-added scores. The outcome the school seeks is 'an educational framework that enshrines our values'.

Mandarin A level on offer from 2021.

Learning support and SEN: No statemented students accepted, but SEND provision supports milder SENs and intervenes when disparity emerges between a student's potential and ongoing achievement, or a student needs, say, organisational strategies or exam-stress support. Extends to students who develop mental health issues. Parents speak well of the expert sensitivity of the support given to their children. Mobility impaired students accepted where possible, but the school's architecture is a constraint.

The arts and extracurricular: Art and design happen in and around a refurbed dorm. Fine art good, photography especially strong just now, as is textiles. Healthy numbers, decent results. Design technology in a good place, partnerships with local industries, lots of energy input from staff. Sixth form has its own DT workshop, equipped to industry standards.

Music universally praised. Inspirational head of music also performs with singing group Opus Anglicanum. No elitism here when it comes to genre: anything goes from Gabrieli to grime. In cases of indie genres his smart ploy is to offer 'hands-off facilitation', thus enabling students to retain ownership of their sounds. High-end choral tradition longstanding and outstanding, biennial opera, multiplicity of ensembles, concerts formal and informal, for they love to go live and give others 'an experience of the sublime'. Two, yes two, musicals every year, all singing, all dancing – one parent said, 'Never a duty date, I simply can't believe the standard they reach.' Music here reaches all parts and catches up those who never knew they could. There's an inter-house music competition including student-rehearsed house song in which everyone sings and thereafter dwells on, marvelling fondly, for the rest of the year. A level numbers small, but of these a good number go on to top music colleges. Chapel choir is 90 per cent day students who come in at weekends to sing at mass. What does that tell you?

Drama's right up there with music (let's call it a dead heat). Up to 14 productions of all sorts a year, much of it high-end stuff. Staff (superb) all come from professional theatre, that's what makes the difference. Fabulous Julian Slade theatre largely funded by Cameron Mackintosh's foundation – he's a former student – palpably redolent of the magic created in it down the years by dint of passion, sweat, discipline, creativity and self-discovery. It's the real thing all right. Mackintosh also funded the excellent dance studio.

You get to do your after-school activities in school here. Recreational options, both lunchtime and after lessons, are multifarious and eclectic, embracing a diversity of endeavours from tricky physics to knit-and-natter – more than 60 to choose from. Saturday (morning) Active programme spans street dance and cookery. There's a CCF – voluntary sign-up from year 8 upwards – and DofE. 'It is fun,' one student told us wistfully during lockdown, 'especially the innings [house evenings] and outings.'

Music universally praised. Inspirational head of music, and no elitism when it comes to genre: anything goes, from Gabrieli to grime

Sixth formers have their own after-school (ad) ventures. They concoct a social programme – film nights, music nights, BBQs etc. The charities committee coordinates competitive fundraising for good causes and the best house wins a cup. Then there's Prior Concern, which sends forth students to do their bit for the homeless, nursery-age children and the elderly. Catholic values in action.

Sport: Parents like the way the school 'encourages everyone to give it all a go regardless of ability'. Hockey's what they do best in shop-window terms (national champions recently). Netball is strong, rugby has an ex-England international coach, the rest competitively respectable given the size of each year's intake. Spacious playing fields,

The grade one listed architecture may be stunning, but notwithstanding, the social climate here isn't the least snooty; this is a grounded, unpretentious place where ordinary people go to school

plentiful Astroturf. Sport for all, they say, greatest involvement by the greatest number, borne out by number of teams per sport sent forth to battle for their school every Saturday – around 10 on a good day but, according to one parent, girls' sport does not get the recognition that the boys' does. Maybe, but girls' tennis was ranked second in the country in 2020. Individuals regularly play at regional and international level. One of the lessons we learn from sport, they say, is humility. That's so Prior Park. No, it's emphatically not a philosophy of loser takes all – they love to win. Sports centre, source of great pride, includes multi-sport gym, fitness suite, you name it. It's been a boon for the less sporty types.

Boarding: Some 140 students board from age 11, around a third of them girls. Of these, around 50 are weekly and flexi boarders. Compulsory residential course early in year 7 and team building day for year 8 students underpin community values. Roughly 90 full-time boarders are international students. Stopover beds for day pupils. We had initial reservations about the boys' accommodation in St Paul's – gorgeous as the building may be on the outside, its bigness seemed inimical to snugness on the inside. This is an adult perception; the students reckon it does very nicely. Boys live alongside residential staff and their families. Girls occupy the unarguably cosier Priory nearby. Prep is supervised by a teacher. Weekend activities, the bugbear of any boarding regime, continually addressed. Weekend mass (Saturday evening or Sunday morning) is compulsory.

Ethos and heritage: The stunning Grade I listed Palladian mansion, set on a hill overlooking Bath, was built by quarry owner Ralph Allen to advertise the golden glories of Bath stone. The estate was purchased by Bishop Baines in 1829 and first opened as a school in 1830. Run by the Christian Brothers until the 1980s, it's now under lay management. Inside, 17th-century architectural grandeur doesn't always adapt readily to the needs of a 21st-century school and can play the part of an awkward host. 'Don't agree,' say the students as you fight for breath up an endless spiral staircase; 'it's quirky, it's part of the charm.' A parent concurred: 'Yes, all right, it's a bit shabby in places but in the nicest way – a bit basic but kids love it.' Lovely chapel, lovely name, Our Lady of the Snows, used also for weekly assemblies – all get in, just. Science block purpose-built.

Refined architecture notwithstanding, the social climate here isn't the least snooty; this is a down-to-earth place where ordinary people go to school, a place whose unpretentious personality answers the values of the sort of parent who celebrates 'a school that doesn't set itself apart from the city but participates in local events'.

Pastoral care, inclusivity and discipline: In a Catholic school with over 70 per cent non-Catholics, staff unabashedly decree Catholic values of kindness, service and 'being the person God wants you to be'. None of these values is objectionable to parents of a broadly secular disposition, and no subject is off-limits, including the exploration and expression of gender. A letter from former students in 2020 asking the school to decolonise the curriculum was met with what one parent considered 'a fair response'. There's a culture here of looking out for each other, teachers for students, older students for younger ones – one parent said, 'They got to know my daughter very quickly and genuinely appreciated her as a person.' Intervention is prompt. One parent said, 'It is a fantastic strength of the school that they are so diligent with the students' wellbeing. This doesn't all come about by wishing it so or generating policy docs, it derives from expectations, watchfulness, example-setting and buy-in. It works because it's hard work.' That excellent provision has continued through lockdown, with daily get-togethers with tutors, online sessions, wellbeing surveys and a listening service laid on.

Boundaries are set and are the same for everyone. 'There is no room for anyone to bend the rules,' said one parent. 'This has created a school of pupils who take pride in how they are being perceived by everyone.' Another said: 'We are constantly amazed by the school's ability to encourage and maintain an exquisite level of behaviour and compliance without the need to instil enormous amounts of discipline.' Major concern over any issues raised by social media; sexting, by way of example, is a regular assembly topic and parents join in the discussion. One parent commented, 'It's a constant conversation.' Bullying is dealt with robustly and the school does not shrink from expulsion in extreme cases.

Pupils and parents: Co-ed since 1982, almost 50:50, boys slightly more numerous. Common rooms are same-sex, lessons and dining mixed. Sizeable contingent of parents are dahn-from-Londoners, who have colonised Bath in recent years – yes, even raggle-taggle Walcot Street has capitulated to the hipsters. Monocultural tendency is mitigated by international students, never more than 10 per cent of the roll. With two outstanding (Ofsted) state schools and four rival independents in Bath alone, the education market locally is working well, with competitive pressures driving up standards and heightening distinctiveness.

For day students, buses from all corners up to 30 miles away. Parental involvement welcomed: twice-monthly coffee mornings hosted by Parents of Prior, which even has its own private Facebook page. Weekly newsletter. Listings of parent phone numbers by year group (voluntary) a nice touch. Businesslike, highly functional website. Parents really like the 'wonderful feeling of community'.

Money matters: Customary range of scholarships up to a value of around 10 per cent. Bursaries can be standalone or added to a scholarship. School likes to help where it can and, in another clear-cut case of walking the talk, an examination of the accounts reveals that it awards roughly half as much again in bursaries (as a percentage of income) as other Bath independents. Discounts for siblings. Lunch bundled with fees but not transport. Taking account of the long school day and the 4-6pm activities programme, good value for money. 'We recognise that we have a lot of working parents who stretch themselves to afford the fees. We don't want to let them down.'

The last word: Confident in its Catholic values, happy in its own skin and distinctive in its commitment to a genuinely all-round education, this is a school which inspires esteem and affection in equal measure.

Queen's College (Taunton)

Trull Road, Taunton, Somerset TA1 4QS

01823 340830 | admissions@queenscollege.org.uk | www.queenscollege.org.uk

Ages: 11–18

Pupils: 400; sixth form: 112; Boarders: 160

Fees: Day £16,185 – £19,695; Boarding £27,585 – £34,500 pa

Head of College: Since September 2021, Julian Noad, formerly head of Oswestry School in Shropshire for seven years and before that deputy head of Rydal Penrhos – like Queen's, a member of the Methodist Independent Schools Trust (MIST). He also spent 12 years at Clifton College in Bristol, including six as a housemaster. Has a long history of playing and coaching rugby, football, squash and fives, but has more recently concentrated on cross-country running and running. Still coaches. Also loves sailing, including yacht racing. Married with two children, both at university.

Entrance: About 60 per cent of senior school entrants come from the junior school without let or hindrance, unless they are trying for a scholarship or have specific learning difficulties. Others arrive from local primaries at 11, yet more from the odd prep school at 13+ and all sit tests in English, maths and verbal reasoning. At sixth form, the bar looks quite low at five GCSEs at 5+ with 'preferably 9-6' for subjects chosen for A level, but hopefuls are also required to take two papers in their likely A level subject choices. Children from overseas take a paper in English as an additional language.

Exit: Around a third leave after GCSE but almost all sixth form leavers go on to their chosen degree courses up and down the land – Nottingham, Exeter, UCL, Swansea, Durham, Bristol, Bath, Birmingham, York, Liverpool, Sheffield all feature. Some gap years. Two to Oxbridge in 2021.

Latest results: In 2021, 65 per cent 9-7 at GCSE; 59 per cent A*/A at A level (77 per cent A*-B). In 2019 (the last year when exams took place), 44 per cent 9-7 at GCSE; 40 per cent A*/A at A level.

Teaching and learning: Not particularly academically selective. Pressure to achieve top grades is not the way Queen's goes about things. Class sizes average 17, and there's a choice of 24 subjects for GCSE and A level. A modern foreign language is compulsory at GCSE; business studies and ethics & philosophy more unusual options. Students are grouped by ability for core subjects but mixed for options. At A level, option blocks are changed yearly in an effort to accommodate individual subject choices, and the school's flexibility at the start of sixth form while A level choices bed down is appreciated. Critical thinking, EPQ and TUG (top universities group) offered alongside these. One parent we spoke to chose Queen's specifically for its academics, another because her child 'did not shine academically, but has not been made to feel inferior by staff or pupils'. Stand-out subjects for the students are geography, chemistry and maths – 'but the sport and music are also amazing,' our guides reported.

Learning support and SEN: SEN support is provided through an integrated approach with the learning development unit [sic], where an electronic register shared with teaching staff records and tracks the needs of the high-ish proportion of SEN students. 'We haven't and don't wish to acquire dyslexia-friendly status,' says school, but it appears to serve its SEN population well, maths support in particular provided by the same teacher throughout the school, using traditional methods. Active EAL programme for the 100 or so overseas students. New timetable introduced, including one-hour lessons.

The arts and extracurricular: Performing arts shine – school boasts largest performing space(s) of any school in the south west: two theatres and a studio big/smart enough for more intimate productions. Even has its own makeup and crew clubs. Recent shows include Seussical, Coram Boy, Macbeth and Storm Boy, adapted from the book by the head of drama, a published playwright. Dancers extremely well looked after in terms of facilities and the school's own academy of performing arts, which attracts the likes of Birmingham City Ballet to give classes; strong on contemporary dance too, such as street jazz. Musicians jolly fortunate, too, to have a dedicated concert hall as part of the music school, complete with Steinway and 30-stop organ, plus music tech facilities. Choirs and ensembles abound – we were intrigued by the 'exuberant arrangements' apparently played by Sound School, a sax ensemble. Trips for local and international (recently Germany and Italy) performance and trophies from Taunton Festival round off an extensive, if traditional, musical offering.

Art of all kinds is housed in a gorgeous art school overlooking the cricket pitches; students are exposed to all media, techniques and materials so that they are well prepared for GCSE art and design. Painting, ceramics and textiles are areas of particular expertise, but all benefit from trips here and abroad (Barcelona and New York, inter alia) as well as the influx of visiting practitioners at the annual Quartz Festival. But despite the range of diversions to choose from, some parents still feel it's too narrow, and that a shove could usefully be applied to the idler students to sign up to more of them.

Sport: Sport is important – more a question of a game for all than winning at all costs. Just the place for sportsmen and women, but 'equally okay for incredibly anti-sports daughter,' according to one mother, who added that it is 'much more geared towards music, drama and the arts than the other Taunton schools'. Nonetheless, Queen's excels at sports and now has academies for both hockey and cricket (for which Taunton is famed), not just for its own promising players, but also for high-flyers locally. Thirty acres of pitches, two Astros, an indoor pool – swimming is a strength here – and well-equipped sports hall make for a comprehensive offering. 'Rugby and hockey have been fundamental to my son's time here,' stated one mother. Off site, riding, sailing, canoeing, climbing and caving in nearby Mendips suits those with less of an eye for a ball, but everyone is encouraged to explore the great outdoors: almost all do at least bronze DofE, and a high number complete gold.

Boarding: More than a third of students board, and some parents, at least, appreciate the finishing time of 4pm, which suits those who come daily. The absence of Saturday school does not mean a fallow day, however: au contraire, there's a full programme of activities or rehearsals in the morning, with sports fixtures and expeditions in the afternoon.

Founding Methodist values still prop the place up today: tolerance, friendliness and a lack of pretension underpinned by Christian principles and practice define it

We felt some of the senior boarding accommodation was on the cheerless side of acceptable; doubtless legally compliant, but the bare walls and lack of personal touches in some of the dorms were a bit bleak – and a bath list a relic from an earlier age. Continuing refurbishment is putting a change to all this, though, while the evident warmth of the staff and close friendships between year groups compensate for any dreary living quarters awaiting tarting up.

Food generally reckoned to be good: a tasty choice of stew with Yorkshire pudding, cheese and onion pie, breaded chicken or salad bar the day we visited.

The boarding community enjoys eating together in the evenings and the tweaking of boarders' teas with extra carbs and meat to suit sportsmen/women is appreciated.

Ethos and heritage: Originally and fabulously named the West of England Wesleyan Proprietary Grammar School and founded in 1843 by local Methodists dissatisfied by the kind of schooling accessible to nonconformists, Queen's was renamed for Queen Victoria's golden jubilee in 1887. A run of imposing Victorian Gothic buildings redolent of the timeline along a stretch of road leading out of Taunton to the village of Trull; modern additions are concentrated behind the original buildings, leaving a view across the extensive sports facilities to the distant Quantocks. A super sixth form centre has been created from a former rather ugly civil service club, now greatly appreciated by its new occupants who enjoy areas for silent study, as well as space to chill, chat and rustle up those staples of British education – toast and coffee. In the view of one parent, it gives students 'independence, self-respect and responsibility'. Sharing the same stretch of road and major facilities as Queen's College, if not its architectural merits, is the junior school.

Largest performing arts space of any school in the south west. Dancers are extremely well looked after in terms of facilities and the school's own academy of performing arts, which attracts the likes of Birmingham City Ballet to give classes; strong on contemporary dance too, such as street jazz

Founding Methodist values still prop the place up today: tolerance, friendliness and a lack of pretension underpinned by Christian principles and practice define it; a full-time chaplain is on the staff. Individuals are valued, quirks and diversity welcomed: 'We looked at several schools,' one mother told us, 'but this one had a good feel and was right for both my very different children. My son was initially shy but has really grown into himself.' Other parents praise the school's 'gentle approach' which builds confidence in the diffident, as well as 'the lack of social/wealth/class issues'. Hurrah for that.

Notable alumni include Sir Nick Harvey (long-standing MP for North Devon), Lord Widgery (former Lord Chief Justice of England and Wales), and clutch of other luminaries across the professions, armed forces and arts, including a prime minister of Newfoundland and Elephant Bill, an army officer known for his work in Burma in World War II.

Pastoral care, inclusivity and discipline: Pastoral care highly rated by students and parents alike, from the tutors to the house staff. Close attention is paid to every child – 'We notice if anyone is off-colour.' Two in-school counsellors. 'There are just so many options of people to talk to,' said one girl we spoke to.

An extensive reward system recognises not only achievement but also students who have triumphed over adversity in some form. Discipline was not a word we heard much – we suspect that it doesn't rear its head that often – but 'to incur the disappointment of the head is a crushing blow,' one mother told us. Prefects have the power to administer 'fatigues' for minor infringements of rules or poor behaviour.

Pupils and parents: Mostly pretty local (Somerset, Devon and Dorset), augmented by a contingent of overseas boarders such as Forces' children and an array of nationalities, with Russian and SE Asian predominating. 'Queen's wouldn't suit very competitive sporty, hearty, Sloaney families,' we were reliably informed. Parents tend to be loyal and to involve themselves in the life of the school, but some think school communications need a kick in the posterior: poor grammar and six copies of the same email are just two examples.

Money matters: Fees about 10 per cent lower than comparable schools for UK students, but work out about the same for those from overseas. Lunch is charged separately for day students; learning support, EAL and any kind of extra tuition cost extra. 'Singing lessons are a bit steep,' remarked one parent. Usual range of scholarships on offer, more bountiful than many at a maximum of 25 per cent for a major academic award. Sibling discounts more generous than some we have seen, too.

The last word: A Taunton institution which distinguishes itself from the local competition by its family feel, yet continues to cut the academic, sporting and artistic mustard year after year, Queen's is a welcoming, inclusive, unpretentious place which could sell itself better. A lick of paint here and there wouldn't go amiss either.

Rendcomb College

Rendcomb, Cirencester, Gloucestershire GL7 7HA

01285 831213 | admissions@rendcombcollege.org.uk | www.rendcombcollege.org.uk

Ages: 3-18

Pupils: 402; sixth form: 71; Boarders: 45 full, 18 weekly/flexi

Fees: Day £6,750 to £24,450; Boarding £29,325 to £37,950 pa

Headmaster: Since 2015, Rob Jones, previously deputy head at Shiplake College. Educated at Swansea (economics), Worcester (PGCE) and Buckingham (MEd). After a brief period mixing banking with elite rowing, he became a teacher and has taught economics and business at Canford, Clifton College, King's Worcester and Dauntsey's, as well as coaching rugby and rowing and running boarding houses. Teaches business economics to sixth formers at Rendcomb.

A keen sportsman, parents say he is an excellent head teacher. One explained, 'When we first met he told us that if there wasn't a lot of noise and laughter in the corridors there was something wrong… [He] runs a caring, happy, pupil-focused school.' Another added, 'He has a compelling vision for the future of the school, with the interests of the students at its heart, and isn't scared to innovate and modernise.' Lives in the college grounds with his family.

Head of junior school: since 2017 is Gavin Roberts, previously deputy head. Before that he was senior tutor (academic) at Cathedral School, Llandaff, for 11 years. Teaches year 5 English and is 'warm, down to earth and approachable,' parents told us. 'The children absolutely love him to bits; he allows them to be who they are… There is always a lot of fun when Mr Roberts is around.' A rugby man, he is a qualified WRU referee. Lives in the village with his wife.

There is a One College approach at Rendcomb, one ethos and one vision for juniors and seniors. The two heads are very much united on this and we get the feeling that this team are steering Rendcomb College towards a bright future.

Entrance: Nursery from 3. For junior school entry, taster days plus assessments in English, maths and verbal/non verbal reasoning, plus school reports.

For senior school entry, entrance exam and interview with the head. Automatic entrance for juniors, but all pupils must sit the exam for assessment purposes. Entrance day tests include exam in the morning followed by an outdoor education session so children can be observed working in teams in a relaxed, fun environment. Overnight stays available.

Transition is seamless from junior to senior school. 'New pupils settle in quickly and are not judged by whether they are good at maths, music or throwing a ball,' parents told us.

Boarders' committee decides on evening and weekend activities. These include dance, yoga, craft nights, laser tag or canoeing down the River Wye

Sixth form entry is based on GCSE results, an interview with the head and school reports.

Exit: Majority of juniors go on to senior school, others to Pate's Grammar, Marling School, Cotswold School and Stroud High. Around 60 per cent stay on to sixth form with 90 per cent then going on to university. Manchester, Sheffield and Bath popular.

Latest results: In 2021, 46 per cent 9-7 at GCSE; 56 per cent A*/A at A level (81 per cent A*-B). In 2019 (the last year when exams took place), 36 per cent 9-7 at GCSE; 28 per cent A*/A at A level (54 per cent A*-B).

Teaching and learning: Twenty-three A levels offered including a new design and technology option and a travel and tourism BTEC. EPQ optional. Consistently strong subjects are the sciences and maths. Oxbridge applicants are supported well with external business experts conducting mock interviews and providing feedback. Bespoke courses for overseas pupils available.

French is taught from nursery along with some Latin and German in the later junior years.

French, Spanish and German are the main languages in the senior school. Specialist teachers teach art, music, drama, PE, English and maths from year 3. Talented junior pupils are encouraged to take part in senior school activities. One parent told us, 'Our son has gone from struggling/being somewhat disenchanted with school to really finding himself. His academic side has picked back up extremely well and he has taken up new hobbies (rock band, film club) and the school has been great at helping him open up and grow.'

Technology is taken seriously. Computers are upgraded every three years, and the juniors have been crowned Gloucestershire's coding champions

Technology is taken seriously. Computers are upgraded every three years, the latest have facial recognition and touch screens. There is a maker-space full of bits and bobs – we saw game consoles under construction and 3D-printed prosthetic limbs have been created in the past. There is also a computing laboratory, 3D printer and Oculus virtual reality headsets. This forward-thinking department won the ICT Facility Award at the Education Business Awards in 2017 and were shortlisted for the ICT Innovation category for the use of technology across the school's 230-acre campus. Even the juniors have been crowned Gloucestershire's coding champions and are ranked first place in the Discover Education coding league table.

Learning support and SEN: SEND department caters for the whole school. Provides one-to-one support as well as catch-up programmes in small groups. Needs include dyslexia, dyscalculia and dyspraxia. Specialist dyslexia teachers teach pupils from 4 to 18. The department has a quiet room. More complex needs are considered on an individual basis.

The arts and extracurricular: Forest school is one of the stars of the show at Rendcomb (the other is the Griffin Theatre). The site has been in the grounds for 10 years, run by four fully trained staff and used by everyone. Every week nursery pupils have two sessions and juniors have one afternoon up to year 4. After that it's an extracurricular option. Nestled amongst the trees they have a fire pit, several dens, rope swings and an eco toilet. Senior pupils have their own dedicated space as part of the outdoor education curriculum.

Art, music and DT are in one building with art studios, textiles and a design technology studio. A small exhibition area at the entrance confirms the standard is high. Upstairs is the music department; plenty of practice rooms and pupils told us they can practise whenever they like. Four concerts a year include both staff and pupils. Around 50 per cent learn an instrument. Plenty of music clubs and particularly talented juniors are welcome to join senior groups.

In 2017, the £3.3m Griffin Theatre opened, the first development in almost 30 years (Godman boarding house in 1989 was the last). An impressive building, it has a 350-seat auditorium plus a dance studio and drama classroom, and will undoubtedly inspire pupils to take part in performing arts. First production was Agatha Christie's And Then There Were None, next will be Les Misérables. Past senior productions include Macbeth, Jerusalem and Footloose, whilst the latest junior production was Porridge. All juniors get a part (even the head) and all year 6s get a speaking part. Next up is Pirates of the Curry Bean.

Classical ballet is offered from 3 years and contemporary dance from 11 years. Royal Academy of Dance and Contemporary Dance Association exams and grading. Stretch and tone classes offered to grade 3 pupils and above. Performance group club encourages pupils to choreograph pieces and enter dance competitions such as the great big British Dance Off and Cheltenham Festival of Performing Arts.

Good range of extracurricular clubs including debating, sailing, dissection, martial arts and gardening. Juniors can opt for mixed year and ability sports or music clubs, knit and stitch, scrabble, or clay pigeon shooting (ammunition is extra). Sixth formers can choose an in-house leadership programme, a buddy scheme or DofE.

Funds for expeditions to places like Patagonia must be raised by pupils. Other trips are kept affordable, including a trip to Norway for hiking and trekking, a sports tour to Netherlands, language exchanges and outdoor challenges in the UK. Junior trips include a year 6 outdoor challenge residential, and a biennial French trip for years 5/6. Day trips include Bristol and Cheltenham Literature Festival.

Sport: Not the sportiest of schools. As it is small, teams are mixed ability and often mixed year groups. However, the school ethos is that everyone tries their best and gets the opportunity to represent the school. Outdoor facilities, including the 10-acre sports park known as Top Pitch, are excellent, but parents would like to see indoor facilities to match.

Pinewood

'Rendcomb is probably not going to be first choice for the highly competitive, sports-mad child,' we were told, but parents would still like to see more than just the traditional sports on offer. Badminton and basketball fixtures are arranged throughout the year but these are minor sports, offered as clubs. Equestrian club and clay pigeon shooting are offered from year 5. Shooting teams 'hold their own' against larger and more experienced schools like Harrow and Eton. An athlete development programme supports pupils competing at county and national levels. Junior pupils have swimming lessons from reception. From year 5, in the summer, the outdoor swimming pool is used.

Boarding: From year 7. Around 45 per cent board either on a full, weekly or flexi (up to three nights a week) basis. Only about 10 per cent of years 7 to 9 board, meaning numbers at weekends are low (four to 12 in each house). However, numbers increase in the older years with around 55 per cent of years 10 and 11 boarding and 70 per cent of sixth formers. At weekends there are around 30 to 40 pupils in these houses. Some 75 per cent of boarders are from overseas covering some 14 nationalities. Year 11 students from Germany do short stays.

The Griffin Theatre is an impressive building with a 350-seat auditorium plus a dance studio and drama classroom, and will undoubtedly inspire pupils

There are five houses, all on campus. House system is horizontal rather than the traditional vertical. All have common rooms with pianos, table football, projectors, TVs, X-Boxs, private Skype rooms and kitchens (used for cooking as a family at the weekends). We were impressed with the homeliness of the houses; rooms are well looked after and the houseparents are friendly and caring. Gap students help out in the younger boarding houses.

Years 7-9 are in Godman House – a newly refurbished and extended coeducational boarding/day house that can accommodate up to 115 day/boarding pupils and can sleep up to 40 students in its dormitories.

Years 10 and 11 boys are in Lawn House, and the girls are in Stable House. Here, boarders have individual bedrooms with a study space. In the boys' house there is a large media room for quiet study, and in the girls' there is a library, a hobbies room and a gym. Plus two house dogs.

Park House is the mixed sixth form house. Again, all rooms are individual. A short stroll away is Garden House, a cottage in the village. All sixth formers spend two separate weeks here; they budget, shop, cook, wash and get to school on their own as an introduction to university life. Some fare better than others, we were told, but the excitement around this was ubiquitous.

A boarders' committee decides on evening and weekend activities. These include dance or yoga, craft nights, laser tag or climbing on the grounds, shopping and cinema trips, roller discos or canoeing down the River Wye.

Plenty of socialising between boys and girls, and across year groups. Years 10 and 11 have The Barn and sixth formers have a bar, open twice weekly. This is tucked away in a basement with sofa snugs, a snooker room, poolroom and a dance room. Think, no windows, flashing lights, graffiti walls – every teenager's dream; they absolutely love it. No place for parents, but rest assured this is a fully supervised, responsible zone.

Ethos and heritage: Founded in 1920 by Frederick Noel Hamilton Wills as a boys' school with just 12 pupils; girls were introduced into the sixth form in 1972 and the school became fully co-ed in 1992. The junior school was added in 2000 and the nursery five years later. Around 30 per cent of pupils are from overseas.

Set within 230 acres of parkland in the Gloucestershire Cotswolds, the school is in, and very much part of, the small village of Rendcomb. Cheltenham and Cirencester are nearby. Within the beautiful grounds lies a deer park, home to over 70 fallow deer and classified as an 'ancient tree hotspot' by the Woodland Trust. This is an 'outdoor' school that makes the most of its setting, with regular events like treasure hunts for the juniors and laser tag days for the boarders. 'Our children come home with pink cheeks and muddy trainers and yet still excel in the classroom,' parents told us.

A traditional school steeped in history, it takes great pride in the 'Rendcomb family'. Not just a marketing strapline, we were told by parents; 'Rendcomb has an amazing community spirit... an all-round, family inclusive, friendly feel.' Pupils are often seen chatting sociably with teachers over lunch, and 'the children all mix and play together regardless of age.' Smart blue uniform with a touch of red. Sixth formers wear business dress.

The main house is stunning inside and out. The staircase has stained-glass windows that beautifully illustrate Aesop's fables. The school recently held a concert here (yes, this is no ordinary stairwell), taking full advantage of the acoustics and backdrop. Heating and maintaining a building like this with its huge windows and stone corridors must be challenging and the school reflects this; it is practical and far from flashy.

The deer park is home to over 70 fallow deer and is classified as an 'ancient tree hotspot' by the Woodland Trust. This is an 'outdoor' school that makes the most of its Costwolds setting

The grand dining hall is used solely for dining. Huge floor to ceiling windows and ornate ceilings give a sense of tradition and old-fashioned splendour. Next door is a large reading room and beyond that is a library with a 150-year history; it doesn't get more authentic than that. New sixth form centre opened in 2020.

Juniors have the luxury of sharing the senior facilities. Junior school is attached to the main building and classrooms are based around a quad with the nursery ('excellent,' reported parents) tucked snugly in the middle. Rooms are large, overlooking the outdoor swimming pool or gardens, and class sizes are small (16 max). Large art, design and technology classroom is upstairs next to a modern and rather grown-up science lab. Daily assemblies are run by 'the very funny' head of juniors. Achievements are celebrated and parents happily join too. 'When they have been awarded a distinction they go up and tell the school and the parents why they were awarded it.. a clever way to get used to public speaking at a very young age!'

Boarders and day pupils share the same boarding houses. All pupils register at their houses to 8am daily. Most day pupils are still on site at 4pm and, for a small fee, can stay on for evening activities or supper. No lessons on Saturdays just sports fixtures.

Notable Old Rendcombians include Issy Bailey, Paralympian (shooting); Jonathan Suffolk, technical director at the National Theatre; Richard Dunwoody, jockey; David Tyler, chairman of Sainsbury's.

Pastoral care, inclusivity and discipline: Excellent pastoral care. 'During some challenging health issues... the children now view the school as a part of their extended family,' one mother told us. Another added that the nurturing environment 'brings out the best in each pupil regardless of their abilities or likes/dislikes. It instils confidence, encourages and builds an all round sense of respect for fellow pupils and staff.'

Pastoral care is further reinforced by the family ethos, including big sister and big brother events when younger pupils are shown around the houses. This sense of 'looking after each other' is not exclusive to these events, we were told. 'I am really impressed with how many students across all years know each other and support one another,' parents said.

Services once a week in the listed St Peter's Church on site are conducted by the school chaplain, Reverend Bob Edy, an old Rendcombian with many a story to tell.

Pupils and parents: Day pupils commute from Gloucester, Swindon, Stroud, and as far as Oxford. 'The parent community is really friendly, refreshingly unpretentious and richly diverse,' one new parent confirmed. Another added, 'The teachers and students have very strong relationships and the parents are welcomed into the community as well.' Communication with parents has improved under the current head.

Inclusive too. 'With its Noel Wills ethos of offering an inclusive education – even to a child who would not otherwise be able of afford it – we felt much less intimidated and genuinely welcomed and valued in the Rendcomb family,' one parent confided. In 2015, the school reduced sixth form day pupil fees and numbers have since doubled.

'We love the way the school not only provides the children with academics but teaches them manners, confidence and to be all round great children.' Based on the pupils we met, this is definitely true. Interests and passions are encouraged rather than stifled, resulting in a real mix of children here. Rules are of course in place, but this isn't a strict school in the traditional sense. More of a place where pupils will be 'steered by conversation' as a parent would at home.

Money matters: Scholarships are awarded at 7+, 11+, 13+ and 16+. Noel Wills Scholarship and the Rendcomb Scholarship are offered at 11+.

The last word: A small family-focused school where everyone knows everyone. One parent summed it by saying, 'When it comes to kids, nothing top trumps the development of character, and on this metric I haven't seen a school in the area that comes close to Rendcomb.' Set in amazing grounds, this outdoorsy school is traditional with some modern twists – an impressive performing arts centre and a forward-thinking ICT department. Not for competitively sporty types, but Rendcomb is a bit of find if you're looking for a school that nurtures individuals.

Royal High School Bath

Lansdown Road, Bath, Somerset BA1 5SZ

01225 313877 | admissions@rhsb.gdst.net | www.royalhighbath.gdst.net

Ages: 11-18

Pupils: 550; sixth form: 150; Boarders: 122 full, 8 weekly/flexi

Fees: Day £13,983 – £14,595 pa; Boarding £27,465 – £32,286 pa

Head: Since January 2020, Kate Reynolds MEd LLB PGCE (early 50s). Previously head of Leweston School. Read law at Bristol, followed by two years at a top London law firm. She then did 'the best thing I ever did' and decided to become an English teacher. After a PGCE at Bath Spa University, she taught English and drama at Gillingham School, then Sherborne School. Joined Leweston in 2002, became head of EAL in 2013 and was appointed as head two years later.

Entrance: Competition for year 7 places is less intense than you might think. Around 100 girls a year apply and the school offers 80 places. The entrance assessment takes place in January – an interview first, then English, maths, verbal and non-verbal reasoning tests a few days later. Around 95 per cent from the junior school progress to the senior school via a transfer test.

Up to 15 girls join in year 9 and 35 or so in year 12. Sixth formers need six 6+s at GCSE, including 7+s in subjects they want to study at A level or the IB.

Exit: Around a quarter leave after GCSEs, either for a change of scene or to do other subjects. At 18 almost all to university, plus a few to art foundation courses and drama school. Wide range of courses including maths, chemistry and engineering. Cardiff, Birmingham and UCL currently popular. Two to Oxbridge, plus five medics in 2021. Four overseas in 2021 – to California, Berkeley, Hong Kong and Toronto.

Leavers join the GDST's Alumnae Network, which offers mentoring for GDST alumnae and sixth formers, university advice, career development and networking opportunities. The Royal High encourages former pupils to inspire and mentor their younger counterparts – old girls return to talk about their careers and many offer work experience.

Latest results: In 2021, 79 per cent 9-7 at GCSEs; 72 per cent A*/A at A level (87 per cent A*-B). Average of 40 at IB. In 2019 (the last year when exams took place), 67 per cent 9-7 at GCSE; 46 per cent A*/A at A level (75 per cent A*-B).

Teaching and learning: Excellent teaching and very good results. One parent praised the Royal High's teaching as 'the very highest calibre' while another told us that girls achieve their potential without the element of pressure sometimes found in girls' schools. 'They are expected to do well but they don't seem to be stressed about doing well,' she said. School has offered the IB since 2008 and girls achieved an average score of 40 in 2021. Lots of help and guidance about the respective merits of the IB and A levels, including an IB/A levels-themed Any Questions event. Sixth formers are encouraged to take the EPQ too. Most girls do 10 or 11 subjects at GCSE, including two or three sciences and at least one language.

Strong focus on STEM (science, technology, engineering and maths) subjects, with impressive numbers choosing sciences at A level (when we visited, a quarter of the sixth form were taking chemistry). 'We do lots of experiments and practicals,' a year 10 girl told us. 'My favourite lesson was when we made toy helicopters and flew them off the balcony. Science is so much fun.' Maths is the most popular A level subject, with year 13 girls giving extra help to younger pupils during their lunch break. Languages are particularly strong – French, German, Italian, Spanish and Mandarin on offer, plus Latin from year 7. Head girl told us she did four languages at GCSE, as well as Mandarin AS. Pupils are keen on Vocab Express, an online vocab learning challenge, and at the time of our visit a group of year 10 and 11 girls had been placed eighth nationally. Lots of language and exchange trips. A sixth former waxed lyrical about a recent trip to China, where she'd taught English in a primary school.

Learning support and SEN: School is broadly selective, but probably not the place for girls with extensive learning needs. Learning support ranges from in-class support to one-to-one help (girls are never withdrawn from core curriculum subjects).

As the school says, 'The majority of girls we currently support are those with specific learning difficulties such as dyslexia. We also have some girls with ADHD, autism and a few girls with sensory impairments such as hearing difficulties.'

The arts and extracurricular: Performing arts are big at the Royal High. Dynamic director of music (a composer who previously worked for EMI and the BBC) encourages musicians of all standards and abilities to have a go. All-inclusive music programme features 35+ events a year, performed by five choirs, orchestra, swing band, strings group, woodwind ensemble, rock bands and more. Carol service at Bath Abbey is the highlight of the year for many parents. All year 7, 8 and 9 pupils get an hour's classroom music a week, learning about different styles of music, performance and composition, plus taster lessons to help them decide the instruments most suited to them. Around 300 instrumental lessons per week, with 14 girls a year taking GCSE music and up to eight doing A level. We met a talented sixth form singer who has already released two EPs of her own. The new Steinway Music Hall was opened in 2019 plus two new recording studios.

Lots of language and exchange trips. A sixth former waxed lyrical about a recent trip to China, where she'd taught English in a primary school

Wonderful art produced in the light, airy art school, with four studios and panoramic views to inspire girls' creativity. We particularly admired a sculpture made of wire, tights and teapots representing pattern and rhythm and a remarkably accomplished series of countryside paintings by a sixth former who brought in bags of twigs, sticks and leaves for inspiration. Up to 40 girls a year take art GCSE, 20 take A level and four or five take art as part of the IB. Well-equipped DT department has an ultra-sophisticated 3D printer and a four-axis router. Head of DT says he's 'constantly surprised' by the girls' ideas, showing us a student's stunning faux-leather backpack inspired by an armadillo. Drama and dance in the Sophie Cameron Performing Arts Centre and school's dance studio. Loads of successes in the Mid-Somerset Festival and LAMDA exams. Year 13 girls run a drama club for year 7s and there's a plethora of school and house productions throughout the year. Recent shows include The Tempest, The Wizard of Oz and The Crucible, with rehearsals for Oliver! taking place when we visited.

School has a strong international focus and links with schools as far afield as New York, Kenya and Sydney. Year 9 girls get the chance to do a five-week exchange with Australian girls – 'the most fantastic experience,' a parent told us. An enterprising sixth former set up a charity project, designing and producing cards and gifts to raise money for a school in Kenya. Year 8s take part in an enterprise day with nearby boys' state school Beechen Cliff and older girls do Model United Nations debates with Kingswood and King Edward's School, Bath. There's also the Aspire programme, an academic enrichment programme featuring after-school lectures, activities and debates.

Sport: Pupils are proud of the school's sporting successes, notably in hockey, netball, athletics, swimming, fencing and taekwondo. 'We hold our own,' says school. At the time of our visit a year 13 had just been selected for Bath Rugby ladies' team after a year of playing the sport. Sports facilities include sports hall, outdoor swimming pool, fitness suite, hockey pitches, netball courts and new Astro opened by Olympic gold-medal winning hockey player Kate Richardson-Walsh. The school also uses the University of Bath's sports pitches.

Boarding: Boarding numbers are growing steadily. Head of boarding joined from Benenden and is responsible for the development of boarding at the Royal High. Around two-thirds of boarders are from overseas – from China, Hong Kong, Spain, Germany, Brazil, Kenya (30 nationalities in all). Boarding from year 7 (also available to year 5 and 6 girls from the junior school). Two boarding houses – School House for younger girls and Gloucester House for sixth formers. Full and weekly boarding only. Flexi boarding is available subject to availability of beds. Lots of weekend activities, including pottery painting, baking, zumba, spa days, expeditions to places like Harry Potter World and theatre and cultural trips. Girls are allowed to walk the mile down the hill into Bath – year 7s are escorted while year 8s go in groups of four.

Boarding houses are comfortable, homely and chic, so much so that day girls jump at the chance to do the occasional sleepover. Youngest girls are in wholesome dorms of four or five while sixth formers get doubles or singles. Sixth form boarding house is 'a stepping stone to university', with girls able to cook and do their own washing if they wish. Sixth form café attached, where day girls and boarders can relax and chill.

Ethos and heritage: Bath is a Unesco World Heritage Site and the first glimpse of the school is an impressive Victorian stone monolith at the top of a steep drive off the city's picturesque Lansdown Road. Extensive refurbishment programme in progress when we visited on a blustery October day but the school's listed Grade II buildings are stunning, especially when viewed under a glowing orange sun. Many of the classrooms, dorms and the head's office boast panoramic views across the school's 11-acre site to the city and beyond. The Royal High has blazed a trail as the only GDST school to offer boarding – a legacy from the amalgamation between Bath High School and the Royal School back in 1998. It admitted boys for a brief period but has been all-girls since 2010.

Sixth formers wear business suits rather than uniform. Younger girls are very happy with their new navy blazers and tartan skirts. Unlike some schools, no over-the-top make-up – 'we don't do contouring here,' grinned a year 9 pupil at lunch, to the merriment of her friends. Food, provided by catering company Holroyd Howe, is very good. Lots of choice, including vegetarian and gluten-free options, all carefully labelled, pasta, salads, sandwiches and hot meals.

Famous alumnae include baking supremo Mary Berry, Baroness Elspeth Howe and entrepreneur Emily Brooke, who designed a pioneering laser bike light.

Pastoral care, inclusivity and discipline: Girls are well looked after and look after each other well. No behaviour problems – just the occasional social media or friendship issue typical of girls of this age. Parents like the school's size ('not too big, and not too small so everyone knows everyone') and say that if an issue arises the school 'is on it very quickly'. 'We talk to the girls all the time about who they are and what they want to achieve. As a girls' school we want to be a positive place where girls can flourish and grow.' All pupils have a one-hour PSHEE (personal, social, health and economic education) session per fortnight and school also runs Your Daughter, a programme of talks for parents on topics like developing resilience and happiness, surviving social media and the dangers of illegal drugs and legal highs. When suitable, girls attend these talks with their parents or hear their own version in school.

One of the most popular members of the school community is Spitfire, a black lurcher, who belongs to the student welfare coordinator (she also teaches biology and is known as 'Spitfire's mum'). A wellbeing dog, Spitfire is a comforting presence when girls feel stressed, worried or tired. When the registrar announced to a group of year 9s that Spitfire had just become a father to seven puppies, a unanimous 'aaaaah' went round the room. He even got a round of applause on a recent open day.

Wonderful art. We particularly admired a sculpture made of wire, tights and teapots representing pattern and rhythm

School is keen on encouraging leadership and responsibility. It hosts the annual GDST Young Leaders' Conference, where year 13 student leaders from all 25 GDST sixth forms get the chance to network, take part in teamwork challenges and hear a host of inspiring speakers. The sixth formers then feed back to the rest of the school in assemblies. Head girl, boarding deputy, day deputy and four additional prefects – all voted in by staff and pupils (year 10s and up). Year 13s mentor younger girls and everyone takes pride in belonging to one of four houses named after impressive women – Austen, Bronte, Wollstonecraft and Du Pré.

There is a pastoral project underway – includes development of a 'reflection room'.

Pupils and parents: The pupils are sparky girls who throw themselves into lessons, music, sport and extracurricular activities with enthusiasm and panache. We particularly enjoyed lunch with a group of chatty year 9s, who, with the amused registrar in attendance, talked about everything from the 'great' integration of boarders and day pupils to the 'reasonable' amount of homework they get. They were funny, charming and keen to extol the virtues of their school. 'We feel like we can be ourselves here,' said one girl. Another said that that everyone was 'so accepting' and she didn't feel any peer pressure.

All agreed that the Royal High is not a snobby school. Parents come from all backgrounds, including business people, medics, media types and ex-Londoners. Sixty per cent of day pupils live in Bath, others are from Somerset and Gloucestershire – some walk to school, some commute by bus and train.

Money matters: Good value for money, especially as textbooks, stationery, most extracurricular activities and sixth-form laptops are included. Boarding fees are cheaper than many other boarding schools due to GDST economies of scale. A raft of scholarships and bursaries available, including academic, art, dance, drama, music and sport. STEM scholarships offered in year 9 and year 12. Means-tested bursaries (up to 100 per cent of the fees) for students demonstrating 'outstanding all-round academic ability'.

The last word: A happy, high achieving, very go-ahead school with a distinctive ethos, sense of community and impressive results. For parents looking for a single -sex school (day and/or boarding) we can't think of any girl who wouldn't thrive here.

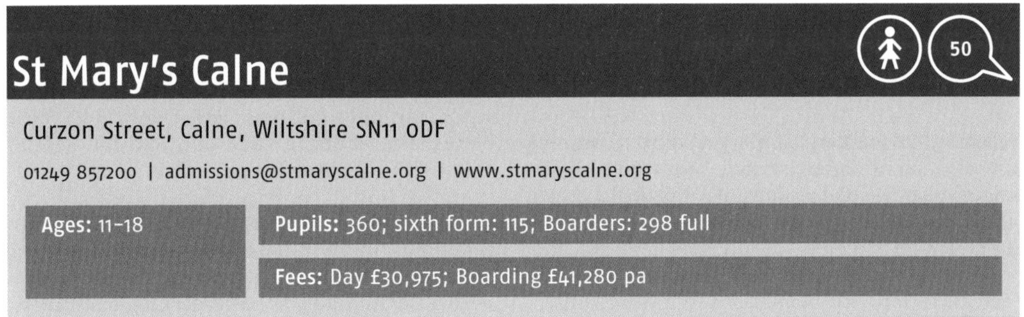

St Mary's Calne

Curzon Street, Calne, Wiltshire SN11 0DF

01249 857200 | admissions@stmaryscalne.org | www.stmaryscalne.org

Ages: 11-18

Pupils: 360; sixth form: 115; Boarders: 298 full

Fees: Day £30,975; Boarding £41,280 pa

Headmistress: Since 2013, Dr Felicia Kirk MA PhD. Born and grew up in Maryland, USA. Her distinguished academic career in languages took her to the University of Maryland, Brown University and then the École Normale Supérieure in Paris to study for her PhD on the 19th-century novel and its relationship to 19th-century painting. She met her husband there and moved to the UK with him. She always knew she'd go into teaching and her first job was at the Royal Hospital School in Suffolk, where she became head of languages. 'I loved the boarding way of life – the fullness and the richness,' she says. After ten years she headed to Wycombe Abbey as director of higher education and then became head of sixth form at Ipswich High School GDST ('my only day school').

Convinced of the benefits of girls' schools, she loved St Mary's Calne from the outset and describes it as 'small, yet ambitious'. 'The brilliant thing about Calne is that there is no one type of girl,' she says. 'We are all about individuality and girls being themselves.' She has led an ambitious building plan over the last decade, including a stunning new library and a beautiful garden with bronze sculptures, water features, benches and swings – 'a lovely place to vibe in,' mused a cheery sixth former. Parents give the head the firm thumbs-up. 'Her attitude is that "we can always do better", which I find so refreshing,' one mother told us. 'I'm very impressed by her.'

The demands of headship mean she doesn't teach on a regular basis these days but she gets involved in pupils' EPQs, does the occasional French or Latin session and holds meetings with the 14-strong head girl's team every week. Her study is quite the nicest we've seen in years of visiting schools – an oasis of calm, with stunning artwork by pupils, French windows opening on to a pretty garden and Lily, her golden retriever (named after the school's emblem), snoozing peacefully on a rug. Her husband works in finance and they live in a cottage on the school site. During the holidays they head to Suffolk, where she keeps her retired 26-year-old eventer Sparky. Outside school her main interests are reading, cooking (she's a fan of Ottolenghi), working out (step, spin and aerobics) and going for long walks in the country.

Entrance: Thirty girls join at 11 and another 30 arrive at 13 to make year groups of 60. Early registration is advised (the school is oversubscribed at 13+). Prospective pupils attend an entrance day, which includes team building, critical thinking and creative exercises, an interview and numerical ability, verbal and non-verbal reasoning tests, after which conditional places are offered subject to satisfactory performance at CE or St Mary's own exams. Bright sparks are invited to apply for scholarships. At 11, a third of the cohort comes from St Margaret's, the school's own prep next door, London schools like Thomas's and Garden House, Scottish schools like Cargilfield and Belhaven Hill and local primaries. At 13, they arrive from a multitude of preps, including Farleigh, St Hugh's, Hanford, Sandroyd, Knighton House and Beaudesert Park.

Five or six new girls join the sixth form each year. Places depend on GCSE grades – pupils need sparkling results in the subjects they wish to study at A level.

Exit: Up to 20 per cent leave after GCSEs, mainly to co-ed sixth forms or to do subjects that aren't offered here. After A levels, the majority progress to university, with Durham, Exeter and Edinburght current top choices. Seven to Oxbridge in 2021. Growing interest in US and Canadian universities. 'We encourage girls to aim high,' says the head. 'We are also trying to promote careers where girls are under-represented, like engineering and materials science.' Interestingly, gap years are becoming more popular again.

Latest results: School is not publishing 2021 results. In 2019 (the last year when exams took place), 82 per cent 7-9 at GCSE, 64 per cent A*/A at A level (86 per cent A*-B).

Teaching and learning: St Mary's Calne is first and foremost an academic school. 'We aren't highly selective but we really add value,' the deputy head academic told us. 'There is a culture of working hard.' The girls get lots of individual attention and wax lyrical about their teachers, saying they go 'the extra mile' to help them. We were shown round by a sixth former who had been offered a place to study engineering at Cambridge and she told us: 'If you are passionate enough about your subject you can get to Oxbridge. Calne has given me so much support.'

Girls are encouraged to be interdisciplinary thinkers, coming up with pioneering ideas of their own. 'Girls are told how to think, rather than what to think,' we were told

All the usual A level choices are on offer, plus economics (currently the most popular subject), government and politics, history of art, PE, psychology and theatre studies. The head introduced computer science in 2016 and eight to ten girls take it every year. 'The portfolio of subjects we offer allows girls to go to any university,' a teacher told us. Many do the EPQ, plus the new Donaldson Award, which includes leadership, scholarship (plus debating and critical thinking), global awareness, skills for life (everything from basic cookery to money matters), giving to the community and preparation for higher education and careers. They can also work towards the Advanced European Computer Driving Licence and some do an advanced communication course run by RADA (Royal Academy of Dramatic Art). Pupils are very proactive, starting their own societies (from geology to history of art) and launching a magazine called Kaleidoscope.

Classes are small – around eight to 12 at A level and maximum of 15 down the school. Setting for languages and maths. Languages on offer are French, German, Spanish, Mandarin and Italian, plus Latin and Ancient Greek. At GCSE pupils do double or triple science (some keen linguists do double science so they can take three or even four languages and double science results are particularly good). Girls are encouraged to be interdisciplinary thinkers, joining the dots between subjects and coming up with pioneering ideas of their own. 'Girls are told how to think, rather than what to think,' we were told. A mother who moved her daughter from a London school to St Mary's said: 'We wanted an academic school but not a hothouse and it ticks both those boxes. She is doing very well and has lots of friends. We are very happy with it.'

Learning support and SEN: The school says its curriculum is 'more suited to the needs of the more able pupil' but there is provision for students with mild/moderate specific learning difficulties, such as dyslexia, dyspraxia, ADHD and autistic spectrum disorders. Everyone is tested on entry and up to 10 per cent have an identifiable educational need catered for. Some receive targeted support in class while others have one-to-one help from the learning support team.

The arts and extracurricular: Art is seriously impressive, with up to 17 a year taking GCSE, up to 13 taking A level and some opting for art foundation courses after they leave. When we visited girls and staff had just completed a project called Voices on the Wind, drawing and writing on flags about what was important to them. The blue and white flags were displayed in an eye-catching outdoor installation, fluttering in the summer breeze for all to see.

Drama is integral to the school, with an annual drama competition, drama club and a senior play performed by year 10s and up. Music facilities are top-notch, including a purpose-built, four-storey music school, recital room, recording studio and 15 practice rooms. The chapel is the main concert venue, with performances by choirs, ensembles, orchestras and a big band. Much of the singing harks back to the English choral tradition, to be expected in a school where chapel is central to its life (pupils attend chapel four mornings a week).

Vast array of activities – something for every taste, whether it's codebreaking, aerobics, yoga, eco group, DofE or Young Enterprise (Calne pupils made the national final in 2017). Work experience, often facilitated by alumnae, is encouraged at the end of years 11 and 12.

Sport: Sporting facilities include a 25-metre swimming pool, sports centre, dance studio, fitness suite and a full-sized floodlit Astro. Lacrosse is the main winter sport and girls have represented

Much of the singing harks back to the English choral tradition, to be expected in a school where chapel is central to its life

the Welsh and English lacrosse teams in the past. 'They love their sport,' a mother told us. 'You aren't seen as uncool if you play lots of netball and lacrosse.'

Other sports are netball, hockey, tennis (there's an award-winning tennis academy), swimming, athletics and fencing. No horses kept at school (some pupils keep them at a local livery) but showjumping and eventing are an important part of the sporting calendar. Lots of individual and team triumphs at the St Mary's Calne Horse Show, which is held every summer and attracts teams from 22 schools. Riding is offered as an extracurricular activity too. In normal times girls take part in the annual British schoolgirls' ski races in the Alps, training at Bristol's Avon Ski Centre.

Boarding: This is a proper boarding school and 80 per cent board. Unlike most schools, St Mary's organises boarding on a horizontal basis according to age, with each year group living together in one of seven boarding houses. 'It means no cliques and gives girls the chance to make firm friends,' says the head. 'It has massive advantages,' a parent told us. 'It means the girls can always find a group of friends of their own age group to be with.' The girls get to mix with different age groups via five vertical 'companies', all named after former bishops of Salisbury. In years 7, 8 and 9 they sleep in cosy dorms (mostly of four girls) while from year 10 up they get their own rooms (with ensuites in the sixth form, lucky things).

We loved the bright, airy year 7 common room where girls sit and chat, knit, bake and play the piano (each boarding house has one). Meanwhile the two sixth form houses are a cut above others we have visited. The upper sixth house is a vision to behold with zingy green tables and walls in the common room, lots of plants and a reading nook underneath the stairs. Younger girls change dorms regularly to avoid cliques. Strict policy on mobile phones – the youngest are only allowed them for a short time after lessons each day and after 8.30pm they have no access to the internet. 'The majority of parents thoroughly approve,' said a housemistress. By the sixth form they are deemed old enough to self-regulate their phone usage.

Saturday school, with lessons in the morning and matches in the afternoon. Weekend activities sound like fun, from silent discos and quiz nights to baking, crafts and cultural trips to Bath and Oxford and there's much-needed downtime too. Exeats every three or four weeks, when everyone departs but girls can go home in between too.

Day pupils (20 per cent of the school) are very much part of the boarding houses. They can go home at 5pm after lessons but some stay for supper and prep and join in weekend activities too. In years 7, 8 and 9 they have their own futons in dorms and get their own studies from year 10. They can opt to board three nights per week at a cost of £46 per night.

Ethos and heritage: Founded in 1873 by the vicar of Calne as a place where girls would receive an excellent academic grounding and get the chance to develop their individuality within an Anglican foundation, the school delivers on all three fronts. The school site is compact but packs a lot into the space, including the stunning new library – a big hit with the girls. There are plenty of break-out spaces and rooms named after inspiring women like Emily Dickinson, Mary Seacole, Maya Angelou and Mary Wollstonecraft. Pupils are encouraged to read for pleasure – current stand-out choices include Fountains of Silence by Ruta Sepetys and Throne of Glass by Sarah J Maas.

Parents like the fact that Calne is 'quiet and safe' and 'not at all London-y' but admit the town 'isn't the most exciting place'. Some boarders come from the capital but they are in the minority (buses run to London at the start of every term and half-term, stopping en route at Reading services).

Pastoral care, inclusivity and discipline: Everyone we spoke to described Calne as 'a happy school' and pastoral care is highly rated by girls and parents. 'I looked at a lot of schools and this was the first school where I thought, Yes, this is the right place,' recalls one parent. 'All the children were smiling and everyone looked happy. I remember breathing a sigh of relief.' Another mother said her daughter had had problems at a previous school but flourished at Calne. 'They saved my daughter,' she says. 'Her confidence came back and she regained everything she'd lost. The other girls were really welcoming and she's now a happy, healthy teenager.'

Each girl has a weekly one-to-one meeting with her tutor (pupils keep the same tutor until GCSEs although tutors can be changed in the unusual event of it not working out). Housemistresses and tutor teams keep a weather eye out for any problems. They're aware that the pandemic hasn't been easy for youngsters and they're on hand to talk to pupils about what they have been through. A counsellor visits two days a week, many of the teachers are mental health first aid trained and year 9s and up are being trained as peer mentors. Girls often speak to nurses at the school health centre too.

The school sets great store by pupil voice, launching a new parliament where girls will be able to air their views on issues like the environment, sustainability, equality, diversity and inclusion. PSHE encompasses everything from coping with the challenges of modern life (social media for one) to becoming responsible citizens who contribute to society. St Mary's is well integrated into the local community – during the pandemic pupils did their bit, helping the elderly, tutoring the children of NHS staff and making cupcakes for care workers.

When the Everyone's Invited website hit the headlines staff spoke to the older girls in a 'gentle, age-appropriate way' about the issues of harassment, assault and consent. 'It's made me even more committed to making sure that we equip our girls and young women to calling this behaviour out and not putting up with it,' says the head. 'We are not hiding from any of these issues. Our students are bright and switched on and want to make the world a better place so it's important to have intelligent debates and discussions.'

Sixth formers wear their own clothes and say they get more freedom as they get older. Lots of socials with schools like Winchester and Eton (there's even a lacrosse match against Radley) so they get the chance to mix with boys. Those we met said they'd be sad to leave when the time comes. 'It's bittersweet,' we were told, 'but Calne does a really good job of preparing you for life after school.' Younger girls wear simple, stylish uniform of tartan skirts and pale blue blouses although when we visited on the hottest day of the year most were sensibly wearing their sports kit.

Pupils and parents: Everyone sets great store by the phrase 'Calne girls can' and the girls we met were a delight – polite, charming and fizzing with ideas. 'They aren't urban or massively sophisticated,' a parent told us. 'They aren't naïve – they are completely with it – but they are just nice.' The year 7s were chatty and enthusiastic, racing to play on the swings after lunch and talking excitedly about Daisy, a day housemistress's black labrador.

Quite a few daughters of old girls and around 15 per cent from overseas, including the US, Switzerland, Sweden. China, Hong Kong and Nigeria. Day pupils come from Chippenham, Devizes, Hungerford and surrounding villages. Former pupils include GB equestrian Laura Tomlinson, journalist Roya Nikkhah, writers Lucy Hughes-Hallett and Eva Rice, actress Belinda Stewart-Wilson and Celia Pool, who invented the world's first reusable tampon applicator.

Money matters: Not a rich school but one that uses its resources wisely. A variety of scholarships available, including choral awards. The school also awards two foundation scholarships every year – one to a year 7 girl and one to a sixth former. These are worth up to 100 per cent of the day fees and are aimed exclusively at local state-school girls for whom 'reasons of financial restriction' would otherwise preclude them from attending St Mary's Calne.

The last word: A successful, happy school. Girls flourish in this supportive, encouraging and nurturing environment. They achieve impressive results, make lifelong friends and clearly have a lot of fun too.

Salisbury Cathedral School

51

The Old Bishop's Palace, 1 The Close, Salisbury, Wiltshire SP1 2EQ

01722 555300 | admissions@salisburycathedralschool.com | www.salisburycathedralschool.com

Ages: 3-13

Pupils: 221; **Boarders:** 31 full, 14 weekly/flexi (from 7 years)

Fees: Day £9,225 – £16,620 pa; Boarding £24,420 pa

Head Master: Since 2013, Clive Marriott MA BEd. He grew up in mid-Devon; 'my mum worked in a care home and my dad worked in an agricultural mill and I'm very proud of that,' he says. His days at Hayward's Primary in Crediton were 'magical' but he didn't enjoy his secondary school years. 'I'm a sensitive soul,' he says, 'but my experience at school drove me to be the person I am today.' A passionate educationalist, he always wanted to teach primary school children – 'I see in them a vision for the future,' he says. After a BEd at King Alfred's College in Winchester he taught at Landscore Primary School in Devon for eight years and did a lot of community outreach work. He then spent 14 years as deputy head of St Paul's Cathedral School before heading to Salisbury.

Enthusiastic, warm and empathetic, he'd much rather talk about the children than himself. 'It's not about me,' he says. 'It's not my show. It's all about facilitating, empowering and believing in the children. I want to ensure that the young people I work with in my school feel valued and respected as individuals.' True to his word, when we toured the school he greeted every child we met by name, congratulating one on his first house badge, admiring a young artist's textiles work and crouching down to talk to cheery pre-prep children.

His faith is a crucial part of his life. He joined his church choir at 7 – 'the sense of belonging, the camaraderie and the uplifting joy of singing together helped to lift me out of my worries at school and strengthened my resolve to get on and do something with my life.' The magnificent Salisbury Cathedral is visible from every corner of the school and the head doesn't underestimate its impact on pupils' lives. 'It's not just the sense of community and family,' he says. 'It also provides children with a moral compass, a sense of place in a society that is drifting all over the place. It's those subliminal values that the children pick up on.'

He's hugely proud of the school but is keen to emphasise that while music is the school's 'uniting raison d'être' it punches above its weight on many different fronts. Very visible in and around the school, he's outside every morning at drop-off time. The teaching staff sing his praises. 'He really looks after us,' one teacher told us. 'He is very approachable, not stuck in an office. If the children want to talk about something they will often go straight to Clive.' Parents are similarly glowing. 'He's amazing,' said one. 'He knows every pupil and understands their personalities. He has a very clear picture of the ethos he is trying to build.' Another told us: 'He's welcoming, fair and makes time for all the children. The school has gone from strength to strength under his leadership.'

He's currently chair of the Choir Schools Association and lives in a house adjoining the school. In his spare time he enjoys walking, sailing, cycling, church music, musical theatre and urban design.

Entrance: The school is non-selective and children start at a variety of ages. Applicants are invited to taster days to ensure it's the right school for them. Day pupils are mostly local although choristers and boarders often come from further afield. Boarding numbers include some Forces children, Spanish youngsters who join for one or two years and, pre-Covid, two or three South African exchange pupils. The school is 50:50 boys and girls. School minibus service from Andover and a feeder bus from the Godolphin School, ten minutes' drive away.

Tucked away in the stunning cathedral close, with 27 acres to play in and the cathedral a couple of minutes' walk away, the school's location is second to none

Chorister places are highly prized and highly selective. Pre-auditions and informal meetings are held throughout the year, with main voice trials in January for girls and in February for boys (in years 3 and 4). Trials include a short singing piece, aural tests and sight singing. Boarding is not obligatory for choristers.

Exit: A few leave at 11 for local grammars like Bishop Wordsworth's (boys) and South Wilts (girls) but most stay till 13. Dauntsey's, Warminster and Sherborne popular, with choristers often heading to King's Canterbury, Uppingham and Wells Cathedral School. Other choices include Clayesmore, Marlborough, Cheltenham College, Canford, Bryanston and Embley. More than 80 per cent win scholarships, often in music, and in 2020 a boy was awarded an academic scholarship at Winchester. Scholarships are proudly displayed on honours boards in the choristers' lobby.

Our view: Tucked away in the stunning cathedral close, with 27 acres to play in and the cathedral a couple of minutes' walk away, the school's location is second to none. One of the oldest educational establishments in the world, it was founded at Old Sarum in 1091 by St Osmund (William the Conqueror's nephew and the Bishop of Salisbury) to educate choristers. After 150 years the choristers' school moved to Salisbury and in 1947 took up residence in the 13th-century buildings and grounds of the Bishop's Palace. The school went co-ed in 1987, founded the UK's very first cathedral girls' choir in 1991 and merged with nearby Leaden Hall School in 2016.

The Grade I listed Bishop's Palace wasn't built with classrooms in mind but the creaky staircase, ancient chapel, rambling corridors and portraits of beady-eyed bishops give the school a distinct Hogwarts charm. The teaching we saw was genuinely exciting. A year 8 class was reading The Five

People You Meet in Heaven by Mitch Alborn but broke off to tell us about Kes, the play they were rehearsing, and the Key Cup, which involved them all having to learn a poem by heart. A year 6 class told us about the school's environmental work, including planting 2,500 bulbs and creating a rewilding area, while the dynamic head of geography and outdoor learning outlined a project to learn about the eight white chalk horses of the Wiltshire hills. Children walked the terrain, learned about the white horses' history and geography and wrote their own poems.

The head of science told us that his number one aim is 'to make them love science'. 'Did you hear my hydrogen rockets going off earlier?' he asked the head. French from nursery and Latin from year 5. Setting in years 7 and 8 but no scholarship group (teachers run tailor-made sessions according to pupils' strengths and intended destinations). Pupils are prepared for CE but humanities are assessed internally in years 7 and 8. Classes of up to 16 and no Saturday school. The school's eight core values of community, creativity, discovery, leadership, resilience, self-discovery, teamwork and thinking are embedded throughout the curriculum and beyond. 'They push them to their individual abilities and encourage them to be proud of what they have achieved and to keep on going forward,' says a parent.

Around 10 per cent have learning support, for needs like dyslexia, DCD, sensory processing needs and ASD. The head of learning support and her team (three specialist teachers and three learning support assistants) offer help in class, small groups and one-to-one. Additional help for handwriting, reading and PE.

SCS has never been known as an ultra-sporty school but sport is definitely on the up and children have recently scooped sports scholarships to Bryanston, Canford, Warminster, Dauntsey's and Embley. Lots of games pitches (real and artificial) and outdoor swimming pool on site. Children play sport four times a week – boys' main sports are rugby and hockey and girls' are hockey and netball. Everyone plays cricket (mixed teams up to the first XI). Girls can play rugby if they choose, coached by a former England women's rugby player. On Fridays pupils can try their hands – and legs – at different sports, such as tennis, football, volleyball, fencing and dance. 'We want to win but we want the children to enjoy their sport and understand the benefits of exercise too,' says the go-ahead female director of sport.

Music is superb, with five school choirs, two cathedral choirs, 13 ensembles, at least 25 music concerts a year and as one parent put it, 'music floating out of every window'. More than 85 per cent learn an instrument and every genre of music is covered. We enjoyed a spirited jazz band rehearsal – so infectious that two year 8 boys broke into a spontaneous dance. No purpose-built auditorium – performances take place in the 18th-century bishop's drawing room (carpeted specially for the Princess of Wales's visit many years ago). Music outreach programme, with staff running singing sessions for local primary schools. Plenty of opportunities for drama, with plays and musicals staged by all year groups – everything from Big Momma by years 3 and 4 to Great Expectations by years 7 and 8.

Common room with sofas and jaunty Union Jack cushions. The boarders even have their own summer festival, called BoarderFest of course

The head is very keen that the choristers 'don't miss out on anything' and works closely with the cathedral to make sure they thrive. 'It's quite competitive to become a chorister but when they apply we aren't expecting them to be very far along in their musical journey,' says the director of music. 'The crucial thing is that they want to do it.' Choristers rehearse from 8am to 9am four days a week and sing at six services, including three on Sundays, as well as at Easter and Christmas. Unlike other schools, the choristers don't wear different jumpers or uniform so they look like everybody else.

As well as art and DT lessons there are plenty of clubs and drop-in sessions. 'There were 15 in here at 8am,' grinned the head of DT as he supervised pupils making key rings, shields and LED lights. Art room has been revamped and the head of art puts every print, painting, ceramic and textile creation on display. 'We don't cherry-pick,' she says. 'Seeing your work on display makes an enormous difference. That's the kind of school we are.'

Two-form entry in the prep but children also belong to houses and vertical tutor groups. Assemblies held in the bishop's drawing room and in the cathedral. School is CofE but all faiths welcomed. We were fortunate enough to attend a Friday morning assembly in the cathedral, complete with 'Canon Ed', the cathedral's canon chancellor, giving the address, readings by pupils, rousing hymns and a young boy invited to light a candle for advent. 'Even if you have no religion you can't resist this,' whispered a parent. We met loads of pupils as they filed in and they were charming, polite, smiley and fun. A group of boy choristers arrived in their distinctive long black cloaks and a year 7 girl sweetly told us that her mother had chosen the school after reading The Good Schools Guide. 'So, thank you,' she smiled.

Pastoral care is first-rate. Everyone – children, teachers and support staff – looks out for each other here. The school has appointed an emotional literacy support assistant (ELSA) and children can talk to her about their worries, be they friendship issues, low self-esteem and sadly, in Covid times, bereavement. She also runs a wellbeing club, offering activities like meditation and yoga. 'If we have happy, healthy children, they will learn,' she says. No head boy or head girl – everyone gets leadership opportunities. When we visited sports scholars were off to deliver a rugby and hockey workshop to pupils at a nearby primary school. Pupils say the school is 'strict, but in a good way'. Every child has a voice here – even the pre-prep children have their own school council. At the time of our visit a year 8 pupil had just successfully campaigned for girls to be able to wear trousers.

Pre-prep is housed in its own building but is an integral part of the school. Nursery children can attend part-time or full-time and virtually all progress to the pre-prep. Very little separation anxiety – 'We let them settle in at their own pace,' says the pre-prep head. Pupils have specialist teaching in French, PE, music, ballet and computing and there are loads of opportunities to get muddy (play trousers and wellies are part of the uniform). Early years children have a rest for 20 minutes after lunch. The pre-prep recently introduced a new approach to learning in year 1, which means that alongside formal learning the children can pursue their own play-based learning activities. The school says it provides 'a bridge between the gentle play-based teaching in reception and the formalised learning pupils experience in year 2'.

Food is cooked fresh from scratch and eaten in an arched dining hall dating back 800 years. The head of catering (he started at the school at 16 and has been there ever since) and his team cook at least 250 lunches a day, plus breakfast and supper for the boarders. At lunchtime there's always a hot meal, vegetarian option and salad bar, with an emphasis on healthy food and nutrition. Pupils love the roasts, fish and chip Fridays and chocolate Rice Krispie cakes. Wrap-around care, with breakfast club from 7.30am and prep school after school care till 7pm (at additional cost).

The parents we spoke to were glowing about the school. 'What it does really well is create happy children,' said one. Another said: 'The staff are incredible – very dedicated to the ethos of the school and there for their students.'

Boarding: About 40 children board, including a third of the girl choristers, and the boarding house, a five-minute walk across the close, is very much 'home from home'. Full, weekly and flexi boarding and children can board from year 3 (there were two year 3 boarders when we visited). Lovely dorms for three to eight children, with sturdy bunk beds and padded noticeboards made by the director of boarding. One lucky year 6 girl can see the cathedral spire from her bed. Lots of nooks and crannies to play in, walled garden and common room with sofas and jaunty Union Jack cushions. The boarders even have their own summer festival, called BoarderFest of course.

Money matters: Means-tested bursaries available. Forces discounts of 15 per cent off day and boarding fees. Choral scholarships are equivalent to 30 per cent of day fees. Around half of the choristers receive additional means-tested bursaries.

The last word: Set in a historic cathedral close and led by an exceptional head, this is a big-hearted, diverse school that buzzes with energy, enthusiasm and happiness. The music is sublime, as you'd expect, but SCS offers something special. No wonder parents wax lyrical about it.

Sandroyd School

52

Rushmore, Tollard Royal, Salisbury, Wiltshire SP5 5QD

01725 516264 | office@sandroyd.com | www.sandroyd.org

Ages: 2–13

Pupils: 236; Boarders: 110 full, 30 weekly/flexi (from 7 years)

Fees: Day £9,570 – £22,950; Boarding £21,990 – £27,780

Headmaster: Since 2016, Alastair Speers BSc MEd PGCE (40s). Educated at Elstree and Sherborne. Read building engineering at Loughborough and UWE, followed by seven years as a consultant engineer (during which he worked in London, Boston, Mexico and Athens). Inspired by his role as a mentor to new graduate engineers, he started to think about a career in education and decided to do a PGCE at Cambridge. His first job was as a design technology teacher at Oakham – he stayed for 10 years, becoming a housemaster, then senior housemaster and completing an MEd in educational leadership at the University of Buckingham.

He grew up in Dorset so when the headship at Sandroyd came up he jumped at the chance to return, drawn by 'the beautiful setting, wonderful facilities and fantastic staff'. He sees preparing pupils for their senior schools as a key part of his role and his experience as a housemaster at Oakham gives him a unique perspective. 'We want them to make their mistakes here so when they get to the next stage they hit the ground running,' he says. Keen for children to reach their potential academically while developing traits like resilience and organisational skills along the way, so they're well equipped to deal with life's challenges. 'I feel very strongly that being successful and happy in your life is not directly related with academic success,' he says. 'It's to do with your social and emotional resilience and how you deal with being dropped from a sports team or having a difficult day.'

The school is situated up a long, winding drive, surrounded by playing fields, woods and parkland. The head's study has stunning views of open countryside

Positive, energetic and approachable, he still teaches maths and design technology and knows all the prep children by name. 'I look forward to the teaching more than anything,' he says. 'This age group has such energy and enthusiasm.' If pupils have a particular hobby or enthusiasm they're encouraged to pursue it – one boy was an avid coin collector and produced a regular magazine about his coins. 'That's what Sandroyd is about,' says the head. 'Our pupils are the ones who say: "I'll give it a go." Our two mantras are "challenge yourself and try different things" and "respect everything that everyone does".' Parents like his dynamic approach, particularly his unstuffiness and ability to blend the school's traditional values with new ideas, such as a dance studio and cricket for all (not just the boys). 'Sandroyd is a traditional prep school with traditional core values but it's very forward-looking too,' one parent told us.

Lives in a house on the school site with his wife Alice, whose two brothers were pupils at Sandroyd. She teaches English here and is very involved in school life. They have two young daughters, both pupils at the Walled Garden, Sandroyd's pre-prep. Outside term time the head's interests include cricket, sailing and 'renovating a cottage in Ireland'.

Since September 2021, the head of the Walled Garden is Polly Holbrook, previously assistant director of studies at Sandroyd. An experienced pre-prep teacher, she recently put the Sandroyd whole-school reading scheme in place.

Entrance: The Walled Garden takes children from the age of 2 and most progress to the prep. Many children join the main school in year 3 from local primaries or pre-preps, while others relocate from London with their families. Waiting lists in some years but it's always worth checking. Families looking to join Sandroyd are invited to an activity morning or taster session and also take part in an assessment (creative writing, verbal reasoning and maths for prospective prep pupils). The school 'isn't hugely selective,' says the head. 'It's just to make sure they will be able to access the curriculum here.'

Exit: Virtually all stay till 13, when the vast majority head to boarding schools. The head is ultra-knowledgeable about senior schools – he and his wife did 12,000 miles in the car before they started at Sandroyd, visiting as many senior schools as possible. Most popular current choices are Bryanston, Sherborne, Marlborough, Eton, Sherborne Girls, Radley, St Mary's Calne, Monkton Coombe, Canford and King's Bruton.

Our view: Delightfully rural, the school is off the beaten track – situated up a long, winding drive, surrounded by playing fields, woods and parkland. The entire school (except the pre-prep) is based in the original house, although there have been significant additions and alterations over the years – most recently Garden Cottage, with its own performing arts hall, teaching rooms and nursery. Beautiful entrance hall, with open fireplace, cosy sofas and impressive wood panelling. The head's study is vast, with stunning views of open countryside.

The school was founded in 1888 by the Rev Wellesley Wesley as a 'small coaching establishment' for aspiring Etonians and quickly flourished. It moved first to Surrey and then in 1939 to Rushmore House (the Pitt-Rivers' family home) on the Wiltshire/Dorset borders (film director Guy Ritchie owns a country estate nearby). School purchased the house and 60 acres within the 500-acre Rushmore estate in 1966. It went

We liked the sign on one of the lab doors – 'Before you come in you need a pen, pencil and ruler, lots of enthusiasm and a big smiley face'

co-ed in 2005 and there are equal numbers of boys and girls in most year groups.

Average class size is 12 (no bigger than 16) and staff know the children well. Parents particularly like the fact that pupils achieve great things on the academic front while 'being allowed to be children'. 'They've got the balance absolutely right,' a mother told us. 'It's a happy, family-run place where my children have really flourished.' Languages are taught from nursery and most do Latin from year 5. We saw a sparky year 7 French class, with children learning vocab by role playing characters in a French café. They fizzed with excitement about the impending annual year 7 trip to Burgundy, where they are totally immersed in the language. General science up to year 5 and then chemistry, physics and biology taught separately from year 6. Science labs are smart and modern and the philosophy is to get children interested by making science fun (activities include a science club, where children make their own slime and watch teachers exploding film canisters). We liked the sign on one of the lab doors – 'Before you come in you need a pen, pencil and ruler, lots of enthusiasm and a big smiley face.' Around a fifth of children have learning support (school caters for pupils with dyslexia, mild dyspraxia, slow processing speeds and visual issues). One-to-one learning support available, plus in small groups too.

Sport is a big deal here. Children play sport virtually every day and everyone gets the chance to represent the school at some point – riding, girls' hockey and boys' rugby are particularly strong. When we visited, the U12 girls' hockey team had just come third in a national tournament. Swish sports hall, opened by Olympic gold medallist yachtsman Sir Ben Ainslie in 2015, has an indoor swimming pool, gym, squash courts and badminton courts.

All children have class music once a week and 90 per cent have instrumental lessons (they get a term's free tuition at any point between year 2 and year 8 to help them decide what to play). There's a host of groups, ensembles, choirs and clubs to join. Drama and dance take place in the impressive Sandroyd Theatre, opened by Zoe Wanamaker in 2008 – recent shows include Macbeth and Joseph and the Amazing Technicolor Dreamcoat. Dance is increasingly popular with girls and boys, whether it's street dance, ballet or jive. Director of the performing arts is keen to give as many children as possible the chance to appear on stage – 'We try and make sure there is something for everybody,' she says. Art is housed in a converted cart shed and all age groups have at least 50 minutes of art a week. Design technology is impressive too – we watched year 6 children designing and making their own ping pong bats, to be used later, of course. Around 50 extracurricular activities on offer – everything from martial arts to film appreciation to bridge.

Pupils make the most of the grounds, whether they're playing sport, climbing trees (yes, they're allowed to here) or riding (the school has its own riding department, complete with an outdoor ménage, show-jumping paddock and cross-country course, and children are allowed to bring their own ponies). The children appreciate the school's beautiful setting. A year 4 pupil we met enthused about the red kites he could see from his classroom window. Pupils aren't allowed to have mobile phones or tablets in school (a popular move with parents) and teachers highlight the importance of good manners, holding doors open and saying sorry if you're in the wrong.

Children are encouraged to read as much as possible. They have 40 minutes of reading during the day and boarders read for at least 20 minutes in the evening. School is very proud of Strive, a new programme that promotes 'intellectual curiosity and a love of wisdom' (the name comes from the school motto, Niti est Nitere, meaning 'to strive is to shine'). Year 3 pupils and up have four 40-minute Strive sessions a week, with tasks designed to build their self-confidence, questioning skills, teamwork and resilience.

School food is wholesome and nourishing. Everything is cooked in-house and pupils and staff eat together on long, convivial tables. We sat with a charming group of year 7s – one boy told us he'd recently had a practice interview with the headmaster in German. 'In German?' we queried. 'How impressive.' The boy dissolved into giggles. 'No, for Sherborne,' he clarified.

Day pupils tend to live within a 30-minute drive – the school runs minibuses to Sherborne, Warminster, Blandford and Salisbury. Distinguished former pupils include Sir Terence Rattigan, Randolph Churchill, Sir Ranulph Fiennes, Lords Carrington, Gladwyn and Wilberforce, Lord Ramsey (the former Archbishop of Canterbury), Ian Gow and ex-soldier and novelist Harry Parker.

Nursery and pre-prep children are based in the Walled Garden – the building is thus named because it's built on the site of an old walled garden and retains one of the original walls. Children are taught in small classes, often by specialist teachers, with a strong focus on numeracy and literacy. The pre-prep is very much 'part of the Sandroyd family' – children walk up to the main dining room for lunch, often sitting with older siblings, and use the main school's facilities, including the swimming pool, library, games pitches, theatre, gym and IT room. Children get a taste of French, German and Spanish from a young age and make the most of the school's stunning location, from team building and survival skills to literacy and numeracy in the great outdoors. Parents pop in for a host of events – nativity plays, class assemblies and social activities. 'We welcome parents who come and chat to staff in the mornings,' says the head of the Walled Garden, who as well as leading the pre-prep spends half her time teaching all year groups. Some pre-prep children travel in on the school minibuses, others live very locally.

Boarding: Boarding is an integral part of the school. Children are expected to board in years 7 and 8 – it's not compulsory but virtually all do. At least 50 boarders stay in school every weekend and day pupils opt in when there's something exciting going on (such as laser tag or bouldering). Instead of staring at screens in the evenings the boarders play board games and table tennis, build creations out of Lego and Hama beads and take part in quiz nights. Junior boarding house for boys in years 3 to 5 and girls in years 3 to 6, middle boys' house for year 6 and 7 boys and senior house for girls in years 7 and 8 and boys in year 8. Girls and boys housed in separate wings. Around 50 per cent of the staff live on the school site, many with young families.

Dorms mostly of four, with bunk beds and lots of posters and family photographs. Health centre is staffed 24/7. Homely touches in the junior boarding house include a tree for pupils to hang 'happy thoughts' on, hot chocolate evenings and the chance to win dorm stars for the best decorated dorm (the winners get a dinner party hosted by houseparents at the end of term). Pupils can either Skype or phone home from landlines in each boarding wing. Letter writing is encouraged too. Communication with parents is excellent. We particularly liked the weekly Sandroyd Times, a lively amalgam of news, views and even the local weather forecast. A recent edition explained why the grass on Sandroyd's sports pitches is cut to 75mm (as opposed to Twickenham's 35mm).

Seventy per cent of boarders live within an hour's drive (some as close as Sixpenny Handley, four miles up the road), others come from Devon, Cornwall and London. Ten children from overseas, including Russia, China and a Spanish contingent who spend a year at the school.

The last word: Sandroyd is a small and nurturing school that offers a well-balanced education in an exceptional location. The pupils we met bubbled with happiness and enthusiasm for the school, while achieving impressive academic results and having fun (and lots of fresh air) along the way.

Shebbear College

53

Shebbear, Beaworthy, Devon EX21 5HJ

01409 282009 | admissions@shebbearcollege.co.uk | www.shebbearcollege.co.uk

Ages: 4–18

Pupils: 270; sixth form: 50; Boarders: 25 full, 51 weekly/flexi

Fees: £5,670 – £14,235; Boarding – £15,885 – £30,750 pa

Head: Since 2019, Caroline Kirby (early 40s). Very much grounded in the south west in terms of upbringing and education, with a geography degree from Bristol and PGCE from Bath, her career has taken her to a range of independent schools (Dean Close, Rendcomb, Leighton Park, Bradfield) no further than the M40 or M4 until an unmissable promotion took her to Le Régent in Crans Montana Switzerland as deputy head; no coincidence that her husband Robert is a modern languages specialist and that the family are all keen skiers. Deciding that their three children should now be educated in the UK and a desire for headship brought them back. Mrs Kirby was set on finding an all-through, co-ed school with an emphasis on outdoor education to fulfil the family wish list – 'and I have discovered a hidden gem in Shebbear,' she told us.

Warm, approachable and looking like the ski instructor she once was, Mrs Kirby has gone down well with parents – 'terribly efficient' and 'very jolly', we heard. In one mother's view, 'There has not been a massive gear shift so far,' but the arrival of the pandemic shortly after Mrs Kirby took the reins has inevitably meant the delay of any major plans apart from significant changes to the delivery of the curriculum. She is proud that the timetable remained completely unchanged, including games and chapel, but that the inescapable pace of technological change in the face of Covid-19 now means the school is where she hoped it would be in 2023 in terms of digital learning. Scaffolding outside the gracious windows of Mrs Kirby's very tidy study evidence of an extensive maintenance programme in progress while there are very few students on the site. There are upsides to everything.

Free time would find the head of this very rural school outside with her family taking full advantage of the walking, countryside and coast on the doorstep (skiing opportunities limited..).

Since 2017 the prep school has been headed by Matthew Foale BEd MSc, a Devonian born and bred but whose further education took him to Cheltenham and Bristol followed by several years at eminent London prep schools before taking on the headship of Kelly Prep (later Mount Kelly) back on his home turf. The long though beautiful commute from his home in Plymouth is worth it for the 'inspirational' children at Shebbear, many of whom themselves undertake long journeys to get there, 'bypassing other schools' he could not resist telling us with a grin. The happiness of those children is top of his agenda, and he appreciates and contributes to the prevailing values of honesty and courtesy at Shebbear – 'This is a place where children own up to their mistakes and learn by them,' he says thoughtfully. A great advocate of outdoor learning, Mr Foale loves Shebbear's windswept campus and grabs opportunities for outdoor learning – creative writing round the fire pit, anyone? Family life comprises his wife Marie-Claire who runs an end-of-life care home, three children (one at St Andrews, the younger two at school in Plymouth) and a red setter. We uncovered a keen competitive sea swimmer – not the ubiquitous vogueish wild swimming type – and Charlie Mackesy on his bedside table – 'A book for our times,' as he put it.

Entrance: Not academically selective – entrance exam to the senior school is for assessment purposes and scholarships. Any doubtful runners from the prep school (this is rare) are identified early on, giving families time to find alternatives. Open days, visits and taster days, including boarding, plus induction days once accepted. Smooth and carefully managed transition from the prep school, which makes up about 50 per cent of the senior intake. Others come from local primary schools, yet more from other parts of the UK.

On settling in, one family told us, 'Our elder son is not particularly confident. It took him a whole year to settle but we had a lot of help from the pastoral team who went to great lengths to try and make him feel comfortable; they even established a new club based on his main interest.' A parent of a boarder told us, 'The entrance process was simple and straightforward. The settling in time was awful for me as I felt like I had lost a child. The boarding mistress and staff were incredible and made my daughter feel immediately at home. They also gave me regular updates as to how she was doing which made me feel a million times better.'

Sustainability is a priority – two biomass plants provide heat and hot water to the main buildings, and solar panels provide around five per cent of the electricity

Exit: A tiny handful leave at the end of year 6, almost always for financial or relocation reasons. Post GCSE around 60 per cent stay on for sixth form; some head off to college to pursue more vocational options. Most of those who stay go on to university. Popular destinations include Exeter, Southampton and Bristol, alongside the odd one off to specialist music college or Norland. Occasional students to Oxbridge, though none in 2021. Some boarders return to their home country to study.

Latest results: In 2021, 52 per cent 9-7 at GCSE; 63 per cent A*/A at A level (83 per cent A*-B). In 2019 (the last year when exams took place), 21 per cent 9-7 at GCSE; 50 per cent A*/A at A level (77 per cent A*-B).

Teaching and learning: Parents are happy with the teaching, saying, 'Academically, I feel the teachers understand [my] children's strengths and weaknesses and work with them so they achieve their best.' Another agreed, '[My children] may not be grade A students, but they are encouraged to give it their all.'

Seventeen subjects offered at A level. Maths and science are strong with at least half of sixth formers opting for these at A level. One pupil was recently ranked number one in the Maths Challenge UK, and another is now studying at Cambridge. Art and music have produced top marks at both levels. Four BTECs now on offer. Religious studies compulsory at GCSE and in most cases a language – some international students take qualifications in Italian, German, Russian and Cantonese. French is taught from reception and Spanish from year 7. Prep school children benefit from specialist teachers not only in languages but also music (everyone learns a musical instrument), ICT and PE from very early on. Small numbers in the prep school mean that years 1 and 2 are sometimes taught together, but work differentiated to allow for variations in maturity and ability. Online learning delivered over Google Meet and Classroom with live teaching has been widely praised for its mix of screen and off-screen provision and contact with teachers and marking maintained. 'My hat is off to the teachers,' one parent affirmed; another told us that it had been 'such a relief to know that my daughter is being taught well and not missing anything education-wise, although she has missed the daily contact in person'.

Learning support and SEN: Pupils are annually assessed for reading comprehension, spelling and writing skills. Academic support is provided at no extra cost. A foreign language can be dropped if extra tuition is needed. One parent told us, 'She needed some additional help, but wasn't bad enough to get any at the state primary school. Shebbear offered, gave, and are still giving her the additional support she needs.' The learning support department produce Individual Teaching Plans (ITPs) twice a year and Individual Education Plans (IEPs) for all pupils with an EHC plan. The department uses a number of tried and tested methods to help pupils, including a handwriting scheme using music, coloured reading rulers and overlays to help dyslexics. Pupils who find it difficult to retain information and to concentrate are encouraged with multisensory techniques, educational puzzles and computer programmes. This provides structured learning in a playful, fun way. The process for access arrangements for public exams starts early and is well organised. EAL also offered.

The arts and extracurricular: At the time of our last visit, preparations were underway for the upcoming performance of Oliver! – two casts performing over four nights. The art teacher was busily working on an impressive set in the main hall. His great eye for design and passion to match do not make up for the lack of a proper theatre though – parents we spoke to reckon drama is the poor relation compared with sport and music facilities. Plans are in the pipeline to put this right, school assures us. Nevertheless, the school's recent LAMDA results are spectacular, with two-thirds of entrants gaining distinctions in 2021. Past performances include Sweeney Todd and The Rocky Monster Show, plus An Evening of Music Drama and Readings from the First World War. Senior pupils have been lucky enough to take part in a drama workshop with actor Joseph Fiennes. Prep school productions have included Joseph and the Amazing Technicolor Dreamcoat, Panto Pandemonium and Pirates of the Curry Bean.

Strong musical reputation. New music centre with recording studio and Steinway pianos in the concert hall. Plenty of musical activities and groups – choirs, orchestra, flute group, saxophone group, brass ensemble and a string group – give regular performances such as informal chamber concerts, gig nights, and more formal concerts. Recent visits by professional musicians have included Voces8 and Festive Flutes.

Summer is when the school really comes into its own, lovely light evenings and sprawling countryside, perfect for barbecues, picnics or evening sports

Art department is on two levels in the main building, with separate pottery, woodworking and food and technology areas. The top level has a large studio for sixth form use where students can leave their work out in individual work spaces. The downstairs level has another large studio. There is screenprinting equipment as well as a cylinder and roller press, plus a kiln room. Artwork is displayed everywhere, no wall is left uncovered, and good use is made of the ceiling, too, with plenty of pieces dangling overhead. The art teacher is keen on pupils being able to compare and contrast their work, learn from each other, and be able to go back to pieces and give them more attention. We felt this approach gave the space a real creative edge, a great way to motivate and improve. Standards of work were in some cases very high. Regular visits to art galleries, local cathedrals and museums for all, plus A level students visit London, Barcelona and Paris. Weekend workshops and some evening classes are on also offer, including life drawing.

Extracurricular activities include the usual array of sports, science, drama and arts clubs, plus a few more unusual offerings such as archery, shooting and surfing. Outdoor education (not just Ten Tors and DofE but also orienteering and bushcraft), though always popular, has been given a shot in the arm by the appointment of a new head of sport and outdoor education, who is busy integrating it into the curriculum using the new outdoor classroom. Other projects like World Aims and Eco-Schools allow pupils to get involved in events like the Global Student Forum

and Model United Nations, campaigning for War Child, Amnesty International and Christian Aid. There are also Fairtrade fashion shows, plus a daily Fairtrade tuck shop. Recent trips abroad include a trip to Poland visiting Auschwitz, and a sixth form charity expedition to Uganda.

Sport: All the traditional sports are played here. For boys, the major games are rugby, hockey and cricket, and for the girls there's hockey, netball and rounders. Other sports on offer include basketball, football, horse riding, hiking, table tennis and trampolining. The 85-acre school site has plenty of room for playing fields, an all-weather floodlit pitch, cricket nets, a dance studio, a gym overlooking the sports hall and a weights room. For a small school the teams do pretty well; the U15 and U14 rugby teams are strong (an ex-head-girl now plays in the England women's rugby team), and the U14 cricket team recently won the Devon Cup. Some of the older sportier prep school pupils play for teams in the senior school. Latest sports tour travelled to Barbados and St Lucia where the boys and girls played football, netball and cricket. A block of swimming lessons on offer in year 3 – off site (no pool at school).

Boarding: Boarding is available from year 4. Almost half the boarders are from the UK, 40 per cent or so from Hong Kong and China, the rest from all over the globe. Quite a few from Forces families. One parent told us, 'We chose Shebbear because it had such a homely feel and the head of boarding made a lasting impression on both of us. The location was and still is stunning, and the facilities for the boarders are very good. I also felt that the school really understood the needs of military children and in this I haven't been mistaken.' She went on to say, 'When asking for time off in special circumstances, eg bereavement and holiday when dad was back from Afghanistan, the school have been understanding and always honoured my request.'

The boys' boarding accommodation, Pollard, is in the main school building. The girls' house, Ruddle, is across the campus and has around 25 boarders. Most rooms are doubles or triples; sixth formers are offered singles. All rooms have internet connection. Common rooms vary – power hockey and snooker tables in the boys' houses and a decent kitchen in the girls'. The two houses meet for activities during the week and socially at weekends. Parents said, 'I have always been completely happy with the rooms, the pastoral care and the general facilities. My girls have been properly cared for and helped if feeling homesick or angry or just plain miserable. I have been able to ring the houseparents if I've been worried and within minutes they have been with my child and then calling me back with an update.'

Artwork is displayed everywhere, no wall is left uncovered, and good use is made of the ceiling, too, with plenty of pieces dangling overhead

Majority are full-time boarders but families do make use of the flexi arrangements. Weekly boarding is becoming more popular, particularly during the summer term to aid revision and with families where the daily commute is long.

Sports hall and library are open to boarders in the evenings and at weekends. Plenty to do at weekends: shopping trips, National Trust visits, theme parks, cinemas, theatres, paintballing, surfing, cycling, and horse riding by arrangement. No school on Saturdays, just sports fixtures. Annual social events include the summer ball, discos, themed parties and talent contests. Summer is when the school really comes into its own, lovely light evenings and sprawling countryside, perfect for barbecues, picnics or evening sports.

Ethos and heritage: Founded in 1841, Shebbear College is one of the oldest schools in Devon. Originally set up as Prospect College by Bible Christians in 1829, it was re-founded by the Bible Christian Church as Shebbear College over a decade later, and eventually became part of the Methodist Church, becoming co-ed in 1992. Exceedingly rural, so be prepared: nearest cities are Exeter and Plymouth, both about an hour away; nearest town is Barnstaple, about half an hour's drive. The school rents out 65 acres of the land to local farmers but has plenty of room left for the main campus, playing fields and a decent cross-country course, plus a great wooden pirate ship in an adventure playground for the prep school. The campus itself is very flat, open to the elements, ensuring any cobwebs are blown away as pupils make their way between buildings. The main building used to be an old print works and some of the original 100-year-old tables are still used in the dining area.

Great science block and lovely, modern, bright classrooms; we particularly liked the biology lab, with its resident python. Sixth formers have exclusive use of the upper floor of a new block. With views of the Devon countryside on all sides, there's a modern kitchen, sofas, a study room and a quiet area, all divided by glass windows rather than walls, as well as teaching space for small groups. Downstairs, the building opens out onto the cricket pitch, perfect for match teas in the summer. There are also changing rooms and a kitchen as well as toilets with underfloor heating, much to the delight of girls who happily take their shoes off.

Sustainability is a priority at Shebbear – two biomass plants provide heat and hot water to the main buildings, and solar panels provide around five per cent of the electricity. Food is locally sourced and cooked in-house.

Pastoral care, inclusivity and discipline: Pastoral care, which has always been strong, has been put under the spotlight to address the needs of students during and after lockdown. The former medical centre is now the health and wellbeing centre – 'It's not just about physical ailments,' we were told. The size of the school means that every child is known to the deputy head pastoral, who during lockdown visited students struggling with isolation and loneliness at home. Chapel happens twice a week, and although the school's Methodist roots are central to its ethos, students of all faiths and none make up the community – less than 10 per cent of pupils are Methodists. One parent commented, 'Both of my daughters are excelling themselves academically and I have to put this down to the quality of the teaching staff and the environment they live in. They are happy, cared for and have a fantastic group of friends around them.' Discipline does not seem to be a particular issue: children are polite and well behaved. Standing when an adult enters the room and opening doors is the norm. One parent said, 'It is very important that our children should be kind and have good manners and these values are constantly reinforced through example.'

Pupils and parents: Little school gate life; pupils come from far and wide. Free buses are provided to a wide range of local towns and villages at 5pm (4pm on Fridays) so everybody gets the chance to participate in after-school clubs. One parent told us, 'Our daughter was not getting on very well at the local school, always came home very tired and grumpy; despite a longer day at Shebbear she still comes home tired, but is happy and achieving lots.'

Parents are kept up to date with regular letters from the head. 'The school is good at communicating to parents. We have email addresses for all the teachers, who are very approachable and are good at coming back with answers to any queries,' a parent told us.

Money matters: A range of scholarships are offered at year 7, year 9 and sixth form entry, plus bursaries including a Methodist Church bursary scheme, sibling discounts and allowances for old Shebbearians.

The last word: Shebbear is a traditional, historic school set in rural countryside, loved for its 'openness, space and family feel, if not for its bells and whistles,' as one mother said. The new buildings are great assets and the new head and her vision for the school will move Shebbear onwards and upwards.

Sherborne Girls

54

Bradford Road, Sherborne, Dorset DT9 3QN

01935 818224 | registrar@sherborne.com | www.sherborne.com

Ages: 11–18

Pupils: 484; sixth form: 192; Boarders: 435 full

Fees: Day £23,760; Boarding £31,650 – £39,510 pa

Headmistress: Since 2018, Dr Ruth Sullivan BSc PhD PGCE (40s). Educated at City of London School for Girls and then Sherborne Girls for the sixth form (she loved boarding there and says 'a whole new world opened up' when she arrived). Studied geography at Edinburgh, followed by a PGCE at Moray House Institute of Education (Edinburgh). Her first teaching job was at St John's School, Leatherhead, where she became a housemistress and head of outdoor pursuits as well as teaching geography. Moved to Glenalmond as head of geography, then to the Queen's School, Chester as head of sixth form. In her mid-30s she decided to do a master's in population and health, followed by a PhD in non-communicable epidemiology at the London School of Hygiene and Tropical Medicine.

She was appointed as acting head of geography at Haileybury as she was finishing her PhD and was 'thrilled to be back in teaching'. Soon promoted to deputy master and spent six years in the role before moving to Sherborne Girls as head. 'I wasn't actively looking for headship but when this came up I didn't pause for a second,' she says. 'I haven't stopped smiling since. Am I proud to be head? Absolutely – and even more so because I'm a product of this school.' She's a firm advocate of girls' schools. 'There are no gendered subjects,' she says. 'The girls can be themselves – and be nurtured, stretched and challenged. Some of the girls here might feel less confident and empowered at a co-ed school.'

A mother who was at Sherborne Girls herself told us: 'I love the fact that all the stuff I enjoyed is still there – like swimming in the river after GCSEs and picnics in the fields'

The demands of headship are intense so she doesn't teach at present but she's very visible around school, observing lessons, taking assembly every Monday and having supper with prefects every fortnight. 'My job is to have oversight of the school, to have a strategy and to lead it,' she says. Parents describe her as 'utterly brilliant' and say she's very approachable. One told us: 'She's everywhere. She's sparky, bright and she really gets the girls.' She's certainly one of the most energetic heads we've met. In her spare time she travels extensively, swims, cycles, runs half marathons (often 12 a year) and triathlons and competes in Ironman events. She has led countless DofE gold award expeditions to places like the US, Morocco, Iceland and Norway, has climbed Mount Kenya and Mount Kilimanjaro and volunteers for Crisis, the charity for homeless people, every Christmas. She's taking a group of pupils to the Everest Base Camp later this year. 'I work hard and I play hard,' she says. 'I took up singing lessons a year ago and I tell the girls: "You're never too old to do things. Give it a go."'

Entrance: Around 25 girls join at 11 but the majority – around 65 – join at 13. They mainly come from 20 schools, including Hanford, Farleigh, Sandroyd, Port Regis, Sherborne Prep, Clayesmore Prep, Knighton House, Forres Sandle Manor, Hazlegrove and Twyford. The school advises registering at least two years in advance of entry, particularly for girls joining at 13+. Pre-assessment takes place in year 7 for year 9 entry and most pupils also complete CE (pupils not prepared for CE sit school's own entrance test). Up to 20 girls a year join the sixth form (they need a minimum of six grade 6s and above at GCSE).

Exit: A few leave after GCSEs, mainly for co-ed sixth forms or to do subjects that aren't offered here (some of them quickly return). After A levels, the majority head to university, with 80 per cent to Russell Group. Exeter, Bristol, Edinburgh and Newcastle popular choices. Three to Oxbridge in 2021. A few do art foundation courses at places like Central Saint Martins, Falmouth and Kingston. Growing interest in degree apprenticeships and the school recently appointed a head of apprenticeships.

Latest results: In 2021, 74 per cent 9-7 at GCSE; 74 per cent A*/A at A level (93 per cent A*-B). IB average point score 37. In 2019 (the last year when exams took place), 62 per cent 9-7 at GCSE; 45 per cent A*/A at A level.

Teaching and learning: Teachers say the school 'isn't a hothouse' but pupils need to be able to cope with the academic curriculum. The school no longer offers the IB (the last cohort took their exams in 2020) but has widened its enrichment programme to support A levels. A wide range of A level subjects on offer – all the usual, plus classical Greek, economics, history of art, photography and philosophy. Most popular A level subjects are maths, RS, English and chemistry. Many sixth formers take the EPQ, choosing an eclectic range of subjects, from 'How ethical is cotton farming?' to 'How has the etymology of six English swear words developed?'

Most girls take nine IGCSEs/GCSEs, including English, maths, religious studies, either separate sciences or combined science and at least one language (Mandarin, French, Spanish and German on offer, plus Latin). Teaching is lively and engaging. We observed a year 10 English class studying Arthur Miller's The Crucible and every time the teacher asked a question a sea of hands shot up. We particularly liked a poster of book recommendations from the head of English on the wall outside the classroom. Impressive new science labs – three for each science subject. 'We do a lot of experiments,' a keen science student told us. 'I love knowing how the theory applies to what we're doing practically.'

Setting and streaming from 13. All girls have personal tutors, moving to a new one every two years.

Learning support and SEN: Learning support team offers support for needs such as dyslexia and ADHD.

The arts and extracurricular: More than half the pupils play an instrument and there's a host of orchestras (including the Sherborne Schools' Symphony Orchestra and the Sherborne Schools' Sinfonia), chamber groups and five choirs to join. We saw an impressive lunchtime strings concert, which featured everything from Bach to Lennon and McCartney. The Candlemas service at Sherborne Abbey is a particular highlight. Recently opened Merritt Centre includes large recital hall, sound-proofed practice rooms and recording studio. New drama school and black box performance space due to open soon too – ahndy for the joint school productions, small studio-based work and house drama festival. Girls can do drama IGCSE and drama and theatre A level. Art, DT and photography are impressive, with genuinely innovative work.

Girls say the school is 'really well-rounded'. 'They provide you with opportunities and encourage you to do as much as possible,' one said. Another told us she used to be scared of public speaking but found her confidence and recently gave a TEDx talk. The deputy head (co-curricular) says the girls are 'very purposeful', constantly coming up with new ideas – from making a podcast about being a woman in the 21st century to launching an equality and diversity society. Lots of lunchtime and after-school activities, including astronomy, cake decorating, coding, DofE, jewellery, life drawing and Young Enterprise. The school has strong links with schools around the world and girls get the chance to do exchanges as far afield as Australia, South Africa, Qatar and Canada.

Interesting speakers invited to give lectures, including RAF pilot Mandy Hickson, the second woman in the UK to fly a Tornado GR4 on the front line. Pupils are keen on environmental projects – the school is the first in the country to sign up to a conservation and rewilding project for schools launched by conservation charity Operation Future Hope and is turning grass areas near the playing fields into wildflower meadows.

Sport: Asked whether Sherborne Girls is 'a sporty school' pupils told us, 'It's an everything school.' Nevertheless, there are sporting opportunities galore. Facilities include a 25m pool, squash courts, tennis courts, lacrosse pitches, climbing and bouldering walls, floodlit Astroturf, fitness suite and gym. Strongest sports are lacrosse, hockey, cross-country and netball but as well as mainstream sports there are opportunities for pursuits like boxercise, zumba, ballet and Pilates.

Boarding: Sherborne Girls is one of the UK's few true boarding schools, with 90 per cent boarders. They can choose to be either full boarders or day boarders who 'stay overnight on the odd occasion'. A total of seven boarding houses – five mixed-age boarding houses for girls in years 9 to 12, a house for year 7 and 8 girls and an upper sixth boarding house for girls in their final year. Some of the younger ones sleep in cubicles – or 'cubies' – but most have double or single rooms. Girls are fiercely loyal to their houses, exuberantly decorating them at Christmas and throwing parties. A recent party theme in one house was 'things you liked when you were 3', so girls dressed up as characters like Dory in Finding Nemo. Unlike many schools, Sherborne Girls doesn't empty out at weekends. There's a lot going on and around 80 per cent stay. Two exeats per term.

Ethos and heritage: Founded in 1899, when Kenelm Wingfield Digby, MP for North Dorset and the owner of Sherborne Castle, decided to open a girls' school. It moved to its current site on the edge of the pretty market town of Sherborne in 1903. The main building is a rambling Victorian mansion, with six out of the seven boarding houses forming a crescent around lawns and playing fields. The latest addition to the site is the swish Merritt Centre, named after a former member of staff who left her entire estate to the school. It houses a 500-seat concert hall, practice rooms, recording studio and café.

'We do a lot of experiments,' a keen science student told us. 'I love knowing how the theory applies to what we're doing practically'

Sherborne Girls and all-boys Sherborne School market themselves as 'separate, yet together' and parents reckon pupils get the best of both worlds here – lessons in a single-sex environment and co-curricular activities, music, sport, drama and social events with boys at Sherborne School. The two schools are looking to align even further, with joint CCF, debating, a pastoral pupil forum and a joint school council.

The girls eat in their houses, with their own separate kitchens and dining rooms. Sixth formers work out table plans for lunch and serve out pudding but supper is more informal. Girls are back and forth to their houses every two lessons so they don't have to cart heavy bags around with them. Distinctive green uniform (no ties). Prayers twice a week, led by the chaplain, with Sunday services in Sherborne Abbey or the school hall. A mother who was at Sherborne Girls herself told us: 'I love the fact that all the stuff I enjoyed at the school is still there – like swimming in the river after GCSEs and picnics in the fields. They don't all jump on the train to London after their exams.'

Former pupils include soprano Dame Emma Kirkby, violinist Ruth Rogers, historian Margaret MacMillan, writers Sophie Kinsella and Santa Sebag Montefiore, Civil Aviation Authority chairwoman Dame Deirdre Hutton and the late Dame Juliet Wheldon, who was legal adviser to the Bank of England.

Pastoral care, inclusivity and discipline: Parents say the school is 'very nurturing' and that girls are clear who to speak to if anything is troubling them – houseparents, tutors, health centre staff and the school's two counsellors (they're in every day). Older girls act as trained peer mentors (known as 'supporters and listeners') to the younger ones.

Sixth formers, clad in black suits rather than school uniform, say they get more freedom as they get older. They like the fact that 'we aren't in complete isolation' and can go into town between 4.30 and 6pm each day. Two head girls, two deputies and 16 prefects – applicants have to prepare a CV and successful applicants are interviewed by senior staff. School rules are straightforward and based on 'keep safe and consider others'. Robust policies on alcohol, drugs and smoking are aligned with Sherborne School. Upper sixth girls are allowed to drink alcohol – maximum of two small glasses of wine – at social events, but only with parental consent and under supervision. After February of their final year the upper sixth are allowed into selected Sherborne pubs. Random breath tests carried out.

Pupils and parents: Quite a few daughters of old girls and many have brothers at Sherborne School. Around 10 per cent from overseas, including the US, Canada, Spain, France, Lebanon, China, Hong Kong, Switzerland and Nigeria, and 10 per cent ex-pat families. 'I want the girls to have a global perspective,' says the head. The 40 or so day girls tend to be very local (they can go home at 6pm, although some stay for prep until 8pm). Parents range from old west country families to Forces parents, diplomats and Londoners with south-west connections (Sherborne station is a ten-minute walk away and it takes just over two hours by train to Waterloo). Parents praise the school's strong sense of community and say it isn't posh or pretentious. 'When you turn up for events the car park isn't full of Range Rovers,' one told us. Asked to think of anything they'd improve, the only (very minor) comment was that the occasional window needed painting.

Money matters: Revised fee structure for day pupils, with two options – day boarders (with the option of overnight stays) and day girls (no overnight stays, but own space for storage and study in a boarding house). A plethora of academic, art, drama, music, sport and all-rounder scholarships and exhibitions available – with a maximum award of £3,000. Means-tested bursaries (up to 100 per cent of fees) awarded in conjunction with scholarships and exhibitions. Military and foreign office families eligible for 10 per cent fee discount.

The last word: A gem of a school, led by an inspiring, go-getting head. Sherborne Girls is better than ever, achieving fine academic standards and, through its partnership with Sherborne School, giving girls the best of both worlds – an all-girls education with a co-ed lifestyle. A sixth former told us 'it's a place of opportunity' and it really is.

Sherborne Preparatory School

55

Acreman Street, Sherborne, Dorset DT9 3NY

01935 812097 | admissions@sherborneprep.org | www.sherborneprep.org

Ages: 3-13

Pupils: 181; **Boarders:** 7 full boarders, 10 weekly/flexi

Fees: Day £9,060 – £17,130 pa; Boarding £24,750 – £25,800 pa

Linked school: Sherborne School, 274

Head: Since September 2021, Natalie Bone, previously head of Sidcot Junior School. Formerly a houseparent and maths teacher at Millfield and head of maths and houseparent at Millfield Prep, she read economics at Reading. Before going into teaching she was a professional dressage competitor and trainer and worked in the City in investment management.

Entrance: Entrance is by interview and previous school report, plus informal assessment at a taster day before joining – to ensure that the school is the right fit and can meet the child's needs. Most pupils start in the pre-prep or year 3 but there is a steady trickle joining from years 3 to 7 and at least 10 new starters arrive in year 7. School is happy to consider new pupils all year round, not just those starting in the autumn term.

Exit: Around 70 head to all-boys Sherborne School or Sherborne Girls. Others go to Bryanston, Canford, King's Bruton and Winchester, plus a few to Eton, Harrow, Cheltenham Ladies', Marlborough, Blundell's, Dauntsey's, Radley, Rugby, Downside, Milton Abbey, more than a third with scholarships. Some to local state schools like the Gryphon in Sherborne or Thomas Hardye in Dorchester at 13+.

Our view: Founded in 1858, the school moved to its present location, just off a quiet Sherborne side street, in 1885. Went co-ed in the 1970s. The school site combines the best of both worlds – it's five minutes' walk from the centre of town but has 12 acres of grounds (including five acres of sports fields) for children to play in.

The prep merged with nearby Sherborne School in April 2021, 'formalising' a longstanding link between the two schools and enabling it to share the senior school's performance spaces, sports facilities and specialist resources, including its stunning chapel. 'It's a logical move,' says school. 'It brings us under one body, makes us part of a school with 600 full boarders and a huge history and enables the prep to move forward with even greater confidence.' The prep will keep its own identity and autonomy and will continue to prepare pupils for a wide range of senior schools, including Sherborne Girls. 'It's right and proper that we feed a whole variety of schools,' explains school.

Teaching is excellent throughout the prep. Teachers are a dedicated bunch, full of ideas and enthusiasm. One parent described them as 'outstanding, with a diversity of styles and approaches', while another declared that the support they'd given to her son, who took scholarship exams to his senior school during lockdown, was 'phenomenal'. 'The teachers are always available if you need to talk,' she said. 'You really feel included in your child's education.' Exam results are first-rate but a member of staff emphasised that the school isn't an exam factory. 'Exams aren't the be all and end all,' she said. 'They are part of the journey. People get so focused on exams and it's important to realise that they are just a stepping stone.' As well as their form tutors, whom they see every day, the children get to choose their own tutors.

Classes are mixed ability, apart from scholarship sets at the top of the school. Maximum class sizes of 18, but rarely more than 16. Three classes per year group in years 6, 7 and 8 and two per year group for younger pupils in the prep. Learning support (accessed by 13 per cent) is provided by the Learning Hub. Children receive one-to-one help or work in small groups.

Pupils enjoy playing conkers (a previous head thoughtfully planted a row of chestnut trees for precisely that purpose) and the school's own four square game

No lessons on Saturdays. Instead, there's an optional activity programme (95 per cent of pupils attend each week). Children come into school in their home clothes or games kit for a three-hour activity programme and take part in everything from drama and dance to junk modelling, crafts and community action. During the week the school runs an impressive 100 activities and enrichment clubs.

Director of sport is keen for every pupil to get the chance to wear a team shirt during their time at the school. During lockdown he introduced co-ed sport during lockdown, which meant that the children who attended school got to play mixed rugby, football and hockey. 'It was extremely well received by everyone,' says school. Main sports for boys are rugby, hockey and cricket and hockey, netball and cricket for girls (rounders less popular these days). The school generally uses its own playing fields but also has access to the facilities at Sherborne School, just over the road, with weekly swimming lessons there. 'Everyone gets some sort of PE or sport every day,' says a parent. 'As well as focusing on the academic side they get the chance to run about in the fresh air and be kids.' Pupils enjoy playing conkers (a previous head thoughtfully planted a row of chestnut trees for precisely that purpose) and the school's own four square game comprising four players on a square court.

Parents are full of praise for the school's music, drama, art and DT. A father with two older children and two at Sherborne Prep said a year 7 play he'd seen was far better than productions he'd seen at senior schools. Music is integral and the school provides choristers (boys only) for the choir at Sherborne Abbey. Three-quarters of the children have music lessons. A host of opportunities for budding young musicians, including full orchestra, senior choir, junior choir, chamber choir, brass ensemble, jazz ensemble and piano trio. Pupils have weekly drama lessons and each year group has an annual production. Head of drama recently introduced yoga too.

The art room is a vision to behold – light and airy, with views of Sherborne Abbey and the children's work proudly displayed everywhere. Head of art is a professional artist who encourages the children to explore different art forms, including drawing, painting, sculpture, film and experimental media. 'They never have the same lesson,' he says. The art room is always open and pupils can use it at break times and in the evenings. The art department produces a weekly video to showcase children's work, with an artist of the week announced every week.

The pupils are spirited, chatty and well mannered. They stand up when visitors enter the room and are keen to talk about their school. Asked what they like best one said, 'The teachers – they understand you as a person.' Another told us that the teachers have 'a fun way of teaching', while a third described the school as 'small and cosy'. They all gave the Sherborne Prep uniform the thumbs-up (especially the navy blazers with jaunty green trim and assorted badges). Senior schools say Sherborne Preppers are mature, independent and like 'having a go'.

Day pupils come from Sherborne itself and from as far afield as Dorchester, Shaftesbury, Shillingstone, Langport and East Coker. Four minibus routes at present. Parents range from architects and business people to writers and directors, many of whom have swapped London for the west country. A mother told us she 'couldn't sing the school's praises highly enough'. She added, 'It's a very warm, unsnobbish, lovely place.' Another said, 'There's such a friendly, welcoming atmosphere. It's a hidden gem. We loved it from the word go.'

Pre-prep and nursery housed in a separate building on the main site. Head of the pre-prep says there's an outdoor ethos, with children spending lots of time outside (clad in wet weather gear on rainy days). 'You don't know until you try' is her motto – and there's a plethora of after-school activities, including recorder club, ballet, golf and cross-stitch.

Boarding: Full time, weekly, flexi and occasional boarding all on offer. Boarding is from year 3 upwards but few board before year 5. Run by a housemaster and his wife who pride themselves on creating a 'caring, warm, family atmosphere'. Around two-thirds of pupils board; there are around 15 international boarders – around half the boarding cohort. Co-ed, with girls and boys sharing joint common rooms and a plethora of varied weekend activities to sign up for. 'It's easy to make friends here,' said one boarder. 'It's more like a family.'

Money matters: Academic, music, sport, art, DT and all-rounder scholarships available – school says 'talent and enthusiasm are especially sought'. However, scholarships are honorary rather than financial.

The last word: Forward thinking and full of character, Sherborne Prep is friendly, down-to-earth and unsnooty. It achieves top-notch results while ensuring that children have a lot of fun along the way.

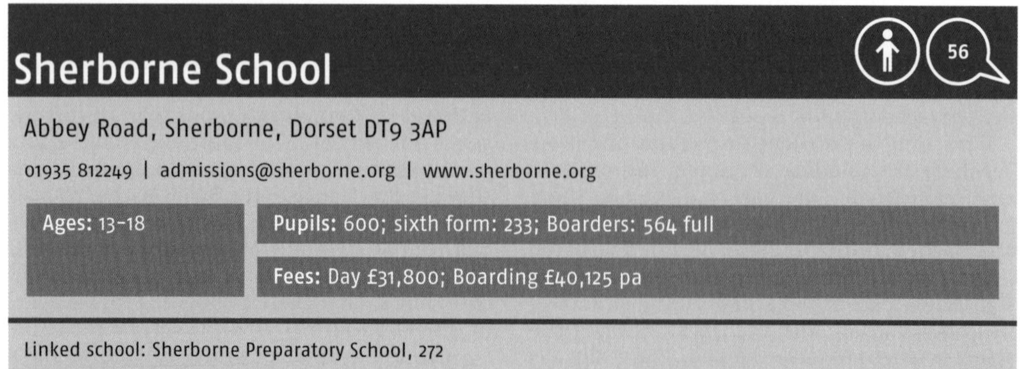

Sherborne School

56

Abbey Road, Sherborne, Dorset DT9 3AP

01935 812249 | admissions@sherborne.org | www.sherborne.org

Ages: 13–18

Pupils: 600; sixth form: 233; Boarders: 564 full

Fees: Day £31,800; Boarding £40,125 pa

Linked school: Sherborne Preparatory School, 272

Headmaster: Since 2016, Dr Dominic Luckett (50s) BA, DPhil, FRSA, FHA, FCCT. Not the product of the kind of school he now heads, as he freely admits, but with a distinguished academic as well as professional track record. Starting with a congratulatory first in history from the University of

Leicester and a doctorate from Oxford, Dr Luckett's career has taken him to Harrow, Worth School as deputy head and Mill Hill, where he cut his teeth on headship. He arrived at Sherborne at a period of trouble and instability at the top, but his unwavering focus on the most important part of the job – headmastering – is undoubtedly paying off. 'He's an educator, not an administrator,' one mother observed approvingly. Since his arrival he has bolstered the links with Sherborne Girls – 'so much more than joint activities, though the boys do learn how to treat girls by doing things together, eg CCF' – and is now CEO of the Sherborne Schools Group, comprising the boys', Sherborne International and Sherborne Prep, recently taken under that umbrella. It all sounds horribly corporate but doesn't feel it – they are still three distinct schools.

The library is exceptional, with its hammer-beam roof and air of quiet scholarship, yet warm and welcoming

We were told he was a very busy man with a diary that only worked in half-hour chunks, so we were heartened that our first sight of him was on the steps of Cheap Street Church at the start of an informal lunchtime musical recital, open to anyone and well attended by parents and locals – of that more anon – and then to chat expansively to him over tea in the hallowed drawing room of his private residence. Some of the chat was too hilariously indiscreet to appear in this review, but he did have some serious points to make about privilege, misogyny and the eye-watering expense of the kind of education Sherborne provides. The boys find him 'attentive, involved, visible, friendly' and appreciate that he knows them by name – he stopped to ask after the progress and recovery of an injured rugby player sporting a moon-boot when we were walking through the courts. Parents rave about him: 'Everyone thinks he's fantastic,' according to one mother, 'even the dads, who don't care that he's handsome and looks good in a suit' (agreed). 'Call me Dominic' and they do – or Dom Luck behind his back. Strict enough though – 'The boys are terrified of him,' one parent told us, so he can clearly fix them with the eye of a basilisk when required.

Married to Cara, a clinical negligence barrister and 'ferociously bright', according to her ferociously loyal husband, they have two daughters, both at Sherborne Prep. Spare time might find him paragliding, hill-walking, skiing – or winding his collection of antique clocks, which temporarily deafened us as they struck the hour.

Entrance: At year 9, but the process starts much earlier, with an online assessment day in the January of year 7. This is the main academic hurdle boys have to clear; Common Entrance, sat at the usual time at the end of year 8, is used for school setting purposes. Allocation of a boarding house happens in year 8; parents can request up to three but requests from Old Shirburnians are given priority. The school has the final say. A few boys arrive at sixth form, having achieved at least a grade 4 in all their GCSEs and a minimum of a 7 in all subjects to be studied at A level, plus online assessment and interview.

Exit: Very little fall-out after GCSE (boys are no longer invited to move on if they didn't get the required grades). Vast majority go on to university, three-quarters or so to Russell Group; a handful of medics and vets and to Oxbridge, though none in 2021, despite stellar results. Exeter, Durham and Bristol the most popular choices, with degree courses tending towards the practical (various aspects of business, engineering, land management) rather than the fanciful. Growing interest in opportunities abroad.

Latest results: In 2021, 76 per cent 9-7 at GCSE; 73 per cent A*/A at A level (95 per cent A*-B). In 2019 (the last year when exams took place), 52 per cent 9-7 at GCSE; 46 per cent A*/A at A level (78 per cent A*-B).

Teaching and learning: Excellent results achieved alongside the kind of array of anything extracurricular that anyone could possibly want must be testament to the quality of teaching ('amazing', according to one mother); not that we witnessed many lessons in progress during our visit, interestingly. Classrooms range from the wonderfully historic (and probably only now used for purposes which don't require smartboards) such as the Old School Room where signatures scratched into the wood panelling date from 1698 (was it considered vandalism then, we wonder?) via the utilitarian 1950s languages/humanities block and Turing labs to the beautiful Pilkington labs with outstanding wet and dry work areas. The library is exceptional, with its hammer-beam roof and air of quiet scholarship, yet warm and welcoming.

Definitely not a hothouse, but 'we wanted a school which catered for the super-bright and the medium bright' one parent told us. Another talked of the breadth of the academic range (all things are relative, of course) and remarked that that the school 'knows when to push and when to encourage the boys to relax'. Academic support gets the thumbs-up from both parents and boys. At GCSE, boys can choose up to four options alongside the core subjects; there is considerable discretion both over the number and choice of GCSEs (no compulsory language, for example): 'the joy of a full boarding environment is that we can make almost any combination of subjects work,' as the school says. The same goes for sixth form, where unusually for a school like Sherborne, three BTECs in sport, creative & digital media and enterprise & entrepreneurship are also offered alongside 24 A level choices. These boys work hard and their prep (halls, in school parlance) is done at set times and places, mostly in boarding houses; younger boys are supervised. Top subjects in their view are sciences, music and art – their alluring facilities may help. Theology gets mixed reviews! Technology seems fully integrated: boys (or doubtless their parents) buy their own laptops equipped with MS Surface Pro, but this does not come at the expense of handwriting.

Learning support and SEN: Its home on the edge of the school belies its importance. A staff of six cater mainly for SpLD, but the head of learning support told us that issues like focus and attention span had come to light during online learning. Referrals to the department can come from class teachers, parents or the boys themselves, who might turn up at the welcoming space with its open door policy saying 'I can't concentrate' or 'My tutor says I should talk to you about revision'. Support is offered either in small groups or one-to-one and links with class teachers are close; emphasis also placed on 'dents or injuries to self-confidence alongside learning needs,' as the delightful head of SEN put it. As to attitudes – 'It's just another thing that boys go off to do,' she reckons. 'The boys are not judgy' – a view borne out by the boys we spoke to. Parents seem pleased with the provision: 'My dyslexic son thrives on pleasing his phenomenal English teacher,' one mother reported. The help the department provides to boys in navigating social situations is well regarded. More detail on the website would be helpful, however.

The arts and extracurricular: Truly extensive, with excellent facilities and opportunities. Music probably top of the pops with a charismatic head of department and fabulous dedicated block with intimate concert hall, plus Sherborne Abbey where the school meets regularly for collective worship and lusty hymn-singing and which provides the setting for a rigorous grounding in the English choral tradition for the abbey choir. The chamber choir has just 22 auditioned members, who are well set up for choral scholarships to the UK's most prestigious universities; the school also recruits its own gap year organ and choral scholars. We were thrilled to visit on a Friday and so able to pop into the weekly Cheap St recital, where musicians of all standards perform. The brass players were by no means perfect but all thoroughly committed to their performance of pieces ranging in difficulty and genre. Q time – an hour after lunch – is set aside specifically for music practice. It pays off: students regularly gain distinctions at grade 8 and some diplomas while still at school.

Drama takes places in the Powell theatre, but there is a strong tradition of house drama too – Sherborne can list some notable names such as Hugh Bonneville, Charlie Cox, James Purefoy, Jeremy Irons, John Le Mesurier and director Richard Eyre among its old boys, plus Charles Collingwood, the infamous voice of that old patriarch of The Archers, Brian Aldridge, and ITV news anchor Tom Bradby. Many productions happen in conjunction with the girls' school. Latest plays include The Turn of the Screw and Incident at Vichy.

Art takes place in its own dedicated light bright space, incorporating the Oliver Holt gallery. Work on the depiction of gender was in progress when we visited, and there is art displayed on the walls all over the school. Both the art school and DT workshop, fully equipped with any piece of kit or machinery you could wish for, are open during evenings and weekends and work closely together.

Sherborne Abbey is the venue for collective worship and lusty hymn-singing, and is the setting for a rigorous grounding in the English choral tradition for the abbey choir

Trips to concerts, plays and exhibitions have necessarily been a casualty of Covid, but in normal times they greatly bolster learning within school. CCF, Ten Tors and DofE provide masses of opportunity to toughen up outside; CCF particularly big here, though entirely voluntary and led by sixth formers: year 10 cadets must earn the right to wear a beret on Remembrance Sunday. Silence is observed all year round on the steps leading up to the chapel out of respect for the Old Shirburnians killed in action and named on the walls. Major General Patrick Cordingley, the distinguished army officer and author, is an OS and former governor.

Sport: As extensive as you would expect for a school of this prominence and location, with acres of pitches surrounding it, some running

Upstairs, dorms were bright, functional and reasonably tidy, with that unmistakeable whiff of trainers thinly veiled with Lynx

right up to the fence with the girls' school. Most venerated of these is the Upper, where only the first XV generally get to muddy their boots. Rugby is huge here but not at the expense of everything else and, refreshingly, offered as part of a carousel of choice right from the start: the game plan (ha!) is to ensure that every boy finds a sport he will carry on enjoying once he leaves the school – not just all about compulsory team games and the trophy cabinet while he is there then, though that doesn't go amiss either. Hockey, football and cricket plus minority sports like golf, fives and clay pigeon shooting of course, but we picked up some gripes about tennis facilities: an imbalance of grass and hard courts and a low-profile tennis pro. The lack of athletics track to complement the rest of the facilities was also mentioned. Gorgeous indoor pool and slightly tired-looking sports hall shared with the town when the school are not using it; a new indoor sports amenity will rise again in the next year from the 'very expensive hole in the ground' we were shown on our tour. Some parents feel that sport plays second fiddle to music, however, and that more recognition could be given to sportsmen outside the first XV or XI for winning less prestigious matches against arch rivals Millfield and Marlborough, for example – a mention in dispatches would be welcome. Those who don't enjoy ball games might try sailing (school has own boats at nearby reservoir), climbing (at the indoor climbing wall at the girls' school) or any of the outdoor education on offer.

Boarding: Full (on) and unapologetic boarding here, with very few day boys (five per cent). Eight houses (soon to be nine, with the reopening of a house previously used by Sherborne International), each with its own distinctive building, character and amount of wisteria, ranging from the historic and ancient School House right in the courts to Lyon, purpose-built 100 years ago and a ten-minute walk away, and the Digby, a former hotel. Large year 9 dorms gradually being subdivided and mixed-aged corridors in the boarding house we were shown; housemasters have considerable autonomy in the way they run their houses, but thankfully the rule of senior boys is a thing of the past; that said, we heard some parental disquiet about 'ridiculous and old-fashioned hierarchy' among boys which the school is addressing. Accommodation is cheery, well-maintained and homely – we were charmed by the tangle of bikes, scooters and toys belonging to the housemaster's young family in the hall; upstairs, dorms were bright, functional and reasonably tidy, with that unmistakeable whiff of trainers thinly veiled with Lynx.

Houses engender fierce loyalty rather than tribalism and the school tries hard to achieve a balance of the brainy, the sporty and the arty in each. Parents can shortlist up to three houses at admission. Most are run by a housemaster and family but one has just appointed its first female housemaster (her chosen title). A team of matrons and tutors, some of whom live in, complete the staff. Boys eat in the central dining hall, a huge echoey space, now showing its age somewhat. A new catering contractor was still bedding down at the time of our visit and, we'd say, still has some work to do. The Friday offering of fish and chips, veggie/vegan gumbo or salad bar was okay, but not comparable with the food at other schools of Sherborne's calibre. The boys did not comment, but the parents we spoke to certainly did: 'The amount they spend on pizza is ridiculous,' and 'We are paying a flipping fortune and they need to get it right.'

Ethos and heritage: Four laughing boys tumbling arm in arm into the street was our first sight of the school and those impressions were not dispelled during our visit. Time and time again we heard how happy the boys are, sometimes from impartial observers. Previous reviews remarked that Sherborne was a place for robust characters only, but this seems to have changed for the better, and more delicate, perhaps initially homesick, flowers can survive, nay thrive. Although it has always had the run of the town whose (bounded and safe) freedom boys and parents simply love, the much closer links with the girls' school, trumpeted by a big new marketing push highlighting the best of both worlds for secondary education, makes the school feel a much more normal place than some of its traditional rivals. Uniform helps: no tailcoats or wing collars here, but a practical everyday uniform of blues – woolly jumper and shirt – and suits for sixth formers, plus an array of sports kit in house colours.

This despite great antiquity: founded in 1550 as part of the monastery and retaining many sumptuous golden buildings from the time, it has gone through a few iterations, reaching its present one in 1850 owing to the vision of its then headmaster and the arrival of the railway. But it remains true to its founding principles of all-boys education with a Christian ethos and its own chapel and the glorious abbey, sitting foursquare in the centre of this small prosperous Dorset market town, are central to school rhythms, even if some boys 'struggle with the amount of chapel and abbey,' according to one mother. They will certainly be grounded in Christianity and, if the school gets it right, will leave with the virtues of compassion, kindness, integrity, leadership and service. As one mother put it, 'I want my boys to come out of Sherborne as nice young men and to aim as high as they possibly can.' It has often been said that you never meet a Shirburnian you don't like – we certainly haven't, past or present. The Bow award, given to a boy who has made an outstanding contribution to the welfare of other boys, is the most prized accolade at Commem, the annual rather grand speech day. Any unsavoury attitudes to girls are swiftly jumped on: our senior guides told us of a recent incident at CCF where a few boys suggesting that girls weren't up to it were immediately called out. 'It's not all weird and woke, but the head does create expectations of being nice,' a parent reflected; but one boy said plaintively, 'I felt I was being told off for being a boy – and I'm only 13!' in the light of fall-out after the launch of Everyone's Invited.

Pastoral care, inclusivity and discipline: The welfare of the boys in this busy environment is placed centre stage, and was particularly vital during lockdown and the return to school. We heard from both boys and parents that there was always someone to talk to, whether housemasters and motherly matrons whose cosy rooms piled with mending and ironing are a refuge, or tutors, generally swift to spot anyone engulfed by too much work, play or both. One mother of a very homesick boy greatly appreciated the daily phone call and photos and videos of him having fun with other boys, sent by the housemaster.

Rules are enforced on the hoof: 'Tuck your shirt in!' and 'Phone!' (not allowed in public) barked a housemaster with a wink at two boys in the street

Gone, thankfully, are the days when being gay meant living out your schooldays in the closet. These days, not fitting the mould of a traditional English school boy is not an issue: 'There is no mould!' we were told by the boys we spoke to, who went on to tell us about the progressive atmosphere at the school and the active equalities group. We also unearthed a 13-page transgender policy. 'The hope is for differences to be of no particular consequence,' in the crisp words of the head. Such a far cry from the school days of Alan Turing, surely the school's most eminent old boy (even counting Chris Martin) who, having changed the course of recent history, went on to commit suicide rather than submit to chemical castration. A fine bust now adorns a corner of the courts.

Discipline – more about carrot than stick – is implemented by a system of merits (awarded for effort as well as achievement) and issues, which can be removed if improvement (or remorse?) is forthcoming; the expectation of good behaviour and consequences of less than good are spelt out. Rules are enforced on the hoof: 'Tuck your shirt in!' and 'Phone!' (not allowed in public) barked a housemaster with a wink at two boys in the street. Academic support is offered for unsatisfactory work where appropriate. Matters such as vaping are being clamped down on – it now comes under the umbrella of drug paraphernalia. Enlightened attitudes to alcohol permit it for sixth form only (and nothing stronger than beer or cider) at specified school occasions and permission to visit local pubs for those over 18; everyone is breathalysed on return to his boarding house.

Pupils and parents: Mostly comparatively local: 'This is not a place where you dump your son and drive off,' we were told; many from traditional Dorset families, gentry of the south west, Shirburnian dynasties or London – but not exclusively: 76 boys count English as an additional language, the majority being Chinese; some first-time buyers. Seemingly less ostentatious than families from similar schools: 'There aren't thousands of helicopters or Bentleys,' in the words of one mother. The boys we met were charming, open, friendly, candid and grateful for the friends and experiences they have at school.

Money matters: Boarding fees in line with comparable schools and day fees 75 per cent of those. Some extras such as art materials sneaked on to the bill, plus purchases from the school shops and barbers, bookshops and cobblers in town. Scholarships (academic, creative, musical and sporting) carry no more than a 10 per cent reduction; additional financial help can be applied for alongside or outside scholarship provision. Open bursaries exist for bright boys likely to be in the top third of entrance assessments, but amounts awarded depend on the competition in any given year. Scholarship assessments are held each January.

The last word: A traditional boys' boarding school in an ancient golden setting busy embracing and marketing the best parts of single-sex and co-education with Sherborne Girls, without losing its identity or appeal: 'Boys will be boys – and girls are welcome,' as a previous head told us. A kinder place than it once was, with excellent teaching, a mass of opportunities, and a spectacular backdrop that instils a lifelong appreciation of beauty and history.

Sidcot School

Oakridge Lane, Winscombe, North Somerset BS25 1PD

01934 843102 | admissions@sidcot.org.uk | www.sidcot.org.uk

Ages: 3–18

Pupils: 617; sixth form: 130; Boarders: 154 full/flexi

Fees: Day £8,700 – £19,530; Boarding £29,490 – £35,280 pa

Headmaster: Since September 2021, Catherine Dykes. She joined Sidcot as head of early years foundation stage in 2018 and was also assistant head pastoral.

Entrance: All junior school hopefuls attend a two-day taster session, including assessments in maths, reading and spelling, non-verbal reasoning plus an informal interview with the head – but the policy is non-selective. Children are welcomed in at all stages; quite a few arrive in year 5. Scholarships on offer from year 1, 'both talent and academic'.

Academically non-selective so transfer is automatic (and highly praised) from the junior to the senior school; otherwise applications are taken at any stage except into years 11 and 13, and places offered on the basis of previous school reports and interviews at the school.

Exit: The majority of juniors automatically to the senior school (around 80 per cent). Baseline assessments for setting and monitoring purposes. Some 35 per cent move on after GCSEs for a change if they have been there since nursery, some to a greater range of courses and subjects post 16, and quite possibly the brighter lights of Bristol. Destinations include old and new universities up and down the land to do an array of courses, with a leaning towards art and design; some gap years. Popular current destinations include Exeter and Warwick. Three medics in 2021. Often a few to Oxbridge though none in 2021.

Latest results: In 2021, 50 per cent 9-7 at GCSE; 56 per cent A*/A at A level (75 per cent A*-B). IB average point score 37. In 2019 (the last year when exams took place), 39 per cent 9-7 GCSE; 62 per cent A*-B at A level. IB average point score 31.

Teaching and learning: Non-selective at junior and senior level – 'We think labelling children according to their intellectual ability is counterproductive,' says the junior school. But that is not to say that the teaching lacks rigour or focus. 'We follow the national curriculum, but are not slaves to it, and we certainly don't expect children to come in and conform to the way we teach. We look for a learning style that suits each child.'

Closer tracking to monitor progress in the junior school. Languages are strong: there is even a competition to recite a poem in a foreign tongue. Forest school from the nursery onwards, with benefits including managing risk, getting up close and personal with nature, teamwork, cross-curricular learning and making an Iron Age round house. Phew! Alongside the three Rs, children here also learn emotional intelligence, to have a voice and to learn independently: each pupil has to research a topic to present on a double-page spread in any way which appeals – writing, pictures, photographs, diagrams. Anything goes and is peer-reviewed. Work is often marked by two stars and a wish – the stars for things done well, a wish for something to be done better next time. The friendliness of the school is noted and appreciated by the children and SEN support is extensive and totally without stigma.

Results are solid if not stellar. That said, maths is acknowledged as being exceptionally well taught. Year 11 Pathway (up to seven GCSEs taken in a year) scoops up students who need GCSEs, and fast – perhaps because they have bombed elsewhere, perhaps because they plan to do A levels or IB and need the groundwork, or because their English requires a shot in the arm. IB taken up by about one in five. Resolutely not an academic hothouse, which is a large part of its appeal – 'Being force-fed academically just because she is bright would not suit my daughter,' remarked one mother – yet parents are confident that bright children will be inspired and well enough taught.

Sixth Form Passport, comprising the CAS elements (creativity, action and service) of the IB syllabus has been introduced for all sixth formers, plus 'post-school survival skills'; EPQ is also encouraged.

Learning support and SEN: SEN students with mild to moderate learning difficulties, as well as social and emotional issues like anxiety and (a lack of) social skills, are well provided for by qualified staff in a light and colourful room; school has CReSTeD status, and staff work closely with English and maths depts. Integration and acceptance are total here – everyone is screened on entry, and periodic assemblies on dyslexia to raise awareness mean it's just part of school life. The undiagnosed are also welcome to ask for support, for example at exam time, and 'Everyone who needs support, gets it,' according to one parent. 'The teachers will help you hundreds of times till you get it right,' affirmed one child.

The arts and extracurricular: Visual arts, drama and music are housed in a new light, airy centre. We witnessed the most controversial A level art exhibit we had ever seen, depicting the conflicting duality of Muslim women, the siren beneath the burqa. Ceramics and textiles also noteworthy. All manner of artistic media are on offer, and those not studying art are welcome to scratch any creative itches at a club or society. DT and product design stand out too: from a man-powered bushfire extinguisher to an iPhone-powered record player – a range of practical, aesthetic and downright eccentric projects are realised.

DT and product design stand out: from a man-powered bushfire extinguisher to an iPhone-powered record player – practical, aesthetic and downright eccentric projects

Seven drama productions a year; recent ones include Into the Woods and A Midsummer Night's Dream (directed by students) performed in the grounds; facilities exist to make film and radio also. International students are encouraged to take part, partly to improve their English – but Struwwelpeter in Chinese was surely not to be missed. School takes a show to Edinburgh every other year. Sidcot's music, the school readily admits, would appeal more to fans of One Direction than the Endellion Quartet, resulting in some of the school's most talented classical musicians choosing to take their lessons in Bristol rather than at school – but they don't half sound impressive at concerts. The auditioned choir (all girls, necessarily limiting the repertoire) tends towards 'the Gareth Malone end of the spectrum', quite possibly because there has never been a tradition of church music. Facilities and tuition designed rather for music tech, creativity and composition.

Plenty besides sport for those unmoved by ball games or horses, such as trampolining, archery, TV production, debating and so on. Outdoor stuff on offer such as DofE, and good use is made of the extensive grounds for gardening, beekeeping and the construction of a nature trail, inter alia. Trips include a French exchange, Tanzania, Vienna for culture/art/language. PASS – Programme of Activities for Sidcot School – 'a co-curricular initiative based on our key values of integrity, stewardship, self-reflection, adventure and community'.

Sports and music are junior school favourites: everyone adored composing music for Tom and Jerry on the computer and the pop choir is – well, popular. Separate PE for girls and boys from year 3. Trips, laid on every year for each year group, also get thumbs-up: a camp-out in the grounds for the littlest, progressing all the way to outdoor pursuits camp in Okehampton for year 6.

Sport: Twenty acres of pitches, including new all-weather pitch, and a multipurpose sports hall with the nicest school pool we have ever seen – base for lifeguarding and kayak tuition – mean there is plenty on offer at Sidcot. The size of the school causes some parents to bemoan the strength and depth of rugby talent – but naked aggression is not the Quaker way. Sidcot is not, perhaps, the place for an elite sportsperson – more serious players often belong to local clubs. The equestrian centre open to the public for livery, Pony Club and equestrian studies. All benefit from an indoor and outdoor school (floodlit) and 160 acres of glorious country to hack in.

Boarding: Majority full but a few flexi boarders; around half from overseas. The five boarding houses are sprinkled through the grounds, facilities are clean, tidy yet homely; we were struck by the warmth and knowledge of each boarder the house staff displayed. Three or four share a room in the younger years; sixth formers in ones or twos. Usual range of sporting and artistic activities after school and at weekends, plus trips to eg cinema, ice skating rink, local festivals.

Ethos and heritage: Everyone, nay everyone, we spoke to singled out the atmosphere at the school as being the reason for being there. The school's proud Quaker origins (dating from its founding in 1699), history and traditions are lived out every day, giving it a curiously contemporary feel which is so much more than lip service. The school's first ever founding director of peace and global studies has recently been appointed, with a brief to 'bring 21st century Quakerism to life' right through the curriculum, weaving in themes such as social justice, conflict resolution and global responsibility. Sidcot is now a 'change-maker school', as a member of the Ashoka movement, which aims to 'empower the next generation to lead social, environmental and economic development'. Specifically, the atmosphere is one of respect and tolerance – for those of all faiths and none, for different nationalities, for different gifts, skills or shortcomings, for each individual. Quaker half hour is held every week and presided over by sixth form elders, at which teachers and students have equal rights to speak and to be listened to.

The school's proud Quaker origins, history and traditions are lived out every day, giving it a curiously contemporary feel which is so much more than lip service

We had never met a more thoughtful bunch of young people. 'The children look out for each other, and the school does its best to bring out well-rounded young adults'; 'a home from home for your child, with similar principles to the ones we have brought them up with at home'; 'the teachers are accountable to the children' were just some of the views we heard. One mother described her daughter as a 'bruised and tender plant when she arrived at Sidcot', but who 'had turned into a strong, forthright and confident young woman, which is moving to see'. We heard of several parents choosing Sidcot for its ethos (dread word) over other schools whose academic, sporting or musical prowess was more notable. Learning is conducted in a calm and conducive environment, where 'punishment is not a word we use,' said one member of staff; some parents though feel on occasion that the benign Quaker view of children needs to be tempered with a dose of realism when it comes to high jinks in class.

The Quaker foundations and conventions are not lost on the juniors, either. 'The elders are year 6 and we sit silently in a circle with our teachers at our Wednesday assemblies. We think about stuff like keeping secrets.' Perhaps because the children and their achievements in every field are fêted, there is no need for anyone to feel undervalued: 'We absolutely do not brag at this school,' said one perceptive year 6.

Conveniently situated just beside the A38 running south from Bristol, the school's main façade is a pleasing white stucco building, with the inevitable less sightly additions behind it. Some charming gardens, covered in brightly coloured gazebos on the scorching summer day we visited, to represent each of four virtual houses. We were enchanted by the ponies grazing beyond the fence bordering the garden to one of the girls' (physical) boarding houses, with a tantalising glimpse of the Mendips behind. New sixth form in the making.

Notable alumni include Sir George Trevelyan (dubbed the hippies' champion), geologist Robert Shackleton, founder of Macmillan Cancer Support, Douglas Macmillan, Zoe Wanamaker, Justin Webb and Deborah Warner.

Pastoral care, inclusivity and discipline: Respectively, exceptionally good and deploying the lightest of touches. We did not uncover any rebels, tearaways, lads or ladettes, and when quizzed, students listed acts likely to attract reproof as 'not listening, disobedience, laziness, doing what you want'. Hardly hanging offences. Censure from one's peers would be a greater deterrent, we sense. According to parents, the head is adamant about drink and drugs in school – one strike and you're out. Sidcot has no bar, unlike most boarding schools with a vibrant sixth form.

Pupils and parents: An intriguing mix of individuals conforming to shared expectations and outlook, but card-carrying Quakers a small minority. Though the students look conventional enough, with uniform on the posh side (striped shirts, blazers), we suspect that Sidcot families conform to fewer than usual independent school stereotypes. When asked what sort of parent would send a child to Sidcot, the head replied, 'Guardian readers indifferent to sipping sherry on the lawn on speech day, whose children see diversity as a strength, who are prepared to stand up for what they believe in.' A few locals, refugees from Bristol schools and nearly 20 per cent from overseas thrown into the mix.

Money matters: Fees are stepped according to year group, and a loyalty discount (about 12 per cent for boarders, seven per cent for day) applies to anyone staying on to sixth form. In general, fees are noticeably lower than local boarding competition in Bristol, but more expensive than the Bristol day schools. Ten per cent sibling discount. Quaker families on occasion receive 100 per cent remission of fees. Scholarships awarded for academics or talent; level of funding is discretionary.

The last word: A school more likely to produce the head of an NGO than a merchant bank. For those untroubled by notions of social pretension or academic snobbery, yet for whom a considerate altruistic atmosphere really matters, this is just the place

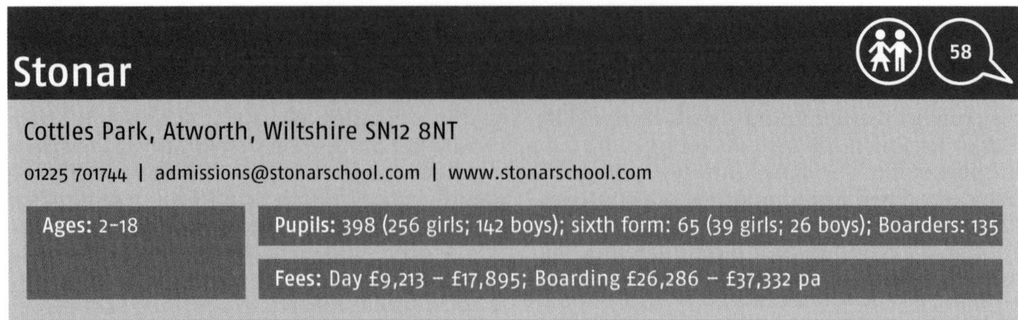

Stonar
58
Cottles Park, Atworth, Wiltshire SN12 8NT
01225 701744 | admissions@stonarschool.com | www.stonarschool.com
Ages: 2-18
Pupils: 398 (256 girls; 142 boys); sixth form: 65 (39 girls; 26 boys); Boarders: 135
Fees: Day £9,213 – £17,895; Boarding £26,286 – £37,332 pa

Head: Since 2019, Matthew Way BSc (Econ) (50s), previously deputy head of Milton Abbey. Educated at Pangbourne College and then read history and politics at Swansea University. Served as an infantry officer in the army for six years, followed by a one-year stint as a management consultant, before realising he wanted to teach. 'My last job in the army was training recruits of 16 or 17 who were away from home for the first time,' he says. 'It was a very pastoral role and was part of my move towards teaching.' He taught at Pangbourne while waiting to do his PGCE at the University of Bath, then moved to Kelly College (now Mount Kelly), where he became a housemaster. Spent six years at Stowe as a housemaster and head of boarding and another five years as deputy head at Milton Abbey. 'I didn't start teaching till I was 28,' he says. 'I haven't scrambled up the greasy pole in education in a mad rush. I've done good chunks of time in schools and through that I've gained on-the-ground, hard-nosed experience of running boarding schools.'

When he visited Stonar for the first time he was immediately struck by its 'lovely, unique charm and warmth'. He doesn't ride ('I have never been on a horse,' he says, adding that friends presented him with a pair of jodhpurs when he was appointed but he hasn't used them yet). He knew of the school's strong academic record and exceptional equestrian prowess prior to joining and is determined to build on these. The school has increased in size since his arrival (but will never be bigger than 445) and after going co-ed in 2016 the ratio of boys to girls is now almost 50:50 in the prep school and year 7. A third of the sixth form are boys and two-thirds are girls.

During subsequent lockdowns the head ran an online weekly quiz for pupils and their families, making sure it appealed to pupils aged 8 and up and their parents from all over the world. 'It was good fun and it helped to retain that sense of community, character and spirit that connected with me at Stonar from the outset,' he says.

Parents are full of praise for him and say he's very visible around the school. 'He is very proactive,' one told us. 'He's a very respected figure but is incredibly approachable and always takes time to talk to the children.' Another told us, 'He is very personable and his ethos resonates with parents. He is a good guy who seems to have done a lot in his life. He's the right man for the job.'

Married to Kate, an intensive care nurse at the Royal United Hospital in Bath, with three children, all pupils at Stonar (a son in year 12 and two daughters). The family lives on the school site. Ultra-sporty (he played hockey for Wales and is a passionate cricket fan), he still finds time to teach history to year 8 and GCSE pupils. In his spare time he enjoys long-distance walking and reading American political biographies.

The head of the prep: since 2019, Rob Cunningham, was previously deputy head of the Mead School in Trowbridge.

Entrance: For prep school entry, literacy and numeracy are assessed in addition to social interactions and approaches to learning through a taster day in school. The learning support team will assess on a second visit if necessary. Nursery from 2, open all year round. For senior school entry, entrance exam to assess strengths and weaknesses. 'We select on character and contribution,' says the head. For sixth form entry, school reports and an interview with the head. If English is a second language pupils must take an EAL exam.

Exit: More than 90 per cent of pupils move from the prep to the senior school (they're on the same site) and 80 per cent stay on for sixth form. Around 95 per cent of sixth formers go to university – 60 per cent to Russell Group. Durham, KCL, UCL, Cardiff and Exeter all popular. Forty per cent of students do science-based degrees.

Latest results: In 2021, 54 per cent 9-7 at GCSE; 53 per cent A*/A at A level (74 per cent A*-B). In 2019 (the last year when exams took place), 52 per cent 9-7 at GCSE and 21 per cent A*/A at A level (31 per cent A*-B).

Teaching and learning: School prefers 'selection based on character and contribution, with a broad academic intake' rather than 'non-selective'. Value-added scores are more important than grades alone (Stonar was recently placed in top 1.5 per cent of schools for value added at GCSEs and top 2.5 per cent at A level). The school uses the Yellis and Alis system from Durham University to keep track, helping pupils to reach their full potential. 'They are really good at getting children to join the dots about why learning is important and how it creates a pathway to progression,' a parent told us. Pupils are encouraged to take three A levels. Sciences are popular at this stage, with most opting for at least one science or maths or psychology. The arts are strong, particularly photography and art. Vocational courses include level 3 diplomas in horse management, sport and fashion design and textiles.

For horse-lovers this is a dream come true. The equestrian centre (British Horse Society approved) is impressive. Pupils with their own horses are up at 7am to muck out. Equestrian staff are 'highly knowledgeable'

With a staff-to-pupil ratio of 1:6, classes are small, usually around 15. Pupils agree that this is one of the advantages of Stonar, especially at A level when there are some groups of four to six. Parents told us the teaching staff are 'incredibly supportive and inspiring'. High praise for the careers advice – an aspiring doctor told us it's 'amazing'. Parents were impressed with the school's 'exceptional' provision during the pandemic. 'They provided online school from 8.30am to 4pm every day,' said one. 'The children were very engaged and inspired and they had after-school clubs too.'

In the prep school parents are invited into school at the end of each topic and pupils 'teach' them what they have learned. There's a culture of 'growth mindset' across the school, with successes celebrated in assemblies and the weekly newsletter. Pupils are taught in mixed-ability classes and aren't streamed. 'We want to nurture a love of learning, not turn them off and create reserved, demoralised children,' say staff. Senior school specialists teach languages, drama, sport and music to prep children.

Learning support and SEN: Prep pupils receive learning support in the form of extra maths and English lessons and/or a teaching assistant in class. In the senior school, around a fifth of pupils have support, though one-to-one isn't currently offered. Needs catered for include ADD, ADHD, ASD, dyspraxia, dyslexia and speech and communication difficulties. More complex needs are considered on an individual basis.

The arts and extracurricular: Main art studio is kitted out with a kiln and there's an adjoining photography studio and darkroom. Separate sixth form studio. High standard of art and photography on display. Latest addition is a DT suite (DT is now a curriculum subject).

Traditionally, the school has alternated the main annual production between musicals and Shakespeare plays but the head of drama is shaking things up a little. Speech and drama available as well as LAMDA and RADA qualifications. The prep school has a classic nativity play every year, plus a large summer production for years 3 to 6.

Plenty of music groups, including choir, chamber choir, wind band and orchestra. The annual Globeducate music festival is a highlight, bringing pupils from around the world together to perform. In the prep school there are termly musical assemblies and larger theatre performances twice a year. Formal carol concerts take place in Bath Abbey, plus musical concerts in the music school.

Extracurricular activities aplenty. Sixth formers must do at least one club, younger years two. There's everything from sports to debating. DofE is popular. Sixth formers run lunchtime science and maths clubs to help younger pupils.

Sport: For horse-lovers this is a dream come true. The equestrian centre (British Horse Society approved) is impressive – stables for 65 horses, BSJA jumps, a floodlit, outdoor all-weather manège, a cross-country course and schooling field with a wide variety of different fences and a large indoor school with a viewing gallery and lecture room. The Olympic-sized outdoor arena with seats is used for jumping and dressage as well as seasonal shows. Competition squads regularly compete on and off site, including British

Showjumping, British Dressage, National Schools Equestrian Association competitions and Stonar's own inter-schools one-day event championships.

Parents say the equestrian staff are 'highly knowledgeable'. Pupils with their own horses are up at 7am to muck out. Horses can be loaned or pupils can earn a riding lesson by working as stable helps. Around 50 per cent of pupils ride, but at various levels: some own a horse, take qualifications and compete; others just have a weekly riding lesson. And it's not just about the riding – stable management skills are taught too. However, the main priorities at Stonar are academic studies and pupils told us that however passionate they are about horses, their schoolwork can't suffer.

Main sports for girls are hockey, netball, cricket, athletics and swimming, while boys do rugby, football, hockey, swimming, cricket and athletics. Good sports facilities, including a swimming pool, with lessons from pre-prep upwards. The annual Globeducate Sports Olympics offers an opportunity for pupils to compete alongside peers from other schools around the world.

A mother told us, 'I have a daughter who wants to be prime minister and a son who'd like to be a YouTuber and they are encouraged in exactly the right way for them'

Boys' sport has flourished since the school went co-ed. 'Our son plays county hockey and loves rugby so the sports provision had to be right – and it is,' a parent told us. 'They are still growing but they have combined year groups for teams and the boys are taking on other schools and beating them. Some of the sport scholars could have had their pick of schools but they chose to come here.' In the prep there's a progressive sports programme, with lessons up to four times a week in football, rugby, tennis, hockey, cricket, athletics, swimming and gymnastics. Plus there's a sports performance programme for talented older pupils.

Boarding: Stonar offers full or flexi boarding. Mainly full boarders, with few below year 7. Just over 55 per cent from overseas, including Europe, America, Canada, China, Nigeria and South Africa. Around 15 per cent of these (mostly from France, Germany and Spain) are short-stay boarders, from one term to one year.

Three boarding houses, all of which have had a makeover. Ganbrook is above reception and houses younger pupils. York is the sixth form girls' house and Hart, a Grade II listed farmhouse with a new boys' boarding wing, is a short stroll away. All houses have decent-sized doubles or singles for sixth formers and dorms of three of four for younger pupils. Common rooms are large with plenty of sofas and a TV. Good kitchens for snacks. Parents speak highly of houseparents and 'the caring environment'. Plus, they told us, there's lots of fun – 'baking cakes, playing games, talent shows, movie and pizza nights. Even when we relocated to be closer to the school, they still wish to board as they love school life so much.'

Day pupils often stay for evening activities and everybody gets two free sleepovers per term. No Saturday school or exeats. Pupils are free to go home any weekend. School weekends are filled with trips to Bath, Laser Quest or Cotswolds Water Park. Younger pupils have to join in but older pupils get more freedom. Sixth formers can go out for up to five hours alone, and from year 10 groups of four can go to Bath for the day.

Ethos and heritage: Stonar was originally established at Stour House in Sandwich in 1895. It relocated to its current location in Wiltshire at the beginning of the Second World War. Cottles Park is a Grade II listed mansion set in rural countryside about eight miles from Bath. Riding was firmly established back in 1934.

Since 2013, Stonar has been part of the Globeducate schools group, an international educational group with 55 schools across 10 countries. As the only English boarding school in the group, Globeducate has been funding Stonar as its flagship English school. New buildings and refurbishments have transformed it, giving it a modern edge and an international feel. Pupils can participate in a programme of cultural and academic exchanges and events with other schools in the group, including a biennial trip to a sister school in Barcelona for years 5 to 8.

As the number of boys grows, upgrades and developments are inevitable but the aim is to keep the school 'family-sized', remaining flexible and providing individual support. One pupil may be passionate about riding, another an aspiring musician, another may need learning support; all can be looked after well at Stonar, we were told. The addition of boys is undoubtedly changing the dynamics of what was a 'traditional girls' school' but the change is being fully embraced by pupils and teachers alike. 'The integration of boys has been so smooth,' a mother told us.

Parents say the school's size gives it 'a family feel' and means it isn't too overwhelming. Prep school and nursery are very much part of the school. Facilities are shared and younger children play out on the front lawn of the main house every lunchtime. The main hall is used for assemblies, performances and drama, with classrooms adjoining. Upstairs on a mezzanine level is the library, fitted out with cosy beanbag areas under the wooden rafters. Outside there are playgrounds, a play area with sandpit, a nursery sensory garden and a forest school for the younger years. The whole school comes together for celebrations, carols and the summer fete. 'The grounds are amazing and my girls go for lovely hacks around the school parkland,' a parent enthused. The campus is a mix of old and new. Traditional wooden-style chemistry labs contrast with the modern physics labs.

Technology has improved dramatically in recent years. Wifi works well across the site and mobile signal has improved. In the senior school year 7 to 11 pupils aren't allowed to use their mobile phones during the day. Several ICT suites, plus iPads available in language and science lessons. In the prep, the ICT suite is used for a computer science curriculum that involves programming and robotics. Hymns and prayers in assembly but pupils told us this is 'not a particularly religious school'. A strong house system carries pupils from prep to senior school. Prefect system, school council and 'committees for everything', we were told.

Pastoral care, inclusivity and discipline: 'It's a nurturing environment,' a mother told us. 'I have a daughter who wants to be prime minister and a son who'd like to be a YouTuber and they are encouraged in exactly the right way for them.'

Discipline is based around asking pupils to question their actions and consequences. Another parent said, 'I really like it that there aren't reams of ill-thought-through rules – rather, the children are really encouraged to think about values instead.' Nurses hold daily drop-in sessions at the health and wellbeing centre. Counsellor available once a week.

Pupils and parents: The head says there's 'a unique, innocent charm' about the pupils. 'If you're a rider then we have brilliant facilities but 50 per cent of our pupils don't ride. No one just does one thing. If you have a child who is outdoorsy, bright and wants to work hard they'll thrive here.' Parents praise the community feel and say the school 'brings out the best in children, regardless of their academic or sporting ability'. One mother told us, 'We've seen our son's confidence grow. It's incredible that a school can unlock that in children.' Good communication between school and parents. 'Be it from the head to the tutor and everyone in between, we feel we have had all matters dealt with quickly and professionally but in a friendly, supportive and helpful manner,' a parent told us. Weekly newsletter plus visibly present heads and teaching staff at drop-off and pick-up.

Former pupils include big names in riding, including junior and young rider gold medallist Georgie Spence and international event rider Lucy Wiegersma, as well as actor Romola Garai and writer and journalist Gitta Sereny.

Money matters: Academic scholarships offered for entry into years 7, 9 and 12, plus art, drama, music, sport and riding. Sixth form scholarships also available.

The last word: Stonar is a small school that treats pupils as individuals and has transformed itself from a traditional girls' school into a modern co-ed with a strong international influence. It has embraced change without losing sight of what makes it special. You don't need to be horsey here but with facilities like this you will probably end up having the odd lesson – why wouldn't you?

Stover School

59

Stover, Newton Abbot, Devon TQ12 6QG

01626 354505 | registrar@stover.co.uk | www.stover.co.uk

Ages: 3-18

Pupils: 462; sixth form: 50; Boarders: 35 full, 8 weekly/flexi

Fees: Day £8,460 – £13,890; Boarding £19,740 – £28,875 pa

Head: Since 2014, Richard Notman BSc. Studied finance and stats at Birmingham University but soon discovered he was not made to be an auditor. After taking his PGCE in Manchester, he spent the next eight years in inner-city comps before teaching maths at Withington Girls School

SG

and becoming head of maths at Alderley Edge School for Girls. From there he went to Longridge Towers, Northumberland as deputy head, and finally Cundall Manor School, Yorkshire as head teacher.

'A breath of fresh air,' said one parent. Some major changes are under way and parents have been impressed so far. 'He has focused the staff on the bigger picture and has given a renewed energy across the school.' Pupils are 'very inspired by his assemblies and messages he is getting across'. Lives on site with his wife and two children who attend the prep school.

Head of prep school: since 2016, David Burt, previously head of primary at Compass International School, Madinat Khalif, Qatar. He has a degree in geography and sociology and a PGCE in primary education. Originally from the Isle of Wight, he is a keen fisherman, sportsman and avid gym-goer. Married with two young children.

Entrance: Main entry points at 4, 7 and 11. By interview, school reports, and a taster day where academic ability and attitude to learning are assessed in an informal manner.

Clubs mainly take place at lunch time and in addition to the usual offerings include bushcraft, astronomy, Dragons' Den, raving reporters, knitting club and 'Man Choir'

One parent told us, 'New pupils are embraced.' Another agreed, saying, 'We all found the entrance process very good. The older two started halfway through the year but they didn't seem to have any problems fitting in and finding their feet. The staff were welcoming, helpful and informative and communication with us was good. Since starting we have not had one single morning that they haven't wanted to go to school.'

A system of parent class reps helps new parents settle in too – 'one parent per class keeps a database of details so that round-emails can be distributed with details of coffee mornings, birthday parties and play-dates – you soon feel like part of the furniture even when you've only been at the school for a matter of months!'

Exit: Most prep school pupils move up to the senior school, with a few peeling off to local grammars. Around 60-70 per cent leave after GCSEs, mostly to non-fee-paying alternatives. Popular university choices are Exeter, Gloucestershire, Staffordshire, Manchester Metropolitan, Bath, Cardiff Metropolitan, Plymouth, Essex and Bournemouth. No Oxbridge in 2021. No medicine. Leavers to Bath, Durham, Warwick, York, Exeter. One to Norland College NQN Diploma

Latest results: In 2021, 40 per cent 9-7 at GCSE; 65 per cent A*-B at A level. In 2019 (the last year when exams took place), 18 per cent 9-7 at GCSE; 16 per cent A*/A at A level (28 per cent A*-B).

Teaching and learning: BTECs offered in home economics, sport, ICT and performing arts. Maths is a strong subject with top grades at both levels. Stover has performed well in recent regional Maths Challenges. Chemistry another strong subject with three students recently winning places at the prestigious Salters' chemistry camps. Photography very popular at A level. Spanish is taught from reception and French from year 3.

Stover welcomes pupils of all abilities. One parent said, 'It's a non-selective school and does very well in terms of exam results given its mixed ability (and after the grammar schools cream the top academics off).' A boarding school with 15 per cent of overseas students, and English is not everyone's first language; this is sometimes reflected in the grades.

Stover is setting up 'bring-your-own-device' and is planning to invest heavily in a new (and safe) server instead of upgrading equipment. The ISI inspectors reported that 'teaching was excellent', but we heard some concerns from parents about its quality. One said, 'I think there should be a review of the current teaching staff to ensure any weaker members of the team receive up-to-date training to help them improve their methods.'

Learning support and SEN: Parents speak highly of the learning support department: 'When extra help is required they have the staff to support your child and our daughter was given her own "adult" in maths to sit with her and help her on a one-to-one basis, which helped hugely.' One-to-one specialist support for autism or Asperger's is available.

The arts and extracurricular: Good music department. One parent said her daughter 'has been inspired by the head of music... they have nurtured her talent; she was very disengaged with it when she first joined.' Most pupils learn an instrument – the ukulele is popular in the prep school – and there are plenty of concerts and groups to join: the orchestra, brass and jazz bands and choirs. Another parent explained, 'Stover has several choirs and is very good at singing and music. They win almost everything in local and regional competitions. My son's year even went to Bruges Cathedral after winning one competition.' Productions, assemblies and concerts all take place in the dome-shaped Jubilee Hall, which also houses a recording studio and practice rooms (more rooms recently added).

As well as music, performing arts and public speaking are strong themes throughout the prep and senior school. Regular productions and plays, including one each year for the prep and pre-prep. 'The ones I have seen are very well produced. I went to Bugsy Malone the other year and the Match Girls last year. So, very different ones,' said one parent. Stover also offers LAMDA speech and drama lessons with Stagecentre plus performance exams.

The boys are in the original part of the building with high ceilings, ornate cornices, and great views. It's very tidy; the military background of the houseparent keeps them in check, apparently

The art department is in separate building with art downstairs (sixth form area at the back) and photography upstairs. Art studio the latest add on. Pupils 'love being able to go outdoors to learn – in science and art they will often make use of the natural world around them.' Great displays and some impressive work including a John Lennon mural, and large fish sculptures inspired by a recent trip to the aquarium. We were particularly impressed by the photography upstairs, including some portraits taken on a trip to Brick Lane. Good take-up for A level art.

Clubs take place at lunchtime, with a late-ish school finishing time of 4.30pm. Mixed messages from parents on this. It suits some, but not all. When we were there we saw the Ukulele Club doing karaoke, and the Ready Steady Fry club had just finished making dough in the well-designed home economics room. Other activities, apart from the usual offerings, include bushcraft, astronomy, Dragons' Den, the Raving Reporters, knitting club and Man Choir.

Day trips from reception, residential trips from year 4, with a night away, then a three-day trip to Cornwall in year 5, three days in Mount Batten for year 6. As well as language trips abroad, there are regular theatre trips, art trips to galleries locally and in London, field trips to Dartmoor, history trips to Flanders, and a recent sixth form expedition to Tanzania.

Sport: Extensive grounds and good sports facilities. Pupils 'relish the 60+ acres at Stover'. There are six all-weather floodlit tennis courts (some recently resurfaced), netball courts, a gym, plus football, rugby, hockey and cricket pitches. The only drawback is that Stover is a small school and there aren't always enough players of the same standard to make winning teams. One parent said, 'They seem to punch above their weight and have won hockey and netball leagues recently against much bigger schools.' However, other parents agreed that there's room for improvement: they would like to see 'a bit more sport and a few more fixtures in the senior school' as well as 'investment in a school swimming pool'. Extracurricular activities include table tennis (big here), judo, fencing, clay shooting and more recently a Stover riding team. With the school on the edge of the moors, DofE and Ten Tors are popular. Links with the Devon Schools Sports Partnership enable other local schools to make use of the grounds, and they recently hosted the Devon Schools cross-country championships.

Boarding: Stover is not as 'regimented' as other boarding schools, head told us. Admissions criteria now focus more on language (interviews by Skype). There is a mix of nationalities (currently 17), with pupils coming from Bulgaria, Serbia and Russia, as well as China, Vietnam, Spain, Germany and Cuba, though Brits are now in the majority in both houses. The plan is to recruit mainly full boarders and offer the flexi option in a limited and controlled fashion – they don't want it to 'feel like a motel'. Short stays will still be offered during the summer as these serve as good tasters, and day pupils will still be able to take advantage of the wraparound care.

Girls board on the opposite side of the main school building to the boys. Both areas have been recently refurbished. The boys are lucky to be in the original part of the building with high ceilings, ornate cornices, huge bay windows with shutters, original fireplaces, domed ceilings, arched hallways and great views. It's very tidy; the military background of the houseparent keeps them in check, apparently. He's also known for getting the boys together for regular evening chats round the dining table. Cheerful rules boards dotted around – live, laugh, love etc – make it feel homely. The large dorms feel light and spacious.

The girls' side, without the original features, is less impressive. The common room felt stuffy, and although it was equipped with PCs, a Wii, a drinks area and dining table, it didn't have the same inviting feel as the boys' room. On the plus side, the girls do have single, double and treble rooms as well as dorms. When we were there the girls were obviously getting ready for the prom, dresses proudly displayed on most wardrobes. Good-sized showers and bath facilities. In fact all the facilities are good – kitchen areas, drinks area and laundry facilities all promote independent living as much as possible.

Usual rules for mobile phones and such, but all seemed pretty relaxed. The boarders here really get to know each other, and the staff, well. Parents say it has a 'friendly, family atmosphere'. Some students even come back for more. Gap year students help out with admin duties, evening activities like football or tennis, and weekend trips to the cinema, the beach, shopping and just recently Stonehenge and Thorpe Park.

Ethos and heritage: Stover School is set in beautiful grounds, 64 acres of parkland located between Dartmoor and the sea. Founded in 1932 by two sisters on the Stover estate, the object was to help pupils lead independent lives. Boys and girls have been in the prep school since it started in 1996, and boys in the senior school since 2005. The Clock House, built in 1843 and housing the prep, was originally stables and is set around a charming cobbled courtyard. Several of the classrooms have interconnecting doors and are linked by very narrow hallways and stairs. It's small, characterful and some might say cramped, although major refurbishment has led to some bigger classrooms, a new beautiful library and new dining space.

The main house, built of granite ashlar, is an impressive sight as you drive in. With its double flight of portico steps it wouldn't look out of place on a film set. Inside, the grand entrance hall continues to impress with high ceilings, beautiful plasterwork and ornate fireplaces. The school is proud of its heritage and cups, plaques and photos adorn the corridors. The rest of the school is housed in various well-designed buildings and wooden outbuildings in the perfectly manicured grounds.

The Millennium building is modern and bright with science labs downstairs and maths upstairs. Floor-to-ceiling windows, new equipment and colourful murals by a teacher make the labs cheerful and inviting. Small class sizes also mean that there is always enough equipment. Fish, gerbils and even an adopted stray ginger cat add to the happy vibe here. Recent trips include the Big Bang and the Eden Project. Upstairs are two bright and sunny maths rooms, linked by a large balcony, also used as form rooms. Separate wooden buildings or cabins are used for English, humanities and modern languages. All freshly painted; we could still smell it.

Amongst the acres of land, there's a large playground with a sandpit, a wooden pirate ship, a football pitch and even an outdoor chess board. The new outdoor classroom has replaced the forest school that was destroyed by bad weather. There's a pond, a fire pit and parents have recently planted fruit trees. They are keen to make as much use of the grounds as possible with activities like bushcraft and gardening club. The nursery is next to the playground and is a homely space for toddlers.

Stover School is set in 64 acres of beautiful parkland located between Dartmoor and the sea. The main house, built of granite ashlar, is an impressive sight as you drive in

All pupils agree full-heartedly on two things at Stover. Firstly, it's friendly. And secondly, the food is excellent. We saw long queues of hungry pupils looking forward to the curry of the day. One said, 'I love Roastie Wednesday and Fishy Friday!' and apparently lots of pupils happily get dropped off early in time for the boarders' breakfast.

One parent told us, 'We chose Stover for a number of reasons – yes, the grounds are lovely and the buildings beautiful but a school needs to give more than that. We were inspired by the ethos of the school as a whole. You don't have to get the highest scores in maths and they aren't going to force your child into a shape they don't naturally fit. [Stover] helps them to excel in the areas they have a passion for.'

Former pupil Debra Newbury awarded the MBE for her services to transatlantic rowing.

Pastoral care, inclusivity and discipline: Well-behaved, well spoken and polite. Good behaviour is part of life here and is instilled at a young age – walk into any prep class and they will all stand. The pupils we spoke to seemed happy and proud of their school. Due to its small size, problems are spotted quickly and dealt with swiftly. Everybody knows everybody, but there is a solid support network of house parents, tutors, the school nurse, the school counsellor and the school chaplain if needed. The chaplain takes an active role in school life as well as regular collective worship and running the Christian Union group.

The house system runs throughout the prep and senior school and gives pupils a sense of belonging. There are three houses, but strangely they are then split into boys and girls, making it six houses in all. The pupils we spoke to had no idea why it was like this as the only aspect they are separated for is sport. Presumably this is just a hangover from days gone by when boys and girls didn't mix. Strange that it hasn't changed with the times.

Pupils and parents: Day pupils from Newton Abbot, Exeter, South Hams, Torbay, Bovey Tracey, Plymouth. Boarders mainly from overseas. Parents mostly in professional occupations. Good bus service. Wraparound care offered from 7.30am to 6.30pm for 6-year-olds and above.

Communication is good, there's even a parents' app for news, events and photos. Plus Soundcloud to access all the latest music. Friends of Stover are always busy fundraising, and the upcoming Summer Ball was causing a bit of a buzz. 'There is also a monthly Friends of Stover coffee morning where parents meet with the headmaster and his wife, and can exchange information, chat and generally catch up, which is lovely,' said one mother.

Money matters: Academic, music, art and sport scholarships available at most ages, up to 20 per cent of day fees. Two means-tested scholarships at year 10 and sixth form, the Maurice Key and Laurus scholarships offering up to 100 per cent of day fees. A maths scholarship is available to international sixth form students covering 25 per cent of fees at Stover and 10 per cent of fees at Plymouth University. Armed forces and police force are offered a 10 per cent discount.

The last word: Stover is a small, friendly school. It's for mixed abilities, and for those that wouldn't suit a larger mainstream setting. It's undergoing some major changes. For the better. Everyone agrees there are 'exciting times ahead'. As one parent put it, 'It was a good school in many ways, but now I think it has the chance to be really outstanding.' And having met the heads, we think this is just the beginning. One to watch.

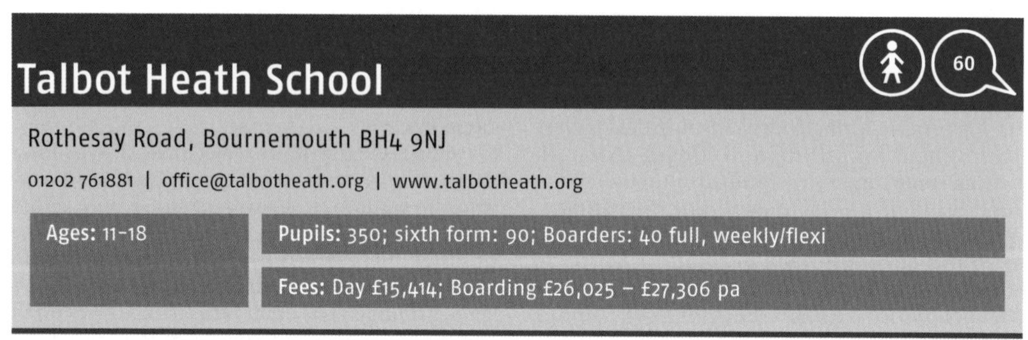

Talbot Heath School

60

Rothesay Road, Bournemouth BH4 9NJ

01202 761881 | office@talbotheath.org | www.talbotheath.org

Ages: 11-18

Pupils: 350; sixth form: 90; Boarders: 40 full, weekly/flexi

Fees: Day £15,414; Boarding £26,025 – £27,306 pa

Head: Since 2010, Angharad Holloway BA PGCE (40s). Educated at a state comprehensive near Cardiff, followed by St Maur's in Surrey (which later merged with St George's Weybridge). Read German and Italian at St Anne's, Oxford, where she was a choral scholar, and then did a PGCE at Queens' College, Cambridge. She originally wanted to become a classical singer but says: 'I couldn't leave my books behind. I couldn't imagine a future for me that didn't involve scholarship.' First teaching job at Sir William Perkins's in Surrey, where she became acting head of the MFL department in her first year. 'My mentality has always been to say yes,' she says. 'If someone asks me to do something I will rise to the challenge.' Later taught at Broadlands School (now Broadlands Academy) in Keynsham – 'challenging but the most rewarding' – and Clifton High School. Then became head of MFL and the IB at the Royal High School, Bath, prior to becoming head at Talbot Heath.

Despite the multiple demands of headship she still teaches for two or three periods a day, including global citizenship to year 7 and German to students wishing to study it (the school doesn't offer it officially). One of the most dynamic heads we've met, she was a runner-up in the recent i25 Awards, which recognise the top 25 leading influencers and innovators in the independent school sector. A parent told us: 'We're lost in admiration for her. She has tremendous drive to get things done.' Another described her as a 'visionary' while a pupil commented, 'You can approach Mrs Holloway with anything.'

She's clearly an inspiration to Talbot Heath pupils. 'I want the girls to be themselves but to explore, discover and be curious. I say: "Don't passively experience life. Don't let life wash over you." I want them to have a spark, a spring in their step and a smile on their face.'

She has two daughters, both pupils at the school, and in her spare time enjoys music, art, books and birdwatching (she keeps a pair of 'bins' in her study so she can watch the nuthatches outside her window). She sings in the staff band, the Talbot Heathens, and often plays table tennis with pupils at lunchtime.

Entrance: Pupils starting in years 7 to 10 take the school's own entrance exam, with six papers in English, maths and verbal reasoning. Around 10 arrive in the sixth form.

Exit: Up to a third leave after GCSEs although some return having discovered the grass isn't greener on the other side. 'I missed it so I came back,' one girl told us. At 18, most to higher education, with Royal Holloway currently the most popular uni. One medic in 2021, and one overseas to Campbell University in North Carolina to study business marketing. Degree apprenticeships are growing in popularity.

Latest results: In 2021, 66 per cent 9-7 at GCSE; 67 per cent A*/A at A level (95 per cent A*-B). In 2019 (the last year when exams took place), 52 per cent 9-7 at GCSE; 44 per cent A*/A at A level (76 per cent A*-B).

Teaching and learning: 'A first-class education for girls,' say parents. Most girls take nine GCSEs, including English, maths, a language (French and/or Spanish), a humanity subject and either double or triple science. Latin taught from year 8. Three forms per year group. Small class sizes (maximum of 20) and school is small enough to offer tailor-made timetables. Flexible teaching accommodates those with training and competing commitments or musical talent. For instance, those on the tennis academy programme may have a reduced timetable.

When the governors asked the head to devise a vision for education she consulted widely and decided that in order to keep pace with technological change all pupils should have a thorough grounding in subjects like design thinking, material science, engineering and ethics. 'Our pupils need to be creative, adaptable, resilient and able to problem-solve so we have completely reworked the curriculum for everyone from three to 18,' she says. 'My educational vision is an integrated one, where schools, higher education and business work together and we now have a resource bank of companies and universities who support us. We've devised a curriculum and we are identifying where we want them to come in and co-deliver.' The school's new £7.6 million STEAM Hub, with a 600-seat auditorium, art studios, design workshops and interactive wall and floor, is integral to the new curriculum. 'There is a real sense of excitement about it,' says the head. 'I'm a passionate advocate of excellence in education – but always forward thinking. I set great store by intellectual curiosity and rigour but value every aspect of the curriculum.'

School motto is 'honour before honours' (definitely has a Malory Towers feel to it). Smart uniform of navy blazers and tartan skirts; sixth formers can wear their own clothes

The STEAM Hub is a vision of beauty, with a sculpture at the entrance signifying wave dynamics and the girls' names engraved on the base. Inside, it gives pupils the chance to experience virtual reality, immersive projection, holographic studios, computer aided design (CAD), animation tools and green screen facilities. 'It inspires us to be creative,' one girl told us.

The head likes the idea of 'interdisciplinary learning' and science and technology are woven throughout the curriculum. For example, when pupils learn about the Normandy Landings during the Second World War they get the chance to design and build pontoon bridges and test them in the school swimming pool. Sixth form chemistry students can plot and point the structure of molecules digitally, see them transformed into a 3D hologram and walk inside them.

Plans are underway for an interdisciplinary day on gunpowder, where chemistry teachers will make gunpowder in front of the students and explain the chemical compounds while the history and English staff look at the history of gunpowder and set creative writing assignments. 'When the Dorset police explosives team came in they said that no other school had ever asked for a licence to make gunpowder,' says the head. Every pupil is issued with an iPad (parents don't pay for this; the girls hand them back when they leave). Girls are allowed to stay at school till 5pm and do their prep.

Learning support and SEN: Learning support department offers individual support to girls with specific learning difficulties such as dyslexia (no additional charge for this).

The arts and extracurricular: Two modern art rooms, a textiles room (pupils knit scarves, hats and gloves for the homeless) and a DT department kitted out with laser cutters, lathes, saws, drills, 3D printers and CAD suite. Music is taught in the music school in the woods, complete with concert hall, teaching rooms, electronic music studio and practice rooms.

Drama and theatre studies offered at GCSE and A level and there are lots of extracurricular opportunities, including a whole school production every year (rehearsals for The Wizard of Oz in full swing when we visited). 'If you have a talent they encourage you to build on it,' a keen thespian told us.

Sport: Swimming, tennis and netball are exceptionally strong here. New indoor pool within the STEAM Hub and the school has opened an elite swimming academy, enabling pupils from across the UK and beyond to train at the highest level while getting a great education. Tennis academy too – a girl reached the second round at Junior Wimbledon in 2019 for the second year running and the school recently reached the final of the national school championships.

Boarding: One boarding house – St Mary's – with weekly, full and flexi-boarders. Some international boarders from mainland China, Hong Kong and Europe. Other boarders are tennis whizz kids or elite swimmers who combine top-flight training with their academic work. Wholesome shared dorms for year 7s and 8s while older girls get their own rooms. Boarders have lunch in the main school but eat in the boarding house dining room the rest of the time. Youngest girls have to hand in their phones at night. Boarding staff run loads of activities, including yoga, baking, movie nights, a Christmas fancy dress party and theatre trips to London. Facilities include a 'hygge' space, music room, craft room and a visitors' lounge. The boarders even have two guinea pigs – Peppa and Pig.

Ethos and heritage: School was founded in 1886 by Mary Broad to provide a first-class liberal education for girls. Originally known as Bournemouth High School, it moved to its current woodland site in Talbot Woods, a mile from Bournemouth beach, in 1936 and was renamed Talbot Heath. The original red-brick school buildings remain at the heart of the school, complete with cloisters, quads and an oak-panelled library. Four Second World War air raid shelters in the grounds and one, known as 'the bunker', has been restored for 'living history' lessons.

School motto is 'honour before honours' (definitely has a Malory Towers feel to it). Smart uniform of navy blazers and tartan skirts for years 7 to 11. Sixth formers can wear their own clothes (they must look smart; no denim and no midriffs on show). Two head girls, two deputies, prefects for each subject department and two form leaders for every class. House system – the four houses are named after inspirational women (Lovelace, Franklin, Shelley and Earhart). When we asked a group of girls if there was anything they'd change about the school, the only complaint was 'Stop putting raisins in the salads.' Apart from the raisins, they give school food the thumbs-up and approve of meat-free Mondays.

Former pupils include Dame Shirley Williams, Judge Cosgrave, Lady Faithful (social worker and reformer), showjumper Pat Smythe, internationally renowned cellist Natalie Clein, opera singer Kate Royal, actresses Louise Clein and Nicole Faraday, engineer Caroline Gledhill and geneticist Frances Ashcroft.

Pastoral care, inclusivity and discipline: Parents praise the school's 'nurturing environment' and say it's a friendly place where everyone knows each other. 'It's very close-knit,' a sixth former told us. Older girls train as peer mentors and recently started a club called There for You to support year 7s. Every year group gets a block of lessons about e-safety.

Parents like the way the school has kept its traditions (pupils celebrate the school's birthday every year) while being innovative and forward-thinking too. A father told us his daughter had 'come on leaps and bounds confidence-wise' at the school, while a sixth former said, 'I was very shy when I got here but they find something you're good at and help you flourish.' Usual system of sanctions for unsatisfactory work or behaviour but girls' behaviour is generally excellent.

Pupils and parents: Many day girls live in Bournemouth and Poole but some come from as far afield as Wimborne, Ringwood, the New Forest and Swanage, either by bus, train or one of the school's minibuses.

Money matters: Academic, music, sport and all-rounder scholarships offered, as well as tennis academy scholarships and swimming academy scholarships. Means-tested bursaries available, as well as bursaries for daughters of CofE clergy and discounted boarding fees for pupils whose parents are in the Forces.

The last word: A gem of a school that is making waves in the education world thanks to its inspiring head and exciting approach to learning. Girls get a first-class education in a safe, caring and encouraging environment – and the school excels at supporting talented sport and music specialists too.

Taunton Prep and Pre-Prep School

Staplegrove Road, Taunton, Somerset TA2 6AE

01823 703307 | admissions@tauntonschool.co.uk | www.tauntonschool.co.uk

Ages: 0–13

Pupils: 396; **Boarders:** 47 full, 1 weekly (from age 7)

Fees: Day £7,950 – £16,635; Boarding £15,885 – £27,570 pa

Linked school: Taunton School, 295

Headmaster: Since 2017, Andrew Edwards BA PGCE. Early 50s. Also an all-rounder: degree in French and German, coaching qualifications in football, tennis and cricket, cellist to diploma standard, school inspector – and solicitor. Two years of lawyering in the City just didn't do it for him so he pluckily bundled sports kit, French text books and a cello into the boot of his disreputable Nissan Cherry and went peripatetic until snapped up by Cottesmore. Here he is 20+ years later having done time at Port Regis, Dumpton and Castle Court. Previously head of Park School, Bournemouth for the last six years.

He likes things just the way they are here, so no major engine rebuild planned, fine tuning only. Not a believer that an eye-catching USP is everything – 'There's nothing wrong with doing what other schools do, the important thing is to do them extremely well' – so no hey-look-at-us joy-riding, either. Not so much a continuity candidate, more a continuous improver. Parents feel that following recent restructuring and staff departures – for the best, all agree – a period of calm is in order. Mr Edwards is a believer in rigour, challenge and respect, but his educational philosophy has it its heart the s-factor. Smiles. The more the merrier. Sound a tad, we don't know, mawkish? Okay, so what better way to measure a school? Our view: Mr Edwards is a Good Thing, a good fit. As an all-rounder, he's exactly what his new school is. Following two relatively quickfire headships here parents will be pleased to know that he has his eye on a decent innings. Married to Robyn, also a teacher. Two boys.

Entrance: Non-selective. Start at 0 in the nursery or come any time from a local school or other prep schools if (big if) there's room. Overseas students join when they're ready from Taunton International Middle School. Taster days on request.

Exit: Pretty much everyone to the senior school, many with scholarships. It's a natural progression and for most parents the whole point. No one is de-selected; this is a cradle-to-adulthood school.

Our view: Taunton isn't one of those towns that tops any tables for loveliness, wellbeing or up-and-comingness. Closer inspection reveals that it's no-one's best kept secret, either. When you discover that the town is the beneficiary of a regeneration scheme your expectancy levels may droop some more, leading you to suppose that its schools aren't necessarily going to be anything to write home about. And there you'd be bang wrong. Just as we were. The town is home to a couple of blisteringly good state schools ('outstanding' in Ofstedspeak) and three independents. When it comes to education, the good people of Taunton and environs are spoiled for choice. So how do you choose? One parent we spoke to chose Taunton Prep School – TPS they call it in everydayspeak – because 'We liked the way it made us feel.' Much to be said for that.

TPS occupies its own self-contained campus bang next door to the senior school in the leafy northern outskirts of the town, bounded by the railway to the south and the A358 to the north. It has none of the huddledness of so many town schools, while the spacious playing fields further mitigate any urban vibe. It feels like its own place. Buildings a mix of Victorian and later, nicely maintained. That's not all: we have never seen a cleaner school nor have we met cleaners who so much enjoyed their work. Shares its chapel with the senior school. Established to educate the sons of dissenters but not Methodists. In place of foundational sectarianism we found only indulgent broad church values. An international contingent, around 10 of them, feed through from the international middle school – TSIMS (tee-sims) – when their English is up to it.

Demographically there's no pinning TPS down. It's popular with hardworking local entrepreneurs and businesspeople wanting the best for their children and for whom this is their first experience of private education. They told us that the school didn't talk down to them like others they looked round, it's not 'grand and intimidating'. TPS is also attractive to parents for whom private is second nature and who like the (relatively) wide social spectrum here. TPS has long been attractive to Forces families, for whom the school very much sets out its stall – to officers and other ranks equally. The draw for them, as for other nomadic families, is that TPS, together with the pre-prep and the senior school, gives them a fixed point from 0-18. So: not a muddy-welly school, nor a set-apart school, but a modern school very much part of, and involved in, the local community. To use a word du jour, inclusive.

TPS has none of the huddledness of so many town schools, while the spacious playing fields further mitigate any urban vibe. It feels like its own place

Academically a very safe pair of hands across the board – just the right blend of extra-mile dedication and judicious professionalism. Every subject is well resourced. Parents of bright children tell us their child is stretched but not to snapping point; parents whose children need support tell us that's what they get, and never in such a way as to make them feel like dawdlers. Lots of praise for the teachers. One parent said, 'You fire off an email last thing at night and get an almost instant reply – it can be embarrassing.' Plenty of celebration of achievement according to your lights – a word oft-repeated by parents is 'nurturing'. One pupil told us she'd really taken off at the school and showed us written work which demonstrated sound understanding of the parenthetical comma. You don't see them very often these days. Maths exceedingly strong – terrific showings in Maths Challenge and an inspirational head of department who left one of your profoundly innumerate reviewers feeling there may still be hope. DT especially strong. Thinking skills a new addition to the academic mix. The head speaks of the children being on a 'GCSE continuum' which makes sense when pretty much everyone goes on the senior school. Lots of dialogue with the senior school and, big strength, some teacher sharing, especially in languages, classics and sport. Currently working on a joint IT strategy with senior school, a bring-your-own-device scheme 'the intention for the future'. IT has just enjoyed a £600,000 investment. Good blend of male:female teachers, roughly a third male. Saturday school till lunchtime for years 7 and 8.

Special educational needs addressed by a team headed up by a head of learning success (neatly standing a downside on its head). The full spectrum of SENs, mostly, note, on the mild side – 10 per cent on the register. Architecturally wheelchair-unfriendly but they're willing to put themselves out for visually and hearing impaired children and wobbly walkers – head expresses a willingness to 'address the needs of any prospective pupil and see what reasonable adjustments could be made'.

Former England batsman Marcus Trescothick coaches cricket here and former England netball team manager Lisa Manley coaches netball so yes, this is a school that takes its sport seriously, generates good stats and crowns a sportsperson of the week at every Monday morning assembly. A very few parents feel sport is taken a bit too seriously, worry that it distracts from the academics and don't relish traipsing in of a Saturday evening and collecting their child from a bus. But maxing out every daylight hour in the week is what a good prep school does; it's all bang for your buck, and busy children who do lots, studies show, get the best results. Around a dozen of the best children rise to county level. No also-rans if they can help it: they try to give everyone the chance to play for their school at least once. It doesn't matter a bit if you're not sporty, if a thing's worth doing, it's worth doing inexpertly, it's meant to be fun. Decent mix of other sports on offer. Facilities are on the amazing side, many their own, some shared with the senior school.

Not many prep schools have their own performing arts centre but TPS does – including a newly refurbished theatre. Not many prep schools have quite such a passionate head of performing arts, either. We were particularly beguiled by five little French hornists parping away pluckily. The French horn is a frightfully difficult instrument at any age and to see so many seemed to set an aspirational benchmark. One mum we spoke to was taken by surprise when her son, having previously evinced neither interest nor aptitude, suddenly took to the trumpet, and this after a daughter had been identified as having an unsuspectedly good voice – 'They spot talents you never knew they had.' Here's a thing: in years 4, 6 and 8 everyone plays a part in a musical for which a whole week of all-day rehearsals is set aside. Everyone. The whole week. Don't parents march on the school demanding proper lessons? No they don't, they reckon the benefit outweighs any academic impact, they trust the school completely. Given that this is not a school whose parents are the sort to allow it to play fast and loose with scholastic attainment, what does that tell you? Lots of performance opportunities, formal and informal, at some of which parents join in. Senior choir sings in churches abroad. All in all, a rich and very classy mix. Heaps of lunchtime and after-school activities on offer. Go home at 4pm or stay to 5.30pm for clubs and prep (homework) periods.

Parents praise pastoral support and rapid response to glitches arising. First port of call is the form tutor. Head's door is ever open – stride on in. No prefect system; it was abolished by the previous head to universal crossness and dismay – a parent told us, 'It's the only time I went to the school and complained' – and replaced by year 8 councillors. Senior pupils apply for a role in writing then stand for election by everyone, including teachers. All are trained in peer mentoring. And it has all come good, making for a kinder environment with higher mutual respect levels and without saying goodbye to leadership opportunities. Parents praise the way the school celebrates kindness and 'is quick to support self-esteem'. You quickly pick up on the social atmosphere here because everyone is so naturally nice and courteous, welcoming of strangers, and that's not something you find everywhere by any means. Try this: flip through the photos in the school magazine – the unstaged ones. Don't all parents want their children to look like these?

The nursery and pre-prep is self-contained on the prep school site. None of the higgledy-piggledness that characterises some pre-preps, no sense of being an architectural afterthought. Described by one parent as 'the jewel in the crown'. Lovely atmosphere, really good staff, brilliantly led. Intelligent use of teaching materials, the best of the new plus golden-oldie classics. Huge pride in their forest school – outdoor areas where the children can play, hunt for bugs and bumble about. Aftercare till 5.45pm at no extra cost.

Boarding: Some 20+ children are full boarders, around 10 per cent of the roll, a number small enough to make you justly jittery. Aren't these simply left-behind children? Lots of schools couldn't make this work, not with so few. But TPS does. The accommodation is clean and snug. There's access to senior school facilities. The staff are brilliant, that's key, and the children are clearly well looked after and happy. Our misgivings evaporated. In the course of the year around a third of all pupils board. All flexi options available down to sleepover, and if you're caught late at work the boarding staff will look after your child till you come to collect.

Money matters: Range of scholarships at 11+ for entry to year 7.

The last word: Marmite schools are schools with a highly distinctive personality and probably a stand-out specialism. These are schools that some children love and others don't. TPS is not a Marmite school. So, a very good ordinary school, then? Well, if you want to put it that way, yes, this is a school for every child, a place where values of humanity come first, where happy children find out who they are and what they can do and then go on and play out of their socks. Ordinariness at its best, then. Extremely personable. A terrific all-rounder.

Taunton School

62

Staplegrove Road, Taunton, Somerset TA2 6AD

01823 703703 | registrar@tauntonschool.co.uk | www.tauntonschool.co.uk

Ages: 13-18

Pupils: 593; sixth form: 279; Boarders: 241 full, 16 weekly/flexi

Fees: Day £20,880; Boarding £35,760 pa

Linked school: Taunton Prep and Pre-Prep School, 293

Headmaster: Since 2015, Lee Glaser MA BSc PGCE, deputy head since 2009. Educated at his local comp in Blackpool and Liverpool University (maths). Qualified as a chartered accountant with Coopers & Lybrand, then turned his back on bean-counting and trained to be a teacher. Millfield for 14 years, maths teacher, senior master and director of sport; he's a diehard sports enthusiast rather than a dead good player. By general agreement he has made a very decent fist of taking over from a bouncy, charismatic head with a silver tongue and a penchant for continuous change. There's been enough of that; Mr Glaser's here to get the trains running on time and bed things down. Doesn't mean innovation is off the cards by any means, mind. Spent his first year appointing a new senior management team and agreeing vision and strategy which is expressed graphically by five pillars – see website – and is, we find, very definitely not a confection of buzz words and blah. If 'challenge, inspire, nurture' is what you want to hear, Mr Glaser is right behind them. A realist (as well as an accountant) he's a big believer in sound finances. Everyone likes him – he's 'approachable', a wysiwyg kind of a guy, 'good sense of humour', 'accessible, a good listener', 'right person at the right time', 'a nuts and bolts person', 'sticking to the knitting'. Very visible, his door is open to students first thing every morning. Oratorical skills reckoned to be improving. When he eventually steps down he hopes the consensus view of his bottom line will be that he 'improved everything'.

Wife Liz is a practising accountant. Two girls, both at the school. Chocolate lab, Lola. Mr Glaser enjoys music and drama. Faced with shipwreck on a desert island he would lunge for Sympathy for the Devil (Stones) and Sebastian Faulks's Engleby.

Leaving in July 2022.

Entrance: Essentially non-selective. Assessment test and interview. Years 9 and 12 the customary boarding points but any other time if they've got room. Go to an open day or schedule a personal visit.

Exit: Between a quarter and a third leave after GCSE, lured by the excellent local (free) sixth form college. A number of these, missing the nurturing, find their way back to the mothership, postponing installation of the new dream kitchen back home for another two years.

Zero sock odour in the boys' houses, testimony to regulated lifestyles and the care of terrific support staff whose pastoral role is crucial. 'One big family,' say the teachers

Pretty much every sixth form leaver to university, half to Russell Group. Given the international intake, there's expert advice available for all students looking abroad. Some British students go on to Harvard, UCLA, etc and the school is a national SATs centre. Plenty of support for anyone opting for vocational training or apprenticeship – eg hospitality, design at NABA Milan. School prides itself on parity of support for all routes from academic to apprenticeship. Two medics in 2021; sometimes a few to Oxbridge.

Latest results: In 2021, 52 per cent 9-7 at GCSE; 53 per cent A*/A at A level or equivalent (76 per cent A*-B). IB average score 36. In 2019 (the last year when exams took place), 43 per cent 9-7 at GCSE; 37 per cent A*/A at A level or equivalent (67 per cent A*-B).

Teaching and learning: Results are sound considering the non-selective intake. GCSE results broadly strengthening. Good range of subjects offered in the sixth form resulting in some very small class sizes. In terms of national averages strong in maths, history, biology, geography. Fewer top grades in physics, economics, business studies and psychology but signs of recent improvement. Curriculum well judged to accommodate a relatively wide range of abilities. Subject range embraces the usual suspects and includes, classy touch, Latin to A level. Open-minded about adding vocational subjects (eg BTECs in business as well as sport and exercise science) to the mix if sufficiently broad-based to act as a springboard to a spectrum of career choices equivalent to three A levels, and laying the ground for a variety of employment sectors. Just under half of the first cohort achieved three triple-starred distinctions. Performance table data shows expected progress at A level and BTEC while IB students do rather better. Saturday school popular with working parents.

Classrooms bright and well equipped, students engaged even as lunchtime became imminent, teachers giving it plenty. A good number of teachers here did something else first. Lovely library – the new name for a learning resource centre – staffed by specialists and open till 9 every evening. Design technology blinking brilliant, masses of kit – oscillating spindle sander, inverted trend router, plasma cutter, you name it.

Huge efforts to retain students post-GCSE, some of which redound to their benefit – ah, the joys of a highly competitive market. Outstanding guidance in opting between A levels, IB and BTEC, choosing the right subjects and thereafter making university and careers choices.

Learning support and SEN: Learning support – 'educational progress', they call it – delivered by a staff of five who also support children in the prep school, offering continuity for long-haul students. The customary range of interventions spanning long-term SLDs to short-term study support. SLDs on the mild side – you've got to be able to keep up. Typically professional, all learning assistants are graduates. Head of department told us it's all about 'celebrating the differently gifted'.

The arts and extracurricular: 'This is a school that really values breadth,' a parent told us. Another: 'Taunton students have absolutely no

Design technology blinking brilliant, masses of kit – oscillating spindle sander, inverted trend router, plasma cutter, you name it

understanding of boredom.' All parents agree that when lessons are over there's masses to do.

The school's minibuses carry the strapline 'Offering more'. There may be something in it. The music offer is multifarious, everything from chamber music ensembles to big musicals – in recent years Phantom, Evita, Cats. There are choirs, overseas tours – in short, around 40 public performances a year. The busy drama department offers courses at GCSE and A level in addition to productions for which anyone can audition. The art studio is similarly open-house and evidence of the quality of work made here surrounds you. Students spoke glowingly of working relationships with their teachers as we gazed.

Outside the classroom there are heaps of clubs and activities on offer, many of them student-generated. There's a fully fledged rationale behind the co-curricular programme – Horizons, they call it. It's all about reaching out beyond the confines of the classroom, it's self-directed and it embraces all abilities. There's a CCF, compulsory for years 10 and 11. And for fresh air fans there's a thriving DofE scheme. Is there enough range? Students told us unanimously yes; parents told us that their children are operating at the outer extremes of busyness, and cited by way of verification the way they sleep for much of the first week of every holiday. One parent said, 'They are trained to cope with lots to do.' Lots of cultural, sporting and exchange trips worldwide reflecting the school's global outlook.

Sport: This is a sporting hotspot that takes a characteristically professional approach to maxing out the talents of all students. Cop these coaches: Pete Sanderson, ex-Somerset CCC first team coach; Marcus Trescothick, ex-England opening batsman; Nic Sestaret, ex-France, Exeter Chiefs and Toulouse rugby player; and Lisa Manley, ex-England netball development squad manager. Yes, blimey. If you're any good you'll go all the way. That's not all. For students whose enthusiasm outruns their innate gifts there are B and some C teams where you can do your bit. Famous victories and lean spells alike are recorded in the Courier, the excellent weekly e-mag that records dash and enterprise in all areas of school life. Exhaustive coverage allows for the greatest number of students to be namechecked, a source of pride and joy to doting parents. As well as progressing to regional and national levels, students also play for local clubs, with some of whom the school shares facilities. All in all, impressive.

Some parents say the focus on sport has got a bit much, others disagree. One said, 'If your child is not in one of the top two teams [As or Bs] you don't get value for money'; others disagree. One said that there's a danger that a sporty child will do nothing but sport and miss out on everything else on offer; others point to manifold achievements on a broad and eclectic front by their own child. Given the strength of the sporting culture here, what is the fate of the non-sporty? Do they shiver on the wing only to be hooted at on the rare occasions the ball reaches them? We spoke to the parent of a resolutely non-sporty child. After popping in for a constructive talk with the right people, a personal fitness programme was agreed. Very civilised, all happy, no stigma. Putting this in context, another parent remarked: 'This is a school which is far more interested in the welfare of every one of its children than it is in looking good to the outside world.'

Boarding: Around 45 per cent board, of which roughly the same percentage are girls. House system in discrete houses, visitors need permission, so privacy (which tends to be in short supply in boarding schools) is safeguarded. Not a hotel school awash with pampering and fine fittings (though refurb ongoing) but students perfectly content with comfort levels; girls' dorms softer and tidier than boys', it goes without saying, for most chaps are strikingly insouciant in matters of interior decor at this age. Zero sock odour in the boys' houses, testimony to regulated lifestyles and the care of terrific support staff whose pastoral role is crucial and, well done Mr Glaser, officially recognised. Happy campers, all. 'One big family,' say the teachers, as they do; 'home from home.' When you hear the children say this too you give it credence. Eventide hunger pangs, long the bane of boarding, sated by after-prep snacks – we liked that. Busy weekend activities programme. Big boys look after little ones. Young people these days really are so much kinder to each other (sigh), the more so when vigilantly and benignly overseen as these are.

Ethos and heritage: Began life in 1847 as the West of England Dissenters' Proprietary School supported by the Wills family, Bristol ciggie kings, who built the chapel. Original neo-Gothic flagship building imparts an image of tradition at modest cost. Target market was nonconformists – manufacturers, industrialists, tradespeople. Within 40 years the sectarian rationale had largely evaporated, denominational differences not being what they were, and the school moved into the public school mainstream, competing directly with eg the two other Taunton indies, Queen's and King's. Never a supertanker sort of school, the sort that can sail serenely through economic bad weather, it has looked disaster in the face a few times, most recently the late 1990s. Existential peril has arguably been the school's greatest friend, compelling it to look repeatedly to its wits and jolly well deserve to exist, denying it the doubtful luxury of complacency. Ever-adept at identifying new markets it went co-ed in 1976 – one of the first – and has offered IB since 2007. Business savvy – in the holidays there's a thriving venue hire business including weddings.

A standout feature of the school is that it will take your children and educate them from 0–18. Their market research tells them this is what parents want

A legacy of this adaptive mindset is the global outlook of the school today built on an admirably enterprising business model. Two separate international schools between them take overseas students aged 8-17, bring them up to speed and feed them into either the prep or senior school – somewhere around 45 different nationalities. This makes Taunton fundamentally different in spirit from schools that look abroad opportunistically to top up ad hoc. There's a fully developed rationale behind this in tune with that of other international schools, yet Taunton remains essentially British because that's what its overseas parents want. Another standout feature of the school is that it will take your children and educate them from 0-18. Their market research tells them this is what parents want, and parents we spoke to concur – 'I didn't want my son to lose all his friends at 13.' One parent, new to town, was only looking for a nursery. One thing led to another; her third child has just started as the eldest gets ready to leave. Taken together, the cradle-to-adulthood model and the international model account for the fact that the head girl who showed us round had been at the school for 16 years, the head boy for just two (he's Russian). Striking for us, perhaps, not a big deal for them. Point is, it works. 'The friendships my daughter has made,' said one parent, 'have made the world a smaller place.' How chill a wind Brexit is going to be is yet to be seen. Taunton students emerge as global citizens, definitely not citizens of nowhere.

The campus, on the northern outskirts of Taunton, embraces also the prep and the pre-prep. The 15-17-year-old international students are semi-detached, just over the A358; the 8-14s are 10 mins to the north in Kingston St Mary. None of the crammedness you get in many town schools, the spacious playing fields and unnecessarily blue artificial pitches of the 50-acre site give way to agriculture. Architecturally there's nothing here to take your breath away, though the Loveday building may elicit a low whistle. At the same time, there's absolutely nothing to make your heart sink. No, there's one of everything and everything's eminently fit for purpose – deceptively so in the case of the theatre which, as performing arts spaces go, is a piece of work. It's all at one with the down-to-earth nature of this place, a school that has no truck with servicing bank loans or wowing have-yachts. One parent said, 'The facilities meet its needs. In real life most people don't have pots of money to spend.' Another said, 'One of the best things about the school: it's not in the least up itself.' Our observation: this is a school you quickly feel at home in.

Very much a part of its local community, the school issues invites to university fairs, talks, etc. There's a community choir. The head enjoys good relationships with local state schools and sixth form college. Townsfolk come in and use the fitness suite. Taunton parents highly approve; they definitely don't want their children growing up aloof and apart. Confident in its identity and values, very much its own place, wholly free of minor public school hangups.

Pastoral care, inclusivity and discipline: Of all the school's greatest hits, pastoral care stands at no. 1. However hard we tried (and we did, we did) we could lure no one into uttering a bad word. First up, this is, in the words of one parent, 'a school where teachers really like kids' – which, interestingly enough, is exactly what the teachers told us when we asked them why they love working here. There is praise for rapidity of response times and sensitive, effective nipping in the bud of problems as they arise. One parent, worried about an unsupervised party planned for a weekend, went to share her misgivings with the deputy head. Sorted. Discipline is reckoned judicious and firm; a parent praised the way the school 'doesn't pander to parents' in this respect. Another parent observed, 'Family values are important to Taunton parents.' A new parent was rung by a teacher in the first fortnight to tell her how well her son was doing, point being this teacher didn't even teach him. We fielded countless 'extra mile' plaudits and enjoyed 'this is the biggest family ever'.

If the school looks big, 'it's not when you're there; the house system divides it into manageable chunks.' There's praise for the way year groups mix, look out for each other and integrate the newbies. There's peer mentoring. Year 9s share their space with year 11s. One parent told us they reckoned the house groups socially too small. All parents see this as an open-door school, they'll always make themselves available and listen to you. You can drop in and taste the food anytime – dished out from a 'spectacular new facility'. It's an inclusive sort of place; a parent told us, 'You'd struggle not to fit in.' Another said, 'There's never been a day when my children have not wanted to go to school.' It's an open-hearted sort of a place, too: there's a pupil-led feminist society open to the full spectrum of LGBT students.

Pupils and parents: Especially popular with hard-working local entrepreneurs, business people and professionals for a number of whom this is their first experience of private education – a higher proportion than you'll find at many independent schools. Not so different, then, in terms of values, from the school's original nonconformist parents – attributes of enterprise, thrift and social responsibility score high with them. They're looking for a return on investment, they like the school's groundedness and professionalism – and they bust a gut to pay the fees. We also encountered a number of seasoned veterans of private education who'd always seen themselves sending their child to a major-brand flagship school but, having found Taunton – in one case because their child was unhappy at a big-name school – count their blessings and have become passionate, even fierce, advocates of the school's virtues. Worth noting the relatively high proportion of state-educated teachers here, too, including the three most senior managers. Most children come up from the prep school, some from local preps, some from state schools. Longstandingly popular with Forces families. Buses bring day students from a 30-mile radius from all parts of the compass – Yeovil, Exeter, Weston-super-Mare.

Money matters: The usual range of scholarships for year 9 entrants. Same for sixth form entrants plus IB scholarships up to 100 per cent of fees. Extras include books, food, daily bus and some trips. Big ongoing investment in bursaries. Application process as far as possible business-like, never an ordeal. Help for students at all ages who exhibit 'talent and determination'.

The last word: Most of Taunton's hard-headed, analytical parents choose the school because it 'feels right', something that leaps out at them. It does. You quickly pick up on the professionalism – the admin systems are superfast. Never a school to fall in love with its own reflection, the new senior team, with its 'improve everything' agenda, is tweaking underperforming areas with precision. What makes the school so likeable, so agreeable, is its individuality: kind, hardworking, ambitious, terrific fun, very much its own person – a great fit for everyboy and everygirl.

Trinity School
63
Buckeridge Road, Teignmouth, Devon TQ14 8LY
01626 774138 | registrar@trinityschool.co.uk | www.trinityschool.co.uk
Ages: 11-19
Pupils: 156; sixth form: 41; Boarders: 35 full, 6 weekly
Fees: Day £13,005; Boarding £37,060 – £29,355 pa

Headmaster: Since 2016, Lawrence Coen BSc PGCE NPQH (40s). Educated at Bromsgrove which he 'absolutely loved' and which shaped his lifelong approach to education (more of which later), he studied marine biology at Aberystwyth, spent a year trying to become a professional rugby player before admitting injury-blighted defeat and, instead, worked his way up the graduate management scheme of Enterprise Rent-a-Car. Four years in, he had a mid 20s crisis and so – pining for outdoor adventures – he ran away to Belize as a Raleigh International group leader where he met his wife-to-be and, in a jungle based moment of life affirming clarity, decided to retrain as a teacher. On his return, he headed to St Luke's in Exeter for a PGCE in secondary school science.

Convoluted though this backstory may be, it is essential in understanding the head teacher he has subsequently become, rooted in determination to broaden children's horizons and decisively manage a school with this as its aim. Was initially attracted to Trinity's small size, taking on his first post as residential boarding tutor 15 years ago and working his way up through ranks from teaching biology and sport to head of sixth form, director of sport and then deputy head before finally taking the helm. Believes in exploring and inspiring the 'whole child' – his ethos that 'success outside of the classroom breeds success inside it' resounds across the whole school, say parents.

Married to Natalie, with three children, all of whom went through Trinity at prep age – one currently still there, though the older two are at different senior schools (helps maintain a healthy space between school and home life, he says). Popular with pupils and parents alike: 'A young, sporty and enthusiastic head' was repeated by many parents, who added that his 'family-man approach' earns him parental respect while the fact that 'he gets stuck in with everything' means that the pupils think 'he's pretty cool'.

The curriculum is rewritten every year to ensure they have current cohort's wish list on offer, and they recruit external teachers to deliver subjects they can't offer in house

Out of school, it is all outdoor action from coaching and chairing the local surf lifesaving club to kayaking, windsurfing, walking Dartmoor and coaching local rugby; his enthusiasm for life's adventures is impressive.

Entrance: Around 70 per cent of the onsite prep school moves up to the senior school and it also pulls in new pupils from across Devon as day pupils, and both UK and internationally as boarders. Not academically selective but CAT4 testing and existing school reports guide expectations of the new cohort, together with an informal assessment day, which includes a discussion with the head. School is keen to encourage new boarders from across the UK and has seen a surge in applications from parents seeking strong academic and social recovery opportunities following the recent lockdowns.

For sixth form entry (when they take eight to 12 on average), applicants need five GCSE passes at 5 or above. Overseas students must complete a personal statement and English skills assessment test.

Exit: Around 20 per cent leave after GCSEs, almost all to vocational colleges, topped up by new pupils joining the sixth form.

After A level, around 65 per cent to university. A solid handful take up places at Russell Group (recent destinations include Exeter, Warwick, UCL, LSE, Bristol and Newcastle), but they insist that each pupil chooses their next step without being pigeonholed, ensuring an understanding that 'university is not the only thing to do after school'. No Oxbridge places or medics in 2020.

Latest results: In 2020, 29 per cent 9-7 at GCSE; 33 per cent A*/A at A level (55 per cent A*-B). In 2019 (the last year when exams took place), 11 per cent 9-7 at GCSE; 54 per cent A*/A at A level (67 per cent A*-B).

Teaching and learning: Teacher-pupil relationships are very strong and the school prides itself on knowing each and every pupil, ensuring that nobody slips through the net. 'We are not the type of school to allow academic middle ground pupils to cruise along unnoticed while we focus on pushing the high flyers or helping those finding things tricky – everyone is given an individual spotlight and celebration,' says head. Proudly standing by its oft repeated commitment to not being 'an exam factory', learning is designed at an individual level, with the emphasis being on engaging every child in the room.

For all its non-selective appeal, the school has steadily raised academic standards, outcomes and expectations under the current headship, and while parents caveat a recent rise in A level results by stating 'it is never going to be the most academic school in the area', it is certainly on a winning streak.

Class sizes are small and teachers pride themselves on their ability to juggle requirements. Parents applauded the method, one delighted that 'every one of my children has reached their full potential and more at this school' and another expounding that 'the small classes instil confidence and belief in the children – they work in a wonderfully uncompetitive, accepting and individual environment.'

Setting in maths, English and science from year 10, when classes become even smaller. The curriculum is rewritten (a two-month process) every year to ensure they have current cohort's wish list subjects on offer and they go as far as recruiting in external teachers to deliver requested subjects that they can't offer in house. With an attempt to allow everyone to choose their desired options, some classes can be in low single figures.

More innovative GCSE subjects include psychology, business, Mandarin, Cantonese, Russian,

Italian, Greek and Latin. A levels benefit from up to 20 subject choices with travel and tourism, economics and business being popular choices, with BTEC options in music, performing arts, ICT and business.

Learning support and SEN: Pupils in need of support work with the Learning Success team, who parents praised as 'really helpful'. Focusing on 'early identification to avoid frustrations and provide the right help so they have no space to drift', teachers are trained to pick up on any initial signs and immediately refer children on for assessments. The school welcomes pupils on funded SEN places via the local authority and, for those, specific permanent teaching assistants are assigned. Mild needs are easily catered for in class, with specific seating plans, coloured paper and continual conversations between parents, staff, LS team and the pupil to ensure all is going well. For those with a greater requirement, one-to-one specialist tuition with qualified SEN teachers is an additional charge, working steadily at the pace of the pupil in any curriculum area in which they need support. Currently 20 per cent of the school has some form of LS involvement. Experienced with dyslexia, ADHD, pragmatic and semantic disorders, ASD, non-verbal language difficulties, dyspraxia and general learning difficulties. Complex needs and some behavioural issues may not be catered for.

The arts and extracurricular: This school comes into its own out of the classroom. 'What we offer so uniquely here is a holistic education where the broader stuff is valued as highly as the academic opportunities,' says school. In practice, it means there is not much that isn't on offer here.

CCF is compulsory in years 9 and 10 and optional thereafter – meets once a week, and there are also weekend activities and holiday camps. 'Very few go into the armed forces from here but they all love the outrageous opportunities,' laughs the head. Cadets can play in the National CCF Band, enjoy live firing, gain their competent crew sailing qualification and attend events at Dartmouth Naval College, to name a few. DofE popular. Ten Tors is important due to the school's proximity to Dartmoor, with fierce competition to gain a place on the 35 and 40-mile options. Year 11 and sixth formers can also join World Challenge Expeditions around the globe – 'There is so much more to school here than sitting in a classroom,' raved a parent.

Good art facilities including a kiln and a printing press. Fantastic studio – a huge diamond-shaped window almost fills one end of the room. Some of the sixth form pieces on display were particularly abstract and demonstrated thinking beyond their years. No surprise that Trinity won two first places in the last ISA national art competition and they have regular showcase exhibitions in local galleries.

Extremely proud of their recent first place ISA award for innovation in STEM, won for a unique approach to scientific learning – Science Buskers. Via a club open to years 5-13, pupils learn and perform science experiments – they took their 'show' to local primary schools, the Devon County Show and into town to busk their science skills to passers-by. Created by the head, who explains the concept as 'learning without realising it'.

CCF is compulsory in years 9 and 10 and optional thereafter. 'Very few go into the armed forces from here but they all love the outrageous opportunities,' laughs the head

Music department is well equipped with the latest Apple computers, a grand piano, drum set, keyboards and electric guitars. Wide range of individual music lessons available, with good take up, plus regular forming of small bands and an annual concert. This is a small school however and parents explained, 'The music department is very good but the school's size means there are not big choir or orchestral opportunities so for highly musical pupils there are sadly not enough challenges.'

There is a performing arts showcase every year for pupils up to year 10 – the latest was a whole-school production of Annie, and strong momentum to learn the 'performing on stage life skill... it gets their blood pumping!' laughs the head. Every student has to write and perform their own poem for World Poetry Day, celebrating the value of creativity and emboldening pupils.

We couldn't review Trinity without mentioning the food, which by all accounts (pupils, staff and parents) is simply amazing. Three-course meals with superb choices and all immaculately presented are eaten in the refectory, as a whole-school experience. Themed tasting sessions linked to topics such as World Book Day or Chinese New Year are hugely popular, as are skill training events, the latest being sushi-making classes. Still on the 'whole child, whole experience' theme, the catering is fully integrated into the school ethos and community.

Sport: 'The best thing about Trinity being a small school with excellent coaching is that pupils get the chance to play every sport and feel that they can excel – they are all big fish in this small pond,' said a parent. There is lots of sport going on and children can compete in many events with strong results at regional and national levels across the board. Rugby, football, netball and athletics all strong, as is swimming, with a newly covered pool enabling pupils, some of whom compete nationally via the south west team, to train at all hours or apply for the newly introduced swimming scholarship. Facilities onsite include indoor and floodlit tennis courts and there is a tennis academy based here run by former junior international player Mark Syms with several nationally ranked players amongst the pupils, plus an indoor cricket academy. Pupils can sign up for individual, group or squad training in both. Trinity takes full advantage of its coastal location and pupils can take part in surf lifesaving, rowing, sailing, scuba diving and other water sports. The school is home to Dawlish Swimming club with associated scholarships for boarding pupils.

Boarding: Boarders make up 25 per cent of the cohort and currently range from 10 to 19 years old with a 60:40 boy/girl mix and 80 per cent international, who are often surprised at the level of pastoral support shown by the staff – a German student wrote in his thank-you note when he finished at the school that what he most valued was the fact that 'the teachers really care about us'.

Set in a stunning location, it has views over Lyme Bay and the English Channel. Not far from Dartmoor and the beaches of Devon, it takes full advantage of both

The majority of boarders are full-time, with occasional flexi-boarders and some European short-termers. A good mix of cultures and nationalities – a third from the Far East, a third from Europe and a third from elsewhere. Around 50 per cent are sixth formers.

Two mixed-gender houses – one for year 11 and below, and one for sixth formers with a more university-style vibe. The boarding accommodation is part of the school building and as such pupils don't leave school 'to go home' – for some this may make a difference. Rooms are nearly all doubles and boarding houses are locked from 8.30am to 5pm to ensure integration with day pupils.

Activities in the evenings and weekends can be five-a-side football, cinema, climbing, go-karting, paintball and endless water sports, including the ever-popular surf trips. Each house votes for their house captains who then assist the boarding staff in the running of the house. All activities are compulsory for the younger ones. From year 9, pupils can go into Teignmouth, and from year 10 they can go to Exeter, back in time for supper. Occasional evenings out are allowed if arranged in advance with set home times.

Regular calls home to parents, plus great updates from houseparents. One parent said, 'Houseparents are simply the best. They looked after him so well and he loved them. They would send me emails to tell me how he is doing without me asking. They are really excellent.'

Ethos and heritage: Founded in 1979, Trinity used to be a girls' convent school. Set in a stunning location with beautifully kept grounds in Teignmouth, it has views over Lyme Bay and the English Channel. Not far from the rugged moors of Dartmoor and the surf beaches of Devon, it takes full advantage of both.

At the very top of the building, aptly named The Attic, is the sixth form area. Ideally located away from everybody else it has a kitchen, café style furniture, table tennis table, quiet study area, common room and amazing views across Teignmouth and out to sea.

The school is a mix of old and new architecturally, with some of the buildings being traditional and atmospheric. 'There is a very definite Hogwarts feel,' parents joked, alluding no doubt to the central winding staircase and wood-panelled corridors in the original convent buildings. 'It is characterful in part but we are already seeing lots of investment from the new owners,' explained another parent. The school was acquired by Alpha Schools Group in November 2019, a British owned and based company that is run by former heads of leading schools. It has already funded a refurbishment of the swimming pool, built changing rooms, begun work on a new onsite nursery building and has plans to install a fitness suite. Building works for a bespoke sixth form centre are currently under way.

Pastoral care, inclusivity and discipline: Pastoral care is a vitally recognised and deeply instilled part of the school, with every teacher having a pastoral role and an allocated period where pupils can come and have a chat. Half-termly, every pupil is discussed at an 'academic pastoral review meeting', with all staff involved. The deputy head laughed that when she first started at the school she was astounded that a child's guinea pig dying was a vital part of such a meeting.

Tutor groups are kept small to foster strong bonds with pupils. Prefects have a key role to play in ensuring that even the youngest members of school have a voice and place to raise concerns; they run a breaktime 'brew club' where anyone can chat through concerns or ideas with the older pupils over a cup of tea. One parent mentioned, 'We hugely appreciate the triangle approach pastorally, where we, our children and the school are all working together with fantastic lines of communication'.

There are clear behavioural guidelines but equally clear support to get back on an even keel when things go wrong and handled, at every stage, in partnership with the parents. One parent reflected, 'When she went through her rebellious teenage behaviour stage, the school allowed her to be a free spirit – but with reins – so that they could gently edge her back on track. It was handled so perfectly and with such compassion that she soon ran out of anything to rebel against and went back to her lovely self.'

Pupils and parents: Parents of day pupils are a mix of mainly local professionals that one parent summed up as 'a wonderfully eclectic and welcoming bunch, truly representing the community here. We are tirelessly invited to everything that is going on at school and feel utterly included in our children's experience.' A train station virtually on the doorstep and the good road links across the county mean pupils attend from right across Devon. There is an escorted airport bus service for boarders. International students give what the deputy head calls 'an enhanced global experience to pupils, offering a microcosm of the globe and the chance to meet and interact with a huge range of people and cultures', important in a relatively parochial part of the UK and demonstrated by the forging of strong international friendships here.

Money matters: Scholarships available at 11+, 13+ and 16+ with average values of around 15-20 per cent of fees but some larger awards are made depending on performance. Range of scholarships – academic, sport, creative arts and the Notre Dame award for all-rounders.

The last word: Rooted in a love of adventure and giving ample opportunities to get stuck in at every level, this is a school that genuinely develops the whole child and gives them a great time along the way. As one parent put it, 'Trinity gives them an incredible grounding in life.'

Truro High School For Girls
64
Falmouth Road, Truro, Cornwall TR1 2HU
01872 272830 | registrar@trurohigh.co.uk | www.trurohigh.co.uk
Ages: 11-19
Pupils: 282; sixth form: 62; Boarders: 60 full, 4 weekly/flexi
Fees: Day £14,805; Boarding £30,414 pa

Head: Since 2018, Sarah Matthews (40s), previously interim head of St Mary's Shaftesbury. Degree in philosophy and RS from Lancaster; PGCE from St Martin's College. Spent 12 years at Stamford High School as pastoral head of year and housemistress before moving to Hong Kong for three years at Harrow Hong Kong, again as housemistress alongside teaching philosophy and RS. Moved back here to give her children a more British education, her daughter is at the school and her son at a local primary.

A warm, approachable figure with a reputation for nurturing and protecting every child in her care. Several of her former charges from Hong Kong followed her to Truro High as boarders and many old girls remain in touch to ask for advice and guidance way beyond her school remit.

Enthusiasm for travel and anthropology has taken her around the world as a volunteer and she regularly sends pupils out to Cambodia to work at a village school that Truro High has partnered with. Incredibly proud of all her pupils' results, she sings the praises of those who get a B after a D prediction or have discovered a love of engineering after being 'virtually dragged to the club'. She revels in the achievements of each child and her pupils are encouraged to the do the same with each other, recognising personal successes at every step. 'We focus on progress not perfection.'

'She knows her girls inside out and is on top of literally everything across both the prep and senior schools,' said a parent, while others extolled her ability to remember important family details and her close ties with the girls.

'She has the most wonderful presence about her and is a great mentor,' said one.

A calm, friendly, maternal force, then. But don't be fooled – it's all accompanied by a determined ambition to be the best, as Truro High's recent awards (Independent School of the Year in 2020 and Top Small Independent School in England in 2018) attest.

Entrance: Most girls arrive from the prep, with a similar sized additional intake from across Cornwall or internationally. It's a source of pride that some head teachers of rival schools choose to send their daughters here. Applicants are invited in for a taster day, occasionally one or two may be advised to look elsewhere at this stage if they seem unlikely to fit with school's ethos or are 'too hard around the edges' (school is clearly protective of its 'nice girls' reputation). All sit an entrance assessment, attitude to learning is key. Once in the school, there is a buddy system partnering new year 7 girls with a year 10 'big sister' to help them find their feet.

Year 11 Spanish students were chatting away in Spanish about the best food they had experienced on last year's trip to Spain, while learning how to cook tortilla

For sixth form, most are already pupils. New applicants (on average 10-15 a year) need at least seven passes at GCSE (8 or 9 in their chosen A level subjects).

Exit: Around a quarter go elsewhere at the end of year 11, mostly to the state sixth form college in Truro but some to larger boarding schools elsewhere in the country, all in search of a bigger pond. A few progress to vocational courses: one was recently offered a Williams Formula One 16+ apprenticeship, another accepted a full scholarship at the Italia Conti Academy of Theatre Arts.

Of those that stay into sixth form the majority go on to Russell Group universities, with occasional students to Oxbridge. UCL, Durham, Edinburgh, Exeter, Loughborough, University of the Arts recently popular. On the arts side, some have been able to skip the entire foundation year of degrees based on the strength of their A level portfolios, no mean feat. Girls left last year to study everything from astrophysics to performing arts. Four medics in 2021.

Latest results: In 2021, 65 per cent 9-7 at GCSE; 74 per cent A*/A at A level. In 2019 (the last year when exams took place), 55 per cent 9-7 at GCSE; 59 per cent A*/A at A level.

Teaching and learning: School says it stopped entering results into league tables at the request of the pupils who, apparently, deemed their use in school marketing materials 'hypocritical of our anti-comparison culture'. Is school's readiness to act upon this gripe an example of the mutual respect between pupils and staff or were pupils pushing at an open door? Whatever its motivation, the decision has not come without its issues – tricky grade sharing conversations took place with rival schools to ensure that Truro High could still claim the 'best in county' title. They may not want to be overly competitive but they're damned if they'll be beaten.

A level students can choose from 21 different subjects; most begin with four, taking an AS Level in one at the end of year 12 and studying the rest to full A level. All sixth formers are encouraged to study for an EPQ plus DofE, Young Enterprise, Golden Arts Awards and TEFL. AT GCSE, 10 is the average number – seven compulsory (including one language and triple science) and three choices from a 12-strong traditional list. Students from China and Russia can take GCSEs in these language subjects though they are not formally taught. Quirkier options include ancient Greek and astronomy (the school partners with Roseland Observatory and is the first UK school to have a solar observatory). Setting in maths from October half term in year 7 and science for GCSE, reviewed every half term.

Classes – maximum of 22 in each – are calm and studious, with a happy buzz during discussion time. Girls we saw were silent and attentive when the teachers were speaking, keen to answer questions and nodding along to ideas given by their peers. When we visited, the year 10 English class was split into small groups creating games and puzzles to set their friends as a key to better understanding the various themes in Romeo and Juliet; year 11 Spanish students were chatting away (in Spanish) about the best food they had experienced on last year's trip to Spain, while learning how to cook tortilla (the Spanish teacher also happens to be a cordon bleu cook).

Pupils are engaged; staff are encouraging. 'There is not one pupil who thinks themselves too cool for school; it is a haven for girls who want to embrace and excel at learning without the distractions of others with a different attitude, or boys,' confirmed a parent.

Staff turnover is low – many have been there for decades and several old girls have come back to the school to teach or form part of the pastoral

Every parent we spoke to, bar none, sang the praises of the pastoral care, describing the approach as 'kind', 'perceptive' and 'down to earth'

care team. There's a healthy mix of male and female staff of all ages; recent recruits include a male Latin teacher, fresh out of university.

The sixth form has its own building with a common room, kitchen, quiet study area and two rooms of carrels (high-sided desks). We saw girls beavering away and others quietly talking or reading. All smiled when we entered and, again, there was not a noisy or grumpy rebel in sight. With only 50 girls in the sixth form, classes can be as small as two with the largest (sciences) being 15. At a sixth form tutor session, we listened as girls quietly discussed topics for their EPQ, whilst the tutor guided another pupil through university choices. The girls came across as mature, dedicated and determined.

All teaching is set up and ready to go online at any point with parents praising the seamless switch to Microsoft Teams classes throughout the Covid-19 lockdown and children responding well to delivering work online.

We like the sound of a new business project the school has recently launched – Trevean Café Project involves girls being given a building on site and a business loan to run it as a commercial enterprise.

Learning support and SEN: Roughly a quarter of pupils have some form of educational need from mild dyslexia or dyspraxia to more moderate ASD. The school has a highly-praised SEN unit, a dedicated room in the centre of school with two permanent members of staff. 'The support that my daughter received from the SEN team has been exemplary' said one parent, with others praising the speed with which any learning difficulties were identified and the positive approach to SEN: 'Having a learning difficulty is not seen as taboo here, there is such a normalcy placed on needing some extra help that those not requiring it feel as though they are missing out.' Girls can receive help in or out of class.

With a growing number of international students comes the requirement to teach English as a foreign language and there is an EAL supervisor in house. Specialist support is provided and most girls can catch up within a year of starting at the school.

The arts and extracurricular: The academic day runs from 8.45am to 3.45pm but all pupils are encouraged to take advantage of the impressive array of extracurricular activity and stay the full 8am-6pm. Those finishing late have the option of the 'boarders' tea'. With a regular choice of over 23 clubs, varying from sports and arts to the more unexpected (such as philosophy, ukulele or seismology), the only complaint was that timetabling does not allow the girls to try them all. They will be even more spoilt for choice, now that there's a new outdoors education centre with clubs for sailing, stand-up paddleboarding, climbing and surfing and survival skills (new ecology area also recently opened with polytunnels for gardening and rewilding schemes).

Fulfilling the head's theory that 'if you don't see it, you can't be it', there are hands-on 'aspiring programmes' for those wanting to become medics, veterinarians, lawyers and engineers. Guided practical sessions with industry professionals complement the academia, from amputating limbs off animal corpses under the instruction of top surgeons to running a courtroom debate with a leading lawyer. School also boasts the only Motorsports UK recognised school car club in the country with its 'green car' initiative, where engineering club pupils race their self-designed cars at the country's top race tracks – and win.

According to parents, the art teacher 'has a brilliant knack of discovering an artistic excel point for every child – if it's not sketching then could it be photography, pottery or woodwork?' Textiles is a popular choice at GCSE and A Level, thanks in no small part to the school's investment in a professional textile printer. 'We haven't had lower than an A at A level textiles in over eight years.'

Full range of peripatetic music lessons with more added by request, bagpipes being the newest arrival and two-thirds learn at least one instrument. There are multiple orchestras and three choirs, performances are well supported and lauded by parents.

Dance is popular, with a bespoke studio and plethora of classes. The annual dance show is a highlight with every girl up to year 9 taking part. 'The standard is literally incredible,' said a parent. Ditto for all other types of performance, they told us, from nativities to dramas. Theatrical ability and confidence is encouraged and in no short supply.

Sport: 'Give it a go, girls!' is the oft-repeated mantra referred to by parents whose daughters had access to choices from touch rugby to trampoline and were encouraged to find one in which they excelled. Nonetheless, we heard a few parent gripes – they want more gym apparatus, greater use of the pool and lacrosse to be taught. This may not be the school for a child whose prime focus is sport, we heard, with many of the girls above year 9 saying they were 'too busy studying' to do much of the sport and outdoor clubs on offer.

We're not sure if the sixth form's ban on publishing exam results extends to sports successes, but quietly the school does rather well (in hockey they are county champions in all age groups and national champions for U16 Tier 3; whilst in netball their U14 team qualified for the regionals). Strong teaching team – the hockey teacher was 2019 England hockey coach of the year. At the lesson we watched with her, the coaching was relentlessly inspirational and the girls were (happily) immersed. Team selection is fair, with all given a chance if you attend the club.

One parent told us that sports facilities are 'spot-on for what the girls need': 22.5-metre indoor swimming pool, three immaculate tennis/netball courts, an Astro, field sports arena, small gymnasium and several grass pitches.

Boarding: Keen to ward off provinciality by attracting a broad range of international students, the boarding houses are home to 12 different nationalities and boarding has seen a 45 per cent growth in the three years since Mrs Matthews took over the headship. Girls are expected to speak English (although we did hear a couple chattering away in Cantonese) and there are a few boarders from elsewhere in the UK – predominantly the Scilly Isles.

School boasts the only Motorsports UK recognised school car club in the country with its 'green car' initiative, where pupils race their self-designed cars at the country's top race tracks

The two, recently updated, boarding houses are split by age (Dalvenie up to year 10 and Rashleigh years 11-13). Communal areas feel like comfortable common rooms with well equipped kitchens. Bedrooms range from four in a room to single ensuites, age dependent. Live-in house parents provide pastoral care, along with other members of staff. Boarders have strict curfews on internet and social media access, all within the tight firewall of the school.

Friday nights are famed for fun (eg inflatables in the pool or roasting marshmallows on the fire pit) and weekend trips take full advantage of the outdoor and cultural adventures that Cornwall is famous for: everything from kayaking to pony trekking, galleries in St Ives to the Eden Project. Boarders are free to visit day pupils' houses or explore Truro in pairs after school hours, returning for 6pm supper. Houseparents step in as in-loco-parentis taxis, collecting boarders from cinema trips or driving them to extra dance classes.

Boarders are accepted as part of the school family with no apparent segregation from the predominantly day pupils: 'I only realised one of my great friends was a boarder after being friends for ages, it makes no difference here,' said one pupil. Day girl parents offer those boarders unable to return home welcome holiday breaks with their friends.

Ethos and heritage: School was built in 1880 by Archbishop Benson (who also oversaw the construction of Truro Cathedral, which the school overlooks) and is within easy walking distance of the city centre. The main building is Gothic, castellated Cornish granite.

Not a sparklingly immaculate, state-of-the-art school, so if outward appearances matter it may not impress at first sight. Paint is peeling off classroom walls and many of the extensions are glorified prefabricated boxes. But there is a general feel of much-loved antiquity. The grounds are a great feature, spacious and light with pockets of wilderness, ripe for development. There are plans to convert the abandoned nursery building into a business centre that the girls will manage entirely; its garden will become a new outdoor learning hub.

Notable former pupils include comedian Morwenna Banks and political journalist Vicki Young.

Pastoral care, inclusivity and discipline: Every parent we spoke to, bar none, sang the praises of the pastoral care, describing the approach as 'kind', 'perceptive' and 'down to earth' and 'what stands this school apart'. The school lives and breathes its ethos of kindness, nurturing and encouraging at every stage. 'They take great care to fully understand each girl and their family so that they can give the right support,' explained one parent. 'Any issues are dealt with immediately and sensitively, often before parents are even aware anything was amiss.' When asked who they can talk to if they have a worry or problem at school, the list from pupils was never-ending, with all girls saying that they felt safe and supported at all times.

Behavioural issues are few and far between. 'The respect between staff and pupils is fostered early, there is literally no need to rebel,' laughed one parent. Acceptance and celebration of diversity is inherent.

St Mary's Calne

Pupils and parents: Dressed smartly in kilts and blazers, enthusiastically eloquent and with engaging and polite attitudes, Truro High girls struck us as delightfully genuine. Any lack of premature sophistication is probably a big selling point for most parents.

Families are predominantly professionals, mostly dual income, from the breadth of Cornwall. Some parents have relocated to the county expressly for the school. One explained, 'Once you have looked around Truro High and seen the kind, confidence-instilling encouragement at the foundation of its first-class education, it is very hard to choose to send your child to the hard-hitting, pressure cooker environments of similarly high-achieving schools in London and the south east. They may look more impressive and polished, but I know where I'd prefer my child to go.' New parents are rapidly welcomed with WhatsApp chats and social gatherings.

Money matters: Around 20 per cent of the school's income goes into fee assistance. One in six pupils is on a means-tested bursary, with several fully funded by the school. Mrs Matthews is set to launch a new scheme where alumni donations fund pupils from lower income backgrounds.

The last word: This school could not do more for its girls if it tried. They are nurtured, coached and encouraged to achieve their personal best at every step. Academic achievements are a credit to the girls' work ethic and the boundless enthusiasm and dedication that the teachers put into their pupils. A wonderfully happy haven, a small school full of girls gently encircled with unwavering support to work hard, achieve high and be kind. What more could you ask for?

Truro School

65

Trennick Lane, Truro, Cornwall TR1 1TH

01872 272763 | admissions@truroschool.com | www.truroschool.com

Ages: 11–18

Pupils: 760; sixth form: 190; Boarders: 70 full, 10 weekly, flexi varies

Fees: Day £14,985; Boarding £25,575 – £29,775 pa

Headmaster: Since September 2020, Andy Johnson MA PGCE (40s), previously deputy head academic at St Dunstan's College, London. Born in Wales and raised in London, he was educated at Westminster School, where the spark was lit on viewing education as a journey of inspirational curiosity. After reading history at Cambridge he toyed with the idea of a career in law but a bit of soul-searching brought him to teaching. Following his PGCE at Leeds and a stint at Berkhamsted School, he spent 13 years at his alma mater of Westminster teaching history, serving as day housemaster and coaching football, tennis and cricket before taking arguably the biggest leap of his career, founding a sixth form free school, the London Academy of Excellence, in the deprived London borough of Newham. As deputy head he spent almost three years establishing and challenging his own views of what makes a great education, describing it as 'exhausting, bonkers and amazing', seeing first-hand how extraordinary aspirational outcomes are possible for all if the academic and pastoral support sparked and supported the students. The restrictions of sixth form only education led him to take his holistic educational approach on to a five-year stint as deputy head academic at St Dunstan's College, Catford where he fully developed his evolving teaching philosophies and from where he was fuelled with the desire to lead a school. Truro School held immediate appeal – childhood holidays in Cornwall had fostered an early love of the county, coupled with the offer of taking over the helm of a highly successful and ambitious school. Not to mention the lure of bringing up his own two young children with wife Pamela by the sea.

We found him considered, analytical and enthusiastic – a true advocate of a learning journey that isn't merely focused on the outcome. He holds deeply rooted and practically explored philosophies on the development of young people where the words 'holistic' and 'pastoral' aren't merely brochure buzz and his plans to ensure that this school is the beacon of success as an curious, inspiring and socially happy hub are enlightening. 'Impressively conscientious,' say parents, with with an 'extraordinarily balanced approach between education and mental health'.

A keen runner, he has two London marathons under his belt. Also speaks of his lifelong interest in history (including teaching it), art and sport (he played and enjoyed coaching football, tennis, cricket and real tennis). An eclectic musical taste too – 'everything from a childhood playing the French horn and adoring classical music through a teenage heavy metal phase to the house music of university in the 90s.'

Entrance: Around 60 per cent come from the prep, the rest from a range of state and independent schools. 'It is such a happy school and I felt settled and made friends here really quickly,' said a year 7 pupil. Moderately selective (around 120 applications for 110 year 7 places) with main entry points at 11+, 13+ and 16+. Entrance exam, school report and interview although, as numbers are burgeoning, the head is exploring an 'experience day' thereby facilitating 'attitudinal rather than merely academic' selection. At sixth form, 18-25 new starters are assessed via GCSE grades, school report and interview.

Exit: After GCSEs, 40 per cent head elsewhere, many to the mighty Truro and Penwith College four miles away, something the head acknowledges as 'healthy choice' but is also addressing competitively via the introduction of a new sixth form diploma – more of which later. After sixth form, 91 per cent to university with 10 per cent taking a gap year beforehand. Top destinations are Exeter, Edinburgh and Cardiff plus a good handful to Oxbridge – three in 2021 (plus two medics, both encouraged by the aspiring healthcare professionals programme). Foreign universities have growing appeal with three pupils gaining 2021 scholarships for sport at universities in USA and Canada.

Latest results: In 2021, 67 per cent 9-7 at GCSE; 74 per cent A*/A at A level (89 per cent A*-B). In 2019 (the last year of exams), 57 per cent 9-7 at GCSE; 45 per cent A*/A at A level (70 per cent A*-B).

Teaching and learning: Pupils are encouraged and celebrated for working hard and engaging in lessons, and they really do. The level of enthusiasm and eloquence from pupils throughout the lessons we sat in was striking, made easier by inspirational and upbeat teachers who are also very open to comms with parents, with one parent laughing, 'I have learned not to send them a message late at night as they always reply straight away and I feel guilty!' Parents also like the regular progress reports and half-termly assessments: 'We really know how are children are doing, both academically and pastorally.'

Sciences and maths stand out. The school is one of only 230 in the country to offer geology – 'We've got a department that isn't far off a small university department.' Pupils were clamouring to be able to study it younger than the current year 9 pre-GCSE taster.

A new sixth form diploma aims to extend the limitations of the A level academic pathway by 'validating the strength of personal choices and co-curricular success'

Though not compulsory, vast majority take at least one (sometimes three) languages at GCSE (pupils can study a third language from year 9 in extra twilight sessions first thing, at lunchtime and after school). Mainly French, German and Spanish but the school will do its best to accommodate other requests (pupils have taken Mandarin, Dutch and Russian in recent years). Exchange trips for younger pupils and work experience in France and Germany for older ones.

More than 20 subjects on offer at A level, including business studies, economics, PE and psychology. Thanks to a bit of timetabling wizardry, students can take any combination. EPQ on offer too. We loved the English A level lesson we observed – a small class of calmly enthusiastic and fully engaged students sharing ideas with mutual respect and impressively articulate language with a teacher that gently guided, stretched and inspired them.

A new sixth form diploma is available from autumn 2021, with a view to extending the limitations of the A level academic pathway by 'validating the strength of personal choices and co-curricular success'. Covering everything from life skills topics such as driving theory and personal development courses, it will also enable pupils to gain 'recognition from the school for service and leadership' that, according to the head, aims to 'shape and define ambition with evidence'. There are high hopes that the diploma will bolster the sixth form retention and selection.

Homework considered sensible by parents and pupils – starting at 20 minutes a night per subject (up to three subjects a night) and rising as youngsters get older.

Learning support and SEN: Learning support department is run by team of full-time head and two part-time staff who across both the prep and senior school with all pupils diagnostically tested during their first year within the school. 'Hugely enlightened and reassuring,' said a parent. Extra support given individually or in small groups (no extra cost). School caters for dyslexia, dyspraxia, dyscalculia, dysgraphia and ASD, with parents describing the support as 'fantastic, intuitive and sensitive'.

The arts and extracurricular: The creative arts have huge prominence at this school with facilities and enthusiasm to inspire even the most creatively wary. Works of art hang from every wall, combining respected local artists' and pupils' creations with a confidence that makes it hard to spot the difference. The school's own onsite Heseltine Gallery hosts exhibitions and talks by established artists, often in conjunction with Falmouth University, and gives pupils immeasurable opportunities to gain from their expertise.

The art and DT block is room after room of tantalising equipment and award-winning samples of recent work. One student was diligently assembling a 3D printed model aircraft 'just for fun in my lunch break', another finalising groundbreaking A level design approaches to cycle safety, in amongst working models of a marine wind training system. Watch this space for a new option to study architecture within the design and technology A level.

Works of art hang from every wall, combining respected local artists' and pupils' creations with a confidence that makes it hard to spot the difference

Impressive music. Truro School is the Truro Cathedral choristers' school, an honour which not only acknowledges the school's music provision but also gives access to the school with a 25 per cent scholarship to those choristers. The music department buzzes with activity from dawn till dusk. A third of pupils take instrumental lessons and there are orchestras, choirs, bands and jazz bands to join with endless performance opportunities. Pupils frequently selected for National Youth Orchestra and National Youth Choirs. Music GCSE is popular and around four to six a year take it at A level.

School has its own theatre opened by Sir Tim Rice, which is used by both prep and senior pupils, with productions throughout the year both by the school and touring companies. The drama staff are true professionals and the department is run as if it were a theatre company. 'Phenomenal,' say parents. We watched auditions for a Wind in the Willows production where giggling pupils were full of jangly nerves and boundless enthusiasm. Those preferring to be behind the scenes have a full technical remit to explore, from light and sound to set design, with the aim being for as much as possible to be student led.

The icing on the cake is the bespoke cookery school, opened by (and named after) Prue Leith. Runs cookery classes for all ages, including Leith's certificate for sixth formers – perfect for that gap year spent chalet hosting in a ski resort.

Wednesday afternoons are given over to extracurricular activities including sport, art and music right through to astronomy, horse riding, debating, surfing and sea fishing. Truro pupils certainly don't lack fresh air. DofE is huge (over 100 take part each year) and there are always school teams in the gruelling Ten Tors Challenge across the wilds of Dartmoor. World Challenge on offer, plus a raft of expeditions at home and abroad.

Sport: A very sporty school, with a refreshing focus on creating good all-round sportsmen and women who genuinely thrive from the game and the spirit, not just the results. Having said that, or maybe because of it, they are usually top of their locality: team county champions in rugby, hockey, netball, cross-country, tennis and cricket. Individual success abounds too, one pupil crowned champion at the European Life Saving Championship, two pupils representing GB at the European Youth Fencing Championship, four top-five placements across the Junior English Surf Championships and another pupil winning the U19 World Champion title in windsurfing.

But Cornwall has its downsides, with teams often having to travel long distances to compete – a gripe among pupils and indeed staff, who bemoaned the long journeys to and from matches. But travel they do and, once up-country, they have excelled against the likes of Millfield with national school achievements including first for U16 football in Independent Schools FA, second in squash National Schools Finals and first in sabre fencing at Public Schools' Fencing Championships.

The jewel in the crown of the extensive and well-maintained facilities is the Sir Ben Ainslie Sports Centre, opened by the man himself, boasting an eight-court sports hall, two squash courts, fitness suite and dance studio not to mention the triple aspect views over Truro. The school excels at fencing and runs an elite academy programme which sees competitors travelling the breadth of the world to compete. Water pursuits a given with sailing, kayaking, surfing and snorkelling all on offer.

Boarding: The three boarding houses (two for girls, one for boys) are small and homely, each with resident housemistress or housemaster. Currently a 50:50 boarding split between British nationals and international students, with 15 different nationalities represented. EAL is included in the fees via one-to-one or small group sessions.

Busy weekends include kayaking, coasteering, surfing, cookery, laser quest etc. Parents spoke of feeling absolutely in touch with what was going on. 'I cannot speak highly enough of the housemistress, who spent so much time and effort with my daughter, helping her totally fit in with exemplary kindness,' added one. Some flexi-boarding available and no apparent segregation, with a pupil telling us, 'We all have friends across day and boarding, it makes no difference.'

Boarders eat in the main school, although they can make toast, pasta, hot drinks etc. in boarding house kitchens.

Ethos and heritage: While not on the same site, both the prep and senior schools have enviable hilltop positions, two green havens on opposing edges of Truro. The distance between them is only a few miles but 'it is an unpredictable traffic nightmare,' according to parents with children at both. The school does its best to alleviate this with a shuttle bus between the two, enabling parents to drop siblings at one school.

The senior school dates back to a Methodist school founded in 1880, which opened with 35 boys and two teachers in a schoolroom in the centre of the city and moved to its current site in 1882. Original Gothic building in local stone has been much added to, with every building housing a separate department, the result of which is a university campus feel. School went co-ed in 1990 and is now a 'pretty even' split between girls and boys.

Food gets resounding approval with lunch included in the fees and decidedly not your average school fodder – we had an impressive Indian curry. 'As a vegan, it's like having an awesome private chef,' laughed one pupil. Sixth formers have their own café and sixth form centre, complete with common room and study area.

Former pupils include government Chief Scientific Officer Patrick Vallance, former M&S chairman Lord Myners, actors Robert Shaw, John Rhys Davies and Nigel Terry, baritones Benjamin Luxon and Alan Opie, sopranos Lynette Carveth and Saffron Jones, quadruple Olympic gold medallist sailor Sir Ben Ainslie, chess grandmaster Michael Adams and Queen drummer Roger Taylor.

Pastoral care, inclusivity and discipline: 'They really walk the talk on being utterly caring and full of compassion,' said a parent, typically. Part of the Methodist Independent Schools Trust, Christian values underpin its approach, something that parents applaud: 'Pupils have a very clear moral compass and spiritual guidance that doesn't feel awkward.' Pupils and parents alike spoke warmly of 'the Rev' – the school's Methodist chaplain who is a vital member of the pastoral team.

School has clear expectations of pupils but everyone we spoke to reckoned it's a fair, equitable place. 'There are lots of rules but they are reasonable ones,' said a year 8. Parents praised a 'sensitive approach to discipline where children are gently guided without being labelled or shamed for mistakes'. Most lower sixth pupils do a 16-week peer counselling programme. Prefects are trained to play a big brother/sister role to younger counterparts and there's particularly good support for new pupils, with sixth form prefects taking them under their wing.

Food gets resounding approval with lunch included in the fees. Not your average school fodder. 'As a vegan, it's like having an awesome private chef,' laughed one pupil

Deputy head is responsible for pupil progress and welfare. Tutor groups organised by year and tutors are pupils' first port of call if there are any problems (they can also go to their head of year, chaplain, medical centre, school counsellor and sixth form peer counsellors). Head boy and head girl, plus deputies and a raft of senior prefects, and a house system in place. Pupils are well turned out in smart uniform, sixth formers wear business dress.

Pupils and parents: Pupils are engaging, modest, warm and enthusiastic about their school. In the place of arrogance or entitlement there was a refreshing sense of inclusivity, opportunity and friendship.

They come from all over Cornwall – around half from Truro, others from up to an hour away and as far afield as St Austell, Bodmin, St Ives and Penzance. Many travel long distances by train (a fleet of double-decker buses ferry them from the station) and parents have organised minibuses from places like Helston.

The boarders include weekly boarders who live in the Scilly Isles, children of expats and a small number of international students who provide a healthy multicultural environment. Everyone mixes – 'What stands this school apart is the lack of judgment, you are warmly accepted for who you are and encouraged to be yourself,'' a sixth former told us.

Parents are an eclectic group, some local to Cornwall but many more from families moving down to the area. The school goes out of its way to help incoming families working in tandem with an active parent network that reaches out to welcome and include new parents. 'Many of us are acutely aware of how isolated and alienating a new start in Cornwall can feel when you first arrive so we make a point of helping others through this – we're a ready-made bunch of friends!'

Money matters: Scholarships at 11+, 13+ and 16+ awarded to both internal and external applicants in academic, art, drama, fencing, music and sport (plus modern languages at 16+) to a maximum of 10 per cent of the fees, offered via relevant auditions, interviews and assessments. Sibling discounts across both schools and means-tested bursaries and Foundation awards.

The last word: A friendly, high achieving school with a truly holistic approach to education delivered via an enlightened balance of academic and co-curricular studies, inspiring a real sense of purpose and opportunity. Refreshingly lacking in arrogance but quietly setting itself up as the place to be schooled in Cornwall.

Wellington School

66

South Street, Wellington, Somerset TA21 8NT

01823 668803 | admissions@wellington-school.org.uk | www.wellington-school.org.uk

Ages: 11-18

Pupils: 661; sixth form: 164; Boarders: 165 full, 12 weekly (from 11)

Fees: Day £14,805 – £16,785; Boarding £25,275 – £33,990 pa

Headmaster: Since 2019, Eugene Du Toit, previously senior deputy head at Trinity School, Croydon. Degree from the University of the Witwatersrand, Johannesburg and an MA in educational leadership from the Institute of Education. Began his teaching career at King Edward VII School in Johannesburg before moving to England and taking up a position at St Paul's School, London as a teacher of economics and mathematics, undermaster (assistant head), and head of house. A keen sportsman who has coached rugby, water polo and athletics. He is married to Angela and they have two young daughters.

Entrance: Main entry at year 7, everyone sits school's entry test in January. At year 9, tests in Eng, maths + paper of own choice. Post-GCSE they'll have you as long as you got three 6s and three 5s. So, not fiendishly selective. International students from year 7 (who take tests in maths and English).

Exit: Varying numbers – around 25 per cent – leave at the GCSE watershed. Of these, most to vocational courses, especially Taunton's Richard Huish College. Some parents make a strategic decision to fund just years 7-11. Majority of leavers go on to uni. Two to Oxbridge in 2021, and seven medics. Popular destinations UCL, Durham, Edinburgh, Bristol, Leeds, Reading, Manchester and Liverpool. Occasional apprenticeships, eg BBC.

Latest results: In 2021, 61 per cent 9-7 at GCSE; 44 per cent A*/A at A level (75 per cent A*-B). In 2019 (the last year when exams took place), 49 per cent 9-7 at GCSE; 35 per cent A*/A at A level (65 per cent A*-B).

Teaching and learning: Typical grammar school curriculum, all the subjects you need for a top university and the right ones to suit the full range of students here – 24 of them. Actually, more than enough, uptake varying from 40+ to, in one or two subjects, zero, so some very small class sizes. Four modern languages including Chinese and two ancient ones (Latin and Greek). BTEC sport level 3 recently introduced. Maths and sciences an enduring strength. Results at A level commendable by any standards. Value-added score admirable. Best of the best: geography, maths (historically strong), Eng lit and classics. Less strong: business studies, economics and physics (improving). Notable: the number of B grades attained by students who might otherwise have got Cs.

Broadly, strong on all fronts, physics especially so. Sixth form foundation course for international students.

Doesn't score five stars for luxury, more like a solid three, though we hear five star things about newish girls' boarding house – and all have had a recent refurb

Careers counselling and course guidance highly rated. You see the evidence for that in the well-chosen universities students go on to, from the highly academic to the best of the rather more doable. As a flagship achievement this is as impressive to us as Oxbridge triumphs: they're bringing out the best in all their students. Head of sixth form much admired and strongly liked by students and parents.

Learning support and SEN: Exceptional special needs provision addresses everything from classic special needs (dyslexia et al) to support for students who have hit a wobbly patch, to a few with mild behavioural problems. Some of these (120 when we visited) have an eye kept on them remotely (they don't know), monitoring mechanisms having registered a blip. Hugely impressive SENCo, masses of experience, wise and thoughtful. He told us: 'Our relationship with our students is key; there's a pastoral element to this. Our department is a good place for a time out, especially for those struggling with sociability.' Big believer in empathy exercises for teachers to give them some idea what dyslexia feels like.

The arts and extracurricular: Music exceptionally strong, much raved about by the mother of a scholar: 'The head of department is inspirational.' Rich range of ensembles and styles and a choral tradition that spans all-girl a capella group and a chapel choir that sings choral compline in local churches. Drama 'could be bigger,' said one parent. Happens in the converted old school hall, ideal for big musicals; also in the South Side studio theatre opened by alumnus David Suchet. Director in residence, thesp background, aims to drum up numbers for GCSE and A level, presently on the low side. Club for techies under the watchful eye of a BBC-trained overseer. Art department buzzy as can be, lots of big ambitious work in progress, everything from paint through ceramics to digital. Well impressive.

Heaps of extracurricular activities likely to render students paralysed for choice. On offer Saturday mornings too, but only compulsory for boarders. Head very keen on outdoor ed, so DofE has enjoyed a recent shot in the arm. CCF hugely popular – very Wellington, this; it's an esprit de corps sort of school. Attractive adventurous activities on offer including arduous Ten Tors trekking event. CCF comes with enhanced outcomes here: you can put your service towards a BTEC level 2 diploma in uniformed public services or an Institute of Leadership and Management qualification. Lots of holiday expeditions home and abroad, some educational, some recreational and some downright gruelling. Brilliant initiative, student generated, enables boys and girls to get their Amateur FA basic refereeing badge. Absolutely not the sort of school that lets anyone skive off but, as a student told us, 'They try really hard to cater for what you want to do.'

Sport: Novel approach to physical exercise – may even be trend-setting. Wellbeing, they call it. Potentially confusing, too, when you're told, in the school's words, that 'The wellbeing programme... replaces the subject that schools have traditionally called physical education.' Acting on a perhaps understandable misunderstanding, The Sunday Times shouted 'zumba puts team games on the bench at top school... Wellington School in Somerset has abandoned traditional PE lessons... and replaced them with "wellbeing" classes.' But it's simply not true. The new and pioneering look for PE here is 'evolved'. 'There is plenty of physical activity but also classroom sessions based around nutrition, mindfulness and leadership, which links into our PSHE programme. Our aim is not only to increase fitness and confidence at school, but also teach pupils how to look after themselves long after they leave school.' In other words, there's as much traditional team sport here as there ever was (heaps), but also a recognition that 'it is... important that an increasingly sedentary generation understands the importance of physical fitness in their working lives.' We can testify that the splendid sports hall was not reverberating to a chant of 'Om' when we visited, and while some might regard the way the school addresses mindfulness as a tad narrow, we were struck by the benevolence of the PE staff, their borderline-messianic dedication and their concern to find something for everyone. One mum told us that her daughter had become sporty for the first time in her life. Strong girls' cricket and rugby. Head of sport is an ex-pro rugby player and ex-county cricketer. Team sports are compulsory to year 10; thereafter you get to choose. The one thing you can't choose is nothing. To the gratification of many parents, mainstream sports have been boosted: 'Wellington needed to up its game.'

Boarding: Around 150 board, roughly 50 per cent of them international students from all over, mainly Russia, China and Europe – 25 nationalities when we called in – numbers of any one nationality limited in order to spur integration. Good systems for boarders to make their views heard. Weekend activities, always a bugbear in boarding schools, have been beefed up. A parent we spoke to who'd sent her son elsewhere entertained a lasting sense of regret that she had not opted what she described as 'Wellington's smelly-socks boarding'. She may have been misinformed. No odour of hosiery when we dived in, everything clean and gleaming. Doesn't score five stars for luxury, more like a solid three, though we hear five star things about newish girls' boarding house – and all have had a recent refurb. The point is the students like it, enjoy their relationships with house staff and express contentment.

Ethos and heritage: Founded in 1837 as Wellington Academy, offering a commercial, mathematical and classical education. That 'commercial' tells you something about the target clientele, still a sector today. In 1879 it rebranded as the West Somerset County School. During WW1 the pupils grew vegetables on the playing fields and made munitions for the front line in the school engineering shop – and the name was changed to Wellington School. In 1945 it became a direct grant grammar school. On the abolition of that scheme in 1976 the school's application to join the state sector was refused, so it went independent. As it has grown it has spilled over into a hodge-podge of handsome buildings bisected by a traffic-calmed road. The main campus is altogether more unified, blessed for space and recognisably public-schooly with its chapel and commodious playing fields. Well resourced throughout, money carefully spent. Most recently, a new sixth form centre, library, study centre and café. Never the sort of school to be seduced by the spirit of the present age and blow cash on fancy-pants prestige buildings. Opened its doors to international students in 1904 and girls in 1979.

The school sits squarely in the midst of the architecturally handsome market town of Wellington, once a wool town, now more of a dormitory for Taunton. Nice Georgian townhouses, a branch of Waitrose and a Wetherspoon pub named in honour of the Iron Duke whose link to the town is in fact notional. He visited just once. His brother chose his territorial title for him when he got his dukedom – the great man was tied up with the Peninsular War at the time – and plumped for the name Wellington for no better reason that that he thought it sounded a bit like Wellesley. A lofty if decayed obelisk celebrating Waterloo stands just outside the town. The town itself nestles on the banks of the M5, enjoying excellent transport links, so much so that some parents to the east of Taunton find it easier to get to Wellington than its competitor schools in Taunton itself. Not to be confused with the namesake college in Berkshire, obviously, except that a surprising number do. The realisation dawns at some point when they're looking round, by which time they have lost their hearts and signed up.

We were struck by the benevolence of the PE staff, their borderline-messianic dedication and their concern to find something for all

The social climate of the school is influenced by the level at which it sets its fees – some 20 per cent or so lower for day students than local competitors (the difference for boarders is less than 10 per cent). This broadens its social base, opening it up to local families who would otherwise be unable to afford an independent education. It also opens it to sneery jibes, eg 'the state school you have to pay fees for', precisely the sort of remark that makes it attractive to affluent folk who don't want their children to be infected by hauteur. We spoke to a number of such parents who had chosen Wellington rather than the sort of school they had been to themselves, who spoke of their pride in the down-to-earth, unpretentious nature of a school whose students go out into the world with an ability to relate to people of all sorts with absolutely no sense of entitlement. We spoke to a working mum for whom finding the fees is a heroic struggle. She told us, 'I never feel intimidated when I go up there', and rejoices that when her daughter leaves 'she will be sure of herself, not full of herself'. One parent talked of a 'school happy to be itself' and there's no doubting its strong sense of identity; we've rarely encountered such ardent loyalty from both students and parents.

Parents also like what one described as 'a thoroughly traditional ethos' and 'Christian values unashamedly proclaimed'. Another said, 'It's the sort of school where it's cool to work hard and make something of yourself.' This is widely endorsed: 'Wellington is good at finding out what your child is good at.' Yes, this is a meritocratic environment whose grammar school inheritance lives on.

Pastoral care, inclusivity and discipline: Sound and recently reinforced systems for pastoral care. Principal guarantor of wellbeing is good relationships among students and between them and staff, whether 'teachers, who really care' or support staff. Some intermingling of year groups; sixth formers pretty good at looking out for the youngest. Parents report rapid response to problems and feel their views count. Though this is a school notable for its camaraderie it is, in the words of a parent, 'not overly conformist'. A student told us 'character is valued; some need more leeway'. For all that the climate is notably orderly. A problem with good schools is that there's so little to rebel against.

Pupils and parents: Most day students come in by bus from Exeter and Chard to the south, Minehead and Dulverton to the north west and beyond Bridgwater to the east. Good social spread of down-to-earth parents. 'Not a posh school by any stretch of the imagination,' one told us. Another: 'No one judges you by what car you drive, only by how nice you are.' And another: 'A good solid cohort of decent parents. Lots of doctors.'

Money matters: High value, especially for day students. Fees what they say on the tin, none of the mum's-the-word discounts you can haggle at other schools and no sibling discounts either. Scholarships up to 20 per cent. Top-up bursaries to 40 per cent subject to means test. The school is committed, according to its means, to educating local boys and girls. Notably astute money management.

The last word: Down to earth. Punches above its weight. No sense of entitlement. Good value for money. Not our words, those of a parent. Says it for us, too.

Wells Cathedral School

The Liberty, Wells, Somerset BA5 2ST

01749 834200 | main-office@wells-cathedral-school.com | www.wells.cathedral.school

Ages: 2-18

Pupils: 754; sixth form: 188; Boarders: 256 full, 15 weekly

Fees: Day £8,310 – £20,442; Boarding £22,098 – £34,212 pa

Head: Since 2018 Alastair Tighe MA (early 40s). Very much a product of the kind of school he now heads, Mr Tighe's career is distinguished not only by its musical but by its academic eminence also. Scholarships both to Downside and to Cambridge for a degree in English and theology preceded teaching and housemasterly posts at Oundle, where he won his teaching spurs on the (then) Graduate Teaching Scheme. Appointments to other notable independent schools (Eltham College, Bedford) followed, leading eventually to Wells Cathedral School, a place Mr Tighe had been aware of since his musical youth. And what attracted him to it, other than the obvious draw of the music? 'The history, the traditions, the family feel,' he told us, then more thoughtfully, 'Respect and humility in the face of many talents. The school is very good at what it does in an all-round way.'

Mr Tighe's face lit up when extolling his school's many virtues, a degree of animation and warmth at odds with his rather austere appearance (shirt and tie, rimless glasses, muted delivery) at assembly earlier. Students appreciate his visibility, open door policy and his efforts to get to know them, especially over sixth form suppers in his home. Parents largely in agreement, acknowledging that he has a lot on his plate, taking over from a very longstanding head and in the aftermath of an unsettled period at the cathedral, to which the school is inextricably bound. 'Not one to be dictated to!' one mother told us. He has brought in a few changes since his arrival, though he assured us he had not 'come to make radical changes, but to make Wells the best version of the school it can be: creative, exciting, spiritual'. According to one straight-talking source, 'He needs to sort the academics out'; daily tutor periods are a step in the right direction, and parents like the renewed emphasis on good manners (eg making eye contact when spoken to) and tackling sartorial scruffiness.

Mr Tighe lives in Wells with his husband Gavin. Any leisure hours in term time will find them walking their dog, gardening or strolling down Vicars' Close to evensong; during holidays they take to the road, drawn inexorably to Italy for the culture, food and architecture. 'I'm a rusty musician!' he admitted ruefully, 'but if I had to save one piece of music from the waves, it would be The Dream of Gerontius.'

Head of junior school since September 2021 is Jody Wells, previously head of Forres Sandle Manor Prep School in Hampshire since 2018. He began his teaching career here as houseparent and class teacher, later becoming head of boys' games then head of boarding at All Hallows School before joining Forres Sandle Manor in 2011 as deputy head. He is an ISI Inspector.

Entrance: Academically non-selective, though everyone is interviewed and undergoes CAT4 screening, and the English of non-native speakers will be tested. Transfer from the junior to the senior school is pretty well automatic, unless significant barriers to life there come to light. At sixth form, where about 50 new students arrive, a minimum of six subjects above a grade 4 at GCSE will be expected, with at least a 6 in chosen A level subjects. A range of scholarships on offer including one for maths. Musical scholars can apply whenever; their auditions take place either at the school, at one of its audition centres round the world or over Skype. Chorister entry is by audition: 'A pure voice and a good ear is what we want; sight-reading we can teach,' we were told. Plus bucketloads of commitment.

Exit: Most stay till the very end, especially if they are heading for music conservatoires and colleges, though around 20 per cent leave post-GCSEs. The majority of music specialists pursue their studies in the UK, an increasing number to European conservatoires and the odd student heading across the pond to the Juilliard or Berklee. The rest almost all head into higher education, many to Russell Group universities up and down the land and a sprinkling to Oxbridge – four in 2021. Degree courses range from accounting and finance to Russian. Gap years rare.

Latest results: In 2021, 61 per cent 9-7 at GCSE; 61 per cent A*/A at A level (80 per cent A*-B). In 2019 (the last year when exams took place), 46 per cent 9-7 at GCSE; 36 per cent A*/A at A level.

Teaching and learning: Non-selective at entry, so results perfectly creditable. 'Academic results are... the result of a good education, not the target,' states the school sagely, though they must have been thrilled with the offer of six Oxbridge places announced in assembly the day we visited. A wide curriculum embracing Latin, politics and, unusually, geology, taught by a true enthusiast in a room furnished with wooden drawers full of meticulously labelled fossils, expands the horizons of the specialist musicians and indeed everyone else. Not overburdened by whizzy technology, in fact in the opinion of one teacher parent, 'Some teachers are hopeless in this regard. The kids are never asked to make a film or a podcast; the teaching is just not very exciting.' School operates a voluntary policy of 'bring your own device' which means its use is patchy: in one class we saw students in pairs working with two different kinds of tablet or no IT support at all. The head later informed us that a review of ICT use is under way. At sixth form, laptops will be expected. Surprisingly small senior school library but we were assured that each academic department has its own.

Music is not everything: one parent who cheerfully admitted that his children were all but tone deaf chose the school for the sport

Our tour was tightly managed: time constraints meant we could poke our heads only into some lessons and only certain students had been selected to speak to us. Analysing methods of characterisation in Hamlet was undoubtedly engaging learners; writing up the common properties of some elements from the periodic table not so much. The science labs hail from some time in the last century but this does not deflect enthusiasm: biology came in for particular praise.

Junior school classrooms bright and colourful, with work of all standards on display. We loved the cross-curricular learning where littler ones were making a model of the layers in a rainforest inside a cut-out shoe box, their uniform carefully protected from glue and paint by Velcro-ed navy smocks. Even if teaching appears to range from the inspirational to the lacklustre, dedication is not in doubt and the quick response to any concerns is much appreciated by parents. Top subjects, according to the students we spoke to, are maths, history, psychology and academic music.

Learning support and SEN: Our previous report judged SEND to be well catered for and this is still the case. New parents are asked to declare any known educational needs on application and all students are screened using CAT4 on entry to assess cognitive ability. SEND support is a whole-staff responsibility and we heard more than one reference to ROCs (record of concern forms). Help comes in three 'waves', starting with targeted in-class support for a particular difficulty and ending with one-to-one sessions in the learning support centre. Mental health as a special need is mentioned in the school's policy document.

EAL prioritised here too, with higher than usual numbers coming from overseas as musical specialists. An attitude of acceptance of a range of physical and mental special needs (including several kinds of neurodiversity) prevails. Despite its sixty different buildings, its antiquity and its cobbles, the school is fully wheelchair accessible at ground level.

The arts and extracurricular: How could we start with anything other than the music? Wells is one of only five specialist music schools in the UK, providing pre-professional training to those seriously considering a career in music in almost any discipline or instrument. Its ancient walls have breathed music for 1,100 years. These days, about 80 of the 150 specialist musicians study under the government-funded Music and Dance Scheme or under specialist provision, where there is a significant focus on music in their daily lives, but not the kind of commitment required of a specialist. To quote the website, this is 'ideal for students who may be looking to see where music takes them and wish to keep their options open'.

Musicians' timetables are personalised to accommodate lessons and practice times. Choristers start every day at 7.45 am with a rehearsal for the day's services in the cathedral in the beautiful new song school off the cloisters with its practice rooms for girls and boys: our visit could not have started more gloriously than hearing them bash effortlessly through a Mendelssohn motet and punctiliously pointing psalms. Our day continued in similar vein, with a young violinist delighting everyone in assembly with a piece he will be taking to the extremely prestigious Menuhin competition in the US, one of only 22 players selected from his age group worldwide. Snatches of melody could be heard wherever we walked; the lunchtime concert in the medieval Quilter Hall (named for a previous headmaster, rather than a bygone artisan) gave us the chance to wonder how a voice of such contralto richness could issue from such a slip of a girl. But there is truly music for all at Wells, with all the instruments, disciplines, ensembles and opportunities anyone could wish for.

Dramatic arts are well served too and are initially taught as part of an integrated approach taking in visual and culinary arts as well. It was heartening to hear that musical theatre is alive and probably high-kicking: Grease was the word at the commercial theatre in nearby Strode recently – and sold out. The junior school timetables weekly drama and dance lessons and collaborates annually with local primary schools to stage a festival of Shakespeare, as well as Christmas and summer shows. Dance in all disciplines massive here too and up to competition standard; students set up their own street dance troupe Blanc.

Visual arts well provided for both in terms of studio and exhibition space, with the foyer of the magnificent Cedars Hall and entrance to the art school dedicated to hanging works. Sixth formers have personal studio space, meaning they do not have to tidy work away at the end of sessions. We shared one student's satisfaction at being able to render the recent experience of a remarkable trip to Everest Base Camp in oils, and another's in the depiction of the architecture of her home in Hong Kong on a huge oblong canvas.

Wells is one of only five specialist music schools in the UK, providing pre-professional training to those seriously considering a career in music in almost any discipline

Life outdoors, from the safe confines of the nursery forest school within the grounds, the neighbouring Mendips and all the way to Sierra Leone or Everest Base Camp (plus Europe of course) is a feature of Wells life. The youngest members of the school community, aptly named Little Wellies, spend time outside in all weathers. Outdoor learning has a whole dedicated department headed by a former Royal Marine; we met the formidable CCF instructor who is closely involved with DofE, a popular activity. A Wells student was recently selected for the National Marching Band of RAF Air Cadets – two worlds collide. Trips go all over the place – as well as the usual sporting/musical/ battlefields tour and ski trip, the school has a long-running link with a project to share music and language with youngsters in Sierra Leone, and scientists recently went to Japan. There's plenty of scope for adventure, just as long as the parental pockets are sufficiently deep: 'Quite extravagant!' remarked one.

Sport: Music is not everything: one parent who cheerfully admitted that his children were all but tone deaf chose the school for the sport, certainly an aspect which has been greatly beefed up in recent years in terms of facilities (gorgeous new cricket pavilion, Astro etc) and staffing, including the appointment of a former professional cricketer to head the sports department. 'It all stops us bleeding people to Millfield and not being pigeonholed as music school geeks, plus it gets the musicians to do other things,' reckons one father. The swimming pool has a retractable roof, making it a more pleasurable experience in the summer (such a good idea, we wonder why more schools don't build them); some discontent that there is no senior swimming team 'but the head is on to it,' we were told. We were glad to hear cross-country runners enthusiastically applauded in assembly for recent successes and 'I am delighted to see choristers kicking a ball about – it's not all about winning, though that is nice!' the head conceded. One young badminton player at the school is now ranked no. 35 in England. Additional Astro available for hire at local comprehensive the Blue School when needed. New MUGA and refubished tennis courts.

Boarding: Offered from year 4 up, the starting age for choristers, not that all junior boarders are. Beaumont house is a former family home in whose welcoming kitchen at a long pine table all the dozen or so younger boarders eat breakfast and supper brought over from the main kitchen. It strives to be a home from home, with a resident family, cosy spaces to relax, a walled garden and girls' and boys' dorms on the same floor (not that they are allowed into each other's territory). A second boarding house for this age group is the newly refurbished Claver Morris.

Senior boarders from year 7 are assigned to single-sex houses dotted around neighbouring roads, into which day students are fully integrated, until their last year when the upper sixth move into a mixed house of their own as preparation for university life. Accommodation definitely errs more towards functionality than luxury ('The boiler breaks down annually,' one resigned parent told us) with quite an emphasis on tidiness, that is until we entered a boys' dorm which was reassuringly messy, with that unmistakable smell of sweaty sports kit thinly veiled by Lynx. Very few single rooms – 'Most of our boarders prefer to share,' we were told. Nearly half of the senior students board; flexi and last-minute boarding available. House staff struck us as very warm and deeply committed to the young people in their care. 'What is on at weekends dictates whether she comes home or not,' one former chorister's mother told us.

Ethos and heritage: The 13th-oldest school in the country and still going strong, Wells Cathedral School was set up at the same time as the cathedral was built to educate its choristers and those destined for the clergy. This duality abides to this day: the elite music provision sits comfortably alongside a school for ordinary mortals, enriching all. Who could dispute that exposure to all kinds of music nearly all day long explodes the horizons and ears of the non-specialist? And for the specialists, the chance to play, sing or rub shoulders with those less gifted than themselves is not an opportunity found at the specialist music schools, but is likely to be a reality for many of them in their future careers. One father chose the school for his double bass player son as he wanted him to be in a 'normal environment', and the students we spoke to during our delicious sandwich lunch (on which they fell like wolves) assured us there was no 'us and them' between musicians and not. The atmosphere is not particularly rarefied, but the school combines ancient and modern quite beautifully, from the medieval Quilter Hall and Vicars' Close to the bang up-to-date Cedars Hall, with its sophisticated acoustics, music tech facility and recording studio attached. Students stride cheerfully between buildings all over that part of the tiny city, music cases strewn below coat pegs everywhere the eye could see. Not a place for fancy shoes – never have we encountered so many cobbles!

Everyone mentioned the firm line taken on bullying: 'They come down on it like a ton of bricks,' one father told us

The acknowledgment of immense talent or its absence spreads into a general sense of acceptance, partly expressed in the school motto Esto quod es – be what you are, a medieval injunction adopted by the school only in the 19th century. The head assured us that this is not some complacent mantra for contemporary snowflakes, but is more in the spirit of 'become the best you can be'. We were glad to know from the students we met that difference is absolutely fine at Wells – some of it arrives in the form of the many music specialists from overseas (24 nationalities at the last count), many of whom do not share the Christian faith (immersed in it though they may be) and those who can be open about their sexuality, taking their lead from the top; Spectrum is the aptly named LGBT club.

Recognition of all talents comes across loud and clear; we picked up no sense that the musicians were singled out for special accolades. 'No one talent should stand above the others' was the head's interesting reflection. The applause we witnessed greeting the winner of the short story competition was warm and prolonged, the citations so engaging, we wish we had been on the judging panel.

Pastoral care, inclusivity and discipline: Voted outstanding by all we spoke to: 'the children are very well cared for', 'proactive, staff know early signs [of problems]', 'a pastoral school and a nurturing environment' were comments which came our way, echoed by the students we lunched with and evident in the interaction we saw with staff. School adopts a 'team around the child' approach, involving student leaders as well as tutors, house and medical staff. Child protection taken extremely seriously – to the point where a volunteer chaperone attends each chorister practice, as the staff leading the practice belong to the cathedral rather than the school, but teddies on top of the grand pianos distract from this sobering thought.

'Better pastorally than academically,' one mother remarked baldly. Everyone mentioned the firm line taken on bullying: 'They come down on it like a ton of bricks,' one father told us. This zero tolerance extends to drugs (immediate suspension); we picked up concern from parents about the rise of drugs in the city and possible county lines. A balanced approach is taken to alcohol; 'we're allowed it under controlled circumstances,' sixth formers told us. The school is also strict about parties at weekends, particularly for the boarders in its care. The need for discipline does not seem to loom large: the new school policy details pastoral infringements (eg unkindness) alongside academic ones. One parent though thought that 'the kids need to understand discipline and boundaries; it's too free and easy and the school motto is taken too literally'; others deplored general scruffiness. Time will tell if new clarity of expectations will sort out these shortcomings.

Pupils and parents: Quite a mixed bag, from the music specialists, some of whom have come from across the world to be there, others who have moved to the south west to be close, to more local families wanting smaller classes and better facilities; buses serve a 30-mile radius. Economically mixed too – 'Some families are minted!' observed one mother – but it's not the kind of place where kids are regularly picked up by helicopter, if ever: more a case of 4x4s of varying vintage and the odd tractor. Many make considerable financial sacrifices to be there, and all chorister families make considerable personal ones to meet its demands: 'People need to accept sacrifices such as sport and birthday parties,' one chorister mum affirmed. 'It has implications for family life.' A proportion of first-time buyers with musically gifted children have found a warm welcome at the school 'when it could have been so daunting'. We found all the students we met congenial and forthcoming without a trace of arrogance – admittedly all hand-picked sixth formers, but the junior school pupils were friendly, chatty and keen to show off their work. 'I'm afraid I can't!' the head replied when we asked him to describe a typical Wells student.

Money matters: Commendably clear policy on the specialist scheme funding, scholarships and bursaries. Choristers get financial help from the start; as of 2020, girl choristers will receive funding equal to the boys. Parents we spoke to found tricky discussions around their personal finances sensitively handled and necessary support forthcoming. Active PA funds extras.

The last word: An exceptional school where the talents of musicians and non-musicians enrich each other's experience and which wears its antiquity lightly, while staying faithful to its founding principles. They shall have music wherever they go. 'I thank my lucky stars for this school,' said one grateful parent.

West Buckland School

68

West Buckland, Barnstaple, Devon EX32 0SX

01598 760000 | headmaster@westbuckland.com | www.westbuckland.com

Ages: 3-18

Pupils: 600; sixth form: 167; Boarders: 91 full, 36 weekly

Fees: Day £8,310 – £16,455; Boarding £31,320 – £33,735 pa

Headmaster: Since 2016, Mr Phillip Stapleton BSc MA Ed MBA (40s). Educated at Bishop Stopford School in Kettering, followed by Durham University, where he read biochemistry and immersed himself in music, drama and sport. Several university friends became actors (including Alex Macqueen of Peep Show and The Inbetweeners fame), but he modestly says, 'I wasn't good enough.' Initially set on a career in molecular genetics, he stayed on at Durham to take part in a show, embarked on a PGCE and discovered he loved teaching. 'It brought everything together – working with inquisitive minds, a passion for my subject and the chance to perform,' he says. First teaching post was at Stonyhurst, followed by Charterhouse, where he taught chemistry and became a housemaster. Then moved to Ardingly, where he was deputy head for five years. He is also an ISI inspector.

Head was struck by West Buckland's friendly atmosphere and beautiful location the instant he arrived for his interview. 'The sun was shining and a group of students were setting off for a run,' he says. 'It was a breath of fresh air to see their sense of enjoyment. There was a real buzz of opportunity and potential.' The school is selective but he's determined that the school should cater for children from all backgrounds. He's very proud of West Buckland's decision to offer 100 per cent bursaries to local youngsters whose families don't have the financial means to send them to the school (there are currently 17 children benefiting from this programme). During his first year at the school he focused on teaching and learning, observing every teacher in the classroom and broadening the extracurricular opportunities on offer. He's determined to raise the school's profile, citing its academic results, musical prowess and emphasis on character development.

The school's annual Exmoor run was described by school archivist as 'the oldest, longest, roughest, toughest, regular scheduled, compulsory school cross-country run in England'

Energetic and approachable, he still teaches (many heads don't). This year he's got a year 12 A level chemistry set. Married to Jules, who teaches maths at West Buckland. They live in a house on site and have three children, all pupils at the prep. Keen on sport (he once ran four ultra-marathons in a year – respect) and has recently taken up the double bass.

Prep school head since 2018 is Nick Robinson MSc PGCE, previously deputy head of Dunhurst, Bedales's prep school. PGCE at the University of Portsmouth in 2002 and a master's in leadership and management in 2013. Before this, he pursued his passion in swimming as a high performance coach and was head coach for the 1996 Zimbabwe Olympic team and placed three swimmers on the 2000 Great Britain Olympic team. Has also been assistant head at Castle Court. The younger two of his four children will join the senior school.

Entrance: Entry into reception isn't selective. After that, those joining the prep higher up spend a taster day at the school and meet the prep school head. Entry into the senior school is selective, but not dauntingly so. Pupils joining year 7 from other schools take English, maths and verbal reasoning tests in the preceding January (but pupils in the prep don't need to take entrance tests for the senior school). Children can start at multiple points so it's always worth talking to the school.

Some new pupils join in the sixth form (27 in 2017), many from local secondary schools finishing at 16. A minimum of five grade 5s required by all, although it's not set in stone. Those aiming to do maths A level need at least a grade 7 in maths and a minimum grade 6 is required for A level biology, chemistry, physics and modern languages.

Exit: Around 10 per cent leave at 16, for a change of scene, to take the IB (not offered by West Buckland) or to do vocational subjects. At 18, around 90 per cent head to university, nearly 60 per cent to Russell Group. One or two to Oxbridge most years. Most popular universities are Bristol, Cardiff, Bath and Southampton, with subjects like engineering, geography, business, English and biology leading the pack. Eight medics in 2020. A few opt for apprenticeships and the world of work. Pupils get plenty of guidance about university and careers. Youngsters are encouraged to get some work experience from year 10 onwards – everything from working at local law, marketing and architecture firms to volunteering at a children's hospice in Barnstaple.

Latest results: In 2021, 65 per cent 9-7 at GCSE; 62 per cent A*/A at A level (83 per cent A*-B). In 2019 (the last year when exams took place), 48 per cent 9-7 at GCSE and 74 per cent A*-B at A level.

Teaching and learning: Results are good. Most pupils take 10 subjects at GCSE, including at least one language (French or Spanish) and two or three sciences (the majority take three). School is the highest-performing sixth form in north Devon, with around 20 subjects on offer at A level. Chemistry, maths and biology are the most popular A level choices, followed by geography and economics. A small number took the EPQ in the past but now AS exams have been ditched all pupils will do it. Other options available to sixth formers include a BTEC in applied science and core maths (a new level 3 qualification). No Saturday school.

Reading for pleasure is encouraged throughout the school. Imposing new library has 14,000 resources and pupils can use it whenever they like, whether they're studying or curled up with

All sixth form boarders have their own ensuite rooms – far more salubrious than many university rooms we've seen

a good book. Favourite authors at the time of our visit included Sarah Crossan and Kim Slater for younger pupils, Emma Cline, Deborah Levy and Ta-Nehisi Coates for sixth formers.

Prep school is housed in a separate building. The head boy, one of our tour guides, reminisced nostalgically about his days at the prep and said he'd be very sad to leave the school. Prep teachers work closely with the senior school – children learn French from nursery and get the chance to use the senior school's art department and science labs (the prep has its own lab too). Ninety-five per cent of prep school pupils progress to the senior school. Pre-prep has its own building, with views across fields full of grazing sheep – no wonder parents race to get their children's names down. It's not all splashing paint and building sandcastles though. When we visited, a group of year 2 children had just learned the meaning of 'onomatopoeia' and were excitedly coming up with their own examples.

Learning support and SEN: Unusually, the school doesn't charge extra for learning support (now called personalised learning and development). Around 100 children have help in some shape or form and the dynamic new head of department has brought in a wealth of ideas and strategies, including coloured reading rulers to reduce visual stress, pencil grips, spell checkers, prep diaries and a quiet room for children who might be having a difficult day and want a bit of peace and quiet.

The arts and extracurricular: Pupils are encouraged to get out into the fresh air as much as possible. The school has its own forest school, where pre-prep pupils – under strict supervision – play in the woods, build bivouacs, make fires and learn to tie knots. The older ones take on challenges like the gruelling Ten Tors hike across Dartmoor and the school's annual Exmoor run, once described by school archivist Berwick Coates as 'the oldest, longest, roughest, toughest, regular scheduled, compulsory school cross-country run in the length and breadth of England'. Around two-thirds of pupils do the run each year (the length of the run varies according to age), while others mark the course, administer the race and cheer their pals as they run across Exmoor's hilly terrain, through muddy streams and over rugged moorland. Staff, parents and old boys and girls take part too and as one of our young tour guides told us: 'The Exmoor run defines the school.'

Music is an integral part of the school, led by dynamic director of music Emma Kent, who's also musical director of the award-winning North Devon Sinfonia. Pupils and staff queue along the corridor to join her lunchtime choir rehearsals – we watched the junior girls' choir singing their hearts out before heading off to afternoon lessons. Music department comprises a recital room, teaching room, computer suite, recording studio and eight practice rooms. Everyone does music till year 9. Up to 25 pupils take the subject at GCSE and around six a year do A level music. Musicians get plenty of opportunities to perform in public – everything from Verdi's Requiem at Exeter Cathedral to Guys and Dolls in the Queen's Theatre, Barnstaple.

School is rightfully proud of its stunning timber-clad 150 Building, built in collaboration with former West Buckland parent Damien Hirst and opened in 2010. As well as the school theatre it houses the art and DT departments. Sixth formers have their own art studio – and their own individual space within it. 'If you treat someone as an artist, they'll work as an artist,' says the head of art. The standard of artwork is inspiring – we were particularly taken with a vast painting of the Exmoor run being painted by a sixth form art scholar as a gift to the school.

Lots of extracurricular options, everything from astronomy to jazz. Enterprising head of sixth form is keen to develop 'academic enrichment' and youngsters are encouraged to take part in the STEM Club, Phoenix Society (debating) and Aldiss Society (guest lectures). Outdoor learning is the jewel in the school's crown. Many youngsters do DofE (bronze, silver and gold) while CCF is compulsory for year 9 pupils (optional after that). New head of outdoor learning encourages pupils to challenge themselves. 'We've got enough tents to put 100 people under canvas,' he told us with a note of pride in his voice. Outdoor activities are voluntary but most take part, whether they surf after school or try their hands at coasteering. There's also the aptly named Adventure Society, which gives pupils the chance to experience new outdoor pursuits. Pupils excel at climbing, with two brothers gaining places in the GB bouldering team in recent years.

Sport: West Buckland is a sporty, outdoorsy place, with acres of playing fields and excellent facilities. The sports centre (named after distinguished old boy and Olympic triple jumper Jonathan Edwards) boasts a vast sports hall, fitness suite and 25m indoor pool. Boys' main sports are rugby, hockey and cricket and girls' main sports are hockey, netball and tennis. Lots of pupils play for local and county teams. The school also offers specialist performance and development programmes in tennis and dance. Sport is compulsory till year 11 and optional after that – but around 98 per cent continue with it, whether it's mainstream sports or activities like squash, swimming or dance.

Boarding: Pupils can board from year 7, and occasionally younger ('we are always open to discussion,' a member of staff told us). Three boarding houses – one for years 7 to 11 girls, one for years 7 to 11 boys and a brand new sixth form boarding house, with separate wings for girls and boys. Sixth form house (Parker's) is very civilised. All sixth form boarders have their own ensuite rooms – far more salubrious than many university rooms we've seen. They're encouraged to do their own laundry and learn to cook. Stylish common room on ground floor is open to all sixth formers. Lots of activities for boarders at weekends, including cultural visits, shopping in Bath and Bristol, cinema trips, surfing, running, kayaking and paintballing.

Ethos and heritage: The school is set in 100 acres of idyllic countryside on the edge of Exmoor, 220 metres above sea level and eight miles from Barnstaple. Initially known as the Devon County School, it was founded as a boys' boarding school in 1858. The school's enterprising founder, the Rev JL Brereton, thought that the boys could do lessons in the schoolhouse in the morning and work on the school farm in the afternoon. They would then sell the produce and the income would pay for the school's upkeep. The school was renamed West Buckland School in 1912.

West Buckland is a sporty, outdoorsy place, with acres of playing fields and excellent facilities. Sports centre is named after old boy and Olympic triple jumper Jonathan Edwards

Imposing main building dates back to the 19th century but in recent years there have been many new additions, including the Michael Morpurgo Library (the celebrated War Horse author has a farm 20 miles away), the 150 Building and the sixth form boarding house.

Notable alumni include novelist RF Delderfield of To Serve Them All My Days fame, former Whitbread boss Alan Parker, science fiction author Brian Aldiss, triple jumper Jonathan Edwards, former England rugby players Steve Ojomoh and Victor Ubogu, and Somerset and England cricketers Craig and Jamie Overton.

Pastoral care, inclusivity and discipline: Universal praise for the school's friendly and welcoming ambience, with just the 'right balance of formality and friendliness'. One parent describes it as 'a hidden gem' while others say it produces 'grounded, socially aware and respectful individuals with a positive self-assurance'. Pupils particularly like the house system (everyone belongs to one of four houses and there are lots of inter-house competitions).

Plenty of people to talk to if problems arise, including personal tutors, housemasters and housemistresses, the school nurse and a school counsellor who comes in twice a week. School has its own chaplaincy team – a school assembly with a spiritual dimension takes place once a week and the carol service at South Molton Church, six miles away, is a highlight of the autumn term. Christian values are part of school life but students of all faiths or none are welcomed and encouraged.

Most day pupils travel to school by bus so they are allowed to bring phones to school but must put them away during lesson time, unless asked otherwise. Pupils' behaviour is excellent – murmurings about the occasional minor misdemeanour but that's all.

Pupils and parents: Day pupils come from within an hour's drive away, mostly from Barnstaple and north Devon villages. Some choose weekly or flexi boarding (parents can book online up to 24 hours in advance). A fleet of school buses ferries pupils (and sometimes staff) in from areas as far afield as Chawleigh, Tiverton and Winkleigh. Buses start as early as 7.30am to allow for the winding country lanes. Senior school day fees include travel costs but prep school fees don't. Around 20 per cent of pupils are boarders – a third of the boarders are from the Far East, a third from Europe and a third from the UK, mostly the south west.

The pupils we met were enthusiastic, unpretentious and refreshingly down-to-earth. No quibbles about the smart navy school uniform (sixth formers wear business suits) or the food, served in the newly refurbished dining hall. Parents range from families who've lived in the area for generations to those who've moved out of London in search of a better work-life balance – plus the chance to surf at nearby Putsborough Sands after work.

Money matters: Mindful of the tough economic climate, the school has kept its fees as low as possible, with learning support, travel, exams and books all included in the senior school fee. Academic scholarships available to year 7, 9 and 12 pupils, plus music, art and sport.

The last word: A gem of a school in an exceptional location. West Buckland is an impressive all-rounder school with excellent facilities, great teaching and a real sense of community. Children work hard, get lots of fresh air and don't grow up too fast. Best of all, they seem to have a whale of a time while they're at it.

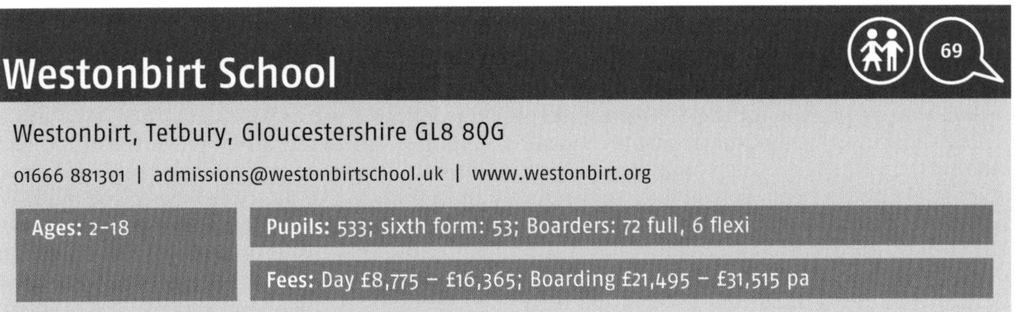

Westonbirt School

69

Westonbirt, Tetbury, Gloucestershire GL8 8QG

01666 881301 | admissions@westonbirtschool.uk | www.westonbirt.org

Ages: 2-18

Pupils: 533; sixth form: 53; Boarders: 72 full, 6 flexi

Fees: Day £8,775 – £16,365; Boarding £21,495 – £31,515 pa

Head: Since 2013, Natasha Dangerfield BA QTS (40s). Degree in PE with English from Brighton. Her career has taken her through various roles in several of the UK's top girls' boarding schools: Downe House, North Foreland Lodge and Harrogate Ladies, plus a spell at Gordonstoun. As a promising schoolgirl lacrosse player, she had played at Westonbirt; her youthful verdict was 'Crikey! This place is really spooky!' but this has mellowed into an appreciation of its rural situation, its heritage and not least, its commercial possibilities. Her first three years, she readily admitted, were a question of 'keeping the place going: we had boilers breaking and waterfalls down the stairs!' but since then she has turned her attention to the longer-term sustainability of the school, embracing the sale to the Wishford Group, looking closely at affordability and recently, the introduction of boys after 90 years as a girls' school. Resolute in her determination to keep Westonbirt academically inclusive – in fact, puts 'driving the academics up' at the top of her priority list.

Despite the kind of name which belongs to the dashing heroine in an airport paperback (along with a fabulously flamboyant signature), Mrs Dangerfield is refreshingly candid, self-deprecating and funny, not half as formidable as her name might suggest – though 'when she teaches us, she can be strict,' according to students. Parents universally rate her: 'compassionate', 'emotionally intelligent', 'approachable', 'professional', 'energetic', 'fiercely determined' and 'a force to be reckoned with' were just some of the compliments we heard, the only minor flaw being a tendency to micromanage on occasions, possible only in a small school. Married to Matt, a firefighter working in Oxford, with three teenage children of her own (two at the school), Mrs Dangerfield is still a country girl at heart and loves walking in her idyllic surroundings and refereeing lacrosse when required. Her chosen reading veers from Sapiens via Wolf Hall to Why French Children Don't Throw Food and she enjoys running a book club for international students.

The prep school has since 2016 been headed by Sean Price BA PGCE (30s), an unmistakable and proud Welshman with a degree in English from Cardiff. Mr Price has made his home and career across the bridge in England, starting in the state sector and moving to Westonbirt as pastoral head for three years before taking on the top job. Voluble and immensely likeable, with a propensity to laugh at himself, he has gone down very well both with his young students and their parents. 'A phenomenal maths and games teacher,' one mother raved and one who was nominated for a local 'teacher of the year' in 2017. Youngsters necessarily see less of him now but our hearts were gladdened by the clamour and press of children wanting to talk to him when he showed us round. Clearly extremely child-centred: 'the children come first every time,' one parent stated. Married with a son in the school.

Entrance: Academically non-selective all the way from nursery up, where the youngest children are informally assessed at individual taster days, plus school reports and references from previous schools for older ones. From year 4 onwards, children wishing to join the prep are assessed on CAT scores 'to ensure they can access the curriculum', states school, and 'on character and potential'. Barring disaster, it appears that the transition from nursery to sixth form is seamless. New starters appear to be welcome at any time, but the main entry points for the senior school are year 7 and to a lesser extent year 9; they come from the prep, Wishford Group's other prep schools and a slew of local prep and primaries. Any learning support needs are assessed on a case-by-case basis.

Exit: Not every child goes on to the senior school from the prep (usually around three-quarters) and there is no obvious pressure to do so. Parents reckon the preparation for the 11+ for the prestigious Gloucestershire grammar schools is good, but that the prep school could usefully gen up on other local senior schools. Popular universities for sixth form leavers include Exeter and Newcastle. The weekly careers lesson (to include apprenticeships and options apart from degree courses) and UCAS preparation gets the thumbs-up from sixth formers. Retention rates post-GCSE seem to be improving, a habitual problem for girls' schools. The introduction of sixth form boys may well help here. One to Oxbridge in 2021, and two medics.

Latest results: In 2021, 62 per cent 9-7 at GCSE; 59 per cent A/A* at A level (78 per cent A*-B). In 2019 (the last year when exams took place), 37 per cent 9-7 at GCSE; 33 per cent A*/A at A level (61 per cent A*-B).

Teaching and learning: The curriculum here really is, in that well-worn phrase, 'broad and balanced' with enough options at GCSE and sixth form to cater for the wide range of ability the school attracts. French, Spanish and Latin are compulsory to start with. Six GCSEs form the core of the course, including a 'gateway combined science course' (triple science for stronger candidates) and – unusually for these secular times – RS; no compulsory language though. Options extend as far as a level 2 BTEC in child development. At sixth form, an even broader choice is on offer, comprising 20 A level subjects, five BTECs, one Cambridge Technical in dance and that gap year jolly-useful, if not must-have, Leith certificate in food and wine.

Exceptional results in further maths, physics and drama. Business studies BTEC particularly successful with 90 per cent of entries being awarded a distinction. For some years, the school has been in the top five per cent of Durham University's national measure for value-added.

Several tests were in progress when we visited and the male teachers in suits gave the senior school rather a formal impression, dispelled somewhat by a lively drama class warming up for their modern melodrama. Laboratories not quite the age of the house, but almost – we heard no complaints, however. We were heartened to see an A level classics set with just two takers. A geography lesson on the Greenwich meridian delivered remotely by a teacher in isolation (another was in the room to oversee order) lost little in translation and students were interested and attentive. Our last review described the IT as 'somewhat prehistoric' but school has now implemented a 'bring your own device' policy, which sees students with their own iPads – though not at the expense of handwriting, we were assured. Prep school teaching takes place in two permanent buildings and some light, bright refurbished temporary ones. 'But please get rid of them!' at least one mother begged. We were delighted by the enthusiasm of the girls learning the dagger speech from Macbeth; the boys seemed keener on maths. Most parents greatly appreciate the apparent lack of academic pressure – 'the children are pushed enough to get the best out of them,' one father told us; another added that 'they do just enough in the prep school to get them into the senior school of their first choice', yet we also heard that staff are receptive to parental suggestions that their little darling could be pushed just a bit harder. Brighter sparks are generally reckoned to be well served, and they are encouraged to be academically ambitious (scholars are provided with 'extension and enrichment activities'), but we wonder whether an outstandingly clever youngster would find enough of an intellectual peer group. Communication with individual members of staff seems to be open, swift and two-way.

We were delighted by the enthusiasm of the girls learning the dagger speech from Macbeth; the boys seemed keener on maths

Learning support and SEN: Making it possible for children to access the curriculum is the watchword here, so the highly experienced and respected head of learning support and her team address a wide range of educational needs, including social skills to navigate school life. Classroom support is provided through differentiated work and homework, rather than through dedicated classroom assistants. English language training for those students whose first language it isn't is prominent and at sixth form; they are entered for the IELTS qualification, essential for entry to a UK university. The parents of children needing learning support that we spoke to were unstinting in their praise, not only for the way academic barriers such as dyslexia are broken down (eg one child was relieved to be told, possibly by a teacher who makes no secret of his own dyslexia, that he could listen to his English books, rather than read them) but also for the way in which less confident or anxious children are gently encouraged to come out of their shells. 'The learning support staff are proactive, and ambitious for the children they teach,' one mother told us. 'I found it hard to accept my child's diagnosis – and they helped me with that too.'

The arts and extracurricular: From the imposing great hall via the orangery to the intimate camellia house, there is somewhere to stage drama of all types at Westonbirt. It is central to the curriculum both in the prep (where, alongside music, a combined offer of performing arts is laid on and everyone has a chance to appear on the stage during the year) and in the senior school. ESB and LAMDA exams are an extracurricular option. Budding thespians perform – and win – at local festivals and take shows to Edinburgh some years. As well as ambitious productions at school (eg Les Mis in 2018), students enjoy the opportunity to showcase their talents on a smaller scale: we heard them excitedly discussing an outdoor staging of Antigone in the school's very own amphitheatre.

Music also hits the top notes, with two-thirds of students playing an instrument and again, a sensational concert venue in the great hall with its Victorian organ. Music is timetabled right up until year 10 and students learn all genres from baroque to pop, as well as having the chance to compose their own works in the technology suite. Instrumental and singing lessons are provided by a team of peripatetics. Singers are well catered for, with several choirs. Occasional services at Gloucester Cathedral are a highlight.

School provides its own counsellor and listening ear service. 'There's always someone to catch the kids who might fall down the cracks,' according to one father

We loved the art studio, a beautiful light space where sixth formers are glad to have their own place to leave their work out. Fine art and photography are frontrunners here. The standard of drawing is high – one of a foetus in utero would not have been out of place in a biology text book (if anyone still uses text books…). GCSE and A level exam pieces are put on show as an exhibition every summer. Masses on offer too beyond timetabled arts: national schemes such as DofE and Model UN but also the Westonbirt Baccalaureate for sixth formers which aims to round out their academic work and doubtless contributes to good UCAS personal statements, plus opportunities to explore leadership. Plenty of trips laid on too: 'I know we live in the middle of a field,' the head acknowledged, 'but we do go to Bath, Bristol, Oxford and Cheltenham in search of plays, concerts and galleries.' Further afield, students can sign up for the biennial ski trip or older ones for service projects to India or Sierra Leone.

Sport: A longstanding lacrosse school through and through – and proud of it ('My daughter couldn't possibly leave after GCSEs because of her lacrosse!' one father told us), but seemingly adapting well to the necessary addition of rugby for the boys. It's clearly catching on – we were amused to see an informal game of mixed rugby in the sunlit prep school playground. Parents and students alike all crying out for an Astro though. One parent furnished us with a list of upgrades the school should, in his view, also have: a new block of changing rooms and floodlit tennis courts, for starters. Happily, plans for all these are well advanced under the eagle eye of Heritage England, who guard the historical and environmental integrity of Westonbirt very zealously. Space and grass it has in abundance – there's even a nine-hole golf course. Netball and cricket on offer at all ages; hockey just in the prep school. Sporting provision greatly beefed up by the leisure centre just beyond the prep school, comprising a multi-use sports hall plus viewing gallery and lovely pool (ecstatic 3-year-olds from the nursery were jumping in and swimming a width under the watchful eye and vocal encouragement of their former Olympian teacher when we visited), open to the public at weekends only. Fixtures are held against local schools and because numbers are small, everyone gets a game. Westonbirt girls have gone on to play lacrosse for England and Wales. A strong equestrian team, as befits this very horsy part of Gloucestershire with the Beaufort Polo Club across the road, completes the sporting array.

Boarding: Offered to girls in the senior school, and to boys from 2021, but every permutation (weekly, flexi, full) is possible, with each day student getting a night a week free of charge. Below sixth form, two houses are accommodated on the rather grand upper floors of the main building. Glorious views right into the trees from dorms which four to five junior girls share. Combined sleeping and study spaces make it slightly claustrophobic in our view, but the communal spaces are cosy enough. We heard that some parents consider that it is 'scruffy and needs sorting', however. Sixth form boarding occupies a separate building designed for the purpose, with university-standard accommodation, kitchen and study hub. Their café also serves alcohol (no spirits) on set occasions and doubtless under close supervision.

Ethos and heritage: The wow factor starts to build as soon as you turn in through the narrow gate and make stately progress along the long one-track drive, designed for carriages rather than the wider and ubiquitous 4x4, through the expansive Victorian parkland. The main house (now the senior school), completed in 1871 by Sir William Holford, who also founded the world-famous arboretum across the road, owes its grandeur and flamboyance to the Jacobethan fashions of the day. These days, its gracious rooms are still warmed by blazing fires and have been put to good use as a school since 1928. Certain parts though have a distinctly below-stairs feel with narrow staircases, red lino and the finest collection of household bells we have ever seen (preserved as a curiosity and out of bounds). But it is heartwarming to see such an imposing monolith so purposefully used, with youngsters scurrying about and revelling in the expanse of gardens – not one officious notice about keeping off the grass in sight. 'I love the fact that my son's free time is spent outside climbing over various monuments instead of being glued to Fortnite,' one mother remarked.

In terms of an ethnic mix, Westonbirt is more diverse than the rest of Gloucestershire – not hard – and the head strives for a balance of nationalities

The prep school surrounds are more modest but skipping through the Italian gardens (filled with magnificent dahlias when we visited) to get there is a treat. It might be lost on the students, but parents are alive to the beauty their offspring inhabit every day – more than one told us how they encourage them to 'Look at the trees! Look at the colours!'

An exclusive setting, certainly, but we kept hearing how inclusive the school is, how academics are not the only measure of success and how the students are 'not numbers or pay cheques'. All the parents we spoke to reckoned their children were not only well known by all members of staff, including the heads, but also that they were always treated as individuals. Not a pushy place, but one where great efforts are made to find out what makes each child tick or could do – one mother told us that her not very out-going daughter had been asked to captain a sports team, not just play in it. 'And they don't give up on anyone,' one father added, 'they take on some difficult kids and do well by them.'

Pastoral care, inclusivity and discipline: Top marks here for pastoral care and wellbeing generally. 'Happy children thrive,' as the policy puts it – and there's a health and wellbeing centre to address ills of body and mind. We heard moving tales of difficulties that the school had supported not just the child but the whole family through. Students we talked to consider their mental health is well looked after and that there is always someone to chat to, starting with tutors. School also provides its own counsellor and listening ear service. 'There's always someone to catch the kids who might fall down the cracks,' according to one father. Diversity and inclusion is discussed in tutor sessions – and words such as 'fat', 'skinny' and 'retarded' are not tolerated. Order is maintained through a system of credits (for good work and deeds) and debits, with the emphasis on credits (some inconsistencies with debits, our interviewees reported). We did not sense that insubordination and poor behaviour were particular issues, however.

Pupils and parents: Such splendid surroundings might give students a misplaced sense of entitlement, but the ones we met seemed to be very grateful for their lot, and inclined to concentrate on the positives. Apart from a unanimous wish for an Astro, gripes concerned clocks telling different times all over the school and 'that weekly meat-free day!' as one young libertarian protested. Uniform is unflashy and practical. We got the usual spiel about a wide economic mix of families, one mother assuring us that it did not matter what car you drove, another that 'you don't have to have a Range Rover and acres, but it helps'; plus there is somewhere to land a helicopter, if need be (the school boosts finances as a wedding and party venue). In terms of an ethnic mix, Westonbirt is more diverse than the rest of Gloucestershire – not hard – and the head strives for a balance of nationalities. So who wouldn't it suit? we asked parents: possibly a child who wanted just to be left to get on with things, a child who might struggle with the pace of a busy school, urban sophisticates and serious hockey players, they responded.

Famous old girls include children's author Georgia Byng, TV presenter Ruth Watson and founder of ethical fashion brand Beulah, Natasha Rufus-Isaacs.

Money matters: Fees at the lower end of the scale both for day students and boarders; the head lists making the school more affordable as one of her achievements since taking over, and a bonus of joining the Wishford Group. Scholarships (10 per cent fee reduction) and exhibitions (five per cent) offered at years 7, 9 and 12 for all the usual attributes, but from 2021, two major academic scholarships also to an exceptional 50 per cent of the fees. Means-tested scholarships for entry to sixth form from local schools 'open up a wide range of opportunities'.

The last word: 'A very posh-looking place with very normal children' (in the words of one mother), but one which is moving with the times and managing that most unusual move to co-ed from a girls-only with finesse – just as long as they keep those boys' numbers up. Memorably described as a 'greenhouse, not a hothouse' by the previous head, we cannot disagree. 'If my daughter was a stick of rock, she'd have Westonbirt running through the middle!' declared one dad – such is the love and loyalty it inspires.

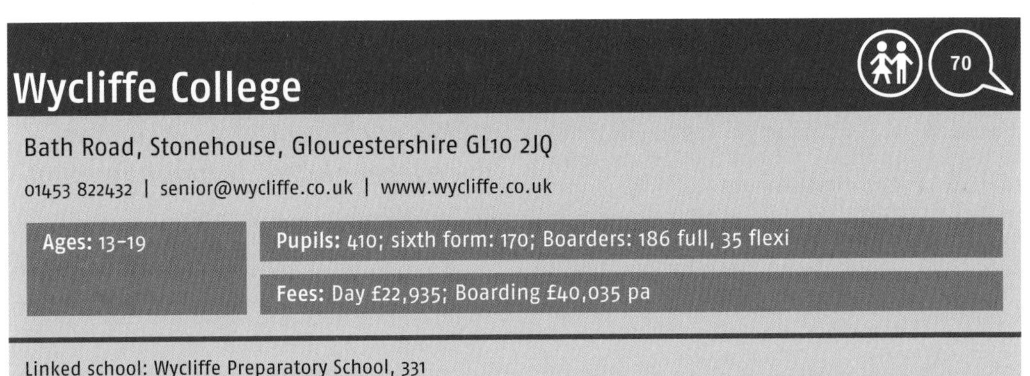

Wycliffe College
70
Bath Road, Stonehouse, Gloucestershire GL10 2JQ
01453 822432 | senior@wycliffe.co.uk | www.wycliffe.co.uk
Ages: 13-19
Pupils: 410; sixth form: 170; Boarders: 186 full, 35 flexi
Fees: Day £22,935; Boarding £40,035 pa
Linked school: Wycliffe Preparatory School, 331

Head: Since 2015, Nick Gregory (50s). Attended Ipswich School where own 'inspirational' father worked for 47 years, 28 as deputy headmaster. Graduated in French and Spanish from Nottingham, having spent time in Argentina fine-tuning language skills and pursuing twin passions for rugby and cricket. Not wanting to be 'predictable' and follow in father's footsteps, accepted a job with Barclays where linguistic talents enabled him to return to Spain and qualify as a banker.

On reaching the milestone age of 30, he acknowledged he had 'an itch he couldn't scratch' and supported by wife Helen, abandoned banking for teaching. Spotting potential, Barnard Castle School engaged him while he completed a PGCE. Knowing leadership and management was the end goal, and to enhance credibility, his next post was at Merchant Taylors Northwood, followed by a stint as housemaster at Old Swinford Hospital where he was 'humbled' to work at an establishment that has such a 'profound impact on people's lives'. Thence to Mill Hill, London where he spent seven years, rising to deputy head (pastoral).

For the Gregorys, Wycliffe College is a family affair. Mr Gregory is frequently accompanied by Helen to recruit international students from Hong Kong, Nigeria, Russia and Europe. 'They want to speak to her – what it is like to be a mum, the practicalities of living away from home.' Back at school they visit boarding houses together regularly for a meal or cup of tea, chatting to pupils informally 'in their own environment'. Two of their three sons have attended the school, giving a fully rounded perspective.

In the headmaster's wood-panelled study an antique grandfather clock strikes each quarter as it surveys the cricket pitches through mullion windows. The room has a timeless quality which could evoke any era in the college's 139-year history, but its current occupant is anything but 'old school'. Mr Gregory is effervescent, loquacious (in his own words) and enthusiastically on brand; he even wears the Wycliffe purple, both tie and (we noticed) socks. Commenting on a fragrant wisteria clambering the Cotswold stone walls he declared, 'It has flowered in the school colour just in time for your visit!' Clearly, building his school's profile is a mission: 'We want the Wycliffe purple recognised on sports pitches and at events.' Thus the new Astro is flanked in purple and according to one sixth former, 'Even the squash court lines have been re-painted purple.' Another conjectured that the headmaster 'would probably love it if I dyed my hair purple!' Amused, we suggested that might be a step too far.

Looking over the grounds Mr Gregory observed, 'Our layout is such that you could put your arms around and hug it.' This epitomises his approach: 'personable', 'professional', 'visible' and 'aware of his market', say parents, but fundamentally he 'cares deeply' about his school and pupils. One boy summed up the fine balance, 'I've never seen it, but he is strict when he has to be.' Another noted, 'He is always smiling, comes to talk to you and remembers everyone's birthdays!' No timetabled teaching but will step in if needed. 'I have watched as other heads have taught and never seen it work; children always get short changed.' So far in his tenure Mr Gregory is proudest of the 'much-improved culture where pupils' best interests come first and aspiration, high expectation and drive are the norm'.

Entrance: Automatic admission from Wycliffe Prep accounts for majority of year 9 entrants. Recent 30 per cent upturn in day pupils thanks to increasing interest from local state, grammar and preps. Headmaster attributes this to Gloucestershire 'word of mouth in response to our achievements, and our ethos'. External applicants (including to sixth form) sit exam and interview to assess requirements and award scholarships.

Exit: Some natural fallout after GCSE, majority continue to sixth form. School has excellent international university programme. Most head to UK universities, a number to US (one to Harvard in 2021). Others to eg Canada, Australia, Europe. Occasional Oxbridge places (one in 2021).

Latest results: In 2021, 46 per cent 9-7 at GCSE; 47 per cent A*/A (69 per cent A*-B) at A level. In 2019 (last year exams took place), 35 per cent 9-7 at GCSE; 34 per cent A*/A (63 per cent A*-B).

Teaching and learning: Headmaster keen to stress that while the school's academic bar has been raised, this has been achieved without compromising pastoral care or breadth of extracurricular activities. The gifted are stretched, those who need it are supported; all are nurtured and encouraged to fulfil individual potential. Results speak for themselves: 2017 and 2019 respectively saw the best GCSE and A level grades in school's history. Number of parents praise school's remote provision during lockdown, one pronouncing it 'exceptional – straight off the starting blocks teachers worked hard to engage the children and kept them fully engaged throughout all lockdowns'.

Pupils can progress from nursery to sixth form without entrance assessments or exam. Parents applaud this, both practically, when accommodating several children, and for prioritising welfare and development over league tables. 'A lot of schools talk the talk but Wycliffe really delivers,' said one. 'You could have three children with different interests and abilities and all would be well catered for,' said another.

Classes small, usually no more than 14, often fewer. We like the way one parent put it: 'Big enough to create interest, small enough to be personal.' Streaming in core subjects begins in year 9. One teacher explained, 'Setting and class sizes are decided by subject, ability, individual needs and year group.' An approach to be applauded but we feel for the person in charge of timetabling.

In the headmaster's wood-panelled study an antique grandfather clock strikes each quarter as it surveys the cricket pitches through mullion windows

At GCSE, geography, sciences and languages are best performers – latter not surprising with significant international presence. We thought the labs looked a little worn, possibly in need of updating in near future.

A level choice impressive with art, maths, psychology and business most popular. There are BTEC options too in business, digital media and sport. EPQ uptake has grown significantly, headmaster sees this as more evidence of school's raised academic aspirations.

Pre-A level 'development year' to tutor international students in English or GCSEs is thriving and around 30 enrol annually. Sharing rooms with existing pupils improves English, forms friendships and gives valuable insight into other cultures. Around 20 or so stay on for sixth form.

Headmaster sees room for improvement in career provision across his and all schools. 'It is not good enough to tell pupils they'll be doing jobs that don't yet exist. More needs to be done to help explore careers and alternatives to university.' We agree and will be watching to see how this develops.

Learning support and SEN: Some 50 SWANs (students with additional needs) receive tuition, mentored by five learning support staff. Situated in the eaves of main school building, a parent qualified that the 'characterful' attic space with beams and sloped ceilings has 'a lovely atmosphere'. Each child has bespoke provision created with parental and staff input. 'Together we choose a subject from the curriculum to replace rather than take children away from recreation or lunchtimes,' says head of learning support.

Headmaster expands, 'The key is not just extra provision, but the culture that every member of staff makes adjustment for pupils in their classroom.' Teachers have 'identified additional needs profiles' with strategies to help individuals who require extra assistance.

Experience assisting dyslexia, autism, ADHD and dyspraxia. 'As long as the child can access the GCSE curriculum, we will support them as they progress,' head of learning support explains. Wycliffe is accredited by CReSTeD; headmaster member of their council of trustees.

The arts and extracurricular: Art, drama and music creativity is in abundance under their enthusiastic and talented department heads. Walls of the large, lofty, light-filled art studio evidence pupils' talent and inspiration. Tutors are professional artists in their own right. Outstanding A level results. Music department hosts 'live lounges', 'gigs', ensemble groups, a 45-strong choir and the invitational Vox choir. Several take music A level each year. Head of drama fondly describes the school's Sibly Theatre as 'our mini National Theatre', by virtue of its 1960s design. Growing number take drama GCSE, encouraging more to consider A level. Pupils involved in every element of ambitious school productions, 'a real showcase of our talent'.

Extensive co-curricular activities – beekeeping, drone flying, fencing, debating, and more. CCF and DofE too. Exciting programme of tours including Costa Rica, hockey and netball trip to Sri Lanka, Europe for languages.

Sport: Wycliffe's strong reputation for sport is, headmaster confesses modestly, 'probably more than we deserve'. Pupils suggest this may be because school is adept at championing and facilitating many 'niche sports'. Talent regularly shipped off site to train with local academies, GB squads (currently sailing, rowing, equestrian, polo) and compete in national and international competitions.

Prospective families enticed from across the world by outstanding squash and rowing programmes. There was an unprecedented sweep of national titles in squash for boys U15, U17 and U19s in 2019. Rowing boasts one of top female sculling programmes in the country and recent highlights include first place in national head of river, quarter finals at women's Henley regatta and more silver and bronze in British and national competitions. Boys' rowing reputation also growing fast. Netball 1st VII enjoyed unbeaten seasons in both 2018 and 2019 and girls' hockey A teams were recently U16 and U18 regional finalists. Boys' rugby not top-flight but 'good standard' and a handful are taken up by Gloucester rugby academy each year. Fencing produced county junior and senior champions in 2018 and 2019. Pistol shooting boasts regional and national medalists. Tennis U18s and cross-country both reached national finals in 2019.

Director of sports oversees senior school and prep. Overview ensures younger players are not disillusioned or intimidated by contact sports, so 'post growth spurt they make balanced choice'. Sees role as helping those not in the top tier, 'the great majority', to find a sport they enjoy – not just at Wycliffe, but for life, harnessing 'health and mental benefits'. Pandemic taught benefit of paring back sport to skills. 'For example, A squad play contact, B team touch, building confidence, focusing on fun.' Years 9 and 10 follow traditional: rugby, hockey, football, netball, athletics; years 11-13 choose from a wider variety: yoga, fencing, strength and conditioning and zumba.

Sports facilities are excellent, particularly for girls. Girls' cricket pitch sits alongside boys'. Two indoor netball courts plus Astro. Plans for viewing pavilion overlooking rugby and football pitches. WASP (Wycliffe advanced sports prog) for scholars includes one-to-one coaching, strength and conditioning. Pool on prep site – recent IAPS success. Options well balanced between genders. Girls' football and rugby options. 'If there's a sport they'd like to try, we'll give it a go.'

Classes small, usually no more than 14, often fewer. We like the way one parent put it: 'Big enough to create interest, small enough to be personal'

House sports competition 'tribal' and 'great fun' – flags and face paint daubed for keenly contested cups. 'Friday Night Lights' becoming regular event, showcasing sports. 'Creates buzz and excitement while inspiring younger pupils.'

Boarding: Eclectic group of international pupils brings diversity and richness to school. Houseparent says school 'teeming with activity at weekends'. Day pupils frequently stay late and welcomed to join at weekends. One chirpy boarder went so far as to say they 'prefer being at school than at home'. Regular cohort of Forces children continues long tradition.

Eight houses comprise seven boarding with a mix of full, flexi and some day pupils (three girls', three boys', and a co-ed sixth form) and one co-ed day. Perhaps not surprisingly, our tour arrived at the newest, award-winning boarding house,

Wards-Ivy Grove, accommodating boys downstairs and girls above. Each floor has vast common room with table tennis, pool table, flat screen TV, plus kitchen and laundry area. There's also an outdoor terrace with seating and pizza oven. Younger pupils share, older pupils occupy single rooms. All are high-ceilinged, many ensuite and some enjoy outstanding Cotswold views. The tight itinerary of our tour did not take in any of the remaining seven houses, so we can only wonder if they compare favourably.

Number of parents praise school's remote provision during lockdown, one pronouncing it 'exceptional – straight off the starting blocks teachers worked hard to engage the children and kept them fully engaged throughout all lockdowns'

A parent or two expressed sadness at lack of sixth form bar, often considered a 'perk'. Sixth formers confirmed they are permitted 'a couple of drinks at socials' and can visit Stroud, Gloucester or hop on the train to London on a Sunday – curfew 6pm. Little in the way of alcohol and related issues. Pupils sanguine: 'It's not a problem. If we want to go out, we stay with day pupils off site' – all prearranged with parents and school, of course.

Houses host array of events – singing, drama, quizzes, barbecues, sport etc. 'House song is the best time of year – and the Christmas meal,' enthused one pupil.

Ethos and heritage: Leaving behind the busy dual carriageway of Bath Road, the visitor is drawn in by Wycliffe's immaculate green cricket pitches fanning out ahead. At the centre of a horseshoe of buildings in a parade of styles is Georgian Haywardsfield House. Beyond, the glorious Cotswolds seem to enclose what feels like a tranquil Wycliffe bubble.

Founded by the Sibly family in 1882, school was named after pioneering Christian John Wycliffe. This pioneering ethos has clearly rubbed off on pupils who espouse 'taking advantage of all opportunities' and 'trying everything you can'. School has been fully co-ed for more than 30 years and according to parents has 'got the balance just right'. Notable former pupils include Mark Blundell (Formula One driver), Jamie N Commons (musician), Ananda Coomaraswamy (philosopher and artist), Mark Porter (TV doctor) Charlie Stayt (BBC Breakfast), Jun Tanaka (chef and restaurateur).

Pastoral care, inclusivity and discipline: Parents praise 'exceptional pastoral element'. Pastoral deputy comments, 'We believe that a child can only achieve their potential if they are fundamentally well adjusted and happy.' Pupils say problems sorted 'often between us, just talking', or through timetabled tutor time.

Pupils are smart, polite and well mannered, yet clearly relaxed and happy as they mill around campus. During our visit the headmaster remarked on a pupil he had reprimanded, for a second time that day, for failing to tuck his shirt in. 'He knows there will be consequences if we speak again, I'll be keeping an eye out.' Later on, headmaster spied offending pupil and raised an eyebrow. In lovely display of respectful jocularity said pupil smiled and flashed open his blazer to display a neatly tucked shirt.

Boarding and teaching staff liaise, ensuring flow of information, enhanced by online system for safe sharing, reporting and updating the welfare of pupils, increasing opportunity for early intervention. Students say there is little or no bullying: 'It's just not what we do and absolutely not tolerated.' None of the sixth formers we met were aware of Everyone's Invited or similar websites, and eschewed the notion that such incidents happen at Wycliffe. Headmaster affirms that he and the governors are 'acutely aware and working together to ensure we continue to educate and have systems in place should such behaviours emerge'.

Pupils united during lockdown with early-morning 'tea and toast' chats and afternoon house quizzes online. Communication cited again and again by parents as 'first rate'. 'I feel at ease with approaching staff or going straight to the head,' one commented. Boarding staff regularly contact parents via WhatsApp or email. Serious problems initiate immediate parent discussion: 'This way issues dealt with quickly and nipped in the bud.'

We observed that international pupils, boys, girls and year groups seem to integrate well, demonstrated by the general mix kicking a football, playing tennis or relaxing at breaks. During a delicious lunch in the unusually serene dining room (head attributes serenity to carpet installed to muffle dining din), an engaging and smartly attired group of sixth formers, a mix of international, day, boarders, Forces pupils, chatted openly, respectfully engaging with each other's viewpoints. 'It's a small school so we keep an eye on each other', 'really your house is your family', 'there's always someone to talk to', they told us.

Peer mentoring is formalised with coaching and safeguarding training, providing opportunities for pupils of all ages to help and support each other.

Global citizenship is embraced at Wycliffe. Teachers say whenever possible opportunities sought to explore multiculturalism and to 'hold up a mirror to themselves', appreciating similarities and differences. School is candidate for Round Square membership to develop.

Chapel, the 'heart and soul of Wycliffe', is where whole school comes together several times a week. Rebuilt after World War II by pupils and staff, all feel genuine connection to this beautiful and atmospheric building. Open and inclusive – all faiths catered for.

Pupils and parents: With international and Forces families, boarders and day pupils, parents are 'eclectic mix'. Headmaster notes increasing 'relocators to Cotswolds', sending children to flexi-board, citing excellent train links for families around Cirencester and Gloucestershire. Parents' association 'not about parent socials, there's no pressure to be involved,' we heard. Local parents told us they enjoy hosting boarders, some extending invitation to visiting families: 'There's no air of entitlement at Wycliffe; the boys and girls are refreshingly down to earth, kind and supportive of each other.'

Money matters: Scholarships available at 13 and 16 for academia, art, music, DT, ICT, drama and sport (10-20 per cent). School offers three Royal Springboard bursaries and 'significant' support is available in exceptional circumstances.

The last word: As GCSE and A level results rise, the college is increasingly gaining a foothold over academically selective local grammars and a grip on the UK and international boarding market. Sporting facilities are top notch with more in pipeline but some other departments require a bit of TLC. What with the Gloucestershire parent grapevine and the current London relocation trend increasing day pupil intake, we wonder whether the 50/50 day-boarding balance will tip. Small but mighty, Wycliffe College is raising its head above the parapet, newly confident that its balance of academic, pastoral and co-curricular provision is the key to successful growth.

Wycliffe Preparatory School

Ryeford Hall, Stonehouse, Gloucestershire GL10 2LD

01453 820470 | prep@wycliffe.co.uk | www.wycliffe.co.uk

Ages: 3-13

Pupils: 287; Boarders: 38 (from age 7)

Fees: Day £10,005 – £17,370; Boarding £14,355 – £23,370 pa

Linked school: Wycliffe College, 327

Headmistress: Since September 2020, Helena Grant BEd (50s). Her parents were career accountant and librarian, a fact that belies an 'incredible childhood growing up in Hong Kong and travelling with my hobby anthropologist and explorer father'. TEFL course during A levels confirmed her vocation and after graduating from the University of Plymouth she took up her first teaching post in Devon. However, wanderlust swept her first to Greece, then on to Tanzania where she met husband, Steve. Mrs Grant kept education at the heart of her work, launching East Africa's only educational children's magazine, Jifunze. She then set up her own nursery school and developed a conservation education programme for an NGO called African People and Wildlife, which is still thriving. Moving with their young family to Kenya, she worked in IAPS District 4 Prep School, Hillcrest as deputy head academic.

As deputy head at Monkton Prep in Bath, she was neither looking to move, nor for headship, but visiting Wycliffe College knew instinctively that she wanted to be part of this 'very real, authentic and special' school.

Lives on site with Steve and their two sons, both pupils at the senior school. Whenever possible, the family return to Nairobi where they own 150 acres of bushland and live a 'simple life outdoors'. In her spare time she loves to read and runs a book club with some girlfriends, 'who are the mainstay of my life'. Harking back to days in Hong Kong watching the Sevens, she loves rugby and enthusiastically supports Western Samoa!

Mrs Grant's study speaks volumes about her character – undeniably British yet blended with international influences: a feature wallpaper of crested cranes in the long grasses, lush lemon and lime trees in rotund earthenware pots (plus thick pile carpets that 'children like to kick off their shoes and feel beneath their feet'). Enthusiastic, open and outgoing, parents say she is 'easy to talk to', 'encouraging and supportive of staff', 'leads by example' and is a 'highly effective communicator'. Pupils say, 'she's always smiling', 'we've all been to her study to get to know her' and delight that 'everyone gets a birthday gift from her present box'.

We met a group of pupils enthusiastically spray-painting a huge canvas outside the art studio, while inside walls are a cacophony of colour and tremendous talent

Despite arriving at the height of the pandemic, Mrs Grant seamlessly integrated into school life. A parent appreciated her greeting the children dressed head to toe in colourful robes on international day, engaging them in tales of African culture, 'both wowing and putting them at ease'.

Entrance: From 3+ into newly situated onsite nursery. Head stresses that although they have an open door policy, entrance tests and taster days (via Skype for international pupils) give insight into a child's ability and they do not accept those who would struggle to access the curriculum.

Exit: Most pupils move directly up to senior school at the completion of year 8 (age 13). Some depart for local grammars at age 11 but places are usually filled.

Our view: There's a tangible energy coursing through this little prep. Despite sitting cosily in its corner of the Cotswolds, it is anything but parochial – armed forces families and international boarders provide a platform from which to leap into different cultures. It's small enough that 'everyone knows each other', yet – as one teacher explained – 'big enough to field teams in each year group and have a wonderful cross-section of pupils.' Add to that the security that a child can join at nursery and move seamlessly to the senior school and families feel they have found, as one parent put it, 'the best around'.

School renowned for pastoral care but headmistress noted, 'being a humble school, we don't shout loudly enough about our academics'. As such, recent restructuring of prep's senior management has installed a deputy head academic to fine tune the Wycliffe prep baccalaureate, align the curriculum with their ongoing commitment to pioneering spirit and global citizenship and tie in to Wycliffe College's Round Square nomination – which, headmistress underlines, 'encompasses everything we are and seek to develop further'. Having chosen the prep over local grammars and 'hothouse' independents, one parent commented, 'Wycliffe won hands down' with their balanced, 'non-pressured' approach to academic, pastoral and co-curricular life.

The gates of Wycliffe Prep open to the traditional Ryeford building with its striking stone entrance, an eye-catching theatre and the sleek modernity of Etheridge Hall. Tucked out of sight, a number of classroom blocks in a confusion of architectural styles sit around a quad with central lawn. Overall the school offers a sizeable footprint for its 210 pupils. Ryeford houses a myriad cheery, bright and colourful classrooms spilling off a grand Victorian staircase. Two well-stocked libraries welcome emerging bookworms to read, study or just take some quiet time. Etheridge Hall, a spacious, crisp classroom block for year 7 and 8 pupils includes large common room and kitchenette for its older cohort. Science master advocates making lessons 'fun, hands on and as practical as possible', there are two fully resourced labs and IT suites easily provide a computer per child.

Learning support widely acclaimed especially for its dyslexia programme (including CReSTeD and recent ISI inspection). 'They really go above and beyond,' a parent reflected. 'We want to get it right. We're really honest with parents about how we can help their child,' head of learning support told us. Around 30 per cent of children have some level of additional support; EAL also available. School has experience with physical disabilities. TAs offer individual support where needed – NAGC recognises its provision for gifted and talented pupils. All teachers and boarding staff have pupil profiles to assist both in and outside the classroom. Coordination with senior school and visits to ease transition.

We met a group of pupils enthusiastically spray-painting a huge canvas outside the art studio, while inside walls are a cacophony of colour and tremendous talent. Professional artist instructs. DT stacked with sewing, woodwork and engineering projects. The theatre, a parent enthused, 'is a real wow!' – outstanding for a prep. Staggering four plays in production at time of our visit. 'My son was reluctant to join in but the drama department really brought him out of his shell,' said one parent. Pupils fully involved, from acting and makeup to lighting and stage sets. Music department well equipped, rooms overflowing with instruments. Individual tuition booths. Active choir (mainly girls) and orchestra.

Although there are pockets of green space and (rather lacklustre) sensory garden for quiet reflection, there is nowhere to really let rip and run off steam in break times. Pupils claim they can go over the foot bridge to the Astro or a playing field beyond if accompanied by teacher for more wholehearted exertion.

The bright, well-equipped interior of the nursery sits in contrast to its exterior space which, though plentiful, could benefit from a little imagination and sprucing up. Over the footbridge there are plans for outdoor teaching areas, forest school, DT and a cookery block. We look forward to seeing finished results.

Sports structure recently reviewed to encompass college as a whole. Assistant director of sport oversees prep to 'foster development throughout a pupil's time at Wycliffe, setting them up for life'. Though standard 'isn't top of table', parents say it is 'improving' and 'everyone is given a chance'. Girls play hockey, netball, cricket. For boys, 'football stronger than rugby', and cricket. Both compete against 'sporty'' schools such as Cheltenham College, Clifton College, King's Gloucester. Year groups field 'strong' A team, with development squad encouraging 'challenge for places'. Prep shares pitches with senior school, creating sense of 'being part of something bigger'. Prospective team captains apply in writing – we questioned whether more timid children might shy away, but pupils seemingly enjoy the process and assured us, 'Teachers have a word if they think you should put your name forward.' Swimming pool is another wonderful asset but some parents disappointed by 'tired changing rooms' and 'slightly shabby sports hall'. School confirms these facilities scheduled for upgrade due to be completed within two years. A smart new Astro sits across the road next to four serviceable tennis courts. We cannot elucidate as they did not feature on our tour, but children mentioned playing fields and cricket nets situated near boarding houses.

'Every evening there's the opportunity to get out of the classroom and play sport,' celebrated a parent, with a myriad extracurricular options reserved for Thursday 'activities'. When we asked how the less sporty respond to this, we were offered open-faced assurance by pupils that, 'We are all sporty at Wycliffe!' Headmistress qualifies that those who find sport challenging work in smaller groups to learn skills so all access 'the mental and health benefits'. Thursday activities include a sweep of sports: squash, rowing, fencing, cross-country, sevens, yoga, capoeira, tennis, trounders (cross between tennis and rounders), plus girls' rugby and boys' hockey. Non-sporting options include forest school, crown court, green power, sewing, languages… the list goes on. Prep can be done during after-school club with help from staff. Parents told us they delight in this complementary option, allowing children to get home, 'kick their shoes off and relax'.

Usual prefects and captains, with addition of 'subject leaders' – able children, recognised for ability, encouraged to assist others in class. Head boy and girl rotated per term, giving more opportunity for leadership experience. Pupils compete resolutely for their houses, mainly in sport and academia, but misconducts result in removal of credits – so all are forewarned. Year 8s undertake the 'Kirby' challenge – a significant personal assignment, documented and presented to peers and staff. Residential outward-bound trip planned for year 8, visit to York for younger pupils and many local excursions in glorious Gloucestershire countryside.

The boys and girls have unsophisticated yet utterly charming accommodation: rooms adorned with pictures, posters and home comforts

Concerned that children may have fallen behind during lockdown, headmistress was relieved to discover, 'not as much as I thought'. Chorus of parents attribute this to 'excellent remote online provision'. Her main concern on return was pupils' wellbeing and making sure teachers' expectations were adjusted for a 'reset' back to school life. Cross-section of strategies put in place helping children understand, 'You're in control. You can manage yourself. Find what works for you' – supported by staff, who always 'notice the small things'. Pupils praised lockdown teaching as 'really imaginative'. One delighted in being encouraged to 'raid the kitchen, taking utensils and piling them into a jug of water to illustrate displacement'. Another member of staff initiated a 'beat the teacher' challenge with various tasks undertaken live on Zoom, to the delight of all.

Communication with parents has increased since pandemic. Headmistress records weekly vlog to complement email newsletters. She contacted pupils directly during remote learning, for which parents are 'hugely grateful'.

Head of pastoral care has accessible, welcoming office or else there's a letterbox for those who would prefer to write down worries rather than approach face-to-face. Children told us there's no bullying: 'You can't because Wycliffe's a nice school,' chirped one. Zero tolerance and a real sense that older pupils understand responsibility to take care of younger ones make it 'a bit like a family,' another attested. Parents confirm that the 'merest sniff' of trouble is dealt with.

Food 'had gone a bit pear-shaped but has got better with the new chef,' gushed one grateful pupil. 'Great', 'delicious' oft repeated. Consensus that 'roast potatoes are perfect'. Pupils invited to proffer suggestions to adapt menus.

Parents are a real mix, with armed forces, international, London-based and local. Head reports emerging trend for families to move out of London and settle nearby. Parents' association 'not desperately sociable', but WhatsApp groups keep connectivity. Local families invite boarders to stay during exeat weekends. Day parent reports that children blend well – 'My son has lots of international boarders as friends.' Pupils are 'lively, happy, supportive of each other', 'down-to-earth' and with 'no sense of entitlement, which is exactly what we want,' say parents.

Boarding: Crossing the footbridge and the end of the day is like 'going home', say boarders. 'Completed homework and any of the day's issues left behind' provides 'good sense of separation from home and school' say parents. The interconnected boarding houses – Penwood accommodating 27 boys and Windrush home to 20 girls – burst with colour, activity, and a lively bunch of charming and grounded children, proud of their 'home from home' where it's like 'having a sleepover every night'.

A merry band of boarders of all ages, accompanied by housemaster, toddler with football and baby on hip, greeted us for our accommodation tour. Huge property, with central, communal area nicknamed 'the middle' comprising common room, kitchen, chill-out area, music room – 'for singing!' – and a computer room. Either side, the boys and girls have unsophisticated yet utterly charming accommodation: rooms adorned with pictures, posters and home comforts. Every corridor boasts multiple blackboards, noticeboards or pin boards for scribbling messages, displaying photos of smiling faces or announcing the raft of evening or weekend activities. We liked the 'fake away' night – kitchen staff rustle up burgers or pizzas, inserting them in takeaway boxes to deliver to houses. A 'Forces board' (the majority of boarders are Forces children), including map showing where parents are posted, is a thoughtful touch. Boys' side has a very cool 'cave', previously a storage area and now a camouflaged movie screening room complete with bean bags and 'often, our duvets'. We were charmed by a number of height charts scribed on the walls, 'only by our housemistress,' explained one girl resolutely with a tap on our reviewer's arm. Amusingly, boarding house tuck shop was, until recently, run by pupils, but due to portion control issues housemaster has taken charge.

Superheroes for boys, 'inspirational women' for girls denote dorms with 'very comfy beds' for up to six, fewer for older pupils. Mixed ages means it 'feels like a family'. Hotch-potch of functional shower and wash rooms – each pupil has own basin surrounded by accoutrements. Spacious kitchens for cereal and toast snacks alongside more common rooms with sofas, toys, games. Phones limited to half an hour in evening, encouraging socialising and downtime. Flexi boarding welcome, many of the pupils we spoke to are keen to give it a go – we don't blame them.

The last word: Refreshingly relaxed yet bursting with activity and energy, Wycliffe offers a 'wholly child-centered, holistic education', balancing academic, pastoral and extracurricular with aplomb. A place where children can revel in their childhood and at the same time are given a foundation on which to build, question, challenge and endeavour. Some parts of the school may look a little scruffy, but what goes on inside is anything but. A small prep with big ideas.

Home Counties West

Berkshire
Buckinghamshire
Hampshire
Isle of Wight
Oxfordshire

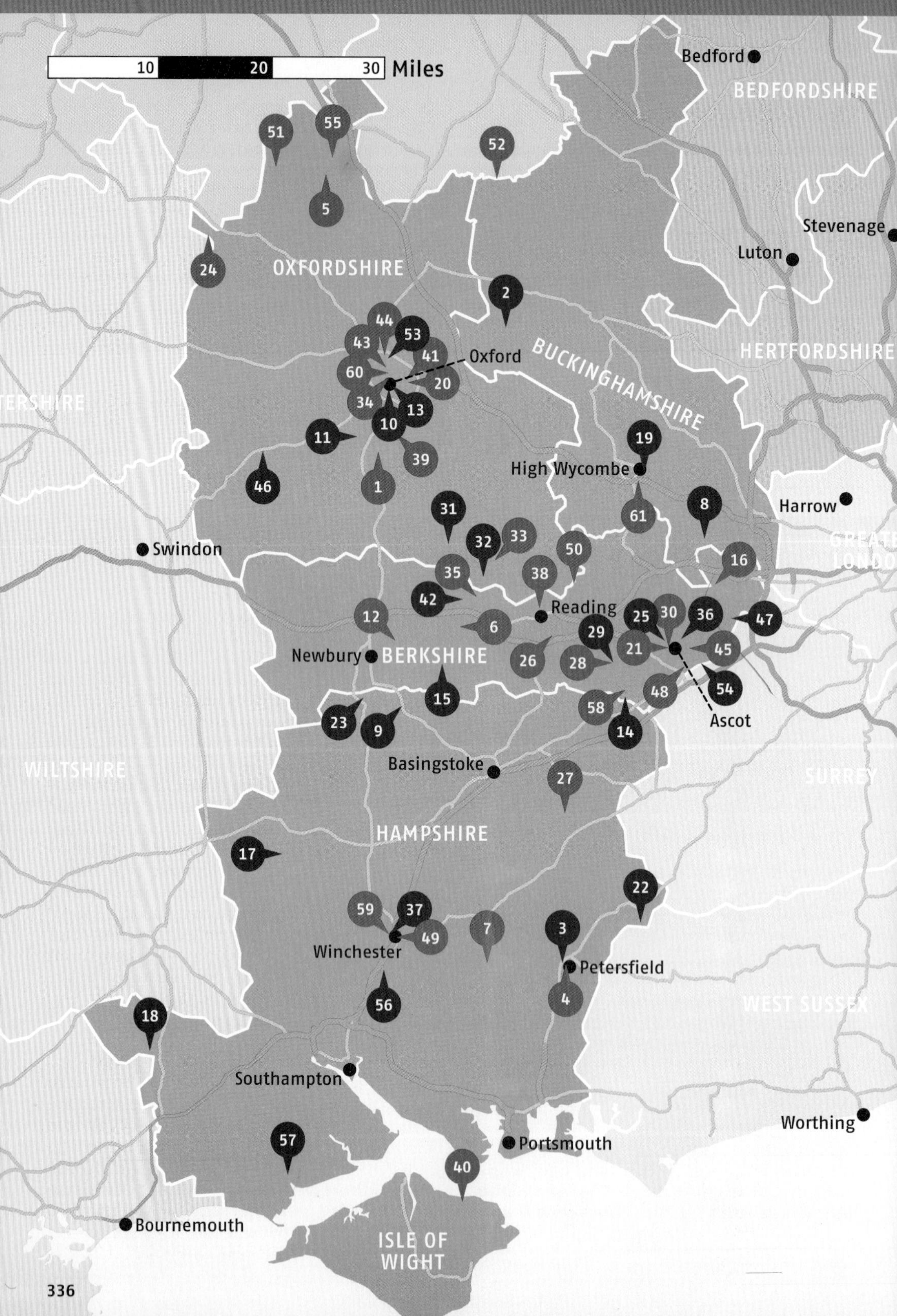

10
20
30
Miles
Bedford
BEDFORDSHIRE
Stevenage
Luton
OXFORDSHIRE
Oxford
BUCKINGHAMSHIRE
HERTFORDSHIRE
High Wycombe
Harrow
GREATER LONDON
Swindon
Reading
Newbury
BERKSHIRE
Ascot
WILTSHIRE
Basingstoke
SURREY
HAMPSHIRE
Winchester
Petersfield
WEST SUSSEX
Southampton
Worthing
Portsmouth
Bournemouth
ISLE OF WIGHT

HOME COUNTIES WEST

1 Abingdon School 338
2 Ashfold School 342
3 Bedales Pre-prep, Dunannie and Bedales Prep, Dunhurst 344
4 Bedales School 346
5 Bloxham School 349
6 Bradfield College 353
7 Brockwood Park School 358
8 Caldicott 362
9 Cheam School 365
10 Christ Church Cathedral School 367
11 Cothill House 370
12 Downe House School 372
13 Dragon School 377
14 Eagle House School 380
15 Elstree School 382
16 Eton College 385
17 Farleigh School 392
18 Forres Sandle Manor School 394
19 Godstowe Preparatory School 396
20 Headington School 400
21 Heathfield School 404
22 Highfield & Brookham Schools 408
23 Horris Hill School 411
24 Kingham Hill School 413
25 Lambrook School 417
26 Leighton Park School 420
27 Lord Wandsworth College 424
28 Luckley House School 428
29 Ludgrove 432
30 LVS Ascot (Licensed Victuallers' School) 434
31 Moulsford Preparatory School 439
32 The Oratory Prep School 442
33 The Oratory School 444
34 d'Overbroeck's 449
35 Pangbourne College 453
36 Papplewick School 458
37 The Pilgrims' School 461
38 Queen Anne's School 463
39 Radley College 466
40 Ryde School with Upper Chine 471
41 Rye St Antony School 477
42 St Andrew's School 481
43 St Clare's, Oxford 483
44 St Edward's Oxford 487
45 St George's School (Ascot) 490
46 St Hugh's School, Oxfordshire 493
47 St John's Beaumont School 497
48 St Mary's School Ascot 500
49 St Swithun's School 503
50 Shiplake College 507
51 Sibford School 511
52 Stowe School 514
53 Summer Fields 519
54 Sunningdale School 521
55 Tudor Hall School 524
56 Twyford School 527
57 Walhampton School 530
58 Wellington College 532
59 Winchester College 539
60 Wychwood School 544
61 Wycombe Abbey 548

Abingdon School

Park Road, Abingdon, Oxfordshire OX14 1DE

01235 849041 | admissions@abingdon.org.uk | www.abingdon.org.uk

Ages: 11–18

Pupils: 1,063; sixth form: 356; Boarders: 111 full, 27 weekly

Fees: Day £21,600; Boarding £35,970 – £44,070 pa

Head: Since 2016, Michael Windsor, previously head of Reading Blue Coat School. The son of two linguists (his father was a lecturer at the University of Bristol and his mother taught French and German at Badminton School), he was a chorister at Bristol Cathedral School. Thence to Durham University and first-class honours in French and German. Worked briefly in publishing before heading to Bologna where he 'toyed with the idea of becoming a professional musician' and making a living from his double bass. That lasted until he got hungry, at which point although he 'knew he definitely didn't want to be a teacher', he gave up jazz for teaching English as a foreign language – and met his future wife. On his return he did a PGCE at the Institute of Education and then joined King's College Wimbledon to teach foreign languages and become the first director of its IB programme. He describes his work introducing the IB as 'an amazing project' but has no such plans for Abingdon (we checked). Moved to RGS Guildford where he was deputy head (pastoral) and after five years there took up the headship at Reading Blue Coat. Has coached rugby, hockey and athletics and was involved in CCF and World Challenge expeditions. That's three academic boys' schools (okay, two have co-ed sixth forms) and Abingdon makes it four. Must be habit forming.

Mr Windsor also has an MA in modern German studies from Birkbeck and is an ISI inspector. He's a keen musician, plays the double bass in classical and jazz ensembles and recently surprised (and delighted) boys and parents with a guest appearance playing bass guitar in the school's Big Band (jazz). Married to Shanti, who works at Reading University; they have two daughters.

He says he 'felt drawn' to Abingdon, especially the culture of 'exceptionally high expectations' that pervades all aspects of school life. He's also enjoying working with the prep school. Even without the prep, Abingdon is much larger than his former school and he concedes his new role is 'less hands on' and he doesn't have time to do any teaching, although he says he would like to.

Abingdon has been through a period of significant growth – both in terms of pupil numbers and building projects – and Mr W feels that the school is now 'as big as it will get'. He does have plans; he's keen to 'develop more areas of collaboration' (academic, pastoral and extracurricular) with St Helen and St Katharine, the neighbouring independent girls' school (where his daughters are pupils). We wish him good fortune. There have been attempts in the past to take things beyond sharing actors, musicians and school buses, but as one boy put it, 'timetables never seem to match up.'

Academic, musical and sporty – Mr Windsor is such a good fit for Abingdon, embodying three of the school's great strengths. He's also down-to-earth, good humoured and at ease with himself – very much a head, rather than a figurehead. The boys think he's 'great' and love the way he seems to turn up and enjoy everything – quite an accolade considering just how much goes on at the school. We felt a genuine groundswell of goodwill and support for Mr Windsor – boys, staff and parents, even those parents we spoke to who have yet only 'seen him in the distance' are right behind him.

Entrance: At 11 candidates from local primary schools and some preps, such as Chandlings, are tested in English, maths and reasoning. On the basis of performance in the test boys are then selected for a 'friendly' interview. Year 7 pre-tests for 13+ entry. For entry to sixth form a minimum of 6 in all I/GCSEs, and 7 in the subjects to be studied at A level (8 for further maths) required.

Exit: Around 10 per cent leave after GCSEs. Nearly all sixth formers head for mainly Russell Group universities to study serious subjects. Bath, Bristol, Exeter, Durham, Nottingham, Manchester and Leeds all popular. Lots of engineers, chemists, economists and theoretical physicists as one would expect, but also historians, classicists and philosophers – it's that kind of school. Three medics in 2021, plus 17 to Oxbridge and two to study overseas – Waseda University, Japan, and Yale, USA.

Latest results: In 2021, 91 per cent 9-7 at I/GCSE; 80 per cent A*/A at A level (94 per cent A*-B). In 2019 (the last year of exams), 88 per cent 9-7 at I/GCSE; 69 per cent A*/A at A level (90 per cent A*-B).

Teaching and learning: Academics matter hugely, but not exclusively. I/GCSE headliners are English, maths and sciences, but A*/9-8 by far the most common mark in all subjects apart from art, RS and drama (where the A/7s have it). In addition to IGCSE maths, boys in the top sets also sit the free-standing OCR additional maths qualification – and take it in their stride with the vast majority gaining top marks. French, Spanish and German are the core language options with Russian and Chinese offered as additional subjects. Healthy numbers and outstanding results for Latin, ancient Greek and ancient history (Latin is compulsory in years 7 and 8). Only a very few marks at grade C/4 or below, but the boy who gets a grade 6 in one or two subjects won't feel alone. Not a school that kicks unexpected underperformers out post-GCSE either

Academic, musical and sporty – Mr Windsor is such a good fit for Abingdon, embodying three of the school's great strengths: very much a head, rather than a figurehead

Most popular A level by far is maths (followed by chemistry and physics); over half of sixth form boys take maths and the vast majority get A*/A, further maths is an option. Parents generally very pleased with A level maths teaching, but one or two felt that boys in lower sets didn't always get sufficient support. Word on the local tutor grapevine confirms that some feel the need to buy in external help.

Large take-up and excellent results too for history, economics and geography. Pre-U exams only for French, German and Spanish (results outstanding), but as elsewhere, modern foreign languages are a minority interest – there are more takers for Latin. Indeed, classics department is thriving (described to us as 'inspirational'), sending annual small, but perfectly formed contingent of brightest and best to Oxbridge. High praise also received for history teaching. Psychology has been a fairly recent introduction to previously 'ology' allergic A level menu. Jury is still out – as yet the subject's popularity and exam record are on a par.

Lessons are fast paced and challenging – setting for maths and science from year 9, but selective intake means all are working above and beyond. Good staff mix of male and female, old timers and recent graduates; sensible creative latitude given to non-standard teaching styles – much appreciated by boys, parents and (we assume) the teachers in question. Great engagement and rapport between boys and teachers in lessons we saw – lots of fun and sparky ideas in year 9 English where boys were coming up with literary foods: apple pie for Paradise Lost, pina colada for Robinson Crusoe and our favourite, a 'saucy stir-fry' for Chaucer's Canterbury Tales.

Learning support and SEN: Abingdon is an academically selective school, but it's a broad enough church to accommodate bright boys with mild to moderate SEND (mostly dyslexia and dyspraxia). In-class, small group and one-to-one help provided by well-regarded learning support department. Pupils who are identified as needing short-term help with, for instance, study skills, receive six one-to-one sessions free of charge. Parents tell us that the department is 'on the ball' and that staff are extra vigilant at high pressure times such as school and public exams.

The arts and extracurricular: Music, art and DT don't attract huge numbers at A level, but are well resourced and get good results. Dynamic music department will seek out and nurture every kind of musical talent – from pipers, choristers and countertenors to, famously, all five members of Radiohead. Every boy is encouraged to take up an instrument when they join the school if they don't already play one. Unsuspecting parents may find their son coming home drooping under the weight of a French horn or bassoon in an ever-optimistic effort by the school's director of music to uncover a virtuoso in these vital, but less popular, orchestral instruments. A plethora of choirs, bands, orchestras and chamber groups, plus an ambitious programme of concerts for all abilities, equals quite a few nights out for supportive parents. Regular organ and choral scholarships to Oxbridge and music colleges.

Annual drama productions for lower, middle and senior school boys plus house drama and joint ventures – and theatre studies A level – with girls from St Helen and St Katharine. Theatre design workshops, modern foreign language plays and a podcasting club add to the repertoire. Newly refurbished Amey Theatre is the main venue for concerts, plays and other whole school events. The addition of a projection screen and surround sound has made it a popular local venue for films, live theatre and opera screenings.

All the above and much, much more is included in the school's famous Other Half programme. You won't hear music, art, DofE, CCF, community service or the 120+ clubs and societies referred to as 'extracurricular activities' here. At Abingdon such things are not optional extras, but essential parts of a well-rounded education. Close harmony singing? Lego architecture? Ceramics? Entomology? Code-breaking? Take a look at the school's (excellent) website and you'll wish you could sign up for one or two options. Worthy of note are debating – the debating society is believed to be the school's oldest non-sporting society and the dinner debates with local girls' schools are a big draw – and Abingdon Film Unit (AFU). The AFU is quite possibly unique, a semi-autonomous organisation run by professional film makers to enable secondary school pupils to make short films – mostly documentaries and stop-motion animations. Since it was set up in 2003 over 120 films have been produced, a number of which have been screened at national and international festivals and won awards.

Sport: Abingdon's sporting alphabet runs from athletics to water polo, taking in a wide range of team and individual pursuits along the way. The letter 'r' gets more than its fair share of kudos, with rugby and rowing being two of the school's chief glories, along with hockey. Full-on fixture list for these and other sports – regular opponents include Marlborough, Radley, Bradfield, Wellington and Eton. Fine sports centre with swimming pool, several grass pitches and popular climbing wall on site; more extensive facilities including athletics tracks and a 4G pitch just down the road at Tilsley Park. Much success too in less mainstream sports such as fencing, cross-country, sailing and shooting.

Abingdon's pupils have been rowing on the town's stretch of the Thames for nearly 200 years and boys in their pink and black kit jogging down to the beautiful wooden boathouse are a familiar sight on summer afternoons. Rowing laurels have suffered a few soggy seasons lately, but boys told us excitedly that the coach was 'making huge changes'.

All boys, including sixth formers, must do at least two sessions of sport a week, but most do many more, including Saturday training and matches. Lots of tours and specialist development camps (some abroad). Boys who duck when they see a ball coming (yes, such boys do exist) are expected to have a go at different options and find something they enjoy – karate and canoe polo have proved popular recent additions to the sports mix.

Boarding: Majority of international boarders are from Hong Kong and China. Small weekly contingent from local families. The three boarding houses (School House, Crescent and Austin) are home to roughly equal numbers of boarders and day boys – ensures good integration. Communal areas we saw were well cared for and rather clubby (pool table, stag's head on the wall); bedrooms are, well, just like those in all the other boys' boarding houses we've visited: two or three beds, floor garnished with huge trainers, lots of Lynx and stashes of snacks. Not overly tidy – always a plus point. Each house has a resident housemaster and his family, at least one resident tutor, and a matron. Other house tutors live nearby. School has its own health centre with a nurse on call overnight and an on-site counselling service. Four meals a day, plus a school café; sixth formers can cook their own lunch in the house kitchen or forage in Abingdon's shops and takeaways.

Boys in their pink and black kit jogging down to the beautiful wooden boathouse are a familiar sight on summer afternoons

Excellent range of joint and individual house activities and trips, making full use of Abingdon's proximity to Oxford and London. Socials and sixth form dinners with girls' boarding schools such as Westonbirt, St Mary's Calne and Headington. Boarding 'enrichment programme' aims to equip boys with vital life skills such as cooking, cleaning and ironing plus information about English law, taxes and applying for student loans. Attendance at boarders' chapel services is compulsory and we heard one or two polite grumbles about this ('a bit boring'). School says it has listened to boys' comments about this and services are now less frequent.

Ethos and heritage: One of England's oldest schools, Abingdon was 'officially' founded in 1256 when the Abbot of Abingdon, John de Blosneville, left money for the support of 13 poor scholars. Earliest references date back to 1100 when a school was likely to have been established alongside Abingdon Abbey. Having survived the dissolution of the monasteries its fortunes waxed and waned over the ensuing centuries, according to the generosity of benefactors and the quality of headmasters. School moved to its present site, adjacent to an elegant crescent around a park, in 1870 and proceeded to buy up more land and some of the crescent's houses. Architecture is sturdy Victorian red brick and running up and down stone staircases between lessons keeps boys and staff pretty fit, but could present a challenge to those on crutches (most of the school except Big

School, the oldest part, is wheelchair accessible). Original library in Big School is a bibliophile's delight and the 21st century additions such as the arts centre, sports centre and the new Yang Science Centre have been thoughtfully designed and well executed. Brand new Beech Court houses sixth form centre plus a library, UCAS resources and careers office.

The Yang Science Centre is a superb addition to the school – three floors of labs and work rooms with an extraordinary metal tree-like sculpture, the Fusion Tower, that fills the stairwell, ascending and morphing into a representation of the science pursued on each level. Apparently, the only drawback of this is that 'physicists have nowhere to drop things from.' (Surely they've got gravity sorted out by now?) At the sculpture's base are 1,256 discs, one for every boy in the Abingdon foundation at the time of the piece's creation.

On the ground floor is a large, dedicated 'outreach' laboratory where pupils of all ages from local schools and organisations such as Scouts and Guides can come for science clubs, projects and subject extension activities. The work tables and seats are designed so that they can be adjusted to fit proto-scientists and there are mini-lab coats and goggles too. Abingdon boys also go out into local primary schools to run science clubs as part of their service activities. This exciting and generously resourced venture has really taken off and the Abingdon Science Partnership (ASP) co-ordinator told us that the school is now a centre of expertise for science continuing professional development, running teacher-training workshops for Oxfordshire and neighbouring counties. School has a burgeoning partnership with Fitzharrys, a local maintained secondary, and the classics department has a long-standing tradition of teaching pupils from other local secondaries too.

With three other independent schools in the immediate vicinity and several others very close by, this corner of south Oxfordshire is rather a hotspot for educational privilege. That being said, Abingdon School isn't regarded as snobby and despite impressive facilities seems to retain the faintest, pleasingly meritocratic whiff of an old-style grammar. Uniform is fairly standard (grey trousers, blue blazer) and most components can be bought from M&S; there's also a second-hand uniform shop, run by the parents' association. Ties are another matter, almost 50 possibilities at the last count: house ties, half and full colours, scholars, societies, prizes, and so on. Boys know what they all mean, but parents usually lose track after the first few.

Old Abingdonians include Francis Maude, former MP and cabinet minister, Sir Kim Darroch, British ambassador to the US, Tom Kempinski, playwright, Thomas Dolby, musician and producer, actors Tom Hollander, Toby Jones and David Mitchell, all five members of Radiohead, lots of rowers and rugby players and centuries of churchmen, soldiers, academics, lawyers and all-round good chaps.

Pastoral care, inclusivity and discipline: Parents tell us that the house and tutor system works well to ensure all boys receive individual academic and pastoral attention – vitally important in such a big school; staff are 'very observant', a parent told us. Boys who arrive at age 11, many from local primaries, join Lower School, which gives them two years to ease in to things before another influx at age 13 from preps, including Abingdon's own. In common with other schools, much more attention is now paid to pupils' mental as well as physical health. Boys can book directly or through the health centre to see a counsellor (on site, four days a week). PHSCE sessions – in class or during tutor time – cover a multitude of age-appropriate topics including healthy eating and body image, bullying, drugs, alcohol and relationships.

The Yang Science Centre is superb – three floors of labs and work rooms with an extraordinary metal sculpture that fills the stairwell

High expectations, both from the school and parents, and long, busy days, generally ensure good behaviour. Rules are sensible and consistently enforced. There's a lot of 'banter', but boys tell us that most know 'how far they can go'. There's no stereotypical Abingdon boy and school has enough alternative milieux for the unusual or eccentric to find their tribe.

Pupils and parents: School buses (all morning and some evening routes shared with the St Helen's girls) bring pupils in from as far as Reading, Newbury, Fairford and Bicester. Parents are fairly typical Oxfordshire mix of medics, academics, IT professionals and business people – not conspicuously wealthy, probably because they're paying school fees. Active parents' association organises socials and fundraisers, runs a popular second-hand uniform shop and a car share scheme. Boys themselves are the most persuasive advert for their school – prospective parents attending open days are allocated a current pupil as a guide and most are ready to sign on the dotted line by the end of their tour.

Money matters: Range of scholarships which confer more prestige (and ties) than dosh. Means-tested bursaries available for part or all of day fees.

The last word: Bigger, yes, and even better. We were delighted to revisit Abingdon and see how it has skilfully managed significant growth and development without compromise to its traditions, ethos and humanity. An outstanding school for bright all-rounders.

Ashfold School
2
Dorton House, Dorton, Aylesbury, Buckinghamshire HP18 9NG
01844 238237 | registrar@ashfoldschool.co.uk | www.ashfoldschool.co.uk
Ages: 3-13
Pupils: 264; Boarders: 45 part-time (from age 9)
Fees: Day £2,070 – £18,225; Weekly boarding £22,500 pa

Headmaster: Since 2018, Colin MacIntosh (40s), previously deputy head of Beaudesert Park School and before that a 15-year run teaching English in various preps. English degree from St Andrews. Warm, unassuming and quite reserved, he admits he felt 'slightly nervous' about his first headship, not to mention superseding an extrovert predecessor with a 21-year reign. 'Definitely not gregarious or a schmoozer – in fact, I get the impression he finds group settings quite awkward and intimidating – but he's incredibly personable one-to-one and most importantly he is exceptionally child-centred,' summed up one parent. Others raved about how he's injected a whole new level of empathy into school life: 'It's not just the predictable kids that get celebrated;' 'You can see how much he cares about the kids' etc. 'In many ways, I'm an overgrown prep school boy and so I always start with the child's point of view,' he told us (one of his fondest memories was how he was encouraged to speak publicly despite his stammer). Pupils lap it up, with 'kind' the winner word from those we asked to describe him, albeit with the caveat that he 'can be strict when needed'.

Particularly popular (besides his sports coaching, of which he does a fair whack) was his commitment to carrying out 50 Ashfold-centred challenges thought up by pupils during his first year – taking part in the annual pancake race, dressing up on World Book Day etc. Number 50, he told us with a twinge of cringe, was singing Bohemian Rhapsody with the choir on speech day. For the few remaining parents still on the cusp of being won over by him, this (coupled with his reportedly 'amazing' speech day address) was the clincher.

Married to Anna, who teaches science at the school, they have two children – a son at Ashfold and a daughter at boarding school. Their home ('a monstrosity from the outside, but lovely inside') is smack bang in the middle of the site – handy, at least, for his regular dinner parties for selected members of year 8s 'to help increase social skills'. A keen sportsman ('though I watch more than play these days') and something of a theatre buff ('I used to act'), he is also involved with the church.

Entrance: Non-selective, with most joining reception from nursery. Prospective pupils for all year groups are invited to an assessment day. Most join at reception, with spaces harder to come by later on, although there was only a waiting list for one year group when we visited.

Exit: Leavers to a wide variety of schools including Stowe, Bloxham, Harrow, Rugby, St Edward's, Headington and increasingly Marlborough and Abingdon. Plus the odd one to Eton. Around half head off to board. Lots of scholarships and awards. Parents praise the effort that goes into finding the right destination, including for the less academic. Around 10 to 15 leave aged 11, usually for financial reasons, and although not considered ideal this isn't the kind of school to blank such parents at the next sports day – 'we want parents to be open with us'.

Our view: The cross-country drive through rolling hills and farmland and rising fear that the satnav is playing tricks on you is well worth it for the first sight of Ashfold's stunning Jacobean mansion set in 33 acres of fields and woodland.

But don't be fooled by the grandeur (it's really not pretentious) or the magnificent rugby pitches in the foreground. It's not a traditional prep in the sense that it's rugger all the way – just take a peek behind the magnificent building where you'll find three hard tennis courts, a heated outdoor pool, full size Astroturf, netball courts and lovely adventure playground.

Wood panelling, winding and creaking staircases and cobbled stable blocks bring Hogwarts to mind. Meanwhile, the rosy-cheeked, windswept and slightly dishevelled children walking, running and skipping through the grassy play areas give an overall impression of an idyllic country school – worlds apart from the London tarmac many of its commuter families have left behind. 'The children are like free-range chickens – able to explore, climb trees and have real freedom,' said one parent.

Purpose-built pre-prep houses nursery to year 2, who are taught in a light, spacious and colourful setting with its own well-equipped playground and large field, complete with bug hotel. Junior department housed in main wing of house, while most senior lessons take place in the courtyard classrooms. Newest addition is the swish art and design centre for DT, cookery, art, ceramics and textiles.

This last building aside, it's probably not the place for those who expect dazzling showcase features and a preoccupation with neatness. Fortunately, for most parents, that's part of the pull: 'This is an unaffected school where everyone getting stuck in matters more.' The result is an inspiring, functional and nurturing environment which puts children first.

Academically, a solid option but much to parents' delight there is considerably less pressure than there once was, eg less testing, more time for other activities. The two (occasionally three) forms per year group are taught in classes no bigger than 20 (usually 18 max), with specialist teachers introduced from the off, then from year 6 children move around the school for all their subjects. Setting in English from year 2, all other core subjects from year 6. Top two year groups all get their own iPads. Parents say pupils have a 'real rapport' with the teachers, whom they describe as 'enthusiastic' – many have children at the school, which 'all adds to the family feel', according to one parent. Many lessons are outside, including forest school.

All children screened for dyslexia aged 7 or whenever they join the school. Currently around 12 per cent of pupils under the SENCo for mild needs (SpLD, dyslexia or dyspraxia). Pupils receive in-class support, small group work and/or one-to-one lessons with the school's SEN specialist, but you won't see the same children getting the same help for years on end – 'idea is to only give as much as is needed, not to create a culture of dependency,' says school.

Children produce a huge amount of both 2D and 3D artwork using just about every material imaginable (coffee filters when we visited; but never oil paints – 'Have you ever tried getting them off uniforms?'), with head randomly selecting art from across the year groups to display periodically in his office (not always the best – we like that). We were wowed by a display of photography from across all year groups, while pupils we met unanimously agreed their best ever project was pop art in year 4 ('I liked mine so much I put it on my bedroom wall,' said one; 'me too,' piped up another). Lots of cross-curricular – eg one class was learning about WWII bombing of Warsaw in history and painted scenes in art.

Rosy-cheeked and slightly dishevelled children walking, running and skipping through the grassy play areas give an impression of an idyllic country school

Over half of pupils learn a musical instrument, with pre-prep children all taught the violin and ukulele while year 1s learn the recorder; instrument fairs encourage pupils to try out some of the less mainstream instruments. Music masterclasses and workshops with senior schools also popular. There's a junior choir and two senior choirs (one auditioned), with the spring concert (held at a church in Thame) a highlight of the school calendar. Music department collaborates with drama teacher to produce some exciting musical theatre – recently The Lion King. Lots going on in the drama department too, with LAMDA seen as 'transformational' at bringing shyer pupils out of their shells. 'There's never any negative energy in drama and everyone is seen as equal,' lauded one pupil, although all agree there's a need for a better performing space (now in planning stage).

Once children reach prep, there's an extended day, ending at either 5 or 6pm, depending on age (a sticking point for some parents – 'challenging if you have three different pick-up times,' explained one). The idea is for the curriculum to include daily sport for all, which although applauded by most is 'a struggle' for some of the less sporty ones, according to parents. Not, however, a school to shout about its trophy cabinet ('There's not a lot in it, mainly because other schools are so much bigger,' says head) although rugby had an exceptional year prior to our visit and gymnastics, triathlon and clay pigeon shooting often do well. 'Top notch' (say parents) specialist coaches for rugby, hockey, netball and football, but head also calls on teachers who happen to be sporty (himself included) because 'it's no good encouraging the children to be all-rounders, then not modelling the same.' Good sized, if a little tired, sports hall.

School has a Christian ethos (we saw tiny tots chanting the traditional grace, 'for what we are about to receive...' with hands firmly clasped, drooling over their plates of roast beef) but accepts other denominations and pupils told us 'it's fine not to be religious'. Mantra here is 'everything is pastoral' and the devil is in the detail, right down to spelling tests ('we don't administer them in that classic way that makes children fear it all week, then feel wretched afterwards'). Three houses compete in eagerly contested competitions (not just sports) with each term culminating in a house cup. Pre-prep pupils presented with star of the week awards for effort and attainment in weekly assemblies.

Largely rural catchment from surrounding villages, with majority of children from middle-class families, many dual income, who travel up to 30 minutes to school (most live east of the M40). Be prepared to get involved, parents told us – 'This is not a drop and run school.'

Boarding: The part-time (not flexi) boarding is considered 'an opportunity not an ideology'. Seventy per cent of year 5s and over have a go, picking a regular day of the week, sometimes upping that to three or even four as they get older. After supper, activities range from rifle shooting or fishing to robotics and cookery. Dorms, all with up to eight beds, are basic but cosy, but gender stereotyping is alive and well with bright blue for boys and powder pink for girls. Common rooms well kitted out and snug, opening onto the houseparents' accommodation. Cooked breakfasts a huge hit. Parents say 'it's on the expensive side' but praise how 'the kids get to see teachers in a different light'.

Money matters: Small number of scholarships, including the Stowe-Ashfold scholarship which covers up to 100 per cent of fees. Other awards up to 30 per cent, available for pupils 'who show outstanding academic, artistic, sporting, musical or all-round ability' for the last two years at the school.

The last word: A happy, vibrant and unstuffy prep that's ideally suited to outdoorsy types and where children who are middle-of-the-road academically are as likely to shine as the very bright. Extremely nurturing too – 'Like one, big warm hug,' said a parent.

Bedales Pre-prep, Dunannie and Bedales Prep, Dunhurst

Alton Road, Steep, Petersfield, Hampshire GU32 2DR

01730 711733 | admissions@bedales.org.uk | www.bedales.org.uk

Ages: Dunannie 3-8; Dunhurst 8-13

Pupils: 279; Boarders: 16 full, 19 flexi

Fees: Day £10,485 – £19,725; Boarding £26,205 pa

Linked school: Bedales School, 346

Head: At Dunhurst since 2017, Colin Baty BEd NPQH (40s). Education degree from Waikato University in New Zealand. Comes from a family of teachers – grandfather, father and brother all heads and his mother is a retired teacher. Originally worked in business but he taught swimming and cricket in his spare time and was told: 'You should be a teacher.' Taught in New Zealand for four years, then decided to travel the world for two years – known in New Zealand as OE (overseas experience). During his travels he worked at Bryanston for a term, then at Bedales, where a three-week stint turned into six years. He later became deputy head of Moreton Hall Prep and head of Great Walstead Prep. Married to Debbie, who is head of wellbeing at Dunhurst, and they have three children, two at Bedales and one at Dunhurst. In his spare time he enjoys surfing, tennis, walking, swimming, cricket, film and theatre. He still teaches sport and year 4 humanities.

At Dunannie since March 2021 Fiona Read. Educated at Clayesmore School and Kingston University, she also studied a postgraduate degree in psychology from the Open University. First teaching job was at Latchmere Infant School which was followed by a jet-setting career including teaching at British International School Jakarta, Indonesia, head of early years at the International School in Nice, France and junior school vice principal at United World College of South East Asia. Speaks Italian, French, Spanish and Bahasa Indonesian. Enjoys the outdoors and sport and has coached netball, cross-country, badminton, swimming and tennis. Also loves photography, drama and community service.

Entrance: Dunannie and Dunhurst are non-selective. Main entry points are nursery, reception and year 3 at Dunannie and year 4 and year 7 at Dunhurst. For entrance to years 1 to 3, informal assessment of reading, writing and maths. For Dunhurst, English and maths assessments, reasoning papers and interview. Prospective pupils spend time with their peers during assessment days so the school gets to know them.

Exit: Most Dunannie pupils progress to Dunhurst and then to Bedales. Last year Dunhurst pupils scooped five academic scholarships, two music scholarships and an art scholarship at the senior school. Common Entrance isn't taught here (Bedales doesn't require it) but even so pupils have won places at Marlborough, the International Community School and Gordonstoun in recent years without any problem.

Our view: The prep dates back to 1902 and the pre-prep opened in 1953. Both schools are on the Bedales campus but have their own entrance and loads of space to run around in. Dunhurst and Dunannie are all about 'the whole child'. Outdoor work is an integral part of the curriculum, with everyone in the prep doing more than an hour's work outside every week – everything from planting trees and bulbs and growing fruit and vegetables (including pumpkins, runner beans, garlic and raspberries) to beekeeping and looking after the guinea pigs, chickens and ducks. 'It's always work-based,' says the head of outdoor work. 'Children are a lot more willing to try things outside.' As well as connecting with nature Dunannie children become proficient writers, fluent readers and sound mathematicians, with the ability to apply these skills to a range of practical problems and theoretical challenges.

'Practical and very hands-on' science in light, airy science labs, with biology, chemistry and physics taught separately in years 7 and 8. French and Spanish taught in Dunannie and Dunhurst. The school is very keen on reading – years 4 to 6 have 30 minutes dedicated to reading for pleasure every week and everyone takes part in the Drop Everything and Read scheme. Maximum class size of 18 in the prep.

Outdoor work is an integral part of the curriculum – everything from planting trees and growing fruit and vegetables to beekeeping and looking after the guinea pigs

Learning support given one-to-one (pupils aren't taken out of class; they access learning support during free study periods, known as 'greens'). Saturday school for years 7 and 8. A space called The Well is used for drama and assemblies (whole school assembly is known as 'Jaw') and external speakers are invited to talk about subjects like Fairtrade, animal cruelty and world events as part of the school's enrichment programme. Head of drama gives each year group a play, then puts the whole thing together in the space of a week. 'It's very impressive,' say parents. More than 90 per cent of Dunhurst pupils have singing or instrument lessons and there's a host of groups to join – from orchestras, choirs, rock bands and ensembles to jazz band, African drumming and samba. Most of these are taught within the curriculum.

Art and design are exciting and creative. Children design their own T-shirts, make props for plays and paint landscapes of places 'that mean something to them'. We watched a year 5 group having a whale of a time making jugs and teapots. 'It's not so much about making pots but encouraging them to be creative,' a teacher told us. DT is a delight; we saw year 5 bird boxes, year 6 siege engines and year 8 lampshades that looked good enough to feature in the Conran Shop. 'There's no such thing as silly ideas,' the DT teacher tells pupils. Lots of opportunities for sport, with all pupils using the school's Astroturf, swimming pool, floodlit tennis/netball courts, sports hall and vast playing fields. Children have weekly swimming lessons from the age of 4. Average of 16 teams play fixtures against other schools each week, with a good track record of success. Some children play district and county level sport.

Pre-prep and prep children have lunch in a light, airy dining room. Children serve themselves at a food bar at their own level, where they can also read inspirational quotes dreamed up by the catering supervisor. What a great idea.

Pastoral care is excellent across both schools, with children encouraged to talk to class teachers, tutors, boarding staff and counsellors if they have any problems. Strong relationships are developed early at Dunannie, with teachers available to talk to parents daily. At Dunhurst year 8 children volunteer to train as peer listeners (they're called the Raktivators). When we visited during national Anti-bullying Week (called 'harmony week' at Dunhurst) all the pupils were wearing 'you can sit with me' wristbands. Like the senior school, children call teachers by their first names and there's no uniform. 'It's a lot nicer to be able to dress how you want,' a boy told us. Pupils can do community service on Wednesday afternoons; some help local primary school with their IT skills while others visit a school for children with learning difficulties. Head runs school council so pupils can air their views.

Day pupils come from places like Winchester, Portsmouth, Chichester, Petworth and Guildford (the school runs a raft of minibuses). The head stands on the school steps every morning, ready to chat to pupils and parents. He even shadowed a pupil for a day (complete with backpack and hoodie) so he could get a child's perspective of the school. 'I had to do a science test and even got prep,' he says. 'I was exhausted at the end of it and it was a good reminder of the fact that these children are on the go all day.'

Dunannie adjoins the Dunhurst building but has separate grounds, so the smallest children can whizz around on tricycles and potter about outside to their heart's content (the nursery is separate, in a beautifully converted old barn). Children have busy and structured days, learning by doing. Teaching is child focused and there are lots of opportunities for creative learning, including dance and drama. Many of them learn at least one instrument and there's a variety of after-school clubs.

The pre-prep is 'all about the outdoors.' The children spend time learning outside in the grounds and on the substantial Bedales estate. They visit the pigs, measure the size of trees and watch the way the natural landscape changes over the year.

The Dunannie garden is idyllic, with an orchard, pond, willow tunnels, castle, potting shed and even an old boat for children to play in. They grow their own fruit and vegetables, then use them to make carrot cake, pizza and soup. Inside, everything is child centred, with relaxed classrooms, immersive lessons and happy children. 'They allow the children to have a childhood,' a parent told us. 'It's a fantastic environment.'

Boarding: Children can board from year 4 but most boarders are in years 7 and 8. Girls and boys live in different wings of the school, with houseparents, assistant houseparents and matrons on each wing. Flexi and weekly boarding offered and the school runs escorted train services from nearby Petersfield for boarders heading home at weekends. Some arrive back on Monday mornings, which means they can spend the whole weekend with their families.

The last word: Parents are full of praise for the school's approach and ethos, evidenced by the fact that many year groups are virtually full. 'It's very nurturing, a real community,' one told us. 'They treat the children with real respect, not as adults, but as equal human beings.' Like the senior school, they aim to educate 'head, hand and heart' – in other words, provide a broad education and focus on developing children's personal qualities as well as their intellectual prowess.

Bedales School

4

Church Road, Steep, Petersfield, Hampshire GU32 2DG

01730 300100 | admissions@bedales.org.uk | www.bedales.org.uk

Ages: 13–18

Pupils: 472; sixth form: 188; Boarders: 326 full

Fees: Day £29,970; Boarding £38,130 pa

Linked school: Bedales Pre-prep, Dunannie and Bedales Prep, Dunhurst, 344

Headmaster: Since February 2022, Will Goldsmith (previously acting head). MA in English lit from Edinburgh. Joined the school as deputy head (academic) and before that director of teaching and learning and head of English at Latymer Upper, which followed teaching in both state and independent schools. Brought up as the child of expats in Africa, the Middle East and Far East; speaks fluent French, having lived in Paris for five years after graduating.

His partner, Andrew, is an English teacher who has been at Highgate School for over a decade and who divides his time between London and the Bedales estate. Big on diversity, working closely with students in supporting LGBTQ+ rights in school and beyond. Enjoys singing, having spent much of his life in a variety of chamber choirs.

Entrance: School is 'inclusive and non-selective'. Maths, English and general ability tests for 13+ entry 18 months before entry. Around 25 to 35 students join in the sixth form. At this stage they need a minimum average of grade 5 at GCSE/BAC or equivalent. External sixth form candidates also attend an interview day. School's view is that the school has a responsibility to let internal students continue into the sixth form, even if they haven't got the required grades. 'If you let them in at 13 it's morally dishonest to kick them out at 16. If there's a sixth form programme that's right for them they can stay, although we obviously have a minimum threshold for subjects like maths.'

Exit: School loses a few pupils after GCSEs – mainly to sixth form colleges like Peter Symonds College and Bishop Luffa Sixth Form to do courses not offered by Bedales.

A parent told us that Bedales 'is very good at helping young adults and kids work out what they want to do'. At 18, virtually all head to universities, music conservatoires, drama schools and art colleges. A small number to Oxbridge (one in 2021) and many to Russell Group universities. Edinburgh, Bristol, Exeter, University College of London and Oxford Brooks all popular. Plenty overseas – recently to George Washington, University of Washington, Dartmouth College and Columbia University (all USA) and Vrije University Amsterdam. Wide variety of courses.

Latest results: In 2021, 49 per cent 9-7 at GCSE; 65 per cent A*/A at A level (65 per cent A*-B). In 2019 (the last year when exams took place), 60 per cent 9-7 at GCSE; 21 per cent A*/A at A level (61 per cent A*-B).

Teaching and learning: Bedales prides itself on offering 'a progressive, liberal education', with the emphasis on developing inquisitive thinkers with a love of learning who cherish independent thought.

At A level, English literature, art, history and maths are the most popular subjects. In years 10 and 11 pupils study a mix of IGCSEs, GCSEs and Bedales Assessed Courses (BACs). Most take five compulsory core IGCSE/GCSE subjects (maths, English, sciences and modern languages) and four BACs. BAC options include global awareness (very popular), English literature, philosophy, religion and ethics, outdoor work, digital game design, theatre studies and sports science. Designed by Bedales teachers, BACs are recognised by UCAS and well regarded by universities, with assessment by written assignments, presentations, projects and an exam at the end. 'We find they are a better preparation for A level,' says school, adding that Bedales students receive as many university offers as those elsewhere. In another letter to The Times the school urged fellow heads 'who decry the lack of educational authenticity in GCSEs' to 'have the courage of their convictions and provide something else in their place'.

One of the school's founding aims was that it should 'foster individuality and encourage initiative, creativity and the appreciation of the beautiful' in pupils – and it does

Uniquely, there is no 'dead time' after IGCSE/GCSE/BAC exams. Pupils start their A level courses as soon as they've finished their GCSEs. If they change their minds about their choices they can swap in September. New sixth form centre recently completed.

Vertical tutor system. Each pupil has a personal tutor to oversee their academic progress, either one-to-one or in small tutor group meetings. Half-termly review by teachers of each student's effort and attainment. Homework generally fitted into free periods during the day. 'I am very impressed by the academic side,' a parent told us. 'They look at each child individually and the courses are really exciting. I'd like to do them myself.'

Grade I listed Memorial Library, designed by Ernest Gimson to commemorate those who died in the First World War and considered to be one of the finest Arts and Crafts buildings in the country. Year 9s get two reading periods a week and the library, open from 7am till 10pm, is full during exam season. Favourite authors when we visited were Holly Bourne for younger pupils and Jean-Paul Sartre for older ones.

Learning support and SEN: Students with specific learning difficulties get one-to-one support on a weekly basis with a specialist teacher (team of eight). Learning support usually takes place during study periods; students aren't withdrawn from academic lessons.

The arts and extracurricular: Bedales is renowned for its music, art and drama. One of the school's founding aims was that it should 'foster individuality and encourage initiative, creativity and the appreciation of the beautiful' in pupils – and it certainly does. Music is glorious, with a school choir and a plethora of orchestras, ensembles and groups. Elite musicians often have a bespoke timetable where they concentrate on honing their skills and take leading roles in instrumental and vocal ensembles. The annual rock show is a much-anticipated event, usually sold out on three consecutive nights. Drama is genuinely exciting. Students can opt to do the school's BAC theatre course and theatre studies is offered at A level. Lots of opportunities for extracurricular drama, including a whole school show performed on three nights in the 320-seater Olivier Theatre. Art is taught in a stunning art and design building that won a national RIBA award. Around 30 to 40 students take A level art each year, getting the chance to do fine art, graphic design, printing, photography, ceramics, illustration, fashion design and much, much more.

Lots of opportunities for outdoor work, both within the curriculum and beyond. The school has its own farm and pupils plant trees, keep bees and learn about livestock management, blacksmithing, hedge laying, timber framing and wood whittling. We met a group of year 10 outdoor work BAC students preparing sheepskins, ready to send them to a tannery. Another lot were cooking pizzas to sell in the pizza shack at lunchtime. Pupils also make chutney, honey, blankets and Christmas puddings to sell. No CCF but many do DofE and take part in charity initiatives. The school has raised thousands for charities like FitzRoy, which supports people with learning disabilities and autism, and the Rural Refugee Network, which helps Syrian refugees settle in the UK. A Syrian student who attended Bedales is now studying biological sciences at university and another is a current pupil.

Sport: The school says that sport isn't 'industrialised' here but there are plenty of opportunities for keen sports players. 'It's driven by interest. Pupils understand the importance of exercise and they want to be outside but it's about choice rather than compulsion.' Main sports are hockey, tennis, netball and football (school has strong links with Portsmouth Football Club) but activities like Pilates, yoga and boxing are on offer too. Excellent facilities – full-size Astroturf, swimming pool, floodlit tennis/netball courts, sports hall, fitness studio, gym and acres of playing fields, all

Students call teachers by their first names. 'We see teachers more as equals – someone to help us rather than tell us what to do'

used by the local community. Pupils told us it's virtually impossible to try everything because there are so many opportunities at the school.

Boarding: Around two-thirds are boarders, many from London and the south east but others from Suffolk, Norfolk, Devon and Cornwall. Ten per cent from overseas – 18 countries, including China, Italy, Spain and France. Three boarding houses (known as 'flats') – one for girls, one for boys and a co-ed house for year 13s (boys and girls live on different floors). Steephurst, the boarding house for years 9 to 12 girls feels like home from home, with a stylish common room, kitchen, surgery and cosy, mixed-age dorms. Year 13 boarders do their own laundry – good preparation for university. The youngest aren't allowed phones during the day and must hand them in at night. If older pupils use phones too much the devices are confiscated for 24 hours.

Ethos and heritage: Bedales has always been ahead of the curve. Founded in 1893 in Sussex by John Badley as 'a humane alternative to the authoritarian regimes typical of late Victorian public schools', it aims to educate 'head, hand and heart' – in other words, provide a broad education and focus on developing students' personal qualities as well as their intellectual prowess. The school has been co-ed since 1898 (it was the first non-Quaker co-ed boarding school) and moved to its current 120-acre site in a pretty village two miles outside Petersfield in 1900.

The school famously has no uniform and fashion trends are far less of a thing here than at many schools, with most students clad in jeans and trainers. 'They aren't interested in high street fashion,' says a parent. 'There's no designer clothing and no pressure.' The school has started a 'give and take' scheme, where pupils can hand in clothes they don't want and borrow other previously owned items. When we asked if there are any rules on clothes pupils said they have to wear shoes, pyjamas aren't allowed and no excessive skin on show. Students call teachers by their first names, which adds to the informal, friendly ethos. 'We see teachers more as equals – someone to help us rather than tell us what to do,' a sixth former told us. Several said school rules tend to be around health and safety and that zero tolerance rules on drugs, alcohol and smoking are far stricter than at other schools. 'I have never seen or heard of anyone taking drugs and smoking is no more of a problem here than anywhere else,' a sixth former said. Bedales is currently piloting a 9.25am start – research shows that teens learn better when they start later.

Former pupils include a galaxy of well-known names, including David Linley (the Earl of Snowdon), Kirstie Allsopp, Daniel Day Lewis, Gyles Brandreth, Lily Allen, Sophie Dahl, Arabella Weir, Julian Trevelyan and Alys Fowler. Parents tend to be open-minded, with a strong interest in education, many of them entrepreneurs, lawyers and creative types.

Pastoral care, inclusivity and discipline: Bedales recognised the importance of pastoral care more than a century ago; founder John Badley was determined to shape the school around what was considered best for the individual's educational welfare and happiness and his vision still holds true today.

Pupils can talk to their tutors, boarding staff, nurses at the health centre and the school counsellors. 'The pastoral care is wonderful,' a mother told us. 'It's a really inclusive school, a place where you can be what you want to be.' When year 9 pupils join the school their induction incudes a series of Outward Bound activities with tutors and sixth form mentors, enabling everyone to get to know each other as a year group. Year 12 students get their own studies away from the boarding houses while year 13s work in their rooms. Busy student council, run by the four head students (two boys, two girls) and attended by the head, deputy heads and three reps per year.

Pupils and parents: Pupils are 'diverse in terms of personality and nationality,' says school. Two-thirds of year 9s move up from Bedales Prep, Dunhurst; the rest come from a vast range of schools, including Beaudesert Park, Cheam, Newton Prep, Notting Hill Prep, Walhampton, Windlesham and Westbourne House. Day pupils tend to live within a 40-minute drive, arriving from places like Winchester, Chichester, West Wittering, Petworth and Midhurst (the schools runs a variety of minibuses). Parents spoke of the school's 'sense of community' and told us that communication between school and home is good. One told us: 'When Bedales started it was very visionary and radical and my experience is that it's got better and better in recent years. The core ethos is still there and they have tightened up the academics.'

Money matters: School is committed to broadening access by offering financial support (more than five per cent of its fee income is allocated to this). Means-tested bursaries range from part fee contributions to 100 per cent bursaries. Scholarships offered in art, music, drama, sport and academic subjects (scholars can access a research fund to support 'scholarly projects' but there's no reduction in school fees).

The last word: Most children would thrive at this lovely, forward-thinking school. Bedales is the biggest it's ever been and seems to be on a roll right now, with other schools taking a keen interest in its initiatives. For teens this is a wonderful place to develop a strong sense of self, stretch their minds, develop a love of learning and make lifelong friends.

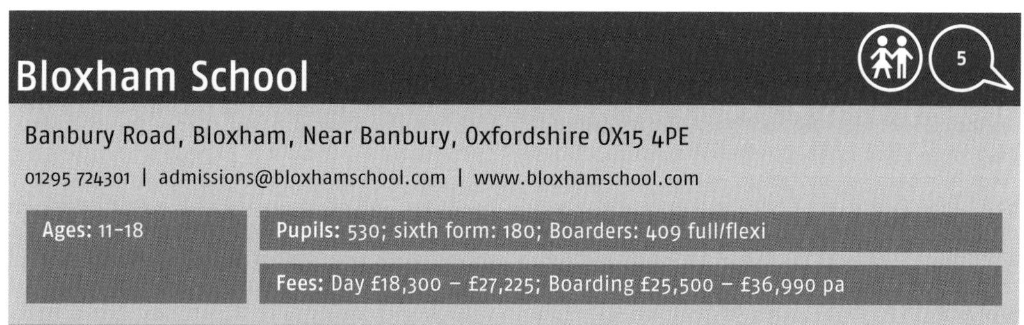

Bloxham School
5
Banbury Road, Bloxham, Near Banbury, Oxfordshire OX15 4PE
01295 724301 | admissions@bloxhamschool.com | www.bloxhamschool.com
Ages: 11–18
Pupils: 530; sixth form: 180; Boarders: 409 full/flexi
Fees: Day £18,300 – £27,225; Boarding £25,500 – £36,990 pa

Headmaster: Since 2013, Paul Sanderson BSc MPhil (40s). A native Ulsterman who graduated in biology from St Andrew's before training as a teacher at Oxford, then did an MPhil at Cambridge. Early posts in the science department at maintained schools including Lancaster Royal Grammar and Carr Hill High before moving to director of curriculum and deputy head at Gordonstoun. Genial and at ease in his comfortable study, he expounds on the wider remit of the school: 'Our job is to educate, body, mind and soul... We're trying to prepare kids for when they are 35, not for 18.' He has improved the exam results, 'not by being selective, but through teaching and learning and making sure resources are available' and has developed links to businesses by encouraging degree-level apprenticeships and direct consultation. 'We asked employers like Deloittes, "Are we producing kids you would want to employ?"' The result is a broadened curriculum and community service at lower sixth.

'A nice man, very approachable to parents, and the kids often say they've had a chat with him,' said a parent. Another told us he's 'very genuine, very determined, readily available if you need him'. Married with three school-age children, he continues to referee rugby matches, lead the school climbing club and teach – we were delighted to find him chasing woodlice round the lab in the upper sixth biology lesson.

Entrance: Three main points of entry but children are accepted for occasional places too. At 11+ children sit the school's own exams in English, maths and verbal reasoning and are interviewed as part of the assessment morning. At 13+ the ISEB common entrance procedure. At 16+ (when around 15-20 join), GCSE results must include six 5s with a 6 in A level subjects to be studied (or 7 if studying maths and sciences). Internationals arrive at 13+, 14+ and 16+.

Exit: Around 10-15 pupils leave after GCSEs. Ninety-five per cent head off to university, with popular choices including Exeter, Bristol, Durham, Loughborough. Others to Sandhurst, professional sports, art foundation and degree level apprenticeships.

Latest results: In 2021, 59 per cent 9-7 at GCSE; 40 per cent A*/A at A level (74 per cent A*-B).

Teaching and learning: In lower school (years 7 and 8), small classes are taught by subject specialist teachers, with sets for maths. A broad grounding in academic subjects – including Latin, either French or Spanish and sciences – is accompanied by a wide choice of creative activities. Numbers expand in the senior school (year 9 up) when children are taught in classes of 20 maximum, with sets in some subjects. The emphasis is on preparation for GCSE, with students taking triple or double science, a choice of French or Spanish and additional maths for some. A level options include computer science, economics, PE, photography, psychology and theatre studies, with some popular vocational courses such as BTec sports science or hospitality and a CTec in business. There's also the chance of an EPQ, mini MBA or psychology programme (mini MAPP).

It's a long day – 8.15am to 6pm – with obligatory Saturdays (optional sports in lower school) but supervised homework sessions and a dizzying number of activities are included in the timetable, and children appear unfazed. However, one parent reckoned, 'It wouldn't be for everybody.'

In the cookery class the chef was rustling up a pasta sauce. 'It's the best lesson. Sometimes he shouts – like Gordon Ramsay, a good shout – and you get to eat it afterwards'

We eavesdropped on an English class celebrating a successful spelling test with a box of chocolates, before moving on to discuss Sir Gawain and the Green Knight. Pupils enthusiastically raised their hands to take part in the informal brainstorming. Another English lesson we saw involved older students in quiet discussion about classical hero, Jason of Iolcos. Elsewhere we visited the cookery class, where the chef was rustling up a pasta sauce. 'It's the best lesson,' said one boy. 'Sometimes he shouts at you – like Gordon Ramsay, a good shout – and you get to eat it afterwards.'

The school adapted quickly and well to the first lockdown of the Covid crisis, issuing individual laptops to all. 'We locked down before the national lockdown,' said a parent – 'the transition was very smooth and they were straight onto Zoom.' Some of the advantages of virtual classroom continued when doors were re-opened, eg joining for lessons with the partner school in Africa. Good teacher to pupil ratio, we heard.

Learning support and SEN: 'The days of having a defined learning support department have gone,' says school. 'Learning support is for everyone. Every member of staff is expected to differentiate. You are meeting every child at where their needs are.' All children have a laptop to work on from day one and provision for dyslexic children includes specific resources, eg reader pens and exam concessions. A parent was fully satisfied with her child's dyslexia support: 'They managed to do it all within the class, which didn't separate her out.' Curriculum adaptations meant the student substituted a foreign language for individualised study skills sessions. The school accommodates mild difficulties in attention, communication and interaction, and has experience of hearing impairment and looked-after children.

The arts and extracurricular: Music is massive, we heard, and not just from the enthusiastic music staff. Music lessons are timetabled to year 9 and all children take an instrument in year 7. As well as playing in one of the two orchestras or many ensembles (the chapel choir has sung at the Vatican) there is a house music competition – 'the biggest school event of the year,' according to one pupil (A-lister musician parents drop in to adjudicate – this year's theme, Glastonbury Headliners). Music GCSE is popular, with double the national average taking A level, and each year some opt for degree level. A band room and several practice rooms accommodate the 200 individual instrument lessons each week.

Drama available at both GCSE and A level. The school has employed an actor in residence to encourage thespians, resulting in several students acting and writing for the National Youth Theatre. LAMDA on offer, and there is a house drama competition although our guides felt this was less inclusive than house music.

Artworks by students are displayed in the dining room, and recent award-winners found their creations in the Royal Academy and top of a national cartoon competition. A bed of red and purple ceramic poppies, inspired by the Tower of London's display, was outside the chapel when we visited, while wacky textile designs were on show in the Raymond Technology Centre's wonderful steel and glass building, where we got a bird's eye view from the gallery, watching the green-aproned students learning to use a soldering iron.

The school puts on a crazy number of extracurricular activities and clubs, some under the banner of the Euanoia (beautiful thinking) Society. Clubs include Future Young Female Leaders club and a politics society where young parliamentarians can find their voice. The more classically inclined can study Homer and the Greats in their lunch hour, while younger scientists get their teeth into making a new toothpaste formula in the bronze CREST award. Trips include DofE, climbing club and CCF, last year visiting the Breacon Beacons and night-time sea kayaking in the Highlands.

Sport: A fabulous sports hall with its own moniker, the Dewey, hosts a huge range of physical activities – all the usual team sports of rugby, hockey, cricket, netball and tennis in the top schools' league, as well as alternatives such as fives, squash, badminton, golf and the rarefied clay shooting, plus riding. A pool allows for swimming, water polo and recreational swims (we heard 6.30am was a popular booking) and there's a mean-looking fitness centre for strength and conditioning, along with a climbing wall. Sport or PE is timetabled three times a week across the school and many choose to play more often as part of the enrichment opportunities. One mum told us, 'My son is very sporty; he's been allowed to follow his passion, doing horse-riding and rugby,' but added, 'My daughter is not a great lover of playing hockey and netball week in, week out… though they do have yoga and dance, now.' Head celebrates individual and team successes alike: 'The bit I'm most proud of is that every child will represent the school in sport over the year. It's equally about your fifth team player as your internationals.'

Boarding: Bloxham's boarding structure is adapted for the 21st century, with permutations to suit every lifestyle. Seven boarding houses, four for boys and three for girls, allow students to choose full or day boarding, the latter including at least two nights' stay per week. 'We find that's a good mix, they get to sit and do their prep at school and get a chance to hang out with mates and do a social in the evening. When they come home, it's home time,' said a parent. That said, we heard a lot of flexis convert to full boarding as they rise up the school.

We spotted a pool table, pingpong and Xbox handsets to pass the time – and there's a yearly competition to keep a plant alive

Every house has a mix of year groups and international students are also distributed across various houses. Variety of dorms and bedrooms: we saw eight beds for year 3 and three-bed rooms with bunks for year 4; sixth formers get a single room with shared bathroom. There are kitchens on every floor for snacks, plus large sitting rooms with TV and sofas – we spotted a pool table, ping pong and Xbox handsets to pass the time and there's a yearly competition to keep a plant alive! Many full boarders depart for home after Saturday sport. The boarding staff say there are always groups available for evening and weekend activities: 'The most important thing is that the boarding houses are busy every night or you could lurch into Travelodge country,' said the deputy head. As for homesickness, 'It's less than you think because of the flexi-boarding,' we heard.

High praise for the matrons. 'They are wonderful, they are like surrogate mums to the kids,' said a parent. Another reckoned the school's greatest strength is 'the quality of the houseparents' who 'foster a real sense of the house spirit'.

Ethos and heritage: Just outside Banbury lies the substantial village of Bloxham, which boasts houses in honey-coloured stone and a Gothic Revival church with the highest steeple of Oxfordshire. GE Street designed both church and Bloxham school, which has an ecclesiastical flavour to its old stone schoolhouse and chapel. However, since its founding in 1860 by PR Egerton, who established the boys' school in the Anglo-Catholic tradition, it has gradually increased and expanded into the extensive grounds and village beyond, though is by no means big. 'It's a small school, they see the individual,' said a parent. 'We can compete at the top level in sport and drama but its not too big that we don't know you,' agrees the head.

Convivial dining rooms, where we indulged in freshly cooked fish and chips with minted mushy peas. 'Have as much as you can of anything,' a boy recommended

Our tour started at the neo-Gothic chapel with stained glass and well-polished pews, where pupils have weekly services from the chaplain, and many opt for confirmation in year 9. Sympathetic additions have been added to the original building to provide kitchens and convivial dining rooms beneath, where we indulged in freshly cooked fish and chips with minted mushy peas ('Have as much as you can of anything,' a boy recommended). Dodging the raindrops, we ran a short way to the Great Hall, equipped with a proscenium theatre for the annual school production and twice-weekly assemblies. Humanities and languages classrooms upstairs were arranged with seats and tables according to teacher preference, some in rows, some as horseshoes. Egerton's original mullioned library has been superseded by a modern, glassy structure, where we found well-stocked shelves, racks of journals, and imaginative reading lists for each year group. The corridors of the nearby science block had been joyfully updated with chemistry symbol wallpaper and motivating quotes: 'Science and everyday life should not be separated' (Rosalind Franklin). The classrooms either side revealed students working in small groups at lab benches and on screens. Outside manicured lawns and an arboretum in the inner court lead off to several grass pitches, an Astro and an informal garden with picnic benches. We visited the day pupils' house, Exham, and strolled through the quiet village to find the sports hall and distant cricket pitch. The sixth form are free to use the local shops and to carry out community service at the primary school and care home, as well as further afield.

We met the children on Compassion Day, which involved a catwalk of youthful mufti (mostly jeans and PJs) but usual uniform is smart black blazer, white shirt or blouse and dark skirt or trousers, with a house tie for boys, business suits for sixth formers.

Pastoral care, inclusivity and discipline: The size and structure of the school, as well as the tried and tested house system, lends itself to pastoral care. Small tutor groups meet daily, house captains meet regularly with the houseparents and a school council sees the headmaster for more formal complaints. Tutor group meetings cover a programme of issues, such as drugs, eating disorders and bullying. 'Drugs, there's no problem,' said one housemaster. 'Teenagers now drink less than they ever have done and we have a very clear behaviour policy.' Bold claims too (unusually) that inter-years bullying doesn't happen. 'With boys, it's more constant point scoring – we deal with it quickly.' A parent concurred: 'The message goes out, if you misbehave, you are not welcome here.' As to the Everyone's Invited social media revelations that have hit so many schools, 'We've not had reason to believe they are weak on that sort of thing,' one parent said, 'though it's very hard for schools to police parties that go on outside school.' Anglican values of tolerance, kindness, service and respect are valued: 'Having a mindset as a giver not a taker,' sums up the head.

Ninety per cent of activities on offer are taken by permanent staff, with a few visiting specialists, eg Mandarin teachers. Means staff know the pupils really well and get to know different aspects of the school. We heard that the physics teacher played organ in chapel, an assistant housemaster worked in the marketing department and senior management regularly did lunch duties. The chaplain, school nurses and a counsellor are on hand all week to support pastorally.

Pupils and parents: 'Every school has its characters but on the touchline at weekends, you realise you are talking to people like you,' said a parent. Apparently this means not the super-rich but everyday working parents. Day boarders come from as far as Oxford, Stratford and Buckingham in a fleet of minibuses, boarders from further afield, including London – and currently around 25 from overseas. The students we met were unspoilt and enthusiastic about school, as well as open-minded about their ambitions in life. 'How mature and grounded and decent the guys are!' exclaimed one parent.

Parents are happy with communications, favouring email as the best method to reach houseparents or matrons. 'It was dealt with appropriately,' said a parent about a complaint she made. 'I was heard and it was resolved.' There are formal parents' evenings to cover a child's progress and more informal meetings with houseparents in the local pub to get to know one another. Many parents attended the school themselves, and we were delighted to meet a fourth-generation Old Bloxhamist, now working at the school.

Money matters: A tiered system, depending on age and boarding type, with a few activities extra. Scholarships and means-tested bursaries up to 100 per cent of fees.

The last word: Once seen as a school for local farming families, Bloxham has been discovered by parents looking for an all-round experience, an antidote to the hothouse Oxford independents and one that produces challenging and free-thinking team players. Bloxham provides the best of both worlds – a small community school with a broad curriculum. Extensive grounds and a competitive spirit make it ideal for outdoorsy children and the versatile boarding system meets the modern family's lifestyle. Unsurprisingly, families keep coming back.

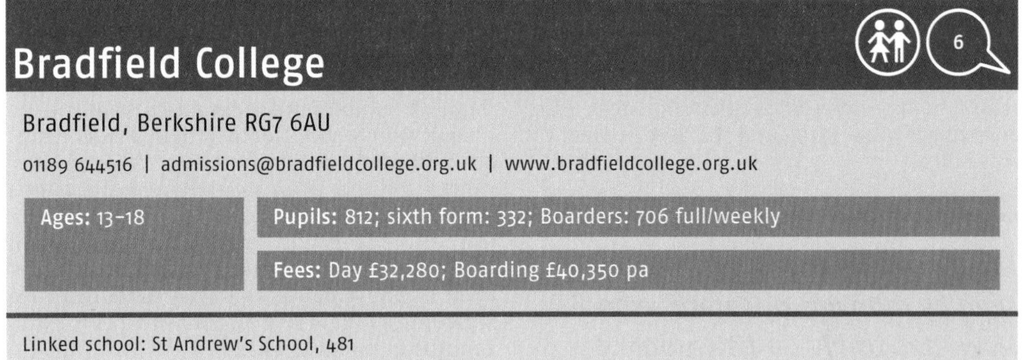

Bradfield College

6

Bradfield, Berkshire RG7 6AU

01189 644516 | admissions@bradfieldcollege.org.uk | www.bradfieldcollege.org.uk

Ages: 13–18

Pupils: 812; sixth form: 332; Boarders: 706 full/weekly

Fees: Day £32,280; Boarding £40,350 pa

Linked school: St Andrew's School, 481

Headmaster: Since 2015, Dr Chris Stevens MA DPhil (50s). Educated at Tonbridge School, then read modern and medieval languages at Caius College, Cambridge before researching Italian literature for a DPhil at Oxford. First experienced working in education as a gappie at Brambletye Prep, and then at Ashdown House where he split the year in half: six months at Ashdown establishing the Ashdown château in France and the rest of the year studying for his doctorate. Began his proper 'career' at age 29 when he joined Uppingham. There he taught French, Italian and history of Art, became a housemaster and was master-in-charge of cricket over his 14 years in residence. Moved on to be second master at Marlborough College. Wife Helen is associate professor of English at Corpus Christi, Oxford. They have three school-age daughters – two of them at Bradfield and one at nearby St Andrew's Prep.

Previous two heads pulled the school up the academic and reputational league tables. So Dr Stevens inherited a school in fine fettle which he has buffed to an opulent glow. Fond of 'mantras' like 'stretch without stress', 'a rising tide floats all boats', and 'teaching up while scaffolding down'. Parents approve, while noticing the shift towards heightening the academic standards.

Loves reading, theatre, opera, ballet. Used to play a lot of sport but became a 'lockdown runner' and thinks he'll stay that way ('it's replaced driving as my thinking time!'). Rugged-bearded when we met him, easy to talk to, a natural orator. Makes a point of meeting every pupil every year, one way or another.

Entrance: Register during years 5 and 6. Take the ISEB pretest between November and Feb of year 6. Pupils with satisfactory prep school references are invited for interview plus team problem-solving assessments between September and March of year 6. First round of offers are made in the summer of that year. Selection criteria are 'attitude, character and potential for happiness,' says head. In year 8 everyone sits either the school's own admission test (January) or CE (June), but these are effectively a rubber stamp. Total of 90 boys and 65 girls enter Faulkner's in September.

Be warned that the school can be a bit quick to dismiss late enquiries for places. If you are delayed to the party, but dead set on the school, then do persevere! Occasional places arise in year

10, and there are around 25-30 places in the sixth form. English and maths tests plus academic and pastoral interviews in November before year of entry into year 12. Minimum of six GCSE grade 6s are required with at least 5s in English and maths.

In December 2021, the school is joining with St Andrew's School, a nearby prep, to establish the Bradfield Group – the two schools, which are just two miles apart, have long shared close ties and the idea is to share expertise, strategic thinking and deliver greater cost efficiencies. Each school will retain its individual identity but be overseen by a combined governing body.

Exit: Few leave after GCSE. 'My daughter will definitely stay through sixth form,' a parent told us. 'She'll be gutted when she has to leave. She'd like it to be her university!' Around 90 per cent of sixth formers go on to university, but the choice is not taken for granted. 'Horizons' (careers) supports youngsters in looking outside the box eg at top-flight apprenticeships or employment. Also encourages networking and the development of soft skills.

Not very long ago Bradfield was seen by many as a 'safety' school. Now, it is firmly on the radar of aspirational parents

Most popular unis include Durham, Edinburgh, Bristol Birmingham and UCL. Occasionally, a student to Oxbridge though none in the past couple of years. Lots more humanities and business degrees than STEM subjects. Increasing numbers head for US universities (some with sports scholarships) and European ones. One medic in 2021.

Latest results: In 2021, 66 per cent 9-7 at GCSE; 52 per cent A*/A at A level (79 per cent A*-B). IB average of 38. In 2019 (the last year when exams took place), 60 per cent 9-7 at GCSE; 34 per cent A*/A at A level (67 per cent A*-B).

Teaching and learning: Last time we were here we said, 'A school that is, without question, on the up.' We can now report that 'up' has been reached, surpassed, and left stranded in the rear-view mirror. Not very long ago Bradfield was seen by many as a 'safety' school. Now, it is firmly on the radar of aspirational parents, with several we spoke to choosing it over offers from heavy hitters like Marlborough, Wellington and top London day schools. 'It was our number one choice,' said one London mum. 'We took him off the other school lists as soon as we visited. Bradfield is the perfect modern education.'

All that said, this is, above all, a school that welcomes – nay honours – the 'all-rounder'. If we had a tenner for every Bradfield pupil, parent or teacher who mentioned 'all-rounders', we could buy a Lamborghini. Academic breadth begins in year 9 when children are given a chance to sample almost everything before committing to GCSEs. 'I'd never been interested in tech or computers,' our guide told us, 'but after we had computer science in our first year, I ended up choosing it for GCSE.' Pupils normally take 10 GCSEs; English results far better than maths.

Business, economics and maths are perennially the most popular A level subjects. Less common subjects on offer include history of art, film studies and photography. Around 25-35 per cent of sixth formers opt for the IB rather than A levels, with parents telling us the six-subject IB is a 'natural fit' for Bradfield, very much in keeping with its all-rounder emphasis. While some schools reserve the IB for their most able students, at Bradfield it's open to everyone: 'The extra classroom time and clearly specified requirements can actually be helpful to some less-independent learners,' explains Dr Stevens. This is apparent in its IB results which display a gargantuan range of abilities. The school is not hugely communicative regarding its exam results, publishing only broad summaries on its website.

Learning support and SEN: Bradfield has eased away from its reputation as a good destination for children requiring SEN support. However, the support is still there. Total of 77 children currently receive individual SEN lessons; lots more have been identified as needing extra time and the like. No specialist unit to cater for extreme needs and, to quote the school, 'The campus is not ideally suited for pupils with mobility issues.'

The arts and extracurricular: In what now seems like a description of a different school, we once commented that the arts played second fiddle to sport. No longer. Music, fine art and drama are all thriving and 'children are firing on all cylinders,' said a parent. 'The kids who do the best here are the ones that get most involved,' said another. Even sports scholars told us that one of the things they liked best about Bradfield was the ability to fully take part in other endeavours, like drama and music. 'Sport doesn't own you,' one explained.

Music is housed in a spacious building with two large classrooms, a concert hall and plenty of practice rooms. Recently restored organ brightens the school chapel. Around 280 pupils learning a musical instrument, from complete beginners to ABRSM Performance Diploma standard. Lots

Lively drama: the college's oddly beloved Greek theatre, the 'Greeker' – a concrete 1,000 seater – has mythic status at Bradfield

of groups and choirs – jazz, contemporary and classical. 'Inspiring,' say parents. That said, not a single music A level entry in 2020 or 2019, and only one in 2018. Three IB musicians in 2019. Art is popular; students like the teachers as well as the subject and art A level results are impressive. The art rooms are tucked away on the other side of a brook in a delightfully separate, rustic Mill-on-the-Floss-style collection of cottages. Photography, sculpture and printing are in interconnecting rooms, plus ample space for 3D design (no one says DT here). Lively drama with three big productions a year (one only for year 9). No dedicated theatre, but a drama studio, a hall with seating, and the college's oddly beloved Greek theatre – the 'Greeker' – a concrete 1,000 seater that has a sort of mythic status at Bradfield.

Beyond the arts, children are busy, busy, busy! 'Millions' of extracurriculars on offer, to quote a parent. The school ring-fences time for them every day of the week and all pupils are expected to take part, whether through the journalism club or the wine appreciation society (year 13 only!). This is not the place for a youngster who wants to hunker down in his room and play Fortnite. Ever keen to ensure breadth, the Bradfield Diploma gets year 10 and 11 kids to try things outside their comfort zone, even if only as a member of the audience. Elements include public speaking, service, and reading five books (of different genres). CCF for all from the summer term of year 9; most continue into year 10 (though volunteering is also an option). All of year 9 strides out along the Brecon Beacons for four days in the summer term (no phones!) and lots enrol in the bronze DofE award at the start of year 10.

Sport: Football rules, ok? The head, a keen rugby player in his day, looked pained as he explained that it's hard for a school to do both football and rugby really well. 'Football,' he points out, 'is a great co-ed sport.' And more: 'If rugby didn't exist, I'm not sure you'd invent it – it's under scrutiny and that will only increase.' Football ferociously strong: Bradfield won the Independent Schools Football Association cup for the first time in 2018. 'No rugby is a huge plus for us,' said a parent. 'Rugby can dominate a school's culture and create a hierarchy among the boys.'

Sport 'works seamlessly with the academic side,' say parents. 'They actually coordinate, unlike at some schools.' Games three times a week plus Saturday matches. Boys' major sports are football and hockey; same for girls plus netball and lacrosse. Summer term is more co-ed with everyone involved in cricket (girls we spoke to loved it), tennis and athletics.

Lots of sports tours in pre-Covid days. One of the most enticing ranges of minor sports we've seen. The school website reads like a highly exclusive action-packed adventure camp. From clay pigeon and rifle shooting (school has its own ranges for both) to zumba and yoga, with fives, real tennis, dodgeball, sailing, canoeing, shooting, riding, polo and golf.

'It stands out a mile for its sports facilities,' said a parent explaining one of the reasons she chose Bradfield. Lush acres of green sports fields as far as the eye can see, splendid indoor tennis courts, a nine-hole golf course nestled towards the end of the games pitches. Massive Astro adorned with 16 outdoor tennis courts when we were there. Water polo takes place in the glistening 25-metre pool that forms part of the swanky sports complex. 'It's not for a kid that hates sport,' one boy told us solemnly. A parent of a non-sporty girl told us, 'It's not her forte, but they're all made to take part in some form. There's something for everyone.'

Boarding: Weekly boarding is a 'defining feature' of the school, say parents. From Monday morning until after matches on Saturday Bradfield operates on full-tilt as a traditional boarding school. On Saturday afternoon, over 80 per cent of the children decamp home, returning bright eyed and bushy tailed on Sunday night or Monday morning. Only around 15 per cent are day pupils, but most of these remain at school late into the evening, departing around 9pm (or later). All day pupils have a desk in a shared room. Up to 15 per cent are full boarders (many, but not all, from abroad). Flexi-boarding not really a Bradfield thing, but local children may also pop home on Wednesday nights, with permission.

In 1998, Bradfield took the brave decision to invest in its youngest boarders – a leap of faith at a time when schools were madly constructing lavish sixth form boarding houses. Faulkner's – the mixed house for the whole of year 9 – is a Bradfield triumph. The idea is to weld the year group together so that as they branch off to their different (single-sex) houses in year 10, everyone will know each other and there will be less scope for cliques. Pupils move dormitories every half term to expand friendships. It's a jolly, cosy and gentle start to boarding life. Parents remarked on how much their children's confidence grew throughout the year, although inevitably we

Caldicott

heard the odd case of difficult relationships, particularly among the girls.

The Faulkner's building is modern, functional but attractive. Comfortable and tasteful common rooms on each boys' and girls' side, and a place in the centre where they can all gather to play games and hang out. All rooms have an ensuite, the larger rooms with two showers! Prep is done in dorm rooms each evening – with doors open. Phone policy among the best we've seen: 25 minutes in the morning and 45 minutes in the evening (turned in by 9pm, along with any other tech) and otherwise locked away. Older pupils are allowed phones for two hours in the evenings. No restrictions in sixth form.

Four senior girls' houses; seven for boys. Many of the study bedrooms have ensuite bathrooms, two or three to a room, with a kitchen on every floor. Currently, D House said to be the sportiest while A House excels in music. Faulkner's children eat in their house with some senior pupils. Others eat in the main dining room. Pupils will make the effort to stay in for a particular event, like the famous Michaelmas Goose weekend, packed with an interhouse riot of a competition which includes a 'total wipeout' style water and inflatables obstacle course as well as dodgeball, debating, dancing and singing ('very raucous, and loud,' warned a student).

Ethos and heritage: A quaintly pastoral and pristine setting that feels more like a movie location or a medieval manor than a school. Founded in the 1850s by Thomas Stevens, lord of the manor and local rector, as a choir school for his church, Bradfield may not have a long sweeping drive or a grand central building, but it is nonetheless a rural school. The village and the school are one and the same: there is no high street, no post office, no pub, not a single shop. Here children have a chance to be children for longer, and there is not much to distract them from all that is available to do at school. It is at once isolated and conveniently located. Forward thinking (and big thinking – is joining with St Andrew's School, a nearby prep, in December 2021 to share expertise, vision, save costs etc) but imbued with romanticism. On the fringes, and at the centre: just off the M4, 30 minutes from Reading, 45 minutes from Heathrow, a pleasant commute from Theale to Paddington Station.

Lovely vistas and unexpected charm at every turn among the flint and brick buildings and sloping roofs. A highlight is the tranquil Thai Garden, named after Bradfield's first student from Thailand. In good nick throughout, the science block stands out as a thing of semi-modern beauty: well equipped, glassy and airy, it is used by pupils after lessons as a distraction-free study space. The Stunt Pavilion, perched on the edge of the games fields, was formerly a dilapidated sixth form bar. Now serves as a swish school café, used by pupils and staff alike; a walk down from the boarding houses for an ice cream on a summer afternoon is a cherished pastime.

As the school has grown more popular, it can be more selective, and an intellectual blossoming is in the air. Increasing numbers of academic societies now flourish. The school has moved from tutor groups to individual tutorials and improved staff's skills at teaching with differentiation so that all abilities can be stretched. The complete renovation a 14th century church, currently being purchased by Bradfield, is the school's next big project. The finished product will be a striking glass and stone learning centre comprising a 21st century library, collaborative learning spaces, 'brainstorming pods' (!) and a café.

Weekly boarding is a 'defining feature'. From Monday morning until after matches on Saturday Bradfield operates on full-tilt as a traditional boarding school

School's have-a-go ethos comes through in its website which is voluminous, joyful... and sprinkled with typos. Straightforward school uniform in the first three years gives way to own-choice smart suits (and ties for boys) in sixth form. Boys still outnumber girls 60/40. Former pupils include politicians Lord David Owen and Sir John Nott, authors Louis de Bernières and Richard Adams, cricketer and broadcaster Mark Nicholas, actor Claudia Harrison, astronomer Sir Martin Ryle, jockey Nico de Boinville, explorer Benedict Allen, comedian Tony Hancock, and Made in Chelsea stars Sam Thompson, Frankie Gaff and Olivia Bentley.

Pastoral care, inclusivity and discipline: Pastoral care lauded again and again by all we spoke to: 'The fact is there are some troubled children at these boarding schools. Many have experienced divorce, mental health challenges or even the death of a parent. Bradfield does a great job for those that need extra TLC.' 'Pastoral care was our biggest priority,' a mum told us. 'That's why we chose Bradfield.' Parents mentioned weekly calls from tutors during lockdown: 'It was huge.' School communication is 'incredible'. 'We get instant replies to emails and there is constant feedback and reports.' Faulkner's children are awarded merit points for kindness and rewarded with treats ('McDonalds!' enthused a pupil; 'a nice touch,' said a parent). Veritas, the newish LGBTQ society, welcomes all. Pupils in years 9-11 have a timetabled wellbeing lesson each week covering resilience, health, equality, community, communication and reflection. Staff too are looked after, and some have completed a mindfulness-based stress reduction course.

Disciplinary incidents of some kind come up most years. Relieved that Bradfield barely featured in the Everyone's Invited exposé, but no school can be complacent, and staff have renewed efforts to make sure this is a school with a culture of speaking up. All of the Bradfield parents we spoke to had confidence in the school's grip on 'boy-girl relationships'. An episode involving a nude photo resulted in culprits immediately exiting the school. Ditto for drugs.

Pupils and parents: M4 corridor and west London loom large. Forty per cent of families hail from a 30-mile radius, 25 per cent have an address in London (some of these also have a more local home). Only eight per cent are based abroad. Far fewer international pupils, and a much more English flavour, than most boarding schools, mainly owing to the preponderance of weekly boarding (only 10 children currently have EAL lessons). A good sprinkling of Old Bradfieldans. Loads of siblings – this is very much a one-school-fits-all place. 'I chose it because it suited both my children – one's super-academic, the other's more relaxed,' said a parent. 'Very academically-pushy parents won't take the risk on the all-rounder education Bradfield provides; they'll most probably look elsewhere.'

A quaintly pastoral and pristine setting that feels more like a movie location or a medieval manor than a school

Pupils come from 60 different prep schools. Among the preps sending larger cohorts (though all send fewer than 20) are Cheam, St Andrew's, Lambrook, Northcote Lodge, Broomwood and Twyford. We have previously said, 'Bradfield remains a broad church and under the current leadership will continue to do so.' So far this holds true...

Money matters: Although lots of scholarships awarded (including academic, sport all-rounder and music) a fee reduction is only available with means-testing. The school is a charitable trust and provides bursary support, from anything from 100 per cent of fees to one per cent. Surprisingly, no sibling discounts.

The last word: An all-rounder's nirvana. Bucolic setting, weekly boarding, co-ed, IB, football, first year mega-boarding-house: these are Bradfield's USPs. A mature, confident school at its peak. 'We have complete trust in the school,' a parent told us. 'A feel-good school,' said another. Delicate swots or single sport obsessives may look elsewhere.

Brockwood Park School

7

Brockwood Park, Bramdean, Hampshire SO24 0LQ

01962 771744 | enquiry@brockwood.org.uk | www.brockwood.org.uk

Ages: 14 -19

Pupils: 82; sixth form: 25 (7 boys, 18 girls); Boarders: 71 (22 boys, 49 girls) full

Fees: Day £6,836 or £7,719 pa; Boarding £23,300 or £30,700 pa

Principal: Since 2015, Antonio Autor. Principal by name only: there is no hierarchy here; everyone has a voice and is heard, and everyone has the same salary, from cleaner to principal.

Antonio has the still presence of a mountain or deep water. Here is someone who seems remarkably free of ego or any sort of push; and yet, astonishingly, he had a previous life as a professional footballer. He has a BA in business and has studied English at Cardiff, Brighton and London. He joined Brockwood Park in 1987, and his jobs have ranged from gardener to teacher.

Students 'love' him; 'above everything, you can go to [him] if out of control'; '[I'm] really comfortable talking to him – normal conversation without having to fake adult and know everything.'

Dr Gopal Krishnamurthy, founder and previously co-principal, stepped down in 2018.

Entrance: Students attend a prospective week before they sign up to the school, so they know what to expect, though Covid means this has been replaced by a two-stage interview process until further notice. Non-selective.

Inwoods Small School, a 10-minute walk away, is a junior school run by the same Krishnamurti Foundation, but few children come from there.

Exit: Five per cent left after GCSE in 2020. 'You will leave education here with a set of questions – with uncertainty,' said the principal. More reassuring is the fact that most students leave to continue their education somewhere in the world. Some depart for gap years or jobs: one student went on to train as a chef and works in one of the only vegetarian restaurants in Italy – she is 'well balanced; well in her basket,' said her father.

Latest results: In 2020, 43 per cent A*/A at A level (77 per cent A*-B). In 2019 (the last year when exams took place), 75 per cent 9-7 at GCSE; 17 per cent A*/A at A level (47 per cent A*-B).

Teaching and learning: 'A way of education which is rare and original,' said a parent, and completely different to traditional education, dismissed as 'academic memorising'; or as Krishnamurti (school's founder) put it: 'education [is]... not merely transferring what is printed on a page to your brain. Education may mean opening the doors of perception on to the vast movement of life.'

No small task and certainly not an easy option for student or teacher. Students are encouraged not just to accept what they read or are told, but to inquire into it themselves: we saw a group of students on the lawn, attempting to get a solar panel working again so they could charge their mobile phones on a camping trip; we have never seen a teacher so alertly attentive, but silent, as students worked it out. 'Right education is a mutual task demanding patience, consideration and affection,' said principal, and this is evidently so at Brockwood Park.

The only common courses here are inquiry time and human ecology. At inquiry time, the school meets to discuss the way we live our lives – '[my son] seems to find it valuable for sorting issues out.' Students said they felt listened to: 'space to speak,' said one. Human ecology is the study of our home in its broadest sense, recognising that we all share the responsibility to care for the planet. Students might work in the kitchen garden, eco building or observation: giving full attention to the world outside and, during inquiry time, to the world within.

There is a large element of personal decision-making in the curriculum, greatly appreciated by students: 'I learn something I want to learn; do what I want to do'; and to some degree by parents: 'Students invest in what they are doing with choice', but 'I would like them to insist a bit more in academic matters.' Another said, 'I'm not sure [my son] is applying himself properly... I think he is challenged, but only if he is interested.'

At Brockwood Park they have their own way of getting people interested in things. Nothing is forced, but a pupil who doesn't like maths can expect to spend a lots of time exploring why. As a parent put it, 'If a student doesn't want to study, they discuss and discuss and discuss...'

We saw a group of students trying to get a solar panel working so they could charge their mobile phones; we have never seen a teacher so alertly attentive, but silent

Those under 16 take three core courses: science and mathematics, humanities, and arts and crafts. The focus, in each, is on learning through first-hand experience. Described by the principal as being 'the roots of literacy... getting them to think for themselves... [where] not knowing is a vital point of departure.'

Topic courses are also available, which enable students to explore issues in much greater depth: the teacher introduces a topic, such as 'movement of humans', and after a few weeks, students determine their own specific area of exploration.

Languages are taught organically, depending on the skills of the staff at the time. There's always a lot of support for them in this international school: Italian, French, German and Spanish are being taught at the moment. English as an additional language (EAL) is highly successful: a French speaker told us he was confident in English after only three months at Brockwood Park. 'Learning English is easy here. Even if I make a mistake, I don't mind. If you say something stupid it doesn't matter.'

Lessons are usually with six or seven students, 10 at the most, with teacher and teacher apprentice present, which allows students to 'work more deeply in the subject,' said a dad who felt that a big class would have no time to divert from the programme. There are no year groups: 'Even young ones help older ones sometimes,' said a parent.

Students can develop their own projects if their proposal is approved by the teachers' group, which will choose an academic adviser to support the project for the year. It's a bigger, tougher version of the EPQ with 'a sense of excellence for its own sake'.

Those coming here from traditional environments can have some 'unlearning to do', often lacking original thought or vitality. We were given the example of a student who arrived with a long list of A*s at IGCSE: 'It took a lot to get her to ask questions or disagree with me – but now she says, "I don't want you to help me".'

They're not against traditional achievement here, but it's a by-product. '[We] do think exams are important, but not as a reflection of worth or learning. They are what you've done, in a particular direction, according to certain criteria. Academic success should not be confused with excellence.'

Some students take A levels and the mock exams are often the first exams students at this school have ever sat; they also have a pre-exam intensive study week with the aim of building a sense of confidence in their own work: 'It's a game – we want them to play it well.'

Students can take IGCSEs if they want to, although it was clear that the principal couldn't really see why anyone would want to: 'an easy option'.

Learning support and SEN: There are students here with dyslexia, dyspraxia and ADHD, but they do not like labelling students SEN: each student has their own programme, and the whole curriculum supports the special needs of each student. No extra charge for one-to-one unless help from outside is necessary.

The arts and extracurricular: The art barn with its curved windows contains a pottery studio, darkroom and Mac suite. Textiles are popular – students used a Japanese manual dyeing technique on old sheets, before making them into clothes.

'Words have limitations,' said Krishnamurti, so music, with the harmony it brings to body and mind, is very important at Brockwood, where regular informal concerts take place.

Sport: Exercise is important here, and students spend two afternoons a week playing games, but not games as you know them. Games are played for the pleasure of the movement, for the beauty of the shot, with 'heart [and] everything in the game', but not for the winning.

A couple of students who had tasted the joys of competitive sport missed the adrenalin, although they do play friendly football with local schools and the farmers. Netball, basketball, yoga (naturally) and hockey are also available. There are plenty of opportunities for long walks and orienteering: 'The need to finish together and take care of the team is a substitute for the team spirit of games,' said a parent.

Boarding: This small school is a boarding community, roughly a third British, the rest international.

'[It is] intense to live with people, but beautiful to share all your day. Your whole life in this amount shared with all these people,' said a parent. Another said it is an 'intense social life. [My son] is thrilled at this.'

A student described how she has come to realise that washing up is part of life: at home, it just happens. Here, everyone has to pitch in, or it doesn't get done

Girls board in the main house, with single rooms for older girls, and large rooms for two or three younger ones. Students arrange furniture how they like it, some making their views clear from their door decoration: next to a picture of a cow, 'Not your mum, not your milk.' Bathrooms are elderly but clean.

Boys are in the cloisters, a 70s add-on around a square of grass and trees with teachers living on the corners; this accommodation was described by one parent as 'adequate': his son will opt for the pavilion next year. The pavilions are very grand indeed: oak framed with underfloor heating and glass-topped roofs, fragrant herb gardens outside; a wing each for girls and boys.

Students have to be in their rooms by 9.30pm and are now allowed smartphones, but only in their rooms. TV is not much of an event here; students generally spend more time in the sitting room: a grand old room in the main house, with sofas, grand piano and wood burner in the old fireplace, for staff and students alike.

Students may catch the bus into Winchester at weekends, and go away for the weekend if they seek permission first ('They're on top of their game for safeguarding,' said a parent).

Wifi is in a particular corner of the school, and otherwise not easy to locate; apparently there's one spot up a particular tree, but use of devices is not encouraged – 'beneficial to be starved of it for some time,' said a parent hardily.

Ethos and heritage: '[It's an] interesting way of living – fantastically beautiful,' said a parent, who was enchanted by his first visit to Brockwood Park. '[We] discovered the ambience and the liberty of the students.' The school is run on the basis of collaboration, not competition, an atmosphere in which all sorts of students thrive: '[They] don't judge you here... [I] feel more open. Better for you: to love yourself and feel more confidence,' said a student.

This school is about learning to live, and understanding yourself as something worthy of inquiry – 'very challenging for the student; not an easy way,' said a parent. Students have to learn about responsibility; or, as one parent put it, 'the capability of everyone to be response-able in a situation... what [they can] do to contribute to the world.' It starts in small ways here; a student described how she has come to realise that washing up is part of life: at home, it just happens; at her old school, there were cleaners. Here, everyone has to pitch in, or it doesn't get done.

'[It's] very challenging for parents to have children at this school. Questions raised with the students touch the parents: about the future, human beings and existence... I am educated by my kids, by their education at Brockwood Park... for some, it is difficult to accept this,' said a parent.

The strength of community here is something students were keen to talk about: 'everyone is open to know you'; 'after only four months, I have found a way I like of having relationships – I enjoy them, even if I don't like the person.' A wide sociality is encouraged, both in terms of the Brockwood community (exclusive relationships are frowned upon), and in terms of being part of a worldwide community: time is devoted to exploring social and political crisis.

Different faiths are tolerated, but if you follow a particular religion, others need to be free to ask questions of it and you. 'If there is a God, find him for yourself,' said Antonio.

Many of the buildings are beautiful: the elegant main house, the assembly room with its beautiful wooden roof and a grand piano, and the study with cream carpet and wood panelling: morning meetings take place there every day – 10 mins of quiet time to start the day. As you walk around, you can feel how much this school is cared for: it is not just a collection of buildings which serve as a shell to house those within.

The school sits in 40 acres, including the original kitchen garden, where students have human ecology lessons, and the head gardener works with the head chef to grow seasonal produce for the kitchen. All food at Brockwood Park is vegetarian; on the day of our visit a delicious lentil bake, a fresh salad from the garden with flowers, and fruit, students spilling out of the dining hall to eat lunch on the lawn.

Pastoral care, inclusivity and discipline: Understanding discipline at Brockwood Park is best done by considering these words: 'After all, discipline means resistance... Do you think resistance will bring about understanding, thought, affection?... Discipline is always exclusive, whereas understanding is inclusive. Understanding comes when you investigate, when you enquire, when you search out, which requires care, consideration, thought, affection.'

There is, however, no absence of rules or agreements as to how to behave. Students sign a contract on entering the school, committing to the curriculum and caring for each other, and agreeing not to smoke, drink alcohol or eat meat (no sneaky bacon butties in Winchester at the weekend, either). Parents are convinced by the school's approach: 'Brockwood Park is the safest school to grow up a teenager that we know.'

Dealing with each breach of rules will be different, emphasises Antonio, but there will be a process, which will involve talking with teacher, student, tutor, and pastoral coordinator. It's an 'opportunity for learning', he says, and much depends on how the student responds to the process. An action plan for drinking alcohol might be for the student to investigate how alcohol attacks the body and mind, and share it with the school. 'Troubles with kids doing forbidden things [are] dealt with in a peaceful way; [they] awaken responsibility in kids,' said a parent.

The gentleness of this school does not mean that there are no consequences for actions. Students will be suspended if a habit needs to be broken. Expulsion can happen, and has, for drug and smoking offences. 'I understand that a firm message has to pass on to the children, and it is slowly dawning on [my son] that he cannot act in any way he pleases.'

Students sign a contract on entering the school, committing to the curriculum and agreeing not to smoke, drink alcohol or eat meat

Another parent told us that his son had admitted to having an unsmoked joint in his room. The consequences were daily discussions with Antonio for 15 minutes every morning – for months. The parent had the impression both quite enjoy the chats now...

Agreements are settled between students and teachers about lesser matters, such as hairstyles and tummy rings, although a determined Mohican lasted out his time without changing his hair: agreements are not rules, but students wishing to flout them should expect a lot of discussion.

Students, asked to describe the best thing about the school, described their relationships with teachers: 'teachers look at you like a person'; 'chat any time'; 'someone, always, has an ear for you. Always.'

Bullying is not a problem here, say students and parents. Students agreed that some people are popular; 'but not better, or of more consequence,' pointed out another.

Pupils and parents: Many students are ex-Waldorf, said a parent, have already opted for this sort of education, and are 'mostly thrilled at what's offered' here.

Parents receive two detailed observational reports a year. Communication varies, with dates for events sometimes communicated rather late in the day, but pastoral communications are good. Parents can come and stay in the area for the weekend, and meet their child's academic adviser and tutors.

Money matters: Bursaries are available from seven to (exceptionally) 100 per cent of the fees. Around 15 per cent of the fee income is available for bursaries.

The last word: Parents think it wouldn't suit a very competitive child, or one who comes from a rigid background – 'Where are the instructions?' 'Great for creative types, artists and musicians'; 'A child needs to be independent in character – you need to "be an actor in your learning".'

This extraordinary school is not for those who want to purchase an off-the-shelf education with the assurance of a clutch of academic certificates to match, but for families who are willing to risk exchanging the bland safety of traditional education for something more real and exciting.

Caldicott
8
Crown Lane, Farnham Royal, Slough SL2 3SL
01753 649300 | admissions@caldicott.com | www.caldicott.com
Ages: 7-13
Pupils: 250; Boarders: 116
Fees: Day £18,738 – £20,901; Boarding £27,732 – £30,813 pa

Headmaster: Since April 2018, Jeremy Banks, previously headmaster of Beachborough School. His mother was a headteacher and having realised relatively young that he too had a way with children, he subsequently did a degree in education studies and geography at Warwick University and an MA in educational leadership (distinction) at Buckingham. Spent his first 10 years at Dulwich Prep; joined Beachborough as deputy head in 2006, becoming head in 2013.

Now gently guiding Caldicott, this most traditional of preps, towards the 21st century (school's first ever head with an active Twitter account). One of his first wins was to completely overhaul the way boys are prepared for pre-test and secondary school interviews, including bringing in external people (cue applause from parents). 'They bus them off to their Wellington interviews en masse where they arrive like a squad with no nervous parents hanging around them and they nail it. Same with Harrow,' said one parent. School is reported by parents to be in a 'period of transition' on account of him being the 'polar opposite to his predecessor' who reigned for 19 years – 'a difficult act to follow as he was a very out-there character, but Mr Banks is less black and white, with more grey areas, and really listens to parents,' said one.

The sea of trophies in reception that smacked of 'Welcome to Caldicott – we win stuff' has been replaced with comfy sofas – a reflection, say parents, of his emphasis on 'inclusivity and developing character, not just the top tier of talent'. Communications have reportedly been 'streamlined' under his headship too. Doesn't shy away from awkward conversations.

When time allows, can be seen running through Burnham Beeches in an effort to get his 5k time below 19 mins. Married to Sophie, also a Warwick graduate and prep school head (a nice change, we noted, to see a prep school head's wife not expected to perform the usual vicar's wife role of pastoral duties and match teas). They have three daughters.

Entrance: Two-form entry in year 3, grows to three in year 5. There is a short formal academic assessment plus an opportunity to meet other pupils and teachers and there are open days in October, March and May. Though still a far cry from the London 7+, boys do get turned away for not being sufficiently academic, although the cohort is comparatively mixed ability.

Exit: Not an obvious choice if you have your eye on the Bucks grammars (or any other school with 11+ intake) as nearly all leave at 13, mainly to traditional boys' boarding, and parents told us those that do leave earlier are not supported to do so (though school disputes this). Harrow (it used to be Eton) most popular, then St Edward's, Charterhouse, Stowe, Wellington and Winchester College. Sometimes ones and twos to eg Marlborough, Uppingham and Tonbridge, plus occasionally to day schools like Merchant Taylors' or Habs. Usually plenty of academic, sport, art, music, drama and all-rounder scholarships.

Our view: Founded in 1904 by Heald Jenkins who named the school after his new bride, a Miss Theodora Caldicott Ingram. The school and its wonderful Harrison Harrison organ (now restored and residing in the chapel) moved from Hitchin to Farnham Royal in 1938.

Blessed by geography, Caldicott sits on top of a wooded escarpment with views down to Windsor; 40 acres of prime Bucks real estate adjoining beautiful Burnham Beeches, yet just half an hour from London, which is where half the pupils come in from (the other half being local) every morning on the 7.30am Caldicott express (school claims to have 'invented' bussing in from west London).

Perfect, billiard table-esque pitches extend as far as the eye can see – 'It's a proper honour to play on the top pitch,' our guide said, staring at it longingly. Sport is the tour de force here and fetishised by all, especially rugby (U13 As remain unbeaten) and cricket that have – when numbers allow – A-E teams ready to take on all comers at all levels. Indeed, parents of unsporty boys do not find them swinging round the corner posts while the A team triumphs on a distant pitch – 'If the A team is playing, so are the rest.' Some grumbles that while they do play football, 'none of the teachers seem to really like it', and some pupils told us that tennis isn't as valued as it could be, with courts also needing attention. But the head is on the case with trying to up the game on these and other less obvious sports, having – for example – recently introduced colours for squash and swimming. 'I'm trying to inject the spirit of the 2012 Olympics where the notion of major vs minor sports simply doesn't exist,' he said, though good luck to him getting this past the rugby-loving alpha parents (yes, there are loads of them – the west London crowd bring heat with them and drive the competitive nature of the school). A new, state-of-the-art structure over the swimming pool means that swimming is on offer all year round.

Anyone that says no teacher is indispensable clearly hasn't met Ma'am (everyone is called sir and ma'am here) Naidoo (senior deputy head, academic), who gets amazing results at CE by really driving the boys in year 8, with the scholarship list going from strength to strength. That said, teaching along the way is said to be 'mixed' – one parent said that early on, 'you wonder whether they are learning anything at all apart from how to open doors for adults, shake hands and be jolly nice chaps', with school admitting 'that's not altogether unfair, but we're on top of it now, with a lot more problem solving introduced earlier on'. Things pick up later, say parents, although even then 'some teachers are better than others' (science, maths and English get biggest votes) and some (though less than in the past, says school) jacks of all trades rather than specialist, so you could find the same person teaching geography, English and RS, for instance. No native language teachers, although not to the detriment of language teaching, it seems, with Latin 'particularly good' and Greek also a shining star, if only for its innovation (the pattern recognition is similar to coding, claims school, so they're sometimes taught hand in hand).

Anyone who says no teacher is indispensable clearly hasn't met Ma'am (everyone is called sir and ma'am here) Naidoo, who gets amazing results at CE

Average class size is 16, maximum 18, and setting in maths, science and languages from year 5. The lessons we saw were dynamic, with boys clearly engaged – there is recognition, say parents, that boys learn kinaesthetically. Yet still, plenty of parents tutor their sons outside school. School used to be slow to pick up SEN, but the new SENCo (from the state sector) is lauded and we heard how teachers now take more responsibility for complex needs in the classroom.

The arts are the school's 'weakest area', say parents, though one boy recently got an art scholarship to Harrow. Heads of music and art 'have been there forever', said one, with art described as 'unimaginative' – 'It needs to be totally overhauled to inspire boys.' Music 'equally drab', said a parent

– 'performances are slowly improving but generally joyless – a recent choir trip to Wellington College saw a take-up of only three boys, which I think speaks volumes' (school says this was because it was during the very popular 'project week'). Watch this space, says school – for the first time there's a school orchestra and the junior choir is no longer audition-only. There's also a chamber choir, ensembles and 200+ weekly lessons from peripatetic teachers, plus more opportunities to perform including three whole-school concerts a year. DT, previously marginal, now injected with new life by increasingly teaming up with robotics (our guides couldn't have been more enthusiastic about their award-winning STEAM projects). Head of drama hugely popular, with LAMDA available and 'some outstanding performances' (recent examples including My Fair Lady, A Christmas Carol and Two Gentleman of Verona abridged to be a homage to the 80s) but 'there's not enough of them,' said a parent.

Boys are charming, chatty and perfectly mannered – 'They all shake hands with the dads when they go for playdates – brilliant,' said a parent, although they do seem moulded. 'Individualism is not heavily encouraged'

Days are long (so are holidays), with many boys staying until 6pm (although younger ones can be collected at 4.15pm). But boys seem to take it in their stride and point out there's no homework apart from spellings, reading and basic maths until the last two years (when all boys board). Saturday school (not for years 3 and 4 from September 2021) is proper, with lessons until 12.15pm for all and matches in the afternoon for the older boys, when London parents are just as visible on the sidelines as locals.

Deputy head (pastoral) considered one of the best things about the school – 'He does it all from the heart,' said a parent, while one told of how 'Caldicott was a real sanctuary for my son while we went through difficulties at home.' 'CaldiKind' has been a massive focus of the PSHEE programme. New 'well-being room' popular. Mixed views on discipline, though, with some parents saying minor transgressions are often handled too severely and more serious ones not severely enough.

There are schools with shinier buildings, but everything is fit for purpose, with bright classrooms, well-equipped labs and lots of techy stuff. And it's incredibly – perhaps uniquely – neat for a prep. Even the art room, usually reliable as a haven of creative chaos, was shipshape. Breakfasts and lunches reported by boys to be 'excellent', although suppers 'could have more choice'.

Boys are charming, chatty and perfectly mannered – 'They all shake hands with the dads when they go for playdates – brilliant,' said a parent, although they do seem moulded. 'Individualism is not heavily encouraged,' confirmed a parent. We heard tale after tale of initially shy boys coming out of their shells – 'My son used to be a "oh no, someone's going to ask me a question" type and now he wants to be prefect,' said one. Boys praise the 'mixing of year groups' and parents are a sociable bunch too – 'It's a bit of a club,' said one, with another saying she made 'great friends even though I came into the school very late'.

Few, if any, preps this close to London can boast such a rural feel and we think Caldicott stands out for its values too – decency, fair play, regard for others and courtesy, among them.

Boarding: All boys in years 7 and 8 board Monday to Saturday, no exceptions – seen as integral to their preparation for the likes of Harrow, Eton and Radley. Optional flexi and occasional boarding available for years 3-6. Refurbished dorms are upstairs in the main school building – clean, bright with home duvets, a few photos and posters. Evenings are busy with golf, kayaking, rock climbing, model making, fondue nights and (you guessed it) more cricket nets, among others. Weekends for the 20-odd full boarders include outings such as Globe Theatre, Liquid Leisure water park and football at Wembley. 'It's not exactly like a sleepover, but it's really good fun,' said our guide, raving about the after-school swims in the outdoor pool. New boarders get a buddy, an experienced boarder in the same dorm to help him settle in and houseparents (as with many staff) live on site. 'My son struggled at first – Christmas term was hell, but they were phenomenal, keeping me updated and supporting him through the crying – I couldn't fault them,' said one parent.

Money matters: The Caldicott Foundation was established in 2020 to fund free places – there are currently two boys benefitting in this way.

The last word: Overall, a cracking prep for confident all-rounders who love sport and being competitive – and although not an obvious choice for softer souls who prefer to be inside reading a book, we suspect that might change under the current headship.

Cheam School

Headley, Newbury, Berkshire RG19 8LD

01635 268242 | office@cheamschool.co.uk | www.cheamschool.com

Ages: 3–13

Pupils: 380; **Boarders:** 90–120 weekly/flexi

Fees: Day £11,925 – £22,035; Boarding £24,525 – £29,325 pa

Head: Since September 2021, Tom Haigh (acting head). To be replaced in summer 2022 by Will Phelps (40s), currently head of The Beacon School, the largest boys' day prep in the country. He has worked in senior and prep schools, covering co-ed and single-sex education, spending over 10 years at Abingdon School, where he taught theology and went on to become senior housemaster and head of boarding. First headship was at the British International School of New York in Manhattan in 2010. Comes from a large 'clan' and something of a teaching dynasty. He was brought up in Oxford where his father was a maths don, attended the Dragon School (where his brother is now deputy head) and Clifton College, Bristol where one of the boarding houses had been run by his great grandfather. Studied theology at King's College London. Has huge enthusiasm for Tolkien and JK Rowling and hobbies include walking, cooking (Sunday roasts and barbecues a speciality) and watching cricket and rugby: 'I support, I don't play. I was never any good.' He's married with three children, two at Marlborough and the youngest at Godstowe. Latest additions are two puppies, Merlin and Luna.

Entrance: Popular with waiting lists in every year group. Broadly selective – must be able to access curriculum but few turned away. Entry by date of registration. Attend familiarisation day – reading, reasoning and maths with time in class – before place is confirmed. Main entry points at reception, year 3 (15 added each time), plus another 10 in year 4. A few places in year 7, rare in years 5, 6 or 8. No feeders – mix of state primaries, London preps and former locals, now returning home. Most live within 20-mile radius. Currently no EAL or overseas pupils.

Exit: One size fits most. 'At Cheam we are preparing your child for their future senior school which will probably be full boarding,' says the school. Every top name, every year, with Wellington most popular recently, followed by Marlborough, Bradfield, Eton, Radley, Downe House and Sherborne. Others to St Mary's Calne, Pangbourne, St Edward's, Winchester College, St Helen and St Katharine, Wycombe Abbey, Bryanston, Cheltenham, Bedales, Canford, St Mary's Ascot and Harrow. Nice mix of awards, most academic, but others in music, drama, sport, DT and general.

Our view: Easy to pre-judge clientele by tweet congratulating 'former Cheam parents HM The Queen and Prince Philip on the birth of their Great Granddaughter'. That, and winning entry in sandcastle competition – a 'multi-storey mansion' – plus prevalence of cast iron titles among the old boys. Viscounts, barons, HRHs (UK and overseas), politicians. (Also John Michell, 'writer and esotericist': ask for details.)

Boasts (in poshly understated way) gold-plated 17th-century provenance, founded in (then) quaint olde world village of Cheam in 1645. Moved to current 100-acre site in 1934, just in time to set up local Home Guard platoon and host 21st Tank Regiment in 1941 (tank rides offered as an after-class treat).

Despite online images of ballet club, all pink tutu-wearing girls, biggest success is former (boy) pupil, a rising classical dance star

Added girls and day places in the 1990s to overcome, as in 18th and 19th centuries, significant money troubles (one financial crisis per century isn't bad).

But despite all this (and the names of pupils, rich on Florences, Allegras, Orlandos and Fredericks), school community stresses social mix. While not exactly drilling down into the deprived underbelly of the nation, rather more diverse – and infinitely more welcoming – than appearances might suggest. 'We came from state school – everyone is down to earth,' said parent.

Lots of earth, too, courtesy of splendiferous site with lakes, formal gardens and fountains; 'an awesome sight,' said parent. Traffic noise well damped down, replaced by gentle smack of tennis balls on the all-weather surface (pupils' complaints of running track deformed by slope, tree roots and 'little frogs' not substantiated by school…).

Little of the original main house remains (two mega rebuilds in 19th and 20th centuries) and modern extras include the Duke of Edinburgh building (powered by geothermal energy), home to pre-prep, art and DT, and a new kitchen area.

Space well used. 'Something for everyone' boasts the website of the extracurricular activities (most free) – including Greek and German as well as extra enrichment for scholars.

Gender stereotypes are being put to one side. Despite online images of ballet club, all pink tutu-wearing girls, biggest success is former (boy) pupil, a rising classical dance star. Membership of sewing, Sylvanians, Jedi and Lego is (often) similarly mixed.

Former sports inequality has also been addressed. Boys and girls play football and cricket, for example. Plenty of co-ed sports including cross-country (masses of prizes), athletics, shooting, fives and swimming (outdoor but no indoor pool – on the wish list).

Performing arts similarly varied, though limited purpose-built spaces, including fab productions (regulars at Edinburgh Festival) and wonderful selective choirs. Two music lessons a week for all pre-prep pupils with tasters in recorder, strings and brass in year 2 (individual lessons from year 3). Well over half the pupils learn some of 17 instruments on offer, with lessons and (for boarders) practice sessions timetabled – impressive string quartet whizzing, unsupervised, through repertoire (snazzy Pink Panther theme). Drama, isn't taught in years 7 or 8 (some parents and pupils would like as an extra), though school points to showcases including soirées and full-blown shows.

Impressive emphasis on pastoral care – parents felt recently improved, especially for youngest; bullying minimal. Staff are all being trained in mental health first aid. Also staff mentors – pupils can request any teacher – prominent displays and emotional tracking (asking same, simple questions twice a year can help predict child's resilience level). One pupil we talked to was movingly open about how school had supported him through family crisis.

But it's the academic fare that really appeals. 'All learning should be fun,' says the school. Confirmed by parents who praised 'magical' teachers – recruitment boosted by staff housing in 'Cheamville'. New recruits with ultra-serious outlook (several 'worryingly young' – though average age is 37) are encouraged to lighten up. 'All seem to get the same principle which is that… if you can't have a laugh in prep school years, good luck to rest of your life,' said mother.

Splendiferous site with lakes, formal gardens and fountains. Traffic noise well damped down, replaced by gentle smack of tennis balls on the all-weather surface

Pre-prep head, Mrs Marriott, praised for warmth, ability (and dressing-up costumes – 'have seen her in more than any teacher should have to wear,' said mother). She presides over bright classrooms with fabulously inventive displays – teachers clearly arrive with A* skills in transformatory foil-wrapping. Admirable fusion of fun and learning – on day of visit, reception pupils were busily chalking planets on courtyard paving stones.

Homework isn't daunting, with light reading, emphasis on key words and writing practice in pre-prep. Twice-yearly reports, plenty of informal contact encouraged while colourful, detailed newsletters (pre-prep has its own) fill in any gaps.

After gentle step up from year 2 to 3, pace increases from year 4, non-stop from 8.15am assembly to end of prep (attended by all) at 6pm – later for top years – and a no-concessions full day of Saturday school.

Well staffed (teacher to pupil ratio of one to six in prep and one to four in pre-prep) and smallish classes – 18 official max, smaller for French and maths, and setting generally left to year 5.

Plenty of interesting things to do, from hatching butterflies to investigating the contents of owl pellets (rather them than us). Numerous subject-related trips (history, geog, French) plus culture (theatre, ballet, museums) sweeten the pill.

Main focus, though, firmly on CE preparation in key subjects (English, maths, science, French, Latin, history, geography and RS). Less academic are, say parents, never made to feel like lesser mortals and subject popularity spans the ability range. Favourites include science – pluses the breeding colony of stick insects, minuses the paucity of labs (on the wish list) – plus DT and history. 'I love the Black Death,' said cheery pupil.

'Behind the scenes they are pushing as much as they can but aren't making them feel that academics is the be all and end all,' reckoned parent.

'People say it's so competitive but I haven't found that in any way, shape or form.' Pupils agreed. 'So supportive about everything, in and out of lessons – may as well be my family,' said one.

If teaching is good – inevitable tutoring, with or without school's blessing, does go on – learning support is 'brilliant', says parent. Issues quickly identified, up to two sessions charged for but anything extra normally isn't. Academic support also there if needed. Currently some 54 pupils receive some form of learning support in prep school, with one-to-one, group lessons and in-class support. 'Really good at helping the ones who struggle as well as the ones at the top end,' said parent. 'Half of these have a diagnosed condition (dyslexia etc) while the others need a little help with spelling, writing and maths,' says the school.

Boarding: Boarders, from year 4, are up at 7am, lights out at 8.15pm for juniors, an hour later for the oldest. ('Sweet dreams' says the timetable.) No mobiles – payphone and email only. Weekly, flexi but no full boarding, so everyone goes home on Saturday afternoons. Fluctuating numbers mean, said some pupils, that they could be on their own. School qualifies this as 'not with their friends... they would never be on their own in a dorm.'

Parents couldn't fault the boarding organisation or the 'super energetic' staff who make it 'so much fun that everyone wants to board', though our girl guides (who hadn't seen boys' quarters before) lambasted perceived inequalities, refrain of 'We don't have that!' prompted by everything from bigger hanging spaces for clothes to bed frames (some metal in girls' dorms, 'which rattle'). Even the disinfectant-filled jar for boys' combs got an envious look...

The last word: While growth in the 1990s was helped by mergers with two other less successful establishments, school's continued success is not down to establishment credentials: plenty, including David Cameron's old prep, have failed to survive. Instead, it's about ensuring that excellent results aren't achieved at the expense of fun. 'A little piece of heaven,' said one parent. But definitely not a metaphor.

Christ Church Cathedral School

10

3 Brewer Street, Oxford, Oxfordshire OX1 1QW

01865 242561 | registrar@cccs.org.uk | www.cccs.org.uk

Ages: 3–13

Pupils: 152; Boarders: 21 choristers (from year 4)

Fees: Day £9,990 – £18,075; Boarding choristers £11,400 – £12,615 pa

Headmaster: Since 2014, Richard Murray BA MA PGCE. Educated at Bradfield College – a 'profoundly inspiring' experience which sparked his realisation that teaching was 'one of the most important things a person could do' – and Durham (English, history and philosophy). PGCE from Magdalene College Cambridge. Arrived at Christ Church after a 14-year stint at Teddies (10 as housemaster) to find a school with a 'lovely, warm atmosphere' – a palpable feeling that he has grasped and built upon. Staff and parents agree that 'kindness has come to the fore and filtered down the school' under his leadership. Has raised school's profile, as well as the aspirations of the senior pupils, and built academic focus and rigour to create 'a serious prep school'. Describes himself as a 'choral music junkie', just one of his cultural addictions; the other is reading (a passion evidently shared by the whole school).

Married with three sons; one at Magdalen College School, one off to Harrow where Mr Murray's wife teaches classics, and another at Orley Farm School.

Entrance: Majority of day boys fairly local and enter from nursery or reception in a steady stream until year 3. A handful of girls in nursery. Assessment by participation in class for younger boys and academic tests for the older years. Cathedral choristers often (although not always) come from further afield and generally join in year 4, frequently having participated in one of school's 'chorister for a day' events and been bitten by the bug. From there they are required to pass a voice trial and academic assessment. One parent made the point that even with the necessary skill set in hand, it is imperative for cathedral choristers to be 'kind, generous, easygoing and from a stable family background' due to the pressures of being part of such a small, hard-working boarding community ('it can have a negative tidal wave effect if not'). Full boarding for 'made up' cathedral choristers compulsory from year 5.

Exit: At 13 boys to a range of day and boarding schools including d'Overbroeck's, Our Lady's Abingdon, Magdalen College School, Abingdon and St Edward's, Oxford. Also to Eton, Shrewsbury, Cokethorpe, Wellington College and The Oratory School. Cathedral choristers generally win music scholarships or exhibitions, many with generous bursaries to boot. Non-music scholarships on the up – school now has a dedicated master in charge – although some parents commented that, when it comes to sports awards, success is driven by them. Twelve scholarships in 2021.

Our view: Tucked away in a historic corner of Oxford, linked to the college itself by a small courtyard garden and under the imposing gaze of Christ Church Cathedral just over the road. Born from Henry VIII's charter of 1546 which established the education of eight boy choristers and a master for the cathedral. Very much an urban school – and a totally different proposition to its local competitors with their vast acreage, muddy knee ethos and 'something for everyone' approach. Every available nook and cranny used and most drenched in history; buildings include the original Tudor residence of Cardinal Wolsey. Newer additions include a bright new classroom block and drama studio named for old boy (composer) William Walton. The net result is a cosy warren of surprisingly spacious and unsurprisingly characterful classrooms, labs and play areas.

School's raison d'être is to supply the cathedral with its choristers and although this absolutely pervades the school we didn't get the feeling that it defines it

Recent renovation programme has given school a bright, cheerful feel and there's not a tatty corner, chipped skirting board or malodorous dorm in sight. Outside space would be top of boys' wish lists if they could wave a magic wand, but although playing fields are not on site, they're just a short walk away and – overlooked by the dreaming spires of Magdalen and Christ Church – are more than worth the journey. Adventure play equipment recently added to the school's courtyards for use at break time, but there's no chance of muddy knees outside of games periods.

School's raison d'être is to supply the cathedral with its choristers and although this absolutely pervades the school we didn't get the feeling that it defines it; one parent commented that it runs almost like 'two parallel schools'. Pupils fall into one of three camps: cathedral choristers, a minority group of up to 20 boys in years 4 to 8; Worcester choristers, day boys selected to be part of the Worcester College choir (approximately another 20, viewed by many to have 'the best of both worlds'); and the remaining cohort of around 110 boys who have varying degrees of musical interest or, occasionally, none at all (although in the main 'music is just what you do,' says head, adding that there are 'more peripatetic music lessons per week than there are pupils'). All benefit from the school's bijoux size and its 'tailored education – our size is the clue to everything'.

Cathedral choristers start their commitment aged 8, when they join school as weekly boarding 'probationers'. From year 5 they operate as professionals, singing in up to four services almost every weekend, including religious holidays such as remembrance, Easter and Christmas when they stay in school until they have sung both at matins and the eucharist services (games socks hung up on Christmas Eve and filled by matrons a lovely touch and 'loads of fun and games' in the lead up). Demanding rehearsal (up to three hours a day) and performance schedule means no exeats but there are 'out' weekends where they can go home from Friday afternoon until Saturday afternoon. We arrived for our visit wondering if it was a somewhat niche existence for boys of such a tender age, and left at the end of the day convinced that the discipline, patience and concentration instilled in them during the course of their time as a chorister ('so often lacking these days,' pointed out head) would set the right kind of boy up for life. With all musical commitments taking place outside of curriculum time, though, it's a rarefied existence and not for the faint of heart. With a requirement to study two further instruments (compulsory piano and one orchestral) on top of choir commitments, academic studies, sport and other selected activities (one chorister parent told us his son had a total of just 60 minutes' unscheduled time a week), boys' hearts need to be absolutely entrenched in their music and the journey needs to be driven by them alone in order to be a happy and successful one. International tours during school holidays are part and parcel (recently China and USA) and boys are constantly photographed by tourists as they process to the cathedral in their Tudor-style caps and gowns. Too much pressure and

What better way to incorporate all the languages spoken at the school than by learning carols in as many as possible, even Korean

responsibility? For an average boy, undoubtedly. But the choristers we met were extraordinarily mature and self-assured for their years ('10 going on 19,' said one parent – our thoughts exactly), although still with broad smiles, tousled hair, wonky ties and the occasional untied shoelace. Their outstanding achievements infuse the entire school: 'All our pupils aspire to that excellence in whatever they do,' says head, and school aims to relieve pressure when the heat is on at the cathedral.

Seamless transition into reception for littlies from the idyllic nursery setting, with parents praising the teaching that 'borders on individual tuition' in tiny classes (seven in reception when we visited). Trad curriculum, with French and Latin in the languages department, plus now Spanish and Greek as clubs. And what better way to incorporate all the languages spoken at the school than by learning carols in as many as possible – even Korean? 'We like to celebrate diversity,' says school. Teachers are 'most brilliant' and 'fantastic', say parents – particularly head's newer appointments. Regular off-timetable themed days, recently focusing on WWI with an animals-at-war workshop, trench digging and an insight into the German side of the conflict. Proximity to Oxford's wealth of offerings maximised with trips and outings, and visits from fascinating academics are the norm. Programming recently introduced to curriculum and IT, French, art, DT and games all specialist taught from reception. Reasoning on curriculum in year 5 to ensure boys' readiness for ISEB pre-test. With 10 per class, 'they have to knuckle down and can't get lost,' say parents – some of whom (delightedly) report dramatic turnarounds in academic achievement having moved their son from larger preps or state primaries: 'Christ Church picks up their potential.' Head says success is due to the 'family atmosphere – we really know the boys.' Those at top of academic heap are sometimes working up to two years ahead of their age. School experienced in managing mild SpLD and makes good provision for a variety of SEN children, with a full-time SENCo plus three TAs who are assigned where needed.

Atmosphere 'not testosterone-fuelled' – boys participate in two games afternoons a week. Cricket and football fight for top popularity ranking depending on who you speak to (cricket: the head; football: everyone else) and boys also play rugby. The beauty of school's size is that everyone who wants to can play on a team and often it's whole year groups rather than just an elite group that get on the school minibus hoping for glory at inter-school tournaments. Although some parents feel that their boys are often outclassed on the sports field by larger schools, results are respectable considering the limited number of boys from which to choose; the CCCS A team will sometimes play others' B or C team to ensure a fair match. One dedicated full-time games coach, now supported by a part-time colleague (a professional football coach) and some 'very solid' members of the academic faculty, but families with the mindset that boys, like puppies, need to be rigorously exercised daily, should probably look outside of school for their sporting fix. Clubs take place as part of the school day. Real tennis hugely popular, as is chess, which is played 'seriously' and to a very high standard. The 'herd energy' of the choristers also drives excellence in musical performances by orchestras, bands, choirs and groups for every instrument going. An art room festooned with props and canvases and DT lab homed in a charming former stable block testify that the creative child is well catered for and although there's no drama on curriculum, thespians are kept busy with bespoke plays often written by head of drama with particular pupils in mind for key roles.

Renewed focus on pastoral care recently: 'It's much better organised now,' says head. 'Well used' counsellor visits one day a week and staff are all made aware of children on the red or amber lists who may need extra pastoral support or just a close eye. Boys understand the disciplinary code and in the main commit only minor transgressions, the result being conduct cards to be carried for a week. Bullying a rarity but relationships between boarders can occasionally become 'explosive' due to the intensity of their living and working relationships. Older boys noticeably nurture and mentor the younger. Houses named after dignitaries associated with the school: Carroll, Wolsey and Sayers. Fiercely fought house competitions include enterprise day, music, sports, merits and prizes and, as culmination, the Dean's Cup. Parent association reportedly 'a lovely group and very organised'.

Boarding: Formerly down-at-heel boarding accommodation now sparkles with pristine paintwork, funky lighting and squidgy sofas and a delightful common room, packed with musical instruments, has a stunning dual aspect of Christ Church College. Pool table hosts 'hotly contested' tournament. Pianos litter the school – an antique Steinway positioned unceremoniously at the top of a back stairwell just par for the course. Food has reportedly 'improved a lot' too and boarders look forward to the weekend chef who whips up 'beautifully presented' fare.

Money matters: Cathedral covers generous portion (sometimes 100 per cent) of choristers' fees as well as associated international tours. Cardinal's Scholarship for up to three year 3s who are expected to achieve well academically.

The last word: With boys from all backgrounds, many from hard-working, dual-income families, plus a range of cultural origins (more than half are fluent in another language), Christ Church offers what the head calls a 'unique educative experience' that sets it apart from the other local options. One parent described it as 'really normal and grounded with just the right set of values' – we agree. For an affable chap who would benefit from life in a tight knit community with intensely focused academics, provided he can either fulfil his sporting ambitions outside of school or has a limited need for such rambunctious frolics, then Christ Church might just fit the bill.

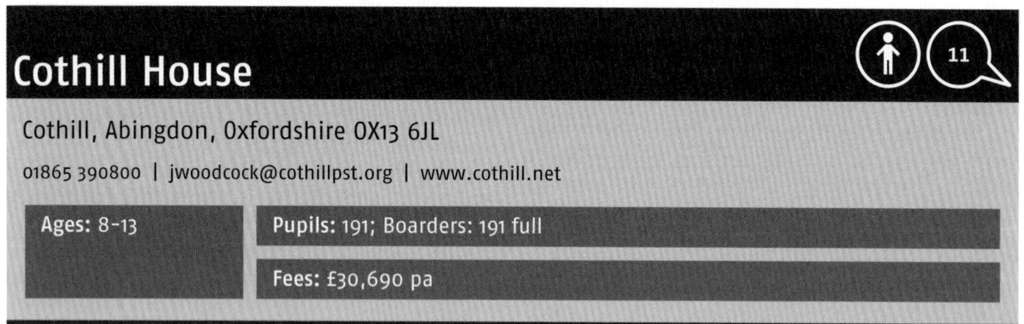

Cothill House

Cothill, Abingdon, Oxfordshire OX13 6JL

01865 390800 | jwoodcock@cothillpst.org | www.cothill.net

Ages: 8–13

Pupils: 191; Boarders: 191 full

Fees: £30,690 pa

Headmaster: Since 2011, Duncan Bailey (40s). A natural leader, Mr Bailey bears a slightly Waugh-esque CV at a time when increasing numbers of independent school heads arrive armed with MBAs in educational management and the like. Educated at Cothill and Eton, he read French at Manchester and German at the University of Vienna. Had planned to become a Jerry McGuire-style sports agent, but 'fell into teaching' games and then French at Eton. Was Directeur of Cothill's Château de Sauveterre for eight years before returning to his Cothill roots as headmaster.

'This is my school,' Mr Bailey told us, making plain that his own reputation is nailed to the mast of this very special school. Still takes a schoolboy's pleasure in a hard-fought game of table tennis or a summer evening of pyjama cricket. Candid. Genuine. Speaks from the heart. Is guided in all he does by the simple awareness that 'they only have one opportunity to be 10-year-old boys'. When we asked if pupil guides might show us around the school, Mr Bailey invited us to select any two boys at random. It is rare, if not unique, for a head to have such confidence and pride in each and every one of his pupils.

Wife Maria, originally from Austria, is head of boarding, pastoral matters and TLC. 'Home' for couple and their two teenage daughters is in France.

Entrance: Academically quite broad; socially quite narrow. It has recently begun offering custom-made bursaries from year 5 for 'talented, deserving' boys. In exceptional circumstances, year 4 bursaries are available. A 20 per cent Forces discount comes in handy for many families. Boys typically enter in year 4 or 5, but can join at (almost) any age and, frankly, any term (although the school recommends September or April). All children are assessed via a gentle and informal process ensuring they will thrive at Cothill and enjoy all that is on offer.

Fifty per cent of parents live or work in London, 30 per cent hail from elsewhere in the UK (a good chunk local), 20 per cent from abroad, mainly China, Thailand, Spain, Nigeria and Russia. EAL available for non-native English speakers, but boys still must be fluent before arriving – though even here, the very occasional exception is made.

Exit: Seventy per cent to Radley, Harrow, Eton, Sherborne, Winchester and St Edward's, with a strong scholarship record. Marlborough, Stowe and Oundle also feature. Some grumbles from parents that the school is overly fixated on trad boys' boarding schools at the expense of excellent co-ed options. No one leaves at 11. The school's superb and phenomenally informative website publishes over seven years of leavers' destinations.

Our view: Plonked deep in the heart of the British private school heartland: nine other independent schools reside within a 10-minute drive – and that's without entering nearby Oxford. So what makes Cothill stand out? It's traditional, but never stuffy. Posh, but down to earth. Low profile locally, but well known to the cognoscenti. Proudly full-boarding, but surprisingly flexible. 'There's no hierarchy in the school,' a beaming parent told us, 'and that includes among the staff.'

We arrived at break to find ourselves in a sea of tousle-haired mini-Prince-Harrys – mainly British, but with a good mix of international pupils: sparkling-eyed, chatty, polite... a bit muddy. They struck us as unspoilt boys who, we hear, agonise over how best to spend their weekly stipend of £1.10 at the school grub shop and are quick to help one another. Main building is a large country house with later additions nestled in 26 acres of grounds, playing fields and woodland. Cothill Fen conservation area is on the doorstep. Sports and leisure facilities include a 15-metre indoor pool, six all-weather tennis courts, a nine-hole golf course, and a somewhat shabby, albeit well used squash-court-cum-table-tennis room. The school's 150th birthday in 2020 kicks off a campaign to fund a long-coveted new sports hall.

Cothill takes in a slightly wider ability range than some similar schools, but do not mistake this breadth for a lack of academic excellence. Boys are set for maths and English from the start – no pussyfooting around this. A scholarship stream firms up from year seven. Small class sizes throughout. The head takes quite a lot of trouble to hire inspirational teachers who are not too precious to muck in. 'We're looking for role models – that's more important than their qualifications on paper.' Parents gushed to us about the teachers, calling them 'amazing' and 'approachable'.

The recently refurbished science area stands out among mostly standard classrooms. Head of science is reputed to have once been the youngest member of the Magic Circle, and there's certainly some hands-on, if not sleight of hand, teaching. This includes quite a bit of dissecting: 'Boys like to bring in things that they've shot,' he explains in passing. Superb computing facilities are on offer, but no hand-held devices allowed except Kindles, no mobile phones, and no social networking. 'We don't communicate with the boys by email; we go and find them,' smiles the head. Boys in the top two years have Chromebooks for school work which they carry from lesson to lesson. SEN support two or three times per week is available for learning difficulties, but also provides maths acceleration for the clever-clogs.

We admired the way excellence is accommodated and nurtured here, even if this sometimes requires bending the school norms. At the time of our visit, two gifted pupil musicians were allowed to miss Saturday school in order to be taught at a London music college. Similarly, the school carves out time for a hotshot tennis player to receive 17 hours of extracurricular tennis training every week.

The star draw is Sauveterre, Cothill's château near Toulouse, where all year 7 boys spend a term immersing themselves in French language, culture, food and sunshine

Sport runs like a wick through the flame of the Cothill experience. There are games of some kind, at every level, every day. When asked what sort of boy might not be suited to Cothill, Mr Bailey paused before replying, 'a boy for whom playing sport is a chore', but he seemed doubtful that such a being truly exists. The range of sport on offer is immense. If the main games, rugby, football, hockey and cricket, are not your thing, then perhaps golf, polo or the climbing wall? Tennis is a particular strength with the LTA supporting provision and five Oxfordshire-area coaches teaching at the school. As well as having its own nine-hole golf course, the school is forging a relationship with a private golf course. Rock-climbing teacher visits every Thursday. Ski team is the current IAPS champion.

Superb after-supper activity programme offers fun, from cooking to canasta. The school now employs a head of outdoor activities (and boasts the slightly cringeworthy strapline 'HQ for boys' adventures'). New, flash electronic scoreboard doubles as a screen for outdoor film nights. 'Tree Tops', an enormous elevated adventure playground, provides fun, especially for the younger ages.

All this outdoors activity does not come at the expense of more refined pursuits. Some 80 per cent of boys learn an instrument, from bagpipes to bassoon, taught by 19 visiting music teachers (early morning practice runs from 7-7.45am). All the main classical instruments are on offer at a high standard, but rock and jazz deserve a special shout out – nice to see them given respect, rehearsal time and performance opportunities. The Rockhill Music Festival – Cothill's version of Glastonbury – rounds out the summer term. Plenty of art, pottery and DT – all open on weekends. Woodwork still taught by former copper and permanent fixture 'PC' (who taught Mr Bailey here back in the day). Boys 'can make literally anything' our guides assured us gravely. Junior, middle and senior plays are part of the lesson timetable, so all boys are involved. Two poetry competitions each year.

The star draw though has to be Sauveterre, Cothill's unique French château outpost near Toulouse, where all year 7 boys spend a whole term immersing themselves in French language, culture, food and sunshine. Parents evangelise about the benefits of this, not only where tipping the balance at CE is concerned but in terms of an unforgettable life experience.

Boarding: Years 4 and 5 may now go home after games on Saturday and return on Monday morning if they wish. School doesn't see this as a dilution of the boarding ethos, but rather an expansion: 'We want to make it easier for those full boarding families who aren't quite ready.' Boarding accommodation for ages 8 to 12 is based in the main school building, with the youngest children under the direct care of Mr and Mrs Bailey and a houseparent. Dorm rooms compete for a coveted weekly tidiness award. Year 8 now reside regally in 'Bowlers', a swish outpost across the games field where boys say they develop a bit

The headmaster still takes a schoolboy's pleasure in a hardfought game of table tennis or a summer evening of pyjama cricket

of independence. Even in this new facility, boys sleep in (roomy) dorms of up to 12 beds. 'Tis the Cothill way! Twenty minutes' reading time for all each night; reading prefects may read to the younger boys. Homesickness – usually brief if it occurs at all – is dealt with sensitively and boys may phone home whenever they like. Mental health issues are addressed by the school counsellor (unusual to find in a prep school) and Cothill has been able to support boys with a range of challenges.

The last word: Cothill is something of leap of faith and might not suit families keen on the more bureaucratic trappings of 21st-century school life. Health and safety are observed, but not worshipped, and much is accomplished on trust. For those it suits, the school provides a magical five years and a superb underpinning for all future education.

Downe House School

12

Cold Ash, Thatcham, Berkshire RG18 9JJ

01635 200286 | registrar@downehouse.net | www.downehouse.net

Ages: 11–18

Pupils: 585; Boarders: 561 full

Fees: Day £31,305: Boarding £42,090 pa

Headmistress: Since 1997, Emma McKendrick BA PGCE FRSA (50s). Educated at Bedford High School (now Bedford Girls' School) and then read German and Dutch at the University of Liverpool. She spent a year working in a German school during her degree and found she loved teaching so decided to do a PGCE at Birmingham. Her first teaching job was at the Royal High School Bath, where she taught German, ran the boarding house and became head of the sixth form. Later promoted to deputy head, she was appointed as head at the remarkably young age of 29. Four years later she became head of Downe House.

Her office is stylish and calm, right in the heart of things, with views across the school. 'It gives me a real sense of what's going on,' she says. The spirit and ethos of Downe House haven't changed in her two-plus decades at the helm. 'It's modernised and moved forward – and I hope it will always continue to do so – but the spirit and ethos are very much as they've always been, with the focus on the individual and on the community,' she says. 'They are the two key things that have always been part of the school's DNA.'

The head is firmly committed to girls' schools. 'It gives girls the freedom to grow up at their own pace,' she says. She knows Downe House girls well, sees new pupils individually after they have received their first set of grades and has one-to-one meetings with older girls to talk about subject choices and their day-to-day lives. Staff are glowing in their praise. 'Emma is the reason I'm here,' one teacher told us. 'She is the most amazing head. She doesn't just know the girls' names; she knows their pets' names.' Parents are equally effusive. 'She is understated and incredibly calm but she is very forward thinking and full of compassion and belief that everyone can achieve,' said one mother. Another commented on her sense of humour and told us: 'She's very good at finding out what's going on in a very subtle way.'

Her husband is a HR director and they have two sons. They live in a house on the school site. The head's interests outside school include spending time with family and friends, theatre, cinema and travel.

Entrance: Mostly at 11, 13 and 16. Around 50 girls join at 11 and 35 at 13 (a few start at 12), arriving from up to 200 preps and primaries. A year prior to entry girls attend an assessment day, which includes activities like drama and DT, team-building workshops, an academic test and an interview with the head. Conditional offers are made after a successful assessment day and girls then take either CE or an academic scholarship. For 13+ entry standard assessment point is year 8 but early assessments are also offered in year 6 and year 7. Unconditional offers are made after the assessment day and CE is used for setting purposes.

For sixth form entry girls take three exam papers – two subjects they are already studying or wish to study at A level and a general paper. Applicants need a minimum of seven grade 6s at IGCSE/GCSE, preferably with grades 7-9 in subjects they want to take at A level. Successful candidates are then interviewed by the head and head of sixth form.

Exit: A few leave after GCSE, usually for co-ed sixth forms or day schools. At 18, virtually all to higher education, including art colleges and music conservatoires. Four to Oxbridge in 2021; others to UCL, Durham, Exeter, Warwick, Edinburgh, LSE, Imperial, KCL, Courtauld Institute of Art, Birmingham Conservatoire and Central St Martins. Two medics in 2021. Up to 15 pupils a year head to university in US, Canada and Europe – recently to Berklee College of Music, Georgetown, University of Southern California, Boston University, UCLA, University of North Carolina and Rhode Island School of Design (all USA), Glion, Switzerland, and University of Toronto, Canada.

Latest results: In 2021, 89 per cent 9-7 at GCSE; 84 per cent A*/A at A level (98 per cent A*-B). In 2019 (the last year when exams took place), 84 per cent 9-7 at GCSE; 61 per cent A*/A at A level (86 per cent A*-B).

Teaching and learning: All the usual subjects offered at A level, as well as business studies, classical civilisation, economics and politics. We saw some exciting teaching – a year 10 history class discussing what they'd learned about Lenin's New Economic Policy and a sparky year 8 physics class learning about pressure in liquids. Everyone does French from the start and from year 8 girls can take a second language – Chinese, German, Italian or Spanish. Most girls take all three sciences at GCSE.

The school has introduced a raft of inspiring initiatives including yoga classes, scented diffusers in the boarding houses and puppy therapy to help girls unwind

Blissfully small classes, with teachers highly praised by parents. 'The head has a very loyal band of teaching staff,' one told us. 'There isn't a huge turnover but the teaching definitely isn't stodgy.' Effective tutor system, with pupils seeing their tutors one-to-one every week. Sixth formers can choose their tutors, all of whom are trained to advise on higher education. The school is a Microsoft Surface Showcase school, one of 51 schools in the country. Years 7 to 10 pupils have their own Microsoft Surface – 'It makes learning fun,' one girl told us.

The Château de Sauveterre in south-west France is home to their school in France – lower fourth girls get a term there in non-Covid times. A sister school is opening in Muscat. Parents describe the experience as 'the jewel in the crown of Downe House' while a pupil says, 'You don't only improve academically, you also make close friends.' As well as that, the expanded Global Schools Exchange Programme gives girls the chance to take part in exchanges with 16 partner schools across five continents.

Learning support and SEN: Five-strong learning skills team offers one-to-one support for pupils with specific learning difficulties, such as dyslexia, dyspraxia and attention deficit disorder.

The arts and extracurricular: A wealth of musical ensembles to join – everything from classical orchestras and choirs to jazz bands and an a capella group. There's even a Downe House young musician of the year competition. Drama opportunities include house drama and musical theatre competitions, large productions (including Billy Elliot complete with wire-flying) and theatre trips. Dance is hugely popular, with chances to do ballet, contemporary, hip hop, tap and more. Art is inspiring, housed in a slightly down-at-heel building the girls love. As well as art and design, textiles and DT are offered at both GCSE and A level. Photography on offer at A level.

Plenty of opportunities outside the academic curriculum too – DofE, Young Enterprise and the elective programme, where year 10 girls get the opportunity to develop lateral thinking skills and scholarly independence and discuss complex ideas. Around 12 sixth formers do global internships around the world each summer. Sixth formers can take an introductory certificate in food and wine run by Leiths Academy.

Sport: Traditionally a lacrosse school (lots of girls have represented the country at lax over the years) but they are very good at hockey too. For keen tennis players there's a tennis development programme (more than 350 girls take lessons every week). Other sports include netball, swimming, squash, gymnastics, athletics, dance, cross-country and trampolining. Sport played almost every day, with matches on Wednesdays and Saturdays. Great facilities, including playing fields galore, tennis courts, huge sports hall and a 25-metre indoor swimming pool. The school promotes a 'sport for all' ethos. Sixth formers still have to do sport but they can choose options like yoga, aerobics, spinning and golf if they wish. A girl recently introduced tag rugby and staff say: 'If a girl wants to do a particular sport we'll go out of our way to try and help them.'

Boarding: All but a handful of local day girls are full boarders. Eleven boarding houses – four lower school houses (including Veyrines) for years 7 and 8, five upper school houses (years 9 to 11) and two sixth form houses.

Parents particularly praise boarding in the lower school, telling us that girls who start at Downe House at 11 'get a very precious two years'. For most lower school girls it's their first experience of boarding and staff are in frequent contact with parents. 'We're in constant communication,' a housemistress told us. 'We feel it's a partnership.' Each house produces a weekly newsletter and tweets house news and views too – great for parents to keep up to date with what's going on. The lower school house we visited was charming, providing a sheltered introduction to boarding life. Wholesome dorms, with family photographs and cuddly toys. Lots to do at weekends – including bike rides, cake-baking and tree-climbing, trips out and Sunday breakfast in the house, when girls are allowed to come down for croissants and pancakes in their pyjamas.

'Emma McKendrick is the most amazing head. She doesn't just know the girls' names; she knows their pets' names'

Some closed weekends but there are also fixed long weekends when girls can go home. Downe House girls socialise with boys from neighbouring schools. Scottish dancing at Elstree School (a prep near Newbury) for younger girls and events, dinner parties and debates with boys from Radley, Eton, Harrow and Winchester for the older ones.

Ethos and heritage: Founded as an all-girls boarding school in 1907 by Olive Willis, the first headmistress. Originally located in Down House, Charles Darwin's home in the village of Downe, Kent, it moved to its present home in Berkshire in 1922. Miss Willis wanted the new school to be in the countryside, on a hill and yet within reach of a town and a railway station – so a house called The Cloisters was perfect. Situated on a high ridge in the village of Cold Ash, four miles from Newbury, it was built during the First World War for an order of Spanish nuns who named it the School of Silence. The historic cloisters, with white walls, arches and terracotta pantiles, and the chapel remain but there are many new buildings – boarding houses and teaching blocks – nestling in the woodland and neatly planted gardens.

The swish, new Murray Centre (named after old girl Dame Rosemary Murray, the first female vice-chancellor of the University of Cambridge) sits in the heart of the 110-acre campus, complete with a new library, collaborative learning areas, seminar room, performance space, gallery area and coffee shop. It's a popular meeting place; when we visited girls were eagerly queueing up for hot drinks, all served in eco-friendly bamboo cups. The ultra-modern library has stunning views of the woods and we particularly liked a display of books that the staff were reading. 'There's a big focus on reading,' our guides told us.

The uniform has recently been updated. Sixth formers wear a black suit (with skirt or trousers) and a shirt of their choice while younger girls look smart in green blazers, pale blue shirts and tartan skirts.

All girls get the chance to take on leadership roles. In the sixth form a head senior (Downe

Cheam School

House head girl) and deputy, plus seniors (prefects) and ambassadors and there are leadership opportunities for younger girls too. The sixth form houses are run like university hall of residences. 'There's more freedom,' a girl told us approvingly. Sixth form programme includes lectures on everything from personal and online safety to nutrition, sleep, risk-taking and personal finance. Pupils told us they like being in a single-sex school. As one girl said: 'It's easy to concentrate without boy-drama.'

Wholesome dorms, with family photographs and cuddly toys. Lots to do at weekends – including bike rides, cake-baking and tree-climbing, trips out and Sunday breakfast in the house, when girls can come down for croissants and pancakes in their pyjamas

Famous alumnae include the aforementioned Rosemary Murray, Geraldine James, Clare Balding, philosopher Mary Midgley, Elizabeth Bowen, author Priscilla Napier, Sophie Conran, Lulu Guinness, Miranda Hart, broadcaster Fru Hazlitt, barrister Hannah Wright, the pioneering civil servant and Oxford don Jenifer Hart, archaeologist Aileen Fox – the list goes on and on.

Pastoral care, inclusivity and discipline: The school has clearly put a lot of thought into pastoral care, educating pupils about issues like consent, pornography and social media. Parents describe the standard of pastoral care as 'second to none', with girls encouraged to talk to tutors, housemistresses, school nurses, matrons and peer mentors. Two school counsellors – so there's always one on site. A mother described the school's female chaplain as 'one of the most outstanding people I have ever met' while another said the school is 'very cosy but doesn't wrap girls up in cotton wool'.

Wellbeing is key to the girls and staff and the school has introduced a raft of inspiring initiatives – yoga classes, copies of The Positive Bullet Diary for pupils, scented diffusers in the boarding houses and puppy therapy to help girls unwind. 'It's the girls' home,' says the boarding deputy, 'and it's really important that they feel secure. They need to get good grades but we want our girls to become women who are comfortable in their own skin and who won't be afraid to stand up for what they believe in.' Sanctions for smoking, alcohol and drugs very clearly set out in pupils' handbook. Few discipline problems although the head admits that the girls, like young people everywhere, test boundaries and inevitably get things wrong sometimes. Two areas she worries about for this generation are vaping and social media – and pupils are educated about these. Speakers like independent safety expert Karl Hopwood and the Digital Sisters talk to the girls about the importance of maintaining 'a healthy digital lifestyle'. Tips offered on making screens less enticing by switching them to black and white, turning off WhatsApp and Snapchat notifications and useful mindfulness apps.

Zero tolerance to bullying. 'It's something we take very seriously,' says the boarding deputy. 'When you know pupils really well you can see any changes in behaviour. The girls can contact me or the head at any time.' School has clear rules about mobile phones. 'We take a staged approach,' a housemistress told us. Year 7s aren't allowed their phones for the first two and a half weeks of school while year 8 girls can't have their phones outside the boarding houses.

Lower and upper school girls eat all their meals in the lovely main school dining room and say the food is good. We particularly liked the round tables for six, all with tablecloths and aiming to encourage girls to take time over meals. There's a separate dining room for the sixth form.

Pupils and parents: There isn't a Downe House type ('Downe House girls are spirited in the best possible way,' says the boarding deputy). Girls come from all over the UK and beyond, with a number of daughters of alumnae. Around 25 per cent, some expats, others from mainland China, Hong Kong, Thailand, Malaysia, Nigeria, Japan, Kenya, Switzerland, Italy and Spain. 'It's fairly diverse,' says the head. 'The health of the community is having a whole variety of characters. The girls need to enjoy community living but they can be quiet and reflective as much as extrovert.'

Money matters: Scholarships offered for academic ability, art, sport, music and drama (they don't carry any remission in fees). Full and partial means-tested bursaries are available at all points of entry and depend on family circumstances.

The last word: A delightful full girls' boarding school that has definitely moved with the times. Downe House is an impressive blend of traditional and modern and produces spirited, able and go-ahead girls who achieve good academic results and go on to make a significant contribution to the world. As a parent told us: 'Downe House has an exciting vibe.'

Dragon School

Bardwell Road, Oxford, Oxfordshire OX2 6SS

01865 315405 | admissions@dragonschool.org | www.dragonschool.org

Ages: 4–13

Pupils: 793; **Boarders:** 160 full and weekly; 90 flexi

Fees: Day £16,719 – £22,419; Boarding £32,793 pa

Head: Since September 2021, Emma Goldsmith, previously head of Winchester House School. Warm and stylish. Born and educated in Durham before reading English at Manchester. As a fourth generation teacher she was at first adamant 'teaching was the last thing I was going to do'. Happily, her rebellious instincts were soon quashed, and she landed first teaching job at Oakham where she threw herself into coaching netball. Later, recruited to help set up sixth form girls' boarding at Rugby. Fell in love with Bloxham School when visiting for a sports fixture and was hired to manage the transition to co-ed, including the first girls' boarding house. Ended up as deputy head, and her husband (with whom she has four children) is still there as director of rugby and a maths teacher. She is an ISI inspector and vice chair of ISEB.

Entrance: First come, first served in early years. Register as early as you can, school says 'about a year in advance'. Usually full, with a waiting list, but Oxford is a dynamic city 'so it's worth going on'. Prospective parents urged to visit: 'We really like to meet them.' While we were there several hopefuls with babes in arms were waiting in reception to do just that. Boarding places possibly slightly easier to come by. Non-selective-ish but does assess English and maths to ensure candidates can cope.

Exit: Near: St Edward's, Oxford, plus Abingdon School and Magdalen College School (boys), Oxford High, Headington and St Helen and St Katharine (girls). Far: Boarding schools including Eton, Harrow, Winchester, Radley, Cheltenham Ladies', Wycombe Abbey. Co-eds – Wellington, Marlborough, Stowe, Rugby. Big numbers, big names and plenty of scholarships too. Of those, in 2021, St Edward's, Eton and Rugby were most popular. Majority stay until age 13, 'relatively few' girls leave for day schools at 11.

Our view: This is one of the largest preps in the country with almost 800 pupils, more than any of its neighbouring senior independents. And yet, somehow, it doesn't feel like it. Established as a boys' school in 1877 by a group of Oxford dons, it moved to its present north Oxford site in 1894. Enviable grounds run down to the river Cherwell, 'but we're not allowed to go further than those trees,' said our guides, pointing. 'Mollycoddling!' Old Dragons huff and puff as they reminisce about learning to swim there.

Went fully co-ed in the 1970s and really feels it, although boys still outnumber girls, especially for boarding. Original name was Oxford Preparatory School, became known as Dragon in honour of St George – one of the principal founders was a Mr George. And those dragons are everywhere, etched into glass, wrought into ironwork and decorating the floor of the dining room. School motto is appropriately fiery: 'Arduus ad Solem' (Reach for the sun).

Fierce rules about mobile phones and other electronic devices. Pupils are resigned. Parents can't believe their luck

Average class size is 18, subject setting for science, maths and French. Parents told us that school manages setting flexibly and makes great efforts to mitigate academic divisiveness: 'The atmosphere is not competitive and boasting about good grades is frowned on.' However, this view wasn't unanimous and we heard some grumbles about setting in maths in years 7 and 8 (by this time there are nine maths sets). Other parents we questioned about this were happy with the status quo although there were a few mutterings about 'lack of aspiration' in lower sets. School acknowledges some further clarification is required and says it has already improved information about its subject setting policy in response to parents' concerns and tried to make the process more transparent, adding, 'Open communication is very important, parents are given staff email addresses and are encouraged to contact them directly with any concerns or questions.'

All do Latin from year 5, school's eight-strong classics dept has designed its own teaching materials; Greek offered years 6 and 7. We enjoyed sitting in on some very active and diverting lessons, including a team vocab game in Latin, a year 6 English class who were looking at Betjeman poems (he was a pupil here) and a year 4 reasoning class who were all on their feet doing some pretty complex numerical sequencing which involved jumping up and sitting down (completely beyond us, but it looked great fun). In DT construction was underway of a wooden boat to go on the river. Prototypes had already been tested: 'Everyone's sank apart from ours!' Library was full to bursting with an author visit, we passed by twice and he was still going (with a different year group), keeping his audience in stitches. Apparently, a pupil had won him for the day in a national competition. Did he know what he was taking on? A gig at the Dragon isn't for the faint of stamina.

Library was full to bursting with an author visit, and he was keeping his audience in stitches. Apparently, a pupil had won him for the day in a national competition

Learning support 'excellent', particular praise for the way they keep parents informed. Eight staff plus external specialists as necessary provide help for pupils with mild to moderate SEND; EAL also offered (around 30 pupils receive this). School says it looks for potential and takes a range of abilities, but the norm is 'above average'.

Saturday academic lessons recently replaced by 'DragonQUEST' for years 4 and 5, with 90 per cent take-up despite being optional; will extend up to year 8 in September 2021. Families choose from 22 different activities each led by a teacher, with activities as varied as paddle boarding, bike mechanics, visit to a working farm and a cultural walk around Oxford.

Teams fielded in a huge range of sports. Girls' hockey is on a high, the 1st XI were undefeated in 2018, as were the U13 A and B rugby teams. Dragon athletes also topped the medals table in the National Championships. Riverside location is great for sculling and school has its own regatta. There's a 25-metre swimming pool and Olympic-size Astro for hockey. Football and cricket for boys and girls. Teams play a whopping 900 fixtures a year and players are bussed off to away games on Wednesday afternoons; a couple of parents told us they thought it was sometimes a match too far: 'Two hours' travelling either side of a match is exhausting, they should restrict it to schools within an hour's drive away.' Sporting glory is the norm, rather than the exception – a win against Dragon is always cause for big celebrations at smaller preps!

Mass participation in music of all kinds to a very high standard, but facilities struck us as pretty cramped – dark, narrow corridors, particularly small practice rooms. Temporary classrooms ('pods') augment space and provide soundproof recording studios. Pupils don't seem to mind, telling us that competitions such as Battle of the Bands and house singing are 'fantastic'. Fundraising has begun for a new music school. Drama 'phenomenal', with plays, musicals, improvisation games and play writing opportunities for all. Around 150 pupils take LAMDA lessons. Leavers look forward to the 'A block' (year 4 upwards known as E-A blocks) end of term revue: 'We have a few songs and take the mickey out of teachers.'

Energetic charity fundraising – 'We're very into charities,' our guide assured us – reaches a peak with the Dragon Sale, a huge festive market held in December: 'There are stalls all over the school, it's amazing.' And it really is amazing, the last sale raised £169,000 for good causes (all family and children related) nominated by pupils. Raffle prizes donated by parents included use of a 10-person ski chalet (bids over £20,000). 'It's really the only time I've been aware of the income disparity here,' said one of our interviewees.

While traffic on Bardwell Road isn't heavy (except at pick-up and drop-off), the school day requires a fair bit of travel across it, hence watchful member of staff in a kind of sentry box. Even so, we thought some Dragons' road sense looked perhaps just a little blasé. Younger pupils do not cross unaccompanied and are escorted to and from houses. School is part of the Oxford Schools Bus Partnership but for some that's an extra expense too far.

Lunch is staggered, youngest eat first and classes sit with their form tutors. 'They don't run out of food, there's always enough to eat,' our guides said, favourites being lasagne and treacle tart. Apparently, lunch used to be 'a bit dodgy' but is now 'really nice' (previous head changed the catering arrangements in response to parent and pupil feedback). We certainly enjoyed a delicious creamy stroganoff. No clubs at lunchtime, they're all after school – cookery is 'really popular', as is judo; we liked the sound of 'Toast and Translation' (Latin club). Friday afternoon lecture programme, Spectrum, has a pretty impressive

Dragons everywhere – etched into glass, wrought into ironwork and decorating the floor of the dining room. School motto is 'Arduus ad Solem' (Reach for the sun)

line-up: 'There's no problem getting speakers (many from deep pool of illustrious former pupils) or audience questions,' says school. Day pupils can stay for tea and do homework until 6pm. Long-established exchange programmes with schools in New York and Tokyo sound pretty special.

Surprisingly low-tech, with fierce rules about mobile phones and other electronic devices ('We've held firm for many years'). No portable screens at all in boarding houses or in school (apart from in IT suites), iPads available but 'not the default'. Day pupils must hand their phones in at the lodge every morning. Boarders are allowed Kindles but must ask before they download material; Skype or Facetime used to contact parents with permission. 'It takes away the pressure,' we were told, 'and it encourages children to talk to each other. There's no social media, no comparing of latest devices. Everyone is in the same boat.' Pupils are resigned: 'I'd prefer to have my phone, but it's never been any different.' Parents can't believe their luck: 'My mum just loves it.'

School's founding values are kindness, courage and respect and it seemed a very friendly place to us. Pastoral system 'incredibly well-coordinated and responsive', house parents, teachers, tutors and a buddy system for younger children all mesh together to ensure that no one feels lost in the crowd: 'They handle integration of new pupils very well, the buddy system also fosters friendships between year groups.' A large team of gappies (most from Australia and South Africa) work as boarding assistants. Female members of staff are known as 'Ma', plus their surname; chaps used to be 'Pa' but are now 'Sir'.

There's a parent portal, lots of events for new parents and Saturday morning parent forums, but probably because it's mainly a boarding school, no PTA or class reps. This has clearly left some parents believing that their voices are not heard. School says it is looking at ways to improve this situation. Dragon parents are a pretty tough and diverse crowd and it's unlikely that school could please all of them all of the time. Nevertheless, even if the vast majority of parents are delighted (and that was overwhelmingly the case among those we spoke to), it looks like there's still room for improvement when it comes to communication and transparency (school doesn't disagree with this point). Any other criticisms? A couple of parents said they'd like some kind of senior schools event, 'choice can be a bit overwhelming' and a pupil declared, 'I would make the lost property system work better.'

The starry quality of its alumni network must make school reunions quite an occasion and many former pupils return to support fundraising events. Thespian Old Dragons alone could form their own branch in Hollywood: Hugh Laurie, Tom Hiddleston, Tom Hollander, Emma Watson, Dom Joly, Jack Whitehall. Big names in the literary world too including John Betjeman, James Runcie, Alain de Botton, William Fiennes, Nevil Shute, Nicholas Shakespeare, John Mortimer and Antonia Fraser. It's tempting to go on, but let's finish with just two more: Metropolitan Police Commissioner, Cressida Dick, and former London Mayor hopeful, Rory Stewart.

Boarding: Boarding from age 8, although only a few start this young. Boarding options are full, day (between one and four pre-arranged nights per week) and now, in response to parental demand, flexi (occasional nights arranged a few days in advance). Ten houses on either side of Bardwell Road, most single-sex but one co-ed for flexi/day boarders. All domestic scale with a home-from-home feel – guinea pigs and a bug hotel in the garden, lots of teddies and own duvets and a smell of baking rather than disinfectant. One Beano fan had papered his wall in covers! 'We try very hard to make it a family atmosphere,' said a houseparent and that's exactly what it felt like to us. New boarders are asked to agree house expectations, good behaviour is incentivised, points are awarded and add up to treats such as movies and hot chocolate. International boarders 'feel very welcome' and are encouraged to share their cultural traditions. Friends who are day pupils can come round: 'They're always intrigued.' Always '100 or so' boarders in at weekends to enjoy activities such as paintballing, laser tag and shopping in the Westgate Centre.

Money matters: Means-tested bursaries available from year 4.

The last word: Thus far we've held back from mining the fertile seam of dragon-related metaphors, but the force of nominative determinism is strong. The school does have a somewhat mythical status and we were keen to see the reality for ourselves. Big? Yes, but friendly and big-hearted, not scary. High-profile? Yes, but definitely not flashy or corporate. As for magic, there's always something magical about a really good school and the Dragon is no exception.

Eagle House School

Sandhurst, Berkshire GU47 8PH

01344 772134 | info@eaglehouseschool.com | www.eaglehouseschool.com

Ages: 3-13

Pupils: 383 (164 girls; 219 boys); Boarders: 60 (from year 3)

Fees: Day £6,750 – £19,275; Boarding £25,905 pa

Linked school: Wellington College, 532

Headmaster: Since 2006, Andrew Barnard BA (50s). Educated at Christ's Hospital and Sheffield University (archaeology). Joined Eagle House to teach English and history, becoming head of history before moving to Heath Mount School as housemaster and head of English, followed by deputy headship at Winchester House, then back to Eagle House as head. Ably assisted by wife Sarah who fulfils hands-on role as trad headmaster's spouse as well as teaching French and EAL. Their three adult children are all Old Wellingtonians and two have followed their parents into the teaching profession.

Relaxed, warm and highly personable; on the door every morning and visibly thrives on the hustle and bustle of a busy prep. Throws himself into the daily fray whether teaching history or playing an ugly sister in the annual staff panto. Has collected strength and depth around him during the course of his tenure with an outstanding staff that parents describe as 'seasoned, but not too seasoned'. Keen to keep school's independent identity and protect position as feeder to many schools, whilst acknowledging the obvious benefits of close relationship with Wellington College. Leads a 'welcoming community' where 'those who opt in, thrive'. School holidays see him heading to his home in France: 'We've been doing it up for twenty years – it's the most therapeutic thing.'

Entrance: Pre-prep: trial day and usually automatic progression to prep. Prep: trial day, copies of reports and a reference from current head. Prep relatively non-selective but pupils 'expected to be able to cope with the school's academic course'. New class added in year 5. Year 7 entrants are tested in English, maths and reasoning.

Exit: Around 65 per cent to Wellington College, making it the top feeder by some way. Head assures us that entry requirements are the same as for other preps but 'good discussions' take place when considering applicants and assessment day 'feels like a home match'. Bradfield, Eton, Lord Wandsworth College, Charterhouse, Wycombe Abbey, Radley also get solid numbers.

Our view: Nestled in woodland between Crowthorne and Sandhurst, school was founded in Hammersmith in 1820 and has been on current site since 1886. Owned by neighbouring Wellington College yet manages to avoid a corporate feel and – for now at least – successfully hangs on to its own identity. Around the main mock-Tudor school house, with its panelled entrance hall (complete with roaring fire on the day of our wintry visit, and setting for school's 'legendary' match teas), sit a number of additions. These vary in architectural style from ultra-modern (the Golden Eagle Centre, housing the drama studio and enviable sports hall, and the design lab with its robots, laser cutters and 3D printers) to tired portakabins (music centre and pool) – although head assures us that the end of these is in sight with plans afoot for a new music centre. Stunning modern library. We loved the maths classroom with writeable-on walls and swanky new science labs with their space-age work stations. A stroll past the pretty memorial garden leading to the quaint chapel with its stained-glass windows (see if you can guess which one was designed by a pupil) reminded us that despite all these whistles and bells we were still at a traditional prep school – albeit one that is not just moving with the times but ahead of them.

Delightful pre-prep department with outdoor spaces mirroring the classrooms within. Child-led teaching in the early years (recent question 'How do you ride a unicorn?' answered beautifully with the help of hobby horses): 'It's not the same old ideas coming out of the cupboard every year,' smiled one staff member, 'it keeps us fresh.' Amen to that. From nursery, children take turns to prepare snacks for the rest of the class and join school lunch in the (recently refurbished) main dining room. Pencil skills taught one-to-one and phonics and maths in small groups from reception – and what 5-year-old wouldn't want to start penning their first novel in the enchanting indoor 'writing den', draped in toile and festooned with fairy lights? Years 1 to 4 mainly class taught (class size max 20) and follow International Primary Curriculum, which 'finds common ground between rigour and enjoyment' and means subjects, other than English and maths, are taught thematically around topics such as chocolate or fashion ('brilliant,' say parents). Each topic has a 'wow' entry point (think chocolate workshop) and 'knowledge harvest' at the start to engage pupils and set the direction of learning. The 'exit point' often sees pupils' work showcased to parents.

School has released itself from the shackles of traditional CE, with years 5 to 8 benefiting from greater breadth under Curriculum 200 – 'a new, rich, robust, assessment-led curriculum that will furnish senior schools with a valuable portfolio of academic data,' according to school. All lessons an hour long ('it can be a bit hard to concentrate that long,' admitted pupils). First school we've ever visited where pupils decreed Latin their 'most fun' subject; 'science experiments in the dark' a close second.

Inviting 'extra learning' classroom is the hub for two full-time SEN staff who work with pupils with mild to moderate SpLD, in a combination of one-to-one and group work. Six hours a week spent in pre-prep supporting eg development of fine motor and social skills. One full-time EAL teacher.

Compulsory Saturday school now on alternate weeks, comprising two academic lessons followed by Golden Eagle activities which focus on either service in the community or teamwork and leadership; head 'very proud' of service ethos – an excellent example of school's 'joined-up thinking with Wellington'. We asked pupils of which of the holy prep school trinity – drama, music and sport – they were most proud. Drama was the hands-down winner: 'amazing' they chorused; 'it's the really cool thing to do here.' Inspirational head of drama 'really pushes us,' they told us. Parents say he doesn't mince his words and 'gives them a really hard time' when drawing the very best performance out of his cast members (the maestro himself told us 'we're not really trying to do a school show – it's got to be better than that – it's more about youth theatre'). Such pursuit of excellence draws auditionees in droves, with 150 pupils across the school signing up to audition for a recent production of Joseph – 55 of them gunning for main parts. Up to three productions in rehearsal at any one time, plus an annual trip to perform at the Edinburgh Fringe. LAMDA taught by Wellington's drama coach. Music also shines and is on curriculum to year 8. Ninety pupils are part of senior choir, and with a thrilling repertoire including rock, pop, gospel and world music – as well as international tours, most recently to Holland – we're not surprised. Some 85 per cent of cohort take peripatetic music lessons and showcase their talents at local care homes as part of the Golden Eagle programme as well as informal lunchtime concerts and larger termly performances.

We asked pupils which of the holy trinity – drama, music and sport – they were most proud of. Drama was the hands-down winner: 'amazing' they chorused; 'it's the really cool thing to do here.' Inspirational head of drama 'really pushes us'

Sport every day. Boys play half a term each of football and rugby (some said they would prefer a greater focus on one or the other), followed by hockey after Christmas and cricket in the summer term. For girls it's netball, hockey and now cricket rather than rounders as main summer sport (cue delighted cheers). School all for mixed-gender teams and predicts there will be female players in the first cricket team within two years. Watch this space. Some matches played on Wellington's pitches and everyone participates. Is it important to win? we asked. Surprisingly, the reply was 'not really – we just like to enjoy it'. Some parents grumbled that the sporting ethos could be more competitive but school takes pride in its inclusive ethos and concurs that enjoyment is the number one factor. Despite this, trophy cabinets are far from empty and 'school hits nationals most years in one sport or another'. Specialist sports teaching from reception and timetable has now been rejigged to ensure that top coaches, including a pro London Irish rugby coach, train all pupils, not just the elite. Biennial sports tours – netball and cricket to Antigua, hockey to Holland and football in the UK. Thirty sports on co-curricular list, from fencing or karate to laser clay pigeon shooting and roller-skating. Huge extracurricular programme takes place at lunchtimes and after school with around 60 activities on offer every week and pupils in year 6 and below expected to participate in one a day. If it all gets a bit much, those seeking quiet time can retreat to the library for 'colour, chat and chill' time during the lunch break. Pupils love the activities fair that takes place at the beginning of every term.

Learning for Life programme (PSHE) covers all matters pastoral, including SRE, well-being, mindfulness, feelings and emotions. 'We make it relevant the whole time,' says head. 'Pupils know that people here have their backs.' Pupils who had experienced significant family events told us openly and with staggering maturity how supportive school had been in helping them through difficulties. Many schools say they're like a family but Eagle House palpably feels like one; a recent year 7 joiner told us he'd 'never felt more welcome anywhere'.

Boarding: Flexible boarding model can accommodate up to 70 pupils from year 3 from two to five nights a week in lovely spacious dorms. Girls' dorms, of course, are adorned with personal effects and boys' rather bare; gender stereotypes are hard at work with pink and blue everything respectively. Gorgeous newly renovated common room with cushy sofas makes a cosy hub for evening down time and boarding parents are 'brilliant', say parents who love the weekly boarding newsletters that keep them informed of their children's activities.

The last word: Whether your sights are set on increasing the odds of a place at Wellington several years hence or you're keeping your options wide open, your child can't fail to enjoy his or her journey through this progressive, kind and buzzy school, described by one parent as 'a beating heart that just doesn't stop'. Sounds like win win to us.

Elstree School

15

Woolhampton, Reading, Berkshire RG7 5TD

01189 713302 | registrar@elstreeschool.org.uk | www.elstreeschool.org.uk

Ages: Boys 3-13, girls 3-7

Pupils: 265; Boarders: 20 full, 60 weekly

Fees: Day £12,300 – £22,200; Boarding + £1,770 – £8,100 pa

Headmaster: Since 2013, Sid Inglis (40s). After Radley and Newcastle Universities, he began teaching at Ludgrove, took a break to complete a PGCE in London imagining he would move into secondary teaching, but ended up returning to Ludgrove, eventually becoming joint head with Simon Barber (who runs Ludgrove still). Mr Inglis and his wife Olivia – who is also a member of the senior team – soon showed their enthusiasm for developing pupils in the broadest sense. 'I've lots of energy and ideas and I hope that permeates down to the staff.'

Besides the established and well-regarded Elstree Award (like a junior DofE), he has introduced the Headmaster's Project (like a junior EPQ), in which year 6s are invited to devise a project they'd like to undertake, and then use whichever school resources they need to deliver it over two terms. Projects have ranged from developing an app to building a chicken house. 'It could have gone either way,' confesses one senior colleague cheerfully, 'but it's been brilliant.' He has also moved the school to co-ed in a two-step process, with girls initially invited up to year 5, then to the end of the school.

Mr Inglis and his wife are universally liked and respected. 'Both lovely, and they're not just about the academics,' says one parent. 'I do feel I can email and expect a very quick reply.' 'A brilliant team, and Olivia has a wonderful relationship with a lot of the mums.' Both of them teach year 8 (him Latin, Olivia teaches French, though Spanish is a new modern language option too) alongside other roles ranging from social media, parent communications, the school magazine and more.

Mr Inglis is considered extremely skilful when it comes to secondary school applications: 'I've had amazing support as a parent and he is very tactful at guiding you gently in the right direction.' Parents know they can rely on him to pick up the phone and make the case for a good boy who – for whatever reason – seems in danger of falling through a crack. 'I know the registrars well and can tell them straight when a boy on a waiting list is really flying,' he says. 'But with integrity,' adds his wife.

'Parents think I have an encyclopaedic knowledge of senior schools. There's no magic wand, but I do invite them [senior staff from target

Parents feel the cultural mix is 'about the same as in peer schools and better reflects the world children will go into'

secondary schools] to be involved in our enrichment programme, to give talks, referee matches and so on.'

A keen sportsman and fundraiser, Mr Inglis is an ardent supporter of the children's mental health charity Place2B – a sketch of Elstree by a young beneficiary takes pride of place on his study wall – and persuaded 20 prep school heads to tackle a kayak, cycle and yomp triathlon in his home county of Pembrokeshire to raise over £105,000.

Entrance: Almost all those in the charming pre-prep (currently around 85 up to year 2) join Elstree proper. Others start in year 3, though entry at other points is welcome too, and there is a clear increase in numbers in year 6. Entry is non-selective but those joining from year 3 up will do a taster day and some low-key assessments in English, maths and cognitive ability. 'The academic pace is quick here,' says Mr Inglis, 'but there are less able pupils here too who have the resilience to thrive.'

Exit: Head's assertion that it's not just about getting children into the 'best' school but 'the right school for them' is borne out by the fact this small prep's alumnae regularly disperse to almost 20 destinations. A large carousel of school prospectuses in one corridor further testifies to a lack of pigeon-holing. He 'cannot remember' anyone having left in year 6, and only time will tell if the incoming girls will stay the course or leave sooner given that girls public schools, and some first-rate girls' independents in nearby Reading, take girls from year 7.

Good numbers currently secure places at competitive schools including Radley and Eton, with similar numbers going to Bradfield. Regular successes in a good array of scholarships, with art and DT a particularly strong area.

Our view: Elstree's pink and navy school colours might have been made for the move to co-education, but they are not the only eye-catching feature of this school. The somewhat unusual layout – with all subjects taught in satellite buildings around the lovely Georgian main building at its heart of its 150-acre site – evidently works well, and certainly helps pupils top their target daily step count: '15,000 a day excluding games,' according to our young guide. With dorms, library, offices and dining room etc in the main building, 'There's a clear distinction between work and home,' as Mr Inglis puts it. Lessons are 30 minutes with a five-minute period between them in which to scurry from one location to another.

With more than eight Elstree families living on site with their assorted offspring and pets, there's a truly homely feel to life here. The vast majority of parents live in the local area – much evidence of camaraderie within the parent body – with six per cent international families and six per cent in London. A brief influx of boys with EAL raised eyebrows among parents. But head is proud of the links he is building with Korea, Spain and elsewhere and other parents feel the cultural mix is 'about the same as in peer schools and better reflects the world children will go into'.

Class sizes are small, the average is 12, but some year groups have only eight or 10 in a class, and parents speak glowingly of a range of favourite teachers, and credit Mr Inglis with some deft pruning of the weaker elements. Perhaps because of its boarding roots, the school day is quite long – 8.15am to 5pm for years 3 and 4, and to 6pm for everyone else. But this includes sport six days a week, and all prep is done in school hours, which parents love ('it's timetabled throughout the day and not just after lessons when they're tired'), with the last portion of the day made over to clubs for the year 3s and 4s. These range from reeling to Lego and the intriguing-sounding Jamaica club, with others – eg judo, music technology, golf coaching and fencing – chargeable.

Elstree's pink and navy school colours might have been made for the move to co-education, but they are not the only eye-catching feature of this school

Streaming starts in a gentle way in year 3 for maths and spelling, and by year 6 there are three sets, though care is taken to avoid calling the top one a scholarship set, in case it encourages complacency. Secondary school preparation has been given a shake up with an excellent year 5 and 6 weekly academic enrichment programme and pre-testing preparation mornings. 'They have definitely upped their game,' says one parent. Besides preparing them for the ISEB and other tests, the programme includes talks from visiting guest speakers such as an Apache pilot or big cheese from Microsoft, to team building activities of the kind they'll now find at some public school assessment days. 'I've tried to widen the children's horizons beyond what they are taught,' says the master in charge. 'You don't want to over prepare and sacrifice many [other] lessons, but we have to be doing as much, if not more, than other schools,' adds Inglis.

'They are really good at pushing pupils to the right degree,' says a parent. 'They do lots of revision in school and are never as stressed as some of my friends find happens in London.'

The pre-prep, on the edge of the main school campus, is a fusion of the rustic and cutting edge, with first-rate (and partially covered) play facilities outdoors, including a living willow tunnel and playing field. Pupils nip through the gate to the big school next door for PE, drama, computing and lunch, and follow the lead of its big brother in other ways too – through its own poetry declamation for example.

If dorm sizes edge towards the high side this does not seem to bother pupils; one of the biggest, with nine beds, is the most popular on account of its lovely views and location in a former ballroom

On woodland Wednesdays, teaching moves outdoors for the early years children, punctuated by sandwiches and hot chocolate by the fire. Charmingly, pupils may earn stars for pleasing behaviour, and award them to staff too if they've been especially good. The delightful Alice Bond [now married], head since 2019, is clearly smitten with country life (having come from Garden House School, Chelsea), right down to fitting a woodland trail camera: 'It even filmed a badger.'

The Pre-Prep is now full with a secondary Nursery class added 'It's a wonderful little pre-prep and I'd love to see it thrive,' says another. 'A wonderful setting, fantastic teaching and very nurturing. My boys all left with amazing – and identical – handwriting.'

We can only speculate if the happy din in the dining room has much to do with the Elstree tradition of handing out sweets to children who've eaten well at lunch. But quiet is swiftly restored when Mr Inglis rings the end of lunch bell, after which comes a timetabled rest period for reading, or catching up or music practice.

Though 80 per cent of pupils learning an instrument is lower than some preps, parents are effusive about the regular concerts and unflagging music department. '[Head] has definitely taken music and sport up a notch or two.' Cricket is an Elstree speciality and many have noted the development in hockey since the laying of an all-weather pitch.

Though, according to the last ISI report figures, Elstree has a higher percentage of pupils with SEN assistance than most (over 20 per cent), Mr Inglis puts this down to teachers being attuned to spotting which pupils need help with organisation etc, plus a happy lack of stigma in seeking support. 'If a child has significant learning disabilities we're not necessarily the right place.'

With weekend sports matches becoming harder to arrange as more schools dispense with Saturday school, and some parents reluctant adopters – 'it eats into family time and leaves them quite tired on a Sunday' – Mr Inglis admits he sees a future at Elstree without it and, by association, without full boarding.

Boarding: Roughly two-thirds of pupils board to some degree from year 4 ('same bed, same nights, it's not a hotel option'), and since it's entirely optional, there's scant homesickness: 'If money was no object, my boys would certainly board more,' says one mother. 'The summer term in particular is phenomenal with cricket nets, pizza oven suppers and headmaster's picnics.'

The very tidy dorms have a slightly less nested feel than in a full boarding school, perhaps due partly to the fact clothes are kept in cupboards on the landings. If dorm sizes edge towards the high side this does not seem to bother pupils; one of the biggest, with nine beds, is apparently the most popular on account of its lovely views and location in some sort of former ballroom, complete with ornate plasterwork and fireplace.

By year 7, three nights is a required minimum. Only 15 pupils board full time, mainly overseas students, but the number of weekly boarders is growning and the risk of rattling in a large house is mitigated through a well-adopted 'take a boarder home for the weekend' programme and Big Weekends. Eight of them are run a year, with different year groups invited to spend a weekend in school enjoying activities from casino nights to an alternative olympics. Free to full borders and £38 for non-boarders, they're a hit with parents and children alike: 'Our pupils have loved them; they're a definite priority on the calendar.'

The last word: With such support among parents for the current head's plans and management, Elstree seems certain to thrive as it evolves: 'Our children have been happy and fulfilled there – I cannot fault it.'

Eton College

16

Eton, Windsor, Berkshire SL4 6DW

01753 370611 | admissions@etoncollege.org.uk | www.etoncollege.com

Ages: 13-18

Pupils: 1,340; sixth form: 540; Boarders: All full

Fees: Boarding £44,094 pa

Head master: Since 2015, Simon Henderson MA PGCE (30s), previously head of Bradfield College. Educated at Winchester College, followed by Brasenose College, Oxford, where he read history. Teaching career started at Windsor Boys' School, thence to Eton in 2001, where he was a deputy housemaster and head of history, and on to Sherborne School in 2009 as deputy head (academic). Married to Ali, with four young children.

Mr Henderson has the impeccable manners, inscrutability and cerebral acuity generally alleged to distinguish the man who's been to Winchester, but in our experience also common to many heads of senior schools. But he has, too, the aura of serene composure and mastery of self that Betjeman mocks, gently, in his poem, The Wykehamist: 'It's something too to know your wants/And go full pelt for Norman fonts'. We strongly suspect that Mr Henderson's equivalent of Norman fonts is schools and teaching. Of his own education he says, 'I loved school – it was dynamic, exciting and vibrant.' His first experience of teaching was in South Africa on his gap year; 'I absolutely loved it.' His vocation was confirmed by a spell doing corporate internships in the City ('awful').

Does being head master of Eton leave any time for teaching? 'The unpredictability means I can't commit to any formal teaching, but I make guest appearances.' He says he has 'plans to get back into the classroom', but in the meantime is making a 'conscious decision to be here as much as possible'. That must be hard when his presence is expected at so many events – 'I go to lots of dinners,' he says somewhat ruefully. 'Schools are big communities of people, it's so important to make personal connections.'

In any large boarding school it will be housemaster, rather than headmaster, who is pupils' day-to-day influence and whom pupils and parents know best, so it was perhaps unsurprising to find that almost all of the many parents we spoke to had had no contact with Mr Henderson. 'He holds lunches after games on Saturdays but we haven't been to one yet.' 'My son says he sends cards to all the boys on their birthdays and they sometimes meet him if they've won a prize.' And what do the boys think of their 'head man'? 'He's nice, but he seems quite strict.'

When we met Mr Henderson, his mind was on the role of technology in the classroom. Eton's Tony Little Centre for Innovation and Research in Learning is at the forefront of developments in this field, working in partnership with education technology firms and also pursuing its own ventures. The centre's aims are to take this expertise beyond the school gates and make it available to its state school partnerships, local education authorities and the wider world. Interestingly, Mr Henderson sees this as Eton's virtual version of other schools' overseas franchises. Eton itself, he believes, cannot be replicated, but the school's approach to education can.

Access to Eton may one day become needs blind, but it's unlikely to become gender blind on Mr Henderson's watch

Does he foresee a time when Eton's beaks (teachers) can stand down? 'Technology is changing what happens. For example, if there are 20 pupils of broadly the same ability in a maths set, computer programmes can be used to detect areas of weakness and generate questions that consolidate or extend learning, but they will never be a substitute for human interaction.' He believes that this kind of personalised learning will free teachers to concentrate on higher-order work – spending more time with individuals rather than generating questions. 'Technology will enable teaching in schools to become similar to that in universities – with a mixture of small classes, online courses, set-piece lectures, time spent on individual study and more fluidity between year groups.'

Every Eton head appointed in recent years must surely have pondered at the start of his tenure whether or not he had the stomach to go down in history as the barbarian who consigned the school's world-famous uniform to the archives. Mr Henderson was touted as a moderniser, just the sort of chap who might actually do this deed. Not that he's ever said as much, naturally. In an early press interview his answer to this predictable question was, 'Well, I'm not getting rid of the uniform this week', accompanied by a photograph of him sporting chinos, a linen jacket and a slightly casual shirt (with tie, of course). Several years on, and despite moving headmaster HQ from traditional study to a studiedly modern office, in sartorial matters at least he appears to have gone native. No doubt the tailors at Eton town's four (yes, four) gentlemen's outfitters have decided it's safe to go ahead and splash out on new tape measures.

Mr Henderson is one of the school's youngest ever heads, so perhaps donning the armour of the uniform each day makes it easier to inhabit such a huge role. Not that he seems to need any help, as anyone who heard him being questioned by MPs from the Education Select Committee inquiry into 'exam integrity' will know. Completely unruffled, his answers were eloquent and precise and there was no doubting his resolve that such a thing (boys seeing material that later appeared in exam papers) would never happen again.

'When all is said and done, a boy is not coming to Eton simply to earn a set of qualifications.' But exams are exams and even Etonians must jump these trifling hurdles

So where, beyond his new office, is the evidence of Mr Henderson's promised 'modernisation'? After all, he taught here for eight years so must presumably have identified things that could be improved. He has made half-term holidays longer to bring them into line with other independent schools and banned mobile phones for boys in F block (year 9). He told us that he wants to continue the school's work to broaden opportunities and access – long-term commitments include sponsoring nearby Holyport College (a state boarding school) and the London Academy of Excellence, a state sixth form college in East London. Eton's famous Universities Summer School has been running since 1981 and provides expert subject tuition to pupils from state schools who are applying to top universities. Mr Henderson says that he shares his predecessor's ambition for access to Eton to become 'needs blind'. 'We spend around £7m on means-tested bursaries and most of that money has been given by former pupils for this purpose.'

Access to Eton may one day become needs blind, but it's unlikely to become gender blind on Mr Henderson's watch. He told us, with just a hint of impatience, 'There's too much focus on whether a school is single sex or co-ed; what matters most is whether a school is good or not.' Adding, 'Young people feel under more pressure to conform to gender stereotypes at co-ed schools.' Women teachers are still in the minority at Eton, but the appointment of the first female lower master (the senior deputy head) is a good sign.

We were interested to get the head's take on the public perception of Eton and the way the school is portrayed in the press. 'We must not be defensive, we need to engage with our critics. Pupils who have been educated here should never feel guilty, but they must be aware of their good fortune and responsibilities.'

We doubt Mr Henderson has much in the way of spare time, but what he has is reserved for his family (he has four young children) and golf. And supporting QPR. Favourite writer? Thomas Hardy. Regrets? Giving up on the piano and clarinet.

Rather than headline-grabbing attempts on the superficial, one gets the impression that Mr Henderson has addressed himself to Eton's internal workings, adjusting the calibration of its doubtless Byzantine ancient mechanisms. 'I think he's probably making subtle changes,' one father told us. 'Subtle changes' can be hard to spot, even for a Good Schools Guide writer, so thank you Eton parents for your help and all your insightful, robust and sometimes contradictory opinions.

Entrance: You might think that all Eton has to do is to sit back and wait for the world to beat a path to its door, so when we met the director and deputy director of admissions we were surprised, and delighted, to find two scholarly Indiana Joneses. As they spoke we had a vision of them in pith helmets, enthusiastically navigating roads less taken to discover new talent for their school. With around five applicants for each of 250 places, you don't need us to tell you that getting a place at Eton is tough, but it's reassuring to know that the admissions department is equally rigorous in seeking out the 'right' candidates.

This is an academically demanding school, but a place depends on much more than getting all the right answers in tests. Eton looks for that extra je ne sais quoi – a quality that is more about character and personality than bolt-on achievements. Parents who believe they can play the system by forcing their son to memorise War and Peace, making him practise the harpsichord until his fingers bleed and drilling him to say that his favourite leisure pursuit is calculus, do not generally prevail. Of course, if your son willingly does this kind of thing he's probably in with a chance.

Parents marvel at the beautifully written and minutely detailed termly reports – each accompanied by a two- or three-page letter from the boy's housemaster and tutor

All applicants are assessed in year 6 (register by 30 June in year 5) – verbal reasoning, numeracy, perceptual potential, interview and school report. School recognises that pre-testing may penalise late developers, so stays in touch with school heads and gets feedback on near-miss candidates. Just think for a minute of the amount of work that assessing and interviewing 1,200 10-year-old boys involves – a five-strong committee spends two days considering the candidates, and places offered are conditional on passing CE or, for boys at state schools, Eton's own exam in year 8. A further 80 names go on the waiting list.

And what about the prep school baccalaureate? We asked knowing that a kind word from Eton would cheer its champions in prep schools up and down the land. The Indiana Joneses morphed back into tail-coated Etonians: 'We still like CE; CE is the right foundation, it covers all the core areas of the year 8 curriculum.'

Scholarship boys include 14 King's Scholars (decided on academic merit alone), plus New Foundation scholars (boys joining Eton from state schools) and many more.

Minimum of six grade 7s at GCSE needed for entry to sixth form, not much of a hurdle at a school where the majority get 10 or 11 GCSE 8-9s. Twelve sixth form scholarships a year for boys from state sector or independent schools lacking sixth form provision.

Exit: One or two may depart for co-ed or day schools post-GCSE, but after A levels almost every boy will be headed for university. Eton has in the past been inexplicably coy about its leavers' destinations, keeping information on their website that is several years out of date. But no more! Perhaps they have listened to prospective and current parents' views. Maybe, ahem, they took heed of our comments about how unhelpful this was. Whatever the reason, we welcome the new spirit of openness. No more 'ball park' figures for us: in 2020, 41 to Oxbridge, five to UK medical schools. Rest to the likes of Durham, Edinburgh, Exeter, UCL, Imperial and Bristol. Thirty-seven headed off overseas in 2020, including to Yale, Harvard, Stanford and Princeton.

Really impressive numbers to Ivy League and other prestigious colleges in the US (30+). School says: 'There continues to be strong interest in applying to the US with a high percentage of those applicants ultimately choosing to attend US universities. The vast majority of boys apply in their final year, with only a few opting for the US route in A Block after leaving Eton.'

Latest results: In 2020, 96 per cent 9-7 at I/GCSE: 80 per cent A*/A at A level. In 2019 (the last year when exams took place), 93 per cent 9-7 at I/GCSE; 76 per cent A*/A at A level.

Teaching and learning: Parents think teaching staff (known as 'beaks') are 'exceptional', but not without exception, and those we met lived up to such billing – deeply knowledgeable about their school and delighted to tell visitors about its past and present. Eton must be a great gig – not just for the kudos of working in the world's most famous school and the resources and opportunities it offers, but also the intellectual challenge of teaching a carefully hand-picked selection of the (mostly western) world's sparkiest young men.

The deputy head (academic)'s introduction for new parents sets a certain tone: 'When all is said and done, a boy is not coming to Eton simply to earn a set of qualifications.' But exams are exams and even Etonians must jump these trifling hurdles. They do so hardly putting a foot wrong. IGCSEs for most of the core subjects; nine languages on offer in addition to French and Spanish including Mandarin, Russian, Arabic, Italian and Japanese. Considerably more opt for classical Greek and Latin than for drama, DT and music. Most boys take 11 subjects and gain top marks in all.

A level results do spread a little beyond the first two letters of the alphabet, with occasional Cs, Ds, Es – even, gasp, a couple of Us. Most popular subject by a considerable margin is maths, followed by economics, history, religious studies, physics, further maths and chemistry. Further maths garners the highest percentage of A*s along with fine art. Only a handful of takers for drama and DT, much better news for the oft-beleaguered modern foreign languages – particularly Spanish – but more opt for Latin than French.

Small classes and setting for all in most subjects ensure teaching is precisely targeted and boys' progress is extremely closely monitored

– any falling off is brought to the attention of tutors and housemasters. Several parents thought it is the combination of great teaching and competition between the boys themselves that keeps academic standards flying: 'They learn so much from their peers.' Clearly understood and immediate sanctions for work submitted late or sub-par. Parents marvel at the beautifully written and minutely detailed termly reports – each arrives accompanied by a two- or three-page letter from the boy's housemaster and tutor.

Full boarding means a different shape to the school day, with lessons (known as 'schools') following afternoon sports activities at least three times a week. We sat in on several late afternoon sessions: computing, Spanish and F block (year 9) divinity. As they mustered and spread themselves out, waistcoats and hair somewhat dishevelled, the older boys could have passed for weary ushers at the end of a particularly gruelling society wedding. And notwithstanding all the high-powered goings on in the Tony Little Centre for Innovation and Research in Learning, the lessons we observed would have made perfect sense to any shades of beaks long dead – books, pens, questions, answers, discussion, testing, checking and a bit of good-humoured banter (though we're not sure what they'd make of laptops, Google and interactive whiteboards).

'Eton encouraged me' was a phrase we heard several times, not necessarily in relation to extraordinary achievements

In 2017 Pre-U candidates in economics and art history had their marks disallowed by the examination board after evidence of questions being leaked in advance came to light. In the case of art history there was no evidence of Eton pupils or staff having done anything wrong, but this was not so for economics, where the revelations led to the departure of the head of economics, who was also deputy head (academic) elect. The school dealt with these matters swiftly and openly, but it makes one wonder under how much pressure teachers feel to produce top results in their subjects.

Dismissal of a popular English teacher in December 2020 for refusing to remove an online lecture entitled 'The Patriarchy Paradox' recently made headlines. As ever when it comes to Eton, gleeful press coverage generated more heat than light. Many parents did not agree with the head's decision at first, but support has gradually shifted in his favour. No more than a storm in a teacup perhaps, but the row mirrors wider tensions in both academia and society at large between so-called traditional and progressive views.

Learning support and SEN: Well-resourced and highly professional SEN provision and staff. Around 50 to 60 boys receive regular learning support for mild to moderate dyslexia, dyspraxia, dysgraphia – either one-to-one or in small groups (charged as an extra). All boys assessed during their first term and any whose results give cause for concern get extra help, either from their tutor or the SEN unit.

The arts and extracurricular: How long have you got? It is surely impossible for any boy to have a go at all the opportunities Eton offers in a five-year school career, but the message from pupils and parents is that the school does its utmost to foster and support boys' interests and ambitions. 'Whatever the talent or interest, school will do all it can to enable boys to make it their thing.' 'Eton encouraged me' was a phrase we heard several times, not necessarily in relation to extraordinary achievements but, for instance, performance opportunities for keen but far from concert-level musicians. Co-curricular programme includes CCF – Eton's was founded in 1860 – community service, and over 50 'societies', nearly all established and run by boys, including debating, comedy, Orwell (described as 'left wing'), cheese and wine (these last two are not held together). Meetings, many with visiting speakers, take place in the evenings.

Over 1,000 individual music lessons a week, splendid facilities for teaching and concerts, eight (yes, eight) organs, and a hierarchy of orchestras: symphony orchestra for the best, chamber orchestra for string players from the symphony orchestra, concert band for wind and brass players plus junior versions of all these. Smaller groups such as piano trios, quartets, jazz and rock bands get the chance to perform at events organised by the school, houses or boys themselves. Audition-only College Chapel Choir sings three times a week at services, tours abroad and has produced nine CDs, but there are also plenty of opportunities for keen but less exquisitely musical voices to be heard.

Of all Eton's many strengths, it was drama that parents singled out for particular praise: 'stupendous', 'phenomenal', 'as good as West End productions'. The Farrer theatre has 400 seats and there are two smaller venues. 'It's not exclusive, there are so many opportunities to get involved – not just acting but on the technical side.' What with whole-school plays, house plays, and productions written, produced and directed by boys themselves, it's perhaps understandable that relatively few boys feel the need to choose GCSE and A level drama.

The large numbers of art GCSE and A level A*s are nurtured in the light-filled Drawing Schools, home to teaching expertise and superb facilities for painting, drawing, printmaking, photography, computer graphics, sculpture and ceramics. Each year a different artist in residence is invited to set up an open studio, produce and exhibit their work.

Sport: School playing fields, with evocative names such as Agar's Plough and Mesopotamia, used for football and rugby matches in the Michaelmas half (term), rugby and hockey in the Lent half and cricket and athletics in the summer. With up to 16 teams fielded for a particular sport at any one time, a parent told us that sometimes two opposing schools are invited so that everybody gets a game. On match days there can be up to 40 teams competing. Even the least sporty boys will play in house and inter-house competitions. A parent told us, 'Sport is important, but it doesn't dominate school life; it's just one aspect of the boys' development – like music and drama.' Another observed, 'Even if your son was in all the A teams at prep school, he probably won't be when he gets to Eton – it can come as a bit of a shock when they find out how many boys are better than them!'

Eton also has its own unique version of football, 'the field game', but since no-one else plays it these matches are entirely home affairs. Another unique sporting tradition is the 'Eton wall game', a version of rugby played between Collegers (scholars) and Oppidans (rest of the school) on a narrow strip of ground adjacent to a brick wall. Nearly all matches, entirely organised by the boys, appear to result in goalless draws, but the rules and vocabulary are so esoteric and confusing we can't comment further. Suffice it to say that Boris Johnson was a keen player. Rowing takes place at Dorney, with superb facilities developed for the rowing and canoeing events of the 2012 Olympics. One or two parents (presumably not parents of rowers) thought that investment in Dorney had been at the expense of other sports (although watch this space for their forthcoming acquatics centre and sports hall). Huge range of minor sports including rackets, fives, golf, shooting and sailing. While lack of stabling means you can't bring your horse to Eton, school has thriving polo and eventing teams.

Boarding: Eton has 25 boarding houses, mostly located in historic buildings throughout the town. Each is home to 50 boys (exception is the scholars' house, College, which has 70). Every boy has a single study bedroom – no dorms or sharing. Rooms we saw were pretty standard-issue boys' boarding school – relatively unadorned apart from large shoes. Several parents mentioned that the quality of the mattresses left a lot to be desired.

Around half the houses have their own chefs and dining rooms; boys from houses with no catering have their meals at Bekynton, the college dining complex, eating in house groups together with their housemaster and other house staff. According to boys, the main pro of a catered house is 'not having to dash down the street for breakfast on a cold, rainy morning'. One parent suggested that because Bekynton offered a wider choice of food, a non-catered house could suit a boy who is a 'picky eater'. We enjoyed a delicious lunch in Bekynton's staff dining area where the food was, we were reassured, exactly the same as the boys were getting (but with added napery).

Despite it being an outfit that flatters just about anyone who wears it, boys shed their uniform double quick once the school day has finished

Meal times seem to be more formal affairs than at other boarding schools. A member of staff told us, 'Eating in house groups is important for strengthening the relationship between staff and boys.' In addition to three main meals, all boys are provided with morning and afternoon drinks and snacks in their houses (breaks known respectively as 'chambers' and 'messing'). And if they're still hungry they can forage at the school shop or those in the town.

When it comes to choosing a boarding house the unanimous advice from school and parents is to keep an open mind, 'Don't get fixated.' Do your homework, visit at least three, rank them in order of preference and the 'vast majority' will get a place in one of their choice. Everything will depend on parents' (and boys') rapport with the housemaster and also the dame (responsible for domestic arrangements, health issues etc). One mother advised, 'Trust your instincts; if you really don't think a housemaster is going to get the best out of your son then it's better to go back into the pool.'

Housemasters are in post for 13 years and in addition to the housemaster and his family, there will be a deputy housemaster and two assistants, the dame and her assistant, plus domestic staff.

Boys also have responsibilities – every house has a house captain and a captain of games. Eton provides all teaching staff with accommodation, so boys' tutors will live only a short distance away.

While boys arriving from prep schools may at least be accustomed to boarding, message from parents is that the very long, full days are quite a 'gear change' for new boys – more so for those coming from state schools. Some housemasters hold events such as barbecues or football games over the summer for those joining in September. New boy integration is, apparently, 'very good' – housemasters are 'incredibly observant and always contactable'. In addition to standard holidays, boys can go home after commitments on Saturday until Sunday evening.

Eton is a small, charming Thamesside town, not unadjacent to Slough and a bridge away from Windsor. It also just happens to have the world's most famous school

It's perhaps inevitable that over 13 years a housemaster will shape the 'character' of his house and as a consequence houses may 'collect boys in the same mould'. Accordingly, some houses will become known as, for example, 'sporty' or 'musical'. Several parents thought there were ongoing 'power struggles' between senior management and housemasters (such tensions are not uncommon in boarding schools). While everyone was overwhelmingly supportive of the 'federal' status quo and utterly loyal to their own sons' housemasters (all 'fantastic', 'indefatigable' and 'inspirational' to a man), one or two conceded that 'a degree of uniformity' might keep accusations of fiefdoms at bay.

Ethos and heritage: Eton is a small and charming Thames-side town, not unadjacent to Slough and a bridge away from Windsor. It also just happens to have the world's most famous school attached. This makes it somewhat atypical, with its three art galleries, gunsmith, four gentlemen's outfitters and any number of restaurants and cafés. At least some of the latter should be applauded for having resisted the temptation to mine the rich and apparently inexhaustible seam of school-related names. No-one but tourists and the occasional nervous prep school boy visiting with his parents looks twice at the tail-coated pupils and teachers as they stride up and down the high street between boarding houses and main school.

On arrival we were made very welcome in the porters' lodge, wood panelling decorated with framed personal photos of the royal family (princes William and Harry were pupils here – it is their local school, after all). Royalty or not, Eton's front of house staff are charming and friendly to deal with – in person or over the phone; quite an accolade when you consider just how busy the world's interest in its most famous school must keep them.

The school was founded by in 1440 by King Henry VI to provide free education for 70 poor boys, but his ambitious building work stopped (the chapel, though fine and large, is considerably smaller than planned) and the school lost many of its original endowments when Henry was deposed by Edward IV in 1461. Records from the 16th century show pupils had a pretty tough day – lessons finished at 8pm and there was only an hour of 'play'. The school's history lives on in its language – terms are 'halves' because there used to be only two three-week holidays a year; 'oppidans', from the Latin for word for town, refers to pupils (originally from the nearby town) who, unlike the scholars, did not live at the school. Now it means all pupils who are not scholars.

Eton has two superb libraries, a huge collection of fine and decorative art including works by Sir Joshua Reynolds and JMW Turner, and no fewer than three museums. The Natural History Museum contains material from botanist and Old Etonian, Sir Joseph Banks, who sailed with Captain Cook; the Museum of Antiquities has a particularly fine collection of ancient Egyptian artefacts and there's also a Museum of Eton Life. All three are open to the public on Sunday afternoons. Most recently, The Queen's Schools Science Department was re-opened by the queen after a major refurbishment – includes seemingly endless labs, science project room and STEM centre.

Until the late 19th century boys at Eton could wear pretty much what they liked, although the upper-class monoculture at that time probably ensured they all looked fairly similar. When uniform was introduced it appears to have taken its first breath and dived into a vat of aspic. Top hats and cropped jackets may have been shed along the way, but what message do tail coats and white collars have for the 21st century? Pride in tradition and the confidence to follow one's own path, or outdated fancy dress, preserved because it distinguishes the members of a privileged club? The answer will be down to the politics of the observer.

Ironically, egalitarianism Eton-style means boys and (male) teaching staff wear pretty much the same costume, with subtle distinctions of hierarchy such as patterned waistcoats and silver buttons for exalted members of Pop (sixth form prefects). Such uniformity may be why the issue of uniform is less pressing than one might imagine. Despite it being an outfit that flatters just about anyone who wears it, boys shed their uniform double quick once the school day is done.

Another unique sporting tradition is the 'Eton wall game', a version of rugby played on a narrow strip of ground adjacent to a brick wall. Nearly all matches appear to result in goalless draws. Boris Johnson was a keen player

The term 'old Etonian' has of late become something of a knee-jerk pejorative shorthand for posh, wealthy and privileged, indiscriminately applied to the relatively small number of alumni prominent in public life – from David Cameron and Boris Johnson, numbers 19 and 20 in the list of British prime ministers educated at Eton, to actors such as Eddie Redmayne, Damian Lewis, Hugh Laurie and Tom Hiddleston. The reality is that you're more likely to have encountered Etonians unknowingly as they quietly get on with doing their professional thing in journalism, medicine, education, law and the arts. Before them came centuries of soldiers, including 37 holders of the Victoria Cross, explorers, novelists, sportsmen, poets, politicians, academics, philanthropists and the odd ne'er-do-well (ancient and modern). Fictional OEs include James Bond (expelled), Bertie Wooster, Lord Peter Wimsey, Mark Darcy and that old crocodile-phobe, Captain Hook.

Pastoral care, inclusivity and discipline: By all accounts the house and tutor system works powerfully well to ensure that despite the size of the school, no one is overlooked – 50 boys in each house means only 10 of each year group. Boys are encouraged to discuss social and health issues; the house dame deals with minor medical problems and school has three doctors, a psychiatrist, two psychologists and a counsellor. Honourable mention goes to the multi-denominational chaplaincy team in this context too. We heard mixed reports of peer support – some say that there's a strictly observed hierarchy of age, but we also heard that members of B block (sixth form) are assigned to look after younger boys. Like so many things at Eton, this seems to vary between individual houses.

Eton is a demanding school, 'very much into the pursuit of excellence in every field', but it is also very good at choosing boys who will thrive in such an atmosphere – robust self-starters who want to take every opportunity offered: 'It puts a lot of trust in boys and treats them as adults from the word go.' Parents describe it as 'surprisingly meritocratic' and 'very comfortable with difference'.

While appearances would suggest that the school doesn't sweat the small stuff (things like hair etc), one parent sounded a word of caution. 'They have their own way of doing things which is fine when all is going well, but if you come up against the system it can be pretty inflexible.'

In 2020 a former teacher and housemaster was jailed for sexual offences against pupils. Parents say school's handling of this matter was open, swift and sensitive.

Pupils and parents: Cast your preconceptions aside: families from all walks of life can, and do, send their sons here. Name down at birth has long gone and now around 60 per cent of Etonians do not have any family connection with the school. We heard from lots of parents who had plenty to say about the school they had chosen for their sons; they were as interesting, non-standard and off-message as we could wish, but all were convinced that though demanding, an Eton education was the very best choice they could have made.

As for Etonians themselves, many are super talented, most are charming, but once you become 'uniform blind' (and because nearly everyone is wearing it this doesn't take very long), they're reassuringly just schoolboys of the scruffy hair, doodles on hands and scuffed shoes variety.

Money matters: Indeed it does, and school remains determined as ever that lack of it should not be a barrier to any boy who is offered a scholarship. Currently around quarter of boys receive some form of financial support – still a way to go before Eton reaches its stated goal of being 'needs blind'.

The last word: As George Orwell definitely didn't write about his alma mater, some schools are more equal than others. Eton is an extraordinary place, and like many of England's institutions it's a misunderstood mass of contradictions – ancient and modern; exclusive and accessible; liberal and exacting; loved and hated; formal and eccentric; hierarchical and meritocratic. And though it sounds counter-intuitive, somehow these traditions, formalities, rules and hierarchies harmonise, allowing 1,300 tail-coated flowers to bloom.

Farleigh School

Red Rice, Andover, Hampshire SP11 7PW

01264 710766 | office@farleighschool.com | www.farleighschool.com

Ages: 3–13

Pupils: 481; **Boarders:** 125 full (from year 3)

Fees: Day £5,865 – £21,405; Boarding £23,685 – £27,840 pa

Headmaster: Since 2004, Father Simon Everson BA cert theology (50s). Educated at Caterham School and then spent a year working as an auxiliary nurse. 'It was the most formative year,' he says. His parents weren't churchgoers but he studied theology at Leeds Collegiate, followed by a three-year certificate in theology awarded by the University of Oxford. He spent 13 years as an Anglican curate and vicar in south London, first in Rotherhithe and then in Kennington. 'I couldn't have enjoyed it more,' he says. 'The people were so warm and welcoming.' He took a keen interest in local schools (he was chaplain and governor of Archbishop Michael Ramsey Technology College in Camberwell) and when the opportunity to become senior chaplain at Hurstpierpoint College came up he jumped at it. Following his conversion to Catholicism he was asked to apply for the role of chaplain at Farleigh and he became head five years later.

Thoughtful, enthusiastic and engaging, he's determined that children should enjoy their time at Farleigh – and they clearly do. He recently gave an assembly about the 10 things he hoped an ex-Farleigh child would say about the school. They included the following: 'Here people believed in me. Here I was listened to. Here I was understood. Here I was given the best possible start in life.' He attributes the school's success to three things – having a clear vision, recruiting the best possible staff and having 'utterly supportive families'.

He enjoys teaching this age group because of the children's openness and lack of cynicism. 'I feel completely energised by them,' he says. He's adamant that the school should be inclusive and ensures that every pupil represents the school in sport every season. Parents say he is an outstanding head. One told us: 'He is an amazing and very unique man. He is very approachable and understands how parents think. The children highly respect him.' Another explained that the ethos of the school 'comes primarily from the headmaster, who is the most remarkable exemplar of a decent man. He is an inspirational headmaster who imbues the school with his values.'

He is certainly busy. As well as his headship role, he's the school chaplain and teaches RS to years 7 and 8 and PHSE to years 6, 7 and 8. He also celebrates Sunday mass, baptisms, weddings and funerals in the school chapel. He tells the children they can ask him anything they like and is constantly surprised by their insightfulness. Nevertheless, he was taken aback when a child asked him if his dog collar was 'bolted on'. He ensures that pupils are grounded and aware of what is going on in the wider world, from Syria and Iraq to the local community. 'We are always trying to look away from ourselves,' he says. Pupils visit homes for the elderly in Andover and he was delighted when a 100-year-old woman imparted her tip for a happy life to them. 'Don't bear grudges against anybody,' she said. The school also has a long-standing relationship with a local special needs school.

Head's wife Gail is immersed in school life – one parent described her as 'an unsung heroine, always smiling and very caring'. A qualified nurse, she is part of the learning support team. They live in a house on site and have two daughters, one at college and one at university. Asked about his hobbies, the head answers with one word: 'Italy'. Passionate about music (Wagner in particular), he used to play (and teach) the cello and hopes to take it up again when he has time.

Entrance: Non-selective. No formal assessment for entry into kindergarten and the pre-prep but pre-prep joiners are invited to spend a taster morning with their peers. 'We don't really turn children away,' says the pre-prep head, 'as long as we feel this is the right place for them.' Virtually all pre-prep children transfer to the prep.

Informal assessment for prep school places. Priority to practising Catholics (40 per cent of pupils are Catholic), boarders, siblings and children of former pupils.

Exit: Most prep pupils stay till 13, although a few leave at 11. An impressive number of children gain scholarships – 20 in 2021. Year 8 leavers go to a host of schools – sometimes over 20. Most popular choices are Canford, Ampleforth, St Mary's Ascot, Marlborough, Radley, Sherborne and Sherborne Girls. The school makes a huge effort to stay in touch with former pupils, with a thriving Farleigh Society and regular reunions.

Our view: Founded as a school for Catholic boys at Farleigh Wallop near Basingstoke, it moved to its current location in 1982 and became co-ed. The heart is a magnificent Georgian house set in 70 acres of sweeping Hampshire parkland with a landscaped arboretum. On the day we visited the head pointed out a glorious red maple tree, its leaves glowing in the autumn sunlight. Despite its rural setting, the school is only five minutes' drive from the A303 (very handy for London parents). It has grown over the past years but the head doesn't want it to get any bigger than it is now. Average class sizes of 14 in the prep and rarely more than 18.

The house has been sympathetically adapted to school life, while retaining much of its original charm. The elegant drawing room is used as a common room and the ballroom is now the chapel, recently extended so it easily seats the whole school. 'You can come into the chapel and have a quiet moment any time,' our young tour guides told us. A variety of new buildings, including a modern science and food tech department and a swish music block, complete with a stunning recital room, 12 practice rooms, recording studio and rock room.

Subject specialists from year 5 (French and PE from reception and Latin from year 6). There's an annual week-long French trip for year 6s. Pupils are set for maths from year 3, English from year 4 and science from year 6. Science is taught in three ultra-modern labs, with circular fixed benches with gas taps, electric points and circuit points. Everyone does ICT – an hour a week in years 1 to 7 and 30 minutes in year 8. Teachers can book iPads for younger children but year 7 and 8 pupils are provided with their own by the school. Everyone learns to type and the children learn coding from scratch. 'Someone left with a typing speed of 82 wpm last year,' said our awestruck guides. Year 5 pupils and up create their own e-portfolios – a record of their work and a useful revision tool. Four classes per year group in the prep (around 60 children in each year). Saturday school for years 3 to 8. Learning support is free, provided one-to-one or in small groups and very well integrated into the fabric of the school. Well-stocked library – all pupils have a library lesson and a reading lesson each week. School has also introduced a 20-minute 'drop everything and read' session every day. Assembly is held every day, either in the chapel or the theatre.

The music is 'extraordinary'. Three-quarters of the pupils play an instrument and there are plenty of opportunities to join orchestras, bands, groups, specialist ensembles and choirs. Several rock bands and three jazz ensembles, including the Thundering Herd Big Band, Five Foot Six traditional jazz band and Green Shoots. Piano is popular and every pianist gets the chance to play in public at the annual piano festival. Programme of 50 to 60 musical performances each year, plus regular informal concerts. New head of drama is continuing the focus on public speaking, regarded as an invaluable skill for the future. The school excels at debating, regularly winning the prep schools' debating competition at Marlborough and elsewhere. Myriad opportunities to act in plays and musicals, all performed in the well-equipped theatre. Annual dance show and school recently introduced an arts festival, with a street piano, concerts, outdoor science laboratory and a Bake-Off competition.

The Catholic faith is at the school's core and the head aims to keep faith enjoyable and contemporary. At mass children of other faiths 'come up and receive a blessing'

Art and DT departments pride themselves on discovering pupils' talent – often when the children themselves had no idea. 'It's the sheer, raw pleasure of a child finding that they could do something that was completely unknown to them before,' says the head. The head of DT (wearing an apron emblazoned with the words 'epic DT teacher', which he hastened to explain was given by a parent) says he is constantly surprised by the children's inventiveness, whether they are making 'wiggly wooden snakes' or building bridges – yes, literally.

Sport is important. Games on four afternoons a week, with matches on Wednesday and Saturday afternoons. Vast expanse of playing fields, plus a 22-metre indoor pool, sports hall and an all-weather pitch. PE curriculum includes dance, gymnastics, life-saving, fitness and leadership/team-building. Boys do football, rugby, cross-country, cricket, athletics and tennis and girls do hockey, netball, cross-country, cricket, rounders, athletics and tennis. Notable successes include the U12 netball team winning the IAPS national finals in 2018 and recent U13 rugby team unbeaten in five years and 55 matches at Farleigh. Tennis is popular – two-thirds of pupils have lessons.

Plenty of opportunities for pupils to air their views – a pupil from every class represents their peers on the school council.

The Catholic faith is at the school's core and Sunday mass is open to all. The head aims to keep faith enjoyable and contemporary and members of other churches say they never feel left out. At mass children of other faiths 'come up and receive a blessing'. Parents praise the school's pastoral care – 'It's why we chose the school,' said one mother. We were impressed by the buddy system, whereby younger children team up with older buddies. We spotted pairs of intertwined butterflies woven into the hedge – depicting each pair of buddies.

Most live within 15 miles of the school, including villages around Andover, Basingstoke, Romsey, Stockbridge, Salisbury and Winchester, while some come from near Alresford, Devizes, Marlborough and Newbury. The school runs minibuses on three routes. Parents are a mix of locals, Londoners and Forces families – all hugely supportive of the school. 'Farleigh creates very unique children,' said one. 'The kids are really grounded and unspoilt. They are taught that the most important thing is to be kind.' Another parent concurred. 'In this day and age Farleigh does something remarkable,' he said. 'The children it spits out at the other end are by the standards of their peers remarkably well-adjusted and thoroughly decent and kind.'

The pre-prep is based in its own spacious building on the school site, with two classes per year group. We arrived at 4pm, with excited children pouring into after-school activities like yoga and sewing. Pre-prep opens its doors for breakfast club at 7.30am and an after-school club runs till 5.45pm.

Boarding: The school offers flexi boarding up to the summer term of year 7, when children either revert to day or convert to weekly or full boarding. The boarders include a cohort of four or five children from Madrid, who spend three terms at the school. Boarding is well organised, with junior (years 3 to 6) and senior (years 7 and 8) boarding houses. Larger and very wholesome dorms for youngest while older pupils are housed in twos and fours. Children are encouraged to bring photographs and posters from home, all adding to the cheery atmosphere. The school has its own 24/7 surgery, complete with a brightly coloured model skeleton to explain the parts of the body ('We call him Nelson,' the senior nurse told us with a smile). GPs from nearby Andover Health Centre visit twice a week. Children eat all their meals in a light, airy dining room. At lunch there's lots of choice, including vegetarian and vegan options, plus salads. Boarders have high praise for the breakfasts – they can have a cooked breakfast every day if they choose.

Money matters: The school offers a 15 per cent discount to full or weekly boarding children of Forces families. Bursaries are available on a means-tested basis. The school has partnered with the Royal National Children's Springboard Foundation, the boarding school bursary charity, to offer means-tested, 100 per cent bursaries to two children from disadvantaged backgrounds. It recently launched its own bursaries programme – the St Theresa Fund – for year 7 and 8 boarders.

The last word: Farleigh is an outstanding school and we aren't in the least surprised that parents go into raptures about the place. 'Ah, lovely Farleigh,' mused one father. Children, teachers and parents extol its virtues, its academic success, its beautiful grounds and its prowess at everything from music to sport. But above all, it's a happy school, led by an exceptional head who's determined that every pupil should be listened to and understood. He wants children to be given the best possible start in life – and they really are.

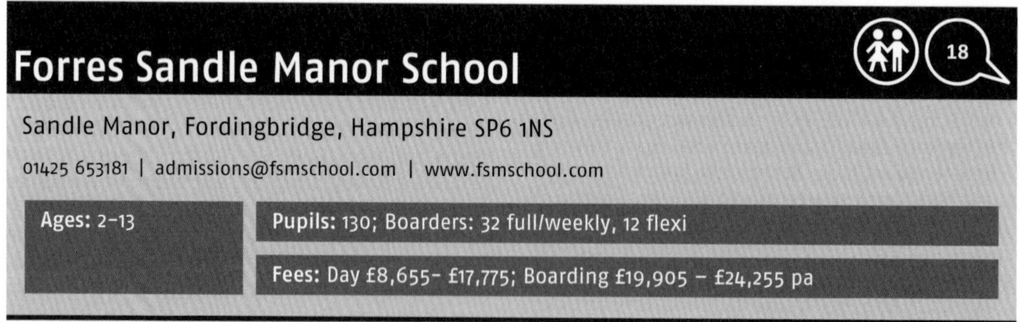

Forres Sandle Manor School

Sandle Manor, Fordingbridge, Hampshire SP6 1NS

01425 653181 | admissions@fsmschool.com | www.fsmschool.com

Ages: 2–13

Pupils: 130; Boarders: 32 full/weekly, 12 flexi

Fees: Day £8,655– £17,775; Boarding £19,905 – £24,255 pa

Interim Headmaster: Since January 2022, interim head is Robert Tasker.

Entrance: Pupils arrive in all years, with boarding from 7. Non-selective but the school works from the premise of 'will a child be happy here?' No formal entrance exam but applicants attend a taster day.

Exit: Year 8 leavers go to a host of different schools, with Bryanston, King's Bruton, King's Taunton, Marlborough, Canford, Cheltenham College, Clayesmore, Millfield, Walhampton, Sherborne and Dauntsey's among the current favourites. Usually double figures of scholarships.

Our view: Two schools – Forres School (originally in Swanage, Dorset) and Sandle Manor – merged to form Forres Sandle Manor in 1993. Set in 35 acres on the edge of the New Forest, the school is centred around an elegant Jacobean manor, with a lower school (complete with a pirate-ship playground and forest school) and glorious grounds. The wood-panelled entrance hall is a welcoming space for children and parents, with a log fire, sofas and toys for young children to play with as they wait for their older siblings. We visited during maths week and found a 'crime scene – do not cross' tape in reception, part of an exciting maths puzzle for year 7s to solve.

The school offers a broad academic curriculum (two parents told us that senior schools said how well their children had been prepared for their next school). Like many preps, it no longer does humanities at CE, preferring to take a 'flexible and creative approach' to teaching history, geography and RS. Children now do 'learning-based inquiries', which are graded internally and externally (the results are sent to their senior schools). French and Spanish taught (Latin is optional) and all pupils have two computer lessons a week. Twenty-three children have learning support, either one-to-one or in lessons, for needs like dyslexia and ADHD. Younger children have class teachers but from year 6 up pupils are in tutor groups of four which meet three times a week. Maximum of 18 to a class but usually smaller. Some setting but the school says it's 'quite flexible'. Science is exciting – the head of science recently got pupils to design a rocket and see who could keep theirs in the air the longest. The slightly down-at-heel science lab (also home to two pet gerbils, Pegasus and Capricorn) is due for a refit this year.

The school recently made Saturday school optional for years 3, 4 and 5 and now offers Saturday enrichment instead of formal academic lessons (older pupils can also choose academic enrichment, such as studying a subject in greater depth). The school thinks it's important to get children used to the idea of making choices, ready for choosing GCSEs at senior school, so they choose from a variety of modules, including forest school, art, DT, textiles, photography, cookery, music, drama and first aid. The youngest pupils can opt in and out as they wish while older pupils relish the chance to try their hand at something new. Year 8 children recently asked if everyone could wear home clothes on Saturdays and after giving the matter some thought the school agreed.

Lots of classical, jazz and rock groups to join, with fun names like Flute Pastilles, Stradivarius Strings and Fabulous Fiddles

Lots of sport – facilities include football and rugby pitches galore, Astroturf, netball courts, an outdoor swimming pool and a multi-purpose sports hall. Hockey is particularly strong and a year 8 girl is currently playing for Rounders England. All year 2 pupils and below do ballet. Music is a big part of the school and 70 per cent of pupils play an instrument. Lots of classical, jazz and rock groups to join, with fun names like Flute Pastilles, Stradivarius Strings and Fabulous Fiddles. Upper and lower school drama productions every year. Art and DT are impressive – year 6 DT pupils make lamps, year 7s design storage for urban living and year 8s make their own speakers. When we visited rehearsals were under way for Bugsy Malone and a play based on the Horrible Histories. Children can stay for activities after school – including coding club, Lego engineering (one boy invented a machine to solve the Rubik's Cube), cookery, Cubs and Brownies. Regular group debates cover subjects like 'should mobile phones be banned in schools?' and 'what is a superhero?' Year 8s get the chance to do their own TED talks. Four school houses, with children competing to be 'star of the week' and for a house trophy at the end of term.

Key staff are mental health first aid trained. 'We know the children very well and they come and talk to us if they have any concerns,' says the head of boarding. 'Sometimes they tell me "it's only a silly thing" and I say to them: "There's no such thing as a silly thing."' The school also runs the PSB (pre-senior baccalaureate) skills programme, helping children to develop six 'learning powers' – collaboration, communication, independence, risk taking, reflection and GRIT (which stands for guts, resilience, initiative and tenacity). PSHE is known as 'life skills', with children from year 5 and up learning about everything from emotional well-being to careers and finance. Year 8s are mentors to children in years 3 to 6 (deputy head trains them, ensuring they know when issues should be escalated to an adult).

Parents like the school's 'huge community feeling' and say boarding and day pupils mix together well. Many day pupils are very local but some come from places like Ringwood, Salisbury, Poole, Bournemouth and Tollard Royal – 45 minutes' drive away at most (the school runs its own subsidised minibuses). Slightly old-fashioned uniform – boys sport green tweed jackets while girls wear tartan skirts and bottle-green blazers, plus ties for all – but the children say it's comfortable and 'not scratchy'. They give the food the thumbs-up, particularly the spicy chicken and millionaire's shortbread. Meat-free Mondays have been introduced. Active school council, with spirited pupils keen to make suggestions and reque sts.

Boarding: Boarders are housed on the first floor of the school, boys at one end, girls at the other. All but five of current year 8 pupils board and two year 3 girls have recently become boarders. Ten residential staff and empathetic head of boarding lives at one end of the house with her family. 'I've never met a more genuine person,' says one parent. 'She deserves a sainthood.' Many boarders are from military families and the school runs a Supporting Active Service group to support children whose parents are away on deployment – everything from helping them to keep in touch with their parents to a countdown sweetie jar to count the days till they come home. As one military parent put it, 'We didn't choose boarding. Boarding chose us because we needed stability for the girls and we couldn't be happier with the school.'

A few international boarders from China, Norway and Spain and some flexi-boarders. Everyone's kept busy at weekends and parents say FSM doesn't empty out like some schools. Sundays start with a full English breakfast, with children in their dressing gowns if they wish, followed by writing letters home (proper letters, not emails), plus trips to places like Paultons Park and Lulworth Cove, on-site pursuits like archery and zorbing and a Sunday roast in the evening. Lots of midweek activities, including silent discos and 'FSM's Got Talent'. Boarders are allowed to use their phones for set periods during the evenings – apart from 'tech-free Tuesdays and Thursdays'. Very wholesome dorms (ranging from four to 11 beds, plus junior rooms for the younger boarders).

Money matters: Means-tested bursaries and discounts for Forces families.

The last word: A small and friendly school, where everybody knows everybody and children can grow up in their own time. Neither posh nor pushy, it focuses on developing happy, confident, well-mannered children who enjoy being at school in an idyllic location. As one parent told us, 'The school produces nicely rounded children who are confident but not arrogant. They have a spark in their eye and a spring in their step.'

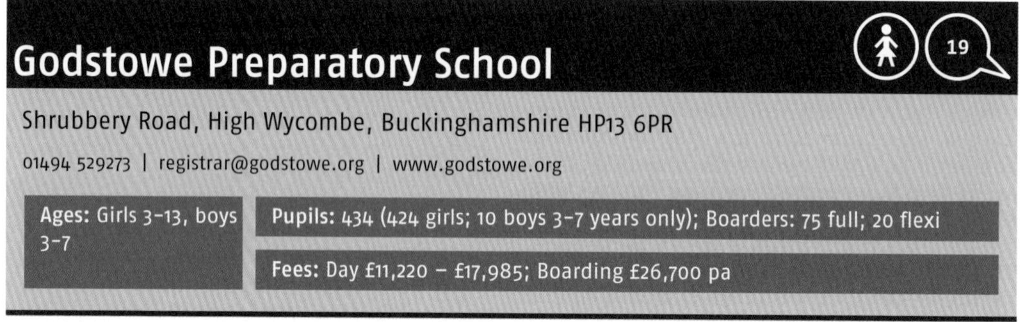

Godstowe Preparatory School

Shrubbery Road, High Wycombe, Buckinghamshire HP13 6PR

01494 529273 | registrar@godstowe.org | www.godstowe.org

Ages: Girls 3-13, boys 3-7

Pupils: 434 (424 girls; 10 boys 3-7 years only); Boarders: 75 full; 20 flexi

Fees: Day £11,220 – £17,985; Boarding £26,700 pa

Headmistress: Since September 2017, Sophie Green (40s). Warm, serene and so glamorous that we wondered if she was off to the opera after our visit. Previously head of Herries School in Cookham. She has also been director of studies at St George's Windsor Castle, where she prepared pupils for scholarships and was involved in the demanding boarding life of the choristers. She is an ISI inspector.

Ask anyone, pupil or parent, to describe her and we'd put money on them using the word 'calm'. 'I like the fact that she was in no rush to make a big show of making a difference when she joined – she just calmly gets on with doing a great job,' one parent told us. 'She's quietly spoken but make no mistake – everything she says is calmly and carefully considered and usually spot on,' said another. Admired for being a good role model to the girls, regularly using examples of strong females from history in her (very well received) speeches. 'And she's a real listener,' one parent enthused, telling how some families grumbled about parking – 'so she spent two mornings from 7.30am in the car park and then made the necessary changes.' Pupils like her 'emphasis on well-being' and that 'she's always reasonable and never raises her voice'. But, most of all, they love her black lab, 'Meg the celeb', as she is affectionately known, who – when not being walked by pupils – lies peacefully in the head's elegant study.

Lives on site with her two teenage sons. Enjoys dog walking, reading, meeting friends and travelling.

Entrance: Despite Godstowe's popularity, school is adamant that it will remain 'first come first served', non-selective. Entry to pre-prep The Lodge (boys and girls) at 3+; most girls move up to the prep (100 per cent the year we visited), with a third class opened up for newcomers in year 3. Other main entry points are years 5 and 7 but girls join all the way through from a variety of local prep and state schools (space permitting) and boarders (who can join from year 3 onwards) from further afield.

Exit: Not a specific feeder, with girls heading off to a range of senior schools notably Wycombe Abbey, Cheltenham Ladies', Queen Anne's and Downe House; others to eg St George's Ascot, Rugby, Wellington, Stowe, Haileybury, Tudor Hall, Oundle, Uppingham, Pipers Corner, St Edward's, Bradfield, Millfield, Headington, Heathfield and Marlborough. A handful leave for local grammars at 11.

Our view: England's first girls' boarding prep school and Enid Blyton's inspiration (though not the only contender) for Malory Towers, purpose built in 1900. The grounds make excellent use of a hilly, if a little blustery, site overlooking High Wycombe, with the original pretty Virginia creeper-clad buildings now housing years 3 to 8, plus The Lodge and nursery buildings. The few boys in pre-prep, mostly siblings, move on at the age of 7.

The airy atrium-style reception building (buzzing at pick-up and drop-off times – 'we want parents to really feel at home here') is a more modern addition to the more rustic Victorian buildings and has a gallery-like atmosphere, setting the tone for the rather artsy feel of the whole school. It also gives a flavour of the wholesomeness that abounds, from the display cabinet of ceramic teapots (year 6) to the fresh-faced girls beaming from the 'Godstowe in Iceland' photobooks on the large oak coffee table. As if on cue when we arrived, a teacher practically skipped through reception humming a song from Beauty and the Beast; another walked through with a box of pom-poms; and the girls actually curtsied when introduced to us.

When you ask them what a Godstowe girl is, they practically sing in unison, 'well-mannered, happy and successful.' Not that girls here are taught to follow the crowd

We found Godstowe to be jolly hockey sticks without the plums in mouths. That's not to say all the girls are from well-heeled backgrounds, but that they have the boisterous enthusiasm and excitement with very traditional (some might say old-fashioned) manners while remaining thoroughly grounded. Definitely not a school placing importance on hushed tones, girls dash about chatting noisily (we even heard screams of exhilaration in the nursery playground) and when you ask them what a Godstowe girl is, they practically sing in unison, 'well-mannered, happy and successful.' Not that girls here are taught to follow the crowd – far from it, they're encouraged to value their uniqueness and to find the thing(s) they're good at.

Non-selective it may be, but success is in the air. Minority (about 15 per cent) peel off at 11 to local schools (parents have to 'opt in' to 11+), but unlike many prep schools in the area which hothouse pupils for the sought-after Bucks grammars, this is a true 3-13 establishment, feeding its post-CE alumni into a heady mix of top day and boarding indies, many with scholarships. Which are pretty abundant, by the way, with the current record for one year standing at 54, to 20 different schools. School puts this down to 'commitment and dedication of staff, who provide quality teaching and know the girls really well' and is proud not to share the pushy reputation of some of its competition. Godstowe Diploma – a three-tier award scheme that recognises soft skills for year 7 and 8 girls – recently launched.

French is taught from reception, Latin from year 6 (plus Latin and Spanish as options from year 7) in creatively themed classrooms. Classes in pre-prep school 'subtly' streamed, with a maximum class size of 18. Formal setting in maths from year 3 and in all academic subjects from year 6. Girls stay in form rooms for lessons in years 3 and 4, after which they start to move around the school for individual subjects. We saw as many

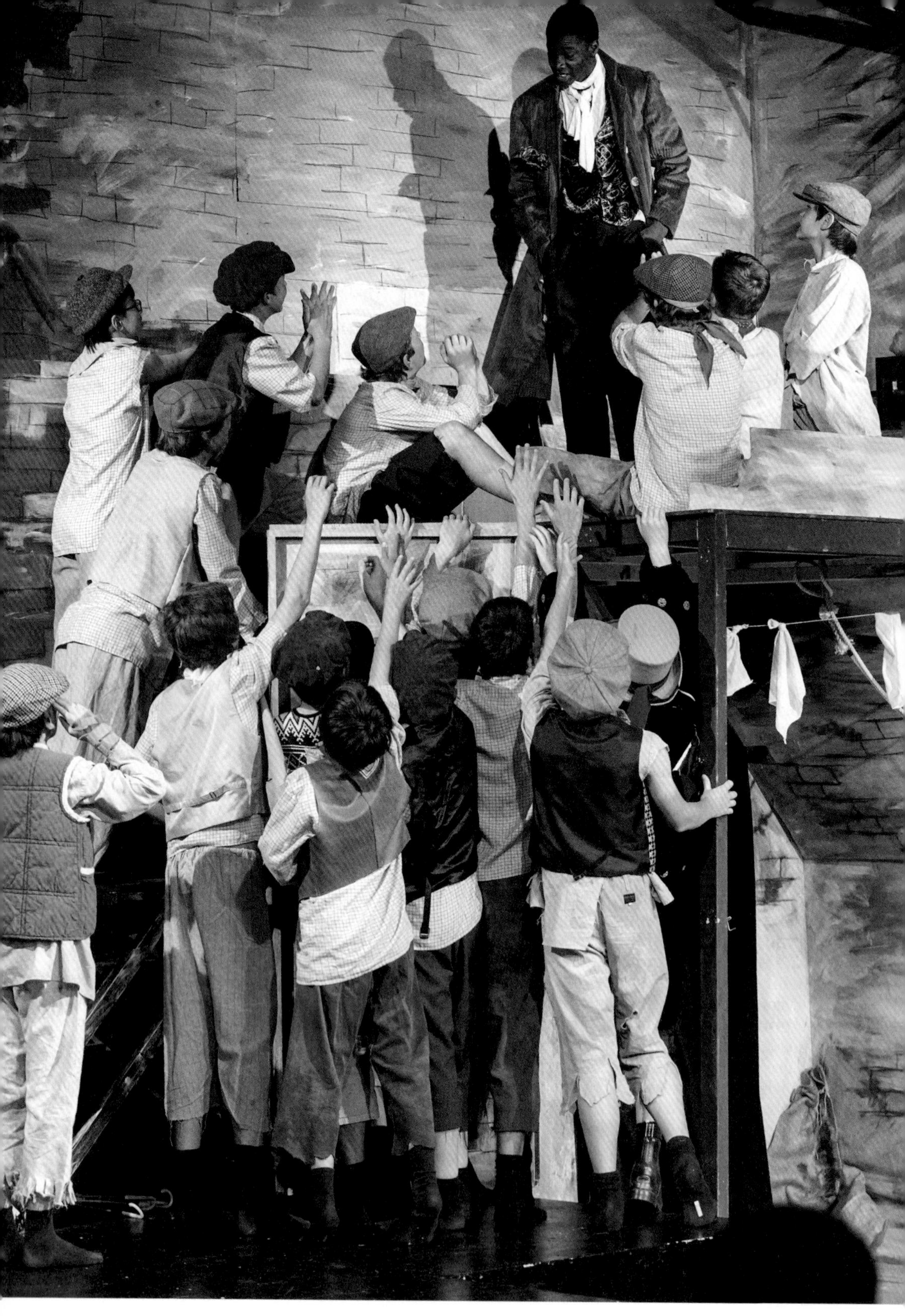

girls learning on their feet and interactively as we did staring at talking teachers. Science particularly exciting, say girls – 'especially when you get your Bunsen burner licence in year 5'.

England's first girls' boarding prep school and Enid Blyton's inspiration (though not the only contender) for Malory Towers

General acceptance that everyone learns differently and SEN is all in a day's work rather than marginalised. Two dedicated SEN staff in place and an excellent EAL programme that we saw in action – mostly for those boarders from the Far East and Spain, with girls' needs assessed upon entry to the school and timetabled to meet their specific requirements. 'My daughter has dyslexia and it's been a complete non-issue getting her the support she needs,' one parent told us.

Creative pursuits are well catered for, with a dedicated sewing room in DT where girls knock up skirts and dresses for the years 7 and 8 fashion show ('the highlight of the year,' said one pupil). Large, bright and airy art room a joy to visit – we saw girls getting messy and smiling from ear to ear as they worked, with every nook and cranny (along with much of the rest of the school) displaying arts and crafts in just about every form you can think of, from glazed sweet packets and shoes to life-size papier-mâché humans that wouldn't look out of place in a GCSE exhibition. Head of art considered something of a legend and her specialisation of 3D work is welcomed. Food technology centre opened in 2017 by Mary Berry.

Some 300 girls learn musical instruments and practise daily in bright, well-equipped studios. Parents say the standard is 'incredible'. 'It is not unusual for me to give out certificates for grade 8 with distinction in assemblies and we have two pupils currently working towards a diploma too,' says head. All pupils are encouraged to participate from the age of 3 in regular recitals and choir is compulsory in years 3 to 6. JK Theatre is used for music concerts, as well as the three major annual drama productions, in which pupils can also get involved backstage. Drama is now on curriculum in the upper years.

Sports – for which there's plenty of outside space, plus £2m sports hall – include the usual suspects (netball and lacrosse) taking centre pitch, all to a high competitive standard. Athletics and rounders are also on offer, as are ballet, gymnastics and dance. New competition-sized swimming pool will doubtless put swimming back high on the agenda. 'It's a bit gendered,' criticised one parent, although cricket and indoor football are available as after-school clubs. Some parents feel the A and B teams are a bit exclusive.

The mobile phone arms race was stopped by the clever acquisition of 100 bog standard phones (yes, these do still exist) into which girls can insert their own SIM cards to call home. Thursdays are 'no go gadget' evenings in the boarding houses to further encourage those old-fashioned skills, reading, conversation and game playing. Girls say the best thing about Godstowe is 'everyone is happy all the time' – future careers in PR await. Food considered 'great' but uniforms (well, the cloaks anyway) are a sticking point for some parents as 'it's so impractical in the winter' (head says it's on her list).

For day girls, early drop-off plus breakfast (7.30am) and late pick-up plus supper (7pm) is available for day girls at low cost and the 'enrichment curriculum' (that's after-school clubs in old money) offers up to 50 options. These range from the traditional sports, LAMDA and wind band to Mandarin, politics and yoga, with up to 100 girls staying for these. Post CE, year 8s are given a lifestyle crash course to prepare them for a less cosseted existence. Includes classes in self-defence, internet safety and relationships, charitable works, trips out and visiting lecturers. Overall behaviour very good, with LOFT (loss of free time – again, in old money that's detentions) for misdemeanours – 'very rare,' say girls.

The mobile phone arms race was stopped by the acquisition of 100 bog standard phones (yes, these do still exist) into which girls can insert their own SIM cards to call home

Families hail from a 20-mile radius for day girls, with minibuses servicing three routes. Friends of Godstowe (FoG) organises the usual fairs, cake sales and coffee mornings etc, though one parent felt 'there's less of a community than I've experienced at other preps'.

Boarding: From year 3. Can be full time or flexible with many day girls choosing to try it in years 7 and 8 as a taster for senior school. Parents say boarding is 'exemplary'. 'It's an extremely caring, nurturing and organised environment – you know they'll get all their prep and music practice done and you also know they'll have fun,' said one parent, while another told us, 'They make me feel very much part of the school even though I'm hardly there.' Boarding facilities homely, albeit in need of a lick of paint in places, with dorms (sleeping between four and eight), cosy common rooms and homely kitchens. All have their own large gardens with plenty of outdoor equipment. Newly appointed head of boarding and housemistresses are non-teaching staff, leaving them free to focus on girls' pastoral care. Good mix of full, weekly and flexi boarders, with strong international mix – some 40 per cent from overseas. Weekend activities keep boarders busy, many of which take place off site (bowling, skating, theatre, cinema etc). 'I found it hard when I arrived as I missed home, but everyone was so lovely that it was soon okay,' one pupil told us.

The last word: This is a school with energy, where girls are lively to the point of effervescent and focused but not pressured. A passion for creativity is also bred into the core of this traditional school and latent talent is drawn out of those who didn't even know they had it.

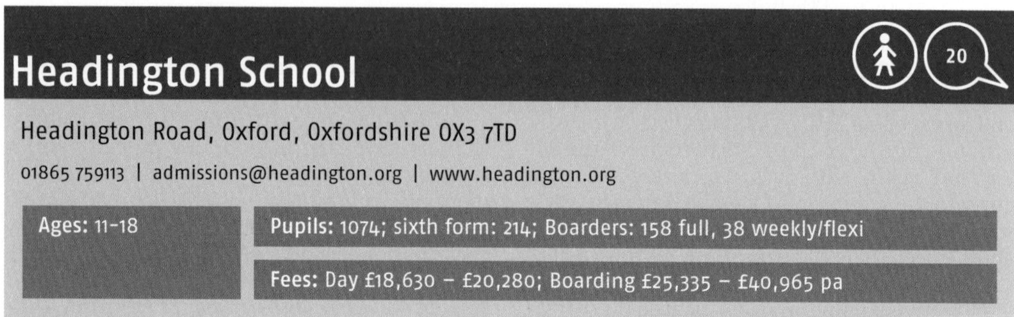

Headington School

Headington Road, Oxford, Oxfordshire OX3 7TD

01865 759113 | admissions@headington.org | www.headington.org

Ages: 11–18

Pupils: 1074; sixth form: 214; Boarders: 158 full, 38 weekly/flexi

Fees: Day £18,630 – £20,280; Boarding £25,335 – £40,965 pa

Head: Since 2011, Caroline Jordan (50s). Previously head of St George's Ascot and before that spent 10 years at Wycombe Abbey where she was head of sixth form and deputy senior housemistress. Currently vice chair of the Independent Schools Council.

A local girl, she was educated at St Helen and St Katharine in Abingdon, read geology at Oxford and did her PGCE (science) at Manchester. Plain-spoken and businesslike, it came as no surprise to learn that she'd built up and run her own company before turning her hand to teaching. Nor, with her brazen go-getting approach, that she regularly reminds pupils she 'might wake up tomorrow and want to do something completely different again'. Headington girls know well that there are many paths you can follow in life.

As in many large secondaries, pupils don't claim to know her well, but describe her as 'inspirational' and as having 'high expectations – very good for us'. Parents, for the most part, agree, telling us that she 'commands authority while still being friendly' and 'always has an eye on the bigger picture – there's nothing she doesn't know about the wider world of education and she knows exactly where the school is headed'. One, however, felt 'she doesn't really know the girls, or value them on an individual level, and that comes across.' Only teaches ad-hoc when required – 'I'd be an expensive teacher – my time is definitely better served elsewhere.'

Lives on site with husband Richard, retired; has an adult son and a stepson. Holidays are spent at their 500-year-old house in France.

Entrance: Several applicants for every place (but bear in mind that girls will be sitting for other schools too). For entry at 11+ girls sit papers in English, maths and non-verbal reasoning and have an interview. Prep school candidates (13+ entry) come for an interview and taster day after the pre-test; all others at 13+ sit papers in English, maths, science and a modern European language and have an interview. Sixth form entrants sit exams at Headington in the November before their proposed entry.

Exit: Around 40 per cent depart post-GCSE, most to local co-ed sixth forms. School says rising cost of living is the major factor and that 'for a small number of girls, our sixth form is not the right academic fit'. But girls we spoke to felt the lure of co-ed was stronger – that, or they want to brave the wider world. 'Bear in mind,' pointed out one, 'that some have been at the school since they were barely out of nappies and they simply feel ready for a change.' Nearly all sixth form leavers to university, around 85 per cent to Russell Group. UCL, Durham, Bristol, King's College London and Nottingham recently popular. Oxbridge, medicine and veterinary hopefuls get application support and so do girls applying for architecture. The latter receive specialist lectures and help with

A parent told us, 'If I ever have problems with teachers, I go straight to the head of department and get a call straight back'

portfolio preparation – must account for the unusually high number of Headington girls accepted to study this oversubscribed subject. Usually several to Oxbridge – two in 2021, plus 15 medics.

Latest results: In 2021, 85 per cent 9-7 at GCSE; 76 per cent A*/A at A level (92 per cent A*-B). IB average 41. In 2019 (the last year when exams took place) 77 per cent 9-7 at GCSE; 50 per cent A*/A at A level (78 per cent A*-B). IB average 37 in 2019.

Teaching and learning: Grades on a piece of paper are only half the story here. 'When girls go on to interviews at the likes of Deloitte, they need to evidence their skills in creativity, teamwork and innovation and we want them fully prepared,' says head – hence the big push on girls learning to think in the round. We met year 7s who had been looking at flight not just artistically, but from a science and even maths perspective; and watch this space for the new creativity and innovation centre, completion due 2021.

Girls say they feel stretched, but not under pressure, although one did tell us of her friend who 'suffered from depression under the weight of GCSEs – the school counsellor really helped her, though'. 'They are expected to work hard and take responsibility for their learning, but support is very much there if you need it,' reckoned a parent. We observed engaging, well planned teaching delivered in a multitude of ways (multimedia, collaboration, traditional lecturing etc), with girls describing their teachers as both 'positive' and 'reinforcing rather than critical'. A parent told us, 'If I ever have problems with teachers, I go straight to the head of department and get a call straight back.' Top tip: expect to get stuck in if you tour during lesson times; we were invited to join in fascinating critical thinking class, then later tackle A level chemistry problems (help!). Setting in maths from year 7 and science and languages from year 8.

Languages are on the up; school bucks the national trend here – 'simply down to a push on promotion,' claims school, though we wondered if girls are also lured by the trips, eg Cologne to the Christmas markets, exchange trips to Spain, joint trip to Germany with Abingdon. Mostly native teachers immerse girls from the off, with a term each dedicated to French, German and Spanish from year 7; they drop whichever one they like least in year 8 and take at least one at GCSE. Surprisingly no Mandarin, although it is offered as an after-school club. Latin and coding (counts as a language here) taught for two years to all from year 7. Ancient Greek available at GCSE.

Girls take 10 GCSEs max 'because there is so much else that we want them to do', with decreasing number of IGCSEs. Changes to curriculum now allow more choice – so besides the core English, maths and science, they can build their timetable from the 26 other GCSEs available – school says it gives pupils more chance to specialise eg in creative subjects, languages, sciences, classics, and more unusual combinations to suit each individual. At A level, pupils choose three (sometimes four, occasionally five) from 25 subjects including fine art, computing, psychology, politics and most recently dance. About a third do EPQ. About 20 per cent take-up for IB – 'great teaching,' report girls, although a few feel there could be more cross-over with A level teaching eg in languages – 'I literally never see my friends who are on the A level course,' complained one IB pupil.

Learning support and SEN: Around 10 per cent on the SEND register, with support above and beyond, according to parents (all one-to-one, never in the classroom itself). 'I was worried that as it's such a big school, they'd overlook my daughter but I couldn't have been more wrong – the support is phenomenal and is seamlessly linked up with pastoral and medical team too,' said one.

'Everyone thinks good portraits are about using the right colours, but actually it's all about the right tones' was one nugget of wisdom we heard in a year 10 art class

The arts and extracurricular: 'I sit there with my mouth open at these young ladies who produce these amazing concerts,' said a parent about the music, which nobody could accuse of being an add-on here. Even before we'd set foot in the swanky and well-equipped music centre, we were met with a vibrant 'on this day…' music fact sheet displayed on a podium like a menu in a restaurant. All girls participate in music during their first two years and the opportunities don't stop at classical, with ensembles including jazz, soul train, music tech club and big band. Girls write their own music and record it in the recording studio. Visits from composers and conductors are plentiful, as are break and lunchtime concerts.

Drama too is compulsory for years 7 and 8 – 'good for getting girls out of their comfort zone', with backstage opportunities also for the taking including lighting and wardrobe. We would love to have hung around to see the end result of the almost deafening drilling by workmen to create a stage for the latest play in the 240-seat theatre complete with box office – 'Oh, believe me, it will be amazing,' our tour guide shouted excitedly over the din. Recent examples of the biannual whole-school productions include Legally Blonde and Alice in Wonderland. 'Turns out my daughter is quite an actor – I'd never have known,' said one parent.

'Everyone thinks good portraits are about using the right colours, but actually it's all about the right tones' was just one of many nuggets of wisdom we heard in a year 10 art class. Finished products (and many in the making too) are terrific, with fine art and textiles (both of which are offered at A level) displayed along with ceramics and installations all over the school, including in the head's office. We were amazed to hear that art is due to move out of the magnificent double-height art building – the facilities are enviable. But there are plans afoot to turn this into a state-of-the-art food and tech building, while art will move into the new creativity hub.

Rowing facilities include a fabulous modern space packed with the latest rowing machines and the icing on the cake will be the new riverside boathouse

CCF (from year 9 upwards) is popular and DofE attracts good numbers too. Charity expeditions to the likes of Ethiopia and Cambodia, history trips to Russia, classics trips to Italy, just to name a few. 'There's Costa Rica and Iceland available for next year,' added a pupil. For parents worried about watching their life savings fritter away, school reassured us that 'we try not to make them too expensive', adding that they also run residentials closer to home, eg creative writing course in Shropshire.

Sport: 'Sport for all' was deemed a weak point in our previous visit. Not so now, with the school having completely changed the way it delivers sport, dedicating (as so many schools do, yet strangely rarely in girls' schools) one afternoon a week to it. It's paying off both in fixtures, competitions and tournaments (we heard how girls now seem to have more stamina to fight to the end in those last crucial games and moments of the game to see them through to the next level) and for keeping girls fit and healthy. With over 30 different sporting activities, ranging from the main players of hockey (autumn term), netball (spring term) and swimming and athletics (summer term) to the less obvious fencing and cheerleading, there is no shortage of pursuits to try out – nearly all in world-class facilities. Many of the sports feature in clubs. Dance particularly strong – one girl told us it was one of her main pulls to the school and that she's since started up a club teaching younger ones (many of the clubs are student led here).

Current South African head of rowing credited with bringing the school national and international success on the water – in the year we visited, girls won one gold, two silver and two bronze medals in the National Schools Regatta and two girls were rowing for GB. Girls start training in the summer term of year 7 (bear in mind that boys generally don't begin until age 13) as part of a programme run in conjunction with Oxford Brookes, in which everything is carefully monitored. Facilities include a fabulous modern space packed with the latest rowing machines and the icing on the cake will be the new riverside boathouse, due to bring them on par with other notable Oxfordshire rowing schools such as Abingdon – a far cry from the current portakabins they share with St Edward's School.

Boarding: About a quarter of pupils board, either full time, weekly or (increasingly popular) half-weekly – 'We initially thought it would help attract more girls into the sixth form, but actually it's the younger girls who love boarding for either the first or second half of the week because they get to do all the extracurricular, as well as getting their prep done and getting more sleep as they can get up later,' says head. When we visited, three-quarters of the junior boarding house (one of five in total) was made up of half-weekly or weekly boarders.

The five boarding houses, all very different in architecture, are cheerful, with plenty of home comforts and personal touches. Dorms range in size from four for younger ones to single bedrooms for the upper sixths. For those who stay on weekends (mostly international pupils) we saw sign-up sheets for Westfield shopping, Christmas card making, rock climbing, panto and canvas bag printing, among others. Sixth form boarders have modern kitchens and may cook for themselves as long as they ask in advance – enables house parents to be sure girls aren't missing meals. They

Some of the newer buildings are magnificent – the award-winning library is among the most inviting we've ever seen

can also go to parties and stay over with school friends – parents are emailed for permission.

Ethos and heritage: Founded in 1915 by a group of evangelical Christians to provide a 'sound education for girls to fit them for the demands and opportunities likely to arise after the war'. Occupied various houses in the area, trading up as it grew from 18 to today's 1,000 (including 280 in prep school). Present main school was built in the 1930s in a sharp-edged, neo-Georgian style. Set in 23 acres just off Oxford's busy London Road, it's right next to the hospitals, and ambulance sirens lend it an extra urban edge. But despite its town site there's a sense of space, and plenty of greenery remains undeveloped. Some of the newer buildings are magnificent – the award-winning library is among the most inviting we've ever seen: a striking, innovative and contemporary space with floor-to-ceiling glass and separate areas for reading, quiet study and computer work in addition to the main space. Dazzling new sixth form centre with sunken lighting, angular sofas and plentiful green plants. The design included a traffic light system that means pupils have green areas to sit, socialise and eat, amber where they can work collaboratively and red for silent working. The Hive, a creativity and innovation centre, opened in 2021 – includes art studios, photographic studio, 3D workshop, darkroom, textiles studios, seminar room, lecture theatre and double-height gallery. New food and nutrition centre due to open in 2022 featuring teaching kitchens plus demonstration kitchen.

We saw year 7s charge full-throttle into the lunch hall – bags hurled down in a huge (but surprisingly neat) pile. Was it (a) that they are really hungry or (b) that you have to fight for space, we asked our tour guides – neither, they said, it's just that they're really excitable, although nobody denies that feeding 800 girls in an hour-and-a-half is no mean feat. With food this good (and varied too), we weren't surprised to hear of the in-joke among staff about the Headington stone, which most newbies (staff, not pupils) put on once they start on the lunches.

OGs include Baroness Young, Julia Somerville, Lady Longford, Christina Onassis, Emma Watson and Lily van den Broecke.

Pastoral care, inclusivity and discipline: This is a large and busy school, but there are two tutors for every form group and two part-time drop-in school counsellors. Each class is also allocated two elected prefects who get to know the girls and alert staff if they think a girl is struggling in any way. But for every one parent we spoke to that praised the pastoral care, there was one that felt there was room for improvement – one was 'horrified' by an incident in which 'the girls were put into rooms and asked to sign statements'. School should do more on sex ed, felt one parent.

On the strict side, report pupils, with a detention system for most infringements and usually a couple of temporary exclusions per year. 'I find the heads of year quite bullish, handing out penalty points, which lead to detentions, a bit too easily – you have to be able to fail and these girls need nurturing,' voiced one parent.

Pupils and parents: Wholesome, polite, swishy-haired girls. Quite, but not very, posh. You feel they'll survive well in the outside world. Not a shrinking violet in sight, with some very vocal in their views of wanting more opportunity for self-expression: 'You have to wear your hair up, no scrunchies, only one piercing in each ear, no shaped eyebrows, no jewellery except for a cross – it's quite annoying,' said one. Pupils would also like to see more integration between different year groups.

Parents mainly medics, lawyers, academics, IT professionals etc. 'It's very friendly – I've made a lot of mum friends in my year,' said one. Fewer full-time working mothers than you'd expect, said a parent, but growing numbers work part-time. International students from 47 countries, vast majority from the Far East, but lack of integration is apparently much less of a problem than it once was and IB and rowing reputation are attracting more Europeans.

Comms between school and parents reportedly excellent – 'We get told things far in advance and get Show My Homework,' said one.

Money matters: Academic scholarships of up to 10 per cent of fees. Free tuition in one instrument is offered for music scholarships. All scholars, including for art, dance, drama and sport, also benefit from a structured scholars' programme, offering masterclasses, specialist coaching and mentoring. Means-tested bursaries of up to 100 per cent of fees.

The last word: A school with high expectations, but coupled with a recognition that achievement doesn't come exclusively from academic areas. Super facilities and spacious grounds too.

Heathfield School

21

London Road, Ascot, Berkshire SL5 8BQ

01344 898343 | admissions@heathfieldschool.net | www.heathfieldschool.net

Ages: 11–18

Pupils: 230; sixth form: 45; Boarders: 110 full, 40 weekly

Fees: Day: £23,520 – £24,000; Boarding: £37,950 – £38,850 pa

Headmistress: Since January 2021, Sarah Wilson (40s). Previously senior deputy head at Cranford House and before that director of sport and head of year (sixth form) at St Helen and St Katharine. Prize-winning first in education with geography and PE from Brunel; MA (Open University) in educational leadership. Chairs GSA Sports and Wellness Committee. Has a daughter in lower sixth and a son at a nearby co-ed.

'Personable', 'always happy to chat', say parents, whose daughters 'absolutely love her'. 'Very kind', 'empathetic', 'a good role model'. A self-professed 'eternal optimist', she joined the school just as that gloomy January lockdown began. 'I got to know people in a very practical way,' she says, finding the 'huge focus on community' invigorating. 'We did lots online together, including dancing on Zoom.'

A 'huge advocate of an all-girls education' and describes 'a sense of coming home' when she got the job. Loves the relaxed interaction between staff and pupils. Plays flute in the orchestra ('I'm not a fantastic flautist but I love it') and one mum recounts the moment when she 'went into school to find her in her trainers playing rugby with the girls'. Competed at British gymnastics championships in 2016 (pretty awesome, we thought), sadly no YouTube evidence forthcoming.

First task was to introduce more flexible boarding model. 'We now offer modern boarding and the flexibility that families need,' she says, keen to 'underpin Heathfield's values whilst moving forward and evolving'. No doubt it will broaden their market, with interest from London having already grown. For a school that was exclusively full boarding until 2015, it's a big change – now roughly half-half day and boarding in years 7 and 8 with more boarding weekly. Boarders outweigh day from year 9 up.

Entrance: 'Brilliant' admissions process praised by parents – 'They knew exactly who she was from the off'. Taster days give potential candidates 'a good feel' for the school. Assessments for 11+ and 13+ in November before entry. Online CEM test, interview with the head and reference from current school – 'not strenuous', we hear. Happy for year 6s to go through the process for a year 9 place and get it all done and dusted. Interview and reference for 16+ applicants, too – offers conditional on GCSE results.

Most from local or London prep schools. Numbers up a quarter since 2015, with bigger cohorts making their way up through the school (but they promise to expand beyond 280).

Exit: Up to 15 per cent after GCSEs for reasons you'd expect (boys, sixth form colleges, change of scene). For year 13s, Newcastle and Exeter popular recently with ones and twos going everywhere from Bristol to Brookes, St Andrews to Salford. Handful each year to art, design or fashion foundations and degrees. No medics or Oxbridge since 2018 and 2016 respectively, though there's interest in both.

Latest results: In 2021, 63 per cent 9-7 at GCSE; 65 per cent A*/A at A level (86 per cent A*-B). In 2019 (the last year when exams took place), 45 per cent 9-7 at GCSE; 38 per cent A*/A at A level (67 per cent A*-B).

Teaching and learning: Gently academic, the school expects ambition and does well with broad intake. No longer seen as a finishing school for Etonians' charming sisters. Girls we met chatted happily about their lessons ('drama's fun because we get to do improvisation'; 'bit too much mapwork in geography'). Teachers eclectic – 'If you put the RS teacher and the textiles teacher and the history teacher together, the only thing they have in common is their passion,' says one mum. Good at hooking pupil interest, says another – 'The girls enjoy calculating fabric lengths in maths or examining One Direction in economics; it's not all coal mining and steel construction' (perhaps new STEM development will change that?). We saw some lessons that were livelier than others, though parents not shy if something's awry – 'God help you if you're a teacher who isn't up to par,' laughs one, 'because the WhatsApp groups are very active.' Sets from year 7 in maths and English; from year 9 in science and languages.

'We were put off by other schools that chucked exam stats at us,' said one mum, 'because I didn't want her to be a stat.' Indeed, stats not the focus, and results superficially seem a mixed bag – at GCSE, plenty of 9s in art and drama, with options (geography, RS) doing better than core subjects (lots of 5s in combined sciences). Art also shines at A level, with photography and PE up there too. It's all in the value added, though, and parents told us that they 'really get the best out of the children'. Tiny classes – average of 14 in lower school, more like eight or nine at GCSE. Encouraging and supportive to those who need it; academic girls who like being top of the class are stretched, but it's not competitive.

Big STEM investment – snazzy new science block, snazzy new teachers – should start yielding results in next couple of years. This will require a shift in culture, or perhaps it will create one. Shool says lower years are already showing interest. International design challenge for Water Intelligence running when we visited. We watched a busy physics lesson with girls getting hands-on with circuits and a very jolly, high-energy biology lesson where girls were improbably excited about a quiz on pathogens. Lots of targeted advice on what Mr or Ms Examiner will be looking for.

Bastardised school uniform was a glimpse of old-school Heathfield naughtiness – 'must marry well; trust fund baby; poor little rich kid' declared the boater's sash. Touché

Library well stocked and welcoming; librarian runs lunchtime club for those who enjoy stamping, shelving and cataloguing (lots do, apparently). Quiet reading room with comfy chairs and knick-knacks on the walls to make it feel homely.

Next big spend is on new sixth form centre, due autumn 2022. New programme to accompany it – mentoring with alumnae, leadership development, broader learning beyond the curriculum. Sixth form can take the Leiths Introductory Certificate in Food and Wine, a five-term course in cooking and entertaining – jointing poultry, filleting fish and making meringues all on the menu. Upper sixth also do a course in how to spot a nice bottle of wine (and drink it, presumably). Parents approve – 'Whenever you go to an old Heathfield girl's dinner party, they can make a soufflé and a gravy.'

Learning support and SEN: Culture of the school in general lends itself beautifully to supporting girls with SEND, and parents rave about support. Around 25 per cent on the register, many receiving timetabled one-to-one lessons. One grateful mum told us that her daughter's prep school had written her off – 'She's so dyslexic, we thought she probably wouldn't do GCSEs, but now she's on track.' Another appreciated the school's guidance: 'It's been life-changing for her.'

Thirty-two receiving English language support with qualified teacher. One-to-ones or small groups, working towards IELTS.

The arts and extracurricular: Art rooms are next-level cool, stuffed with projects past and present. A bejewelled skeleton perched on top of some drying racks; a dress made from mussel shells and leather on a mannequin in the corner. A lot of very feisty work, unsurprising given department's attitude that every project should be 'bigger, better and more interesting'. Bastardised school uniform was a glimpse of old-school Heathfield naughtiness – 'must marry well; trust fund baby; poor little rich kid' declared the boater's sash. Touché. A well-established tradition of excellence in fashion and textiles, and a touching tribute to the late Isabella Blow, alumna and muse to Steve McQueen. Partnership with Falmouth College gives GCSE and A level artists the opportunity for undergraduate-level experiences.

Musicians well catered for. More than half learn an instrument and there are choirs, orchestra and ensembles aplenty. Digital recording studio stocked with iMacs and one of those clever mixing decks – electric and acoustic guitars looked very nonchalant just lying around.

All-mod-cons 220-seat theatre, with lots do LAMDA as well as RADA Shakespeare Certificate. Drama scholars run clubs for the younger ones; there's also costume and stage make-up club and technical theatre club. Art and textiles students now involved in school productions on the creative side.

Sport: Thirty-six acres of glorious greenery. Six netball and tennis courts, five lacrosse pitches, fitness suite (on an old squash court), studios for spin and dance. Not particularly flashy, but a great offering for a small school and who needs flashy, anyway? The 25-metre swimming pool has 'leisure centre' feel, and boarders love getting the inflatable canoes out 'for silly fun' at weekends.

Sport central to school life with focus on lacrosse, netball, cricket, tennis, athletics and rounders. All year 7s represent the school – every one of our lunch companions was off to play lax that day. Fixtures organised to ensure they don't just get thrashed by A teams from big schools. Not a walkover, though – seniors won division one at recent lacrosse nationals. Rosy-cheeked girls running around in their skorts on the chilly autumnal day we visited – a wholesome, get-outside attitude. Lots of tennis year-round and trampolining popular.

Equestrian life big, though we didn't find it 'horsey'. Girls ride at Berkshire riding centre; doesn't matter if you have a pony or not. Heathfield Diamonds polo team get lots of goals off Eton, Marlborough etc – won SUPA UK Schoolgirls' National Open Championship 2020. Not all too gymkhana and jolly (recreational) hockey sticks, though. School has links with Ascot FC and a couple of girls have joined the youth ladies' team there; visits from England rugby players and a trial at Maidenhead RFC has encouraged some to pursue rugby.

Boarding: Accommodation cosy and characterful, endearingly scruffy after the rather clinical, anonymous rooms that we see so often nowadays. Colourful duvet covers, fairy lights, photos and lots of teddies add to the effect. Proper tweenage bedrooms – a bottom bunk made into a den, handbags hung over the bedpost. Noticeboards shout about 'tidiest dorm' competitions, birthdays and new year's resolutions ('to play with my new friends'; 'to try and listen more in maths'; 'to learn how to play lacrosse'). All very innocent stuff. Boarders each have their own tuck shelf – apple juice, pot noodles and Turkish delight the poisons of choice. House parents try to mix up friendship groups – 'They always get told, if you don't get your besties this term then you'll get them next term,' chuckles one mum, adding that 'of course, by then your besties have changed'.

Lots of evening activities including mindfulness Monday, honey and oat facemask making, meditation. No wonder they all look so well. Weekends more high energy – girls were off to do laser clay pigeon shooting (mind boggling), ice skating and Go Ape when we visited. Day girls often join in too. A quarter of boarders from overseas, drawn in part by proximity to Heathrow (biggest numbers from Spain and China).

Relaxed approach to going home at weekends, or parents coming to visit: 'If I want to take her out for dinner, I can just email and ask – I could never do that at my son's school.'

Every day girl attached to a boarding house, and can pop up there to hang out with friends – a nice touch, 'eroding any division between boarders and day girls,' say parents. Sixth form house more independent and separate from the rest where girls develop important life skills by doing their own laundry and ordering the odd takeaway.

'The girls enjoy calculating fabric lengths in maths or examining One Direction in economics; it's not all coal mining and steel construction'

Ethos and heritage: Founded in 1899 by Eleanor Beatrice Wyatt, of whom a rather humourless portrait hangs in reception. Miss Wyatt already ran a school in South Kensington for 'the lower-middle and lower classes', but had a change of heart, deciding that what she really ought to do was teach those who could in turn educate others (ie poshies) and that she fancied some country air. A move to Ascot was just the ticket, and Heathfield was born. School absorbed St Mary's Wantage in 2006 and started admitting day girls in 2015.

A 'good, clean environment', say parents, delighted by how the school pushes the wholesome fun – 'We have a laugh,' girls agree. One popular outing involved going to Tesco with the gappies and getting their own trolley (presumably Ocado brings it to the door at home); roller-discos and water-skiing also recent offerings. 'My daughter was wary of joining in until the school suggested indoor skydiving – you can't turn that down as a 12-year-old.' All harmless stuff but, for these girls, the ideal way to break the ice and reduce social anxiety post-lockdown.

A close-knit community. 'The other day her head of year called just to say hello and check in,' one mum tells us; communication is 'fabulous', says another. Parents feel that teachers are accessible and eachers say there is no distance between them and the girls; girls feel safe and looked after by this cohesive team of adults around them.

Pretty chapel with 'hysterical' chaplain (funny, we assume, not panicked) means that girls look forward to the services. Inscriptions of every old girl have overflowed from the wooden pews onto the wall paneling and provide a snapshot of the school's history (Betty, Diana and Joan have given way over time to Katerina, Flora and Grace). A nice sense of belonging for current girls, who tell us that they feel part of the school's story.

Famous alumnae all style and sass. Interior designer Nina Campbell, actress, ex of Jude Law and everyone's-pin-up Sienna Miller, Jimmy Choo CEO Tamara Mellon, polar explorer Rosie Stancer, and cousin-of-the-Queen Princess Alexandra, the Honourable Lady Ogilvy. Almost certainly never all in a room together, but nonetheless the list conjures irresistible notions of cocktail parties,

Chelsea dives and Marlboro Lights. More recent alumnae serve to demonstrate how the school has changed since the 90s, of course: one recent leaver just finished army officer training at Sandhurst and another worked on the front line as a newly qualified nurse during Covid.

Pastoral care, inclusivity and discipline: Exceptional pastoral care and a culture of looking after one another. Parents much more interested in talking to us about this side of school life than the academics. No eye-rolling here about teenage girls. School unfazed by 'everyday trials and tribulations' and girls talk about 'hippo time' ('it's fine to wallow – as long as you've got a strategy to get out of it'). 'If she's having a wobble, I can email one member of staff and it all gets filtered down,' said one mum. Another described how when granny wasn't well recently the school gave her daughter a card and some stamps so that she could write – 'so kind, so thoughtful'.

Everyone's Invited 'such a moment in time', says head; school 'gave the girls the opportunity to respond in whatever way they felt most comfortable'. Curriculum deals with issues around consent ('it doesn't have to be sexual; we introduce the concept of consent within friendships too') and use of alcohol and drugs. Girls can speak to staff anonymously, if they'd prefer, using an online help line accessed through a QR code. Small size allows staff to be very hands-on ('the biggest challenge of lockdown was not being able to check in with them all informally, not seeing them in a passing moment'). No formal LGBTQ+ group, but 'everybody is accepted for who they are'.

Accommodation characterful and endearingly scruffy. Proper tweenage bedrooms – a bottom bunk made into a den, handbags hung over the bedpost

Girls hang out in common rooms at break times. Welcoming spaces, all a little different – bulging bookcases trendily organised by colour, pretty fireplaces, squishy sofas. Year 8s swarmed to show us the tuck they'd bought (lollipops the snack du jour). Good old-fashioned tuck shop sells good old-fashioned sweets; none of that Jamie Oliver nonsense here, thank you very much.

Oak-panelled dining hall bustling at lunchtime, French doors opening onto garden. We visited on Mexican 'Day of the Dead' and found the array of goodies totally overwhelming (it's not often that we get buffet paralysis). Mountains of guacamole, tacos, chilli con carne and – whisper it – churros for pudding. We took a couple for the road, clinging on to them all afternoon like a child with a party bag.

Boarding organised by year-group, not vertically. Four vertical houses run independently and engender great loyalty. Lots of photos around of girls being silly in the name of house competition.

Discipline taken seriously, though school recognise that 'they're going to push boundaries, that's normal'. Vaping pre-Covid has calmed down; annual drugs searches ('we get the dogs in') yield nothing, school says. Misuse of social media results in suspension and rehabilitative safety session. Parents mentioned classroom disruption in the lower years ('room for improvement,' said one). Majority of naughtiness seems to be talking after lights-out, though, and we can forgive that.

Pupils and parents: Minibuses bring in day girls from Bracknell, Windsor, Virginia Water etc. Weekly boarders can jump on board at South Kensington and Chiswick on a Sunday evening, returning on a Friday night.

We were surprised by the international diversity of pupils – not all born and bred in the home counties by any means. Nor do they seem particularly high maintenance – a few glossy ponytails, of course, but generally low-key in the glamour stakes. Introduction of day girls has reinforced the socio-economic diversity, the school told us as we walked into the car park to see an enormous Bentley arriving for pick-up. We do believe them, though – much less old-school posh than it was. Mums say, 'It's not obvious who has cash and who doesn't.' 'It's not a cheap school, and there are going to be some parents who want the network', but 'a nice, normal, family feel', with no pressure to dress up for the school gate – less glitzy than elsewhere in the area.

Money matters: Academic, art, drama, music and sport scholarships at 11+, 13+ and 16+. Equestrian at 11+ and photography at 16+. Means-tested bursaries of up to 100 per cent awarded for financial or compassionate reasons.

The last word: A nurturing school with a popular new head who unashamedly prioritises all-roundedness. Parents appreciate the traditional skills and values – 'It's no good being a lawyer if you don't know how to poach an egg,' said one. But school keen to push the academics and leave that culture behind. We can't see why they're incompatible, and look forward to watching this generation of Heathfield girls work their way to the top of whatever field they choose, equipped with the life skills to ensure they're as happy cooking up ideas in the boardroom as they are in the kitchen.

Highfield and Brookham Schools

Highfield Lane, Liphook, Hampshire GU30 7LQ

01428 728000 | headspa@highfieldschool.org.uk | www.highfieldandbrookham.co.uk

Ages: 2-13

Pupils: 440; Boarders: 52 full, weekly/flexi

Fees: Day £11,775- £22,725; Boarding £25,800 – £28,425 pa

Head of Highfield: Since 1999, Phillip Evitt MA (Hons) Cantab, PGCE. Educated at Kimbolton School where he says he was taught by some remarkable teachers who inspired him to follow in their footsteps and changed the course of his life. Read history at Cambridge and began his teaching career at Monmouth School for Boys before spending 14 years at Dulwich College, latterly as head of history, and then on to Highfield. He never expected to get the job and has loved every minute. Married to Jo, a former lawyer and now a homeopath, she is very involved with the school in an unofficial capacity and they have four adult children who were all educated at Highfield and Brookham. They live on site and retreat to their house in Pembrokeshire during the holidays where he tinkers with his elderly Morris Traveller. He has lost none of his enthusiasm after 20 years at the helm and there has been a steady programme of improvements during his tenure. He is always looking at how to do things better and has recently hosted a conference on the future of the 13+ Common Entrance.

A highly cultured man with effortless charm who loves music and history and 'for whom nothing is too much trouble,' says a parent. He says that the school's great strength is adding real value and finding the magic in every child. He describes the school as dynamic and positive with a can-do attitude and great energy and encourages children 'to give it a go, don't listen to what others say but find out for yourself.'

Head of Brookham since 2015, Sophie Baber BA (Hons), PGCE, PG Diploma (psychology), 40s. She was head girl at Millfield and took her PGCE at Cardiff University. Her first teaching position was in a specialist school for children with behavioural problems. She then worked in two challenging state schools in London where she had her five minutes of fame on television in the documentary The Unteachables, before moving to Singapore where she spent five years at the Tanglin Trust and a further two at Marlborough College, Malaysia. She is married to Guy, a chartered surveyor, who is estates manager at the school. They have three sons who are all at Highfield and Brookham. She says she can't believe her luck and pinches herself every morning. 'It is a little slice of heaven and it is such a privilege to work here.' She is famous for her trademark gold and red spangly shoes and one parent described her as 'soft but steely' which she takes as a compliment. 'She interacts effortlessly with children on their level and enthrals them with random facts,' says a parent.

Entrance: Nursery from 2 for combo of morning and/or afternoon sessions, up to full time five days a week (subject to available days). No entrance tests for the prep, they rely on detailed reports from the child's current school and a report from the head. Most come up from Brookham pre-prep, others from local primaries as well as those who have moved to the area from London day schools. School wants to be confident that children will flourish and be happy.

Entrance for foreign nationals is via the UKiset test and a reference and report from the child's current school.

Exit: Most move on at 13+ but a few go at 11+ and school supports them. Sends to a huge range of schools including Wellington, Marlborough, Cranleigh, Charterhouse, Eton, Harrow, Winchester, Harrow, Radley, Sherbourne, Royal Grammar School and Guildford High School. The headmaster has built strong relationships with the senior schools and great care is taken to find the right school for the child; parents are involved with the decisions from early on. Good scholarship record across the board most years and children are well prepared for the ISEB pretest. Six scholarships in 2021.

Our view: The school was founded in 1892 in Southampton and bought by the Mills Family in 1904. It moved to its present purpose-built site in 1907. It is now owned by Bill Mills, the grandson of the founder; he is chairman of the board of directors of both schools and is very involved.

Always forward looking, the school went co-ed in 1978.

On the borders of West Sussex, Surrey and Hampshire, in prime commuter belt, you enter the school off a quiet country lane and down a rhododendron avenue. It is set in 175 acres and the Edwardian main building is light and airy with views across the playing fields and the school's own nine-hole golf course to the woods beyond. There have been additions over the years, some more elegant than others, and the light, bright atrium is the hub of the school, 'where you go if you want to find out something,' says a pupil. There is a constant programme of refurbishment and everything is immaculate inside and out. One parent described it as an oasis where children can have an old-fashioned childhood but still be aware of the outside world.

Small classes with a maximum of 18. Children are set for maths from year 5 and streamed for English from year 6. The top set in year 7 and the separate scholarship stream in year 8 have extra classes to broaden their thinking through discussions on politics and philosophy and current affairs.

Science is taught in well-equipped labs and is 'really fun with lots of experiments,' say our guides, and some biology lessons are taught outside. Well-stocked library and reading for pleasure is promoted. All have to read for 20 minutes a day and boarders always read before lights out. Good mix of youth and experience among the staff including the occasional PGCE student. The school is strong on staff development and all are encouraged to look beyond the curriculum and all who leave move on to promotions.

Head describes school as dynamic and positive and encourages children 'to give it a go, don't listen to what others say but find out for yourself'

Regular CAT and other tests give the teachers an insight into learning profiles so that learning can be tailored to each child and the curriculum is reviewed regularly. Two EAL teachers for the 30 or so foreign nationals who need support. Some arrive with only a basic level of English and have total immersion supported by one-to-one or small-group tuition; 'They learn incredibly quickly at this age,' says the headmaster.

The SENCo is an advocate of growth mindset and learning support runs across both schools. Teachers know the children well and can spot potential problems without the need for blanket testing. Some children have in-class support and others have about 10 minutes a day of one-to-one support. We spoke to a parent of a child with learning difficulties who said that the school really understands inclusion and has enabled their child to take part in everything.

Sport is played five afternoons a week, there are acres of playing fields and a nine-hole golf course together with a 20-metre indoor pool, recently refurbished sports hall, squash court and mirrored dance and drama studio. Most recent is the addition of a brand-new, floodlit all-weather Astro. The usual major sports including rugby, cricket, hockey, football and lacrosse and girls' cricket as well as a range of minor ones. 'Everyone can play in a match if they want to' and 'you don't have to be that brilliant,' said our guides. 'No one is excluded,' says a parent and children take just as much pride being in the fifth team as the first. They are taught to 'win with dignity and lose with grace', although the trophy cabinets groaning with silverware suggest that they have more practice at the former.

All have a weekly music lesson and can create their own sounds using GarageBand on a bank of computers. About two-thirds learn an instrument with increasing numbers achieving grades 6-8. External musicians come to work with pupils and recently performed Vivaldi's Gloria with the senior choir. Numerous opportunities to perform in public including weekly cushion concerts, the rock concert, the termly formal concert and other informal events open to all abilities.

Drama and dance lessons every fortnight and each year group puts on an annual play with year 8 doing theirs after Common Entrance. The school has its own theatre with retractable tiered seating. Lots of opportunities to stand up in public like LAMDA, debates, poetry recitations and public speaking.

Weekly art lessons and an impressive end-of-year art exhibition. Pottery especially popular and we admired a fine display of clay cottages and Greek pots. Year 4 make the clay poppies for the Remembrance Day service. Well-equipped DT room with laser cutter and 3D printer – children are encouraged to experiment and work together and share ideas and were making stickers for their iPads on the day we visited.

Huge variety of clubs including Greek, Mandarin, debating, dance (ballet and modern), quidditch, cookery and bridge and a range of sports as well as mountain biking and running in the National Park. One-hour lesson a week on Highfield Keys Programme, a sort of mini DofE award which helps develop soft skills and creativity and aims to introduce children to lifelong interests. They learn about the environment, interview techniques and problem solving, as well as touch typing, first aid and cookery. Regular trips include the much-anticipated year 7 adventure trip to Scotland at the beginning of the summer holidays, year 8 trip to France and the year 6 trip to the Dorset coast.

The school's eco credentials are excellent and it is almost carbon neutral with a biomass boiler fuelled with wood from the estate. Environmental studies are part of the curriculum for year 4, year 6 learn bushcraft and the eco-committee, with two reps from each year group, meets fortnightly.

Strong involvement with Mental Health First Aid England which promotes the importance of mental health in schools. Highfield and Brookham took the lead and hosted a conference and helped kick-start mental health awareness in prep schools. Two mental health first aid teachers train other members of staff so that every teacher in the school is trained in mental health and wellbeing. 'Everyone needs to be aware and to know what to do,' says the headmaster. They also run a two-day programme for parents. Internet safety talk for children and their parents in years 7 and 8. Year 8 can train as peer listeners and our guides said that so many people want to do it that there won't be enough people to listen to. 'Pastoral care is brilliant across the board and children feel listened to and respected,' says a parent.

The High Reach Programme takes children out of their bubble and makes them aware of the wider world. Years 7 and 8 visit and help in two local special schools and an old people's day centre. 'There is an emphasis on actually helping people rather than just raising money,' says a parent, although the school does raise over £70,000 a year for charity.

Children can take on positions of responsibility such as form captain in all year groups and year 8 act as role models and can be part of pupil leadership team – head boy and girl, deputies, house and boarding house captains. The headmaster says he can take the pulse of the school from his conversations with them. The children are confident and good conversationalists.

Many parents are successful professionals and there is an increasing number of working mothers. Often privately educated, they have high standards and 'know what good looks like,' says the headmaster. His door is open for parents and he will always listen and respond, but may not necessarily agree. Parents are active and engaged and very supportive of the school; they can walk and run in the grounds and there is a lot of socialising. One new parent who had moved down from London said she felt scooped up and welcomed as soon as she arrived and had a ready-made set of friends within a few weeks.

Alumni include: designer and restaurateur, Terence Conran; Downing Street chief of staff under Tony Blair, Jonathan Powell; Lord Justice of Appeal, Sir Andrew Moylan and actor, Rupert Vansittart.

The school is almost carbon neutral with a biomass boiler fuelled with wood from the estate. Environmental studies are part of the curriculum for year 4

Brookham is the nursery and pre-prep school for Highfield. The schools share a site but have separate buildings and are autonomous. The head reports directly to the proprietor but works closely with the headmaster of Highfield.

Brookham was founded in 1992 on the same site as Highfield and is a series of light-filled interconnecting octagons. Everything is painted in tasteful muted colours and the outdoor play equipment is made from wood from the estate as head says that too many primary colours and clutter distract the children. Soothing music is played at the start of the day and there are no large laptops or iPads in the classrooms as 'they overstimulate the children and there is a time and a place for IT.' 'The atmosphere is very calm,' says a mother, and 'you feel soothed when you go in.' Maximum class size is 18 and there are two or three classes per year. Children go to the main school for lunch, music, theatre, swimming and sports pitches and so get the best of both worlds.

'Risk and challenge are vital,' says the head, 'and children learn from mistakes and how to ask for help.' Teaching is interactive and children are encouraged to question things and 'wonder if' and 'let's have a go and see what happens'. The wonder wall with a word of the week is covered with interesting facts and questions such as, 'What colour would a zebra be if it didn't have any stripes?'

The culture is a mix of tradition, freedom, challenge and exploration and parents need to buy into this and understand the ethos. Plenty of collaboration with parents who are invited to work with the children and spend a morning at the forest school. There is not much homework as parents might muck it up says head, who, by her own admission, is very pedantic.

Not the right school for anyone who doesn't like their children getting dirty. As much teaching as possible takes place outside and children can play in the mud pit in the garden and waterproofs and wellies are part of the uniform. Each year group has its own section in the forest school for building camps and campfires and there is even an outdoor cinema. Children can grow their own vegetables and have put up a barn owl box and watched the chicks hatch.

There is much talk about being kind, courageous and the best you can be and children are encouraged to solve their own problems and have to take responsibility for themselves from nursery upwards. They talk through problems and learn how to work on emotional wellbeing from a very young age.

Boarding: Boarding numbers at a current high, with half of all pupils now boarding. Means that for the first time in years, the senior boarding house is full, with around 130 boarders from years 6, 7 and 8; the junior boarding house, for years 4 and 5, is home to around 13 children, with space for a few more. Usually around 30 who stay at weekends, but that can go up to 80 if there is a popular activity. Numbers tend to be biggest in summer term as parents think about preparing their children for senior school. Junior boarders have their own self-contained co-ed house which is cosy and homely. The older boarders live in the main house with boys and girls in different wings. All dorms well decorated and immaculate – the matrons give prizes for tidiness. Elegant dining room adorned with honours boards and paintings – cafeteria-style eating with very good food and masses of choice.

Money matters: The school runs a bursary scheme for children whose families would not be able to afford the fees. Highfield and Brookham collaborate with senior schools to make sure pupils are supported in their teenage years with similar bursaries.

The last word: Highfield and Brookham have really got it all – a beautiful setting but within commuting distance of London, happy children who are allowed to enjoy their childhood but are aware of the outside world, good academic results and two inspirational and innovative heads.

Horris Hill School

Newtown, Newbury, Berkshire RG20 9DJ

01635 40594 | registrar@horrishill.com | www.horrishill.com

Ages: 4–13

Pupils: 110; Boarders: 55 full/weekly

Fees: Day £11,850 – £21,300; Boarding £21,750 – £29,925 pa

Headmaster: Since August 2021, Dr Steve Bailey BEd PhD FRSA (50s). Taught at Winchester College for 29 years, housemaster for the last 12; has also been headmaster at Twyford and interim head at Westminster Under. Born and raised bilingually in Hong Kong. Born in Hong Kong, he was educated at Kent College, Canterbury, Southampton University and St Paul's College of Education. Is a fellow of the Royal Society for the Arts, boarding team inspector for ISI, research fellow of the International Olympic Committee, author of six books and has an international reputation as a historian of sport and the Olympic Games. Played hockey at county and regional levels and enjoys tennis, water polo and surfing.

Entrance: Tour of school, familiarisation and assessment day, interview with head. Not overly fastidious. Since 2021, school has been part of Forfar Education.

Exit: Nearly all to senior boarding schools, nearly all at 13. Recently: Winchester, Harrow, Eton, Radley, Charterhouse, Marlborough and Sherborne. But loads of other schools on the leavers lists – often over 20 and a more eclectic bunch than you might expect. Seven scholarships in 2021.

Our view: Founded in 1888 to prepare boys for entry to Winchester, Horris Hill is set in 80 acres of wooded heathland on the borders of Berkshire and Hampshire. School's entrance is somehow hidden in plain sight (watch for the Swan pub). Don't trust your satnav to get you there – ours took us, unrelentingly, to the non-existent back 'entrance' and thence to navigation purgatory. The vast grounds create a cocoon of safety and separation from the Newbury bypass beyond. Low-profile locally – one could live down the road and never know it was there. The recent opening of a lower school aims to address this by extending the school's age range down to 4 – an idea popular with parents who previously had to stash their littlies elsewhere before they could ascend to HH.

We think it is fair to call the school 'old fashioned', though much less so than in the past. No mobiles or tablets, although year 8s have recently been granted access to smartphones on Sundays. Parents mainly happy as things stand. Bit posh. The only school ever to have replied to our query about pupil backgrounds and languages with 'UK upper middle class and multicultural' (around a quarter of the boys come from abroad; 10 receive EAL help). Old boys include Richard Adams, who set his book Watership Down near here, controversial cricket captain Douglas Jardine, and pop star Will Young.

This is a prep school in the true sense of the word with boys assiduously prepared for future study. Many boys join at age 10 or 11 with this in mind, and subject classrooms are named after destination schools: Winchester, Harrow, Eton, Radley etc. The traditional subjects are taught and form orders are published every three weeks, giving each boy his mark, position and effort grade by subject. French for all, but boys can also study Mandarin and German off timetable. Exams twice a year. Boys with SEN – mostly dyslexia and dyspraxia – receive support, but this isn't the place for those with more than mild difficulties. School has responded to pre-testing in year 6 by providing interview practice and reasoning lessons.

A prep school in the true sense of the word with boys assiduously prepared for future study: subject classrooms are named Winchester, Harrow, Eton, Radley etc

One of Horris Hill's idiosyncrasies is that it doesn't do year groups, it does 'termly remove'. Boys are placed in small classes (average 11.7 (!) but much smaller in the final year) according to the progress they are making and remain there until they have mastered all their subjects to the requisite level. It's an unusual (possibly unique) system and only feasible in a school of this size (max 135) and age group. Besides accommodating summer birthdays, advantages are no B stream, no individual subject setting and ongoing challenges for all. Arrangement is only for academic work; boys are grouped by age for sport, dorms etc.

Beautiful framed photos in the head's office show HH boys engaged in games, boating, music, drama – all that the school offers outside the classroom. It is these pursuits – the crown jewels of the HH experience – that are 'all that'. In the face of changing senior school requirements, pre-testing in year 6, government dictates and parental whims, the school will continue to offer 'all that'.

The small size means that all boys will have a go – whether on the sports field, the stage or the music hall. Sport every day but Sunday. Main sports are rugby, football and cricket, but almost everything gets a look in. Super facilities including sports hall, Astro, nine-hole golf course (golf pro visits once a week). Outdoor pool, but serious swimmers can train at Newbury Swim Club nearby. Keen climbers are taken to Reading once a week. For a one-off charge, the school provides all sports kit, does all the labelling and laundering, supplies larger sizes as needed, replaces lost kit – why don't more schools do this?

Drama is exceptional – one of the brightest stars in the Horris Hill firmament. The school is in the final throes of fundraising for a new theatre slated for opening in 2020. Nearby professional Watermill Theatre is involved and the facility will be shared with the local community. 'We take our music very seriously,' our guide told us earnestly. Almost every boy learns a musical instrument. Boys can 'choose' to be in choir. Dedicated music school loaded with two floors of practice rooms. All boys, all years, have an academic music lesson once a week. Ditto art.

Activities every night after supper. Long list, from judo to knitting. Friday night is a whole-school activity, often based on a game show like Dragon's Den, Just a Minute or Who Wants to Be a Millionaire? Train room tucked up a stairway, with huge layout and space for Warhammer. Chess popular and a grandmaster visits for weekly coaching. Boys can play in the woods; younger boys have their own smallish adventure playground. Bikes allowed in summer. Grub Cupboard dispenses limited tuck where boys can spend their pluses. You can be 'taken off grub' if you've too many minuses.

We enjoyed the good, traditional school nosh doled out by teachers who sit at the head of table. Boys take turns stacking and wiping. Organic kitchen garden, run by boys and parents, provides fruit, veg, eggs and pork – the school raised five Hampshire Black piglets last year (resulting in an agreeable hog roast at the father-son cricket). Loads of fruit about. Indeed, the historic Cocoa Passage now dispenses mainly fruit and water.

Usual prospectus etc, but we love the fabulous comic-book-style pamphlet, 'Coming to Horris Hill'. It will tell you everything you need to know, and we defy any boy to read it and not be amused and intrigued – 'Hello Luke, I'm your Pater' (Paters are the eldest boys). Parents say communication with day families is improving but day parent class reps might help.

Boarding: Boarding can be full, weekly or transitional (four nights a week – or even less), or boys can attend as day pupils. Currently only one day boy in year 8. Most weekends, full boarders can choose to go home after Saturday matches and return on Monday mornings, but over half are in school every weekend, many lured by the superb activities and Sunday outings. Boarding is extremely well done, starting as an extension of the head's own accommodation and ending with the sort of independence the boys will encounter when they enter senior school.

The last word: Horris Hill is such a distinctive school it's unlikely you could choose it by mistake; proud to be different, though a little less so than in the past. Courageously striving to protect a childhood of conkers, match teas and the sheer joy of semi-illicit tuck from a world of Facebook, iPhones and health and safety risk-assessment templates. This is a unique, traditional prep coming to grips with modern ways and choosing the best while being buffeted by the winds of change.

Kingham Hill School

24

Kingham, Chipping Norton, Oxfordshire OX7 6TH

01608 658999 | registrar@kinghamhill.org | www.kinghamhill.org.uk

Ages: 11–18

Pupils: 345; sixth form: 102; Boarders: 113 full, 42 weekly

Fees: Day £18,525 – £21,090; Boarding £26,235 – £35,550 pa

Headmaster: Since 2008, Nick Seward BEng MA (early 50's). Educated at Millfield; degree in aerospace engineering from Imperial College and master's in theology from Durham. He brings a powerful combination of strong Christian values, really positive energy and a love of intellectual curiosity to the school. Born in Zambia, his formative years were spent in Papua New Guinea where his father managed the national football team.

After work with the homeless in Blackburn and London and four years as a curate, he joined Magdalen College School in Oxford, where his roles included Chaplain, house master and head of theology. At MCS he saw at first-hand how the right encouragement could lead to remarkable results and this culture of confidence-building is very much the hallmark of what Kingham does so well. His belief that reading is the single most important determinant of academic outcome is reflected in the school's £1.5m investment in a new library. As well as teaching economics and preaching both in school and at the local church, he has built up a successful scheme for mentoring pastoral assistants and has also introduced Kingham to his love of motorsports through the Kingham Hill Racing Club. Pupils love the opportunity to experience the thrill of motorsport and to compete at national level, all at the same time as being exposed to the fundamentals of engineering. An immensely popular and revered head, particularly amongst sixth formers at weekends when he runs the school's bar as a way of introducing them to responsible drinking.

He masterminded Kingham's development 'vision' which has delivered (ahead of schedule) new facilities including a £4m maths and science block and an impressive new £6.2m sports block. Plans are also in place to increase pupil numbers whilst remaining true to the charitable and inclusive Christian ethos of the school. Mrs Seward is also a key part of the school community; head of English, director of the school choir and mother to three sons and a daughter, she is frequently described by her husband as 'the brains of the outfit'.

Entrance: Non-selective, no formal entrance exams but prospective pupils sit the hour-long MidYIS test to provide a measure of 'typical' performance. School offers a huge range of opportunities to children of all abilities. Head meets with all families before joining. Taster days available. Just under 17 per cent international pupils, ESOL offered. German exchange group join for a term in Year 10. US High School Diploma available. About 40 US students join each year. Numbers higher than ever before so early registration advised.

Exit: Some 20 per cent of pupils depart after GCSE to pursue vocational courses or due to redeployment of military parents but most continue through to the sixth form. Three quarters of leavers go on to Russell Group universities. Warwick, Exeter, Loughborough, Bath, York, Imperial, UCL, LSE, Bristol, Nottingham, and Edinburgh are popular choices. One Oxbridge place in 2021. US students generally head home to universities in the States.

Latest results: In 2021, 61 per cent 9-7 at GCSE; 80 per cent A*/A at A level (94 per cent A*-B). In 2019 (the last year when exams took place), 49 per cent 9-7 at GCSE; 45 per cent A*/A at A level (or vocational equivalent).

Teaching and learning: For a non-selective school to be rated amongst the top five of schools in Oxfordshire for academic results and in the top three per cent of sixth form providers nationally is a huge achievement. 'A combination of small class sizes (average 15 pupils), individual attention and staff who have time to listen characterises the academic environment at Kingham'. Curiosity for learning is very much what the school strives to achieve and is at the heart of its ethos. Strong support structure creates confident pupils who enjoy learning and positivity abounds. One parent, heralding the transformation of his son since joining the school felt 'he would have been lost in the London day school system but is instead thriving and loving school'. Whiteboards and interactive learning all in place, but the emphasis is on traditional teaching and handwritten work rather than technology. Major investment in laboratory facilities in the new maths and science block reinforces commitment to STEM subjects. Setting in maths only. History, DT, animal management and engineering are popular amongst the 31 subjects currently taught with A levels, BTec and CTech offered to suit all abilities. Relationships between pupils and teachers are strong, pupils are often seen walking to lessons chatting happily to staff.

The Octagon Society is where the most academically curious meet to discuss ethical and philosophical issues and challenge their beliefs, it encapsulates the inclusivity of the school as pupils of all levels of academic ability are welcomed. Being curious is what matters here, reflecting the school's mission to broaden horizons. 'Everybody is encouraged to have a voice'. The international feel of the school, together with its US Middle States Association accreditation, adds a global dimension.

Learning support and SEN: CRESTED registered, Greens, the school's dedicated learning support department, offers 1:1 support (at an additional cost). Considered good value by parents. Around 16% of the pupils receive some form of additional learning support with careful monitoring of all pupils taking place. Support either in the form of drop-in sessions or dedicated lessons on a regular basis. Some just enjoy dropping in to chat to the staff and that is welcomed. Pupils interviewed spoke of the tools they have been given to deal with challenges that will benefit them for the rest of their lives. Confidence building and examples of huge improvements in learning outcomes reported. Head of department 'goes the extra mile' and always has time for pupils who need help.

The arts and extracurricular: It's not the broad extracurricular offering per se that is so noteworthy, but the engagement and enthusiasm that is remarkable. CCF (compulsory for form 3), art and drama facilities are brought to life by the energy and enthusiasm generated in the pupils by the school's dedicated staff. New heads of art and DT have reinvigorated these subjects and the latter is now one of the school's most popular subjects – pupils love designing with CAD technology. The former sports hall has been transformed into a 150-seat performing arts centre where the school's drama academy on Monday evenings allows those interested to become involved on or behind the stage. Animal management is also very popular, pupils enjoy learning to look after the stock on the school's own farm.

The headmaster's enthusiasm for motorsports has resulted in active participation in the national karting championships and two national champions for the school

Forms 1 and 2 learn a musical instrument for free and often then join the school orchestra or one of the ensembles. Singing is part of the chapel service three times a week with a gospel choir and music tech also available.

One parent marvelled that her son could be so excited by CCF drills, and several parents wonder if there is 'something in the water at Kingham' that promotes such fun and enjoyment from previously unengaged children. Pupils throw themselves into the many activities on offer because they are enjoying themselves without worrying about the need to be 'cool'.

Sport: One hour of sport/activities per day timetabled, with all pupils encouraged to be active and

Heathfield School

take part, making full use of the school's glorious site. Rugby, football and cricket, hockey and tennis as well as athletics, netball and rounders, badminton and cross-country on offer. Regular fixtures with local schools on match afternoons. The impressive new sports hall houses a climbing wall, squash court, four-court hall with fitness suites and a viewing pavilion onto the Astro and tennis courts. A 25m swimming pool and additional gym are on offer and available for parents to use. For those not so keen on team sports, mountain biking, fencing, riding, golf and clay pigeon shooting are to be enjoyed, not to mention the real one off, the school's karting team. The headmaster's enthusiasm for motorsports has resulted in active participation in the national karting championships and two national champions for the school. There's definitely something for everyone to enjoy here.

Boarding: About half of Kingham's pupils board, with 50 per cent weekly boarders; occasional boarding is also possible. Seven dedicated single sex boys' and girls' houses on campus. No Saturday school so a varied programme of activities and trips is scheduled to ensure weekends are busy and fun for the relatively small number of full boarders. Pupils speak enthusiastically of visits to the local trampoline centre, Alton Towers and of team building days when everyone in the boarding house (maximum 33 pupils) gets to know each other. The boarding houses are clean and fit for purpose, with a big emphasis on promoting a family feel that is 'fun, friendly, homely and happy'. Staffed by two resident house parents and three tutors per house; recent university graduates also help out. Boarders are allocated housekeeping tasks and expected to keep their rooms cleaned, providing excellent training for life after school. Sixth formers enjoy separate boarding accommodation and the weekend bar.

Ethos and heritage: Situated in 100 acres of beautiful Cotswold countryside, 80-minutes by train from London and 10 minutes from Daylesford House, former home of Kingham Hill's founder, Christian philanthropist Charles Edward Baring Young. He founded the school in 1886 to provide orphaned and destitute boys with a family home and an education. With plenty of room for the school community to thrive, there is space and time to live life at a healthy pace. Parents are invited to make use of the school's facilities and take an active part in the life of the school. Christian ethos aims to promote qualities of character, kindness and empathy through its guiding principles of responsibility, humility, resilience and integrity but the religious message is used more to frame a code of behaviour rather than as

Being curious is what matters here, reflecting the school's mission to broaden horizons. 'Everybody is encouraged to have a voice'

indoctrination in any way. The school's charitable mission involves the support of its bursary programme and giving to many other causes.

Pastoral care, inclusivity and discipline: Pastoral care is at the heart of everything that Kingham does. Parents are astonished at the achievements of their children and attribute them to the small numbers and individual attention pupils receive from excellent caring staff. When questioned about discipline, parents and pupils alike felt that the school deals appropriately with issues and problems and that behaviour is generally kind, compassionate and inclusive. The international diversity as well as the mixing of ages breeds a happy community. Many talk positively of Kingham's protective bubble while recognising that learning to deal with the less benign aspects of the outside world is necessary. Many parents referred to the head of sixth form's exceptional understanding, empathy and ability to offer advice about making subject and university course choices as well as decisions relating to future careers. The school celebrates diversity, embracing the many cultures its pupils as well as the diverse talents and challenges of its pupils. Everybody is welcomed into the Kingham family.

Pupils and parents: About 15 per cent of the school's British pupils have parents in the Forces or the Foreign Office. In the words of one local estate agent 'the school is on the up' as it is 'discovered' by families moving out of London in search of the rural idyll. Parents seemed to us to be less competitive and results driven, genuinely seeking a holistic education. Interestingly however, the school's less pushy approach is paying dividends in terms of academic performance. Alumni or 'Hillians" as they are known, are great ambassadors for the school and actively engaged – on the day of our visit a former navy and commercial pilot was having lunch with a 16-year- old boy with dreams of becoming an airline pilot who was already learning to fly. A plan was being enthusiastically but realistically hatched. The Hillian waxed lyrical about the school as do current parents, those we spoke to who had visited many schools in the area had opted for Kingham 'because it gets the important things very right'. Pupils of all abilities are accepting of each other, kind and full of positivity. The international contingent is from all over the world with 20 nationalities represented, 10 per cent are American students, mostly from families with embassy or government connections. Happy and engaged children make for happy parents.

Money matters: The school's strong Christian ethos and charitable mission is reflected in the 15 per cent of revenue which is allocated to concessions and school bursaries. Means-tested bursaries (up to 50 per cent) and 100 per cent sixth form scholarships available for able pupils.

Scholarships of up to 25 per cent of fees for academic, art, performing arts and sport and at sixth form, one 50 per cent organ scholarship and three 75 per cent academic scholarships. The governing body of experienced professionals and senior management team are impressively strategic and have delivered ahead of schedule on the school's ambitious development plan without recourse to debt. Importantly, parents report channels of communication with management are open and transparent. Trustees oversee the Kingham Hill Trust, a grant making organisation set up by the school's founder.

The last word: A growing number of families moving out of London are discovering this very special school which has quietly been quietly evolving over the last decade under its talented leadership. Not only does it offer ample space and facilities, but more importantly it is run by a headmaster who understands that inspiring confidence and curiosity can change lives. Proximity to the likes of Daylesford Organic and Soho House may be fortuitous but is unlikely to disrupt what is down to earth and special about the school. Thriving, happy, resilient pupils and happy parents.

Lambrook School

Winkfield Row, Nr Ascot, Berkshire RG42 6LU

01344 882717 | info@lambrookschool.co.uk | www.lambrookschool.co.uk

Ages: 3-13

Pupils: 610; **Boarders:** 278 weekly/flexi

Fees: Day £13,167 – £20,997; Boarding £25,440 pa

Headmaster: Since 2010, Jonathan Perry. BA in theology and history from Gloucestershire before PGCE at Cambridge. Four years as head at Kingsmead, housemaster at Monkton Combe, head of RS and philosophy at Wheatley Park.

Wife Jenny, part-time pharmacologist, works with pastoral team. Sitting together in his immaculate-yet-homely study, they radiate calm, warmth and a sense that everything's going to be okay with the world. Sofas covered in perfect neutrals; painting of the school (by a parent, naturally) hanging above the fireplace; huge windows looking out onto parkland. Jenny pours a winning cup of tea from one of those personalised Emma Bridgewater teapots ubiquitous in kitchens across the home counties and yet still somehow classy. Heaven.

It may feel like stepping into Homes and Gardens, but Mr Perry is far from complacent. Very socially conscious and keen to modernise by increasing bursary provision and outreach – 'Our role mustn't be tokenistic', he says, 'and we need to sow seeds then water them.' May fund a languages teacher at a local school and recently launched Lambrook Foundation on the bursaries front. School has no endowments but 'significant fundraising' will allow school 'to serve more individuals'. 'We are really, really committed to building a healthy surplus,' he says sincerely, and we believe him: we don't sniff any cynical marketing chat here. Parents call him 'charm personified' and 'a really good frontman': 'There'll be hundreds of people at a match tea and he'll say, "Ah, Mrs X, would you like an egg sandwich?".'

Strapline is 'feathers to fly', a concept which Mr Perry returns to often. 'We give them feathers to fly so that when they leave us, they will spread their wings and take flight,' he says. Fits with gentle, encouraging approach, informed in part by his Christian values. 'We are not a sharp-elbowed environment,' he says, despite the school's increasing popularity with Londoners. Embodies the school with his softly spoken and twinkly manner, with no rough edges or ego.

Entrance: Mainly into nursery, reception, years 3, 4 and 7. Register ASAP. Not formally selective in younger years but 'meet with all families to ensure that we are the best fit for their needs' (yes, they're interviewing you too and they are 'not afraid to turn away' parents who don't fit with the ethos). Formal assessment for year 4 and up: academic but also 'interests, character and general behaviour'. Biggest feeders in recent years have been west London preps. Fifty-five per cent boys overall, though varies year to year.

Exit: Handful leave for 11+ schools, but huge majority stay until 13+. Leavers to 40 schools each year, almost exclusively boarding, mainly co-ed but significant minority to single sex. Recent favourites are Charterhouse, Bradfield, Wellington, Eton. 'Future schools' conversation starts in year 5 with parent meetings. 'Very, very few parents will say they must go to this school or that school,' says head (not a pushy bunch). School is 'quite firm about not allowing 13+ to turn into a circus,' say parents, and keeping pupils calm. Separate scholarship class from start of year 7; 14 scholarships in 2021.

Our view: Breadth and balance in the curriculum prepare spongy young minds for whatever the common entrance has in store. All the usual, including French, RS, design and technology and, from year 5, Latin. We saw an RS lesson come to life as pupils competed to recall their bible stories, squealing as their names appeared on the interactive whiteboard. Teachers strike balance between relaxed and fun but totally in control – unflustered by the hustle and bustle. Academics gentler than at pushy local and London preps, but yield effective results. 'They're getting more out of her by not sitting right on top of her,' says one mum. 'At our London prep they made a point of being a year ahead in English and maths – what's the point of that?' says another, knowing full well that this would be sacrilege in Battersea.

Littlest are structured from the off, covering phonics, literacy, maths in their pre-school year – we saw a lively phonics session (sausage! stick! star!). Moving imminently to new, purpose-built centre. Thence to self-contained pre-prep zone – easy flow between classrooms, colourful displays about happiness and reminders of character values (kindness, respect, independence, manners, courage, responsibility) on the wall. Specialist teachers in PE, swimming, music and French. Saturday school from year 5 gets mixed reviews from parents, particularly those less local ('we just suck it up'; 'it's just one of those things').

Modern classrooms housed in single-storey, wooden-clad buildings with big windows that let in lots of natural light. Strikingly clean-smelling and up-to-date teaching spaces – no dusty corners or tired paintwork. All feels chipper – serious capital expenditure in recent years, and it shows. Science labs a little more tired (though really, this is relative), with strip lighting and slightly saggy inflatable planets dangling from the ceiling – but totally fit for purpose and well looked after. Pretty chapel at the school's physical and emotional heart hosts four services a week – families join on a Saturday morning and often outside speakers, too.

Fifty-two acres in which to run and run – total freedom to explore, provided you've got your wellies on. At least one mum mystified by how they get pupils back for lessons

DT studio well organised, tools stored under wooden benches – working clocks, a year 8 project, proudly displayed. Art room similarly pukka, with colourful paintings of water lilies on display and a wonderful tutu made from ballet slippers on a mannequin in the corner, plus elaborate Venetian masks ready for the kiln. Welcoming library heaves with books (not to be taken for granted, we find) and student book reviews, beautifully illustrated ('It is a story about friendship and many things its young readers can relate to,' writes one year 7 – warrants many heart emojis). Walls lined with names and photos of first XVs and XIs back to 1905 – one suspects today's teams don't look dissimilar. We saw diggers in action developing the dining room, newly extended to reduce waiting times and accommodate more boarders. Food delicious.

A whopping 178 LAMDA lessons each week and 420 individual music lessons. Diamond Jubilee Centre one of the best prep performing arts facilities we've come across – we saw year 8s studying film scores, boys tap-dancing (yippee), bagpipe teacher in action. Extracurricular choirs and ensembles galore. Lambrook Festival of Arts Week culminates with house choral competition. Senior chapel choir has performed in Notre Dame and Windsor Castle. Listening to them trilling away about badgers and hedgehogs in preparation for upcoming harvest festival was a total delight.

Fifty-two acres in which to run and run – total freedom to explore, provided you've got your wellies on. At least one mum mystified by how they get pupils back for lessons, but like clockwork they tumble in, ruddy-cheeked and full of fresh air. A nine-hole golf course, 25-metre swimming pool, huge Astroturf and sports hall.

Volunteering and charity prominent. Year 7 don't just go canoeing on the lakes in Sweden – everyone raises £500 to enable an underprivileged child to do the same (through Teenage Wilderness Trust). Mum and dad aren't allowed to get the cheque book out: 'They have to feel like they're raising the money, making cakes or washing cars,' says Mr Perry, giving their time, not just their money. Pupils also visit partner school outside Durban, 'playing lots of cricket' with pupils there and taking practical donations like pens or toothbrushes. 'They come back as better individuals,' says head. Mountains of food donations awaiting donation to two local food banks (much of it organic, of course). 'We want them to be leaders, want them to be outward-looking,' says Mr Perry. 'We'd be really sad if our children were arrogant so-and-sos.' Prints from Charlie Mackey around the school – 'The mole says to the boy, "I'm so small", and the boy tells him, "Yes, but you make a huge difference."'

Sustainability important – children planted 300 saplings last year. Recent development has been emergence, rather organically, of school orchard. Pupils collect eggs from rescue chickens, newly restored to good health and refeathered, Lambrook-style (don't point out that chickens are hopeless flyers); beehives produce Lambrook honey (a particularly nice going-home present); pupils come to stroke the rabbits of a lunchtime. Every class has a veg patch. Excellent teaching resources on ecology and food industry; we were less convinced by the educational value of the bunnies, but they're very cute and no doubt good for everybody's general zen.

Pastoral care excellent. This is a big school, but pupils feel known and staff quick to take action where there's a concern. One challenge, says head, is how busy pupils can become with the sweetshop-esque timetable of extracurricular fun. 'They need time to be on their own,' he says, 'to just stop and be – ensuring that as we go forward we still find moments in a busy weekly schedule.'

Fifty receiving support from LDC, either long-term or for a short-term confidence boost. Nice big classroom devoted to it, cupboards neatly labelled, 'handwriting', 'visual skills' etc. 'Children with dyslexia, dyscalculia etc might find academic learning challenging', but their 'many strengths' should be 'viewed positively'.

Minibuses bring pupils from affluent areas of south Oxfordshire, Bucks, Surrey, as well as Chiswick and Brook Green. 'They love the bus,' say parents, raving about the 'cheerful' and 'avuncular' drivers. Lots of locals too, of course, most of whom drive. 'The car park is a sight to be seen,' we hear, 'literally Lamborghinis, Ferraris, very smart Range Rovers.'

London market growing quickly, 'but we won't be the London school in the country,' says head. A bit of London vs not-London awareness amongst parents – logistics mean that there are London-specific socials at the pub in Brook Green – though dedicated London rep encourages people to get involved and lots of Londoners make it to Saturday chapel and match teas. Buses leave too early for London pupils to take part in most after-school activities, 'but they pack a huge amount into the rest of the day,' say parents, delighted that their children get home 'at 6pm having done their homework and their running around'.

'Welcoming, thoughtful, warm' induction for newbies including handwritten card from new buddy. 'There are so many WhatsApp groups,' said one mum, 'for our year, for our area, for our minibus.' 'If there was anything I didn't know at the beginning there were five different people I could ask,' says another. A sociable school – 'there's always great cake at match teas' – and every parent we spoke to seemed to be off to a Lambrook get-together soon.

Boarding: Only weekly boarding; no overseas boarders. Houses very cosy with colourful bedspreads, mini ping-pong tables and bookshelves packed with David Walliams and Roald Dahl. Boarding numbers have grown, particularly flexi. 'It's competitive for a Friday night,' school says – and boys' houses are about to be expanded and developed. Almost half the school boards at some stage each year, predominantly year 4 and up but the odd year 3 who's there with an older sibling. 'We don't insist that you board from a particular year group, and so parents don't have that anxiety that their child might not be ready.' In their experience, though, those who manage senior boarding best have done it before they get to 13+. Tries to recruit couples as houseparents where possible.

Money matters: Means-tested bursaries available; school has recently started working with Springboard to give 100 per cent bursary.

The last word: 'My son's the classic prep school candidate – he loves the muddy knees,' says one mum – and in Lambrook they've indeed found the classic prep school. Big and shiny, yes, with facilities that would make many senior schools green with envy – but we also found a heart of gold. Busy children having a whale of a time, running through the woods, singing their socks off or having a giggle in the lunch queue. A bit of a bubble, naturally, but when the bubble's this nice, what's not to like?

Leighton Park School

Shinfield Road, Reading RG2 7DE

01189 879600 | admissions@leightonpark.com | www.leightonpark.com

Ages: 11–18

Pupils: 523; sixth form: 148 (87 boys and 61 girls); Boarders: 88 full, 43 weekly/flexi

Fees: Day £20,235 – £24,660; Boarding £27,525 – £40,455 pa

Head: Since September 2018, Matthew Judd (40s). Cheerful and, judging from his almost scarily ordered office (even the pencils in the pot are equally spaced apart), ultra-organised. Grew up in Crawley and was the first person in his family to go to university (geography at University of Wales followed by teaching qualification from Cambridge), having attended the local comp in the shadow of Gatwick airport: 'If you were a boy, you went into baggage handling; if you were a girl, you went into duty free.' Started his career at Haberdashers' Aske's boys in 1993, moved in 2005 to be principal at MPW college in London before rejoining Habs five years later as second master and executive head of its prep. Also an ISI inspector and it was this role that brought him here: 'Every school I inspect claims it's unique but I could see this one really was – it was a compelling calling.'

Matthew's (everyone is on first-name terms at Leighton Park) office provides other clues about his philosophies. Interior designed down to every last inch, with a magnificent vista even on the bleak winter day we visited, he explains that it looked very different before his arrival – a nod to his firm belief (which he put in action back at Habs prep) that building design can add real value within schools. 'I don't just mean a lick of paint, but beautifully designed spaces where you can be creative and nooks that double up as opportunities for interaction.' Latest examples for students range from a new Quaker (more of which later) room with comfy low stools and wellbeing-focused colouring books through to stunning new music and media building.

Describes Leighton as 'a school with a soul', although thus far nobody seems to have got much of a window into his. Pupils say he's 'nice' and 'friendly', but none of them or the parents we spoke to seemed to have any real sense of him as a person (although this is not not unusual among students in senior schools): 'I just don't know him'; 'I haven't had a lot to do with him' etc. Reportedly clamped down on discipline ('it's stricter'), upped the ante academically ('it had slipped a bit') and transformed boarding ('now all single-sex'). Majority of parents are on board, although a couple we spoke to fear it's a ploy to attract more traditionalists, 'which misses the point of the ethos of the school'. 'Take the logo change,' said one, 'it used to be an oak leaf, simple and understated like Quakers themselves, but now he's put a shield around it which really isn't us at all.' Almost universally unpopular are his structural changes to the day – 'One of the best things about this school was the emphasis on social time and the new timetable takes most of it away,' said a student.

Pupils like calling teachers by first names ('makes them far more approachable')

Lives on site with his partner Ian and is often seen on his old-school (complete with basket) bicycle around the grounds. A keen musician, he also enjoys travel and fitness.

Entrance: Online entrance tests in English comprehension and maths, plus creative writing exercise and interview in the January preceding entry for years 7-10. At 11+, 130 apply for 48 places; at 13+, 35 apply for 15-20 places (although remember this is not first choice for all these families). At sixth form, around 20-30 places become available, with around four applicants for each. Entry criterion is five GCSEs at grade 6 or above, although some subjects require higher grades, eg for maths you'll need grade 7. Plus interview. Year 11 is a 'pre-sixth' year for overseas students. Second-language speakers sit an EAL test. 'Parents often want to come back several times – on their own, with the child, then a taster day etc, and we're fine with that,' says school.

Exit: Around a third leave post GCSEs, many lured by vocational courses at local colleges. Half of sixth form leavers to Russell Group. Birmingham, Edinburgh, Exeter, Kings' College London, Loughborough, Royal Holloway and UCL all popular. One to Oxbridge in 2021. Eighty per cent study STEAM related degrees, including one medic in 2021. School told us it's appointed a head of careers but bizarrely, we were met with confused looks, even from sixth formers, when we asked about careers advice. Turning to each other blankly, one eventually voiced, 'I guess we must have a careers advisor, but I've no idea who it is.'

Latest results: In 2021, 53 per cent 9-7 at GCSE; 72 per cent A*/A at A level (91 per cent A*-B). IB average score 35. In 2019 (the last year when exams took place), 55 per cent 9-7 at GCSE; 31 per cent A*/A grades at A level (56 per cent A*-B). IB average 35 in 2019.

Teaching and learning: Push without the shove. Teachers cajole and bolster rather than drill and it's one of the things the parents like the most about the school, reporting that work is taken seriously and pupils strive for success but 'thankfully without being results driven'.

Maths, science and creative subjects the current stars of the show at GCSE. In sixth form, three-quarters of students take A levels (usually three plus EPQ). The remainder do the IB. Despite relatively low take-up, there is an impressive commitment to the IB because 'its values are so much those of the school'. Useful cross-fertilisation – IB and A level languages often taught together in year 12. Top three per cent in England for added-value.

Maximum class sizes 22 in the lower years (top set maths only) and by sixth form some have only one or two students. Setting in maths from year 7. Spanish and Mandarin from year 7, with the potential to swap the latter for French or German in year 8 and all take at least one language at GCSE, 'except for those who will clearly struggle'. GCSE offerings include dance, engineering and food tech (lemon meringue pies in full swing when we visited). Plus, most recently, a compulsory GCSE in global perspectives – 'These students are going to be the change makers, they need to know what the world will look like,' says head. As at many schools, maths A level is having its moment in the sun; humanities also popular. Strongest results in science and maths. Latest A level offering is business studies – hasn't cannibalised economics, reports school. BTec in creative digital media available in years 10/11, as is music tech in the sixth form.

Parents say the teaching is 'excellent' and 'child focused', but not without exception – 'the languages department is on the weaker side,' reckoned one. All hail the annual parents' evening, 'where you realise how well they know your child'. Pupils like calling teachers by first names ('makes them far more approachable'). Lessons we observed were meticulously prepared and engaging – we sat with year 8s working out the best way to start a book (English), year 10s learning about the coffee trade in Ethiopia (geography) and sixth formers being quizzed on social influence (psychology), among others. Very much a school for joiners-in and those prepared to question.

Many staff live on site and have boarding duties. 'They are all extremely hands-on and so kind with the kids that my daughter very quickly felt totally at home'

Learning support and SEN: EAL classes for small number of students who need them, with preparation for FCE and IELTS exams available. School has strong reputation for supporting additional educational needs at the mild to moderate end, with overwhelming acclaim for the individual learning centre ('they're so helpful', 'they always reply to emails straightaway', 'they sort exam arrangements' etc). Perhaps surprising then, to find only 15 per cent on the SEND register when we visited. No EHCPs.

The arts and extracurricular: Music is a serious business, with annual house music reportedly louder than a football match – 'It doesn't finish until after 10pm, so loads of people stay over that night, it's awesome,' said a student. Head of music considered a 'legend'. Around 180 learn an instrument in school, many beyond grade 8. 'Concerts are astounding,' said a parent. New all-singing, all-dancing music and media centre has led to increased connectivity with media – Pinewood and Disney, both with large local presence, taken full advantage of. OL David Lean was a huge champion of the school.

Rather less dazzling is the jaded-looking art block, but the three studios are spacious and well equipped, and most importantly it's a real hub of talent, which more than one student told us is their favourite hang-out area. Students told us they develop a real sense of self through their art, and have a good time doing it. We noticed they took time to appreciate each other's work – hard not to, particularly the installations (with our tour guides we lingered for some time around a piano, every inch imaginatively decorated with music, quotes and photos). DT provision enhanced by laser cutter, CNC router and 3D printer in one of the largest DT rooms we've seen. 'The best year 7 project is when you get to make and design your own chocolate bar with branding,' a student told us.

Musicals are the centrepiece of the drama department (they were practising for Chicago when we visited – 'you have to see it, it will be amazing,' enthused one student). But there's serious acting too, now with the opportunity to perform in the round in the school hall.

Big range of clubs and activities and masses of space for them all. Young Enterprise, DofE, trips of all kinds but no CCF, of course.

Sport: Sport is about the taking part. Even those that enter the school feeling lukewarm about PE wind up wanting a slice of the action – who wouldn't on this large and beautiful site, with fields, pitches, courts and tracks which positively set your muscles aquiver? Not to mention the indoor pool. The week before we visited, the rugby coach replaced a strong player with a weaker one to make it more even against the opposition – this pretty much sums up their inclusive approach that may, as one parent put it, 'not appeal to traditional parents wanting their sons to play rugby with the best of the best'. That said, school recently joined ISA to get more competitive fixtures. At the elite end, one recent leaver got a professional rugby contract, others have rowed and kayaked for Team GB. Sports hall, a rather meagre old gym, considered something of an embarrassment by students.

Boarding: Boarders make up 30 per cent of the school community; of those, 70 per cent are full boarders, the rest weekly/flexi. As with many schools, biggest growth area is weekly boarders from London, but with two-thirds of boarders present at weekends, there is a lot going on – from abseiling to shopping visits to Bicester village.

It's been all change (not altogether popular) when it comes to gender, with the school recently moving the three co-ed boarding houses to three single–sex – two for boys and one for girls. But with day boarders (as the day students are known here because they can stay until 7pm or even 9pm) each allocated to one of these three houses regardless of their gender, the school argues there is still an overall co-ed feel in the downstairs common areas (only upstairs, where boarders go, is single sex). For day students in the younger years (7 and 8), there remains a co-ed house.

Décor-wise, we found the houses more YHA than Premier Inn (disappointingly, not even a poster or any other evidence of personalisation in the dorms we saw). But school is currently investing £2m into boarding facilities – so far, Fryer House (year 7s and 8s) has had a facelift. Rooms are spacious enough, even the dorms of four, and all houses have ample facilities – sofas, tellies, table games etc. No singles except for sixth formers, and none with ensuites.

New all-singing, all-dancing music and media centre – Pinewood and Disney, both with large local presence, taken full advantage of

Many staff live on site and have boarding duties, the head's modest house is also on site – adds to the sense of community. 'They are all extremely hands-on and so kind with the kids that my daughter very quickly felt totally at home,' said one parent, 'so although they're not very new or amazing rooms, who cares? I'm just happy they're so nurturing.'

Ethos and heritage: The spacious green site has generous planting and low-rise buildings; even better, most of it is pedestrianised, with no vehicles to interrupt the soothing sounds of nature. A sense of calm pervades the place – your shoulders drop as you step out of your car and breathe out. Hundreds of mature trees, several garden areas and a large reedy pond – all give the impression of being much more rural than it really is.

The campus is made up of buildings of all eras, little of astounding architectural merit though the aforementioned music and media building is a spectacular addition and cleverly designed to provide floor-to-ceiling views of the green spaces from the rehearsal and performance rooms. There's also a fully equipped media suite, hi-tech recording studio and main hall. Oakview, though now a little dated, also provides glorious views – this time from the canteen, which serves fresh and varied food (turkey fricassee, followed by home-made granola and yoghurt for us – yum). Everything is so well ordered here – no mess, no peeling paint, no stained carpets and no litter. Someone must be a big fan of straight lines – display boards are hyper-neat, without a rounded edge or sloped piece of paper in sight. Science labs on the retro side but it doesn't seem to put students off. Lovely library spread across the upper floor of the main house. New sixth form in the making – due to be completed Sept 2022.

The main building, an elegant 1850s white house, was bought by an earlier incarnation of the school in the 1880s and more land was donated by the Reckitt family – the aim being to educate Quaker children for Oxbridge. Although only half the remaining governors are Quakers, and none of the staff or student body, the school continues to live by and exude its gentle, civilised and socially responsible values. No parent we spoke to claimed to choose the school on this basis – 'I didn't know anything about Quakers, really' was a common refrain – but few families leave taking nothing from it and many consider it a guide for a healthy life. 'I really like it because it's based around common decency and finding the good in other people,' said one student; 'Respect and equality are at the heart of it – it can be no coincidence that we hardly have any bullying here,' said another (head claims, bravely, that there's none). Many like the mindfulness aspect ('I often say the Quakers invented mindfulness,' claims the head), especially the silence (weekly assembly, called collect, ends with 10 minutes of silence and there's a weekly meeting for worship). During lunch, anyone can ring a bell to bring about a silent moment of pause, reflection and gratitude; equally, anyone can ring it to break the silence. Students say Quakerism is never pushed and is more of a 'calm wisdom that seeps into your consciousness'. The Peace Pole, a handsome carved wooden column visible from most parts of the school, enshrines these Quaker principles, as do the many examples of pupil creativity – benches etc carved from fallen trees on the site and a daily quote on the blackboard outside the canteen: 'No act of kindness, no matter how small, is ever wasted' (Aesop), when we visited.

During lunch, anyone can ring a bell to bring about a silent moment of pause, reflection and gratitude; equally, anyone can ring it to break the silence

While Leighton Park is certainly a different kind of school, it is not 'alternative'. Head is keen to make the distinction: 'It would be easy to confuse the free thinking for free behaviour. It's actually a very disciplined school where we focus on achievement but with values, character and community.'

Old Leightonians include Sir David Lean, Sir Richard Rodney Bennett, Jim Broadbent, Laura Marling, Eliza Bennett, Michael Foot, Lord Caradon, Lord Frederick Seebohm and a fair clutch of MPs plus Rowntrees, Cadburys, Clarks, Reckitts, Morlands and Frys.

Pastoral care, inclusivity and discipline: Discipline historically light touch, but a growing undercurrent of low-level disruption and sometimes worse (there were a number of exclusions for drugs the year before our visit) has led head to take a firmer line. But while 'no student will tell you they want their school to be more strict' (as one pointed out), this student body is surprisingly on board: 'To be honest, sanctions weren't very consistent before with some students getting multiple warnings and others getting only one or two, so it's a lot fairer now,' explained one. If your offspring have had mishaps elsewhere, fear not, the school still seems to be able to turn most into model citizens and welcomes deserving second-chancers. More rules than you might expect – no eating while walking around, no use of mobiles during the school day – but all designed to consider others and to maintain the peace.

Pupils and parents: Not a school where you'll be fighting off the Land Rovers and Q8s. Of course, some families are minted, but most work hard to send their children here – more dual-income than ever. Internationally eclectic – some 72 per cent are UK nationals (most local or local-ish), the rest encompassing 36 nationalities at the time of our visit – largest number from China, then Germany; school's current push is for more Latin American students. 'Lovely for my daughter to have friends from so many corners of the world,' raved a parent. The first groups of students we met seemed solemn and untalkative – where is their zest for life and sense of fun, we wondered. But a later bunch cracked more smiles, and we even got them chuckling at our jokes (not everyone does). Some parents think school communications could be improved: 'You get a lot of half-baked messages,' said one; school says it's introducing a new comms tool soon.

Money matters: Decent amount of money available for bursaries. Emphasis on enabling those who otherwise couldn't afford the fees, with most recipients on awards of 50 per cent or more and robust mean-testing and assessment of income/commitments/assets etc. Usually around six on 100 per cent bursaries at any one time, plus a few on 80 per cent. Scholarships mostly worth 10 per cent. Head has brought in new exhibition scholarships with £500 awards.

The last word: Uniquely straddles free thinking with more conventional parameters. Not for hustlers, bustlers and takers but great for thinkers, makers, givers, be-ers.

Lord Wandsworth College

Long Sutton, Hook, Hampshire RG29 1TB

01256 862201 | admissions@lordwandsworth.org | www.lordwandsworth.org

Ages: 11–18

Pupils: 660; sixth form: 190; Boarders: 42 full, 217 weekly/flexi

Fees: Day £22,020 – £25,890; Boarding £28,200 – £36,840 pa

Headmaster: Since 2015, Adam Williams (40s), previously deputy head of Glasgow Academy. Has also been head of geography at Bradfield (his alma mater) and Oakham. Impressive cricketing and golfing skills in his youth took him into national teams both at school and university (Durham, where he studied geography). Speed golfing is his latest fad – if it's anything as quick as his wit and fast as his talking, trophies await.

Born Down Under, he is unaffected and laid back, with an open face and the hint of a twinkle. 'He's the reason I chose the school,' said more than one parent about him and, unusually, some pupils too: 'He came to our school and did this amazing talk on how friendly and fun the school is – me and my best friend decided right there and then,' remarked one. Parents say he is 'pragmatic', 'down to earth' and 'incredibly good with the kids, pretty much knowing them all by name'. But it's Project Beanstalk – his securely financed 10-year strategy – that has really tickled them pink, not least because it came straight off the back of parent feedback. 'When I joined, we asked them what needed changing and they told us classrooms needed updating, pupils needed more stretch, more teachers needed to be specialist and the fees were too high.' Tick, tick, tick and tick, say parents. And because Mr Williams was on a roll, he also got to work increasing student numbers (which he's still doing), improving teachers' CPD and building a fabulous new dining room (one of the nicest we've seen), plus a glass-fronted science centre. He has improved outdoor learning and digitisation, increased parental involvement and boosted the pastoral care for which the school was already renowned ('Actually, I didn't think it was that great,' he says).

As for Covid, Mr Williams told us he spent the first summer sitting under his desk sucking his thumb and rocking gently. 'Rubbish!' laugh parents, who are well used to his self-deprecating sense of humour. The school was 'brilliant', they told us, with online lessons tweaked to 10 minutes shorter so as not to overwhelm students, 'and there were all sorts of imaginative challenges for the likes of sport and art'.

His wife is a busy medic; the two eldest of their three children are at the school, the youngest has already eyed up her future dorm. They live not in the eight-bedroomed, drafty house allocated to previous heads – 'where I had to write reports in a ski jacket and woolly hat' – but a new Arts-and-Crafts style one he had built in the middle of the campus.

Entrance: Lightly selective, with equal numbers joining at 11+ and 13+ via CE pre-test. Minimum score of 105 required, plus interview and reference. Most from Danes Hill, others from St Neot's (which has a formal link with the school), Yateley Manor and Edgeborough, with Hall Grove and Bishopsgate sometimes featuring. A few from local primaries. Oversubscribed but waiting lists aren't mammoth. Around 20 join at sixth form, for which applicants need six 6s at GCSE (7s in the subjects to be studied). 'All along we are looking for pupils who are naturally curious and want to get stuck in.'

Exit: A third leave after GCSEs, either to other independents (for a change or because they offer other courses) or more commonly to one of several excellent state sixth form colleges in Hampshire, usually for economic reasons. Most sixth formers to university, nearly half to Russell Group. Bath, Cardiff, Exeter, Oxford Brookes and Royal Holloway recently popular. Wide range of courses include arts and sciences. Two to Oxbridge in 2021, plus four medics. Increasing numbers of degree apprenticeships, eg Rolls Royce and PWC. Some decide to bypass university altogether to start their own businesses – fully supported by school.

Latest results: In 2021, 59 per cent 9-7 at GCSE; 56 per cent A*/A at A level (79 per cent A*-B). In 2019 (the last year when exams took place), 53 per cent 9-7 at GCSE; 30 per cent A*/A at A level (63 per cent A*-B).

Teaching and learning: As is so often the case with one-time weak spots that schools hone in on, stretch and challenge is now on fire. 'There is a philosophy of investing in dynamic teachers who are utterly, ridiculously passionate about their subjects,' we heard. A further culture shift has been towards it being cool to want to learn. 'The older ones are good at role modelling this,' said a parent. Not overly pressurised, though – this will never be a hothouse, a major factor for parents choosing it.

Setting in maths and English from year 7, then sciences and languages from year 9. All pupils take one or two languages at GCSE, having learned French and Spanish (plus Latin) from year 7. A few take eight or nine GCSEs, but vast majority take 10 – 'certainly never more than that as I'd rather these stronger students used their time to focus on the extracurricular,' says head. Art and science do well, and history is having a resurgence. At A level, business, economics, psychology and biology are popular, while art and French get stellar results. A special mention should also go to English, both at GCSE and A level – previously an underperforming department, it is now soaring both in terms of engagement and results. The View from the Bridge class we dropped in on was punchy and entertaining, with bright-eyed pupils confident to express their views – teaching at its best. Meanwhile, a geography A level class reminded us how meticulous lesson planning always pays dividends. Three BTecs now available: enterprise and entrepreneurship, creative digital media and PE. 'Students who would have got an E at A level are getting distinctions at BTec – it just goes to show they are not for weaker students, just a different way of learning,' says head. EPQ started by around 35 students and completed by 15-20.

Busy 'head of futures' organises everything from industry round tables to mentoring programmes, degree apprenticeship talks and one-to-one sessions – although disappointingly some students had no idea.

Learning support and SEN: Those with SEN used to have to trot off to a scruffy room in a dilapidated building but those days are long gone, with the department now boasting a central spot – ideal for the 18 per cent of students with a learning support need, though most are supported in the classroom. Majority have dyslexia, for which all students are screened in years 7 and 9, and again in lower sixth. 'Incredibly detailed support, and they do all their own cognitive tests too,' lauded a parent, while a student told us, 'I have weekly one-to-ones for maths support and it's been brilliant' (literary sessions equally popular; both cost extra). Currently no EHCPs.

The arts and extracurricular: Saturday morning extracurricular options attract large numbers from the arty, sporty and (in older years) those keen to fill academic gaps – these are in addition to all the usual after school clubs (and some less usual ones: 'My favourite is BBQ club,' said a pupil; 'you cook up some meat and eat it!'). Lots of takers for bronze and gold DofE (they don't do silver), while the possibility of taking to the sky in a glider is a strong card for the CCF, with the added draw of yomping in wilderness far from tidy, cultivated Hampshire. A quarter of students do both. Debating thinner on the ground than you might expect.

Stretch and challenge is now on fire. 'There is a philosophy of investing in dynamic teachers who are utterly, ridiculously passionate about their subjects,' we heard

Music is run by a professional composer – 'the most modest and coolest dude on the planet,' we heard. Pupils love how he has digitised performances, and music tech is a popular AS. Greater numbers of younger children are coming up through the department, helped by the fact that you don't need to be accomplished when you join – one boy had never picked up a cello two or three years ago and is now at grade 7. Practice rooms are full all week, there are different choral groups and ensembles, plus bands and an orchestra. 'This year's carol service is outside and if it rains, it rains,' the head told us, proving that the pandemic doesn't have to stop play.

Drama is going great guns under a new department head and with the newly refurbished black box theatre. Our tour guide hardly drew breath as she raved about the We Will Rock You rehearsals and the Shakespeare Festival too. 'Oh and cabaret evening is coming up.' Technical workshops available for the more stage shy and they'd just had a visiting workshop and performance from Paper Birds when we visited. Dance increasingly important – it has its own mirrored studio which one student told us she headed off to twice a week for four hours. LAMDA available, with many students doing grade 6+.

'This is where the magic happens,' exclaimed a pupil about the spacious art department. Ceramics was the highlight for us – the school doesn't just have its own kilns but a massive ceramics studio where a student was busy wheel throwing and where the quality of the work is gasp-worthy. Plenty of other working spaces, one of them packed with paintings depicting the theme of 'versions and diversions'. Photography available as an A level. 'We believe in scale,' the head of department told us, as evidenced by some large installations and canvases displayed throughout the school, including in a permanent exhibition space where the crème-de-la-crème serves to inspire others. The annual art competition is popular – this year's theme was 'musical journeys', last year's was 'me and my world'. Over in DT, we watched a lively year 9 lesson on modelling, where students transformed lacklustre shoeboxes into thriving mini businesses using recycled materials.

Sport: Hockey and cricket dominate for both boys and girls, with plenty of club and county level players, though school still struggles to shake off its rugby-is-king reputation. Head said he might even move poor Jonny Wilkinson's jumper from reception to get the message across. 'I won't buy in academy players just to get the wins,' he added (though school still does very well at rugby). Football is on the up, which has pleased students no end, and there's also netball, tennis, swimming, cycling and badminton on offer, as well as yoga to rock-climbing or riding, among others. 'Inclusive,' say parents, 'they will put out four teams in some cases.' Impressive facilities include pitches as far as the eye can see, a decent sports hall and pool although the gym could do with an update, reckon pupils.

Boarding: 'Everyone is a boarder' is the school's philosophy, with day pupils (40 per cent of the school) all allocated to one of the boarding houses. They often stay for activities, prep and supper, especially on Fridays when the real fun happens eg pool party, arts and crafts, dodgeball etc. 'It definitely blurs the distinction between day pupils and boarders although I'd still say day pupils wind up making more friends with other day pupils and the same with boarders,' said a pupil.

Flexibility is the name of the game – 70 per cent are flexi (up to three nights a week), 15 per cent are weekly and the remaining 15 per cent (mainly international) are termly. All reside across eight onsite boarding houses – the co-ed year 7 and 8 Junior House, plus three for senior girls and four for senior boys. Some are modern, some are old, but families don't get to pick their house – school prefers to ensure a mix of interests across them all, as well as matching personalities with the right houseparent. We visited Park, a delightfully cottage-style girls' house packed with wooden beams and fairy lights, and a quirky open plan desk area up in the eaves. Next door, Sutton – with its monochrome tiled hall, rows of school photos and leather sofas – smacks of masculinity. The views of rolling hills from the vast windows are, we were pleased to note, not lost on the boys – 'Imagine waking up to that every morning,' said one. Rooms we saw were meticulously tidy though one boy later admitted his room gets so untidy that it's not unusual for the sea of clothes on the floor to get mixed up with his room-mate's, which can cause some embarrassment when either one goes to open his games kit.

Termly boarders all stay in the same house so weekends don't get too quiet. Not much chance of that on Saturdays in any case, with masses of pupils in for activities and/or sports. On Sundays, boarders report a 'family atmosphere' and there's always an optional activity – up next is a shopping trip to Guildford. 'Canoeing, climbing and orienteering are on offer,' added a pupil.

'This is where the magic happens,' exclaimed a pupil about the spacious art department. Ceramics was the highlight for us – the quality of the work is gasp-worthy

Pastoral care is 'pretty phenomenal,' said a parent, with particular praise for the houseparents. 'Last Sunday night, I had a note from my son's housemaster saying he'd got 20 house points and where he ranks in the year,' said one. Matrons also come in for high praise – 'You walk in and they know who you are – they foster a really lovely vibe,' said a parent. 'In the end,' said another, 'most of them want to board a bit even if they live locally, and you really can't blame them' (though sixth formers said they'd like a bit more freedom in the evenings, if only to pop into another house).

Ethos and heritage: The century-long transformation from farming orphanage to present-day independent school began in 1912 with the bequest of Sydney Stern (the one and only Lord Wandsworth), a wealthy playboy turned Liberal politician. For the son of a Victorian banker buried in the Balls Pond Road it was rather an odd choice as a memorial, but due to the financial ability of the foundation trustees it turns out to have been a wise one. The school motto, 'perseverantia vincit', was taken most literally by the redoubtable Scot Sandy Henderson, headmaster from 1943 to 1968 (25 years of perseverance), who inspired the metamorphosis from agriculture to academics, though it remains surrounded by the original farm. Students (60 per cent boys, 40 per cent girls) value the 1,200 acres, with one year 7 telling us 'the space to run around in' was one of 'the best things about the school'.

A surprisingly pompous arched entrance is a reminder not to judge a book by its cover as this is not a school with architectural pretensions. The feeling is more of a friendly village as you drive past the 60+ staff houses dotted about ('sometimes I feel more like a landlord than a headteacher'), although the now pedestrianised campus means you'll have to park up before entering any of the neat, mostly low-rise brick buildings where teaching takes place. New additions include stunning dining room (with quality of food to match, although the chefs may want to go easy on the chicken – 'It's nearly always chicken,' groaned pupil after pupil) and the glass-fronted science centre, the biggest investment in the school's history. But don't hold your breath for more, with head insisting, 'I refuse to play the shiny buildings game.' Students hope he makes an exception for the sixth form centre, which is decidedly out of date, and we thought the library (converted old gym) was a bit disappointing.

Pastoral care, inclusivity and discipline: 'Teachers know the children and care about them, and they go well beyond the call of duty,' said a parent (though there is a sensible rule of no emails after 8pm). All staff are trained in mental health first aid, and there's lots of peer mentoring – both formal and informal, with the house system meaning younger ones naturally talk to older ones. An open, honest and transparent culture means pupils feel they can speak out. School has won four recent national awards – for transition, wellbeing of pupils, looking after vulnerable children and character education; next up, it's going for the Diana Award in recognition of its approach to bullying, about which you see notices everywhere.

When school was mentioned on the Everyone's Invited website, the head picked up the phone, asking what they could do? 'No idea,' came the response, so he set about educating the pupils themselves via eg PHSE and assemblies as well as an inspired parent workshop on how to run a teenage party (bouncers, how to limit drinks, right to search etc). We also liked the sound of the parent workshop on unconscious bias, all part of the focus on ensuring an inclusive culture. Pupils told us there's a lively Pride group.

Far more rewards than sanctions, and even the latter starts with 'flags' that lead to a coaching conversation rather than automatic finger wagging. Detentions, when used, 'must be meaningful – if I had my way they'd be working on the farm,' says head. Pupils feel rules are fair and like that they are dealt with on a case-by-case basis and include wiggle room for grey areas. But school won't stand for nonsense either, with around 25-30 fixed-term exclusions and a couple of permanent ones most years. Sniffer dogs are brought in every term. 'As I tell parents, it's not that we have a drugs problem but random tests give students a way out so they are able to say to their friends, "I can't risk it as we get tested".'

The views of rolling hills from the vast windows are, we were pleased to note, not lost on the boys – 'Imagine waking up to that every morning,' said one

Up there with the best of them when it comes to pupil voice. Not only were they consulted about the newest building additions, they were also closely involved in the design. They feel listened to on smaller matters too – 'We said we needed a PlayStation in our boarding house and it has arrived within a week!' said one student.

Pupils and parents: This is a local school – 90 per cent of families live within 40 miles, stretching up to Guildford and down to Winchester, although enquiries from London are on the up since Covid. The small number of overseas families come from all over, including Europe, Asia and South America – 'We are careful not to focus on one place,' says school. Parents – who appreciate the lack of pretension of the school – are mainly dual income and from a range of professions. Pupils are a delight – chatty, engaging and appreciative. The Sternians' Association, with its deliberately rustic (covered in tractors) website, encourages parents to muck in and even make fools of themselves at the Santa Dash, a charity run started by the head.

Money matters: Eight per cent of pupils are supported by the foundation, which offers means-tested awards restricted to British children who have lost the support of one or both parents through death, divorce or separation, and whose surviving parent (if there is one) has not formed a new relationship. 'It's been amazing for our family,' said one parent, and pupils told us, 'We don't stand out in any way, which is a good thing.' Academics, art, performing art, sports and all-rounder scholarships at all the main entry points (11+, 13+ and 16+) – majority are honorary but a small number carry up to 10 per cent reduction in fees.

The last word: Continues to benefit from dramatic transformation under current leadership. The kind of school where children make friends for life, don't have a minute to spare and are likely to look back on their school days very fondly indeed.

Luckley House School
28
Luckley Road, Wokingham, Berkshire RG40 3EU
0118 978 4175 | registrar@luckleyhouseschool.org | www.luckleyhouseschool.org
Ages: 11 – 18
Pupils: 328; Boarders: 20 full/weekly
Fees: Day £17,811; Boarding £24,750 – £31,164 pa

Head: Since September 2020, Areti Bizior BSc BE. PGCE from University of South Africa. Seven years at St George's Ascot, three at Queen Anne's, Caversham, thence to Downe House as deputy head in 2013. ISI inspector; former governor of nearby Holme Grange School; on executive committee of Boarding Schools Association.

Learnt 'an incredible amount' at Downe – now pleased to 'make a difference', bringing the good practice that she's seen along the way. Wants to capitalise on 'sense of momentum', focusing on 'aspiring to your personal best', an aim which we feel encapsulates the ethos here. Quotes a prefect who, in recent assembly, 'talked about working towards your goal little and often – before you know it, you've climbed the mountain.' 'Everyone comments on how happy the children seem here, but to be happy you have to be resilient, flexible, content with yourself.'

Inviting, unintimidating office with fresh flowers, gas fireplace and pupil art hung tastefully above the desk. Pupils find her calm, easy manner reassuring – no wonder they just pop in. 'Some come for a chat, others to visit Copper the dog – she's so popular we're going to need a sign-up sheet. They know there's always cakes up here too.' The other day a group swung by to sing her a Bee Gees song – 'I think they thought that's my era,' she laughs. Emotionally astute: 'Younger ones come in pretending it's just for a chat, and then they'll say, "by the way…" and I know I'm getting the real reason why they're here.' Big windows overlooking school grounds: 'I love seeing them go about their day.' We take a moment to do just that, observing pupils milling around, many lugging sports kit towards after school activities. When she spots one boy chatting to a new friend, she comments, 'It's lovely to see him branching out.'

Ten years ago, school faced an existential crisis when numbers got perilously low, dipping below 200. Mrs Bizior's predecessor turned things around (there are now over 300 'lucky Luckleys', as one parent termed them). Even then, some feel the school had begun to lose direction again before Mrs Bizior joined, 'bringing renewed energy and vision'. 'She's got a business head on her,' say parents – indeed, currently doing an MBA at UCL. Objective is to grow slightly but 'it's important that Luckley remains small in number, big in opportunity,' she says.

Keen netballer in her schooldays and will still always 'grab a ball if I'm passing the courts and see boarders playing in the evening'. Also practises karate at a local club. Lives on site with husband, in IT, and teenage son, at a nearby all-boys school – 'He loved his taster day here but having mum as head was just too much.' Parents appreciate that she's a mum – 'She knows how it is.'

Entrance: Usually 40 places in year 7 and 15 in year 9, though numbers can be flexible if demand high. Pupils from huge range of primaries and preps, and with a broad range of ability. Taster days for all those interested. Cognitive ability tests, plus English for overseas applicants. Head interviews everyone. The 11+ hopefuls create an autobiographical storyboard in advance – 'some are covered in photos and glitter; others have just a few words on them', but 'if they're a bit shy, it's a way to get them talking'. Characteristic of student-centred approach. Ultimately looking for pupils with diverse skills and interests.

Exit: Half leaves after GCSEs, usually for BTecs or bigger settings. 'The reasons people leave are the reasons people stay – Luckley's a small school and everybody knows your name,' say staff. University destinations vary with cohorts, which are too small to establish patterns. Royal Holloway,

Reading, Cardiff come up. Odd few medics and students to Oxbridge, though none in 2021.

Latest results: In 2021, 61 per cent 9-7 at GCSE; 66 per cent A*/A at A level (86 per cent A*-B). In 2019 (the last year when exams took place), 30 per cent 9-7 at GCSE; 25 per cent A*/A at A level (51 per cent A*-B).

Teaching and learning: Gentle academics. 'Teachers get to know you really well,' said a pupil. Until year 11, groups of up to 18 (12 in practical subjects). GCSE options as small as four. Happy to run an A level class of one. 'Means we can tailor teaching to the group,' say staff.

Curriculum starts broad, with 21 subjects in year 7. Three languages in year 7 whittled down to two in year 8 and one or two in year 9. Year 9s choose their practical subjects and there's an optional HPQ research project. Pupils particularly love food tech (as, we suspect, do parents – seriously delicious-looking focaccia being rustled up when we popped in). No subject snobbery – 'If you're really good at photography they make a big deal out of it,' says one pupil, 'rather than going on about how you need As in maths and English.'

Unusually flexible – anything possible. The school's size allows for bespoke experiences and timetabling and has the capacity to tailor a student's academic diet to fit them. While most take at least the standard nine GCSEs, some do just six. Majority take three A levels but the school can accommodate students taking just one, perhaps with a practical EPQ alongside it.

The head quotes a prefect who, in a recent assembly, 'talked about working towards your goal little and often – before you know it, you've climbed the mountain'

Small sixth form, which has pros and cons – having one or two in humanities subject may limit debate, though 'we get better at countering our own points, which is what you need for the exam anyway,' says loyal pupil. Head emulating breadth of year 7 at the top of the school, introducing classical civilisations and politics. Largely taught in dedicated centre, newly refurbished in parts and due for further development. Bright, fresh classrooms with seminar-style table, big whiteboards and flatscreen TVs. Sixth form retention a focus – parents all told us that their offspring would stay if enough others did so. Everyone's hoping for a snowball effect.

Learning support and SEN: 'We're better now at knowing what we can offer for pupils with SEN,' says academic deputy, who looks carefully at ed psych reports and talks to families in depth when they apply. Twenty-five on SEN register. One-to-one support provided, progress carefully tracked. Many more access study skills provision laid on by learning support. 'We didn't look anywhere else,' says mum of a girl with dyslexia, 'because of the school's reputation for SEND.' 'Proactive' support and lots of 'coping strategies'. Placement test identifies those who'll need EAL support. Can work towards IELTS with specialist teacher.

The arts and extracurricular: Beautifully designed music room with wacky acoustic-enhancing ceiling. One-third have individual lessons. Recording room and music tech facilities too. Many music scholars also members of national choirs and orchestras – we watched soulful rendition of Snow Patrol.

Theatre small but perfectly formed in glassy new development complete with smart foyer for interval drinks. We saw sixth formers rehearsing with great maturity – characteristically, school offers A level in lighting and sound for those who don't fancy the stage. Lots of prizes in ISA lockdown monologue competitions, including first place in two categories. Musical this year is Wizard of Oz, seniors doing Pride and Prejudice – pupils hotly anticipating outcome of auditions when we visited.

Art and design provision broad up to A level. Colourful pupil work imaginatively displayed around the school (monsters made from cheese-graters a first for us) – genuinely decorative rather than 'we ought to have some pupil work up'. Studios appropriately well-loved – tables painty, printing press inky, shelves heaving with pottery due for the kiln. At A level, photography, fine art and graphic design students work happily alongside one another. Where numbers are small, years 12 and 13 come together, with second year A level students acting as mentors to first years. 'We work hard to make sure that everybody can do what they want to do. It makes it dynamic – fine artists learn from photographers about slow shutter speeds and then go away and recreate the effect themselves.'

Wide range of other activities, from rock school to robotics, available as part of extended day provision.

Sport: New director of sport has big ideas and the confidence to 'knock on the head's door until she says yes' ('He's very competitive,' she chuckles). Provision not previously a priority – self-fulfilling, of course, because school didn't attract traditionally sporty children. Strong athletes (recent accolades in cricket, trampolining, horse-riding, kayaking) predominantly got their fix at external clubs. Now proactively engaging and nurturing talent. New Athlete Development Programme is 'elite pathway' for scholars or promising individuals. We saw year 9 ADPs doing some exhausting-looking coordination and agility work. Full-time strength and conditioning coach devises tailored fitness plans and talks about oxygen deficits and other such elite athlete things. We didn't fancy a bounce on the new AirTrack but heard that it's ideal for jumps and flips. Annual sports dinner being held the evening of our visit. No hierarchy of skills here, and sporting success is celebrated just as much as academics.

For mere mortals, 'sport for all is still there'. Priority is making it fun, with small teams (eg nine-a-side football) creating more contact with the ball. 'Level ups' and 'special powers' engage those who'd rather be in front of a PlayStation. And here's that flexibility, again – judo and fencing introduced for current year 9s, because department reckons that they'd enjoy them. Cross-country well attended by students and staff. Other options include climbing, volleyball, dance, trampolining.

Sports hall houses most of the action, with ergs and bikes on the mezzanine. Large multi-use games area in development (diggers hard at work): all-weather pitch and floodlighting will allow year-round fixtures. Handy app now posts matches and results, though parents wish there was a bit more warning about logistics and away matches ('We might want to go and see them!').

Boarding: Twenty full or weekly boarders as we write (plus flexis) – plan is to grow this to forty. Nationalities and languages mixed within rooms – most full boarders east Asian. Rooms freshly painted in neutrals with space on the walls for reminders of home. Bathrooms spotless.

New head of boarding has come from Milton Abbey (where 95 per cent board), and is putting into place jam-packed activity programme for the weekends (no Saturday lessons or fixtures here). Two trips go out every weekend – every boarder must go on at least one of them. Theme parks, waterparks, cinema trips – nothing too worthy. More day students now staying for evenings and the odd night ('when she fancies a sleepover with friends'), as well as joining weekend activities. Boarding community thus feels bigger than it really is, and at under £50 a night, parents are slowly realizing that a night at school is 'cheaper than a babysitter', laughs head.

During the day, boarders are day pupils – 'they wave goodbye to house parents in the morning and don't return until after activities'.

Full-time strength and conditioning coach devises tailored fitness plans and talks about oxygen deficits and other such elite athlete things

Well integrated with day pupils. Parents and pupils welcome the international diversity that boarders bring.

Ethos and heritage: Founded in 1918 by one Miss Bertha Drake, a 'deeply religious woman', 'to provide a broad-based education, based on Christian principles, to allow girls to develop their full potential' (according to charming 1970s history). Various guises since: became Luckley-Oakfield School in 1959 having merged with another girls' school; rebranded to Luckley House in 2013. Ethos hasn't changed, though – 'girls were given considerable freedom of choice regarding work and activities', meaning there was 'no typical "Luckley girl"'. Since 2015 there have been Luckley boys, too, but those values remain.

Main building a neat 1907 red-bricker – a touch of period charm but no danger of any nasty drafts or rickety staircases. Inside it's warm and welcoming – log fire smouldering in the oak-panelled fireplace, thick carpets and smelly candles that you'd choose for home ('Frosted Zest with a Hint of Mint', if you're interested – much nicer than it sounds). Other buildings more modern, lots of glass and colourful statement walls. Classrooms inviting and lively – top marks to Spanish for the rainforest-themed garlands ('because they speak Spanish in lots of places where they have rainforests,' explains our young guide earnestly) and textiles, where we saw lampshades mounted on the wall with real lightbulbs inside. Lots of gardens to explore including a zipwire ('where you'll find year 8 at lunchtime,' we are reliably informed).

School feels more modern even in the short time since Mrs Bizior joined. 'The general look of the school has been refreshed,' says one parent, adding, 'If I'm paying school fees it's reasonable to want to sit on a nice bench and look at nice signage.' Some grumbles about systems moving faster than the staff who are meant to implement them, or information coming home at the last minute. 'All homework is meant to be on Doddle,' says one mum, 'but gaps in what's been uploaded mean we spend a lot of time emailing teachers to check.'

Flexibility a big appeal to parents who are looking for a school that does not put academics front and centre – 'It's very balanced between academics and life skills,' says one mum, who 'wasn't that interested in how many Oxbridge candidates they had'. 'They've really got it right' when it comes to pressure, says another, comparing it with other schools where they 'talk the talk but don't actually do it'. 'Parents and children are looking for those transferable skills now, rather than just grades,' and pupils seem to be developing those in spades. Bonfire night laser show this year organised by a pupil – 'he put together a plan and presented it to the committee' – and prefects take on a lot of responsibility.

Christianity remains central too, though you won't see crucifixes in classrooms. 'It's more about a way of life,' says head; 'love and service are core values, good human values.' Visiting chaplains once a month, often from parent body – 'I tell them that assembly must be based on a feelgood message about life.' Popular Bible & Cake club, part of wellbeing programme, provides opportunity for Bible study and games.

Very 'normal', say parents. We felt that, too – lots of staff have worked in the state sector; lots of pupils have been to primary schools rather than preps; fees are low compared with other schools in the area. We came across a number of families who had moved to Luckley House having found their child struggling in a big comprehensive, or who had felt let down by state provision during lockdown. Very unfusty and accessible – a long way from some of the big, formal schools in the Royal County.

Pastoral care, inclusivity and discipline: 'Phenomenal', we hear. Head engendering 'sense of belief', 'making aspiration more overt'. Marketing material peppered with pupil quotes around this theme: 'I believe I can help world leaders'; 'I believe I can win a BAFTA' etc. 'They really did write those themselves!' says head, who thinks a lot about 'how we can get them to believe'.

Some year groups in the middle of the school girl-heavy; oldest and youngest evenly balanced. Arrival of boys 'changed behaviour', say staff: 'The girls came out of their shells, became more expressive, shared opinions more quickly.'

New prefect-run mentoring scheme – year 13s paired with younger students ('not like Tinder!' prefects hasten to add) who want someone to chat to. Prefects given significant responsibility (they'd run assembly that morning) and represent student voice, acting as role models to younger students, who feel that they know them well. Lots of vertical integration – we saw nice interactions between older and younger students. Socials encourage cohesion within sixth form, including bowling and lasertag in Wokingham, black tie soirée and Christmas trip into London to see a show.

PSHE, or 'life skills', recently restructured. Students feed into what's covered ('gives them ownership') and school supplements as necessary. Pupils not as socially sophisticated as counterparts at glossier schools – Everyone's Invited website didn't hit their radar though school ran sessions around the issues raised. Hotchpotch of personalities and types, with no pressure to conform. Students discussed starting an LGBTQ+ group recently, but 'the more they discussed it, the more they realised they didn't need one,' say staff. Support sessions for those approaching public exams. 'Safe Drive, Stay Alive' programme in Reading for year 12.

Food very good – 'a full, balanced, meat and two veg approach,' say happy parents. Excellent salad bar and range of hot options in bustling canteen. Chicken burgers a particular favourite. As we tucked in, boys peered at our plates to check out what was for lunch – 'Oi!' staff scolded in jest – rapport between teachers and pupils respectful with a smattering of humour. Sixth form share well-equipped kitchen with boarders; huge jar of biscuits gets filled every morning (and demolished by lunchtime).

Christianity remains central too, though you won't see crucifixes in classrooms. 'It's more about a way of life,' says head

School counsellor available for students and staff. Form tutors first port of call for pastoral concerns, though pupils feel comfortable talking to any member of staff if they're worried about something.

Pupils and parents: Minibuses cover 20-mile radius: Maidenhead, Farnborough, Windsor, Fleet etc. Buses run once in the morning but twice in the afternoon, so that parents 'can cherry-pick the length of the day,' says head. 'We are really flexible about suiting the family' – lots of busy working parents who appreciate that support.

Parents generally have no assumptions about privately educating their children or worries about keeping up with the Joneses. The school has a history, but it's not a Latin-songs-and-glory-on-the-rugby-pitch sort of place. Perhaps it's adding boys to a girls' school, rather than vice versa; perhaps it's relatively low fees; perhaps it's the school's size. Whatever the reasons, Luckley is a grounded, local school rather than a status symbol, and parents are self-selecting.

Money matters: Means-tested bursaries available. Fee remission for children of clergy. Scholarships for year 7, 9 and 12 entry (academic, sport, music, art, drama) worth between five and 20 per cent. Exceptional GCSE performance rewarded with £100 to spend on something inspired by their academic studies.

The last word: A school on the up – hence this, its first inclusion in the Guide. Parents rave about the flexible, caring provision that this 'little gem' has to offer. What kind of child would Luckley not suit, we wondered. 'Someone super academic, perhaps?' says one mum, before pausing – 'Actually, I know some really clever children who would benefit from the social skills they'd pick up.' A completely contrasting offering from the better-known schools in the area, and all the richer for it. With a zingy head and modern approach, we have high hopes for this new era of Luckley House.

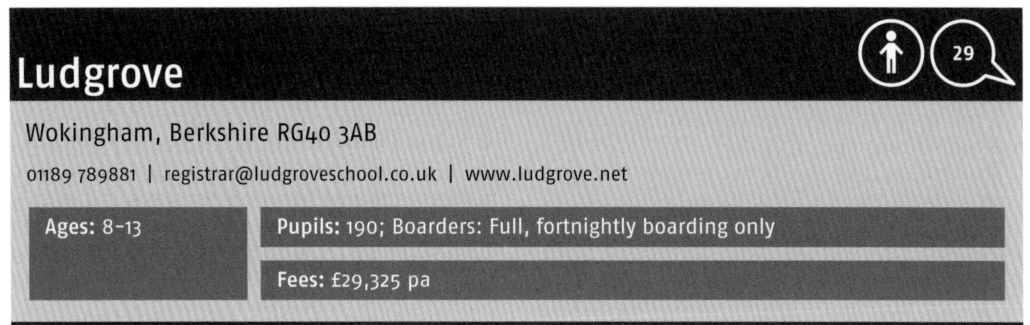

Ludgrove

29

Wokingham, Berkshire RG40 3AB

01189 789881 | registrar@ludgroveschool.co.uk | www.ludgrove.net

Ages: 8-13

Pupils: 190; Boarders: Full, fortnightly boarding only

Fees: £29,325 pa

Headmaster: Since 2008, Simon Barber, BA (50s). Many schools like to portray themselves as 'one big happily family' but few do so as convincingly as Ludgrove. For one thing, Mr Barber is the third generation of Barbers to take the role, and lives barely 50 metres from the main building. He was a boy here, as was his own son, and found he took instantly to teaching. After Eton and Durham University, he cut his teeth in state and independent day schools, then worked for a spell in the City before bowing to the inevitable and following in the family footsteps. 'It was difficult not to come back, but I wanted to feel this was definitely the right choice.' He still teaches 'seven or eight' lessons a week because 'I enjoy knowing the boys. The beauty of Ludgrove is its size – I can put a spotlight on every boy.'

You'd be forgiven for wondering if his actual name was 'Simon-and-Sophie' so regularly do parents couple his name with his wife's; she is completely involved on the pastoral and domestic side and the pair are universally appreciated by parents: 'Incredibly charming, and they really know their stuff.' Family loyalties to the school run deep, too, with sometimes almost a third of the intake siblings.

In an age when pre-teen boarding is an ever-harder sell, some parents commit to Ludgrove's fortnightly boarding model under sufferance, but the school is firm about enforcing it. 'We're certainly an outlier [in the boarding commitment required] but if it's fair, people love it,' attests Barber. Parents all appear to warm to the old-fashioned boy fun enjoyed at weekends and 'extremely nurturing' care: 'You really do find boys in the evening with their duvets and teddies having stories with Sophie by the fire.'

Entrance: With ever fewer families looking for boarding from age eight, the 25 to 30 joining in year four (known here as 'Sixes') are not beating off hordes of applicants. Entry is non-selective at this stage, which appeals to the steady trickle of families who transfer children from state primaries ('saving a few pennies for later,' as one mother put it), though all sit low-key tests on arrival for streaming purposes. Strong links exist with London feeders such as Garden House and Eaton House Belgravia. The senior year groups swell to around 40, but joining later is more stringent, involving an English and maths assessment plus a taster day.

Exit: Ludgrove's reputation is built upon its consistently strong teaching and small classes (typically 12 to 15), resulting in impressive output. Every year, they send 70 per cent of year 8 boys to Eton, Harrow, Radley and Winchester. Other school destinations include Marlborough, Sherborne, Charterhouse, Bradfield and Stowe. By year 8, English and maths are split over four streams (from three earlier in the school), the top one being the scholarship class.

While London parents in particular choose this school to give their sons space, exercise and an escape from the hot-housing prevalent in London preps ('they never bring homework home in the holidays,' says one mother approvingly), Mr Barber and his team are terrier-like in pursuit of places for their charges at their target schools. 'Much as we believe in climbing trees, we want our guys to go to amazing places. You have to put more firepower into literacy and numeracy – you'd be mad if you don't.'

Assessment preparation lessons are timetabled from year four, with more specific preparation by year six. One newer initiative Mr Barber rates highly is an outside company which comes to film boys doing mock interviews to show them how their body language comes across.

Our view: 'Very traditional but constantly evolving' is one parent's summary of Ludgrove, which very much hits the mark. Good schooling is combined with good fun in the beautiful 130 acres of grounds, and the pressures of getting into top public schools are clearly balanced with ample time to build camps, play sport and hang out with your friends rather than your iPad.

The traditional elements are very much in place, some of them delightfully quirky. Boys all yomp the 400m 'cart track' after breakfast each day, considered indispensable to revving young brains up for action. Another idiosyncrasy is 'sets football', an inter-house event involving every member of a house at once. 'You'll get some crazy scores, and small boys brazenly tackling big ones' – also a good time for the latter to demonstrate their grasp of the school's 'be kind' mantra.

Each boy's name is painted up in the dining room as soon as he arrives (there are shutters with new panels over old ones, so no shortage of space), and lovely glass cases in the main corridor house an ancient hooks and tags system to show team selections, and where you will be playing. Plenty of parents visit twice a week to watch matches ('I'm there so often there's really no time to write,' said one). Exeat weekends begin at Friday lunchtime, enabling families to get home before the end-of-week rush hour.

Parents are vociferous about the standard of teaching; several teachers were mentioned in dispatches, with a good balance between male and female: 'I'll have entire history lessons played back to me because my son's been so caught up in it.' Though we had the impression that the conversion of Pringle packet into a hydrogen rocket was done largely for our benefit, the master in charge undoubtedly had the easy knack of informative digression – in this case the invention of the Davy lamp to detect methane in mines – as we waited for take-off.

Mr Barber is convinced that creativity will become increasingly vital in the careers of tomorrow, hence the new £2.5m exploration centre housing housing science, coding, art, CDT and ceramics facilities.

Being a small school, masters muck in far beyond the classroom, coupling teaching with sports coaching, drama, dormitory duties and more, and perhaps this drives a pleasing sense of interconnectedness around the school. In pottery boys were making a large urn destined for the new Chelsea-style garden under construction; in DT, boys laser engraved homemade wooden tuck boxes to take to their next school.

Mobiles and personal devices are largely verboten (how many schools still have call boxes, let alone a vintage red one, under the stairs?). One pupil from Hong Kong insisted, 'It's torture!' although – or perhaps as a consequence – 'parents quite like it,' says Mr Barber. Overseas students are allowed devices at certain times to call home.

In counterpoint, there has been a massive push in IT investment, ranging from increased use of technology in classrooms to improved systems for parental communication (noted by many with gratitude) through the use of systems like SOCS (for sports fixtures) and ISAMS. A noticeably professional social media feed relays everything from a boy's birthday 'cakes' made from favourite flavours of ice cream, to special events and swimming pool muck-around sessions on soggy Sundays. 'They've got sharper while still retaining muddy wellies by the door feeling of a family home,' says one parent.

Traditional elements very much in place, some delightfully quirky. Boys all yomp the 400m 'cart track' after breakfast: indispensable to revving young brains up for action

'Ludgrove is so incredible at how well they know your boy, and quickly,' says another, the product perhaps of a six-to-one boy-teacher ratio, and that mingling of staff and boys both inside the classroom and out.

Learning support is readily available – around 30 pupils may be having one-to-one help at any one time – and there are three full-time specialists covering all the specific learning difficulties. Help with things like dyslexia and dyscalculia is included within the fees; help from other visiting specialists for things like occupational and speech and language therapy are charged as extras.

The theatre, completed in 2014, hosts house and school plays, assemblies and guest speakers, and the recently spruced-up music department, its walls now adorned with a vast musical timeline, are abuzz. Over 80 per cent of pupils learn an instrument, and a third of them learn two: 'We even have two bagpipe instructors.'

General stampede for seconds after lunch that we witnessed on our visit supports the notion that the very appetising photographs on Twitter fully represent the standard of fare. Lunch is eaten at small tables with a teacher on each, a rota ensuring every boy takes turns to sit and chat with them.

Impressive though the academic achievements of the boys are, there's a palpable understanding of what a boyhood should involve, and no shortage of humour... see the definition of 'Boy' on one classroom wall: 'A noise with dirt on it.' And regardless of the gleaming swimming pool, gym complex and nine-hole golf course, it's clear teachers are equally happy for boys to lark about on the 'monkey house' climbing frame or 'camps' (den-making area). 'Both my boys are now very competent with a pen-knife and getting a bonfire going,' says one approving London mother.

Unsurprisingly, the sporting focus here is on traditional English sports, from rugby to clay pigeon shooting, archery to Eton fives, through cricket is the school specialty, and a portrait of WG Grace smiles down over the main corridor. Parents confirm that every team plays and is coached with equal fervour and has the chance to play away matches.

A semi-apologetic assertion from the head of marketing that 'we're all about the product, not the packaging' seems rather mystifying: this purpose-built building with its vast south-facing windows may be Victorian but doesn't feel at all tired. It is bright, warm and welcoming.

Boarding: Roughly half of parents are Londoners, another 40 per cent live within two hours of the school and around 10 per cent are from overseas. They appreciate the fact that emails to the matrons go into a shared account 'so they don't fester in one person's inbox'. Teachers comment that fellow pupils will immediately spot and cheer up a homesick room-mate, though one ex-Royal Marines teacher spoke with endearing earnestness about a squirt of lavender (sent from home) on teddy working well for one boy.

The dorm carpets are thick, the paintwork fresh, and an ongoing investment programme is progressing at full speed.

Money matters: School now has a small number of boys on free places through the matchmaking charity the Royal Springboard foundation, and a handful of full or partial bursaries, means-tested annually through a third-party assessor. Curiously though for a school with illustrious royal connections (Princes Harry and William both came here before Eton), the fees are at the lower end for boarding preps in the region.

The last word: Ludgrove may be bucking a trend in offering only boarding, and requiring boys to stay in every other weekend, but it remains a prince among prep schools by doing it so well. As one parent put it: 'The only crying we've had is because he has to leave the school next year...'

LVS Ascot (Licensed Victuallers' School)

30

London Road, Ascot, Berkshire SL5 8DR

01344 882770 | admissions@lvs.ascot.sch.uk | www.lvs.ascot.sch.uk

Ages: 4–18

Pupils: 809; sixth form: 142; Boarders: 143 full/weekly

Fees: Day £11,160 – £20,010 Boarding £28,545 – £35,160 pa

Principal: Since 2010, Christine Cunniffe BA MMus MBA. After university, had close brush with the law (professionally speaking, that is), securing postgraduate traineeship with Slough-based legal practice only to succumb to alternative role as pianist to fashionistas and London high society (think white baby grands and late nights in plush hotels). Four years later, she put aside renewed yearnings for law when husband-to-be pointed out years of study ahead and tried her hand at teaching instead. Loved it from the off, going straight in as head of music, first at a Stevenage school, then St Bernard's, a selective co-ed grammar school in Slough. Joined LVS Ascot as ambitious director of music in 2003 (school, which had no choir when she arrived, was performing Vivaldi's Gloria at Eton College chapel just two terms later).

Personable, laid-back and quietly assured, she has an unusual (if not unprecedented) openness for a head, which she feels sends useful message to pupils. 'If I have self-doubt, I admit it – children are going to face problems in life, so why pretend it doesn't happen?' Lives on site with her husband and youngest child, who attends the school (the two older ones have now left for uni) – all three regularly feature in conversations. 'I am very honest about my experiences of parenting; I want parents to know I understand what they're going through.'

She's clearly nailed it, with parents describing her as 'empathetic' and 'understanding'. All parents are given her email address and she doesn't shy away from criticism. Runs the parent-staff choir, 'which is tremendously good fun and a good way to encourage bonding.' 'There's no superiority about her – she doesn't swoop in with the "I'm the principal" look,' one parent told us, while others point to her strategic prowess: 'She knows her stuff and is very strong on where she wants the school to go.' Pupils keen – juniors practically hugged her when they saw her – but some seniors told us they rarely see her except at assemblies. Doesn't have time to teach, she says, but steps in when needed. Is something of a TV celeb in the headteacher world, regularly appearing on programmes such as ITV's This Morning to debate topics ranging from back to school stress to whether there should be homework in the holidays ('yes, definitely – a little each day is no bad thing').

Entrance: Most children arrive at junior school in reception (single form to year 2) or year 3 (two forms to year 5). At 11+ majority from school's own junior department with assorted state and private schools supplying the rest. Around 35 places become available at sixth form; students will need GCSE grade 6 or better in chosen subjects though vocational courses such as ICT and sport also available for those of a more practical mindset.

Exit: Around half leave after GCSEs. Nearly 90 per cent of sixth formers to university, with courses ranging from the solidly academic – philosophy, business and maths currently popular – to the more vocational, including sports studies, film production and nursing. Remainder enter a variety of apprenticeship schemes and jobs. Massive breadth of universities, roughly 20 per cent Russell Group. Bristol, Royal Holloway, UCL, Winchester, Harper Adams, Southampton, Oxford Brookes, Surrey and University of the Arts London have all featured recently. Two medics in 2021.

Latest results: In 2021, 39 per cent 9-7 at GCSE; 34 per cent A*/A at A level (56per cent A*-B). In 2019 (the last year when exams took place), 33 per cent 9-7 at GCSE; 16 per cent A*/A at A level (35 per cent A*-B).

Teaching and learning: Non-selective, but no easy ride – 'We think like a grammar school and that means knowing when to put the pressure on and turn it off to get the best results.' Expect multiple retakes, for example, if your child gets lower than their predicted grades in their mocks. But it's no hothouse, say parents – 'Children generally reach their potential happily and the school seems to know the best way to respond to each child.'

There's a pick and mix approach to national curriculum and everything is seasoned with welcome dash of carpe diem flexibility so teachers can go off piste if appropriate

Mission in junior school is to ensure that no child is left to languish in educational no-man's land; regular meetings picking out those 'falling below or zooming ahead'. Favourite subjects among pupils include literacy (popular library-based reading scheme, which carries on into main school, tests comprehension rather than merely rewarding headlong dash for the last page) and science in year 6 – where, joy of joys, 'you get to light the Bunsen burner'.

There's a pick and mix approach to national curriculum – used or modified where it works, ditched if it doesn't – and everything is seasoned with welcome dash of carpe diem flexibility so teachers can go off piste if it's deemed appropriate. Subject-specialist teachers in most subjects from year 5. Setting in maths and English from year 3 and science from year 7. Class sizes average at 13-15, with a maximum of 20.

Children's progress is well ahead of national averages and exam results are good for a non-selective school, let alone for one so large. Nine or 10 GCSEs the norm, selected from around 20 subjects – no Latin or classics, but there is law, psychology, PE and media/business studies – and RS recently changed to philosophy. Wide range of BTecs are popular (everyone has to take at least two sciences), but languages (students choose two from French, Spanish and German from year 7) are not.

Luckley House School.

Around 65 per cent stay on to sixth form – more than in the past, no doubt partly due to jazzy new sixth-form block with swish study areas that top businesses would be proud of and 30 wide-ranging courses, including law and psychology.

Scholars programme run by vice principal for the gifted and talented.

Learning support and SEN: Those with SEN on the rise – 'as long as they only need a maximum of one hour of additional help each week in addition to in-classroom support, that's fine; any more than that and they'd struggle to keep up with the curriculum,' says head. 'The school doesn't pretend they have all the answers, but they're willing to try new things and are incredibly open,' said one parent with a child with more complex problems.

The arts and extracurricular: Drama a joy, with every parent we spoke to praising the slick performances – 'It's lovely to see the ones who get stuck into lighting or directing praised just as much as the performers,' said one. Plenty of signs of artistic talent and spacious studios to work in. Music (as you might expect, given the head's background) is strong, with three choirs, numerous ensembles including rock school and jazz band, and around a third of pupils learning instruments, some to diploma standard. Whizzy music tech studio adored by students, a couple of whom were enjoying a working lunch in the recording studio when we visited.

Sport: School's sports philosophy is that there's something for everyone – 'We are not all about boys' rugby and girls' netball; in fact a popular sport at the moment is boys' hockey, great for boys who are less keen on contact sports,' says head. Team sports are favoured, though, and compulsory for all, including sixth formers – 'What we want is for them to leave here with a love of sport for life, not give up on those who aren't the very best.' Inevitably, there are moans and groans – 'You do see kids who stand on the side with their arms crossed, but most are keen,' one parent told us.

Cracking facilities including two games halls, the larger with climbing wall and cricket nets, the smaller with cushioned floor for happier landings in judo and high-impact sports. Enticing heated pool is well used, offering all-ability training at 6.30am three times a week, while thumping pop music makes well-equipped fitness suite even more inviting for youngsters. Elite golf academy for sixth formers, which combines coaching at a nearby club with a BTec in sports science. Plenty of wins against other schools in rugby, football, netball and hockey; school also competes in athletics and swimming.

Boarding: Boarding houses are homely, yet practical, with plenty of leather seating and welcoming photos in the spacious communal areas, while the comfy carpeted dorms sleep between one and five. 'I came to England two years ago and settled so much quicker than I thought – they make it so easy,' one student told us. Experienced boarding house staff are experts at sidestepping homesickness and are enthusiastic, friendly and forward-looking (one recently introduced the digital Reach system that means staff and parents can keep tabs on students at all times).

'If you want the manor house boarding experience, this isn't for you, but look past the buildings and see the phenomenal time they have here,' one parent told us

Keeping idle hands (and brains) busy is the priority, with a steady but not relentless stream of activities. After school, it's free time from 4pm-5.50pm (usually a club or, for year 9s up, going into Ascot), then dinner, prep and finally an hour more free time before winding down for bed at 9.30pm. Weekend minibuses, booked by the hour, swap returning sports teams for boarders off on assorted excursions (shopping, cinema, bowling, walking in Windsor Great Park, go-karting and paintballing all popular, with some trips further afield to eg Portsmouth) with departures and arrivals as precisely coordinated as flight control at Heathrow. Laminated sheets stating, 'This dorm is too untidy to be cleaned,' spotted in pile on the side, are mercifully rarely needed, say staff.

Polite reminders in the common rooms for international students to speak in English – a world map on the wall reveals the vast breadth of countries they all come from. In fact, the large international contingent helps explain why most boarders are full time, but increasingly flexible options are available – and day pupils can also cross to other side by signing up for occasional one-off boarding sessions. 'Out of the nearly 200 boarders, around 120 are here any one weekend,' one housemaster told us.

'If you want the manor house boarding experience, this isn't for you, but people need to see past the buildings to see the phenomenal time they have here,' one parent told us. 'In my son's boarding house, they have such a great mix of international students, kids from brewery trade, from the military and families who are just minted – and in true LVS style, they keep them all completely equal.'

Ethos and heritage: Site was formerly home to Heatherdown, an ultra-traditional prep school for chaps and David Cameron's pre-Eton alma mater, with own miniature steam railway. It was demolished in 1982 after Licensed Trade Charity (LTC) – which was founded 200 years ago to support drinks trade employees and now runs school – made such an advantageous sale of previous premises in Slough to well-known supermarket chain that could fund construction of what prospectus claims is the 'most modern boarding school in the UK'.

School houses, originally named after major drinks brands, were changing – 'It was a nice link to LTC, but would you call houses after cigarettes?' explains head

And although the thoughtful layout of 80s red-brick buildings may no longer be the cutting edge of school design, it still manages to look surprisingly contemporary and the fundamentals still apply, noticeably the way space-intensive subjects like performing arts get the room they need in central location rather than being consigned to outer reaches of site, while related subjects are housed together making navigation a breeze. The whole place has a small university campus feel, with a rolling refurb programme ensuring facilities stay up-to-the-minute. Massive recent investment in new dining room to provide restaurant-standard space, complete with booth seating and natural lighting, where everyone eats together. Sports department has also had a complete facelift. Outside, there's 25 acres of grounds with oodles of sports grounds and rustic bridge spanning small but perfectly formed lake.

Junior school is vibrant and colourful, with good-sized infants' play area with buddy bench (hardly used, though, say pupils, because nobody gets lonely) and lots of sturdy wooden equipment to climb and balance on. Year 3s and up enjoy scaled-up versions in adjoining area, separated by unmarked but universally recognised boundary line. Reception also has smart outdoor classroom and cheerful playhouse, starting point for innumerable let's pretend games.

Atmosphere throughout is surprisingly laid-back, despite the hard work – no mean feat. Youngsters are encouraged to ask questions and question thought processes, and lesson bell abolished after it broke five years ago, ending mid-sentence rush for the door and making teachers so happy that it was never reintroduced.

School houses, originally named after major drinks brands such as Guinness and Carlsberg, were in process of changing when we visited – 'It was a nice link to LTC, but would you call houses after cigarettes? Anyway, some of the breweries don't exist anymore anyway,' explains head.

Added flexibility with extended day, including meal and the run of learning resource centre, popular with working parents.

Alumni include Holly Tucker, co-founder of Not on the High Street, Simon Cowell and Tracey Ullman.

Pastoral care, inclusivity and discipline: Highly regarded pastoral focus is a tutor group system, with same teacher responsible for child's well-being throughout school career. 'I've been blown away by the quality of individual care,' said one parent, while another points to the way 'they hand out so many awards in assemblies – and it's not just the predictably clever ones.' Students say reformed Horrid Henrys stand as much chance as card-carrying Perfect Peters of getting their day in the sun.

Head's own experiences make her sympathetic to late developers. 'I experienced problems at about 13 and it's made me passionate about not giving up on a child until we have exhausted all areas.' She believes some children 'need to test boundaries, but they also know the security of knowing those boundaries don't shift.' Usual hierarchy of detentions, Saturday morning ones being the worst – and if that doesn't do the trick, the student is sent home and brought back in only on contract. 'I don't think twice about asking students to leave for anything such as misuse of social media or bringing alcohol on site, where a second chance is not warranted, although I've only ever had to do it three or four times,' says head.

School brings dogs in two or three times a year for random drugs checks, but nothing has ever been found – 'The kids actually love it when they see the dogs,' laughs head. Zero tolerance to bullying – 'I was bullied as a child and take a very firm line. Thankfully, the students are real heroes when it comes to reporting any unkindness.' Asked if they knew of anyone with eating disorders or who had self-harmed or been bullied, one student said, 'I personally don't know of anyone, but I'm not stupid enough to think that means it doesn't happen because it can happen anywhere' – suggests it's not just the staff that lack complacency. Students said they'd like to see more consistency among teachers, with regards to sanctions – 'You do get much stricter teachers than others,' said one.

Pupils and parents: A friendly, un-showy and straightforward bunch, pupils are thoughtful rather than introspective, articulate but not glib, and fond of school without the kind of gushing that makes us suspicious. Start of term, said one, 'feels like you're going home rather than just going back'. Families have historically covered socially and economically broad spectrum from royalty to socially deprived, although there's been a noticeable shift towards more 4x4s lately, suggesting greater affluence.

Catchment area extends 15-20 mile radius or so to Reading in west and Maidenhead up north, compass points ably covered by seven school bus routes (some oversubscribed, so worth checking). That said, families from London fringes and deepest Berks and Bucks are on the rise. These 'locals' form large proportion of the clientele and, while job mobility means some degree of coming and going each year, there's not as much as you might suppose. Some expat families, mainly in Forces, and there's a fast-growing international component.

Money matters: Ten per cent discount for siblings (only third child onwards, but discount applies even if first or second subsequently leave), 15 per cent off for MOD and diplomatic service employees, including five per cent early payment discount and a 20 per cent reduction for anyone who has worked in the licensed drinks trade for five years or more.

Scholarships – academic, music, art, drama and sport – all worth up to 50 per cent off fees. School tries to keep budgeting simple with many senior school clubs and activities included in the fees – rowing, riding, sailing and ballet plus individual instrumental lessons and one-to-one language or learning support are the main extras. Means headline fees are just that, with minimum of extras, although brace yourself for the big school trips to the likes of South Africa and Brazil – but again head tries to keep these to a minimum and plans them at least a year ahead so you can dust off your piggy bank.

Read terms and conditions carefully: has unusual policy of retaining acceptance deposits, plus payment for bus transport for the next term, if pupils decide to leave the school, even when a term's notice is given. Only exceptions are if the child leaves at end of year 6, year 11 or year 13.

The last word: Families are attracted to the all-through co-education in this well-equipped, welcoming and unpretentious school. We particularly like the university campus style, modern layout and the fact that non-selectivity is seen as the starting point for success rather than a justification for its absence. The strong results prove it works.

Moulsford Preparatory School
31
Moulsford, Wallingford, Oxfordshire OX10 9HR
01491 651438 | admissions@moulsford.com | www.moulsford.com
Ages: 4-13
Pupils: 370; Boarders: 45 weekly/flexi
Fees: Day £12,600 – £18,825; Boarding £23,550 pa

Headmaster: Since 2014, Ben Beardmore-Gray (40s). Educated at Ludgrove (where his father taught) and Ampleforth. After history degree at Newcastle he trained as a lawyer and worked in the City, but the lure of the family business was too much for him and he succumbed to teaching. Back he went to Ludgrove where he gained his QTS, thence to Farleigh Prep as deputy head followed by seven years as head of Mowden Hall School in Northumberland.

Mr B-G is a huge fan of boarding. He and his wife, Sarah, have done a stint as houseparents and he also ran boarding at Farleigh. While the majority of pupils at Moulsford may be day boys, the small Monday to Friday boarding community is 'key to the school's ethos,' he says. He sees weekly boarding as 'dynamic' and 'forward thinking' and believes it could well be the future for schools like his.

Boarding also 'draws staff' who are enabled, courtesy of the school's staff flats and houses, to live in what could otherwise be a prohibitively expensive part of the country.

After time spent 'observing' and consulting parents, Mr B-G has exciting plans for Moulsford's future. The school already had a deservedly strong reputation for sport when Mr B-G took over, but after time spent consulting parents he was determined to raise its profile in other areas, particularly the performing arts and extracurricular programme. Hence forthcoming redevelopment of the theatre and music school – cue more plays, ensembles and concerts. He wants Moulsford boys to enjoy breadth of opportunity in as many different areas as possible. All this, we were assured, will not come at the expense of sporting excellence.

Mr B-G is a progressive head, he wants to know what parents and staff think. He conducts regular surveys and has an open-door policy (parents confirm he is 'very approachable' and genuinely interested to hear their views). With no link to any one senior school, Moulsford parents can reserve judgement on senior school decisions until they know what will best suit their son and Mr B-G plays a major part in helping them to decide the best fit.

Mr and Mrs Beardmore-Gray, who met at university, both hail from this part of the world. The couple have three children plus the standard-issue black lab. Down time is for cricket, golf, tennis and cycling.

Entrance: Main entry points are reception (for pre-prep) and year 3 (for prep) although admissions enquiries are accepted in all year groups subject to places being available. One or two pre-prep classes, expanding to three in year 3.

Entry to reception is first come, first served. Assessment day in October for following September's year 3 applicants. School says it's not 'overtly academically selective' but paucity of boys' prep options in Henley area means a scramble for places.

From September 2022, the all-boys pre-prep will be accompanied by a co-ed pre-school from age 3.

Exit: Abingdon takes the lion's share of day boys followed by Pangbourne. Others to Radley, St Edwards, Oratory, Bradfield, Eton, Shiplake, Oundle and Stowe. Fourteen scholarships in 202 and two exhibitions.

Our view: Moulsford and its eponymous village sit on the banks of the Thames just outside Wallingford in south Oxfordshire. Fast rail links to the capital make this picturesque area attractive to London escapees with young families (and deep pockets). The school has always been popular with locals; its distinctive red blazers and caps give chaps a retro Just William charm and make for great free PR in Waitrose. The strange dearth of boys' preps in and around Henley is Moulsford's gain – about a third of the school's pupils come in from there by coach (about half an hour each way).

Sport acknowledged by everyone to be Moulsford's forté. 'Rugby is our best sport, but the school isn't 'just about rugby,' boys told us

Before Moulsford took up residence in 1961 the Victorian red-brick building at its centre was a private house and subsequently the boarding accommodation for Cranford, the girls' school across the road. It sits, high and dry, on top of a steep bank overlooking the Thames. Lush water meadows at the foot of the bank do their job if the river floods and the rest of the time accommodate a fire-pit, camps and the school's fleet of river craft.

Head's study and front of house admin are downstairs and boarding accommodation is upstairs. The library occupies what must have been a delightful drawing room with bay windows overlooking the river. Room and contents have been completely refurbished and there's a new librarian to go with the new reading material.

No Saturday lessons but extensive programme of matches demands attendance. Boarding starts at age 10 and is Monday to Friday only. Flexi boarding parents must commit termly in advance to minimum of two consecutive nights a week. 'Day boarders' can stay until 8pm. As we looked through the dorm windows we wondered if the occupants were inured by familiarity to the priceless view of river and water meadows so charmingly framed by Virginia creeper. We hope these lucky boys remain blithely ignorant for as long as possible of the hours they would have to slave in order to open the curtains onto such a vista as adults.

Dorms sleep up to 13 and are fresh, bright and very comfortable – likewise the communal areas. As part of the school's general revamp of boarding provision the head of boarding looked at senior school boarding and 'asked what do boys need to prepare them for the move to senior school'. Consensus was that organisational skills were key so these are now getting extra emphasis. Over half of Moulsford's pupils will board at some time and, as Mr B-G points out, even if they're not going on to a senior boarding school 'those boarding skills are very useful.'

General consensus from parents is that teaching is 'brilliant'. There has been a major overhaul of the curriculum to promote interdisciplinary themes and links between subjects, coinciding with a move away from the traditional Common Entrance exam. Head believes extending boys' skillsets by means of problem solving, lateral thinking, collaboration and presentation skills will support their academic and social development and help the transition from prep to senior school.

School takes e-safety extremely seriously and ICT lessons in years 6-8 include a programme specially designed to help boys understand technology and the wider issues surrounding its usage. 'Boys need to learn how to self-regulate,' says head.

First on our tour was an inter-house maths challenge in the multipurpose hall with stage, retractable seating and very impressive lighting gantry. Small groups of boys, the 'top two or three from each house', were tackling maths problems in a relay. Later on the whole school (including staff) gets involved. Apparently it's very entertaining although we have yet to be convinced regarding the dramatic potential of equations.

Next stop was a year 6 class in the rather swish ICT suite. Boys were learning how to select and export images for use in the picture books they were designing for young children. By way of contrast we also saw little year 2s who were learning to tell the time in a reassuringly hands-on and low-tech style.

Top set French was a hoot. An inspiring teacher, a bag of props and imaginative use of the interactive whiteboard kept everyone on their toes. No 12-year-old boy should be without the ability to say 'There is a stain on the pillow' or 'The mini bar is empty' and these chaps (according to our notes they were all called Henry or Monty) could bandy such useful phrases with Gallic gusto.

Science labs and art rooms are in good shape and we loved the stylish stand-alone classrooms, all cedar and glass, topped by a living roof, that are now home to the pre-prep (though construction of the new pre-prep is now in full swing – due to open September 2022). Music and drama are tackled with typical enthusiasm. There are several choirs, an orchestra and a jazz band; parents said that music had improved 'hugely' in recent years and all supported head's plans to raise the status of the performing arts.

The provision of after-school clubs was something parents felt needed addressing on Mr B-G's arrival and it certainly has been. An impressive extracurricular programme makes full use of the school's 30 acres and riverside location with options such as archery, bike maintenance, cyclocross, gardening, geocaching, sailing and paddleboarding. Other clubs include real tennis, golf, yoga, 'magic and cards' and even stand-up comedy.

We mostly heard praise for Moulsford's approach to SEN though there were one or two grumbles about cost and how out-of-class support timings didn't always fit in sensibly with lessons. 'Little and often' is the mantra and whether it's help with motor skills, speech and language or handwriting, the school provides support from in-house or external experts. 'Come and talk to us' if you're worried, the head of SEN tells parents.

And so to sport – acknowledged by everyone to be Moulsford's forté. Cricket, rugby, football, hockey, tennis – courts and pitches are tip-top. 'Rugby is our best sport,' boys told us, but added that the school isn't 'just about rugby'. School says all teams get expert coaching and plenty of matches against rivals such as the Oratory Prep, Dragon and Caldicott. It's not all about being in the A team though, boys of all abilities who show exceptional effort on the sports pitch are recognised with 'lionheart' prizes awarded in assembly. Moulsford is also a top judo school (came joint first in recent IAPS championships) and offers trampolining, fencing, gymnastics, a climbing wall and 'wonderful match teas'.

We wondered if the occupants of the dorms were inured by familiarity to the priceless view of river and water meadows so charmingly framed by Virginia creeper

Plenty of opportunities to make the most of Moulsford's dampest asset. Canoes, kayaks and dinghies are launched from the school's own creek for expeditions upriver to Goose Poo Island and as many as 40-50 boys can be out on the water at any one time. Since our visit many more vessels have been added to the Moulsford fleet, including 12 stand-up paddleboards courtesy of the parents' association. Plans are afoot for a new pontoon to launch rowing boats and the ever-generous parents have provided eight ergo rowing machines. By the time they leave boys should be pretty handy around boats of all kinds – great for those heading to rowing schools such as Abingdon, Eton or Harrow. Forest school, camping in the tepee, bows and arrows, fire building and whittling are all part of the fresh-air fun.

We asked a group of boys enjoying their riverside barbecue, What did they think of the head? 'He's lively,' we were told. And what should he do for the school? 'Make it more famous, not enough people have heard of it.' Other boys were keen to add to Mr B-G's to-do list with requests for a retractable roof for the outdoor pool (parents echo this one) and loos on the far pitches (portaloos are now brought in for the cricket season).

The cricket nets are, apparently, fine for fast bowlers but too low for spinners. Several boys were very keen to see fishing reintroduced as a hobby and we're pleased to say that it has been.

Boarding: About 35 boys board at any one time and school will do its best to accommodate 'ad hoc' requests if numbers allow. Boarders we met were keen to tell us how much they enjoyed the experience: 'There's so much freedom. After prep and supper you can kayak or go in the pool and in winter there's movies.' Food – especially fish and chips – got the thumbs up, the only exception being 'something like couscous'. We certainly enjoyed sharing the boys' riverside barbecue lunch. We hear that the boarders' annual Master Chef competition is keenly fought.

The last word: Mr B-G told us his favourite book is The Great Gatsby but parents can be confident that under his leadership Moulsford will most definitely not be 'borne back ceaselessly into the past'. With a loyal crew and experienced captain at the helm, the good ship Moulsford is steaming ahead.

The Oratory Prep School

Goring Heath, Reading, Oxfordshire RG8 7SF

01189 844511 | c.atkinson@oratoryprep.co.uk | www.oratoryprep.co.uk

Ages: 2-13

Pupils: 347; Boarders: 12 (+30-40 flexi)

Fees: Day £10,200 – £117,550 pa; Boarding: £22,470 – £26,070pa

Headmaster: Since 2017, Robert Stewart (40s) BA PGCE. Educated at Dragon School and St Edward's, Oxford then theology degree from Durham followed by PGCE at Queens', Cambridge and later a masters in education management at King's College London. First post at Ampleforth before moving to Eton in 2001. During his tenure of some 16 years he coached rugby and cricket, was head of divinity and ultimately a housemaster and master in charge of Roman Catholics. Open and businesslike, still with shades of public school formality but on his way to getting to grips with the cosy charisma required of a seasoned prep school stalwart. 'Sincere, highly visible and approachable,' say parents.

Was 'immediately impressed' by staff upon arrival, so was it a case of a new broom doing the proverbial at this well established local favourite? Reportedly more of a gentle (but thorough) spring clean. The big – and surprisingly controversial – news was the scrapping of compulsory Saturday school in favour of a voluntary programme of enrichment activities, with pupils from years 6 to 8 able to join for some or all parts, or not at all. Following the initial parental protests from a significant, vocal minority though, it's actually gone down rather well – try as we might, we couldn't find a pupil who missed it and even some of the most vehement protestors have performed a volte face after trying the new arrangement.

Introduction of hot snacks – sausage and bacon sandwiches – at morning break also a hit, 'a bit like scoring a hat trick', and report cards are just twice termly now – a popular move with staff. High on mid-term agenda is retaining more girls in years 7 and 8, a strategy kicked off with a brand new Astro in 2017, lending itself beautifully to netball and hockey, and an 'absolutely superb' new head of girls' games, 'crucial in creating a sense of being genuinely co-ed'.

Head still teaches RE to years 4 and 6 and English to year 7. Lives on site with wife, Sam, a GP, and their three children – two daughters and a son – all now installed at OPS. Full-time dad in holidays, oft found at the family home in Somerset, either cheering on Chelsea FC or dreaming of finding the time to train for his fifth marathon.

Entrance: Non-selective, although tinies now moving up to reception in numbers from on-site nursery, Little Oaks, established 2014, makes it worth getting names down early as most year groups oversubscribed. Assessment morning and report from current school for entry to pre-prep and prep.

Exit: Parents say school 'does not encourage' departure at the end of year 6 so don't expect tons of coaching for 11+ entrance exams. But a small handful of boys leave at 11+ bound for local day schools, with now about a third of girls choosing to stay put and numbers rising. Despite boarding angle, parents mostly want co-ed day schools next. Just over 60 per cent of boys move seamlessly up to the Big O, with Abingdon a popular single-sex option. Bradfield College also features. Others to eg Pangbourne College, Radley, Eton, Harrow, Headington, Malvern College, Marlborough College, Oundle, Queen Anne's, Sherbourne, Shiplake, St Edward's Oxford, St Helen and St Katherine, St Mary's Ascot, St Mary's Calne, Stowe, The Abbey, Warwick School and Wellington College. Usually some relocations to Spain.

Our view: Approached down a seemingly endless drive that winds through some 65 acres of grounds, before opening out to reveal the lovely Arts and Crafts main school building, with its wealth of original features including oak staircase and panelled, Hogwarts-esque, dining hall. Modern additions from assorted decades, the most recent a beautifully designed wood-clad nursery for pupils from 2+ set in the heart of the woodland. Pre-prep housed in former stables with top-notch outdoor facilities and jolly classrooms adorned with examples of pupils' written and artwork. Outdoor learning, including forest school, strongly in evidence with an enviable abundance of fields, ponds and woodland lending itself beautifully to the cause.

With just 35 per cent of the cohort RC, it's catholicism with a small c: 'Parents buy into our strong pastoral ethos and we're keen to make the school as accessible as possible to all religions and cultures,' says head. Daily prayers, hymns in assembly and the charming Father Ken – also chaplain at the senior school – are the only obvious indications of school's religious foundation, although all pupils attend mass once a week in delightfully compact school chapel (termly for pre-prep). Parents praise the overwhelmingly 'kind and thoughtful' culture of the school, streaming down from a number of 'genuinely spiritual' senior staff members modelling Christian values. Any pastoral issues reportedly ironed swiftly out with parents 'impressed' by the way things are dealt with. New cognitive screening tool helps identify any pupil concerns and anxieties to allow for early intervention.

Surprisingly, since boys outnumber girls two to one, school has genuine co-ed vibe, and the girls certainly make their presence felt. This is helped by uplift in those continuing into year 7 (over 30 girls in combined years 7 and 8 at the time of our visit), who operate as single entity for sports and social events and 'really have each other's backs'. 'Not a glitzy school,' according to head, with large number of first-time buyers and a down-to-earth feel, pupils coming from a radius of up to 30 minutes. Little racial diversity (less than 10 per cent non-Caucasian) and head says there are 'occasional issues' amongst pupils reacting to difference, but all faiths are represented in (sometimes very) small numbers.

Catholicism with a small c: 'Parents buy into our strong pastoral ethos and we're keen to make the school as accessible as possible to all religions and cultures,' says head

Solid academics in classes averaging 16. Pupils couldn't choose a particular favourite department, just that 'whatever your favourite subjects are, you can be sure they're covered well'. In the languages department it's French from reception, with two native speakers on staff, Spanish in years 3 and 4 and Latin from year 6. Mandarin on offer as a club. Setting for maths from year 3 with 'plenty of movement', and thereafter in year 7 when a small scholarship set is formed. New perspectives course taught by head to years 7 and 8 – everything from historical facts about British society to rules of law and ethical dilemmas around freedom of speech. Parents report 'incredibly high' workloads for the most able pupils – 'a great deal is expected of them' – with a far more nurturing approach to those less academically inclined. Technology used lightly where appropriate – pupils love the 'pebble pads' voting tool in history as well as mathspace on the school iPads. The upside of a very long school day (8.15am to 5.00pm including a compulsory hour of prep, followed by optional activities until 6.00pm) is that very little work goes home – a great relief for parents.

Two dedicated learning-support teachers in prep school and one in pre-prep offer extra one-to-one lessons up to twice weekly for pupils needing SEN support, charged as extra. Parents describe department as 'a supportive constant in the background – always there to help'. School can support mild to moderate dyslexia, dyscalculia or dyspraxia and mild ASD. Excellent EAL provision offers eight hours of specialist integrated teaching per week for international (mainly Spanish) boarders who typically join for year 8. Performance 'a big thing'. 'Almost everyone' sings in the non-selective senior choir, although choristers, of course, audition and 'are quite another thing altogether'. We loved the fact that music department (described by head as 'very inclusive' and parents as 'incredible') embraces imperfection with its 'beginners concert' for new instrumentalists, and experienced musicians are inundated with opportunities to perform. Orchestras and bands abound; there are numerous music practice rooms and many pupils achieve at least grade 5 in an instrument by the time they leave. Drama 'really fabulous', according to parents. Senior pupils take a play annually to the Shakespeare Schools Festival and there are combined plays for years 3 and 4, and 5 and 6.

As at the Big O, it's mostly about rugby for boys, although footie results are not too shabby and cricket's also big. Definitely one to beat on the fixture list. Director of sport told us it's 'sport for all', sometimes with two fixtures a week and as many as six teams fielded in years 7 and 8. Parents less convinced that quality coaching is 'for all', though, with grumbles that C and D teams tend not to benefit from the outstanding instruction on offer to the more able players and are often lumped with an inexperienced gappie: 'not a very encouraging message'. Football and cricket also for girls alongside netball, hockey and rounders, now with fixtures and, on occasion, girls playing on boys' teams. Additional options, including tennis, athletics, triathlon, darts (darts!) and recently a mini mudder, mean that even the most comfortable of couch potatoes should find something to float their boat. According to pupils, though, it's the co-curricular opportunities that are the real cherry on top of the OPS pie. Unashamedly 'outdoorsy', according to head (thank goodness for the sensible winter uniform of roll neck jumper atop shorts and kilts rather than shirt and tie), a plethora of activities awaits pupils at the end of their school day and if that's still not enough older years can choose to take part in the optional Saturday morning enrichment programme that offers everything from talks on philosophy and climate change to visits from senior school heads to three or four weekly modules run by teaching staff on eg cookery or upcycling.

Prefectships galore for top two years – compulsory duties assigned to pupils according to their interests: art, music, class, ICT, library. Minibus routes morning and afternoon from Reading, Shiplake and Henley. Active parents' association (FOPS) organises coffee mornings, fundraisers and class reps.

Boarding: Boarding totally flexible, with all boarders having their own bed, regardless of how many nights they choose to stay and the majority, living locally, doing it 'just for fun'. Boarding houses in main school building, with boys on one side of the staircase and girls on the other. Lovely quirky dorms with up to 10 beds get top marks from us for decoration – unusually, even on the boys' side. Cosy common rooms offer both mixed and single-sex socialising areas and are kitted out with table football tables, air hockey, board games and TVs. Quite the most inviting san we've ever seen – and house staff of matrons, nurse and gappies give the place a happy family feel. There's 'loads to do' for the international full-timers who get trips to local attractions at weekends.

The last word: In the words of one parent: 'OPS is a school for all sorts of children.' A place with a palpable buzz and vibrancy that gets the balance between giving children the freedom to be themselves, whilst maintaining a focus on traditional values, excellent manners and respect, absolutely spot on. No longer a 'boys' school with girls' but a truly co-ed option, one for the list for parents of boys and girls who want their children to reap all the opportunities that a genuine 13+ prep can offer.

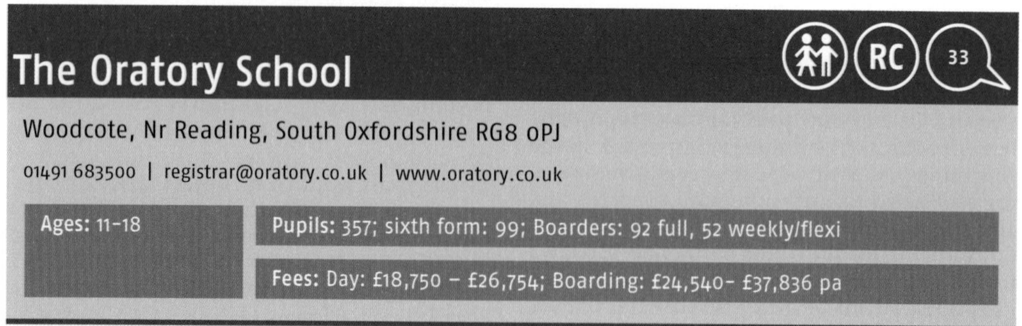

The Oratory School
RC
33
Woodcote, Nr Reading, South Oxfordshire RG8 0PJ
01491 683500 | registrar@oratory.co.uk | www.oratory.co.uk
Ages: 11–18
Pupils: 357; sixth form: 99; Boarders: 92 full, 52 weekly/flexi
Fees: Day: £18,750 – £26,754; Boarding: £24,540– £37,836 pa

Head Master: Since 2016, Joe Smith BA PGCE MEd (40s). Studied English at Liverpool, PGCE at Brunel, MEd at Buckingham. Taught at Colfe's School and Monkton Combe before becoming head of The Oratory Prep in 2010. Governor at Downe House and Berkhamsted. Very popular within the school community, with everyone we spoke to citing him as a reason for choosing

OS – 'absolutely brilliant', 'everybody loved him at the prep', 'a big factor in why lots of people are joining' etc. His vision? 'To be a great co-ed smaller school,' he tells us, smiling. The big BBQ at the start of term is 'typically Joe Smith', we heard – a relaxed welcome to the new school year, 'a really nice family day'.

Parents told us he's 'very fair, very organised' and 'doesn't bow to parent pressure'. 'The kids don't mess around' – 'you need someone like that with teenagers.' Not strict, though – far from it, he is known as compassionate and caring. Is visible, involved and engaged, with staff and parents appreciating the 'direct line of communication'. One recalled how he'd ribbed her son's muddy knees on open day, 'making him feel instantly at ease'.

A school on a journey, with first girls having arrived in September 2020. 'I'm co-ed down to my boots,' he told us – 'why be single sex?' Move is shifting school's standing locally – 'I always said there was no way we'd look at The Oratory, despite living down the road, but its reputation began to change. Now people ask me about it all the time, in a good way,' said one parent. Negative gossip about discipline and reports of historic abuse left parents 'with the sense that it was just another of those all-boy Catholic schools' but today's school is unrecognisable and becoming an active choice for families looking for a small, nurturing environment.

Lives on site with wife Debbie and three children – one still at the school, the rest grown up. Shares study with Purdey, a friendly and inquisitive 'sprocker' spaniel. Persian rug, mahogany furniture and one of those huge, leather-topped writing desks that we always lust over.

Entrance: Gently selective, with 30 places at 11+, 45 at 13+ and 20 at 16+. The 11+ involves online test, written maths and English. ISEB pre-test in year 6 for 13+ hopefuls with offers conditional on CE. At 16+, online IQ test and GCSE grades. Separate scholarship papers at 13+ and 16+. Pupils come from a range of local primaries and preps at 11+ and 13+. Year 12 intake from nearby single-sex options, state and independent. Numbers currently up to 360 after a few precarious years; aim is to hit 450.

Part of the same association as the Oratory Prep until the latter was sold to private equity in 2019. The schools remain friendly but the prep is not an official feeder and there are no formal links.

Exit: A few leave after GCSE to bigger sixth forms. Half of year 13s to Russell Group and the rest all over. Exeter, Nottingham Trent, Oxford Brookes popular with ones and twos to Warwick, Bristol, UCL. No Oxbridge for years now, but application numbers slowly rising – due an offer soon? Significant minority to art or design foundations and degrees.

Latest results: In 2021, 60 per cent 9-7 at I/GCSE; 73 per cent A*/A at A level (89 per cent A*-B). In 2019 (the last year when exams took place), 42 per cent 9-7 at I/GCSE; 34 per cent A*/A at A level (55 per cent A*-B).

Teaching and learning: 'Expectations were too low,' says head, 'and the academic temperature is rising,' though school will remain 'proudly holistic'. Classes average 15 in years 7 to 9, up to about 20 at GCSE. RS compulsory at GCSE; computer science, Latin and ancient Greek offered ('the fact that we've kept Latin tells you something about our self-image').

A school on a journey, with first girls having arrived in September 2020. 'I'm co-ed down to my boots,' the head told us – 'why be single sex?'

Rigorous monitoring. Parents praised quarterly reporting system (not something actively raised with us, usually) – 'you can track their progress very easily', 'not too much jargon' etc. 'You always know who you need to contact,' parents also told us, with tutors and house parents easily reached. Pupils aware of setting but not fazed by it – 'Mine's in the bottom maths group and he's just pleased that he gets lots of help.' School 'very quick' to respond to concerns or questions – 'really proactive in talking it through with us and outlining a plan of how they could support her'. Supportive environment universally appreciated – 'he's so happy; his peers elsewhere are very, very stressed'; 'academically it's been amazing, his flight path is totally different from what it would've been' etc.

'Some teachers are brilliant,' we heard, particularly the newer faces. Head has made good recruiting decisions, particularly in management and core academic subjects. 'Common room is almost unrecognisable,' he told us, with newbies experienced in transitioning to co-ed and academic tracking.

Most popular and successful A level is art. Photography and 3D design also offered. Business and maths attract steady numbers. Broad results reflect intake: a healthy smattering of A*s but lots of As, Bs, Cs too. Latin, Greek, drama, PE, psychology all offered – wide range for a small school. Busy academic life beyond curriculum: silver awards recently in RSC Olympiad and Cambridge Chemistry Challenge. Everyone follows Loquitur programme of enrichment, volunteering, careers talks and PSHE, including cookery lessons and managing finances. Investment in new sixth form annexe, due for completion soon, should boost retention into year 12.

Saturday school still going strong. Although the school has recently introduced new later start time, it doesn't feel like much of a lie-in to a teenager: fine for boarders, less popular among day families. 'It's a hell of a long week,' said a parent

Saturday school recently reviewed but still going strong. 'It took mine a while to get used to it, but they come home feeling great after a big match,' said one mum. But although school has recently introduced new later start time on a Saturday it doesn't feel like much of a lie-in to a teenager: fine for boarders, less popular among day families. 'It's a hell of a long week,' said one parent.

Learning support and SEN: Around 20 per cent on SEN register, with school supporting mild to moderate learning difficulties. Full-time SENCo and team of part-timers deliver in-class support or sessions in the learning support department. Progress shared with relevant teaching staff: parents report lots of joined-up thinking. Ten per cent receive EAL support, including timetabled one-to-one lessons; pupils can be prepared for IELTS and second language IGCSE.

The arts and extracurricular: Art department a hive of energy, where everybody finds their niche. The director of art and design would happily have kept us there all day showing off the brilliant stuff that's going on – 'he's so great,' enthused one pupil. His philosophy? 'Anyone can learn to draw, we get them all involved.' We got a demonstration of the camera obscura in the photography studio and saw the clay room, 3D room and print studio in action, properly kitted out and plastered with lively student work. We enjoyed bold, Banksy-style political statements, a feistier side to Oratorians than we saw elsewhere (anti-Boris, anti-capitalism, anti-lockdown). 'There's no way he'd have done art before – but it's really fun there,' said one mum.

Music also important, with 100 peripatetic music lessons taking place each week. Schola Cantorum (main choir) and Consort (by audition) perform regularly throughout the year. We heard beautiful, resonant voices ringing out through the chapel in four parts. Strong jazz presence – big band seriously funky – and we saw the corps of drums rehearsing, too, using just sticks on desks but making an irresistibly toe-tapping noise. Healthy GCSE music numbers.

Most complete bronze DofE though numbers drop at silver and gold. CCF also popular, among girls as well as boys. Dance studio being developed – sixth formers currently brushing up their ballroom dancing in anticipation of upcoming ball.

Busy LAMDA timetable. Steady take-up of GCSE and A level drama. Large theatre hosted glamorous post-lockdown production of Bugsy Malone; many splurge guns featured. Lots of opportunities for involvement behind the scenes if stage doesn't appeal.

Sport: A huge part of school life. 'It used to be all about rugby,' says director of sport, but things are moving on. Nonetheless rugby still looms very large, along with cricket and girls' hockey. We wondered how it was possible given small size. 'Often A teams are unbeaten, but B or C teams won't be as strong,' said one mum whose 'sport-obsessed' son has 'thrived'. Golf very successful too.

Lots of pupils play at club level outside school, particularly London Irish RFC – school not squeamish ('we're benefiting'). 'They accommodate talent,' say parents. Two recent leavers play professional rugby, and Sir Ian McGeechan, Sir Clive Woodward and Andrew Triggs-Hodge OBE all gave virtual talks during lockdown. Annual tour to Ireland and sometimes to sunnier climes.

Girls' sport shines. U14A cricketers captained by a girl and both netball and hockey teams won first ever fixtures. Positive, can-do attitude, with coaches having seized the opportunity to train and train while external fixtures were off due to Covid. Staff lead by example – 'On Saturday it was hammering it down but they were all out there in their waterproofs.' As girl numbers grow, opportunities will present themselves to hire further specialist coaches, says school.

Has long punched above its weight in racket sports (perhaps since 1896 when alumnus John Pius Boland won a tennis gold at the first modern Olympics). Nowadays, one of only five schools nationally that offer real tennis. Coached by reigning ladies world champion, pupils give as good as they get against much bigger boarding schools. We watched year 8s whacking balls with great gusto on the indoor court. Outdoor court sits in a blissful walled garden. Squash and badminton also very active. It's a clever tactic – racket sports scoop up those talented sportspeople less keen on muddy pitches.

Boathouse at Hardwick and erg room on site ('Pain is only temporary but victory is forever', reads one of the motivational quotes on the wall). Padel courts (tennis/squash hybrid, since you ask) and full-size Astro in the pipeline. Horseriding at nearby Checkendon.

Sporty culture. Big crowds, supportive atmosphere and sideline BBQs for major fixtures. For one girl with 'ADHD tendencies, playing an hour of sport every day really calms her'. Parents thought that OS may not be the right place for someone who is 'awful' at sport – it's a bit of a social currency here. Most find their niche, though, whether on pitch, court or river.

Boarding: Parents love the ability to 'dip in and out of boarding' – truly flexible. Boarding houses run with extraordinary efficiency. Flexi-boarders book in as late as that morning – somehow staff maintain a grip on who's in which bed (we hope). 'Blue-chip organisation,' say parents. Boarding staff praised for speed of response ('she must have email built into her brain') and parents given mobile numbers, meaning house mums and dads are 'just a WhatsApp away'. Weekly or full boarders tend to come from overseas, particularly Mexico and Spain (school limits numbers).

A boarding school week, Monday to Saturday. Pupils do majority of prep in school. Flexi-boarding allows everyone to join in without worrying about getting home. School has become 'more day, more local,' says head, but most seem to do at least a night here or there.

Boarding houses clean and warm, not swish. Rooms well-appointed with lots of clever storage and bunks in the bigger dorms. Common rooms bright and tidy with kitchens dotted around the houses. A little institutional, we felt, but pupils happy and comfortable. Girls' house felt cosy and welcoming, more so than the boys' house we saw, though lots is being done there to encourage camaraderie, starting with a tuck shop. Junior boarding house – for year 7 and 8 boys – due to be refurbished imminently.

Ethos and heritage: Pretty Queen Anne house, added to over the years. Sits on edge of Woodcote village – unremarkable but for its claim to be the second-highest place in the south Chilterns – a dubious brag but nonetheless makes for some lovely views over the hills. The 100-acre site creates sense of space and quiet. Tidy, well-kept gardens and grounds look out onto open countryside – very pleasant, green, unintimidating surroundings. Parents say that facilities are 'amazing', 'really high spec', 'nicely done'. They're well-loved, and some areas could use a lick of paint – definitely a school rather than a swanky hotel (as you can find elsewhere), though parents like that about it.

Catholicism 'part and parcel of school life,' say parents, but not in an evangelical way. Old chapel is charming, all old beams and wooden pews. Two priests on staff described as 'really good role models'. 'We've tried to soften the tone in terms of the Catholic thing – a Catholic education is good principles, looking for Christ in every child and never writing them off,' explains head. School's patron saint is St Philip Neri, he points out, better known as the apostle of joy – 'It's meant to be fun, not austere or forbidding.' 'Doesn't matter if you're not Christian,' parents tell us – 'everyone enjoys the bells and smells at mass.' Catholicism also inspires more links with local state schools, with OS finding partners in the diocese with which to share UCAS sessions, co-curricular days etc. Covid put this on hold but it's on its way.

'We've tried to soften the tone in terms of the Catholic thing,' explains head. School's patron saint is St Philip Neri, he points out, better known as the apostle of joy

Parents have really welcomed the move to co-ed – it seems to have gone more smoothly than anyone dared hope. 'I was expecting there to be a bit of "bear with us, we're finding our feet",' says one mum, 'but they have it sorted.' Staff, pupils and parents all tell us that it's hard now to think of the girls not being there and year groups are evening out in terms of numbers. Their boarding house, Wootten, is in a very old part of the school, so feels central and purposeful, not a bolt-on. A 'sisterhood' has developed here (perhaps that intimacy will fade as numbers grow), with a real sense of togetherness for these 'pioneers', as they are known. 'It's a very special time to have joined as a girl, and my daughters wouldn't have it any other way,' says one mum who had been worried about them being guinea pigs.

A lovely innocent atmosphere to the place – teenagers not growing up too fast. It's not old-fashioned (or at least, not in a bad way), but definitely wholesome. The buzz around the weekly Rose Bowl competition sums it up for us: it's the place to be on a Monday night with houses competing in everything from badminton to tug-of-war. Everybody gets involved – 'That boy who's never going to represent the school, he's out there on a Monday night competing and participating,' said one delighted teacher. It's a big deal, agree parents – 'Since joining the school, she's excited about hanging out at the pavilion after the Rose Bowl, rather than worrying about who's invited to which party on a Saturday night.' Speaking of which, typical birthday parties are low-key, not too sophisticated and certainly not blingy, with parents often welcome to hang around rather than the 'drop and run' culture found elsewhere.

Alumnae include England rugby international Danny Cipriani, poet Hilaire Belloc, actor Jonathan Bailey and cricketer Benny Howell.

Pastoral care, inclusivity and discipline: School nurse 'warm and caring', say parents. Teachers approachable and accessible. Wellbeing built into the curriculum. Going co-ed has given head the chance to ensure that pastoral approach is 'different, inclusive, diverse' and put in place new systems to track concerns. PSHE sessions address respect and tolerance; pupils shocked by Everyone's Invited website but say that relations between boys and girls here are balanced.

Sports coaches seized the opportunity to train and train while external fixtures were off due to Covid. Staff lead by example – 'On Saturday it was hammering it down but they were all out there in their waterproofs'

Food fine, not ground-breaking. Pupils seem okay with it, though some parents describe it as 'a bit dated' and wonder if teenagers could cope with something more challenging than fish fingers. Pupils have access to kitchens in houses – toast, jam, scones, cereal – during the school day. No one comes home hungry.

Where discipline is required, school acts swiftly and decisively, calling parents in as appropriate. Carrot used more than stick, though, and success celebrated. Prizegiving a 'lovely experience', even when online. 'They are very good at giving rewards for going above and beyond in anything,' says one mum, pleased that 'even my more chaotic child has already had three this term.' House cup awarded to student who demonstrates the school's core values.

Uniform straightforward. Expectation is that pupils are smart, though enforcement seems fairly relaxed – one mum pleased that her daughter 'doesn't get pulled up for wearing a couple of bracelets', while another was jokingly horrified that hers 'sometimes comes home looking like a barmaid'. Some boys rocking trendy haircuts, which we took as a good sign about unstuffiness – 'Happiness is more important than hair length,' confirms head.

Pupils and parents: Children of farmers, local businessmen and London commuters mix happily. Minibuses bring them in from as far as Oxford, Newbury and High Wycombe, though majority live nearby. 'Quite a local catchment,' say parents, 'so you get a sense of community.' 'There are three families in our village – you wouldn't get that elsewhere.' An exceptionally welcoming crowd, from what we can gather – 'The first time we met we all swapped numbers and I immediately had back-ups for the school run.' 'There's a nice social buzz around the school; at our other son's school, we never saw anyone.' 'Everybody gets out of the car and says hello at drop-off.' Very multicultural, particularly given the area – 'much more so than my other son's school even aspires to be'. Most families dual-income and not interested in money and who has it. Lots have been to village primaries nearby. Much more low-key than many of the glossier schools on the south Oxfordshire-Berkshire scene – 'The cars in the car park are noticeably muddier at OS,' we hear.

Active PA, known as FOS. Newbies thrilled to discover that cheese and wine night was 'literally cheese and wine rather than an opportunity for the head to schmooze us'.

Money matters: Scholarships (10 per cent remission) or exhibitions (five per cent) available for academics, sport, art and design, music and drama. Means-tested bursaries available as well as significant discount on boarding for service families.

The last word: Families in this area are spoilt for choice and until recently, The Oratory was not a go-er. Now, 'We're back to our A game,' says head. Parents agree – 'it's like a new school'; 'Joe Smith has really caught the community – we all want to be on board'; 'they're excited, so we're excited – it's a joy to be a part of that'. A happy little school with old-fashioned values and a modern approach that has emerged from a rough patch with its sights set firmly on the future. With excellent leadership and now girls on board too, The Oratory seems to be thriving.

d'Overbroeck's

333 Banbury Road, Oxford, Oxfordshire OX2 7PL

01865 688600 | sixthformoffice@doverbroecks.com | www.doverbroecks.com

Ages: 11-18

Pupils: 700 (inc 100 in International School); sixth form: 390; Boarders: 285 (in sixth form)

Fees: Day £18,975 – £30,450; Boarding £13,500 – £18,450 pa

Principal: Since July 2019, Jonathan Cuff BA MSc (40s). Educated at Gresham's School, Norfolk (father was head of the prep), Brunel University (religious studies and PE) and Leicester (education leadership). Always aspired to become a head teacher and had 'a clear route in his head'. Immaculately executed it was too: first post at Framlingham College where he was assistant housemaster and director of hockey; on to Worth as a boarding housemaster; thence to Mill Hill where he ran the boarding and hockey, followed by a spell at Hampshire Collegiate as deputy head pastoral before joining d'Overbroeck's in 2017 as deputy head pastoral and senior deputy head. Propelled into headship following the unexpected departure of the former head due to ill health and swiftly set about formalising internal structures to 'empower staff to make decisions' in a what had formerly been a more autocratic culture.

It was love at first visit to the school when he realised he just couldn't get the students to say anything negative: 'Our student questionnaire is stupidly positive.' Having cut his teeth in more traditional environments, how did he adapt to the more relaxed ethos and atmosphere? 'I was dubious,' he admits. 'But without the little challenges around things such as strict uniforms and haircuts, we can focus on what really matters.' Bravo. We take our hat off to this obvious man's man for falling in love with his school because of, rather than despite, its lack of 'macho bravado issues'. Says the 'main players' at d'Overbroeck's are the creatives – the actors and musicians – and that he, ardent supporter of Welsh rugby that he is, is 'a complete convert'.

Still teaches RS to year 7s ('the best part of my week'). Married to Kate, head of boarding at Lord Wandsworth College in Hampshire, with whom he has a young son. Lives in Oxford during the week – no time for local culture or socialising, though, as he is a self-confessed 'weekday workaholic'. When he does manage to tear himself away, he fits in some golf in the summer months and spends time at his home in Cognac during the holidays.

Entrance: Main entry points are years 7, 9 and 12 and entry is selective, although not intensely so. Applicants into years 7 and 9 are tested in English, maths and non-verbal reasoning plus interview and reference from current school. For sixth from, students need six grade 6s at GCSE with maths and English compulsory and minimum of a 6 in the subjects to be studied at A level. Students wishing to take A level maths need a 7 at GCSE and an 8 or 9 for further maths. International students must have very strong English skills (minimum level 6-6.5 IELTS) and are asked to sit written tests in English and maths if applicable.

Exit: A majority of around two-thirds of students from the lower school progresses to the sixth form (we await with interest to see whether this increases over the coming years now that the facility is so appealing). The remainder move either to the state-maintained sector such as Cherwell or Cheney, with some of the girls choosing Magdalen College. Sixth form leavers mainly into higher education with top destinations including UCL, King's College London, University of London, Manchester, Nottingham, Edinburgh, Newcastle, Bath, Exeter, LSE and SOAS. Four to Oxbridge, and one medic in 2021. A handful to art colleges and drama schools (including the biggies) most years. Refreshingly, apprenticeships are also on the agenda with specialist talks and trips to eg the National Apprenticeship Show on the enrichment schedule.

Latest results: In 2021, 69 per cent 9-7 at GCSE; 67 per cent A*/A at A level (88 per cent A*-B), In 2019 (the last year when exams took place), 60 per cent 9-7 at GCSE; 51 per cent A*/A at A level (81 per cent A*-B).

Teaching and learning: It would be impossible for parents doing the rounds of the local independent schools not to wonder what conclusions to draw from the urban location and lack of sprawling fields at d'Overbroeck's. Head is quick to tell us, 'We use it to our advantage – our teachers have no choice but to bring their A game to every lesson.' And bring it they do, with school consistently boasting the highest value-added score in Oxfordshire (not to mention ranking in the top 30 on a national level), against some not inconsiderable competition.

Some 35 subjects on offer at A level – all the usuals plus eg media studies, photography, music tech, film studies and textiles. Maths by far the most popular A level, with economics, biology, sociology and psychology also topping the popularity charts. Refreshingly, students can choose any combination of subjects they like and school not averse to running courses for lone students if necessary; this quite often the case in eg Latin, history of art, textiles and some of the less popular modern languages. Good take up of EPQ – around 90 students most years. Crucially, students told us that 'teachers love what they are doing' and parents concur that even though it's a fairly mixed academic bag, even in the sixth form, 'it's a very stretching environment for bright pupils'. Those hoping for an easy ride courtesy of the relaxed vibe can think again – there are exams every term right from the start of year 12 to keep even the most reluctant students focused and working.

Staff are called by their first names and the ethos is very much about encouraging students to 'be the best you can be' rather than 'be better than other people'

'An individual approach to learning' is a phrase we heard time and time again over the course of our visit. In the lower part of the school, it's not just class sizes that are small but the whole school itself, with a total of less than 200 pupils in years 7 to 11. All teachers know every pupil well; teaching groups can sometimes be as small as eight (we saw this in action with a year 10 English class working on a collaborative project with the art department on graphic novels) and in exceptional circumstances, gifted pupils receive one-to-one teaching in the same way as those requiring learning support, occasionally even taking GCSEs and A levels years early. GCSE grades also impressive for a school that describes itself as 'quite academically mixed', with most students taking 10, including three sciences and a compulsory modern language for the majority.

Teaching styles are, as you would expect, reasonably relaxed. Staff are called by their first names ('We like to interact like human beings,' says head) and the ethos – for which most parents choose the school – is very much about encouraging students to 'be the best you can be' rather than 'be better than other people'. Pupils told us that maths was the standout department, borne out by its results. Students taught by the same maths teacher from years 9 to 11. 'We can really get to know not only the students but also their parents to create a true partnership.' Perfect. We observed a GCSE maths class where the most able who had finished their work were coaching their peers. In the languages department, it's French and Latin from year 7 with the addition of Spanish in year 9. Chinese, Japanese, Russian, Italian and German offered at A level.

Learning support and SEN: All students screened on entry for additional needs, with school able to support those with mild SpLD, usually within the classroom setting but with some one-to-one (usually included in fees). The cosy learning support centre with its fish tank, fairy lights and biscuit tins is a refuge for all students, not just those on the learning support register. Those who need support beyond years 7 and 8 may be given a reduced timetable from year 9 but crucially school is focused on 'getting curriculum right for each student' and 'skilling people up in the right way, whether it's socially, emotionally or academically'.

The arts and extracurricular: Thriving extracurricular programme focuses on 'choice, engagement and fun'. Years 7 to 9 have two periods off-timetable each week to pursue enrichment activities, with these changing constantly to suit different year groups' passions and preferences. Debating and public speaking consistently strong, with school represented at Oxford Youth Parliament amongst other competitions. Lower sixth formers have a compulsory enrichment programme two afternoons a week, comprising mainstream sports and everything else you would expect, plus the likes of knitting, psychology, film, polo (the fledgling team recently victorious at Eton) and aerial silks. In short, something for everyone. 'If a student discovers just one thing they are passionate about, we're happy,' says school. The 'Plus' programme encourages A levels students to broaden their academic learning around their chosen subjects. There's also Young Enterprise and DofE plus myriad external speakers ranging from university professors and admissions tutors to writers, scientists and entrepreneurs.

In true d'Overbroeck's style, a positive spin is put on the absence of large performance spaces for music and drama: 'We're so fortunate to be able to perform at the Sheldonian and other amazing

Preparation was underway for a 'myths and magic' concert with a programme set to include music from Debussy and Metallica (the latter accompanied by the orchestra wearing horned masks)

venues around Oxford.' Having sat through our fair share of draughty school hall productions, we can see the upside. There's a 'good musical vibe' according to departmental staff and talent is nurtured at the lower end of the school, with about half of year 7-11 students taking part in peripatetic lessons and plenty of opportunities to join the orchestra, chamber choir or other ensembles. At the time of our visit, preparation was underway for a whole-school 'myths and magic' themed concert at the Sheldonian with a programme, tailored to the strengths of the performers, set to include music from both Debussy and Metallica among others (the latter accompanied by the orchestra wearing horned masks). 'It will really encapsulate what we're all about,' beamed the director of music. We suspect he was referring specifically to the music department but would apply his comment to the whole school ethos. More traditional performances include an annual musical or abridged opera, most recently The Marriage of Figaro; 'We have a great tradition of singing.' Music and music tech available at A level with small numbers taking them up.

'Drama coheres the school,' the departmental director told us. There's a focus on modern works and quality performance rather than laboriously designed sets. The 'constant struggle' faced without the luxury of a performing arts centre 'breeds creativity and great performances'; strong links are being forged with the world of professional theatre and we loved the fact that the entire cast of a recent production of Macbeth was given professional sword fighting training which then played out to spectacular effect on a catwalk style stage. No auditionee is turned away from a performance and texts are reinterpreted to accommodate if necessary; a whole coven of junior witches, orphans from the battle against Macdonald, appeared as a chorus in Macbeth. Drama on curriculum in years 7 to 11 and is a reasonably popular GCSE and A level choice.

Sport: Not the most obvious choice for the super sporty and even the head told us that 'if school team games are your thing then we're probably not for you.' That said, school works hard to ensure pupils are active and engaged in a wide range of sport and activities and although it doesn't have its own playing fields it has access to sports facilities at both Oxford University and Oxford Brookes, plus extensive facilities across the city. Years 7 to 11 have two timetabled slots per week with sports, including football, basketball, rugby, netball, handball and lacrosse, rotating half-termly. Fixtures are focused on participation and pupils described the overall sporting ethos as 'laid back' and 'really inclusive'; boys not keen on the rough and tumble of the rugby pitch can, for example, play netball instead. Activities such as yoga concentrate on helping students 'release their happy hormones'. New sports scholarship introduced in 2017 to attract outstanding athletes to the school to act as ambassadors and encourage enthusiastic participation by others, and an elite tennis programme has recently launched to attract global talent to the sixth form with 10 hours of coaching a week.

Boarding: Not a conventional boarding model as it's for sixth formers only. With about half of the 370-strong cohort boarding and about 80 per cent of boarders international (52 nationalities across the school at the time of our visit with the largest numbers from China, Russia, Ukraine and Turkey), it has more the feel of (a very cosmopolitan) university than school. Two co-ed boarding houses host the lower sixth formers; the super-modern Islip House – built the same time as the new sixth form building in 2017 – is directly opposite school and boasts light, bright and modern facilities with mainly twin rooms. The second house, St Aldates, is across the city with the upside of single rooms for those that prefer but a ride on public transport of around 20 minutes to school. Unusually, in the upper sixth the vast majority of students board with local families rather than staying in school accommodation, an arrangement which parents we spoke to described as 'okay'. That said, students do get to choose their family as well as a friend to home board with. No choice of room mate is given to lower sixth formers, however, and we heard of a occasional issues of incompatibility and suggestions that school could do more in the way of match-making before term starts. Once in situ, however, students are allowed to switch around if they so wish and the house had a homely and harmonious atmosphere to it. Majority are full-time boarders; weekly boarding introduced in 2019.

Ethos and heritage: A 'mushroom-shaped school' which grows in size with each year group. Founded in 1977 as a sixth form college by French and Spanish teacher Malcolm van Biervliet who was head of languages until his retirement in

2007. The lower school was opened in 2005 and the whole operation was purchased in 2014 by the Oxford International Education Group. Split across two sites, with the years 7 to 11 homed in a compact site more akin to a state primary school (which in fact it once was), albeit one that makes excellent use of what little space it has. Its ingeniously designed main building boasts a galleried library and a social area with a vivid pink wall, café tables and glossy blue lockers (never locked and apparently there's no need – staff and pupils looked shocked and horrified when we asked whether there was ever any theft). The original school hall next door is used for lunch, assemblies and theatrical productions. Numbers in years 7-11 are now pretty much on capacity at around 200, typically with two forms in years 7 and 8 and three from year 9. Sixth formers mill around a gleaming sixth form centre on Banbury Road that sells the offering to potential students without even trying. Light, space, whistles and bells (well, any academic facility an A level student could wish for anyway) meld together to make for an extremely appealing – and quite adult – offering that transformed the landscape of sixth form education in Oxford when it was built in 2017. Although the two sites couldn't be more different in appearance, each suits the age and stage of education of its own students and is integrated with the other through ethos and teaching style as well as some shared activities such as concerts and productions.

Happiness is core to school's culture; its founder used to listen for laughter in lessons as a sign that students were enjoying their work. A real buzz everywhere you turn

We had already picked up a far more relaxed vibe than we generally do at other Oxford schools from our visit to the lower school. The sixth form students we met later confirmed that we were right, describing their school as 'a chilled place' where 'everyone's calm' and 'teachers love what they're doing'. Happiness is core to school's culture; its founder used to listen for laughter in lessons as a sign that students were enjoying their work. There's a real buzz everywhere you turn – lots of lively chatter and an informal and energetic atmosphere throughout – energy, fun and achievement encapsulate the ethos. The catering team based in the sixth form centre provide meals for students throughout the school, including dinners for boarders. Some students stroll up to M&S or Taylors in Summertown to buy lunch – they're spoiled for choice.

Pastoral care, inclusivity and discipline: 'Pastoral support is crucial,' says school. Form tutors are first port of call in the lower school, with tutor groups meeting every day and staff holding a meeting every week to discuss pastoral issues. Sixth formers are all assigned their own director of studies (universally known as their DoS), and we witnessed many chatting casually to students in nooks and crannies around the site. They are the embodiment of school's 'focus on the individual' and are on hand for all matters pastoral and academic – pretty much in loco parentis for boarders – also providing frequent updates to parents. Counsellors are on hand across both sites for a total of 40 hours per week. Also for sixth formers, there's the wonderful 'Hannah', the only dedicated 'pastoral mentor' we've met in any school. Head of Islip house, she's not a teacher and not exactly a big sister either, but both rolled into one. So many students mentioned her that by the time we met her for ourselves we almost expected a hug. It seemed to us that d'Overbroeck's has its priorities right; rules around hair and clothing are relaxed, rules on drugs and alcohol are firm with transgressors immediately asked to leave and the expectations around punctuality and work ethic are all clearly in place.

Pupils and parents: Pupils notably unassuming, charming and low key. Those from wealthy or well-known families, of which there are many, wear it lightly and there's no sign of bling or obvious status. Year 7 pupils generally come from local primaries, with year 9 entrants coming in numbers from Chandlings (around a third of the year), Dragon and New College School. UK sixth formers generally from local single-sex independents who are looking for co-education, a broader range of subjects or a more realistic transition between school and university. Some escapees from local pressure cookers, seeking a more relaxed approach. How do internationals and UK students mix? School assured us that it was a melting pot, although we did sense from our observations in the dining room that some ethnic groups were more exclusive than others. The temperature was definitely low, however, and parents we spoke to concurred that although some nationalities do tend to congregate together, in general each is tolerant of others and any conflict tends to be inside normal teenage boundaries. School agrees that its broad open nature is a strong feature.

Parents themselves are an eclectic mix of creatives, professionals, academics and medics which makes for great fodder on careers evenings when up to 50 volunteer to attend to help students understand various career paths and start their networks.

Money matters: A range of academic, art and performing arts scholarships for pupils entering years 7 and 9 (up to 20 per cent of tuition fees). Academic, sports, art and performing arts scholarships available at sixth form level (up to 40 per cent of fees).

The last word: In a local market crowded with historic educational institutions, academic powerhouses and well-established single-sex schools with decades of solid results, it might seem like a leap of faith for parents to choose such a small and unassuming school for their 11-year-old. But strip away the aesthetics and we can't think of a school with a more nurturing environment and superb quality of teaching. At sixth form, for the quirky, the artsy, the bright, late developers and just those who need a change of scene, d'Overbroeck's is one for the list, although it should be noted that 'a level of maturity is required' to thrive in this environment and is definitely not for families looking for a trad public school with armies of prefects and frequent chapel services. In the words of one happy parent, 'It's a very big hole that can accommodate many different shaped pegs.'

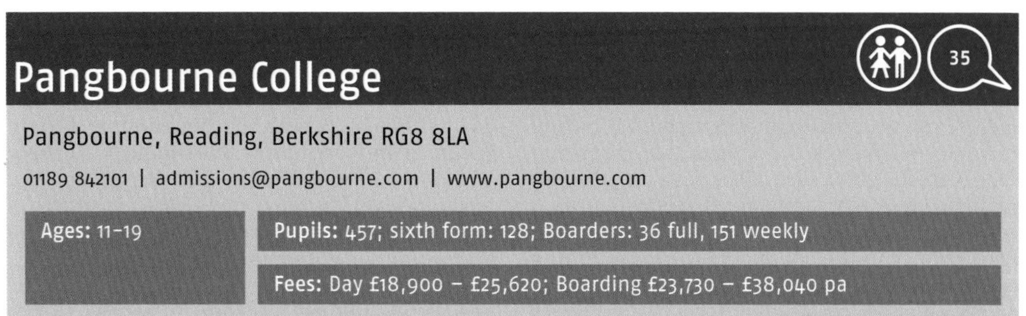

Pangbourne College
35
Pangbourne, Reading, Berkshire RG8 8LA
01189 842101 | admissions@pangbourne.com | www.pangbourne.com
Ages: 11-19
Pupils: 457; sixth form: 128; Boarders: 36 full, 151 weekly
Fees: Day £18,900 – £25,620; Boarding £23,730 – £38,040 pa

Headmaster: Since 2005, Thomas Garnier BSc PGCE (50s). Educated at Sandroyd and Radley, read physics at Bristol and was a seaman officer in the Royal Navy for seven years. He left the navy after meeting his wife Alexandra (who's also very involved in school life, including running events such as an annual piano festival) and trained as a teacher. Did PGCE at Oxford, followed by first teaching job at King Alfred's, high-performing state school in Wantage, Oxfordshire. Spent 10 years at Abingdon School, where he progressed to housemaster and then head of boarding.

We found him – sporting traditional attire with socks that Jon Snow would be proud of – animated, affable and reassuringly enthusiastic about students having their say, which made it all the more surprising that the ones we met seemed cautious of telling us anything even vaguely critical about their school (this happens sometimes when we visit schools and it's quite possible they couldn't think of anything on the spot). We were also struck by how willing he is to adapt, constantly reconsidering the school's policies – he recently, for example, decided to trial a partial mobile phone ban 'in light of what is emerging about their effect on young people's mental health'. Students describe him as 'tall' (he really is), 'well-respected' and say 'he knows all our names – amazing, really'. But although he occasionally manages to fit in some rowing coaching and is involved in the naval section of Pangbourne's CCF, they said 'you don't see him much'. Parents agree: 'You don't have much contact with him, but you can always get a meeting if you need one.' 'I think he's just the right balance of intimidating, which a head should be, and approachable,' said one parent, while a student told us, 'He's friendly, but you wouldn't make too silly a joke around him.'

Has two sons, both educated at Pangbourne (one still there). A firm believer in 'lifelong learning', he took up the flute again after a 25-year gap, passed his grade 8 with ease and has since done the same with piano.

Entrance: Students come from a host of state and prep schools, including Brockhurst, Moulsford, Thorngrove, St Andrew's, Pangbourne and many more. Main entry points are at 11, 13 and 16. At 11 and 13, admission is by school's own entrance exam or CE (interview and head's report taken into account too). Pupils joining sixth form (up to 20 a year) also sit an entrance exam and must have at least five good GCSE passes, including English and maths.

Exit: Forty per cent leave after GCSEs (most are replaced by new joiners), mainly to do subjects not offered here or 'just for a change'. Vast majority to university, most to Russell Group. Edinburgh, York, Exeter and KCL recent big hitters. One to Oxbridge in 2021, plus two overseas – to Whitman College and Salve Regina College, both to study liberal arts. Subjects are wide ranging, including more vocational ones like agriculture, accounting and sports science. Apprenticeships growing in popularity and a handful go into the Forces.

Latest results: In 2021, 43 per cent 9-7 at GCSE; 45 per cent A*/A at A level (75 per cent A*-B). In 2019 (the last year when exams took place), 36 per cent 9-7 at GCSE; 20 per cent A*/A at A level (40 per cent A*-B).

Teaching and learning: School welcomes a wide range of ability, although says it has 'become more discerning about only taking students we feel we can genuinely support without it having too much of an impact on others' (the idea being that everyone gets a slice of the pastoral cake, not just a needy few). Head agrees that Pangbourne is sometimes perceived as being 'for the less able' (particularly in the context of the surrounding selective schools) but is vexed, claiming they do a very good job for academic children (there's a 'high potential achiever' programme for the most able) and parents agree: 'We've got one child who is really bright and another who is a bit slow with processing, but they've supported both brilliantly,' said one (and most families we spoke to said they send all their children here because of this).

Setting in maths, science and French from year 7 and English from year 10. Students get a taste of French, Spanish and German in year 7, then most pick one for GCSE (although it's not compulsory). Eight or nine GCSEs is the norm here, including IGCSE English language, English literature and maths.

Students choose between combined science and two or three separate sciences. Latin is offered as an additional extra, despite small numbers. At GCSE, strongest results in English and maths.

Around 25 A levels offered (popular ones include maths, English, geography, economics and business studies), plus BTecs in sport, music tech and DT – 'great for the less academically focused students or those who find exams stressful'. School says some of the most heartening performances are found among those who worked tremendously hard to secure Bs and Cs – 'We take real pride in these.'

Tracking data used extensively by teachers; students get 'heatmaps' to highlight their strengths and weaknesses. 'There's been a big push on helping student take greater ownership over their learning and students talk about their work in a much more reflective, positive way now,' says school. Students say teaching staff (two-thirds male and a third female, half of whom live on site) keep most lessons lively, 'but even when the lesson is boring, you do learn,' said one. Good mix of experienced and newly qualified teachers (school has links with teacher training departments at universities of Buckingham, Reading and Oxford Brookes). One parent told us, 'The teaching level has fluctuated a bit and there have been complaints, but latterly they've really upped their game and got some really good new ones in.' Staff hold regular academic clinics and students can also email their teachers.

No more academic lessons in Saturday school (there will still be sports and activities) – one parent wondered if the cheers could be heard the other side of Berkshire. No loss of teaching time, though

From September 2019, no more academic lessons in Saturday school (there will still be sports and activities) – one parent wondered if the cheers could be heard the other side of Berkshire. No loss of teaching time, though, as lessons will be moved into the week.

Learning support and SEN: Learning support available for students with minor learning difficulties – individual lessons offered at extra cost, 'although for most, it's a case of making sure their teachers know how to go the extra mile for them.' School works hard to identify those whose SEN hasn't yet been picked up.

The arts and extracurricular: Terrific music school houses recital hall, recording suite and 10 practice and teaching rooms, as well as four prized Steinway grand pianos – 'I practically live in here,' beamed one student. Around a third of pupils take individual music lessons, with brass, drums, guitar and singing leading the pack. Loads of musical groups to join, including orchestra, jazz band, choirs and a marching band. Performing arts are on the up with a variety of college productions, theatre trips and drama workshops. Three drama studios and pupils encouraged to take Trinity exams. Everyone does CCF for at least a year and DofE is compulsory in year 9, with three-quarters of students doing silver and a third doing gold. Spectacular art and DT spaces, with healthy numbers taking subjects at GCSE and A level and some mind-blowing work displayed throughout – some of the most imaginative we've seen, including large 3D installations.

Relatively few clubs and societies – school feels that after DofE, music, drama, sport etc, 'the week is already well filled'. All the usual day and residential trips, including to far-flung places such as New York (academic) and South Africa (joint rugby and hockey).

Sport: A very sporty school, with at least an hour a day spent exercising, with plenty of wins against other schools especially in hockey and rugby; the school's size means virtually all get the chance to represent it. Pangbourne boathouse is a mile from the school, on the scenic banks of the Thames, and school has won the Princess Elizabeth Challenge Cup at Henley four times. Unlike some schools where pupils drop sport in the sixth form, everyone keeps it up here: 'I'm a firm believer that you learn so much on the sports field or hall or in a boat,' says head. Main boys' sports are rugby, hockey, rowing and cricket while girls do netball, hockey, rugby, rowing and tennis. Lots of equestrian enthusiasts – riding popular. One parent told us, 'Initially, it was hard for my son to settle because he wasn't that sporty – thank goodness for the hockey, which he did like – but he's at the top of the school now so that may have changed.' School insists it has and students agree: 'It's really okay not to like rugby – I don't,' said one, while another said, 'The increase in breadth of sports means there's pretty much something for everyone.' Decent facilities, including newly refurbished open-air pool and a new Astroturf, though students said hockey pitches need updating.

Boarding: Four boys' houses and two for girls (with another one in the pipeline for around 2024), integrating day and boarding students ('the day boys and girls are very much included as part of the boarding ethos,' said one parent). Just over half of students board – around a third of these are full boarders while the rest are either part boarders (Monday, Tuesday, Thursday and Friday) or weekly boarders (introduced in 2017 as a third option). The latter two options grow in popularity as the students move up the school – by sixth form around 70 per cent board. 'We don't actively push boarding,' says head. 'It's a natural phenomenon.' No flexi boarding, although school offers parents chance to buy 10 extra boarding nights a year per student. Houses are functional, with some homely touches and dorms ranging from single bedrooms to those housing four. Pupils eat breakfast, lunch and supper in the central mess hall. Boarding staff praised by parents for being 'very nurturing' and 'genuinely caring'.

The youngest pupils (years 7 and 8) are housed in Dunbar, a detached red-brick house with its own garden (loads of space to play football, jump about on the trampoline and catch up with friends). Lower school lessons take place in the main school, but the rest of the time students make their way back to these cosy environs. Students told us how students are divided into four 'watches' (Port, Starboard, Forward and Aft), each with their own 'watch captain'. Capacity for 22 in Dunbar, with around 16 beds taken up when we visited – generally larger dorms than for senior boys.

New life has been injected into the boarding programme in the last couple of years, say students, who cite comedy evenings, magic evenings, Come Dine With Me house competitions ('the food was good – surprisingly good,' says head), among others. 'It's more exciting than it used to be.'

Ethos and heritage: School is set in 230 acres ('half an acre per student isn't bad,' laughs head), in an area of outstanding natural beauty. Founded in 1917, Pangbourne's aim was to prepare boys for service in the Merchant Navy and Royal Navy. In 1969, however, the school was established as a charity, with a similar curriculum to other schools, and these days only two or three leavers a year join the Forces. Even so, Pangbourne prides itself on maintaining many of its original traditions and is the only school in the UK where students wear Royal Navy officer cadet uniform every day.

Has its own distinctive vocabulary, much of it nautical. Study bedrooms are cabins, house common rooms are gun rooms, and casual clothes are always referred to as scruff

Students parade in their number one (ceremonial) uniforms six times a year, with practice every Friday morning. Uniforms have to be immaculate and shoes polished. A guest of honour inspects the whole school on the vast parade ground and takes the salute as pupils march past. Head says Pangbourne's parades are an integral part of school life and help to develop self-discipline (pupils have to stand still for 15 to 20 minutes, often with a biting wind whistling across the parade ground), confidence, teamwork, leadership – 'and above all, a community spirit.' 'It's not always massively popular with the younger ones, but the older ones start to realise what an amazing thing it is and the pride really kicks in,' a parent told us.

Pangbourne has its own distinctive vocabulary, much of it nautical. Study bedrooms are cabins, house common rooms are gun rooms, the dining hall is the mess hall and casual clothes are always referred to as scruff. Current head introduced 'flag values' – kindness, integrity, industry, moral courage, selflessness, resilience, initiative and most recently added respect – and students are urged to display them throughout their time here. Chapel is a key part of Pangbourne life, including 'congers' (Saturday morning congregational practice), reflecting the school's firm Christian ethos with a 'forthright and challenging' chaplain (although students tell us 'it's fine to be atheist'). Many services are held in the Falkland Islands Memorial Chapel, opened by the Queen (who has visited the school five times). The rest of the extensive campus is a mixture of buildings, some in need of updating (eg labs) but most on a rolling programme and everything is fit for purpose. Food good – we enjoyed a hearty roast on a frosty day.

New life has been injected into the boarding programme, say students, who cite comedy and magic evenings, and Come Dine With Me house competitions ('the food was surprisingly good,' says head)

School has been fully co-ed since 1996 (the boys-girls ratio is now approaching 4:3). Lots of student committees, including boarders, food and general student councils. Very inclusive Team Pangbourne feel to the place and pupils are fiercely loyal to their school. All students expected to greet everyone they walk past – 'It can get tiring, but I can see why they insist on it,' said one. Sixth formers can apply to train as peer mentors. Raft of prefects – called cadet captains – chosen by head and senior staff. Lower sixth pupils take leadership course in readiness for their responsibilities in the upper sixth.

Pastoral care, inclusivity and discipline: 'Happiness' is a word you hear a lot here, the ethos being that if youngsters are happy then their self-worth and academics will follow. The main vehicle for the pastoral care is the house system, with weekly meetings among staff using a traffic light system for all students. School counsellor is well used – students self-refer. Growing emphasis on mental health, including outside speakers. Sixth formers have their own bar (Medway), which is open for soft drinks on Thursday evenings and pizzas and beer/lager (strictly limited) on Saturday nights.

There's a feeling you can make mistakes here – 'Everyone makes mistakes,' points out head. But there are 'crystal clear' policies on everything from boy-girl relationships (PDAs banned) to bullying and drugs, alcohol and cigarettes. All have caused issues at one time or another, admits school, with one or two permanent exclusions a year, most recently for substance abuse or 'inability to reform bullying behaviour'. Around 10 suspensions a year, 'usually for inappropriate, offensive or unpleasant behaviour'. Less serious sanctions include the 'sin bin' – a kind of mini-detention for failing to produce prep or applying yourself in class – while Saturday detentions are for repeat offences or more grave misdemeanours. An equal emphasis on praise means positive input is also rewarded.

Strict uniform policy. Students must need hefty trunks to pack all their kit, though – list includes number one uniform (jacket, trousers/skirt and cap with badge for Sundays and ceremonies), number two uniform for every day (trousers/skirt, navy jersey, epaulettes, beret and Dr Martens shoes), and recreational rig (known as 'rec rig') for social occasions and away matches (sixth formers may now wear suits instead). And that's before they even think of throwing in games kit and weekend clothes. Trousers only offered as an alternative to skirts from September 2019 – surprising to us that it took so long, though seemingly not to students who are also fine with the strict 'not too long, not too short' haircut rule (questioning societal 'norms' doesn't seem to feature highly among students here).

Students say it's 'a caring, friendly school' and that it's easy to settle in.

Pupils and parents: Fleet of minibuses brings day pupils in from as far afield as Basingstoke, Newbury and Maidenhead, with bus routes also now offered from Henley-on-Thames, Wargrave and Ascot. Majority of boarders live within an hour's drive. Around six per cent from overseas (including the Far East and Germany). Despite school's naval associations, only around 20 youngsters from Forces families. Families mainly hard-working – 'You get the odd child picked up in a Lamborghini but plenty of VWs like ours too,' one student said. Former pupils include the late film director Ken Russell, Olympic gold and silver medallist sailor Andrew (Bart) Simpson (a sailing foundation was set up in his name after he drowned whilst training for the America's

Cup), motorcycle racer Mike Hailwood, hedge fund founder David Harding, former Second Sea Lord, Admiral Sir Michael Layard and Dazed & Confused founder and journalist Jefferson Hack.

Money matters: Not a rich school, but a significant number (16 per cent) receive some help with fees. Means-tested bursaries are available from 10 per cent upwards, with around 6 to 10 students receiving 100 per cent or more. Scholarships include academic, music and sport at each entry point – no monetary value, but means-tested bursaries available for those who need help.

The last word: A small, distinctive, grounded and family-oriented school that puts huge emphasis on self-discipline, teamwork and leadership. Caring and supportive, Pangbourne buzzes with activity and encourages every pupil to have a go.

Papplewick School

36

Windsor Road, Ascot, Berkshire SL5 7LH

01344 621488 | registrar@papplewick.org.uk | www.papplewick.org.uk

Ages: 6–13

Pupils: 211; Boarders: 76 full/flexi (from 9 years)

Fees: Day £17,790 – £24,705 ; Boarding £32,160 – £35,940 pa

Headmaster: Since 2004, Mr Tom Bunbury (50s). BA (Hons) in law from Durham, criminal solicitor for four years, PGCE (Cambridge) and a year at Woodcote House. Joined Papplewick in 1993.

Absolutely adored by the school community. 'Funny', 'sincere', 'caring', say parents; 'totally charming, not in a dreadful smooth way'. Really, really understands boys ('little itchy scratchy creatures'). Has given his life to the school ('totally dedicated, but not a loser,' one parent suggests), and still finds huge joy in it: 'The whole thing should be fun.' Unafraid of boys-will-be-boys approach: 'They need exercise and food, like puppies.' Invests a lot in recruiting tremendous teachers 'who see the world through children's eyes'.

Confident balance between carrot and stick, independence and structure, work and play: 'in amongst the madhouse, they get the results'. Boys given unusual responsibility in terms of managing themselves, but safety net provides a soft landing if need be. Boys tumble from activity to lesson to fixture, but staff know exactly what they're doing: 'We set the guidelines and then let them out of the trap.' Their glorious freedom is thus carefully orchestrated, creating a uniquely spontaneous-feeling environment from which boys emerge having learnt an awful lot.

Married to Sallie, teaching assistant and 'mother figure', say parents; 'absolutely lovely'. 'During lockdown she sent a birthday card and a Milky Bar– he felt he hadn't been forgotten.' Four children, boy-girl-girl-boy, arrived in consecutive years after Mr Bunbury became head. 'The governors said we needed to fill the house they'd given us,' he laughs. Now they babysit staff children; oldest is a gappy.

Entrance: No academic selection. Mr Bunbury spends a couple of hours with each boy, looking for kindness and character: 'I choose the nicest boys I can and surround them with other nice boys; we couldn't run the school with so much freedom if they weren't so nice.' Ten in year 2 grows to 40 by year 8. Majority join at 6+, 7+ or 8+ from local or west London preps and state primaries.

Exit: Almost everyone to boarding. Greatest number go to Eton (10 awards in last three years including two King's Scholarships) followed by Harrow (10 awards), Winchester (two awards) and increasingly co-eds like Bradfield, Charterhouse, Wellington. 'Lots of you seem to be scholars – is it difficult for those that aren't?' we asked the boys: 'Not really – so many people are scholars that it's not a big deal.'

Our view: 'Set the bar high and they really go for it,' says Mr Bunbury. Indeed, lessons are go go go, teachers and pupils firing on all cylinders as they try out new ideas and learn from each other. Exceptionally sparky – constant back and forth, whether in scholarship Greek or year 5 maths. 'What's your favourite subject, apart from maths?' we asked the latter group. 'History!' cried

Books stuffed sideways into overflowing shelves. Boys hanging out at break time working through huge box of Lego

one, launching into an explanation of tanks at Cambrai in 1917. By the time we left, a book about tanks had been retrieved and the maths lesson had taken an unforeseen turn (sorry, sir). Average class size of 13. Streamed from year 3. Parents describe 'healthy competition' between the boys.

Whiteboards in classrooms covered in notes or reminders. One 'Quote of the Day', scribed in unmistakably small-boy handwriting, was from West Indian cricket commentator Ian Bishop: we imagine a lot of father-son test match viewing goes on. Year 7s and 8s soon to get laptops, 'to prepare them for senior school', but not as a substitute for writing. Library chockablock, every wall covered with posters of eg Terry Pratchett and Roald Dahl (apt, given that we felt like we'd walked into a Quentin Blake illustration). Books stuffed sideways into overflowing shelves. Boys hanging out at break time working through huge box of Lego.

Six per cent have EAL support. Twenty per cent on SEN register including dyslexia, ADHD, dyspraxia. Teachers differentiate within lessons; small groups allow for it. Targeted support in Learning Support department too.

Almost three-quarters learn a musical instrument and over 10 per cent identified as potential scholars. Supervised practice slots from dawn till dusk; minimum of two weekly. Around five scholarships each year, mainly to Eton, Harrow and Bradfield; growing success in music tech, too. Bassoon club to flute ensemble via 'junior toots'. Chapel choir sublime, though 'the chaps at the back give it some welly in chapel' too. In art room, pupil work piled perilously high on every surface, clay dragons on top of painted tiles on top of beautiful, mature acrylics on canvas. Lots of art scholarships.

Thursday afternoons a cornucopia of activities. Herpetology leads the way ('a knowledge of creeping animals,' one boy helpfully translates from the Greek). We met a corn snake coiled on a desk chomping lazily through a baby chicken; a thick black millipede creepily crawling over orange peel; bearded dragons ('beardies' to the boys) feeling perky after a mid-morning cricket snack. For anyone that gets the heebie-jeebies, the bibliomaniacs visit London fairs to sell antiquarian books (punters must swoon), military buffs to Airfix, Potterheads to Harry Potter club and budding adventurers to pioneers, Papplewick's version of Scouts. Props in last year's leavers' photo included chess sets, wickets, science goggles, snakes as thick as your arm and a clarinet.

Loads of sport, masses of fixtures (amongst the most at any prep, school claims): 'The best way to learn the importance of respect, teamwork and being gracious in both winning and losing.' Football, rugby, cricket. Written on old-fashioned whiteboard daily – seven teams out playing on the afternoon we visited, including first XI vs Eton. Staff had given boys a run for their money the previous evening, drawing three-all only after a late equaliser. Year 3s summed it up saying grace at lunchtime: 'Thank you, god, for friends and family and, um, good luck in the matches today. Amen.'

Pastoral care and discipline thoughtful but not cotton-woolly. 'They are carried, but they don't know they're being carried,' says Mr Bunbury lovingly. Year 6s assigned to a tutor in small groups and stay with them until year 8: again, quite senior-school-y ('This term seems mainly about listening to David Bowie,' one parent told us approvingly). PSHE delivered throughout; lots of focus on consent post-Everyone's Invited. 'There's more work to be done,' says Mr Bunbury, who's keen to establish further working partnerships with girls' schools rather than just the odd awkward social: 'It's crazy that we don't do more.' 'Papplewick words of wisdom' peppered around the school: 'Be like a pineapple!' proclaims one poster: 'Stand tall, wear a crown and be sweet on the inside.'

We met a corn snake coiled on a desk chomping lazily through a baby chicken; a thick black millipede creepily crawling over orange peel; bearded dragons

'We don't mind untucked shirts; it's just not necessary here,' say staff. Head agrees: 'If they smuggle in a pot noodle, good luck to them – the water's not hot enough.' Give out 'masses' of house points. Boys feel sheepish about a minus: 'It's not something they look forward to telling us that evening,' says one parent whose 'spirited' son quickly got the hang of what was expected of him. Rolling Bloomberg-esque screen in foyer shares the latest house point news, both positives and minuses. 'Getting technology wrong' taken seriously, as is any breach of the golden rules: 'no theft, no vandalism, no unkindness'.

Headmaster's detention on a Sunday the ultimate horror for these boys: they really admire him.

Unassuming driveway opens up to reveal fairly ordinary red-brick architecture, the odd dollop of pebbledash; don't be fooled, though, there is nothing ordinary about this school. Facilities 'the right side of too scruffy', say parents, who universally tell us that this is part of the charm (we agree, for the record), like everyone's too busy having a whale of a time to mind. And they are: we have never laughed so much on a school visit. 'Expectations of the boys are really high,' say parents, 'but it's all done with a joke and a sense of fun.' 'They're all characters,' say staff, 'and we have great back and forth in the lessons.' Affectionate nicknames, in-jokes: lots of the warm humour that ensures boys feel part of the gang. An exceptionally cohesive gang, too:

Papplewick words of wisdom peppered around the school: 'Be like a pineapple!' proclaims one poster: 'Stand tall, wear a crown and be sweet on the inside'

staff living on site don't come up for air during term time, with partners and kids mucking in too. 'As long as you bring something to the party, it doesn't matter what it is,' says Mr Bunbury of the whole community.

Traditional, but not stiff. The best bits of 'old-fashioned' without the canings or the cold custard (food's delicious, in fact: yummiest pudding apple crumble, according to connoisseurs), like Enid Blyton without the casual racism. A myriad of special ties for extracurriculars, responsibilities, sports tours. Saturday school 'alive and well' for year 3 upwards. Staff use surnames for the boys. Ripsticks (those skateboards that wiggle) lie all over the place, used and then dropped between lessons. Very few screens around. Year 6 common room a multisensory 90s timewarp: dark, Trekkie-style space scenes covering the walls, red velvet seating and a dishevelled rabble playing a furious game of table football. Bookshelf stuffed with boy-friendly paperbacks from 'Stig of the Dump' to Bear Grylls' 'Mission Survival'. Bliss, if you're 11.

Relaxed and open to parents. One mortified after recent slip-up: 'I'd completely forgotten to collect him! He was very happily reading in the library, and lovely staff said, "don't worry, you can never be late at Papplewick".' Londoners (a quarter of pupils) have opted out of that more frenetic landscape. Buses ('jolly drivers,' say parents) ferry them from Chiswick, Brook Green, Gloucester Road. Lots of involvement for those that want it – boys vs mums in football and cricket, dads-and-sons camp outs – but not as glossy a social scene as elsewhere. No return school bus on a Saturday, encouraging parents to come to Saturday chapel and then 'chaotic family lunch with grannies and siblings and boys rushing off to play matches'. 'Your whole Saturday quickly becomes Papplewick,' parents tell us; most, though not all, delighted by it. Lower key than some preps and parents feel they're an unflashy bunch – 'no snobs' – though fees hardly bargain basement so we wouldn't take this for granted.

Boarding: Compulsory boarding from summer of year 6. Many flexi-board earlier. Evening activities compulsory throughout winter and spring but optional in the summer, when boys would rather run around building dens or playing cricket into the evening. No smartphones allowed – only 'old bricks'.

Dorms bright and boyish with manga-style cartoons, retro Batman posters, Arsenal duvet covers, paintings of sharks on surfboards wearing suits. 'Fun fact,' our guide announced: 'my duvet cover's dad's old one from boarding school.' Smart new block houses the oldest boys. Hot chocolate for all before bed. Winning 'tidiest dorm' gets you 'cool rewards', our guides tell us, 'like spending £12 as a dorm at Londis'. Excited to have a toaster in year 8 – gets them used to endless toast at public school. 'We wouldn't be doing our job if we didn't prepare them for Eton,' says Mr Bunbury.

Money matters: Scholarships up to 15 per cent 'for a really great all-rounder'; means-tested bursaries add a further 35 per cent. Work with Springboard; Forces bursaries too.

The last word: A mock-up Penguin book sleeve in the foyer sums it up: 'Papplewick School: snakes, ripsticks and other great adventures for boys'. Many of those adventures happen within the classroom, where boys given the freedom to think, challenge and explore with funny, passionate teachers. It's horses for courses, though, and don't expect glamour: a school with its knees out all winter and a big, crooked smile.

Rarely do we spend our drive home mulling over a relocation to Berkshire (lovely though it is). Indeed, it's our policy not to fall in love: professional distance, don't gush. Papplewick tested our mettle and seems to have the same effect elsewhere: 'I can't get him out of the place!' said one mum, whose son had announced midway through a trip to the circus, 'This is fun, but I wish I was at school.' The truth? At a school like this one, we don't blame him.

The Pilgrims' School

3 The Close, Winchester, Hampshire SO23 9LT

01962 854189 | admissions@pilgrims-school.co.uk | www.thepilgrims-school.co.uk

Ages: 4-13

Pupils: 244; Boarders: 100 full/weekly (from year 4)

Fees: Day £11,742 – £20,457; Boarding £26,064; Choral scholar £15,639 pa

Head: Since 2020, Dr Sarah Essex, formerly deputy head academic at Fulham Prep. She attended St Mary's Convent School in Worcester, then Worcester Girls' Grammar School. Her very impressive CV includes a first in natural sciences and a PhD in theoretical inorganic chemistry, both from Cambridge. She had a distinguished career as a senior partner director and chief financial officer of a number of international strategy consulting firms but switched direction after learning that UK primary schools didn't have enough qualified science and maths teachers. 'It really bothered me as a scientist,' she says. She took Fridays off and began voluntary teaching at her local parish primary school and other primaries in London and further afield. Eighteen months later she decided to teach full-time and at the age of 45 did a PGCE in primary education at UCL Institute of Education. 'Everyone thought I was a little mad,' she adds with a smile.

A few misguided heads told her she was too over-qualified to teach but The Hall School, a boys' prep in Hampstead, snapped her up as a maths teacher. Within four years she'd risen to head of maths, head of data, assessment and reporting and even head of GDPR. After two more years at The Hall and then two years at Fulham Prep she was appointed as head of Pilgrims'. 'Coming here felt like coming home,' she says. 'I walked in on the first day and music was pouring out of every window. I loved the fact that the boys here can be whatever they want to be. Everyone is celebrated. We help them to find their passions and nurture them. It's a very joyful place.'

She teaches non-verbal reasoning to year 6 boys and spends as much time in the pre-prep and prep classrooms as she can. 'Our school is very verbal,' she says. 'Lessons here are like conversations.' She firmly believes that dialogue with and between pupils drives learning – at her first prizegiving she quoted a line from Professor Christine Harrison of King's College London: 'Fostering dialogue and orchestrating discussion should be at the heart of what teachers do on a daily basis.'

In her spare time she enjoys running, Pilates and musical theatre, is a keen mono-skier and has taken up improvisational comedy. Warm and professional, she's highly praised by teachers and parents. 'She's really skilled at managing a team and taking leadership,' a mother told us. Another said: 'She really takes time to know the pupils. I'm very impressed.'

Entrance: Main entry points are reception, year 3 and year 6 but a growing number are joining in year 5 to prepare for ISEB pre-tests, as well as other years. Before being offered a place boys sit assessments in maths, English, verbal and non-verbal reasoning to ensure they will thrive. Older boys have interviews with subject teachers. Choral scholars join in year 4 (choristers) and year 5 (quiristers).

Boys joining the pre-prep are invited to 'stay and play' sessions, where staff chat to parents and see how children interact with their peers. The intention is that boys joining the pre-prep will stay at Pilgrims' till year 8 – and virtually all do.

Exit: Pilgrims' is not the prep school for Winchester College but enough families see it as a route for there to be a separate form in year 8 (13 went there in 2020). Winchester exams are earlier and different from Common Entrance, which accounts for another form, as well a third group for scholarship candidates. Prepares scholarship boys very specifically and successfully for the academic requirements of other major schools. Unsurprisingly, music awards and exhibitions are also plentiful.

Remainder to Eton (10 in 2020) and Sherborne (five in 2020), with one or two to eg Canford, Portsmouth Grammar, King Edward V, Harrow, Charterhouse, Wellington and Marlborough.

Our view: Pilgrims' is an academic school ('we want the boys to excel,' says the second master) but learning here looks like fun. We visited a host of lively lessons where boys were brimming with enthusiasm. 'Has everyone got their goggles on?' quizzed the head of science as he guided year 6 pupils through a practical experiment on the states of matter. We observed a rapt English class where year 8 scholars were keenly analysing William Wordsworth's sonnet, Composed upon Westminster Bridge. 'The teaching is amazing,' said a parent. 'The teachers are really passionate about their subjects and get the boys excited about them too.' Another described teachers as 'reassuring and nurturing' and said queries and worries were always acknowledged and acted on promptly. In years 3 and 4 boys do English, maths, history and geography with form teachers (plus science, sport, music, French, art and DT with subject specialists) but from year 5 up they have specialist teachers for every subject. French taught from reception and Latin and ancient Greek from year 6.

Classes are small – never more than 16 and often fewer. Pilgrims' boys are able but there is a range of attainments and all are taught to achieve above and beyond their potential. Eighteen have specialist one-to-one weekly lessons for difficulties in areas like reading, spelling, comprehension, maths, attention, motor skills and coordination, processing speeds, working memory, executive functioning and anxiety. 'Our son is dyslexic and was falling behind in the state-school environment,' a father told us. 'We moved him to Pilgrims' and he has absolutely thrived. It has been transformative and wonderful.'

Pre-prep has its own purpose-built centre between the prep and the deanery garden, with a tributary of the River Itchen running alongside (fenced off for safety). The pre-prep playground has a superb view of Winchester Cathedral and boys play out in all weathers. 'We are outside as much as we can be,' says the pre-prep head. There's also a forest school – we met a bunch of cheery boys collecting autumn leaves ready to paint them. Pre-prep has launched a drive to use natural resources where possible, with a concerted effort to reduce plastic, use less paper (the boys have digital learning journals) and recycle and reuse. Classrooms have hessian display boards – both practical and beautiful. Buddy system means the transition from the pre-prep to the prep goes smoothly. 'The pre-prep is a really great place to start a child's journey through education,' said a parent.

Not surprisingly, with two professional choirs and a plethora of other choirs and orchestras, music is a joy. Twenty-two cathedral choristers, sing with the Winchester Cathedral choir and 16 college quiristers sing with the Winchester College chapel choir. Known as the Cs and Qs or 'the reds and the blues' (choristers wear red jerseys, quiristers wear blue), they sing daily to the highest standard. A chorister's parent told us: 'It's a bit like Charlie and the Chocolate Factory. When our son became a chorister it was like winning a golden ticket.' Eighty-seven per cent learn an instrument, and many boys learn two. Head of music asks year 7s and 8s to 'sell' their instruments to year 3 pupils – in other words explain why the younger boys should take them up. 'We offer four free taster lessons and this year five of them went for the double bass,' he told us proudly. 'It's fine until their parents say: "But our car is a Mini."' Music lessons are arranged on a rota basis to minimise disruption to lessons. A plethora of musical groups to join – senior and junior choirs, chamber choir, orchestra, big band, sinfonietta and many more. 'We try to give boys the opportunity to be in two groups – one in their comfort zone and another to extend and challenge them,' says the head of music.

Lots of after-school activities, known as 'commoners' – everything from computer coding to knitting. Chess is big too

Drama is on the curriculum but there are plenty of other opportunities to perform on stage, including plays, musicals, Pilgrims' Got Talent and the Christmas cabaret. Large, airy art room where enthusiastic head of art has devised an exciting array of artistic pursuits. We admired Rothko-inspired paintings by year 3s, landscapes by year 5s and pop-art self-portraits by year 8s. 'I embed art history in everything they do,' he says.

For a smallish school Pilgrims' fields an astonishing number of sports teams – soccer, rugby, hockey, cricket and athletics. PE all year round and swimming lessons in the open-air pool in the summer and up until the October half-term. Other sports offered through the co-curricular programme, including judo, karate, fives, rowing, squash, sailing, tennis, golf, fencing, fishing and water polo. Extensive games pitches have views of the Bishop's Palace and the ruins of Wolvesey Castle. Lots of after-school activities, known as 'commoners' – everything from computer coding to knitting. Chess is big at the school – there's an outdoor chess board with giant-sized pieces and boys compete against other schools. The aim is for boys to follow their passions – 'be it Tiddlywinks or first XI football,' says the second master.

The school, tucked in a quiet close between Winchester Cathedral and Winchester College, has been on its present site since 1931 and is a wonderful mix of ancient and modern. Light, airy classrooms and library blend with the neighbouring medieval and Georgian houses. We were very taken with the Pilgrims' Hall, used for assembly and dating back to the 14th century. The school has services at Easter and Christmas in Winchester Cathedral and in the chapel at Winchester College.

Very sensible policies on mobile devices. Day boys can't bring mobile phones to school but boarders can use them for 40 minutes in the evening. After that devices are locked away. Device-free nights on Mondays and Thursdays. If they want to ring home at other times they can use the school's iPads or landlines. Boarders write postcards home every Sunday. Pastoral care very well structured – mainly through form teachers until the last three years, when boys are in tutor groups of up to nine. 'There is a real camaraderie and sense of happiness here,' a mother told us, while a father said: 'Kindness and consideration are woven through the school like a stick of rock.' PSHE for all year groups and head nurse has recently introduced 'Group' for year 7s, an informal 45-minute gathering where they share thoughts, feelings and concerns. 'It helps to develop the boys' emotional literacy,' she says. House system – boys belong to one of five 'sets', with lots of inter-set competitions.

Food gets the thumbs-up. Breakfast and supper for boarders (and day pupils if they want it) is cafeteria-style while lunch is table service, with a member of staff sitting at each table to encourage good manners and conversation. Option of wraparound care from 7am to 6pm fits in well with parents' working hours. A tuck shop – the delightfully named Num Nums – is open twice a week for boarders. Year 8 boys have an annual social with girls from St Swithun's although one parent said they'd like to see more interaction with local girls' schools – either drama productions or a joint sports day perhaps.

Past pupils include novelist Patrick Gale, comedian Jack Dee, broadcaster Jon Snow and four BBC choirboys of the year since 2000.

Boarding: Boys can board from year 4 (Forces children are occasionally allowed to board in year 3). Full and weekly boarding available, but no flexi. By year 8 three-quarters board. International boarders from the US, Hong Kong, China, South Korea, Nigeria, Luxembourg, Turkey, Spain and Italy. The two boarding houses originate from the choristers' and quiristers' needs, with choristers in the main school and quiristers in Q school. The dorms are the nicest you'll find anywhere – six or eight bunk beds in imaginatively decorated rooms (themes include sports, Dr Seuss, Superheroes, Tintin and Beano). The sports dorm, for instance, has a vast mural of a football pitch painted on one wall and bookshelves made from skateboards above every bed.

Teaching houseparents, with their own boys in school, create a family atmosphere, and the three paediatric nurses are very approachable. The san has recently been renamed R & R, short for rest and recuperation (it was named in a competition by a boy). Choristers who stay on over Christmas and Easter for choir clearly have a whale of a time – with a Christmas story on Christmas Eve, secret Santa and Christmas stockings. 'It's full-on but it's magic,' we were told.

Money matters: Choristers and quiristers are awarded choral scholarships of 40 per cent of the full boarding fee. Means-tested bursaries sometimes available.

The last word: A stunning, distinctive and very caring school, Pilgrims' combines a forward-thinking outlook with an incredible heritage and history, excellent academic results and breathtaking music. There's something special here for almost every boy, especially for those who are bright, intellectually curious and eager to learn.

Queen Anne's School

38

6 Henley Road, Caversham, Reading, Berkshire RG4 6DX

01189 187300 | admissions@qas.org.uk | www.qas.org.uk

Ages: 11–18

Pupils: 450; sixth form: 140; Boarders: 225 full/weekly/flexi

Fees: Day £25,110; Boarding £36,750 – £41,775 pa

Headmistress: Since January 2022, Elaine Purves, previously head at St John's International School in Belgium. She has also been head at Rossall School and Ipswich High School, as well as deputy head at the Royal High School, Bath, GDST.

Entrance: Girls join at 11 from a large number of prep schools and state primaries. Tests in maths, English, verbal and non-verbal reasoning and a group interview. Recommendations of help required for girls with SEND made in offer letter.

For entry into year 12, there's an entrance exam and requirement of minimum six GCSEs at grade 4 or above (including English and maths) and 6 in subjects to be studied at A level.

Exit: Around a quarter head off after GCSEs in search of co-ed sixth forms or to local colleges. Those who stay move on to a range of universities including Manchester, UCL, Exeter, King's College London, Leeds, Durham, St Andrews, York and Nottingham to study a wide range of subjects including politics, philosophy and economics, fashion management, medicine, law, physics with astrophysics and international business. One or two to Oxbridge most years.

Latest results: In 2021, 80 per cent 9-7 at GCSE; 72 per cent A*/A at A level. In 2019 (the last year when exams took place), 60 per cent 9-7 at GCSE; 44 per cent A*/A at A level (68 per cent A*-B).

Teaching and learning: Solid results, especially given mixed-ability intake. Excellent outcomes in sciences, languages and the humanities at GCSE. Biology, maths, chemistry, psychology and economics most popular A level choices in recent years; just tiny numbers choosing languages. Strong added value, with pupils adding between one and three grades to results. Smallish take-up of EPQ.

One of the most imaginative arrays of A level art we've seen, from intricate hanging installations to the imaginary office of Kim Jong Un's head of propaganda

School says academics are 'critically important, but we'll make sure we get there holistically'. So while they have some medics, lawyers, vets and straight stars, school insists 'that's not for everyone.' Indeed, the beauty of QAS is that it takes girls of all academic abilities and works hard to get the best out of them, quietly measuring and assessing all the time. School has been working for some years alongside Reading and Goldsmiths universities to develop research into what makes the brain tick with its BrainCanDo project to enable staff and girls to understand the science of learning. Such initiatives notwithstanding, the teaching we observed was basically what we see in good schools everywhere: small classes, engaged pupils and plenty of audience participation. Crucially, 'girls are able to access real learning strategies,' according to school. Students say their teachers are 'passionate' and parents, with only a few exceptions, agree. The A level economics class we sat in on was buzzy and interactive with state-of-the-art classroom technology being used to full effect.

Girls set for core subjects in year 7 and progress is 'carefully tracked from the moment they arrive,' says school. E-learning is a major focus, sending message to students that 'tech is cool'. Collaborative working facilitated with access to OneNote and areas of the school (notably the 'study pods' in the sixth form centre) have their own mini Wifi zones to enable students to share ideas and projects. Touch typing taught as 'a tool for life'. We approve. Visits from eg leading artificial intelligence companies and programming masterclasses reinforce the message and participation in fun Bebras computational thinking competitions ensures that technology 'is not seen as too geeky'.

Learning support and SEN: SEND support provided in class wherever possible with individual sessions (additional charge) available if required taking place during the (extra long) lunch break to avoid 'counter-productive' withdrawal from classes. Around 15 per cent of cohort on SEND register, with about nine per cent receiving support at any one time. Subject clinics praised by students. School has experience working with mild dyslexia, dyspraxia, ADD and hearing impairments. Much of site, especially the newer parts, wheelchair accessible. 'There's absolutely no stigma to SEN,' school assured us, 'but girls have to be able to pass the entrance exam.' EAL taught in place of MFL or Latin.

The arts and extracurricular: And so to where the school truly shines – and where to begin?

Clubs galore at lunchtimes and after school, and double-period lunch break enables girls to take part in activities as well as eat. Fabulous art department – 'creativity happens here' announces a trompe l'oeil splashed across floor and entrance. One of the most imaginative arrays of A level art we've seen, from intricate hanging installations to the imaginary office of Kim Jong Un's head of propaganda. DT absorbed into art ('we don't do technology, but we have technology'), with super equipment including 3D printers and a laser cutter enabling the focus to be 'career focused, not airy fairy' according to staff. Ceramics teacher recently appointed. With such riches in terms of facilities and an inspirational departmental head, no wonder so many girls choose art as GCSE and A level options (25 at A level in 2018) and many head off to study product design or architecture at university.

Drama too is 'a big subject' according to school. How do they choose what productions to stage? 'We look at what the girls will be good at.' So sometimes it's Shakespeare, sometimes a musical. Music taught in the gleaming new music centre (2018) which, from a grand piano to a fleet of state-of-the-art iMacs, has whistles and bells and then some. On curriculum from year 7, pupils work on projects such as writing advertising jingles to creating soundtracks to short movies. Beats scales and arpeggios any day of the week. Over 300 peripatetic lessons take place each week and year 7s all sing 'whether they like it or not', although with whole-choir trips to destinations including Washington, New York or Rome, we suspect that 'like it' they mainly do. Chamber choir is unauditioned (there is a consort choir for elite songstresses) and with bands aplenty from jazzabelles to saxaholics there are informal performances every week.

Sport: Super sports facilities, including 25-metre pool, fitness suite, sprung-floor dance studio, climbing wall, squash courts, plus loads of tennis and netball courts means there's something for everyone. Even girls who hated sport before they arrived at QAS 'love it here' and there's a 'culture of being active', says school, whether it's a sponsored charity walk to Botswana (the distance, not the actual route), yoga, meditation and Pilates or fiercely competitive games. Known for outstanding lacrosse (despite the sloping pitch – soon to be levelled, much to the delight of all – school has five girls who play for England and ranks in national top eight), and netball also strong. Fixtures for everyone in years 7 and 8 with A-E teams and from year 9 there are still C team matches most weeks, with 'incredible' sideline support from the parent body, and girls giving the thumbs-up for fair team selection.

Dance is 'huge', with three-quarters of students taking dance classes and in 2018 150 ISTD dance exams taking place in school. Stunning annual dance show (we were blown away by video clips pinged to us by glowing parents) to an almost professional standard, often fully choreographed by the girls themselves. Rowing ('very strong') is coached by a former Olympian. Plenty of fun as well as serious sport – sports day is 'for everyone', with highlights including a flag relay race (flags designed by pupils) and a capture the flag competition organised by sixth form. Ballroom dancing lessons for sixth formers with boys from the Oratory – with whom they also play mixed tennis and go on a ski trip – culminates in a summer ball, eagerly attended by almost everyone ('It's a rite of passage,' says school).

Boarding: If it's possible in the boarding world to be all things to all girls, QAS has it sewn up. Day girls, full boarders and everything in between all rub along easily together. Flexi is just that. One night a week? No problem. Full boarders are treated to a range of weekend activities and if the plan sounds like fun, day girls are welcome too. Four smart boarding houses are mainly purpose built, well kitted out and beautifully decorated with squidgy sofas and stylish fabrics in communal areas. No poky kitchenettes – the hubs of the houses are spacious home-style kitchens, complete with farmhouse table and chairs as centrepiece for girls to gather round in the evenings. The houseparents we met were just the ticket – friendly and approachable but no-nonsense – and many houses have a four-legged resident. Upper sixth girls are based in Michell, slightly separate from the main cluster of buildings to give them peace and a degree of independence. Day girls have (slightly scruffy, very untidy) rooms with desks and lockers.

Ethos and heritage: Set amongst 34 acres of prime Caversham real estate. The handsome ivy-clad Victorian brick pile belies what lies beyond: not the usual melange of low-rise horrors from the decades that architecture forgot, but an aesthete's dream collection of facilities (fit for a capital F if only our editors would allow it) to rival any we've seen. The Space, home of the brand-new sixth form centre plus dining hall, is a triumph of glass and stainless steel, complete with Café 6, the bright, stylish in-house eatery serving hot snacks and proper coffee to sixth formers, who relax in leather upholstered booths or outside in their own charming courtyard area. Atop this are flexible classroom spaces (we loved the writable-on walls) and themed breakout rooms decorated in the style of eg Central Park (Astroturf carpet, skyscraper mural and park benches), Big Ben or theatre. The female chaplain performs services in the galleried chapel for lower and upper school several times each week. Food gets the thumbs-up; breakfasts are 'amazing' and good old fish and chips on Friday is top lunch. Queen Anne's is part of the Westminster Greycoat Foundation and was established on its current site in 1894. Historic links with Westminster and the Abbey remain. Between head and her marketing department there's plenty of buzz around school with initiatives (mostly linked to BrainCanDo) such as the recent week-long experiment allowing sixth formers to sleep until 10am before starting their school day. We wonder whether parents buy into such non-curriculum-focused initiatives. The jury's out amongst those we spoke to, but our advice is not to not get distracted by all the spin and fluff – everything you expect to get from a school with boarding fees well north of 10 grand a term is here, and more besides.

Pastoral care, inclusivity and discipline: Long days (8.00am to 6.15pm) but prep is completed under supervision at school and tea is provided, so quality time at home is, in theory, just that. School transport includes coaches with flexible routes, taxis and minibuses to ship girls from up to an hour away to school each day. Pastoral care praised from the rooftops by parents and pupils and there are not many schools we have visited that have such a relaxed atmosphere and 'hardly any peer pressure,' according to pupils. Problems can be taken to housemistresses ('really approachable,' say girls), tutors, independent listeners or fellow pupils from year 10 upwards, trained as part of the peer mentor team. 'Families' are akin to vertical tutor groups; newbies are given a 'sister' in the year above when they join, and girls clearly appreciate the strong inter-year group relations.

Uniform rules 'have got really strict recently,' say girls (shorter skirts and more earrings high on their wish lists). Sixth formers allowed the dreaded 'smart business' mufti (it didn't look all that smart to us, but to be fair it was exam season). The distinctive red hooded cloaks are no longer compulsory uniform but are still worn at formal events, eg carol services and the biennial service of thanksgiving at Westminster Abbey. Not an obviously diverse community but school does run an annual LGBT week with special assemblies and talks and there's a diversity noticeboard highlighting different sexualities. Misuse of social media results in immediate suspension (enforced a few times in recent years), but the usual drinking, drugs and smoking transgressions are few and far between. Low incidence of serious mental health problems rife in some girls' schools – 'we're very hot on intervention,' says school, and houseparents eat all meals with girls to keep an eye on healthy dietary habits. Well-being programme has replaced PSHCE recently and is now delivered by a dedicated team to tutor groups in years 7-10, covering issues such as relationships, friendship and social media. Pupil well-being ambassadors 'make such a difference,' says school.

Food gets thumbs-up; breakfasts are 'amazing' and good old fish and chips on Friday is top lunch

Pupils and parents: Girls we met were down to earth, articulate and chatty. Majority are reasonably local, with boarders and day girls living up to an hour away. Sixteen per cent overseas (including students from over 15 countries, Forces and expats) with the remainder mainly a mix of entrepreneurs and City workers. Increasing numbers from London who see it as an alternative to the ferocious London school scene and, after all, Paddington is only a 25-minute train ride away.

Money matters: Boarding fees as expected and in line with local competitors. Day fees not too painful considering extended school day and access to boarding perks. Scholarships for art, music, drama, sports and all-rounder at 11+ and 13+. Foundation generous in the case of hardship or support needed by less wealthy families.

The last word: Cut through the marketing blurb and you'll find a school where you can be a star without being an academic whizz. 'There's something magical about the place,' said one parent; 'it's as much about life preparation as academics.' And with such an array of first-class facilities, tip-top pastoral care, plus a culture of female empowerment, we think it's definitely one for the list of any parent for whom happiness and roundedness are top priorities.

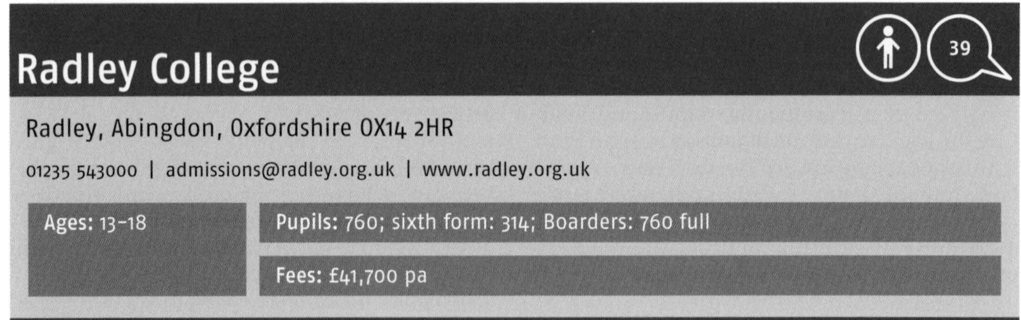

Radley College

39

Radley, Abingdon, Oxfordshire OX14 2HR

01235 543000 | admissions@radley.org.uk | www.radley.org.uk

Ages: 13–18

Pupils: 760; sixth form: 314; Boarders: 760 full

Fees: £41,700 pa

Warden: Since 2014, John Moule MA (40s), previously head of Bedford School. Educated at a Telford comprehensive and sixth form college, he won a history scholarship to Lady Margaret Hall, Oxford and left with a first. Refreshingly atypical background for a post like this. Taught history and politics at Dean Close, Cheltenham, moved to Stowe as head of history and became housemaster, then senior housemaster. Perhaps it's Radley's proximity to Oxford but we thought Mr Moule had a little of Laurence Fox's (aka Sgt Hathaway in Lewis) lean, pale intensity. This impression only somewhat dampened when we learnt that pallor was a result of his 'feeling under the weather'.

He seems to have made a very favourable impression and was described to us as a 'brilliant' speaker, able to hold an audience of parents and boys simultaneously. 'He's very visible and really involved,' one mother told us. 'He drops into Socials (Radley-speak for boarding house) and plays chess with the boys.'

Married with three children, his eldest daughter is a veterinary student, his son is finishing A levels at Bedford School and the youngest is at a girls' day school nearby. Having worked in medical research, his wife completed a second degree in maths and now divides her time between the many and varied duties of a head's spouse and teaching at a school in Oxford.

Like so many heads, Mr Moule claims to have 'fallen' into teaching. (Watch out, there must be a huge and cunningly disguised hole somewhere designed for just this purpose.) It goes like this. He was all set to study for a PhD in 16th century English theological history but the grant-awarding bodies had other plans and chose this moment to withdraw the financial support that had hitherto been awarded to arts students with first-class degrees: 'You could say that I was saved by lack of funds.' At a loose end in Oxford, someone inevitably suggested he try teaching. 'I'd never set foot in an independent school but after two weeks I knew it was right.'

Of course Mr Moule is convinced of the benefits of a full boarding school. 'It fosters strength of character and independence.' He goes on, 'The 24-hour culture is hugely creative, it allows teachers to develop boys' genuine interests beyond the classroom.' He describes the 'powerful' triangle formed by the school, the parents and the boy, 'all have to buy into it', he says. For fee-paying parents that is both metaphorically and literally the case.

Since becoming warden Mr Moule has done a great deal of observing. Not only has he dropped unannounced into lessons and watched every don (Radley-speak) teach, he also shadowed pupils throughout their day (including late afternoon and evening) to learn more about their experience as well as the school's 'flow'. And what were his conclusions? He was seriously impressed by the variety he found but felt some lessons were rather too teacher-led. We imagine it can be hard to avoid in a school full of bright boys who for the most part will arrive having had eight or more years' listening and learning in prep school. We saw some young hopefuls during our visit, serious little chaps wearing polished brogues and tweed jackets – just like the fathers accompanying them.

He wants to do more to raise boys' awareness of the world beyond Radley's 800 prime Oxfordshire acres and has also told parents, and boys, that he intends to 'wage war on teenage apathy'. While acknowledging that every day should still contain a little time for creative boredom, he says boys have a tendency to do 'just enough' and feels this should be challenged. When he's sorted that one out perhaps he could let us know.

He wants to do more to raise boys' awareness of the world beyond Radley's 800 prime Oxfordshire acres and has said that he intends to 'wage war on teenage apathy'

His plans for the school itself are well underway. The website has already been improved beyond recognition – it's now (fanfare) welcoming and informative – and the college's famously esoteric ('mystical' was how the warden described it) entry procedure has been revised. It used to be the case that if you had to ask Radley how to apply then you were probably too late. The process is now more open, in line with other, similar schools, though the 'List' remains and is an advantage for those who want to sign up early. Increased bursarial support is another target, as is 'careful' recruitment of applicants from beyond (even far beyond) the home counties.

Mr Moule's strong Christian faith means Radley's timeless tradition of whole school chapel four times a week is in safe hands. Boys 'love' chapel, he told us, 'especially as they get older', and indeed this was borne out by those we spoke to. Of course it's important to the 'sincerely spiritual' but it's also valued by chaps who just want a bit of peace and quiet, or 'separated space', as the warden puts it. It may not be as fashionable, but perhaps this is mindfulness, Radley style.

When not wardening Mr Moule says he is an 'avid' armchair sportsman and enjoys a spot of golf or real tennis. Reading is, naturally, another recreation and favourite books include Wilkie Collins' The Woman in White and PG Wodehouse's classic, The Mating Season. Box sets are also high up on this warden's list, especially The West Wing and the US version of The Office. And if he hadn't so carelessly 'fallen' into teaching? Journalism, the law and the church are all the poorer for his stumble.

Entrance: Still the forward planner's choice. Radley remains loyal to those who register early and 'conditional' offers are made three years in advance to boys on 'Provisional' and waiting lists. Subject to interview and ISEB common pre-test results, they will get firm offers on 1 March of year 6. No open days, individually arranged visits all through the year. Friendly and approachable admissions staff will explain system.

Radley puts 'much emphasis' on candidate's performance at interview and head's report when assessing applicants. From 2019 onwards, after offers are made to boys on the 'Provisional' list, there is an open entry system whereby all interested candidates are first asked to sit the ISEB common pre-test in year 6 and send a school report; interviews will be offered to shortlisted candidates and offers made in June of year 6.

Few (around eight) places at 16 + but on the whole this is a settled community and there's not much movement.

Exit: Edinburgh, Durham, Newcastle, Bristol, Exeter and the London universities hoover up most of Radley's leavers. Regular 15–20 boys to Oxbridge every year (though number not provided for 2021) – mock interview exchange scheme with nearby Abingdon School seems to benefit both sides. School's university entrance team recently expanded to integrate expertise in applying to universities in North America, Europe and beyond. Five medics in 2021, and three overseas – to USA, Canada and Spain.

Latest results: In 2021, 93 per cent 9-7 at GCSE; 84 per cent A*/A at A level. In 2019 (the last year when exams took place), 82 per cent 9-7 at I/GCSE; 59 per cent A*/A at A level.

Teaching and learning: Even with the recent changes to its entrance procedure Radley is not a school that selects solely on academic ability; excellent GCSE and A level results stem from fine teaching and staff who don't think their job is done when the lesson finishes. Recent reintroduction of the linear, two-year A level has proved that Radley wasn't so maverick after all when it held out against AS levels being taken at the end of the first year sixth. We did detect a certain quiet satisfaction that the rest of the country has finally come into line. Sixth formers sit three or four A levels, a fourth subject is generally one that contrasts with the other three. All will also do an extended project.

Particularly strong GCSE results in, well everything, but also some lower grades. At A level, most popular subjects history, maths and English literature followed by sciences. Notable proportion of A* in art and English lit. Nice to see decent numbers taking classics, languages and geology too. While maths and further maths are very popular, Radley has always stood apart from the overwhelming science/maths dominance so commonly found in boys' schools and we're glad to see this remains the case.

Radley still has that slightly separate feel of an Oxford college, enhanced by the sight of boys rushing to and fro, gowns billowing behind

Teaching in the lessons we observed was of the tried and tested sort – a fast pace and lots of quick-fire questions kept everyone on their toes. Very clearly exam focused. However, despite adding a distinctly scholarly air, gowns didn't seem to make Radleians any more elevated or less prone to muttering at the back than their non-gowned counterparts at other schools.

We met some really amusing and inspiring dons who just seemed to love their jobs (less jobs, more way of life, we thought) and the very stones of the place. Good mix of ages and lots of women among teaching staff. Dogs seemed to be part of the package too – that explained the water bowls we'd wondered about in some of the classrooms. All dons and their families live on site.

Much talk of efforts to 'learn from other schools and widen diversity'. Strong links with local primaries and a Maidenhead secondary school; some exchange of teaching staff but latter a little too far away for frequent activities. Closer to home the warden hopes to further develop joint academic extension activities for A level subjects such as music, English and geography with Headington School. There are links for the scholars with St Helen and St Katharine and plans for 'ambitious extension days' with Oxford High School. Lest we get too carried away by all this talk of diversity, at Radley take-your-dog-to-work day is unlikely to be joined by enrol-your-daughter day any time soon.

Learning support and SEN: Latest ISI report called learning support 'exceptional' and parents are in agreement. All boys have to meet the entrance criteria to get into the school but once there SEN support is extensive and lacks stigma. Individual and small group sessions are arranged according to need. Some take place during what is known as 'central hour' (1.30-2.30pm daily), time set aside for relaxing, working, music lessons, extracurricular activities etc.

The arts and extracurricular: Art school, complete with rather cool gallery space, is in Clocktower Court. Pupils' work, paintings, ceramics and photography, not confined to here, it's all over the school – eerily lifelike papier-mâché boys peer down from beams in the library. Ambitious projects undertaken in DT include surfboards and a rather spectacular trebuchet. Once again, facilities lack for nothing and are open late into the evening and at weekends. Nine or 10 boys take art or DT at A2 with creditable results.

Large chapel choir with trebles from local primary schools and preps sings at services and evensong in chapel and elsewhere, including Oxford colleges. Weekly concerts in the school coffee shop, house and college concerts give boys as many solo and ensemble performing opportunities as possible. The music school is open until 10.15pm and boys are expected to organise their own practice although a member of staff is on hand to help. Just one or two doing music at A level despite high profile of music in the school – theatre studies more popular option.

Inter-house competitions and endowed prizes are great motivators and boys take to the stage for such keenly fought contests as the part song competition, debating, declaiming, battle of the bands, piano and percussion trophies. The legendary Piano Extravaganza featured, most recently, 91 players from age 6 upwards (under-13s are dons' children) playing on eight pianos. The Silk Hall is school's premier music venue and next door is the theatre where college and year group plays are performed as well as A2 drama devised pieces. Parents rave about the drama at Radley; even shy boys take to the stage. No reluctance from boys to take on female roles but every so often school puts a 'Girls wanted' advert in the local paper if the production requires the genuine article. Warden told us he directed several plays at his former school and might be tempted again.

CCF compulsory for removes, fifth form do community service and sixth formers can choose enrichment activities such as opera, film or cooking. Couple of parents thought a few more 'life skills' wouldn't go amiss at this stage. Seriously impressive calendar of visiting speakers including WW2 RAF hero, Auschwitz survivor, scientists, authors, journalists, MPs and members of the clergy. Vast array of trips – theatre in London, art in Florence and music tours (singers and instrumentalists) to America. Energetic fundraising for variety of good causes including partner school in Tanzania and Christian Aid.

Sport: All rather civilised. Manages to maintain a creditable sporting reputation without the ruthlessly competitive atmosphere than can prevail at boys' schools. We got the impression that the disinclined to run are not regarded as also-rans. Rugby is main game of Michaelmas term – around 20 separate teams do battle every Saturday.

When it warms up the 'wet bobs' row; 'dry bobs' play hockey, fives, cricket or tennis in the summer term. Boathouse on the Thames is 10 minutes away and those wet bobs are usually up there with near neighbours Abingdon and rivals Eton and St Edward's during the Henley Regatta and head of the river competitions.

Twice weekly so-called 'minor sports' include swimming, golf (there's a course on site), fives, squash, real tennis, cross-country, rackets, tennis, badminton. Those who wish to can do a spot of beagling. Alternative sports programme (ASP) is a circus of different sports for boys (remove upwards) who don't take to rugby. Sixth formers can choose which sport they want to play.

Boarding: Boarding houses at Radley are known as 'Socials' and Socials are distinguished by letters of the alphabet (A Social, B Social and so on). First years ('shell') have curtained 'cubs' or cubicles with a sink and cabin bed. Apparently Radley was the instigator of this arrangement that affords pupils some degree of privacy within a dormitory. It caught on and can still be seen in many prep and senior boarding schools. From removes (second year) on, it's single study bedrooms. In typical boarding boy fashion these were all rather tidy, noticeboards generally unadorned by photos, posters and the like. Our guides told us they liked the busy, structured days at school and appreciated the relative freedom of home life all the more for it. 'We probably take Radley for granted,' one added.

Pupils' work, paintings, ceramics and photography not confined to art school – eerily lifelike papiermâché boys peer down from beams in the library

Boys may buy uniform, stationery, tuck etc in school's shop (known, wait for it, as 'Shop'). Card system for purchases in Shop or coffee shop; 'jam account' (upper limit of £60 per term) for tuck. One parent thought it was a shame there was no opportunity to buy second-hand uniform, sports kit etc.

'Oxford leave' allows boys (mostly sixth formers) to travel into Oxford (by bus or taxi). Upper sixth chaps may spend Saturday evenings there as long as they're back in Social by 10.30pm. Quite a restricted regime for boys of this age, although exeats and privis allow a few slightly longer Saturday nights out elsewhere.

Ethos and heritage: In the quartet of boys' full boarding schools (first violin Eton, second violin Winchester, cello Harrow), Radley would be the viola – less frequently played ('mystical' entrance requirements), smallish solo repertoire (690 boys), confident, necessary, but unflashy (low profile) and so on. It's also the newcomer, having been founded by Oxford Movement devotees, the Revs Sewell and Singleton, in 1847 to 'provide a public school education on the principles of the Church of England'.

The founding Revs organised their school along the lines of colleges at the University of Oxford, hence some of the nomenclature: warden, dons etc. Indeed, Radley still has that slightly separate feel of an Oxford college, enhanced by the sight of boys rushing to and fro, gowns billowing behind. Last vote saw proposal to do away with gowns defeated by 95 per cent. Daily choral services were, and remain, a key aspect of the school.

It was believed boys' minds and souls would be improved by learning in a beautiful rural setting and well-designed environment. Shades of William Morris perhaps. School motto is the succinct, Sicut Serpentes, Sicut Columbae ('Be ye wise as serpents, and harmless as doves'), and these creatures appear on the coat of arms – with the crossed keys of St Peter, to whom the college is dedicated, safely between them.

Radley College is neither overwhelmingly grand nor intimidating. Reception is small and unpretentious, seating would indicate that they do not expect more than three people to arrive at any one time. Reception staff friendly, but appeared to be fighting a losing battle to stop the office becoming overwhelmed by online delivery packages. 'Radley boys keep Amazon in business,' said a long-suffering voice from behind a pile of boxes.

School originally occupied the Mansion, an 18th-century house that belonged to the Stonehouse, then Bowyer families. This rather elegant building with grand panelled reception rooms is now home to admin and the warden's offices. Other parts are usual mix of charming and slightly less charming additions. Wide vistas, generous lawns and paths are another great advantage of a large, rural site. The grounds were by laid out by Capability Brown and some features of his design remain visible. Many trees, looking especially lovely on the golden autumn day of our visit. Immaculate pitches (delightful cricket pavilion) stretch into the distance.

Queen's Court (aka the Doughnut), opened by Her Majesty in 1997, may dominate aerial views of the college but we were rather taken with the inside, which seems to have stood the test of time. It's home to maths, economics, biology, geography and geology and the communal space outside the classrooms is full of fascinating natural history specimens and large tanks containing turtles, scorpions and cockroaches. Members of the animal society come here to get up close with reptiles and snakes, if not doves. New science block completed in 2019.

Rather sweet little handbook sent to boys before they join includes useful advice such as, 'Bring more tuck. Most don't bring enough'

Former pupils (ORs) include Andrew Motion, poet; Sir Clive Stafford Smith, human rights lawyer; Lord Wilson of Dinton, former cabinet secretary; Peter Cook, comedian; Sandy Nairne, former director of the National Portrait Gallery; Christopher Hibbert, historian; Ted Dexter, Andrew Strauss and Jamie Dalrymple, England cricketers; Sir Charlie Mayfield, chairman of John Lewis; Lord Wolfson, CEO of Next. And many other actors, writers, lawyers, engineers, sportsmen, clergymen and public servants of all kinds.

Pastoral care, inclusivity and discipline: The tutor (housemaster) is the key figure in a boy's life at Radley. He oversees the boys in his Social along with sub-tutors and pastoral housemistresses (PHMs) – the latter come in for particular praise from mothers of younger boys. Form masters monitor academic progress. Boys in the first two years also have a lower sixth mentor. Cocoa at 9pm every night is a chance for all the boys in a Social to meet up and chat about the day; this and other activities help blur year group hierarchies. Boys are expected to help with the running of their Social: shell do chores such as collecting post; sixth form house prefects supervise prep and bedtimes. Parents all praise dedication of Social staff and say that any enquiries are dealt with 'by return'; they also like the regular progress reports.

Two exeat weekends per term and boys earn 'privis' or privilege weekends for good behaviour, work etc. On 'Sunday outs' boys can go out with parents or a friend after chapel for the day. One mother lamented, 'My son doesn't take his privis, there's too much going on at school to miss.' Rather sweet little handbook sent to boys before they join includes useful advice such as, 'Bring more tuck. Most don't bring enough,' and, 'If you are lost, confused or unhappy don't be afraid to ask for help.' Information about who to ask (both in and outside college) and how to do this is also included.

School places great emphasis on tolerance, kindness and manners. Biggest crime, according to new boys' handbook is 'to be rude to a cleaner, a member of catering staff, the ladies who help you in Shop or any other member of the College staff.' This is not intended in a de haut en bas way – as the Warden says, 'We discourage any sense of entitlement or arrogance.'

School is keen to enhance the quality of social activities with girls' schools. Shell still get the chance to disco with the likes of Wycombe Abbey, but older boys now join girls from St Mary's Calne, Tudor Hall, Headington and St Helen and St Katharine for dinner and discussion or joint theatre trips.

Pupils and parents: The warden describes a Radleian as 'civilised, friendly and engaging, in short, good company' and all the boys we met lived up to his definition. He also debunks a commonly held myth (that may stem from former entrance procedure) that most boys are sons of former pupils. 'It's 15 per cent,' he told us. Seems that the lower sixth drama group we had spoken to where all but a couple were second or third generation Radleians was just a blip. 'Most people find out about us through word of mouth,' continued the warden. 'They've met and liked a Radleian at work or university and think of us as a possible school for their own son.'

Even so, the hour has arrived to tweak what school describes carefully as its 'cultural variety'. Don't expect a revolution, or a rainbow nation – it'll be a while before the grain of truth packs its bags and departs from school's nickname, 'Ra Ra' Radley. Change will happen, carefully, in Radley's own time, and it will most certainly be for the (even) better.

Money matters: Cheapest of the quartet (no viola jokes please) but there's barely a gnat's crotchet between them. Uniform requirements less painful on the purse – parents told us that suits, shirts etc can be bought from high street. Gowns aren't expensive and, look on the bright side, might save on jacket dry cleaning bills (and they cover books if it's raining, boys told us). Sports kit will cost you, but then it does everywhere. Lack of coffee shops (or indeed any shops) in immediate vicinity looks promising but remember the Amazon-overwhelmed reception desk...

Scholarships of up to 10 per cent off fees awarded annually at 13+ and can be topped up to 100 per cent with means-tested bursaries. Foundation awards enable boys from state system to attend a prep school for two years before admission. Armed Forces Fund provides assistance to boys from Forces families. All very clearly explained on school website.

The last word: In our last review we said that Radley was the connoisseurs' choice; this remains the case. Yes, it's traditional, but it's utterly unstuffy. Like the serpent and the dove in the coat of arms, respect for tradition lives harmoniously with tolerance, intellectual curiosity, humour and humanity. Radley provides boys with an immersive education of the highest quality and a strong moral and spiritual core.

Ryde School with Upper Chine

40

Queen's Road, Ryde, Isle of Wight PO33 3BE

01983 562229 | school.office@rydeschool.net | www.rydeschool.org.uk

Ages: 2.5 -18

Pupils: 801; sixth form: 158; Boarders: 53 full, 11 weekly/flexi

Fees: Day £7,935 – £14,190; Boarding £30,795 – £31,260 pa

Headmaster: Since 2013, Mark Waldron (40s). Previously head of the English College in Prague, deputy head of Sherborne, and taught at The Leys School and Radley College. Hard to imagine a better fit – he is impressive yet laid back, traditional yet progressive, and globally focused while never losing sight of the individuality of pupils that make up this enviable community of islanders. Pretty much sums up the school itself which (also thanks to him) is now a Round Square School. Ten out of 10 for listening skills too – not always a forte of headteachers (we forgive them because they're so used to commanding an audience), he practically invites interruption and interaction (even on a Zoom). 'I think he makes the school,' said a parent. 'He's pushed the school in a fantastic direction.' Another told us, 'He's open and honest and says when he doesn't know the answers.' About as hands-on as you can get – not only does he teach A level politics (having also taught German and maths in the past), but he also runs the Oxbridge entry course and even cooked Christmas lunch for all the boarders who stayed at school due to the travel restrictions during Covid. Never misses an opportunity to engage with parents either – via YouTube Q&A sessions during the pandemic which, by the way, they prepared for with a practice run before lockdown – 'They had a plan, it made all the difference,' said a grateful parent. With staff, his big thing is encouraging them to think about the potential for creative and independent thought when planning their lessons: could the lesson take place without the pupils? 'The school I took over was basically a non-selective grammar with aspirations to be the best school of the island – we've grown away from that into something much more creative,' he says. Doesn't give much away about his private life but has learned to sail since joining the school (as does everyone) and is a politics junkie and devotee of the races. Likes pub quizzes too.

Head of senior school since January 2020, Philip Moore, who joined Ryde School 2014 as deputy head (academic) before moving on to being head of junior school. Has been around the houses, having formerly been director of studies at Bilton Grange Prep School, Rugby and prior to that head of maths at Kimbolton in Cambridgeshire. Started his teaching career at St Columba's College, St Albans before taking up his first head of maths post in Norfolk. Studied maths at Hertfordshire and has a master's in education management from King's College London. Set up DofE in two schools and is currently a gold award leader.

Head of prep since January 2020, Ed Marsden, who has been at Ryde since 2016 and was previously deputy head (pastoral). Before that, head of boys' sport and geography at St Michael's Prep in Sevenoaks, Kent for nine years, and head of sport at the British School of Vila-Real (Spain). Studied sports science and exercise at Greenwich and a PGCE. His wife Georgina works in the learning support department; together they have two young sons, both at Ryde.

Head of Fiveways (nursery and pre-prep) since 2017, Emily Willetts, previously at Llandaff Cathedral School, Cardiff and as head of lower school at Riverside International School, Prague. Married to Jim who is head of RS in the senior school and together they have two children in the prep with another new baby, born in 2020. Studied music at Durham, taking on the role of chapel warden for her college, Hild Bede, as well as earning a choral scholarship at the college during her three years there.

There was a huge basin of conkers in the science lab – year 3s were finding out whether size and shape have an impact on strength

Entrance: Non-selective (head prefers 'all ability'). Main entry points are 4+, 11+, 13+ and 16+ though increasingly at other points too (the year before we visited, they'd had newbies join in every single year group). From year 5 upwards, there's testing in English, maths and non-verbal reasoning – 'a basic hurdle not to try and catch children out but to ensure we can offer a curriculum to suit them,' says head. Interview with head for all; IQ test for those for whom English is not first language. Around 10-15 join at sixth form – criteria are the same as for current pupils (at least five GCSEs with 6s in the subjects to be studied).

Exit: Over 90 per cent go through from the prep to the senior school, the rest increasingly to Winchester and Millfield (usually on academic and sport scholarships respectively). Just over a quarter leave after GCSEs. The majority of sixth formers to university (a quarter to Russell Group). Exeter and Southampton popular ('They want to move away from the island, but not the sea,' says head), with Bath and Bristol also featuring. One to Oxbridge in 2021 and three medics. A few to art colleges.

Latest results: In 2021, 57 per cent 9-7 at GCSE; 58 per cent A*/A at A level (86 per cent A*-B). Average IB score 37. In 2019 (the last year when exams took place), 41 per cent 9-7 at GCSE; 25 per cent A*/A at A level. Average IB score of 33.

Teaching and learning: Good solid academic results for a non-selective school, which parents say gives a 'degree of assurance'. Mix of GCSEs and IGCSEs, and they also run the vocational IB (IBCP) alongside the IB. It is in the privileged position of being virtually the only independent mainstream school on the island (the other is very small), and island state secondary schools do not rank highly in the league tables.

Children from nursery to year 2 are taught at Fiveways, a separate campus across the road. Mixed ability classes of 14-16, though teachers will hand out work of differing levels within classes. Pupils read with a teacher or teaching assistant every day. For all that, a surprisingly small library. Mandarin taught weekly. Parents couldn't say enough about how great this part of the school is.

Prep school, covering years 3 to 6, is on the main site, though distinctly separate. Two or three classes a year, size 14-18. Spanish from year 3, Latin from year 5. Setting in maths and English from year 4. There was a huge basin of conkers in the science lab when we visited – year 3s were finding out whether size and shape have an impact on strength in a very joyful conkers experiment. STEM is a growing focus. A nice emphasis on creativity too – not always the case in through schools with an eye on the end results – year 4 write a story or poem every week, and after their trip to the Amazon World, wrote stories about the Amazon in geography. Plenty of monitoring and the school will do everything and anything to help children falling behind.

In senior school, maximum class sizes of 22 at GCSE and 8-14 at A level. As with prep, there is a strong work ethic – the classes we saw were almost universally heads down, working hard, the concentrated effort almost palpable. 'It's not something that you get teased for – it's actually cool to be clever,' said a pupil. Setting in French, maths, English and science from year 7. Maths and science are popular – due in part, says the head, to the large number of doctor parents; and illustrated by year 10 turning the whole periodic table into cupcakes in the school bake-off. The head has come from a school where students were studying in their third or fourth language, and firmly subscribes to the saying 'if you only speak one language then you can only live one life'. From year 7, all learn French plus either German or Mandarin (in addition to the Spanish and Latin that are introduced in prep). Everyone takes at least one language at GCSE, with a quarter doing two or more. Italian and Dutch are available at 16+.

Roof terrace in the art block with lovely view out over the sea – it's made full use of for parties – and a few beds of weeds which apparently have an eco purpose

Alongside GCSEs pupils study one of global perspectives, arts award, science CREST award or informatics. This emphasis on enrichment and a global perspective is woven throughout the school. It is not unusual, for example, to see pupils collaborating with students across the world – during lockdown, year 9s had regular online seminars with home working boarders, swapping information about daily life. Teamwork, reflective learning, independent research and presentation skills are also biggies here. Particularly popular is the mini-EPQ in years 7 and 8 – one group of pupils had used theirs to work out how to renovate Ryde's theatre for full use with the island, while older students had just presented their findings on how the (presumably very happy) bursar could save money on water bills. Up until exams hit, pupils are encouraged to take risks in their learning and you are left in no doubt that they leave armed with the kinds of skills employers genuinely want.

Nine or 10 I/GCSEs is the norm, with creative subjects attracting high numbers – around half take DT, a reflection perhaps of island industries. At A level (half the pupils take these; the rest do IB), three subjects plus an EPQ is the norm (or four minus the EPQ if they're doing further maths), with all doing an elective IB standard level or enrichment subject such as sports leadership ('to balance out the workload with the IB pupils,' explains head).

Parents receive mini monthly report cards detailing effort and progress until GCSE, when this turns into attainment, and predicted and target grades – to flag up any problems with work. Focus on praising effort: merit badges worn on blazers, like awards for courage under fire, are awarded entirely for effort. When the school as a whole has achieved 2,000 efforts there's a mufti day.

Learning support and SEN: Shared SENCo for whole school 'to ensure good continuity between prep and senior school', with provision offered both inside and outside the classroom. Around 15 per cent of pupils here have special needs, all mild to moderate. Support for English and maths is available as separate curriculum subjects alongside GCSE options. All included in fees.

The arts and extracurricular: Music is super here – our tour guides, neither of whom were taking music A level, said their happiest hours at school were spent in the music block. The teaching inspires a real love of music, with a new music teacher from Manhattan having brought a more contemporary feel, while not losing sight of the classics. Around a third of pupils learn an instrument and there are all the usual choirs, orchestra, ensembles etc. A poignant moment for the school was the music concert in March 2020 as it was the final school event before lockdown. Everyone looks forward to the annual outdoor concert and there's an annual music tour, most recently to Croatia and northern Italy.

Pupils relish the joys of the annual Global Rock – an international dance competition.

They put together routines and costumes themselves; parents describe the results as 'incredible'. Separate annual drama productions for senior (most recently Les Mis) and prep (most recently Bugsy Malone) are both highlights of the school year. New head of drama ensured productions continue during lockdown.

Grand DT and art rooms in the predominantly glass block. 'If I get them in year 7, they stay,' said the DT teacher with a smile; and indeed both our guides expressed huge enthusiasm for the subject, and remembered with affection their first task of designing an insect in year 7. Roof terrace with lovely view out over the sea – it's made full use of for parties – and a few beds of weeds which apparently have an eco purpose.

Very high take-up for DofE – school proud to have continued bronze, silver and gold in the July of lockdown. CCF available. Full range of clubs – everything from the usual sport and music options to quirkier croquet (school made it to the national finals) and beekeeping. Growth in more intellectual clubs and societies such as diplomacy (which the head runs) and bridge. Model United Nations has become increasingly student led, with some lively mock elections. Trips include sports tours to eg South Africa, Malta and Argentina; annual ski trips for juniors (with parents – very popular); and senior and geography trips to Iceland. Round Square School status has led to lots of exciting exchange potential, with plans for Tanzania, Germany, Colombia and South Africa.

Light touch discipline. The one student who was suspended during Covid was asked to come into school – 'How else do you suspend a pupil during lockdown?'

Sport: Emphasis is on participation. But while in the past this meant it was not an obvious choice for top sportsmen or women, there are now more elite pathways too. Sailing, as you'd expect, is huge – by year 7, everyone gets the chance to reach level 1/2 and the pupil body includes some international sailors from eg Germany and Thailand, as well as UK. Rugby, hockey, netball and cricket are the other main sports but although cricket for girls is on the up, everyone agrees there is some way to go with the girls' rugby (at least it exists, though – more than can be said for many schools). Easier than it used to be to find schools to play against, eg Portsmouth and Gosport, and they play an annual cricket match against a school in Guernsey. Particular success in golf. New netball coach recently joined – 'I'm looking forward to seeing the impact on fixtures,' says head.

Boarding: Nearly all boarding is now on site – a big change since our last visit. Millfield is a refurbished Victorian villa that opened in 2020. Home to around 30 boarders in years 7-10 (well, year 6 too, but hardly anyone does board from prep), there are two to three pupils to a room. Even newer (April 2021) is the purpose-built new boarding house (no name yet) for 60 year 11-13s, with Solent views and ensuites (upper sixths get single rooms, lower sixth and year 11s get twin rooms). There's a third small house, Spinnaker, a pre-university Georgian townhouse in Ryde for 10-12 sixth formers who want a more independent light-touch boarding vibe, though they will need to get used to doing their own ironing and washing – 'My son absolutely loved getting more freedom and it was great to see him encouraged to be more self-sufficient,' a parent told us.

Lots of confidence from parents regarding the boarding set up. They told us their boarding offspring are happy and that any minor issues arising are dealt with successfully. There's a very strong sense of community and good diversity too, with a carefully maintained split of a third Asian pupils, a third from UK and the final third a combination of European and north American.

There's an informal feel to boarding – it's run by a young cohort of staff, including a lovely Argentinian couple who whisk pupils off to sports events across the island. Boarders set up their own clubs – cheesy Tuesdays (the cheese on toast club) and the Coco Pops club – foodie clubs popular for obvious reasons. They make good use of the kitchen facilities, and can cook as they please – there's plenty of fruit and cereal available at all times, and a Tesco run every Friday night (no energy drinks allowed).

Ethos and heritage: A school surrounded by stunning scenery – how lovely to sit in the library and stare out at the picture postcard view over the sea. Venerable main building with nondescript (but well cared-for) adjuncts. Lots of recent upgrading including new classrooms, gym, tennis and netball courts and a new coffee shop for parents. A new performing arts centre is due in 2022. The advantages of attending school on the island are clear – it is safe, secure and beautiful. The counter to this is perhaps an element of complacency born of isolation. But all agree the head has done a great job of ensuring pupils are not limited by the stretch of water.

The junior school is on the main school campus, a cluster of unremarkable buildings to one side – nicely kept and feels safe and secure;

Papplewick School

definitely separate from the senior part of things. Reasonable size library, where pupils can do prep after school. Not loads of room to run around at break time (year 6s look forward to using senior school playing fields), and the children would like a bit more interest in their playground. Fiveways is located over the road.

A traditional environment – although surprisingly pupils are allowed to use mobile phones in class for task-related research. CofE but with a light touch – close links with All Saints church, with vicar the school chaplain. Prayers at the end of assembly, because that's just what happens; much like a full stop at the end of a sentence. Parents are happy with communication levels, and reaction to complaints (which are rare). Uniform is the usual fare.

The headmaster is about as hands-on as you can get – not only does he teach A level politics, but he also runs the Oxbridge entry course and even cooked Christmas lunch for all the boarders who stayed at school due to the travel restrictions during Covid

Pupils are friendly and polite (although this is not a leap to your feet place) and clearly enjoy being at school – one who transferred to Ryde from a local school commented how good it is to be at a school where he actually wants to stay and do activities, just because it's nice to be there.

Pastoral care, inclusivity and discipline: Parents view the pastoral care at Ryde as exceptional and describe the advantages of a small school where staff know all the pupils and their families. Community and family are important words here, with one parent from prep telling us how a teacher delivered a birthday cake to her daughter during lockdown and another called in to check a pupil was okay when her pet died. The new health and wellbeing centre is well used and we love how most staff are trained coaches. 'We used to be told we do a great job at putting people back on together when they fall apart, and the coaching is a pre-emptive pastoral measure to help stop them falling apart in the first place,' explains head. In a nutshell, it means working with pupils to ensure they start from the heart, then get pragmatic and reflective in working towards their own solutions with guidance. Some of the staff are now qualified to train others in coaching, with the courses for parents on eg how to speak to your teenage child, having been a huge hit. There is a move to involve sixth formers more with younger years, and prefects now wear listener badges, so pupils have an obvious person to go to if they want to talk to someone other than a teacher. Any bullying occurs is dealt with properly – 'sensitively and appropriately,' said a parent. Mindfulness walks, bee hives, an outdoor yurt and a Victory Garden – where pupils grow vegetables for the school kitchen – recently introduced.

Light touch discipline, with a largely well-behaved pupil body that responds well to the relaxed feel of the school. Perhaps more tolerant than other schools with trying to work things out when they go wrong, though head has asked people to leave for eg bullying and drugs. 'I believe people deserve a second chance, but I'm less forgiving the second time,' he says. The one student who was suspended during Covid was asked to come into school – 'How else do you suspend a pupil during lockdown?' he said. Well, quite.

Pupils and parents: Parents range from fish and chip shop owners to medics. Large numbers scrimp and save to send their children here. They come from all over the island, along with commuters (by ferry) from Portsmouth and a growing number (especially since lockdown) of DFLs (Down From London's). The islanders in particular are a sociable bunch – school even ran an online cocktail party for them during lockdown. Two-thirds of boarders are international. Pupils we met were polite and articulate, although they didn't quite have the polish you might encounter in some mainland independent schools – the relaxed vibe rubs off.

Money matters: Head decidedly unimpressed with the trend towards independent schools becoming ever more inaccessible to the 'squeezed middle'. Wants to keep fees affordable and provides support where possible. Scholarships open up means-tested bursaries. Academic scholarships are available for entry into years 5, 7, 9 and the sixth form with sailing, music and sports scholarships also available for entry into years 7, 9 and the sixth form. McIsaac scholarships also available and some HMC scholars are placed at Ryde.

The last word: A school distinguished by its strong community, set in beautiful surroundings with solid academic provision. Last time we visited, we said it was not somewhere you are likely to encounter unscheduled exuberance – no longer the case. 'This is a place where everyone has a chance to be themselves – what more can you ask for?' said a parent.

Rye St Antony School

Pullen's Lane, Oxford OX3 0BY

01865 762802 | info@ryestantony.co.uk | www.ryestantony.co.uk

Ages: Girls 3-19, boys 3-11

Pupils: 287; sixth form: 35; Boarders: 20 full

Fees: Day £10,275 – £17,055; Boarding £25,200 – £29,415pa

Head: Since February 2020, Joanne (Jo) Croft. Previously deputy head, head of sixth form and head of languages, having been at Rye for 17 years before getting the governors' nod. Had always aspired to it, 'though I never thought it would happen here' – but when her predecessor stepped down at short notice, 'I thought, "OK, I can do something really good here for the school."' Spontaneous pupil applause when she announced the news in assembly that morning; parents feel it was a good decision, that 'she'd earned her stripes'.

'I'm happy to throw my hands in, I don't want to be stuck in an office'. True to her word, she's out in the car park every morning greeting pupils, busy and visible around the school. We got the sense that she really cares, and pupils clearly feel it too, happily popping into her office for a chat (and the pastries). Office decorated with pupil artwork (including hand-painted lampshade) – de rigueur, of course, but Miss Croft unusually excited to share the stories behind each piece. Not a Catholic herself, 'but you don't need a faith to show respect, dignity, tolerance'.

Very positive about the school's place in the market. It hasn't been an easy time for Rye – very long-standing head Miss Jones ('cult-like status'; 'Rye's Alex Ferguson', we heard) retired in 2018. 'Always a dangerous tipping point', parents point out. Successor was not the right fit, by all accounts. Thus Miss Croft found herself as head quite suddenly in February 2020, and we all know what came next, don't we? Microsoft Teams set up 'in hours', say parents – 'they didn't miss a beat'. Boarding numbers fell as international travel dried up. The change of leadership created staff turnover, always noticeable in a small environment. Miss Croft has 'responded magnificently' to the various obstacles she's faced, say parents, and certainly things felt stable when we visited.

One objective is to modernise, albeit sensitively. Processes and systems being put in place to ensure consistency in terms of pupil experience and to make things a bit more streamlined and efficient – spreadsheets seem to be a relatively new concept at Rye. A 'bit more health and safety than there used to be', we also hear from sceptical parents. Long-standing families miss the old 'eccentricity – it was a bit wacky' but recognise that there's a balance to tread between maintaining traditions and ensuring that Rye can compete in increasingly challenging times for the independent sector.

Lives outside Oxford (as do most staff). Devoted to all things French and Italian, and to travel generally. On a mission to see the northern lights: 'I went to the darkest depths of Svalbard and still didn't catch them!' Easy company, straightforward, warm – we can see why the community has welcomed her into the post so readily.

Head of prep (since January 2021), Mrs Alexandra Prockter. Previously deputy head of lower school at Harrow International School, Bangkok.

Entrance: For nursery and 4+ entrance, a visit and registration form; for older prep students a taster day too. Gently selective at 11+ upwards with papers in maths and English, group activities and interview; GCSE predictions and interview at 16+. Reference from current school for every age group.

Exit: Boys leave at 7+, 8+, 11+ to Oxford preps or all-throughs including Abingdon and Magdalen College School. Year 13 destinations vary from year to year: Cardiff, UWE Bristol, Oxford Brookes, Bristol, UCL all popular. UCAS support bespoke and practical rather than sausage-factory. None to Oxbridge in recent years.

Latest results: In 2021, 64 per cent 9-7 at GCSE; 77 per cent A*/A at A level (89 per cent A*-B). In 2019 (the last year when exams took place), 39 per cent 9-7 at GCSE: 18 per cent A*/A at A level (38 per cent A*-B).

Teaching and learning: 'The Rye Way', as the school terms it, creates 'resilient young people with a positive outlook'. 'We are building more challenge into what we do day-to-day,' says head, though nothing cut-throat – teaching nurtures pupils' self-esteem rather than battering it. In a landscape crowded with big names (or hothouses, according to many Rye parents), we were struck by Rye's confidence in not being all about grades – 'it's not about the stream of 9s and A*s', says head, though she does want 'our girls to be going out and winning competitions – seize Oxfordshire first, then the world'. 'Pupils get brilliant grades, but percentages don't look as impressive as elsewhere because they take a broader ability range', one mum wisely points out.

Nursery and reception have French, PE, music, drama all taught by specialists. Weekly Forest School. Rye Bear Nursery up a narrow staircase – train and hot air balloon murals say, 'little people, come this way', but it's not the most child-friendly of approaches. Some discussion of moving nursery downstairs to facilitate indoor-outdoor flow and interaction with reception – this would improve things. Wraparound care from 7.30am until 6pm for nursery to year 6.

'We are building more challenge into what we do day-to-day,' says head, though nothing cut-throat – teaching nurtures pupils' self-esteem rather than battering it

New 'booked-based' curriculum for KS1 and KS2. Enquiry-led, topic-driven – all very 'now' and encourages joined-up thinking. Year 6 read 'Journey to Jo'burg', study the ancient kingdom of Benin and discuss issues around refugees in their enquiry about freedoms. Prep classrooms in their own zone (except year 6, located in a different building) though in reality it's all on a small scale and felt quite integrated to us. 'We see the little ones around the whole time', older students told us, and they share music and sports facilities. Boys prepare for 11+ (though most have moved on by year 6, it seems) while the majority of girls will stay – parents we spoke to reported no awkwardness around this.

Onwards to senior school, where broad range of GCSEs includes business studies, graphic communication, food and nutrition, computer science, drama and music. RS compulsory. Sixth form choices equally varied – business BTEC and psychology alongside the usual suspects. As ever in a small school, some classes end up being tiny, but parents and pupils have actively chosen this intimate, safe environment and recognise that it's the compromise that has to be made. Sixth form retention always an issue in this kind of set-up: a big focus for new head of sixth form, who describes the offering as 'like entering a tailors: we can design the programme around you'. Pupils can take two creative subjects at A level, 'if we've had that discussion about going on to foundation art' and if parents are on the same page. Library light and welcoming with lots of space to browse, work and chill (though empty when we visited other than a teacher getting on with some marking).

Lots of sixth formers take Leith's course in food and wine. Modern, business-like approach to food and nutrition – not a doily in sight and lots of talk of marketing, food science and product development. GCSE foodies were making 'bomboloni' (Italian filled doughnuts, to the uninitiated) when we poked our heads in – we were amazed that they weren't already licking the bowls but were instead getting on with it conscientiously.

Parents feel that teachers are available and easy-going – 'they're friendly, with an 'I'm a normal person' manner'. A mixture of some very experienced staff and others who are younger. Lots are recent additions.

Learning support and SEN: Learning support up in the eaves ('there are lots of stairs – are you sure?', warns our guide). A thoughtful set-up, once you've got your breath back: small classrooms for group work and a warm snug for counsellor sessions complete with comfy sofa and throws. Careful consideration goes into applications from girls with SEN – 'we need to be able to deliver for the individual,' says school, and they will be honest if they feel they cannot support your child's needs. Inclusivity appreciated by parents, who say that school is 'respectful', 'totally accommodating' and will give 'all the time and support that you ask for'.

The arts and extracurricular: A warren of art rooms, with dedicated spaces for years 12 and 13. Sixth formers beavering away on the computers were happy to chat to us but equally keen to get on with the task in hand. Photography studio with dark room. Year 6 pottery lined up ready for the kiln; brightly-coloured still lifes on display. Purpose-built drama studio has lighting rig that pupils can operate themselves; music rooms busy, violins and ukuleles lying about the place. Not the swankiest arts facilities, but all feels welcoming and well-loved. Lots of excitement around upcoming production of Into the Woods, to be performed alongside prep school fairytale mashups. Major production annually.

Girls taking the initiative with charity work more than previously, getting their hands a bit dirtier. Plans to get out into the community

Lots of excitement around upcoming production of Into the Woods, to be performed alongside prep school fairytale mash-ups

more – 'rather than raising the money, let's go and work there, serve at the food kitchens', says head – particularly at the Porch Day Centre, a homeless shelter with whom the school has links.

Sport: Not particularly sporty – tricky with small numbers – though, as one grateful mum puts it, 'they make you be active however much you feel like not being active'. Focus on lifelong fitness rather than team glory. Hockey, netball, tennis, athletics, rounders, badminton all on offer, plus riding, dance, swimming, rowing. Playing field, full-size Astro, sports hall, heated pool, fitness studio onsite. Victory never taken for granted and success varies between year groups, though they do get some great results: third place in recent U15 hockey tournament ('you've done really well – now, what can we do to get first next year?', said Miss Croft); parents satisfied that girls recently 'trounced' more glamorous rival school 'on their own posh floodlit court'.

Boarding: Boarders have their own front door to the boarding area to encourage a sense of coming home in the evenings. Well-maintained courtyard garden with a pretty fountain – table and chairs for al fresco living when it's warm; fairy lights for winter evenings. 'Boarder of the week' an effective pat on the back and encourages those who need a boost. Common room is 50 shades of brown, but the pile of well-thumbed novels in the corner, power-hockey table and blackboard on which somebody had written 'I heart U' all suggest that the girls have a nice time in there. Small kitchen doesn't get used much – boarders well catered for in dining room downstairs.

Bustling activities programme – we were disappointed to have missed Thorpe Park, campfire fun, laser quest and 'Boarders Got Talent'. A different activity every Saturday and Sunday – compulsory to sign up for at least one each weekend. Optional weekday activities run on a timetable – 'nobody's signed up for my knitting!', bemoans housemistress, but lots get involved in arts and crafts, fitness and prayers and reflection. A low-key, unpressured boarding environment which offers a home-from-home feel. A few local girls will do flexi or occasional boarding: 'the odd night of Malory Towers is really fun', says a local parent.

Ethos and heritage: A lay Catholic establishment (no monks or nuns to be seen) and fewer than a quarter of pupils are Catholic – so yes, a Catholic school, but at the relaxed end of the spectrum. Display in the library wished us a 'Happy Hannukah!' as we arrived; prayer room set aside in boarding house for Muslim girls. Assembly hall set up for advent when we visited – candles, purple cloth, little nativity set but nothing in-yer-face. Established by Oxford teachers (and Catholic converts) Elizabeth Rendall and Ivy King in 1930, who were apparently so inspired by a visit to the Church of St Anthony in Rye, Sussex ('a little gem of magnificent beauty', says its own website), that they returned to Oxford and founded a school in its name (almost – history doesn't relate the dropping of the 'h'). A family vibe – the great-great-niece of one of the founders recently got in touch to say 'hi'.

Started life at a small house in Summertown, then a bigger one on Woodstock Road before moving to the current site in 1939. Sits in 12 charming acres of Headington, a stone's throw from the hospital and the busy high street but you wouldn't know it sitting in the peaceful wooded gardens. Calming, campus-like feel, all nicely organised and well-kempt. Based around two sensible 19th century red-brickers called The Croft and Langley Lodge, originally occupied by an Oxford don and a publisher respectively, back in the good old days when dons and publishers could afford Oxford property. Everything feels safe, solid, a tad institutional (you know those dropped ceilings with the square tiles?) but in a reassuring way.

A school with a sense of fun and 'a really positive attitude to being silly,' according to parents. Christmas a big deal: Christmas jumpers, dodgy cracker jokes, pantomime, nativity, you name it... 'raucous' tangerine party involves huge Christmas cake, cut by the youngest and oldest pupils, and lots of singing, every year group taking a line from '12 days of Christmas' with 'five gold rings' reserved for year 13, obviously. Last year they even hired a snow machine – 'it fused immediately', laughs Miss Croft.

Pastoral care, inclusivity and discipline: 'Be well, do well', runs one school mantra. 'Covid has reinforced the importance of wellbeing and the individual', says head, 'parents know we're good at pastoral care'. We came across lots of pupils who had come from bigger schools where they'd felt lost in the crowd or found the atmosphere too rough-and-tumble. Parents praise 'brilliant communication' and the sense of working as a tight team with staff when things get tough – 'they have been utterly brilliant', said one. Will build whatever support is needed around the child, involving outside organisations (eg CAMHS) as appropriate. All-through structure lends itself to pastoral care. 'We get to know the children so well, their interests, what motivates them', says head of prep. Year 13s listen to prep pupils read; year 12s help out with their art classes. Vertical houses mean that events are mixed: think teenagers in the throes of adolescence cheering on five-year-olds in the sack race.

Long tables in dining hall, big jugs of water and the words of the grace on the wall, said together by younger pupils before they tuck in. Sixth formers have separate lunch space (used by boarders for breakfast and supper) – round tables and fresh flowers give an air of sophistication. Food less sophisticated – 'not dreadful, but a constant complaint', says one parent – with limited options, though we heard that girls have a good relationship with eating, reinforced by effective PSHE curriculum.

Established by Oxford teachers (and Catholic converts) Elizabeth Rendall and Ivy King in 1930, who were so inspired by a visit to the Church of St Anthony in Rye, Sussex ('a little gem of magnificent beauty'), that they returned to Oxford and founded a school in its name

'God gives our pupils their talents', staff say, 'and our job is to nurture those talents'. A beautiful pair of portraits hanging in the corridor are by 'a girl who came to us as an athlete and left as an athlete and an artist', having discovered a gift that she never knew she had. Rye girls getting feistier, more determined. Miss Croft leads the way on this: 'being ambitious is really important – if somebody says you can't, go out and do it'. 'Girls are empowered to thrive in STEM subjects here', says a teacher; recent sixth form mug-decorating session saw one girl covering hers in complicated-looking formulae.

No staff attend school council – 'it's great for the children to have that open voice' and for head girl team to learn 'how to negotiate, delegate, manage those difficult conversations'. Increasingly confident, happy to express themselves. What about when this gets targeted at peers? Fallings out over eg Young Enterprise ('nobody likes my idea!') build resilience, school says, and anyway there are remarkably few bust-ups. Parents say that dramas do happen, quite regularly ('it's natural, right?'), but that girls encouraged to talk to each other and rebuild bridges.

Everyone's Invited followed up in PSHE; girls felt safe to respond individually. Links with local boys' schools have dropped (partly Covid, partly other schools going co-ed); school recognises the need to revive them. Lots of pupils questioning sexuality, gender, identity – pupils and parents seem unfazed by it but feel that school errs towards conservatism, unsurprisingly given relationship with the diocese. 'I get a sense that the ethos of care and concern is genuine, though', says one parent.

Small cohorts ensure that there's little room for manoeuvre, behaviour-wise, but we didn't feel there was much of an appetite for rebellion anyway. Uniform and day-to-day discipline have got tighter in recent years ('Miss Jones was more relaxed about how long your skirt was or the colour of your hair bobble' says an old-timer). School told us that 'alcohol, drugs, vaping are not part of the culture here', though parents suggested that girls have a healthy social life, lots of house parties, not over-squeaky. Plenty of good clean fun too – sleepovers, shopping, cinema trips etc.

Pupils and parents: Some pupils have jobs outside school to earn a bit of extra pocket money, and we got the impression that many families are dual-income, though there's some serious cash around too. Majority at the school gate are mums rather than nannies, some dads too. A sociable school and a small community: parents buy into the ethos and come together often, perhaps unusually so in the senior years where this tends to tail off at other schools. 'We really missed it during lockdown', said one mum. Tea on the lawn a particular highlight – proper traditional stuff with sandwiches and scones.

Money matters: Can give means-tested bursaries and considering how to develop this offering further. Patsy Sumpter Scholarship is awarded at 16+ for girls who excel in the humanities.

The last word: 'Be ambitious, be curious, be yourself', reads the school's strapline. We saw girls and boys being all three in this straightforward, loving little school where academic success is not incompatible with happiness. Comfortable, relaxed teenage girls are not two-a-penny in these parts, but Rye seems to have cracked it: girls can explore the world and work out who they are with a safety blanket in place should they need it. Relatively under the radar until now, but Miss Croft is determined to spread the word. Watch this space.

St Andrew's School

Buckhold, Pangbourne, Reading, Berkshire RG8 8QA

0118 974 4276 | taylorj@standrewspangbourne.co.uk | www.standrewspangbourne.co.uk

Ages: 3-13

Pupils: 307; Boarders: 20 (Monday-Thursday)

Fees: Day £11,670 – £19,575 pa; Flexi boarding + £3,750pa

Linked school: Bradfield College, 353

Head Master: Since September 2021, Ed Graham, previously deputy head at Westminster Cathedral Choir School in London. During his nine years there, he was head of English, head of sport, led on pastoral provision, and taught history and ancient Greek. Married to Olivia, with two children, both in the pre-prep.

Entrance: Mainly from local nurseries and primary schools or families relocating from London. Admissions ethos couldn't be simpler: St Andrew's is 'a family school which offers places to children who will be happy and thrive academically'. That all sounds lovely but remember, it's also a popular school that receives many more applications than it has places. Main points of entry are at ages 3 (the half term of their third birthday), 4 and 7 although places may become available in other years. Younger children invited to spend a taster session in the school; older children spend a taster day and sit 'short' informal tests. Priority given to siblings and children of former pupils.

In 2021, the school joined Bradfield College to establish the Bradfield Group – the two schools, which are just two miles apart, have long shared close ties and the idea is to share expertise, strategic thinking and deliver greater cost efficiencies. Each school will retain its individual identity but be overseen by a combined governing body. Parents can expect additional investment in St Andrew's facilities eg there are plans to transform the Old Hall into a contemporary, performing arts centre, and develop the boarding provision.

Exit: Mainly all over (the home counties). Co-eds Bradfield College and Pangbourne scoop up the majority. The odd one to Shiplake College, St Edward's Oxford, Queen Anne's Caversham, Canford, Abingdon, Marlborough and Radley. School says it loses 'a few' girls to day schools at age 11 but can sometimes arrange 'deferred places'. Good spread of academic, sport and music scholarships.

Our view: St Andrew's motto is Altiora Petimus ('we seek higher things') and this is certainly the case as one ascends the steep hills of the Thames valley in search of the small village of Buckhold. School occupies a rather delicious Gothic revival pile designed for Herbert Watney (of the brewing family) by Alfred Waterhouse, better known as architect of the National History Museum. Not all parts of the school building are by him – no prizes for guessing those in which he didn't have a hand. Lawns roll down to meadows and woodland, in total 54 acres of greenest Berkshire, where Buckhold birds do their best to drown out the persistent hum of the M4 – a reminder that less pastoral regions (Reading and Newbury) are close by.

Not a school with ancient lineage, it opened in 1934 under joint heads. Two heads may be better than one but this was somewhat over specified considering the inaugural page of the register runs to eight boys. First girls were admitted in 1971. At just over 300 pupils it's comfortably full yet with room for some growth. Parents will be relieved; several told us that they chose the school for its size. 'We looked at bigger preps but felt that our child might get lost.'

Our visit started with a walk through the dining room, worth a visit if Royal Doulton tiled panels are your thing (they are ours). Then it was out and over to the cluster of modern buildings housing nursery and pre-prep. Up to year 2 children are taught by stage, not age, we were told as we tiptoed past a group working hard on their phonics. Adaptable multi-purpose conservatory with small cookery area was lovely and bright (though we wondered if it didn't get a little warm in summer). Specialist teachers for French, music, PE and swimming. Parents told us that pre-prep was 'on top' of the basics such as reading, spelling and times tables and aimed to get these 'out of the way' before move to prep.

Some parts of the pre-prep looked in need of a revamp, but they've done a grand job with a lovely new adventure playground. Future plans include opening up the reception class and extending the indoor/outdoor space with a canopy.

Some of the forest schools we've seen stretch the conventional meaning of the word 'forest', but with 50 bosky acres St Andrew's isn't one of them and outdoor activities, rain or shine, have always been a big part of the school day – whether it's collecting bundles of 10 sticks for maths or going on a 'shape hunt'. Each child plants a tree on arrival and sees it grow as they move through the school. All-in-one waterproofs and wellies hang in the cloakroom and get a lot of use. 'We love the fact that children can play and explore in the grounds. They're encouraged to be bold and enjoy the freedom.'

Outdoor activities, rain or shine, have always been a big part of the school day – whether it's collecting bundles of 10 sticks for maths or going on a 'shape hunt'

Independence is the aim and even the youngest are expected to dress themselves, use knives and forks and pour their own milk or juice at break; some parents take a little convincing, especially if they have to wash the aftermath. We loved the noticeboard in the nursery cloakroom which had a filthy shirt pinned to it with labels pointing to each stain reading, 'I'm sorry that my uniform got dirty today but this shows that I have been learning x.'

After-school provision has been beefed up for all age groups. Equestrian skills are honed at the next-door stables. The summer bike ride club has been a huge success: 'We weren't sure if parents would want to bring their children's bikes into school, but they love it.' (Preponderance of 4x4s may be a factor.) Pupils learn cycling safety via the 'bikeability' scheme and the course culminates in an Enid Blyton style group ride and picnic.

We came across a group of pupils (according to our notes they were all called Daisy, Harriet or Freddie, but surely that can't be right) enjoying their morning break 'squash and bs (biscuits)' outside and conducted a quick vox pop. What did they like about their school? 'We have two breaks every day and you can climb trees, it's just amazing.' 'Everyone can be in a team; no one is left out. And everybody cheers.'

Next stop was year 5 history and pupils arrived, sorted out their seats and were ready to work in double quick time. It was an enjoyable, pacy lesson based around interpreting portraits and every pupil got to contribute their ideas. Teaching style seems to be fun – hands on with lots of activities and trips – but also rigorous. None of the parents we spoke to thought it was an academically pushy school, instead they used words like 'intense' and 'thorough'. Science labs are pretty trad, with specimens in glass cases and stuffed alligators; pupils told us that they really enjoyed all the practical work. Latin recently introduced to year 5s, and together with year 6s, they are now given senior school preparation lessons – verbal/non-verbal reasoning, team building, interview skills etc.

Learning skills (no longer known as learning support, 'everybody decided on the name change') steps in quickly if necessary, whether for short-term confidence building or extended help for pupils with mild SEN such as dyslexia. Focus is on individual, rather than group, work and the approach is holistic – children are taught relaxation techniques and staff are vigilant for signs of stress. Parents say homework 'not excessive, just a bit of reading or spelling until year 6, unless there's a test coming up'.

'We're quite sporty,' a pupil told us, modestly. In fact St Andrew's, though small, is a big player. Hockey was described to us by one parent as 'phenomenal' – recent achievements include girls' team getting to the national finals and boys' team winning the county championships. School orienteering team are also national champions. Swimming, tennis, lacrosse and equestrian also enthusiastically and successfully pursued. One of our guides was glad she could now play cricket instead of rounders but thought that girls should also get a chance to play rugby (not yet on the cards). Fantastic new sports centre with swimming pool and climbing wall.

Drama lessons, now on the curriculum, take place in the rather small studio – lots of lighting equipment but no actual stage. After-school drama club is popular and there are regular productions (performed in sports hall). Pupils may work towards the LAMDA grades and several have won drama scholarships to senior school.

While drama may be playing catch up, music at St Andrews is in a class (in fact a music block) of its own. A quick look at the noticeboards revealed three recent grade 8s and even a diploma, not to mention a range of individual instrumental lessons that started with bagpipes and, for all we know, ends with xylophone. Three choirs (plus one in pre-prep), a full orchestra, a string orchestra, big band, jazz band and concert band and any number of ensembles. Parents of musical children are delighted with the provision but we did hear one or two mutterings about (almost inevitable) music/sport timetable clashes. The sporty and musical child might be stretched rather thin here, given the predominance of both.

No house system; school has 'sections' distinguished by colour (red, blue, green etc). 'It's a bit boring but that's the way it's been since the beginning,' we were told. Parents confident that pastoral care system would pick up any problems early on and also praised home-school communication, 'Teachers respond very quickly.' Chapel (can just about seat whole school) three times a week; 'it's a buzz when everyone is singing,' said our guide; Christmas carol service is held at Bradfield College. When asked about food the pupils were very keen to share: curry Mondays and chicken in barbecue sauce are firm favourites; rocky road and chocolate brownies are top puddings. Opinion sharply divided as to whether macaroni cheese was best or worst.

Families live within 45 minutes' drive and are mostly long-term local or London escapees. Parents, many both working, appreciate the improved after-school care. Very active parents' association, FOSA (Friends of St Andrew's) arranges social events such as pub nights and charity fundraisers. 'It's not a cliquey school,' we were told, 'there's a really good mix.' While this is undoubtedly true, it's worth bearing in mind that the 'mix' doesn't have that many different ingredients ... Former pupils include author David Cornwell (aka John le Carré); broadcaster Adam Hart Davis; artist Sir Howard Hodgkin; actress Emily Bevan and, wait for it, James and Pippa Middleton and their sister, Catherine, Duchess of Cambridge. Apparently it was at a hockey match on the fields of St Andrew's that Prince William, then a pupil at Ludgrove, first saw his future wife. All credit to the school for not overplaying this particular connection.

Boarding: Boarding (Mondays to Thursdays 'as we believe that weekends are precious for families') is increasingly popular. Accommodation is up in the eaves of the main house (boys at one end, girls at the other and a sensor alarm between) and preponderance of beams and wood give the space rather an alpine feel. Small numbers (12 beds for boys and 12 beds for girls) make for comfortable and homely arrangements, dorms spotless but not at all institutional. Boarders love the experience – hot chocolate and toast in the common room, summer evenings playing tennis, swimming or 'just lying on the grass talking'. School looking to grow and evolve its boarding as part of the merger with Bradfield.

The last word: Many of the parents we spoke to had looked at larger or better-known schools before choosing St Andrew's. 'It's a little gem' was a phrase we kept on hearing. The fact that it has been below the radar appeals to some, rather like that favourite, 'unspoilt' holiday destination. One mother said, 'I don't really want to tell my friends [about St Andrew's]; it won't be so unique and special.' Er, sorry about that. School's relative youth means that some founding old boys from the 1930s are still on the mailing list. The school told us of one chap who, at nearly 90, loves to come back and visit. And his verdict? 'Yes, it's changed, but the magic is still here.'

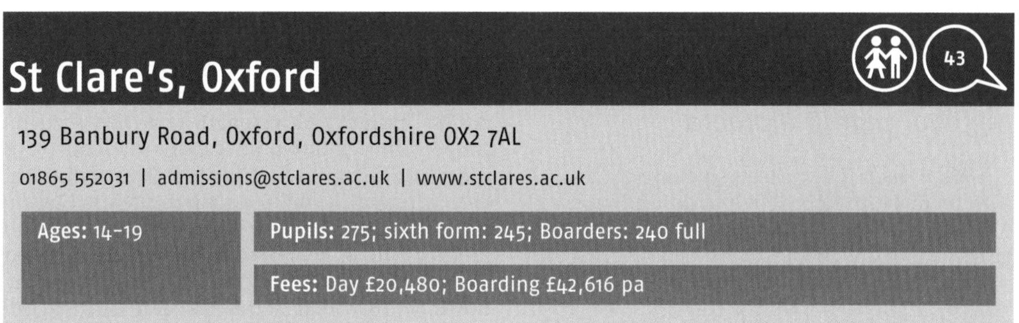

St Clare's, Oxford

139 Banbury Road, Oxford, Oxfordshire OX2 7AL

01865 552031 | admissions@stclares.ac.uk | www.stclares.ac.uk

Ages: 14–19

Pupils: 275; sixth form: 245; Boarders: 240 full

Fees: Day £20,480; Boarding £42,616 pa

Principal: Since 2017, Andrew Rattue MA PGCE (50s). Formerly head of King's College, the British School of Madrid, and prior to that head of RGS Worcester. Read English at Brasenose, Oxford and later Victorian studies at Birkbeck before nailing the hat-trick with a PGCE from King's College, London. Says teaching was 'the last thing I wanted to do,' but following a postgraduate stint working in a school in Thailand, and there discovering that he possessed that rare and fearless quality of enjoying the company of teenagers, his destiny was sealed and his career has seen him teach English at Mill Hill and Haberdashers' Aske's (including a sojourn as a Fulbright exchange teacher in Dallas, Texas), become head of English at Highgate and second master at RGS Guildford. Joined St Clare's 'at an important time,' he says: 'we represent the polar opposite of the Brexit mentality.' Parents say he has brought 'a different presence' to the school and is 'very involved' with the progress of every student.

Married to Jacky, currently training to be a careers advisor, with three grown-up sons and a daughter, all accomplished linguists. Self-confessed 'frustrated thesp' (career highlights include directing Matt Lucas as Mr Hardcastle in She Stoops to Conquer during his Habs days); lover of theatre, cinema, walking and travelling. Governor at nearby Rye St Antony School and the Oxfordshire Hospital School, and trustee of the Alliance Française in Oxford.

Entrance: Semi but not overly selective. Word of mouth is St Clare's secret weapon and most students have links through friends or family. Conversion once families have visited is 80 per cent. Majority join in UK year 12 (just 45 pupils in the pre-IB year when we visited). Placement tests in English and maths marked whilst the potential student is still in the building and if they pass muster at interview stage – enthusiasm for the IB being number one criteria – offers made on the spot. A four-day induction programme for newcomers is supported by senior students. Fluent English a necessity.

Exit: Majority straight to higher education – about half to UK universities. Popular choices include London colleges (LSE, UCL, Imperial) as well as many Russell Group and new universities. Four to Oxbridge in 2020, and seven medics.

St Clare's is all about the IB and students come from the world over (48 different nationalities at the time of our visit) to study here for the two-year IB diploma

We've seen a few careers departments and, with its in-depth knowledge of destinations and courses that other schools are unlikely to have even heard of, plus online tracking system covering everything from research and applications to offers from institutions in multiple countries, we've yet to see one better. 'They guide you every step of the way,' glowed one student. Recent alumni have headed to diverse destinations such as Harvard (one on a 'full ride' scholarship), Bocconi and the elite World Bachelor in Business course at the University of Southern California. St Clare's Connect (like a private version of LinkedIn) ensures St Clare's alumni continue to benefit from global networking opportunities even after they leave the school.

Latest results: In 2021, IB average point score was 39 (36 in 2019).

Teaching and learning: St Clare's is all about the IB and students come from the world over (48 different nationalities at the time of our visit) to study here for the two-year IB diploma. The first school to offer the IB in England and over 40 years' experience, plus consistently high results, mean that St Clare's is more than able to compete with the many top public schools now offering the IB. Impressive results given the non-academically selective intake and rigorous demands of the diploma: three subjects at standard level, three at higher, including mother tongue and English, a humanities subject, science and maths. Not forgetting the compulsory theory of knowledge course, extended essay and community, activity and service (CAS) programme. Makes A levels look like a walk in the park – one of the reasons St Clare's claims it has the edge over schools that offer both routes: 'When pupils realise the continuous academic rigour required to do well in the IB, there can be a disastrous temptation to quit and jump across to A levels for the wrong reasons,' said one senior staff member.

Students report high standards of teaching and praise school's internationality as a major benefit: 'We're very open minded and willing to share different views which means a broader range of conversations.' Parents say that excellent teaching is a given but also that 'nowhere else can you learn such tolerance by living with such a diverse group of people.' Relaxed approach to numbers needed to run a course: if one pupil wants to study eg Mandarin, then study it they shall (and most likely be roomed with a native speaker to help with tricky homework to boot).

Those too young to commence the IB course (UK year 11) or who need to brush up their English language skills can spend a year in the school before the IB course proper starts, studying the pre-IB. This is flexible in length, up to one year, and can be joined at any time to bring students up to speed before starting the core subjects at diploma level. Despite the fabulously international teaching staff (literature must be taught and studied in mother tongue, so individual tutors are recruited from all manner of local and worldwide institutions), all tuition (collaborative and informal; no chalk and talk in evidence) is in English and class sizes average 10 to 12, sometimes fewer. Languages – unsurprisingly – are the star turn, with maths and science departments also 'outstanding', according to head. Economics and business strong, and psychology 'charismatically taught'. History and global politics 'well taught and popular'.

Learning support and SEN: No dedicated SEN department but mild to moderate learning difficulties catered for by an LDD coordinator, and

The head delights in the eclectic range of musical instruments that arrive amidst luggage from farflung corners of the globe

school has experience with students with ADHD, ASD and hearing impairment.

The arts and extracurricular: Music, drama, dance, writing, debating and Model United Nations all excellent. We'd gladly offer up a prize for anyone who can find a school better qualified to excel in the latter, in fact. Pupils describe director of music as 'incredible' and head delights in the eclectic range of musical instruments that arrive amidst luggage from far-flung corners of the globe: 'Our concerts are remarkable: epiphanies of international culture that nowhere else in the UK could deliver.' Not a huge uptake in peripatetic lessons – flute, piano and violin dominate – but school will arrange tuition in instruments of pupils' choice and many musical pupils use the practice rooms in their free time. Drama smaller scale to what's on offer in many other independent schools, but performances do take place on high days and holidays and there's an annual musical production. The CAS programme also involves community service, which takes the form of charity work in local shops, visiting the elderly, wildlife conservation projects or helping at local schools. A personal tutor is on hand every week to monitor progress and offer advice.

Pupils report 'loads of freedom' to explore the city and its rich cultural offerings: free lectures at the university as well as the local shops and cafes of Summertown which is just a five-minute walk away ('The Italians like to go there to smoke,' the head told us. 'That, and apparently the pasta is cooked more to their liking than ours'). The exception to the freedom rule (curfew at 11pm on weekdays and midnight at weekends) is for the pre-IB students who have compulsory weekend excursions on Saturdays. Grumbles from those concerned, who said they would like weekends to be more relaxed, although we think if they were dropped into a trad public school they'd have more gripes on that front. Fewer major international trips than some other schools (eg no rugby tour or ski trip).

Sport: Sport at St Clare's is a totally different proposition from the usual independent school formula, with no PE on curriculum but sport falling under the 'activity' banner of the mandatory CAS module of the IB. No playing fields – all students have membership to the swish Nuffield sports centre and pool in nearby Summertown, and other facilities are a short minibus ride away at other local schools or Oxford Brookes University. Boys' and girls' football teams use the Astroturf pitches at Oxford City FC grounds, and rugby teams use nearby Oxford Harlequins ground. The walls of the 'covered way' showcase the multitude of sporting activities on offer – from badminton to meditation. There are so many activity options that one pupil even saw it as a negative: 'team sports suffer'. Football (both sexes) popular.

Boarding: Almost all students board full time. Fifteen boarding houses – all single-sex – within a short stroll of one another and teaching facilities. All pre-IBs and younger IB1s (year 12s) housed in the stunning '121' – an architect-designed, oak-clad collection of modern cubes sensitively adjoining a Victorian frontage, each housing two students, with picture windows onto the grass quad and art studio. Others dotted amongst the Victorian villas – all rooms we saw were extremely spacious and well furnished, many full of Victorian character, some with own showers and all with safe and Wifi. All IB1 students doubled up with another nationality and disagreements are, apparently, very rare. IB2s (year 13s) can choose to share with a friend or take a single room. All houses have residential warden in charge of general well-being of students, who must text their warden at 7pm each evening to let them know where they plan to be that evening – 'wardens run the houses with a light touch,' parents report. Curfews are generous (11pm week nights and midnight at weekends) but rigorously enforced. Those over 18 are allowed to drink 'but with care', those ever-sensible students told us. Party animals 'so rare they go down in history,' said one parent. Day students allocated a house and able to stay one night a week with no additional charge and can also take all meals in school, seven days a week.

Ethos and heritage: In head's words: 'There's only one St Clare's.' It would be wide of the mark to agree that other independents are 'samey' in comparison but his observation that there are 'several genuine USPs here' rings true – and it would certainly stand out amongst local IB sixth forms to those on a tour of UK education options. An 'extremely' international cohort is just the start of it – some nationalities with numbers in 20s or 40s, many with under five and several with just one: 'Nobody stands out,' one (Swedish) pupil told us: 'we all do.' No uniform and first-name terms between teachers and students. Parents say school doesn't have a brand, rather a culture. Prefects?

No. Many pupils are offspring of former St Clare's students who met at the school and what the head calls the 'small, human scale touch' is in plain sight. Founded after World War II by visionary educationalist Anne Dreydel (portrait looms over reception area) with the motto 'to advance international education and understanding', St Clare's was a pioneer in establishing exchange opportunities for German students. Recognised with an OBE and the German equivalent, her cultural olive branch towards international peace has evolved – via a stint in the 1960s at a 'posh girls' finishing school' ('Old Etonians in their 50s still blush at the mention,' chuckled head) – into a thriving sixth form for around 265 students. There's 'still a sniff of the slightly alternative atmosphere,' says head, but there's certainly no whiff of eau de party school in the air – the vibe is studious, and students are mature and sincere. 'There's a lot of focus on studying,' our guides assured us.

There's 'still a sniff of the slightly alternative atmosphere,' says head, but there's certainly no whiff of eau de party school in the air

Fabric of school lends itself well to collegiate feel, with a collection of 27 Victorian villas set amongst prime north Oxford real estate, providing boarding accommodation and classrooms: 'We get to live in this amazing city, not just our school,' one student raved. Buildings are Tardis-esque, with spacious gardens to the rear and quirky touches such as red telephone boxes dotted about. Three meals a day taken in the canteen (standard-quality school fare with an international twist) or school coffee shop (the delightfully un-PC named Sugar House), which serves up coffees, teas, paninis and cakes all day (although not at the end of the day when it's most needed, some students complained). Pamela Morris building (2015) is home to several laboratories and maths rooms, as well as being base camp to the 'pets and plants' club (that's rats and snakes to you and me). Breathtaking purpose-designed art studio with bi-folding doors onto a grassy quad and optimum north facing light, plus darkroom for budding photographers, and one of the loveliest libraries we've seen (and certainly the most diversely stocked).

Pastoral care, inclusivity and discipline: With 270 15 to 18-year-olds thrown together so far from home, what could possibly go wrong? Well, not a great deal, says head. School apparently 'reads the riot act' when pupils arrive and thereafter works on the basis that open channels of communication and lashings of trust go a long way to keeping teenagers on the straight and narrow – and when trouble does rear its head, clear consequences are set in motion. 'There are very few rules, but they are strongly enforced,' say parents. Pupils respond well to this: 'It feels like home. There's very little we can't do – it allows us to be independent and find our way in life.' Lateness or poor behaviour results in loss of free time, confinement to the library or house. Those who fall off the study wagon made to attend compulsory supervised study. Zero tolerance of drug use, transgression resulting in immediate suspension and expulsion for a second offence – school maintains right to drug test students at random. Sex possibly a bigger (although not major) issue: 'We have strict rules and education in place but can't stop the students having relationships,' sighed one senior staff member. Liberal environment makes for high tolerance of any differences relating to sexuality: 'There are possible issues with acceptance amongst some nationalities,' says head, 'but it's seldom discussed; just not an issue.'

Parents love the fact that 'everybody is new – so there are no cliques.' School admits it has its 'fair share' of mental health issues to deal with, particularly anxiety, perfectionism and eating disorders, and has 'beefed up' pastoral support system with the appointment of a counsellor on staff to support the house wardens and trained peer mentors who 'actively seek out' homesickness. Families praise the 'incredibly serious' approach to supporting affected pupils. The new weekend activities programme also attempts to keep possibly homesick younger students busy with trips to football matches, theatre trips and shopping outings to eg Bicester Village. Students meet with their personal tutor on a weekly basis to cover pastoral and academic issues. Open channels of communication between parents and staff – parents invited to email their child's tutor or teachers at any time. Reports and test results viewed electronically via the parent portal.

Pupils and parents: Not the usual international boarding crowd. St Clare's is less of a global brand than many public schools scooping up the progeny of the global elite, so appeals to a different market. Head describes the typical St Clare's parent as 'discerning, intelligent and ambitious', drawn to the school not only by the rich opportunities but also by the fact that it's 'part of the real world'. Italians are the largest group, followed by Germans, Russians ('We are still very much open for business to Russia,' says head) and British (who although significant in number make up just eight per cent of the school community). Parents see the total lack of their own group presence around school as the only downside: 'a bit strange'. Brits – as with other nationalities – often join from international schools overseas ('an easy transition,' say pupils), but some simply have an interest in the IB. Around 10 per cent are day students with parents working locally at the university, hospitals, BMW or similar businesses. In a round table scenario, they are disarmingly mature, serious and erudite. Around 18 scholars each year, some on full bursaries, 'set the tone of the school,' according to head. A 60/40 girl/boy split.

Money matters: Generous means-tested bursary scheme for around 30 promising students. Day fees reasonable especially considering their inclusive nature.

The last word: A perfect stepping stone (for suitably mature and motivated students committed to the IB) between school and university. A real sense of turning out not St Clarians but global citizens – with these girls and boys as our future world leaders, there is hope after all.

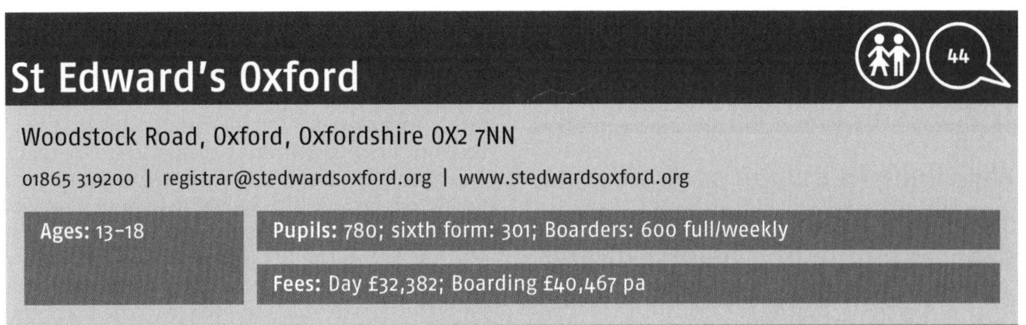

St Edward's Oxford

Woodstock Road, Oxford, Oxfordshire OX2 7NN

01865 319200 | registrar@stedwardsoxford.org | www.stedwardsoxford.org

Ages: 13–18

Pupils: 780; sixth form: 301; Boarders: 600 full/weekly

Fees: Day £32,382; Boarding £40,467 pa

Warden: Since September 2021, Alastair Chirnside, previously deputy head at Harrow. Brought up in Oxford, he attended the Dragon, winning a scholarship to Eton where he later taught. Took a congratulatory first in classics and modern languages at Merton College, Oxford, where he also won a lightweight rowing half blue. Married to Zannah, with whom he has two young daughters.

Entrance: The school takes children via Common Entrance from prep schools all over the south and midlands. Others take the school's own entry test in January of entry to year 9 and there are a limited number of places for year 10s. For internationals, the UKiset screening test can be sat abroad; from 2022, 11+ children will take ISEB tests. Sixth form entry requires Teddies' own exam and at least six GCSEs 6-9, or equivalent.

Exit: Around 10 per cent leave after GCSEs. Post A-level/IB most head off to Russell Group universities with Exeter, Edinburgh, London universities and Bristol popular choices. Four to Oxbridge in 2021. Impressive number of respected art, drama and music destinations and a few entrepreneurs who take off to set the world alight, going straight to start-ups and media careers. A professional head-hunter runs the careers programme. Some head to overseas universities.

Latest results: In 2021, 60 per cent 9-7 at I/GCSE; 61 per cent A*/A at A level (83 per cent A*-B). Average IB point score 33. In 2019 (the last year when exams took place), 53 per cent 9-7 at I/GCSE; 45 per cent A*/A at A level (79 per cent A*-B). Average IB point score 34 in 2019.

Teaching and learning: 'Traditional' and 'down to earth' were phrases we heard repeatedly at the school, but in reality we found the once traditional curriculum has transformed into an Aladdin's cave of enlightened choices. A mounting number of GCSEs and IGCSEs ('my son had to do 11,' complained one mum) led to solid results. However, all change from 2020, students sit only eight core GCSE subjects, including a modern language, along with the virgin Pathways and Perspectives courses. These have been devised at Teddies and are aimed at awakening an individual's passion or refining a particular interest. 'More like real life and what they will be doing at university' explained the warden. The courses, accredited by the University of Buckingham and graded like a GCSE, are assessed by a range of measures, including presentation and reflective log. Exciting options include Global Society, Big Ideas for the deep thinkers or courses with a practical element, like Sports Science Pathway or Design and Entrepreneurship Pathway. They are aimed at eliminating hidebound aspects of GCSEs which stifled enquiring minds. 'We are going for high end thinking,' said one teacher. 'Kids fear the failure of GCSE but we want, like James Dyson, not to worry about failing but to build on failure – it's so important.' One mum was annoyed there was no computing GCSE.

Sixth formers are also spoilt for choice, between three (or four) subjects at A level in addition to an EPQ title, or IB with its wider range of academic subjects, and creative and active-service curriculum. IB has proved a hit, with over 50 per cent of students choosing it. 'I wanted to continue as many subjects as possible,' we heard from one girl. 'It's got wider grade boundaries,' explained a teacher. 'You've got your eggs spread across more baskets.' Results are solid at A level/IB. One parent commented diplomatically, 'The logistics of running IB and A levels have not been easy for them.'

We witnessed a pupil perform a quick-change from sensible school shoes to pirouetting pointes during an after-school dance class in the wonderful, mirrored studio

Eight forms are created from the 145 new pupils in the shell (year 9). The intake is broad and the school prefers not to use sets in the middle years, except for maths, in which the top two groups follow extension work. Languages also require some filtering due to a wide variety of language skills arriving in the lower years. Sixth form numbers increase by 45 and the emphasis is on self-motivated learning, supported by a coaching model of teaching.

Learning support and SEN: A small learning support department nurtures children with mild specific learning difficulties like dyslexia, supported in class rather than by individual sessions.

The arts and extracurricular: This is a school with its own professional 1,000-seat venue for concerts, performances etc. Darcey Bussell had visited the week before, to open a photography exhibition in the foyer-gallery. We witnessed a pupil perform a quick-change from sensible school shoes to pirouetting pointes during an after-school dance class in the wonderful, mirrored studio. Alumnae include Sir Lawrence Olivier, Oscar-nominee Florence Pugh and Emilia Clarke of Game of Thrones, so no shortage of drama role-models, and a few lucky students get to perform at the Edinburgh Festival each year. 'It's really exciting, you learn so much, the teachers are professionals,' said our guide. Music has recently been rehoused in a fabulous new temple to the muse, the Ogston Music School, where we found two floors of concert-standard studios and recording equipment. Instrumentalists can practise anything from the violin to the bagpipes in one of 20 sound-proofed rooms. An elegant concert hall, warmly resonating in Douglas-fir panels, allows for choir rehearsals (full choir, chapel or chamber choir) and orchestral performances. A mum commented, 'My son signed up for music tech, he wanted to live in that building, he wanted to immerse himself in it.'

Above the noise of lathes and electric saws, we tracked down the head of design in his workshop. 'It's more creative than straight DT', he tells us. One class were making skateboards as part of Design and Entrepreneurship, which involved developing a brand. 'It's the entire process of production, how to sell, how to market.' We were shown an Arts and Crafts style steam-bent chair, made from ash-wood felled in the school grounds. Jewellery design is popular with boys and girls, who get to use the 3D printer and wield a blow torch. The shell have art in their own room, the old boiler house (not a reference to the teachers, we heard) and upper and lower sixth have dedicated studios. 'We literally have everything we need,' a student told us, 'and everyone we need.'

An exuberance of riches is on offer in the form of clubs, societies and boarders' weekend activities, from debating club to dressage, from making a fortune with the investment society, to making honey with the beekeepers; lunch hour extends to 90 minutes to accommodate it all. 'It's very easy for a school to put everything on for the pupils,' explains the head, 'but isn't it better that the pupils put it on?' Media-savvy students have developed their own TV channel, Teddies TV, which broadcasts wonderful short movies and reportage of student life. Binge-watch them via the newsletter on the website or on Teddies TV Vimeo channel – we were completely hooked. One boy was recently allowed to film the England rugby team, in a coaching session on the school's sports fields.

Sport: Vistas of green fields around the quad tell you Teddies is a sporty school and the glittering-prize walls of the dining room, lined with tin shields from 1929 to the present day, celebrate their sporting heroes (known as Martyrs). Opportunities to take part are myriad. Regular fixtures in team sports, netball, hockey, tennis, rugby, football and cricket are played against formidable independent schools. Teddies' large numbers of athletes mean the school can field several teams per event, so everyone gets to play

Thriving CCF, the school has links with the RAF and boasts Douglas Bader and Dambusters' Guy Gibson as alumni

up and play the game. Where the school excels is in the facilities for more unusual sports: a boathouse on the Isis trains the rowing and canoeing teams; use of the Nuffield Health Centre in the grounds allows for indoor tennis, squash, swimming and fitness, and if you still have the legs, try a round of golf on the school's six-hole course. 'If you've got a dim sporty child, they'll be very happy there; if you've got a clever sporty child they'll be even happier,' said one mum. One parent we spoke to had seen her son become the captain of rugby, another proudly declared that her's skippered the football team, while an international pupil from a desert country, who had 'never in his life rowed' had joined the rowing crew. As one pupil said, 'There's no shame in being interested in things here.' The only gripe we heard was the lack of girls' football.

Boarding: Thirteen houses, six for boys, five for girls and two co-ed. Some sited quad-side, popular with children who rate food a higher priority than sport. The newer houses on field-side are accessed by a tunnel under Woodstock Road. A far cry from the dorms of Malory Towers, the girls' house we visited was stylish and spacious. Inside was a living room with squashy sofas for evenings chilling in front of the TV, with nachos and cheese, after communal prep at one of the many desktops; there was a spotless dining room with kitchen facilities and several floors of bedrooms. First-year students share four to a room, fewer in the upper years and a single bedroom with whiteboard, basin, desk and wardrobe for the sixth. Students return to house at break for a quick round of toast, but eat meals together on the main site in a communal dining room. (Food was excellent, especially the cakes, and always available, we heard. Shame about the single-use cups!) Housemasters/mistresses (HMs) live in-house and are a line of communication between parent and offspring: 'They encourage you to keep in contact. Email and they'll always get back to you,' said one mum. Another parent added, 'You get a very respectful and professional response to emails.' Day children are allocated a house, finish prep with their housemates and depart for home at 6.30 or 9pm. One mum felt the introduction of weekly boarding had changed the inclusive culture of the school. As to the tricky process of selecting a house, all students we met had joined the house they were directed to, on their initial visit to the school; no sorting hat procedure needed! 'All houses have their own traditions,' a student remarked. 'You form strong relationships with the people you are living with. I literally have 10 sisters.'

Ethos and heritage: Occupying a prominent site in Summertown, a genteel suburb of north Oxford, St Edward's has the edge over other independents in its position on the threshold of a vibrant university town – an aspect which appeals to parents, while having a back gate to local shops and artisan bakeries, popular with the youngsters. The school's Victorian Gothic façade is complemented by many splendid horse-chestnut trees which line the road dividing the school from its acres of green fields. Within stands a central quad, suggestive of an Oxford college, with stained-glass windows of library and chapel glinting at one side, tall mullioned windows of refectory and warden's rooms on another, all planned in 1873 when the school moved from the centre of Oxford. The original Christian ethos, established by the school's founder, continues today in services three times a week in chapel, where the choir's voices rise to a vaulting apse and the school's war dead are remembered by commemorative plaques on the walls. Meander with the students along the gravel walkways between neat lawns and through the subway, however, and you leave tradition behind to discover a small settlement of modern boarding houses, a bright new sports pavilion, Astros and pitches stretching as far as the eye can see.

We visited at midweek, when the school is a hive of activity. Students in their navy and gold-trimmed kit were hurrying to sports, sixth formers in dark suits were head-down over books in the hushed library, while others in cadet force fatigues strode across the courts to parade. (The school has links with the RAF and boasts Douglas Bader and Dambusters' Guy Gibson as alumni.)

We made our way to the not-so-gorgeous workblock where we found traditional design classrooms with encouraging slogans on the walls. We particularly liked the English department's 'One's vocabulary needs constant fertilising or it will die', mulched by a helpful Word of the Week. Newer Christie Centre is, however, gorgeous – incorporating university-inspired sixth form reading room, a library, flexible classrooms, break-out spaces and new café for social learning.

Pastoral care, inclusivity and discipline: As well as a formal structure of pastoral care, supervised by the HM, the boarders can talk informally to a peer listener, an in-house sixth former who can empathise from a student's perspective, or call on matron, nurse, chaplain or personal tutor as need be. The health centre is open seven days a week and a counsellor is on the staff. Parents were happy with the pastoral provision: 'It's very important for parents not to worry, for example, if a child gets hurt during a match.' Another mother discussed a past drugs incident, which saw a number of boys expelled: 'It's not something considered cool or edgy.' A parent added, 'I was impressed that they don't hide things. It's very important for everyone to know the repercussions of this sort of thing.' We heard from parents, 'They emphasise kindness a lot; ambition and kindness don't often go hand in hand.'

Pupils and parents: Day children come mostly from Oxford – 'You wouldn't want to live far away,' we heard. Boarders from 60 different schools, but the day children and boarders were indistinguishable, even the teachers couldn't tell. A coach now runs between London and Oxford via Beaconsfield for weekly boarding. Head is keen to keep the traditional character of the school and maintains the international intake at 15 per cent. The highish fees naturally create the demographic. Parents come from academic, professional, medical and banking careers and are all invited to meet up at weekend activities, quiz nights and dinners. One London parent had joined the St Edward's Singers, made up of parents, staff, neighbours and friends, 'from grannies to teenagers,' she told us.

Money matters: It's not cheap maintaining 100 acres of prime Oxford estate and these academic standards but, 'if you really make the most of what's on offer,' a teacher told us, 'it's worth the money.'

'Lots of bursaries,' said one mum, 'to get clever children to Oxford and Cambridge; it gives a chance to people unable to afford private education.' At 13+ and 16+, academic and music scholarships and exhibitions, plus sports and arts awards. At 13+, there are arts awards covering drama, dance, art and DT, while at 16+ they cover drama, dance and art. Scholarships attract £2,000 fee remission per annum; exhibitions and awards attract fee remission of £1,000 per annum.

The last word: A happy, fizzing school plumb in the middle of an inspiring city. St Edward's takes a broad mix of children and grows a community of successful, interested and energetic young people by offering them a clever mix of choices. 'I have three very different kids, and they have excelled in different areas and failed in different areas,' said one mum. They will tell you it is very 'down to earth', we thought it was flying high.

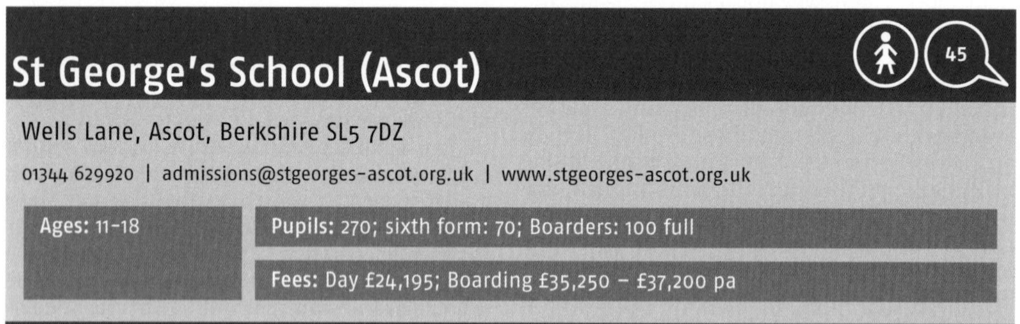

St George's School (Ascot)

Wells Lane, Ascot, Berkshire SL5 7DZ

01344 629920 | admissions@stgeorges-ascot.org.uk | www.stgeorges-ascot.org.uk

Ages: 11–18

Pupils: 270; sixth form: 70; Boarders: 100 full

Fees: Day £24,195; Boarding £35,250 – £37,200 pa

Headmistress: Since 2016, Liz Hewer (only just 40s), two children, one dog. Destined for pointer and whiteboard from the cradle; her mother taught special needs. A brief flirtation with the financial world before and during her Cambridge career but back there for her PGCE. Relaxed, friendly, very sporty, captained the women's hockey team at Cambridge and won two half-blues for cricket. She comes here from literally just down the road as she did seven years as deputy head at St Mary's Ascot, but plenty of other top schools on her CV, including Marlborough.

Supporters are vocal and enthusiastic; she has taken time to understand the workings of the school ('she turns up for everything' and 'meets questions head on') before she makes too many changes. There's obviously much more going on inside both her head and the school, but the hot topic now is the introduction of traffic lights on the way to the car park, not ground-breaking but a jolly sensible step. She lives happily on site, finding 'going home to be mum helps me switch off'.

Entrance: Described by one parent as 'pretty much non-selective', intakes are at 11+, 13+ and into the sixth form. At 11+ admission is by exam, interview and report from current school. Pre-assessment operates for 13+ entry with exams in maths, English and verbal reasoning plus an interview. Entrance at 11+ and 13+ also now includes a CEM (Centre for Evaluation and Monitoring) test. Access to the sixth form requires a minimum of six 9-4 grades at GCSE and at least a 6 in any subject to be taken at A level. There is a wide variety of feeder schools including local preps such as Lambrook, Upton House, Godstowe and Coworth Flexlands and local primaries. Some also come from west London schools including Thomas's schools, Knightsbridge, Broomwood Hall and Garden House.

Exit: Around 30 per cent leaves after GCSEs, girls tempted by the lure of co-ed and parents by the savings made if the move is to a sixth form college. Durham most popular in recent years, followed by Edinburgh, Exeter and Leeds. Sometimes a few to Oxbridge, but none in 2021.

Latest results: In 2021, 78 per cent 9-7 at GCSE; 77 per cent A*/A at A level (90 per cent A*-B). In 2019 (the last year when exams took place), 45 per cent 9-7 at GCSE; 35 per cent A*/A at A level (61 per cent A*-B).

Teaching and learning: LH is confident that the balance of teachers – average age early 40s – is correct, and there was no mass exodus at the end of her first year in office. Our impression was plenty of younger faces amongst the staff, and the girls said they liked the variety of teaching styles. A new academic deputy head has been brought in to ensure that all levels of ability are catered for, as there had been some intimation from parents that the most able were not being stretched enough. Small classes in the first years, a maximum of 20, but more usually 15 or 16 are reduced to 10 for GCSE courses and often single figures at A level.

Setting starts from day one in maths, followed by Latin, French, science and Spanish in the third year and English at GCSE. Monitored twice a term, pupils say they are happy with the flexibility, confident that the staff are on it. One pupil told us that she had moved from the bottom to the top set at exactly the right speed.

You have to get your beauty sleep here because there is a deliberately long day; starting at 8.15am, it's pretty full on until the end of prep, which varies from 6.15pm for the younger ones to 6.45pm for the sixth form. If they add in other activities or clubs it can often be a 12-hour stretch before the day girls get home. Despite the long hours, the format appeals to both boarders and day girls because it means that they can chill when the school day ends with homework out of the way.

At present, but undergoing review, the lessons are only 35 minutes, which elicits the odd grumble but means they fit in nine lessons and slot in one more for A level students. The average number of entries for each girl at GCSE is nine or 10 with the occasional super-bright spark taking 11. The majority of students in the sixth form take three A levels plus an EPQ in the lower sixth. Some of this year's entry were not entirely convinced that they had sufficient time to do the extra work needed for an EPQ, although LH contends that it is becoming a valuable source of content for UCAS personal statements and interviews.

The food is both gastronomic and healthy; one parent said it was so good that she was moved to write a thank-you letter

We left feeling that there was a high level of satisfaction with the teaching although there does not appear to be one particularly outstanding academic area. A more accurate evaluation might be the across-the-board added value (GCSEs average a grade higher than expected at entry level). The impression is that they are trying hard to raise the academic bar and their results are very consistent.

Learning support and SEN: The 10 per cent or so of the school who have special educational needs, mainly dyslexia, speak highly of the SEND provision. One pupil told us that her problems had been so well dealt with that they no longer existed, and another that her only gripe was that she was limited to 25 per cent extra time in exams. Equally, a mother said that they had 'bent over backwards' to make her dyslexic daughter's life as easy as possible. Any girls who want or need that little bit extra can attend clinics, often with one-to-one teaching at no extra charge, which were described as 'brilliant' by one parent. After consultations with parents they also have the option of calling in the nearby Helen Arkell Institute, one of the UK's leading dyslexia centres.

The arts and extracurricular: There is a mass of popular options when it comes to out-of-school activities, including a surprisingly oversubscribed ukulele club. The older girls are fully involved and often run clubs for the younger lot. The only negative was a mention from a boarding parent that there was 'too much knitting club'.

The arts are another example of how this school refuses to be limited by the small number of pupils. There may have only been two sixth formers in the art room but their work was colourful and accomplished. An indication of how seriously they treat the subject was the presence of the artist-in-residence as well as a new young art teacher who has taken over from a Georgian legend.

The music department is headed up by a long-term, much-praised contributor who twinkles at the new enthusiasm for the flute among the possibly less talented pupils but also helps the very able to move on to specialist establishments, such as the Royal Northern College of Music. The choir is 'so good', according to parents, that they regularly sing in public, including in the Albert Hall and with the BBC Symphony Orchestra.

Drama and music for all is the guiding principle and serious time and effort go into carrying this out through inter-house drama and music competitions, LAMDA exams, the opportunity to take drama at GCSE and A level and even a theatre director in residence. They recently staged a production of Cats involving over 80 girls.

Sport: The head certainly has all the right sporty qualifications and seldom misses turning out to cheer them on.

In the summer the outside lacrosse pitches turn into tracks for athletics and the six netball courts magically grow into eight tennis courts. You can play everything from badminton to squash in the sports centre, which incorporates a viewing balcony for fans. Lower down everyone gets a chance to be in a team, but further up participation becomes more focused and the teams more competitive, with one parent commenting that 'the coaching was second to none'. One of the results of all the hard training has seen them crowned Small Schools Lacrosse Champions two years in a row, but they don't just cater for sporting heroines. On top of the daily offerings they can provide private coaching for everybody from wannabe ballerinas to polo players. A 25-metre indoor swimming pool opened in 2019.

Boarding: The balance tips more towards boarding as they move up the school with only 20 per cent full-time boarders in the first two years but increasing to nearly 50 per cent in the sixth form.

The formal stairs out of the main hall lead up to cheerfully decorated, cosy dormitories for the first two years, 'deceptively spacious' in estate agent speak; we liked the look of them and believed the assurance that they were 'always that tidy' was down to a daily vetting. Sensibly, they mix up the first and second years so that there is an experienced old hand around if it all seems daunting to begin with. The number sharing diminishes as you go up the school with the upper sixth having their own room in a separate house. This is a bit dingy at the moment with strange 80s wallpaper in the passage and rather depressing ex-bedrooms used as studies by day girls. Staggered improvement here is next on the list and due to start soon.

Out-of-school activities include a surprisingly oversubscribed ukulele club. The only negative was a mention from a parent that there was 'too much knitting club'

One parent felt that full boarders were quite often left to their own devices and that it was more a school for free spirits than girls who needed a lot of TLC; having said which, there was strong confidence in the house system and that the older girls looked out for the new intakes. Parents speak highly of the flexibility on offer: 'If she wants to stay for dinner, she can stay for dinner.'

The food is win, win all round, being both gastronomic and healthy; one parent said it was so good that she was moved to write a thank-you letter. The only eating problem might be avoiding the temptation to want seconds of everything. Day and boarding pupils all muck in together, which is another way that the school avoids barriers springing up.

Ethos and heritage: Originally a boys' prep, until it went bust in 1904 despite having Winston Churchill as a pupil. After a sex-change into a girls-only establishment it continued on surprisingly strongly through two world wars, thanks to an air raid shelter enterprisingly built at the start of the second.

This tiny kingdom lies down a lane only a short canter from the finishing post at Royal Ascot. The main circle of buildings crowns the top of a steep hill, guarding the green lawns and well-tended playing fields below from the encroaching hordes of modern houses. The original Victorian house grew over the years with the most obvious additions of more classrooms, a chapel, labs, music rooms and a sixth form house, all built in the 1980s. Later buildings include a technology block, a sports complex, a performing arts centre (no prizes for guessing that it was opened by the Duke of York) and, most recently, an imaginative, light new library complete with a feisty librarian ('she was part of the package') and swanky new £5.6m swimming pool tucked under the hill.

Once past the intercom and the keypad, the modern sentries of scholastic establishments, you find yourself in a large entrance hall, bedecked with trophies, cups and futuristic fashion. The centrepiece is a splendid flower arrangement distracting your attention from the friendly ladies on reception (not there at weekends) sitting beneath a board listing the names of the school's head girls, past and present. As in almost all buildings that have evolved over time, the rest of the layout is slightly confusing to the outsider but poses no problems to its inhabitants who all talk of its 'homely atmosphere'.

Pastoral care, inclusivity and discipline: LH's ease with social media means lots of communication with parents, which goes down well. She is quick to tweet praise and encouragement and parents feel they are kept in touch with their children's progress on all fronts. The school has a pastoral deputy who deals with petty disciplinary problems quickly and efficiently and there is no evidence of serious issues. This is a school that takes modern dangers seriously, and blocks the use of social and streaming media for older girls during lessons; younger girls have zero access.

The pupils now have a clear structure of authority, with the head girl supported by a team including a group of peer mentors; girls in the lower sixth who choose to undergo formal training with the school counsellor so that they can offer a friendly shoulder to lean on or even cry on if necessary. This format works really well, according to parents, with the inevitable odd grouse being sorted out so discreetly that the original sufferer is only aware that the problem is no longer there. Members from all years are elected to take part in a school council where they can air their ideas or their moans, and the sixth form has its own separate version.

Pupils and parents: As with so many similar schools, the evolution from the days of old-school parents (who dropped their children off at the beginning of term and picked them up at the end) to present-day parents (who prefer them to sleep in their own beds) is almost complete. High earning, mainly very local parents of both sexes drop their children off before they go to work for the rest of the day, thankful that they can arrange for sleepovers if they are still chained to their desks or stuck on an aeroplane.

A large number of pupils live locally but some are bussed in from as far away as Chalfont St Giles and a smaller number come from west London, often on a school bus that operates at weekends. Some 10 per cent come from international families spanning the globe from Mexico to China with the occasional Russian or European.

Money matters: Academic, music, art, sports, performing arts and all-rounder scholarships available at 11+, 13+ and 16+, all offering up to 10 per cent off the fees. In addition they offer a limited number of means-tested bursaries.

The last word: As with their equine counterparts on the racecourse across the road, careful attention is paid to each well-bred individual, persuading them to give of their best. However, it is done in a spirit of camaraderie and they are actively discouraged from being academic know-alls, bullies on the games pitch or divas on the boards. Old-school tradition meets 21st-century sensibilities to turn out intelligent, civilised young women proving that the Georgian formula continues to work.

St Hugh's School, Oxfordshire

46

Carswell Manor, Faringdon, Oxfordshire SN7 8PT

01367 870700 | registrar@st-hughs.co.uk | www.st-hughs.co.uk

Ages: 3–13

Pupils: 352; Boarders: 30 weekly, 110 flexi (from 7 years)

Fees: Day £12,555 – £21,675; Weekly boarding + £4,245 pa

Headmaster: Since 2019, James Thompson, BA QTS. Previously head of Royal Russell Junior School, Croydon, has held posts at Ardingly College Prep and Kingswood Prep in Bath. Educated at Dulwich College Prep and Cranbrook School, he has first-hand experience of both boarding and day schools. His grandfather was deputy head at Marlborough House Prep for over 30 years so education is very much in the blood. Actively involved in numerous sports throughout his career, he specialised in PE while teacher training at St Mary's University, Twickenham. With a background teaching maths, geography and even KS1 French 'the lure of being able to lead the whole school community as opposed to just one part of it' was always his dream.

Mrs Thompson ran the Minors Nursery in Notting Hill and is now director of early years education for Chatsworth Schools. The couple have two daughters, both boarders at Cheltenham College.

Mr Thompson is very visible around school, not just due to the colour of his trousers. He is enthusiastic, approachable, and popular with pupils, parents, and staff. Pupils applaud his love of odd socks and pink trews, and how he approves of muddy knees. There is enormous pride in his voice when he pinpoints what is at the core of St Hugh's: 'We are a proudly non-selective, high achieving, all-inclusive school with the opportunity for everyone to develop their own talents.' His understanding of the mindset of London relocators is seemingly also paying dividends for a prep with no full-time boarding or Saturday school.

The headmaster, Mr Thompson, is very visible around school. Pupils applaud his love of odd socks and pink trews, and how he approves of muddy knees

The head's office is an ordered yet homely sanctum, complete with dog bed and tasteful eau de nil sofas, overlooking the grounds. During a lengthy sandwich lunch he barely drew breath in his impassioned praise of the school, and his child-focused ethos. He explains one of the key roles of the head is to work with parents in deciding the right senior schools for their children – sometimes this may entail balancing expectations.

Entrance: Non-selective. Early registration is recommended as priority is based on the date of registration (although school will do its best to accommodate families). Taster days for prospective pupils include assessments in English and maths for entry into year 3 and above. Majority join in reception (28 places) though pupils can be integrated throughout the year if space allows. Weekly boarding available from year 3.

Exit: Advice about progression to senior schools is rated 'excellent and spot on' and the broad spectrum of over 20 destination schools bears this out. About 60 per cent go on to board and popular destinations are St Edward's, Oxford, Radley College, St Mary's Calne, Marlborough, Eton, Winchester, Wellington College, Cheltenham College, Abingdon, Headington and St Helen & St Katharine. Seventeen scholarships including four to Radley (academic, music, sport, art) in 2021.

Our view: Established in 1906, St Hugh's moved to Carswell Manor, a pebble-dashed Jacobean house set in 45 acres of Oxfordshire countryside, in 1945. Once home to the Niven family and the birthplace of quintessentially English actor David Niven, initial impression of fading grandeur is quickly erased on stepping into the immaculate oak-panelled interior with its views of well-manicured playing fields as far as the eye can see. Impressive modern buildings house superb facilities and the setting provides a rarefied rural bubble for this small (350 pupils, balanced number of boys and girls) nurturing school. 'Family' and 'community' are descriptions frequently used. 'St Hugh's is a very kind place,' explained one parent, herself a teacher, 'where children are encouraged to be the best that they can be. The standard of teaching is exceptional. Timetabling is very consistent, it's well organised and led by consistently outstanding practitioners.' A parent from London describes the lack of pressure and stress at the school, noting 'St Hugh's is more relaxed than London, but the same stuff gets done.' And yes, there is something rather special about this school, summed up by comments from a couple of prospective parents who were 'completely blown away' by their visit to the school. 'The grounds and buildings are incredible, and we couldn't wait to tell our children about the Harry Potter style dovecote, what a magical place to have a library, and the new gym and swimming pool facilities. But above all, it was the children who made our trip so fantastic.'

Our visit on a busy day during the summer term left no stone unturned. We were accompanied by the head girl and boy who provided an impressive example of the St Hugh's end-product: self-assured, enthusiastic, articulate, considerate children, ready to take on the world without a sniff of arrogance. In fact, everyone we met during our visit was equally keen to showcase their school's many opportunities – we absolutely failed to uncover any dissenters.

The Cottage Nursery is the first step of the St Hugh's journey. It opened over 10 years ago in response to parental demand and offers two sessions per day for 20 children each. Recent influx of children from families where both parents are working and those who have moved out of London is in keeping with an emerging demographic shift that also includes more first-time

buyers than used to be the case. With acres of space, including a large forest school and adventure playground, children are encouraged to enjoy being active outside. The vibrant classroom is equally stimulating and fun; pupils we saw were engaged, relaxed and content. Specialist teaching in music, PE and ICT with access to the phonics programme used throughout pre-prep. French is introduced via croissants and chocolat chaud. A rest room is provided for 'time out'. Children look forward to frequent visits from the head and attend whole-school assembly.

Pre-prep (ages 4-6) is housed in the adjacent stable block with classrooms positioned around a central space offering flexibility for small group work. The average class size is 15. Cross-curricular teaching is impressive; we witnessed children in year 1 eagerly imagining what creatures found in the forest school might like to eat. Each year tends a raised vegetable bed, proudly growing their own produce which sometimes ends up on the lunch menu. Having achieved model status for phonics programme Read Write Inc, there is a high ratio of qualified teaching assistants (HLTA) with maximum literacy groups of eight. In the words of one parent, 'The school encourages excellence, where any ability is nurtured and where there is no capping at the top or bottom.'

Everyone we met during our visit was equally keen to showcase their school's many opportunities – we absolutely failed to uncover any dissenters

Years 3 and 4 enjoy lessons taught mainly by form teachers in their own 'middle school' teaching block. Maths and English, set from year 3, are taught first thing in the morning with remaining subjects taught throughout the day in mixed-ability groups. Upper school starts in year 5 with specialist subject teaching the norm. Year groups are divided into three sets; Latin introduced in year 5; scholarship set from year 7.

The provision of online learning during the pandemic gave parents an insight into their children's enthusiastic participation and interaction during lessons, reassuring them of the inclusivity and quality of education provided. Keeping IT provision up to date is one of the head's priorities.

Focus is placed on detecting learning challenges early with fellow pupils taught to respect different learning styles. The SEN team carry out assessments and provide support, either individually or in booster groups, at no extra charge. Children can dip in and out as necessary.

Much time spent outside in all weathers, with waterproof trousers and wellies on the uniform list and at least one hour of sport per day timetabled. Facilities are outstanding and pupils are encouraged to play at their own level with sportsmanship held in high regard. Equal attention paid to general fitness for pupils of lower sporting ability, promoting both physical and mental wellbeing. Every pupil in years 3-8 participates in school fixtures, day and residential trips; A,B,C and D teams equally involved in Wednesday matches. Core sports plus basketball, tennis, lacrosse, synchronised swimming, water polo, gymnastics and dance; very strong equestrian team. Excellent sports scholarship record with many playing at county and national level. Trips abroad offered to all in years 7 and 8 with the Barbados cricket and netball tours very popular. The year 8 post-exam trip involving camping, coasteering, surfing and beach barbecuing in Devon is a highlight of the school calendar, with the leavers' programme providing a memorable end to their time at St Hugh's. Pupils enjoy making a music video, learning first-aid and life-saving and an Apprentice-style entrepreneurship competition.

School is 'a great believer in the crucial role of co-curricular learning, whether through sport, music, drama, or the creative arts.' Some 80 per cent of pupils play a musical instrument and there are numerous choirs and orchestras. Performing arts and debating a particular strength and seen as key skills in confidence building. Songs from the musical Joseph echoed across the grounds as we completed our tour and the enthusiasm and enjoyment of the pupils was evident. Light and airy art block inspires creativity and imagination, number of leavers with art scholarships is testament to its success.

Drop-off is from 8am with the option for late pick-up after prep on weekdays, at no extra charge. No weekend boarding but Friday night boarding with pick-up after prep on Saturday morning is very popular.

Wellbeing is integrated into the curriculum. Examples include pupils choosing a member of staff as their mentor, campfire sessions in the forest school and the pre-prep one-minute pause for silence at the start of every lesson. Support for staff wellbeing is also strong with turnover exceptionally low throughout the school.

Policy of no mobile phones (brief use allowed for boarders) recognises that constant screen time is detrimental to a child's development. 'Above all, St Hugh's offers the space for pupils to learn physically, academically and socially.'

Parents we spoke to have confidence in a school that 'has seen it all before'. It is understood that young people make mistakes, but it is how they react to and learn from them that is important.

Boarding: Highly flexible weekly boarding. Flexi package is for three nights or more, availability for occasional boarding published weekly. Boarding takes place on two floors of the manor house. Recently refurbished dorms and sitting rooms are tasteful and cosy, with a genuine home-from-home feel. House parents are 'cool', according to boarders, who enjoyed telling us about fun Friday evenings of movies and popcorn, face mask nights and silent discos. For those in year 8 weekly boarding is seen as a stepping stone to full boarding at 13.

Money matters: Meals, all trips (home and abroad, with the exception of the optional Barbados sports tours) and SEN support are included in fees, making surprises on the termly bill unlikely. Full means-tested bursaries available.

The last word: Very well run, excellent teaching and a focus on being active in the great outdoors. With professionalism and quiet confidence St Hugh's guides pupils and parents skilfully through from nursery to year 8. The end result? Happy, achieving, energetic, children who are more than ready for their next adventure.

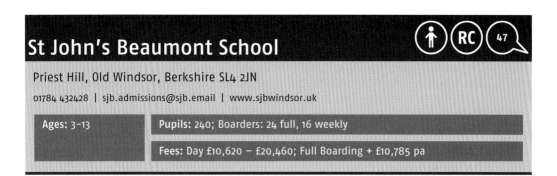

St John's Beaumont School

RC 47

Priest Hill, Old Windsor, Berkshire SL4 2JN

01784 432428 | sjb.admissions@sjb.email | www.sjbwindsor.uk

Ages: 3-13

Pupils: 240; **Boarders:** 24 full, 16 weekly

Fees: Day £10,620 – £20,460; Full Boarding + £10,785 pa

Headmaster: Since 2006, Giles Delaney (40s). Educated at Hereford Cathedral School and Cardiff University (music – his instruments are French horn and organ – and psychology). After a PGCE at Cambridge he responded to an ad for post of music teacher at St John's Beaumont (apparently with the caveat, 'not for the faint of heart'). Clearly lion-hearted, he lasted the course and was appointed deputy head three years later before being catapulted to headship upon the sudden death of his predecessor. After so long in post, we wondered whether he had any plans to move on. 'As long as I get out of bed with a spring in my step,' he says, 'I will stay.' We were delighted to hear this and so, no doubt, will be the parent body who describe him as 'the heart and soul of the school'. Far from sitting back and enjoying the status quo, he recently undertook a postgraduate research project at Oxford to help him – and the school – understand boys in the broadest sense; 'it's easy to create a bunker mentality,' he says; refreshingly, he acknowledges the need to move with the times and respond to the extraneous challenges that face independent schools.

Like many RC schools, SJB has a reputation for being very disciplined, although Mr Delaney is anything but a martinet. If the ethos and personality of a school flows downwards from its head, then the disarmingly kind and civilised vibe that permeates the very fabric of the school is testament to his character and leadership. Sharply dressed, quietly but precisely spoken and absolutely clear that it's the 'sense of relationship' that's important to boys, and that he always encourages them to ask 'What else can I offer in life?' In the same vein, he 'can't abide boys being judged by what secondary school they go to,' but instead asks, 'What will our 13-year-olds be doing when they're 28?' Aims to visit boys at senior school in their first year to check on progress and ask whether they were well prepared for their new environment. Our guess is that they almost always answer in the affirmative. Certainly, when it comes to the importance of context, relating academic subjects to the real world and building a humane, outward-looking stance into the very core of education, it seems that Jesuit schools were there long before the educationalists.

Lives on site and shares a keen interest in medieval history with his wife, Katie, who teaches in a school in north London. They have four daughters – must be something of an antidote to life at SJB.

Entrance: Intakes into nursery at 3+ and reception at 4+ with boys entering after attending a taster session. Parents also interviewed by head and although not selective, school will turn away families who 'appear disengaged in our values'. Further small intake into year 3, when boys take school's own assessment (English and maths) to establish their level and they also consider previous school records. Some spaces available in other years. Boarding applicants complete a taster stay of one or two nights in boarding. Priority given to practising RC families, siblings and applicants with connections either to St John's or a Jesuit education.

Exit: Only a handful leave at 11+ to eg Hampton, Reading Blue Coat. The remainder head far and wide at 13 in ones, twos and threes rather than in huge groups to any one destination school – a fact of which the head is proud. Mainly to boarding at this point, with big names such as Harrow, Eton and Wellington most popular recently. Others to Charterhouse, Winchester, Worth, The Oratory, Stonyhurst, Bradfield, Oundle and Radley. Respectable clutch of scholarships most years – eight in 2021.

Our view: There's nothing a Good Schools Guide writer loves more than a school that surprises them. As a parent on the same fixture list as SJB, this writer had shivered in all weathers on the school's 'flats' (pitches) on numerous match days over the years but apart from lingering in the foyer to the sports complex sampling the undistinctive match tea (albeit in the shadow of a fabulous climbing wall), had never ventured further and, in honesty, had always thought the red-brick Gothic buildings somewhat austere, bordering on intimidating. Coupled with the school's Jesuit foundation and reputation for strong discipline, our expectations were duly set when we arrived on the day of our visit. Happily, we left with them blown out of the water. Serenity and respect pervade the grand corridors (which, true to first impressions, could never be described as cosy) and the staff we met oozed empathy and enthusiasm.

St John's Beaumont sits atop 70 acres (complete with outdoor theatre in the woods) of playing fields and woodland on a hill overlooking Old Windsor. Designed by John Francis Bentley (also responsible for Westminster Cathedral) and opened in 1888, it was the first purpose-built prep school in England, built for 60 boys (the lovely chapel still has 60 seats, each with individually embroidered hassock, plus just four seats for masters). The huge reception hall, hung with portraits of old boys and next-door neighbour Her Majesty the Queen, does set a rather formal tone, but tucked behind the Victorian edifice are recent additions: a fine sports centre with aforementioned vertigo-inducing climbing wall, music, science and art departments, a theatre and the Nicholas Owen pre-prep block complete not only with STEM room for practical science experiments and baking room but – and arguably more importantly – a menagerie of guinea pigs, hamsters, a bearded dragon and occasionally chicks, which 'keep the big boys coming back to visit,' according to pre-prep head. Smart new science labs have given boys the space and facilities they were lacking to experiment to their hearts' content.

Indoor rowing quite a thing, with boys winning silverware at regional and national finals most years, and now school makes good use of its proximity to actual water by getting out on the Thames too

Lessons take place in high-ceilinged classrooms (apparently kept deliberately chilly to allow for boys' high body temperatures) with quiet concentration the order of the day. Head passionate about difference between 'teaching the curriculum and learning the curriculum – we don't teach the Battle of Hastings from a textbook, that's for sure'. Pupils class-taught until year 6, with specialists for just art, music and sport and teachers sharing their subject expertise between classes to create an effective balance between a primary and prep school model. Parents of very able pupils speak highly of the academic rigour of the school, particularly for the teaching of maths. Reasoning on curriculum from year 5 to help get boys ready for that increasingly important pre-test. Although, thankfully – given the long days which stretch from 8.00am to either 5.00 or 6.00pm depending on the age of the boys – there's very little homework given, parents we spoke to felt that thrice-yearly examinations were overkill: 'The boys are literally on their knees.' That said, when we asked boys whether they thought lots were tutored outside of school, there were nods all round. 'Yes, too many,' sighed head, and school has increased timetabled English and maths in years 4 and 5 to try to curb the trend. A small but strong SEN department, all of whom are ex-class teachers ('crucial,' says head), with school able to support mild to moderate SpLD plus high-functioning ASD, of which there are a small number, all diagnosed here.

Badminton, basketball, hockey, cycling, climbing, sailing, skiing and tennis – SJB boys pursue and excel at all kinds of sport, but rugby still rules. Football only recently became a major sport – school gradually moved from two full terms of rugby via a six-week break for football, to the beautiful game now having its very own term of fixtures, and it's cricket in the summer term. The best tennis courts we've seen at any prep school greet visitors on arrival. The usual parental grumbles about lower teams not benefiting from the same quality of coaching as their A team counterparts but boys just seemed delighted that they all get to play so much (every day plus Saturday matches for year 6 up) and told us that it wasn't unheard of – or especially unusual – for a boy to make his way from the D team to the As. Swimming now a major sport following the appointment of a dedicated coach who has transformed reluctant water babies to accomplished swimmers, elite swimmers to IAPS medallists, and also takes a squad on tour to South Africa. Indoor rowing also quite a thing, with boys winning silverware at regional and national finals most years, and now school makes good use of its proximity to actual water by getting out on the Thames too. Noticeably, though, sport is viewed as a mere part of the SJB journey – equal but not superior to the arts or academia. And definitely not a vehicle for machismo.

The fantastically airy art studio is now used by the whole school rather than just the senior pupils and presided over by an inspiring figure who acts as artist in residence and has taken a formerly solid but traditional offering totally boy-centric. The studio is stuffed with everything from miniature hot air balloons and gargoyles to self-portraits in clay. Art tied closely to literature and art history – a recent project was papier-mâché bird skulls wrapped in the text of The Raven by Edgar Allen Poe. Music too has recently been overhauled. Previously seen as somewhat elitist, the appointment of a new choirmaster (himself a coach with the National Youth Choir of Great Britain) with the brief to 'open up' choral music has changed all that. Hymn practice now starts with fun, physical warm-up exercises that get the boys firing on all cylinders. The chapel choir is now fast becoming a 'choir of leaders' rather than one with a couple of stars, and there's also a 'cambiata' choir for boys at the top of the school whose voices are changing (definitely not 'breaking', we were told). Two 'jubilate' choirs for junior and senior pupils use games and actions whilst singing modern music to enthuse boys and help them learn about the physicality of singing. And if that's not enough, there are orchestras and bands for all levels of musicianship. A recent concert ('breathtaking,' said parents) saw school's top musicians conducting the orchestra; 'We want our high performers to inspire the next generation, rather than take all the limelight,' says head. Drama seemed to have a lower profile, although LAMDA is on curriculum in years 4 and 5 and A Midsummer Night's Dream and Treasure Island have been recently performed in the outdoor theatre. Perhaps upping the theatrical ante is next on head's to-do list.

Animal-themed house system engenders keen rivalry for 'TYE' points (Tiger, Yak and Emu) and all things competitive are 'inter-animal' rather than 'inter-house'. Around half of boys come from RC families but school has a light touch from a religion perspective, although saintly effigies and crucifixes are present in most rooms. Parents unanimously praised the pastoral care and the way the school welcomes diversity. Innovative AS tracking system, a computer-generated survey aimed to detect early signs of psychological or mental health problems, provides early warnings to help school identify boys who might be struggling. School's view is that they welcome boys of any faith or none but those who join, 'join a community' and must play their part, including attendance at weekly mass. Boys felt that the Jesuit Pupil Profile, effectively their code of conduct, 'makes us better'. We agree.

Animal-themed house system engenders keen rivalry for 'TYE' points (Tiger, Yak and Emu) and all things competitive are 'inter-animal' rather than 'inter-house'

The scholarship boards provide a record of the school's evolution. Thirty years ago practically all went on to Catholic schools such as Stonyhurst, The Oratory, Ampleforth; today's scholars are just as likely to be bound for Eton, Winchester and Wellington. They're also stretched by the school's impressive Magis programme; senior boys have weekly lectures from visiting speakers, parents and members of staff and are also encouraged to present talks themselves. Lots of fundraising to support a sister school, St Rupert's, in Zimbabwe; all funds raised by both boys and the active Friends of SJB parent committee donated to charity rather than the school.

Day boys come in from a 10-mile radius (bus service operates from Chiswick and Maidenhead). About 40 per cent of boarders from overseas. Parent body is 'like a battenberg cake,' says head: a mix of trad Windsor and glossy Middletonshire (or, as someone put it, those who have Wentworth membership and those who don't). Their sons are commendably oblivious to such pigeonholing and there's a great sense of camaraderie; boys are proud of their school and its traditions. One recent former parent told us: 'Once a St John's boy, always a St John's boy.' In our book that can only be a good thing.

Boarding: Fifty or so boarders – around half from overseas – enjoy a full weekend programme of activities, including paintballing, tank driving and trips to Windsor Castle and the Science Museum. Weekly and 'tailor' boarding (two or three nights a week) also offered.

Like the chapel, boarding accommodation is in its original format: two long and regimented dorms with well laid-out, comfortable curtained cubicles down either side to sleep exactly 60 boys, all with jolly matching planet duvet sets and ceilings festooned with flags representing all boys' nationalities. Smart, recently renovated bathrooms. The 'play room', used for assemblies, doubles up as boarders' common room in the evenings and provides an excellent space for them to play pool, table football or relax – when they're not bounding around outside, that is. 'We worry that parents see so many photos of their sons building dens, cooking or toasting marshmallows in the woods, they'll think they live there,' laughed one staff member.

The last word: One of the most contented and civilised boys' preps we have ever had the privilege of visiting.

St Mary's School Ascot

RC 48

St Mary's Road, Ascot, Berkshire SL5 9JF

01344 296600 | admissions@st-marys-ascot.co.uk | www.st-marys-ascot.co.uk

Ages: 11–18

Pupils: 390; sixth form: 120; Boarders: 375 full

Fees: Day £30,465; Boarding £42,780 pa

Headmistress: Since September 2019, Danuta Staunton BA MA PGCE. English degree and masters in Renaissance literature, both from York. Worked in publishing before joining St Mary's English department in 2010, and has been here ever since, as year coordinator, deputy head of house and then part of the senior management and education team. She spent a year as headmistress elect, working closely with the outgoing headmistress, prior to taking the helm.

Entrance: Selective but not awesomely so. Siblings, while favourably viewed, need good dose of what it takes to secure a place. School gives preference to girls who are Roman Catholic (nearly all pupils are). Many from bilingual backgrounds, though no formal support offered. Special educational needs geared towards those with 'generally mild' dyslexia, with learning support lessons and workshops.

Main entrance points are 11+ (English, maths and general knowledge/intelligence tests) and 13+ (English, maths, science, religious studies, history or geography, MFL, Latin). Feeder schools many and various (300 preps and maintained primaries); so oversubscribed that inevitably there will be some disappointments.

For the unsuccessful, there's another chance in the sixth form (test in proposed A level subjects plus general paper). Chances of success are diminutive though. The maximum new intake is just five, though in reality often fewer.

Exit: Not much fall-out after GCSEs (eight per cent in 2021). Seventy per cent to Russell Group universities. Durham, LSE, UCL, King's, Imperial, Exeter, Edinburgh, Bristol, Manchester, Cardiff, Sheffield, Newcastle, St Andrews, Bath and Goldsmiths all popular. Ten to Oxbridge in 2021. Subjects range from sciences to languages, law to art. Several overseas most years.

Latest results: In 2021, 95 per cent 9-7 at I/GCSE; 88 per cent A*/A at A level. In 2019 (the last year exams took place), 95 per cent at I/GCSE; 77 per cent A*/A at A level.

Teaching and learning: All-round excellence, helped by well-stocked staff room (overall pupil-teacher ratio of six to one). Class sizes average 16 up to year 9, 15 for GCSE years and seven at

A level. Three in a class not uncommon for more rarefied subjects such as further maths.

School is keen to dispel the suggestion that their classy results are easily come by or a foregone conclusion. While they may suggest highly academic intake at 11+, with the vast majority at the top end of spectrum, behind the scenes number crunching (school uses MIDYIS) tells a very different story. Pupils span just about everything from the mid-range and below to the giddy super-bright heights.

A well-managed process steers a careful line between encouragement and pressure. The universally cheerful and confident demeanour of sixth formers about to enter final preparation for final A level exams indicated that it was working. Pupils rated supportive ethos – 'It's cool to work,' said one – and extensive out-of-hours access to staff. 'So many of the teachers stay late that it's easy to meet up with them,' confirmed another. Well-structured lessons where peers, as well as staff, assist with problem areas are a boon, too, say pupils. Transformation of geese to high-flying swans isn't lost on parents, who talk of being 'staggered' by strings of GCSE top grades achieved.

Subject range, though not vast, is well chosen and augmented only after considerable deliberation. Religious studies a non-negotiable core subject at GCSE. Latin (taught like French from year 7) taken by around half the year group at GCSE, well ahead of Spanish, German, Italian (added year 8) and Greek (year 9).

Three cheers for science, a particular strength, with five well-equipped labs and surging physics numbers post-16 (head takes some classes) on a par with biology and chemistry. Over 40 per cent take science subject to A level. Computer science and psychology recently added at A level.

Maths also has consistent numbers of fans, though broad sweep of subject popularity (English literature, politics and French all make an appearance in the top five most years) means most tastes are well catered for. 'There's no subject that's a no-go area. When people ask me, I'm really proud to say what I'm doing,' said a further maths and science star.

The arts and extracurricular: 'We're academic but with lots of extracurricular activities,' a pupil told us. 'The school encourages you to thrive.' And how. Being not just good but 'brilliant' at everything, including sport, drama and music, is the goal, though not easy in such a small school.

As with sport, the arts boast range of spaces that would be outstanding in a school with double the numbers. With its studio, full-size theatre, enormous green room (partitioned for girl/boy casts), bar and extensive costume room, the Rose Theatre is a budding thespian's dream. Many work towards LAMDA exams, gaining the full set by the time they leave. Productions every term, some girls-only, others involving other schools. Production of The History Boys featured an all-girl cast, apart from the French mistress, who was played by an Etonian. A sixth form group took its own play to Edinburgh Festival, gaining good reviews into the bargain.

Art, housed with textiles (DT, though not a GCSE option, is taught as a carousel subject in years 8 and 9) is terrific. In some schools, head of department's hand often all too visible in strikingly similar interpretations of GCSE/A level coursework theme: here, variety (including burqa-clad, slogan-adorned figures in entrance) suggests pupils really do think for themselves. Quality is so impressive that you almost forget where you are and start peering for red spots. Portraiture wonderful – not surprising as school, in one of many go-ahead moments, offers life drawing. Here as elsewhere, school's decision to go its own way has left it ahead of the game. 'We stick to traditions worth sticking to,' a senior teacher told us.

Music is a high-profile affair. Well-equipped recital room, numerous practice rooms (including one, doubly soundproofed, for drums), concerts also in the chapel to capitalise on 'wonderful' acoustics. Head of music who grows her own compositions is now inundated with requests for new works following première of spine-tingling Easter Story and also plans to up numbers taking subject at GCSE and A level (scant handful currently).

Animal friendliness is a big thing. 'Only this school would put a damaged pigeon in a taxi and send it to the only vet open on a Sunday,' said a member of staff

Activities provide outlet for girl power in every form. For younger pupils, few delights trump pet club housed in mish-mash of cages and runs. Hamsters and rabbits dominate, with talent shows featuring animals in natty little homemade outfits. Animal friendliness is a big thing generally and mercy dashes aren't unknown. 'Only this school would put a damaged pigeon in a taxi and send it to the only vet open on a Sunday,' said a member of staff.

Wide range of clubs and societies, from the mind-expanding (human rights, music appreciation, current affairs) to DofE, London theatre trips and upscale wine-tasting (upper sixth only). Born movers and shakers (and there are many) can hone their organising skills in assorted forums, from influential school council ('what we recommend gets done,' say girls) to range of committees. Old girls regularly pop up to widen careers horizons as part of a programme that kicks in from year 9.

Sport: Sports facilities positively glistening with new honed and toned additions. In addition to swimming pool, the Orchard Centre has a big sports hall, two squash courts and a dance studio. One of few girls' schools to have own 400-metre running track, green instead of customary red. Polo available, courtesy of local stables.

While there's a steady crop of outstanding individuals and teams at county level and above (tennis a particular strength), any lingering perception that the keen but hopeless are left to languish is out of date, says the school. All shall have matches (if not prizes). Team sport ceases to be compulsory post-16 but there's enough to inspire even the most sedentary-minded to stay happily active. Body conditioning, universally (though to official disapproval) known by girls as LBT (legs, bums and tums), particularly popular.

Boarding: Modernising elsewhere in the school has seen large-scale abolition of big dorms (mostly no more than five to a room). Top favourite, however, was blast from the past curtain-partitioned 'cubies' in year 8 dorm, voted the best fun, with last night of term midnight feasts.

Catholicism defines the school, sweeping in the committed and the less so. Morning chapel compulsory for all while regular weekday masses are optional

Upper sixth boarding courtyard recently opened – consists of five townhouses and a pastoral centre and lecture theatre around a landscaped courtyard, with each house containing 12 ensuite study bedrooms, a kitchen and open-plan living area.

Sixth form privileges include no uniform (pupils were delighted by this, some parents less so), a separate queue at meal times and annual ball. Biggest perk is separate living quarters, away from main school hurly burly, circle of little homes corralled around own courtyard. Decent kitchens are well used (fruit and veg high on request list, adding to menu staples of toast, pasta – and chocolate crispie cakes). Entertaining is encouraged, with guests treated to more elaborate fare (visiting Etonians haven't thus far reciprocated in kind. 'They don't have the same facilities,' say the girls).

Multitude of house-organised weekend activities helps to dispel any boarding blues. Staples include mass pizza ordering as well as rare forays into deepest girly territory (nail decoration a favourite) and specials like St Patrick's Day marked with cookery (Irish potato scones) and crafts (shamrock felt jewellery).

Weekend activities have greatly expanded in recent years. They now include things such as ice skating, visits to galleries and museums, sailing, rock climbing, and trips to waterparks and trampoline parks, as well as socials with other schools. Onsite activities include house competitions, expert cookery, chocolate making, giant inflatables, craft activities, quizzes and games, festivals and funfairs. Recent evening events have included an Abba tribute band and a stand-up comedy night.

Ethos and heritage: School was founded in 1885 by the Institute of the Blessed Virgin Mary (IBVM), a religious order begun by Mary Ward (1585-1645). Her dreams of founding a Jesuit-inspired apostolic women's order (she even crossed the Alps on foot to put her case to the Pope) came to nothing in her lifetime. Undaunted, followers continued to plead her cause, though it was 2009 before her 'heroic virtue' was recognised by Rome.

Catholicism defines the school, sweeping in the committed and the less so. Morning chapel compulsory for all while regular weekday masses are optional, attracting anything from a dozen to 60 just before exams. Houses take it in turns to organise mass and pick the hymns, the more rousing the better. The election of the current pontiff greeted with huge excitement. 'Someone started screaming "white smoke!" – I had coursework to do but the Pope comes first,' a sixth former told us.

School makes the most of its 55-acre site. Main buildings, some on Gothic revival lines, go up rather than out, with long but not unfriendly corridors, helped by warm terracotta and mosaic tiles and a riot of gleaming staircases (some now adorned with essential if unattractive anti-slip edging).

We were the first outsiders to experience the gorgeousness of school's former concert hall, now transformed into a terrific new senior library (juniors separately and snazzily catered for). Nicer than many universities, say pupils. No wonder, with its curvy window seats, acres of bookcases and wonderful first-floor curved ceiling. Café, complete with morning papers. No learning resource centre faffage here. Pupils can take in iPads and laptops but the printed word is

Transformation of geese to highflying swans isn't lost on parents, who talk of being 'staggered' by strings of GCSE top grades achieved

definitely the star of the show. 'Books betoken silence.'

Pastoral care, inclusivity and discipline: A little light rule-bending aside, few serious offences recently. Sanctions, when they do occur, are now consistent from house to house (just about the only minor imperfection found after recent inspections). Internet misuse would lead to merit-cancelling red ticket. Drink and smoking, almost unheard of, would result in suspension and 'you'd be out' for drugs.

Day to day, six heads of house have the biggest pastoral responsibility. They're considered mainly excellent. Praise too for boarding. Inevitable beginner homesickness well handled with the help of older buddies and kindly boarding staff, vast majority of whom don't teach. 'They're lovely and very sympathetic if you say you have too much work,' said sixth former. Residential chaplain is mentioned by almost everyone as inspirational force for good and a multi-tasker to boot.

There's a fair bit of moving around, which stems from a sensible desire to head off anything that could lead to cliques forming. Sleeping arrangements changed at least once a term and occasionally twice to mix and match the personalities. As a result, happiness tends to rule, and on the rare occasions it doesn't, there's a swift resolution of problems. Sixth form exceptionally strong, with friendships that often endure for life.

Pupils and parents: Around a third from London, a third within an hour's travel, a fifth from overseas (half non-British) and the remainder from elsewhere in the UK.

In times of yore, vibe was a bit Frost in May, with slight sense that the very grandest of old Catholic families had a more exalted cachet than others. Now, though they're still represented, and anyone paying full fees needs to be 'mega rich' to afford them, there's a more egalitarian spirit abroad.

Increasing numbers are funded by bursaries, and though there's lots of emphasis on socialising with other top-notch schools (Eton the top favourite) there's careful control of the trappings of excess. Nickames, amongst them Biggles, Squeaky and Booey, are plentiful and once bestowed are generally there for life.

Parents are a happy bunch. Not hard to see why, given the St Mary's effect, resulting in girls who emerge ready to subdue the world with charm, intelligence, confidence and poise. 'I think anyone in my year could stand up quite happily in front of 500 people and speak,' one former pupil told us.

Money matters: Standard range of scholarships at 11, 13 and 16 on offer (five per cent reduction on the fees). Music scholarships include free tuition on up to two instruments.

The last word: Catholic education at its best. So popular that when it comes to getting a place, faith may not be enough.

St Swithun's School

49

Alresford Road, Winchester, Hampshire SO21 1HA

01962 835700 | admissions@stswithuns.com | www.stswithuns.com

Ages: 11–18

Pupils: 519; sixth form: 146; Boarders: 132 full, 86 weekly

Fees: Day £21,918; Boarding £36,339 pa

Headmistress: Since 2010, the contained and cogent Jane Gandee MA (40s). Read French and Spanish at Girton College, Cambridge, then a local government accountant until she went into teaching (OU PGSE) at Lord Wandsworth College, Oakham, Queenswood and finally director of studies at City of London School for Girls. The stamina and thoughtful tactics that make her a successful athlete (represented Cambridge at athletics and cross-country, captained the women's football team) are combined with a rigorous passion in her stewardship of the girls here. She teaches Spanish in the lead-up to GCSEs and speaks at two out of the five assemblies each week, finding raw material in books ranging from Freakanomics to Daphne du Maurier novels.

Proud of the expanded co-curricular and sport options ('she's got the place buzzing'), determined to open the pupils' eyes to a real range of issues via external speakers – John Humphries, Michael Portillo, Sir Ranulph Fiennes, Laura Bates (Everyday Sexism) – so they can make their own decisions. Committed to developing girls' resilience and confidence – they once took the mickey out of her for her frequent championing of feminism, but now they join in.

Entrance: Main intake by pre-test, January 11+ and CE. Places offered on pre-test and reference from current head – no longer in order of registration. Everyone must pass CE, whether from state, private, or school's own junior school. The latter provides about a third of the intake, others from London day schools and local preps. Note that 11+ candidates are no longer required to sit a science paper. About 20 more enter at age 13 with a pre-test 18 months before (can be taken overseas) and then a firm offer; if there is a crisis and they don't make the necessary 60 per cent at common entrance then there is leeway – occasional places further up the school. About 20 join the sixth form with own entry and test in November; a summer year 10 report is necessary before registration – very competitive.

Exit: Around 20-25 per cent leave after GCSEs, bound for the local sixth form college or for other co-ed sixth forms. Almost all the others go on to university, mostly the old-established ones, with Oxbridge (four in 2021), UCL, King's College London, Durham and Exeter among destinations. Sciences unsurprisingly popular (seven medics in 2021). A few to study overseas in some years.

Latest results: In 2021, 89 per cent 9-7 at GCSE; 88 per cent A*/A at A level (96 per cent A*-B). In 2019 (the last year when exams took place), 80 per cent 9-7 at GCSE; 59 per cent A*/A (86 per cent A*-B).

Teaching and learning: Brilliant exam results, up in the dizzying thin air at the top of the league tables. How a relatively unselective school like this one manages it is mysterious and must drive the London hothouses – with their exacting entry testing of pupils from the age of 4 – around the bend. Parents say, 'They don't cream off the top of their applicants; they help girls reach their potential.' Famed for hotshot sciences (three floors of dedicated labs) and maths; English is just as impressive, even if pursued by fewer girls – pupils say teachers are great, 'no duffs'.

Psychology, politics and art history offered at A level (with art history lessons also on offer for parents). Compulsory GCSE subjects are English, maths, plus a foreign language and at least two sciences. Setting in maths and modern languages. French and German both studied to the end of year 8 when Spanish enters as an option. Most take (only) 10 GCSEs, and just French taken early – a strategy that produces few results below a 6.

Parents report that teachers expect a lot and the girls push themselves, which means that confidence must be built elsewhere if not academically strong. The whole of the lower school enters the Maths Challenge, which encourages different ways of thinking. The Stretch programme helps put academia in perspective – a compulsory hour per week of a loosely cerebral activity for every pupil, eg film clubs, music composition, chess, Amnesty International.

The timetable is in half-hour units but most lessons are an hour; each A level choice has an hour of each subject per day for balance and to mitigate risk when missing a day. The light and warm library is used for study periods mostly by the sixth form, although whole classes can book out the IT area. In the upper sixth both day and boarding girls can return to their one dedicated house to study and hang out.

Brilliant exam results. How a relatively unselective school like this one manages it is mysterious and must drive the London hothouses around the bend

Careers fair annually in Harvey Hall with parents and old girls and speakers ranging from architects to philosophy teachers. Families report that careers advice strong on well-trodden paths such as medicine and Russell Group universities, yet quirky directions need more research initiative from home.

Learning support and SEN: One full-time SENCo, part time assistants and outside support if necessary. An SEN child can still access the curriculum.

The arts and extracurricular: In the lower years there is an hour of art, drama and food tech each week. Very enthusiastic art team with a regular life model, Rosa Verloop inspired sculptures (stuffed tights), nominated desks and eventually cubby holes for A level students – DT floor just as sparky with electronics, laser cutter and Green Power car (has to be fast, green and involve good team) racing every year at Goodwood, but no A level take-up at present. Amazing aromas sandwiched on the floor between the other choices, cooked up in the professional tech kitchen. Textiles popular too with A level newly on offer.

Performing arts centre provides a lively hub for music and drama in the school (and doubles as the venue for morning assembly). Drama studio backs on to the main stage and is used for lessons (no A level at present). Girls do plays on their own initiative too, inviting Winchester boys in for male parts (and vice versa) eg Alan Ayckbourn's Bedroom Farce. Recent joint performance of Oliver! with Winchester College, and more planned. Parents would like more academic links to Winchester College, but it plays quite hard to get; lots of local girls' schools would like to be partnered with it more closely.

Great range of orchestras, bands, ensembles and choirs – chamber, gospel and a capella – some open to all, others more selective. Music school houses practice rooms and an IT suite with Sibelius for composition, basic Cubase skills for recording performances. Around 75 per cent of pupils learn a musical instrument and some 215 candidates are entered for external music exams each year. Senior choir sings evensong each term in the cathedral and tours overseas every other year.

Sport: Lacrosse is the strongest sport with a fixture every Saturday in both the two terms it is played, attendance at the nationals and amazing international tour a highlight. Conscious effort to broaden the range of sports – netball and tennis are on the up in terms of competition; also swimming, archery, golf, fencing, squash, scuba diving, badminton, cheerleading, football, polo, skiing, Pilates. Some of these are only on offer as one of the 30 or so co-curricular choices, others have emerged into the fixture list. The pool is 25 metres with an Olympic-standard diving board (Winchester residents use it too), stables are 10 minutes away and the sailing squad heads off most Sundays. Location in South Downs National Park means limited permanent floodlighting for sports pitches but play continues regardless through temporary arrangements. Early morning swimming popular until studying gets really serious in sixth form, and equipment has been recently updated so apparently girls watch The Big Bang Theory while running.

Boarding: Separate boarding and day houses until a single combined one for upper sixth; the latter are the only ones allowed to go back to their house to work during the day. The seniors do prep duty for the younger ones and there are clusters with a 'mother' in the sixth form and younger 'sisters' or 'cousins' in other years, a 'family' that looks out for each other. A race back to day houses for a hot chocolate made for the girls at break – and letter delivery for the boarding girls; day and boarding girls become less separate as they move up the school. Different nationalities are more likely to hang out with their own at the weekend – the balance is well set between cultural comfort and integration.

The pool is 25 metres with an Olympic-standard diving board. Early morning swimming popular until studying gets really serious in the sixth form

Initially Toblerone-shaped dorms with equal sections under Velux windows, flexible boarding and school bed linen for the youngest, a single room for most from 12+ with a hand basin, useful essay quotes and posters on the wall. Each house has thoughtful inclusive touches that soften the necessary (safeguarding) communality – word of the week board for little ones, movie night, pool table, Wii, piano – as well as the vital drudge of learning to do laundry. Everyone sits around the breakfast bar at the weekend in their pyjamas and the houseparents make sure that full boarders keep busy with three activities during week nights and three at weekends, eg a trip to the zoo, decorating your mobile phone cover, making gingerbread men, skating or music practice.

Ethos and heritage: Founded as Winchester High School in 1884 by Anna Bramston, daughter of the Dean of Winchester, who remained as school secretary for over 40 years – the dean, the headmaster of Winchester College and the mayor are still part of the governing body. Changed its name to St Swithun's in 1927 and moved to the present 45-acre site in 1931. Vast, intimidating, red-brick, Queen Anne style building with blonde parquet flooring, large windows and long corridors (and a new sixth form from 2021) – girls learn to look up and smile as they pass each other rather than hold/avoid gaze as they approach from either end.

A tight community of supportive girls with a culture of 'go for it' rather than 'too cool' to join in, eg minority of girls remain in normal clothes on dress-up days. Flip side of this is the pressure for good results that they can exert on each other. Boarders and day pupils retreat to different houses for break but all eat together at lunch, and head girl team runs the school forum and instigates a school-wide and term-long game of tag. This has everyone searching for their targets, who in turn dye their hair, swap uniforms and even hide in cupboards – all for glory, chocolate and side effect of integration. Pupils give regular assemblies and topics range from Beyoncé to the Khmer Rouge, while the school forum has input to subjects as disparate as the air con in the gym and more tenor timbre in the hymns. Fundraising Friday is another equaliser, as money is raised for the voted annual charities, and some girls do EdClub, a worldwide initiative that uses Skype to encourage disadvantaged children (many in slums) to learn using broadband.

Vast, intimidating red-brick building with large windows and long corridors – girls learn to look up and smile as they pass each other rather than hold/avoid gaze as they approach from either end

Winchester the town is important for the freedom it offers only 15 minutes' walk away – and usually a cab ride back uphill. Provides an opportunity to meet up with Winchester boys; the seniors can eat out or go to a play. The outgoing ones say it is very relaxed, no-one puts on make-up, they are all just a group of friends with about 20 per cent in relationships and many of the day girls knowing the boys from local life; the less confident ones mention a pressure to add the boys as friends on Facebook as soon as they return – yet all monitored (some girls reckon too closely) by the housemistresses and house assistants. Both have a reduced teaching timetable so that they can concentrate on the emotional temperature in each house – there is a health centre on site and a clinical psychologist offers discrete appointments in the old chapel; the whole school benefits from her years of experience of the lives and issues of teenage girls. The leavers' ball is usually just for the girls alone (their choice, no Winchester boys); that, and the singing of Jerusalem, is guaranteed to cause some tears to be shed.

Alumni range from actor Emma Chambers (Alice in the Vicar of Dibley) to journalist and radio presenter Fi Glover and Emma Walmsley, CEO of GlaxoSmithKline.

Pastoral care, inclusivity and discipline: Houseparents are first point of contact for issues from homesickness through bullying to A level choices – although a form tutor is vital for the latter too. Parents feel everything is dealt with swiftly and sensibly; avoiding a before-bed phone call can give both parent and child a less weepy night. Phones are used for email nowadays, particularly useful for older girls looking at timetables and emailing essays, restricted for the younger ones.

An art project of smiles photographed around the school has found a permanent home on the wall of the modern (2013) chapel – all full boarders and staff attend every Sunday, optional for the upper sixth. Over-indulging in alcohol the most common serious disciplinary issue – and that not very, if girls' shock at relaxed attitude observed in their visits to boys' or co-ed schools is anything to go by.

New Thrive programme for all years 'aims to inculcate the habits of good mental and physical health, and to prepare students for the world outside the school gates'. Lessons designed around 'real world' experiences have included year 7s trying out setting up a new community after a plane crash on a desert island, year 10s practising empathetic listening through role-play and year 13s taking part in a student survival programme including cooking and cycling.

Pupils and parents: Down-to-earth parents who value education; armed forces, businesspeople, diplomats, lawyers, doctors and parents of bright children working in less lucrative professions; four wheel drives rather than Bentleys. Over half are day pupils – school bus services are getting better after unflattering comparison with King Edward. Twenty (and rising) per cent of boarders from London, often with more local weekend houses – weekly boarders make up 20 per cent of the school. Heathrow is less than an hour away and Southampton airport only 20 minutes, so 16 per cent of boarders from overseas, range of 17 countries. Occasional international guest pupils come for a term from France, Germany, Spain, Czech Republic – must be fluent in English.

Money matters: One in six pupils has a means-tested bursary, an academic scholarship, sports scholarship or a music award (available at 11, 13 and 16). All scholarships are for up to 20 per cent of fees and based on the calibre of the applicant, rather than need. Bursaries are means-tested and available for 50 to 100 per cent of the fees. Music awards include free music lessons.

The last word: Academic powerhouse with bluestocking reputation now widened into great co-curricular and sports options. Girls egg each other on to great results and fun too.

Shiplake College

Shiplake Court, Shiplake, Henley-on-Thames, Oxfordshire RG9 4BW

01189 402455 | registrar@shiplake.org.uk | www.shiplake.org.uk

Ages: 11–18

Pupils: 487; sixth form: 202 (142 boys, 60 girls); Boarders: 33 full, 134 weekly/flexi (from 13 years)

Fees: Day £20,010 – £25,125; Boarding £28,050 – £37,350 pa

Headmaster: Since September 2019, Tyrone Howe (early 50s). Degree from St Andrews (German and international relations) followed by a masters in European literature from Oxford. Formerly a housemaster at Uppingham, Shiplake is first headship. Began teaching career at Marlborough before a stint playing professional rugby for Ulster, representing Ireland, the British and Irish Lions and the Barbarians. Spent five further years in industry before returning to education, coaching all levels of rugby at Uppingham on top of teaching duties. Describes himself as 'hugely into fresh air and exercise'.

Rugby may be his sport, but we think poker should be his game. 'Any thoughts about going fully co-ed?' we asked on our visit. 'Possibly at some point in the future,' came the reply. But given the school's commitment to its sixth form girls, we were not surprised by his announcement just weeks later that from 2023 the school would take girls from year 7.

Described by parents as 'a natural communicator' who orchestrated a 'phenomenal effort' during Covid lockdowns, which he viewed not so much as a baptism of fire but an opportunity to showcase his strengths. Demonstrating his characteristic ebullient positivity he described it as 'my single biggest opportunity'. Teaching barely skipped a beat and parents really appreciated his weekly assemblies, focus on pupils' mental health and pre-empting of questions, 'heading them off at the pass'. The school's online lockdown pub quiz is the stuff of legend and a quick look on YouTube will demonstrate how seamlessly the music and drama departments transitioned to online performances. Has effortlessly picked up the baton from former head continuing strong focus on pastoral care. 'Fundamentally, I want to be the head of a kind school,' he told us. He's doing okay so far: we hear there were lumps in throats all round when he told latest new cohort of year 7s to remember to pack not their pencil cases or calculators on the first day but their kindness.

Describes Shiplake as a 'personal best' school. On arrival, he found exactly what he hoped for: 'explicit core values' and staff that blew him away with the quality of their teaching. Most important to him is school's 'positive dynamic' and that pupils enjoy the experience. Says success to him is when he can look out of his office window onto smiles, laughter and interaction. But it's not all touchy feely; the future success of the school lies in 'marginal gains', he points out. Says he has 'turned dial up' on academic rigour in a bid to 'raise and build aspiration'. In fact, first job was to rewrite the KS3 curriculum, teaching fewer topics in greater detail and adding the vocabulary of GCSE and A level as early as possible. Also assessed 'reading fitness' of entire cohort on arrival, subsequently introducing accelerated reading scheme to years 7 to 11.

Married to Alex, also a teacher, with school-aged twins and a golden retriever.

Assessment is thorough, taking a day; head wants hopefuls to 'bring a bit of magic with them'

Entrance: Forty-five pupils join in year 7 from a mix of prep and state primary schools and there's a further intake of around 30 into year 9 (assessed in the autumn of year 7). The number of girls in years 12 and 13 is now 60+ and head is clear that they are 'part of the whole school, not just the sixth form'. Incomers at this entry point require five GCSEs including in English and maths, with occasional exceptions. Will rescue those burnt out from (or shot out of) Thames Valley swot-houses.

Assessment is thorough, taking a day and enabling school to see 'the whole picture'; head wants hopefuls to 'bring a bit of magic with them'. Candidates assessed in numeracy and literacy and participate in a group activity, are interviewed by the houseparent or deputy and finish the day with a sports activity. From 2023, in response to the constant parental wish, 'if only there was a Shiplake for girls', the school will welcome girls as day pupils into year 7, a move head describes as 'a natural evolution for the school'.

Exit: Between 15 and 20 per cent leave after GCSE, swiftly replaced by newcomers into sixth form. Around 90 per cent to higher education most years, 40 per cent to Russell Group. Exeter and Loughborough currently popular. One most years to a world leading university including, recently, Yale, Oxbridge and one to Princeton in 2021. Two medics in 2021.

Latest results: In 2021, 47 per cent 9-7 at GCSE; 70 per cent A*/A or equivalent BTec at A level (85 per cent A*-B). In 2019 (the last year when exams took place), 24 per cent 9-7 at GCSE; 37 per cent A*/A at A level (64 per cent A*-B).

Teaching and learning: Parents told us that school's success lies in the strength of its senior leadership team, all of whom have remained in post since head's appointment. Head fiercely loyal to this able crew: 'They have a sense of mission to get the best out of every child.' Very small class sizes, maximum 16, allowing each child to get individual attention and creating strong value-added scores. The consensus from parents was that pupils arriving from prep schools in year 7 might cruise a little bit until the pace picks up in year 9, although school says it's addressing this.

Atmospheric theatre in the Old Tithe Barn area, painted black, with black wooden floorboards and black stone walls, complete with old wood smell

At GCSE it's either double or triple science (even when small numbers choose the triple option, the school will support it). French and Spanish on offer; no Latin or Greek. All the usual suspects at A level as well as sociology, photography and politics, with history, biology and chemistry the stand-out departments in terms of results. BTecs in criminology, business, sport, music performance and travel and tourism, all achieving strong results (92 per cent distinction or above most recently). Majority of sixth formers complete either an EPQ or a sports leadership qualification.

A school that celebrates its 'all ability' intake, Shiplake is creative and innovative in how it instils a healthy learning attitude in its pupils. The Shiplake Seven is a mantra engraved in the breast pocket of every maroon, black and gold striped blazer (curious, open-minded, motivated, reflective, determined, creative, independent). This is enforced and reinforced throughout the academic curriculum, as well as the co-curricular. Major focus on digital literacy, with all pupils expected to bring their own laptop and learning is managed and curated using Google Classroom. School has also designed cyber skills course, taught at KS3 in addition to computing.

No allowances made for laziness or hiding behind sporting excellence – head is crystal clear on this and threats to place match bans on even the most highly prized sportsmen if their academics aren't up to scratch are followed through.

Learning support and SEN: Shiplake has long had a reputation for excellent provision for those with SEN and the support provided by the learning development department for pupils with diagnosed dyslexia, dyspraxia and mild ASD is exceptional. Percentage receiving additional support is 12, in line with national average.

All pupils are screened on entry at which point school asks itself whether the child can function in the classroom independently of an LSA, otherwise support may be individualised with pupils attending up to four small group lessons per week (charged for) to support literacy needs. These are additional to timetabled subjects for years 7 and 8 and replace a modern language from year 9. Pupils receiving learning support in years 10 and 11 take eight GCSEs rather than nine. At sixth form, support moves to guided study support with a focus on preparation for university life. Subject clinics on offer across all departments.

No stigma, and head says he has 'never heard a teacher label a child'. There is a definite drive, nonetheless, to diminish the understanding that this is Shiplake's USP, with numbers of pupils requiring support in year 7 limited to 'a handful', rising in year 9 to 16 of the 75-strong cohort.

The arts and extracurricular: Art housed in spacious beamed roof space in the eaves of one of the modern buildings, photography in the adjoining space. Lots on display around the school. Busy ceramics department and large DT space, four rooms with capacious work stations.

Music described by parents as 'second to none'. Camerata (chamber choir) and auditioned-for First VIII a capella group. Big band, numerous choirs and several rock bands for performers of all ages. Winter, spring and summer concerts give them a chance to perform. Music technology with all the gear – Macs and keyboards – takes place in

Rugby may be the headmaster's sport, but we think poker should be his game. 'Any thoughts about going fully co-ed?' we asked on our visit. 'Possibly at some point in the future,' came the reply

the comfortable new John Turner building. Lots of individual practice rooms and all overseen by an energetic and inspiring director of music. Budding musicians of all genres should check out YouTube for an idea of what's on offer. 'One of the exceptional things about the school,' observed a parent, 'is the ability to find something in which a boy or girl can shine.' Singers emerge who never knew they could sing, and the same applies to drama and all areas of school life. Atmospheric theatre in the Old Tithe Barn area, painted black, with black wooden floorboards and black stone walls, complete with old wood smell.

Enthusiastic and popular DofE, community service and CCF as well as an all-singing, all-dancing array of extracurricular options.

Sport: The focus on sport here is evident. Rowing, thanks to its elite training programme, currently outstrips even rugby in its competitive achievements, with both genders taking on (and mainly beating) all-comers with aplomb at local and national regattas. Current pupils and Old Vikings (former pupils) regularly represent GB at junior and senior levels in the European and World Championships. In 2021, two girl quads qualified to race at Henley Royal Regatta with one bringing home the Diamond Jubilee Challenge Cup. The spectacular new Davies Centre opened in 2020 and nestles on a grassy slope right on the bank of a bend in the Thames. It includes a boathouse, an indoor archery/rifle range, a climbing wall, weights room and an ergo room, which transforms into a function room with a balcony overlooking the river.

The Lynch, the island beyond owned by the school, is ideal for adventure, rafting and camping exercises. A lot of enthusiastic rugby, football, cricket, netball, hockey and tennis players too. Games sessions place a strong emphasis on inclusivity, although those who want to compete needn't worry. Shiplake plays to win with head even intent on 'silverware within five years' for the newly formed croquet team.

Boarding: Five core houses from years 9-12, mixing day and boarders (though full boarders predominantly live in Burr House). In addition there is a sixth form girls' house (Gilson), as well as a house dedicated to the year 13 boys (College House). Years 7 and 8 join Olympians, Titans or Spartans, and attend the majority of their lessons in their house group. Some senior girls lucky enough to have ensuite bathrooms. Younger boys normally share their room with two or three others.

Boarding comes in all varieties here and is tailor-made to meet the demands of the families. Far more weekly and flexi than full boarding pupils, though, with the school feeling relatively local. Flexi-boarding is particularly popular and attractive to busy families where both parents work but can have quality time with their children at weekends. Not a lot of pupils stay at school at the weekends, but a boarding activities co-ordinator and dedicated team of housemasters and teachers make sure that there is plenty to do for the few who are in. Trips to Liquid Leisure in Slough, as well as enjoyable nights out at the local curry house, top the charts. Each house is comfortably equipped with sofas, kitchens and games rooms with, when we visited, a delicious smell of clean laundry and the lubricated sense of being well run.

Ethos and heritage: Situated in luxurious Oxfordshire countryside on the banks of the Thames, only a couple of miles from Henley but far enough from the bustle of Reading to feel secluded and remote, Shiplake Court began its existence in 1895 as family home and farm. In 1959 it became a boarding school and has always been smaller and a more nurturing environment than many schools of similar ilk. The site, mainly red brick and flint, has been tastefully developed through the years, modern buildings and windows blending with the old (newest addition is 2020 sixth form block with café).

Parents praise the communication. It's frequent, inclusive and inescapable for everyone – the receptionist to the head – and covers everything from discipline to rewards and merits. Not a school for a fire-and-forget parent. Some parents, comparing to (high-profile) schools of siblings, say they never knew what they were missing in terms of communication until they joined Shiplake. No Saturday lessons, just sports fixtures to allow more family time at the weekend for day pupils and weekly boarders.

Notable alumni include Nick Jones, Soho House proprietor, Alex Pettyfer, actor, Chris Standring, jazz musician, Jonty Hearnden, antiques expert and, unsurprisingly, a handful of Olympic rowing medallists including Will Satch, Ben Hunt-Davis, Richard Lester and Malcolm Carmichael.

Pastoral care, inclusivity and discipline: Shiplake's reputation as having an exceptional standard of pastoral care is justified (we couldn't find anyone to disagree). This is founded on high teacher-to-pupil ratio (roughly 1:6), and a highly effective school chaplain, the Rev, who doesn't teach but is the pivot of the pastoral system. Even parents go to him with their troubles. A strong system of tutors, as well as houseparent, matron and various support staff within the house. Years 7 and 8 are cocooned in a lower school house, complete with 'wonderful' matron who nurtures 'her' boys until releasing them fully fledged into the main school in year 9. Parents warmly praise the extent to which the staff get to know their students and understand any difficulties. Quite apart from the structures, however, there is also a strong set of principles running from the top down. From growth mindset and the Shiplake Seven to mindfulness clubs and good old-fashioned exercise and fresh air, constant care and attention is given to the wellbeing of the students.

The focus on sport here is evident. Rowing, thanks to its elite training programme, currently outstrips even rugby in its competitive achievements, with both genders taking on (and mainly beating) allcomers with aplomb at local and national regattas

The food is delicious and there is plenty of it (one parent was delighted that her son eats six sausages for breakfast), with a wide choice in the wood-panelled Gothic great hall plus piles of toast back at the house. Mentoring – responsibility taken by the sixth formers for the new year 9s – is both popular with the students and an effective way to break down hierarchies. Bad behaviour not tolerated – from drugs to bullying – and the school will not accept children with behavioural difficulties. However, school is prepared to recognise potential and give people a second chance.

Thorough PSHEE and RSE programme for all years, including visiting speakers to talk about matters such as consent, illegal substances, wellbeing and resilience, as well as addressing such topics in assemblies and tutor time along with other current themes in the media. Sixth formers recently received a hard-hitting talk on consent, harassment and sexual assault, with a recording sent to parents, with pre- and post-presentation surveys for all.

Pupils and parents: Set in the heart of shiny Range Rover, well-heeled territory. Most parents work, a lot are in business. Some are demanding and discerning, some completely hands off, and school prefers the former – we lost count of the times we heard mention of the 'Shiplake community' or the 'Shiplake family'. Most parents share a balanced view about exam results, and while they want their children to flourish, are not obsessively competitive about how they are performing academically. Not a smart or fashionable school ('no fancy airs and graces,' said one former pupil), parents here are grounded and practical, with sound middle-class values and concerned more about the right fit for their children than brand.

A few Forces children, but mostly families live close enough to be day or flexi boarders. Only five per cent of families from overseas. Most of the catchment is east of Reading (navigating Reading during rush hour puts a lot of people off) and a fleet of coaches whisks pupils to and from school from near (Goring, Sonning, Watlington) and far (Gerrards Cross, Beaconsfield, Bourne End, Windsor). There's also a coach from west London for weekly boarders. The only major downside of a Shiplake education, according to the parents we spoke to, is the long day for those who live at the end of the coach routes – the earliest sets off at 7am and returns at 7pm. That said, pupils have done all their prep and had supper before leaving school.

Money matters: Art, drama, music, rowing and general sports scholarships awarded but more for prestige than pounds. Sixth form academic scholarships assessed by a written exam in a subject they will take at A level as well as interviews to determine suitability as an academic ambassador. Means-tested bursaries awarded at the school's discretion with small pot to assist existing pupils, should financial hiccups occur.

The last word: We used to say that Shiplake was not a place for the brainy but now we beg to differ. Pupils of all academic abilities can make their mark at this inclusive school, from those who need some extra support to brainboxes who also value being nurtured, developing empathy and becoming rounded adults. Under the guidance of its dynamic head, the only pressure pupils face is 'to turn up with a positive attitude'. Any doubters should go back to YouTube in search of the 'Shiplake Shanty' for reassurance that this is a school comfortable in its own skin and on top of its game.

Sibford School

Sibford Ferris, Banbury, Oxfordshire OX15 5QL

01295 781200 | admissions@sibfordschool.co.uk | www.sibfordschool.co.uk

Ages: 3-18

Pupils: 426; sixth form: 81; Boarders: 17 full, 15 weekly/flexi (from 11 years)

Fees: Day £10,086 – £16,191 pa; Boarding £31,467 pa

Head: Since 2016, Toby Spence. Joined from Greensteds, a British curriculum boarding school in Kenya. A Quaker by upbringing, his career has included a five-year stint as head of history at another Quaker school, Bootham in York: 'I'm a late medievalist and it was a joy to see York Minster out of the window.' He also had the delicious experience of returning to his old school – King's School in Tynemouth – as deputy head, and as the boss of a teacher who had disliked him in his schooldays. 'We got on better as colleagues,' he says.

Toby is married to Jill and they have three young children, all providing proof of the pudding by being at Sibford School. They are a super-sporty family, and Toby is something of an action man, with swashbuckling tales of paddling a sea-kayak with killer whales off Vancouver Island, making a number of first ascents of mountains in South America, and sailing tall ships around the coast of Australia. He has brought a fervour for triathlons to the school, with much excited chatter about one held earlier in the week when we visited.

A new emphasis on sport is at his instigation, as is a greater emphasis on the academics, although not to the detriment of those requiring learning support, he assured us robustly. His watch is bringing not quite a new broom – not the Quaker way – but rather a dustpan and brush to some dusty corners.

Parents told us he is 'inspiring to students and parents' and they felt confident Sibford was in good hands for the future. 'He's open to opinion and change,' said one. Others appreciated his deep involvement in helping sixth formers to secure university places.

Entrance: Will Sibford's changing focus alter its intake? 'Early days,' says Toby. 'But the numbers coming to see us doubled last year.' There is now a formal assessment day in January for year 7 entry (before it was come when you like). However, he says, 'There is no bar to jump, no Sats, no 11+. Pupils take CATS tests, do some outdoor learning and ceramics. We are a non-selective mainstream school, so as long as the child can cope and thrive in this environment they will be offered a place. It might be more tricky where we feel we might not be able to meet needs.'

Progression from the junior to senior school is as good as automatic. For more academic sixth form courses they ask for five or six 6s at GCSE for externals taking up A level courses – for vocational courses that would be more flexible.

Exit: About 40 per cent of pupils stays on into the sixth form. Leavers include those who may move on to something more vocational; a few who want a more rigid academic focus; and a few who are seeking a bigger sporting offer.

The majority of sixth form leavers go on to university, and to a wide variety including King's College London, Warwick, Cardiff, Oxford Brookes, Royal Northern College of Music, Birmingham Conservatoire and Royal Agricultural University.

Latest results: In 2021, 26 per cent 9-7 at GCSE; 90 per cent 9-4 in both English and maths. At A level, 40 per cent A*/A at A level (58 per cent A*-B). In 2019 (the last year when exams took place), 22 per cent 9-7 at GCSE; 18 per cent A*/A at A level (45 per cent A*-B).

Teaching and learning: Sibford has a long-held reputation as the go-to school for the child who needs a little extra nurturing and support. Toby insists it will remain that way; but that he also wants to develop its academic offer. 'Sibford has an unfair reputation as warm and cosy, but not particularly strong academically. For me they are not mutually exclusive,' he says. Work is underway on what he terms 'rebalancing'. There's a director of learning and teaching, and a fresh tracking and monitoring system. There are working groups looking to build on good practice, and to deliver improved added-value results. 'My expectation would be 0.5 on value added, so if you are predicted four Bs you would get two As and two Bs,' he says.

The junior school is small – 90 pupils – with the majority joining the school at year 4 or above. Years 1 and 2 are in a joint class. Subjects are mainly class taught, with specialist subject teaching for music and PE. There is setting for English and maths. We looked in on a year 5 maths class, and received an unprompted chorus of 'We love maths' from the children. Learning is frequently taken outdoors – we saw a troop of little ones coming through the mist in their orange boiler suits, looking like a tiny chain gang. Reception parents spoke fondly of welly walks and forest school.

In the senior school there is setting for English, maths and science. Pupils can choose the dual award or separate sciences. The language choice is French or Spanish, with German as an extracurricular option. Numbers are higher in the senior school, with 46 in year 7, split into three teaching groups averaging 14 to 16 pupils.

There's a choice of 28 courses in the sixth form, ranging from traditional A levels to textiles or product design, as well as BTecs at levels 2 and 3 in subjects including business studies, sport, ICT and media. Courses will be laid on for small numbers, as one parent said: 'My daughter's French class has just two pupils. I had worried about whether this would work, but it does and the teachers respond well to any class size.' Sixth form is 'led by an outstanding head who knows all the pupils well. The sixth formers are encouraged to be young adults and provide leadership to younger pupils and amongst themselves,' according to a parent.

Founded as a co-ed boarding school by the Quakers, to find 'that of God' in everyone. 'The way I interpret that today is finding the good in everyone,' head says

'We have lived in three different countries since my daughters began their education, and so far the teaching staff and experience at Sibford has been far superior to anywhere we've been before,' said a parent. 'My daughters have all had an excellent connection with their teachers, and I have felt that they quickly understand their learning styles, strengths and weaknesses, and work with them individually in the ways that motivate them best. The teachers at the junior school make it fun and engaging to learn, and they have been quick to see where they can stretch and encourage them to push themselves to work harder and excel.'

There's extension work for more able children – one parent told us her child was in a small group having additional English to stretch them further.

Learning support and SEN: Around 20 per cent of pupils receive learning support for any combination of literacy, numeracy, fine motor, attention and focus, and speech and language needs. Children typically come out of language lessons for support, and in years 7-9 receive three hours per week. For years 10 and 11, it's two hours, and sixth formers have one-to-one for an hour or two. It's possible to have additional one-to-one on top. The learning support department is well regarded – one parent said it had given her child 'confidence and belief in her abilities'. And it is not restricted to those timetabled sessions out of class. 'My mantra is we are all in the support for learning department,' Toby says.

The arts and extracurricular: Plenty of bands, orchestras and ensembles, and an egalitarian approach to performance opportunities. There's a dedicated drama studio, and the school gets a strong showing in LAMDA exams. The head of drama is RSC-trained, and a number of sixth form leavers have gone on to production and acting careers.

Sport: 'We tend to do better in the younger rugby teams,' said our honest guide, when asked about sporting wins. 'Sport is not all about winning, culturally we are more into full participation and giving our best,' is the head's take.

As a small school, and one with a contingent of children there for gentle nurturing, it wouldn't be the place if league-leading teams and dazzling matches are top of your requirements. But you can expect it to claw its way up the fixture lists under this sports-mad head – we did notice his eyes straying out of his office window to the rugby pitch conveniently in view when the 1st XV were playing.

And it can be a joy for pupils shunted to the sidelines at previous schools. 'I'm now in the 1st XV rugby team when I wasn't in a team at my other school,' one boy told us proudly. A parent concurred: 'At her previous school our daughter wasn't great at sport, didn't get into any of the school teams, and felt left out of sport generally. At Sibford the school finds sports that everyone can participate in, and everyone gets a chance to be on school teams. She has been much more sporty, doing swimming, hockey and netball, and representing the school in enthusiastic teams.'

From year 7 there is a sports carousel so if competitive sport is not your bag you can do other things. On our visit we watched a mixed-sex group having a ballet masterclass with two male dancers. A new climbing wall adds to the options, and there's a recently formed equestrian team. Triathlon, swimming, hockey and cross-country are the strongest sports.

Boarding: Around half of boarders from overseas (predominantly Asia, a few from Europe). There are three boarding houses – one each for 11-16-year-old boys and girls, plus a co-ed sixth form house – all with games rooms and quiet areas. Sixth formers have one or two to a room, in the younger houses it may be up to four to a room. Rooms are standard boarding fare.

There is plenty of flex – some pupils will board only one night a week, to tie in with after-school clubs or early morning swimming, or as a chance to sleep over with friends. 'There are always things to do,' one boarder said, and the sixth form girls assured us the presence of their friends meant that they often got more studying done than they might at home alone.

Boarding is for seniors only, but occasionally they will take a year 6 when an older sibling boards.

Ethos and heritage: It's a long wind through tractor-muddied lanes to a bigger campus than you'd expect for the number of pupils. It sits in 50-acre grounds with an orchard, woodland and pond. The original manor was sold off, and the campus is now a hotchpotch of purpose-built blocks including the more recently added music and art blocks and a sixth form centre.

It was founded as a co-ed boarding school by the Quakers in 1842, with an ethos to find 'that of God' in everyone. 'The way I interpret that today is finding the good in everyone,' Toby says. 'Our role is to find the talents and qualities in each individual and develop and celebrate it. At this school you don't have to be one type of person, or one particular fit. We talk about the three Rs but for us that means respect, resilience, and relationships.'

There are meetings for worship twice a week, where the community sit in silence, but anyone can speak or give a reading. Fewer than five per cent of families are Quakers, but the rest are drawn here for the values, and many more parents attend the meetings. 'No parent should be put off Sibford for a moment because it is a Quaker school – it is an entirely positive and largely benign influence,' one parent said. Our pupil guides told us that meetings were a nice time to reflect. 'Like walking into another world, it's beautiful,' said learning support head.

The use of Christian names for all children and adults, and the meetings, result in excellent relationships across the school, parents said. One commented that the sense of community means that teachers often stay for many years, giving tremendous continuity and commitment.

Pastoral care, inclusivity and discipline: 'Always believe you might be mistaken,' is Toby's starting point, meaning errant pupils always have an opportunity to speak in their defence. 'Let's hear, listen and understand. We look for the good in anyone; however bad has it been, we ask, where's the good in here?' Discipline mainly comes in the form of positive reinforcement and praise, but there are 'full sanctions if need be' which has included pupils being asked to leave.

Set among the mellow stone of the Cameron-Clarkson Cotswolds, but 'not a yummy mummy brigade, you don't have to dress up for the school run,' said one mother

This approach means they will consider pupils who may have gone off track in other schools. 'We are open to discussion, and we say if you want to come in these are our expectations. We have some real success stories.'

A parent commented: 'I have occasionally felt that sometimes staff, particularly in the junior school, are less strict with certain children who might require more discipline. They work very hard to support children through kindness and patience (living the Quaker values demonstrably). The senior school is firmer, which we recognise and appreciate.'

Two well-being counsellors are on site two days a week, and the school offers training for parents in identifying and supporting mental health problems. For children with autism or other needs who may need emotional support at any time, they will put together a timetable of key people who are free throughout the day. 'It needs as immediate a response as possible; after the event isn't good enough,' says the learning support head. Where children have social communication difficulties, learning support sessions may include coaching on strategies they can use in class.

A few pupils are transgender or gender questioning. 'Our senior leadership team is reviewing what we need to do to get it right. Our school community understands why this school is at the vanguard here – equality, tolerance, and liberal values are very important to us.'

'Peer relationships are very accepting,' parents said.

Pupils and parents: The school is set among the mellow Cotswold stone of the Cameron-Clarkson brigade, but pushy parents are a rare breed here, we're told. Those choosing it are like-minded, in putting equal store by the values a child will gain to the certificates they leave with. 'Not a yummy mummy brigade, you don't have to dress up for the school run,' said one mother.

Others love the mutual support, and lack of jostling over which set or which team your child is in. 'There's a big fan club if a match is on, and they'll be shouting for all the year groups, not just their own child's,' one parent said.

Another praised 'the inclusive manner of the school, where all ages mix frequently, and there are no groups of girls who exclude others from their circle. Everyone gets on very well, regardless of age, ability, background, etc.'

Money matters: There are academic, sports, music, drama and arts scholarships worth 5-10 per cent of fees, and means-tested bursaries covering up to 80 per cent of fees.

The last word: One of the few schools which is genuinely all-ability, in every meaning of the word. There's a place here for those who need learning support, and those who might apply to Oxbridge; for those who want to perform on stage, and for those who want to quietly contemplate; for those who've made teenage errors of judgement, and those who need cosseting. It's a great option if your brood all need different handling. You won't come here if a slick and shiny public school is what you are after; despite having an international contingent, the feel is more of a local school. However, if competitive parents and league table chasing turn your stomach, you will find your ilk here.

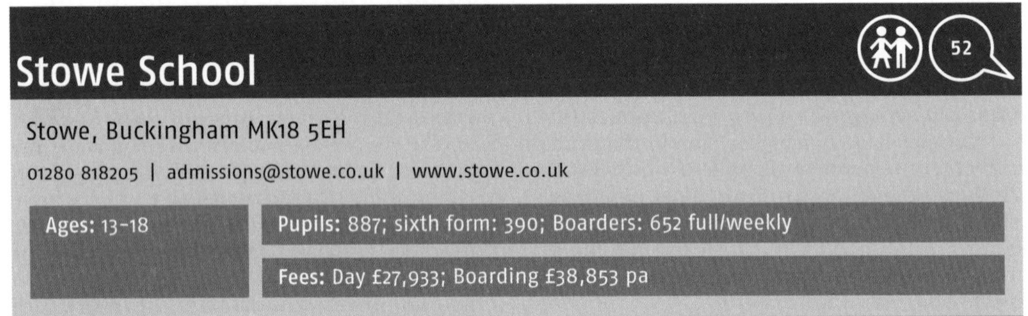

Stowe School

Stowe, Buckingham MK18 5EH

01280 818205 | admissions@stowe.co.uk | www.stowe.co.uk

Ages: 13-18

Pupils: 887; sixth form: 390; Boarders: 652 full/weekly

Fees: Day £27,933; Boarding £38,853 pa

Headmaster: Since 2003, Dr Anthony Wallersteiner MA PhD (50s). History at Cambridge, doctorate in art history and theory at University of Kent. Taught history at Sherborne, St Paul's and Tonbridge before arriving as head.

Passion for art, progressive approach to pedagogy and irreverent humour – all very 'Stowe', an uncannily good fit. Enlightenment values evident in the school's architecture inform 'the genius of the place' today, he says; teaches year 9s a visual education course about the significance of their surroundings. His study is the house's old library, a mini replica of Henry VII's chapel in Westminster Abbey – totally OTT until you learn that it's a rare example of Sir John Soane doing Gothic revival (seriously cool, if you're into that sort of thing). PhD on Cornish artist Peter Lanyon led to involvement in Tate St Ives. Erudite (but not pretentious) and a natural teacher – we would happily have spent our hour together listening to his analysis of Tudor propaganda if we hadn't had to talk shop.

Very proactive, driving the school forwards even after two decades. Parents appreciate lack of complacency – 'When we went to look around Stowe, his attitude was "this is what we can do for your child" rather than the approach elsewhere which was "your child will be lucky if we offer them a place".' Hands-on, too – 'Talked to us personally on results day when our daughter had messed up an A level,' said one grateful mother, while another praised his involvement when her son was going through a rough patch.

Lives with wife Valerie. Three children, all Old Stoics now pursuing wildly different careers in politics, creative consultancy and rock stardom – typical of school's diversity. Dr Wallersteiner 'quite alternative' by his own admission – dreams of 'giving away everything I own and windsurfing around Portland Harbour with a VW camper van,' he says, only half joking. Strikingly organic, almost symbiotic, relationship with the school – embodies a lot of what Stowe is about while school, in turn, has grown around his vision. Won't stay forever, of course, but if or when he does decide to move on his legacy will be a thriving school confident of its place in the landscape.

Entrance: For 13+, interview two to three years before entry. Then ISEB CPT in year 6 (day) or year 7 (boarding) and school reference. Offer conditional on CE, PSB or Stowe tests. Big intake at 16+: papers in two chosen subjects plus essay paper and interview. Scholarship papers at each level. Fed mainly by prep schools, in particular Beachborough, Dragon, Caldicott, Winchester House, Swanbourne House (latter two acquired by the Stowe Group in January 2021).

Exit: Around 15 per cent leave after GCSEs. For year 13, range of destinations reflects range of academic profiles. Newcastle, Oxford Brookes, Exeter, Edinburgh all popular recently. More study business and management than anything else. Four medics and four to Oxbridge in 2021.

UCAS support depends on tutor – some more experienced than others, we heard from parents. Head of sixth form keen that students understand the range of offerings out there when identifying the right course for them.

Head previously vocal about the hot potato which is independent school admissions to Oxbridge. Says now that he's 'pretty philosophical' about it – 'We've always had reasonable numbers but that's not what we trade on.' Harvard grad helps Stoics navigate 'maze of the American application system'. Europe, particularly Holland, an increasingly 'attractive alternative'. 'We talk about the Global Top 200,' he says, rather than Oxbridge and Russell Group.

Latest results: In 2021, 56 per cent 9-7 at GCSEs; 60 per cent A*/A at A level (87 per cent A*-B). In 2019 (the last year when exams took place), 45 per cent 9-7 at GCSE; 33 per cent A*/A at A level (68 per cent A*-B).

Teaching and learning: 'Education is about drawing out – teachers are coaches and mentors,' says head – 'the guide on the side' rather than 'the sage on the stage'. 'Dead Poets Society is the worst film ever about teaching – Robin Williams stands on a table and the only voice you hear is his.' He's got a 'chaotic brain' himself, he says, showing us his notes for a recent whole-school assembly which were indeed indecipherable. Wants to 'stop putting perfect work on the walls, favouring a particular personality type'. Processes not outcomes key – it's like those David Attenborough programmes, he says, where everybody really loves those behind-the-scenes bits at the end about how they filmed it.

Strongest A levels are art, English, history of art. At GCSE, smaller, self-selecting subjects like music and Latin get more 9s and 8s than core subjects taken by the whole year group. Not an academic hothouse and has no intention of becoming one, but those that are academically inclined are 'nurtured', say parents – confidence-boosting to be a big fish in a smaller academic pond, with lots of invitations to extension groups etc. Works well for those who enjoy learning but would not thrive being mid-table at a more competitive school. No shame in doing well, as one mother explained: 'She worked hard – not everyone did, that's for sure – but she never felt out of place for getting good grades.'

'Education is about drawing out,' says head. Teachers are 'the guide on the side' rather than 'the sage on the stage'. 'Dead Poets Society is the worst film ever about teaching'

BTecs now complement the traditional A level offering – a pathway for those who may have gone elsewhere for vocational qualifications and a way to attract new, fresh talent to the sixth form. First was in engineering – a partnership with Silverstone UTC, where students go for welding and machine manufacturing. BTecs in business, creative digital media production and sport since added.

Science centre recently transformed to include 18 labs, six lecture theatres and dedicated sixth form zone. We watched a cracking physics lesson, every pupil chipping in to a discussion of Galileo in a lively, unselfconscious way. Major new DT and engineering centre to be completed for 2023, the school's centenary.

New sixth form centre – pared back aesthetics with tiered seating area and café-style set-up. Lots of pupils in there tapping away on MacBooks or having a coffee. Dubbed 'Stowe-ho House' by witty teenagers who know a thing or two about what's hot right now.

Learning support and SEN: Twenty-seven pupils receive specialist support from 'skills department'. Group or one-to-one sessions as needed, all included within fees. Around the same number receive EAL support from specialist department.

The arts and extracurricular: We could only get superlatives out of parents when it came to arts. 'Outstanding', 'worlds apart', 'superb'. Relatively recent Chung Music School houses 24 Steinways including a grand in the recital hall. A third of

St Hugh's School, Oxfordshire

pupils learn an instrument, many up to diploma level. Opportunities to perform almost every day.

Drama based in the Roxy, named after the school's first head. The Beatles played here in 1963; rehearsals for Oliver! in full swing when we visited. We loved chatting to sixth form artists in the art department (big north-facing windows offer the best light for art, head of department tells us – they've thought of everything) and saw sophisticated and varied work. Every year 13 gets their own little section of the studio to use as they see fit. Pupils can take Arts Award, a holistic qualification that encourages participation as well as appreciation of the arts industries nationally. Stowe Arts forms part of outreach with local youngsters getting involved in front of house, marketing productions etc. Arts are dying at schools around the country – not so here at Stowe.

Climate action group leading on conservation from a scientific standpoint – 'It can't just be polar bears and seals,' says head. Cameras set up for monitoring badgers and bats (Stowe's Springwatch). School recently hosted inaugural national assembly for Schools' Climate Action, committing to becoming carbon net zero by 2040: mock COP 26 and talks by Michaela Strachan, Sir Ed Davey and John Sauven, executive director of Greenpeace.

One of the top golf schools – ninehole course with views over 18th century monuments and follies, including the dog-leg over water towards the ancient Fary's Oak

Volunteering becoming more meaningful – less fundraising, more action. 'No longer a box-ticking exercise,' say staff. Not just care home visits, but dementia training too; discussions with local organisations about providing experiences for the vulnerable using Stowe's facilities. Hard to get hands dirty from the middle of a 700-acre estate, though, and we couldn't help but think that the 'fill a shoebox for Africa' scheme required little more than access to mum and dad's Amazon Prime; nonetheless, moving in the right direction. Pupils choose between DofE and CCF – good take-up from girls and boys in both. Change Makers week to finish school year – film-making, empathy workshops, lectures and coaching in core transferable skills for the future workplace.

Sport: Rugby main sport for the boys, with five senior teams. Lacrosse for the girls, played across two terms. We watched girls putting Radley boys in their place on the pitch – far from a jolly, it looked seriously competitive out there. Weekend fixtures coordinated against one school – we visited in the run-up to a Rugby School away weekend. Girls going up on Friday night to play hockey under lights, livestreamed on YouTube (553 views and counting); rugby cup match on the Saturday was set to be a season highlight (for completeness: first XI girls won; first XV boys lost). Charming cricket pitch hosted first recorded school match in 1928. Five hundred pupils regularly representing the school, 'regardless of level'. Girls' teams for football and rugby too, 'if there's demand'. Lots of basketball. One of the top golf schools in the country – nine-hole course with views over 18th-century monuments and follies, the highlight of which is the dog-leg over water towards the ancient Fary's Oak (not our area of expertise but, we suspect, pretty awesome).

Enormous number of options for everyone, from badminton ('very popular') to 5km Stowe Stroll through glorious parkland. Kudos to those who have a go ('the D team is the coolest, really,' say pupils). Not just sporty, but wholesome generally – traditional outdoor pursuits include a 'small but solid' number involved in both beagling and fishing. Equestrian centre is cherry on the cake (or one of many cherries) – cross-country course designed by Captain Mark Phillips, British equestrian royalty (and ex of actual royalty). As we pulled up in the car we saw a pupil galloping across the parkland seemingly without a care in the world – a Jilly Cooper paradise without the smut.

Indoor facilities less lovely – parents identified swimming pool as tired, though redevelopment of sports complex is imminent and will house new classrooms for GCSE, A level and BTec sport as well as dance studios, bigger gym, viewing facilities and smarter changing rooms. Third Astro and a big indoor dome will allow for more hockey, netball and tennis year-round.

Boarding: School has recently relaxed the approach to full boarding so pupils can go home every weekend. Parents' reactions mixed (though current parents hadn't, of course, signed up for a weekly boarding school): 'We liked the fact that they wouldn't be traipsing down the Kings Road every weekend,' they told us. Saturdays busy with lessons and fixtures regardless. Those who stay in can take minibus into Buckingham or, sometimes, to the bright lights of Milton Keynes ('But why would we?' say pupils). Seventeen per cent of boarders international.

Houses we saw were fresh, homely and well kitted out with USB chargers, underbed storage etc. Others are more oak-panelled but equally comfortable, we hear. Common rooms strike the right balance between modern and characterful with comfy sofas and house silverware on display. Sixth form do their own laundry. Day students all have a desk in their house which they can use during the day, many adorned with fairy lights and photos of friends. Day houses close at 9pm though a lot of the younger ones leave at 7pm.

We found the atmosphere in the boarding houses warm, cosy, intimate. School engages couples as house parents to create a home-from-home feel. We saw girls doting on house parents' newborn; 'We've got 60 babysitters on tap,' chuckles the new mum. Very relaxed, easygoing relationships ('ooh, miss, I like your dress'); pupils join staff to walk their dogs at the weekends.

Ethos and heritage: We've seen some serious school buildings in our time, but this takes the biscuit. We knew we were in for a treat (the school famously occupies the Grade I listed Stowe House) but the National Trust-owned parkland around it – ornamental lakes, monumental columns, temples – is extraordinary in its own right, inspiring stunning pupil landscapes. No time now for the detail, go and see for yourself, but suffice to say there aren't many schools that boast an 1803 Egyptian Hall (sphynx – tick; sarcophagus – tick), a marble saloon modelled on the Pantheon (Roman-style victory frieze – tick) and a 17-something library with ornate plaster ceiling (views of Capability Brown gardens – tick). It's testament to how impressive it all is that we were shown the chapel – flanked by Ionic columns and complete with 18th-century panelling – as an afterthought. A few parents observed that some of it could do with tarting up but realised that it's the price you pay to go to school in one of Britain's finest neoclassical piles (along with the actual fees, that is).

No longer a playground for the rich and racy – culture has changed. Growing day provision has pushed up academic standards and cultivated a more 'normal' demographic (a relative term, of course). Stoics nowadays by no means goody-goodies, thank heavens, but more aware of their privilege. Great company without being smarmy, with a confidence which comes, we reckon, from having the chance to be good at a whole host of things. We found their easy manner and good humour endearing: a welcome change from the precociousness of their peers elsewhere. Not kids who've continuously been told that they're headed for Oxbridge or that the world owes them A*s. They're more real than that, and a lot more fun for it.

A country school, not as cosmopolitan as city-based co-eds and socially softer. One teacher described her 'ultimate success story': 'She came to us with a tough exterior and said she was never going to join in and now she plays badminton

The school occupies the Grade I listed Stowe House, but the National Trust-owned parkland around it is extraordinary in its own right

for the school and is so relaxed, so comfortable in herself.'

Alumni united by passion and a twinkle in the eye: Richard Branson (ever the disruptor, apparently forcing total rethink of the canteen); David Niven (one-time Bond and classic English gent); Matthew Vaughn (director and producer); Marilyn Okoro (GB runner and Olympic bronze-medallist).

Pastoral care, inclusivity and discipline: Eight boys', four girls' and one co-ed (for sixth form) house – all central to pastoral care for day pupils and boarders. PSHE programme delivered (unusually) by subject specialists and augmented by staff from medical centre, chaplaincy, peer support group and school counsellor. New Wellness Centre in Queen's Temple.

Everyone's Invited prompted four 'town hall' meetings, not least because school was named (along with almost 3,000 others). 'We are looking more at consent, focusing on what boys need to think about.' Fits with the school's approach to gender anyway – 'challenging those exaggerated masculine stereotypes, those tropes of masculinity: it's fine to be male and to prefer ballet or fashion,' says Dr Wallersteiner, ever the aesthete, adding that, 'We could all benefit from leafing through Vogue.' Girls need 'to understand why some boys are interested in football and gaming – it's competitive and interactive, it gamifies social interaction.'

Classic navy blue uniform up to year 11; business suits for sixth form. Mostly in hoodies when we visited (an own-clothes day for Amnesty) but probably the 'right' hoodies. Lots of gum-chewing and floppy hair on the boys – staff don't seem to mind a bit of superficial scruffiness provided that everybody's showing respect and getting their work done. Some more debonair: 'They want to get to Henley because they want the blazer'; 'His personal grooming went from 0 to 100 per cent when he joined,' say parents.

Food is 'acceptable', according to parents who suggest that school could buy more locally and seasonally. Pupils happily tucking into proper hot lunches when we visited ('wild boar sausages – yum,' we noted) and meals are a sociable affair. Breakfasts delicious, apparently – avocado on toast makes the odd appearance at Sunday brunch.

What about discipline, in a school once renowned for drinking, smoking and heavy petting in the bushes? We found it hard to get an answer on this one. Some parents unaware of any mischief, others could reel off recent misdemeanours and subsequent sanctions. 'Lots of penalties' for those caught vaping, for instance, though approach seems to be pragmatic rather than punitive and depends on house parents. School doesn't attract disciplinarian families – 'I hope they're a bit naughty,' laughs one mum. 'They're allowed to be creative within a sensible set of rules without overpowering them with legislation,' says another. Major offences dealt with appropriately and Stoics certainly not running wild – a 'pick your battles' approach?

Pupils and parents: Day pupils now make up a quarter: lots coming in by minibus from across Bucks and Northants (no public transport to speak of here). Parents with a creative bent, looking for something a little different to the more traditional offering or just living locally.

There exists a wealthy set, for sure, particularly among the boarders – international, London, home counties, sometimes all three – but 'they all eat the same food,' points out one mum. Seems that even where there's 'money swilling around', pupils don't bring swank or swagger to school with them.

Parents we spoke to were down-to-earth, balanced, realistic. 'If he ever goes on a superyacht, it'll be as crew.' 'My expectations weren't accurate – we've found parents to be inquisitive, motivated, not interested in money.' 'I've edited a few parents out but I can't get over how inclusive and fair-minded my son's friends are.'

Money matters: Academic scholarships along with music, art, drama, sport, equestrian, design, golf and original thinking. Change 100 bursary programme aims to raise £100m to fund 100 places in perpetuity – first cohort of boys and girls already benefiting.

The last word: Stowe has left the sex, drugs and rock 'n' roll behind while maintaining its sense of fun and developing a thoroughly modern approach to learning and pastoral care. Plenty of opportunity for first XV or Oxbridge if that's what's right, but your child will not be forced down that path; space for the unconventional and eccentricity too. An enlightenment 18th-century setting for the enlightened 21st-century parent. We think it's a winner.

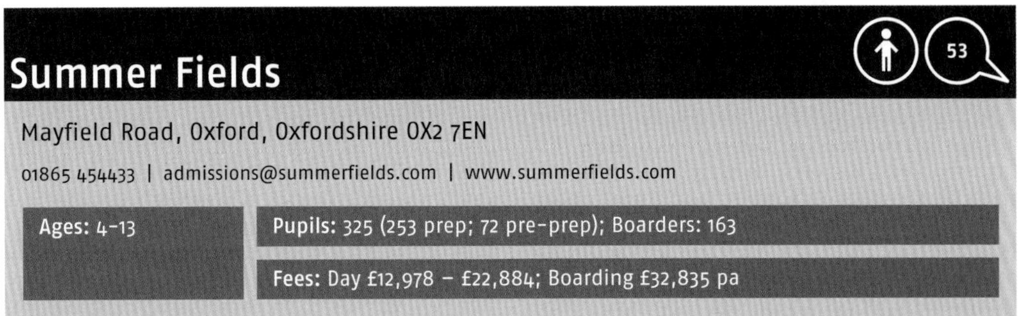

Summer Fields

53

Mayfield Road, Oxford, Oxfordshire OX2 7EN

01865 454433 | admissions@summerfields.com | www.summerfields.com

Ages: 4-13

Pupils: 325 (253 prep; 72 pre-prep); Boarders: 163

Fees: Day £12,978 – £22,884; Boarding £32,835 pa

Headmaster: Since 2010, David Faber MA Oxon (50s); came to Summer Fields as old boy; former parent and governor, as well as grandson of illustrious alumnus, Harold Macmillan PM. After Eton and Balliol, became a Conservative MP from 1992-2001, including Opposition spokesman on foreign affairs (recently secured schools minister as a speaker for a meeting of prep and public school heads). A keen cricketer (sits on MCC committee) and has introduced new cricket nets to the fields; also referees boys' football matches.

Interesting appointment as not originally from a teaching background. Urbane and reserved in manner until on the subject of the boys' achievements – fond collector of past medals, 'sporting caps' and historical mementos of the school. Uses his experience as a historian and author (two books on modern history) in teaching history to the older years and lecturing on Appeasement and the Munich Crisis to public school history societies. Popular with parents ('dream headmaster'), who have seen him institute 'a lot of changes for the better, one thing at a time'. Makes himself available to the parents and appears to know the boys by name and character. Married to Sophie, not on school staff, with two school-aged daughters and a son at Oxford University.

Head of the new pre-prep is Joanna Chapman, previously head of junior school and pastoral lead at Knightsbridge School, with degrees from Exeter and Winchester.

Entrance: Into the pre-prep by 'very relaxed and informal' assessment. Prep school 8+ entry assessment day includes written tasks (English, maths and non-verbal reasoning) and informal interview, along with an all-important report from current school. Early registration necessary, but occasional late entry places and mid-year starters also accepted. Head refers to it as a 'national' prep school, with most coming from within an hour's drive of Oxford; some overseas and regular group of Old Summerfieldian sons. Previously thought of as upper crust, and hasn't entirely shaken off the image. Head disagrees, but one parent regretted the narrow social compass. No plans to take girls.

Exit: About 60 per cent to Eton, Harrow, Radley and Winchester. Lots of scholarships in recent years offered by Eton, Harrow, Bedales, Wellington, Radley, Harrow and Oundle. They covered academic, art, sports and outstanding talent. Head maintains, 'Proof of the pudding is that the less academically able boys still get into public schools.' Others to St Edward's, Marlborough, St Paul's School and Stowe. Parents like the fact that it doesn't feel like a 'feeder' but still gets great results.

Our view: Set in over 70 acres of stunning grounds in the heart of north Oxford, the school is unremarkable from the front, but boasts a stately bow-fronted building with fields, woods and river at the rear. Founded by Victorian educationalist husband and wife team, Maclarens, in 1864 and still conscious of its Christian traditions with (recently refurbished) Victorian chapel and oak-panelled hall. There are more modern additions of several smaller houses along adjoining road; two pools (indoor and outdoor); a sports complex, Eton fives courts, a climbing wall, new all-weather tennis and Astroturf courts, as well as nine-hole golf course and cricket nets and relatively recent very large sports pavilion. Most recently, they've added a 6m tree house providing a classroom in the trees, which includes two viewing platforms connected by solid bridges.

Very long day for both boarders and day boys starts with whole school convening for chapel or assembly. Lessons in small classes (10-17) and early setting promote strong academic results at CE. Scholarship class in last two years given Greek, and Latin and French learnt by all. New DT and ICT suite and science labs, where boys encouraged to 'design your own experiments and make things pop', as well as large, busy library. Boys genuinely motivated by trips to Oxford museums and field trips, including to France. Teaching staff visible round school, as most live in, some of long standing (30+ years); 'most staff leave to become a headmaster somewhere else'. Academic success earns boys personal and house points which can be enjoyed by tangible rewards in the school shop (Buzzer) and a house feast. A staff of six for learning support, with some experience in EP support and statements. One parent felt that it was particularly good for boys who aren't particularly socially confident and so may experience difficulties elsewhere.

Music is a strength, with a dedicated music block and theatre. They recently hunted down a marimba (eastern xylophone) teacher in Oxford for a lad from the Far East

Music is a strength, with a dedicated music block and theatre. Three choirs, one with adult voices, sing in Oxford colleges and on tour (Rome recently). Specialist music staff allow boys to take up to three instruments (we heard of a 10-year-old playing four), ranging from conventional to electric guitar, even quirky. They recently hunted down a marimba (eastern xylophone) teacher in Oxford for a lad from the Far East. Drama productions for different year groups from Twelve Angry Men to We Will Rock You, open to all those who risk taking time from their scholarship clubs. Sport is plentiful and all-inclusive; parents like the fact that all boys make the teams, which play twice a week. Football has recently had its best season since 1937; rugby and hockey also strong, with some players in county cricket and rugby teams. Prolific art and ceramics studio, obviously not PC – fantasy coats of arms and big game trophies made from papier-mâché adorn the walls.

Boys emerge from lessons brightly but quietly. They are articulate and confident, although suspiciously neat and clean in brightly coloured shirts and sweaters. Parental niggle that boys were 'a bit too polished'. However, children appear kind and supportive – 'when you are in the third year you know everyone's names' – and a nice touch that both staff and children refer to the school as 'We…'. Boys don't seem fazed by formality or overt competition – academic progress bulletins are posted on the board every two weeks for all to read – but seem to enjoy it as 'healthy rivalry'. There is a wealth of extramural activities, spanning spiritual (Time for God group), sporting (fencing, shooting, polo) and more earthy interests (cookery and Adventure

Quest – bushcraft-style camps – for handy skills in lighting the campfire and skinning a rabbit).

An appreciation of the school's history is encouraged with scholars' boards lining the walls of the hall; and a moving Remembrance Day service, when choral speakers read out names of the fallen alumni. Boys follow this up with a trip to the Somme. Old Summerfieldians include generous helpings of baronets, colonial civil servants and military leaders, as well as Dick Francis, who set one of his detective novels at the school. Active old boy links suggest happy memories.

New pre-prep in a converted boarding house in the grounds. School is also nearing the end of a big new development for the older children including new classrooms, learning support rooms, library and refurbishment of the chapel.

Boarding: Lodges (boarding houses) for boys of same year group; run by husband and wife team and kept apart from the teaching rooms (no homework or dining in lodge). Newly refurbished and remarkably neat dorms sleep four to six boys, with effective in-house incentives for boys to change own sheets, polish shoes and tidy up. One parent commented, 'What I like is that Summer Fields doesn't smell like a school.' Weekend leave for boarders regularly throughout the year. Pastoral care is managed with a three-tier 'belt and braces' approach. Lodge parent claims, 'Homesickness is more of a problem for the mums' than the boys, who are kept busy in the evenings with board games, computers and giant chess sets. Parent of a young boarder was hugely relieved how easily the youngest were settled in. Discipline maintained by healthy competition and withdrawing privileges rather than anything more gruelling. Boys appear to appreciate this.

Money matters: Special assessment day for the Maclaren Scholarship – up to 100 per cent bursary for a year 6/7 boarder given to a high-flyer, usually from a state primary. Academic and music scholarships at 8.

The last word: A small and cosy school, in a serene and beautiful setting, successfully eases a boy into a boarding career. It provides a breathtaking array of sports and music facilities as well as being reliable in placing boys in top public schools. Sense that boys work hard, play hard and turn out to be happy, considerate and polite, if slightly formal. Not for Just Williams.

Sunningdale School

Dry Arch Road, Sunningdale, Ascot, Berkshire SL5 9PY

01344 620159 | headmaster@sunningdaleschool.co.uk | www.sunningdaleschool.co.uk

Ages: 7–13

Pupils: 110; Boarders: 65 full, 30 weekly

Fees: Day £20,520; Boarding £26,250 pa

Headmaster: Since 2005, Tom Dawson MA PGCE – and recent distinction in grade 1 piano (40s). Previously taught at Harrow before taking over the shop (school is fully owned by the Dawson family), inheriting headship 'because I'm the boy,' he jokes (slightly).

Family-run is understatement and a half. Wife Elisabeth, fellow modern languages graduate, is highly organised director of studies, garnering almost as much praise as husband. 'Lovely', 'kind' and their ilk crop up in conversation with parents with Swiss railway regularity.

Amy, a jolly Dawson sister, one of three (others educationally occupied elsewhere), runs high-quality art department and masterminds school productions, more fulfilling than previous career as mural painter (only so many David Beckhams you can glorify on child's bedroom wall without spot of existential angst).

Also living and working on site are Mr Dawson's own parents and uncle, who acquired school as going concern in 1960s and are a genial background presence, mother putting final touch to colossal flower arrangements, father waving from ride-on roller. 'Keeps them going,' says their son.

We wondered about sotto voce presence of school parents, who don't, currently, have own association. 'Don't need one,' says Mr Dawson, who points to numerous 'meet the Dawsons' opportunities at well-attended matches, concerts and exhibitions. Parents, professing ardent faith in his leadership, fall over themselves to deliver several carillons' worth of ringing endorsement apiece. 'Exudes incredible values', 'outstanding personality' two among many.

Mr Dawson, while amiable, is reckoned to miss nothing and parents felt that he wouldn't shirk from tough decisions. 'If there's one super-naughty boy in the school then I guess somebody has to be expelled, as in all schools,' thought one. Impressive networking skills don't go amiss either. 'I know a lot of people,' he says, and what a useful crowd they are. Barnaby Lenon, former Harrow head, extols virtues of pupils and school at length on school website. Mr D cultivates contacts through cricket – a predictable passion. Another – repairing pre-digital Roberts radios (impressive range neatly arranged in his study) – possibly less of an obvious social asset.

Entrance: Register at birth for one of 22 places, waiting list if full (as, increasingly, it is). Mr Dawson understandably hates putting up 'no vacancies' sign – 'don't want to be known for it' – but is currently 'turning down a lot. It's a cosy, happy place and I don't want to get any bigger.'

Long the place where old money arrived as small change. Cricket commentator Henry Blofeld, Duke of Westminster, horse trainer Sir Henry Cecil – list of old boys says it all

While it has plenty of high flyers, entrance requirements aren't stratospheric. School expects fluent reading and writing and grasp of basic arithmetic. May ask for report from current school and very occasional pupil is directed elsewhere.

Prospective pupils spend day at the school year before they join when sit short papers in maths, English and VR. Also attend music, art and sport workshops. Main purpose is to work out forms ('we don't really operate in year groups,' says school). Some scholarships available as well as means-tested bursaries. Weekly boarding available for the first three years. Also takes maximum of 10 day boys through the school, all locals, inherited by Mr Dawson who has 'just stuck with them'.

If you miss the boat, there's a diminutive chance of place or two in year 7 – 'incredibly rare for anyone to leave,' says Mr Dawson – offered after cognitive ability tests (though non-academic strengths also taken into account).

No linked feeders; elite London mob – Garden House, Thomas's, Eaton House – increasingly feature, as do old boys' offspring – at 10 per cent and rising, says school, which stresses that fees 'are kept as low as possible'. School buses to London at exeat weekends, long leaves and end of terms.

Gaps increasingly filled by international families – one boy we met saw family only three times a year – though school has recently started live feeds for concerts. Otherwise, pupils come from all over the country 'except Cornwall'. We were hoping for some ancient West Country vs Home Counties blood feud. Disappointingly, down merely to poor transport links.

Exit: Mr Dawson not a fan of serial entrance exams and suggests maximum of three senior schools, two aspirational, one 'a safer bet'. To most of major, trad names in south-east. Leavers to Eton, Charterhouse, Wellington, Tonbridge, Stowe, Harrow, Sherborne, Marlborough.

Our view: Long the place where old money arrived as small change. Cricket commentator Henry Blofeld, Duke of Westminster, horse trainer Sir Henry Cecil – list of old boys says it all. All it takes is names of first two heads – Girdlestone and Crabtree – to know you're in the presence of Tradition, with capital (and gold-embossed, gothic-lettered) T. Would make a fine detective series title as well. Additional helpful pointers come by way of slightly fly-blown pictures of Victorian worthies in visitors' loos – OBs Duke of Marlborough 1893; Lieutenant the Honorable FHS Roberts VC, killed Colence SA 1899.

Scratch the surface and you'll find... more tradition, bookcase packed with Biggles, Worrals and even a Henty or two (remnants of old library) adorning the morning room – or, more prosaically to those of less gentle birth, the school office. Makes statement architecture of curved library – first building visitors see and the newest – the more startling by comparison. Accoutrements – refectory table and two sternly positioned sofas – are set off by glow-in-the-dark bright blue carpet (also a dormitory feature), bare walls crying out for some splendiferously mustachioed OBs, picture windows giving vistas not of bosky woods or slumbrous streams but cars approaching up the drive.

Shelves reassuringly weighted in favour of fiction, wooden blocks with school number marking borrowings, one per boy. And if you want to borrow two books? 'Two?' asked Mr Dawson, experiencing mild Beadle-like moment. 'Why would anyone want to read more than one at a time?' It's the hallmark of a school with a strong sense of its own place in the world, conventional yet not in thrall to crowd mentality. Summer half term, for example, happens a week later than normal. Trade off, with school taking strain of final revision for CE exams, worth hassle of arranging two sets of holiday activities for offspring elsewhere, reckoned parents.

Class structure, average size 12, also takes a bit of getting used to. Ability rather than age-based, so while nobody is ever moved down, brighter boys will go up a year, sometimes two, never more. In top years, carefully planned scholarship work ensures there's no 'here's one I made earlier' duplication.

From animated debate on how to stop extinction of coral reef in science – 'tries to make it as visual as possible,' said star pupil – to year 6 pupils reading (beautifully) extracts from end of year English exam, a 'do-able' past CE paper, impression was of willing learners enthusiastically taught. Bright, super-engaged staff, majority male and with average age of 39, includes several of distinctly young fogey-ish disposition and bouffant charm – Boris Johnson recast with auburn and brunette tresses.

Impressive commitment to pupils with SEN. One, with ASD, initially reluctant to attend lessons, supported with one-to-one help, funded by parents, 'fully integrated,' says Mr Dawson. More usual needs (mild dyslexia) respond – miraculously so, thought one parent – to small classes and skilled teaching without intervention. Head 'isn't a big believer in throwing tons of time and money at extra tuition,' said one parent. 'Because the classes are so small, and teaching so good, you don't really need it.'

Staff praised not just for ability to inspire love of learning – 'never did we expect such commitment,' said mother – but for reinforcing universally wonderful manners and behaviour. One parent thrilled when master told son to 'stand up and show the way for your mother.' Compliments, convertible to house points, awarded for the dutiful, complaints doled out for the untidy or overly chatty lead to writing out code of conduct.

Had been very slight relaxation in discipline, now checked, thought one pupil (like peers, a charming lunchtime host) and all to the corporate benefit. 'Wasn't working so well before – now good for the school but bad for the individual.'

Minor transgressors write out school code of conduct; serial offenders lose 'privs' for a week, part of plentiful school jargon that includes 'going across' (signals need for comfort break rather than deepening interest in spiritualism), 'grub' (sweets) and 'lemonade' (a generic term covering hot chocolate, juice and even cake).

Parents universally thrilled by restricted presence of i-anythings out of lessons, and tactical use within. Rather than mass breaktime retreat into solitary cyber universe, pupils here whizz energetically about in real time with friends. 'Really important because children become so addicted to these games that they don't interact with their peers,' said relieved mother.

Plenty for them to enjoy, from lovingly tended plots with courgette flowers and tomatoes to three Gloucester Old Spots, sensibly not named, bees ditto – though for logistical rather than emotional reasons. Other tucked away treats include shaded mini-adventure playground for first years and personable wood-panelled and colonial-style chapel, consecrated 1880 after arriving in kit form (so many identical labradors on site that you start to wonder if assembled in similar way).

Universally wonderful manners and behaviour is reinforced by staff. One parent thrilled when master told son to 'stand up and show the way for your mother'

While academic success is all well and good (and often very well and very good), school also does best to find ubiquitous spark. Music a strength, with 80 boys learning at least one instrument, variety of ensembles to play them. Many cheering examples of mild reprobates transformed by gift for singing (there's a queue to join the choir, say parents).

But whichever formerly dark area of the curriculum light of budding talent might illuminate, helps to have at least nascent interest in sport. Not for everyone, one OB recently describing it as 'an acquired taste', but for most, it's a way of inculcating right values, particularly as school size ensures participation by all. 'Perfect because even the boys who are mediocre at sports all get to make the teams – nobody gets left out,' said parent. Year to year, results vary considerably – inevitable consequence of small size. One cricket and rugby team had been undefeated all season; others with less enthusiastic cohort won't do half as well.

In addition to big three (football, rugby, cricket), tennis, Eton fives (since 1892), golf and swimming are all provided on site. Five pitches (four multi-use and a new Astroturf) appear to stretch away into far distance, courtesy of clever landscaping that makes the most of stand-out planting, including massed rhododendrons (Mr Dawson has sole pruning rights over favourite). Provides effective masking of more functional buildings including vast sports hall (for basketball, fencing, air rifle shooting and much more) and gives 25-acre grounds feel of something much bigger.

Sport, inevitably, dominates the summer term after school activities list, replaced in winter by idiosyncratic range that currently includes Warhammer and fly-tying (teachers, all required to take at least one sport or activity, encouraged to indulge own enthusiasms). All adds to the fun.

Boarding: Seemingly endess activities seen as essential (particularly for new boys) in helping to acclimatise to full boarding lifestyle. Weekly an option in the first three years, though 'half full board from the word go,' says school.

In addition to two long weekends (Friday to Monday evening), a couple of bonus Sundays and half term, there's much anticipated treat of year group excursions to school/family-owned house in France. Icing on the cake (almost literally) is first-class food prepared by Mrs Dawson Snr. One boy 'asked why I can't cook like that,' said mother.

School points out that boarding for all hurts parents far more than the boys – 'always rather sad for the mother,' agreed one, 'but we just knew they'd be so happy.' Also ensures a full house at weekends for Saturday film nights (no lonely minority waiting for life to start again on Sunday evenings) when all but first years, who have own small-scale version, pile into theatre with pillows and duvets.

All happens within or next to main building, dorms six to eight-bedders, comfortable rather than haut couture ('they're nice, cute, small, humble,' said parent), possessions neatly arranged, pinboards sometimes rather sparsely filled. Bathrooms and loos clean, fragrant and hygienic – bar single cracked tile surround in need of repair. Most pupils in top two years enjoy additional privacy of individual cubicles (new arrivals will start off in dorm). Buddies take settling in duties seriously – 'boys were all waiting and had his bed made,' said parent, leaving son for taster weekend.

For the very youngest there are separate quarters with common room (reassuringly compact) and playroom (ditto – Hide and Seek games a non-starter) and own live-in matron, one of five, three full-time, notable for reassuring names (Miss Turnball and Miss Foynes – yet another detective team, surely?) and a guaranteed presence on the touchline at matches.

The last word: Education here is all about bestowing resilience, self-awareness, realism and courage (fairy godmothers might blench). 'Finally and most importantly, pupils must learn to love life…' says website. If they don't while they're here, won't be for want of trying. Parents are in no doubt they succeed. 'We put our trust in Mr Dawson,' says mother. 'We've been so incredibly impressed with the results.'

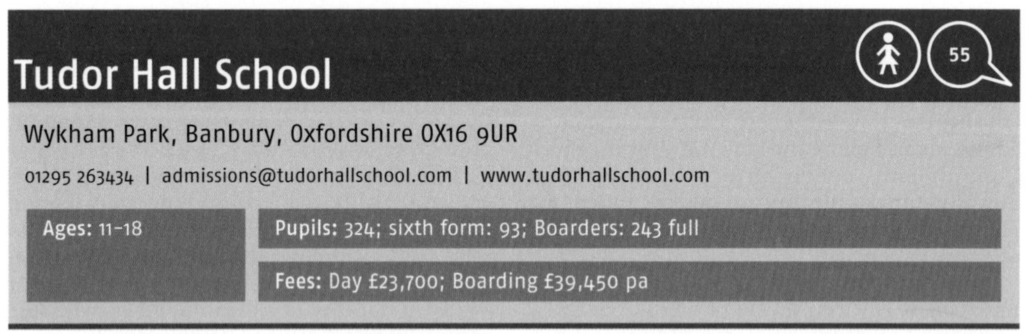

Tudor Hall School

Wykham Park, Banbury, Oxfordshire OX16 9UR

01295 263434 | admissions@tudorhallschool.com | www.tudorhallschool.com

Ages: 11–18

Pupils: 324; sixth form: 93; Boarders: 243 full

Fees: Day £23,700; Boarding £39,450 pa

Headmistress: Since January 2022, Julie Lodrick, previously head at Kent College, Pembury for five years and before that head at The Mount, York for six years.

Entrance: Candidates for 11+ and 13+ invited for 'taster day' (or day and night for prospective 11+ boarders) and assessment days with tests in maths, English and verbal reasoning. The tests are to 'ensure girls are compatible with academic pace' of school. Girls applying for entry at 13+ offered conditional places dependent on outcome of CE. Sixth form entry by general and subject-specific papers. All candidates are interviewed – school says it is looking for 'character' and girls who are 'sparky about something.'

Exit: Edinburgh, Exeter and Newcastle are current favourites. STEM courses popular – biomedical sciences, biological sciences, chemistry, biology and psychology. Other choices include specialist institutions such as Central School of Speech and Drama, Central St Martins and Royal Agricultural University.

Latest results: In 2021, 76 per cent 9-7 at GCSE; 73 per cent A*/A at A level (89 per cent A*-B). In 2019 (the last year when exams took place), 61

per cent 9-7 at GCSE; 35 per cent A*/A at A level (75 per cent A*-B).

Teaching and learning: Gradual upward trajectory of academic results is testament to small classes (average 15), plenty of individual attention and by all accounts, dedicated and inspirational teaching. Top performers at A level are geography, economics and maths. That maths is one of the most popular A levels speaks volumes for the teaching – school told us with regret how girls continue to arrive from prep schools saying they 'can't do' it. In addition to A levels, vocational courses in psychology, business and sport are available.

Innovative work to inspire girls to stay engaged not just with maths but also science subjects. Super new labs for exploding jelly babies as well as more serious experiments. We saw girls in smart red lab coats investigating their own cheek cells under the microscope. Lively programme of extracurricular science clubs, visits to science fairs and National Space Centre etc.

We shared a delicious lunch with girls who had very different and exciting plans for their future – lots of gap years followed by courses from criminology to drama. No sense that sixth formers are all expected to board the non-stop university express – one told us how much support she'd had for her decision to go straight into interior design rather than take a degree in the subject.

Visiting speakers widen horizons as does head's initiative, 'Tudor in three continents', which includes travel scholarships for girls to participate in projects in India, Cambodia and South Africa whilst at home the school has added a project that doesn't involve epic amounts of air travel: mentoring children at the Bolton Lads and Girls (sic) Club. Meeting less fortunate children in their own country, rather than thousands of miles away, has been a very profound experience.

Parents told us staff keep an eagle eye on each girl's progress and are quick to intervene if she appears to be lagging. 'Teachers work so hard to get the right results; if there's a problem they really drill down to find the root cause.' Girls love the fact that teachers are so accessible: 'There's always a subject teacher who can help if you're stuck on homework or revision.' What parents love is the individual attention given to their daughters' academic progress; all those we spoke to said they were confident no child would be allowed to struggle or fall behind.

Learning support and SEN: SEN or EAL support provided individually or in classes but head says this is not the place for a girl with serious needs; 'we want all pupils to be able to participate fully in the curriculum.' Dynamic learning support team uses variety of approaches including latest educational technology such as iPad apps.

The arts and extracurricular: Drama is offered at GCSE and A level but TH girls love to perform, whether or not they are pursuing it as a subject option. Great results in LAMDA speech and drama exams too. Regular participation in Shakespeare Schools Festival, plenty of theatre trips and a choice of stages – newish studio theatre has eye-catching neon sign. Dance is accorded greater status here than at other schools and can be taken as a GCSE. Reaction, the audition-only school dance group, has been going for over 20 years; the house dance title is as keenly fought as house singing and drama competitions. Music, too, offers girls of all abilities the chance to perform – whether at school concerts, carol singing at care homes or carrying off trophies at Banbury Young Musician of the Year competitions.

Regular socials with chaps from Radley, Eton and Harrow. The young gentlemen from Harrow are current favourites, but apparently this changes from year to year

The quality of the art, both in the studios and (perhaps a little infrequently) displayed throughout the school, fair took our breath away. Quite the best we can remember seeing anywhere. Likewise textiles and photography. Style and subject matter went from traditional to unexpectedly edgy and challenging. The textile and art rooms stay open into the evening and at weekends and girls love the freedom this gives them to work on their projects outside lessons. Textiles currently housed in Portakabin but purpose-built studios are in the offing. Leavers regularly go on to art foundation and fashion design courses.

Extracurricular options encompass just about everything from Model United Nations to the very popular dissection club. It seems not only can a Tudor Hall girl address a crowd and whip up a soufflé (if she's done the Leiths course), she can also eviscerate a frog. Parents approve of the way girls are kept very busy lower down the school, gradually developing independent study skills as they approach the relative freedom of the sixth form.

Sport: School has put considerable efforts into improving sports provision and parents say that it's much better. Facilities are all present and correct including glass-roofed outdoor swimming pool (not used in the winter) and plenty of pitches. Girls told us that a 'bigger gym' and a 'pavilion on the top pitch' would be great. Larger schools' A teams are likely to have the advantage so notable and sustained recent successes at county level in hockey and cross-country are all the more creditable. Individual talents in tennis (lovely courts in former walled garden), skiing and riding are well supported and a wider range of non-competitive options such as swim fit and zumba are offered in the sixth form. Girls also work with Carrdus School (Oxfordshire prep owned by Tudor Hall) and local primary schools to provide pupils with coaching and taster sessions in eg lacrosse.

Boarding: The full Monty – two exeats per term and no flexi or weekly. Saturday school with lessons until 1pm and games in the afternoon, trips, activities and down time thereafter. Boarding is arranged horizontally – ie by year group – meaning that everything (activities, bed times etc) can be tailored to the age group. Works especially well at exam times – much easier if everyone around you is revising.

Year 7 boarders and day girls are based in Todd (named after the school's founders), a charming house with a large peaceful garden on the edge of the school grounds. It's as uninstitutional as possible with a large family kitchen, colourful soft furnishings and lots of toys and games. And, when we visited, a body on the sitting room floor. 'Just step over it, we're doing first aid,' the housemistress told us. Todd girls love putting on plays and concerts for their captive audience, they also enjoy 'special breakfasts', baking and Sunday excursions (day girls can go too). Todd girls have lower sixth buddies, described to us as a 'big sister support system'.

Dorms vary from two to six cabin beds; bathrooms are clean but on the functional side. Apparently they're 'due for a refurb'. Personal technology at this end of the school limited to mobile phones for 10 minutes a day. Skype etc always available, 'we never stop a child speaking to their parents'. Glad to hear it. Housemistress has set up a Facebook page for Todd parents who get daily photos and updates on their girls' activities.

Other houses (known as The IIs, The IIIs and so on) are spacious and well equipped. Girls need no encouragement to personalise their space; walls were papered with photos, letters, bunting and many, many rosettes – plenty of keen horsewomen here.

Each boarding house has its own character and traditions so there's a real sense of progression through the school. Sixth form accommodation is designed as a halfway house to prepare girls for living independently. They can cook, are responsible for their own laundry and organise trips and activities. One such is the Christmas shopping trip to Paris (plus Disneyland Paris); no shortage of teachers signing up to chaperone that one, we imagine.

A great summer treat for the older girls is, we were told, to walk to the nearby farm shop, buy a picnic and eat it in a field

Ethos and heritage: One of the oldest girls' boarding schools in England, Tudor Hall was founded in 1850 by Rev T W Todd and his wife. In 1908 the school moved from London to rural Kent and on the outbreak of the Second World War it decamped to Burnt Norton, a small Cotswold manor house, to escape the air raids. Pupils, teachers and parents stayed here, even during the holidays, and old girls remember those times with great affection. It was a visit to the gardens at Burnt Norton that inspired T S Eliot to write his eponymous poem, a meditation on time, memory and original sin. Perhaps he would have penned something a little jollier than 'Garlic and sapphires in the mud clot the bedded axle-tree' if he'd visited a few years later when the Tudor Hall girls were in residence.

Surrounding area predominantly rural – grazing cows more common than passing traffic – but access to Oxford, London, Stratford and Bicester etc pretty easy. A great summer treat for the older girls is, we were told, to walk to the nearby farm shop, buy a picnic and eat it in a field. Wouldn't suit a committed urbanite, but that's not really the demographic which is, we suspect, one that is accustomed to town and country living and has the right shoes for both.

First-time visitors may be surprised to find no busy reception desk; the entrance hall, with its bergere furniture, beautiful flowers and polished wood, is rather reminiscent of an exclusive hotel – but the welcome is warm and personal. Usual mix of buildings (including a new £5m teaching centre) – not everywhere is country house gracious – but all well tended. School magazine and publicity material are similar – high production values but nothing boasty or brash. Come to think of it, that probably sums up the Tudor Hall pupil.

Old Tudorians include Katherine Hooker, tailor to Duchess of Cambridge; Cleo Barbour, shoe designer; Julia Peyton-Jones, director of Serpentine Gallery.

Pastoral care, inclusivity and discipline: Tudor Hall has long had a reputation for the highest standards of pastoral care, but don't confuse caring with soft. Yes, it's a nurturing environment, as all the best small schools are, but within that environment girls are encouraged and tested; challenged to overreach their own boundaries and try new things. All the parents we spoke to felt that their daughters were in the safest of hands and cited many examples of occasions when tutors or other members of staff had gone above and beyond to help or advise them. Day and boarding parents get a weekly update from tutors about what's been going on and home-school communication in general receives nothing but praise.

A couple of people we spoke to thought the downside of year group boarding was that it contributed to a somewhat stratified hierarchical atmosphere, but we didn't feel this was the case. Vertical house system, not to mention the mix of different clubs and sporting activities, must go a long way to defuse this. Day girls are very well integrated and can join their boarding friends for trips and weekend activities, but it's a long day and, with Saturday school, a long week. Even year 7 day pupils don't finish until 6.45pm or later, although they will have had an hour or so's break, a snack and done their homework.

Regular socials with chaps from Radley, Eton and Harrow. The young gentlemen from Harrow are current favourites, but apparently this changes from year to year.

What do you gain from boarding, we asked a group of sixth formers? They all cited strong and lasting friendships; others valued the 'accessibility' of teaching staff and the fact that there's always someone around to help with academic work. 'It helps you become responsible and independent – and it stops you taking home for granted.' We like that last one but doubt it survives the summer holidays.

Pupils and parents: Most recent ISI report described Tudor Hall pupils as 'overwhelmingly positive in outlook', which sounds rather alarming – a posse of Pollyannas, perhaps. It would be so easy to fall back on the old stereotype of Tudor Hall girls as darling daughters of the home counties, what with Leiths, polo, doing the ski season, etc – but that wouldn't be fair or accurate.

The girls we met were friendly, thoughtful, comfortable in their own skins and definitely not the identikit result of an educational production line. There's no arrogance or sense of entitlement and definitely no hair flicking. Girls know they are fortunate and are very aware that the world beyond Banbury is considerably less shiny; it certainly won't be any the worse for having Tudor Hall alumnae in it.

Pride in one's school is not usually compatible with the teenage psyche, but Tudor Hall girls aren't too cool for that. Lots of daughters of old girls – always a good sign.

Money matters: Fees at the slightly less eye-watering end of the boarding range; day fees look like good value considering time spent in school. Academic, music, art, drama and sport scholarships (up to £1,000 pa) available at 11+, 13+ and 16+. Also textiles and dance at 16+. Means-tested bursaries to support new and current parents in financial need.

The last word: Leave your preconceptions at the door and prepare to be bowled over. Whether your daughter is headed for fashion design or Oxbridge, Tudor Hall deserves a place on everyone's shortlist.

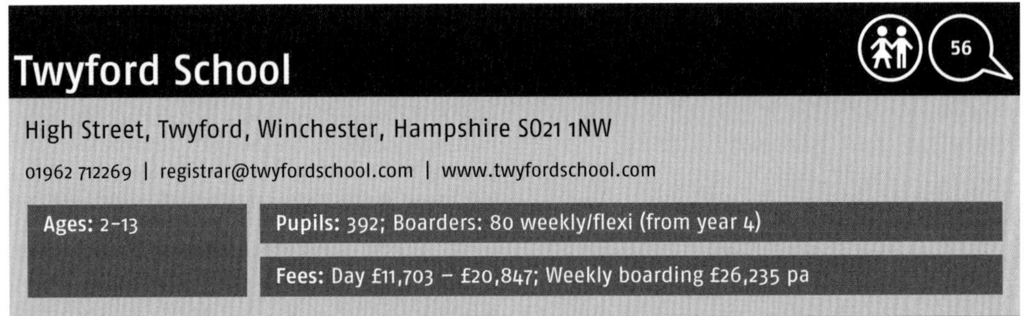

Twyford School

56

High Street, Twyford, Winchester, Hampshire SO21 1NW

01962 712269 | registrar@twyfordschool.com | www.twyfordschool.com

Ages: 2–13

Pupils: 392; Boarders: 80 weekly/flexi (from year 4)

Fees: Day £11,703 – £20,847; Weekly boarding £26,235 pa

Headmaster: Since September 2020, Andrew Harvey, formerly head of The Paragon, an IAPS co-educational junior school in Bath. Studied theology at university, followed by a PGCE and has previously taught at Perrott Hill School, Chafyn Grove School and Sherfield School where he was head of pastoral care. He was appointed deputy head of Lambrook School in 2007, before becoming head of The Paragon in 2012. Married to Anna, the couple have two daughters.

Entrance: Main entry points are nursery, reception, years 2 and 3, although places are occasionally available in other years. Nursery places allocated according to date of registration; siblings have priority on waiting lists at other times. Short half-day assessment in November for those joining later, which school says is 'not a rigorous hurdle – just an informal day to check they're willing to have a go, are respectful and respond to teachers'.

Exit: Most stay until 13, with an average of six to 10 (two-thirds girls) leaving at the end of year 6. At 13, pupils head off to around 17 schools, with many to Marlborough ('because they're the closest senior school to us in terms of feel,' says head). Winchester College by far the most popular boys' school, with Eton and Radley College also regularly featuring. Girls-only schools include St Swithun's and Godolphin. Other popular co-ed destinations include Bradfield and Canford. Lord Wandsworth and Sherborne have featured recently. Around a third get academic, sport, music and drama scholarships.

Our view: Main school building, a beautiful Queen Anne house, is set in over 25 acres and surrounded by the South Downs. Moved to its present location in 1809 from premises in nearby Twyford and can probably trace its origins back to the mid-17th century, making it one of the oldest prep schools (possibly the oldest – a Latin grammar book has turned up bearing the inscription 'Twyford School, 1775'). Boarders still live in original house, which has a pretty Victorian chapel, oak-panelled library, atmospheric old school hall and large modernised refectory – though Orchard Close has now been added to these facilities. Teaching takes place in a collection of modern buildings dotted around quadrangles, with modern, bright and spacious classrooms.

There's a 'fun, sleepover feel', according to pupils – 'you get to do things like dodgeball or hang out watching TV with your mates on the beanbags – it's brilliant'

Academically stronger than ever, which parents attribute to current head and 'an injection of younger teachers who teach effectively and interactively and make it both fun and relevant'. Lots of hard work going on for CE when we visited; most pupils aim to sit level 2 in subjects across the board (some level 3 if appropriate). Setting in maths from year 4; in year 8, pupils are divided into two CE sets and one scholarship set. French is taught from nursery and Latin from year 6. The bespoke 'learning qualities programme' (recently revitalised) encourages children to think more independently and take responsibility for their own learning. Pupils told us the workload can 'feel pressurised at times' but that 'lessons are rarely boring'. Class sizes average 16-18, with Chromebooks for every child, used regularly in lessons and preps (plus iPads in pre-prep – 'so they can do things like take pictures of their castle made from kitchen rolls and record it on the system'). Lessons now finish earlier so individualised learning via clinics, support groups and extension groups can be squeezed in, but overall teaching time increases in year 6 ready for pre-tests.

Two full-time members of staff offer learning support in the 'hub'. One-to-one sessions for around 30 prep children with SEN, and pupils can also self-refer, for example to learn a bit of algebra they didn't understand, and there's small group work for things like help with French vocab. 'The reputation for SEN support wasn't great, but the hub has transformed it – they're really forward thinking and inclusive now,' said one parent.

Very sporty. Main winter sports are netball and hockey (girls) and football and rugby (boys, with some girls also playing football); summer sees cricket for all, with some rounders. Matches most Wednesday and Saturday afternoons, with a good sporting record in fixtures, especially for netball and cricket, with teams often reaching national level. Pupils also compete in swimming, water polo, athletics, tennis, lacrosse and girls' tag rugby, with individual champions in skiing, fencing and sailing. School is a 'centre of excellence' for girls' cricket in Hampshire. 'They love their trophy cabinet, but it can feel a bit too focused on promoting excellence and talent rather than celebrating enthusiasm and getting involved,' said one parent. Large gym and indoor 25-metre swimming pool sit side-by-side, with 25-metre traversing wall outside. Has two all-weather courts for tennis and netball, plus Astroturf for hockey and football.

Dazzling art department, with stunning displays of refurbished chairs, gargoyle masks, gigantic fish and clay silhouette self-portraits, among others. DT also stands out, with imaginative work such as complex ballbearing games.

Music block a hive of (ambitious) activity. More than 80 per cent of children learn at least one instrument, including the less usual, eg harp, drums and bagpipes. School is a centre for ABRSM and Trinity College music exams and many pupils pass these at higher grades. Two school choirs, school orchestra and various ensembles give occasional concerts. One parent told us, 'The sheer love of music isn't celebrated enough, though – sometimes it feels they prefer showing off the good ones.' Weekly drama is taught by specialist teachers. LAMDA popular. Dance (ballet, modern and tap) also on offer. Annual Shakespeare workshop for year 8 takes place after CE.

Structured outdoor education programme, called Twyford Explorers (Come Rain Come Shine in pre-prep), includes navigation, orienteering, shelter building and survival techniques. Saturday mornings now dedicated to mountain biking, robotics, school newspaper, young sports leader award, gymnastics, badminton, bushcraft, leadership and cookery, among others. Two sessions for years 4 and 5; one session in rotation with a guest speaker for year 6 upwards. One residential course away for each year group every year; in school there is a treehouse complex with outdoor classroom and advanced adventure playground. The range of after-school clubs has recently been increased – art, cookery, judo and street dance etc – running up until 6pm daily.

Superb food (school even produced its own cookbook for parents, whose offspring were apparently regularly asking, 'Why can't you make it like they do in school?'); dinner staff know all the children by name and are part the pastoral support (they report if a child looks sad, isn't eating etc). Assembly or chapel service every day ('they can be a bit boring,' admitted one pupil), but some like the tradition. A combination of PSHE lessons, a specific 'bullying@' email address and multiple whisper boxes mean bullying is, according to school and pupils, rare. Everyone belongs to one of four houses, with end of term team feast for house with the highest house point scores; individual high scorers are 'sent up good' on Fridays for jelly babies from the head (a Twyford tradition). Astonishingly, the children we met didn't know what the sanctions were for bad behaviour – 'people don't really misbehave here,' shrugged one; head says there have been only two detentions in last 18 months. Lots of parent involvement and regular themed days such as French (everyone dresses up and only speaks French, with French food) and WWI (including re-enactment with full-size cannon) – 'they're so fun,' enthused one pupil.

Pre-prep is described by parents as a 'cosy, wonderful start to the school', with much praise for the pre-prep head although the little interaction we noticed between her and the children felt a bit on the stern side. One class in nursery, two in reception and three each in years 1 and 2; attractive wooden building added much-needed space – windows at child height is a nice touch. French and music learned from an early age. Mainly play-based learning, with homework limited to spelling, reading and topic work, eg polar bears. Lots of outdoor play and who cares if it's raining (they certainly don't) with such fabulous outdoor settings, including wooden covered outdoor classroom, a wooden train, outdoor drums, a theatre stage and an outdoor adventure play area and bike track. Opportunities for little ones to show off their music, ballet and ESB exam preparation to parents, and separately to grandparents. Clubs include the bunny club, street dance, Lego club, cookery, Pilates and mindfulness.

Superb food (school even produced its own cookbook for parents, whose offspring were apparently regularly asking, 'Why can't you make it like they do in school?'); dinner staff know all the children by name and are part the pastoral support (they report if a child looks sad, isn't eating etc)

Most families (increasingly dual income) live within 30-mile radius (60 per cent in and around Winchester), with six free buses ferrying in the children – a good job, given the groans about the parking (although school says it is working on a 'development masterplan' to address parking problems). Means-tested bursaries available from year 3 onwards; sibling discounts are limited to five per cent for third and subsequent children. Old Twyfordians include Alexander Pope, Douglas Hurd, Hubert Parry, Mark Tully, Thomas Hughes and, more recently, The Apprentice winner Tom Pellereau. Very active Twyford Society keeps ex-pupils in touch.

Boarding: No full boarding, but small number of long-distance boarders stay with local guardians (other school families) on Saturday and Sunday nights. Flexi-boarding available from summer of year 4 and most at this stage board one or two nights a week; by year 7 some are boarding two or three nights and by year 8 some are weekly boarding. Welcoming, beautifully kept dorms for younger children; cosy two-bed cubicles for year 8s to allow for more privacy and the chance to room with a friend (78 beds in total). There's a 'fun, sleepover feel', according to pupils – 'you get to do things like dodgeball or hang out watching TV with your mates on the beanbags – it's brilliant.' Parents praise boarding houseparent, also head of sport. Facilities now also include Orchard Close, a property with 2.3 acre site adjacent to the school.

The last word: This is a friendly, happy co-ed prep with high academic standards and where parents enjoy being part of the 'family'. But with the older children staying until 6pm daily and spending many Saturdays at school, the children can be – as one parent put it – 'flipping exhausted by the holidays'.

Walhampton School
57
Walhampton, Lymington, Hampshire SO41 5ZG
01590 613300 | registrar@walhampton.com | www.walhampton.com
Ages: 2–13
Pupils: 357; Boarders: 18 full, 4 weekly
Fees: Day £9,750 – £19,395; Boarding + £7,860 pa

Headmaster: Since January 2021, Jonny Timms, previously senior deputy head at Caldicott where he developed academics and pastoral provision, as well as being safeguarding lead. English and history degree Edinburgh and Toronto universities. Began teaching through the Teach First scheme at the Harris Academy in Peckham, and after two years moved to Merchiston Castle School in Edinburgh where he taught English and ran a boarding house. Has an MA in educational leadership and is an ISI boarding and team inspector. Married to Sophie who works in international development and is also actively involved in the school; they have two children.

Entrance: The school is non-selective. Children attend a trial day for informal assessment. One pupil told us she enjoyed her trial day so much she started at Walhampton the very next day.

Exit: Year 8 leavers go to a whole host of schools, with King Edward VI Southampton, Clayesmore, Ballard, Bryanston and Canford leading the pack. Other popular choices include Winchester, Eton, Radley and Marlborough. Usually around a third achieve scholarships.

Our view: Founded in 1948, Walhampton has an idyllic setting, with a Grade II listed house at its heart, four lakes, ancient woodlands, 100 acres of grounds and a very distinguished history. Queen Victoria once stayed there and the house was requisitioned by the American Air Force during the Second World War so airmen on leave could use it as a holiday home. An Italian terrace and sunken garden designed by celebrated architect and garden designer Harold Peto was recently turned into a garden of remembrance, with a bronze sculpture created by one of the art teachers.

In the last few years there has been a big push on the academic front – 'to ensure the standards of teaching and learning are A1,' says school. Parents praise the 'academic rigour' and the teaching we saw was exciting and vibrant – a year 7 classics class acting out a Great British Bake-Off for the gods, year 8 artists making eccentric pottery shoes (including one with a zany, squirrel-shaped heel) and year 5 scientists clad in professional white coats using the principles of chromatography to work out who had written a fictional murder note. Physics, chemistry and biology taught separately from year 6 and pupils are clear that 'if you can't see it, it's physics', 'if it smells it's chemistry' and 'if it runs away it's biology'. Maximum of 20 per class and setting for English and maths. A total of 39 children receive learning support from a four-strong team, mostly one-to-one and charged as an extra. Tutor system for years 6, 7 and 8 (children have a say in who they want to be their tutor). History is big at Walhampton and the school has strong links with the veterans of the Battle of Arnhem. The head takes year 7 and 8 children to Arnhem every year and a group of veterans visit Walhampton every November for an outdoor remembrance service. 'We want them to honour the older generation and understand that history and tradition are important,' says school.

Light and airy library, with reading sessions for all, story-time and author talks. The school librarian, a former runner-up for a national school

Light and airy library, with reading sessions for all, story-time and author talks. One boy told us the library is 'the happy place'

librarian of the year award, fizzes with ideas and is also a school tutor. 'I try to make the library really welcoming and exciting for everyone,' she says. The pupils clearly feel the same, with one boy telling us the library is 'the happy place'.

Pupils have sport four days a week, including matches on Wednesdays. Boys' main sports are football, rugby, hockey and cricket while girls play hockey, netball and cricket. Girls' football is growing in popularity too. Reception up to year 6 have a swimming lesson every week and the outdoor swimming pool is used from April to October (everyone can join the swimming club in the summer term).

Around 120 pupils have riding lessons at the school's equestrian centre, which has its own arena and cross-country course. Five children keep their own ponies at school while others borrow school ponies. Non-riders are welcome to come and groom the ponies, muck out the stables and sweep leaves. 'It's really inclusive,' says the head of riding. Drama is big at Walhampton, with lots of LAMDA exams and annual junior and senior plays (including promenade performances, where the audience follows actors round the school). Impressive art, pottery and textiles (there's even an 1859 printing press) and more than half of pupils learn a music instrument. As the head of music took the senior choir through its paces in the chapel one of our young guides whispered: 'She's an amazing teacher.' The school supports two charities every year and has recently helped to fund the building of a new school in Cambodia.

School wanted to make the grounds 'magical' – and the staff have certainly done that. The school feels like something out of Swallows and Amazons, with Portmore Pond for sailing, Sandwalk Pond for fishing and a jaunty shepherd's hut on the lawn. Pupils spend as much time outdoors as possible, for learning as well as play. We spotted a year 6 class learning about teamwork and communication in the outdoor classroom (a vast open canopy with a log fire and benches) in the woods. There's plenty of space to run around in, the New Forest on the doorstep and breathtaking views of the Solent and the Isle of Wight from the grounds (some pupils get the ferry to school while several boarders arrive on horseback at the start of the week). There are scores of outdoor activities to choose, such as kayaking, sailing, gardening and beekeeping. Escape from Colditz is a Walhampton institution, a winter game where children volunteer to escape from an area of the grounds in the dark, make their way to the head's study and ring the bell while staff wearing miners' lamps as headgear try and stop them. Asked if there was anything he'd change about the school a boy told us he'd like to play Escape from Colditz more often.

Pupils are encouraged to take an interest in wildlife, learning the names of butterflies and birds (everything from cormorants to oystercatchers). Other highlights include the chance to re-enact famous moments in history outdoors, including the Battle of Trafalgar on the lake, and learning Shakespeare on bikes. Children are allowed to climb trees during break (as high as the former head of maths, who is 6ft 6ins) and there's a tree-climbing club run by the head for those who want to go higher. Visitors are advised to bring wellies and mud is part and parcel of school life. Children aren't afraid to get dirty and take risks.

The school feels like something out of Swallows and Amazons, with Portmore Pond for sailing, Sandwalk Pond for fishing and a jaunty shepherd's hut on the lawn

Lessons start at 8.30am and finish at 5pm, followed by clubs and activities. Voluntary Saturday progamme for boarders and day children (no Saturday lessons, apart from year 8 pupils approaching exams). Medical centre, staffed by three nurses, works closely with the boarding and pastoral teams. They also provide a sympathetic ear for children who want a chat and a mug of hot chocolate. Every child belongs to one of four houses. Pastoral care is excellent and children know exactly who to contact if anything is troubling them – teachers, tutors and/or a member of the safeguarding team. Parents say that Walhampton is 'very nurturing'. One told us: 'It lets them be who they are – and lets them be children.' No phones allowed (apart from boarders who can use them for 30 minutes in the evening). Regular assemblies, often led by the head. When we visited six mums had delivered three-minute talks on 'inspiration for life' and six dads were about to follow suit. Friday afternoon chapel is a highlight of the week, often attended by parents.

Nursery and pre-prep children are based in their own purpose-built building a short walk from the prep. The classrooms all have their own verandahs and children clad in wet-weather dungarees and wellies spend a lot of time outdoors. Forest school in the woods once a week for all pre-prep children.

Boarding: Parents describe the boarding as 'cosy and calm'. There are 26 full boarders, including some from Spain and mainland China, and 35 flexi-boarders. Some boarders catch the 'Walhampton Express' from nearby Brockenhurst to London on a Friday afternoon, accompanied by a member of staff. The boarding houses – girls on the first floor, boys on the top floor – are beautifully kitted out. The sturdy grey bunks in the girls' dorms are stunning, with lots of storage and space for sitting, designed by the head's wife and an interior designer parent. Year 6 boys' dorms have the best views in the school and boys gather there on Thursday evenings to watch boats racing in the Solent. Lots of weekend activities for boarders, including beach school at nearby Milford on Sea. Day pupils tend to live within a 40-minute drive, with buses ferrying them in from places like Ringwood, Christchurch, Lyndhurst and New Milton.

The last word: The only regret we heard from parents was that pupils have to leave Walhampton at 13. Children, teachers and parents extol its virtues, its academic success, its amazing outdoor provision and above all, the fact it's a happy school. 'It sends children home happy – and that's a joy,' a parent told us.

Wellington College

58

Duke's Ride, Crowthorne, Berkshire RG45 7PU

01344 444013 | admissions@wellingtoncollege.org.uk | www.wellingtoncollege.org.uk

Ages: 13–18

Pupils: 1,090; sixth form: 475; Boarders: 860 full

Fees: Day £31,140 – £35,760 pa; Boarding £42,630 pa

Linked school: Eagle House School, 380

Master: Since 2019, Mr James Dahl MA (classics at Cambridge). Married with a daughter who is currently at the school. Joined as head of admissions and marketing in 2013 before becoming second master elect and deputy head (pastoral care). Worked with the now legendary Anthony Seldon here and at Brighton College, where he started his career ('an utter privilege… [my] biggest influence apart from my mother') becoming head of classics at 23, then head of sixth form. Moved to Repton in 2006 where he was a housemaster.

Family tradition narrowed career choices down to teaching, medicine or the church. Feedback suggests that he picked the right path. Parents like his lack of obfuscation, particularly evident during the twists and turns of government guidance during the pandemic. 'Letters so informative, doesn't try to hold anything back.'

Any downsides? 'I haven't heard a bad word about him,' said one. Nor indeed, did we, no matter who we asked and meeting him simply confirmed that he is, indeed, disarmingly nice, from conversational interjections of 'bless you' to the smart suit accessorised with Breton-style stripy socks.

Famed for in-depth knowledge of pupils (all invited to dine at the Master's Lodge). Remembers names, siblings, scholarships, previous schools and successes. 'He probably even knows what I ate for breakfast,' says one. Inevitably, down to sheer hard work. Essential, he says. 'Every child has a need to be known and loved and cared for… my heart sinks when other heads say they don't have time [to learn] their names.'

Given the school's rip-roaring success over the last few years, his leadership is of the even keel rather than apple-cart overturning variety. He'd said that he couldn't 'wait to start writing the next chapter in the college's illustrious history.' Several paragraphs well under way. What matters is 'Wellington genuinely being the school we say it is'.

Educational excellence is constantly under review. Also examining social impact, wider role in 'the world of education beyond teaching the pupils' and equality, diversity and inclusion.

Support has been extensive – half a million pounds (which otherwise would have funded a fab new swimming pool) has gone to state schools (school has links with 29) to help with Covid catch-up.

The master, Mr Dahl, is famed for in-depth knowledge of pupils. 'He probably even knows what I ate for breakfast,' says one

Newly revamped Prince Albert Foundation programme will double the number of scholars on socially transformative awards to 40 by 2025 (100 pupils already have means-tested bursaries). While fee-paying pupils will be in the majority, since 2014 all scholarships are now honorary ('felt it wasn't right to give a millionaire a small amount off the fees').

Planned new wellbeing centre is probably the project closest to his heart. Will offer the works, from dedicated classrooms to yoga, therapy dog to onsite professionals, stigma-free so completely natural for any pupils to come forward to seek help – so a rise in numbers will signal success.

Musical and sporty (Peloton has been a well-used lockdown purchase), he's also a demon touch typist (essential for keeping notes as an ISI inspector) and enjoys attending concerts in London.

Entrance: Takes 200 pupils into the third form (year 9). About five applicants for every place, most from UK prep schools (Eagle House, Lambrook, Dragon School, Thomas's Group, Cheam School and Godstowe all significant feeders), others from secondary schools, state and private. Other senior schools considered by families ranged from Harrow to Brighton College, though many of those we spoke to felt single-sex schools hadn't been an option.

More mythology attached to the entrance process than for any other school we've encountered. Did charm and social skills trump academic performance? We heard tell of prep school heads training candidates to break away on assessment day and circulate, circulate, circulate.

School keen to demystify the process – helpful website admissions section entitled 'our selection criteria' well worth a look. Mr Dahl stresses that while everyone has to be able to cope with the brisk pace here (so not the place for anyone switching off and tuning out after the last lesson bell goes), they are looking for a mix of personalities – some extrovert, others quietly confident but not temperamentally inclined to make themselves the star of any social gathering. 'We're not just looking at charming, alpha [characters]... because if we filled the school with sharp-elbowed kids, my goodness what a school,' says Mr Dahl. Confirmed by parents. 'Not just for shining stars,' says one.

Sit ISEB Common pre-test – current head's perspective also taken into account. Assessment days in Jan/Feb of year 6 'let us get to know the child as a person'. In March of year 7 school reviews those on the waiting list (and late entrants) for additional places. Final assessment day, held in September of year 8, is for very late entrants for a place on the waiting list.

Three-stage assessment for 50 sixth form places including short exams in three subjects and further assessments for shortlisted candidates – many 'fun!' (school's exclamation mark).

Exit: In 2021, 16 to Oxbridge, 26 to US universities. Other top UK destinations include Edinburgh, Durham, Exeter, Bristol, UCL, Bath, Imperial College and Manchester. Huge range of courses – medicine to music, business to biochemistry, as well as photography, criminology and fashion.

Latest results: In 2021, 94 per cent 9-7 at GCSE; 80 per cent A*/A at A level (96 per cent A*-B). IB average score 41.2. In 2019 (the last year when exams took place), 83 per cent 9-7 at GCSE; 58 per cent A*/A at A level. IB average score 40.

Teaching and learning: Parents see this as a progressive school (and it's won several awards for its approach). There's a refreshing willingness to rethink the way it does things. Take GCSEs. While 10 or 11 currently the norm, as elsewhere, it's under review. May drop down by at least one to make more of everything else on offer here (after all, why provide so much if access is constrained by needlessly weighty academic timetable).

Sensible homework, much online, with independent research encouraged. If it all gets too much, 'you just email the teacher and they come straight back,' says pupil

School was swift to respond to the 2020 lockdown, transitioning to a full online timetable within what felt like hours. Talking about silver linings seems somewhat insensitive but the legacy – fewer textbooks than ever before, virtual access to just about every resource and the ability for any child unable to attend lessons to log in and participate online – has undoubtedly streamlined what was already a responsive approach.

Up to GCSE, all pupils study core subjects in classes no larger than 24, average 16 up to GCSEs and 10 in the sixth form. High staff-to-pupil ratio of six to one. Parents praise the balance between teachers' ages and experience (average age is 35-45, with around 50 staff here for 10 years or more).

There's minimal setting though some streaming in maths and languages. Mandarin, with own delightful little bright red, temple-like building, is one of five languages on offer. Dance, design engineering and computer science are also popular options.

Sixth form, says head, is 'humming under the bonnet'. Equal split between A levels (always taken with an EPQ) and IB – the perfect balance, thinks Mr Dahl. Philosophy, psychology, economics and business studies all offered, with around two-thirds of pupils taking maths (the single most popular subject) and sciences. School bullish about popularity of sciences among girls – ahead of national averages, on a par with many girls-only schools.

A focus on real world problems. We watched sixth form chemistry pupils creating their own giant molecules to demonstrate how accidental transposition can spell disaster (as with the thalidomide scandal)

Predicted grades very often comfortably bettered. Sensible homework, much on-line, must help, with independent research encouraged. If it's all getting too much, 'you just email the teacher and they come straight back,' says pupil.

Many lessons have an absorbing focus on real world problems. We watched sixth form chemistry pupils creating their own giant molecules to demonstrate how accidental transposition can spell disaster (as with the thalidomide scandal); others in an IB class explored data linking weight and diabetes diagnoses.

Where the approach was more conventional, as with year 9 pupils engaged in parallel line equations, there was an excitingly anarchic touch, with calculations covering not only the pull-down screen but escaping down the (wipeable) walls on either side as well. Pupils' attention and focus notable – these are children who want to be here.

Learning support and SEN: Last inspection identified 140 pupils as having some form of SEN, notably SpLD and three with an EHCP. Most common learning need is SpLD, some pupils have ADHD, a few high-functioning autism.

Highly rated head of learning support supports new pupils who arrive with a diagnosis and arranges for assessments to take place where SEN is suspected but undiagnosed. 'Role is to see who can cope and thrive.'

Annual reviews for anyone needing extra time in exams, some pupils may skip a language in favour of additional English support. Offer academic support ranging from help with organising prep to prioritising and planning. Pupil led. 'Will come to us because they need support in a particular subject at a particular time.'

Regular meetings with houseparents. Liaise with teachers where a pupil, for example, needs pre-learning – so consolidate before moving on to something new. Helped by online system – they have access to all lessons so can work together with pupils.

Given that good organisation essential to make a success of life here, there are inevitably limits to what is doable. Sustained one-to-one support isn't. Would be concerned if pupil needed a reader – pace of life here just too fast. That said, have previously supported children with medical needs and visual/hearing impairments. Direct access to psychiatrists, psychologists and speech and language therapists so that assessments can be undertaken on site. Staff team currently working on ADHD – particularly in girls, an underdiagnosed group.

Key concern is whether 'students can cope given the size of the campus – they have to be on top of it... It's about working out whether they will thrive and be happy.'

The arts and extracurricular: The works. Often the deal-breaker for prospective pupils, promise amply fulfilled on joining. Willingness to give everything a go – 'things you like, things you don't,' says pupil – is essential (don't leave home without it).

Thus equipped, pupils, whether round, square or even four-dimensional pegs, can't fail to find their niche here. 'So many extra things on offer.' 'Wellington just seemed to be more colourful – more music, sport and random societies.' 'You have the chance to be what you want to be.'

Art ranges from delightful ceramics to what appeared to be freely unravelled anatomical study of stomach and intestines, while extracurricular activities include the unmissable 'glass fusing with Mrs Carr'.

School champions individuality – if pupils want to set up a club, they'll be backed all the way – while tutors help with sometimes difficult choices – history society, fireside talks with outside speakers, 3D printing or all three? Online calendars help with organisation together with physical reminders. 'Will have people in assembly telling you who, what and where instead of getting 15 emails,' says pupil. Inevitable clashes normally resolved with email to coordinator.

Dad-like puns abound, from the Wellingtones a capella group (one among many ensembles catering for the 500 or so pupils who have instrumental lessons here, around 10 per cent at grade 8/diploma level) to the DukeBox radio station, a pupil initiative that broadcasts live to all Wellington College schools, here and overseas (let's hope they don't fall foul of Chinese censors) as well as Welly Telly (officially WTV), again entirely student led and impressively slick. Just wants house dance competition (hugely popular, choreographed – with varying degrees of idiosyncrasy – by sixth formers) to be re-named Welly Shoes. We live in hope.

CCF and DofE awards both offered. Volunteering (with local groups of differently abled or elderly people) is a popular option, school community impressively united when swift action needed – created 1,250 welcome packages (with clothes, food and other essentials) in just a week for Afghan families arriving in the UK in autumn 2021.

One parent wondered if the general brilliance was disheartening for rank amateurs. 'Sometimes you think... I'm not going to give it a try because the standard of everything is so high,' commented one. Firm disagreement from staff and pupils. 'We've had a big push to ensure that there's something for everyone,' countered member of staff. 'Absolutely not just the elite.'

Sport: One of the myths is that if charm and academic ability doesn't get you a place here, team sports talent will do the trick. Not a prerequisite, stress current parents. 'My child is very much an individual sports person and unbelievably happy,' says one.

Facilities vast and extensive, with a permeable area on the edge of the site, enabling carefully timetabled public use of some of the facilities (swimming pool, tennis court and health and fitness centre). Not just one sprung floor for dancers but two (can also practise in main theatre). Sports hall does its best to ring the changes outside (design features metal ribs in alternating colours) while the vast Robin Dyer centre, used for cricket, netball and tennis, is so huge and sub-dividable that you could probably lose several smaller schools in its curtained-off recesses.

While every team sport you'd expect – rugby, football, hockey, cricket, netball – is offered and extensively catered for, with informed coaches who 'see if we're doing too much sport or if need a break or a rest,' says pupil, they're not compulsory. Alternatives – golf, badminton, swimming and rackets among them, and one pupil was delighted to have discovered shooting – can be chosen instead.

Dad-like puns abound, from the Wellingtones a capella group to the DukeBox radio station, a pupil initiative that broadcasts live to all Wellington College schools

An enlightened and sensible approach, think parents. 'If you hate rugby, you're going to do your best to skive,' pointed out one. Approach clearly pays off, particularly with top teams for rugby (one of the strongest sports here). A teams routinely do well – success for Ds and beyond more variable though we were impressed to see that even some netball E and F teams (based on last matches pre-lockdown) had decent sprinkling of fixtures – and wins.

Recent adjustments to the timetable – previously sport for all on the same two afternoons a week, plus Saturdays; now staggered – and recruitment of more pro sports players ensure that every team has its moment in the sun and a session with a top coach at least once a week (we heard one comment that golfers could benefit from slightly more attention). 'Don't want to be seen [just] as catering for the elite – participation is really important,' says the school.

Boarding: Officially, this is a full boarding school – 80 per cent board – though vast majority of pupils go home on Saturday afternoons, returning on Sunday evening, some on parent-organised minibuses (the SW London route is particularly popular). A flying visit but 'enough to catch your breath and do your prep,' says parent (about two hours a night is the norm up to GCSEs).

Mass exodus means the school might feel rather empty on Saturday nights when total numbers in each house can be down to low single figures and entertainment is of a homely nature. 'You can stay in, chill out and order a takeaway,' says a pupil.

The 17 houses (more for boys though ratio will change as number of girls increases) come in a glorious variety of styles, from Victorian villa to 20th-century red brick (website tour bravely attempts an exposition of each house's unique qualities and values, all set to pounding music).

Names honour history and heroic military men (something that could well be under review as first co-ed house for sixth formers and new day house are completed?).

Over 90 per cent of families allocated first or second-choice house, preferences submitted after places have been offered (early registration boosts chances of success). Centrally located houses are 'in', others 'out' (school terminology), some a brisk trot away (no wonder 'golf buggy for each house' was on one pupil's wish list). A few have a smattering of day boarders (welcome to outstay their official welcome – officially leave at 9pm but can be later). All are staffed 24 hours a day. Sixth form house prefect looks after new pupils.

More mythology attached to the entrance process than for any other school we've encountered. Do charm and social skills trump academic performance? We heard tell of prep school heads training candidates to break away on assessment day and circulate, circulate, circulate

Much attention is given to small and well-thought-through details. Atmosphere is as homelike as possible. Pupils can return to collect forgotten possessions and – in the three houses with full kitchens – eat breakfast and evening meal here. Regular deliveries of fruit, milk and comforting snacks, though toast and toasties about the limit of pupils' self-catering aspirations. We liked the noticeboard in girls' house with brief sticky note announcements: 'I failed my physics test.' 'Lucy bought me a coffee when I didn't have time.'

Bedrooms (a few larger dormitories, but mainly up to three share in junior years, double or single for older pupils) range from functional to imaginative: one high-ceilinged girls' house has a little staircase in each bedroom leading to mezzanine study level. Common rooms ditto, some so formal that visiting cards and silver salvers wouldn't look out of place. Regardless of vintage, considerable effort goes into making them attractive places to be, with matching sofas that work with the prevailing decor and available space rather than fighting other furnishings for colour chart supremacy and location.

Other customs and traditions are largely down to the houseparents. Take Stanley (64 boys), where vertical house families are called 'blessings' (collective noun for a group of unicorns, the house symbol) and the floors are named after journey through school – a sort of Pilgrim's Progress in reverse: 'Heaven' for younger boys, 'Passage' for years 10 and 11 and 'Hell' for sixth formers – 'because we're taking exams,' explained one.

Rich social life all round with lots of activities like Maniacs – where pupils get up early, swim two lengths of the outdoor pool (staff sometimes adding ice to enhance the experience) then 'run off shivering for bacon rolls in the dining hall'. Mini chocolate bars as prizes. Other – more conventional – events range from games of football in the gardens to regular socials with other houses.

Ethos and heritage: Ignore the uncooperative online map that attempts to usher you in through the more workaday entrance where sports centre meets industrial park and you'll approach the school as intended, along the Kilometre (nobody could explain surrender of imperial measurement) that runs the length of the 400-acre grounds.

They're beautiful, impressive, with wild areas (woodland nature reserve is home to protected spiders), a lake, nine-hole golf course and beautifully tended pitches stretching to the horizon. The road is open to the public and a popular cut through is patrolled by a security team, sometimes in dauntingly shiny four-by-four (complete with school crest) – otherwise 'We're on a bike,' they say.

Entrance to the school, halfway up, is through a grand arch (style, apparently, is French Grand Rococo). Opens onto a series of attractive courtyards, all beautifully maintained and Grade II listed, making the occasional antidote to tradition – like the V and A café, interior a surprisingly successful riot of pastels – particularly striking by comparison.

Modern additions are dotted around the original site. Star attraction, appropriately, is the wood-faced, circular performing arts building (also the venue for whole-school gatherings as the chapel, beautiful but surprisingly diddy, is long outgrown). Science blocks are attractively low-rise (biology has its own greenhouse), other buildings are tucked into corners of the undulating site. The humanities building, notable for squat form and vast metal flue, appears to be hiding, and we can't blame it, given the competition.

Was grandeur also intimidating to pupils? Can be daunting at the start but quickly overcome and transforms into 'What can I do to live up to it?' says pupil. There's a lot to live up to. Conceived by Queen Victoria as a memorial to the Duke of Wellington, the school was intended to offer a subsidised education for orphaned children of army officers. First pupils – Foundationers in the

majority, the remainder fee-paying – arrived in 1859. Girls 'allowed' into the sixth form in the 1970s (we hope they were appropriately grateful) and the school went fully co-ed in 2006.

Strong connection with the services endured into the 20th century (700 pupils were killed in WWI alone). With Sandhurst just one rail station along (Broadmoor is also close by), pupils could – and did – move seamlessly from school to officer training – first alumni were almost all seasoned military men.

After years of being distinctly so-so, school was rescued from the doldrums thanks to transformational leadership and a radical reappraisal of its purpose. Now enjoys stratospheric popularity among parents who see it as being in the top tier.

Part of its success is that it lives comfortably with its layers of history without being overwhelmed by them, think parents. Heritage matters but only so far. 'It wasn't about how many prime ministers they'd produced but about what we can do for your children – it felt modern whereas other schools were a bit old-boysy.' 'You're not going to end up sleeping in the same bed your grandfather slept in.' (A dubious recommendation at the best of times, we'd have thought.)

The school has a clear sense of its market – 'a thriving, co-ed, academic school not far from London'. Goldilocks zone location undoubtedly helps – rural-ish but a doable commute from SW London and swathes of the home counties. Pushes values on-line (we were full of admiration for videos featuring, among other delights, prefects bouncing in through the school gates on space-hoppers, maintaining dignity and poise throughout).

Part of its success is that it lives comfortably with its layers of history without being overwhelmed by them, think parents. Heritage matters but only so far

Transition to a school described to us several times as 'libertarian' would – perhaps – have the Duke spinning in his wellies. 'So many freedoms,' says parent. 'Respects your individuality and your age.'

Pastoral care, inclusivity and discipline: Nobody has yet suggested changing name to Wellbeington College but may only be a matter of time. Can't move for hearing about wellbeing, thought parents. Prize-winning too, school picking up gold award for mental health support. Timetabled wellbeing lessons for most year groups, covering everything from getting a good night's sleep to coping with adversity. Spontaneously mentioned by pupils as a strength, whether or not they'd sought support.

Health centre is well staffed, pupils are listened to without judgement and (unless safeguarding is involved) in confidence. 'Treated as adults so any issues they have, there will be someone that they can talk to.' Also offer a parents' programme online.

Issues often spotted by houseparents (eating disorders aren't unknown here) or by pupils and parents – staff felt to be quick to act when alerted. While anxiety (before and after the pandemic) is inescapable, school's ethos can be liberating, suiting some pupils down to the ground. 'It was as if a burden had fallen off [their] shoulders,' says parent, though 'I don't how it would work out for a child who doesn't have the same work ethic.'

A particularly good school for girls, felt one parent, as mixing with boys gives valuable sense of perspective. 'Need them to cut through the nee-naw overthinking that can go on in girls' heads.'

Commendably open approach to Everyone's Invited – no shirking, no defensiveness. When Ofsted report appeared, 'had to accept that it is happening here even if it's not reported.' Social care team from local authority were invited in to interview staff and students, concluding that there were some 'low level' issues.

Extensive programme now developed with sex and consent expert. For girls, includes what harassment looks like, how to ensure it's not normalised and how to say no. Can also report incidents anonymously. Boys learn about respect for girls and 'what consent is'. Also running parent education programme, while staff can self-report incidents that they're worried about. Concerns about staff (who complete online safeguarding course each year) can also be reported to new values guardians.

Pupils and parents: A smart school with well-groomed children (long, glossy, effortful hair still the norm for majority of girls) in neat uniform (herringbone jacket and black trousers for boys, blue and black tartan skirt and black blazer for girls, navy V-neck jumper for all). Suits that exude appropriate values – 'smart, businesslike, respectful' – for sixth formers.

Parents come across as confident and hugely articulate – no diffidence here about flagging issues. ('Silver-tongued,' says one). Sociable – physical meetings pre-Covid, WhatsApp groups during the pandemic. 'Form tight-knit groups.'

Money matters: Offers academic and music scholarships and exhibitions during the 13+ entrance process, with sport, art, dance and drama scholarships awarded at the end of first year at the school. Similar range of scholarships at 16+. All are honorary with the exception of music, where scholars receive free tuition (two instruments, composition and Alexander technique).

Help with the fees now comes in three forms. Fee-assisted places cover between 10 per cent and 100 per cent of the fees (average is 50 per cent). Also 20 current Prince Albert Foundation scholars from low-earning families with strong reason for seeking boarding 'who would not normally be able to access independent education'.

Will continue to educate children of deceased servicemen or servicewomen and 'orphan children of persons who, in the sole opinion of governors, died in acts of selfless bravery' free of charge.

The last word: One of the great educational transformations, from small-bore to big gun in under a generation. Thoughtful, contemporary education and first-class leadership ensure that bright confident extroverts and quieter types alike with the drive to make the most of opportunities here will flourish. Just a shame there isn't room for them all.

Winchester College

College Street, Winchester, Hampshire SO23 9NA

01962 621247 | admissions@wincoll.ac.uk | www.winchestercollege.org

Ages: 13–18

Pupils: 700; sixth form: 291; Boarders: All full

Fees: Boarding £43,335 pa

Headman: Since 2016, Dr Timothy Hands (60s), previously master of Magdalen College School. Affable, relaxed and extremely charming, one is aware of his formidable erudition but not overawed. Comes from something of a teaching dynasty – his father was head of four schools (not at the same time). His has been quite a long and winding educational road, albeit undeviating. Educated at a London state school he went on to study music at Guildhall; his main instrument was the violin but although we spied a music stand in one corner of his rather fine study, he claims not to have lifted a bow for 'a long time'. Thence to King's College London where he read English and on to St Catherine's College, Oxford, as a graduate scholar. After a stint as English lecturer at Oriel College he left higher education, closing the circle with a teaching post and then housemastership at the King's School Canterbury; 'I loved it from the word go, I was astonished at how good a school could be.' Went to Whitgift School as second master and was appointed to his first headship at the Portsmouth Grammar School where he stayed for 11 years before returning to Oxford as the 61st master of Magdalen College School in 2008.

His teaching career has covered the independent school board: co-ed, single sex, day, boarding, musical and academic excellence and long tenures have added depth to breadth of experience. Continues to teach lower sixth English and has written and contributed to a number of books, including several on Thomas Hardy. Fascinated by Winchester's many literary connections – Keats wrote 'Ode to Autumn' here, Matthew Arnold was a pupil, as was Anthony Trollope (whose autobiography is less than elegiac about his schooldays). Some Trollopian graffiti is preserved under Perspex. College archives are a bibliophile's delight and Dr Hands is keen that Winchester's treasures be shared.

What a pleasure it is to meet a head who knows his mind (not uncommon) and speaks it (somewhat rarer) without a trace of edu-jargon. Firm views on topics from how and when to teach Shakespeare (wasted on the under-16s) to gender, 'there's much more to an individual than gender, let's pay attention to the multifold', to bursaries. Has gained from the sale of some college land for housing, the proceeds to be spent 'exclusively on bursaries'. The college does not concentrate exclusively on 100 per cent awards, focus is on 'social mobility, not extremes' and the average is 60 per cent.

Parents think he's a good thing. We heard there were concerns that he would be too much of a moderniser ('Winchester parents like the school's traditions'), but consensus is that changes so far have been timely and necessary.

Very keen on sport and has relaxed rules to enable boys to play county matches on Sundays. His own sporting endeavours are now vicarious and he enjoys watching anything, 'from cricket and rugby to Gaelic hurling'. Spare time is for 'listening to music and writing things'. Married, his wife is now 'retired from law', with two sons in their twenties.

We felt it was probably a bit unfair to ask such a literary man for his favourite pieces of writing, but he took our request in good part. George Herbert's 'Love'; Wordsworth's 'Elegiac Stanzas' and Thomas Hardy's 'At Castle Boterel' were Dr Hands's impeccable poetic picks.

Entrance: 'Our aim is happiness' states the school in its commendably clear admissions literature. Well, yes, no one could argue with that except perhaps the 400 or so whose applications for the annual 140 places are unsuccessful. Recent review of procedures has increased the number of open days and shifted interview focus to take into account potential as well as prior attainment via a 45-minute 'discussion' and 'short maths test'. According to Dr Hands, 45 minutes is 'long enough to find out what the boys are really like'. Parents describe the process as 'rigorous' but had nothing but praise for staff: 'So experienced, they know exactly what they're looking for.'

What a pleasure it is to meet a head who knows his mind (not uncommon) and speaks it (somewhat rarer) without a trace of edu-jargon

Invitation to interview determined by pre-test results and reports from prospective candidate's school. Unlike Eton, Winchester is happy to consider boys from prep schools who teach the PSB (Prep School Baccalaureate) rather than Common Entrance: 'We assess the whole child.'

Parents are advised to start the application process when their son is in year 4 (age 8-9). In the year after a boy has been offered a place the school now invites him and his parents back at least three times to 'drop into sport, music or Div'.

School will be welcoming girls as day pupils to the sixth form in September 2022, and as boarders in the sixth form from September 2024. The admission of girls (and the increasing number of day pupils), will significantly increase the size

School will be welcoming girls as day pupils to the sixth form in September 2022, and as boarders in the sixth form from September 2024

of the sixth form since there are 'no plans to reduce the number of boarding boys'. Over time school plans to admit a minimum of 30 day pupils (approximately half of these will be girls) and up to 50 girl boarders into the sixth form.

Exit: UCL, Edinburgh, Imperial, Durham and LSE are top of the Russell Group choices, but largest number by far go to Oxbridge, 18 in 2021. An increasing number attend premier US universities, eg Brown, Chicago, Columbia, Dartmouth, Duke, Georgetown, Harvard, MIT, Princeton, UNC, UPenn and Yale.

Latest results: In 2021, 94 per cent 9-7 at GCSE; 92 per cent A*/A equivalent at Cambridge Pre-U. In 2019 (the last year when exams took place), 88 per cent 9-7 at GCSE; 67 per cent A*/A equivalent at Cambridge Pre-U.

Teaching and learning: Has maintained a 'proudly Pre-U' stance and results are consistently outstanding – while still leaving room for a smallish tail of lower grades (well, mostly B/C equivalent). But since 2020, pupils in year 12 study linear A levels (three), plus EPQ. News that the Pre-U has been retired caused inevitable consternation, but school has had a few years' grace in which to grit its teeth and reacquaint itself with A levels. Nineteen exclusively 'proper' subjects on offer; history of art makes the cut, as does philosophy & theology, but no class civ and the only other 'ology' is biology. Most take three Pre-Us, but some may do four or even five. Maths the runaway favourite followed by sciences; respectable numbers too for languages, history and economics. I/GCSE results equally lofty, with almost nothing below a 5.

Central nervous system of the curriculum is 'Div'. Unique to Winchester and non-examined, Div could be seen as defining the school's academic ethos. It is a truly educative and inspiring constant in pupils' lives throughout their time here. Topics broadly based on history, culture and current affairs ('from Henry II to Brexit') are researched and debated – all are expected to speak. Dons 'direct' rather than teach, 'It's not about right answers, it's about exploring ideas'; for sixth formers the format is 'less syllabus based'. On Saturday evening all complete a Div task on what has been studied during the week. We observed an MP (second year) lesson: 'There can never be another artistic renaissance because we have lost the Medici ideals.' Boys got busy with research, full of ideas and contextual knowledge. Discussion ranged from Elon Musk and Tesla ('feels similar') to the rebuilding of fire-damaged Notre Dame ('It's pointless to put 700 million euros into a building when people are starving'). At the end boys were asked to what extent they agreed or disagreed with the original statement by placing their post-it note along a continuum line. Apparently, 'If it's a good question the answers should be split.' An impressive amount of ground was covered in half an hour (lessons are 35 minutes' long, 'just the right length for boys' concentration').

Seems like Winchester's former reputation for lagging behind the digital times has gone the way of its infamously terrible old website. All boys have laptops, OneNote is used for homework setting. 'Of course it's yes to technology, but only if it makes things better. Handwriting is still important.' Work experience – always an interesting one for boarding schools – is a 'new thing' and takes place after GCSEs. New emphasis on a more global context within teaching.

Learning support and SEN: SEN provision is there and personalised for those who need it, with mild to moderate dyslexia, dyspraxia, hearing and visual impairments catered for. Learning support staff run study skills sessions and specialist one-to-one tuition as required. Boys can also email tutors to request 'task time' if they need help with a particular subject or an essay hasn't gone as well as expected.

The arts and extracurricular: 'Nothing apart from lessons is compulsory,' we were told. 'No one is forced to do anything.' But dull would be the boy who declined to take full advantage of the cultural and sporting opportunities at Winchester, and Winchester doesn't do dull.

Wednesday afternoons are for CCF (founded in 1860) or community service – care home visits: 'we play cards and serious dominoes'; work with disabled children; musicians give mini concerts in primary schools, 'we have a phenomenal network.' Some boys undertake training so that they can visit patients in specialist dementia care.

When it comes to music, whatever the instrument the school will find a way and a teacher. Two-thirds of boys play at least one instrument – hence 50 practice and teaching rooms – and there are choirs, ensembles and orchestras for every interest and level of ability. Winchester's chapel choir sings at services much as it did when the school was founded 600 years ago; boys and staff are joined by 16 quiristers from Pilgrims' School (just over the road). Music and choral scholarships fund free tuition in two instruments (includes voice), candidates must be at grade 6 level in more than one instrument to apply.

Boys can prepare for LAMDA exams but there's no drama on curriculum and while there are several drama clubs, most have 'play reading' as a qualifier. According to website this means that boys' 'appetite for theatre is resultantly all the more passionate', a somewhat niche justification for not offering a subject. There is, however, a head of drama who coordinates dramatic projects, productions and workshops. Beautifully refurbished art school and great DT facilities are open in the evenings and at weekends; art and art history offered at Pre-U.

Fresh air enthusiasts can join Natural History Soc and try clay pigeon shooting, sub aqua and fishing – head told us boys can land trout from the Itchen and have their catch cooked for lunch

Boys are encouraged to join at least a few of the many clubs and societies. In addition to all that play reading, these include lots of subject-based academic clubs, Kenneth Clark Society (the art historian was a former pupil) and other enticing activities from bell ringing to book binding to the intriguingly named 'Make-up Society'. Lots of opportunities too for would-be journalists to work on a range of very well produced publications. Fresh air enthusiasts can join Natural History Soc and try clay pigeon shooting, sub aqua and fishing – head told us boys can land trout from the Itchen and have their catch cooked for lunch.

Sport: School's 'not very sporty' reputation truly is a thing of the past ('we're now beating Marlborough'), although judging by the dogged PR drive in this direction, nothing is being left to chance. It's all the more impressive when one considers that no sport is compulsory and things like chess can be options. Golf seems to be quite a favourite, there are four golf bursaries, recently introduced and funded by alumni keen to 'up the standard' of Winchester's golf. It appears to have paid off and one chap we spoke to was hoping to go to a US university on a golf scholarship. Fact that college owns its own golf club may be pertinent. Football and cricket are 'for all abilities'. Football described by one boy as a 'a great leveller and v good for social cohesion' – important when around a quarter of boys are from abroad. Sports fields in general and the cricket pitches in particular are breathtakingly lovely, to play there must soften any defeat. Winchester also has its own, unique, variations on both fives and a mash-up of football/rugby (known as Winkies). Work has begun on a new sports centre that will provide, among other facilities, a 25-metre swimming pool, squash and fives courts and a dojo where the college plans to host 'major martial arts tournaments'. Not just new facilities, but newly launched sports scholarships underline school's commitment in this area.

Boarding: Boarding houses are all near the main school and most are in fairly old buildings – creaky, quirky, domestic scale, nothing much purpose built, but comfortable and charming in their way. Houses are officially named after their founding masters but referred to by nicknames; they also have letters. Thus, Moberly's (official name) is known as Toye's and its house letter is B. All clear? Seventy scholars live in school's original 14th-century buildings and, somewhat confusingly, both they and their accommodation are known as College. Each house has its own library equipped with all the text books the boys are studying as well as music practice rooms. There are 60 boys in a house, 12 per year group, 'very cohesive, friends for life,' said a parent. Dorms for JP and MP (first and second years), then double rooms; single rooms for all in their final year. Head of house gets a large room of his own – the one we saw had a sofa and a rather nice window seat overlooking the quiet street below. This well-appointed den also featured a surprising blast from the past – there on the wall we spotted what we will refer to as the infamous Athena tennis girl poster. Younger readers can Google it. Was it a family heirloom passed down from Wykehamist father to son or something more meta – a sophisticated, ironic challenge to the male gaze? The boy in question wasn't in, so we shall never know.

Two hours' homework every evening (with a 15-minute snack break) is the norm for most – something parents would struggle to enforce at home. First and second years do supervised prep in their own curtained study cubicles known as 'toys', where 'we let them show off their own personality in terms of mess until it drives us mad'.

No mobiles after bedtime; use of laptops and mobiles in boarding house at housemaster's discretion, onus is on trusting boys' 'self-discipline'. After the second year boys can sign out if they want to go into town, they don't have to ask permission.

Unique to Winchester, Div could be seen as defining the school's academic ethos. Topics broadly based on history, culture and current affairs ('from Henry II to Brexit') are researched and debated – all are expected to speak

Not a huge number of resident staff, usually just housemaster and his family, matron and assistant housemaster, 'that way it's more like a parental role'. Tutors are also attached to each house to assist boys with academic work and offer additional pastoral support. All meals eaten in house, 'means we see every boy several times a day'. We enjoyed a delicious lunch in one house's 'grubbing hall' (dining room), preceded by a lightning quick prayer, a flourish on the piano and a round of 'Happy Birthday' (the birthday boy gets a cake at dinner). Different members of teaching staff are invited to lunch in houses – helps to get to know everyone. Every house has three full-time chefs and a pupil representative from each of the years meets with them to discuss the food. Several parents thought that quality of food was 'variable', with some houses serving up better offerings than others.

Two exeats a term, bit more time off for prefects; local boys can go home on Sundays. But really it's all about working and living in school; as one boy told us, 'It's nice being close to friends, although there's not much spare time.'

So, what about that vexed issue, choice of house? Parents say that it used to be partly 'luck of the draw'. No one ever gets to see all ten houses but new, 'improved' system means most parents now have the opportunity to visit up to six. One parent thought it would be easier if the school had an open day where you could visit all the houses and then arrange to re-visit the ones you favoured. In the end though the parental consensus was that even under the old system there wasn't a huge disparity and once boys are settled in a house, 'they all think theirs is the best'.

Ethos and heritage: Founded in 1382 by William of Wykeham, Bishop of Winchester (busy chap, he also founded New College, Oxford), this is one of the oldest schools in the world, though overshadowed in age and presence by near but unrelated neighbour, Winchester Cathedral. Main entrance is tucked modestly down a quiet side street, visitors state their business to friendly porters (they were feeding a resident robin when we dropped in to the lodge) and there, behind the flinty walls, are quads, ancient buildings, magical secret gardens and playing fields that run down to the River Itchen with a view of hills beyond. It really is quite breathtakingly lovely. 'Yes, but you do get used to it,' said our guide.

All schools have traditions, but they run particularly deep here – boys and parents seemed very protective of them too. Rather like a remote island, behind the high walls customs and habits have evolved, largely uncompromised by the vulgar brutalities of the world beyond. Boys and dons peppered our conversation with unfamiliar words, not to enforce exclusivity but because they had forgotten not everyone speaks fluent Winchester. Win Coll vernacular, its history, language and traditions, are known as 'Notions' and in the bad old days new boys were subjected to a proficiency test by their older peers. The test may have gone but getting to grips with vocab can still be daunting: 'It took ages to learn all the language,' one of our lunch companions told us.

Classrooms (or those that we saw) are nothing fancy – utilitarian tables, blue plastic chairs, rather nasty strip lighting. Two old wooden desks huddled against the wall – one got the feeling they were on borrowed time. School says much classroom refurbishment has taken place since our visit. The young don (assortment of suits meant we briefly thought he was a sixth former, only the wedding ring gave it away) seemed to be perching on a piano stool. Not that any of this matters, it certainly doesn't to the boys and parents are unanimous in praise of the teaching, 'just exceptional'. The Moberly Library is a gem, atmospheric and stuffed with books, artefacts and the odd chess set. According to our notes it even smells lovely. The Cameron Bespolka Outdoor Classroom, which overlooks the river, was opened in 2019 – includes amphitheatre-style seating and a pontoon.

Chapel can accommodate half the school. Weekly midday service for each year, services for all on Sunday. Remodelled after WWI, on the left hand of Christ is the mother of a soldier and on his right is a soldier to commemorate the 513 Wykehamists killed in that war. The beautiful and very moving War Cloister, completed in 1924, is the largest private memorial in Europe and 'nearly bankrupted the school to build'. Its position was chosen so that boys would pass it every day as they walk to and from lessons.

In recent years there have been efforts to make the school more visible, appear less introspective, though our taxi driver said he thought local people didn't have much idea about it. Parents also felt communications were still a bit patchy (while acknowledging they are 'a lot better' than they were): 'The onus is on the boys to tell parents what's going on so it can be a bit hit and miss,' said one. Another felt school wasn't interested in parent feedback: 'It's all about the boys, which is good, but parents can feel peripheral.' Top marks for reports though, described as 'incredibly detailed, so good'.

Old Wykehamists (former pupils) include bishops ancient and modern, poets, lawyers, soldiers, scholars and a couple of first elevens of gentleman cricketers including Douglas Jardine. Also, Seumas Milne (Jeremy Corbyn's spin doctor), comedian Tim Brooke-Taylor, novelist Patrick Gale and Joss Whedon, film maker and creator of Buffy the Vampire. Lots of MPs, but no prime ministers (yet). Two rather delicious fictional Old Wykehamists are Sir Humphrey Appleby, the consummate mandarin in Yes, Minister, and Basil Fawlty (who apparently sports an OW tie).

Pastoral care, inclusivity and discipline: Great emphasis on trust and self-regulation in keeping with school's low-key liberalism, but we observed quiet vigilance on the part of dons – easy enough in small classes. Parents concur: 'The staff and housemasters really do know the boys as individuals, they notice everything.' No centralised rules re things like uniform – boys wear their own suits and plain shirts with house ties; academic scholars wear gowns. Ditto length of hair (certainly nothing that could be put up in a ponytail, but quite a lot of shaggy thatches well below the collar). Parents say this and much else, such as use of electronic devices outside lessons and whether or not boys are allowed to order takeaways on Saturday nights, is down to housemasters. Dons are 'sir', boys go by their Christian names.

Behind the high walls customs and habits have evolved, largely uncompromised by the vulgar brutalities of the world beyond

Each new boy is paired with an older boy who shows him around and looks out for him in the first few weeks of term – seems to work well, according to parents. Nearly all the parents we spoke to said their sons found the intensity of college life and the evening homework load pretty exhausting at first. School is aware and warns parents, 'Don't book anything for that first half-term holiday.' Parents agree, one described the academic demands as 'rigorous and relentless', but went on to say that boys adapt quickly and that the resulting work ethic was 'unbeatable'.

Parents felt school would not suit mothers (or fathers) of the helicopter persuasion: 'You need to back off and let the boys be, it's hard for some at first but you get used to it.' Most are confident that the school knows what it's about, 'They're up front about the way things are done, the focus is completely on the boys, not hand-holding parents.' One or two dissenting voices though: 'Families are spending a lot of money, their goodwill matters.'

Pupils and parents: We met a carefully curated group of sixth formers – all different, all eloquent, all devoted to their school and fulsome in its praise. What distinguishes a Wykehamist we asked? 'Individuality' said one, 'humility' said another. 'Good etiquette' too – school motto is 'Manners Maykth Man' after all. 'We know not to eat in the street or be seen on our mobiles.' Hmmm. If time allows, Good Schools Guide reviewers always try to do a bit of casual loitering outside before their appointments with schools. As chance would have it, but half-an-hour earlier we had been diverted by the sight of an impeccably suited sixth former deftly managing to cross the road, scoff baked goods and text at the same time... Needless to say, this rebel was not among the boys we met. And what about girls? Yawn. 'That's the top question we're asked at open days. The school has been this way for 700 years, it won't change.' All-girls establishments Goldolphin, Calne, St Mary's Ascot and St Swithun's are the local suppliers for socials, plays and charity concerts.

Parents we spoke to – and we spoke to lots – were a delight. Forthright, devoted to their sons' school of course, protective of its traditions, tolerant (if not exactly fond) of its eccentricities, realistic about its 'could do betters' and generous with their advice for prospective parents – much of which appears in this review. There is a parents' committee that organises social events (two per year) and fundraiser balls every second year. Not much use if you live thousands of miles away, but pretty good for a full boarding school.

'V V international,' said one boy. School maintains that its proportion of students from abroad (just under a quarter) has been constant for 15 years, but also says there's no quota: 'We always respond to quality.' Parents seemed under the impression it was higher than this.

Money matters: Fees just tipped over the £40,000 mark. Lots of financial help available and ambitious plans for more. Around a third of boys are in receipt of some means-tested bursarial support, from five per cent to 100 per cent. Bursary provision planned to increase by 25 per cent (150 pupils) by 2024. Scholarships and exhibitions are awarded for 'exceptional' abilities in sport and music and cover the cost of specialist tuition.

The last word: Winchester is sometimes described as 'very traditional', the implication being that this is not necessarily a good thing. The reverse is true. It is the college's enlightened (but not unquestioning) commitment to the enduring principles of a 'traditional' liberal education, as embodied by Div, that parents, dons and boys value the most. Ironically, Div's cross-curricular, discursive and research-led ethos now seems strikingly modern. Those calling for education to be re-invented to provide young people with skills fit for our brave new world might find that Wykehamists are, with typical good manners, quietly ahead of the game. Announcement that sixth form is expanding to take girls and day pupils, starting in 2022, seems absolutely on brand. Lucky girls, we say.

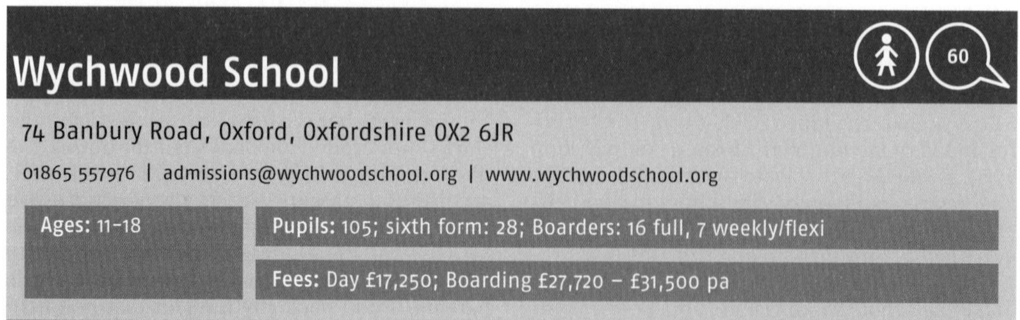

Wychwood School

60

74 Banbury Road, Oxford, Oxfordshire OX2 6JR

01865 557976 | admissions@wychwoodschool.org | www.wychwoodschool.org

Ages: 11–18

Pupils: 105; sixth form: 28; Boarders: 16 full, 7 weekly/flexi

Fees: Day £17,250; Boarding £27,720 – £31,500 pa

Headmistress: Since 2012, Mrs Andrea Johnson BSc (early 60s). Comes from a family of teachers and doctors and intended 'never to do either'. She was educated at Sherborne School for Girls, read chemistry at Durham followed by a PGCE there 'because it might be useful', and then, unexpectedly, fell in love with teaching. Began teaching at a large comp in Sunderland, then on to head of science at Battle Abbey School, and then 20 years at Tudor Hall where she was head of physical science, housemistress and eventually assistant head. The first head of Wychwood not to be an old girl. Teaches chemistry to year 7 and at GCSE. Married to a retired scientist, her two adult children haven't fallen far from the tree: son is a teacher in Bicester; daughter is pursuing higher education in theatre and drama writing, while also temping here at Wychwood.

A big believer in the magic of small schools. 'Everyone knows everyone – and you can be part of their families if they need you to be. I know every single child here!' Straight-talking and very friendly, but the word parents most often used to describe her was 'sensible'. 'She's easy to talk to and willing to listen,' elaborated a mum. Told us that she sees her role as 'taking children with a bit of sparkle and placing them where they should be'.

Investor Simon Tyrrell became a 51 per cent owner of Wychwood in 2020. Some disquiet from baffled parents who feared the new ownership could change the school's character. In reality, the school might not have survived Covid without him. Keen to preserve the school's quirky past, while embracing the future. 'Oxford is unique,' he explains. 'There are a lot of academically selective independent schools. But not everyone is cut out for an academic juggernaut. Some need to take the country route instead of the motorway to reach the same destination.' Mr Tyrell sees Wychwood as the maiden investment of his newly-created Albion Schools. Takes a personal interest, 'not a private equity approach,' he says – a fine match for the school's unconventional character.

Entrance: Girls join at 11 from local primaries/preps; there's another official intake from preps at 13, but girls are able to join at almost any age, so do ask. Prospective year 7s spend a day at the school and are tested in maths and English. Assessment day includes science labs, games, drama and art. 'It's a fun day; school should be exciting, fun and interesting!' Girls may now sit for year 9 place in years 6 and 7 (as well as in year 8). Open to a very wide range of abilities, 'but we won't take anybody who will bump along the bottom,' says head. External candidates for sixth form need a minimum of six GCSEs at grades 9-4 with 9-7s in A level subjects.

Exit: 'We help them develop their confidence and intellect, and then they decide they want a bigger pond, or boys,' laments the head about the number of students that leaves post-GCSEs, although there were only seven of them in 2021 and a number of those were international students who left due to uncertainty around travel restrictions (more than this number took their place). New 'cool' head of sixth form certainly seems to be helping retention. One to Oxbridge in 2021, with popular destinations including Durham, Bristol, Leeds, Exeter, Birmingham, Bath and Manchester. Sometimes students also head off to University of Art London and London College of Fashion. Weekly 30-minute careers lessons start in year 8 and provide time and guidance for work on personal statements and the like in sixth form.

A mum told us, 'A teacher overheard me joking to another parent that Wychwood reminded me of Enid Blyton's Chalet School, and she earnestly replied, "Thank you!"'

Latest results: In 2021, 68 per cent 9-7 at GCSE; 70 per cent A*/A (82 per cent A*-B). In 2019 (the last year when exams took place), 56 per cent 9-7 at GCSE; 27 per cent A*/A at A level (47 per cent A*-B).

Teaching and learning: A genuinely personalised approach to learning – many schools claim to offer this, but few really deliver. Wychwood excels in accommodating a vast range of academic prowess, with the top end as bright as you might find at any local independent school (and in Oxford that's saying a lot). The school will ('within reason') run a course for just one student, even at GCSE. In the sixth form, some A level classes will be two or three strong – more like the tutorial teaching that goes on at the university down the road.

'It's tiny,' said a mum, 'but there's nothing missing. It offers everything. It's exceeded our expectations.' 'All subjects are strong,' said another. 'Excellent across the board,' said a third, 'but it really excels in drama, music and all the creative arts.' One teacher per subject with the exception of English and maths: fantastic if your daughter clicks with the teacher; bummer if she doesn't. We watched an innovative geography class that was working on a 3D weather printing project representing the central England temperature record going back to the 1700s – part of the school's partnership with the Royal Meteorological Society.

Girls take a maximum of nine-and-a-half GCSEs, and different strengths and interests are accommodated: double or triple science; both

Englishes or just English language; psychology; art, textiles or photography; French or Spanish (other languages available privately); PE, music, drama, computer science, geography, history, and RS also offered.

Tiny sixth form packs a lot in its punch: 'Our range of A levels is as good as anywhere,' says Mrs Johnson. Curriculum has been renewed and refreshed, now called Wychwood Global, with hopes of incorporating online courses. At A level the most popular subjects are maths, the sciences, photography and history of art. BTec in business now offered.

Learning support and SEN: Around 30 per cent of pupils have SEN requirements of some kind, and many families choose the school for its excellence in this area. Numbers are small enough that much learning support for dyslexia and dyscalculia can happen in regular class time, but there is also one-to-one help. Site not set up for mobility issues, but in such a small place anything is possible. EAL lessons provided for international pupils who may need them. One girl we spoke to was having three 30-minute sessions a week; around 10 a year get EAL support from the dedicated EAL department.

The arts and extracurricular: 'The school is driven by the arts,' a girl told us proudly. Lots of drama for different age groups, from form plays (girls are given a title and then free rein to create a 15-minute play in a fortnight) to a whole-school extravaganza. The Wychwood Factor is a much-loved student-organised talent show. 'Other well-known schools in the area boast about their performance opportunities,' a parent told us, 'but 100 talented girls will be auditioning for six parts in the school play. Here, the plays are genuinely open to everyone and there's lots of encouragement.'

The school's new co-owner is tremendously keen on rowing. Whole school took part in a Big Row 2021 charity challenge to kickstart the school's rowing programme

Not only can keen thespians shine, but shrinking violets can be coaxed out into the limelight. 'There's a lot of support and nurture here,' a girl told us. 'It's like learning to drive: it's better to start out in a car park than on the motorway.' 'There's an opportunity to stand out – in things like plays and sport – that doesn't exist in bigger schools,' another pupil told us. Drama is also a vehicle for outreach to the wider community. The school has launched a Saturday club in partnership with the Oxford School of Drama; school drama scholars help to run it.

Around 80 per cent of pupils learn a musical instrument, sing in a choir and/or play in an ensemble (ad hoc music groups are created depending on the talents present in the school at the time). Art, photography and textiles are housed in a lovely, light space. DofE is offered up through gold; Model UN too. There is a core of regular clubs like the girl-run Inklings (creative writing), but small numbers can make it hard for them to gain momentum. 'They tend to fizzle,' admitted one girl, but the Harry Potter club was going strong when we visited. Lots of fundraising for charity.

School is small enough that whole-school events are possible, and there really is a retro, Malory Towers vibe to the school picnics and sleepovers. 'They took the entire school to the anniversary of the first day of the Battle of the Somme,' exclaimed a mother. 'Marvellous!'

Sport: More likely to win the sportsmanship sticker than a first-place trophy. Even parents who gush about every other aspect of the school concede that sport is not its forte; very keen sportswomen will want to top up with outside training. One mum of a very sporty girl told us the limited sport was 'the only downside' of Wychwood, but was made up for by her daughter being able to shine on all the school teams. 'The sporty girls get to do everything,' beamed a girl who loved her sport and was on school teams for netball, hockey and rounders.

Plenty of physical activity, however, to keep mere mortals satisfied. Some year groups buddy up to turn out viable teams against well known schools (the pride of Wychwood usually play against B and C teams elsewhere). Netball, hockey, tennis, athletics and swimming all offered.

The school's new co-owner is tremendously keen on rowing. 'Rowing was once a big sport here,' he points out. It's now part of the curriculum and everyone is involved. Whole school took part in a Big Row 2021 charity challenge with Hinksey Sculling School to kickstart the school's rowing programme. Signalling its commitment to the watery depths, Wychwood has recently begun offering rowing scholarships.

Boarding: A few full boarders, mainly from abroad; more weekly and occasional boarders, parents often dodging Oxford's notorious traffic. One international boarder we spoke to had randomly happened across the school's website online, selected it 'because I wanted to be

Nothing flash here, no plate glass or modern architecture, but everything is well loved and homely. Smallness is part of Wychwood's DNA

in Oxford', and was thriving here. Small kitchen allows girls to cook or warm up takeaways on Sundays and such. Friendships flow freely across day and boarding girls and there are occasional sleepovers. 'Our big worry when we joined was that there'd be a divide between day and boarding girls but there's none whatsoever,' said a parent.

When we describe the boarding as 'homely' it's a compliment as well as a reality check. Years 7-9 have large first-floor rooms – sash windows and high ceilings – with three to four beds in each. School says mixing the age groups helps foster sisterly ethos; colourful curtains and duvets, bedside clutter and lots of family photos and posters add to the family feel. There's wardrobe and underbed storage but no desks – homework takes place elsewhere under supervision.

Ethos and heritage: The school was founded by a Miss Lee and Miss Batty in 1897 and has always been on Oxford's busy Banbury Road. Miss Lee, the younger of the two, was a pioneer, obtaining a first-class degree in English at St Hugh's and going on to lecture and become vice principal. She funded the school from her earnings and continued to lecture in both Oxford and London. The school was named after Oxfordshire's Wychwood forest in 1918, having formerly been known unofficially as the Battery or Battery Lees, and a uniform of forest green was adopted. One of the early teachers, the redoubtable Miss Rendall, went on to found another Oxford school, Rye St Antony.

Today's Wychwood is still domestic in scale, the original brass plaque on the door modestly announcing its presence in an area where a Latin primer, carefully launched, is bound to hit a venerable educational establishment. There's nothing flash here, no plate glass or modern architecture, but everything is well loved and homely. Smallness is part of Wychwood's DNA. Even at full capacity, the school would only accommodate around 165 pupils, and it is currently running well under this maximum (only 18 in the lower sixth when we visited).

Behind the original building is a (somewhat) more modern addition where we were delighted to encounter a dog in the history classroom.Tennis court, basketball, and playground with swings. Six more tennis courts, swimming pool and playing fields off site (walk or minibus ride). The surprisingly formidable climbing tree marked with red lines indicating to what heights the girls can scramble. Each year group has a form room with lockers; the sixth form area is particularly good. Girls mostly complimentary about the food which is served in the below-ground canteen. We partook and can formally report that the chilli con carne and salad lunch we sampled was endearingly old-school and tasty. Day children can be dropped off for breakfast and can stay for (free) clubs and prep up to 6.45pm.

Might the school be described as old fashioned, we enquired timidly? 'We absolutely are!' boomed the head. 'If you mean polite, kind, demonstrating respect. Sadly, these are seen as old fashioned values! We do make them write thank-you letters – they will need it when they leave here!' One mum told us, 'A teacher overheard me joking to another parent that Wychwood reminded me of Enid Blyton's Chalet School, and she earnestly replied, "Thank you!".' Lots of beloved old-fashioned touches, eg morning break is 'bun break'.

Yet it's also modern: the tiny classes and bespoke approach make for a nurturing, holistic, democratic environment that some famously alternative schools could only dream of. Staff are all very accessible and 'reply to emails immediately,' say parents, 'even on weekends!' 'They put in so much extra time for the girls, they really do,' enthused another. 'We had a lower school Covid research project. All subjects – science, history, maths were involved; very forward thinking.'

Bizarrely – almost freakishly – low profile. 'It's a well-kept secret,' said a parent, leading us to wonder if some school families might be conspiring to keep this gem hidden. 'Once people see it, they tend to be impressed,' said the head. Huge hopes hang on the marketing nous of the school's new co-owner. 'We have plenty of room,' says head. 'We have A level classes of two girls. We could easily go up to ten and wouldn't need any new building.' Much frank acknowledgement that Wychwood 'needs updating for the next generation of learners'.

Former pupils include Margaret Casson, architect, designer and photographer; Joan Aiken, writer; Vicky Jewson, film maker; Rebecca Stockland, opera singer; Matilda Leyser, actor and aerialist; Dame Ottoline Leyser, scientist; Dame Honor Fell, zoologist (school records refer to Honor's ferrets, which populated the garden); Florence Pugh, actor.

Pastoral care, inclusivity and discipline: All schools say that they nurture every child as an individual, but this is easier to achieve in a school of 110 rather than an academic supertanker of 800 or more. Kindness is encouraged at every turn here; interpersonal problems are dealt with. 'Friendship group issues can seem amplified because the school is so small,' said a parent, 'but that also helps girls push through them. Girls learn to change and grow. Ultimately, everyone has to get on because you see the same people every day and there's nowhere to hide.' None of the hierarchies you often find at girls' schools: friendships genuinely extend across year groups. Year 11 girls act as 'house mothers' to year 7s. New joiners are given a 'house sister' to help them settle in.

Not a school for children who failed the Oxford High or Headington entrance test, or for severe behavioural problems. 'People assume this is where all the weirdos go,' says the head. 'But coming here is a positive choice, not a stopgap.' Hugely inclusive, aiming to get the best from each girl without comparing them. Three pupils self-identified as transgender when we were there, including the head 'counsellor' (the school's term for a prefect) – made easier by there not being a uniform in sixth form. We visited during pride month which was celebrated with vigour. A couple of parents expressed concerns about 'social contagion': 'it feels like half the school are LGBTQ,' said a mum. 'Could use a bit less rainbow and a bit more focus on women's sex-based issues, like how I lost my job when I got pregnant!'

Pupils and parents: This is a school for girls 'who don't have sharp elbows,' as the head puts it. 'Girls here don't want to trample others; kindness and compassion are valued – you don't need 13 GCSEs.' Girls we met were thoughtful, independent-minded and fiercely loyal to their school and its ways. Rough and tumble girls – no make up, little self-consciousness – 'almost feels like another century,' said a parent. Lots of summer-borns, adopted children, refugees from schools that were too big or competitive, girls going through upheaval at home, the shy, the anxious – all seeking a safe harbour. 'My daughter was nervous about going to a big school,' a parent told us. 'Wychwood felt small, friendly and not overwhelming.' And then there are girls who visited on an open day and simply 'fell in love' with Wychwood. 'I'd never heard of the school,' a parent told us. 'But a neighbour's daughter went there, and we saw her transformation from shy to very confident.'

Majority of local parents are Oxford professionals – lawyers, doctors etc. Parents 'mostly very lovely,' said a mum, 'they prioritise nurture.' Twenty per cent from overseas.

Money matters: Day fees on a par with local equivalents – okay, you're not getting the sports facilities but you are getting something pretty close to a customised education. Boarding comparatively good value. Small scholarships (£500–1000) available at 11+, 13+ and 16+ to new joiners and current pupils: academic, art, creative writing, drama, music (including an organ scholarship), sports, rowing plus an all-rounder award known as the Lee Scholarship. The 49 per cent of Wychwood that remains in the hands of the Wychwood Charitable Trust will continue to provide limited bursaries including one for MoD families.

The last word: A traditional, quaint girls' school whose tiny size and individual approach make it feel crisply modern. A much-needed alternative to the academic overdrive of some other Oxford area independents. What a pleasant surprise that such an original and eccentric school can still exist in this era of grinding uniformity. Girls who thrive on competition may look elsewhere.

Wycombe Abbey

61

Abbey Way, High Wycombe, Buckinghamshire HP11 1PE

01494 520381 | admissions@wycombeabbey.com | www.wycombeabbey.com

Ages: 11–18

Pupils: 660; sixth form: 200; Boarders: 595 full

Fees: Day £30,945; Boarding £41,250 pa

Headmistress: Since 2019, Jo Duncan (40s) previously head of the Royal High School, Bath. Hails from Northern Ireland ('still home') where she attended a girls' grammar school before St Andrews (English and theology), sights set on a career in the law. A prophetic A level RS teacher predicted her future career in education, one she initially eschewed, before stints working at schools in Hungary and Romania during her degree turned her head. A PGCE at Homerton College, Cambridge followed, then a four-year stint at The Latymer School where she 'mastered classroom management' before moving as head of department and deputy housemistress to Benenden. First headship, at (the now defunct) Princess Helena College followed, then onwards to the Royal High School, the GDST's only boarding school.

When the Wycombe job came up, she couldn't turn down the opportunity to lead a school at 'the pinnacle of girls' boarding education'. On arrival, found it 'slightly softer' than anticipated, 'with a really strong sense of community'. And what of areas for development? No surprise to hear that research showed school's greatest weakness was – and from our conversation with parents, remains – perception. Not so much hothouse as nuclear bunker is the word on the street. The 'bright, hardworking, goal-driven' girls she describes bring their own pressure. Not to mention the high expectations of the parents. But, she assures us, things are changing with the new focus on mental health: 'We work with perfectionists to get perspective.'

The latest to enter through the spinning door of Wycombe heads (for some girls at the school she will be their third), Mrs Duncan is planning 'transformational' change to school over the next decade; another brand new boarding house, along with full refurbs to two others, wellbeing spaces and ensuring that academic buildings support teaching needs. We do hope the lovely art deco tiling in the main school survives the revamp and that Mrs Duncan, with her warm smile and easy manner, hangs around long enough to see it all through. She has, after all, landed one of the plum jobs in girls' boarding education; at time of writing, our Instagram feed informed us she was about to jet off to Monaco to sell the benefits of a British education.

A CEO-style head, supported by stellar team on the ground, no longer teaches but takes a weekly assembly and chapel twice termly. Occasional evening visits to boarding houses for Q&A sessions and hosts various social events – cookies and juice evenings and prefects' barbecues feature – across year groups. Does running the country's leading girls' boarding school leave any time for leisure? 'I love to travel,' she says – Vietnam and Wycombe's Chinese outposts are on the wish list. Speaking of which, she has good relationships with Wycombe's schools in Hong Kong and mainland China.

Married to Murray, a London lawyer, with whom she has two school-aged children – a son who is a full boarder at a school in Northern Ireland and a daughter at Wycombe Abbey. Completed the family vignette with the lockdown acquisition of a black lab, surely the envy of his litter with the vast and rolling Wycombe Abbey woodlands and fields at his canine disposal.

Entrance: Competitive, although less so than you might think, especially for those also considering London day schools. Around 300 apply for 80 places at 11+, about 160 for 20 places at 13+ and 190 for 20 places at 16+. School now writes own exam papers rather than using Common Entrance. Worth a call if you're applying outside usual admissions cycles – places occasionally come up.

In the exam results Olympics, Wycombe goes for gold. Parents report (mainly, but not exclusively) 'faultless' teaching. 'Gazing out the window just isn't an option'

What is Wycombe looking for in a future pupil? 'They have to be bright and interesting with a curious mind and be willing to take risks,' says school. 'Also, kind.' 'It's a myth that they only take the top academic superstars,' parents told us. 'It's how they manage the talent that's their forte.' To be successful, however, a hardy work ethic is prerequisite. With 11 GCSEs and four full A levels plus EPQ the norm, girls need to be prepared to put the hard yards in.

Around nine per cent from state primaries. Currently 19 per cent of entrants on Tier 4 visas – mainly from South East Asia but also Europe, Russia and Middle East.

Exit: About 15 per cent leave after GCSEs most years, usually in pursuit of coeducation, with the largest number of these heading to Westminster and others to a mixture of co-ed boarding and occasionally high-performing state schools. But with 16 Oxbridge places taken up in in 2021, plus 21 medics, two vets and a dentist, as well as eight overseas (including University of Chicago, Columbia, Georgetown and Stanford) why risk chances elsewhere? UCL, Imperial College, Kings College London, Cambridge, Oxford, Edinburgh recently popular.

Around a quarter apply overseas. Professional USA university counsellors on staff offer a long-term programme starting in year 10. 'To do it right takes time; if girls think they want to go overseas we encourage them to decide early and build towards it, essentially modelling the US high school experience from year 10.'

Very few to art college, drama school or music conservatoires. No degree apprenticeships and none so far have set the world alight as entrepreneurs. Despite characteristically thorough preparation for adult life, some parents felt that 'school gives pupils a fairly narrow view of what girls can do later'. We couldn't help compare this with the schools attended by some of Wycombe girls' tailcoated and boatered brothers – where entrepreneurs, actors and musicians (even a combination of all three) populate alumni lists. 'School encourages professions and doesn't necessarily prepare them for the fact that they are not always an easy path for women,' thought one parent.

Latest results: In 2021, over 99 per cent 9-7 at GCSE; 94 per cent of A levels A*/A (99 per cent A*-B). In 2019 (the last year when exams took place), over 97 per cent 9-7 at GCSE; over 80 per cent of A levels A*/A (95 per cent A*-B).

Teaching and learning: In the exam results Olympics, Wycombe goes for gold. Parents report (mainly, but not exclusively) 'faultless' teaching, with the overriding aim to deliver a clean sheet of stellar grades at GCSE and A level. 'It doesn't happen by accident,' reckon pupils. 'Gazing out the window just isn't an option – the teachers are totally on it.' Mock GCSEs taken well before Christmas, to allow a full six months of tweaking, honing and micro-monitoring in preparation for the real thing, with no slightly below-par result given the benefit of the doubt. Teaching to the test? Yes, but there's plenty of extension study for girls who want it, with well over half taking the optional EPQ in sixth form and prizes in Oxford and Cambridge essay competitions most years. 'The academic experience is bespoke,' says school, 'it's not a production line.'

Forensic examination of exam results couldn't throw up any weak areas. Around 80 per cent of cohort takes maths at A level ('they're not afraid of it and even further maths is no big deal'), with the sciences, history and economics in the second tier of popularity. Very small numbers of art, drama and languages at A level, although school commits to running most courses if even one girl wants to take a subject – a lone classics scholar flies the flag for ancient Greek most years.

Provision of support for higher education – a 'high emotion' area for pupils and parents – recently reviewed. 'The traditional Oxbridge model that used to work needed an overhaul,' says school. 'Our approach has become more scholarly and less focused on knowledge.' Time spent on preparation for most competitive universities and courses has tripled and starts after Christmas in year 12. University preparation now a timetabled lesson, narrowing academic focus and teaching critical thinking as well as the necessary TSA and BMAT skills for those that need them. 'It's not just about watching a few Ted Talks; we are introducing genuine difficulty into the curriculum.' Same staff support local state sixth forms with Oxbridge and med school applications.

What's most important – academia, sport, music or drama, we asked? The answer was unanimously in that order, and no surprise that academic studies always come first

'Workload is immense,' was overriding theme from parents; 'it's hard for girls to fit it all in.' Conflicting parental views on whether school allows a rounded education. We heard of some girls with such full CVs they didn't have space for that small matter of DofE gold on the UCAS form and others who had limped through seven years with no time for anything other than hard graft. School seems to do its bit, though, departments working together to ensure homework is evenly distributed throughout the week and nothing set for exeats. Reading week introduced for whole school with no prep set and book clubs taking place in houses. 'It's not a gimmick,' says school. 'We are genuinely giving time back.' How pupils take it upon themselves to use that time to relax is a different matter altogether.

Trad curriculum. Compulsory Latin and Greek for year 7, with girls able to choose two modern languages from French, Spanish, German and Chinese, one to be taken at GCSE. Maths set early on, with those who were top in primary sometimes finding themselves at the bottom. 'It's about pace,' says school. 'Girls in lower sets frequently get 9s and go on to take A level.' Loads of academic enrichment with creative and critical thinking on curriculum in years 7 and 8. 'Great fun,' thought school.

Learning support and SEN: Department busier than one might expect. All girls screened on entry with just a small number diagnosed at this point. Pupils this bright are masters of working around issues and school says more come to light as they progress through school – particularly at A level when the pace escalates dramatically and previously masked eg ADHD, dyslexia or dyspraxia bubbles to the surface. As with all things Wycombe, support is individualised and school assures us there's 'absolutely no stigma' attached to visiting the learning support department. 'In fact, lots of sixth formers go there by choice.'

The arts and extracurricular: Everything you'd expect on offer and a super array of facilities in which to carry out chosen endeavour, with little hand-holding or coercion; onus very much on girls themselves to go and grab the opportunities. Some parents grumbled that girls can 'get away with doing nothing', but we didn't feel that was part of the broader culture. What's most important – academia, sport, music or drama, we asked? The answer was unanimously in that order, with drama considered to have a significantly lower profile than the rest and no surprise that academic studies always come first.

Music on curriculum in years 7 and 8 with a small number of between 12 and 17 taking it at GCSE and up to five at A level. Some 600 peripatetic instrumental lessons, delivered by 39 visiting teachers every week with substantial numbers hitting grades 7 and 8 each year, some diploma standard. Myriad opportunities to perform; three orchestras plus multiple other jazz, stage and concert bands, as well as a thriving rock scene. 'Glastonabbey' a summer highlight (audience rocks out in the 'posh pit') and the Rock Soc hosts an annual battle of the bands jointly with Harrow. 'We try to have music all over the place,' says school. Several choirs – from trad to gospel – and house choirs to cater for those who prefer to exercise their vocal chords to the tunes of Rick Astley or Elton John. Parents of less elite musicians praised school's approach of encouraging and engaging girls, allowing them to play 'for pleasure' rather than constantly pushing them towards exams.

Drama taken from year 7 and 'quite popular' at GCSE, also recently re-established at A level for a small handful of students. At the time of our visit the whole-school musical, Sister Act, was in rehearsal and there are annual non-musical plays for every year group. Sixth form production is run by drama prefect – recently The Sweet Science of Bruising, a play about female boxers in Victorian times. Plenty of opportunities for backstage contributions – lighting, sound, costume and make-up and filming all led by students.

Societies and clubs aplenty – 50 led by sixth formers – and we were pleased to see not all had an academic twist – there's fashion, bees, embroidery and film to distract girls' minds from studies, as well as visiting speakers, recently beauty entrepreneur Liz Earle. Model United Nations is characteristically stellar and when Wycombe hosts conference the event includes a diplomatic dinner and highland ball ('not the usual disco').

Full array of weekend activities (most included in fees) launched every Monday morning and ranges from mocktail flare masterclasses, magic shows and archery to cinema or escape room outings. Popular socials (with eg Eton, Radley, Royal Grammar School) are frequent and although the trad fixtures such as the Caledonian Ball remain, there's been a recent move away from discos towards activity evenings with male counterparts. Girls also allowed to venture beyond the gates to sample the delights of High Wycombe at weekends. The main attraction, as far as we could gather, is the two-storey Costa Coffee which girls earnestly told us is (you guessed it) 'a great place to catch up on work'.

Sport: Hugely busy sports department, delivering the full spectrum of offerings from elite to inclusive. Fab facilities from breathtaking outdoor pitches to a fully equipped sports centre (Olympic-sized pool, climbing wall, fencing salle, squash courts, need we continue?) mean there's no excuse not to find something to enjoy – at any rate, sport is compulsory throughout so girls have plenty of time to seek their passion. Major sports taken seriously – particularly lacrosse (baskets of lax sticks are a feature of almost every spare corner in boarding houses), where school is a regular at national finals. More exciting than that though is the annual Wycombe vs Eton match, complete with major poster campaign in lead-up ('Hate the patriarchy? So do we. Let's get Eton beaten' and '75% of our team have kissed an Etonian. Watch it be awks'). Careers in media surely await.

The annual Wycombe vs Eton match comes complete with major poster campaign in lead-up ('Hate the patriarchy? So do we. Let's get Eton beaten.') Careers in media surely await

'Quite kind' to non-sporty girls, one of whom beamed, 'We're allowed to play netball inside in winter.' Parents felt lack of forced misery was key to encouraging 'even house cats, who hate cold and rain, eventually putting themselves forward for rowing'. Weekly house games session, where girls of all ages play together, reportedly 'quite terrifying' for some of the younger ones, although the general positive feeling from pupils and parents is that such girls are not labelled 'non sporty', but encouraged in the things they do like, whether it's ballet, yoga, golf, riding or one of the mainstream sports.

Boarding: Full boarding or day (for a minority), nothing in between. Less 'all or nothing' than it used to be, with school now quite flexible about girls going home at weekends. Some of the loveliest boarding accommodation we've seen is spread across the entirety of the dramatically undulating campus, with benefits to each location. Daws Hill girls get views, own dining hall (chandelier, frescoes) and superior lower body strength from the uphill hike; those in 'out houses' get cosy fireplaces and proximity to lessons and Pitt and Rubens girls, modern facilities including ensuites. Oldest and youngest pupils have own houses. Year 7s have chickens for extra homeliness, upper sixth ditch poultry for taste of independence in Clarence House with own kitchens and weekly grocery budget, and wear their own clothes (standard uniform: track pants, hoodies, zero make up).

Quite the quietest school we think we have ever visited. No marauding hordes charging to lunch or between lessons – at times we wondered where they were all hiding

Years 8 to 11 in mixed-age houses. Housemistresses we met seemed impossibly young (more like big sisters than parents – not always the case, we are told), although reportedly keep a handle on discipline with 'coaching conversations'. Mixed views from parents on their ability to keep one step ahead of 'highly intelligent teenage girls'. Dorms rotated half termly, 'not always popular, but definitely broadens their horizons,' thought one parent.

Ethos and heritage: Readers familiar with High Wycombe's Marlow Hill will understand when we say that first sightings of the school from this aspect are at best, austere and at worst, bleak. Happily, mere moments after a sharp right turn at the foot of the hill, eyes are opened to a vast and undulating site, resplendent with woodland, fields and lake where, according to our student guides, swans nest and hatch their cygnets. 'Abbey' is a misnomer – it is, and always has been, a nun-free zone, named for status purposes only, the main school building an 18th-century former mansion.

Founded in 1896, school was an experiment by pioneering headmistress (and one of Girton College's test batch of girl students), Miss – later Dame – Frances Dove. Her aim was to create a girls' education that was every ounce as good as boys' through pursuit of excellence, development of talents, godliness and an understanding of the needs of others. Not much has changed there and it's quite the quietest school we think we have ever visited. No marauding hordes charging to lunch or between lessons – at times we wondered where they were all hiding.

The suitably inspirational site, originally belonging to the Carrington family, was expanded in 1929 by purchase of next-door estate, Daws Hill, large enough to house a school in itself and now home to three boarding houses as well as a WWII underground bunker, annexed after school was requisitioned as HQ for US Eighth Air Force. In addition to the stunning array of facilities, girls have myriad spaces, such as the 'hub' or the Courtyard Café, as well as at least two libraries, for down time and independent study. And if you're concerned about your dd being cosseted away in an ivory tower, fear not. The elevated position of the school means that the delights of downtown High Wycombe are never far from view – whether the hospital maternity unit entrance or the local branch of Office World, it's all there reminding girls to keep their feet on the ground. Community service also a keystone of Wycombe life, notably with girls heading out to read with local primary school children on a weekly basis.

Pastoral care, inclusivity and discipline: Outstanding pastoral care isn't the first thing you think of, and not every parent we spoke to sang its praises, but for those with daughters who had genuinely needed intervention during their time here (with eg mental health problems, eating disorders or SEN diagnoses), the plaudits gushed forth.

It all starts in house, where a triumvirate of housemistress, matron and tutor have their work cut out ensuring the balance between the girls' high expectations and their wellbeing. 'The pressure comes from the girls comparing themselves to their peers,' school told us. 'Our role is to get them to do nothing sometimes and to help them realise their own strengths.' The trust, encouragement and mutual respect that form the cornerstones of Wycombe's ethos run through the house system. On arrival, new girls become 'daughter' to a 'mother' in the year above. Mixed age group dorms (years 7-12) ensure that there are no cliques or hierarchies in house and older girls show the newbies the ropes. Each dorm head has her eyes peeled for signs of homesickness or work-related stress and the prefect team undergoes child protection training.

In these pandemic times, how has school adapted to girls' changing needs? 'Our day-to-day job has totally changed,' says school, 'it's much more focused on looking after mental health now.' To this end, there are now two dedicated counsellors, a 24/7 health centre right in the middle of the campus and a team of peer listeners trained by MIND. Some members of staff are mental health first aid trainers and were about to commence teaching others at the time of our visit: 'It will revolutionise our offering.'

One of the most diverse and inclusive girls' schools we've seen. Hugely impressive approach to those questioning gender identity or sexuality; there are openly gay teachers of both genders, the Identity (LGBTQ+) Society is chaired by the school chaplain, Rev Penny (likened on multiple occasions to the Vicar of Dibley), and girls are encouraged to be the truest version of themselves both by their peers and by staff. Barriers are down; when school embarked on a review of its gender identity protocol recently, pupils were invited to contribute, although head quipped, 'I'm not going to stop calling them girls any time soon.' Equally, pupils that might quite simply be 'square pegs in round holes' in other schools find themselves accepted here. Open conversations 'take place constantly', according to parents. In light of recent press coverage relating to peer-on-peer abuse, school has revisited the way it teaches consent, starting with age-appropriate material – focusing on friendship – in year 7.

Discipline meted out for all the usual boarding school hijinks – vaping, drinking and inappropriate use of social media (plus the odd dip in the lake) – but very few serious transgressions. Parents tell us that such issues are dealt with fairly and quickly, usually with a firm but supportive hand by school and often with more senior girls used to give their younger peers a 'dressing down' when required.

One or two parental grumbles in relation to 'unstructured and unsupervised' mealtimes. School has a unique – and we thought ingenious – timetable structure of 12 periods a day that includes 'frees' right from year 7 to allow 'extras' – peripatetic music, dance or drama etc – to be plugged in so that girls don't miss curriculum lessons. To fit in with this, lunch runs from 11.45 to 2.00 with girls dropping in at any time during that window to fit in with their commitments, hence it can feel a bit like they eat on the run. What their parents think they miss in etiquette and table manners is no doubt made up for in music grades and LAMDA certificates.

Pupils and parents: By and large, a school with more than its fair share of wealthy parents. Not so much the green welly brigade (although there are some), more the global elite: hard-working, successful with clear ideas about education; discerning, highly educated buyers who want more of the same for their daughters. The girls we met were the kind we mothers of boys would love our sons to invite home for supper. A distinct lack of made-up faces and rolled up skirts – 'they stay young much longer than their London day school friends,' we were told – although also *whispers* of a crowd who 'escape to the bright lights of London, swanning around spending their huge monthly budgets at any opportunity'.

Mrs Duncan is planning 'transformational' change to school over the next decade. We do hope the lovely art deco tiling in the main school survives the revamp and that Mrs Duncan, with her warm smile and easy manner, hangs around long enough to see it all through

Markedly diverse. Large contingent of girls with South East Asian heritage (school says about 15 per cent, we – and parents we spoke to – thought more), others from every corner of the globe. 'We're an international school – that brings something exciting to the classroom,' says head. 'Nobody stands out for the colour of their skin,' said one mother, although parental muttering persists about certain groups 'feeding the tyranny of the league tables' (and populating the top sets). Despite global feel, majority of boarders have a home within a 90-minute drive of school (this may be one of a few dotted around the world). Tolerance and acceptance of difference is palpable and we lost count of the times we were told of girls 'celebrating each other's success' or 'being fiercely protective of one another'.

Money matters: Fees tipping over the £40K mark not an issue for most parents. Seven per cent of cohort (around 30 girls) on full bursaries; head has ambition to triple this by 2026. Academic and music scholarships ('not a big thing – we ask parents to put discount back into bursary fund'), available at 11+ and 13+, are for kudos and access to scholars' programme.

The last word: Grafters, self-starters and competitive Carolines will get from Wycombe Abbey exactly what their parents sent them there for: A-stars, a glittering array of achievements for their personal statement and a place at a world leading university – not to mention the grit to take on all-comers and the work ethic to tackle the most demanding careers. Such girls will emerge from the experience with a high-flying army of friends for life (and possibly an Etonian boyfriend). Parents of the 'just want Camilla to be happy' school of thought, however, should look elsewhere.

London and South East

City of London
East Sussex
Greater London
Kent
Surrey
West Sussex

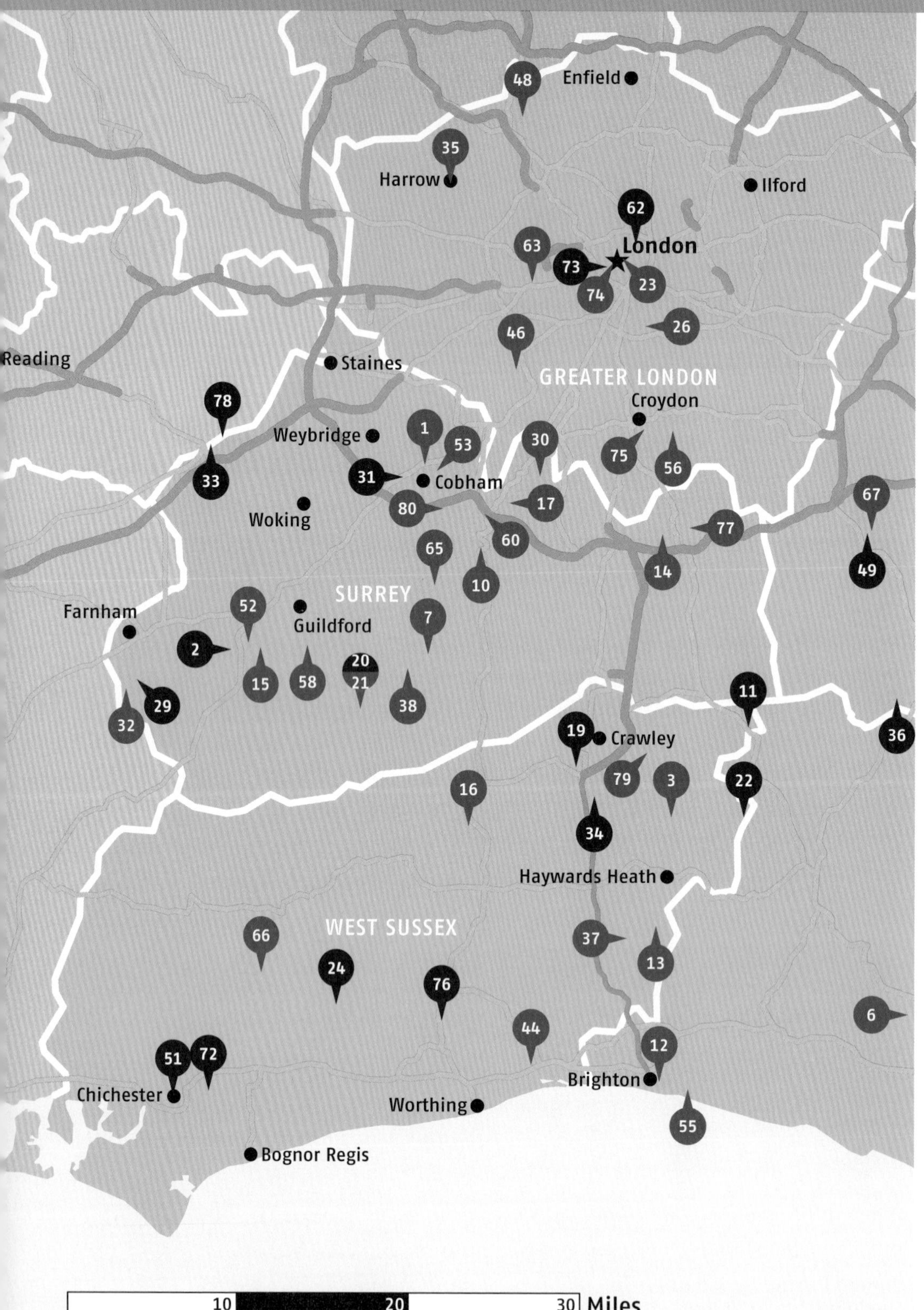
Enfield
Harrow
Ilford
London
GREATER LONDON
Croydon
Reading
Staines
Weybridge
Cobham
Woking
SURREY
Farnham
Guildford
Crawley
Haywards Heath
WEST SUSSEX
Chichester
Worthing
Brighton
Bognor Regis
10
20
30
Miles

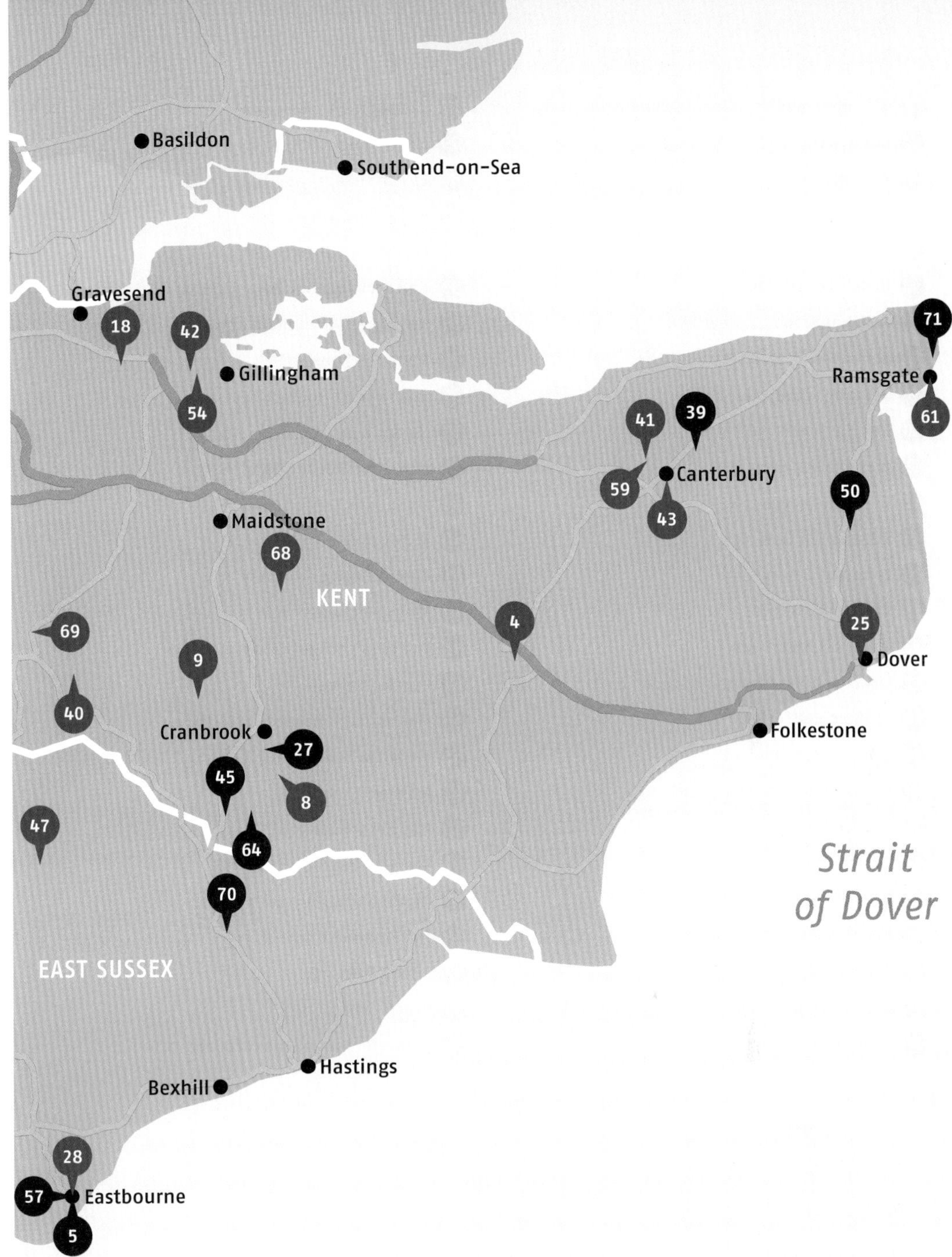
Basildon
Southend-on-Sea
Gravesend
18
42
Gillingham
54
71
Ramsgate
61
41
39
59
Canterbury
43
50
Maidstone
68
KENT
4
25
Dover
69
9
40
Cranbrook
27
45
8
Folkestone
47
64
70
Strait of Dover
EAST SUSSEX
Hastings
Bexhill
28
57
Eastbourne
5

LONDON AND SOUTH EAST

ACS Cobham International School

Portsmouth Road, Cobham, Surrey KT11 1BL

01932 867251 | cobhamadmissions@acs-schools.com | www.acs-schools.com

Ages: 2-18

Pupils: 1,323; sixth form: 316; Boarders: 152 full (from 12 years)

Fees: Day £8,230 – £28,760; Boarding £41,200 – £49,790 pa

Headmaster: Since summer 2019, Barnaby Sandow, previously principal of Jerudong International School in Brunei. Read engineering at Durham and did a PGCE at Exeter, having discovered his sense of purpose as a schoolboy sailing instructor. Taught physics at Abingdon and Stowe before heading off to SE Asia, progressing from academic director to principal over 14 years at Jerudong International, where he led the introduction of the IB. He still teaches young children to sail.

Entrance: Inevitably, because of the transitory national side of the school, places can crop up at different stages. So it is always worth trying. Academic records examined and references required, but no testing until 13+, when English is assessed. However, school adds the caveat: 'We will take any child at any stage providing we have space and can meet their needs academically and socially.' In the last two years, they will only take IB pupils if they are already following the programme and their courses can be matched. Any child can join the American programme, even, occasionally, for their last year. But they do have to stay for at least one semester.

Exit: To a wide range of universities including Durham, St Andrews, Sussex, Exeter, Brunel, King's College London, Queen Mary University of London, Imperial, SOAS and LSE. Lots to USA and France is also popular, eg Ecole Européene Supérieure de l'Image; Ecole Supérieure des Techniques Acronautiques et de Construction Automobile; Esmod Paris; Paris College of Art; The American University of Paris; Vatel International Business School Hotel and Tourism Management. Also Canada, Spain, Switzerland and Netherlands. Every student assigned a college counsellor at high-school level.

Latest results: In 2021, average of 37 points at IB. In 2019 (the last year when exams took place), average of 33 points at IB.

Teaching and learning: Non-selective so a real mix of ability throughout. A truly international school – 72 different nationalities represented and a multitude of different languages spoken.

In the early childhood years pre-schoolers are prepared gently for the future. They build their social skills and interact with each other, developing their language and communication abilities through play. With such a large range of backgrounds, we were delighted to see them chattering away together and enjoying participating in group discussion and activity.

The lower school contains grades 1-4 and the majority of core lessons are classroom-based. They largely follow the American curriculum, but elements of the International Primary Years programme are also included. These are the preparatory years, when teachers discover strengths and weaknesses and begin to unearth any particular talents. All classes are mixed-ability. No formal exams or tests at this stage, though parents say general testing is continuous – presumably because MAP (Measure of Academic Progress) begins in grade 2.

At around 10 they move into the middle school for four years. This is when their futures begin to be mapped out. Timetables are based on the individual needs of the children, who are grouped by ability within their own age groups. Each child begins to follow a curriculum based on his known strengths and weaknesses. Classrooms are now subject-based, and it's the pupils not the teachers that move. The school is determined to provide a solid grounding and ensure that pupils can work together in teams, sharing their ideas and listening to each other. Exceptionally able children will sometimes be transferred to work with older pupils for particular subjects, thus assuring that they are being properly stimulated and working at their correct levels. Middle school children can be found studying their native language several grades higher than their ages.

At 14 it's high school, still in the same building as the middle school. They are separated by a large marble hall where these older pupils have

Wifi access and the use of computers. The curriculum is wide and mixed, with 17 languages currently available. Timetables are based on each child's needs, exams are coming into the picture – decisions will soon have to be made. Some opt to study IGCSEs for a year, though they don't sit external exams in all subjects. For their final program(me), some decide to follow the International Baccalaureate, others take a variety of AP courses (18 available), and the rest work for the American High School diploma and SATs. Much depends on whether they are heading for university in the UK, the USA or continental Europe. This school prepares them for all, thus really meriting the international label. Results not bad for a non-selective school.

Learning support and SEN: With such a large range of nationalities, there is a huge need for EAL support, particularly in the lower and middle schools. So EAL numbers are capped. Children are initially assessed by EAL teachers and given as much support as they feel necessary. Depending on need, this can be in class or out of class, either in small groups or individually. iPads are used for translation and general help.

Whether pupils are heading for university in the UK, the USA or continental Europe, Cobham prepares them for all, thus really meriting the international label

About 250 pupils have some form of mild to moderate learning difficulty or EAL need. Each one is looked at individually, 'one-to-one case management', and a programme devised for them. Learning support numbers are capped each year and children are only accepted if the school feels it can support their particular needs.

Parents report some communication problems over learning support, as teachers are not always ready to listen but, on the whole, happy with the situation. The holistic approach adds extra dimension, treating the whole child. Excellent occupational therapy room, and imaginative ways of helping. Enthusiastic, sympathetic teachers with specialists at even the youngest age groups.

The arts and extracurricular: Theatre, drama and music are 'a big deal'. The amazing new performing arts centre provides everything budding thespians and musicians need. Several drama studios and music practice rooms; a music technology suite and an amazing high-tech theatre which some drama schools would die for – even has an automated fly-tower. Instrumental and choral groups to suit all tastes. For those who want it, it's all there. No wonder the middle school singers have won their category in the Godalming Music Festival at least twice and drama students have been selected to participate in the National Theatre Connections project. Plenty of opportunities for students studying theatre for the IB. And for the musicians, it's all there for them as well – there is even a large lift so that a grand piano can take its place on the stage for a special recital. Good artist in residence programme when, for instance, a visiting band spends time with all instrumentalists, working with them and introducing them to new concepts.

Art on display all round, certainly appears to be plenty of talent. Imaginations run riot. Well-equipped studios enable experimentation, self-expression and developing talents to thrive.

Plenty of expeditions and field trips within UK, Europe or worldwide – exploratory, educational or languages involved. Around 100 working for the DofE, at all levels. Recently two current students got their golds – a significant achievement given that most don't complete this till university.

Sport: At a school sitting in 128 acres of country, with plenty of playing fields (new ones recently added, plus new Astroturf) and its own a six-hole golf course, you'd expect the sports to be good. And they are. Not only outdoors, but in the all-singing, all-dancing sports centre as well. We were fascinated by the swimming pool with its computerised touch pads, enabling the raising of the pool bottom or adjustment of water temperature at will, depending on activities of users. And with the dance studio/gym with a professional sound system and sprung wood flooring; the fitness suite for older exercisers where the equipment is card controlled; the international-sized basket/volleyball show court and the café for spectators and participators alike – these children have no excuse for being unfit. PE is compulsory for all the whole way through the school.

From middle school up, all take part in a good mix of indoor and outdoor sports, competing against other schools and, once in high school, in the ISST (International Schools Sports Tournaments) programme Europe-wide. A varied selection of different sports each season, something for everybody. A parent said, 'Sport is a big deal. Even the less sporty children find something they enjoy doing.'

Boarding: More than 100 boarders aged 12-18, most full, with equal numbers of boys and girls. About 80 per cent from overseas. Boys and girls in separate wings, but plenty of chance for social mixing. A banner in the entrance hall reads: 'Because we are all different, we are all the same.' Jolly, caring, head of boarding says, 'We are a home from home and, with children representing so many nationalities, this is a great opportunity to understand and embrace different cultures. All are well integrated, no cliques.' New boarding house with single rooms for grade 12 (year 13) students plus twin rooms for grade 11s.

A banner in the entrance hall reads: 'Because we are all different, we are all the same.' Jolly, caring, head of boarding says, 'We are a home from home'

Trips organised every Saturday. Supervised prep every evening between 7.00pm and 9.00pm; the younger ones in a study room, the older ones in their rooms with the door open. Rooms look clean and comfortable. Seniors given personal privacy and do their own washing.

Ethos and heritage: Originally built in the 13th century, the main house at Cobham went through a variety of owners, from the aristocracy to businessmen, until it was acquired by ACS in 1975 in order to create their first American school in England. They now have two others in Surrey and Middlesex, and one overseas in Doha. Originally aiming to provide an American education for families living and working here, they have now become 'international' and the curriculum has been broadened to include the IB programme and enable pupils to attend universities worldwide. Looking round at the huge mix of nationalities represented, 72 at present, the change is merited. And you certainly notice it as you walk round this ultra-modern, high-tech school where classroom and studios are fully equipped with every possible learning aid. This is the 21st century.

No uniform, but a code, for both pupils and staff, and those not sticking to it are in trouble. Some parents told us they would prefer to have one, and felt staff should perhaps be stricter on the boundaries, but they also agreed that their children are perfectly happy with the way it is. We noticed no extremes: most pupils we saw looked neat, tidy and relaxed. The school says having no uniform 'means focusing on the child'.

A closed campus, surrounded by its own land, no entry without a pass; this is a safe place for children of all ages. The early childhood village cossets the very young, giving them a sense of security before they move on to the lower school building. Here floors and classrooms are colour coded, all mixed ability, light, bright and welcoming; they only move for specialist classes. Great library, where language books are plentiful and some are colour coded to lend variety to different reading levels. For the first two years children are each lent an iPad for class use; from grade 3 onwards, they are given their own to take home. Both lower school and early childhood have their own playgrounds, while the middle school has its own playing fields, and the high school pupils have their own designated areas during break times.

The technology is blinding in the middle/high school building. From the interactive learning centre in the basement where they appear to be able to reach out all over the world, to the science labs where they can work together with their iPads, to huge divisional libraries again filled with books in a multitude of different languages, you could say the atmosphere buzzes.

And as for fuelling the inner child – the new dining area is high tech. Canteen style, children collect their food from a range of options, in coded containers, which are then scanned and a thumb scan identifies the child – no money changes hands, and parents are digitally informed what their children are eating. Or, at least, what they are taking to their tables. Big Brother is definitely watching over these children. Selections are such that no-one can get away with eating unhealthy food, and staff are watching carefully for any secret non-eaters.

Pastoral care, inclusivity and discipline: School says substance abuse problems rare and dealt with quickly and efficiently on a case-by-case basis. Can't realistically control what happens outside the school grounds, but does not believe anything serious. As school is in own guarded grounds, cases of bringing forbidden items rare. No toleration of antisocial or unkind behaviour. Rules are there to be obeyed.

Pupils and parents: A multi-national, multicultural school. Around a third are American and about a third of the rest are from the UK and other English-speaking countries – the remainder cover Europe and the rest of the world. Inevitably, turnover quite large in the early years. Lots of expats from various different walks of life, some in transit, some who have decided to settle here – at least while their children are at school. Truly representative of today's mobile world. Excellent bus service, covering a huge area from Godalming to Hyde Park Corner, before and after school, means that quite a few travel from London. Beware the fleet of buses at arrival and departure times.

Parental involvement huge, as you would expect from a largely American school. Also makes relocation and transition easier. Plenty of charity support, organised social gatherings and careers advice.

Students appeared relaxed and happy. We asked one what he would change about the school: 'Nothing really, but maybe lessons could be shorter?'

Money matters: Well, it's certainly not the cheapest. But just a look around will tell you why. That said, fees cover pretty well everything, including curriculum-related field trips, all books and those iPads. Private corporate owners of all four ACS schools. Means-tested bursaries available, and has introduced 16+ all-rounder scholarships with a 10 per cent fee discount.

The last word: If you are looking for a large, lively, international school with a multitude of opportunities and facilities to die for, or if you are in transition round the world, then this could be perfect for your child. Shy, retiring children might just get a bit lost, but then again the holistic approach could also help them. Anyone looking for a traditional, structured, English establishment, however, should probably look elsewhere. That said, this school has a huge amount to offer any child prepared to think outside the box.

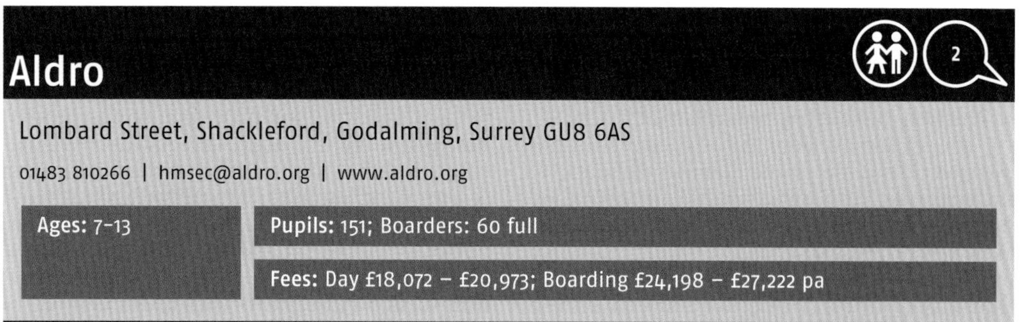

Aldro
2
Lombard Street, Shackleford, Godalming, Surrey GU8 6AS
01483 810266 | hmsec@aldro.org | www.aldro.org
Ages: 7–13
Pupils: 151; Boarders: 60 full
Fees: Day £18,072 – £20,973; Boarding £24,198 – £27,222 pa

Headmaster: Since September 2019, Chris Carlier. Degree in modern languages from Oxford, PGCE from Cambridge and a masters in educational leadership from Buckingham. Formerly head of French and senior housemaster at Bradfield where he started his teaching career over 20 years ago. Drawn to the prep sector because it 'tees children up for life'. Genuinely delights in the vitality and innocence of childhood and 'the privilege of shaping characters and minds that transcends the curriculum'.

Having led the school firstly through a pandemic and now to co-ed for the first time in the school's 120+ year history, he almost fell off his chair laughing when asked what is next for Aldro. 'This period now is about bedding in.' Of the move to co-ed he muses, 'There is a charming simplicity about single sex education, but is it the best preparation for modern life?' Firmly believes prep schools have a critical role to play in teaching mutual respect between boys and girls, 'especially in light of Everybody's Invited'. Consequently, Aldro's historic 'bringing out the best in boys' strapline is replaced with 'freedom to flourish'. Other shifts include renaming the school squads. The previous six 'inappropriately named after former colonies' have been streamlined to four more acceptable geo-historical references to the school. Parents describe him as 'dynamic', adding, 'He has bought a real buzz to the school, it feels like Aldro is on an upward trajectory.'

Wife Nicky has a pivotal role in the school's pastoral team. Together they greet every child and parent by name each morning. 'They are nice, vibrant, caring people. They've energised the school,' said one parent. Three children in their teens and two dogs, keep the couple on their toes. Relaxation is escaping to their Cornish bolthole to catch lobsters and paddleboard. A signed Reading football shirt in his office and Reading FC cufflinks reveal his guilty pleasure.

Entrance: Personal tours by the head and open days lead to an assessment day involving some verbal and non-verbal reasoning tasks, reading and creative writing. Two to three forms in each year group. Numbers increased dramatically in 2021 but class sizes remain no more than 16. The demand for girls surpassed all expectations with almost four times as many joining than was forecast. A combination of the co-ed offering and post-pandemic London relocations have resulted in peak interest. 'We might have to get more selective,' admits head.

Exit: Boys have exited to over 25 'academically aspirational' schools in the last two years including Eton, Harrow, Cranleigh, Sherborne, Tonbridge and a small number to Royal Grammar School after year 6. Charterhouse remains a firm favourite for around a third, largely by virtue of proximity. Head at pains to stress Aldro is not a feeder for the school, adding, 'we prepare the boys for boarding here so that we may cast our nets wider geographically'. Girls are expected to follow suit with Downe House and Wycombe Abbey on the radar already. Eleven scholarships in 2021.

Our view: Despite its tranquil location deep in the Surrey countryside, Aldro is anything but sleepy. An education here is full of pace and purpose. The school day is lengthy finishing at 6pm for years 7 and 8, and Saturday morning school is compulsory from year 4. All prep is completed on site. Each day is jam-packed, peppered with a plethora of enrichment activities plus masses of sport. It's no wonder that Aldronians are described as 'have a go children' by so many senior heads.

The addition of girls this academic year has injected a fresh energy and 'lightness of touch' to the erstwhile 'boys' own paradise'. When we visited, staff were twinkly eyed and still adapting to their arrival, reminding us of a family captivated by the birth of a baby girl into an all-male family. One teacher swiftly corrected herself after referring to a group of mixed pupils as gentlemen – old habits die hard. The substantial library has been overhauled to include books about inspirational women, but 'not too many pink and fluffy' titles and head assures that history is not taught from an exclusively male perspective. Female speakers are booked to inspire and 'boys no longer need to wear wigs' in forthcoming drama productions. Parents told us the move to co-ed has been seamless. A new head of girls meets with her 38 charges over hot chocolate to ensure any teething troubles are identified early. One mother of two new girls explained, 'I don't have a single worry about them. They are so happy to be there and get the opportunities their brother had.' Another with sons added, 'Just two weeks in and it feels like it has always been co-ed.' One boy however, when asked what he'd change about Aldro, quips 'no more girls'. Very much a lone voice, he was soon shot down by his peers.

Off long, narrow, wood-panelled corridors, lessons are underway. Some are heads down, quiet and focused. Others are buzzy, with raised arms and pupils darting around classrooms. All are engaging. Specialist teachers from year 5. Setting begins in year 4 for maths. One parent says, 'Aldro is not a hothouse but they get very good results along the way.' SENCo department with five-strong team undertakes 67 one-to-one lessons each week. 'Very visible and very busy,' said one parent of the department. School can cope with moderate needs but child must be able to 'cope with the pace' at Aldro.

The addition of girls this academic year has injected a fresh energy. Female speakers are booked to inspire and 'boys no longer need to wear wigs' in drama productions

Pupils are a delight. Polite and charming, with a hint of mischief. Bad behaviour is uncommon and understood rather than chastised when it occurs. Head explains, 'The best discipline is delivered compassionately. We focus less on who they are now and more on who they are going to become.' The school's core values of kindness, respect, integrity, humility and service underpin everything and align with Aldro's Christian ethos. Children attend morning chapel most days of the week. All faiths are celebrated and welcome. Children are encouraged to be children, not constrained into behaving as mini-adults. Head laughingly apologises for the 'fancy dress' of mismatched uniforms – a result of supply chain issues. Some shirts were untucked, hair was a little ruffled and according to one mother 'they always come home covered in mud'. At break time we were almost knocked off our feet by boys darting through the playground to queue up for their mid-morning snacks served by prefects. We too had to give the 'magic password' to one small boy guarding the pathway.

Lunches are hailed as 'amazing' and 'the best you'll get' by a group of children we interview, as they demolish a pile of biscuits quicker than we've ever seen. We can report they are not wrong. The parents tell us of deserts emblazoned with the Aldro logo. One says, 'They are fed all the time!' Food is central here.

A sport-for-all policy with incredible facilities. As far as the eye can see there's sports pitches. New netball courts, all weather tennis courts, a croquet lawn, rifle and pistol ranges and a rowing lake reached only by rowing boat or wobbly rope bridge. An outdoor pool too, which according to one parent is used for 'larking about more than galas'. Impressive multi-purpose indoor sports hall complete with climbing wall. Sport is a daily feature on the timetable. The school fields A-E teams so that every child gets to compete. New head of girls' games was delivering a bespoke programme to her small cohort so that all have a chance to succeed too. Netball and riding have been added to the already impressive roster of sports. Extracurricular clubs include Pilates, cheerleading, judo, fencing and sailing. For the less sporty, there's the model railway club and Warhammer. Chess is part of the curriculum with pupils winning many national titles.

Strong too in the arts. One parent described the offering as 'a different level'. Eighty five per cent of pupils learn a musical instrument, there's singing for all three times a week and termly drama productions. At least half the school take LAMDA exams.

Parents are the school's biggest cheerleaders. One describes it as 'a little bit magical'. 'You feel part of something,' says another. Mainly professional and from the surrounding towns and villages. A friendly, sociable bunch who particularly enjoy the annual regatta day and match teas.

Boarding: Boarding on a flexible basis. Boys only for now, with plans to extend to girls in 2022. Seen as an important part of the 'prep' experience and fundamental to the school's 'homely' feel. Trial boarding sessions available and decision is often child-led. One mother told us her son 'practically begged to board'. All of the children we speak to either did or wanted to. Mostly attracted to the food. After the 'yummy dinners', studying, music practice, games and sports fill the evenings with excursions to theme parks, beaches and football matches at weekends. 'Like a big sleepover' according to one boy, although 'certainly not seen as such' in school literature. The breakfasts are 'better than any hotel buffet' apparently.

Money matters: Ten to 12 full bursaries a year. Some set aside for candidates who approach the school via the Royal National Children's Foundation; and in line with the school's Christian foundation, some are earmarked for the sons of people in full-time Christian work. School is keen on social mobility and is delighted to be able support a boy who could not otherwise afford to come here.

The last word: A place where energetic children do indeed have the 'freedom to flourish'. Aldro promotes the innocence of childhood, alongside academic rigour and sporting excellence.

Ardingly College

3

College Road, Ardingly, Haywards Heath, West Sussex RH17 6SQ

01444 893000 | registrar@ardingly.com | www.ardingly.com

Ages: 2–18

Pupils: 1,080; sixth form: 268; Boarders: 127 full, 125 weekly/flexi

Fees: Day £17622 – £25,184; Boarding £31,000 – £37,656 pa

Head of College: Since 2014, Ben Figgis, MA (Cantab), (50s). Married to Joanna, with three children – all educated at Ardingly. Head of the entire school, and soon to be a super-head, with day-to-day head duties being passed to deputy James Johnson. Education is Mr Figgis's second career; his first was in broadcasting, which he left after concerns about ethical compromises in newsgathering. He indulged his passion for history in his first teaching job at Abingdon, then after a stint as housemaster and head of boarding, became deputy head at Oakham.

Parents describe him as, 'reassuring and competent', indeed it is difficult to imagine Mr Figgis ever being ruffled: he has the enviable skill of being able to turn disaster into opportunity. A pupil who didn't get the necessary A level grades was told, 'this will be the making of you', then supported through a year out to achieve the second time around. Really cares for his pupils: 'he knows everyone, and has your best interests at heart'; 'you really listen to what he says'.

He has increased the number of girls in the school to nearly 50 per cent and now he wants to hear from them. 'Well behaved women don't make history,' proclaimed one of the many signs about women covering the lawn for International Women's Week. What misbehaviour would he encourage, we asked? 'Pupils will be expected to work cooperatively with teachers,' said the head prudently, 'but not to conform', going on to explain that they have noticed girls are less willing to speak up in large groups. 'There is a danger of women being self-silencing,' said the head. 'We want girls to engage and have their voices heard.'

Head of prep since 2018, Harry Hastings, BA (Hons), MEd (Oxon) (40s), married to Kate, with three children at the school. Previously head of Brighton College Prep, and taught history at the Dragon School and Cumnor House.

Mr Hastings has a warm, eager energy and a wholehearted interest in his pupils: he knows their strengths and their foibles. Parents are delighted: 'I can't sing his praises enough'; 'thoroughly invested in those kids... an educator'.

High point of the week is the head's celebration assembly, loved by parents and pupils alike. It's not just for the glorious best, the F team are as likely to be team of the week as the A team: 'Assemblies aren't boring any more,' said a pupil. Mr Hastings loves what he does, his greatest aim is for Ardingly prep to make a lasting difference to pupils' lives.

Applies his characteristic energy in and out of school; a keen sportsman, he runs and plays golf, and is an avid supporter of Brighton & Hove Albion FC.

Entrance: For prep, a taster day plus tests in verbal reasoning, English and maths. CAT around 105. For year 7 entry, there is an 11+ assessment day including exam and interview, and applicants also need reference and school reports. For year 9 admission, ISEB pre-test in year 6. For admission into year 10 or fifth form, assessments in English, maths and science, plus interview. Admission into sixth form by assessments in English, maths, verbal reasoning and critical thinking.

Exit: A handful leave after year 8 – those who don't make it into the college or fancy a change. Around 20 per cent leave after GCSEs. Over 80 per cent of sixth form leavers to Russell Group. UCL, KCL, Warwick, Durham, Bristol and St Andrews all popular. Five to Oxbridge in 2021, plus five medics (three of whom are studying overseas). Lots overseas including recently to UCLA, Munich, Budapest and Milan.

Latest results: In 2021, 91 per cent 9-7 at GCSE; 82 per cent A*/A at A level (97 per cent A*-B). IB average 41. In 2019 (the last year when exams took place), 65 per cent 9-7 at GCSE; 54 per cent A*/A at A level (86 per cent A*-B).

Teaching and learning: School declined to give us a breakdown of results, neither would they tell us the numbers of pupils choosing each option. We cannot, therefore, offer parents our usual insights into which subjects are performing best or worst, which are popular or otherwise, and in which subjects results hold steady.

Of course, exam performance isn't everything, but many prospective parents are (quite understandably) keen to know what lies behind those headline results. What follows isn't first-hand information but it's the best we can do: the school is ranked around seventh in the UK for the IB with roughly 45, mostly international pupils taking it each year. The majority of sixth formers take A levels and overall results have remained broadly similar for the last four years. That all sounds pretty good so we're not sure why the school met our request for details with such a dusty answer.

Parents say the academic level is good and the teaching 'excellent'; IB excellence is a definite pull factor for overseas families. They describe a school with a strong work ethic; 'they will ask the students to make more effort,' said one approvingly. 'My daughter wasn't so motivated at her previous school.' Senior pupils describe teachers as 'very supportive', commenting that they 'try to connect subjects to the real world'.

Pressure increases as pupils progress through the college, but gradually, said a parent, adding that teachers help children balance their workload, and there are rigorous evening study sessions at school. 'So glad I'm not having evening rows about homework,' said another candidly.

Admittance to the college is now decided in year 6 for internal and external candidates alike (no CE since 2021). The transition from prep to senior was a bit of a shock workwise, said one parent, but efforts are being made to increase continuity with a curriculum that runs through prep and senior.

Excellent teaching is evident in the prep school, with classes around 18, and strongly focused lessons; concentration and participation required of all, no relaxing in the back row. Or, as a pupil put it, 'always on your toes'.

Excellent teaching is evident in the prep school, with classes around 18; concentration and participation required of all and no relaxing in the back row

'It's the first school we've come to where every teacher intimately knows my child... it's reassuring,' said a parent, describing staff willing to go to considerable lengths, one learning chess to connect with a shy child. Another, whose child was below average when they joined the school, 'found the teachers really positive, not disparaging... they picked out anything done well to praise her and spur her on.'

Each term in pre-prep pupils choose a topic and every skill is learnt through their chosen area – dinosaurs or space are always popular. 'They're

One pupil chose to come here for the glorious view from the terrace across nine acres of playing fields to the countryside beyond

so encouraging that the kids want to learn,' said a parent, enthusiastically describing how the reception teacher is 'always dressing up'.

Learning support and SEN: The SEN department is situated centrally between the college and prep, not hidden away in a backwater. Staff assist pupils with mild to moderate dyslexia, dyspraxia, dyscalculia and some ADHD. They are also, newly, offering support for children with mild autism and say that fellow pupils have shown great kindness and are tolerant of differences. Twenty-five per cent of pupils receive help, often just needing a strategy to cope with something they are struggling with, such as focus, or memory. Pupils have great faith in the SEN support: while we were there, a child brought a friend along to his session, confident the unit would also be able to help him with his problems.

A lot of class observation goes on in prep and pre-prep, SEN staff pointing out that it can be hard to spot problems with children who are well behaved and keen to please, a parent confirmed that they are 'very, very vigilant'. Individual and small group sessions available, but the aim is to help children in class as much as possible.

The arts and extracurricular: Music is a 'real release' from academic pressure, said a parent. The head of music (described as 'inspirational') is determined to make music relevant school wide. In GCSE music, pupils were exploring how conflict is depicted in the unsettled and strained notes of Tristan and Isolde and learning to recognise a half diminished seventh. 'I hear Love on Top, and think half dim,' said the teacher enthusiastically; 'So the Tristan chord is like Beyoncé?' asked a puzzled pupil.

In a year 10 physical drama lesson pupils were quickly immersed in movement and emotion. The teacher exhorted them to enter an exhaustive state – 'you show raw emotion when you are tired and committed' (something that pupils at high-performing senior schools can vouch for). A good number of pupils take GCSE drama; just a handful take A level. A dance studio has been built and head of dance appointed, with a variety of dance options are on offer.

Prep pupils described their head of drama as 'always enthusiastic... very calm and positive... just takes it gently'. Just three or four weeks to put on the Grinch, said pupils with approval – 'and she looks after the bunnies... that's a really hard job.'

Colour and vibrance are on show in the large light rooms devoted to art. We saw an outspoken display from IB students, who choose their own theme. 'Voting Tory will cause your wife to have bigger breasts and increase your chances of owning a BMW M3,' proclaims one banner, next to a mangled President Trump and selection of Angela Merkels.

'Lots of random stuff going on,' said a prep pupil happily, and there is, from futsal or bushcraft to robotic Lego. Plenty of opportunities for enrichment in the college too, from the solar car project, now conducted jointly with a community college, to taking a service trip to sponsored schools in Kenya, India or the Gambia. A couple of boys described a reluctant trip to the ballet, and their awed surprise at 'the athleticism'. Pupils could learn beekeeping or sign language, and DofE, (bronze, silver and gold) is popular here.

Sport: Sports have always been a focus – 'the most competitive school we came across,' said a parent. All the regulars, and the less so, such as sailing or rowing on the nearby reservoir. A new sport and conditioning centre opened a few years ago and talented athletes in the Elite Sports Programme benefit from coaching and highest level competition. PE at GCSE and A level, and a BTec in sports and exercise science.

The prep school has seven national champions in an array of sports, but at this inclusive school it's not just about the elite, all prep pupils participate in lots of matches, whatever their ability, to gain from the experience of being in a team – there are often thirty teams playing on match day!

Boarding: Around half of the pupils at the college board (full, weekly or flexi) and both pupils and parents love it: 'feels like joint parenting,' said a parent in relief; 'relaxed, laid back, lots of freedom,' said a pupil.

Around a quarter of pupils are from overseas. Ardingly is well placed for quick transfers to Gatwick and is popular with those working overseas and parents looking for a 'British education with an international feel', one parent telling us her Spanish child 'adapted well and settled quickly'.

Modern and colourful decoration in the recently refurbished girls' houses. Girls can embellish their rooms as they please – no obsession with pristine paintwork. A common room with comfy sofas, a drum kit, the Daily Telegraph and table football; smaller area called the snuggery for quiet moments. Kitchen facilities are available for pupils to make tea and toast when they want; the common room table was ready for break with deep boxes of biscuits (so no one knows how many you take, said the housemistress) and fruit.

Boys' houses are mid-renovation, with common rooms completed – boys were consulted as to colour and style. Bedrooms haven't yet been done, but furnishings are in good condition and each room has a basin; slightly elderly, but still, a boon. Bathrooms are clean and fittings up to date. A brew room on each corridor.

Around 150 pupils are present at weekends. There are sports fixtures on Saturday mornings and a busy activity programme for those who want it, including trips to shops, cinemas and a shuttle bus to take pupils into Haywards Heath. Older pupils, with permission, can visit London or Brighton.

Boarding in prep is available for two to four nights each week, with 37 regular boarders. 'Boarding specials' are tremendously popular, giving children a taste of boarding by spending the night at school, playing in the pool and feasting on pizza.

Ethos and heritage: Handsome red-brick Gothic revival buildings, alongside utilitarian red-brick new. One pupil chose to come here for the glorious view from the terrace across nine acres of playing fields to the countryside beyond; this green belt certainly enhances the feeling that Ardingly is a protected and protective space. 'Bubble' is a word often mentioned by parents, who partly desire their children to be insulated from the world outside but also worry that too much bubble wrap could be a bad thing. The head shares their concerns and in response he has constructed the World Ready programme. Senior pupils enjoy a week during the summer term learning practical stuff: 'drills and paella,' says the head. But World Ready is also about finding experiences for pupils that are 'genuinely purposeful' to their lives beyond school: a psychology student might work for a level two counselling qualification; a prospective accountant might work for financial services qualifications. Parents are sold. Pupils enjoy it and appreciate the opportunities, though 'it's not changed things drastically', one adding, fairly, that they won't really know if it's worked until later in life.

In prep, the equivalent programme is called Shaping our World, with the aim of getting pupils to engage positively with their environment. Skills range from understanding sustainability and being able to name to trees, to the ever-popular practical lessons (sewing on buttons not proving quite so much fun as learning to put up shelves).

Pupil numbers have increased by over 100 under Mr Figgis and while there's room for growth they are keen to keep the family feel: it's one of the things parents value most about the school, many referring to the warmth of their welcome at Ardingly in contrast to other schools in the area.

Ardingly is well placed for quick transfers to Gatwick and is popular with those working overseas and parents looking for a 'British education with an international feel'

The schools feel uncluttered and calm. While not a place for laden walls and lavish display, pupils' excellent artwork is around the place, and posters of women scientists filled the stairwell of the science building. The library is well stocked, with extensive online resources, including journals, and audiobooks. It has a most determined aim: not just to instil a love of reading, but also to ensure all pupils know how to research, from finding the Mr Men books at age 2, to writing a proper bibliography at age 18. New Café 150 celebrates school's 150th anniversary.

Pastoral care, inclusivity and discipline: Thorough approach to ensuring good mental health for pupils. A parent told us that academics don't dominate: 'It has that side, but it is more about the pastoral side, and we liked that a lot.' A third of teachers are trained in first aid mental health, and the health centre staff also provide support. Day houses now have house supervisors to look after fabric of house and pupils – 'very successful as early warning system'.

Anxiety is a problem, as it is at all schools now, but the head disputes the connection between this and high expectations from school. 'It comes from different directions – online, parents, the number of 'likes'... pupils have a permanent open invitation to come and talk.' Similarly, in prep, pupils are encouraged to just tell someone, 'a friend, a member of staff, head of welfare... write it down, leave a note – as someone from year 8 did, about a friendship issue. We go them together, sorted it out,' said the head.

Quite strict, agree pupils and parents, but 'they're fair and want the best for you,' said a pupil; kind and caring too, said a parent. Pupils feel it is a school which gives second chances: 'they will try and keep you here'.

Bullying is not much of an issue, said one pupil; 'the atmosphere seems to shut it down,' said another. Of course things happen, but they are dealt with promptly; a boy who made an inappropriate post online was disciplined and soon writing letters of apology, the post immediately removed. (Pupils are allowed to take phones into school, but they must be left in houses during the day.) In PHSE lessons, pupils explore the difference between bullying and banter, the difficulty of finding the line.

Care for pupils goes beyond 9-5, even for those who are not boarders. A parent planning to serve alcopops at her underage daughter's birthday party found herself in receipt of a courteous email requesting she didn't. Parents approve – '[the head is] really sensible'. Sixth form boarders can have two drinks a week, carefully policed.

Pupils and parents: Senior pupils are friendly, articulate, and unassuming. A parent told us how confident her child has become in social situations; the deputy head recalled his first week at Ardingly, walking home and bumping into a pupil who was at pains to ask how he was settling in and put him at his ease.

Prep pupils are eager to talk about their school and beamingly happy. Boys and girls mix here, 'unlike my old school,' said one. 'This school is unjudgy,' said another.

Parents from the locale (bus routes cover the area), London and abroad. Broader social mix than might be expected, from wealthy Russians to taxi drivers, the culture of the school does not encourage 'flexing' (flaunting wealth), said a parent. Communication is excellent; emails and calls receive prompt responses.

School hours support the many working parents: 8am-7pm is included in the fees, and can pay more and drop off at 7. Nursery available from 7am-7pm, 50 weeks of year. Parents report some difficulties with car parking; prep school has introduced 'kiss and drop' which has eased congestion somewhat, and planning permission is being sought for a new car park.

Money matters: Academic, music, art, drama and sports scholarships available, between five and 25 per cent. Can be supplemented by a bursary award.

The last word: Community is vital here and pupils need to participate: no loners, even high performing ones; everyone is busy and involved. Often picked by parents as a particularly caring all-rounder, but this school is ambitious for its pupils and eager that they excel academically: they usually do.

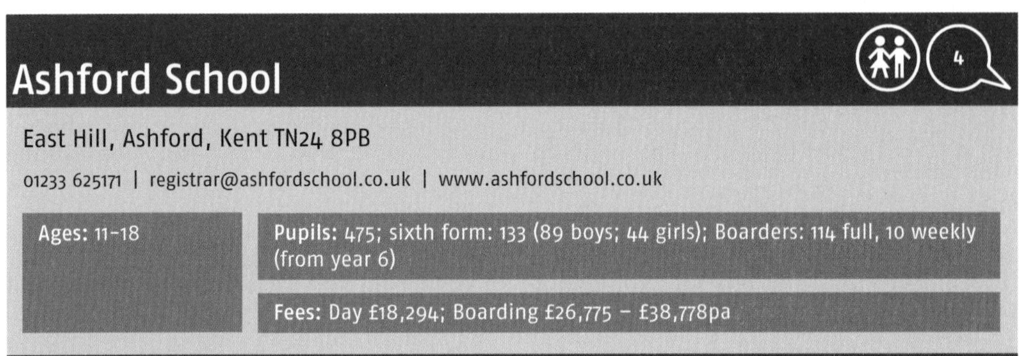

Ashford School

East Hill, Ashford, Kent TN24 8PB

01233 625171 | registrar@ashfordschool.co.uk | www.ashfordschool.co.uk

Ages: 11-18

Pupils: 475; sixth form: 133 (89 boys; 44 girls); Boarders: 114 full, 10 weekly (from year 6)

Fees: Day £18,294; Boarding £26,775 – £38,778pa

Headmaster: Since 2018, Michael Hall (40s). Previously CEO and principal of GEMS Wellington Academy in Dubai (possibly the largest British school in the world, with 4,100 pupils). Economics degree from Liverpool and a master's in education management. 'Who are you trying to kid?' he asked himself after applying for a career in the City – 'In my mind, I thought I'd earn a lot of money but the truth is my heart wasn't in it,' he admits. Reverted instead to plan A – teaching. Having felt some of his own teachers 'could have tried harder' and experienced co-curricular that was 'very hit and miss', he'd long thought to himself, 'Surely it could be better than this.' Started as a boarding master and economics, geography and sport teacher at AKS Lytham, ending up as head of sixth form; deputy head at Kingston Grammar, then eight years as head of Bedford Modern where he'd 'happily have stayed for 20 years, but it wouldn't have been good for me or the school'.

Tall, temperate and compassionate, he struck us as a gentle giant – though make no mistake, he has a core of iron and is a man with a plan. Top of his list is building developments, with ambitious new sixth form centre first in the queue (due summer 2021) then a new pool (they have two already, one on the prep site, but are determined to become world class in this area). Keen to blow the school's trumpet harder too – 'About time, because even some people who live in Ashford don't even know we are here,' pointed out a parent. We particularly warmed to his focus on forging new community links, which already includes sixth formers helping with maths and mindsets in local primaries – in shared foreign language where relevant, eg Eastern European.

Says he's 'very visual and present in all parts of the school', though some students we met would like to see a bit more of him. Seems well liked enough, with parents saying he's 'always around for the concerts' and 'really approachable – you'd have no hesitation going up to him'.

Lives onsite at the prep with his wife – a choral director, teacher and singer – and their three sons, all at the school. Enjoys trekking and cycling, though admits to working more hours than he should – 'I'm the person who always says to staff and pupils take time for yourself and for wellbeing but I'm not so good at doing it myself.'

Entrance: Sixty to 70 per cent come up from the prep school, others from local primaries and prep schools, eg Dulwich and Spring Grove. Intake set to increase from 1,000 to 1,300 over the next five years. Wide ability range – some very bright, others who struggle, but all must have the ability to pass at least six GCSEs. Almost automatic entry from prep school but must be within the academic range. Children joining from other schools sit assessment tests in English, maths (and science from year 10) and non-verbal reasoning and take part in a team-building exercise. Preference given to siblings where possible. A further 15-20 per cent join at 13+ via school's own tests, and there's an influx of 15-20 students in year 10, predominantly international students. Sixth form entry tested in proposed A level subjects and must have six GCSEs at 6+, plus English proficiency test if appropriate. Lots of foreign nationals come for sixth form as well as several each year from local state schools.

Exit: Around a third depart after GCSEs, mostly to local colleges. Manchester, Durham, and Surrey all feature. London unis including UCL and LSE increasingly popular too. One to Oxbridge and two medics in 2021 – plus four overseas, to McGill, University of British Columbia and University of Hong Kong.

Latest results: In 2021, 57 per cent 9-7 at GCSE; 57 per cent A*/A at A level (84 per cent A*-B). In 2019 (the last year when exams took place), 32 per cent 9-7 at GCSEs; 38 per cent A*/A at A level (66 per cent A*-B).

Teaching and learning: Broad intake, results improving year on year. Particularly good results in science, maths and art.

No chance to snooze at the back of the class here – the whole place is a hotbed of interaction and debates. 'What was the main reason the English civil war happened? Money, power or something else? Discuss,' we heard – and discuss they did. Another classroom door opened into a dispute around why it was considered so controversial that Macbeth engaged in the supernatural. And if you think that's controversial, you should have been in the class where we spotted two fingers stuck up at the front – but don't panic, it was just a slide of an incensed trade unionist in the 1960s, forming the backdrop to a discussion about unions v government back in the day. Plenty of opportunity to learn kinaesthetically too – we watched young biologists dissecting lamb hearts, while wannabe chemists dissolved jelly cubes in different temperatures of water to learn how to control variables. Lovely library, in muted tones, forms the centrepiece of the school and its welcoming vibe pays off – students fill every corner.

A hotbed of interaction and debates. 'What was the main reason the English civil war happened? Money, power or something else? Discuss,' we heard – and discuss they did

Caters for the whole shebang when it comes to ability – 'my daughter has friends who are really high achievers, those that need learning support and those like her who are middle of the road,' said one parent. 'My daughter isn't particularly academic, but she's flying here,' voiced another. Setting in maths and English from year 7; banding in most subjects (except the arts) and setting in science from year 9. French, German and Spanish taught on a carousel from year 7; students pick their two strongest from year 8 and take one (possibly two) at GCSE. Students from abroad can also take GCSE in their own language, eg Chinese – popular as virtually all the 180 boarders have EAL (often a strength – it's not unusual for students to speak several languages fluently). Art, DT and history popular at GCSE and there's a 50:50 split of students taking double or triple science. A good range of 20+ A levels includes business studies, psychology and Chinese, plus a BTec in sports studies. Most take three, with about 20 per cent take up for EPQ. Russian, German and Spanish also offered as a business language (mostly conversational) to sixth formers – this is a truly global school. Very accommodating timetable – 'I only had a couple of other people in my music A level,' said our guide.

Low staff turnover – this is a loyal bunch who love the challenge and freedom to innovate and use their initiative. But there's no shortage of new blood – school runs a leading and innovative graduate teacher training programme. A very tech savvy school – all children have a device and we saw them in (supervised) use to enhance the curriculum in almost every other classroom. IT-based pedagogy is particularly strong (school's mantra is that 'IT should support not lead'), eg lots of digital analysis of sports performance. Lots of language exchanges and trips that help bring learning to life. Popular Adventurous Learning programme gets staff and students out of their comfort zone, personally as well as academically, eg speaking in front of the whole class and then the whole school. The Oxbridge Club provides extra coaching in problem solving and analytical and critical thinking.

Learning support and SEN: Vast majority of the 20 per cent with SEN have mild dyslexia, dyscalculia or dyspraxia, though some have more complex needs and school can support children with physical disabilities. 'You get regular updates and they really customise the support they give,' one parent told us. International students in year 9 have access to a one-year intensive English language course, plus transition into the British system.

The arts and extracurricular: 'I'm not very good, but I love it,' beamed one student about art, listing the Photoshop, lino and ceramic projects she'd recently got her teeth into. 'You can really express yourself and the department is always open to all at lunchtimes.' And what a department it is, with two large, motivational spaces where we'd have gladly have grabbed a few paints and brushes and got stuck in ourselves. In one, GCSE students were refining their sketchbook skills, while in the other we were captivated by an A level student marching round a carriage clock, egg timer and tape machine – 'I'm going to do a piece focusing on the rearrangement of time,' he explained. In a separate project area space, two students were making a film about lights and shadows. Nothing is deemed too adventurous or indeed too big – students here have created installation art including a lift to a mirror maze. Staff are all working artists and hold their exhibitions here 'to help enthuse students' ('very nerve-racking actually – probably more so than exhibiting anywhere else,' confided one) and there's always an artist in resident, currently a digital artist.

Lots going on in the drama department – house plays and speech and drama recitals, lower school productions and the much-anticipated whole school summer musical (next up, Beauty and the Beast). National Youth Theatre was in doing auditions when we visited, and there are plenty of workshops by eg Paper Birds, Frantic Assembly. We watched year 9s critically analysing their own scenes from Daisy Pulls it Off on iPads and heard all about the active junior drama club, plus technical club for 'those who prefer to stay out of the spotlight'. Loads take LAMDA and drama GCSE and drama is run as an A level too. 'I spend half my life watching my kids perform,' said one parent.

Each boarding house has a computer room but presumably rules around tidiness are devolved – could play 'spot the carpet' in Alfred, yet military neatness in Brooke

Head of music is a colourful character who won't let any tuneful talent lie dormant. You name it, you can learn it (about half do) – organ, bassoon, harp, and the school has only Steinway pianos as part of the Steinway schools programme (one of only 17 schools in the UK to be all Steinway). 'Pretty much the only instrument we don't teach is the banjo.' Lots going on: concert band, chamber music groups, string quartet, rock bands, string ensembles, an 18-piece orchestra – not bad for a smallish school. We saw posters for newcomers' concert, harvest festival, cello teatime tootles (in the atrium), guitar showcase and keyboard kavekade, although head of music confided that 'Beauty and the Beast is my big sweat of the moment'. Visiting orchestras too – Whitehall Symphony Orchestra were due in the month our visit.

Mammoth range of extracurricular activities – from debating (school regularly represented at competitions) and cooking to Lego robotics and Scrabble, though disappointing absence of student-led ones even in sixth form (school says it's on to it). While not exactly compulsory, they might as well be, reported younger students – not that they mind. CCF popular and each year about 12 pupils complete their DofE gold.

Sport: 'My daughter isn't very sporty but does lots of sport out of choice, so it must be good,' said a parent. Some told us they'd chosen the school on the back of the sports offering alone – 'it's not just the facilities, they also get to pick from this ridiculously long list of every sport you can think of,' raved one. Hockey, netball and cricket are core sports for girls, while for boys it's rugby, hockey and cricket, and in addition there's swimming (to a high level), climbing, fencing, yoga and table tennis, to name a few. Lavish sports centre, two (not so lavish) gyms, as well as a fitness centre and dance suite, indoor swimming pool and all-weather basketball court. Pitches, including AstroTurf are few minutes' walk away. 'Fantastic team of sports staff.' School has national strength in pentathlon and swimming and does well regionally in rugby, show jumping, netball and cricket, but school's baseline position is very much sport for all, which has head's full backing: 'I was that boy in the B team that only got good when I was 15 – you should never give up on a child because you never know when they'll develop and grow,' he believes. And it's clearly not just lip service, with D teams for hockey and F for netball and school has policy of not just putting strongest coaching with the top teams, eg director of sport takes the U13 C hockey team. Plus – and this has to be a first – the trophies were displayed not in some well lit, dutifully dusted glass cabinet but stuffed on shelves in the sports staff room. 'My son gets frustrated because sport is his thing and he wants to win, but the school insists on mixing different levels of children so everyone has a go, which I think is excellent,' said one generous-spirited parent.

Boarding: Boarding from year 7 (with the very occasional year 6 bussed over from junior school). Four houses – Brooke for junior boys, Alfred for senior boys, Brabourne for girls and Judith Webb House for sixth formers – all very close to main school facilities, although students are not allowed back there during the day, which means plenty of interaction with non-boarding majority. Judith Webb House, the newest, has a corporate feel in reception and is upmarket youth hostelesque elsewhere. The others, especially Brooke, could do with some TLC (especially the bathrooms – yikes) but school has pledged to prioritise. Each house has a computer room but presumably rules around tidiness are devolved – could play 'spot the carpet' in Alfred, yet military neatness in Brooke. Children from abroad spend the first weekend of term with a day pupil – helps integration, although we heard of cliques among the international students – 'definitely needs addressing, especially with the Chinese and Russians,' said a parent.

Birthdays always celebrated and activities include fishing, shopping, go-karting, Thorpe Park, though one parent felt 'they're a bit hit and miss in terms of regularity'. Lots of leadership opportunities running house events and activities, from community work to the house play. Day children always happy to come in and it means the boarders are kept busy. 'I was quite scared in year 7 when I came in, but they make it really welcoming,' one boarder told us, while older ones appreciate 'the freedom to go into town if you show you are responsible enough'. 'Food is a bit naff – that's the number one complaint I get,' said a parent.

The senior school is a green oasis in the middle of busy Ashford but tricky to find if you don't know where to look

Ethos and heritage: Founded in 1898 with the aim that the pupils should play an active role in the life of the town and with an emphasis on 'training and development of character', the school moved to its present site in 1913 and became part of United Learning in 1999 (a group of state primary and secondary as well as independent schools). This brought a welcome injection of cash resulting in new buildings springing up all over the place, though some are now starting to look tired. Senior school is at the foot of the High Street, approached by a narrow lane and enclosed by high red-brick walls with lawns and greenery stretching down the hill. It's a green oasis in the middle of busy Ashford but tricky to find if you don't know where to look.

Brightly painted Atrium café a popular meeting place, also open to parents at pick up and drop off time, with larger refectory – bog standard fodder, say students, fish and chips gets a thumbs up while the mere mention of the paella invites some contorted expressions. Strict on uniform (instant detention for an untucked shirt), but school perhaps needs a reminder that it's the 21st century as trousers are still not allowed for girls.

Pastoral care, inclusivity and discipline: The beating heart of the school. Strong vertical house system ensures mixing of year groups, including peer mentoring of year 7s by sixth formers. All new joiners have a specialist tutor – high praise from parents. There's a whole raft of training for students around mental health, including visiting speakers and workshops; ditto for staff so they can spot early signs; parents are invited to attend talks too. Frequently used health centre – note not just medical as also encompasses mental health and wellbeing, including well used counsellor. 'My daughter is quite anxious, but she's really blossomed here,' said one parent.

Soft-touch discipline – forgetting homework and being late are about the size of the behavioural problems here. Very occasional temporary exclusions, usually relating to social media, and permanent ones once in a blue moon. Prepared to do random drug tests if and when necessary. Students appreciate their freedoms here – 'We get to go on our phones at break times, which I don't think they do at other schools,' said one, excitedly.

Pupils and parents: About 70 per cent day pupils, with catchment forming a perfect circle around the school, incorporating up to an hour's travel (minibus service available). That said, families are increasingly from Ashford itself, where 7,000 new houses are currently being built. Boarders (all full) nearly all international, over 30 nationalities and particularly popular with Chinese, Eastern Europeans and Nigerians. Most parents are hard working, grounded peeps, many dual income, for whom a big selling point of the school is that it is 'not snobby' and that it 'lacks grandeur'. Families are sociable – lots of WhatsApp messages likely to ping up on your phone to the tune of 'Fancy a curry?' but 'absolutely no pressure to go if you don't want to'. No airs and graces among the student body either – just nice, polite, easygoing youngsters. 'They know they're lucky to be educated privately – you don't get the sense they grow up thinking the world owes them anything,' said a parent.

Money matters: Academic, music, art, drama and sports scholarships offered – usually up to 30 per cent of day fee. Means-tested bursaries available, including short-term emergency ones.

The last word: A forward-looking, unstuffy school with a strong international contingent and increasing links with the fast-growing community of Ashford. Pastorally, it's moved forward leaps and bounds in recent years and we loved watching them gently encourage kids out of their comfort zones, whether in the classroom or on the sports fields.

Bede's Preparatory School

Duke's Drive, Eastbourne, East Sussex BN20 7XL

01323 734222 | prep.admissions@bedes.org | www.bedes.org

Ages: 3 months – 13 years

Pupils: 253; Boarders: 19 full, 16 weekly

Fees: Day: £10,440- £17,970; Boarding Supplement: £8,940 pa

Linked school: Bede's School, 575

Headmaster: Since September 2020, Mark Hammond, previously headmaster at Skippers Hill Prep since 2015 and before that deputy headmaster at Skippers. Has also been head of pastoral care at the Geneva English School.

Entrance: Not academically selective. Entry by interview and screening for SEN.

Exit: Most (85 per cent in 2021) to the senior school. Others to Eastbourne College, Brighton College and Millfield. Three scholarships in 2021.

Our view: You can't beat it for location. At the upmarket end of the grassy Eastbourne seafront, where the land curves and rises to the great cliff of Beachy Head, perches an attractive five-storey, mock-Tudorbethan pile, its long windows facing the sea. Surrounded by fields on all but its southern aspect, with a cluster of smaller buildings round about, it sits like a benign hen comfortably supervising its offspring, assured that all can run about safely in a healthy, beautiful, open space.

Space is a key asset and to anyone used to, for example, an urban prep or primary, Bede's is a revelation. There are more fields five minutes up the hill and another five minutes inland – all facilitate the range of sports available to these lucky children, who have the look of relaxed freedom that inhabiting such openness gives. Space also in, for example, the dining hall, one wall of which is just large windows fully open on warm, sunny days, so that the outside and the inside blend.

Two main buildings. Holywell Mount – a large Edwardian house to the right of the main building if you face the sea – houses the pre-prep and nursery. We visited at the end of a long day and were astonished by the bright-eyed vitality of the teachers. They told us of the new topic with which each term is launched in each classroom: 'It's so exciting – they can't wait to come in and see what we're going to do!' And on offer in just some rooms were: Under the Sea World, Ice World, Out of the Egg (and you should have seen the egg!) and Knock Knock – imaginative stuff, inviting exploration and discovery of all kinds.

Sports are exceptional – and not just because of facilities – at both ends of the spectrum. Says school: 'We're the best cricketing prep in the country' and, as parents told us, 'even the non-sporty get enthused – and they have elite schemes for the really talented.' 'They do wonderful trips, especially for sports and languages.' Children concur: 'We went to Portugal and got trained by Benfica.' They have a clifftop walk to reach their playing fields – a walk many remember with great affection years later – but many sports are now played up at the senior school. They do, though, have their own swimming pool on site. Several teams in most sports for all years so that all but the child with thumbs glued to his iPad get a look-in, though some sense that more could be done for the less than athletic. Dance is serious – remember that Bede's is home to the Legat dance school – so all do dance up to year 5 and many continue. Teachers seen as 'brill'. Music has a relatively new director and is set to sparkle; art and drama well on the way.

You can't beat it for location. At the upmarket end of the grassy Eastbourne seafront, where the land curves and rises to the great cliff of Beachy Head

An overhaul of maths has affected learning and results, and is starting to influence other subjects, as the effectiveness of the new method becomes evident: before studying in the abstract, a subject is examined from every angle and thoroughly embedded – no racing from topic to topic to tick the boxes of rapid progress. 'Maths lessons are now noisy,' said the head; in fact one was quiet, but the next was, indeed, noisy – 'That's better,' said the head. Parents enthuse: 'The teachers are wonderful – so imaginative and approachable!' – and especially about individual needs and pastoral care: 'superb – any problems or hint of bullying are dealt with at speed' and 'they answer emails practically before you've sent them.' Weekly staff meeting to discuss and act on academic or pastoral concerns with head of learning support on hand if needed. Pupil praise too – 'They push you to your potential and we are only 10 in some groups so they can really help you.' Small group specialist work in eg fine motor skills, writing, reading, phonics for tots who seem to be falling behind. All lower classes have a TA to support individuals but some feel this should continue into upper years, 'where they need it just as much if they are struggling with a subject'. As a pupil told us, 'When I'm stuck, if they take time to explain it to me, I really get it!' Individual support – and around 25 per cent on the SEND register here – described as 'good but pricey'.

All staff are being trained in first aid mental health. The school says anxiety is sometimes a problem for pupils coming in from hothouse schools – pupils can be school phobic and need to be reintegrated into school. For pupils feeling pressured, the school counsellor runs 'chill and chat' drop-in sessions at break time. 'Health and safety are taken very seriously,' parents tell us, as are efforts to integrate newcomers, especially into year 7 when there is a fairly substantial intake.

And there is masses to do. 'My daughter was very shy but there are so many performances and so on – her confidence has grown unbelievably.' No shortage of facilities, inside and out – big sports hall, 18m pool, climbing walls, decent library – 'they'll get books you want if you ask' – good theatre and lovely, light rooms with the downside that 'if I'm facing the sea I just go into a daydream,' as one youngster confessed.

Most are local, though word is spreading and pupils now bus or car in from a wider range of villages. School runs its own bus service on eight routes.

Bede's prep and senior are increasingly one school, the heads busy building strategies to ensure smooth academic and co-curricular progression through the schools. Service is a mantra senior school head returns to again and again, and he's determined to make it school-wide – 'Year 1 can be collecting for the food bank and the sixth form can volunteer there.'

Boarding: There is a small number of boarders, in a family house over the road from the school. Lovely warm houseparents and Molly the dog, of bounding, bouncing love, a garden big enough for football, and blankets to snuggle down under to watch TV. Rooms allocated sensitively, the quiet girls who like their sleep separate from their noisier peers.

The last word: A happy school – 'It's good at turning out all-rounders,' said several. 'It's pretty unsophisticated and relaxed – you don't get awful pushy parents there – they trust the school to know what it's doing.' And, in the words of a pupil, 'My parents wish they could have come here.'

Bede's School

The Dicker, Upper Dicker, Hailsham, East Sussex BN27 3QH

01323 843252 | admissions@bedes.org | www.bedes.org

Ages: 13–19

Pupils: 817; sixth form: 325; Boarders: 176 full (girls: 73 / boys: 103), 143 weekly (girls: 55 / boys: 88)

Fees: Day £23,400; Boarding £35,100 – £37,350 pa

Linked school: Bede's Preparatory School, 573

Headmaster: Since 2016, Peter Goodyer (Rhodes, BA; Keele, MBA), previously deputy then acting head at Colston's School, Bristol. First came to this country from his native South Africa as a teacher of history and geography to a school in Leatherhead, and never went home. Dad was a vicar, and there is something of the pastor with flock about Mr Goodyer: he wants his pupils to make a difference in their community and the world, and understand what it means to give of themselves.

Pupils are very enthusiastic about him: 'easy to talk to'; 'knows us all'; 'down to earth'; 'his priority is our well-being… and the teachers' well-being… and the bus drivers' and the cleaners'…'. Pupils find Mr Goodyer 'accessible', in what he says and how he says it, and although some parents might miss the smooth charm of his predecessor's oratory, pupils prefer Mr Goodyer's straightforward approach. They believe him, and think he believes in them.

Parents like Mr Goodyer too: 'Extremely friendly, always smiling, easy to talk to, good sense of humour. Good psychology – about finding the talent in your child and helping them to grow.'

Entrance: Not academically selective. Entry to prep (except for year 6) by interview and screening for SEN. Those applying to year 6 and senior school must attend the Bede's experience day: MIDYIS test, discussion and problem-solving tasks with prefects, then choice of activity. The head seeks diversity and balance – a year group will not consist solely of the loudest voices with best academic scores.

Exit: Some 20 per cent leave after GCSEs, mostly for sixth form colleges. Leeds, Oxford Brookes, Warwick, Brighton Met, Exeter, Winchester, Bath, York, Sheffield, University of the Arts London, Nottingham, Queen Mary, Lincoln, Bristol, Sussex and City University London all popular destinations. Lots overseas – in 2021 to Fordham (San Antonio, USA), Göttingen (Germany), Nebrija (Madrid, Spain), ArtsFX (Montpellier, France), Quincey (Illinois, USA) and Parsons (USA). Usually a few to Oxbridge, but none in 2021. Three medics in 2021. Gap years recently popular and art foundations at Brighton Metropolitan College.

Latest results: In 2021, 56 per cent 9-7 at GCSE; 64 per cent A*/A at A level (83 per cent A*-B). In 2019 (the last year when exams took place), 39 per cent 9-7 at GCSE; 48 per cent A*/A at A level (70 per cent A*-B).

Teaching and learning: A pupil who left Bede's returned a term later – 'the difference was in the teaching – at the other school things were just presented, with no engagement… [here] they care.' Both pupils and parents praise the dedication of teachers, one describing chatting to her German teacher during the holidays over My Bede's (a sort of firefly); another saying her son emailed a teacher at 11.45pm, and he answered at midnight.

'Bede's has a reputation as not terribly academic, but from what we've seen, he's not held back at all,' said a parent. Results are good, sometimes exceptional (maths is a consistently strong subject), and a parent said that both the prep and senior school have become more academic, 'but not scarily so'. There are some extremely academically bright pupils here, but they're not all like that, and Bede's wouldn't want it so. The best mainstream independent school in Sussex for value added; evidence of the strong culture of growth mindset here for the pupils.

A good range of subjects on offer, and seven BTecs, including animal management. No feeling that they are a second class option – a pupil who wanted to study marine biology at university, but struggled with A levels, got to the same place by doing a double BTec in animal management. As the head says, 'BTecs can get you where you want to go.' Psychology recently introduced as an A level.

Class sizes 15-20, eight or nine classes per year, with pupils from the prep making up a third of the first year.

The first year creative carousel is very popular, and, says the head, very important – 'Once a child understands by what it is they are fulfilled, motivation will follow... You don't have to be successful to be happy – you need to be fulfilled.' Carousel subjects range from graphic design to sculpture. First years also take 21st century studies, which teaches important skills like personal finance, psychology (taught by the head) and cooking – 'My child can make a Mexican breakfast and an omelette,' said a parent.

The Bede's diploma is for sixth form pupils, and includes the EPQ; a lecture series, much approved of by parents – 'from Oxbridge to the New York school of dance'; leadership and teamwork competencies; and community service, options ranging from Meow Mondays at the Cats Protection League to assisting at a local primary school. A junior version of the diploma is in the pipeline.

Learning support and SEN: Learning enhancement is much praised by parents for its 'really really good support... he was not achieving in other schools'; another said that his bright dyslexic daughter has done better academically here than in her academic prep. Individual, small group and in-class support available. Parents report good liaison between LE and class teachers.

The arts and extracurricular: 'Co-curricular is extraordinary,' said a parent. Activities take place three times a week, chosen from a vast range, from the BEden project (creating a sustainable, organic healing garden using recycling and freecycling), making a homebrew in wine-making (sixth formers only) and UK space design. Pupils say that strong community groups which span ages develop in different activity areas, and that trying new things is one of the best things about the school; but those who want something calm and low key are also catered for: in reading for pleasure, pupils sit peacefully in the library with thermoses of tea and coffee and a plate of digestives – no feeling that this is a choice for second class citizens. In animal management, pupils look after a range of zoo animals, and help with the dormouse breeding programme to increase numbers in the wild. One activity must be something physical, but determined games haters could choose walking, along the seafront or across the downs.

Art and DT are superb here, some of the most popular subjects in the school, from fine art, to weird and wonderful photography, to furniture that would not look out of place in Heals. Pupils consistently attain top grades in art and photography, and serious art lovers will receive the encouragement and help to take their studies further.

The first year creative carousel is very popular, and, says the head, very important – 'Once a child understands by what it is they are fulfilled, motivation will follow'

Drama is another strength – 'productions are fantastic – if you close your eyes... on a par with X Factor,' said a parent. The theatre on site is small, but the school uses Devonshire Park Theatre in Eastbourne for big productions, such as the recent Oliver!, described by a parent as 'simply fabulous. Evidence of fantastic teaching and mentoring... Such teamwork and commitment demonstrated.'

Not many take music as an examination subject, but there are plenty of choirs, orchestras and bands, and for those keen to dance, Bede's is home to the Legat dance school – the head boy of the prep dances every day.

Sport: Many pupils are attracted by the choice of sport – others by not having to play it. The main sports are hockey, cricket and football because both sexes can and do play, in mixed and single-sex teams. One family was attracted to Bede's by the tennis academy, which is excellent. (Not a school for rugby devotees, but rugby 7s available for those who like a taste.) Sports facilities which could serve a small town – 'second to none,' said a parent – and the sports coaching is outstanding, say parents and pupils. BTec sport is popular.

Boarding: 'A real atmosphere of family... brotherhood,' said a pupil. In large boarding houses of around 80, pupils are organised into family groups of 10, spanning the year groups, who look out for each other. It works, one pupil saying, 'I've got really good friends who are older than me.' A parent commented that the houses are run in a very inclusive way, with all sorts of events to bring them together; there is certainly a vigorous house system, with fierce competition ranging from cross-country (most run, but one pupil strolls, reading a book) to pumpkin carving.

Some 40 per cent of senior pupils board, weekly and full time only (for the same cost

– pupils can choose whether to stay weekends). Day pupils can join in boarding activities at weekends if they book in advance, and there's always plenty going on, from target rifle shooting to South Downs photography, with Sundays for lie-ins and shopping trips.

Boarding houses range from converted houses to modern and purpose-built. The girls' house decorated in pink and bunting, the boys' with flags of all the different nationalities in the house. The houses we saw were in excellent condition – a pupil said some of the others are bit tireder, but good in essentials. New boys' boarding house to open in early 2021.

Younger pupils are four or five in a room, lower and upper sixth one or two. Kitchens with toast and fruit freely available. Kids have to hand in tech at 9.30pm, recently tightened up to ensure compliance, and Wifi is turned off at night. Sixth formers can keep phones.

Day boarders also belong to boarding houses, with a place there to stay and study at school in the evening – 'quiet and comfortable,' said parent. 'More support, a belonging feeling.'

'Good communication from tutor and housemaster,' said a parent who lives abroad. 'They really look after my son... he's very secure in the boarding environment.' If parents have a concern, they need to be proactive – 'You need to be a partner, don't sit back,' said a parent.

A parent commented that the houses are run in a very inclusive way, with all sorts of events to bring them together; there is certainly a vigorous house system

Such a variety of views about food it is difficult to believe they are talking about the same meals. Delicious on the day of our visit, with a good range of choice. Breakfast is 'the best meal of the day,' said a boarder – full English is available, plus fruit, cereals, and homemade yogurt and bread. There is the usual boarding takeaway pizza community, and boarders are keen supporters of the village shop, but the pupils' food committee talks directly to caterers, and suggestions are implemented.

Ethos and heritage: 'Its location is a real plus... beautiful, surrounded by green... got a bit of a wow factor,' said a parent. A first impression of the school is one of great size, with school buildings a mish-mash of styles – some old and charming, some modern and splendid, and a few huts.

Plenty of international students – 'It's exciting to hear the variety... makes you tolerant of everyone... you can be yourself in that,' said a pupil – and a similar variety of religions.

School buses cover a 35-mile radius, and you may well see their philosophy quotes darting past on their way in to Bede's. There is some real effort to be true to these sayings, pupils saying, 'You don't have to fit the mould.' The appreciation of individuals is clear, not just in their choice of activity, but also their choice of appearance, with no attachment to traditions empty of meaning: boys can have long hair, providing it's kept neat (though the head doesn't particularly like 'those top knots'); boys can put their earrings in once they get back to the boarding houses in the evening; and with clear-sighted ease, the head put uniform changes to the vote: girls voted to wear trousers, then chose the design, and a tie in house colours, loosely tied (in truth, slightly BA style). But, most importantly: the head asked the pupils, and they decided.

Bede's prep and senior are increasingly one school, the heads busy building strategies to ensure smooth academic and co-curricular progression through the schools. Service is a mantra Mr Goodyer returns to again and again, and he's determined to make it school-wide – 'Year 1 can be collecting for the food bank and the sixth form can volunteer there.'

Pastoral care, inclusivity and discipline: '[They] make the kids feel good about themselves... [with] emotional support as well as academic support,' said a parent, another adding she has noticed a real difference in her child since going to Bede's – body image, clothes and make-up matter less, and her daughter told her to 'embrace who you are – don't worry about how you look'.

Another parent told us they chose Bede's in the hope their introverted son would gain social skills; he's now 'coming out of his shell, more confident, speaking up... Bede's is the right place,' she went on; 'it identifies the weakness of a child, and finds ways of taking them out of their comfort zone' (her sports-loving son is encouraged to organise competitions).

A pupil transferring from another school said she couldn't believe how well behaved everyone was, and pupils agreed it might not suit someone with really challenging behaviour – 'but lots of chances are given,' said one earnestly. Misbehaviour is not generally a problem here: 'Pupils are really happy, so they don't need to misbehave,' suggested one.

There is less bullying than at many schools due to diversity and increased tolerance, thought one pupil – 'from year 9 you have to accept difference.' The online Whisper programme allows pupils to report concerns anonymously; pupils are encouraged to blow the whistle, and have done in an incidence of sexting, which was dealt with thoroughly.

Mental health is 'quite forensically managed,' said the head, with an online system of recording anything of concern, from behaviour which is slightly out of character upwards, with regular reviews. A parent told us that when her daughter had anxiety problems, the head of house was 'straight on to it', and she praised the good relationships with tutors – 'very supportive, know the children really well'. There are two school counsellors, and a mental health nurse.

Pupils also mention getting support from the chaplain, and from attendance at chapel – a message or moral, or a reflective piece of music. 'We try and touch on all religions,' said the head.

At prep school all staff are being trained in first aid mental health. The head says anxiety is sometimes a problem for pupils coming in from hothouse schools – pupils can be school phobic and need to be reintegrated into school. For pupils feeling pressured, the school counsellor runs 'chill and chat' drop-in sessions at break time.

Pupils and parents: Social variety. 'Not typical public school, as you imagine them to be,' said parent. 'Bede's has more variety… it has the diversity that a modern school needs.'

'Caters for all sorts,' said a parent of three very different children who are all happily accommodated at Bede's.

Money matters: Scholarships of up to 25 per cent and a good and growing bursary fund.

The last word: Bede's fosters individual strengths and helps individuals with weaknesses. As a parent said, 'You don't have to be good at everything… if they thrive at something it spills over into the rest of life.'

Belmont School (Surrey)

Feldemore, Holmbury St Mary, Dorking, Surrey RH5 6LQ

01306 730852 | schooloffice@belmont-school.org | www.belmont-school.org

Ages: 2–13 (gradually expanding to 16+ from 2020)

Pupils: 194; **Boarders:** 67 weekly/flexi (from 7 years)

Fees: Day £10,740 – £17,820; Boarding £17,235 – £21,450pa

Headmistress: Since 2006, Helen Skrine BA. Following a music degree at Exeter, she took up posts teaching music, English and Latin at Wrekin College, Greenacre School and Chinthurst Prep and was deputy head at Highfield School, Liphook.

A sound business head comes across when she describes how she has steered the school through the challenges of the recession, but there's also a strong maternal streak. On our tour we came across a boy with a bloodied knee being helped in by his friends. 'Oh my darling boy,' she exclaimed. 'Let's get that knee up. Matron is coming with her blue light on.'

Described by parents as 'very hands-on and responsive' and 'a strong but caring leader'. Much praised for pastoral care. 'She has even offered support to our son whilst he struggles to adjust to secondary school,' said one mother. Another said: 'She is completely honest and open when it comes to issues with bullying. We were approached by her regarding our daughter being upset in school, something we found most refreshing.'

Her home is next door to the school building, not even a stone's throw away. She's not remotely tempted to move off site for a more private off duty life, as some heads are. 'Last evening the children were all outside here playing,' she said. 'Some boys came to borrow the dog. I love it. It's a life, not a job.'

Entrance: 'First and foremost I look at the parents,' says the head. Yikes. No need to brush up on algebra though – she means she wants to be sure that they are buying in to the school's ethos, which is not of the all-stations-to-Oxbridge variety. 'We want parents who understand what the ethos of this school is,' she says. 'We do a really good job academically but we are also interested in developing the co-curriculum areas and developing the children as people. I really believe school should be fun, not weighed down in endless testing, stress and strain.'

Who wouldn't it suit? 'Some of the tiger mums I met in my daughter's previous school,' says one mother. Another parent concurs, telling us: 'I haven't met any overly pushy parents at Belmont but I imagine that they would struggle to fit in.'

Next on the head's selection list is: 'Does the child have a spring in his/her step, will they throw themselves into everything and will they fit academically in the range of the year group?' Assessment is through reasoning tests and classroom observation. 'We won't take children outside the average range, but we will take low average pupils – sometimes it's just that they're not thriving in their current school,' the head says. Once in, school says the children are now guaranteed a place until 16, unless any serious learning difficulties arise. However we've heard from one or two disgruntled ex-parents who felt the school was unhelpful when their child proved to have additional needs, and they had to move them elsewhere.

Key points of entry are at 2, reception, year 3 – and some come from other preps at 11. In line with increasing their age range to 16 years, 13+ entry also now offered. Entrance mid-school is well catered for. A mother told us: 'The parents in my daughter's year have been extremely welcoming. A barbecue and trip to Legoland were organised by the class rep before the start of the academic year so the new children could meet everyone before their first day. Mothers were quick to give me tips and advice about matters such as games kit.'

There's a two-form entry per year, and that's the limit. 'I won't go to more than 32 to a year group,' says the head. 'I don't believe big is beautiful.'

Exit: Most parents are buying in to private education for the duration – it's rare for a child to leave at 11 for local state secondaries. The head is a big fan of boarding and so far children have spread their wings far and wide. Hurst, Ardingly, Wellington, Worth, Harrow and Gordonstoun have also featured recently. Since 2020, though, they have been able to stay on as school expands gradually to 16+.

Our view: The campus is a glorious 65 acres, with children's playtime roaming through nooks and glades – only constrained by dots on the trees, which indicate when they are out of hearing range of the bell. The main school building is based around the one-time home of Edwin Waterhouse (of the Price Waterhouse Cooper accountancy firm), and although the original 1880 house was rebuilt after a fire, it retains its grandeur, with high corniced ceilings, lots of wood paneling and deep window seats. Classrooms for the older children are based here, while younger children have their own building, while the foundation stage pupils have The Mews arranged around a courtyard, patrolled by three cats. Since 2021, there has been another new building including DT suite.

Children can board for an occasional night or up to five nights per week. All of this can be done on an ad hoc basis, so there is great flexibility for the working parent

Specialists for French, music, drama, art and sport are involved from the early years onwards and from year 5 pupils are split into two sets for all CE or scholarship subjects in years 5 to 8. This is flexible, with lots of movement between the sets, and pupils feel it's no big deal to be in a lower set. 'It's exactly the same work – they just slow it down to your speed,' they explained to us.

Parents are overjoyed by the fact there is little homework until year 7. Up until then most prep is timetabled in a daytime session. 'This is where Belmont differs from most prep schools,' a parent told us. 'They actively keep the pressure off the children and parents right up until year 7. The work handed in is theirs alone, and not the parents'.' In addition, the school never sets time consuming projects for the children where the parents end up spending endless hours making models of Egyptian vases or the like. 'It's such a relief, as a working parent.'

Feedback to parents comes in the form of half-termly grades, full written reports twice a year and parents' evenings. There's lots of informal reporting. 'Every parent has the email address of every teacher,' says the head. 'I encourage email and we have a policy of getting back within 24 hours.' There's also afternoon tea with the head on a Friday afternoon, which parents say is a great way to meet other parents and have an informal chat with the head and teachers.

'We get lots of awards for things such as work of the week, good manners, boarder of the week,' said the children. During our visit the head's table was strewn with rosettes and certificates – all being sorted ready for prize giving at the weekly assembly. 'Winning a commendation certificate from the headmistress is a most sought-after prize,' said one parent.

An array of clubs. These can be mixed and matched, most having no requirement to commit for a term – no battles then to haul a recalcitrant child along to a club which he didn't like by week two. Invitation clubs for the most talented run alongside general access clubs.

Sport is very much an all-inclusive affair. The commitment to involve everyone may mean that if a prestigious A team is high on your list, it may not be the place for you. 'Some may feel it does not have enough children to pick teams of excellence,' said one parent. 'We feel our daughter plays major sports at county level, so for us she is learning to be a team player, to lose sometimes and enjoy sport.' That said, the school is keen to point out it has an excellent record of success on the small-schools circuit, with a number of invicti seasons in recent years.

Head also points out that the school fields U13, U11 and U9 teams that are selected on ability, and says they 'win many more games than they lose'. Parents praise the school's willingness to embrace individual needs – timetabling cricket and tennis sessions with the boys' teams for a very sporty girl, for example.

On the arts side, the head says 'every child is on stage in front of the parents at least once a year.' Bands, choirs and string groups, with teaching from a professional opera singer and a director of drama. The school has its own biennial festival, Belartis, where visiting professionals lead workshops for children, culminating with an evening of performance.

The school shares the site with Moon Hall, a specialist school for dyslexia. The two have separate governing bodies and are separate companies running separate academic programmes for their pupils, but there's much crossover outside academic lessons. The Moon Hall children wear Belmont uniform and join Belmont for playtime, assembly, lunches and extracurricular activities. They can be in a school play and board alongside the Belmont pupils. Superb option if you have a dyslexic in the family.

Children can be dropped for breakfast from 7.30am and parents have a broad range of pick-up times to choose from – at the end of the school day at 3.30pm or 4.30pm, after clubs at 5.45pm, after supper or extended day care at 6.30pm, after prep at 7.45pm, or there's always boarding.

Boarding: Children can board for an occasional night or any number up to five nights per week. All of this can be done on an ad hoc basis, so there is great flexibility for the working parent. 'Our daughter begs to board as often as we will let her,' a mother told us. 'It is a wonderfully warm and friendly environment with the boarders doing lots of interesting activities and going on trips.'

The last word: The head is passionate about ensuring that it's not just academic achievement that carries kudos here. And there's certainly no shortage of extracurricular activities in which to shine. A real all-rounder of a school that caters to children's individual interests and talents, wherever they may lie.

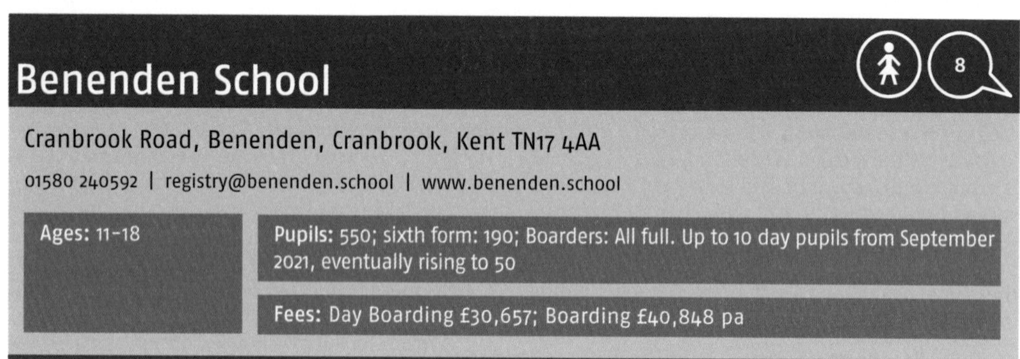

Benenden School

8

Cranbrook Road, Benenden, Cranbrook, Kent TN17 4AA

01580 240592 | registry@benenden.school | www.benenden.school

Ages: 11–18

Pupils: 550; sixth form: 190; Boarders: All full. Up to 10 day pupils from September 2021, eventually rising to 50

Fees: Day Boarding £30,657; Boarding £40,848 pa

Headmistress: Since 2014, Samantha Price MA (40s). Always thought she'd like to be a headmistress and when a visionary housemistress saw her potential, she blossomed. After a degree in history of art from Edinburgh came a job in development at the Tate in London, until an ad for trainee teacher (history of art and history) proved irresistible. First teaching post at Reading Blue Coat School, then King's Canterbury and Hereford Cathedral School. First headship at all-girls Godolphin School in Salisbury.

Her days are packed – takes assembly, meets prospective parents, staff and governors and deals with Girls' School Association matters (she's the 2021-22 president). Priorities when we visited included opening of first overseas incarnation of the school in south China in 2023 (no compromises on school values, promises Mrs Price), completion of mega building project and overseeing the first intake of day pupils, known as day boarders (rising to 50 in years 9 and 12) from September 2021. This follows long-term campaigning by local parents, understandably miffed that it was board or nothing. 'We need to listen to what the market is saying,' says Mrs Price. Including meals, activities and Saturday school, it's as close to boarding as it gets and thus felt to be completely compatible with the 'all girls, all boarding' mantra.

Soft-voiced but exuding assurance and authority, she oversees the school from a nicely proportioned study overlooking some of the rolling acres that make up Benenden's green and pleasant estate. Parental approval of her leadership has remained sky high throughout. 'Makes the right decisions at the right time.' 'Open and candid.' 'Charming, engaging, articulate – everything you'd expect from someone at the top of their game.' During the pandemic, she secured top-of-the-range Covid-testing technology at an early stage, offering tests to two local schools – this impressed parents so much that they crowd-funded a second machine. 'Leadership… has been phenomenal,' sighed one parent. 'If only the country was run so well.'

Good at garnering cool points with pupils – she'd just led pre-exam, stress-busting zumba session when we visited, her choice of footwear brand the big talking point ('Vans!'). Pupils also praise her approachability. 'Some heads can seem inhuman,' said year 7 pupil, with feeling. 'She's really kind.' Older pupils relish being listened to – 'Having that transparency where she'll sit down and chat like we're adults, that's really important,' says one. Recent sundae-making session at her house – arranged after sixth formers asked to spend more time getting to know her better – particularly enjoyed.

Married to Iori, an army chaplain. Two children – a daughter, who's a pupil here (and who 'deserves a medal for coping with having me as a head as well as she does') and a son. To relax, she runs or hikes and spends time with her family and two dogs. Has a seaside retreat, far enough away to ensure that she isn't recognised, so far at least.

Entrance: Oversubscribed, with around three applicants for each of 45 year 7 places; same again for 13+ admissions when there are 50 places. A few places offered at 12+ and 14+. Pupils come from numerous prep and junior schools in London and across the south-east, as well as overseas. Some parents still put daughter's name down at birth (leaving it till year 5 is fine).

Pupils start with preview weekend (held in October for 11+ candidates and in May at 13+), combining assessments, activities and overnight stay. If successful, offered a conditional place. Sit either ISEB exam (11+, 12+ or 13+ version) or school's own entrance tests (combined entrance and scholarship paper at 11+). Looks for scores of around 116 (11+) or Common Entrance mark of 70 per cent. Sample papers published online. Just 10 external sixth form places are offered when candidates sit papers in two of their proposed A level subjects.

Exit: Around 12 per cent of departures post-16, though the right to remain isn't automatic. While the school doesn't set formal targets, any girl likely to fall short of a string of good GCSE grades (unusual) can expect a conversation about whether it's the right place for sixth form. Support if alternative school needed – also offered on the rare occasions that girls are asked to leave for drink or drugs offences (a handful since Mrs Price has been in post).

During the pandemic, the head secured Covid-testing technology at an early stage. 'Leadership has been phenomenal,' sighed one parent. 'If only the country was run so well'

Vast majority to university – around 80 per cent to Russell Group. Durham, Edinburgh, Exeter, Imperial, UCL, LSE and St Andrews all popular, with four to Oxbridge in 2021. Plenty overseas – recently to Columbia, Cornell, McGill, NYU, Stanford, Trinity, Trinity/Columbia, UBC Canada and Yale. Pupils are encouraged 'to follow their inclinations,' said a parent, whether Norland nanny training or (in one case) opening a bakery. Whatever you want to do next, the school 'will find someone who can help you get started,' says a pupil.

Latest results: In 2021, 89 per cent 9-7 at GCSE; 83 per cent A*/A at A level (97 per cent A*-B). In 2019 (the last year when exams took place), 78 per cent 9-7 at GCSE; 55 per cent A*/A at A level (80 per cent A*-B).

Teaching and learning: School's focus on 'a complete education' may sound glib and, reckoned one parent, even be slightly ridiculed by pupils (surely not?) but is a thorough, well thought-out approach. It's 'a philosophy that underpins everything that goes on,' says school. Looks beyond classroom success and evaluates pupils' progress across five areas: creativity and culture, mind and spirit, global awareness, skills for life, physical health and wellbeing – all 'crucial to personal development,' says school. Ensures no regrets later. 'Allows you to explore before going on to next stage of your life… You don't leave thinking, I wish I'd explored that,' reckoned a pupil.

School's innovative solution to evaluating the heart-warming but slightly imprecise goals (eg ensuring that girls leave with a love of learning) is to track them for 20 years after leaving school. If at 38 they're succeeding professionally, giving back, learning and happy, school, says Mrs Price, will have 'thoroughly prepared them for life'.

Animated curriculum – expect climate change to be covered in geography, economics and science, for example. Highly rated trips – to Belgium (year 9s) covering English war poets as well as history syllabus – can be similarly multifaceted. Others include visit to Shakespeare's home (English) and Cordoba (Spanish). Several times each year, school suspends the normal timetable for years 7-9 to focus on a single theme designed to connect subjects like 'lasting change' involving external speakers and taking in everything from poverty to female equality. They're also big on original research, particularly in the sciences. While many sixth formers take the EPQ, resulting in ambitious original work such as a solo photography exhibition and a complete symphony, the school also offers a GCSE version, while years 7/8 complete a foundation version as part of the Benenden Diploma. 'Wonderful,' said a parent. 'At the end of it they come out having covered six areas of study.'

Most girls take 10 or 11 GCSEs, a few 13, fewer still (such as exceptional sports stars requiring substantial extra training) might sit eight. Triple science for all, plus a modern language. Spanish, Mandarin, French and Greek and Latin on offer, with German, Russian and Arabic possible as extras. Dance recently added following pupil requests. Sixth formers choose three (out of 26) A levels, with English lit, maths, history, politics and economics the most popular. Considering introducing vocational qualifications, eg forensic science with criminology. Maximum class size 20 (lower school) and 16 (sixth form). Some setting in maths and languages from the off, with a few subjects added from year 9. Otherwise it's down to painstaking differentiated teaching, ensuring appropriate challenge for all.

Pupils praise teachers' non-stop commitment and energy. In one class, exceptionally animated physics teacher won our admiration for determined attempts to rev up rather low-key year 10 class with revision bingo – we'd back her ability to enthuse them after we'd left our (admittedly short) session there. Staff even manage to lure most sixth form leavers back to school after A levels for a two-week life after school programme, including qualifications in teaching EFL. Teachers praised for interspersing online learning with bonding breakout sessions and fun stuff like 'sock cricket' during lockdowns. 'Excellent teaching that has lived up to expectations – and I have very high expectations,' agreed parent. Individual tutors are the front line in ensuring that girls aren't understretched or overloaded (homework can be on the weighty side), often the person girls will go to rather than subject teacher if there's a problem.

Exceptionally animated physics teacher won our admiration for determined attempts to rev up rather low-key year 10 class with revision bingo

Everyone puts in the hours here, with day divided into six periods, going through to 5.30pm – can be a shock to the system though school now considering an earlier start and finish.

Learning support and SEN: In addition to specific learning difficulties, ADHD is creeping on to the radar in a small way – several senior girls recently diagnosed, though not the school for anyone requiring more than minimal support and no pupil with an EHCP currently. Learning needs team (badged 'academic support') is located in rooms off the wisteria-clad cloisters, close to the main teaching areas. Help with study skills and literacy, some one-to-one, with ten-minute sessions to unpick a knotty problem felt to be particularly useful. While it can be difficult to admit to a difficulty, inhibitions quickly disappear. 'They explain that not everyone thinks the same way, that learning is not a straight line but a curve and suggest different ways of learning to work around it until you get it so you're never ashamed to ask for help,' says senior girl, who'd had help with essay planning and organisation and had seen her grades improve as a result.

The arts and extracurricular: Even the youngest fit a lot into their days, one packing a clarinet lesson into morning break with squash at lunchtime. Consensus is that 'it's busy but not in a bad way.' Offers around 150 activities, some charity or community linked. Girls can pitch for funding to support a cause close to their heart, while compulsory personal and development programme sees everyone given seed capital to turn an idea into profitable reality. Clothing – 'I heart Benenden' T-shirts and Benenden joggers – particularly

Ardingly College

popular. CCF is run (as part of co-sponsorship programme) with Ashford-based state school, and particularly popular with younger pupils. Most interests catered for, though school welcomes suggestions for more, with recent additions including Amnesty Youth Group (inspired by continued detention of Nazanin Zaghari-Ratcliffe).

One of the warmest boarding experiences anywhere. Not the glitziest rooms but who cares when staff work so hard to make this a place that's as homelike as it can be

Performing and visual arts bristle with facilities. Fun too. Drama 'a jewel in the crown,' said a parent, who praised high-quality productions with proper stage and lighting. 'Felt as if I was performing on Broadway,' says child quoted in school online prospectus. Music, slightly peripatetic while new building is under construction, carried on through the pandemic (meant no teachers were furloughed), with individual lessons delivered online, some girls adapting so well 'that they actually made more progress,' according to head of music. Three choirs – one is auditioned and tours all over the place (New York, Paris and Venice have all featured). Meanwhile, musicians in search of an ensemble (and with over two-thirds of pupils having individual lesson there are plenty) are paired with others of equivalent standard. Symphony orchestra plus jazz, brass and concert bands for larger scale music making. One pupil talked about taking her breakfast over to the music centre; we saw another almost swamped by her double bass (encouragingly popular here) as she carried it back to base after an informal recital – these pupils are committed.

Sport: Core sports are lacrosse ('our game – in gaggle of top schools winning national tournaments,' said staff member) and, increasingly, cricket (has made it into top twenty girls' schools), with netball also on the way up. Parents draw favourable comparisons with boys' schools – sports 'laced through the itinerary,' said one. Only request was more coaching for the keenest to add to trophy haul, though families recognise that with so much on offer it's hard to know when pupils would fit it in (as it is, many practices are held at lunchtime). 'Not enough time in the day,' said one.

Strong competitive feel if you're in the mid to top teams, otherwise can just enjoy playing for its own sake – there are 1,000 matches or fixtures each year. Sport compulsory all through, sixth formers able to choose from gamut of individual sports – aqua aerobics to zumba – rather than team games.

Ginormous all-weather pitch, complete with grandstand, is unmissably splashed across school videos. Also sports complex – open up to 14 hours a day – and well-lit fitness gym with prime views across green fields. 'You don't often set foot there when some of it isn't in use,' said parent.

Boarding: One of the warmest, most reassuring boarding experiences anywhere. Not the glitziest rooms – 'homely and cosy rather than flashy,' described a parent – but who cares when staff work so hard behind the scenes to make this a place that's as homelike as it can possibly be, and involve parents every step of the way? 'When your child goes to boarding school you have that fear that you're sending them away. [Instead] we were taken with them on the journey,' said a parent. Little touches add a massive 'aah' factor, eg Christmas trees that pop up round the school in December and 'big sisters' in older year groups offering tips for new boarders 'like putting your laundry in a mesh bag and not bringing too many home clothes,' according to one junior.

Of the 10 boarding houses, four are for sixth form, five for years 8-11 and one for year 7s, who so loved being in a Covid bubble together that it became a permanent arrangement. Houses range from Hemsted, part of the older main building (star attraction, Princess Anne's old room), all wood panelling, high ceilings and imposing Gothic windows, to purpose-built Guldeford with its red-carpeted, white-walled, porthole-windowed corridors – less Instagrammable but somewhat cosier. The older you are, the fewer pupils you share with; average around four (one sought-after dorm sleeps eight). Sixth formers have their own rooms unless request to share (most don't). Matrons sleep in but houseparents (all academic staff) don't, though they're always close by. While they come in different styles – some strict, some not – 'all are brilliant,' said parent. Housemothers' offices are informal gathering points, for 'chatting, playing music and biscuits,' said a pupil, as well as the place to go for help with homesickness, inevitable but bearable and (generally) short lived. 'You do [get homesick], I don't know one person who hasn't but it's manageable,' says pupil. Marmite the labrador particularly effective at banishing the blues.

Younger years have much-decorated dorms (we liked essential items checklist on one door asking, 'Have you remembered your friends?') which are regularly inspected. ('Floor clear, please,' was one of the firm comments.) Sixth formers' communal kitchens must be kept tidy or they're locked for a day.

Boarders can go home every second weekend though around two-thirds of pupils stay in, some out of necessity, other enticed by activities of which knife-throwing, cited by one pupil, was a new one on us. More conventional options include visits to Harry Potter World and the seaside, pamper sessions and plentiful animal visits (photogenic tenrec – looks like baby hedgehog – stars in several school videos).

Ethos and heritage: School's setting in deepest Kent, seven miles from the nearest station, often gets equal billing with the quality of the education. Though spacious – 250 acres in total – the buildings occupy a relatively compact area, upper sixth pupils whizzing between them on beribboned scooters (a much-anticipated perk) that merit their own warning road sign. This antithesis of the bright lights, big city vibe appeals to many families who, while not wanting their daughters to miss out on London life, are happy to put the unboxing process on hold.

Girls enjoy award-winning food beautifully presented in artisanal containers; despite numerous funky menu options, chunky chips remain a perennial favourite

It comes with an impressive back story. In '1216. Robert of Hemsted built the first house on the site,' starts the school history. Now that's what we call establishing your credentials, leaving aside the minor detail of a 700-year wait before the school – founded by three Wycombe Abbey teachers – arrived in 1923. In the intervening centuries, assorted owners came and went, some bringing the wrecking ball, one marrying Kitty Fisher (of nursery rhyme fame) whose ghost reputedly haunts one of the site's oddities – a miniature tunnel to nowhere, approached by nicely planted grove and much favoured by art and photography enthusiasts. The Elizabethan house went in 1860, new owner Lord Cranbrook replacing it with a neo-Gothic pile slightly to the east (he also removed all the houses on the village green to create 'the first village cricket pitch' – cause for celebration, implies the school website, though Benenden residents whose homes were sacrificed in the process might not have joined in the huzzahs).

Apart from a few decayed window frames – instantly fixed post-visit, we're assured – and some run-of-the-mill corridors, most of the school buildings are in tip-top condition with white walls, subtle, effective lighting and smart stripped flooring much in evidence. The dining room is a particularly attractive pale wood oasis where girls enjoy exceptional, award-winning food beautifully presented in artisanal containers (despite numerous funky menu options, chunky chips remain a perennial favourite). Mix of old and new continues elsewhere, with picturesque cloisters housing well-lit art rooms on the upper floors (cheerful paintings of cakes, dragons and magpies on display). Contrasts with striking, modern additions including DT block – brick interspersed with four chimney stack shaped pillars of glass – and the science block, whose ground floor atrium doubles as a concert venue (venue delightful, spine-searing seating slightly less so; 'first complaint we've had,' says the school). It's particularly busy while the new music school and assembly hall (distinctive circular shape – think spaceship crossed with a Roomba vacuum cleaner – no doubt ensuring superb acoustics) take shape.

Pastoral care, inclusivity and discipline: Warmth of approach shines particularly brightly when it comes to medical care, where the school goes not one but several extra miles. Exceptional staff include in-house team of matrons who 'genuinely adore the girls – my daughter has got very close to them', while medical centre is staffed 24 hours. Parents kept in the loop at all times, removing nagging 'what if?' worries. When daughter was ill, 'We were blown away,' said one family. 'We saw the system kick in in a way that we had never seen before.' Parents also praise size of school – 'So many of the boarding schools my friends' children go to are double the size and I do think it's easier to get lost,' said one, 'but here you know where all your friends are.'

Recent toughening up of rules about when phones can be used; pupils would like to have a greater say when other similar decisions are being made. But absence of make-up relished, particularly by those from schools where pressure to look good was unrelenting. Here, 'roll out of bed, brush teeth and I'm out,' says one. 'You can be yourself.' Uniform worn by all, with prefects singled out by (and known as) 'grey jumpers'. Smart and comfortable, it now includes trouser option though still some way from the 1970s, when jeans were added to the uniform list.

Has been touched by Everyone's Invited scandal, with former pupil going public about an experience at a private party involving pupils from a boys' school. Staff and senior pupils from Benenden and another local single-sex school have been working together to 'change our acceptance of what's acceptable', encouraging girls to 'feel stronger, not allow themselves to be taken advantage of and speak out,' says the head.

Pupils and parents: Still regarded by outsiders as properly posh though with ever increasing number on 110 per cent bursaries, diversity is increasing. 'All to the good,' said a parent. Around a third hail from Kent, Sussex and Surrey, similar proportion from London and elsewhere in the UK and 80 from Hong Kong, Singapore, Malaysia, Thailand, Dubai and Switzerland, plus 30 overseas Brits, some from MOD. Friendly to newcomers, with virtual parent get-togethers replacing face-to-face events during the pandemic.

We wondered how much Princess Anne would have in common with pupils today. Given the bright, motivated and down-to-earth girls we met, probably quite a lot. School describes them as 'confident, positive young women truly prepared for the future'. Or, in Mrs Price's own portmanteau word (that trundles rather than rolls off the tongue), 'humbitious' – ambition plus humility.

Many pupils spoke warmly of support from others. One junior's struggle with end of year exam prep was effectively managed by her friends who made her revise with them. 'It really helped me.' A level drama students had a full audience for assessed performance at the height of the pandemic. 'There's a feeling of everyone uplifting [everyone else] that I have never felt in any other school,' said one.

Money matters: Bursary support sensitively handled to ensure that all the extras are covered will be an increasing focus in years to come. 'They're some of our most outstanding pupils,' says head.

The last word: Top-notch education delivered with exceptional warmth in a beautiful corner of England. Brilliant for bright girls with an appetite for learning, backed by reassuringly thorough pastoral care.

Bethany School
9
Jarvis Lane, Curtisden Green, Goudhurst, Kent TN17 1LB
01580 211273 | admissions@bethanyschool.org.uk | www.bethanyschool.org.uk
Ages: 11–18
Pupils: 356; sixth form: 71; Boarders: 45 full, 34 weekly
Fees: Day £17,910 – £19,785; Boarding £27,810 – £33,750 pa

Head: Since 2010, Francie Healy (50s). A graduate of Trinity College, he remained in Dublin to teach in an inner-city school before moving to Bethany as a maths teacher in 1989, subsequently progressing to head of IT, director of studies, academic deputy, houseparent then deputy head. He doesn't, however, plan to stay quite as long as two previous heads who are buried in the grounds!

'Jovial, upbeat and down to earth', according to one mother who didn't even realise who he was when he first became headmaster. Does two duty days a week and enjoys chatting to pupils in the lunch queue, often joining a table at mealtimes. In fact, he is known for chatting to everyone – 'sometimes nonsense and sometimes serious,' laughed a pupil, 'and he always seems to know what we are doing'. 'Very visible, friendly and welcoming,' reckoned a parent, 'the children love him, even his terrible jokes.' Discusses GCSE options with pupils before their parents.

Says kindness, tolerance, courtesy and respect are the key values of the school and 'the child is at the centre of every decision we make'. Believes in looking for the positives even in a negative situation. Children are encouraged to find something they are passionate about and to take part even if they are not very good – small roles can always be found in the school play for enthusiastic actors. 'If we identify strengths, a child's confidence will increase. Children must be given strategies to deal with difficult subjects and must be able to see the point of them.'

Lives onsite with his wife Frances, who teaches English at the school; they have three adult children. No longer teaches (not enough time) but takes PSHE lessons when he can. Enjoys walking, reading and sport – 'more watching than playing nowadays,' especially football as a self-confessed 'Manchester United Nut'.

Entrance: Mostly into years 7 and 9, with all applicants assessed in non-verbal reasoning, reading comprehension, creative storytelling, maths and spelling. 'Assessments, not tests,' stresses the head. Maths and English assessments for those going into year 10. All have a 'chat rather than an interview' with the head as he believes it's the best way to learn more about a child and look at the overall picture – 'can we do right by this child?' is at the crux of it, he says. For sixth form entry, applicants need five 4s at GCSE with a 6 in subjects to be studied at A level (with some flexibility); international students sit papers in subjects to be studied at A level. All must submit reports and references from current school and details of any SEN.

Exit: About 30 per cent leave after GCSEs. Some to the grammars they didn't get into at 11+, others to further education colleges or higher level apprenticeships. About 90 per cent of those staying on go to university. Oxford Brookes is currently top of the pops, with others heading off to eg Exeter, Leeds, Loughborough, UCL and Portsmouth to read a variety of subjects – anything from biochemistry to civil engineering and from sports management to computer animation. Several every year to art and drama schools. Very few to Oxbridge but school can pull out the stops when required and one student went to study medicine at Cambridge in 2021. One or two to degree apprenticeships with numbers increasing each year.

Latest results: In 2021, 54 per cent 9-7 at GCSE: 37 per cent A*/A at A level (64 per cent A*-B). In 2019 (the last year when exams took place), 32 per cent 9-7 at GCSE; 29 per cent A*/A at A level (56 per cent A*-B).

Teaching and learning: Bethany is a mainstream school with a specialist learning support department and about 30 per cent receive some sort of help. As part of the wide range of abilities, there are some very bright pupils have floundered elsewhere but thrive in this small nurturing environment.

Twenty subjects offered in sixth form, either A levels or BTECs, including economics, photography, media studies, business studies, drama and politics as well as the traditional subjects. No pressure to take the 'right' mix of subjects and pupils are free to take three creative subjects if that is where their strengths lie. The EPQ is also offered.

Twenty-one subjects at GCSE or equivalent including computer science, hospitality and catering and media studies. Science is taught in well-equipped labs and is offered either as a single award or as three separate subjects. The school gets involved in the Big Bang Fair, a STEM based project, and usually sends a team to the finals in Birmingham – quite an achievement for such a small school.

All pupils take food technology in years 7-9 and sixth form offered a cooking course to prepare them for independent living at university.

All year 7s are introduced to Mandarin and can continue this as an option – 8-10 students take Chinese GCSE with impressive results.

Project based learning in years 7-9 – pupils are divided into groups and given tasks to solve which cover several disciplines, for example they might be asked to cost, design, make and market a pizza for a blind person. All pupils have laptops and there is a team of technicians to support them.

Bethany is a mainstream school with a specialist learning support department. Its primary specialism is dyslexia but learning support is woven into all aspects of school life

High expectations from teachers who are used to teaching a range of abilities in a class and can offer different learning styles and different ways of doing things. The staff, many of whom have been at the school for a long time, are a loyal and committed team, we heard.

Average class size in GCSE years is 12-13, smaller in sixth form. Setting for core subjects. Progress as well as achievement is celebrated and pupils are encouraged to take risks and make mistakes and to learn from them.

Pupils can stay at school to do their homework in the library, a godsend for working parents. Sixth form have their own sixth form centre with dedicated study areas.

Pro-active careers department organises an annual careers fair as well as talks from visiting speakers and visits to external careers fairs and events. Much trouble is taken to make sure that the pupils choose the right course for them.

The school was very quick off the mark during the pandemic and face-to-face remote learning was in place from the start, helped by the fact that all pupils were already familiar with Microsoft Teams.

Learning support and SEN: The school has been CReSTeD registered since 1994 and its primary specialism is dyslexia but learning support is woven into all aspects of school life. Those with mild difficulties have one lesson a week in small groups and those with moderate difficulties have three lessons a week instead of Spanish or French. The school does not give learning support outside lessons because, as one parent put it, 'the kids work hard and need a break.' About 25 pupils have EAL support and are taken out of French or Spanish.

The arts and extracurricular: The arts are a particular strength at Bethany, with a specialised programme for scholars. The music department has been been re-energised and about a third of pupils now learn an instrument and music technology is increasingly popular 'because it is fun', according to one pupil.

Busy drama scene with annual whole school and junior plays, as well as GCSE and A level productions and LAMDA exams. Planning permissions has been granted for a performing arts centre which is due to open by September 2023. Performing arts events every half term, both formal and informal, and anyone who wishes can take part. The aim is to bring pupils out of their comfort zone by incremental steps until all are confident to stand up in public. Annual festival of scholars celebrates achievements across the board from drama, music, art, DT, sports and academic with canapes provided by the food scholars.

No Saturday lessons but activities are compulsory for years 7–12 and upper sixth are encouraged to learn to manage their own time in preparation for university

Impressive art, with a wide range of options including ceramics, photography (the school has its own dark room) and textiles which are popular with both boys are girls. They take part in thought-provoking art projects like the UN competition on sustainability and climate change and 'only the rich profit from war'. A number of students move on to top art schools each year. Thriving and well-equipped DT department including a 3D printer, a mig welder and a small forge. Very enthusiastic teacher who allows pupils to choose their projects – when we visited the A level students were refurbishing a Morris Minor.

Lunchtime and after school activities every day. 'Everyone loves activities as they are so much fun,' our pupils guides told us. Optional for sixth form but most take part. Huge choice from symphony orchestra, chess, life saving, golf, biking in Bedgebury forest, cake decorating, academic enrichment, and the high ropes – the list goes on. Team building activities across year groups enable different age groups to get to know each other and provides leadership roles for sixth form. They might be asked to prepare a meal or put together a public speaking presentation and it is all about the team and not personal glory.

Bethany is an accredited DofE centre and about 20 pupils achieve gold each year. Extensive programme of international trips and expeditions, including an exchange programme with a school in mainland China, IT trip to San Francisco and Silicon Valley, business studies visit to New York, geography trip to Iceland, art to Rome, as well as adventure holidays to South Africa and the Himalayas.

Sport: Whole school games afternoon each week as well at least two games lessons and other sports sessions during activities. All have a chance to play in a team not just the crème de la crème. Although not known as a super sporty school, Bethany holds its own in matches against other schools and keen hockey players can join the Marden Hockey Club. Good variety of individual sports and school has a climbing wall and new indoor pool as well as a dance studio and fitness suite. Pupils increasingly health conscious as they get older and all sixth formers take part in the Body for Life health and fitness programme.

Boarding: Strong family feel throughout the school and no more so than within the boarding community. There are about 45 full boarders who are mainly international or children of ex-pats, as well as 35 weekly boarders and a small number of occasional boarders. No Saturday lessons but a programme of weekend activities and outings. Saturday activities are compulsory for years 7-12 and upper sixth are encouraged to learn to manage their own time in preparation for university.

Four boarding houses including a co-ed sixth form house where all have their own ensuite rooms. Houses all have their own individual styles; they all have kitchens and common rooms and are run by live in house parents. Boarders can use some of the school facilities in the evenings and prep is supervised for younger pupils.

Ethos and heritage: Founded in 1866 by Joseph Kendon, a Baptist minister, the school still has a strong Christian ethos and a resident chaplain but welcomes all faiths and none with the mantra to treat others as you would like to be treated. Whole school chapel once a week for each key stage with a headmaster's assembly and house assemblies and tutor meetings on other days. The school is set on a rambling rural campus three miles from the nearest village and children are ferried to and from school on a network of minibuses from as far afield as Sevenoaks, Tunbridge Wells, Tenterden and King's Hill.

Each year group chooses a charity to support and raises money throughout the year – the highlight is the whole school charity walk each September. Pupils also visit old peoples' homes and hospices to cheer up residents.

Good food with plenty of choice and a salad bar. The school council is the vector for any complaints and 'they really do listen', said our guides. All have to wear uniform until GCSEs and sixth form must dress smartly as if they were going to the office.

Pastoral care, inclusivity and discipline: 'Children feel supported and know who to talk to and staff are genuinely interested in the pupils,' said one parent. 'There is a kindness about the school that permeates everything,' remarked another. All teachers have a pastoral role managed by the head of year who reports to the pastoral deputy head. Twice daily pastoral meetings continued online during the pandemic in addition to lessons. There is also a school counsellor whose hours can be increased as necessary. All teachers have received training on Everyone's Invited mental health first aid and dealing with cyber bullying and issues are dealt with quickly. Parents and pupils are invited to talks from outside experts. There is a strong community feel and good inter year mixing helped by the vertical house tutor groups.

Clear policies implemented swiftly and fairly with a zero tolerance of bullying and a philosophy of 'punish the act not the child'. Random drug testing is used when appropriate and drugs dogs come in once a term – none have ever been found but acts as a deterrent.

Pupils and parents: Broad mix of families, many of whom make great sacrifices to send their children here. Parents share the school's holistic approach and must buy into the philosophy. In a county where the grammar schools cream off the brightest, many parents are attracted by the size and know that their children will be nurtured and supported and their strengths channelled.

Lots socialising among the parents including barbecues, quizzes, the summer fete and the music festival and there is an active Friends of Bethany School group. Loyal and supportive parent body who say they feel involved, even if sometimes their children receive news and information before they do!

About 10 per cent of pupils are foreign nationals, mainly from Hong Kong, Nigeria, Spain and China. A handful join in years 7 and 8 but the majority arrive in years 10, 11, 12.

Money matters: A range of scholarships for entry into years 7, 9 and sixth form valued at between 15–25 per cent. Means tested bursaries of up to 50 per cent for current parents and 30 per cent for new parents. Consideration given to how much a pupil can contribute to or gain from a Bethany education. In addition, there is a 10 per cent fee reduction for children of armed forces families, children of the clergy and siblings of existing Bethany pupils

The last word: A small rural school with a personal touch. While not the obvious choice for academic, confident all-rounders, it caters for all academic levels and particularly suits children who might get lost in the hurly burly of a bigger school. Summed up by one mother who said, 'I was delighted to find a school where my child is happy at last – once a child is happy everything else follows.' There are still more boys than girls and although this is evening out in the lower years, it is worth checking with the school about a particular year group.

Box Hill School

Mickleham, Dorking, Surrey RH5 6EA

01372 373382 | admissions@boxhillschool.com | www.boxhillschool.com

Ages: 11–19

Pupils: 425; sixth form: 106; Boarders: 140 full

Fees: Day £18,525 – £19,935; Boarding £23,985 – £36,000 pa

Headmaster: Since 2014, Corydon Lowde BSc MEd NPQH, previously school's deputy head – as such has 'spent my entire 40s at the school'. Before that, nearly three years' handy overseas experience in similar role at British International School of Boston, preceded by seven-year stint at

Hampshire Collegiate School, starting career at large state comprehensive.

A teacher from the off (management, part of his degree, was the career that got away), he is mild-mannered and slightly quirky with the kind of self-deprecating British humour (honed, no doubt, during own schooldays at Dragon and Frensham Heights) that must make international parents want to take him home gift-wrapped in a Burberry bag. (Should really be Duchamp, he says, a loyal fan of their ties, socks and, indeed, 'pochettes'.)

Unusual in this area, as it welcomes the all and sundries who wouldn't necessarily get a place in the harder-nosed, results-driven schools

Pupils interact easily with him – no sudden straightening of backs or rabbit-in-headlight smiles when they spot him approaching. This is not wasted on the parents, with one commenting, 'In other schools we visited, it felt like the pupils were on parade, but at Box Hill they are completely comfortable around him.' Doesn't teach ('my schedule doesn't allow it') but regularly pops in to lessons ('to make sure they are friendly, fun and focused') and is never far from sight during break times and at the beginning and end of the day. 'Very down-to-earth' and 'really interested in us as individuals,' pupils report, while parents laud his commitment to the 'development of character education'. A walking, talking accounts spreadsheet, there's nothing he doesn't know about every recent and planned spends, reeling off figures almost as often as he uses the word 'holistic'.

When not headmastering, follows sport. Was British karate champion in the 1990s (not an Olympic sport – down to international wrangling) but jokes that any sport participation these days is 'usually with the sole aim of fighting the ageing process'. Lives onsite with his partner – each has two children (one of hers currently at the school; his two are grown up). They recently got a dog, so are 'embracing all the joys of walking in the Surrey Hills – you can literally walk any direction out of the school grounds and be in an area of outstanding beauty. So lucky.'

Entrance: Main intakes into years 7 (40 places), 9 (20 places) and 12 (variable) but there's a lively and continuous recruitment cycle, with five recently having joined in year 8 and 25 in year 10 when we visited. Majority of pupils from 10-mile radius though extending. Kingston and Horsham (as well as thriving metropolis of Nork) all now within reach thanks to 15 school buses (6.55 am start for furthest-flung locations). Micklefield, Downsend, Reigate St Mary's, Chinthurst, Aberdour, Priory Prep and Kingswood House among preps sending pupils, though no official feeders. Local primaries also well represented. Increasingly attracting the London market – 'I've had conversations with three families recently about moving house so their children can come here,' said head.

Exit: Up to 70 per cent leave after GCSEs, often to grittier experience at local sixth form colleges while others go to local co-ed schools. Not a criticism of the school but tribute to confidence-building, believe parents. Of those who stay on, university entrance for most, mainly Russell Group. City, University of London, Queen Mary, Royal Holloway and Cardiff all popular. No Oxbridge currently but aiming for one or two a year – no special department as 'we're small enough to personalise timetable where needed.' Courses in anything and everything – from biomedical sciences to business management. A couple to art college most years. The school employs consultants to help girls with SAT applications to US universities. Six overseas in 2021 – to Berlin, France, Switzerland and Penisacola USA. One medic in 2021.

Latest results: In 2021, 28 per cent 9-7 at GCSE; 26 per cent A*/A (56 per cent A*-B). IB average of 34. In 2019 (the last year when exams took place), 20 per cent 9-7 at GCSE; 19 per cent A*/A at A level (46 per cent A*-B). IB average of 31.

Teaching and learning: A marmite option – and certainly unusual – in this area of the Surrey hills, on account of welcoming the all and sundries who wouldn't necessarily get a place in the harder-nosed, results-driven schools. Unlike near neighbours that seek solid A grade glory, this school is of the opinion that 'the equivalent to an old-fashioned C grade can be a huge success for some and we celebrate that'. That's not to say pupils underperform or that the pupil cohort doesn't include extreme cleverness – far from it, value added is first-rate and we met some very able and bright youngsters with high aspirations. And although only minimally selective with a relatively broad ability range, it's worth noting that candidates need to be capable of passing eight or nine GCSEs. Exam results are proof of the quality of teaching. 'Just because it's not a selective hothouse doesn't mean they don't take the academics seriously,' a parent told us, echoing others.

Tons of tracking, mentoring, small group (and sometimes individual) teaching, lunchtime clinics, giving out of teacher email addresses and relationship-driven steering all help. So does the fact that school promotes pupils focusing on their own growth, learning and success instead of comparing themselves to others. Ethos derives in part from membership of Round Square group of schools, linked to ideals of eccentric but hugely influential educationalist Kurt Hahn, who stressed compassion coupled with 'just do it' mentality. Teachers' bonds with pupils have clear in loco parentis feel and you are left under no illusion as to their commitment to the well-being of each and every child. 'The teachers are the reason I stayed on after GCSEs,' one pupil told us – 'they understand what makes you tick as an individual and do everything in their power to ensure you succeed.'

Around half of sixth formers do the IB, where overall scores are a point above the world average. Rest do (usually three) A levels from a choice of 10 – maths, further maths, sciences, humanities and business are the most popular, but no languages are available – 'if pupils want to study languages, we steer them towards the IB'. No EPQ.

Learning support and SEN: Supports around 100 pupils with SEN, from mild dyslexia to school refusers – 'though we're not a special school,' says head, and pupils must be able to access curriculum. Helped by lowish pupil-to-teacher ratio (nine to one) and small class sizes (average of 14 and much smaller higher up school, although classes occasionally reach 22 lower down). Support includes one-to-one specialist help (normal maximum of an hour a week, mostly maths or literacy focused) and multi-sensory teaching. Will also try to help those (often with ASD) struggling with social communication.

'I am committed to how boarding can change a young person's life thanks to the band of brothers and sisters around at all times,' says head. Parents say he gets it spot on

Majority of the 145 EAL pupils (the school community represents 37 nationalities) follow mainstream syllabus, with English studied at a range of levels, with around 20 pupils attending the International Study Centre where they can choose from three courses, most aimed at the 14-16 age range. Its one-year intensive GCSE programme (also marketed as pre-IB) which springboards straight into sixth form is particularly popular.

The arts and extracurricular: If we had a pound for every time a school told us it offers a truly holistic education, we'd probably have our head office in the Maldives, but whole-character education really does seem to be the raison d'être here. It won't be for everyone – the single-minded academic or ultra-competitive, for example – but for a good all-round education to find, unlock and nurture key strengths, this is a safe bet.

Talented musicians, some at diploma level, welcome practice rooms being open all hours (seven in the morning till nine at night) and free instrumental taster lessons encourage the curious to have a go. There's an active choir and a brass and jazz band and the school offers everything from piano masterclasses to sound recording training, but one pupil felt more could be done: 'There are enough people for a small orchestra and for more ensembles – I think there are missed opportunities.'

The colossal painting of Hugh Laurie and graphically designed (using only straight vertical lines) portrait of Barak Obama in the head's office are testament to the artistic flair of some pupils. Such was the concentration of the year 10s in their sketching class that they didn't even notice us on our tour, although the arts classroom is underwhelming (with nowhere near enough natural light) so we were pleased to hear that a new 'creative arts hub' is next on the wish list.

Drama facilities are also lacking, but the tired hall was due a facelift when we visited – blacked-out practice and performance areas that the pupils are excited about. Exceptional tuition and choreography, say pupils, and some imaginative performances (a recent immersive, in-the-round enactment of The Great Gatsby involved characters freezing at certain points, with others appearing on stage to interpret their emotion through dancing – 'mind blowing,' said a parent). Winter performances are open to all who want to get involved – 'my absolute favourite thing in the school year,' said one excited pupil – apparently it's such a big deal that the show affects the vibe of the whole school for days afterwards (perhaps lucky we didn't visit in the melancholy days following the recent production of The Crucible). 'Drama is very inclusive – you never feel left out or second best,' said one pupil.

Sport: All major sports on offer (main players are netball, rugby, football, cricket and rounders) and lots of minor ones (table tennis, badminton, tennis, horse riding, among others), with strong teams which, crucially, are regularly readjusted to encourage widespread participation. 'Most of us get a go in a top team,' said one pupil proudly, with school favouring a professional approach over the win-win-win mindset of some other local schools. 'It's not that wins against other schools go amiss, but results can fluctuate fairly widely so if you want your child to bring home every trophy, it's probably not the school for you,' said one parent. From year 10, the focus is on more individual fitness. Noticeable improvements on the gender front – no longer a much pinker shade of sport for girls, school now offers girls' football and rugby, for example, but one girl told us the two-to-one boy-to-girl ratio meant that in her class 'there weren't enough girls to get a hockey team together'. Swish new £5m sports hall with courts and fitness areas, plus MUGA and Astro outside.

Boarding: 'I am committed to how boarding can change a young person's life thanks to the band of brothers and sisters around at all times,' says head – parents think he gets it spot on. The large numbers of full boarders (making up around a third of the school) are spread across six boarding houses, four in the grounds, two across the (quiet) village road. House names, though full of meaning to school, have certain random quality for outsiders, Constantine and Ralph among them. Dorms vary in size from six to singles, with the décor generally getting plusher the older you get. Pupils we met raved about the freedom, eg after prep on Saturdays, seniors can travel into London, though must be back by '2230' (time rather than century, we assume); also popular is the excellent range of trips, eg ice skating at Somerset House, Chinatown, paintballing, Thorpe Park etc. 'No them-and-us culture,' assured a pupil, with parents confirming that boarders and day pupils are well integrated, although all boarders we talked to waxed lyrical about the 'boarding family'. Homesickness dealt with promptly, say pupils – one remembered 'a girl who was really missing home, so they organised an evening themed on her country so she felt more at home – it worked really well.' Minor niggles about mealtimes – 'occasionally, it would be nice to be able to use the kitchen in the house' or 'just to miss breakfast – I never eat it anyway' etc.

Ethos and heritage: School boasts idyllic village setting in Mickleham, between Dorking and Leatherhead and about 20 miles from London. As pretty as they come, main building once private Gothic-revival Victorian house with aspirations to grandeur, full of delightful stained-glass biblical scenes, plush purple carpets, floor to ceiling oak, stately home scents and gigantic roaring fire. Newer wings tacked on at the back sufficiently sympathetic to keep the charm intact though some more elderly stand-alones have their work cut out and there are some portakabins. Stand-out facilities include modern music block, new sports hall and spacious sixth form centre. Dining hall (which serves good choice 'and plenty of it', according to pupils – we had a delicious mushroom risotto although salads could be more imaginative) should be praiseworthy, but wind tunnel outside can make for a chilly dining experience.

Head boy and girl are known as Guardians: the superhero connotations are a highly successful recruitment tool

Original grandeur belies school's relative youth. It was established in 1959 by a former Gordonstoun housemaster on principles inspired by Gordonstoun's founder and inspirational educationalist, Kurt Hahn. Much emphasis on whole-pupil development, democracy, environment, adventure, leadership and service – with whole-school activity week in September involving camping, canoeing and rock climbing in Wales or New Forest. DofE – closely linked in ethos – from year 9 and just about everyone takes bronze.

Pastoral care, inclusivity and discipline: Very open and honest – doesn't sweep things under the carpet. Example is alcohol policy. If over 18, boarders can purchase but are 'carefully monitored' – to ensure any headaches are admin, not consumption, related. Zero tolerance towards pupils who seriously transgress, however, with widespread knowledge among pupils that a small number of students were recently excluded for drugs. And head won't hesitate to temporarily exclude for less serious offences – 'usually one every half term, generally for things like serious disruption or unpleasantness – it's difficult to define but you know when it's passed a certain line,' he says. A detention system, including newly introduced Saturday detentions, deal with the more minor stuff. Complete mobile phone ban in school, except for sixth formers – a relief to some parents.

Pupils don't consider the school strict. 'Nurturing', 'caring' and 'sensitive' are more common descriptions – 'you get second chances here,' said one, with restorative justice widely used (and appreciated by pupils) to ensure they can learn from mistakes. A full-time counsellor is on hand and anonymous whistleblowing is encouraged. 'This school gets teenagers and education comes secondary to their mental health and wellbeing and that's paramount to me,' said one parent.

Commitment to democracy and leadership is visible. Boarders nominate two reps from each of the six houses to discuss issues – often food related. Head boy and girl lead a 13-strong pupil syndicate who supervise breaks, administer tellings off for minor uniform infringements. Known as Guardians, the superhero connotations are a highly successful recruitment tool. Handover speech to successors an annual tear-jerker.

Communications have improved dramatically, say parents – notifications of matches and music events no longer last-minute.

Pupils and parents: Parents range from diverse international community (84 per cent of boarders are from overseas) to ecstatic locals – most thrilled with what school has done for their children. Once considered the wrong postcode for some Reigate mums, the school is increasingly considered a first choice for holistic education. Start saving now for the many later life reunions which take place all over the world (although plenty of alumni stay put, careers covering eclectic range from surveyors to musicians and authors). We found pupils a laid back, but motivated bunch – pleasingly comfortable in their own skin.

Money matters: Half a million pounds of school fees (the school's only source of income) is reinvested every year and put towards awards which include scholarships and bursaries (often quite widely spread out – fluctuates each year).

The last word: Warm-hearted, low-key, unpretentious and exceptionally encouraging school that would be very easy to overlook in favour of (sometimes false) assurances of top grades elsewhere. Best for more liberal-minded families.

Brambletye School

Lewes Road, East Grinstead, West Sussex RH19 3PD

01342 321004 | registrar@brambletye.com | www.brambletye.co.uk

Ages: 2.5 -13

Pupils: 278; Boarders: 46 full, 31 weekly/flexi (from 7 years)

Fees: Day £8,130 – £22,305; Boarding: £26,580 – £27,195 pa

Headmaster: Since 2015, Will Brooks BA (Durham), in tweed and pink (Brambletye's colour). Started by teaching maths and English at Bruern Abbey, where he was promoted to deputy head, followed by two more deputy posts at Sunningdale and Port Regis; glad now to be in a cosy family school and determined to keep it that way: knows all the names, addresses groups with 'Hello rascals', and wants to extend childhood for as long as possible; encourages children to build dens in the woods, and when a child knocked on his door to say 'Come and see our den, we've just finished the second floor', did so with alacrity. ('Children need to make mistakes... but we're not reckless.')

Parents gush about Will and his wife Amelia: 'great having a younger team with loads of energy and ideas'; they've brought 'new vitality to school... really encourage the children.'

Pupils approve too: 'nice and fun', 'easy to talk to' and 'always involving us in his problems,' said one to general hilarity of the rest, clarified to 'he wants our opinions about things' (and indeed has changed homework in response to criticism from pupils).

Entrance: Light-touch assessment and interview.

Exit: Children depart for a wide range of destinations, with Hurst, Charterhouse, Ardingly, Bede's, King's Canterbury, Worth, Tonbridge, Eastbourne College and Bennett School all featuring recently. Head emphasises the importance of children flying into the right senior school in the middle or top of the cohort.

Our view: An old country retreat in the Sussex countryside with views over Ashdown Forest that stretch out into forever. Described by one parent who chose it over a place at a desirable London prep as a 'school in the woods' – 'How could any child not love it?... [there are] trees to play in...' Inside, panelled walls, wood fires, a strolling sausage dog (Hercules) and comfy sofas. A stately home with pupils lounging happily by the fire, as if they were at home; which of course they are, pupils telling us it feels like a 'big family'.

Academically 'a real mix of kids,' said a parent at the this lightly selective school. 'High expectations,' said the head, 'but plenty of support if necessary.'

A pupil told us, 'It's different to other schools because the teachers help you so much', another saying, 'You can give your opinion... a different opinion is not wrong.' Special praise for the maths teacher who 'makes it really clear', and for IT, a parent commenting, 'It could be desperate, but it's fun and creative.' The Latin teacher rewards full marks with a turn on the zipwire – an effective incentive for most.

'No one slacks in year 8,' said a pupil, 'you're too scared', but the head makes no assumptions; he has introduced 'how to revise' for pupils to engage with what they know, don't know, and how to learn most effectively: 'They won't all be up all night before their finals when they're 21,' says the head ruefully.

Inside, panelled walls, wood fires, a sausage dog (Hercules) and comfy sofas. A stately home with pupils lounging happily, as if they were at home – which of course they are

Smart new labs following a recent refurbishment, with the academic space to one side, practical to the other. Even newer is the library, plus art and debating chamber space.

Communication is 'excellent', say parents, with a new website, parent zone, and effort and attainment grades fortnightly. 'If a child gets a C3, a member of staff will call to discuss.'

A flexible approach to those with different needs – 'excellent to all its students,' said a parent, describing how her fidgety son in pre-prep was allowed to sit under his desk provided he would listen. 'Beautifully managed, no-one bats an eyelid.' A pupil of high ability with poor writing skills and a need to move around sits on a movement cushion (as do several others), has pencil toppers and wrist things on which to chew, is being taught touch typing, has a scribe in the meantime and is, said his mum, treated as an individual. Bored with history, he has been given a special project on WW1 propaganda and time to discuss it with the head of history. '[They] accept pupils as they are.'

Around 20 per cent of pupils have extra learning needs, and most learning support is free of charge, provided in small groups or in-class support. Where one-to-one support is necessary, this is charged as an extra.

It's a long day here, with day pupils being dropped off at 8am and picked up at 6pm, or 7.10pm if they have activities, but all work is completed at school (very popular with parents). Saturday school lessons recently replaced with a hearty breakfast followed by sport, a very popular move. 'Allows it to be a proper boarding school... keeps it alive at weekends,' said a parent.

'Strong, nurturing care – confidence building,' said a parent, describing how her nervous son has gained a natural sense of confidence through drama, music and giving presentations; another told us her children's senior schools have said children from Brambletye are 'not daunted'.

Changes to pastoral care under the current head. The traffic-light system moves pupils with pastoral needs to an amber light, which kick-starts a process with their tutor and gets parents involved. Tutors are 'very, very vigilant and know of children's niggles,' said a parent, but children can also speak to a school listener or a counsellor.

Generally 'children respect each other and are kind,' said a parent, fresh from helping with school trip to Lord's, but when there are problems between children ('not really bullying, but unkindness,' said a pupil), parents say they are dealt with quickly and throughly, one telling us her daughter's problems were dealt with 'sensitively and discreetly'. The school's approach, said a parent earnestly, is that the bully needs as much attention as the victim – they address the problem rather than handing out punishments. 'You're always given a second chance,' said a pupil.

Amelia is always standing outside to greet the children in the morning, notepad and pen in hand to jot down any concerns. 'I feel I can really trust the school – and thank God we're not in this alone as parents.'

Pupils take real pride in the house system with discipline minuses and credit pluses contributing to the inter-house contest – 'it really works, they take responsibility,' said a parent. Pupils get to know everyone in their house – 'younger pupils do talk to us about upsets... or just anything,' said a year 8.

Children are not allowed phones, and are not bothered. 'We manage time better without them,' said a pupil, but older children would like more daytime access to computers and email (windows and iPads are lesson specific). The head works hard to help pupils understand their digital footprint, recommending that if they wouldn't be happy to show their grandparents, they shouldn't post it.

No one goes hungry here – fruit is always available in the dining room, and 'grub' is available every evening until 8.30pm: toast, cereal, fruit, sandwiches. A parent told us how hard the school worked to help her fussy child to eat normally, emailing the parent every day with progress.

'Music and drama are exceptional,' said a parent, describing the musicals in the school theatre as 'like West End productions' and an 'enormous pleasure'; another saying her child who didn't want to do a play was 'nearly jumping off the stage with enthusiasm'.

The standard of art here is exceptionally high for a prep school – 'amazing', said a parent, and they've had 180 art scholarships to senior schools in the last 20 years. 'Second to none, the teacher cares so much,' said a parent whose unartistic son is slowly developing confidence and enjoyment.

Sport every day for an hour, and activities on top of this, although an extremely musical child who wanted more practice time for a music scholarship was allowed time off games – no rules for rules' sake at this flexible school.

'Not so many to pick from [for teams] but we punch above our weight,' said a pupil, another adding, 'If you're good at sport it earns you enormous respect.'

Girls have been in both cricket and football teams, and the first girl on the rugby team apparently 'played a blinder' – but there's 'not been a boy in the rounders team,' said a parent thoughtfully (although all pupils play in interhouse rounders). Hockey is now included on the curriculum for boys, who will soon play their first fixtures.

Pre-prep is described by a parent as 'so nurturing... a really safe space to hold the children as they grow.' Pupils have a great affection for their exceptional head – 'Mrs Atkinson, I love you a lot,' said a child, arms flung around her knees, and it's the first head we've seen invited on a sleepover.

Golden leaves for kindness fill a tree in the entrance hall and jewels are handed out for good work. Lots of time outside, pupils wearing their all-weather muddy puddles. Growing boxes for each year (for outdoor maths), plants in wellies, two enormous rabbits (Moonbeam and Paddington) and a proper hobbit hole. A jolly nursery filled with happy busy tinies – 'George cries on the day he doesn't go to nursery', sighed a parent.

Boarding: A domestic and international boarding community includes pupils from Russia, France and Thailand. Flexi boarding is available from year 3, and is used by many local parents, who like to be able to just pop in to school. Years 7 and 8 have to choose between weekly boarding (opting in or out of weekends as they wish) or day; most board, with just three of year 8 remaining day pupils.

Dormitories for up to nine with bunk beds, old and quirky rooms for boys, a modern wing for girls, but all recently refurbished to a high standard. The most extraordinary views to wake up to. All dorms named after flowers and trees, and thank goodness for a school that doesn't think it detracts from boys' masculinity to sleep in Tulip.

Between 50 and 90 pupils stay at weekends, and enjoy trips out, such as go-karting or trampolining, or mucking around at school – a slope outside turns into a water slide in summer and snow slide on rugby tackle pads in winter.

The last word: The head says Brambletye wouldn't suit a child with a flat learning curve, or one who never gives anything back – they need to engage with what's on offer. Parents thought reserved children might struggle, but pupils said that shy children will develop confidence, one year 8 telling us she was 'quite timid' in year 4, but 'it's small, everyone is welcoming and you get used to school quickly'.

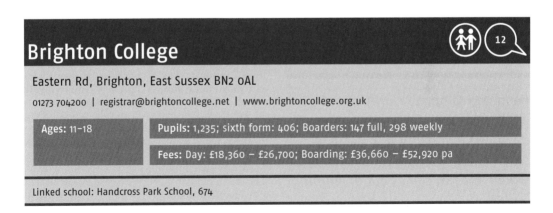

Brighton College

12

Eastern Rd, Brighton, East Sussex BN2 0AL

01273 704200 | registrar@brightoncollege.net | www.brightoncollege.org.uk

Ages: 11–18

Pupils: 1,235; sixth form: 406; Boarders: 147 full, 298 weekly

Fees: Day: £18,360 – £26,700; Boarding: £36,660 – £52,920 pa

Linked school: Handcross Park School, 674

Head master: Since 2006, Richard Cairns MA (first-class history degree from Oxford). Previously Usher of Magdalen College School Oxford (1999-2005). Before that, head of history at Stewart's Melville College Edinburgh, which he joined from the Oratory School.

A quiet, authoritative leader who's very much in charge, masterminding operations from a gorgeous office in the main building. He's also a first-class publicist for the school. 'The Cairns touch', as it's described in school literature (and elsewhere), has ensured the college's reputation has rolled inland to reach those affluent London families who now make up a growing proportion of the pupils here and (increasingly) are in the majority at open days.

Headline hitters include introduction of gender-neutral uniform policy and compulsory Mandarin (school was a trailblazer for both). 'Like John Lewis, we never knowingly undersell ourselves,' Mr Cairns was reported to have told alumni (he doesn't disagree when we ask for confirmation).

Behind the image, the reality is a head who commands huge respect from parents, some won over almost in spite of themselves when they meet him. 'Avoids platitudes'; 'a deep thinker'. Even his round robin letters are well read – and praised (a real rarity). 'Find myself touched and quite interested,' said surprised-sounding mother. 'Legendary,' says one. 'As good as you think he is.'

We heard also of great kindness behind the scenes in supporting families in distress. 'Genuinely inspirational and as approachable as he can be in a school with a lot of kids,' says parent.

He has complete clarity about what ensures the school's success. It's down, he says, to making it 'a place of scholarship, inspiration, excitement,' where 'the fun comes out of learning'. Essential to have top class teachers (buildings, however lovely, come a distant second). Canny recruitment includes advertising in Oxbridge college bars and offering would-be teachers a decent salary, no need for a PGCE and, says Mr Cairns, 'bigging up' Brighton's cool vibe. Throw in accommodation (school owns and rents out some nearby houses at a bargain price) and it's been a huge success – the school now gets up to 50 applications for hard-to-fill STEM subjects.

Head has complete clarity about what ensures the school's success: it's down to making it 'a place of scholarship, inspiration, excitement,' where 'the fun comes out of learning'

In person, softly spoken and understated (in contrast to high-profile public image) and he clearly adores the job. The best moments 'are with the pupils'. He dines regularly with them to help understand what they worry about and asks what they'd like to change. Focuses on making them feel 'loved, valued and safe' – and instilling a sense of curiosity – a legacy from his late grandmother. 'She said the reason she lived so long was that she kept asking questions.'

Pupils are impressed that that he goes out of his way to spend time with them when he's on site – and by his phenomenal memory. A week after he saw a pupil looking for his phone, 'I bumped into him and he asked if I'd found it.'

They describe him as akin to the CEO of a large firm – recent initiative has been the creation of a wildly successful state sixth form college – the London Academy of Excellence – in East London, which selects students based on background and ability and gets sponsors to offer financial support.

'He is the vision – staff are there to enact it,' said one. 'Innovative, every time you speak to him he's thinking about a way he can improve the school.' 'Asks us what's not quite right, very engaged.' 'Really connects with people.' Summed up in three words? 'Passionate, forward thinking, engaging.'

Entrance: Competition for places is very different from London pressures, says Mr Cairns. School is looking for pupils 'on the bright side of average… Anyone in top two sets at [leading London prep] would stand a good chance.' Potential counts – much is made of government data proving that pupils make more progress here than at top schools to achieve top A level results. Has 45-50 'main' feeders, including school's own preps – Brighton College Prep, Handcross Park and St Christopher's. Thomas's (Clapham and Battersea) and Fulham Prep feature among the London schools. Local schools in Surrey, Sussex and Kent include Sevenoaks Prep, Westbourne House, Windlesham House, Cumnor House, Bede's Prep, Feltonfleet, Hazelwood School, Holmewood House, Marlborough House and Pennthorpe.

Always has some spare places put by, says Mr Cairns, 'because I want a mix. We keep places aside for late developers, summer birthdays and anyone recommended by a prep or primary school who may not be good at a pre-test but is a lovely person or a real giver or good at maths.'

Pupils sit ISEB pre-tests and the school's own exams (maths, English, NVR and VR) and have two meetings with member of staff. Prep school pupils take CE or CAS.

At 11+ (when pupils join lower school) 50-55 places are available. Pupils are assessed in VR, NVR, English and maths – look for a standardised score just above national average (110). Main intake of 180 is at 13+ – pupils made conditional offers after sitting ISEB common pre-tests in year 6 (if not offered at current school, can take them at the school in year 7). Places confirmed after have sat Common Entrance.

Potential sixth formers sit reasoning, maths and a general paper, followed by interviews. Conditional offers (based on GCSE grades) made in December of year 11. For overseas candidates, arrangements can normally be made to sit assessments at current schools.

Exit: Once here, pupils are never asked to leave before their time. 'We guarantee every 13-year-old a sixth form place,' says Mr Cairns. Pupils agreed (other schools, it was suggested, were in the frame for rumour-spreading – references to 'annual culling', say the school and pupils, are completely inaccurate). 'I do not know a single person to whom that's happened,' said sixth former. When they do leave (usually around 10 per cent), it's from choice. Stay on into the sixth form and there's no question that you'll be helped to do well. However, they 'do tell you what to do,' said a pupil. While this undoubtedly adds huge reassurance to many families, it can feel like golden handcuffs to others who want something a bit less intense.

Bath, Bristol, Cambridge, Durham, Edinburgh, Exeter, Manchester, St Andrews, UCL and Warwick all popular university destinations, with 28 to Oxbridge in 2021. Lots overseas – nine in 2021 to Columbia, Hong Kong, IE (Spain), NYU, Queensland and University College Dublin. Twenty-two medics in 2021.

Latest results: In 2021, 98 per cent 9-7 at GCSE; 95 per cent A*/A at A level. In 2019 (the last year when exams took place), 94 per cent 9-7 at GCSE; 83 per cent A*/A at A level.

Teaching and learning: You don't have to arrive here as a fully formed boffin. 'We're definitely not as selective as top London schools,' says Mr Cairns. Desire to do well, having a spark, being funny, quick and kind (mentioned repeatedly, something of a school mantra) can certainly help during the admissions process.

That said, this is a fast-paced environment. 'My mum says school is on speed, there's so much going on,' says a pupil. Laurels are added to, not rested on, a strong work ethic is a given and impressive turn of phrase a notable feature (not surprising that staff team includes a head of critical thinking). 'Is there a direct correlation between economic growth and free will?' we heard one a year 9 pupil ask another during a lesson.

Self-starters have a definite advantage. 'If a child is going to need to be pushed to get anything done, there will be years of strife,' says parent. Levels of homework demand considerable weekend sacrifice, for example. Add in a few activities and working days can easily stretch over 12 hours.

Parents, similarly, expect great things. 'Oxbridge is in many people's sights,' says one. Some express concerns about the pressure though school felt this could give the wrong impression. While pupils set their own goals, it says, 'We don't put pressure on the pupils if they do not have a goal themselves.' Every pupil we spoke to felt that while you work hard, you do it for yourself. One stressed that she'd never felt overwhelmed and put it down to 'an atmosphere of niceness which isn't seen by other people'.

This is a fast-paced environment. 'My mum says school is on speed, there's so much going on,' says a pupil. Laurels are added to, not rested on

With GCSE results like these, nobody (unsurprisingly) has anything much but praise for the quality of the teaching – though parents did wonder how the staff coped with what must be a fairly high-pressure working environment. Class sizes are kept to maximum of 22 (halved for languages, arts and DT), but considerably smaller in the sixth form, with a low pupil-to-staff ratio (five to one).

Helps, think parents, that many teachers (average age around 40, 21 who have been at the school for a decade or more) are young, including some fresh out of university, love their subject and are willing to put in the extra hours – fast response to emails, available to talk to during prep sessions and subject clinics laid on (maths probably the best attended). Ad hoc help also available if needed. 'Asked if teacher would mind teaching me on Saturday morning and he was just so willing. It's amazing to have teachers who are willing to arrange timetables to help you,' says pupil.

Parents report that normally taciturn offspring 'come home talking about what they've learned'. (Must be helped by the presentation skills lessons, compulsory for all). Stand-out subjects (English and chemistry feature on best of the best list) can be 'beyond outstanding' and vast majority of lessons are 'lively and interesting', often moving well beyond the curriculum essentials. The Creative Learning Centre is banked with cameras, so lessons and presentations can be filmed and shared (one history session which – we were told – used wheelie chairs to re-enact battle formations, surely deserves a wider audience).

Art and DT equally exciting. We watched year 10 pupils creating a group work in the long, light art room, chalking their response to music on a

Brighton College

large sheet of paper while, in DT, year 9s created Easter egg holders out of cardboard, origami masterpieces that (bar one wonky lid) would have reassured the most anxious of Humpty Dumptys. 'Everyone has a creative spark,' insisted dynamic teacher, surrounded by entries for the Leonardo competition, which suggested that some might need to dig deeper than others – one entry (a gorgeous blend of kittens, rainbows, enhanced with a row of little lights) contrasting with another – a full size traffic cone.

Pupils (boarders in particular) can become deeply involved in the volunteering programmes, like the group of six who travelled to Calais to work with refugees

Interests, even if niche, are catered for. With linguists able to study up to three languages at GCSE including Russian and (of course) Mandarin and dance, photography, PE and computing are also on the menu, making that final choice can be agonising.

At A level (choice of almost 30), sixth formers follow their interests, leading to an eclectic mix of subjects – one had opted for biology, history and drama. All choose four subjects (unusually, can drop one from the second term onwards) and everyone studies school's own history and politics course, Our Human Story (modified version, Story of Our Land, is taught in the lower school), which attempts to decipher impact of current events on pupils' futures (and must have the fastest-changing content of any subject). Stunningly successful.

At this stage lessons have a substantial input from pupils. 'It feels very student led [with] the pupils involved in deciding where and what you do in addition to the curriculum.' Reasons for choosing subjects many, varied (and occasionally tongue in cheek). Politics: 'Get to have debates – great because I like the sound of my own voice.' Drama: 'Fun, awesome class.' Economics: 'Interesting how the logic and reasoning impacts on people's decision making.'

Budding business innovators are currently supported with skills development and a Dragons Den style competition and the goal for the future is to up the number of more vocational sixth form courses so the school can appeal to 'quirky, entrepreneurial children for whom doing three or four A levels is not of interest,' says Mr Cairns.

Learning support and SEN: Over 100 pupils have additional learning needs including profound hearing loss, others with ADHD, autism and specific learning difficulties. All will have IEPs (individual education plans). Much English and maths support, provided either by specialist teachers at the learning centre (timetabled small group lessons) or as add-on sessions with college teachers.

Ad hoc one-to-one assistance with study skills and organisation offered but pupils – who stressed that bright children who struggled shouldn't be put off from applying here – felt that social skills support in particular stood out, making sure pupils 'feel included, know how to respond... and don't struggle socially.' We also thought inclusivity was well served by making touch typing lessons compulsory for all younger pupils, not just those with SEN.

Previous rave reviews for dyslexia provision were backed up by a current pupil who urged others with specific learning difficulties to apply. 'People should realise that as someone with learning differences who has struggled quite a lot you can thrive here.'

The arts and extracurricular: Outstanding range of activities spanning the conventional to the highly original. Two additional activity periods are timetabled each day, though much also goes on before and after school. With so much choice, the onus is on pupils to organise themselves with help from personal tutors if they're feeling overwhelmed.

Music is high profile, with 25 ensembles and 680 music lessons each week (beginners to diploma level), 70 performances and events each year. Groups range from boarders' rock group to swing ensemble (featuring sax-playing head of music), extra inspiration provided by masterclasses for top performers, and musician in residence, one a recent Young Musician of the Year winner.

For rehearsals, there's a recently added suite of 10 practice rooms, acoustically separate, music only audible in linked corridor. For performance, there's an attractive hall, recently completed, with gorgeous lighting and flexible raked seating.

Subject-related clubs, dissection to drama, offer 'options for everyone'. Pupils' own initiatives are also encouraged, currently ranging from the appeal of conspiracy theories (understanding, not joining in) to crosswords (concise or cryptic). Other current highlights (with teachers, too) include 'Werewolves', involving deductive skills and hidden killers.

Many pupils are impressively motivated to give back. 'An important statement of what we're about, we're part of society, not apart from it,' says Mr Cairns. All pupils undertake some form of community work. This could be CCF or DofE, while others opt for volunteering programmes where initiatives range from involvement in Make a Difference (MAD) week (pays to avoid clashes with other schools as 'communities can only take so much goodwill at once,' says witty sixth former) to supporting the homeless and dementia sufferers, to teaching maths and English to Syrian refugees.

Pupils (boarders in particular) can become deeply involved, like the group of six who travelled to Calais to work with refugees. And when the school recruited a drama coach to boost new debating society's success (they reached a competition final in the first year) one sixth former, realising that state schools could potentially lose out, was awarded a grant from the school to make free online resources available to all.

Sport: Games feature large – compulsory through the school and taking up around three hours a week. Onsite space isn't huge so most pitches (rugby, netball and football) are a five minutes' minibus away – not that it gets in the way of success. While the school doesn't hand out special blazers to top teams as 'they are part of what we do,' says the head (and temptation to print DofE progress figures on the back might in any case be overwhelming), results suggest it's doing just fine with the normal kit. Particularly strong in netball (top team holds regional and county titles) and rugby (last major title, according to school literature, was in 2016 – updates presumably on the way).

Ethos, says school, is 'sport for everyone', with 90 per cent of year 9 and year 10 pupils playing in school fixtures. With teams running A to F, anyone who loves a sport but isn't a shining star should get a match but, mercifully for those who don't, school will offer alternatives for anyone 'who really [does] not want to play a particular sport'. Given that options span the gamut from athletics to zumba, chances are that everyone can end up within (mobile) comfort zone.

Communal areas boast floor-to-ceiling bookcases in contemporary light greens and vast, custom-built sofas. Even the bowls of fruit look as if they've been curated

Most teams, bar water polo and athletics, are single sex but 'gender divide is breaking down – now part of day to day life,' says pupil. There's growing enthusiasm for dance, highly rated by growing numbers of boys (100 currently dance) and girls for combination of power and flexibility – and, under dynamic head of dance, it wins awards – recent 'best choreography' win at local dance festival.

Boarding: The number of boarders, vast majority weekly but can stay for Friday nights at no extra charge, has increased. Now up to six houses, all but one on site, with plans to open two more. About 40 per cent of sixth formers board – overall there's a 50/50 split between day pupils and boarders.

Every pupil is part of vertical boarding family (single sex), each with its own idiosyncratic name (Lellikelly and Hurricane Laura) featured in homemade posters up the stairs and become so close-knit that though sixth formers can opt for their own co-ed boarding house, most don't.

While we only saw one boarding house (pressure of time), we're assured by pupils and parents afterwards that its general gorgeousness and glamour is the norm, courtesy of rolling refurb programme.

Bedrooms (maximum three beds, upper sixth have single rooms) have plentiful pale wood storage (termly room change ensures that social mix is given a regular stir). So coordinated is the look that duvet covers, boarders' own, inject a note of almost shocking individuality. Near perfection marred only by slightly clouded appearance of main-road-facing windows but it's sea salt, not traffic pollution, we're assured.

Communal areas boast floor-to-ceiling bookcases in oh-so-contemporary light greens and vast, custom-built sofas (none of your mismatching and end of range fill-ins here). Even the bowls of fruit look as if they've been curated. Instagram friendly? Not a doubt. 'Very home like,' says staff member (this reviewer's home, however, several taster pots short of the full colour palette).

The boarding experience is a box of delights. Pupils have the run of the place, with weekend access to practice rooms, and activities spanning (over one weekend) yoga, water polo and zumba to volunteering, a trip to the Harry Potter Experience and a cinema night (with hot chocolate).

Pastoral care is sensible rather than overbearing, with a strong phone policy. Years 7-11 have free use of phones only between 4.30 and 9.30pm (not overnight). Any calls to parents during the day must be made from boarding parents' office. Beyond desire to scrap compulsory breakfast and allow older pupils to make their own, little in the way of complaint. Nice additional touches include mentoring for new pupils and opening the school earlier for boarders to ease travel arrangements.

'Excellent balance between standing on own two feet and right amount of pastoral care,' thought one parent.

Ethos and heritage: One of what feels like a magic circle of schools exercising almost mesmeric effect over parents. Was one pupil really heard to say (as reported by parent) that, 'The school is my destiny'? We wouldn't be surprised, given pupils' extreme positivity. 'Nice and sunny even when it's raining,' says one. Even a cracked glass door (a rare imperfection) was cause for celebration and it's catching. We found ourselves agreeing that, yes, the all-over crazing 'actually does look better'.

It can all feel a bit cult-like – not that prospective parents are put off. 'When you walk around the senior school you can just see interactions between staff and pupils, between pupils, the way they speak to each other, the language they use. I want my child to experience that,' says one.

The college is a Victorian Gothic jewel designed in the 1840s by Sir George Gilbert Scott (of St Pancras station fame), in what we'd originally described as quite a gritty part of Brighton. (School, less than keen on our choice of vocab, agrees that while the bingo hall next door 'can misleadingly give this impression… Kemptown is filled with boutique shops and local food suppliers' and property prices are some of the highest in the city.)

Arrive at the school and you'll instantly realise that you're in the hands of branding experts when you're greeted by the friendly front of house team sporting suits in can't-miss-it school blue, yellow waistcoats and even shiny buttons with the school crest. Recently revamped – all staff are delighted. 'Less security staff, more concierge,' extolled one. And if that's the goal, it's been triumphantly achieved.

The main entrance gives onto a lawned quad, a fine weather favourite at lunchtime, though there are plenty of other places to relax in, including Smith's Café, which serves light snacks as a space filler before dinner (spring rolls and buns feature on eclectic menu).

The attention to detail is a marvel, tidiness at epic levels, original buildings like the library (galleries and Gothic window, well stocked and well used) and the chapel (where visiting former pupils search for their old seats) an attractive oasis of calm. But what makes the layout so pleasing is the way newer buildings have been thoughtfully integrated. Opened by politicians from varied shades of the political spectrum – Charles Kennedy and Ed Balls among them – they're varied, gorgeous and all beautifully appointed, thanks to a one-in, one-out buildings policy (no Portakabins or 60s buildings rotting gently in the shade here).

In addition to the Confucius Centre and the Yeoh Building, a focus for creativity, the current star of the show is the new sports and science building that runs, long and low, up the side of the sports field and is already a darling of the architectural press. Opens up activities quite literally – interior and exterior glass walls mean that everyone is on public view.

Pupils' doubts about 'doing zumba and seeing rowing machines next to you' are now banished. 'Thought it would be odd but you can focus.' Fitness suite, in so many schools a rather dark, uninviting place off to the side, is light, well laid out (equipment is thoughtfully placed, rather than squashed in) and – while currently attracting more boys – exponentially increasing appeal to girls. 'Not hostile, a gym for everyone,' says pupil.

Was one pupil really heard to say (as reported by parent), that 'The school is my destiny'? We wouldn't be surprised, given pupils' extreme positivity

Serious learning also goes on here, though science labs (purple and black) could be mistaken for ubercool cocktail bar). Other highlights include a sky garden (TellyTubby-ish bright green grass and flying saucer domes – actually for ventilation) and – very popular with boarders – a small cinema with super-comfortable chairs and stunning views (officially 'an auditorium – connecting to universities across the globe', a worthy purpose that, strangely, came a distant second to the prospect of hot chocolate and Netflix).

And there's more, much more. With other highlights including indoor sprint track, heated pool (delightfully tropical on day of visit owing to faulty thermostat), Camper Van café, and a sports hall that's genuinely different (a first), ditching tyranny of the right angle for geometric variety, you could have a great day out and never leave the building.

University campuses, in consequence, are starting to feel distinctly underwhelming by comparison. 'Older sister has warned me not to expect too much,' says sixth former.

Next on the agenda is ambitious plan to be carbon neutral by 2023. Fleet of electric minibuses is on the way, food waste is already properly recycled (instead of the bin bags of shame, destined for landfill). Beef may disappear from the school menu (biggest environmental despoiler) and a heat exchanger is reducing reliance on fossil fuels. Will it prove another headline grabber? We'd take a small bet on it.

Plenty of alumni from the worlds of sport and art, ranging from Sir Michael Hordern (actor) and David Nash (artist) to Matt Prior (England cricketer).

Pastoral care, inclusivity and discipline: Supportive vertical house system (separate houses for girls and boys and day and boarding pupils) works well, with housemasters/mistresses in charge of teams of tutors, each leading a 15-strong group of pupils. 'Can't fault it,' says parent.

Small site a huge benefit. Room to get away if it all gets too much ('It's like having 80 sisters here – so many people you can rely on… Sometimes it can get a bit much but there's always space to get away.' However, if you're struggling, it will be picked up, feel pupils, who cited head of house, matron – and older pupils ('often the first to talk to rather than friends') as first ports of call if they had a problem. Prepared to take direct action, too – one matron all set to protest, pupil reported to us, after she was shouted at during CCF training.

We met several pupils who had started off at other schools, moved here and were deliriously happy, as were others who had opted for the school over top single-sex alternatives. They felt listened to, able to be themselves and express this with an impressive maturity. 'We're encouraged to have beliefs and develop an understanding of the consequences,' says pupil. In particular, they praise the absence of labels. 'At other schools there's someone who is the gay kid or the autistic kid… here there's such a great awareness of what's socially acceptable to say. Children are comfortable in their own skin.'

Ambitious plan to be carbon neutral by 2023. Fleet of electric minibuses is on the way, food waste is already properly recycled

Mr Cairns recently asked a group of sixth formers 'if there was anything they had done in their life that nobody knows about. One pupil came out as gay over dinner, got a round of applause, and conversation carried on as if nothing had happened.'

But while tolerance is a feature of life here, head stresses that the school's approach is rooted in tradition – 'Forward thinking but not liberal.' So, while in theory there's freedom of choice over uniform (trouser and skirt option available to all), the vast majority stick to convention.

Rules overall aren't harsh and are generally observed, though we heard, from parents, of the occasional infringement – school thought to turn the occasional blind eye. Pupils couldn't possibly comment on whether, for example, they ever visited the beach, strictly out of bounds for all (though we'd hazard a guess that the school has a clear idea, whether acknowledged or not).

'Good and prompt at dealing with bullying,' say parents. Teachers make a huge difference – one parent felt there were many examples of 'when they've intervened in situations, or personally looked out for a child and gone way beyond the extra mile'. Pupils look out for others, too. One teacher, who'd been on crutches, was 'blown away by how many people offered to help'.

Pupils and parents: Former pupils don't (so far) include many big names from the world of business, but they undoubtedly will – many social entrepreneurs among them, if current pupils are anything to go by.

Families today are a mix of locals (Sussex, Kent and Surrey) and, increasingly, Londoners. Most have what the school describes as 'a broad British background', though they embrace many cultures and many pupils are 'fluent in multiple languages' – and, if the ones we met were anything to go by, highly articulate in all of them. A few expats (currently under 30), with around 160 overseas pupils from the USA, Canada, Europe, Hong Kong, Russia and Singapore.

Manners are universally good, praised by locals. 'Always move off the pavement [for parents] walking with a buggy.' Many of the girls – as so often in co-ed – looked as if they had spent hours on their appearance though the school stresses that girls can't wear makeup unless they're in the sixth form. Those we spoke to, however, stressed absence of pressure to achieve daily perfection. 'There's no expectation to look any way at all. The only makeup I wear is mascara and mostly I don't bother,' says one.

Expect greater diversity in the future as school's ambition to widen access takes off, through the Opening Doors scholarship programme (currently reserves 20 free day sixth form places for local, disadvantaged children).

Money matters: Weekly boarders who stay on for the odd weekend aren't charged for the privilege. All 11+ candidates automatically assessed for academic scholarships as part of the process. Sport, music, art, dance or drama choral and (unusually) a chess scholarship also offered.

Similar awards at 13+ (180 places) with the addition of DT, plus Millennium Scholarship for all-rounders. Sixth formers offered academic, sports, creative arts and scholarships for disadvantaged local children. Has recently supported two Syrian refugees with scholarships, one going on to Oxford.

The last word: Glowing with self-confidence and success but with a strong social conscience (and brilliant at self-promotion), this is a school that knows precisely what it's about. Energetic, motivated and hard-working children will breathe in the ethos along with the ozone and feel instantly at home. Not the place for passengers.

Burgess Hill Girls

Keymer Road, Burgess Hill, West Sussex RH15 0EG

01444 241050 | admissions@burgesshillgirls.com | www.burgesshillgirls.com

Ages: 2.5–18

Pupils: 456; sixth form: 57; Boarders: 51 full, 1 weekly

Fees: Day £5,100 – £20,850; Boarding £27,300 – £36,750 pa

Head: Since 2017, Liz Laybourn BEd. Gained her BEd in PE and maths at Dartford College, joined Burgess Hill Girls as a newly qualified PE teacher in 1986 and has been there ever since. Loved the ethos and feel of the school from the moment she arrived and became head of PE within a year. Before long she was promoted to assistant boarding housemistress and then deputy head in 2006. Says she has 'lived and breathed the school and grown up with it,' and is a passionate advocate of all-girls education. 'Girls must feel happy and enjoy their education, it is about empowering young women and discovering what they want to do. Whether it is art, engineering or fashion, the school will support them to achieve their dream.' She says that the school does not have a narrow view of success, girls are celebrated for who they are as people and soft skills are equally as important as academic qualifications. 'She still has plenty of new ideas and has a very good team around her,' says a parent. She likes girls to work things out for themselves and wants them to feel that they are being listened to. When the girls on the school council asked for the netball courts to be painted purple (the school colour) this was done. Pupils in the prep school redesigned their playground and got involved with the budgeting, but she drew the line at purple Astroturf. Knows every girl in the school, her door is always open to parents and pupils and she is highly respected by the girls. 'She is wonderful leader,' says a parent, 'everyone looks up to her.'

Married with two adult daughters, one of whom works at the school. She is also a governor at a maintained secondary school and an ISI inspector. When not working she enjoys spending time with her family, reading and walking.

Head of the prep school: since 2011 is Heather Cavanagh, who is also deputy head of the whole school. Studied at Canterbury Christ Church University and is doing a part-time masters in educational leadership.

Entrance: Entrance into reception to year 2 is via informal assessment at taster days; those entering year 3 and above sit written tests but school looks beyond the academic. Will accept girls mid-year if there is a place.

Almost all prep school pupils move on to the senior school – this is automatic as long as the head feels a girl will cope with the work. External candidates joining in years 7 or 9 sit school's own exams in maths, English and a CAT test and generally come from local prep and primary schools including Great Walstead, Copthorne, Handcross, Cumnor House and Brighton and Hove Preps.

About 15 join sixth form from local state and independent schools and from abroad. Entry is via a CAT test, interview and report and applicants must have a minimum of six GCSEs at grade 6 or above. All international students sit tests in English and maths.

Exit: Around half leave after GCSEs for state sixth form colleges and local co-ed schools. Girls go on to a range of universities – mostly Russell Group with King's College London, Southampton, UEA and Birmingham recently popular. Girls study a wide range of subjects, including nutrition, civil engineering, computer science and a couple to art college most years. The school employs consultants to help girls with SAT applications to US universities. Often a few medics and a few to Oxbridge and overseas.

Latest results: In 2021, 75 per cent 9-7 at GCSE; 73 per cent A*/A at A level (91 per cent A*-B). In 2019 (the last year when exams took place), 76 per cent 9-7 at GCSE; 43 per cent A*/A at A level (78 per cent A*-B).

Teaching and learning: Pretty impressive results for an almost non-selective school. Good value added according to Durham University's CEM measurement and girls achieve on average 1-2 grades higher than would be expected for their ability.

Offers 26 subjects at A level although not all subjects are taken every year. The school will run a subject for one or two pupils and most subject combinations can be accommodated. Chinese, further maths, ancient Greek, Higher Project Qualification, EPQ and statistics offered off timetable via the enrichment programme. Most popular subjects at A level in 2018 were maths, biology, chemistry and English.

GCSE courses start at the beginning of year 9 and 26 subjects are offered, all fairly traditional – some parents say they would like to see one or two less academic subjects as options. Science taught in well-equipped labs and can be taken as a combined award or individual subjects. Handful take GCSE computing and in 2018 all grades were 9 or 8. Good proportion of male teachers and a wide range of age and experience among staff. Some have been at the school for many years and others are newly qualified and bring energy and fresh ideas. 'The teachers really know how to get the best out of the girls without making them feel pressured. They are approachable and always reply to emails,' said a parent. Digital language labs with brightly coloured chairs and tables where girls can work at their own pace and talk to the teacher without everyone else hearing.

Busy learning resource centre (aka the library) is open from 8.30am to 6pm, well stocked with books as well as computers, and is a popular place to work. All age groups are encouraged to read for pleasure and 'the librarian is really friendly and helpful and knows us all by name,' said our guides.

About 17 per class and a maximum of 20 in the senior school and about 18 per class in the pre-prep and prep school. Fewer than 40 girls in each year group in sixth form with nine to 10 pupils per tutor group and sometimes very small numbers in subject lessons.

Girls encouraged to think about their futures from early on and are given formal careers advice from year 8. Maths and science departments work with the careers department to promote STEM-related careers and career events are supported by successful female role models. School has developed links with businesses and girls can attend careers conferences with global companies including Roche, Porsche and IBM. Year 10 are invited to business breakfast meetings organised by the sixth form and sixth form take part in a networking dinner which often leads to work experience and internships. Lots of help with university applications and girls are encouraged to apply for subjects they enjoy and not just follow the crowd.

Support also provided for applications to higher level apprenticeships and school leavers schemes.

Learning support and SEN: Two part-time SEN teachers in the senior school and two more in the prep school and would bring in additional staff if necessary. Less than 10 per cent need some sort of help, mainly for dyslexia and dyspraxia. One or two sessions a week can be incorporated into the curriculum and individual or small group support is also offerered. Currently no wheelchair users but the schools says it would consider moving classes around if necessary. One EAL teacher – 36 of the boarders are international students and EAL is built into the timetable.

The arts and extracurricular: Modern performing arts centre with a 320-seat auditorium and practice rooms. About 200 girls learn an instrument and are taken out of lessons on a rotational basis so they don't miss the same subjects. Years 7-8 have one music lesson a week and music is offered at GCSE and A level. Girls can also learn conducting and composition. Numerous opportunities for performance including choirs, an orchestra, a jazz band and ensembles for all abilities and even an African drumming group. Pupils in the prep school have two music lessons a week and their own choir, orchestra and various ensembles.

Girls helped choose new house names. Out went the dead male poets and in came Williams, Pankhurst, Austen and Watson – all feisty and successful women

Busy drama department. Drama clubs for years 7-9 run by sixth formers, lunchtime shows throughout the year and inter-house performing arts competitions open to all girls in the senior school. Workshops hosted by visiting professional theatre companies and girls who prefer not to be on stage can get involved in lighting and technical theatre. Regular theatre trips to London and Stratford and girls have been to Broadway and Hollywood. Big production every year alternates between a musical and a more serious play. Drama offered at GCSE and A level. All the prep pupils learn drama as part of the curriculum and stage their own productions.

High standard of art with all A level and GCSE students in 2018 getting an A* or A. Design and technology offered as fashion design and resistant materials – years 7 and 8 rotate between the two. Wonderful exhibition space with very high-quality works on show – the lamps were particularly impressive. School takes part in a festival of quilts and some beautiful pieces are hung around the school – we saw some fine appliqué cushions and waistcoats on display in the reception area.

Trips include visits to the House of Commons for Prime Minister's Questions, a debating competition at Durham University, French and Spanish exchanges and outward-bound activities.

Sport: Wide range of lunchtime and after-school sports clubs for all levels from recreational to elite, including hockey, netball, dance, football, cricket and trampolining. Good fixture list for major sports and also teams for equestrian, polo, athletics, skiing, sailing and swimming, to name a few. Floodlit netball and tennis courts and Astro as well as a fitness suite; swimming takes place at the local leisure centre. While it may lack the facilities of larger schools every effort is made to support the girls in whatever they want to do. Team sports are compulsory until the end of year 9 but all have to take some form of exercise – could be dance, boxercise or zumba. Annual ski trip and big foreign sports tour every other year with netball and hockey teams going to Sri Lanka in 2019. Wide range of sports in the prep school including netball, hockey and rugby as well as water sports on Ardingly reservoir.

Boarding: Around 50 boarders from year 7 upwards are housed in two homely and comfortable Edwardian villas in the grounds. Meals are eaten in the main dining room but both houses have kitchens for making snacks, games room, common room, music practice space and gardens for summer barbecues. Younger girls share, most upper sixth have their own rooms. Majority are full boarders with a large proportion from Hong Kong and mainland China. Handful of weekly boarders mostly from London. Day girls can stay the night after a late rehearsal or concert if there is room. Cosy family atmosphere and all age groups mix well. Younger girls do supervised prep in the main school and older girls usually do theirs in their rooms.

The school works hard to integrate boarders 'although they do sometimes stick together a bit,' says a parent. There's a three-week induction programme for international boarders to learn about British culture, plus a conversation club. All are expected take part in activities. Weekend outings include shopping in Brighton, theatre trips, ice skating, go-karting and film club.

Ethos and heritage: Founded in 1906 by the pioneering Miss Beatrice Goode who wanted girls to have an equal education to boys. Moved to its current location in 1928: 14 acres on the edge of Burgess Hill town, five minutes' walk from the railway station and 20 minutes' drive from Gatwick. School is housed in a series of Victorian and Edwardian villas with cleverly designed additions – the assistant bursar is a talented architect and his skills have been put to good use. Modern sixth form centre with lecture rooms and space to relax. Head is keen to develop a separate sixth form identity and has recently appointed a new head of sixth form.

Pre-prep and prep school are housed in two Edwardian villas with their own playground. Emphasis is on building confidence. Equal weight is given to academic rigour and developing strong social skills, especially courtesy and kindness. Purpose-built nursery takes boys until 4 and is open 51 weeks a year.

The school works hard to integrate boarders. There's a three-week induction programme for international boarders to learn about British culture

Visitors are greeted by a large sign at the entrance saying, 'Welcome to Burgess Hill Girls – Tomorrow's Women'. Girls are taught to feel empowered from a young age and to follow the school motto: 'I am, I can, I should, I will'. This message is reinforced in lessons and pupils in the prep school have recently done a project on brave and brilliant women of the second half of the 20th century.

Girls helped choose new house names and had to justify them. Out went the dead male poets and in came Williams, Pankhurst, Austen and Watson – all feisty and successful women. Friendly rivalry between houses including sport, public speaking, debating and performing arts competitions.

Strong sense of community and identity and a good balance between academic work, recreation and volunteering. The charity committee votes on which charities to support and girls are encouraged to have their say. They are taught the value of giving something back to the community and put on concerts for local people at the school and sing in local churches. Senior girls help in the town's charity shops. Year 9 girls help out at the school's annual carers day for registered carers.

The school wants every girl to be noticed and makes a huge effort to find out what each pupil is good at. Girls are encouraged to follow their own path, be themselves, have their say and organise activities. One group asked to put on a play and then took it to the Edinburgh Fringe. 'Girls are given their independence but with backup when necessary,' said a parent.

Most parents we spoke to hadn't planned to send their daughters to an all-girls school, but 'there is something about it and it is head and shoulders above the other local schools' was the refrain from several. There is a calmness about the school and in an age of anxiety an all-girls environment can take away some of the pressure. Girls are encouraged to develop the confidence to stand up for themselves and become independent young women.

Former pupils include television presenter Holly Willoughby and her author sister, Kelly; diversity champion and lawyer, Funke Abimbola MBE; cricketer, Caroline Atkins; professor of neuroscience, Francesca Happé and triathlete, Kate Mactear.

Pastoral care, inclusivity and discipline: Girls know where to get help if they need it but are also taught how to solve problems on their own, build resilience and support others. Strong pastoral team includes school counsellor, tutors and pupil mentors. 'Happiness is the key to success,' says the head, and 'there is a culture of approachability throughout the school.' Older girls support younger ones and act as role models.

Girls are allowed to develop at their own pace and the school sets high expectations for good behaviour. Rare cases of bullying are 'hit head on,' says a mother, and parents are involved. Regular internet safety talks for children, parents and staff. Medical centre and sick bay with registered nurse. The nurse visits the prep school to talk about hand washing and medicines, participates in year 4 science topics and speaks to year 6 about puberty.

Transition from the prep school is carefully managed. Heather Cavanagh, head of the prep school, is also head of pastoral care for years 7 and 8, which gives a sense of continuity. 'There is still a firm dividing line between the two schools so it is a big thing to move up to the senior school,' says a parent.

Pupils and parents: Most families live within a 30-mile radius – some very prosperous but most working hard to send their children here. School is very supportive of working parents and children can stay until 6.30pm for supervised prep and activities. Minibuses ferry children to and from school. Burgess Hill Girls does not produce a particular type, but former pupils are known as 'Bold girls' which probably says it all. Bold girls go on to a wide range of careers and are hugely supportive of the school – there are even a few Bold girls on the staff.

Money matters: Means-tested bursaries of up to 100 per cent of fees. Academic, art, drama, music and sports scholarships plus sixth form technology scholarships. Academic and music scholarships available in the prep school.

The last word: The school is almost non-selective and yet achieves better results than many more competitive schools. The holistic approach to education, where equal value is placed on academic achievement and softer skills, produces extremely confident young women who grow up to believe they can be whatever they want to be.

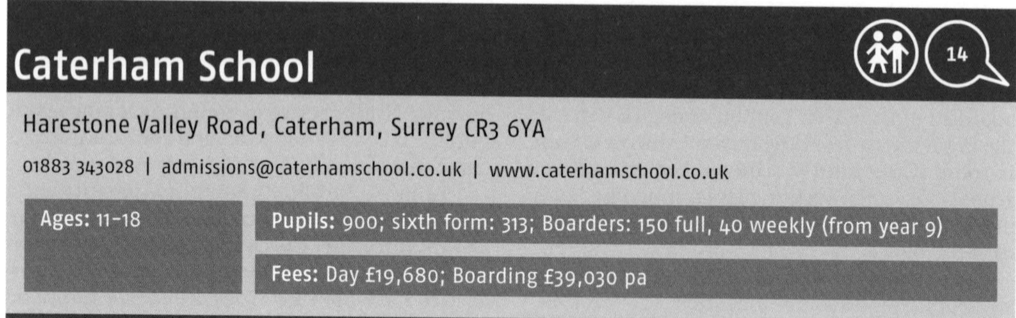

Caterham School

14

Harestone Valley Road, Caterham, Surrey CR3 6YA

01883 343028 | admissions@caterhamschool.co.uk | www.caterhamschool.co.uk

Ages: 11–18

Pupils: 900; sixth form: 313; Boarders: 150 full, 40 weekly (from year 9)

Fees: Day £19,680; Boarding £39,030 pa

Headmaster: Since 2015, Ceri Jones (40s). Attended Nab Wood Grammar (now the Samuel Lister Academy) in Bradford, which had already turned comprehensive by the time he started, then read history at Fitzwilliam College, Cambridge. Went into teaching straightaway because he loved his subject. Began his career at Godolpin and Latymer, then Bancroft's, then joined Caterham as head of history. Left to take up post as housemaster at Tonbridge, where he stayed for 11 years. During that time he rose to become deputy head, and was seconded to run the Marsh Academy in the Romney Marshes. Returned to Caterham because he liked the quiet confidence of the students – 'they were all very different, very assured, but not arrogant.' Married to Kay Moxon, head of politics at Tonbridge, and they have two daughters.

Unlike many heads we meet with similarly glittering credentials (he has a master's in educational leadership), Mr Jones impresses as a very human headteacher with his feet firmly on the ground. With his kindly energy and soft-spoken manner, he is clearly popular with parents. 'An excellent head, and a very clear and intelligent thinker,' said one; 'he is definitely a doer, and we can all see positive changes and improvements.' 'We really appreciate that he's passionate about education being holistic, and not all about academic achievement,' said another. Manages to fit in some football in his spare time (he played for Cambridge), still teaches A level history. Runs the Accelerate and Access Foundation, a charity which helps bright children from disadvantaged backgrounds in the south east.

Has no wish to change the ethos and values of the school, but is a skilled moderniser – he introduced the policy of issuing all Caterham students with iPads.

Entrance: Around 90 places at year 7, a third of which go to children coming up from the junior school. Others come from a range of local schools, both state and independent: The Hawthorns, Hazelwood, Oakhyrst Grange, St Mary's CofE Junior School, Sevenoaks Prep, New Beacon School, Copthorne School, etc. Fifty additional places in year 9 to pupils coming from preps, either via year 6 deferred entry or standard year 8 route. Some additional places available in the sixth form, but almost everyone stays on and, very commendably, the school doesn't weed out: the threshold of six B/6s at GCSE is 'a discussion point, not an ultimatum'.

Exit: A very small number after GCSEs, mostly for financial reasons. After A levels, the overwhelming majority to university. Popular destinations include Bath, Durham, Edinburgh, LSE, Imperial College, Warwick, York. Some overseas too. Vocational courses also becoming increasingly popular, and the head is currently in discussion with at least one high-profile financial company about apprenticeships. Eight medics in 2021.

Latest results: In 2021, 92 per cent 9-7 at GCSE; 83 per cent A*/A at A level. In 2019 (the last year when exams took place), 79 per cent 9-7 at GCSE; 62 per cent A*/A at A level (86 per cent A*-B).

Teaching and learning: Impressive, with results putting it comfortably in the top 100 independent schools in the country.

Class sizes in first three years around 20-24, dropping to 15-20 for GCSE teaching and usually 8-12 for sixth form. Broad curriculum, with core subjects supplemented by Latin, philosophy and theology, computer science, 3D design, all the usual creative arts, and a good modern languages offering: French, German, Spanish and, from year 9, Italian.

We particularly liked the Davey Building, home to the science departments, which had a real buzz about it. A biology teacher clad in brilliant pink lab coat and blue trainers saluted us with great good cheer, thoughtfully cradling the departmental mascot, Buffy the bearded dragon, as jazz drifted out overhead. The skeletons in the labs wore Jack Sparrow headscarves, and it really did seem refreshingly unstuffy.

A biology teacher in brilliant pink lab coat saluted us with great good cheer, cradling the departmental mascot, Buffy the bearded dragon, as jazz drifted out overhead

Lessons universally praised as lively and interactive. 'My daughter has been inspired by the teachers' love of their subjects,' wrote a mother. 'The teaching standard is of the highest quality at Caterham,' wrote another; 'our son has blossomed in all subjects, making his choices for GCSEs even harder.'

The key note here seems to be approachability. One sixth former thought the best thing about Caterham was 'the relationship between staff and students – I've never seen anything like it. They're incredibly supportive and happy to give up their free time.' School introduced iPads for all its students in 2015, and is formally accredited as an Apple Distinguished School. Parents approve. 'The iPad use for school communication for the children is excellent, both for homework and for keeping in touch with what is going on in school,' observed one parent. 'I was sceptical at first, but have been proven wrong,' a father was happy to admit. 'I've seen how it allows the students to embrace technology as a great medium for learning.' At sixth form, digital inquiry course now taken alongside A levels – idea is to prepare young people for the digital world covering problem solving, design thinking, digital skills such as coding, web design and video editing.

Learning support and SEN: Full-time SENCo (here called the assistant director of learning and teaching), aided by two teaching assistants, offers support to the 15 per cent or so of pupils who need it – dyslexia, processing difficulties, the occasional high-functioning autistic student – mostly in a classroom setting. 'There is one-to-one support, but it's not the bulk of what we do. Otherwise I'd become a crutch, and we want them to be independent,' commented the SENCo, whose office was decorated with reassuring posters of celebrities with SEN – Daniel Radcliffe, David Beckham and the like. This is an academically selective school, however, and they were keen to stress that it's unlikely to be suitable for pupils with more than mild difficulties.

The arts and extracurricular: Performing arts has its own thriving centre. Drama has upped its game, with the opening of a new dedicated studio theatre in 2016 supported by full-time theatre technician – who also runs the Humphries Theatre, the large multi-purpose space across the foyer – with a strong team of tech enthusiasts drawn from the students. Annual shows for both senior and lower school pupils – 'I don't think I can count the number of things I've done in the drama department!' beamed a stage-struck sixth former. Recent productions include Grease, Les Misérables and Our Day Out. Fabulous new air-conditioned dance studio – 'Dance is big here,' confirmed a male student, who praised the way the school encouraged both boys and girls to get involved. Annual MADLive dance performance showcases the students' achievements. Music department is lively and busy: orchestras, ensembles, concerts, choirs, and lessons on almost any instrument you can think of.

Girls' boarding house boasts a beautiful dining room with oak panelling and a rather lovely Positive Message Tree in the corner, which could have been tacky but simply wasn't

As you'd expect, visual arts are well resourced, and we liked the textiles area – a pleasure to see sewing machines in a school in this day and age. However, the work on display, whilst stylish, didn't strike us as particularly inspired or visionary – perhaps there just isn't much creative angst at this down-to-earth, affluent school – and it's probably no coincidence that the only negative feedback we received concerned this part of the school's provision: 'I would pick out art as an area of weakness,' wrote one parent, bluntly.

DofE and CCF are flourishing, and there are dozens of extracurricular societies catering for every taste. Of particular note is the Innovations Centre, where pupils can play and experiment with all things digital and robotic, and home also to the film club, where pupils have access to their own Green Screen room and Mac editing suite for creating special effects.

Sport: Strong on all fronts, and superbly well resourced: almost the first thing visitors see as they approach the school is what impresses as a Wembley-sized brand new Astroturf. Dual approach to sport: elite athletes go onto the Caterham Programme, where top-class coaching pushes them to their limits. But everyone is encouraged to have a go, and the school works to ensure that no one is left out. Rugby, hockey and cricket are the main sports for the boys, lacrosse, netball and tennis for the girls, and school has invested heavily in the coaching and facilities for these. It struck us as a rather traditional delineation, but the girls we spoke to liked it, praising the 'community feel' of lacrosse – something we couldn't remember about the game, frankly, so it's good that times change. There's also sixth form girls' rugby, synchronised swimming in the school's own magnificent pool, and a myriad other exciting things to try, from horse riding (the school has its own equestrian team) to judo, archery, golf, fencing etc. Splendid sports hall the size of an aircraft hangar is open to the public, and the English hockey regional training team uses the facilities here. The Wildcats Adventure area, a woodland paradise of treehouses, ropes and zipwires, looked like every child's dream.

Boarding: We thought the boarding pretty special. Houses are comfortable, spotlessly clean, light, modern in feel and attractive. In addition to everything you'd expect, girls' boarding house boasts a beautiful dining room with oak panelling and a rather lovely Positive Message Tree in the corner, which could have been tacky but simply wasn't. The boys are housed in equal comfort, and are about to get their own kitchen. Bedrooms are for four or two students in the lower years, then single rooms for lower sixth formers and single with ensuite for those in their final years. Good number of live-in staff, and a team of matrons are on site from 7.30am until 10pm.

Nearly 90 per cent are full boarders, mostly international students who do the IELTS (English language learning) programme on Saturdays. Weekly boarding introduced in 2016, and is attracting UK families – numbers small at present, but school hopes to grow them. However, now offers boarding from year 9 only (previously from year 7). Lots of trips and things to do – and a nice leisurely 10am breakfast on Sundays. The boarders we met struck us as a thoroughly happy and well-adjusted lot, and, as a student confirmed, 'the boarder and day pupil relationship is really good.'

Ethos and heritage: Founded in 1811 to provide a boarding education for the sons of Congregational ministers – William Wilberforce was one of the school's first governors. Moved to its present lovely site in the wooded Surrey North Downs in 1884. Even then the school was a forward-looking place. The main building, a beautiful late Victorian red brick and terracotta affair, was the height of modernity for its time, with the heating being provided by circulating warm air through the Hare Stone Tower, now long gone. The school maintains its links with the United Reform Church – bursaries are available for children of URC clergy – but now describes itself as 'multi-faith' and welcomes children of all faiths and of none.

Lots of new buildings, all of them practical and most of them tasteful, and astonishingly well-equipped and extensive outdoor areas – playing fields, woods, bridle path, you name it. With 200 acres to play with, space is not an issue, and the students move about with an air of confident purpose, smartly dressed in their business-like uniform. Co-ed really works here. The boys aren't loutish, and the girls aren't cliquey. More than anything, they're just themselves. 'For me, it's the most natural environment,' observes the head, and everyone we spoke to agreed. Students work hard, but are encouraged to play hard too and take advantage of the many opportunities on offer. 'Both my children find the school environment positive,' wrote a mother, 'and it's been a place where we've seen them develop. We cannot ask more from a school as we watch our children grow into young adults.'

Pastoral care, inclusivity and discipline: Universally praised for being a caring place that nurtures the whole child, and this is shown in lots of small ways rather than anything obvious. One such that impressed us was that boarding house prefects are there simply to support the younger students, not to discipline them – the house staff do the latter, so relationships between older and younger pupils remain friendly. Students appear confident without being arrogant, ready to have a go at anything, and really did come across as keen to serve the wider community. Behaviour throughout is lively but courteous.

Across the school, the words that kept coming up were 'approachable' and 'welcoming'. 'An unstuffy, happy school where the children do really well without being highly pressurised' was one parent's verdict. Another wrote, 'There have been a couple of occasions when our circumstances have meant that the children needed some extra care and I found the school and staff incredibly helpful, and very swift and ready to offer and provide sensitive and genuine care for them.'

Universally praised for being a caring place that nurtures the whole child. Boarding house prefects are there simply to support the younger students, not to discipline them, so relationships between older and younger pupils remain friendly

Form the top down, the school seems to have got the work-life balance right, and the result is a sane and kindly place where people have room to look about them. 'The school leadership at all levels seems genuinely to be on the watch for pupils in need of support and then deliver this in a sympathetic manner,' wrote a parent. A member of staff commented, 'People are nice to each other, because we're given the time to be nice to each other. We're valued by both leadership and parents. It's busy here, but we're not pushed to the limit.'

Pupils and parents: Parents are a grounded lot, mostly dual-income and working hard to give their children a Caterham education. Supportive of the school, and very much involved, turning out in great numbers for sporting fixtures and other school events. School works hard to include them, running a lively programme of talks – Revise Like a Champion was aimed at parents wanting to help their children – and putting at their disposal an amazing hospitality suite complete with terrace overlooking the playing fields. Pupils are level-headed, proud of their school, very happy to be here.

Money matters: About a third of pupils on some form of financial assistance. Bursaries of up to 100 per cent available for pupils from low-income families. Academic scholarships at 11+, 13+ and 16+ can be worth up to 50 per cent of fees. Broad range of 25 per cent scholarships offered in specific areas: sport, music, drama, science, art and design, all-rounder and boarding.

The last word: A traditional yet innovative school offering all that's best in modern independent education, both day and boarding, without putting its students through the mill. 'Caterham's one of the best schools in the country already,' the head told us proudly at our meeting. We're inclined to agree.

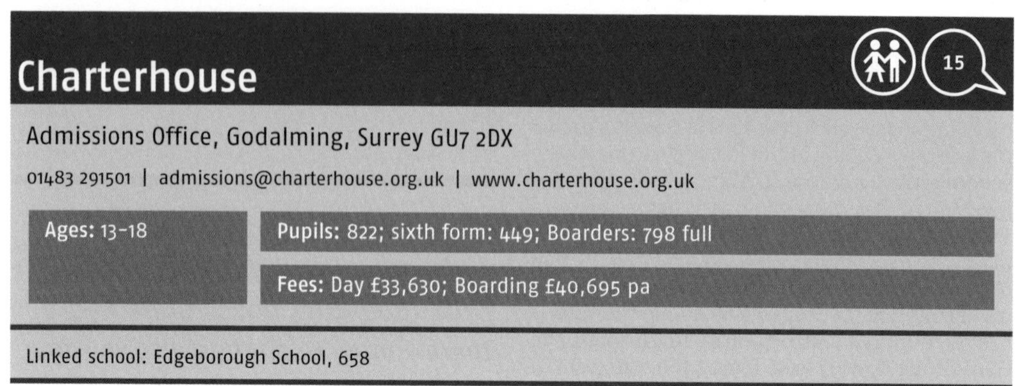

Charterhouse

15

Admissions Office, Godalming, Surrey GU7 2DX

01483 291501 | admissions@charterhouse.org.uk | www.charterhouse.org.uk

Ages: 13-18

Pupils: 822; sixth form: 449; Boarders: 798 full

Fees: Day £33,630; Boarding £40,695 pa

Linked school: Edgeborough School, 658

Headmaster: Since January 2018, Dr Alex Peterken (40s), formerly head of Cheltenham College. Educated at The Prebendal School, Chichester where he was head boy and head chorister, thence to Eton College as a music exhibitioner. BA in theology from Durham, MA in educational management from London and a doctorate in education from Surrey. Previous head's tenure was short and not without controversy. Dr Peterken frankly acknowledges that when he started: 'Morale was low, there was lots of work to do to galvanise everyone, to renew confidence.' It's quite possible that with his delight in and optimism for the school he could have done all the galvanising himself, but in fact he is supported by an impressive and loyal team – several of whom upped sticks and followed him here from Cheltenham (he's keen to point out that 'they're not disciples!'). His biggest project, of course, is to implement the school's move to fully co-ed (he did the same at Cheltenham College): 'I've seen how brilliant co-ed can be, this is the most exciting project in independent education.' Despite his excitement he's taking things slowly: 'We've spent 18 months reviewing and listening, we've looked at all the case studies and learned all the lessons, we're planning every single detail.' Pupils told us, 'He's definitely stricter, but he's also very approachable.' Parents unanimously declared, 'Exactly the right man at the right time.'

His first move was to restructure existing sixth form girls' boarding. Previously girls had their own separate accommodation, but it was not much more than a place to sleep, there was no house identity, instead they were assigned to existing boys' houses. Establishing a girls' house with housemistresses, 'great, positive role models' has, apparently, 'changed the atmosphere in the school so much'. Girls who have lived through this mini-revolution have found it a bit of an upheaval – not much time to gain perspective if you're only here for two years.

Head's biggest project is to implement the school's move to fully co-ed: 'I've seen how brilliant co-ed can be'

Leaving the small matter of co-education to one side, Dr P has also reviewed the timetable, 'to make the day work for teenagers, not systems'. This does not mean everyone gets a lie-in: 'Morning break now is a break; it used to be used for tutorials.' Something that teenagers probably think doesn't work for them is the robust crackdown on mobile phones, our guides said it had been pretty unpopular (previous policy allowed use at housemaster's discretion). Dr P says he's happy to take the flack: 'Technology is great for communicating and in the classroom, but we don't want unrestricted screens in boarding houses, we want pupils to enjoy school and socialise.' He adds, a little defensively, 'The school as a whole has to have a view and not be afraid to stand by it. We do know best, thank you very much.' Current crop of sixth formers are particularly feeling the burn, Dr P says he's listening and 'may tweak'.

School rules have come in for scrutiny, 'I read 20 pages of rules and they were all about what not to do, but we also need to be clear about what the school's values are.' And they are? 'Kindness, moral courage, responsibility, perseverance and open-mindedness.' 'It's easy for boys to lose their empathy between the ages of 13 and 16, we need to change the culture so that it's okay for them to call out unkindness if they see it. We're always battling to encourage them to come forward about things like bullying, it's not easy, we've got to keep working at it.'

He acknowledges that his first 18 months were hard work: 'The school needed to modernise, it was looking for leadership and change', but there's no sign of weariness (although we noticed he was wearing his Monday socks on a Thursday); his vision and enthusiasm are driven by a genuine, clear-sighted sense of purpose. Determined to get a bit of teaching in (RE): 'I taught half a GCSE course last year; this year I will teach year 9, they will get taught by me.' We believe they will. He sings with the Charterhouse Choral Society and 'keeps an eye on music in general'. Also, he 'tries to run' and has done the Godalming 10K – that sounds like a bit more than trying to us. Lives on site with his wife, Henny, they have six children, youngest is 3 – 'It helps with perspective' – and escapes to Cornwall for the holidays.

Entrance: About 125 places in year 9. Candidates sit the ISEB common pre-test in the autumn of year 6 at their current school. Boys (and now girls) invited for interview and activity afternoon in spring term and close contact maintained with prep schools. CE pass mark of 60 per cent expected. A few places not dependent on pre-testing remain for late applicants and exceptional cases. One parent described the admissions process as 'really relaxed, they try and make it fun for the children.'

Houses matter (although after a few weeks every pupil thinks theirs is the best). Families visit two or three, meet housemaster/mistress and staff and boys, they then select their preferred house – but don't always get it. Family connections with a particular house are respected if possible. Once places have been offered, school organises events such as an overnight camp out so that pupils get to meet before starting.

At sixth form, 75 girls and 30 boys come, most as boarders and a few as day pupils. Admission by competitive examination, school reports and interview. Offers of places are unconditional but high proportion of GCSE 9-7s are expected. Houses are allocated rather than chosen at this stage.

Exit: Fewer than one per cent left after GCSEs in 2021. Careers advice has gone up a few gears since our last visit: 'We get emails every day,' said a sixth former, 'they really encourage us to look outside the conventional group of UK universities, to consider applying to the US or specialist colleges.' UCL, Exeter, Durham and Bristol all popular. History, biomedical sciences, business and finance, law, politics and, bucking the trend, modern foreign languages, are the most popular degree subjects. Five to Oxbridge in 2021, and three medics.

Parents say the quality of the teaching is 'absolutely excellent' and that pupils are challenged to do well not only by the beaks (teachers) but also by their classmates

Latest results: In 2021, 83 per cent 9-7 at I/GCSE; 66 per cent A*/A at A level (88 per cent A*-B). In 2019 (the last year when exams took place), 71 per cent 9-7 at I/GCSE; 50 per cent A*/A at A level. IB average of 34 in 2019.

Teaching and learning: Offers A levels (Pre-Us in a few subjects, will change as the qualification is phased out) and the IB. Nearly all pupils will do four subjects or three plus an EPQ and choices from a non-examined electives programme. Not huge numbers opting for IB (around 20 per cent) but parents say the programme is very well resourced and taught. 'It's great for academic all-rounders who aren't ready to specialise,' said one, adding, 'Some [IB] classes only have two or three pupils so everyone benefits from the extra attention.' Fairly trad range of A level/Pre-U subjects on offer plus business and management, theatre studies and philosophy and theology. School amalgamates IB, A level and Pre-U results on its website which isn't particularly user-friendly for those in search of specifics.

Parents say the quality of the teaching is 'absolutely excellent' and that pupils are challenged to do well by each other as well as the beaks (teachers). Several mentioned how dedicated staff were – nearly all run extracurricular clubs and societies too. 'The fact the beaks live on site and run clubs means that pupils see them in lots of different contexts, and vice versa.' Another told us, 'We really like how the beaks will go with boys' curiosity, they're encouraged to question things. It's so much more than just getting through the curriculum.' Good mix of male and female staff and Dr P has recruited more with specific co-ed experience. Facilities all well-provisioned or being refurbished – we admired the rather sleek science block: 'It's filled with labs and that sort of thing,' said a sixth former, clearly not a scientist.

One or two parents felt that academic reports could be more detailed: 'If you're far away it can be hard to get a sense of how your child is really getting on.'

Learning support and SEN: SEND support is 'incredibly well coordinated', small educational support team works with all staff to ensure that the approach is multi-pronged. Some one-to-one, but school says its focus is on providing whatever additional support is necessary in lessons. Study skills sessions offered to all pupils.

The arts and extracurricular: Art dept is deliberately studio space rather than classroom – 'We want to encourage risk taking' – and staff (all professional artists) are on hand every day, including weekend afternoons and two late evenings. Head of art was a big fan of the Pre-U: 'It's more rigorous and accommodates cross-medium creativity'; we hope he isn't too disappointed that its days are numbered – IB and A level will no doubt fill the gap. Work we saw here and across the school was bold, imaginative and extremely skilful – no wonder school's reputation is particularly strong in this area. Pupils can also join Beerbohm – a drawing society named after former pupil, the cartoonist Max Beerbohm. It's just one of around 60 clubs and societies that encompass everything from aeronautics to Scottish dancing.

The hallowed turf, the 'Big Ground', is right at the heart of the school, a football pitch impeccably rolled and dazzlingly green where only the top teams' boots may tread

Charterhouse has produced some notable musicians, from Ralph Vaughan Williams to Peter Gabriel (and the other founding members of Genesis) and parents say the music department is 'Absolutely superb, they're enthusiastic, collaborative and work so hard – the drive is always towards quality.' Another said, 'It's so much more than "school music" and the range of what's on offer is huge, there's something to fit everybody.' Concerts are well attended by parents who live close enough, and outreach activities in local care homes and primary schools (playing carols, introducing young children to different instruments) build players' confidence and broaden horizons. A quick flick through the school calendar reveals a packed rehearsal schedule – chapel choir, chamber music, symphony orchestra, evening recitals, jazz band, house singing. There's even Concert Choir in which pupils, staff and family members get to sing together.

Lack of whole-school play mentioned as a downside by some, but there's plenty of drama to be had via houses or year groups with seven or eight major productions a year – 235-seat Ben Travers Theatre (named after the playwright, who was a pupil) is certainly well used. Pupils can also prepare for LAMDA exams. Artifex is the whole-school arts festival, held in June, which showcases every conceivable talent: inter-house debating, academic symposia, cinema in the chapel, sketch shows and even a pop-up restaurant. Plugged, Unplugged and Lack of Talent are annual, pupil-run occasions where the school's many bands and solo performers get to show off their creative artistry.

Sport: It was at Charterhouse (jointly with Westminster) that football was first developed and in the early years of the FA Cup teams were largely composed of ex-pupils from these schools. We were shown the hallowed turf, the 'Big Ground', right at the heart of the school, a football pitch impeccably rolled and dazzlingly green where only the top teams' boots may tread. Not being followers of the beautiful game we were probably a bit underwhelmed by the pitch's historical significance, but hats off to the groundskeepers. 'This is such a football school, people are obsessed,' we were told, 'rugby really struggles' (15 football pitches and only one rugby pitch would seem to confirm this). Girls' sport, which thus far only concerned sixth formers, has been a bit underdeveloped, 'You could get away with not doing much.' A new director of girls' sport is already in post and looks set to change all that. What about girls' football, we asked one of our guides: 'It's quite big, but it's never played on the Big Ground.' In fact, we discovered later that some girls' matches are played here.

Football, of course, is not the only sport (though some feel it does dominate a bit too much); hockey and cricket are the other majors, played by boys and girls. Minors include sailing, shooting, water polo, tennis (there are 24 courts), fencing, lacrosse, netball and golf – there's a nine-hole course on campus.

Boarding: Charterhouse is a full-boarding school, with only a handful of day pupils. Around three-quarters of pupils go home on Saturday afternoons and return on Sunday evenings. This can leave boarding houses depleted but there's still loads going on for the 200 or so who stay in, including theatre and cinema trips, socials, takeaway nights and karting. School day is a long one, with some societies, rehearsals and other events starting at 9pm several nights a week.

New mobile phone rules are prominently displayed; housemaster told us that since their imposition 'board games have become much more popular'

There are currently 14 boarding houses, 'Old Houses' at the centre of the school and, wait for it, 'New Houses' further away on campus (two new ones due to open soon). Each has three resident staff including a matron, plus a team of house tutors. Move to fully co-ed has given school a once-in-a-lifetime opportunity to review all provision and create bespoke facilities for 21st-century boarding; head describes this as a 'game changer'. There's a hugely positive feel about the ambition and enthusiasm with which all concerned are working on every detail – from design to location. Plan is to have boys and girls living on both sides of the school so one of the two new houses being built on the edge of campus is actually for boys and the oldest boys' house at the centre of the school will become a girls' house.

No more 'halls of residence' for sixth form girls – back in the day these (rather nice) blocks were where the girls worked and laid their heads, but they weren't 'houses', instead, in a rather awkward arrangement, sixth form girls were assigned to existing boys' houses. Now there are three girls' houses (currently just for sixth formers but by 2023 will be home to girls from all year groups as co-education develops), with housemistresses and identical status to the boys' houses. A fourth girls' house opened in 2021. And the one we saw looked fantastic, nearly all single rooms with ensuites too – luxury! The kitchen-diner looked very inviting, lots of plants and flowers and the table was decorated for an 18th birthday party – cake and a little bottle of prosecco.

The boys' house we visited had just been refurbished and looked very smart. Good to see the old honours boards still in pride of place on newly painted walls. General tightening up of boarding procedures means all comings and goings are visible from ground floor office. New mobile phone rules are prominently displayed (they didn't look that draconian to us), housemaster told us that since their imposition 'board games have become much more popular'. Extremely shiny brown leather sofas in the common room – suppose they have to withstand more wear and tear than the softer velvet ones in the girls' house.

In-house dining persisted at some of the farther flung houses until recently, but all from New Houses are now fed in a very fine, open-plan central dining room. The ceiling of this dining room is perforated with many thousands of different sized holes – they look like they should be back-lit to produce a starry effect at night, but apparently this is not a feature. Those boarding in Old Houses will soon also be able to eat meals at a nearer café/ social space. Pupils gave a somewhat cautious welcome to this change but appreciate the thinking behind the move to central dining: 'It may be positive, it's meant to boost whole school rather than tribal, house loyalty.' Parents report their children saying food is 'great at first but can get a bit boring ' ots of chicken.' We thought our lunch was delicious – plenty of choice, excellent salads and the puddings looked great. Vegetarian and other special diets are well catered for. For other hungry moments there's 'Crown', the school tuck shop and boarders can make snacks and drinks in their house butteries.

Ethos and heritage: Founded by Lincolnshire coal baron Thomas Sutton in 1611. He endowed a hospital in London on the site of the Charterhouse and left money in his will to maintain this, a chapel and a school. Moved to its present 250-acre site on top of a Surrey hill in 1872, main buildings were designed by architects of the Royal Albert Hall, the Lucas brothers. Craftily concealed behind the busy streets of Godalming, but when one arrives congested, suburban sprawl is instantly forgotten. Staff and monitors (pupils who are head of their houses) bicycle to and from lessons and houses, giving the place a rather timeless air, but main routes across campus are shared with quite a lot of cars; 'It's all going to be pedestrianised,' we were told. Nevertheless, feels safe, the campus is beautiful – there's even a farm – and the atmosphere (as one parent put it) is 'just very calm'.

Chapel by Sir Giles Gilbert Scott (he also designed the red telephone box) is a fine place – interior is quite plain and very tranquil. It's dedicated to the 1,050 Carthusians who lost their lives in the in the two World Wars, and subsequent conflicts. There is also a separate Catholic chapel on site, but the door was locked and currently there are no Sunday services: 'The previous priest left and hasn't been replaced.' We sensed some unhappiness about this. Pupils attend services four times a week, a longer service on Friday afternoon to replace compulsory Sunday evening attendance has proved to be one of Dr P's most popular changes.

Sixth form became co-ed way back in 1971 (those brave first girls were billeted with the good people of Godalming). It's fair to say that the school really didn't rush to accommodate (in any sense) its female pupils but is certainly making up for that now.

Yearlings (year 9) and other new pupils will need to learn to speak Lingua Carthusiana. 'It's quite hard at first,' said one. 'Quarters' are terms (Oration Quarter, Long Quarter and Cricket Quarter make up the Carthusian academic year), morning break is also known as a 'quarter', a lesson is a 'hash', a classroom is a 'hashroom', teachers are 'beaks', and so on.

Move to fully co-ed has given school a once-in-a-lifetime opportunity to review all provision and create bespoke facilities for 21st-century boarding; head describes this as a 'game changer'

Tremendously fascinating list of notable former pupils (Old Carthusians). Among the many deans, bishops, MPs, brigadiers and major-generals we were particularly taken by Andrew Amos (1863-1931), 'England international footballer and clergyman'. Footballing vicars aside (there's more than one), there doesn't seem to a field – sports or professional – without a significant Carthusian presence. In addition to the founding members of prog rock band Genesis, Charterhouse has given the world poet and novelist Robert Graves, composers Ralph Vaughan Williams and Rachel Portman, sculptor Sir Anthony Caro, a brace of Dimblebys (David and Jonathan), William Makepeace Thackeray and Frederic Raphael (writers) and actor Graham Seed, famous for Nigel Pargetter's long, anguished cry as he slipped to his death from the roof of his ancestral pile in The Archers.

Pastoral care, inclusivity and discipline: According to parents, pastoral care has been 'revolutionised' and is, apparently, 'unrecognisable' from where school was three or four years ago. The tutor role is now 'holistic' rather than purely academic and heads of year have been appointed. Dr P says the aim is 'proactive pastoral care with a vertical and horizontal double lock to ensure no one slips beneath the pastoral and academic radar. The school has to know every child.' Deputy head academic told us that the new system should 'coordinate academic and pastoral tracking'. Lots more tutor group time, discussions, external speakers and sessions on, for instance, relationships and eating disorders for both boys and girls separately. Tutor groups are single sex but some topics are delivered to larger co-ed groups. Parents involved too: 'It's very important that there's fluid contact between parents and tutors, the expectation should be lots of contact.' All the parents we spoke to had noticed the difference and heartily approved.

Sixth form girls told us that some found the first few weeks quite hard: 'It is weird, there's lots of showing off, but the school is brilliant and staff pick up on any comments or behaviour that goes too far.' The culture change that going fully co-ed brings will hopefully soon mean an end to this difficult transition. Talking to former pupils we got the impression that things were possibly a little liberal in the not too distant past, but that door has closed. The rule forbidding 'intimate sexual relationships' is two sentences long and the consequences of breaking it are crystal clear.

Every new pupil is allocated a 'father' (presumably soon to be joined by 'mother') from the year above who helps them learn the ropes – and the language. Surprisingly, we were told that the majority of pupils are new to boarding and need some help at first with things like organisation: 'We have to teach them to board.' Not everyone finds it easy to settle in and the first term especially is very tiring, so there's an option for year 9 pupils to return to school after the weekend on Monday morning and go home for one night in the middle of the week, 'Not many take it up, but it's a safety blanket.' This isn't an option for international pupils, one parent felt that it was hard for them watching the others go home for weekends.

Pupils and parents: 'Quite a few' pupils are following in the educational footsteps of fathers, mothers and grandfathers. One of our guides was a case in point: 'I like the continuity, I was always going to come here.' Several parents told us that the school is what you make it, 'They positively encourage parents to get involved, they want you to come to all the events and to visit at weekends, but you don't have to.' Communication with parents used to be, well, 'just bad, you really had to dig for information', but is now 'so much better'. We heard very happy reports of housemasters sending parents regular, detailed newsletters and one or two less happy reports about the opposite kind (irregular, less detail). Nevertheless, old hands say that what you get to know depends largely on how communicative your child is. Just under 20 per cent of pupils are from abroad, this rises to around 25 per cent in the sixth form when there's an influx from Europe – particularly Italians – for the IB.

Money matters: Offers a limited number of means-tested bursaries, up to 100 per cent of fees in year 9 and year 12 with the preference given to those who gain scholarships. Two year 9 bursaries are awarded every year on the basis of academic performance in year 6. Scholarships and exhibitions of various kinds are awarded solely on merit – the recognition is greater than the money involved.

The last word: It may have played a long game (nearly 50 years in fact), but Charterhouse is about to make the very best kind of fashionably late entrance into the world of co-ed boarding. The school we saw was eager for change, dynamic and crackling with expertise, energy, optimism and unashamed ambition. Dr Peterken has said that he wants Charterhouse to be 'the best co-educational boarding school in the country'; from what we saw the future looks very bright indeed.

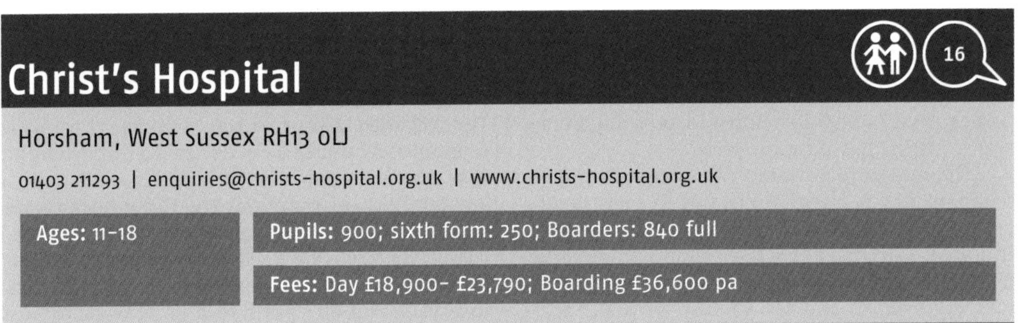

Christ's Hospital

Horsham, West Sussex RH13 0LJ

01403 211293 | enquiries@christs-hospital.org.uk | www.christs-hospital.org.uk

Ages: 11–18

Pupils: 900; sixth form: 250; Boarders: 840 full

Fees: Day £18,900- £23,790; Boarding £36,600 pa

Headmaster: Since 2017, Simon Reid, a South African who read English at the University of Witwatersrand. Married to Michele, who is French, with two grown-up children. Previously head of Gordonstoun; before that, an English teacher and housemaster here. The unique territory of disadvantage brought him back: CH is a school attended variously by those who pay full, part or no fees, enabled by the 1552 foundation.

Pupils like Mr Reid; for many in this big school he is viewed from some distance, but he 'talks to everyone in the queue at lunchtime', and gained enormous respect from pupils by admitting when he made a mistake in excluding two pupils, and changing his decision.

He still teaches English: 'There can be a riot in my class, but I'll be in control' (no doubt he will); 'dry and witty, firm and fair,' reflected a former pupil. Runs a very tight ship; older pupils baulk sometimes, but Mr Reid makes no apologies: 'We hold them carefully, tightly – but with some sensitivity.'

The head has a clear direction for CH: to challenge pupils, then, in turn, ask them to challenge, and take this spirit forward to contribute to society.

Parents are impressed by his level of involvement: 'He's at everything we go to. This guy is part of the school'; 'was filled with joy that he taught here before… he gets it'; 'he is interested in feedback… really keen to listen and improve'.

Entrance: Most join in year 7, when there are some 780 applicants for 110 places. A raw ability test whittles this down to around 300, who then come in to sit tests in English and maths, and have a one-to-one interview. Around 25 join in year 9, and 25 in sixth form. They are looking for above average ability, aiming for a balance of abilities, characters and level of support needed, but always fitting the formula which allows CH to function: the right number of full bursaries, part bursaries and full fees, with 10 per cent from overseas.

Exit: One parent chose CH as 'the best preparation for life and working life and gaining financial independence'. Careers are discussed from year 7, stretching minds forward to consider life, while those at prep schools are getting their heads down for CE. Careers talks take place every week; even reluctant pupils are nudged to attend. Up to 20 per cent leave after GCSE.

A recent focus on careers and university means pupils consider not just course but cost of living, societies and student satisfaction. This informed decision-making has resulted in a greater breadth of destinations and subjects. Manchester, Kings College London, Exeter, Bristol, Loughborough, Warwick and UCL all recently popular, with students studying subjects ranging from law to yacht design. Six to Oxbridge and three medics in 2021.

Latest results: In 2021, 70 per cent 9-7 at GCSE; 62 per cent A*/A at A level. Average IB point score 40. In 2019 (the last year when exams took place), 63 per cent 9-7 at GCSE; 35 per cent A*/A at A level (61 per cent A*-B). Average IB score 34.

Teaching and learning: 'They work for [their] own achievements... take nothing for granted,' said a parent, and the self motivation of pupils here is evident from a glance at the extraordinary news in the latest release: two pupils received awards in the John Locke essay competition, two more received Arkwright engineering scholarships, and one pupil (not a native Japanese speaker) was highly commended in the Stephen Spender prize for her translation of an eighth-century Japanese poem. Another parent said that it is 'definitely competitive, but not in a horrible, pointing finger way... [they] all want to do well.'

The desire to succeed can result in pupils feeling pressure, say parents, but there is plenty of support: 'Teachers are on hand, also tutors in house... always a teacher around outside the classroom. [They] seem to have a 24/7 role... you can drop in and see them... very supportive.' They're aware of the whole student, another added, saying she sometimes receives an email saying her son is working very hard, and needs to get a balance. A pupil commented, 'There's a lot of pressure, but they are lenient with people who need it. Mental health [care] is really good – you can leave a lesson and go back to house if things are getting on top of you.'

There is plenty of challenge to be found in the academic curriculum; lower down the school this includes two modern languages and Latin for all, and an HPQ in the third form (year 9), in which pupils independently research and present a project on any subject of interest to them.

The head is keen to connect subjects with a philosophical base, so that education at CH is more than attainment in individual subjects. He would like children here to like learning, drily assuring us he is not so rash as to hope they will love it. A new director of teaching and learning is touring classes to make sure what happens in the classroom is 'delightful'; we didn't see many delighted faces on our tour, but as the head says, '[we] can teach inventiveness. [It's] early days, but [we are] learning how to be better teachers.' There was a good buzz in science, but most lessons we saw were those of quiet concentration.

IB and its philosophy suits this school well, and about a third opt for it; the others, clear about their choices, choose A level and Pre-U – 'so we invent a philosophy for A level students,' said Mr Reid, and pupils are encouraged to build diversity into their four subjects (pupils can drop a subject if four is too much). No psychology or politics at A level, but there's plenty of debate for those with a political bent.

Learning support and SEN: LS supports 98 pupils with dyslexia, dyspraxia, ADHD, ASD, SEMH. A parent of a dyslexic daughter said support is 'excellent' and her daughter's confidence has increased. Prospective pupils must meet the school's selective academic criteria, with reasonable adjustments made during the assessment process. Support is one-to-one and in small groups, out of class, at no extra charge. A parent whose child was helped with revision methods commented that this department isn't just about labelled conditions, but about helping 'every child get better'.

The arts and extracurricular: 'Each year I find out so many new things I can do,' said a pupil, adding that the vast range of opportunities and facilities are the best things about the school; there are over 60 clubs including Arabic, fencing, girls' rugby and Model United Nations. The CCF travels the world. CH hopes pupils will develop lifelong interests, and one pupil told us, 'I want to be a photographer, not because of any lessons, but because of the photography club.'

Plenty of challenge to be found in the academic curriculum. The head wants children here to like learning, drily assuring us he is not so rash as to hope they will love it

Challenge is one of the head's favourite words, and in this vein he is keen to introduce more outdoor education, such as walking, kayaking and cycling. 'Put them on a moor, and they will understand how to work together to survive' – like a DofE for all.

The community action programme runs throughout the week, and is limited only by the number of minibuses that can fan out from the school, with 200 pupils visiting care homes and primary schools, and running a club for disabled people, Ready and Able, in the sports centre.

Pupils are involved in every aspect of productions in the large 70s theatre, with a junior and senior show each year. Drama lessons provide a space for pupils to explore difficult emotions; workshops have explored immigration and the Grenfell Tower tragedy. The recent production of West Side Story showcased both dramatic and musical talent; 'musical opportunities are amazing,' said a parent. The marching band make a joyful noise with the precision and skill of professionals; their gigs include the Lord Mayor's show, Lord's cricket ground, and Whitehall on Remembrance Sunday.

The art teacher enthuses about the rigours of art Pre-U – pupils need to be independent and committed to spend a year developing a portfolio. History of art is also available at A level, and increasing numbers of pupils go on to study art after school. The current artist in residence makes rugby balls, footballs – in fact any ball – in plaster. He does some teaching, too, and pupils benefit from having a real artist working alongside them.

Sport: 'Sport is excellent,' said a parent, and with games every afternoon, they get plenty of practice. Sports are compulsory, but with more flexibility higher up the school. At this Rainbow Flag Award school, there are mixed football and cricket teams, and rugby 7s for both sexes. The Bluecoat sports centre is very swish, with memberships available for the public when not in use by pupils.

Boarding: Nearly all pupils are full boarders, but this is less radical than it used to be: pupils go home every third weekend, leaving school at lunchtime on a Friday and returning on Sunday evening. Two boarding houses are kept open for those who can't or don't want to go home.

Rooms for four for the first two years; single rooms for GCSE and above. Desks in rooms, where pupils complete their homework – once they have shown that they are responsible enough to do so. Just eight new pupils in each house each year; a manageable number of new faces, said a parent, another saying, '[it's a] big family. Older ones relay experiences to younger ones.'

Phones are taken away at night in the first year (known as second form), and they don't encourage contact at the beginning, said a parent, who wistfully wished she had received some voluntary updates on how her son was settling in, 'but if you don't hear anything, it's fine'. Another said, 'You can pick up the phone anytime and speak to the housemaster – they'll make you aware if there's a problem.'

At weekends, pupils in year 10 and above can go into Horsham on their own. Pupils really appreciate Saturday nights; sometimes the theatre turns into a cinema; there are discos, house pizza, 'great attention to detail... makes you feel you're having a good time.'

Sixth form house is a release of grip, says the head. Spacious rooms contain basin, ample wardrobe, large desk and shelf. There are modern bathrooms, and a shared kitchen – 'If you don't clean up it gets locked,' said a pupil, resignedly washing up. Pupils can choose to do their own laundry; some do.

Ethos and heritage: 'Once she saw it, she wanted it,' said a parent about her daughter, although it was very different from her small rural primary school; 'such diversity... quite a change'. Pupils are from a range of backgrounds, and as such, wealth is not a subject of conversation; it's rare to hear conversations about the latest family skiing holiday or new car. This diversity is one of the great and unusual attributes of CH, and evidence of a school holding fast to its founding purpose: to care for and educate those from disadvantaged backgrounds.

Rooms for four for the first two years; single rooms for GCSE and above. Sixth form house is a release of grip. Pupils can choose to do their own laundry; some do

Tradition is very important here; '[It's] wonderful to be part of something so warm and timeless,' glowed a parent, and there is a real sense of strength and purpose flowing from the past to power the present. Pupils and parents are in no doubt of its value: it unifies. The startling uniform of Tudor-style breeches, white shirts and bands and long housey coats 'levels the playing field socially,' said a parent, or as pupils put it, 'You all feel so odd.' Girls have a smart fitted jacket for the summer months; boys wear half-housey, shedding the long coats. 'Like joining a very special club,' said a parent.

A huge green quad; 'Keep off the grass' (although pupils recently camped on it for charity). Pupils march in to lunch military style in houses to the music of the excellent band, and are judged on who makes the best marching noises (shout the loudest with clearest commands, we clarified). Pupils say, 'It's quite fun'; they like the way it brings houses together and structures the day.

Buildings of red brick add warmth to the grandeur; there's a splendid dining hall and good range of food (new kitchens are under construction, for kitchen staff and pupil use). CH is the only school who have calmly taken this reviewer to the end of the lunch queue, which says something about equality at this school, and at the schools that don't.

This is an energetic and rather loud school, but there are plenty of rules which tend towards strict, in lessons and otherwise. No loose hair (though we saw plenty of it, awaiting the reprimand we were confident would follow). No hoop earrings. Pupils must not be seen holding phones in uniform, though it's allowed once they have changed into civvies in the evening. Some disorder allowed: sixth formers zip around on bikes, left in disarray outside buildings, one dumped hastily in a flowerbed.

Departing pupils are read the charge: a grave request to consider the benefits received and give back where possible. These words are recalled by many old blues, one saying, 'The fine words of the charge have been constantly in my mind ever since they were addressed to me in July 1949. My education at CH shaped my future life in every way.'

Pastoral care, inclusivity and discipline: Eleven is young to start boarding school; 'not if they've not done camps or sleepovers,' suggested a parent, but 'the school are experts at it... I don't think they take those who wouldn't cope.' A discovery programme for new year 7s includes essential skills such as campus orientation, friendship and food nutrition, moving on to sex and relationships, and wider world skills such as road safety and managing money, later in the year. 'Very good at helping with puberty,' said parent appreciatively.

A huge green quad; 'Keep off the grass' (although pupils recently camped on it for charity). Pupils march in to lunch military style accompanied by the excellent band

Bullying is taken seriously, and dealt with at deputy head level, with a restorative justice approach which aims to protect the victim and help the perpetrator who often, too, has been bullied. A parent whose son was being picked on said it was dealt with very quickly, and did not recur; another that there was 'some unpleasantness in early years, [but they] were on it... spoke to both, brought together, was sorted in days. Communication amazing.'

CH works hard to reassure parents that the school is a completely different place to one lambasted in the press for past abuse: the rules are detailed and thorough, from the phone and list of child support numbers in each boarding house, to a houseparent team and matron – 'all easy to contact,' said a parent, 'very good and knowledgable' – and three full-time counsellors. Staff receive regular training; pupils too, in weekly PHSE lessons and assemblies. There seems to be a confidently open culture; a parent said her daughter, spoken to inappropriately at a choir festival by men from another choir, reported the incident, which was dealt with immediately. 'They regularly update us. Systems are good. Children are aware of their rights. They are doing the best they can do,' said a parent earnestly.

Two pupils have been excluded in the last year, for disciplinary and drugs offences. Pupils who are old enough to visit Horsham might indulge in crafty drinks and drugs on Saturdays, but the school will breathalyse or produce the sniffer dogs if they suspect anything. The tightness of control in this area is not always appreciated by pupils: pub pass has been removed, to the disgust of upper sixth, who speak with slightly curling lip of the two drinks allowed on Saturday nights with half an hour in between, and feel their views on this are not heard. Parents are happy with this containment – 'not saying no, but allowing a bit' – and the head says pupils need to be held, even as 17/18-year-olds. '[They've] got their whole lives to make use of drugs,' said the head. '[We] want them to be able to make a half sensible decision.'

Pupils and parents: From every walk of life, but few are helicopter parents. One said, 'We realise as parents the need to step back and let school do as they do.'

Money matters: Full fees are the usual eye-watering independent boarding school levels, but only 17 per cent of boarding pupils will pay them; the rest are subsidised, fully or partly, and this doesn't just cover fees, but also travel costs, sports kit, music lessons, pocket money, house funds and school trips. Uniform is free to all.

Each bursary case is means-assessed on its own merits, considering earnings, commitments and outgoings, capital saving and investments. This school keeps its founding purposes in mind: when it can possibly help, it does, and has found last-minute places for those in extreme need on full bursaries.

A range of scholarships of up to 20 per cent of fees.

The last word: Pupils here say, 'You need to get on well with other people, be determined and willing to work hard.' It is the getting on with others that is most important. As a parent said, it is 'for those who welcome difference, not for those who want the security of wanting something like themselves'.

'Not,' said the head bluntly, 'for those who need to step on others to succeed, or need to establish themselves above others in society,' for at this school, as former pupil T S Surr said, 'no rich dunce can rise on bags of gold' (Christ's Hospital, a poem, 1797).

City of London Freemen's School

Ashtead Park, Ashtead, Surrey KT21 1ET

01372 277933 | admissions@freemens.org | www.freemens.org

Ages: 13–18

Pupils: 526; sixth form: 230; Boarders: 57 full/weekly

Fees: Day £20,895 – £21,525 pa; Boarding £32,835 – £36,993 pa

Headmaster: Since 2015, Roland Martin (early 50s). Grew up in a council house and won a Foundation scholarship to Rendcomb College in Gloucestershire, where he loved boarding. Read English at York, 'where everyone said I should be a teacher, but I was stubborn and male and didn't want to do anything I was told to.' So worked as an assistant manager in a bar instead until his boss sat him down after a shift 'to help me work out what I wanted to do'. Was about to embark on PGCE when he was offered a job at Newcastle-under-Lyme School and learned on the job instead. Six years later, he got 'another lucky break', this time at Eton, 'which is not known for taking people like me but they said I had one of the best references they'd ever seen.' And so it was he taught English and drama there for 13 years, as well as being head of year 11 and a housemaster. Returned to his alma mater Rendcomb in 2011 as headmaster, so well versed in the demands of the role before moving to Freemen's four years later.

Spin is not his thing, so while some heads are PR-ed to the hilt, this one is as honest, authentic and reflective as his rows of framed pupil pictures depicting their future dreams. Intellectual but not fanciful, he must be the first head we've met whose office is in a purpose-built classroom, still complete with whiteboard – 'I moved because it's more central.' Still no-frills, though well-loved sofa has replaced the desks. Well-liked by parents and pupils, though is more behind-the-scenes than some would like. 'Clearly very bright and has lots of ideas where he wants the school to go but gives the impression of being uncomfortable speaking to large groups.' 'Goes to lots of conferences and very out there in that sense, but doesn't seem to know the pupils well.' Pupils agree that 'you rarely see him', though perhaps the tide is turning as he's currently directing Twelfth Night with a sixth form cast, plus a few from years 10 and 11. We were struck by his kindness – 'balancing mental health and aspirations' is a major post-Covid focus. Collaborative too, increasingly partnering with other schools to 'solve the sticky problems that schools have, eg how to bring on boys' learning in a co-ed school.'

Thinks that if he hadn't become a teacher he might have chosen to be ordained ('never say never'), and certainly feels that teaching is a vocation. Has two children and loves theatre and all things 18th century.

Entrance: At 13+, nearly all join from the junior school with automatic entry. An additional 20 (soon to be more) places for outsiders are keenly competed for via tests in English, maths and non-verbal reasoning, plus an interview and report. These applicants come mainly from local preps such as Downsend, Danes Hill, Cranmore and Homefield Prep and the process is described as more selective than local competition. 'We are looking for spark and creativity,' says head. At sixth form another 20 join, including overseas boarders. Applicants need 58 GCSE points or equivalent, with additional subject-specific criteria, plus interview and school report. International students sit papers in November in maths and non-verbal reasoning.

Exit: Between 10 and 20 per cent leave at 16+ for all the usual reasons – financial, they fancy a change or, increasingly, to the excellent local colleges such as Reigate College. At 18+, around 80 per cent to Russell Group. Popular destinations include Birmingham, Bath, Durham, Bristol and Exeter. Nottingham increasingly popular, as is York. Six to Oxbridge and six medics in 2021, plus three overseas – to McGill, Princeton and Trinity.

Latest results: In 2021, 89 per cent 9-7 at GCSE; 81 per cent A*/A at A level (95 per cent A*-B). In 2019 (the last year when exams took place), 83 per cent 9-7 at GCSE; 65 per cent A*/A at A level (86 per cent A*-B).

Teaching and learning: Stellar results at both GCSE and A level give the school the reputation as the best in the locality academically, although any suggestion of hothousing is quickly scorned. 'It's a clever child's school but doesn't feel intense or pressurised,' said one parent. Students report 'excellent support' from the teachers, as well as 'a good rapport – you feel respected.' School also praised for teaching the independence – 'I have very little to do with the school because the kids just get on with it, it's a brilliant skill that the school teaches them,' said one mother. Head was delighted when a students in a recent unscripted film raved about the fun involved in learning here – 'That's what we really want to hear, and that was even with the pandemic,' he exulted.

Head was delighted when students in a recent unscripted film raved about the fun involved in learning here – 'And that was even with the pandemic,' he exulted

Classes are small, the tutorial group system works well, and students we saw were motivated and well-prepped for lessons. Expressive too, frequently disagreeing in academic debate. In an English lesson on dystopian texts a sixth form girl was so insightful and eloquent we wondered if she was the teacher. Not much setting – 'We don't think pupils benefit from being pigeonholed and we know they learn better when there is more of a spread of intellectual capacity.' Broad curriculum, with sports studies and business studies recently added at GCSE. French, German, Spanish and Latin taught from year 9. History, geography, drama and art all popular at GCSE. All take 10 and all get first choice of subjects – 'We have resisted blocking the timetable to make students do a certain number of humanities, languages and creatives (a) because it would be difficult logistically and (b) that's not what we're about – we want students to tailor their choices towards their passions,' says head. Maths dazzles at all stages but chemistry teaching can be lazy, say students.

Not a school where you start off with four A levels, dropping one later on – all take three, except those taking further maths. Leaves room for EPQ and Free Minds programme, the latter providing seminar-style exposure to teachers' hobbyhorse subjects, eg Shakespeare's tragic comedies, the importance of 19th-century architecture, origins of the Middle East crisis, seven inventions that changed the world, DH Lawrence etc. If they're lucky they have them in the so-called James Bond room which boasts an entire wall of tellies via which different visuals can be shown simultaneously, as well as people from around the world joining remotely. The room is one of many magnificent learning spaces based in Main House. We have seen some sixth form centres in our time, but these sympathetically restored yet modern spaces are sensational.

Learning support and SEN: A team of three SEN teachers across the junior and senior schools supports a small number of students with mild SEN, mostly dyslexia and ASD. 'Both of my children have had one-to-ones and I feel confident the school keeps a close eye on them, which is very reassuring as I don't want them to struggle. All included in the fees too,' said a parent. However, this isn't the place for more than a minor level of need, and one parent added, 'If you had really high expectations of every teacher understanding exactly how your child should be supported I think you'd probably be disappointed, but overall it's good and better still if your child has already found their own coping mechanisms.' Specialist EAL teacher visits three times a week to support mainly the international boarders.

The arts and extracurricular: DofE is massive – only four year 9s didn't do bronze this year, and lots go on to silver, then gold. CCF (army and RAF) small by comparison with a contingent of around 100 but again it's available from year 9, and impressively the head himself is undergoing training. Over 90 clubs and societies post-Covid, when head insists they've been 'more important than ever because the students are passionate about doing things they've missed'. Everything from Minecraft to debating (the latter is big and getting bigger) and from philosophy to eco society.

We've lost count of the number of schools that make do with some musty old hall as their musical performance space. Not so here, where the purpose-built music block contains its own professional acoustic concert hall (where we persuaded our grade 8 pianist tour guide to play for us on the Steinway grand – a real treat, we can tell you). The department also contains recording studio, live room for band practice, Mac suite, practice rooms galore and music classrooms. Orchestras, choirs, ensembles – always plenty going on, including collaborations with the other City of London schools and the chance to play at venues such as Milton Court and St John's Smith Square. But one parent commented, 'My children play instruments but don't participate in any groups – I'd like to see more encouragement there.'

Drama takes place in Ferndale Theatre, where we watched GCSE students immersed in small play practice – stirring stuff and in the spirit of a true fourth wall, they seemed completely oblivious to us. 'Teaching is really high class, as are the facilities and opportunities for light and sound,'

said a student. There's even a club for special effects. 'I went to see Alice in Wonderland and it blew me away – they do brilliant Shakespeare too,' said a parent. Lord of the Flies recently performed in the new outdoor classroom. Regular trips including to Edinburgh Fringe.

Large, double-storey art department is industrious, varied and inclusive. Textiles, ceramics, painting – you name it, there's an example or 10 displayed around the school. 'We work to their strengths,' we were told, and strengths they most certainly have. Over in DT, students were watching a live streamed annual lecture from London that in non-Covid times they'd normally attend. Glass cabinets are packed with metal, wood and plastic exhibits of varying usefulness, though the first prize must go to the beautiful pair of slatted chairs that slot inside each other, having been made from equipment the DT teacher bought from 'another school that didn't embrace it'.

Sport: Every parent we spoke to described sport as the school's weak point. 'The coaching could be better', 'they're not massively successful' and 'they seem a bit disorganised with sport – for example, putting students into an athletics day with no build up training,' were among common grumbles. On the positive side, 'there is plenty of opportunity to represent your school', 'lots of variety including fencing, squash and Pilates' and 'fantastic facilities including the beautiful swimming pool'. Students thought it all a bit harsh – 'They really encourage you in sport and the teaching is strong, although I agree there are not as many elite young sportspeople as at some other local schools,' said one; another told us, 'It is true we lose a lot, I'm not sure why that is.' School responded by sending us a long list of near wins (but no first place spots), as well as country and regional representation among individual students. Boys do rugby, football and cricket and have the option of hockey and football. Girls do hockey, netball, tennis and cricket. Basketball, badminton, squash, cross-country and table tennis also available at a competitive level. Excellent facilities include hockey Astro, magnificent new pool, vast pitches and cracking gym and fitness suite. Ski trips highly rated by students.

Boarding: The school was founded to care for orphans, so boarding is part of the original statute and must be provided, these days to a maximum of 30 boys and 30 girls. Around 70 per cent are full boarders (mostly international, until recently hailing almost exclusively from China and Hong Kong but now also from eg Russia, Nigeria and Kaszakhstan), the rest weekly and the odd few flexi ('where you have to bring your own duvet, which can be a bit annoying,' according to a parent).

The floor-to-ceiling glass entrance doors of the centrally located contemporary boarding house open straight into a manned reception area and open-plan IKEA showroom – sorry, common room. More private (still IKEA-like) spaces upstairs where girls' and boys' rooms are at opposite ends of the corridors. 'That's usually where you'll find me, I love cooking,' said a pupil when we passed the well-equipped kitchen space. A new creative hub has been set up with keyboard, paints etc. Students share two to a room until the sixth form, when they get a single. Bedrooms tidy to the point of military precision ('they remind us it's a life skill'), but don't lack personality and one girl's room looked interior designed. Just two ensuites (the golden tickets?) but multiple and spotless bathrooms. Laundry facilities good – 'I prefer to do my own although you don't have to,' said one sixth form boarder, music to the ears of most parents.

Bedrooms tidy to the point of military precision ('they remind us it's a life skill'), but don't lack personality and one girl's room looked interior designed

Weekend activities include ice skating, cinema and for shopping and – these must be a first – Sainsburys and the local service station, both surprisingly popular! Massive noticeboard and display of leaflets dedicated to mental health. Two live-in staff, supported by a day matron and other assistants, who have succeeded in integrating boarders with day pupils, not always the case in the past.

Ethos and heritage: The second of the three City of London schools to be created, Freemen's opened its doors in 1854 with a remit to educate 'orphans of the Freemen of the City of London'. Housed originally in Brixton, it could accommodate up to 65 boys and 35 girls aged 7 to 15. So whereas many schools have added on boarders, girls and junior-aged children in order to survive economically, Freemen's welcomed them all from the off. In 1924, the school relocated to the 57-acre Ashtead Park estate, when fee-paying boys started to also be admitted, then fee-paying girls from 1933.

Entrance is so unremarkable that we wondered if we'd taken the tradesmen's route by mistake. It belies the space (and, in the case of Main House, the beauty) within. Most of the teaching areas are in modern buildings in a fairly tightly packed campus, with the Haywood Centre the hub of the school. Junior school also central, rather than tucked away, with year 7s and 8s (still officially juniors) making especially good use of senior facilities – all helps with seamless transition. No danger of anyone feeling cramped, though – there is space and green fields in abundance, stretching far into the distance. And the main house, built in the 17th century and given the Bonomi treatment in the 18th, is flanked by Palladian balustrade, topiary, manicured lawns and is simply gorgeous – what lucky sixth formers getting the whole thing to themselves, orangery and all. 'It was all set up for dorms when I joined but I said, "Why would you only want 30 people to experience this?"' said head, who set to work on a restoration bonanza. Junior school and dining hall next on the list for ambitious development.

Uniform more sensible and smart than posh, with sixth form boys still wearing school ties. Food good – we had a lovely curry – plus there's a tuckshop in a red converted bus.

Pastoral care, inclusivity and discipline: Latest remembrance service demonstrated just how supportive, reflective and respectful these pupils are – almost complete silence throughout and smiles, pats on backs and whispers of 'don't worry' to those feeling nervous about laying wreaths. 'Friendly' was the single most uttered word used to describe the school by students, while parents report that their offspring are 'happy'. 'Kind' and 'non-judgemental', we also heard, with 'support on tap'. 'My daughter suffered from extreme anxiety and they have been brilliant with her – access to the counsellor whenever she wants and all staff know to look out for her but not draw attention to it, and if she can't handle school one day they're okay with that,' was a particularly heartfelt testament we heard. Another told us how 'well the teachers understand the children'. Tutor system helps, as does the fact that most teachers teach years 7 and 8. House system helps build positive relationships across the school.

Despite the many grumbles we heard about student voice – 'They only ever get past consideration stage most of the time and they even vetoed sanitary products in the toilets for ages,' said one student – everyone agrees the head acted quickly when students told him the school was stuffy on the topics of sex, sexuality and consent. He was equally quick to react to a mention on Everyone's Invited – 'We went straight to pupils and surveyed key year groups.' Was all over Black Lives Matter too, so far addressing aspects of the curriculum and reading material in the library. 'When I walked into the kitchen recently and someone said, "Happy Diwali!" I felt that was a real breakthrough,' says head.

Rules are clear, but watch this space regarding uniform and haircuts: 'In all honesty, I couldn't care less if boys have their ears pierced and I'd rather nobody wore a tie – I hate wearing one myself,' admits head, who is soon to meet SLT to gauge other views. No permanent exclusions recently, although there are usually a couple of temporary ones a year; generally the school prefers a more restorative rationale to discipline.

No danger of anyone feeling cramped, though – there is space and green fields in abundance, stretching far into the distance. The 17th century main house is flanked by Palladian balustrades, topiary, manicured lawns and is simply gorgeous

Pupils and parents: Pupils are sparky, polite and easy company. 'I just had a load of them over for a party and what a cracking bunch of kids – polite, nice and really able to communicate with adults,' lauded one parent. Parents mainly professional – finance, doctors, lawyers through to entrepreneurs – but from a range of backgrounds, not all affluent. Catchment widening, now reaching up to Guildford, Reigate, Dorking and up into Wimbledon and Kingston, with a school bus service (and a shuttle bus from Ashtead station) much appreciated. Has led to greater ethnic diversity, though this is still rural Surrey. 'Some of the parents are helicopter-esque and slightly exhausting – inevitable at an academic school, perhaps – but the majority are sensible,' reckoned one parent. 'Communications could be better,' was a common gripe, 'you email the school and it goes into a void.'

Money matters: Fees are competitive alongside other comparable schools in the area. Academic and music awards at 13+ and sixth form available to current pupils and incomers. Means-tested bursary awards, sponsored by the City livery companies.

The last word: A down-to-earth, friendly school that's comfortable in its own skin rather than relentlessly trying to show off its most polished side – and is all the better for it. Just the ticket for parents after a high-quality, stress-free route for their academically bright sons and daughters from age 7 right through to 18. Almost unique around here.

Cobham Hall

18

Cobham, Brewers Road, Gravesend, Kent DA12 3BL

01474 823371 | admissions@cobhamhall.com | www.cobhamhall.com

Ages: 11–18

Pupils: 136; sixth form: 24; Boarders: 32 full, 5 weekly/flexi

Fees: Day £20,412 – £24,738; Boarding £30,837 – £38,493 pa

Headmistress: Since September 2020, Wendy Barrett. Previously deputy headmistress for three years, having originally worked her way up from part-time maths teacher when her daughter was a tot. Following her BSc in maths and physics from Royal Holloway College, she initially trained as an engineer and worked for Thorn EMI Instruments in Dover, Kent, eventually specialising in sales and marketing, then moved to the DTI then the Royal Fellowship of Engineering as a manufacturing engineer. After a career break, she retrained as a teacher (PGCE in secondary maths education from Canterbury Christchurch), teaching both maths and physics. Held both academic and pastoral roles at Cobham, including as a Round Square representative, which involved taking girls on Round Square trips to South Africa, Botswana, Australia, Europe and the USA.

Entrance: Entry into years 7, 8, 9, 10 and sixth form via tests in English and maths and an interview with the headteacher in the autumn before entry. International students can either take the school's own tests or apply via UKiset. A taster afternoon and sleepover can be arranged at any time and parents are also given the opportunity to get to know each other. Main feeder schools are Steephill and St Joseph's at Gravesend, Pointers in Blackheath and south-east London preps and local state primaries – the school runs a minibus service as far as Sevenoaks.

Some 10-20 join from abroad for the increasingly popular one-year pre-A level course.

Exit: Around a third to half leaves after GCSEs, mainly to larger co-ed schools, local grammars and sixth form colleges. For those who stay on for the sixth form, great trouble is taken to choose a course and university that is right for each girl. Around a fifth to Russell Group universities; art foundation and business courses popular as are eg criminology and biomedical sciences. Growing expertise in helping girls with the process of applying to foreign universities including Australia and the US – the school is able to help with SATs. Odd few overseas and to Oxbridge, as well as medics.

Latest results: In 2021, 55 per cent 9-7 at GCSE; 40 per cent A*/A at A level (67 per cent A*-B). In 2019 (the last year when exams took place), 33 per cent 9-7 at GCSE; IB average point score of 33.

Teaching and learning: The IB was introduced in 2009 and A levels phased out at the same time: however, this has now been reversed. The results reflect the wide range of abilities within the school. All girls take at least eight GCSEs and most do 10. Girls setted in maths, English and science from year 7 and sometimes in other subjects depending on the size of the year group. 'Girls generally do better than expected,' says the school. Class sizes up to 20 in the lower years with an average of 12 and no more than 12 per class (and some much smaller) in sixth form. One parent said that she was concerned about the small classes before her daughter started but added, 'the brightest girls are stretched and encouraged.' The teachers are a 'good combination of the homely and the vibrant and dynamic' – about half are male.

French, Spanish, German and Latin offered at GCSE and A level. Science is popular and most take three separate sciences at GCSE although dual award is available – 'Girls are braver about sciences in a single-sex school.' Computer science, film studies, drama and PE are all A level options. The small size of the school means that they can be 'reactive to demand and flexible with the timetable'.

Cobham offers a pre-A level course and girls joining this for the year have the option of sitting up to five GCSEs. Many join for only one or two terms to brush up their English or as preparation for the sixth form at Cobham. They are taught separately in most subjects but may join the school's GCSE students for sport. They live in Main Hall with the other GCSE students.

About 60 girls need help with English and the EFL programme is tailored for each girl. Girls joining in years 10 and 12 need good English and will generally study the English B qualification

(English for non-native speakers). The school is a registered centre for ESOL exams but not IELTS.

Girls offered careers advice from early on: via PSHE in the lower years and are then help with interview technique before work experience in year 10. They take part in the Big Business Pitch, a two-day event where girls learn about starting and marketing their own business. Year 12s attend a higher education fair and an Oxbridge conference. Plenty of help with personal statement and university choices. The school also belongs to the ISCO which, for a fee, offers girls individual interviews and career profiling until the age of 23 – most sign up to this.

Learning support and SEN: The school is CReSTeD registered – about 20 need some sort of learning support. Much emphasis on inclusivity; girls offered one-to-one support to develop strategies and there is good support for teachers in the classroom to enable them to get the best out of students. Occasionally have to turn a girl away if the school feels they cannot meet her needs.

The arts and extracurricular: Impressive artwork displayed around the school reflects the internationalism of the pupils. Photography popular and school has its own darkroom as well as a suite of Apple Macs for digital work. One photography student invited to exhibit at the Royal Academy. Ceramics and sculpture particularly dynamic under the tutelage of the 'legendary clay man'.

Sixth form boarders can eat breakfast and cook supper in their houses – they have a weekly visit to supermarket and are taught about food hygiene

The school has a fully equipped drama studio, but the magnificent Gilt Hall is often used for productions and everyone has to take part in the inter-house drama competitions. One whole-school play a year and girls do well in LAMDA exams.

The school fosters a spirit of adventure and leadership – girls encouraged to take assemblies and stand up in public, and about 20-30 attend the Model United Nations each year. Trips and expeditions all over the world as part of the Round Square – conferences and exchanges, usually for three to four weeks but sometimes for a whole term, and involvement in international projects working with students from other Round Square schools.

Duke of Edinburgh compulsory in year 9 – most do bronze and a good number do silver, some start gold at school but complete it at university.

Ambitious head of music who previously worked in Barbados 'pushes the boundaries and has got the choirs going'. The school has links with Rochester Choral Society and the chamber choir has recently returned from a trip to Poland. About half the girls take individual music lessons in the music wing with nine practice rooms, a recording studio and digital music suite. 'It's a small, lively department – not that many do music, but those who do are very good and into it,' according to one girl.

Sport: Sport has come on by leaps and bounds in recent years; 'it was at the egg and spoon race stage when I arrived,' said the previous head. 'Now we have girls trialling for the England U18 hockey team, the Kent County Schools show jumping champion, a girl in the South of England eventing team, finalists in the National Biathlon Championships and an Elder (old girl) headed for Rio with the modern pentathlon team' (she won the event in Tokyo). Good links with local hockey club – some county hockey and netball players and a girl training with the girls' U16 West Ham football team. All girls up until year 11 have to take part in team sports two or three times a week and sixth form have to take some exercise – zumba and yoga are popular. Indoor heated swimming pool with swimming coaching twice a week.

Boarding: About 50 per cent board, mostly full with a few weekly and flexi boarders – school is very accommodating but likes 24 hours' notice unless there is an emergency, and charges accordingly. The younger girls sleep in Main Hall in bright light dorms of two to five. Two sixth form houses – Bligh and Brooke – with single and double rooms, many ensuite. All boarding houses have kitchens and common rooms with large televisions.

Sixth form boarders can eat breakfast and cook supper in their houses – they have a weekly visit to supermarket and are taught about food hygiene. 'We have a lot of fun in the boarding houses and boarding makes you learn how to rub along with people,' said one girl. Girls have genuine friends in different year groups and it really does seem to be a 'home from home'.

No Saturday school, but day girls have to come in on some Saturdays for activities, project work, and some school trips. 'My daughter sometimes asks to stay in for the weekend as the boarders have such fun, especially if there is a trip to Bluewater shopping centre,' said a mother. Cookery club runs on Saturdays: girls cook a meal and eat together in the evening

Ethos and heritage: The school is housed in a Grade I listed Tudor mansion complete with turrets and chimneys and set in 150 acres of parkland between Gravesend and Rochester, about 30 miles from London and 10 minutes from Ebbsfleet station, with Eurostar connections to mainland Europe. Built for the 10th Baron Cobham in the 16th century and sold to the earls of Darnley in the 18th, it remained their family home until 1957. Often used as a film set, including for the Hetty Feather BBC series by Jacqueline Wilson and feature film Tulip Fever, as well as weddings and conferences. The school was opened in 1962 by Mrs Bee Mansell as an international boarding school for girls where they could enjoy the same education as boys. Cobham joined the Round Square in the early 1970s and was the first girls' school to do so. The name comes from the Round Square building at Gordonstoun, one of the original member schools where the first RS conference took place in 1967. Everyone given a map on arrival but girls quickly get used to their stunning surroundings – the ornate fireplaces and plasterwork ceilings and the glorious Gilt Hall complete with an 18th-century organ soon get taken for granted.

Girls quickly get used to their stunning surroundings – the ornate fireplaces and plasterwork ceilings and the glorious Gilt Hall soon get taken for granted

Elders, as the old girls are known at Cobham, are hugely loyal to the school and include Mishal Husain, news presenter, Olivia Graham, bishop of Reading, journalist Alex Crawford, jewellery designer Francesca Amfitheatrof, Princess Antonia, Duchess of Wellington and Kate French, who won individual gold in the modern pentathlon at Tokyo.

Pastoral care, inclusivity and discipline: The Round Square philosophy, 'there is more to you than you think' and 'education through experience', underpins everything the school does. 'It is only when girls step out of their comfort zone that they truly discover themselves.' Girls given a lot of autonomy and encouraged to use opportunities and 'they seem genuinely to care about the Round Square programme,' said one mother. 'Girls want to do well and we put so much pressure on ourselves – it is important to make time for yourself,' said our guide. Girls are trained and expected to take part in the running of the school and all staff and girls vote for the Guardian (head girl).

Older girls very supportive of younger ones and everyone is given a 'big sister' when they arrive; the mixed-age tutor groups in each house mean there is good mixing between year groups. 'Everyone is very kind and my daughter and I both felt part of the Cobham family from the start,' said a mother. Years 7-11 have their own common rooms with kitchens, which encourages mixing between day girls and boarders. Weekly 'family lunch' when girls sit in tutor groups and practise their conversation skills. Bullying rare but nipped in the bud and restorative justice applied. Automatic suspension for drugs or alcohol – not that it is an issue here – and repeat offenders would be asked to leave.

Community service involves anything from visiting old people's homes and collecting food for food banks to helping out in local primary schools and youth clubs. There is a Christian Union group within the school and those of other faiths are encouraged to worship locally – there is a Sikh temple, mosque and synagogue nearby. Good communication between staff means any problems are picked up quickly

Pupils and parents: About 40 per cent of pupils are foreign nationals, rising to about 60 per cent in the sixth form, with increasing numbers of Europeans. No one nationality dominates; 'girls really do mix' and integration taken seriously – no two girls of the same nationality are allowed to share a bedroom and there are 'small sanctions, like kitchen duty, if you are caught speaking your native language during the day,' said our guide. Day girls come from as far afield as south-east London. The school turns out girls who are 'confident and worldly-wise, who are keen to get involved and tend to be quite adventurous. The girls don't grow up too quickly and there is no need to yank up your skirt or slap on the make-up as no one is going to see ...They are more likely to be seen chatting in Lady Darnley's garden or swinging on "the branch".' 'Turns out confident and beautifully eloquent girls,' said one mother. The girls all see themselves as global citizens and have no fear of travel – 'The Round Square network means they have friends all over the world,' said a parent.

Money matters: Art, drama, music, sport and Round Square scholarships by application, and general (academic) scholarship by invitation only – identified through the entrance assessments. Means-tested bursaries are available for up to 100 per cent of fees.

The last word: A small, truly international school which turns out compassionate and adventurous global citizens.

Cottesmore School

Buchan Hill, Pease Pottage, West Sussex RH11 9AU

01293 520648 | office@cottesmoreschool.com | www.cottesmoreschool.com

Ages: 4-13

Pupils: 200 (121 boys; 79 girls); Boarders: 108 full (from 8 years)

Fees: Day: £10,080 – £18,870; Boarding: £28,650 – £31,650 pa

Headmaster: Since 2008, Tom Rogerson, married to Lottie, with two small sons, Wilf and Bear. Cottesmore runs in the family (grandad and dad were heads before him) – 'I've been quietly planning to take over since I was 17,' said the head. Routed via other schools (Ludgrove, Eaton House and Broomwood); his dad wouldn't let him take the headship too early. Quite right, dad.

Articulate and thoughtful, focuses on each pupil and knows them all – they chatter away happily with him. A strong team with Lottie, who provides ballast for the head's lively energy.

Parents like him – 'He's a warm guy, easy to talk to, and always there when I pick up and drop off from exeats.' Another: 'A school derives its culture from the head – and I like its culture. It places emphasis on traditional Christian values: kindness, courtesy, honour and fair play.'

Entrance: Pre-prep: taster day, during which prospective pupils will do a piece of work assessing English and maths. Prep: English and maths tests, interview (children need to be 'interested and interesting') and head's report from previous school. UKiset test for non-English speakers.

Exit: To many of the more magnificent public schools: Eton, Downe House, Harrow, Cheltenham Ladies', Radley, Benenden, Winchester, Wellington, Marlborough, Charterhouse, St Edwards.

Our view: Approach the school past towering rhododendrons, lawns mown to velvety smoothness, golf flags, the fragrance of flowers and hedges. Cottesmore is a stately Victorian pile – enter through the heavy wooden door carved with mischievous sprites. Wood-panelled walls, stately hall with minstrels' gallery; fishing rods leaning casually against the wall in a corridor. Things here are orderly, but it's not an institutional tidiness: there's a feeling of a home, where places for things arise organically and become established through habit.

Grounds which beg to be played in: climbable trees everywhere, from 'the monkeys' – a cave of under rhododendron/tree branches – to the hollow oak: climb its ancient trunk in a circular direction (teacher present, and only up to a certain height). Bamboo for forts and den making – so popular here that it occasionally has official activity status. A parent said to his wife of their son, who had fallen out of a tree and was limping towards them on the last exeat – 'He's having a childhood and that's wonderful.'

Children here are bubbling, confident and eager, so keen to tell us about their school that we hardly needed to ask questions

Children here are bubbling, confident and eager, so keen to tell us about their school that we hardly needed to ask questions. They happily fill their own skin: we've rarely met a group of children so content to be themselves. Some bounced up to say hello and give their views; easily said, in front of their head, what they didn't like about school (the chairs are too low and they want new showers).

We also met quieter introverts, busy with the library and their model railway in the basement. They've started their own after-supper library lecture series ('tea' was exceedingly popular). Not so likely to bubble eagerly about the things they love, but no hesitation in expressing their views, and total confidence in their value. Geekiness is certainly not frowned upon – 'They're lauded for loving the library,' said Lottie.

The head said, 'We're a family school,' then chuckled; whether this is a good thing clearly depends on how dysfunctional the family. Certainly the warmth and care seen here must exceed what many families experience at Christmas. ('Beautifully small,' said a mum.)

Broad church here – which means chapel isn't optional. Cultural Christianity, whose values informally underpin the community, but 'we go about it quietly'.

An academically rigorous school – 'rigour balanced with fun,' said the head. A flamboyant fashion-designer-to-be is celebrated, but 'he has to be good at maths by the time he leaves'. Lack of endeavour here would be a problem – 'that's not an option'.

In this small school, there are no separate boarding houses: everyone just troops upstairs to bed, the matron's flat situated between the boys' and girls' dorms

'Not a pressure cooker,' said a parent who has experienced the hothouse of London preps, '[and] notches up in balanced and useful lives.'

Small classes, no bigger than 14. Single form entry until year 4, then double form entry, finally splitting in three in the final year. Pupils are streamed (but not labelled) and set within those streams. This school does extremely well at enthusing its pupils: they showed a keen interest in Latin, eagerly pointing out Latin in the roots of words and telling us their favourite myths.

Maths lessons have been transformed by new IT (iPads, Chromebooks and a Raspberry Pi). Pupils were whizzing through tables on iPads – less time marking means more time teaching; or 'connecting', as the head likes to say. Excelling at maths is something this school particularly prides itself on: the head has increased the number of maths teachers and seen CE scores soar.

A geography teacher was enthusiastically making geography pertinent to the real world: 'What are the pros and cons of building a Tesco in the Cottesmore grounds?' (The head's smile became a little fixed at this point…)

Learning support helps students who have mild dyslexia, dyspraxia and dyscalculia, also those with speech and language difficulties. Ten to 20 per cent of pupils receive one-to-one help, and in-class assistance (charged as an extra). The fact a child has SEN doesn't make any difference to attainment here, says the head.

Behind a glass-panelled door is pre-prep, the colour and liveliness evident through the glass panels. Coloured cellophane hung from the ceiling in strips – 'we're doing under the sea at the moment'. Around 10 per class, children seated at round tables, doors in each class opening onto the lawn: a much more relaxed, crazy colour atmosphere than on the other side of the door, but a similarly high standard evident from the written work in displays. A parent told us that Cottesmore was the only school they visited which was more interested in the child than the parents: Lottie got right down to her daughter's level – 'so, do you like spiders?' And off they went to find one.

A large array of sports on offer: 33, including all the usual major sports, as well as the less usual: archery, shooting, billiards and paddleboarding. Pupils of all abilities play in matches, and even the C and D teams play a good number of fixtures. They win plenty of matches and get plenty of support – Danish housekeeping team take great joy in waving their pompoms in support of the third XI. 'It is competitive – they care a lot for sport, but they know they have all types, and encourage and get the best out of everyone.'

Houses here are called sets, and there's plenty of friendly inter-set competition. A parent, commenting on the set dash, said, 'The whole school cheer each other, particularly the useless ones… To be very kind is to be very Cottesmore,' he added.

Plenty of clubs, from real tennis to fishing for carp in the pond – 'The film club is just the best,' said one girl. Chess compulsory for two years – it's taken very seriously here (under-11 girls champs).

Music is strong, with 80-90 per cent learning instruments; there are three choirs, including the chapel choir, which often tours abroad. The head of music is also head of drama, so every play tends to be a musical, said a parent: Oliver! was described by another parent as 'excellent – my quite shy son volunteered for it…'

Each class sends a rep to the school council and food committee – a food committee board in a classroom simply stated 'BETTER BURGER'; but they don't have much to complain about: they've won awards for their food, which a parent described as 'brilliant'.

The children's happiness is testament to how well they are cared for – and indeed the school Happiness Charter is on the wall of every room. A parent described the school as 'gentle'; they chose Cottesmore for its rounded, happy pupils and nurturing environment. Easy for pupils to speak to staff here – they're all out in the hall at break time accompanied by their coffee trolley.

Certainly the best mannered children we've met at a prep, leaping to their feet if we so much as glanced over, opening doors, shaking hands. Watching the children, it seemed evident that the respectful environment influences how they treat each other.

Time-out area on a wooden chest in front of the study – pupils who've been a bit rowdy perch there until they've calmed down. A clear bullying policy: the one incident a parent described to us was 'clamped down on quickly'.

Pupils from London, home counties, and abroad, including expats and diplomats (about a third of boarders from overseas).

Boarding: Everyone in the prep has a bed and boards to some extent: around 80 per cent full time, everyone else up to four nights a week (must stick to chosen nights). In this small school, there are no separate boarding houses: everyone just troops upstairs to bed, the matron's flat situated between the boys' and girls' dorms.

Large dormitories for eight, three per room for older pupils, the usual is six. Pupils wake to music – the latest charts.

'Palatial since my day,' said a parent; but actually they're mid-renovation – decoration of some rooms is a bit tired. 'It's all going,' said the head briskly, although the parents we spoke to were happy with it as it is.

Year groups take it in turn to occupy the drawing room in evenings (music, piano, chess, Wii dance), other year groups spilling out into hall, library and ICT room, playing ping pong or snooker. Children here flow everywhere – no feeling of being penned in to a particular area.

Lots of activities at the weekends: Saturday morning school, then matches; trips on Sundays – children talked with great joy of a trip to Brighton Pier, when older pupils were allowed to go off in groups of four, and told us how much they love the independence – 'At my last school they never stopped watching us,' said one, impatiently. 'Here, they trust us.'

The last word: A parent from London told us he looked at 20 prep schools, and Cottesmore had the best combination of options one could get: 'A* in all the things that really matter in life.'

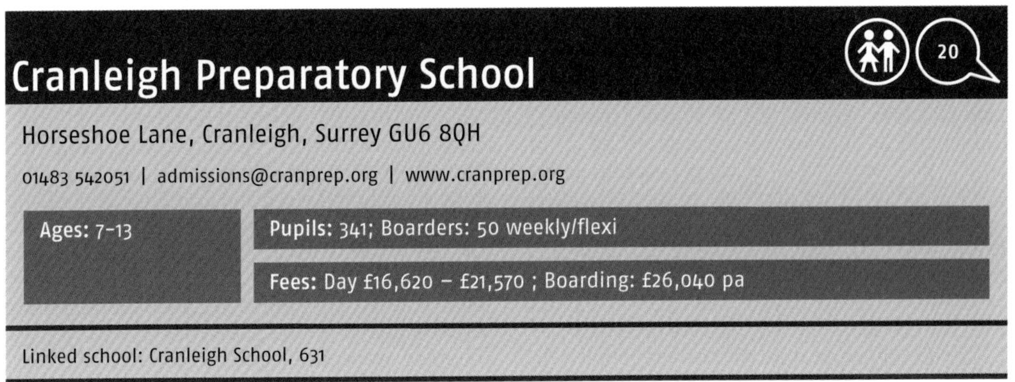

Cranleigh Preparatory School

Horseshoe Lane, Cranleigh, Surrey GU6 8QH

01483 542051 | admissions@cranprep.org | www.cranprep.org

Ages: 7-13

Pupils: 341; Boarders: 50 weekly/flexi

Fees: Day £16,620 – £21,570 ; Boarding: £26,040 pa

Linked school: Cranleigh School, 631

Headmaster: Since September 2018, Neil Brooks BA QTS (early 50s). Read geography and PE at Warwick University. Unusually (to say the least) for a head, he spent his 20s as a 'soldier' – a British army officer serving in an airborne unit in Northern Ireland and Bosnia. Plunged into the world of education by becoming a housemaster, and then headmaster for eight years, at Cothill House. He and his wife then embarked on an Elysian project to reopen the recently shuttered Old Malthouse Prep in Dorset as a venue for science courses. Courses and boarding experiences were designed for inner-London children, in affiliation with the Natural History Museum and London's Pimlico Academy. Most recently, had a spell at Fulham Prep where he was hired on the quixotic errand of launching a senior school. Spent two years on the project before being snapped up by Cranleigh. An outdoor education enthusiast, he spends much time running and cycling.

Emanates competence, experience, calm. Thoroughly direct and down to earth, with an engaging, self-deprecating sense of humour.

Entrance: Main entry point is at 7+. The assessment day consists of an informal group interview, English papers in comprehension and creative writing, a maths paper and 'fun team building activities'. Parents promise us it's nothing to stress over. Around 38-45 boys and girls enter at this stage. Most come from independent schools like Glenesk, Duke of Kent, Longacre, St Hilary's and Belmont, plus local infant and primary schools like Ewhurst, Wonersh & Shamley Green, Shere and Peaslake. Some 10-15 pupils join at 11+, many from London preps, and here the process is more competitive. These late applicants sit the ISEB pretest in year 6 and attend a holistic review day. Strong sibling policy: this is very much a family school.

Exit: Vast majority, some 85 per cent, move 'across the road' (an oft-used phrase here) to Cranleigh School, many with scholarships. CE taken in core subjects with school's own tests in the humanities. However, promotion isn't (quite) guaranteed, and children aiming for other schools are given equal support and advice ('but they certainly push the senior school,' noted a parent wryly). Those who move go on to a wide range of public schools including Wellington College, Charterhouse, Millfield, St Catherine's Bramley, Prior's Field.

Our view: A flourishing school with two forms entering year 3, expanding to five forms by year 8. Specialist teachers from day one for French and science. Spanish has been introduced in the top two years, and there are murmurs of Mandarin following suit. Every child in year 8 now has a school-issued iPad; year 7 will come on line next. Wide ability range but, as usual with trad preps, we found some parental grumbles about the scholarship stream separating children for the last two year. Proto-scholars have all lessons together and, as a by-product, can end up socially separated from former friendships (school points out that scholars have all games sessions and breaks with the rest of the school). 'It's unnecessary,' the parent of a child who is now 'way ahead' of his peers at his senior school told us. 'They get them so far ahead, they could polish off a couple of GCSEs – the pump is primed too early.' Long days ending at 5.45pm after two preps or an optional activity; bit earlier on Wednesdays (school day formally ends at 4.35pm; the prep sessions and activities are optional).

Good SEN support for mainstream pupils who do not require specialist assistance: 55 children currently receive this additional help, mainly for dyslexia and dyspraxia. Parents we spoke to heaped praise on the support their children received. Access ramps and accessible toilet facilities mean the school can cater for children with mobility issues. The new buildings are equipped with lifts.

Reading and literature boosted by Cranleigh's very own Awesome Book Awards, an annual prize that honours the best new fiction for young readers aged 7-10. Thousands of pupils from schools across the south-east read the five books on the shortlist and vote for their favourite. Winner is announced at a celebration at the senior school and the winner becomes the school's 'Reading Patron' for the year: Awesome!

Sport sits firmly at the heart of education here. It's timetabled every day, with matches midweek and on alternate Saturdays – all levels. 'It's the reason we moved our daughter here,' said the parent of a girl attending one of the area's many girls' schools. Head has tipped the balance a smidge towards the arts, and perhaps a scintilla away from sport, but the latter's heft continues to be felt. Aims to marry the goals of 'sport for all' (encouraging the duffers) with 'competitive excellence' (pushing the natural athletes). Lots of minor sports, like fencing, judo, swimming and fives, are a welcome alternative for children who don't excel at team games. The senior school's equestrian centre looks after keen riders, and a few children keep their own horses or ponies at the school. Prep shares all the senior school's sports coaches, pitches and its indoor swimming pool.

Although day pupils hugely outnumber boarders, the daily routine of late finishing, prep at school and Saturday school on alternate weeks permeates the ethos

Annual stage performances for each year group include nativity, panto, musical and Shakespeare. Dance part of the curriculum years 3-5. DT in lovely new building from year 5; food tech too. Music is particularly strong, and musicians benefit from a programme called Cranleigh Music 7-18 through which music teachers work at both Cranleigh Prep and Cranleigh School and the most able musicians play in ensembles across the age range. Around a third of children learn an instrument. The art room is stuffed full of current projects by pupils of all ages, including some really unusual ceramics, textiles and sculptures. Talented artists could find the perfect niche here.

Lunchtime has been extended and now includes a 'protected' half hour for enrichment activities like orchestra and choir, so children aren't rushing off mid-chew or missing out on play and social time with their peers. Middle and upper school children have optional 'priority time' activities at the end of the school day, which include hobby-based activities such as Airfix modelling, brain games, chess, crafts, family history, patchwork and stone masonry.

Pastoral care is 'as important as what we do academically,' says the head. Kindness valued above all things. Some years ago the school was occasionally faulted for not always handling bullying with sufficient vigour. Children accused of bullying received understanding and rehabilitation, when parents were really looking for an iron fist. We found no complaints from parents on this score now, and nary an iron fist in sight! Mobile phones are not allowed, and the head pleads guilty to being 'slightly old fashioned'. One of the advantages of having a well-seasoned head is he can take the long view. He worries about children as young as 10 or 11 suffering from anxiety: 'It never used to be the case.' The school runs lectures on mental health for parents and children. Wants the prep to be a place where children can be children, and where play is valued ('not always easy in materialistic Surrey,' he murmurs).

Not what you might call an international or multicultural melting pot; the school roll included zero children of expats or of overseas nationals at the time of our visit, though one child was receiving EAL support.

The great outdoors is what defines Cranleigh: acres of grassy pitches, Astro, tennis courts and netball courts. Lovely play area for the youngest Cranleighans. The school even has its own little woods: the Copse. The buildings are a mix of Edwardian and a hotch-potch of newer. The glass-and-wood Townsend building was inspired by African game lodges (previous head grew up in Kenya) complete with viewing deck overlooking the cricket pitch. The senior school across the road dominates the views, keeping that future option ever in mind.

Boarding: Smallish numbers of boarders, especially under age 11. The school is always fanning the boarding embers, but continues to attract take-up of around 15 per cent (though this percentage is now growing rapidly). Increasingly popular with south London families who find the weekly option handy indeed. Big plans to refurbish boarding accommodation have been stalled by Covid. Super-flexi boarding means children can board from one night a week up to five (no boarding offered on weekends) or even on an odd night when parents will be out or away. The head calls it 'a gentle introduction to boarding rather than Cothill-type full-on boarding'. Two matrons are always on hand. Although day pupils hugely outnumber boarders, the daily routine of late finishing, prep at school and Saturday school on alternate weeks permeates the ethos.

Money matters: A few scholarship awards are given to exceptional candidates at 11 for academic, music and sport, nothing earlier. Scholarship winners may apply for means-tested bursaries. Sibling discounts are available for third and subsequent siblings.

The last word: A traditional co-ed prep with an outdoorsy atmosphere radiating space and freedom. Strong links to its senior school. A good choice for a broad education, less academically pressured than many others and with plenty of learning support for those who need it. A school for children firing on all cylinders and keen to get stuck in: it's all here.

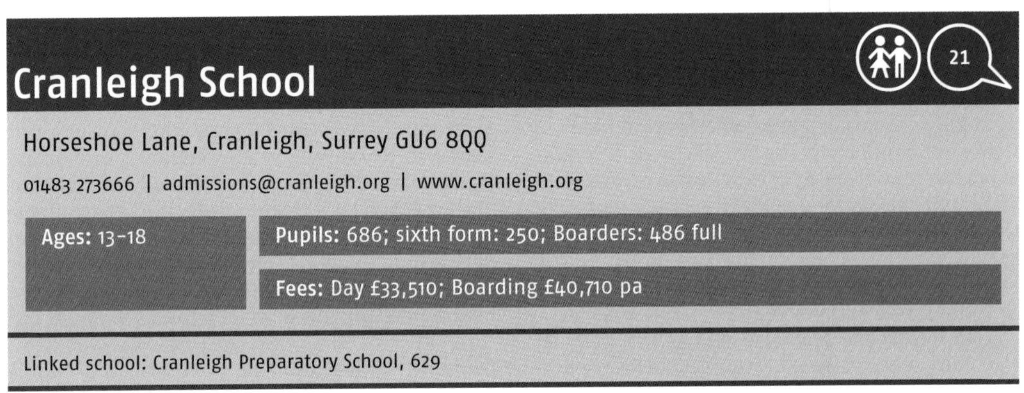

Cranleigh School

21

Horseshoe Lane, Cranleigh, Surrey GU6 8QQ

01483 273666 | admissions@cranleigh.org | www.cranleigh.org

Ages: 13-18

Pupils: 686; sixth form: 250; Boarders: 486 full

Fees: Day £33,510; Boarding £40,710 pa

Linked school: Cranleigh Preparatory School, 629

Headmaster: Since 2014, Martin Reader (50s). Previously headmaster of Wellington School in Somerset for eight years. Brought up in Orpington and attended St Olave's Grammar School. Thence to University College, Oxford where he was an exhibitioner in English and English lit and played lots of rugby. Stayed on for an MPhil in English studies (1100-1500); later an MBA in school leadership. Began his teaching career at St Edward's in Oxford before moving to Oundle and then to Reigate Grammar where he was senior deputy head. Warm but formal; parents call him 'sensible'. Son in upper sixth; daughter has finished university; wife Amanda runs the careers department.

Sees himself as a 'modernising' head – has no interest in wrapping the past in cotton wool. Believes he has met his aim of getting Cranleigh's academic and co-curricular offerings in balance. There's more breadth, eg wider subject choice, but also depth, eg longer lessons and the ascendancy of the EPQ for (almost) all. Digital learning has also been in the spotlight. Everyone in the school now has his or her own school-issued iPad which must be brought to all lessons. It's the culmination of a thoughtful three-year project ('Eton followed our model. They came to see how it was done!'). Thanks to this head start, the school was able to sail on serenely when lockdown struck, an advantage that was highlighted by all the parents we spoke to, especially those with other children attending less well-prepared schools.

Drama is a particular jewel in the crown: ambitious, multimedia, immersive. 'We try to compete with the West End,' a pupil explained to us solemnly

Modern Mr Reader may be, but parents we spoke to described him as a champion of old-fashioned good character: 'He's as likely to give a commendation for someone doing a good deed as for achievement at academics or sport.' Describes himself as 'owl-obsessed', and indeed he is the only HMC head who is a trustee of a wild birds of prey conservation charity, the Hawk and Owl Trust. Started an eco club at the school, has installed bird boxes and is keen on projects to increase biodiversity over the school site.

Entrance: Around 120 join at 13+, half from Cranleigh Prep across the road. Others arrive from Highfield, Cumnor House, Thomas's, Westbourne House, Feltonfleet, Windlesham – and a number of nearby schools. Register when your child is in year 4 or 5. Applicants sit the ISEB pre-test in year 6, but the school doesn't evaluate the results until after applicants attend one of its assessment days. Cranleigh runs a whopping 10 of these 'holistic review' days per year, each one hosting around 50 kids. CE, or Cranleigh's own entrance test, is sat in the summer term of year 8.

NB Pupils can now also join at 11+: they sit the ISEB pre-test in year 6, attend a holistic review day in January of that year and start at the prep in year 7. They then have no further testing to move up to the senior school.

A few places are available at 16+ but competition is strong. Candidates should be predicted 9-7 grades at I/GCSE and must sit verbal and non-verbal reasoning papers and submit an essay. Interview and reference also required.

Exit: Nearly a quarter leave after GCSEs – usually to sixth form college or perhaps nearby Hurtwood House. Diverse set of university destinations and courses. Bristol, Exeter, Durham, Leeds, Edinburgh, Manchester, York, UCL and Imperial all popular. A few overseas, especially to the States (recently to Colgate, George Washington and Harvard). Instituto de Impresa in Madrid also featured in 2021. Two to Oxbridge in 2021, plus three medics.

Latest results: In 2021, 74 per cent 9-7 at GCSE; 68 per cent A*/A at A level (91 per cent A*-B). In 2019 (the last year when exams took place), 39 per cent A*/A at A level.

Teaching and learning: The rare school that can truly cater for both the Mensa candidate and his or her less gifted younger brother. Strong sibling policy means the school will always have a broadish range of abilities. Fourth formers (year 9s) take the usual broad range of subjects, with the less common compulsory addition of either Latin or classical civilisation. No surprise, then, that the school makes a strong showing in Latin at GCSE, with a few souls even braving Greek (Greek is also available as an AS). Most pupils will take 10 GCSEs, to include at least one language – current range includes French, Spanish, German; looking at introducing Mandarin.

Pupils we spoke to gushed about their teachers, though art, drama, English, economics and history seemed particularly gush-worthy. Fifty minute lessons seen as an improvement over the short and bitty lessons of the past. English lit, maths, business studies, geography and economics are the most popular subjects at A level. DT is a serious subject here and A level pupils can choose between product design or design engineering.

All sixth formers do either an EPQ, a fourth A level or a two-year AS. Cranleigh's director of learning, teaching and innovation is one of the pioneers responsible for the national development of the EPQ and is a chief examiner of the qualification. An enrichment programme of lectures and debates for academic scholars gets mixed reviews from the scholars themselves. Perhaps think twice before pressing junior to slog for a scholarship.

Learning support and SEN: Over a third of pupils have been identified with some level of SEN; 71 of them receive additional support. Inspirational learning support: 'made my son feel able,' said one parent. 'She became confident because of the support, they managed it beautifully,' said another. Year 9 students may take one fewer subjects to access learning support. Whole school is now wheelchair and mobility scooter accessible. Recent pupil with cerebral palsy was national wheelchair tennis champion in his age group.

The arts and extracurricular: 'Pupils should be able to do everything – sport, drama, music – and not have to specialise narrowly; it's the Cranleigh way,' said the head, and we saw plenty of evidence. Drama is a particular jewel in the crown: ambitious, multimedia, immersive. 'We try to compete with the West End,' a pupil explained to us solemnly. And what we observed really was at the cutting edge for a school. Up to 95 per cent of year 9 pupils choose drama as an option. Fabulous theatre tech is housed in the antique Speech Hall (c.1905). 'Dangerous Minds', a pupil public speaking programme inspired by Ted talks. Students have to memorise their speech.

Music 'was very highbrow' when Mr Reader arrived. Much more broad-based – and 'cooler' – now. There is now a head of contemporary music, and music technology is an A level subject. We noticed larger than usual numbers on the lists for guitar lessons, but also lots learning ... church organ. A generous donation from an Old Cranleighan made possible the purchase of a high quality three-manual pipe organ in the chapel. There is now an organist in residence and a slate of pupils learning to play the thing. Plenty of lusty congregational singing. Art facilities include printmaking, photography, ceramics and kiln. Large, and high achieving, uptake of art at both GCSE and A level.

Many parents spoke highly of sport's inclusiveness here. Still, 'it might not be the right school for a boy who literally cannot tolerate rugby,' said the head drily

CCF cadets can be seen robustly marching about the place with flags and camouflage, and there's no awkwardness about turfing all of year 9 outdoors for weekly drill (DofE is an alternative).

Sport: Cranleigh has 10 grass pitches (including an international standard 1st XV pitch), three Astros, 21 tennis courts, eight netball courts, four squash and six Eton fives courts, a nine-hole golf course, a 25-metre, four-lane swimming pool, and a full-fledge equestrian centre. So, it's a bit fit. Some families choose the school for sport alone – 'It's a great selling point.' Rugby not quite god, but at least a minor deity. 'We're not a rugby academy,' the head told us sternly, before listing the Daily Mail trophies and other silverware the school's rugby teams had made off with over the past 18 months. Director of rugby proud that the 1st XV has been almost entirely nurtured through the school ranks rather than being poached from elsewhere along the way. Calls them, with perhaps a nod to James Brown, 'the hardest working school squad in the country'.

Girls' top sport is hockey, and Repton (unaccountably) are arch-rivals. Boys' hockey also outstanding, and an Olympic gold medallist runs the boys' 1st XI hockey team. Sixteen girls' teams and 17 boys' play on Saturdays. Frequent national finals winners or runners-up in several age groups. Top sportsmen and women will train in their main sport all year round.

'Sport for all' is more than an empty phrase here. This is the sort of school that can rustle up D and E teams without turning a hair. Sport four afternoons a week (including Saturdays). Loads of minor sports, with choice expanding as pupils move up the school. Many parents we spoke to said their own children were more of the squash and yoga ilk rather than big into team games and spoke highly of sport's inclusiveness here: 'There are no grim hierarchies – boys on A teams help coach D and E teams.' Still 'it might not be the right school for a boy who literally cannot tolerate rugby,' said the head drily. Football being deliberately rehabilitated, with a full fixture card against some worthy opponents.

Sports hall does the business, but we particularly liked the 'Cricket Bubble' and the 'Woodland Fitness Centre'. Nine-hole golf course is used by locals as well as students. Outdoor education centre with a focus on kayaking, a climbing wall and DofE. Equestrian centre has two all-weather arenas and 60 acres of grazing and riding land. Pupils may bring their own ponies; those without learn on the school ponies. Riding lessons are also available to the wider community outside the school.

Boarding: This is the classic, authentic boarding school experience, but with 21st-century flourish and plenty of TLC. At least 70 per cent of pupils board, but it feels like even more since the day pupils get with the programme. 'It's a pain in the backside to be a day pupil here,' said a parent whose son started as a day pupil but swiftly changed over. A brim-full day that doesn't end until almost 9.30pm, Saturday lessons followed by matches, and very little blue sky between day and boarding fees – all these things help keep boarding robust. 'They want Cranleigh to be a strong community; they don't want people disappearing at 6pm.' All that said, Cranleigh is largely a weekly boarding affair. Sure, there will always be some pupils in school of a Sunday – particularly international ones – but even they will often have a bolt hole in London or with a family friend.

Now four boys' and four girls' houses – the newest girls' house, Martlet, opened in 2019. The school is, steady as she goes, sailing towards its ultimate goal of 50/50 boys/girls (currently 42 per cent girls, up from 30 per cent when Mr Reader took over). No flexi boarding ('yuk!' commented a pupil at the very idea); day pupils are fully part of boarding houses and have a cabin desk in boarders' rooms – it's their 'centre of gravity' within the school where they do prep, get changed for sport, make toast and drinks and take part in house activities. Much loyalty and mutual support within houses; much competition between them. Every pupil we spoke to said their house was best – always a good sign. One boy referred to his housemates as a 'brotherhood'. Girls' relationships, as elsewhere, can be trickier. All girls' houses have an 'affiliated' boys' house – 'It fosters co-ed spirit,' we were told – and join them for activities.

Ethos and heritage: Founded in 1865 by George Cubitt, MP for West Surrey, and Rev John Sapte, who decided that what Victorian Surrey needed was 'a public school for the education of the middle classes'. The school was to 'provide a sound and plain education… for the sons of farmers and others engaged in commercial pursuits'. The Surrey County School, funded by public appeals, was built on eight acres at the top of a hill just outside the village of Cranleigh. As the school grew to its present 280 acres, neighbouring farms were gradually acquired, remembered only in names such as The Butts (a sixth form café).

This is the classic, authentic boarding school experience, but with 21st-century flourish and plenty of TLC

Most of the original buildings still flourish. The quaint original 1865 quad is now mostly administrative offices. But pupils all eat and chat across the original 19th-century tables in the dining hall. They worship three times a week in the Victorian chapel built in 1869 – all faiths and no faiths – the whole school still fits! Unique and ghostly war/peace statue designed and sculpted by former Cranleighan Nicholas Dimbleby, brother of Jonathan and David, looms outside the chapel window. It is one of the most moving artworks we have ever seen in a public school.

Among newer buildings is the Van Hasselt Centre, a grey, Siberian larch and aluminum clad teaching monolith which provides a public-school-industrial aesthetic to the school. We guarantee that anyone describing this building will at some point use the adjective 'Marmite'. Light and airy, it comfortably houses 24 classrooms wrapped around ancient squash courts, the latter now used as a café space and a small lecture theatre. The building gives prominence to the superb learning support department. 'I wanted it at the heart of the school, not hidden down a dark corridor,' says the head. Also Cranleigh Futures (careers) and a new sixth form centre. Another swish recent addition, the Emms Centre, houses modern foreign languages, science labs and IT, its double-height atrium, flooded with natural light, provides a brilliant space for group study.

Former pupils include numbers of successful sportspeople, a fair few military types, plus Patrick Marber (actor, director, screenwriter); actors Julia Ormond, Laurence Naismith and Michael Cochrane; film producer Eric Fellner (co-chair of Working Title Films); historian Andrew Roberts; England cricketer (and great-great-great-great-grandson of Cranleigh's first headmaster!) Ollie Pope; Will Collier (England Rugby) and former editor of the Guardian, Alan Rusbridger. Cranleigh was used as the location for Prince William's school, Ludgrove, in the fourth series of The Crown and was the setting for a rugby match.

Pastoral care, inclusivity and discipline: 'Zero tolerance' for drugs in school. Sixth formers found to be taking drugs in 2019 are 'no longer at the school'. 'We don't want drugs to drift in; the school has to be a safe place.' However, will go to lengths, via testing and counselling, to support kids who may have strayed outside of school. School bar open twice a week for 'a couple of beers'. Smoking a rarity. Refreshingly strict on phones. Mobiles are banned in the first year, end of. Then permitted on 'highly restricted' basis in years 10 and 11.

Bullying a bit more of a challenge as it's harder for teachers to detect, and young people are reluctant to report it. Some parents felt that Cranleigh 'may not be as tough on bullying as other schools'. That said, parents we spoke to singled out pastoral care as the very best thing about the school, and it struck us as superb. 'Houses are everything' at Cranleigh, both academically and pastorally. 'Returning to your house should be like coming through a family door,' we were told.

Housemistresses, housemasters and matrons are 'so available' and 'really nice people who look after the whole child'. 'During lockdown, we got phone calls from tutors, matrons, subject teachers and the learning support department – all to check on our son's wellbeing.' All of this is essential in such a full-on and fast-paced school. 'Cranleigh is a busy place with very little let-up,' said a parent. 'Everyone is on their knees by the end of term.'

Despite the superficial homogeneity of the pupils, diversity lurks within. School welcomes the occasional Springboard Bursary child (national charity for children who have suffered trauma). The Alliance Society welcomes LGBTQ pupils. And the 'iron clad' sibling policy means there will always be a range of personalities.

Pupils and parents: Waspy. Local. Vast majority of pupils come from a 35-mile radius, covering Surrey, Sussex, Hampshire, Herts and south London. 'Loads of people live within a half hour of the school,' a parent told us. 'It's great because it means the children can get together easily during school hols.' One or two parents (of boarders!) we spoke to described themselves as living 'almost walking distance from the school'.

Not really on the expat circuit, though there is a tiny handful of children of overseas Brits. Forty 'tier 4' children (non-EU international) – much lower than most other schools of its ilk, and the school would like a few more. Only two pupils currently receive learning support for EAL. Wide range of nationalities: Nigeria, China, UAE, USA, India, France, Portugal, Switzerland, Iran, Cayman Islands, Greece, Hong Kong were all mentioned. More from the Emirates since Cranleigh opened its sister school in Abu Dhabi (2014). Remains to be seen if its new branch in China will have the same effect.

Money matters: Fees broadly in line with similar schools, though day fees are snapping at the heels of fees for full boarding. Wide range of 13+ scholarships (here called Excellence Awards) includes one for design engineering. These can be supplemented by means-tested awards: 11 per cent of pupils are currently receiving bursaries. At 11+ only music scholarships can be applied for. However, a few academic scholarships will be offered based on exceptional results in the Holistic Review.

The last word: Busy, English, local, sporty, humane – a lovable weekly boarding school firing on all cylinders. An all-rounder's paradise, yes, but the academic offering can stand up to almost any school in the land. 'The school is viewed as very, very sporty,' a teacher almost lamented, 'which is actually a problem, because there's so much more to Cranleigh.'

Cumnor House Sussex

22

London Road, Danehill, Haywards Heath, West Sussex RH17 7HT

01825 790347 | registrar@cumnor.co.uk | www.cumnor.co.uk

Ages: 2-13

Pupils: 360; Boarders: 11 full, 43 weekly/flexi

Fees: Day £9,495 – £20,625; Boarding £24,570 pa and flexible options available

Headmaster: Since September 2020, Fergus Llewellyn. Previously headmaster of St Andrew's Prep School, Turi, Kenya and prior to that was at Cheltenham College for 10 years, serving as housemaster and head of English and drama. Earlier in his career, he was at King's Bruton and Haslemere Preparatory School. He attended Sherborne School and graduated from the University of London with a BA (Hons) in English. Married to Tamsyn, the couple have three children.

Entrance: Non-selective in early years; thereafter selection of those most likely to be fully involved in school life. Taster day for all, and interview for years 6 and above.

Exit: To a wide range of schools, both local and further afield. In 2021, to 17 senior schools with 21 awards and scholarships. Brighton, Eton, King's Canterbury, Charterhouse, Ardingly, Hurst, Cranleigh and Eastbourne all featured. In directing children towards schools, considers not just whether they can meet the academic requirements, but also whether they're sufficiently emotionally robust to cope with life at the school in question.

Our view: Beautiful setting in the Sussex countryside overlooking the downs. Buildings range from the charming to the unremarkable, in a village-like cluster. Lush green grounds, and large pond to row over in the Cumnor boat, or swing over on a rope (it's drained and cleaned and carefully tested for any virulent bacteria first, assured the head's wife).

Main entrance has been recently modernised and leads into the slightly scuffed country house hotel-type interior – parquet floor and log fire, and a few Famous Five books on a windowsill by a sofa. Lego table and 70s sweets jigsaw on the go. 'Another genius from Cumnor' cushions – to reassure existing parents, or perhaps tempt prospective ones?

Common room with a log fire, couple of pool tables and newspapers (including Times and Independent). Award-winning artwork on the walls, and a long piece of paper where pupils had drawn self-portraits in the style of Quentin Blake to celebrate World Book Day.

Pre-prep is a cosy separate entity that particularly attracted one mum, who remembers fondly the special mothers' day celebration in reception, children presenting mums with handpicked flowers wrapped in foil, then escorting them into school for special cakes and poems – 'very simple and lovely'.

In-house custard creams and jammy dodgers were startlingly yummy to those of us used to the pedestrian version (they've got an award-winning pastry chef)

Nursery open 7am-7pm 50 weeks a year, available to the whole community. Pyjama-clad children can be delivered in time to have breakfast alongside the older boarders and then picked up ready for bed at night.

'Academic, but not pushy academic,' says school. Certainly a school which achieves a goodly number of scholarships, but not, in atmosphere or method, like a prep with an eye on the prize for the duration.

Careful consideration of the timetable, which is broken up so kids are not using their brains in the same way for long periods of time – pre-prep dance outside before each maths lesson. No one model fits all, so if there is good reason for the usual school curriculum not to apply to a child, then an exception will be made.

Not much prep until year 7 (when pupils start preparing for scholarships and CE): just vocab and spelling, which could be learnt in the bath or around the dinner table, and reading, occasionally left undone – 'I don't read on Friday nights as mummy and daddy have gin and tonic,' said a child in year 1.

Year 7s and 8s all have iPads for use during lessons, purchased by parents in an optional scheme ('you didn't have to sign up, but if everyone else was going to have one...'). No social media or unsuitable apps.

Learning support is excellent, and not only provides help to (around 30) pupils with special needs, but also to those who just need a bit of extra now and then. There's an educational psychologist on the staff, who observes classes, and deals with any emotional problems suffered by pupils which may be exacerbated by school, from separation anxiety to bereavement. No extra charge for counselling or one-to-one learning support. Additional charges for extras such as speech therapy.

Saturday school on alternate weekends, which children seem happy with (though some parents would prefer a lie in, and more family time).

School motto – 'aim high, be kind and dare to be different' – permeates everything, said one parent: apparently the head girl's and boy's job is to make sure everyone is happy at break time, and no one is being left out; so it comes as no surprise that the pastoral care is very thorough: regular full staff pastoral care meetings where every child's name is read out, and their welfare considered, and a new well-being curriculum programme. Form teachers are the first port of call for difficulties until year 5, after which each child has a tutor whom they meet weekly to talk about everything and anything. School policy on bullying is to make sure children understand what bullying behaviour is, and ask them to blow the whistle: senior children attend the ABC (Anti-Bullying Committee) every week to report on anyone they are worried about. One parent whose child experienced bullying behaviour said it was dealt with quickly and efficiently, and also praised the presence of 'gappers' (gap year students), who she said could pick up on things teachers might not get to hear.

CofE, but not evangelically so. Exposure to the most valuable tenets of faith with a bohemian touch: daily prayers described by head as also a school silence – a time for a loud school to be silent and consider things.

The school shares facilities in the local community, and links with a local primary each year. The head is setting up the Cumnor certificate (own-brand DofE), which will involve years 7 and 8 working in the local community, and being part of drama workshops with younger pupils from local primaries.

Food is 'amazing', say kids – apparently there are no adjectives which can do justice to the wraps. In-house custard creams and jammy dodgers bulge with cream and jam and were startlingly yummy to those of us used to the pedestrian version (they've got an award-winning pastry chef).

Occupations, as clubs are called at Cumnor, range from boules to calligraphy, and vary each term. Cinematography described in detail by enthusiastic kids – 'it makes you look at films in a completely different way.' There's a waiting list for cooking, but everyone gets a turn eventually. Year 8 learn to cook a three-course meal as a post-exam treat.

The 'co-curriculum' (sports and arts) is given equal rather than ornamental value here ('They find out what every child has going for them,' said a parent).

Sport is for awareness, commitment and health – and everyone: a poor, enthusiastic player will be in teams all the way through, playing matches most weeks. 'It's nice to win,' said a pupil; but it's not the only or main purpose of sport here. No A, B or C teams until year 7: teams change from week to week, and the make-up of teams depends on whom they are playing.

Art is 'exceptional', said one parent. Housed in a barn-like room with high beams, glass doors and space to hang strange colourful objects. All learn a musical instrument – it can be dropped in year 7 to make way for the demands of common entrance and scholarships, though many continue. Each year from year 3 upwards does an annual production, Shakespeare being the year 8 remit to be performed in the mossy green outdoor theatre.

The uniform and sports kit is good quality but expensive – one parent complained indignantly at the cost of school sweatshirts; but there's some secondhand provision in the uniform shop. Sports kit is laundered by the school, much to the joy of parents.

Parents around 30 per cent London, the rest local, mostly professionals or City types. Not cliquey, said one parent, outgoing and sociable, inclusive of newcomers, with a buddy system to match new parents with old.

Boarding: Boarding is possible from year 7: full-timers, who all go home every other weekend, weekly and flexi boarders, who spend a few nights every week at school. 'They are completely flexible,' said one grateful parent. Tremendously popular with pupils, several of whom commented on their difficulty persuading their mums they were old enough – 'but it's so fun.' Lots of activities: preparations for Dragons' Den were under way, not to mention Marlborough Murders; Friday night is magic night and day trips at the weekends.

Rooms are for five, and cosy: four beds at ground level, and one bunk. Bathrooms are clean and up to date. Parents like the proximity of houseparents (described as 'warm and welcoming' and 'extremely efficient'), and the easy access pupils have to gappers, who have rooms on each corridor, and are the first point of call in the night.

Fruit is always available, and there's a pantry where boarders can make tea, toast and hot drinks (with gappers' help). Obligatory weekly letter writing, and phones available for making calls in the evening or at break time – parents and pupils were happy this was sufficient. No Skype, iPads or mobiles allowed ('they get technology soon enough,' said one parent). Currently no overseas boarders.

Money matters: Two full means-tested bursaries for talented (academic and/or sport and creative arts) pupils joining year 4, covering 100 per cent of fees up to 18 at one of the partner schools – (these are Ardingly, Benenden, Eastbourne College, Hurstpierpoint College, King's Canterbury, Lancing College, Mayfield, Radley, Roedean, St Mary's Ascot, Sevenoaks, Tonbridge and Worth) – apply by April to join in September.

The last word: Many parents fresh from pressurised London preps may struggle initially with the comparatively relaxed Cumnor environment – 'You don't know at what level everyone else's child is reading,' said one startled mum. No constant testing. 'Trust us,' claims the school – 'Children are meant to be enjoying themselves and having fun.' Few parents wind up being disappointed.

DLD College London

23

199 Westminster Bridge Road, London SE1 7FX

020 7935 8411 | dld-admissions@dld.org | www.dldcollege.co.uk

Ages: 14–19

Pupils: 330; sixth form: 272; Boarders: 191 full

Fees: £24,670 – £31,930 pa; Boarding + £19,500 to £27,990 pa

Principal: Since 2018, Irfan Latif BSc PGCE FRSA FRSC (40s). Educated at Emanuel School in south London, he went on to study chemistry at King's College London, where he also did his teacher training. Taught at Haberdashers' Aske's Boys' School in Elstree, followed by stints as senior

Kent College Canterbury

housemaster at Whitgift School, deputy head (academic) at Bedford School, and five years as head of state boarding school Sexey's in Somerset. At which point, he was approached to head DLD. 'I relished the challenge of running a boarding school in London,' he says. A natural urbanite, decisive, fast-talking and energetic, he has quickly brought DLD into line – 'There were some pastoral issues in the past which needed addressing; things needed to change' – and is already planning ahead for expansion to 600 students.

Married to a teacher, with two school-age daughters, in his spare time he enjoys cooking, reading, music and adventurous travel. (He has, in the past, led a school trip to Everest base camp and is currently planning another one to Nepal.) He used to coach rugby, cricket and tennis, but his busy schedule now only allows time to give masterclasses in chemistry.

Entrance: DLD is the only central London 14-19 college to offer onsite boarding, so unsurprisingly the demand is global, with over 50 nationalities represented. UK sixth form entrants – mainly escapees from boarding schools and London independent day schools 'looking for a different experience, something more academic or a different structure' – require at least five GCSEs at 5+. Overseas applicants must prove a minimum standard of English. All are interviewed to establish their motivation, work ethic and something about their home life. Below sixth form, by school report and interview.

Exit: Nearly 20 per cent leave after GCSEs. One of Mr Latif's objectives has been to raise the academic bar, introducing an assistant principal with dedicated responsibility for UCAS and careers. Results have been encouraging. Russell Group numbers up. Popular destinations include UCL, King's College London, Queen Mary, University of the Arts, City and Westminster. Lots overseas – most recently to Hong Kong, George Washington University (USA), Seoul, EHL (Switzerland), Bocconi and Luiss (both Italy), Concordia (Canada) and UCLA (US). 'Our job is to create aspirations, encouraging pupils to believe they can do it if they put their mind to it.'

Latest results: In 2021, 62 per cent 9-7 at GCSE; 56 per cent A*/A at A level (82 per cent A*-B). In 2019 (the last year when exams took place), 28 per cent 9-7 at GCSE; 26 per cent of A levels were A*/A (54 per cent A*-B).

Teaching and learning: What DLD offers is intensive attention. Class size is kept to a maximum of 16, with most A level classes about 8-12. All are mixed ability. Teaching – in a day that extends from 8.50am to 5pm – is notably strong, as is 'value added' (in the top five per cent in the country). Staff are well qualified, many from Oxbridge, quite a few with doctorates. 'They know how to unlock potential,' declares Mr Latif. Many, too, have been at DLD for some time. 'I love teaching here,' said a long-serving art teacher. 'The student-teacher relationship is strong and I love the atmosphere.'

What DLD offers is intensive attention. Class size is kept to a maximum of 16, with most A level classes about 8-12. Teaching is notably strong, as is 'value added'

Over 30 subjects available, though some only when there is sufficient demand. 'If subjects aren't recruiting, we won't teach them, but I have resisted the temptation to consolidate,' says the head. Good sweep of languages (German, French, Spanish, Italian, Mandarin), plus EPQ and bespoke DLD diploma for those who want to work along similar research lines without external pressure. Unusually for an independent boarding school, DLD also offers the more vocational BTecs. ('My daughter really enjoyed her BTec in media studies,' said one parent. 'She gained hugely in confidence.')

As well as A levels and a two-year GCSE course, DLD teaches a one-year intensive GCSE programme for UK students who take a minimum of eight subjects (including maths, English, double or triple science, a humanity and a creative subject). Not necessarily the ideal option for those starting mid-stream. 'It's very structured,' said one parent whose daughter had done one year of GCSEs elsewhere. 'They go through the entire syllabus, starting at the beginning. She was looking for something more tailored.' Overseas students hoping to continue to sixth form can also take a one-year pre-A level course, with a smaller basket of GCSE subjects. 'As well as four to five GCSEs, we ensure their academic English is at the standard necessary to get them into a UK university and teach them about British culture and values, taking them on plenty of trips and visits.'

Learning support and SEN: Strong 'learning support' department – 'We don't believe in labelling,' says the head – provides one-to-one attention, liaising with subject teachers and monitoring progress. The college also boasts a reigning Dyslexia Teacher of the Year. Site well adapted to physical disabilities, with a lift serving all parts of the building.

The arts and extracurricular: DLD has a particularly strong art department, offering graphics and photography alongside art. They have a 100 per cent success rate in placing students on art foundation courses (Central St Martins, Goldsmiths, Ravensbourne, Kingston) and students proceed to art-related degrees that range from fashion photography and illustration to interior design and animation. They are also regular prize winners in the Independent Schools Association's art competition. There is also an energetic music department offering an interesting range of music qualifications, including the subsidiary diploma in music tech and a foundation programme in music. Plenty of extracurricular music too, with band club, Christmas concert, and DJ night. Drama too is lively, though not necessarily a reason to choose DLD.

At weekends, boarders are allowed out by prior arrangement. Those remaining in situ (the majority) are kept entertained with cultural trips and outings

Facilities for everything are excellent, with bright, well-equipped science labs, three large, light and airy art rooms, a spacious restaurant. A digital learning lab, a new library and a well-being centre have recently been built.

Over 50 extracurricular activities provided on site, from creative writing to Model UN and DofE.

Sport: Own basement gym and pool and weekly games afternoon, but the super-urban location means no onsite playing fields. Main sports are football and netball played at nearby Archbishop's Park, in the lee of Lambeth Palace. Beyond that, 'London is our playing field,' says the head.

Boarding: Nearly 200 boarders – housed in smart, individual ensuite hotel-like rooms and shared well-equipped kitchen-cum-common room – are overseen by ample staff (seven on duty every evening), who operate a 'huddle' system to ensure everyone gets sufficient personal attention.

Those of compulsory school age remain on site during the evening with an early evening dinner at 6.30pm, followed by fun activities, such as marathon film nights, themed dinners and games, before a 9.30pm curfew. Sixth formers are allowed off site, but must be back by 10.30pm. At weekends, boarders are allowed out by prior arrangement. Those remaining in situ (the majority) are kept entertained with cultural trips and outings, including to football matches and the ballet.

Ethos and heritage: Launched as a small private sixth form college in the early 1930s, Davies Laing and Dick's original purpose was to tutor applicants for Oxbridge entrance and the Colonial Service exams. Still focused on helping individual students reach their potential, it is now one of 21 schools owned by private education company Alpha Plus and is primarily a boarding school, offering a safe bridge between school and university.

In 2015, DLD merged with Abbey College and moved from its long-time base in Marylebone to a bespoke modern building a few minutes' walk from Waterloo and Westminster stations. Designed around a spacious central atrium used for meeting and group activities (drama productions, concerts, musicals), the centrifugal space extends upward in rings, with spacious classrooms offering London views of the former Eurostar hangar, the Thames and the Houses of Parliament. Good-sized outside garden-cum-playground on ground level; sunny, well-supervised terrace higher up used for barbecues and social events.

Pastoral care, inclusivity and discipline: Student well-being and mental health are central to the ethos – 'That's our raison d'être,' says the head – and staff have been carefully recruited to further this objective, with two counsellors, a life coach, a head of well-being, a head of co-curricular, an attendance officer, plus 40 staff trained in mental-health first aid. 'We're not too worried about league tables,' says the head. 'We want them to be comfortable in their own skin. If mental, physical and emotional needs are addressed, the grades will follow.' Parents appreciate what's on offer. 'The reason my son came here is that he was miserable at his previous school. Both he and I have been delighted with the support he's received.'

Discipline is structured but not authoritarian. 'In general, they're nice kids, very respectful.' There are, of course, still those who push the boundaries, and the head has dealt with four permanent drug-related exclusions since his arrival. Those not making sufficient progress (ie not working hard enough) may also be asked to leave. Overall atmosphere is relaxed and informal. 'We treat them as young adults, with some independence, but not too much.' Staff are called by their first name, but the head is suited (if sans tie) and uniformly addressed as 'sir'.

Pupils kept a close eye on inside and outside the gates, with double-guarded single entrance ('We're hot on safeguarding') and Reach tracking software used to identify movements of sixth formers. Years 10 and 11 not allowed out during the day.

Encouraging student involvement is also key, and a popular student council – 30 applications for 12 posts – is invited to senior leadership team meetings. Actively involved in charity, academic and well-being, members organise the summer ball and suggest ideas – such as last year's 'graduation' ceremony, which took place in a committee room at the House of Commons.

Pupils and parents: Large percentage of boarders from overseas (some 60 per cent) aided by well-administered visa system. A hefty cluster from China, but also significant numbers from Europe. International outlook celebrated in a United Nations of flags ornamenting the atrium, and global feast days – such as Turkish New Year – prominently displayed on noticeboards. DLD's well linked-in location means day pupils also come from far and wide.

Money matters: Not the cheapest place on the planet, not even in London, but fees reflect up-to-the-minute accommodation and pupil-teacher ratio. Ten scholarships, three a year, awarded to those from the local area.

The last word: This unique educational environment seems to capture all the best things about a college environment, combining them with the pastoral care and motivational structures that are more typical of school provision. All this takes place in small classes, with one-to-one help when required, in a state-of-the-art, purpose-built building in the heart of London, where students have the option to board on-site. The result is an informal atmosphere with an underlying structured regime where everyone is kept up to scratch. A fantastic place for the very bright, as well as remotivating the disaffected, although not for young people who want a more traditional boarding school experience.

Dorset House School

24

The Manor, Bury, Pulborough, West Sussex RH20 1PB

01798 831456 | info@dorsethouseschool.com | www.dorsethouseschool.com

Ages: 4–13

Pupils: 135; **Boarders:** 43 flexi (from 9 years)

Fees: Day £9,315– £18,954; Boarding + £1,258 – £4,488 pa

Headmaster: Since 2017, Matt Thomas, formerly deputy head of Moulsford, and previously taught in two challenging comprehensives 'where you need a huge box of skills'. Degree in PE, geography and education studies from St Luke's Exeter. Married to Julie, with two children. The head was attracted to the school by the mud – 'It's outdoorsy – how schools should be.'

The head's most important quality for pupils to gain at DH is confidence. He's by the gate every morning to greet the children – just as important is for them to return his greeting, and make eye contact; pupils are expected to shake hands firmly each Friday before they receive their tuck voucher. The emphasis on manners and respect is matched by a warm friendliness between pupils and head, pupils saying: 'the head will sit next to you and ask what you're doing'; 'gets involved in everything we do'; 'he always helps'. The head teaches RS to years 7 and 8, which he loves – 'the highlight of my day'.

This open-door policy also applies to and pleases parents, who describe him as 'warm and friendly'; 'in the fabric of the place'.

Entrance: Non-selective, entrance on the basis of a taster day and school reports. In-house nursery is not part of the school but supplies around half of reception entrants.

Exit: Sends pupils to a wide range of senior schools, in particular Brighton College, Christ's Hospital, Frensham Heights, Hurst, Lancing College, Our Lady of Sion, Roedean, Seaford, Wellington and Worth. Four scholarships in 2021.

Our view: Dorset House seduces at first sight. Set on the banks of the Arun with views over the downs, its ancient buildings (a 12th-century manor house at its core) are surrounded by lawns, walled garden, woods and an amphitheatre. A parent said, 'You walk through the grounds and feel that idyllic childhood memories could be created. It took my breath away a bit...'

Beyond the stunning grounds, what immediately strikes a visitor is children having fun – when we arrived a group of girls were giggling, elbows digging into a tub of fruit – 'trying to get their snack without their hands,' explained the head. It's a school where you hear laughter and see children playing as well as learning – as a parent said, the attraction is in the 'joy that the school creates'.

In this small family school there's lots of mixing across year groups – it's not unusual to see a year 8 holding hands with a 6-year-old. One parent said her son loves its size because he's a worrier, '[he] feels safe and contained'.

This school listens and cares, but the head is keen to equip pupils to cope rather than resolve all their difficulties for them; one parent described how her daughter was given 'coping strategies' to help with a problem with peers, and how much this helped – 'She understood what was going on and how to deal with it.'

The science teacher was described as 'barmy – in a brilliant exciting way', and was keen to describe the delights of blowing up jelly babies in the fume cupboard

Pupils said they would talk to a teacher or gap student if they had a problem, and pupils can request a session with the independent listener, described by a pupil as 'a comfortable and supportive experience'.

Punishments here are proportionate and rare. You get the feeling that they're not often necessary. When Ds (detentions) happen, they generally doing something useful – cleaning up a classroom or picking up litter. Or so pupils have heard.

It's small, relative to some of the preps in the area – 'not for those for whom huge grounds and the best facilities are essential,' said a parent – but the head is keen to make both pupils and school the best they can be. A 'boutique class act,' said a parent firmly. It really is.

Sports lessons follow the usual gender divide, but girls have played on the cricket team – 'It's a very flexible school, no hard and fast rules,' said a parent.

A small school means fewer teams, and one parent suggested it wasn't the school for someone who 'wants to be always on the winning team'. But, parents and pupils insist, there is an upside to being small: everyone has to take part so everyone has a chance; a mixed ability team brings out the best qualities in all players, and those who excel can be a big fish in a small pond – or play for the team in the year above for more of a challenge.

A parent who described his daughter as a 'lazy socialiser' said this has gradually changed in the world of Dorset House. She did one-night boarding, and is now asking to do more, and wouldn't say this unless she was really happy – 'she loves to sleep'.

Homework is contained at Dorset House: half an hour to an hour, completed at school. Only in year 8 does it overflow the school slot, with French and Latin vocab to be learnt at home, and essays to write over the weekend. Some of the usual worry about CE, but pupils are well supported by teachers and the independent listener – 'not a hothouse,' says the head firmly.

Science and English were repeatedly mentioned by parents and pupils as exceptionally well taught, the science teacher described by one as 'barmy – in brilliant exciting way', and indeed we have seldom met a more enthusiastic teacher, describing humans as 'scientists from the moment we're born' and keen to describe the delights of blowing up jelly babies in the fume cupboard (to show how cells use energy).

There's a large selection of books in the English classroom and the boarders' common room, but no library as such; neither pupils nor parents feel this is of concern. 'The kids read relentlessly,' said a parent.

Class sizes have increased a bit, now up to 22 in the upper part of the school, but this has meant TA support has increased, so the child-teacher ratio has improved.

Learning development (LD) in the pre-prep involves lots of movement – a pupil was happily engaged on a wobble board during our visit. The LD teacher brings her old camper van to school in the summer, and pupils love popping to the van for lessons. A more formal approach in prep, but a gentle switch when pupils are ready during years 4 or 5.

Pupils can have up to two sessions of support outside class, and support in class too. Assistance is flexible, pupils can have just half a term of support if that's all that's needed. In-class support is included in the fees, one-to-one is charged as an extra. Parents say the support is good, and like the fact sessions are integrated into what's going on in class and the curriculum – 'a very holistic approach'.

The head gives year 6s and 7s test interviews for senior school, each pupil having to make their appointment to see him – 'It's all about soft skills and taking responsibility,' says the head. One parent said her son was set up well for his large senior school – 'learnt great values, how to speak to people and be confident, to look out for others – it's been a smooth transition.'

Music is a particular strength, described by a parent as 'amazing'. The music director follows the Kodaly approach from Hungary, and enthuses about children's inherent musical ability 'which they all have in their DNA'. Drama has less focus, felt one parent, but there is LAMDA, drama clubs and various school productions.

The most recent ISI report awarded the school an 'excellent' for the quality of pupils' academic and other achievements and 'excellent' for the quality of pupils' personal development.

The pre-prep building is separate but proximate to the prep, and filled with light, colour and joy. The head (Sarah Hobrow) is a dab hand at making up songs for learning, the hokey-cokey now the maths doubling song, pupils in both schools often eager to set her another challenge.

During our visit, half of reception were squeaky clean and making buns, the other half were outside, happily filthy, in head-to-toe wet-weather gear, making a dinosaur family comfortable in sand and mud. It is difficult to imagine happier 4-year-olds.

Children learn through topics, the year 3 classroom transformed into a chocolate factory, huge sweets hanging from the ceiling, children relishing learning about chocolate with Willy Wonka, the Aztecs, and chocolate fudge, then running a chocolate museum to teach their parents all about it.

Boarding: Praise for the flexi and weekly boarding (there's no full boarding) was common to all the parents we spoke to, in particular the warmth and care of the houseparents. Boarding is available Monday to Thursday, and there is competition for places, which are allocated in as fair a way as possible. Large dormitories (six to eight) nestled under the eaves, each bed with a reading lamp. 'Buns' before bed (not actual buns anymore, but toast, fruit and cereal). An attractive common room with packed bookshelves, a pool table overlooking the downs, and a piano and squashy sofas, with a pile of soft blankets to snuggle under to watch a film. '[They] love being with friends... never in a hurry to come home,' said a parent.

The last word: Many are attracted to the sense of children having a traditional upbringing – 'they're allowed to be children for a lot longer,' said a parent, another saying, '[my son] has rosy red cheeks and muddy kit every day... nonstop chatter and always saying how good lunch was... so bubbly and enthusiastic.'

Dover College

25

Effingham Crescent, Dover, Kent CT17 9RH

01304 205969 | admissions@dovercollege.org.uk | www.dovercollege.org.uk

Ages: 3–18

Pupils: 300; sixth form: 59; Boarders: 60 full, 3 weekly

Fees: Day £9,225 – £17,850; Boarding £25,500 – £36,750 pa

Headmaster: Since September 2020, Simon Fisher. History degree from Exeter. His first teaching post was at Wycliffe College in Gloucestershire, where he climbed the ladder to head of department then on to the senior management team. Thence to Worth School in West Sussex as assistant head then deputy head (academic). Governor on the board of Effingham Schools Trust and a member of its academic committee. Married to Abigail, with whom he has two young children who both attend Dover College Prep. As a keen amateur photographer, you'll often find him with a camera in his hand in his spare time.

Entrance: Non-selective academically, and with every intention of remaining so – 'It's one of our great strengths.' Instead, the school looks for potential, and a willingness to fit in to the school environment and contribute to its ethos: 'Pray together, stay together, eat together.' In the older children skills and aptitudes are always of interest – arts, sports, etc.

Happy to admit into most year groups and at any point in the academic year. Largest intake is into year 12, when a lot of international boarders join them, plus a 'surprising' number of local day pupils, often those whose grammar schools have rejected them for sixth form. Very small numbers in the infant year groups, but increasing thereafter as parents get stressed about the upcoming Kent Tests.

Exit: A few head off to grammar school after year 6 having passed the 11+, and 15 per cent leaves after year 11. 'Our parents are not rich,' reflected the head. At 18, recent destinations include UCL, Warwick, Leeds and Surrey to do courses both academic and vocational. International students often return to their own countries for university. Art foundation courses also a popular choice.

Latest results: In 2021, 44 per cent 9-7 at GCSE; 53 per cent A*/A at A level (79 per cent A*-B). In 2019 (the last year when exams took place), 21 per cent 9-7 at GCSE; 27 per cent A*/A at A level.

Teaching and learning: That most refreshing of things in this county, a non-selective school and pleased to be so. The school slogan is 'think differently', and from juniors up to GCSEs, teaching is delivered via themes, eg 'coffee, tea and chocolate', 'war and peace' or 'two thousand years ago'. What children learn across the subjects is therefore interconnected, and they're encouraged to debate and discuss. It's an approach similar to the IB, and it's no surprise to learn that the school introduced an IB-inspired curriculum across the school in September 2019. To be clear, the IB itself won't be offered: the school doesn't want to stop teaching A levels and its small size puts offering both beyond its reach. Instead, sixth form students will choose an academic or a vocational pathway alongside a 'thinking differently' course, a 'leadership and skills' course and the EPQ. 'We liked the IB, and wanted to take the best parts of it whilst not disenfranchising the UK market,' says school. 'We feel our bespoke curriculum gives the best of all worlds.'

School insists that they have the full ability spread, including the very able, although their exam results reflect the diverse intake. High praise everywhere for the value-added: students who came to Dover College because they'd failed the Kent Test often leave with better A level grades than their friends who passed it. We spoke to one such sixth former in receipt of offers from two excellent universities, who confirmed, 'the academic support I've had from all the staff here has been absolutely fantastic.' Extra lessons routinely offered in the evenings, at weekends and even in the holidays for students who need them.

One small class per year in the junior school, rising to two per year in the senior school – usually between 10 and 15 students per class. Setting from year 9 in science, maths and English. Languages taught are French, Spanish, Mandarin – a slightly narrow provision in a school that's so proud of its international connections, particularly the number of German students who come here. Latin was recently introduced for pupils in years 7 and 8. Very good range of subjects on offer at both GCSE and sixth form, commendable in such a small school.

High praise for the value-added: students who came to Dover College because they'd failed the Kent Test often leave with better A level grades than friends who passed it

The lessons we saw in both junior and senior schools were lively, enjoyable and expertly taught. The head of science shares her teaching space with fish and guinea pigs – 'I like to have live animals in a lab, it reminds us of what we're here for' – presided over by a cheerful, white-coated skeleton sporting goggles. We liked the French class where the teacher had put photos of her own family up on the board and invited students to identify 'ma soeur', 'mon père' etc – so eager were the children to put their hand on the correct photos that they kept knocking them off the board. Being able to see France from the classroom windows is especially motivating, perhaps? Junior school history class was immaculately behaved but full of vim and vigour, a pleasure to watch. At the time of our visit, not the most glittering dynamic intellectually – triple science GCSE was only introduced comparatively recently, suggesting that the school's expectations of its students may once have been too low – but the staff are now working tirelessly to raise the game in this area and the pupils everywhere struck us as confident and keen to participate. Pleasant learning resources area, but the library was disappointing – small, not many chairs (suggesting few linger here), rather bare and drab; lacking a dedicated librarian, and we thought it showed.

Learning support and SEN: Parents raved about the learning support, which here is called individual needs. 'Sending our children here was the best thing we ever did'; 'The help we get for our son and his dyslexia has just been above and beyond.' School keen to stress, however, that it isn't geared up for more than a mild level of need. Study skills – organisation, prioritising tasks, time management – are taught to all students as part of the curriculum.

The arts and extracurricular: Drama facilities currently rather moth-eaten, but the school's 150th anniversary is approaching and celebrations include an entirely revamped creative arts centre, to be run by the school's director of performing arts, a recent appointment intended to expand the provision in that area. 'The key thing in a school is creativity,' says school, which is keen to re-establish creativity 'at the heart of the curriculum'. Regular productions – we looked in on an animated rehearsal of Scrooge, where the children were clearly having a whale of a time – and school is happy to send students interested in lighting and sound on technical enrichment programmes at eg the Gulbenkian Theatre in Canterbury. The Minerva Club offers an excellent programme of theatre trips, around eight per year.

The chapel is at the heart of the school's music-making, and choir is especially strong – we thought the standard of part-singing really fine. Other events include concerts, recitals and competitions. Art is lively and popular, and the art block is a hub of focused creative calm, with photography, fine art and textiles all offered at A level. 'My son has really been brought out of himself by the art and the music here,' commented a mother.

Very strong emphasis on charity and community work, with all students taking this very seriously – recent appeal for shoeboxes filled with presents was so successful that when the Christmas Child charity reps turned up to collect same they couldn't get them all in the van. DofE has had variable take-up in the past, but is now reinvigorated and growing in popularity. School is also in the process of joining Round Square, a network of schools worldwide that all sign up to founder Kurt Hahn's six ideals: internationalism, democracy, environment, adventure, leadership and service. For the pupils, this will bring increased opportunities for overseas exchange and community projects.

Sport: Under new leadership, sport here is impressively varied and the approach is entirely inclusive: recently every single pupil in years 7 and 8 played in at least eight fixtures for the school, making this an excellent place for children who want to get involved. 'We're fostering that participation culture,' said the sports director with relish, a man who leads the 6am sessions in the fitness suite; 'We celebrate excellence and we've got some great individuals who are exceptional, but the guy who plays for the U13B team is equally important to me.' Rugby, cricket, athletics, cross-country, hockey, netball, tennis, basketball and rounders are all on offer, plus swimming, squash, sailing and horse riding. Football is flourishing: the boys recently did a football tour to Germany, and the girls countered with one to Holland. The school's Eton fives courts have been refurbished and put to work, and the Astroturf laid across the Priory's old burial site is in constant use. The monks slumbering below would surely approve – laborare est orare and why shouldn't the same be true of playing soccer?

Boarding: Available from year 7 upwards. Around a third of the students here board, and about two-thirds of the boarding community are from overseas and board full-time (the UK boarders tend to go home at weekends). The school works to keep a good balance of nationalities – it's popular with European students because of its location – but doesn't have quotas. The price of flexi boarding has been slashed, and the result is a much higher take-up: recently, for instance, a number of day pupils opted to stay over at the school after returning late from an evening theatre trip to London. How sensible is that?

Boarding houses are warm, comfortable and characterful: lots of light, views of Dover Castle. 'Every single child here gets their shirts ironed!' beamed the matron

Boarding houses are, according to the students, 'really family orientated'. Students share in threes until they reach year 11 when it drops to two, and only upper sixth formers are guaranteed a room to themselves. Accommodation is homely, bordering on shabby – utilitarian furniture and a washbasin is the norm here rather than fitted wardrobes and ensuites – but is warm and comfortable and characterful: lots of light, views of Dover Castle, potted geraniums at the entrances, cheerful common rooms equipped with games and coffee machines, and clothes lines strung across the laundry room ceilings in the basement – 'Every single child here gets their shirts ironed!' beamed the matron. It struck us as more genuinely cosy and welcoming than some schools we've visited, whose boarding houses may have been smart but had all the ambience of a motel. The boys have an excellent kitchen for their own use, and the girls are getting something as good very soon. Prefects get first pick of bedrooms in exchange for responsibilities: organising rotas, tidying the common room, supervising the younger ones, etc.

Unusually, no official exeats, although students can go home if they wish. Every weekend here is staffed and, according to students, chock-a-block with things to do. Saturday programme of trips – cultural, sporting, shopping – plus fun activities such as Quasar. Older students can opt instead to do supervised study. Sundays are relaxed and the emphasis is on winding down. Staff universally praised for their kindness and hard work – 'They're always there for you,' said a year 8 boy.

Ethos and heritage: Built on the site of the 12th-century Benedictine St Martin's Priory, Dover College was founded in 1871 by a group of local businessmen who wanted the town to have its own public school. In 1958 the then-headmaster Alec Peterson opened an international faculty in the sixth form before going on to help create the IB. The school has maintained proud and strong international links ever since. Originally for boys, it became fully coeducational in 1974, opened the junior department in 2001 and its own nursery in 2009.

The chapel is simply lovely, with white crumbly walls that put us in mind of Caerphilly cheese

Many buildings have been patched on down the years, but there's still a wonderful sense of history everywhere. We passed the remains of the original priory on our way to the junior school – two Victorian houses knocked together – and were given coffee in the barrel-ceilinged dining hall, which happens to be the oldest working school refectory in the UK. At the heart of the school is the chapel, which is simply lovely, with white crumbly walls that put us in mind of Caerphilly cheese, and timbered beams – a kindly, mellow, peaceful place. 'We're proudly Christian. It's our absolute moral compass here in the college,' affirmed the head, and who wouldn't feel the same in such a place? The school welcomes children of all faiths and of none, but everyone must attend chapel twice a week. For the seniors, this is formal worship, but for juniors, it's more like an assembly – we watched certificates and house stars being given out for reading, progress, courage, enthusiasm etc to children who were chatty, articulate and beautifully well-mannered. Evensong is held every Friday – parents are welcome to attend, and can also come along to assemblies: we spotted several rows of them at the back of the chapel smiling proudly at their offspring, before they headed off to the refectory to chat over tea and buns laid on by the school.

There are currently around 300 students on the roll for the entire school, ie from reception to year 13. The aim is to increase this to 350, but the school is keen to keep the sense of personalised education that is its USP, and class sizes will stay at a maximum of 15. Lots of integration between juniors and seniors – it really is one school. At mealtimes children sit in houses rather than year groups, to encourage a family atmosphere. A member of staff eats with them at the head of each table, and judges competitions such as 'who can eat the most vegetables'. It seemed a very happy ship to us. All the staff we spoke to expressed great satisfaction at working here, and a number also opt to send their children here. Great sense of loyalty to the school amongst Old Dovorians, many of whom play an active role in fundraising and development. 'We love the family feeling here,' said one mother. 'It's like a prep school that goes all the way up to 18.'

Pastoral care, inclusivity and discipline: In many ways, the teacher we spoke to summed up the appeal of this likeable school as we strolled across the beautiful old college green, dotted with junior pupils having a kickabout: 'In three years, I've never had to raise my voice. The children are fantastic, and there are are no discipline issues, so you can get on and teach. It's a wonderful place to work.' Parents agree. 'There's a very high standard of nurturing and care'; 'It's a real family atmosphere'; 'The communications are excellent'; 'Since coming here, the improvement in my children's confidence has been amazing.'

House staff are proactive in mending any broken friendships, and well-being is taken seriously. PSHE is taught throughout the school and carries a high profile. 'It doesn't have a chance to fall out of favour here,' according to deputy head. Pupils feel happy, safe and free to thrive. 'I haven't experienced any bullying here – the culture is not fostering of it,' asserted a sixth former. 'Compared to my old school, the bullying is none, non-existent,' said a younger student firmly.

The food used to be a source of unhappiness, but school has listened, created a student food council and appointed new chefs. Results are now 'massively improved' according to students, and we thought it excellent, one of the best school lunches we've had. Arriving on a Friday, we were offered a choice of four hot main courses: traditional fish and chips that wouldn't have disgraced an East End chippy, some thoroughly appetising smoked haddock and potatoes, rather excellent local sausages, and an inviting chicken curry. Unusually on a school visit, we really were hard-pressed to decide what to have. A visiting speaker who came to give a talk on the tea business liked the school so much that he offered to mix a blend especially for them, taking into account the particular chalkiness of the area's water. We can report that Dover College tea makes a most refreshing cuppa, inducing a mood of tranquillity and reflection.

Clear rewards and sanctions policy, but amongst both children and staff the overall feel here is a peaceable one. 'Every pupil here will have an opportunity to lead because of the school's size, but they also need to learn how to follow,' was a remark of the head's that impressed us. Students here combine both roles with warmth and composure.

Pupils and parents: Day pupils drawn mostly from a 20-mile radius – Canterbury, Ashford etc – ferried hither and yon by network of school minibuses. Predominantly Caucasian demographic of these reflects the area, but strong international intake ensures diversity and balance.

Many parents here are first-time buyers of private education, and show enormous support for and commitment to the school, actively involved in fundraising and helping out. 'We're just lucky to have our daughter here, and we'll help with whatever we can,' was a typical comment.

Money matters: Fees are extremely reasonable: weekly boarding here will set you back less than a day place at one of our leading London schools. A range of scholarships available at 11+, 13+ and 16+: academic, art and DT, drama, music, sport and all rounder. Means-tested bursaries available for those who need them.

The last word: Excellent value for money, something we don't often say in our line of work; sending your child here will genuinely set them up. But also a place that is human in its outlook: healthy, kind, and vigorous in its quest for excellence. As one student put it, 'I love it at this school, and I feel privileged to be here.'

Dulwich College

26

Dulwich Common, London SE21 7LD

020 8693 3601 | info@dulwich.org.uk | www.dulwich.org.uk

Ages: 11–18

Pupils: 1,633; sixth form: 492; Boarders: 140 full/weekly/flexi

Fees: Day £21,672; Boarding £42,408 – £45,234 pa

Master: Since 2009, Dr Joseph (Joe) Spence BA PhD (50s). Previously headmaster of Oakham School. Before that, 10 years as housemaster to the King's scholars at Eton College. Studied modern history and politics.

Grammar school educated, Dr Spence is vocal on education as a vehicle of social mobility – on a 'social mission' to attract pupils and staff from every background. Inspirational (not a word that we bandy around), sincere (without a hint of worthiness) and ambitious (but for the school rather than for himself). Generous in his praise for his team and quick to give credit where it's due. Parents describe his approach as 'grown-up', 'level', 'considered'. Appears to wear his responsibilities lightly, though, and brings a sense of fun to even the meatiest of topics – gives a rousing assembly, we hear.

Very excited by the 'fantastic cauldron of south London' that the school sits within. Leads the Southwark Schools' Learning Partnership, a network of independent and maintained schools collaborating to provide opportunities for students and teachers to learn from each other. Also works closely with Springboard charity to broaden access – 'Only with social mobility will come social amelioration,' he says. Proud of bursary candidates' Oxbridge success, but is 'not trying to make people into little bourgeois imitations – we want boys to keep a bit of where they're from.' 'Diversity within staff is coming,' he says, 'and candidates of colour are now coming through fields successfully.'

Married to a lawyer, with two sons and daughter, he still finds time to keep his own intellectual life alive – book-lined study bears testament to his love of history, drama, music, art and literature, and particularly all things Irish. Writes creatively ('happy to write a libretto overnight for the right commission' – one played on Radio 3 just recently). Mentors extended projects from SSLP and state-school educated Art History Link-Up students. Describes commitment to 'free learning' as 'my vision of what an independent education can be' – embracing 'those supra-curricular opportunities, that intellectual hinterland free of the constrictions of curriculum'.

Entrance: Not ultra-elite, but a high bar. 'We're committed to the top 15 per cent or so academically', students bringing different strengths, who will 'take hold of and enjoy the co-curricular'. At 11+, half of the 75 boys arrive from Dulwich College Junior School, others from primaries and preps. Letter from a registered professional needed to ensure appropriate SEN arrangements for entrance exam. At 13+ mainly prep feeders.

Exit: Less than 10 per cent leave after GCSEs. Majority who stay progress primarily to Russell Group universities. Imperial, King's College London, LSE, UCL, Bristol, Bath, Durham, Edinburgh, Exeter and Warwick all popular recently, in addition to drama and art foundation courses and degree apprenticeships. Nineteen to Oxbridge in 2021, plus seven medics. Increasing focus on global destinations, particularly the US. In 2021, students headed off to University of Virginia, University of Hamburg, Hong Kong University, University of Leiden, University of Canterbury (New Zealand), IE (Spain), University of California, Georgetown University, Georgia Tech, La Salle College of the Arts (Singapore), Penn State University, McGill NYU, ETHZ (Zurich) and Nanyang Technological University (China).

Latest results: School not releasing 2021 results. In 2020, 97 per cent 9-7 at I/GCSE. In 2019 (the last year when exams took place), 84 per cent 9-7 at I/GCSE; 63 per cent A*/A at A level/Pre-U (86 per cent A*-B).

Teaching and learning: Academic culture thriving. Focused on a love of learning for its own sake. 'We don't strain for everyone to get nine 9s'; accordingly, plenty of 7s at GCSE and the odd 6 too. Sciences, English, maths, history and art all do well. At A level, maths most popular by far (large numbers add further maths), followed by physics, history, economics, chemistry. Lots of A*s in chemistry, English literature, geography, Latin and further maths. Over a third of teachers there for over 10 years though new faces get the thumbs up from parents, who describe staff as 'hugely committed': 'they understand a boy's potential' and 'set the bar high'.

Free learning underpins everything – 'free from the syllabus, free from the constraints of the curriculum and freely engaged in by boys and teachers'. 'It's the interesting bits that usually happen in the crevices of the timetable,' Dr Spence explains – essay projects, competitions, debate – 'but embedded within the school day.' Thoughtful approach to teaching and learning, with boys researching a new topic independently before discussing it in a 'flip' lesson; individual mini-whiteboards enable teachers to assess understanding at a glance.

Free learning underpins everything – 'free from the syllabus, free from the constraints of the curriculum and freely engaged in by boys and teachers'

Only setting is in maths and languages. 'Idea of mixed ability pervades everything,' says deputy master, who believes that setting stifles potential growth by pigeonholing students. Separate sciences for everyone up to IGCSE. Boys seeking further intellectual stretch between years 7 and 11 can enrol on the lively scholars' programme.

Languages strong. French, Spanish, Chinese and Latin taught in lower school, with German, Italian and ancient Greek added later. Japanese, Arabic, Russian and Turkish off-timetable. Appealing language trips, including exchanges, with boys considerately settled in host families in pairs. School supports National MFL SCITT (School Centred Initial Teacher Training).

Quirky academic opportunities abound in sixth form. Dulwich Diploma encourages A level depth with something more like IB breadth – boys produce a 2000-word independent essay. All pupils take A level Plus, a programme of university-stye cross-departmental electives including American studies, gender studies, Page to Stage. Pupils engage in subject extension classes, cleverly branded eg 'further physics' rather than 'Oxbridge physics' to encourage wider engagement. Boys take advantage of national and international competitions, essay prizes and the lectures and provision that London offers.

Liberal studies taught alongside girls from JAGS and Sydenham, allowing everyone to learn in a co-ed environment – modern poetry, bookbinding, Italian cinema and ballroom dancing available. Annual Symposium comprises keynote speakers and workshops around a theme, recently 'Consumption', 'Tradition and Innovation' and 'Uncertainty'.

Learning support and SEN: Four well-qualified learning support teachers shared with the junior school, providing support to those 20 per cent of boys with a diagnosed learning difficulty. Eight per cent receive EAL support via two dedicated teachers.

The arts and extracurricular: Arts, music and co-curricular are outstanding. Offering has been rationalised recently – 'The breadth has always been there, but consistency of approach was needed.' Philosophy behind it is voluntarism – 'boys are there because they want to be there', though the school tracks who's been turning up to what.

A rich theatrical tradition (Edward Alleyn was a big name in theatre). Won a performing arts award in 2019. Lots of London theatre trips, plus three drama festivals and 24 performance pieces annually. Work ranges from low-key and topical (year 8 'ocean pollution'-themed puppetry) to colourful, energetic crowd-pleasers (like Guys and Dolls and Grease). Photos of past productions suggest enormous fun was had.

Sophisticated art department engages on a high academic level and balances use of new technology with recognition that hand drawing remains key. No gimmicks. We saw exuberant classes housed in light, bright facilities. Students use film, photography, printmaking and sculpture alongside canvas. Pieces are consistently thoughtful, often thought-provoking. Comic club and blank canvas club open to all. Artists-in-residence series, currently Anne Desmet RA (wood engraver) and Cecilia McDowall (composer).

Numbers learning instruments peak in the lower school at 45 per cent. All musicians celebrated, from enthusiastic beginners to leaders of section in the National Youth Orchestra or principals at Glyndebourne and the ENO. Shiny suites for music technology and acoustic percussion; small and large practice areas. The fully sound-insulated electric 'shed' would be a great place to let rip with the electric guitar, if only we were cool enough to know how.

Smallish rooms unlikely to worry teenage boys intent on studying and playing hard surrounded by friends. Common rooms with large screen for movie nights

Myriad clubs and societies during long lunch breaks and after school. Debaters consider issues of justice, equality, and equity in global and local contexts, learning the art of influence in meaningful and purposeful ways. Busy competitions programme – boys debate these issues with peers from a variety of schools and backgrounds. College continues to produce world class debaters who win major tournaments and are often included in the England team. Debating also seen as a place where everyone who is interested can find community and voice, building confidence.

Work around community and sustainability is now embedded into the wellbeing syllabus rather than being an optional add-on: 'It's fundamental to the foundation of the school.' College is building local partners 'rather than supporting them for a term and then disappearing' – boys and staff take these responsibilities seriously. College off-timetable for 'service day' each year, from DUCKS all the way up to sixth form. Boys involved with the usual visits to primary schools and care homes, but also support the council with upkeep of local parks and graveyards.

Sport: Year 7 is considered a time when skills are built and sports tried for the first time; rugby, football, hockey and cricket are all compulsory. By year 8 choices emerge, eg can drop rugby for fencing. No single sport is compulsory in the middle school but a plethora of teams lure lots in – skiing, rowing, fives, squash, cross-country and basketball, to name but a few. Boys can try golf, rock-climbing, self-defence, taekwondo and rugby 7s. Sixth formers still very involved, sometimes even officiating or coaching; they can also try croquet, horse riding or sailing. Cyclists use the superb facilities at Herne Hill velodrome.

Seventy acres of playing fields. Although rugby is the highest profile, the school points out that it is just one of many successful sports. High Performance Programme compulsory for sports scholars but open to all who demonstrate ability and potential. Boys represent GB in a range of sports. House competitions encourage everyone to take part.

Boarding: Two-thirds of boarders are in the sixth form, majority from China and Hong Kong but also Eastern Europe. Parents praised integration of overseas boarders and day boys, who are invited to fun socials including a Chinese New Year dinner. Four boarding houses are all on campus: modernised period houses decorated with OA sporting team photos. Quite basic in our view, smallish rooms with less than luxurious ensuite bathrooms, but unlikely to worry teenage boys intent on studying and playing hard surrounded by friends. Common rooms with large screen for movie nights, table football and toasters. Now offers flexi-boarding.

Ethos and heritage: Founded in 1619 by wealthy actor and businessman, Edward Alleyn, who set up and endowed the foundation, which includes Dulwich College, JAGS and Alleyn's, on a rolling manorial estate which William Blake later enjoyed visiting.

The college moved to its present site in the 1870s – a gracious and intriguing south London landmark. The Grade II listed buildings, designed by celebrated architect Charles Barry Junior (his father designed the Houses of Parliament), are rather lovely – a handsome Palladian structure with some twiddly bits added. The modern buildings forming a large part of the teaching spaces are functional if lacking in charm – possibly a bit depressing on a grey day. The Lord George Building which houses the Upper School Centre feels fresher, including the youthful and trendy Ned's Place, spacious and bright common rooms and popular 'work room' which is well stocked with banks of computers.

Stripy 'colours' blazers awarded in recognition of achievement. Ties come in all sorts of jazzy designs depending on society or event. Boys wear the uniform with pride

The Laboratory, costing over £21m, opened in 2016. Led by prestigious Grimshaw Architects – Cutty Sark, the Eden Project – it includes a 240-seat auditorium, five IT suites and 18 glassy labs. 'Boys can embark on their own adventures in learning' in this space, which is intended to unite arts and sciences. The Landscape Plan, already underway, is redeveloping the centre of the campus, replacing the car park with 'reflective spaces for the boys'. A wildlife boundary on the edge of the site has been established and 1,000 trees now grow across the campus. Ambitious plans are now also underway to regenerate the lower and junior schools.

Dulwich College International now consists of seven schools across China, South Korea and Singapore, as well as two more established in conjunction with Chinese schools. The 2019 Dulwich Olympiad was a celebration in London of sport, drama, music and art with 900 students representing all the Dulwich schools. The master is clear, though, that Dulwich in London is his absolute focus and 'has delegated all but top-level sign-off'.

Sartorial traditions are big but not taken too seriously. Boys and OAs enjoy the complexities of who wears which blazer or tie, but not in a pompous or snobbish way. Stripy 'colours' blazers awarded in recognition of achievement. Ties come in all sorts of depending on society or event. Boys wear the uniform with pride (though plenty of untucked shirts, of course – they're still teenage boys).

School lunches have had a makeover. Salad bar, jacket potatoes and pasta available every day with a rota of more exotic main courses including shakshuka, stroganoff or curry.

Alumni include Chiwetel Ejiofor, Raymond Chandler, PG Wodehouse, Nigel Farage, Lionel Barber, Sir Ernest Shackleton (would be quite the school reunion).

Pastoral care, inclusivity and discipline: Although the school is large, boys feel they know each other within their year. Transition points handled thoughtfully, ensuring boys get to bond with each other, for instance on a Welsh adventure when joining the lower school. Those that have known each other since DUCKS or the Juniors mix well with new joiners. Houses named after great Tudors, a rich collection of swashbucklers, romantics and men of letters. Wooden boards throughout the school see Drake, Spenser et al jostling for position – house competitions facilitate both friendships and rivalry.

We visited at a very challenging time for the school, just as the Everyone's Invited website hit the press and pushed Dulwich, alongside others, into headlines with anonymous accounts of sexual harassment by students from the school. The school has been happy to discuss it; Dr Spence confronted it head-on both in public announcements and in communications with current parents, who praised him for his 'characteristically balanced, level-headed, non-hysterical' approach. We spoke to parents about the school – are they aware of a 'rape culture', as the website claimed? We got the sense that the school was once quite a macho place but had softened. Rugby does not rule as it used to, and the behaviour sometimes associated with it seems not to be an issue; perhaps it once was, but the school is a different place now. The concept of 'positive masculinity' has been discussed within wellbeing sessions for a while, long before Everyone's Invited emerged.

Pastoral team switched-on and relatable. Warm, sensible (female) pastoral head told us that 'one of the positives of being a boys' school is the boys can be precisely who they want to be – there are no genderish subjects'. Dedicated head of wellbeing, 'excellent' school counsellor and five division heads make up her team. Every form tutor delivers wellbeing lessons weekly. 'Consent, teenage drinking, feminism, sexual health – if you're having those conversations with your form tutor then it's not embarrassing to bring it up if you're worried about yourself or a friend,' the school told us even before Everyone's Invited broke. School considering introducing a sports psychologist and CBT.

Annual Dulwich College Identity Awareness Month – DC I AM – involves a series of events around 'who we are and our respect for difference'. Big focus on LGBTQ+ issues with 'powerful' boy-led events showing 'it's okay to be out'. This year's ended with a community curry cookalong during lockdown: 'We got this guy who runs a community curry club to cook a five course curry – the whole community, parents, boys, staff, were on screen cooking together – such a funny night.' Diversity and Inclusion Alliance created in response to BLM ('we had always quietly thought about it but we'd not properly grasped what needed to be done') – run by an English teacher who also sits in on every staff recruitment interview. School has started 'looking at the opportunities [candidates] didn't have' when assessing CVs, and actively looking to recruit a diverse teaching body, 'to allow boys to feel represented positively'.

Expectations around behaviour and respect are high. School takes a tough line on bullying. Any problems with punctuality, organisation or effort are flagged very quickly with the daily report system. Gross misconducts such as possession of drugs or bullying would result in consideration for exclusion, whether fixed-term or permanent, rather than an automatic exclusion.

Pupils and parents: Socially inclusive. A culturally and ethnically diverse population, augmented by the boarders though lots of multilingual day children too. 'It takes boys who are sporty, academic, musical, artistic and a mixture of all those things. If your child is gifted in one area, they will soar here. If they are a good all-rounder they will be encouraged to be a great all-rounder,' said a parent. It may come as a surprise to find that parents describe each other typically as 'a good bunch of mixed, non-stuffy parents', 'un-snobbish and not cliquey'. Many families local, but Foundation coaches come from as far as Notting Hill, Canary Wharf, Wimbledon and Chislehurst.

Money matters: Nearly a third of boys have some financial assistance – two-thirds of these from scholarships, the rest from bursaries. Up to 105 per cent fee remission available on a means-tested basis. Parents feel the school offers excellent value for money. Exciting times ahead as a needs-blind future, championed by the master, will see up to 50 per cent of students on financial support. A protective measure against becoming a school for the global super-rich, certainly, but Dr Spence freely admits it is 'enlightened self-interest', too. Partly funded by OAs keen to give something back, it sits very well in this already socially enlightened place.

The last word: Don't be fooled. Dulwich may be 400 years old, but the approach to learning and co-curricular is bang up to date. PG Wodehouse (known as 'Plum' to his schoolmates) described his time there as 'six years of unbroken bliss' – thanks to an ambitious bursary scheme, this privilege will now be available to the brightest from all backgrounds. Academic, yes, but not elitist. A super school for busy boys with inquiring minds.

Dulwich Prep Cranbrook

27

Coursehorn, Cranbrook, Kent TN17 3NP

01580 712179 | registrar@dulwichprepcranbrook.org | www.dulwichprepcranbrook.org

Ages: 3–13

Pupils: 400; **Boarders:** 29 weekly/flexi

Fees: Day £6,465 – £19,965 pa; Boarding £40.00 – £44 per night

Headmaster: Since 2010, Paul David (50s) with a BEd in maths and PE from St Luke's, University of Exeter (he grew up in Cornwall). He taught at the City of London Freemen's School in Surrey, where he was housemaster, prior to becoming deputy head of St Paul's Juniors. He also taught maths at St Paul's. Became headmaster of Eaton Square School in 2002.

Although his rugby playing days are behind him, he is still a keen skier and walker. He also plays the trumpet in the school orchestra. Married to Nicky who teaches PSHE at the school. They live in a house in the grounds and have two older children, both of whom were at Dulwich.

'He is besuited and business like and likes order but is very approachable and his door is always open,' says a parent. 'He has the children's best interests at heart and believes in what he is doing and won't bow to parental pressure,' says another. He is always out and about around the school – even more so now that the family has a dog and is a regular visitor at the Star of the Week and the special assembly at Nash House.

He says children are encouraged to try everything to see where their talents lie and are then stretched and supported in equal measure. He says it is very rare for a child not to fit in at Dulwich and 'quirky kids' will find their niche. He has worked hard to put child mental wellbeing at the centre of everything the school does and the school is a leader in the area – see more below.

We're pretty sure that every school we now visit will have its art compared to the benchmark of Dulwich Prep Cranbrook. Leavers were making a flock of porcelain Matisse-inspired doves. 'Dulwich has the best art in the south-east,' says a mother

The remote learning during the pandemic was 'pretty phenomenal' says a parent and was up and running from March and improved over time and included not only academic work but yoga and singing and children were given a chance to chat to their friends in between lessons.

Entrance: Nash House is for 3 to 5 year olds, Little Stream for those aged 5 to 9 years and the Upper School for pupils in their final years. Unconditional offers for children joining nursery to year 2; children who start in the term in which they turn 3, join Fledglings, based in the nursery. Children can and do join at any stage, but main entry points 4+ and 7+ and school is popular with families moving out of London. In years 3 to 8, children sit an assessment and spend a day at school.

Exit: All parents are invited for a discussion about senior schools in year 5 and Dulwich is equally supportive of those who leave at 11+ or 13+ and the headmaster has built good relationships with senior schools. About 40 per cent of pupils leave at 11+ for Cranbrook as well as other grammar and independent schools. Destinations at 13+ include Cranbrook, The King's School, Canterbury, Benenden, Tonbridge, Sevenoaks, Mayfield, Sutton Valence, Eastbourne College and Claremont. Usually a high number of scholarships, often with top academic scholarships to Tonbridge and Benenden – 23 in 2020.

Our view: The headmaster describes the ethos of the school as 'a world of possibilities' where self-belief and confidence can be nurtured and there is an emphasis on kindness. There are benefits for those who stay on until 13+ as they have a chance to shine and get into the top teams. Years 7 and 8 are setted in small groups with the flexibility to move around. They follow the Dulwich Colours Programme, an innovative curriculum for languages and humanities encouraging independent and collaborative project work alongside the basic Common Entrance course.

Teachers a good mix of 'lifers' and younger staff and 'their commitment and enthusiasm is unbelievable,' says a parent. French is taught from Little Stream, Latin from year 6 with Spanish added in years 7 and 8. Late joiners may play catch up with languages not encountered before. Personal tutors monitor progress of children in years 7 and 8 as well as acting as mentors.

IT is well integrated within the school. Each pupil in years 7 and 8 has personal ownership of an iPad which just becomes part of their pencil case – the head describes a textiles project in which students used their iPads to record progress from start to finish with time-lapse photography. The library is large with a full-time librarian and boasts some 7,000 titles.

Plenty of dressing-up days in Little Stream and Nash House: on Egyptian day they mummified a member of staff. As well as form teachers, subject specialists for maths and science. Very ordered, bright and inviting classrooms with tortoises in the science room. Children smiley and chatty and teachers are thrilled to work in the building they had input into designing. Plenty of individual attention. A mother having observed her children learning through play in the initial years told us: 'It is obvious great care has been given by the teaching staff to establish a curriculum which suits the children both academically and emotionally.'

This is a school which places an emphasis on 'oracy' – standing up and speaking well is all part of the school's effort in developing socially confident individuals. Several parents credit their children's flourishing independence to the school. Some testing lower down the school, then more of an emphasis on twice-yearly exams from year 5 – the children we met about to sit them said they were used to testing and it was no big deal.

Every child plays sport and everyone in year 3 and above plays in a match against other schools. From year 4 children must be available to play in Saturday matches. There are also Tribe (house) fixtures for each age group and the specialist coaches and gap students are shared around teams of all abilities. Girls play netball, hockey, lacrosse, rounders and tennis, also taking part in cross-country, track and field events, triathlon and swimming. Boys take part in these too and play football, rugby, hockey and cricket. Outdoor swimming pool is used during the summer months.

Those who don't enjoy team sports can take part in the Dulwich Inspires! programme which includes sailing on the local reservoir and biking in the forest. The school has hosted IAPS and national cross-country competitions, the under-13 lacrosse team were the only one from a prep school to reach the last 16 of the national championships and the school boasts handy table tennis players too.

Sixty per cent take instrumental lessons. Taster music lessons are available to children in year 3 on a wide range of instruments from the kinder horn to the ukulele. Some attend the Junior Royal College of Music on Saturdays. Children play at regional festivals such as the Hastings Music Festival and musical ensembles have toured Prague and Italy. The Tribe music competition, performed in front of the whole school, is a highlight. There is a string orchestra in Little Stream and a senior orchestra, percussion groups, woodwind ensemble, Rock School, Stringcredibles, jazz band and choirs.

Drama is timetabled. Each year group performs annually, whether straight plays or musicals such as Grease or The Sound of Music. Performances, musical and dramatic, are spectacular according to parents, who if they appear windswept it is because they all report being so frequently 'blown away'.

We're pretty sure that every school we now visit will have its art compared to the benchmark of Dulwich Prep Cranbrook: truly stunning from the earliest beginnings in Little Stream to the beautiful scholarship work that to our eyes easily compared to GCSE projects elsewhere. Leavers were working on a sculpture project making a flock of porcelain Matisse-inspired doves (there are two kilns) holding bundles. The director of creative arts conceives new projects every year, so year 4 does not always do X and year 5 Y, and says much is child-led. 'Dulwich has the best art in the south-east,' says a mother.

There are trips relating to every subject, ranging from visiting Lullingstone Roman villa to outings to the West End for drama and geography field trips to the coast. In Nash House all classrooms have an outdoor learning area (under a retractable roof) leading onto the playground. Little Stream enjoy forest school activities and from year 5 start camping in the grounds, progressing to a full week in Snowdonia by year 8. Teachers with a passion run clubs, most included in the fees. Huge range including coding, thinking skills, art, drama, Dulwich entrepreneurs and a variety of music and sports.

Dorms of four to eight, some in bunk beds. Resident tutor and a games room and common room. Pupils say they board 'because they love it' and all bring their teddies

An hour from London by train, rather more by car, the school is set in 50 acres of glorious Kent countryside and has beautifully groomed playing fields. It has a charming history – Dulwich Prep London (DPL) evacuated its 300 boys by train to Cranbrook at the start of World War II, setting up in huts in the headmaster's orchard, and after the war remained as a separate school. The two schools are still linked and are run by the Dulwich Preparatory Schools Trust. It became fully co-educational in 1975.

Buildings are not as beautiful as some prep schools in the area. However, the pre-prep resides in a stylish new-build, with the same architect as DPL – a wooden exterior, fabulous in and out spaces and a large soft-surface playground. Classrooms are vast by metropolitan standards and every inch looks fun. Little Stream also has use of the outdoor heated swimming pool.

Parents praised the pastoral care as 'excellent', 'impressive' and 'thoughtful' and there has been a move towards further developing this aspect of the school's provision. The head places an emphasis on nurturing self-confidence but says, 'You don't need to be "robust" to do well here.' All new children have buddies. The head attends all the pastoral meetings and says he has never before worked with 'staff who are so attuned to children'. Mental health awareness is high on the agenda and everyone is delighted with the recent partnership with Place2Be for one-to-one counselling and group sessions. The school introduced the iSpace and iWonder programmes in 2019 to help children build emotional resilience. Children are encouraged to talk about mental health in a normal way and to distinguish between big issues and little problems. The aim is to help children develop a deeper understanding of 'self'. They are already becoming better equipped to identify situations that are likely to cause them stress and they are learning how to self-regulate and regain control when their emotions take them close to tipping point.

Learning support is provided for approximately 170 pupils. As well as dyslexia and dyspraxia a wide range of other needs such as maths, sensory processing, or speech and language difficulties, hearing or visual impairment and complex medical conditions can be catered for. The school is quick to pick up on children who are working behind the curve and SEN is taught in small groups and occasionally one-to-one. Some withdrawal, some in class. All learning support is included in the fees, not always the case elsewhere.

Food highly praised, with cowboy pie being particularly popular (we didn't ask about the ingredients). Cafeteria style system for the older children and younger ones sit at tables with their teachers in the Morrison Gallery next door.

New extended day care options – a choice of breakfast and after-school clubs. Day boarding is available until 8.00 pm for year 5 and above and year 4 siblings: includes tea, supervised prep and an activity.

Most families live within a 20-mile radius of the school and many have recently moved to the area from London. 'It is a real mix from the creative industries, doctors, finance, and farming.' Large numbers are dual income families and some are very rich, said a mother, 'but it is not at all snobbish'. The friends group organise lots of events, new parents are made to feel welcome and there is a strong sense of community.

Boarding: There are 29 boarding places in The Manor with boys and girls accommodated on different floors in dorms above the headmaster's study – beamed and very homely with some up in the eaves. Dorms of four to eight, some in bunk beds. Flexi-boarding offered from one night to full weekly boarding. Resident tutor and a games room and common room. Pupils say they board 'because they love it' and all bring their teddies. Lobby full of tennis racquets and cricket bats, overflowing bike shed, boarders' fire pit.

The last word: One long-standing parent told us: 'The quality of teaching has been excellent across the curriculum and in many areas exceptional.' Recent migrators say: 'outstanding' and 'the standard is high'.

Eastbourne College
28
Old Wish Road, Eastbourne, East Sussex BN21 4JX
01323 452323 | admissions@eastbourne-college.co.uk | www.eastbourne-college.co.uk
Ages: 13-18
Pupils: 650; sixth form: 300; Boarders: 290 full/weekly/flexi
Fees: Day £24,735 – £25,230; Boarding £37,695 – £38,280 pa

Head: Since 2016, Tom Lawson (PPE Oxford), married to Jessica with two children and adored boxer dog Roy. Previously deputy head at Christ's Hospital, and a 16-year stint at Winchester.

At Eastbourne College (EC), the head has found his fit. He looks back wistfully to a time when public school was about becoming a balanced human being, not hitting the top of the league tables; his primary aim for pupils: to be good people other people want to be with – 'they come out really nice...'

Loved by pupils, who smile when they think of their head: 'great guy – decent sense of humour'; 'modern – bringing EC into the 21st century'; 'really nice... witty... makes an effort to know us all'. Tells great stories in assembly, which always start, 'So there I was...'

Parents like him too: 'really approachable... very jolly'; 'highly intelligent... great business acumen'; 'will look at each child... understand that kids can have a bad day'.

Entrance: Lightly selective. Pupils from the allied St Andrew's Prep, with which EC is working on a bridging curriculum for years 7-9, and other prep and state schools. EC now accepts pupils on the basis of school report, CAT scores and reference in year 6; the head seeing no point in the CE, or putting year 6 pupils through the stress of a test.

Exit: Around 20 per cent leave after GCSE. At 18, most to university, the majority to Russell Group. Exeter, Cardiff, Durham, KCL, Warwick and Newcastle all popular. Five to Oxbridge in 2021, and five medics. Usually some overseas – seven in 2021, all to the USA including Vassar College and Parsons New York (school has a strong reputation for sending good numbers of tennis player to

US universities on scholarships). Often a few into business apprenticeships, specialist art or drama colleges such as Guildhall School of Speech and Drama, ACM and University of the Arts.

Latest results: In 2021, 65 per cent 9-7 at GCSE; 58 per cent A*/A (80 per cent A*-B) at A level. In 2019 (the last year when exams took place), 60 per cent 9-7 at GCSE; 40 per cent A*/A at A level.

Teaching and learning: Pupils head down in quiet concentration. Is it always like this? In maths, mostly, but not when it doesn't need to be. Not in English, said our guide, people talk non-stop in English. And in economics – which the head teaches.

A largely traditional subject offering, including classical civilisation, Greek and Latin, but politics have made it onto the curriculum and the school is open to offering other subjects where there's demand – 28 subjects now offered in sixth form. Desire to study non-curricular languages is accommodated wherever possible.

EPQ or the Gold Arts Award available to supplement A levels. The head is also introducing an online passport to ensure pupils are on track for life, to include skills from cooking, driving and finance to team work, charity and resilience. By the time they come to fill out UCAS, these pupils will be ready, as will macaroni cheese and a balanced bank account.

An excellent level of high-end results at this lightly selective school. Science and maths are particular strengths. The head is keen to increase academic results, but says he will do this with better teaching and learning, not by becoming more selective. '[They] work twice as hard because it's not selective,' said a parent, who added that this comment could apply equally to teachers and pupils.

One parent said her above-average son thrives at the EC 'because of the nurturing approach, and their kind, gentle way of getting results'. Another described the teaching as 'on the whole good', others commenting on the 'spectacular teachers', in particular in science and music. There is the odd bit of home tutoring here and there, but extra sessions are also provided at school.

Two reports a term, achievement and effort grades; tutors go through reports with pupils, who add their comments and targets, before the report is posted online for parents. Feedback in report cards is very helpful, said a parent; they are 'on top of it all the way'.

Saturday morning lessons have been replaced with a programme of optional guided enrichment sessions.

A head of futures is in post, and sixth formers are delighted: one told us careers advice used to be 'nothing much', but now they have someone to help with university, careers, and skills; 'very good news,' said a parent. There's no point going to an event if you can't go up to someone, shake hands and introduce yourself, says the head of futures, fresh from a lesson on communication skills and year 9 pain at having to stand before their classmates and say their name and what they love doing.

Head wants to ensure pupils are on track for life. By the time they come to fill out UCAS, these pupils will be ready, as will macaroni cheese and a balanced bank account

School of Pre-Medicine (series of seminars for sixth formers) is popular, and the school is one of only a few in the country to be fully trained up to teach the Chartered Institute for Financial Securities & Investment (CISI) level 2 award in fundamentals of financial services.

Learning support and SEN: Learning support help with a broad range of conditions, but not at the severe end of the spectrum. Out of class, one-to-one assistance, charged as extra. Parents are very happy with support, one saying the head of learning support is 'approachable, helpful and great at communication'; another that her dyslexic son has had 'phenomenal results'. All year groups screened.

The arts and extracurricular: There's space every afternoon for co-curricular activities (although we have never seen detention listed as such before): games, service or creatives.

Service starts in year 10 with CCF for all; not all are keen, but school is enthusiastic about the opportunities for challenge and teamwork. Some continue with CCF, while other year 11s learn the skills to go out into the community. By years 12 and 13, pupils are volunteering in charity shops, schools and old people's homes.

The creatives' options include all things musical and artistic, from the Gold Arts Award (an arts alternative to the EPQ) to singing with the Decibelles or Testostertones. Parents comment on the 'amazing art and music departments', with a 'standard of professionalism [that is] wonderful'.

Art exam work is displayed in the Birley Centre and is of a very high standard – pupils regularly obtain top grades here. The art department is rich with works of the imagination, and lively with challenge, a teacher describing with enthusiasm the reward of life drawing without looking at the paper. We loved the innovative work in textiles, projects showing the meticulous care taken by pupils, one considering a 'communion of threads'; we particularly liked the map dress, cut to a figure and a landscape.

A parent described the musical talent at EC as 'unbelievable'. There aren't any foreign music tours (unlike sports and arts), but plenty of domestic performances, and 'standards are incredible' at school open concerts, say parents.

There's a lively drama department, with productions ranging from School of Rock to The Crucible, and a small group performing at the Edinburgh Fringe in 2019.

Sport: 'It's a very sporty school,' said a parent, and they play everything, the girls excelling in tennis and hockey, the boys at rugby, which is the major boys' sport here (football is classed as one of the many 'other options'). 'Hockey is excellent,' said a parent, whose son plays for England, and says the school is very flexible about time away training, and helping him catch up with work afterwards. A girls' cricket team is just starting up, and the school will accommodate any girls who want to play football. The school is very proud that 93 per cent of pupils represented the school in teams last year, believing that team play is one of the best things about sport. The aquathalon (swimming in the sea, then running along the prom) was only cancelled because of stormy seas – but the whole school was steeplechasing across the downs...

Boarding can be full or weekly and there's odd nights in for day pupils in Arnold Lodge; they really cater for all. 'Flexibility makes it what it is,' said one parent

The school has just completed £33m worth of works – Project 150 (that's how many years they've been here); they have 'enhanced how [my daughters] feel about [school],' said a parent. It's top class stuff – not just a big swimming pool, but one with Olympic training pads at the end of each lane; the ballet studio even has a raised roof for those high leaps across the centre. Dry changing rooms and wet; everything a sporty person could desire. DofE too, with the highest rate of gold awards in Sussex.

Boarding: Around 45 per cent of pupils here board, with three boys' and two girls' boarding houses. They cross the age range and pupils form small families who look out for each other; it works really well. International boarders come from a range of countries, and make up 15-20 per cent of the boarding community.

Parents describe strong teams in the houses, from matrons who 'really look after them' to 'the housemistress [who] couldn't have done more to help my daughter settle,' said a parent, admitting it was hard but saying they give plenty of individual attention, and the housemistress was 'amazing – dealt with issues before they became issues'. Another described her son's housemaster as 'absolutely brilliant... slightly disorganised... it's quite endearing... he needs a nap now and then'. Her weekly boarding son has learnt to be very organised, but there are prompts – 'They don't expect complete self sufficiency,' said the parent.

Spacious, colourful common rooms with a constant supply of fruit, and kitchen for toast and drinks. Own ensuite room from year 11, spacious shared study bedrooms in years 9 and 10; no choice over room mates – pupils don't seem to mind. 'If girls don't get on, they will be thrown in together; they will press on through difficulties by getting to know each other,' said a parent. 'They don't shy away from problems.'

'Flexibility makes it what it is,' said one parent. Boarding can be full or weekly and there's odd nights in for day pupils in Arnold Lodge; they really cater for all, with some obligatory community weekends in ('a good thing,' said a parent).

Matches on Saturday afternoons, and trips on Sunday – Thorpe Park, Harry Potter World and the like.

Saturday nights on the town for upper sixth until 10.30pm. A two-drink limit, supposedly, but sensibly enforced – 'providing you're not wobbling or vomiting, no one's going to breathalyse you,' said a sixth former; they appreciate being treated as responsible human beings, and behave accordingly.

Ethos and heritage: The thing about Eastbourne, said a parent, is that it's actually 'not that far'. It feels like a peaceful backwater, but is only an hour and half away from London, a seaside town with its broad streets and bracing air. EC was described by a parent as having 'a public school, traditional feeling'; there are old flint buildings that fit this description nicely, but it is an indisputably modern school, with new classrooms and sports facilities to prove it. Popular new Wifi café and a new Futures Centre too.

One parent chose EC because of its intimate size: 'It feels like a close family. Everyone knows each other.' The head describes a 'confident, calm community' where there is space for fun, and this

'What's your favourite colour?' asked the head, and the ceiling of the smart new dining hall glowed red in response

seemed almost exactly right. There's chatter, but no rowdiness (though year 10 can be a bit wild, say sixth formers; 'that was a good year,' said a year 11 nostalgically). There is a feeling of competence and organisation, pupils who know where they're going and what they're doing. 'Both girls feel quite special being there... If it wasn't warm, relaxed and efficient, they wouldn't cope with the long days,' said a parent.

The pupils we met were friendly and unassuming; not much arrogance here, and it's difficult to imagine these modest pupils bragging about their achievements (might need to practise a bit of this before those university interviews).

The school is part of the Eastbourne Schools Partnership, which involves local schools getting together to benefit all, activities ranging from digital workshops to community orchestras, and Roy's homework club, where EC sixth formers – and the head's dog – tutor struggling GCSE pupils from partner schools, with both tutor and tutee benefiting hugely.

House feeling is strong; houses are homes in a school with a boarding atmosphere, even for day pupils, and pupils go back to their houses during break times or free lessons. We saw a fantastic boys' day house, with table football, pool and ping pong, and thought the girls might like some of this in their houses too. The boys even had an Astro with floodlighting in the back garden for football. Apparently the girls do come over sometimes, and use it for hockey.

An active school council make members' voices heard: complaints about too-long lunch queues have led to staggered intake, and girls requested and voted for trousers, now part of the uniform.

'What's your favourite colour?' asked the head, and the ceiling of the smart new dining hall glowed red in response. The food consumed in it has 'massively improved', said a parent, and we hear fine things of breakfast – 'best meal of the day'. There's a café, which can be used by sixth formers during free lessons, bringing something of a university feel for the upper years.

Pastoral care, inclusivity and discipline: 'Brilliant pastoral care,' said parent, 'tutors will call just to say how things are going', another parent telling us the school identified and told her about a problem with her daughter before she knew anything was wrong; this seems typical of this vigilant and proactive school.

Care begins in the houses, and parents report close relationships with housemistresses/masters, one describing a housemistress as 'very caring, very prompt in all queries, seeks opinion if unsettled. Really on top of things. Keeps things in proportion.' House structure can vary a bit, said one parent, whose son's current head of house is 'caring, but doesn't command respect'.

The non-hierarchical house structure promotes friends through the year groups, and this helps prevent bullying, say parents. 'Really like a family – what you want when you hand children over to an institution – [that they] have child's interests at heart.' One described a bullying incident – 'ragging' – dealt with thoroughly through the house system, and says small issues are efficiently dealt with this way.

Certainly a school for second chances, agree head and pupils, a parent commenting that 'the school really makes the effort' to involve them in education about mental health for teens, and is 'very open about drink and drugs': drug users will have to submit to a testing regime, sellers will be out. 'It's more what goes on at home that is the problem,' says the head, who tells parents they have to develop a 'digital spine'. What happens out of school certainly counts, whether in uniform or not.

Pupils and parents: Mostly local middle-class professionals and quite a few old boys; 'down to earth parents,' said one. 'Everyone welcome,' said another, describing a parent community which is 'as strong as you want it to be'. An ex-state school parent said he 'sometimes feels like the hick cousin', but that his children have not felt this at all and settled easily.

Parents and pupils agree that it would suit a wide variety of children, and, said a parent, 'would sort out disruptive kids'. Lots of siblings at this family school. One parent chose it because she wanted mixed sex, mixed ability for her non-alpha oldest son, but has also found it right for her highly self-sufficient second son too.

Very efficient school buses, 'so many routes... bend over backwards to help'.

Money matters: Scholarships from five to 20 per cent of fees. Means-tested bursaries of up to 60 per cent.

The last word: This is a friendly, down-to-earth school which, as a parent said, 'thinks about the whole person... the roundedness of the individual'. Hard workers will thrive here, and relish the great opportunities available.

Edgeborough School

Edgeborough, Frensham, Farnham, Surrey GU10 3AH

01252 792495 | admissions@edgeborough.co.uk | www.edgeborough.co.uk

Ages: 2–13

Pupils: 361; Boarders: 80 weekly/flexi

Fees: £11,571 – £18,789 pa

Linked school: Charterhouse, 610

Headmaster: Since April 2022, Mr Daniel Cox. Formerly deputy headmaster and 'future schools lead' of Lambrook School in Berkshire. Prior to joining Lambrook, Mr Cox spent 11 years at Churcher's College in Hampshire, a school for pupils aged 3-18, most recently as senior teacher and a member of the senior management team. While there, he completed an MSc in education and management

Mr Cox's early teaching career had a strong sports focus, and he was both head of rugby and director of sport at Churcher's College. He has played representative rugby at a regional level and is a keen sailor, cricketer and golfer. Unsurprisingly therefore, he is a strong proponent of a rich and varied co-curriculum that provides children with the broadest range of opportunities. He also has a firm belief that to be truly successful an independent school needs to be outward-looking, and he was been responsible for developing Lambrook's very effective outreach and partnership programme.

Entrance: Gently selective. Around 20 pupils join reception each year and there's another intake at year 3 to form three classes for this age group. Will accept applications into other year groups if vacancies occur. Since August 2021, Edgeborough is part of the Charterhouse family of schools.

Exit: Some pupils go at 11+ but most leave at 13+ to a good variety of day and boarding senior schools including Charterhouse, Lord Wandsworth College, Cranleigh and Wellington. Eleven scholarships in 2021.

Our view: Edgeborough started life as a 'coaching establishment' in 1895 and opened in Guildford as a boys' boarding school in 1905. Moved to its current site – 50 wooded acres that look out over the Surrey hills – in 1939. Main house, Frensham Place, is a sturdy Victorian mansion that was once home to newspaper magnate and founder of the Daily Express, Sir Cecil Arthur Pearson. The head's secretary at the time spotted the building and thought it might be suitable; shortly afterwards it was purchased by the school for £7,000. Co-ed since 1992.

Nursery and pre-prep are housed in Scandi-style wooden chalets with generous covered outdoor play areas, little raised gardening plots and extensive grounds beyond. Every other Friday the youngest children head off into the forest for 'woodland activities'. Apparently, London escapee parents (of whom there are increasing numbers) can't get over how much space their children have to play and learn in.

'You're never hungry here and our match teas are the best,' we were told. We can vouch for both friendly atmosphere and delicious food

A feature of the nursery classrooms was pointed out to us (if an absence of something can be called a feature): there are no teacher desks, everything is at child level. It sounded like a good idea at the time, but what's the theory behind it? Is there proof that full-size furniture inhibits early learning and, if so, how did we all cope? Perhaps it's nice for the children, if they actually notice, but we felt a bit sorry for the teachers. Those tiny chairs must take a toll on adult backs.

Parents can find out what their children are up to (and comment) via the Tapestry App, an online early years 'learning journal'. Mini trips to investigate things like the postal sorting office or supermarket (Waitrose, naturally) are followed up by role play and other activities. We crept in to get a preview of rehearsals for the nursery nativity play – confident singing and a very good year 8 narrator.

Big emphasis on sharing 'positive praise' – not just from teachers, parents can also give stars when their child does something noteworthy at home. Recognising individual achievements, however 'normal' they may seem to others, is a big part of the Edgeborough culture and starts early.

Everything we saw in the prep was as it should be, from the merry, paint-spattered art room to the very impressive science labs. The labs (one brand new) are designed so that they can be reconfigured every term according to which science is being studied; wooden benches appear to have made a comeback, apparently 'it's a much better surface for chemistry'. Upstairs is food technology and science equipment used by the younger children when they come over from the pre-prep. In DT pupils were working on a sofa for the new year 8 common room and we admired Ferris wheels controlled by computer programmes, all designed and built by the children. Testing for SEN as and when required from reception onwards; parents say problems are picked up quickly and learning support (known as Leap) is very good.

Music teaching described as 'absolutely incredible', one even went so far as to call it 'miraculous', with reports of harmonious noises being coaxed from the most unpromising sources. Every single reception pupil learns the violin but there's no need for parents to buy earplugs: 'They don't have to practise at home,' we were told, 'it's done to get them all playing something together.' Music for all is the theme, but there's plenty of scope for variations and solo talents with four choirs and lots of instrumental ensembles. The same goes for drama – we heard no complaints about parts always going to the select few.

Sport is a big part of Edgeborough life and as one might expect the onus is on fun, fitness and team effort; on playing the game as much as hammering the opposition (fortunately both are achieved). 'Children are developed and stretched, whatever their ability,' one parent told us. Girls and boys play hockey and cricket; rugby, football, lacrosse and netball divide along gender lines. There's specialist sports coaching for all from nursery upwards. Dance (street, tap, modern and ballet) is a popular extracurricular option as are judo, gymnastics and climbing. Plenty of pitches, an Astro and an adventure playground, pool is outdoors and getting that covered seems to be high on children's and parents' wish list.

Nice old-school dining room (rather dramatic fireplace, honours boards, long tables); 'family style service' – prep children can choose where they sit and staff 'dot about'. 'You're never hungry here and our match teas are the best,' we were told. We can vouch for both friendly, informal atmosphere and delicious food. Days are fun, busy – and quite long, with a 4.20pm finish; older pupils can stay on for prep, supper and activities until 7.30pm. 'Great for logistics,' said one mother, 'but exhausting at first.' She felt that children needed to have 'lots of energy' and to be 'well organised'. Nothing but praise for school's pastoral care: 'staff know the children so well', 'they really help children grow in confidence and self-esteem'.

Rooms, named after leaders, Nelson, Drake, Churchill etc (great chaps all of them, but bit of a boys' school hangover, we wondered?), are warm and brightly decorated

Close to Camberley and Aldershot but no significant numbers from military families – 'we're not reliant on that,' says head; more likely that one or both parents are working in London. Quite a lot of parents were brought up round here, moved to London for work and have returned, hoping to give their children a bit more green space and a lot less school pressure. They approve of Edgeborough's traditional values, several singling out pupils' smart appearance and good manners: 'they look you in the eye'. They love the small classes (average of 14) and want their children to do well – but not at any cost. That's why they're so supportive of the school's attitude: 'Teachers tell children not to worry about exams, that they'll get into the school that's right for them. They want pupils to work hard but also to learn from things that go wrong. It takes the pressure off them.'

Boarding: No Saturday school, boarding is Monday to Friday only. Can board from year 3 although majority start from year 5. Most do from one to three nights but odd night's 'hotel boarding' also available. Everyone has their own bed, even if they only stay one night a week. As usual, dorms occupy what were once servants' quarters at top of main house, boys and girls at either end. Rooms, named after leaders, Nelson, Drake, Churchill etc (great chaps all of them, but bit of a boys' school hangover, we wondered?), are warm and brightly decorated; corridors feature lots of photos and well-kept, informative noticeboards. Rule is no individual screens – phones are handed in; contact with outside world is via landline. Nice, homely kitchen with sofa where boarders can make tea and toast. After supper there's a choice of indoor and outdoor activities (day pupils can stay for these) until 7.30pm after which boarders can watch films in the common room, 'do baking' or just spend time with friends; 'there's always someone to talk to'.

The last word: 'Make the most of every opportunity and enjoy every second,' staff tell pupils, and Edgeborough is just the place to do it. Inclusive, ambitious, just the right balance of traditional and modern – and a huge amount of fun.

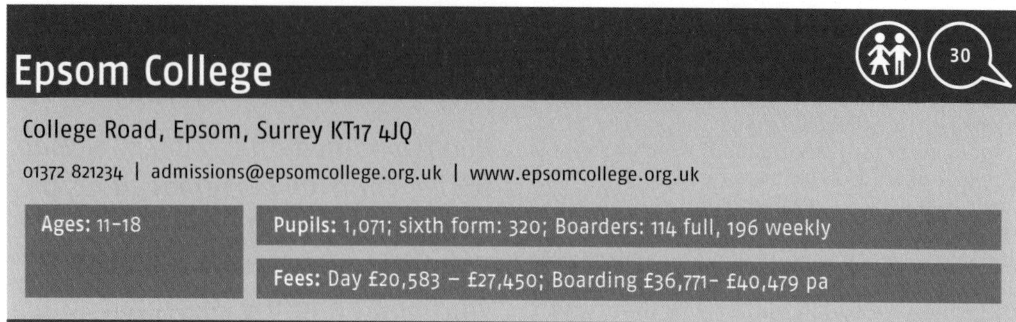

Epsom College

College Road, Epsom, Surrey KT17 4JQ

01372 821234 | admissions@epsomcollege.org.uk | www.epsomcollege.org.uk

Ages: 11–18

Pupils: 1,071; sixth form: 320; Boarders: 114 full, 196 weekly

Fees: Day £20,583 – £27,450; Boarding £36,771– £40,479 pa

Headmaster: Since 2012, Jay Piggot BA MA PGCE (50s). Previously headmaster at alma mater Campbell College, Belfast between 2006 and 2012, and, before that, put in 17 years at Eton (clearly a hard place to leave), starting as assistant master in 1989 and becoming housemaster 10 years later. Not bad going given that it was only his second teaching job: his first, immediately after completing his MA in English Renaissance literature at Liverpool, was at Millfield, where he taught A level/Oxbridge English.

Modestly dashing, this is one smooth operator and lordy, lordy, what a popular man he is, especially among parents, who claim he 'has given the school a personality'. 'He has charisma and exudes a wonderful air of power without being intimidating.' 'He is utterly lovely and completely has the children's interests at heart.' Students told us they 'don't see all that much of him' but he does assemblies, teaches a bit and comes to matches, as well as inviting students to breakfasts and lunches – seen as golden ticket. Also great excitement about his personally signed birthday cards – 'and can you believe he gives us Christmas cards too?' one enthused, wide-eyed.

All his high-profile changes (of which there are many) seem to be popular among students and parents alike, particularly his Eton-inspired reintroduction of matrons into the houses – 'a mum away from home,' said one parent. 'Matrons are the pillar of the house – you can talk to them about anything and they'll listen and even if they're not interested, they pretend to listen,' said one student. His academic shake-up, still ongoing, has seen an introduction of heads of year and – as one student put it – 'a lot more vibrant and often younger teachers'. 'They've brought in new energy and ideas – it's been transformational,' says head (70 per cent live on-site or within a few minutes' walk). Biggest change of all was opening lower school in 2016 (competitor schools were 'sweeping up the stronger pupils earlier on', he explains), with year 7s and 8s taught in own shiny new premises ('I know they share some of our facilities, but we don't see them much,' said a senior).

Lives on site with his wife, two dogs, cat and three children. Oldest (son) went great guns at Eton, then Oxford and is now doing a masters at UCL, the middle (son) is at Bristol University, and his youngest – a girl – attends Epsom College.

Entrance: School is after all-rounders with several strings to their bow and fair share of the bright students. No longer a second choice regular, the school is increasingly a bill-topper, recruiting from over 40 preps and state schools, likely to increase as it extends reach (Danes Hill, Downsend, Shrewsbury House, Aberdour and Feltonfleet feature prominently though no official feeders).

At 11+, entry via maths, English and VR tests plus interview in January of year 6. Second intake into year 9, with January pre-test in year 6 (VR – scores of around 118-120 the norm).

If no joy at 13+, small number of places at 14+ (three to five only; English, maths and VR tests). Second biggest influx is post-GCSE with 45 joining the sixth form, following VR, NVR and numerical skills tests plus interview. Students at this stage need minimum of seven GCSEs with at least grade 6, and a minimum of grade 7 in their chosen A level subjects (or 8 for more technical subjects like maths, science and modern foreign languages).

Exit: Fewer than 10 students (often none) leave after GCSE; school feels it has a 'moral obligation to take them all the way through'. Vast majority to university and of those 70 per cent to Russell Group. No shortage of ambition, most achieving first-choice unis – UCL, Nottingham, Exeter, Manchester, Bath, KCL, Loughborough,

Birmingham, Durham, Leeds, Imperial, Liverpool and York all most popular in recent years. In 2021, four to Oxbridge and 12 medics. Lots overseas, most recently to ESSEC Business School in France, UHK, NYU, USC, UC San Diego, Tusculum University and Grand Canyon University.

Latest results: In 2021, 88 per cent 9-7 at GCSE; 80 per cent A*/A at A level (96 per cent A*-B). In 2019 (the last year when exams took place), 74 per cent 9-7 at GCSE; 67 per cent A*/A at A level (90 per cent A*-B).

Teaching and learning: One of formerly mid-ranking schools to have substantially upped game, Epsom retains a prevailing sense of progression. Data and pupil intervention have nudged their way up the priority ladder, with subtle testing carried out every three weeks which appears to be tackling underperformance and ensures no report ever has any surprises for parents. Meanwhile, more layers in the academic management team have focused minds on more engaging teaching ('though some teachers still give boring lessons,' one student us).

Parents like how the school doesn't 'steer them in a direction that wont suit them – if a child doesn't want to go to university, they are fine with that'

Selective to a degree, but with breadth of intake, staff have to pass muster in proving they can teach a range of abilities, 'which ultimately means having a range of strategies at their fingertips to capture all hearts and minds, not just teaching to the top end,' says head. Innovative approach to CPD, with staff not sent off on courses ('generally winds up being a bit of a jolly') but instead invited to pick from half-hour power-learning sessions, which they then have to prove they've linked to their teaching. 'All teachers here know they have to work on their craft,' says school.

Though class sizes have grown – average 23 for GCSE and 16 max at A level – school is consistently good when it comes to value added (it's in the top two per cent in the country), with banding in languages (all do French, Spanish, German and Mandarin from year 7 then pick one, ideally two, for GCSE when Latin and Greek also become available) and setting in maths and science (where small group of less able students might do GCSE dual sciences rather than IGCSE triple – although not enough for students' liking, it seems, with one telling us, 'some of my friends absolutely hate science and find it so confusing yet were told they have to do triple').

Most do 10 GCSES and, in sixth form, three A levels (75 per cent also do EPQ). Results generally very good given relatively mixed intake. Largely traditional subject range, almost ology-free. Maths, science, art and PE do well at GCSE and art, sciences, economics and business studies are the dazzlers at A level.

Plenty of emails and reports to parents ensure that everyone is kept informed, although one parent told us 'one parents' evening a year, which is always a bit rushed, seems a bit on the mean side' (school says there are numerous evenings each year, but not all called parents' evenings – information evenings, choices evenings etc). Lengthy school day (lessons start at 8.20am, finishing at 6pm for seniors) incorporates sufficient free periods for the organised to get their homework out of the way ('good preparation for using time sensibly at uni,' says school).

Students are challenged but not pressured, say parents. One told us, 'My son was skimping on his revision at one point – he got a bit lazy really – but the housemaster took him aside and said, "Look, you're a clever boy, don't blow it" and it worked a treat.' Other parents like how the school doesn't 'steer them in a direction that doesn't suit them – a child doesn't want to go to university, they are fine with that'.

Careers advice could be better, feel parents, with one student telling us about a 'very uninspiring' careers aptitude test 'that told my friend she should be a librarian and me a maths teacher'. School points out there are 'multiple workshops, evenings, societies, world of work evenings, careers fairs etc'.

Learning support and SEN: Extra scaffolding where needed, with clinics in all key subjects and teachers not just present (many live in) but in many cases 'always available'. Of the 140 or so pupils with SEN, SpLD is the overwhelmingly dominant need and all SEN is at the milder end. 'They've managed our daughter's extra needs very well,' said a parent.

The arts and extracurricular: Music, drama and arts have a louder voice than in the past (at one time it was little more than a whisper, from what parents told us), thanks to current head pushing their weight. New head of music has introduced greater breadth so jazz, pop, classical, you name it, are all celebrated, with 'extravaganzas' every term. 'Sometimes you see the ballet dancers from the lower school dancing with the 18-year-olds – not always on the money but they get the claps and that's what it's all about,' says head. There are

King's Rochester

junior and senior choirs (it's cool to be in the choir here – 'even the rugger buggers get stuck in') and a strong orchestra (they get professional musicians to come and play with them to 'ginger them up a bit'), plus all the usual ensembles. Drama 'improving', say parents, although head would like to see the 'great culture of musical theatre that seems inevitable in co-ed senor schools' to be balanced with some more serious acting. Art also attacked with relish, with lovely facilities and a university art school feel.

Buddy system helps combat homesickness, while matrons add much appreciated extra tea and sympathy layer

DofE prevalent. CCF feather in school cap – one of oldest and biggest in country. Clubs aplenty – we met one student who'd introduced a film club, another University Challenge. Everybody gets out a lot on trips or to matches – a fleet of minibuses awaited students when we visited. DT excursions to real factories (MINI to New Holland tractors) popular among staff and students.

Sport: Sport is successful, 'but could go up a level,' believes head, who has introduced live-in sports graduates (those who play top flight hockey or netball, for instance) to come in for two-year stints – 'there's been a quiet revolution in sport due to the gapees'. Boys' and girls' rugby VIIs regular regional winners, lots of post-school success too. Ditto hockey (girls' first XIs through to fourth XIs lost only two of their 40 games the season we visited). The word 'unbeaten' features widely but never with expectancy or smugness – in fact, school wears success surprisingly lightly: numerous impressive sports cups casually behind bars with the guns. 'Nobody is on the bench at Epsom,' says head; parents agree. Golf is strong – just over the fence is Epsom golf course; two students were recently awarded golf scholarships to US universities. Shooting and climbing popular; riding available off site. Facilities generous – two cracking sports halls, one giant sized, six squash courts, a swimming pool and a fencing salle, among others. Most recently, an Olympic-standard all-weather hockey pitch. But while rugby 'is still king' and this is a very sporty school, 'you're not penalised if you're not really sporty and it is no longer a rugger bugger school,' a student told us. 'Sport is very important, whether you're A team or D/E/F team material,' agreed a parent.

Boarding: Most boarders are weekly, but full boarding numbers aren't far behind. Boarding houses, five in total (plus another eight day houses) are all dotted round the site and are spacious, colourful and homely. Kitchen in the girls' boarding house we saw looked as if it had been taken straight out of a showroom, though a student told us that 'certainly isn't the case for all of them', with 'some houses much snazzier than others'. Dorms, on the small side and rarely with more than four beds in, functional and with varying degrees of tidiness.

Sensible trouble-preventing measures include optional half-termly dorm swaps and plenty of weekend activities for full boarders, from trips to Thorpe Park to house evenings and bowling. Buddy system helps combat homesickness, while matrons (whose offices are welcoming and cosy) add much appreciated extra tea and sympathy layer. Students told us each house is very different, both in terms of feel and rewards such as town leave (at the discretion of the housemaster or housemistress), but all rules are the same.

Ethos and heritage: 'I thought it might be a bit stuck up, but it really isn't,' deemed a parent. Though patron is HM the Queen, we agree it's definitely not a high-society institution. Altogether a very civilised place to be, though, with sprawling campus rich with lush green lawns and fields, buildings – most completed between 1850s and 1920s, with tasteful modern extensions – and imposing chapel at its heart ('a place where you get a chance to be quiet and reflective, though services can be boring,' admitted a student). Started life as the Royal Medical Benevolent College, a charitable Good Thing, helping the relatives of deceased impoverished medics. Modern additions – humanities building particularly palatable – don't jar and there's plenty of social areas for sixth formers. Lovely, spacious library – 'I stay until 9pm some nights,' an older boy told us.

Took only boys for the first 120 years or so (sisters presumably expected to marry their way to economic success); girls added in sixth form in 1976 then throughout the school in 1996. Now, of course, school wouldn't be without them and the intake of year 7s in 2017 was 51 per cent girls – the first year they'd had more girls than boys in a class, though they remain minority partners in other years. Desired ratio (for now) is 45:55.

Pastoral care, inclusivity and discipline: 'If your child worries – which mine does – there is so much support both available in and out of the houses in terms of their emotional well-being,' said one parent, although another told us she felt school isn't for 'the less robust child'. Generally speaking, pastoral care is 'light touch', says school, though behind-the-scenes monitoring ensures problems don't get missed. Deputy head reeled off impressive lists of mental well-being speakers and workshops; form tutors, matrons and school counsellor tend to be first port of call for those seeking support. Seniors a strong force and take turns to lead assemblies and, as one student told us, 'won't tolerate seeing students picking on others'. Could be more freedom in sixth form, say some. 'In upper sixth, there's very little change in school life from earlier on and so the boys push against that when they're 18,' said one parent, but students told us it 'really depends what house you're in – some matrons are stricter than others'.

Little in the way of serious misbehaviour, with the odd student 'withdrawn by parents' (expulsion by face-saving euphemism). Two or three temporary exclusions per term, increasingly social media misdemeanours. Day to day, class silliness and late homework the main issues, reckon students, with escalating sanctions – lines, notification of tutors, warnings, departmental then school detentions. Lots of rewards, too – from pizza or chocolate for work-related merits and distinctions to privileges of seniority.

Pupils and parents: 'You don't get a lot of Ferraris and designer suits, put it that way,' said a parent, using her barometer of wealth, though it's fair to say families are well off (perhaps just not showy with it). Used to be predominantly local intake with vast majority of pupils, including 95 per cent of UK boarders, living within 10 to 15 miles – that's now expanded to 25 miles, with more bus routes to cater for them. Many staff have own children here.

Cosmopolitan feel added by international component, although this has dropped from 20 to 15 per cent in recent years – a proactive measure as school not keen to lean too heavily on the international market: 'We know that local parents don't want their weekly boarders exclusively living with youngsters speaking another language.' For those who are non-native English speakers there is a structured EAL programme in place, but they're fully integrated into the curriculum, says the school, 'right from day one'. Sister school opened in Kuala Lumpur in 2014 – first foray into pastures new, with all profits ploughed back into widening access back at Epsom College.

Money matters: Annual bursary spend just over £1m on up to 100 per cent of fees. Possible additional financial support for families with medical connections through the Royal Medical Foundation, based at the school, though since 2000 a separate legal entity. Scholarships for academic, sports and performing arts (drama and/or music) at all entry points.

The last word: 'You feel you're part of a school that's really going places – a bit like what it was like at Wellington 10 years ago,' said one parent. Led with real vision, this school offers an exciting learning environment within an extensive, top-notch campus and the students are among the most inquisitive and delightful we've come across.

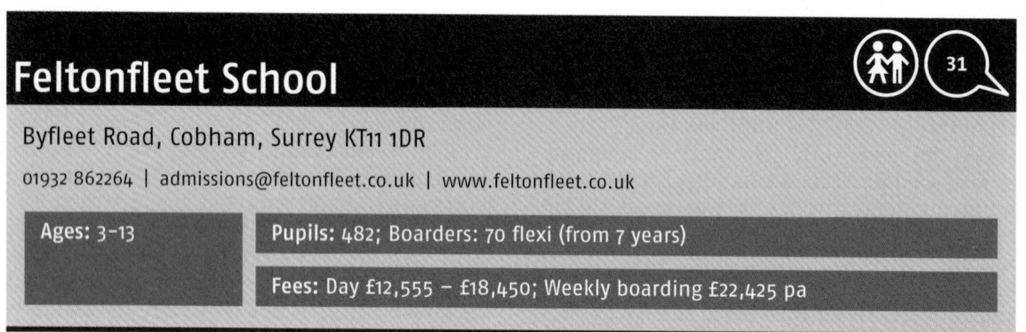

Feltonfleet School

31

Byfleet Road, Cobham, Surrey KT11 1DR

01932 862264 | admissions@feltonfleet.co.uk | www.feltonfleet.co.uk

Ages: 3-13

Pupils: 482; Boarders: 70 flexi (from 7 years)

Fees: Day £12,555 – £18,450; Weekly boarding £22,425 pa

Headmistress: Since January 2018, Shelley Lance, previously deputy head. Theology degree from King's College London; began her teaching career at Alleyn's, then taught at Whitgift, where she was head of lower school and responsible for the school's pastoral care provision. She joined Feltonfleet in 2010.

A self-confessed 'reluctant head' – 'I love the frontline coalface interaction, which can very easily be squeezed out when you're leading a school,' she explains. So she teaches RS and mindfulness, as well as sitting in on other classes, including in pre-prep, and doing gate duty every morning. 'It can mean long days and be exhausting, but it pays dividends because I know all the teachers, children and parents, which facilitates easy communications and means I sense frustrations and know when changes are needed.' Charismatic, grounded, gutsy and highly articulate, she has certainly not shied away from making changes, including a major rebrand, replacing compartmentalised learning with a more thematic approach and moving away from common entrance towards 'the equally rigorous model' of the Prep School Baccalaureate. Plus – and this is the real biggie – a major expansion of pre-prep. Parents call her a 'natural leader', 'responsive', 'phenomenal' and 'everything you could want in a head', while pupils say she's 'fun' and 'very involved'.

Married to Ed, head of lower school at Epsom College, they have a young son, Henry. Enjoys family time, the great outdoors, skiing and reading.

Entrance: Largely non-selective, the pre-prep works on a first-come-first-served entry basis which means, says the school, that 'broad range of ability inevitably comes through'. Two-form entry means competition for places is less of an extreme sport than it was, although parents are well advised to bag one of places by registering at birth. Further external places available for year 3 entry, when you can expect border controls in form of maths and English assessment plus interview 'to search out character and enthusiasm for learning'. (Own year 2 children aren't tested.) Occasional places also crop up, including in year 7 following a few post 11+ departures at end of year 6.

Exit: To around 20 different senior schools. Most popular in 2021 were Epsom College, St John's School, Leatherhead, St George's College in Weybridge, Reed's, Charterhouse and Brighton. Hurstpierpoint, City of London Freemen's School, Claremont Fan Court School and Eton are among others that have featured in recent years. Good guidance on future schools, and school has right connections, reckon parents; scholarships across the board for art, drama, DT, music, sport and academic usually in the early 20s.

Our view: The swish, modern and airy reception area makes for a grand entrance. We could almost have imagined ourselves in an upmarket corporate establishment until we spotted a pile of pencil cases on the floor and a procession of boys and girls in their smart blue blazers. On the left is a stunning performing arts centre and dance studio (a joy to see the little ones tap dancing); on the right, the vast glass walls frame a striking view of the main prep building (mid-19th century Gothic), which you loop round the corridor to get to. Here you are met with yet more stunning interiors, this time more traditional, including the head's designer office – think interior magazine-worthy grey armchairs, orchids, scented candles, beautiful art (one by an upper school pupil, the rest by the school's art teacher) and – reflecting her approachability and transparency – a new glass-fronted door. From this sun-drenched room (even on the January day we visited), you get a panoramic view of the sweep of green stretching away down a gentle slope towards the grass pitch, idyllically bounded by woods and dipping pond much used by all year groups, plus the very popular treehouse now complete with slide ('The children begged for one for three whole years!' says head).

From the sun-drenched head's office, you get a panoramic view of the sweep of green stretching away down a pitch, idyllically bounded by woods and dipping pond much used by all year groups

On both sides are the learning blocks for year 2s upwards, including new science labs. Plenty of idiosyncratic charm throughout, from revamped lower school block classrooms with winning cosiness, colour and light to seniors' French classroom with miniature shop and restaurant, much used for role play. Calvi, the separate pre-prep building across the road, is also winningly equipped, from own hall to shaded play areas (trees a feature everywhere) with big sandpit and marked-out scooter track. Plentiful wildlife, too: some guinea pigs, available for cuddles, and tadpoles, who aren't.

At one time, the school was known locally as one of the less academic; no longer, with a strong and dedicated staff cohort and ever-enhanced strategies to ensure the curriculum and its delivery are top notch. Parents generally delighted with academic running – 'There were some weaker teachers, but they've been weeded out – I'd say they are all good to very good now,' said one (even more expertise has come in since the school has grown in size). Maximum class sizes of 20 (occasionally 22), optimum size for lively classroom atmosphere, reckons school. We saw pupils crawling around a lab in the dark with torches (studying how shadows work), younger ones gleefully playing in a recorder group and the DT lab ready for pupils to make the likes of mood lights and rulers; this is a bustling, engaging environment. Specialist teaching for French, PE, swimming and music from year 1, when they get a shot at DT and digital learning too. Options grow with age and by year 5, all subjects are taught by specialists. Setting from English and maths from year 3 and in science and French from year 7. Prep

School Baccalaureate has been introduced to year 7s. SEN and gifted and talented provision overseen by the four-strong learning enrichment department who use an integration model as much as possible; one parent told us, 'It's fine and certainly better than it was.'

Strong range of sport on offer: netball, hockey and cricket basic range for girls; football, rugby, hockey and cricket for boys; swimming, cross-country and athletics for both. Fab facilities too in the 25-acre estate, including indoor swimming pool, Astroturf, yodelling-quality sports hall, hard surface tennis courts and two rifle ranges (air and .22) on top of scenic sports fields. Strategy is to seek out challenge, everyone representing the school regardless of talent, although some parents feel 'girls' sport isn't taken quite as seriously' – a view not lost on the head, whose prep school district meetings often involve fighting for sporting equality via a more varied fixtures model. 'Bottom line is we're on it and we've added two more sports coaches to add to our own depth of expertise.' Plenty of tolerance for the rugby-averse – not the case elsewhere. Mega results in shooting – teams beat everyone everywhere, including older siblings in senior schools (Wellington and Epsom College). Coach, who travels here from Wales 'because he likes us', secret weapon.

'I wondered how much homework my son would actually get done, but it's tightly monitored, followed by the fun stuff in the sports hall,' one parent said

Drama popular – it would be hard not to be enthusiastic about performing in the swanky theatre. Parents describe the performances as 'outstanding' and, impressively, drama is also used for raising serious issues such as bullying and gender wars. Good collaboration with music department, the head of which has an exceptional reputation – 84 per cent of pupils learn an instrument here and well over half are in one of the five school choirs (junior and senior), with the 15 single-instrument ensembles also popular. Year 2s went off to sing in an old folks' home when we visited. A welcoming and well-equipped art room is a haven for the creative, with iPads used to photograph all work – 'It gives me an opportunity to give feedback actually on their work,' explained teacher.

Rigorous pastoral system (now with new role of deputy head, pastoral) is subject to routine interrogation, with frequent dedicated meetings and an emphasis on staff accountability. Pupils told us, 'We all have a favourite teacher so that's the first port of call for most of us.' Impressive focus on mental health, including from outside speakers. 'Every child knows every child, so the younger ones grow up knowing it will be their job to take care of the newer ones later on,' said one parent. 'They take their leadership responsibilities, like being prefect, very seriously,' said another. Unusually, pupils told us there's 'no bullying'; head wise not to make such bold claims, but all can list a whole bunch of prevention policies that, as one pupil put it, 'stops friendship fallouts turning into anything worse'.

Behaviour good, with pupils reporting that strictness increases as you get older – 'It's always fair and good preparation for your next school,' said one. Pupils we met (there's a pretty equal gender split) were lively, happy and comfortable in their own skin. And although we arrived at drop-off time to a sea of black Range Rovers, school says (and parents agree) that families range from the very wealthy to those who 'really work hard to get their children here'. Most hail from Weybridge, Cobham and Esher, although there are some groans about growing numbers from London – 'I think the school should set their cap as to whether they're a local school or not. The big increase has changed the dynamic for the school, especially for playdates,' said one. Food good – that hasn't always been the case, say parents. Ditto with affordability of uniform – this was a major gripe in the past.

Boarding: Weekly and flexi, plus day boarding options from year 3 – latter can include a full boarding day without the sleepover. In reality, it's only a handful that weekly board; much more popular are the one, two or three times a week flexi options which parents use for helping prepare their offspring for senior school, encouraging greater independence or simply because their children 'want nothing more than to stay over at school with their friends, despite us living 10 minutes away,' as one parent put it. Homely dorms (though pink for girls' dorms and blue for boys' seems outdated) with 46 beds in total. 'Trial nights' are popular, say pupils – themed nights encouraging pupils who haven't stayed overnight before to have a go. A good programme of activities, the opportunity to mix with pupils across the years and a much-loved matron are all part of the pull. 'I wondered how much homework my son would actually get done, but it's tightly monitored, followed by the fun stuff in the sports hall,' one parent said. Here, as elsewhere, essential to shut ears to competing clamour of A3 that borders one side of site, though pupils oblivious.

The last word: From an already strong base, this is a school that feels on the up and for a prep, it takes an impressively long-term look, preparing children not just for their next school but for life. All this in a happy, positive – not to mention immaculate – environment.

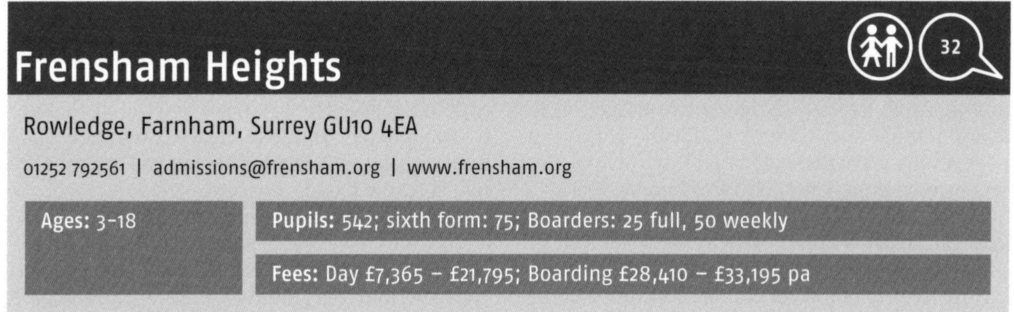

Frensham Heights

Rowledge, Farnham, Surrey GU10 4EA

01252 792561 | admissions@frensham.org | www.frensham.org

Ages: 3-18

Pupils: 542; sixth form: 75; Boarders: 25 full, 50 weekly

Fees: Day £7,365 – £21,795; Boarding £28,410 – £33,195 pa

Head: Since January 2019, Rick Clarke BA PGCE (40s). Previously deputy head at Warminster School. Born and raised in South Africa, his career choice must have delighted his parents (father was a teacher and mother was an ed psych; he did his degree in English and psychology at the University of Natal then PGCE). Worked his way up the ranks in South African schools to head of English at St John's College in Johannesburg before heading to the UK where he became a protégé of the transformational head Sir Anthony Seldon when he was head of English at Brighton College and housemaster at Wellington College. But parents (and there were some) who worried he was going to Wellington-ise Frensham need not have fretted. 'He's just the breath of fresh air we needed – pulling the school back from becoming just a bit too laissez faire, while still hanging onto its core values,' summed up one.

Understated, softly spoken, considered and, as one parent put it, 'possibly a teensy bit shy'. An intimidating head this is most definitely not. But that's the whole point. 'I've always valued relationships above all else in the classroom – I'm not autocratic and I've never been one to shout or give detentions.' Must have jumped for joy when this post came up. Parents like that he has 'aligned the junior and senior schools' and 'made the reports much more thorough'. Office door wedged open, with students frequently popping in eg for ideas on how to minimise the queues for break time snack and requesting an A level in film studies (coming soon).

Embarked, during his first year, on a USA road trip to discover the roots of progressive ('I steer away from the word liberal – sounds too political') education, upshot of which is that he's considering how to inject even more breadth into the curriculum and explore what the oft used expression 'the Frensham way' really means in an educational climate where co-ed, student voice and even no uniform are becoming more normalised. 'In other schools, you get the crest, the Latin motto and the values, but we have historically been more fluid and I think we need to be clearer on what we're all about.' Keen also to ensure watertight foundations – 'Schools that allow students to have greater freedom need even clearer rigour and structures underneath,' he believes. One parent surmised, 'I think Rick will make the school and the school will make him.'

Lives on site with wife Natalie, an artist and art teacher in the junior school, and their young children, also at the school and whom he insists 'provide all the work/life balance I need', although he is also a keen runner.

Head of junior school: since September 2019, Katherine Bluck MA PGCE (30s). Educated at Berkhamstead School then Cambridge, where she read geography and education; PGCE also from Cambridge. Previously deputy head of junior school at Stephen Perse Junior in Cambridge and before that worked across the state and independent sectors including Lambrook for many years as their head of lower school. Youthful, savvy and with enough innovative educational ideas to fill a book, we also liked her unperturbed manner and unpatronising way with the kids.

Entrance: Entry into nursery in term of 3rd birthday (16 places) or the following year to reception – assessment done by informal observation during a visit. Years 1-6 take one or two more – roughly two apply for each place. Candidates spend a day with peer group during which they are assessed in reading, spelling and maths. 'We look for those who are curious, good at communicating with their peers, respectful and all-rounders.'

In year 7, two apply for each place. All candidates are interviewed in groups of four or five. Exams a week or so later – 11+ tests in reading, writing, spelling, maths and verbal and non-verbal reasoning. Reference sought from current school. Ditto plus a science test for 13+ candidates (when there are 1.5 applications for every one place), though pre-testing in year 6 for boarding year 9 places available on request. Sixth form places (up to two apply for each place at this stage, often fewer) require six GCSEs at 4+, ideally with 6s in A level subjects (with some flexibility). School also sets its own papers for sixth form entry.

Exit: Half leave at 16, mostly to the several large state (free) sixth form colleges round about, some for the IB or for subjects not on offer here. 'Some have been here since they were three and just want a bit more urban grit,' said one parent ('some return the following term,' says school). Around 30 per cent of sixth form leavers go to Russell Group universities, the rest to one of the widest range of tertiary education establishments we've seen. Many to creative courses – arts, design, music – and odd ones to Oxbridge or overseas. Nottingham, Liverpool, Bristol, Exeter, KCL and Sussex currently popular. UCAS support phenomenal, say parents.

Latest results: In 2021, 61 per cent 9-7 at GCSE; 62 per cent A*/A at A level (85 per cent A*-B). In 2019 (the last year when exams took place), 31 per cent 9-7 at GCSE; 23 per cent A*/A at A level (45 per cent A*-B).

Teaching and learning: It would be disingenuous to suggest Frensham is anything other than selective, but they are more interested in you fitting in with the school's broad-minded ethos than helping them soar to league-table-topping prominence. 'We are frequently reminded that becoming the best version of ourselves is more important than striving for all A*'s,' a student told us. Doesn't mean they don't achieve highly however.

We were initially struck by the sheer amount of chit-chat in lessons but it's not a case of the tail wagging the dog – students are encouraged to learn as much from each other and via brainstorming, negotiation, teamwork, co-operation etc as via the teacher standing at the front (in many cases the teacher wasn't even doing that, instead weaving through the class – all 18 max). We dropped in on a year 6 class on slam poetry where youngsters were discussing ideas ready, as per their instructions, to 'read out loud, cut the fat, read again, and flavour'. Vibrant labels surround the interactive whiteboard reminding students to eg plan, rethink, question, co-operate, risk etc, while huge (non-interactive) whiteboards at the back act pose questions of the day ('If you could invent something that would make life easier, what would it be?' was one – 'a money tree!' one student had astutely suggested). In a year 9 geography class on climate change, students frequently (but respectfully) interrupted the teacher to question her statements, ask for more detail etc – the teacher's answers showed striking subject knowledge and typified how news-driven the curriculum is. You snooze, you lose here – 'Somehow they make it that you're always engaged and analysing,' a student said.

Even pre-prep is child-led, with structured adult input – we watched reception children following a dragon topic with a mixture of construction, role play, drawing, cutting and pasting. 'What are scales?' piped up one, prompting a teacher to dash off to the library to find a relevant book. Junior lessons also novel – year 3s entered their classroom to find everything everywhere as they were learning about hurricanes, meanwhile forest school gets littluns outside come rain or shine.

We dropped in on a year 6 class on slam poetry where youngsters were discussing ideas ready, as per their instructions, to 'read out loud, cut the fat, read again, and flavour'

But Summerhill this is not. There's setting in maths from year 7, English from year 8 and sciences from year 9. French from nursery, with Spanish and German introduced on a carousel from year 7. If the demand is there for eg Italian, they might employ a teacher. Smallish school but a wide range of GCSEs – no classics, Latin or Greek, for instance, although they do offer photography and business studies (both popular) and are soon to launch philosophy and religion. Geography and history get good numbers, the latter boasting some of the best results in recent years alongside visual arts. Most students take nine, some more. 'Rigour at sixth form has improved,' said a parent. Three A levels are the norm, with history, drama and fine art all popular and increasingly ('a surprise to some parents given that we're an arts based school,' says head) psychology and sociology, with growing numbers going on to study these subjects at uni: 'They have catered tremendously for my daughter whose strengths are in the sciences,' said one mother. Around a third do EPQ, with stunning results. 'One or two teachers are a bit lazy, but there is far more brilliance than bad,' remarked a parent.

Learning support and SEN: Mixed views on SEN support, which is only really for milder end (moderate and beyond are often referred to More House down the road) and mainly classroom based. Several parents raved about it ('In his last school, my dyslexic son felt thick and his self-esteem was down the toilet, whereas the enthusiasm of teachers and the bigging up of his questioning techniques, along with the one-to-one support, have made him shine here'); others feel there's some way to go ('I think they could be a bit more clued up on latest evidence'). EAL available, though rarely required.

The arts and extracurricular: Arguably, the most impressively led art department in the country, offering oodles of GCSEs and A levels (eight in total). Art school vibe – and it looks like one too, with the students relishing every inch from the newly covered outside space ('great for spraying') to the rows of kilns. Artwork, displayed throughout, is of an astonishing standard, with the diverse work exposing just how much freedom students are given to develop their ideas. We loved the gigantic portraits, out-of-kilter wardrobe installation representing a stream of consciousness and the mock GCSE 3D designs. Ceramics, textiles, wood, metals, jewellery, furniture, lighting – you name it, these students use it to go off in their own directions. A 'hope or concern' themed year 9 exhibition offered a particularly fascinating window into the minds of teenagers politically, personally and environmentally. Photography has a long history here, under inspirational leadership, and school still has its own darkroom (always a joy in this digital age).

Next door, A level drama students were preparing their devices to the sounds of The Clash in one of the two studios, with the main theatre a spectacular space in which to perform. Again, creativity and freedom are order of the day – students write and perform at the likes of the Edinburgh Fringe Festival, while back at school there are alternating annual junior and senior musicals (Mary Poppins up next), plus biannual dance concerts.

'Everyone is musical in some way,' we were informed by the extrovert head of music, and the music block, complete with recording studios, is certainly a great space to hang around in to find out. Lovely to see one boy completely lost in music playing one of the many grand pianos; around half of students learn an instrument, including three harpists and a couple of instruments we'd never heard of when we visited. No orchestra – 'we don't have the economies of scale,' says school. Would be easy to nit-pick but we rather like the supply and demand model over slogging through a term with meagre numbers (and anyway, there are ensembles for that). It's the buzz that matters here and there was plenty of that with all the student-led musical prep for the years 4-8 Mary Poppins production. Rock choir and chamber choir.

Grounds are immaculate and campus is huge. Newer buildings nestle in trees and witty sculptures sprawl on the lawns and in foyers – we loved the wax mushrooms

Extensive menu of extracurricular options should tempt the most sluggish teenager – bike maintenance, parkour, eco warriors and even reading Harry Potter in German in addition to the more predictable sports, chess, debating etc. Dance much praised and popular. The Edge programme sees sixth formers signing up to the likes of first aid, cooking and driving theory. Visiting speakers range from Holocaust survivors to a hairdresser for the homeless. And masses of trips, with the two weeks in west Scotland for year 9s the real highlight (where all start their DofE bronze).

Sport: Sport, as an old OF recently reminded the head, is a far cry from the 1940s when students had to run five miles at 6am. Many heads have come and gone since then – some similarly hardcore; others who shuddered at the idea of enforced exercise or sport. 'I thoroughly dislike uber-competitiveness, where winning matters too much and I would never force kids to do what they don't want to,' current head told us, suggesting he is of the latter mindset. 'But,' he added, 'I do believe in the value of exercise and staying active and I do think we have a duty to cater for those who are keen on more competitive sport,' and as such there's now an annual sports day and more fixtures (though rarely on Saturdays). Students hold their own even against much bigger schools like Weydon and Bedales with girls' netball and boys' football getting best results. Facilities, indoor and out, are certainly conducive to performance although, as is the case with most endeavours here, we got the impression the main focus is on breadth and creativity – badminton, table tennis, basketball, rowing, fencing, golf, tennis are all for the taking. Student-led too – 'We're not a rugby playing school, but some year 8s wanted to play it so we got together a team and a fixture list,' says head. One parent summed up, 'We were playing a school the other day and the coach on the other team was screaming at his lot, whereas I knew ours would walk off having had a great time whether we won or lost – they know how to encourage each other but nobody gets silly about it.'

Boarding: Around 100 board, half flexi (most of these weekly), the rest full-time. Around a third are international, though school has wise policy of not taking more than four pupils who speak the same language into any senior year. So penny numbers from eg Russia, Germany, Spain. Hamilton House is for juniors, while years 10 and 11 reside in the upstairs of the main house and sixth formers in Roberts House (also base for day students). All co-ed, with boys and girls housed on different floors or wings, sharing modern kitchens and exceptionally welcoming sitting rooms. Good sized bedrooms, although singles are compact – all clean and tidy (ish for the older ones – a few unmade beds). Plenty of workspace and outdoor space. Evening activities, as we saw from wall-mounted picture collages, include baking, gymnastics, skating, dinner dances and making sushi (well, this is Surrey) while weekenders do anything from dinner at Nando's, shopping in Guildford, Winter Wonderland and Harry Potter World (those who attend aforementioned club posing as Germans, perhaps?). Older children can trail 10 minutes through the woodlands to the village with its supermarket and sweetshop. 'Vertical friendships common and all unbelievably homely,' said a parent, although a few niggles there aren't more boarders 'and the beds could be comfier'.

Ethos and heritage: Charles Charrington, the brewer, acquired Fir Grove House on the edge of Rowledge village, overlooking a panorama of Surrey woods and hills and transformed it into Frensham Heights – a striking Gothic red-brick residence with turrets, leaded lights and stained glass, splendid Georgian-style interiors (they still do readings of Dickens round the fire), cornices, architraves, fireplaces – the lot – in 1902, as a would-be ancestral pile. Alas, the First World War intervened and the house became a military hospital and, as the old order changed, was reinvented as a school by three redoubtable women: Edith Douglas-Hamilton and joint headmistresses, Beatrice Ensor and Isabel King. Ensor, an early proponent of Montessori education, was a theosophist, a vegetarian and an anti-vivisectionist. The school's liberal credentials, being coeducational and progressive, were integral to its ethos from the first. Strangely, every head since its founding pioneers has been male.

Grounds are immaculate and campus is huge – 'feels more like a mini-university,' said parent. Newer buildings nestle in trees and witty sculptures sprawl on the lawns and in foyers – we loved the wax mushrooms. Nursery to year 3 learn in sunken single-storey junior school with good-sized classrooms full of attentive, relaxed looking tots and interesting activities going on, accompanied by good junior playgrounds with lots of different surfaces and play equipment. Lots shared with seniors, including sports facilities, some staff and the dining room – lovely to see 3-year-olds and 18-year-olds eating together, and it's good fodder too (we even got a sticker for choosing some deep fried cauliflower from the 'try something new' table). Middle school (years 7/8) share even more senior facilities. Aesthetically, art and drama blocks are the real dazzlers (complete with café for parents – well used when we visited) but the regular classrooms are nicely done out too – beanbags in psychology and English classroom decorated with literary chat-up lines. Library a bit tired – welcoming enough, though, and includes every journal you could think of plus (nice touch) tea and coffee.

Evening activities, as we saw from wall-mounted picture collages, include baking, gymnastics, skating, dinner dances and making sushi (well, this is Surrey)

Notable Old Frenshamians include performers Bill and Jon Pertwee, Jamie Glover, David Berglas, Rufus Hound, Hattie Morahan; also Sir Claus Moser, Noah Bulkin (Merrill Lynch, Lazard, now entrepreneur) and uber-fraudster, Edward Davenport.

Pastoral care, inclusivity and discipline: No uniform and teachers called by first names. Reasonable expectations and modelling of good behaviour substitute rules, all accompanied by heaps of personal responsibility. Even extends to falling in or out of love, although you'll rarely see anything more than a hug or linked arms. 'If you like rules and formality, it won't be for you,' said a parent, although there's been a (much praised) tightening up of discipline under new head. 'I love it that they have a chat to unpick reasons rather than give a meaningless detention but if the chats don't work, there has to be a next step and now there is,' said one parent. Now up to a handful of suspensions a year and a couple of permanent exclusions in the last year too. Zero tolerance on drugs and a hard line on drink. 'For more minor things, they spend time helping you so you don't make the same mistake again – more reflection than punishment,' mused a junior student. Mutual respect part of school's DNA, right down to teachers not barging ahead of students in the lunch queue. Bullying minimal, although one year 6 boy did mention that 'in my year, you get teased if you play with a girl, which I think is silly' (school says they are aware of it and currently scratching their heads about how to solve it as it's not an issue they've come across in any other year group).

Pupils and parents: Day students, who make up around three-quarters of school community, come from an ever-shrinking (school isn't sure why) radius of about 20 miles in all directions. We noticed how comfortable they are in their own skin and they really appreciate being able to express themselves – we met one goth sixth former, although most opt for jeans and hoodies. Even younger ones are noticeably articulate and, one parent reckoned, braver – 'When I go out with my friends, it's my children who will go up to the counter while theirs sit nervously refusing to make eye contact.' Parents, we heard, are 'a right old mix', although another added that, 'You do wonder why some of them chose Frensham – seems like Charterhouse might be more their bag.'

Money matters: Ten per cent discounts for third and subsequent siblings. Means-tested bursaries in case of need but school has no endowments so not plentiful. Scholarships in academics, performing arts, creative arts and sport but all glory and no gold and note they are awarded a couple of months into years 7, 9 or 12 'when we've got to know them a bit'.

The last word: If the thought of rigid teaching, endless tests, petty rules, school uniform and calling teachers Sir and Miss all leaves you cold, this could well be your educational paradise. The huge breadth of opportunities, impressive campus and thoroughly lovely, erudite staff win many over. But it's the freedom for your child to grow into the person they are meant to be – all within a safe, caring and mutually respectful environment – that clinched it for us. As one parent put it, 'They say youth is wasted on the young – well, it's not here.'

Hall Grove School

London Road, Bagshot, Surrey GU19 5HZ

01276 473059 | office@hallgrove.co.uk | www.hallgrove.co.uk

Ages: 3–13

Pupils: 383; **Boarders:** 15 weekly/flexi (from year 7)

Fees: £11,100 – £15,900 pa; Boarding + £4,050 pa

Headmaster: Since September 2021, Neil Tomlin OBE. Degree in geography and PE and master's in international relations. Fresh from the British Army, he has swapped a battalion of 750 soldiers for a troop of 400 children at Hall Grove and so far it is 'living up to all expectations'. But, following in the footsteps of the 30+ year tenure of the previous head (now principal), is he? Parents – 'a difficult crowd to please' – are positive about the mostly 'spit and polish' changes he's implemented so far. One mother commended his regular presence on the sidelines of their children's non-school-related sports fixtures at weekends – 'He seems to turn up everywhere,' she marvelled. As for the parent who queried his lack of experience in the education sector, he's unfazed, insisting that the role of headmaster is 'the same as the army – all about people'. He is working closely with the principal and seems to us to have got the hang of it. Children love that he dresses up in assemblies and say he's 'around much more'. He teaches current affairs and has his own tutor group.

Praise too for his exuberant wife Eugenie whom we catch rollerskating around the playground at break; she sings in the Military Wives Choir in her spare time. Principal Mr Graham confirms the couple, complete with their labrador puppy and Instagram-famous house bunnies, have 'bought a sparkle to the school'.

Very much still in the military mindset and inspired by his own 'amazing' prep school head, he wants to embed in his charges 'strong academic, physical and moral values that together provide a compass that intuitively kicks in through life'. His approach is to 'give the weaker nothing to fear and the stronger something to challenge'. Staff are falling in line nicely. 'It's good to have direction and targets,' says one.

Dismisses flash competitors, adding 'not all needs to be delivered by 13'. 'We don't need a weights room or running machines. We have a lovely walled garden,' he says before musing that 'a new indoor pool would be nice though.' Despite describing Hall Grove as 'not all fandango', he believes it still needs to 'be a bit more chest out'. Parents however are content that the school is 'humble' and 'not in your face'. On his radar is the lucrative west London brigade which he hopes to enlist with the expansion of the boarding provision, which 'frankly, needs massive improvement'. He'd also like investment in infrastructure (to include that pool), development of the co-ed offering and more commitment to diversity throughout the school.

Billed as a traditional country prep, it comprises a farm with grazing sheep, an apple orchard from which we are presented with crisp Hall Grove juice, and beehives galore

Principal is Alastair Graham, son of the founder, who himself was educated at Hall Grove. Many describe the school as his 'life's work' and while he's handed over the baton on the day-to-day job, he is very clear to us that 'it's still my school'. Outspoken and critical of other schools that 'have a lot of slack' in their finances, he runs a 'tight ship' in a challenging market where parents get 'great value for money' and 'raised aspirations' for their offspring.

Entrance: The Barn (early years), offers places after discussing child's current development with parents. Main intake at 3+ is non-selective and also embraces a sibling policy. Children from pre-school move up to reception where they are joined by a class of new entrants at 4+. In year 3, the expansion to three forms allows room for an additional 20 children, who take tests in maths and English at the school. At the beginning of year 7 the upper school replaces any leavers (mainly girls going to a school where the intake is at 11+). At this stage, potential pupils spend a day at the school and are assessed to help confirm that they will fit in with their peer group.

Exit: After year 8 into mainly aspirational co-ed and single-sex schools. Dialogue starts with parents in years 5 and 6. Families report a boosted exit preparation in recent years including a specific residential 'to unshackle the shackles' and mock interviews with parent volunteers. School has an excellent record of matching children to seniors and can only remember 'one or two in the last 13 years' who failed to get into their first choice. New head up to speed on the options, having visited 17 senior schools around the country in his summer break.

Wellington is first choice for more academic pupils, probably partly on proximity grounds, but children also go to a wider range of both private and state schools, often fairly local. Favourites include Charterhouse, Tonbridge, Eton, Cranleigh, Lord Wandsworth College, St George's, Weybridge, Bryanston, Gordon's, Sherborne School for Girls and Sherborne School. Plentiful academic and co-curricular scholarships most years.

Our view: Tucked away behind possibly the most tangled roundabout system on the Surrey/Berkshire border, Hall Grove emerges like an emerald oasis. Parents tell of 'minds made up' the minute they pull up. Billed as a traditional country prep, it comprises a farm with grazing sheep (that pupils wean as lambs), an apple orchard from which we are presented with some crisp Hall Grove juice, and beehives galore which produce Hall Grove honey. There's a vast lake and a magnificent walled garden, tended to by an RHS-trained gardener. Playing fields meld into the manicured greens of adjoining Windlesham Golf Club, while an outdoor pool, Astro courts, forest school, low ropes course, mountain bike track and pony stables tick the outdoor pursuits boxes nicely. 'What a place to come to school,' sums up one teacher. Parents like that the school is 'inclusive and genuine'. 'It holds old-fashioned values but isn't stuffy,' says one.

Classrooms are a charming mishmash of styles, scattered haphazardly across the site. The Hall Grove experience begins for pre-preps in the purpose-built 'from natural materials' barn. A chalked path of doodles and daffodils potted in preparation for Mother's Day lead into an expansive double classroom. On one side a French lesson is underway, on the other The Wheels on the Bus is ringing out. One parent expressed her sadness that due to lockdown, her child had missed out on 'such a lovely start to school life' in the space. Elsewhere classrooms are large, airy and all spick and span. On the walls impressive displays of work and learning techniques. 'Classic maths mistakes' catches our eye in one. A smattering of subject-specific Scandinavian wood cabin classrooms for senior pupils from year 5 include a fully equipped cooking cabin where the annual school bake-off competition is fiercely fought. Specially designed surfaces in the science labs allow pupils to draw diagrams straight onto tables, walls and windows. There's a bit of a stench in the one we visit where year 7s are dissecting onions to study their cells.

For many, the pièce de resistance of the Hall Grove journey is the annual residential to the school house and farm in Devon

'They're always learning in weird and wonderful ways,' says one mother. Immense and industrious art room jam packed with displays from gravity-defying sculptures to printed T-shirts. IT facilities are good, all pupils get a Chromebook in year 7. Adequately equipped DT block is in the firing line for a revamp. Classes range from single half hour lessons to quadruples for seniors. We witness a number of small, focused tutor groups on our visit. Latin and maths are favourite lessons amongst the pupils we meet. 'It doesn't try to be elite, but the highest standards are certainly there,' a parent said. 'The harder you work, the more fun it is,' declared a pupil.

In the younger classes shoes are neatly lined up as children learn barefoot. 'It feels nice,' explains one. Wellies outside each class too – at least once a week all children enjoy gardening classes and lessons in the outdoor classroom. There's the odd battle re-enactment for history and large-scale science experiment too. Getting outside 'is just part of the culture' here. 'Hall Grove's USP is that it puts to use every inch of land,' added a parent.

And so to sport. School has a good score sheet with numerous successes and scholarships over the years. Despite going on to be an international athlete, the director of sport was never picked for the school team himself and so is passionate that all children compete in some shape or form. School working hard to level up the playing field for both boys and girls. Football is on the agenda for girls this year, with netball open to boys 'if they wish'. Most don't. School has 'moved on' from Chelsea FC football coaches as the 'standard was not as high as we have in-house'. There's mixed hockey and cricket. Rowing is taught by Eton coaches and sailing and judo are also popular. Olympic swimming champion Adam Peaty MBE recently dropped by to coach some swimmers and modern pentathlete Kate French gave an inspirational talk on becoming a world champion. Cross-country runs two mornings a week attract a certain crowd – the group we talk to were unanimous in their dislike. A fun mix of extracurricular clubs, from shooting and fencing to pony and magic club.

Performing arts high on the agenda. There are four choirs, eight ensembles and informal concerts every week. Over 160 children learn an instrument. Multiple music scholarships each year and the choir have sung on Radio 4. In drama children enjoy year-group productions ranging from Macbeth to musicals. In the summer, Robin Hood was performed outside in the woods. Year 8s recently wrote and performed their own Windrush inspired speeches to mark Black History Month. One pupil was disappointed 'we only have half an hour a week'.

Pupils fill in daily diaries to chart progress. Form tutors monitor at first, then study tutors after year 5. Parents are 'super impressed' with all the teachers. 'No weak links,' said one. Younger children are motivated by the Hall Grove bees – striving to be 'bee of the week' or earn the cuddly bee to take home. Some parents wondered if discipline could benefit from 'a more mature approach' higher up the school and others said it might not be the school for a family expecting an authoritarian environment. Head admits consistency among staff may be lacking and that he doesn't want 'children running out of my office feeling like they'll never recover'. The children we meet are polite and responsible, switching off lights as we leave empty rooms. 'Teachers encourage us to be independent,' explains one. At lunch a group of year 8 girls swarm around us, chatting away easily – not a queen bee among them. Eyes are rolled a little when it comes to boys. 'They're all nice, just a bit annoying at times,' says one. Lessons from Everyone's Invited have been incorporated into a new PSHE curriculum rebranded 'The Hall Grove Journey'.

For many, the pièce de resistance of the Hall Grove journey is the annual residential to the school house and farm in Devon. One boy's family seriously considered cancelling a scholarship opportunity because it clashed with the long-awaited trip. Referred to as 'the real Famous Five bit' by one member of staff, it was acquired by the principal in the 1980s for field trips. From year 4 children enjoy den building, rock pooling and constructing egg catapults. Senior years use the opportunity to brush up on interview techniques and leadership skills. It's 'an exceptional place', says the principal. One parent claimed her son came home 'smelly, muddy and four inches taller'.

Lots of praise from parents on a bolstered and refined SEN provision. One family said the school had identified their child's issues almost instantly. Another with an earlier diagnosis said, 'We led the process but the support has been amazing.' Head committed to ensuring 'our supply meets the demand now we are looking for these things more'.

Boarding: Limited provision currently accommodates just two weekly and a handful of flexi (mainly single night) boarders at any given time. Accommodation is just across the hall from the headmaster's quarters in the main house. There's a decent sized common room in the rafters with stunning views of the school grounds. Carpets are well worn, furniture a bit battered and well used bean bags. A TV and pool table for rare time inside. The four boarders' rooms are comfortable and clean, with the air of somewhat forgotten spare bedrooms. Various cartoon-themed bedding looks like it's kept more than a few children warm through the nights. Whole year group taster nights get a bit cramped but look like great fun. Grand plans afoot to revamp and extend the offering.

Money matters: Parents are mainly dual income and currently very local. 'You don't need to be multi-millionaires to come here,' explained one.

The last word: Hall Grove is a humble but assured school where children reach their fullest potential in the most idyllic of settings. A family school in the truest sense, albeit with an eye on a more distant market. It will delight traditional families with no appetite for snobbery or showiness. Let's hope there are plenty of those amongst the west London brigade.

Handcross Park School

34

Handcross, Haywards Heath, West Sussex RH17 6HF

01444 400526 | registrar@handxpark.com | www.handcrossparkschool.co.uk

Ages: 2–13

Pupils: 379; Boarders: 33 full, 21 weekly/flexi (from 7 years)

Fees: Day £10,335 – £20,625; Boarding £17,505 – £42,255 pa

Linked school: Brighton College, 595

Headmaster: Since 2016, Richard Brown MA, who lives on site with his sons. Previously head of Dorset House School, with a stint before that as housemaster at Pangbourne College. Five years in the army are not immediately apparent in this head, who likes best to spend his free time writing or walking. Was a 'tennis parent' and understands parents getting a bit twitchy about teams. His most important qualities to inspire in pupils: love of learning and kindness.

'Bent over backwards to help us,' said parent seeking urgent places for her four children mid year, 'transition was incredibly easy'; another said, 'one step ahead and always thinking about what needs to be done' (passing places appeared on the drive as if by magic). A bit more traditional than his predecessor, thought another, explaining that he has introduced grace before meals, and increased the emphasis on manners. Parents appreciate the well-attended surgeries the head has introduced for the parents of each year group, and say he is at his best one-to-one.

Following an adored predecessor has its challenges, but most appreciate his ideas: 'The... leadership programme is brilliant,' say pupils, and his busy programme upgrading facilities is very popular. He's good at focusing on children's abilities, said a parent – he 'makes a point of telling a child if they're doing well'.

'I like his different approach – more focused on academics,' said a year 8 pupil thoughtfully. A boarder told us, 'He's really friendly; comes and chats at lunchtime and visits boarding houses... helps with maths.'

Entrance: By one or two-day taster experience including English, maths and reasoning assessments and interview, plus reports and references from previous school. Remote assessments and Skype interviews possible for overseas applicants. Pupils come from local nurseries and preps, but with expansion of boarding the catchment area is widening to Brighton, Crawley, Haywards Heath and London. Boarders mainly from London, Forces families, a few from Europe.

Exit: Brighton College is most popular, with Hurst College not far behind. Others to Ardingly College, Worth, Charterhouse, Eastbourne College, Lancing College, Wellington, Epsom, The Perse, Harrow and Culford.

Our view: A parent told us the school's 'culture is to do with the magic of childhood'; or perhaps the magic of how we think childhood should be, with acres of green on which to run around, ancient trees to climb (plus new wellbeing garden), and teachers who say, how about doing this lesson outside in the sun? Children seem young here compared to city schools, and the head aims to extend childhood for as long as possible (whilst of course preparing pupils for senior schools). It's impossible to resist the happiness of this place, and this reviewer received more random smiles in corridors from children here than at any other school; a tribute not just to their politeness, but to the genuine warmth and friendliness which seem to fill this school.

It's not selective, but parents say it's an academically challenging school: 'we joined the school for more academic stretch,' said one; 'the bright are well challenged,' said another. Parents say teachers are as the best thing about Handcross, and feel that its small size means they know teaching staff well: 'The teachers are very inspiring – particularly… in English and science,' said a parent, relaying her surprise when her son, enthused by science for the first time, talked about time and black holes the whole way home.

'Teachers are kind,' agree pupils, one commenting that English has become less scary because the teacher uses her own stories and experience; a year 3 pupil said of the history teacher, 'He tells wonderful stories… and they're all true!'

Handcross is a Google reference school, and a lot of academic learning here is through this medium. Pupils start using Chromebooks in pre-prep, and have their own from year 5 of prep school (although not to the exclusion of using a pen). Parents and pupils are enthusiastic: revision notes and homework are all detailed there and pupils can email the teacher if they're not sure about a topic. In Spanish, Chromebooks mean that each table can be doing something different; in the class we saw one group answering questions on a video, another translating, others practising conversation.

Google Chrome 'works across so many different things,' say pupils, who particularly love the multiple choice Caboodle. Google expeditions mean pupils can travel the world in geography and history – 'so amazing', said a pupil, enthusiastically recalling a virtual trip to the theatre to see Lincoln die. GoGuardian means teachers can see whatever pupils are doing on screens – 'so they know if you sometimes look at the football scores,' said a pupil feelingly.

Learning support has been transformed here in the last year, with parents and pupils bubbling over with enthusiasm for the wonderful staff in the 'dairy'; '[My son's] self confidence has soared,' said a parent. Innovative thinking in this unit: there are no desks, but beanbags, a ball to lounge over and wobble boards; a teacher may well say, 'Let's do our half an hour of English walking among the trees': they understand here that dyslexic children need to move while they learn. Dyslexic pupils were using tweezers to move dinosaurs from bowl to bowl to increase their dexterity – a fun way to improve handwriting; a pupil struggling with maths was using a toy horse rider and jumps to learn his four times table (four faults every time you knock down a fence).

Part of the Brighton College family, but not a back entrance to the college; pupils must hit same standards as other applicants

Around 20 pupils receive regular support (one-to-one charged as an extra), but this is a department with school-wide relevancy, a parent telling us that any pupil who feels 'flaky' about exams can do them in the dairy instead of the school hall, and in this friendly environment feel more confident and do better.

Handcross is part of the Brighton College family, but is no back entrance to the college; pupils must hit same standards as other applicants. The link provides a quality standard, and staff throughout the family share best practice.

Pastoral care is a particular strength. The head is keenly aware of the mental health issues which can assail young children, and is keen to increase pupils' resilience to life's knocks. If pupils have a problem they will talk to their tutor or the deputy head (pastoral), loved by pupils and parents alike, and pupils can also talk to an independent listener. Random acts of kindness are rewarded with kindness bands, on the day of our visit for handing in money, helping a younger pupil find their parents and for lending someone shin pads.

Parents say that complaints of unkindness or bullying are dealt with quickly – 'same day, took seriously, dealt with it discreetly. School investigates misdeeds, doesn't jump to conclusions.' This school is up front when things go wrong: an incident was dealt with 'head on… in a mature manner… and avoided the school gate gossip,' said a parent; 'they allowed children to make a mistake and be helped rather than punished. Their way of dealing with the situation made me feel we're at the right school.'

The usual sports, and gorgeous grounds to play them in, with an indoor pool too. Chances for all in A-E matches every week, and a celebration of the less able in the 'Be Trewe festival' where the D and E teams play other schools. Girls and boys play football, cricket and rounders (which gives every player a chance to play – unlike cricket, which favours the strong few).

Most pupils here learn instruments, and music lessons are an energetic business: shoes were in a scruffy pile at the entrance, pupils were sitting on the floor, drums and other instruments between legs, singing and playing with gusto. It's a traditional set up musically, which one parent thought could benefit from some street dance and hip hop. More than 70 pupils do LAMDA exams, with drama lessons and annual productions for all year groups.

The swish new art and design centre houses art of all sorts, including pottery, textiles and photography. Music played as pupils practised watercolour techniques; next door in woodwork, pupils were turning recycled wood into flags and making plastic coffee containers into Christmas bells.

The lavish range of clubs includes pig care; despite calling them Thing One and Thing Two, the field-to-plate scheme didn't work out, and the pigs look set for a long and happy life at Handcross.

Pre-prep is headed by Mr Gayler – 'a big kid at heart; throws himself into everything,' said a parent. It's set in what would once have been the walled vegetable garden, now a magical place of willow arches, cherry trees and every sort of adventure equipment. The children make full use of the surrounding woods in their forest school lessons, and on the day of our visit, reception, all in pjs, were about to take a magic trip on a bed to a jungle.

Communication is good ('to the point of saturation', said a parent), by email and text; not just if matches are cancelled, but even if a road is closed that might be a problem on the school run. Parents are confident of quick response when they contact the school.

Boarding: Around a quarter of years 5-8 do some sort of boarding, with full, weekly and flexi available. An international presence, with boarders from Spain, China, India and more. The varied activity schedule at the weekend always includes a trip; Thorpe Park, laser quest and the shopping centre are all popular. Day pupils can join boarders for breakfast at 7.15am for small extra fee, and can stay for supper until 6.30pm. 'Takes the pressure off if you're both working,' said a parent (pre-prep also provides wraparound care for 50 weeks of the year).

Boarding facilities are of a very high standard, and 'sensible bedtimes', said a parent approvingly. Food is equally good, and pupils enjoy food from around the world on Tuesdays – a taste from home for overseas boarders.

The best thing about boarding is the freedom they get compared to home, pupils agree. Phones were banned a few years ago, and for a few days boarders didn't know what to do with themselves. Now they're up and out, involved in sport or drama or watching a movie. 'We can interact with friends more.'

Money matters: No scholarships but about one fifth receive some kind of bursary. One means-tested bursary, virtually 100 per cent, and one free place in nursery. Offers sibling discount – five per cent off first, 10 per cent off second. Over and above that you test your negotiating skills with the head.

The last word: 'Believe the advertising,' said one parent earnestly. 'Its very welcoming, very kind.' 'Scatter kindness' is a sign which appears all over the place at Handcross, and it seems that everyone here has taken this to heart. No average family, say parents, but it wouldn't suit 'someone overly aggressive or full of their own importance and abilities,' said a parent crisply.

Harrow School

35

5 High Street, Harrow on the Hill HA1 3HP

020 8872 8007 | admissions@harrowschool.org.uk | www.harrowschool.org.uk

Ages: 13–18

Pupils: 830; sixth form: 333; Boarders: 830 full

Fees: £43,665 pa

Head Master: Since 2019, Alastair Land MA (Cantab) (youthful 50s), formerly head of Repton after three years as deputy head at Harrow. Educated at Manchester Grammar School and Trinity College Cambridge where he was awarded a first-class honours degree in natural sciences. The 'inspirational teaching' he received at MGS piqued his interest in academia, later cemented by a gap year teaching in Kathmandu. First teaching job was nine years in the biology department at Eton and from there to Winchester where he was master in college and senior housemaster. Quite the most immaculately attired head we have ever encountered; we were not surprised to learn that he served as a CCF officer for his entire school career (surely it was here that he acquired his pristine style), had a close call with a career in the armed forces and is commanding officer at Harrow. Still hoping to be ordained into the Church of England when he feels his work as an educator is done – his vocation is clearly to serve.

Upon return to Harrow, had 'very few' surprises ('I knew when I opened a door whether it was a corridor or a cupboard') and a 'positive and energetic' start. Says school benefits from 'phenomenal common room of talented masters,' (and mistresses, we assume), so primary task was to conduct a top to bottom curriculum review to ensure school equipped to deliver 'what boys need to be real-world ready', focusing on digital, cognitive and social literacy. Had a short run into leading a school in lockdown and remained unphased by the challenge. 'Like a true Mancunian, you play the cards you're dealt. We stayed on track and boys continued to thrive.' Parents concur and sources tell us that school barely missed a beat; pupils even wore uniform throughout the homeschooling period.

Applicants to Harrow can be in for the long haul – and it's the whole family under scrutiny (insider tip for dads – leave your mobile phone in the car)

Not a huge character but nonetheless commanding. Parents describe him as 'night and day' from his predecessor, with greater visibility around school – often spotted, in the early days, pitch side with a baby strapped to his chest. 'Very measured'; 'focused on community' and 'down to earth' were recurrent comments and he is intent on instilling humility in his charges: 'it's a privilege to be here, but not everyone is privileged'. No major cultural shift noted by parents or boys since his arrival; 'he was already part of the fabric of the school and highly respected by boys,' thought one parent. Concerned rumblings from a few stalwart families that some of the school's more rumbunctious traditions are being tamed by the 'fun police'. His thoughts? 'Traditions are ties that bind, but they have to be built on friendship and trust. We're a value-led organisation and boys' behaviour has to be consistent with that.' Speaking of traditions, at the time of our visit he was about to embark – as a relative 'new boy' himself on a tour of houses to participate in new boys' house song solos, naturally planning to be the first voice up.

Married with three young children, the elder two attending nearby prep school, Orley Farm.

Entrance: Are you sitting comfortably? Applicants to Harrow can be in for the long haul – even the registrar admits he arguably runs 'the most complicated process of any boarding school' – and we won't beat around the bush, it's the whole family under scrutiny (insider tip for dads – leave your mobile phone in the car). 'We need to be sure we can work with the parents – it's a team effort,' says school.

Competitive entry, although the right prep school helps smooth the path. Top feeders are Caldicott, Summer Fields, Cothill, Papplewick, St John's Beaumont, Dragon and Wetherby. Potential parents describe 'impeccable' tours – friendly yet slick, with staff 'out in force'. Around 700 apply for the 160+ places on offer at 13. Prospective pupils should ideally register by the end of year 5. Stage one of the selection process is the ISEB common pre-test, plus detailed reference from the applicant's school, in year 6. Very few fallers at this first hurdle. Sufficiently strong candidates invited to tour two houses for an interview which, depending on housemaster, ranges from 'a casual family chat whilst touring the house to a formal grilling,' according to parents. We should point out here that OHs tell us that boys very much join house first, school second. If the housemaster likes the cut of their jib, the family then receives 'house interest' – an offer to meet the candidate for a second time when he sits the Harrow test (online maths, English and – 'the most important bit' – two interviews) in the autumn of year 7 when they're 'a little bit older – the last thing we want to do is filter out superb boys who haven't developed yet'.

This is where the nail biting begins. Only about 50 per cent of applicants not offered a place are given a flat rejection at this stage – the rest are placed on ranked waiting lists and kept hanging, sometimes until the bitter end (we've heard of offers on speech day) and sometimes brought back on multiple occasions, only to find themselves back on one of the many waiting lists. Parents of those not successful in the first round describe the lengthy process as 'excruciating – worse than a flat no.'

Rather than zooming in on academics, school looks for a rounded picture; 'We're not trying to be St Paul's.' Boys who are average or above academically and 'get stuck in and take the fruit off the tree,' fit the bill. 'And they have to actively want to board.' What of sons of OHs – are the days of legacy shoe-ins over? Just 12 per cent of all current pupils have fathers who attended the school. 'We have to be cruel to be kind now,' says school,

Feltonfleet School

'we don't offer to boys who won't be able to keep up. Likewise with siblings.'

Total of 20 new pupils a year into the 340-strong sixth form. Candidates need at least seven or eight 9-7s at GCSE or equivalent but many will have straight 9/8s. Candidates write a CV, plus letter to the head explaining why they want to come to Harrow, and take preliminary tests in two of their proposed A level subjects. The best attend a day of interviews and assessments.

Exit: Boys leaving after GCSEs is rare and almost all sixth formers off to university, usually with good numbers to Oxbridge (14 in 2021). Other top destinations include UCL, Imperial, King's College London, LSE, St Andrews and Durham. US very popular – 27 students to eg Harvard, Yale, Brown, Chicago and NYU in 2021. School now has a master in charge of North American universities ('they really know their stuff,' say parents) specifically for the 25 per cent who apply, and offers bespoke help with the necessary SATs, ACTs and essays required.

Latest results: 95 per cent grades 9-7 at IGCSE in 2021. 80 per cent A*-A at A level and 91 per cent A*-B. In 2019, the last year in which exams were taken, 83 per cent 9-7 at IGCSE; 62 per cent A*/A at A level (87 per cent A*-B).

Teaching and learning: Not a 'league table' school – Harrow doesn't believe in presenting a one-dimensional image of itself (for what it's worth, we agree) – but we suspect that if it were, it would sit comfortably in the upper echelons, a few rungs below Eton and Winchester but above Radley and most of the co-ed boarding schools. Those keen on close examination of such matters, however, should remember that Harrow's entrance criteria allow for a wider range of ability at entry than at these other schools; applicants are judged on their own merits and character, not just a CATS score.

Parents told us unanimously that they give a 'big tick' to 'outstanding teaching' and that 'boys love the beaks' (Harrow lingo for teachers) who 'really enthuse' them. Even those with sons who, at prep school, 'mainly enjoyed sport and getting into trouble' report emerging academic excellence thanks to instilled passion for learning. Head's recent curriculum overhaul has incorporated a progressive focus on digital and cyber skills, woven through all elements of the curriculum, to deliver a truly 21st century education, and the tradition of Harrovians walking between lessons hidden behind huge piles of folders and books has been replaced by one of neat bags containing laptops over shoulders as school moves towards a more (although not entirely) paper-free existence. Terrific range of subject choices at A level – all the usual suspects as well as business, politics, history of art, music technology, photography, drama and theatre as well as a dazzling array of languages. Over half take four full A levels – maths is most popular with over 60 per cent choosing it.

Head's curriculum overhaul has incorporated a focus on digital and cyber skills, woven through all elements of the curriculum, to deliver a truly 21st-century education

Head's introduction of the Harrow Diploma, reflective of the North American commitment to a liberal arts education, sees sixth formers choosing from a range of electives in addition to their A level subjects – a chance for them to experience meaningful university-style teaching in specialist areas over eight periods per fortnight, with options changing three times termly. These range from mountaineering or programming to evolution of the human species (taught by head) or psychoanalysis and are 'taken seriously', say parents. Boys are strongly encouraged to enter external essay competitions and Olympiads to gain credits towards their Diploma. Class of 2023 will be the first cohort to complete the HD, with the majority expected to achieve it.

Learning support and SEN: Sector-leading SENDCo heads team of three learning support teachers, including two specialist assessors, with around 25 per cent of cohort under their watch. Boys with, for example, dyslexia, dyspraxia, ASD and ADHD are supported on an individual basis with a bespoke plan established – from one-to-one or small group sessions to additional help with study skills – as required. Parents, housemasters and teachers work alongside boys to form a cohesive plan.

The arts and extracurricular: With options so numerous it left us exhausted just hearing about them, it would be quicker to report what isn't offered. Every second of the day is filled ('we're just getting going when we see pupils from other schools going home,' school told us) leaving boys with just a few breathless moments to speak to parents before dashing off to another activity at 9pm. Even 'down time' back at the house sees them making use of their own flood-lit five-a-side pitch (every house has one), practising their instruments or playing board games. It almost came as a relief to us that to hear that they still find time to watch Love Island and play on the house gaming console from time to time. The pace doesn't let up at weekends. After Saturday fixtures, there's a full programme of clubs and societies plus informal tournaments for eg football or water polo, cookery classes or trips out with tutors or matron – one group of Shells had just been ice skating and for hot chocolate at the time of our visit – to fill the rest of the weekend. Evenings are for movies, takeaways or socials with other schools.

Those who enjoy a bit of rough and tumble will love Harrow football, a game with a pork-pie shaped ball which absorbs water and can be propelled by any part of the body

Founded on a strong tradition of singing, the Hill is, indeed, alive with the sound of music. Harrow songs are unique, mainly written in Victorian times, and covering aspects of school life ranging from the lights of Hampstead to cricket. A huge part of the bonding experience, they are sung in the Speech Room amphitheatre, resplendent with panelling, stained glass and deep sense of history, as part of the head's assembly on a Monday morning. Such is their nostalgic, binding power that the Royal Albert Hall plays host to some 5,000 OHs every five years, who return in droves to sing Harrow Songs en masse. In November each year the whole school assembles in Speech Room in honour of its most famous alumnus, Sir Winston Churchill, for the Churchill Songs. Elite peripatetic music teachers come from eg The Guildhall and Royal Academy, with around half of all pupils learning instruments, including bagpipes and the organ for those so inclined, as well as all the usuals. Choirs, ensembles and orchestras aplenty, with around 100 concerts performed every year.

Drama, no second fiddle, is 'key part of pastoral experience'. First major project for Shells (new year 9s) is house drama festival – recently Aesop's Fables with a twist – with all taking part and major roles often offered to those who may not previously have considered acting. House drama performances alternate annually with whole school play, recently The Bloody Chamber and Chariots of Fire respectively. The Ryan Theatre seats 300 and is used for school and professional productions, with annual Shakespeare productions taking place in the Speech Room which boasts authentic Globe-style staging. Strong tradition of Shakespearean performance sees pupils welcoming peers from local schools for masterclasses with actors from The Globe, culminating in a biennial performance there, most recently Twelfth Night. Wonderful art and, befittingly for a school where photography pioneer William Fox Talbot was a pupil, photography. DT, sculpture, art and photography taught in a bright and airy facility that also includes a new digital design suite.

Personal statements enhanced by compulsory service via school's community outreach arm, Shaftesbury Enterprise, a full-time operation. Every Harrovian supports the local community by eg working with local elderly, reading with pupils or running sports coaching in primary schools.

Sport: With 28 sports 'done properly', from the major (rugby, soccer, cricket) to fencing, fives, water polo and countless others, there's no doubt that this is a phenomenal school for sporty boys and, arguably, the one to beat on the southern public school circuit. Coached games sessions take place five afternoons a week and fixtures on three, and even those with aversion to major team sports are encouraged to find something that suits them. Those who enjoy a bit of rough and tumble in the mud will love Harrow football, a unique game with a pork-pie shaped ball which absorbs water and can be propelled by any part of the body. Played only in the depths of winter and only amongst current and former Harrovians, it makes rugby look tame. And clean. Everything done to elite standard; the football tour is to Argentina, the first XI cricket team is coached by Mark Ramprakash and judo is encouraged for serious rugby players. Sporting traditions are numerous and include Long Ducker: 'a long run or a very long run', carried out annually for charity. In 2021 pupils raised a quarter of a million pounds which was used to buy ChromeBooks for local primary schools during the Covid-19 lockdown. Vast playing fields, 25m indoor pool and sports hall, courts for tennis, rackets and squash, a nine-hole golf course and Olympic sized running track will soon be joined by a brand new sports centre with 1,800 hours per year of community use built in.

Boarding: Full boarding. No day pupils and no flexi. Parents, pupils and OHs unanimous that the twelve houses are 'like twelve different schools', each with its own culture, atmosphere and fiercely loyal members, although school does a good job of bringing them together 'like a big, extended family'. Evidence strongly suggests that the culture of houses recruiting certain 'types' (sporty, artsy, academic etc) remains, although school insists this is not deliberate and scholars of all disciplines are distributed across houses. Housemasters dictate the ethos of each house, with parents describing them as ranging from

Housemasters dictate the ethos of each house, with parents describing them as ranging from 'very formal' to 'totally relaxed'

'very formal' to 'totally relaxed'. 'Some matrons are better than others', thought parents, but the best are outstanding, 'like a mum', many are highly qualified nurses and most unphased by anything. They are central to the boys' happiness and wellbeing, baking with them, organising fun evening events such as bingo and, crucially, keeping parents in the loop with photos and frequent informal updates. Inter-house sporting fixtures – and competitions of all kinds – are 'hugely competitive,' say pupils, and are taken even more seriously than those against other schools.

Houses vary enormously in their fabric and locations; older ones such as The Head Master's and Druries, which dates back to the 1790s, are central to the main teaching buildings, with the ultra-modern en-suite Lyon's, built in 2010 (monikered by some wags 'The Holiday Inn'), and West Acre at the opposite end of the High Street, more outliers. Some more recently refurbished than others (one boy told us that not only was he sleeping in his father's former dorm but that it had barely changed in over thirty years). Boys' view is that proximity to the central dining hall and ability to get back to house in time for snacks at break is crucial; parents should look for best fit with housemaster and matron. Each house has its own charm; many, stunning architecture; all have common rooms, music practice rooms, games rooms with plasma TV, pool and table tennis tables and garden, some with facilities such as cricket nets. Rooms shared until year 11 and room mates rotated half-termly to build bonds and 'make sure each gets his fair share of views of Wembley Stadium,' in the words of one housemaster. All pupils' names etched on wooden house boards with head of house's name picked out in gold.

Meals eaten centrally in a surprisingly unassuming dining hall where boys are seated in houses at breakfast and lunchtimes but have free rein to join other friends at dinner. Food gets the thumbs up and we can report most favourably on the chicken curry. Boys allowed out for a meal with parents on Sundays and there are two weekend exeats in the autumn and spring terms and one in the summer. Parents warmly invited to watch fixtures and houses maintain close links with families with dinners, socials and, like any school, WhatsApp groups.

Ethos and heritage: Harrow will surprise the uninitiated with its range of contradictions: fiercely traditional yet progressively outward looking; unashamedly elite yet wholeheartedly inclusive; simultaneously conservative whilst unmistakably diverse. One of a dying breed of only four (soon to be three now that Winchester has broken ranks) all-boys, full boarding schools in the UK and a heavyweight pillar of the establishment since 1572. Founded under a royal charter granted to local farmer John Lyon by Elizabeth I to provide free education for 30 local scholars.

The approach to the school is via some of west London's least salubrious neighbourhoods – a stark contrast to the bubble about to be entered – which morph quite suddenly into the picturesque, steeply climbing and rather narrow (we wonder how it copes with fleets of 4x4s that no doubt transport its pupils to and fro) High Street, opening onto Harrow-on-the-Hill which is essentially the school campus. We were rather breathless at the end of our visit, partly owing to the spectacular panoramic London views but mainly because the undulating nature of the school means that flat shoes and cardio fitness are a must. Unless granny happens to be Jane Fonda, probably best to leave her at home on speech day.

Steeped in tradition and history. The 17th century Old Schools are home to the mesmerizing Fourth Form room, former pupils' names (we were thrilled to spot Byron and Churchill) carved into every centimetre of panelling. The War Memorial Building commemorates the 642 OHs who died in WWI. We adore a library and Harrow boasts possibly the loveliest we have ever visited (and there have been a few), built over three floors into the hillside and featuring spiral staircases and more magnificent views.

Almost every parent and pupil we spoke to used 'friendly' as their first Harrow adjective. Housemasters and head are approachable to parents; boys are kept focused and are 'very tightly managed' but have 'huge fun'. In relation to equivalent schools parents may be considering, we were told by one family that 'nobody gets lost and all boys are known – it's definitely not sink or swim.' Lots of jargon to learn on arrival; uniform comprises 'bluers' (jacket) and 'greyers' (trousers), 'Skew' is a punishment, 'tosh' is a shower, 'tolley up' is permission to work late – the list goes on.

Long and distinguished roll of former pupils – seven former prime ministers (including Sir Winston Churchill), 19th century philanthropist Lord Shaftesbury, King Hussein of Jordon, Lord Cardigan (who led the charge of the Light Brigade) plus countless other men of military renown (20 holders of the Victoria Cross and one George Cross holder). The arts and sciences are equally well represented, with dazzling luminaries including

Lord Byron, Richard Brinsley Sheridan, Anthony Trollope, Terence Rattigan, John Galsworthy, Cecil Beaton, Edward and William Fox, Richard Curtis, Benedict Cumberbatch and James Blunt, plus Julian Metcalfe (founder of Pret à Manger) and cricketer Nick Compton.

Pastoral care, inclusivity and discipline: Noted by parents as 'a great sized school' with a 'cosy' feel. The 'well cared for' ethos all starts in the house – a home from home where housemasters are very hands on, dictating the entire culture and ethos. New boys are given 'shepherds' – boys in the year above – to guide them in their first few terms, as well as sixth form mentors. Older boys, in the main, are 'not scary', we were told by younger ones; keeping an eye on them, coaching house sports and activities and acting as role models. On the academic front, weekly meetings with tutors ensure that laziness is pulled up with a mixture of carrot and stick; parents say 'well tested systems are in place to get the best from the boys.'

Full boarding. Boys allowed out for a meal with parents on Sundays and there are two weekend exeats in the autumn and spring terms and one in the summer

Definitely (metaphorically and physically) a 'short hair school' and we couldn't find anyone to tell us that individuality is strongly encouraged. Known for its distinctive straw hat, compulsory attire when moving around school (we marvelled at how they remained in place on the blustery day of our visit), an air of conservative uniformity permeates the site. On the subject of uniform, parents should brace themselves for the hefty price tag of almost £2,000. 'Tell them they don't need to buy everything on the list,' cried parent after parent we spoke to. Consider yourselves told. Pupil prestige and achievement indicated by an array of ties earned by participation in clubs and societies, excellence in sport. The sixth former with whom we lunched sported a natty striped – and impeccably tied – bow tie for outstanding achievement in music. Senior monitors (prefects) upgrade their straw hats for top hats and canes, worn on formal occasions.

Minor misdemeanours – shabby shoes, uncut hair, broken hats and other 'boy things' (school's words not ours) – are dealt with by the delightful 'Custos', a former army sergeant major and fount of all knowledge – a firm but kindly great uncle figure, to whom transgressors must report every morning to have their uniform checked before school. We suspect they quite enjoy their visits to his office and emerge with smiles on faces as well as corrected attire. Parents we spoke to report a definite tightening up of serious discipline under the new head, with matters formerly dealt with by house masters now escalated far more readily to deputy head; a step change some parents are finding rather 'heavy handed.' Zero tolerance of drugs and alcohol, with occasional random drug testing and room searches.

Formal hierarchies within house thankfully now a thing of yesteryear and we watch with interest to see whether new head successfully stamps out the few remaining undesirable traditions, described by parents we spoke to, linked to pecking order. That said, we were told there is 'very little serious bullying' and that when it happens it is dealt with fast and effectively, often by older boys stepping in, and with anything relating to protected characteristics referred to deputy head. Parents were unanimous that discipline was 'robust' and that school takes a 'reflective' approach to punishment. Absolutely no sense of a 'boys will be boys' approach; RSE provision reviewed post the Everyone's Invited campaign in 2021, with the programme rebuilt 'from the bottom up' in September 2020 and parents drawn into process with educational workshops on issues such as pornography and consent to ensure consistent messaging. There are designated monitor leads for EDI (equality and diversity) and groups welcome frequent visitors and guest speakers, recently Aaron Phipps, Paralympian; Toni Fola-Alade, Old Harrovian, former president of the Cambridge University African and Caribbean Society and member of the vice-chancellor's advisory group on the legacies of enslavement, and Soma Sara, founder and CEO of Everyone's Invited. Conversations with all parties left us unconvinced that Harrow would be the most comfortable environment for a boy questioning his sexual identity – there is no LGBTQ+ society yet – but initiatives such as celebrations of Pride month in the Vaughan Library with recommended reads and sports teams being invited to wear rainbow laces in their shoes are a start.

Compulsory chapel for Anglicans twice weekly, with a weekly mass and catechism classes available to Catholics and separate provision for those from non-Christian faiths. Director of pastoral care oversees all pastoral matters, although boys are surrounded by a triumvirate of housemaster, deputy and matron to support them when needed and the health centre is open 24 hours. Pastoral support committee meets four times weekly to discuss boys with live issues and includes the school psychologist and three chaplains.

Pupils and parents: What most surprised us was the down to earth feel. Social and ethnic diversity is palpable, with recent OHs telling us how strange they found the relative uniformity of 'type' when they went to university. Although school as a whole is founded on Christian values, head is working on expanding spiritual provision for other faiths and has recently employed a Jewish chaplain, with a Muslim counterpart to follow; 'we don't want our boys to have to leave their culture and heritage at home.' One parent confessed to being so surprised at how grounded the boys were that she asked her son where all the posh people were hiding. Wealth and privilege worn lightly – the heir to a hereditary peerage barely distinguishable from the son of a state educated entrepreneur or a boy on a full bursary – and pupils are 'quietly proud' of their school. We were assured that there is no sense of the pink trouser-wearing 'old guard' and that parents new to the system don't feel like outsiders. Parental friendships are formed pitch-side, often leading to dinners, lunches and, sometimes, bonds that last far beyond their sons' time at Harrow. Pupils come from near and far, around 20 per cent from overseas (some expat, others from a range of about 40 countries), around 25 with EAL needs. Boys we met were unassuming, well-mannered and appreciative of their educational opportunities.

Money matters: School franchised in Beijing, Bangkok, Hong Kong and Shanghai; all successful enterprises which fund generous bursaries at home and carefully monitored by Harrow. Harrow online launched in 2020, offering further access to a global audience. Huge range of scholarships (mainly around 5 per cent) and bursaries of up to 100 per cent available at 13 and 16. Four scholarships awarded each year for boys from state primary schools to cover fees for feeder boarding preps for years 7 and 8 followed by Harrow. Full time access officer manages outreach programmes to primary schools not only in Harrow and Brent but also in the Midlands and Lancashire, 'we go out to find boys who will benefit from a Harrow education,' says head. 'We will make it happen for boys who want to come.' By 2026 school aims to have 100 boys on full bursaries and 200 on part.

The last word: Premier league. For families who value an outstanding 360 degree education soaked in tradition, and energetic boys happy to throw themselves into everything, Harrow ticks every box. Not the obvious choice for softer souls, individualists or disrupters. Turns out a close-knit tribe of polished, confident young adults whose hearts will always be on The Hill. In the words of one veteran mother, 'I can put my boys in front of anyone and feel proud. Even the grungy 16-year-old.'

Holmewood House School

36

Barrow Lane, Langton Green, Tunbridge Wells, Kent TN3 0EB

01892 860006 | welcome@holmewoodhouse.co.uk | www.holmewoodhouse.co.uk

Ages: 3-13

Pupils: 445; Boarders: 30 full

Fees: Day £9.120 – £20,100; Boarding £23,985 – £26,985 pa

Headmaster: Since September 2017, Scott Carnochan, previously head of Sedbergh Prep in Cumbria. Degree from Heriot-Watt University and postgrad from Nottingham. Has taught at Hillcrest Prep in Nairobi, been housemaster at St John's College School, Cambridge and head of boarding at Repton Prep. Boarded from the age of 11 while his parents were abroad and says his 'inspirational housemaster had a huge part in shaping my career choice'. Played international rugby, representing Scotland at U18 and student level.

Enthusiastic and affable, he has made the school more transparent and sees parents' input as part of the school's 'triangulated approach', although parents tell us he's also clear when they need to step back – a good job, it seems, as 'it used to be a case of the tail wagging the dog,' according to one, with practically every parent we spoke to making reference to the significant cohort of 'very pushy parents'. 'When I arrived, I thought, "You're kidding me" and I'm from London! Some even contradict the referees on the pitch,' a parent told us, while another said, 'Some of them used to look through me as a working parent.' 'Based on feedback we heard before we arrived, it felt like the parents came with a health warning,' laughs the head, but insists he's found them 'lovely' and parents agree there's a more laid-back attitude taking hold.

Parents say it's helped that the 'school communications, which we'd been moaning about for years, were up and running within his first month' and that 'he acts on what he says and promptly'. Parents also like the way he 'stood back and watched what was going on, changing things slowly but effectively' and in a 'really forward-thinking way' – including a five-year strategic vision focusing on the likes of well-being, a full curriculum review ('to include not just knowledge but skills like collaboration, research and resilience') and a reputational shift ('the perception was that the school is more academic than pastoral'). Has also introduced three school values – self-belief, aspiration and kindness. Pupils say he 'runs a tight ship' but 'you can have a laugh with him'.

Married to Kate, a youthful, energetic woman who heads up the school's marketing; they live on site with their two young children. Together, they enjoy travelling and sport plays a big part in the family too.

Entrance: For nursery and reception, it's first come, first served and entry into the pre-prep is non-selective, although informal assessments will ensure the child 'can keep up and be happy here'. Around 15 children join at year 3, when prospective pupils take tests in maths, reading and spelling, plus there's an interview, and reports from the previous school are considered. Ditto for year 7 in terms of numbers joining and the entrance process (these children replace those who leave for grammar schools).

Exit: Previously frowned upon when kids took the 11+ and left for grammar school, but school now supports any child, with around 12-15 heading off at the end of year 6. No bespoke 11+ tuition (not allowed to under Kent policy), but school says the preparation all children receive for secondary school entrance and Common Entrance pre-tests is relevant (and many are tutored at home too, according to parents). Parents say school has become less 'tunnel visioned' about Tonbridge and Sevenoaks to include Eastbourne and sometimes Eton, Benenden, King's Canterbury, Charterhouse, Ardingly, Brighton College, Wellington, Hurst etc. But some feel the school still has 'a way to go in promoting a wider range of schools, as well as managing parents' expectations, as some still feel only Tonbridge and Sevenoaks count'. A roadshow with 20 senior schools held every two years helps. School harvests a good crop of academic scholarships, as well as in music, sport and drama – 20 in 2021.

Our view: Tucked away in a leafy residential area of Tunbridge Wells, the main house (rebuilt after the original burned down in 1837) first belonged to Sir Charles Locock, gynaecologist and physician to Queen Victoria. School opened here in 1945 with just eight boys. In 1990, it became co-ed and the boy-girl ratio is now 55:45.

Outside, the 32 acres are spectacular, including fields, pitches, walled garden, beehive (school sells its own honey) and a soon-to-be orchard and pond

The main house (with headmaster's swish office and staff rooms downstairs and boarding upstairs) aside, it couldn't be said to be the prettiest prep, with a hodgepodge of buildings, a few a little tired and poky. But everything is fit for purpose and a £4.5m building project has added some superb facilities including spacious contemporary new classrooms in the Collings and Cloisters buildings, with the money also going on new learning hub, digital library and enrichment centre, plus three refurbished science labs. Sensational new pre-prep playground and a dedicated parents' area with free Wifi. With three different pick-up times, parents will be able to 'go and get a decent cup of coffee and socialise, catch up on emails or do spellings etc' – a novel idea, if ever we heard one. Both pre-prep and prep libraries could be more inspiring aesthetically and pupils told us there is no dedicated librarian (English teacher does it). Nobody was in either when we visited (not unusual, say pupils).

Outside, the 32 acres are spectacular, including fields, pitches, walled garden, beehive (school sells its own honey – money goes into the PA pot) and a soon-to-be orchard and pond. No accredited forest school, but they do have their own similar Discoverers. It's one of very few prep schools with its own 20-metre rifle range and the pupils are champion shooters among English schools. There's also a 25-metre indoor pool (open to the local community and primary schools), squash courts, a climbing wall, and a snazzy sports hall. Lots of sporting success at county and national level, especially in netball, rugby and hockey. Also in swimming, judo and squash. Some parent niggles ('If a child is in the A team for football, they tend to be in the A team for everything' etc) but school says 'participation rates are up'. We like the fact that the non-sporty don't get it rammed down their throats as much as in some other prep schools – whilst there are three afternoons of compulsory team games, on the other two they can choose drama, music or craft activities, or individual sports instead.

Drama is popular – the impressive stage set in the 350-seat theatre was all ready for the upcoming Bugsy Malone production when we visited, one of many big productions. Treading these boards launched the careers of old boys actors Dan Stevens of Downton Abbey and Tristan Gemmell (Casualty and Coronation Street). More remarkably, perhaps, Shane McGowan of The Pogues was also here.

Art is head and shoulders above most preps, with history of art embedded into lessons. We saw children in the throes of creating mosaic-decorated clay pots and there are fabulous displays throughout the school including abstract artwork that we'd have gladly hung on our walls. DT also a hive of activity, where we saw pupils making wooden iPhones, name boards for their horses (yes, many have them) and a lovely bird box ('for Mother's Day,' said pupil), with all the whizzy equipment such as 3D printer and laser cutter in full use. Music also strong. Parents consider the concerts a 'real treat' and the school boasts two orchestras (one for pre-prep alone), a swing band, jazz ensembles and three choirs (junior, senior, chamber).

This is a high-achieving, ambitious school, with an academically full-on timetable, but most prep is done in school, which parents appreciate. In the junior school, years 3 and 4 are classroom-based with a form teacher, although they go to music, art, DT and science in dedicated classrooms and they have subject specialist teachers for music, French, ICT and sport. From year 5, all subjects are taught by subject specialists. At this point, children can expect two periods a week of Latin, and scholars (a scholarship class is introduced in year 6 for the brightest sparks) can also do ancient Greek. There's also Mandarin in year 6 and critical thinking, problem solving and reasoning (taught by the head) in years 5 and 6, a Spanish option from year 6, and French from nursery. Setting in maths from year 3 and in French from year 6. The seniors get Christmas and summer term exams in every subject, although only in English and maths for year 5s. CE in geography, history and RS now scrapped, with pupils producing projects instead.

Teaching is excellent; the children learn a lot and are pushed quite hard, parents told us, while pupils told us, 'They're very good at making sure you're not left behind.' We saw faces so attentive that they barely noticed us and weren't surprised at the head's story of having a similar reaction even when he walked into classrooms dressed as Miss Trunchbull on World Book Day. Not that these kids don't have fun – there's a reassuring playfulness about them, despite their impeccable manners. Pre-prep have a separate block, which parents report has improved – 'There was a need for it to be brought up to speed as there was inconsistency among teachers, with some pushing the children a lot more than others,' said one.

The tone for SEN support is refreshing, with learning support now called 'learning strategies' in recognition of 'the fact that some of the most able children have learning barriers'. Parents praise the school's move towards more classroom-based support and are generally impressed with, for example, 'the work they've done on self-esteem and encouraging children to be able to articulate what they need'.

Ninety per cent of parents live locally. Working parents (once a rare breed here) are grateful for the seven minibuses and wraparound care 7.30am-6pm, including plenty of after-school clubs. There is also a health centre staffed by nurses between 8am and 7pm, which can manage complicated medical regimes.

Boarding from year 3. Majority flexi, with some weekly. Activities include swimming, drama, baking and – the favourite – dodgeball on a Thursday night, run by the head

Weekly pastoral staff meetings, values-led assemblies and drop-in sessions with the well-being lead (no stigma, say pupils) all make for strong pastoral scaffolding. Major focus on treating others as you'd want to be treated – result is very little bullying, claim pupils. Self-reflection document brought out for misdemeanours so children 'learn from their mistakes'. Food gets mixed reviews – 'it's not to everyone's liking,' admitted a pupil. Strong parent community – the 230 tickets for the ball were hotter than Coldplay tickets, selling out in just 21 minutes. Fees around £1,000 a term higher than neighbouring preps, but school has deliberately narrowed the gap in recent years.

Boarding: Boarding from year 3. Majority flexi, with some weekly; rest are full (half from London, the rest from overseas). Cosy, refurbished dorms are six or eight bedded and there's a combined games room. The two houseparents are 'really kind', say pupils, with activities including swimming, drama, baking and – the favourite – dodgeball on a Thursday night, run by the head. Sunday trips to Go Ape, London museums, ice skating, local castles etc.

Money matters: Academic scholarships, which can be topped up with bursaries, are available from year 3.

The last word: For a school that used to be known for its air of elitism and rather scary parent cohort, we were pleasantly surprised to find a different reality – inclusive, buzzy and busy, with friendly, likeable people. 'The school has got its mojo back,' said one parent.

Hurstpierpoint College

37

College Lane, Hurstpierpoint, West Sussex BN6 9JS

01273 833636 | registrar@hppc.co.uk | www.hppc.co.uk

Ages: 4–18

Pupils: 1253; sixth form: 359; Boarders: 450 weekly/flexi (from age 13)

Fees: Day: £9,660 – £25,485; Boarding: £29,670 – £31,620 pa

Headmaster: Since 2005, Tim Manly (Oxford, LSE and Cambridge), married to Henny with four children. Abandoned a career in commerce to teach, first at Sevenoaks, then as deputy head at Oakham School before joining Hurst. The only head we've come across where pupils gave an audible 'aaaah…' when asked for their views: 'the best head'; 'respectful of us as pupils… makes the effort and knows all names'; 'not scary… you can have a conversation with him'. The head likes to keep teenagers busy and expectations of pupils are high, said another, who described the head as 'a man of boundless energy; always there, always visible… who is very engaging as an individual. [He] takes every opportunity to include parents in what the school is thinking and intending.'

Head of prep and pre-prep since 2013, Ian Pattison (chemistry, Southampton), married to Janina with one son at the prep. Joined Hurst as a chemistry teacher in 1997, and became a housemaster in 2006. This warm, enthusiastic head loves hockey and cycling up mountains; no surprise, then, that he wants his pupils to be ready to take on the world. 'Not a place for children who just want to turn up to do lessons and go home.' A head pupils can go and talk to about anything.

Entrance: Not aggressively selective, but recruits better than average. Those joining from outside take ISEB pre-test in year 6 for year 9 entry and need to get over 55 per cent in maths, science and English, 50 per cent in other subjects at CE. Hurst prep year 8s make up less than half of year 9: there is a big intake from outside at this stage which 'avoids stagnation', says the head of prep.

At prep, most pupils join in reception, year 3 and year 7 (which, like year 9, is oversubscribed).

Exit: A handful leave the prep school for other local senior schools. Around 20 per cent leave after GCSEs. Rest primarily to Russell Group universities. Exeter, Bristol, Bath, Durham and Leeds all popular. Three to Oxbridge in 2021, plus eight medics. Large variety of courses including theatre, art, musical, film, dance and acting.

Latest results: In 2021, 92 per cent 9-7 at GCSE; 83 per cent A*/A at A level (96 per cent A*-B). In 2019, (the last year when exams took place): 83 per cent 9-7 at GCSE; 51 per cent A*/A at A level (84 per cent A*-B).

Teaching and learning: 'Pupils are well taught and achieve their academic potential,' said a parent. '[It] does its core purpose brilliantly.' Sciences and maths are popular high performers.

No IB takers in the current cohort, but the door isn't closed to those keen to take the IB in future years. A good range of subjects available, including BTec in business and sport, though pupils felt media studies was a noticeable omission from the list. The head initiated dropping from four A levels to three, with all pupils doing the EPQ.

Results have gone up in the last four years: parents speculate that this is partly due to a more selective intake, partly due to a change of staff – 'It's a very quality staffroom now,' say staff. Parents told us there has been a tightening up of academic standards: 'If pupils don't engage academically, there will be more and more supervision to ensure they do engage and get the grades they are capable of getting,' said parent. Some 'disquiet at new rules', with a few parents expressing concern that Hurst might be edging into the territory of the local high-flying competitor, but things have settled down, and parents are delighted by the new regime for Oxbridge.

Hurst has a challenge grade system, which means that each child's performance is assessed according to the challenge set for them: tick is on target, +1 exceeding target, -1 falling short. There are no comparisons between pupils, and a parent commented that she likes the fact that a very academic child can get minus marks because they're not achieving their potential. There are frequent reviews under the challenge grade system, and teacher comments are 'thoughtful, personal and helpful', said a parent. It certainly works for pupils, with Hurst in the top 10 per cent nationally for value added. 'Academic performance is not the be all and end all,' said a parent, but her child 'achieved more than she thought she would achieve.'

One-hour lessons and a longer school day means there is a steady pace, said a parent, but expectations are in accordance with your abilities: 'You are recognised and supported as a person.' Parents describe great support from staff – 'happy and willing to work incredibly long hours,' said one appreciatively; 'they make it easy to catch up if you fall behind,' said a pupil.

iPhones are allowed in the senior school: the school is strict about usage, and pupils generally keep them switched off when they're meant to be. Pupils in years 9-11 have MacBooks, and iPads are frequently used in the prep, which one parent said has made a 'huge difference [to her son's] learning and confidence'.

Hurst is described by the head of prep as 'a genuine through school', and it works hard to ensure continuity between prep and senior school: a single deputy head academic covers both schools, and any change to the college curriculum will result in changes all the way down; for example, the introduction of Spanish GCSE means that this is now taught in years 7 and 8 of prep.

Year 8s take exams before leaving prep; it's not the CE, but there is a ritualistic formality about them, and all the frisson of results in envelopes. Pupils want to do well, though not through fear of failure: all progress to the college (the few whom it is felt would not thrive there are told in good time). The absence of CE frees up the curriculum – year 8s spend time doing a presentation and essay on a topic of their choice.

Learning support and SEN: The learning support department provides mostly one-to-one support for pupils with mild learning difficulties. A parent described how their unconfident dyspraxic son turned into a different child at Hurst – 'he didn't feel a misfit anymore'. He was assessed straightaway, and the parent was asked how her child learned and what worked for him; her advice was forwarded to all her son's teachers and has been every year since.

The arts and extracurricular: One parent said what she liked best about Hurst was 'the sheer level of opportunity and encouragement. Everyone has a go and gives everything they've got. Whether you're good at something or not doesn't matter – everyone will support you. That's what you're paying for…'

The wide range of co-curricular activities here includes dissection, mechanics, environmental conservation, CCF and DofE (silver for all). 'They encourage anything which enthuses the kids,' said a mum, describing how her chamber music loving daughter was encouraged to create a group.

Parents choose Hurst because they feel it provides something more than an academic education: 'we wanted the children to be themselves'

Music is a popular pastime, though numbers taking A level are small, and every taste is catered for; there's a huge non-audition choir of 160, and a selective one too. A lively outreach programme sees Hurst musicians entertaining the local community: the Big Band playing for village pensioners at Cake at the College, and the brass group playing festive music for the WI in the village. Updated facilities mean there's now even more space including additional music classroom and music lesson rooms.

There are a great number of dramatic performances every term, from Cabaret to Titus Andronicus and Lord of the Flies (by the prep), now in the new theatre. 'It's better to do lots, than one Barbican level performance a year,' says the head, and this means that performers include both the experienced and novice at this school which champions 'give it a go', regardless of ability.

Art is displayed throughout the school, in beautifully mounted neat and tidy style. Standards are high, and facilities have recently expanded to include a printing press and textiles room, in which pupils used wax and sewing to produce a mixed media hanging exploring man's impact on the environment. Only a handful take A level, but GCSE is more popular, with most pupils achieving high grades.

Sport: A rugby school in the main, with just a couple of teams giving a nod to football. Netball is strong for girls, and both girls and boys play hockey and cricket. There are 'isolated moments when rugby comes first, netball second… but girls' sport has come on tremendously and does extremely well,' said a parent. A school with an inclusive sports ethic: a parent said her son is in a D team, but still enjoys matches every other weekend. 'You can't tell which team they're in on the basis of enthusiasm,' says the head of prep.

A flexible approach to sixth form games – you can do what you want three times a week, and games haters can do yoga instead. Even lower down in the school, there is a humane quality to games here – a parent told us how her son, rugby hater, joined Hurst prep, and was immediately allowed to do kayaking, rock climbing and orienteering instead.

Boarding: A strong house system here with separate houses for day pupils and boarders. A parent described their child's house as 'a refuge, not just a place to leave books': there are homely common rooms, cosy bedrooms with bunkbeds or studies for day pupils, and kitchens ('for cookie baking,' said a parent).

'Care is extremely good,' said a parent, who added that on the odd occasion her daughters had had problems with girls they roomed with, the housemistress had listened, and switched the girls' rooms.

Pupils are together with 10 or so others in their year group, and form a really strong bond: their 'own clan', said a parent. 'It's the main way you make friends,' said a pupil, and they evidently enjoy much lively inter-house competition, including house water polo.

St John's is the sixth form boarding house, and popular with parents and pupils alike. 'St John's is brilliant,' said a parent, 'a good step up towards university… but still well monitored and controlled.' Individual rooms at St John's mean pupils can sleep during the day if they want to; the head is evidently not speaking lightly when he says, 'It's a busy place, pacy – pupils need some stamina.' School no longer offers full boarding in the sixth.

Currently no prep school boarding, but plans to introduce this soon for years 7 and 8.

Ethos and heritage: Parents choose Hurst because they feel it provides something more than an academic education: 'We want [them] to do well academically but not as an expression of everything else… we want them to be brought on as people'; 'we wanted the children to be themselves'. Seen, then, as a holistic educational experience by parents, it is no surprise to hear the head say, 'I don't want to win everything, it's not healthy.' Learning here comes from many different angles, and the school is loyal to its pupils – 'Anyone who is in the school can stay. We will back them. We always take siblings if we can…'

School buildings of grand old Sussex flint walls, draughty cloisters surround a courtyard, and Grimm's fairytale windows. Gorgeous grounds – 140 acres of them, but they are not the main pull for pupils. 'I fell in love with Hurst,' said a pupil. 'It was the atmosphere, everyone was involved.' Pupils have friends across the year groups, a sixth former proudly telling us, 'Younger pupils are often disregarded in other schools, but not here; younger pupils can have leading parts in plays.'

Homely common rooms, cosy bedrooms with bunkbeds or studies for day pupils, and kitchens ('for cookie baking,' said a parent)

Prep buildings sit alongside the college, surrounded by play areas, including a wooden adventure climbing course, and woodland school for outdoor education.

Chapel – 'the still place' – was named as a favourite place of many (dining hall, with its delicious food, and the rugby pitch also figuring). 'Chapel,' said a pupil, 'is where we consolidate the week. The whole school gathers.' The head gives a thought for the week, pupils are recollected – there is no feeling of piety at this school, but weekly chapel evidently plays its part in drawing the community together.

Uniform: smart navy for boys, and a lovely tartan skirt for girls (though ending at a troubling mid-calf length). Once pupils reach year 7, they get college blazers – quite a milestone. Sixth form must wear suits, can choose the colour and must look smart – 'to match the work ethic,' said a pupil gravely.

Pastoral care, inclusivity and discipline: The head is well aware of the whitewater nature of adolescence – 'it's all about the speed of turnaround after a dip' – and whilst this school works hard to try and keep children from vulnerable situations, there are good support networks in place to support pupils: houseparents, tutors, staff and school counsellors. 'It really is a fantastic community,' said a parent. '[A] strong culture, and out of this, children support each other. Problems are addressed and dealt with swiftly.'

A parent described the effective support given to her child, whose friend suffered serious trauma: counsellors provided 'what she needed'. They are very aware that some pupils might suffer from anxiety, said another, and are 'right on' in their support of pupils. Counsellors give advice and talks to pupils on mental health issues, and although one parent felt that there is not enough work done with pupils about knotty life issues such as consent, others felt this was dealt with adequately.

Tutors are the first ports of call for pupils with difficulties in prep, but they are happy to extend support to whatever is necessary, including family therapy or a life coach.

House guardians (pupils) regularly meet to discuss anyone who might be in distress, at both the prep and senior school. Bullying is discussed a lot – 'The school have a firm grip on it… and my son is ripe for it,' said a parent. Pupils were very clear that incidences of bullying could result in suspension or expulsion: not harming others or self is evidently a mantra they have absorbed.

There's careful education about what constitutes bullying and how to form positive relationships with each other (boys, in particular, sometimes don't even realise they've upset someone, says the head) and creating an environment where children feel they can talk about problems. The head has, and will, suspend or expel pupils for being unpleasant to others.

The head, said a parent, is 'almost Victorian' in his laying down of the rules: the Big 12. Parents say everyone knows what they are, and the disciplinary consequences of breaching them. 'It's strict,' said a parent, 'which is a good thing…'

Rowdy pupils will have a bumpy ride here. 'Not a school for second chances,' said another, 'though punishment is about trying to educate and improve.' 'What you do at the weekend does matter,' say pupils. 'Particularly if there might be photographic evidence,' one added feelingly.

Pupils and parents: Hurst feels like a local school in its intake, said a parent who likes this, and the typical Hurst family consists of the upper-middle-class white professionals who live in the area. School buses serve the local area, Chichester and London.

A parent told us this is not a school for those who want to fly under the radar and just get to the end of their schooldays: 'The thing you do at this school is engage – it can be anything, there are endless opportunities.'

Day-to-day communication is good, confirm parents, and the views of parents on teaching and pastoral care are sought regularly.

It's a long school day with a six o'clock finish, which can be tricky for parents collecting day pupils – 'We moved to be close to the school,' said one. Prep school day finishes at 4.20pm, but with after-school care (included in fees), can run until 6.00pm to match the college day.

Money matters: Academic bursaries from 11+.

The last word: Parents are clear why they chose Hurst: '[It has the] right balance… the right direction, the right balance of pastoral and academic. Our four very different children have thrived there. [There's] lots going on and it's very inclusive.' 'It's a good time to have kids here,' said another. 'It's hitting a high – and Tim Manly is inspiring for kids.'

Hurtwood House School

38

Holmbury St Mary, Dorking, Surrey RH5 6NU

01483 279000 | info@hurtwood.net | www.hurtwoodhouse.com

Ages: 15-18

Pupils: 340; sixth form: 340; Boarders: 300

Fees: Day £30,339; Boarding £45,513 pa

Joint headmasters: Richard Jackson MA (80s), originally an English teacher, is the founding head. Having conceived his school back in the late 1960s, it still bears the stamp of those heady, idealistic and experimental days although 'the old man' (as he is now affectionately known by his son and joint headmaster) has a more governing role, 'dropping in daily but his relevance significantly reduced'. Don't be fooled by his softly spoken and understated manner – he has an almost statesman-like presence of a man who made his remarkable dream a reality for these privileged students.

Cosmo Jackson BEd (50s), son of Richard and a more effervescent version of his father, took over the day-to-day running of the school in 2004. An alumnus of Charterhouse, he spent two years at Bristol University not enjoying economics and thence to the University of the West of England to do his – perhaps inevitable – BEd. He was, in all senses, to the manor born, as were most of his siblings and their spouses (and until recently his mum), all key personnel at Hurtwood.

We met Cosmo (we're all on first name terms here) in what must be up there with the most impressive headmaster's offices on the planet – a vast drawing room with coffered ceiling, grand fireplace, sink-into sofas and lots of warm lined oak. But the grandness belies the convivial vibe – the door, just to the left of the entrance, is all glass and there's no gatekeeper if you want to pop in unannounced, which students and parents frequently do. With his main duties centering around incoming students, you'll more often than not spot a hopeful-looking teen perching on one of said sofas, their parents leaning in even more hopefully from a sideline seat. Considers his role 'more akin to a prep school head' than the big I ams of the public schools that these students often hail from. All the bigger shame, we felt, that he doesn't teach, but he's firm on the matter: 'The idea that you can claim, as a head, that you're completely hands on and know every student just because you encounter eight students in one class a week is a laughable notion to me.' Parents say they have 'little to do with him' but that he's 'easy to talk to', while students say he's 'super-friendly' and 'takes an interest'. 'Because every student gets a grade in every subject every week, I know more about them than they probably realise,' he smiles.

Entrance: Around 175 vacancies up for grabs ever year. No open days; personal tours only (most by housemaster Ted, another Jackson brother). Most come from the big public schools and are, as one parent put it, 'tired of the hierarchies and authoritarian rules'. Others from smaller private and state schools; many first time boarders. In most cases, it's the student who has found the school, with many parents admitting nervousness until visiting, upon which they tend to declare, 'Do you take grown-ups?'

Stunning late Arts and Crafts house, overlooking the North Downs and set among 50 hilly acres. 'I wish it was less hilly,' said one student, 'although it does keep you fit'

Parents and prospective pupils are seen by the head for about an hour-and-a-half – he looks for enthusiasm and whether you'll fit in and make the most of the opportunities. A few obviously outstanding applicants are offered a place on the spot, subject to reference; the rest register and apply and wait until later in the year to hear ('partly to save us the embarrassment of saying no on the spot,' admits head). Oversubscribed and currently a waiting list of around 50-60. Places not dependent on GCSE results (except for eg the sciences and maths).

Exit: Wide range of universities and colleges and courses for the aspiring actor, dancer, film director, artist, fashion designer, photographer, musician, singer or composer. Others do something completely different, eg engineering and business management degrees increasingly popular. Ninety per cent to their first choice. Many Russell Group and a few to Oxbridge some years. Bristol, Nottingham, Bath and UCL all popular.

Latest results: In 2021, 61 per cent A*/A at A level; 87 per cent A*-B. In 2019 (the last year when exams took place), 53 per cent A*/A (83 per cent A*-B).

Teaching and learning: 'I always thought of it as an artsy, theatrical school so almost didn't even consider it for my more academic child,' said various parents we spoke to in one form or another. The perception, though wrong, is not helped by the school itself heavily promoting the arts as its obvious point of difference. In reality, results across the whole range of subjects are uniformly starry and the 22 A levels on offer include all three sciences, economics and further maths, although most popular are drama, media, English, maths and psychology. Fine art and textiles do particularly well – a sneaky peak at the students' thick black portfolios reveals some extraordinary talent in everything from acrylics to life drawing, every page a testament to sheer dedication. Most students do three A levels, although some kick off with four to dabble between, say, psychology and sociology before picking their fave. Around a third do EPQ. Particularly strong value added.

The biggest asset here is the teaching staff. 'Who cares about a £5m sports hall when you can invest the money into great teaching?' exclaims the head, who is rightfully proud of his devoted, high-calibre and long-standing team. Students, who are taught in average sized classes of eight to 12 and often less, are equally extravagant in their praise – 'I've been struck by how much they care about each person,' said one.

Absolutely no coasting, largely thanks to weekly grades for all students in achievement and effort doled out by all teachers, who in turn are cross-examined by the head in weekly meetings – 'What is it that Lily did this week that made you give that grade?' etc. 'Not that we go silly on any one grade as we'll have new grades in five days' time – what we're really looking for are patterns,' he says. While in most schools, the nuances of monitoring systems are largely lost on parents, there wasn't one we spoke to who didn't wax lyrical about them – 'It's a measure for them and us and yet somehow it doesn't impact on the relaxed atmosphere,' summed up one, with students too pointing to the 'friendliness' and 'intimacy' of the lessons helping to motivate and engage them. Bottom line, claims school, is the cosiness of a prep with the academic rigour and maturity of a university.

Learning support and SEN: No SEN dept as such – among such creative people, the 'dyses' are inevitably common and most have learned the strategies and techniques to manage their challenges, believes school. But a SENCo ensures any recommendations in ed psych reports are being carried out.

The arts and extracurricular: The real glory of Hurtwood, and at the heart of its ethos, is arts and media. The place fizzes with fervour around it and everything is slick and professional, largely thanks to the teachers themselves (a full-time staff of 20, plus visiting teachers, in the performing arts department alone) being true pros, straight from the likes of the BBC and West End, all top of their game and all up with the latest techniques – in acting, dancing, lighting, set and costume design, you name it. It really sets Hurtwood apart and we were instantly wowed watching A level students performing in a moving play based on verbatim quotes of homeless people; the set, made entirely from graffiti-ridden cardboard boxes by an art student, was also exceptional.

Even academically minded students find it hard to resist as an extracurricular offering. Whereas in their previous school, there might have been one or two productions per year, here there are productions, films and videos galore – many of which wouldn't look out of place on mainstream telly – in which some are constantly involved. The elite too are catered for via an acting company, film academy and dance company; the best dancers are put through four to five hours' extra dance every week in preparation for applying to top conservatoires, while wannabe film makers get to make thrillers and pop videos, as well as creating documentaries from scratch. We watched a snippet of one about life in the navy (students had to get permission from the MoD) and heard about another based on an orphanage where a student had volunteered in Nairobi (the school sent five students and two teachers out to film it). Project YouTube is popular – once a month, a YouTube celeb collaborates with students to make live videos, with the last one getting half-a-million hits.

There's no swanky performing arts centre, but the 180-seat theatre is of professional quality, albeit with little backstage or flyroom/wing space, and there's a TV studio complex. 'Better quality than some West End shows I've seen,' reckoned one parent about the performances (of which there are 10 for the Christmas musical alone), and those who go on to media courses usually find they've covered everything they do in the first year.

Musically, singing stands out, with at least a third taking singing lessons, while around a quarter learn an instrument and a sixth take dance. Peripatetic teachers are in a league of their own – the drum teacher is the drummer from Hamilton. Music tech is a big deal with two tech rooms plus recording studio; the school even has its own record label.

If there was a Good Schools Guide food award, this would surely bag a gold – our roast beef with all (and we mean all) the trimmings, was up there with the best of gastropubs

Art is rich and varied, with students raving about the small studio down the track through the woods with its 'university art school feel'; for some, it's a second home (but mind your head on the beams). Textiles is a specialism and the results are striking.

There's pretty much nothing that doesn't appear on the extracurricular calendar in some form – first aid courses, Lego club, wine tasting (yes, really) among them. Can't decide? Simply hop on the weekly mystery bus, where surprise destinations range from Denbies for a cream tea to the BFI.

Sport: 'I chose this school for the sport,' said nobody from Hurtwood ever. It's just not why you come. But there is rugby and football for the boys and netball and rounders for the girls, with mixed hockey the most popular – including weekly matches against other schools for those who want to compete. There's a football pitch, all-weather hockey/basketball pitches, two tennis courts and sports pavilion, and students told us about going off site, eg to Dorking Wanderers home pitch.

Boarding: All but around 50 of the students board, split across the upper floors of the main building (girls only) and five shabby-chic (some more shabby, some more chic) country mansions (all mixed, with girls and boys on separate floors) within two miles, from which they are shipped in and out via minibus. Bedrooms – a mixture of singles, doubles and triples – have unrivalled character – 'all feels a bit like a faded gentrified house,' described one parent. On paper, it's full boarding only, but students are free to go home at the weekends with permission and about three-quarters do, though less so in the thick of theatre productions. No structured programme of weekend activities, but sporadic jaunts include paragliding, powerboating and mountaineering in Snowdonia, as well as local cinema and paintballing. School runs buses into Guildford and Cranleigh for shopping etc. 'Boarding is my favourite thing here – everyone is so friendly and it's so homely,' said one student.

Ethos and heritage: Not the easiest school to reach. The darkening, narrowing lanes winding through and over wooded hillsides are a reminder of just how rural Surrey can still be and the school is not big on signage. But the view from the car park is a worthy reward. Although not Hurtwood's original home (the school spent its first three years in a building rented from the National Trust), the house too was worth the wait – a stunning 1900s late Art and Crafts house, overlooking the North Downs and set among 50 hilly acres (we reckon the guys we saw building outdoor steps might just have a job for life).

Bedrooms – a mixture of singles, doubles and triples – have unrivalled character – 'all feels a bit like a faded gentrified house,' described one parent

Downstairs is gorgeous – the inviting drawing room, the library with its wondrous ceiling and well-stocked books and periodicals; even the loos are posh. The rest of the school is made up of a mishmash of outbuildings – some more aesthetically pleasing than others – housing various subjects and classrooms, common rooms etc. 'I wish it was less hilly,' voiced one student, 'although it does keep you fit.'

If there was a Good Schools Guide food award, this would surely bag a gold – our roast beef with all (and we mean all) the trimmings, was up there with the best of gastropubs and there's an ice-cream machine, barbecue bar and outdoor pizza oven. 'They get steak for lunch,' marvelled one parent.

Notable former pupils include Harry Lawtey, Viviek Kalra, Kate Burns, Nikki Amuka-Bird, Emily Beecham, Phoebe Boswell, Emily Blunt, Amelia Brightman, Ben Chaplin, Amelia Curtis, William El-Gardi, Edward Fox, Sam Harrison, Jack Huston, Tom Mison, Leah Wood, Hans Zimmer, Hannah Herzsprung.

Pastoral care, inclusivity and discipline: It was always to be a 16-19 school, GCSEs being, for Richard, 'the absolute natural breaking point'. And so it has proved. Students see it as 'the perfect bridge' between (especially traditional public) school and university and parents concur. 'They treat them like adults and my son was really ready for that'; 'He'd had enough of being told what to do'; 'She is independent and wanted to be treated as such', etc. And yet, says school, 'when the students get here, we admit we've tricked them, in that we do hold their hand because they're not quite ready for university'. It's a 'fine balance and one they get spot on,' said a parent. Indeed, while students and staff are on first-name terms and the lack of uniform (girls can be seen in black leggings and hoodies; for boys, it's mainly skinny jeans, trainers and hoodies) can give the impression of a liberal free-for-all, students told us it's 'well disciplined so you always know where you stand' and the school is quick to 'gate' students who play up or fail to work. Very strict regs on smoking and drinking and even more so on drugs (random drugs tests), bullying and stealing – 'anyone remotely involved gets hoofed out sharpish,' says school. Around six suspensions a year, plus the odd expulsion – we spoke to the parent of one student who'd recently been suspended and she was fully on board with the school's decision. Low-key counselling provided by nurses, plus trained counsellors available onsite.

Pupils and parents: Approximately two-thirds are British, mostly from London and the home counties, the rest from 30-40 countries. Around 60 with EAL whose needs are supported by a specialist department. Cliques somewhat inevitable, believes school – 'If I went to Shanghai to study, I'm sure I'd cling on to other Brits at least at first,' says head – but an even distribution of international students across the school helps stop it becoming entrenched and no student we spoke to felt great distinctions were made between home and international students, nor day and boarding students – nor, for that matter, those who drip wealth and those on scholarships.

Money matters: Famously and unashamedly expensive. A few performing arts scholarships are available – usually up to three worth 50 per cent of fees and around two more at 25 per cent, although there is fluidity and occasionally a student will get 100 per cent of fees paid, with the Jacksons using their discretion (up to a quarter of a million pounds a year) to support those who deserve and need it.

The last word: Incomparable, which is a shame because the world could do with more Hurtwoods. A breath of fresh air for teens who've had enough of what can seem like a straight-jacketed world of education. Particularly well suited to arty and media types, but not to be ruled out for more mainstreamers.

The Junior King's School

Milner Court, Sturry, Canterbury, Kent CT2 0AY

01227 714000 | registrar@junior-kings.co.uk | www.junior-kings.co.uk

Ages: 3–13

Pupils: 365; **Boarders:** 79 full (mainly years 6–8)

Fees: Day £11,640 – £19,575 Boarding £27,270 pa

Linked school: The King's School Canterbury, 707

Head: Since September 2017, Emma Károlyi, previously deputy head and director of studies at Loretto. She has a degree in classical studies and ancient history from St Andrews and is married to Julian, a modern languages teacher at King's. They live on site with their two children, both at King's, and the school dog who is much loved by all.

We met her on World Book Day, dressed up in full garb, reflecting parents' claim that she 'is all about the children, engaging with them on their level at every opportunity'. 'She's not into gaining PR points with the parents, although that's not to say she isn't approachable,' said another. Astute, but with a soothing mumsiness about her, pupils say she's 'kind' and 'so interested in us'. Teaches Latin to year 6 – 'From day one, I knew I couldn't be a head and not teach,' she says. Parents like the way 'she spent a year watching everything pretty closely, but now she really owns it,' as one put it, with modifications – when they were made – including developing a more open and inclusive atmosphere (including better communications with parents), celebrating more non-academic achievements ('Now, in a newsletter, you're just as likely to read about a charity walk as the latest scholarship,' explained one parent) and restructuring the management to include two deputy heads – one academic and one pastoral ('because both are equally important'). The third deputy is the registrar. Has also improved links with the senior school, although pupils we met felt strongly about wanting 'to spend more time there before actually going' – head says she's 'on it'.

A keen viola player, she is involved in music and orchestras in Canterbury – she played in Brahms's German Requiem in the cathedral the week after our visit.

Entrance: Most join nursery and reception, and increasingly year 3. Other major intakes in years 5 and 7 when extra classes are added (two forms until year 5, when there are three, then four from year 7) and occasionally into year 8 for CE if trying for King's. Younger children have a taster day and informal assessments; from year 3 children assessed ('tested is too strong a word,' says school) in English, maths and non-verbal reasoning. 'We are looking for appropriate behaviour and potential to manage at an academic school.'

Exit: Between 85 and 95 per cent go on to King's Canterbury. Others to Eton, Brighton College, Cheltenham Ladies' College, Cranbrook, Lancing College, Tonbridge and Wycombe Abbey, while in previous years destinations have also included Bedales, Taunton and Westminster. A few leave for the grammar schools at 11+. Scholarships to King's Canterbury every year. Parents are given plenty of advice if it is thought a child might not pass CE to their chosen school.

Our view: Founded in 1879 as the prep school for The King's School, Canterbury and spent its first 50 years in the precincts of the cathedral. Boys were known as 'parrots' because of the noise they made and houses are still named after parrots. Moved to current site in 1929 when Lady Milner gave Sturry Court, an Elizabethan manor house, together with the Tithe Barn, in memory of her husband. It was opened by their friend Rudyard Kipling. Two miles from the centre of Canterbury, it is set in 80 acres of grounds and playing fields with the River Stour running through the middle. Despite arriving during drop-off mayhem (parking is a 'nightmare', according to parents, although we thought the school did well keeping traffic flowing), the scene was picturesque thanks to the spectacular estate and beautiful buildings.

This is an aspiring school academically, but 'not at the cost of creative pursuits or with the work, work, work mentality of London preps,' as one parent put it (one of several we spoke to who'd made the move from London precisely to get this kind of academic rigour without the hothouse feel). Parents told us the head is promoting a culture of less pressure than previously, although they feel it has become more selective in recent years. Very occasionally, it is suggested tactfully that a child might do better elsewhere.

Average class size 15-16, max 18. Setting in maths from year 5, English and languages from year 6 and science in year 8. Separate year 8 scholarship class. French from nursery, Spanish from year 5 and Latin from year 6. Greek offered to scholars. Teachers 'really get to know what makes your child tick', said one parent; pupils told us they are 'friendly and rarely shout'. Much more attention given to SEN in recent years, about 10 per cent with some sort of learning support – system of monitoring and referrals means problems picked up early, although we're talking mild-end problems here. 'The SENCo is fabulous – she rings you up and say what they're going to do, then they do it,' said one parent. EAL support if required, and these pupils in year 7 get an EAL-trained teacher for English lessons.

Boys get a common room and games room, including computers and playstation; girls get a common room and computer room – 'and yes, there is some envy there,' one girl said

Year 3s and 4s have their own building, with spacious, welcoming classrooms and stunning displays, plus own library, changing rooms and pet tortoise – 'it all helps with the transition from pre-prep'. At this stage, 70 per cent of lessons are with the form teacher, while French, DT, computing, drama, art, sports and music are taught by specialists. From year 5 – where children are taught in classrooms dotted around the school – the number of specialist teachers increases. Bright, sunny library (with weekly bookshop) central to main school with regular visits from authors. Lovely large, light dining room with popular food; long, hour-and-a-quarter lunchbreaks mean children don't have to rush and can fit in a club, should they wish.

Sport 'less elitist and divisive' than it was, say parents, but school still likes to win, with children competing at national level in netball, athletics, hockey, swimming and cricket. Superb facilities, here and at King's. Rowing an option from year 7 and squash offered at King's. Floodlit Astro means hockey now a major sport for boys and girls. Huge galleried sports hall and five tennis courts. Heated outdoor pool for fun but serious swimming taught at the King's recreation centre, but pupils we spoke to felt swimming 'could be better' – 'I know people who pretend to be sick for swimming' (school is trying to get an indoor pool sorted, 'but these things take time'). Fencing strong and a number of international fencers started at Junior King's. Inter-house competitions give everyone a chance to take part and attract friendly rivalry. Golf, sailing, riding among sports on offer among the seemingly infinite evening and weekend activities. Saturday school with lessons in the morning and sport in the afternoon from year 5. Pupils told us, 'If sport isn't your thing, you can do arts instead of matches from year 5.'

Performing arts take place in the Tithe Barn. When we noticed a glass cabinet stuffed with silverware, a teacher explained, 'It was rather embarrassing as we hosted the Kent drama festival and won most of the trophies!' Drama part of the curriculum from year 3 and everyone has the chance to get up on stage at least once a year, with much excitement about the recent Mary Poppins performance, although an older pupil told us they'd like 'less old-fashioned plays' (a recent example being The Canterbury Tales). Good numbers for LAMDA.

Music is never far from your ears; over 300 individual lessons a week from peripatetic teachers (all of whose photos appear in the dazzling new music centre – a nice inclusive touch) and we saw ensembles for guitar, saxophone and flute in action (there are many others too) before the school day had even started – impressive stuff. Range of bands and a junior house choir, middle school choir and (audition only) chapel choir. Plus, more recently, a parent choir. All pupils get to sing in the cathedral three times a year and there are music scholarships to King's senior most years. Regular music workshops from professional musicians free-of-charge.

Busy art department, where we saw year 7s making clay masks. Current teacher has a specialism in textiles. DT from year 3 is extremely popular; gorgeous displays including striking pompom-covered stool and illustrated flipflops.

Activities most afternoons and evenings, dozens to choose from (some charged for), everything from bushcraft to debating, dance to riding. Annual Spanish exchange, year 6 weekend in Normandy, much looked-forward-to post-CE jaunt, sports trips to mainly European destinations which do not put too much strain on parental pockets.

Strong Christian tradition with weekday and Sunday services at the village church but all faiths welcome, and parents say school 'isn't pious'. Pastorally on the up, say parents, and discipline policy is based more on merits than sanctions, although children are sometimes suspended and very occasionally asked to leave. Bullying rare, with updated anti-bullying policy – 'You don't feel like you're telling on someone if you do spot anything,' a pupil said.

Pre-prep housed in the Oast House with own hall and delightful library. Seven classrooms – among the most stimulating environments we've seen for this age group with displays that are second to none, with examples of themes including plastic on the beaches, polar explorers and the history of Canterbury. Children learn PE, French, dance and music from nursery onwards with specialist teachers and use the prep school facilities – sports hall, Tithe Barn, sports fields and dining hall. Accredited forest school in the grounds; children reeled off lists of what they'd made there, although older children told us with disappointment that outdoor learning time is minimal further up the school. Weekly visits to local residential home for the elderly part of emphasis on community links. Nursery in Swiss-style chalet known as Little Barn with a free flow to attractive outdoor area with Astroturf – a busy, happy place with guinea pigs and a tortoise. Head of pre-prep a real hit among parents.

Day children from up to 40 minutes away. Accompanied train from Wye and the school uses a fleet of taxis but is considering minibuses. Most from professional families – doctors, medics, lawyers and City and creative types. Of the total pupil population, 17 per cent are international. Strong links with the Foreign Office. Active Friends' Association has weekly coffee mornings, committee mornings and social events such as Burns Night. Alumni include former Olympics minister Hugh Robertson, actor Orlando Bloom, Commonwealth Games president Tunku Imran Ja'affar, ceramicist and writer Edmund de Waal, pianist Freddy Kempf and international rugby player Huw Jones.

Boarding: Boarding (mostly full-time, with a few staying only the odd night) from year 5 cared for in two houses: Kipling (boys) and Juckes (girls), 90 beds in total. Local children often ask to board and most don't even want to go home on Sundays – 'Why would you when there are things like beach trips, Dreamland and panto on offer?' said one; children told us there is no time to get bored or homesick. Around three-quarters of boarders are international, especially from Asia, Russia, Spain, France and Nigeria. Various sized dorms, some with sinks and some with their own bathrooms are cosy and tidy, albeit with dated pine furniture. Boys get a common room and games room, including computers and playstation; girls get a common room and computer room – 'and yes, there is some envy there,' one girl said.

Money matters: Means-tested bursaries available from year 7 for up to 100 per cent of the boarding fee. Academic scholarships offered at 11+ for new joiners and children already in the school – worth a max of five per cent of fees. Additional bursary support available.

The last word: Best suited to bright children with a 'have a go' ethos, this traditional prep school brings out strengths, both academic and creative, so that by the time they leave they're prime fodder for the fast-paced senior school.

Kent College

40

Old Church Road, Pembury, Tunbridge Wells, Kent TN2 4AX

01892 822006 | admissions@kentcollege.kent.sch.uk | www.kent-college.co.uk

Ages: 11–18

Pupils: 380; sixth form: 80; Boarders: 70 full/weekly

Fees: Day £22,575 – £24,150; Boarding £28,200 – £35,970 pa

Headmistress: Since January 2022, Katrina Handford, previously senior deputy head at Nottingham Girls' High School where she also had a stint as acting head. In her spare time, she has helped build a coastal path with the National Trust in Scotland, mentored girls suffering from abuse and led the Nottingham branch of the Women's Equality Party.

Entrance: One hundred or above on standardised scores, leeway for those from state primaries. Feeder preps: Sevenoaks, Derwent Lodge, Dulwich, Wallyhall junior. Fifty per cent of intake from own prep.

Exit: Over half leave after GCSEs. Around half of sixth formers to Russell group. Bath, Durham, Nottingham, Manchester, UCL and Exeter all popular. One to Oxbridge in 2021, plus two medics and two to study overseas.

Latest results: In 2021, 69 per cent 9-7 at GCSE; 62 per cent A*/A at A level (82 per cent A*-B). In 2019 (the last year when exams took place), 62 per cent 9-7 at GCSE; 37 per cent A*/A at A level (72 per cent A*-B).

Teaching and learning: 'Not a hothouse,' said a parent, 'but they will make the most of your child's talents, and get the best out of them academically.' Results are consistently creditable. English is popular, with most pupils receiving top grades (it makes a difference having published authors on the staff, says the deputy head), and geography, with its 'fantastic teachers', is one of the most popular GCSEs. RS is compulsory at GCSE; parents could opt their kids out, but none do.

KC excels at drama: they have a 300-seat theatre in which they run a theatre academy, and drama is one of the most popular options, with pupils achieving top grades

Plenty of traditional subjects here (options include classical civilisation, Latin, ancient Greek and history of art), but psychology, the new kid on the block, is very popular with pupils, and heeding pupil suggestions, sociology is now available. This school prides itself on making any combination of subjects work – the deputy head here is a timetable mastermind.

Teaching is good, say parents and 'what a nice bunch of teachers... it's not so long since they were young'; ' [They're] in touch with kids' lives, very committed, hard working... know my child... I'm very pleased.'

Maths is the one area of concern, parents worrying about staff turnover and inflexible teaching styles of new teachers, high levels of tutoring, and the best teachers teaching the top sets – 'They should be good all through,' said one indignantly. KC points out that pupils achieve good results in maths, and a new head of maths will be starting soon.

This school emphasises that ability is not fixed, and all have the potential to grow, which is evident in their superb value added: MidYIS data shows that KC adds at least a whole grade per GCSE; and, more remarkably, a further grade at A level: BBB to ABB can often make the difference between Russell group and non-Russell group, points out the deputy head. KC achieves this by placing girls in small classes with focused teaching, and constructing classes around individuals: this is not a school which unquestionably follows the same pattern year after year.

ICT is under review, and developing: the VLE now live, and there's Wifi throughout site. There are six dedicated computer rooms, and laptop suites.

Parents describe a school which is very attentive to learning styles: one said her daughter was upset because she seemed to make no progress; the school suggested a mentor: 'Now she has a learning support journal; can see the progress she is making, and is learning to organise herself.'

Sixth form can feel like relentless pressure, and parents feel KC is a listening school on this: one who emailed the school to report a daughter in meltdown over the amount of homework said it all eased up the following week. Pupils say the deputy head has an open door so you can 'just go and vent' when it gets too much.

There's lots of support with UCAS, although a parent suggested there could be more interview practice for university and jobs. The head's push on developing a global mindset means more visits from inspirational speakers, talks ranging from apprenticeships to Cambridge.

Learning support and SEN: The SEN unit supports mild difficulties, in one-to-one and group sessions (extra charge for one-to-one). One parent described excellent support from the unit for her daughter's problems with processing, and the 'amazing change in [her] grades'. The unit will support any pupils who need extra help, from those with gaps in knowledge to those struggling to engage with lessons.

The arts and extracurricular: KC excels at drama: they have a 300-seat theatre in which they run a theatre academy, and drama is often one of the most popular options, with pupils achieving top grades. Parents told us of the magic effect drama has had on their shy offspring – 'she's always laughing and confident now' – one pupil telling us that she had been painfully shy when she arrived at the school, and probably still would be but for the enthusiastic support of the drama teacher: one word well uttered felt like an achievement.

Music is housed in a purpose-built centre, complete with drum studio and Apple Mac suite. Musicians play a crucial role in the success of the school annual productions, and recently performed The Marriage of Figaro, complete with guest professionals.

Activities are compulsory until year 11, and the girls have a fine array to choose from, including beekeeping and fencing. A popular option in lower sixth is the Leiths course: 'You get a knife

Lancing College

set and a chef's uniform,' said a pupil with enthusiasm, 'and two times a week you can forget all about work.' It's also rather nice having children who can come home and cook a good supper…

Textiles is big here: KC hosts and often wins prizes in the Young Fashion Designer of the year. Photography a full A level, and is now more popular than fine art.

Sport: Games at KC was what drew one parent to the school: she described visiting as the parent of a child on an opposing team and noticing the rapport of the girls with their sports teacher; a pupil challenging the teacher to a race, and 'the joy they both experienced'. The humane quality which runs through KC penetrates even sports, pupils commenting that the head of sport is 'so endearing, completely understands that some [pupils] hate it, but her enthusiastic approach makes even haters optimistic…'

Lots of special boarding community events, such as the boarders' international evening to celebrate every boarder's culture with food and performances

The sports department has grown in the last four years: there are more teams, more matches and more specialist coaching. KC runs specialist academies in gymnastics and swimming, and gymnastics is a particular strength here, with national and individual team successes.

Everyone who turns up to training gets included in matches, and pupils told us the school doesn't get miffed if you want to play out of school – '[they're] really flexible with everything'.

Boarding: 'It's very important for the girls to feel cherished,' said the head of boarding; the boarding house 'needs to feel like home'. A parent told us: 'My girls loved boarding; they made it fun for them. [The girls were] very much at home [and staff were] very attentive to their needs.'

There are some 85 boarders, including flexi boarders – on regular nights, just during exams or when parents have a last minute work crisis: popular with parents and pupils alike. Around a quarter from overseas (China, Hong Kong, Europe, Africa). No real divide between day pupils and boarders, say the girls, though the Chinese/HK pupils do form strong friendships within their community. UK boarders tend to go home at weekends, but there's a full programme of activity for stay-behinds.

Around 35 of the boarders are juniors (years 4-9), mostly weekly; but Saturday activities are so popular that some parents take home their child on Friday and drop them back on Saturday morning so they can join in (trips to trampoline parks or castles) and stay Saturday night.

Juniors are in rooms of around six (which change each term); no bunk beds, and facilities are clean and well kept. There's a comfortable common room and kitchen where they can make toast or help themselves to fruit.

Seniors are in double rooms, with single study bedrooms for upper sixth. Rather more substantial kitchens than in the junior house, and grown-up feeling common areas. More freedom for seniors, who can take the 15-minute walk to the farm shop on the other side of reservoir, but no wandering around in the woods on their own. Buses into Tunbridge Wells are organised for girls in years 10-13, and weekend trips to theatres and shops might go to Bath or London.

Lots of special boarding community events, such as the boarders' international evening to celebrate every boarder's culture with food and performances, and the leavers' BBQ – 'we hire inflatable things,' said head of house – an assault course last year. The leavers' bag includes university essentials: an adult colouring book, fairy lights, a mug and a rose.

Ethos and heritage: Pupils describe a school of strong family feeling – 'like a bunch of sisters'. Biscuits are put out for the girls at the end of the day: 'all the girls in happy chatter,' said a parent. Not cliquey, say pupils, who told us they could happily sit down to lunch with over half the year. Although one parent commented it would be nice to see someone at the front of the school to say hello in the morning, pupils here have strong relationships with teachers, one telling us it is the best thing about KC – 'I can go to [to them] with any problems or personal issues. A friend in grammar school has one teacher she can go to with problems – here, there are many.'

A girls-only environment is a grade enabler, says school; a STEM subject enabler too, and no worries about fitting the box and behaving a certain way. 'They can roll over and over down the grass,' said a teacher, 'which wouldn't be cool with boys [present]: they can be children for longer.' One pupil told us the best thing about the school was 'how comfy I feel… but not babied or hand-held'.

A Methodist school, but welcomes all faiths or none; though the John Wesley prayer about doing all the good you can is part of daily conversation here. The chaplain is always available for a chat, and leaves chocolate outside his door.

The main building is a Victorian manor house set in beautiful Kent woodland, surrounded by a miscellany of other buildings and styles: the new Walker building 'is amazing', say pupils: arts and textiles have their own space, and the new library is great (though we never quite got the bottom of the body outlined on the floor in tape...). Pupils would like more infrastructure improvements, and work is on the cards, but even the older buildings here were well cared for.

There is a house system (Celts, Danes and Saxons), with all the usual inter-house sport, drama and quizzes, but the girls weren't very engaged with it: 'It could be improved,' said pupils.

The uniform is basically blue, and has been through a few changes: the plain version made the girls look like cadets at Hendon police college, said one parent, and others say the current blouse reminds them of toothpaste: we rather liked it. Sixth formers wear a suit (skirt or trousers), and are pleased to be relieved of the need to choose what to wear.

Pastoral care, inclusivity and discipline: One parent described KC as an 'extremely caring small community' where 'teachers genuinely care a lot what happens to girls'; it was chosen by another because she felt her daughter would get a good education in a small-class environment, but be more nurtured than at a grammar school, where 'middle of the road can get a bit lost': 'Both girls came out really believing they can achieve – and having achieved academically.'

The school takes a pastoral approach to disenchanted pupils, which, says school, is usually due to lack of confidence: 'We need to unpick the reasons why a pupil cannot engage'. They will talk to the pupil and parents and provide a huge amount of extra support to help resolve problems.

KC has a good eye for pastoral care: a parent told us about the lovely change in her daughter, who found it difficult to make friends at her old school: chocolate club, run by the learning support team, gives pupils who struggle socially practical help, for instance suggesting ways to open a conversation; other support includes the buddy system, ensuring that nervous girls have someone to walk with to the bus stop, and to sit with at lunchtime, until they are confident they can manage on their own.

Bullying is dealt with effectively, though the head is quick to point out that long, targeted bullying campaigns are very rare; problems are more likely to be the small tiffs typical of childhood, which are quickly resolved by talking; and in fact a parent whose daughter received unpleasant texts from other pupils said it was dealt with within half an hour of her phone call, and there have been no further problems. The school counsellor will help both pupils and families if necessary, a service described by a parent as 'very, very subtle'.

A parent described a school that is 'good at spotting what happens', and communication is good – 'brilliant at responding to telephone/email queries'; 'oh yes, grades all the time'.

Pupils and parents: Parents range from extremely wealthy to those making sacrifices for fees. Parents agree that this is not a school for very pushy parents or children who are only interested in work (go to a grammar). Eleven different bus routes around local villages and beyond; most pupils from east Sussex or Kent.

Money matters: Means-tested bursaries, and scholarships of up to 10 per cent of fees.

The last word: The word parents use most to describe KC is 'happy'; next up is 'all-rounder'. 'They will make the most of what your child is good at, whatever it is,' said a parent.

Kent College Canterbury

41

Whitstable Road, Canterbury, Kent CT2 9DT

01227 763231 | admissions@kentcollege.co.uk | www.kentcollege.com

Ages: 0–18

Pupils: 800; sixth form: 198; Boarders: 215 full

Fees: Day £17,391 – £19,995; Boarding £26,901 – £37,017 pa

Head: Since January 2022, Mark Turnbull. Attended Marlborough College; BA (geography) from Liverpool and MA from University of London. First teaching role was at Sevenoaks, where he went on to become head of boarding. In 2008, he moved to Eastbourne College as deputy head before taking up the headship of Giggleswick in 2014.

Junior school head: since September 2020 is Simon James, previously deputy head, a role he has held for two years. Before that head of business and economics at the senior school, as well as the houseparent for Guilford boarding house for many years.

Entrance: About half of the children from the garden cottage nursery move on to early years, all the early years pupils stay on for junior school and from there almost all go to the senior school. A further 35 or so pupils join year 7 from the feeder prep school Lorendon or other local schools. Second large entry point at sixth form. Interview and placement assessments (interview by Skype and extra online English assessment for international students) to decide on sets when pupils first arrive, otherwise non-selective – 'we are unable to accept only a small percentage of applicants' – though they won't take pupils if they don't think they can accommodate their special needs. One junior pupil said 'it wouldn't suit a person who minds about mud'. Ten places for students coming just for a term or two ('it introduces them to what the school offers and most stay on or will come back as full-time students later').

Exit: Around a quarter leave after GCSEs. More than three-quarters of sixth formers to university, with over half to Russell Group. Some overseas or to Oxbridge in some year groups. Particularly wide range of subjects including medical biosciences, architecture, music, business studies, maths and psychology. Three medics in 2021.

Latest results: In 2021, 48 per cent 9-7 at GCSE; 56 per cent A*/A at A level (78 per cent A*-B). IB score average 38. In 2019 (the last year when exams took place), 36 per cent 9-7 at GCSE; 43 per cent A*/A at A level (73 per cent A*-B). IB score average 37.

Teaching and learning: Junior school has brand new pre-reception 'garden cottage nursery' for 0-3 years (fully subscribed). One-to-three ratio supports children in homely environment with kitchen, playroom, soft play areas and generous outside space. Food cooked on the premises, spotlessly clean and fresh. The ultimate in childcare with little ones staying for mornings, afternoons or whole days (can be from 7:30am-6:30pm). Early years provision for nursery and reception with separate creative areas and learning areas. Big windows and generous space inside and out, good facilities – dressing up, lots of creativity, specialist music and art.

Year 1 is a transition year – 'this is a most important year for us to consolidate learning and skills'. Homework from year 1. Setting in maths and English from year 2. Afternoons for creative subjects or themed learning – humanities, sciences, art and expressive art. Year 6 for exam preparation and developing in other ways. Healthy mix of age and gender of teachers.

In the senior school personalised timetables (300 separate timetables currently) allows for setting, choice of curriculum pathways, extended teaching time and accelerated learning programmes where appropriate. Year 7-9s in sets for core subjects; some are ready to take GCSEs early in languages or digital arts. They then may start a new language or A level language syllabus. The enormous flexibility in timetabling allows pupils to choose up to 12 subjects in almost any combination. Pre-sixth form course in year 11 possible for international pupils to improve English and take five or six GCSEs with the main student body. Sixth form sees a choice of three pathways – IB (taken by 25 per cent of students), A levels (taken by 70 per cent of students) or vocational courses (Cambridge Technicals).

Fully working farm is a special feature of the school, with a number of pupils from farming families. Year 4s upwards can help with lambing, grooming horses etc

Results are impressive for a non-selective school. The school highlights the strength of maths. Also does well on value added. Pupils said, 'Teachers genuinely care and give you all the time you need to succeed.' Extension tuition for GREATs (gifted, really enthusiastic, able and talented).

Learning support and SEN: The in-house international study centre (six teachers) gives intensive EAL tuition in small groups or individually to help both with English and with their studies. Learning support in dyslexia centre (three teachers) – mostly individual sessions. Awareness and testing for dyslexia was commented on by parents – 'They identified my child within weeks of arriving at Kent College though no one had mentioned it at the old school.' Needing extra help doesn't seem to have negative connotations here – 'You can be strong at lots of things even if you find writing difficult.' The individualisation of the timetable really helps – those struggling with English don't need to do another language; some do extra GCSEs.

The arts and extracurricular: Options mentioned enthusiastically by both parents and pupils – 'I chose the school for the range of different activities'; 'the school provides good life experiences and opportunities that enhance their time in school and afterwards'.

Fully working farm is a special feature of the school, with a number of pupils from farming families. On the timetable for years 7 and 8 as part of eg science and geography. Year 4s upwards can help with lambing, grooming horses etc. But this is a real working farm providing the school with its pork sausages and lamb.

Plenty of impressive art round the school including a striking ceramic installation – a poppy shape of terracotta tiles with the names of Kent College students who fell in 20th-century conflicts laid out in the quad. Spacious DT room with plenty of kit including a 3D laser printer.

Music a big feature (the executive head being a music graduate must help) with several bands (including staff bands and a folk group) and several choirs. Choristers have been on BBC Songs of Praise, pupils have entered Young Musician of the Year, been to Eisteddfod and on music tours. There is a summer opera in the grounds. Some 2019 Canterbury Festival events took place in the new hall with students performing.

Drama can be taken at GCSE and A level. Oh! What a Lovely War was the big school musical for the WWI centenary. Media and film studies popular and degree course choices include film and media, musical theatre, media production and creative music production.

Clubs and societies plentiful in junior and senior schools. Many run by students as the service part of IB curriculum, but also by teachers who, students tell us, 'will do anything for you and always offer to help'. Alongside sports there are eg electronics, enamelling, farming, gardening, debating, coding; years 7-9 must do at least two a week.

Trips include skiing, geography ('You don't have to be doing geography to go on the trip – they go to great places,' we were told), choir tours, sports tours, physics trip, language exchanges, history trip, and DofE gold went to Italy for their final hike ('much less wet than the Lake District').

Sport: Junior school has sport twice a week on the spacious playing fields or up at the senior school Astroturf. There is a heated outdoor swimming pool for the summer term; all juniors learn to swim. Fixtures and every three weeks the school hosts an athletics meeting open to other local children. Emphasis in the junior school on everyone to 'having a go' – so large numbers of teams and pupils told us that there was no shame in being in the E team: if you weren't very good at sport, then you would simply get extra help until you got better. 'They never get angry,' we were told by kids. 'You don't have to be the best to be in a team,' said one parent. 'They take it in turns to be captain – no one is excluded.'

Pupils take pride in their rooms and wanted us to see the views, the pictures on their walls. Main meals taken in school; kitchenettes in boarding houses for snacks and weekends. School library and sports facilities open in the evenings and at weekends

Senior school students mentioned sport as a selling point. Hockey, football, netball (for girls only), cricket, tennis, swimming, athletics. Endless sports run as lunchtime and after-school clubs (including dance and archery) in 26 acres of playing fields. And talented sportspeople get extra tuition, strengthening and conditioning and practice time – tennis, horse riding (a team reached the Hickstead finals), football, hockey (a couple of students representing England). Very well equipped fitness room.

Boarding: Very flexible boarding arrangements – around a third of pupils board, with others using occasional wraparound care. Parents tell us that houseparents vary, though the two we met were very cheerful and warm and just the sort you would like as role models for your child. Six boarding houses with live-in staff, many of whom are also teachers. Separate junior boarding house for pupils as young as 7, but most from 9 years. Kitchens, sitting rooms, single and shared bedrooms with study areas (newer boarding houses have ensuite shower rooms). Pupils take pride in their rooms and wanted us to see the views, the pictures on their walls, the desk spaces, the way they had dressed their rooms. They said that if you act responsibly, you are given freedoms, but abusing the rules results in repercussions like having your phone taken away. Main meals taken in school; kitchenettes in boarding houses for snacks and weekends. School library and sports facilities open in the evenings and at weekends. Pupils seem happy with weekend activities

– sports fixtures on Saturdays, then they can walk into town, and Saturday night is takeaway and film night. Outings every Sunday – Westfield, bowling, London Dungeons, IMAX, hiking, beach, even Disneyland Paris once. Junior school holiday clubs.

Ethos and heritage: Founded in 1885, senior school is walking distance to the centre of town and set in generous grounds. The junior school is a little further out, with ancient trees and views of rolling hills. Both schools have grand old buildings which, whilst elegant, may not be ideal for a modern school. So a bit of a maze of old and newer, added-on buildings. All clean and warm and more cosy than shabby. Part of the Methodist Independent Schools Trust group of schools and whilst 'you would be hard pressed to find many Methodists here amongst pupils or teachers', pupils still go to chapel twice a week. But very inclusive: 'Two pupils from my boarding house had meals made to take to their rooms for after the fast during Ramadan.' New 'grand hall' opened in 2019 – 600-seat auditorium for the performing arts, plus new art department in juniors and new science department for seniors with forest, stream and pond dipping area for biology.

Music a big feature (the executive head being a music graduate must help) with several bands (including staff bands and a folk group) and a variety of choirs. Choristers have been on BBC Songs of Praise, pupils have entered Young Musician of the Year, been to Eisteddfod and on music tours

Lunch cooked on site with plenty of choice: 'they have vegan options because four children in my year are vegan'. Teachers and pupils eat together. Popular snack shop very well used by parents and pupils at break times. Teachers a very stable cohort – possibly too stable – with 20 and 30 years of service not uncommon.

Pastoral care, inclusivity and discipline: The school houses help to build bonds between age groups and between boarders and day pupils. A sense of family pervades. Pupils have a range of adults they can, and do, speak to about concerns – boarding house staff, the chaplain, the head of pastoral care, their tutors, the school nurse; or they can self-refer to the weekly school counsellor.

We witnessed immaculate good behaviour as we toured the school – no pushing or shoving, doors opened and plenty of pleases and thank yous. Junior pupils told us that there is no bullying and 'we are kind to each other', and senior pupils felt they all look out for each other. Teachers said that pupils need to learn from their mistakes and may be put on a pastoral support plan or are expected to work out their own suitable sanctions. Some irritations between girls in boarding houses, according to parents, but nothing the houseparents couldn't sort out. Parents said they 'are bombarded with information from the school – good if your children don't always tell you what is going on'. One working mother would have loved to have earlier notice of events so as to be sure to attend.

Pupils and parents: About two-thirds from Canterbury and surroundings, with school buses serving seven different routes and shuttle buses from Canterbury station. A third international – about a third of these from Europe, a third from Asia, with some 42 nations represented in all – a different country's flag hung outside the school each day. The new fast train to London has changed the demographic, with parents working in London and appreciating the long day cover (7.30am to 6.30pm possible) and the possibility of flexible boarding.

Money matters: Fees include meals and individual MacBook but not specialist lessons in the dyslexia support centre, EAL lessons or music. However, pupils told us that teachers are always available to give you extra help at any time: 'There are fixed clinics but teachers will always find a time to see you – and I don't think they are even paid for it.' Scholarships of 25 per cent (art, drama, music, academic, design, sport) and bursaries up to a maximum of 50 per cent (Forces allowance gives a 90 per cent reduction).

The last word: Waiting lists just starting to form and we can see why. An excellent choice for those wanting a wide range of options. Praise from pupils for the music and for the business studies, for the sports and for the great English department. Room to be an all-rounder at this school but no space for the arrogant or madly pushy (though good added value results). Teachers and students need to buy into the importance of egalitarianism as an ethos, and both the pupil who gets 45 out of 45 for IB and the pupil who loves hockey and squeezes into university for sports science are equally valued.

King's Rochester

Satis House, Boley Hill, Rochester, Kent ME1 1TE

01634 888590 | seniorschool@kings-rochester.co.uk | www.kings-rochester.co.uk

Ages: 13-18

Pupils: 239; Boarders: 32 full

Fees: Day £20,700; Boarding £33,840 pa

Principal of King's Rochester and headmaster of the senior school: Since April 2019, Ben Charles BA PGCE (40s). Previously second master (senior deputy head) at Portsmouth Grammar. He has been director of music at Chigwell and Millfield, and joined Portsmouth as deputy head in 2009. Music degree from Exeter and PGCE in music from Durham. As an experienced choral conductor and singer joining this most traditional of schools, you'd think his first public solo in the cathedral to parents and pupils would be suitably highbrow but 'in fact, he burst into song with Reach for the Stars accompanied by a pupil on the banjo – it was epic,' a pupil told us. Worked a treat at breaking the ice and making his mark and, given his quite reserved persona, must have knocked his audience for six. Has also won brownie points among pupils for introducing birthday teas (tea and cake in his office in your birthday month) and team of the week awards ('for effort, not achievement, so the last winner was a hockey team, even though they lost the game – brilliant,' said our guide). 'The future will be rosy in his hands,' thought a parent. 'He's young and modern, but not too young and modern.' 'It sounds silly, but I love the fact that he brought in a tiddlywinks competition – my son isn't at all sporty and he just loved that.' A head, it seems, who is full of surprises.

Save for a short-lived flirtation with the idea of a singing career, he only ever wanted to go into teaching. 'Where else can you incorporate sport, drama and music into your working day and make a real difference at the same time?' he says, reflecting his firm belief that learning doesn't only happen in the classroom (has recently introduced drama and sport scholarships on the back of it). Doesn't teach but plans to. Mammoth consultation of governors, pupils, parents and staff has culminated in some serious strategising with aims here and strands there, all of which trip off his tongue at record speed (the short version is that parents can expect the prep and senior to feel more seamless, as well as seeing more co-curricular, a bigger emphasis on wellbeing and outreach work and tapping into alumni, among other things).

Lives on site with wife Helen, also a teacher but currently taking time out to care for their three young children, the eldest of whom is at the pre-prep; he also has an older son from a previous marriage. He's a huge sports fan, particularly offering support to teams from his native city of Leicester. Also enjoys concerts and reading – currently dipping into four books (a good sign that he's a multitasker): Bill Bryson's The Body, a James Bond by Ian Fleming, a comedy by David Mitchell and a classic William Boyd.

Entrance: Broad ability intake but children are expected to be able to take nine/10 GCSEs and three A levels (a few do four). Almost all move up from the prep school where summer exams are taken mainly for setting purposes. Entry from other schools at 13+ via common entrance or school's own tests; pretesting in year 6 now also available. Occasionally spaces in year 10. For entry into sixth form, candidates need five GCSEs at grade 5 or above and 6+ in subjects to be studied at A level.

Exit: Down to under 10 cent drop-out rate post GCSEs (reasons for leaving mainly financial, seeking more vocational courses or they just want a change); most places are filled by external applicants. After sixth form, destinations include Exeter, Bath, Gloucestershire, Leeds Conservatoire, Warwick and Reading. Occasional students to Oxbridge, though none in the last couple of years. Four medics in 2021, and one to study overseas (Amsterdam to study fashion). Good on apprenticeships – to Morgan Stanley and AB Group in 2021.

Latest results: In 2021, 58 per cent 9-7 at GCSE; 41 per cent A*/A at A level (61 per cent A*-B). In 2019 (the last year when exams took place), 44 per cent 9-7 at GCSE; 31 per cent A*/A at A level (58 per cent A*-B).

Teaching and learning: There are 26 grammars within a 25-mile radius so the last thing anyone around here needs is more of the same. Instead, King's raison d'être is catering for a wide range of academic ability from average to Oxbridge, though a few parents felt 'it's probably not the first choice for the super academic' and head says he'd 'like to see more aspirational thinking across the board'.

Advice for university and beyond has been beefed up and alumni are increasingly involved in providing mentoring and work experience to current and former pupils

Art, music and English do very well at A level, with particularly pleasing results in economics, DT, English and music. Psychology is the new kid on the block at this level. Strong on value added across the board. Setting in maths, English and science. Pupils choose from French, Spanish or German (German is most popular as they learn it in nursery), with around half taking a modern language at GCSE. Small numbers do Russian. PE, classical Greek and Russian are among other subjects offered at GCSE and all take RS. DT, art and music are popular; IT numbers also expected to pick up thanks to new head of digital learning. Economics, government and politics and fine art feature in the 24 A level offerings and school won't shy away from running a class for as few as three pupils – timetabling logistics must be a military operation. A quarter to a third do EPQ and school is currently working on developing its own equivalent – 'research is key for university entrance,' insists head. Watch this space too for a shift from all A level diet to the addition of a few vocational qualifications in sixth form.

Thumbs up from pupils for small class sizes (20 max for GCSE, 15 for A level), dedicated teachers ('they really care') and what they feel to be the strongest departments of economics, English and art. But universal thumbs down (and this goes for parents too) for the science department (dogmatic textbook teaching where you regularly have to stifle yawns, we gathered).

Classrooms, labs and other work spaces all fit for purpose but charming, tucked away library is depressingly under-utilised. Pupils told us, 'Nobody really wants to bother with the walk,' and 'No teacher ever encourages you to go.' One even confided that she didn't know there was a library 'until I'd been at the school for a whole year'. Advice for university and beyond has been beefed up and is seriously good. We saw sixth formers working intently in a CV writing clinic and alumni are increasingly involved in providing advice, mentoring and work experience to current and former pupils, as well as help with interview practice and technique.

School is now an Apple Designated Leader School.

Learning support and SEN: Team of qualified SEN teachers – mainly for mild dyslexia, although school accommodates those with greater needs where possible. Pupils assisted both in class and through withdrawals. 'I'm dyslexic and got English intervention instead of having to do German and lots of support to get things like extra time in exams,' a pupil told us, though one parent wasn't convinced the support was quite up to scratch: 'They're left to their own devices a lot more than I'd have expected and it's in stark contrast to the prep.' Dedicated staff members available for EAL.

The arts and extracurricular: A thirst for music is contagious here, even when it comes to hymn singing, say pupils – 'You mumble them under your breath when you join, but by upper years everyone loves getting stuck in,' said one. The prep is a cathedral school so the choristers (age 8-13) are part of the school and the chapel is Rochester Cathedral. Choir trips all over the place and they had just made a CD when we visited. About half learn at least one instrument, several up to grade 8, and there are plenty of choirs, orchestras and ensembles, a wind and jazz group. When we visited, a few pupils were in the Kent County Youth Orchestra, one was in the National Youth Orchestra, three were in the National Training Choir, one played in the Junior Guildhall every Saturday and a number go on to study music most years, two recently to conservatoires (Guildhall and Birmingham Conservatoire). All classical, although head is keen to shake things up a bit to expand the contemporary offering which currently includes the popular termly open mic night and even more popular annual house music competition.

Pupils we met reckon 'it's the best art department in the country' and although that may be stretching things a bit far, it's bloomin' good, with photography, sculpture and fine art offered – product design particularly popular and pupils often go on to art college. Facilities are spacious and well equipped and there are plenty of exhibition-worthy pieces lining the walls to inspire (or intimidate). Our favourites included a huge black canvas with floating pink cuboids and a remarkably good self portrait done with oils and pallet knife (more great examples to be found in the head's office). No shortage of freedom of expression, then, and the head of art prides himself on not even knowing the exam board syllabus – 'I know how to teach them how to be artists and designers, embedding a firm foundation of skills, then I let them fly.'

One major drama production per year – alternates between a musical (eg Titanic) and a more serious play (eg Macbeth). Plus plenty of smaller ones – for instance, sixth formers recently performed a re-contextualised version of Jane Eyre. One pupil, who was about to embark on her LAMDA grade 8, couldn't get enough of this department, literally leaping to the middle of the blackened studio and talking us through a flip chart that she'd used in her last lesson to produce and perform a short piece about bipolar. 'The teaching is so good – they really spend time on the techniques, then let you run with it, keeping a watchful eye,' she said.

'My son's in the fourth team and manages to get regular matches because they're good at finding other schools with B to D teams,' said a parent

Clubs a bit thin on the ground unless you're musical or sporty, according to parents (pupils we met reckon they're too busy for them anyway), although debating and chess are popular and ballet gets take-up throughout the school, some up to grade 8. No student-led clubs, though, or a single society. Lots of trips and outings, open to all – we loved that our guide was going on a classics trip to Rome and Pompeii 'even though I haven't done classics in years'. Ski trip sells out 'within about 20 minutes'.

DofE popular and 10-15 do gold each year. CCF offered in all three services – compulsory for the first two years and many keep going. A charity is chosen by pupils each year, currently a local children's hospice, for which impressive amounts of fundraising are achieved – and there are plenty of other good works, eg upper sixth boys had done Movember, raising £2k for men's charities.

Sport: Introduction of sports scholarships is reflective of school's growing commitment to sport. Young, dynamic head of sport considered a great asset, but some facilities – notably the Alps sports fields and pavilion, a five-minute walk away – are in need of an upgrade. King's Rochester Sports Centre with adjoining Holcombe Hockey Club is a 10-minute walk or short minibus ride from the school. Free membership for King's parents and open to the general public too. Strong on team sports – core offerings are hockey and cricket plus rugby for boys and netball for girls. Long success in cricket, with usually at least one match a day being played on the school field. U15 hockey team remains unbeaten and netball gets increasingly good results. Small size of school means most pupils get a chance to play fixtures. 'My son's in the fourth team and manages to get regular matches because they're good at finding other schools with B to D teams,' added a parent, although one felt the sport 'is more geared towards boys'. Rowing from the school's own boathouse on the Medway near Maidstone – 18 boats and five large canoes. Swimming popular in 25m indoor pool, as is cross country. School very supportive of outside achievements, eg many pupils represent Kent in cricket, play rugby through Saracens. And if you don't like sport? 'There's no getting away with standing at the back trying not to get noticed, but not in a bad way – they really want to get you to like it,' said a pupil. And anyway, there's always the headmaster's tiddlywinks.

Boarding: Capacity for 65 boarders – 24 girls in St Margaret's, an attractive white Tudor home in the grounds of the prep (although only just over half full currently); the rest, all boys, in School House, a refurbished Victorian red-brick about a 10-minute walk away nearer the senior school campus. About half come from overseas – some 14 different nationalities, although Chinese dominates, and school admits there is 'work to be done on integration'. Start off in small dorms (three max in boys; two max in girls), and sixth form and most of fifth form have their own room with ensuite bathroom. Girls and boys eat and do weekend activities together, but otherwise keep to their separate houses. Each run by resident housemistress/master and house tutors, at least one of whom is also a resident.

Both are homely, with two common rooms in the girls' house and three in the boys' – handy if older ones want to watch a 15 rated movie. School sports facilities available every evening. Always something organised at weekends, eg shopping, theatre, London Eye, ice skating, Go Ape, go-karting. Some have a more personalised timetable, eg one girl does riding, another tennis lessons.

Mobile phones allowed, but not during prep and handed in at bedtime (except for sixth formers); Wifi stops at 11pm. Youngsters taught how to wash up, sew, use washing machine etc – all good practice for uni, with girls' house hoping to soon get a hob and oven so they can add cooking to the list. Food unpopular – 'When we say we want better food, they give us fancy stuff that reads like some ridiculous Parisian menu, but we just mean we want the classics like spag bol done well,' said one pupil – although the menu we saw looked appetising with everything from curry to fish and chips to pork chops.

Ethos and heritage: 'The whole thing's nuts – it's absolutely wonderful,' exclaimed the head, producing a recent photo of senior pupils dressed to the nines in all the regalia they dig out for high days and holidays – various coloured gowns, silk scarfs, ties, boaters and even canes, according to their specific leadership roles. Like the head, you get the impression pupils don't take it too seriously (who could?) but they lap it all up nonetheless, with our guides taking time to explain it all in great detail. Bottom line is they are fiercely proud of being part of a school with such history and that forms such a central part of the community.

Part of the Foundation of Rochester Cathedral, the school was founded in 604 AD at the same time as the cathedral and re-founded under Henry VIII in 1541 when the monastery at Rochester was dissolved. Right next door is the Norman castle and Charles II spent his first night in England at Restoration House on his return in 1660, while Queen Elizabeth I is rumoured to have stayed at Satis House (now the school administration building). In total, there are a whopping 26 buildings (we were glad we wore flats) from the medieval cathedral to Georgian, Victorian and 21st century, with St Margaret's Street running down to the high street. An unexpected and peaceful oasis in the middle of the bustling Medway towns. One of the few co-ed independent schools in Kent which offer a seamless education from 3-18 years.

Youngsters taught how to wash up, sew, use washing machine etc – all good practice for uni; girls' house hoping to soon get a hob and oven so they can add cooking to the list

There's plenty of the traditional – standing up in class when we walked in (well, sometimes), calling teachers sir and miss, no trousers for girls and 'absolutely no dodgy haircuts' (as one parent put it). But overall, it feels a forward-looking school and there's certainly no shying away from dealing with modern day challenges – we walked in on not one but two PSHE classes on porn.

'More healthy food please!' is not a plea we hear too often in schools, but it's loud and clear among pupils here, who say healthy options not only cost more but are few and far between in both Bob's café and the refectory. 'And please can they go cashless!' add parents. Grumbles too about lack of lockers. Surprisingly few moans about the sixth form common room, though, which is basically a bog-standard computer room with nowhere to chill out.

Former pupils known as Old Roffensians and are hugely supportive. They go on to follow a variety of careers and include surgeons, musicians, authors, artists and poets. Alumni include Prof Sir Derek Barton, who won the Nobel Prize for chemistry, John Gummer, former Conservative cabinet minister, Pete Tong, Radio 1 DJ and Matthew Walker, professional cricketer.

Pastoral care, inclusivity and discipline: Exceptionally warm and caring – the kind of school where teachers know your child even if they don't teach them. Concerns are shared quickly among staff and pupils look after each other too, including those in prep – our sixth form guide did weekly peer mentoring there. Size of school helps ('means you pretty much know everyone'), as does vertical house system (two boarding houses, plus four day houses, although one girl boarder felt a bit short changed on eg sports day and house music, with a mere 14 in her house). Strong Christian ethos; the cathedral is the centre of school life and the service held four mornings a week is a period of quiet reflection before the day begins. But all faiths and backgrounds welcomed and pupils said, 'it's even fine to be atheist, you just have to respect the religious traditions'. Chaplain trained as an independent listener and there's a visiting counsellor, although shame it costs extra (means pupils can never self-refer). Mental health training for all staff. If there are difficulties at home, pupils can come and board for a bit to take the pressure off.

Pupils and parents: Over half of parents are first-time buyers, although conversely there's a number of families where several generations have been King's educated. Not a wealthy area and many make huge sacrifices to send their children here. Lots are dual income. Parents and pupils are down to earth and grounded, with a refreshing lack of sense of entitlement. Accents far from affected. While not unworldly exactly, there's a charming naivety and wholesomeness about the pupils – you get the sense they are allowed to be children, yet they also thrive on the independence they get from navigating a school based in the heart of a city. Some come from the Medway towns and villages, others as far as SE London and Bromley, Whitstable, Sevenoaks and Maidstone. 'I travel an hour to get here,' we heard from several pupils; parents must be grateful for the high speed train and extensive minibus service. Good ethnic diversity, largely thanks to the international contingent. Parents say they feel involved but some say communications from the school could be better.

Money matters: Offers sports, academic, music (including organ) and (most recently) drama and art scholarships worth up to 30 per cent of fees which can be topped up with means-tested bursaries up to 75 per cent of fees. Discounts for clergy, Forces families, siblings and staff. Head adamant not to increase fees – 'I'm keenly aware of how hard people work to send their children here.'

The last word: An antidote to the plethora of Kent grammar schools, this is a non-selective school with a warm family feel and an excellent pastoral and spiritual backdrop. Located in the shadows of the cathedral, it's a special place to grow up and seems to inspire lifelong loyalty among pupils.

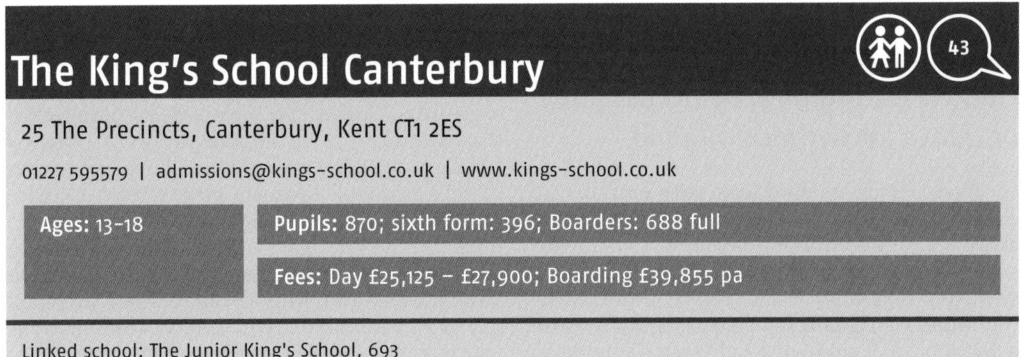

The King's School Canterbury

43

25 The Precincts, Canterbury, Kent CT1 2ES

01227 595579 | admissions@kings-school.co.uk | www.kings-school.co.uk

Ages: 13-18

Pupils: 870; sixth form: 396; Boarders: 688 full

Fees: Day £25,125 – £27,900; Boarding £39,855 pa

Linked school: The Junior King's School, 693

Headmaster: Since 2011, Peter Roberts MA PGCE (50s), previously head of Bradfield College for eight years. First in history from Oxford followed by a PGCE at London Institute of Education. Started teaching career at Winchester as head of history, then also as master in college.

You can bet your bottom dollar that any descriptions of him will include the word 'eccentric', which, a parent told us, 'suits King's perfectly' – 'through his ability to be fun and himself, he seems to permit everyone else to be themselves too, with all their idiosyncrasies.' Indeed, this is not a school that's afraid of characters, and it has a certain edginess where quirkiness and difference are celebrated. Always immaculately dressed, he is known as 'the head man' among pupils who say he is a 'highly intelligent', 'thoughtful', 'non-authoritarian' school leader. Attends every play, recital and concert and even the matrons' meeting, describing his job as 'vastly enjoyable'. Teaches the Shells (year 9). 'Great at networking but not everyone's cup of tea' was the general consensus among parents, 'and perhaps not the most polished of public speakers,' said one, but most agree that once you get him on his own, 'his interactions with individuals are absolutely on the ball'.

He feels the school 'gives a strong sense of belonging, a realisation that King's helped to make them [the pupils] what they are' and 'this creates the wish to give something back in return' and sees the atmosphere of the school as 'like a massive confidence-building machine'. Expects very high standards from the children at every level. Each week the Robertses invite 16 different pupils, one from each house, to lunch in their private dining room.

Married to Marie, an elegant and accomplished Frenchwoman who was head of department at two large state schools and, in addition to playing an active part in school life (mainly pastorally), is also a harpist. They have three daughters. They enjoy spending time in France where he sails, and they both practise calligraphy and paint watercolours – helping to uphold the renaissance ideals of what is technically the oldest school in the country.

Entrance: At 13+ by Common Entrance. School assesses and interviews those who have not been prepared for CE. Occasionally spaces in year 10, when applicants take school's own exam. Just over a third come from Junior King's who go through the same process as everyone else; rest from a range of 110 Kent, Sussex and southern prep schools and London day schools ('we try to work collaboratively with all of them so that our assessment accords with the way they prepare pupils for seniors and common entrance,' says head). Pass mark is 60 per cent but school likes to keep families together and takes an enlightened view if someone is borderline. It is also possible for pupils to take an entrance exam to Junior King's at 11+ which would guarantee entry to the senior school, although they would still have to take CE for setting purposes. From 2020, for entry in 2023, applicants will be required to sit the CE pre-test at their prep school in the autumn of year 6, as well as provide a school reference, with formal offers (subject to academic and behavioural progress) given over years 6-8.

'Everyone finds a passion here' – and in the true King's way, that could just as easily be kite surfing, chess or accordion playing as rugby or dance (or perhaps all five)

About 50 join at sixth form with entrance by competitive exam and interview in Nov before entry with minimum of seven 6s at GCSE, with some A levels requiring a higher grade in same or related subject at GCSE – also required of current pupils, although school insists 'there is no cull – almost all our own pupils get a higher level than they need'.

Exit: Very few leave after GCSE and if they do, it's usually due to family relocating. Vast majority of sixth formers depart to top universities – 15 to Oxbridge in 2021, with Bristol, Durham, Edinburgh, Exeter, King's College London, Newcastle and UCL all popular destinations. Increasing numbers to American and Canadian universities and usually around five to 10 to music college, drama or art school. Eleven medics in 2021. Languages, sciences and economics/business management most popular degree subjects recently. Occasionally, degree apprenticeships.

Latest results: In 2021, 77 per cent 9-7 at GCSE; 71 per cent A*/A at A level (89 per cent A*-B). In 2019 (the last year when exams took place), 70 per cent 9-7 at GCSE; 54 per cent A*/A at A level (79 per cent A*-B). A levels include Pre-U results converted. IGCSEs for two-thirds of subjects.

Teaching and learning: 'You have to want to learn,' we were told by multiple parents and there's no doubt the pursuit of academic excellence is at the heart of everything here, although co-curricular activities are given equal weight and as such pupils have an astonishingly busy day – one of the first lessons they learn is how to plan their time to include both. 'You never stop,' said one, while another added, 'Everyone finds a passion here' – and in the true King's way, that could just as easily be kite surfing, chess or accordion playing as rugby or dance (or perhaps all five). 'I think of it as a David Gower school – everyone knows he's a great cricketer, but they probably don't know he was a keen musician and actor when he was at King's,' says head. School claims pupils are 'clever enough to get into the London day schools, but choose to come here, often precisely because of our rich programme'.

Expect a fast-paced academic environment which parents say 'is not for wimps', although pupils say teachers are 'good at picking you up if you're struggling' and it's not as if anyone takes silly numbers of GCSEs, with majority taking nine or 10 including a creative subject like art, drama, IT or music (art and music are the most popular non-core GCSEs). Strong results across the board, with chemistry, Spanish and maths the shining stars. Good numbers of girls doing physics. Astronomy GCSE is available, as are many languages (most taught by double linguists, able to build up those wanting to go on to study languages at university) including Latin, Greek, French, German, Spanish, Italian and Mandarin (minority also do Japanese and Russian and school will accommodate any others if requested). Most subject combinations are possible, even if some have to be taught outside the timetable. School always looking at ways to stretch the most able and curriculum constantly adapted. Pupils told us strongest departments are English and science but felt 'history and drama are on the weaker side'. Setting in maths, sciences and languages from the off.

Offers 32 A levels and Pre-U subjects, including six Pre-U subjects. Geology and, most recently, psychology, on the menu. Strongest results in English, maths, French and art, with most popular including economics, maths, biology and chemistry. Pupils encouraged to think about their broader academic profile and alongside A levels there are enrichment subjects such as critical thinking, perspectives on aesthetics, globalisation and science and EPQ (we met a pupil who'd done theirs on 18th-century France and another on Cornish history). Careers advice starts in the first year on a drop-in basis and fifth form have timetabled careers periods to help with A level choices and beyond.

Stunning William Butterfield designed library (1848) is centre of academic life with a hushed and studious atmosphere and combining the best of the old and new with 30,000 books, along with periodicals, European newspapers and DVDs – they even have dogs to stroke around exam time. This well-staffed library is a great source of pride and open every day until 10pm and at weekends, although pupils told us they 'wish we didn't have to wear school uniform as it makes the library less inviting when you've got a free period'. Somerset Maugham and Sir Hugh Walpole both left their personal libraries to King's.

Learning support and SEN: About six per cent need extra help, mainly for mild dyslexia, in The Hub, and any pupil can ask for help with study skills. Wouldn't suit anyone with bigger difficulties. EAL for a handful of pupils but all must be fluent on arrival.

The arts and extracurricular: Long tradition of excellent music and anyone involved is definitely awarded 'cool status'. New performing arts centre in former Victorian malthouse in 2019. Symphony orchestra plus numerous bands and ensembles; the pupil-run jazz club is particularly popular. Plenty of choral groups, from the Crypt Choir which tours annually, most recently to Rome, to the choral society which is open to anyone who enjoys singing, including parents and staff. Pupils were preparing to play Brahms's German Requiem in the cathedral when we visited, without a professional in sight. Drama both on and off the curriculum, with plenty of performances and regular theatre trips to London, although pupils feel drama 'could be improved'. Busy art department housed in 12th-century priory has a different artist in residence each year. Photographic studio and pottery centre opened by old boy Edmund de Waal.

Oodles more activities, continuing into sixth form, from academic societies with visiting speakers to mountain biking, cryptic crosswords, debating and the Model United Nations. Pupils told of us of clubs in Japanese cooking, Sanskrit and even pole vaulting, plus student-run Jewish club ('popular, not least because of the food'). CCF gets decent numbers and community work and volunteering are central to school life – often part of DofE (around 20 golds are awarded annually), but which also include teaching science and, more recently, music, in local primary schools.

School says it offers 'family-based' boarding, insofar as it's seven days a week, 'but you can get off the bus along the way' – in other words, go home when you want

The famous King's Week at the end of the summer term is the highlight of the year and is a festival of music, drama and dance with events being staged in all corners of the school every day for a week – parents and friends come bearing picnics, with every B&B and hotel in Canterbury booked out for the duration. 'It's a garden party for all involved and there's something going on until 11pm every evening.' Expect Shakespeare, classical concerts, jazz, house harmonies, a Chariots of Fire dash round the green, serenade in the cloisters at sunset, poetry slams etc, all culminating in Commem Day and the leavers' ball. 'The sun's out, exams are over, jazz is playing, vintage bikes are everywhere and you're sitting with your friends – it doesn't get better than King's Week,' said one pupil.

Sport: Acres of playing fields about 15 (head insists, with a wink, that it's 11) minutes' walk away as well as a modern sports centre incorporating pool, indoor courts, climbing wall, café and gym – more akin to a posh private leisure centre. A democratic approach to sport means most pupils get to represent the school in matches, if they want to. Top performers are rugby, rowing, cricket and fencing (boys) and hockey and cricket (girls), with girls' lacrosse and swimming also on the up. School has produced several international fencers. But parents told us of 'a general lack of oomph in sport'. One said, 'You're not playing to the highest level here – more Eastbourne than Eton and occasionally Tonbridge at rugby, but even then our A team will play their B team, so if your child is terribly sporty, you might feel disappointed.' However, the emphasis on 'fitness, health and fun' and the sheer breadth of sports mean most people find something they enjoy, though pupils curious as to why they can't do 'more co-ed sports, including lacrosse'. Sporting trips all over the world.

Boarding: School says it offers 'family-based' boarding, insofar as it's seven days a week, 'but you can get off the bus along the way' – in other words, go home when you want. It's never empty at weekends, though, and some won't take all exeats, with school often having to suggest parents come for a weekend to Canterbury instead of trying to tear their offspring away. Six boys' and seven girls' houses (latest, Lady Kingsdown, for girls, opened in 2017) – three are day, the rest boarding, with some bigger than others to cater for 50:50 boy:girl ratio. Half the houses clustered round the cathedral and the other half across the road on the St Augustine site where they have their own dining hall. Pupils generally have a preference for one or the other and the most popular houses get booked up years in advance. All in a variety of architectural styles from the 13th-century Meister Omers to 21st-century Grange, some have received a much-needed recent refurb. Small dormitories for younger children and individual study bedrooms for sixth form. Huge praise for housemasters and housemistresses, described by parents as 'deeply pastoral', although one felt 'there could be more consistency in how houses deal when it comes to discipline'. Large and popular social centre open for the whole school during the day and for sixth formers in the evening.

Ethos and heritage: Set in the shadow of Canterbury Cathedral (which pupils can visit any time – 'it's so calming,' one told us) and part of a World Heritage Site, this has to be one of the most inspiring settings for a school. Founded in 597 when St Augustine arrived in Canterbury and then re-founded as The King's School during the reign of Henry VIII after the dissolution of the monasteries – not many schools can produce a list of headmasters going back to 1259. Beautiful ancient buildings and cloisters and immaculate gardens with the busy city life going on just beyond the gates. Pupils enjoy the contrast and the fact that the city with its shops and cafés is on the doorstep.

Set in the shadow of Canterbury Cathedral (which pupils can visit any time – 'it's so calming,' one told us) and part of a World Heritage Site, this has to be one of the most inspiring school settings

Latest additions include girls' boarding house and day house and the school has also acquired Beerling Hall by the Marlowe Theatre, now their art block, as well as the refurbished historic Malthouse as a performing arts centre – a 334-seat theatre, complete with art, dance and photography studios.

Next up is a brand new science building, ready in 2021. Dining facilities have been extended to include three options. 'Food is amazing here – everyone gets particularly hyped on chicken night and I've never seen more of an opera than when they got rid of spicy goujons,' a pupil told us. Took girls into sixth form in 1970s and went fully co-ed in 1990. Former pupil Michael Morpurgo said, 'King's is like a university designed for younger people.' Some parents feel it's best suited to more robust children although one pupil told us her sibling was 'really quite shy and loves it'.

Pastoral care, inclusivity and discipline: Ultra-smart, traditional uniform – pinstripes, wing collars and a jacket, and a brooch for the girls. 'They tried to modernise and take away the brooch, but we were having none of it,' one girl told us, although girls do now have the option of trousers. Monitors, known as Purples, wear striking purple gowns with huge pride; one told us they are regularly stopped for photos by tourists. Woe betide pupils whose incorrectly worn uniform is spotted by the Beadle, usually found lingering around the entrance in his top hat and tails – sharp (often loud) words will ensue.

Strong Christian tradition, with main school services held in the cathedral, but different religious and cultural backgrounds welcomed. Mental health is a key focus pastorally – everything from reformed PSHE programme to talks from outside speakers to mindfulness, and this is a Stonewall school, championing LGBT rights. Children have a healthy respect for each other and are generally self-regulating regarding bullying; honesty and integrity are highly valued. Several staff/pupil committees to ensure all have their say and we noted respectful communication between staff and pupils – this, together with mixed-aged tutor groups and trained older pupils mentoring younger ones, ensures good interaction between year groups; day children and boarders also mix well. 'But please can we stop this silly expectation that you have to have a date for lunch, which involves organising meeting them first,' said one pupil. 'It's a pain logistically and sometimes you just want to chill out alone, so us Purples are starting to go alone to set a trend.' Strict rules and punishments regarding drugs, alcohol and parties and children know where they stand. Around half a dozen temporary and one or two permanent exclusions every year.

Pupils and parents: Popular with locals, London and county sets alike, plus Foreign Office and expat families and increasing numbers from abroad. About 20 per cent foreign nationals, with a 25 per cent cap. Doesn't really produce a type but pupils are articulate, well-rounded and appear to genuinely to relish others' achievements. Charming, undeniably posh and among the most confident we've seen, pupils also have a glint in their eye reflecting a sense of fun and have a huge sense of ownership over their school. 'King's pupils are not slow in coming forward,' smiles head. We heard tales of parents arriving at the school in a helicopter, but pupils assured us not everyone is so well-heeled and we saw for ourselves an ethnic mix.

The King's Society, a cultural, social and educational society for parents and friends, comprises over 300 families. Old boys and girls include potter and writer Edmund de Waal, astronaut Michael Foale, Patrick Leigh-Fermor, Christopher Marlowe and William Somerset Maugham, supermodel Jacquetta Wheeler, Olympic silver medallist and world champion rower Frances Houghton and Anthony Worrall-Thompson.

Money matters: Twelve King's Scholarships. Ditto with music scholarships and around three to five in art, DT, dance and sport, all with a rigorous selection process and worth up to 10 per cent of fees. Three or four sixth form scholarships awarded for outstanding performance in the sixth form entrance exam. Greater emphasis on bursaries – the King's foundation has been set up to fund both scholarships and bursaries and allocates over £2 million a year. Parents means-tested annually and can receive up to 100 per cent of full boarding fee.

The last word: Thriving academic school in exquisite surroundings steeped in history, with highly motivated pupils who are hungry to learn and where there's very little room for slack and never a dull moment – rarely, in fact, even a moment to stand still, such is the busy programme of engaging activities.

Lancing College

Lancing, West Sussex BN15 0RW

01273 452213 | admissions@lancing.org.uk | www.lancingcollege.co.uk

Ages: 13–18

Pupils: 600; sixth form: 262; Boarders: 336 full, 29 flexi

Fees: Day £26,340; Boarding £32,400 – £38,550 pa

Head master: Since 2014, Dominic Oliver MPhil (40s). A grammar school boy who read English at Sheffield before spending a decade forging a sterling academic career at Oxford (specialising in Shakespeare). Edited the Longman School Shakespeare edition of Richard III, which garnered very favourable reviews. Eventually, wanting a less narrow life ('the bit that really excited me was teaching students'), took a post at the Royal Grammar School in Worcester. Three years as head of English at Malvern College followed, then four years as managing head of Bedales School, before he settled into the top job at Lancing. Married to Lydia, a psychoanalyst, with two sons, one at Oxford and the other currently in the sixth form.

'Approachable and visible,' was the verdict of parents. Head and school seem to be a particularly good fit; he brings insight and genuine scholarly radiance to the relationship, Lancing provides history and warm-hearted Woodard-style Christian ethics, and both exude silver-haired distinction. A real marriage of true minds.

Entrance: Selective. At 13+, about 100 places on offer, with around 20 to 25 per cent of these usually going to pupils from the school's own preps at Hove and Worthing. A few places also available at 14+. At 16+ an additional 40 or so places. School looks for 'academic crunching power', but also for a wide-ranging and diverse school community – 'a willingness to give, and a wish to participate in a broader kind of life'.

Exit: Up to 20 per cent leave after GCSEs, but school insists it doesn't cull. 'We have an academic bar, but it's administered humanely. If you take someone at 13, you have a duty to look after them.' At 18, 65 per cent to Russell Group universities. Bristol, Cardiff, Durham, Exeter, Imperial College, Leeds and UCL all popular, with others off overseas. Three to Oxbridge in 2021, plus two medics. Art, design and architecture are all popular choices – a love of beauty, perhaps, being a happy side effect of living on this ravishing campus.

Latest results: In 2021, 62 per cent 9-7 at GCSE; 41 per cent A*/A at A level (87 per cent A*-B). In 2019 (the last year when exams took place), 46 per cent 9-7 at GCSE; 44 per cent A*/A at A level (71 per cent A*-B).

Teaching and learning: Lancing is less punishingly selective than (at least one of) its nearby competitors, and this is reflected in its results, which are nonetheless very creditable.

Make no mistake, however, there is some real scholarship going on here. In 2017 the school set up the Heresy Project to celebrate the anniversary of Martin Luther nailing his articles to Wittenberg church door and to encourage Lancing lower sixth formers to challenge orthodoxy. They did, and we thought the resulting essays were impressive examples of coherent and independent thinking. How does the school achieve this in its students? According to the deputy head academic, by placing a high value on intellectual joy and curiosity. Year 9 students, for instance, come off timetable for a week each year to write a dissertation on something that interests them; half a term prior to this is spent learning how to amass and assess information. The head himself teaches the skills of parliamentary debating and integrating quotation into argument. Lucky students, we thought, who seemed to take all this for granted, praising the lessons simply as 'really enjoyable'. The classes (average size 18, smaller in the sixth form) we saw were teacher-led and traditional, but friendly and relaxed with good student input. 'Exceptional and dedicated teachers,' according to one parent.

Languages offered include French, Spanish, German and Mandarin. One parent lamented that compulsory Latin had been phased out for the year 9s. Excellent science facilities, although the physics class we saw were gleefully piling outdoors to launch water rockets. Learning everywhere is purposeful, calm and undertaken with satisfaction. Superb library is open seven days a week – strict silence rules, but there is also a seminar room for collaborative work and plenty of computer workstations.

Learning support and SEN: Two full-time and one part-time SEN teachers support the small number of students with mild dyslexia, dyspraxia, slow processing, etc. 'The school was able to accommodate my son's additional needs beautifully, enabling him to shine in the areas he loved, and he is now at a top university,' wrote a grateful parent. International students must already have excellent English and are screened for this on application, but once here, they receive regular EAL support.

The arts and extracurricular: One of the best programmes of extracurricular activities we've come across anywhere with facilities and staffing to match. Lancing's farm provides a refreshing alternative for those who want to get their fresh air and exercise off the sports field. Run by the estates manager with two part-timers and an abundance of student help, there are lots of ways to get involved. Would-be vets learn to give injections to animals, and anyone who wants to gets to bottle-feed the lambs – or even to get up in the night to help deliver them.

Music here is 'unrivalled' and we thought that outside of a specialist music school, you'd be hard-pressed to do better. Wealth of opportunities includes orchestras, choirs, a cappella club, Big Band, rock music workshops, conducting classes, improvisation workshops, composition lessons and a full programme of chamber music coaching. Between 30 and 40 concerts each year ensure that everyone gets plenty of chances to perform. Instrumental lessons offered on practically anything, 'including Chinese flute'. Masterclasses and professional recitals are common, as are visits to concerts and opera. The chapel is home to no fewer than three organs, and the chapel choir and choral scholars sing evensong at major cathedrals across the country.

The Heresy Project, celebrating the anniversary of Martin Luther nailing his articles to Wittenberg church door, encouraged lower sixth formers to challenge orthodoxy

Drama is popular and well-resourced – 'outstanding,' wrote one parent – with around 10 events a year including productions. There's even an open air theatre, opened by Agatha Christie in 1960, where the Founder's Day play is performed every summer term. Dance is also offered – ballet, contemporary, street jazz. Art is very big here, and we thought the work on display was superb. 'The art department is wonderful and full of happy, enthusiastic teachers,' wrote a parent. Now offers photography GCSE as well as A level. Busy calendar of community service includes DofE and the outreach programme for sixth formers. Lots of school trips – recent destinations have included Malawi, Germany and Iceland. 'It's been brilliant,' said an upper sixth former; 'I've got involved in so many different things and I've loved them all!'

Sport: The one-word question 'Sports?' to a group of students received an universal exhalation of satisfaction. 'What's great about Lancing sport is that it really is for everyone, and you can find your level.' 'The range of sports here is just ridiculous!' Main ones are football, hockey, netball, tennis (on both hard and grass courts) and cricket. One student we spoke to relished his place in the 6th football team, playing twice a week for enjoyment; his friend in the 1st team practised four times a week and received regular professional coaching. Even this unathletic reviewer thought the football pitches were amazing – 'As school pitches go, this has to be one of the best in the country.' Cricket is also strong – Mason Sidney Crane is an OL. Excellent swimming pool, used by locals as well as school community, since 2018 home to LC Swim Club affiliated with Swim England. Endless list of more niche sports includes sailing, squash, basketball, riding (brand new equestrian centre), Eton fives, golf, fencing, badminton, water polo and aerobics. CCF also popular; we witnessed a boy being awarded an enormous trophy for success in target rifle shooting.

Boarding: Some 60 per cent of the students board and boarding is very much the school's ethos. Seven of the nine houses are for boarders: four for boys and three for girls, reflecting the slightly boy-heavy intake (which school is working to address); new co-ed day house. Full, weekly and flexi options and free boarding for day pupils if an activity goes on past 9pm. Of the day pupils, half stay over regularly and it's not uncommon for there to be 280 pupils in school over a weekend.

All houses are for the full age range of students from years 9 to 13. No separate sixth form accommodation, but they have their own corridor and common room and the students said they preferred the resulting age diversity. On entry, pupils generally share in pairs, threes or fours, but two to a room is standard in year 10 and single rooms by year 11. The rooms we saw were spacious and neat, although the lad who declared that 'coming down here is a breath of fresh air' might well have been referring to the wintry interior temperatures. All houses have a matron and, say students, 'They're all welcoming.' 'Our second mum!' Some 70 per cent of teachers live on site and involve themselves in the school, meaning that there are lots of activities and socialising in the beautifully furnished and well-equipped communal areas – 'There is SO MUCH to do!' was a comment echoed by many.

Everyone we spoke to agreed that boarding, even if it was part-time, enabled them to get the most out of being here. 'You're more involved'; 'It's easier to work.' As the head put it, 'For me, it's the logical extension of educating the whole person. Who wouldn't want to live here? I wake up every morning and feel that. And that's the experience of the vast majority of people at Lancing.'

Ethos and heritage: Traces its origins back to 1848, but on the present site since 1857. There can scarcely be a lovelier school approach anywhere. Emerging from woodland, the road opens out onto the astonishing prospect of the school chapel: 90 feet of soaring Victorian Gothic in Sussex sandstone, crowning the rolling grassland that slopes gently down towards the coast. Nathaniel Woodard, the founder, built some cracking schools, but knew he was on to something special with Lancing chapel, insisting that it was built to its full height at one end first, so that if he died before completion the proportions couldn't be cut down to save money. So from the outset, perhaps, the Lancing principle was to put beauty before profit, and it doesn't seem fanciful to say that the benign effects of this are perceptible throughout the school.

Consider the light and airy art department (with sea view), bursting with imaginative work, the wonderfully high-ceilinged library or the working farm with its programme dedicated to the reintroduction of the grey partridge. Lancing impresses as a place where creative thinking is encouraged – or rather, where creativity grows and thrives by itself, because the soil in which it's planted is so good. 'Lancing allows for the eccentric,' as one pupil put it. 'It's about giving them the time to stand and stare,' affirmed the deputy head. 'Relaxed, friendly, a happy school,' said a parent, more prosaically.

Lancing welcomes those of all faiths and of none, but Christian values underpin the school and are made flesh by the chapel. Long, thin, vaulted – and chilly – it's the only space large enough to house the whole school community. Everyone has to attend college eucharist on Wednesday morning, as well as on one or two Sundays each term, but the approach is inclusive. All the students we spoke to loved it and insisted it was part of what made their time at Lancing unique. 'The chapel remains to our whole family as a very special and emotional place,' wrote a mother.

Emerging from woodland, the road opens out onto the astonishing prospect of the school chapel: 90 feet of soaring Victorian Gothic in Sussex sandstone, crowning the rolling grassland that slopes gently down towards the coast

'It's an honour to be at a school this pretty,' and 'I've loved the look of Lancing since I was little,' were comments echoed everywhere. But this is also a busy, bustling community that buzzes with purpose and activity, and perhaps the real beauty of the place lies in the equilibrium and sense of sanity that the school manages to achieve. 'The school is really excellent at putting eggs in different baskets,' thought a younger pupil. 'The first time I came here I knew this was the school for me – it was the balance,' said another. 'It's such a family feel,' said our tour guide, as we passed a tabby cat washing itself contentedly outside the piggeries.

Alumni include Evelyn Waugh, Sir David Hare, Peter Pears, Tim Rice, Christopher Hampton, Jan Morris, Tom Sharpe, Jamie Theakston and Sir Roy Calne, pioneer of liver transplantation.

Pastoral care, inclusivity and discipline: Housemasters and mistresses are the first point of call for parents. 'I cannot praise my son's housemaster enough for the support he offers to both the young men under his care and their parents!' wrote one mother, and all the parents we contacted concurred. 'Housemistress is extremely kind with a lovely family'; 'Always approachable'.

Long-established peer support scheme is also highly valued, with over 50 students applying each year for the 18 or so places. Those selected spend over 16 hours being trained by the school counsellor in skills such as listening, confidentiality and dealing with homesickness. No restrictions on phoning home, we were relieved to hear.

Surprisingly, a couple of parents whose opinion of the school was very positive nonetheless murmured that they weren't entirely satisfied with how the school had dealt with issues around bullying: 'We've found that the school policy on this doesn't match up with our children's experiences.' The pupils we spoke to, however, insisted that bullying was rare and that instances were dealt with swiftly. Certainly behaviour around school appeared excellent and parents report that the discipline is 'firm but fair'. The attractive dark blue uniform is smartly worn and gives way in the sixth form to equally smart business attire.

Catering has changed recently and there is now much praise for the food, served up in a magnificent dining hall reminiscent of an Oxford college. 'Healthier', 'nicer', 'plenty to eat', say students. We ourselves were served a delicious lunch so can only agree.

School operates a six-day week with Saturdays being given over to a mixture of lessons and extracurricular activities. Day pupils have to be in school by 8.15am and must stay until 6pm so it's not the place for those with a busy life outside school. A few complaints persist from parents of day pupils that they're not always kept fully in the loop regarding events and fixtures. Inevitable, perhaps, in a school as energetic and bustling as this where the mindset is primarily boarding.

Pupils and parents: Accepting of difference and encouraging of resourcefulness, the school suits all sorts but is very much for those who like to keep busy. Around 25 per cent of boarders from overseas. Parents are hard-working, professional, aspirational, successful. Bus service covers a wide area and there's a shuttle between Lancing College and the preps. New London bus serves those needing to get back from the capital on a Sunday evening.

Money matters: Scholarships available in all the usual fields – sports, drama music, academic, all-rounder – plus, more unusually, an organ scholarship for Y12s and the Peter Robinson Cricketing award, which in 2017 was won for the first time by a girl. 'Owzat!'

Scholarships are worth between five and 10 per cent of the fees, and students who achieve one can then apply to the bursary fund for further assistance. Commendably, school is currently fundraising to create 25 'Foundationer' places by 2022, enabling students from poorer backgrounds to access full-fees assistance. 'It's important that we have a mix of students, not just the very wealthy, and it's making everybody here think about what education is for.'

The last word: A truly beautiful school where the upward spaces encourage students to reach for the skies whilst keeping their feet on the ground. As one parent put it, 'Lancing is wonderful, and has given my children such a positive start to their lives.'

Marlborough House School

Hawkhurst, Cranbrook, Kent TN18 4PY

01580 753555 | registrar@marlboroughhouseschool.co.uk | www.marlboroughhouseschool.co.uk

Ages: 3–13

Pupils: 250; Boarders: 45 (Tuesday–Thursday)

Fees: Day £9,345 – £18,690 pa; Boarding £35 per night

Head: Since September 2020, Eddy Newton (50s). Rapidly steadied the ship after what parents describe as a 'rocky 18 months' for the school following the sudden departure of last head and a year with an acting head in post. 'I knew from about age 17 that I'd be a teacher,' says Mr Newton, even before he started his classics degree at Jesus College, Cambridge, and he has never deviated from that path. This is his third headship after Felsted Prep and Chafyn Grove in Salisbury, and a stint as chief executive of the Cothill Trust.

Any impression that this 'gnarly old veteran', as he jokingly calls himself, has come here for a cosy pre-retirement job is immediately dispelled by his honesty, warmth and dynamism – his own children may be teenagers but he's an ultra-marathon runner and cyclist. He's also been an immediate hit with parents: 'He's grasped straight away what Marlborough House is about, but he's quite no nonsense,' and 'We've been very impressed – he's straight talking, consistent, and having older children himself, he gets what we're all aiming for.' Communications are much improved and everyone was impressed with his grand tour of local secondary schools and ensuing presentation.

His wife is a graphic designer and the family has a home on the school grounds.

Entrance: 'No type it wouldn't suit,' says the school. Most start in the universally loved nursery and pre-prep. With pupil numbers increasing again with a new head and very real Covid-driven exodus from London, there is capacity for more than 300 so it's possible to join the school in most year groups. There is soft touch testing so they know where pupils are and can monitor development.

Exit: Another school with the slightly irksome habit of listing all forward destinations rather than giving you hard numbers on its website. In fairness, though, with fantastic state and independent options in the region, MHS feeds to a really broad range, which parents appreciate. Most popular in 2021 were Eastbourne College (nearly half with scholarships), Hurst (a third with scholarships), Cranbrook (doesn't offer scholarships) Brighton College (all with scholarships) and Battle Abbey (all with scholarships). The diminishing financial value of scholarships in the area does not seem to have dulled parental interest in winning them.

Our view: Marlborough House enjoys elegant Georgian buildings, gravel paths and mature trees, though many feel it could use a lick of paint here and there. This will start with the extension and refurbishment of the art and DT facilities in summer 2021 (in place of a rather expensive and now-ditched plan for a new Innovation Centre). As with all good schools, though, character matters more than decor, and this is a caring, tight-knit community.

The school is divided into nursery, pre-prep, middle and upper school, with separate buildings for pre-prep and nursery. The transitions between these are, according to one mother, 'really well handled – there's a real emphasis on resilience'. A jolly nursery, with children learning to care for rabbits, guinea pigs and giant snails. Quiet area behind ribbons is a place to snuggle down for a nap or quiet time.

The pre-prep prides itself on its innovative, ambitious teaching to develop character and problem-solving skills alongside knowledge. The building has a communal hall at its heart for assemblies and clubs, and there's a 'children in charge' approach to learning in a very fluid way. Pupils may access the outdoor learning spaces (under awnings), pre-prep library and three learning hubs (with computers etc) to investigate ideas further. 'The world has become so noisy for children – our philosophy is to give them space and time to go find out who they are and start their learning,' says the pre-prep head.

Boys' dorms named for sport, mostly skiing, with the black-run stairs (roped for safety) down from their top-floor dorms; girls' dorms named after flowers and bubbles

Regular 'carousel days' allowing children to buddy up across the year groups – paired by interest and ability – to work on certain projects have been a great success and naturally led to more inter-year group working. Also interesting are EWOC (Everyone Writing in Our Class) and ERIC time (Everyone Reading In Class) – in which pupils and teachers all take time to do some creative writing or reading, without being marked, to experience and develop the sheer pleasure of doing so.

The forest school is well used and well loved – 'you can see the kids' shoulders going down,' says a teacher – and expanding outdoor learning is another area on the head's radar; they are shortly to plant 200 new trees and build a new outdoor classroom beside the lake.

While a few staff left through MHS's 'wobble', things now very much more stable and academic teaching here is rigorous. This, coupled with maximum class sizes of 16 in the pre-prep and 18 in the prep, 'seems to do a huge amount for confidence levels,' says one mother. With pupils sitting either the 11+ and ISEB pre-test (and sometimes both), preparation for such specialised tests starts in year 4, with practice lessons and BOFA online tests. 'I claim no credit but our VR scores in the 11+ are fantastic,' says head.

Families who were nervous about moving to the Pre-senior Baccalaureate curriculum and assessment model for years 7 and 8 – helping children to leave with, according to school, a 'toolbox full of skills not a briefcase full of grades' – have now fully embraced its coursework and continual assessment. The leavers of 2021 complete it first, but cleverly the school has opted for a hybrid in that all pupils still do CE maths and English: 'We understand the need for a common assessment in those key subjects,' says head, who is a convert to the PSB. 'I'm another who feels CE has probably had its day... I really like the philosophy of the PSB.'

Both the very able and those towards the middle of the pack thrive here, bright pupils being stretched with extension classes run weekly by each head of department. Commenting on the atmosphere, a parent says, 'It's not wholly laid back; but [doing] the best you can do is perfect.'

The forest school is well used and well loved – 'you can see the kids' shoulders going down,' says a teacher – and expanding outdoor learning is another area on the head's radar

Lockdown provision better the second time around, when parents declared the school's live lessons 'fantastic', while maintaining the school's care for the individual: 'Online form time has been really helpful and warm.'

A well-established tutor system (involving weekly tutorial group meetings and less frequent one-to-one tutorials) has been further developed through the adoption of the PSB. Most pupils say that they would go to their form tutor if they had a problem, one shyer pupil saying he would rather use an independent listener box so he wouldn't have to talk in front of others. 'It's a very caring school,' confirms a parent. Another parent whose son experienced bullying at his previous school says he was 'brought back to life' by MHS.

The learning support team – made up of two full-time specialists – is there for everyone, including those who just want a chat and some reassurance. They help those with a variety of needs, including severe dyslexia. Most support is offered in groups of up to six (the dynamic is better in small groups, they say, and it's more fun for pupils). One-to-one help is also available, charged as an extra. 'We're not selective but we are very occasionally de-selective,' says head. 'If someone needs three or more hours a week one-to-one, we're not the right school.'

MHS is often chosen by parents and children for the happy, comfortable atmosphere that pervades the school, one parent adding that it is 'neither as clinical or feral as other independent options in the area'. Another was attracted by the respectful interaction between staff and children and describes the role modelling by staff as 'exceptional'.

Sport every afternoon from year 6 upwards, with lots of pupils saying that sport is their favourite thing about the school. They punch above their weight in many areas, and girls' cricket has grown well, with some pupils now in county squads. But there is a pleasing emphasis on sport for all, with an approach that highlights enjoyment, inclusion and effort: coaches also focus on the bottom teams, with most parents and pupils saying that everyone gets a regular chance to represent the school in matches.

School's comprehensive music programme evidently fosters a real love for the subject. Various instrument and vocal coaches are from illustrious stables such as English National Opera and the Globe Theatre.

There is a middle school play annually as well as a modern take on a Shakespeare classic performed by the year 8s, plus enthusiastic use of external LAMDA teachers. However, a move to extend the school day from 4.10 to 4.30pm is driven partly by a wish to accommodate more art, drama and sports clubs. Current clubs include philosophy in the forest and theatre make-up but head adds, 'We'd like to get back into sailing and mountain biking and.22 rifle shooting' – MHS has its own rifle range. It must also be one of the only schools with a permanent indoor maypole, children learning that the important thing is to keep smiling merrily, even if the ribbons are getting in a frightful tangle.

'Good manners cost nothing but mean a lot,' says a notice on a door. 'Are you looking as smart as you could be?' says another. Respecting self and others is the theme which runs through this school from nursery to year 8, with much of the system of rewards and sanctions being tied into this ethos. Bad marks may well land you in the reflection room to consider the impact of your behaviour and what you might do differently in the future.

Though pupils are predominantly white, roughly 10 per cent have north European family heritage and speak a second language such as Dutch, Swedish etc.

The pandemic has encouraged the school to 'look harder at local poverty,' says the head, including fundraising for local families who could not otherwise afford a decent Christmas lunch.

Parents are diverse: city, professionals and business, old money, and 'just working hard to get them through school'. That not all of them can afford private secondary schools at least one parent declares as 'actually really nice... there's a down-to-earth attitude.' A very parent-friendly school and the welcoming parent group (some mothers even use the courts for morning tennis coaching) quickly scoops up newcomers.

Boarding: Offered from Tuesday to Thursday, with an average of 25 boarders over the course of a week. 'The best club is boarding,' said one boy, who has finally persuaded his mother that he should have one night a week at school. Last minute requests for boarding will be accommodated if there's a space. Parents all report the school is very flexible and accommodating. Pupils can board from year 4, but most are older.

Evening activities are popular – laser guns and throwing marshmallows into a bucket are recent hits, and pupils enjoy roaming the grounds. A nice supper for boarders – 'pitta bread things, and hot chocolate or milkshakes,' said one boy with enthusiasm (no kitchen for snacks at present).

Rooms with bunk beds, mostly for six; cosy, but not cramped. Ample bathroom facilities in good condition. Blue sheets for boys, pink for girls; but white provided to older girls who asked. Boys' dorms named for sport, mostly skiing, with the black-run stairs (roped for safety) down from their top-floor dorms; girls' dorms named after flowers and bubbles (pupils chose dormitory names a few years back).

The school promotes boarding as great experience for secondary school – with even state boarding an option down the road, over half go on to do some at their next school.

Money matters: New for September 2021 is a year 7 scholarship package – involving extra tuition and fee discounts between 5 and 20 per cent – for academic, art, design and technology, drama, music, sport and all round ability. Open to internal and external candidates, no doubt they're also useful in encouraging pupils to stay to year 8. A high proportion of candidates won them in the launch year.

The last word: With a focused head at the helm, and now embedded PSB programme for the final two years, the spirit and strengths of this school are secure: 'We're small, but everybody mixes with and knows one another, whatever their year,' says one parent. Strong academically, parents agree with Mr Newton's assessment that 'the warmth is genuine here and individual attention to each child is fantastic; that's where we excel.' The school goes far beyond academic results and prides itself on the development of the whole child – very much the ethos behind the PSB.

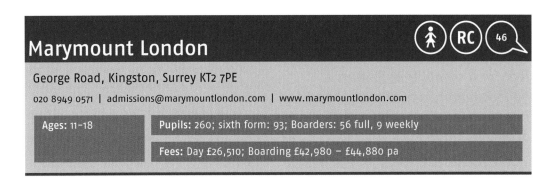

Marymount London

RC 46

George Road, Kingston, Surrey KT2 7PE

020 8949 0571 | admissions@marymountlondon.com | www.marymountlondon.com

Ages: 11–18

Pupils: 260; sixth form: 93; Boarders: 56 full, 9 weekly

Fees: Day £26,510; Boarding £42,980 – £44,880 pa

Headmistress: Since January 2021, Margaret Giblin, previously deputy head at Woldingham Catholic School for Girls, which she joined in 2012. Experience in education spans over two decades in both UK and Ireland. MA in Catholic School Leadership from St Mary's and Higher Diploma in teaching and a BA in theology and English from National University of Ireland and St Patrick's Pontifical University, respectively. Married with two teenage children.

Entrance: Applicants encouraged to visit school via open day or arrange individual tour. All sit English and maths test but school essentially looking for a good fit and students committed to IB programme. Interview with head is key. Open to admissions throughout academic year if space allows.

Exit: Majority to Russell Group. King's College London, UCL, Imperial and Edinburgh all popular. One to Oxbridge in 2021 (plus one other offer, but the student decided to go to Stanford). US applications on the rise, especially since Brexit we heard. Girls can sign up separately for SAT and ACT prep course; staff prepare in-house for any UK tests. Eleven overseas in 2021 to Stanford (English lit), NUY Stern Business School (business), UC San Diego (computer science), Amsterdam (psychology), Glion Institute of Higher Education (hospitality), EBS (business and law), Waseba Japan (liberal arts) and UCLAN Cyprus (advertising, marketing and communications). Two medics in 2021.

Latest results: In 2021, average IB point score of 38. In 2019 (the last year when exams took place), average IB score of 37.

Teaching and learning: Marymount was one of the first adopters of the IB and has been following the programme now for over forty years. It remains the only girls' Catholic day and boarding school in UK to do so. Results on the rise. No mean feat for a school that favours a holistic admissions process: head's interview all-important rather than academic smarts.

Girls join Marymount at the start of the seven-year IB programme in grade 6 (aged 11). The first five years or 'Middle Years Programme' provide the foundations with project work, assessments and termly school tests. There are no external exams in this period (hurrah, no GCSEs) and it is grades 11 and 12 (ages 17-18) which culminate in IB exams and award of IB Diploma. Girls are encouraged to think for themselves and explore ideas and connections between varied subject groups. The IB style of learning is 'a breath of fresh air,' said one parent, whose daughter joined after being 'taught to the test' in her 'pushy' prep. Another parent: 'My daughter was suddenly asked what she actually thought – it took a while to get used to.'

Results on the rise. No mean feat for a school that favours a holistic admissions process: head's interview all-important rather than academic smarts

Collaborative and independent work features across the curriculum and teaching is student-centred. To 'really thrive' girls ideally will have completed at least one year of Middle Years Programme before moving on to the Diploma Programme, advises a staff member.

Class sizes are small, with around 12 students. Teaching we witnessed was engaging, relaxed and cheery. Girls use their own laptops in lessons: study plans, research, homework and progress are coordinated via school's intranet. Girls are guided but not spoon-fed: in a physics class groups were discussing conflicting results from a previous experiment: Why? What did it mean? Views shared, the teacher referred them back to their textbooks. A geography session on grid references for younger students was turned into an entertaining computer game with teams competing against one another. We also dropped in on some top-notch Mandarin Chinese teaching; an energetic teacher was imparting key food vocabulary, and students grappled with correct pronunciation of their favourite dishes.

Girls are attentive, confident learners who seem very tolerant and respectful of each other. No hand raising required as students spontaneously take turns to speak. Teachers will prompt but there seemed little hesitation or self-consciousness in these students coming forward. Small class sizes mean lots of attention and no question goes unanswered, although girls may well be encouraged to figure it out for themselves. 'They don't over-react,' says a mother who recognises her own daughter's propensity for 'robust' discussions, 'but they don't curb enthusiasm either.' Rapport with teachers appeared respectful, warm and friendly. 'I get good and helpful feedback on things,' said one student. 'Teachers are dedicated and devoted to their work,' says a father. 'Very caring and attentive to the child's strengths and weaknesses,' said another. Director of studies explains that the bespoke nature of the IB means all students can and do succeed.

Remarkable range of languages on offer as befits a diverse student body where 40 per cent opt for a bilingual diploma: school always keen to accommodate, even if tuition is via Skype or individually with a visiting 'external' tutor. Thai, Polish, Turkish, Korean, Dutch all currently on offer along with more regular fare such as French, Latin, German, Spanish and, of course, Chinese. Library about to undergo minor refit to make way for more foreign language books but clearly already a well-stocked and popular student resource.

Prep is 90 minutes per night. Boarders can do it before or after supper, depending on activities. Parents feel that demands of IB in final years significantly increase workload and local girls often choose to board then to maximise study time.

Learning support and SEN: A handful of girls have learning difficulties and school says it offers differentiated work in classroom as well as individual or small group help on a 'needs' basis. One mother felt that while learning support had definitely been upgraded under current head, there was still room for improvement as quality of differentiated classroom teaching could be variable.

The arts and extracurricular: Dance and theatre are popular options and offered at diploma level. Sparkly brand-new dance studio open for business and although exterior looks rather utilitarian in arcadian Marymount setting, interior is tiptop. Girls were gently being led through a modern jazz routine on our visit: clear mix of abilities on the dance floor and no refuseniks. Royal Society dance exams available and LAMDA taught too. School assembly previewed upcoming musical with high-kicking dance routine garnering much enthusiastic applause. Last year's offering of Hairspray proved a triumph, its success prompting a switch to yearly rather than biennial productions.

Girls were gently being led through a modern jazz routine on our visit: clear mix of abilities on the dance floor and no refuseniks. Royal Society dance exams available

Music per se clearly enjoyed, especially choir with over 40 girls taking part, and is seen as intrinsic to spiritual life of school. Instrumental tuition catered for and five practice rooms available but musicians hankering after the full symphony or big band experience should look elsewhere: current orchestra numbers just 10.

Art is taught as part of IB and not all about the portfolio but also marketing and presentation skills culminating in girls organising a show in a London gallery. Emphasis is on conceptual art: one student made a life-size plaster cast of a horse. Art rooms are well-equipped, light, spacious and artistically messy in a good way.

Creativity, Activity, Service (CAS) is one of the three essential elements that every student must complete as part of the Diploma Programme. All grades participate and are obliged to write up a 'meaningful reflection' afterwards. School operates on a Monday to Friday week but every Saturday morning in term time 15-20 local primary children are picked up by Marymount bus to attend 'enrichment' programme. Organised and taught by girls (under supervision): a recent session tempering chocolate had apparently been 'a lot of fun'. Community clean-up events, imaginative charity fundraising and individual projects flourish: one student collected unwanted spectacles and teamed with a local optician to offer free eye tests and glasses for the homeless. We noticed boxes of sanitary products in one corridor that girls were donating to charity: a house competition was in play to see which could supply the most.

For a small school, Marymount packs a big punch with an impressive range of student-led activities. Numerous committees and societies to get involved with and if nothing appeals the Marymount can-do attitude prevails and girls encouraged to set up a new one. Lots of badges proudly worn on blazers testify to membership of different groups.

Sport: No yawning expanse of green playing fields to contemplate, but decent tennis courts and a large sports complex accommodates volleyball, soccer, basketball and badminton. Teams compete internationally and with other London schools: trophy case is full, says school. Perhaps not quite up to the cut and thrust of some competitive sporty secondaries, with at least one girl underwhelmed on arrival according to her mother: 'She came from a really large independent and it did not compare well.' No lacrosse or hockey and no pool on campus, but despite this the school does have a swim team with day girls training elsewhere and competing under Marymount banner. Group of upbeat boarders we spoke to insisted trips to local municipal pool also an option and likewise horse riding, golf and fencing are all possible by arrangement.

Boarding: About a third board with biggest uptake in later years. Full, weekly and even occasional sleepovers catered for. Out of bounds during class time, accommodation is modern and comfortable and like everything else at Marymount, all spick and span. Girls room primarily in twos, but some threes; in IB years they can get an upgrade to single room with shared ensuite bathroom. Students do their own laundry (apart from uniform blouses) and change their own beds. Blazers conveniently handed in for a dry clean at end of every school year. Rooms we saw were filled with family photos and study aides-memoires. Lots of international boarders, head of boarding told us: 'It can be hard for some girls to be so far away from parents and we try and make it a home.' Weekend activities include a recent Harry Potter trip, and the school chefs are sometimes roped in for impromptu cupcake icing or even a risotto-making session. A boarding council organises regular themed weekend dinners with quiz afterwards – girls divide themselves by age into 'families' and fierce but enjoyable competition ensues to claim winner's crown – staff lend a hand and provide token prizes.

Sunday morning service obligatory in school chapel. No students allowed off campus without express parental permission: shopping trips in nearby Kingston popular. Overwhelming perception of Marymount from appreciative parents is a safe, protective and nurturing place: 'My daughter is very happy and quickly built up a sense of belonging,' said one. 'Staff foster a very warm and caring environment,' summed up another.

Ethos and heritage: Marymount is part of an international Catholic network of schools founded by Sisters of the Religious Sacred Heart of Mary. The congregation started in 1849 in Beziers, France, formed by Father Jean Gailhac and Mother St

Jean Cure. First school established in 1907 in Tarrytown, New York and since then around the globe. Marymount retains close links within the network and girls regularly visit Rome and Paris schools.

School sits on Coombe estate, a wealthy enclave of Kingston upon Thames. Sisters bought site in 1955 and lived there for over sixty years. In 1988 they hosted Mother Teresa of Calcutta, who arrived by helicopter and joined students in prayer and hymn singing. Marymount is now under lay leadership, but Sisters retain an advisory capacity as governors.

The original property has undergone many changes: chalet-style classrooms and light wood interiors all add up to a clean Scandinavian feel while the six-acre manicured gardens make for a very English backdrop. Climbing trees is allowed and classes often held outside in warmer weather. Attractive dining hall equipped with fold-back doors makes al fresco dining a regular summer treat. Location is a handy one for international students with easy access to Heathrow and also good rail links into central London.

Atmosphere is happy, relaxed and friendly. Girls go about their business without fuss and seem to rub along amiably together. Lunchtime scrum in canteen however was slightly alarming when our reviewer got caught up in the maelstrom. Not typical, says school, it was unusually busy due to lunchtime talk. Attendance at all meals is obligatory and decidedly worth entering the fray for, judging by our tasty vegetarian haul. Girls decided to implement meat-free Monday and consensus on food is generally favourable. No puddings in evidence but large mound of fruit available. Mid-morning savoury snacks too, pizza on day we were there, plus a sweet treat in the afternoon.

Pupils present as fresh-faced and good company. Uniform is worn comfortably, if a little crumpled round the edges, skirt lengths all very respectable. Room for individuality too, with one student clearly attached to her pompom hat indoors and out, albeit a regulation school one. Gentle enquiries uncovered no serious hardships. 'I was told to change my earrings – a bit too big,' one girl concedes. 'Only natural looking nail varnish allowed,' volunteers another. Celebrations and festivals punctuate the school year: onesie day coming up soon and Halloween always an occasion. Summer graduation ceremony follows Catholic high school tradition with girls donning white gowns and carrying bouquets. Older girls we spoke to were perceptive and remarkably down to earth. Focused on their final exam year, they felt they had been well prepared and were waiting to hear back about university offers with a mixture of trepidation and excitement.

Pastoral care, inclusivity and discipline: Teachers act as a sounding boards for girls, but parents impressed by non-teaching staff too: 'pleasant, kind and reliable' is the prevailing view. 'I know one of the canteen servers looks out for my daughter,' said a grateful mum. 'Always keen to look after the girls and very helpful,' was another comment.

Marymount is not run at the helter-skelter pace of some other institutions and the girls appear all the happier for that. Each grade has an annual retreat for a few days of inner reflection. 'The school has the rare ability to nurture the individual,' believes one parent. 'Definitely know what's going on and take an interest in each individual girl,' echoed another. 'They [staff] are watching you,' said an older pupil, 'they want to help you out.'

Out of bounds during class time, accommodation is modern and comfortable and like everything else at Marymount, all spick and span

Very detailed behaviour policy published on website. One mum recounted her daughter being pulled up for use of a swearword; another agreed that boarders' movements are 'very strictly regulated', but parents are delighted with pastoral care and girls seem at ease.

Pupils and parents: Rolling admissions and international clientele result in student flux: one girl had just arrived mid-term, but peers clearly welcoming. Students appear genuinely proud of cultural diversity and international friends they have. Around 40 per cent are British and broad spread of nationalities makes up the balance. International Day is a highlight where everyone shares their culture and cuisine and parents are welcomed into school for the celebration.

Parents' association hosts a fundraising summer barbecue and Christmas fair. School throws a party at the start of academic year allowing day and boarding parents to get together. Invitations to talks at school roll out throughout the year and the day we visited parents were invited to the same internet security presentation their children had just had. Alumnae are also invited to share in Marymount celebrations and girls have been known to return to school to marry in chapel. Wikipedia throws up a couple of vaguely interesting old girls but school prefers not to mention names.

Money matters: Some means-tested bursaries are available up to 100 per cent of fees. 'We want to be generous,' says school.

The last word: Marymount is not a school in a rush. Girls are allowed space and time to mature emotionally and intellectually at a gentler pace than elsewhere. Lack of GCSEs might be a problem if anyone wanted to spread their wings for sixth form but evidently few opt to do so. 'My daughter went from being miserable to super-confident,' said a very grateful mum. Another just said: 'Thank God for Marymount!'

Mayfield School
RC
47
The Old Palace, High Street, Mayfield, East Sussex TN20 6PH
01435 874600 | registrar@mayfieldgirls.org | www.mayfieldgirls.org
Ages: 11-18
Pupils: 406; sixth form: 104; Boarders: 149 full, 17 flexi
Fees: Day £23,250; Boarding £36,750 pa

Headmistress: Since 2008, Antonia Beary, previously deputy head here, and before that at New Hall, Ampleforth and The Leys. Read English at Cambridge. Devoted to the school and its pupils, and determined to inspire her girls to do anything: 'they don't have to be something safe or obvious [in their careers]'. Hear hear.

In assembly, challenges Britain's Got Talent as lamentably failing to model good behaviour or taste; in fact, encourages the girls to challenge lots of things on a regular basis. Parents are confident that she handles the school well, and impressed at her knowledge of every child. 'Delightful head... very professional,' said one; 'slightly eccentric... has helped us so much,' said another. 'Girls like her, but have a healthy respect for her,' said a dad, adding that his daughter is happy to write or speak to the head if things go wrong.

Entrance: At 11+, 13+ and 16+. Gently selective, but largely on the basis of fit: pupils attend a two-day assessment, which includes papers in English, maths and verbal reasoning, and fun activities (ISEB pre-test for 11+). Less good performance in one area can be compensated for by excelling in others.

For sixth form entry, pupils take exams in two of the subjects they wish to study at A level, and a general paper. Pupils must get at least six GCSEs at 6+, with 6+ in the subjects they wish to study at A level.

Exit: Up to 20 per cent leave after GCSEs. Most popular university destinations include Bristol, Durham, Edinburgh, Exeter, Imperial, Leeds, Manchester, UCL and York. In 2021, one to Oxbridge, one medic and one overseas to University of Groningen.

Latest results: In 2021, 87 per cent 9-7 at GCSE; 79 per cent A*/A at A level (94 per cent A*-B). In 2019 (the last year when exams took place), 68 per cent 9-7 at GCSE; 56 per cent A*/A at A level (75 per cent A*-B).

Teaching and learning: 'Some absolutely amazing teachers,' said a parent, who told us about staff who have 'engaged and enthused' her daughter in subjects she didn't like. 'I feel that teachers really know my children,' added another. A good number of top end results at this gently selective school. The school is in the top 20 per cent of value added schools, adding at least one grade onto pupils' expected scores.

Maths, chemistry and biology are very popular here, determinedly bucking the trend for girls to choose more humanities. The head says it is important to create an environment where girls can make mistakes, and the approach to learning maths at Mayfield is based on this: 'Maths is brilliant,' confirmed a parent. Geography is also a favourite – 'we're evangelical about geography'. RS is 'very lively', say the girls, and a parent who described herself as a committed atheist said how much her children enjoy this subject: plenty of challenge and discussion.

Lessons of quiet, determined concentration, though an excited physics teacher showed us a burst of air pinging out of a bucket, to the slight embarrassment of our guides.

Most pupils take 11 GCSEs, which must include a language. Class numbers in lower school are up to 15, with up to 12 in A level classes.

Pupils here happily mix subjects, splitting their time between sciences and arts, for instance, and the school prides itself on not labelling pupils and persuading them to choose options accordingly. One parent felt that that girls should be guided towards studying their strengths, but other parents like the open choice at A level – 'I knew the girls would struggle to choose, but it was important it was their choice.' We love the idea of the subject fair, with teachers pitching their subjects to girls. A wonderful way of keeping teachers on their toes (as is their habit of getting girls to help interview new staff).

One parent said she was 'worried they wouldn't push kids enough', but they have been 'brilliant at handling different levels of maths, and pushing them where necessary'. Subject clinics are open door and well attended, and pupils describe teachers willing to put in extra time. New sixth form enrichment programme with options ranging from global perspectives to farming and land management to diploma in culinary skills and the art of effective communication, plus an Erasmus research project.

Small lower school library, much liked by the younger girls, who felt that the upheaval of changing schools was helped by having their own safe area away from the rest of the school, and a well-stocked main library for years 9 upwards (New Scientist, Psychology Review, Pharmaceutical Tech and The Tablet).

The head wants to create an environment where girls can make mistakes, and the approach to learning maths is based on this: 'Maths is brilliant,' said a parent

Swish new sixth form centre, complete with kitchen and 'friends' common room'. Lovely views over the countryside, study rooms with designated desks, and intimate classrooms. Own clothes for sixth formers, but no jeans or leggings. A small room overlooking the chapel with beanbags and candles for quiet moments of reflection.

Lower school diploma recently introduced for years 7 and 8 to develop 'soft' skills including teamwork, problem solving and resilience, alongside their academic education.

Learning support and SEN: Around 40 pupils receive SEN help, which in this school can be anything from assistance with a particular problem, to help for dyslexic pupils or extra work for gifted and talented. 'No extra time in the real world,' says the head, and the unit aims to give pupils strategies to deal with and make the most of their talents. A parent whose friend's daughter attended the unit raved about it: 'They have a very practical way of helping with difficulties.'

'No negativity smudge,' said a parent; 'so many use [the unit] one way or another.' Help is usually on a one-to-one basis out of class. Charged as an extra. Dyslexic pupils achieve at the same rate as other pupils.

The arts and extracurricular: Plenty of trips, including one to Cambodia to teach children English – 'an extraordinary initiative,' said a parent, with teachers managing to fit teaching TEFL to pupils into the school day. 'I was gobsmacked,' said a parent, who said the trip has led on to so many things, such as designing a T-shirt, and a video workshop so that pupils could compile video libraries while away.

Two-thirds of pupils here learn an instrument, and many play them in the orchestra. Several choirs, the more selective ones singing at illustrious venues, such as Westminster Abbey. Regular school productions, and both LAMDA and GCSE drama are popular, though there are fewer takers at A level. It all takes place in the new music and drama centre.

A vast range of options available, with activity sessions built into each school day – compulsory down time. There's even a farm club with livestock – though the last residents have just been eaten.

Food and nutrition is 'quite splendid', said a parent, and compulsory in years 7-9, on the basis that however brilliant your mind, you can't function in life without a healthy body. There's a session every Saturday morning for boarders, and how to eat well on a budget is part of the life skills course for sixth formers (roux sauce and making bread – no white slice at uni for Mayfield girls).

Exceptionally beautiful artwork on display around the school, with some lovely ceramics: a pot modelled on church architecture captures the feeling of a soaring church roof, and butterflies fly from the edges of a ceramic goldfish bowl. A dress inspired by WWI is made of teabags and luggage labels; a half-decomposed shirt shows the stress and texture of the material.

Sport: Sports are extremely popular, and there's everything imaginable here, though some, such as football, are extracurricular options. The usual compulsory sports in years 7- 9, with free choice after that (Pilates, fitness room and zumba become options at this stage). Girls decided they wanted to learn kickboxing, and a couple of months later it was up and running – 'an incredibly responsive school,' said a parent. Cricket now an option with coaching by a former England player. Riding is immensely popular: pupils can bring their own horse to school, or take part in a horse share. Fabulous equestrian facilities on campus – pupils ride at national level. All have a chance to represent the school in matches if they want to, and netball is popular even with the girls who find it difficult. One parent described how her daughter was awarded a muffin when she scored in netball – 'Her ball skills were so abysmal,' she cheerfully explained, 'they didn't think it would happen again.'

Boarding: Around 50 per cent of pupils are boarders, divided into four houses by age. 'The school is ultra flexible about adding extra nights,' said an appreciative parent. Junior houses have comfortably sized rooms for two, three and four, with beds for anyone who boards more than two nights a week, bunkbeds for the odd night flexi boarder. All rooms have basins. Common room of colourful squashy sofas, Wii and TV; lovely to see a dressing-up box.

Catholicism underpins the supportive, caring atmosphere. Pupils have to attend liturgy (some think it's boring; some like the space to be quiet and think), and boarders must go to mass on Sundays. But the Catholic ethos is applied gently, and often with cake

Plenty going on: a crammed noticeboard includes details of a trip to the Harry Potter studios and an animal rescue centre, and Pride and Prejudice catch-up night; two-thirds of boarders are around at weekends to enjoy activities. Fruit, toast and cereal are always available in the kitchen, where a map of the world – 'where do you come from?' – shows a wide spread of flags.

'Rooms are quite nice,' said a parent, 'but it's the personalities that make [the boarding experience],' describing his daughter's slightly eccentric housemistress who enjoys extreme sport – 'a great role model,' he said with enthusiasm. 'They love and respect her in equal measure.'

Sixth form boarding, in St Dunstan's, is spread across the top floor of the old school in four areas, with around 20 pupils in each. Over 60 sixth form boarders, of whom 50 or so are full time. (Anything over three nights is full time, because this encourages pupils to stay for the weekend, which makes a better atmosphere.) Good-sized individual study bedrooms. Considerable freedom and responsibility for sixth formers, who are allowed up to London at weekends, and into Tunbridge Wells by bus.

No work on Friday night – movies, popcorn and mocktails; 'food is important to these girls,' said the housemistress. Brunch in house on Sundays: pupils turn up in their pyjamas for waffles and eggs of all sorts.

Laundry is done for younger ones, with pupils gradually assuming more responsibility, until they are doing their own in sixth form.

An overseas parent was full of praise for the care her homesick daughter received from the housemistress: she was confident that the school would email her straight away with any problems, and they respond immediately to any emails from her. Her daughter keeps in touch by telephone and Skype (mobile signal comes and goes). Transport home is arranged well.

Ethos and heritage: One parent said that the moment her girls walked into the site they loved it: 'They saw the school in action and were enchanted by it.' It offered something to both her girls, the more academic and the less so. Another said that the surroundings and small size of the school attracted them – 'everyone knows each other'.

The religious backbone of this Catholic school underpins the supportive, caring atmosphere. Pupils are of any or no faith, but they do have to attend liturgy (some think it's boring; some like the space to be quiet and think), and boarders must go to mass on Sundays. But the Catholic ethos is applied gently, and often with cake – the history teacher described attending mass at a church in France on a school trip, and the delight of going to the patisserie next door for cream cakes afterwards.

Community service, in the Actions not Words programme, is 'a fundamental part of who we are,' says the head. This sees girls working at a local primary school or an old people's home, or helping with riding for the disabled. 'I think they benefit more from doing it than the people they help,' said a member of staff thoughtfully, explaining how important it is for girls to look beyond themselves.

Most parents are happy with the single sex environment, one saying that she felt girls don't want to appear cleverer than boys – 'I don't want them to have to bother to look after male egos…' The head says the girls value the space to be themselves, and they also have social and academic engagement with nearby boys' schools. But it's not exclusively female here: there are male teachers in nearly every department.

'Food is important to these girls,' said the housemistress. Brunch in house on Sundays: pupils turn up in their pyjamas for waffles and eggs of all sorts

Plenty of smiles and good manners from pupils. 'They develop the whole person,' said a parent, who felt that girls from other schools are not as well rounded or comfortable with themselves and adults. 'They are good academically, but there is not too much pressure,' said another. Girls here are competitive, and there is certainly vigorous competition between the houses, but 'resilient, not bloodthirsty', said a member of staff.

Food is good: since the new chef arrived 'they come home raving about it'. Changes are made in response to suggestions in the food comment books: the request for savoury snacks at break time resulted in the delights of cheese scones and sausage rolls.

Beautiful buildings and grounds, once a palace for an archbishop, discovered by the school's founder when she took her girls on a picnic from the school, then situated in St Leonards. The chapel is ancient and movingly plain. At Christmas, the village cluster in for the live crib – baby, donkey and all, the angel Gabriel singing from a balcony. The Hub (café) is the centre of the school, and many pupils' favourite place (for good reason: deluxe hot chocolate, doughnuts, and blue raspberry slush, with healthy snacks besides).

The school puts itself out for parents – one parent said that when they were unable to make the last parents' day, the school gathered all the teachers for a tailor-made alternative meeting. Another confirmed that 'if we're unhappy about anything, an email or phone call gets an immediate response'.

Pastoral care, inclusivity and discipline: Pastoral care is the particular responsibility of the deputy head, who is quick to point out that actually it is a responsibility of each teacher here. This works, emails shooting around between teachers, boarding mistresses and parents so that any problems are quickly picked up. There are plenty of people for pupils to talk to: tutors, the head of pastoral care, the school counsellor, the chaplain – and two members of staff additionally trained in counselling, one in CBT, the other a humanist. 'Care of pupils here gives stability. I feel teachers will listen to any problems they have,' said a parent.

Tutor groups in the middle school stay the same for three years, which means the eight girls get to know each other really well. Girls are good at looking out for each other, one teacher telling us that some girls came to see her, anxious that one of their friends was skipping meals. This school is extremely aware of the various conditions which can affect teenage girls, and staff are ever vigilant.

The head is keen to teach girls coping skills – 'In the real world they are going to meet difficult and dominating people… if they're wrapped in cotton wool, they won't be able to cope.' True to this, a parent said bullying behaviour is often 'cut off at source by the girls'. But systems are also in place to capture anything untoward, from general unhappiness onwards – 'they're very vigilant,' said a parent, who described a conflict between girls, efficiently sorted out by the housemistress.

Disciplinary measures are rarely needed here, though accumulated bad marks would result in detention, where you sit in silence and consider the implications of your crime. No one has been excluded in the past year, though persistent disruptive behaviour could lead to a mutual conclusion that a girl would be better placed elsewhere. Selling drugs would result in immediate exclusion; a contrite drug user would probably be given a second chance. Behaviour out of school must be as responsible as in, and things that happen out of school will have implications inside.

Pupils and parents: 'You won't find old girls on the cover of Hello,' said the head. 'They will be influential, but this is not the cult of the celebrity.' The large variety of families at this school is reflected in the mixed entry, with 50 per cent from state primaries and the rest from local preps, with a small number from overseas.

Money matters: Seven full bursaries, one in each year group, and scholarships worth 10-20 per cent of fees.

The last word: A great all-round school with high academic standards, extensive extracurricular and the outward-looking expectation that its pupils will enrich the lives of others, both at school and beyond. A parent said: 'They get so much right. Would recommend to anyone. Sheer awe…'

Mill Hill School

The Ridgeway, Mill Hill Village, London NW7 1QS

020 8959 1176 | angela@millhill.org.uk | www.millhill.org.uk/?utm_source=goodschoolsguide&utm_medium=review&utm_campaign=millhill

Ages: 13–18

Pupils: 885; sixth form: 347 (boys 227; girls 120); Boarders: 90 full, 19 weekly

Fees: Day £22,830 pa; Boarding £31,140 – £36,900 pa

Head: Since December 2018, Jane Sanchez BA PGCE. Raised in the Midlands, she studied geography and qualified as a teacher (in geography and PE) at Sheffield University. After a stint at a community college, she taught in Argentina for four years, then, for nearly a decade, headed the PE and careers departments (while teaching geography) at top-flight girls' grammar school Henrietta Barnett. This was followed by a time as director of sport at specialist sports college Whitefield School, as school facing 'extra challenging circumstances'. 'There aren't many areas I haven't had to deal with,' she says, 'and that helps me understand what's needed is balance.'

Since her arrival at Mill Hill in 2003 as pastoral deputy head, her experience has been extended in a wide range of roles, but always with a strong emphasis on the wellbeing of pupils. Considered very down-to-earth, visible and approachable, she clearly also has a good sense of fun, starring in an April Fool's prank as a concert pianist. 'I like her a lot,' says one parent. 'She's very sensible.' Two adult children, both of whom attended the school.

Entrance: At 13+, 176 enter – including 130 moving up from the prep school, Belmont, 70 of whom join in year 7. Common Entrance no longer required for those transferring, but the 140 or so who apply for 30-40 available year 9 slots are pre-tested in year 6 (by computerised tests and interview). Most stay on for sixth form, when entrance for existing students in line with external candidates, but evaluated on a case-by-case basis. Incomers – after positive feedback from their current school – are invited for interview and expected to achieve at least two grade 7s and three grade 6s with specified grades in their intended A level subjects.

Exit: Recent destinations include Bristol, Nottingham, Manchester, Exeter, Imperial, UCL, Birmingham, Leeds, Edinburgh, King's and LSE. Usually several overseas – recently to Chapman University, USA; Vrije Amsterdam; Hong Kong University of Science and Technology. Subject choice unusually wide-ranging, from traditional professions like law and journalism to aeronautics and film and directing. Two to Oxbridge, and four medics in 2021.

Latest results: In 2021, 97 per cent 9-7 at GCSE; 66 per cent A*/A at A level (89 per cent A*-B). In 2019 (the last year when exams took place), 57 per cent 9-7 at GCSE; 35 per cent A*/A at A level.

Teaching and learning: Very solid exam results throughout. No weak spots. Since her appointment, the head has rethought the timetable, reducing lessons from 50 to 40 minutes to aid concentration and allow an extra period in the day. 'It gives more time for each subject,' says the head, 'and has allowed us to make RS, very popular here, a stand-alone subject.'

At GCSE, English (lang and lit), maths and science (just under half take all three) are the compulsory core, with French, German and Spanish the language selection. After that, as well at the regular range of humanities, students can opt for classical civilisaton, computer science, PE, music, DT and ICT. At A Level, popular choices include: business, economics, geography and psychology. The EPQ is available but not widely taken as the most academically able are steered to a subject-specific Oxbridge preparation programme.

Teaching overall considered challenging and stimulating, and warm and supportive relationships between staff and pupils encourage the shy or reticent to find their voice. 'Extension' supplied by challenging in-class work, regular lectures, debates, workshops and participation in the Sir James Murray Society (where a recent student-led debate analysed the statement 'We should not be at the mercy of our emotions'). The particularly able or interested are given mentoring and regular challenges. 'There are many bright, motivated pupils and I've seen that they stretch them in the right way,' said one mother. Some parents, however, (and the last school inspectors) consider not every lesson is as exciting as it might be and marking could occasionally be more focused to maximise progress.

Learning support and SEN: SEN is a strength, with a full team including head of learning support, two part-time teachers and four assistants, who occupy four well-resourced rooms and oversee individual and small-group support as well as liaising closely with teachers to ensure they receive appropriate intervention in lessons. English language instruction for international students is supportive and positive, and those we spoke to, who'd often started out with very basic skills, had acquired a strong command of the language.

The arts and extracurricular: Music, art and drama are vibrant. Energetic participation in music at individual and group level. Singing notably strong ('Mill Hill,' says a recent magazine entry correctly, 'is a school that sings'), and there is a multitude of opportunities to give voice, from the 'Big Sing' building community spirit with an inspiring new hymn book, to the Farrow singing competition and the annual school musical. School orchestra performs significant works, such as Vivaldi's Gloria, and future maestri and maestre encouraged with annual composition prize. Instrumentalists participate in instrumental competitions, chamber groups, masterclasses, jazz soirée and twice-weekly informal coffee concerts, while school clubs extend performance opportunities with jazz band, percussion, shout band, music tech, wind band and ukulele. Music scholars – who've gone on to glory in the National Youth Orchestra, National Choir and National German Music competition – get specialist attention, with masterclasses taken at the Junior Guildhall. 'The music department is like an extension of my family,' said one. 'They've supported and encouraged me in everything I've done.'

Drama lively, with a carousel of theatre trips, including to productions featuring Old Millhillians. Art and DT have spacious, well-equipped space, and art extends well beyond the studio with year 9's self-portrait ceramic heads – à la Antony Gormley – on show in the school chapel to become a focus for services and sixth formers' work vaunted in dedicated private view.

Creative thinking encouraged for all in the 'Big Idea', an inter-house competition to improve school life assessed by Dragons' Den-type finale. More than 150 clubs and activities cater to virtually every interest, from feminism and Model United Nations to horticulture, Hispanic theatre and touch typing. CCF particularly strong with about 150 smartly clad cadets filling the campus after lessons, and annual general inspection, chapel service, and holiday camps. Endless relay of work-related and pleasure trips – business studies to China, physics to CERN, DT to Jaguar Land Rover, ski trip to USA. Annual summer-term activities week offers a further multitude of adventures to expand the mind. 'There's so much to do here, it sometimes feels like it's hard to fit it all in,' said one year 10.

Sport: Mill Hill has a well-deserved reputation for developing the whole pupil through its outstanding extracurricular offering, but sport is the jewel in the crown. As one Oxford-bound sixth former accurately put it, 'Sport here is huge.'

International boarders appreciate the school's proximity to central London – 'We love going shopping on the weekends,' said one – and its cosmopolitan atmosphere

The department has recently been boosted by the catch-your-breath energy of director of sport and the introduction of 11 impressive new coaches (including two professional women rugby players from Saracens Women). National aspirations abound. Until a few years ago, the school had a Saturday timetable combining lessons and sports fixtures, but the academic side is now confined to GCSE and A level workshops and weekends (including Sundays) have been freed for fixtures. Virtually all participate in competition, with 95 per cent of year 9s involved in a school team. Main boys' sports are rugby (with national level players), hockey, football and cricket. Girls' sport as strong as the boys', and girls play hockey, netball, rounders and cricket (with old girl Sophia Dunkley recently selected for the England squad), but not football. Girls, like the boys, also excel at fives, with U14 and U15 players ranking in the top 10 in the country. Girls' aspirations and achievements recognised in girls' sports dinner, and (perhaps!) encouraged by mums' netball competition.

Talented sportsmen and women – identified through sports scholarships at 13 and 16 – are carefully nurtured (with specialist instruction in nutrition, strength and conditioning, video analysis, golf and tennis academies), and pupils participate at high competitive level in individual sports including riding (at nearby stable), shooting, golf, tennis, bouldering (GB junior team member) and sailing. Less common team sports like basketball and volleyball (in which the school recently fielded a team in the England volleyball U18 national championships) offer a broad scope for enthusiasm. Excellent facilities for everything with a multitude of pitches (including Astroturf), courts, golf centre and pool, and impressive sports trips (rugby to Japan, for example) provide exceptional opportunities, particularly for what is predominantly a day school.

Boarding: Mill Hill started life as a boarding school, but as local boarding teetered on extinction, a sustained campaign abroad led to a powerful resurgence. Now boarding houses are full again with international as well as weekly boarders. Five boarding houses (girls-only, boys-only and mixed), a short walk from the main buildings, are comfortable and up to date, furnished with triple, double and single bedrooms (depending on seniority). Meals are taken in the school dining room, but each house has a kitchen for snacks. International boarders appreciate the school's proximity to central London – 'We love going shopping on the weekends,' said one – and its cosmopolitan atmosphere. 'Before I came here, I went to a boarding school in the country where I was the only non-English pupil; I felt very uncomfortable,' commented one. 'I am much happier here.'

Ethos and heritage: Founded in 1807 by non-conformist reformers, the Mill Hill School Foundation now encompasses a family of schools – pre-prep (Grimsdell), prep school (Belmont), and international boarding (The Mount, Mill Hill International) – that provide a smooth transition to the senior school. Together the schools occupy 150 acres of green belt and, though only half an hour from central London, offer a semi-rural refuge of green and pleasant space and fresh country air. Now overseen by a single CEO, the foundation schools share a united mission – to produce 'a strong sense of community in which the academic and co-curricular provide a challenging and stimulating environment in which to learn the skills which play a key part in future success and happiness'. 'The modern working world is not just about exams,' says the head. 'Employers today are looking for the ability to lead, to tackle challenges, to live with integrity, honesty and fairness.'

If a physical environment can contribute to these objectives, then pupils here are particularly blessed. The original school house of 1825 – by London Royal Exchange architect Sir William Tite – provides an elegant neo-classical centre, where pupils meet for meals in the tall-windowed dining hall. This is complemented by an impressive catalogue of satellite buildings, ranging from the Basil Champneys-designed chapel with its soaring coffered ceiling to the delightful arts and crafts library and thoroughly modernist humanities and modern languages building. The gardens, too, are undoubtedly 'worth a detour', containing specimens originally planted by renowned 18th-century botanist Peter Collinson, including Britain's first hydrangea.

Sports department recently boosted by the catch-your-breath energy of director of sport and 11 impressive new coaches (including two professional women rugby players from Saracens Women)

Mill Hill originated as an all-boys boarding school, introducing the first girls into the sixth form in the 1970s; today, it's primarily a coeducational day school (with full and weekly boarding also available), but the girl-boy balance remains weighted two-thirds in favour of boys. 'You notice it, but it's never an issue,' says one girl. Some subjects (like science and history) still boy-dominated, but languages, maths and English fairly evenly split. 'It's realistic, like in the real world,' said a pupil. Both sexes feel the mix works. 'There's a really good relationship between the boys and the girls,' said one boy. 'It's a lot more relaxed, less intense in the classroom,' said a girl – 'competitive, but in a healthy way.'

Numbers continue to grow and in 2014 Mill Hill launched The Mount, Mill Hill International, its own self-contained international school, where students from nearly 30 countries (including the UK) come to sit GCSEs (in one year or two) or undertake an intensive English programme, in many instances proceeding to the main school for sixth form. Taught in their own attractive building (a former girls' school) less than half a mile away, pupils here use many of the main school facilities and boarders share boarding houses.

Still a non-conformist Christian foundation with timetabled weekly chapel, today the school welcomes all faiths and none. 'Giving back', however, remains very much part of the ethos and pupils are involved in regular fundraising activities and community action, much of it delivered through the school-wide charity committee. Strong links, too, with the London Academy of Excellence, a state sixth-form college in Tottenham, and neighbouring girls' comprehensive Copthall School, who share joint enrichment activities, and with overseas partnership schools in Tamil Nadu and Zambia.

Pupils generally happy and upbeat. 'It's a very happy place,' commented more than one parent – and few complaints even on traditional peeves. 'You're supposed to hate the food, but the food is really good here,' said one year 11, after being pressed on any dislikes.

Pastoral care, inclusivity and discipline: Eighty-five per cent of pupils arrive daily and are looked after through a day-house system, with eight mixed houses of 80-90, each with a games room, quiet study room, lockers and housemaster or mistress's office. House tutors take responsibility for the pastoral care of about 15 pupils. Wellbeing very high on the agenda, and a recently opened wellbeing wing is now its hub, home to two school counsellors, the director of PSHE, and head of pupil development, as well as the wellbeing room, a comfortably furnished, plant-filled space with soothing views of the rolling hills beyond. 'Mill Hill Minds', the student-led society formed to raise awareness of mental health, campaigned for the centre to be moved from a distant outpost. 'It used to be quite isolated, now there's a safe space where you can come at lunch, before school and after school.' Pupils very much involved in its operation, interviewing, for example, the new school counsellor. Mental health also promoted through wellbeing week and cross-school endeavours such as the Mill Hill Minds mural painted by pupils throughout the school.

Fairly traditional approach in other matters, so head boy and girl, heads of houses, smart uniform (business black for sixth formers, navy blue and tartan for younger years), and formal manners. ('Sorry sir,' was immediately forthcoming as we squeezed past a sixth former on a staircase.) Upper sixth given the freedom to leave at 12.30, timetable permitting, and, for those with a licence, parking is permitted.

Pupils and parents: An extensive bus route fetches and carries day pupils from affluent homes in a large swathe of north London. Eighty per cent come from no further than Hampstead, with outliers arriving from St John's Wood, Potters Bar and Northwood. Quite a few have a long-time family link with the school, and quite a few do the full stretch from nursery to 18. Pupils are confident, articulate and poised, very much a credit to the school's holistic approach.

Money matters: Scholarships and exhibitions (academic, sports, music, drama, art and design technology), available at 13 and 16, currently limited to 10 per cent fee reduction (though this is under review), but bursaries (for new entrants and those experiencing hardship) can make this up to 100 per cent. Some extra funding, too, for non-compulsory trips, courtesy of the generous Old Millhillians Association.

The last word: A vibrant, buzzing school, with a solid academic underpinning and an outstanding extracurricular programme producing confident, articulate, mature young people, who start adult life solidly grounded, positive and well informed. 'A very happy place to be' is the consensus of parents and pupils.

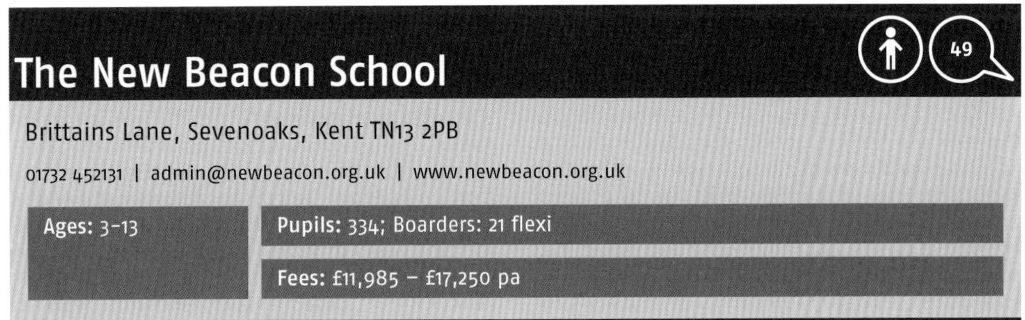

The New Beacon School

49

Brittains Lane, Sevenoaks, Kent TN13 2PB

01732 452131 | admin@newbeacon.org.uk | www.newbeacon.org.uk

Ages: 3–13

Pupils: 334; Boarders: 21 flexi

Fees: £11,985 – £17,250 pa

Headteacher: Since 2008, Mike Piercy BA (50s). Read English at Leicester. Two headships prior to this one – Moor Park Prep in Ludlow and Dunhurst, Bedales Prep, where he loved the liberal ethos. Previously deputy head at Forres Sandle Manor. Teaches English to all year 5s and runs a weekly drama activity group – 'a natural teacher,' said one parent. 'He's relaxed and well in control, popular, fair and a good speaker,' said another. Skilled at managing parental expectations. 'He is very professional but approachable and is a master at never crossing the line,' said one parent, 'and he is tough when he needs to be.' Another added that he is 'adept at managing high achieving parents with opinions and quietly sticks to his guns in a non-confrontational way.'

When not at his desk he enjoys going to the theatre, reading, skiing and armchair sport. He says that manners, kindness and respect are the keystones of the school and 'happiness breeds confidence and we all perform better when we are happy.' Not only did he get the online schooling up and running smoothly during the pandemic, but also allowed the school to facilitate a Covid testing assessment centre, used the school minibuses to deliver prescriptions and donned a high-vis jacket to help with the parking at the local vaccination centre.

Married to Lucy who teaches senior music; they have four children between them and live in a house in the grounds.

Entrance: Co-ed nursery with 24 places, available for children aged 3+. Most boys join in reception where entrance is non-selective and on a first come, first served basis. Tends to be oversubscribed so worth registering boys as soon as possible – occasionally a third reception class can be added if there is space. About 60 per cent of boys do the full nine years. Selective entry from year 3 with testing in reading, reasoning and maths. Those entering in year 5 are expected to commit to stay until 13+.

Exit: Sends to a wider range of schools than in the past, but Tonbridge (with which the school merged in 2021) then Sevenoaks are still the most popular, with increasing numbers to Caterham and a few each year to King's Canterbury, Sutton Valence and Eastbourne. Boys have moved on to 21 different schools in the past five years. About 20 per cent leave at 11+, mainly to the grammars and a few to Sevenoaks. 'The teachers are very good at talking to parents and choosing schools (and managing expectations) and take great trouble to get the school right,' said one parent. Impressive list of scholarships including academic, sport and music scholarships to Tonbridge for the last couple of years – all displayed on the boards in the dining room.

Our view: An all-boys school founded in 1863 at St John's Road, Sevenoaks and moved in January 1900 to its present purpose-built site in 21 acres on the outskirts of Sevenoaks. It stayed put during the war and even admitted girls for a while. The school was ahead of its time in many ways and introduced a pre-prep department and science, languages and maths laboratories as well as a parent-teacher association long before other schools in the area.

Everywhere well maintained with a rolling programme of refurbishment. The school makes good use of its relatively small site and the latest addition is the New Beacon Centre, a swanky new sports, arts and media centre with an auditorium, gallery, activity studio and technology zone. The chapel, built in 1912, only holds 100 boys – Friday evening service is compulsory for years 7 and 8

Varied extracurricular activities include chess taught by a grandmaster, model making, photography, shooting and athletics

and includes a talk from a visiting speaker, often from a senior school.

The school is proud of its academic tradition and has high standards and expectations. 'We ask boys to strive for personal excellence,' says the headmaster, but the school 'caters for all and boys are taught at the level they need,' said a parent. Boys don't feel 'over-pushed', said another. 'They get used to working hard and playing hard but they never feel under pressure; the school is very good at tailoring to an individual boy's needs.' 'Expect a lot and boys will surprise, expect a little and they will disappoint,' says the headmaster. Parents say it is 'very annoying' that the school has a reputation in the area for being a 'bit of a hothouse' as it is 'simply not true and there is a very good level of emotional and academic support'. The school works hard to develop confidence and self-belief and is good at spotting potential – 'My son would not get on the stage when he joined but now has the main part in the school play,' said a mother.

The online offering during the pandemic was 'very impressive', said a mother – 'There were lots of live lessons and assemblies and they got it just about right and were realistic about expectations.'

Pre-prep and reception housed in bright, airy purpose-built block with their own Astroturf playground. Some 14-16 per class and two members of staff – around half of all teachers are male. Specialist teachers in music, ICT, swimming and games. High expectations and firm boundaries and boys taught to respect each other's opinions from an early age. Taught health and hygiene and given a sticker for eating their veg. Good communications with staff mean parents feel they know how their children are progressing. Early years highly praised by the inspectors, who say all teachers have a good understanding of how young children learn.

The prep school is divided into three distinct sections: the junior school for years 3 and 4 with its own building, the middle school for years 5 and 6 and the senior school for the top two years. Usually about 45 boys per year group with an average class size of 15, but sometimes up to 20. Streaming from year 5, but flexible approach and movement between streams if required. A scholarship class is added in year 8 and the high achieving Common Entrance boys are streamed, with the other two classes being mixed ability. Boys have specialist teachers from year 4 and are given increased independence from year 5, when they start moving classrooms for lessons. ICT ties in with all subjects and 'it's fun,' said a boy. French introduced in year 5 and the brightest start Latin in year 6. Classical Greek and Mandarin offered as after-school clubs from year 6. Sciences taught separately in well-equipped labs from year 5. As many senior schools are moving away from Common Entrance, the school has become increasingly creative in its teaching for the top two years, including critical thinking and philosophy as well as an extended project and live presentations. There is lots of debate and discussion around discernment and judgement and how to spot fake news but exam technique and work ethic are still firmly on the curriculum. The staff are a good mix of age and experience and about 75 per cent have been at the school for at least 10 years. The teachers know the boys well, said a parent, and the reports are very 'insightful'. 'The teachers are very open,' said a boy. 'We can ask questions and they don't bite your head off if you get it wrong.' 'I like the fact there are no girls around – it is more relaxing and it means the teachers focus on you.'

The boarding master runs a tight ship and boys do prep and music practice. 'My son gets much more done than he does at home,' said one mother

Well-used and well-stocked library in what was a 23 bed dormitory, headed by a librarian and assisted by a team of pupil librarians – boys are encouraged to read for pleasure. Wide range of outings including history trip to the National Portrait Gallery and Canterbury Cathedral, a geography trip to Iceland and the year 8 trip to France includes visits to Agincourt, Crécy and the Somme battlefields.

One full-time SEN teacher and two part-timers a well as maths specialists, EAL and others brought in as required. About 60 boys need some sort of SEN help and emphasis is on identification and support in the lower years – all are tested for dyslexia in year 3 although there are few surprises. Most taught in small groups but a handful has one-to-one support in year 5 and above.

Sport taken seriously with the usual rugby, football and cricket and the recent introduction of hockey on the new floodlit Astroturf (also used by the local community). Inevitably more focus on team than individual sports but some recent additions to the fixtures including inter-school swimming. Specialist teachers brought in for minor sports like judo and fencing, and sailing offered at a local reservoir. School works hard to find fixtures for the lower teams so everyone has the opportunity to play in a match. Loyal and enthusiastic bunch of parent and staff supporters. Sporting etiquette taken seriously and woe betide any boy who argues with the referee. 'The school has a good record of success in matches as is demonstrated by the abundance of silverware on display in the entrance hall. The school has produced some fine sportsmen in recent years including England cricketers Zak Crawley and Sam Billings, England rugby player Ben Earl and Olympian and modern pentathlete, Joseph Choong.

The head's particular interests are music and drama and these have come on in leaps and bounds, but not at the expense of sport. The school aims to develop a love of music in the boys, most learn an instrument and all sing – 'It is part of the culture, there is always something musical going on,' said a parent. Two lessons a week starting with the recorder in year 3 and the ukulele in year 6, and boys can learn to compose their own music from year 5. Purpose-built music and arts centre with space for whole-class teaching and smaller rooms for individual lessons and rehearsals. Wide range of ensembles including woodwind quintets, percussion groups and string quartets as well as the big band – boys get the chance to perform in all three parts of the school, with informal concerts most weeks and three big ones a year. Two choirs in the middle school, one inclusive and one selective, and year 6 and above can audition for the chapel choir. Choir trip every other year – boys have sung in St Mark's, Venice and at St Peter's, Rome. Each part of the school puts on a production once a year, with everyone involved. Lots of opportunities for standing up in public, including poetry recitations and debates, and the senior boys hold a Question Time.

Busy art department with its own kiln and opportunities for litho and screen printing. Some impressive artwork displayed around the school. The art room is well used and always open at lunchtimes. Well-equipped DT room including a laser cutter.

Varied extracurricular activities include chess taught by a grandmaster, model making, photography, shooting and athletics. 'It is not all about sport,' said a parent, and 'helps boys appreciate and respect different skills'. Strong sense of community and boys appear to genuinely celebrate each other's talents. Bullying is rare and is dealt with quickly and effectively and boys know who to turn to if they need support. Mental health is a central pillar of the school and boys are encouraged to talk about their feelings. Younger children can voice their concerns via a worry box and there is a confidential email address for older boys.

About 30-40 foreign national children whose parents have moved to the area or have been posted to the UK. 'The school is traditional but has quite an international feel,' says a parent. About 50 speak English as a second language and a handful need EAL assistance.

Early morning breakfast club from 7am to help working parents and after-school club until 6.30pm and boys are encouraged to do their prep at school.

Active parents' association puts on two or three events a year, including a summer ball, which give parents the opportunity to get to know each other. Old boys include high court judge Sir Guy Newey, ambassador Sir Sherard Cowper-Coles, First World War poet Siegfried Sassoon and Vice Admiral Sir Tim Laurence.

Boarding: Boarding offered from Monday to Thursday with space for 18 boarders – just a handful stay the full four nights. 'It's so civilised,' said a boy. 'It's just like home.' The boarding master runs a tight ship and boys do prep and music practice and take part in a well-structured evening activity programme. 'My son gets much more done than he does at home,' said one mother.

The last word: Many parents 'high achieving, aspirational professionals who drive large 4x4s and who are ambitious for their boys'. They choose New Beacon because it is clear about its mission of high expectations and academic tradition – there are very few unhappy parents here. 'There is not a day when I don't feel lucky to have my boys here,' says a parent.

Northbourne Park School

50

Betteshanger, Deal, Kent CT14 0NW

01304 611215 | office@northbournepark.com | www.northbournepark.com

Ages: 3-13

Pupils: 189; Boarders: 49 full/weekly/flexi

Fees: Day £9,105 – £17,346; Boarding £21,834 – £26,514 pa

Headmaster: Since 2015, Sebastian Rees (40s), a prep school man through and through. Attended Cumnor House and Cranleigh, and describes his time there as 'the best school years you could have'. Read languages at UCL, did his PGCE in primary education, lived in Spain for three years as an English teacher, then returned to England for a spell as assistant head at neighbouring Northbourne Primary before joining Junior King's School, Canterbury as director of studies. After six years he took up the post of head of prep at Seaford College, before the headship at Northbourne beckoned. No plans to move on – this is 'the dream job'. Married to Gillian, the head of the pre-prep here, with four grown-up children scattered hither and yon.

His mother is German, and his interests have always included languages, 'the value of which,' he says, 'is immeasurable'. Also likes making things, eg furniture, and even a swimming pool, and renovating anything broken. May well have spent hours as a child tinkering with his father's radio set. Thoroughly engaging, he comes across as both thoughtful and down-to-earth, completely on the wavelength of his young charges and in his element at this rural but outward-looking school. Parents report themselves very happy, reassured that the school has lost none of its essence under his leadership and that numbers are increasing. 'A fantastic man for the job,' was a typical view.

Entrance: Twenty-four into the nursery at 3+, of whom between 50-75 per cent usually move up to reception (some leave for the state sector at this point). School is one-form entry with a maximum class size of 20, so not too many places available at 4+. Occasional places in other year groups – always worth checking.

The head likes to meet all applicants initially – happy to Skype those from overseas if this is a problem. Specifically looking for two things: can the school meet the needs if a child requires learning support? And behaviour – 'We're a happy ship, and one child can make a big impact. Above all, we're looking for children who want to be here.'

Children are then invited to a taster day during which 'low level' assessments will be made of their academic ability – ethos is non-selective, but school points out that as a prep school their focus is on preparing pupils for the Kent Test and Common Entrance, so children need to be able to cope. School also looks for how they fit in with their peers and engage in class.

At year 7, healthy numbers of overseas children apply to join the French programme, replacing the gaps left by those who jump ship for grammar schools at this point. International applicants have their level of English assessed and sit papers in English and maths.

Exit: A number pass the Kent Test and leave at 11 for the local grammar schools. ('I'd like to lose none of them,' comments head, ruefully.) The majority, however, stay on to sit Common Entrance at 13+. Destinations are diverse, reflecting the intake, and include King's School Canterbury, St Edmunds Canterbury, Dover College, Tonbridge, Eton, Harrow. Usually a handful of scholarships. Most of the overseas pupils go back to their original lycée, but a few stay on in England.

Our view: Set in 100 acres of beautiful landscaped grounds and approached via a quiet wooded lane, Northbourne is pretty magical, especially on a blustery autumn day with leaves swirling about. The large, grey and honey coloured house, finished in 1845 and looking all chimneys and inglenooks, became a school in 1936 and the current Lord Northbourne was one of the first pupils. He still takes a keen interest in the school, and has been known to take year 8 pupils to tea in the House of Lords.

Dotted around the estate are the Old Rectory, now home to the pre-prep and nursery, and the Church of St Mary the Virgin, aka the school chapel. The Christian ethos is integral to the school and service is held every other Sunday. Attendance is not obligatory, however, and a current Muslim pupil does supervised Koran studies during chapel time. The head and his wife live in the old head gardener's house, complete with walled garden – 'The dog thinks he's in heaven.' Children can go sledging when it snows, and even in September a big pile of wood was in preparation for the traditional Guy Fawkes bonfire.

With some 175 children on the roll and no plans to increase to two-form entry, this is a small school with a family feel. What lifts it above similar schools is its remarkable languages programme. For over 20 years Northbourne has offered a unique provision: at age 11, French and French-speaking Spanish children can join the school's Section Française Bilingue and continue on the French curriculum for years 7 and 8 (Sixième and Cinquième in the French system). Taught separately by French staff, they follow the French national curriculum in history, French and maths – the exams are ratified by the Lycée in London and monitored by the CNED in France, so that pupils can slip seamlessly back into French education when they leave at 13. However, they're taught science, music, art and geography in English, and come together with all the other Northbourne students for sports, art, music, socialising, etc. Meanwhile their English counterparts have been learning French from the nursery and Spanish from year 5 – 'It's very hands-on and completely immersive,' said a parent proudly.

The result is something rather wonderful: an international, open-minded, happy, diverse community, where everyone really does speak each other's language. It's not uncommon for children to leave here trilingual, effortlessly switching between French, Spanish and English. 'The languages are taught brilliantly,' affirmed one English mother. 'Most children who've been through Northbourne will do French and Spanish GCSE early, and many of them will do A level as well.' 'It's been so much easier for my children to pick up French and Spanish because they hear these languages spoken all the time, it's not a big deal here,' said another. 'There were many opportunities for my children to travel abroad. It gave them huge confidence and a massive head start when they moved on to senior school,' was a further comment.

Set in 100 acres of beautiful landscaped grounds and approached via a quiet wooded lane, Northbourne is pretty magical, especially on a blustery autumn day

In addition to the languages, there's a broad curriculum for both English and international pupils, covering all the usual subjects. Most classes are taught in beautiful old Northbourne House, skilfully put to use as a school. We liked the science lab in particular. 'We try and keep things as hands on as we can,' beamed the teacher. 'We're currently growing rocket plants from seeds that Tim Peake took into space,' although it seems that micro-gravity took its toll on these – 'They flopped over!'

School operates a two-week timetable with Saturday school on the middle weekend. The lessons we saw were purposeful and focused, but also lively, bubbly and highly enjoyable. 'I still find maths really, really, really, really fun,' said one young year 5 pupil who seemed to speak for many, and the history teacher was dressed up in a crown and sword when we met her, to the children's evident delight. Pupils with additional needs supported by full-time SENCo and team of teaching assistants. School approach is to give support in the classroom wherever possible, rather than taking children out of lessons.

Loads to do here. ('In England you do so many more games!' enthused our Spanish tour guide.) Sports are high quality but inclusive – 'Excellent,' according to a mother; 'the sports teachers have totally inspired our children.' Football, rugby, cricket, hockey, netball, rounders, athletics all on offer, plus swimming, volleyball and cross-country. Outdoor education is also a big part of the school's provision, with opportunities to build shelters in the grounds, spend the night therein and cook breakfast on open fires in the morning. There's a policy of encouraging tree-climbing, although children must stick to trees that are no more than twice their height. 'I love the Broken Bone Tree!' one little girl told us cheerfully – no broken bones in evidence at our visit, however. We loved the notice in the main entrance, 'You may go into the woods today – take care!' Next on the head's wish list is an onsite organic farm and a chicken coop.

Remarkable languages programme. School offers a unique provision: at age 11, French and French-speaking Spanish children can join the school's Section Française Bilingue

Music is 'absolutely exceptional', 'off the scale', say parents, 'and other prep schools are in awe of how good it is here'. (Old boys include the composer Sir Richard Rodney Bennett and the concert pianist Freddie Kempf.) Some 70 per cent of pupils can take singing and a wide range of instrumental lessons, and take part in an excellent array of orchestras, choirs and ensembles. At least two annual productions, a senior and a junior one, performed in the sports hall. LAMDA exams also popular. 'The music and drama here changed me! There's so much to do,' said a French student.

As many as 18 clubs on offer at any one time, among them Lego, junior chess and fencing, needlework, yoga, music enrichment and French ciné. Plenty of residential trips, eg kayaking in the Ardêche. Well-used table football in corridor.

The pupils are put into one of four houses, Nelson, Drake, Wellington and Marlborough – all famed, ironically, for licking the French or Spanish. Any disputes these days are dealt with kindly and swiftly, however, and the head personally makes sure that every incident is resolved satisfactorily. No issues with social media, and access to mobiles and iPads strictly limited, both for day pupils and boarders. Smart grey and navy uniform is worn proudly, and behaviour is excellent. 'The children are all brought up to be incredibly polite – they open doors, stand aside in the corridors, and are so courteous!' confirmed a parent.

The head has shortened the school day – 'Some children were finishing at 6pm when I joined. I felt it was too late for children this age' – but working parents can use the breakfast and after-school clubs, and a shuttle bus means that they can drop off to either the pre-prep or the prep – a godsend for families with a child in both. Indeed, kindness and common sense are the keynotes here. Birthdays are celebrated at lunchtime when the whole school sings Happy Birthday! and Mr Rees personally delivers birthday cards. 'It's wonderful here, the teachers are so kind!' was a typical pupil comment, and a French lad added, 'For me this is a beautiful school and I love the teachers here.' All the children struck us as self-possessed, healthy, confident and chatty. A mother wrote, 'Northbourne has been a total antidote to the whole selective school treadmill. They help children hold on to their childhood and look after their emotional wellbeing.' Vigorous and articulate, the children had no difficulty criticising the food, however, and as a veteran of school lunches we confess we didn't think it up to standard for a boarding school. School dismayed to hear this, and contends: 'Since your visit we have spoken to many of the children at mealtimes and monitored what they eat and leave behind and it does appear that overwhelmingly they enjoy the food.'

Many parents here are buying into the independent school system for the first time and working hard to put their children through. Others, particularly those from international families, are from quite privileged backgrounds. The children, happily scrambling into their boiler suits and rubber boots (on the uniform list) to go outdoors, seem genuinely and blissfully unaware of any difference. Who wouldn't like it here, we asked them. 'Someone who didn't like to be outdoors,' was the unanimous opinion.

Boarding: The boarding community is mostly international and full-time, although there are a few London children who go home at the weekends and flexi-boarding is popular among the day pupils. Girls live in a modern building in the grounds, the boys are housed in the old school where the rooms open onto a corridor replete with stained-glass skylights. Facilities in each are comfortable and well equipped, with dedicated lounges and kitchens for the children and ensuite bathrooms in many of the rooms. Beautiful views from the windows abound. Unusually, there are no official exeat weekends, but the school organises Eurostar trips every few weeks. Parents are allowed to call every day on the boarding house phone (not on the pupils' own mobiles) and time is rationed to 20 minutes each. Boarders are 'thoroughly happy', according to parents. 'I'm never homesick!' said a French year 7 boy, 'and I love the countryside here.'

Money matters: Means-tested bursaries available from reception upwards, usually up to a maximum of 50 per cent. Scholarships available for sport, creativity (art and drama), music and academic excellence. Sibling discount of 10 per cent.

The last word: For children lucky enough to come here, this is the most lovely school. 'It's been brilliant for my children, a really special place, completely magical,' was one mother's verdict, and everyone we spoke to agreed. A happy and well-adjusted child told us, 'Wherever you go, Northbourne is your home. I sometimes talk about going home and I mean Northbourne.'

The Prebendal School

52–55 West Street, Chichester, West Sussex PO19 1RP

01243 772220 | office@prebendalschool.org.uk | www.prebendalschool.org.uk

Ages: 3–13

Pupils: 130; Boarders: 20 full, 7 weekly (from 7 years)

Fees: Day £8,850 – £16,500; Boarding £23,700; Choristers £11,850 pa

Head: Since 2017, Louise Salmond Smith BA (East Anglia), MMus (Hull), PGCE (Gloucestershire), Keele (MBA). Previously head of junior school at Tormead School in Guildford and the school's first female head. Plain-talking, feisty and a virtuoso on the recorder. Has introduced hot chocolate at Bill's as the termly treat for pupils with the most pluses, this replacing a book token; her parish is wholly convinced by the wisdom of this move, and all aspire to join her.

Pupils say she's 'really nice' and that they see a lot more of her (than the last head): 'She's a lot friendlier.' The children seem to appreciate that they don't have to leap to attention when they see her around the place; a small child, post music lesson, saw the head with relief and gave up her private battles with the timetable to ask for help.

Stands up for children, and refused to remove from the classroom a child with SEN who was, a parent complained, disturbing her child's learning. The complainant and her children departed, the other parents appreciating that lessons of the classroom are not just those found in books.

Parents are very enthusiastic: 'brilliant… knows every child's name… speaks in a way they can understand'; 'a doer… not full of bluster. Has great ideas and is interested in the children themselves.'

Entrance: Non-selective. Testing for bench marking and setting purposes. Taster day for prospective pupils. Auditions for choristers, boys only.

Exit: In 2021, 80 per cent of year 8s got scholarships. Popular senior schools include Charterhouse, Christ's Hospital, Eton, Lancing, Portsmouth Grammar, Portsmouth High and Seaford. The head is keen for parents to expand their horizons.

A small number leave after year 6 for state schools.

Our view: This is a school of sounds. Children move through corridors at their own pace, making their own noises, from chatter, to sung snatches of anthems, to an odd experimental mixture of the two: children finding and expressing themselves by voice. Music is a way of life at this school; virtually all the children learn one instrument and many learn more, and each year there is a clutch of music scholarships to senior schools.

School buildings range from ancient to modern, but it's the old ones that arrest you: the curved classroom doors off a spiral staircase; the jail from the old magistrates' court (now storage behind bars); the cavernous old kitchen in the Bishop's Palace, used for band practice and drama. The Prebendal is as old as the cathedral (1100s), and was founded as its song school, with its first head listed simply as John. To be in these buildings is to feel centuries peeling back around you; teachers say to children: 'this room was here when...' Pupils are sitting in time, and this is something they are very aware of – 'I can feel it in English when the windows rattle as a bus goes past,' said one pupil: history shaking down through the centuries.

The Prebendal is as old as the cathedral (1100s), and was founded as its song school. To be in these buildings is to feel centuries peeling back around you

Pre-prep is the modern part, full of light and colour; but from its playground the cathedral arches up, ancient behind modern. The school treats the cathedral as its chapel – 'but we let them use it for other services', said the head kindly. Pupils say it's a religious school, with lots of prayers and services (they quite like the ritual of it), and parents like that the children get used to talking in cathedral assemblies; 'not arrogance, just what they do...' New Pelicans nursery is now open 7am-7pm.

The divine sound of the choristers comes at a cost: 23 hours of practice and services a week; like having a part-time job on top of the full-time job of school and being a kid. Asked if he would recommend it, a chorister said, 'only if you like life very hectic'. But if you love singing, this is a chance to be part of a professional choir, with the cathedral paying 50 per cent of fees, and there's topping up if needed. It's boys only, and there's no prospect of a Prebendal girls' choir in the near future; funds only run to one professional choir, and a girls' choir instead of the boys' one would be a radical step too far.

A mix of abilities at this non-selective school, the very academically able and those that just 'muddle through', said parents. 'No divide or distance between them,' said another, they all mix, and pupils from the state sector comment with pleasure on teachers who focus on all, not just those at the lower end.

Teachers know the children well, one parent describing how her son's teacher approached her at the end of his first week at Prebendal – 'This is how I am thinking about teaching [your son]...'

Prebendal follows the CE syllabus, but also the pre-senior baccalaureate, which focuses on skills rather than spoon-feeding. It's a great idea, and parents feel it will set pupils apart, but it hasn't really kicked in yet, and pupils would like more time to talk in lessons; a teacher pointed out that both pupils and teachers have to get used to a different way of being. But we saw some lively lessons, a year 8 pupil standing on a chair to work out an equation in blue marker on the window to the encouragement of her peers; scribbling on windows during lessons is encouraged here.

Learning support staff are 'on it', said a parent, describing how they read with her dyslexic son daily, and provide extra in-class support free of charge (one-to-one sessions are charged as extra).

Beach school fortnightly for the little ones, the head saying she would rather they are learning their letters outside, with a stick in the sand, than a pencil on paper inside. On the day of our visit, year 2s were finding things, man made or natural, then building them into castles (this term's project). It is difficult to imagine a happier place for children to learn.

Pupils describe the school as 'strict but friendly'. Bullying is 'taken quite seriously', said a pupil, and the head says they encourage snitches. Pupils say they talk to both sides, but there are not always evident consequences for the person doing the bullying, and things can recur. System of pluses for all things good, comments for the bad, with three comments getting you a detention – this might be copying out a portion of an encyclopaedia, or some Mandarin. Parents report prompt dealing with pastoral concerns; the form teacher or school chaplain is usually first port of call, 'but anyone passing would help...'

A playground big enough for break-time football, tennis and hen coop; the rescued factory hens have nearly all their feathers now, and Vera, the bravest, enjoys cuddles at break time (two pupils at a time in the hen coop only) and has braved the hen swing (who knew?).

There's a new outdoor classroom with wood chips underfoot (year 8 patiently pick up the ones that get away), and a more informal area called the amphitheatre: a circle of wooden benches with a fire pit at the centre (a wise head prioritises toasting marshmallows).

They have their own entrance to the Bishop's Gardens from their playground, where they can climb trees – to a certain point. At night, after the gardens are closed to the public, boarders use the garden for manhunt in the dark.

For a small school, there is a vigorous programme of sports, and parents think this is probably the only element of the school that feels really competitive; but they read both losses and wins out in the cathedral, and no-one holds it against those who haven't achieved on the sports field, added a parent earnestly.

One pupil told us how wonderful it feels to play cricket on their pitch next to the cathedral – it is the backdrop to their lives here, and gives great pleasure. Girls are pleased they now have opportunities to play cricket, and football too, but want to keep playing all their traditional sports as well. In some years there are cool kids and it's not always the sporty ones who get the kudos; we were met with a bemused shake of the head from a chorister at the thought that his status might command any admiration from his peers.

Parents like the long school days, and the flexibility, geared for working parents – 'they will keep children if you're late to pick up… I've picked up at 9pm.' It's a friendly, busy parent group, with nearly all parents working (lots of professionals); 'no one has time for bitchiness'.

Pupils agree that the food is okay, though not up to home cooking: 'main courses packed with mushrooms, puddings packed with raisins,' said a pupil resignedly, but compared to his old school, it's really good.

A girl who likes her skirt gravely told us that she still thinks there should be the choice to wear trousers, and the boys were very clear that they would like to wear shorts in summer. A sympathetic shudder from all at the requirement for pre-prep boys to wear shorts all year round. Some pupil uncertainty as to whether using Pupil Voice (their council) makes a difference, but the head is keen to change this; she has refurbished the girls' changing rooms, and the pupil who suggested a zip wire over to school from the cathedral wasn't all that surprised it was turned down.

Boarding: The boarding here is mostly weekly or flexi; only the 11 choristers and a couple of international pupils are around at weekends, when it is very quiet, said a chorister, although there is a family feel to Sundays, when the families of choristers join the school for Sunday lunch.

A dormitory (of 14) with old wood panelling has ancient graffiti, carved into it by pupils long gone; pupils of the present day are allowed their own graffiti, by pen not penknife, on the wall of a tight spiral staircase. Dormitory numbers shrink as pupils get older, to three for year 8s. Bathrooms are clean, sometimes elderly (when did you last see a wall-mounted cistern and chain?).

The last word: Most people are attracted to Prebendal by its small size and family feel, and describe the school as gentle and nurturing – 'they won't shut your kids down, judge them for being dyslexic, or anything else…' Prebendal would suit all, we heard time and time again, from the really sporty to the meek and mild. 'It looks very traditional, but the thinking is new,' said a parent. 'Not that it's Bedales,' she added.

Prior's Field

52

Priorsfield Road, Godalming, Surrey GU7 2RH

01483 810551 | admissions@priorsfieldschool.com | www.priorsfieldschool.com

Ages: 11–18

Pupils: 425; sixth form: 70; Boarders: 31 full, 54 weekly/flexi

Fees: Day £19,800 – £20,250; Boarding £29,775 – £33,150 pa

Head: Since 2015, Tracy Kirnig (50s). Born and brought up in London, she ventured to university in Aberystwyth, reading RE and philosophy. Ms Kirnig was never in doubt about a teaching career and returned nearer to her roots to take a master's in education at King's London and then a PGCE at Lancaster before working in both the state and private sectors. Her interests in music and travel were re-enforced by the scaling of Mount Kilimanjaro, particularly impressive as she admits to being a latecomer to the joys of climbing. Moving here from her last job as deputy head of co-ed Caterham school, she is noticeably happy in her own skin with a firm belief in the worth of her school and in particular of the girls in her care. Married to a geo-technological engineer with a sideline in potting.

Entrance: An open morning or a pre-arranged 'Meet the head' coffee morning plus school tour are followed by a taster day in November and an exam in January. The school is oversubscribed at 11 and 13 but they don't just go on exam results. Rather, they try to find girls who are 'sparky, curious about life and learning and want to get involved with everything on offer'. A genuine effort is made to determine whether this is the right place for each individual and they're pretty good at it, judging by the great attitude of the present lot.

Exit: Up to 60 per cent leave after GCSEs, a percentage of which are replaced from outside. We suspect that affordability is the major reason (plus the school's location), but the assumption that life is more 'real' in a co-ed still attracts a proportion to either private school sixth forms or state colleges with good A level results. One medic in 2021, but none to Oxbridge. Other students (in ones and twos) to Cardiff, Durham, Kingston, Oxford Brookes, Bath, Birmingham, Exeter, Leeds, Northampton, Nottingham, Portsmouth and Surrey.

Latest results: In 2021, 76 per cent 9-7 at GCSE; 65 per cent A*/A at A level (77 per cent A*-B). In 2019 (the last year when exams took place), 64 per cent 9-7 at GCSE; 34 per cent A*/A at A level (59 per cent A*-B).

Teaching and learning: An academically selective school, although not generally in the high-flying category. There has been a noticeable recent attempt to redress the balance away from the arts, with around half the year taking one or more maths and science subjects at A level. Languages are not an obviously strong point, but they make a great effort to find outside teachers if pupils voice sufficient interest in a language outside the fairly narrow choice on the core curriculum of French, Spanish and Latin at GCSE. Everyone takes one or two of these at this stage and recently up to 20 per cent have taken at least one language at A level.

Sixth formers all have larger rooms with good work space, the upper sixth even having their own bathrooms – a very much appreciated luxury

The average class size in the early years is 18, reducing to 15 as they move up the school and six in the sixth form. Setting takes place on arrival at both 11+ and 13+ for English and maths and later in the first term for science, MFL and sport. The girls speak of flexibility and are confident that they will be moved up or down rapidly if it appears necessary.

The staff, with a ratio of one teacher to eight girls, have a relatively high average age but, as the head says, 'this brings a wealth of experience,' 22 of them having been at the school for more than 10 years. Despite this statistic, she feels that there are plenty of younger members and promotes them on the basis that 'they are old enough if they are good enough'. Certainly, on our visit, the enthusiasm and interaction with the pupils was noticeable with plenty of young faces and absolutely no stuffed shirts in evidence. It may be a smallish school but the determination to help each girl reach her academic potential is clearly evident.

Learning support and SEN: The staff and pupils are confident about the SEND provision; it appears to be handled efficiently and sensitively, although they admit that they might dissuade a parent from sending a child with problems that would prevent her from coping fairly easily with the school's academic expectations. However, one parent told us that they were 'great about accepting my very dyslexic daughter' and that the SENCo was 'fantastic'. One-on-one help is available, if necessary, at an hourly rate.

The arts and extracurricular: Clubs and activities are a big deal, meriting their own brochure, and are often free, although if you're into creating Funky Food, not surprisingly, you have to pay for the ingredients as well as persuading your parents to eat the results. In a nod to the country, you can go riding after school, or if you're a home bod, you can get into knitting and crochet, of which we saw an imaginative, if eccentric, example in the making.

Completely unsurprisingly given the school's Arts and Crafts heritage, there is a major emphasis on art, music and drama. The art rooms are designed for people taking it seriously, with sixth formers each having their own space that fills up with imaginative work during the year. The result is that several girls go on to art college and a high proportion of alumnae make it a career. They mean what they say about encouraging talent, as one girl with a natural bent for photography persuaded them to add the course to the GCSE curriculum. New music rooms encourage even the less musical to give an instrument a go, whilst the more gifted are nurtured carefully. Drama is definitely front stage with brave large-cast musical productions, entry in the Shakespeare Schools Festival and popular LAMDA and RADA classes.

Sport: A surprisingly sporty school despite its size. Netball, hockey and athletics tick the most boxes and teams compete locally and nationally. Rugby and cricket now available, the latter becoming popular after the successes of the England women's team. Tennis is huge; they even run to a tennis academy (complete with a permanent coach), which paid off recently in the Surrey U15 championship and with their first tennis scholar having her pick of American universities. At a more achievable, if slightly wacky, level the inter-house cross-country competition last year had an underwater theme, with the girls sporting

Roedean School

mermaid tails; it may not have increased their speed but it was good for a laugh.

Boarding: About a quarter of the girls board but increasingly this is on a weekly or flexible basis rather than full time. At weekends the school can seem a little empty lower down as only around seven to eight board full time in the first two years, but further up the school the percentage increases to 50 per cent in the fifth year and up to 60 per cent in the sixth form. One parent was a bit unhappy and thought that her daughter lacked supervision, but this was contradicted by several of the present cohort.

Conan Doyle sent his daughter here and the germ of the idea for a short story entitled The Adventure of Priory School must have come from his knowledge of Prior's Field

The younger girls are up in the attics in cosy if slightly cramped quarters of up to four in a room, but it feels cheerful and there was no griping when asked if they had enough space. You wouldn't want to be a budding fashionista with a lot of frocks as the hanging space is strictly limited, but there are lots of drawers for 'stuff' and you are encouraged to make it as personal as possible. The bathrooms looked newish and were pretty spotless, a nice cleaning lady telling us they had a 'really good go twice a week'. The sixth formers all have larger rooms with good work space, the upper sixth even having their own bathrooms – a much appreciated luxury. The general consensus was that there was plenty to do out of school hours and some of the day girls would love their parents to come up with the cash so that they could board.

Ethos and heritage: Prior's Field nestles in a hidden corner of leafy Surrey, just out of sight of the London hubbub. A rather surprising unicorn-themed advertisement for the school is squished on a small roundabout off the A3, but the tree-lined road leading off it soon reveals a pebble-dashed, beetle-browed Arts and Crafts set of buildings. The original 1900 house, designed by CFA Voysey, has grown since through the addition of convincing fakes and the whole ensemble fits happily into its surrounding acres.

The founder, Julia Huxley, was related by blood, marriage and proximity to the intellectual and educationally passionate giants of the Edwardian age. You could not dream up someone more suitable to start a school than the granddaughter of Dr Thomas Arnold (the Rugby legend), niece of Matthew Arnold (the poet), wife of Leonard Huxley (a Charterhouse schoolmaster himself before becoming an important literary figure) and friend of Conan Doyle. Her children, Julian, a scientist and director of UNESCO, and Aldous, author of Brave New World, provide further evidence of why she was the perfect person to run a school based on moral philosophy and forward thinking. There is a brilliant photograph of her in the hall, hand on chin, glasses slightly skew-whiff, with her ample successor, Ethel Burton-Brown, sitting at her feet, made more touching by the fact that she died a year later aged only 46. Conan Doyle sent his daughter here and the germ of the idea for a short story entitled The Adventure of Priory School must surely have come from his knowledge of Prior's Field, although the plot is not exactly an advertisement for pupil care.

The slightly labyrinthine layout of a turn-of-the-century house is not ideal for a modern school, but a newbie told us that despite getting lost frequently for the first two weeks she had quickly learnt the necessary shortcuts to make it everywhere on time. Again surprisingly, the interior, whilst a tad scruffy, is not as dark as you would expect and is greatly improved by art on every available wall as well as impressive displays of textile work for which the school is justifiably famous. Amongst the newer buildings, they are proudest of their pristine science, technology and music centre, which manages to be light and attractive inside despite its folksy exterior. The area at the front of the school is cramped, but the back opens up to a wide green space, a new all-purpose Astroturf pitch, several tennis courts and woodland beyond.

Grandparents will be thrilled that Enid Bagnold (National Velvet) was an old girl, watchers of Netflix will know of Victoria Hamilton (the queen mother in The Crown), and others will be encouraged that Baroness Mary Warnock was at the school.

Pastoral care, inclusivity and discipline: This side of the school was high on the head's agenda when she took over and she has changed the structure so that now there is one person responsible for the emotional development of each individual, separate from the person in charge of checking whether they've got the right tights on. PSHE is not just an acronym here but built into the whole workings of the school, and the result hits you straight on, all the girls we talked to genuinely appearing to put helping each other above being competitive. The school has definitely got across their belief in moral welfare but it is not heavy handed; common sense rather than a set of rules is the order of the day. With her philosophical background, the head also wants to broaden awareness and a series of talks on mindfulness are scheduled, the first one being given by a Buddhist nun. Zero evidence of wrongdoing: the head girl sounded puzzled when we asked her if she had to discipline the younger ones.

The beautifully presented food (think huge Moroccan bowls of salad and a bread offering that would challenge a trendy London bakery) is seriously yummy, one girl giggling that it was much better than her mum's. Being allergic or just fussy is not a problem, a non-gluten pupil telling us that there was masses of choice and they were 'really helpful about it', and teachers seem very aware of any potential problems.

Not the smartest of schools in terms of uniform, but this is being remedied with major input from the pupils who, slightly to our surprise, actually want to wear blazers with badges to show off where they come from.

Pupils and parents: Majority of day girls bussed in from all points of the compass, increasingly from nearer London as parents turn away from the capital's pressure-cookers and look for an academically competent school with an individual flavour. Some 10 per cent from a wide range of foreign countries; these, when asked, said that they had settled in straight away, and certainly all had smiley faces. Parents' backgrounds are as diverse as the children's ambitions but they say that they feel fully involved with the school via personal contact and email communication as well as the PSA.

Money matters: Plenty of scholarships and bursaries; academic, sporting, musical, artistic and dramatic abilities are recognised by an award which equates to between £250 and £1,000 per term. One or two exceptional tennis players are awarded a place in the tennis academy, with coaching costs fully funded by the school. A handful of foundation awards (100 per cent bursaries funded by parents, alumnae and friends of the school) are awarded each year and a 20 per cent discount on the fees is given to the daughters of parents in the Forces.

The last word: A century may have passed but the aim to turn out resilient young women, capable of achieving the maximum possible in the outside world, remains the same. It is still a school where 'it is cool to try out new things', and the head is confident that the well-equipped young adults that leave are recognisable as the children that arrived five or seven years earlier. The school is also long on charm and good at detail, winning us over immediately by giving us a car parking space with our name on it.

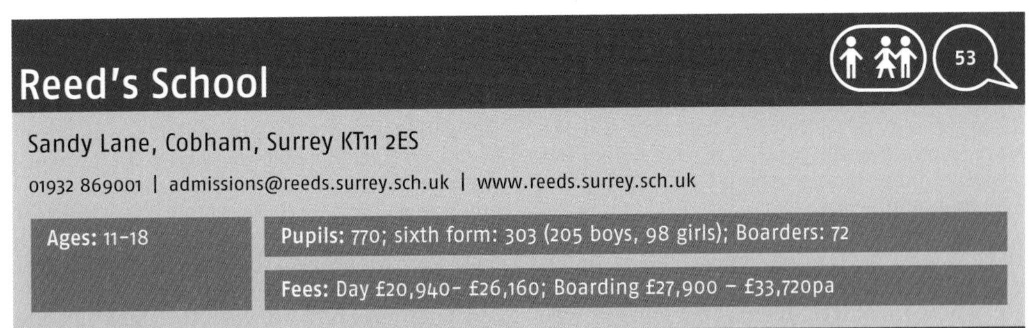

Reed's School

Sandy Lane, Cobham, Surrey KT11 2ES

01932 869001 | admissions@reeds.surrey.sch.uk | www.reeds.surrey.sch.uk

Ages: 11–18

Pupils: 770; sixth form: 303 (205 boys, 98 girls); Boarders: 72

Fees: Day £20,940– £26,160; Boarding £27,900 – £33,720pa

Head: Since 2014, Mark Hoskins BA MA MSc (50s). Previously second master at RGS Guildford for nine years. Before that, spent eight years at Whitgift, starting as head of economics and business studies in 1997 and then becoming head of middle school. First posts were in highly regarded maintained schools – two years apiece at Rosebery (comp, girls) and Wilson's (selective grammar, boys). Mixed sixth form here first foray so far into coeducation. Has two master's under his belt, the second in economics from the University of London, accomplished post-marriage with small children and combined with full-time teaching.

Laid-back, unassuming and very much at home with Zoom – good news for parents (and us) who need to chat to him online during lockdowns. Equally at ease, we noted, with admitting when he doesn't know something or feels something's not perfect – the epitome of authentic leadership. Praise from parents comes thick and fast. 'I think it's safe to say he's unanimously liked by all of us.' 'Always available.' 'Actually listens and always takes things on board.' 'A good speaker, personable and relates to people.' Credited with upping the ante academically without losing the ethos of the school. State educated himself and with a strong moral purpose, he's also upped the numbers of foundation places for disadvantaged pupils. 'Surrounded by a fantastic team,' we also heard.

Lives on site with wife Sharon and two children – a son (at the school) and daughter (not quite old enough). An able sportsman, he coached soccer in US during gap years.

Entrance: At 11+ (and 13+ from 2023), ISEB common pre-test, taken at school in January for entry in September. For 13+, register a good three years in advance, pre-test in year 6, CE in June if at prep school. Other candidates sit English, maths, science, modern language and VR papers. Around 50 places become available in sixth form – hopefuls do entrance tests in the subjects they want to study (for which they need 7s at GCSE, with some exceptions, eg for siblings), plus interview.

Ham-fisted, two left feet or otherwise, everyone will have talent, however limited, coaxed out of them. Kung fu among latest offerings

Heavily oversubscribed at all entry points, but while greater competition inevitably means more able applicants achieving well beyond pass mark, head doesn't go by grades alone. Good relationships with prep heads mean that the reference of the headteacher, previous attainment is also taken into account if the child has had a bad day. More good news for parents is that school has grown so takes more pupils (75-80 at 11+; 50 at 13+) than in the past.

Can flex entry criteria for siblings, and the 10 per cent of foundation pupils – that is, pupils who have lost the support of one or both parents and where there is a financial hardship as well as the need for strong pastoral support. Need to sit entrance exams and will also have home visit. Siblings also get preferential treatment (though no guaranteed entry) – over half the girls coming in to lower sixth were siblings when we reviewed the school.

Exit: Less than 10 per cent exit post-16 – fewer each year – freedom offered by local sixth form colleges ('longer hair and earrings,' says head) being the main lure. Those who want to stay almost always can – even if shy of required GCSE grades, though substitute subjects may be imposed (DT rather than physics, say): 'We are not a school who asks pupils to leave in order to enhance our A level league table position.'

Translates into gamut of places: Bath, Birmingham, Bristol, Durham, Exeter, Leeds, Loughborough, Nottingham, Warwick and King's College London recently popular. Wide range of courses – classics to chemistry, economics to engineering, modern languages to music. Good numbers of medics – three in 2021, plus two to Oxbridge. Sometimes a few overseas.

Latest results: In 2021, 88 per cent 9-7 at GCSE; 78 per cent A*/A (95 per cent A*-B) at A level. In 2019 (the last year when exams took place), 74 per cent 9-7 at GCSE; 50 per cent A*/A (78 per cent A*-B) at A level.

Teaching and learning: Academic performance has soared under current headship, with 9-7s at GCSE up by around 75 per cent and A level results at all-time high. As such, school is edging ever closer to nearby powerhouses like Hampton and RGS. No wonder locals are waking up to educational excellence on their doorstep and, in growing numbers, starting to make this their first choice. Elsewhere, pupils' brilliance polished till it shines but personalities remain unchanged. Here, parents feel pupils' characters have room to grow, too.

'Good at catering to all academic capabilities – they find and nurture the potential,' said parent. Many have more than one child at the school, often streets apart in terms of brains and motivation, and told us they cater well for both. 'The pace has definitely picked up, but it's avoided the hothouse feel,' said another. Whether you're a budding medic or haven't found your forte yet, the staff (one to every eight students) will do you proud. 'We're not a grammar and don't try to be.' Self-confidence and self-esteem are seen as key building blocks, and there is more assessment for learning and feedback than there used to be, with boys awarded bronze, silver and gold grades for effort as well as achievement. 'They spend time teaching boys how to work too, making sure they do study plans and use them – has certainly helped organise my boys,' said parent.

Small class sizes – 17 up to year 11, 10 in sixth form. 'Fairly fluid' setting in maths and science from year 7; English from year 10. Pupils pick between French and Spanish in year 7 and German is currently (but this is being reviewed) added in year 9. Latin also from year 7. A language is 'strongly encouraged', but not compulsory, at GCSE. Japanese, Mandarin and Arabic available as extracurricular, plus Italian as a non-exam course in sixth form. Nine GCSEs is the norm, with the top two maths sets adding further maths. Around two-thirds do triple science. Geography, history and computing popular. Post-16, there are 24 A level options – all the traditional ones, plus graphic design, media studies and psychology. Maths is most popular, followed by geography, sciences, history and English. Will also keep subjects going for tiny numbers. Most take three A levels, plus EPQ (around a third take this) or additional courses such as AS in photography or PE. School also runs its own study programme for sixth formers, covering everything from politics to cooking for university.

Trees know their place – confined largely to the perimeter so space can be given over to cricket, rugby (big and little pitches), two Astros and tennis courts

Staff enthusiasm is boundless – you'll encounter your history teacher on the hockey pitch or your English teacher in choir, all making for stronger relationships with pupils. You can teach, motivate and inspire until the cows come home, but the magic dust – says head – lies in knowing pupils as individuals.

Lots of subject stretching by way of societies, eg medsoc. Futuretech programme popular – DT reimagined to give free rein to 'what if' projects linking STEM subjects. DIY model wind turbines created by second years and visit from Tesla among the many highlights. Careers advice praised – cascades right down to year 7s and kept going right through pandemic. In fact, school hit the ground running with online learning, largely thanks to appointment of new head of digital in 2016, but also due to its focus on interactivity – online lessons with cameras on right from day one, along with tutor groups making breakfast and ensuring no overload of screen time with eg treasure hunts in biology. 'Well ahead of other schools in the area during Covid, from what I can gather,' said parent.

Learning support and SEN: School is notable for quality of support – currently offered to around 80 pupils, vast majority with assorted dys difficulties, and very small numbers with ADD, ADHD, ASD, visual or speech and language issues. Just under 20 with EAL are supported individually or in small groups. Academic support classrooms are deliberately located smack, bang in the middle of the school. No stigma – in fact, school has opposite problem of tearing some pupils away from this supportive environment. Lovely to hear of eg dyslexia talked about in positive terms by staff – what it can bring to the table, not just the obstacles it creates; one dyslexic pupil recently gained a place at Oxbridge. 'My son struggled with some sensory processing issues and the support he was given was staggering,' said parent.

The arts and extracurricular: Strength of arts – performing and visual – particularly impressive, from scale of ambition to levels of investment and numbers involved (over 200 individual music lessons each week). Music increasingly a reason parents choose the school – 'It's gone from strength to strength and everyone adores the concerts,' said one parent. Teachers crack on even when limited to online learning, with a full schedule of rehearsals and lessons – 'My son is up in his room every week doing jazz band, wind band, virtual song writing and more,' said parent. Plenty of choirs, orchestras and ensembles, and a good dose of rock and roll too – one band recently released an album on Spotify and has gigged all around London. Foundation pupils often find taking up an instrument life-changing, reports school.

While smaller scale than music, drama is also popular. New drama studio provides a decent professional space, though a larger performance centre is on wish list. Whole-school plays, plus year group performances; good numbers at GCSE and A level.

No end to the imaginations of budding artists here – an installation of a door recently bagged a top grade at GCSE. Breathtaking quality across a range of styles. More space too these days, thanks to head having doubled the size of the studios. At A level, you can take fine art or graphics and there's an AS in photography.

Ham-fisted, two left feet or otherwise, everyone will have talent, however limited, coaxed out of them. Clubs – 100 plus, ranging from archery to golf and robotics to silk painting – cater for dabblers as well as enthusiasts. Pupils are compelled to do at least three. Kung fu among latest offerings, while parent raved about film club ('my son gets to eat pizza and talk about the film's theme – brilliant'). Popular DofE (bronze is compulsory) and good numbers for CCF. Doesn't neglect social skills either, with everything from debating club (including during Covid) to Toastmasters for older pupils. Many new sixth formers, compelled to try previously hated activities (two a week in years 11, 12 and 13; three to year 10) converted into fans. Brilliant for bonding even if not, thought pupil. Charitable endeavours part and parcel of school life, even in lockdown – staff made visas for NHS, while sixth formers wrote to elderly people in care homes, with younger ones sending pics. 'Lots of collections for food banks too,' added parent.

Sport: Along with music, sport is a huge selling point for families. Recent winner of Times

Educational Supplement sports award, beating the likes of Wellington and Repton. On the achievement side, tennis, golf and skiing are top dog – all have their own academy, offering elite coaching (every major sport comes with own professional), flexible timetable and extra training (before or after school and – in case of skiers – sent off to the snow), plus strength and conditioning department. Plenty of individual successes at national and county level across a range of sports; ditto for stonking team triumphs. Hockey does increasingly well – current national U18s champions – not bad given that all are home grown, demonstrating that value added isn't confined to the classrooms. 'My son arrived not even knowing how to hold a hockey stick and they got him in a match that weekend that he loved – says it all about inclusivity and encouragement,' said parent.

Whatever your specialist interest, facilities excellent, packed in on relatively compact site. Trees know their place – confined largely to the perimeter so space can be given over to cricket, rugby (big and little pitches), two Astros and tennis courts. Whole shebang has accolade of being accredited by Tim Henman Foundation as model primary school outreach programme for others to follow. Wow-factor indoor cricket centre is available to outsiders as well as pupils; includes system that 'combines motion tracking and video analysis'.

Youngest sports scholars enjoy substantial perk of all-day trackies to avoid frequent changes of clothes. Sixth formers allowed to devote some private study time to sport – strength and conditioning programme particularly popular for this age group. Sixth form girls far from sidelined – six girls' netball teams and four each for girls' cricket and hockey. Impressive levels of cooperation between academic and sports staff – can be the make or break of sporting success, we've learned. Another secret weapon is sizeable number of teachers so blessed with charm that can even make punishments a laugh a minute. 'If we forget our kit, coach makes us run and touch all the lines on the pitch – there are about 500,' said junior pupil, chortling at the very memory. 'Makes it so funny.' You probably had to be there.

Boarding: 'Doesn't feel like a boarding school as boarding element is so small,' said parent, and that was from a parent of boarders. Of the 15 per cent that board, juniors are housed in The Close, seniors in School House, sixth formers upstairs in own courtyard block (recently refurbished and now unrecognisable with glassed-over study area and café – 'I'm sure there are grander, but it's given it a wonderful lift,' said parent). Sixth form girl boarders, a particularly minuscule group (under a handful in upper sixth), flock together and take pleasure in niche status, downstairs common room a homely oasis of papers and possessions. Offers full, weekly or occasional B&B – a boon to any child with a late finishing match or parents with work commitments. Despite low numbers, school rarely feels empty, say pupils, all of whom talk about the sense of community.

All-action weekends are filled with sport, cinema trips, shopping and doughnutting (descending Sandown Park's dry ski slope in rubber ring)

Accommodation is spick and span, white and magnolia the prevailing signature décor, eye-catching touches headed by world's reddest kitchen in School House, neon signs and slinky bar-style seating for its 36 year 9-11 boarders. Elsewhere, communal areas are businesslike rather than breathtaking, though as long as there's space enough to pack in the crowds for must-watch TV (usually matches, we'd assume), pupils clearly don't mind.

Tempo of life is exceedingly brisk and a marvel of logistics, junior boarders showered and powered into breakfast in just 30 minutes – even faster when bacon's on the menu (food – bar some evening meals – generally excellent) – while all-action weekends for everyone are filled with (more) sport, mixed age cinema trips, shopping (in groups of three, one phone compulsory) and doughnutting (descending Sandown Park's dry ski slope in rubber ring).

Pace of life here may account for absence of personal touches. Some pinboards stay empty because there's just no time to unpack. 'Too much to do,' said pupil, who'd had initial reservations about absence of down time. No longer. 'Now realise that being busy is perfect.'

Cheerful matrons keep everything ticking over, washing machines permanently on spin cycle (18 loads of laundry in one day a personal best), aided and abetted by thoughtful, compassionate houseparents proffering small-hours hot chocolate and DVDs when homesickness strikes and with welcome ability to tread the fine line between firmness and latitude.

Ethos and heritage: Founded in 1813 by Andrew Reed, social reformer, minister and serial setter-upper of charitable institutions (and upsetter of fellow trustees), but the only school to survive intact, discounting change of name (originally the

London Orphan Asylum), location (arrived here via Clapton, Watford and – briefly during WWII evacuation – Totnes), and financing (fee-paying pupils first admitted 1950s, though charitable focus on foundationers has never changed).

Handy for M25 and with Gatwick and Heathrow just a 30-minute drive away, it's a cinch to get to, as long as you avoid rush hour and don't take address too literally (says Cobham but actually in Oxshott – it's a postal area thing).

Heart of the school is restored Arts and Crafts building, home – among other areas – to attractive chapel and library, surrounded by separate music school, labs, classrooms and airy sixth form block with lecture theatre which doubles as venue for film screenings. Packs a lot onto 40-acre site, with most recent additions including drama studio, cricket suite and sixth form centre, while next in line is a vast extension to the science labs which will link up other departments including art and humanities.

Overcoming pupil/space dilemma by corralling outside areas and roofing them over – small courtyard is now a conservatory-style dining hall extension while The Close boasts an impressive stretch reception, 100 or so tennis balls trapped on the roof a happy reminder of previous incarnation as impromptu sports pitch.

Pastoral care, inclusivity and discipline: Cordial relations between staff and pupils ensure that lines are clearly drawn, usually toed and rarely crossed. Mild misdemeanours seen as part and parcel of growing up, though – 'children make mistakes and school should be a safe environment for that to happen,' says head. Flexes disciplinary muscles for serious breaches (as with other schools, drink and drugs the main culprits) – offenders likely to be asked to leave. Not a shouty school – 'I can't abide that,' says head.

Everyone very much at home here, much emphasis on age-appropriate three-day induction programme. For year 7s includes onsite camping and games of chubby bunnies ('See how many marshmallows you can get in your mouth and still say "chubby bunnies",' said pupil – well, of course). Activities for new sixth form girls include rather more sophisticated (and confectionery-free) meal out in Kingston.

For first two years, The Close, a separate building, is a world in miniature. 'Opportunity to settle very well without being overwhelmed – a home away from home,' said parent. Have own houses, games, activities and responsibilities, plus quality pastoral back-up from sixth form mentors, a high profile and popular presence, who dispense quiz questions and chocolate brownies, organise house drama and deal with acts of minor unkindness.

School tracks emotional health – 'useful for detecting issues before they arise'. And there is a whole raft of professionals waiting in the wings when needed – counsellors, psychologists, behavioural therapist and good links with eg bereavement charities. Pastoral care 'outstanding' during Covid, say parents – everyone gets tutor time, opportunities to socialise, weekly comms with parents, cameras on during lessons etc.

Pupils and parents: With just a handful of expats and generally no more than six international students (half from Hong Kong), most families are UK-based Brits living maximum of an hour's travel time away, network of school bus routes reading like estate agent's bumper book of desirable destinations (Putney, Richmond, Wimbledon and Guildford).

End product includes plenty of high-grade sportspeople (Tim Henman most glorious example), though crop of musicians, actors and entertainers is almost as substantial. One 1980s batch (they organise alumni by decade here) yielded two opera singers, an art dealer and a Jordanian prince. Plenty of somethings in the City as well. Sports, arts or royalty, Old Reedonians stay in touch. 'Once a Reedonian, always a Reedonian.' Partners, we were told, like to swap notes, finding ORs nicer and gentler than the common herd.

Youngest sports scholars enjoy substantial perk of all-day trackies to avoid frequent changes of clothes. Sixth formers allowed to devote some private study time to sport

Judging by today's happy mixed-age lunchtime throng, pupils impressively (and unusually) relaxed about talking about their feelings, oldest pupils encouraging the youngest to speak, everyone giving strong impression of liking everyone else, nothing much has changed. No surprise, then, that foundationers, some with traumatising early life experiences, are painlessly absorbed. There's room for all here: 'Nerdy, quirky, eccentric, they all fit in here – you don't really get the cool gangs except in the younger years and they quickly grow out of it,' said parent.

Money matters: Bursaries for foundationers up to 110 per cent of fees – these numbers are on the up. Also range of scholarships – DT and drama at 13+ and in the sixth form – also open to existing pupils, plus headmaster's award for able but not quite scholarship level candidates at 11+ and CE;

additional scholarships awarded to existing pupils during school career if merited. Some grumbles about fees – 'I feel we pay boarding fees, when there aren't many boarders,' said one. Worth noting, though, that they include majority of extras from meals to choir tours.

The last word: One parent equated school to post-privatisation Jaguar – took a while for shift in quality to be recognised. 'Took years for prices to catch up, but they did.' With current head in the driving seat, this revamped model is definitely proving an all-terrain winner.

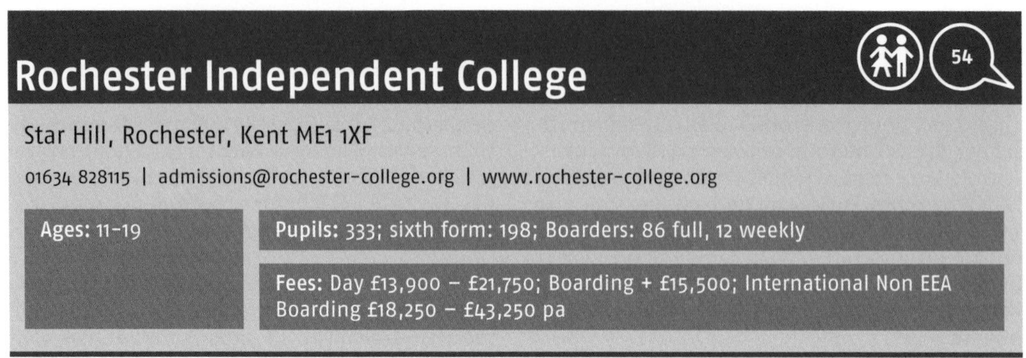

Rochester Independent College

54

Star Hill, Rochester, Kent ME1 1XF

01634 828115 | admissions@rochester-college.org | www.rochester-college.org

Ages: 11-19

Pupils: 333; sixth form: 198; Boarders: 86 full, 12 weekly

Fees: Day £13,900 – £21,750; Boarding + £15,500; International Non EEA Boarding £18,250 – £43,250 pa

Principal: Alistair Brownlow MA (St Andrews) MPhil (Glasgow) in English. Joined as a new graduate in 1997 after teaching English in Russia and Romania, working his way up to co-principal in 2002 and sole principal in 2016.

Adept at putting others at ease and bouncing with enthusiasm like Tigger, he expresses the school's beliefs and methods with an articulacy which backs up his reputation as an ace English teacher. Winces at the term 'headmaster' on account of the school's flatter leadership model – in fact, he refuses to take any more credit for school's success than the other 'principals', aka heads of lower school, sixth form and pastoral and welfare.

Parents say he's 'always available', 'very understanding' and 'he listens'. 'You never feel like you're going into an old schoolmaster's office where your feelings will be belittled – he makes it clear you have the right to feel however you do and he takes swift action too,' said one. 'He's intuitive when it comes to responding to each individual and is also pragmatic, both of which make him very skilled at fitting the right courses for the right child,' said another. Pupils told us he's 'often wandering around, usually with prospective parents' and that he has a 'good sense of humour'.

Tends towards relentless comparisons with 'other' schools, presenting a somewhat unrealistic view of the big, bad world of education – though to be fair, he hears many tales from pupils who have become completely disillusioned with their previous schools. Some pupils go further still – 'All state schools are rubbish,' one told us, although school says this view is 'regrettable and we believe it is not representative of the views of most students here'.

Entrance: It's non-selective in that there's no entrance exam for children joining at 11 or 13, and there's no minimum GCSE grade requirements for sixth form entry. You don't even have to have done a history GCSE to do a history A level ('We get that some 14-year-olds are put off history but want to come back to it later on'). But every prospective student is interviewed ('it's as much a consultancy session as anything'), and the principals say they do turn some away.

Direct entry into any year group at any point in the academic year is possible, and places can be secured in the short gap between exam results and the start of a new term. Around 60 students join each year, either to retake their A levels having completed two years of A levels elsewhere, or directly into year 13 after disappointing results in year 12 elsewhere. Welcoming boarders from 13+ (previously 15+) from September 2022.

Exit: Over half leave after GCSEs. Those that stay for the sixth form go on to universities including UCL, Manchester, Leeds, UEA, Bristol, Newcastle and Loughborough. Courses reflect a very wide range of interests from law, maths, medicine and classics to animal behaviour, film studies, marketing, photography and midwifery. In 2021 six medics; no Oxbridge.

Latest results: In 2021, 37 per cent 9-7 at GCSE; 55 per cent A*/A at A level (79 per cent A*-B). In 2019 (the last year when exams took place), 25

per cent 9-7 at GCSE; 29 per cent A*/A at A level (60 per cent A*-B).

Teaching and learning: There's no uniform or dress code and the teachers are just as likely as pupils to be wearing a hoodie. Everyone goes by their first name and there are no school bells. Classrooms mainly consist of large tables with chairs grouped round collaboratively, where small groups of pupils learn via discursive tutorial type teaching. So far so hippy – until you notice the hush that has descended in the classrooms and the fact that pupils (younger ones, at any rate) are just as likely to do traditional spelling tests and times tables as any other school, while older ones follow strict exam-oriented curricula. 'People try to place us in the progressive/alternative mould, but we're not,' says Alistair. 'It's common sense; small classes, good teaching, and an informal but ordered and respectful atmosphere.'

The next surprise comes in the teaching methods where – certainly higher up the school – it's teach-test-teach-test, with A level students getting a test a week in every subject. The idea that testing thwarts children gets short shrift here and both pupils and parents seem to welcome it. 'It's not testing in the sense of passing or failing; it's testing to spot the areas where you need more support,' one pupil explained. 'The ethos is that if you get something wrong, the teacher needs to work with you and if the whole class gets something wrong, the teacher needs to sort themselves out – it highlights the school's dedication to personalised learning and genuine accountability,' said a parent. Pupils say it also reduces exam wobbles ('we're so used to tests that we just get on with it') and that it's confidence-boosting to watch your grades go up (many students transfer here after poor progress elsewhere and the effect can be dramatic).

Couple this with an unashamed concentration on exam techniques and you could be forgiven for assuming this is an exam factory, but it really isn't. 'The teachers here have real passion for their subjects and the two-hour lessons at A level mean you can really explore a subject from all angles,' said one sixth form pupil. The whole shebang attracts, as you might imagine, the kind of teacher that prefers 'more teaching, less bureaucracy' model and many have higher degrees. Some have attended the school themselves, as have many admin staff – 'You'll get no sharp-suited admissions department here.'

There are three pathways through the sixth form, mainly set in different teaching groups. There are those doing a two-year A level course through the school; students who have transferred here for year 13 after a disappointing year 12; and those who have done two years elsewhere and are doing retakes. The A level programme, which involves 40 options including global perspectives, music technology and fashion and textiles, is flexible with no option blocks, and students can do speed courses in a new subject to complement retakes. The school is in the top five per cent in the UK for student progress at A level. Maths is the biggest A level subject and English literature and film studies are also strong departments. School says pupils are increasingly joining from IB schools either half-way through or after completing it because 'they personally find A levels a better route to their chosen university'.

'The teachers here have real passion for their subjects and the two-hour lessons at A level mean you can really explore a subject from all angles,' said one sixth form pupil

At GCSE, most students take seven or eight subjects. English and maths are taught at IGCSE level. Languages on offer include German, French, Spanish and (by student demand) Mandarin, but it is not compulsory to take a language. Pupils can also take subjects such as astronomy, film studies and most recently classical civilisation has been added. Many take art subjects, sometimes two or three. Nobody cares about EBacc here. English and the creative arts get the highest grades.

Learning support and SEN: There's no highly developed SEN department and school is up-front about being suitable for milder end problems, where support is in-class. A dyslexic pupil told us, 'I definitely get all the help I need and haven't had to miss a single lesson', while a parent of a child with ADHD said 'socially, it was a nightmare at her last school but she has blossomed here'. EHCPs are few and far between, usually around issues like anxiety or school phobia, nothing complicated. Some pupils come from neighbouring SEN school Trinity to be more stretched academically. Parents appreciate the efforts made to ensure each pupil gains the best possible grades, with extra lessons available before exams and in the holidays, none of which is chargeable. 'You'd have to be mad to get an out-of-school tutor here,' said a parent.

The arts and extracurricular: It would be hard to find better provision for the artistically inclined. GCSEs are offered in six disciplines – fine art, graphics, photography, textiles, ceramics and 3D. Some students take three to A level, enabling them to bypass a foundation year. The art rooms have a welcoming, university feel, with much of the work on display of university standard with real individuality and flair. We also like the cross-curricular approach.

No school orchestra or choir, but pupils describe the music here as 'sick' and rave about the music technology opportunities and their bands, which they can showcase at the summer festival. There are musical opportunities within drama too – the first ever whole-school performance, Bugsy Malone, was in rehearsals when we visited. The drama theatre is a rich cultural hub, according to pupils, hosting visiting theatre companies while the school's onsite cinema regularly hosts the National Schools' Film Week. 'For those of us that come here because of issues at our previous school, drama can be a great way of building up confidence,' said one.

Sport: Not for the super-sporty – unless your child is prepared to pursue their sport outside school, for which they will be flexible around commitments for elite sportspeople. And while some pupils say 'it can be frustrating when they try and fail to set up sports teams for the likes of rugby or football', the school had brought in football teams when we visited. The main stumbling block is space – there just isn't the infrastructure to provide serious provision. But they do use local facilities and they have a small gym and outside court, where we saw pupils kicking a ball around. Main PE provision is, however, more activity based – things like ice skating, sailing, self-defence and climbing.

Boarding: Beds for 119 pupils aged 15+ (from aged 13+ from September 2022) across seven terraced houses, full to capacity when we visited. All have small, single rooms – some with a small 'pod' ensuite, otherwise it's shared bathrooms until the school completes its rolling programme. Georgian high ceilings and big windows add light and space and each house has a common room with comfy chairs and a study for quiet work. Décor is welcoming and modern, IKEA style, with some houses still awaiting refurb. Teenage-friendly touches include pool tables. School describes it as 'lighter touch' boarding, so no housemasters or mistresses, but parents praise the school nurse – 'she's responsive and relates to them,' said one, although a few we spoke to said the food can be bland and get repetitive. Boarders say they settle in quickly and one praised the way boarding staff 'respect teenagers' need for independence, while also setting appropriate boundaries – I will be well prepared for university life.' Currently some 40 per cent of boarders are from the UK, 11 per cent from Europe, and the remainder from countries including Canada, USA, Thailand, China, Russia, Nigeria and South Africa.

Ethos and heritage: It started as an A level college in 1984 and extended to take pupils from year 7 in 2007. Bought by Dukes Education in 2016 which has given a cash injection to facilities, including new canteen (although some students say food isn't great) and higher-spec boarding interiors. Plus, members of the Dukes team visit regularly to give advice and talks on the likes of Oxbridge, medical and US admissions.

Boarders say they settle in quickly and one praised the way boarding staff respect teenagers' need for independence, while also setting appropriate boundaries

The campus is as unique as the school. It started as one terraced house, but as the school expanded, it gradually bought up 14 properties in adjoining roads, including the seven terraced boarding houses. What would once have been the back gardens to these houses now form the grounds with ancient apple trees and wild garden areas, paths to secret nooks and crannies, a viewing platform to climb – and the oversized 'maths shed' where we saw a business studies class in action. Students work on garden projects such as the allotment as part of their DofE award, and the gardens – a hide-and-seek nirvana for younger ones – have won awards. The £100,000 steel sculptural musical gates, on which you can play three octaves, are an art installation created by Henry Dagg. These gates, like many other areas of the school, feature flying pigs – a wry reference to a cynical comment made when the school opened. Younger pupils said they'd like to do 'more outside learning – there's a wasted opportunity there'; older pupils said they'd welcome a main library (there are subject-specific ones) and better sixth-form common room space. Those niggles aside, pupils appreciate their surroundings. Lower school has its own block.

You'll find no Latin mottoes here, no mahogany-rich headmaster's study and no suave head in a handmade suit. No pupils with collars and lips firmly buttoned. No assemblies and no pupil 'type'. No manicured rolling hills and no school hymn. For many, all this is a blessed relief. Pupils can be themselves, with or without piercings and alternative haircuts (all of which we saw), while parents can (and often do) breathe a sigh of relief they'll never have to attend a PTA committee or fundraising ball again. As for parents who worry it will be Lord of the Flies in the making, the school points out that 'it is still school and actually quite old-fashioned in the sense of being exam oriented'.

Numbers lower down the school are small, starting with around 13 pupils in year 7, who have deliberately opted for a small and different type of school. These are added to over the years, generally by pupils who have been disaffected or haven't thrived in other schools, to numbers in the mid-20s for GCSE years. By sixth form it grows to 70 in year 12, and 130 in year 13/14. This is something to consider in the younger year groups, especially as the gender split can be very uneven. The flipside is less of the gender division that you see in big schools – all pupils are clearly relaxed in each other's company and there's much more mixing between year groups.

Pastoral care, inclusivity and discipline: Some of the pupils have been labelled as bad apples or having limited prospects in previous settings, but have quickly turned things around here, where they are free from discipline based on minutiae. Other pupils have come from grammars where they felt under too much pressure, or from large schools where they felt overwhelmed, and they have also flourished here. Parents speak highly of the pastoral care: 'The way they handle each pupil as an individual is striking and they treat them as young adults, so it's more a case of negotiating than imposing regimes, which motivates them enormously,' said one. A level students have one-to-one meetings with a personal tutor every couple of weeks, more frequently if they wish, and pupils lower down the school have individual meetings every term. Parents get regular reports, and never any with surprises.

You'll find no Latin mottoes here, and no suave head in a handmade suit. No pupils with collars and lips firmly buttoned. For many, all this is a blessed relief

School is strict about turning up on time, behaviour and homework and pupils told us detentions do get handed out for 'swearing, distracting others in class and too many warnings'. Some pupils believe the school is too rigid about being 'even two minutes late', but overall they recognise and respect the trust they are given and the way 'you get a second chance if you mess up' although there is zero tolerance to drugs, with regular random testing. Three or four students a year are excluded or encouraged to go elsewhere but school doesn't believe in temporary exclusions.

Pupils and parents: Local pupils form 70 per cent of the cohort and come from a wide catchment area – there are four minibuses from towns including Tonbridge, Tunbridge Wells, Maidstone, Ashford and Sevenoaks, and the train station brings pupils from Bromley and London. A further 15 per cent come from elsewhere in the UK, and 15 per cent from overseas, including Thai government scholars (who tend to be very high performers, often ending up at Oxbridge). Around half the pupils come from the independent sector, the rest families with no tradition of private education. 'It's genuinely diverse,' said a pupil.

This is a place for individuals. There's a lovely air of tolerance and warmth between the pupils – many of whom seem relieved to have found a home among other square pegs – and the vulnerability of the ones who have had negative experiences of previous schools is palpable. 'They look after each other and genuinely celebrate each other's successes – not just good grades but perhaps a moment that highlights they've grown in confidence or self-esteem,' said one parent, who added that the school's emphasis on the arts means there's 'equal respect for successes in art or academia'.

Money matters: Around £100,000 per year goes into means-tested bursaries, which are awarded not on academic ability, but 'if we think they'll make a good contribution'. Scholarships include the Ralph Steadman Art Scholarship, which offers a two-year full scholarship for A levels. Extras are kept to a minimum – music lessons, buses and exam fees are extra, but extracurricular trips are kept deliberately modest.

The last word: This won't be one that sits on your shortlist and you can't make up your mind about. As one parent put it, 'It's a Marmite option.' Nor will it be the type of school you'll be boasting about your child going to at the west Sevenoaks dinner parties. Your money won't buy the trappings of a public school, but you'll get that warm buzz in your heart when you recognise your kid in the personalities here – or not. That might be one of several types we saw – the quirky one, condemned to be picked on in an average school; the fiercely intelligent, who has rubbed teachers up the wrong way by being too smart for his own good in other settings; the kid whose education got derailed by too much focus on petty rules and discipline. It won't suit sporting jocks, but it's money well spent on children who don't suit more conventional schooling, but whose parents still prioritise the best possible grades.

Roedean School

55

Roedean Way, Brighton, East Sussex BN2 5RQ

01273 667500 | enquiries@roedean.co.uk | www.roedean.co.uk

Ages: 11–18

Pupils: 686; sixth form: 158; Boarders: 283 full, 56 weekly/flexi

Fees: Day £17,970 – £23,490; Boarding £31,770 – £42,135 pa

Headmaster: Since 2013, Oliver Blond (early 50s) married to children's author Helen Peters, with two children. Mr Blond has excellent girls' school credentials, having previously been head of Henrietta Barnett in London, and deputy head at North London Collegiate. Joined Roedean to turn around a school that was failing, and has done so; the days of needing to consider the admission of boys to save the school are long gone: Roedean is proudly and decidedly about educating girls.

The head's aim is for happy children and high academic standards, but, importantly, not to 'compromise the journey for the outcome'. Parents agree: if children are happy, results will follow. So have pupil numbers, with the school doubling in size during Mr Blond's tenure.

'Amazing… [I'm] really inspired about what he says about women… he seems to empower the girls,' said a parent. Another said, 'he's immensely impressive… his whole approach lifts the girls. Education there has far exceed our expectations, and they were high.'

'He's on your side, knows names and says hello,' said a pupil; 'very human… talks to people, chats and is friendly,' said another. A new girl, not used to this friendliness in a headmaster, said, 'He came and smiled and shook my hand, and I thought – what's his agenda?'

Entrance: A variety of 'experience days' to catch the attention of prospective pupils, from rockpooling to science challenges. Then tests in English and maths and an interview. Oversubscribed, so entrance is increasingly competitive, but candidates don't need to be excellent in every area emphasises head, good potential counts for much.

Exit: Some leave after GCSEs to attend the local sixth form college; the number of overseas pupils in sixth form increases correspondingly. At 18 most depart to university in the UK, with a few heading abroad or taking a gap year. UCL, LSE, Manchester, King's, Edinburgh, Bristol, Cambridge, Durham, Imperial and Loughborough all recently popular. Five to Oxbridge and six medics in 2021. Annual handful to art foundation at Central St Martins.

New director of higher education helps pupils focus on which university and how to get in, with mock interviews and entrance exam practice. Sixth formers are advised that fulfilling their academic potential is the most important thing – 'Get a good degree in a good subject and you can do anything,' a sixth former told us confidently.

Latest results: In 2021, 90 per cent 9-7 at GCSE; 82 per cent A*/A at A level. In 2019 (the last year when exams took place), 68 per cent 9/-7 at GCSE; 55 per cent A*/A at A level.

Teaching and learning: 'I actually understand (Mr X's) teaching methods,' said a tag written on the kindness tree, and you can imagine the relieved delight of the writer. This school, like many, claims to have innovative teaching methods; in this case, the maths teacher puts all the questions in a new topic up on the board to see what girls can do by using their initiative and puzzling things out, the aim being to engage the girls and make them think. We saw a lesson with girls on their feet, working out problems with words and actions; called to silence by the teacher, they were asked for feedback on the exercise. A hand shot up. 'It's hard,' said a girl feelingly. Each teacher has their own method; many have drama training from RADA, to broaden their repertoire of teaching styles.

One parent described her daughter, who wasn't engaged at primary school, being transformed at Roedean: 'She joined the physics club just for fun.' 'Teachers are exceptionally passionate about their subjects,' said another. Pupils are asked for feedback on teachers once a year and say that the senior team shadow lessons to ensure they are up to standard. A few teachers are 'less good', said a parent, but most are 'superb'.

Younger girls are engaged by the Head, Heart and Hands curriculum, which aims to introduce them to new things, such as philosophy, self defence, British Sign Language or farm club. At the other end of the school, sixth form work includes independent research projects, which can be extended into the EPQ. Flip learning in sixth form (preparing a new subject before the lesson, so pupils start from an informed position) means open-ended preparation, 'but we're told to cap it at three hours,' said a pupil casually. Pupils respond well to homework entitled 'insane challenge'; 'it's about making it exciting,' said the head. They borrow the best parts of the IB to supplement A levels: pupils study the theory of knowledge, and everyone does community service.

The school has grown quickly in the last few years: some parents voiced concern about class sizes increasing, and both parents and pupils said they could do with more space inside. The school says in fact class sizes have decreased in the last few years, with an increase in the numbers of staff: the average class size at KS3 is 18, and they are creating more space in other areas of the school.

'If you're just a set of results, you're just achievement, which, like glass, can shatter. There needs to be more,' declares head. Results are only one element of what matters at Roedean, but they do rather well, all the same. A level grades have held steady for the last few years, as have the numbers of those achieving top grades at GCSE (9-8) (around 50 per cent). Consistently good results in maths and sciences; economics and politics are also popular at A level. Results in economics are a bit less shiny, but on the up this year, with a new economics teacher in post.

Individual bedrooms from year 8 are the nicest we've seen. Top floor in each house is called 'heaven' – with amazing views over the sea

Until recently Roedean was only lightly selective, but with growing popularity entrance is becoming harder: the academic profile of the school is likely to change as a result. 'They don't work children to the bone,' said one parent, but '[they] push academically as far as they can,' said another. Her daughter was behind in maths when she joined; they put her in a lower set until she had caught up, then moved her up three sets, and the parent was delighted with this 'very supportive approach'.

Learning support and SEN: The head of learning support is assisted by five TAs, who give in-class support in core subjects. Around 35 pupils have one-to-one sessions, but learning support offered to any pupils who need help at 'pinch points', such as assistances with revision or exam technique.

The arts and extracurricular: Co-curricular offerings are varied and plentiful, from Lego engineering to the astronomy club, where pupils wrap up warm on clear winter nights to be guided around the sky using one of the school's five telescopes. The sea swimming club meet at 6am and go through Roedean's private tunnel to the beach for their swim, no wetsuits allowed; they've signed up to relay swim the channel.

Round, well fed and happy – the sheep in Roedean's farm that is, their happiness reflected in the glowing faces of their pupil carers.

Pupils use the lovely original art studios; picture tiles on the walls were painted by pupils decades ago and light pours in from the glass panels in the roof. An elaborate woven model from an A level artist sits alongside one of the oldest printing presses in the country (they have a more up-to-date model for regular use). Pupils excel at art here and achieve high grades at A Level and GCSE.

Performing arts are popular and there is a variety of workshops and performances, both traditional and less so: in an Indonesian gamelan workshop, new year 7 pupils learnt music which is only passed by oral means, to emphasise the importance of community. Older pupils performed a dance showcase on Instagram vs Reality, interpreting the pressures on teenagers in modern society. One parent told us how delighted she was that her daughter's talent on the piano was recognised and celebrated, even though she had taught herself. Other schools rejected this home-made effort, but 'Roedean embraced it'.

Roedean may be placed in splendid isolation on a clifftop, but it takes its role in the community very seriously; the purpose and value of outreach here is considerably more than gloss for a university application. Girls take on many different volunteer roles, from working in charity shops to helping at the Royal Institute for the Blind. The school also has an excellent relationship with a local primary school, described by the head as both 'privilege and opportunity'. Minibus loads of girls are dispatched weekly to St Mark's to help with reading, sports, maths and buddying, and last year Roedean raised £30,000 to build a new library there, each girl donating her favourite book. The girls feel strongly about homelessness in Brighton, and support the local homeless charity Off the Fence: 50 extra portions of lunch are cooked every Thursday and are taken, piping hot, directly to this charity.

Sport: Twenty-six sports on offer, all the traditional girls' ones and most of the boys', including tag rugby. Two dance studios, indoor pool, new all-weather pitch – there's even a golf course.

Boarding: You could be staying in a boutique hotel. Following a £9m refurbishment, boarding houses are modern and elegant, the design celebrating old features, such as fireplaces, and introducing the new and fun, like the hanging teapot lights. Individual bedrooms from year 8 and they are the nicest we've seen, with soft grey wooden fittings for desk, bed and wardrobe – 'You can always pull a mattress into a friend's room if you want a sleepover.' Pupils tried out the new rooms and found the polished wooden floors too cold under toe, so they've been carpeted. The top floor in each house is called 'heaven' – with such amazing views over the sea, this is not far off.

Roedean makes a vivid first impression in its grand clifftop position. But more notable is the atmosphere, one of lively purpose. It is immediately compelling

Houses mix day pupils and boarders: around half of the 630 pupils board and most are full boarders; no feeling of an abandoned ship here at the weekends. Day pupils can board for the odd night with prior notification and anyway can come to breakfast and stay to supper. Weekly boarders from London are chaperoned back and forth to Victoria.

Saturday mornings are busy with sports, then there are trips to cinemas, shops and trampolines and activities such as cooking or making balloon stress balls (no, we're not sure about these either). Special days are marked in special ways: Remembrance Sunday by a service, and showing of War Horse in the theatre; Halloween by a maze made by sixth formers, who dress up and lurk in dark corners to jump out at people. Each house has a piano, a common room with comfy seating and TV, and a kitchen where girls can make snacks in the evening; fruit is always available. 'They [the house parents] have dogs,' said the girls, with evident approval.

The parent of a first-time boarder said communication is good and she receives regular emails from housemistress, who is 'very, very efficient… nothing goes unseen, unsaid…' Her daughter has settled really well, 'she's so happy'.

Ethos and heritage: 'We thought it was incredible the moment we walked through the door,' said a parent. Roedean makes a vivid first impression: of bold determination, certainly, in its grand clifftop position to the east of Brighton, and in its size, with its large fireplaces and wooden floors softened and shined by decades of feet. But more notable is the atmosphere, one of lively purpose. It is immediately compelling.

Roedean was started in 1885 by three sisters to educate girls for entry to the women's colleges at Oxbridge. It was a strong statement about female education: girls swam in the sea before breakfast, played cricket, and showed the world they could do anything boys could do. In many ways this is still the case (although the sea swimming is optional). Successful women, including Olympic gold medalists and a professor of space physics, come into the school as ambassadors six times a year to encourage and inspire.

The atmosphere of the school has profoundly changed in the last few years, due in large part to the influx of UK and local pupils, which has trebled in the last five years, many of whom receive bursarial support. 'State school pupils come with openness, creativity, determination and thirst,' said the head. 'There's no sense of value [here] associated with status and wealth… it's a very inclusive environment.' Parents echo these thoughts, describing the ethos as inclusive, and the environment as encouraging (though they all know who's going on the fabulous holidays, shrugged one). It's an 'intenser school', said a sixth former.

Pupils were articulate and forthright – and they love it there. 'It's hours on the bus every day, a 12-hour day… but it's worth it. It's their life,' said a parent. 'They appreciate it every day… know we make sacrifices [to pay for it],' said another.

House feeling is strong; houses aren't named, but numbered from one to four, (after 1-4 Sussex Square, where the original school was situated), plus two sixth form houses, Keswick and Lawrence. There's plenty of inter-house competition, from the usual sport to a recent competition celebrating extraordinary women.

Chapel is compulsory, unless pupils choose not to go for religious reasons. It is deliberately inclusive; one Muslim pupil gave a talk in chapel during Ramadan, and girls of other faiths speak about their religions. Much is pupil led: girls talk in chapel and assembly more than adults, and introduce speech day.

The weather was mentioned by all the pupils we spoke to; they are intimate with the wind, and it's the one thing many would like to change. 'The wind… it has a personality… it is out to get me, particularly me,' said a pupil from Nigeria feelingly.

Girls like the food most of the time, and the school says surveys show that the food is considered exceptionally good. There's always fruit available in houses, and pupils can make tea and toast or other snacks after school. One parent beamed as she told us, 'the food is so good... I don't cook at night because they're so well fed at lunchtime.'

The school is in the midst of a multi-million-pound refurbishment, boarding houses and sixth form centre complete and extremely smart, the library next up: the original library, already quite ample and well stocked, is about to have a mezzanine level added. The old reference library, with its learned bookcases and tiptoe hush has very good acoustics, and is now used for recitals.

Pastoral care, inclusivity and discipline: They don't want boys here, not even slightly, said the girls we spoke to. 'It's the perfect place for women to grow and develop,' said a sixth former firmly, 'perfect as it is.' 'Girls are less kind to each other when boys are around, and more competitive,' added another. Pupils are asked to bring in family and friends for various events, and boys turn up at Roedean that way, without fanfare; no bussing them in from Harrow for parties.

A parent said her daughter had 'blossomed beyond imagining' at Roedean, and that her aspirations and expectations of herself are much higher than at her previous school. '[They are] encouraged and supported to take opportunities... [they] quickly recognise what the girls are good at.' Good behaviour is rewarded with responsibilities, such as farm prefect – 'I love it!' said a girl, face glowing, arms around a goat. Poor behaviour results in focus points, 'half help, half sanction', said a pupil who had collected a fair few. Some horrified faces when we mentioned drink and drugs; not identified as a problem amongst those we spoke to.

'They don't let pastoral problems escalate,' said a parent. There are three pastoral managers on the main corridor; the girls like the fact they are situated here, not squirrelled away in a secret corner. Pupils describe them as fast and efficient; peer listeners can be helpful and the counsellors in the health centre are available for drop-in sessions. 'They're really on it,' according to a parent, who said the health centre provided amazing support for her daughter following a broken limb; they even thought to let her out of lessons 10 mins early: empty corridors and stairs for easier passage.

School recently introduced vertical tutor groups meaning that girls get to know pupils from all years. Apparently this has given them a greater sense of familial support: 'There's a good community feel.'

The odd incident of bullying is sorted out quickly, one parent saying the school dealt with an incident before she'd heard about it, and that the agreement between the girls to be 'civil and friendly' was effective.

Many sixth formers are balancing a heavy workload: academic studies, school offices, sports commitments and university entrance, and parent views vary about the support offered by sixth form leaders. One said her daughter received excellent reassurance and help from the head of sixth form to set up a balanced working structure, another that support is insufficient and there isn't enough communication between different departments to make sure her daughter isn't overloaded. A flying trip to the Peak District, two nights away, was a controversy of almost Marmite proportions with parents: 'ill timed' and 'too far', said one; 'important time to relax and enjoy themselves,' said another (activities included abseiling, cycling and mindfulness sessions).

The weather is the one thing many would like to change. 'The wind... it has a personality... it is out to get me, particularly me,' said a pupil from Nigeria feelingly

Roedean has recently decided to detach mobile phones from pupils: phones must now be handed in on arrival at school (apart from sixth form). Head was braced for a backlash, but there was none: apparently pupils were relieved to have the social pressure removed and find the experience liberating (boarders get their phones back for a short time each evening).

Pupils and parents: 'Posh, state [school] and Chinese,' said a parent briskly when asked about pupil demographic, adding that there are no problems with mix of privileged and less so, but Chinese pupils could be better integrated. International pupils make up 20 per cent of the pupil body, and are mostly Chinese, though there are pupils from 40 different countries.

Money matters: Full fees are the usual eye-watering amount, but Roedean is very generous in its financial support, offering means-tested support to around a third of pupils, and bursaries of up to 100 per cent, particularly for local families. Help also available for the daughters of clergy, FCO and services families. Academic, sports, drama, dance, art and music scholarships available.

Parents whose children receive bursaries warmly praise the school's generosity, one saying that when she can't afford a school trip, they ask her to pay what you she can – 'My daughter has never missed out for lack of money.' Uniform is pricey, but secondhand gear is available.

The last word: This is a school where girls make a noise and get their hands dirty; a school determined to help girls realise their value and erase the limitations to which they often subject themselves. Selective, but no longer on class or even cash. The diversity at Roedean has revitalised the school: it seems healthy, and crisply alive.

Royal Russell School

Coombe Lane, Croydon, Surrey CR9 5BX

020 8657 4433 | admissions@royalrussell.co.uk | www.royalrussell.co.uk

Ages: 3-18

Pupils: 1100; sixth form: 258; Boarders: 181 full

Fees: Day £11,661 – £19,986; Boarding £39,504 pa

Headmaster: Since 2011, Chris Hutchinson BMet. Second headship – first was at Newcastle School for Boys, which he joined in 2007. 'Teaching is in the blood,' he says. Opted for metallurgy degree but decided against engineering career. Worked for family owned and run school in Wales for two years, followed by formal teacher training at Cambridge and posts in top schools, starting with Clifton in 1990 where he met wife Alex – also a scientist. ('Some unfortunate Cliftonites were taught a lot of Hutchinson chemistry and physics.') Left as head of physics, moving to Wellington in 2000 in same role where was also a boarding housemaster.

Had completed full cycle (years 9 to 13) at Newcastle School for Boys when post here came up. Was encouraged to apply and felt instantly at home, compatible ethos of 'getting to know people well, giving them an individual opportunity to shine and supporting, rather than pushing them, on their journey' the clincher. He fits in a bit of energetic teaching and has advanced child recognition skills. 'Knows them – every one,' said staff member in full on Tiny Tim mode. Pupils equally chuffed. 'So, so good – really engages,' said one. 'Makes the effort to get to know you.'

Mr Hutchinson's hobbies include singing, gardening, Herefordshire, old Land Rovers and exercising his pets: dog Scrumpy and Linus the cat. Reflective, funny and kind, Mr Hutchinson is a major attraction for parents. Staff ditto. 'I took the job because of him,' said one, who praised mastery of details – 'Reports broken locks, picks up the rubbish' (he does, too – only gave up on stray banana skin on walk round because of its advanced stage of decomposition). 'Nothing is too trivial.' On day of visit, had just written 71 congratulatory notes to cast and backstage team of school production.

Headmaster of Royal Russell Junior School: since September 2019 is John Evans, previously senior deputy head at Haberdashers' Aske's School. Studied English and education at Cambridge; has taught English at Dulwich Prep London. Married with three children.

Junior and senior school reviews, previously separate, are now combined, with blessing of the school. Reinforces sense of togetherness that emanates from the top.

Entrance: Popular and currently at capacity in every year group. Undaunting entrance process. 'Very gentle,' says school. Junior school entrants arrive the September after third birthday, are observed in small groups (no interview or formal test). 'We're looking to see if children are on track with development, communications and ability to interact.' More formal assessments further up the school – all joining in years 3 to 6 must be senior school shoo-ins.

Around 90 per cent go on to the senior school, with places offered to junior school pupils in year 6; they sit exams only if they want to be considered for awards, often scooping the top scholarships, though there's no favouritism, stresses school.

For senior school, main entry point is year 7, when 96 places are available – around half of these are secured by the junior school pupils. External candidates sit entrance exams in maths, English and VR. A further 24 places available in year 9. Varying numbers in year 12 – no entrance exam, with places based on GCSE performance.

Popularity means the school is selective, but makes the effort to know each child and assess what they would contribute to the community. 'The assessments are important. However, we also want to see pupils reflect the school values and be open, ambitious, courageous and distinctive.'

Exit: Loses a few juniors to local grammars and other independents such as Alleyn's and Caterham. A bit drop recently in numbers leaving post-GCSE – down to five per cent in 2021. Manchester, Nottingham, Kings College London, UCL, Warwick, Edinburgh, Exeter and Southampton all popular university destinations. None to Oxbridge in 2021, but there were three medics. Courses wide ranging, including architecture, business, computer science, economics, English, history, music production, maths, sport and exercise science, film and TV, and philosophy and psychology. A number of pupils also go on to study abroad. Some apprenticeships, eg PWC at Birmingham University.

Latest results: In 2021, 67 per cent 9-7 at GCSE; 65 per cent A*/A at A level (88 per cent A*-B). In 2019 (the last year when exams took place), 53 per cent 9-7 at GCSE; 44 per cent A*/A at A level (68 per cent A*-B).

Teaching and learning: Known as a gentler alternative to more selective schools in the area, though 'we do get the brightest students,' says school. Now positioning itself as 'the family school of choice in south London' (plays better than Croydon, 'a sell too far' for gentrified sunny uplands of Nappy Valley, Wandsworth and Balham).

Entry requirements may not have shifted but winds of change are definitely well above zephyr level, starting with results. And government-issued value added table recently put school right at the top of the country.

Heads have trimmed, rather than hacked, their staff teams, felt by parents to be stronger, if a work in progress. 'You'll hear some rumblings and grumblings in the car park and it's usually about staff,' said one. Thirty, average age close to 40, have completed first decade (one cheery and popular geography teacher on way to notching up ruby anniversary). For seniors, maximum class size is 24, average 18 to year 9, 15 for GCSE years and just eight for sixth form. Junior class average is 17 (parents make feelings known if numbers pass 20 in busy year).

New generation of vibrant staff newcomers love it here. One raved about mentoring ('have grown as a person'). Energy exemplified by new junior school librarian who has created oasis of great charm with imaginative use of lighting – Chinese lanterns, netting studded with fairy lights, even reading by torchlight sessions.

Despite school togetherness, juniors have own staff temperamentally suited to this age group. Combines specialists (music, computing, French, Spanish, sport and science) from nursery upwards with dedicated class teachers. Continuity and security means pupils 'retain their childhood for as long as they can'. 'System works,' agreed parent. 'Always somebody to hear you out and help you.'

In senior school, star subjects include A level biology, as popular with boys as girls. History, though, is the chart-topper, converting the marginally interested into passionately keen. Differentiation is a key part of the process, teachers praised for willingness to explain a topic in limitless different ways until it clicked ('and if that doesn't work, will ask someone else to explain it to you'). While 10 GCSEs are the norm, will adjust if necessary, provide after-school sessions and generally do what it takes. 'Always there to help,' said pupil. Nurturing qualities appreciated by parents – 'You won't get that in some [other] schools,' said one. International pupils similarly feel exceptionally well looked after. Though English isn't mother tongue for around 20 per cent, who can arrive with large gaps in learning, expectation is that all will take GCSEs and A levels. Support is flexible, generally at no extra cost and often yields rapid results. One new international sixth form boarder was delighted to have passed GCSE maths in first term. Junior school support similar, with one pupil attending local centre part time.

Ten minutes by tram from east Croydon, green and pleasant site, complete with own deer herd, offers antidote to crowded London senior schools

Parents also praised efforts with very able. 'School invests in children that need more time either because they're slightly behind or ahead – they have different programmes and challenges,' said mother of junior school pupil.

Learning support and SEN: School's reputation for SEN remains undimmed. Currently, very few students have EHCPs. Have experience of autism, ADHD, and specific learning difficulties. Support includes additional literacy and numeracy sessions, assigned teachers who work with pupils in and out of lessons, though with just one full-time member of staff in the senior school, there's a limit to the numbers they can help.

The arts and extracurricular: Junior school activities range from numerous informal concerts (music is timetabled from nursery) to residential trips from year 3 and over 40 activities (pupils pack in up to five a week), including coding club, swim squad and media club (filming and editing).

Tonbridge School

Same again for seniors – one year 10 pupil involved in choir, extra sport, Mandarin and popular CCF (night exercises more of a draw than drilling). Model United Nations vast – school hosts annual international conference and gamely lends other local schools placards for their own events.

Bar slight glumness from one senior school pupil analysing recent production rather than doing it ('Interesting work?' we asked. 'Not particularly,' was the response), enthusiasm for the arts abounds. No wonder, given trips (West End to New York for thesps) and lavish facilities including auditorium in performing arts centre, the base for regular productions (Importance of Being Earnest, Wind in the Willows). Pianists, among the 200 or so musicians, have new Bechsteins – 'I live in this practice room,' said one – with concerts in venues including the Royal Albert Hall for those who do make it outside.

Sport: 'All the space a child could need to run, jump and cartwheel,' says junior prospectus, with 110 acres well used by all, from nursery school pupils walking the 1.3 km cross-country circuit (in a morning) to boarders taking it at a rather faster pace 'for fun' (takes all sorts). Bar an all-weather surface that, frustratingly, needs duvet day if there's a hard frost, facilities and options are top notch, including new pavilion (not picturesque but home to host of extras including gym and physio suite) and two swimming pools.

Little, indeed, that isn't offered, to parental (and inspectorial) approval. 'Everything is there so children don't need to spend lots of time away from education by driving to swimming,' said one. Sports successes could go up a notch or two, think some, though limited by smaller pool of talent to draw on, compared with single sex schools. Rugby, notable by absence, heads the parents' wishlist (and likely to remain there), hockey felt to get fair share of resources and then some. Overall, though, 'win more than we lose,' thought a pupil, results pages revealing impressive football success (teams reach semi-finals of London and national contests) but mixed fortunes elsewhere.

Boarding: Most of the full boarders in the senior school stay on for weekends and must attend at least three activities (fireworks and go-karting among them) a term. Other perks include after-school exploration of the fleshpots of Croydon and exclusive access to swish-looking coffee machine in dining hall. Homesickness still strikes but 'keep talking' was advice from one boarder, and will pass. For anything more serious, school has medical centre staffed round the clock.

Girl boarders have one house that backs onto junior school (new building for 160 girls). Boys do better with two (Oxford and Cambridge, now in two wings under one roof), all with day pupils too. Further six houses for day pupils only; flexi-boarding so day pupils can stay on for extra sport or rehearsals. Rooms and bathrooms are generally tidy and pleasant and happy, trusting atmosphere prevails with personal possessions left out, not locked away.

Though British boarders are substantially outnumbered by Chinese and other nationalities, school ensures that everyone mixes in multinational social groups

Though British boarders are substantially outnumbered by Chinese (majority in sixth form) and other nationalities including Russian, Armenian, Bulgarian and Ukrainian, school, unlike many others, ensures that everyone mixes in multinational social groups. Horizons are impressively expanded for all pupils, with boarders enjoying tea with local families. Website features overseas students (Bogdan from Romania and Yizhou from China among others) extolling the virtues of the school in their mother tongues.

Ethos and heritage: Ten minutes by tram from east Croydon, green and pleasant site, complete with own deer herd, offers antidote to crowded London senior schools. Originally a charity, founded by City of London clerks to support a colleague's orphaned children in 1850s. Grew into a school named for its first president, former PM Lord John Russell. Moved from New Cross to Purley in 1866, acquired this site in 1924. Sir Aston Webb – best known for Buckingham Palace façade – responsible for regal design. Added Royal to mark 1953 coronation and in 1961 became co-ed on single site. Upped numbers of fee payers in the 1970s to avoid closure (previous philanthropic desire to educate pupils FOC laudable but ruinous). Since then, has gone from strength to strength.

Buildings mainly very easy on the eye (and being attended to where they're not). Oldest is group of 1850s cottages with octagonal tower. Grander elsewhere including mirror image staircases that face each other across flashier of two quads, joining original building and later additions. Latest renovations include extension to science facilities.

'Top of agenda was to turn this into a single school journey,' say heads. So junior school pupils get to know senior school early, using theatre, chapel and swimming pool and, from year 3 up, have lunch in the blue, vaulted dining hall (featured in TV hit show The Durrells). Plenty of space for traditional library and 'practical' block – DT room filled with sound of merry hammering as year 7s enjoy high volume metal beating. And despite lack of riches, site is smart, ditto pupils in recently revamped uniform that's high on practicality (largely washable) and low on crested shirts.

Similar neatness round the grounds (bar pair of school bags languishing, Hansel and Gretel-like, in undergrowth). Even food ingredients painstakingly handwritten on blackboard. Salad Nicoise contents – 'fish, sulphites and egg' – helps those with allergies. 'Learn how to manage them,' said parent. Thirsty have choice of squash in every conceivable flavour. (Milk, also offered, is 'not that popular', thought pupils.)

Pastoral care, inclusivity and discipline: A happy place. 'It's a punishment to keep son off school,' said junior school mother. 'My child absolutely loves it,' agreed another. Teachers supportive if families hit difficult patch. 'Will go above and beyond,' said parent. Pupils similarly complimentary. 'Does take time to settle in but you do feel welcome,' said one. Tutor groups help new pupils settle into school with older senior school pupils providing informal help to younger. Chaplain another source of support, chapel open all day for anytime prayers.

Heart of multi-layered friendship groups is strong house system (juniors have their own) which promotes cohesion and competition – usually at healthy rather than arms race levels. Add forms and streamed subject groups and 'you can have social groups that extend through the school – it takes some getting to grips with,' said parent.

Around one senior school pupil a year withdrawn or asked to leave (normal issues…) but it's sensitively handled, Mr Hutchinson often asking 'headmaster mates' to take a pupil who has lost their way. It's then, he reckons, that you discover just how much of an educator you are. 'They make awful decisions but shouldn't be punished for the rest of their lives.'

Most focus is on rewards for the triers. Even the prefects, who told us they can impose detentions (head says otherwise), never do ('though we might remind everyone that we can,' said one).

Pupils and parents: Slightly more boys, many locals among day pupils (80 per cent from Croydon), rest from south London and into Surrey and Kent borders, lots of diversity, cultural and financial. 'Pretty much all walks of life,' said junior parent. 'And when you're doing reading at night, books aren't just about pink-skinned children, which is great.'

Junior and senior parents tend to tread separate paths and organise own events. It's a heterogeneous mix – cars ranging from second hand to luxury marque, some parents dwelling in marble halls, others scraping school fees together. Wraparound care offered to increasing numbers of working couples. Not flash, thought parent. 'Have quite a wide breadth of people there, and I think that gives it a nice atmosphere.'

Only mystery is where leavers end up. Not into the limelight, at least so far. 'We have a great many success stories, but nobody famous,' says school.

Money matters: No endowment to speak of but prudent management and fundraising keeps things ticking over nicely. Offers scholarships (academic, sport, music and drama) and bursaries of up to 100 per cent (income shouldn't exceed £40,000).

The last word: Think fab site, rising results, unified and inspirational leadership (and the odd deer) and get on that tram.

St Andrew's Prep
57
Meads, Eastbourne, East Sussex BN20 7RP
01323 733203 | admissions@standrewsprep.co.uk | www.standrewsprep.co.uk
Ages: 1-13
Pupils: 357; Boarders: 21 full, 5 weekly
Fees: Day £10,695 – £18,750; Boarding £23,535 – £26,745 pa

Head: Since September 2021, Tom Gregory, a former pupil and previously head at Ashfold School. Other senior roles include deputy head at Vinehall. Started his career in the City working in investment banking; 10 years later, he followed his heart and moved into teaching. He is joined by his wife Esther (who has a long-standing 23-year teaching career in both senior and prep schools) and their two children.

Entrance: Non-selective, to any year group and in any term (where there is space); as many taster days as required.

Exit: Majority to Eastbourne College – 42 students in 2021. Others to King's Canterbury, Bede's, Box Hill, King's Bruton and Brighton College. Usually plenty of scholarships – 17 in 2021.

Our view: There is a cheerful noise as pupils move around and the children seem very confident, but the school ensures that there are quiet places for those who need them, and parents assure us that shy introverts also thrive at St Andrew's: 'our youngest was not gregarious; what St Andrew's do very well is give kids a voice. They will have a conversation in a room of people which they wouldn't have done before… they have the confidence to get things wrong now'; another described her children's confidence as 'sky high' since moving here.

A new wellbeing hub called the Snug opened in 2021 – a quiet area in the heart of the school where children can talk privately or in groups with one of the school's 15 staff listeners. One said her children just pop in to get things off their chests; another that her daughter has regular weekly sessions, which have helped her cope with all the worries of changing school.

St Andrew's responds sensitively to circumstance. Following a spate of parent deaths a few years ago, the school planted a memory garden, with commemorative benches – a place for pupils to sit quietly and listen to the running water and wind chimes. Teachers were trained to support the children, and on learning that death and grief are best talked about openly, death and bereavement have become part of the PHSE curriculum.

The disciplinary system is 'absolutely right… [we] don't hear about it much,' said a parent. A sensible and humane flexibility – difficulties will be resolved by talking if possible, with teachers praising in public, discussing difficulties in private. There are some absolute rules – phones must be handed in to the office in the morning ('if you get caught [with your phone] it's not good,' said a pupil). Unresolvable bullying would result in exclusion – none in recent years. There's a sensitive and active approach to handling differences amongst children – when there were communication problems amongst the girls in one year, the school arranged for the NSPCC to come in and run a course to help pupils understand how their actions impact on others.

A mish-mash of buildings reflect the school's history – once a farm, now a school. Pupils play table tennis in an old wooden panelled hall with parquet floors softened by centuries of feet, learn music in a 1970s block, and play sport in a superb state-of-the-art sports hall.

A house system, with annual competition, and points awarded for merit and industry. The winning house each term gets a cinema trip, although pupils don't think house feeling runs particularly high at this school.

Sports here used to be just about being the best and although success of top teams is still significant, now it's also about enjoying it, taking part and recognition of each child. There are lots of teams, with members being regularly rotated. Sports day is a house competition and pupils are healthier and happier.

'Everything comes alive!' In history, children studying Henry VIII play the 'take me out' game (whether that concerns dating or lopping off heads was not clear)

Sport offerings include badminton, fives and shooting, as well as all the regular ones, and there's increasingly equal provision – girls play cricket, football and tag rugby, and the hockey provision for the boys is increasing. The school has notable successes in girls' hockey and table tennis, and boys' rugby and cricket and a structured development programme helps the more able to excel. Eastbourne College, with which the school shares a governing body, helps with training and shares facilities.

Forest school up to year 2 – small people in top-to-toe green wet weather gear had just finished a Christmas hunt though the woods and were settling down to toast marshmallows. The weekly session includes studying bugs and trees and pursuing the pond life. Teachers say pupils who are very shy 'come alive' in the forest.

Beach school for juniors, whatever the weather, who use whatever they find to create a mythical creature, and tell its story. 'Children who struggle to write in the classroom, can find it easy to tell a story with their tongue,' said a teacher. 'Sometimes when it's rough we just sit and look…' Pupils say the best thing about St Andrew's are the opportunities, 'a fantastic thing', and love the range of extracurricular activities, from sailing to Piglet's pantry (cooking) and chess.

'Even on a quiet morning, there is music all over the department,' said the head of music, who maintains links with West End. There are large-scale productions every year, and the children remember High School Musical with great enthusiasm. School orchestra, rock bands and choirs perform regularly in public, in their own high beamed hall, in local churches and in EC's ample facilities; this year the choir will perform in Venice and Lake Garda. A parent described the music as 'brilliant… blown away by quality of productions and quality of the choir'.

Children produce some beautiful artwork, and enjoy trips out to paint the sea and downs. The school hopes to see even more trips out as they invest more in this department.

Pupils say, 'Teachers are good, they know what they're talking about,' and parents feel St Andrew's provides for all – 'The middle are not ignored.' A bit of tutoring does go on in maths, as it does in most preps, and the school is keen to recruit more staff with innovative and fresh ideas. Parents emphasise that 'the academic child is well catered for', with extension tasks and a scholarship set – although all parents were clear that this is not a pushy school and they do not want it to be so.

A parent commented on the difference in teaching style compared to her children's last school – 'Everything comes alive!' In history, children studying Henry VIII play the 'take me out' game (whether that concerns dating or lopping off heads was not clear); in a lively year 3 maths class, enthusiastic mathematicians stretched elastic bands around toy cars and measured their distance of travel across the classroom floor. Years 5 and 6 learn thinking skills with the help of the debater-in-residence. Mind matters also runs for years 5 to 8, teaching pupils how to form opinions and listen to their peers. 'The children talk all the way home,' said a mum.

A parent who moved his children from a high-pressure school said, 'Performance wise, my kids are now living up to their potential.' Industry awards place great emphasis on effort, which is 'really important and hugely encouraging', he added.

The day ends at 5.30pm, with all homework done at school, to the great relief of parents (apart from weekend tasks for years 7 and 8, to get them used to doing work at home). If you're working parents, St Andrew's is great, said a parent. You can drop off from 7.30am and pick up at 6.45pm after clubs; early morning sports are possible too.

The year 7 cohort of 2019 were the first not to take CE. St Andrew's has worked with Eastbourne College, the senior school destination for 75 per cent of its pupils, to replace it with a bridge curriculum for years 7, 8 and 9. This means reduced anxiety for year 8s and, according to the school, a more exciting, dynamic and effective preparation for the demands of GCSEs and beyond. The brightest pupils will still tackle the common academic scholarship.

The popular nursery takes babies from 9 months, and has nearly 80 children on its role. Learning is entirely child led, and children can happily make a mess. An art sensory room for little ones and big – anyone who could benefit from it, said the head of nursery cheerfully, including parents. Little ones leave nursery able to swim and ride a bike, and ready for the pre-prep.

Early years up to year 2 have their own building, complete with hall, ICT suite and a lovely large library. Magical classrooms, with every bit of the ceiling hung with Christmas. Letters to Father Christmas were not just wish lists, but carefully asked after him, and the well-being of the elves.

The SEND unit is staffed by two full-timers and one part-timer, with one-to-one charged as extra. 'Fantastic support,' said a parent, whose son was very unsure of his ability when he arrived at St Andrew's – now 'he's really flying'. Other support, such as the LEXIA programme for those who are mildly dyslexic, is popular with parents, one saying it has transformed her son's learning. A pre-learning programme helps children who struggle by introducing them to difficult words and concepts before lessons, to help them keep up.

Most day pupils join boarders for optional activities on Saturday. The 'early morning march' has a utilitarian ring to it, but plenty of kids take part in this yomp across the downs. A busy programme of trips for Sundays, from museums to skiing and go-karting.

Most parents at St Andrew's are local, and this is a strong supportive community; very different, parents say, to London-type schools, where the parents are vying for position. Lots of parents are involved in the school and the parent body, Friends of St Andrew's, raises funds, runs socials and helps new parents settle in.

Boarding: The boarding house, Colstocks, is mid-renovation – the 'done' bits are lovely. Full and flexi boarders (ad hoc nights accommodated where possible) from 14 nations, with numbers rising in the summertime with international short stays. Pupils say it's a very friendly community, one describing it as 'a break from my parents…'

Rooms for two to six, with full-timers getting beds and flexis bunks, all of which were very tidy – children are keen to win the tidiness competition. A comfy common room, and a kitchen for making snacks, complete with seating and TV – although the catering here is excellent.

Pupils are allowed mobile phones for half an hour in the evening to call parents, and a little more time at the weekend, but phones spend most of the time locked away, and pupils do other things.

The last word: St Andrew's is about having a 'wonderful childhood… [they] learn, play and make great friends… [are] not stressed out,' said a parent. Another described the ethos as being about positivity and kindness, and happy smiling children seem to fill this school.

St Catherine's School

Station Road, Bramley, Guildford, Surrey GU5 0DF

01483 899609 | admissions@stcatherines.info | www.stcatherines.info

Ages: 11–18

Pupils: 635; sixth form: 160; Boarders: 135 full/weekly

Fees: Day £19,755; Boarding £32,865 pa

Headmistress: Since 2000, Alice Phillips MA Cantab (50s). Educated at Kendal High School, then read English at Cambridge. First teaching post was at the Royal Masonic School, Rickmansworth, where she rose to be head of English. Thence to deputy headship at Tormead in 1993. Understands young people. As a boarding school brat – Mrs Phillips' father was a housemaster at Sedbergh – she 'grew up with 68 surrogate brothers and four natural ones'.

Mrs Phillips impresses at once as being full of brisk common sense, good humour and get-up-and-go. But she is also super-bright, super-articulate and super-focused on the highest of standards for her staff, her charges and herself. 'She is utterly determined for her girls,' one mother told us. And this blazes forth in her dedication to the job of equipping them for the future – 'Girls need to be in an environment which demonstrates that there's nothing you can't do.'

Back in the saddle after a few years of cross-pollination as president of the Girls' Schools Association (GSA) in 2014, which took her out of school three days a week, and then vice chair of the Independent Schools Council 2015-17. Now busy directing the school's next phase of physical development – rebuilding part of the sixth form boarding house ('we're not going for luxury ensuite' but comfortable, practical and home from home) and replacing a time-worn teaching block with a whizz-bang new one dedicated to science, technology, maths, digital learning and independent research.

No plans to go anywhere for now, but if retirement should beckon, feels the school is firmly on its rails come what may – 'If I went under a bus the rest of the management staff would keep the ethos going without a hiccup.'

Entrance: Entry by academic selection, using St Catherine's own assessment. Eleven-plus candidates take papers in English, maths, science and verbal reasoning. A few places at 12+ and 13+ – papers in English, maths and reasoning. Reports from existing schools. Sixth form general paper, tests in A level choices, verbal reasoning and predicted GCSE grades – 7s expected in A level subjects. Interview for potential sixth formers (in person or via Skype). Roughly 1.5 applicants for each 11+ place – about 90-100 enter at this age and six to nine more boarders at 13+. Around 70 apply for the 10 or so annual places in the sixth – they can afford to be very choosy. School flexible and helpful – happy to interview via Skype if you're abroad. Not a school for anyone with less than fluent English. The few internationals who need help are offered it long-distance in the summer before they join the school.

Exit: Around a quarter of girls leave after GCSEs – mostly to co-eds or to state sixth forms. Just under two-thirds of sixth formers to Russell Group universities. Eight to Oxbridge in 2021 and five medics, with four overseas (Brown, Cornell, Pratt Institute in New York, and Sydney).

Latest results: In 2021, 91 per cent 9-7 at I/GCSE; 85 per cent A*/A at A level (94 per cent A*-B). In 2019 (the last year when exams took place), 83 per cent 9-7 at I/GCSEs; 64 per cent A*/A at A level (88 per cent A*-B).

Teaching and learning: A level results excellent across the board – no weak areas. Maths the most popular A level by far: 60 per cent of girls do it in sixth form. No other subject has even half as many takers. Greek and German surviving alongside shiny sixth form ab initio subjects like business, economics, history of art, psychology and photography. Sixth form enrichment programme includes advice on higher ed and interviews, healthcare and citizenship issues. No plans to bring in the IB diploma: 'By the time they're in sixth form they're ready to specialise,' says the head. All girls start sixth form with four A levels and around half drop a subject after the first year. Some sixth formers may do another GCSE, add a language or work on an EPQ.

IGCSEs in most core subjects, with GCSEs for the arts (art, DT, drama music, textiles) and fringes (Greek, Latin, PE). All girls do an IGCSE in French, German or Spanish. Italian an option in sixth form. Food and nutrition available as a GCSE (some girls' schools have dropped this) and all girls participate in cookery lessons in the first two years, rotating with art, drama, DT, textiles and music. Most girls sit one GCSE, plus an RS short course, one year early.

SCAGS – tracking tests for every subject every term – keep the flames licking at the girls' heels in the years leading up to GCSEs. 'They let you see where you are within your year,' a girl told us earnestly. Academic extension programme for years 11-13. Lots of options, lots of opportunities – real education takes place here. Sensible system of sixth form subject mentors.

Established in 1885, this is a school with a proud tradition (only seven heads in its 130+ year history) which, unusually, has grown and developed all on the one site

Embraces technology, but not naive. Parents are required to supply iPads for their daughters from year 5 up – yippee, if that's your thing. Google classroom used for notes/prep. At the same time, the school advises parents to purchase phone contracts with minimum data, and the library remains well-stocked. 'We have literally every book,' our guide gushed.

Learning support and SEN: Parents unlikely to zero in on this school for its SEN provision. Girls with only mild dyses likely to be able to stand the heat. 'We pride ourselves on our tracking system,' says head, 'and on spotting any late-emerging problems.'

The arts and extracurricular: A 'busy' school. Music, dance and performing arts particularly shine. A ton of music on tap and standards are high – over 600 individual lessons are taught every week through the senior and prep schools, and Mrs Phillips has been a governor of the Yehudi Menuhin School since 2009. The list of ballet/dance lessons available at school is as long as your arm. LAMDA too. Lively art in many media. Lots of clubs, and girls can start their own, eg this year's Medical Reading Club(!).

DofE thrives and produces a surprising number of golds. Excellent outside speaker programme, sixth form lectures, and lots of stimulating trips.

Sport: Games important – a bit jolly lacrosse sticks – and more inclusive than in the past. Lots of opportunities for those less than Olympian in prowess – 'I'm on the fourth lacrosse team!' a girl told us brightly (there are five). Guildford High are the arch rivals (Benenden for lacrosse). Meanwhile, sports hotshots fulfil their destinies – county and national finals places in several sports and stellar showings in swimming, tennis and – especially – lacrosse. Usual range of sports on offer, and excellent facilities, plus equestrian team, and lots of individual success in non-mainstream sports, eg ice skating.

Boarding: Boarder numbers start slowly in the younger years but work up to over a third of the sixth form – around 125 boarders all told. Around half of boarders are full, half weekly – the boarding fee is the same either way. Occasional boarding also an option. Half of boarders are from international families (either expat or foreign). Big concerts, productions and lectures are streamed online so that overseas families can tap in. No Saturday school, but plenty of activities offered, plus sports matches. And, in case you're wondering, the admissions requirements are exactly the same for boarders and for day pupils.

Bedrooms and dorms are spacious enough, welcoming and homely. Most in two-bedders, often with a third bed for occasional boarders. Even sixth formers mostly share (there are new sixth form boarding facilities). Boarders encouraged to invite a day girl friend to board on a Friday night once a term, and are invited out at weekends in return. NB The school can accommodate a few boarders from the prep school across the street – hugely handy for a few parents.

Ethos and heritage: Established in 1885, this is a school with a proud tradition (only seven heads in its 130+ year history) which, unusually, has grown and developed all on the one site. Set in a leafy village 10 minutes south of Guildford and smack in the centre of a private school nirvana, with girls' schools Guildford High, Tormead and Prior's Field, co-eds Cranleigh and Charterhouse, and boys-only Royal Grammar School all within five miles.

Snug and compact, the school makes a tidy footprint surrounded by playing fields. At the centre is a humongous £15 million complex – the 125th Anniversary Halls with a dazzling auditorium (seats 300 and has 'better acoustics than the Barbican') plus music practice rooms, a recording studio and other spaces, which segue into the sports hall, gyms, changing rooms, dance studios and a single squash court. All fits ingeniously under one roof ('it's great, we can avoid the rain'). Indoor swimming pool. Science labs a mix of old and new. 'University style' sixth form study centre, due to be upgraded in 2022.

Strong house system – girls are allotted to houses aiming for a mix of abilities and interests in each. Strong ethical dimension to energetic charity work – includes toilet twinning with a loo in Africa. Food has improved – salads particularly praised – though it has not reached the Michelin star quality of a few girls' schools we have visited.

The school's website is succinct rather than ostentatious – an apt reflection of the school.

Notable old girls include Francine Stock, Juliet Stevenson, Elizabeth Beresford, Zena Skinner, Davina McCall, UA Fanthorpe, Dorothy Tutin, Elinor Goodman, Isabel Hardman, Ali Dowling, Lily Travers, two ambassadors and legions of academics and other high flyers.

Pastoral care, inclusivity and discipline: 'Lovely dedicated staff' universally praised. A sense that all girls can fit in and do well here – whatever their aptitudes, enthusiasms, personality – something to which all parents we spoke to attested. 'It can be a bit full-on for some of them,' one parent admitted – and others agreed: 'the girls themselves push themselves to the limit – the atmosphere makes them want to be the best of the best.' 'They do the best they can,' another said, 'but they do it while looking after each other.' All that said, this is not the Kew Gardens Palm House, and a few girls have decamped here from the most sizzling of hothouses (Wycombe Abbey, North London Collegiate?) and thrived in the slightly lower temperature.

Worship once a week for each year group in the Gothic style chapel – splendid Kempe stained-glass windows celebrating notable female saints, fabulous rose window and Willis organ. Uniform dropped starting in the spring term of the upper fifth on through the sixth form.

Pupils and parents: Attracts bright berries from Guildford and surrounds plus south London, and overseas boarders. Locals come from everywhere but mostly the school's own prep and from Haslemere, Midhurst, Farnham, Guildford, Godalming, Cranleigh, Woking, Esher, Oxshott, SW London. Overseas pupils predominantly English with some EU nationals. Full boarders from eg China, Taiwan, Nigeria, Hong Kong, Russia, Malta, Korea, Ireland, Latvia, Estonia, Moldova – aiming for a wide blend. Lots of old girls' daughters. Middle class and comfortable backgrounds, in the main.

Money matters: Four scholarships available at 11+ cover 10-20 per cent of fees. More of the same ilk at sixth form. Music awards include the esteemed Jennifer Bate organ scholarship, offered in conjunction with Guildford Cathedral. A few bursaries covering up to 100 per cent of fees for the bright broke at 11+ and sixth.

The last word: If you want convincing that girls-only education is the right and modern way for your bright and motivated daughter, go and look. This is as good as it gets.

St Edmund's School

59

St Thomas Hill, Canterbury, Kent CT2 8HU

01227 475601 | admissions@stedmunds.org.uk | www.stedmunds.org.uk

Ages: 3-18

Pupils: 571; sixth form: 115; Boarders: 80 full, 17 weekly/flexi (including 25 choristers)

Fees: Day £10,185 – £22,200; Boarding £26,745 – £38,538, Choristers £25,818 pa

Head of school: Since 2018, Ed O'Connor, previously deputy head since 2013. Welcoming and likeable. Read history at Peterhouse, Cambridge followed by a masters in international relations at Oxford. Spent five years in investment banking before deciding that teaching was all he had ever wanted to do and took an MEd at Cambridge. Reckons his banking years toughened him up and are useful when he is talking about careers with sixth formers. Joined St Alban's School as head of history and politics, thence to Sutton Valence as director of sixth form and head of history before moving to The Perse as head of sixth form and politics and a history teacher. Believes this school stands out for its pastoral ethos. 'We look at what is special about a child and work with it – we celebrate their strengths and strengthen their weaknesses.' Adds that a sense of humour runs through the school and the staff are a delight to work with and will always go the extra mile for the children – especially so during the pandemic.

Popular with parents, pupils and staff: 'He runs a happy ship.' 'He is approachable and has a good rapport with parents and children and is liked and respected by staff.' 'He knows all the children by name and really seems to care about them.' 'He delivers his speeches without notes and has the gift of making everyone he talks to feel special and he is also very entertaining.'

Lives onsite with his wife Jude, who works at the university, and their two children, both at the school. He teaches history and English when he can and when he is not working he enjoys walking on the beach and being outdoors.

Head of junior school: since 2020, Andrew De Silva, previously head of Fair Oak Junior School in Hampshire. Started his teaching career in Peterborough, progressing rapidly to his first deputy headship at Southfields Junior School. He has a BA in primary education (QTS) NPQH and an MSc in educational leadership. The son of a priest, he attended King's School Peterborough as a chorister and his earliest ambition was to be an astronaut and failing that, head of a choir school. While he has yet to fly to the moon, he has achieved his second as Edmund's educates the Canterbury cathedral choristers. He was attracted to St Ed's by the singing, the faith and the music and has brought pace and energy and lots of new initiatives from the state sector – 'his boundless enthusiasm is contagious,' said parent. Feels that children should be able to see that grownups can have fun too though he can be quite strict and is a stickler for good manners, insisting that shirts are tucked in, ties are straight and rules are not negotiable.

Entrance: From local primaries and prep schools such as Spring Grove, Northbourne Park, Lorenden and Wellesley House and sometimes from the grammar schools at 13+. Main intakes into years 3, 7 and 9 and the sixth form but will take into other years if there are spaces. Informal assessment day for year 3, assessment day and some tests for years 4, 5 and 6 and more formal tests for years 7 and 8. Year 9 entry is via Common Entrance or the school's own tests as well as a reference and report. Sixth form entrants need six 4s GCSEs with at least 5s in subjects to be studied at A level plus reference and report. International applicants interviewed via video and those not taking GCSEs tested in chosen A level subjects plus English if not their first language.

Exit: Around five move elsewhere after the prep – and a small number after GCSEs – usually to local state schools. Almost all go on to university with about half to Russell Group to read anything from maths, history and law to agriculture and international relations. Exeter, UCL, Bath, Warwick and Oxford Brookes are most popular, followed by KCL, Bristol and Edinburgh. A couple to Oxbridge most years – two in 2021. Oxbridge candidates and medics are well prepared with pre-reading seminar groups interview practice. Some go on to top drama and art schools and conservatoires. The careers department is open to ideas other than university – a couple a year move on to degree apprenticeships and others to internships and vocational training colleges. The school runs the Prue Leith Programme in the sixth form and one boy moved straight to a training position in a restaurant.

Latest results: In 2021, 52 per cent 9-7 at GCSE; 45 per cent A*/A at A level (76 per cent A*-B). In 2019 (the last year when exams took place), 36 per cent 9-7 at GCSE; 29 per cent A*/A at A level (59 per cent A*-B).

Teaching and learning: The school caters for all abilities and children are stretched to achieve their best, whatever that may be, and no one is expected to fit into a mould. The headmaster has upped the academic ante and university destinations are increasingly ambitious.

Children are stretched to achieve their best. The headmaster has upped the academic ante and university destinations are increasingly ambitious

Twenty-two subjects offered at GCSE including computer science, food preparation and nutrition, sports science (GCSE equivalent) drama, dance, art and design and ceramics. Most pupils take combined science but can also take three separate subjects. Twenty-five subjects offered at A level including computer science, sports science, photography and product design. Most start with four A levels and drop one at the end of the first term.

Class sizes usually 15-16 and sixth form classes often very small and more like university tutorials. There were only three pupils in one biology lesson we visited.

Successful EPQ programme mentored by PhD ambassadors from the University of Kent. The school also runs an internal EPQ, The Durrell

Essay named after Lawrence Durrell who was at the school. Sixth formers can take the leadership and management diploma. All learn cooking from year 9 which includes diet and nutrition and the Leith's course is offered in the sixth form.

A dedicated team of teachers most of whom are in their late 30s/early 40s with a few more venerable members of staff and a handful of NQTs who come with new ideas and challenge practices. Supervised prep can be done at school, a boon for working parents and children can come in for subject clinics on Saturday mornings.

Weekly programme of talks by visiting speakers known as the Curiosity Shop on a wide range of subjects from power and freedom to fine art.

Children in the junior school learn how to navigate the internet and are introduced to machine learning and AI, as well as being taught to search on Google for what is true and what's not. The ICT genius lab gives a real life context to ICT. They are taught to see a link between the past and the present with questions like 'what do the Romans tell us about today – who were the Tik Tokkers of ancient times?' French taught by native speakers and years 7 and 8 learn Spanish for a term. Children take a St Edmund's Diploma to introduce them to the concept of an original research project. They are gradually prepared for the move to the senior school and years 7 and 8 take on leadership roles. They are taught by specialist teachers in a separate block in the senior school from year 6 and use the art and DT facilities and use the science labs where they make fireworks for bonfire night. Forest School also on offer in juniors.

Learning support and SEN: Two full-time members of staff and a director of learning enhancement monitor all students with additional needs. Problems are identified early and staff work closely with subject teachers to ensure the right support is in place – could be either one to one or in small groups and includes English, maths, organisational and social skills, revision and exam techniques. Usually a couple of EHCPs. The able, gifted and talented are stretched through academic clubs and societies like debating and the curiosity shop. About 10 pupils have EAL support either individually or in small groups.

The arts and extracurricular: The excellent music, art and drama provision is the reason that many parents choose St Ed's and almost all children get involved in it in some form or another.

Music has been at the heart of the school since its foundation and the cathedral choristers are a big part of the school. Some have been selected for the National Children's Orchestra, the National Youth Orchestra and Kent Youth Choir but there are ensembles for all talents and abilities and some take part just for the fun of it. Music and music tech are both offered at A level. The school has its own 450 seat tiered theatre as well as a recital hall, practice rooms and music tech suites. 'The music and drama are exceptional,' said a parent, 'and the teachers are phenomenal and will help pupils with their audition speeches to drama school even after they have left.' 'The plays are National Youth Theatre standard – everyone was blown away by a recent production of Chicago,' said another. A production of 'A Midsummer Night's Dream' staged in a glade in the woods at the end of the summer term was magical, we heard. As the stage set was made of paper mâché there was some trepidation about the English weather though thankfully the rain held off. The junior school puts on one big production a year and sometimes take part in senior plays and musicals.

No Saturday school but activities are organised for boarders and day pupils often come and join in the fun. Outings on Sundays but pupils often prefer to stay in school to relax

Busy art department where pupils can do anything and everything from photography, ceramics and textiles to fine art and stained glass. The school has its own dark room and printing press. DT is another hub of creativity where pupils are encouraged to design things for the real world; they visit the design museum in London and take part in London Design Week. The GCSE and A level art exhibition was in full swing when we visited with a beautifully curated display of portraits, masks and photographs – a rival to any commercial art gallery.

A wide range of clubs and activities includes riding, chess, mindfulness and debating and the hot chocolate club (a good excuse for a chat). Busy outdoor education department which includes CCF and DofE – about 100 children take bronze every year and five to six achieve gold annually.

Sport: Sport for all and sport for fun with all the usual team sports except rugby. The school has started an elite athlete development programme for the most able and is flexible with the timetable to fit in training sessions. School is supportive of outside sporting interests and has developed a link with Chelsea Football Club's Foundation department for super talented footballers, as well as with Kent and Boughton golf club. Despite this, some feel that sport could be celebrated a bit more. Strong individual sports but difficult to compete at team sports with the much larger schools in the area, we heard. Sports pitches are all on site and there are two ex-professional cricketers on the sports staff. Heated outdoor pool for summer use – a cover is on the headmaster's shopping list.

Boarding: About 80 full boarders from 20 different countries as well as a number of weekly and flexi boarders. About a quarter are British ex-pats and Gurkhas. Occasional boarders are welcome if there is space – useful for parents who have to travel for business.

Pupils are encouraged to develop an awareness of their community and a social conscience and St Ed's has longstanding links with local charities

Junior boarders (aged 10-14) live in School House in small dorms with their own common room. They have supervised prep and evening activities. Senior boys live in the main school building with the younger ones housed in cubicles which have been carved out of the huge nineteenth century dormitories – popular as no one gets left out. Older pupils share two to four to a room with ensuite bathrooms, while sixth form have either double or single rooms. Several common rooms and games rooms with PlayStations and computers and kitchen areas for preparing snacks. The sixth form girls have their own house.

No Saturday school but Saturday activities are organised for boarders and day pupils often come in to join in the fun. Outings to museums, theme parks and shopping trips on Sundays but pupils often prefer to stay in school to relax and catch up with work. School encourages boarders to mix with day pupils but some tend to 'keep themselves to themselves,' according to a parent.

The choristers (all boys aged from 8 years) live in Choir House within the cathedral precincts. All are full boarders due to Sunday commitments. They sing in the cathedral six days a week and most learn two musical instruments and take lessons in the theory of music. They come up to St Ed's by minibus and enjoy a normal school day before returning for evensong and rehearsals.

Ethos and heritage: St Edmund's was established in Yorkshire 1749 as the Clergy Orphan School and following a move to London, it settled in Canterbury in 1855. It is centred around the original School House, a monument to high Victorian exuberance with chapel attached. It is set in 45 acres on St Thomas's Hill with views to the Cathedral. Not all buildings are architectural gems but there is a rolling programme of refurbishment and the newly built academic hub contains eight bright and airy new classroom with more planned. The grounds are immaculate and include a meadow and a pond for studying biodiversity. The junior school has its own modern self-contained building with bright, colourful classrooms and its own playground within the grounds of the senior school and can share many of the facilities.

The chapel is the physical and spiritual heart of the school and there is a strong Christian ethos but all faiths and none are welcome. All eat in the panelled dining room which offers a good choice of home cooked food including a vegetarian option

Head has increased community involvement and the school is part of East Kent Schools Together. They share facilities with local schools and pupils help with reading in primary schools. Pupils are encouraged to develop an awareness of their community and a social conscience and St Ed's has longstanding links with local charities including Pilgrim's Hospice and Catching Lives, a homeless centre in Canterbury.

All pupils, day and boarding, are assigned to one of the four houses named after local historical figures. Strong house loyalty and friendly competition enables friendships to form across year groups.

Well known alumni include actor, Orlando Bloom; concert pianist, Freddie Kempf; businessman Sanjeev Gupta; vaccine manufacturer, Adar Poonawalla and middle distance athlete, Alexandra Millard as well as a number of first class cricketers, church and military men.

Pastoral care, inclusivity and discipline: 'The school does pastoral care to perfection,' said a parent and everyone else we spoke to agreed. 'Pastoral care is the bedrock of a successful education,' reckons the head, 'and if a child is happy everything else follows.' Each pupil has a personal tutor who oversees their development throughout their time at St Ed's. All staff are trained in safeguarding including business services and administrative staff. There is a strong family atmosphere and everyone knows who to turn to for help, with posters all over the place. There are two school counsellors, one full one part time, and an independent listener as well as a peer listening programme for sixth formers – pupils are well trained and know what to do and it is very popular for both sides. In juniors, children meet their form tutor every morning and afternoon so that a close eye can be kept on wellbeing including friendships, e-safety and nutrition.

Misdemeanours are usually minor and dealt with by a mixture of rewards and sanctions. Zero tolerance of any form of bullying, with all issues taken seriously and with swift action. E safety officer monitors internet activity and all sign an ICT code of conduct. Everyone knows where they stand.

Pupils and parents: St Ed's attracts creative and arty families, many of whom run their own businesses or work for the university. 'Hardworking middles' was how one parent described them and many make great sacrifices to send their children here. They are generally very supportive of the school and there is a strong sense of community which was strengthened during the pandemic. We found them down to earth, without airs and graces. Active PA runs all the usual events eg summer ball, coffee mornings and quizzes. There is a palpable sense of family and parents feel involved with school life. Staff are quick to respond even for small things. About 15-20 per cent of families are international.

Pupils are natural and charming without a hint of arrogance. Some have had a difficult start elsewhere but have blossomed at St Edmund's and felt lucky to be there.

Money matters: Academic, art, drama, music and sports scholarships of varying values as well as a small number of means tested bursaries for new and existing families. Twenty-five per cent discount to children of clergy and employees of Dean and Chapter of Canterbury Cathedral. Boarding discounts for children of members of the armed forces and sibling discounts for third and subsequent children who are at the school at the same time.

The last word: A school that has upped its game in recent years. Particularly strong on pastoral care, with children telling us they feel safe and well cared for, while its relatively small size means that children are can progress at their own pace. Ultimately, it's about doing your best, whether it is in the classroom, the stage, the art room or the sports field. The school motto 'Be all you can be' sums it up nicely.

St John's School (Leatherhead)

60

Epsom Road, Leatherhead, Surrey KT22 8SP

01372 373000 | admissions@stjohns.surrey.sch.uk | www.stjohnsleatherhead.co.uk

Ages: 11–18

Pupils: 838 (478 boys; 360 girls); sixth form: 259 (159 boys; 100 girls); Boarders: 167 weekly/flexi

Fees: Day £19,785 – £24,810; Boarding £25,035 – £31,365

Head: Since September 2017, Rowena Cole (40s) BSc PGCE MBA. Educated at Exeter University (biology). Drawn to teaching by her own experiences: 'It saved me – I loved all those little bits of school life like DofE and could never imagine myself sitting behind a desk.' Has taught in both the state and private sectors: Howard of Effingham and City of London Freemen's followed by a deputy headship at Guildford High School before taking the reins as head at Dunottar School in Reigate. Parents love the fact that she's a local – 'I really wanted to lead a school in the community I grew up in,' she says. Relished the opportunity to take the helm as a female head of a traditional public school.

First job was to do away with the dusty tomes and leather wingback chairs in the head's study ('I didn't want to be that kind of head') and now presides from a serene minimalist oasis of calm in soft, monochrome grey where pupils can feel at ease and the Surrey mums can try to work out which shade of Farrow and Ball paint is on the walls. Parents say she has 'a big job' to do to really make the major changes made by her predecessor (introduction of girls and entry at 11+) work properly. Keen to continue sharpening the focus on academics, although adamant that it won't be at the expense of breadth; 'we want every child to achieve as much as they can but have no plans for the school to become more selective' (thank goodness: the area doesn't need another highly selective school) and says the plan is to continue 'placing equal value on everything and staying genuinely broad in outlook and interest'.

Married to Alistair with whom she has two young children and a menagerie of pets. Lives on school site during term time and enjoys adventure travel when time allows.

Entrance: One of the head's questions to self when we met her was, 'How do we run admissions to make it a more emotionally intelligent process?' We'll watch with interest to see what changes in the coming years, but for now it's fairly standard. There are 80 places available at 11+, with applicants required to take maths, English, reasoning and an informal interview. No major feeders at this point and plenty from state primaries. At 13+ (year 9 entry), a further 45 places open up and offers are made on the basis of a report from head of current school plus a pre-assessment taken in January of year 6, after which unconditional offers are made, with CE no longer required. Feeder preps include Danes Hill and Felton Fleet.

The look of the school reflects its character. It comprises a splendid, immaculate Victorian building with cloisters running around the quad and an imposing panelled dining room used by everyone for all meals

Entry to sixth form is now selective, with about 30 places available. Applicants sit an assessment and interview in November of year 11, plus report from current school; places are confirmed by GCSE results. 'Co-curricular strengths are taken into account.' At 16, lots of girls come from nearby Manor House, and a few boys and girls wanting a change from local state schools or other independents.

Exit: Around 15 per cent leave after GCSEs. Most to first choice of university, with a good handful taking gap years. Most popular recent destinations: Nottingham, Birmingham, Exeter, Durham and Bath. Two or three to art foundation courses. Usually a few into medicine and/or to Oxbridge. Degree apprenticeships 'pushed quite hard' but few are attracted to them; parental aspiration is definitely for university. Parents report 'a pretty robust system' in place when it comes to university guidance – in fact sixth formers given so much help with university applications that parents told us they didn't even need to look at at the form. Tutors lead the process and there's a series of lectures plus trips to Reading, Surrey and Portsmouth universities.

Latest results: School not releasing results for 2021. In 2019 (the last year when exams took place), 76 per cent 9-7 at GCSE; 46 per cent A*/A at A level (78 per cent A*-B).

Teaching and learning: Not renowned locally as stiff competition for the top Guildford schools, although parents who may formerly not have bothered looking here for their bright child are starting to think again. Academics 'better than we thought', according to parents and results now coming to bear after a strong push on academics in recent years. League table watchers will still note that St John's sits way below the lofty likes of Guildford High and RGS, but considering its far gentler admissions policy, output is testament to (mostly) strong teaching and belief that academic success goes hand in hand with pastoral care. Is it cool here to work hard these days? 'We're well on the way – there's been a big shift, and it's definitely cool to be involved,' says head.

With a host of new academic societies and external scholarship pages on pupil intranet, the message is certainly out there. School notes that girls' academic work and success helps to pull the boys along, although by the sixth form they are equal. Looking around at A level classes, we wondered whether certain subjects were biased towards one gender; boys currently outnumber girls in A level subjects such as chemistry and DT, for example. School says rather that it reflects the imbalance of the sexes at the top end of the school than any latent gender stereotyping – and was fast to point out the large number of girls taking A level maths. Worth asking the question if gender neutrality is high on your wish list, however. Parents praise staff as top notch role models, not just taking pupils in hand when it comes to curriculum based learning but also in life skills, eg what colour socks or tie to wear with which shoes or suit.

Trad curriculum, with French, Spanish and German all on offer in the languages department, plus Latin and Classical Greek. Top performers at GCSE are English, maths and humanities (particularly RS). Twenty-seven subjects available at A level; all the usual suspects plus classical civilisation, politics, psychology and business. Maths, psychology, economics and English are top choices, with solid results across the board. Smatterings of C and D grades noticeable at both A level and GCSE, although not in any particular subject. EPQ taken by over one-third of year 12 cohort, with solid results. All take three A levels, along with a core curriculum covering political thought, philosophy and finance ('extremely practical').

Learning support and SEN: All pupils screened on entry to identify any additional needs. Four full-time learning support staff work with the 10 per cent of pupils currently on the register who are also catered for by teaching staff (there are no TAs), small group sessions and one-to-one classes where necessary. 'Our job is to remove barriers,' they say. The small number of pupils with EAL have flexible, small group provision alongside support from tutors.

The arts and extracurricular: All additions to the academic curriculum taken very seriously and highly valued; school places equal value on sport, drama and music as on academia.

Trophies aplenty – in recent years St John's has won the Rosslyn Park National Schools Sevens for rugby and the National Independent Schools League for football

If sport (see below) flies high, in our opinion music soars. We were fortunate enough to be treated to a lunchtime recital on our visit and would rank what we saw as some of the best school music around (a special bravo to the oboe teacher who is clearly outstanding, judging by his pupils' performances). Around a third of pupils learn an instrument and several pupils also play with national orchestras and ensembles as well as the many taking place in school. We loved the fact that pupils clad in games kit turned up to watch their friends perform along with parents and teachers in exactly the same way they would to cheer on a sports team. On the pop front, school supports pupils creating their own rock bands. Senior school musical – most recently Legally Blonde – is a highlight, but according to pupils nothing eclipses 'congers', the whole-school hymn practice, which is apparently 'the most fun ever'. Drama also well represented with plenty of opportunities for the thespian community to throw themselves into a variety of school productions. More prizes won at the Leatherhead drama festival and several pupils belong to National Youth Theatre.

Good art and DT facilities are housed in a modern block with a reasonably high standard of work on display, although again art seemed to us to be a 'girl' subject (boys we spoke to felt the type of work was more focused on female aptitudes) and DT had a distinctly male flavour.

CCF compulsory (and 'massive' according to pupils) in year 10, and many continue beyond; 'significant' community service and DofE, involving challenging activities and trips. Evening activities, lectures, rehearsals and concerts can all be demanding on pupils' time, although their take on it is 'we're really well rounded'.

Sport: Sport 'riding high', says head (her comment that they recently 'smashed' Blundell's at rugby confirmed how seriously competition is taken here). Facilities all present and correct, plus a 'very glamourous' new sports centre including swimming pool, conditioning suite and multipurpose studio. There are A-D teams in most years so everyone gets a chance to represent the school and there's a high standard of coaching across the board, including ex-All Black rugby player who not only takes a broad range of rugby teams but also the U12 girls' netball team. Moreover, pupils uniformly felt that the standard of coaching was high regardless of the players' level. The usual suspects (rugby, football and cricket for boys and hockey, netball and rounders for girls) are on the roster for lower years and year 10 and up have a range of choices including tennis, athletics, cross-country, yoga, pilates and baseball too. Trophies aplenty – in recent years St John's has won the Rosslyn Park National Schools Sevens for rugby and the National Independent Schools League for football as well as multitudinous accolades for county hockey and netball. School also features annually in The Cricketer magazine's list of top 100 cricketing schools.

Boarding: If we had a pound for every parent who told us St John's offers 'the best of both worlds' we'd (almost) be able to afford the fees. Although not a viable option for those who need full boarding, flexi-boarding flourishes, with nights spent at school increasing as pupils reach GCSE and A level (about 40 weekly boarders at the time of our visit and 'loads' two to three nights a week). Lower school (years 7 and 8) can now board four nights a week and with such delightful accommodation on offer – spacious, colourful modern rooms with characterful period fireplaces, bunks and central sofas (far better than the bedrooms of any 11-year-old we know), who wouldn't want to? One enthusiastic year 7 boarder described it as 'just the best'. Senior boarding accommodation has similar, albeit more traditional, appeal with tidy corridors and rooms for up to four in the younger years. Twin or single rooms with small ensuite loos and showers are the privilege of sixth formers and all boarders can grab fruit on the go from the generously laden bowls in the corridors and snacks from the small kitchens. Model is totally flexible and much loved by working parents: 'You can ring in the morning if you need last minute cover; it's great when you have breakfast or dinner meetings in London.'

Ethos and heritage: Imposing building on the outskirts of Leatherhead. Enter through the wrought iron gates (if you're very fortunate you might be directed by the utterly charming grounds staff) and watch the school open up Narnia-like as you walk into reception and gaze out through the floor-to-ceiling windows onto the main quad. The look of the school reflects its character. It comprises a splendid (immaculate – try as we might we couldn't find any shabby corners) Victorian building with cloisters running around the quad and an imposing panelled dining room used by everyone for all meals (and rumoured to have been a potential set for Hogwarts). Beyond are other newer buildings including the terrific classroom, art and DT block, a new science centre and a very attractive modern new boys' house plus a new boarding house for girls. Plus the stunning modern chapel – one of the loveliest we've seen. Pupils required to attend daily chapel as well as Sunday evening services with their house once every half term, at which parents are also welcome.

Lower school (years 7 and 8) can now board four nights a week and with such delightful accommodation – spacious, modern rooms with period fireplaces, bunks and sofas

Very much a local school with the majority hailing from within a 15-mile radius. Trad environment (head only recently inadvertently overturned an archaic rule that only allowed prefects and staff to walk on the central path in the main quad), providing a safe and wholesome education that's 'genuinely broad in outlook and interest'. Initial impression is of a conservative (big and small c) and somewhat squeaky clean bubble; definitely not for those looking to give their offspring a healthy dose of gritty reality (this is deepest Surrey, after all). But despite this, there's a definite feeling of acceptance for anyone who might not quite fit the typical mould (we met one or two) and sixth formers assured us that they were well equipped to tackle the 'real world' (although we couldn't help but wonder what they'd make of the average digs in a northern university city). Girls now take up 50 per cent of places in year 7, so the culture shift from 'boys' school with girls' is as good as complete, although parents (and, we are told, some boys) said that some still see it as just that (glorification of the 1st XV named as a factor). Barely any trace of former diehards lamenting the loss of Saturday school or arrival in the 21st century, though; we heard nothing but positive remarks about school's metamorphosis and parents we spoke to were looking forward to embracing further developments when they arise; 'we haven't changed the value set,' says head. No changes in the house structure, around which pupils' lives revolve: the day start and ends there, their tutor is to be found there and studying and socialising takes place there.

Pastoral care, inclusivity and discipline: House system is key to school's pastoral success ('so strong' say parents), with almost every staff member a tutor to a small number of pupils. Loyalty to houses runs deep and pupils will support their house/matron/prefects to the hilt to an extent not seen in siblings' schools. Now that girls are just part of the furniture, plans in pipeline to forge links between boys' and girls' houses to create brother/sister relationships for sport and other competitions, which are numerous and include a house pancake race around the quad on Shrove Tuesday. Any bullying (rare) kept in check by house system ('sixth formers step in if we see anything going on,' one told us.) Older year groups mentor the younger, forming genuinely supportive relationships. Fairly strict mobile phone policy – years 7 to 11 have to hand them in at the start of the day. Year 7 and up bring their own laptop for use at school and we are informed that the Wifi is 'absolutely amazing'. Disciplinary issues are, unsurprisingly, 'very limited'. No LGBT+ society but there are openly gay staff members (both sexes) as well as a few pupils, and in the interests of 'walking the talk' a member of staff has been open in assembly with their own experience of depression to encourage pupils to seek help should they need it.

Pupils and parents: Boys still just about outnumber girls but the overall imbalance is not particularly noticeable. Pupils describe school as 'a real community' and note that the integration amongst members of the same houses forges strong ties between year groups. Families are typically well-heeled middle-class professionals ('we're definitely not glitzy or glamorous,' one mum told us) but hold a happy middle ground of being generally more down to earth than parents at many of Surrey's flashier boarding schools – and bit more relaxed than those at the day schools. St John's suits pupils who can cope with a fast paced and busy environment, Saturday sport and Sunday chapel included (be ready to relinquish weekends away and lie-ins). Pupils we met were charming but not smooth, well-spoken but not posh.

Notably (in the words of a particularly sparky year 7 boy), 'everyone is smiling'.

Money matters: A little bit pricier than most local day schools. Scholarships available in music, drama, art, design and technology, sport, academic and all-rounder, at 11+, 13+ and sixth form entry, worth 5-10 per cent. Means-tested bursaries and grants available, including up to 100 per cent of fees for children of Anglican clergy, foundationers, reflecting the school's foundation.

The last word: Safe as houses. A school that recognises the value of Tradition (upper-case T), family and good manners, and genuinely values roundedness as much as academic success.

St Lawrence College

College Road, Ramsgate, Kent CT11 7AE

01843 572931 | admissions@slcuk.com | www.slcuk.com

Ages: 3-18

Pupils: 590; sixth form: 120; Boarders: 176 full (from 7 years) and 1 weekly

Fees: Day £7,995 – £17,025; Boarding £28,320 – £37,455 pa

Head: Since April 2020, Barney Durrant. Previously head of Harrow International School in Hong Kong and before that, geography teacher then housemaster at Stowe for 14 years. Studied geography at UCL and also has PGCE from Cambridge and master's in educational leadership and management from Nottingham. Has an athletics blue from Cambridge and is still very active, playing and coaching rugby to a high level, as well as competing in triathlon and cycling endurance events. Lived all over the world as a child, boarding from the age of 7, which helped mould his adventurous spirit and cosmopolitan outlook.

He took over the reins during the pandemic and, having already had experience of lockdown in Hong Kong, was able to offer online lessons from day one and help with the boarders, most of whom stayed in school throughout. Says the ethos at St Lawrence fits well with his own philosophy of growth mindset and high performance learning. Also happy to be working in what he believes to be a genuinely international school that prepares pupils for a globalised world and has a true understanding of diversity though adds its potential is not yet fully tapped. 'He is quite formal,' said a parent, 'but has a great sense of humour, is very calm and a good listener and open to new ideas.' Lives on site with wife Charlie (also a teacher), their three children (all at the school) and Tara, the golden doodle.

Head of junior school: since 2016, Ellen Rowe BA PGCE. Previously head of Haddon Dene prep in Broadstairs. Geography degree from Sheffield; worked for her local authority then for Shelter before turning to teaching. Has taught at state secondary and independent prep schools, including as director of sport at Spring Grove prep in Wye. Married to Adam; they have twins who are both at St Lawrence.

Entrance: Just about non-selective. Entry for all applicants to the senior school via tests in English and maths plus an interview and report from current school. Entry to junior school via meeting with head for parents and child plus taster day and report from child's current school, and sometimes an assessment if there is concern a child might not be able to cope. Will take children at any stage if there are spaces. International pupils can join in year 11 for a one-year unexamined course before they start their A levels. German pupils sometimes come for a year. About 75 per cent of senior school entrants come up from the junior school, others from a range of state and independent schools like Wellesley House – they have a big primary school engagement programme. Some transfers from local grammars. Around 15-20 join in sixth form – international pupils will be tested in English and all will have to submit a report from their current school.

Exit: Automatic transition from junior to senior school and some three-quarters stay on – the rest mainly to grammars and non-selective state schools. Reasoning is part of the curriculum and so children are well prepared for the Kent Test, but some parents still get outside coaching. Around 15 per cent leave after GCSEs, either for financial reasons or to take vocational courses. Most go on to university, with Loughborough and Kent most popular recently, with others to eg UCL, King's College London, Bath and Exeter. One medic in 2021.

Latest results: In 2021, 58 per cent 9-7 at GCSE; 54 per cent A*/A at A level (74 per cent A*-B). In 2019 (the last year when exams took place), 33 per cent 9-7 at GCSE; 19 per cent A*/A at A level (38 per cent A*-B).

Teaching and learning: Exam results not bad for a non-selective school with quite a few EAL pupils, and good value added. As well as the usual subjects, music, PE, photography and Latin offered at A level – 24 subjects in all, plus sports BTec and EPQ. German A level available for native speakers. Pupils do particularly well in history, maths, economics and psychology. Class sizes are small with an average of 15 often with fewer in A level lessons. Science offered as dual or triple award at GCSE and taught by young and enthusiastic team in stunning new science labs based in the Canon Perfect Centre (opened in 2018). Popular science and engineering week and science lecture in conjunction with the Royal Society of Chemistry. Maths and science clinics for anyone who is struggling. A number of foreign trips including geographers to Iceland, physicists to CERN and classicists to Pompeii. Healthy mix of new young teachers and those have been at the school for many years. Several new members of the senior leadership team as both deputies moved on to be heads of other schools. There is a focus on staff development and teachers look at performance mindset to make sure pupils are aiming where they should be. 'The school allows different abilities to be nurtured and pushed in equal measure,' said a parent.

The sports excellence programme attracts pupils from all over the world. The school has two Astroturfs, one with an Olympic standard water base, a rarity in schools

Careers centre open every afternoon; careers programmes for years 9 and 11 and sixth form – seminars, lectures and group sessions and one-to-one advice about higher education.

Saturday morning lessons and afternoon sport from year 9 upwards, with years 7 and 8 doing activities on Saturday mornings. Years 7 and 8 taught separately in Kirby House but by senior school teachers, and can use the other specialist facilities. One lesson a week of thinking and study skills and ICT incorporated into core lessons.

Learning support and SEN: About 10 per cent need learning support. One-to-one coaching and small group teaching is available alongside in-class support, with focus on inclusion to make sure pupils do not feel pigeonholed. Head of department, a former head teacher who was previously head of learning support at UWC Singapore, is assisted by four part-time staff. About 60 pupils receive some EAL support with a determined focus upon integration; now offers intensive EAL course for lower sixth entry. Lots of support tailored to individual needs, most take English GCSE and a few do ESOL. IELTS offered for university entrance.

The arts and extracurricular: Music part of the curriculum for years 7 and 8 and also offered at GCSE and A level. A number of bands and ensembles including rock, jazz, samba and concert band as well as various sixth form bands outside school, and school has its own recording studio. Regular music trips in the UK and abroad and school has invested in instruments for children to borrow.

Has a 500-seat multipurpose theatre with specialist lighting and sound equipment, with seats that can be covered so it doubles as the examination hall. Everyone has a chance to take part in major productions, either on stage or behind the scenes. Drama part of curriculum until year 9 and also offered at GCSE and at A level. Enthusiastic head of drama gets everyone involved.

Beautiful new art rooms at the top of the Canon Perfect Building take advantage of the wonderful light in the area and the school has close links with the Turner Contemporary gallery at Margate and there are regular trips to London art galleries.

Good range of activities including maths and science club, chess, musical theatre, various minor sports and debating society. Extended school day available for juniors, from 8am to 5pm – a boon for working parents. After-school activities for reception to year 2, while years 3-6 can take part in optional (and very popular) Saturday morning activities ranging from scuba diving and computing to play rehearsals.

Sport: The sports excellence programme is not only attracting more local families but pupils from all over the world. The school has two Astroturfs, one with an Olympic standard water base, a rarity in schools. It has recently employed an Olympic hockey player as elite performance director who spots potential elite athletes and looks at all aspects including individual training schedules and diet and nutrition.

Wide range of sports available though school's real strength is in mainstream sports, particularly boys' and girls' hockey. Cliftonville hockey club has its home at St Lawrence and a number of old Lawrentians are in the team. School brings in additional outside coaches and runs a cricket and netball academy during the winter, and several pupils train with the Kent squad. Some parents say they would like more competitions in minor sports.

Everyone takes part in team sports and the school is keen to encourage an ethos of sporting achievement and a healthy lifestyle beyond school. 'They like to keep you fit and active,' said one boy, and many day children stay on to exercise in the evenings – the mirrored dance studio and the climbing wall are both well used. DofE popular and several gain gold each year. CCF compulsory in year 9 and many carry on. Juniors can use the sports centre and theatre, indoor heated pool, Astroturf and games pitches and have plenty of sport and fixtures against other local schools. The recent introduction of girls' cricket is proving popular.

Boarding: Around 175 full boarders and a handful of weeklies. Sixty are from abroad, the rest from the UK – and the school stays open for exeats. Four boarding houses all with common room, kitchen and tuck shop and ensuite study bedrooms for senior pupils. House kitchens closed at lunchtimes to make sure pupils eat a proper meal. Years 7 and 8 boarders and day children live and learn in Kirby House, a light, modernist building with a glass atrium and a library which is housed in what looks like a large blue pottery chimney – inspired. All junior school boarders sleep here too. Large bright common room area with sofas, table tennis, a piano and a large television and 10 five-bed dorms with ensuite bathrooms and two flats for resident staff. Pupils allowed into Ramsgate at the weekends and some activities organised although often pupils want to 'chill and relax' at school.

Ethos and heritage: Founded in 1879 as a boys' boarding school with the purpose of combining 'careful religious training with a sound, liberal education'. The college was incorporated as a public school in 1892 and went fully co-ed in 1983. It is set in 45 acres of walled grounds in the middle of Ramsgate and within walking distance of the sea. The Virginia creeper clad main building, complete with towers and turrets, is a monument to muscular Christianity. Inside it is all panelled corridors and sweeping staircases. The chapel, with its beautiful stained-glass windows and fine organ, was built to commemorate the lives of 140 Old Lawrentians who died in the First World War. Impressive 19th-century dining hall decorated with portraits, shields and silverware. Major investment in building projects in recent years including new science, art and design technology building which is light and bright and modern and contrasts well with the Victorian Gothic of the original buildings.

Pastoral care, inclusivity and discipline: The strong Christian ethos of the school underpins its religious and spiritual life. Chapel services for everyone twice a week, as well a Sunday service for boarders, helping to maintain an ethos of consideration for others and moral values. One of the stated aims of the school is to encourage 'a sense of serving others as a source of personal satisfaction'. The popular chaplain is a whizz with technology and 'makes the services interesting', according to the children. He lives on site and plays an important role in the boarding community. All major world faiths are represented within the school; Jewish pupils can attend the synagogue in Ramsgate and Muslims can observe Ramadan and attend the local mosque. The head meets regularly with the chaplain and head of the junior school.

The Virginia creeper clad main building, complete with towers and turrets, is a monument to muscular Christianity. Inside it is all panelled corridors and sweeping staircases

Strong house loyalty and plenty of friendly inter-house rivalry – plays, matches and singing competitions. All houses have live-in house parents and a resident tutor. Head believes in positive justice but takes a hard line on bullying, drugs, alcohol and won't tolerate antisocial behaviour.

Pupils know where they stand and who to turn to. There is a clear pastoral structure of tutors and house staff who all know the pupils well as well as a system of buddies, mentors and prefects. There are two part-time counsellors and school can call on more if needed and several members of staff are trained mental health first aiders. The headmaster has rewritten the mental health and wellbeing policy which includes AS tracking, an emotional wellbeing tracker which looks at personality traits. 'Positive wellbeing in year 2 improves academic performance in year 6.' The school is on top of the small things, says head.

Good food with plenty of choice at lunchtimes, including a salad bar, and can cater for special diets and allergies. Food committee made up of pupils and staff and meets regularly to make recommendations. Some boarding parents say that the food is less good in the evenings and weekends. Coffee shop open at break time, evenings and weekends – also popular with parents at drop-off time. Lots of interaction with the local community – children from nearby schools invited to watch plays and the Chemical Magic show and take part in the annual science and engineering challenge; pupils pick up litter and visit old people's homes and the school has close links with the local church.

Pupils and parents: A big range: traditional families from local prep and primary schools, a number of first-time buyers and first-generation immigrants who are aspirational and ambitious for their children. Popular with the arty crowd moving down from London – high-speed railway means it is just over an hour to St Pancras. School prides itself on its internationalism and 30 per cent of pupils are foreign nationals from 30 countries including a sizeable contingent of Nepalis from the Gurkha barracks in Folkestone. Strong Nigerian connection and lots of Germans in sixth form. Children generally integrate well, although some say there could be more interaction between boarders and day pupils – school says it is working on this.

'Relaxed yet respectful' relationships between pupils and teachers. 'I love the way the children are treated like young adults,' said one parent. 'Everyone is respectful of everyone else and it is a very caring and supportive school.' 'My son joined for the sixth form and felt welcome from the start – sending him there was the best thing we ever did.' 'As parents we felt welcomed from day one and have made friends for life,' said another. A very loyal team of former pupils – successful businesspeople and entrepreneurs who help with work experience. Pupils are 'natural, friendly and unpretentious' and very supportive of each other.' Lots of mixing between year groups, helped by the house system. Parents feel listened to and are encouraged to get involved. High praise for school comms too, particularly the parent portal where they can view their children's marks, teachers' notes and homework.

Money matters: All-rounder, academic, sporting and music scholarships offered at 11+ and 13+ – worth up to 25 per cent of fees. Sixth form scholarships for up to 25 per cent of fees for academic, arts, music and sport. Also means-tested bursaries, and special bursaries for Forces families who qualify for the Continuity of Education Allowance. Generous sibling discounts.

The last word: The school is going from strength to strength and the high-performance learning and growth mindset, together with the sports excellence programme and the close attention paid to emotional wellbeing, is a hit with parents. Its international and outward looking approach attracts pupils from all over the world. No wonder word has got out that this school is definitely worth a closer look.

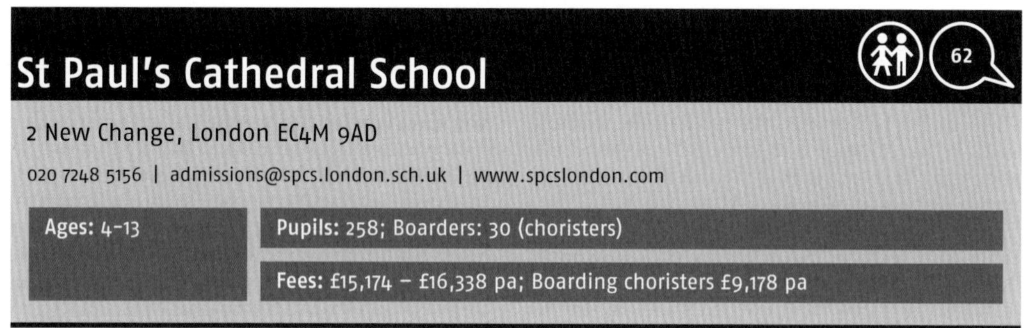

St Paul's Cathedral School

2 New Change, London EC4M 9AD

020 7248 5156 | admissions@spcs.london.sch.uk | www.spcslondon.com

Ages: 4–13

Pupils: 258; Boarders: 30 (choristers)

Fees: £15,174 – £16,338 pa; Boarding choristers £9,178 pa

Headmaster: Since 2016, Simon Larter-Evans (50s). Eclectic career to date: trained at Rambert and became principal dancer with Janet Smith & Dancers then, via commercial management, to teaching. Prior to SPCS, head of boarding and head of English at the Yehudi Menuhin School. Parents value his accessibility: 'If there's anything simmering, tell me, call me,' he says. 'Charismatic', 'practical' and 'empathetic' are some of the universally positive comments we heard. He is credited with creating the 'warm, family atmosphere' conveyed, among other things, through interactive assemblies and his Friday letter. The letter covers thoughts on everything from tutoring (okay if you have to, but let's work together) to internet safety (devices handed in on arrival). 'I don't mind being wrong,' he says with disarming humility, 'but we all need to try things out, make mistakes, and have the discipline to learn from them.' On the day of our visit, he exchanged funny faces with giggling children darting in and out of view at his study window, and sorted out a friendship issue in the playground. The array of funny hats on his bookshelf suggests a penchant for dressing up but, more seriously, he feels 'a burden of responsibility' to help the children understand their role as global citizens. The prep school experience, as he sees it, is preparation for life itself. 'The anxiety of the next school pervades. The destination is core to what parents are buying, but this must not distract from what it is to be a child.'

Simon and his wife Dawn, a managing director at Accenture, live above the shop. Along with their lively Airedale terrier, Parker, they escape to the country most weekends. In addition to studying for a master's in coaching and practising the trumpet, he enjoys photography (his black-and-white photographs line the walls of the music corridor), cooking and cycling. He and Dawn recently cycled 1000 miles from Land's End to John O'Groats to raise funds for food banks.

Entrance: Early registration essential. Eighty children assessed informally (enthusiasm, curiosity, social interaction) for 34 places at 4+. Around 12 places available for 7+ entry: pupils are selected through a range of activities, both academic and interactive. Further openings at 11+ after assessment in maths and English. Priority given to siblings.

Boy choristers, about 6 per year, may be admitted as boarders from 7+, up to year 5. They are auditioned by Andrew Carwood, director of music at St Paul's Cathedral, who looks for 'quality of voice' and potential musical ability rather than formal training. Choristers need to be 'academically on top of things' to be able to cope with the demands of the schedule.

Exit: Wide array of destinations, at both 11+ and 13+: City of London (girls and boys), Forest, Queen's College, Francis Holland, North Bridge House Canonbury, UCS and Westminster; many academic and specialist scholarships offered. Just under half the year 6 cohort leave at 11+ for London day schools. Those who stay on go to a range of schools, including boarding schools: King's Canterbury a favourite. Excellent track record of music/choral scholarships alongside other awards.

Our view: Although the Great West Door of St Paul's Cathedral is just a stone's throw away, there is no grand entrance to the school. Children arrive unassumingly (no blazers for discretion) on foot, on scooters and on the back of bikes. On the morning of our visit, strains of 'In the Bleak Midwinter' greeted us from the hall below. Nothing bleak about this impressive chamber choir rehearsal though (four-part harmony), a reminder of the nearly 900-year-old choral tradition of the school. In 1123, eight boys in need of alms were given a home and education in return for singing in the cathedral. The original school was destroyed in the Great Fire of London and, after a number of reincarnations, the current brutalist building has been home to the school since the 1960s. Non-chorister day boys arrived in the 1980s, the pre-prep opened in 1998, and the school has been fully co-ed since 2002.

Mudlarking on the banks of the Thames is a less obvious prep school discipline, until you see a boy beam at the discovery of 'disposable clay pipes with beautiful engraving'

Numbers have now grown to about 260. Any fear that the governing body (seven lay and five chapter members, chaired by the dean) might be a tad austere is quickly allayed. 'They are permissive in the very best way,' says the head, allowing the school to use the cathedral, affectionately known as the school chapel, as a focal point and a valuable teaching resource – art, maths, history, classics: 'You can try to decipher the Latin inscriptions in assembly if your mind wanders,' says one thoughtful child. 'You really feel as though you are part of something special.' How many children have the privilege, in weekly school assembly, of gazing up at mosaics in the quire?

Simon Larter-Evans came on board in time to oversee an ambitious £8million building project. Echoing the architecture of the cathedral, it has created an exciting multilevel playground, a larger dining room and an ICT suite, the latter to be used as outreach in the City. A very fine new boarding house has been built 'in harmony with St Augustine's tower'. The history of the ancient site was brought to the fore when skeletons, exhumed under the former nave of St Augustine's church, were blessed and re-interred. 'Thankfully no Roman mosaic floor was discovered,' said the relieved bursar.

Former alumni – Simon Russell Beale, Charles Groves, Walter de la Mare to name a few – are testimony to the arts being central here. Alongside the outstanding individual music teaching (350 scheduled music lessons a week), there are six choirs (160 children sing), two orchestras and 10 ensembles. We watched a lively rendition of a cha-cha-cha from the percussion ensemble, complete with conga drums and cow bell. Some parents who expressed initial quiet concern about the emphasis on music are won over by their offspring's enthusiasm. 'They just want to join in the fun, and they soon realise that it brings its own rewards,' enthused one. Against the background of outstanding musical talent, 'Everyone is encouraged to have a go, music is celebrated at all levels.' Dance and drama are timetabled from the get-go. We watched 8-year-olds perform an energetic street dance and an elegant 17th-century Scottish reel. The cross-curricular, theme-based International Primary Curriculum is taught from reception to year 4. Specialist teaching in academic subjects begins from year 5 when Latin is added to the mix; Greek and Spanish from year 7. The head is keen to stress that, even in this 'unashamedly academic' school, 'exams are the outcome rather than the goal'.

Routine is, perforce, strict: after singing there's instrument practice, a 10-minute slot for phoning home, shower, the news, and 20 minutes' reading before lights out

Pupils mention teachers who are 'kind' and 'available'. They 'don't just teach, they make learning enjoyable' and 'involve everybody'. They also enthuse about the science lab, as much for the mobile fume cupboard (an unlikely gift from the PTA) as for the resident leopard gecko. Mudlarking on the banks of the Thames is a less obvious prep school discipline, until you see a teenage boy beam at the discovery of 'disposable clay pipes with beautiful engraving'. One scientific experiment tested the river water 'which was incredibly clean, even with the mini eels!' said an excited child. One of many parents who gained an insight into the classroom in lockdown agreed that 'even with the bells and whistles stripped away, the teaching was phenomenal'. There is a refreshing absence of setting; instead, 'positive mixed ability groups' to keep the curriculum broad. SEN issues are, we hear, picked up quickly 'with a light touch' and followed through by one of two learning support teachers. Standardised CAT results analysed and tracked from year 2. In the older years English and maths is 'destination based'. Parents like the absence of hot-housing, preferring the 'strong push to inspire and learn'.

'The whole child is looked after from the minute he is greeted on the door,' one mother tells us; 'bumpy moments are addressed quickly.' Older pupils can book a slot with the school chaplain if they need someone to talk to. Vertical tutor groups help familiarity across different age groups. We liked the idea of a 'bus stop' in the playground where children can stand if they feel a bit lonely and somebody picks them up. The library may not be flash but is a much-loved hub: the librarian keeps a basket with strands of wool on her desk 'for a bit of quiet knitting or crochet'. 'Nostalgia with substance,' as one mother said. Good behaviour is rewarded with positive house points and, occasionally, the converse applies 'for minor misdemeanours'.

Outdoor space is indisputably limited, but not a limiting factor when it comes to sport. 'No kids complain about the lack of space generally,' according to one father, surprised at his son's acceptance of the rabbit warren of narrow corridors and the lack of playing fields. Understandable pride from popular head of PE in fielding competitive teams from year 3 in football, cricket and netball against much bigger, single-sex prep schools. Coram's Fields, Finsbury Leisure Centre and Archbishop's Park are used for games lessons, although this does involve travel. A fencing coach has an enthusiastic following, as does the new head of girls' PE 'to give girls' sport a boost'. There is a laudable ambition to broaden sport in the community.

Parents, mostly dual-income, live predominantly in Barbican, Islington or east London and appreciate new 8am-6pm wraparound care. 'A lovely parent body with an international feel', 'friendly and inclusive'. 'We drop off our children on the way to work, and then bump into each other in the Temple,' says one enthusiastic dad. That's not to say that it's only lawyers and bankers; arts, media and medicine are well represented, and all, it seems, liberally-minded, 'the sort of parents who encourage their children to ask questions'.

Boarding: The new boarding house is home to up to 36 boy choristers. The 17th-century spire of St Augustine Watling Street forms part of the wall of the comfortable common room. It is homey and tasteful, equipped with pool, air hockey, table footie and a popular old-style Pac-Man machine. Not that there's a lot of downtime. On top of the normal school week, there are 21 hours' singing: two rehearsals and a cathedral service every day apart from 'Dumb' Thursday, and three services on a Sunday. Boys are allowed to go home for five hours on a Saturday and from Sunday night to Monday morning if distance allows. We had the honour of being shown in through the back door of the cathedral where there was a formidably energetic rehearsal of Britten songs before school. Bright treble voices resounded around the crypt, limbs and sinews moving with rhythmic intensity. Nothing short of a professional training, which, as one chorister parent said, sets up these boys for life. The boys themselves are bright-eyed and chatty, enthusing about the simple pleasures of jam sandwiches (by special request) and the 'almost' full English breakfast (bar the black pudding) on a Saturday. They proudly show us the smart, well-ordered six-bed dorms, each with air filtration unit, airport-standard windows against City noise and a panic button should they need to raise the alarm in the night. There is a sense of each boy and every member of staff (three at any one time, including a resident nurse and a first aider) being there for each other. In lockdown, they missed playing football with 'loads of brothers'. Routine is, perforce, strict: after singing there's instrument practice, a 10-minute slot for phoning home, shower, the news, and 20 minutes' reading before lights out. 'We encourage them to brush their teeth with all the singing and smiling they have to do.' One boy, with prescience, says, 'I think I'll be bored for the rest of my life after this.'

Money matters: A few means-tested bursaries to children in year 3 and above, and sometimes to newcomers in year 7. Choristers' school fees are covered by the cathedral, boarding costs by their parents or the Chorister Trust.

The last word: Brutalist 1960s architecture belies the warm, caring atmosphere within. Friendly and family-focused. Dog-eared Latin texts, battered cello cases and well-thumbed hymn books (Ancient and Modern, of course) sit alongside the sparkling new boarding house and playground. 'We've won the golden ticket to a non-London school in the middle of the City,' says a happy parent. Indeed, the celestial dome glistens up above and is an ever-present reminder of this exciting location.

St Paul's School

63

Lonsdale Road, London SW13 9JT

020 8748 9162 | admissions@stpaulsschool.org.uk | www.stpaulsschool.org.uk

Ages: 13–18

Pupils: 988; sixth form: 413; Boarders: 35 full, 17 flexi

Fees: Day £26,556; Boarding £39,966 pa

High Master: Since 2020, Mrs Sally-Anne Huang. Degree in classics and English from Oxford followed by an MA and an MSc. Married to Alexis and has two adult sons. Previous headships at James Allen's Girls' School (there for six years) and Kent College. Before that, roles as deputy head at Roedean and housemistress at Sevenoaks School.

Opted for teaching out of love of her subject after realising that first choice – journalism – involved extracting stories from people 'at a difficult time in their lives'. Education proved a wise move, swift promotions quickly leading to first headship. She was 'thrilled' to be appointed high master. 'After a certain point, you know there are only certain headships that would provide the right level of challenge.'

She had the hardest of all possible starts, contracting Covid at the end of her first term. She describes it, however, as a 'surprisingly positive experience', providing valuable insights into the workings of the school. 'When you're in crisis management you get to know your team really well, what they can do and you see the pupils rise to that challenge.'

A good communicator and a confident speaker, say parents (chaired excellent online debate when in-person events were in abeyance). Substantial management experience is also welcomed: 'That always wins trust – that she can handle a big organisation and isn't fumbling about.'

Pupils rate her – 'Very sympathetic, personable, stresses wellbeing – sense that she really cares.' 'A visible presence and not intimidating.' Teachers are similarly positive. 'It's an exciting time… to have a woman in a position of authority – good for school and for students to see that,' says one. 'She leads but listens and lets people have their own style.'

Her other big roles – a former chair, then vice-chair of HMC – have given some of her recent tweets a politicised perspective, felt one parent – she'd advocated vaccinating teachers ahead of other groups, for example. 'She doesn't hold back on her views. It's a bit of a departure from previous heads.'

Hasn't thus far made any drastic decisions – conscious (as anyone in this role must be) that 'you are a steward for a finite time and have a responsibility to the people who will follow you.' Changes must benefit the school and pupils. 'If it's not improving the learning for pupils, I'd question whether it needs to be done.'

Inclusion is a long-term interest. She's aware of the gap between very wealthy and 'just about managing' parents that can impact on their children's confidence. 'It's important that this disparity is acknowledged,' she says. School wants to increase the number of bursaries from 143 to 'beyond' 153 so that 'we are welcoming to families who assume we are not for them.'

As the school website puts it, 'the real academic strength of St Paul's is that discussion in the classroom is not constrained by the examined curriculum'

Had missed teaching during the pandemic – delighted to be back in the classroom (teaching classical civilisation to junior school pupils). To relax, she walks her two dogs and has recently taken up tenor sax, achieving grade 3 and finding jazz and swing 'a lifesaver' during lockdown.

Come back in five years' time and, she says, the school will be broadly the same, though with improvements to St Paul's Juniors and boarding. 'Fundamentally, we'll still be a school for very bright boys.'

Entrance: Admissions pages must be the most studied on the school's website. Each year many, many boys – hundreds at least (school was not prepared to share the figures) – compete for 80 external places in year 9 to join the 104 moving up from St Paul's Juniors, who now transfer automatically. Successful candidates will 'comfortably meet' academic standards and boys, unsurprisingly, are naturally extremely bright – the latest ISI inspection puts around half in the top three per cent nationally.

Most come from independent schools in SW and NW London (those applying from state schools generally apply for a year 7 place in the junior school). For year 9 places, helps to attend a school with an in-depth understanding of what's covered in years 7 and 8 here.

Candidates visit before sitting the ISEB online pre-test in year 6. Report from current head teacher. Additional assessments and interviews in successive rounds. Definite and reserve places offered within three weeks of final assessments.

Candidates for 20 external sixth form places sit exams in chosen A level subjects, problem solving and critical thinking skills plus interviews.

Exit: Never ask a boy to leave in the rare event that they underperform in GCSEs 'because we believe it's in their interest to remain'. If pupils do leave, almost invariably because of relocation. Occasional departure at other times for the usual reasons but 'infrequent', says the school and because 'every situation is different', support for family in finding an alternative school would need to be discussed.

Preparation for university entrance is very thorough. While Oxbridge policy of ever-increasing offers to state schools may become more of an issue, it will take a lot more for families to consider moving sons to the state sector to improve the odds. A fraught topic, says a parent. 'It's quite harsh to tell your son you have to move schools to increase your chances for Oxbridge.'

In 2021, 39 offers from Oxbridge, 35 places at top US colleges. Ten to study medicine. Around 95 per cent to Russell Group universities. Bristol, Imperial, Durham, Edinburgh, Exeter and Warwick all popular, with favoured subjects including economics, English, history and maths.

Latest results: Not found in any league table – too narrow a measure of educational success, says St Paul's. In 2021, 97 per cent 9-7 at GCSE; 95 per cent of A levels were A*/A or equivalent. In 2019 (the last year when exams took place), 96 per cent 9-7 at GCSE; 80 per cent of A levels were A*/A or equivalent.

Teaching and learning: As the school website puts it, 'the real academic strength of St Paul's is that discussion in the classroom is not constrained by the examined curriculum. Examination success is important, but for gifted boys it should be a by-product of their broader intellectual development.'

Pupils agree: 'It's about the width of education… making links between subjects.' 'A healthy mix of enjoyment and pragmatism.' One (citing a former high master) likened the approach to the conveyor belt in a sushi restaurant. 'You choose what you want and can make a delicious meal.' We attended a thrilling EPQ presentation by head boy to politics and economics society on the complex forces at play in Yemen – a Michelin-starred example.

So how do you keep these 'pre-selected ambitious and intelligent young men,' as a parent put it, interested and engaged. A lot is down to the boys themselves – 'They feed off each other and that's what propels them to excel,' says parent – coupled with exceptional teaching, essential given that many boys 'are so advanced that they finished the GCSE curriculum months ago and it bores them to death'.

Class sizes are around 20 for a lower school class and 10 for a senior class. Maximum 24 at GCSE, 14 at A level. Smallest classes are for slower-paced lower ability sets (temptation to add inverted comments almost irresistible – though the school aims to add an average of half a grade, sometimes more, to their GCSEs). 'It can be tough if you're not up there with the academic elite,' says a former parent. Most advanced in years 10/11 might spend 20 per cent of the time of exam content, judiciously administered in small doses to ensure it stays fresh.

Calibre of staff essential. School looks beyond normal recruitment channels to ensure that teachers can cope and may take eg PhD students or former City high-flyers. 'Quite agnostic about background... [as it can be] quite a job keeping up with those kids,' says school insider. 'Work with us' section of school website describes school as 'a great and fun place'. Must be – there weren't any vacancies when we looked, even for hard to fill STEM posts. Offer of (admittedly limited) staff accommodation no doubt helps.

Boys eloquent about universal quality of teaching at every stage. By the time we'd dropped in to some of the lessons – year 12 pupils debating Satan's seductive but dangerous humanist perspective in Paradise Lost; A level drama students uncovering the superobjectives of their characters in a Sam Shepard play, while boys in year 11 Latin worked out who killed Germanicus (definitely not Colonel Mustard in the library with a revolver – illness rather than foul play the likely cause) – so were we.

Yes, teachers are focused on ensuring that everyone nails the grades but 'they do it engagingly,' says pupil. Some take you 'wildly beyond the syllabus' others 'know how to keep us engaged and get us through'. But while the teaching style varies, passion for subject is universal.

Boys disputed recent criticism of the schools curriculum in England – presented in the media as restrictively narrow. Here, at any rate, what you get, regardless of specialisation, are the tools of scholarship – curiosity, love of learning and research. 'As somebody who studies humanities it is about learning the skills... the critical thinking, the flexibility, sorting the wheat from the chaff,' says senior pupil.

Maths was widely mentioned as fuelling interest well beyond the demands of the syllabus while ensuring that boys are still motivated to do well at GCSE and A level. 'Incredibly stimulating and motivating for bright pupils,' says a parent. There are university-level whole-class problems; online quizzes, problems that reflect current events – like allegations of electoral fraud in the US elections – and a maths-off (think bake-off with absolutely no cakes) where two pupils volunteer to solve a maths problem against the clock with animated support from the rest of the class. Why do it? 'There's glory to be had,' one boy told his parents.

Because most pupils have a wide range of talents, decisions on which subjects to continue with can be fraught, though school recognises this and does its best to offer advice and accommodate much-loved subjects where possible.

Everyone takes Eng lang and lit, maths, three sciences and then chooses five more, one creative or technical subject (engineering vies with art, music and drama) and a language – extensive range offered. At A level, 22 subjects offered. No psychology. Can choose three or four A levels (must do EPQ with three, optional with four). History and economics are the only non-STEM subjects to achieve similar pupil numbers. In such a high-achieving school it must be hard for sprinkling of pupils who do less well.

Homework a well-thought-out combination of reinforcement and appetite whetting. 'A mixture of summarising the lesson and taking thinking on further or preparing for next lesson,' says a senior pupil. 'And if you feel stressed, you can email the teachers.'

With so many strings to their bows, pupils often lead clubs that plug the gap if much-loved subjects have to be dropped. Arts specialists run STEM groups and vice versa

Covid handled well so far, parent confidence high. 'Some of the boys would have liked to take exams to show what they could do. My son's a [typical] teenage boy – do you think he minded not having sat exams?' says one parent, with commendable frankness.

Learning support and SEN: Support is perhaps surprisingly strong. 'People assume that when you have very academically able children you don't have neurodiversity, [yet] there are aspects of neurodiversity that go with being very able,' says the high master. In reality, specific learning difficulties are most common, though high functioning autism certainly not unknown.

Support headed by popular staff member. 'Boys feel comfortable opening up,' says a parent. Impressively, managed to keep support lessons going during the pandemic using virtual classrooms/Google Meet.

Pupils with EHCPs few and far between. Teachers 'guided' to provide class-based support, some small group and one-to-one sessions with learning support teacher can be offered, though always in break or before/after school – will never miss lessons. Talk about pupils overcoming 'weaknesses' by harnessing their strengths.

The arts and extracurricular: 'You're bound to get kids with exceptional ability – so you have to be good at something, earn your stripes, get some respect and recognition,' says former parent. Range – eclectic – includes champion juggler and cup stacker. Pupils' advice is not to overreach. 'You need to invest your energy into a few things you really care about,' says one.

No shortage of volunteering opportunities. Pupils (from here and from St Paul's Girls' School) run enrichment classes at local state schools.

Boys encouraged to become familiar with the washing machine in preparation for life at university and beyond. Dishwasher, routinely requested, is always turned down

As with sport, performers are extensively provided for, with the Wathen Hall (large enough for decent sized ensembles with a foyer opening out onto the Thames, much in demand for commercial recordings) and the Samuel Pepys Theatre (large stage, classrooms and even showers).

Top singers audition for the 30-strong Recital Choir, instrumentals start with the training ensemble, graduate to the full orchestra and join string, wind and big band groups. Around a fifth learn an instrument in school – occasional support for those learning 'endangered' instruments (like French horn, double bass, viola – there's even a harpsichord room).

Art is well resourced (own gallery, photography room and darkroom) with attractive examples of pupils' work dotted round the school, from covetable Grayson Perry-style vases to triptych of paintings interspersing bars of colour with tree-like images. Portrait of bosomy lady – mentioned by previous reviewer – still hangs at the top of a staircase...

With so many strings to their bows, pupils will join and often lead clubs and societies that plug the gap if much-loved subjects have to be dropped. Arts specialists run STEM groups and vice versa, performing spaces stuffed full of professional-quality kit that attracts technicians as well as performers.

If there's nothing that appeals, pupils set up their own groups or get involved in external competitions and events, often high profile, sometimes world-changing. In just a few weeks (life seems to happen at an accelerated pace here – perhaps there's a prize essay in it) pupils have won competitions, one entry on the theory of roulette – 'a lesser-known branch of mathematics,' said judges (we'll say). Another invented a cough analyser that works out whether patients are asthmatic, potentially saving 100 million patients from misdiagnosis.

Sport: Intensive, fast moving, packing a huge amount of high-quality training into the school day (deliberately long lunch break helps). Inclusive too – unusually, while sport is compulsory, team games aren't – around 50 per cent or so play competitive sport, numbers declining with seniority.

Something to appeal to interested novice and elite performer alike, with 27 sports on the menu, from traditional to esoteric (aikido and ultimate frisbee). Large and larger sports halls, several fitness suites (enthusiastic, welly-wearing teacher running session for rowers), good-sized pool offering Sunday family swimming and a fencing salle. Own rackets court – 'like squash on steroids,' apparently (essential to approach the open viewing area with extreme caution).

Outside, 11 pitches, all bar one grass, stretch into the distance. Built over Thames Water reservoir tanks, some in use so weedkillers are banned, though grass radiates herbaceous good health, kept in trim by a dedicated team of groundsmen so crucial that new pupils have a formal introduction 'so they understand that we're a community looking after the pitch together,' says staff member.

Rugby the traditional main sport and remains a big part of the sports menu, with 400 pupils representing the school and teams down to F. Director of rugby's encyclopaedic knowledge of opponents' skill levels ensures that teams 'can win with grace, lose with dignity – and then have tea,' says staff member.

Given the school's river frontage (boathouse ramp was briefly home to tragic Freddie the Seal), rowing is, predictably, high profile and successful. Old boys regularly feature in the Oxford and Cambridge boat race, Olympic squads and Ivy League crews.

Boarding: Boarding hasn't always had the highest profile – one member of staff spent his first term unaware that it existed. But for the weekly, full and now flexi boarders, from year 9 though most in the sixth form, it's a real oasis, combining

St Andrew's Prep

educational riches within and delights of London without.

Most full boarders are international, mainly from America/Asia and around 60 per cent stay in on any given weekend. Interests range from scholarship (one pupil regularly travels to British Library to access rare Chinese manuscripts for his EPQ) to sport – gym and basketball are top favourites. Trips include paintballing, go-karting and Leiths cooking classes to learn 'how to cook an actual slab of meat,' says staff member. Any budding bakers? 'Absolutely not – I've tried.' (Boys encouraged to become familiar with the washing machine in preparation for life at university and beyond).

Two boarding houses, with a second, West House, which opened 2021 for flexi-boarders. Original boarding house best described as functional, with single bedrooms and shared bathrooms for all, though welcoming head of boarding had spent much time ensuring that new sofas were homely in scale and design (not easy when also have to meet ultra-strict fire regulations). Bar a small duvet mountain – spares in case any boys forgot their own – all was spick and span tidiness.

Boys can return at lunchtime (not between lessons) and bring two after-school visitors, weekend breakfasts are served later (no pjs and slippers in the dining hall). Meals tailored to needs of individuals (elite sportsmen can have extra meals if failing to thrive on standard regime).

Starting point is support, not sanctions, so pupil who struggles with organisation would be encouraged to be packed and ready for lessons, rather than returning to the boarding house after breakfast.

Boarders are involved in much of the decision making, voting on equipment (recent additions include top-of-the-range coffee machine, floor-length mirror and a whiteboard – for recreational maths problem solving) and snacks (Twirl, Twix and Quavers feature currently). Dishwasher, routinely requested, is always turned down. '[It would] just fill up and sit there.'

Ethos and heritage: So good they founded it twice. First time was in the 12th century, as a place to train choristers for St Paul's Cathedral. The second time round was in 1509 when John Colet bequeathed the bulk of his fortune to educate 153 boys 'from all nacions and countres indifferently'. His statue, flanked by the figures of kneeling pupils, greets visitors en route to the main entrance of the school, set in 45 acres by the river in Barnes, the school's home since 1968.

In theory the school is easily reached, in reality hampered by the long-term closure of Hammersmith Bridge to vehicles. Until re-opened (or rebuilt or replaced by a ferry), parents have adapted. 'Pupils north of the river are being dropped at the bridge and walking over, and parents are supportive of this until the bridge is fully repaired,' says the school.

Old and new work effortlessly together here – most recently in austerely beautiful new building in brushed concrete and glass (and so solid that there's pretty much no mobile signal), that completes a rectangle around the central courtyard. Incorporates a library with views of the Thames, classrooms, a chapel and a hall. Its name – GTB2 – is the only aspect that doesn't do it justice (as well as being easily confused with R2-D2, or perhaps that's just us) together with the vintage engineering building that slightly spoiled the architects' vision of a striking and distraction-free vista.

'Our history is the kind that inspires bold ideals for the future,' says the school and aides memoires – if needed – are two a penny here. One former high master gazes approvingly from a vast gilded frame, every inch at home on the bend of an ultra-modern staircase. Others, immortalised as stone busts, look out over the stunning new atrium.

Old and new work effortlessly together here – most recently in austerely beautiful new building in brushed concrete and glass, so solid that there's almost no mobile signal

Comprehensively demonstrated in roster of illustrious former pupils, a compendium of the great and good through the centuries, spanning politics (former Chancellor of the Exchequer George Osborne), science (astronomer Edmond Halley), to sport (cricketer Sam Cato), the arts (writer GK Chesterton to TV presenter Nicholas Parsons) and alternative thinkers (yogi and guru Aurobindo Ghose). Unlikely to be joined by any women as, despite media speculation, co-ed sixth form won't come to pass any time soon. Instead, 'we are intending to work more in partnership with our partner schools so that our pupils can work alongside girls.'

Pastoral care, inclusivity and discipline: The importance of wellbeing and happiness the 'very bedrock' of all that happens here, says the school, which was a leader in training all tutors in mental health first aid.

Not every boy feels under pressure – many appear to have an instinctive grasp of the school's modus operandi almost from the off. 'He doesn't cheat but he knows when to focus and how to fit into this culture,' says a parent. You can't help but wonder if it's these insights, acquired early and presumably honed over a lifetime, that might as useful as any number of glittering prizes.

Vertical tutor groups with pupils from all five year groups work well (in abeyance during the pandemic but will be back, says the school), while the extensive co-curricular programme ensures that even the newest pupils can expand their social circle within weeks of joining the school.

School's assumption, felt parents, is that boys have the intellectual wherewithal to manage their time. 'There's no babying,' says parent. 'They do treat them as older than their age, which has its plusses and minuses.' Where there are problems, however, the school felt to step in quickly and effectively. Two well-regarded counsellors are easy to access – very busy in lockdown supporting boys with mental health issues.

Strong safeguarding team includes undermasters, chaplain, medical staff and learning support team. 'Good, generous, caring and professional if something requires medical specialists,' says pupil. 'I was constantly made aware of where pastoral care was, you don't have to search for days and you're definitely aware that the school cares about it,' felt another.

For others, a small warning shot across the bows may suffice. 'I realised that when the school actually intervenes, that spells a problem, so no news is good news,' says a parent, whose son's minor rule-breaking was effectively nipped in the bud with a single sanction.

Strict on drugs – those bringing in drugs or 'tempting others to use' 'can' face expulsion, though 'will always support pupils who ask for help'. School says that 'consent is sought before searching pupil or possessions for drugs or alcohol but can go ahead without if necessary, in accordance with Department for Education guidance.'

We sensed a degree of frustration that while sexual abuse scandal involving former teachers at the school has receded in public arena, Everyone's Invited has taken its place. While recognising how important the issue is, the high master stresses that many other schools – state and independent – have also been implicated. It's being comprehensively addressed. Boys 'overwhelmingly felt it was not appropriate and wanted to see change'. Top two years have set up a committee with counterparts at St Paul's Girls'. New roles – head of character education and head of inclusion – created and the school has also taken part in the Ofsted review – 'a very positive experience'. Determined to be part of the solution, though high master stresses that 'it's not simple and [won't happen] overnight.'

Pupils and parents: Many delighted families. 'My son is so happy that I often think that when John Colet founded it he thought of what he would like,' says parent (also a staff member).

Pupils come from all over – destinations stretch, tentacle-like, though great swathes of London and out into Surrey and Middlesex. Some celebrities among parents (and sometimes pupils), significant numbers of international families and – though having two parents working full-time is increasingly the norm – inevitably attracts a high percentage of wealthy families. Shouldn't put boys at a disadvantage – but it can. 'My son [felt he] wasn't able to compete on a socio-economic basis and wasn't part of the in-crowd,' says past parent. In all other respects, diversity is seen as a huge benefit. 'It's really opened up my son's friendship groups and opened up his mind – it's a big improvement from his predominantly white primary school,' says another parent.

Pupils describe groups as 'blurred, interconnected, multiplistic… we might not be the best of friends but we rub along well.' Speedy access to the co-curricular programme helps forge new friendships – new boys spoke enthusiastically of finding kindred spirits within weeks. Thriving LGBT+ group (Nigel Owens was a recent speaker).

Excellent range of get-togethers for parents – walks and talks in normal times, webinars during the pandemic. 'I've met people I would never normally have contact with,' says a parent. 'You can form lasting, long-term relationships which also sustained us during lockdown.'

Money matters: Academic scholarships are honorary, music awards give free tuition on two instruments (one instrument for music exhibition) plus honorarium.

Priority is founding commitment to take all academically eligible boys 'regardless of their economic or social circumstances'. Offers free and subsidised places. All pupils gaining a place eligible to apply. Parents provide full details of income and capital – website has worked examples. Don't offer 110 per cent bursaries though stress that award will be enough to cover 'exams, school buses, music lessons, most educational trips, and allowances are made for smart devices, uniform and book costs.'

The last word: If, like a top-grade electrical appliance, you had to give St Paul's an energy efficiency rating, it would be A++++. It would do the pupils an injustice to say that their exam grades are achieved effortlessly – they aren't. But they're achieved with enough power in reserve to undertake just about everything in life that they set their hearts on. A world-class incubator for the future great leader, doer or thinker in your life.

Saint Ronan's School

Water Lane, Hawkhurst, Kent TN18 5DJ

01580 752271 | info@saintronans.co.uk | www.saintronans.co.uk

Ages: 3–13

Pupils: 450; **Boarders:** 77 flexi, 4 weekly (from year 4)

Fees: Day £11,184- £19,164; Flexi-boarding £40.15 per night

Headmaster: Since 2003, William Trelawny-Vernon (50s), only the seventh headmaster in the school's 13+ decades. Very much a joint enterprise with wife Emma (she's the Trelawny, he's the Vernon), who is both registrar and teaches PSHE. They are known as Mr and Mrs TV to pupils and parents, who describe them as 'fun', 'kind' and 'an open book', with one mother beside herself that 'he was the first head to look me in the eye instead of automatically turning to my husband'. The couple – whom we found relaxed, down-to-earth, straight-talking and broadminded – met at Exeter, where Mr TV read biology. Previously at Stowe School for 12 years, including posts as a biology teacher, and seven years as housemaster of Chatham House. Teaches year 5 history – 'largely in preparation for "the chat"' (senior school choices).

The business is in the blood – his father was head of Hordle House (now Walhampton) in Hampshire – and the oldest of their four children is teaching at Stowe, making her the fifth generation of teachers in the family (the other three are at university). Both grew up in a four-child family, and with their own gang of four have that deep respect for fairness and equality of treatment which comes from big families – as well as that willingness, or in their case eagerness, to get stuck in. 'There's no sitting in an ivory tower here – you get the sense that they can't wait to get away from the office and be involved with the children whom they see as members of the community rather than people to go through an academic treadmill,' said one parent – and we noted that they made our tea rather than (as at so many preps) getting their minions to do it (served in chipped mug with posh teabag – like the school, grounded with no airs and graces but first-rate results).

The couple, who moved off site in 2005, eschew the parental dinner party circuit, believing it's important to maintain a distance – parents think they get it 'just right'. In their spare time, both are content with home and hearth and socialising with the wider family, while holidays take them to the West Country, home of Emma's ancestral seat (her brother John inherited the Salusbury-Trelawny baronetcy).

Many preps claim a family feel but this is the real deal, with the head's secretary Mrs TV's sister, known as Aunty Amanda. Even in these admin offices, say parents, there's the 'sense of happy chaos that is the Saint Ronan's way' – 'It wouldn't suit parents who like everything neatly diarised,' said one. 'It looks disorganised, but it works.'

Entrance: No open days – head shows parents round personally. All children attend a taster day, and from year 3 are assessed by the class teacher and do a free writing exercise. Intake covers wide-ranging abilities, but all are expected to behave in the free-range learning environment and pass common entrance or the Cranbrook grammar tests, so school is honest when they believe child's needs are not going to be met.

Exit: Forget it if you have your sights on the local grammars, with the exception of Cranbrook which has recently dropped entrance from 13 to 11. Also popular are Bethany, King's Canterbury, Hurstpierpoint, Lancing and Tonbridge. 'Since I've been head we have fed into over 60 different schools,' says head. Parents say they are good at helping you choose – the TVs visit a clutch of senior schools each term so they are well informed. Often 30+ scholarships.

Our view: The Enid Blyton-esque, what's-not-to-love campus is the perfect setting for this school that sees fun, adventure and creativity as the best way to achieve strong results and create enviable childhood memories. The spectacular 249 acres include ancient, spreading trees, inspiring views, fishing lake, roaming peacocks, meditative garden, pupil allotments, Treetops adventure playground (opened by staff dressed as monkeys) and wonderfully non-PC swings. There's even a farm with pigs, alpacas, chickens and (handy for the Nativity plays) donkeys. The emphasis is on old-fashioned, wholesome fun, making full use of this natural playground, including bushcraft and mountain biking, as well as forest school, in the 100-acre wood. The Tempest was in rehearsal when we visited, with the audience cycling to the different scenes around the school ('a bit bonkers, but that's Saint Ronans').

Even the parents get a generous slice of this rural cake, thanks to the Walled Garden coffee shop that many pile into after drop-off and we saw parents walking their dogs in the grounds (they all rave about the school's close interaction with the parent body – 'it's more come hither-ish than the other local preps,' we were told). Everything is named for Boy's Own adventures – there's the Gulch, an area around a stream ideal for making mud pies, the Saltmines, an overgrown area with secret pathways, and even the pitches have names, such as Timbuktoo (because it's a long journey to reach it). A classroom on the edge of the woods is the Hobbit House and a converted horsebox called Doris is the grub (tuck) shop for pupils, doubling up as a prosecco bar for parent events. Thank goodness for the uniform, among the most relaxed we've seen – corduroy trousers, skirts or pinafores, topped with school sweatshirts in a choice of pink, green, red, purple, light blue and navy. There's a formal uniform for Fridays, key days and trips out.

Main building is Tongswood House, a grand Victorian mansion built by an Oxo magnate, with original features including a sprung floor ballroom (now the main hall which head's study overlooks through an interior window), where frescoes of semi-naked nymphs on the ceiling liven up assemblies. A wood fire burns in the reception hearth and parents can buy free range eggs from the basket (you can also pick up school produced pork and apple juice). There's wood panelling and grand staircases aplenty, but it all feels lived-in and every room, from classrooms to loos, is eccentrically named, such as Drury Lane, 10 Downing Street, The Zoo and Windsor Castle. Children scrape to their feet as adults enter – initially it seems at odds with this otherwise laidback environment but manners are hot, hot, hot here, along with being kind and honest. And that goes for the staff too. 'If we heard a teacher shouting at a child, they would have to come into the office and explain why.' Prefects are elected by the children in a secret ballot 'which means they go for someone who is kind in the changing rooms, not necessarily just one of the first XV'.

The pre-prep is in a separate bright and modern building (where a corridor poster advises on 20 things to do before leaving pre-prep, such as dam a stream, make a mud pie and hold an animal), shared with music, and there's a cosy nursery in the former headmaster's house. New buildings for computer science, art and DT ('so pupils can make a beetle in art, put an engine underneath it in DT and programme it to work robotically in computing') – aim is to be leading prep for STEAM. Large nirvana of a library complete with cheery-looking jars of book suggestions and a book tree. Delightful chapel.

Three-form entry, with maximum class sizes of 18 and four-way setting in English and maths from year 4 ('deliciously small groups'); setting also in French from year 5 and science and Latin from year 6 ('we used to have the scholarship class, but it just produces a sense of entitlement'). Subject specialists from reception in music and sport, from year 3 in computer science, art and DT and sciences, and from year 4 in everything. Teachers need not apply unless they get the job done with humour, compassion and love and prioritise energy, enthusiasm and the example they set; many had previous careers, eg deputy head was a former hot shot in the Met police. 'Time after time, I've seen teachers getting down on their knees to talk to a child – there's a real connection,' said one parent. Long school day – 8.30am to 5.15pm, with prep afterwards at home or at school from year 5 until 6.00pm (6.30pm for years 7 and 8). Homework selected from 'walk, jog, run' levels, with most choosing 'run' – 'psychologically clever as you hook them into the most challenging without forcing it on them'. 'I don't think you realise quite how strong the academics are until you leave because the children never feel pushed,' said one parent.

This is the biggest boarding prep in Kent. Rooms are up in the eaves, and you wouldn't be surprised to find the Famous Five up there having lashings of hot chocolate

Pupils say you ask what musical instrument someone plays rather than if they play one, such is the popularity of the peripatetic teaching. There are oodles of choirs (year groups, chapel and chamber), a 40-piece orchestra and 19 ensembles, with performance opportunities ranging from musical breakfasts to Rye Festival. Drama part of the curriculum until year 5, with senior productions thereafter, including backstage opportunities. School was first prep to put on Chitty Chitty Bang Bang. Art has breadth but heavy on ceramics, the teacher's specialism.

Core sports are hockey, lacrosse, rounders, cricket, netball (girls) and football, rugby and cricket (girls and boys), but tennis, athletics, swimming and cross-country also strong and fencing, golf and sailing on offer too. Plenty of silverware – unbeaten first team in rugby in the season we visited ('and it's not a Micky Mouse circuit down here') and finalists for IAPS national cricket (mixed set team), although some parents say it's less easy to get matches since the school's got bigger and one reckoned 'if you've got a really, really sporty child, they might struggle as they have such a rainbow of children' (school disagrees). There are other options on extras afternoon for the non-sporty, including farming, funky dance, fishing, beekeeping and touch typing. 'The school excels at finding strengths – not just academic,' said parent.

Pupils are friendly, spirited and chatty with a twinkle in their eye. They're supportive of one another too – as likely to pat others on the back as punch their own fists in the air at exam results time. Lots of mixing of year groups. Mental health a priority, with an online tracking system giving staff an insight into, for example, how much each child is prepared to disclose about themselves and how much they trust others.

Parents are a mixture of City and media types, doctors and farmers – all very inclusive and friendly with no social divides, say parents. All describe the school as 'magical', with many claiming an immediate 'gut feeling' that this was 'the one': 'I thought it would be quite stuffy, but straightaway it reminded me of St Trinians,' said one. Not the anarchy, she was at pains to add, but 'the eccentricity and fun'. Some grumbles around school's recent growth, but all agree 'the family feel has remained'. Minibuses bring children in from Staplehurst, High Halden, Burwash, Wittersham and the villages en route. Alumni read like a fantasy dinner party guest list: BBC security correspondent Frank Gardner, spy Donald Maclean, MP Airey Neave, Olympic rower Matthew Parrish, and the late Mark Shand, travel writer (and brother of Camilla, Duchess of Cornwall).

Boarding: This is the biggest boarding prep in Kent, with around a third of pupils sleeping over at least one day a week (maximum four nights) from year 4. 'Really fun – like one big sleepover,' reckon pupils. Rooms are up in the eaves, and again you wouldn't be surprised to find the Famous Five up there having lashings of hot chocolate. Boarders do supervised prep for up to an hour, followed by supper then options such as swimming, singing and playing outside. 'Motherly' matron Julie ('Me Julie') a big pull ('when my eldest, who has left, goes back she always goes to see her') as is food (although school lunch gets mixed reviews).

Money matters: Scholarships available for academic, music, art and sporting talents, and there are means-tested bursaries.

The last word: Roald Dahl, eat your heart out. This quirky rural prep encourages kids to be kids, without trying to squash their imaginations or sense of the absurd and mischief. A far cry from PR-led schools where everyone stands on ceremony, this place fizzes with warmth, gusto and authenticity. A joy for curious, energetic kids and parents for whom education is about more than just grades.

St Teresa's Effingham School
RC
65
Effingham, Surrey RH5 6ST
01372 452037 | a.charles@st-teresas.com | www.st-teresas.com
Ages: 5-18
Pupils: 635; sixth form: 65; Boarders: 50 full, 16 weekly/flexi (from year 6)
Fees: Day £12,405 – £19,365; Boarding £26,535 – £32,985 pa

Headmistress: Since 2019, Dr Claire McShane (30s). At the school since 2013, firstly as assistant and then deputy head. State school educated, a love of literature propelled her to read medieval literature at Oxford and then a MPhil at Cambridge, before completing her PhD at Edinburgh. Bright as her dangly button earrings, there's clearly a razor-sharp academic brain beneath the chic beehive updo. Always wanted to be a teacher because it allows her to be in touch with literature every day.

Began career at Merchiston Castle School, a boys' boarding school. Has found her vocation teaching and leading girls who 'need a bit more confidence boosting' to thrive. Sartorially and scholarly sharp, she is an excellent role model for her Gen Z girls, who say her classics classes are great fun. Parents describe her as 'inspiring and captivating' if a 'little whacky'. 'She electrified the room' at a recent talk, enthused one. Whilst her passion can't be doubted, we found her vision for the school a little hazy. It's 'all about the girls', she says. Empowering them to be 'emboldened but not arrogant'. Committed to continuing to raise academic standards but 'not at the expense of the child'. 'A St Teresa's education is underpinned with love,' she explains.

Her recent marriage made national press as the last wedding before lockdown. She found a free period and was waved off by pupils

Teaches English, Latin, classical civilisation and ancient Greek, runs a couple of academic after-school clubs and even undertakes the odd boarding duty. This erudite Mary Poppins seems practically perfect in every way, except for a small cohort of parents who worried that she was not entirely across everything. To counter, others said she 'gets stuck in' and has a 'can-do attitude'. Currently enjoying a 'post-Covid theatre and cinema bender', The French Dispatch receives an incisive review. Her recent marriage made national press as the last wedding before the country locked down. Organised in hours because 'filing wins wars', she found a free period to carry out her nuptials and was waved off by pupils lining the route out of the school. 'It's a moment I will treasure forever,' she says.

Head of prep since 2015, Sarah Conrad, previously head of New Hall Prep School in Chelmsford. BA in English, German and Theology from University of Durham and a passion for music. From a family of teachers, education is in her DNA despite her best efforts to avoid it, flirting with banking and fashion buying before completing her PGCE. Career has included four years in Singapore at renowned British international school, Tanglin Trust School. More businesslike than her senior counterpart, she is an inspector for ISI as well as a section 48 inspector for both the Diocese of Brentwood and the Diocese of Arundel and Brighton and a committee member of the national Catholic Independent Schools' Committee (CISC). Unsurprisingly then, there's no time for day-to-day teaching duties but she does run a choir, and assemblies and gate duty are immutable.

Exuding efficiency and warmth in equal measures, her role, she explains, is 'not just about being an academic leader for the girls, but being there for the entire family'. Parents have nothing but praise for her. They tell us she is 'very kind and approachable' and 'does an excellent job of instilling values into the girls'. Married to the school's deacon Simon, they share two grown-up daughters and enjoy ballroom and Latin dancing.

Entrance: Following recent merger girls now start co-ed nursery 10 minutes down the road at Cranmore where, under the new diamond model, they stay until year 2. Entry into the prep is by report and informal assessment during a welcome day, plus references from previous school. The main criterion is whether the child is likely to cope in the senior school as the ethos is 'once you're in, you stay'. Can lead to wily parents putting girls in the prep at year 5 or 6. Numbers double in year 7 and the senior school has a waiting list. More girls at the top end of the academic spectrum have been applying, so the academic standard for entry at 11 is now similar to an 11+ pass or level 5 in national curriculum tests. Other talents can prevail, however, and head thoroughly enjoys interviewing every applicant personally to see if 'they're a jolly, kind, good egg'. All current pupils are accepted into the sixth form 'as long as we can offer them a programme', while incomers need six 6s and a 7 at GCSE – particularly in those subjects they are studying. Although the school is Catholic there is no requirement to be so.

Exit: Vast majority of prep school girls move on to the senior school with automatic entry and a large number of scholarships. Almost half leave after GCSEs to go to a variety of sixth form colleges. For post A-level leavers, onward destinations include law at Warwick, archaeology of the historic world at Durham, maths and statistical science at UCL, physics at Edinburgh and ceramic design at Central St Martins. One to Oxbridge in 2021.

Latest results: In 2021, 52 per cent 9-7 at GCSE; 65 per cent A*/A at A level (84 per cent A*-B). In 2019 (the last year when exams took place), 49 per cent 9-7 at GCSE; 46 per cent A*/A at A level (68 per cent A*-B).

Teaching and learning: Amidst the academically competitive Surrey independent school sector, St Teresa's has historically been perceived as the 'pastoral' school. Some might say an 'easy option'. But the results are in and they're looking good. In the prep, girls are performing well above the national average. At senior level, grades are on the up. 'Every school is academic,' laughs the head before explaining, 'It's our bread and butter.' This is a nurturing, values-based education. 'We're a greenhouse, not a hothouse,' claims the school. Many parents we interview say their daughters have risen from bottom of the class to top thanks to the school's 'gentle handling'.

In the prep there's a holistic approach to teaching through immersive cross-curricular topics. Wall displays illustrate 'our frozen kingdom' where year 6 experimented with 'blubber gloves' and learnt how the Inuit people live, and we love the giant marshmallow Stonehenge model being built in year 5. Children tell us about standing on the edge of Mount Vesuvius, thanks to virtual reality headsets. There's a 'super-duper fun' code-breaking maths escape room workshop underway in the hall and the school also brings in external companies to teach entrepreneurial skills.

The largest Catholic independent girls' school in the country with over 630 girls. Around a quarter of pupils are Catholic and faith underpins everything

At senior level, the arts shine. We saw some outstanding ceramics and textiles; many girls go on to art and fashion colleges. Maths is the most popular A level closely followed by psychology and English. Dr McShane's literary salon for avid readers and ancient Greek clubs are big hits. Double and triple science available at GCSE. Enrichment in the form of MedSoc for those interested in studying medicine at university and a lighter BioSoc where girls enjoy fun practicals. French, German and Spanish are taught in rotation through year 7, reducing to two until GCSE when students are expected to study one and most choose two. Language assistants are available for pupils to practise their speaking skills and there's a foreign language film club. Weekly lectures on a range of subjects by visiting academics. Most recent promised 'Eight Things to Make You Live Longer' and was packed to the rafters. Academic scholars must attend three enrichment lectures a term.

Learning support and SEN: School supports almost 100 girls across the prep and senior using mix of tactics from one-to-one lessons and help with study and planning skills, to aids like reading pens and pedagogical teaching strategies such as providing visual to supplement auditory. Department strives to get the girls learning independently, adding, 'we celebrate the uniqueness of any additional learning needs'. One parent said, 'The progress my daughter has made is phenomenal. There's no blanket approach.'

The arts and extracurricular: Performing arts and music departments are vibrant in both facilities and output. Sizeable performance theatre with tiered seating and professional standard equipment allows ambitious large-scale productions. The forthcoming Wendy and Peter Pan production will employ a flight system. In previous years an immersive Christmas Carol began with Scrooge's coffin being carried through the school chapel, and circus skills involving aerial silks and hoops were incorporated into A Midsummer Night's Dream. One drama and one whole-school musical every year, plus end-of-year performing arts evening. The big draw for wannabe thespians is the school's association with a leading talent agency which has led to girls securing roles in TV and film productions from Eastenders to The Secret Garden.

Both heads of music (prep and senior) are RCM-trained professional musicians and between them have over 35 years of service at the school. 'The girls know we are musicians first and foremost, so they go with us. We don't just get them playing the notes.' Suite of AppleMac computers for GCSE and A level composition, plus a recording studio, a designated drum room, and numerous practice rooms 'you can just nip into at break time'. All girls are encouraged to learn an instrument with 24 visiting musicians providing lessons. Ethos is 'excellence and inclusion'; all are nurtured, 'not just the cream'. Big on singing with countless choirs throughout the school. Led by the head, prep girls enjoy Young Voices and have performed at the Royal Albert Hall. Sadly impeded by a pandemic, the annual senior choir tour across Europe, depicted on a vast photo display in the department, looks a hoot.

Extracurricular warrants its own glossy brochure, declaring 'there's something for everyone' and all are expected to partake in enrichment activities. For the prep, a balanced but extensive mix of sports and performing arts with a smattering of technology, chess, art and photography. There's a popular eco gardening club, poetry and debating too. Added to the roster for seniors are coding, mindfulness, public speaking, and a most auspicious virtual investment club where pupils learn about money management and delve into the stock market. Even more convenient, the school has just partnered with a driving school to offer lessons to sixth formers.

Sport: Girls receive a standard three hours a week of PE, but thanks to the breadth of extracurricular sport it's easily tripled for many. 'All our girls love sport,' says department head who guarantees that if they commit to a club, they will make a team. Gymnastics, dance, zumba, spinning, orienteering, badminton, canoeing (head of PE represented GB in canoeing) and water polo on offer as well as the traditional sports. Strong in netball and hockey. There's a partnership with Guildford Hockey Club and a former English international and New Zealand under-21 star are PE teachers. Swim squad taught by Surrey Swimming head coach resulting in the U11 medley relay team securing first and second places in the leading schools swimming competitions last year.

Football also gaining momentum under the tuition of the Chelsea Football Academy with regular matches for U9 and U11 teams in the spring term. Parents say department has enjoyed 'much needed boost' in recent years, although it's worth checking out how well organised fixtures are if this is your daughter's raison d'être as we also hear some grumbles that post-lockdown matches were 'very slow to non-existent starting up'. The facilities are indisputable: 25-metre indoor pool, onsite tennis academy with six floodlit courts, a further three floodlit netball courts and an Astro pitch. Huge indoor multi-sports hall and a fully equipped fitness suite. Lots of pupils enjoy the equestrian centre which has many horses, 'if the girls don't have their own'. Managed independently of the school, one parent lamented that staff had been known to 'simply forget' to enter girls into events but the accolades suggest they do alright with girls regularly cantering to victory in the National Schools Equestrian Association and British Show Jumping Association competitions. One rides for team GB.

Boarding: Capacity for up to 80. Three zones each with own common room and dorms of between four and five. Single rooms with perfectly appointed views for years 10 to 13. All remarkably tidy for teenage girls, with sweet personal touches and we spotted just the one stray sock. There's a sleepover room for five that can be booked out in advance by groups of flexi boarders and a mindfulness room with twinkly lights and fluffy cushions for girls that might need a bit of restorative time. Games room has table tennis, an abundance of books and DVDs (no terrestrial TV) and even an Instagram-friendly flower selfie wall, though strict phone policy sees devices collected half an hour before bed. Décor is a little dated in places but ambience is relaxed and warm. We spotted at least two pianos and a noticeboard full of excursions from ice skating to 'the most popular' Friday shopping trips to the local supermarket.

A mix of nationalities with girls from Spain, Nigeria and Uzbekistan who bring a 'wonderful roundness to the school'. They enjoy sharing their national dishes at international boarding suppers and the school ensures national commemorations are marked. There's currently a large contingent of Mexican girls so school threw a Day of the Dead celebration. Nurturing (but no-nonsense) new head of boarding is planning board game nights to get them through the somewhat discombobulating darker nights of their first British winter.

Ethos and heritage: Set in 55 acres and atop a hill ('a bit too steep,' according to one girl), St Teresa's was founded in 1928 by the Religious Order of Christian Instruction with just four pupils. It is now the largest Catholic independent girls' school in the country with over 630 girls. Around a quarter of pupils are Catholic and faith underpins everything. Chapel once a week and daily prayers in the prep school. We spot crosses in every classroom – sometimes numerous – and the school's church-led values are evident on most available wall space. One mother felt it was a 'little heavy-handed' in the prep school, expounding a recent Easter service where a child was 'literally put on a cross to die and then covered over with a sheet'. We wonder what the talent agency made of that performance. Others said it 'only takes all the good from religion'. Inclusive and celebratory of all faiths, school undertakes numerous charitable endeavours. Big into eco, recently awarded an Eco-Schools silver award.

There's a sleepover room that can be booked in advance by groups of flexi boarders and a mindfulness room with twinkly lights and fluffy cushions for a bit of restorative time

The original house forms the main senior school and is surrounded by numerous purpose-built blocks that have been added over the years, including the spacious prep in 2009. Most recent is an award-winning architect-designed sixth form building. All wood and windows, it houses a vertiginous lecture hall and bright, airy classrooms with stunning vistas of the school's woodlands. For added wow-factor it wraps around a silver birch tree planted in a central courtyard. The common room smells of freshly popped corn and is teenage bedroom messy when we visit. With the youngest now shipped off to the Cranmore site, the old nursery building is being transformed into a whizzy tech hub, complete with four 3D printers, green screen and funky gaming area. Beyond this, the recent merger with Cranmore doesn't seem to have affected the day-to-day life of the school as yet beyond the odd joint disco; it may never. Head says she hopes when boys do eventually join the sixth form 'the girls won't turn a hair'. Lessons on 'consent and banter were well embedded in the curriculum before Everyone's Invited blew up,' she adds.

Pastoral care, inclusivity and discipline: Impressive pastorally. New pupil-led wellbeing hub in the senior school – a safe, quiet space that is dimly lit and softly furnished. In the prep there are wellbeing boards where girls can discreetly let staff know of concerns. Pupils tell us they feel safe and able to share their problems with staff. Lots of peer-to-peer support from top down throughout the school. Some year 11 girls have been trained as mental health ambassadors, an initiative the school will further roll out. There's an online wellbeing hub too which provides content in all formats for pupils, staff and parents alike. A visiting school counsellor, a therapy dog and a dedicated pastoral support programme for those affected by bereavement and loss. LGBTQ+ society in senior school.

Pupil voice is mighty. One prep girl explained, 'If we want something we just ask at student council,' before another clarified, 'We do have to need it of course.' Independence encouraged through responsibilities. From classroom monitors to prefects, there's a job for everyone. At sixth form, however, some of the girls – who are still expected to wear a version of uniform, albeit with conspicuously shorter skirts – complain there's a lack of freedom because they can't leave the school site due to its secluded location. Prep pupils say teachers are 'fun and friendly', not strict, but they 'don't dilly dally'. 'They support our hopes and dreams,' one enthused. Parents concur.

Behaviour was exemplary for our visit. One group lining up excitedly for lunch perceptibly hushed as we passed by. In the senior feedback is mixed – a small cohort of parents believe that 'the prep is far superior to the senior'. Reports of a minor exodus in one year group because discipline 'dropped massively' after lockdown are downplayed by the school as being for 'financial or practical reasons'. Most of the lessons we observed appeared to be in order. Class management was a little slack in one we passed by and we witnessed one incident of adolescent disrespect behind the back of a teacher. But one bad egg does not ruin the cake and the overriding impression is of diligent, considerate, well-behaved girls who are achieving. Reports of some 'niggles between girls' in the middle years of the senior are tackled readily by head: 'When the shifting sands of friendship kick in, so do we.'

Pupils and parents: Girls are wholesome, mostly makeup free, with sensible school bags and shoes. Head describes them as 'compassionate with some oomph'. Those we met all sang from the same song sheet, or in the case of the prep girls a laminated crib sheet of key messages. They spoke of feeling safe and supported. We found them to be confident, not precocious. Thoughtful, kind, driven and focused. One parent tactfully explained, 'It might not suit the more streetwise, boundary pushing girl.'

In what is an incredibly privileged enclave of Surrey, parents describe themselves as 'not stuck-up'. We're told the mix includes builders and celebrities alike. WhatsApp groups are 'very vocal, but positive' and there's lots on socially if you want it. Recent influx from abroad told us the school had 'grounded them as a family'.

Money matters: Scholarships are awarded for academic excellence, art, drama, music and sport.

The last word: Parents describe the school as a 'beautifully self-contained world'. For those seeking a gentle values-based education, where girls can be inspired and remain unaffected for as long as possible, it's worth taking a hike up the steep hill.

Seaford College

66

Lavington Park, Petworth, West Sussex GU28 0NB

01798 867392 | jmackay@seaford.org | www.seaford.org

Ages: 13–18

Pupils: 643; sixth form: 235; Boarders: 144 full (90 boys, 54 girls)

Fees: Day £10,995 – £22,785; Boarding £22,908 – £35,250 pa

Headmaster: Since 2013, John Green. Background in professional rugby – he teaches the first team, donning wellies with suit. Taught previously at Barry Boys' School, Ardingly College and Hurstpierpoint, before becoming deputy at Seaford. Married to Sîan with three children.

Tiggerish energy, staunch and unapologetic supporter of the underdog, with a clear vision of how he wants Seaford to be. Works hard to install a sense of value and self worth in all his pupils: A* pupils at Seaford now consider Oxford; BTec pupils are told 'you could be employing those

A* pupils in a few years' time'. Quality he most desires for his pupils: pride in self.

Entrance: Fifty per cent of year 9 from Seaford Prep, the rest from a range of preps and local primaries. ISEB pre-test in year 6. Non-selective until GCSE; thereafter need 45 points to enter sixth form. Screening for SEN on entry.

Exit: Just over 20 per cent to local sixth form colleges, usually for financial reasons. Around 20 per cent to Russell Group. Oxford Brookes most popular destination by far. Kingston, Exeter, Bath Spa and Gloucestershire also feature. One to Oxbridge in 2021, and one medic.

Latest results: In 2021, 53 per cent 9-7 at GCSE; 55 per cent A*/A at A level (71 per cent A*-B). In 2019 (the last year when exams took place), 29 per cent 9-7 at GCSE; 33 per cent A*/A at A level (53 per cent A*-B).

Teaching and learning: Good solid results. Judged on its place in a league table, unremarkable. But the remarkable exists within these figures at this non-selective school. The most able are achieving the high grades you would expect; but so are a good number of those of more average abilities, Seaford generally adding at least one grade to pupils' attainment.

New pupils at Seaford all have a data interview: a detailed meeting showing parents and the pupil their CAT scores and the national picture of attainment for someone of their abilities. 'Children in the middle can achieve highly and shouldn't put a ceiling on expectations.' Top grades can suddenly seem like something attainable. One parent told us about her son, told by his previous school that he was a no hoper, whose confidence has soared at Seaford: he's predicted good grades at A level, and led Young Enterprise last year. When he went up on speech day for an academic prize, 'it was worth every penny'.

'Seaford was seen as a school for dunces,' said a parent who was initially dubious about the school, thinking it was a 'too relaxed environment'. On meeting the head, the parent quickly felt that things had changed. Rigour is now a word which could apply to Seaford. One parent described how her son did a mock paper which went wrong: 'They were all over it and him, in a supportive, but thorough way.'

There's a new focus on high flyers here; a head of enrichment now guides the Oxford application process, and an enrichment programme selects high performers in each subject and adds a layer on top of syllabus stuff – masterclasses in maths this term with lectures on chaos and infinity. Lecture doors are open to anyone truly interested (while trying to exclude crafty prep dodgers).

The head has made several staff changes, to the relief of parents: 'The dead wood's gone,' said one briskly. There was a lot of praise for the effort put in by teachers: 'what makes this school special is its staff'; 'teachers go above and beyond to help failing pupils... three extra sessions a week to help my son get a pass'.

A long driveway, past golf flags waving in the breeze and ancient trees up to the mansion house: stately home turned school. Seaford College sits at the foot of the downs

An extremely active tutor system, with a weekly meeting of an hour, and daily catch up of five to 10 minutes every morning. Pupils are also part of vertical tutor groups spanning year groups.

Homework is marked with comments, not grades – 'If pupils get a grade, they immediately want to know what their friend got.' Effort grades have been abandoned – only pupils can really know. Instead, effort and attainment have been absorbed into the challenge grade system: grades set are a indication of potential – what a pupil could achieve if they work hard. Different colours indicate how well they are progressing towards their challenge grades, from significantly underachieving red, through amber, green and gold to extremely high-achieving platinum. Challenge grades are set with tutors and can be upped by pupils if they feel the challenge is not sufficient (hollow laughs from students).

A good array of subjects on offer at both GCSE and A level, plus BTecs (most recent additions hospitality and countryside management) and EPQ. Most subjects have a spread of attainment in grade terms, with grades in English, history and maths clustering towards the top end.

Learning support and SEN: Learning support here is done extremely well by a staff of nine specialist teachers, five full-time, four part-time. Nearly half the pupils at the school use the unit at some point, by teacher or self-referral. Seaford proudly locates learning support in the centre of the campus, 'not the usual broom cupboard under the stairs,' said a parent wryly.

'I've been to a lot of schools who say they are good at SEN,' said a weary mum, 'but here it isn't just a soundbite.' The unit describes an approach that involves nurturing and developing individual potential, working hard to increase confidence, by pointing out what's right, not wrong, and how to improve. High degree of joined-up thinking to enable dyslexics to access the curriculum, with the unit meeting with other teachers regularly.

And their approach yields results. A parent described how her severely dyslexic son 'changed overnight' here. He was told at his prep that he wouldn't be able to sit GCSEs, but is now at the school of architecture in Oxford, having left Seaford with three A levels and an EPQ. If things weren't working, Seaford always looked for alternatives which fitted him better, she explained.

Mild to moderate dyslexic pupils in general, though the door is not closed to those at the severe end of the spectrum if they have a high IQ or good underlying ability, but they need to be able to access the mainstream curriculum with the help available. The unit assists pupils with dyspraxia, speech and language problems, slow processing speeds and memory problems. Would consider mild Asperger's, but not the place for autism. Help also given for ADHD (experienced but not specialists in this).

Head soloist describes 'music coming up through my toes' – it's no surprise that she and the choir were selected to support Gary Barlow on the last night of his tour

There is one guaranteed one-to-one session a week (which is charged as an extra). Extra sessions are offered to pupils if they become available, on the basis of need. There is a little in-class support.

Seaford has had a number of high-achieving dyslexics, one achieving his eight As and one B at GCSE with the help of a scribe; another part of the current small group of high flyers trying for Oxford.

The arts and extracurricular: Music at Seaford is glorious. Singing is outstanding here – the head of voice is also head of voice at junior Royal Academy in London. The head soloist describes 'music coming up through my toes' – it's no surprise that she and the choir were selected to support Gary Barlow on the last night of his tour. The music block is all white paint and new wood – smooth, calm surroundings to complement the mellifluous sounds.

Not as great an emphasis on drama as music ('not enough,' said one parent bluntly), but drama is now part of the year 9 carousel, some pupils do LAMDA, and there are productions each year: Dr Faustus the last, a dyslexic pupil taking the lead part, learning his lines by drawing pictures.

Compulsory CCF in year 10: the parades are dull, say pupils, but CCF camp was a favourite memory. DofE also available.

Art here is superb, with a big range on offer, from fine art to creative media production. Exam work included dresses of balloons and feathers; curvy wooden speakers and fabric stags' heads (they look so much better in tartan). Ghoulish sci-fi heads in the animation area; a fabric prawn (Shaun), life-like and eerily huge, hung casually from the ceiling. Sixth form art students almost live in the block – there's even a kitchen so they can brew – 'We look after them,' said the head of art, comfortably. Students depart for art colleges across the country.

Sport: A new focus on games with the rugby-playing head: hockey's always been strong here (county winners); now rugby's just as good. Girls were languishing behind the boys a year or so ago, but head has given girls' sport a new emphasis: hockey and netball are flourishing. Cricket and tennis for both girls and boys are taking off.

Teams for all, the best playing every week, less able around six times a term. Specialist coaching for all ability levels here; and it's not just the top performers who get the accolades: recent team of the term was the U14 hockey C team.

Boarding: It's particularly nice here, and one of the nicest things is its lack of uniformity. The four boarding houses are all different, each with a strong sense of home. Most are weekly, full timers largely being international (10 per cent of boarders are from overseas). Flexi-boarding is also available, and it's usually possible to get a room at the last minute by emailing houseparents.

Boys (years 9-12) are in a crisp new building (which parents love), run by houseparents with fluent ease. Basket drawers for shoes as soon as boys come through the door – they generally remember: it's nice to walk around in socks with underfloor heating. If they don't – hoover duty that night. Rooms for two, with temperature gauges in each room and a sofa which can turn into another bed. New wood furniture, built in above bed lights. Rooms compact, but not tight. Worth getting the big jobs – head of house gets a comfy chair and ensuite, TV and fridge (wow).

Wifi throughout (indeed, throughout the campus), and a system so houseparents can see if pupils are online when they shouldn't be (after 11.30pm); younger pupils hand in tech at bedtime. Comfortable common room, kitchen for snacks, fruit and toaster. Homework is supervised, houseparents pleased that their only niggle ('haven't got any homework, sir') has been resolved by the internet site which makes it clear what everyone's got. A house mum bakes pancakes and fudge crumpets for movie night. Houseparent dogs bounce into the common room in the evening. The kids love it.

Sixth form girls live in a bungalow, well-mown lawn with gnomes out front, patio with BBQ around the back. Some feeling of arriving in antipodean suburbia

Girls in years 9-12 are housed in the Mansion: rooms of all shapes and sizes for one or two, some extremely spacious – elegant windows, dreamy views. Graceful spiral staircase up to the boarding floor. In various states of paint, just done and needs doing ('needs to be modern and fresher,' said a parent). Good quality wood furniture, the usual kitchen provision.

Sixth form boys housed in what parents and pupils refer to as 'the youth hostel' (aka Hedon Hall) – 'but the boys are all happy in there and love the housemaster'. The fabric is old, and inside it is painted lime green (gulp), but the furniture in bedrooms and common room is smart and new, bathrooms are clean, and the common room is decorated with sports paraphernalia, donated by past and present sixth formers. Residents have a fierce affection for the house and its head, who is a staunch supporter of them. He enforces an hour's leisure reading every afternoon in the winter term (proper books, not magazines), having found out that dyslexic commuters do better because they read on the train.

Sixth form girls live in a bungalow, well-mown lawn with gnomes out front, patio with BBQ around the back. Some feeling of arriving in antipodean suburbia. Scottish giant of a house dad, casually consuming his Magnum, showed us a bright pink sitting room with golden buddha in the fireplace – teenage heaven. Kitchen and seated area – they can go to the dining hall for breakfast, but most prefer to eat 'healthy girly breakfasts' in house. Cosy rooms, with the usual high quality fittings. A warm friendly relationship between pupils and houseparents.

Plenty going on for boarders at weekends, with the Sainsbury's trip on Friday evening, sports and shopping trips on Saturday, and trips to places of interest on Sunday.

Ethos and heritage: A long driveway, past golf flags waving in the breeze and ancient trees up to the mansion house: stately home turned school. Seaford College sits at the foot of the downs, wooded hills rising immediately behind it, mists caught in the trees on the drizzly day of our visit – brewers' dubbin, said the head of English dreamily. A beautiful flint chapel nestles in the grass behind the school. Compulsory weekly service, but all beliefs welcome.

Stately elegance mixes with old cottages and swish new build. A few tatty portakabins, due to be ripped down soon. Most parents we spoke to would like things to be a bit smarter – 'there shouldn't be peeling paintwork – it needs a bit more polish'; and the head is working hard to spruce up buildings as well as pupils. Manners are of the old-fashioned variety, and include standing up for visitors and handwritten letters of thanks.

There's an emphasis here on giving something back: community service activities every week, and community action day once a year, which includes activity programmes with local primary school children, or clearing beaches.

It would not suit a child who was full on academic with no other interests, said a parent. 'Very intelligent children will thrive there if they do other things… it could be a very lonely place for those just absorbed by maths and physics. Everyone's outside at the end of the day – you need to be able to mix and be a bit independent.'

Pastoral care, inclusivity and discipline: Pastoral care at Seaford is 'unbelievable', said a parent, as she described the extraordinary level of kindness and understanding from the school when facing family tragedy. And they're very aware of the pressures of growing up. Staff in the Pink House provide a listening ear at any time – pupils can even ask to be excused in a lesson, and staff will email the Pink House to say a pupil is on the way. It's staffed by one full-time director of care and welfare, a part-time safeguarding officer, the rev, a counsellor and Poppy the dog (who is particularly busy in September helping homesick pupils). At least 10 pupils turn up at the Pink House every day, but problems can be also be picked up by phone, tutors or peer mentors. Any bullying is dealt with promptly, confirm parents. One described how her daughter would pop in to the Pink House to get some perspective on school squabbles – 'so and so's being a bit nasty, I'll go the Pink House and see what they think'.

In discipline terms, rules are firmly based on traditional good manners and strict enforcement of standards. No more easygoing Seaford; the head is ensuring the school is up to the mark, from looking smart to the top 10 rules: break them and you risk exclusion (interestingly, dishonesty is ranked outside the top 10 as a less serious offence, alongside chewing gum…). No second chances for sex or drugs (although first time joint users might get a managed reprieve, depending on the circumstances). And to make sure no one flouts the rules, sniffer dogs (a crazy spaniel and a labrador) check the lunch queue. They're much loved by kids – and have never actually found anything. Two exclusions in the last year: for persistent disruption, and bullying. No surprise, in this caring school, that those suspended or excluded can go the Pink House for a chat with support workers 'to feel the love'.

Delicious lunch served for us in the head's study – is it always this nice? 'It doesn't look quite like this,' said the head boy carefully, regarding a swirl of purée, 'but it tastes good.'

Pupils and parents: Posh, and not – 'I know someone with a jet, and others working three jobs to get their kids through.' Lots of weekly boarders from London, and school buses serve the surrounding area.

Fewer girls than boys (around a third), but the head is keen to attract more, and ran an everywoman conference to provide aspirational role models for girls.

Parents are happy with a good level of communication, with frequent emails from school, and teachers letting parents know if there's a problem – 'in the past we'd have had to work this out for ourselves'.

Money matters: Fees good value for money, said a parent; but she wouldn't want them to be any more. Means-tested bursaries; range of scholarships available at 13+ and 16+.

The last word: A happy, exceptionally caring school, which strives to do well by all who cross the threshold, whatever their ability.

Sevenoaks School

67

High Street, Sevenoaks, Kent TN13 1HU

01732 455133 | admin@sevenoaksschool.org | www.sevenoaksschool.org

Ages: 11–18

Pupils: 1005; sixth form: 468; Boarders: 393 full

Fees: Day £25,020 ; Boarding £39,960 pa

Head: Since September 2020, Jesse Elzinga. BA in comparative religion from Harvard, MSt from Oxford on a Rotary International Scholarship. Previously at Reading Blue Coat School – his first headship.

The latest in a long line of fearsomely well qualified and multi-talented heads, he doesn't just pack an academic punch but is a highly talented sportsman as well – a three-time national champion rower at Harvard and Oxford who then switched to competitive cycling, twice racing against Sir Bradley Wiggins at the British Time Trial Championships.

To fill in any spare moments, he's also an Ironman triathlete and marathon runner (and a dab hand at welly throwing, judging by video on website). Out of school, enjoys cooking, BBQing, travelling, opera and supporting England Rugby Club with wife Elaina. Though with three daughters – youngest born during the pandemic – spare time must be at a premium.

Teaching experience, unsurprisingly, is suitably high powered. A summer school rowing coach and housemaster at Eton in the early noughties, his first teaching post (theology), was at Whitgift, where he qualified as a teacher, set up the school's first rowing programme and subsequently became assistant head of sixth form.

Two director of studies posts followed, first at St Edward's School in Oxford (joining in 2006 as head of religious studies, promoted in 2009), next at Harrow School where he worked for five years from 2011 before his move to Reading Blue Coat School in 2016.

Knew he wanted to work with children at age 10. Had initially planned to be a paediatrician but after gruelling work experience in a children's ward turned to teaching, unwavering even when his peers opted for masters of the universe careers in banking, investment or law (they now call him for education advice).

No AI-generated background during Zoom call from his office. A traditionalist, he's already overpainted previous statement fuchsia stripes on the walls and leather chesterfield sofas are on the way, while marble fireplace, currently captive behind high-gloss cabinetry, is shortly to be released back into the wild.

Relish for the role unmistakeable. Leadership style, he says, is about remaining positive and determined 'really important… especially in difficult times.' Still teaches (year 9s) and has thrown himself into school life.

Trained with the first XI when normal life was still possible (though 'was reminded I did not make the top football squad in my school') and among other things made ecobricks (with the rest of the school) when it wasn't.

Confesses to being spotted in the nearby Waitrose 'more often than I'd like' as well as enjoying a daily run round Knole Park to give him 'the moment of stillness.' Post-pandemic, he believes, there'll be greater appreciation and gratitude ('an important aspect of wellbeing') for schools and teachers from families.

He's passionate about ensuring that school opens up to more children from all walks of life, in part because of the scholarships that made his own education possible. (His father, a fruit farmer in the Midwest, 'never grew enough apples to pay my tuition fees.')

Points out that school's founder, William Sevenoke, set the school up 'to support social mobility'. Following a little mission creep through the centuries since, Mr Elzinga's ambition is to 'create a culture of philanthropy' by setting up an endowment fund (school, despite appearances, is not plump in the pocket where means-tested bursaries are concerned) to ensure that one day there is needs-blind admissions for all. May take several generations of headteachers to come to fruition but with sufficient determination (and a concerted campaign to persuade alumni to give generously) will be worth the wait.

While he's so energised that he avoids coffee before meetings (effects unspecified but we're guessing scorch marks on the meeting notes), his video messages are gentle, understated, thoughtful (singles out the cleaners for all their efforts during the pandemic) and upbeat. All delivered in a pleasant accent which is part UK, part US, with the occasional slight tussle between the two.

He's made a favourable impression with parents who praise his commitment and straightforward communications style and (when briefly possible) was a friendly presence in the car park at drop-off time (and no doubt will be again).

'Doesn't rely on long words and technical terms,' says one. 'Talks in a very human way.' Stays in touch. 'We know he's there and what he's up to.' Praise for passion for education and respect for his straight talking – if he doesn't have the answers, he'll say so.

Hard-to-impress pupils, meanwhile, are also (in a more understated way) pleased with their new head. Approachable, thought one. 'A good bloke,' felt another – considered to be high praise. Based on Zoom call this reviewer would certainly agree.

Entrance: At 11+, 80 places, and 100 at 13+. For year 7 place, entrance tests in maths, English and VR, references, group interviews and reports. Numerous local prep feeders. Rumour that state school entrants may be favoured if tie break for a place. 'Only a rumour,' stresses school. School stresses that parents should not worry that lockdown means that candidates with limited access to online learning will be disadvantaged – will look at all results (maths, English and CAT scores) and talk to previous schools before making a decision.

Pupils leave, says school, with 'enlarged capacity for independent thought' – and without, as far as we could see, acquiring swollen heads on the way out

Applicants for 13+ entry take maths, English and VR tests in year 7, plus 40-minute group interview and reference. Unconditional offers made in June of year 7. Those at prep schools asked to aim for 70 per cent at common entrance (used for setting purposes).

For sixth form entrance, when another 75-80 pupils taken in, tested in three proposed IB higher level subjects plus maths and English if not native language (high levels of fluency essential though can offer a session a week to 10 pupils needing short-term boosters).

Exit: Vast majority (95 per cent) stay on into sixth form. Countdown to UCAS form completion handled extremely well with teachers pitching their own degree subjects. Also 'how to' personal statement talks, coaching for US SAT tests and support if predicted grades don't work out quite as planned. School baulks at our description of talking near misses on to foundation places at desired uni as doesn't want to create the impression of dark arts string-pulling – but if they can support pupils they will.

Many offers from highly prestigious unis here, there and everywhere – many to US and Canada, few to anything other than Russell Group or top international equivalents. 'Work really hard to support them, in the end it's what you pay them for,' said parent. As a result, destination list tends to resemble a global best of higher education list, with 28 to Oxbridge in 2021, and 42 to US and Canada (including Chicago. Toronto, Brown, Northeastern, Berkeley, Pennsylvania, Yale, Columbia, Dartmouth, CalTech and Stanford) and nine to Europe and Asia. Around half study arts and humanities courses, a third STEM and the rest mainly liberal arts and combined programmes. Fifteen medics in 2021.

Latest results: In 2021, 94 per cent 9-7 at GCSE. Average diploma score of 41.

Teaching and learning: Not so much a case of getting down with these kids but scrabbling up to their level. Regardless of mother tongue, notable for gift of gab and desire to avoid muscular Christianity (or contortionist's pantheism) in favour of secular education that builds curiosity, creativity and critical thinking. They leave, says school, with 'enlarged capacity for independent thought' – and without, as far as we could see, acquiring swollen heads on the way out. This despite evident brightness starting early, year 7 packed with top of their year types – no surprise given school's entry criteria: grammar school level or better. 'Other girls took five lessons to learn something; I took one,' says typically bright 11-year-old. Most pupils find flocking with similar highflyers an easy transition, though brilliance of plumage can be dazzling. 'It was hard at first,' said one recent leaver.

By sixth form, IB is natural extension of school's way of thinking, most pupils revelling in mind-stretching approach that's been their lot so far. It's about 'developing brain muscle'

Unquenchable sense of purpose the norm. 'A lot of people had very strong opinions about where they'd be in life in the next five or 10 years' time,' said ex-pupil. (And you can probably assume they aren't thinking middle-rank pootling with safe pension in Basildon.)

But while spreading a little zappiness throughout, school doesn't ramp it up to mind-blowing levels. Don't sit exams early – why spoil the pleasure of discovery? Staff lay on homework with a light touch rather than trowel – if not necessary, won't set.

Curriculum, naturally, is robust. Three sciences from the off, second language added in year 8. Most teaching is mixed ability – maths and languages the exceptions – sometimes adjusted instead for gender balance. For years 10 and 11, formulaic in the sense that these very bright children have only to be shown the way to strings of 9-7 grades at GCSE and it happens (87 per cent in 2019). Norm is 10. New Middle School Diploma for years 9-11 records co-curricular and skills based learning.

By sixth form, IB is natural extension of school's way of thinking, most pupils revelling in mind-stretching approach that's been their lot so far. It's about 'developing brain muscle so can frame an argument,' said upper sixth English teacher leading typically lively, interactive lesson. Intellectual weightlifting produced 39 point IB average in 2019.

The head, who's had substantial involvement in the IB in previous schools, is a proselytiser for the way it covers all the main academic bases, incorporates 50 hours of community service and keeps options open. 'Sixteen is too young to be closing those doors and professional careers,' he says.

Maximum class sizes sound large (24 to GCSE, 15 in the sixth form), but average is far lower (16 to age 16, and between eight and 10 in final years), with overall teacher to pupil ratio of one to nine.

Stable core of middle management reflected in average staff age of 41, with 55 notching up 10 years plus. Inevitable turnover of younger mob to more senior positions elsewhere (around 10 headships in recent years). Staff team so strong that (unusually) parents and pupils couldn't name a single weak area and inspection accolades agree. 'Can go away and think about it,' offered recent leaver. 'Used to being at the top of their game,' confirms parent.

Just as well, given need to move swiftly to an online platform during lockdown, learning 'how to teach online from scratch, look at safeguarding [and] health and safety and leap into being new teachers again in world that they hadn't ever experienced.'

Results impressive, with some nice touches to compensate (where possible) for absence of corridor conversations – the day-to-day stuff of normal and much missed interaction. There's deliberate latitude, with extra minutes in breakout rooms so pupils can enjoy a bit of chat and laughter 'so hard to recreate,' says parent.

Learning support and SEN: While around 10 per cent of pupils have some form of learning need, it's mild only for dyslexia, dyspraxia, dysgraphia, ADHD, Asperger's Syndrome and visual impairment. Only exception is hearing impairment. Not suitable for anyone needing substantial support in class. Once in (and admissions process incorporates extra hand holding where needed) support is felt to be thorough and effective.

The arts and extracurricular: Visitors might find numbers of events and activities almost overwhelming. Not so pupils, busily adding more, from coding to Middle Eastern society, at a rate of knots. Others enter – and win – high-profile competitions, one group snaffling £15,000 prize after developing app for autistic children.

Haven't let the pandemic slow their efforts with pupils involved in potentially world-changing initiatives. One group is synthesising molecules (as you do) as part of an open source project seeking a cure for fungal disease affecting Indian farmers. Other pupil initiatives include an app that shows people exactly how their choices damage the planet and another, 'Get well soon, world', that focuses on support for mental health.

Overdoing things isn't an issue, says school. Can mean hard choices – some pupils (reluctantly) give up drama in the sixth form, and school keeps watchful eye on the ultra-active, though approach, ladling on the encouragement rather than activating the brakes, is distinctly hands-off. 'If you feel you can cope, you probably will,' says pupil. Latest initiatives are three institutes – teaching and learning, service and social impact, and higher education.

Performing arts impressively housed in The Space, with vast, acoustically advanced theatre that takes staging challenges in its stride (pop-up orchestra pit for Les Mis a doddle) and umpteen practice rooms for 750 weekly individual lessons. Very talented flourish (conductor Andrew Gourlay is a former pupil) with symphony orchestra, jazz band, gospel choir and song writing groups among many ensembles on offer, though 'have a go' spirit sees all abilities from virtuoso to enthusiast rapturously received when they take to the stage.

Sport: Lavish facilities the norm. For sporty, substantial outside spaces supplemented by great indoors of Sennocke Centre – just lapping its three tennis courts, pool and giant sports hall probably enough to meet daily exercise requirements. With some international pupils completely new to team sports, hasn't been high profile area in the past, though recent successes – U14 hockey and U16 netball teams making national finals – could signal a change, achievements recognised by must-read authority, School Sport Magazine. Individual sports generally more popular – sailing especially so. However, numerous parents and pupils testified to star ratings for CCF, available from year 10, khaki-clad mob milling prior to drilling, rugged in T-shirts despite below-zero temperatures on day of visit.

Boarding: Sensible pandemic planning enabled international boarders to stay on during autumn half term 2020. Plaudits from parents for Mr Elzinga's fleet footed acquisition of highly accurate rapid response Covid testing equipment (funded by parent donations and bought only when certain that it was not at patients' expense).

Has minimised unnecessary self-isolation time, essential when one child's symptoms can impact on an entire boarding house, though pupils have been exceptionally sensible, one selfless soul staying outside boarding house with a temperature, alerting housemaster by knocking at his window so when he did test positive for Covid, nobody else was affected. Similar behaviour par for the course in every house, so don't worry which one you're allocated, says pupil. 'They're all just as friendly and happy.'

Pupils involved in potentially world-changing initiatives. One group is synthesising molecules as part of a project seeking a cure for fungal disease affecting Indian farmers

Sensible to book your place early – not easy to change to boarding later on and even a few sixth formers (house captains excepted) share rooms. Not that pupils mind, enjoying companionship and, according to one sixth former, preferring in any case to study in three-level, attractively nook-filled library, which like Sennocke Centre and practice rooms is open late. 'Less distraction as you don't have your stuff round you.'

Cleanliness comes as standard (a spot of stuffiness in one bedroom was nothing that open window or two wouldn't solve), ditto entertainment (TV/DVD, Sky, snooker or table tennis, Wifi) and bulk deliveries of bread, fruit and milk (sensible refrigerated dispensers).

Considerable variation otherwise. Sixth formers have International Centre (boys) and Girls' International House. Then there's gorgeous Johnsons, one of seven houses for year 9s to upper sixths, all early 20th-century Agatha Christie-whodunnit-style fixtures and fittings except from the two new ones. No longer offers boarding to years 7 and 8. Construction has started of a new girls' boarding house for 2023.

Newest boarding house, Aisher, opened in 2019 for 60 middle and upper school boys and is much sought after. 'Incredible – newest, cleanest facilities,' says parent who extolled the homely feel and sensitive use of colour palette (a mustard and yellow – warm and welcoming rather than hot stuff). Each of the single and two-bed rooms has an ensuite, with an enormous TV and lounge area – university accommodation likely to be a distinct letdown.

Some non-negotiables. No solo travel to more distant boarding houses regardless of age and, if late, with accompanying teacher. Y9/10/11

Benenden School

boarders have their mobile phones removed at respective lights out (parents predictably thrilled to be let off this particular hook).

Otherwise, trust and flexibility dominate, from lockers (unlocked) to negotiated later bedtimes for older pupils if vital world events like US election intervene. 'About compromise,' says warm houseparent, who teaches ironing and cooking as university preparation. Previously laundry seemed to happen, magically off stage, but no longer, with parents stressing that ways with spin cycles are now imparted to all.

House rivalry low key to point of invisibility. 'Children have to compete with the outside world, they don't need to compete with each other,' is parent's take on school's philosophy.

No 'them and us' between day and boarder, local or international pupils – 'seamless', said pupil, of integration between the two (national groups split up, factions/combatants eg Russia/Ukraine brought together). House events include Valentine's meal (partners can be blind date, same sex, day or boarding pupils – one boy invited his best friend).

In normal times, around three-quarters of sixth form boarders remain at weekends (it's half or so in other years). Home clothes allowed though if inappropriate will be 'sent home at the boarder's own expense...' (not a regular occurrence). Sunday excursions enjoyable if not cutting edge (a liking for Laser Quest definitely useful), but a welcome change from frantic pace of life in the week. School prefers parties for younger pupils when hosted out of school to be alcohol-free – and provides useful hints and tips including checking water bottles for vodka – though sensibly stops short of laying down law (impossible to enforce, we'd have thought).

Ethos and heritage: Given awe-inspiring prospectus – fabulously well written, slightly tongue in cheek self-praise in vignette form – school could have work cut out just living up to it. For the most part, succeeds – triumphantly, even if tiny imperfections (like smeary bin in visitors' loo) are the more jarring by comparison. And though it comes with over 500 years of history – was one of the earliest secular school foundations in the country – and literary references in works by everyone from Daniel Defoe to Charlie Higson, isn't weighed down by it, with plenty of space, physical and philosophical, to let in plenty of fresh thinking and the odd bit of quirkiness.

When back on site, pupils benefit from what one described as a 'wonderfully happy location', thought pupil. Also Sevenoaks's biggest employer, owning substantial chunks of the high street (all pupils must use underpass – severe sanctions if they don't). Waitrose, appropriately, marks the boundary line. Most of 100-acre site, which backs on to Knole House, isn't visible from the road, though year 7s and 8s initially operate on a smaller scale for registration and break while are finding their way round the school's '30 buildings, 107 classrooms, 14 sports pitches, 12 lawns, six ponds and thousands of trees'. Recent additions to bump up the numbers are science and technology and IB global study centres, newest are the biology pond and school allotment – one area converted into nature reserve, from building site. More environmentally focused initiatives on the way soon.

Sensible to book your place early – not easy to change to boarding later on and even a few sixth formers (house captains excepted) share

Each modern language merits own room off long corridor, the world in miniature, while English scores paved courtyard with baby olive trees and silver birch – a grove in the making – just needs own Muse. In the meantime, plenty of inspiration from works of art dotted around, many by teachers and former pupils. One orange sculpture is featured in nuts and bolts parent handbook, together with similarly toned handbag. Possible reimagining of lost property cupboard? 'Probably to give sense of scale,' thought sensible guide.

All well worth a look given that one talented sixth form artist (product of satisfyingly messy art room, complete with artist in residence and pile of larger than life-size clay busts) flogged one of own works for £1,000...

Pastoral care, inclusivity and discipline: Copers will thrive here. 'You shape up pretty quickly,' said parent. Big on nurture in year 7 but given pace of life here, in other years best to get with the programme pronto. Plenty of help around and one parent felt it's kept semi-structured so that pupils feel that 'they can go to any teacher who feels like the right fit for them.'

Daily meetings with tutors reckoned to be a good safety net, staff normally quick to respond to parent queries. Counsellor also well used – sometimes making appointments difficult but school had been planning more. Sensible approach – though school has made much of the importance of exercise, taking breaks and putting pupils' – and staff – families first (online lessons often start with wellbeing check in).

Robust but not unkind sanctions for eg alcohol misuse. For drug use, possible that might be allowed back but would have to agree to random testing for remainder of school career.

Common sense advice issued on everything from pocket money allowance (keep it sensibly low to avoid 'over-reliance on material goods' – nice thought, though we can't help wondering if that boat has already sailed – even recent lower school cake sales raised over £1,000) – to cases of bullying: rare, according to school surveys, but acknowledged to rear head now and again.

School sensibly quotes examples of nastiness: 'You've got no friends, you're fat/gay…' and urges telling at all times. One parent agreed that unkindness happens but room to escape the tormentors helps. 'You can breathe here,' thought pupil. Minor problems tend to work themselves out, school on the whole reserving its energies for coping with more serious problems – has fair share of mental illness including eating disorders and self-harm. 'Very on the ball,' thought mother.

Parents are also expected to behave. Don't expect leave to remove children in term time without a very good reason (weddings or funerals might just about hack it but little else). And as for taking unilateral decisions to run holiday of lifetime into first few days of term? No way. 'School holidays are fixed at the absolute maximum consistent with good learning,' says school. In contrast, an empty school is the goal at exeat weekends though pupils 'in real need' can stay.

Pre-pandemic, we'd heard that a bit more approachability 'would make it a better place for parents and allow better communications'. Views may well have shifted given school's ability to follow shape-shifting government guidance and keep everyone calm in the process. 'They'd always say this is our best guess at the moment, then we'd get a letter saying rip up yesterday's letter, more information has come in and we need to change our advice,' says a parent.

Pupils and parents: Has always been cosmopolitan, first international pupil arriving in the 18th century. Currently 175 international pupils from Australia to Azerbaijan, Serbia to Singapore, Malaysia to Moldova – greater proportion further up the school, plus 70 expat families. Walls of vast dining hall serving quality food that even Italian tour guide, initially sceptical, was happy to endorse, decorated in a sea of flags representing every pupil nationality.

Sizeable numbers of local-ish families (Kent, Sussex and accessible bits of Surrey plus some Londoners). Can join popular parents' choir. Friends' organisation, recent innovation, going great guns with monthly drinks and cultural excursions.

Some parents reckon that small proportion of pupils – Londoners in particular – afflicted by sense of entitlement. Absolutely not, we were told, indignantly. 'We're grounded, also there's so much cultural diversity.' School's down-to-earth outreach programme (two pupils diligently sorting stock in local charity shop, medics putting in time at local school for the disabled) doubtless helps.

Money matters: At least five full bursaries at 11+ (may trickle up to year 9 if funds permit), some partial bursaries and offer of temporary support if difficult times strike existing pupils. Scholarships of up to 10 per cent. Head is keen to attract more disadvantaged, 'intellectually voracious, go-getting' children – those out there would be well-advised to get in touch.

The last word: Exhilarating, immersive education that's ideal for bright, organised, go-getting types – perhaps less so for those seeking a more gentle voyage of discovery. Those eager for new worlds to explore with a team of top-class guides to help them along the way can't really go wrong.

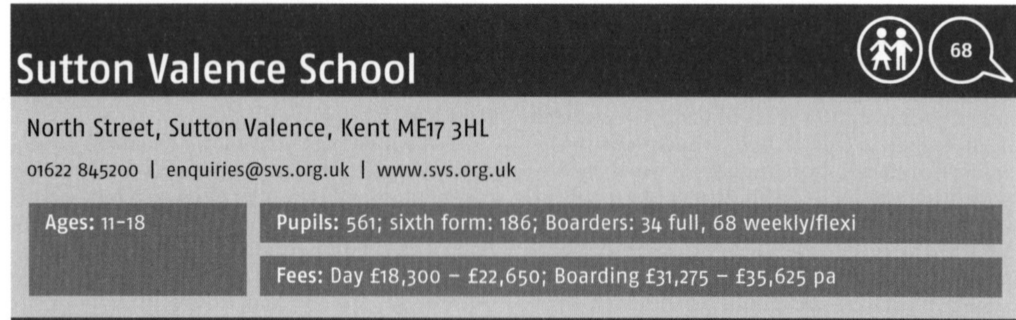

Sutton Valence School
68
North Street, Sutton Valence, Kent ME17 3HL
01622 845200 | enquiries@svs.org.uk | www.svs.org.uk
Ages: 11-18
Pupils: 561; sixth form: 186; Boarders: 34 full, 68 weekly/flexi
Fees: Day £18,300 – £22,650; Boarding £31,275 – £35,625 pa

Headmaster: Since September 2021, James Thomas, previously head of senior school at the British School in Tokyo. Educated at St Paul's, he has a degree in theology from Trinity Hall, Cambridge and an MA in educational leadership from University of London. Also holds the

National Professional Qualification for Headship. He has been head of theology and philosophy at both Dulwich College and Wellington College, where he was also in charge of Oxbridge applications, as well as director of studies at Harrow International School Hong Kong. Enjoys music, choirs, sport, travel and current affairs.

Married with three young boys who attend the prep. Spare time is spent with them and their faithful old labrador. Interests include music, choirs, sport, travel and current affairs.

Entrance: Main entry points are 11+, 13+ and sixth form but will take pupils into other years if there are spaces. For 11+ tests in English, maths, verbal and non-verbal reasoning. Children at prep schools are expected to take Common Entrance; others, including those from abroad, can take school's own tests. New sixth formers will need a minimum of five GCSEs at grade 6 plus an interview. Foreign students have to pass an English exam. The school is on the radar of heads of local preps, eg Wellesley House, St Ronan's, Marlborough House, Dulwich Prep, St Michael's Otford, Sevenoaks Prep and the New Beacon.

Exit: About 15-20 per cent leave after GCSEs either to go to state schools or because they are not A level types and want to take BTecs and NVQs elsewhere. Most sixth formers go on to higher education to study a huge range of courses. Range of courses including engineering at Durham, liberal arts at Exeter, natural sciences at Nottingham, mathematics at Bristol, linguistics at Manchester, English at York and fine art at UCA. The odd one to Oxbridge, though none in 2021. Two to study medicine in 2021.

Latest results: In 2021, 51 per cent 9-7 at GCSE; 49 per cent A*/A at A level (72 per cent A*-B). In 2019 (the last year when exams took place), 41 per cent 9-7 at GCSE; 60 per cent A*-B at A level.

Teaching and learning: Some 25 subjects offered at A level with geography and business studies being the most popular. A wide range to suit different abilities including economics, psychology, media and film studies, sport and photography and can also offer Chinese and Russian. EPQ available. As well as the usual subjects, the school offers media studies, computing, photography, drama and sport at GCSE.

Impressive value added – something that the headmaster is particularly proud of. The improved results are partly due to pupils being made to realise they can do it and keeping them engaged. The top 30 per cent can be stretched and achieve A* and A grades, for others a C is a brilliant achievement – staff know the pupils well and so know what they should be aiming for; attainment and effort levels are reviewed half-termly. Class sizes up to 18 in the junior years and as few as four in some A level classes.

The school takes on one new young teacher each year for on the job training: they bring academic passion and energy and reinvigorate the staff room.

CV writing and interview skills part of the curriculum from age 11. Annual careers convention in lower years and all year 11s have individual interviews about their career aspirations – the head librarian has a master's in careers education. Plenty of help with UCAS forms – sixth formers attend a higher education convention at the University of Kent, lectures are offered on degree subject choices and extra support available for prospective vets and medics. The few not going to university are given help with job applications and interview technique.

Strong sense of community. The school has close links with Maidstone's Gurkha community and raised £60,000 to rebuild a school in Nepal flattened by an earthquake

Numerous opportunities for academic enrichment; the school has close links with the local section of the Royal Society of Chemistry. Debating and public speaking are particular strengths, pupils can take part in the Model UN, take courses in financial services and personal effectiveness and leadership, and join the philosophy club.

Learning support and SEN: Full-time SENCo plus two full and two part-time teachers. Pupils either given in class support or withdrawn from lessons for small group or individual tuition and are helped to develop their own learning styles and coping strategies. About 190 on the register for concern but not many need extra help. All juniors take part in a study skills programme and all are offered help with stress, resilience and exam technique. About 40 need help with EAL and have two or three lessons a week instead of languages, unless close to native fluency, and can take an IGCSE in ESL and IELTS for entry to British universities.

The arts and extracurricular: All do bronze DofE in year 9 and about a quarter achieve gold before they leave. CCF is part of the curriculum in year 9 – all three services but army by far the most popular; can learn to fly in the RAF and take a BTec in leadership as part of the course, and the shooting team does well at Bisley. About 10 per year take part in the Young Enterprise scheme.

Music has gone from strength to strength. About 200 learn an instrument and there are a number of formal and informal concerts. The chapel choir is a central part of the school community and has sung evensong at Canterbury, Cologne and Winchester cathedrals and performed at the Pantheon and St Peter's in Rome, and top singers can attend a masterclass at the Royal Academy of Music. Large variety of musical groups including the chamber orchestra and string ensembles and quartets, several pupil-run rock groups and there is a suite of computers for composition. The band has accompanied Jools Holland, toured Paris and Disneyland and played in concerts with the Gurkhas and several pupils are in the Kent county youth orchestra.

Drama at GCSE and theatre studies at A level, and several achieve gold in the LAMDA exams each year. A junior and a senior play each year – either a big musical or something more serious.

Art housed in a beautiful old church in the village. Everyone introduced to a range of different styles when they arrive and 'you are given the freedom to create what you want in DT,' say the pupils.

Boarding for three or four nights a week is popular and a godsend to working parents. 'You always have the same bed and can change nights,' said a pupil

Numerous trips and visits throughout the year have included sports tours to South Africa and Canada, a camping and trekking expedition to Morocco, a ski trip to Italy and a visit to the Neeja Modi School in Jaipur, Rajasthan as well as CCF trips to Belize, Brunei and Malaysia and DofE expeditions.

Sport: Excellence, endeavour and discipline are the buzzwords of the Sutton Valence sports department and everyone expected to aim for their personal best. Some join the talented athletes' programme, others play for the fun and the exercise. Sport for all in major and minor sports and about two-thirds play in weekend matches. Higher up the school sport isn't compulsory but must take some form of exercise. Dance, aerobics and badminton popular among the less team minded. Pupils also encouraged to train as umpires and coaches. The school also has an equestrian team but you have to provide your own horse and transport.

Boarding: Boarding for three or four nights a week is popular and a godsend to working parents. 'You always have the same bed and can change nights,' said a pupil. Four boarding houses all under major renovation: junior boys and girls live in a large residential house a few minutes away and are housed in five small dorms, all with ensuite bathrooms, and there's a small five-a-side football pitch. 'It's like a large family,' said a pupil – 'we all eat supper together in the kitchen and then have to do supervised prep before free time.'

Two senior boys' boarding houses of about 55 each and a girls' house of 44. Younger pupils share, whilst upper sixth have their own study bedrooms and all can use the school's facilities at evenings and weekends. The girls' house is below the main teaching blocks and must have one of the best views in Kent.

Saturday morning lessons and afternoon sport for all, and movie nights, pizza evenings and kitchen cook-ups are organised for the full boarders. All houses have a houseparent and a team of tutors and house prefects and new arrivals are teamed up with a buddy so there is always someone to talk to and 'matron is like a second mum,' said one girl.

Ethos and heritage: The school was founded by William Lambe, a London clothworker, in 1576 and the Worshipful Company of Clothworkers ran it until 1910, when it was transferred to the Westminster School Foundation (which also includes Queen Anne's Caversham, Grey Coats, Emmanuel and Westminster City School). Girls were admitted in 1983 and it is now fully co-ed. They have recently opened a prep school in China.

Built into the hill just above the village of Sutton Valence and with wonderful views over the Weald of Kent, the Virginia creeper clad main buildings, including a lead clock tower, dominate the skyline. Surrounded by immaculate lawns and flowerbeds and the acres of playing fields stretch out on top of the hill – it can be pretty windy watching winter matches. The Lambe's library, formerly the school dining hall, contains 11,000 books ranging from first editions to Kindles and DVDs. Four day houses alongside the boarding houses, and the co-ed junior house for years 7 and 8 where children can find their feet before moving into the senior school at 13+.

House-based charity work is overseen by the chaplain. The school has close links with Maidstone's Gurkha community and raised £60,000 to rebuild a school in Nepal flattened by an earthquake.

Strong sense of community with whole-school chapel service every Monday and a weekly headmaster's assembly where sports results are read out and achievements celebrated. Leadership opportunities in all year groups and younger pupils take part in a leadership course and help out in prep school and in village community projects, whilst lower sixth take part in a community service programme. Positions of responsibility are keenly fought over and lower sixth have to write a letter of application for prefect positions and are interviewed by the headmaster. The prefects wear gowns and the Sutton Valence Blue – a dark blue gown – is awarded to those who make a major contribution to school life.

Well known Old Suttonians include journalist Robert Fisk; GB hockey player and gold medal winner at Rio 2016 Susannah Townsend; BBC journalist Ben Brown; England cricketer Mark Benson; actor Peter Polycarpou; and painter Terence Cuneo.

Pastoral care, inclusivity and discipline: The school is small enough for everyone to know everyone else and prides itself on picking up any problems quickly. Each house has a houseparent and house-based tutor groups which meet daily. These are arranged vertically so that year groups get to know each other and sixth formers can act as mentors and role models, and tutors are the first point of contact for parents. Needle-sharp inter-house competitions, plays and quizzes, as well as celebrations, generate house loyalty.

Zero tolerance on drugs and pupils sometimes put on a contract (including random testing) if drug use suspected outside school. Vaping not allowed. School promotes the philosophy of growth mindset which encourages pupils to believe that they do not have a fixed ability and therefore create glass ceilings for themselves, but that with perseverance and encouragement they can improve. 'Once confidence comes, children achieve more than they ever thought they could,' says school.

School is very aware of mental health issues and pupils can talk to the two counsellors or the school chaplain, who is kind and down to earth, and school has set up a new mental health strategy, 'Can I have 10 (minutes)'. Pupils can choose a member of staff they feel comfortable with and talk to them at any time. The usual cyber problems – social media issues generally happen outside school but parents are given guidance on how to manage them.

Pupils and parents: A 60:40 boy-girl ratio – would like it to be 50:50 but lose a lot of girls to the single-sex grammars. A stable nine per cent from abroad. Others from a 20-mile radius including a number of Gurkhas. A network of school buses brings children from Ashford, Hurst Green, Hawkhurst, Kings Hill, Sevenoaks, Tenterden and the edge of Tunbridge Wells.

Excellence, endeavour and discipline are the buzzwords of the Sutton Valence sports department and everyone expected to aim for their personal best. Some join the talented athletes' programme, others play for the fun and the exercise. Sport for all in major and minor sports and about two-thirds play in weekend matches

Eclectic bunch of parents – lots of City workers and entrepreneurs, first-time buyers and local farmers – generally down to earth, hard-working types. Some struggle to pay the fees and others are very rich – it is not unknown for a pupil to be given a sports car for their 18th birthday. The headmaster describes the pupils as 'charmingly confident but not arrogant, self-disciplined with a desire to please,' and his prefects as a 'ministry of talents'.

A very sociable school with an active PTA and 'there always seems to be something going on – which is great if you have just moved to the area,' said a parent. Busy Old Suttonian Society with 4,500 members worldwide who hold regular reunions and an annual dinner, and offer advice and mentoring to current pupils.

Money matters: Academic, music, drama, art, sport and DT scholarships – those who do well in the entrance tests are invited to sit the scholarship exams and prep schools can put pupils forward for 13+ scholarship. The Westminster Scholarship available for sixth form. Bursaries are at the discretion of the headmaster and can be applied for via the bursary committee.

The last word: Now very much a first-choice school which has grown in size and reputation under its inspirational headmaster. Can accommodate a wide range of abilities from the very bright to the less so and all are tolerant of each other's strengths and weaknesses. 'It embraces all types,' said a mother, 'and you can try everything, don't have to be pigeonholed and the school is determined not to be a sausage factory.'

Tonbridge School

69

High Street, Tonbridge, Kent TN9 1JP

01732 365555 | admissions@tonbridge-school.org | www.tonbridge-school.co.uk

Ages: 13-18

Pupils: 802; sixth form: 331; Boarders: 462 full

Fees: Day £33,363; Boarding £44,835 pa

Headmaster: Since September 2018, James Priory, previously head of Portsmouth Grammar School. Read English at Oxford before his first teaching post at Bradford Grammar School, moving on to PGS in 2000 as head of English, from where he climbed the ranks. Governor at various local prep schools. Three children. A very nice, unassuming, amusing man who puts one at ease. Talks with such passion and warmth about the poetry of Edward Thomas that we are inspired to read some of it for ourselves. We weren't surprised to hear that he gives a cracking school assembly.

Parents told us that he's 'very approachable and not at all self-important' and 'there for every event and always comes to say hello'. Spends Saturdays cycling round the pitches so that he can see a few minutes of every fixture. Liked and respected by parents, staff and pupils, who trust him completely and enjoy spending time with him.

Entrance: Most join at 13+ from 50-60 prep schools. Computer based ISEB pre-test and assessment afternoon in year 6, plus school reports including CAT scores where available. Assessment afternoon 'allows us the opportunity to see what the boy's like as a person'. School makes unconditional and provisional offers, maintaining close contact with prep schools. Overseas students expected to demonstrate excellent fluency in English and a willingness to integrate. Around 6 join in year 10 and about 12-15 join in lower sixth. Sixth form entry via tests in subjects to be studied at A level. Process of choosing a house starts when boy receives unconditional offer, though 'days of the housemaster running his own fiefdom have gone,' we are told, so parents need 'not get too stressed' about the decision. Admissions team's 'unusually human approach' praised by grateful parents – 'Superb registrar was pivotal to our decision,' we were told. The school merged with the New Beacon Preparatory School in August 2021.

Exit: Popular destinations are the usual suspects – Oxford, Cambridge, St Andrews, Durham, Bristol, Warwick, Imperial, UCL. Mostly to read traditional academic subjects, but some for art foundations or other creative subjects. Good relationships with European and American universities and provide onsite training for SAT exams – in 2021, four to the USA (Cornell, Marshall, North Carolina, Boulder) and one to Hong Kong. 'World class university destinations matter to us – they're a sign of intellectual health,' says the head. Four medics and 22 to Oxbridge in 2021. Head acknowledges that Oxbridge becoming more competitive, 'but boys benefit anyway from the experience of application'. No unhealthy level of expectation.

'Masters are funny, treating the boys like university students,' we were told – and the boys 'love them'

'Phenomenal' careers department provides guidance using psychometric testing to suggest suitable routes for the boys and helping with work experience – 'really empowering' for the boys.

Latest results: In 2021, 95 per cent 9-7 at GCSEs; 87 per cent A*/A at A level/Pre-U (97 per cent A*-B). In 2019 (the last year when exams took place), 92 per cent 9-7 at GCSE; 68 per cent A*/A (91 per cent A*-B).

Teaching and learning: Very impressive. Sixth form curriculum recently re-evaluated to ensure depth and breadth. Twenty-four subjects offered at A level including computing, theatre studies and business studies. Most popular is maths, with economics also attracting big numbers. Boys still find time for further academic work, excelling in national essay competitions and maths and physics olympiads each year. One parent commented that her son, 'brilliant at prep school', had 'a bit of shock' – not a place for those not thriving academically.

Most take 10 GCSEs, mostly IGCSEs. Among the best results in the country. Science offered as dual award or individually – particularly good showing in individual sciences. A language compulsory at GCSE – French, German, Spanish and Mandarin offered at GCSE and A level. Art GCSE offered as fine art or photography. All do non-examined course in divinity – largely discussion based and includes critical thinking – and seminar programme in years 11 and 12 also encourages debate. Everyone takes digital creativity (ICT) in three fab digital creativity labs. EPQ launched in 2020 with around 75 boys taking it up. Lots of support when choosing GCSE and A level options.

Good liaison between teaching departments – very dedicated team, 18 of them female, 'who really seem to care,' according to the boys. 'Masters are funny, treating the boys like university students,' we were told – and the boys 'love them'. Teachers also involved with coaching sport. 'An unusually close, respectful rapport' between boys and staff.

Learning support and SEN: All boys screened for learning difficulties on arrival – around 15 per cent on SEN register, mainly mild dyslexia and dyspraxia. Study skills and metacognition programme offers all boys help with note taking, essay writing, memory and organisational skills. Learning mentor programme trains boys up to help each other. First year dyslexic pupils trained as dyslexic specialist mentors to help in partner primary schools. Two EAL teachers support with technical language. Reasonable adjustments made to meet accessibility needs wherever practically possible.

The arts and extracurricular: Growing numbers involved in music. Around five take music A level each year and over 40 per cent learn an instrument, including the Marcussen chapel organ – one of the best in the country. Organists play to a high standard, winning Oxbridge scholarships and performing at recitals in London. Steinway status means top-quality pianos in every practice room. Excellent facilities include two recital halls, a suite of teaching practice rooms, music library, designated rock and percussion suites, and a double recording studio. Director of music a professional conductor with links to the Bournemouth Symphony Orchestra – 'a really wonderful, generous person'. Wide range of orchestras, bands and ensemble groups for all musical styles including flourishing jazz and pop groups and thriving choral music. Numerous opportunities to perform – Octagon concerts feature a different instrument each week. Sell-out performance of all seven movements of Holst's The Planets pre-Covid. House music competition an annual highlight – great gusto from performers and attendees alike.

Drama thriving, with 11 productions a year staged across three venues including the 380-seat EM Forster Theatre (complete with orchestra pit and studio). Three major school plays, with girls from local schools taking part in most productions. Boys get involved with all aspects of production including set design, stage management and lighting – industry professionals show them the ropes. Drama competitions and house plays, put together by the boys, give everyone the chance to have a go. Performances in Spanish, French and German. Covid has meant lots of monologues recently; a major production of Sondheim's Into The Woods has been in the pipeline since before lockdown. Boys enter the National Theatre's playwriting competition and upper sixth take a play to Edinburgh Fringe each year. Annual Short Films competition, organised by an Oscar-winning OT, culminates in glamorous awards ceremony.

Growing numbers involved in music. Numerous opportunities to perform. Sell-out performance of all seven movements of Holst's The Planets (pre-Covid)

Whole school in activities and clubs on Wednesday afternoons – set programme for first years, who have a go at all sorts, while older boys choose what they do. Boys involved in a huge range of cultural, political, scientific and sporting societies, anything from investing to Formula 1 design. Rocketry club launches working model rockets. Popularity of the conservation unit, which includes beekeeping and rearing pigs, demonstrates boys' commitment to green initiatives; when we visited they had been helping with the management of ancient woodland on behalf of the local council. Arts workshops by visiting professionals include street dance, masks and puppetry – parents say art is done 'brilliantly well'. Creative writers visit the Arvon Foundation. Varied programme of lectures by visiting speakers; recent virtual Tonbridge Science Conference attracted students from Australia, Mexico and the USA as well as across the UK and included sessions on nuclear power and climate change.

Seminar programme in years 11 and 12 encourages boys to question their assumptions and see things from a different perspective, eg sustainability in business or organ transplants. Around 200 take part in CCF across all three services. DofE also popular – approximately 12 achieve gold each year. Numerous foreign visits and exchange trips during the holidays.

Sport: Long tradition of sporting excellence, but ethos of participation by all. Everyone has the chance to play in a team – sport is for life here, and for all to enjoy. 'It's more about taking part than being a first XI god,' say parents. Truly outstanding sports facilities (a training venue for London 2012 Olympics). A hundred acres of immaculately groomed playing fields, three Astroturfs, clay tennis courts and an all-weather athletics pitch. Sports centre with cricket nets, 25-metre swimming pool, climbing wall and a swanky fitness suite – membership open to general public. Hockey, rugby and cricket academies – one of the best school rugby sides around and produces county and international cricketers. However, as the school points out, even stellar sportsmen do not have to be 'lads' – current England rugby international Ben Earl 'loves reading Jane Austen and playing chess', says the head; England cricketer Zak 'Creepy' Crawley did very well academically. Every imaginable sport – fives, ultimate frisbee, fencing, water polo, sailing – with novi encouraged to have a go at everything. In short, plenty of choice if you're not first XV material.

Boarding: Seven boarding houses. Youngest ('novi') start in small dorms of up to six. Older boys have their own rooms. Strong system of pastoral care. Housemasters seen as 'father figures' who get to know boys and their families very well. Aided by assistant housemaster and tutors, with whom boys have regular meetings. During the week boys eat in their houses but at weekends boarders eat together in the Orchard Centre. Most boarders are local – majority go home after games on Saturday, but have to be back in time for Sunday evening chapel. 'For London parents, it's long enough to have their boys home; for overseas parents, it's short enough to know that their son won't have an empty weekend'. About a quarter of boys left in each boarding house at the weekend – if there's a social event, more will stay. Most boarders seem to spend the odd weekend in school anyway, 'catching up on work, playing their instruments, watching Match of the Day with their friends'. Trips and outings organised to ward off loneliness for full boarders. Compulsory boarding weekend at the start of term and for Remembrance Sunday.

Ethos and heritage: Founded by Sir Andrew Judde in 1553, the school still has close links with the Worshipful Company of Skinners – Skinners' Day celebrated each summer. The school grew rapidly in the 19th century and has been rebuilt twice on the original site. Dominated by the fine rebuilt Edwardian chapel (gutted by fire in 1988), the school is set in 150 acres grounds behind the not-so-glamorous Tonbridge High Street. Imposing Victorian buildings combine with tasteful, modern additions to blend tradition with up-to-date facilities. The Vere Lodge Centre for DT and art, with its spiral staircase and light-filled space for exhibitions, is particularly impressive. Well-used library – recently extended and refurbished – with 23,000 books, a number of which date from the 17th century, as well as the 1479 Jensen Bible. Boys seem to get most of their information online, though – plenty of digital technology here too. All boys bring their own devices into the classroom (purchased by the family unless the boy is supported financially). Gleaming new science centre, shortlisted for RIBA award in 2020, puts Tonbridge at cutting edge of school science. New classrooms and very latest technology juxtapose with original architectural features, aiming to modernise the way science is presented, learned and understood.

The perception that boys' boarding schools tend to be alpha does not ring true. Yes, of course there's a lot of testosterone pumping through the place, but there's no Tonbridge 'type' and it doesn't feel macho like it perhaps used to

A long list of famous old boys includes EM Forster, Frederick Forsyth, all members of the band Keane, Vikram Seth, Patrick Mayhew, several generations of the Cowdrey cricketing dynasty, Dan Stevens of Downton Abbey fame, Tim Waterstone and Kit Hesketh-Harvey.

Pastoral care, inclusivity and discipline: Boarding and day houses run along the edge of the playing fields and the high street, each with about 60 boys. Houses lie at the centre of pastoral care and close friendships are formed – 'You don't join as one of 800, you join as one of 12.' 'Superb' matrons are 'really on it with the boys,' parents say. Strong sense of belonging in houses helped by range of inter-house competitions in art, music, film, sport plus house plays and concerts, though school ensures that it stays friendly – 'You want healthy competition but you don't want it to be tribal.' Socially, as wide a mix as possible in each house – boys from the same prep school split up to stop cliques forming. Good food on the whole (with grace before lunch) – we heard excellent things about the boys' table manners too.

No 'command and control' culture here, and the perception that boys' boarding schools tend to be alpha does not ring true. Yes, of course there's a lot of testosterone pumping through the place, but there's no Tonbridge 'type' and it doesn't feel macho like it perhaps used to. 'Because we're in a town, and we have day boys, there is fluidity of movement and a sense of boys being able to be who they are and who they want to be,' says school. Boys are grounded and natural, happy to get involved. Wear their achievement lightly. Parents comment on how accepting the community is of difference – 'They just get on with it and find their niche.' Student-led Bridge the Gap society celebrates diversity.

Mindfulness meditation embedded within year 10 PSHE and all boys can pursue it as a Wednesday afternoon activity. Life skills programme for senior boys includes emotional literacy and cookery in a new dedicated classroom (fajitas with homemade guacamole, anyone?). On-site school counsellor.

All boys attend weekday chapel services four mornings a week, and other faiths encouraged to attend their own places of worship for special religious festivals. Local community is very important to the school and sense of social responsibility is something that parents praise – 'We are synonymous with our town, we're on the high street,' says the head. Large numbers of boys involved with Tonbridge Community Action, helping in local primary schools, supporting disabled children with swimming lessons or playing their instruments at local retirement home. Primary children come to use the labs in the science centre and enjoy inter-school sports days on the school's grounds – whole school community day sees hundreds of local children on site with Tonbridge boys running the show. Tonbridge has close links with The Marsh Academy at New Romney, a fellow member of the Skinners family – boys act as e-mentors to provide help and support to Marsh students, and Marsh students come to Tonbridge for practical science work in the labs. Gap year boys can also work at Marsh Academy for a term.

Boys very driven and there are not many problems on the behaviour front. Zero tolerance drugs policy (and school has not been afraid to use it in recent years). These boys work hard and there's much less of the fast-living party environment than you might find elsewhere – even socials with nearby Benenden are fun for all but do not get out of hand. Headmaster has clamped down on mobile phone use. Where things do go awry, school is sensitive and low key – one mother described how pleased she was that the school had given her 'very sociable' son some 'wise words of wisdom' about his behaviour.

Pupils and parents: Most boys live within about an hour and a half of the school. School describes the typical Tonbridge parent as 'understated and low-key'; parents themselves say that they are a 'measured', 'professional' group. The boys have a quiet self-assurance – 'We don't want the pointy-elbowed kinds,' school tells us, 'but boys who are capable of listening and empathising, who are comfortable with themselves.'

At weekends boarders eat together in the Orchard Centre. Most boarders go home after games on Saturday, but have to be back in time for Sunday evening chapel

Sport dominant, but boys admired more and more for other things and music and culture increasingly important. 'A much more tolerant and a kinder place than it was some years ago,' we also heard. There doesn't seem to be a typical Tonbridgian – some sporty, some less so, some musical, some not – but all seem to enjoy themselves, and the key seems to be to take part in everything. They have a keen sense of fun, demonstrated at the annual Pink Day when all boys dress up in pink in support of breast cancer charities with some very imaginative and outrageous outfits.

About 15 per cent foreign nationals from 36 countries, who are generally well integrated. Each house twinned with a house at Benenden for socials, restaurant outings and quizzes. Parents encouraged to get involved, and there is always strong support for Saturday matches with lots of 'touchline friendships' forming between families. Many parents, particularly of local day boys, are members of the Parents' Arts Society, which organises cultural and social events each term, everything from private views at art galleries, theatre trips, wine tastings and lectures to weekend trips to Europe. 'Healthily sociable,' said one mother, 'with no pressure to get involved if it's not your thing.'

Money matters: A well-endowed school which offers numerous awards. A big push on Foundation Awards (bursaries). About 10 boys with significant Foundation Awards in each year – Tonbridge aims to double this by 2028 (the school's 475th anniversary). Foundation Awards can also help fund years 7 and 8 at prep school, followed by a guaranteed place at Tonbridge. Keen to recruit able boys from local primaries. Dedicated person for Foundation Awards in admissions – 'word is getting out there,' says school. Up to 45 scholarships offered at 13+ – academic, music, art, drama, technology and sport. Academic and music scholarships offered in sixth form. These scholarships open the door to Foundation Awards of up to 110 per cent of fees. Parents say that the school was 'very generous and sympathetic' about financial hardship during Covid.

The last word: A brilliant school that somehow remains totally unsnobby. Boys make the most of world-class opportunities to learn and have fun, but that's not the best bit – Tonbridge's modern, proactive approach to social responsibility and bursary funding ensures that they stay firmly grounded whilst doing so. These rounded, engaging young men are destined to go far, we feel – but without a scrap of the entitlement that so often accompanies a top-notch education. Top marks to all involved.

Vinehall School

70

Mountfield, Robertsbridge, East Sussex TN32 5JL

01580 880413 | admissions@vinehallschool.com | www.vinehallschool.com

Ages: 2-13

Pupils: 180; Boarders: 16 full (from age 7)

Fees: Day £10,350 – £19,290; Boarding £22,575 – £25,125 pa

Headmaster: Since 2017, Jonathan (Joff) Powis (BSc geography, Leeds) married to Liz with four children at Vinehall. Previously deputy head at Papplewick. A family man – we saw assorted wellies lying on their sides in his study. Opens school doors to families too – welcomed everyone to play in the grounds when it snowed.

One of his first priorities was to find more time for pupils to play, which he has done by extending break times and cutting back prep (quality, not quantity). Parents approve: 'Brilliant… new energy, new ideas'; 'Very present… can talk to him. Open door policy… encourages people in'. Pupils say assemblies are fun and describe Mr Powis as 'kind and supportive'. More importantly still: 'he brought conkers to the school'.

Entrance: Non-selective. Taster day or overnight stay, as relevant. Informal testing in English and maths from year 3 to ensure academic needs can be met.

Vinehall is looking to join Repton School. 'Discussions are ongoing,' the head told us. 'I know that Vinehall's pupils would benefit hugely from collaboration with specialists within the Repton family of schools, broadening horizons both academically and in co-curricular activities of all kinds. Enhanced training and development opportunities will help us maintain the quality of our staff body, and shared use of resources will promote operational efficiencies.'

Exit: Recent destinations include Battle Abbey, Bede's, Benenden, Brighton College, Claremont, Cranbrook, Eastbourne, King's Canterbury, King's Taunton, Lancing, Roedean, Sevenoaks and Tonbridge. Six scholarships in 2021.

Our view: Vinehall is non-selective, but feeds a number of the big name senior schools by focusing, the head says, on high quality teaching, small classes (around 15) and high expectations. 'We are incredibly strong with slower attainers.' Parents too were keen to emphasis this: 'Irrespective of level, they cater for your child… differentiate [between abilities].. and the kids are unaware.' Pupils are clear that ability doesn't matter: 'As long as you do your best and are improving, it doesn't matter where you are.'

As a small school, there are no subs on lines; all pupils are playing, and in mixed-ability teams

The head has shaken up the curriculum, replacing CE humanities with thematic learning of social and natural history for years 7 and 8: 'More relevant and stimulating,' he says, adding that the changes will give children a sense of place and purpose. Year 7s are currently studying conflict, planet Earth and equality and rights, 'really fun topics', say the children, instead of battling through the Tudors yet again.

Prospective engineers would find a home here, with STEM subjects introduced from year 5, and the head is keen to introduce a STEM method into all subjects – 'to have time to go back to the design if things aren't working out'. It seems pigs might fly here – a papier-mâché porker certainly appears to be in the lobby next to the slick new science labs.

Pupils of all ages enjoy working in the outdoor classroom, a tepee in the woods. Children particularly enjoy the teamwork exercises – 'making dens and setting up tents in the pouring rain,' said one enthusiastically.

Parents say teachers know their children well; pupils describe them as 'supportive and friendly – within limits'. 'You're expected to get it once it's been explained twice,' said another, 'but you can always ask your friends.'

Pre-prep is bursting with colour; it's set in a building on its own, and makes full use of the surrounding outside space for play and growing vegetables. It's a place of fun and exploration; they have stories and marshmallows on camp fire Fridays, and all sorts of adventures in between – on the day of our visit, smiling older pupils in wellies waited to greet tiny pre-school visitors, and assist them on their bear hunt in the grounds. Learning is evidently rigorous too: year 1 were learning how to structure an essay, and insert the right key words; a year 2 maths class were diligent and industrious. 'They get really good results, but don't feel stressed and pressurised,' said a parent.

There are around 20 pupils on the SEN/EHC register, some of whom have dyslexia. One parent describing how their child's quirky spelling was remedied by extra spelling sessions for a term. Group help and one-to-one are available, and they'll also help at parental request. The unit is justly proud that five children with LS help got scholarships to their senior schools last year.

The main house is 19th century with some modern additions, such as the library. It's a lovely place to work, with its high gallery and light pouring in from the skylight above. 'Equations are painted on the steps in the library... someone thought about it,' said a parent with pleasure. Pupils' art is widely displayed; 'every child has something somewhere,' says the head.

The dining hall is not the most elegant part of the school, but we liked the bright autumn leaf print oilcloths on the tables and the happy chatter of the children enjoying good food. Grace depends on the teacher – a singing grace with one, a Latin grace with another. Not all pupils are happy with healthy food revisions, some feeling carrot sticks and hummus are not substantial enough a snack, but winter break-time soup is very popular.

Pupils change from smart uniform into scruff at break time: trainers, wellies and tracksuit for mucking around and getting muddy. They all tumble out of doors, those seeking quiet preferring the melon garden, with its trees and pond, others racing around the lawns.

Children protested at the planned demolition of the monkey bush, their favourite climbing tree, fort and lair (an old spreading rhododendron), and the new adventure playground will be built around it. 'They tell us if they want something,' said the head. Indeed the food committee got results: their request for more fruit was answered by kiwi fruit and dragon fruit at break time the next day. School council successfully bid for water fountains, a PJ day and a toy shed: 'They listen most of the time,' say pupils.

Pupils enjoy working in the outdoor classroom, a tepee in the woods. Children particularly enjoy the teamwork – 'making dens and setting up tents in the pouring rain'

Parents also feel this is a listening school, and appreciate the way the head dealt with an unfortunate school advertisement involving a Jaguar: a quick formal apology, then renewed focus on the school's real message, described by a parent as, 'Not about showing off the school, but making the child happy and confident.'

This school works hard to encourage children to be kind. In the Lenten friends scheme, everyone picks a name of another pupil or teacher from a hat, with the job of being subtly kind to that person for the duration of Lent. The spring term is full of children glancing both ways before hanging dropped coats on pegs, or secretly tidying lockers. Things are a bit harder if you get a teacher...

Children choose which charities they want to support, and will soon be participating in a scheme to cook for the homeless in Hastings, though there is, says the head, too much poverty there for them to deliver it themselves.

One child has been excluded in the last year, a last straw offence concerning online material. Bullying is dealt with promptly, says the head, the sanction depending on child's understanding. He prefers a light touch. Detention is a time for a reflection, and might be spent writing a letter of apology to the person offended. Pupils said they would report bullying directly to teachers; one, who thought this would be daunting, said she would put any concerns about bullying in the worries box. Or get her parents to email in. 'You can feel safe at school,' she said.

Children are well cared for by the pastoral team, which includes external counsellors and a full-time school nurse. We heard examples of careful and attentive support. One parent described how her child, new to the school, was struggling, and the school's immediate response was to organise lunchtime social groups to encourage friendships to grow. A prize won outside school was presented to him in assembly so he became the new kid with the gold medal. 'Remarkable,' said the parent. 'Handled organically and socially and with optimism.'

There is a house system, and pupils sit on house tables at lunchtime, but as the head said, 'We don't overplay it.' Still, there are house matches at the end of term, and at this sporty school, pupils have games every afternoon. Parents say they are good at most sports, and exceptional at athletics, gymnastics and swimming. As a small school, there are no subs on lines; all pupils are playing, and in mixed-ability teams (they have close communication with rivals about ability levels to make matches enjoyable, says the head). Everyone can choose between cricket and tennis in the summer term, and girls play football, although not yet in fixtures.

Dorms have glorious views over the Sussex countryside, and good quality fittings, with beds and bunks for younger ones, and seven or eight to a very tidy room (marks out of 10 daily)

Several families were attracted to the school for its range of opportunities – 'They try so much as well as academic.' There's an indoor heated swimming pool, and nine-hole golf course; a dance studio and even carpentry sheds– it's extremely popular here, part of the curriculum, and there's a club too, if you're quick off the mark. We saw year 4s carefully making bedside tables, although one boy said cheerfully, 'I'm rubbish at woodwork, so I'm making a pirate ship.'

There are plenty of opportunities for drama, and other varieties of performance: pupils in the pre-prep do English Speaking Board tests, and the final of the poetry by heart competition in the prep is in front of the school. 'You do worry about people judging you,' said a pupil, 'but you're told to be a nice audience, and people are quite generous and supportive.'

Musicians are well catered for; there's an orchestra of 100 that accommodates a wide range of abilities. Everyone is in the school choir, even reception children, and the non-selective senior choir includes teachers and children. One parent whose child wasn't enjoying learning the violin any more was about to end lessons, the school suggested he practise with another pupil and he started to enjoy it again. 'Quite a personal touch,' said the parent, '[they] take a lot of time unpicking things.'

Parents think most children would thrive here and that it is great for busy families: 'I have a complex working life – Vinehall are remarkably flexible and make it possible. It's a very easy place for modern life.'

Boarding: It's a small boarding contingent, but one to which the school is committed; of the 35 full-time boarders, 25 are from overseas. '[The] mixture of culture and languages adds a lot to the community,' says the head. 'It's the future workplace.' Most start in years 5 or 6, but they will accept younger boarders with older siblings. A year 3 boarder, homesick at first, now flings arms around matron whenever he sees her. Part-time and flexi-boarding also possible, last minute availability pleasing busy parents. Many pupils opt to board on Wednesdays for movie and tuck night. At weekends, pupils take over the home economics room to cook their home country's cuisine, and enjoy trips out of school, such as scavenger hunts, ice skating and cinema.

Dorms have glorious views over the Sussex countryside, and good quality fittings, with beds and bunks for younger ones, and seven or eight to a very tidy room (marks out of 10 daily). They are in the process of revamping; plush new carpets and tables in those done. A boy who likes to sleep alone has a room to himself, with only occasional flexi-boarders in the other beds. Parties in the common room on your birthday, with a golden ticket for boarders to give a free night's stay to a day pupil friend.

Money matters: Bursarial awards of up to 50 per cent available from year 3. Scholarships up to 10 per cent.

The last word: Many parents are attracted to Vinehall as a rural prep school, but it's more than this: 'I had a visceral reaction,' said one mum, 'I had to send children there. [It was the] combination of intellectual curiosity, and [their] interest in the children.'

Wellesley House

114 Ramsgate Road, Broadstairs, Kent CT10 2DG

01843 862991 | hmsecretary@wellesleyhouse.net | www.wellesleyhouse.org

Ages: 2-13

Pupils: 125; Boarders: 25 full, 30 weekly

Fees: Day £8,925- £19,917 pa; Boarding £26,331 pa

Headmaster: Since September 2017 Gavin Franklin BA (40s). Previously a housemaster at Wellington College, from which he 'unashamedly plagiarises' when it comes to approaches such as reflection instead of detention. Sport degree from Durham; represented British Universities at cricket and went on to play for Staffordshire and Warwickshire. Spent five years at the Oval, as performance manager in charge of elite player development, becoming a level 4 cricket coach, before moving to Wellington as assistant director of sport and English teacher.

Hands down the homeliest head's study we've seen – hardly surprising since it doubles up as the family sitting room, complete with sizeable telly, heaps of framed photos and the kind of sofas that invite you to curl up on with feet up. Needless to say we didn't, although there is evidence that his gorgeous black lab Freddy may do so, and who can blame him? Merely a few steps from the school's main entrance, this family couldn't live closer to the school if they tried. All somehow works a treat, what with his warm and elegant wife Claire – also a Durham graduate and teacher with an interest in sport – reportedly 'essential to cultivating the parent community', and both their young sons attending the school.

We loved the way our guide described Mr Franklin not with words but actions. With arms outstretched and grinning ear to ear, he eventually engaged his vocal cords to explain that 'his personality is larger than life' and that he's 'just really friendly, really funny and, well, really amazing' which, we later learned, was pretty much the general consensus of all pupils. Meanwhile, from the parent cohort, we learned that he 'always has time for you and knows every child and parent by name' and is 'affable, knowledgeable and kind but with a core of iron'. Widely commended for his 'modern thinking', 'good vision for the school', and 'having a real team spirit'; we were also won over with his classically British self-deprecating humour and seeming ability to get involved in every aspect of school life, minus the micromanaging. In his spare time, sport still looms large, most recently golf and running.

Entrance: Pre-prep opened in September 2019, so children now able to join from two upwards, with automatic entry into prep. Entry into all year groups thereafter, but be warned it can be difficult getting up to speed for Common Entrance if you join after year 7. Non-selective but entry via interview and reports and examples of work from the child's current school. Would only test if there were concerns about learning support or that a child might not thrive.

Surprisingly large catchment area, as far as Deal, Canterbury, Faversham and Whitstable, with a handful from London (an accompanied minibus runs to Battersea at half term and exeats).

Exit: Around a third to King's Canterbury. Rest to huge range of senior schools all marked and labelled on an enormous wall map in the corridor – the odd drawing pin denotes schools as far as Scotland and Wales while Harrow, Rugby, Charterhouse, Bryanston, Chelthenham College, Shrewsbury, St Edmund's Canterbury and St Lawrence College also feature – a daily reminder to these youngsters of potentially very bright futures. Trouble taken by the head to find the best school is heavily praised by parents. Nine scholarships in 2020. Currently hardly any leave at 11+ but they are expecting some Kent Test leavers with the introduction of the pre-prep and are happy to prepare pupils accordingly.

Our view: Avert your eyes as you drive through the cabbage patches and retail parks of Thanet – it is worth it. Parents spend up to 45 minutes in the car each way to send their children here, passing other good prep schools en route. While schools often claim to be one big family, this one lives up to the hype and it's great fun too, with idyllic beach themed photos of pupils getting well-deserved top spots in the marketing materials. Learning here is a far cry from chalk and talk – we sat in a French lesson where year 3s sang their hearts out about

French colours accompanied by the teacher on the guitar and an ICT class where children were having a terrific time coding a guessing game on Python. On warmer days, the children are often taught outside – from hunting for insects and collecting leaves to check for starch to painting a scene of the cricket pavilion or writing nature poems – plus, of course, making use of that fabulous coastline. No wonder the Old Welleslians, who feature in the old whole-school photos that adorn some of the corridors, are famously nostalgic; many stay in touch or even marry and good numbers send their own offspring here. 'It's busy, it's happy and most importantly, it's kind,' summed up one parent, while another told how consideration for others, tolerance and being a thoroughly nice person are as celebrated as academic effort (and it's always effort over attainment here) at the annual summer prize giving.

Girls live over at the Orchard, set in its own grounds and – as the name suggests – surrounded by apple trees. 'Like one big sleepover,' said a pupil

Originally located in Ramsgate when it was founded in 1869, the school moved to its current purpose-built site in 1898, merging with St Peter's Court in 1969 and going co-ed in 1977. Slow down when your sat nav says you're nearing your destination – the entrance, a gravel driveway that leads to the red-brick building, is easy to miss. Lots of adding onto over the years, including some standalones, but the overall scene remains appealing and although the grounds don't boast the rolling acres of some preps, there's enough room for den-making, vegetable plots, shooting range and playing fields. Everything is immaculate despite being well utilised by these bouncy, spirited youngsters who have an endearing sense of ownership and pride. Blazers and ties are only for best here – house coloured aertex shirts, many hanging out from under their navy jumpers, serve as far more sensible attire for such an energetic schedule.

Inside, the maze of corridors leaves you in no doubt that you're in private school territory – Farrow & Ball painted tongue and groove on the bottom, and white with neat displays of children's work at the top. Classrooms are inviting – 'Geography Rocks!' we were reminded (literally, with rows of interesting stones) as we entered one classroom, while labs await eager young scientists with white coats and colourful test tubes. There's a large, welcoming library with plenty of comfy seating and each year group has its own common room. Boddington House, adjoined to the main school, is home to the new pre-prep where we were sorry to have missed the Goldilocks Crime Scene. If that kind of endeavour is not enough to lure in the punters (tiny-tot numbers were quite low when we visited, but it's still early days), the free wraparound care from 8am to 6pm is bound to tempt working parents.

Average class size is 12, with 16 max – 'means the very able can be stretched and those needing extra support get it,' reckoned a parent. Streaming and setting from year 6 in maths and languages; scholars are taught separately for the last two years, including extra sessions with the head on Tuesday evenings (debating anything from a poem to a piece of journalism). Latin and French both on the curriculum; Spanish by private arrangement. Around 15 per cent on the SEN register – most support is in the classroom. A parent: 'School is great for things like dyslexia, but I've seen those with more serious problems go elsewhere.' EAL provided for around 15 per cent of pupils. Real push on reading throughout, with timetabled reading lessons for middle school.

Tons of sport – 'almost relentless,' according to one parent, 'which is truly brilliant if you're a sporty kid, although those that aren't might feel a bit stuck.' While they may not have the pick of children that larger schools do, coaching is second to none, we heard from parents. 'They send every child out the best equipped they possibly can,' said one. 'You see these kids that you wouldn't think would shine and yet over time, they pull it out of the bag,' remarked another. Cricket historically strong (huge excitement about a forthcoming tour to Cape Town when we visited), though they get fewer IAPS wins than they once did. Lovely dance space with vibrantly painted walls. Golf is popular – there is a putting green in the grounds and the lucky few are allowed to play at Royal St George's nearby (cue parental envy). Clubs include photography and art, board games and chess, boys' hockey and girls' football, judo, fencing, riding at the local riding school, archery, cooking, needlework for boys and girls, even scuba diving, with the 'shrimp' course taking place in the school swimming pool – although one parent grumbled that it's more set up for boarders than day pupils.

Music – once a classical-only domain (though there is still plenty of that on offer, with a recent choir trip to Venice) – is now 'cool' and 'modern', we heard, with music tech, song writing and even a DJ-ing club. Over half learn an instrument in school and our tour guide, who was in a band, was itching for the forthcoming recording studio to be built – funded by Friends of Wellesley House. Singing is huge – we lost count of the number of choirs, including staff choir ('Look how our headmaster can't sing, yet still gives it a go,' head of music bravely announced in assembly).

Huge paint-splattered black tables form a circle in the middle of the art studio, providing ample room for experimenting, while the walls are packed with inspiration and examples of pupil work – from Mona Lisa to year 3 portraits. Cross-curricular work prevalent, eg totem pole design accompanied children learning The Indian in My Cupboard. Imaginative DT work – puppet making always a highlight. Two school plays a year – one from middle school, the other from seniors, although neither are quite as popular as the form plays in which each class writes and performs its own 10-minute production – lots of silly wigs and no parents allowed.

Chapel twice a week and the full choral service on Saturdays – all parents welcome, with soup and sandwich lunch laid on. Team of the week celebrates everything from choir to netball teams – prize is much sought-after cake and squash in head's study. House system encourages cross-year friendships, although pupils felt some peers 'take them far too seriously – crazy'. Food good – toad in the hole and banoffee pie firm favourites, although mention of meat-free Mondays invited some groans.

Pupils are considerate (we lost count of the number of 'After you's) and comfortable chatting to adults (they even quizzed us about our work – a rarity) but all with a charming naivety – 'There's no doubt these children are wrapped in cotton wool which I absolutely love, but it won't be for all,' said one parent. Friendly banter with staff – 'Look, sir, it's a real moustache,' insisted one little boy sporting a piece of white paper under his nose. Pupils clearly care for each other too – minimal bullying is nipped in the bud. Parent comms could be better, say some.

Boarding: Upstairs in the main house is boys' boarding – great big dorms with up to nine beds (no bunks) would win military points in the tidiness stakes, yet are surprisingly homely, with personalised bedding ranging from Marvel to nautical themes. Girls live over at the Orchard, set in its own grounds and – as the name suggests – surrounded by apple trees. 'Like one big sleepover,' said a pupil, while another chooses to board despite living within spitting distance of the school. Still, boarding numbers are on the decline, to the disappointment of some parents – 'My son was the only full boy boarder in his year, which was a bit of a surprise,' voiced one.

About 40 per cent of boarders come from overseas, mainly Chinese and Spanish – these, plus some from the UK, form the half of the boarding cohort that stays for weekends (around 23 when we visited); the other half is weekly. Parents like that it's 'a phone and iPad free zone – they don't even watch much telly because they're too busy having fun,' and that 'they're just so well looked after – pastorally it's outstanding'. Sunday outings (there always is one) range from bowling to beach time and paintballing to cinema; and the top year is allowed 'down town' into Broadstairs, pocket money usually spent on ice cream.

Money matters: Means-tested bursaries up to 50 per cent are available for sports and academic scholarships (on average one of each a year). Discounts for army families.

The last word: A small, caring, traditional and outdoorsy prep in which everyone knows everyone, all children get a chance to shine and nobody gets lost in the crowd.

Westbourne House School

72

Shopwyke, Chichester, West Sussex PO20 2BH

01243 782739 | admissions@westbournehouse.org | www.westbournehouse.org

Ages: 3–13

Pupils: 369; Boarders: 9 full, 42 weekly/flexi (from 7 years)

Fees: Day £10,980 – £18,900 pa; Full-time Boarding £25,335 – £27,000 pa

Headmaster: Since 2011, Martin Barker (BEd Exeter), deputy since 2007, previously at Papplewick in Ascot. Married to Helen, with two children. Keen to equip pupils with a broad range of skills and open minds to cope with the unknown world to come, and says, 'It's not the super pushy school people say it is. We do our best in all areas to be as good as we can be, but inclusivity really matters.'

Parents like the headmaster, describing him as 'fair'; 'kind... follows through and listens'; and 'solid, reliable and trustworthy'. They say that their children 'respect him and have the right level of awe... they wouldn't mess with him'. The word 'scary' did come up when pupils described their headmaster, but also 'nice', one adding that as you get older you can 'sit next to him at lunch and talk to him like a normal person'. And year 6s weren't too scared to throw custard pies at him at the end of their school play.

Entrance: Non-selective. Prospective pupils attend a taster day.

Exit: Feeds a wide range of senior schools. In 2021, majority scooped up by Seaford College, followed by Hurstpierpoint and Lancing. A few each to Bedales and Brighton College. Nineteen scholarships in 2021.

Our view: 'There's grass!' said a parent, asked why they chose the school, and indeed the immediate impression is of an elegant house, and grounds which stretch in every direction, including a woodland playground (no, they can't climb trees). '[It's an] amazing environment with lovely energy', said another. 'The kids always run into school. All three of them love it.'

The headmaster likes pupils to 'have a go' and hopes that confidence will flow from doing so. Personal development interests him more than anything else, a parent commenting, 'building happy, confident children is their theme'.

There are activities of every sort, from debating (against parents) to music of all sorts, and 'amazing drama productions' in their splendid theatre. Each year has a play, and everyone takes part, the headmaster's wife commenting, 'If children are shy, [they] get so used to performing and taking part, [they] don't seem so.' New performing arts centre to house it all.

Westbourne is of hothouse repute, but it's not so one-dimensional. Certainly, there's an atmosphere of determined concentration in lessons, and they 'do push for excellence and scholarships,' says the head, 'but it's just as satisfying to bring on the non-academic child. We're pretty diverse, and keen to emphasise personal bests.' Parents will send their children here to get them into the big named public schools, but Westbourne House, to its great credit, is non-selective and 'a much more healthy community' for it, says the head. Achievement matters, but effort also gets recognised, say pupils. There is no doubt that the culture here is one of working hard: a notice on a board says, 'Work hard until you don't need to introduce yourself.'

School chosen by one parent because they were 'impressed by the special needs support'. The

Parents send their children here to get them into the big named public schools, but Westbourne House, to its great credit, is non-selective

Individual Needs department supports around 20 per cent of pupils who have academic, emotional and/or behavioural problems, in one-to-one or small group sessions, and is chargeable only if parents ask for support, not if the school identifies the need.

'I try to get brilliant staff. The rest takes care of itself,' says the head, and parents report 'more strength within teaching staff than ever'. There are extra sessions during reading prep at the end of the day for pupils who need extra help, and personal tutors for years 7 and 8 pupils. By the time pupils reach CE, they are, say parents, 'not daunted or nervous'. '[It's a] really clever machine... [they're] so ready for it.' Parents feel the school is 'well structured with... goals in every different area'; 'focused' was also a word which came up quite a lot, one saying it is 'driven, but also nurturing'. 'We want results,' said one parent firmly.

There's opportunity for down time in the art department, a relaxed loft space where the teacher encourages children to express what makes them individuals. Gaily coloured boats made from driftwood sail across the wall, and the picture of the week was pop art bearing the legend: 'Women who seek equality with men lack ambition'.

Pre-prep, from nursery to year 2, is housed in a separate building, with a magic-filled nursery. Someone was teaching Read Write Inc phonics, as in many schools, but every part of this exceptional teacher was engaged in communication: she seemed to use her voice and whole body to illustrate the sounds, so you felt that there was a story behind each one – the 3-year-olds and your reviewer were mesmerised. The reception classroom is as much outside as in, a group of boys dragging around mathematical shapes in full wet weather gear and determination. 'They need to be out, and that eases things for those who want to be in,' said the teacher. Things are steadily more formal from year 1, and children are ready for the move to the big school by year 3.

Pupils say, 'everyone's really busy', and indeed these are some of the busiest children this reviewer has met, with lessons finishing at 4.55pm, followed by reading prep until 5.30pm, optional activities until 6.30pm. Parents say, '[It] sets them up well for senior school. They organise themselves very young.' Saturday school now abandoned – much to pupils' delight.

Patrols, the house system here, are 'one of the best aspects of the school,' said a parent, commenting on the happy mix between the years in each. A parent said, 'It's a warm caring school... got really nice atmosphere... kids are very caring to each other, and for younger children.'

Behavioural expectations are high; holding open a door is expected, say parents. Children say it's 'quite strict if you do something wrong', and one parent said her daughter was a scared about getting a 'note' for eating a biscuit in the changing room. But, parents say, 'it is weighed towards credits and they can be for anything... or having a smile...' Pupils are all aware of the process for reporting bullying, and say, 'It does get sorted out.' A parent said a problem was taken seriously, and both she and her child were happy it was properly dealt with.

This is, in the main, a listening school, although one member of pupil council said precisely, 'They listen, not necessarily implement.' But the monkeybars were the result of council suggestion, as was the easing of the no fleeces in school rule, it being persuasive when pupils said, 'If we can't wear fleeces, you need to turn the heating up.' Girls now also allowed to wear trousers and shorts, this traditional school taking an enlightened approach to this basic question of equality, comfort and choice for girls that other closed-minded schools would do well to heed.

Facilities are fabulous, and pupils play games every day. The standard of sports is very high, one parent saying, 'They won't necessarily make the top sets at senior school, but will make the A team at sport.' Teams here win most of the time, one parent even suggesting that it might be good for the A team to know what it feels like to lose. The vexed question of teams provokes much comment from pupils and parents, but the headmaster says, 'We pick the A team on merit, but the lower teams are rotated strictly – if the children don't play one week, they are included in the next fixture.' Parents describe their touchline behaviour as supportive, noisy, passionate – but respectful. 'Westbourne House has a reputation for cliquey, scary parents,' said one. 'It's not fair. They are there, [but] there are lots of people. [It's a] very good community.'

Pupils love the activities, particularly in the summer – 'sometimes bouncy castles, slip and slide, and go-karts', and the Boarders' Adventure Badge, where they learn survival techniques, including night navigation and outdoor cooking. Parents like the fact that children learn to be organised and independent.

Pupils are enthusiastic about the food, which they say is 'really nice, particularly pudding', one pupil telling us seriously that, 'There are all the food groups... it's a healthy meal, and you can get seconds; but not of pudding.' Pupils eat 'crusts' at morning break; almost literally so, bagels with or without butter, but also fruit and carrot sticks.

Boarding: 'Boarding houses are so nice,' said a pupil, 'like a real house', and indeed, there is a row of houses as if lifted from a nearby town, each complete with garden and slide. Older pupils sleep in these 'outhouses', while younger pupils board in the main house. Pupils like the fact you can submit a list of requests in the morning, asking for bread, butter and honey, and it is delivered in a basket to the house in the evening – 'like a stocking'. Boarding accommodation is light, comfortable and high spec.

The last word: Head says school best suited to children who want to get involved, and parents agree that the school is brilliant for a sporty child, or one into drama and music. Non-selective, high standards and great teaching – a winning combination.

Westminster Cathedral Choir School

RC 73

Ambrosden Avenue, London SW1P 1QH

020 7798 9081 | office@choirschool.com | www.choirschool.com

Ages: 4-13

Pupils: 261; Boarders: 23 weekly (choristers, from 8 years)

Fees: Day £17,937 – £21,612; Boarding choristers £10,692 pa

Headmaster: Since 2007, Neil McLaughlan (40s). For a man with a truly Catholic background (large C), a Catholic boarding school and posts in all the obvious schools, including Stonyhurst, Worth and Downside (only Ampleforth missing), he is engagingly undoctrinaire and also extremely good company. On our last visit he told us that he hopes to be here 'for the duration' and there's no change here, in fact it would be hard to imagine the school without him, he does literally appear to be part of the fabric. Parents are equally convinced: 'he picks up on everything'; 'totally approachable'; 'understands my son'; in fact it's lucky that he loves living in London and is definitely not heading out the door any time soon. Prodded over any further ambitions for his hugely successful school, he admitted that only a lack of cash was stopping his dream of a senior branch of WCCS turning into a reality and we hope that help from above may solve this problem for him.

Entrance: Reception class of 30 boys join via an assessment, described as 'very relaxed' by a parent, in groups for an hour to find out how they interact and respond. Entry at 7+ (16 places) and 8+ (12 places) is heavily oversubscribed with three to five boys trying for each place. Tests in maths, comprehension and composition, punctuation and spelling in the January before September entry.

Satisfying the Master of Music's accurate ear is only the first step for choristers who also have to make the same academic grades as the day boys.

Exit: Today's parents (almost all major players in the financial and legal world) set their sights on the internationally famous English public schools, with Eton firmly at the head of the boarding wish list and City of London, Dulwich and St Paul's the main choices in London. Charterhouse, Harrow, King's College School (Wimbledon), London Oratory, Radley, Stowe, Thomas's Senior School, UCS, Wetherby and Winchester College have also featured recently. The choristers also tend to head in the same directions. One choral exhibition in 2021, plus one music scholarship and a sports scholarship.

Our view: WCCS is as close to being a school inside a church as is physically possible: only a Westminster version of the Bridge of Sighs (thankfully, a happier outcome for its occupants) separates the school building from the cathedral's interior. In contrast to the solemnity of the surroundings, there is a wondrous space outside with an Astro pitch and running tracks as well as room for all the off-letting of steam.

Luckily, they found a building for the pre-prep just across the playground. Deeply suitable, having been home to Franciscans amongst its various incarnations, it is an architecturally surprising building, reminiscent of a galleon, with a rather sad St Francis serving as an off-centre figurehead. This unusual, one-room-deep layout has been sensitively turned into a great teaching space, with light classrooms, a playground and a tempting covered porch for rainy days. The teaching is 'pacy' even at this level and the competition (using numbering fans) was fierce to be number one fan of tables. Music is already part of school life and one tiny violinist was spotted concentrating hard on his individual lesson.

As close to being a school inside a church as is physically possible: only a version of the Bridge of Sighs separates the school building from the cathedral's interior

The prep itself is unflamboyant inside (in contrast to the stripy brick exterior), the colour provided almost entirely by the cherry red of the boys' blazers and the occasional sparkly shoes of a female teacher. The corridors are lined with red and blue lockers, more than usual due to the number of instruments, and music stands replace works of art on the walls. Darth Vader appears, in poster form, offering an unlikely exhortation to earn points towards stars, described by our extremely articulate guide as 'an unlikely paradox'. These stars are serious stuff: they don't just stop at gold as in most other schools but also have an exalted platinum and diamond level – 'everyone gets gold but the others are quite hard'.

The curriculum, 'begged, scraped and borrowed from every possible source', according to the head, is 'not fogeyish in any way' despite its structured feel. There is obviously an extremely successful attempt to marry the 'grammar – logic – rhetoric' classical approach to a more modern, integrated way of learning. This is proper joined-up teaching and the combination of art/RE teacher who starts each RE lesson with a religious painting is typical of their modus operandi. Very little streaming is necessary because, as they explain, there is a narrow range of ability here, but there is a SENCo available to offer one-to-one or group sessions to anyone struggling, and also the odd boy with educational needs. However, it is made very clear that it is essential for everyone to be able to handle the speed of the teaching.

The art teacher explains that her life is made far easier by the fact that she has a large number of the most exciting galleries in the world on her doorstep, which eases the task of embedding art into the school's curriculum, and there is a kiln and a printing press to extend her creative options. Naturally, music is part of life here but not just for the choristers: one day boy told us that if you can hold a tune you can sing in non-chorister choirs and even perform outside the school. The choristers all play the piano and one other instrument, but the majority of boys also have individual music lessons and there are several orchestras of differing abilities (if all rather better than average).

The number of names signed up for football on the tidy noticeboard says it all and they have been winners of the Thomas's five-a-side tournament at both U10 and U13, but the size of the school makes it less sporty than some of its competitors (one boy wrinkled his nose when questioned on their cricketing prowess) – still, two sports scholarships recently (one to Winchester) is pretty impressive. Lots of alternatives to football on the clubs list with the boys responsible for suggesting magic, mad science and even British military fitness, all of which have takers.

WCCS families have changed over recent years and there is now a much higher percentage of Catholics amongst the day boys (up from 50 per cent to over 80) but there are Anglicans and several non-Christian families. We felt convinced by both parents and head that the spiritual element was an addition rather than a handicap and was not forced down the boys' throats: instead they got a buzz out of their connection to the cathedral and its faith.

Boarding: The top two floors are home to the chorister boarders and it's a pretty good sanctuary for such incredibly hard-working boys, who have to combine their full-on musical life (singing in the cathedral on a daily basis and honing their skills) with a packed academic timetable. The head says that their welfare is his 'biggest single headache' and that sometimes he has to tell them to take time out 'when they are bushed'. Anyway, the dorms, whilst not exciting and amazingly tidy, have a cosy feel and apparently the matrons and cleaning staff make sure that 'Teddy is on the right bed'. A big common room is equipped with pool and football tables and a chorister assured us that there was plenty to do at weekends – the most popular pastime being 'ripstiking' (a form of skateboarding) which looked extremely difficult when demonstrated and that was minus cassock... However, full boarding has given way to weekly, with boys returning home from Friday evenings to 9am on Sundays, which will preclude families who live further afield.

The last word: Last time we wrote a review, we concluded by saying 'this is just about as near perfect as it gets' and we would endorse that sentiment today with only one caveat; this is now a school for seriously bright boys and it would be wrong for any parent to overestimate their son's academic ability when considering putting him up for the entrance exam.

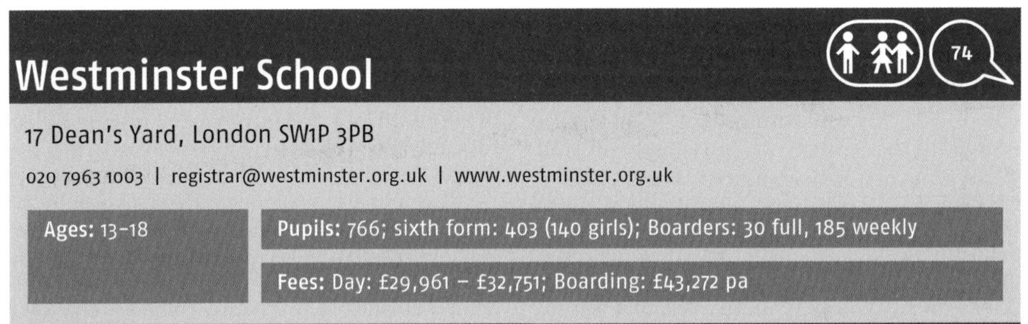

Westminster School

17 Dean's Yard, London SW1P 3PB

020 7963 1003 | registrar@westminster.org.uk | www.westminster.org.uk

Ages: 13–18

Pupils: 766; sixth form: 403 (140 girls); Boarders: 30 full, 185 weekly

Fees: Day: £29,961 – £32,751; Boarding: £43,272 pa

Head Master: Since September 2020, Dr Gary Savage, formerly headmaster of Alleyn's School. Previously head of history and master-in-college at Eton and before that under master at Westminster. Grew up in Suffolk and read history at Cambridge, taking a double first before doing a PhD on the political culture and foreign policy of later 18th-century France. Married to Natalie and enjoys history, the arts, studying German, walking his two Jack Russell terriers and following the fortunes of Ipswich Town FC.

Entrance: Register by the end of year 5 for 13+ entry (boys at state primary and other schools that finish at 11 may apply to Westminster Under School). Computer pre-tests in English, maths and reasoning in year 6; high performers who also have a good report from current school called for interview, which includes short maths and English tests. Those with conditional places sit either the Challenge scholarship exam or CE (pass mark 70 per cent) in year 8. Entry from 2021 onwards will not depend on passing the CE but on 'continued good conduct and academic progress at their existing prep school, including an unreserved reference of support from their school in year 8'.

For 16+ places, register between summer and October of the year before entry. Applicants – boys and girls – take exams in their four most likely A level subjects, and are interviewed.

Exit: Excellent and detailed preparation for Oxbridge, where 75 went in 2021. 'The school has been very supportive from an early age,' said a student, 'keeping us up to date with when to take subject tests and when to visit colleges.' Good preparation too for medicine, which is amongst the most popular degree subjects (17 medics in 2021) alongside liberal arts. Growing numbers to the US (again with excellent preparation, including school trips to visit east coast universities) – in 2021, one to Harvard, two to Yale and two to Stanford. Lots to the London universities, especially UCL and Imperial.

Latest results: School is not releasing 2021 (or 2020) results. In 2019 (the last year when exams took place), 98 per cent 9-7 at GCSE; 83 per cent A*/A at A level/Pre-U (93 per cent A*-B).

Teaching and learning: With these very bright pupils, 'you can teach for the love of the subject and focus on the exam when need be,' says head. 'It's a breath of fresh air,' said a parent. 'Intellectual risk taking is encouraged. They're never not challenged.' Many of the teachers are experts in their fields, encouraged to follow their interests. 'I cannot believe there is a more stimulating place to teach in the country,' said a teacher. 'It is so much more liberal than at my previous school,' said a sixth form student. 'It's not constrained by the syllabus – it's learning for the sake of learning. It really allows you to get a proper understanding outside the exam baselines.' Pupils tend to internalise that love of learning. 'They read and they question and they challenge,' says the head. 'In my first lesson one asked me, "Where is the evidence?" I'd never been asked that before.'

Everyone encouraged to include a practical subject like art, electronics, drama or music at GCSE. Huge range of languages includes Dutch, Arabic and Portuguese. Several parents commented that inspirational teachers had sparked their sons' interest in subjects they had previously hated. 'He'd always been a bit of a maths boy but now he is flying at English and languages too. They've understood how to teach in a way that suits him.'

Top exam results are, nonetheless, part of the package. Thinking skills course – designed as a more challenging alternative to critical thinking A level – introduces sixth formers to the elements of informal logic, and helps prepare for university entrance skills tests such as the Oxbridge Thinking Skills Assessment.

Many of the teachers are experts in their fields, encouraged to follow their interests. 'I cannot believe there is a more stimulating place to teach in the country,' said one

Links with local state schools Grey Coat Hospital and Harris Westminster Sixth Form – the latter sponsored by Westminster School – see sixth formers from these schools joining in German, Latin, art history and drama lessons. 'They've done a really good job at integrating us,' said a Westminster sixth former. 'I'm as good friends with students from outside as anyone else in the class.' Joint senior management meetings with Harris Westminster staff: 'We are going to learn from each other.'

Learning support and SEN: High academic ability is obviously a prerequisite, but study skills coordinator works with all those who need support for mild dyslexia, dyspraxia or Asperger's or just lack of organisation, helping them with the skills needed to cope with learning at different levels as they move up the school.

The arts and extracurricular: An almost overwhelming range of extracurricular opportunities. Societies often stem from the particular passions of both staff and students, ranging from feminist to secular to geography. English society may see Simon Russell Beale answering questions on playing King Lear at the National, whilst Piyush Goyal, national treasurer of the Indian Bharatiya Janata Party (BJP) party, tells the political society about Indian public affairs. 'I set up a society and had an ambassador from Panama come to talk,' said one student. 'Staff are really supportive when you want to set up new things.' Huge range of journalists and politicians, scientists and thinkers drop in to give talks; poet in residence inspires creativity. Trips everywhere: climbing in Cataluña, Beijing exchange, art history in Venice. Years 9-11 go off for a week's climbing, sailing, hill walking or camping at home or abroad.

'Phenomenal' music, with professional standard orchestral concerts at St John's Smith Square and the Barbican, carol service in Westminster Abbey, masterclasses, eminent musicians from Nicola Benedetti to Ian Bostridge giving evening concerts. One parent felt that 'unless you are excellent you won't get a look in', whilst staff point out there are house concerts and ensembles for the less stratospherically talented. 'We like to think there is room for everyone.' Drama equally high performing – Guys and Dolls a recent sell-out but much cerebral fare too, plus house drama and GCSE/A level pieces – and again huge talent required to bag a role in the large-scale school productions.

Art, too, 'wonderful', with much emphasis on traditional drawing and painting skills, life classes, film making facilities and a darkroom. Plus, of course, easy access to all of London's galleries and museums. 'My son had no artistic ambition when he arrived, but is now doing art A level. They have totally inspired him,' said one parent, whilst another commented: 'They let these academic boys be so creative – they feel free to explore.'

Volunteering taking on increasing importance with head's passion for outreach, with nearly all Westminsters teaching music or setting up debating societies in local primary schools, working on Hampstead Heath or learning sign language to communicate with deaf children. 'People are really involved and really making a difference,' said a student. 'Staff have the time, passion and faith in us to let us get on with things.' Phab week – where year 12 Westminster students host young people with physical and/or mental challenges, taking part in creative activities and seeing London together – is a 'life-changing experience'.

The last Anglican monastery in London now houses Purcell's, a girls' boarding and boys' day house with attached chapel. Many rooms surprisingly spacious

Old Westminsters span the centuries and the professions: the massive list ranges from Ben Jonson, John Dryden, Robert Hooke, Lord Lucan, Kim Philby, AA Milne, John Gielgud, Tony Benn, Corin Redgrave, Helena Bonham-Carter and Imogen Stubbs to Dido and Mika.

Sport: Sports – known as 'Station' – take place on Tuesday and Thursday afternoons, mostly on the enviably large playing fields in nearby St Vincent Square plus adjacent sports centre (in a previous life one of the Royal Horticultural Halls). In Westminster liberal fashion, no particular sport is compulsory, with a huge range of choices from sailing to judo to golf to girls' football. 'You wouldn't send a very sporty boy to Westminster,' thought a parent, who was grateful that her keen but not-particularly-athletic son had been in teams which he would have been unlikely to make at a more overtly sporty school. However, particularly successful at rowing (and was basking in the glow of recent success at National Schools' Regatta when we visited), fields nine football teams with 'at least respectable' results, and 'we do very well at niche sports such as rock climbing and fencing'. Often dominates the London School Cross-Country Championships and the Westminster Secondary Schools Swimming Gala, with pupils representing Westminster in the London Youth Games, and is successful at fives and real tennis. 'You are encouraged to try lots of things and find something you are passionate about,' said a student.

Boarding: The last Anglican monastery in London now houses Purcell's, a girls' boarding and boys' day house with attached chapel. Five other boarding houses, all in or near Little Dean's Yard and all of which include some day pupils. Many rooms surprisingly spacious; younger boys in College, the scholars' house, in dorms of up to eight, whilst upper years have their own rooms and those in between may share with one other. 'Because these are all old buildings, the room arrangements can be random, and sometimes we have to improvise.' All boarders are cared for in relaxed fashion by the housemaster (male or female), some with own family; resident tutor and matron also on site. Breakfast and supper in College Hall, the medieval dining room of Westminster Abbey, which day pupils may also join.

The only full boarders are sixth formers, and Saturday evenings tend to be quiet, though school is increasing organised weekend activities, particularly for the 10 per cent or so of overseas sixth form boarders.

Boarders have supervised prep sessions, and there are evening activities in the sports and music centres after prep, but those after a full-on boarding experience jammed full of organised activities may want to look elsewhere. 'He likes it for the independence and to be with his mates,' said a boarder parent, whilst another said, 'It feels like a convenient B&B. Much better than having to pick him up at late after a rehearsal or lecture.' However, a sixth form boarder commented on the 'serious sense of community you can only get from living with others. The people in your own house become quite special to you.'

Ethos and heritage: Whilst some other great public schools overshadow their environs, Westminster is an integral but discreet part of central London, largely located in the walled precincts of the former medieval monastery of Westminster Abbey. Its main buildings surround the square of

Little Dean's Yard, known as Yard, where pupils spill out after lessons to chat or kick a football or practise basketball. The Abbey, next door and with its own private entrance, serves as the school chapel, used for twice weekly services plus carol and other concerts.

'It is an incredibly tolerant and civilised atmosphere,' said a parent. 'Unlike other schools, they don't try to mould pupils into a particular product. They are quite laissez-faire'

Westminster had become a school by 1179, with pupils taught by monks of the Abbey at Westminster. It survived Henry VIII's dissolution of the monasteries in 1540 and has been in continuous existence since the 14th century, with Elizabeth I celebrated as the school's official founder.

'It is an incredibly tolerant and civilised atmosphere,' said a parent. 'Unlike other schools, they don't try to mould pupils into a particular product. They are quite laissez-faire.' Parents of quirky students are relieved to find a school that is very kind and accepting of eccentricities. 'If he was at any other school he'd be toast,' said one. 'Some schools can be so unforgiving: Westminster is the complete opposite.' Another reported that it has 'catered brilliantly' for each of her very different children. 'It's so wonderful to see these kids spark off each other.'

Has signed an agreement with Hong Kong education company HKMETG to set up six bilingual 3-18 schools in China by 2028, with 10 per cent of places free to less affluent families, and consultancy fees contributing to the Westminster bursary fund.

Pastoral care, inclusivity and discipline: Tutors attached to each house oversee the academic side, whilst housemasters look after all else. One parent felt that both have too many charges to know her son well. 'I feel his well-being is my responsibility, not the school's. I don't think anyone there knows him well in the round.' Others, however, described the pastoral care as 'exceptional', and a student said, 'I have always found the school really responsive. Your housemaster is always there and will take care of everything from not feeling well to having too much work.'

Pupils expected to be proactive, motivated and organised, with very full timetables but no compulsion to take part in organised activities. 'But anything you want to try, there's some way of doing it,' said a student.

The school, among others, was recently implicated on the Everyone's Invited website regarding allegations of peer-on-peer sexual assault and sexual harassment. The head told us the testimonies 'have made for difficult and distressing reading'. He said, 'We condemn and abhor all discriminatory and abusive attitudes and behaviours and have brought to the attention of the relevant authorities every specific allegation in line with our safeguarding responsibilities. We are determined to expedite positive and lasting change as quickly as possible. To this end, the governing body has commissioned an independent review led by an experienced QC. Her report will make concrete recommendations on the school's policies, procedures, wellbeing curriculum and staff training to ensure we are equipped further to address, tackle and ultimately eradicate discriminatory and abusive attitudes and behaviours so that every single child at Westminster may flourish.' The Guide views this as a national rather than a local phenomenon and will be taking a close interest in the effectiveness of schools' responses to it.

Pupils and parents: Westminster families undoubtedly tend to be wealthy, intellectual, metropolitan, cosmopolitan and no doubt demanding, but most parents are extremely supportive of the school. 'It is very hard to withstand this full on praise and delight.' 'I am a real believer.' 'Fantastic on every front.' And from an initial sceptic: 'I am increasingly fond of it.'

Girls entering the sixth form report a much easier ride than they might have expected. 'I had heard rumours about the boys being awful and arrogant – but they weren't,' said one. 'Some would show off in lessons to begin with, but they calmed down pretty quickly.' 'I suspect they look for a certain confidence,' said another. 'If you were insecure you might find it intimidating.' 'It was quite a shock to the system at first,' said a third, 'but we can hold our own.'

'Westminster imbues in you a sense that it is fine to talk to anyone on equal terms,' said an ex-student. 'You have a real feeling of being special.'

Parents – nearly all are Londoners, with even boarders mostly coming from within the M25 – offered a cornucopia of outings to Dulwich Picture Gallery, tours of Westminster Abbey and the Houses of Parliament, plus quiz nights, drinks parties, concerts in the Abbey, and the opportunity to attend expert lectures with their children. 'Parents very friendly and there's a good sense of community and involvement,' said one.

Whitgift School

Money matters: A number of means-tested bursaries of up to 100 per cent of fees available at 13+ and 16+; applicants must live in London. Bursaries also available at 11+; boys spend two years at the Under School before moving on automatically to the Great School. Eight Queen's Scholarships awarded at 13+; recipients must board, and the scholarship covers half the boarding fee. This can be topped up by a bursary in case of need. Five exhibitions at this level. Up to eight music scholarships at 13+ worth 10 per cent of day fee and four 16+ music scholarships, plus free instrumental tuition. Four 16+ Queen's Scholarships now available for girls.

The last word: One ex-student commented that Old Westminsters of her acquaintance have gone into a far wider range of careers than those from other schools. 'They seem to be following their passion. Westminster instils a belief that you can do whatever you want to do.'

Whitgift School

Haling Park, South Croydon, Surrey CR2 6YT

020 8688 9222 | admissions@whitgift.co.uk | www.whitgift.co.uk

Ages: 10–18

Pupils: 1,550; sixth form: 380; Boarders: 105 weekly/flexi (from age 13)

Fees: Day £21,240 pa; Boarding £34,260 – £41,550 pa

Headmaster: Since 2017, Christopher Ramsey (50s). With two headships already under his belt (King's Taunton and Chester), Mr Ramsey could be described as a 'career head' in some ways, but he also enjoyed a successful career as a modern languages teacher at the Leys, Shrewsbury and Wellington. Arriving here, he has faced the formidable challenge of succeeding an exceptional and long-serving (26 years) head, Dr Christopher Barnett, but is full of calm praise for his predecessor. 'I was lucky: not merely did I take over an excellent school, but it was one which Dr Barnett had acclimatised to accept change as part of the inevitable drive towards excellence.'

With more than 1,500 pupils and 200+ teaching staff, Mr Ramsey might look at a glance like the supreme technocrat, but he's personally approachable and low-key. 'A headmaster has a licence to be nosey,' he muses – he is certainly trying to be visible in all areas. 'He comes to lunch,' said one pupil, matter-of-fact. 'Often he says hello; sometimes he tells us to tuck in our shirts.' Married with three children (teens and early 20s), he still somehow tries to find some time to enjoy theatre and football – these days as a spectator.

Entrance: Notwithstanding the huge numbers on the pupil roll, Whitgift is a highly selective school. Around 800 applicants at 11+ last year for the 180 places on offer. It evidently welcomes boys who are able, but likes them to be willing to contribute in a whole raft of activities. Entrance process inevitably emphasises the academic and the school is equally glad to receive pupils from independent or state schools. Main entry points are at 10+, 11+ and 13+ but a limited number of places are also available to boys at 12+ and 14+. The entrance examination concentrates on mathematics, English and verbal reasoning for younger applicants, while older ones sit papers in mathematics, English and science. Section Française applicants will also sit a test in French. Some overseas applicants may take EAL exams. If all goes well enough, they then come for an interview, although application process is currently fully online for all entry levels. For 13+ entry from 2022, pre-test in year 6 for prospective day and boarding students, with offers subject to continuing 'satisfactory academic progress'. Prospective sixth form entrants need seven GCSE passes at grades 9-7 and sit the entrance examination in two of their subjects choices for A level or higher level IB.

Exit: There is no formal bar for getting into the sixth form for internal pupils; however, up to a third decide to move elsewhere at this point. Around 85 per cent to Russell Group – London universities popular, plus Bath, Bristol, Durham, Edinburgh, Exeter, Leeds, Loughborough, Nottingham and Manchester. In 2021, 11 to Oxbridge (would have been 12 but one student who had an Oxbridge offer decided to go to Harvard instead). Whitgift boys, once launched in life, often do exceptionally well – often far outstripping those pupils from schools with results even glitzier than theirs. Maths and chemistry results seem particularly strong, with a slight but perceptible bias among students towards STEM subjects – so often the default setting for ambitious pupils these days.

Latest results: In 2021, 93 per cent 9-7 at GCSE; 82 per cent A*/A at A level. For IB, average score of 41 points. In 2019 (the last year when exams took place), 82 per cent 9-7 at GCSE; 66 per cent A*/A at A level. For IB, average score of 39 points.

Teaching and learning: A place rich in ability and steeped in high endeavour. All-out effort seems to be the default setting, and this is reflected amply in the results. 'Unlike some,' said one parent, 'this school has really integrated IB into the life of the school.'

Delving below these very strong performances, it's possible to detect hints of the underlying academic culture. Competence and hard work abound: pupils and staff are ambitious for success and share in the prevailing ethos that academic attainment is a huge part of school life, but emphatically not the whole deal.

Those who join the Section Française follow the French Ministry of Education curriculum in French lessons, and must be more-or-less fluent French speakers.

'The work ethos is excellent,' says the head, 'and the school has for long tried to maximise its pupils' potential to deliver: good teaching, enough homework, proper marking – all that.' He is also clear that, by taking careful incremental steps, the school must encourage its pupils to become ever more independent learners. 'It's tantalising,' says the head; 'we all want them to have that independence. But, of course, that involves loosening the reins a bit. Naturally, that can feel scary. So, we'll just move at a sensible pace, learning as we go.'

It's hard to believe Whitgift won't confront the challenge with its customary energy and integrity – a description which applies as much to the staff as pupils. School is, famously, a nursery for future heads. About 15 are doing teacher training at any one time. 'The only downside,' says the head, 'is that they then get a promotion and leave us.' Mainly a young staff body, with 12 old pupils currently teaching.

Learning support and SEN: Great care is taken of those needing learning support, with five specialist staff catering for them – at no extra cost in the normal way.

The arts and extracurricular: Thoroughness and ambition shape the school's cultural life: breathtaking music, with a symphony orchestra and a concert orchestra. There's also the Whitgift Chamber Orchestra, an ensemble composed of both Whitgift pupils and other talented boys and girls from the London area, which performs regularly at major national venues alongside the Royal Philharmonic Orchestra. There are two big choirs: the Whitgift Chamber Choir and Minster Choristers. Orchestras and choirs tour internationally, and play at major venues, including the Royal Albert Hall, Royal Festival Hall and Cadogan Hall.

Cracking drama, and a lot of it. 'It's as good, at least, as its sport,' said one parent, whose children have experienced both. The main assembly hall converts to a tiered-seating theatre for major productions; there is also a separate performing arts centre and concert hall for smaller productions. Very democratic feel: opportunities for boys of all ages, with some productions confined to particular year groups. Informal links with film companies have seen Whitgift boys take leading roles in TV productions and the West End. Some boys are also members of the National Youth Theatre. Recent plays include The Government Inspector, The Lion, the Witch and the Wardrobe, and Doctor Faustus. The school sponsored a boy in his last year to run his own theatre company. 'We try to make everything possible,' says the head, 'if that seems consistent with good sense.'

'The work ethos is excellent,' says the head, 'and the school has tried to maximise its pupils' potential: good teaching, enough homework, proper marking – all that'

More than 80 clubs meet at different times during the week. As well as over 200 pupils engaged at any time in DofE, there is also a CCF with over 400 pupils in its ranks. Worth mentioning that two local state schools take part in this – a very natural way to achieve outreach. One recent trip involved boys spending a week at a marine commando training centre. Service culture runs deep within the school's DNA: there are currently 38 Old Whitgiftians serving in the army. The school also pioneered an exceptional (surely unique) exhibition Remembering 1916 – Life on the Western Front: a homage to the sacrifice of lives (of old pupils among others) made during the First World War, brilliantly showcasing its social sensitivity, historical skills and an acute awareness of its own past.

Sport: Big numbers have helped to make Whitgift a home of serious schoolboy sport, but participation and teamwork run right through the school's DNA. Teams have won more than 120 national titles in the past five years: stalwart rugby and football, hockey and cricket – with nearly 30 school teams fielded in each. The participation levels are impressive, with more than 1,200 boys playing in 2,000+ fixtures annually. Over 40 sports are available, including superb athletics, modern pentathlon, tennis and golf. The sports facilities are magnificent – top-of-the-range everything: fitness centre, squash courts, indoor Olympic swimming pool, indoor and outdoor pitches of every kind. Only rowers are forced to take a coach ride. 'We can offer many things,' head acknowledges, 'but not our own river.' Many boys represent their country in a wide variety of sports, or go on to top-level sporting careers.

Boarding: Whitgift's decision to open a boarding house in 2013 was an eloquent statement of self-belief. Many established boarding schools have come to rely increasingly on overseas boarders to make their existing establishments viable, but Whitgift has catered for a versatile market – over 50 per cent of whom live in the UK. The house is superbly comfortable and well-equipped (top-flight IT equipment, study areas, en-suite bathrooms and spacious, communal social areas with kitchen facilities), but feels a considerable social success as well. Full boarding for some (mainly from overseas) but also weekly boarding, which between them account for over 100 pupils, of whom about half stay over the weekends. There's also flexi-boarding for interested day pupils between 13 and 18. As well as the housemaster and tutors, there's also a head of boarding who represents boarders' interests within the school's senior leadership team.

A strong sense of identity and conviviality seem to have evolved over the past years in this fledgling boarding community. This has no doubt been helped by the school's determination to ensure that its facilities are made available for boarders out of hours, and to exploit the endless resources of London: the result has been to foment a palpable energy and excitement.

Ethos and heritage: Strong sense of a place at ease with itself. Great investment of time and energy from all constituencies for local causes – visits to primary schools, elderly and disadvantaged – as well as energetic fundraising. Pupils and staff communicate an aura of being glad to be here, but no grand public school airs and graces. 'That was what sold us,' said one father. 'We wanted our son to have a busy and fulfilling life, but the sense of entitlement one sees in some schools was completely alien.' Manners are easy, with evident fondness as well as respect for others. All staff we met emphasised the diversity of the intake – socially and ethnically: middle-class affluent children from the Surrey and Sussex borders, but plenty from south London who are anything but. Nearly 50 per cent of the children here are being financially supported.

The decision to open a boarding house was an eloquent statement of self-belief. A strong sense of identity seems to have evolved in this fledgling boarding community

Excellent concentration by pupils evident in each of the classes visited, but with a style of comfortable interaction that made it all believable. Head is currently two-thirds of the way through marathon one-to-one interviews with all teaching staff and says, 'One theme recurs, time and time again. I ask them "What should I change?" And they, virtually every time, say "Don't change the kids".'

Screeds of distinguished old pupils – Chris Cook, previously editor of Newsnight, is a recent notable, and also Martin Jarvis and Derren Brown. Back in the day, Sir Bernard Crick and Lord Tedder also attended.

Pastoral care, inclusivity and discipline: Form tutors are the everyday go-to teacher, especially for the younger pupils. These feed concerns into heads of year who work alongside heads of upper and lower school. It's a tried and trusted structure, but what really seems to make it work is the calibre of pupil-staff relationships. Head is quick to praise his predecessor who was 'way ahead of the game in pastoral matters, and a big support of counselling, long before it was fashionable'. The school currently has three counsellors. All pupils are also members of a house which has come to be a vehicle for much more than just competitive sports. 'Increasingly,' says the head, 'it's a focus of all kinds of activity – plays, concerts and so forth – but also of identity.' One or two parents wondered out loud at the intensity of life. 'Mainly I'm delighted,' said one, 'but there is a cost: my children are pretty often exhausted.'

A conservative society – no doubt about that. Zero tolerance on drugs and, the head adds, 'We make it perfectly clear that, when you're a member of Whitgift, you're a member seven days a week, 365 days a year. Boundaries are important at any time.' As he acknowledges, that tough line can risk that 'the chop falls on someone more unlucky than anything else'. No recent exclusions, however. There is a 'headmaster's detention' on Saturdays for medium-serious infractions – something which, Mr Ramsey admits, with a twinkle in his eye, he is not called to supervise.

Pupils and parents: Full communication between home and school: termly reports, and at least one major parents' evening annually for each year group. In a school with a much broader socio-economic constituency than some independent schools, the accessibility and approachability of staff is much valued.

Money matters: The school allocates significant resources for means-tested bursaries. These are targeted at day pupils, but the school has made boarding awards available for boys of exceptional talent who might benefit from boarding. There are art/design/engineering and music and drama awards, as well as academic scholarships. Nearly 50 per cent of the students here are on some form of financial support – a consequence of generations of philanthropy and of the massive contribution of school luminaries and well-wishers.

The last word: An outstanding school, through and through. Despite the peacocks parading on the lawn, nobody round here is preening. We happened to bump into a great throng of pupils at the local train station and were struck by their combination of energy, cheerfulness and calm courtesy. The head's confidence in them, the staff and parents is a good augury. Yet he is also alert to the irreducible truth that the school is massively privileged. 'We do need to keep helping them see the extent of the privilege they enjoy,' he admits, 'so that we help them become more automatic givers.'

Windlesham House School

76

Washington, Pulborough, West Sussex RH20 4AY

01903 874700 | whsadmissions@windlesham.com | www.windlesham.com

Ages: 4–13

Pupils: 300; Boarders: 100 full, 18 day (from year 3)

Fees: Day £9,555 – £24,522; Boarding £27,102– £29,580 pa

Headmaster: Since September 2020, Ben Evans, formerly head of Edge Grove. A Devon lad (mother still breeds Dartmoor ponies there) with a love of all things country. Head boy at Bramdean School before Exeter University where he read history and archaeology. Returned, armed with his degree and PGCE, to Bramdean where he 'learned to teach', before taking up the post of head of history at Brighton College, later returning as deputy head to his alma mater.

Had a 'now or never' moment before hot footing it to Sri Lanka to teach at the junior school of the British School in Colombo, Sri Lanka, where he served a total of six years, the final four as head. Returned to the UK and Edge Grove following the birth of his first child – he and his wife Alex now have two young sons.

Entrance: Non-selective. Academic assessment from year 1 upwards for setting purposes plus night's stay from year 3 upwards. Waiting list for many years.

Exit: Pupils move on to over 35 different schools, including Marlborough, Oundle, Bryanston, Lancing College, Uppingham and St Edward's Oxford.

Our view: Gorgeous grounds, movingly beautiful even on the miserable day of our visit, with the elegant Queen Anne house standing at the end of a long drive past a mixture of woods, playing fields and golf course. Game rambling around (they don't shoot it here – just clay pigeons). Beautiful entrance hall with roaring fire adds to the impression of arriving at a country house hotel; one specialising in modern art – it's everywhere, and extremely good.

Feels happy and free – described by one parent as a 'tree-climbing education centre'. The amazing grounds are fully used by the children; one parent described how the matrons have to drag them in to bed during the summer months, and how kids are out playing golf and cricket before breakfast – 'kids have the freedom to be children' (children with a nine-hole golf course).

Parents and children all comment on the strong community at Windlesham – 'it's an incredibly kind place' – which aims to be a family home away from home. No uniform promotes the homey feel, although the strict dress code prevents a grungy look. There's no label competition here – 'They ruin clothes at school, so don't send them in anything good,' said one parent wryly.

Huge amount of energy devoted to pastoral care. Many staff live on site: one parent said 'they never clock off'. One parent described the 'brilliant support' from the school after a family death – they have a 'genuine love of children' here.

High level of responsibility and support shown between children. Peer listeners appointed from the top class, peer mediators in each year – described lavishly by one of our guides as 'unpaid spies', but a peer mediator calmly countered with an example of a love/hate triangle successfully resolved by her and her counterpart. Any help from adults? 'No, of course not – confidentiality,' she said in a shocked tones. For prep age children, they are astonishingly responsible and outward-looking. This is one of the school's aims, with the head's mantra firmly in mind – be kind, be kind, be kind. Any bullying nipped in the bud early. 'There's not a great deal of it,' said a parent, whose daughter experienced bullying which was dealt very efficiently.

Huge emphasis on good manners here: children pay good heed to the head's warning – 'Get your greeting in before I do.' Good evidence of this on our tour: all pupils held open doors, flattened themselves against walls as we passed and leapt up in classrooms.

Parents say school is just not the same for day pupils as boarders, who don't have the same access to activities or teachers as them. Boarding is particularly useful as work steps up in preparation for common entrance, parents say – early bird lessons start at 7.15am, and work ends at 6.30pm, so it's a long day for commuters.

Academically, parents and pupils are happy with most subjects, exceptionally so in English and science, but French is 'not that popular', say the kids, and parents agree, citing a reliance on worksheets. School says it has taken on new teachers since our visit.

Another parent suggested maths is also a key subject that could be taught better, although the children we spoke to gave maths teachers a glowing report – 'If you listen carefully they're really funny – very sarcastic.' One teacher apparently tells stories of his life in mathematical fantasy (difficult to imagine how this might go…).

Rigorous reporting for parents: monthly progress report with attainment and effort, both child and parents get a copy, and a full report at the end of each term. Annual parents' evening (termly for juniors). 'Amazing level of communication,' say parents: written letters from kids every week, emails and phone calls. 'School responds promptly to any query, over and above what you would expect.' Another parent commented how welcome she felt at weekends – you can attend Saturday chapel, watch a play rehearsal or recital. '[You] never feel excluded as a parent – always welcomed.' Parental portal has live stream of events, also available for catch up, ideal for parents who aren't local.

Homely girls' dorms, with posters, cushions, bears; spartan boys' fare, with coloured duvets the most cosy touch (despite the school's best efforts)

Three computer rooms, one reserved specially for junior use. Dell laptops and iPads to book out, also available to assist those with mild learning difficulties (about 15 per cent of children here). Learning development unit with head and team of assistants. Bright, well-stocked library, open from before breakfast until bedtime, news with a Tory bent – Telegraph and Times, with the honourable exception of the i.

Perhaps a bit hunting, shooting, fishing, but doesn't feel exclusive. Sports are the usual public school fare. Parents are delighted that sports kit left hanging around at school is returned washed and pristine. New sports hall and swimming pool get good use.

Most boarders are around at weekends (though it's possible to go home four weekends a term). Everyone's around on Saturdays: morning school, matches in the afternoon. Plenty of activities available – Capture the Flag is extremely popular at the moment; but also debates, mountain biking, gardening in the walled garden, shows and games – pupils can keep extremely busy if they want to (though some kids just want to live in the woods, and that's okay too). All love cooking club – you have to run fast if you want to sign up.

All have drama lessons, three productions each year – everyone who auditions is included in some way. Own theatre, the Malden Family Theatre, with visiting productions every term. Some rumblings from parents who are a bit tired of seeing the super-duper children starring again. Music compulsory all the way, but popular even with those who are not musical because of the inspirational director. Over 80 per cent play an instrument. Vast array of music groups of all complexions, from marimba to rock choir.

Early years housed separately at Little Windlesham (reception to year 2), currently undergoing major renovations. Relaxed setting, emphasis on flow and play. Tapestry method of contacting parents, who receive a video stream of their children in class directly to their email at work, which parents love. Described by a parent as being 'part of [the] big school – but very gentle, with a lot of time [spent] in their special oasis'.

The head says Windlesham would suit most types of kids, providing they join in and have a go at things. One parent suggested it would not suit a child who needs to be totally organised by others, nor is it a place for shrinking violets, although conversations with shy pupils suggested they could find their feet and flourish here. One parent emphasised that those who want their children to be day pupils should avoid Windlesham – all kids here will want to board eventually.

Parents from the Foreign Office, business, Forces, professions, and lots of expats. Some 20 different nationalities in the school, around 12 per cent non-British. Assesses language skills on entry, but will give special assistance to learn English as a foreign language. Some 50 per cent of kids local, 50 per cent from abroad or other parts of the country. Parents like the mix of children from different countries, and to a degree, backgrounds – and no judgement, say parents, although four-wheel-drive likely to be parent vehicle of choice.

Boarding: Pupils can board from the age of 7 – has now introduced more flexible options including part-time boarding of two or three weekday nights for years 3-6, with full-time available from year 4. Around half are full boarders, 18 per cent from overseas. 'Boarding provision is exceptionally good,' said a mum, whose kids started as day pupils, and all ended up boarding at their request. Pupils agree – 'It's a sleepover that doesn't stop.' Homely girls' dorms, with posters, cushions, bears; spartan boys' fare, with coloured duvets the most cosy touch (despite the school's best efforts). 'It's the girls who need One Direction posters,' said one of our guides loftily. Girls also get bedside tables and lights – boys don't because of their tendency to play cricket in the dorms. Dormitory phones for goodnight calls to parents (time restricted to give everyone a chance).

Twelve is the biggest boys' dorm, six the smallest, nine and three for the girls. A little unfortunate that the girls' dorms are named after colours – Azure, Saffron etc (to suit their delicate natures?) – whereas boys' dorms are sturdily named after senior schools – Wellington et al. Unfortunate indeed, but no other whiff of sex discrimination here.

Bathroom facilities extremely clean, but not all that new. Nightly showers, although boarders can relax in a birthday bath. Each year has a comfy room, reduced to cheerful bedlam for the boys, ordered comfort for the girls.

Money matters: No scholarships, but a few means-tested bursaries available.

The last word: Several parents of leavers said their children are homesick for Windlesham: the move from this caring environment to senior school can be quite tough; but as a parent said, no one would want Windlesham to be less fabulous.

Woldingham School

RC 77

Marden Park, Woldingham, Surrey CR3 7YA

01883 349431 | registrar@woldinghamschool.co.uk | www.woldinghamschool.co.uk

Ages: 11–18

Pupils: 611; sixth form: 159; Boarders: 175 full, 135 weekly/flexi

Fees: Day £22,710 – £24,750; Boarding £32,850 – £40,710 pa

Headmaster: Since September 2020, Dr James Whitehead, previously head of university strategy at Rugby. He is Woldingham's first male head in the school's long history. Educated at Stonyhurst College and Hertford College, Oxford, he completed further degrees at Stirling and Manchester universities. Kicked off his school career teaching English at Radley College and joined Worth School as second master before becoming head at Downside, a Catholic day and boarding school in Somerset.

Entrance: There are 80 places available at 11+, 30 at 13+ and 20 at 16+. Occasional places at 12 and

14+. Candidates for 13+ may apply in year 6 for deferred entry (same online test as for 11+) or in year 8 for standard entry. Assessment day includes an English writing paper, group interview and fun creative activity. The school is looking for pupils with interests beyond the academic, with reasonable adjustments for SEND. Sixth form candidates are examined in two of their chosen A level subjects and a general paper.

Exit: Around 15-20 per cent leave after GCSEs, with places filled by incomers. An incredibly broad range of university courses, which speaks of inspiration well beyond the purely academic – quite a few budding criminologists, digital media specialists, vets, anthropologists, electrical engineers, land economists and art historians. Durham, Edinburgh, KCL, Liverpool, Manchester and Warwick all popular recently. One to Oxbridge in 2021, plus three medics. One student to study in the US (MIT).

Latest results: In 2021, 80 per cent 9-7 at GCSE; 90 per cent A*/A at A level. In 2019 (the last year when exams took place), 63 per cent 9-7 at GCSEs; 47 per cent A*/A at A level.

Teaching and learning: Highlights at GCSE include Latin and all of the sciences, with consistently good results across English and maths. Popular subjects at A level include English literature, maths, biology and history, whilst the artists in particular shine.

Girls are expected to study a language (not necessarily modern, could be Latin) to GCSE; Mandarin is a club. Most sixth formers take three A levels. Further specialism introduces A levels in textiles, psychology, media studies, government and politics and classical civilisation.

Oxbridge support starts in the lower sixth with girls assigned a teacher to support their applications one-to-one. There is no fear of being made to feel like a 'geek' for being good at something, say parents. Girls interact with their subjects outside of the grounds: a lower sixth student was joint winner of a recent Cambridge history prize, with successes also in 'teen tech' and poetry competitions.

Almost 25 per cent of staff have been working at the school for more than 10 years. A parent commented: 'The girls seem to relate well to both the male and female teachers. They respect them and feel that they can easily approach them if they need further explanation with a subject that they find tricky.' A girl we met thought, 'They are here to support you as a person, as you grow into yourself.' We watch an upper sixth economics class where the teacher sits inside the circle of desks giving detailed essay feedback.

Maximum class size is 22 up to GCSE then 14 in the sixth form. Lower sets have smaller numbers so that students can receive more support. One mother said, 'During the first three years they do not believe in setting pointless holiday homework, they believe the girls work hard enough during term time.' Hurrah.

Learning support and SEN: An experienced learning enhancement department provides support for standard numbers of girls with SPLDs such as dyslexia but also small numbers with ADHD and autism spectrum disorder. All are screened on entry. The majority receive 'light touch' support, only a few receive direct support and a reduced curriculum.

There is a significant programme of carefully thought-through support for girls with EAL needs. Unusually, some one-year GCSE students (usually girls from Spain and Mexico) are prepared for the Cambridge English ESOL examinations.

The arts and extracurricular: Slightly less than half the school have individual music lessons, including singing. Some stand-out performers have places in national orchestras. Musicians gave two concerts on a tour of Prague recently.

We saw the work of one published poet, also an artist, in the stunning art studio, quite the biggest we've ever seen, allowing each upper sixth student to have their own 'nest'. Fascinating projects in progress include one from a student developing her own religion and researching curses and another who was building a 'city to the lost creativity of children' in wax. Naturally, several are heading to art school.

One-third of girls are Catholics, but almost more integral to the school are the values of the sacred heart: faith, intellect, community, personal growth and social justice

With Carey Mulligan a notable former pupil, it's not altogether surprising to find drama facilities of such a high standard: the 550-seat theatre is stunning, with a flexible stage and space for a full orchestra. Helping girls to settle into year 7, everyone takes part in a production, most recently Roald Dahl's The Twits and The Witches. Very professional-looking production posters from former years line the staircase. Higher up the school the number of shows is limited but there are opportunities to take part in backstage work. Drama available at GCSE and A level.

Pupils are far from just sequestered away in their valley. Computer science students have recently returned from a trip to Silicon Valley; year 11s and sixth formers spent four days in Berlin; year 9s visit the battlefields of Ypres and geography students enjoy an annual trip to Iceland. Eighty clubs on offer: Mandarin, archery, tap dancing, coding, darkroom photography, rock-climbing and dissection caught our eye. Day girls are encouraged to stay for extracurricular activities but are free to go home from 4.30pm. Sports matches and supervised study with friends until 6.30pm. Transport is provided to facilitate this and many stay. On Saturday mornings, Saturday Active for years 7 to 10 boarders provides a range of activities.

Sport: Sports facilities are not lavish given the space – plans are afoot – and a parent's view that 'sport is average, but music and drama are outstanding' and artists in particular shine, does seem to fit with the picture of the school on view today, although there are some noticeable sporting successes, recently in hockey and netball. Main sports also include swimming, tennis and athletics, with aerobics, lacrosse, table tennis and squash added in higher up the school. There is a dance studio and an indoor tennis dome. The school is notable in supporting its elite athletes, currently including cross-country, skiing, lacrosse, modern pentathlon, carriage driving – enabling them to take part in term time without falling behind. No timetabled football but soccer club is popular and cricket is coming.

Boarding: Years 7 and 8 boarders have a separate block, Marden. It's tidy but plain, plentifully kitted out with sofas. Décor-wise, if we had been told the over-50s lived here we would have believed it, but what does that matter when you have all of your friends here to crowd around I'm a Celebrity and share in the odd yoga class? The upper sixth block is next door and they've recently initiated a year 7 movie night so that the older girls don't seem in any ways remote or intimidating. Years 7, 8 and 9 share a room, from year 10 girls have their own, with sixth formers getting en-suites: compact, but modern, fresh and functional, perfect for studying. Boarders are free to go home at weekends from 4.30pm on Friday. There are often boarding house pets, whether that be elderly Doris or a new, highly anticipated puppy. Flexi-boarding on hand: simply sign up for one to two nights a week a term in advance.

Ethos and heritage: Founded in 1842 by the Society of the Sacred Heart, 100 or so years later at the end of the Second World War the school of 100 pupils moved to Woldingham from Roehampton. Main house is all highly decorative Victorian red brick without and dark panelling within. Plainer 20th-century additions and conversions form a courtyard and then a Millennium building smartly houses arts.

The grounds, with cattle, horses and deer, extend to a staggering 700 acres, a secluded wooded valley on the edge of the North Downs

The grounds, complete with cattle, horses and the odd deer, extend to a staggering 700 acres, a secluded wooded valley on the edge of the North Downs. Along the two-mile drive you're likely to encounter only the odd rider. The school does feel quite isolated, even if in reality it is not. Sixth formers are allowed to take the train into London at weekends (with planning) and clearly relish the privilege.

It no doubt adds to the family feel, which the girls we meet are emphatic about. When the head tells us about a year 7 pyjama day we imagine the whole school wearing pyjamas to lessons every day – who would know? As for snow days, we can't think of anywhere better. As the head says, 'We're good at relaxing – staff v girls Would I Lie to You?, pancake race, inter-house go-karting…' A mother confirmed, 'There is a charming sense of fun about the school – even amongst sixth formers if they think no-one is looking.'

A perusal of old girl careers throws up a number of mum-preneurs as well as a varied clutch of famous names. Interior designers including Neisha Crosland, also Louise Mensch, Vivien Leigh and Clarissa Dickson-Wright. And Carey Mulligan. Old girls may get married in the school chapel and come in for business breakfasts to share their experiences.

Pastoral care, inclusivity and discipline: 'We are absolutely a Catholic school,' says the head – just the odd statue and religious painting on view. One-third of girls are Catholics, but almost more integral to the school are the values of the sacred heart: faith, intellect, community, personal growth and social justice – 'It's very tangible for us, it's how we make decisions,' says the head. Girls no longer wear uniform to mass on Sunday but all faiths attend, even if it is just for a moment of quiet reflection.

Day and boarding pupils are allocated to one of four houses and tutor groups are also arranged by house. The first Saturday of the autumn term is a house festival of dance, music and costume making.

The health centre is staffed by qualified nurses and a counsellor is available. With gender in the news we quiz the head on gendered vocabulary: 'I say "girls", but I would say that I'm aware of this every time I use it, which was perhaps not the case a year ago.' Each parent mentions the relative lack of pressure their daughters find here. Marden has an adventure playground and the head agrees girls may be able to 'stay younger for longer'.

Parents are all praise for the pastoral care: 'Excellent. If there is an issue the problem is dealt with with kindness and discretion. Invaluable,' is typical. Little need for sanctions. Digital matters are the greatest challenge now, with posting something inappropriate online warranting an immediate suspension. In years 7 and 8 the school takes away devices, from year 9 girls are allowed to self-monitor, and boarders in years 7-10 hand in their devices at night. Sixth formers enjoy some uniform privileges such as their own suits, shirts and jumpers as well as taking on responsibilities as 'ribbons', one of the most charming traditions of the school, where they wear sashes and take on house or school leadership roles.

Pupils and parents: Who might the school suit? 'Not one stereotype of girl,' says the head. Parents agree upon 'girls who respond to encouragement rather than pressure'. A predominance of west Londoners and those from nearby Surrey and Kent. More than 100 from overseas, predominantly from Hong Kong and China but comprising 30 nationalities. 'A complete mix of backgrounds, ethnicity and relative wealth, from the daughters of Russian oligarchs downwards, but all part of the school community,' said a parent.

Money matters: Not prodigiously well endowed so bursaries and scholarships unlikely to play a major role. Academic and co-curricular scholarships are offered at 11+, 13+ and sixth form, designed to recognise exceptional achievement, intellectual curiosity and persistence. Awards typically cover five to 20 per cent of day fees. No need to be stratospherically accomplished for music scholarships as potential also recognised. One scholarship to a local girl each year and two in science. Bursaries are intended for girls who demonstrate strong academic potential and where the financial circumstances of the family would make attending Woldingham impossible. Forty students are in receipt of a bursary, a few up to a life-changing 100 per cent of fees.

The last word: Girls are sure to find a home from home in this Catholic school which welcomes all and promises fun, fabulous dramatic and artistic opportunties, strong academics and the chance to be young for a little longer.

Woodcote House School

78

Snows Ride, Windlesham, Surrey GU20 6PF

01276 472115 | Admissions@woodcotehouseschool.co.uk | www.woodcotehouseschool.co.uk

Ages: 7-13

Pupils: 100; Boarders: 25 full, 40 weekly/flexi boarders

Fees: Day £18,900; Boarding £25,350 pa

Headmaster: Since September 2016, David Paterson. Tall (but not at all imposing) and quietly spoken. His grandfather, Douglas, acquired the school in 1931, apparently buying the elegant Regency property together with its 30 acres on a whim as the village shared the same name as the prep school where he had been teaching. David's parents, the legendary Mr and Mrs Mark, succeeded Douglas as heads. David took over from his brother Nick after serving for some time as deputy head. The family are still proprietors, with an 'advisory board' made up of family, friends and ex-parents, who oversee the management of the school. As well as being on the advisory board, Nick is still a strong presence on the ground, teaching Latin and scholarship classes, with his rambling study full of books and wisdom tucked behind the school dining hall. Nick's son Oliver (OP to the boys) is a Renaissance man – Woodcote, Eton, Durham – and is waiting in the wings for his turn at the helm. OP has an array of talent, sporting, musical and artistic, and is involved in everything from running the school play to playing the organ in the tiny jewel of a chapel in the grounds, as well as cricket (Woodcote's own yard cricket is still a favourite pastime of his) and maths. Although David still calls the shots, and will no doubt still be present after he hangs up his boots, there is no doubt OP will be fast out of the blocks as soon as David fires the gun.

Entrance: No formal exams; a taster day instead. Often applicants come individually, occasionally in pairs, never in groups. They are assessed in the round, in the classroom, at lunch and at play. 'We are not selective academically,' says head, 'but we do need to be sure that successful candidates will get the most out of their time with us.' Some will have been on the lists since birth, others might arrive mid-term needing a place having relocated to the UK from abroad. There are no feeder schools. Growing numbers from London since the arrival of the London bus which ferries boys to school by 8am from Putney and other parts of south London. The head's son drives the bus and sometimes you might be lucky and be chauffeured by the headmaster himself. A core number remain local, within a 45-minute drive. (Very flexible) boarding from year 3. Most choose to board in their final two years.

Exit: At 13+ almost all to leading senior schools, mainly boarding. Sherborne, Bradfield, Marlborough, Wellington, Canford and Tonbridge recently popular. A handful each year to Winchester, Harrow and Eton. Preference is for full boarding though there is a realistic understanding from all parties that the days of genuine full boarding have passed. One of the many advantages of a small school like this is that the quality of advice and guidance given by the headmaster and his team is superlative. 'They really know our son, have a thorough understanding of the schools and ensure the match is right,' said a parent. Woodcote is a school that is far more concerned with substance over style and form, we heard – 'We parents are encouraged to be grounded as much as the boys are; David Paterson is a good listener and won't just tell you what you want to hear.' As a result, most parents are largely prepared to accept that their son might not suit the school de jour.

Our view: School mottoes, in our experience, can feel tired or pretentious or both. But the Woodcote motto of 'Live to learn and learn to live' is spot on. It's like entering the pages of Conn Iggulden's The Dangerous Book for Boys – but substitute dangerous for adventurous, playful, fun, messy and muddy. In an age of screens and childhood stress, Woodcote provides the antidote. In fact, apart from the occasional hour of PlayStation on a Sunday or in the sixth form house – or perhaps the odd film night in the dorms – no screen activity is allowed. Even in lockdown they carefully managed the timetable so that it was limited. Upshot is that boys play conkers, climb trees, hurl themselves along the zip wire and build dens in the woods. At break they can choose to play a few holes of golf or a quick game of tennis. But it's not all outdoorsy, with some preferring to do extra art or music – and after lunch they enjoy quiet time, which means silent reading at your desk. We were impressed with how many boys were eager to discuss the novel they were reading – increasingly rare. Cooking is another popular pursuit, with a new kitchen suite complete with several hobs, ovens and grey worktops. A games room with table tennis and snooker tables, as well as air hockey, was humming.

In an age of screens and childhood stress, Woodcote provides the antidote. Boys play conkers, climb trees, hurl themselves along the zip wire and build dens in the woods

You won't just hear the patter of schoolboys' feet down Red Lane (the main artery of the school, so named because of the ancient red flagstones that line the floor) – dogs are another comforting feature that contribute to the warm family feel, as well as the shabby chic sophistication of the place. All staff are encouraged to feel part of the fabric of the place, their dogs too.

A very small school, with about a hundred pupils, Woodcote punches well above its weight in every area. In their almost comically vintage brown and yellow uniforms, the boys burst with a fresh enthusiasm and energy that carries them onto the sport fields, hurling themselves against the competition whether it be football or rugby but especially cricket, which the school prides itself on.

The same vigour is evident in the classroom where numbers are small (between 10 and 14 and sometimes even fewer in scholarship lessons) and attention is focused. Boys can't hide behind their neighbours or their jumpers here. The head is a stalwart proponent of CE and they have fine-tuned preparation for the pre-test to keep in touch with the times. Politics has recently been added to the timetable for years 7 and 8 as well as LAMDA and a subject incorporating the school motto, which covers community, when to be a team player and how to lead. There is an unusually high number of male teachers, especially further up the school, and all staff – including marketing and admissions – roll up their sleeves and get involved with each aspect of school life.

The school day is long with a 6.15pm finish (in the senior years it can be as late as 8pm) but all work is done at school – there is no 'home' work, avoiding the potential for parents to interfere as well as ensuring that holidays live up to their title.

The school is steeped in charm, history and a heavy dose of myth and legend (think Dick Turpin and the original incarnation of the school as the Pelican Inn in the 18th century and ask the boys about Mr Mark's famous rounds in his golf buggy). From the moment you enter the very short drive it feels as if you are in the heart of the countryside despite being only a 40-minute bus journey from the capital. Not polished or sparkling with swanky facilities, Woodcote's proudest recent investment has been a new central heating system – 'We miss the wrought iron radiators,' the head confided, 'but I think everyone is happier to be warm.' On almost every wall, in practically every common space, hang sepia-coloured portraits of every boy who has attended the school. Whether they were taken in 1940 or 2020 every photograph bears the same yellowish hue, a black and white photo of a boy, wide eyed and full of promise. We couldn't help wondering whether the photograph tradition alone would force the school to modernise to make more gallery space. The head was quick to point out that their regular annual investment has recently yielded new Astroturf pitches, as well as a theatre – but he agrees, 'We will never be swanky.'

Boarding quarters are housed in the main building. Matrons wreathed in smiles and clad in informal T-shirts go a long way to making the dormitories feel safe and cosy

Art is one of the jewels in the Woodcote crown. The teacher is gold dust and 'though her art room may look like a bombsite' (head's words), we know from experience that this usually reveals a creative lack of inhibition. No mean feat to engage all the boys and not just the talented few. Some find their way to the art room to seek the mental release drawing and painting can bring but all of them love seeing their art displayed on the walls. Several art scholarships are won each year and there have also been several prestigious prizes won including second prize in the Saatchi competition.

Drama is vibrant. When we visited years 7 and 8 were rehearsing A Christmas Carol. Boys get involved in every aspect of the production – we watched some constructing and painting the set of The Marley Arms. Past productions have included Titanic, Sweeney Todd and Spamalot! Don't expect any girls to get involved (although the school's relationship with Cowarth Flexlands, a local girls' prep, is starting to flourish).

The dining room – where every boy sits and is served together with members of staff – is overflowing with silverware, a plethora of cups and shields, the most striking of which is a huge sword used to cut the house cake awarded to the winning house at the end of each school year – 'our Harry Potter moment,' winks the head. No wide and colourful choices of food or salad bar here (though we were assured that there is salad tea), but we enjoyed a beef stroganoff followed by roly-poly pudding and custard. Another bow to traditional excellence. 'Boys are encouraged to eat what they're given,' we were told.

Like so much about this school, you cannot put the parents in any kind of box except one that is marked 'very supportive and enthusiastic about the school'. They fly the Woodcote flag with enthusiasm, commenting on how well their sons behave, how proud they are of their progress through boyhood to teenager and how confident they are in the process of making the transition to senior school. The longstanding tradition of the final year group clubbing together to give a present to the school (which has included a zip wire, pizza oven, and a climbing apparatus, as well flashy professional lighting for the theatre) is concrete evidence of the devotion and affection for the school held among generations of alumni.

Boarding: Boarding quarters are housed in the main building. High ceilings, carpets barely concealing the thud of wooden floors, and beautiful large Georgian windows. Fairly spartan but well-kept dormitories, as is so often the case with flexi-boarding when boys rarely put down roots. Matrons wreathed in smiles and clad in informal T-shirts go a long way to making the dormitories feel safe and cosy. Some senior dorms have a flat-screen TV discreetly positioned on the wall, used for the treat that is film night and the occasional Sky sports.

Weekends are punctuated with a chapel service after lessons on a Saturday. Parents are invited and many come – standing room only – followed by drinks, lunch, a match and tea, confirming the view of many parents we spoke to of how involved they feel – and perhaps more so than they would in a day school: 'We are given so many opportunities for informal chats with key members of staff,' said one. For the few who stay in school for the whole weekend, the school will always provide some form of entertainment, eg bowling, Thorpe Park. The latter is hugely popular with the boys but the head can barely conceal his grimace

– 'a ghastly place but the rides are rather fun!' As frank and open as ever, the school is keen for parents to understand that although they do offer full boarding as well as part boarding and part day, boys tend to be pretty thin on the ground on a Sunday. This does not stop them from catering to the requirements of all three sectors, however, and each one gets equal attention.

Money matters: The Patersons reserve funds for families in need though they prefer not to give them the formal title of 'bursaries' and there is no formal means testing. The money is 'awarded at my discretion,' says the head, his soft eyes twinkling. Scholarships are awarded 'for outstanding ability of any kind and we will offer a reduction as an award, regardless of means.' Old style, and as with so much here, a tonic.

The last word: An enchanting place for boys to grow and learn. If you are tired of marketing speak and glossy presentations and yearn for a school that takes pride in its roots, looks you in the eye when it has to tell you any uncomfortable truths and is unashamed about an infrastructure that can seem a bit threadbare, then look no further. Woodcote is that rare breed of school, family owned and run with a warm and authentic heart.

Worth School
RC
79
Paddockhurst Road, Turners Hill, Crawley, West Sussex RH10 4SD
01342 710200 | information@worth.org.uk | www.worthschool.org.uk
Ages: 11–18
Pupils: 630; sixth form: 240; Boarders: 325 full/weekly/flexi
Fees: Day £16,890 – £25,080; Boarding £36,480 pa

Head master: Since 2015, Stuart McPherson MA (40s). Educated at the University of Western Australia and took an MA in literature and religion at Newcastle. He had not planned to be a teacher but joined Sydney Grammar for a year, ended staying for 10 and did his teacher training on the job. He came over to the UK on a short-term teacher exchange with Eton and spent 15 years there, where he taught English and coached rugby and cricket and was a housemaster for the final five years. He is married to Johneen, who is deputy head academic at St Mary's Ascot, and they have four children. He says it might sound like a cliché but he spends any spare time reading and enjoys walking and camping – but definitely for no longer than 24 hours.

He has a strong Catholic faith and says the 'key aims of the school are rooted within the Benedictine tradition – it's about the formation of character and values and not just jumping through GCSE hoops. There is something special about the place; the ethos is tangible.' He is the third lay head and also, by coincidence, the third Australian head. 'He is a good communicator,' said a pupil, is willing to listen and is very approachable – 'he always has his door open in the morning and you can drop in.' 'He looks over our personal statements and is not a scary figure and you see him a lot around the school.' 'He hasn't raced in and changed lots but he has improved the general ambition of the school – and the food is much better,' said a parent.

A lot has been going on behind the scenes – he has reorganised the senior leadership team and now has a team of nine, some new recruits and some from within the school, and in his second year, about 20 per cent of staff are new. He has appointed a deputy head (academic) and introduced a system of target minimum grades which, once set, are not allowed to go down, as well as peer reviews and lots of scrutiny. He says this gave teachers a shock to start with but he has encountered surprisingly little resistance, and teachers say that they feel listened to. He will walk into lessons unannounced and feels it is important to be seen to be interested, and there is a sense of co-operation between teaching staff and the senior management team. He is raising the profile of the school and has upped the marketing, and says that 'while humility is important, it does not have to apply to the way we market the school'. 'He is spreading the net a lot wider,' said a parent. 'Previously the school used to rely on word of mouth.' 'The school is much more efficient and there is more of a buzz about the place,' said another.

Entrance: Pupils come from a range of local prep schools as well as Catholic prep schools in London.

Most join in years 7 or 9 or for sixth form, with a few places available in years 8 and 10. Eleven-plus assessment tests at Worth in January year of entry – online English, maths and non-verbal reasoning – and informal interviews and small group tasks plus report from current school. Overseas pupils can sit the tests in their home country.

Thirteen-plus entry via the common pre-test plus assessment day with informal interview and group tasks in the spring of year 7. Common Entrance is for setting purposes only.

Some international pupils join in year 11 for one-year pre-IB course leading on to full IB diploma in sixth form. About 25 join sixth form – reports, references and interviews plus at least six GCSEs at grade 6+.

Exit: A handful leave after GCSEs, usually to go to sixth form colleges. Most popular universities are UCL, KCL, Durham, Warwick, Nottingham, Bristol, Southampton, Loughborough, Lancaster and Exeter with a wide range of subjects. One to Oxbridge in 2021 – to study medicine. Sometimes a few to US universities – school can help with applications but pupils often get outside tuition for SAT exams. Happy to look at alternatives if pupils not keen on university. A handful to art and drama school each year.

Latest results: In 2021, 59 per cent 9-7 at GCSE; 58 per cent A*/A at A level (80 per cent A*-B). Average IB score 36. In 2019 (the last year when exams took place), 50 per cent 9-7 at GCSE; 28 per cent A*/A at A level (66 per cent A*-B).

Teaching and learning: The school's fairly broad intake is reflected in the results. The headmaster insists that the school is not becoming more selective, but as more clever children apply there are more to choose from. About 25 per cent do the IB, which is popular with the Europeans – average point score was 35 in 2019. Most teachers teach both. Good range of subjects offered at IB including German and Italian at AI, psychology, philosophy, music, theatre and visual arts. Offers 24 subjects at A level, including business studies, psychology, politics, DT and photography. Those doing A levels also take the EPQ. There can be as few as three pupils in the IB classes and about 19 in the average English GCSE class.

All juniors learn Latin, which can be dropped in year 9. All year 9 pupils have lessons in Christian living, and all have to take an RS GCSE. French, Spanish and German offered as part of the curriculum and Italian, Polish, Russian and Mandarin may be available via private tuition, but depends on the availability of a tutor. Native or near native speakers of French and Spanish can take the GCSE at end of year 10. Forest school programme.

Rugby is the main winter sport for boys. The school still basking in the glory of Tom Mitchell's silver medal at Rio as captain of the GB rugby VIIs

Plenty to keep the more academic on their toes with a range of academic societies including medical, philosophy and debating as well as challenge workshops and lectures. Careers advice much improved but still a 'work in progress'. Well stocked careers library and useful 'how to apply to university' guide and annual careers fair. Old Worthians very helpful with work experience and shadowing and offer careers lectures and talks. Year 13 pupils offered a course in interview technique.

Library with a large study area and IT suite is open seven days a week and before and after school. Librarian and assistant on hand to help with research skills.

Learning support and SEN: Learning support provided by a small team of specialist teachers, mainly for mild difficulties and study skills, and taught either in small groups or one-to-one including in the sixth form if needed. EAL provision for about 40 pupils either in group or individual lessons, some only for technical language. Intensive tuition sometimes a condition of entry. EAL pupils also taught British traditions, life and culture. All those without a recognised English qualification have to take IELTS exam required for entry to British universities. Pre-IB course available for overseas students not ready for the full diploma.

The arts and extracurricular: Very busy music department based in the performing arts centre with a recital room, teaching room and practice rooms and a suite of Mac computers – about half learn an instrument or have singing lessons and the abbey choir performs at Thursday worship and Sunday mass. 'There is always something musical going on,' said a pupil – regular instrumental and choral concerts and the very noisy and keenly contested annual house music competition as well as Battle of the Bands and Worth Unplugged. Students encouraged to form their own groups and soundproof rock room is available for band practice. Two former pupils currently reading music at Oxford, one with an organ scholarship and another, who is in the Sistine Chapel choir, arranged for the Worth choir to sing alongside them at a papal mass.

Lively drama in superbly equipped theatre and other venues around the school. Every year group has the opportunity to be part of a play, either acting or behind the scenes, and pupils can learn the technical aspects from the full-time theatre technician, as well as costumes and make-up.

New art school opened in 2016 – spread over two floors with junior and senior art rooms, photography studios and darkroom, ICT and research facilities and a stunning gallery and light-filled exhibition space with some pretty impressive artwork on show – drawing a particular strength as well as sculpture and large-scale installations. Open-door policy so students can come in whenever they want. All year 9s have to have a go at DT and photography, DT is a new GCSE subject and both are available at A level.

Huge array of afternoon and evening activities, ranging from the usual cooking, drama and sport to Minecraft and code breaking, scuba diving, pedal cart design and street and modern dance. Arabic club assisted by two Syrian refugees; the African Science club produced materials which were taken out by the school group visiting Irundu in Uganda. Polo offered at a local club and riding, as part of the equestrian club, at a nearby yard, where you can also keep your own horse, and school has fielded its first equestrian team. About 10 pupils per year take part in Model United Nations and Young Enterprise. The Wednesday community service programme can be linked to the CAS element of the IB and to the DofE – about 30 achieve gold each year. 'The headmaster has encouraged more uptake in activities so children have much less time for hanging around,' said a parent.

Sport: Sport compulsory in lower years with most continuing into sixth form – sixth formers have to do four hours' exercise a week as well as activities. Many of the coaches have played at professional level including the head of cricket who was a first-class player. Huge investment in girls' games which, until recently, were considered the poor relation – hockey now coached by a women's premier league player (who also teaches biology) and girls often train with the East Grinstead hockey club. Rugby still the major winter sport for the boys and school fields 12 teams, which means keen players of varying talents can play in matches. Boys' hockey has also been introduced. Huge range of facilities including squash courts, a golf course, floodlit Astro, two fitness suites, a couple of gyms and a fencing salle but no swimming pool – keen swimmers train at the local sports centre. The school still basking in the glory of Tom Mitchell's silver medal at Rio as captain of the GB rugby VIIs.

Boarding: About 55 per cent of pupils are boarders. They are allowed home most Saturday nights, but about half the boarders are in most weekends. 'I am surprised how many stay in,' said a parent. 'We only live 10 minutes from the school but the children like to board as they have so much more fun.' Flexi-boarding an option for boys in the first two years only; girls board from year 9 upwards. Seven boarding houses with space for 60 boarders each – all have their own character and each is a home from home within the school. Many of the houseparents have young children which adds to the family atmosphere. The younger pupils share rooms but most sixth formers have their own study bedrooms and the lucky ones have ensuite bathrooms. Increasing number of girl boarders: they have moved to a larger house where everyone in years 11-13 has their own room with ensuite bathroom, whilst the younger ones share. The upper sixth have traditionally had their own house, but now stay in the same mixed age house all the way through.

About half the boarders are in most weekends. 'I am surprised how many stay in,' said a parent. 'We only live 10 minutes from the school but our children like to board'

Cinema and theatre trips as well as in-house socials and film nights held on Saturday evenings and an outing offered every Sunday, anything from paintballing, bowling or a shopping trip to a visit to the Tower of London, and there is supervised access to the school sporting facilities and fitness suite.

Ethos and heritage: Founded in the 1930s when Downside Abbey bought the Paddockhurst estate from Lord Cowdray and founded Worth Abbey and an adjoining prep school. Worth broke away from Downside in 1959 and by the mid-1960s the prep school had morphed into a senior school. The first day pupils arrived in the 1990s and the first girls were admitted into the sixth form in 2008 with the school becoming co-ed throughout in 2012. Although the abbey still owns the buildings, the school is now a separate charity with an independent board of governors and a lay chairman. The original sandstone Victorian house, together with a mock Tudor model farm and whimsical clock tower, was built for Robert Whitehead, the developer of the first rocket-propelled torpedo. Set in 500 acres of farm and parkland and approached via ornate iron gates and a long sweeping drive, it must be one of the most impressive approaches to a school – and it is only seven miles from Gatwick

Airport and 30 from London. It still has the feeling of a grand country house with wood panelling and a faint scent of beeswax polish.

Ten houses, some in the main house, some in the old farm buildings and the more modern ones dotted around the grounds. All have a common room for each year group, a small kitchen, a computer room and library. New sixth form centre and library. Rectory has been given a facelift, as have the school menus. The remarkable flying saucer shaped chapel designed by Francis Pollen and opened in 1974, with new pews designed by the Thomas Heatherwick Studios, is central to the school: whole-school worship held once a week and a mass every Sunday.

About 60 per cent of the children are Catholic and 'there is quite a lot of religion,' said a mother, 'but the ethos is very inclusive and the children accept it as part of the school. It makes them think of other people and that there is more to life than who has the best mobile phone.'

Younger pupils wear uniform, sixth form boys and girls a matching suit and academic staff wear gowns.

Very much a boarding school which takes day pupils, and despite there being more than 40 per cent day pupils, the headmaster is determined to keep it this way – the day pupils are involved in all aspects of school life and activities and have to attend Saturday morning lessons and play in matches if they are in a team. A network of school buses brings pupils from as far afield as Guildford and Tunbridge Wells.

Remarkable flying saucer shaped chapel designed by Francis Pollen and opened in 1974, with new pews designed by Thomas Heatherwick Studios, is central to the school

Strong ethos of service and everyone expected to undertake some community work, culminating in Worth in the Community Day at the end of the summer term – anything from helping in primary schools, gardening for old people and work in local homeless hostel to drama productions and concerts in local care homes. Pupils encouraged to take on challenges and each year a small group attempts the cross-Channel swim; five have made it so far.

Well-known old Worthians include actor Robert Bathurst, art dealer Philip Mould, comedian/actor Harry Enfield, England rugby player Nick Walshe, racing driver Henry Surtees, after whom the pupils' café is named, and Tom Mitchell, who captained the silver medal winning GB rugby VIIs team at Rio. As the girls come through, we expect to see their names up in lights as well.

Pastoral care, inclusivity and discipline: 'Pupils are very well cared for here,' says the headmaster. 'We don't tolerate drugs, alcohol or bullying,' and the school runs a programme of lectures and seminars on the dangers of drug and alcohol abuse. Every house has a houseparent and deputy, there are house-based tutor groups which meet at least twice a week and every house has a chaplain. The school is small enough for everyone to know each other, and tutors and houseparents know pupils well and spot problems early on – it is hard to slip through the net here. Counsellor in three days a week – busy but manageable. The chaplaincy sits at the centre of the school and has a mixed team of monks, teachers and young Catholics known as the Forerunners, plus a part-time Anglican chaplain. 'The monks are very special; they are always around but quite low key,' said a pupil, 'and you can call in at the chaplaincy whenever you want – and they often have cake.' The chaplaincy promotes pilgrimage and service and organises trips to Lourdes, Camino de Santiago, and the Taize community in France during the holidays, and everyone is expected to go on a retreat. Annual trip to Worth Abbey's charitable outpost in Peru which runs children's homes in the Andes.

House and school prefects act as mentors to younger pupils. 'The seniors are so nice to the juniors and there is good mixing between year groups, especially through the societies,' said a parent. Everything you need to know can be found in the school magazine Worth Knowing; 'I could not resist the pun,' says the headmaster.

Pupils and parents: Most day children live within an hour of the school and boarders mostly from London and the home counties. About 20 per cent from abroad, mainly from Catholic countries of Europe and South America with a dozen or so from Asia. The school is improving integration between IB (mainly foreign) and A level students, who now have mixed tutorial groups. Quite a broad spectrum of parents but a large number of prosperous City workers, often with both parents commuting. Strong Catholic ethos, but families from many different religions who like the sense of community and responsibility to the wider world, and don't feel religion is being imposed on their children.

Active friends' group gives parents a sense of belonging: 'You can get as involved as you want – there are a lot of social events and the school is generous with its hospitality, which can lead to the development of a Worth Girth,' said one parent. The school likes to involve the whole family via annual parents' meetings and seminars and family mass as well as the parent portal. Although only about a third of the pupils are girls – 40 per cent in some years, and school plans to achieve this throughout – they more than make up for it in energy and ambition and 'keep the boys on their toes,' said a parent. We were pleased to hear that International Women's Day is celebrated.

Former pupils tend to stay in touch and the strong sense of being part of a community carries on afterwards – a blend of confidence and humility without the public school swagger.

Money matters: Academic, art, drama, music and sports scholarships offered, plus exhibitions. Max award of 40 per cent goes to the top scholar in each category and other scholars may receive 20-30 per cent – additional means-tested bursary can take this up to 50 per cent of fees. St Benedict's scholarship of up to 100 per cent of fees for local children from families who are in full communion with local church but can't afford fees – a child must be capable of achieving a scholarship in one of the categories.

The last word: This school has everything going for it – beautiful setting and only 30 miles from London, good sport, music and art and improving academic performance, and an ambitious and energetic headmaster.

Yehudi Menuhin School

80

Stoke d'Abernon, Cobham, Surrey KT11 3QQ

01932 864739 | reception@yehudimenuhinschool.co.uk | www.menuhinschool.co.uk

Ages: 8–19

Pupils: 80; sixth form: 39; Boarders: 69 full

Fees: Day £43,111; Boarding £44,252 pa for those not on music and dance scheme

Head: Since April 2020, Ben Gudgeon, previously deputy head pastoral at Sherborne Girls'. Mr Gudgeon read music and French at Bristol University and at the Sorbonne. Following this he undertook graduate studies in vocal performance, conducting and piano in the USA, where he also taught undergraduate music theory and piano. Before turning to teaching, Ben spent 10 years as a freelance musician, working as a tenor lay-clerk, animateur, accompanist, musical director and jazz pianist. Prior to his current role, he was head of the faculty of performing arts at Churcher's College, and then director of music at Dauntsey's School. Married to Melissa, a teacher of religious studies, the couple have a 6-year-old son.

Entrance: No set entry point. The process is long and thorough: preliminary audition, then main audition, then a three-day residential assessment during which they take part in all aspects of school life including instrumental lessons, academic lessons and boarding. Children have to be robust. A rejected recent candidate played incredibly but wasn't ready socially. Academic ability not important.

Students who join the school in the sixth form must stay on for year 14, continuing with their instrumental tuition plus academic music and possibly another AS. This could be seen as another example of the school's determination to control its end product, but the year 14 students we met were positive about the experience, and felt it to be of benefit to their musical development.

A child must join before their 17th birthday, but otherwise a student's age isn't taken into account and the year groups aren't even. School won't admit into year 11, but happy for students to repeat a year and go into year 10.

Exit: The overwhelming majority to music conservatoires around the world: at this rarefied level, they choose the teacher with whom they want to study and apply to the institution where that teacher is based. Destinations include Royal College of Music and Guildhall School of Music & Drama. In 2021, overseas destinations included Hanns Eisler Musikschule in Berlin, New England Conservatory and Universitat der Kunste in Vienna and in Berlin. Occasionally a student wishing to pursue broader academic options will leave at 16.

Latest results: In 2021, 71 per cent 9-7 at GCSE: 53 per cent A*/A at A level (71 per cent A*-B). In 2019 (the last year when exams took place), 54 per cent 9-7 at GCSE; 62 per cent A*/A at A level.

Teaching and learning: 'It's not the best, but it's okay,' was how one student described the academic provision. Results are certainly more than okay. No-one is here for the academics, but that said, the ability profile here is above the national average, and students want to do well on all fronts.

Music is the school's raison d'être, and at least half of each day is devoted to it. Pupils receive two one-hour lessons per week on their principal instrument

Most students take seven GCSEs from a narrow range of subjects: music of course, then maths, English, single or double science, history and German, the school's main language because conservatoires in Germany and Austria are popular leavers' destinations here. Other languages are also taught when the need is there, and Russian, Japanese, Turkish, Mandarin have all been offered. At A level everyone takes music, and then chooses one or two further options from English, history, biology, chemistry, maths, further maths and German. No physics, because the low demand makes it hard to justify employing someone to teach it. 'That's a tricky one for us, and we'd love to be able to offer it.' Art taught throughout the school and some lovely work on show, but not usually taken as an examined subject. 'I wish there were more options,' was a concern voiced by one student and echoed by others. But the school's academic music programme, a longstanding jewel in the YMS crown, was highly praised by everyone. 'It's incredible!' 'Amazing!' 'Inspiring!' 'Harder than at Juilliard!' were typical comments.

Impossible to build year groups as such, because of very small numbers. Instead, learning is organised in four groups based on key stages. D group is made up of pupils in years 3-6, C group of those in years 7-9, B group years 10-11, and A group years 12-14. Classes are very small, and all students get a high degree of individual attention.

Learning support and SEN: No SEN teacher, but the school's few dyslexic pupils receive ongoing support from the regular staff and teaching assistants; one-to-one tutorials where necessary. Strong EAL support, with students who need it given regular lessons with dedicated EAL teacher. 'I couldn't speak English very well when I came,' one student told us, 'and the school has really helped me.'

The arts and extracurricular: Music is, of course, the school's raison d'être, and at least half of each day is devoted to it. Everyone has a daily practice target to meet, and it's perfectly usual for the older students to do four or more hours a day. Younger students do less and their practice sessions are supervised. Pupils receive two one-hour lessons per week on their principal instrument, and half an hour on their second study, and everyone learns composition. There are also courses in classical improvisation, choral singing, aural training and general music studies. The result is a landscape of really stellar music-making in which the students live and grow. The orchestra is stunning, and chamber music is wonderful. Huge programme of concerts, including twice-weekly ones at the school given in the beautiful Yehudi Menuhin Hall, all blond wood and gleaming Steinways, and dozens across the UK and abroad. The three pupils we saw in concert had excellent posture, were compellingly confident on the platform, and gave virtuoso performances of great beauty and taste.

Art is much loved and drama has always flourished at the school: shows are staged in the Square Room, and a recent production of The Tempest was set quirkily in a boarding school. Plenty of trips to concerts, theatres, art galleries, museums, etc. DofE scheme.

Sport: Pupils have two hours of timetabled sport per week, chosen from a range of swimming (in the school's own indoor pool), football, PE, badminton, tennis, cross-country running and dance. Yoga is optional but encouraged, and an Alexander technique teacher is always available for those who want or need to see her. Annual football fixture with the Purcell School for Young Musicians in Hertfordshire. The latter usually win, it has to be said, perhaps because they number brass players and percussionists among them who tend to come up beefier.

Boarding: Boarding has been intrinsic to the school's ethos since its inception. The tiny number of 'day boarders' are in school from 8am until 6.30pm and are regarded as boarding pupils who sleep at home. The youngest students are weekly boarders and can go home at 4pm on Fridays. The rest stay on for Saturday morning school, after which they can go home if they choose, although many of them come from too far away for this to be possible.

The girls and the youngest boys live in Music House in quarters that we thought well-appointed and attractive. Students are grouped in 'pods' of broadly similar ages; same-age room mates can't be guaranteed because numbers are so small. Younger pupils share two or three to a room, older ones may get an ensuite to themselves. Pianos everywhere – Debussy's L'Isle Joyeuse drifted out dreamily from under the door of one room as we passed – and practice sessions are timetabled throughout the day. We'd heard reports of students practising themselves into a decline, but the house staff and students we spoke to denied this. 'We patrol the corridors and we do stop students over-practising,' said the housemistress, 'but they learn common sense.' 'It's very busy here during the day, and we want to sleep,' agreed a soignée young violinist.

The boys live in Harris House, which has a brand new extension providing seven ensuite rooms and a kitchen for student use. Like Music House, it was clean, orderly, cosy and dotted with pianos. We liked the wall of clocks showing the current time in different countries around the world – 'We have pupils from every time-zone and it was a way of making them feel at home,' explained the housemaster.

As a rule, boarders have to be at least 9, but the school conceded that this wasn't rigid, and they have taken children as young as 8; we heard from one mother for whom this hadn't worked, possibly because children of that age are the exception here rather than the rule.

Ethos and heritage: Founded in 1963 by Yehudi Menuhin to give musically gifted children the chance to develop their potential to the full through a sympathetic curriculum, enhanced practice opportunities and superlative teaching in an immersive environment. Initially only for pianists, violinists and cellists, the portfolio has since been expanded to include double-bass players and guitarists. The YMS approach has had its detractors and historically the school has known darker times, but some truly world-class musicians have come out of the place, although 'it's not the purpose of this school to produce lots of little Yehudi Menuhins'. Tiger mums, please take note.

Beautiful Victorian mansion setting in Surrey village suggests peace and harmony. Once inside, the feel is a curious mix of very relaxed and rigidly controlling. There's no uniform, the dress code is informal, and staff and pupils are on first-name terms. But as a seasoned schools reviewer, it was clear to us as we went round that this school doesn't like criticism, or what it perceives as criticism, and that it keeps a tighter grip on the way its pupils make music than the other specialist music schools. Unlike Purcell, Chetham's and Wells students, those at YMS can't choose to continue on programmes at Saturday junior conservatoires, for instance (indeed, the school's Saturday morning programme would make this impossible). The only exception is the double-bass players, whose teacher also teaches at RCM junior department. And despite a packed calendar of performance opportunities, the system by which pupils are chosen for the most sought-after of these is a closed one (at other music schools it's often done by audition), and several pupils told us that they felt consistently excluded. 'They choose the students who are a safe bet,' said one, a remark which had everyone nodding vigorously, and others said, surprisingly, that in the time they'd been at the school they'd had hardly any chance to perform chamber music. 'We have to give pupils the opportunities that are right for them,' was the school's response. 'If you have a high-profile concert, you have to put the people in who will pull it off. It's not always easy to be fair on paper.'

A wall of clocks showed the current time in different countries around the world – 'We have pupils from every time-zone so it was a way of making them feel at home'

However, students were adamant that the atmosphere between them all was supportive, and not destructively competitive. 'There's actually not much competition; I've never felt it here,' was a comment that everyone agreed with, and their relish for the musical experience here was unstinting. 'It's the best you can get for the age we're at'; 'It really prepares you for music college'; 'They are such good teachers!'; 'My violin teacher is like a mother to me'; 'For practice, it's so much easier to be here, everything is so close' – etc.

No parents' association. School's reason for this is that parents come from too huge a radius for such a thing to work. Ex-parents told us that they had felt kept at arm's length, with one even telling us that they never felt welcome. But the only current parents to contact us wrote, 'Headteacher and indeed other teachers are approachable and welcoming even though they must be under pressure also.'

Alumni include Nigel Kennedy, Tasmin Little, Nicola Benedetti, Kathryn Stott, Melvyn Tan and Colin Carr.

Pastoral care, inclusivity and discipline: Yehudi Menuhin believed in the importance of a homely, family atmosphere in his school, and we saw children playing contentedly in the school's leafy grounds, cheering on their friends in the lunchtime concert, and generally appearing happy and at ease. Students attested to the kindness of the staff. 'The school's been really patient with me,' said one, philosophically. 'When I first came, I wasn't a well-behaved child. Anywhere else would have asked me to leave.' In this small, artistically-driven community, the kind of misbehaviour most schools have to deal with is rare. Pupils have worked hard for their place here and want to keep it.

Staff-to-student ratio is low, and there are regular weekly meetings about pastoral issues. 'If someone's falling through the gaps, it's picked up,' affirmed housemaster. However, all the staff we spoke to put much emphasis on pupils 'self-managing': 'There's a lot of autonomy here'; 'They just get on with it'; 'They're surprisingly mature'; and we did wonder if this sometimes meant pupils were left to flounder. The school emphatically denied this – 'I have never taught in a school which discusses, and, yes, cares for pupils at this level.' The students themselves offered slightly ambiguous observations, such as, 'We do a lot of our stuff on our own in this kind of school'; 'The older ones usually take care of the younger ones'; 'The boarding staff are doing the best job they can.' However, inspection reports have consistently rated the school's pastoral care as excellent, and the only parents to respond to our appeal for feedback wrote, 'Pastoral care is very important to us since we live far away but have been happy with the attention so far in that area.' We could not find any other parents of current students who wanted to talk to us, although we were contacted by parents whose experience of the school had been negative and who had taken their children away. New medical centre since 2021.

Pupils and parents: Just over half are from the UK (although this figure includes a few international families who have relocated so that their child can attend the school), the rest from overseas. Very broad range of backgrounds and nationalities makes for a truly cosmopolitan school community: students currently hail from the UK, Ireland, France, Germany, Switzerland, Spain, Poland, Bulgaria, Bosnia-Herzegovina, Serbia, Turkey, Morocco, Tunisia, China, Taiwan, South Korea, Singapore, Japan, Thailand, Brazil and Mexico. It's a musical hothouse and has its fair share of eccentrics, but it's impossible not to be won over by the results. The young people we met were all really lovely: articulate, thoughtful, intelligent, personable, good-mannered and good fun.

Money matters: Inevitably one of the most expensive boarding schools in the country, given all the top-calibre specialist tuition, but hardly anyone pays full fees. Families who have been continually resident in the UK for at least two years receive means-tested funding from the government's Music and Dance Scheme. For those ineligible for the scheme, the school has its own bursary fund: it has a good endowment, and fundraising is ongoing. Where they can, they match what the Music and Dance Scheme would pay.

The last word: This is as unusual a school experience as it's possible to get, and one that parents need to choose with their eyes wide open. Don't send your highly academic teen here and then complain that they can't do triple science. Don't put your 8-year-old here if you want them to have lots of friends the same age. Try not to send your child here in the secret hope that they'll be the next Fritz Kreisler. But if the music offered here is what your child wants with all their being, and you believe that they couldn't be as happy anywhere else as they could be here, go for it.

East of England

Bedfordshire
Cambridgeshire
Essex
Hertfordshire
Norfolk
Suffolk

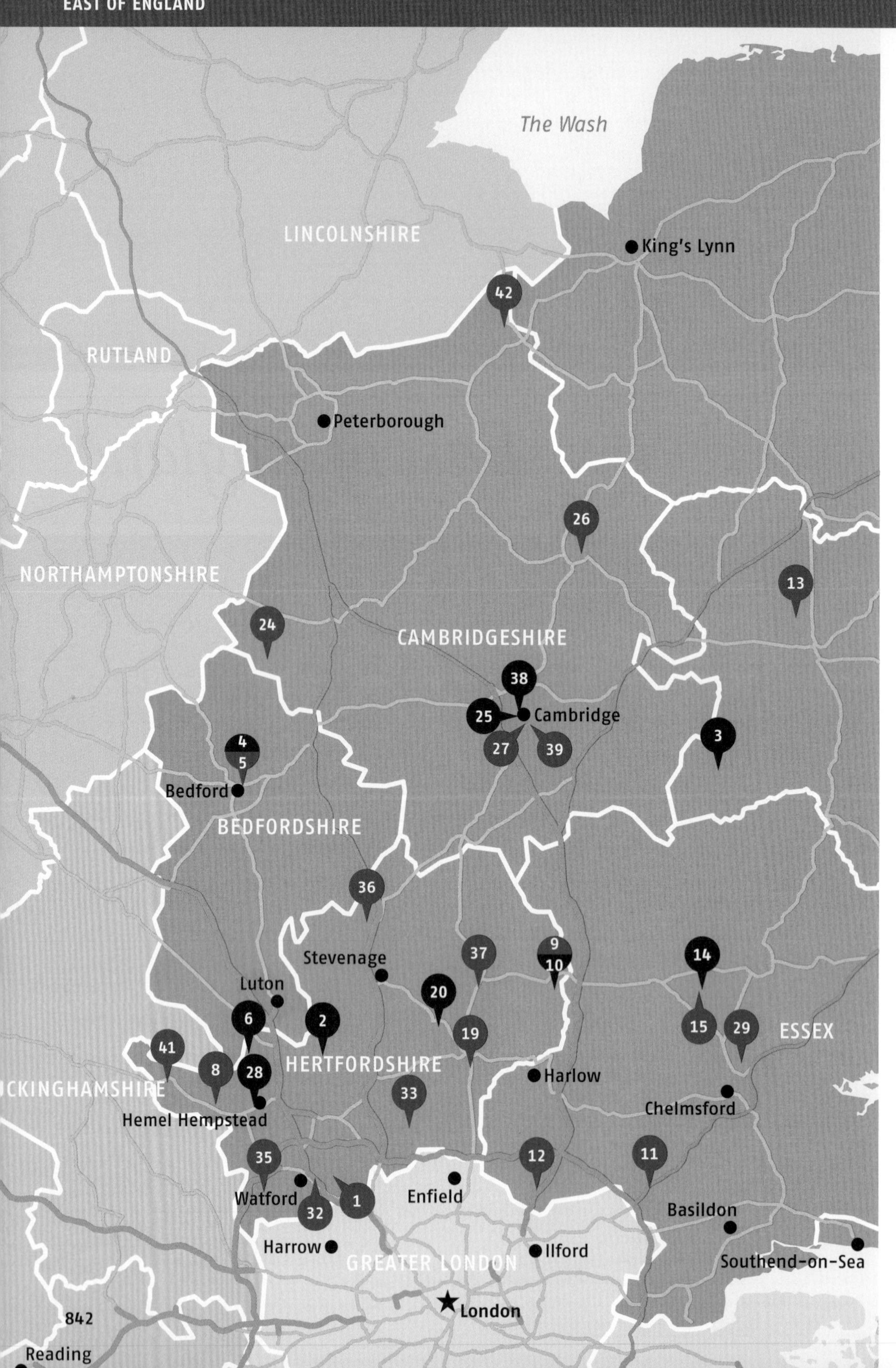
The Wash
LINCOLNSHIRE
King's Lynn
42
RUTLAND
Peterborough
26
NORTHAMPTONSHIRE
13
24
CAMBRIDGESHIRE
38
25
Cambridge
27
39
3
4
5
Bedford
BEDFORDSHIRE
36
Stevenage
37
9
10
14
Luton
20
6
2
19
15
29
ESSEX
41
8
28
HERTFORDSHIRE
Harlow
CKINGHAMSHIRE
33
Chelmsford
Hemel Hempstead
35
12
11
Watford
1
Enfield
32
Basildon
Harrow
Ilford
Southend-on-Sea
GREATER LONDON
London
Reading

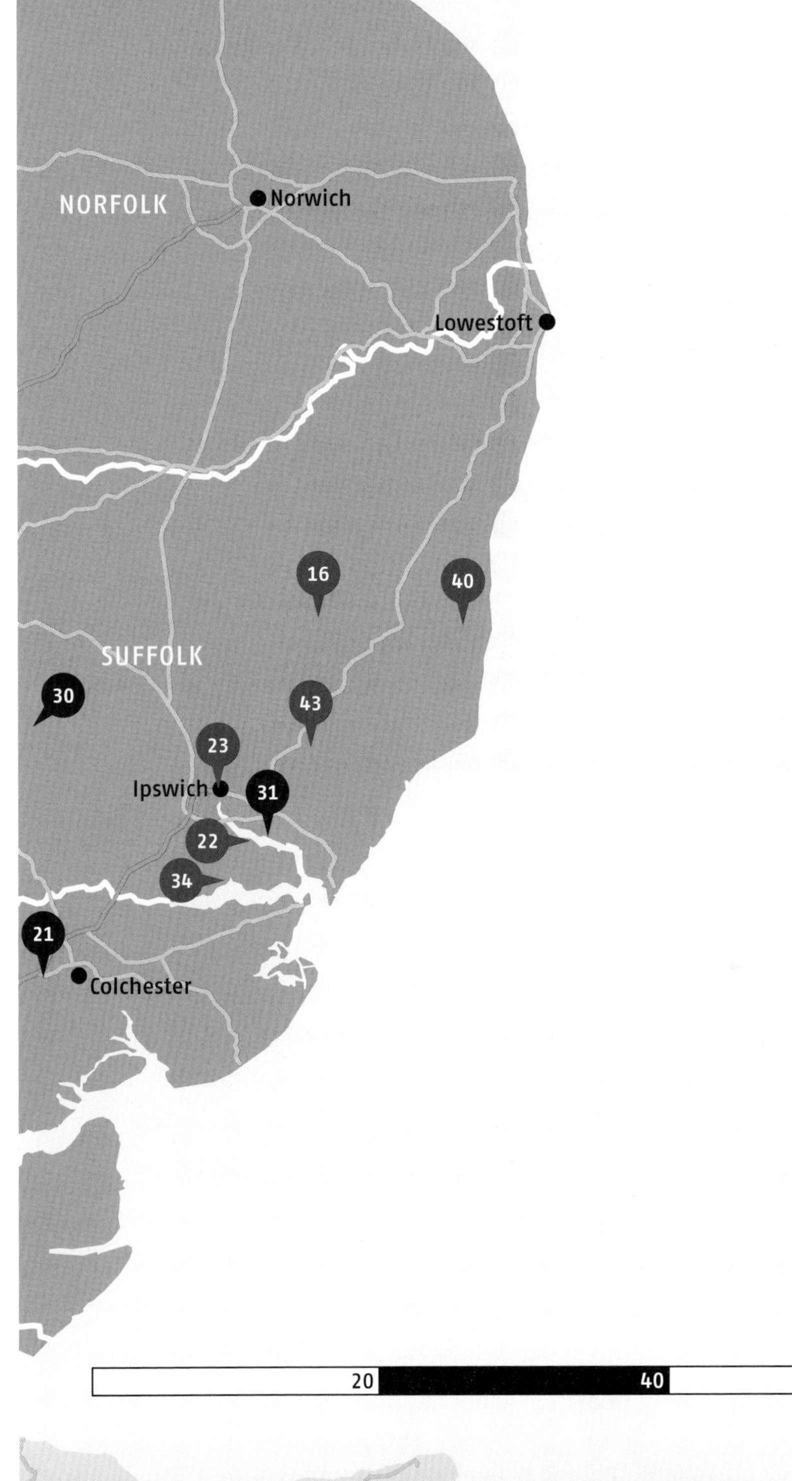
17
Holt
18
7
Cromer
NORFOLK
Norwich
Lowestoft
16
40
SUFFOLK
30
43
23
Ipswich
31
22
34
21
Colchester
20
40
60
Miles

EAST OF ENGLAND

Aldenham School

Elstree, Borehamwood, Hertfordshire WD6 3AJ

01923 858122 | admissions@aldenham.com | www.aldenham.com

Ages: 11-18

Pupils: 645; sixth form: 173; Boarders: 17 full, 126 weekly/flexi

Fees: Day: £17,841 – £23,964; Boarding: £35,346 pa

Headmaster: Since 2006, Mr James Fowler MA PGCE (50s). Educated at Merchant Taylors' School, Northwood and New College, Oxford where he was a choral scholar. Previously head of sixth form at Brentwood School and deputy head at Highgate. Now head of the whole Aldenham Foundation (which includes Aldenham Prep School and St Hilda's Bushey), he has moved into a more CEO type role (no longer teaching, for example) but it is still a school that takes its cultural tone from the top and he permeates every facet of school with his relaxed charisma and understanding of what makes parents and pupils tick. Unusually, interviews every candidate with their parents before admission. Is he interviewing the parents as well as the child, we asked? 'Of course,' he says. 'I spend a lot of time helping people understand what we are and are not.' And it's to this level of mutual soul searching that he attributes the happy, enthusiastic nature of his cohort in evidence all over the school, almost all of whom he knows not just by name but all about them – 'their families, what subjects they're doing, what motivates them and their interests,' said parent. 'He is a phenomenal head and I can't imagine a better one,' said another, though she will have to as he is retiring in summer 2022. 'We'll miss him – he's at every event and I've never met a single parent that doesn't like him,' remarked one parent, with more than a hint of emotion in her voice.

Definitely not a head chasing glory in the league tables, and one totally at ease with this status – a breath of fresh air in the ferociously competitive north London landscape. Keen to provide a totally different experience to his urban competitors and single-mindedly focused on school providing 'the best possible pathways' for each student, regardless of academic prowess – 'We celebrate successful entry to art school in the same way as entry to Oxbridge.' Trust in the model has, it seems, increased, with school having witnessed a steep hike in applications from the more academically able in recent years.

Lives on site with wife, with whom he has two adult sons. A sailing, skiing and golf man, he also has a penchant for classical music and has dabbled in conducting over the years.

Entrance: Main entry point now at 11+, when there are four applicants for each of the 85 places available, with between 15 and 20 of these taken by children coming up from on-site prep school and the rest made up of children joining from the state sector (up to half) and local 11+ preps (over 130 schools in total). About a third are girls. Another 20 to 25 join in year 9, when there are three applications for every place, from a vast array of preps, notably Lochinver House, Orley Farm, St Martin's, St John's, York House, Lockers Park and further afield The Beacon, The Hall and Davenies. Applicants at 11+ take papers in maths, English and reasoning with the addition of science and a language at 13+.

Late arrivals come from other, more pressured, local schools – not always because they can't cut the mustard but mainly because they are looking for a school that's about more than exam results. Around 30 places available in sixth form, when applicants need 6s (or 7s in the case of maths, sciences and economics) in the subjects they want to study at A levels.

Exit: No clearing of the decks after GCSEs – this school commits to an 11-18 education, though around a quarter leaves to follow vocational courses or A levels elsewhere (mainly state schools or colleges) or to employment. A broad spectrum of destination universities reflects mixed academic intake, with about a third to Russell Group. Birmingham, Bristol, Cardiff, Durham, KCL, Leeds, Liverpool, Nottingham, UCL and Warwick all popular. Around a third do a STEM degree. A couple each year to art schools (often Central St Martins) and regular success with applications to top drama schools. One to Oxbridge and one medic in 2021.

Latest results: In 2021, 47 per cent 9-7 at GCSE; at A level, 54 per cent A*/A (73 per cent A*/B). In 2019 (the last year when exams took place), 30

per cent 9/7 at I/GCSE; 21 per cent A*/A at A level (49 per cent of A*-B).

Teaching and learning: Situated in the heart of UK's spiritual home of secondary academia (Habs, Merchant Taylors', North London Collegiate et al), Aldenham stands apart with its unpressurised vibe and mixed ability cohort. Perhaps not a destination for the single-minded scholar, though all pupils are strongly encouraged to hit their personal best and that includes those bright enough (of which there are more than ever) to get into Russell Group universities and occasionally Oxbridge. Bottom line is it's the journey that defines Aldenham rather than the destination.

'The reason we chose the school,' said a parent of the music department. Bands, orchestras and choirs galore are run by 'fantastic' and 'passionate' musicians

Nice balance of gender, age (average age 36) and ethnicity among the teachers who really buy into the school's ethos – you won't get the best teachers allocated the top sets here; it's often quite the opposite with the head of maths, for instance, insisting on taking bottom set maths in year 7 to give them the best start (there's also setting in sciences and English from year 9). Small class sizes of maximum 22 and often down to 10 in sixth form. French and Spanish taught in year 7, from which students elect one to take them through to GCSE from year 8. Latin and classical civilisation taught in year 7, with an option to continue in year 8, and a handful of the brightest take ancient Greek too. Ten (11 for the half that take triple science) GCSEs the norm with a broad range of subjects including drama (particularly popular), textiles and DT. Brighter students are also recruited into small study and discussion groups such as Les Philosophes with visiting speakers, including Anthony Grayling, enabling them to exchange ideas and broaden horizons. In sixth form, most choose three A levels from the usual traditional fare, with psychology, media studies, government and politics, and computing also on the menu. Parents and pupils appreciate extra revision lessons at lunchtimes, after school and even on Saturdays laid on in the run up to public exams. University conversations start in year 12, with a series of events including visiting professionals brought in to 'give insights' into the world of work. Pupils feel well supported and guided through uni application process.

Impressively comprehensive training for teachers in the pandemic – 'Teaching online is a world away to teaching in the classroom if it's done properly,' says head. 'Aldenhome', as it's affectionately become known, has continued to go from strength to strength during times of online schooling, with eg interhouse drama, music and sporting events all continuing.

Learning support and SEN: Like many mainstream schools that offer outstanding SEN provision, Aldenham has become something of a victim of its own success, having landed itself the (incorrect) reputation of having a specialism. In reality, around 10 per cent are on the register – mainly mild dyslexia, dyscalculia and ASD – who are catered for via one-to-one and group lessons by full-time SENCo who meets all children with their families before they join 'to both get a flavour of whether school can cope and work out best ways to support them'. Conditions rarely stand in the way of students reaching their potential here, with one such child recently heading off to Cambridge. Parents gush and gush about this department, with some having taken their children out of other schools where they felt 'desperate' only to find they 'thrived here.' 'They look at your child and think, what does this kid really need? How can we get her confidence up? How can we pinpoint the areas of need? She's gifted in this subject but struggling with certain aspects of others.' No TAs, which some parents griped about, 'but they are honest with you about what they can provide and you're never off the SENCo's radar.'

The arts and extracurricular: Two compulsory activities a week, ranging from bell ringing, horse riding and film club to a popular CCF, make for a long school day which for most ends at 5.30pm. This gives school a unique boarding atmosphere, even for those who do not take advantage of the marvellously flexible boarding on offer. Aldenham is 'synonymous with trips', according to pupils, who enthuse about the 'amazing experiences' they have had on CCF trips to Holland, language trips including a Spanish trip to Cuba, cricket tour to Barbados, geography to Iceland, choir to Rome and a three-week charity volunteering trip to Malawi. Lockdown, then, has taken its toll. 'Just before the first lockdown, we had students in three continents – Cape Town on a cricket and hockey tour, a junior ski trip in France and senior ski trip in USA – yet a month later we couldn't go to the end of the drive, and that has taken its toll,' admits head.

Outstanding art department, unanimously acclaimed by everyone from head to parents and pupils, with superb art cabin accommodating the bulging numbers electing to pursue art A level.

Fabulous work on display: huge canvasses, three-dimensional installations and sculpture with as much rigorous preparation and development of concepts on show as final works. Pupils say that head of art won't accept anything less than excellence and parents report offspring joining school 'unable to draw' and emerging with A grades. Dedicated textiles room also displays high-quality fashion design and DT labs are hives of industry, complete with 3D printers in motion.

'The reason we chose the school,' said a parent of the music department, which has bands, orchestras and choirs galore, run by 'fantastic' and 'passionate' musicians, according to pupils. As with sport, there are opportunities for musicians of all levels to participate, with pupils enthusing that the fiercely competitive annual house music event (compulsory participation for all) is one of the highlights of the year ('you can't get more than one ticket even if you beg, borrow and steal,' said parent). All year 7s offered opportunity of one term's free music lessons on the orchestral instrument of their choice, leading to many taking it up more seriously. Futuristic music technology equipment puts department very much in the 21st century.

Drama department drives excellence and pushes boundaries both on and off curriculum. School refreshingly veers away from the usual hackneyed shows and rarely produces musicals, mainly delivering productions of the Sophocles and Brechtian variety, oft performed in the purpose-built 150 seat theatre, but sometimes out in the grounds or as a promenade, which are 'mind blowingly good,' according to parents. 'One of my daughters has been in every play there is and the other loves getting stuck in back stage – it's West End standard stuff.' A handful of students are members of the National Youth Theatre, some take part in the Edinburgh Fringe and it's not unusual for one or two each year to head off to destinations including Central School of Speech and Drama or LAMDA.

Sport: In a setting that needs to be seen to be believed – over 110 acres encompassing woodland, playing fields plus full-sized Astro hockey pitch, tennis courts, dance studio, well-utilised weights room and an enormous sports hall (recently resurfaced) plus manicured cricket pitch that lies literally at the heart of the school ('the pavilion is one of my favourite spots,' says head) – sport is integral to life at Aldenham and thrives at all levels, from the most elite to the 'just for fun' ('You can have two left feet and they'll still include you,' said parent). It's football, hockey and cricket for the boys, no rugby, while girls focus on netball, hockey and rounders. School known for its footie prowess – U15s have been the independent schools national champions for two years running and the U13s would have played in the final in 2020, had it gone ahead. A handful of boys train with top academies and there are links with Southgate Hockey Club. 'What I like is that they think of centre, so if you're not good at the main sports, you can ski at Hemel or, if you're not sporty at all like my daughter, you can go to the gym.' Other options include zumba, archery, sailing, tennis, athletics, Eton fives, judo and climbing on its climbing wall. Some groans that they don't have enough numbers for a second netball team and about the lack of swimming pool (but school still manages to have among its cohort national swimming champions).

Boarding: Around 30 per cent of the school community (some two-thirds boys) participates in boarding life at some level – enough to lend it a 'proper' boarding ethos without any trace of 'them and us' between boarders and day pupils. Boarding starts in year 7 in a small co-educational junior boarding house with 25 beds. No full boarding at this stage, meaning that cohort tends to be exclusively UK based with vast majority never having boarded before. 'On day two, my daughter told me she wanted to try boarding and by day four she didn't want to come home – I hated the idea of it but it's really homely and they really do have so much fun,' said parent. Enough rules and regulations to reassure parents in the younger years, 'with things getting a bit more relaxed in year 9' when they move into one of the four main single-sex boarding houses – three for boys and one for girls. ' 'I think the students push the boundaries a bit at bedtimes, but they deal with it well,' said parent.

Most popular nights to board in sixth form are Tuesdays and Thursdays when the bar opens and pizza is served in the wonderful sixth form centre

Head keen that students 'experience boarding as part of their overall education', hence provides excellent flexibility with boarders able to stay from just one night to, for a minority of mainly older, overseas students (some 25 per cent of boarders), full time. Up to sixth form, majority are reasonably local though, with boarders heading home at weekends to homes in north London, Herts and Bucks. 'Terrific' live-in houseparents supervise their charges in spacious houses – not the most luxurious we've seen, but all recently renovated and functional (well-equipped kitchens and study spaces) and welcoming with plenty of nooks and crannies for down time and socialising. Boys dorm in fours until year 11 when they double up, with girls mostly in twos and threes then single rooms in sixth form.

Evenings see boarders participate in the clubs or activities of their choice, or gather in the art block, library, media suite or gym. Most popular nights to board in sixth form are Tuesdays and Thursdays when the bar opens and pizza is served in the wonderful sixth form centre. Sunday brunch is 'the best meal of the week', attended by most staff who live on site, plus their families, as well as weekend boarders, and whilst there are weekend outings, trips and activities on offer, quite often students, having had a long week and sports fixtures on Saturdays, just 'want to chill'.

Ethos and heritage: Founded by brewer, Richard Platt, in 1597 after Queen Elizabeth I granted him letters patent to build 'the Free Grammar School and Almshouses' at Aldenham for elementary children. The Brewers' Company then had a controlling interest in the school and links remain strong. Original Tudor buildings demolished in the 19th century to make place for two new schools – one providing an elementary education for the local population, the second a grammar school for fee-paying boarders. School now occupies a prime position in protected green belt, attracting pupils from affluent local villages like Radlett and Sarratt, London suburbs such as Edgware and Stanmore and increasingly north London, with parents attracted by the fabulous country campus, handy coach services and inclusive ethos.

Majority of families from a 20-mile radius. 'It's a really good community – everything from daily WhatsApp chatting to amazing balls and quiz nights,' said parent

Main school building is Hogwarts-esque Victorian gothic with gables, tower and turrets, with additions – some more appealing than others – from subsequent decades. We loved the fabulous sixth form centre – all white walls, squidgy sofas and sliding glass doors offering panoramic view of cricket pitch – complete with its own coffee shop and bar where years 12 and 13 can socialise, study and generally commune outside of school hours. A few tatty corners in other areas, but plenty of up-to-date Mac technology and a luxurious feeling of abundant space. Newest addition is the former prep school building, providing useful additional classrooms.

An extraordinary chapel (the largest consecrated building in Hertfordshire after St Albans Abbey) which can host entire school – and frequently does – lies across the road that bisects the school. Surprisingly welcoming, the Stanley Spencer altarpieces of yesteryear are but a part of school history now (sold to raise funds during the desperate 1990s) and an attractive ironwork cross and dove now dominates the altar. Despite the diverse religions of the school community (about 60 per cent Christian, 20 per cent Jewish and all other main religions represented), all attend chapel twice weekly to underscore the 'feeling of one community' that's so integral to the school. Beautiful panelled library complete with mezzanine level, spiral staircase and view of cricket pitch and miniature replica statue of old boy Alfred Gilbert's Eros. There's an annual run on the last day of term for those brave enough, from Eros in Piccadilly to the school's statue, just one of the many traditions that pupils say are 'a huge part of the school'.

Break times see pupils congregate en masse on the field with cross-year-group socialising in evidence everywhere ('we're like a family – everyone knows everyone,' said one happy pupil).

Pastoral care, inclusivity and discipline: Pastoral care is a USP, including throughout Covid when everything from after school meditation, chapel services and assemblies were heavily promoted – appreciated not just by students but parents too ('gives us a window we wouldn't usually get'). All students belong to a vertical house (day or boarding), with staff keeping a close eye on everyone's well-being. Good sign that many boarders we spoke to live locally and board 'because we love it'. Good teamwork between health centre, counsellor, chaplain and safeguarding team mean few things get missed. Over half of staff have mental health first aid training. LGBTQ+ and Black Lives Matter are discussed regularly and openly – in the case of the latter, black parents and students appreciated being asked their opinion about how school should respond ('thoughtfully and sensitively, not just jumping in with knee-jerk reaction'). Curriculum regularly reviewed from diversity perspective – black history is more than just a month here. The usual disciplinary issues but in the main very few incidents. Suspensions for major breaches of rules (eg boarders driving off campus) and exclusions for worse (a few youngsters were asked to leave recently due to drugs) but in the main little need to transgress as students given sufficient freedom to spread their wings.

Pupils and parents: Although not the most polished cohort we've ever seen, pupils without exception seem totally at ease with the school and are arguably one of the most sociable and understatedly confident bunches we've met. Quite possibly one of the happiest too, again making lockdown so much more than an inconvenience. Majority from a 20-mile radius, with two extra coach roots meaning that most can be transported without the need for parents to sit in traffic. Lots of busy, professional commuters and London parents attracted by the flexible boarding uniquely on offer here – as well as the atmosphere that they say gives their children 'space to breathe', both literally and metaphorically. Mixed financial demographic – plenty of first-time buyers and parents stretching themselves to afford Aldenham – with these children fitting comfortably in with those who can easily cover the fees. 'Really good community – everything from daily Whatsapp chatting to amazing balls and quiz nights,' said parent.

Overseas boarders tend to be in higher year groups. Of these, around 30 per cent from Germany, then handfuls from China, Hong Kong and ones and twos from elsewhere. All are well respected and well integrated – boarding pupils embrace and relish the diversity of their peers. Around 40 boarders stay in school at weekends.

Money matters: Scholarships at 11+ in music, sport and academic and 13+ in all those plus art and DT, with a maximum of 15 per cent off fees awarded. Means-tested bursaries available.

The last word: Head describes Aldenham as 'an extraordinary school for ordinary children' and we concur. An unpressurised environment such as this makes for some of the most contented pupils we have met, and self-motivated children can fare well academically too. If it's a rounded and happy child you're after, then Aldenham's definitely one to consider.

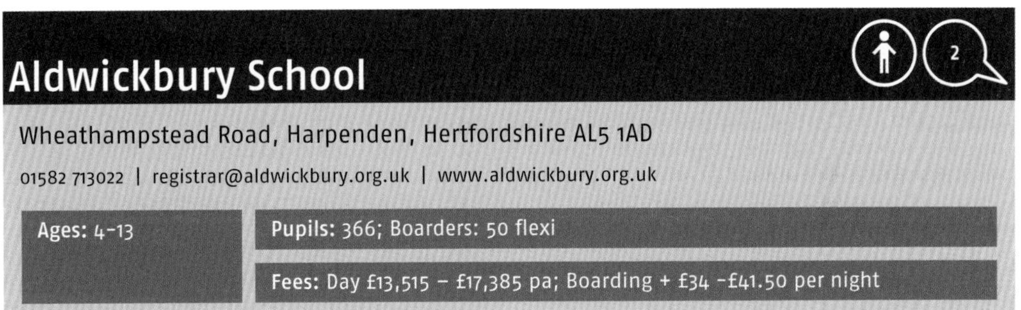

Aldwickbury School

Wheathampstead Road, Harpenden, Hertfordshire AL5 1AD

01582 713022 | registrar@aldwickbury.org.uk | www.aldwickbury.org.uk

Ages: 4–13

Pupils: 366; **Boarders:** 50 flexi

Fees: Day £13,515 – £17,385 pa; Boarding + £34 –£41.50 per night

Headmaster: Since September 2021, Paul Symes, previously senior deputy head at Belmont School (part of the Mill Hill Foundation). Attended East Bergholt High School, Colchester Sixth Form College and Brunel University (Borough Road). Started his teaching career at Isleworth and Syon School for boys, followed by various other secondary state schools in Suffolk teaching up to A level before moving to the independent prep sector in September 2010, returning to London as head of boys' games at Belmont where he progressed to senior deputy head.

Entrance: Boys join from a range of local nurseries in St Albans, Harpenden, Wheathampstead – staff go out and visit before joining to smooth the process. Twins are generally separated, following discussion with parents – Aldwickbury's reception classrooms are interconnected so twins can peek at each other for reassurance. Three-form entry, no more than 16 to a class. Head is happy with the roll of around 380 – 'we fit well on the site'. A few spaces at the bottom of the school but otherwise full. Non-selective at 4+ but boys joining higher up the school are invited in for an informal assessment (English, maths, reading – not a test) with relevant year group staff to ensure they can cope with the curriculum. Means-tested bursaries available; no scholarships. Boys' sisters often at Wheathampstead House, St Albans High School for Girls Prep, St Hilda's.

Exit: A handful of boys leave for state system at end of year 6 but – unlike many other preps – the intention is to reduce in numbers slightly for years 7 and 8 to allow for more individual focus and positions of responsibility; 'more elbow room,' says school. St Albans is a key year 9 destination – 'good local school which ticks lots of boxes for our pupils' – Bedford also popular. Others to Haileybury, Berkhamsted, Habs, Harrow and The Leys. Single numbers to Oundle, Aldenham, Uppingham, Merchant Taylors', St Christopher's, Stowe, Shrewsbury, Millfield, Oakham, Rushmore, Shiplake, Bishop's Stortford, Greshams, Brighton College, Culford, Dulwich College, Eton, Framlingham, Oratory, Westminster, Winchester and Worth. Most want day or the opportunity to grow into boarding. Majority of academic scholarship candidates aim for St Albans; music, art, drama and all-rounders an even spread. School invites in parents to discuss next steps; 'alternatives are politely suggested' to those aiming unrealistically high. One parent told us the school believes 'that if your son needs excessive coaching to get into a particular secondary school, then that probably isn't the right school for him – not a message that every parent in Harpenden wants to hear.'

Our view: Aldwickbury Mansion, a character Victorian house just a stone's throw up the hill from Harpenden's second high street in Southdown, became the school's home in 1948. Now surrounded by a collection of sympathetically designed more modern buildings as well as playing fields, an Astro and 25-metre indoor pool, this leafy 20-acre site makes for a friendly and well-functioning school campus of the ideal scale for prep school age children – big enough to stretch your legs in but small enough to know your way around. Planning application in for a new-build sports hall on-site.

'Sport' was the reply when we asked what was the best thing about school. Football, rugby, hockey, basketball in winter; cricket, athletics, tennis, swimming in summer

Pre-prep has its own little world – a self-contained, purpose-built base secured with a large, squeaky gate. Three classes of 12 to 14 per year in reception, years 1 and 2. Pre-prep day is 8.30am-3.15pm, though 3pm finish for reception. Wraparound care morning and afternoon. Head of pre-prep welcomes all in the morning and answers questions to nip any misunderstandings in the bud, and reception parents have their own parents' evenings. Exempt from early years curriculum, children go at their own pace, some on a play-based regime. Each class has a teacher and dedicated teaching assistant. Large classrooms well suited to the age of the children and with plenty of storage (teachers' delight). Much recent investment in the pre-prep outdoor learning environment and adventure playground with outdoor areas differentiated by age, stuffed with bikes, trikes etc for engaged play and fewer incidents. Little distinction in reception between learning time and playtime. Swimming from reception, all year round, plus drama and music taught by specialists. Instrumentalists on the rise from year 1, particularly piano and violin, though some take on cellos, guitars, drums; later woodwind and brass. French from year 1 with popular annual Languages Day, focusing on pupils' mother tongues. Year 2s use school art room, DT studio and library and have clubs for choir, recorders, drama, football, tennis, eco. Regular Celebrations of Learning showcase children's work for the admiration of parents and family.

Junior department for years 3 and 4 has a year per floor in three classrooms. Class teacher for all subjects, bar specialist ICT, art, DT, music and drama in dedicated rooms. 'They're taught to walk sensibly between lessons by the teacher,' explains school. 'Then in years 5 and 6 they know how to do it on their own and take all the relevant equipment with them.' Fifteen to 18 per class, which our guides judged just right – 'You don't want too many but enough that you can choose your friends.' Good point.

Subject classrooms for seniors (years 5 to 8). Tasters in Spanish and German added to the mix in year 5 and Latin from year 6. Individual needs met in mixed ability classes until end of year 5 and plenty of small group work; teaching assistants dotted around the timetable and gappers help with reading, as do year 8 boys who support year 5s and 6s through the Reading Lab programme (those who have benefited from help are often keenest to repay later). Setting and streaming introduced from year 6, with two or three classes and a scholarship class in year 8. SEN all in a day's work – full provision within the classroom and also one-to-one, ranging from a few weeks to constant. 'The right support helps them to flourish but we might find a passion as a trumpeter, or an artist, to give them self-esteem,' says school. Early discussions with parents of strugglers.

Clocktower clock recently stopped ticking and needed repair, so head seized the moment to refurb the upper floor of main school building to create a new music room, now hanging with computers for Mixcraft and traditional instruments. Whole of year 3 learn the violin and all in years 4 and 5 may try out a brass instrument with the aim of keeping up the flow of trumpeters and euphonium (really) players. Practice rooms well used for individual lessons with visiting peris. Ambitions of dynamic music teacher with choral background being realised – 14 music ensembles, from choir and orchestra to school rock and samba bands, some for all-comers, some auditioned. 'I don't expect them to be able to play

'Boarding is really fun – you can stay when you want,' grinning boarders told us. Superhero Night and Nerf Night always fully booked

a Mozart piano concerto when they leave here,' he says rationally, 'but I do want them to be able to tell me why they do or don't like it.'

DT studio well-equipped – strict rules re which year groups are entrusted with which tools (hacksaws from year 3). Art department on two floors – year 5s intently recreating Gaudi's mosaics when we visited – concentration etched on young faces. At least an hour of art on the timetable every week and popular art club. New kiln.

Hall named for a former headmaster with raked seating, the venue for assemblies for years 3 to 8 and chapel on Friday afternoons, school plays – this year the Wizard of Oz. Auditions open to all, and also opportunities for essential behind-the-scenes involvement. Well-used library stocked with 'every book you could possibly think of,' confirmed our guide sagely. Large dining hall – pre-prep eat lunch first, followed by years 3 and 4, and 5 to 8. Rotating menu, now with the popular introduction of soup in the winter. 'Breakfast and supper are the best' – unlimited eggs, bacon, sausages, toast for the largest of appetites.

'Sport' was the quick reply when our guides were asked the best thing about school. Football, rugby, hockey, basketball in winter; cricket, athletics, volleyball, tennis, swimming in summer. Specialist teaching twice weekly from year 1 and boys from year 3 up have a daily games lesson (what a lot of boys crave – clever). School ski teams and squads compete in English Schools events and around 90 boys involved in the school's ski programme. Fencing now major with 70 or 80 boys regularly en garde (old boy in national team). Some 12 to 15 teams from years 5 to 8 regularly represent the school in Wednesday fixtures. Everybody in years 3 and 4 plays for the school; more selective higher up but by the end of term all who want to have played. Boys not in teams may opt for photography, climbing or sailing. Cyclo-cross added recently. Two nights a week after supper in summer boys may play on the nine-hole par 3 course which surrounds the school.

Colours system recently overhauled – boys awarded Half, Full or Headmaster's Colours when they have earned enough Wheatsheafs, which are awarded for notable deeds in any areas of school life including sports, arts, academics and citizenship. Prize-giving in a marquee at the end of term kept under the hour – 'it's important that every boy in the school is there and that's as long as it is reasonable to expect the youngest to engage,' says school.

Huge choice of clubs and activities – 'busy boys are happy boys,' says school. Chess, tech club, general knowledge, debating, skiing and fencing top the bill. School makes full use of being on the capital's doorstep, with trips to art galleries and theatres. Curriculum-related trips all year round with the more fun visits saved until the end. Annual ski trip run by head of maths, year 7 to France, year 8 football tour to (exotic) Eastbourne, year 4 camping on-site. Year 7s throw themselves into a two-day on-site camp as part of their leadership programme which also comprises team events such as crossing the river blindfold and talks from professionals about leadership in later life. 'In seven years I've never had any of my three boys not wanting to go to school,' declared a parent. 'I put that down to the stimulating environment they find themselves in. That can be in the academic work or in the extracurricular activities, that are legion and legendary – there is something for everyone to grab and enjoy and the breadth is quite remarkable. In sports, the desire to win is always finely balanced with the Corinthian spirit of gentlemanliness and amateurism.'

World of Work talks for years 7 and 8 – doctors, airline pilots etc – and informative parent talks throughout the year too, recently 'why 13+ is better than 11+' for those with children in years 5 and 6. Great loyalty to 'sections' (houses) – Highlands, Midlands, Uplands, Lowlands. Competitions ranging from the sporty (eg football) to the silly (eg foam rocket launching and 'tunnelball' – passing the ball through a tunnel of everyone's legs). Plus points for good work and behaviour. Sanctions not really a thing here. 'Boys want to please,' says school; 'you tell them off and you move on.'

Day boys may join boarders for breakfast and supper for a small cost – handy for commuting parents. All boys from year 5 up may stay after school for prep and there is an after-school club for pupils of any age which runs until supper time at 5.50pm. Post-supper activity until 7.30pm.

A local school – half the boys in the school have the same home postcode, within a 20-minute drive. School buses not needed – mum or dad's taxi does the job; carpools are common. Parents 'invested in and engaged with their children's education,' says school. Accountants and other professionals, many with offices in London thanks to easy commuting and family-friendly semi-rural environs. School recently moved breakfast forward 10 minutes to 7.30am to help parents make the 7.50 to St Pancras. A sociable bunch, by all accounts, many are committed members of the Aldwickbury Friends Association – 'a real force for good,' says school – committee meetings 'fun'; parties 'late and loud'. Money raised through events and social occasions split between charity and school wish list purchases, eg adventure playground equipment – school presents ideas but AFA also suggests in line with its remit to 'raise friends and make memories'.

Boarding: A day school run along boarding school lines, but no full boarders currently or recently. Flexi boarding best suits local families – a good chance for boys heading off to senior day schools to experience boarding, or a run-in for those boarding full-time from year 9. Boarding starts at year 5, with taster nights beforehand. Thirty beds with 50 boys currently booked in to board once a week. 'Boarding is really fun – you can stay when you want,' grinning boarders told us. Popularity of the boarding week night tends to be dictated by the activity laid on after supper – Superhero Night and Nerf Night fully booked. A fun sleepover in reality. Matron is on hand in the bright and welcoming boarders' house, along with two New World gappers. Lounge has TV and Wii; several large and comfy four- to seven-bed rooms – bring your own own duvet or sleeping bag. Boarders usually sleep in the same bed whenever they stay. Large windows with lovely views across the school fields and woods, to which boarders have privileged access.

The last word: Certainly, those lucky enough to be educated here will look back on a golden childhood few today experience. A warm, well thought-out school, genuinely for and about boys, producing good eggs of the modern variety.

Barnardiston Hall Preparatory School
3
Barnardiston Hall, Nr Haverhill, Suffolk CB9 7TG
01440 786316 | registrar@barnardiston-hall.co.uk | www.barnardiston-hall.co.uk
Ages: 6m–13
Pupils: 214; Boarders: 24 full, 12 weekly/flexi
Fees: Day £8,880 – £14,760; Boarding £20,430 – £22,155 pa

Headmaster: Since 2017, Colonel Keith Boulter, Cambridge theology graduate and hockey blue (60s) and the owner of the school. Barnardiston is one of several schools and institutions run as a family business.

He was, in fact, headmaster from 1990-2012, before stepping into the role of principal and passing the reins of day-to-day management over to the previous headmaster (Tim Dodgson who, while no longer head, remains at the school as a history teacher).

The Colonel has always been a force within the school, teaching mathematics, helping with games and choir work and followed everywhere by children, like the Pied Piper. He retains a certain bluff, military manner with great geniality and is greeted with wild enthusiasm and respect wherever he goes in the school. 'Who has camped in the garden with their teacher?' he asks. A forest of hands goes up. 'Who acted in the play? ' – hands up again (slightly different lot). 'Who wants more homework?' Groans and shouts of 'Not me!' His early career in the Royal Army Educational Corps and, later, administering Gurkha schools, has helped shape the school's philosophy. Married, with a grown-up family, and lives in the grounds of Barnardiston. His daughter is head of the pre-prep department and his three grandchildren all attend the school.

Entrance: Non-selective. Pupils accepted at all stages through the school. A number come up from the nursery (six months – three years) to pre-prep. No formal exam but previous school reports are looked at and the children meet the head. Taster days are arranged for older children who attend classes, whilst particular needs are noted, and referrals/advice given to parents. The school has provision for educational support and few children are not accepted.

Exit: Most go on to a range of local independents at 13 – Felsted, Framlingham, Uppingham, Gresham's, Finborough and Culford among them. One or two leave at 11 for local state schools. Good guidance is given to parents. 'We suggest they visit three schools, two likely ones plus a wild card,' says the head. Pupils all get to where they want to go – a few scholarships each year.

Our view: A country prep with a strong, slightly quirky character, very much the creation of its owner, Colonel Boulter. With a rural setting, agricultural rather than chocolate box picturesque, it has a splendid indifference to the customary marketing gloss. Boarders live in the main building, an Edwardian villa, alongside the headmaster and his family.

Announcements are made over a PA system, known as the 'bing-bong', that operates all over the school; slightly disconcerting at first

Subject teaching takes place in the converted stables which surround the courtyard, and the purpose built pre-prep department. A series of Portakabins are still in use, though no one appears bothered; in fact, the pupils see the strengths; as one pointed out in the 'temporary' science lab, 'We never have to worry about dropping liquids on the benches – they are so old!' The decorative theme throughout is inspired by the Colonel's travels including elephants and giraffes, displays from Tutankhamen's tomb, wooden carvings, ornamental ponds and, unexpectedly, two full suits of armour standing guard at the end of a passage.

Indoor sports and ballet take place in a marquee (heated), supposedly temporary but no plans to change this. School has a small theatre with raked seating and facilities for sound and lighting – 'We all learn to do it as well as act' – and productions are all-out efforts of the whole school rather than an elite group. Music, a particular interest of the Colonel, is well taught and popular; around 50 per cent learn an instrument.

No formal gardens or prefects' lawns here; the grounds resemble an adventure playground. Approached by a drive full of potholes ('We know the fees aren't wasted on tarmac,' said a parent, approvingly), skateboarding is allowed, as are tree climbing and den building, there is a miniature railway, a bouncy castle – all tastes catered for. Announcements are made over a PA system, known as the 'bing-bong', that operates all over the school; slightly disconcerting at first, rather like a tube station, but pupils like it and think it is sensible.

A lot of parents are commuters and chose the school 'because the pupils seem so happy and relaxed, very different from London schools,' said one. 'Mine have all made tons of friends and have a crack at anything going,' said another, though also warning that 'it's not a place for namby-pambys.' (We think that remark is directed more at parents than pupils.) Adventure and independence encouraged from the outset with form sleepovers. 'We camped with our teacher in the garden when I was 6!' said one pupil, and this spirit continues up the school. Orienteering very popular (Prep National Champions), camping expeditions, and all team sports played with gusto. Long-awaited Astroturf is now installed. Parents welcome the unfussy attitude but warn: 'If you like things just so and organised months in advance then it might not suit.'

Classes are small, average 14, and setting begins early in the key subjects. Latin and French from early on, though Latin is dropped in the top three years by some. Those who might struggle in other schools find areas where they can shine. 'The staff are brilliant at building confidence,' say parents, who approve of the less stressful approach. Educational learning support is provided in the special needs department (known as The Bridge). Needs range from an extra boost to cases at the mild end of the autism spectrum, dyslexia and dyspraxia. There is also EFL and support for gifted children. A few children have statements and are LEA funded but the school won't take pupils they cannot help.

Boarding: Boarding facilities are on the top two floors of the main building. Though approached by a slightly depressing staircase, the facilities themselves are comfortable and homelike. Boys and girls occupy separate floors. Bedrooms, mostly four-bedded, are light, well decorated and some have en suite bathrooms. Rather posh bathrooms in fact – think department store loos – good lighting, warm and clean. Friendly matrons, who remain on duty until the younger boarders, at least, are in bed and asleep. Boys, who form some two-thirds of the boarders, also have a common room on their boarding floor with an enormous screen for weekend viewing. The girls have one in their bedroom but, I was assured, there is no signal so can only be used for DVD watching. Mobiles, for all pupils, are looked after by the school during the day and boarders are allowed to use them for only limited periods. 'Can be hard for some, at first, especially those from abroad, but we want them to join in real life here,' said the headmaster. Weekend outings to local towns/places of interest are arranged for those, largely from overseas, who stay in school. With notice, it is possible to remain through the half-term holidays also. Occasional boarding is popular and encouraged towards the top end of the school, especially for those moving on to board at senior schools.

Money matters: Limited bursarial help for overseas pupils and siblings.

The last word: This is a tremendously jolly school where a sense of adventure is encouraged. Most pupils thrive and go on to do well at senior schools. 'We often hear of former pupils becoming prefects or house heads,' we were told. Perhaps not suitable for those with hearts set on scholarships to the top-flight schools, but definitely worth looking at for those who appreciate a less stressful, unstuffy, purposeful atmosphere and a staff dedicated to the needs of its pupils.

Bedford Preparatory School

De Parys Avenue, Bedford, Bedfordshire MK40 2TU

01234 362216 | prepadmissions@bedfordschool.org.uk | www.bedfordschool.org.uk

Ages: 7-13

Pupils: 405; **Boarders:** 26 full

Fees: Day: £13,575 – £17,790; Boarding: £23,028 – £28,692 pa

Linked school: Bedford School, 857

Headmaster: Since 2013, Ian Silk (40s). Previously deputy head of Bishop's Stortford Prep School and former housemaster at Ardingly College. An English and drama specialist, brims with enthusiasm about all aspects of the school – most particularly the spectacular theatre shared with the upper school and the town.

There aren't too many heads we meet who kicked off their career in Buckingham Palace (he was in the office that organised the re-opening after the fire); also unusually, he had a marketing stint with the London Philharmonic Orchestra. But it was teaching (which he'd done briefly in Greece) and his love of English that really floated his boat, leading him to top up his English degree from Lancaster with a PGCE at Worcester.

Quite the biggest ears we've ever seen. 'I am supposed to be able to hear for 25 miles with them, but the truth is they're just blocking my hearing,' he confessed, removing them from his head and placing them on the desk. This was World Book Day and he was the BFG. Always a treat to find prep school heads that don't take themselves too seriously, even more so when they add a big dollop of humility into the mix ('That's very kind because I don't feel I get out enough,' he replied when we told him parents we'd spoken to were impressed with how 'present' he is). Knows most boys by name – lots of heads do but this is a large prep – and has lunch with all new joiners in small groups. Familiar with parents too, helped by the fact that he does all prospective parent tours (an hour-and-a-quarter each) himself. 'Easy to talk to', 'friendly and open', 'very measured and not a bit flashy', they told us.

Three favourite words of the moment? Future skills curriculum. Might sound like yawn-worthy edu-jargon, but apparently there are 30 skills – from productivity to resilience – that school believes are key to boys' futures and it's Mr Silk's job to embed them into assembly, classes, prizes etc. 'Not rocket science, but having a major impact,' he claims and parents concur.

Parents report boys are 'pushed' academically, 'but never at the cost of a more all-rounded education'

We're guessing there's a lot of shop talk at home as he's married to Sarah, who teaches at the school; they also have two sons there. Was training for a marathon when we met him; also enjoys walking the dog and skiing.

Entrance: Mainly at 7+, 8+ and 11+. A little more oversubscribed than at our last visit, though still not heavily. Looking for the right fit, ability to keep up and fully participate in school life. 'If a boy isn't there by 7, it's absolutely fine to try again later,' says head. Assessments in English, maths, NVR, creative writing, an in-school day – and that all-important report from current head. Large contingent from nearby pre-prep and fellow Harpur Trust member Pilgrims and around 30 per cent from local state schools. Buses from Luton, Milton Keynes, Hitchin broaden catchment.

Exit: Almost all (92 per cent in 2021) transfer to Bedford School with the odd exception departing for the state sector or, for international boarders, their mother country. No prep for CE or formal advice on other destination schools, but existing pupils sit the same test as external candidates for setting purposes. Parents report a seamless transition to upper school, with boys better prepared for workload than those joining from other preps.

Our view: Tucked away in the corner of the vast Bedford School campus, one of the biggest pluses of this prep is unfettered access to the wealth of facilities of its big brother school. Boys rave about the 'rec' (huge sports hall and swimming pool with additional squash courts, gym, table tennis area etc) and the theatre is among the most stunning we've seen, shared with the town and able to seat over 280. The immense modern dining hall serves popular, plentiful food with lots of choice (we enjoyed delicious sticky ribs and were even shown to our table by suited and booted maître d'). Fields, as you'd expect with the school's sporting kudos, are immaculate and vast. The prep's own amenities are noteworthy too, including a mix of traditional and modern purpose-built classrooms centred around an Astro play area where boys let off steam at break. A separate adventure playground adds to the fun. All feels surprisingly cosy despite the scale of the wider surroundings. The well-equipped science labs are packed with so many creatures (animal care is one of the most popular clubs) that it was almost another school tour for the science technician to take us round them all: gerbils (they breed them), snakes (one recently hatched), guinea pigs and geckos. All in all, simultaneously feels separate from and integral to the upper school and offers everything young boys could hope for, whatever their interests.

Parents report that boys are 'pushed' academically, 'but never at the cost of a more all-rounded education' and that 'learning is brought alive' (literally, with those animals in the science lab) at every opportunity. We saw boys constructing rivers out of modelling dough to learn about eg drainage basins and years 4, 5 and 6 hanging on the every word of a visiting author. Even doing past science papers (potentially the dullest of dull activities) was made into a game – each boy had to run to the front of class and rip off a piece of kitchen roll exam paper after completing each one. Twice-yearly testing enables school to keep a beady eye on progress and one parent reported that 'they're very good at explaining to the boys that their homework doesn't benefit anyone except them – has helped with my son's motivation hugely.' Teachers ('nearly all good, with the odd exception,' said a parent) are praised for their 'commitment' – all run a club in addition to their academic duties. Tons of sharing of good practice, with head reporting that 'the best inset days are the internal ones because we love learning from each other.' Streaming from year 6, with two top sets and two mixed-ability classes; another mixed-ability class added from year 7; setting for maths – not all keen on this system, though, with one parent saying, 'I'm not sure they've got the streaming and setting 100 per cent right.' French from year 3; Latin (new) from year 6; half a term each of German and Spanish from year 7, from which boys choose two to learn in year 8. 'Particularly towards the upper end of the school, they bring out the intellectual curiosity – you can really see them getting ready for what's coming in the upper school,' reported a parent.

Science labs are packed with many creatures (animal care is one of the most popular clubs): gerbils (they breed them), snakes (one recently hatched), guinea pigs and geckos

Small-group lessons and one-to-ones on offer from dedicated SENCo and two supporting specialists. And not just for those with (generally mild) SEN (about 10 per cent) as school prefers a wider approach, offering booster classes to eg anyone who finds punctuation or a particular area of maths tricky. Strong emphasis on training whole staff to support individual needs. Close communication with upper school a great strength and leads to nobody slipping through gaps in the transition. Strong ESOL team caters for overseas students.

Prepare to be buying washing powder in bulk for seriously muddy games kits – rugby, hockey and cricket ('huge' according to head) top the sporting agenda, with one parent telling us, 'everyone gets to regularly go out and get covered in mud and they absolutely love it.' An inclusive approach means school puts up as many as 18 competitive teams for fixtures, so everyone gets a ride on the bus and a post-match tea at least once a term, whatever their ability. School has some really good tennis and badminton players, plus swimmers, and cross-country does well too. Breadth is huge as we learned when we asked a large group of boys to shout out the favourite sport they do at school and practically every one was different. School pushing for even more bottom-up opportunities in future tournaments – 'we want the boys to play these sports when they're in their mid 20s just purely because they love it,' says head. 'They managed to produce a swimmer out of my very nervous son in just one term,' raved one parent, while another told us, 'If you'd have asked me before my son started the school who it wouldn't suit, I'd have said the non-sporty, but I've changed my attitude completely.' But you might want to give parents of boys who are moved into lower teams a wide berth – 'some show more disappointment than the boys, and certainly shout louder about it,' one of our contacts observed.

Spacious (and exceptionally tidy) dorms sleep between four and eight boys, some of whom make them their own with pictures, posters and duvet covers from home

Not a macho culture – boys are just as likely to wield a bow and play the violin as run around a freezing cold field, indeed some do both. Sometimes they find it hard to fit it all in, though school says it helps the boys prioritise. Tons of music, all hugely popular, includes the (crucially, non-selective) junior choir, plus chapel choir for years 5 and up, and there are instrumental lessons on curriculum for years 3 and 4 with around half going on to learn an instrument after that (everything from bagpipes to sax). Positive, energetic and fun. 'They encourage performance even if you're a real beginner so you have everything from the slick and confident to those who can only play a few notes,' said a parent. Best event of the year is the house singing, said another – 'The boys look immaculate and amazing in their white shirts and ties and sing really complicated notes absolutely beautifully, all conducted by a year 8 boy and properly judged externally.'

Great excitement on the dramatic front too (especially for the forthcoming Wind in the Willows performance when we visited – whole choir was to be included) as all major performances now take place in the £7m theatre (thanks to a legacy donation). 'My boys are naturally shy and definitely not extrovert, but drama has really helped them come out of their shell in a way I'd never have imagined a few years ago,' told one parent. Musician in residence must surely be an insomniac – he's just written his fourth school musical; last one was a Western, this one is based in space. Year 6 boys get chance to learn backstage skills.

Fabulous art space, where we watched youngsters finalising landscapes to show contrast, although head of art keen 'not to get boys to see art as just the ability to draw,' telling us about one boy 'who would have struggled on paper but made the most wonderful sculpture'. Boys told us about favourite projects including 'bending wire into Olympian stances such as Javelin throwing' and self-portraits.

Over 100 activities a term and upper school boys help run the weekly activities programme eg coding club. Lots of trips – some of the boys had just been to South Africa – and there are bi-annual trips to Ickwell, a nature reserve owned by the school.

Bullying rare – a no-nonsense policy and zero tolerance attitude helps, but most of the work is preventative, teaching boys how to eg be 'an upstander not a bystander'. Strict on kindness, uniform, politeness etc – 'means bigger things take care of themselves'. Gold coins given out for conduct merits – put in house 'tubes' ready for big weekly count-up which leads to house flag flying outside head's office. Parents a relatively grounded bunch, many OBs themselves.

Boarding: Boarders inhabit the purpose-built Eagle House, a quick skip (and many of them do) across the playground. Sleeps up to 32 boys (though never more than 26 at one time) from year 3 and up, although most start after year 5 as either flexi, full or weekly boarders and the vast majority are from years 7 and 8. All very homely with nicely furnished, comfy spaces including separate areas for chilling, games, prep and kitchen (where they'd been making banana cake the night before) with lots of personal touches for boys to hang out after school hours. Wicket, the house dog, laps up all the fuss bestowed on him. Spacious (and exceptionally tidy) dorms sleep between four and eight boys, some of whom make them their own with pictures, posters and duvet covers from home, while others keep them surprisingly bare. Around half the boarders are from overseas (mainly Russia and China), so there are plenty around at weekends once Saturday school (compulsory for all from year 6) and Sunday chapel are out of the way. Enjoyable outings such as go-karting, escape room, high ropes and bowling are often followed by a takeaway or one of the housemaster's legendary barbecues. Year 7s and 8s can go into town, just 200 yards away – 'gives them a real world feel as you can get isolated in boarding houses.' 'The boys really look out for each other,' said a parent.

The last word: Parents here are signing up for the long haul, happily waving goodbye to the stress of the 11+ or CE in favour of a seamless transition into the reputable senior school. A happy, thriving start on this journey where, as one parent put it, 'they find whatever is your thing and then fly with it.'

Bedford School

De Parys Avenue, Bedford, Bedfordshire MK40 2TU

01234 362216 | admissions@bedfordschool.org.uk | www.bedfordschool.org.uk

Ages: 13-18

Pupils: 708; sixth form: 266; Boarders: 123 full, 76 weekly

Fees: Day £20,949; Boarding £34,257 – £35,430 pa

Linked school: Bedford Preparatory School, 854

Head master: Since 2014, James Hodgson (50s), educated at Wellington College and Durham (classics) before being scooped up on the milk round by Ernst and Young and spending a couple of years as a trainee accountant. In his 20s, a cricketer hovering around the fringes of the professional game (and uninspired by the world of finance), he wrote to Cambridge on the off-chance of a late place on its PGCE course and turned up trumps, meaning he could pursue his long-term ambition of running a boarding house as well as playing regular top-class cricket, ultimately earning a blue.

Spent six years teaching in Sydney before joining Tonbridge School as boarding housemaster and director of admissions. Latterly senior deputy head of Magdalen College School, Oxford. Oft told story is how he fell for Bedford on the basis of rapport between pupils and staff – 'completely at ease with other – wonderful to see,' and was also impressed with 'every boy shaking my hand and looking me in the eye'. At peace with Bedford not hitting the dizzy academic heights of Magdalen but has upped the ante for pastoral reasons ('good for self-worth and opens up choice for the next step'), gaining best-ever A level results three years into his headship (the same year Oxbridge numbers hit double figures for the first time) and best-ever GCSE results four years in, though there have been blips too. While fiercely proud of vertical pastoral system across houses and tutor groups ('so younger ones have plenty of time with older ones, an atmosphere that pervades the school'), he has recently introduced academic year heads 'to ensure no boy gets missed'.

Gives impression of being younger than his years – boyish looks and demeanour help as much as dynamic approach. But a more measured, outward-looking and educationally savvy man you couldn't find. Boys describe him as 'warm and welcoming' and 'an instant leveller which was great for me because it's easy to feel initially intimidated by the grandeur of the school.' Genuine open-door policy, they told us – 'you can go in and talk about anything'. 'Very good with names and he remembers what you're good at too,' added another. Praised by parents for tightening up systems, lifting expectations and improving communications. 'He exudes openness and kindness at the same time as upholding discipline,' felt one, while another said he was the reason they chose the school.

Recent areas of focus include digital learning. Has brought in director of digital learning 'to work out what 18-year-olds need and work backwards' – paid off when school took a team to London to enter a competition about blockchain technology (a subject they knew nothing about until 48 hours before) and wound up coming third (two major banks came first and second). Also keen on entrepreneurial thinking, with many boys leaving already running businesses. Service is high on his agenda – 'Every boy will have had a meaningful relationship with the local community by the time he leaves,' he promises, with nearly 100 out of 140 volunteering in local primary schools, old people's homes etc. Lovely story of one overstretched music teacher at a local primary now having a Bedford boy as pianist for the choir – 'completely revolutionised her life'. Keen to learn from state sector too, which has led to some strong local partnerships.

Married to Rachel, with four children – oldest a theatre director, two at uni (Sydney and Oxford) and youngest at Oundle. Cricket still runs deep in his bones, although loves 'all sport' and now skis and sails more than ever, the latter in Chichester harbour and Isle of Wight, where he and his wife originally hail from.

Entrance: Around 60 per cent of the 140 boys who join year 9 come up from the prep. Feeder preps for the remaining 50 or so additional places include Aldwickbury, Beechwood Park, Kingshott and Lockers Park; others from the state sector. Optional ISEB pre-test in year 6 or 7 potentially leading to conditional offer, confirmed by school's own online entrance examination in year 8. A few extra places at 14+ then around 25 join in sixth form, when hopefuls will need six good GCSEs with at least 6s in the subjects to be studied at A level (7+ grades in maths and sciences). Not ferociously competitive for day boys, albeit more selective than in the past; same is true for boarding. Overseas pupils often offered places conditional to taking ESL, billed as an extra.

Exit: Nearly 20 per cent heads to pastures new post-GCSE. Handful to Oxbridge every year (four in 2021) and two-thirds to a wide range of Russell Group – Durham, UCL, Bath and Exeter currently popular. Lots study sciences and a few to medicine each year (11 medics in 2021). Two off to the US – Harding University, Arkansas and University of San Diego. Others to Universität Mannheim and Ludwig-Maximilians-Universität München in Germany, and HKUST Business School in Hong Kong.

Latest results: In 2021, 77 per cent 9-7 at GCSE; 75 per cent A*/A at A level (90 per cent A*-B). IB average score 37. In 2019 (the last year when exams took place), 66 per cent 9-7 at GCSE; 43 per cent A*/A at A level (72 per cent A*-B). IB average score 34.

Teaching and learning: Decent results, especially given the broad intake. 'Academic without being pressurised,' thought parent. Much looser setting than in the past – now only broadly at the very top and bottom for maths and English. Class sizes capped at 24, shrinking to a pleasing eight or nine for many A level subjects. Pretty much all take 10 GCSEs. Particularly good results in English; computer science and DT popular. In sixth form, around 15 per cent take IB (school would like it to be a third, but not overly fussed as 'it is so important to match individual pupil strengths to courses'); rest start with four A levels, dropping to three at various stages of the sixth form (menu felt by some to be a bit too narrow and traditional, though – 'would be nice if they offered something like psychology,' said a parent). Maths and sciences get biggest take-up. Bedford School Independent Project (BSIP) taken by all boys in year 12, with about 20 per cent going on to do EPQ – one boy told us about his project on the physics behind Interstellar ('I love physics and I love movies – couldn't suit me more'). German, Spanish, French and Latin on offer in the languages department, with Mandarin available as a twilight option, but rather low take-up of these at A level. Some boys told us they'd like a get out of jail card around languages at GCSE – 'I struggle even with English, so to take French too is really hard,' said one. Head takes two Greek classes on Saturday mornings – 'was originally requested by Latinists who I fully expected not to turn up after a few weeks but is still going strong two years on and I'm now taking their protégés,' he says.

DT among the highest calibre we've seen – and imaginative too, with boys encouraged to think about solving real needs with eg laptop cooler and self-heating baby bottle

Good to see chalk and talk widely replaced by more stimulating, interactive approaches, eg we saw one class experimenting with guppies to see if fish can recognise colour. 'The teachers really engage with their subjects – they go above and beyond,' said a boy; goes for outside the classroom too, with pupils clearly appreciative of eg head of academics recently travelling to Stowe to watch them play rugby – 'makes you feel he really cares'. A few grumbles around consistency of homework – 'sometimes you get five pieces of prep in a day, other days none,' said one boy.

Two careers specialists, with UCAS application process highly praised. Lots going on off-timetable – pretty much every day, one or other of the academic societies (many run by boys) has a meeting, speaker etc.

Learning support and SEN: Around 10 per cent SEN (mainly mild dyslexia or dyscalculia), all given bespoke care. Good at diagnosis too, felt parent – 'and they've put everything in place to help my son while never making him feel different'. Strong ESOL team caters for overseas students, who are offered extra English language sessions in place of another language and about half of them take IGCSE ESL instead of English.

The arts and extracurricular: Super modern music centre designed by award-winning architect Eric Parry and word has it that it's positioned opposite the pavilion so that the director of music can keep one eye on the cricket scoreboard whilst conducting the school orchestra. All the choirs (including a 50-strong chapel choir, which our guide described as 'amazing, just amazing'), orchestras, bands and ensembles you'd expect and there's a music technology suite, recording studio, rock room and recital hall where the grand piano was being tuned during our visit ready for the weekly performances by pupils and recitals from visiting professionals. Annual house singing a hugely anticipated event on the school calendar – expect raucous chanting and cheering from housemates. Music regularly released by boys onto Spotify. Inclusive approach means all are welcome – all the more surprising to find music just wasn't on the radar of some families we spoke to.

Seriously wow factor theatre, built on the site of a former Moravian church, is architecturally stunning with own box office and reception complete with bar, seating area and grand piano. Shared with the town, and able to seat over 280, it is a hub of dramatic activity with at least two or three events a week ranging from BedFringe (mini Edinburgh festival that often sees participants move on up to the real deal) to a 10-day festival in July that celebrates everything from comedy to jazz. Drama available at both GCSE and A level, with good results. Many productions in conjunction with Bedford Girls' School, while boarders get invited to all external productions by visiting companies. A full-time technical director takes care of special effects and shows boys the ropes with lighting and scenery.

Mind-blowing work on show in the art department and indeed all around the school; boys clearly very at home with the printing facilities. 'A very calming place – a real haven for my son,' said a parent. DT among the highest calibre we've seen – and imaginative too, with boys encouraged to think about solving real human needs with eg laptop cooler, bike work stand, thermo-kettle and self-heating baby bottle, plus our two favourites – a lamp designed for a children's hospital and beautiful wooden box made by a boy for his grandfather with dementia containing sections for pills, notes, visual reminders of family members etc. No wonder so many move on to study engineering at university. History of art an extracurricular option; parents, have your paintbrushes at the ready as there are adult classes available in evenings.

A non-stop merry-go-round of extracurricular activities keeps boys busy – 'my son's only two terms in but already does CCF, shooting club, electric guitar, debating society plus sports clubs,' said parent. Popular DofE; CCF in all three branches, run in conjunction with Bedford Girls'. There's always some sort of trip or tour in the planning whether for sports or choir, along with academic excursions and some just for fun.

Introduction in recent years of colours for art, drama and academia in addition to sport – a welcome addition signified by a colourful array of scarves and pockets – and special striped blazers for those awarded cricket colours.

Sport: Sport has always been the lifeblood of Bedford. And while the trophy cabinets are bursting at the seams for all sports from rugby and cricket to rowing and golf, the overall ethos is far from elitist, including when it comes to training – the input and expertise from the directors of all major sports filtering down to even the lowliest teams. All get fixtures – they must surely one of very few schools who can lay claim to 35 rugby matches on a single Saturday (shortly before our visit), with 700 boys (includes prep boys) playing against other schools. Unusually, all major sports tours are non-selective, giving every boy the opportunity to go.

Rugby, hockey and cricket are the core sports, as is rowing (school has its own boat house on a beautiful stretch of the river Ouse). But there's plenty more besides: you name it and Bedford offers it, from archery or rifle shooting to pilates and fencing. National and international honours in all main sports plus golf and fencing, and boys have gone on to play for their universities and even their country; the main challenge for staff is finding competitor schools strong enough to give them a good game. Outstanding cricket – the CEO of Lord's went to Bedford, as did most of the bigwigs at Northamptonshire County Cricket Club, both on and off the field.

Decent results, especially given the broad intake, 'The teachers really engage with their subjects – they go above and beyond,' said a boy; same outside the classroom too

Facilities unsurprisingly splendid, including a weights room that would give many private gyms a run for their money, plus 25-metre swimming pool, well kept sports hall and squash courts. Outside are vast fields, tennis courts and a cricket pavilion opened by England captain and Old Bedfordian, Alastair Cook.

Boarding: Six senior boarding houses – four on site and two just a short walk away – all adapted Victorian villas, each with own character and all bright and roomy. Home from home in every sense, all with a fraternity house feel. We were reassured rather than put off by the huge pile of muddy boots in the hallway and unmade beds and towels hanging here there and everywhere – boys must feel very relaxed to be quite so slovenly. Each house has between 32 and 54 boys, with dorms sleeping between one (for upper sixth) and six, and has a housemaster with family and assistant housemaster with family ('couldn't praise them more if I tried – you can call them about anything, no matter how minor,' said a parent). Communal areas are attractive – no mean feat to manage such cosiness with 10+ sofas in a single room. Enough Xboxes, pinball machines, pool tables, chess tables etc to please the most discerning of young gamesmen. Plenty of roll calls to keep boys well informed and two hours of prep a night, divided into two slots. Many of the boys – all of whom have the freedom to come and go during the course of the day – are former day boys fed up with the daily commute. And around 65 per cent are full boarders (half of whom are local and half international – from 24 countries across Europe, Asia and Russia) so plenty of buzz at weekends although some feel 'there could be more outings'. Compulsory Saturday school for all.

Ethos and heritage: If you can, get your satnav to take you to the school via the grand wide avenues of Victorian villas (two boarding houses among them) that lead down to the attractive river bank (the less-posh half of Bedford includes the somewhat run-down high street – definitely not the scenic route). Once through the gates, it's impossible not to marvel at the manicured sports fields to your left and pleasing mix of old and new buildings mainly to your right. The main building is all turrets, spires and a bell tower, with a magnificent hall as the central point and classrooms on four levels.

We were reassured by the huge pile of muddy boots in the hall and unmade beds – boys must feel very relaxed to be quite so slovenly

Difficult to choose a stand-out feature or department as each and every addition to the school has been made with care and deliberation to fuse function and form effectively. From the professional-looking cricket pavilion to the super modern glazed music school (who could fail to be inspired in here?), stunning library full of gleaming new books – but with the antique ones carefully displayed – and the cottage-like art building, set in its own sculpture garden, the whole campus gives the aura of a school offering roundedness in the purest sense of the word. The word chapel doesn't quite do justice to the glorious building where weekly services are held – 'one of my favourite places in the school, which is not at all what I expected as a non-Christian, but the singing and the atmosphere is very special,' said our guide.

No complaints on the food front (although several about the 'chaotic lunch queues'), 'and they go out of their way if you have a dietary requirement,' said a boy. We were touched to see a boy call out to the dining staff as he walked past, 'Smells good, as always.'

An enviable community where boys look out for each other across the year groups – a truly brotherly atmosphere. Made even more amiable by the good manners and open chattiness of the boys. All open doors and all have a ready smile.

Alumni, as you might expect, include some seriously influential Britons including Sir Alistair Cook (cricket), Budge Rogers (rugby), John Holland-Kaye (Heathrow CEO), Miles Young (master, New College, Oxford), Lord Naseby, Will Gompertz (BBC arts correspondent), Paddy Ashdown (politician), Al Murray (comedian), Archer Martin (Nobel prize winner in chemistry), John Fowles (author), Quentin Skinner (political theorist), Krishnan Srinivasan (Indian foreign secretary and deputy secretary-general of the Commonwealth of Nations) and Harold Abrahams (athlete).

Pastoral care, inclusivity and discipline: Tutor is first port of call in moments of difficulty; teachers also available to parents via email. Timetable collapsed five times each year to focus on PSHCE with age-appropriate focus on drugs, internet safety etc. Tight on discipline – 'I'm quite tough,' says head. But there's give where appropriate – school understands that this is a place for boys to grow up in and that some mistakes will be made along the way. No movement on eg haircuts and facial hair, though (except for Movember) – a 'bit petty,' thought boys until the debating society battled it out verbally against the 'strictest teacher in the school' who had such a plausible argument that in the end the pupil vote went to him. Usual zero tolerance when it comes to dealing with drugs, either inside or out of school – does crop up from time to time. Suspensions and exclusions? 'Probably too many,' admits head – wouldn't be pinned down to number of former; around three to six a year of the latter, 'the vast majority mutual removals by the time we get to that stage.' Bullying rare and stamped on quickly, with school reassuringly uncomplacent.

Pupils and parents: Boys are a delight, their trademark being an ability to mix with any age group with easy, understated confidence. Buses from Luton, Milton Keynes and Hitchin and easy access from Harpenden by train makes for a broad catchment, with most living within a 40-mile radius, commuting for up to an hour. Parents range from old money right through to first-time buyers who have their own businesses or London-based professionals. Over 50 boys on lifetime bursaries help keep school from being a bubble. 'Not much of a parent community, though,' felt one. Good ethnic diversity, reflective of the area and topped up by the international contingent. Many OBs in parent cohort – it's hard to exaggerate how proud these men are of their old school.

Money matters: Good clutch of scholarships and bursaries for entry into years 7, 9 and 12, with art and more recently drama added to the list and golf scholarships in conjunction with nearby Woburn Golf Club. Generous – up to 35 per cent of fees, non-means tested, up for grabs 'for boys with exceptional talent' – and buoyant reserves in the hardship fund. Just under 200 boys across the school currently hold awards, with around 10 per cent of these on 100 per cent.

Part of the Harpur Trust but financially independent and benefiting from an extremely active and benevolent OB network.

The last word: A solid option for a single-sex independent school where boys can reach their academic potential without undue pressure and kickstart their adult lives with a real love of sport and/or the arts. Boys are among the nicest and most outward looking we've met, helped by school's (and particularly the current dynamic head's) strong sense of service. Softer skills a real point of differentiation.

Beechwood Park School

6

Pickford Road, Markyate, St Albans, Hertfordshire AL3 8AW

01582 840333 | admissions@beechwoodpark.com | www.beechwoodpark.com

Ages: 3-13

Pupils: 544; **Boarders:** 60 flexi (from year 5)

Fees: Day £12,285 to £18,165; Flexi boarding plus £4,320 pa

Headmaster: Since 2015, Edward Balfour (50s). Educated at Pilgrims prep in Winchester, then King Edward VI School Southampton, a 'state grammar that went independent as I arrived. It was quite rough in some ways,' he reflects. The son of solicitors, he read English at Cardiff and taught at RGS Worcester, before doing a PGCE at Homerton College Cambridge. Then taught English at Uppingham, followed by Whitgift and 13 years at Bradfield. His first headship was at Northbourne Park School in Kent, whose substantial bilingual (French) cohort no doubt equipped him well for Beechwood, also hot on French. Why the move from secondary schools? 'It's so much more interesting – you don't get as much chance to make an impact in five years as you do in 11.'

Opening the massive front doors for us in an open-necked shirt, the overall impression is of someone in full control of his ship and eager to explore new waters with it. He's also got a long passenger list — pupils numbers have risen from sub 500 to 557 during his tenure: 'The surplus created supercharges our development plan.' This has ranged from a drive to become more tech-forward ('there wasn't even Wifi here when I arrived') to reviewing timetables and reporting systems: 'We do a huge amount of analysing data now, putting into place interventions and tracking progress' — as noted approvingly by the latest ISI report. Data is widely shared with parents, for whom communications have also improved with the adoption of iSAMS information system.

Parents find him progressive, involved and readily accessible. They approve of his teacher appointments and feel he really listens — surveyed after lockdown, they saw clear responses to their input second time round. Though he doesn't teach, he lives on site with wife Emma (head of year 5), leads assemblies and was spotted reading to a nursery class during our visit. With his three children grown up, he also eats frequently with the boarders: 'It's so important heads are not on a pedestal.' He enjoys supporting his football-playing son, gardening, cooking and reading.

Entrance: Most join from nursery, with reception and year 7 other key entry points. But applications are welcome at any stage, space permitting. Children are not appraised for nursery, and are given a 'light touch' assessment from reception. From year 2, they are invited for a group assessment and interview, and their current school work is considered. 'We're looking for interaction and enthusiasm — not just academic ability.' School report required for joiners into year 5 upwards.

Aldenham School.

Exit: A double-edged sword for any good Hertfordshire prep is losing a number of your pupils after year 6 to great local state options like St George's in Harpenden or St Albans Girls. Year 7 entry for the highly academic St Albans High School for Girls is also popular, and St Albans (the boys' equivalent) the top pick for boys at 13 (though precise numbers are not spelt out on the website). Committed as he is to co-ed, the irony is not lost on Mr Balfour that many go to single sex secondaries 'because that's the provision round here'.

Thereafter, Berkhamsted, Bedford, Abbot's Hill and Haileybury regular choices, though there is a broad output, with the occasional pupil going to Oundle, Eton and Harrow. Good scholarship success with 13 in 2021 from St Albans alone.

Our view: The tone is set in Woodlands nursery, the newest part of the school. Bright and spacious, indoors and out (the nearby long jump doubling as a sandpit), there's a long Forest School tradition which our year 8 tour guides remembered vividly. Main nursery building accommodates two classes of 20, divided by a partition, but our concern that this might be noisy seems unfounded — one class is often away anyway doing PE, music etc. Beechwood's child-centred approach is visible from day one with individual interests logged on a white board to be integrated into exercises on phonics etc. The staff here want every child to feel 'safe, secure, known and loved' and are touchingly mindful that many lately have had limited socialisation through the pandemic; a detailed knowledge, care and affection for pupils permeates everywhere.

Pupils split into four classes of 15 in reception in the junior department building, with fantastic self-portrait wall tiles, then three classes of 21 for years 1 and 2. Specialist teaching kicks in from the word go for PE, music and French, then for TPR and art, and streaming now starts in year 3 instead of 4 — one impact of all that additional data. Year 2 handwriting is impressive, testament to the head's drive to develop fully cursive handwriting throughout the school. Regular contests for 'handwriting heroes' and entries to the SATIPS national handwriting competition. Year 3 marks the move into the fabulous main Queen Anne building, for many years the home of the Sebright family (Queen Mary visited several times), overlooking farmland. School's history goes far beyond that, though, and archaeologists have found artefacts dating back to Tudor times and beyond. Became a school in the Sixties, saving it from dereliction, and incorporating two other prep schools as it rose from the ashes. It has been fully co-ed for almost 30 years. Rolling programme of refurbishment extends to the many music practice rooms, a sports and playground in a former walled garden, lofty dining halls and stunning panelled library. It couldn't fail to bring out the reader in any child, particularly as local children's authors come in to give readings and run workshops.

The head had warned us that lessons here are loud and the maths class we joined was exactly that — lively teaching and lots of discussion. And we love the school policy of writing reports directly to children rather than parents – at start of term too so the points stay fresh in the mind. 'It's hugely powerful,' agree teachers. Every school has weak spots in its staff but favourites far outnumber them in parental feedback, the head of French particularly adored. Something of a longstanding speciality here, Beechwood runs annual soirées amicales for year 6s and above, involving songs, plays and recitals in French. Rumours abound about Beechwood pupils being 'practically GCSE standard' when they leave, though one parent was cynical about the ratio of French lessons to computer science (which is taught weekly from year 1). Ever ambitious linguists, Latin plays are also tackled too — Latin is taught from year 5.

We love the school policy of writing reports directly to children rather than parents – at start of term too so the points stay fresh in the mind 'Hugely powerful,' agree teachers

Plenty of enrichment, with children in years 3-5 taking part in the future skills programme – includes puzzle solving, presentation, interview skills and is great secondary school application preparation. Senior pupils can work towards the optional Beechwood Park leadership through service award, involving four levels, to encourage thinking about and working with others in line with Beechwood's 16 well-publicised values (illustrated in various posters around school). As one parent put it, 'There's a lot going on to remind children there's a real world at the end of that long drive.' School recently raised the vast sum of £250,000 for a local hospice. Those who stay to year 8 are given extra responsibilities — eg as link monitors for younger forms — and a lot of 'transition training' including early career guidance, contact with secondary school teachers, advice on conflict resolution and more. Blazer lapels therefore often laden with achievement and responsibility badges, and pupils positively burst with pride in the place. Inter-house activity has been beefed up to encompass competition in everything from sport to academics and music to community action. Everyone pounds their feet in a drumroll at Monday assembly as the latest point tallies are announced. Parents report that any instances of unkindness are handled swiftly and in a way that encourages children to step forward and take responsibility.

Parents agree no stone is left unturned in ISEB preparation — 'loads and loads of Planet BOFA' besides the future skills programme. 'It's total rubbish that you can't prepare for VR and NVR tests,' attests Mr Balfour, and around 65 per cent of pupils now sit them at 11 or 12. However, several parents say they'd like more information and reminders about open days, entry processes, key dates etc for schools beyond St Albans. Almost no one sits CE at 13, though this can be accommodated when needed.

Each child has a daily 20p allowance for the tuck cupboard and given that Beechwood is a mobile-free zone (hurrah!), there's a free mobile any child may borrow

The Learning Support team works with about 10 per cent of pupils, mostly with dyslexia and ADHD, led by two full time specialist teachers and a TA. They run group and one-to-one sessions and have two grad assistants. A counsellor visits weekly (though this is chargeable, unlike other LS help). 'The children we help are not necessarily on the SEN register, but need support in the context of Beechwood,' explains the LS lead. 'Many of them may not even be identified in another school. We're a big, busy, school and you need to be able to cope.' Beechwood occasionally takes children who are acquiring English, and with LS support, the last ISI report noted they make 'particularly rapid progress' here.

A new head of art is making the most of refurbished art rooms in the old coach house, where we found children happily absorbed in sketch books. All kinds of media are explored here including print making and weaving, and the cellars house a pottery studio. DT similarly well equipped (3D printer, laser cutter etc) and was the scene of a riveting Micky Mouse robot dissection on our visit.

Technology and arts collide happily in the music department which has new software for recording and manipulating sound. We've rarely seen a school with quite such a high percentage of pupils (around 90 per cent) taking private music lessons, but judging from the groove coming from one young rock band, who could resist? Lessons at the more expensive end, though year 2s may try a range of instruments for two terms in small groups at a reduced rate. There's a percussion room packed with drums and xylophones, six choirs (with the selective chamber choir the most prestigious) and over 20 different music ensembles. 'We don't have a school orchestra — we want the children to hear themselves playing,' said head of music.

Like music, drama is taught right through to year 8, with a host of productions staged annually which children discuss rapturously. There can have been no shortage of great outdoor locations for a recent Wind In the Willows (performed on camera rather than stage due to Covid).

The sports facilities — including a large sports hall with viewing gallery, Astro turfs, cricket nets, covered swimming pool etc — would be a credit to a secondary school. Parents describe sport as 'huge' while our pupil guides reckoned football and cricket are Beechwood's specialities. Every child has the chance to compete for the school and there's a thriving, parent-run equestrian team, and a ski team too (run in part by parents, part by school). Children appreciate that senior pupils may opt out of team sports in favour of alternative options like sailing.

Almost everyone lives within 40 minutes of the school, and feels very involved, including via a lively PA. Working parents who don't take up the boarding option have a sports-rich array of after-school clubs for children to use and may pay for tea and after school care until 5.30pm.

Boarding: The fact that most pupils live extremely locally has not impacted on the popularity of boarding — so oversubscribed at the time of our visit that it was only open to year 6s and above, instead of year 5, as usual. The model here is for a boarding place to be paid for Monday to Friday, whether or not your child chooses to stay every night — two or three seems most popular – so no hot-bedding.

Bright, welcoming dormitories sleeping up to 11 in the eves enjoy terrific views. Partitions with built-in reading lights are used cleverly to break up larger spaces and belongings are either stored on shelves in the laundry — dirty clothes are never sent home — or in a truckle under the bed.

Each child has a daily 20p allowance for the tuck cupboard and given that Beechwood is a mobile-free zone (hurrah!), there's a free mobile any child may borrow who wants to call home.

After prep and music practice, children are let loose on activities that make the most of these terrific grounds. Sport features heavily but there's also a lounge-cum-games room well equipped with table football, table tennis etc for hanging out in, plus a range of fantastic themed nights from bug eating to laser tag.

On-site houseparent declares himself 'a boarding evangelist' and with potential boarders able to have a two-week free trial, it couldn't be much easier to work out if boarding life is for you, either now or in the future.

Money matters: Some means tested bursaries available from year 3 upwards.

The last word: 'We have some of the best state schools the country round here but still chose Beechwood,' and 'Our children feel loved and part of everything,' are typical parent comments. Particularly strong reputation for trad subjects like French and music but also nurtures and educates children in the wider sense. The result is sparky, confident children who exude pride in their school and are incredibly happy learners.

Beeston Hall School

West Runton, Cromer, Norfolk NR27 9NQ

01263 837324 | office@beestonhall.co.uk | www.beestonhall.co.uk

Ages: 4–13

Pupils: 151; Boarders: 40 (from year 3)

Fees: Day £20,070; Boarding £26,970 pa

Headmaster: Since 2016, Fred de Falbe (50s). Eton (same vintage as D Cameron), followed by theology at Manchester. Was previously head of St Richard's, a boarding prep in Herefordshire that has since closed. His varied career has taken him into the film business, property management and a spell as a 'jackaroo' in Australia, as well as eight years teaching in state schools close to the family farm in north Devon, where, among other things, he carried out most of the maintenance work and raised Tamworth pigs. Was drawn back into full-time teaching at Knightsbridge School, a popular day prep in London.

His style is exceedingly hands-on – definitely not just a man in a suit, think parents. 'He's very visible around the school and pupils like that,' said one. Easy to talk to with understated charm, has already established good rapport with staff while pupils say he's interested in all of them, not just the stars. 'You don't have to be the best in something for him to talk to you,' said one.

Has strong views about the need to nurture confidence and self-reliance. His advice to parents to 'give your child a broken Hoover to take apart and try and fix in the holidays' provoked media interest and he is happy to be associated with the idea of 'directed purposelessness'. Believes children should look forward to coming to school: 'Learning takes many forms and some of the best schooling is done when children are having fun.'

Is very pro 'the small country prep school where we all know each other', and is not looking to expand the school greatly. His wife Juliet is immersed in everything going on at the school. A trained artist, she was able to fill in teaching art for half a term. Very much a partnership. Three children, now almost through school and at university stage.

Entrance: Non-selective. Numbers increase steadily throughout the school with year 8 the largest age group. Older pupils attend an informal assessment day. Can accommodate mild to moderate learning difficulties but all must be able to follow the curriculum. Not for those with behavioural problems.

Exit: Almost all stay to the end of year 8. Ampleforth, Bedales, Eton, Gresham's, Oundle, Rugby, Stowe and Tudor Hall all feature. Careful guidance is given and pupils all get where they want to go, many with awards. Fourteen awards in 2021.

Our view: Children create a good impression. Respectful but 'at ease' relations with staff ('none of that giving them The Look,' as one mother put it), unforced good manners – standing up for visitors and holding doors open for each other as well as adults. Mobile phones are not allowed in the school. Head feels pupils should be better occupied. 'We stick to the tried and tested phone box in the hall,' he says. Close supervision of computer use in the evenings and off duty; very aware of online risks and need to educate pupils. Traditional lunch (served at tables, grace is said, water jug passed round) for the whole school, including staff. 'We are improving the acoustics in the dining room – the noise is unbelievable, you can't hear yourself speak at times,' says the head. Daily organised games and lots of off-duty playtime punctuate the day. No prep before year 6 ('developing a good reading habit matters most,' says school) then it's 20 minutes a day, increasing in year 8, especially for scholarship hopefuls. Dog-friendly with several around and about in classrooms with their owners (staff) and spectating at matches. Humans (and no doubt dogs as well) are agreed on the benefits.

Idyllic setting, close to north Norfolk coast and nearby National Trust Felbrigg Estate. Sweeping lawns and a Regency house are the centre of a mixture of newer builds. Extensive sporting, music and art facilities. Everything spick and span with notices such as 'Please walk ON the grass' and, 'Why not hold the door for someone?' Walls crammed with details of daily happenings, pupils' work, art, photographs and achievements.

We visited on World Book Day, taken as seriously by staff as pupils , and were greeted by Captain Haddock (the head) plus the Gruffalo (DT master)

Small, mixed-ability classes until year 4, when there's flexible setting for English, maths, science and languages. French starts in year 3, Latin from year 6 and Greek (for some) in years 7 and 8. The year 8 scholarship form gives intensive preparation for senior school awards, focusing on individual requirements rather than hothousing a group. Staff flag any problems straightaway via emails and parents are encouraged to have informal chats with them at pick-up times, though effort grades are issued and more formal consultations can be arranged.

An educational support unit, based in an attractive suite of rooms, with excellent interactive displays and hard to resist games, is run by a sparkling and vivacious teacher who makes attending a session fun and even a privilege. 'We have drop-in sessions and parties and children really do see coming here as a treat.' Parents agree. 'My daughter only needed help for a year but kept on dropping in to see staff there as it was such a happy place,' said one. Roughly a quarter receive help of some sort, usually in English and maths.

A well designed and stocked library with wonderful squashy sofas to recline on is staffed throughout the day, including breaks and lunchtime. Pupils have timetabled library lessons for changing books and quiet reading. We visited on World Book Day, taken as seriously by staff as pupils, and were greeted by Captain Haddock (the head) plus the Gruffalo (DT master, helped by 'easy access to the materials'), as well as Matilda and Cruella de Vil – and not a single Disney princess to be seen. Art is taught in a barn-style studio, mezzanine floor devoted to pupils' scholarship work, each with own desk and work area so they can come and go in their spare time and leave work in progress undisturbed. Music a school strength with 90 per cent of pupils learning an instrument in timetabled lessons, lots of space for rehearsal and practice and a host of choirs, bands, ensembles and plenty of performance experience. Focus on encouragement – all pupils join the junior choir, auditions only introduced in the higher forms.

School does all the usual team sports and one of the benefits of being a relatively small school is that 'everyone gets regular match play,' said a parent. Games every afternoon, played in 'spirit of enjoyment; competitiveness is important but should not be the last word,' says the head. Also sailing on the nearby Broads (they have their own fleet of Toppers) and shooting instruction (prep league champions). Plenty of choice for after-school and weekend activities: fencing, beach picnics, fashion shows, cookery club, trips to local attractions such as Bewilderwood, theme days as well as Beeston's got Talent, a well established contest, though highlight of the week for many pupils remains 'the visit of the ice-cream cart' in summer.

Boarding: The school retains a strong boarding feel; many day pupils stay on into the evening for activities and supper (no extra charge). Very often the pupils themselves want to change. 'My son began as a day pupil, saw the fun and wanted to board – it was his decision,' said one mother. 'Mine both boarded and when family circumstances changed, we asked them if they would like to become day pupils – but they refused.'

Predominance of pupils from county boarding families who know what to expect and settle quickly. 'The atmosphere is so welcoming and friendly, lots to do,' said a parent. 'Older pupils look after younger ones, it is not hierarchical at all.' They make friends for life,' felt another. 'My daughter has done her gap year travel with old boys.' Lots stay in at weekends (30 is usual) and there are regular exeats at least once each side of half term. The recent introduction of flexi-boarding on designated nights is popular, though full boarding remains the choice of many, especially higher up the school. By year 8, virtually all are boarding full time. Parents chorus approval for the way pupils are prepared for senior schools. 'By the time my son left, he had developed the confidence to cope in a much bigger school.' Year 8s are integrated into the boarding houses with other years but have certain privileges (such as access to an all-important toaster). Mr de Falbe feels the opportunities to befriend and offer leadership to younger pupils in that final year stand pupils in good stead, besides promoting a strong community.

Money matters: A plethora of scholarships (up to 20 per cent of fees) offered for academic excellence, art, music, sport and general all-round ability for all ages plus some means-tested bursaries and help for parents who fall on hard times. Encouraged by former pupils, a drive to fund a greater number of bursaries is underway. The head is determined to encourage the widest possible access to the school. Sibling discounts on a sliding scale are available if two or more children are at the school at the same time.

The last word: A traditional, but not hidebound, country prep with vitality and warmth and a well-deserved reputation for nurturing its friendly, confident pupils who are 'willing to give things a try,' said a parent. Solid grounding ensures they go on to make the most of their senior schools.

Berkhamsted School

8

Overton House, 131 High Street, Berkhamsted, Hertfordshire HP4 2DJ

01442 358001 | admissions@berkhamsted.com | www.berkhamsted.com

Ages: 11-18

Pupils: 1,291; sixth form: 386; Boarders: 43 full (from age 16), 7 weekly (from age 13), 8 flexi (from age 11)

Fees: Day £18,330 – £22,170/ Boarding £29,850 – £35,610 pa

Principal: Since 2016, Richard Backhouse, educated at Cheam and Marlborough followed by Selwyn College Cambridge, where he read economics. From there, took a gap year teaching sailing in Dorset and skiing in the Alps, and was promptly bitten by the teaching bug: 'I was fizzing after my first morning with the feeling you get when you take a child from "I can't", to "I just did".' Decided at that point to teach 'just for a year or two', which led to six years at Oundle teaching economics and ultimately becoming head of year 9, followed by a stint at Bradfield as head of economics and politics, director of pastoral and extracurricular and head of a 'difficult' boarding house which, under his watch, became oversubscribed. From there he moved as principal to Monkton Combe School in Bath where he spent 10 years before joining Berkhamsted. As principal overseeing the six schools in the Berkhamsted group, he is more chief executive than managing director these days, seeing parents 'if they're unhappy about something the heads haven't resolved – a rarity' and pupils 'when I do the rounds and speak in assemblies.' Despite ivory tower nature of his role, is also frequently pitch side on match days, at concerts and other school events. 'Inspirational' and 'good on communications,' say parents. 'Gravitas is the word I'd use,' voiced another. Lives on Castle Campus with wife Debbie and has two adult children. Loves skiing, sailing, gadgets and Southampton FC.

Since 2014, head of the girls' school (years 7-11) is Liz Richardson, previously deputy head. Bubbly and savvy, she teaches English and PSHE to all year 7s. To be replaced in September 2022 by Emma Watson, currently deputy head of Berkhamsted sixth form, having joined the school in 2018. Spent six years in the Army Air Corps as a pilot and flight commander and has taught at Stowe, Harrow and Wycombe Abbey, where she was a boarding housemistress. Originally from County Down, she read aerospace engineering at Manchester and has a PGCE from Buckingham University, and is currently undertaking an MBA part-time at Salford

University. She is also trained in Graydin coaching and restorative approaches.

Since January 2022, head of the boys' school is Tom Hadcroft. Previously senior vice principal at DLD College London. He has also been head of department at St John's Leatherhead an senior boarding housemaster at College Alpin Beau Soleil in Switzerland, where he was also responsible for technology enhanced learning. Degree in modern European studies from Lancaster, masters from Leicester De Montford, Lancaster and Buckingham. Is a qualified Graydin coach and enjoys football, athletics and rugby.

Since September 2017, head of the mixed sixth form is Martin Walker. Previously house master at Harrow, he combines straight talking with compassion. Keen to ensure sixth form is a bridge between school and university, he has created a more independent vibe in this part of the school, but with excellent pastoral scaffolding. Teaches French and German.

Entrance: No longer a safe bet for those who didn't quite make the grammar school grade at 11. Oversubscribed at both major entry points (11+ and 13+), with places sought after by bright and talented pupils from far and wide, looking for more breadth than the local grammars can offer, without the hothouse feel of some schools closer to London. Around 80 move up from prep each year.

Every year group does its own annual production and – as with music – there's a lot of mentoring by the older ones of the younger ones. Big take-up for LAMDA

Around 100 external applicants for the 30 girls' places in year 7 and around 120 for the 40 boys' places; all take the ISEB (English, maths and VR), plus interview. Around 30 per cent from state primaries. Siblings largely accommodated provided they reach minimum academic standard. Same application process for year 9 entrance (when a minimum of 40 boys' places become available), girls places at year 9 are subject to availability as it is not a main entrance point for girls, but these hopefuls take the school's own exam (similar to ISEB plus NVR and a language paper), plus interview. Around 60 new students admitted into sixth form, who join similar numbers from the girls' school and 100 from the boys'. Entry requirement is 43 points including at least a six in the A level subjects to be studied (in some cases a 7 and, for maths, an 8).

Exit: A handful leaves after GCSE and despite local coffee shop chatter, school assures us that anyone not expected to make the cut for sixth form is advised to seek alternative options well in advance – 'it should never come as a shock.'. Vast majority to university – around half to Russell Group. St Andrews, LSE, Imperial, Durham, Loughborough, UCL, Bath and Warwick recently popular. Wide range of courses, with economics and business studies increasingly popular. Degree apprenticeships valued by school – recent blip in applications, though, which they are looking into. Five to Oxbridge, and eight medics in 2021.

Latest results: In 2021, 74 per cent 9-7 at GCSE; 63 per cent A*/A at A level (88 per cent A*-B). In 2019 (the last year when exams took place), 65 per cent 9-7 at GCSE; 47 per cent A*/A at A level (79 per cent at A*-B).

Teaching and learning: You won't find Berko showboating at the top of league tables but head and parents alike are totally fine with that, all focused on broader offering. With around half of the senior cohort joining from the prep – many having been there since nursery – and a host of hungry grammar schools in surrounding area snapping up many of the most academic 11-year-olds, value added is king. Grammar school results with a mixed ability intake – impressive. 'The first term is quite a shock to the system,' reported one parent, 'but there is support.'

The other thing you won't find here is complacency, as their latest inspection attests. There are no weaker subjects and parents, pupils and staff talk about a constant redirection of energy to keep everyone on their toes. Online learning, when in place, is regularly surveyed by both parents and pupils – meant that the fun and collaborative work which got squeezed out of learning in the early days was quickly reinstated thanks to eg break-out rooms and more social experiences. The online history, drama and English classes that we dropped in on were entertaining and absorbing – pupils, many in their beanies, were right on task, without a monotone response to be found.

Every pupil has their own tutor to help them develop as an individual and understand how they best learn – they spend daily group time with them, plus regular one-to-ones. Pupils write their own reports and set their own targets, reflecting on the skills they've picked up, as well as the new ones they need; they're also in the driving seat at parents' evening. 'Research shows young people are much more likely to do better if they're in control of their own learning and we've seen the benefits of that,' says school. Leadership theory taught in year 10.

Setting in maths and some languages from year 8. Pupils choose two out of French, Spanish, Latin and Mandarin to study from years 7 to 9, with a language at GCSE 'strongly advised.' Newcomers in year 9 may not take up a new language. Nine is the default number of GCSEs, with these pupils also taking the school's 'learning pathway' or HPQ; triple science and further maths can take total up to 11. History and drama popular at GCSE, as is food technology, thanks to outstanding facilities on both campuses – we were thrilled on our visit to find eight boys diligently preparing a caramelised goats cheese and red onion tart as part of their GCSE coursework. With 28 subjects to choose from at A level (all the usuals, plus sociology, media studies, photography and most recently computer science), plus the option of EPQ, it's clear to see that school is really walking the walk when it comes to providing the breadth expected by its parent cohort. Pupils effusive about support given during university application process and familiarisation trips to universities available to some from as early as year 10. Weekly careers lunches for year 12 pupils with visiting speakers from all walks of professional life, many of them old Berkhamstedians.

Learning support and SEN: Caters for hearing impairments right through to dyslexia, processing needs and ASD, though all must be able to access curriculum. Various drop-ins for help with core subjects available, as well as one-to-one specialist sessions from year 10 at no additional cost. Some pupils drop a language for timetabled support. Main emphasis, though, is on differentiated classroom teaching. Each year group has an SEN co-ordinator who has significant input to wider staff meetings. Very little EAL outside boarding, and even then most have a good grasp of English. 'Good at spotting learning problems,' reckoned parent. Wheelchair access not an issue, with majority of campus accessible and timetables tweaked to ensure inclusivity if necessary.

The arts and extracurricular: Music on the up – 'better than five years ago,' thought parent. Word on the street is that it's all credit to new teachers, plus a new structure so that there's now one staff member each for solo, academic music and ensembles. Almost half take peripatetic music lessons and there are bands, choirs and orchestras galore. 'Music online has been one of the best things about Covid – listening to my son tap out beats on the table on Monday mornings has been really nice,' said parent. Strong links with the drama department – few events evoke quite such excitement as the annual whole school musical. 'Every single person who sings does so with real confidence and with a wonderful big band to back them up,' we heard. Every year group does its own annual production and – as with music – there's a lot of mentoring by the older ones of the younger ones. Big take-up for Lamda (including during online learning) – many sail through the grades, reaching grade 8 by year 10. Sixth formers head off to the Edinburgh Fringe Festival every other year. For those who prefer to stay backstage, opportunities abound in set design and backstage technology.

You won't find a definitive Berko style when it comes to art – everyone is encouraged to go off in their own direction and the results are all the richer for it. Plenty of mediums, from meticulous fine detail in textiles through to whopping great installations.'

You won't find Berko showboating at the top of league tables but head and parents alike are totally fine with that

Endless extracurricular opportunities, with CCF and DofE, both run in house, at heart of school and strong uptake of both. DofE happily non-selective, with a 99 per cent take up for the bronze award in year 9 and one of the UK's highest number of gold awards achieved year after year. Monday afternoon includes a slot for everyone to do something extracurricular, with the rest of the clubs taking place before and after school and at lunchtimes. Multitudinous trips punctuate pupils' time at school. Football tour to Bolton and Liverpool right through to lacrosse tour to the West Indies – near and far, there's something for everyone, including curriculum based. Even managed (unusually) to squeeze in an expedition in the summer following the first lockdown.

Sport: Recently ranked third in the country for sport by School Sport magazine. 'Why?' we asked, mindful that the trophy cabinets that groan with silverware probably provided the obvious answer. 'We'd won a lot,' confirmed head, though other staff members interjected that actually it was down to sport for all approach too, with school boasting A-J teams in football in some years (though some parents told us the exceptional standard of coaching means that competition for the top teams, which get most of the matches, is 'very hot indeed'). We wondered if the sheer breadth might also have helped nail the award – we're not just talking rugby, netball and lacrosse (although pupils play all of these – and jolly well too) but skiing, equestrian and climbing are part of the enormous array. Eton fives stands out – 'We win an almost embarrassing number of matches,' says head.

Sports facilities definitely worth writing home about, including most recently six repurposed netball courts, 3G lacrosse practice e area and two additional grass pitches. Jewel in the crown is vast sports complex housing a huge multi-purpose sports hall, well equipped gym and pool. Shame the sports fields, including Astro, are slightly out of the way, though. There also exists (uniquely in the area as far as we know) a dedicated, three-strong outdoor education department poised to scoop up not only the gung ho pupils who want to have a go at everything, but also those who, on arrival, purportedly 'hate' sport – and thrust them into the great outdoors. From high ropes to Nordic walking to kayaking and bushcraft, it's all here, with a genuine focus on getting absolutely everyone to find something they enjoy.

Relationships with tutors, formed as part of the vertical house system, are highly praised both for their 'coach-like qualities' and the 'sheer amount of interaction'

For year 10s, activities include the likes of zumba and pilates to keep in shape if competition isn't their thing. At the other end of the scale, elite young sportspeople get time out from timetable to pursue training if required, with some allowed to take fewer GCSEs. During lockdown, the whole school (pre-prep to sixth form) collectively ran the entire aggregate circumference of the world in an 'around the world' event aimed at keeping everyone fit and healthy during lockdown – a huge success. 'Sport has been the making of my child,' said more than one parent, although one warned that 'if you muck about in your team, you're dropped like a hot potato – it's about attitude, not just ability.'

Boarding: Less a boarding school than a school with boarding. Two large, comfortable boarding houses, indistinguishable from residential properties, are situated a stone's throw from either campus. Houses boast large and beautifully furnished common rooms, mainly single rooms (lots of ensuite bathrooms in girls' house) and a well-equipped games room for the boys, plus kitchens where boarders can prepare meals at weekends. Occupied almost exclusively by international boarders (from Hong Kong, China and increasingly Eastern Europe, with a smattering of British sports professionals) who tend to join in year 12 for A levels (though can now join in year 10), often to prepare for British university. Best suited to older, independent pupils – and a good stepping stone to university life – as there is no separate schedule of activities, and organised weekend outings are sporadic, although sixth formers are allowed to venture as far afield as London on Saturdays.

Pupils can flexi or occasionally board from year 7 – the latter sometimes used by pupils staying late for an activity or rehearsal – you don't even need to give 24 hours' notice. Weekly boarding from year 9 and full-time from year 12 (year 10 for international students), but they are usually almost exclusively used by sixth formers. Some parents feel more could be done around integration of boarders.

Ethos and heritage: Very much integral to the smart commuter town of Berkhamsted, its two campuses sit astride the pretty high street and the boarding houses and principal's office are dotted around town, yet in its entirety, school has a totally cohesive, integrated feel. The Castle Campus, which houses the boys and the sixth form, dates back to 1541 and has all the hallmarks – in scaled-down version – of a traditional public school. The main school building is built around a grassy quad with cloisters at the side leading to house rooms where pupils from years 7 to 11 congregate for a spot of table tennis, pool or just to chat at break times. A tour of this part of the school will also take in the beautiful, two-floor vaulted library and possibly the archive room where the historic green baize door referred to by Graham Greene (Greene was a pupil and his father a former head) leads you into an archive space dedicated to all things Berkhamstedian, from old uniforms and sports kit to books. The Kings Campus, a brisk 10-minute walk from Castle and base camp for girls from years 7 to 11, is a far more modern affair, boasting a fabulous modern double-height dining room (we can vouch for the fish and chips) and sports centre. Both campuses have well-equipped classrooms and super art rooms.

School follows a 'diamond' structure with a fully co-educational preparatory section, boys and girls taught separately from years 7 to 11 (although trips, productions, events and performances – as well as DofE and CCF – are mainly joint) and then together again in sixth form. Male and female sixth formers move freely between the two campuses and choose to use either library (books can be withdrawn in one and returned to the other) and eat in either dining room (where a few parents said the quality of food could be improved). Coffee and tea is served at break times in sixth form common room on Castle Campus with rooms for quiet study above (a new sixth form centre is in the planning). The very embodiment of leafy suburbia, school has a safe, sociable and happy feel – pupils are chatty, smiley and conventional and its diversity lies far more in the breadth of its

Two large, comfortable boarding houses, indistinguishable from residential properties, are situated a stone's throw from either campus

academic and co-curricular offering than in the ethnicity of its pupils (although this is on the up).

Pastoral care, inclusivity and discipline: Relationships with tutors, formed as part of the vertical house system, are highly praised both for their 'coach-like qualities' and the 'sheer amount of interaction'. Pupils also appreciate the way it mixes up the year groups, with older ones acting as role models and helping out with younger ones informally when needed; everyone is expected to be a mentor here. 'Very much a family feel,' we heard a lot. Mental health prioritised – came into its own during the pandemic, with pupils expected to have cameras on for online lessons and the counsellors, nurses and chaplains working round the clock to make sure nobody slips through the cracks.

Restorative approach to misdemeanours means fewer detentions than in the past. 'We want pupils to develop empathy and prevent resentment,' says school. Around four temporary exclusions a term and one permanent a year – 'reasons are reflective of the endless inventiveness of teenagers,' says head, with raised eyebrow. School takes strong anti-drugs stance (while not a common sight, sniffer dogs are not unheard of), for which parents, who talk of a thriving party scene, are grateful. Pupils expected to toe the line with uniform, haircuts and time keeping. Quirkiness is embraced and, in the main, differences in terms of sexuality, race or religion accepted as par for the course.

Pupils and parents: Pupils travel in literally by the coach load, mainly from within a 40-minute radius of school. Healthy mix of first-time buyers alongside more affluent – but is definitely in the 'private' rather than 'public' school bracket. Parents report a 'strong community feel.'

Thriving OB association with regular sporting fixtures against the school, meetings with fellow professionals, reunion dinners and charitable events, and busy Friends' association, that organises well attended balls, quiz nights and Christmas bazaars.

Money matters: Cost of extras considered reasonable – particularly outdoor pursuits, expeditions and DofE which are startlingly good value as run in-house. Academic, drama, music and sports scholarships available at 11+ and 13+, usually representing a 10 per cent reduction in fees, although means-tested bursaries also available. School has links with Denbigh High School, taking on eight leavers into sixth form on full bursaries every year.

The last word: Solid, safe and exceptionally well-rounded in its offering. Diamond structure at its best – a winning formula as boys and girls are free to concentrate on their educations 'without distractions' (their words) until sixth form and yet have sufficient exposure to the opposite sex to forge good social skills via extracurricular activities and trips.

Bishop's Stortford College

9

10 Maze Green Road, Bishop's Stortford, Hertfordshire CM23 2PJ

01279 838575 | admissions@bishopsstortfordcollege.org | www.bishopsstortfordcollege.org

Ages: 13–18

Pupils: 582; sixth form: 238; Boarders: 63 full, 63 weekly/flexi

Fees: Day £20,910 – £21,096 ; Boarding £32,610– £35,838 pa

Linked school: Bishop's Stortford College Prep School, 875

Head: Since September 2020, Kathy Crewe-Read, formerly head of Wolverhampton Grammar School. Originally from the Isle of Man, went to school in England and took her degree (maths) at Aberystwyth. Taught at King William's College, St Swithun's and Yarm school and was senior deputy head at the King's School, Chester before joining Wolverhampton. She is a school inspector for ISI.

Personable and with great warmth of manner, she is clearly revelling in her role. She admits that arriving in the middle of the pandemic made it difficult to 'feel the pulse of the school and get to know people as I would have liked', but she has been making up for lost time, greeting families at the gates, dropping (unannounced) into lessons and activities and generally 'being around,' for pupils to waylay her, which they do. Parents too say she is 'present', also describing her as 'very approachable,' 'dynamic, but a good listener,' 'someone really informed about the world our children will be living in.' Wholehearted enthusiasm for the school being led by its first woman after 25 years co-ed. 'The school will fly even higher with such an ace role model,' said one parent, who adds that 'education is obviously her passion, she is not just a manager'.

School offers one, two, three and four night weekly boarding packages too and families can opt for one or the other on a termly basis

Keen to build on the solid foundations the school enjoys, particularly the 'quality of teaching which is really high. Every lesson I have been into has been good or better'. Is reviewing school structures, the timetable, subjects and exams and is looking ahead to a time, hastened by the online teaching and assessments of the pandemic, when many exams, starting with GCSEs, will be abandoned. 'We must prepare pupils for the world as it is and as it will be,' and is au fait with current developments in AI. 'AI will ultimately mean pupils will be able to choose their own method of assessment'. Brave new world indeed. Thinks that as 'technology takes over much of our work, it will be our qualities of humanity and creativity that distinguish us and these take time and space to develop.' Is very aware that to be an effective leader means 'not necessarily repeating what worked in a previous school'. Loves teaching maths but is not doing so at present – 'it's not fair on the pupils if I have to unavoidably miss lessons,' she told us, adding that she feels it's more effective getting to know the wider school body by being around, dropping into classes, attending school events and being accessible. Thinks the different 'phases' of the school (pre-pre,,prep and senior) all offer pupils the opportunity to experience the school differently.

By her own admission, she is not the best at relaxing but off duty she likes to spend time with her grown up family, gardening (especially flowers), cycling and walking her cocker spaniel, Charlie.

Entrance: Academically selective, though takes a range of abilities not just high fliers. Selection is via entrance assessments and tests (appropriate to the age group), school references and interviews. Pupils are admitted throughout the pre and prep school years with 20-30 joining at senior stage (year 9 and 10) plus another 30-40 in the sixth form.

Exit: Up to 15 per cent leaves after GCSE to study A levels elsewhere. Nearly all sixth formers head to universities: six to Oxbridge in 2021, with Exeter, Imperial, Bristol, Nottingham, UEA, York and Durham all popular. One overseas in 2021 – to Bates College, USA, to study anthropology and sociology. Lots studying history, psychology, business and management and economics, plus a sprinkling for law and medicine. Each year a few go on to study acting, music or art and design at the various specialist colleges. None to overseas universities in recent years.

Latest results: In 2021,79 per cent 9-7 at GCSE; 67 per cent A*/A at A level (87 per cent A*-B). In 2019 (the last year when exams took place), 76 per cent 9-7 at GCSE; 50 per cent A*/A at A level.

Teaching and learning: Standards have risen steadily in recent years. This is partly due to the presence of girls who, it could be argued, tend to develop good habits of work early. But it's also down to the rigour and quality of the teaching which parents describe as 'outstanding.'

Though not super selective, pupils tend to come from homes where education really matters. 'It suits all types, even if not academically at the top of the tree,' remarked one parent. 'The school tries hard to find out what makes them tick and what motivates them,' said another and pupils agree that, 'working is normal here.' The habits of hard work and application are begun right from the off in the prep school. Pupils know who the prize winners are but they 'also know the class average so they can see the bigger picture and their place in it,' said a parent.

Setting starts in prep and continues up to GCSE in all the core subjects and parents feel this offers the best chance for individual abilities to be supported and challenged. Pupils move sets when necessary, though the pastoral situation is taken into consideration – 'My daughter was more comfortable near the top of a lower set and that was fine,' said one parent. Class size average is 20.

Girls' cricket has made the top 100 schools in the Cricketer magazine and the school is thinking of offering rugby for girls

French, German and Spanish taught from prep up to GCSE; Latin for all from year 6 onwards and 15-20 take it as an option at GCSE. Maths is the most popular subject studied at A level, followed by English, art, history, business studies and economics. About a quarter of pupils take EPQ.

Digital learning advanced dramatically during the pandemic-related lockdowns when all teaching was online and parent consultations and meetings with staff on Zoom. 'There is no substitute for classroom learning,' says the head, 'but that is not to disparage online learning or the plus points of holding meetings with parents on Zoom'. Parents agree, with one telling us, 'We hope it continues. I found it much easier to get to the point and to speak confidentially without a queue of parents waiting behind me, probably listening!'

Learning support and SEN: Three full-time and two part-time staff run the department which ensures a lot of help is given within the class as well as individually or in groups. Pupils are referred by subject staff and form tutors (plus parents) are closely involved. Around 100 pupils, drawn from the whole school, receive help at any one time, quite often for a short term problem. For many, it will be for difficulties such as dyslexia or dyscalculia with a few on the autism spectrum or ADHD. There is no sense of stigma around receiving help, which is free. All international pupils are offered EAL lessons if necessary, to get them through the IGCSE in English (required for university entrance) and for this there is an extra charge (included in the overseas boarding fee). The school site itself is largely accessible though some of the older buildings are still awaiting improvements which the school has committed to.

The arts and extracurricular: Music is encouraged at all levels of the school. About 50 per cent learn individual instruments, often spurred on to learn after being introduced to a variety of string, wind and keyboard instruments in class music lessons in the prep school. Various opportunities to perform with regular concerts and recitals, some taking place in a nearby church to which local people are invited. Confidence is built with small, class based, 'soloist,' performances for parents, in the pre and prep schools (streamed online during the pandemic) and many pupils belong to one or more of the school's orchestras, bands and ensemble groups. Several choirs, including an auditioned senior choir, provide lots of scope for choral concerts and light opera performances (Pirates of Penzance in 2019) and the extremely popular house music events. Lots of practice and rehearsal rooms in the music centre, pianos in all the houses and a resident college musician (usually a post-grad student) to accompany and support pupils in exams.

Around half take art as a GCSE option and the high standard is evident in displays of their work in the art studios and foyers, including sculpture, pottery, photography, clay and graphics as well as fine arts.

There is a comprehensive programme of trips and tours around the world together with field trips, DofE expeditions (this is the leading school for number of gold awards in East Hertfordshire) community work and debating competitions.

Sport: Unbeaten seasons in rugby, hockey, netball and cricket seem to be the norm. In the past 10 years the college's U16 teams (both boys and girls) have been national indoor hockey finalists six times. Regular games afternoons, serious coaching (often given by ex-international players) and every opportunity to compete both locally and nationally mean pupils can develop their particular skills. Sports scholars and talented players receive master classes and training sessions from Olympians and professional players and the school has good contacts with the Saracen's RFU academy programme. Swimming, water polo, tennis and athletics all on offer. Girls' cricket has made the top 100 schools in the Cricketer magazine and the school is thinking of offering rugby for girls, alongside netball and hockey. Recognising that team sports are not everyone's 'thing,' the school offers running, yoga and pilates in the higher forms with the emphasis on encouraging good exercise habits for life.

Boarding: Of the four boarding houses (two for boys and two for girls) Trotman house (girls) is the most glamorous – only four years old, light and spacious with well-designed common and recreation areas and individual bedrooms rooms with en suite facilities. Two resident dogs for company and fun. Of the other three houses, two of the boys houses have been revamped to a high standard and the other two girls' houses are next in the queue. The school is aware of the discrepancy and say that they try to put full boarders, particularly those from overseas, in the new houses.

Heads of house, resident staff and matrons are praised by parents for the homely atmosphere they create and the attention paid to helping pupils settle in when new. Wednesdays (sports fixtures) and Fridays are the most popular for 'flexi' boarders. School offers one, two, three and four night weekly boarding packages too and families can opt for one or the other on a termly basis though school try to be as accommodating as possible if circumstances change. Siblings are offered the choice of joining the same house as elder members of their family.

Ethos and heritage: Originally on the edge of Bishop's Stortford, it is now part of the town as it has expanded but the lawns, playing fields and woodland that make up the 130 acre site mean the school retains a 'country,' rather than, 'city,' feel. It was founded in 1868 as a non-conformist school for the offspring of those of moderate means who wanted a good education for their sons and this principle remains current today, although the school has been fully co-educational since 1995 and numbers of boys and girls are pretty evenly balanced. Though relatively few pupils board (around 15 per cent), the school has a strong boarding 'vibe', which stems from the strong house system, the basis of pastoral support and the wide range of extracurricular opportunities made possible by the long working day and Saturday school for all from aged nine onwards.

In an area of high population density, close to both Cambridge and London, the school has plenty of interested families, many of whom have moved from London

Despite an unprepossessing approach up a long tarmacked drive and a main building (now reception, admin and classrooms) like rather grand council offices, the school is an interesting mix of older, adapted buildings and newer purpose-built ones. The high ceilinged library (1930s) with its long windows and balcony has the ideal atmosphere for reading and study. The original Memorial Hall (1920) is a much loved and used space for assemblies, concerts and formal occasions while the sports hall is large enough to contain the whole school. Interesting art, music and sixth form buildings, a stunning swimming pool and three brand new boarding houses (the others are being updated). Grounds are well maintained and pupils enjoy their 'promenading' between buildings at change of lessons and at lunchtimes, as well as making the most of the extensive sports pitches and courts. Despite school numbers, as the prep and senior occupy separate parts of the site, it does not feel too big and parents all remark on this aspect – 'It is large, but staff know pupils all by name and the parents too,' said one. 'Everyone knows everyone'.

The dining room, rather overcrowded and noisy, is used by both prep and senior schools in separate sittings and the school has improved the food after some chopping and changing of catering companies and pressure from parent representatives – 'Foodgate,' as one referred to the process. The traditional uniform is worn well and the girls' ankle length tweedy skirts remain surprisingly popular, though one parent suggested they resembled picnic blankets.

Lots of distinguished former pupils including writer Dick Clement ('Porridge'), several former MI5 heads and Peter Wright, the author of 'Spycatche,r' together with a string of sporting successes and several musicians of note (especially if you are under 30!).

Pastoral care, inclusivity and discipline: The house system provides the pastoral base. There are 10 houses (four boarding and six day) and pupils use their house for registration first thing and as a place to re-charge – 'I know where I can flop, if I need to,' said one. Most return to their houses at break times for snacks and drinks and house staff keep an eye out for anyone needing help. 'It is mostly friendship difficulties, especially in the younger years, but struggles with a particular subject may also come up,' said a house head, 'and of course we keep a careful look out for the usual adolescent problems with low moods, or food or family matters.' Vertical grouping helps create a sense of 'family' with older pupils looking out for younger ones and this aspect was very much missed during the pandemic. But during the lockdowns, house assemblies were held online and competitions and quizzes held regularly to keep everyone in touch and maintain some esprit de corps.

Great care is taken to help pupils transition from prep to senior school and settling in those from elsewhere. Parents describe the school as 'nurturing' and several said the pastoral nature of the school decided their choice. Wellbeing of pupils was a particular priority during lockdowns. There is a school counsellor, to whom pupils can refer themselves, a chaplain and a medical centre.

Zero-tolerance on drugs and alcohol but few discipline problems. Having good relationships in the first place mean it is rare to get a situation that cannot be worked through satisfactorily, according to the school. School is very aware of the various pressures on pupils, in and out of school, and a questionnaire was set up (with the help of sixth formers) in the wake of the social media campaign 'Everyone's invited.' House staff and tutors deal with day to day trip-ups, contacting parents if necessary and senior staff rarely need to get involved. Pupils are motivated and well behaved and know where to turn for help if needed.

Pupils and parents: In an area of high population density, close to both Cambridge and London, the school has plenty of interested families, many of whom have moved from London to take advantage of an all-through school that operates a long school day and has a boarding offer. 'We had several children, all really different, and we moved out of London so they could come here. It has worked out for them all.' Minibus pick-ups have just been introduced but most parents deliver and collect, 'which can be really slow at the end of the day – mine often arrange to meet me in the Waitrose car park!' Mixed parent body with a predominance of business and finance, farming, scientists and other professionals – mostly two-career families. Quite a high number of pupils are offspring of former pupils and the school is popular in the town and surrounding area. Most full-time boarders are from overseas, both Europe and the far East and parents feel this gives the school a greater ethnic diversity than it would otherwise have.

Money matters: Academic, music, art and sport scholarships offered at 13+ and a considerable proportion of school income goes on means-tested bursaries (currently 34 pupils receive one). School tries to keep fees down as far as possible.

The last word: This is a flourishing school with a head who really understands the direction education is going in and will see to it that pupils are prepared for the world as it is. Unburdened by (relatively) fewer centuries of tradition than some more high-profile schools and now completely co-ed, its strong work hard/play hard ethic and excellent pastoral care of pupils make this a deservedly popular, oversubscribed school at all stages. It recruits by the best means – word of mouth.

Bishop's Stortford College Prep School

Maze Green Road, Bishop's Stortford, Hertfordshire CM23 2PH

01279 838607 | psadmissions@bishopsstortfordcollege.org | www.bishopsstortfordcollege.org

Ages: 4–13

Pupils: 635; Boarders: 11 full (from age 9); 16 weekly/flexi

Fees: Day £9,960 – £16,728; Boarding £24,942 – £26,238 pa

Linked school: Bishop's Stortford College, 871

Headmaster: Since 2013, Bill Toleman BA MSc FRGS. Previously head of Yarm Prep School and before that deputy head of King's School, Worcester. Read geography at Nottingham University, later studying for an MSc in educational management and leadership and becoming a fellow of the Royal Geographical Society. Still very much a geographer – pointing enthusiastically to the large aerial map of the school and the grounds on his study wall to explain the school's position in the town. In non-pandemic times he accompanies field trips but feels, as many heads do, that he gets to know the pupils throughout the school better by being available, visiting classes unannounced and being a, 'presence,' at changes of lesson and drop off and pick up times (which parents all mention, with approval). He is cheerful and easy with pupils and staff alike, completely un-pompous and fortunate to possess that, 'Pied Piper,' quality that children naturally respond to. On our visit he spoke to every pupil we met around school by name. Pupils approach him directly, 'they can drop into my office if they want, if I'm not here my PA will make them an appointment'. Parents full of praise, 'he gets on with everyone,' 'you can talk to him about anything, he is friendly and practical'. The head's natural warmth contributes significantly to the atmosphere of the school with well-motivated pupils who come to school with a zest for the day's happenings in and out of class, 'He shines out,' a parent commented. He is a man of broad interests but sport remains an abiding love, 'all the team sports and I run, and we have a boat down in Devon for the holidays'. Keeps up with professional reading but enjoys detective fiction

(Lord Peter Wimsey a favourite character). He is married with three grown-up sons and a dog called Jessie.

Entrance: For the pre-prep (4-7) there are informal assessment sessions. Admission to the prep at 7+ (20 places) is via the entrance exam with tests in English, maths and reading. These are taken within a morning spent at the school, in class, and the process is kept as unintimidating as possible. Head meets all parents. A further 20 places are offered at 10+ and another 20 at 11+ (when academic and music scholarships are available). By the end of the prep, pupils are in a year group of 100.

Exit: Great majority move straight up to the senior school. A handful to other boarding schools (Uppingham, Stowe, Benendon) and a few to local state schools at 11+. If it is thought a pupil will really struggle in the seniors parents are given plenty of notice and other schools are recommended – but this is rare. The school prides itself on helping under-achievers fulfil their potential rather than casting them out.

Our view: Shares the attractively lush, green and wooded 130 acre site on the edge of the town with senior school, but has a clear identity of its own. As the head points out, 'In the end, pupils often spend more time in the prep than the senior school so this is where the good habits of work and behaviour are established'. Traditional naming of classes, so lower and upper shell is followed by forms 1 and 2. Pre-prep (age 4-7) has a rhythm of its own and is set in its own grounds and lower and upper shell have a separate building too so pupils are accustomed to the space they occupy, but also become familiar with the wider school. In the higher forms pupils move around the whole prep site with certain lessons in years 7 and 8 taken in the specialist facilities of the senior school. Parents praise the school's handling of the transition from one stage to another, 'it was done really sensitively, they were so well prepared for moving up,' and another spoke of how, 'when the time came, my son was keen to move.' Despite the relatively small numbers who board (available from year 3 up), the school has that boarding 'feel'. The longer days (5pm finish) plus Saturday school from year 3 mean lots of opportunities for drama, sport, music and other activities which also allow staff to get to know their pupils really well away from the formal classroom setting. Several parents spoke about this aspect, 'one of ours boarded, the other didn't but they both had the same sense of belonging to a community that exists beyond the school day,' 'there is time to develop relationships.'

The main prep school building is contemporary, lots of glass and acres of carpet – the entrance foyer somewhat akin to an art gallery. Though the buildings, of varying ages and styles, are not on the whole architecturally distinguished, they are updated and well designed for their purpose. Art studios, science labs, a superb library (permanently staffed) and assembly hall, are all positioned to make the most of the site's splendid views; the vistas are quite distracting from certain vantage points and even the rooftops, visible from some classrooms, are intriguing. Moving about the site gives pupils a chance to relax in between lessons and get some fresh air. Setting for maths begins in year 4. French, German and Spanish are introduced to the pupils, as, 'taster,' lessons initially, with Latin added for years 7 and 8. Drama and DT from year 3.

The prep boarding house, Grimwade (rather aptly named as it is large and gothic) has five resident staff, including gap students

Sport makes full use is made of the excellent facilities, both the prep's own courts and playing fields but also those of the senior school for rugby, hockey, cricket, netball and tennis. The school competes at the highest levels in all sports – often national finalists- and promising pupils receive professional coaching. Girls play cricket, also reaching national finals, and there is talk of them beginning rugby. Music is encouraged and pupils try out a variety of instruments in class, often leading to their learning seriously. Lots of choirs and ensembles and solo performances encouraged from pre-prep onwards, 'It helps build confidence if you start young.' Plays and musicals performed regularly (in non-pandemic times) in the large hall, most recently 'Armageddon outa here'. Pupils belong to one of four houses for sports, behaviour (merit points), music and maths challenges and other competitions. The houses also run various fundraising efforts such as a teddy bears' picnic and film nights which help raise awareness of the need to, 'give back to society'.

Great attention is paid to pupil's wellbeing. During the lockdowns, there were weekly assessments (scoring from 1-10) to check on moods and attitudes and parents speak of the efforts the school made, 'staff kept in close touch and quizzes and competitions were held regularly to keep them together as a class'. There is a specially designated garden for quiet reflection and yoga and other forms of relaxation are taught in the activities programme. The form tutor is the key person for parents to consult, followed by heads of year, senior teachers, finally deputy head and head but it is rare for problems to rise to this level as the school encourages communication rather than waiting for parents' evening to air a worry. There is a school counsellor and medical team available. As with the seniors, families often move out from London to take advantage of the school's extended day and the boarding offer. Most are dual-career with many in business and finance, farming or the professions.

Boarding: The prep boarding house, Grimwade (rather aptly named as it is large and gothic) has five resident staff, including gap students. Relatively small boarding contingent of ten or so full-time boarders (majority from overseas) plus around 15 flexi boarders makes for a strong sense of being in a real home. Equal numbers of boys and girls board with Wednesday and Friday the popular nights. Pupils sleep in four and eight-bedded dorms furnished with the usual bed-cupboard-drawers combo but each has a pinboard for display of pictures and personal mementoes and rooms look cheerful and comfortable. Boys' rooms slightly bigger than the girls' on the (debatable) grounds that, 'they need more space'. Bathrooms all in good nick and there are plenty of games, TV and recreation areas for off-duty times. 'We try to keep up the, 'fun,' side of boarding, even with pandemic restrictions,' says the housemaster, explaining the presence of a large tent pitched in the middle of a common room. 'They couldn't do the usual expedition this year so we pitched camp in here and they enjoyed an evening under canvas playing games'. The slightly, 'Malory Towers' sounding, 'Matron's sewing room', is the central, 'hub,' and place to go if a pupil needs help or company and efforts are made to create a family feeling at weekends with breakfast cooked in-house on Sunday mornings. Pupils' colourful hand prints (signed) cover a whole wall of the dining room, 'they all look for their own when they come to visit,' says the housemaster. Bedtime is between 8.45 and 9.45pm and mobile phones are not allowed except for full boarders at the weekend. There is lots of support with prep and great attention is paid to helping overseas boarders, 'settle,' when they first arrive.' We send pictures of weekend activities and keep closely in touch with parents.'

Money matters: Academic and music scholarships at 11+ and bursaries (currently 11) are offered where possible to support an applicant who might otherwise be unable to accept a place. No sibling discounts.

The last word: An extremely well-run prep. It would suit a wide range of pupils but offers the greatest opportunities to those motivated to work and take advantage of the outstanding extracurricular offer. Nurtures good relationships and looks after its pupils, laying the ground well for the move at 13+ to the main college.

Brentwood School

Middleton Hall Lane, Brentwood, Essex CM15 8EE

01277 243243 | admissions@brentwood.essex.sch.uk | www.brentwoodschool.co.uk

Ages: 11–18

Pupils: 1,329; sixth form: 371; Boarders: 67 full

Fees: Day £20,598; Boarding £40,365 pa

Headmaster: Since 2019, Michael Bond, previously vice principal (education) of Berkhamsted Schools Group. Classical studies degree from Liverpool and PGCE from Newcastle. Has taught at RGS Newcastle, Merchant Taylors' School (head of sixth form) and Christ College Brecon (head of history and housemaster). A keen sportsman with an interest in football ('a long-suffering supporter' of Newcastle United), skiing and fitness. Married to Suzanne; they have two sons. Described by parents as 'happy, kind and personable' and 'a motivational leader – encouraging students to do their best, not to impress their teachers or parents, but for themselves', he is clearly excited by the possibilities Brentwood has to offer. 'It has all the ingredients to be one of the most forward-thinking schools in the sector,' he says. 'My job, and that of my colleagues, is to realise this potential.'

Has 'hit the ground running', putting into practice his vision to 'prepare Brentwood students for life well beyond the step they take after they leave us; for jobs that don't yet exist, as well as those that do.' Also keen to build on Brentwood's long history of widening access.

'Brentwood Online' – their remote learning programme – delivered a full academic and co-curricular timetable during the recent part-closure of the school. 'Very little has been missed, within or beyond the classroom,' says head. Experience has 'made us think differently in a number of areas,' he says and has prompted a step forward in the use of technology for student engagement. 'Virtual Music Land', a student concert broadcast on YouTube every Friday night during lockdown, has made a strength of music technology and garnered the school a recording studio. Similarly, the necessary development of individualised learning pathways has had a positive impact. 'This has shown me what a community like Brentwood's is capable of,' says head, 'and it's very rewarding.'

Entrance: Up to 200 places available for year 7, just under a third of which are taken by pupils moving from up school's own prep. Both external and internal candidates sit the same entrance exam in maths, English and verbal reasoning. Interviews under some circumstances. An additional 50 places available at sixth form – entry by interview and 50-72 points from a student's best eight GCSE/IGCSE qualifications for IB Diploma or A level pathways; 40-72 points from a student's best eight GCSE/IGCSE qualifications for BTEC Extended Diploma pathway.

Exit: Around 15 per cent leaves after GCSEs. Those who stay mainly head off to universities – Exeter, Durham, LSE, Imperial College London, Edinburgh, Nottingham and USA (scholarships) popular. Sometimes a few to Oxbridge though none in 2021. Seven medics in 2021, and two students overseas – one to Yale and one to Northern State University, South Dakota, both on scholarships. Degree apprenticeships also becoming an established route.

Latest results: In 2021, 70 per cent 9-7 at I/GCSE; 70 per cent A*/A at A level (91 per cent A*-B). IB average 40. In 2019 (the last year when exams took place): 62 per cent 9-7 at I/GCSE; 37 per cent A*/A at A level (65 per cent A*-B). IB average 35.

Teaching and learning: 'Our task is to ask "how is this student intelligent?" rather than "how intelligent is this student?", explains head. 'At Brentwood we genuinely celebrate a student who gets three Cs at A level if that represents fulfilment of their academic potential, especially given that they are likely to have excelled in one or more areas beyond the classroom, just as much as someone who gets a clean sweep of A stars.'

Co-curriculum is where the school 'really shines,' says a parent, and there is certainly an impressive range of activities, from Trivial Pursuit to Spanish film club

Selective on entry but not a hot house, though there are high academic aspirations even for those whose talents may lie elsewhere. Learning is not for its own sake here, but for real-world application, and this is seen across the curriculum, from physics to PE; hands-on engagement and flexibility of thinking is key. 'How can schools prepare students for jobs that don't exist and for the multiple careers most of them will go on to have?' asks head. 'By ensuring we teach the skills that won't be replaced by computers (as well as the competences and content in traditional and emerging subjects) – problem-solving, enquiry-based learning, communication (verbal and non-verbal) skills, teamwork, independence and interdependence, critical thinking and so on.'

Girls and boys taught separately in years 7 to 11, then mixed for classes in the sixth form – the diamond model, relatively unusual for a one-campus school. 'The decision was made purely on educational grounds,' explains head. 'We track the statistics and find there is a marginal improvement on the take-up of certain subjects, but the main advantage is that the classes are more relaxed if students feel they can be themselves during the early years of adolescence. There are no strong educational reasons to separate younger children for academic lessons, and there are good broader reasons to provide full co-education for sixth form students as they prepare for life beyond school.' All trips, plays and concerts co-ed. A good balance.

From year 7, all learn critical and creative thinking, as well as Latin and two languages (French or Spanish, and German or Mandarin). Global Perspectives, Human Universe and HPQ courses help develop transferable skills. 'We teach the students to make connections between the things they do within and beyond the classroom as part of our belief in metacognition as one of the most impactful interventions we can make as teachers,' says head. Teachers are 'always available and happy to help students with their learning on an individual level', say parents.

Unusually for an independent school, sixth formers have a choice of three pathways – A levels (choice of 26 subjects in any combination), IB, and two new BTEC Extended Diploma programmes (sport or business), which the first cohort has found a very positive experience and all have secured places at Russell Group universities. On top there are plenty of activities, including law, Italian, peer-mentoring training, sports leadership and cooking.

Educational visits and trips are exciting and take Brentwood students as far afield as Iceland (to examine the volcanic landforms first-hand) and Tokyo (to experience a contrasting culture).

Learning support and SEN: Dedicated learning and development team provides support to around 50 students with needs including dyslexia, dyspraxia, ADD, ADHD and ASD. Individual education plans, one-to-one tuition, subject support and lunchtime drop-in sessions, which result in such 'good and exceptional progress' that they 'sometimes outperform their peers', noted the ISI on a recent inspection. Usually around 35 pupils receive EAL support, largely from teachers who have lived and worked abroad.

The arts and extracurricular: Appreciation for the arts even by those pupils who don't consider themselves arty is encouraged here; many opportunities for those who do consider themselves so to demonstrate their talents.

Annual art exhibition is crammed with high quality work for all to admire and competitions throughout the year – water-colours and sculpting, for example – draw a large number of entries. Well-equipped design centre named for Hardy Amies (an alumnus) is the venue for art, DT, ICT and food tech. All who take part are encouraged to think creatively and find solutions.

Performing arts traditionally strong and boosted recently by partnerships with elite organisations. One of 14 Steinway Schools in the country, Brentwood has top-notch equipment for young musicians and even runs an extensive endangered instrument scheme – encouragement for students to take up instruments not considered fashionable, such as French horn and double bass. School happy to loan instruments free of charge to beginners. Several organs around the school for aspiring university organ scholars. Music tech recently taken to another level through remote learning and the new music recording studio has had plenty of use, including for the production of a weekly student podcast. School symphony orchestra, big band, choir or choral society all well-attended and more than 60 concerts staged annually, involving over 300 pupils. Unsurprisingly, Brentwood musicians regularly achieve places to study music at top conservatoires.

Three major annual drama productions cover every genre from musicals to comedy to classics, often with a creative twist – Macbeth intercut with video clips of war in the Middle East, modern ballet version of Antigone choreographed by a student, for example. Dance showcases include tap, jazz and street. All put on in school's own 400-seat auditorium.

The co-curriculum is where the school 'really shines,' says a parent, and there is certainly an impressive range of activities, from Trivial Pursuit to Spanish film club (Cine & Literatura) – everyone must choose at least three. 'Something for everyone and very inclusive,' nod parents – 'I rarely pick my children up from school on time,' offers one, 'there is so much to do'. Guest speakers invited by The Sir Antony Browne Society to hold forth on a wide range of political, financial and medical hot topics. DofE popular as is the CCF, one of the longest established in the country at more than 150 years old and with over 500 members. Community service is entered into willingly and raises thousands for charities locally and internationally.

Sport: Great reputation as a breeding ground for elite sportsmen and women, most notably footballers (Frank Lampard et al). More than 100 school teams in a huge range of disciplines (cricket, football, squash, tennis, water polo, netball, fencing and athletics to name but a few) compete at inter-house, inter-school, county and national level – every Saturday in term-time around 400 pupils pull on a Brentwood sports strip.

Unusually for an independent school, sixth formers have a choice of three pathways – A levels, IB, and two new BTEC Extended Diploma programmes (sport or business)

Sport is for all here though and the benefits of a healthy and active lifestyle run though the PE curriculum, which takes advantage of extensive sports facilities including acres of pitches and playing fields, a running track, an indoor sports centre, a 25 metre indoor pool, a fitness suite, a gymnasium, a dance studio, glass-backed squash courts and a fencing salle. Brentwood School was an official training venue for the 2012 London Olympics.

Several experienced coaches on the PE staff, many of whom have had successful sports careers of their own. Gifted young athletes are nurtured on the Brentwood School Elite Player Pathway, which prepares them for potential progression to professional sport. BTEC National Extended Diploma in sport emphasises vocational skills and covers such topics as anatomy and physiology, fitness training and programming, sports leadership, coaching, sports performance, sports psychology, and rules and officiating.

Boarding: Around 90 per cent of Brentwood's boarders are international students who have the benefits of being fully integrated into a large, vibrant day school and then 'go home' to a warm, family-style environment in the two boarding houses. Houseparents put in place regular routines for homework, bedtimes and activities and provide a link between parents and school.

Ethos and heritage: In 1557, during the English Reformation, Brentwood's Weald Hall and land was bought as an act of penance by one of Queen Mary's magistrates, Sir Antony Browne, in recompense for ordering the burning of a 19-year-old protestant. A boys' grammar school, principally boarding, was established there, and in 1622 it received its motto from the pen of John Donne, dean of St Paul's. Girls were admitted into the sixth form in the mid-1970s and into the main school in 1988.

Gifted young athletes are nurtured on the Brentwood School Elite Player Pathway, which prepares them for potential progression to professional sport

Not much is left of the Weald Hall save a few ruins, but the 75 acre site in the heart of Brentwood is still a significant landmark, right across the road from the impressive cathedral. The Old Big School, built in 1568, still has the original front door and is used for lectures, meetings and discussions, and there's a beautiful Victorian chapel.

A strong sense of the traditional alongside the modern – bright and lively classrooms, decorated with pupils' work, are housed in both 19th and 16th century buildings. Beautiful chapel dates from 1868. Art and science are taught in an old stable block

A number of notable former pupils including Douglas Adams, author of The Hitchhiker's Guide to the Galaxy; Sir Hardy Amies, couturier and dressmaker (he designed the school uniform); Lord Black, Deputy Chairman of the Telegraph Media Group (and Chair of the Royal College of Music); Frank Lampard, footballer; and Jack Straw, former lord chancellor and secretary of state for justice.

Pastoral care, inclusivity and discipline: This is a school whose values 'are not just posters on the wall,' says head. Parents agree – 'The school has put so much thought into the well-being of students, with a genuine understanding of current needs,' approves one, singling out for particular praise a card system that allows children with, for example, social anxiety to skip the queue for lunch without question. Classrooms are often organised to best suit individual learning styles.

This is certainly a large school (with all the resources and facilities that brings) but the structures within it lend it a small-school feel. Individual students and their families are well known and genuinely valued, say parents. Supporting others is key here, and the peer mentoring scheme is a successful one – younger pupils share their troubles with trained sixth formers over a hot chocolate in a welcoming space.

Pupils have good relationships with their form tutors and teachers – 'there is always an open door for students, with a friendly approachable member of the pastoral team for anyone who needs it,' confirms a parent.

Pupils and parents: Pupils 'articulate, kind, driven and resilient,' in the view of one perspicacious parent. Indeed, they are clearly confident, polite and respectful and proud of their school. Parents are mostly local professionals, with a small number of international student boarders, mainly from Eastern Europe, Central Europe and the Far East. Friends of Brentwood School does a good job of bringing families together with a calendar of well-attended social events. Flourishing Old Brentwoods alumni network keen help with work experience, placements and careers advice.

Money matters: A good variety of scholarships, including academic, art, chess, dance, drama, music (including singing) and sports. Typical fee reduction 10 per cent. Sixth form scholarships offered on the basis of performance in a two-hour critical thinking paper. Means-tested bursaries up to 100 per cent available – more than at many other schools, to the tune of £2.5 million.

The last word: A genuine focus here on seeing each student as an individual and helping them discover and develop the skills and knowledge needed to steer their own individual future trajectory.

Chigwell School

High Road, Chigwell, Essex IG7 6QF

020 8501 5700 | admissions@chigwell-school.org | www.chigwell-school.org

Ages: 11–18

Pupils: 439; sixth form: 178; Boarders: 24 full

Fees: Day £19,485; Boarding £33,975 pa

Headmaster: Since 2007, Michael Punt MA MSc PGCE (late 40s), a physicist. Previously deputy head (academic) at The Perse School, Cambridge. Grew up in nearby Brentwood, did his physics degree at Oxford and his masters at Imperial. 'You know, Michael, there's always teaching,' his mother used to say, which of course meant he set out to do anything but and originally headed for the electronics materials industry. But the calling was too strong and when he finally did embark on a teaching career at St Dunstan's College – later moving up to head of year and head of physics – he once again surprised himself 'by falling for not just the teaching of my subject but the wider pastoral role.'

One of a rare breed of heads that made us a cuppa himself (the majority call on their minions), you feel this is a man who'll take no persuading to roll his sleeves up and get stuck in whenever needed. 'No airs and graces, no superiority,' 'Loads of gravitas but never in an "I'm better than you way,"' 'Tells you we're all in it together and you believe him,' say parents. 'We loved him from the beginning,' 'He knows every family' and 'Our only worry is that he'll ever leave,' voiced others. Pupils agree that he's a thoroughly decent, jolly nice chap that only the hard of heart could pick fault with – 'In four years, I think I've only ever heard him properly tell one person off,' 'He knows all of us, not just our names but what makes us tick,' they told us. Still teaches, as well as doing mock interviews, and clearly adores the school, practically skipping round the beautiful, sun-drenched grounds during our visit.

Lives on site with his wife Gill and their three sons, all of whom attend the school – a fact that many parents say 'keeps him in tune with pupils.' In his spare time, you'll find him supporting school events, serving as a school governor elsewhere, being a school inspector, or cycling, walking or sailing with his family.

Entrance: Half of the year 7 intake is made up of junior school pupils (the vast majority move up), with the other half from a wide variety of local prep and primaries. Around 400 apply for these 50-odd places (it used to be 40 but has slowly risen). Assessment by interview (separate ones for pupils and parents), along with tests in English and maths. Small number of vacancies at 13 (English, maths and a modern foreign language tests). At 16, those moving up within the school are joined by around 10 local entrants as well as around 14 overseas boarders. Entrants to the sixth form need 8s in the subjects they are studying at A level (occasionally 7s by discussion).

Exit: Up to 10 per cent leaves post GCSEs and vast majority of sixth formers head to university or music and other specialist colleges. UCL, Nottingham and Birmingham are currently top of the pops, with others heading off to eg LSE, King's College London, Loughborough, York, Warwick, Manchester and Leeds. Popular degree subjects include economics, sciences, English and humanities. Odd ones into degree apprenticeships – we met a sixth former considering one who felt well supported in his choice. 'While the majority will go to university, I want them all to consider the alternatives, which we don't see as a soft option,' says head. Usually a few to Oxbridge.

Latest results: In 2021, 90 per cent 9-7 at GCSE; 73 per cent A*/A at A level. In 2019 (the last year when exams took place), 80 per cent 9-7 at GCSE; 47 per cent A*/A at A level (88 per cent A*-B).

Teaching and learning: A more positive, conscientious bunch of pupils you'll be hard pushed to find, as we learned when we watched some of them going into an exam (flicking through text books outside the hall for that one last revision boost) and coming out again afterwards ('What did you put for question 3?' 'I really hope I got it right,' etc). The hard-working group of skilful, collegiate, and caring teachers (all of whom are also involved in extracurricular activity) are also clearly ahead of their game and widely appreciated. 'I have never come across any that you'd think, "I hope we don't get that one," and many are exceptional,' said a parent. Both factors contribute to the excellent results, which have risen steadily.

Best suited to independent learners, although have no fear if your offspring isn't at that point quite yet – 'they get them all self-reliant one way or another, they're brilliant at it,' said a parent. Those allergic to relentless testing will be pleased to hear the school has done some trimming back on this front, but you'll want to be sure they can cope with the fast academic pace. 'It's quite stressful at times, I won't lie. They're under constant scrutiny, so it's not for the faint hearted, but most are fine with it,' a parent told us. Teachers, too, are under the microscope, with a coaching system helping to keep teaching standards high (eg around developing their questioning techniques, stretching the most able or use of debating in class). Lessons are interactive and busy, and pupils looked reassuringly captivated during our tour (some sixth formers were so glued to live election results as part of a politics lesson that they didn't even notice us at all). Huge drive on reading, with all pupils having daily time put aside to get stuck into their latest book.

Good to see risk taking, not just polished pieces – 'Art is a great way to embrace uncertainty and find a new way through, an alternative kind of problem solving'

On entry, five classes of 22 maximum, sometimes just a few in a class by A level. Latin and French from year 7, and all try German and Spanish at that stage too. French, plus one of the other three, from year 9, with at least one picked for GCSE. Some take Greek alongside Latin, and Mandarin is available as extracurricular. Gentle setting in maths from year 7, and a little bit in languages from year 7, then English and sciences from year 10. 'But setting is all quite light touch and even in English, it is not by performance but dynamic in the group,' says head. Homework manageable.

All take 10+ GCSEs, including triple science, and the lack of option blocks keeps choices nice and wide. Computing is the latest offering at GCSE and psychology has recently been added at A level, with economics, maths, sciences, geography and English among the strongest performers at this upper stage. Drama and DT popular at both GCSE and A level, enforcing Chigwell's reputation as a place for the all-rounder. Around a third do EPQ – Will robots take our jobs? To what extent are changes in the cerebellum responsible for autism? etc. In fact, independent research is a biggie here at all levels, with HPQ pushed at GCSE and the school is piloting something similar for years 7 and 8 'where younger children can follow their nose and dig deep into a topic.' Other enrichment opportunities include essay competitions and Olympiads and there's umpteen academic societies eg law, social sciences, medics etc. University preparation good, but there's room for improvement with wider careers advice, report pupils (although school points to new careers advisor and programmes including Unifrog and careers testing for all). A few parent grumbles about the growing private tutor culture (not exclusive to this school, of course).

Learning support and SEN: Some mild dyslexia and processing skills and occasional cases of mild ASD, ADHD, but that's about it. All pupils screened in years 7 and 12. Learning support, if needed, generally happens outside the classroom (no extra charge). School bases its offering on three tiers of support – those who check in for study skills support; more regular support eg weekly or more; and having a TA (though only one EHCP when we visited). 'SENCo is actively involved, knows the children, listens to parents and gives just the right input,' remarked a parent.

The arts and extracurricular: Head seemed concerned during our tour that the theatre in the eye-catching drama centre was looking a bit tired but we were having none of it – this large, professional space is enough to make a thespian of anyone; even we were tempted to leap dramatically onto the stage. No wonder local drama groups jump at the chance of borrowing it and that drama GCSE and A level are both popular. The foyer is big enough for pre-theatre drinks receptions and – when we visited – an improvisation drama class was taking place. 'People come and watch anything and everything we do – it's a very supportive environment,' said a pupil. Related subject areas, such as theatre make-up and costume design, are also taken seriously, and the centre is used for public speaking, debating and LAMDA. But some parents feel there could be more drama overall – 'There's usually only one big show a year and that means there's not room for everyone,' said one (school insists there's at least one and everyone can be part of them), while others would like to see more linking up with the music department (school says it was on the case, then COVID struck, so results yet to be seen).

'The music department is almost like a conservatoire,' claimed a parent of a music scholar. 'It has been transformative for my child – simply outstanding.' The sheer number of music groups

No need for intrusive bells to mark the change of lessons, with pupils making their way around the school in an ordered fashion

meant we couldn't scribble them down fast enough in our notebooks, with all musical tastes catered for, from swing bands to string bands, as well as rock and pop. The chapel choir, an elite choir for 40-odd students, performs regularly at the likes of St Paul's, Westminster Abbey and Canterbury Cathedral. But it's inclusive too – 'It doesn't matter how good you are, you're encouraged to have a go,' grinned a pupil, with a particularly big push on years 7 and 8 'who don't think they're any good at music' to get involved. A joy for us was seeing the practice rooms in full use during break time.

Spacious art, DT and graphics (which is also available as a standalone subject at GCSE) studios. We watched year 12s in their German expressionism class, while younger pupils were itching to show us their colourful 3D pencil holders. The roomy central exhibition space housed everything from junior robots project to A level fine art pieces during our visit. Political views, mental health, physics concepts – you name it, you'll find it all spilling over into art. Good to see some risk taking, not just polished pieces – 'Art is such a great way to embrace uncertainty and find a new way through, an alternative kind of problem solving,' as the art teacher himself pointed out.

School rarely closes before 6pm, thanks to a full programme of extracurricular activities, from DofE (including gold, carried out in the wilds of Scotland) and scouts to the inspiring and thought-provoking talks on everything from evolution to restorative justice for schools. A seemingly infinite amount of trips, including French and Spanish homestays, hockey tour to South Africa, scout trip to Switzerland, annual ski trip to France, along with smaller-scale trips including activity weekends in the likes of Wales and the Lake District, as well as to their partner school in India.

Sport: Is it a sporty school? We were met with a pregnant pause when we posed this question to pupils. There's no shortage of it, they all agreed, and school punches above its weight in competitions, regularly getting through to regional and even national finals especially for football and hockey – but it's more about mass participation than fighting tooth and nail to be seen as the best of the best in everything. Core boys' sports include football (first term), hockey (second term) and cricket (third term). For girls, it's hockey (first term), netball (second term) and football (third term). Athletics is big and there's also golf (played at nearby club), swimming, basketball and badminton, among others. Outdoor facilities are vast, with 100 acres of playing fields, including Astroturf, plus new sports hall but parents have been hankering after an indoor pool for years (to be addressed, says school). Pupils are also coached out to Redbridge and Nuffield sports centres. A couple of parents felt girls' sport takes second fiddle, but school says senior girls' teams are growing year on year.

Boarding: Sixth form only boarders live across four boarding houses, two on the school site and two just over the road. Inviting and homely, though fairly no-frills. All adds to the family feel of the school. Mostly international students, from around 16 countries, mainly central and Eastern Europe and China (no two boarders who share a language share a room). House parents reported by boarders to be 'lovely' – they tend to stay years and their children, if they have them, get involved. Curfews are 10.30pm on weekdays; 11.30pm at weekends. Evenings and weekends are spent doing all the usual – cinema trips, London shopping etc, although you'll just as often find these pupils studying. 'Quite a self motivated bunch,' reports head. A boarder told us, 'There's no them and us culture – everyone is really welcoming.'

Ethos and heritage: This leafy suburb is spoilt for choice education-wise, with several good fee-paying schools on the doorstep and some of the best grammars in the country a short hop on the train away. Even Old Chigwellians admit to investigating the competition before signing up their offspring (common practice), but the school still wins people over with its ability to develop not just academic success, but confident, well-rounded people, as well as having a 'more local, family feel'.

The school started life in 1629 by the Reverend Samuel Harsnett, the local vicar, who became Archbishop of York and Chancellor of Cambridge University. Today the original red-brick schoolhouse, which is located on the approach road to the historic high street, forms the centrepiece to this pretty village of neat buildings, punctuated by gardens, blooms and trees. The surrounding playing fields stretch towards Epping Forest and give a rural aspect to the school and some lovely views from the windows of the attractive, low-rise teaching blocks. Buildings all kept up to date, with sixth form centre, floodlit 3G football pitch and dining hall extension the latest additions. The 1920s chapel was built in tribute to fallen alumni and is a mainstay of life here. Beautiful library, the original school, was full of silent readers when we visited – and we love the old school tradition of leaving prefects being able to carve their initials in the wall next door.

No need for intrusive bells to mark the change of lessons, with pupils making their way around the school in an ordered fashion. Uniform is smart and sober – kilts (none rolled up, we noticed) or plain trousers with a navy blazer (soon to show off new school crest), though sixth formers wear office attire. Food is plentiful and, agree all, excellent – our roast beef lunch was pub standard. Whole families are invited to have breakfast whenever they want – a nice touch. Communications from school to parents could be improved, say parents – 'too much reliance on parent WhatsApp groups,' remarked one.

So what's a Chigwell child? School claims it's a youngster who works hard, is a decent individual and takes advantage of all the opportunities on offer

Distinguished alumni include William Penn, Sir Arthur Grimble, Sir Austin Bradford Hill, Sir Richard Dales, Col Bob Stewart and Sir Bernard Williams.

Pastoral care, inclusivity and discipline: All praise to the transition from junior to senior school, according to parents – 'couldn't be more seamless,' said one. No doubt helped by years 7 and 8 almost acting as a middle school/halfway house, still falling pastorally under the junior staff that know them so well. Pastorally strong for older years too, with one pupil pulling us aside to tell us about a personal tragedy that 'the school could not have been more brilliant about' – we were almost moved to tears. Not a school to bury its head in the sand around mental health issues, with head chatting openly about self-harm and eating disorders – discussions with students around drugs could be more nuanced, thought student.

Little poor behaviour to speak of but head reassuringly unfazed by any youngsters that do push boundaries – all par for the course, as far as he's concerned. As such, school plays the long game with regards to discipline, with a highly structured but light touch approach that gets vast majority through unscarred. Where there are more serious sanctions (Saturday detentions and internal exclusions), it's usually because of repeat low level stuff eg homework failure, persistent talking in class etc rather than one major scandal. No permanent exclusions in recent years. School on the ball when it comes to bullying – tries hard to track it, ensures pupils are good at coming forward etc.

All the diversity groups you'd hope for – Black Lives Matter, LGBTQ+ etc, with pupils reporting that it would be 'a non-issue if someone came out as gay' and parents of children from ethnic diversities telling us their kids have 'never felt uncomfortable in any way'.

Pupils and parents: Around a third are British Asian – the younger classes the most ethnically diverse. Expect to see your fair share of Porsches and Range Rovers in the car park as parents are mostly an affluent bunch, although change is afoot here too and we were impressed with the school's commitment to less well-off families – there's a broader intake than you might think, with some families who would be on pupil premium in the state sector, including many single parent families. Most live within a five-mile radius, although there's a growth in the number coming in from East London, with six school bus routes. Lots of socialising – breakfast get-togethers and afternoon teas etc, as well as the programme of social events put on by the Friends of Chigwell PA – one parent warned that you have to 'get past the cliques.'

So what's a Chigwell child? School claims it's a youngster who works hard, is a decent individual and takes advantage of all the opportunities on offer. And to be fair, that's exactly what we encountered. If your child is the type to say, 'Yeah, I'll have a go at that, why not?' they'll probably fit right in. We weren't in the least surprised to hear a local GP report that, 'You always know a Chigwell child because they're polite, pleasant and have a certain quiet confidence.'

Money matters: We've lost count of the number of heads that wax lyrical about wanting to create more bursaries to level the playing field, only for us to revisit a few years later and find nothing has really changed. Not so here, with almost one in 10 children now on a means-tested bursary and half of those on full bursaries and best of all, you'd never know – everyone mingles, everyone is seen as equal. Academic scholarships available at 11 and 13 years; scholarships for art, drama and music offered at 16.

The last word: Anyone who spends time in this school couldn't fail to pick up on the academic rigour, family feel and have-a-go ethos. Possibly wasted on bookworms who rarely look up from the page or tunnel-visioned sporty types (although they do have both), but for those who want to take advantage of the widest possible education, it's a clear winner.

Bishop's Stortford College

Culford School

Culford, Bury St Edmunds, Suffolk IP28 6TX

01284 385308 | admissions@culford.co.uk | www.culford.co.uk

Ages: 3–18

Pupils: 800; sixth form: 139; Boarders: 215 full, 18 flexi (from age 7)

Fees: Day £9,465 – £20,685 ; Boarding £32,280 – £34,470 pa

Headmaster: Since 2004, Julian Johnson-Munday (50s). MA in English at Leicester followed by MBA at Durham. Toyed with joining the advertising industry but ended up at Cranleigh, where he became hooked on teaching. Rose through the ranks to be a housemaster, 'the best job in the world,' headed to London (Mill Hill) but decided a small rural boarding school 'where I knew all the children' was for him. Very settled at Culford and well liked by parents and pupils. Accompanied everywhere by his two dogs, 'they slow the children down,' who are greeted with enthusiasm by pupils, parents and staff. 'He has a lovely way about him,' said one parent. 'Very paternalistic and knows the children.'

You can tell he did English: slightly dramatic, very witty, warm, possibly a bit of a luvvie, who we imagine enjoys his time 'on the stage' as head, but in the nicest way, with a self-deprecating sense of humour. Smartly turned out. Runs the school with great efficiency and warmth. 'He's completely aware of what is going on, but is happy to let his very efficient management team cope with the day-to-day minutiae,' was one parent's view. 'Pragmatic and takes difficult decisions at times, but deals with them with great empathy,' from another. Keeps in close contact with parents via email and social media. 'Very much on the ball,' was said more than once. All fourth form (they use the old fashioned descriptions of year groups here) pupils have tea with the head, and his dogs, who enjoy hoovering up crumbs.

Prep school head: Since 2008, Mike Schofield (50s). Studied history and sport at Bedford College; has been at Culford for 19 years, arriving as a housemaster from the state system. Still coaching local rugby teams and referees matches at Culford. Chatty and likable, knows all children well, again very paternalistic. 'Watching them perform on stage, it's like being a parent 22 times over.'

Entrance: Entry into nursery via taster sessions, pre-prep by day's assessment and taster session. Prep by entrance exam, entry to senior school automatic from prep, entrance exam if external student. Sixth form requires seven GCSEs including maths and English, grades 5+. Flexibility is key. Unusual for a sibling to be turned away if they don't make the grade; 'we are a family school.' Largeish intake at year 7, mainly from the state, and larger again in year 9 from local prep schools, including the Cambridge contingent.

Exit: Very, very unusual to have a pupil not make the grade for transfer to senior school. The odd one leaves to board elsewhere, usually following family tradition. About 30-40 per cent leaves after year 11, most to vocational courses or, again, to board elsewhere. Entry to sixth form denied if attitude doesn't fit. Most go to university, the odd one into Forces or family business. Arts and dance courses quite popular. Interestingly, apprenticeships not on the horizon. Some gap years. Odd few medics, and a few overseas some years.

Latest results: In 2021, 56 per cent 9-7 at GCSE; 48 per cent A*/A at A level (77 per cent A*-B). In 2019 (the last year when exams took place), 44 per cent 9-7 at GCSE; 26 per cent A*/A at A level (53 per cent A*-B).

Teaching and learning: Good results for a school that does not claim to be highly academic. Spanish, French and Latin available at GCSE and A level, and taught in prep as well. Latin for the top set only in prep. All senior school pupils do one language, not many do two and unusual for all three to be taken. Maths is most popular subject at A level. Children set from year 5, gifted and talented spotted early and nurtured. No parent could fault academic progress and all spoke of being kept well informed of progress and problems. Extra help available if needed, and problems quickly spotted. IT well embraced. Old fashioned IT rooms have disappeared, it's all about laptops here, note the trolleys in the corner of classrooms loaded with laptops. Pupils encouraged to try all subjects, including art and DT, which proves popular further up the school. Good to see boys do textiles as well. Mention must go to the drones that are now being used in the grounds.

Excellent facilities including shared new science block, fabulous new £2.2 million library and refurbished art and DT blocks; alumni have proved generous benefactors. Sixth form centre with kitchen, used by groups quietly working. The new library is more popular for quiet study. Prep school has its own excellent library, well used with plenty of workshops and visiting authors. All seniors bring their own laptops.

A school full of energy. Happy children, relaxed teachers, all keeping busy and enjoying life, but don't be fooled, they are working hard. Saturday morning lessons for all in senior school. Senior school finishes at 5.30pm after clubs and sports practices, or prep for non-participants. Extended day runs to 9pm at no extra cost. Supervised prep and supper provided. Popular with many hard-working parents as no dreaded homework to be done at home.

Good to see there are teams for all, it's not just about the elite. Sports participation encouraged in the prep school; 'the unwilling are gently, but firmly encouraged'

Small classes mean there's nowhere to hide, and teachers know pupils well. Parents appreciate this and most said it was one of the main reasons for choosing the school. 'You can see the rapport on parents' evenings and it's good to hear the banter between teachers and your child; this reassures us that all is well.' We can vouch for this from our tour of the school. Average class size in prep is 17, 20 in senior and 10-12 in sixth form. UCAS preparation exemplary with one-to-one help for all. 'Amazing advice offered including what to look for on open days,' said one parent.

Learning support and SEN: No pupils with an EHCP but 55 on the list for extra help. 'Learning support is excellent, staff are supportive and reassuring.' 'They know what is needed. My child was supported throughout the school to A levels and got excellent results.' Lots of one-to-one teaching if needed, or two-to-one where suitable. Plenty of feedback for parents. EAL pupils also well supported. Mainly group lessons, but individual if needed. Lots of long-serving staff.

The arts and extracurricular: Music and drama are both popular. Music centre in the beautiful old building, lots of rooms available for quiet practice. Many have individual singing and instrumental lessons. Loads of choirs, ensembles, orchestras and productions. 'Pupils are made to feel important whatever their role in the play,' said one parent. 'There are no divas; everyone's contribution is treated equally.' Loads of clubs and practices during lunchtime and after school.

New arts centre unveiled in 2019 – a glass-fronted, modern and dynamic space for lessons and exhibitions. Both here and throughout the rest of the school are excellent works of art. Plenty of options, including art, textiles and ceramics separately available at A level. Plus a new digital media course. All pupils welcomed us with open arms, happy to chat and proud to show work.

DofE and CCF well supported. 'Children are brought out of themselves and encouraged to try things,' said one parent. 'The children are encouraged to take ownership of the opportunities they are offered.' Plenty of school trips for all including a freshers' week for lower sixth with a trip to the Peak District for team building. Sixth form life seems to be very sociable, lots of dinners in the magnificent main house, the Highland Ball and numerous other occasions. 'We get through lots of dresses,' said our guide.

Sport: Sport is king at this school, particularly tennis. Rated the best co-educational school in the country for tennis by the LTA, Culford attracts pupils from all over the world because of it. Elite athlete programmes on offer for tennis, golf, swimming and now football; these pupils have extra coaching and strength and conditioning classes, but never miss academic lessons. This lot are up with the lark and in the gym. Some 120 pupils play tennis all year round using the excellent facilities, including a four-court championship standard indoor tennis centre. There are six grass, six hard and six Astro courts as well as numerous other pitches. Mention must go to golf as well, a new indoor studio with simulator and radar technology attracting golf scholars. More regular sports such as rugby, hockey and cricket (girls too) also extremely successful. Good to see there are teams for all, it's not just about the elite. Sports participation encouraged in the prep school; 'the unwilling are gently, but firmly encouraged,' says the head. This attitude prevails throughout the school. Large sports complex, lots of pitches and pavilions, excellent swimming pool, gym, studios – you name it, they've got it.

Boarding: Boys' boarding full, girls' growing rapidly. Flexi-boarding popular throughout. Pupils staying three nights a week always have the same bed. Offers 10 nights a term, part boarding of three nights a week or full boarding. Parents appreciate that there is always a bed available if necessary.

There are two houses for boys and two for girls. Co-ed house for prep school. All houses mix day and boarding pupils so strong friendships develop throughout. Extended day option available: pupils stay until 7pm, popular with many parents.

Newly refurbished prep boarding has eight in a dorm, four bunk beds, with years 7 and 8 mixed together. Very neat with pupils bringing their own duvets. 'We change our sheets weekly and sort our washing out,' we were told. Pupils' dorms checked daily by prefects. 'We stand by our beds and are dismissed only when our space is tidy.' Phones taken away every night. Lots of outings and trips for boarders: roller skating, cinema etc, and they have the run of the grounds as well, though younger pupils have to stay within certain areas. Supervised prep for all boarders.

Pupils are smart with the senior girls in long, extremely long, skirts. 'They are brilliant,' said one of our guides; 'we can wear our pyjamas or tracksuit bottoms underneath'

Senior boarding houses not quite as tidy, a bit shabby, but homely. The tidiness instilled in younger years seems to slip a little, but teenagers will be teenagers. Years 9-13 in together, with upper sixth having their own rooms. Most younger pupils share, and there is one dormitory of 16 for the year 9s which is very popular. Plenty of facilities for tea and toast making, and comfy common rooms. Sixth form flexi boarding very popular as Paddy and Scott's Café opens on Friday night for sixth formers. Pizza and snacks served here, very popular for socialising. Some sixth form boarders have their own cars. School fairly relaxed about toing and froing; they sign in and out using an app. Very much a family atmosphere with houseparents having dogs, pupils keen to walk them – it covers their DofE service module. Mention must go to the resident parrot as well. Boarders encouraged to have day pupils to stay. Plenty of trips, which day pupils can also join; Alton Towers particularly popular, London shopping and buses run regularly to Bury St Edmunds, making excursions to local town popular and encouraged.

Ethos and heritage: Located not far from Bury St Edmunds, the school is situated in beautiful grounds, just shy of 500 acres. Entering through impressive gates you drive through the estate past a very pretty church, used by the school and very popular for marriages of alumni, before rounding a corner to a 16th century magnificent mansion house, previously owned by the Cadogan family. The new buildings flow well and blend in, with plenty of space around them. The prep school is in the old stable block, built around a quad with the library in the middle. The nursery is housed in a separate building, cleverly located nearest the main gates so parents coming and going aren't noticed. Parents, staff and locals seen walking their dogs in the grounds, which are so large that pupils are easily absorbed, as are the large sports pitches and buildings. The 'Culford bubble' that parents and staff talk about is suddenly apparent. Easy to forget there is an outside world whilst cocooned in this cornucopia of beauty. School well aware of this, as are pupils, who appreciate how lucky they are.

Founded on strong Methodist beliefs in 1881, the school is strong on moral values and there is much talk about the Culford Way. It is a relatively small school so a family atmosphere prevails; pupils and staff are friendly, jolly and welcoming. Everyone seems to know everyone. The school knows not just their pupils but the families as well. Pupils are smart with the senior girls in long, extremely long, skirts. 'They are brilliant,' said one of our guides; 'we can wear our pyjamas or tracksuit bottoms underneath when it's cold and no one knows!' Pupils encouraged to join in and try everything. 'Be the best person you can be each day,' is the prep head's mantra and it seems to work its way through both schools.

Pastoral care, inclusivity and discipline: Every parent we spoke to praised pastoral care. To be honest they raved about it. 'They pick up on problems – even at home – so quickly and are incredibly proactive,' said one parent. All spoke about the 'paternal' atmosphere and the sense of security the pupils, and parents, feel. House staff praised, and their dogs. Mental health problems quickly picked up on. School has focused on mental health for many years, 'long before it was flagged up,' says the head. Counsellors are well used, 'a good release valve'. Half of all staff are mental health first aiders, plans for every single member of staff to be trained.

Drugs have reared their ugly head in recent years and this is where the head comes into his own. 'Deals with problems empathetically, fairly but firmly,' was said by parents. Pupils and parents are kept well informed, nothing is swept under the carpet. Some miscreants leave, others given a second chance but have to agree to random drug tests. The head has had to have some fairly

Founded on strong Methodist beliefs in 1881, the school is strong on moral values and there is much talk about the Culford Way

uncomfortable conversations with some worried parents. All parents spoke positively about discipline: 'They are tolerant to a certain extent but the children know where the line is drawn.'

Pupils and parents: A strong community of parents who are focused on a good all-round education. These parents aren't just concentrating on exam results but on the development of well rounded individuals. Most parents are working hard to afford the fees and very grateful for flexibility school can offer with regards to boarding and late pick ups. Many second and third generation pupils, some even fifth. Most pupils live within an hour and a half from the school. Quite a large Forces contingent. Pupils happy and relaxed and do not show any signs of being under any undue pressure, but are obviously putting in the hard work. Mention must go to one of our charming guides, who had a disconcerting ability to walk backwards at full speed and hold a sensible conversation – we are convinced senior pupils practise this skill in the evening.

Money matters: Academic scholarships and exhibitions available offering 25 per cent and 10 per cent off fees for years 7, 9 and 12. Sports and music awards. Discounts for siblings and discounts for Forces families.

The last word: This small school, housed in beautiful surroundings, really is a family-orientated place; note the dogs and pets making it home from home. Happy children and parents. The school takes much of the strain away from busy parents. The Culford Bubble could be a disadvantage, but pupils are well aware life exists outside the grounds. Its strengths are small class sizes, excellent pastoral care and tremendous facilities. Once a Culfordian, always a Culfordian, it would appear.

Felsted Preparatory School

Braintree Road, Felsted, Essex CM6 3JL

01371 822610 | prepadmissions@felsted.org | www.felsted.org

Ages: 4–13

Pupils: 491; Boarders: 7 full, 89 weekly/flexi (from 9 years)

Fees: Day £9,870 – £19,335; Boarding £25,065– £26,625 pa

Linked school: Felsted School, 892

Headmaster: Since September 2016, Simon James BA PGCE (40s), whose degree is in history. Previously head of Chigwell Junior School and Rossall School, Lancashire. Prior to that, director of studies at King's School, Chester, following various teaching posts at KS2. Has a warm and friendly manner with just the right amount of brisk cheerfulness to reassure and encourage pupils, without overdoing the heartiness. Has the build of an ex-rugby player (which he is) and impresses parents with his open door policy and general accessibility, 'He is usually about at drop off time in the morning,' and 'is easy to approach,' we heard. 'He was so helpful when my daughter began at the school and I always felt able to speak to him,' commented one parent. Respected for his firmness – 'he doesn't avoid straight talking when it is needed' – but geniality is his hallmark.

His wife (also a teacher) and his two children began at Felsted four years before he did. 'It was a very easy move for me,' he admits and is obviously an extremely good,'fit,' as head of prep. He lives with his family a short drive away and enjoys cooking and playing cricket. His youngest daughter is at Felsted Prep, with the eldest having left the senior school two years ago.

Entrance: Pupils enter at various points but chiefly at 4+ and 7+ with the biggest intake at 11+. Not overly selective. All entrants attend a 'taster' day and are interviewed. Tests in English, maths, verbal and non-verbal reasoning, together with a confidential report from current school. Numbers joining the school increase year on year and by the top of the prep school there are 80 or 90 in the year group.

Exit: Well over 90 per cent proceed to the senior school, many joining older siblings. 'We thought it was important to ask them all if they wanted to move elsewhere at 13, but they were all keen to go up to the seniors. Fine with us!' A sprinkling opt for other boarding schools, the local grammars or occasionally, overseas.

Our view: Despite its size, this is a school with a sense of intimacy, probably due to the way buildings are assigned to one of the four 'phases' through which pupils move in their journey up the school. In rural Essex, the school is set in extensive grounds on the other side of the road from the senior school. A series of buildings, more functional rather than beautiful, have been built and added to over the years. Year 2s and under occupy Stewart House, a contemporary two-storey building with its own play areas and wonderful outlook. The emphasis is on creating a happy learning environment and establishing strong links between home and school – 'that relationship is so important and remains so,' says head. On registration to the school, pupils are given a teddy bear, a 'FelsTed,' to take home and keep. A giant version is in the reception area. Frome Court is the base for years 3 and 4 again, with its own play area though pupils can venture out to the larger green spaces with older pupils. Years 5 and 6 are based in The Cloisters, so-called for obvious reasons though the walkways are now enclosed creating a sequence of interesting learning spaces with nothing predictable or dull – 'one of the things we like about it,' agree pupils. Top two years, 7 and 8, are in Courtauld House which includes facilities for science, DT and music (including practice rooms) and a common room. This is a really attractive building – with lots of light and a galleried upper floor, it has the spacious feel of an art gallery. Assemblies and performances happen in Ross Hall and there is also an ICT suite and art block. Everything is well maintained and pupils move confidently around the site, making the most of the interesting courtyards and covered ways around the school as well as the vast expanses of playing fields.

As with the senior school, parents choose the school for its approach where – as one put it – 'children can be children; they don't put the pressure on.' Some also mentioned the 'great mix of opportunities in things such as music and sport – they have time to develop interests that they can take on with them later.' 'A really buzzy, full-on place.' Extracurricular activities include golf, Mandarin, LAMDA, cookery classes (extremely popular) and judo. The school's commitment to the Model United Nations and Round Square programmes provides whole-school initiatives that pupils in years 7 and 8 join in with. (They also go over for sport and to eat in the senior dining hall).

Class sizes of up to 18 until year 3; 20 thereafter (but smaller for sets). Specialist teaching and setting begin in year 4 for English, maths and science. Parents approve – 'My daughter arrived at the school finding maths a struggle, but once in the right set, she recovered her confidence and made tremendous progress. She felt able to ask to have things explained if she needed to,' said one. Progress is under constant review and pupils are moved regularly – and not just up. We spoke to one parent whose child chose to stay put rather than go up -'She liked the teacher and was learning well where she was.' The focus is on personalised learning, the move online during the pandemic hastening a development already underway. The director of learning thinks 'it has transformed the ability of teachers to gear lessons to specific needs without children standing out in any way. It is an exciting time to be in education.' Pupils say teachers 'like us asking questions.' Provision for SEN is mostly on a one to one basis in half hour sessions with one of the designated learning support team. The difficulties are mostly dyslexia, dyscalculia and the milder end of the autism spectrum, although 'for many, the issue is confidence and individual help can resolve problems,' according to school.

The extended day means that a lot of pupils choose to 'flexi' board, especially in the higher forms and the 'three-night package' is a popular choice

Spanish, French or German from year 6 and Latin added in year 7. Homework from year 5, mostly reading and learning a few spellings, with 'proper' homework from year 6 and above, three times a week. It is taken seriously; handing in late, 'forgetting' books and so on is not tolerated and parents approve. They certainly work hard, with a school day that gradually extends from 3.30pm (year 2 and under) to 5.45pm for older years plus Saturday school – optional for years 5 and 6, compulsory for years 7 and 8. Rather cleverly, this comes across as a privilege for older pupils that most look forward to it – 'mine couldn't wait for Saturday school!' said one parent.

Parents speak highly of the school's pastoral care. 'They know the children really well, both tutors and subject staff'

Drama is taught weekly and plenty take the extracurricular offering that leads to performance. Art, including textiles and pottery is taught in one of the two large art rooms, full of various enticing projects and works in progress – a favourite place for many. The plays each year are whole school efforts with the art department helping make props and scenery. Music is taught in every year and roughly 60 per cent have individual tuition on a variety of instruments. Lots of practice rooms so pupils can fit that in during the day, as well as playing in one of the many ensemble groups or bands – everything from jazz to steel drum groups. Singing in several choirs, the chapel choir for those selected by audition.

Sport centres on rugby and hockey (boys) and hockey and netball (girls). Everyone plays cricket in the summer and girls love it – 'it's my favourite sport,' said more than one. Several sports are played at county level and hockey and cricket (girls) nationally. There is no denying the kudos that comes attached to success in a team sport, 'but they aren't silly about it,' we were told. Great efforts are made to see everyone enjoys playing at whatever level and teams from A-G work through the terms fixture list. Parents are encouraged to support matches and the headmaster of the seniors often umpires or referees a prep match, 'I think it's brilliant of him,' said a parent, 'he certainly isn't a distant figure.'

Parents speak highly of the school's pastoral care. 'They know the children really well, both tutors and subject staff, and everyone seems to know who to go to with a problem and feels comfortable with it,' say parents. The care taken to help new pupils settle was frequently mentioned, especially for those slightly older who have been to other schools first. 'We felt they really worked to help my daughter settle, even with the small things such as where she sat in class,' said one. The four phases of the school each have a head who is responsible for the pupils in their section and in the higher forms, pupils have the same tutor for those three years. It means pupils have someone who knows them really well, especially for the years leading into the teens and the move up to seniors. There is a matron and everyone is taught mindfulness so that they know when to press the 'pause' button; 'we learn to relax.' A system of reward cards and house points encourages good behaviour (of the holding doors and not running in the corridors variety) and pupils are friendly, with just the right amount of door holding. Pupils exchange cheerful greetings and badinage with staff – no flattening themselves against the wall.

Outdoor classrooms, some under cover on the verandas or canvas, have been well used in times of pandemic and the school is generally outdoorsy, Thursday afternoons being given over to a scaled down version of DofE. Pupils make full use of all the sports facilities and in year 7 and 8 begin to use the senior provision.

Boarding: Though relatively small numbers board, this is a school that definitely has the special 'tone' that boarding provides. The extended day means that a lot of pupils choose to 'flexi' board, especially in the higher forms and the 'three-night package' is a popular choice. Hamilton House is a co-ed boarding house but girls' and boys' sleeping accommodation is quite separate. Good sized, mostly four or six bedded rooms, all well decorated and with own duvet covers and other homely touches. Bathrooms are perfectly functional, if a bit drab, and are undergoing a gradual programme of updating. Common rooms well decorated and lots of comfy seating for 'film nights' for the different age groups and a separate one for years 7 and 8 to give a chance for boys and girls to mix socially, in readiness for the seniors. 'By then, they are getting to the age of wanting to mix more, outside class,' said a house parent. House parents live in an adjoining flat and there are a range of other live-in staff and a resident matron so 'there is always someone close by at night.'

Day starts with showers and breakfast at 7.45am and evenings have designated times for prep between supper and evening activities. These activities, often instigated by the pupils themselves, include sports, craft projects (very popular), ICT and the library for quiet reading or revision. 'The summer term is the best for boarding though – we can be outside lots more.' One night a week is 'tuck' night and pupils are allowed to spend up to £2 when visiting the village shop (agreed in advance with parents). General emphasis is on healthy eating and no food is allowed from home. There are 'suggestions' boxes on each floor, notice boards and post-it notes on bedroom doors from staff which all make for easy communication between pupils and staff. The house merit system is largely used to support respectful and thoughtful behaviour towards each other. 'We encourage them to stop and think about what they are doing, but every day is a fresh start,' say house staff.

Money matters: Academic, music, sport, art, design and technology, and drama scholarships offering up to 20 per cent off fees are available at

11+ entry. Top up bursaries are available alongside some assisted places up to 100 per cent, on a means tested basis for pupils who would benefit and make the most of a place at Felsted.

The last word: With pupils who are lively, full of questions and from quite a wide ability range, the school manages to be both an exciting place to learn and somewhere that reassures and nurtures its pupils. Despite its rural setting, this is not a sleepy backwater but a school very much on the front foot with current thinking and practice. Very different children from the same family can all develop and do well here, it really is a, 'family' school. Though the school has its own, 'feel' and identity, most go on to the seniors. A vibrant, happy place where pupils learn and do well.

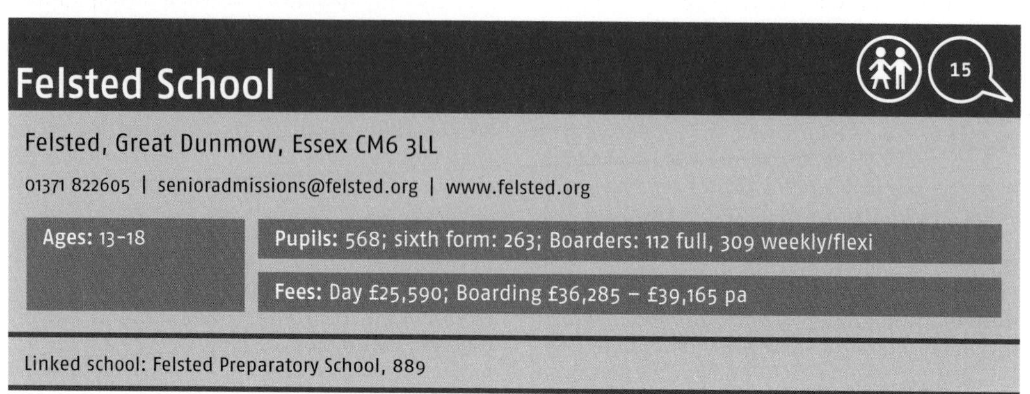

Felsted School

15

Felsted, Great Dunmow, Essex CM6 3LL

01371 822605 | senioradmissions@felsted.org | www.felsted.org

Ages: 13-18

Pupils: 568; sixth form: 263; Boarders: 112 full, 309 weekly/flexi

Fees: Day £25,590; Boarding £36,285 – £39,165 pa

Linked school: Felsted Preparatory School, 889

Headmaster: Since 2015, Chris Townsend BA (Oxon) PGCE (40s). Previously deputy head. Read classics at Oxford and, having also won three cricketing blues, had potential for a professional career in sport – 'it was tempting, but I had already enjoyed playing top class cricket and was discovering the pleasure of teaching'. His first post at Dean Close (his old school) quickly led to his becoming a housemaster, which was followed by a stint at Stowe as head of boarding before joining Felsted as deputy head in 2010. His appointment as head was greeted with wild rejoicings from both staff and pupils – they, and parents, speak highly of his approachable manner: 'No airs and graces, he knows who we all are and greets the children by name.' 'Not at all aloof, he doesn't hide away and just come out for the big occasions – he is around the school and often at games fixtures.' He is a good listener and this means people feel able to tell him things. He is sensitive to diversity too and recently set up a committee for diversity and inclusiveness, more of which later. He believes Felsted offers an education with breadth and the opportunity to discover and develop a range of interests – 'we aren't just in it for the A*s, good as they are.' He thinks parents are looking for a school where their child will be, 'happy, of course, but will have their abilities discovered and fostered.' He admires the entrepreneurial 'giving things a go' spirit and thinks school should be a place that encourages pupils to take chances. 'Success in life will depend on more than a string of exam passes.'

His wife Melanie teaches in a local school and they live on the site with their children, one a former pupil and the other currently at the school. 'Walking the dogs' (two red setters) is his main relaxation in term time, plus reading. He keeps up with professional writings, enjoys history and biography. Continues to play cricket and other sport. Very 'at ease' with himself and his role as headmaster.

Entrance: A hundred pupils, split into four classes, enter year 9. Roughly 70 per cent come up from the prep school (having been assessed and tested in preceding two years), with remainder coming largely from neighbouring preps including Holmwood House, Heathmount, Orwell Park and Edge Grove. Close relationships with feeder preps are maintained and there is no encouragement to 'jump ship' before year 8 if pupils are happy and working well.

Not overly selective; a 50 per cent pass mark in Common entrance although most now do pre-testing to provide assured places anywhere from Year 6 to 8. Tests are in maths, English and verbal reasoning. All pupils are interviewed. The same process applies for entrants in the higher forms (where places are available). At 16+ another 40 students are admitted and they must have achieved 32 points in total across their best six subjects, with a grade 6 in the subjects they wish to take at A level or IB (at Higher Level). If English is not the first language, a prospective pupil will be assessed by EAL staff to be sure they have a sufficient grasp of the language to follow courses, though extra support is on offer.

Exit: Around 15 per cent leaves after GCSEs, with another 30 joining. After A levels/IB, over 85 per cent leave for university, over 50 per cent to Russell group. Durham, Exeter, Nottingham and King's College London all popular and an increasing number overseas – 10 in 2021 including British Columbia, Northeastern, Tampa and Syracuse. One to Oxbridge in 2021, and eight medics. Subjects studied weighted towards business, marketing, politics and international relations, plus a few drama and music courses each year.

Latest results: In 2021, 57 per cent 9-7 at GCSE; 57 per cent A*/A at A level (84 per cent A*-B). Average of 37 points at IB in 2020. In 2019 (the last year when exams took place), 47 per cent 9-7 at GCSE; 27 per cent A*/A at A level (55 per cent A*-B).

Teaching and learning: Without being highly selective, and despite the lure of local grammar schools, pupils do very well in exams with a solid cohort getting top grades across the board at GCSE and A level. Results in English, maths, history, and all three sciences stand out at GCSE, with languages and the creative subjects (especially drama, music and DT) also doing well. At A level, there is a high take up for economics, politics and psychology and results in these subjects are particularly good. Maths, further maths, history and languages all popular too. The IB runs alongside and is taken by roughly a third of pupils. 'Two of mine opted for the IB and one for A levels. It is great that both options were possible in the same school,' said a parent.

Spanish is the core language taught from year 9, with French, German and Latin all available as options from year 10 and other languages possible for IB if self-taught (Mandarin, Russian and Italian all recent examples). School believes the presence of international students (many from European countries) has a positive influence on the study of modern languages and parents also praise the number of native speaking language teachers.

Small class sizes – between 15 and 20 up to GCSE, close to 10 in sixth form. Setting from year 9 in maths, English, sciences and languages; pupils are regularly assessed and can be moved, though 'my daughter chose to remain where she was and not move up as she liked her teacher and was confident in that set,' said one parent. Being in a set for certain core subjects leads to groupings for other subjects, such as history. Pupils say this does not mean 'you are labelled and lumped with the same people,' but one wonders. Subject staff are all involved pastorally and know pupils well – 'they are a really committed and able bunch,' say parents. The move to online teaching during the pandemic speeded up digital teaching methods already underway and now, 'we have incorporated so much that we learnt during that time into our regular classroom practice,' says school. It helps in tailoring personal work programmes and sometimes means pupils can ask for help without drawing attention to themselves. Homework can be tailored to take account of where pupils are, including further extension work for the most able.

Traditionally good at games 'but not one track minded,' as a parent put it. No sprints before a cold shower and breakfast, it leans far more towards developing talent

Constant opportunities to study beyond the main curriculum are offered via the enrichment programme, formalised through the Felsted diploma project in year 10 and the EPQ in sixth form. The Roberts Society (years 9-11) and the Andrew Society (sixth form) are intended to provide those holding scholarships, or who express a particular interest, with further opportunities through lectures and discussions to foster intellectual and cultural development. The Felsted diploma is a school award that formalises the principles of the Round Square IDEALS (Internationalism, Democracy, Environmentalism, Adventure, Leadership and Service) and those who wish to can submit their work for an external 'Cresta' award.

Learning support and SEN: Many pupils receive help with various mild to moderate difficulties (mainly dyslexia, dyspraxia, ADHD, and those on the autism spectrum) at various times throughout the school. But 'support for learning' can be accessed by all pupils, many of whom simply need a bit of extra help in a subject at a particular stage, others with longer term needs. Help is offered on a one-to-one basis or in groups and there are drop in sessions (open to all) for help with prep. There is no stigma – far from it, with one pupil telling us, 'few of us don't need support or help to do our best at some point.' A separate department specialises in EAL for the 20 per cent of pupils who need it, although pupils must have a reasonable grasp of English before admission otherwise a language school is suggested for initial learning. The school makes every effort to accommodate pupils and visitors with physical disabilities, though the many historic and listed buildings mean it is not necessarily straightforward.

The arts and extracurricular: Music, art and drama are given every chance to flourish, whether a pupil is gifted or not (plenty are). 'They are all encouraged to give things a try,' said a parent. Drama is taught to year 9, then it's an option with plenty of takers for GCSE and through to A level. A small number qualify for drama school each year. There are regular school productions, a mixture of musicals and other plays ('Goodnight Mr Tom,' a recent effort) geared to offering all ages opportunities. Pupils not wanting to tread the boards get a chance to learn and develop skills in stage management, costumes, special effects and make up – all vital parts of the production.

The Felsted diploma is an award that formalises the Round Square IDEALS (Internationalism, Democracy, Environmentalism, Adventure, Leadership and Service)

Participation in music is encouraged and the majority of pupils play at least one instrument, several more than one. Percussion is popular, including the marimba (something like a xylophone, with a rich, deep sound). Dame Evelyn Glennie gave one to the school after performing there and opening the new music school. Some outstanding musicians are selected for a place at the highly competitive junior Guildhall music courses (held on Saturdays in London) or for the National Youth Orchestra. Many are studying at grade 8 and beyond in readiness for professional study. Singing is popular throughout the school and there are a variety of choirs – some, such as the chapel choir, with an audition, others more relaxed. The chapel choir leads singing in the chapel and the 'house shout' competition is a popular event. There are regular musical evenings, many show-casing individual talent and overseas tours most years.

Art is taught in the old school laundry, which is well equipped with facilities for teaching in a variety of media. In addition to the GCSE /A level teaching, extracurricular opportunities include a weekly life drawing session. A good clutch leaves each year to study art in a variety of disciplines including fine art and architecture.

The longer school day (8.15 – 6pm) allows time for over 50 clubs and societies to operate – Model United Nations, the academic societies, many charity projects, film clubs etc. Everyone does DofE up to bronze, with many going on to gold in the upper sixth. CCF popular throughout the school and this feeds into the Round Square promoting of IDEALS. There are links with charitable projects and enterprises in in Uganda and with Felsted's own mission church of the Ascension in the Victoria docks, London.

Sport: Traditionally good at games 'but not one track minded,' as a parent put it. No sprints before a cold shower and breakfast, it leans far more towards developing talent and giving everyone a chance to enjoy team sports at some level. The range on offer is impressive with an extensive fixtures programme in all key sports including rugby, hockey (girls competing at national level), netball and cricket (girls recently in the national finals). There are partnerships with professional clubs eg Saracens rugby and netball, Essex cricket and Blue Hornets hockey, with several pupil signings each year. There are a number of professional players among the staff. The 80 acre site includes 12 pitches, nine cricket squares, two floodlit Astroturf fields, 10 hard courts, squash courts, gym, weight training and a swimming pool (in need of an update). Focus is on enjoying exercise and developing habits of fitness for life so lots to choose from including show jumping, polo, badminton and basketball. Running is encouraged and a recent marathon challenge, where teams of parents, pupils and OF's battled it out in a relay (beating Mo Farrah's time) raised money for several charities. Parents are encouraged to support matches and several mentioned how important the contact was, 'apart from watching our children, it is a chance to have a casual word with staff and meet other parents.'

Boarding: The house structure is fundamental whether a pupil boards or not, but around 80 per cent do, mostly on a weekly or the popular three-nights-a- week basis (rather oddly known as 'contemporary' boarding). Full boarders are mostly international, though not exclusively. Many pupils start with the 'contemporary' offer and increase to weekly over time, largely to spend more time with friends. There are two day and eight boarding houses (five for boys and five for girls) with separate houses for the upper sixth. This means their houses have more of a university feel with own rooms and greater freedom. Heads of the main houses are drawn from the lower sixth – 'they have the chance of leadership before their final year,' said a housemaster who thinks the presence of senior pupils in the houses contributes to the family atmosphere and good interaction between the years. Most bedrooms are three and four bedded, with some singles for older pupils. House styles vary from the '60s building that needs (and is getting) refurbishing to the very well designed, open plan new girls' house – but all are well maintained and comfortable with common rooms and kitchen areas for the ubiquitous toast. Food is good – snacks of fruit and sandwiches are freely available at break times. House parents live on site with their families, together with matrons and other house staff. Pupils register in the house at 8.15am each day, a chance for notices and reminders to be given out by house staff before everyone goes off to lessons.

Ethos and heritage: Founded in 1564 during the reign of Elizabeth 1 by a local boy, Richard Riche (later Lord Riche), who rose in service at the courts of the various Tudor monarchs to be Lord Chancellor. He was a wily operator, patronised first by Thomas Cromwell (beheaded by Henry VIII) but he survived those politically turbulent times and Elizabeth rewarded him. The school he founded at Felsted (the original Guildhall is still in use) expanded and flourished and in the 17th century even had the distinction of educating all the three sons of The Other Cromwell, Oliver. Plenty of history to relish but, like its founder, Felsted has adapted and embraced change, 'They are not into maintaining pretentious traditions for the sake of it,' said a parent,'it's definitely forward looking'.

Food is good – snacks of fruit and sandwiches are freely available at break times. House parents live on site with their families, together with matrons and other house staff

The school buildings, set in extensive grounds in a charming Essex village, vary from the listed historic buildings through to the new builds of the 21st century, some more distinctive than others but all well maintained and positioned in a pleasing way around the vast green playing fields. The most recent additions include the music department, the sixth form centre and a girls' house, Follyfield but others are in the pipeline (including a sixth form boarding house and an academic learning centre). Parents say, 'We didn't choose it for being camera ready, it is not a "shiny" school. It could do with a spruce up here and there but then we didn't make our choice on the basis of the facilities.' Lots of outside spaces to gather and socialise and the coffee shop, which is open to all but only sixth formers allowed to work there. The quality of the food 'is pretty good – lots of choice,' say pupils. Lunch is the main meal and for lots of boarders the cooked breakfast is king, 'I get up and go over to the dining hall even when I could just make toast in the house.'

The school is a Christian foundation (C of E) and there is a school chaplain on the staff, with the chapel at the centre of the school. Pupils attend weekly worship ('We enjoy singing hymns!'), but religious affiliation is not a requirement. 'We are not a religious family but our children have all loved the chapel and the part it plays in school life. It brings everyone together.' One parent recalled the recent animal service, 'with everything from a snake to a horse'. The school is one of only two remaining public schools to retain a mission church in London's East end and charitable enterprises here and abroad are woven into school life. 'They do realise that not everyone is as fortunate as they are. Life should be about putting something back,' said a parent. Here is a school with the 'hum' of purposeful, happy pupils. 'No one is left to manage by themselves,' a pupil said, and parents agree. The school's USP is that staff really know the children.

Notable OF's include General Lord (Richard) Dannatt, formerly chief of the defence staff, a number of England cricketers and, in 2020, school's first England rugby player.

Pastoral care, inclusivity and discipline: House staff deal with day-to-day issues, looking out for home sickness (boarders) and friendship difficulties, and they are the point of contact for parents with worries. It is a school that expects a high standard of behaviour, with the emphasis on courtesy and taking responsibility for one's actions, and parents support this. Uniform is expected to be smartly worn and pupils accept the fairness of expectations – 'We like knowing where we are.' Pupils carry cards for the recording of any minor misdemeanours; persistent low-level behaviour gets noticed and consequences follow including detentions and temporary exclusions (about 20 a year). Drugs and alcohol miscreants are dealt with firmly and random testing is occasionally employed if the school has reason ('more likely because of a weekend party than something in school,' say parents). No big problems. Parents say it is a happy school, a real community. 'They help raise emotionally intelligent young people – there is a lot of talk'. The new wellbeing centre, a tranquil space with subdued lighting, is permanently staffed by professional, dedicated staff and is a well-used facility. Staff offer one-to-one consultations (pupils refer themselves) and group sessions, including relaxation classes. It is seen as important that the centre is not part of the medical provision. Together with the house staff and school chaplain there is a choice of help and support.

Particular care is taken to help international students settle and find friends. An equality and diversity committee has been set up, tasked with finding out feelings within the school in the light of the Black Lives Matter movement as well as in connection with LGBTQ and gender issues. Bearing in mind the demographic of East Anglia, which the school reflects, the head spoke of the school's awareness of the need for a diverse staff, 'Pupils need role models,' said the head and there is a drive to ensure that recruitment procedures draw from as wide a group as possible. 'It is easy to return to the same pool of eligibles again and again. We need to look beyond the predictable.'

Pupils and parents: The zeitgeist is doing rather than being, and the school attracts parents with an entrepreneurial spirit and high aspirations for their children. Pupils themselves are ambitious learners and 'have a good idea where they are going,' says head. Most families live within a two hour drive, less in most cases, with increasing numbers from London. The close proximity of Stansted airport is an inducement for international students, from over thirty countries but mainly from Europe.

Money matters: Academic, music, sport, art, design and technology, drama and all-rounder scholarships offering up to 20 per cent off fees are available at 13+ and 16+. There are some assisted places up to 100 per cent on a means tested basis for pupils who would really benefit and make the most of a place at Felsted.

The last word: This is a school with an atmosphere conducive to successful learning. The high academic standards reached by many pupils are not achieved at the expense of a broad education, with plenty of time to develop sporting, and cultural interests and friendships. Exceptional leadership from a head who believes 'a successful school career should be a happy one.' Perhaps not ideal for the determinedly un-sporty, but hard to think who would not thrive here. Lucky pupils.

Framlingham College

16

College Road, Framlingham, Suffolk IP13 9EY

01728 723789 | admissions@framlinghamcollege.co.uk | www.framlinghamcollege.co.uk

Ages: 3–18

Pupils: 622; sixth form: 151; Boarders: 82 full, 195 weekly/flexi (from year 4)

Fees: Day £9,495 – £21,657; Boarding £24,724 – £33,678 pa

Principal of the College, Head of the Senior School.: Since 2019, Louise North, previously senior deputy at Oakham School. French and Spanish degree from Durham. Began her teaching career at St Peter's School, York and after stints as a boarding housemistress at both Glenalmond and Marlborough College, joined Stonyhurst College as deputy head (upper school).

Her clear message is that Framlingham is now a single entity with a seamless curriculum from 3 to 18 and says her priority is to 'put academic achievement front and centre – I want pupils to feel the buzz for learning.' She herself is full of energy, with a confident, friendly manner and a lively wit. In raising expectations across the board, she acknowledges that this may mean 'having awkward conversations with parents as well as the pupils, but we are determined to see that pupils are challenged by staff to achieve their best academically.' The winds of change have been noticed by parents: 'Less flannel, there are direct answers to direct questions – very refreshing!' 'The direction of travel is good,' and 'One feels heard.' The decision to invest in staff, rather than in more new buildings, is widely approved of though a note of caution came from one parent who said, 'Of course all schools must evolve but not so fast that the special ethos is lost.'

She is determined not only to raise the profile of the school ('I have heard it called Suffolk's best kept secret') but to bring wider global influences to bear ('The future adult world will be different, we must equip our pupils for uncertainty, for jobs not yet in our sights. Never mind league tables, we want each child to have the spirit to pursue what they really want to pursue, but anyway, good grades are a by-product of excellent education').

Married to Dominic, a dealer in rare and fine books; their two children are at the school. Reading, especially contemporary fiction, along with jigsaws and walking the family Jack Russell, are her chief off-duty enjoyments.

Head of prep: Since April 2021 is Jonathan Egan MA, previously deputy head of Bedford Prep. As the son of a prep school head, he did the inevitable of actively deciding not to follow in his father's footsteps and following his degree in business admin from West of England University, he did a ski season, worked in the treasury department of RBS, became a maths tutor and spent a couple of years in South Africa before finally accepting that, 'teaching was what I must do' (and he still teaches maths). After a brief stint at the Hawthorns, Bletchingley, he moved to the King's School, Wimbledon where he was director of studies and head of maths. Says he is delighted to be in a school, 'with an ethos I believe in, with a family feel and where children are put first.' Quiet, unflashy and a good listener, parents also like that he is a father of three at the school. 'He is about at drop-off times for a quick word,' we heard, but he will always, 'put the best interests of the child first even if that means pushing back against a parent's request.' A keen sportsman, he has run the London marathon twice (though not a patch on his wife who has run 21 times!) and enjoys the theatre, but most of all treasures time with his family. An ISI inspector.

Entrance: For entry to the nursery and pre-prep, pupils come in for an informal assessment. Ditto for year 3 and above although their day also includes an underlying ability test.

For those joining senior school, there are tests in English, maths and non-verbal reasoning, plus interview and school report and references.

Significant numbers also join at sixth form. Minimum of seven 5s at GCSE (or equivalent for overseas applicants), plus interview and school report. Overseas candidates sit tests in English and maths.

Exit: All but a handful transfers from prep to senior school (results help decide setting in year 9). Around 30 per cent leaves after GCSEs. Almost all sixth formers to university. Exeter, Nottingham Trent, Newcastle, Reading, Oxford Brookes Durham and Queen Mary's. all popular. One to Oxbridge in 2021. Others head off to study eg chemical engineering at Lancaster to equine management at the Royal Agricultural College Cirencester and children's nursing at Kingston, plus the odd ones overseas. Separate careers advice and university applications advice.

Latest results: In 2021, 46 per cent 9-7 at GCSE; 56 per cent A*/A (80 per cent A*-B). In 2019 (the last year when exams took place), 31 per cent 9-7 at GCSE; 23 per cent A*/A at A level (52 per cent A*-B).

Teaching and learning: 'Whole college' approach to the curriculum is underway, with subject heads of department becoming responsible for the entire age range of 3-18. Principal says this is both to ensure a cohesive approach and to give staff the opportunity to teach in both prep and seniors, as is already the case with languages, music, sport, DT and computer science. 'It makes sense for the pupils, particularly in years 7 and 8 as it means they get to know subject staff based at the senior school, but it also offers more choice and flexibility to staff.'

Head is determined not only to raise the profile of the school ('I have heard it called Suffolk's best kept secret') but also to bring wider global influences to bear

Having dispensed with CE, school's focus for years 7-9 is a theme-based curriculum with an emphasis on gaining skills rather than amassing knowledge for a defined test. 'We are keeping parts of the CE but want to prepare pupils better for what is to come when they begin GCSE work'. It's all about critical thinking, collaboration, leadership, listening and asking questions. Themes such as identity, the natural world, global citizenship, conflict and enterprise all feature. It's early days, but pupils seem to have cottoned on to the idea that, 'what we learn connects several different subjects, not just one.'

Maximum class size of 20 up to GCSEs and nearer 10 in sixth form. Setting begins early in the prep for English and maths, with others added in seniors. French starts in pre-prep (we saw a class singing rollicking choruses, en Francais), with Spanish in year 7 and Latin offered in seniors – all pupils take at least one at GCSE. 'Subject ambassadors' are recruited from older pupils to spread positive messages and be a reliable source of information.

The new influx of staff – 'the premier league,' as one parent dubbed them – is part of the overall strategy to raise academic expectations and to keep staff on their toes. Targets for improvement and strategies to tackle any academic difficulties are put in place early, rather than waiting to broach matters at the parents' consultation evening. Academic hubs and informal 'drop in' sessions for pupils who need a bit of extra help with a particular subject are run regularly.

The sixth form centre is an attractive work/study/social area with some subject teaching in small classrooms. But he privilege for year 13 pupils of being allowed to work in their own rooms can be withdrawn for any who fool about and waste time. BTECs in music, sports science, computer science and business studies. EPQ offered.

The library, though a fine space and permanently staffed, seems under-used and has a slightly neglected air – school says it's on it.

Learning support and SEN: The focus is on providing help tailored to the individual. Most difficulties relate to dyslexia, dyscalculia, speech and language or ADHD. Some pupils have occasional help with study skills or a particular subject, especially in the lead up to exams. Regular help is timetabled to avoid too much withdrawal from mainstream classes. Pupils are taught by experienced specialist staff in the department, which is next to the library, either in small groups or individually (for which there is a charge).

Full, weekly and flexi boarding available for seniors. Pupils have their own swipe cards and can go back to their houses at break and after lunch

The learning support centre at the prep is off a main thoroughfare and pupils pop in and out frequently – even more so since Walter the lab joined the fold. He is a comforting presence for any child who is, 'perhaps just having a bad day and needs a bit of a boost or a quiet time.' Posters remind pupils of various famous people with dyslexia such as Jamie Oliver and Bill Gates.

The arts and extracurricular: Drama is popular. At the prep, the performing arts centre is housed in the old stable block with a dedicated dance and ballet studio, though larger performances take place in the HPT (Headmaster Porter theatre) at the senior school. For the seniors, the HPT is suited for full scale productions, flexible raked seating, foyer and dressing rooms. It incorporates the music department, which includes space for performance, rehearsal and practice. High take up of drama as a GCSE and A level, far less for music though a handful do pursue the subject, particularly the BTEC in music performance and production. Lots of well attended public performances including concerts in St Michael's church, Framlingham, Ely cathedral and Aldeburgh. Choirs, ensemble groups and band rehearsals are mostly held at lunchtimes so all pupils can take part.

Art is taken at GCSE by half the pupils and a significant number go on to A level, doing very well. The excellent facilities for textiles, ceramics, photography and fine art are in the impressive building shared with DT and the displays of work are there for all to see and be encouraged by. Big take-up for DofE (highest in the country) with considerable numbers reaching gold.

Plenty of clubs and societies for various interest groups also take place at lunch times.

Sport: Excellent provision for all sports (plus parking!) means the school is frequently the host for tournaments and matches. The artificial courts, pitches and the indoor pool and fitness centre are well used and all pupils take part in the team sports. Girls do the same sports as the boys though rugby and football remain a club choice rather than a timetabled activity. Hockey is the most consistently successful sport with several pupils (boys and girls) in the England squad. Seriously high level of coaching across major sports. Parents offer good support on the touchlines on Saturday afternoons (and the get togethers at tea after matches are an important social time for parents to meet). For those not so keen on team sports there are other options higher up the school including squash, tennis, running and serious fitness training. Sports science is a popular choice both at GCSE, BTEC and A level.

Boarding: Prep school boarding is on the top two floors (one for boys, one for girls) reached by a splendid, creaky, oak staircase. The views from the well-decorated dorms (four and six- bedded) and comfy common rooms are spectacular. Plenty of space for games, computers and TV watching although we were assured that 'they spend most of their time playing outside!' All are looked after by live-in staff and matrons. Flexi boarding is popular, especially on Friday nights for years 7 and 8. Full boarders can have a friend to stay – a nice touch.

Senior boarders are divided between four houses for boys and three for girls, with around 55 in each. Two of the boys' houses are on the upper floors of the original building, the others purpose-built across the road. 'We find they rather like having a bit of a walk away from the main school buildings at the end of the day,' we heard, though others prefer the easiness of being on the spot for breakfast first thing. Rooms are well-decorated, the newer ones (especially the girls') more colourful and inviting – although they've rather overdone the consciousness-raising quotes on some house walls. Older pupils, usually year 11 up, have their own rooms if they are full or weekly boarders.

Full, weekly and flexi available for seniors, with day pupils also getting a place in each house. Pupils have their own swipe cards and can go back to the houses at break and after lunch. Snacks (toast and Nutella, as usual, very popular) and drinks are available in the houses though main meals (much improved, we heard) are all eaten over in the school dining room. 'Sunday brunch is my favourite meal of the week,' said more than one pupil.

Lots of activities laid on – quizzes, zumba, film nights etc. There is plenty of inter-house rivalry (most of it friendly!) primarily in sport but also in music and dance, largely organised by the pupils themselves. The school decides on the house placements; great majority goes home at weekend after Saturday sport.

Ethos and heritage: Set on the hill above the town, the college was founded in 1864 in memory of Prince Albert, whose statue stands in front of the school. The original senior building is a fine example of Victorian architecture and the view across the valley to the castle is sublime. Framlingham is a substantial market town with an interesting history and the castle itself was the rallying point for Mary Tudor (Henry V111s elder daughter) and her forces when she made her bid to claim the throne after her brother's death. A variety of other buildings have been added over time, none particularly distinguished, but well planned and designed to make the most of the extensive and beautiful grounds. Three of the boarding houses are over the road from the main buildings but everything is within an easy stroll, including the town which all pupils are given permission to visit once a week after lessons, as well as at the weekends for boarders.

The prep is based at Brandeston Hall, a few miles from the main school down the twisty Suffolk lanes. Of Tudor origin, it was founded in memory of those killed in the First World War and to educate their sons. Remembrance is taken seriously both here and at the senior school and VC citations of former pupils are proudly displayed. The rambling country house with its oak staircases, panelled rooms and glorious grounds is enjoyed to the full by the pupils who are outside whenever possible. Newer buildings have been added including a large sports hall, performing arts centre, along with classrooms for DT and science and a covered link between buildings. Nursery and pre-prep occupy their own purpose-built accommodation and play areas on the same site. The school dining room is traditional, but the food is not. The chefs provide interesting menus, though some say the food could be improved.

This is a happy school with an established tradition of taking full account of talent and character in addition to academic prowess. As a parent commented, 'Academic performance is important, but so are other things – we like the balance struck.'

Pastoral care, inclusivity and discipline: The house system is the bedrock of pastoral care, with housemasters, mistresses and tutors the first point of contact for pupils. Following careful induction of new pupils, they are tracked both academically and pastorally, with tutors keeping subject staff informed about any particular stresses. Strong focus on helping pupils develop the skills they need to overcome particular challenges. Strong home/school relations are maintained with tutors contacting all parents within two weeks of the start of term and staff know pupils well. 'What's comforting at Fram is that when they speak to me about my children, they describe the children I know,' said a parent, while another told us, 'It's a partnership – they are helping us raise our children.' School says, 'Young people exist in an extraordinary, fast-changing world and it is for us to keep up, listen to them and help them navigate their way through.'

Prep learning support centre is off a main thoroughfare and pupils pop in frequently – even more so since Walter the labrador joined the fold

When Everyone's Invited hit headlines, the school initiated a pupil forum which has resulted in twice-weekly tutor led discussions – one with a focus on wellbeing and life skills, the other on matters such as sexting, toxic masculinity and consent. The move to promote a culture where pupils treat each other with respect and kindness also includes the Teen Tips Wellbeing Hub, with resources to help pupils (and parents) chart their way through. There is a prefect responsible for wellbeing and diversity and there are initiatives and campaigns targeting 'casual' homophobia, racism and sexism. Each house has a committee to discuss issues as they arise and meets the principal on a regular basis. Though trying, if possible, to 'offer second chances,' there are clear expectations around behaviour with a firm but fair approach. Random testing may be used, particularly after exeats and holiday times.

Pupils and parents: This is a school held in affectionate regard and lots of pupils are the offspring of former pupils. Strong entrepreneurial and business backgrounds, with quite a few parents working in London who make full use of the school's flexible day and boarding arrangements. Also continues to attract East Anglian farming families and a significant body (20 per cent) from overseas, averaging 17 different nationalities. Pupils are reassuringly cheerful, well-mannered and purposeful. They are respectful and friendly and know their good fortune.

Money matters: Scholarships are awarded at 11+, 13+ and 16+ in academic, performing and creative arts, computer science and sporting excellence. The Albert Memorial scholarships are awarded to pupils showing excellence in two scholarship pathways. 'Top up' bursaries can be added to a scholarship in cases of financial need (means-tested), and there are stand-alone bursaries separately. Reductions for siblings and Forces families.

The last word: This is a school with a long, well-deserved reputation for highlighting the gifts of individual pupils and giving excellent pastoral care. A new and significant change in emphasis is promoting academic prowess It is confidently run by talented staff with a determination to give pupils an education and social experience that will stand them in good stead their whole lives.

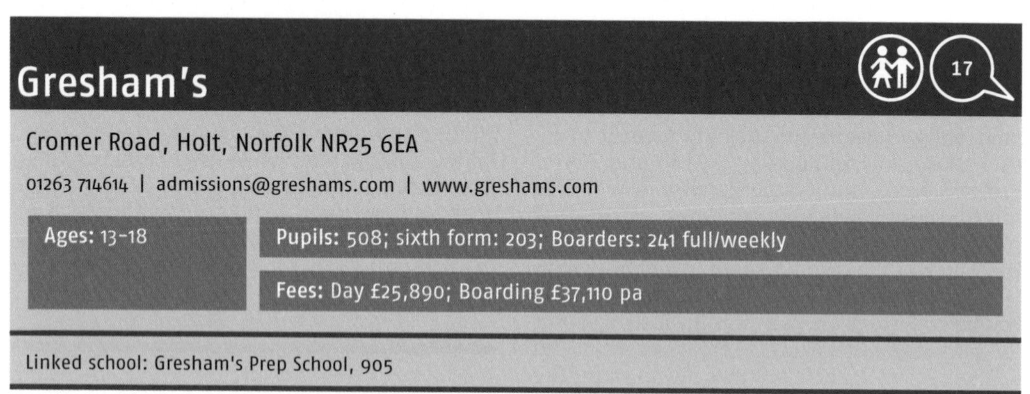

Gresham's

17

Cromer Road, Holt, Norfolk NR25 6EA

01263 714614 | admissions@greshams.com | www.greshams.com

Ages: 13–18

Pupils: 508; sixth form: 203; Boarders: 241 full/weekly

Fees: Day £25,890; Boarding £37,110 pa

Linked school: Gresham's Prep School, 905

Headmaster: Since 2014, Douglas Robb MA (Edinburgh) politics, MEd (Homerton, Cambridge). Previously head of Oswestry School. A post-university spell teaching in Zimbabwe and at Fettes College helped decide his career and, after teaching politics and economics at Loughborough Grammar School, he spent 10 'very happy years' at Oundle as a teacher of politics and economics and housemaster, which 'totally persuaded me of the benefits of boarding'. A former rugby player, has a commanding physical presence, is quick-witted and entertaining; a real live wire. Perceptive pupils note 'he is confident enough to be able to listen to us and sometimes change his mind.' Parents say he is 'not afraid to show his funny side', but is also polite, friendly, helpful to them and very much in evidence – 'I have seen him at literally every public event' attests one. An advocate of the house system as being central to the success of pupils' learning and their integration into the life of the school and for 'opportunities for conversation and friendships, both amongst peers, but also with staff'. Has high expectations of his staff and spells out the commitment at interview; 'I pin them down, no woolly promises to help will do. This job is a vocation.' Is keen to continue raising academic standards, emphasise the central importance of boarding to the ethos of the school and to encourage the creativity and original thinking that 'have always been the cornerstones of a Gresham's education,' he says. 'We are keen to disrupt the established narrative that young people must choose between science and the arts at an early stage of life. By teaching the subjects side by side, pupils see how the knowledge gained from one discipline can be used in a creative way in another.'

Married to Lucinda and they have three children (two are at Gresham's, one has moved on to university). Enjoys north Norfolk life, 'countryside, dogs, getting to know people'. Maintains keen interest in rugby, also golf, skiing; travel and 'proper holidays'.

During the period of remote learning, every aspect of Gresham's life moved online. Parents appreciated the continued 'exceptional' academic provision, pastoral support and a sense of community encouraged by the efforts of houseparents. Pupils new to the school were cleverly integrated and included, say parents.

Full programme of co-curricular and social activities included fitness, skills and wellbeing activities such as morning yoga and HIIT workouts. An online debate was held for the first time in Gresham's Debating Society's 121-year history. Even CCF continued virtually, with pupils taking part in practical exercises and scenarios at home. School chaplain initiated the 'Daily Pause' – a poem of the day accompanied by a piece of music, sent to pupils and staff via email as a reminder to enjoy a few moments of calm and reflection. Parents appreciated the regular communication; 'we felt very lucky that our daughter was at the school at this time,' said one.

Entrance: Roughly 50 per cent of senior school come up from the prep school, others from a mix of day and boarding preps, some from maintained sector. No common entrance; an assessment day is held for year 9 entrants in Lent term for following September. Tests in English and maths plus reports and references from current school. For sixth form, predicted grades (usually a minimum of 6 in six subjects including those to be studied and minimum of C in English and maths) plus school report and interview.

Exit: Around 15 per cent leave post-GCSEs. Post-sixth form, a few to Oxbridge, sizeable numbers to London (Imperial, LSE, UCL) plus the other Russell Group universities. Wide range of subjects studied including a regular few to drama school and music colleges (Central St Martins, Guildhall).

Latest results: In 2021, 58 per cent 9-7 at GCSE; 56 per cent A*/A at A level (81 per cent A*-B). IB average score 37. In 2019 (the last year when exams took place), 43 per cent 9-7 at GCSE; 29 per cent A*/A at A level (58 per cent A*-B). IB average score 34.

Teaching and learning: 'A very modern approach for a 450-year-old school,' says a parent. Plenty of individual attention, in classes of up to 24; sets for most subjects. Parents have noticed a steady build-up of academic 'push' – notes one, 'things are less easy-going than in the past' – and a palpable focus on encouraging independence of thought and learning. French, German, Japanese, Spanish, Chinese and Latin from year 9, building on the MFL foundations laid down in the prep and pre-prep; at least one must feature in the list of 10 subjects generally taken at GCSE. Sixth formers have the choice of A levels, IB or BTECs. Creditable results across the board at A level – most pupils take three. Around half choose IB, though some are put off by the requirement for a language as one of the six subjects studied, and, as head points out, 'IB is an excellent exam and we encourage it, but it is not, and never will be, for everyone.' Pupils may replace one or two A levels with BTEC National Diplomas: currently on offer are agriculture, digital music production and sport.

Learning support and SEN: Around a fifth receive extra help with SEN, mostly dyslexia, dyscalculia, sensory impairments and poor self-esteem. Experienced learning support team of four full-time qualified specific learning differences (SpLD) teachers and two learning support assistants (LSA) is based in a new, purpose-built wing, equipped with the latest technology and facilities, right in the centre of the school. Timetabled 1:1 lessons and prep support with a specialist teacher and/or support with an LSA available (additional charge). SENCo is a qualified assessor and screens all new pupils joining the school, and also reaches out to feeder schools. Special extension programmes for scholars.

The arts and extracurricular: Music is important here and roughly 30 per cent of pupils have timetabled instrumental tuition. Many choirs, ensembles, bands and orchestras and a calendar of performances.

Plenty of individual attention in classes of up to 24; sets for most subjects. Parents have noticed increased academic push, 'things are less easy-going than in the past'

The Britten Building (opened in 2017 by HRH The Princess Royal and named after Old Greshamian composer Benjamin Britten) features the state-of-the-art 140-seat Fishmongers' Recital Hall, along with a recording studio, music practice rooms and teaching rooms. Access all areas for serious musicians as well as those who play for fun. Industry-standard recording studio used by pupils studying A level music tech pupils and BTEC digital music production, but also for recording performances by the school's many bands and choirs (Gresham's Girls' and Guys' charity singles to prep pupils' Christmas album). As a Steinway School, there are top-quality pianos everywhere.

Drama facilities are of professional quality too – perhaps appropriately as the school has produced several household name actors, most notably Olivia Colman. School's Auden Theatre stages at least three major school productions every year and also hosts touring companies. With such a pedigree, this is a springboard for pupils who are keen to tread the boards, but also

Felsted School

for those whose vocations are backstage, with opportunities to develop skills of stage management, sound and lighting. Accredited Private Learner Centre for London Academy of Music and Dramatic Art (LAMDA) exams.

Creativity is a serious subject here and pupils are given the time and the tools to engage in their own projects; in the process, developing their skills of problem-solving, collaboration and decision-making. Donations by another illustrious former pupil, Sir James Dyson, have helped establish a superb new centre dedicated to science, technology, engineering, arts and mathematics (STEAM) education at the school. The Dyson Building is an exciting new hub where pupils can come together to share and exchange ideas in social learning spaces, and is equipped with the latest technology. Art flourishes in this environment and incorporates graphics and 3D Design. Ambition is to propagate success in all fields of design practice. 'We are unashamedly contemporary in our approach to art education,' says head. 'Rather than teaching set projects, we encourage an ethos of individuality and encourage students to explore the impact of creativity on digital forms of communication.' Close relationship with the Saatchi gallery and partnership with Imperial College London for materials research. Top grades at GCSE, A level and IB and the most talented artists head straight to degree courses, skipping the foundation at The Slade, The Ruskin and Glasgow School of Art, for example.

Donations from former pupil, Sir James Dyson, have helped build a superb new centre dedicated to science, technology, engineering, arts and mathematics (STEAM)

Pupils take part in extracurricular clubs three times a week, with a wide range of activities to suit their interests and allow them to explore new ventures. Outdoor pursuits are incredibly popular here, school has its own 21-part armed forces style obstacle course, featuring a 220-metre zip wire, high ropes course, low ropes course, abseiling facilities, two climbing walls and a 25-metre 'Bourdillon Tower'. Also an intentionally basic bunkhouse for use as a dorm or teaching facility for 20 people. Survival course devised for year 9 pupils is based loosely on a military escape and evasion exercise with shelter building, fire building, wild food preparation, open fire cooking and emergency first aid exercises to hone interpersonal and life skills such as team building, leadership, resilience, and self-confidence, and to encourage pupils to care about the outdoors and their local environment.

One of the country's largest CCFs – all three services (Royal Navy, Army and Royal Air Force). Participation is high – 90 per cent of pupils take part in Year 9; 50 per cent continue in the sixth form. Active Duke of Edinburgh's Award programme with the majority of students completing bronze and a high proportion going on to silver and gold; expeditions in the Peaks, Dales and Lakes.

School holds the Eco-Schools Green Flag programme's Gold Award and earned Green Flag Eco-School status in seven months as opposed to the usual two years. Environmental co-ordinator is responsible for exploring and implementing initiatives aimed at reducing waste and ensuring sustainability. All school's electricity now comes from solar power or renewable sources.

Sport: All the usual team sports: rugby, hockey (for boys and girls), netball and cricket, with lots of match play and good coaching for all. Pitches, Astroturf and courts for tennis and squash galore. Riding lessons at local centre offered as a games option, suitable for all abilities, from beginner level to experienced riders who are away for their horses during term time. School showjumping team recently qualified for the NSEA National County Championships at Hickstead. Swimming an extracurricular activity. Cross-country running a popular pastime. 'I often go for an early run; it's one of the reasons I like boarding,' a pupil tells us. Upgraded gym facilities now include a strength and conditioning suite, with a specific coach to nurture pupils on school's talented athlete programme. Alternative activities include sailing, fencing, cycling and swimming higher up the school. School has its own rifle range (several members of the club have been selected for the GB under-19 rifle team and cadet rifle team 'The Athelings' in recent years. During the holidays, school hosts training camps – some residential – in cricket, rugby and hockey.

Boarding: Strong boarding feel, but day pupils are well integrated – each has a shared or single study in their house. Flexi boarding is not actively encouraged, but pupils are 'happily' accommodated overnight on occasions when they are at school late for rehearsals, performances or other events. Many hitherto day pupils choose to board in the sixth form. Houses are comfortable, well lit and decorated with a thought to homeliness; kitchens are large and well used for sociable cooking and eating. Pupils return to their houses at break and lunch-times; houseparents and matrons always on hand. Bedrooms mostly shared between two or four though most sixth formers have individual rooms. Plenty of organised activities for boarders, though not what the head calls 'enforced jollity'.

Ethos and heritage: Founded in 1555, originally as a grammar school, but rejuvenated in 1890s by George Howson, a headmaster with 'advanced' views on education that advocated the teaching of sciences, the abandonment of corporal punishment and (most unusually for the time) the encouragement of pacifist thinking. School's 200 acres of woodlands and extensive playing fields stretch along both sides of the old Cromer road heading out of Holt and its buildings range in style from magnificent Edwardian and art deco halls and libraries (all grand staircases and stained glass), to more ordinary classrooms, but all neat, tidy and well cared for. Edifices of note are the historic Big School and chapel, the famous Auden theatre, and brand new The Dyson Building, an impressive new space for STEAM education. There is plenty of fresh Norfolk air between the buildings and pupils are kept fit walking briskly from lesson to lesson, even crossing the road by means of a footbridge. Robust uniform keeps out the sea breeze – light blue tweed jackets for all but the sixth form, who wear suits; most refuse a coat.

Student-led group called Soc(I)ety aims to 'celebrate the diversity at Gresham's School'. Members recently spoke in chapel about how important it is to be kind, considerate and understanding about fellow pupils' sexual orientation and identity

Former pupils have made their mark, particularly in the fields of the arts, sport, science and technology, including Benjamin Britten, WH Auden, Sir Christopher Cockerell (inventor of the hovercraft), Tom and Ben Youngs (international rugby players), Lord Reith (first director-general of BBC), Prof Alan Hodgkin and, of course, the actor Olivia Colman and inventor Sir James Dyson.

Pastoral care, inclusivity and discipline: 'A caring school with a strong community and a good moral and work ethic', sums up one parent and others agree. Pupils not from the prep who join in year 9 are embraced and well nurtured; a successful 'big brother/big sister' system pairs each year 9 pupil with a sixth former. Year 13 mental health first aiders are trained to provide support and advice to their fellow pupils, focusing on well-being and sharing tips and techniques for looking after mental health, as well as signposting to appropriate help and offering a listening ear.

A relatively small school, staff and pupils all know each other well and there is good vertical interaction between the year groups and friendly, respectful staff/pupil relations. 'I feel that my daughter has people she can talk to at school,' says a parent. Signs of stress are picked up on quickly and there are regular sessions teaching relaxation techniques.

Student-led group called Soc(I)ety aims to – in their own words – 'celebrate the diversity at Gresham's School'. Members recently spoke in chapel to each year group and emphasised how important it is to be kind, considerate and understanding about fellow pupils' sexual orientation and identity. They made their peers aware of their fundraising for The Trevor Project, which provides crisis intervention and suicide prevention services to LGBTQ teens and young adults.

Few major misdemeanours happen here. A clear anti-bullying policy (lots of awareness notices on walls), and counsellors, school chaplain, matrons and house staff all on the look-out. Well understood rules on illegal drugs (zero tolerance), and alcohol: over-18s may 'enjoy a pint' (as the school puts it) in Holt; no PDA (public displays of affection) rule; few overstep the mark.

Pupils' – and therefore parents' – only criticism is the food, which one senses will not be given the benefit of the doubt due to Covid for much longer.

Pupils and parents: Day pupils hail from a large area of north Norfolk, many travelling for an hour each way; boarders from all over the country but predominantly East Anglia. Pupils described locally as friendly, positive and caring, with some 'free-spirited individuals'. Mostly professional and business families with a sprinkling of county boarding families. Many are from London and enjoy the contrast with the competitive city schools; some families even move to Norfolk – parents commute back daily so their children can be day pupils. About 20 per cent from overseas, mostly Europe.

Money matters: Valuable scholarships and bursaries on offer, thanks to a long association with the Worshipful Company of Fishmongers and its generous financial underpinning of the school's finances. Academic scholarships worth up to 20 per cent of fees offered for year 9 entry (can be topped up with a bursary, if financial need is demonstrated), drama, music, art and sport awards also offered, for up to 20 per cent. Sixth form scholarships for those who do brilliantly at GCSE (if not already in receipt of an award). Assistance for families who fall on hard times, at least to enable pupils to get through to the next public exam. Usual sibling discounts for three or more at one time.

The last word: Happy, hardy country boarding school with a deserved reputation for inspiring creativity and developing the skills and confidence to turn ideas into reality.

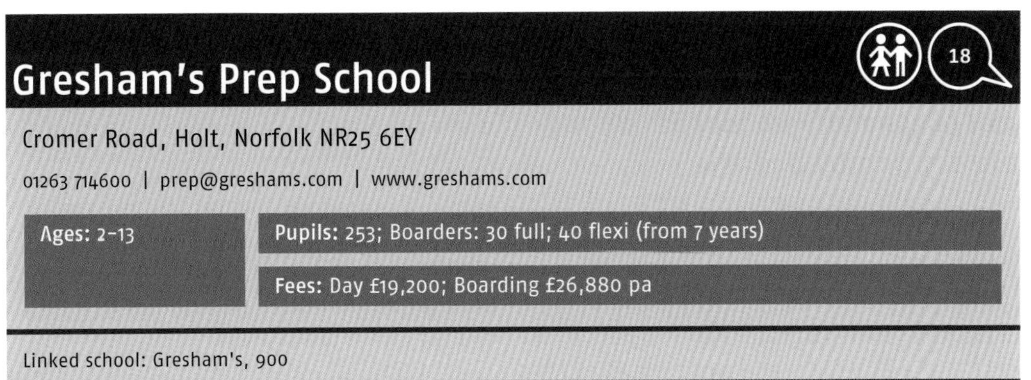

Gresham's Prep School

18

Cromer Road, Holt, Norfolk NR25 6EY

01263 714600 | prep@greshams.com | www.greshams.com

Ages: 2-13

Pupils: 253; Boarders: 30 full; 40 flexi (from 7 years)

Fees: Day £19,200; Boarding £26,880 pa

Linked school: Gresham's, 900

Head: Since November 2018, Cathy Braithwaite BA(Ed) from Exeter, previously deputy head here. Taught in Staffordshire, Norfolk and Northern Ireland and was head of maths and director of teaching and learning at St Francis School in Wiltshire for 10 years before joining Gresham's. She is married to Ollie and they have two sons and a black labrador, Isla.

Head of nursery and pre-prep since 2016 is Sarah Hollingsworth (30s), previously director of pastoral care at Oswestry School. She has had various early years and KS1 roles and is a trained ISI inspector.

Entrance: At all ages and stages from 3 (nursery and pre-prep), 7 and 11 in the prep school, although they will try to accommodate when possible at other times. Some year groups fill quickly, so first come, first served. Accepts a fairly wide spectrum of ability, but admission is not a foregone conclusion. Informal assessment in the early forms, the same plus maths, English and verbal and non-verbal reasoning tests at 11. Pupils from the state sector often join for years 7 and 8 in preparation for the senior school.

Exit: Great majority go through the school to year 8 and move up to the seniors. All take the 'exit' exam, those not likely to make the grade are warned in good time. Those wishing to go elsewhere at 13, and there are a few most years, are prepared individually for the entrance exams for eg Oundle, Royal Hospital and Millfield. Others have recently accepted places at Repton, Culford and Norwich.

Our view: On its own site, though only a brisk walk from the senior school, on the edge of Holt, north Norfolk's stylish market town. Uses certain senior school facilities such as sports pitches, swimming pool and theatre, but in the main it operates autonomously. Parents queue up to praise this relaxed and happy school where 'childhood still seems to last the right length of time'. One parent thought, 'My son came out of his shell here, he became a different boy.' A number of families have both Norfolk and London bases, but choose Gresham's for its 'less pressured atmosphere' over the more hothoused approaches in the Capital.

Common entrance teaching recently abandoned so greater flexibility in the curriculum. Excellent languages with the focus on fun and communication in the early years. French from year 6 with Spanish and Latin options from year 7. Other languages (eg German, Mandarin) can usually be accommodated on request. Science taught in designated labs, sometimes using the more sophisticated facilities of the senior school. There is mixed-ability teaching up until year 4, then setting in most subjects, though 'these are flexible and pupils move up and down', with differentiated targets.

Educational support well resourced, with five specially trained staff (two full-time) who are also class teachers. Caters for mild difficulties such as dyslexia and Asperger's, and emotional problems such as low self-esteem. About a quarter of pupils receive help, either in one-to-one tuition, small groups, or support in the classroom. Brilliant library, bursting with delectable titles, displays, opportunities to enter competitions and with an enthusiastic, full-time librarian. Open all day long (boarders can use it in the evening for project work), the atmosphere is quiet: 'we don't insist on a deathly silence, but purposeful reading does need peace and quiet.'

A mock-up of Giles Gilbert-Scott's classic telephone box houses the real telephone – no mobiles during the day or after bedtime

The performing arts, particularly music and drama, are very well taught both within the curriculum and as extra activities ('one of the reasons we chose the school'). Everyone sings in a choir in the lower forms, with auditions higher up for the senior and chapel choirs (runners up in the national Barnardo's Contest recently). Over two-thirds of pupils learn an instrument, some at the top grades, and there are many bands, ensemble groups and orchestras with frequent performances. Dance is on the curriculum in the lower forms and an extra activity later on. Drama is timetabled throughout the school; some larger productions are staged in the senior school Auden Theatre. Art and design have their own rather eye-catching building, with spectacular displays of pupils' work (including designs on backs of chairs) and every inducement for creativity. 'We do textiles, mosaics, woodwork, mess generally.' Loads of sport, all the usual team games with lots of fixtures, and though 'we understand not everyone is mad keen, but it's also important to have to keep going with something you wouldn't necessarily choose'. Shooting and kayaking available in years 7 and 8.

Mostly new buildings of one or two storeys set in the midst of extensive grounds, adventure play areas and piazzas; 'pupils have to play in sight of the gazebo'. OWLS is the new outdoor learning school with open-sided wooden classroom, spaces for campfires and an outdoor theatre, plus climbing tower, zipwire, obstacle and rope courses in the woods.

Careful attention paid to well-being and happiness. As well as the usual offers of counselling well displayed, there is a worry box to post in 'anything they want to discuss, however small it may seem'. Staff keep a weather eye, particularly in changing room areas, which are always supervised. In the un-canteeny dining room, pupils are helped to make good food choices, picking from colour-coded categories: green (vegetables), red (protein) and yellow (carbs). Early supper ('children are all starving by 5:30pm') which day pupils often stay for if doing activities, and cereal/toast and hot drinks in the houses before bed.

Boarding: Separate boys' and girls' houses, each for 40 or 50 children, in bedrooms of two to four. Exceptionally attractive and home-like decoration (strong Cath Kidston influence) and furnishings. Photographs of children enjoying themselves on every wall, bunting, posters; a mock-up of Giles Gilbert-Scott's classic telephone box houses the real telephone – no mobiles during the day or after bedtime. Houseparents and matrons always around, and pupils return to house at break and lunch.

The last word: This is a happy, well-run prep that benefits from its connection to the senior school, but is definitely separate. Would suit most types but is not specially geared to prepare for common entrance or other highly competitive school entrance exams.

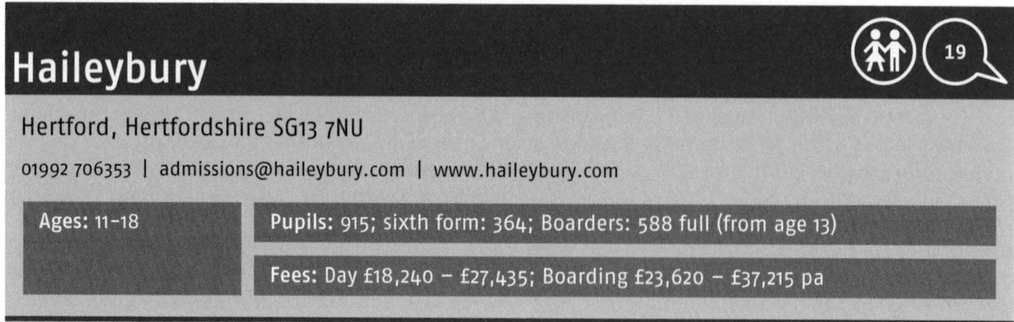

Haileybury

19

Hertford, Hertfordshire SG13 7NU

01992 706353 | admissions@haileybury.com | www.haileybury.com

Ages: 11–18

Pupils: 915; sixth form: 364; Boarders: 588 full (from age 13)

Fees: Day £18,240 – £27,435; Boarding £23,620 – £37,215 pa

Master: Since 2017, Martin Collier MA, previously head of St John's School Leatherhead. He read modern history at St John's College Oxford, followed by PGCE from London University. His first 10 years of teaching were in the maintained sector, at the 'fantastic' Thomas Tallis in south

London and the 'tough' Weavers School in Wellingborough. He then moved into the independent sector and Oundle School, where he worked through roles of head of history, director of studies and second master. He also has many years' experience as an examiner with different boards, has been involved with the Qualifications and Curriculum Development Agency and has appeared as an examinations expert before the House of Commons select committee on education. He is also chair of the Headmasters' and Headmistresses' Conference (HMC) academic policy group.

A famous name in public school education, Haileybury has become equally renowned for its enthusiastic participation in the IB which was launched here in 1998

No extrovert, but quietly impressive and we loved his sing-song intonation and commanding hand gestures that have an almost sermon-like effect. Not the warm and cuddly type, but genial and passionate about getting the best for every pupil. Big on vision (in his wider roles, discussions stretch as far as 'curriculum planning for 2035') but also detail ('schools are all about detail,' he says). 'Some say he's scary, but he's not once you get to know him,' insist pupils, who say they see him regularly around school (no wonder, when he spends three days a week showing prospective parents round) and value 'the way he asks for feedback and acts on it'. Has made 'plentiful changes' including around timetabling, recruitment of new staff, tightening up lesson planning and use of reflection within lessons; parents see it as 'upping the ante academically' and it's gone down a treat. 'I think he will do tremendous things,' mused one; clearly the general consensus.

Married with three older children, he lives (as all masters have since time immemorial) on-site but is the first not to use its tucked-away sitting room as his main office, which has now been moved centre stage to the picturesque quadrangle where 'I see everything, and where pupils can see me.' It is, he says, the 'best view in the school.' We agree.

Entrance: More academically able applicants than in the past, though school won't be pinned down to saying it's more academically selective. Cohort of 65 in year 7, a further 70 in year 9. Unusually, also a healthy intake (20) in year 10. Typically, 70 new pupils enter the sixth form, including about 40 from overseas. At this juncture the school is heavily oversubscribed, with about three applicants for every place. Entrance tests at all levels in maths, English, verbal and non-verbal reasoning. Year 9 entry pre-tested by negotiation with the prep school 12 or 24 months in advance and entrance exam used for setting. 'We are looking for somebody who wants to do their best, is B+ to A* academically and will throw themselves into the co-curricular.' Wide range of feeders including Heath Mount, Duncombe, Lochinver House, Beechwood Park, Davenies, St Joseph's in the Park, St Hilda's and St Faith's.

Exit: No leavers after GCSEs generally. Post A levels and IB, it's mainly to Russell Group universities (most popular choices include Bath, Bristol, Birmingham and UCL). Wide range of subjects, the sciences and maths being most popular. Good specialist advisers, but some parents would like more support for North American and European universities, which pupils are increasingly choosing ('everything is geared to Oxbridge applications and medics,' said one); head says he's addressing this. Two to Oxbridge in 2021.

Latest results: In 2021, 84 per cent 9-7 at IGCSE; 70 per cent A*/A at A level (91 per cent A*-B). In 2019 (the last year when exams took place), 65 per cent 9-7 in IGCSE; 38 per cent A*/A at A level (and 71 per cent A*/B). IB average score 37 in 2019.

Teaching and learning: A famous name in public school education, Haileybury has become equally renowned for its enthusiastic participation in the IB, which was launched in 1998 'to provide a broader curriculum' and continues to flourish here despite floundering elsewhere. About 110 sixth formers (over a third) follow the diploma programme, with about 40 arriving each year specifically to do it. 'The IB is engrained into our culture and we embrace it philosophically, including the individual thinking, lateral thinking and pupil-driven learning,' says head. A levels, however, are still very much on offer and the school does very well in both sets of exams. English, history and drama notably strong; ditto for maths ('if you can do maths, everything else follows,' believes head). Highly qualified staff (including a hefty sprinkling of doctorates) generally teach across both systems. 'The teachers are amazing – they go above and beyond,' said one pupil. Most recently, sixth formers have got the chance to get stuck into the Stan-X programme – a partnership with Oxford and Stanford universities that involves students conducting investigations with fruit flies to advance biomedical research, in hope to find cures for diseases such as diabetes and cancer.

Lower down, IGCSEs in just about everything. Here, all do a compulsory core of maths, English language and science. From year 7, pupils pick two languages from German, French and Spanish and one from Latin or classical Greek – compulsory until the end of year 8, when pupils are 'strongly encouraged' to continue at least one. German and Italian also taught to the native speakers taking the IB. Setting in maths and languages from year 7, science and English from year 9.

Overall high aspirations, with sane expectations. 'It's not uncool to be clever or try your best but it's very unpressurised,' said a parent. 'My son got amazing GCSE results, much better than we expected, but without any stress and hassle,' said another. Parents appreciate the teaching recruits – 'the majority were good before, but certain departments were stronger than others, whereas now it's good across the board,' said one.

Learning support and SEN: All pupils are screened on entry 'to understand how they are as a learner' and as such, learning support is not an add-on but an integral part of education, although typically around 50-80 have a diagnosed SEN (mild to moderate) and get more help than others; a small number, too, have extra help with English as a second language. School has one of the most sophisticated tracking systems we've seen – 'we get to know the pupil first, then the data helps us understand how to tailor their learning.'

The arts and extracurricular: Co-curricular activities are very much part of Haileybury's raison d'etre and for many families it's why they choose the school. 'Both my children have learned to become their true selves and that's a direct result of the school stretching them in all directions. This, for me, is the biggest stand out point,' one parent told us. School says it helps that 95 per cent of staff live on-site – 'they're committed and involved at every level.'

Music out-of-this-world. The school has a 30-year tradition of exceptional choral singing and won the BBC Songs of Praise School Choir of the Year some years back (it has reached the semi-final twice since then too). Practically every parent we spoke to mentioned the head of music by name, describing him as 'charismatic' and 'phenomenal'. 'He's so inclusive too, it's not just about favouring the best,' said one. Chamber choir of about 30, plus larger chapel choir of about 90. Wide range of other musical opportunities, from jazz bands to concerts and musical theatre. Twenty peripatetic music staff, with pupils studying everything from harp to bassoon and from organ to jazz piano.

As with music, art has its own purpose-built, spacious and light-filled building – open seven days a week and in the evenings, regardless of whether you're doing a GCSE or A level. Offers 2D and 3D, print, ceramics, photography and textiles, with exams tailored to individual interests. Stunning works on display. Drama renowned for bringing a whole host of pupils out of their shell who may never have acted before. It's not the same children on the stage every year, confirm parents, and again it's not just about those doing a GCSE or A level (although both are available). Some pupils said they'd like 'a bigger and better theatre'. Dance lessons on offer for about 100 keen participants in jazz, ballet, street and tap, plus an annual dance show. Trips galore, as you'd expect, as well as more modest outings to battlefields and cultural events.

Unusually, a boarding ethos for all, with the opportunity for day pupils to stay until 9.30pm (though most leave at 6.30pm) and some have their own beds

Community service is huge – everything from digging gardens for the elderly to helping in local primary schools. School is particularly proud of being the single sponsor of a local academy which, says head, 'is improving significantly as a result – it's one of the most important things we do.' Wednesday afternoons devoted to DofE, CCF and adventure training for years 9 to 11, broadening out in the sixth form to take in activities like photography and web design. 'I'm not convinced it's the best thing in sixth form, though – we barely have enough time to study as it is,' one pupil told us; some pupils down the school also mentioned the need for 'more free time' with one girl looking completely dazed when listing her activities.

Sport: The school has an outstanding reputation for sport, which is compulsory for all throughout, with games afternoons twice a week and matches on Saturday. Plenty of teams too, often from A-D, so everyone gets a chance to show their mettle. And those who aren't fans of the playing field can do 'something less taxing', with options including aerobics, badminton, trampolining, rowing, rackets, golf and sailing, among others – although pupils told us these never get taken 'anywhere near as seriously as the core sports'. Though boys triumph in hockey and football (where the school plays in the Boodles Cup) and girls in tennis, hockey, netball and lacrosse (competing at county and national level), rugby and cricket remain the 'communal sports' and it's not unusual for the whole school to turn out to cheer on matches played on the front field. Some niggles from parents about girls' sports playing second fiddle, but pupils we spoke to were having none of it ('lacrosse is massive,' laughed one). Facilities out of this world, with a bright, modern pool, two Astroturf pitches and a professionally operated tennis club in the grounds (but another parent niggle here – 'lower school aren't allowed to use it, which is a bugbear,' said one). The rackets court is also considered one of the finest in the world and plays host to the world rackets championship. High Performance Programme (including training and lectures) aims to help talented sportspeople raise their game. Proper physio support and hi-tech fitness monitoring equipment is business as usual here.

Boarding: From year 9, about 70 per cent of pupils board, with a sizeable chunk of weekly boarders who leave late on Saturday and return on Sunday evening or Monday morning (except for five or six weekends annually, when all remain). Opportunities too for flexi boarding in years 7 and 8 and taster boarding (three days a week) in year 9. Unusually, a boarding ethos for all, with an opportunity for day pupils to stay until 9.30pm (though most leave at 6.30pm) and some have their own beds; fewer, though, with the recent spike in boarders – 50 more in the year we visited, bucking the national trend. School attributes it to their location and modern family-friendly approach and the boarders lap it up – 'we're like brothers and sisters.'

Seven boys' houses, five girls'. Four more recently built, with light, bright rooms, the rest older but updated. 'The house personality literally becomes the housemaster or mistress's personality and I love that,' said one parent. A couple of eight to 10 bed dorms in younger years; for the rest (and all from year 11), single or shared rooms – some with military-precision neatness, others in the kind of disarray you'd see in normal homes. Active inter-house social life and plenty of weekend activities for full-time boarders, with Saturday film nights and Sunday trips. Plus 'a lot of people have flats in London' or visit local pupils (with beneficent parents).

Ethos and heritage: The school was designed in 1806 for the East India Company by William Wilkins (also responsible for the National Gallery and Downing College, Cambridge) as a training college for civil servants bound for India. In 1862, after the closure of the college, it was taken over by Haileybury, to be transformed into a public school for families in the professions and services, amalgamating, in 1942, with the Imperial Service College. The first girls were admitted in 1973. Today the school continues to occupy an impressive slice (550 acres) of rural Hertfordshire, complete with magnificent neo-classical buildings constructed round a traditional quadrangle. Later additions include modern, purpose-built buildings which sit surprisingly well amongst the more established architecture, with favourites including the DT centre (easily the best we've seen) and regularly revamped science block (with wildlife documentary showing in lobby). Interestingly it was the domed chapel (more like a full-on church) that came out as the best-loved space in a recent pupil survey. All must attend services there four times a week. Beautiful, well-stocked library. 'If they don't have a book, they will order it for you.'

Not a grand school in atmosphere. Manners are formal (new pupils jump to attention, teachers are addressed as Sir) but not stiff. And despite the pupils' full timetables it's surprisingly calm, not a bit frenetic. 'You see these happy, helpful children wandering around and you realise what good individuals they're producing – what more can you want for your kids?' said one parent. International vibe is celebrated, with around 20 per cent from abroad.

Food comes highly commended; three compulsory self-service meals a day in the mammoth oak-panelled dining room, though parents and pupils say the favourites can run out fast.

School is particularly proud of being the single sponsor of a local academy which, says head, 'is improving significantly as a result'

Long tradition of charity work. The Haileybury Youth Trust, first set up in the East End in 1890 by old boy Clement Attlee, has been working with impoverished Ugandans since 2006. It receives grants from both UN and EU and has even patented a brick now used for building schools, kitchens and water towers.

Two further Haileybury branches operate in Kazakhstan, the first British public schools to be opened in Central Asia, with plans for more international schools. These help underwrite bursaries for UK-based students.

Pastoral care, inclusivity and discipline: The pastoral ethos is central to everything – 96 per cent of pupils said they have an adult to talk to at school in a recent survey. The chaplain (known as 'the reverend') is seen as a particularly key pastoral figure – 'everyone trusts him,' said one pupil.

Lines of communication with parents praised, as is the school's frequent tweeting – 'it means I can always see what my son is up to pretty much all the time,' said one.

Parents have mixed views on the transition from lower to upper school – everything from 'my children were the only ones from the country we came from and they felt so included so quickly, there seem to be no cliques at all' to 'my son had a tough time at first and didn't easily settle but they didn't get to know how to handle it. The housemaster seemed out of his depth.' Parents say the school essentially operates as two schools, a more-or-less self-contained lower school, running as a day prep from 11 to 13; and an upper school, from 13 to 18, which is very much a boarding school, with a full day of lessons and sport on Saturday; older pupils also told us they have 'very little to do with the lower school'. But school insists there's more integration these days, drawing the lower school into the upper 'as we didn't want the lower school to be a holding pen'.

Discipline standards are tighter under current head, whom parents describe as 'no nonsense' but 'not draconian'. Sanctions run the usual gamut from detention to permanent exclusion, of which there have been a handful in recent years, plus around 10 temporary exclusions ('typically a day or two to make a point,' says head). Zero tolerance to drugs, but not enough of a problem (pupils concur) to do random testing (although they reserve the right). Bullying policy clear and pupils adamant strong community spirit prevents it. Strong prefect system.

Pupils and parents: Mainly from the nearest home counties – Hertfordshire, Essex, Buckinghamshire, Cambridgeshire – and it's easily commutable from London too. In general parents are 'City folk, business people, successful professionals' and as most live reasonably nearby, more involved than usual at boarding schools. Large numbers from Europe for the sixth form, particularly Germans and Italians. Pupils seem happy, confident, friendly and balanced.

Money matters: Academic, music, sport, art, and all-rounder scholarships form a complicated system, in addition to a range of (generous) means-tested bursaries.

The last word: A vibrant and busy school set in exquisite surroundings, with a long-established, successful IB diploma programme and an exceptional co-curricular offering. Great fun for those who want to be involved in everything it has to offer, although you might want to look elsewhere if you have a child who burns out easily.

Heath Mount School

20

Woodhall Park, Watton At Stone, Hertford, Hertfordshire SG14 3NG

01920 830230 | registrar@heathmount.org | www.heathmount.org

Ages: 3-13

Pupils: 520; Boarders: 100 flexi (Monday - Thursday)

Fees: Day £12,435 – £19,188. Boarding plus £5,115

Head: Since 2014, Chris Gillam (40s). With his spiky hair style and ready grin, it's easier to picture Mr Gillam playing bass in a band than behind the headmaster's desk. Nonetheless, he is in top gear at Heath Mount, rolling out numerous fascinating innovations and reaping the rewards in pupil numbers: the school is full, with a waiting list.

The son of two teachers (so far, so familiar), his father was headmaster of a state school in South Yorkshire. Mr Gillam studied a BEd at Plymouth University, supplementing his income with tennis coaching on the side (a game he still loves). His affinity with his pupils caught the eye of a young player's dad (himself a deputy head) who swiftly headhunted him upon graduating.

He rose to deputy head of Bishopsgate School in Windsor via posts in three other prep schools before joining Heath Mount as head. Mr Gillam now enjoys one of the grandest headmaster's offices in the country — Heath Mount occupies the main house of the Woodhall Estate, owned by the Abel Smith family.

Since this is a large prep (over 500 pupils) and Mr Gillam shows every prospective family round himself — 'so I get to know them, and they get to know me; I've always believed in that' — he doesn't teach as much as he would like, but headmaster's teas each Friday (and regular year group assemblies) ensure he really gets to know the pupils. Tea attendance is granted by presentation of a headmaster's commendation bookmark awarded by teachers.

Clearly an ideas man, he is proud of the team he's built: 'It's taken six years to get to this point, but the staff are superb. I've quite a young, dynamic SMT, and we're roughly 50/50 men and women teaching year 3 and above.'

Parents see him every day at drop off and pick up, and agree he has put the place on the map: 'I've been impressed by the standard of teaching and Mr Gillam has been behind that,' and 'He's confident to delegate to his heads of year and department — he trusts them, and they are fantastic.'

Underpinning this is an in-house graduate teacher trainee programme Heath Mount has developed in partnership with Hertford University, through which promising graduates are invited to train at the school, with the best offered a job there afterwards (vacancies permitting).

The headmaster's house is elsewhere on the estate (not within the school grounds) and Mr Gillam has a son and daughter currently at the school.

Entrance: Register early, certainly before two-and-a-half. Most pupils join in nursery or reception. If there is space for a child to join later, they will be assessed in English and maths and invited for a taster day, mainly for setting purposes.

The school is non selective, and a child is only likely be turned away if they require constant one-to-one assistance. Some pupils do join the school for the final two years, partly because few other preps in the area go to year 8.

Exit: Haileybury hoovers up roughly a third of leavers each year, with Bishop's Stortford, Felsted, The Leys and Harrow pretty popular after that. Others recently to Millfield, Brighton College, Benenden, Uppingham, Oundle, Rugby, Gordonstoun and Ampleforth. The range points to a lack of typecasting, and each pupil's plan of attack is drawn up in a meeting with the head and future schools manager. Scholarship successes (21 in 2021) are detailed in full on the school's website, and testify to the success of year 7 and 8 scholarship programmes. A 100 per cent success rate in art, drama and music awards is not uncommon.

Our view: The splendid Grade 1 listed grounds and main school building — with magnificent staircases and plasterwork, and the finest print room in Europe — provide a fitting home for a school with a rich history and starry alumnae, including novelist Evelyn Waugh, photographer Sir Cecil Beaton and actor Sir Gerald du Maurier. Dating back to 1796, it began as a boys' boarding school in Hampstead, the Heath part of its name deriving from its then home on Heath Street. As the region developed, the school (its name also evolving over time) eventually outgrew London and moved to its present Hertfordshire home in 1934. Girls were admitted in 1976 and only in the 1980s did the school expand its buildings beyond the main house. The site does appear a little crowded with parked vehicles, one downside being that (served by a busy road) it's really only viable to come by car.

Well-established forest school is clearly popular – even year 8s remember setting cardboard Tudor houses ablaze there in the annual recreation of the great fire of London

The nursery has its own building, with the pre-prep in another next door, an attractive, bright space with a central hall (perfumed with freshly baked croissants on our visit), and a cracking outdoor play area. The lower school (years 3 and 4) are in yet another building adjacent to those — one can see why London emigre parents' eyes shine at space here. While the parent body includes a lot of 'own business, City worker' professionals, people who might not fall into those categories have also felt warmly welcomed. They're also excellent fundraisers; they financed a pirate ship playground behind the pre-prep, and the parent-run Du Maurier society organises all kinds of social events in support of the school and charities with which it has close links.

A well-established forest school is clearly popular — even year 8s remember setting cardboard Tudor houses ablaze there in the annual recreation of the great fire of London — and there was no danger of the drizzle damping a good fire and re-enactment of The Scarecrow's Wedding on our visit.

From the middle school (years 5 and 6), children spend most of their time in the main building, and parents are attracted by the transition between different buildings as you progress through what is a pretty large school.

One of Heath Mount's best attributes is its art department, housed in a network of bright basement rooms. If it charged to tour the Modigliani-inspired self portraits, ceramic collections and textile homages to Zandra Rhodes exhibited on our visit, you'd think it money well spent. One full-time head of department (who's been at the school over 20 years) is supported by part-time specialists, 'so we've a wonderful team of professional artists'. How many prep schools have an animation suite or textile room, staffed by specialists in those fields? 'My philosophy is variety — they are lucky little children,' adds the head of art, with no small degree of understatement. The school regularly has pieces accepted by the Junior Royal Academy and was even offered £3,000 for one recent exhibit by a visitor (gently declined).

Another stand out feature is a commitment to the 'learning power' ethos developed by learning sciences Professor Guy Claxton who has trained the SMT and addressed parents and pupils about it. 'It's a language we use to help give children skills beyond the classroom — particularly collaboration, reflection, respect and resilience,' explains one teacher. Children are all paired with 'learning buddies' with whom they must collaborate, and a regular catchphrase is 'Try three before me' to urge them to solve things with their brain, book, or buddy before having to ask a teacher.

Streaming starts (amusingly) with swimming in reception, followed by maths in year 1, English from year 3, with languages and science from year 5.

The head places much emphasis on the fact that years 7 and 8 are treated as very distinct members of the school, and are at once recognisable by their navy jumpers (the rest of the school has green), 'which seems to mean the world to them, for some reason'. They also have their own gym and hang-out space in the basement.

A definite incentive to stay to year 8 are the scholarship programmes run in sport, academics, art, drama and music. Pupils apply in year 6, and they involve extension classes and special projects, with music lessons provided for free for music scholars. We watched year 7 sports scholars pumping weights to pumping music in a lunchtime conditioning workout, but they're also given free sports kit and extra training in relevant topics like nutrition. Their fitness is documented as it improves and used in secondary school sports scholarships applications, alongside details of their sporting achievements in and outside school.

Facilities include an indoor pool and an astroturf pitch, and professional coaches and international players from cricket, rugby, hockey and netball are brought in for guest training sessions periodically. Girls' cricket is growing, and from year 5, anyone who really doesn't like team sports may opt for a largely off-site alternative sports programme including anything from high rope courses to canoeing.

With ever more secondary schools making unconditional offers, Heath Mount invites pupils to study a broader syllabus in history, geography and TPR (philosophy, theology and religion) than that offered by CE. Called the Libellum (meaning bill or certificate in Latin), this is examined (and externally moderated) through coursework and projects, with only 30 per cent determined by a final exam. Heath Mount has persuaded public schools which still mark these subjects at CE to accept it as an alternative, and year 8s we met seemed very engaged with it.

Yet it's for singing that this school is really on the musical map. There are five choirs, with the Bax choir (selected by audition, competition is hot) chief among them

As befits a school which boasts composer Sir Arnold Bax as an old boy, music is another school focus. Year 1s are all given six weeks of violin instruction and around 75 per cent study an instrument (with many learning two or three), with the option of joining the junior or senior orchestras (the former performed the first movement of Beethoven's Fifth recently), a concert band, wind band, guitar group, jazz group, junior or senior strings group or a string quartet. Ticket demand for the two annual headline summer concerts is such, pupils must do a matinee and evening show. There's also an ensembles and orchestras concert each Lent term, year group production and informal 'rush hour concerts' at pick up time for parents.

Yet it's for singing that this school is really on the musical map. There are five choirs, with the Bax choir (selected by audition, competition is hot) chief among them. The Bax choir rehearses for two to three hours a week under the director of music (herself a classically trained soprano) and have a remarkable record in competitions. In 2019 they reached the finals of the Songs of Praise Young Choir of the Year (a title they won in 2012) and became Children's Choir of the World at the Llangollen International Musical Eisteddfod, becoming only the second English choir to do so.

Dance is an interest here too, thanks in part to ties with a local dance school and the fact Heath Mount has a smart dance studio. In addition to after school ballet classes, there's a popular commercial dance club (boys are well represented) and an annual dance show.

Completing the deck on the arts front is drama. Everyone from years 3 to 8 has a weekly drama lesson, with supplementary sessions on offer to anyone applying for a drama scholarship. The main annual school production (featuring year 6s and 7s) in the very handsome school theatre is supplemented by a musical from the year 4s and a less formal drama show for year 5s. A school podcast instigated during lockdown to offer distanced performance opportunities is doing well too.

The school surveys pupils twice a year about wellbeing to help them identify pressure points and year group trends, and 'Wellbeing Wednesdays' involve things like mindfulness and nature walks. The school even has two trained nurture dogs (owned by one of the learning support team) which may be walked or read to by any child who's finding the going a bit heavy.

There's a full-time counsellor at Heath Mount (one parent we interviewed was very impressed with the support given to their child through a family crisis) a nurse, an occupational therapist plus two learning support assistants to support all kinds of issues such as processing problems, dyslexia etc. There is also a visiting educational psychologist and speech therapist.

There are separate, sizeable ICT suites for the junior and senior parts of the school, and we came across one parent who had jettisoned plans for their child to move schools in year 7, based on the quality of the online learning provision during lockdown.

Boarding: Heath Mount offers boarding or flexi-boarding between Monday and Thursday from year 3, 'a fundamental part of the school and so useful for secondary school preparation,' says the head. The boys' dorms are high within the main building while the girls are in the smart — and very pink — River House a short distance away, from where they are bussed to the main building each morning.

Bright and inviting, the rooms have the slightly impersonal character of all dorms used flexibly but the boys certainly have fabulous views over the park. Roughly one third of pupils board to some degree, with evening activities ranging from swimming to the intriguing sounding 'real life hungry hippos'. Many parents sign up just to let their children make the most of the many resources and space — the best dens built in the grounds may be awarded with a golden pinecone award (produced by the DT department).

Money matters: Some bursaries available from year 3, of up to 100 per cent of fees.

The last word: Heath Mount is a place buzzing with innovation, and scoring notable national achievements in more than one area. 'Every year, it gets better and better,' attests one parent. Though it may feel dauntingly large on arrival, our feeling was that no one could fail to love it, with its confident, sparky pupils the best advertisement of all.

Holmwood House School

Chitts Hill, Lexden, Colchester, Essex CO3 9ST

01206 574305 | headmaster@holmwood.house | www.holmwood.house

Ages: 3-13

Pupils: 237; Boarders: 15-25 per night

Fees: Day £9,900 – £14,580; Boarding £32 per night

Headmaster: Since September 2021, Edward Bond, previously head of lower school at Haileybury where he taught for 20 years. In the (nearly) 100 -year history of Holmwood, he is, remarkably, only the sixth head and the second with no family or previous connection with the founder. Educated at Wellington College, thence to Durham where he did his history degree and PGCE. More recently, he gained an MA in educational leadership at Bath. He was previously a senior examiner in history for the IB, as well as being involved in the IB History Curriculum Review Committee – and he has experience of inspecting schools for the ISI too. A ball of energy, he is excitable and bursting with ideas. Currently teaches history – 'and I might well teach maths next year.' Meets and greets pupils, often pops into classrooms, reads with the younger ones and has been known to play cricket in the yard with the pupils. Lives onsite with wife Kathryn and their three sons who attend a local all-through school. Loves reading (currently an Alex Gerlis spy novel) and sport (is a rugby coach).

Entrance: School nursery (on separate site) from 6 months old and a good clutch move straight up to pre-reception (on the Lexden site) or reception while others leave for local primaries. Majority joins reception at age 4 and increasingly at 11 (especially since 2021, when the school started to expand to 16 – first year 9s start in 2023). Non-selective admissions policy and no formal tests at reception, but entry at 11 is through the school's own entrance tests. Spaces usually available for the higher forms; numbers in years 7 and 8 hold up well.

Exit: 'One of the first questions some parents ask me is, "Do you prepare for grammar schools?" and the answer is yes,' says head, with half the pupils heading off after year 6 to do just that (or to senior independent schools). They are swiftly replaced with new pupils. Rest leaves after year 8 for the nearby day and boarding schools: Uppingham, Framlingham, Felsted, Royal Hospital School, Ipswich School, Ipswich High, Culford and Gresham's. Occasional places further afield at eg King's Canterbury, Ampleforth, Benenden, Eton, Stowe and Gordonstoun. About half win awards to senior schools. Likely to be a different picture in the coming years with pupils now able to stay on to do their GCSEs.

Our view: Set in a semi-rural pocket of north Essex (or 'south Suffolk') handily close to the A12 and two miles from Colchester. The only prep school in the area that offers both day and boarding options. 'We are essentially a day school, with the opportunities of a boarding school, including occasional overnight stays,' says the school. On the same site for nearly a hundred years (2022 is the centenary), the school remains academically broad and prides itself on adapting to and understanding children's needs. 'We prioritise giving children ownership of their learning,' adds the head, who got all the pupils to give a presentation to their mums and dads before the last parents evening 'so they knew what their sons felt about their learning, ready for the discussion with the teacher.'

Extensive wooded grounds are pleasant rather than idyllic. Main building, used largely for administration, boarding and school meals, stands amid a sequence of functional one – and two-storey buildings, set around courtyards and play areas. Much is made of the natural surroundings with well maintained forest trails, outdoor classrooms and games pitches and running tracks as far as the eye can see. Prep school has its own adventure trail and an outdoor learning space called The Spinney.

The day starts at 8.25am (breakfast club from 7.30am) with teaching until 3.25pm or 4pm for all years. Pre-prep and years 4 to 6 can either go home then or opt for tea, prep and activities at school until 6.15pm, and this is popular with many on at least some days of the week. The later time is compulsory for years 7 and 8. Saturday morning school now ditched.

Parents appreciate the flexibility of the school's boarding offer, 'especially when you have several children'

Houses are named after the elements and there are challenges and competitions, mostly charitable or sporting, all year round, notably the 'Songfest' in the first term when everyone spends an hour learning a new song and an outside adjudicator is invited. Rewards system of golden awards and super stars for younger pupils and show-ups and show-downs (sounds more drastic than it is) for older pupils. Behaviour is very good and pupils are well mannered, opening doors and so on, in a relaxed, unforced way.

Pupils in reception get the newest premises, close by but separate from the main building. Lovely, large and well equipped spaces for work and play are set within partly wooded grounds. The main pre-prep department (years 1-3) occupies a new(ish) two-storey building that includes a decent sized hall as well as a series of light, airy classrooms, though 'we like being upstairs best,' admitted our guides. Two forms in each year. French taught from nursery. Interactive and often messy learning right from the off to get kids switched on to their learning – 'you want to get boys excited about, say, the earth so we get them making one out of clay,' says the head.

Over in prep, Spanish is added in year 4 and there's setting in maths and English from year 6. Spark programme in place for year 7s and 8s – focuses on getting pupils to think, analyse, reflect etc. Great enthusiasm for global studies, an amalgam of history, geography and RS: 'We do all about life and death, battles, medicine, Joan of Arc, religions, everything!' Support for SEN is a combination of classroom based and one-to-ones (latter costs extra), with thew new SENCo currently drawing up plans for ever more innovative ways of getting youngsters with eg ASD, ADHD and dyslexia to overcome learning barriers. The individual approach is praised by parents: 'It's about how can we help you be your best.' School stepped up well during Covid, with a seamless move into online learning.

Sport is played on most days. Rugby, football, hockey and cricket for boys; hockey, netball and cricket for girls. Plenty of match experience. 'It's often the same people in the As but we all get a chance in matches as there aren't that many of us.' Twenty acres of the school's extensive grounds are given over to sport, plus a vast sports hall and an indoor swimming pool. The school has the use of the on-site Lexdon rackets club with its tennis and squash coaches.

Drama is a timetabled subject and several productions are staged annually by combined year groups. 'We rehearse the play for a whole week when it's our turn,' a pupil explained. Year 8s have a play all to themselves. Parents feel these opportunities boost all-round confidence. 'They learn to stand up in front of people and perform from an early age, so it feels natural.'

Music is taken seriously with everyone having the chance to learn a stringed instrument in class as a 'try out', with the consequence that some continue learning. There are several choirs. 'I joined the chamber choir because it goes on tour,' we were told. There are orchestras for all abilities and everyone gets to perform in concerts throughout the year.

Parents are usually blown away by the art room – a huge well lit space with lots of room to spread out and get creative. There's a kiln and DT area in an adjoining workshop, equipped to a high standard and individual workstations (fretsaws in action when we called). By the end of year 8 pupils have mastered electronic circuits, animation and food wrapping projects and designed a building.

Enormous library with thousands of books and a balcony that seats at least 60 and is well used. Pupils have library lessons in the lower forms and it is used for supervised prep for all years. It is a year 8 privilege to sit on the red sofas in a corner of the balcony. The Jubilee Hall, used for daily assemblies and staging school plays, has tiered seating for 200, a foyer and exhibition space.

This is a school with an atmosphere. 'Children feel safe and valued,' a parent said and there is praise all round for the 'buddy' system where older pupils act as a friend and guide to a younger pupil. 'It's a relationship that can mean a great deal on both sides.' Form tutors, then the relevant head of 'phase', are the main points of contact for parents and in addition the school arranges regular consultation sessions. The emphasis is on keeping in close touch so that any emerging difficulties can be tackled early on. There is a variety of ways the school keeps in touch with parents (and vice versa): the weekly bulletin (need to know), newsletter (nice to know), email for particular information concerning subjects or year groups, as well as Facebook and Twitter. If all else fails, or there is a serious personal problem to be discussed, 'pick the phone up,' says school.

Boarding: Boarding – two nights a week maximum – available from year 4 with certain nights reserved for particular year groups or for a 'themed' night (Burns Night was a recent jolly). Particularly popular with year 7s and 8s, even more so since Covid. 'Special nights are my favourite, all my friends stay then too,' said a year 8 pupil. Parents appreciate the flexibility of the school's offer, 'especially when you have several children.' Boarders have their own games room with pool and ping pong tables etc, but also use the sports hall and art and music facilities.

Money matters: Fees average for the area. Some means-tested bursaries available.

The last word: A small school experience on a big campus, with extensive grounds and facilities that rival some secondary schools. Lots of parental excitement about years 9, 10 and 11 being added.

Ipswich High School

Woolverstone Hall, Woolverstone, Ipswich, Suffolk IP9 1AZ

01473 780201 | admissions@ipswichhighschool.co.uk | www.ipswichhighschool.co.uk

Ages: 3 -18

Pupils: 445; sixth form: 62; Boarders: 26 full, 26 weekly/flexi

Fees: £10,300 – £16,285 pa. Boarding £28,500 – £36,380 pa

Head: Since 2020, Mark Howe. Began his career as a history teacher in a state school in Hampshire in 2006 and after two years, became professional mentor for all trainee and newly qualified teachers in the school and in the same year he completed the postgraduate certificate of innovation in education at Warwick. Appointed as head of history and secondary teaching and learning co-ordinator at an international school in China, then returned to the UK five years later as head of an independent boarding school in Devon.

Head of prep school: Since April 2019, Lisa Finch (replaced Eileen Fisher, who departed after 10 years in the role for a founding headship in China). Mrs Finch, previously head of Stanway Fiveways Primary School in Colchester, has a background and degree specialism in drama and theatre, a particular interest in PE and numeracy education and is a qualified SENCo. Two daughters, one at Ipswich High, the other now at uni.

Entrance: Boys and girls may join in any year in the prep school where there are spaces; in the seniors, boys are now accepted into years 7, 8, 9 and sixth form (extending in future years), girls wherever. Non-selective pre-prep. Entrance to reception is by informal assessment; informal tests in maths and English during a visit to the school for those joining thereafter. All pupils assessed for SEN. Prep pupils have year 7 places guaranteed and are joined by others from 20-plus feeder preps and primaries. All candidates – internal as well as external – provide a report from current school and together sit tests in English, maths and verbal reasoning in October and then take part in a team-building activity led by sixth formers – 'less stressful for the students,' says head. Handful of joiners at year 9 from regional boarding preps, eg South Lee in Bury St Edmunds, Old Buckenham Hall, Holmwood House in Colchester; potential growth here. Internal year 11 students are automatically offered a place in sixth form; new entrants at this stage require at least five GCSEs at grade 6; 7 for maths.

Exit: Nearly all prep pupils move up to the senior school; a few to boarding or grammars. Some (about two-thirds) post-year 11 leakage to co-ed sixth forms or grammars in recent years. Post-18, Russell Group favoured, particularly Bristol, for traditional academic subjects, though art and design strong. A couple annually overseas, often through family links. Sixth form 'escape' trip visits universities outside the UK as a taster – recently Milan, Edinburgh. Apprenticeships and other options supported. Five medics in 2021.

Latest results: In 2021, 70 per cent 9-7 at GCSE; 39 per cent A*/A at A level (89 per cent A*-B). In 2019 (the last year when exams took place), 64 per cent 7-9 at GCSE; 32 per cent A*/A at A level (66 per cent A*-B).

Teaching and learning: Very much an all-through school so curriculum integrated right across the campus. Self-contained pre-prep section for little ones from the age of 3 in large, airy rooms with dedicated outdoor spaces. Infant and junior pupils – taught by specialists for languages, dance, music and PE; science and maths specialist teaching due to be added. Emphasis on reading – friendly library stuffed with books and comfy places to sit and dip in and teachers who say 'drop everything and read!' during the annual read-a-thon, according to our pupil guides. Class library lessons weekly and all welcome at lunchtimes, supervised by librarian, who organises a stream of author visits. Learning support also cross-school and prep has a dedicated room offering support for 'people who are not quite getting it,' our guides explain.

Among the strongest top results in Suffolk. One of the aims of the new co-ed sixth form is to stabilise numbers to 40 per year, which is beginning to happen.

School recently won an award for their boarding houses – 'they would not look out of place in Architectural Digest.' Busy activity programme at weekends

Strong on maths, which is set from year 6, and also science – GCSE syllabus for both double and triple begins in year 9. Head of science reports a growing interest in the physical sciences and engineering, alongside perennial vets and medics. At least one foreign language GCSE is highly recommended, but otherwise a fairly free choice outside of the core subjects; unusually, no compunction to take something creative. Latin popular. A level – no plans to introduce IB – option blocks 'flexible' and students choose either three or four subjects; further maths an exceptional addition. Choices weighed up in advance in individual meetings with parents and head of sixth form. Wifi everywhere and students may bring a mobile device from year 9, for use in lessons when directed. Half-termly effort grades and regular reports throughout the year groups keep students up to scratch and parents in the picture.

Form tutors begin UCAS discussions in year 12 with a view to early applications in year 13. 'My form tutor is very good at keeping us on track and head of sixth form knows a lot about it,' reports our lower sixth guide. Careers talks by industry professionals, former students or parents every other week, all-comers welcome. Lord Winston

Competitive locally, particularly in hockey and swimming, and nationally in triathlon and aquathlon, even for prep pupils

recently packed out for a talk on Happiness. Work experience after GCSEs in year 11, some in year 12 usually to support UCAS application. Online assessment tools help with careers suggestions and clubs fan the flames – eg MedSoc, STEM Club, engineering and robotics.

Learning support and SEN: School aims to provide support both through differentiated teaching in the classroom and, if required, additional support. Mild dys- and processing needs are picked up early and supported one-to-one or in small groups.

The arts and extracurricular: Music and drama not done by halves. Most students – prep and senior – learn an instrument or sing and regular concerts are staged at nearby Snape Maltings (in artistic Aldeburgh) or in the school's impressive 300-seat Hayworth Theatre. Young Musician of the Year contest, choirs, orchestra and ensembles. Annual musical production and Shakespeare play. Prep school has its own venue – hall with stage – for dramatic and musical performances and a popular dance competition. A whole-school musical and a Shakespeare production each year for year 9 and up.

A level artists each have a designated 'atelier' style studio space in the professional-style art school – so no need to pack away – in preparation for foundation or degree course, a route pursued by a couple every year and the occasional architect. University of Suffolk exhibition as well as showcase for work by GCSE artists – usually half the year group – (catered by food studies students). DT well established – bench-cum-water-butt by one student an ingenious environmentally-friendly seating solution and wooden wall concealing geometric furniture – very forward-thinking. 3D design runs the range from architecture to sculpture in wood, metal and plastics plus other materials – 'we encourage them to work in all sorts,' says teacher as one student focuses on creating a table from rope. Two hours a fortnight in years 7/8 and an option thereafter. Around eight students take GCSE. A level DT newly introduced but already a handful signed up. Impressive sculptures on display in the grounds.

Enrichment sessions at the start of and at 3.30pm every day for seniors includes squad training, horse-riding and DofE (bronze for most of year 10 and silver popular too, with gold on the cards), so no after-school clubs and carriages firmly at 4.30pm. Wraparound care and late-stay homework session available. In prep, enrichment activities in the school day cover 'everything you can dream of,' say our guides – eco warriors, DT club, rock climbing, Lego, skiing at local dry slope and many more. Said a parent, 'The children are worked hard but they also have so much enjoyment through their enrichments and excursions.'

Sport: Acres of playing fields on site as well as Astros, hard courts, indoor sports hall and 25-metre pool... sport is taken seriously here. Competitive locally, particularly in hockey and swimming, and nationally in triathlon and aquathlon, even for prep school pupils. Football and cricket on the curriculum long before the boys turned up, but an expanded fixture list is the hope, and the chance to take part in co-ed tournaments on an equal footing. For the less team-oriented, yoga, pilates, fencing, plus clubs for sailing nearby at the school Neptune Club, skiing at local dry slope and equestrian pursuits. Sixth formers choose from hockey, football, sports hall games (badminton, fitness etc), fitness suite – all mixed lessons. Annual ski trip for prep and senior pupils.

Boarding: Weekly, flexi and full boarding offered. School recently won an award for their boarding houses – 'they would not look out of place in Architectural Digest,' said BSA. Facilities include the Dairy House, a Grade II listed house that sleeps 20 in single, twin and en suite bedrooms, as well as the Barns with an additional 20 twin and single en suite rooms featuring mezzanine sleeping decks, cinema room and big social spaces. Most recently, the Annex completes the boarding offering with another 19 bedrooms and accommodation for the full-time, live-in house parents and matron. Busy activity programme at weekends. Interest already from current parents, many of whom have been asking for boarding for years, as well as international families in Hong Kong, Thailand, Vietnam and elsewhere. Boarding facilities will give greater scope for on-site summer activity clubs too.

Ethos and heritage: One of the country's first GDST schools, Ipswich High School for Girls was borne out of a strong passion for women's education. Established by Miss Sophie Youngman in 1878, originally with 43 girl pupils in the Assembly Rooms in Ipswich's Northgate Street, the girls' day school flourished and by 1905 had outgrown its premises. Brakefield in Westerfield Road was bought for the school by The Girls' Public Day School Company (forerunner of the Girls' Day School Trust), which sufficed until 1992, when continued expansion prompted the purchase of the grade I-listed Woolverstone Hall, set in 80 acres on the banks of the River Orwell and previously a school for boys. Facilities quickly added and in 2007 the school launched Woodland Pre-Prep.

A surprise to many, in 2017 Ipswich High School parted ways with the GDST, was purchased by Ipswich Education Ltd and announced plans to welcome boys from 2018 and boarders from 2019, with the intention of achieving a co-educational day and boarding school by September 2023. Roll is under 500 currently; capacity on the site for 700. 'We won't grow massively if we are to grow,' reassures head. 'Class sizes will remain much the same.'

Pupils 'unfazed', by move to co-ed. A parent told us, 'I wanted single-sex education for my girls but liked the school so much I gave it a chance; so far I am happy'

School's original governing body was retained and, although not the legal entity, their input is 'significant'; head answers to the school's owners, Ipswich Education Ltd, and their board of directors. 'Making a profit' is not their focus, insists school. A lot of investment in the school already apparent: IT infrastructure, purchase of boarding house and review of sports facilities, as well as toilets and changing rooms. Even the school's logo has reverted to a traditional gender-neutral shield design from the previous flowery pink creation.

Students 'unfazed', says school, a comment verified by one prep pupil: 'I always knew that eventually there would be boys here, it was kind of obvious'. Another was less prepared, however: 'When I heard boys would be joining I said "Sorry, what?!"' As did some parents by all accounts. 'I cannot lie and say I was thrilled with the changes,' said one. 'I always wanted a single-sex education for my girls but I liked the school so much I decided to give it a chance, and so far I am happy with it.'

Approached via a tree-lined avenue surrounded by acres of sheep, Ipswich High already has the look of an idyllic semi-rural boarding and day school. The Hall itself, a fine example of Palladian architecture dating from 1776, is flanked by landscaped lawns with vistas of the River Orwell. The grand interior has National Trust standard décor, all ceiling mouldings and well-polished panelling. No wonder it's a popular wedding venue. A highlight is the orangery – no ordinary school refectory – with a terrace for al fresco dining in the summer. A daily hot meal is served, with a vegetarian alternative, jacket potatoes, salads and a 'grab and go' selection of sausage rolls etc. Sixth formers may take lunch to eat in their own sophisticated suite on the upper floors, which has college-style small classrooms, break-out areas and spaces for individual study. Also in the main building is a bright Learning Resources Centre, a library and computer-studded study space for lower years with laptops and iPads to sign out.

Neighbouring Orwell House teaching building is of more practical than architectural interest. Downstairs has two science labs per science, some with traditional horseshoe-shaped benches, others with more modern designated study and practical areas. Upstairs are classrooms for English and MFLs, Latin and maths. All bright and spacious with interactive whiteboards. Distraction-free learning environment with computers at the core. A contemporary glazed entrance hall welcomes visitors to the separate two-storey prep school building – recently made over in bleached wood and glass. Inside, friendly wide corridors lead to spacious classrooms, all with big screens, and a recently reimagined and inviting library area.

Pre-preppers have their own secure outdoor play area, as do the infants, while junior morning and afternoon breaktimes are spent on the large safety-surfaced playground with football area, trim trail and play equipment, bounded by lush hedging. 'Eco hut' outdoor classroom is well used in summer for lessons from science to mindfulness and 'sometimes we just sit here and listen to the birds'.

Outbuildings dot the grounds, most currently used for storage but ripe for renovation – this school has plenty of room to grow. Lord Belstead Cookery Rooms (link to the local gentry) in former stables, beautifully fitted, the envy of the home cook. Another outbuilding is a suitably inventorish home for the DT workshop; inside is a hive of practical as well as brain activity.

Impressive and very white sports and arts building. Theatre with stage and tiered seating fits entire senior school and professional sound and lighting encourages back-stage tech skills; genuine theatrical experience for those in the spotlight. Sports hall has movable wall to reveal staging behind for large-scale events such as speech day. Large indoor pool with spacious changing rooms etc, well used before, during and after school by all year groups throughout prep and senior, and also by local clubs after hours. Girls' and boys' changing rooms already existing for outside use, but girls' now extended (pupils used to use both). Astro for hockey and tennis; hard courts for netball and tennis, some year-round. Super standard.

Pastoral care, inclusivity and discipline: Frequently cited as a strength by parents. Senior houses, named after eminent women, are largely used for social, sporting and charity events; prep houses are mythical creatures and house points are added up every Friday – 'very competitive,' confided our year 6 guide. Winner of highest number has the honour of using the trim trail ('before that we all used to argue about who could go on it'). Main prep corridor adorned with a board of photos of weekly stars in each class, voted for by pupils for good work, acts of kindness etc and pupil suggestion box – 'really works,' confirmed our guides, who had put in a request for two new football goals and were delighted to find that they had materialised over the summer break. School council has two reps from each prep year group and is fêted for initiating a 'buddy bench' for the playground. Throughout the school, good-tempered and respectful relations are the norm between staff and pupils. Few, if any, serious problems with behaviour. 'They deal with any small problem therefore it doesn't escalate,' approved a parent.

Pupils and parents: From an hour's radius – 13 school bus routes extend to Bury St Edmunds, Colchester, the Essex and Suffolk coasts. Mainly professional, business and city commuter families, still a few farming. Pupils relaxed and seemingly comfortable in the supportive environment. Respect, integrity, ambition and courage rightly prized and enshrined in the school's ethos; pupils are encouraged and empowered to be who they want to be.

Money matters: 'Given our beautiful main building, people often assume we are scary and inaccessible, but we're actually quite affordable for working families,' says school. At the value-for-money end locally with exam entries, lunches and text books included in fees. Second-hand uniform shop run by Parents' Association; new kit through Schoolblazer online. Early years funding accepted. Academic scholarships based on entrance assessment achievement – all candidates entered. Art, music, drama, dance and PE scholarships require an interview with staff, multiple entries and awards allowed. Maximum fee remission for scholars 50 per cent; majority receive 10 per cent though often a little more in sixth form (senior scholars must reapply). Charitable fund awaiting approval since transition from GDST – common question posed by clued-up parents. 'Now we are not a charity, our funding is probably more transparent than it was,' says school. 'Fees are reinvested for the benefit of students.'

The last word: With academic and sporting credentials already in place, a lot of potential here to create a successful co-ed boarding and day school on a well-equipped campus. Sure to appeal to international students and those closer to home wanting a modern independent school education of a slightly different flavour to what's currently on the menu in the region.

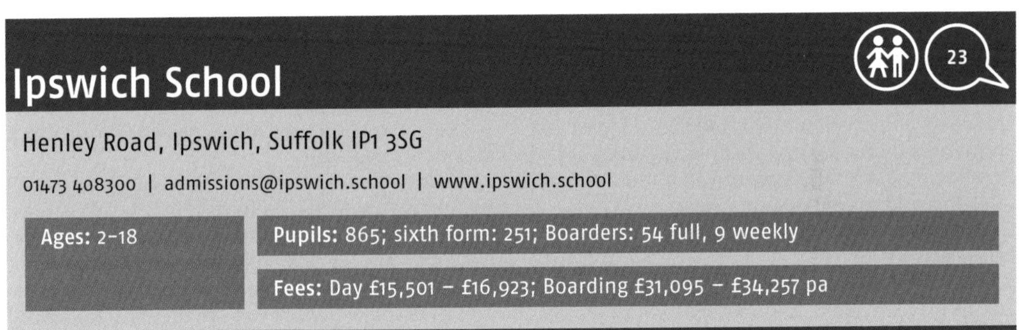

Ipswich School

23

Henley Road, Ipswich, Suffolk IP1 3SG

01473 408300 | admissions@ipswich.school | www.ipswich.school

Ages: 2-18

Pupils: 865; sixth form: 251; Boarders: 54 full, 9 weekly

Fees: Day £15,501 – £16,923; Boarding £31,095 – £34,257 pa

Headmaster: Since 2010, Nicholas Weaver BA. Read engineering at Jesus College, Cambridge. Previously deputy head (academic) at Portsmouth Grammar, and before that taught physics at the Leys School, Cambridge, the Royal Grammar School, Guilford, and Radley College. Urbane and apparently unruffable, married with three children, all pupils at Ipswich School. Committed to developing in his students not just the skills needed for A*s but 'the flexibility of mind to apply their knowledge to novel situations, using those high-level taxonomy skills which transfer across disciplines'. This has called for an intellectual approach to the academic curriculum at Ipswich and also the important and wide-ranging co-curriculum, mostly student-led, which is designed for balance above all else. 'He is incredibly positive, dynamic, determined and clearly proud of the school and everything it stands for,' said a parent. 'I admire his qualities as a head and his views on pastoral care,' added another.

Entrance: Maximum 120 year 7 places. Currently five-form intake (previously four) with no more than 24 per class up to GCSE. Nearly half of year 7 intake from prep – entry on recommendation from prep head. Littlegarth in Colchester and St Margaret's in Gosfield are big 11+ feeders; rest often arrive solo from village schools within an hour's radius. Entry by school's own entrance exam in November, plus a report from current school and a chat with the head. UKiset applications (online testing) for overseas admissions.

Additional 15 to 20 places made available in year 9. Holmwood House in Colchester and nearby Orwell Park provide 13+ entrants. Entry by school's own exam in February, or common entrance (dwindling number).

Entry to sixth form requires six GCSEs with at least 6s, preferably 7s in chosen A level subjects, plus satisfactory chat with the head and report from current school.

Exit: Around 15 per cent leaves after GCSEs for local sixth-form colleges. Vast majority of those remaining head to university with a leaning towards traditional academic subjects at Russell Group establishments. Durham, Bristol, Edinburgh, Exeter, Leeds, Manchester and York popular in recent years. Four to Oxbridge in 2021, plus five medics and three to study overseas (Czech Republic, Hong Kong and USA). 'We are at the high-water mark of students going on to university but I feel degree apprenticeships will increase,' says head, who is on HMC committee pushing for regulation. Much effort on the part of careers and sixth-form staff to identify and recommend suitable worthwhile opportunities. Old Ipswichians currently apprenticed in the aviation, telecoms and property industries.

Latest results: In 2021, 70 per cent 9-7 at GCSE; 61 per cent A*/A at A level (86 per cent A*-B). In 2019 (the last year when exams took place), 65 per cent 9-7 at GCSE; 46 per cent A*/A at A level (74 per cent A*-B).

Teaching and learning: 'We had a choice between sending our youngest daughter to other independent schools and also a grammar school in Colchester but chose Ipswich,' said one clued-up parent, typical of many.

Consistently the top independent school in terms of exam results in Suffolk. 'People sometimes lazily categorise us a as a hothouse,' laments head. 'We are selective but there is huge value-added; the co-curriculum provides a wealth of opportunities for students' engagement.'

Annual Ipswich School Festival of Music brings internationally renowned musicians, including many former pupils, to perform at the school

Growth mindset school, so academic excellence programme rather than gifted and talented, with extra lessons for stretch and a specialised programme of talks and seminars. 'The school is relatively agile while not being over-reactive to fads,' explains head. 'We move with the times.' Eight-lesson school day runs until 4.15pm on a two-week timetable. Paper and pen for most lessons but plenty of computer suites, and Wifi throughout; laptops welcome but not essential other than for those with SEN.

Year 7s are set after their first half term for maths – one set 1, two set 2s and two set 3s; around 20 pupils per set. A wide curriculum introduces all of the major academic subjects, including French or Spanish and philosophy, religion and ethics. Year 8 introduces Latin and the integrated principles of science course gives way to discrete lessons in chemistry, physics and biology.

Year 9 sees the introduction of Russian or German and the start of GCSE courses in some subjects. GCSE choices are fairly unrestricted and there are many revision sessions and subject 'clinics' in the run-up to exams. All year 11s have a period of work experience, facilitated through school if necessary.

Students take four or more A levels (no IB here) with options including business studies, drama and theatre studies, economics, PE, psychology, politics and computer science on top of the traditional academic subjects. Year 12 classes of 10–15 are typical; even smaller the following year. Each student also selects an option from new The Edge programme of enrichment subjects, eg politics, law, EPQ.

A wealth of advice on uni courses, higher level and degree apprenticeships, from heads of sixth form and careers office, with the help of Unifrog. Early UCAS applications encouraged – a finely tuned process that sees the offers noticeboard updated with uni offers from October onwards.

Learning support and SEN: Those with SEN have support outside the timetabled day and lunchtime drop-in sessions.

The arts and extracurricular: Most recent inspection report praised Ipswich as a school where it's 'ok to like rugby and poetry'. Indeed, 'our provision does not limit the students,' says head; students are encouraged to try as many new activities as possible. Our year 8 guide backs this up – 'I love the sports,' she says, 'but here you can do other things alongside. I had never done music before I came here but someone persuaded me to give it a go and now I really enjoy it.'

A third of pupils take individual instrumental lessons from an army of peripatetic teachers (unusual instruments on request) and over half of pupils play in a variety of orchestras, including symphony, plus ensembles and choirs, which perform throughout the year. The chapel choir, besides singing evensong at several British cathedrals including St Paul's, tours regularly abroad (recently to New York). The annual Ipswich School Festival of Music brings internationally-renowned musicians, many featuring Old Ipswichians, to perform at the school in masterclasses and workshops. Britten Faculty of Music is based in a state-of-the-art purpose-built music school, with own concert hall and recording studio. National Youth Orchestra member on roll.

A mix of full-boarding internationals and flexi-boarders who stay a few nights to suit family arrangements, club or training commitments

School drama productions are impressive and professional musicians perform at school's own theatre. Technicians kept busy backstage with lighting and sound. Lower school production annually – most recently Peter Pan – and senior plays all year round. Professional-looking costume department. Art impressive and includes textiles and photography as options. DT compulsory in years 7 and 8 and a popular GCSE and A level option.

'We hear from universities and employers that some young people have all the A*s etc but they are a little underpowered in terms of life skills,' says head, who seeks to rectify this with recently formulated The Edge enrichment programme, drawing together life skills strands and accredited by the Institute of Leadership of Management (level 3). In addition Thursday afternoon sessions for students from year 9 offer a vast range of activities – CCF (army or RAF), voluntary work (eg in local primary schools and the school's own prep), cookery etc. Journalism club produces the weekly (and very popular) school newsletter building on a rich tradition – the school was one of the first in the country to produce a student magazine.

Clubs for all year groups– mostly at lunchtime so as not to disrupt travel arrangements – range from show choir to sub-aqua and drone club. Debating strong throughout the school. Sixth formers have the Athenaeum programme, a lunchtime forum for students to speak about a passion or discuss a burning issue. 'It's not formal debating,' explains the head, 'more – "Here's an interesting question, what are views in the room?" It's cool here to be talking about things from an intellectual standpoint.'

Curriculum related trips for all year groups. Our sixth-form guides were looking forward to a six-day art and religious studies visit to Italy. Adventurous residential visit to Cumbria a highlight for year 8s, while similar in south Wales teaches life skills to year 12s, covering, surfing and other physical activities as well as self-reliance and practical advice on what to do in the event of teenage scrapes.

Sport: Hockey and rugby are the main sports in autumn; netball and hockey in spring; cricket and athletics for all in summer. PE lessons all year round and choice of other games and sports. County champions and national finalists in girls' and boys' hockey and cricket across most age groups, but also non-competitive teams for leisure players and a well-used, well-equipped gym. Four alumni in GB Olympic squad are an inspiration and participation rates are high. Self-contained sports centre has a cavernous hall with plenty of lines for indoor hockey and rounders as well as netball, basketball, badminton, volleyball etc. Courts for fives – school enters nine or 10 teams per year group to national tournaments. Yoga studio. School has acres of playing fields and sports pitches nearby for lessons and training.

Boarding: School has two boarding houses, which accommodate fewer than five per cent of students. A mix of full-boarding internationals and flexi-boarders who stay a few nights to suit family arrangements, club or training commitments. A short walk from the school they have common rooms and kitchens, with breakfast and dinner on weekdays and all meals at weekends. Equivalent of home at this otherwise day school – no popping to and fro during the school day. On Saturdays those not involved in school sports fixtures have organised activities laid on – trips to Norwich or Cambridge, marshalling and taking part in local parkrun, art and craft projects etc – and also plenty of free time to explore the town, or to stretch their legs in the boarding house grounds or on the Astro. The sixth form boarding house is newly refurbished, with ensuite facilities – similar to a university hall of residence.

Ethos and heritage: Only school mentioned by Shakespeare, in Henry VIII – 'Ipswich and Oxford, those twins of learning'. Founded much earlier but no-one knows when – an unpaid bill dated 1399 is the oldest piece of evidence. Henry VIII granted the first charter and school's coat of arms and motto, Semper Eadem (Always the Same), are those of Elizabeth I. School's poster boy for social mobility is Cardinal Wolsey, the butcher's son who went on to become the most powerful man in the country and refounded the school in 1528 as The Cardinal's College. Plans fell with him, and the stone he intended to use to build the school in the 1500s was shipped off to build the palace at Whitehall. All that remains is a gate and the church which he had commandeered as the school chapel.

Concept survived, however, and Ipswich School was established in the town centre before moving in 1852 to new buildings opposite Christchurch Park, which it occupies to this day. Surprisingly spacious campus in a quiet residential area, centring on the original Victorian edifice, but expanded with 20th century buildings, connected by a series of passages, steps and covered ways, all punctuated with well-kept horticulture. Facilities range from the functional (run-of-the-mill classrooms and corridors) to the fantastic (impressive library with windows by John Piper depicting the seasons, and built-in chapel with wonderful organ, played by local church organist if no organ student on roll). You never know what will be behind the next door.

Art department is a professional-style work space and a huge area is dedicated to DT with tools for woodwork, metals, plastics (including 3D printer) and textiles, and a well-used exhibition space. School's own Great School Theatre is open to the public too.

Sixth form centre recently reimagined, now large contemporary relaxation and study zones with a large kitchen. Walls adorned with artwork based on photos of school activities and there is a grand piano for break or lunchtime ivory-tinkling. PRE – philosophy, religion, ethics – has its own building.

Architecture of new music school reflects the school's Snape connection (annual concert there is a highlight) and offers superb acoustics, not to mention fabulous wall art of Benjamin Britten extract notated in stones carved with the names of benefactors. Clever and creative – very Ipswich.

School's poster boy for social mobility is Cardinal Wolsey, a butcher's son who became the most powerful man in the country

School pavilion overlooks immaculate on-site cricket square and there are three more sports sites a short walk away: Rushmere has three new hockey pitches and six netball/tennis courts, most floodlit; Notcutts has playing fields for rugby and football, pitches for cricket and rounders and a grass athletics track; and there is an Astro hockey pitch-cum-tennis court at Westwood, the school boarding house. Several local houses serve as accommodation for teachers.

List of notable alumni starts with Cardinal Wolsey and moves on to author and illustrator Edward Ardizzone, physicist Sir Charles Frank and Nobel Prize winner Sir Charles Scott Sherrington who coined the terms 'neuron' and 'synapse'.

Pastoral care, inclusivity and discipline: Home-school-pupil triangle very robust. Every tutor opens channel of communication with parents within first two weeks of new term – usually a phone call. 'We get everyone facing the same way from the start,' says head. Support 'matrix' ensures that any issues are dealt with first by the tutor, then passed up vertically to head of house, and horizontally to senior leadership team. Staff have half-termly 'care meetings' to co-ordinate approach to individual pupils. Matron and chaplain are central and even school office staff and estates team have a role – 'all eyes and ears that are valuable to the pastoral system,' says head. Parents are appreciative of school's handling of sensitive situations and conditions. Local authority has in the past funded students to attend because they have deemed Ipswich the best environment.

Mental health first aid training for staff is ongoing. 'We have some high-functioning students who are very driven and the skills they need to learn can include not driving themselves too hard,' explains head. 'We focus on encouraging them to enjoy themselves and to take advantage of the co-curricular activities for a balanced life.' Regular reading weeks in the lower school – homework is suspended in favour of a good book.

No lower school houses – all in form groups. Inter-form competition for Cardinal Cup is hotly contested. Seniors from year 9 compete for the Ganzoni Trophy, with points awarded for effort and attainment, sports day, competitions etc. Tutor groups according to house have the same tutor for three years (9 to 11), then a re-shuffle for mixed year 12 and 13 tutor groups, subdivided into three per house, for a five-year journey under same houseparent.

Sanctions ladder, from yellow cards (a note home which explains to parents their child's undesirable behaviour and what has been said about it) to detention (lunchtime, after-school or, worst-case scenario, Saturday). 'We value every student and sometimes we might want to encourage one of them to turn down the volume on a particular behaviour, but turn up the volume on another,' as the head puts it. Exclusions for eg repeated offences, social media abuse, bullying, damage to property, violence. Drugs 'not a significant issue for this school,' says head, but accepts that it is among young people generally, so he recently wrote to parents with information about the local drugs scene and 'to re-emphasise that it is not possible to be a drug user and a member of Ipswich School'. Firm, clear stance.

Recent letter home on mobile phone policy was received warmly by parents. Approach focuses on good manners – lower school students should not use phones in school; years 9 to 11 may carry phones but not use them for more than a minute unless directed by a teacher, though they may plug into headphones to aid concentration (not when walking around) and must put the phone away if passing through a doorway into a new environment. Relaxed for sixth formers. 'It's helpful to take a photo of a notice or a team sheet, or contact home with arrangements for travel, but there's a responsibility to use a mobile phone politely,' expands head.

Pupils and parents: 'The pupils we have met have a good attitude and the parents are sociable and supportive,' said a parent. Ipswichians as a rule thoughtful and down-to-earth, thanks perhaps to the urban, real-world location and feet kept firmly on the ground at home. Less than five per cent international students – Hong Kong, China, some from Africa and Europe. Majority live within an hour's radius, either side of the Suffolk-Ipswich border, and arrive by all modes of transport – trains, public and school buses, parent taxi, bike, on foot. Many from Colchester, served by three school bus routes. Sixth formers find on-road parking nearby.

Parent perceptions survey an 'eye-opener' according to head, delighted by the diversity of parents' values and backgrounds – local businesspeople, farmers and professionals, but also many London commuters. Impressive turnouts for school events and matches. Parent forum selected as a cross-section to discuss school matters, with outcomes reported to parent body as a whole.

Money matters: Scholarships available at 11+ and 13+ – academic (Queen's) are worth up to 50 per cent of fees; music, art, sport, all-rounder, and Arkwright (for DT).

Means-tested bursaries available at 11, 13 and 16 'for pupils of high academic or all-round ability whose parents could not otherwise afford the school fees'. Head keen to coincide 500th anniversary of the Cardinal's College in 2028 with the launch of a new Wolsey Fund for transformational bursaries, working towards 'needs-blind' admission.

The last word: Predominantly an academic day school, but with boarding school style commitment to the development of personal skills that will help take these able students a lot further than exam results alone.

Kimbolton School

24

Kimbolton, Huntingdon, Cambridgeshire PE28 0EA

01480 860505 | registrar@kimbolton.cambs.sch.uk | www.kimbolton.cambs.sch.uk

Ages: 4–18

Pupils: 1,070; sixth form: 205; Boarders: 49 full, 1 flexi

Fees: Day £10,300 – £17,175; Boarding £26,850 – £28,560 pa

Head: Since 2002, Jonathan Belbin (50s). History at Bristol followed by PGCE. Sporty so decided could combine sport and history by teaching. Spent a lot of time as sports coach. Joined independent sector by chance and never looked back. Moved around country expanding his roles before first headship at Kimbolton. 'I liked that Kimbolton was co-ed and boarding and I could see lots of potential.' Very well established and popular with parents, 'a bit of a shining light,' said one parent. 'He's interested in the kids,' was another take. All spoke of his high profile around the school and at matches and productions. 'He's very professional, not gushing or effusive, slightly distant from parents, but in a good way. I don't want a friend, but a professional, which is just what he is,' said one perceptive parent. 'He has good people skills,' was said by another. Has handled tricky situations well according to parents, 'dignified and straightforward, measured in his responses and manages the school well, in good times and bad.'

Has overseen many building projects and refurbishments, bringing facilities up to date over the years, the most recent being the new science and maths block opened in 2015. Numbers have expanded by 150 under his tenure. Still teaching PHSE and history to certain years so knows all the children. Profile high around prep school as well. Smartly turned out, youthful looking, friendly and welcoming. We got the impression of a head very much on the ball and comfortable and confident in his role. His children have all been educated at Kimbolton.

Head of prep: Since 2015, Philip Foley (50s). Studied education, so could spend more time playing sports, before spending a year in industry, then drawn back into teaching, 'the best decision ever'. Kimbolton is his fourth headship. Establishing himself well and knows all the children. 'He is making positive changes, slowly without upsetting anyone.' Parents like what they have seen of him and say he is very accessible, and always outside at the end of the day. Softly spoken and mild mannered, teaches years 2 and 4 so getting to know children well. Daughter joined sixth form on his arrival.

Entrance: Pupils for reception assessed in small groups and teachers visit them at local nurseries to see that they are ready to learn. School happy to say no at this stage. Older children assessed and spend taster morning at school. No automatic transfer to senior school; all pupils take entrance exam. External candidates interviewed as well. Those from prep who won't make grade kindly weeded out in earlier years, but this is a rare occurrence.

Numbers double in senior school 1st year (year 7) with external pupils, 45 per cent, coming from up to 30 local primaries with a small intake in year 9. Senior school full, the odd place in prep. About 20 join the sixth form, virtually all from state schools, the odd one from independents. These pupils all interviewed by head and head of sixth form. Six GCSEs, grade B/6 or above needed including English and maths.

Exit: Up to a quarter leaves after GCSE, mostly to local, excellent sixth form colleges rather than rival independents. The odd one doesn't come up to scratch with GCSEs, but this is unusual. Most leave after A level for top drawer universities – Durham, Edinburgh, Exeter, Newcastle, UCL and Loughborough. Variety of subjects but a leaning towards the heavyweight – law, physics, philosophy, engineering, computers. Seven to Oxbridge in 2021. A sprinkling to study art or music and the occasional one to RAU or Harper Adams.

Latest results: In 2021, 72 per cent 9-7 at GCSE; 68 per cent A*/A at A level (87 per cent A*-B). In 2019 (the last year when exams took place), 56 per cent 9-7 at GCSE; 37 per cent A*/A at A level (61 per cent A*-B).

Teaching and learning: Spanish and French available at GCSE and A level, taught from reception. Not many take two languages at GCSE, nine or 10 a year. Half the year group take all three sciences. Pupils taught in mixed-ability groups apart from maths and languages. Maths is the most popular subject at A level; philosophy, religion and ethics now an A level option. All parents, throughout both schools, spoke of excellent academic progress and close contact with teachers. Academic problems picked up on quickly and help offered in both schools. Lots of subject workshops and drop-ins available and popular with pupils. Prep pupils taught by class teacher until year 5 when

Impressive new science block, please say hello to Colin the fish in one of the classrooms. Lovely new library in prep. Pupils working hard but more than happy to chat

subject taught and pressure ramped up, subtly, with more homework, getting them ready for senior school life. Maths set from year 3 onwards.

Excellent facilities throughout both schools, some – such as halls and sports – shared. Impressive new science block, please say hello to Colin the fish in one of the classrooms. Lovely new library in prep. Pupils working hard and more than happy to chat, pleased to show off their work. Very relaxed atmosphere between pupils and staff, but mutual respect apparent. Parents spoke of 'excellent teaching staff who know our children well and want them to succeed'. Most said, 'staff handled child well, knew them and brought the best out in them,' others spoke of their child 'flourishing'. One parent noted that 'the odd teacher appeared to be marking time and needed moving on,' but was sympathetic to the situation and said, 'these individuals are now a rarity here.' IT embraced, computing and programming taught to a high level and right up to date, so much so that our sixth form guides were slightly at a loss, we completely so. Excellent artwork on display in both schools. DT, textiles and cooking for all, in both schools. Sixth form offers 'life cooking skills' as an extracurricular course, although home economics is no longer available as an A level.

Parents impressed with boarding. 'The house is run really well and weekly and flexi boarders are treated as full boarders, welcome to go on trips and excursions'

Class sizes small, average of 17 in prep, 21 in senior with an average of seven in sixth form, so nowhere to hide, which is appreciated by parents. UCAS support exemplary; staff appear to be very much on the ball. Sixth form common room in basement equipped with comfy chairs. Very much their own space, with large study rooms also available, and well used.

Learning support and SEN: Some 40 pupils receive extra support throughout both schools, but only two are statemented. A handful of pupils bilingual, 18 on the EAL register. One-to-one available for learning and language support if necessary.

The arts and extracurricular: Music and drama popular and well represented. Lots of individual lessons, including over half of pupils in upper prep. Parents spoke of sensible way these lessons are timetabled, particularly in the senior school, so less academic do not miss essential teaching time. Dramatic productions spoken of highly in both schools. Lots of productions, choirs, orchestras, bands and after-school clubs. You name it, they have it.

CCF very popular with vast majority of pupils taking part from year 10 upwards. DofE also popular, up to gold. Lots of school trips, sporting and curricular.

Sport: As expected with two heads who are ex-sports teachers, games plays an important part at Kimbolton. 'We aim to get everyone out at least once a year representing the school,' said the prep head. Lots of silverware in the cabinets and lots of choice, bar rugby, which is not played. Football plays a major part, along with hockey for boys and girls. Prep girls are campaigning for football and cricket teams and head is open to the idea. Swimming on-site with own pool and lots of pitches within the grounds. Lake where canoe practice takes place. Lots of teams for all levels. Plenty of sports clubs and after-school practices; 85 per cent of prep pupils stay after school. Most parents very complimentary about sport and facilities. All other parents spoke about the children being 'taught well and lots of choice'.

Boarding: Boarding available from year 7. It's not a major part of the school, which is predominantly a day school with boarders making up about seven per cent of pupils. Boarders housed in two houses at each end of Kimbolton's High Street (it's not very long) and never the twain shall meet. Girls' house is full, boys' house has the odd space. Full and weekly boarding offered, flexi if space available. Some 45 per cent of boarders from overseas, others based just outside travelling distance, most within two hours. Quite a few children have parents in the Forces as the school is quite close to some RAF bases.

Parents impressed with boarding. 'The house is run really well and the weekly and flexi boarders are treated as full boarders, welcome to go on trips and excursions.' Parents spoke about children being kept well occupied, 'there is always a full term of events, booked in advance.' Parents of girls spoke about 'the mumsy chats' the staff have with their daughters. Curfews upheld and respected, older boarders given more independence. School happy for boarders to visit day pupils, with parental permission.

The two boarding houses are well equipped and modernised; tall boys will need to duck in certain rooms, with low ceilings and ancient buildings. Three in a room maximum, sixth form have own rooms. Communal common rooms for all age groups well used. We get the impression that because there are so few boarders they are a close knit, but welcoming, little unit. Lots of encouragement to participate in sports and extra-curricular life. Supervised prep for younger years, older ones do it in their rooms at set times. They cook their own breakfast at weekends.

Ethos and heritage: Located in the small pretty village of Kimbolton, The Castle, originally an ancient castle and now a magnificent Georgian mansion, dominates the village sitting at the end of the High Street. Very little teaching actually takes place in The Castle, but admin and head housed magnificently, with sixth form in the basement. The prep school, at the other end of the village, an old red-brick purpose-built Victorian school house, was once the senior school. Originally a boys' grammar, dating back over 400 years, the school bought The Castle from the Duke of Manchester in the 1950s for a reputed £11,500, and a further 200 guineas for the magnificent paintings when the governors were offered them at the last minute – they had a quick whip round to raise the money. Since then the school has thrived and succeeded, reflecting rather sadly on the opposite fortunes of the Manchester family. The Castle housed Catherine of Aragon when she was exiled from London. She died in what is now the head's office and historians still pay an annual visit to pay homage. This is not as macabre as it sounds, but do note the secret panelled door into the head's office.

Purple, black and white striped blazers are possibly an acquired taste – not the easiest colour combination for everyone to look good in

The prep school was opened in the 1950s, and became co-ed in the 70s. Both schools are accessible via a brisk walk through parkland. There's lots of space, 120 acres, to absorb pupils, who make the most of their magnificent surroundings.

Very much a family orientated school, and being relatively small, this atmosphere prevails with the school seeming to know parents well too. Pupils know each other, and the staff, well. Parents really appreciate this and, for many, was the reason they chose the school. 'My child isn't lost in large numbers,' was alluded to many times. A jolly, relaxed atmosphere prevails with a warm welcome for everyone. The distinctive purple, black and white striped blazers dominate, possibly an acquired taste, and not the easiest colour combination for everyone to look good in. Sixth formers wear black business suits. Purple dominates the school, it's their school colours and it's everywhere. Even the Christmas decorations are purple on the tree, matching the purple carpets et al. We're sure you get the picture. Food raved about in the prep school and, since recent changes, is equally delicious in the senior school.

Pastoral care, inclusivity and discipline: Every parent praised pastoral care. 'I don't know how they manage it,' said one parent who went on to praise the' kind, patient, supportive, caring teachers,' and believed this atmosphere is absorbed by the children, who behave in the same way. 'They pick up on problems quickly,' was said numerous times. Many parents spoke about the 'feel of the school' when they first visited, the friendliness of pupils and parents, and wanted that for their children. 'The children and parents are nice.' Friendship issues dealt with kindly and effectively. Counsellors available and well used.

Pastoral care and safeguarding so effective that the odd parent feels independence is being lost. But those with older children spoke about 'independence and more freedom in the sixth form'. Sixth formers a familiar sight in the High Street where they congregate at a popular coffee shop. Discipline at acceptable standards. 'They have high expectations which are usually met,' was said. Pupils in prep aware that if attitude unsuitable they will not be going up to The Castle. We are not aware of this happening in recent years so all appear to toe the line. Suspensions incredibly rare and low detention numbers. Pupils and parents happy that discipline is fair and appropriate. Lots of mentoring between pupils and effective school councils in both schools.

Pupils and parents: Most families rural dwellers from surrounding villages and small towns. Traditionally a farming and Forces school, this is now changing with many families moving from London whilst parents still work there. More families now coming from Cambridge's outskirts, so more medics and techy parents joining the fray. Most parents both working to pay fees and want a good value for money, all-round education for their children, 'involved parents,' said the prep head.

Parents welcome flexibility school offers with boarding and late pick-ups. Many children second, even third generation. Pupils happy and chatty and seem very relaxed, but ambitious and not fazed about leaving their rural idyll for urban sprawl; they are being well prepared.

Money matters: Scholarships available in senior school only, up to 20 per cent of fees, the vast majority academic, but the odd sports, leadership and arts available at 13+. The equivalent of six full means-tested awards at senior school per year group, usually given to 8-10 applicants, most subsidised by at least 80 per cent of fees.

The last word: This small school, housed in beautiful surroundings, appears to be a well kept secret, much to some parents' bemusement. 'Why is it not more well known?' said by many. We get the impression that there's no need; the school is virtually full, has an excellent reputation locally and is providing a good all-round education for local families wanting to use the private sector. Pupils can spend their whole education at Kimbolton enjoying the benefits of a happy environment, small class sizes and excellent pastoral care. Not flashy but classy. Those parents in the know appreciate that a Kimbolton education is money well spent. Shhhh.

King's College School, Cambridge

West Road, Cambridge CB3 9DN

01223 365814 | office@kcs.cambs.sch.uk | www.kcs.cambs.sch.uk

Ages: 4–13

Pupils: 420; Boarders: 17 full, 17 weekly/flexi

Fees: Day £13,452 – £17,085; Weekly Boarding £26,460; Choristers £8,730 pa

Head: Since 2018, Yvette Day, previously head of the Chorister School, Durham. She is also Master over the Choristers, in charge of the education and care of the boys who have sung in King's College Choir since the College's foundation by King Henry VI. A musician herself, she holds an MMus degree in historical musicology from the University of London (more recently she also completed a law conversion course with the College of Law) – 'there is something of the delight of the most magical sweet shop in being able to listen to King's singing every day!' she says. Brought up in apartheid South Africa at a time when independent schools opened their doors to a multiracial community and sourced the bursaries needed to pay the fees, 'a phenomenal change to culture' she says, Mrs Day is enthused by the 'vibrant' choir school model as a type of education that has benefits for the whole community. 'We can chuck gazoodles of money at schools and children don't always have a great education; as independent schools we should be championing a creativity about how all children learn.' Described by parents as 'proactive and effective', 'approachable and compassionate' and 'interested in our children's lives in and out of school', she has made an early impression.

Entrance: Registration is recommended by May/June the year before starting reception. Registered pupils are assessed in small groups, and parents meet with the head, following which an offer may be made. Priority for siblings, past pupils and fellows of King's. More formal assessment for pupils joining higher years; King's welcomes children at the age of 7, 8 and 11, with pupils joining at other times when places arise. Pupils from Cambridge and a wide commutable area encompassing Suffolk and Hertfordshire; boarders even further afield. Many parents ex-Oxbridge, academics, medics, City, a good cross-section united by their ambitions for their children.

Exit: A few leave at 11 for the state sector or due to family relocation (Cambridge brains are called for around the world). At 13 to local senior and boarding schools around the country such as Eton, Harrow, Winchester, Westminster, King's Ely, Oundle, Uppingham, Oakham and Rugby. Locally, the Cambridge day schools – Perse Upper the huge favourite, also The Leys, Stephen Perse, St Mary's. More than half with scholarships – 32 out of 45 pupils in 2021.

Our view: Founded in the 15th century to educate the choristers, now set in spacious grounds just a brisk walk from King's College. Although famous the world over for the pure voices of the young choristers who make the exquisite traditional Christmas Eve 'Carols from King's', you don't have to sing like a lark to be a pupil here. Described by the head as a 'musical school' rather than a 'music school', a small but significant number of pupils are choristers (24 of the 400). 'When the choristers are in school, they are just regular pupils,' says the head. However, this being Cambridge, it's hard to find a pupil who is truly 'just regular'. King's pupils – all under 13 – currently number a published author and a pianist who recently won a recital competition in Russia. 'We teach our pupils that being a child is no barrier to achievement.' says head.

King's pupils are undoubtedly a very bright bunch, a fact recognised in the school's refreshingly unpatronising ethos. These girls and boys are levelled with about the demands of the real world – particularly the requirement for commitment and to step up to the challenge of tests and exams by learning to 'be excited and nervous but not unduly stressed' says head. 'This is a very natural school so there's no need for any pretence about anything.' Teaching is differentiated from reception and there is certainly no shying away from setting, with children in groups for spelling from year 2; maths and spelling from year 3; grammar, spelling and maths from year 4; and sets for all subjects in year 8 including a scholarship set. This pays off – the huge number of academic and music scholarships achieved by leavers certainly guarantees an income for

Ipswich High School

the engraver who updates the school's polished wooden achievement boards every year.

Far from a hot-house though – these small sparks are keen to learn and to develop their (considerable) talents. King's pupils from reception to year 4 have their own building (a former rectory, the only part of the school that is not purpose-built), with two parallel classes in reception, years 1 and 2 (all with a full-time teaching assistant) and an extra class added from year 3. Class sizes average 16; room sizes up to year 4 (rather charmingly) vary. We happened to visit on 'King's-on-Sea Day' and found the littlest dressed in beachwear role-playing paddling and sandcastle-making in their playground, cleverly transformed into a beach.

Specialist lessons for all, with French the main language and taught from reception up, Latin from year 4, and Ancient Greek from year 7. Older children have a form tutor, who they meet with each day but all other lessons are in specialist classrooms. Modern science labs and superbly well-equipped IT room with computers for computer science, including coding, as well as independent study. Cupboards on every landing in every building packed with tablets and laptops, charged and ready to go. Dedicated and well-staffed learning support centre, one of the first in the country, described by parents as 'an amazing resource which increases children's confidence and skills.'

Music is key here of course, and not just for the choristers. Most learn an instrument – many learn several. Organ popular (pupils may play in King's College Chapel) as well as bassoon, double bass and harp. Ensembles of all kinds and regular performances. Year 4s were engaged in bright brush-stroked Gustav Klimt-inspired work in the buzzy art room when we visited, while year 7s were designing their own MDF flat-pack furniture in the DT workshop – rare to see such a philosophical attitude towards dismantling a gone-wrong project and starting all over again ('it was meant to be a shelf'). Real-world skills of planning, collaboration, project management all in action.

A source of pride is the £6-million Sports and Cultural Centre opened in 2018 after a 15-year gestation, mainly funded by school's own coffers and fundraising; rest to pay for itself through outside hire. Dance studio and changing rooms at ground level with a first-floor sports hall above (lifts as well as stairs), including electronic scoreboard and basketball hoops that drop from the ceiling, as well as retractable seating and acoustic panels for transformation into a concert hall and theatre (well used here). Clever external access means it can be used by King's pupils during the school day and by university students, external clubs and societies on evenings and weekends. Outside there's an Astro with four pitches (also used for playtime). Main sports are football, rugby, cricket (boys and girls), netball and hockey. Fixtures from year 3 for all abilities. PE lessons too. Two netball courts and squash courts shared with King's College (not at the same time). Outdoor pool.

King's choristers join as probationers (essentially choristers in training) in year 4. An honour and a huge commitment by families as well as the boys, once they become full choristers in year 6 they take part in six services each week at the chapel during university term time and choir practice for an hour and half every day before school in a purpose-built acoustic room. They travel the world touring and, of course, there is that spine-tingling carol service every Christmas Eve and the service on Christmas Day (a long line of LP covers makes a unique school corridor display). Choristers seem to thrive on it – every care is taken to make sure they don't suffer academically or personally or miss out on too many school sport matches. 'Choristers are just like everyone else but when they're on TV their friends are immensely proud of them,' says one pupil matter-of-factly. Some concession made by teachers for eye-rubbing in class after late-night concerts.

Famous the world over for the young choristers who make the exquisite Christmas Eve 'Carols from King's', but you don't have to sing like a lark to be a pupil here

Day pupils battle the Cambridge traffic (handy 'kiss-and-drop' inside the school gate) or take the locally favoured option of two wheels or shoe leather to arrive for form period from 8.30am. A well-used minibus service runs from some outer villages and a local Park and Ride. All but one of the school's buildings are easily accessible to the pupils on roll with mobility issues.

Uniform adapts as pupils progress through the school – blazers replace the rather workaday purple sweatshirts. Second-hand uniform shop appreciated, run by PTA (committee includes three members of staff, vociferous parents), whose prime function is fundraising.

Pastoral care is vital, particularly in a school of this kind and a supportive, family atmosphere pervades. Parents appreciate that the staff know their children well and present them with every opportunity to capitalise on their talents and thrive. 'The staff are very collegiate in their approach and they really understand the children,' says one. Pupils have a great fondness and respect for their teachers and are confident and eager to share their thoughts and ideas. Older children 'buddy' the youngest like big brothers and sisters. Bullying nipped in the bud. For pupils with concerns, school listener on the staff is 'an extra set of ears' in addition to parents, form tutors and boarding staff, and well embedded into the school. Spends Mondays sitting on a sofa in a quiet corner to hear any 'little worries that don't go away' during break or lunchtime. On Tuesdays she can be found helping out in the pre-prep and prep departments, and one evening a week she and her two sausage dogs (one of which is also the talented author of regular articles for the school newsletter) spend an evening with the boarders. 'The message is that there are a lot of people who care about each child and want to support him or her,' she says. King's is an Anglican foundation but all religions are taught and festivals celebrated; philosophy and ethics basis. Huge day surgery with qualified nurses on hand. Dining hall is the most important room in the school, say pupils, who love its multi-coloured chairs and tasty lunches (breakfast and dinner too for the boarders, who are treated to a roast on Sundays).

The round of concerts, music and academic exams, sports fixtures and homework commitments makes life at King's 'hectic' say parents, who speak of tensions between areas of school vying for children's time and attention and the impossibility of engaging with any non-school pastime on weekdays. However all are quick to point out that they are pleased with their choice of school and that their children are happy. 'Our son thoroughly enjoyed his time at King's,' says the parent of a recent leaver, 'and he has moved on with a good bunch of friends, a love of learning and a music exhibition to Eton.'

Boarding: Choristers are compulsory boarders from the age of 8 and their school home-from-home is a bright but traditional boarding house with large dorms of four to eight single beds, rearranged from time to time for balance. Only choristers full-board; day and non-chorister boarding places are available Sunday to Friday or on a flexi basis – beds are assigned to the boarder and are empty when that boarder is not in it. Family atmosphere, with parents included, as they often pop in mid-week and, if local, walk the choristers back from chapel. A few exeats a term, although sometimes shortened for choristers who have to work around chapel services.

Money matters: Means-tested bursaries of up to 100 per cent; all choristers offered scholarships of two-thirds of fees or more, plus free piano lessons, open to any boy in the world if he passes the audition – many try.

The last word: An iconic school, surprisingly pressure-free, where talented young individuals grow their wings.

King's Ely

Old Palace, Ely, Cambridgeshire CB7 4EW

01353 660707 | admissions@kingsely.org | www.kingsely.org

Ages: 2–18

Pupils: 1,006; sixth form: 194; Boarders: 175 full/flexi

Fees: Day £11,109 – £32,892; Boarding £25,017 – £43,476 pa

Principal: Since August 2019, John Attwater. PPE at Oxford with intentions of joining the foreign office. On leaving university still not sure which direction to take so did a PGCE whilst teaching at Wells Cathedral School. Arrived at Ely from King Edward's Witley where he was head. Very musical with great experience of chorister schools as a pupil and teacher; he was one at Chichester. Still very musical ('I love singing') and plans to join school chapel choir 'when we are allowed to sing again and if they will have me.'

Baptism of fire joining King's as only one 'normal' term before dreaded lockdowns reared their ugly heads. 'I can't – or couldn't – wander round the school as I could have ended up being a super spreader.' Hence parents (and some pupils) don't know him well yet but he's acting as a cover teacher and supervises the EPQ in the sixth form so his presence is felt. 'Communication has been good and consistent and we have been kept informed all the way through,' said a parent. 'I've been very impressed by him and he's led the school through a very difficult time,' remarked another. 'He's a thoughtful man,' was one parent's take – 'he's quite quiet and softly spoken so some parents feel he could be more dynamic. I don't agree. He's a completely different character to the previous incumbent and is softly, quietly getting on with stuff which is great. I like that.' Has plans to raise the profile of the school – 'King's is a bit of a sleeping giant sometimes perceived to be in a rural backwater, which is partly true but we are a short train journey from Cambridge so attract a diverse, cosmopolitan set of families who buy into our ethos and this is becoming more apparent every year and enhances the school.'

Parents like that he has children at the school, as do the heads of the senior and junior schools – 'They are one of us, as well as being heads.' Principal happy to have followed his chosen career path – 'I would have made a terrible spy.'

Head of senior school: Since 2018, Jonathan Shaw. Arrived from Guernsey. Down to earth and welcoming, and appears to have a good rapport with pupils. 'I like him; he had huge shoes to fill and wisely stood back and watched then gradually took control.' He also teaches history, which parents like. 'He's a great public speaker, seems really switched on and professional and is modernising the school which is excellent.' 'He's quite dry, is fun when he needs to be but keeps everyone in order.'

Head of junior school: Richard Whymark (apt name for a teacher). Has a high profile around the school and seems to be loved by all – 'I think he's fantastic and is the perfect junior head. He knows the children well and seems to be able to get the best out of them by making everything fun but setting firm boundaries at the same time,' said a parent.

Entrance: Children can start aged 2 in the nursery and continue their schooling until 18, and more than a handful do. Most continue through Acremont with the odd one 'kindly' removed before. Very unusual for pupil not to continue to junior, or indeed from junior to senior, but if felt necessary parents are well aware of what is coming. Not an academic hothouse but potential spotted and all pupils expected to be able to cope and to be aiming for university education; informal testing takes place. 'We like to be as broad a church academically as we can be,' says head. Large intakes at ages 7, 11,13 and 16 – works well as this is when major moves happen within the school anyway. Automatic entry into senior school from junior; scholarship exams sat and entrance exams for external children. Large contingent arrive in sixth form – grades 6 in the A level subjects studied are needed, either from local state provision, single sex independents and quite a large overseas cohort.

One of the main sports is rowing. Pupils can participate from year 8 and many do. It's not all about winning, but they are very good

Exit: Around a third leaves after GCSE (and very few indeed before that), mainly lured to Cambridge sixth forms which are a short train ride away and free, with others seeking a change of scenery having been at the same school since they were 2. Principal wants to slow post 16 leakage and new location in the Old Palace is helping – not many can resist being taught in the bishop's old home. Virtually all go to university. The theatre, arts, fashion and music well represented with places at St Martin's and many other arts' schools in recent years. Many to Russell Groups. Exeter, Edinburgh, Nottingham, Durham, Warwick, Manchester and the London universities all popular. One medic in 2021, and five to Oxbridge. Two overseas in 2021 – business management at Hong Kong and hotel and restaurant management at Cesar Ritz College, Switzerland. Gap years not that common, possibly a sign of the times; apprenticeships barely mentioned.

Latest results: In 2021, 65 per cent 9-7 at GCSE; 69 per cent A*/A at A level (89 A*-B). In 2019 (the last year when exams took place), 56 per cent 9-7 at GCSE; 34 per cent A*/A at A level (58 per cent A*-B).

Teaching and learning: Every parent we spoke to impressed with teaching skills, commitment and diligence of staff. 'They really do seem to care.' Staff seem to know children well and are able to bring out enthusiasm, aptitude, participation and diligence.

Acremont is based across town in a beautiful Georgian mansion within large gardens. Children learn through play initially and the likeable head drums 'independence and development' in from day one. Children expected to stand on their own two feet early including organising themselves and putting their own shoes and coats on. This grounding and early learning stands them in good stead for progression to the junior school.

Pupils set from year 4 in maths and English with science and languages – French, German and Latin – following in the next few years. Academic rigour built throughout time in juniors so by the time pupils head to the senior school they are more than ready for academic pressures ahead. 'We are kept informed throughout our child's school life and we know if a bad report is coming; the school say they have failed if we are not prepared and it rarely comes to that,' said one parent. 'What I like is that effort is recognised, it's not just the academic superstars who get all the credit.' International students from year 6 on the ESOL team, very much integrated into the school when English is good enough.

All pupils closely monitored, high fliers encouraged but those less able brought along at own pace too; and those coasting are quickly spotted and brought back on point. All parents happy with progress, communication and outcomes. 'They know the children, help them realise their potential and seem to be able to do it kindly with very little apparent pressure.' Don't be fooled though – expectations are high. Two or three sciences taken at GCSE, split about half and half. Two languages offered, plus Latin at GCSE. School quickly adapted to lockdown remote teaching and ran a full timetable during the second one. All parents, whatever their views on home schooling (and they vary hugely), commended the school on its outcome and felt that their children had been able to keep up with their education. 'Remote teaching is difficult but they did the best they could, and it was successful.' Real life teaching that we saw showed engaged enthusiastic pupils. Lessons seemed to be pretty relaxed with lots of rapport between teachers and pupils, mutual respect too.

Every sort of band and ensemble you can think of. Mention must go to the award winning King's Barbers, an a capella group made up of ex-choristers

Sixth form housed in the Old Palace. The Long Gallery is the common room, plenty of quiet areas for private study. Helpful staff easily accessible and all parents spoke of 'great UCAS advice, support and help.'

Learning support and SEN: All pupils screened for dyslexia in years 2, 3, 6, 7, 8 and 9 so very few slip through the net. Around 20 per cent of students monitored or supported for potential SEN. Mild to moderate dyslexia, dyspraxia and ASD all included. Unusual for individual lessons but available if needed. Lots of specialist support in small groups. 'We are often unaware of the extra help that is being given to our child during the term as it's so subtle; but it's really effective.' Support for learning and studying skills available too and SEN department well used. Subject clubs available for those 'invited' and invitation expected to be taken up – 'it makes it a lot more subtle, the extra help on offer,' said one parent. Pupils happy to go to clubs to help plug the gaps at their own pace.

When we visited, 74 students were using the ESOL department including 40 on specific programmes such as one year GCSE courses for international students. The aim is for them to become part of the main school curriculum once their English is strong enough.

The arts and extracurricular: Music, as you might expect, is particularly strong here and is the heart of the school. It is a cathedral school with traditional choristers, who we were privileged to hear practising. There's also a girls' choir age 11-16 which runs parallel with the boys', singing daily in the cathedral and performing all over the world. And there is the sixth form choir as well. Every sort of band and ensemble you can think of, and more – includes chamber music. Mention must go to the award winning King's Barbers, an acapella group made up of ex-choristers. Nearly 300 pupils learn an instrument, including drums – good job there are plenty of rehearsal rooms – we enjoyed hearing a trumpet lesson on our tour. Rehearsals and lessons continued over Zoom during lockdowns so no one lost out.

King's is renowned for its arts education and many parents are attracted by this. A tour of the art department was testament to this, with skilled artwork on display – fine art, sculpture work, photography etc and then there's DT and textiles and don't forget cookery. Most pupils participate in some way. Drama productions also spoken of with awe. The non sporty child is allowed to shine somewhere, it doesn't have to be on the playing field. Clubs and societies galore, not just musical – you think of it, it's more than likely that they do it.

Sport: Not traditionally renowned for sports but gaining traction and other schools are sitting up and noticing. First XV rugby unbeaten last season. New principal investing heavily in better facilities including new Astro turf and covered tennis courts. We liked that the games' mistress had her dog with her supervising some practice sessions. Open air (heated) swimming pool well used from April to October and climbing walls found dotted around the place. Lots of space and pitches and less obvious sports also encouraged. Every child will find something active that they can enjoy.

One of the main sports at King's is rowing. From year 8 pupils can participate and many do. It's not all about winning, but they are very good at that. The enthusiastic but less apt equally encouraged to get out on the river. There's a strong rowing community and the school has their own boat house at the forefront of the river community on the Great Ouse. The King's tyros can observe the Cambridge elite teams who have a rather more shiny boathouse just up the river. This year the boat race was held on their patch and it's encouraged even more participation. 'I like that my daughter can get out on the river and enjoy being at one with nature, alongside the swans and ducks and just taking it all in, enjoying the peace – and she gets to compete to a high standard as well.'

The Ely Scheme is well supported. This is a leadership scheme led by older pupils for the year 9s involving lots of outdoor activities, team building, creative thinking and challenges. Develops into DofE, also popular.

Boarding: Starts aged 7. Junior boarders housed in two medieval houses within the cathedral grounds along with girl choristers in a separate house. A popular matron looks after the boy choristers and caters for their every need. They are made to feel special 'because they are' but parents speak of them also 'being grounded.' Flexi boarding now allowed, with local choristers able to nip home overnight when evensong duties allow. Flexi boarding popular with all other boarders. Pupils move to senior houses for years 9-11 and then to separate sixth form houses.

Boarding houses clean and tidy with older pupils encouraged to be independent. The station is down the road and it's easy to hop on a train to Cambridge or London. Most rooms are shared even in sixth form. Good facilities for cooking, lovely outside space and plenty of sofa space. Boarding increases further up the school with a larger international cohort joining. School proud to be host to 42 nationalities (including Welsh).

Ethos and heritage: This is a cathedral school and one of the oldest in the world founded in 970AD. Its relationship with the cathedral is symbiotic. Ely, in the heart of the Cambridgeshire Fens, is a very pretty rural market town completely dominated by the Ship of the Fens which can be seen for miles across the flat landscape. But despite this remoteness there is a regular train service to and from Cambridge, London and Norfolk so the traditional rural community is interspersed with more cosmopolitan outsiders, and this is reflected in the school too. Because of the domination of the cathedral in the town, the school has the same effect – a benign one with townspeople enjoying and accepting the pupils, staff and parents around the town. Initially it feels as though the school sits entirely in the shadow of the cathedral, but it doesn't. It is spread, sprawled really, over 75 acres within the centre of the town and it is beautiful architecturally ranging from the ancient incorporating the Georgian era with modern additions fitting in well. This includes the junior school which is a stand alone building. There are large outside spaces, beautiful gardens and one of the oldest London plane trees in the country can be found in the Old Palace gardens. Look closely and you will notice that it's aided by a few supports ('It's not falling down on my watch,' says principal). Pupils eat in the monastic barn. The tiny school chapel managed to survive the beady eye of Oliver Cromwell, who was born in the town.

Boarding houses clean and tidy with older pupils encouraged to be independent. The station is down the road and it's easy to hop on a train to Cambridge or London

The ecclesiastical background of the church is felt throughout the school. It's a friendly, caring place with all pupils, whatever their background, buying into the ethos. Parents appreciate this – 'it's a caring, friendly school,' we heard. The tranquil atmosphere and time spent in the cathedral and the school's chapel, is reflected by the pupils. But it's not all clerical gowns and organs – it's a dynamic place.

Pastoral care, inclusivity and discipline: 'This is not a school of angels' said one parent. 'But they seem to be on top of discipline with miscreants dealt with quickly and fairly.' Discipline initially dealt with at house level and is usually sorted there. A wellbeing department (new bigger one on the way) well used with both male and female counsellors available, used by staff as well as pupils; it's viewed as quite normal to avail of their services. The school seems to be a very accepting, tolerant place with individuals allowed to flourish and be accepted for whoever they are. All parents agree, 'it's a kind school' was said by them all. Many parents chose the school because of its pastoral reputation. 'What we like is that King's invests in the whole child, not just the academic side which makes for a much more rounded child.' Barber shop acapella group set up to help ease choristers back into more normal life and also to help them cope with maturing voices. Tutor groups in the senior school are single sex with hopefully the same tutor all the way through so they get to know the pupils well. One parent thought this slightly odd as the school is co-ed but agrees it works well. It means that girls and boy groups can be spoken to separately when relevant. Girls on Board approach used to help girls navigate toxic relationships, a similar one for boys to be introduced soon. 'The loud confident types can dominate in the common room,' said one parent referring to the sixth form 'but the school are aware of this and listen to the silent majority too.' Another more outspoken parent said 'the witches covens are dealt with' which quite amused us but good to hear.

'It's a stupid head that says there is no bullying in their school,' the head told us, and he is well aware of the latest 'toxic masculinity' furore – 'Measures are in place to do the best we can.'

Pupils and parents: Traditionally a school for East Anglian farming families, professionals from the town and choristers. This is still true today with many second generations, or more, in attendance. But improved travel links, particularly rail, means that at least half the pupils are now from out of area. A large contingent come daily from Cambridge with many children of medics and the IT and bio industries in attendance. These parents are buying into the ethos of the school and the more rounded education in preference to the academic hot houses in the city. More parents are commuting to London daily and good rail networks from King's Lynn and further afield mean a large cohort come from Norfolk. 'There's a wonderful mix of cultures and religions which is great for the kids,' said a parent – seems to work, with all gelling well.

Money matters: Means-tested bursaries on offer of up to 110 per cent of fees. All choristers receive scholarships including boarding fees. Academic, music, sport, art, STEM, drama and choral scholarships available.

The last word: Pupils are privileged to be educated in such beautiful surroundings, although of course they won't realise this until long after they have left. The tranquil atmosphere seems to be absorbed by osmosis and turns out well rounded, likeable individuals who attain academically but who also realise there is more to life than just results. Parents like and appreciate this and are sailing towards the school in the shadow of the Ship of the Fens and the safe harbour she offers.

The Leys School

Trumpington Road, Cambridge CB2 7AD

01223 508904 | admissions@theleys.net | www.theleys.net

Ages: 11-18

Pupils: 572; sixth form: 204; Boarders: 355 full

Fees: Day £17,025 – £23,835; Boarding £25,965 – £35,610 pa

Headmaster: Since 2014, Martin Priestley MA (Oxon) PPE. He had planned a career in diplomacy but changed course after a Damascene moment sitting at his desk in Westminster – 'I knew I would rather be teaching.' Having written 50 speculative letters to schools and received positive replies, the course of his working life changed. A personal awareness of the possible twists and turns ahead for his pupils has reinforced his commitment to the importance of offering a broad educational experience and the chance to develop serious cultural interests and sporting prowess. As a boarding school in Cambridge, 'our pupils benefit from the outstanding scholarship of the city, planned lectures and events, yes, but also from the atmosphere of learning and discovery with which they are surrounded,' he says.

After a spell teaching at Uppingham and as head of Warminster he came to The Leys and was struck by the level of ambition among his pupils – 'I think our job is to be their Sherpas, to help guide them to reach their own summits. Pressure does not come from above, nor does it need to'. He meets pupils informally, a few at a time, most days at lunch, attends matches and play rehearsals and really gets to know their families and lives. Parents are impressed that 'he has a touch on everything that goes on which really helps when it comes to making difficult pastoral judgements.' Known for believing that 'everyone deserves a second, though not necessarily a third, chance,' he is also praised for 'not shying away from taking tough decisions' and being a good disciplinarian. Has a kindly, understanding manner and pupils know they will be listened to. His communication skills, 'are excellent, the school really keeps us in the loop. Children don't always pass stuff on.' Very true. He lives on the site, totally immersed during term time but, 'enjoying all that Cambridge offers, with the pupils.'

Entrance: All pupils are interviewed and tested prior to entry. Roughly 30 are admitted to year 7, mostly from local primaries, and another 70 in year 9. St Faith's is part of the foundation and a key feeder school but pupils come from all the other Cambridge preps; boarders often from further afield. The entrance tests are competitive. The school sets its own maths and English papers and uses standardised verbal and spatial reasoning tests. Oversubscribed so they can take their pick.

Sixth form entry: five 6s for pupils already at the Leys. Officially, the same for pupils admitted from elsewhere but the reality is that the bare minimum will not secure a place. The school is popular and oversubscribed and can be choosey. References and reports from previous schools also required.

Exit: Up to a quarter leaves after GCSE, mostly to local, excellent sixth form colleges rather than rival independents. The odd one doesn't come up to scratch with GCSEs, but this is unusual. Most leave after A level for top drawer universities – Durham, Edinburgh, Exeter, Newcastle, UCL and Loughborough. Variety of subjects but a leaning towards the heavyweight – law, physics, philosophy, engineering, computers. Seven to Oxbridge in 2021. A sprinkling to study art or music and the occasional one to RAU or Harper Adams.

Latest results: In 2021, 61 per cent 9-7 at GCSE; 72 per cent A*/A at A level (90 per cent A*-B). In 2019 (the last year when exams took place), 83 per cent 9-7 at GCSE: 53 per cent A*/A at A level.

Teaching and learning: The excellent results, showing year on year improvement, are gained through the pupils' own motivation and 'the quality of the teaching,' say parents who are full of praise for the unpressured atmosphere of the school. No one is mealy mouthed about the importance of exam results – 'We all want our children to succeed, it's just a question of how they do it.' The headmaster also acknowledges that 'the Cambridge intake does represent a parent body that really values education,' and the pupils themselves say, 'working hard is normal here'. Parents mention that choosing The Leys partly owes to this balanced approach and as the head remarks, 'I never wanted to run a foie gras force feeding school'.

Several languages on offer – French from year 7, with Spanish, German, Greek and Chinese in subsequent years. Latin for all up to year 9 when classical civilisation can be opted for instead. All languages taught to GCSE and A level. Setting for maths right through the school and in sciences from year 10. Class sizes up to GCSE are slightly under 20, at A level often under 10. Broad spectrum of A levels taught – the emphasis, unsurprisingly, on the heavyweight subjects.

Headmaster acknowledges that 'the Cambridge intake does represent a parent body that really values education.' Pupils say, 'working hard is normal here'

An atmosphere of learning is very apparent. In class the pupils are attentive and interested, the teachers engaging and it is clear the relationships are good whether in a science class (sewage processing in the class we dropped in on, proved to be fascinating) or in the more informal DT (where we saw pupils designing F1 formula racing cars). The main subject areas have their own buildings and movement between lessons is calm but provides a chance for cheerful conversation and a breath of air. All pupils have their own tablets provided by the school and IT facilities in all departments are excellent. However, three cheers for the head for promoting the use of fountain pens – 'They are shown to improve the quality of writing. A good style is still an asset'. Outstanding library with timetabled lessons up to year 9 and free access throughout the day for borrowing and reading for the rest of the school – 'We encourage the habit and in many cases, it sticks'. Saturday school for all years, though years 7 and 8 finish at lunchtime and higher forms have matches and other activities in the afternoons. 'They do work a very full week – just right for teenagers,' said a parent and pupils appear to thrive on their packed schedule. Being in Cambridge means unparalleled opportunities to visit exhibitions and to hear eminent speakers, some of whom may visit the school but pupils can easily attend elsewhere in town and the freedom to do so enhances the experience of pupils in the sixth form.

Not too many schools we visit boast a vision studio but this school opened one in 2021 – a teaching space dedicated entirely to the use of VR and AR.

Learning support and SEN: The learning support department provides pupils with help where needed and about 50 pupils at a time are receiving assistance with various aspects of learning. The department works closely with subject teachers to ensure the same approach and emphasis is being followed across the curriculum and pupils attend both in small groups and individually for extra help. The aim is always to spot any difficulties early on and monitor progress carefully. Pupils may attend learning support in place of Latin in years 7-9. There are drop- in clinics that pupils can attend whenever they feel the need. Sixth formers are helped with independent learning and preparation for university.

Fifteen per cent of pupils come from overseas (35 different countries) and varying numbers require EAL support. Three English lessons a week are offered with extra (privately funded) lessons available, should they be necessary. Care is taken to ensure that language skills do not hold pupils back academically.

The arts and extracurricular: The performing arts building is made full use of, with a theatre of professional standard complete with its backstage world and studios, rehearsal space, class and dressing rooms. Drama is extremely popular, timetabled for all in year 9 and offered at GCSE and A level. In addition, all manner of chances to act, dance, sing or spin on a trapeze in a string of performances throughout the year, both the serious (Arthur Miller's 'The Crucible') and the not so serious ('Sound of Music). Debates, quizzes and charity events are also staged and as we were told by pupils, 'there is always something else we want to squeeze in'. The benefit of boarding is that rehearsals and practice can take place in the evenings and weekends.

This is a sporty school, with outstanding facilities. 'The opportunities are amazing, I couldn't believe all there was to do when I came,' said a sixth former

Music has high status with excellent facilities including a music school, complete with acoustically engineered recital hall (opened by Julian Lloyd Webber) and endless opportunities to play and perform. There are workshops and masterclasses to inspire and the chance to learn practically any instrument to a high standard. Choirs, orchestras, bands and ensemble groups galore. All pupils have a timetabled music lesson in years 7 and 8 and it is an option at GCSE and A level. Many talented pupils including former choristers of local college choirs. The hymn tune, 'Coe Fen', named after the meadow that borders the grounds, was written by a former director of music.

Outstanding examples of art, pottery and displays of pupils' work in DT adorn the walls and other spaces throughout the school. The prevalence of glass in the newer buildings means the opportunity is there to see fascinating lessons underway, notably art and DT – 'It makes you want to try things yourself,' a pupil commented.

Compulsory DofE for years 9 and 10 with CCF a choice from year 10 on Wednesday afternoons. Lots of subject field trips and opportunities to travel further afield, often as part of a sports team or charitable endeavour.

Sport: This is a sporty school, with outstanding facilities. 'The opportunities are amazing, I couldn't believe all there was to do when I came,' said a sixth former. As a small boarding school there is plenty of chance for match play, a plethora of teams at all stages in all the team sports. Cricket is as much for girls as boys, and rugby is increasingly popular for girls too – 'We started with 30 and now there are loads of us,' say the girls who helped get it going. If team sports are not your thing, then there are all manner of alternatives offered in the higher forms – sailing, gymnastics, dance (hip hop and street, as well as ballet) and circus skills among them.

Boarding: Pupils are divided between 11 houses, with years 7 and 8 kept together in Moulton House, moving up to a boarding house (single sex) or a day boarders' house. The houses for day pupils are the same as boarding houses, minus the beds. All houses have a house master or mistress (known as HMs) and are supported by matrons who provide a lot of the necessary day to day care, helping to create the homelike atmosphere. The school offers two types of boarding, full or home. There is no 'flexi' option. Full boarding speaks for itself and home boarders arrive for registration in house at 8.15am and remain at school into the evening for activities, supper and prep, leaving at 9pm, sometimes later. These pupils have a desk and allotted space in one of the boarding houses and follow exactly the same regime as full boarders, save for the sleeping part. It is a popular option with parents and pupils alike – 'It suits us. We wanted them in the centre of a vibrant city but with the much broader offer of a boarding school,' said one parent. It is possible for home boarders to move to full boarding and plenty do, especially in the sixth form – 'Mine will probably board full time in the sixth form. They ask about it every day!' Of the 70 per cent accommodated in boarding houses, 50 per cent are full boarders and 20 percent home boarders. The remaining 30 per cent are day pupils, so the feel of the school is very much that of a boarding school.

Houses are of varying age and have their own distinctive qualities, but all provide a similar standard of comfort and privacy. Younger pupils sleep in mostly two or three bedded rooms, all with their own zone of bed/desk/bookcase; sixth formers have their own rooms. High standards maintained in bathrooms, showers and loos and matrons keep a close eye on morning and evening routines. Meals are eaten in the school dining room but houses have a series of smaller kitchens, usually one on each floor, for the inevitable toast making and drinks.

House staff work to create a family atmosphere. In one house, we saw a collage of house residents faces together with their birthdays – 'we always celebrate with a cake and some fun. It is especially important for any pupils from overseas'. Boarders, for a treat, can occasionally cook a full blown meal in the house kitchen. Relaxed sitting and common rooms, with screens, but staff keep a weather eye on activities – 'No screens or phones at bedtime for younger pupils, and we keep other periods free of them too'. Good to know that board and card games are still encouraged. Prep is supervised up to year 11. Older pupils act as guides and friends to the younger ones and it is obvious that ages mix very comfortably – 'My daughter gained so much from being in a house of all ages,' said one parent. Another mentioned that 'the matrons really do behave like mothers, keeping an eye out for anyone a bit under the weather or just tired and needing a chat and some attention.' There are plenty of arranged activities at the weekend and sixth formers are free to go into Cambridge, so long as they respect the 10.30pm curfew. There is a sixth form club with its own bar that opens occasionally.

Ethos and heritage: As a Methodist foundation, the school has a particularly strong sense of community and the school chapel remains central to its life. Not overly religious (there are no religious credentials required for entry) but there are weekly services for the whole school, whatever their denomination. Parents speak approvingly of 'the sense of community that is fostered' and the way 'conformity is not a goal, they are encouraged to question things,' which is very much a quality of the Methodist movement. It has been praised for its tradition of encouraging independent thought and the head agrees that 'we educate and encourage pupils to think their own thoughts' and adds that 'pupils on return visits to the school always want to visit the chapel. It remains at the heart of the school.'

Having begun in 1875, the Leys is the only co-educational boarding and day school in Cambridge. On a 50 acre site, with views over Coe Fen, the school has a surprisingly rural feel, given how close it is to the centre of Cambridge. Many of the early buildings are of the red brick, gothic style, and the chapel itself is a good example of the Arts and Crafts movement. It is a spacious site. The old and newer buildings, some of outstanding design, are an interesting mix and are positioned to keep plenty of green open spaces and quadrangles, in addition to the extensive playing fields. Everything beautifully kept and facilities in the houses are well maintained.

We wanted them in the centre of a vibrant city but with the broader offer of a boarding school,' said one parent. 'No screens or phones at bedtime for younger pupils'

Often referred to as a 'big, small school,' and one can see why. With a strong foundation and support from generous benefactors, the school has retained its moderate size and with it, 'the sense of belonging to a school that knows the individuals who make it up,' as one parent put it. Pupils have relaxed good manners, but nothing starchy. Good buzz of conversation in the dining hall, with orderly sittings for different year groups. Younger pupils eat first with house staff keeping an eye. Food, rather above the average school offer (we can vouch for the sea bass) and plenty of choice.

Among former pupils are Martin Bell, the broadcaster/politician, and the late Christopher Hitchens, journalist and polemicist. Several from the sporting world including tennis player Jamie Murray, plus the King of Bahrain and the King of Tonga.

Pastoral care, inclusivity and discipline: The house staff are on the lookout for any problems and 'nip them in the bud before they develop,' say parents – and there is praise on all sides for the way staff get to know the pupils. 'It is one of the school's great strengths and a reason that we chose it for our children,' said a parent. 'The staff spend a lot of time getting to know pupils and with their antennae, especially with teenagers, can offer help before things reach a worrying stage.' Good social relations are emphasised and house staff swap roommates around – 'we were sorry at first when my son was moved, but it turned out to be brilliant for both boys. Staff knew what they were doing.' Counselling and support services are available for particular worries and problems. From the top down, 'the place gives short shrift to any nasty behaviour. Bullying is not tolerated,' said a parent. The head is 'a good disciplinarian,' we were told, but equally was 'very understanding when he dealt with a misdemeanour of our son. He was kindly and forgiving and did not make us feel worse than we already did!' Another parent spoke of 'the incredible support the school offered my son when I was having serious medical treatment. They also introduced him to a pupil who had had a similar experience and that really helped.' Pupils themselves speak of the value in keeping sixth formers in the house with younger pupils – 'It's fun but it really helps having older people around who you can talk to quite casually.' Year 9 pupils (day and boarding) spend a 24 hour period of initiation at the school the summer before entry. It gives them a chance to get a feel for the place and to make friends through team bonding sessions and fun. 'The school knows that happy pupils do well and they take the trouble.' Very few behaviour problems and most can be dealt with at house/tutor level. For occasional problems related to drink or drugs there is a clear policy, 'effectively zero tolerance, but there are times when, say, for a small mistake, it is right to offer a second chance'.

Pupils and parents: This is Cambridge and parents reflect it. Academics, entrepreneurs, scientists and medics predominate but there are farming families from nearby and a number of pupils are the second or third generation at the school. Boarders mostly from a small catchment – Essex, the home counties and London, plus the 15 per cent from overseas. Described as 'an international school in an international city', it offers the chance, a parent was frank enough to admit, 'to make connections that are as broad as possible, in a global market.' Several parents spoke of valuing a school that would work as a day or a boarding school and all prize the opportunities Cambridge has to offer – 'They can develop into adults in a city.' 'They are ready for university, no shocks.' The parent body itself is felt to be, 'A nice bunch, not flashy.' 'You tend to know best your children's friends' parents but it is not cliquey'. There is a 60:40 split between boys and girls but this seems of little consequence and neither is the day/boarder a significant divide – 'I board, my best friend is a day pupil,' said a year 10 pupil.

'Conformity is not a goal, they are encouraged to question things,' which is very much a quality of the Methodist movement

Money matters: Academic scholarships offered for year 7 entry with same again at year 9 plus usual music, art and sports awards. Bursaries also available and can be available to top up scholarships to cover full fees. Awards also available in the sixth form.

The last word: With an idyllic setting in central Cambridge, this is a popular school with bright, hardworking pupils. There is a breadth of vision and a great belief in the individual. Pupils feel able to speak up and 'sing their own song.' This is a happy school and pupils know they are lucky.

Lockers Park School

Lockers Park Lane, Hemel Hempstead, Hertfordshire HP1 1TL

01442 251712 | secretary@lockerspark.co.uk | www.lockerspark.co.uk

Ages: 4-13

Pupils: 170; Boarders: 10 full, 50 weekly/flexi

Fees: Day £11,505 – £18,255; Boarding £24,195 – £26,325 pa

Headmaster: Since September 2021, Gavin Taylor. Joined the school in 2008, starting out as form teacher and winding up as deputy head for six years before taking the helm. Has also taught at Haresfoot Prep, now part of Berkhamsted School. Educated at Magdalen College. Big on rugby – played in the Northampton Academy until 18 when he went to the University of Wales in Bangor and was selected for North Wales. Lives on site with his wife Nichola and their daughters,

Sookie and Fleur. Enjoys family walks with their golden labrador, Honey, and cooking.

Entrance: Pre-prep, like the prep school, is a boys' school. A day of 'social assessment' enables school to evaluate 'whether they are going to fit in and enjoy the environment'. Other key intake points are years 3 and 4, with a 'taster morning' assessment for the younger ones and 'low key' assessment day including tests in verbal reasoning and maths for older candidates. Scholarship applicants are observed in music, sport and a fun activity such as a treasure hunt. School doesn't just look for 'academic potential' but children 'who bring something more'.

Pupils come from a mixture of state primaries and other preps, most within a 20 to 30 minute drive. Around half the boys are day pupils, the rest do either flexi or full boarding (available from year 3); about half the full boarders are from overseas, typically Spain, Russia, China and Nigeria. School currently not oversubscribed, but 'nearly full'.

Exit: Bedford most popular, followed by Harrow, then Berkhamsted. Rugby, St Albans, Stowe, Eton, Haileybury, St Columba's, Sherborne, Abingdon, St Edward's Oxford and Aldenham. The occasional one to state grammar at 11+, although 'we don't prepare them for it', warns school.

Our view: Lockers Park was purpose-built in 1874 and sits atop 23 glorious acres of woodland – a boys'-own oasis in a lacklustre Hemel suburb. And boy oh boy, do they make the most of it, from the 40-minute morning break when you see boys tearing around fields and woods to the daily hour-and-a-half of PE, plus fixtures at least once a week. Boys we met were jumping out their seats with arms up as straight as nails, itching to take their turn to tell us about 'the shrubs' where they build dens, go on the bum-slide (down a steep hill) and climb tree trunks – 'it's a world of adventures,' exclaimed one. The Dark Tower night is a highlight of the school calendar – an unlit night-time treasure hunt around the school.

The heart of the school is undoubtedly the stunning, light-flooded oak-panelled dining hall, with the names of alumni etched on its walls. Here we joined laid-back, garrulous boys and their teachers for chicken and noodles and jam sponge with custard ('Wednesdays are easily the best lunch day,' grinned one chap) when suddenly a teacher made a loud noise, prompting all boys to swiftly drop their cutlery and bury their heads in their arms on the tabletop ('you never forget your first grace here,' a teacher smiled). Next up, boys were bellowed at to finish up and go 'up passage' ('means go to the loo,' whispered another interpreter of Lockers Park lingo) before getting ready for sports. Nobody sits still for long here and that's the way they like it – 'boys are allowed to be boys' is the school's strapline and almost every parent seems to have it tattooed into their psyche.

Days here aren't just busy, they're also long – sometimes up to 11 hours for older boys. Pupils can arrive at school from 7.30am and stay for breakfast and supper with no extra charge and no prior arrangement, all of which helps to cement the seamless boarding vibe. Yet it's all some parents can do to tear their offspring away at the end of the day.

Boys we met were jumping out their seats to tell us about 'the shrubs' where they build dens, go on the bum-slide (down a steep hill) and climb tree trunks

Back in the classrooms, the heavy dose of fresh air makes for rosy-cheeked boys ready to learn, usually kinaesthetically and discussion-led by teachers who, as one told us, 'are thankfully no longer all old-boy network, like when I joined, but a wonderful diverse mix'. We observed a lively French lesson (the school's stand-out subject) with every single hand up (boys here are encouraged to have a go, 'even if they give a horribly wrong answer, because that's how you learn,' explains school) and classical music helping to feed the senses. We met Snakespeare the snake and Isaac the bearded dragon in a science lesson, saw fun quizzes keeping things energetic in Latin, and so on. 'It's a full curriculum with academic rigour – my boy is always switched on in the lessons,' said one parent, while others praised how they 'cater for a broad church' – Eton wannabes through to those for whom obtaining 50 per cent in CE is a challenge. Staff know all the boys and are 'extremely accessible,' say parents – 'visible and just a phone call or an email away.'

Setting from year 7 in preparation for CE with specialist teaching across all subjects from year 5. All prep done in school – a popular move with boys and parents. SEN a moveable feast – 'if I can see a journey for a child and if I can work with the parents, I'll explore that,' says school. Most help given in the classroom 'as the best support is teachers being upskilled'; those with greater needs get small intervention groups or (for an extra fee) one-to-one lessons.

Spacious library (divided by glass doors – one side for reading, the other for study) has a cosy feel with armchairs and banks of laptops but we thought it could do with a few more books. Chapel ('a bit boring sometimes as you have to go every morning,' admitted one boy) can house the whole school at a squeeze. There's a large art room with kiln but we saw less artwork on display than in other schools – surprising as standards are high enough to win a senior school art scholarship most years. In DT – housed in separate building – boys told of how they recently 'made robots for robot wars'. Lovely big sports hall, while the 'old gym' is home to popular table tennis tables. Pianists practise on a baby grand situated in the main assembly hall rather than tucked away in a practice room – 'great for getting them used to performing,' says school.

Tousled boys bomb happily around between classes in these and other spaces, with plenty of cheery greetings for staff and visitors. The uniform – or lack thereof – comprising a check or striped shirt of the boys' choice and a pair of navy cords, sums up the collegiate learning environment where the endgame is reached via a path punctuated with a lot of good, wholesome fun as well as academic rigour. 'Best' is when the jackets and ties come out – again the boys' own choice of jacket – reserved for school outings, concerts and away matches. Maximum class size is 16, parents believing that school's bijoux size is its 'true strength'. A short walk through the grounds leads to the modern, light and airy pre-prep whose girls wear navy cord pinafores.

The uniform – or lack thereof – comprises a check or striped shirt of the boys' choice and a pair of navy cords and sums up the collegiate learning environment

Music 'extremely good', report parents, with a music scholarship secured for at least one boy each year. 'When people hear the chapel choir on a national stage, they'll often say, wow, why haven't I heard of these boys before?' Violin for all from year 3 and at least 95 per cent of boys continue with an instrument, some playing two or three, with boys regularly reaching grades seven or eight towards the top of the school. Choirs, ensembles and bands galore. Less praise for drama (on curriculum from years 3 to 5 and replaced by Latin in year 6), which some parents feel 'could be stronger and gets a bit side-lined into extracurricular'.

Sport is integral to the school – besides the daily PE, there are matches on Wednesday afternoons and some Saturdays. Boys lament the demise of the traditional post-match tea in other schools – 'oh not that school, all they give is a sausage roll and squash,' moaned a few during lunch when they discovered who they were playing. Huge emphasis is placed on fair play and sportsmanship, fielding A-E teams wherever possible from year 3 so everyone gets a trip on the bus whatever their ability. Football, rugby and cricket are core sports, but boys also compete in the likes of basketball, swimming, golf, tennis, athletics, badminton, skiing and squash. Facilities include cricket nets, a renovated outdoor pool, tennis courts, and putting green. A few parents have niggles – 'it promotes itself as a sporting school and they do games every day, but it's a small school and I think the coaching could be more rigorous' and 'my boys are average – I don't envisage them getting better than that' were among less positive comments; but others disagree. Tons of extracurricular from chess (very popular) club to year-round skiing at the nearby snow dome. Lockers' own beavers, cub and scout packs thrive, and boys who take part generally stay the night afterwards.

Upon arrival, we'd held the main door open for some boys who darted past with not so much as a thank you, but it was untypical. Still, lucky they didn't get caught as they might have got an amber or even red slip, which mount up to detentions (there are green slips for merit). One boy felt the system was sometimes ill-used – 'I saw someone get two red slips at the same dinner last night and that didn't feel fair.'

Boarding: Boarding house is part of main school, with boys split over two floors according to age and presided over by houseparents and matron. They clearly feel at home in the bright, functional dorms housing two to 12 boarders, as well as in the cosy common room and separate prep room, with action-packed weekends for full-timers including everything from visits to theme parks to movie and pizza nights. Exeats every third weekend, with optional Saturday school on non-exeat weekends, including workshops for all core subjects, plus everything from art to team building, then fixtures (if schools are available; most aren't) in the afternoon. Boarders talk of 'learning independence' and 'having great fun', while parents report that they 'learn to live without ipads, TV and gaming'.

The last word: This small prep is like one big family and ticks a lot of boxes: boarding for those who want it, the academic rigour required for entry to top public schools, support and challenge for those who need it, and lots and lots of fresh air.

New Hall School

The Avenue, Boreham, Chelmsford, Essex CM3 3HS

01245 467 588 | registrar@newhallschool.co.uk | www.newhallschool.co.uk

Ages: 11–18

Pupils: 878; sixth form: 240; Boarders: 98 full, 139 weekly/flexi

Fees: Day £18,936 – £20,502pa; Boarding £26,838 – £32,472pa

Principal: Since 2001, Katherine Jeffrey MA PGCE MA (EdMg) NPQH. Previously an RE teacher at St Mary's School, Shaftesbury, head of RE at Woldingham School and deputy head at The Marist School, Ascot before coming to New Hall as its first ever lay principal and teacher of theology. Now the longest-serving head at the same HMC school. She is also executive head of New Hall's Multi-Academy Trust. Awarded the Institute of Directors' East of England Businesswoman of the Year Award, followed by a national Independent Schools Award for Outstanding Strategic Initiative and the TES Overall School of the Year. She has been a committee member of the Catholic Independent Schools' Conference and a governor of St Mary's School, Hampstead. She is currently a director of The Tablet, the international Catholic weekly, and a member of the Catholic Association for Racial Justice (CARJ). Married with four daughters – all educated at New Hall School.

Making the change from dyed-in-the-wool Catholic convent girls' boarding school of variable academic results to one of the UK's most successful examples of the 'diamond model' (co-educational nursery and prep school, single-sex teaching for ages 11 to 16, returning to co-education for the sixth form) took her a speedy five years near the start of her tenure, and she has continued at a cracking pace of change which has touched every part of the school. The driving force behind New Hall's outreach move to sponsor maintained primary schools, her outreach extends to the local community. New Hall received national commendation as the first independent school to sponsor a primary academy, rescuing it from special measures, a falling roll and near closure; today Messing Primary School is an oversubscribed primary school, praised in its inspections for outstanding leadership and governance and the quality of education.

'Mrs Jeffrey moves with – and often ahead of – the times,' observes a parent, while others describe her as 'a calm professional', 'intelligent', 'approachable' and 'dedicated to the all-round development of the children in her school'. Adds one, 'from the principal to the division heads, subject heads and all other departmental leaders, the picture is one of focus and cohesion'. Her energy for education and for providing a continually evolving and diverse range of educational and co-curricular opportunities is clear, and New Hall is now a veritable village, with everything students could need for a rounded education under one patch of sky.

'We now make much more use of our 70 acres of grade one listed parkland,' she told us. 'Students are discovering parts of the site they hadn't really been to before.' As well as being one of the largest all-through independent schools in the country with a current roll of 1,400 and rising, a stated aim is to be one of the most affordable, having reduced fees by six per cent in September 2020 after several freezes in preceding years. 'There's no compromise on quality,' she emphasises, 'in fact the scale works in our favour and gives us even more opportunity to open our students' hearts and minds and to prepare them for a full and active life in the future.'

Entrance: Year 7 has 120 places – usually three times oversubscribed. Around 40 pupils come up from New Hall's own year 6 and have priority, although they too must go through the same entry procedure as external applicants – papers in English, maths and verbal reasoning plus an interview and report from the previous school. Unusually, keen parents are encouraged to write to the head to put their case for their child's suitability the school. Lengthy admissions preamble – families tend to visit for at least one open day as well as a group tour before beginning the formal application. Lower sixth has 150 places, with new entrants needing two 7s and four 6s at GCSE to be in with a whiff. 'Our A level classes are very fast-paced,' says principal, 'with pupils aiming for A* to B grades.'

Exit: Around a quarter leaves after GCSEs and there is a large external intake at sixth form, many from grammar schools and other independent schools.

Around two thirds of the sixth form to Russell Group. Durham, Warwick, Exeter, UCL and Nottingham currently popular. Each year a number of students also progress to medicine, dentistry, veterinary medicine (seven in 2021) and law courses. Also, places are won regularly for top conservatoires and art schools. One to Oxbridge in 2021.

Latest results: In 2021, 79 per cent 9-7 at GCSE; 75 per cent A*/A at A level (97 per cent A*-B). In 2019 (the last year when exams took place), 51 per cent 9-7 at GCSE; 51 per cent A*/A at A level (84 per cent A*-B).

Teaching and learning: Interestingly, the genders at New Hall are on a par results-wise at GCSE, bucking the national trend for boys to fall behind by 10 per cent. More grist to the mill of the 'diamond model', allowing the teaching between 11 and 16 to be tailored to gender-specific learning styles, with co-ed lessons in the prep and sixth form.

The school farm has been improved with new paths alongside the roomy pens for pigs, Rutland rams, pygmy goats, chickens, rabbits and even young peacocks

French and Spanish are taught from Year 7 through a newly re-developed curriculum centred around the DELF and DELE language diplomas. These allow all students to gain a recognised language qualification and the programme is focused on developing students' confidence in communication. Theology compulsory up to Year 11. Computer science and Latin also taught to all students in Years 7, 8 and 9. In Year 9, students may begin ancient Greek. Theology, English, maths and science compulsory GCSEs, alongside a choice of up to four optional subjects. Most choose three option subjects leading to 9 or 10 GCSEs and also take the level 2 project qualification. Top students achieve 12 GCSEs. Students in all years also follow a tutorial programme including 'life skills' and careers education as well as sports.

'Teaching is dynamic and exciting and not all done the same way here,' says principal. 'It's creative because we don't want to bore children.' Judging by the bright-eyed, smiley and engaged students we met, she's right, and parents are happy – 'our son, a scholar, has felt stimulated and challenged,' says one. 'The teachers are passionate about what they do and this rubs off on the children.'

Sixth form is 'diverse and exciting' say parents, and currently with 250 students, but earmarked for expansion and already with a strong external intake. 'We are very keen to keep going with subjects that are hard and have smaller numbers,' confirms principal. 'It's so important at A level that students study the subjects they want to study.' This means ancient Greek and Latin classes run even if for a class of just one. Music, psychology, economics and business studies are popular, and this is one of the largest centres in the country for A levels in government and politics and theology, with 80-plus in sixth form choosing each. HPQ and EPQ also on offer. Careers service keeps tabs and offers a breadth of suggestions. Guidance throughout is a strength say parents, who appreciate the 'highly personalised approach' – students of varying abilities work together at their own levels while 'maintaining an amazing sense of harmony and inclusivity'.

Learning support and SEN: All staff are trained in differentiation, and the gifted and talented benefit from accelerated learning in lessons and encouragement to find stretch in enrichment opportunities. Academic societies promote scholarly habits (including 'challenge', 'persistence and big picture thinking', 'intellectual courage' and 'metathinking'), and prepare around 20 each year with sights set on Oxbridge.

'I say to parents "please don't worry for a second if your child has dyslexia, dyscalculia or ADHD – we might be the perfect school for you",' says principal. Indeed, one parent told of being shown around the school by a girl who spoke of her dyslexia as if she had been chosen for the hockey team. 'It's a culture here,' emphasises principal, 'SEND is not a negative thing.' School also has a good track record for children who lack confidence, thanks to the homely atmosphere and the focus on finding something at which children can flourish.

The arts and extracurricular: 'Our co-curricular programme is not an add-on,' emphasises principal. One of the few occasions we've come across a choir that's compulsory – year 7 boys and girls enjoy or endure a year before being given the option to remain. 'We have discovered some great voices that way – people who wouldn't have put themselves forward,' says head of music. Choice of choirs for those inclined, including Voces for the broken-voiced, plus instrumental ensembles of all kinds and the occasional rock and pop band. Organ lessons on the restored Norman & Beard organ in the school chapel. Many informal as well as the formal performances. Music remains a popular option at GCSE and A level.

'Teaching is dynamic and exciting and not all done the same way,' says principal. 'It's creative because we don't want to bore children'

Drama and dance a speciality, with the school's Walkfares Centre the venue for all performing arts activity. Annual dance show is a highlight and dance A level popular. Own dance company takes students from year 10 upwards and crosses over with the local community. ESB and LAMDA thrive. Around 30 a year take art A level – working away in a warren of atelier-style studios – and about a third continue beyond, though architecture tends to win out over fine art.

In keeping with the school's focus on community and charity, all pupils heavily involved with the New Hall Voluntary Service, which for many becomes a way of life. Tea parties, lunches and concerts hosted for local groups at the school's own chaplaincy centre, and some students work with sponsored primary school. The Good Hope coffee shop is housed in a friendly wooden lodge in the grounds and serves coffee, cake and panini to sixth formers and staff, with proceeds to a Catholic charity (previously For Jimmy) that supports young people at risk of being drawn into gang culture.

Eight houses – unrelated to the boarding houses – contest in competitions of all hues and there is a clear joy among the students for participation. When the 2020 prom was cancelled, the replacement event on campus was preceded by a cavalcade of the school's golf buggies, festooned with decorations, which were driven on a tour of the school grounds by prom-outfitted former sixth formers.

Sport: Sport is taken very seriously. Hockey now a major sport for boys as well as girls. Girls' rugby up and running. Cricket for all. All sports available to everyone. Income has been ploughed into facilities – sleek, purpose-built gymnasium block stuffed with cardio machines and weights overlooks a sweep of sports pitches (several floodlit), 10 courts for netball or tennis, 400-metre cinder running track and chlorine-free pool in its own block with changing room facilities (also used by the Essex swim squad). A former equestrian arena is now an indoor sports hall with state-of-the-art flooring, while the many horse-related activities take place off-site. New grass-roofed building accommodates rugby changing rooms; one for tennis too, complete with a pavilion.

Pro coaches complement the PE staff, now numbering a former England golfer, who, as well as presiding over the state-of-the-art 12-bay golf driving range, demonstrated his versatility during our visit by focusing the wandering attention of a group of hopping youngsters on the task of dribbling a hockey ball on the Astro.

New Hall provides county and national athletes in many disciplines, including UK independent school golf and equestrian champions, not to mention star swimmers, cricketers, tennis, hockey and rugby players. A New Hallian athlete competed in the last Commonwealth Games.

Boarding: Cream sofas? Cushions? Can this be a boarding house for 7 to 13 year old boys? Quite apart from Petre House's jaw-droppingly ornate cornicing and mouldings worthy of a royal palace, the place is spotless in the face of a most unforgiving neutrally toned décor. The dorms too are a revelation – all belongings stowed neatly into storage compartments hiding behind the ladder treads of ingenious high-sleeper beds, designed by a former New Hallian head of boarding and incorporating a study space underneath. Magdalen Wing in Hawley House, for girls in years 3-8, is more the usual fayre – though rooms for ones and twos rather than the multiples for boys (full boarders usually roomed with the flexi boarders) – and a comfortable lived-in look with cheery interior design scheme chosen by the girls themselves. Four other houses – two for boys and two for girls as they progress through the school – accommodating a third of each year group, who board on a flexi, weekly or full-time basis. Up to 16 reserved places for junior (full and weekly) boarders from year 3 onwards. An influx of weekly boarders from London and across East Anglia anticipated to coincide with the opening of the new mainline railway station at the end of the school's drive, scheduled for 2025.

Ethos and heritage: The original Palace of Beaulieu, ancestral home of the Boleyn family and thought to represent much of the attraction to King Henry VIII of his second wife (beheaded), perhaps with good reason. Henry expanded the existing building to create a most imposing and gargantuan edifice, with eight courtyards behind a 550-foot wide red-brick frontage and two enormous gatehouse towers, apparently the inspiration for Hampton Court Palace. Channel 4's Time Team dug up evidence of the foundations of what was identified as a nursery for Henry's first-born, Princess Mary. Having passed through a few hands (including those of Oliver Cromwell) after Henry's demise, in 1799 the palace became occupied by the Canonesses of the Holy Sepulchre, one of the most ancient orders in the Catholic church, established in Europe long before the English Religious Community was founded in 1642. Forced out of

King's College School, Cambridge

their home in the Low Countries by the French Revolutionary Wars, the Canonesses brought their school to the Palace of Beaulieu with the intention of offering a Catholic education to girls denied this in England in the post-Reformation period. Thus, New Hall is the oldest Catholic girls' school in England.

Today's New Hall is (in terms of footprint at least) a fraction of Henry's pile, but breath-taking nonetheless and approached via a mile-long avenue at the end of which one fully expects a National Trust ticket booth to appear. Perhaps one of the most impressive interiors is the chapel, with its original solid wood door and Henry VIII's coat of arms over the main entrance.

Behind the long façade of the main building, which houses an impressive entrance hall with tastefully interior designed waiting room, the chapel, classrooms and a boarding house, there is a dedicated performing arts block incorporating three large studio spaces (which host the school's popular Saturday dance and drama schools as well as lessons throughout the week). New science centre on the drawing board. The Eaton Theatre seats 210 and is used for productions as well as lectures and year meetings. Large library with study area for all-comers and hanging with Apple Macs. Eight science labs. Spacious refectory reminiscent of the restaurant in an upmarket London department store with a choice of three hot options, plus a salad bar and other cold choices.

All of these facilities are in constant use by the pupil body, which now numbers 840 seniors and 1,400 overall, with capacity for another 100. However, the structure is a family of small schools – year groups of 60, so 300 in the girls' division, 300 in the boys' and a sixth form that is a tight-knit community of 240. Parents see the upside of this rapid growth – 'there are now even more opportunities available both in and out of the classroom for students,' says one, adding 'they're known as individuals and not mere numbers'. Sixth formers have their own wing of the arts centre, plus the atmospheric Denford Bar in one of the most historic parts of the main building – originally a grand entrance and stairwell to the Duke of Buckingham's bedroom, more recently the HR offices – now sympathetically restored and interior designed with leather stools and tapestry cushions and soon to be licensed (student drinks under staff supervision only). The venue for informal student society meetings and also the haunt of teachers in the evenings, who in the daytime frequent the newly refurbished mid-mod style staff room, complete with kitchen and adjoining room of work stations and a big-screen TV (head's weekly briefing takes place here but the school's 400 may tune in virtually from across the school).

Recent bold development of the campus for 2020 and beyond has shone a light on the need for learning in a sensory way outdoors, and has caused certain more exterior projects to be bumped up the schedule. Large-scale structures cover several less-used areas of the grounds, transforming them into semi-outdoor spaces for activities, including dining, play and concerts. The school farm has been improved with new paths alongside the roomy pens for pigs, Rutland rams, pygmy goats, chickens, rabbits and even young peacocks – one of whom obligingly celebrated our visit by showing his colours – all enjoying the rural idyll and providing inspiration for lessons along with instruction on animal husbandry to students of all ages. An historic pond is due to be reinstated for fishing, reviving a traditional manor house pastime, and a 2020 Memorial Orchard is soon to be planted, with a plan to bottle the resulting fruit and sell for charity. Meanwhile, the original walled convent garden is a tranquil spot and has proved useful for on-campus camp-outs with campfires and marshmallows.

Quite apart from Petre House's jawdroppingly ornate cornicing and mouldings worthy of a royal palace, the place is spotless in the face of a most unforgiving neutral décor

A mini settlement of eco-friendly lodges accommodates non-local staff, as well as the occasional visitor, and two semi-detached houses on the edge of the campus have been bought by the school to house eight trainee teachers who are learning their craft on-site, with good prospects of being retained.

The school chapel, with catered receptions in the landscaped gardens, is now a popular place for New Hallians to tie the knot.

Former pupils are automatic members of the New Hallians, an association which numbers many notables, including: international fashion designer Anya Hindmarch; CNN international correspondent Christiane Amanpour; English racing driver, broadcaster and motoring journalist Amanda Stretton; artist and novelist Leonora Carrington; former British Ambassador to Mexico, Spain and Andorra and Chair of Council at the University of Sussex, Dame Denise Holt DCMG; Master of Gonville & Caius College, Cambridge, Pippa Rogerson; neuroscientist and feminist Prof Gina Rippon; opera singer Stefanie Kemball-Read; and Horrid Henry actor Theo Stevenson.

Pastoral care, inclusivity and discipline: Personal qualities, kindness in particular, are recognised and drawn out, and pupils we met were certainly happy in their own skin. This is a Catholic school and although those of all faiths and none are welcome, Christian values are at its core. 'Pastoral care is a quintessential component of life at New Hall and one which pervades each student and parent experience,' approves a parent. Support and care for others, both in school and outside it, are fundamental. 'Corpus' sixth form discussion group focuses on equality and diversity and reports back to principal on behalf of students, while a parent forum has recently been established to discuss issues of racial diversity and inclusion, with recommendations implemented. Parents satisfied that the school's growth has not had a negative impact – 'we feel strongly that the level of care and teaching provided has not been 'diluted' in any way,' says a parent. 'If anything, it appears the school has used this growth to accelerate various improvements in its infrastructure and facilities.' Parents too are comfortable in the fold, and school communication is praised for keeping families in the loop.

Pupils and parents: This is a school surrounded by a changing profile of local parents – from the traditional farmers and professionals to city commuters and the grammar school educated. 'Some have attended the historic Catholic schools such as Stonyhurst and Worth themselves and are now looking to us for their children,' says principal. Being Catholic is not a prerequisite, but engagement with the religious life of the school very much is. 'I would hope that our pupils would leave here well-informed on matters of faith, and that they would have absorbed our core moral and spiritual values,' says principal.

Two new access roads have recently been added to make the site's access and egress a more attractive prospect – one to skip the congestion of a chunk of the A12 and the other to link with the new upmarket housing development under construction on adjacent land and these, together with the proposed new mainline railway station are sure to widen New Hall's net, from London to East Anglia. Long a favourite with overseas pupils – about 35 per cent of boarders, who represent more than 30 countries.

Money matters: Scholarships for Catholics, academic, music (including specific instrumental), all rounder, sport (general) and tennis, plus means-tested bursaries. Proponent of the HMC Scholar Scheme, with 100 per cent fee remission for several students from central Europe.

The last word: One of the largest independent schools in the UK, but smartly arranged for a small-school feel – this is a place boys and girls may contribute to and take from in equal measure, learning to relish individual academic success but also the greater joy of being part of a community.

Old Buckenham Hall School

30

Brettenham Park, Ipswich, Suffolk IP7 7PH

01449 740252 | admissions@obh.co.uk | www.obh.co.uk

Ages: 3–13

Pupils: 239; **Boarders:** 7 full, 69 weekly/flexi

Fees: Day £10,275 – £20,841; Boarding £23,853 – £27,156 pa

Headmaster: Since 2018, David Griffiths, previously head of Daneshill School and before that deputy and acting head of St John's-on-the-Hill (Dean Close). After school and university (BA in history and PGCE from Cardiff), he held posts teaching in Llanishen High, Howell's School GDST and Haberdashers' Monmouth School for Girls, where he met his wife, Becky, also teaching there and a head of house. Despite a great love for teaching his subject (ancient and medieval history) in senior schools, he came to feel that it was the all-round educating of children at the prep stage that he wanted to be involved with – this led to working at, for example, Old Buckenham Hall. Has an MEd from Buckingham.

Was 'immediately taken with the ethos of OBH' and 'knew it was the place we wanted to be as a family'. His relaxed style (tweed jacket and flannels) complements his oak panelled study with roaring log fire, comfy sofas and a large box of toys in the corner ('It helps having distractions to hand for younger brothers and sisters during interviews with parent,' he explains). As a father of three, he knows what's what and he has made no secret of his wish to stay at the school for a decent amount of time. 'Parents need the reassurance that I won't up sticks the minute their child arrives,' and this fact has gone down well. 'He has a firm hand on the tiller – the school is in safe hands.' 'It's our luck that the school is in a really good place with this head.'

Is it a traditional school, we asked him? On this he hesitates, believing the word can imply being stuck in the past. Then again, he muses, it can also be a reference to respect, courage and making a contribution to wider society – all of which he really does associate with the school and which were plain to see when we attended the last Remembrance Day service – included reading the names of former pupils who died in battle, wreath laying and Last Post. The OBH way, he says, signals courage, respect, kindness, pride, responsibility and community and was drawn up after consultation with staff and pupils – all considered by the school as important as academic success, 'though of course we also want our pupils to achieve academically and eventually to move on to schools of their choosing,' he adds.

Still teaches. 'I started off teaching my own subject but that limited me to the higher forms so now I teach PSHE which means I get to know everyone.' Makes himself available for parents at drop-off and favours face-to-face meetings to discuss any issues that arise, 'rather than endless emails.' The school year begins with a massive BBQ for everyone connected with the school – pupils, staff, parents and their families.

Lives on site (as do several staff members) with his family and two cocker spaniels, Dilys and Madog. Hobbies include photography, guitar playing and he is still a big rugby fan. In the holidays the family decamp to their house and small holding in North Wales. Delights in his family's Welsh background but remains modest about his ability to speak the language.

Entrance: Academically non-selective though pupils must be keep up with the curriculum. Prospective pupils and parents are invited to visit the school to meet the head and tour the school. Pupils then have informal assessments in maths and English and parents have the opportunity to discuss things further with the head. 'It is all about getting to know each other and building a relationship based on trust.' School is almost at full capacity, especially higher up the school.

Exit: Pupils move on to senior schools all over the country though the most popular destinations continue to be the relatively nearby. Oundle, Uppingham, Oakham, the Leys, RHS and Harrow all popular. One or two to Eton each year. Plenty of scholarships and awards.

Our view: A country school that revels in its rural Suffolk setting. Wellies, whether green or not, are essential for pupils to rush about and enjoy the grounds which include wooded areas (with climbable trees), ponds, walled gardens and endless green vistas. As the crow flies, not far from Stowmarket or Bury St Edmund's but you will need a decent map or satnav to find it down the twisty lanes.

Parents are 'friendly, not the showy sort,' they told us. Most are dual income, with some ex-Londoners seeking a different pace – mostly professional and business-oriented

The splendid gated entrance, complete with lodges on either side, leads to an avenue of trees – 'It raises the spirits just to drive in each day,' said a parent and everyone spoke of how the school's setting influenced their choice. Originally a boys' school, founded in 1862, it was moved to its present site, Brettenham Park, in 1956. The main building, a mansion with 16th century origins, has been built on over the years, most notably during the ownership of Joseph Bonaparte (ex-King of Spain, brother of Napoleon) in the 19th century. It was he who created a salon in the style of the hall of mirrors at Versailles which really takes the breath away. The room, off the main hall, is not kept in moth balls for occasional show but in regular use for receptions and meetings – a log fire roaring when we visited, and yet another in the oak panelled, galleried main entrance hall. 'We all warm our hands as we go past,' a pupil told us.

Some classrooms and specialist areas have purpose-built premises, none especially distinguished, but many – including science (three separate labs) and DT – are based in interesting adaptations of former stable blocks. Most buildings single storey, connected by brick-weave paths and covered ways with boot racks outside most entrances. The nursery and pre-prep have their own buildings where we met pupils who – though having an after-lunch 'rest' – were only too glad to sit up and talk. Play areas include a massive walled garden, playground with a sky-blue bouncy surface, climbing apparatus and giant chess set, trikes and bikes.

The Britten Hall – built in 2003 and named after OBH's most famous old boy – houses classrooms and a massive, balconied hall that is used for assemblies, performances and gym. The practice rooms and rehearsal space, all well used by the 70 per cent of pupils who learn an instrument. The outdoor swimming pool is used throughout the spring and summer and, mirabile dictu, is about to finally get a roof so swimming will be all year round.

Class sizes are kept small, ranging from 10-18 with setting in core subjects beginning in the middle school (age 7). French begins in nursery, Latin in year 5. We saw a Latin class in action, very lively teaching on adjectives with lots of hand waving from pupils with the right answers. Everyone leapt to their feet when we came into the room.

The library is a large panelled room with enticing sofas to snuggle into to read. Learning for Success (the term coined for extra support) takes place in a large, cheerful room. 'Lots of children need a boost at some point.' Help is primarily one-to-one with mild dyslexia and dyscalculia the most common difficulties. Pupils have their own individual goals to reach and are encouraged to focus on their own path rather than comparing themselves with peers.

Wellies, whether green or not, are essential for pupils to rush about and enjoy the grounds which include woods, ponds, walled gardens and endless green vistas

Once in year 7 and 8 there is a more structured set up, with those hoping to win academic awards kept together in a set. Specific help for entry to certain senior schools is individually targeted with an extra hour or so on a weekly basis. The school makes a point of celebrating varied triumphs including a recent case where a pupil – having repaired an old bike for charity that he found in the sheds at school – found himself a social media star when it was picked up and went viral. 'It's not only about the fast lane,' a parent remarked, 'which is also good for the pupils who generally do well in lots of other things.'

Pupils keep the same tutor from year 6 to 8 so they have continuity. Tutors are the first port of call if there is a problem but there is 'no trouble finding the right person, the head is so often in the car park it is easy to have a quick word,' according to a parent. Head says childhood is a time 'to be able to make mistakes because that is how you learn,' and this is echoed by lots of parents who told us the school is a place where 'children can enjoy a proper childhood.'

OBH was a Forest School long before the term was in vogue. The south lawn has a large pond, currently duck-less (a Defra ruling, hopefully temporary) but with a jetty to do pond dipping from and an arboretum, begun by a former owner and added to recently when a tree for each child in the school was planted. Pupils can climb trees, make dens, do the whole Arthur Ransome number with nothing roped off. One of the three deputies, with a military background, leads OBH Explorers (a kind of junior DofE) and is passionate about pupils learning practical skills in an outdoor setting. By year 8 pupils are ready to tackle the 100 lengths swim and the Gold Survival Expedition. Clearly there are excellent ground staff, also very tidy children because we did not see a single piece of litter anywhere.

The School performance of A Midsummer Night's Dream was staged in the grounds this year with watching parents following the action from scene to scene in the woods. 'It was a magical experience,' said one. Lots of musical opportunities with jazz and samba bands, orchestra and four choirs. Regular concerts in school and the annual carol service is held in Bury St Edmund's. All team sports are played and there is an impressive weekly fixtures list for both boys and girls, though Saturday afternoon matches have been curtailed. Now after morning school, on alternate Saturdays, a programme of voluntary activities includes rock-climbing, fly-fishing and clay pigeon shooting for year 5 and above. 'At least fifty per cent join in,' we heard.

Parents are 'friendly, not the showy sort,' they told us. Most are dual income, with some ex-Londoners seeking a different pace – mostly professional and business-oriented, some established boarding families.

Boarding: Full and flexi options, with two, three and four night packages. Around a third boards, increasingly popular in higher years. In year 3 there are a handful of flexi-boarders and by years 7 and 8 almost everyone boards for a few days each week. The push to board usually comes from the children themselves. 'They see the fun going on and want to be a part of it – in fact, it's so popular it's hard to get in!' said a parent.

Boarding takes place upstairs in the main building and all provision has been recently updated and decorated. Most rooms are six or eight bedded (very few bunks) with splendid views of the grounds. There is a junior boarding house, Spero ('I hope,' the school motto), plus houses for older boys and girls. All have their own common room with plenty of space for activities and table football, not forgetting the little kitchens for toast and hot drinks. Year 8 have a shared common room off the main hall downstairs. Lots of staff live on site and houses all have live-in matrons. Even if you don't board, you can join in activities and stay for supper.

Money matters: Fees are towards the top of the range but include lunch and activities. Individual music tuition is charged separately.

The last word: With gifted leadership, OBH is enjoying a deserved surge in popularity. Pupils flourish academically and socially.

Orwell Park School

Nacton, Ipswich, Suffolk IP10 0ER

01473 659225 | headmaster@orwellpark.org | www.orwellpark.co.uk

Ages: 2–13

Pupils: 250; Boarders: 33 full, 82 weekly/flexi

Fees: Day £8,883 – £17,976; Boarding £25,072 – £27,582 pa

Headmaster: Since 2011 Adrian Brown MA (Cantab) PGCE. Early 50s. Previously spent 20 years at Ipswich School where he taught French and German before being appointed deputy head (pastoral). He thinks, 'It has been invaluable, as a prep head, to have taught in senior schools. I know what they are looking for and expecting. Being "in the know" is something parents can depend on for guidance in choosing senior schools and entering for scholarships.' Wants all pupils to 'discover their strengths and develop skills that will stand them in good stead throughout life'. Believes in allowing pupils to experience the sometimes-uncomfortable feeling of 'not getting things right first time': 'We are becoming risk averse as a society and sometimes we learn best by our mistakes.' Strong advocate of collaborative learning and developing resilience and good communication skills, which are 'essential for life no matter what career path they follow'.

Continues to teach his own subject (French), usually in year 6, and remains a dedicated sportsman; he was a Cambridge blue and played professional cricket at county level (Essex). His wife, Nicole, also a trained teacher, concentrates on organising major events such as the Leavers' Ball and dealing with design and decoration throughout the school. Strong approval from parents for the way the head and his wife greet all pupils as they arrive at school in the morning. 'It is so welcoming for the children and makes it so easy, as a parent, to have a quick word.' They have three grown-up children who have all flown the nest.

Entrance: Main entry points are at 4+ and 7+ but places continue to become available throughout. Year group sizes increase year on year. Nursery and pre-prep places are non-selective (taster mornings in class and a home visit). At 7+ and 11+ tests in maths, English and reasoning plus a report from current school and an interview. Not overly selective but as school only offers learning support for mild difficulties pupils must be able to follow the curriculum.

Exit: At 13+ post CE. Excellent track record for winning scholarships; usually over half the year 8 cohort win an award, some several, and to a range of senior schools throughout the country, including to the top-drawer ones (24 scholarships in 2021). No well-trodden path to favoured schools – fewer than five pupils go to the same school. Current destinations include Harrow, Stowe, Uppingham, Oundle, King's Canterbury, King's Ely, Tudor Hall, Sedbergh, Dauntsey's, Shrewsbury, Framlingham, Royal Hospital School, Ipswich School and Woodbridge School.

Our view: The splendid Blenheim Palace-style wrought-iron gates open to reveal grounds of outstanding beauty with sweeping lawns, wisteria-draped pergola, a ha-ha and the River Orwell glistening in the distance. A Georgian mansion, with significant additions (including an observatory) made by the Victorian philanthropist who then owned the estate, forms the core of the school. Many Downton Abbey features have been retained, including the orangery (now used as an assembly hall), panelled walls, French windows and a roaring log fire in the entrance hall. Pupils revel in their surroundings and 'swimming in the pool and looking up at the trees', 'playing outside on summer evenings', and 'the view from the dormitories' were all mentioned as special; all seem aware of their good fortune. The recently built pre-prep department is a one-storey building in its own grounds close by.

Stepping through French windows from the head's study (size of a small ballroom) onto the terrace is an ageless experience, but the school is thoroughly 21st century. 'We want to prepare pupils for the uncertainties ahead and a job market that we do not yet know.' A recently appointed head of digital strategy oversees the introduction of interactive panels in every classroom, the adoption of Firefly (virtual learning environment) and individual iPads. Use of mobile phones, however, is strictly limited to off-duty times. Each day begins with a tutor period or assembly and a service is held in St Martin's church, close at hand, every week. Serious emphasis on academic attainment with pupils' individual strengths encouraged and targeted support where needed. In the middle school (years 3-5), pupils mainly class-taught with specialists for music, DT, art and languages. Seniors (years 6-8) taught by subject staff and in sets according to potential. Classics continue to have status with Latin taught from year 6 and Greek, for scholars, in year 8. A notice on the classroom door says 'Mistakes welcome here!' and pupils confirm this: 'You learn best if you can say if you don't understand.' There's even a growth mindset co-ordinator to make sure it sinks in. French continues as main MFL.

Den building in the spinneys and copses together with a genuine assault course in the woods provide plenty of opportunity to run free and exercise

Learning support is for all with a drop-in centre open all day and into the evening with plenty of help available, including typing courses, interactive revision sessions and assistance with speech and language development from trained therapists. 'They spotted that my son needed some help without me having to ask and ask,' we were told; and 'there is such an atmosphere of acceptance and support and no stigma attached to receiving extra help.' Those who require more formal support can be withdrawn for one-to-one help and this is charged as an extra. Communication with parents considered vital, as it is with any outside agencies involved such as educational psychologists. Real focus on study skills with pupils encouraged to take responsibility for their learning and personal organisation, particularly in years 7 and 8 as preparation for senior school.

Potential scholars are identified and streamed in year 7 and go on to form the 'scholars' group' in year 8. School well aware of risks in labelling pupils too early as gifted and talented and the enrichment programme laid on to nurture scholars is open to all pupils, parents and the wider community. This programme includes a series of 'Orangery lectures' given on a range of subjects plus scholarship preparation for music, art, sport and drama. Pupils take part in off-site initiatives such as the Uppingham skills day and the Gordonstoun challenge. Debating workshops, musical soirées, plays and careers talks all nourish and support pupils' motivation and widen their horizons. For the same reason a link has been developed with Mayo college in India with exchange visits to take place annually.

Performance culture well established in verse, singing and public speaking, usually as inter-house competitions or with other local independent schools. Grounds perfect for letting off steam at break and play times, the ha-ha providing a natural boundary. Den building in the spinneys and copses together with a genuine assault course in the woods provide plenty of opportunity to run free and exercise as well as more formal games provision of rugby, cricket and hockey. Girls all play cricket these days, there is a nine-hole golf course, squash and tennis courts, outdoor swimming pool and an equestrian and ski racing team. Art scholars have specially allotted areas for their work in the studio which they can continue with in spare time. Extracurricular activities include clay pigeon shooting and a stargazing club run from the school's own observatory. Recent introduction of LAMDA and a STEM focus includes construction of a kit car as an activity. Plus there's a new recording studio in music department.

The recent introduction of the OPS challenge, a sort of mini DofE with long hikes, camp-outs, bushcraft and outdoor pursuits holidays to Normandy in year 7 and the Ardèche post-CE provide opportunities for learning leadership skills – as well as enormous fun. Senior pupils are selected for the responsibilities of prefect, dorm captain, head boarder and house captains and the school has a head boy and a head girl, as well as two senior prefects.

Boarding: Boarding increasingly popular, particularly in top two forms when it is seen as good preparation for senior school, but care is taken not to assume every child is on the path to boarding school. 'My son decided he did not want to board at senior school and we were supported fully in that decision.' Many begin with flexi boarding, later becoming full boarders, even when they live close at hand to the school. 'I like being with friends and we have so much fun.' Dorms, for six to 10, have recently been updated to a high standard.

The last word: In a spectacular setting overlooking the River Orwell, it is difficult to picture more idyllic surroundings to grow and learn in. Top notch academics and so much more besides.

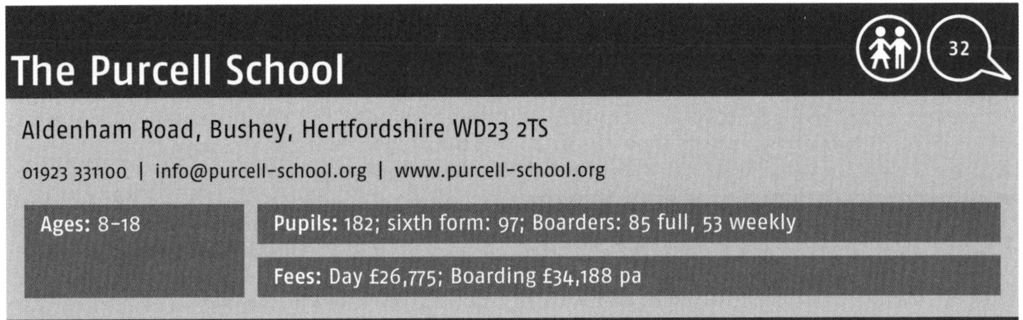

The Purcell School

Aldenham Road, Bushey, Hertfordshire WD23 2TS

01923 331100 | info@purcell-school.org | www.purcell-school.org

Ages: 8–18

Pupils: 182; sixth form: 97; Boarders: 85 full, 53 weekly

Fees: Day £26,775; Boarding £34,188 pa

Head: Since 2018, Paul Bambrough, previously vice principal at the Birmingham Royal Conservatoire, where he also, inter alia, taught in the vocal and operatic studies department and contributed to the orchestra conducting course. Whilst director of music at the Sixth Form College Farnborough, he created the largest A level music department in the country of 500+ students. He has sung at most of the UK's foremost concert halls and cathedrals, is a harpsichordist, organist and pianist and has worked as a repetiteur with some of the world's finest singers. Away from music he enjoys the countryside, architecture and maintains a (largely) enthusiastic fitness routine.

Entrance: Audition season runs weekly between September and March. Prospective pupils come for a preliminary, one-to-one audition and are invited back for a thorough going over by a panel if they are taken to the next stage. Key criterion is not what grade candidate has achieved but how committed they are to a career in music. About half those who audition are offered a place – staff talk about the 'wild glint in the eyes' of the selection panel when they see an outstanding talent. No academic threshold but school 'must be able to cater for them' and numbers for entry into any year group are a constantly moveable feast. The tiny numbers at the lower end of the school (10 pupils in year 6 at time of writing) quadruple by year 12, and there's a large intake post-GCSE.

Exit: Almost all to the great and good of music colleges, top universities to read music, and conservatoires. Strongest numbers to Royal Academy of Music, Royal College of Music, Guildhall School of Music and Drama, Royal Welsh College of Music and Drama and the Royal Conservatoire of Scotland. Several to study abroad – Hochschule für Musik Leipzig (piano) and International Academy of Music and Performing Arts, Vienna (violin) both featured in 2021. One to Oxbridge in 2021. The occasional pupil goes completely off piste and chooses to read anything from history to neuroscience – no trends here, but we're talking one or two per year. Occasional premature departures back to mainstream education – often because families with more academic children struggle with the balance being so enormously in favour of music.

Latest results: In 2021, 77 per cent 9-7 at GCSE: 66 per cent A*/A (88 per cent A*-B). In 2019 (the last year when exams took place), 52 per cent 9-7 at GCSE; 49 per cent A*/A at A level (63 per cent A*-B).

Teaching and learning: Not an obvious place for the academic scholar who also happens to be a musical prodigy, but then again this is not a place pretending to be a one stop shop all for the all-rounder: far from it. 'Music colleges don't require academic excellence ... but we do want parents to trust that the academic side can be delivered.' Public examination results variable from year to year. Subject range limited, and unsurprisingly by far the greatest number of takers are in the artier subjects (English literature, art and music tech consistently most popular), although the diminutive number opting for sciences tend to do quite well. School encourages pupils to take three A levels 'unless performance requirements get in the way'. Cambridge pre-U qualification in music now offered in place of A level music.

GCSEs respectable. Pupils generally take no more than seven or eight subjects (compulsory music, maths, English language and science) – 'our pupils undertake a huge amount of practice; there simply isn't time'. There are so few pupils in years 5 and 6 that they are taught as a single group, and classes throughout are comparatively very small, but increase gradually towards the upper end of the school. Teaching staff vibrant and engaging in the main (occasional parental rumblings that some have been there too long) – with some new appointments really upping the ante. 'The academic side isn't stellar,' say parents (and it's true to say that it doesn't come close to measuring up to other nearby independents in that regard, either in terms of facilities or teaching), 'but it's getting better all the time'.

Theory not taught as a matter of course beyond grade 6 – a cause of consternation for some parents. School adamant, though, that it is offered 'on demand' up to grade 8

But ultimately it's all about the music. Pupils' days begin bright and early with pre-breakfast practice, and continue with instrumental tuition and rehearsals interspersed throughout the day, with supervised practice for the younger pupils. Blessed with music rooms containing two grand pianos apiece and genuinely inspirational music teachers, most of whom also have professorships or senior teaching posts at top music academies and colleges. Having observed one such maestro in action, we are hard pushed to think of a single more dynamic teacher of any subject we have seen (and the pupil was nothing short of breathtaking). Pupils have up to two hours of academic music lessons a day, around two hours weekly of individual instrumental tuition plus between three and (in the final years) up to five hours of timetabled practice per day. Theory not taught as a matter of course beyond grade 6 – a cause of consternation for some parents. School adamant, though, that it is on offer 'on demand' up to grade 8 for those who wish to continue (with exceptionally high results for those who do), and the recent accolade of the Incorporated Society of Musicians' Gold Award for the highest achievement at GCSE music (taken a year early at The Purcell) should give comfort that school has the academic side of music covered.

With one-to-one relationships so fundamental to teaching music, what happens if a pupil and teacher just don't click? 'School is amenable to change,' the parent of one such child told us, 'but parents need to be prepared to intervene.' Abundant performance opportunities, from lunchtime recitals under the discerning eyes of peers and teachers to the full symphony orchestra at Cadogan Hall, and chamber ensembles series at London recital venues (Wigmore Hall, St Martin-in-the-Fields).

Learning support and SEN: Dedicated SENCo works with the 50+ pupils on the register, the majority requiring help with some degree of dyslexia, dyspraxia or dyscalculia but also some ASD (two statemented at time of writing) and ADHD. Assistance also provided to pupils with general organisational and planning skills, particularly around exam time. One-to-one support provided in lessons when required.

The arts and extracurricular: Options vary wildly as there's such a constant intake of new pupils with differing interests, but those with a specific passion are encouraged to start their own club, be it debating, chess or ping-pong. Choir is compulsory, art pursued to a high standard in the delightful stable block atelier adorned with cellos and bicycles hanging from the ceiling and some inspirational two- and three-dimensional work – much of it music themed – on display. A dedicated art technician supports the teaching staff and keen photographers and potters can use the dark room and kiln. Drama 'very good' (and now on curriculum) according to parents, with pupils entering into the spirit with great enthusiasm and delivering some 'highly entertaining' performances.

Sport: Never have we been so reassured by the sight of a boot rack laden with well-worn football boots. Despite the all-pervading musical focus hanging in the air, and only one timetabled PE lesson per week, pupils still enjoy a range of sports including badminton, volleyball and football, mainly of the rather jolly, participative, uncompetitive sort, with the exception of one annual fixture against the Yehudi Menuhin School (the Purcell usually wins). Recent appointment of an enthusiastic young sports teacher has been met with rapturous appreciation. 'He asks the pupils what they want to do, then organises it for them.' Perfect. Sports facilities rather sparse – we were not voluntarily shown the ancient, draughty sports hall (cobwebs present), but see it we did and frankly it does the job, as does the very generous field at the school's rear. Yoga a regular and organised activity to benefit the young musicians' core strength and posture and help avoid injury, and those who wish to are able to use the gym and pool at nearby Bushey Leisure Centre.

Boarding: Majority of pupils involved in boarding life to some degree and they enjoy all the creature comforts of smart, cosy boarding houses. Littlies in years 6 to 8 are in homely co-ed Avison

House, just a hop, skip and jump from the main school building. Run with a true family atmosphere, with its own garden, well kitted-out common room (anyone for table tennis?) and spacious twin bedrooms ('we do have one single, but nobody ever wants it,' the housemistress told us). Accommodation has been designed to be totally flexible, thanks to a clever system of locking doors on the bedroom corridors to allow for fluctuations in the male:female ratio. Full programme of activities runs for these youngsters, including team building at the start of each year.

Sunley House, upstairs in the main school building, is where you'll find some of the girls from years 9 to13 (as well as Rupert, the house labrador), and offers modern rooms, lovely views – and pianos in the bedrooms of sixth form pianists. Peachy. The large, well-equipped common room doubles as venue for film nights, food nights and craft activities (dreamcatchers and crochet recent hits). Gardner & Graham offer the same high quality accommodation for years 9-13, arranged in single-sex corridors. Parents praise house staff as 'wonderfully supportive' and 'so kind', with the only real grumbles relating to the food which, we must agree, was not up to scratch for a boarding school. Tuck box definitely required.

Weekly boarders head home Friday afternoon and the programme for those staying for the weekend is a mix of performance classes, practice and rehearsals with homely activities (baking, takeaways) in the house when time allows. So integral is boarding culture to the school that parents tell us their day pupils can 'feel a little bit out of it' at times.

Ethos and heritage: Not as old as one might expect, despite being the UK's first and oldest specialist music school. Founded in 1962 by Rosemary Rapaport and Irene Forster as The Central Tutorial School for Young Musicians and residing first at concert venue Conway Hall then Morley College in London before relocating to Hampstead. Renamed in 1973 and relocated to its current site – formerly the Royal Caledonian School – in 1998. The drab environs of Bushey and austere Edwardian façade of the school do no justice to the lightness (actual and metaphorical) and vibrancy that lie within. The pristine main school corridors are bathed in natural light and schools with three times the number of pupils would envy the space. First stop on our tour – via a welcoming modern reception area showcasing some 3D artwork – was the coffee shop, frequented by both staff and pupils, and decked out with brightly coloured sofas, tables and chairs. Spacious classrooms, kitted out with all the latest IT equipment, look out over a vast field that could almost fool you it was countryside. The icing on the cake, however, is the fabulous modern music centre at the school's rear with its multitudinous practice rooms, teaching spaces, studio theatre and concert hall. Even for a music school, though, we found the library somewhat lacking in... well, books. Pupils can take out any music score you could think of, but those looking for the latest David Walliams will need to consult Amazon.

So why choose a school like this over a mainstream school with a cracking music department? It's simple, according to the pupils, who are not just mainstream kids with a cracking aptitude for music: 'everyone here is like us.' And if ever a real life school could mirror the Hogwarts wizards versus muggles effect, The Purcell is it. Pupils have often felt 'different' in their former schools and joining The Purcell has enabled them to live, breathe (and probably dream) music in a school where everyone's agenda is the same. Even their senses of humour have a musical slant. Unexpectedly for a hotbed of such great talent, the temperature is pretty low and overall vibe laid back and friendly – pupils told us: 'everyone in the school is a friend... even the teachers'. Lack of uniform underscores relaxed, creative vibe and parents say 'it feels more like a college than a school.' Performance is all part of a day's work – our tour included a lunchtime recital by a trio of year 13s, and nothing could quite have prepared us for the standard of music – we were buzzing for hours afterwards.

Weekend programme is a mix of performance classes, practice and rehearsals with homely activities (baking, takeaways) in the house when time allows

Former pupils include Oliver Knussen (composer and conductor), Nicholas Daniel (oboist and first winner of the BBC Young Musician competition), Catrin Finch (former harpist to the Prince of Wales), Lara Melda (winner of 2010 BBC Young Musician), Janice Graham (leader, ENO Orchestra), and Yiruma (Korean pianist and composer).

Pastoral care, inclusivity and discipline: Crucially, staff:pupil ratio is such that in the event of an issue they have ample time to spend resolving it. Pupils say that bullying is out of the question: 'Everyone respects each other and we're such a small community that a bully would be socially ostracised.' Homesickness in the boarding houses is dealt with 'with incredible patience and kindness', say parents. Despite vast talent pool, school assures us that 'pupils are no more neurotic than other kids', but that the necessary systems are firmly in place to support the pressures, which are different to those experienced by most young people: 'We ask them to work at adult level and need to be aware of the demands that are placed on them.' Pupils say school is very helpful with time management challenges and that they have 'lots of free time' to unwind from performance pressures. School 'extremely firm' around transgressions, according to parents, and alcohol or drug use results in expulsion.

Pupils and parents: Families from all walks of life and social backgrounds, some from the music world, many (around 40 per cent) from other creative industries and occasional bewildered parents who have no idea where their prodigy's talent came from. Tiger parents not an endangered species. A little less than 20 per cent of boarders come from overseas, with largest numbers from Korea and Singapore. Pupils bright and breezy, funny and articulate – totally at ease in this environment with their talent, commitment and work ethic.

Money matters: With boarding fees now comfortably topping £30K it's up there with the top public schools, but very few pay full fees. The majority of places (currently over 140) are funded by the brilliant government music and dance assisted places scheme, school bursary or scholarship.

The last word: In the words of one parent: 'proof that specialist music schools can work'. Not to be entered into lightly – particularly at the younger end of the age range – but here is a greenhouse of a school, providing exactly the right environment for its brilliant young students to flourish amongst like-minded individuals.

Queenswood

33

Shepherd's Way, Brookman's Park, Hatfield, Hertfordshire AL9 6NS

01707 602500 | admissions@queenswood.org | www.queenswood.org

Ages: 11–18

Pupils: 453; sixth form: 92; Boarders: 70 full, 85 weekly/flexi

Fees: Day £21,990 – £25,620 pa; Boarding £26,445 – £36,060 pa

Principal: Since 2016, Joanna Cameron BSc PGCE (40s). Educated at St Stephen's College, Broadstairs where she was a boarder from age 7 (pony in tow) followed by A levels at Moira House School, Eastbourne. Degree in environmental science from St Mary's College, University of Surrey, where she stayed to complete PGCE with specialism in biology. Considered a career in either the RAF or police force, but was 'inspired by my own love of school' to eschew a life in uniform and pursue the path of teaching, firm in the belief that 'every girl should have great opportunities'. First teaching post was at St Mary's, Wantage, where she became head of science, followed by a stint at St Gabriel's, Newbury, before becoming deputy head at Ipswich High School in 2013. Headship of an all-girls' boarding school seemed a natural next step: 'I'm so at home in this environment.'

Was impressed by 'phenomenal' pastoral care and has now improved it further by cementing the structure rather than relying on individuals. Says school is 'passionate about every girl exceeding her expectations, not only celebrating success at the highest level' and keen to communicate that, despite continued uplift in registrations, Queenswood 'will never be an academic hothouse – we get results without tears'. Parents concur that their daughters are 'part of a community that's not just about exams' (perhaps that's why the jungle drums tell us that Q scoops up a fair number of refugees from nearby girls' schools that are found to be either too academically pushy or unfriendly). Exudes a sensible and purposeful aura; parents say she's 'full of determination' and has focused on 'evolution not revolution' since her arrival. All this, wrapped up in a friendly and down to earth demeanour. Says Q has 'such warmth' and seems to embody this herself.

Lives on site with husband, David, a software engineer, and two sons currently schooled at Lochinver House and St Columba's. Entire family visible around campus, often all going to school supper and performances together. 'I want to show our girls that women today really can have it all,' she says. Keen sportswoman – runs, plays hockey and still competes with her horse.

Entrance: Increasing competition for between 70 and 80 places at 11+. Candidates take an entrance exam, attend an interview and do a fun team activity. 'References and spark as important – if not more so – as academics,' we are assured, although school expects successful applicants to be 'at least average or above'. Top feeders are Stormont, Duncombe, Devonshire House, Edge Grove, Heathmount and Manor Lodge. Strong sixth form intake. Candidates must have six GCSEs at 6 or above and 7s in their chosen A level subjects.

Exit: Around 40 per cent leave after GCSEs, mainly lured by co-ed or to experience life outside of the ivory tower. 'Retention into sixth form is tough,' admits head, who is upping the ante to try to hang on to older students – not just with the new sixth form centre on the edge of the site to give it a slightly separate feel, but also with focused events such as talks from eg Tom Kerridge and Clare Balding. Careers department, however, thought to be 'really good' and mirrors school's open-door policy for meetings or CV checking as well as organising careers and networking evenings with OQs and current parents. Majority at 18 to wide range of solid universities – over 65 per cent to Russell Group. Pleasingly broad range of subject choices – no trends. Occasionally some to Oxbridge, though none in the past couple of years. One medic in 2021, and two students heading off overseas (Miami and Massachusetts).

Latest results: In 2021, 67 per cent 9-7 at GCSE; 67 per cent A*/A at A level (81 per cent A*-B). In 2019 (the last year when exams took place), 45 per cent 9-7 at GCSE; 26 per cent A*/A at A level (56 per cent A*-B).

Teaching and learning: Strong results, especially given broad intake. Although these don't place school at top of local league tables (the competition is, to be fair, on the stellar side), few can touch it when it comes to value added. Parents pleased to see the academic ante being upped – science and French reportedly showing marked improvement. Strong modern languages department, with French, Spanish, Italian and Japanese all available up to A level (Japanese increasingly popular partly thanks to a cultural visit to Japan) and Latin from year 7. Chinese GCSE and A level for native speakers if requested. Nine or 10 GCSEs taken by the majority, but the most able can take up to 12, plus the optional HPQ (Higher Project Qualification) which counts as a half. Outstanding GCSE results in maths and science – maths also very popular and reports top results at A level. Psychology, media studies and photography A levels now available – a bid to stop girls looking elsewhere.

At its core a boarding school, though day pupils well integrated ('they are good at discouraging a boarder/day girl split,' one parent assured) and all manner of flexible options

'Gentle setting' in year 7 for maths and English, then science from year 10. Teaching 'aims to be bespoke and individualised' says head, 'all teachers aim to inspire one or two girls every single day' – and with the luxury of a staff/student ratio of 5.5:1 and class sizes never higher than 24 (often smaller), the formula to achieve this is spot on. 'Our USP is that we have time for every girl,' says head. Relationships palpably strong between students and staff and an 'open door' culture pervades: 'my teachers work around me,' one sixth former told us. Trad teaching, although technology well used – all girls have a laptop and google classroom is being 'gently' introduced.

Learning support and SEN: Newly launched personalised learning centre has replaced the traditional SEN department and brings girls with IEP reports, academic scholars and Oxbridge candidates together under one roof 'to get rid of any stigma and ensure all needs are met,' says head. 'It sits nicely with who we are.' Around 10 per cent of cohort are on learning support register at any given time – and are kept on it even after 'graduating' to ensure no slippage. School now aiming to avoid withdrawal altogether and keep support for those with mild to moderate SpLDs as much in the classroom as possible.

The arts and extracurricular: 'Amazing' music department, according to girls, more than half of whom learn at least one instrument, some more. Inspirational departmental head says, 'if they have a talent, I'll try to find it,' and 'anything goes in terms of style – as long as it's good.' Q songwriters are frequently highly ranked in the Amnesty International Protest Song competition – with one recent overall winner. Bands, orchestras and ensembles for every instrument and genre, from percussion band to flute choir. The school CD with performances recorded at Angel Studios we were given to take home made the journey fly by. Plenty of opportunities for international showcasing here too – orchestra and choir tours to destinations including Venice and Florence allow students to perform in world-class settings – next up is Hong Kong in 2020. Drama equally strong, making excellent use of super facilities that include a studio theatre with a full-time dedicated two-man stage crew. Lower and upper school plays are open to all, with girls forming strong friendship bonds across year groups. Recent hits have been Les Mis and A Christmas Carol Gone Wrong (the latter a comedy penned by school staff). Large LAMDA take-up with excellent results.

Sixth formers now have their own centre (currently being extended) with smart studies shared between three or four students, social area and well stocked kitchens

Buzzy art department with artist in residence on hand. We loved the way that art scholars of all ages are brought together to create paintings and installations for display around the school – when we visited they were working on a collection for the new library. Decent take-up of art A level, with a few girls each year heading off to art school. Super textiles too, starting simple with jazzy pencil cases for younger pupils, building up to wedding and evening dresses by senior girls. Leiths cookery course run in preference to food tech (sounds like a good trade to us), taught as a timetabled lesson to years 7 and 8 and as a club thereafter. An abundance of clubs at lunchtimes and after school – girls encouraged to do at least three per week – and even sixth formers pack their schedules with pursuits including Model United Nations and debating, on top of their academic and sporting commitments.

Sport: 'Queenswood's good at everything,' one proud pupil told us. And who are we to disagree? Sport tops the list and it's a battle between hockey and tennis for starring role, parents marvelling at how decidedly unsporty prep schoolers have become passionate sportswomen during their time at Q; 'it's the give it a go attitude that we love,' said one. On the tennis front, school is national LTA clay court centre, hosts the annual national schools' championships, is recommended by the LTA as a destination for wannabe tennis pros and offers tennis-specific sports scholarships. It boasts no fewer than 25 courts – 12 clay and 13 all-weather. New sports hall has replaced antiquated indoor tennis centre. Hockey played competitively for two terms on the impressive Astroturf; tip-top coaching sees many girls reach county and some national level and trophies and cups abound. Students can also choose options including athletics, gymnastics, fencing, swimming in modern indoor pool, sailing, badminton and tag rugby. Football less popular but sometimes played if demand is there, school is a UK hub for girls' cricket – a recent masterclass with former England captain has left girls 'absolutely inspired', say parents – and the recent introduction of a dance scholarship has put that firmly on the school map too.

Elite athletes across all disciplines are carefully mentored; fitness coaches devise bespoke programmes, advise on diet etc and school accommodates external training and fixtures for these high flyers (a GB skier, a GB sailor and a GB tumbler currently in their number). Parents of less elite players report delightedly that emphasis is on health, nutrition and fitness too. Tons of sports tours, recently tennis to Catalunya and Rome, years 7 to 9 hockey to Barcelona and biennial senior hockey to eg South Africa and Sri Lanka. Well-being introduced in year 11, with options including yoga, couch to 5K, boxercise, riding, golf and basketball. Up to six sporting activities on offer every lunchtime: 'it's the rich non-academic life that makes all that maths and physics worthwhile,' quipped one parent.

Boarding: At its very core a boarding school, although day pupils well integrated ('they are good at discouraging a boarder/day girl split,' one parent assured us) and all manner of flexible options, from one to four nights, now in place as well as full boarding (mainly international students, who account for about a quarter of the school population) and occasional boarding too. Majority of accommodation over two floors in main school building. More functional than inviting with very little personal decoration in place and no sign of a tidy dorm policy – perhaps Queenswood girls are so busy they don't have time to hang around and enjoy their dorms, although when we popped in at break time, rooms were awash with girls hungrily getting their morning social media fix. Decorative improvements are afoot, however, so watch this space. Sixth form accommodation is better, with bright and cosy common rooms, views across the rolling hills and playing fields and a full kitchen for students preferring to prepare their own meals. Two staff members live in each house. Very small boarding numbers in years 7, although recent dramatic reduction in boarding fees for these years (now cheaper to weekly board than travel on some bus routes) hopes to see this change. Almost half board in some capacity in year 8. Lively programme of activities for full boarders, with cooking, crafts and trips – often making the most of proximity to London – and sixth formers are allowed into London in pairs, although older girls in particular appreciate 'lots of free time'. Day girls can stay for any meal with no charge.

Ethos and heritage: Founded in Clapham Park in 1894 before moving to current location – a purpose-built neo-Tudor building, set amongst 120 acres of sports fields, woodland and immaculately clipped gardens – in 1925. Rarefied in the extreme. Just two miles from the M25 but still somehow in the middle of nowhere. Passing through the monogrammed, wrought-iron gates the real world is left behind and immersion into a pristine, wholesome universe feels absolute. Rolling programme of improvements keeps things fresh – there's no particular jewel in the Queenswood crown but perhaps more a tiara of equally shining attributes. Sixth formers now have their own centre (currently being extended) with smart studies shared between three or four students, social area and well stocked kitchens. Super theatre with all mod cons and stunning new library – an airy, vaulted art deco affair housed in the Old Pool Hall.

Girls, smart in grey and purple, are friendly and down to earth. There's an air of innocence about them – not a spiky edge in sight. All appreciate the 'immense trust' that pervades school: 'we can leave our stuff around and know that it will be safe,' one told us.

Although this is a reasonably conservative environment, head says 'we don't shy away' from issues with eg sexuality: 'differences are totally accepted'

Carol Thatcher's an old girl, as are tennis ace Naomi Cavaday, actress Helen McCrory and TV presenter Lady Georgie Ainslie.

Pastoral care, inclusivity and discipline: Pastoral care uniformly 'phenomenal', according to parents. In a competitive landscape of academic hothouses and sharp elbows, Queenswood seems elevated to a higher stratosphere permeated by kindness and support. Sure, there are 'friendship issues' like everywhere else, but students told us that anything over and above day-to-day spats 'gets shut down really quickly'. Head describes communication between staff as 'phenomenal' and mental health issues amongst the students such as anxiety or eating disorders are 'few and far between'. Parents rave about 'proactive approach to teenage mental health'. 'We have so many pairs of eyes on them,' says head, 'and the staff operate as one large team.' Girls say they 'go above and beyond' to help one another – demonstrated by excellent mentoring programme with A level students supporting GCSE strugglers where needed. Sixth form students are able to choose their personal tutor and meet with them weekly to discuss progress or concerns.

Almost every dietary requirement imaginable catered for by an outstanding canteen staff, delivering top-notch cuisine morning, noon and night. Although a reasonably conservative environment, head says 'we don't shy away' from issues with eg sexuality: 'differences are totally accepted and the vast majority are really accepting of one another.' But is all this kindness and such a heavily rarefied environment really preparing students for the big bad world out there? Head believes so: 'we actively encourage risk taking and failure, to develop resilience,' she says. Transgressions? 'Very few. I'm lucky,' says head. No drugs enforcements on recent record and just one alcohol-related misdemeanour, resulting in exclusion. Mixed views on socials with boys' schools. Some girls we spoke to wanted more, some none at all. Lochinver's on the dance card for the younger girls, with Bedford and Radley for the older ones. Thankfully, some bright spark did away with the year 7 disco recently and replaced it with a mini Olympics-style team-building event: 'much more fun,' said one attendee.

Pupils and parents: Around half of all pupils board, with a quarter of these from overseas, largely Hong Kong and mainland China, and all continents represented. Increasing numbers of first-time buyers plus north London families looking to escape the hothouses by taking advantage of Q's bespoke transport service. Active parents' association organises plenty of social activities throughout the year and helps with fundraising efforts. All sixth formers awarded a silver Q brooch – presumably to help them identify one another in the 'real' world. The Old Queenswoodians' Association is some 4,000 members strong and branches across the globe in readiness to support and advance its members whatever their location or chosen field. Speech days are attended not just by current pupils and their families, but also a handful of old girls – some in their 80s – who come to socialise and share in the successes of current pupils.

Money matters: Day fees on the high side compared to local competition – and that's without the pricey, albeit bespoke, door-to-door transport service. Occasional means-tested bursaries and discount for Forces families. Majority of scholarships are honorary, offering additional support or training rather than monetary value.

The last word: Pushy parents move along – this is not the place for you. But if you want your daughter to experience all the sport, arts and extracurricular that Queenswood has to offer, whilst securing some pretty decent grades (and staying sane in the process), we strongly advise a visit.

The Royal Hospital School

34

Holbrook, Ipswich, Suffolk IP9 2RX

01473 326200 | admissions@royalhospitalschool.org | www.royalhospitalschool.org

Ages: 11–18

Pupils: 732; sixth form: 101; Boarders: 279 full, 213 weekly/flexi

Fees: Day £17,097 – £19,017; Boarding £26,126 – £35,319 pa

Headmaster: Since January 2016, Simon Lockyer, previously second master at Portsmouth Grammar and housemaster and head of department at Wellington College. Educated at Blundell's School, Devon. Married with three children, all in the school. Affable and pin-sharp, parents describe him as 'approachable, positive, ambitious for the school – and no-nonsense'. He chose headship at RHS for its 'huge potential and the socio-economic diversity of the pupils, which is its strength'.

Entrance: The majority enter at 11 via entrance tests in maths, English and verbal reasoning. At 13+ another 30-40, respectable common entrance performance needed, and there is another influx in the sixth form. A reference from the current school is essential and all prospective pupils have an interview with the head.

Exit: Housemaster jokes 'in the past the RHS alumni organisation was called the royal navy' – over two centuries, 20,000 boys and girls have left the school and joined up but these days about 10 per cent of pupils head to Dartmouth or Sandhurst. 'The rest go on to a huge range of careers and individual pathways – it's a real cauldron-like fire spitting off in all different directions,' says head. Heavyweight universities eg Durham, Exeter, Bath an Newcastle are well represented. Significant numbers take a gap year, often for travel and following courses abroad. Around a third leaves after GCSEs.

Latest results: In 2021, 55 per cent 9-7 at GCSE; 59 per cent A*/A at A level (89 per cent A*-B). In 2019 (the last year when exams took place), 41 per cent 9-7 at GCSE; 26 per cent A*/A at A level (56 per cent A*-B).

Teaching and learning: Head aims high academically and results are taking off. 'We're a comprehensive school in intake,' says head, who has brought greater academic focus to the curriculum and more subject choice. Pupils take nine or 10 GCSEs. Year 13s take three or four A levels as well as an academic elective subject or EPQ. Creditable results, given the wide ability range.

Plenty of scope for differentiation, thanks to the 'dynamic modern learning environment' – iPads all over and recognition as a beacon school for safe and effective digital learning. 'Impressive use of technology in lessons,' say parents. Real-world skills – including interviews, aptitude tests, CVs, personal statements, careers advice, mentoring, thinking skills, teamwork, computing and digital literacy, well-being and coping with stressful situations – are embedded throughout the curriculum from year 7. Newly introduced sixth form options include BTecs in enterprise and entrepreneurship, creative and digital media, and sport. Plus sociology A level. 'Parents tell me they don't want a privileged and entitled education,' explains head. 'They want schooling that will prepare their children for the world.'

Learning support and SEN: Twenty per cent of pupils on roll have some requirement for in-class learning support or receive regular lessons provided by the learning support department and about one in eight pupils have EAL.

The arts and extracurricular: 'The difference the school can make to children's characters – that's the real "value added",' says head and certainly the array of co-curriculars is impressive.

Everyone recommended to take art, DT or music GCSE. Expansive art and design department with superb atrium exhibition space. Art and DT carousel offers a taster. Craft and design skills are encouraged and pupils work on projects outside class time. 'If you have a talent they push you to keep it on even if it's not one of your exam subjects,' said a pupil. Impressive investment in and commitment to music – John Rutter opened the superb music school and is patron of the school's annual concert programme, performed by home-grown and professional performers. Recitals hall has spectacular acoustics and two grand pianos, with 10 others in practice rooms, all Bechsteins and Faziolis. Aspiring organists perform on one of four organs, including a grade 2 organ that is a magnet for international performers. In fact, half of pupils learn one or more of a staggering variety of musical instruments (explains our bagpipe-playing guide).

Music compulsory for years 7 to 9 and a popular choice at GCSE and A level. Recording studio and Mac suite for music tech A level and also a club. Busy choir – charity gala concert, two choir concerts, scholars' concerts, as well as a tour to New York and annual performance at St Paul's Cathedral. Regular concerts and performances, besides chapel, for orchestras, ensembles and bands. A 60-strong marching band accompanies pupils' regular military-style parades, known as Divisions ('Divis' colloquially), which is open to all over grade 3 with drummers taught from scratch, including band marching skills – 'not the same as marching with the squad'. Band and guard tour every three years – previously to Canada; China and Dubai next. Members receive free music tuition in return for learning this tricky skill.

Clubs 4.15-6pm – 'technically you could do a different activity every lunchtime and every evening of the week'. Model UN, scuba diving club, Tycoon in Schools, yoga, golf and robotics club – choices for all tastes. DofE starts in year 9 and is compulsory for all. Overseas trips, excursions and tours are put on by academic departments, CCF and co-curricular activities. Four sections of CCF – royal marines, royal navy, army, royal air force – compulsory in years 9 and 10, but many continue. 'It's not a recruitment tool,' said a pupil, 'there's no pressure.' Parents endorse – 'Whilst our son may not go on to a career in the military, the skills he is learning through this are hugely important and transferable to the modern world.'

Divisions remain a cornerstone of RHS tradition and take place on special occasions, such as Remembrance Day, harvest festival, speech day etc. All pupils wear genuine naval uniform, with band and guards marked out by specific gaiters, and 'chiefs' (heads of school and prefects) with their own variations. Says head, 'It might look a little peculiar to watch at first, but no more than the Eton wall game, for example – Divisions are our equivalent. There is nothing more remarkable than watching 750 pupils, without a single member of staff, on the parade ground and taking an enormous pride in it.' Parents agree – 'Whether you are from a naval background or not, I believe most families embrace the school's heritage and Divisions.'

Sport: Not an elite sporting school, but an emphasis on variety. Three games afternoons a week with all the seasonal team sports represented and chances to taste 70-plus activities, from rock climbing on the school's own impressive indoor wall to squash, shooting and kickboxing. Gigantic sports hall (or gymnasium), indoor pool in another vast building and outdoors 96 acres of playing fields. Not to mention the Graham Napier Cricket Academy for girls and boys, golf course and bowls club. With such facilities on-site there's little need to travel, although several annual sports tours.

There is nothing more remarkable than watching 750 pupils, without a single member of staff, on the parade ground and taking an enormous pride in it.' Parents agree

Unsurprisingly, given the school's heritage and Alton Water only a stone's skip away, sailing is a real strength and produces some elite performers. All year 7s receive a full week's instruction – 'we want to find ability among those who are not "dynastic" sailors,' says school's own director of sailing and water sports who teaches on RHS's fleet of 60 dinghies (from beginners' to Olympic classes), four Cornish shrimpers and four powerboats. Many achieve RYA qualifications, enter national and inter-school sailing competitions and have a recreation for life. Sailing scholars have individual tuition from RYA advanced instructors. Sailing trips to the Med and further afield every year.

Boarding: 'Our house is our home,' said a boarder. Houses remain the hub of RHS life for all pupils, whether day or boarding. The house structure now better reflects family life, with a junior house for both girls and boys – boarding and day together – and two houses dedicated to ad hoc boarders. Sixth form house Nelson is very much a stepping stone to university – 'we gradually remove the scaffolding,' says housemaster. Programme of house refurbishment has seen the creation of open-plan sitting areas, snug TV rooms and spacious kitchens, at the same time retaining 1930s features – lighter and brighter.

Day starts and ends in the house with an early 'roll call', then a return at 'stand-easy' (break) for toast and fruit and to pick up books for next lessons from named pigeonholes. After 'mess' – sittings in the dining hall in house groups – another roll call in-house. Prep for the youngest pupils is done in after-school sessions in the main school buildings, but houses have work rooms for extra study. Free time has to wait until after 'stations' (house duties). 'You can slip into the routine quite easily – there's something quite comfortable about it,' said our guide.

Sixth form house now all single rooms, uni-style, with a shower 'cubi' between two, and kitchenettes and laundry areas for pupils to do their own 'civvie' washing in preparation for studenthood. Take pride in your appearance and look after your belongings to stay on the right side of housemaster, who conducts a routine room inspection – best floor rewarded with Krispy Kreme.

Twenty-six-bed medical centre has a full-time nurse and there's a school doctor and dentist (NHS), plus a counsellor who can be seen confidentially.

Ethos and heritage: Long and distinguished association with seafaring and the Navy sets the tone, although a conscious evolution – 'removal of the anchors,' in head's words – over the past 30 years has loosened some of the practical strictures and focused on applying the qualities and values of service life to 21st-century education. The Royal Hospital School was founded in the early 18th century at Greenwich in what is now the National Maritime Museum, with a remit to educate boys in mathematics and navigation. A bequest from the estate at Holbrook and a generous endowment prompted a move in the 1930s to the current enviable location on the banks of the river Stour and overlooking Alton Water, and bespoke school buildings, replicating the Christopher Wren architecture of the school's original home.

RHS turned co-educational in 1991 and the first day pupils were admitted in 2006. Today 40+ per cent of pupils are girls and full and weekly boarders make up around 50 per cent to the total roll. School's parent charity, Greenwich Hospital, has invested an impressive £18 million in the site over the last decade but 'you would never build a school on this scale nowadays,' points out head. 'What we've got is really fit for purpose and is built to last. I'm not interested in vanity projects – you can spend a lot of money on design plans and consultations and I want every pound to go into creating the greatest impact on educational resources.' Indeed, there's no lack of ideas for the school and, thanks to the recently established development office, the funds to realise them are beginning to be forthcoming. 'We are in a fortunate position as so many alumni had a free education and feel really invested in the school,' beams head.

School was founded in the early 18th century at Greenwich in what is now the National Maritime Museum, with a remit to educate boys in mathematics and navigation

An ambitious programme of refurbishment is well underway, with most houses upgraded, along with the gym, dining hall and many classrooms. Refurbished library includes flexible spaces for learning and collaborating, including extra study areas. Links are being forged beyond the campus, with business, industry and local universities, as well as maintaining the relationship with Greenwich Hospital and the navy. Says head, 'The school was built on a peninsula to be self-sufficient, even with its own water supply, but I am keen on "bursting the bubble" – we don't exist alone.'

Pastoral care, inclusivity and discipline: Nothing but praise for pastoral care from parents – 'school quickly understands students' strengths and areas for improvement and offers them opportunities to challenge and grow,' effused one. Not a huge school – 750 in total – and house system creates worlds-within-worlds, where students say they feel safe and secure and well known as individuals by the adults responsible for their care. 'No one-size-fits-all approach,' noted a parent. Particular understanding of the challenges facing children of Forces families – 'there was a lot of moving about before I joined RHS,' said one such pupil, 'but now I have stability in my life and I feel the school deals with the difficulties really well.'

Saturday school, afternoon sports fixtures, clubs, Sunday Divis and chapel make for a busy life, but staff are on hand to help pupils to learn the skills of time management and to make sure day boys and girls don't miss out. Most boarding schools run on copious quantities of food and the RHS mess hall dishes up a daily full breakfast including granola and fruit compote, lunch with a 'theatre bar' special of the day (eg Szechuan chicken chow mein, potato or pasta dish), mess at 6pm serves up still more, followed by toast and supper snacks available in-house. Anyone still peckish can raid his or her tuck box.

Older students are encouraged to take responsibility. Six heads of school – two heads and four deputies – and around 28 prefects have duties in the mess hall, at Divis and around the school, and the mantle of role models. Sixth formers have the freedom to go out at weekends but often prefer to see what's going on at the in-house bar, which allows the odd drink and puts on themed party nights. All are aware of the school's position on banned substances (expulsion) and relationships (courting allowed outside lessons only). 'There is a clear line on bad behaviour and a consistent approach,' reported a parent, 'which is refreshing after our experience previously where it varied greatly.'

Pupils and parents: Growing local day population mixes with boarders from across the UK and the world (13 per cent of the roll from currently 21 countries). Still a high number of Forces families (10 per cent), with naval families supported by parent charity Greenwich Hospital. London is an hour away and school helps with lifts to the station, airport etc, and provides a 'blue box' repository for travelling pupils' belongings over the holidays. Most staff are East Anglian; 85 per cent live on-site.

Head encourages parents to 'throw themselves in' as much as their children – a recent Remembrance Day service attracted 2,500 people and had to be run twice to accommodate them all – and houses host popular family social events. Parents address staff by first names and vice versa 'which gives a warm community feel and sense of mutual respect to the relationship we have with the school,' said a parent. 'A surprising informality, given the military connections…' Easy access to teaching and house staff either in person or via email and a useful parent forum sounding board gives feedback on recent or suggested initiatives. Social media is a constant link for parents further afield.

Money matters: Complex range of awards and bursaries. School offers a limited number of academic, sporting, drama, music, art and sailing scholarships each year. The value of the award is at the discretion of the headmaster and can be topped up with a means-tested bursary. From five to 25 per cent discount for siblings. Forces families claiming the continuity of education allowance (CEA) are also eligible for discounted fees. Greenwich Hospital bursaries and discounts for the children of seafarers also available, depending on family income.

The last word: A school unlike any other – modern interpretation of naval heritage suits a diverse intake of day pupils and boarders. Super sailing and music. Pastoral care paramount.

Royal Masonic School for Girls

35

Rickmansworth Park, Chorleywood Road, Rickmansworth, Hertfordshire WD3 4HF

01923 773168 | enquiries@rmsforgirls.com | www.rmsforgirls.org.uk

Ages: 11-19

Pupils: 701; sixth form: 186; Boarders: 77 full, 19 weekly/flexi

Fees: Day £19,095 – £19,278; Boarding £30,609 – £33,198 pa

Head: Since 2017, Kevin Carson BA MPhil PGCE (40s), previously co-interim head at The Grammar School at Leeds. Has headed up the English and drama departments at Cheltenham College and subsequently Abingdon School, also taking on the role of resident tutor in boarding houses in both schools. He particularly championed equal opportunities for his female tutees within Cheltenham's co-educational environment.

Original plan was to go into academia, but after spending 'more time in the library than with people' while doing his postgrad, he 'realised a more sociable career might suit me better.' Became so passionate about teaching as soon as he'd tried it that 'friends said I talked about nothing else – not even small talk,' he laughs. Still teaches year 7s and 8s and sixth formers. 'It's absolutely the best way to get to know the students,' he says.

With his broad (by southern standards) Scouse accent and laid-back demeanour, he's certainly not your stereotypical headteacher of a home counties private girls' school, but parents and pupils are thrilled with him. 'Make no mistake, he had big boots to fill,' says one parent, 'but I think everyone would agree he is absolutely dedicated to the children and it shows.' Girls say he is 'around a lot, whether teaching, doing lunch duty or assemblies and sometimes he just pops into lessons – we really feel we know him.'

Married to Sarah, with two daughters, both in the junior school. Outside of school, the family pursues a wide range of sporting and cultural interests.

Entrance: Increasingly selective (but nowhere near as much as some local schools), RMS is seen by more and more parents as a desirable option. Majority join at 11+ but some places are also available up to 14+. Online test in maths, English and reasoning. There's also a creative writing exercise, group activity and group interview. School looks closely at report from current school as well as test results. Candidates for entry in later years sit tests in English, maths and non-verbal reasoning.

Boarders are treated to an outing every Saturday (bowling, cinema, horse riding, theatre, London attractions etc), with occasional trips further afield

Around 170 girls compete for approximately 60 places. About a third come from state primaries; a further third from local preps (Maltman's Green, Charlotte House and Orley Farm are main three feeders); and the final third from school's own prep, Cadogan House (guaranteed entry, making for a mixed bag academically). Good sibling policy – a relief if younger ones aren't as starry as big sister. Around 25 new places are available in year 12, with girls being selected on GCSE results and extracurricular achievements.

In line with its charitable ethos, school offers a limited number of assisted boarding places to disadvantaged children from London boroughs of Hillingdon and Tower Hamlets and (surprisingly) Norfolk. Head says that integration of these girls, and that of the mainly international boarders, is 'fantastic'.

Exit: Around 12 per cent leaves at 16, to local grammars, state schools and college. New year 12 intake balances out the loss. Majority of those who stay the course to university, with around 40 per cent to Russell Group. Exeter, Nottingham, Durham and Warwick all popular. Huge breadth of subjects studied, with engineering and psychology the most popular. Five to Oxbridge (all STEM) in 2021, and three medics.

Latest results: In 2021, 77 per cent 9-7 at GCSE; 64 per cent A*/A at A level (85 per cent A*-B). In 2019 (the last year when exams took place), 57 per cent 9-7 at GCSE; 27 per cent A*/A (53 per cent A*-B).

Teaching and learning: The school does academically better than it's sometimes perceived to. In fact, it's turning formerly dismissive heads and winning more and more parental votes with persistently improving results. Small class sizes (maximum 20) across the board and teachers who 'go the extra mile', with lots of clinics, email correspondence and one-to-ones during lunchtimes where necessary. 'They really get to know us individually and what makes us tick– nobody slips through the net here,' said one pupil. Setting from year 7 in maths and French, with fewer than 10 in some lower sets. More setting (English, science) from year 9 but these are very flexible and it's not unheard of for girls to move from the bottom to top of six sets in the space of a year. Everyone does one modern language from year 7 (out of French, Spanish and German), then in year 8 they pick an additional one (Mandarin and Italian also on offer by this stage). Latin for all from year 7.

Parents say it's a 'good all-round school' where their children get to 'have a go at everything'. 'They are spectacular at finding each child's strengths across the board and then relentlessly nurturing them,' was a typical parent comment. Girls told us they don't feel under pressure, even though homework levels 'can feel very heavy in the upper years'. History by far the strongest department, say pupils ('they just make learning so fun and have so many great staff'), with sciences and maths coming to the fore at A level.

At A level, everyone starts off taking four out of 30 options (all the traditional, plus the likes of psychology, sociology, photography and creative arts). But those taking two A levels in photography or art are treated with as much support as mathematicians and scientists taking four and in any case, three-quarters of pupils drop an A level and pick up an EPQ, whose results are impressive. Handful of BTecs also available, for example in food and nutrition and performing arts. Plus a plethora of non-examined courses in subjects ranging from history of feminism to the more practical cooking at university. Good parent networks mean plenty of top business leaders come in to do one-off talks.

With his broad (by southern standards) Scouse accent and laid-back demeanour, he's certainly not your stereotypical headteacher of a home counties private girls' school, but parents and pupils are thrilled

School claims to cater for the gifted and talented, although a parent said, 'if I had an academically brilliant child – I mean, really at the top end – I have no doubt a more selective school would be better.' Reporting system could be improved, say some parents – 'they give them such good grades that you sometimes are led to believe they're doing better than they are, so it throws you when the exam results come through.'

Learning support and SEN: Excellent on SEN, according to parents, with individual lessons on offer (at extra cost) to girls needing support – around 60 in total when we visited, though none with EHCPs. All pupils screened on entry. Specialist EAL teaching for overseas pupils (again, charged as extra). 'It helps that the school is so transparent and accessible,' said one parent, who claimed her daughter had 'become a different child – so happy and well supported.'

The arts and extracurricular: School has strong artsy feel, with some beautiful pieces peppered throughout the pristine corridors. There's a well-used photography studio and dark room, drama studio and plenty of musical and theatrical productions throughout the year, many performed at the Watersmeet theatre in Rickmansworth. Great excitement about new performing arts faculty opening in 2019 with dance studio, drama studio, music areas and all-new recording studio. Musical opportunities abound, with 300 girls learning an instrument and concert orchestra, various ensembles and choirs, along with an emphasis on jazz groups.

Trips and tours of all sorts and vast array of extracurricular activities, including very popular DofE and cadets, means the school continues to buzz after lessons are over. Girls enthuse over chess and Chinese clubs as much as astronomy (in school's own planetarium – there's an astronomy GCSE on offer too) and taekwondo. Plenty of charitable works, with prefects nominating a charity for the school to support each year.

Sport: Gymnastics, trampolining, dance, squash et al take place in a jawdropping double sports hall. Acres of playing fields, great for cross-country and adventure training, and all-weather pitch, with football, cricket and rugby most recently on the up. Trophies galore for the competitive, especially in hockey, netball (internationally), gymnastics and swimming (nationally). Big push on inclusivity to give the less naturally sporty a love of physical activity (including PE lessons for all including sixth formers and alternative options such as zumba, pilates and yoga on offer).

Boarding: Three boarding houses with most boarders in years 10 to 12. Around 40 per cent of boarders from overseas – Europe, the Far East, Russia and further afield. Also popular with Forces families.

Boarders are treated to an outing every Saturday (bowling, cinema, horse riding, theatre, London attractions etc), with occasional trips further afield, with recent examples including Brighton and to Harry Potter studios. Older girls allowed to London in groups for shopping and lunch and in years 12 and 13 to the cinema in the evenings. 'It's incredibly warm and welcoming, and they get the balance just right about how much independence you get,' one girl told us.

We visited the most newly refurbished house which, like the rest of the school, was spacious, clean and well equipped, as well as being cosy and homely with all the mod cons. Dorms with up to four girls per room in younger years; and up to two for sixth formers. Tidiness clearly not a priority for some, suggesting more lenience on that front than at some schools we visit. Light, bright and modern dining room, where boarders and day girls take all their meals, feels like a hub of chatter at lunchtime, with girls seated at sociably round tables, enjoying freshly cooked meals which are, according to all, 'outstanding'.

Ethos and heritage: Founded in 1788 to educate the children of masons who had fallen on hard times, the current 150-acre site, built in the 1930s, is the school's fourth home. A vast campus, more akin to a redbrick university than a suburban girls' school, with smart, identikit buildings surrounding two quadrangles ('teeming with girls chatting in the summer term,' said one), and the longest teaching corridor in Britain. Became an independent school, open to all, in 1978.

Great sixth form centre – comfortable common room, complete with black and pink sink-into sofas, and café area. Girls describe guidance at this stage of their education as 'excellent', with teachers giving up free time to help with UCAS applications, although some parents said they would like to see 'more emphasis on Oxbridge applications'. Spectacular rotunda library, one of the nicest we've seen, with plenty of space for quiet study. Atmosphere is serene (so much so that you sometimes wonder where all the girls are) and purposeful, but with a good dose of fun thrown in the mix, although girls told us there could be 'more integration between the year groups'.

Small class sizes (maximum 20) across the board and teachers who go the extra mile', with lots of clinics, email correspondence and one-to-ones during lunchtimes where necessary. 'They really get to know us individually and what makes us tick – nobody slips through the net here'

This is a forward-looking school, but with a strong sense of tradition – RMS is the only school in the country still to do 'drill': a spectacle of pinafored girls with pinned-back hair performing something akin to synchronised swimming but without the water (they recently appeared on The One Show). Places in the squad are highly sought after, with dozens volunteering even for the reserves.

Pastoral care, inclusivity and discipline: Often chosen by parents precisely for its pastoral focus, the school is regularly invited to talk about their tactics at national conferences. So what's their secret? 'Time,' says the head – every teacher has enough time to support the individual girls, as well as to bring up issues, no matter how small, during weekly staff meetings. 'She's loving science but is worried about her French vocab test' and 'She's had a fall-out with her friends but worked it all out now' etc. Sixth formers are trained as peer mentors by the school counsellors, with year 9 girls taking on 'big sister' roles to new year 7s. School acutely aware that friendship groups formed in year 7 sometimes break up in year 8 or 9 and on the ball in how to deal with it, with specific friendship mediator on hand. 'It means it rarely turns to bullying,' girls told us.

Behaviour is excellent – girls put it down to mutual respect with staff. Parents add that school has never been afraid to 'take a hard line' when necessary and has even been known to call in police to educate girls on the outcomes of certain scenarios if they rear their ugly heads. School claims alcohol, drugs etc are 'not an issue'; girls concur. On a more micro-level, girls say the school 'isn't strict, but there are a lot of rules, especially around things like uniform'. Detentions aren't as readily handed out as at some schools, though, with a whopping five black marks before one is handed out.

Pupils and parents: For over 200 years, this was a school for families facing hardship and although it's now fee-paying, the culture seems to have stuck, with girls well grounded and grateful to be there. Seemingly younger and fresher than their more streetwise grammar peers, RMS girls are nonetheless confident and articulate too. Ethnically reflective of the local area – mainly white, with a large British Indian contingent and sprinklings of other backgrounds.

Parents – an exceptionally sociable bunch – from all walks of life from the well-heeled to hard working, dual-income, first-time buyers. 'But as a working mum, I'm still a minority,' said one. Some expats and international parents, largely of overseas boarders. Many from across the Chilterns and Hertfordshire, with an increasing north London crowd. The school provides an excellent coach service from all these areas, with the London brigade able to take advantage of the shuttle bus from the tube station. Parents of girls at smaller prep schools reported a bit of a culture shock when their daughters joined this vast establishment, but added that they felt totally at home 'after just a few weeks'.

Money matters: Capital expenditure is underpinned by an endowment set up by the Masons and the school is a tenant of the site. Multitude of scholarships and exhibitions available at 11+ (academic, all-rounder, art, music and sport) and sixth form (performance arts added) typically offering 25 per cent discount on fees. Five per cent discount for siblings and 10 per cent for Forces families. Means-tested bursaries available.

The last word: Academically on the up, RMS is now a serious contender in the competitive local market, with top-notch facilities also a pull for many families. Teachers adept at drawing the best out of everyone, whatever their abilities, and the emphasis on the arts and extracurricular means girls leave well-rounded and confident. Nurturing, but not to the point of being a bubble, this is a school that walks the walk when it comes to focusing on the individual. 'I can tell you about my experience here, but it won't be the same as anyone else's and that's the great thing about this school,' was the kind of comment we heard time and time again from girls, although pushier parents might still prefer some of the more selective local schools.

Queenswood

St Christopher School

Barrington Road, Letchworth Garden City, Hertfordshire SG6 3JZ

01462 650850 | admissions@stchris.co.uk | www.stchris.co.uk

Ages: 3-18

Pupils: 516; sixth form: 62; Boarders: 20 flexi

Fees: Day £11,979 – £19,944; Boarding £22,095 – £34,545 pa

Head: Since September 2020, Emma-Kate Henry, who was deputy head from 2009-2013, thence to lead Hampshire Collegiate School and d'Overbroeck's in Oxford. Has experience in London comps, a selective single-sex independent, a city tech college and co-ed all-through independent schools – a deliberate decision to experience a broad spectrum. Read English lit and African and Caribbean studies at Kent; PGCE from IoE. Went into teaching after a gap year teaching special needs in Jamaica proved more satisfying than an initial foray into IT recruitment in the City after first leaving university.

Likeable, chatty and we imagine quite a forceful personality – she's going to get things done. Despite a tricky start with Covid restrictions and lockdowns, she's already getting on with it. She understands the St Chris ethos and parents trust her because of it, despite very few having met her as yet. 'She's a good fit,' said one parent. 'She will push things on,' said another. Is on a mission to persuade parents that 'being liberal and progressive does not mean academic ambitions aren't met. You can have it all at St Chris. Some parents think they are taking a risk with us, I want to change that.' Plans afoot to retain more at sixth form and increase size of it. Now that school has reopened her mission is to get to know all pupils in person.

Entrance: The school has wonderfully popular open days and many parents visit several times to get a feel of the school. Applications are followed up with a meeting with parents, and a separate interview with the child, to make sure that expectations match. All applicants over year 4 are given cognitive ability assessment which is age related. They aim to accept a small number of pupils with individual needs each year if the school can match a child's needs to school resources. Mild dyslexia well supported with extra individual (paid for) lessons, high-functioning verbal pupils with ASD seem to do well, and especially good for those who may not thrive elsewhere – the anxious child, for example. Head says that some children will benefit from being here, but prospective students need to show cognitive ability at average levels or above. Oversubscribed senior school, and years 5 and 6 generally full too but worth contacting the school directly. Sixth form to be expanded. Children with individual needs must apply by early November for the following year.

No taster days for 2021 entry in junior school; socially distanced assessment mornings are running at the senior school. Sixth form entry via video interview with head or head of sixth form.

Exit: All early years move on to junior school, and almost all move from junior to senior school. Quite a bit of movement at 16 as London students get weary of the commute and move to sixth form colleges in the big smoke, and some are just ready for a change or move to technical colleges.

As for higher education, interesting split between the large number who go on to do art (around a quarter) and those who do engineering, science and maths. Some applying for foundation art courses were offered the degree course directly since they were so well prepared by St Chris. A good range of universities, including Russell Group. LSE, Edinburgh, Bristol, Durham, Manchester, UCL, Central St Martins, Leeds, Arts University Bournemouth and Southampton all popular. Parents spoke of 'strong support with UCAS and uni choices.' A special extension group prepares sixth formers for entry into the most demanding courses. Courses range from electrical and electronic engineering to history and psychology to product design.

Latest results: In 2021, 53 per cent 9-7 at GCSE; 51 per cent A*/A at A level (75 per cent A*-B). In 2019 (the last year when exams took place), 28 per cent 9-7 at GCSE; 29 per cent A*/A at A level (52 per cent A*-B).

Teaching and learning: Not narrowly academically selective, yet clearly a school with an expectation that each child is hungry to learn and participate. Independent learning is encouraged throughout the school by teachers who are enthusiastic, energetic and creative. This helped many when the dreaded home schooling hit win the pandemic. During lockdowns the school provided a full timetable of online lessons, including extra sessions for learning support. All parents pleased with efforts – 'They did a good job under the circumstances,' we heard. Parents happy that teachers and staff kept in close touch offering encouragement and support.

Nursery has more space than usual with plenty of outside play areas – grassed, soft surfaced and a covered 'outside classroom' with lots of equipment clearly being well used for learning. Historically Montessori, so lots of practical learning, playing and making but now following the EYFS curriculum with clear evidence of more formal phonic learning and number work. Children seen in wellingtons in the garden as well as in wonderful fairy dressing up clothes. Nursery and reception children well prepared for reading and writing when they are ready.

The trips get more exotic as the students move up the school – Rajasthan one of the most original we have seen. Hopefully all will be back on the agenda before long

In the junior school, topic-based learning and much creative planning seems to allow students to develop and research ideas, which allows for more independent learning than usually seen in a junior school. Topic learning across all subjects very much in evidence – stretching the topic to music and maths not just in humanities. Small classes (20 average) with a teacher and teaching assistant in each airy classroom. Desks grouped – a sign of collaborative learning with lots of space for carpets, beanbags, making and creating. Early introduction to democracy with class rules and ethos very much child instigated. The junior library is extremely well and widely resourced – a joy in this technology based era – with pupils and parents encouraged to take books out at any time even if the enthusiastic dedicated junior school librarian not available. Interesting to see extension maths allowing for more challenging work. Learning support staff in the junior school take pupils out of class but pupils also given in-class support.

Five one-hour lessons each day in the senior school so no rushing between lessons with bags full of books, and as a result much less tension all round. Extra impressive therefore that they manage to give such a breadth of subjects (though no Latin or RS). Spanish and French expected for all students, where appropriate. Language exchange trips considered a rite of passage and something to look forward to in year 10. Geography trips also popular as is the history war graves trip to northern France. The trips get more exotic as the students move up the school – Rajasthan one of the most original we have seen. Hopefully all will be back on the agenda before long. Creative English learning involving role play, drama, filming and journalism work. Setting in maths from year 7 then more subject setting in year 9. Separate sciences from year 9.

Sciences and maths get particularly good GCSE results, as do English, arts and 3D Design. Parents and students appreciate being able to choose whatever combination of 18 GCSE subjects they want with no timetable limitations or restrictions. Subjects include film studies, additional science, PE and Spanish. At A level there are even more subjects to choose from, with the arts and sciences getting particularly impressive results. Career evenings and seminars to help students from year 11 onwards with choices for further education. Extension classes for Oxbridge candidates and extended project qualification for those with particular interests.

Learning support and SEN: Dedicated learning support staff in both junior and senior parts of the school take students out of classes for extra (paid for) lessons as well as supporting in class – this continued through home schooling. Touch typing taught before school to those that want it from year 5 onwards and we saw several students with laptops as well as having amanuensis (teaching assistant writing for them – particularly useful in exams). The school takes a small number of pupils with individual needs each year but these places fill early with cognitively bright dyslexic pupils and a few with ASD or ADD. Pre-screening for children with SEN, so apply by November in order to be considered to make sure the school has enough provision in place for individual needs. Parents very impressed with SEN department and support offered, including for those slightly anxious about returning to class.

The arts and extracurricular: St Chris is often chosen for its wider curriculum offerings. Art, music and drama not considered soft options but very valued subjects. A very lively music department with practice rooms for individual instrument learning as well as much music creation in music technology suite. Bands and groups abound – some students we spoke to (in pre Covid days) were delighted to go to a gig in a north London pub and see one of their school bands on stage. Plenty of opportunities to perform at weekly Morning Talks. More jazz and rock and small ensembles than classic orchestras, although these too exist. Junior school choir and some singing. Lots of recitals and performances held online but all desperate to get back to 'real life.'

A large theatre building ideal for drama classes and huge annual musical productions. All the school involved in these extravaganzas, and if you don't like to be in the limelight, lots of opportunities backstage, in production and stage management.

This school is well known for its visual art department which is marvellously well resourced – sewing machines, pottery studio, printing room, multi-media studio, woodwork, metalwork, fine art in very mixed media. A whole room dedicated to displays of their work – and one rather wonderfully designed piece of woodwork even ended up in a shop window in Carnaby Street to display shoes.

The school exudes clean orderliness, which is surprising in view of the reputation it has for being liberal. Students wear their own clothes, call teachers by their first names

The Forest School site is generous and gloriously muddy and wooded and well used. An impressive climbing wall up the whole of one side of a classroom block. But there are also trees in the grounds that are specifically 'climbing trees' – any child welcome to climb in break time if they think they can get up and down. Such a joy to see kids climbing trees in these health and safety conscious days. Plenty of fruit trees and others growing in the extensive grounds. The apple trees are picked and juiced in October by the students who get a bottle to take home. Other growing areas including a wormery from which compost is made and sold locally or used here. Nothing wasted from vegetarian school lunches. A garden shed designed and built by students made from recycled plastic bottles and bamboo sticks provides a good greenhouse for seeds and plants before planting out. And the role of food is not only evident in the growing and composting, but of course in the cookery suite. The Vege Centre is a serious part of the school curriculum where students are taught to make meals not just bake scones. The enthusiasm for all these extracurricular activities was brought home, according to one mother whose son came home eager to show off his cooking skills one day and another time wanting to make a board game.

Once a week there is an enrichment programme allowing students to choose an activity to explore – film making, jewellery, yoga, tai chi, philosophy, dependent on the interests and skills of current staff, supplemented where necessary by external tutors. These are across the age groups so give an opportunity for different years to get to know each other and perhaps explains the familial atmosphere.

Sport: Despite the non-competitive ethos, successful sports teams that definitely punch above their weight for such a small school. Everyone is involved and the theory is that this brings up the weaker sportspeople – evidently it works. Matches against local teams and county games. Netball, rugby, football, tennis, volleyball etc. Indoor swimming pool used from early years up – for swimming lessons and fun swim club as well as squad training. It is also an opportunity for older students to obtain a lifeguard certificate so they can work at school or outside in the holidays. Heaven to find a pool with a very civilised and warm temperature of 28 degrees. More sports in lunchtime clubs and after school – rambling, cross-country, cycling, jogging, dance, canoeing, trampolining, athletics and fitness training. Their spacious green fields much in use when we visited for an inter-school football competition with five games going on at a time.

Boarding: Extremely flexible boarding available from year 7 upwards. Where there is space and availability, pupils can choose between 'day boarding' between 7.30am and 7.30pm which includes breakfast, supper and supervised homework, flexi boarding just for the odd night, weekly boarding from Sunday evening to Friday afternoon or full boarding. Inevitably more full boarders as the students move up the school, especially international students. Two boarding areas according to the age of the student, Sixth form students in a very modern and light extension, and younger years in cosy traditional rooms in the heart of the school. Many of the rooms are single ones – privacy being part of the respectful ethos of the school.

Kind houseparents, resident tutors and gap students involved in weekend activities, and each teacher also responsible for one Saturday activity a year. Weekly evening activities available include movie night, cookery, games nights. Weekend activities almost always involve a trip away from school. Cooking facilities for snacks available to students, though older students have a good kitchen and cook for a weekly supper club. Meat meals are available for boarders after the vegetarian-only daytime school canteen. Despite separate boarding areas, it felt very family-like, with older students and younger all hanging out together. We liked the rule that phones were taken away and charged overnight and only returned in the morning once beds were made (something to start in all homes, perhaps?)

Ethos and heritage: Founded during the First World War, this school aims to treat children as individuals, to be non-judgemental and to encourage independence. The Quaker origins of one of the first heads are reflected in Morning Talk three times a week that always involve a period of silence. This opportunity for silence was also seen when we visited: in the middle of a lively lunch, one student rang a bell, the hall fell silent for a moment, and the pupil thanked the hall and the day continued. The right to ring the bell is clearly a privilege allowing for a moment of calm.

Large grounds and airy classrooms with plenty of space also add to the atmosphere of calm. Set in a quiet road in Letchworth, and based around an arts and crafts building with wood panelled rooms, several newer buildings and extensions: a slightly ramshackle group of buildings, with plenty of opportunity to walk outside between classes. Immaculate grounds and planting and freshly painted and very clean rooms despite the fact that many of the buildings are old. The school exudes clean orderliness, which is surprising in view of the reputation it has for being liberal. Students wear their own clothes, call teachers by their first names, are all doing projects and exploring ideas, and there are no bells between lessons, little noise and a great sense of purpose. Teachers appear passionate and engaged, as do pupils. The friendly and efficient catering staff, ground staff and administrators all spoke of loving their jobs. One doesn't sense hierarchy here at any level. Parents said that they appreciate that the school concentrates on things other than uniform and it was one less thing to pay for and worry about. A parent said the school 'has fantastic facilities, is not overly selective and is all inclusive. What's not to like?'

Pastoral care, inclusivity and discipline: You wouldn't necessarily choose this school if you wanted a safe route or wanted to impose on your child, said one parent, but it really works if you trust your child to make their own choices and the school to nurture and empower them. Parents described it as 'non-pushy but allows the child to pursue what they most want to do'. The pupils do choose – their subjects, the direction they want to take and how they work best. Classrooms were busy with students carrying out their own projects and working at their own pace. This is possible because the teachers work hard and there is so much mutual respect. First-name terms with teachers – we saw pupils open doors for teachers and teachers waiting for pupils in the lunch queue. No pushing and shoving. Older pupils making allowances for younger pupils and sitting together at lunch. More like a family rather than exclusive year groups; something which every parent referred to, 'it's like one large family and we feel part of it too.'

There are also trees in the grounds that are specifically 'climbing trees' – any child welcome to climb in break time if they think they can get up and down

Dedicated head of pastoral care who liaises with heads of year, who in turn meet with advisors or tutors. The fact that students meet their advisors every day means that issues are fed back quickly up the school, and students and parents feel that they always have someone to speak to. Parents we talked to all knew exactly who they could speak to or email with questions or complaints or concerns.

Self-government (a way of introducing democracy and ensuring students are totally engaged in the school) is an important feature of St Chris according to students we met. Anyone can attend the school council, at which student representatives can vote. Any proposals that get passed by the school council go up to a meeting of the entire senior school where each student can vote. Resolutions passed by the school are enacted unless vetoed by the head (which almost never happens). Pupils we met loved the fact that even the youngest child in the senior school could make large things happen – like the building of the cookery Vege Centre.

Pupils and parents: Quite a large proportion of pupils commute from north London thanks to trains from Finsbury Park and school buses. Also some from Cambridge, and more who are either local (as are junior school pupils) or move to be near the school. A growing number of international students, especially higher up the school, who tend to be boarders. This is not a narrowly academically selective school and students and parents really reflect this – some making sacrifices to have their children at St Chris, many 'first time buyers' of private education, some second-generation St Chris families, some bursary students, some with special needs, some with multiple strengths and huge academic ability. Ideal for a family with several children of mixed interests and abilities

– how rare to find a school to suit both the artistic child and the mathematician, the reader and the doer, and to value them all equally. 'It sounded a bit tree huggy and off the wall,' said one parent, 'but they are far from that. It works. I'm so happy I took the risk and all of my children can be at the same school, something I thought would never happen because they vary so much in ability and need.' Parents said they are 'encouraged to be involved' and 'can pop in at any time to ask questions'.

Money matters: This school is built on solid foundations with good transparent governance provisions in place. Financially stable and well supported. The facilities show recent and regular investment and maintenance. Despite having to pay for extras like music lessons and individual learning support lessons, parents say that the school does its level best to keep costs to parents down as much as possible. There are some 100 per cent bursaries and small allowances (10 per cent fee remission) for art and academic scholarships for pupils at years 7, 9 and 12.

The last word: Calm and orderly, busy without feeling hectic. Palpable sense of mutual respect between pupils and teachers, between pupils and other pupils and a sense of confident self-respect in the pupils themselves. Passionate, quietly self-confident and articulate students suggested that this was because everyone felt empowered thanks to their role in the school council and self governance. The ethos of respect included the school buildings – extremely well cared-for with interesting wall displays, spotless toilets and no sign of writing on desks or chewing gum under desks. The pupils are given a voice at this school so there is no need for graffiti.

St Edmund's College

RC 37

Old Hall Green, Ware, Hertfordshire SG11 1DS

01920 824247 | admissions@stedmundscollege.org | www.stedmundscollege.org

Ages: 3–18 (boarding from age 11)

Pupils: 899; sixth form: 135; Boarders: 108 (full/flexi/weekly)

Fees: Day £11,583 – £18,990; Boarding £25,020 – £33,606 pa

Headmaster: Since September 2019, Matthew Mostyn, previously second master at Stonyhurst. Educated at Downside; degree from Exeter. Taught French and German at Cheltenham College, then 14 years at Shrewsbury, including 10 as a housemaster. He is a literary translator and amateur organist and pianist, has directed numerous plays and was an officer in the CCF. Sporty too – a level four rowing coach, he has also coached rugby and still enjoys skiing, country sports, dog walking and – in quieter moments – a good book and The Times crossword. A practising Catholic, in common with 35 per cent of his students. 'We're very proudly a Catholic school,' he says, 'it's why St Ed's exists. But Catholicism is something we propose rather than impose. We are saying: here it is, this is what we believe, this is a way of life and a way of thinking that can bring you great joy in life – if you want to find out more about it, we're here to help, but we're not going to force it. It's a gentle Catholicism.'

Parents describe him as 'warm and a good communicator' and are relieved that he has 'fitted seamlessly into the school's ethos' but many agree that his fresh eye was much-needed – he has already drawn up a wishlist of improvements and appointed development groups to make them happen, starting with sport and tailing off into 'wait and see'.

Prep school head: Since 2013, Steven Cartwright. Joined the school in 2009 as deputy head and became acting head before taking up the post of headmaster. Married with two daughters, one at St Edmund's and the other looking forward to joining in future. Interests include squash, climbing, running. 'My wife and I got married here,' he says, 'this place is close to my heart.' The feeling is clearly mutual – 'Mr Cartwright is so nice,' say pupils and the parents 'adore him', according to one, because he 'hits the right note between wit and seriousness and he's often at the school gates chatting to children and parents'. His first experience of independent school, he still marvels that 'the children here are greatly advantaged – it's a small school feel but with all the facilities and even sheep in the nearby fields to feed at lambing time'.

Entrance: Entrance to nursery from the term following a child's third birthday, subject to observational assessment. Places usually found for siblings but not always, to some parents' dismay. One form entry with 24 places available (teacher and teaching assistant in each nursery, reception class and in forms 1 and 2). Half or whole day sessions with wraparound care from 7.30am until 6pm. Eighty per cent of nursery pupils go right through the school to 18. Further admissions at age 4 by interview and informal assessment; taster morning for joiners in year 3 and up (two forms per year group, max 20 in each) and entry on the basis of tests in maths, English and non verbal reasoning. Children joining before year 4 have 'more or less' assured entry to the college at year 7. 100 places in year 7 – a fifth filled by pupils from own prep school. For the rest there's a half-hour interview with parents and an entry assessment in January – 'we are selective but not to the extent of the academic hot houses in London,' says head. Report from previous school also carries weight. Two applicants for every place. Small additional intake at 13+. Sixth form joiners need five 9-5 grades at GCSE with at least 6 in their chosen A level subjects (and for some subjects 7 or 8).

Exit: Ninety per cent of year 6 transfers to the college; the rest mainly to other independent schools with a few to state system. Up to a quarter leaves after year 11 for state sixth form colleges; occasionally other independents. Most choose university – favourites are UCL, Exeter, LSE, Leeds, Nottingham and Southbank. Sometimes a few medics. Apprenticeships increasingly tempting – GSK and Pilot Training with EasyJet recently.

Latest results: In 2021, 63 per cent 9-7 at I/GCSE; 60 per cent A*/A at A Level (87 per cent A*-B). In 2019 (the last year when exams took place), 39 per cent 9-7 at I/GCSE; 35 per cent A*/A at A level.

Teaching and learning: 'We are emphatically a school that is about developing the whole person, and that takes a lot more than just an academic education,' says head. That said, top grades consistently account for at least a third of results in the college. College (senior school) year groups are named after stages of learning in Latin and Greek: Elements, Rudiments, Grammar, Syntax, Poetry, Rhetoric I and Rhetoric II. Years 7 and 8 (Elements and Rudiments) study combined science; separate sciences from year 9. Choice of French, German or Spanish in year 7, plus another language in years 8 and 9 – at least one must be continued to GCSE. Latin also offered. RE compulsory up to and including GCSE, with other options chosen in year 9. Some GCSE courses start before the end of the year to get a jump on year 10. Sixth formers (known at St Ed's as Rhetoric I and II) have a weekly RE lesson and the (popular) option of A level theology.

Across the school, the last period of every school day is given over to co-curricular activities – 'it is part of the curriculum' explains headmaster

Classes of 10 or fewer in sixth form, 24 below. Parents approve of the attention paid to trends in students' grades and the intervention offered when expectations are not met, although, says one, 'students could perhaps be pushed harder academically'. Widespread appreciation of the teaching quality – 'it has been very high in the subjects our children have selected,' nods a satisfied parent. A broad range of abilities catered for and pupils with SEN requirements are well supported, both in class, in the new dedicated learning support room and at homework club, which takes place four afternoons a week in the college. EAL available and IGCSE second language English is offered to overseas students where appropriate. Careers department works mainly with younger seniors – Poetry (year 11) have one-to-one careers interviews and online testing to suggest suitable options. Two co-directors of sixth form stay with the cohort and help with UCAS management and there is a wide-ranging talks programme (one led by an ex-convict made an impression recently). Most of the dark suit-clad Rhetoric students opt for university but there is also support for degree apprenticeships and half a dozen take them up each year. 'You can talk about your next steps anytime,' says our Rhetoric guide, 'someone is always happy to give advice.'

Broad curriculum in the prep, French from nursery; Spanish and German added in year 4 and rotated through to year (known here as 'form') 6; science lessons in the college labs (also fun learning CSI days and rocket design workshops). History and drama particularly popular according to show of hands in year 5, but ICT, games, art, science (and break-time!) close behind.

Pupils are excited by their learning and bursting to talk about it – recent year 6 battlefields trip made an impression, so much so that the pupils shared their experience on TripAdvisor. High level of exuberance all round and impressive knowledge of and enthusiasm for the school and its history (recent 450th anniversary was a big celebration by all excitable accounts). Year

6s take on roles of responsibility (lots, including school council, house captains, chaplaincy) with pride and sashes, and speak seriously of the importance of bonding with the younger ones in the playground – 'you have to give them as much kindness as you can because they adore you'.

Learning support and SEN: A lot of individual support for SEN and 'intervention groups are not really noticed by the other children,' explains a parent, 'so many of them go out of the classroom to be supported or extended in different areas and subject that it is commonplace.'

The arts and extracurricular: Drums and bongos filled the music room at the college when we visited – a big space used by only 12 at a time as lessons are timetabled against food tech or DT. Several practice rooms and a recording suite – invaluable for GCSE (taken by about a dozen) and A level (a few per year). Good take-up of instrumental lessons, including the organ (morning prayers accompanied by a sixth former), which are boosted by whole-class introductions in years 8 and 9. Music has had an overhaul since the arrival of a new director – 'when I joined it was all analysis of Chopin and things like that but now we learn bass guitar and drums,' beams our guide. A few attend junior programmes at London conservatoires. Annual school concert featuring numerous ensembles including a jazz band. Much-loved Schola Cantorum (80-strong) recently led the mass at Westminster Cathedral and has sung in Douai, the school's birthplace in France, as well as at Canterbury Cathedral and the school's own masses. Chapel choir sings on Sundays in term time and chamber choir performs at weddings, funerals and balls. In the prep, piano, guitar, ukulele played widely (one of our talented guides reeled off her five instrumental lessons a week, including singing and recorder) – a musical bunch and choristers sing in chapel too.

College puts on an annual drama production at Spotlight, a professional theatre at Broxbourne Civic Hall – Hairspray, Les Mis, School of Rock and Me and My Girl recently – auditions open to all, for roles on stage and behind the scenes. LAMDA lessons popular. Specialist drama teacher in the prep (who also presides over forest school) co-ordinates regular productions with a cast of all ages – Madagascar, Aladdin and Oliver were well-received. Weekly dance lesson in nursery and many of the littlest have peripatetic music lessons too. Performing arts colours awarded to the most dramatic in year 6.

Senior art impressive and a few go on to art school. In the prep, there's a weekly art lesson with specialist teacher – clay faces and large animal papier mache models loomed over the art tables when we visited, but also evidence of creative drawing, painting, print-making, clay modelling (kiln in the college) and printing. Prep has recently been awarded Arts Mark Gold status.

Across the school, the last period of every school day is given over to co-curricular activities – 'it is part of the curriculum' explains headmaster. In the prep, Aboriginal art and computing as well as the usual crafts and cooking; in the college, CCF (army and RAF), DofE (bronze, silver and gold with expeditions on foot and by canoe – college is a centre) and Model United Nations, as well as activities associated with academic learning, such as sharing reviews of books with a scientific slant, and rehearsals for a small annual play (latest, One Man Two Guvnors). Prep has annual house (named after important figures in the school's history, throughout the prep and college) competitions for music, drama and dance, judged by an external expert. Plenty of visiting speakers, even in EYFS, which welcomes parents in a range of professions to explain their roles. Prep's Eco-Schools Green Flag award recognises school garden and pupil-led campaigns to support and raise environmental awareness (staff now bring in their own mugs rather than disposables and pupils collect the recycling).

'We are emphatically a school that is about developing the whole person, and that takes a lot more than just an academic education,' says head

Many thousands are raised annually for good causes (often chosen by the students themselves) through the usual sponsored events. Strong links with the local and church community – school hosts Lea Valley Deanery Inset for teaching staff and art workshops and higher achievers' STEM day for pupils ('it's about helping those schools that are not as advantaged as our own' says prep head). Recent 'soup day' saw usual school lunches donated to charity. 'We need to burst the Edmundian bubble every now and again,' says head.

Trips throughout the year – highlights are the year 6 outward bound residential in France ('I personally have a fear of heights so I was very scared but I overcame it,' confides one of our guides) and year 5 week at PGL ('short for parents get lost' we're told) as well as curriculum-inspired visits in college. Annual whole-school activities week at the end of the academic year offers days out and trips abroad for all but sixth formers (who work on their UCAS instead).

Sport: Butler Hall is the PE venue for the whole school, the sports hall floor a network of lines marking courts for a multitude of games. A rotating menu of options for seniors including water polo, boxing, cardio training, fencing and golf. 'I'm crazy about badminton so I'm really pleased the school introduced me to it,' enthuses our college guide. Indoor pool is used regularly by all, even nursery. Outdoors, acres of pitches for the usual round of hockey and netball for girls, rugby and football for boys, athletics and tennis for all in the summer. Day-to-day, the atmosphere is serene. Students are courteous and smiley as they make their unhurried way around the main college buildings, which have the feel of a cathedral crossed with a military academy – austere and magnificent in equal parts and requiring near-constant maintenance. The latest refurbishment focused on the science labs and used money raised on the occasion of the college's 450th anniversary. Rugby and cricket coaching by professionals but parents would welcome a keener focus on core sports – grumbles about 'poorly led and attended' sessions in the college and a 'weak' fixture list against local state and independent schools; head says fixture list is being reviewed and a new director of sport has been appointed with a brief to transform sport provision across the College.

Prep pupils have a sports programme that includes cross-country, basketball, girls' football and boys' hockey and there are inter-house sports competitions as well as matches against other schools – 'we win a lot' says our sporty year 6 guide, but points out that 'if you put your full effort into the sport you'll be in the team'. True to the ethos, both the elite and the simply enthusiastic are 'applauded and encouraged equally' approve parents, because 'at St Ed's it's cool to be kind and cheer on your peers'. Bognor Regis football camp for year 5.

Boarding: 'A day school with boarding attached,' says head. Full boarders are mainly international students (20 countries represented) but flexi-boarding is becoming more popular and head expects weekly boarding to grow. One house for boys and one for girls on the upper floors of the main college building (with the best views across countryside as far as Stansted airport and even a glimpse of Canary Wharf on a clear day). Single rooms for sixth formers and twins for the rest. Modern showers and a small kitchen. Staff live alongside, with a matron per floor. In the week, boarders have a snack before evening prayers, supper and study. No Saturday lessons, just sport and weekend activities (shopping, cinema, theatre).

Ethos and heritage: The oldest Catholic school in England, the college counts 20 canonised saints and 133 martyrs among its alumni. Founded in Douai, France by Cardinal William Allen in 1568 as a seminary and Catholic school for boys, it relocated 200 years later in the midst of the French Revolution to the village of Old Hall Green, just outside Ware in the Hertfordshire countryside. In 1874, the junior boys were hived off into Saint Hugh's Preparatory School (now St Edmund's Prep) in a house built by Pugin. Girls from the adjacent Poles Convent were allowed to join the sixth form in 1975 and the college became fully co-ed in 1986.

Full boarders are mainly international students (20 countries represented) but flexi-boarding is becoming more popular and head expects weekly boarding to grow

The idyllic 400 acres and imposing buildings are imbued with this heritage, most notably the jaw-dropping Pugin-designed chapel, worthy of any capital city, which is used for weddings, funerals and baptisms as well as for school services. It's flanked by the smaller shrine chapel, built to hold St Edmund's left fibula that was presented by Cardinal Wiseman in 1863. Overseen by the Archdiocese of Westminster, there is no doubt that this is a Catholic school – iconography is everywhere and the ethos informs everything that is said or done within its boundaries. All students (Catholic or otherwise) are expected to attend mass every two weeks and morning prayers, though other chapel attendance is voluntary, including Friday Mass. Prep pupils use the chapel weekly but also have their own. Chaplaincy plays a significant role and meets every week to discuss all aspects of college life, in a similar vein to a school council ('though more religious,' interjects our guide). Prep and college community comes together on St Edmund's Day (16 November) for a huge, off-timetable, feast day and the culmination of a 30-verse hymn which is sung in the run-up (upper sixth formers prepare for interviews and exams instead).

Day-to-day, the atmosphere is serene. Students are courteous and smiley as they make their unhurried way around the main college buildings, which have the feel of a cathedral crossed with a military academy – austere and magnificent in equal parts and requiring near-constant maintenance. The latest refurbishment focused on the science labs and used money raised on the occasion of the college's 450th anniversary. Also upgraded in recent years, the sports hall, fitness suite and indoor pool are well used by pupils of all ages. The library is functional and well-equipped, music and art rooms are generous, and there is IT throughout, as well as 'bring your own device' scheme and lots of digital learning. Sixth formers (Rhetoricians) have a dedicated study area with computers and a common room. Classroom blocks are arranged around a series of courtyards, with views through the windows of playing fields to the front and an astro at the back (used mainly for hockey), as well as three hard courts (for netball or tennis), athletics track, cricket field and nets. A feature of the otherwise unfussy quads is the pretty Pinot Garden, named in remembrance of a much-loved college priest.

There is no doubt that this is a Catholic school – iconography is everywhere and the ethos informs everything that is said or done within its boundaries. All students (Catholic or otherwise) are expected to attend mass every two weeks and morning prayers

The original 19th century prep building which shares the campus is somewhat cosier thanks to 1960s additions that have created larger classrooms with big windows. Prep children have their own assembly hall, which fits all of them, and a very appealing little chapel, in daily use ('you can just pop in for a quick prayer whenever you want,' our guide informs us). Outside there is plenty of space to play, as well as an outdoor amphitheatre and wooded area, the ideal location for forest school.

Notable alumni include William Scholl the sandal designer, perfumiers James and Robert Floris, and Ralph Richardson.

Pastoral care, inclusivity and discipline: 'We all know people who have led successful lives, but also people who have led good lives and changed the world for the better,' says head. 'The secret to a happy life is to focus on other people.' Parents say with one voice that pastoral care is the key strength – 'the senior staff really live the values of the school'. Pupils too feel the cushion of support – 'there's always someone there for you if you're sad or not feeling well – that's what's nice about this school' a year 6 told us without prompting. In the college, the house system is the main source of pastoral care, and there's also a school counsellor. In addition, year 7 pupils are mentored by sixth formers – 'they love it,' says head. 'We don't have any more issues than anywhere else, but we take it seriously and offer advice to pupils on how to reduce stress levels and help yourself, although we say it's ok to speak up about it and ask for help if you need it. The staff in our on-site infirmary tell the pupils they have been dealing with these issues since before they were born!'

Lunches are prepared by a contract catering team and are appreciated (superb ceiling in the college dining room must be a distraction from the food). On the menu is a main meal plus an alternative and a vegetarian option, with a daily pasta and three salad bars. Cakes and crumbles to follow. Dietary requirements catered for on an individual basis. 'I usually go for seconds' confides our guide – must be tasty. Breakfast and dinner too for boarders. Coffee shop for sixth formers also serves hot snacks and lunch.

Parents are largely pleased with the swift action taken to deal with any disciplinary matters; one praised the close communication during a recent incident which was 'reassuring to the family throughout a difficult period'. Head firm that 'anything that makes another person unhappy is unacceptable'. Sanctions include detentions, short- or long-term suspensions and ultimately expulsion (zero tolerance for bullying and drugs). 'It's a question of what action is right for the person and the community,' head explains. 'Sometimes a new start is what's required.'

Pupils and parents: Vast majority are day students, who come from a 50-minute radius encompassing north London, Hertford, Hitchin, Stevenage, Bishop's Stortford and Cambridge. Most use school buses that criss-cross the Herts and Essex countryside. A wide social diversity, thanks to the numerous excellent scholarships and bursaries, and cultural too – a fifth of the roll is made up of boarding international students, many from Spain and France, eastern Europe (particularly Bulgaria), Africa and Asia. 35 per cent of pupils are from Catholic families, the rest of 'all other faiths and none'.

Former students keep in touch. Edmundian Association organises social and fundraising occasions plus reunions in London and elsewhere. 'There's a lot of goodwill,' says headmaster who welcomes back alumni to give talks (alongside current parents) at the annual careers fair as well as for advice and mentoring.

Money matters: Academic scholarships at 7+, 11+ and 13+, awarded on performance in the entrance exam. Music, art, sport and all-rounder scholarships also available, often in combination with academic awards. Total awards can be extremely generous – we heard from one parent whose child's scholarship was worth 90 per cent of the annual fees. A few sixth form scholarships. Limited number of means-tested bursaries, covering up to full fees.

The last word: A charming school built on solid core values, which looks to be modernising with care and thought.

St John's College School

75 Grange Road, Cambridge, Cambridgeshire CB3 9AB

01223 353532 | admissions@sjcs.co.uk | www.sjcs.co.uk

Ages: 4–13

Pupils: 459; Boarders: 18 weekly, 9 flexi (from age 8)

Fees: Day £13,605 – £16,920; Boarding £26,715; Choristers £8,925 pa

Headmaster: Since 2016, Neil Chippington MA (Cantab) FRCO (late 40s), previously head of St Paul's Cathedral school. After reading music at Gonville and Caius, where he was also organ scholar, he was briefly employed teaching and as organist at Cranleigh (a school he himself attended) and this led to him deciding on a career in teaching. First at Winchester, where he taught music and was housemaster for eight years, then moving to St Paul's, a co-ed choir school, in 2009. As a gifted musician, he understands from experience what is expected of the choristers in his care, although his dedication is very much to the whole school and the education of every pupil. Un-stuffy and easy to talk to, with an engaging, almost boyish appearance and the lean greyhound build of the serious runner (which he is). He thinks education should be about giving children the necessary skills to navigate their way through learning, a life-long process and that St John's offers more than the traditional academic focus by helping pupils to develop enquiring minds and attitudes: 'We want our pupils to keep asking the question, "why?"' he told us, adding, 'We want pupils to be asking themselves, "Where do I go to get to the next bit?" They will become the problem solvers of the future.'

A former chorister himself (Winchester Cathedral) and currently chair of the Choir Schools' Association, he is steeped in the cathedral/choral tradition and all it offers for the 'naturally musical, bright child'. His wife, Leisle, also teaches at the school and they have two sons, both educated at St John's. He is a keen cyclist and runner and regularly takes part in half marathons and triathlons for charity. He attends evensong at St John's as often as possible – 'it is always a great pleasure.' He lives next door to the boarding house with his family.

Entrance: Entry at 4+ is by registration and parental interview (40 places). There is no formal assessment of children at this stage other than to ensure the child is ready for the school environment and will be happy. The wellbeing of pupils is central to the culture of the school; academic achievements come as a result of this and parents must understand and support this view. At 7+ pupils spend half a day in school with informal assessments in English and maths but again, 'we are asking the question, "will this child be happy here?".' So, not highly selective in the formal sense, but this is Cambridge and pupils are, as one would suppose, a bright, motivated bunch. Admission to the handful of boarders (aged 8+) is dependent upon a place being available in the day school. Admission to choristers (aged 8+ when they join the school; all board) is by a voice trial. Pupils are drawn from Cambridge and the environs, some from London, further afield for boarders. Parents mostly come from business, academic and professional backgrounds.

Exit: Apart from the odd pupil leaving at 11, usually for a local state school, the overwhelming majority leave at 13 – 'Having those two years at the top is so valuable,' says head. Occasionally parents are advised to move their child if it is felt they would be happier elsewhere, and help is always given to find the right place. Excellent support and advice about senior schools. 'We sometimes ask, "have you considered so and so school?" Knowing the children, we can suggest schools that may be a better fit'. Large numbers leave for the local independents or the boarding schools within easy reach. In 2021, Perse Upper and The Leys scooped up the most pupils, followed by King's Ely, Oundle, Stephen Perse and then Bedford, Gresham's, Oakham, Rugby and St Mary's Cambridge. Some students (only one to each school) to St Mary's Ascot, Ardingly, Eton, Northstowe College, St Edward's Oxford, Uppingham and Winchester. Eighteen scholarships in 2021.

Our view: Founded in the 17th century to educate the choristers in the choir of St John's College, this core purpose remains at the heart of a school, with music in its DNA. Though musically at the top of the tree, it is the school's approach to learning that attracts parents. -'We chose it over others because we loved the ethos, it's all about how children can learn best.' The refusal of the school to engage in constant assessment and testing of pupils is seen as a strength – 'They are allowed to have a childhood', 'not a school that panders to parents wanting to see a lot of gold stars.' There are no exams until the top two forms. Encouraging intellectual curiosity early on rather than stressing about tests, certainly seems to develop confidence. Pupils tend to go on to do really well at senior stage and 'they look back and realise how much St John's is part of their success,' said a parent. Though the school is immensely proud of the choristers and does all it can to smooth their path, once in school, 'no privileges or star status.' Choristers rehearse from 7.30 to 9am and again after school until evensong at 6.30pm in the college chapel. There are weekend services in term time but St John's does not require the boys at Christmas or Easter except for tours or recording. 'As well as the music, being a chorister has taught me to concentrate and to look presentable,' said one. 'I like the atmosphere in chapel and passing the tradition on.' A professional standard is expected from the boys – and received.

A dazzling array of after school clubs from year 3 up includes rowing, motor skills, musical theatre club, art club, tennis, poetry and debating

On a leafy road in Cambridge opposite the college playing fields (which they share), the school occupies three adjacent buildings, all imaginatively extended and modernised. No architectural gems, but everything well designed for occupation and purpose by the different year groups. Buildings are surrounded by interesting woodland areas (some started from scratch within the last five years) for play and learning in a forest school setting, plus, 'it makes for a far better view from the window than a concrete playground.' Very true.

Byron House, the base for the early years (up to aged 8) is a two-storey building with light classrooms, each with their own cloakroom. Many ground floor rooms lead out onto a veranda that runs around a courtyard full of enticing play and climbing equipment. Byron House has its own hall for assemblies, gym and lunch and a large well stocked library. The pupils' natural interests are key to laying the foundation for successful learning and classrooms are planned for collaborative tasks (writing on desks is encouraged – the tops are made of whiteboard) with carpeted areas for group discussion. The wellbeing of pupils underlies the way they are taught from the outset – 'we want them to give things a try without being worried about getting it wrong,' said the head of learning. We saw a class of 5 year olds learning the rudiments of the shoulder massage (carefully asking permission from their partner first), another discussing their emotions (how to deal with being frozen with fright) to a teacher led class on long multiplication. Technology is widely used to support tailored learning strategies and Chrome books are on hand in every classroom for creative writing or research. There is a cheerful buzz in every room and not much notice taken of visitors – everyone too engrossed in what they are doing.

Senior House is centred on a 1950s era building and others with an attractive mix of architectural styles (some with clapboarding), mainly single storey and positioned to create interesting spaces with quadrangles, piazzas and the (so-called) quiet garden. The role music plays in school life is evident. The purpose built music school is set around a courtyard with a fountain playing, one's ears greeted with the sound of trumpet practice or piano lessons issuing from one of the many practice rooms. The art room opens off the garden and is an enticing space with facilities for every possible kind of creativity, textiles, pottery, weaving, papier mâché and oil painting and an emphasis on recycling – chicken wire, hessian sacks and old mop heads turned (with great skill) into various animals. Older pupils can drop in and get cracking on projects at lunchtimes. Drama is taught throughout the school and the large multi-purpose Hinsley Hall includes a stage and a control room so there are opportunities for pupils more interested in direction or the technical side as well as for acting. Most thrilling of all perhaps is helping with costumes in the Aladdin's cave 'props' room. This interesting space is crammed from floor to ceiling with such items as animal heads, outfits for characters in Alice in Wonderland, a full set of World War 1 uniforms, costumes for fairies, pirates and vicars – a dressing up fantasy world. The wardrobe mistress combines her role with that of librarian in Byron House. 'It's the coolest place,' say the children and

Parents of choristers often attend evensong and drop by at the house afterwards for tea with their sons in the kitchen. At weekends, choristers can go out with their families on Saturdays after morning rehearsal

one can but agree. Costumes are loaned to other schools and organisations. Each year several, 'set piece,' performances take place including two nativity plays and a passion play together with at least seven other productions – 'A Midsummer Night's Dream' and 'The Lion, the Witch and the Wardrobe,' among recent offerings. The library is large and beautiful with mullioned windows and attractive displays of books and seating – exactly the kind of place to encourage reading. Timetabled library lessons throughout the school with provision for independent study in break and lunchtimes. A book week is held each February and authors regularly visit.

Latin is taught enthusiastically from year 5 – 'pupils all benefit from a grounding in the classics, whether they go on to study it or not and apart from it improving their spelling!' Setting in English and maths from year 5 and these sets lead to groupings for other subjects which may be a mixed blessing though it means ' we really get to know each other,' according to pupils. Class sizes are kept to well under 20, with three registration groups to a year. The individual is offered tailored support when it is needed – at no extra cost. 'We try to pick up on any difficulties quickly.' Those trying for scholarships are given extra tuition in particular subjects. The timetable is flexible; an enrichment programme operates each Thursday afternoon for 9-13 year olds which enables cross-curricular work in the arts and sciences, plus the My Mind programme which includes tai chi, yoga and relaxation techniques. Team sports are all played enthusiastically and include fives and squash in addition to rugby, cricket and hockey. Rowing on the river Cam is an option in years 5 and 6 and pupils take part in regattas against local schools. Athletics, both track and field are the main focus of summer PE.

A dazzling array of after school clubs from year 3 up includes rowing, motor skills, musical theatre club, art club, tennis, poetry and debating. As you would expect, a staggering range of musical groups, choirs, ensembles and orchestras that cover every possible interest, the Menuhin string quartet, Rubinstein piano ensemble, chamber choir (invitation) Bluenotes and Rednotes jazz groups and music theory. Clubs finish by 5.30pm.

The school's distinctive cherry red (wool) blazers are worn in combination with kilted skirts or trousers and pupils seem to like them. 'They are warm,' 'My mother doesn't bother to clean mine except occasionally,' (small wonder – dry clean only) 'We like them, this is my sister's!' etc. There is a brisk market in hand-me-downs and lots of siblings share items of uniform that is pricey if you buy the lot brand new. Dress code does not include shoes – 'anything black will do,' say pupils and we saw lace ups, buckle fastenings, even patent leather. Pupils are friendly, clever and fun, happy to chat about a school they obviously enjoy being part of.

Boarding: Choristers (aged 8 and up) all board full time with another 20 or so, mostly older, pupils. Weekly/flexi boarding available. Choir parents agree that though 8 'is young for full boarding, they are looked after so sensitively.' Parents of choristers often attend evensong and drop by at the house afterwards for tea with their sons in the kitchen. At weekends, choristers are allowed to go out with their families on Saturdays after morning rehearsal.

The house has been adapted and decorated in a beach hut-chic style – lots of pale wood, dazzling white walls (painted each year), tip top bathrooms and spacious carpeted landings. Bedrooms are four or six bedded, boys and girls on separate floors though mixed downstairs. A recreation room with snooker, table football, squashy seating and a television for (rare) off duty moments. Lovely uninstitutional kitchen with whopping table round which entire choir can squash for toast and hot drinks after evensong. Meals are eaten in the school dining room. Staff all very aware of helping pupils, especially choristers, pace themselves. 'If one seems particularly tired towards the end of term, I may keep them off games and let them have a catch-up sleep.' Only a few, but strictly kept, rules – no child to enter another dorm, no mobile phones in the boarding house at all and no tuck. This last deprivation is, 'tough, but pupils take it in their stride. They understand the reason behind it.' House parents are loved by their charges and parents alike – 'they really care for the children and will always go the extra mile.' There is a small, quiet room where a child can rest if ill and is waiting to be collected. No off-putting dirty kit or socks anywhere, everything spick and span, a haven to return to.

Money matters: Decisions about bursaries and awards are made by the Governors' Bursaries committee, with guidance from the headmaster and bursar, and are subject to annual review.

Choristers receive scholarships of 66 per cent of the boarding fee which can be supplemented by a bursary of up to100 per cent, depending on financial circumstances.

The last word: This is an unpretentious school where bright, talented pupils receive an exceptional education that encourages intellectual curiosity and artistic integrity, without any surrendering of childhood. Can wisdom be taught? St John's is having a jolly good try.

St Mary's School, Cambridge

RC 39

Bateman Street, Cambridge, Cambridgeshire CB2 1LY

01223 224167 | admissions@stmaryscambridge.co.uk | www.stmaryscambridge.co.uk

Ages: 3–18

Pupils: 646; sixth form: 103; Boarders: 80 full, 5 weekly

Fees: Day £10,923 – £17,031; Boarding £27,600 – £35,301 pa

Headmistress: Since 2007, Charlotte Avery. English degree Oxford, PGCE Cambridge. Taught in various schools, deputy head at Highgate where she oversaw the transition to co-ed. St Mary's is her first headship. One of triplets, all with Oxbridge degrees. A formidable intellect who is determined to get her point across. Dedicated to girls' education. Brisk and efficient but also kind and caring. Obviously stands no nonsense. Well liked and respected by parents. 'She can talk the hind leg off a donkey, but in the nicest way,' said one parent. 'She's brilliant, a whirlwind with great enthusiasm who carries everyone along with her.' Many parents spoke of her great vision and the 'huge changes she has made'. Others spoke of how she has promoted internally. 'A very nice person, tough and a great leader.' Very high profile and attends all school events. Interesting to note that she is an Anglican but head of a Catholic school.

Head of junior school: Since September 2021 is Jo Christian.

Entrance: Entrance tests for all, even the reception children, who have a chat with a member of staff, count, write and sort shapes, 'to see if they will fit in'. Don't be fooled: they are looking for bright sparks. Applicants for years 7 and 9 take the CEM Select online test and a creative writing exam. Skype interviews for those overseas. Most girls are interviewed. The senior school is oversubscribed and the junior school full from year 5. Automatic entry from the junior to senior school, with only one girl in the last five years leaving in year 5. Quite a large intake at year 9 when girls arrive from the local prep and state schools, and from abroad to board.

Exit: Around 50-60 per cent leaves each year after GCSEs, mostly to the excellent state sixth form colleges in Cambridge. The odd one to a co-ed independent, but quite unusual. Sometimes a girl is advised not to return for sixth form, but it's very unusual, and as far as we could tell entry to sixth form was automatic for current pupils as long as they have a clutch of good GCSEs.

London a very popular destination, reflecting the international profile of the girls. Sciences, medical subjects and engineering very popular. One to Oxbridge in 2021, and one medic. The head is embracing apprenticeships and encouraging girls to explore this option.

Latest results: In 2021, 66 per cent 9-7 at I/GCSE. In 2021, 81 per cent A*/A at A level (97 per cent A*-B). In 2019 (the last year when exams took place), 61 per cent 9-7 at GCSE; 51 per cent A*/A at A level (54 per cent A*/B).

Teaching and learning: Impressive results from girls instilled with great self-belief and a strong work ethic. 'The girls work really hard but have great fun too,' said one parent. Lots of support for all, whatever their abilities. Parents kept well informed about academic progress and spoke about 'prompt responses' from teachers. Science and maths very strong with lots of science clubs. Fabulous new science hub, incredibly well equipped. Year 10s were working hard at an experiment and good to see large sixth form groups doing sciences. Spanish, French, German, Latin, Greek and Mandarin all offered at GCSE. Many girls do two languages, though small groups for A level languages.

Inspirational quotes throughout the school from renowned women. Good to see a noticeboard about exam week and preparing for them. 'Don't panic' was one piece of advice. 'A very proactive school,' was one parent's comment. Another parent said, 'How I wish I'd had teachers like that.' Lots of computer suites and iPads filtering through to all pupils. Certain social media sights blocked – good. Food tech and Textile Design offered at A level. A younger age group was cooking when we were visiting – some delicious smells wafted our way.

The junior school is a short walk away in Chaucer Road, in a lovely old house with lots of outside space. One teacher for all subjects, but with specialist input throughout. Again lots of inspirational quotes, particularly from the founder, on the walls. 'They get a very good start here,' was said more than once. French for all and Mandarin taught to all but a few who have extra tuition when needed. All girls actively encouraged: 'You can do it,' is what a lot of parents said their daughters were being told. Average class sizes of 20, smaller in the sixth form. Many teachers long serving.

Learning support and SEN: Learning support lessons for those that need it, about 100 SEN on the register, all with milder needs. 'My daughter needs extra support and time and the school couldn't have been more supportive helping her plan her work and revision as well as extra lessons.' Some 48 students have EAL classes, all in the senior school. Many more from overseas who no longer need this support.

The arts and extracurricular: Drama very popular with lots of productions, clubs and workshops. Parents very enthusiastic about performances. Drama GCSE one of the most successful subjects; most gain top marks. LAMDA popular and encouraged for overseas students.

Art is big at St Mary's and it has a very strong reputation. The art school is situated next door to the main building. Sixth form art scholars' photos displayed in the reception area. Each sixth form student has their own space; we admired the quality of the work, ambitious and eye-catching. Impressive art on display throughout the school.

Orchestras, choirs, bands, ensembles galore, in both junior and senior schools. Our visit coincided with mass rehearsals at the junior school. Every room was full of performers practising. Music as a career actively encouraged.

Numerous sports tours and subject trips. DofE for all, up to gold award.

Sport: Quietly sporty and successful; cabinets full of silverware are testament to this. County cross-country runners, hockey players and netballers. Pitches situated a 10-minute minibus journey away, where there are all new sporting facilities. 'Sport for all and there are no sporting prima donnas,' said one parent. All talk about plenty of teams and 'masses of sports clubs'. Touch rugby and rowing on offer. Gymnastics popular. Sports rotated throughout the year so always something for everyone.

Boarding: The boarding community is international. Some 20 countries represented, with those from south east Asia being the largest cohort. Currently about half the boarders are in the sixth form, and virtually all from overseas. The majority are full boarders, though flexi boarding is offered. All boarders now housed in Mary Ward House, a short walk from the school on Brooklands Avenue. Up to five younger girls in a room, with double rooms for years 10-12 and year 13s in single rooms.

Girls are encouraged to personalise their space and taught to do their own laundry. One father couldn't understand why boarders from year 9 were allowed so much freedom – 'why do they need to go into town to buy sweets?' – but we suspect the boarders disagree with him. They are kept occupied with church on Sundays, optional, and plenty of trips to Alton Towers and the like. Parents keep in close contact and are happy their daughters are 'safe and supervised'.

Squeezed into the centre of Cambridge along a large part of Bateman Street, the 70s façade is quite low key. But once inside the school it's another matter

Disappointing to hear from sixth form day girls that the new boarders don't mix socially with them (school says it's not true). Lots of effort made to include them in sixth form socials but not many takers and very few attend the Leavers' Ball. Doesn't appear to be the case lower down the school: parents spoke of daughters going to stay with friends who are day girls.

Ethos and heritage: Now the only girls' school left in Cambridge. Founded by Mary Ward, an innovator of education for girls, St Mary's opened in 1898. Based on a strong Catholic ethos that is reflected throughout the school. All religions, and none, are welcomed and embraced, with the spiritual welfare of the girls being of paramount importance. There is a resident chaplain, a small chapel where services are regularly held, parents welcome to attend as well, and whole-school services regularly. A strongly Christian school that believes that 'every girl is of equal value and has something to offer.' This belief permeates throughout junior and senior schools.

Outwardly the school is not particularly attractive. Squeezed into the centre of Cambridge along a large part of Bateman Street, the 70s façade is quite low key. But once inside the school it's another matter. Modern additions have been incorporated well, including new science hub opened by Dame Mary Archer in 2016, and it's interesting to tour the school going from ancient to modern: it adds character and works well.

The original building, once a residential house, is beautiful. Now home to the admin and head's office. The magnificent staircase and large bay windows looking out onto large gardens reflect back to another era. The gardens are well used with plenty of benches, an outside gym and table tennis table.

Impressive results from girls instilled with great self-belief and a strong work ethic. 'The girls work really hard but have great fun too,' said one parent. Lots of support for all, whatever their abilities. Parents kept well informed about academic progress and spoke about 'prompt responses' from teachers

Sixth form housed in a separate building that used to be the junior school, across the road. Smaller classrooms for teaching, a dance studio, gym and showers; please note the hairdryers and straighteners. A beautiful building that has recently been refurbished. Comfy-looking common room, kitchen (we spotted the toast and Nutella), and outside space for dining. Interesting to see a sign up in the kitchen to say only English should be spoken. Impressive library with sixth form girls quietly working. Silent study rooms and less quiet ones, but all working hard in them. Good use made of Cambridge and all it has to offer.

The junior school reflects the senior school, with large gardens and an attractive, airy building. Pretty sensory garden and vegetable plots for each year. Both schools are very much 'girls' schools'. The empowerment of women, strong women, is a theme throughout. The girls seem to absorb this. Very little make up worn and no strutting divas to behold – thank goodness.

Pastoral care, inclusivity and discipline: All parents praised the pastoral care. Very few bullying claims. Happiness and joy with strong moral values is their mantra and the girls take this on board. But girls will be girls, and the school knows it. Spats and sniping dealt with calmly and efficiently, usually with very little parental intervention. Parents spoke of a happy school with 'no queen bees or cliques'. A junior school mother said, 'some parents get too involved, collaring teachers at every opportunity. They are too protective to the detriment of others.' But that's junior schools for you. Most parents trust the school and know their daughters are 'safe and happy'. School knows how to deal with girls and their problems. A counsellor and female lay chaplain available if needed, and staff appear to know the girls well.

Instilling self-esteem and confidence is very much an ethos of the school and many parents spoke about it along with the Mary Ward philosophy that they have great belief in. 'My daughter was very shy when she started but they have brought her out of herself and her confidence now is amazing.'

Pupils and parents: Parents are very much 'Cambridge' – academics/medics/professionals. Many are old girls. All spoke about the values of the school and how important that was to them. About a third are Catholic. All very pro single-sex education, even the mother who said, 'I was very anti single-sex education initially, but St Mary's suited my daughter best and she's thrived.' Girls from a 30-mile radius around Cambridge with about 20 per cent from overseas.

The girls were interesting. Charming and unaffected in both schools. It was quite revealing to see the sixth formers, slightly scruffy, but not in a bad way, and minimal make up. As one mother said, 'they don't care what they look like as there's no-one to impress.' Amen to that.

Money matters: Scholarships in years 7, 9 and 12 are usually awarded at a one-off fee remission of £500 (maximum of two per student). Bursaries of up to 50 per cent available. Two Ogden Trust maths and physics scholarships open to lower sixth candidates from the state sector, means-tested and can be worth up to 95 per cent of day school fees.

The last word: A girls' school offering a tremendous education to young women. Being instilled with the belief of the empowerment of women from such a young age, these girls will go far. There'll be no glass ceilings for this lot.

Summerhill School

Westward Ho, Leiston, Suffolk IP16 4HY

01728 830540 | office@summerhillschool.co.uk | www.summerhillschool.co.uk

Ages: 5-17

Pupils: 54; Boarders: 41 full

Fees: Day £6,636 – £12,741; Boarding £14,460 – £21,894 pa

Principal: Since 1985, Zoe Readhead (youthful late 60s) – proprietor, keeper of the ethos and daughter of school's founder, AS Neill. Literally born, bred and educated at Summerhill. Calm, inspiring and probably sees into your soul. Answers as if for the first time questions she has presumably been asked her whole life, her patient vocation to explain her father's educational vision and the school's core values. Gradually scaling down her day-to-day involvement and preparing to pass the baton to two of her four children, all of whom are intrinsic to the life of the school, in which they were also born, bred and educated – 'they'll let me know when they don't want me here any more.' Married to Tony, a farmer. Son Henry presides over the music studio and is joint deputy head with William, who teaches woodwork and metalwork; Amy is an agronomist who helps with the paperwork; and Neill a farmer who offers support and advice. 'Zoe and the staff are great,' enthused a parent. 'I have complete faith in them and the way they teach. Zoe is always at the end of the phone when I've needed her, even in the holidays.' Said another, 'It is a real challenge to change with the demands of the time, but also to keep a safe shield around the school so it can continue to do what it does in the way it does it. Balancing and enabling that is certainly an art and I am very grateful to Zoe for that... and much more.'

Entrance: Entirely on the child's suitability for the school, and vice versa. The impact of a new joiner on current pupils is also considered and over-11s are rarely enrolled, so as not to upset the established dynamic. New children may join at the start of any term. Parents are well advised to read carefully the direct, honest and plentiful information on the school's website, before making an enquiry and visiting.

Exit: Most leave at 17 or 18, the majority for further education and then university, equipped with the skills of independent learning and knowing what they want to do with their lives. 'A degree is not an end in itself,' says Zoe. 'Kids here can adapt in order to get to where they want to go.' Summerhill produces many skilled craftspeople and creatives. Children's writer John Burningham (The Snowman) attended, as did several successful actors, musicians, dancers, artists and scientists. But after the idyll of Summerhill, is adult life a disappointment? 'Isn't it for all of us?' asks Zoe. 'When they move to life outside, the kids are tolerant and understanding enough to deal with it.'

Teaching and learning: Not a priority here, unless decided so by the individual. Nominally under the umbrella of the Democratic School movement particularly prevalent in Germany, Russia, Eastern Europe, South America and India, Summerhill prefers to be known as a 'free' school though certainly not to be confused with the state free schools of the past decade. The central tenets here are that each member of the school – adult or child – has the same rights and value and the school is run by its members, for its members. What happens in school is agreed at a meeting of pupils and staff held three times a week – or more often by request – and chaired in rotation by children. The day we visited had been agreed by the meeting as a Slobbing Day, due to a fireworks party that went on late the night before, so all lessons were off.

However, even on a regular day at Summerhill, academic lessons are entirely optional. As the parents' handbook emphasises, 'remember, at Summerhill your kid could theoretically NEVER go to a lesson – they have that right. Staff members are not going to persuade, cajole or bully your child about lessons.' The student body, aged 5 to 17 or 18, is divided into three classes by age and while the youngest two classes do have a lesson timetable, if no-one shows up at a class after 10 minutes, the teacher goes away again. Class 2 (aged 10 to 12) are least likely to feel in the mood for learning – 'they have more interesting things to do at that age,' says Zoe. Older children sign up for the 40-minute lessons on their timetable but do not need to attend if they prefer not to and they choose whether or not to work towards an exam – GCSE or International O Level – in a subject. Some Summerhillians opt to take several and some none at all. 'When kids decide they do want to learn, they are surprisingly conservative,' says Zoe. 'It doesn't have to be the most exciting lesson, they're focused. They're saying "I'm here, I want to learn – teach me".'

When they're not there and not wanting to learn, these 'free-range' children are hanging out in the woods, or the school library, or anywhere they like, together or alone. They might be being creative in the art room, the woodwork room or the forge, or making music, or perhaps walking on nearby Sizewell beach or in 'downtown' Leiston, a quiet Suffolk backwater. 'It's a bit like microwave cooking,' says Zoe. 'Kids continue to develop when they aren't learning.'

Lessons entirely optional. As the parents' handbook emphasises, 'remember, at Summerhill your kid could theoretically NEVER go to a lesson – they have that right'

Independent learning is just one of the many educational and developmental benefits of the Summerhill approach. AS Neill founded the school in 1921 and virtually nothing has changed, but it dawns quite quickly that in a lot of ways Summerhill is still the education of the future. Conventional contemporary methods of schooling sure have their problems; Summerhill appears not to. It operates in a parallel universe where self-worth, self-knowledge and living harmoniously and respectfully with others are not just the goal, they're the reality. While schools spend millions of pounds and hours of planning on creating opportunities for pupils to learn the importance of risk-taking, for example, at Summerhill children play tag in the trees and gladly manufacture their own knives in the metalwork shop. A lesson on risk-taking comes in the form of a wobbly moment on a high branch or a nick on the thumb. On our visit, Zoe stopped to shoot the breeze with a young girl (helicopter parents, look away now) on roller blades, sucking a lollipop.

Summerhill's nine teachers, including the founder's grandchildren, all live in too and assist those who are houseparents 24/7. 'Of course as an independent school we don't have to employ people with formal teaching qualifications, but we do because it's really the best mechanism,' says Zoe. 'Some job candidates come and say "I would love to live here but I couldn't teach this way".' All the usual safeguarding checks are carried out. Adults as well as children are known by their first names. There is a charming register system in the entrance corridor to Summerhill's main house – a huge peg board divided into three wide columns, titled 'in', 'out' and 'far out'. Each Summerhillian has a name fob to personalise (wild and wacky metalwork planets, plants or abstract objets) or not (felt tip on hardboard) and move across into the relevant column to show the current whereabouts – 'out' the area shaded on a map of the local area as the centre of Leiston, with the fringes marked as somewhere not to go unless you have told someone you're going; 'far out' usually home. Day children – and there are few and only as a precursor to boarding – move their fobs to and fro night and morning. At the end of term someone dutifully moves all the fobs to 'far out' and back to 'in' on the first day back. Typical Summerhill – each individual has a strong identity, is responsible for him or herself and as a member of the community as a whole; it's a simple system; it works.

No wonder then that Summerhill's termly visitors' day is oversubscribed by students of education and open-minded school leaders who want to find out for themselves what makes Summerhill work, presumably so they can take away a gem or two. But surely Summerhill is more than the sum of its parts? 'Yes,' says Zoe, 'but they might use an idea and it could be some improvement.' Such generosity is endemic. Zoe has toured the world to share her father's vision. Beyond the 90 or so children currently at Summerhill, if Neill's vision adds even a modicum of value to the development and education of children wherever they are, it is all grist to the 'free' school mill. Regular requests from fly-on-the wall Educating Manchester style documentary-makers are swatted away – 'the only way we would make a documentary to show our approach would be to make it ourselves, which we could do,' says Zoe thoughtfully. We look forward to it.

Learning support and SEN: Children with SEN are absorbed into the school community. 'We try not to change the way we behave towards children because of SEN,' explains Zoe. 'We rejoice in individuals and so a child with ADHD for us is just another individual and will be treated the same as everybody else. The school community would certainly never let a child behave badly just because they had been diagnosed with something.' The school does apply for pupils to be given extra time in exams if they're eligible.

The arts and extracurricular: 'Adults are not there to create things for the children to do,' reads the parent information. 'They need to create things for themselves. Indoor activities on offer include performance of all kinds – dance, drama and music, including music technology and studio recording – and there's a small theatre. The woodwork shop and new metalwork forge are popular places and many Summerhill kids discover a real passion – 'they mostly make furniture,' says Zoe, 'or weapons.' They can go in whenever a lesson for the younger children isn't in progress. Similarly art, which has a large room, stuffed with imaginative works by pupils, past and present. Computer room – gaming and screens in general (laptops, iPads etc) not allowed on weekdays until 3pm, but fine the rest of the time. Japanese, Chinese, gardening, photography, calligraphy, film-making, crafts, riding, cooking in the café, camping in the grounds, making tree forts etc are all popular self-directed pastimes. A Social Committee is elected by the community in the winter and spring to organise bigger games and activities – such as capture the flag, word games, board games, spontaneous acting, story-telling and cinema trips – for afternoons and evenings. Breeds practical, can-do children who know what they want and get on with it.

Sport: Sports, games and other amusements are all generated by the pupils and adults, according to need.' Facilities are ready and waiting, though the somewhat lumpy football pitch is little used currently – 'we had some German kids here at one point who were keen and put on a match every afternoon, but not much interest recently,' says Zoe. Considering turning the tennis court over to volleyball, which is more popular now. Kids swim in the school's unheated pool or the warmer indoor version at Leiston Leisure Centre. PE lessons are not a thing here. 'If you think about it, in regular school children enjoy sports as their only chance to get outside,' says Zoe. 'Here they are outside whenever they want to be.'

Boarding: Pretty much all Summerhillians – only the very youngest and any very recently arrived don't board. Class 1 children, who can sleep at school from the age of 5 if they like – all are by about 7 – overnight in mixed rooms and then split into separate girls' and boys' accommodation buildings when they move up to class 2. Class 3, age 12 and up, have individual rooms on mixed corridors, sharing bathrooms in the accommodation known as Carriages (originally literally old railway carriages, but now replaced by wooden buildings). Ofsted had a little difficulty taking this on board and recently came to investigate Summerhill's sleeping arrangements. They left enlightened. 'I think they saw that it works and that we just don't have the problems associated with a lack of respect for gender they find in other schools,' shrugs Zoe.

Ethos and heritage: One of the most famous and most controversial schools in the world. Founded in 1921 by AS Neill – described on the school website as 'a Scottish writer and rebel' – near Dresden, Germany, but moved to a Victorian house in Leiston, two miles from the Suffolk coast, in 1927. He decided this would be the ideal place to create a community in which children could be free from adult authority. Neill's ideas became famous through his extensive writings and lectures and were accepted more readily outside of the UK. However, in the 1960s his success at Summerhill was finally recognised closer to home and Neill was awarded honorary degrees from the universities of Newcastle, Exeter and Essex. In 1999 he was named among the top 12 men and women to influence British schooling during the last millennium by the Times Educational Supplement.

This has not prevented the school from being threatened with closure on several occasions, most recently in 1999 after a damning Ofsted report that accused the school of failing the children educationally. Summerhill contested the notice of closure in court and after four days of wrangling and vociferous protest from current and former parents and pupils, the government's case collapsed.

A popular misconception: Summerhill does indeed have rules (or 'laws') – at least a couple of hundred of them, all agreed, amended or abolished at the meeting

The school's idyllic 12 green and woody acres remain as peaceful as ever. On the fringes of the town, Summerhill's main house – interior features sadly wrecked by the army during wartime requisition – is surrounded by a collection of long, low buildings which house the no-frills learning areas, accommodation and facilities, as well as ancient trees including beeches perfect for climbing and rope-swings.

Numbers wax and wane over the course of the year, but there are never more than 100 children and adults in the school community. Long holidays – five weeks at Christmas, five weeks in the spring and nine weeks each summer – no half-terms or bank holidays. Former pupils are welcomed back for a party every five years (the next one being the school's centenary).

Pastoral care, inclusivity and discipline: 'We believe in freedom but not licence,' says the parent information. 'This means that you are free to do as you

Orwell Park School

like – but you must not interfere with somebody else's freedom. You are free to go to lessons, or stay away, because that is your own personal business, but you cannot play your drum kit at four in the morning because it would keep other people awake.' A popular misconception: Summerhill does indeed have rules (or 'laws') – at least a couple of hundred of them, all agreed, amended or abolished at the meeting. 'A lot of society's ills relate to individuals not taking responsibility for their actions,' says Zoe. 'Here each member is responsible for him or herself.'

Bullying doesn't really figure – every individual is confident in his or her own self-worth and the value of others. Similarly sexual harassment – 'if it were to happen, the intended victim would simply look the assailant in the eye and tell him or her where to go,' says Zoe. No problem with women's empowerment here – gender is no barrier to self-esteem.

Such is their confidence that parents accept they must be almost completely hands-off for the sake of their children – there is almost no parental involvement at Summerhill

Those who transgress are 'brought up' in the meeting and a suitable consequence is agreed – usually either a monetary fine (a specified amount, such as 'a fiver for smoking', explains Zoe, or a percentage of the child's 'poc', pocket money dished out by the school) or some kind of community service (such as helping out in the school kitchens). Being 'brought up' in front of peers is often punishment enough. Serious misdemeanours, such as drink or drugs, usually result in the child being sent home for four to eight weeks – 'the worst thing, because they all want to be here,' says Zoe. A parent backed this up – 'I couldn't get my daughter out of bed all through the summer holidays, but on the day she went back to school she jumped out of bed at 7am, screaming at the top of her voice with delight to be going back! And the tears and sadness to be going home at the end of every term is all the evidence anyone needs that the kids absolutely LOVE Summerhill.'

Pupils and parents: An international community. Despite being branded 'crackpot' by sections of the UK media over several decades, Summerhill is well known and respected around the world and 65 per cent of pupils are from overseas, most often Japan, Korea, Holland, China, Germany, France, Poland and Russia. Pupils arrive with varying degrees of English – EAL help is available in a dedicated classroom. British children travel from every corner of the kingdom, though some families make a point of moving to be nearer. Summerhill is a magnet. Children who join after the age of 5 have more often than not been home-schooled previously, or have attended other alternative schools, or have had difficulties elsewhere and arrived seeking sanctuary. 'Qualities we typically see in Summerhill pupils are: Self-esteem, tolerance, integrity, fairness, understanding, sensitivity, compassion, assertiveness, creativity, individuality, humour, self-motivation and common sense,' says the school. The hope and intention is for those who don't arrive with these attributes to leave with them.

Parents of Summerhillians tend to be ardent advocates – no doubt practised in the art of explaining their choice to sceptics; they need to be to put their faith in Neill's educational philosophy and live with the eventual outcome for their child, which could range from enlightenment to illiteracy. Such is their confidence that parents accept they must be almost completely hands-off for the sake of their children – there is almost no parental involvement at Summerhill. 'As the philosophy of the school is to encourage children to live their own lives and make their own decisions, they value their independence and the vast majority prefer parents not to be a part of the school,' says Summerhill. 'Accepting this is part of learning to accept your new independent, free child.' However, parents are treated to a taste of their children's school life on one summer weekend when they are invited to stay for a few days. 'I found it difficult at first, because I'd had lots of involvement when my daughters had attended state school,' said one parent, 'but I quickly understood that it is part of the Summerhill way that children are allowed the complete freedom to do whatever they like without intervention from parents. I am happy with that, I love seeing how much they have changed at each holiday.' Said another, 'The fact that I have no influence on the children is of course a challenge. It requires a completely different way of living motherhood. I see it as my own learning process. The parameter is, and remains, whether the children are doing well.'

Money matters: Mega-cheap – no pricey historic buildings or gleaming facilities to keep up; make-do-and-mend mentality. Discount of 10 per cent or more for children of ex-Summerhillians. Chinese, riding, dancing and music lessons, for example, are charged as extras. School squirrels away funds for the AS Neill Summerhill Trust, which provides limited bursaries for existing pupils.

The last word: An uncompromising, authentic, 'free' education, as true to AS Neill's vision as the day he launched it in 1921. Never capsized or blown off course by the changing tides of educational and political trial and error, Summerhill sails on serenely towards the horizon, the rest of us in its wake.

Tring Park School for the Performing Arts

Tring Park, Tring, Hertfordshire HP23 5LX

01442 824255 | info@tringpark.com | www.tringpark.com

Ages: 8-19 (dancers can do 3rd sixth form year)

Pupils: 355; sixth form: 163 (46 boys/117 girls); Boarders: 208 full

Fees: Day £15,405 – £24,885; Boarding £26,190 – £37,605 pa

Principal: Since 2002, Stefan Anderson MA BMus ARCM ARCT. In his early 60s, Mr Anderson is a highly personable man with a big heart, uncontrived charm and a good dose of self-deprecating humour; surprisingly understated, all considered. A classically trained musician, he grew up in Toronto, Canada and attended Carleton University, Ottawa. Moved to the UK and studied at the Royal College of Music and Emmanuel College, Cambridge, where he was an organ scholar. He spent 12 years at Wellington as assistant director of music, then seven years as director of music at King's Canterbury, before taking up the principal's post (his first ever) at Tring in 2002. 'Didn't think I'd end up in teaching,' he laughs, 'but here I am.' Recalls standing in the hall on his first day watching the students run excitedly into school: 'I thought, this isn't normal' – no wonder he's been here so long. Doesn't teach but can be regularly spotted in the dining room and around school.

Superlatives slip off the tongues of parents and pupils alike – 'the best principal you could ask for', 'the sweetest man', 'the most impressive educationalist I've come across in the performing arts sector' etc. In short, adored and admired universally. 'Just the right amount of gravitas and warmth,' said one parent. 'He knows every kid's name.' 'He comes to all the performances and is involved in everything.' 'He knows the students – it isn't just lip service.' Meanwhile, pupils told us, 'You could ask him anything.' 'He's always chatty and friendly, but very professional.' ''He's incredibly understanding and supportive – there's nothing insincere about him.'

Entrance: Children can join the school from age 8 to 16, but the commonest entry points are at ages 11-13, 14 and 16. School receives around seven applications for every place. One-day audition process at which children show what they can do in dance, drama and singing. They aren't expected to excel in all three of these (although many do) but the school is looking for great talent and potential in dancing for winnable dancers and two out of three for everyone else. Applicants are also expected to evidence a strong motivation to learn. For 2021 entry, auditions are being held virtually.

Exit: Around half leaves after GCSEs. After sixth form, around three-quarters go on to further performing arts training; others progress straight to major companies such as English National Ballet, Birmingham Royal Ballet and Scottish Ballet. Some join the school's own dance company, Encore, for a rigorous third year of touring and performing. 'Because of the short shelf life of a dance career, they tend to peak early,' says school.

Drama schools are a popular destination – Arts Ed London, Guildhall, Guildford School of Acting, Mountview, Bird College and Royal Conservatoire of Scotland among them. Tring also regularly turns out some good classical musicians, although invariably these are singers – recent singing alumni went on to train at Royal Northern Music and Royal Conservatoire of Scotland. Commercial Music students have continued on to the Institute of Contemporary Music, Berklee College of Music, etc.

Some pupils launch straight into professional jobs (Downton Abbey and Cinderella have mopped up several Tring alumni), while others take a bit longer to get their break, with past pupils having worked their way up to appearing in eg Peaky Blinders, Poldark and the Manchester Theatre Festival. A number go to university instead: Durham, Exeter, Kings College London,

Leeds, and Royal Holloway, as well as overseas eg the Juilliard performing arts school in New York and University of Southern California in recent years. Interestingly, two of Tring's dancers recently graduated as medics, having gone to uni in their late 20s.

Careers advice widely praised, 'and they gear children up from quite an early age, encouraging them to get more and more strings to their bow regardless of their end goal,' according to a parent. Because it's a dual curriculum, staff are good at balancing both academics and vocational skills into their guidance and many staff get involved – any one pupil might get direction from the director of musical theatre or dance, head of sixth form, director of academic studies and mentors, 'so you get input from quite a few,' we were told.

Latest results: In 2020 GCSE, 50 per cent 9-7 at GCSE; 45 per cent A*/A at A level (73 per cent A*/B). In 2019 (the last year when exams took place), 33 per cent 9-7 at GCSE; 23 per cent A*/A at A level (56 per cent A*/B).

Teaching and learning: Tring's focus on academics is undoubtedly what makes it stand out against other schools of performing arts and results are proof that for the right children, the chance to do what they love actually enhances their academic performance. Many parents told us they selected Tring for precisely this reason. Pupils are selected solely on their performing abilities (all those who pass the audition sit an academic test, but only for diagnostic purposes) yet results are impressive. And no, they are not made up exclusively of subjects such as drama and dance, they cover the full spread including sciences and languages, IT, history and geography. At A level, three are usually taken out of 23 on offer, except for dancers who supplement a third with the Trinity National Diploma in Dance. English, maths, physics and theatre studies are all popular.

Only half the school day is given over to academic subjects, which makes lessons 'pretty intense', albeit 'nearly always engaging' and 'lively', according to pupils. Pupils who fall behind are offered lunchtime clinics, extra sessions etc, although a pupil told us, 'in the end, your level of engagement is left up to you, but there is a strong encouragement to take full advantage of what's on offer.' For those in prep (years 4 to 6), vocational and academic lessons are mixed up throughout the day, while for remaining students it's a morning of vocational and an afternoon of academics for years 7-9 and the other way round for years 10-12. A long day 'and you can get tired,' pupils told us.

Those of us who remember the days when academic expectations were often consigned to an understudy role at stage schools can only marvel. But then Tring isn't a stage school in the old-fashioned sense, as the pupils were eager to point out, but a heady mix of high-level vocational and academic education, where the two strands rub together to produce very bright sparks. Past pupils have become medics and done PhDs.

That said, it's important to remember that this is a vocational school, one of only eight such in the UK funded by the DfE as centres of excellence for exceptionally talented young dancers and musicians. Tring's remit is to produce highly trained performers who've received a rounded education, not lawyers and doctors who like hoofing.

Only half the school day is given over to academic subjects, which makes lessons 'pretty intense', albeit 'nearly always engaging' and 'lively' say pupils

Learning support and SEN: Around a third receive SEN support in either one-to-one or small group sessions, covering everything from minor difficulties with spelling to dyspraxia and mild autism. One parent said, 'I can't fault them – my daughter has learned some great coping strategies for her dyslexia and gets all the extra time she needs in exams.'

The arts and extracurricular: Everyone agrees the vocational training is phenomenal. 'Unbelievable talent – you have to see it to believe it,' said a parent. 'The breadth of experience was the big selling point for us,' said another. Children in the prep (years 4-6) all receive training in acting, singing and dancing. Thereafter, students specialise in either dance or performing arts. Dance training covers ballet, contemporary, tap and jazz; performing arts training includes both dance (less intensively) and acting, as well as voice, improvisation, and other aspects of theatre technique. And of course, there's musical theatre and singing too. In the sixth form students specialise in dance, musical theatre, acting or commercial music. Tring isn't a specialist music school – aspiring concert pianists would feel frustrated at having to break off and jeté every time they'd sat down to practise – but the music department is strong, with several excellent choirs and all students given the chance to learn instruments and play in ensembles. The chamber choir recently won BBC Young Choir of the Year – all the more impressive when you consider most of the singers are not on the music course. There is setting in dance – we watched a top set in action, a couple of the pupils having just finished a stint in Matthew Bourne's Romeo and Juliet.

At least 100 shows, plays, musicals and other performances are put on every year, all to an astonishingly high standard. 'We go and see pretty much everything, whether our child is in it or not, and they blow me away every time,' said one parent, while another told us, 'Even the prep performances are polished and professional.' No waving to mums and dads from the stage at this school.

Reassuringly, the 'in-your- face', 'me-me-me' types are few and far between, although one parent felt that 'the really strong personalities get away with more'

Sometimes students have a chance to do external work – ballet dancers join English National Ballet for productions of The Nutcracker every year, for instance, while some pupils have received one-off opportunities which the head says it would be unfair to deny them. But the school doesn't encourage students to be absent, and children wanting a school that will act as their agent and find them regular professional work should look elsewhere. 'In the end, the school wants you to have a childhood and education – I think they get the balance right,' said a parent.

Art is offered at both GCSE and A level, with a reasonable uptake – fine art, textiles, photography and sculpting all a hit with the pupils in two new, light and bright (but not huge) studios.

Sport: If sport is important to your offspring, strike this school off your list. There's no time for it and judging from the sweat dripping off the youngsters mid-dancing, your child will get all the exercise they need. With this in mind, we were surprised to spot a couple of football goals. 'That's my legacy,' exclaimed an old boy (who stars in a Netflix series) who was visiting the same day as us – 'I came from a sporty school and wanted a kickabout with other pupils.'

Boarding: Full boarding (although in reality many sixth formers go home for weekends) available for 60 per cent of pupils whose eyes light up as they extol the virtues of living, training and being educated with the same people – life-long friendships in the making. For those that stay at weekends, there is at least one non-compulsory activity – shopping to Milton Keynes or London, theatre trips, ice skating etc, although others prefer to stay put for in-house baking, making use of those football nets etc. 'There is an element of wanting to keep weekends less ordered because so much of their week is regimented,' says head.

Facilities range from pretty basic (but being refurbished) to the shiny (literally) new Elizabeth building with 70 beds and all the mod cons. 'Elizabeth House aside, they are not dazzling, but fine and we all appreciate the work they've done to make them more homely,' said a parent. Largest dorm sleeps six, with most for two, three or four. One parent expressed surprise 'that we had to wait until upper sixth for a single dorm', while others said they'd like to see more integration between boarders and day pupils – 'it could so easily be fixed,' said one. Superb houseparents, report parents – 'very supportive and nurturing'.

Ethos and heritage: Started life as the Cone Ripman School, founded in 1939 and itself the result of a merger between two previous dance schools. Originally located in London, the outbreak of war forced a move to Tring where the school shared premises with the Rothschild Bank at Tring Park Mansion House (strange bedfellows they must have been). In 1941, the school moved back to London but kept its Tring premises as a second school where boarders could be accommodated, and in 1947 both places were renamed the Arts Educational School, to reflect Grace Cone's and Olive Ripman's commitment to a proper academic education for their stage-struck charges. Gradually the two schools diverged, with London becoming more focused on post-18 training, while Tring continued to develop as a vocational boarding school. Eventually they became completely independent and in 2009 the Tring school changed its name to Tring Park School for the Performing Arts, in order to avoid confusion with its former partner. Originally for girls only, one boy was admitted in 1993, 'and that opened the floodgates'.

Still housed in the gorgeously flamboyant mansion in which it took refuge over 70 years ago, Tring Park School literally sings with activity and joy. Half the stunning wood-panelled entrance hall is glazed off as a dance studio, and our tour kicked off to cries of 'Five, six, seven, eight, and right! Two, three, four, and left!' for a jazz warm-up, while Guys and Dolls mingled jauntily with a more demure strain from the ballet class next door. Performance, as you might imagine, is in the very bones of the place – 'every time I walk in, there's performing going on the whole time, even in the playground and in lessons, it's so inspirational,' said one parent.

For years, the mansion's grade II listed status hampered some necessary modernisation, but

At least 100 shows, plays, musicals and other performances are put on every year, all to an astonishingly high standard

school now boasts an impressive array of recently built dance studios, while the new copper and wood themed Elizabeth building is home to some contemporary drama and art teaching rooms. Academic teaching takes place in what's known as the 'new block' (actually 1970s) with classic school décor, including three updated science labs. School has received funding for a bigger and better theatre to supplement the existing 176-seat Markova Theatre – as the head himself points out, the current stage space takes older male dancers a mere three leaps to get from one side to the other. The surrounding tree-studded gardens provide a tranquil backdrop to all the artistic fervour. Pupils would like more spaces dedicated to gym equipment and for day pupils to meet for a drink and snack.

Feathers do get ruffled occasionally, but 'this is not a dog-eat-dog environment,' as one parent put it, with the school working hard to foster a supportive environment in which pupils are taught not to compare themselves to others, but to where they were last term. 'Of course, when the cast list comes out, there is disappointment,' we were told, 'but you always see those with the principal roles comforting those that didn't get chosen' – this outward-looking ethos, along with a very strong work ethic, is what many directors and producers say singles Tring graduates out. 'We've been to a lot of auditions where you see pupils from other schools being really competitive, while our lot just support each other,' said one parent. 'They develop them beyond just being performers so whether my daughter has a career in performing arts or not, they are giving her grit, determination and an ability to manage failure while at the same time being able to celebrate other people's successes,' said another.

School-parent communication on the up, but many feel it's still their weakest point. 'Sometimes messages come through very late in the day,' said one, while another complained that, 'because the school is predominantly boarding, they sometimes forget the day pupils in the communications.'

Pastoral care, inclusivity and discipline: Behaviour at Tring is exuberant but respectful. There are the usual sanctions for infringements (including principal's Saturday evening detention – although we can't help wonder who that really punishes), but the students want to be here and are generally keen not to mess up. Permanent exclusions are almost unheard of, although there are temporary exclusions most terms; accrued merits make for a long list of prizes handed out on Founders' Day.

A full-time counsellor is well utilised and although the school is praised for spotting and discouraging eating disorders, it does happen, especially among dancers – 'if I was sending my child in as a ballet dancer, I'd be a bit concerned, despite all the school's efforts,' said one parent. Another parent felt the school could do more with the dancers around injury prevention and caring for your body – 'some years do Pilates, some don't, so it's hit and miss. They need to do more work on, how do I look after this machine that is my body and which I'm going to be working extra hard?'

Pupils and parents: 'Not just rich kids,' said a parent with an audible sigh of relief, 'although we are still unusual in that we both work.' Families from all over the UK and some from overseas (7.5 per cent of boarders), with EAL help for those who need it. Families who are new to boarding, or independent schools, or to the world of performing arts (some to all three), are nonetheless united by a common ardour. We found pupils (60/40 girls/boys) chatty, dedicated and polite; parents say you can almost measure their growth in confidence year on year, although one added, 'it's perhaps not for more fragile souls.' Reassuringly, the 'in-your-face', 'me-me-me' types are few and far between, although one parent felt that 'the really strong personalities do get away with more'.

Money matters: Stonkingly high fees, as you'd expect with all this specialist tuition, but around 40 per cent of students are on some kind of support. Dancers who join the school at age 11, 12 or 13 can apply for funding from the government's means-tested Music and Dance Scheme. Dance students joining at 16+ may be eligible for DaDA scholarships (Dance and Drama Awards, another source of government funding). Tring has its own scholarship fund for musical theatre and drama pupils, to which families can apply. Many Tring students come from families on modest or low incomes. Up to 100 per cent assistance available for those who need it.

The last word: Like coming home for young theatrical souls, and they feel it the moment they walk through the door. A vocational school where joie de vivre is the beating heart, but where academics don't play second fiddle. The upshot is an excellent and well-balanced education for all, provided they can hack the long, busy days.

Wisbech Grammar School

42

Chapel Road, Wisbech, Cambridgeshire PE13 1RH

01945 583631 | admissions@wisbechgrammar.com | www.wisbechgrammar.com

Ages: 3-18

Pupils: 600; sixth form: 102; Boarders: 12 full

Fees: £9,897 – £14,127 pa

Head: Since 2014, Chris Staley (40s). Studied geography at Portsmouth, MBA from London. No plans to teach, intended to join the army. Got a place at Sandhurst but cracked a cheekbone whilst playing rugby so had to delay entry. Decided to do PGCE whilst waiting and within two weeks was hooked. No regrets about abandoning army career, 'every day is different.' Started in the state sector 'as I wanted to experience it, having been privately educated,' quickly became disillusioned and turned to private sector. Wisbech is his first headship, arriving via Cranleigh and deputy headship at Milton Abbey.

Keen sportsman spending many years as a rugby coach alongside teaching geography. Wisbech a bit of a change, 'it's not in a rich part of the country and numbers were dropping.' He's certainly ruffled a few feathers and given the school a good shake. Lots of changes made. 'Eyebrows were raised at times.' Junior and senior school timetables now aligned, making for a more coherent community; school day also extended with late pick-up and early drop-offs now offered. Teaching improved and academic standards rising. Building work completed in the new refectory, dance studio opened, reception area moved, newly refurbished kindergarten and reception, new netball courts and, most importantly of all (for parents), a new car park that they can access. 'We wanted to make parents more welcome, and moving the staff car park to allow parents ease of access for pick ups and drop offs was a good way to start.'

Parents like him, some more than others. 'I'm a Staley fan,' said by many. Others took a while to warm to him. 'I wasn't sure at first as he seemed quite distant, not being a teaching head. But he is inspirational and I'm delighted my child is at the school.' Parents appreciate what he is doing at the school, 'he was an exceptional choice.' A small number see him more as a manager than an educator but they are very much in the minority. 'Some parents can't see the bigger picture,' said by one wise mother. 'He's driven and motivated and knows where he wants to take the school.' Lots of new appointments since his arrival; all of the senior team are his choice.

Three children in the senior school, which parents like. Initially lived in head's house provided by the school but sold that to raise funds. Happy to buck the trend to get what he wants. A welcoming, forthright character. Friendly and approachable, but we imagine he doesn't stand any nonsense, from staff, parents or pupils; and nor should he.

Prep head: Since 2015, Keryn Neaves. A New Zealander who is a keen rugby fan too, so lots of fun in the staff room, we imagine. Liked by parents: 'she's grown into the role', 'strong but fair and very approachable.' Has a child in the prep school. 'I like that, she is one of us as well as being head.' Parents respect, and like, both heads.

Entrance: The school is selective, but not excessively so. Heads meet every child before a place is offered after they have taken an entrance assessment. School happy to say no to pupils. Entry to senior school for prep pupils not guaranteed and they also have to sit entrance assessment and be interviewed by head. A few each year don't make the grade, but usually headed off at the pass in year 5 and guided elsewhere. Two-form entry in reception, which is full. Numbers almost double in year 7 when a large number come from local state primaries. A few more join in year 9. Head cleverly not hugely increasing numbers, although there is demand, instead he is raising entry standards; parents take note. Entry to sixth form requires all GCSEs at 4+ with chosen A levels needing a minimum of a 6. Five or six join externally a year, usually from grammars in Lincolnshire.

Exit: Virtually all pupils go from prep to senior, the odd one to grammars across the county line. Nearly half leaves after year 11, mainly to impressive state sixth forms in Cambridge (there is a good train link) or other privates in Cambridge. Some, from the farming contingent in particular, to board at big hitters such as Oundle and Uppingham. Head very proud that high numbers achieve first-choice universities. One to Oxbridge and three medics in 2021; others to study eg history of art at Leeds, earth science at St Andrews and business management at Birmingham. Apprenticeships actively embraced, by parents and pupils, many of whom return to family businesses. The odd gap year, but not many.

Latest results: In 2021, 43 per cent 9-7 at GCSE; 54 per cent A*/A at A level (79 per cent A*-B). In 2019 (the last year when exams took place), 28 per cent 9-7 at GCSE; 15 per cent A*/A at A level (36 per cent A*-B).

Teaching and learning: Solid results that are steadily improving. Science taught singly with many pupils taking all three at GCSE, clever appointments with all three heads of department now having PhDs; 'they are so enthusiastic,' said one parent. Maths and English standards improved. RS now taught to A level. French, German and Spanish on offer; every child has to take at least one language at GCSE. Pupils set in English, maths and languages, from year 4 in prep and year 7 in the senior. Pupils happy and focused, chatty to visitors and proud to show off work.

We visited a science hospital where a teacher is present throughout the lesson and any senior school pupil can pop in for advice and help. Good up-to-date labs

Homework every night from year 3, 'but not on Wednesdays as we have matches then,' said our charming guides. Nice to see old-fashioned lift-top desks in some prep classrooms; 'some of our teachers don't like them as they are noisy.' Older children taught in the science block by senior teachers. Some facilities shared with senior school: library, assembly hall and refectory.

Junior and senior parents happy with academic progress and small class sizes, reasons why they chose the school. 'There's lots of parents' evenings, it's easy to see teachers, who care.' 'The children are pushed and compete with each other, in the nicest way.' Parents talked of teachers going 'above and beyond'. We visited a science hospital where a teacher is present throughout the lesson and any senior school pupil can pop in for advice and help. Good up-to-date labs; 'the chemistry lab is the hottest room in the school,' said our guides ruefully, and we can vouch for that. A separate electronics room. Very impressive art studio: do admire the giraffe sculpture, as well as a man on a chair and a gorilla. Very impressive art on display throughout the school. Lots of IT suites including a language lab. DT workshop well used, radio blaring; note the buggy and electric car, both driven by pupils.

Separate sixth form centre offering a kitchen, garden, lots of computers and a common room. Plenty of UCAS support and interview practice. 'We have supportive teachers,' said our guides. 'I can't fault the school academically,' said every parent we spoke to. Some mentioned personality clashes with the odd teacher; school tries its best to counteract this by making sure child not taught by them again. 'Teachers are honest and offer extra support where it's needed.' 'Good hiring choices have been made by the head.' A couple of parents mentioned that communication could be improved but realise that 'paper free is the way to go, so we must read emails.' Bright and gifted invited to join Poyser Group in sixth form, made up of pupils who are scholars and exhibitioners, with extra lectures.

Learning support and SEN: SEN support in both schools help 66 in total but only two currently with EHC plans. Help within the classroom from learning support assistants or one-to-one SEN qualified teacher. Some four children need EAL support.

The arts and extracurricular: School cleverly has a period 5 every day, straight after lunch, which is effectively a free period when children can indulge in sports and clubs, extra help sessions, music and band practice, and the occasional homework session. 'They make sure we aren't doing homework every day in period 5.' This allows every child, however far they live from the school, to join in practices and clubs. Plenty of after-school sports clubs as well. We enjoyed watching a dance session in the new studio.

Lots of drama productions, whole school and year groups as well as successful shows at the Edinburgh Fringe and at the local theatre. Plenty of music clubs on offer; 'What I would like is a club for complete beginners, there's plenty on offer for the knowledgeable but nothing for those of us who can't even read music,' said one pupil.

Plenty of school trips including an icebreaker on the Norfolk coast for year 7 and more exotic further afield ones for older pupils including to the Himalayas and Costa Rica. Lots of sports tours. DofE up to gold.

Sport: Sport has dramatically improved since the arrival of the current head, with the appointment of new staff and coaches. Sport for all, right the way through the school, including compulsory for sixth form – good. Rugby and rugby 7s for boys; 'we want it for the girls too,' said one of our prep guides. Cricket and hockey, for boys and girls, no football for either. Plenty of teams for all. Fitness suite well used with conditioning coach improving the fitness of team members. Parents keen supporters of matches, home and away. One parent would like better communication from the PE staff, 'I'd like to know fixtures and kit requirement sooner.' A happy father remarked, 'coaching has improved dramatically recently, as have the teams' and parents' match teas.'

Boarding: Opened Hazel House (the school's first ever boarding facilities) to international pupils in 2019 and another similar property in 2020 – the first two of seven projects to kick-start the school's international strategy. These two houses – one for boys and one for girls – house 12 boarders each, all with en-suite facilities, with plans to expand the provision to 50 pupils over the next couple of years. Eight other students are in homestay accommodation either with teaching staff or parents of other students.

Not your typical purpose-built, Travelodge-style boarding facility – rather, a converted five-double-bedroom house, with open-plan common areas and separate kitchen. Mainly Asian cohort, with 'executive chef' plucked from an exclusive Burnham market restaurant specialising in Asian cuisine.

Mention must go to the very pretty gardens, all immaculately kept, including the head's garden which pupils aren't allowed to use. There's plenty of seating elsewhere for all

All boarders are studying either a pre-A Level course or A levels, coupled with specialist EAL and EAP. Recreational sports on offer at the weekends, plus trips out to eg Cambridge, London and north Norfolk coast. Boarders can stay during half-term for a programme of academic enrichment, English Language support and cultural trips.

Ethos and heritage: Located in the Cambridgeshire Fen town of Wisbech and founded in 1379, it is one of the oldest schools in the country. Originally two separate schools, for girls and boys, they amalgamated in 1970 with the boys moving across the river to the girls' school on the current site. In 1983 the school became fully independent and increased in size. Newest addition is the sixth form centre, which opened in 2019.

Arriving at the school is slightly underwhelming as the new car park, although very convenient, is all that you initially see, along with the school sign. Walk through to the school and you are surprised by so much space – 34 acres in total – with lots of newish buildings and plenty of pitches. Mention must go to the very pretty gardens, all immaculately kept, including the head's garden which the pupils aren't allowed to use. There's plenty of seating elsewhere for everyone.

Prep school brightly decorated with plenty of outside space and the added bonus of being able to say hello to a couple of horses in the next-door field. The best behaved table in year 4 gets a cup at the end of the day, so behaviour exemplary.

Parents talk about the 'welcoming feel,' when they first visited and 'the happy children we met', wanting that for their own offspring. Our impression too. Surprisingly the school does not seem very well known locally. 'I didn't know the prep existed,' said one parent, but the head is working to make it much more visible with an open-door policy. School does not have strong competition from other privates (there aren't any close by) but the Lincolnshire grammars are on the doorstep, so head aware school needs to 'up its game with what we offer for a broader education'.

Pastoral care, inclusivity and discipline: All parents spoke highly of pastoral care and how problems were handled. Head does not deny bullying exists, but it is dealt with swiftly, effectively and robustly, backed up by parents whose children have experienced it. One parent said that the arrival of the current prep head had improved discipline standards dramatically. All parents said teachers knew their children very well. Lots of help during transition from one school to another. 'It's a happy school where teachers are really helpful, and care.' 'They know the social issues that children are up against, understand the children and use their strengths to help them cope.' Strong mentoring system in place between sixth form prefects and year 7 classes. Tutors have 10 children each so do know them well, and spend a lot of time with them, daily. Forms mixed every year, up to year 11, so friendship groups do not become static and everyone knows each other. Sixth form in the same tutor group for two years, vertically across two years, so lots of support for lower sixth from upper and vice versa. Counsellor and nurse available with mental health nurse due to be appointed shortly.

Pupils and parents: Pupils come from far and wide across the county, and from Lincolnshire and Norfolk as well. Parents happy to travel to access school, up to an hour each way in some cases. Traditionally a school for the children of farmers, there are still many today, joined by Forces families and professionals, many self-starters running their own businesses. Parents working hard, both of them, to pay fees. Many children are second or third generation to come here, at least. Head has extended the school day to include a 7.45am drop off and 6pm pick up, at no extra cost, which parents greatly appreciate. Pupils a friendly bunch, down to earth and unpretentious. Fourteen prefects wear distinctive striped blazers which make them stand out and easily identifiable. Other pupils more conservatively dressed in smart navy blazers. Sixth formers wear 'business wear'.

Money matters: Academic, sports and music scholarships available of up to £1,000, rising to £1,500 in the sixth form. Means-tested bursaries up to 100 per cent in exceptional circumstances.

The last word: The head ruffling a few feathers since his arrival has been for the better; the school had rather sat on its laurels in previous years and dwindling numbers reflected this. We get the impression from parents that the school's purpose and intent has intensified, taking all with it. They have stiff competition from local grammars so have had to up their game, offering a well-rounded education, and parents appreciate this. 'Confident children are what they produce, happy to stand up and speak in front of people; how I wish I had been given that chance when I was at school.'

Woodbridge School

43

Burkitt Road, Woodbridge, Suffolk IP12 4JH

01394 615041 | admissions@woodbridgeschool.org.uk | www.woodbridgeschool.org.uk

Ages: 11–18

Pupils: 523; sixth form: 138; Boarders: 60 full (from 13 years)

Fees: Day £16,626 – £17,994; Boarding £33,684 pa

Head: Since 2020, after a period as acting head, Shona Norman. Attended Wisbech Grammar School in Cambridgeshire, studied English lit at London University and PGCE at Cambridge before joining Woodbridge as a newly qualified English teacher in 2002, and has worked her way up through the ranks. Roles as housemistress, EPQ co-ordinator, mental health first aid instructor, deputy head (pastoral) and senior deputy have all been taken in her stride, as has the recent completion of a master's in Educational Leadership and School Improvement at Cambridge. One of few thirty-something women heads of HMC schools, her appointment was welcomed by 'delighted' parents and staff, satisfied that the role is well deserved. 'She is experienced, well-supported by the staff, kind and compassionate, while being firm in her decision-making,' says one parent. 'She really cares for her students and staff team,' enthuses another. Students describe her as an inspirational leader and outstanding teacher.

Keen to get her teeth into the role, she has a very clearly prioritised agenda. Top is a review of the curriculum from reception to year 13 in order to 'embed the skills that will enable pupils to be ready for future life,' she says. 'The Seckford Foundation allows us to address privilege and how we give back – it's why the school was founded and we mustn't lose sight of that.' This philanthropic theme has prompted an increased bursary provision. Teachers' professional development is another focus, 'to keep on top of the latest thinking and model life-long learning to the pupils', as is keeping the facilities up-to-date and encouraging an evolution of boarding – 'condensing, not expanding' emphasises head.

Under her guidance the school responded sensitively to the period of school closure, minimising disruption. 'The usual timetable was delivered live via Teams at both the prep and the senior school and we also ensured that the co-curricular programme of music, drama, sport and chess continued – through the use of much imagination and ingenuity.' Required to steer the ship through unprecedented choppy waters having only just been appointed as head, she is grateful to have been well established at Woodbridge already. 'Knowing the community was essential,' she says. 'We all worked in our different areas to ensure that school, in its new form, could continue. As the world seemed so uncertain, I took great comfort and reassurance knowing that our school would get through it together.'

Married to Michael who is in the Royal Marines, she 'devours' books and loves going to the theatre when she is able. She is also passionate about wildlife and the environment and feels fortunate to have the River Deben on her doorstep.

Entrance: All candidates invited to a taster day and private meeting with the head. Entrance test, together with a report from present school, and interview at 11+, 12+, 13+ or 14+. Half of intake at 11 transfer from the prep, the rest from local state and private schools. About three-quarters of those tested are accepted. Entry to the sixth form is based on an interview, test and GCSE predicted grades.

Exit: Few leave after GCSEs. Great majority head from sixth form to university – Edinburgh, Nottingham, Birmingham, UCL, Newcastle and Durham currently popular, as are STEM, modern languages, English and business and finance courses. Three to Oxbridge in 2021.

Latest results: In 2021, 69 per cent 9-7 at GCSE; 87 per cent A*/A at A level (65 per cent A*-B). In 2019 (the last year when exams took place), 58 per cent 9-7 at GCSE; 75 per cent A*-B at A level.

Teaching and learning: Academically the right buttons are being pressed, but although results across the board are strong, 'it doesn't feel like a hothouse,' approve parents, and there is an inherent disregard for league tables. The arts, maths, sciences and languages stand out, but the results of middle-range ability pupils reflect solid achievement – always pleasing. Pupils are banded from year 7 and setted in certain subjects, including maths. Classes around 20. All take French in year 7, adding Latin and Spanish or Mandarin in year 8; at least one modern language to GCSE, with Mandarin and Japanese optional extras and classics including Greek available at GCSE and in the sixth form. Sciences popular, practical and taught separately from the start, a term for each, and choice of separate or combined for GCSE. At A level, two groups of around 10 for each science; nearly all continue to study science at university – medicine (thriving weekly MedSoc), vet med, natural sciences. Teachers are lauded by parents as 'highly qualified and experienced'; 'amazing and so helpful' say pupils.

Learning support and SEN: Around 80 pupils have mild learning difficulties; several full-time teachers offer support individually and in groups. The emphasis is on keeping pupils fully integrated into the mainstream classes. Strong EAL provision for overseas pupils. This is a school that works for all abilities.

The arts and extracurricular: Music regarded as mainstream. Half the school learns one or more instruments in a warren of practice rooms and rehearsal spaces in the music department, where classrooms hang with Apple Macs for composition. Symphony orchestra, samba band, strings, percussion, single reeds, choirs (from chorum to 'Vocal Fellas'), swing band, brass ensemble. Regular informal recitals for parents as well as more formal concerts. Recently school musicians performed at the Edinburgh Fringe; regular appearances at the atmospheric Snape.

Buzz around school when we visited was about who had landed the starring roles in the upcoming performance of Grease, to be staged at school's own Seckford Theatre, a professional venue complete with interval bar and ice-creams, which hosts touring as well as school productions; community always welcome.

Cross country running is a real strength with Woodbridge representing England at the World Championships in 2020. The school also has its own equestrian team

Dance increasingly popular. DofE and successful CCF, which has its own facilities in the grounds. Pupils spend periods of up to three weeks at linked schools and the school's international programme provides visits and exchanges throughout Europe, Russia, China and Japan.

Sport: Impressive pitches, all on-site – including a new floodlit Astro for hockey – and courts, plus a sports hall housed in an Eden Project-style Dome, which has plenty of space for several classes to be active together (cricket nets and video cameras out for training when we visited in the autumn). Indeed, sport is for all here and everyone has the opportunity to play competitively in the school teams, often trouncing the opposition (we heard that the girls' hockey team had just won the regionals, under the guidance of double Olympian coach who used to play in goal for South Africa). The Elite Sports programme is devised to encourage the most talented pupils, many of whom catch the selector's eye at county and international levels, and there are dedicated coaches for hockey (parents would welcome similar investment in rugby and athletics). Cross country running is a real strength with Woodbridge representing England at the World Championships in 2020. The school also has its own equestrian team and reaches the national finals every year. Friday afternoon is timetabled for the Seckford Scheme, an extraordinary range of non-academic activities in which the whole school (staff included) joins. All interests and tastes are encouraged. School has its own chess international master. Running club is strong (the school is a key supporter of the Woodbridge 10K road race and also sponsors the youth and mini sections of Woodbridge Rugby Club). Rowing and sailing on the nearby river Deben.

Boarding: A day school with boarding – currently 31 boarders (all but two from all four corners) in one house in the middle of campus, which celebrated its 150th anniversary in 2020 and has spectacular views of the valley and chapel. 'The single house is a strength,' says head, 'it's small and feels like family.' Looking to offer weekly boarding Monday to Thursday but no more houses planned. Boarders are free to visit the town after school and at weekends when excursions to London and Cambridge, for example, are laid on alongside outings to parties, paintballing, the cinema etc. English language top-ups available.

Ethos and heritage: Founded in the 17th century, the school is part of the Seckford Foundation and has occupied its current site in the town since the 19th century. The extensive grounds are on a hilly plot (unusual for Suffolk and great for sledging point out our guides), dotted with a collection of buildings of various vintages, from the Victorian to the strikingly contemporary Seckford Theatre and glass-walled sixth form centre. Top-level all-weather astro pitch recently installed and there is a five-year plan to add further facilities, including a new gym. Fully co-ed for 40 years, there is a palpably studious atmosphere across the university-style campus, with its spacious, fuss-free classrooms, chilled library and many corners set up for independent study. Time wasting is frowned upon and every moment not in class is filled with sports and activities. 'Pupils can have a crack at everything going – there is a niche for everyone,' approves a parent. Pupils themselves are friendly and polite – teachers, if anything, even more so. Unstuffy relations all round, and the staff give praiseworthy loyal service and appear fully invested in the school (many having chosen it for their own children). Large governing body equally on board (chair is ex CEO of Pret).

Pastoral care, inclusivity and discipline: 'One of the school's key values is "kindness to others and to self", which permeates all that we do,' says head. Students themselves reinforce this through societies and clubs, such as MUN and Pupil Support. This commitment does not go unnoticed and parents praise pastoral care as 'excellent'. Says one, 'Every member of the team seems happy and supportive of the pupils, including the catering team, admin support team and grounds staff.' All pastoral staff are mental health first aid trained with a focus upon the individual as central to the pupil experience as their academic studies. 'During the pandemic, tutors called pupils individually to check on them, as well as meeting as a tutor group,' report appreciative parents.

Looking to offer weekly boarding Monday to Thursday but no more houses planned. Boarders are free to visit the town after school and at weekends

Vertical tutoring system works well – years 7 and 8 are kept together and separate from the older years; after that, years 9 to 13 – day pupils and boarders – are mixed for tutor groups. 'They get to know older and younger pupils and gain an appreciation of different stages of school life,' recognise parents. Weekly house assemblies in the chapel, built by students in the 1920s.

Leadership opportunities for sixth formers, who are allowed to wander into the safe and pleasant town centre at lunchtimes ('prepares them for university' says head). Few discipline problems.

Lunches are tasty – meat and vegetarian options (meatballs on the day we visited), pasta, salad, jacket potatoes and choice of puddings. Portions are 'eco-friendly' but seconds given freely. Fruit at breaktimes. Breakfast and supper for boarders as well as day pupils involved in a school activity.

Communication with parents is taken very seriously. As well as the usual parents' consultations, staff are available on a day-to-day basis via telephone or email.

Pupils and parents: Pupils are 'bright, friendly and supportive of one another,' says a parent, who also notes that 'all-rounders do well'. Drawn largely from professional East Anglian families, many have a media background (Aldeburgh, BT close by), but a fleet of buses brings pupils from as far afield as Bury St Edmunds, Felixstowe and Colchester. School is very popular in the town and many parents have moved out from London to the Suffolk riverside – particularly prompted by the pandemic – to take advantage. New pupils and parents integrate well and are made to feel welcome. International students attend for long or short periods and ginger up what would otherwise be a very English school.

Money matters: Scholarships competitive – academic, as well as music, sport, chess, drama, art and all-round. More means-tested bursaries than ever before and up to the value of full fees; must be applied for as part of the school application and demonstrate how the pupil will make a contribution to the school community.

The last word: In a small, cosmopolitan riverside town, a country-style school with a culture of collaboration, community and kindness. Happy pupils of all abilities do well academically and throw themselves into an exceptionally wide-ranging co-curricular programme designed to bring out the best in every individual.

Midlands and Wales

Derbyshire
Herefordshire
Leicestershire
Lincolnshire
Northamptonshire
Nottinghamshire
Rutland
Shropshire
Staffordshire
Warwickshire
West Midlands
Worcestershire
WALES

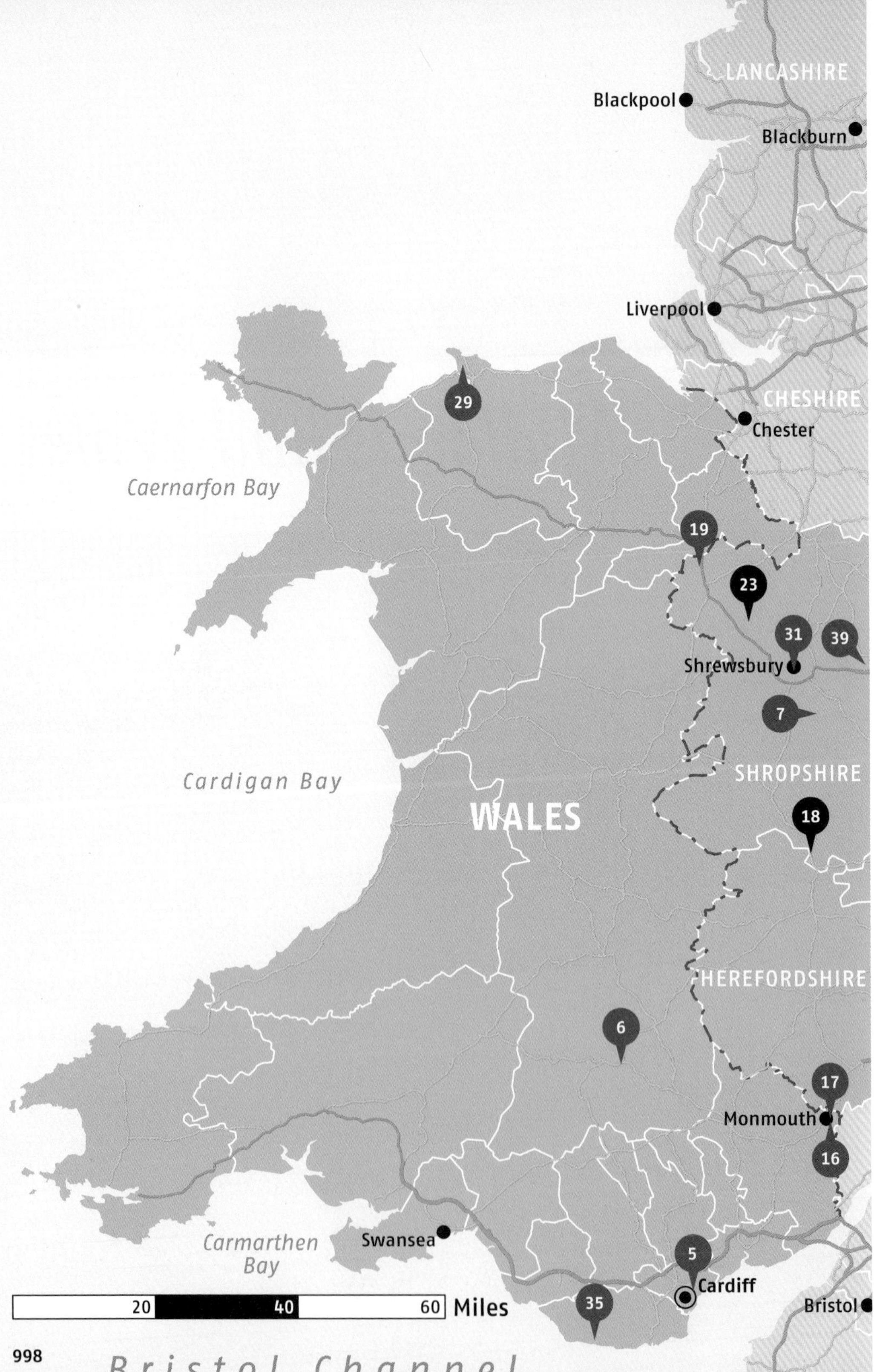
LANCASHIRE
Blackpool
Blackburn
Liverpool
29
CHESHIRE
Chester
Caernarfon Bay
19
23
31
39
Shrewsbury
7
SHROPSHIRE
Cardigan Bay
WALES
18
HEREFORDSHIRE
6
17
Monmouth
16
Swansea
Carmarthen Bay
5
Cardiff
35
Bristol
20
40
60
Miles
Bristol Channel

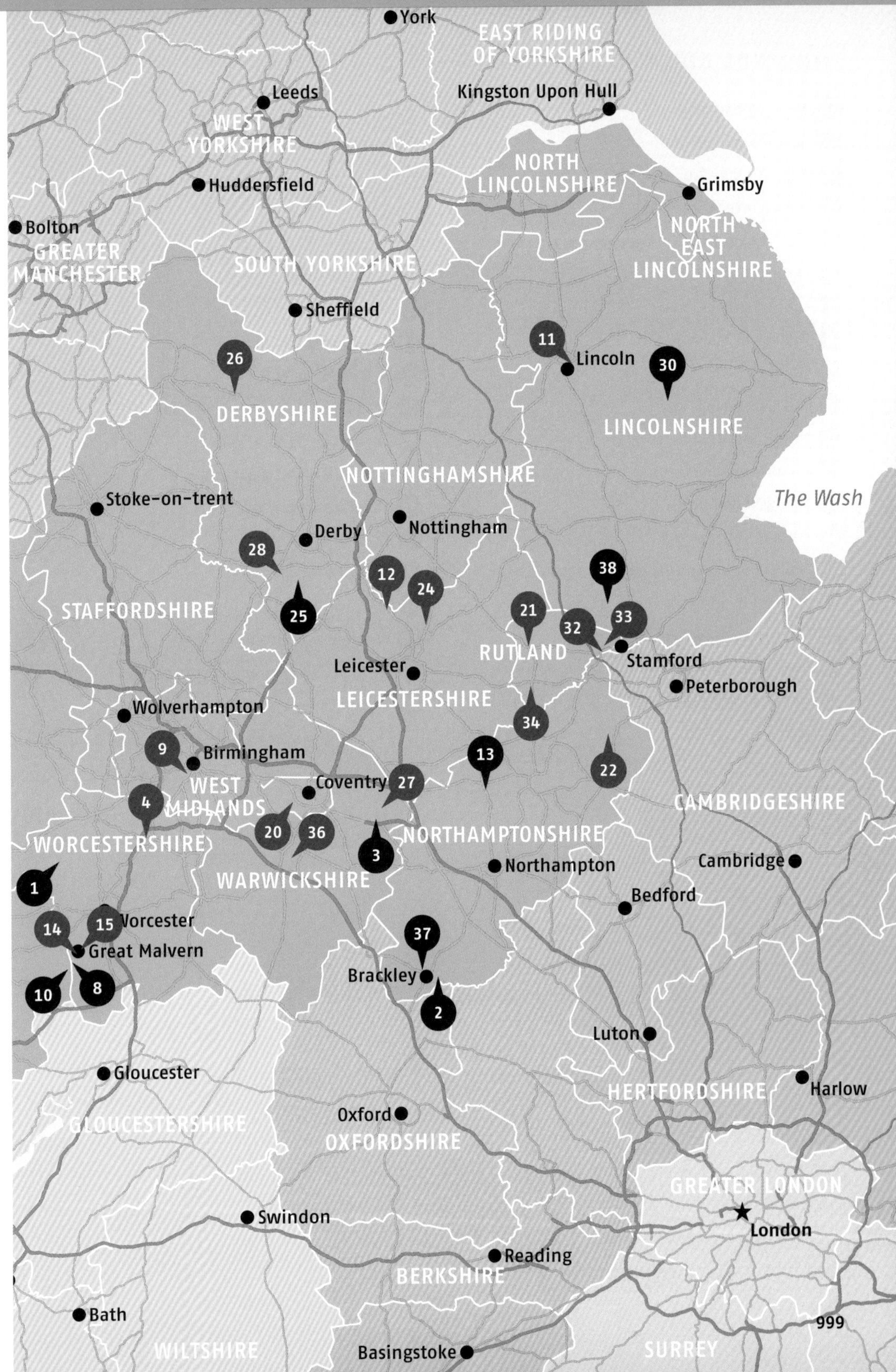
York
EAST RIDING OF YORKSHIRE
Leeds
Kingston Upon Hull
WEST YORKSHIRE
NORTH LINCOLNSHIRE
Huddersfield
Grimsby
Bolton
NORTH EAST LINCOLNSHIRE
GREATER MANCHESTER
SOUTH YORKSHIRE
Sheffield
Lincoln
DERBYSHIRE
LINCOLNSHIRE
NOTTINGHAMSHIRE
The Wash
Stoke-on-trent
Nottingham
Derby
STAFFORDSHIRE
RUTLAND
Stamford
Leicester
Peterborough
LEICESTERSHIRE
Wolverhampton
Birmingham
WEST MIDLANDS
Coventry
CAMBRIDGESHIRE
WORCESTERSHIRE
NORTHAMPTONSHIRE
Northampton
Cambridge
WARWICKSHIRE
Bedford
Worcester
Great Malvern
Brackley
Luton
Gloucester
Harlow
HERTFORDSHIRE
GLOUCESTERSHIRE
Oxford
OXFORDSHIRE
GREATER LONDON
Swindon
London
Reading
BERKSHIRE
Bath
WILTSHIRE
Basingstoke
SURREY

MIDLANDS AND WALES

Abberley Hall

Worcester WR6 6DD

01299 896275 | office@abberleyhall.co.uk | www.abberleyhall.co.uk/home

Ages: 2–13

Pupils: 160; Boarders: 52 full, 35 part boarders (from year 3)

Fees: Day £9,570 – £18,600; Boarding + £6,000 – £4,500 pa

Headmaster: Since September 2020, Jonnie Besley, previously deputy head at Orwell Park in Suffolk and before that, head of boarding and history at Westbourne House in Sussex. Has also taught history and coached sport at Dulwich Prep. Educated at Gresham's School in Norfolk, he studied history, English lit and philosophy at Durham. First career was in events management, but he then retrained as a teacher at Cambridge.

A lover of 'the great outdoors', he enjoys walking, cycling, fishing and sailing and has a lifelong love of carpentry. Married to Tessa, who is head of years 3 and 4. They have two children aged 9 and 11.

Entrance: Non-selective. Children are assessed either before arrival or when they arrive to ensure there is clarity about educational needs and, with older children, to help determine which academic sets are appropriate.

Exit: The vast majority stay to the end of year 8. This is a school that is a serious player in the CE stakes and leavers depart with a significant number of scholarships/exhibitions each year. The head says parents are keen to seek advice on senior schools, which they recognise as objective and in the child's best interests. So although school is part of the Malvern College family of schools it also sends pupils to Eton, Harrow, Winchester, Rugby, Shrewsbury, Radley, Oundle and Stowe.

Our view: Ninety acres of park and woodland surround Abberley Hall, a 19th century edifice of some significance. The bluebells were out along the drive on our visit to add to the idyllic rural setting in which the children grow up. Inside, the first impressions are of a grand but comfortable past. While we talk to the headmaster, a glorious peacock pecks at the window as if he wants to join us. Many of the original features of the old house remain – the headmaster's study is the old library, apparently untouched since an era of leisurely scholarship.

But there is nothing leisurely about the scholarship at Abberley today. It offers a traditional academic curriculum. The older children have 30 hours of lessons a week. 'It would be nice to have a few less lessons,' one or two year 8s said to us plaintively. Languages are a huge strength – Greek is taught from year 6, there are three hours of French a week and two and a half of Latin. It pays off in terms of scholarship examinations, the school tells us. From year 3, the children have twice-yearly exams. It is low key to start with but it means the children are getting used to tests. Science, maths, design and manufacture have a practical, cross-curricular emphasis that is impressive.

The workshops are open at lunchtime and after school for children to work on their own design projects – about a third of the school is engaged on one of these. Art is striking with a practising artist running workshops twice a week – 'It has been a huge help for the children preparing for scholarships,' the head of art tells us. There are textiles, ceramics, print-making, painting onto canvas and use of different media. The head is keen to develop even further the profile and challenge of the creative arts.

The older children told us that the high academic standards were what made the school stand out. 'We can get help from teachers whenever we want,' they say, 'and we can sign up for extra academic coaching sessions.' The school is preparing the children for success in their future education. Parents are enthusiastic about the quality of the teaching. 'They go the extra mile.' Once year 8s have completed all their exams, there is a challenging leavers' programme of events for them. The head says that feedback from senior schools is that Abberley children are notably good at grasping opportunities.

As the school is non-selective, learning support is taken seriously. Class size is kept to 15 maximum, allowing for much individual support within the classroom. There is dyslexia screening in years 1 and 2 and careful scrutiny of ongoing assessments. Where a need is identified, the head of learning support will step in. The school may do its own further assessment or advise an educational psychologist's report to help tailor future learning. What happens next depends on the level of need and is very much individually determined. Parents say that the children take needing extra help as a matter of course – there is absolutely no stigma attached.

Extracurricular life is teeming. Music is highly valued and a big part of the school. Not only lessons but practices are timetabled for the children which, with 200 instrumental lessons going on, must take some doing. There is a lunchtime concert series and the emphasis is on everyone getting a chance to perform at some stage. Many take RSM exams and do very well. A group goes each week to the CBSO Children's Choir in Birmingham. There are lots of instrumental ensembles and choirs. The senior chapel choir is invited to sing around the area, regularly performing at Worcester Cathedral. Parents describe the music as 'sensational' and are delighted by the high expectations from staff. There is a 'phenomenally ambitious' annual musical. 'The staff are not just wanting performance but perfection,' one parent told us approvingly.

'Gumboots and Greek' is school's strapline and it is a good reflection of what life is like. There is no sense that the rugby players are any more valued than the grade 1 flautist

The school is considered to punch well above its weight in sport, which happens every day with matches on Wednesdays and Saturdays and sports tours. Facilities are brilliant. Rugby coaching is exceptional even by standards outside the prep school world. Girls' cricket is taken as seriously as boys' cricket. Lots of the children said sport is a great thing about the school, but even those who admitted to not being particularly keen appreciate the choice they have and the chance to be outside.

There is drama and beekeeping, run by the headmaster, fishing and film making, spy club and electronics; the list goes on. Children can bring their horses from home and ride round the grounds on their bikes. It is a day packed full of intellectual and outdoor activities – 'Gumboots and Greek' is the school's current strapline and it is a good reflection of what life is like. Parents like the lack of hierarchy in school activities. There is no sense that the rugby players are any more valued or respected than the grade 1 flautist. The days are long and, particularly for parents considering boarding, it is important to ensure their child is ready for this degree of activity.

'We are not big on punishment,' says school and indeed the discipline issues with which staff are dealing are low key. The focus is on getting children to think about their own behaviour and how it impacts on others. Parents say that the school's attitude to problems has always been to leave it to school and not encourage parents to be very much involved. The new head seems to be changing this a bit, but everyone we spoke to seemed very confident in the school's ability to sort things out quickly and humanely and follow through on issues. The school is keen on giving the children responsibilities and has created new roles in the last couple of years to ensure the opportunities are there to learn about leadership.

Family backgrounds range from landowners and farming families to professionals and business people, and they are highly supportive of the school, generally living close enough to attend matches, concerts, Sunday chapel and the many other events. There are some children whose family connections with Abberley go back several generations.

The children are strikingly open and unaffected, living witness to the head's belief that prep school children retain their innocence longer. They are unselfconscious, gutsy and ready to talk to adults appropriately.

Boarding: The school says it is not what happens in lessons that distinguishes the outstanding boarding school, but what happens at weekends. Abberley Hall is committed to full boarding. There is no flexi-boarding but there is part boarding, where parents commit to specific days a week a term in advance. One weekend in three is full boarding, one is optional and the third is an exeat, so the most a child would be continuously at school is likely to be three weeks, which we think is right for children at this age and a good preparation for senior boarding schools. Many of the weekend activities, which the children tell us they adore and are keenly anticipated, are open to parents. Just before we visited there had been the annual fun run where everyone dressed up to complete various length runs around the grounds. The grounds are fully used. The children have built an outdoor pizza oven, there are outdoor classrooms and mini DofE style award activities outdoors one afternoon a week. There are clear rules about where in the grounds children can explore but plenty of space for climbing trees and building dams.

The children we spoke to enthused about boarding. The accommodation is very non-institutional, using the variety of spaces in the old buildings. Pastoral support is strong and the turnover of staff small. School has introduced a new tutor system for the older children so years 6, 7 and 8 have their own personal tutor for three years, who acts as a single point of contact for parents and with whom the children have a weekly individual meeting. We think this is an excellent model to ensure no one slips through the pastoral net.

The last word: Pupils here are being prepared for a work hard, play hard culture. They love the outdoor freedom and they also know life is a serious and competitive business, which they are up for. The school has much to be proud of in its past and everything to suggest the future is golden for the children lucky enough to come here.

Beachborough School

Westbury, Brackley, Northamptonshire NN13 5LB

01280 700071 | office@beachborough.com | www.beachborough.com

Ages: 2.5-13

Pupils: 381; Boarders: 58 (Monday - Thursday from year 3)

Fees: Day £9,570 - £17,910 pa; Boarding + £37 - £47 per night

Headmaster: Since September 2018, Christian Pritchard (40s). Previously head of Ranby House Prep School, and before that at international schools in Amsterdam and Taipei. The son of two head teachers himself, and hailing from Northumberland, he consented to following in their footsteps, he jokes, when he realised his dreams of becoming the new Neil Armstrong were unlikely to be realised. His interest in science and technology has nevertheless served him well (his degree was in Technology and IT), being a great fit with Beachborough's highly evolved interest in technology and its use, particularly in the motor industry – a significant employer in these parts. 'We're building real life business connections for the children, and through things like innovations days – to which we also invite local primary schools – we've been able to show local technology in action.'

Mr Pritchard is also a keen mountain biker and walker, and equally keen to see children taking education out of the classroom and off-curriculum – 'Having been lucky to work in two lovely country school settings, I'm a big fan of learning everywhere' – with close up magic a more intriguing hobby.

His wife Zoe also works at the school as head of nursery and kindergarten, and their younger daughter attended Beachborough for two years before secondary school. 'We've always approached our school and career as a family,' he says, which has no doubt helped facilitate the globe-hopping.

How have those years overseas influenced his style of headship now? 'It's fed my concept of preparing children to be world ready — to have an international outlook,' he replies. Increasing the school's diversity is another pleasing focus (the school community appears predominantly white).

Though he doesn't teach regular classes, Mr Pritchard 'helps out when needed', works with older children on debating and of course takes assemblies. 'I'm not a tweed jacket and labrador type of head, but I do spend a lot of time with the children.'

The parent body unanimously agrees – everyone interviewed volunteered that he is all about the children: 'He's so invested in educating the whole child'; 'He's empathetic and kind, on the children's level'; 'He lets the kids show off the school and they absolutely love him.'

Though Mr Pritchard describes his team as 'strong believers in the co-ed system', his own daughter, I observe, chose an all-girls secondary school – 'I'm also a big believer in listening to what your children think!' – more proof of that empathy.

Entrance: Entry is usually in nursery or reception, with years 3 and 5 other natural points of entry, if there is room (and sometimes there isn't). Every applicant comes for a taster day and children with learning support needs will be assessed against their cohort 'to decide if we can meet a need or not,' says the learning support deputy.

Mr Pritchard describes the school as 'broadly non-selective, but we do some light touch assessment'. This includes written assessments for any child applying to join in year 1 or above.

Exit: A school with the annoying habit of listing future destinations in marketing material without divulging how many go to each. In fact, Bloxham and Stowe hoover up almost 70 per cent between them, since most parents seek local options, with pupils dispersing to a large number of schools after that, mainly in and around Oxford, Buckinghamshire and the Midlands. St Edward's, Tudor Hall, Millfield, Eton, Uppingham and Abingdon have featured recently. Secondary schools in this part of Britain offer good numbers of scholarships involving financial assistance, and Beachborough is very good at landing them.

Our view: The key item of uniform at Beachborough is not a blazer (they don't have them, to keep uniform costs down for parents) but their trademark blue 'boiler suits'. Boys and girls pull one over their uniform with a pair of wellies to enjoy the playing fields whatever the weather – a much-loved feature of this beautiful 35-acre school. 'That's one of the first things we saw, and my husband just said, "I'm sold!"' said one parent. Rarely have we heard parents so consistently talk about 'us' and 'we' when discussing their children's school – there is immense loyalty: 'I'm always very proud to be a Beachborough mum,' and 'It has a beating heart. My daughter calls it her second home.'

Beachborough's marketing is certainly slick. Its prospectus is packed with graphics, its cover – like the website – adorned with pupils beckoning you in, as does a personalised poster by the door, greeting by name any visitor or prospective parent.

Northamptonshire is actually the fourth county this school has inhabited. Originally founded in 1910 in Surrey, it landed here after various moves, through Kent (at Beachborough Park, from which the school then took its name), and Hampshire when its Kent home was requisitioned by the MoD in WWII.

The Elysian first impressions of lawns and pitches extending from the charming sandstone manor house (a definite draw for many parents) are backed up with an impressive focus on science – here described not as STEM, but STEAM, to include the arts in the acronym. From learning groups named after famous scientists and astronomers to the beautifully designed TED centre opened in 2017 (all glass, steel and daylight) equipped with a laser cutter, 3D printers, a vacuum former and other kit more usually found in secondary schools, the enthusiasm for science and

Boys and girls wear the trademark blue 'boiler suits' over their uniform with a pair of wellies to enjoy the playing fields whatever the weather

technology is palpable. Connections with the local motor industry are fully utilised – a Formula One fan on the staff and parent in the trade jointly run the Goblin Car Club, for example, in which year 5s and 6s design, build, wire, market and race an electric car. How could any child resist? The five-year plan now is to join the F1 in Schools programme. Pupils study in the TED centre from year 3, with a range of clubs (eg tech club and engineering club) also using its DT workshop, CAD suite and more. Beachborough's tech focus is destined to grow further – a digital music composition is opening shortly, with an augmented reality system for the science labs, and video and image manipulation software planned for the art department.

A child's journey through the school begins in the separate Boardman building (named after a former head) which houses the nursery and pre-prep. Classrooms are set around bright shared central spaces, with excellent gardening, exploring and play areas outside. Some lessons also take place in a well-established forest school with adjacent wetland area – inhabited by two new ducks – ideal for pond-dipping and other ecological (and boiler-suited) investigations.

A commitment to the ACE learning approach (standing for active, creative and exploratory) has led to the development of different zones within each classroom, eg for reading, creativity and wellbeing. Mondays may be used for a scene-setting discovery day from which the whole week's activities unfold, and the system helps children to learn in an enduring way through first-hand experience. The resulting picture is one of utterly engaged, happy children with enthusiastic teachers: 'We've learnt far more about these children through this – it is so much more child-centric.' Certainly we've never seen a cosier scene than one form enjoying snack time to background music and a fire crackling on the giant screen behind them. Also striking is the uniformly excellent handwriting almost everyone seems to have by year 2 – 'a big focus, along with politeness,' attests one parent. Years 3 and 4 are next to the Boardman but begin to take some of their lessons in the manor house, before moving there completely from year 5, when they will also be streamed in English, maths, French and science.

Once in the prep school there's a house system – but here they are called clubs (again named after former heads) – with termly and annual points tallies. Every child from year 5 has a tutor (not their form teacher) they will meet in small groups twice a week, once with a wellbeing focus. Parents and pupils find this creates a strong pupil–teacher bond: 'You'd liaise with your child's tutor before their form teacher – they get to know the children very well.'

Though the school day does not finish until 5.05pm for year 5s and above, there is well-used after-school care until 6.45pm from year 3. This incorporates a period of self-directed time in which children may 'pause, disengage and just let off steam on the lawns' before the familiar mix of tea, clubs, homework or one-to-one assistance if needed from a teacher.

There are three full-time and three part-time learning support assistants in the school who offer small group sessions or provide individual support in class. Termly and annual standardised testing from year 1 helps flag any issues – and any learning support assistance is included within the fees. There is also a wellbeing counsellor who visits two days a week.

Beachborough's reputation – alluded to by parents interviewed – as not the most academic of prep schools is something the school explains by saying, 'We are quietly proud that we are not an academic hot-house but that we are "excellent in all areas" of teaching and learning and pupil welfare as cited by our ISI inspection in 2018.' Yet this same reputation in fact attracts many parents, as does the school's skill in helping children fulfil their potential in a less pressurised way – such as the awarding of effort grades, rather than achievement ones, each lesson. As one teacher puts it, 'Achievement is very important but effort comes first.'

Class sizes are between 16 and 18, with two or three classes per year group. There is a scholarship set from year 7, its recent successes certainly indicating plenty of achievement besides effort. Parents feel the teaching is consistently strong, and no one would or could fail to be gripped by Tudor history in the history classroom decorated floor to ceiling in the style of a castle interior.

Enrichment weeks – at least once a year – are another highlight at Beachborough, with pupils and staff jointly choosing the themes which then direct studies (and dressing-up opportunities) throughout the week. 'They're a chance to turn away from the obvious – eg how do you light a fire when you have no matches? – and take children out of their comfort zone,' says Mr Pritchard. Beachborough has also for some years run its own junior DofE-type awards – increasingly common in prep schools – here called the Beachborough Endeavour award. Offered from year 3, roughly half the pupils pursue it all the way from bronze to gold.

The very smart school theatre affords every child a performance opportunity at some point in the year – for year 7s this is Shakespeare, while the year 6s put on a musical and the year 8s a leavers' showcase. Not quite half the pupils – a smaller percentage than in many preps – have private music lessons, but no one misses out: all year 1s and 2s study an instrument for nine weeks and all year 3s and 4s sing in the junior choir. Senior choir is optional but enjoys 90 per cent uptake, with a chamber choir too for which pupils must audition, and which does concerts, festivals and tours – including a memorable performance at the last post service at the Menin Gate in Ypres. There is a school orchestra, two big annual concerts, and 12 different instrumental ensembles run by visiting music staff, with the Beachborough Rockers particularly popular.

A Formula One fan on the staff and parent in the trade run the Goblin Car Club, where pupils design, build, wire, market and race an electric car. How could any child resist?

On the sporting front, rugby and hockey are perhaps the highest profile games, with numbers of pupils playing these outside as well as within school (hockey being huge in the Midlands). An active partnership with the Northamptonshire Saints rugby club enables the school to enjoy some of their coaching and match tickets, and the best players may try out for the Saints' junior academy. The netball courts have been newly resurfaced, there is a large Astroturf and a really vast indoor sports hall to accommodate PE, gymnastics, basketball and more. Everyone gets to play in away matches and triathlon has lately taken off, driven by a former GB veteran on the staff. Beachborough also hosts various contests, from an equestrian event at Stowe (there are no on-site facilities but plenty of keen riders at the school), a triathlon (also run from Stowe as Beachborough does not have its own pool), and – within its own grounds – two annual cross-country runs, including one for local primary schools. Some parents comment that they'd like to see more team buses organised for weekend tournaments, however, and less reliance on them to chauffeur.

On the top floor of the manor house is a relaxed hang-out zone for year 8s, and a thoughtfully laid out and furnished wellbeing room – part library, part-lounge – for everyone's use (all teaching staff are being trained in mindfulness).

Boarding: On the top floor of the manor house is Kites, the boarding house which accommodates some 45 children a night, Monday to Thursday. Sometimes almost an entire year group opts to stay on a given night – a sure sign of approval – with two to three nights a week the more usual commitment.

Children from up to two different years may share dorms, the time before bed usually spent in the sports hall or fields, or playing manhunt through the manor house – a perennial favourite. The dorms themselves avoid the slightly impersonal feel of most flexi-boarding rooms, having been beautifully decorated by a range of secondary schools, Bloxham's black and white design, and the Narnia-inspired dorm designed by Malvern (alma mater of CS Lewis) being particularly striking.

Money matters: There are some bursaries available from year 3, of up to 100 per cent, which are means tested and anonymous.

The last word: 'Watch out robots, children in training,' says a notice in Beachborough's impressive TED suite, a building which houses so many great clubs and scholarship projects it must be a great recruitment tool in itself. Indeed, the school is working hard to relegate to history its reputation as the destination of choice for the less naturally academic, and to be recognised instead as a place that helps children to prepare for the future and fulfil their potential. Our experience was of cracking, expressive pupils brimming with confidence and happy to interact, even beyond a teacher's earshot. 'I hope you enjoyed your visit!' shouted one girl from the playing fields as we headed back to the car. We absolutely did.

Bilton Grange School

Rugby Road, Dunchurch, Rugby, Warwickshire CV22 6QU

01788 810217 | admissions@biltongrange.co.uk | www.biltongrange.co.uk

Ages: 3-13

Pupils: 320; Boarders: 28 full, 16 weekly

Fees: Day £10,743 – £20,727; Boarding £26,190 – £28, 239 pa

Headmaster: Since September 2021, Gareth Jones, previously head at St Andrew's Prep, Eastbourne for six years. Before that, he was at Dragon (Oxford), where senior roles included director of sport and housemaster. Read English and history before doing his PGCSE in primary education and a master's in educational leadership.

Entrance: Two or three form entry. Slightly more boys than girls (particularly amongst boarders) but it's not obvious looking round. Non-selective, though the school says they are looking for children who can access what is, in an age appropriate way, an academic curriculum. A number come in from London at 11+ for the final two years, to get the boarding experience or just to get away from the London hothouse. School became part of the Rugby School Group in 2020, but the admissions process remains the same.

Exit: Parents felt very well advised by the school about appropriate choices at 13+. A few leave to go to grammar schools at 11 but mostly it's senior boarding and around half to Rugby, with which the school merged in 2020. Others to Repton, Oundle, Benenden, Uppingham, Shrewsbury, Princethorpe and some overseas to Spain. A number of scholarships each year – 18 in 2021. As you might expect, the focus is on 13+ and the head is not keen on 11+. 'It puts a lot of pressure on children much too young,' says school. 'They lose out on years of childhood.'

Our view: Set in 90 acres of countryside and woods, the Pugin designed buildings stand as a symbol of stability, tradition and British cultural heritage. The children can't but be reassured and uplifted by the glorious wooden panelling and carvings of chapel, library and staircases, the huge windows, the period wallpaper sourced from the Houses of Parliament. Within this, modernity in the form of ongoing building development sits comfortably. Not all the 20th century builds are as stunning as the Victorian heart but buildings are being adapted and renovated.

Academically Bilton Grange does very well both by its high flyers and by those who are not going to get the big public school scholarships.

A number of parents who have moved children out of the London pressure cooker told us that while Bilton Grange is less academically pushy than its London counterparts, it does get children to the best schools and even more importantly, it creates highly motivated and self-driven children who succeed well beyond 13+.

The school works positively with those who might be considered to have a mild learning difficulty. Small class sizes (around 12 to 16) allow for a lot of individual support within lessons and the increasing setting as they get older gives further tailoring to meet specific needs. Where difficulties are identified, specialist staff develop an individual learning plan which may involve a range of strategies – one-to-one sessions, in-class support, Saturday literacy enrichment, for example. The school identifies high flyers who might be heading for senior school scholarships during year 7 and is about to look at year 6 as well. The children are offered various opportunities and teachers watch how they respond to the stretch and challenge. We visited as academic scholarship exams had finished, and one group was busy designing Bilton Grange's own Cluedo whilst another was making a trebuchet scaled up from some carefully worked out computer calculated designs. Others were writing policy papers for a forthcoming election in school to mirror the June general election manifestos.

While the curriculum is fairly traditional, the focus is on encouraging what the head calls 'flexible' learners. The school now teaches the three sciences together rather than separately with an emphasis on the applied aspect of science – the children had a talk from a Jaguar Land Rover designer recently and have been creating their own rocket-propelled cars. DT is a real strength. Even young children work on serious machinery and love it. The options and curriculum enrichment programme, which runs after school and on Saturdays, is extensive.

The school is also traditional in terms of its values and behavioural expectations. There is an emphasis on courtesy, respecting one another and the community, but this in no way inhibits the children's enthusiasm, which is celebrated round every corner of the school. Parents, too, are expected to uphold the school values and the head has very little time for those who don't.

The school runs a lecture series for years 7 and 8, their parents and the wider community three or four times a year that aims to bring in leaders from a wide field to help the children become aware of the vast number of opportunities now available. There are other forms of outreach going on – one success is the Scout group, started and still run by the head. It is now the biggest in the district and gets together very regularly with other packs for scouting activities. School welcomes parents in and considers their needs thoughtfully. This is regarded as a huge strength. There is a lounge area in a charming stone-slabbed Victorian conservatory for parents who are waiting to pick up a second child, or just want to chat or browse the senior school brochures, with a little play area for tinies. Talks that are regarded as important for parents to hear are videoed and sent to parents who can't make it. 'The school really understands working parents,' one family told us.

The school is traditional in terms of its values and behavioural expectations. There is an emphasis on courtesy, but this in no way inhibits the children's enthusiasm

Saturday mornings are optional for year 4s, with an exciting new programme called the BiG Saturday that should tempt many back before afternoon sports matches. By year 6, there are some Saturday lessons for everyone as well as the vibrant enrichment options. In years 7 and 8, everyone is in for academic morning lessons and games in the afternoon. If you are not actually in a match, you are in a training session.

We enjoyed the food, which caters for various special diets as well as providing keenly anticipated treats such as roasts and steaks. Matron is on the door to ensure plates contain a variety of colours. Pastoral care is high on the school's priorities. PSHE programme aims to tackle the issues that start to cause anxiety as the children head towards the teenage years. No-one was worried about bullying; yes, normal friendship ups and downs, but nothing the school isn't highly experienced at resolving.

Although it is a school where masses seems to be going on all the time, staff are conscious that children also need quiet times and these, too, are built into the day. Sports facilities are good and school encourages non-team sports (golf, clay pigeon shooting, zumba, trampolining) though the school also wants everyone to experience the community values playing in a team can bring. The children love the fact that they can do sport more or less every day and they like the fact girls play cricket. One family, whose children are clearly sporting stars, felt a bit more of the 'winning at all costs' drive wouldn't come amiss, but that was not a general view, most going along with the sport for all approach. In fact the school does do well in matches and the top players compete at county and, indeed, national level.

The grounds lend themselves to a vigorous relationship with the outside world. Some of this is formalised – a science garden, a gardening club – but probably more important is the tearing about outside that goes on around lessons. Drama thrives and much use is made of the theatre. 'Being able to participate in plays has really given my son the confidence he lacked before coming to Bilton Grange,' one father told us. The head is a musician by training and keen to develop music facilities. Lots of the children play instruments (about 80 per cent have individual music lessons each week) and there is a wide range – the harp as well as the mainstream orchestral instruments. There are many performance opportunities for the various ensembles and choirs, both in the school and outside.

Boarding: Most don't start boarding until year 4. The school is very careful to try to ensure that boarders are emotionally ready for it – and indeed that their parents are. Weekly boarding available but by year 8 most are full boarders. There is deliberately gradual transition.

Boarding accommodation is refurbished on a rolling programme and the rooms, most of which house about six, are fresh and unregimented. Day children are very welcome to join boarders for prep and boarders are encouraged to invite their day friends in for the odd sleepover at weekends.

Money matters: Scholarships and funded places which are now processed in conjunction with Rugby School.

The last word: Bilton Grange is unpretentious despite its splendid buildings. 'Not posh enough for some,' the school told us, with some pride. It has been co-educational for many years and there is none of the alpha male feel of some prep schools. It has a genuine child-centred core – children are not there just to fulfil parental expectations and not allowed to be mini-teenagers plugged full time into the cyber world – they are there to experience and enjoy childhood.

Bromsgrove School

Worcester Road, Bromsgrove, Worcestershire B61 7DU

01527 579679 | admissions@bromsgrove-school.co.uk | www.bromsgrove-school.co.uk

Ages: 13-18

Pupils: 990; sixth form: 459; Boarders: 521 full, 46 weekly

Fees: Day £17,940; Boarding: £26,610 – £40,155 pa

Headmaster: Since 2014, Peter Clague, following a glittering career in New Zealand that embraced the state and independent sectors. Attracted by the school's sense of heritage and purpose, Peter says it was Bromsgrove's challenge to the traditional public school image that clinched the deal for him. He is a huge supporter of IB and believes that its genuinely international spirit suffuses the whole school, bringing with it a progressive liberalism and excitement about modern educational developments. He has introduced more flexibility in the timetable, with longer lunch breaks for pupils to pursue co-curricular interests, and aligned the prep and senior school more closely, but perhaps the biggest changes are in the importance he is giving to the arts. There is more music and drama than ever before and a huge investment in the building of a new theatre at the prep school and concert hall at the senior school.

'He is not as scary as he looks,' said one girl to us, which is more a comment on his height and presence than anything else because he is universally seen as charming and warm. The school is proud of its international leader and feel he mirrors the increasingly global outlook of the school. They like also the way in which he respects the traditions of the school but helps them all to look critically at what works and change what could be better. He is described as a visionary and also praised for being in touch with reality. 'He's not all idealism – he has his finger on the business pulse and is very data focused,' one senior member of staff told us. He is a skilled wood turner and works beside staff and students building stage sets. He is an 'awesome' public speaker, pupils told us: 'We never know where his metaphors are taking us.' His litmus test for everything is 'Is it good for the pupils?'

To be replaced in August 2022 by Michael Punt, currently head of Chigwell School since 2007 and before that deputy head academic at The Perse School, Cambridge. MA in physics from St Peter's College, Oxford and MSc in semi-conductor science and technology from Imperial. Married to Gill with three sons.

Entrance: At 13+, CAT 4 tests and an essay. The largest cohort from the school's own prep. No automatic entry, but parents seem to feel that plenty of warning and advice is given if a child is unlikely to be accepted to move through. At sixth form level, entry depends on GCSE results. A confidential school reference is required for all candidates.

Exit: There is a seriously impressive range of courses, universities and countries in terms of pupil destination that reflects the wide sixth form clientele. Eight medics in 2021, and three off to Oxbridge. UCL, Manchester, LSE, Edinburgh and Bath all popular, and increasing numbers overseas – in 2021, two pupils gained scholarships to Toronto, with other North American destinations including UBC, McGill, UC San Diego, Boston, NYU, Northeastern, Parsons and Georgia Institute of Technology. European destinations include IE Madrid, Bocconi Milan, Amsterdam, the Hague and Leiden and further afield in the world, Sydney, HKUST, HK Polytechnic University. Economics, engineering, business, psychology and law are among the most popular courses.

Latest results: In 2021, 70 per cent 9-7 at GCSE; 62 per cent A*/A at A level (89 per cent A*-B). IB average point score 40. In 2019 (the last year when exams took place), 64 per cent 9-7 at GCSE; 57 per cent A*/A at A level (77 per cent A*-B)). IB average point score 37.

Teaching and learning: This is a school that really does embrace and value the vocational and the academic. A Level, IB and BTec are all on offer in the sixth form and each has its strong supporters. The IB group loves the small, but growing, tightly knit IB community and tells us that they get all the very best teachers – but the other groups said the same, so we assume there are just a splendid lot of wonderful teachers. A level students assured us they get the breadth through all taking the EPQ. Geography is 'amazing', politics is 'brilliant' and both attract large A level groups. Science and maths flourish. There are usually some nine sets taking single maths and three further maths groups. Results are strong. At the end of the sixth form, virtually all BTec results are double distinctions.

The only criticism on curriculum breadth came from parents who wanted the school to be offering much more on the home economics and cookery side of things, but apparently the school is taking this on, and other than that there is an impressive range of opportunities.

There is a popular café, open all day, for older pupils – but we were assured by earnest sixth formers 'it is never a substitute for a proper lunch'

Saturday mornings are not compulsory but a large proportion of pupils are likely to be there, not least because that is when some of the additional academic classes take place – whether in the form of catch-up and support 'surgeries' or Oxbridge preparation. There are plenty of other academic interest groups running too for anyone not falling into those categories. For those who miss a Saturday, there are departmental tweets that keep you interested.

Learning support and SEN: Learning support is highly rated, though one parent gave a word of caution that moderate learning difficulties were beyond the scope of the school. There is a very attractive and well-used learning resources centre on three levels and we were delighted to hear it is open till 10pm in the evening and at weekends. This is the sort of opportunity that makes boarding so attractive to the serious student as well as those who want one long sleepover.

The arts and extracurricular: There is an exciting variety of clubs and societies and the school has invested heavily in staff on the co-curricular side to make a strong offering for all. Everyone was rightly proud of a girl who had entered an international competition to build an electric car and had ended up racing it at Rockingham. Drama is big and lots of departments – including art and DT – contribute to productions. Music is getting stronger all the time with smaller lunchtime concerts as well as the big school showpieces. New performing arts centre (opened in November 2017 by Julian Lloyd Webber) features a Vienna concert grand piano. There is Model United Nations and the school sends pupils to the European Youth Parliament. Pupils and parents were keen to tell us that the school looks for what every individual is good at and helps them find their niche and passion.

All year 10s do CCF. Some continue and others take up DofE awards separately. There are service projects running so everyone makes a community contribution at some stage.

Sport: Everyone was at pains to tell us that this is not just a rugby school. Well it certainly brings home the rugby silverware, winning two recent national finals, but then the girls' netball team are national champions too. There is genuinely a big variety of sport on offer with D teams that inspire just as much enthusiasm as the A teams. The school was ranked fourth in the country recently in School Sports Magazine. The elite senior rugby players do have to make the sort of serious commitment you would expect at national level, so it is not really an option to be in the U18 squad and play the lead in the school play. Sports facilities are excellent as you would expect, with a particularly impressive new indoor arena with pull-out seating for 400 where the national indoor hockey finals take place. The pool and gym are open at weekends for boarders.

Boarding: At first the size may be a little intimidating but it is that which ensures the wide opportunities and it is ameliorated by the house system. Each house has its own internal family structure with older pupils acting as mothers and fathers and the younger ones as children. At the end of year 11, students can move to a sixth form house, but some can't bear to leave their first boarding house, home from home, at that stage. Apart from those in the sixth form house, everyone eats in a central dining room. There are separate day houses and one with day pupils and boarders.

House tutors have about 11 in a group and, with a 50-minute weekly session timetabled, get to know their tutees well. Sixth formers say that if you act like an adult, tutors treat you like an adult. Houses are good at communicating with parents and pupils – there are house newsletters and blogs as well as balls that help create a strong house identity. House competitions are seen as big bonding experiences and we were urged to get onto the school website to enjoy the full splendour of house music competitions.

The medical centre – which now boasts a qualified teenage mental health nurse and onsite residential nurse – is highly praised. The nurses visit each boarding house every night to check all is fine and the focus on wellbeing, which includes bringing in outside speakers, is welcomed. Boarders say it is a 'full on' school. If you want to spend your weekends and evenings on a couch, the Bromsgrove experience would be wasted on you.

Ethos and heritage: Teaching staff come from a range of educational backgrounds – Oxbridge as well as the old polys – and this gives a sense that the school is grounded in the realities of life outside. There is a drive to ensure an authentic connection with the local community, who use the sports facilities and will be enjoying the new performing arts additions. Senior pupils have links with local state schools through CCF, DofE and university preparation. There's a sense of energy and hard work. The days are long for boarders and day pupils but they are full of purposeful activities.

Boarders say it is a 'full on' school. If you want to spend your weekends and evenings on a couch, the Bromsgrove experience would be wasted on you

It is a large campus, 100 acres, in the middle of Bromsgrove, a medium-sized Midlands town. Buildings vary in age and the overall impression is of a site loved, cherished and very well maintained. Teaching blocks are attractive with wide corridors and big classrooms, all well lit. There is a delightful little school museum in the old chapel which is just one of a number of reminders of the school's heritage. There are 13 houses, all but one single sex, some in modern buildings, some in charming older ones; the only co-ed house, in a converted hotel a few minutes from the main campus that was once the home of AE Housman, is a real stunner. The 'new' chapel is very prominent on the school site and there are assemblies three times a week for everyone.

There is a popular café, open all day, for older pupils – but we were assured by earnest sixth formers 'it is never a substitute for a proper lunch'.

We were impressed by the careers department where there has been a serious investment in staffing. Year 11 and sixth form pupils have a number of one-to-one interviews and these are supplemented by a Bromsgrove Futures programme of weekly visiting speakers. The contact with ex-pupils is also strong, so current pupils can get advice on careers and university choices and the chance to practise interview technique. There is a diverse intake and the careers department is well aware it is catering for a wide range of needs – another example of how, despite its size, the school is interested in individuals.

Pupils clearly feel the school is good at listening. The head boy and girl lead regular school forums with no member of staff present and they told us the very positive results from these meetings. Pupil voice is increasingly bedded into all aspects and creates a sense that pupils really are at the centre of this school.

Pastoral care, inclusivity and discipline: The pupils do need a degree of self-discipline to flourish, parents told us. They need to manage themselves to some extent, especially as they get older – which is seen as excellent preparation for life beyond Bromsgrove for those who succeed, but some parents knew pupils who had struggled with it. Discipline is seen as being robust and fair and pupils need to be prepared to accept it without arguing the toss. Uniform regulations are enforced strictly. Punishments for serious breaches of school rules ('but it's very rare,' pupils assured us) are consistent and take sensible account of the culprit's previous history, but there is very little debate round drugs or sex – you are out. The underpinning rule is that you must not stop others from learning.

Pupils and parents spoke very warmly and appreciatively about members of staff both on the academic and pastoral side. The overriding sense is that well-being and the whole person really do matter to staff.

Pupils and parents: The school sits somewhere between highly competitive Birmingham and posh boarding school clientele. Families typically have both parents working and are fairly diverse, but probably not a lot of old money and quite a number of military families. It attracts English families who want an international community – there are boarders from all over the world – and a choice of routes post-16. Bucking national trends, there has been an increase in British boarders and prep boarding in recent years. The pupils we met were delightful and genuine. They were articulate and thoughtful and all quite different from each other, which was refreshing. The situation of the school is an asset – it is in a good central England location, easy to reach from all corners of the country.

Money matters: You are paying for the excellent facilities and opportunities as a boarder or a day pupil. Learning support is included in the fees, as is ESL tuition. The head is very conscious of the need to widen access and play a part in promoting social mobility. He is actively building a bursary fund and currently there are 73 children on life-changing bursaries (worth 75 per cent plus of school fees). He tells us that past pupils are very receptive to raising funds for bursary support. Scholarships are on offer for academic, sporting, artistic and musical talents.

The last word: Bromsgrove manages to combine the feel of a local family day school with an international boarding school, attracting pupils both for its sporting reputation and also its academic offer and results. It is a carefully crafted hybrid that works. There is a culture of hard work and hard play and an earnestness about the pupils that is beguiling, far from the arrogant outcome some parents fear in independent schools. The arts side of the school is definitely in ascendency, both in terms of the huge financial investment and in the mindset of the community. We want to be invited back for performances in the new theatre and concert hall – we expect them to be world class.

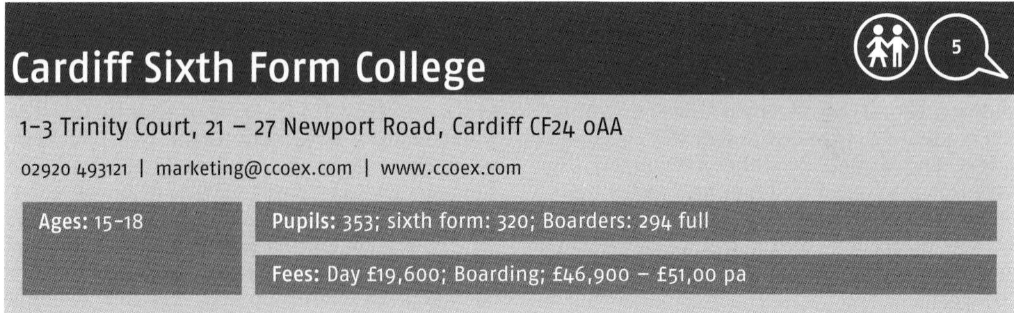

Cardiff Sixth Form College

5

1-3 Trinity Court, 21 – 27 Newport Road, Cardiff CF24 0AA

02920 493121 | marketing@ccoex.com | www.ccoex.com

Ages: 15-18

Pupils: 353; sixth form: 320; Boarders: 294 full

Fees: Day £19,600; Boarding; £46,900 – £51,00 pa

Principal: Since January 2020, Tom Arrand (40s). Theology and philosophy degree from Oriel College, Oxford and PGCE from Homerton College, Cambridge. Spent a decade at the Haberdashers' Monmouth Schools including as deputy and acting head at Monmouth School for Girls. Before that, five years as housemaster, head of religious studies and philosophy, head of Oxbridge and head of KS4 at Colston's School in Bristol. Under his leadership, students gained the top RS results for GCSE in the UK. Resident house tutor and head of rugby and cricket at

King's School Ely, Mr Arrand has also taught at Royal Grammar School in Guildford and Orwell Park in Suffolk.

Entrance: A few on to the one-year GCSE course as a preparation for hitting the ground running for A levels. Good English is a prerequisite: overseas students have to get 6.5 in the academic version of IELTS. 'We're not dragged down by poor English here,' claims school. Or indeed academic weakness: this is an exceptionally selective school. Applicants with GCSEs must have at least six A*/8-9s in total with A*/8-9 in all subjects chosen for A level, plus doing sufficiently well in college admission tests. All sit the GL assessment in verbal reasoning online and are interviewed, either in person or on Skype.

Induction arrangements are good; parents like the fact that students are not thrown straight into lessons, but given a chance to get acquainted and to start meeting, in some cases, a very different set of expectations. Unequivocally a student's choice to come: 'we are very suspicious of pushy parents,' says school.

Exit: Around five per cent leave post GCSEs. A stellar set of UK university destinations. In 2020, 17 to Oxbridge. Heavy bias towards degree courses in medicine, engineering and computer science. Forty medics in 2020. Twenty four overseas in 2020 – Hong Kong, Northwestern University US, Trinity College Dublin, University College Cork, Sydney.

Huge praise came in for the wraparound support underpinning the entire UCAS process both from students and their parents – this extends to a second bash at Oxbridge the term after a student had left – but one parent felt that interview preparation should be more rigorous and taken beyond the familiar surroundings of the college. Occasional gap years. Anyone not getting AAB in college tests at the end of year 12 will be invited to reconsider their choices or directed to other Dukes colleges. Careers advice starts the minute the student starts to ensure correct choices for A level and beyond. Possibly too young an institution to have produced famous former pupils, but we would wager that in years to come, there will be Cardiff Sixth Form alumni at the top of global scientific, political and legal trees. Watch this space.

Latest results: In 2021, 90 per cent 9-7 grades at GCSE; 97 per cent A*/A at A level. In 2019 (the last year when exams took place), 84 per cent 9-7 grades at GCSE; 90 per cent A*/A grades at A level.

Teaching and learning: Its raison d'être – make no bones about it. From the very high bar to embark on the foothills of the one year (and now also two year) GCSE course, or year 12 to the summits of academic excellence scaled at the end of a student's time at the college, students are there to work – and work they do, quite voluntarily. Results are a dazzling array of As and A*s: anything less jumps off the page in the prospectus. The school has topped the Times and Telegraph league tables for the last six years.

Boarding is a means for overseas and further flung students to attend the college rather than an end in itself: provision is functional not flagship

So how do they do it? Well, partly by being pretty picky at the outset, but once students have arrived, they benefit from exceedingly committed and experienced teaching staff (average age 60+: age clearly does not weary them, nor the years condemn) whose time is not spent doing anything other than teach: all other jobs like extracurricular matters, trips and related admin are done by a separate team. 'I demand you teach excellently' is the head's unequivocal requirement of academic staff. Small classes (eight is average) and the high number of taught hours (25 per week) also factors. Close weekly monitoring by teachers, who fix problems in one-to-one interventions; peer one-to-one sessions also common: 'any notions of shame or losing face with teachers is overcome,' we were told, and we were struck by the collaborative approach to learning.

Students and parents greatly appreciate the dedication and commitment to personalised learning shown by academic staff – and that they run revision days on the odd Sunday. Teaching and its environment looked conventional, without the latest whizzy IT, and all student eyes riveted to the front. In a maths class, students were entering findings onto graphs in what looked like exam conditions, but weren't; chemists were looking at double and triple bonds in alkenes. Focus and seriousness of purpose evident throughout. At just 15 subjects on offer at A level and an emphasis on STEM subjects and sciences leading to medicine, dentistry or veterinary courses, there's no place here for woolly A level choices – the college offers naught but facilitating subjects, aiming as it does for the world's top universities. No IB – 'no call for it', according to the head. The library has nary a fiction book in sight, but everyone is enrolled in Cardiff City Library for light relief, if needed.

Learning support and SEN: Significantly, a search for 'special needs' or SEND produced a blank on the college website, nor was there any mention of learning support during our visit, but there is a handful of students receiving help with conditions such as ADHD; nothing that would impede the pace and intensity of academic demands, however.

The arts and extracurricular: Debating got a universal thumbs up from students and parents alike: not only an excellent way to prepare for a career where the ability to string a forcible argument is a necessity (law, politics, parenthood), as well as building confidence in English, especially for non-native speakers, but also 'a means to develop eloquence,' as a proud mum whose son had represented Wales told us.

All work and no play certainly makes Jack a dull boy and Jill a dull girl, so students are actively encouraged to relax and let their hair down singing and dancing in Glee club (recent productions include Hairspray and Mulan, where the mix of nationalities lends more credibility to these shows than is often the case at UK schools) or preparing for the annual Eisteddfod. The cultural evening was mentioned as a yearly highlight by many people we spoke to, an opportunity for every student to showcase national dress and traditions such as music and dance. Balls at Halloween and Christmas, along with the odd team-building trip in the nearby Brecon Beacons blow away any remaining cobwebs.

---

*Results are a dazzling array of As and A*s: anything less jumps off the page in the prospectus. The school has topped the Times and Telegraph league tables*

Art is offered as an A level subject and soon as a leisure pursuit: it would have cheered up the corridor walls to have had more on display. Music ensembles get some airtime, and for the first time lessons in 18 instruments including the harp and euphonium are being offered; the college boasts some seriously accomplished musicians but study comes first. Clubs are limited in number and are sorted into 'hobby' and 'interest', the latter being academic in focus. The NASA club has participated – and done commendably well as finalists in 2018 – in a worldwide competition where students 'propose detailed designs for a future human settlement in space'. Academic trips also keep pace with student aspirations: not just Bristol Zoo but also CERN and the remarkable International Citizenship Experience, which takes students to Malaysia, Tanzania or India to take part in work experience in a variety of settings including government and NGOs, exposing them to team-building and leadership opportunities along the way.

Sport: Look away now if acres of green pitches, manicured wickets, lofty rugby posts and extensive fixture lists are what you are after. Cardiff Sixth Form has none of these, occupying as it does a city centre site on a busy road. Sport is definitely relegated to the second division here, but don't expect any couch potatoes either: sport is encouraged and some (fitness, dance, yoga, swimming) organised through local gyms and other providers (college lays on minibus). Traditional ball games take place on local pitches, and matches are arranged between the college's five (virtual) houses and on occasion with local schools; also DofE. Three hours' compulsory weekly sport for anyone below sixth form. Annual sports day takes place at a local sports stadium. Nonetheless, space and facilities (or lack of) are a source of rare student grumbles.

Boarding: A means for overseas and further flung students to attend the college rather than an end in itself: functional not flagship, though sited in two blocks in former university accommodation for the most part, a short walk from the main building. Students have the choice of studios or cluster rooms, where 5-6 single rooms share a kitchen (for snacks) and hanging out space; GCSE students have a communal dining table. Décor and set-up very contemporary and a useful bridge to university, but with sufficient staff to lend support, both practical and emotional as necessary. Day parents are grateful that there's just enough capacity to offer a place for a student getting back very late or stranded by bad weather to lay his/her head. All meals are provided in the utilitarian top floor canteen in the main building; all dietary needs catered for (all meat is halal, for example), but cuisine was (deliciously) noodle-heavy the day we visited.

Ethos and heritage: Set up in 2004 by the previous visionary, charismatic but now discredited former head as a small private tutorial college where clever, driven youngsters could achieve all they were capable of and get a leg-up into the best British universities, Cardiff Sixth Form has never been sidetracked into amazing buildings or facilities. It makes much of its central location in popular vibrant Cardiff, with its rich intellectual and cultural life (if students have time to enjoy it), easy transport links and fabulous wild country just beyond. After a very rocky patch during which it looked closure in the eye, the college was acquired by Dukes Education in 2017, with all that experience of compliance, finance and marketing galloping to the rescue.

The environment (a former insurance company office block, with tiny rooms and endless corridors) may have absolutely no frills, but the teaching has all the tips, tricks, techniques and tlc anyone could wish for

Its roots, then, are far from ancient or traditional, and it is exceedingly clear about its purpose: 'It is for students who wish to win a place at the best universities to study courses which will provide fulfilment and challenge,' to cite the website. The environment (a former insurance company office block which still looks and feels like it, with tiny rooms and endless corridors) may have absolutely no frills, but the teaching has all tips, tricks, techniques and tlc anyone could wish for. If, however, we were expecting gimlet-eyed automatons clutching laptops, we did not find them, but we encountered focus, drive and commitment to academic demands by the bucketload, in students and staff alike. For the right person – very bright/ambitious/hard-working/determined – fed up with being insufficiently stretched or distracted at school, this place would be a focused heaven of intellectual rigour and endeavour. 'Exam factory' would be an easy but lazy and inaccurate label. Taking the best from the cultures of east and west – the single-minded discipline of an Asian education versus the lateral cross-curricular thinking of a western one – might seem like a convenient strapline, but the students unconsciously echoed the benefits when talking to us.

Pastoral care, inclusivity and discipline: Very sound. It is well recognised that youngsters working as hard as these ones do need adequate support. Teachers are surprisingly 'nurturing rather than pushy' in their approach, one mother told us: 'they love them and encourage them to do well.' Quick to respond to any concerns, above and beyond academic, too. Students meet their tutors one-to-one every fortnight, and student welfare was flagged up as a positive by the students we met, extending to removing errant spiders, one girl recalled with a shudder. Another had received help with a stutter. The Independent Schools Association recently nominated the college for an award in mental health: 'We see a lot of exam anxiety, but we have measures in place to tackle it,' a staff member told us, adding that the stigma over mental health is gradually fading. Some of the trickier aspects of teenage life are covered in PSE lessons, but the ethnic and cultural mix of the college means that some topics are definitely off limits, eg LGBT matters. Though we got lowered eyes and shuffling feet when we raised this with students, some parents reassured us faintly: 'The kids speak to each other, so maybe the school doesn't need to intervene formally,' one mother concluded. The college definition of bullying was written by students. As for discipline, it's hardly a feature here. Sanctions are reckoned to be rare but fair: 'we're redirected on to the right path, rather than being shouted at,' one boy explained. We have never seen a clearer example of carrot over stick.

Pupils and parents: Academically and professionally ambitious: these families know their kids are aiming for the top, and are giving them the means to get there. In the head's view, 'Some are pushy, some appreciative, some have saved all their lives to give their children the opportunity of a UK education.' Of the 320 students, 44 are local, many on astonishingly generous bursaries. Many nationalities (SE Asia, Nigeria, Russia and eastern Europe predominate) are represented, and this came up time and again as a huge strength. We found students to be highly articulate, determined, realistic about the demands of getting top grades, top degrees and top jobs – and a million miles from nerdy geeky types we might have anticipated. There was something rather untypically adolescent about them too: all cheerfully wear school uniform, and do not appear to push the boundaries to explore the wilder shores of teenage or Cardiff life.

Money matters: Fees are right up there with the most expensive schools in the country, attributable to the cost of leasehold buildings, the small classes and high number of teaching hours, the two latter points perhaps making up for the lack of space and facilities. Some very generous bursaries (up to 100 per cent) are offered and all Welsh students receive some kind of subsidy. The college does not have charitable status.

The last word: If the disconcertingly corporate setting and relentless intellectual demands do not deter, this is an ideal place for the very bright, ambitious and motivated. Definitely not for everyone, but should be on the radar of anyone aiming for the stars – with the means to fund the trip.

Christ College, Brecon

Brecon, Powys LD3 8AF

01874 615440 | enquiries@christcollegebrecon.com | www.christcollegebrecon.com

Ages: 7–18

Pupils: 356; sixth form: 119; Boarders: 155 full (from year 5)

Fees: Day £9,582 – £19,584; Boarding £16,278 – £31,110 pa

The head: Since 2017, Gareth Pearson, BEng (40s). Brought up in Dorset, he read mechanical engineering at Loughborough before joining the Royal Marines for eight years. A stint at Millfield saw him through the graduate teaching programme as a maths teacher; a move to Wellington then expanded his career in house-mastering, clearly invaluable experience for headship, which he describes as 'like being a housemaster on steroids – every pupil will expect to have a relationship with you'. His most recent post was senior deputy at Lord Wandsworth College and he let slip that his friends tease him that the reason he got this job was because of his good Welsh name: 'but my wife is Welsh, plus I'm a rugby coach and referee,' he counters. Whatever the process, Mr Pearson seems to be an exceedingly good fit. Parents swoon: 'We absolutely adore the guy!' said one; 'The kind of person you'd like to have round to supper,' added another. Yet more commend his dedication, his visibility, the fact that he knows all the students and latterly, the school's handling of the Covid-19 crisis, which broke shortly after our visit. We reckon the ability to strategise instilled in the military and to react coolly in a crisis has come in pretty handy; other hallmarks from those days are an immaculate appearance (shoes polished to a mirror glaze), firm handshake and uncompromisingly direct gaze. We wouldn't mess with him and suspect the students wouldn't either. Their take on him was less starry-eyed than their parents', praising his approachability and encouragement of feedback, and that he has managed to realign some college traditions without doing away with them.

Mr Pearson describes himself as a busy dad to two teenagers, both in the school. They are, by their own admission, a 'very outdoorsy family' whose perfect day would comprise walking, cycling and canoeing in the sensational landscapes surrounding Brecon.

The junior school, St Nicholas House or St Nick's inevitably, set up only in 2014, has from the start been headed by Julie Lewis, previously deputy head in a local state school. 'Not many people get the opportunity to open a school from scratch,' she told us, 'and we had to integrate sympathetically with a community which had been here for hundreds of years.' We were struck by her warmth, such that lots of tinies rushed up to her to show off their reading books as we passed by. She has two children who went through the senior school, one of whom is training to be a teacher herself.

Entrance: Main entry points are year 3 for the junior school (where hopefuls will spend a day or so with a class undergoing informal assessments), year 7 and to a much lesser extent year 9 to the senior school (where matters become more formal and the school's own entrance tests in English, maths and non-verbal reasoning are taken). At sixth form, where a good clutch join from local state schools, the requirement is at least six GCSEs at a grade 5, but 6s in any subject to be taken to A level. International students sit the school's own papers online in English as an additional language and maths, plus Skype interview with the head. Transfer from St Nick's to the senior school is largely seamless.

Exit: Around 15 per cent leave after GCSEs in search of greater options and freedoms at sixth form, possibly financial reasons also. Main destinations seem to be newish Merthyr College and the longer established and fabulous Hereford Sixth Form (GSG). Vast majority to uni and half of those to Russell Group. Bath Spa, Cardiff, Cardiff Met, Durham, Exeter, KCL, Imperial, Nottingham and Swansea all popular. Two to Oxbridge, plus one medic in 2021 – and two overseas to Toronto and Hong Kong universities.

Latest results: In 2021, 46 per cent 9-7 at GCSE; 54 per cent A*/A at A level (78 per cent A*-B). In 2019 (the last year when exams took place), 41 per cent 9-7 at GCSE; 39 per cent A*/A at A level (69 per cent A*-B).

Teaching and learning: Not the whole story here: 'Academics aren't everything,' as the head states, so recent results are all the more creditable. Subjects are organised into seven faculties, and every student is assigned a tutor who oversees all aspects of their life at CCB. Not the widest choice of A levels but 'not much call for Russian or Italian here,' as one mother put it.

The introduction of three BTecs (sport, ICT and drama) has, however, been welcomed. Students reckon there are no weak subject areas, but history, geography and maths came in for particular praise, as did the science facilities and advice from teachers. Absolutely sensational library with upper floor a dedicated archive and quiet study space. In the junior school, we loved the guided reading we saw, where the more hesitant read to Tegan the golden labrador. Right answers are rewarded by a coloured button in a pot that each child has. Audrey the python lives in her vivarium in one classroom...

Provision of remote learning during the Covid-19 crisis was praised.

Learning support and SEN: SEN – known as additional learning needs here – has had its own dedicated department since 1995, which is now headed by a SpLD specialist. Referrals to it can be made by parents, teachers and students themselves. The website states unequivocally that 'all pupils, including those with identified special educational needs, are expected to cope with a full curriculum at a relatively independent level' and therefore that some students may 'require a level of support that Christ College does not currently offer'. That said, parents we spoke to were unanimous in their praise, not only for diagnosed learning difficulties such as dyslexia and ADHD, but also for supporting students with other serious health problems. We were impressed by what we were told about the school's flexibility in, for example, dropping superfluous GCSE subjects and resitting entrance exams and its 'kind, supportive and thoughtful attitude'.

The arts and extracurricular: Outdoor pursuits in the form of DofE and CCF are predictably huge here – the latter compulsory in years 9 and 10. Brecon is, conveniently, the centre of the army in Wales. The head is commanding officer but delegates day-to-day routines. From September 2020, lucky youngsters can sign up for the Beacons Challenge Programme, designed to 'encourage our pupils' physical, spiritual, social and moral development', through three multi-activity days of mountain derring-do each year.

Music is strong, as befits a school sited in the land of song. Auditioned and unauditioned choirs mean anyone who wants to sing can, and the house music competitions, one for singing and one for instrumental players and ensembles, are hotly contested. About 40 per cent of students learn an instrument and there are ensembles for all standards and most genres. Regular open mic sessions provide an informal setting for musicians to polish their skills before concerts or exams. Close collaboration with the drama department results in some spectacular musicals such as Scrooge and Phantom of the Opera in recent years.

Immensely proud of its heritage but not weighed down by it, the school's origins live on in some of its ancient buildings constructed from the region's pinky-hued slate

Plays and other performances take place in the Neuadd Memorial Hall, a strikingly modern addition to the traditional school buildings, complete with gallery and social space. Every aspect of theatre is possible here, from the usual set design and lighting to the less usual make-up and prosthetics, and most major productions run for four nights with split casts, so more budding thespians can tread the boards. Younger students don't miss out either: their shows are staged there – the latest being Beauty and the Beast. Aladdin is for now metaphorically on ice.

Art has a delightful listed building overlooking the river Usk, where sixth formers have their own dedicated space. Photography is a real strength here with facilities to match, including a dark room – 'It's not all about the digital,' as the maestro told us. Sculpture, textiles and ceramics also on offer.

Sport: We cannot better the words of one mother: 'Being in Wales, the school lives and breathes rugby but hockey is a real strength.' Main competitors are Llandovery College and the Monmouth schools. Cricket has a perhaps surprisingly high profile for girls as well as boys, with coaching throughout the winter. Forty acres of grounds provide enough space for an Astro (due an upgrade shortly), hard tennis courts, an indoor sports hall (incidentally the only place on site where the whole school and parents can fit) and covered 25m swimming pool. Plenty on offer for those not so keen on team games (a compulsory carousel to the end of year 10, however) and full advantage is taken of the school's stunning surroundings with climbing, mountain biking and kayaking laid on in the Brecon Beacons by the school's qualified instructors. Ambitious recent tours for top players – hockey to South Africa and rugby to Japan.

Boarding: Just over half of students board in some way. Boarding is possible in the junior school, where it is accommodated in the one house which is also home to year 7 and 8 day students. Two senior boys' and girls' houses complete the set-up. We liked the warm and welcoming feel of the girls' house we saw, with its young house-parents, bright cheery common space and insistence on phone-free Friday; phones are taken in each evening for everyone below sixth form. Dorms clean and tidy, with singles for sixth formers and double-sized ones for prefects. House loyalty is intense but not tribal, and those who board seem to love it. Parents also broadly supportive (especially of the house staff) but some feel accommodation could do with freshening up, and one overseas parent thought much more could be done to share school life, such as live streaming of major school events and more digital wizardry for parents' evenings. Maybe Covid-19 and its necessary technical innovations will see to that. Everyone eats in the stunning dining hall; we picked up the odd gripe about the food, but the smell and golden crackling of the roast pork proved irresistible over the salad bar the day we visited and it did not disappoint.

Ethos and heritage: Founded in 1541 by Henry VIII on the site of a Dominican priory dating from the 13th century, Christ College became a proper 'public school' in the Act of 1855. Immensely proud of its heritage but not weighed down by it, the school's origins live on in some of its ancient buildings constructed from the region's pinky-hued slate and its jaunty emblem of a crowned H, reproduced in the overwhelmingly green uniform and in topiary in the grounds. Very much an institution in this small but significant market town in mid Wales, the school is proud of its contribution to the local economy as an employer and provider of facilities – it has a mutually dependent relationship with the town and wide swathes of the surrounding area, and refreshingly little town v gown animosity, if any. Its position just across the river means a five-minute walk into town, allowed for senior school students; boarding parents like that small taste of freedom for their offspring. The serenely beautiful chapel sits at the actual and spiritual centre of the school and the prevailing ethos is Christian, but inclusive – 'The chaplain makes the Christian faith relevant to modern life, even for non-believers,' we were told. All are required to attend chapel, however, although the content is sometimes secular. Those values spill over into making a very friendly school, where relationships between students and staff are strong. Again and again we heard words like 'family' and 'community' – this is a small school which caters for everyone. It is not, we were told, 'snooty, elitist, nor ridiculously academic', rather a place where everyone gets a turn. The mid Wales bubble that the school arguably inhabits is popped intermittently by the stream of outside speakers such as 'mountaineers, military people, academics, business people and politicians,' as one mother spelt out. Yet its Welshness is celebrated by means of an eisteddfod for younger students and an option to study Welsh in years 7 and 8. Even the head has had Welsh lessons.

The most famous former pupils are the cool hip young stars of BBC Garden Rescue, Harry and David Rich.

Pastoral care, inclusivity and discipline: Highly, highly rated by all. There are 'layers of people to talk to when things go wrong', according to one mother. 'Mental health support in houses especially good,' students added. Good deeds are acknowledged by gold notes, bad ones by blue. Although some students remarked that they were awarded inconsistently at times, they like the fact that all achievement is recognised, and colours awarded for all manner of success, not merely sporting. But don't think that the school fights shy of serious matters like drugs: offenders can expect the heave-ho.

One parent thought that more could be done to share school life, such as live streaming of major school events and more digital wizardry for parents' evenings. Maybe Covid-19 and its necessary technical innovations will see to that

Pupils and parents: Crisply summarised by one father as rural families from miles around (a few dynasties), city kids from Cardiff and overseas families from SE Asia, Nigeria, Nepal, (Gurkha HQ is in Brecon), Germany and Spain mostly, all of which makes for a surprisingly wide mix for such a rural school, appreciated by parents. The students we met were charming, aware of their good fortune and obediently wearing school uniform right through sixth form. This is not the place for the rebel, show-off or non-conformist, we feel.

Money matters: Noted by us in the past as one of the best value schools in the UK, where the fees comprise almost everything and extras are limited.

Usual range of scholarships and bursaries, the latter likely to be sought as the fall-out from Covid-19 develops. Generous provision for Old Breconian parents and forces families in receipt of Continuing Education Allowance. Local businesses sponsor events at school, a great innovation.

The last word: Think of the place as a magnet: it draws in those needing or wanting boarding or simply added extras from a vast tract of country where independent schools are a rarity for economic or ideological reasons. What's more, it succeeds in providing pretty well everything for pretty much everyone who can stretch to the fees.

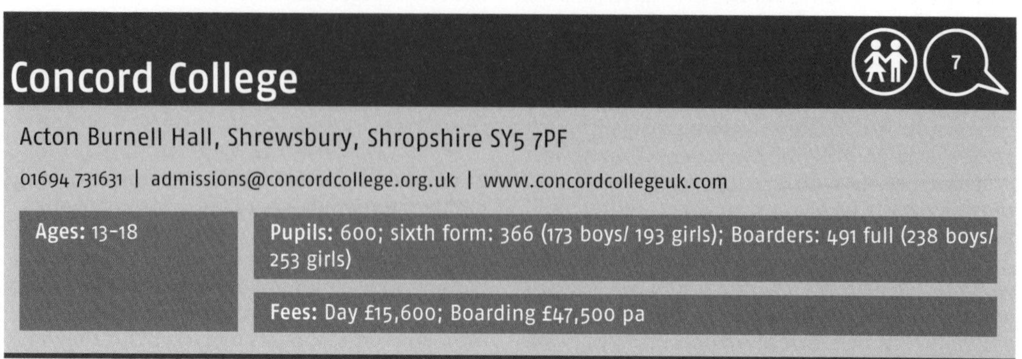

Concord College

Acton Burnell Hall, Shrewsbury, Shropshire SY5 7PF

01694 731631 | admissions@concordcollege.org.uk | www.concordcollegeuk.com

Ages: 13-18

Pupils: 600; sixth form: 366 (173 boys/ 193 girls); Boarders: 491 full (238 boys/ 253 girls)

Fees: Day £15,600; Boarding £47,500 pa

Principal: Since September 2021, Dr Michael Truss, previously deputy head (academic) at Barnard Castle. First class MPhys degree in physics from Oxford and a PhD in theoretical astrophysics from Leicester, followed by post-doctoral research at St Andrews and a teaching fellowship at Durham. Became a maths teacher at Bedales in 2007, where he subsequently became head of academic enrichment.

Entrance: Highly selective and getting more so, particularly at sixth form level. For entry to year 12 spoken and written English has to be competent. Those coming in at 13+ have more time to get it up to standard.

Exit: Sixteen per cent left after GCSEs in 2021. The influence of family background can be seen in pupils' higher education choices. Parents have done well themselves in business and they value degrees in economics, finance, medicine, law, maths and the sciences. Having said that, quite a few go on to study architecture and the art department has considerable success with the London art schools. LSE, Imperial, KCL, UCL, Warwick and Durham are popular. Thirteen to Oxbridge in 2021, plus 26 medics. Usually plenty overseas including recently to Chicago, Toronto and Pennsylvania.

Latest results: In 2021, 94 per cent 9-7 at I/GCSE; 94 per cent A*/A at A level. In 2019 (the last year when exams took place), 85 per cent 9-7 at I/GCSE; 85 per cent A*/A at A level.

Teaching and learning: Whichever league table you choose to consult, you'll find Concord among the top selective schools in the country. Exam results are consistently impressive. Huge numbers take maths, further maths, economics and the sciences. Other disciplines are smaller but achieve equally stellar results. Class sizes are small and the whole emphasis is on individual attention. We visited as A levels were kicking off; teachers had provided a list of all their non-contact time each week so students knew when each teacher was available for individual support.

Whichever league table you consult, you'll find Concord among the top selective schools in the country

Results reflect not only the high calibre of teaching staff but also the fact that students come from backgrounds that are very goal orientated and where education is highly valued. Expectations are stratospheric. After regular Saturday tests teachers are bombarded by students wanting to know how to move their 98 per cent to 100 per cent. Many are aware that this is a very different style of education compared to that offered in the top schools in their own country and they relish the relative liberalism. The pace is fast and teachers find they get through twice the material in a Concord A level lesson that they would expect to in other schools.

Students and teachers were at pains to explain that although the atmosphere is competitive – there are notice boards with the top students from last year's external results featured – it's also highly supportive. The students want everyone to achieve and helping each other is seen as part of the principles of a Concord education. This may be true, but parents did raise questions about how it must feel to be a student who doesn't get all A*s and a place at a top university.

Student after student to whom we spoke was high octane; ideas came pouring out of them. They want a school with a brilliant reputation and results so that they can go on and be significant players on the global scene. They know that it is not just about their sharp intellect, but also about wider awareness and they are just as keen to grab that too with both hands.

A level choices confined to what might be considered the safe traditional subjects and one student commented that there was a limit to the possible combinations. Music is offered as a BTec rather than GCSE and as an EPQ (extended project qualification) in the sixth form, rather than as an A level subject. Rather like sport, music is seen as high quality recreation rather than purely academic study and both the BTec and EPQ focus on a practical approach.

Learning support and SEN: While English language support is available, a student with weak English would undoubtedly struggle because of the pace of lessons.

The arts and extracurricular: There are wonderful performance opportunities for the musically gifted and a lot relish these, unsurprisingly given the number taking individual music lessons. But again the emphasis, particularly in the house competitions and international society cultural events, is on everyone having a go. The day we visited, everyone was talking about a concert the night before that featured student ensembles playing students' own compositions. Like a number of other performances, it was also a fundraising event for a local social enterprise charity. It had been professionally recorded by a music producer – the school has its own recording studio – and CDs were being sold to raise funds.

Performing arts opportunities consciously draw on Concord's international demographic, offering ample opportunities for creative expression within a culture that is familiar but also exposing students to ones that are less so. House arts competition is hugely popular and includes songs, poetry, dance and ensembles.

Myriad of clubs and societies including the important international ones. 'It is good preparation for university where international societies are a valuable anchor for some of our students,' a member of the SMT told us. Many are student led and intellectually based – behavioural economics, CED (Create, Engage, Discover – the Concord answer to Ted talks).

The word 'Concord' means harmony, a value which remains at the heart of what the college is. It may be an intellectual powerhouse, but it's a calm and gentle one

There is a real awareness of social issues in a college where firsthand experience of Third World problems is common. A committee coordinates charity outreach and there is a lot going on which requires a level of business acumen.

Sport: 'Sport,' one teacher told us, 'is not God here. It is a recreation for everyone and something you are expected to manage as part of your daily life.' That said, PE is timetabled for everyone including final year students during the week. In addition to the usual suspects there are probably more minority sports on offer here than at other schools – badminton, table tennis, basketball, volleyball. Facilities are marvellous and going to be further extended with the recent purchase of a large field adjacent to the main school site. Links with local and regional clubs support the elite sports people and the college boasts the occasional national champion. On the other hand, one father told us his son disliked sport and coming to Concord had been a huge relief to him.

Boarding: Boarding has undergone reorganisation to reflect the needs of a larger college. All boarding houses are single sex. Some students are housed outside the main school campus around the village, but all lower school boys and girls are now accommodated on site (not all parents completely comfortable with this arrangement, so getting the younger ones on site has been a popular move).

High quality accommodation with an increasing number of single ensuite rooms; security is unobtrusive but rigorous. Food was praised – lots of variety and not surprisingly, an international or fusion flavour.

After academic lessons finish, boarders' time is carefully structured for younger pupils, becoming less so as they move up through the school. Weekends are pretty packed with the school facilities being well used and plenty of day trips organised. Students spoke warmly of the relationship between staff and students.

One group of boarders commented that it was a very trusting community and speculated on how prepared they would be for the more edgy outside world.

Ethos and heritage: Concord stands in 80 acres of Shropshire countryside, its sympathetically designed modern buildings blending with the 18th century and medieval. The school was founded after the Second World War as an attempt to foster healing between nationalities through language teaching and personal warmth. The word 'Concord' means harmony, a value which remains at the heart of what the college is today. It may be an intellectual powerhouse, but it's a calm and gentle one where community and service are held in as much esteem as individual success.

High quality accommodation with increasing number of single ensuite rooms; security is unobtrusive but rigorous. Food was praised – lots of variety and, not surprisingly, an international or fusion flavour

Not being bogged down in sacred past traditions, the school responds quickly to new ideas and will run with whatever students' passion of the day might be. Recent initiatives include bee keeping and an outdoor movie event as well as a buggy competition.

Parents felt there was a difference between the atmosphere in the lower and upper parts of the school, observing that while lower school had a genuine family feel, the big annual influx of new sixth form students caused a change in atmosphere. One or two felt that the new students saw Concord purely as a means to an end – top universities – and the environment was more hard edged as a result. 'But that's what their lives are going to be like,' commented one parent philosophically.

Pastoral care, inclusivity and discipline: These students want to please. They hold teachers in high regard and behavioural problems, even the low-level class disruption that you often find in years 9 and 10, simply do not occur at Concord. 'The students self regulate,' staff told us. Occasionally, if a new student is not focusing in class, it is his classmates who get him in line. Students wear their own clothes, proving that uniform has nothing to do with inner discipline and motivation. But everyone knows there are boundaries and if drugs were brought into the college, the perpetrator would be heading out.

Impressive, all embracing pastoral structure includes outside counsellors, a psychotherapist, student counsellors and lots of staff training, as well as tutors, house staff and those in the leadership team with pastoral responsibility.

Pupils and parents: Parents are largely from the international business community. They are not families who want or need the social cachet of a traditional English public school. Local Shropshire parents of day students are particularly keen on the cultural, racial and religious mix. Lack of uniform lends an informal air, but underlying ethos of rigorous endeavour is palpable.

Students clearly love the place and can't speak highly enough of what they have gained from it. About 80 of the 550 pupils are from the UK, the rest come from many countries, predominantly Asian. The ones to whom we spoke were articulate, confident but unassuming. Most were very natural and charming, but you could also spy the next mandarins, carefully considering our questions and weighing up their responses!

Money matters: Fees are high but you get the impression no expense is spared when it comes to the goal of academic excellence. Facilities are superb and always improving. School is working on developing its own bursaries and scholarships and some students attend on scholarships from their home governments. Fees include being able to stay at half terms and, for sixth formers, during the Easter holidays. Some bursarial support for day pupils.

The last word: Concord isn't for everyone. It won't suit a child who doesn't want to work or who is made uneasy by a fierce academic pace. It may also not be right for a child who is solely interested in the arts – not because they wouldn't find high quality and wide ranging arts teaching, but because they might not find enough like-minded students.

Concord is, however, as near perfect a place as you could want for the student who is academic. This is where the next generation of global high fliers is being nurtured. If you want your offspring to have a chance in this stratosphere, want them to engage with issues beyond the shores of the UK or just want them to make life-long international friendships, then do look at Concord. It is in a league of its own and one that is increasingly in high world demand.

Beachborough School

The Downs Malvern

Brockhill Road, Colwall, Malvern, Worcestershire WR13 6EY

01684 544108 | registrar@thedownsmalvern.org.uk | www.thedownsmalvern.org.uk

Ages: 3–13

Pupils: 196; Boarders: 35- 40 boarders per night seven days a week (from year 3)

Fees: Day £7,530 – £18,120; Boarding £13,665 – £23,985 pa

Linked school: Malvern College, 1038

Head: Since 2009, Alastair (known to everyone as Sam) Cook. Previously head of Pembroke House in Gilgil, Kenya, he is a graduate from Westminster College, Oxford. There is something of the gentleman's club about his study. The comfortable chairs, old school photos and stirring mountain landscapes speak of a man and school at ease with the world. Alastair Cook certainly is that and much more. He has energetically meshed three schools (The Downs merged with Malvern College Prep in 2008) together into a now seamless unit, worked on relationships with Malvern College to mutual benefit and made himself much respected and loved by parents and the children whom he places firmly at the centre of everything. He teaches, does sport with the pre-preps and runs a swimming club. 'He is always around when the children arrive, there with his dog, at matches, just all the time,' said one parent. He knows all the children, even those who have just arrived. 'You would never worry about approaching him over anything,' said a mother.

Retiring in July 2022.

Entrance: Non-selective – can support all but those with serious learning difficulties. Informal observations and interviews on taster days, combined with discussions with parents, lead to offers. Depending on the age of the child, may also request information from the current school.

Exit: More or less all take CE and 70 per cent move across the Malvern Hills to Malvern College – there is a strong flow through in curriculum terms. A smattering go to other local schools or further flung public schools. Repton, Bloxham, Sedbergh, King's Worcester, King's College Gloucester, Hereford Cathedral School, RGS Worcester and Malvern St James have all featured recently. If there is a problem academically, parents are told at an early stage and alternative plans discussed.

Our view: The school spreads over the Malvern Hills and the only downside we could see were the narrow roads and precipitous bends on the way there. There is a flexibility and breadth about everything. Pick up times are to suit parents not the school, boarding can be when families need it – it is all about individuals growing up in a community that cares, and for which families too care and show respect. The curriculum has all the academic rigour combined with creativity that you would hope for – strong science in suitably equipped labs ('We get to use proper chemicals,' one 10-year-old was bursting to tell us), French is all the way through with Spanish or German in years 7 and 8, Latin from year 6, art has its own kiln and there is masses of music.

Parents and children praised the flexibility and common sense – no rigid rules that stunt children. Fairness is the basis of discipline

All of this spills out of the classroom into the rich extracurricular programme that runs at lunchtimes, after school and on Saturday mornings (not compulsory but much loved by parents). There is sport galore (including girls' soccer), gardening, chess, Chinese, pottery, cookery, world history, computer coding, current affairs, science in the news, touch typing, debating, Scrabble, endless drama and music and so it goes on. Perhaps what best sums up the timeless charm is the little steam train that runs through the school grounds. The oldest miniature light railway in the world, this is a serious educational tool. The children learn to drive and maintain it. The wholesome environment too is fully utilised – the children are outside as much as possible, soaking in subliminally, we would like to think, the awe-inspiring rolling landscape, but also using it for serious geographical and scientific measurements and as inspiration for their artwork, which is of a seriously high standard.

There are plenty of links with the world outside the school. Its own first-rate facilities are supplemented by some use of Malvern College – its theatre, chapel, swimming pool, for instance. The choir sings locally and the school hosts national music and art events for other schools.

Parents say the teachers are very quick to pick up on any individual needs and that they take huge pride in the children's small achievements. 'Go to Friday assemblies,' parents urged us. 'Everyone is invited and we really get a sense of how much the school praises the children, how the discipline works in practice, the clear moral message the school is getting across, and we can see the opportunities all the children get for developing confidence through public speaking.'

The head told us, 'Care comes first and then education.' Parents and children praised the flexibility and common sense – no rigid rules that stunt children. Fairness is the basis of the approach to discipline. Teachers want to find out what the situation actually is by spending time talking to children involved in any difficulties – and then it is a quiet word and a real attempt to equip the children with the skills to move forward.

'So what do you give school out of 10?' we asked one boy. 'Ten+++!' he said with a big grin.

Boarding: About three-quarters of the boarders are from overseas (11 different countries when we visited) and parents commented on how well the school integrates the day pupils and the boarders. The school offers excellent preparation to overseas boarders wanting to brush up their English and understand British values ready for senior school. There are fun and cosily low-key events organised at weekends for boarders – a visit to the circus, theme parks, ice skating, Christmas shopping. The flexi-boarding is popular with parents who want to give their children a taste of boarding before the full immersion as they move on to Malvern College. The boarding accommodation is in The Warren – rightly named as it rambles round the centre of the original school buildings, not smart but very homely.

The last word: The Downs has the feel of a much loved school with bucketloads of unspoilt charm that you find in the very best rural preps.

Elmhurst Ballet School

9

249 Bristol Road, Edgbaston, Birmingham B5 7UH

0121 472 6655 | enquiries@elmhurstdance.co.uk | www.elmhurstballetschool.org

Ages: 11–19

Pupils: 190; sixth form: 59; Boarders: 156 full

Fees: Day £19,503 – £20,214; Boarding £24,999 – £26,949 pa

Principal: Since 2010, Jessica Wheeler BA NPQH (30s). There can't be many people in the world, never mind the UK, who combine professional dance experience with top-notch educational management expertise. But Elmhurst has found it. Laban trained, she then became resident with the Laban dance company. Moved into teaching as freelance and guest teacher. Tough London comprehensive that employed her to teach dance spotted the charisma, energy and determination and she was fast-tracked to assistant headship before moving with a team of super fixers to work magic in one of the worst schools in London.

Aspirations since arriving at Elmhurst are to make it the dance school of choice in the UK and beyond. Her vision is a holistic one – to ensure talented dancers are also healthy and wise – and this is being realised through detailed, methodical planning, management and monitoring. She is stunning in every sense, and warm with it.

Brilliantly supported by artistic director Robert Parker, the driving force behind the increasingly world-class dance side of the school. He had a meteoric career through the Royal Ballet School, into the company and to Birmingham Royal Ballet as principal dancer. He knows the industry inside out and inspires huge respect in the young dancers. Coming from a Billy Elliot background, he is driven and self-disciplined but also hugely charming, brimming with enthusiasm and cares passionately about the experience Elmhurst gives its young dancers. And he has collected a commercial pilot's licence along the way.

Entrance: Entrance is entirely on artistic merit. Auditions are held at various times in the year in the UK and overseas, although the overseas auditions are increasingly conducted via DVD submissions and then by Elmhurst staff travelling to host auditions overseas. Children will have had ballet lessons before they come and the school has links with some of the best local ballet teachers around the country. The school also runs its own associate classes for the under 11s in Birmingham, Sunderland, Manchester and Plymouth as outreach. Also visits some very challenged primary schools to talent spot. Students are reauditioned at the end of the third year (year 9) and fifth year (year 11) and places are either confirmed or not.

Exit: In 2020, 63 left after GCSEs, though most of these leavers go on to further dance training. More than 80 per cent of sixth form graduates enter dance-related employment within six months of graduating – increasingly to join internationally prestigious companies. A graduate placement scheme has been introduced to allow students who don't gain immediate employment to stay at the school to sustain audition-ready fitness. The odd student for whom the idea of a ballet career has palled by the time they are 19 heads to university. In 2020, two to university – both to Oxford Brookes (mental health nursing and physiotherapy).

Latest results: In 2020, 55 per cent 9-7 at GCSE. At A level, 40 per cent A*/A grades; 69 per cent A*-B grades. In 2019 (the last year when exams took place), 32 per cent 9-7 at GCSE. At A level, eight per cent A*/A grades; 23 per cent A*-B grades.

Teaching and learning: Given that admission is entirely done on dance potential, results are good. Academic staff are up against students who say all they want to do is dance, but while they might be guided by their hearts, they are surrounded by adults who know you can't dance forever, however talented you are.

Principal and her team have brought in changes to ensure any dip in academic performance is picked up and acted upon swiftly. She is building a curriculum that will play to the strengths of young dancers who are increasingly getting their GCSE grades. Baseline testing for children coming in to allow individual target setting and tracking of progress year on year. Most importantly, there is now transparency for students and parents about where things are heading.

Most dance schools give up on the academic side at 16 but there is a philosophical commitment here to the value of an academic training

School is rightly proud of its serious A level programme – dance, music, art, English and maths are on offer – and hopes to introduce geography and biology. Most dance schools give up on the academic side at 16 but there is a philosophical commitment here to the value of an academic training, heavily underpinned by the practical consideration that a student who is seriously injured at 17 or has simply grown a bit too tall must have alternatives to a dance career.

Classes are around 20 – smaller once options are chosen. A real strength, parents tell us. Teachers all comment that the discipline and focus of the dance studio infuses academic lessons. The issue is sometimes getting the students to speak at all (they are so used to the silence of dance class). Teachers are very conscious that many of the students are kinaesthetic learners and match their teaching styles to maximise this.

Learning support and SEN: Some streaming for EAL students and English exams are very carefully chosen to meet the individual's best needs.

The arts and extracurricular: This a rigorous training for the most gifted and resilient. The artistic and dance side of the curriculum takes up about a third of the students' time up to 16. Then, as they head towards their three-year National Diploma in Professional Dance, it takes up two-thirds. Training is in classical ballet but there is also a strong emphasis on jazz, contemporary and other supporting dance styles. There is an assessing out process in year 9 and year 11, when students who have not developed as dancers as expected are asked to leave. Process is done as compassionately as possible and warning given in good time for families to find an alternative. About eight per cent of the cohort assessed out across these two key stages; however a percentage leave at the end of year 11 of their own accord to go to dance schools offering a different sixth form curriculum.

Recent major review of the programme drew on the views of the professional dance companies, ensuring students are prepared for the demands of the dance industry today. Increasing number and diversity of visiting artists, directors and choreographers, running workshops, masterclasses and lecturing to enrich the students' experience.

Partnership with Birmingham Royal Ballet (reason why Elmhurst moved to Edgbaston 10 years ago) is the icing on the cake for the artistic side of the school. It means getting top quality dance teachers is much easier than anywhere else outside London and students get the chance to perform regularly with the company. Even the youngest can audition for children's parts in productions like The Nutcracker. Also allows for easy professional exchanges.

Friday afternoons have been developed as an off-timetable fun time for learning new skills and offering enrichment and students love it. Sport, art and craft, academic clubs, drama, student-led choreography projects and yoga. Keen to showcase the students' talents outside dance, the school takes part in a host of national competitions – poetry and short story writing, for example, have seen recent successes.

Heart of the school is the excellent 250-seater theatre where the many performances take place, culminating in the outstanding end of year productions.

Sport: Dancers simply don't do risky contact sports but Elmhurst is keen for them to try everything else and takes its responsibility for overall fitness very seriously. Attractive fitness suite has been created and staff and students are encouraged to use it, and there's a new multi-use games area. They also share sports facilities and coaches with a nearby mainstream school.

With no sports fields, there are no obvious spaces for younger children to run around but school's pretty, landscaped grounds give a sense of openness to the site.

Boarding: Accommodation for the vast majority who board (just under nine per cent from overseas) is excellent, with many single and double rooms. When we visited the girls had set up their own beauty studio for pamper time with the help of a beauty-trained member of the house staff.

Sixth form accommodation has now moved into a purpose-built space nearer the main campus. This better links the sixth form experience with the rest of the school. Prior to this, one parent felt that when the children were younger they were in a very protected, small environment and then at 16 were suddenly launched into independent living. Students and parents commented on the recent increase in weekend activities, making the most of Birmingham, once Saturday classes have finished.

Ethos and heritage: The moment you walk into Elmhurst, you arrive in a huge dance studio, where there is invariably a class going on. From that point, you are in the ballet world. Students move around the corridors as though they are still on stage. They are graceful, hold themselves beautifully and even when they are chatting outside a maths classroom manage to group themselves as though in a corps de ballet. Most of the time they are either in dancewear or tracksuits in which they naturally look elegant and purposeful.

Staff comment on the maturity with which students relate to adults. Students we spoke to were articulate, able to express themselves confidently and had plenty to say. No bells and the atmosphere is calm and quiet. Something about the absolute dedication to a highly disciplined vocation infuses the whole place. Drive is there in academic as well as artistic classes. 'I have never been in classes with fewer discipline problems,' one teacher told us. 'The children succeed more than they would in other schools because all the time they are asking "how can I improve?" They do that in their ballet and they have that attitude to their GCSEs too.'

No bells and the atmosphere is calm and quiet. Something about the absolute dedication to a highly disciplined vocation infuses the whole place

School's recently developed 'live, dance, learn' slogan captures the holistic approach to dance education. This is also underlined by 'the Elmhurst way', four statements posted all over the school to remind students and staff what it is all about – choose the right attitude, be there, make someone's day and have fun. We like the sentiments – they give an adventurous and humane dimension to the gruelling discipline of the ballet world.

Former pupils (known as Old Elms) include actresses Helen Baxendale, Hayley Mills, Juliet Mills, Jenny Agutter and Joanna David, singer Sarah Brightman and ballet dancers Dame Merle Park, Diana Fox and Isabel McMeekan.

Pastoral care, inclusivity and discipline: There has been a huge amount of heartbreak over the years about 'assessing out', the process at the end of years 9 and 11 when students are told if they are good enough at dance to carry on. Elmhurst has done much soul searching as to how they can make this stressful time as bearable as possible for everyone concerned. They have introduced pre-assessment, which allows teachers to give early indication to both students and parents if things are not looking good. In some cases it can be turned around and every opportunity is given, but sometimes, no matter how much they work, it just can't. At least everyone knows sooner rather than later and the school support swings into action, looking for other alternatives (of which there actually are a lot). Pupils may not end up as Giselle at the Bolshoi but they could still have a career in the dance industry.

Overall, Elmhurst has moved way beyond the usual pastoral care. Students' health and well-being is at the core of everything and systems are in place that recognise the unique nature of vocational ballet training. Dedicated medical centre, with qualified nursing staff, on-site GP appointments, physiotherapy services, dance psychology, dance nutritionist, sports massage and chiropractor. New health and well-being centre aims at a holistic approach, fostering 'a closer working relationship between healthcare, artistic and boarding staff'.

Partnership with Birmingham Royal Ballet (reason why Elmhurst moved to Edgbaston 10 years ago) is the icing on the cake for the artistic side of the school

The school is ahead of the game – linking with university researchers to ensure pre-emptive strategies are in place to keep the students dancing at their peak. More in the pipeline – working with international researchers to develop motivational programmes based on the psychology of success. Probably because of the emphasis on well-being, there are virtually no cases of anorexia. Principal told us that during her time at the school there have only been two diagnoses (both of which had positive outcomes) and that this is proportionately far fewer than at her last school (a large comprehensive).

The school holds student inset days, much like those for staff. Outside agencies come in to run workshops and talks on subjects like e-safety, cancer, injury prevention and choreography. Staff make every effort to ensure that parents have the same information to complete the circle and ensure maximum input for the students.

'The children are simply in love with what they are doing,' one houseparent told us in an attempt to explain the enthusiasm and buzz about the boarding experience.

Pupils and parents: Most are encouraged to apply by their ballet teachers and all are there because they want to dance. There is a real warmth in relations between staff and students and between the students themselves. One boy told us: 'I have finally got friends who have the same interests as me.' Everyone we spoke to stressed the very special people here and the friendships made. 'I have become a different person,' said one girl. 'I am independent and confident now that I am doing what I love.' Parents commented on the way the school by its very nature encouraged independence. 'Our son is noticeably more mature and independent that his contemporaries at other independent boarding schools,' observed one father.

Not surprisingly, parents are quite intense. They are acutely aware of both the dangers and the strengths of opting for a specialist vocational education at 11. A number choose the school because they can see that it tries very hard to keep the academic doors open.

Parents are more obviously desperate for their children to succeed than those in other schools (although given the limited employment opportunities with the world top ballet companies, they know that not many can). This gives an edge to how they relate to the school, and one or two thought some parents were reluctant sometimes to approach the school with criticisms. The last thing they want is for their child to be asked to leave. Those with children about to start auditioning for their first jobs were unsure if the school was doing enough to support them, although they recognised it did as much or more than other dance schools. A parent whose child had just had a minor injury wanted to see even more physiotherapy and counselling support. But even the most anxious parents agreed that their child couldn't be happier.

Money matters: Given that the fees include all the specialist ballet tuition, they are reasonable. Many UK families are able to take advantage of two government funded, means-tested, bursary/scholarship schemes: music and dance scheme (MDS) for those aged 11 to 16 and dance and drama awards (DaDa) for the sixth form. Awards are highly competitive but all credit to the government for ensuring highly talented children can get the specialist training they need, regardless of parental income.

The last word: The only purpose-built ballet school in the country, this is the ballet school to watch. Elmhurst isn't afraid to look beyond the intense and sometimes claustrophobic ballet world. It challenges the conventional thinking that young dancers must be silent sponges soaking up the technical knowledge of their teachers. With the school's rising academic profile and development of pupil voice, the dancers coming out of Elmhurst are critical learners ready to take ownership of their own careers.

Elmhurst is not the Royal Ballet School and in that sense it has to fight really hard to prove itself. There are no laurels to rest on here. It reinvented itself when it moved to Birmingham and it has the drive and energy of a young institution hungry for success. The Royal Ballet School is still the first choice for the majority of families but Elmhurst is biting at its heels, offering something new and very special.

The Elms School

Colwall, Malvern, Worcestershire WR13 6EF

01684 540344 | office@elmsschool.co.uk | www.elmsschool.co.uk

Ages: 3–13

Pupils: 168; Boarders: 23 full, 23 flexi (from 8 years)

Fees: Day £7,965 – £14,985; Boarding £23,055 – £26,130 pa

Head: Since 2018, Chris Hattam BA (in comparative religion from Edinburgh), MA (in community justice from Manchester). Educated at Sherborne where he met his wife, Jess, who was at Sherborne Girls and who now works as the school registrar. Unconventional route to teaching via some frustrating years in the probation service – 'red tape meant you couldn't do anything'. Studied graduate teaching programme while working at Sedbergh where he remained for 14 years, teaching PSHE, RS, philosophy and ethics. Also served eight years as housemaster – 'a privilege'. Straight into headship at The Elms, ignoring the deputy rung on the ladder on the advice of friends and colleagues – 'Chris, you'd be bored within two years.'

Amiable, ambitious and brimming with ideas, he is one of those people that makes you wonder what you do with your own time. 'I wake up every morning and jump out of bed to come here,' he says, casually adding that he squeezes in a 10km run before breakfast. Parents describe him as approachable, organised, visible, always around at drop-off, pick-up and every match, with a 'strong idea of his vision for the school'. Teachers say he is 'a true gamechanger' – and indeed change has been the watchword of his three years' tenure.

Five long-serving staff (with over 120 years of combined experience) have retired since his joining ('coincidence') and team Hattam now includes new academic and pastoral deputies, as well as heads of science, English and music. Parents report a new injection of dynamism and edginess. He has also introduced the school to the delights of marketing and social media – 'I just wish that people knew about the Elms, I'd like a loudhailer on the roof.' 'We've got to make ourselves more accessible,' he adds, keen to push for a more inclusive pupil base. Hence the active development of overseas pupil recruitment (capped at 10 per cent of school population), particularly in the Far East, and the addition to the fees menu of a reduced day rate as a complement to their existing day, flexi and boarding rates. The new day fee strips out all but the core daily teaching. What is now termed 'day plus' offers extracurricular activities and access to the longer school day. Such new-fangled ideas ruffled a few feathers among a pocket of parents but, after a small rebellion and some quick-footed politicking, the initial panic seems to have abated. For now.

Changes don't end there. Instead of formal teaching on Saturdays (currently compulsory for years 5 and above), from September 2021 there will be a non-compulsory weekend STEAM programme – we approve! The CE humanities curriculum is also in his sights, to be replaced with an extended learning project which he hopes will create 'hungry learners'. 'Destination schools feel it's the future,' he reassures CE traditionalists. ICT will be removed from the timetable, with use of technology increased and learning engrained within the context of the wider curriculum – sounds sensible. Weekly rural studies classes become an after school club, a seemingly odd decision for a school with a farm at its heart. Mr Hattam explains that the subject is 'given more space' in the evenings and as part of the STEAM offering and already enjoys informal use by the children during breaks and weekends.

We heard from parents and teachers that Mr Hattam has brought a more 'competitive' culture, with the school now 'trying to fit a more academic mould'. But while the majority now seem to accept that 'change is for the greater good' and that the head has to be 'tough, not trying to be everyone's best friend,' there is no doubt that some have found the process a little 'bumpy'.

Mr Hattam says his time at Sedbergh, an all-through school, has given him a thorough understanding of what the next stage is and he takes 'great pride' in being able to direct children to the right school for them.

Entrance: Non-selective. No tests on entry, but previous school reports are requested. A new Elms Seedlings nursery is due to open in imminently, expanding the offering to 6 months +. The early years Montessori department currently caters for rising 3s and above.

Exit: Malvern College is the most popular destination, followed by Rugby, Shrewsbury and King's Taunton. Ones and twos to Eton, Cheltenham College, Cheltenham Ladies, Gordonstoun, Hereford Cathedral, Marlborough, Moreton Hall, Pangbourne, Radley and Tudor Hall. On average 40-45 per cent of pupils gain scholarships to destination schools.

Our view: You wouldn't find The Elms unless you were specifically looking for it. Its unpretentious entrance is nestled under a railway bridge at the far end of the sleepy village of Colwall (one shop, one hairdresser, two pubs) on the border of Herefordshire and Worcestershire. Like siblings who have been separated to keep the peace, its nemesis The Downs School (Malvern College's prep), is situated at the polar opposite end of the same road. Founded in 1614, the school boasts the (rather unsnappy) title of oldest prep school still on its original site. Set in 80 acres, with jaw-dropping views of the Malvern hills, the main building was once a Tudor farmhouse. Although the original exterior is long gone, some interior features remain, including the dining hall, some wonky floors and narrow staircases and the wood-panelled chapel, with vaulted ceiling and obligatory musty scent. At some point in the last 400 years, someone left a saddle on the bannister of the main staircase. This antique lost property remains in situ, awaiting collection, a cautionary reminder to parents of the value of nametaping.

The rest of the site is a rather more up to date affair, with academic buildings and theatre built in the last 10 years, sports hall and pool in the last 15. Modern science labs are twice the size required for the number of pupils, although classrooms in the older parts of the building are more snug. Labs and library both benefit from a wall of French windows, opening on to the endless green of sports fields and that view. At least one dog snoozing in the corner of the class is commonplace. Profiles of all school dogs are available on the school's Instagram feed for those interested. Mrs Tigglewinkle apparently loves cheese, speaks fluent French and is considering dual nationality post-Brexit.

The school's farm is right at the heart of the site and fully integrated into daily life. The farm 'gets children outside and involved'

The school's unique selling point is its farm, right at the heart of the site and fully integrated into daily life. The farm 'gets children outside and involved'. Arrive early and you can muck out, bring the ponies in from the fields, collect eggs and feed the animals, all before 8am. Curiously (or perhaps not), 'It's often the children who don't come from farming families who get stuck in,' says the farm manager. 'The whole school is buzzing' during lambing. Each class has its own allotment plot, with home grown fresh produce often whipped up for lunch by the school chef. We 'push the sustainable agenda' and 'show what field to plate looks like so they can make decisions for themselves.' No apologies then for the large outdoor signage in the yard displaying the individual cuts of a cow. If you didn't get the message from that, then the annual hog roast using their own rare breed pigs gives a 'realistic understanding of where meat comes from'. Children regularly show animals at the Three Counties, Devon and Staffordshire shows, where they compete successfully at the same level as adults. After-school practice moving pigs with boards generated screams of delight from the pig shed during our visit. There's room for 25 horses and two full-time equine staff are on hand. The vast majority are owned by pupils who take advantage of not only having your own pony at school, but favourable working livery rates, an impressive floodlit 50 x 40 foot arena and cross-country trails. 'It's not an elite club,' says the head, 'it doesn't matter if you don't have a horse.' Riders range from 'happy hackers' upwards.

The Montessori ethos creates what the head calls a 'flight path' through the school, promoting independent learning from the get-go. Early years has become more integrated with the rest of the school under the Hattam regime. Previously they would watch, now they participate in inter-house competitions, joining in as equals to their elders. In addition, prefects regularly read, play and perform music and drama with the little ones.

Saturdays now voluntary from year 4 upwards, when pupils get the choice to attend new STEAM project or Humphrey's Club, so named in reference to a camel (it's a long story...). Themed activities include Hawaiian pool parties, wild west cowboys with real ponies in the arena and Hollywood film productions, creating movies using sound and lighting in the theatre. Our seemingly innocuous classroom request to view a club scrapbook caused an immediate stampede of enthusiastic drawer opening and effectively forced the conclusion of an otherwise absorbing year 4 English lesson. Whoops.

Academic content and curriculum have recently been reviewed and made more challenging, and this increased rigour has already been recognised in parent surveys. Average class size is 10 so there's none of the forgotten middle that plagues larger groups. We sat in on a high energy science class of six pupils that felt more like a conversation than a lesson, with children showing real enthusiasm for the experiment and delight in each other's work. No formalised classroom teaching assistant support (unless allocated for individuals by head of SEN/G&T), although a number of live-in post sixth form 'gappies' help out with reading and prep. Some interesting ideas imported by new teaching staff. We particularly liked the excellently titled Stage and Rage, teaching formal debating and public speaking skills – 'We want to embed oracy into the curriculum,' explains the absolutely irrepressible head of English, a larger than life personality who encourages 'proper blue sky crazy thinking'. Integrated humanities with a move away from CE in those subjects.

Strong take up for speech and drama, and musical theatre is a big deal. A recent dedicated end of term concert (in addition to a more general music concert that term) had a packed programme, with no shortage of talented soloists. Professional grade theatre lighting and an attic stuffed full of costumes provide the perfect environment for budding West End stars. We were treated to a highly polished performance of All That Jazz by a year 8 who had stepped off a horse minutes earlier, still sporting muddy jodhpurs – slightly incongruous when teamed with a sequinned top hat and cane.

Sport is a six days a week affair, which you would think was enough for anyone, but hardcore sports fans can also set early alarms for pre-breakfast sessions. All the usual core sports are catered for and there are shiny new cricket nets. Swimming every week for every child and further opportunities for badminton, fencing and taekwando. An air rifle and pistol shooting range in the attic means that the school is one of the few places in the country where tetrathlons (as well as triathlons) can take place on a single site. In summer, lucky boarders might get a surprise wake-up call for an early morning hack. Break time means elastics, roller blades, wobble boards and scooters. 'Boiler suits and outdoor shoes are worn for play in the fields,' explains the head, as we watch boys without either, rugby tackling each other onto the sodden grass. 'A sterile school is not childhood in my mind,' he rapidly follows up. The ensuing mud on the carpets generates little more than an eye roll and a weary tut. Even with all this going on, pupils are currently lobbying the head for longer Wednesday games sessions. We assume they sleep well.

SEN has been transformed in the last few years. The focus has shifted towards getting the right tools to access classroom learning, rather than separation of children with additional needs. 'Most places' in school are wheelchair accessible – 'It's just a puzzle I need to work round,' says the head of SEN/G&T (although we couldn't help thinking of those wonky floors and narrow staircases). Support is 'need led rather than label led' and a well thought out three wave structure determines level of intervention. Dyslexia, ADHD, ASC, physical, visual impairments, social, emotional and communication needs will not frighten admissions. Individual additional paid support is reviewed on a six-weekly basis and new targets set. Numbers requiring EAL vary: 18 last year, but only six at present.

'When you have local children choosing to board, you know you are doing something right'

Pastoral care is 'natural', in fact almost 'taken for granted' due to small classes, reports its director. 'It's not been revolutionised;' there are 'no catchy slogans and programmes, but we do talk to the children.' Mr Hattam has breathed new life into a previously slightly ailing house system. Every child from early years up is now either an Athenian, Spartan or Trojan and attendance at weekly inter-year meetings has had the positive desired impact on pride and inter-year play; parents speak of an 'absence of hierarchy'. There's a focus on good old-fashioned manners. Invitations to weekly Lodge lunches at home with the Hattams (parents love this 'personal touch') must have handwritten replies and subsequent thank you notes. Boarders are encouraged to write letters home as well as call. Mind you, since mobile phones and tablets are not allowed in school, options are limited. Instead there's 'appropriate' use of IT and a Sparks room with nine workstations. The head talks of a sense of duty running throughout the school, whether it be duty to look after the animals on the farm, an allotment, or your house's turn to tidy up around the place. We noticed a culture of eagerness, all pupils were keen to put hands up, jostling to be chosen with no trace of the usual back row eye-rollers.

Mealtimes are genteel. Mixed age tables are politely served from individual platters rather than canteen style, and food is more akin to a decent local deli than a school hall. We were reliably informed that we were there on the best day: sausage plait followed by apple and pear crumble (although debate rumbled throughout as to whether boarders' weekend breakfasts were better). Birthdays are celebrated by a terrifyingly loud post-lunch hakka (our ears are still ringing).

Parents say they 'can't shut the children up on the way out of school'. Previous mutes are now 'full of chat'. 'Mummy, a pig stood on my finger' is arguably more exciting than the average timetable rundown. Families are a mix of local entrepreneurs, professionals, London refugees and weekly commuters, army and farming community: 'Lots pick up in wellies.' A good number have generational ties, some vicariously reliving whimsical versions of their own childhoods. The majority display an affection for the school that goes beyond the transactional payment for education. Small number of internationals largely from the Far East, coupled with Spanish and the odd Italian family. Head describes a 'rural school moving away from that country set,' but equally recognises that he is still 'battling the if-you're-not-into-riding-you're-not-in attitude'. It's a genuine desire to include.

Boarding: Numbers of full boarders are around the 20 mark, but flexi is popular, with another 25 or so boarding two or more nights per week, mainly from year 6. 'When you have local children choosing to board, that's when you know you are doing something right.' The savvy wouldn't volunteer for duty night on a Friday though, when 60-70 boarders are not uncommon.

Definitely cosy, dorms are crammed full of bunks. This is explained by the every-child-has-a-bed policy, which does what it says on the tin, irrespective of day or boarding status of the child (although this won't apply to the new reduced day rate). A curious custom, but a firm favourite with parents and the children who make regular use of their own personal common space in breaks. 'It makes everyone equal,' they report. There's a year 8 in every dorm to ensure order, and to earn their privilege of hot chocolate and biscuits. 'Pupils don't need palatial, lush carpets,' reported one parent. 'Apparently the mattresses are lumpy,' noted another, but it wasn't a complaint – 'just as they should be'.

Full-boarders' Sundays are for paintballing, crazy golf, bake offs, beach days, survival weekends, waterslides and falconry displays. A recent WWII weekend where children shared research about fallen ex-Elms soldiers around the campfire was 'really moving'. Or just marching up the Malvern hills and rolling down again, before heading to the shop with fifty flavours of ice-cream. 'You can organise loads, but it's often the simplest of things,' says head of boarding.

Money matters: Scholarships up to 10 per cent of fees available at year 7 – academic, art, music, equestrian, sport and drama and musical theatre. Bursaries awarded dependent on application.

The last word: The Elms, only recently gradually waning and slightly out of touch, has well and truly pulled up its long, grey socks. An institution with 400 years of history probably won't be quick to change, but this is surely one to watch – a school with progressive leadership, ambitious staff, eager-minded children and a generous helping of fresh air. One parent summed it up nicely: 'The Elms deserves to be better known for academic and pastoral care, not just as the school with the farm.' But for now, it was definitely a missed opportunity for us to get our best tweeds out.

Lincoln Minster School

11

The Prior Building, Upper Lindum Street, Lincoln, Lincolnshire LN2 5RW

01522 551300 | admissions@lincolnminsterschool.co.uk | www.lincolnminsterschool.co.uk

Ages: 2–18

Pupils: 484; sixth form: 90; Boarders: 27 full, 8 weekly/flexi (from year 3)

Fees: Day £10,134 – 14,895pa; Boarding £22,839 – £33,930pa

Head: Since September 2020, Maria Young. Previously head of St Mary's School in Shaftesbury and before that, deputy head pastoral at Worth School in West Sussex. Educated in Kent, studied music at Durham and Cambridge, keeping up her love of tennis, rowing, running and expeditions alongside. Began her teaching career at Bryanston, later teaching in grammar schools and becoming the lead advisory teacher for music in Kent. She has conducted musicals, opera and major choral and orchestral works, touring her school groups all over the world, most recently to Peru.

Entrance: All applicants and parents are interviewed. Reports requested from previous school and prospective pupils offered a taster day prior to joining. Automatic entry to the senior school from junior. Many year 7 entrants from state primaries. Overseas boarders join for sixth form, after entrance exams. Sixth form entry subject to GCSE results: 'grades need to reflect their subject choices.'

Exit: About 15 per cent leave at the end of year 6, many to state grammar schools. School aware of this and does practice 11+ papers. Around 10 per cent leave after GCSEs. Durham, St Andrews, York, Nottingham, UCL, Leeds, Manchester and Sheffield all popular.

Latest results: In 2021, 58 per cent 9-7 at GCSE; 48 per cent A*/A at A level (74 per cent A*-B). In 2019 (the last year when exams took place), 37 per cent 9-7 at GCSE; 25 per cent A*/A (62 per cent A*-B).

Teaching and learning: Solid results for a non-selective school. High flyers encouraged, less able nurtured. French, German and Spanish on offer at GCSE. One language for all, a few do two but, disappointingly, not many. iPads being rolled out for all. Plenty of computers available with up-to-date IT suites. Lessons we observed showed engaged pupils and articulate teachers. Pupils set in year 8 in most subjects. Criminology recently added at A level. Excellent facilities, most of them modern. Parents kept up to date with academic progress and all commented that problems were picked up on quickly. Most spoke about the small classes being a huge selling point of the school. 'We are made aware of any academic problems quickly and support on offer immediately.' The school instils a good work ethic: 'They come home from school and get on with their homework with no fuss,' was said more than once. All parents commented on how well staff knew their child.

Children get a good start here with lots of academic support and diligent, enthusiastic teachers pick up on any learning needs. The non-selection ethos means there's a broad spectrum of abilities, coped with well. Brand new IT suite and well stocked library. Languages taught from an early age by specialist teachers. Spanish in pre-prep, French from year 3, with a chance to sample the more exotic linked in with other subjects: Arabic, Mandarin and even a smattering of Welsh. Children taught as a class with separate subject teachers. Interesting to hear that pupils practise for 11+ papers, but Lincolnshire is a grammar school county.

Learning support and SEN: Pupils in the junior department usually getting extra support if needed so are able to keep up in senior years. Some 82 SEND pupils throughout the school. Individual learning plans after assessment; parents spoke highly of support offered. 'My daughter was struggling at one point, they spotted it, put her into support and she quickly caught up. We much appreciated it.' Support available in lessons for those that need it and staff aware of how to teach these pupils. Parents very much involved. EAL requirements for 28 pupils, mainly sixth form. A minimum of two hours' help a week offered, more if required, particularly in year 11. One-year pre-A level course, including GCSEs in key subjects, offered to international students.

The school instils a good work ethic: 'They come home from school and get on with their homework with no fuss,' was said more than once

The arts and extracurricular: Music very popular here; it is a choristers' school, supplying the cathedral with 25 of its 40 choristers (boys and girls in separate choirs, which sing at separate evensongs). Until recently all choristers at school here; now children from any school can audition. This is happily embraced by the head and some parents. 'It's good to see as there was a bit of them and us from some chorister parents,' said one. It's a big commitment. Practice starts before 8am for an hour every day with evensong beginning at 6.15pm. A long day, with late finishes every other evening. Choristers mostly join the choir in year 3; boys usually out by year 9, girls a little later. Choristers lead the way musically but many more pupils involved as well. Lots and lots of bands, orchestras and other choirs, very keenly supported. Lots of practice rooms including a drum room: drumming very popular, apparently.

Drama also popular. Lots of productions in junior and senior schools, some student-led, others include whole school. Modern theatre with sound and lighting box and new drama studio. Recording studio too. Art students support productions by creating backdrops and props. Excellent art facilities with fabulous views over the city; sixth form artists have their own work space.

Loads of after-school and lunchtime clubs including strong debating club. Sports and music as well as homework club to enable later pick up for parents. DofE to gold and school trips far and wide.

Sport: Sport rapidly improving, helped no doubt by enthusiastic support from the previous head, who rejuvenated the department. All abilities encouraged to take part. Rugby and football for all, girls too. Rock climbing, judo, polo and squash all on offer. Squash team very successful. Lots of silver in cabinets: U15 girls tennis are regional champions, successful hockey teams and cross-country strong with one star ranked first U15 in the country. New sports hall a few years ago including a basketball court and indoor cricket.

Boarding: Boarding offered from year 3 but not many at this stage. Just over half of boarders are sixth formers, with 70 per cent of these from overseas (Brits are all weekly boarders, most living within an hour of the school), in three separate houses. Boarding facilities good. Pretty relaxed for the older children with school friends allowed to stay overnight. The Mount, for younger boarders up to year 8, includes most boarding choristers. Senior girls in Hillside, adjacent to the main school, with panoramic views. Senior boys in Eastgate, a large period house with massive gardens, also a stone's throw from the main school building. Easily accessible to the city. Close links with local hockey and rowing club, with boarders encouraged to join in. Gym on site and weekend trips for overseas students. Use made of Forces links with trips to nearby bases and museums. Lots of social areas with tea and toast making facilities. Pupils eat at the main building. Supervised daily prep for all ages. Younger boarders do lots of baking and competitions. Maximum of three to a room, which are large and airy – and tidy. Older pupils, mainly sixth form, have their own rooms. Boys planning a garden, designing and planting it themselves. Chapel not compulsory on Sundays. Despite numerous nationalities and languages, a cohesive atmosphere prevails and freedoms do not appear to be abused.

Ethos and heritage: Formed in 1996 by the amalgamation of the Cathedral School for Boys, St Joseph's School for Girls and Stonefield House School. St Mary's Prep School merged with them in 2011 to become the junior school. Lincoln Minster is now the only private school in the city, housed on three separate central sites, a stone's throw from the cathedral. The main building, the senior school, is a combination of old and new. Aesthetically pleasing modern building, opened in 2002, which has blended well with the old, offering large church-like windows and sweeping, modern curves. Its curving corridors are particularly attractive. Sixth form housed in separate wing. Good facilities with comfy common room and eating area.

Being a chorister is a big commitment. Practice starts before 8am for an hour every day with evensong beginning at 6.15pm. A long day, with late finishes

The junior school is a short walk away. On this site since 2014, an attractive old building with modern extensions, bright and airy, with a well-used outdoor classroom, sitting rather incongruously within a modern housing estate. It was once a city farm and school has large, leafy grounds and is well hidden from suburban sprawl. Each site has plenty of room around it with outside seating areas and large playgrounds. Pre-prep, up to year 2, on a separate site within a walled garden with the cathedral looming over the wall. Lots of space and play areas within a very secure setting, delightful surroundings.

Close links with the cathedral, not just the choristers, and ties are getting stronger, with work experience offers.

The pupils are easily spotted in their distinctive green, white and blue striped blazers, the junior girls wearing kilts – thankfully with a navy blazer; stripes and tartan would be a step too far. Sixth formers wear smart business suits and look the part. A friendly bunch.

Pastoral care, inclusivity and discipline: 'They know what they can get away with,' said one parent, 'and if they cross boundaries there is retribution.' All parents supported the school's stance on discipline. 'My child was given detention for something pretty innocuous. But they knew the rules, got caught, so fair enough.' Children excluded if necessary or given time out and taught in isolation – doesn't happen very often, but parents made aware of situation. 'What happens in school is dealt with by the school, which is as it should be,' said a parent. All parents commented on quick responses to emails and good communication from the school.

Pastoral care excellent, according to all parents, and the school prides itself on being nurturing. All the pupils are known to every member of staff and their development closely monitored. 'Problems dealt with confidentially and appropriately,' was said more than once. Niggles eased before they have chance to escalate. Support offered and coping strategies put in place for those struggling. Two counsellors and a school nurse available. 'We have a close rapport with our teachers,' said one of our rather earnest but delightful guides.

Pupils and parents: A strong community of parents. Professionals, medics, London workers, academics from the university and a strong contingent from farming and the RAF. All very supportive of the school. All we spoke to happy with their child's progress and would recommend the school. 'If my child is happy then I'm happy.'

Pupils chatty and friendly and willing to engage in conversation. Independent and well rounded and obviously very comfy and happy at their school. We got the impression of a very tightly knit community with firm friendships.

Money matters: Fifty per cent scholarships for choristers whilst they are in the choir; other awards possible afterwards and some have music scholarships. Academic, sports and art awards also available, plus means-tested bursaries; discounts for siblings.

The last word: We feel the school has rather sat on its laurels in recent years, having no private competition, but that is all changing. School is well aware of local competition from the grammars and an excellent academy in the city, and is working hard to raise the profile and standards. The school prides itself on its pastoral care, has excellent facilities, gets solid results and, its real strength, has small class sizes.

Loughborough Grammar School

12

Burton Walks, Loughborough, Leicestershire LE11 2DU

01509 233233 | grammar.admissions@lsf.org | www.lsf.org/grammar

Ages: 10–18

Pupils: 874; sixth form: 211; Boarders: 65 full

Fees: Day £13,920 to £14,205; Boarding £32,880 to £33,990pa

Headmaster: Since September 2021, Dr Christopher Barnett, interim head. Was a lecturer in economics at Brunel University, head of history at Bradfield College and senior deputy head at Dauntsey's.

To be replaced by Dr Daniel Koch in September 2022.

Entrance: Entry into year 6 is small, 17 places, and not publicised; mainly takes younger siblings. Most boys, 131, join in year 7, with a third coming from the affiliated prep school Fairfield, the rest from state primaries. Entrance exam: they are looking for bright sparks. A small number join in year 9. Another 25 or so join the sixth form, 10 overseas boarders, the rest from the state system, mainly to study maths and sciences. Five 6s at GCSE as an absolute minimum are needed for the sixth form, higher for certain subjects including maths, sciences and languages. Most new entrants have a fistful of 8-9s. School happy to turn a boy away if attitude and work ethic aren't right.

Exit: Between 25-30 per cent leave at the end of year 11, mostly to mixed colleges in the town. Virtually all go to university. Exeter, UCL, Durham and Liverpool currently popular. Five to Oxbridge in 2021, plus eight medics; many engineers, 'it's in the genes,' says school. Sometimes a few overseas – most recently to Hong Kong.

Latest results: In 2021, 81 per cent 9-7 at GCSE; 72 per cent A*/A at A level (93 per cent A*-B). In 2019 (the last year when exams took place), 60 per cent 9-7 at GCSE; 48 per cent A*/A at A level (74 per cent A*-B).

Teaching and learning: Excellent results but remember the school is fairly selective, though 'not as selective as you might expect,' says school. French, German, Spanish, Latin and Greek all taught to A level. Head very keen for languages to flourish; 33 per cent of boys do two languages, 35 per cent study classics including Latin to GCSE. Maths is king, with around two-thirds studying it for A level. Sciences also very popular. Results have improved in the last few years with tracking of pupils becoming more effective. This means intervention is more prompt. 'Some boys are naturally lazy if they are not pushed,' says school. Parents back this up, commenting on 'outstanding teachers who push the boys.' Parents kept well informed of progress. Lots of clinics for different subjects. Boys take advantage of these. 'They get lots of homework,' said one parent. School well aware of boys and their foibles. All homework online so no excuses. iPads for all from year 8. The jury is out, with the head and parents unsure about the effectiveness of these as an educational tool. Half of the boys' work is handwritten so still lots of emphasis on 'old fashioned' skills.

Music excellent and parents rave about the concerts. Far too many clubs to mention but a nod must go to bridge and chess, and the slightly more unusual beekeeping

The school is cleverly laid out with defined areas for each subject. Impressive library with spiral staircase in oldest part of the building. Chapel now used as a classroom, but small services still held here. Boys working hard and taking part in discussions in classes we viewed. Each science subject has its own block with impressive labs. Setting in maths. Lots of artwork on display. Mention must go to DT: a massive department, with state of the art equipment, run by a very enthusiastic teacher. Please note the electric racing car, built by the boys. The boys are taken driving round a local race track in the cars they have restored and built. Sports car being restored, and driven on sports day, funded by parents. Many more boys who are not studying DT join in with restoration work. The school has recent UK Young Engineer of the Year winners and many go on to engineering careers, including in motorsport. Some sixth form subjects are taught with the girls from Loughborough High: psychology, music, languages and politics.

Learning support and SEN: Some 40 boys on the SEN register, one boy with an EHCP. Five per cent of these are seen every week by learning support at no extra charge, as yet. Around 120 boys are on the monitoring list. Diagnostic testing for all boys in years 7, 9 and 12. Class sizes average 16 in the main school, 10 in sixth form. EAL support is very good. There is an EAL co-ordinator who works four days a week helping the boarders, in particular, who are offered at least two hours a week support. Day boys can also use this service. Many boys, in line with the ethnic diversity in the area, speak a second language at home.

The arts and extracurricular: Fabulous music school that is shared with the other schools in the Loughborough Schools Foundation. Please note the grand piano in one recital room; this is a Steinway School. Many boys have individual music lessons. As expected, music excellent and parents rave about the concerts and reviews: 'They have an amazing choir.' There are over 40 weekly ensembles. Plenty of orchestras, bands, choirs, most combined with the girls' schools in the foundation. Lots of instruments lying around the school during our tour. Drama and school plays talked about a lot by parents. 'They are well co-ordinated with lots of rehearsal time.'

Far too many clubs to mention but a nod must go to bridge and chess, and the slightly more unusual beekeeping. CCF very well supported, joining forces with the girls. DofE popular and lots of school trips including trekking in Vietnam and plenty of sports tours. As one parent said, 'There is so much available, it's up to the boys to take advantage of these opportunities. They are pushed to try things, which is excellent.'

Sport: Sport is compulsory right into the sixth form; 'it's good for them,' reckons school, and boys are expected to participate and contribute. Rugby very popular and successful. Hockey, cricket and football also well supported, as are cross-country and athletics. Plenty of teams for all. Sport rotated and varied, so even the least sporty boy can find a niche. Excellent facilities a short minibus ride away at Quorn, their 70-acre site where most sports are played. On site are a swimming pool, large gym and cricket pitch. Parents happy that sports stars not favoured; 'they all muck in together,' said one parent. Another said their son 'didn't miss out by not being sporty.' One parent did complain about 'the amount of sports gear we have to buy. Do they really need at least two sets of shorts and so many different tops?'

Boarding: Most boarders from year 9 upwards, nearly half sixth formers. Virtually all of them international, the vast majority from Hong Kong and China. LGS has been an international boarding school for 25 years. There are two boarding houses: Denton House for those up to year 11 and School House for sixth formers. Lots of cultural trips for the boys including visits to London, Oxford University and a pantomime at Christmas, as well as many more local trips to nearby matches. The boys are kept busy, encouraged to join the CCF and take part in the musical activities.

Very experienced housemasters know the boys well. 'The common room is the heart of the house,' said one; during the refurbishment he made sure that there was room to sit all 31 boys together. There is a house meeting every day at

6.30pm, even if it's only for five minutes. The newly refurbished dormitories house up to four boys; sixth formers usually in pairs. Each boy has his own desk. Very cleverly supervised, but allowing independence, doors are propped open between 6.30 and 8pm. Computers and phones allowed but Wifi use closely monitored, any misdeeds picked up immediately.

Sport compulsory three evenings a week, usually basketball, which is very popular. Boys allowed into town, which is a five-minute walk away, in twos or more and out of school uniform. With all this activity it's easy to keep the computer nerd off his laptop. English language classes held in the house. Unlimited supply of hot water greatly appreciated by the boys. Note the chickens in the garden; boys enthusiastically collect eggs for breakfast.

Ethos and heritage: Established within the town since 1495, the school has been at its present site since 1852. A state grammar school until 1974. Sited just on the edge of Loughborough, a town not noted for its aesthetics, the school itself is something of an architectural revelation. Part of the Loughborough Schools Foundation which comprises four selective independent schools, Loughborough Grammar, Loughborough High School, Fairfield Prep and, since 2015, Loughborough Amherst. Loughborough Grammar shares a massive campus with the High School and Fairfield.

Virtually all of the boarders are international, the vast majority from Hong Kong and China. LGS has been an international boarding school for 25 years

This handsome Victorian red-brick school is built around a quad. Modern extensions have blended in exceptionally well. As you enter under an arch, which is a memorial to fallen pupils, the school stretches out in front of you. Neatly mown grass, which only the upper sixth – and your guide – are allowed to walk on. Over the years the school has bought most of the Victorian and Edwardian houses on the opposite road so boys can roam safely in a traffic free environment. It is slightly confusing trying to find the main office; luckily a friendly sixth former took pity on us and guided us in the right direction. Very confusing, we imagine, for visitors. Upper sixth boys have their own car park – the privileges of being in your final year.

A large school, both in number of boys and space. Lots of grounds for boys to let off steam. A school of all creeds and colours, the boys all seem to rub along well together and the atmosphere is cohesive and cordial.

Pastoral care, inclusivity and discipline: School is honest enough to say that in a school of this size bullying does exist but is dealt with rapidly. Backed up by a parent who talked of problems on the school bus 'that were dealt with effectively and fairly'. All parents were happy with discipline, many of them saying, 'The boys are not allowed to step out of line, standards are to be met.' Good. Heads of year play an important part in the boys' welfare and discipline. Parents spoke highly of them and said, 'Staff know my son.' Boys understand sanctions that are handed out and reasons for them.

School very attuned to mental health issues and is proactive and preventative. 'We want the boys to know and like who they are and learn to be good at being themselves.' Very keen to ensure boys have a balanced lifestyle, hence plenty of sport and music as well as studying. Certain parents need to have this balance explained; school happy to do this. Parents happy with pastoral offerings. 'The reverend and his team are always available if necessary.'

Pupils and parents: Boys travel from up to 25 miles away, covering Leicestershire, Nottinghamshire and Derbyshire. Busses from all areas. The school has a broad social and ethnic mix with a number of pupils speaking a second language at home. Families vary from old county families, where a pupil could be the fourth generation to study here, to university staff, academics, professionals, engineers, as per the area, and many medics. All parents want a broad independent education; interestingly, not many expressed a strong preference for boys only. Parents have high expectations and most are working hard to be able to afford the fees. Boys mix well and strong friendships are formed. Good to see that the geeky, quiet boy is as accepted as the rugby stars.

Money matters: Scholarships – music and academic – and bursaries on offer of up to 105 per cent of fees. Fees are excellent value for money, deliberately kept low. The parents appreciate this.

The last word: A large, traditional, urban boys' school offering a good, well-rounded education. It's not just about grades, albeit these are an important part; these boys are turned out as grounded young men with a broad outlook on life.

Maidwell Hall

Maidwell, Northampton NN6 9JG

01604 686234 | headmaster@maidwellhall.co.uk | www.maidwellhall.co.uk

Ages: 7-13

Pupils: 140; **Boarders:** 66 full; 16 flexi

Fees: Day £10,965 – £18,765; Boarding £28,800 pa

Headmaster: Since 2001, Robert Lankester MA PGCE (50s). Educated at Charterhouse and Selwyn College, Cambridge, where he read history. Leapt into teaching after seven years in the City ('the best decision I ever made'). PGCE at Durham then 13 years at Uppingham, 10 as a housemaster. Exudes an air of calm confidence that pervades entire school and his charges (averaging around 127 in number) have acquired in spades his self-assured qualities as if by osmosis. Was responsible in 2010 for the introduction of girls, who are now fully established at around 40 per cent of the cohort.

Adored by parents who say he is 'incredibly all-seeing'. A teacher at heart, still teaches CE history and mingles with pupils at mealtimes. Lives on site with multi-talented wife, Carey ('a very special person,' say parents). With such idyllic rural surroundings, there's probably no need to escape to the country, but when the Lankesters do, it's to their home in Carmarthenshire, where they enjoy walking.

Retiring in July 2022.

Entrance: Merging with Uppingham in September 2022, so watch this space. For now, 15-20 join school into year 4, with handfuls joining each year thereafter, resulting in numbers almost doubled at top of school. Small numbers of pupils join aged 7 and are taught with year 4, repeating the year. Very gently selective ('I can count on one hand the number of children we have turned away over the past 10 years,' says head), prospective pupils assessed in maths, spelling, reading and NVR, plus short interview.

Majority join from pre-preps or other prep schools and live within a 90-minute radius of school. Few London families, Forces 'significant'. Less than 10 per cent international.

Exit: Almost all stay until 13+, progressing to (mainly co-ed) public schools. Greatest numbers to Oundle, Uppingham, Stowe, Rugby, Harrow and Eton with girls only very occasionally opting for single sex schools, eg Queen Margaret's, York or Roedean. Extremely rare exits at either 11+ or to day schools. Some scholarships, although head says, 'We don't push them. They can be a weight around your neck and ruin your last year of prep school. We'd rather good grades at CE than shaky scholarship results.'

Our view: How many prep schools of such modest pupil numbers can boast such riches? Maidwell's gardens, rugby pitches, trout-stocked lake, six-hole golf course and 'wilderness' – where its pupils can climb trees ('only to three times our own height,' we were earnestly assured) and build dens to their heart's content – are framed by spectacular Northamptonshire countryside and farmland as far as the eye can see, the school instantly seducing visitors with its quaint Swallows and Amazons feel. A 17th century turreted hall is the main school building and boarding accommodation. To compare the fabric of Maidwell to other preps would be as to compare Sandringham to Beckingham Palace. Here you will find no trace of architect designed theatres or gleaming new boarding houses but a low-key wealth of facilities that's right in line with the lifestyle of the well-heeled parent cohort.

The overall vibe is wholesome, jolly and humane. No abrasive bells to signal the end of lessons or break: 'This is their term time home,' says head, 'and we try to make it feel as homely as possible.' Also: 'We have less a uniform and more a code of dress, allowing pupils to express their individuality.' The result is a charming array of corduroy trousers or culottes, a striped or checked shirt and tie of choice (boys and girl prefects only), topped off with a jacket tailored in pupils' own choice of tweed. Screen time almost non-existent, save the occasional sports match or the news for prefects. Phone calls home are made from one of a few good old-fashioned landlines situated in nooks around the school and the tradition of a compulsory weekly letter home to parents continues. Free time, or 'muckabout', is spent running around the vast grounds, taking part in one of the plethora of activities and sports on offer or – we were delighted to see – reading. Parents love that their children 'are not just getting an education, but a childhood too'. The 21st century has not bypassed Maidwell, though, and technology is very much alive and kicking in the classroom, with all pupils now taking a standard issue iPad to every lesson.

So, we asked, what kind of 8-year-old goes full boarding these days? Head very clear that Maidwell pupils are not 'sent away' from home as was often the case yesteryear. Boarding here is 'always a positive choice' and 'to be honest, the children clamour for it', he says. All have a 24-hour boarding trial in the summer prior to starting and, as far as we can make out, it's consistently a hit. About half of parents are 'old school', with the rest 'a lovely smattering of everybody else, but definitely not flash', we were reliably informed. Those we spoke to – most having had the debate about the benefits of weekly versus termly boarding – were keen advocates of the full boarding model, grateful that their children are not subject to the weekly upheaval of lengthy travels, the emotional switch between school and home life or constantly exhausted without a chance to fully recharge between Saturday teatime and Sunday evening.

Small class sizes of up to 15. All lessons taught by subject specialists, many of whom are trained secondary teachers, which 'enables us to be teaching at almost GCSE level by the time pupils leave,' says head. Two streams in each year, with pupils set separately for maths. Trad curriculum (languages are French and Latin, with Greek for potential scholars taught outside of usual timetable). Parents of very academic children full of praise for teaching, with staff spending their break times to offer extra tuition to scholarship candidates around exam time. Exam technique covered in detail at frequent revision seminars in the run up to senior school exams and all CE pupils create revision plan with deputy head, with up to eight hours' extra independent study expected at key times: 'we make sure they are always in the right place at the right time,' he says. High praise, too, from parents of the less academically stellar who, if necessary, are 'taken off quietly by the incredible learning support department', often resulting in pupils becoming 'unrecognisable' in their outcomes. Mild dyslexia, dyscalculia or dyspraxia all in a day's work 'but pupils do have to be mainstream,' says head. Mild ASD (mainly undiagnosed) also fine but 'I dislike labels and won't allow them,' says head. 'The structure of a boarding school plays to the favour of children who may have been told they have ADD or ADHD – we work with it as we would anything else.' Specialist EAL teacher supports international students, who are often withdrawn from French or Latin. We loved the vertical tutor system – there are no forms and pupils have the same tutor from the start of their school career to the end and meet weekly in groups of six to eight – 'it engenders a lack of hierarchy among the pupils,' says head. Behaviour and manners a major strength of school: 'we are very strict, although pupils don't really realise it and parents comment on improvements after just a few weeks,' says head. Mothers concur: 'if you want a well-mannered child, send them to Maidwell'.

On top of all the academic subjects, very strong art, led by the 'young, fizzy' head of department, and drama equally impressive. One 'massive' production every year, described by parents as 'brilliant – so slick and fresh'. About two-thirds take peripatetic music lessons in the somewhat makeshift music rooms. 'Not ideal, but it all just happens,' says head. Sport six days a week with 'everyone in the teams' and plenty of match day success. It's rugby, hockey and cricket for boys, and girls – whose sport is 'good now', thanks to new head of girls' games – play netball, hockey and rounders, albeit sometimes in mixed age groups to make up numbers. Great to see girls' football on offer as an activity – how about cricket next? Pupils jet away on fabulous sports tours (eg hockey to Barcelona, rugby to Dublin and cricket to Antigua). Weekly swimming in school's indoor pool, also used for free swims during activity time. Activities aplenty, with two compulsory during the generous 45-minute morning break and three in the evening each week.

Homely dorms sleep six to seven pupils. Spectacular views across the grounds and surrounding countryside (beds in turrets most coveted)

Whole school assembles each morning plus service in the church next door every Sunday, with plenty of parents in attendance. Meals all taken in quite the loveliest prep school dining room we've ever seen. Family style dining ('the food's amazing,' said pupils – and we can vouch for Friday fish and chips) served out by either a member of staff or, for the older ones, a pupil. Lunch fairly formal, with grace at the beginning and end announced by head's hand bell, and the tradition of a box of boiled sweets passed round to finish. At breakfast and supper pupils can sit amongst their friends or siblings in different year groups.

Boarding: Boys' dorms up a sweeping staircase off the main entrance hall and girls (who have to access their dorms via a different route in the evenings) on the charming attic floor above. Pupils allowed to board weekly during their first year – and can even choose to be a day pupil throughout their Maidwell career if they so wish – but very few do. Homely dorms sleep six to seven pupils. Dorm captains – top year pupils placed to keep an eye on their younger peers – in every room 'to make sure everyone's happy – and tidy'. Spectacular views across the grounds and surrounding countryside (beds in turrets most coveted) and the girls' rooms in particular, with their sloping ceilings, lending themselves to festooning with cheerful bunting. When we visited, pupils were buzzing in anticipation of the competition for most festive dorm decorations (whilst on the subject of Christmas, we are told that the carols round the tree, with the tradition of head boy/girl placing the star on top and youngest boarder a glass dove on a lower branch, followed by an 'amazing' Christmas lunch, are 'magical'). No boarding parents per se but head and his wife, a director of boarding, two matrons and three gappies live on site.

Weekends in school are action packed, with Saturday morning lessons generally followed by a sports fixture and relaxed evenings in with pizza and movies. After church on Sundays, there are trips or friendly sports matches. As one parent told us, 'There really isn't time for homesickness.' House system in place with head boy/girl, house captains and fiercely fought competitions for absolutely everything.

The last word: Maidwell parents 'couldn't be more delighted' with their choice. Traditional in the most positive sense, parents describe as 'extraordinary' the extent to which staff know their children and love the fact that school allows its pupils to elongate their childhood, free from the pressures of social media and the internet, whilst packing a hefty academic punch and shimmying them smoothly into their next schools.

Malvern College

14

College Road, Malvern, Worcestershire WR14 3DF

01684 581613 | admissions@malverncollege.org.uk | www.malverncollege.org.uk

Ages: 13–18

Pupils: 663; sixth form: 306; Boarders: 499 full, 22 flexi

Fees: Day £26,952 – £27,084; Boarding £39,954 – £41,145 pa

Linked school: The Downs Malvern, 1022

Headmaster: Since 2019, Keith Metcalfe, previously deputy head at Harrow. He's a local lad – educated at Monmouth School from where he went to Downing College, Cambridge and took a degree in geography, 'the most broad-ranging subject,' and a blue in golf. After graduating he worked for Christians in Sport where he discovered that he 'really liked working with young people,' and so completed a PGCE in Oxford. Joined the geography department at Harrow in 2000. He is married to Clare, a photographer and primary school teacher, and they have three young children, two at The Downs, Malvern College's prep and one at the College. 'I wanted to lead the kind of school I would like my own children to attend.'

This is Mr Metcalfe's first headship and the disruption of Covid soon after he took up the post must have made it a pretty tough debut. He acknowledged this with a wry smile and then paid tribute to his staff, 'I'm so proud of the people here.' Parents told us they were impressed by the way Malvern rose to the challenge of switching to virtual school, 'They were brilliant'. And some measures may be here to stay, 'Online parents' evenings are a big plus.' His role encompasses not just Malvern College, but also the Malvern 'family': two preps, five international schools and alumni. Getting to know four thousand plus pupils worldwide is 'tricky', he says with considerable understatement. Teaching geography to FY (year 9) keeps him grounded, 'If I'm here, it happens. It's in the timetable.'

He disagreed when we suggested that Malvern College must be very different from Harrow, 'No, it's very similar.' Perhaps he meant from a leadership perspective? While we were still pondering this he went on to confess that he had 'stolen something from Harrow.' It's the idea of 'a super curriculum,' the purpose of which is to make teaching and learning more inspiring, 'GCSEs can be quite dull.' Other big things on his to-do list are a 'focus on bursaries' and 'building leadership and collaboration skills into sport.'

He was described to us by parents as 'friendly, approachable, but maybe a bit shy,' and several approved that he was canvassing opinions, listening, 'taking his time and not doing anything drastic.' 'He's in and out of classrooms a lot, he's very astute and knows what he's doing.' We detected some underlying worries about whether changes on the academic front might narrow the all-rounder ethos of the school. We didn't get this impression from our discussions with the head and senior members of staff ('We're not about elites, we want academic strength and challenge for all.') but it was mentioned quite frequently by parents, 'There are lots of rumours about the head's intentions.' Some room for clearer communication on this front? 'Listen to his podcasts, you'll get a good understanding of what he's trying to do,' another parent advised.

Pupils say he's 'really nice but very busy' that he's 'quite sporty, he cycles and runs a lot,' and that he is 'very strict on uniform.' Like parents, they also felt there was a 'bigger push on academics,' but seemed pretty sanguine about things, 'he's left lots the same too so it's okay.' Any changes you would like the head to make, we asked? 'Floodlights on the cricket pitch' was the immediate response. Oh, and could he 'change the fixture list so that the whole school can watch games.' Over to you Mr M.

Life at Malvern is clearly suiting Mr Metcalfe, he loves the countryside and running with his dog and has close family nearby. He's been out with the school mountain biking group and taken up rackets, 'I like to do things really well, I am competitive.' Other interests are music and theatre, both of which abound in his school and the town beyond. He described Malvern College as, 'Friendly. It's big enough so that there's a niche for everyone but small enough for each pupil to be known. Everyone has a chance to shine, either for the school or for their house.' His aim is for, 'Pupils to leave here feeling fulfilled and successful, ready to go out and make a difference.'

Entrance: Register three years before 13+ entry; some houses fill up faster than others. New system of online entrance tests based on verbal and non-verbal reasoning. Around 35 per cent from the linked prep, rest from all over. Some entries into years 10 and 11 for a one-year pre-A level/IB course. About 30 join the sixth form each year and they normally do tests in the subjects they want to study at A level or IB, including an English and maths paper as appropriate. Interviews, school reports and predicted GCSE results also part of the process.

We dropped into a science lesson on isotopes and electrons. Science facilities excellent, with light, modern labs that felt more university than school

All parents (boarding and day) asked to select two or three houses from which they will be allocated one and in most cases they get their first preference. Parents of day pupils are advised to check number of other day pupils in their chosen house (can be low) and ask about what is done to ensure day and boarding pupils are integrated – we heard one or two concerns about day pupils feeling excluded.

Exit: Almost all the sixth form go on to higher education. Durham, Warwick, Imperial, LSE, University College London, King's College London, Exeter, Bristol, Cardiff and Edinburgh all popular. Four to Oxbridge in 2021, eight medics and 28 to overseas universities including some of the most prestigious European, Canadian and US universities: TU Munchen, TU Delft, Columbia, University of Southern California and NYU.

Latest results: In 2021, 72 per cent 9-7 at GCSE; 43 per cent A*/A at A level (71 per cent A*-B). IB average score of 38. School did not publish its results in 2019 (the last year when exams took place).

Teaching and learning: A levels and well established IB programme offered in the sixth form and the different options are 'really well explained' to pupils and parents, 'there's no push either way,' we were told and if they want to swap early on pupils can do so. School is realistic about the demands of doing the IB, 'It's a huge commitment.' Parents seemed to view it as something that was predominantly popular with the international pupils, less so with the UK contingent. There are 27 A level options from which pupils choose three or four, all the standards plus classical civilisation, psychology, government and politics and physical education (the latter should be offered as a BTec, suggested a couple of parents).

A delve into the 'Academic excellence' section of Malvern's website reveals little in the way of useful specifics such as year on year exam results for individual subjects. Even university

Cardiff Sixth Form College

destinations are recorded generally. One can learn much more than headline grades from this kind of information – how popular subjects are at GCSE and A level for instance. Malvern isn't the only school to be coy about such things but it's still rather frustrating for potential parents. 'Exam results are only one piece of the jigsaw', is their explanation. That may be so, but how can we view the full picture if a piece is missing?

We dropped into a science lesson (IB chemistry) where pupils were brushing up on isotopes and electrons – quick fire testing with answers scribbled on laminated cards held up for the teacher to check, much better than hands up. Science facilities are excellent, with light, modern labs that felt more university than school.

'Our job is to find, develop and value our pupils' talents. We don't want them to be constrained by things they think they can't do,' the head told us. Parents agree that pupils are stretched and challenged – 'tutors are very good at picking up slackers' said one. 'Not every teacher is fantastic, some can be quite dry, but others are phenomenal.' 'The teachers are there all the time, they teach all day and then tutors are in houses from 7pm until 9pm in the evenings, they're so impressive.'

Music and drama are 'phenomenal' was the unanimous verdict. Malvern has been awarded the status of All-Steinway School in recognition of its musical excellence

So what's this 'super curriculum' that the head purloined from Harrow? Should it go in this section or under the heading of extracurricular? Both probably. School describes it thus: 'The super-curriculum gives pupils a chance to take leadership responsibility by designing their own individualised and independent curriculum... Super-curricular activities help pupils develop intellectual curiosity beyond the constraints of examination content and create a passion for advancing their own knowledge and bringing their education to life.' That's super as in above, or extra then – academic enrichment as a parallel to the core curriculum alongside co-curricular activities. It will take a while to embed something this ambitious, but early signs are very positive.

Learning support and SEN: About 20 per cent of those who arrive in year 9 receive some learning support. We hear from parents that learning enhancement, as it's now known at Malvern, has improved hugely in the last few years, 'There used to be a stigma about it and my daughter was reluctant to go, but it's so different now, she loves it,' said one. Another told us, 'The department has had a change of location, name and staff and it's absolutely fantastic.' In class, group work, individual support and short courses provided for mild to moderate SEN. Study skills support and EAL also offered. Emphasis is on in-class support rather than withdrawal from classes and if that's not possible sessions are offered at the start or end of the day.

The arts and extracurricular: Music and drama are 'phenomenal', was the unanimous verdict from parents. Malvern has been awarded the status of All-Steinway School in recognition of its musical excellence, there are 30 Steinway pianos at the college, including a performance grand which is used for recitals. It's also the headquarters of the National Schools Symphony Orchestra and a rehearsal venue for several local groups. Choirs of all kinds, multiple orchestras and instrumental ensembles perform regularly, there are 'unplugged' sessions for bands and house singing and music competitions get everyone taking part and are highlights of the school year. Five or so pupils sign up for music and music technology A levels each year and there is a good record of music and choral awards achieved by those going to university or music college.

Great facilities for design, technology and the visual arts – pupils can realise their creations using 3D printing and lasers but also learn the skills of hand and eye doing wood and metal work. Photography is offered as a separate A level. Around 30 pupils opt for these subjects at A level, going on to art foundation courses, to study architecture or other creative degrees at university.

'It used to be quite easy to do very little extracurricular stuff, but that's not the case now,' a pupil confided. Another told us, 'The housemaster will have a word if we're not doing enough.' There's already a huge amount to choose from – dance, film club, debating, creative writing, Model United Nations and the like, but Mr Metcalfe's super-curriculum means that in the pursuit of academic enrichment societies will be pupil-led and subject focused, 'We shouldn't be afraid to get rid of old societies, we want to do things in a different way. We want to facilitate pupils to follow their interests and create new societies. Some may last for just a year, some will endure.'

School has a separate outdoor pursuits department which runs co-curricular activities such as climbing, mountain biking and kayaking, making the most of Malvern's proximity to the River Wye and Brecon Beacons. CCF (Army, RAF and, unusually, Royal Marines) is linked with the DofE expedition programme meaning that it's possible for pupils to do both.

Sport: Excellent sports facilities both indoor and outside and an impressive list of highly qualified coaching staff. Specialist programmes cater for the elite players but not to the exclusion of the rest, their expertise enables pupils of all abilities to raise their game. Core seasonal sports are rugby, hockey, netball and cricket. Rugby is the dominant boys' game in the autumn and lent terms; girls' football is very popular and several players have been selected for the U18 national development squad. Cross country running is also a big deal, first years start with the Ferret's Race; seniors do the Ledbury Run which begins seven and a half miles and some very big hills away from the edge of Ledbury. There's also an inter-house cross country league.

The cricket pitch is right at the centre of the school campus and that tells you all you need to know about the importance of this game at Malvern – several parents told us that the school's cricketing heritage was a deciding factor in their choice, 'It's definitely a cricket school.' Coaches all have English Cricket Board qualifications and many have played professionally. Malvern's cricketers were national T20 U18 champions in 2019 and 2021 (no competition in 2020 because of Covid). Hockey is equally well provided for with a new water-based pitch and large indoor arena – since hockey is mainly a winter game this means play can continue whatever the weather.

Boarding houses are among the nicest we've visited – warm, welcoming and as non-institutional as it's possible to be in a school setting

Shooting range, mostly used by CCF. Very nice swimming pool, 'You can do canoe water polo or just swim for pleasure.' No on-site golf course but pupils play competitively all year round at a nearby club and can practise under cover at school using some fancy equipment donated by the Old Malvernian Gold Society. The traditional independent school games of fives (like squash but without a racket) and rackets, also like squash but with rackets, are both very popular at Malvern. There are just 14 other schools on the rackets circuit and competition is fierce.

Sport is part of the defining culture here and seemed a huge deal for nearly all the pupils we met – we wondered how school life would feel for those less able or less interested, 'It is very sporty, but there's plenty of other things to get involved in so you don't feel you're missing out.'

Boarding: Houses – known by numbers, not names – are based in a mix of characterful old or well-designed newer buildings, boys on one side of the campus and girls on the other. They are among the nicest we've visited – warm, welcoming and as non-institutional as it's possible to be in a school setting. No separate day houses, day pupils (around 25 per cent) are members of boarding houses and day fees include 15 ad hoc nights a year – useful for occasions such as trips, concerts and other events. Parents can also buy additional days. All new year 9 pupils board for their first seven nights which is great for bonding and does not use up the day pupils' annual allowance. Depending on the house there are sometimes proper beds for day pupils or else 'very nice' camp beds if they stay over. First and second years sleep in four or five bed dorms; older pupils have double or single study bedrooms. Day pupils have their own study area. First years have supervised study 'until they get the right merits', usually by the second year. Fifteen minutes of reading time for all first and second years every evening.

We enjoyed our lunch in one of the girls' houses, served by pupils at round tables seating eight or so – all rather civilised and better for conversation than long refectory tables. 'Mixing up the year groups on dining tables means they all get to know each other, it's especially important post-Covid,' said the house mistress.

In-house dining is much less common in boarding schools these days and has its pros and cons – some parents thought it would more sociable if girls and boys from different houses could mix, others liked the idea of children returning to their house for meals. The pastoral advantage is clear, 'It means we see pupils at several points in the day.' Another big bonus of in-house dining is that breakfast can be eaten in pyjamas, 'it's quite quick, eat and leave' we were told (presumably after having dressed). Another is that teachers and visitors routinely lunch in different houses, 'It's great for social skills and getting used to talking to adults.' Cakes, fruit and snacks provided for sustenance between meals and there are small kitchens for making toast and hot drinks.

External company supplies meals and house catering staff do final preparation. Mixed views on food (as ever), ranging from 'terrible' to 'it's mostly okay but depends how hungry you are.' Apparently menus are being trialled so that pupils can choose in advance. Parents mentioned 'too many carbs and not enough protein' but told us they knew that the school is working to address these and other concerns about catering. School shop, known as Grub, sells snacks such as panini and cookies (as well as uniform and other supplies), but apparently 'girls go and buy food in Waitrose' and the boys order takeaways at weekends.

Hymn practice (known as 'Congo') is enjoyed by believers and nonbelievers alike, 'especially when we sing Jerusalem'

We visited House 8 (girls), a rather grandly proportioned Edwardian pile. The atmosphere was relaxed and friendly with girls popping in and out of the ground floor 'hub', the place to go for everything from tea and sympathy to plasters and paracetamol. A large chart was covered with stars keeping track of the (many) extracurricular activities girls had chosen to take part in. Bedrooms were decorated, 'we encourage personalisation,' with photos, mostly of dogs and ponies. Phones are allowed after lessons but pupils below year 11 must hand in their tech before bed, 'We sign phones in and out and there are sanctions for keeping second phones or hiding them.' Day girls can stay for house events such as arts soirees which celebrate creative writing, music and drama (parents are invited too).

Ethos and heritage: The advent of railways made Malvern easily accessible from London and it consequently became a fashionable destination for 19th century travellers in search of pure air and healing waters – we can vouch for the former, if not the latter. Malvern College was founded in 1865 on the outskirts of the town as a boys' school with 24 pupils and 12 masters. The College had a brief spell at Blenheim Palace in 1939 when its premises were requisitioned by the Admiralty and was ousted again, this time to Harrow School, to make way for the war time government's Telecommunications and Research Establishment. It was a great privilege for us to talk to staff in the wood-panelled senior common where vital work on the development of radar took place during WW2. The College went co-educational in 1992 which was also the year the IB was introduced – it was among the earliest adopters for both of these.

Full, weekly and flexi boarding may be on the menu at other schools, but Malvern is holding firm to its full boarding tradition, making it particularly appealing to international and military families, 'We chose it partly because of the proper boarding.' Saturday remains a school day for all but the shape of the weekend has been changed to allow a bit more relaxation time, 'We took chapel out of Sunday,' says the head, 'to allow more time for leisure and the chance of a lie in.' That's not to say that chapel has been side-lined, it just happens on Saturday. 'Some want less, some want more,' a pupil observed, 'but it's more pupil-led now and the talks are really good.' Hymn practice (known as 'Congo') is enjoyed by believers and non-believers alike, 'especially when we sing Jerusalem.' Fabulous library – no danger of books being replaced by electronic devices as far as we could tell.

On their first day all pupils are taken for a walk on the glorious Malvern hills immediately behind the school so that they get to know the landscape (and elements) that will define their next five years. We arrived for our visit in warm autumn sunshine but a few hours later were struggling across the campus in lashing wind and rain. 'You get used to it,' said our guides. The large site is on a slope which means a fair amount of up and downhill walking between houses and classrooms – parents are happy that their children get lots of that healthy fresh air but several pupils confessed they would like a way of getting from A to B that was a bit faster, warmer and drier, 'It's a long way up that hill,' said a girl from one of the houses at the top.

The school bar may have slightly fallen out of favour elsewhere but it's still going strong at Malvern and known as the 'Longy'. 'It's literally a night club' said one sixth former (if this is true then prospective parents might be concerned, but we suspect the pupil in question may not have been to an actual night club). Three beers is the Longy limit and pupils are breathalysed on the way in and out.

We thoroughly enjoyed our visit to Malvern – it was a privilege to be allowed such free range and access to different parts of the school, especially given Covid restrictions. We met and enjoyed talking to lots of pupils as well as members of the senior leadership team. A first for us was hearing unprompted praise and affection for the house domestic staff from a pupil, 'They're really kind, they are sort of an unofficial part of the pastoral team and you can talk to them about things.' Tells you a lot about a place.

Pastoral care, inclusivity and discipline: House staff and tutors are the bedrock of pastoral care and we heard nothing but the highest praise for them from parents, 'My child had a few problems and support from the school was fantastic.' 'The environment house teams create is superb. There are lots of different personalities but the staff know each pupil as an individual, they find out what a child likes and build on that.' Another parent commented on what good role models the senior pupils were for the younger ones. Appreciation too for the 'calm and helpful' way the school deals with parents' anxieties, particularly during Covid.

Discipline was described to us by parents (approvingly) as 'Firm, they will follow through if a pupil breaks the rules, but they also understand that young people have lapses.' Very strict on vaping, a persistent problem in all schools, 'they are working really hard to stamp it out.' Sixth formers are allowed to go into Birmingham or Worcester on the train and over-18s can have up to three drinks in a town pub (with parental permission). Apparently school employs security guards to ensure pupils out in Malvern stay on their best behaviour. Occasional isolated incidents of bullying have been 'resolved straight away.'

When it comes to friendship problems, relationships between pupils or other anxieties there are many different sources of help and advice, from specially trained peer mentors ('house buddies'), to personal tutors, school counsellors and (unofficially) house dogs which are 'good for a cuddle if you're feeling sad.' Parents describe the interaction between boys and girls as 'well balanced, it's mostly about close friendships rather than romance.' School says, 'Any relationships are expected to be discreet. Pupils know the rules and that they run the risk of being expelled if they break them.' House parents 'have a little conversation' as necessary and keep a watchful eye.

We asked pupils about the issues raised by Everyone's Invited, 'There's been a really big push to get discussion going – it's mostly been initiated by pupils but staff have really encouraged us. We think individuals could speak out now if they had a bad experience.' School has 'audited' both its curriculum and disciplinary processes with the pupil-led Black Lives Matter Society. A programme of peer-to-peer talks covers subjects such as racism, sexism and co-education, 'There has been a massive increase in pupil voice,' we were told, 'which is the foundation of strong pupil teacher relationships.'

Pupils and parents: 'Down to earth', 'grounded', 'mainly middle class, not super rich' is how parents described themselves. The head agrees, 'It's not a city school, pupils are less sophisticated – their biggest thrill comes from things like house singing, silent discos and firepits!' Several parents said they chose the school because the linked prep made it an all-through option, others said it was the location and emphasis on outdoor activities. Around 30 per cent international pupils (quite a few ex-pats) from 50 different countries. IB has long been a draw for European families and according to the school remains so post-Brexit.

Former pupils include Sir Chris Whitty, epidemiologist and chief medical officer during the pandemic, Jeremy Paxman, Monty Don, actor Denholm Elliott, sports commentator Mark Pougatch, novelist C S Lewis, the occultist Aleister Crowley, and two Nobel prize winners (economics and chemistry). Plus a pavilion full of eminent cricketers including Reginald 'Tip' Foster, the only man to have captained England in both cricket and football, and ranks of distinguished politicians, diplomats, clerics and soldiers. Back in the here and now, 'Our Malvern Stories' is a very interesting read (website or book) about what more recent leavers, girls and boys, have gone on to do.

Money matters: Means-tested bursaries and scholarships for a wide range of talents, just over half of pupils receive some fee assistance. Learning support and EAL tuition come as extras.

The last word: Malvern's motto is 'Sapiens qui prospicit' (Wise the one who looks ahead), it's a fitting epithet for such a well run, dynamic and forward thinking school. Just the place for families in search of a top flight, all round education with plenty of fun and fresh air. As one parent put it, 'Each of our very different children has flourished here. When you come over the hills and see the school, see the houses, you feel that you belong.'

Malvern St James Girls' School

15

15 Avenue Road, Great Malvern, Worcestershire WR14 3BA

01684 892288 | admissions@malvernstjames.co.uk | www.malvernstjames.co.uk

Ages: 4–18

Pupils: 400; sixth form: 116; Boarders: 130 full, 66 weekly/flexi

Fees: Day £7,650 – £19,740; Boarding £14,115 – £40,410 pa

Headmistress: Since 2016, Olivera Raraty, a historian (Leeds) with impeccable girls' school credentials. Senior deputy at Notting Hill and Ealing High, assistant director of studies and head of history and politics at Wycombe Abbey, history specialist at Francis Holland NW1. With a warmth that has captivated the whole community, Olivera has brought the academic clout of her former roles with her, and while she loves the breadth of the ability range at MSJ, she is determined to build on the intellectual force blossoming in the school.

The girls say there has been a bit of general tightening up since Olivera's arrival but no worrying dramatic changes. 'She is there at everything,' they note. She has got the staff on board because they can see she puts in the hours, loves the school already, has masses of exciting ideas for focusing the academic life of the school and the confidence to move things forward. 'She is just great to work with,' we heard over and over again from her colleagues. Parents are pleased to have a mother of two daughters with whom to share the ups and downs of adolescence (both Olivera's daughters are now safely through the teenage years).

Entrance: There is an element of selection but it is not ferocious. Up to year 3, the girls are invited in for a day to see how they get on. After that there is some assessment through tests. The juniors sit the same 11+ tests as external candidates but if teachers think they won't cope with the step up, there are early discussions about where would be more suitable. Nearly all of the juniors do move up, forming about half of the new year 7. Eleven-plus and 13+ entrants are often moving from co-ed preps. Sixth form entrants take papers in their three A level subjects, plus an EAL paper if English isn't their first language.

Exit: Very little drop-out post GCSEs. Two to Oxbridge in 2021 (one of them a medic). Diverse range of interests. Bristol, Cardiff, Durham, Edinburgh, Exeter, Imperial and UCL all popular. Careers advice also for students not going to university (worryingly not enough of this at some schools we visit) with enterprise education lead who helps find work experience placements and jobs.

Latest results: In 2021, 74 per cent 9-7 at GCSE; 75 per cent A*/A at A level (90 per cent A*-B). In 2019 (the last year when exams took place), 55 per cent 9-7 at GCSE; 44 per cent A*/A at A level (70 per cent A*-B).

Teaching and learning: GCSE results have been improving steadily – impressive for a school that is by no means highly selective. Nearly 90 per cent of sixth formers are studying one or more STEM subjects (60 per cent are doing maths A level) and an unusually high number go on to study some form of engineering. An MSJ team got into the finals of the UK Maths Challenge in 2016. There is computer science on offer at GCSE and A level as well as DT product design. In fact the sixth form offer is unusually broad and undoubtedly one of the strengths of the school.

School is proud of its tailored approach to the individual in all areas of academic and personal development and is working on building an active learning approach where girls take responsibility for their own attitude to school work. In the classes we watched there was a sense of real engagement in learning and teachers were enthusiastically promoting creativity and challenge. Prep also fosters independent learning, so the girls who move up already have a strong basis which is then developed through a new year 7 curriculum that includes a Philosophy for Learning course.

Stunning library, well stocked and with long opening hours. The librarians are enthusiastic and fully involved with curriculum innovation across the school

The offer for the most able pupils is being refined; there are academic enrichment opportunities for everyone who wants them and some who may need a bit of initial prodding. The extension programmes include exciting outside lecturers, the prestigious Somerville suppers and various debates. New mentoring and coaching programmes have also been established.

Staff report it is an exciting place to teach and they feel free to try out innovations. The impressive senior team is keen to take the school's enthusiasm and expertise outside its grand walls and is busy plugging gaps in the local area by providing all sorts of opportunities for local primary schools – modern languages days, maths challenges, technology workshops – that get out the message that academic rigour can be fun and creative.

Careers education is far reaching, including an increasing input from alumnae. With various old girls in the Debretts/Sunday Times 500 Most Influential Britons list, the girls can connect with women who are at the top of their careers and wanting to give back to their alma mater. 'My friends at co-ed schools always have to sit through talks from lots of old boys,' one of the sixth formers told us. 'Our alumnae are all important women.'

Stunning library, well stocked and with long opening hours. The librarians are enthusiastic and fully involved with curriculum innovation across the school, in particular critical literacy

– vital for independent learning, and understanding and interpreting information sources.

The prep department is at the heart of the school, not just physically but also in its ability to access high quality facilities and specialist staffing. Not that the movement is all one way. A recent Toy Story theme allowed the girls to get to grips with mechanics while the woodland school lets them get messy and use serious tools to make tree dens. We spoke to a number of parents who had moved girls from state primaries for the range of opportunities the prep department offers.

Several much loved traditions endure, including the exchanging of prefects' gowns ceremony, the annual staff pantomime and ships (house) events

At the other end, the sixth form is going from strength to strength. Tutors and tutees are matched as far as possible by interests and support is coherent – enough to ensure they learn how to maximise their potential without floundering when they leave. The size (about 60 in each year) means the school can be fleet footed when change and innovation are needed. EPQs are increasingly popular and topics reflect the diversity of interests – How to Organise a Tough Schools Day, Training a Racehorse, The Drawbacks of Volunteering Abroad.

Learning support and SEN: Learning support operates at various levels. There is a drop-in session for juniors during prep. All staff have training on learning difficulties and there are two full-time SENCos in addition to literacy and numeracy specialists. Support is provided within a graduated framework after a problem is identified. This may include short-term focused group work as well as one-to-one lessons (extra charge) – all designed round the needs of the individual.

The arts and extracurricular: Interest groups abound. Quest, a liberal religious literacy group, got a special mention. Model United Nations is popular and MSJ works with state secondary schools to help them get involved. Year 9s ran a mock election for the whole school and the staff are keen to develop the girls' confidence in public speaking. There is a STEM club where much of the enthusiasm for all forms of engineering is born. MSJ is really doing its bit to redress the gender imbalances. 'Coding is boring until you see the application,' one enthusiastic teacher told us, 'hence the STEM club.'

Drama is flourishing and much loved. Some girls and parents say music is the strongest department in the school – there are lots of performance opportunities including choirs, orchestras and ensembles. Visual arts are vibrant; we saw lots of evidence of ambitious, high quality pieces. Textiles is also strong.

Sport: Given the size of the school, its sporting success is remarkable, and the head is determined to take it still further in line with some parents' views that there could be even more wins. There are a number of elite national athletes – at hockey, lacrosse, rounders, golf, cricket, fencing, athletics, eventing – and the school receives lots of accolades for its willingness to support individuals when they are off competing. The excitement around sport is reflected in the girls' very small wish list, where bigger sports facilities came pretty near the top. We thought they were very generous already.

Boarding: One junior boarding house for years 3-8, two for years 9-11 and two sixth form houses, one of which is in the main school building. The latter is much coveted by those who want to stay in bed a bit later and those who want to burn the midnight oil in the library. Other houses are in nearby Malvern, lovely properties with large country gardens, high ceilings with light and fresh air flowing through.

Weekend activities are highly rated and compulsory up to year 9. Girls are very positive about relationships between day girls and boarders.

There is a strong and experienced pastoral team. Pastoral care plans are put in place quickly and unobtrusively when necessary to provide additional support to girls. Parents say that considerable work has been done on improving home-school communications.

All pupils eat together in the newly designed dining hall and the food is fresh and diverse, catering for a cosmopolitan set. There was a healthy eating week when we visited that certainly sold the concept to us.

Ethos and heritage: Malvern St James is the result of the 2006 merger of Malvern Girls' College (founded in 1893) and St James's School (founded in 1896). The school is located opposite the railway station (good links to Birmingham and London) in buildings that were formerly the Imperial Hotel and which lend a certain grandeur and spaciousness to the bustle of school life.

Having the prep department in the centre of the school gives a light and fun atmosphere – this is certainly not a school that feels dominated by teenage angst. The younger girls dart around a glorious copper beech, reminding everyone in the summer term when we visited that there is a life outside GCSEs and away from computer screens. 'They look up to the seniors who they see around all day – it gives them something to aspire to,' the prep head told us. While it is clearly a whole school and everyone loves that, each phase has its own distinctive features. 'We dress up a lot in the junior department and parents are in and out all the time.' Senior girls get involved with the juniors in lots of ways: prefects from the senior school are attached to the pre-prep, there are house links, and junior girls sit on the school anti-bullying and food committees.

Although it's not a school weighed down by its past, several much loved traditions endure. These include the exchanging of prefects' gowns ceremony, the annual staff pantomime and ships events (the competitive houses – as distinct from the boarding houses – are called 'ships' here and run from the junior department right through the school). It is a place with the imagination to go with the creative ideas that the girls come up with, celebrating the quirky as well as the more mainstream.

'It's warm but not fluffy,' says the head and we think that just about sums it up.

Pastoral care, inclusivity and discipline: The school prides itself on its tailored, personal, family feel. There is a lot of careful, professional attention given to defining and meeting individual needs and the decision to offer an unusually broad range of options, particularly at sixth form level, supports this principle. Girls tells us that they stay at the school because its size means everyone looks out for everyone else.

The growth mindset philosophy is being well bedded in for both girls and staff and builds on the can-do mentality the school has historically cultivated. A new year 10 course looks at negative and positive coping strategies and the school intends to encourage parents to get to grips with current mental health theories, recognising that in such matters school and home need to be giving the same message.

Mental health issues are discussed very openly. There is a 'brilliant' health and well-being centre, the girls tell us, and staff are complimentary about how well the centre communicates with the rest of the school. Girls have access to an external counsellor.

Behaviour is exemplary, as you find in so many girls' schools. Staff and girls scratch their heads to think of naughty actions, but if they find something, there is a range of the usual sanctions – detentions, withdrawal of privileges. Staff say an awful lot of listening and talking works as prevention.

The management team has been looking at extending leadership opportunities for everyone. This is just as true at year 6 as at year 13. The girls appreciate this and relish the chance to try new roles in a fairly small and safe environment.

Pupils and parents: Pupils here have that unique quality you can find in non-city girls' schools – a gentleness combined with a sassy competitiveness. These are girls who know what is trending globally on social media, but who also love a hike in the rolling Malvern Hills. These are girls who are comfortable in their own skins, they are accepted for who they are and give others the same respect and kindness. It is not nerdy to like science, we were told, and even if you are no good at sport you can still have fun on the games field.

These are girls who know what is trending globally on social media, but who also love a hike in the rolling Malvern Hills

While families are in the main pretty well-heeled, bursaries and scholarship dilute this a little. There are old farming families, those working in the new Worcestershire high-tech areas, businesspeople and professionals from the local vicinity and overseas.

Money matters: Range of scholarships (academic, sports, music, art drama etc) of up to 10 per cent of fees offered in years 7, 9 and 12. Some means-tested bursaries up to a total of 40 per cent. The prestigious Founders' Awards Scholarships are for top-notch scholars and all-round ambassadors, there are additional assessments and interviews for these. Wraparound care is available at no extra cost.

The last word: While MSJ may not be smart and shiny, there is something of a Bloomsbury feel about it, but a Bloomsbury fit for the 21st century. Operating in a competitive area, MSJ continues to carve out a niche for itself as being at the forefront of thinking on girls' education. The fact the new head has come from the GDST stable is helping this still further. The school feels driven and full of girls who are going to change the world, but keeps a sense of a small, close knit community. Undoubtedly brilliant for the all-rounder, but increasingly meeting the aspirations of the high flying academics.

Monmouth School for Boys

16

Almshouse Street, Monmouth NP25 3XP

01600 713143 | boys.admissions@habsmonmouth.org | www.habsmonmouth.org

Ages: 11–18

Pupils: 524; sixth form: 261 (156 boys and 105 girls); Boarders: 150 full (from age 9)

Fees: Day £16,599; Boarding £31,467 – £34,167 pa

Linked school: Monmouth School for Girls, 1052

Headmaster: Since 2020, Simon Dorman. Previously the school's second master and, say pupils and parents, as engaged with the boys now as he was back then. Softly spoken and playfully self-effacing, he's right up there in the popularity stakes, coming in for particular praise for his 'very open ears', 'calmness' and 'humility'. 'Makes a real effort with parents in a down-to-earth, I'm-a-dad-too kind of way,' lauded one; 'Helped scoop up our son when he broke down on assessment day,' said another.

Hails from Northern Ireland, where he was educated at a Belfast grammar school, boarding from 11. Loved school so much that teaching was really the only career that could fill the hole after leaving at 18. And so, armed with his degree in German and philosophy from Jesus College Oxford and MPhil and a PGCE from Queen's University in Belfast, he set off to the wilds of Scotland to kickstart his career at Gordonstoun – 'an amazing place' – followed by a year in Seville, where he worked on his Spanish while teaching English and German. Returned to the UK as head of German at The Leys School in Cambridge and became housemaster of a boarding house before joining Monmouth in 2010.

Married to Miranda, who teaches learning support at Monmouth School for Girls, where their youngest of two daughters is still a pupil. Reads a lot (mainly Spanish and German literature), plays the piano (is having lessons again, having previously stopped when he was 16), walks and runs. We happen to know he has a penchant for Erasure too (it was his 50th birthday when we visited and he was off to see them that night to celebrate).

James Murphy-O'Connor became the first overarching principal of Haberdashers' Monmouth Schools in September 2019.

Entrance: The Monmouth schools have taken on a diamond structure so the prep is now co-ed, followed by single sex at senior school, then a co-ed sixth form. Most of the boys at the prep move up to the senior school where they are joined by almost as many again from outside – mainly state primaries reaching as far as Hereford, Chepstow, Cardiff and Bristol, along with a few boarders.

Selective but not frantically so – only a few are turned away each year. At 11+, online exams in English, maths and verbal reasoning, plus interview and a current school report. At 13+, by Common Entrance or the school's own exams in maths, English and French, plus interview and report. Emphasis on spotting potential more than test performance. Worth asking about entry in other years too. Entry into sixth form requires five 6s at GCSE, with 7s in the subjects to be studied, along with interview and report. Non-nationals must speak reasonable English, although the school does offer EAL support.

Exit: Up to 15 per cent leave post-GCSE. Vast majority of sixth formers to university, 60 per cent to Russell Group. Cardiff and Swansea always popular, Bristol and Bath increasingly so. Durham, Reading and Southampton usually feature, plus a smattering to the London universities. Four to Oxbridge in 2021, plus three medics and four overseas (California, Netherlands and two to Spain). Maths and science-based subjects are popular, as are business studies, economics, history, psychology and PE.

Latest results: In 2021, 74 per cent 9-7 at GCSE; 66 per cent A*/A at A level (86 per cent A*-B). In 2019 (the last year when exams took place), 55 per cent 9-7 at GCSE; 40 per cent A*/A at A level (66 per cent A*-B). A level results are combined with the girls' school.

Teaching and learning: 'They get boys – they understand how they learn,' said a parent, approving of the movement, games, challenges, humour and light-touch sense of competition that underpins learning here and leads to impressive results, especially when it comes to value-added. Maths is successful and popular, with teachers adept at making the most lacklustre of equations and fractions relatable – 'makes it feel relevant, not just maths for maths' sake,' said a boy. Sciences hold a special place in these boys' hearts – no wonder, we thought, when we happened upon a chemistry lab with flaming Bunsens, fizzing test tubes and boys' cheerful but purposeful chatter. The school collaborates with Monmouth state schools on the Monmouth Science Initiative, which brings young people together regularly to work with specialists in the science world, who come and speak at the schools, plus twice-yearly visits to Cardiff University. Computer science is a growth area – we sat in on a class on cookies vs viruses with hands popping up here, there and everywhere among boys hungry to acquire more nerdy know-how. In English, groups of chaps were writing speeches on 'the environment in crisis' to world leaders. Pupils make 3D maps in geography, re-enact battles in history, go outside to practice mindfulness and use clay to express their creativity.

The school believes that single-sex academic classes up to GCSE mean the boys are free of the distractions of girls in their adolescent years and are less likely to be self-conscious, especially in creative arts and languages. The jury is still out among the boys on the sixth form going co-ed (across both the boys' and girls' schools) but it certainly makes for a lovely long list of A level choices – 31 at last count – including philosophy, RS, Russian, Latin and Greek. Typically, students do two A levels at their school and one at the other – with maths, sciences and history getting the best results. About a dozen complete an EPQ.

Not much by way of setting, just maths from year 8 and English from year 10. 'Our ability band is narrow enough not to need it,' claims school. French and Latin from year 7, German and Spanish added in year 8, then boys choose two of the four in year 9 with vast majority expected to do a language at GCSE. All start with triple science, with up to 16 boys dropping down to double post-mocks. Ten GCSEs is the norm, with history, DT, geography and RS among the most popular non-core subjects. Classes average 20, classrooms are well-appointed though not huge, and most departments have their own library. 'The history library had all the books on Disraeli and Victorian politics that I needed for a project – it saved me masses of time by not having to go to public libraries,' raved one sixth former. Academically and pastorally on the ball during Covid, we heard – 'They learned a lot from the first lockdown,' said a parent. We picked up a lot of negative vibes among pupils and parents around the existence of Saturday school – 'I literally can't stand it,' declared one mother (though school says it is popular with some and not with others).

Learning support and SEN: Around 10 per cent of pupils are on the learning support register, mostly for mild SEN, with the learning support department run by one full-time and two part-time members of staff. 'I wouldn't say they're brilliant at it, but their pastoral support sort of makes up for it,' said a parent. Some group sessions available to help with such difficulties as time management and organisation; occasional one-to-ones for longer term programmes (costs extra). A few boys have physical disabilities – some parts of the campus are more wheelchair friendly than others, but school is happy to adapt timetables to make use of ground floor classrooms where it can.

The arts and extracurricular: Full-on, which can take a bit of getting used to. 'He's absolutely exhausted!' laughed a mother of a boy in year 7. Cerebral societies are on the up under the current headship, plus there's DT workshops, reading groups, science clubs etc. CCF is growing; DofE historically weak but new head of outdoor pursuits soon to be on the case.

Sciences hold a special place in these boys' hearts – we happened upon a chemistry lab with flaming Bunsens, fizzing test tubes and boys' cheerful but purposeful chatter

Music on par with sport in the pecking order of extracurricular, spanning the more classical symphony orchestra to a modern jazz band, with plenty of ensembles and choirs to suit all tastes. Animated head of department steers his ship from just across the road, with plenty of (recently renovated) rehearsal and classroom space and easy access to instruments ranging from organ to drums. Performances and tours aplenty, including overseas, although we were surprised that only a third of boys learn an instrument with a peri. 'Too much writing and not enough practical music in the early years,' grumbled a few boys, but older ones reckon it sets good foundations.

Drama gets less air time, although decent numbers are suitably impressed by their taster year in year 9 to pick it as a GCSE and a few at A level too. 'I like the way the drama teachers work with you, not just telling you what to do – there's so much creative freedom,' said one boy; another chortled as he told us about a slapstick play he's involved in as part of drama club. Performances (many written in house) are often joint with the girls' school, including a biennial musical as well as the big drama classics. The school theatre, the Blake, is a brilliant resource for the town as well as the schools, showing NT Live streams and hosting a number of touring companies as well as local arts groups.

Art is a dazzler of a department – two whole floors of pleasingly cluttered studios right in the heart of the school, including one dedicated to all things ceramic: poppies, birds, fish, you name it. Decorating skateboards and detailed watercolours feature among the boys' favourite projects, with screen printing a specialism. DT is another spacious hub of activity – we saw year 8s cutting wood for a box project and sixth formers using sophisticated machinery for metalwork. Not unusually, the DT teacher told us he attended the school himself.

The fact that Monmouth is such a small and safe town 'means the boys get to enjoy a wonderful freedom that you don't get with more bubble-like boarding schools'

Lots of the residential and overseas trips are joint with the girls. We loved the framed photos of pupils whitewater rafting in Sri Lanka and sitting on jeeps on the beach in Morocco.

Sport: 'The reason we chose the school,' we heard time and again. Already great, now outstanding, thanks to current head boosting coaching resources and staff, as well as ensuring all boys now have access to strength and conditioning. 'You get two to three teaching staff per session,' said one youngster, clearly in awe; 'You get advice on mindset and technical side of things as well as the more obvious practical side,' piped up another. Although the jewels in the crown continue to be rugby and rowing ('I wish football was on offer before year 9,' said more than one parent), other sports are getting a look in and gaining considerable success. Some, such as swimming, are now putting out mixed teams. The A teams win regularly both regionally and nationally ('Clear your diary if your son gets into one!' advised one mother), but the impressive fixture list puts out up to three teams per year group most weeks. Boys praise the 'balance between having fun and playing seriously' and told us you don't have to be sporty to be in the in-crowd. Badminton, squash, kayaking, tennis and climbing, among others, mean most boys find something they like.

The sports centre is open day and night and incorporates a private members' sports club for the public and parents. It is home to a canoeing club, pilates studio, fitness suite, huge all-purpose sports hall and gym. An impressive sports pavilion overlooks the playing fields that fall away to the Wye river. 'But the pitches – although professional – are sacrificial lambs for flooding,' said a pupil.

Boarding: A major factor in parents picking this school is the fact that Monmouth is such a delightful – but more importantly, small and safe – town which, as one put it, 'means the boys get to enjoy this wonderful freedom that you simply don't get with more bubble-like boarding schools.' Half the boarders are British, the rest international – around half from Hong Kong, then Germany and Spain, plus a few each from eg mainland China, Japan, Russia, Nigeria and Eastern Europe. All are split up to help avoid cliques, though 'can be hard to avoid,' we heard. House parents, who are also teachers – something parents value – are totally devoted to the school and boys.

The five (all recently renovated) boarding houses comprise one for juniors in years 5-8, three for years 9-12, and one for year 13s, the latter designed as a stepping stone to fully independent university life. Here the boys learn how to cook on a budget and how to operate a washing machine. They also all have their own en-suites. The houses range from Georgian townhouses to a 60s block, with tidy-ish (some more than others) dorms of anything up to six. With most staying put at weekends, there are plenty of activities to get involved in – cinema, paintballing etc – often joint with boarders from the girls' school.

The school is proud of its boarding, but some parents told us that culturally it feels more like a day school with boarding attached. 'You go to some boarding schools and everything clearly centres around the boarders – the structure, the timings, the food – but here, the boarders slot in with the day pupils,' said one. It's not a problem, they said, just something to be aware of (although we did hear a couple of tales of boarders having been forgotten when it came to packed lunches on school trips and lists being sent home of things pupils need to bring in the next day).

Ethos and heritage: Founded in 1614 by William Jones, a member of the Haberdashers' Company, the school expanded its boarding throughout the 19th century, a period that also saw a major rebuild in magnificent Jacobean style which 20th and 21st century buildings have since added

Set in a chocolate box part of town with perfectly maintained cottages in one direction and jawdropping scenery in the other

to. Upshot is a campus that embraces a mix of architectures from the almshouses, now offices, to more modern builds, to the sensitively refurbished chapel, now a (non-silent 'as we want it to be welcoming') library.

Set in a chocolate box part of town with perfectly maintained cottages in one direction and jaw-droppingly stunning scenery in the other, the school is a source of great pride locally. Absolutely none of the tensions you get between local school children and residents in some market towns (probably helped by school being the town's main employer). On the day of the annual commemoration service, there is a much-loved tradition where the school parades through the town to church, and all the key local dignitaries are invited to events such as the carol service. But while the school is doing its best to create more links with the girls' school, pupils feel there's still some way to go.

The school feels friendly and fun, particularly coming to life in the dining hall. So much so that we wound up feeling rather sorry for the boys who had to sacrifice their banter-ridden, laughter-filled tables to eat (a delicious chicken curry) with us (though they did get to jump the very long queues because of it – a silver lining for sure).

Pastoral care, inclusivity and discipline: Parents speak highly of the school's 'family feel' and several reported a huge growth in confidence and self-discipline among their sons. More formal pastoral tracking systems have been put in place since Covid – means that pupils who are deemed cause for concern on the mental health front are now numbered 1-4 on the pastoral barometer, updated each week with support put in place accordingly – anything from a few more gentle chats with a favoured teacher to a recommendation to visit one of the two part-time counsellors, and lots in between. Recent mental health first-aid training for all (already supportive, according to parents) staff means they know better than ever what to say and what not to say – especially important in encouraging boys to open up. We were impressed at how openly the boys discussed emotional problems that can occur, as well as the benefits of the mindfulness sessions they get. School also bigs up the importance of physical exercise for warding off serious mental health problems.

While school rules fit on a single sheet of A4 and are by and large a sensible mix of common sense and good manners, they do sweat the small stuff here and are especially hot on uniform, haircuts and punctuality. 'They don't slack on the discipline and it's all better for it!' said one parent, though another admitted it drove her son up the wall. Temporary exclusions usually happen in outbreaks, according to the head, with boys doing stupid things on eg social media. No permanent exclusions in over three years.

Not a school to brush the knottier aspects of teenagers under the carpet – gender politics, Everyone's Invited and racism are far from taboo and explored in assemblies, PSHE and – for example – art exhibitions, with one being set up on Black History Month during our visit. Diversity and inclusion group covers both LGBTQ+ and racism. Bullying carefully rooted out by staff who, for example, understand that it's more likely to happen in eg year 7 when 'boys are grouped together for the first time and trying to assert themselves in the pecking order.' We like the school's approach to always reconciling bully and victim, 'with both explaining their experience to the other and encouraged to see the good in the other; just punishing the bully isn't enough.'

Pupils and parents: This is a school that inspires a lot of loyalty from pupils, parents, staff and the wider Monmouth community. Many old boys send their own sons here. Catchment mainly covers Herefordshire and Monmouthshire but can stretch down to the Forest of Dean and Gloucestershire, with school bus routes adjusted each September, though some parents grumble about the cost – 'and if your son does sports after school, it can be a nightmare,' added one. Relatively wide socio-economic mix (helped by a third of boys being on some kind of fee support), with teachers and parents praising the easy social mix. 'We loved that it's not up itself!' said one parent. Boys are unpretentious and comfortable in their own skins, welcoming to newcomers and proud that, as one said, 'everyone can fit in'. They feel fortunate to come here and don't mind saying so.

Money matters: For escapees from the southeast the comparatively low level of fees brings tears of joy to the eyes. This school offers excellent value for money. Bursary support stretches to 100 per cent and scholarships – academic, music and sport – typically shave off 10 per cent of fees.

The last word: 'We work and play hard,' say the boys, and it all happens in the most magnificent setting, far away from the city scramble but not isolated socially or intellectually. Probably wasted on those who abhor sport or are such die-hard scholars that extracurricular proves a rude interruption. But otherwise this very friendly, aspirational school is an absolute gem where boys – more often than not – come out with skills, talents and interests they never even knew they had.

Monmouth School for Girls

17

Hereford Road, Monmouth, Monmouthshire NP25 5XT

01600 711100 | girls.admissions@habsmonmouth.org | www.habsmonmouth.org

Ages: 11–18

Pupils: 455; sixth form: 261; Boarders: 106 full/flexi

Fees: Day £15,507 – £16,599; Boarding £30,366 – £34,167 pa

Linked school: Monmouth School for Boys, 1048

Headmistress: Since April 2019, Jessica Miles MA PGCE (late 40s), previously head of Queen Margaret's School in York. Educated at girls' boarding school Farnborough Hill in Hampshire and a scholarship student at Oxford, graduating with a degree in modern languages. Worked for short time in arts administration, then did PGCE at King's College, London. First teaching post at Dulwich College, where over 11 years she became head of Spanish, deputy head of upper school, head of sixth form and director of rowing. After a move to Dorset in 2007 and a year teaching Spanish and French at Sherborne School, she moved to Leweston School as deputy head. She joined Queen Margaret's in 2015.

At Oxford was a member of the university drama society touring in Japan and Russia; she also rowed for her college. Fluent Spanish speaker, who once wanted to be a flamenco dancer. Married to Paul, a former teacher who now works in cricket development for Help the Heroes; two young sons.

James Murphy-O'Connor became the first overarching Principal for Haberdashers' Monmouth Schools in September 2019.

Entrance: The Monmouth schools have taken on a diamond structure, so the prep is now co-ed, followed by single sex at senior school then a co-ed sixth form. About a third of girls join from the prep, a third from other independent schools and a third from state schools. Entry is by entrance exam, interview and junior school report. At 13+ by own exam or Common Entrance. Some join at sixth form following an interview and good GCSE results.

Exit: There is less of a problem than some girls' schools face with large numbers of year 11 leaving for mixed schools. A few go for financial reasons or because A levels really aren't for them, but around 65 per cent stay on for the final two years. Sixth formers and parents say the school prepares girls very well for university and beyond. There are lots of links with old girls – staff meet up semi-formally with those who are London-based very regularly. There are plenty of opportunities to visit universities and the girls are starting to think about apprenticeships. At the moment virtually everyone goes to university, the majority to Russell Group universities. Birmingham, Exeter, UCL, Reading and Swansea all popular. Others to do niche high quality courses such as stage management and technical theatre, agri-food marketing, anthropology and media. A number study science, including medicine and engineering. A few go overseas. Three to Oxbridge and nine medics in 2021 (these numbers are joint with the boys' school).

Latest results: In 2021, 75 per cent 9-7 at GCSE; 66 per cent A*/A at A level (86 per cent A*-B). In 2019 (the last year when exams took place), 65 per cent 9-7 at GCSE; 39 per cent A*/A at A level (68 per cent A*-B). A level results are combined with the boys' school.

Teaching and learning: The results at GCSE and A level are very good and the school says it achieves this without putting the girls under too much pressure. Art, modern languages, maths and science are popular choices. Now co-ed at sixth form, allowing 29 subjects to be on offer, which ensures virtually everyone gets the combination of subjects they want. The girls say they like the different perspective the boys bring to subjects and comment on an often-repeated observation that it is noticeable that the girls think before they speak, unlike the boys. Three new A level options include photography, music technology and digital technology.

Parents say that the school doesn't heap unreasonable amounts of pressure on the girls, but that doesn't mean that HMSG has any lower expectations that the big London day schools, with which parents were often comparing it. The girls say teachers will always make time for them if they need a bit of extra help on a less formal basis. Most departments run surgeries for individual help, too.

Links with outside organisations enhance the academic work. Renishaw plc sponsored a STEM competition recently that led to further work supported by the school staff, which led in turn to two girls exhibiting their invention at the NEC, pitching it on Dragons' Den and selling to national retailers.

Learning support and SEN: Learning support is available on an individual/shared basis from suitably qualified staff.

The arts and extracurricular: Drama and dance are popular, music is strong with 50 per cent taking some additional music lessons, all housed in the new performing arts centre which includes a recital hall, dance and drama studio and a rock room. The annual inter-house eisteddfod gives an extra frisson to these activities. The glass atrium is hung with house flags on such occasions. Art is popular and high quality – lots is displayed around the school. Parents praise the standard of the drama productions.

Girls struggled to think of naughty things that anyone did. The worst seems to be not doing your kitchen duty or being late to breakfast (punishment – go in early next day)

At senior level, most of the extracurricular performing arts are done with the boys' school along with CCF, shared visiting speakers and a number of societies. It would be nice to have even more, the girls tell us. DofE and other local community service opportunities as well as fundraising for overseas projects. Girls are committed to these ventures both for their own personal development and also, we felt, out of a genuine desire to serve others.

Sport: The school has a deserved reputation for being very sporty, and clearly even the girls who aren't games mad are very proud of the reputation. There is a tennis club across all the Habs Monmouth schools, and they compete at softball, rowing, show jumping and eventing as well as the more traditional sports. Girls regularly play for the region and Wales, and there are sports and dance scholarships. One parent told us that her daughters had asked the PE staff if they could start a gym club. Within a few months they had it – well resourced and competing nationally.

Boarding: The boarding houses are on the school site and are purpose built. They are strikingly attractive and friendly in feel. From year 11 up, girls have rooms of their own. Below that they share in twos or threes. There is a lot organised for the boarders outside lesson time, some trips including the boys' school. Much sport goes on at weekends and in the evenings. There are cinema trips, shopping, salsa evenings, BBQs and generally a purposeful but relaxed atmosphere, which is very appealing and might account for the very low incidence of illness, despite the attractions of the medical facilities – there are soft toys on every bed. It might also account for the equally low level of law breaking. The girls really struggled to think of naughty things that anyone did. The worst seems to be not doing your kitchen duty or being late to breakfast (punishment – go in early the next day).

Boarding is flexible but that hasn't meant the school opts out of providing after-school and weekend activities. This is an active school with high-energy pursuits on offer throughout the days and weekends. The meal menu is wide and quality good with meals served in an attractive extended dining room.

Ethos and heritage: Founded in 1892, to offer girls the opportunities that Monmouth School for Boys had provided since 1614, the girls' school was funded by the original bequest of a local man, William Jones, a member of the Haberdashers' Company who made his fortune in Russia. The livery company is responsible for the school and provides financial support and stability, which reassures staff and has allowed for continual development of facilities. Although the boys' school is not far away, the girls' school has its own extracurricular facilities such as an Astroturf and swimming pool. The original Victorian buildings have been enhanced by imaginative, modern expansions such as a glass atrium and sixth form centre.

The school – now one element of a diamond structure – works hard at being a part of the Monmouth community and seems liked and respected. We arrived in the middle of the Monmouth Literary Festival – Carol Ann Duffy had been speaking the night before – which is organised entirely by the sixth forms of the local Monmouth and Habs schools. A remarkable achievement involving contacting agents, organising programmes, ticket sales and so on. There is another serious collaboration through the Monmouth Science Initiative, where state and independent schools work together with Cardiff University to bridge the gap between A level science and university science.

A much-anticipated annual satirical review is put on by staff as part of the sixth form Christmas entertainments – a good indication of strong relationships

There is a lovely sixth form centre with study areas and a cool common room café – 'The boys love it,' the girls tell us. 'We have to remind them that they are here for lessons not to drink hot chocolate all day.' Sixth formers still wear a uniform, suits, and tell us that they like it as they don't want to feel separate from the rest of the school. The dropout rate between year 11 and the sixth form is quite small – girls can't wait to wear suits and go to the café, we are told.

Former pupils include Dr Jenny Harries, Lisa Rogers, Sandra Huggett and Jackie Ballard MP.

Pastoral care, inclusivity and discipline: The atmosphere is one of calm and sunny good manners. The relationships between the girls and staff are universally praised and we saw lots of warm and relaxed exchanges. 'They are interested in you and what you want to make of your life,' sixth formers say. We heard about the much-anticipated annual satirical review put on by staff as part of the sixth form Christmas entertainments, a good indication of strong relationships. There are anti-bullying ambassadors and a buddy scheme working between year 7 and year 13. The girls tell us they would like even more integration between year groups. Prefects apply for their role and are eager for an opportunity to give back to the school. 'It is the school empowering us to experience responsibility,' we were told by a successful applicant. The school covers the effects and dangers of social media and bullying. It is less focused on punishment and more concerned that the girls understand the ramifications.

A coloured card system operates for minor disciplinary infringements throughout the school – three yellow cards for something like late homeworks leads to a detention. 'It is really to help us get caught up,' the girls say. There are orange cards for uniform matters – zero tolerance for nail varnish: it gets that naughty. Parents say problems are nipped in the bud early and the staff are open and honest in their communications on pastoral issues. Pastoral care is outstanding, we were told.

Pupils and parents: Pupils come from a wide local area. There are buses from Cardiff, the north Bristol area, the Monmouthshire border, Hereford, Newport and the Ledbury area. The bursary scheme ensures a good social mix. There are émigrés from the home counties, old Monmouth families, families with very little in the way of income and lots with both parents working hard to afford the fees. Staff commented to us that you find none of the sense of entitlement that some schools engender – pupils seem grateful to be here.

The school takes parents' surveys very seriously and we were impressed by the positivity about parental criticisms to help with raising the game. School council is valued by staff as well as by the girls: it pays more than lip service to parent and pupil voices. Parents complimented the school on its proactive approach to keeping them aware of current problem issues such as e-safety. 'They are taking care of my education as a parent,' one mother told us. Parents' view of the HMSG 'product' is one of engaging, confident, interesting girls who are keen to try new things, unaffected and enthusiastic. We would agree.

Money matters: One in five receive financial assistance through a means-tested scheme that reassesses every year from endowment income.

The last word: Habs has been in Monmouth for 400 years and reinvented itself over that time. The current diamond structure is a selling point, parents tell us. They like the all-through concept with co-ed for the little ones in Agincourt and The Grange and at sixth form level. Parents frequently used the word 'honest' when describing the school. You feel the fresh, clear air from the Welsh hills permeates the whole ethos. The location is very inspiring. From the sports fields you look out along the Wye valley and from anywhere in the school you have views down to the rest of Monmouth and beyond. It is a lovely place to live.

We wondered if it was all a rather awful shock when girls had to move outside the Monmouth bubble, but we were assured that the school was anything but parochial. There are lots of visits to far-flung parts of the globe. Having said that, there is no doubt that Monmouth feels a very long way from Cardiff or Bristol, where a number of day girls live – no doubt part of its appeal for many families.

It has the ambitious feel of a big city school without any of the traffic jams and tower blocks.

One parent summed up the feel of the school well: 'Monmouth School for Girls may lack a little of the pomp, ceremony and glitz of some public schools, but what you get is genuine care and a commitment to help your child reach her potential, whatever that may be.'

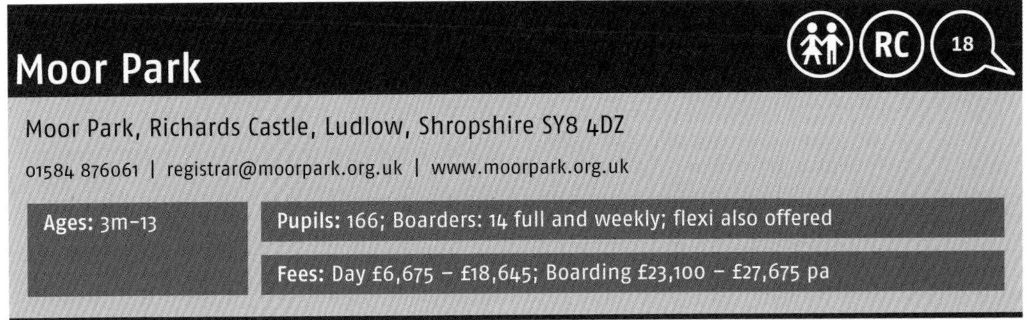

Moor Park
RC
18
Moor Park, Richards Castle, Ludlow, Shropshire SY8 4DZ
01584 876061 | registrar@moorpark.org.uk | www.moorpark.org.uk
Ages: 3m–13
Pupils: 166; Boarders: 14 full and weekly; flexi also offered
Fees: Day £6,675 – £18,645; Boarding £23,100 – £27,675 pa

Headmaster: Since 2015, Charlie Minogue BSc (biology), PGCE, MEd. Previously deputy head at Aldwickbury. Landed at Moor Park after family decision to up sticks and quit the commuter belt in favour of the 'more centred' culture of rural Shropshire. Less of an obvious frontman than some heads, he emits a relaxed, informal politeness. No stiffening of bodies or sudden hushed conversations in corridors when he passes. Children unhesitatingly bound up to him to share their enthusiasm. 'We all got smelly stickers in drama!' gushed an obviously delighted year 6 as we passed by. Described by parents as 'fair', 'level-headed', consistently highly encouraging of his staff ('There was a good staff when I arrived, now it's exceptional') and, most importantly, 'always around'.

Head's multitalented wife also totally immersed in school life, organising social media, teaching music, running grounds and maintenance, studying and – when we met her – pushing a pram from the school's on-site nursery, Tick Tock. Both passionate about music, he a violinist, pianist and one-time member of St Paul's Cathedral choir, and she a double bass player. Holidays in Scotland provide the perfect backdrop to indulge his interest in sea kayaking and to use his qualification as a mountain leader. Thanks to the wonders of the internet, video evidence also reveals some rather dangerous Scottish dancing.

Spent much of the last couple of years working alongside staff to develop an array of mindsets on which to base teaching. Every teacher has now completely rewritten schemes of work to encourage confidence, creativity, resilience, critical thinking, independence and curiosity. From the nursery child who gets the 'resilient rabbit' or 'curious cat' award to the year 8 who is set a deliberately flawed science practical, so that they have to work backwards to discover what's wrong, everyone is well drilled in the new mantra, including parents. Head says, 'It's not mutually exclusive to prepare kids for the world of work and Common Entrance.'

Next couple of years will see a bedding down of the new mindsets within teaching. Although happy with a small amount of growth in pupil numbers, head doesn't want to lose 'care for individuals'. Describes a culture where staff 'fundamentally believe in finding what each child is good at'. Parents agree, reporting children succeeding at interests they would never have suggested.

In the meantime, he's not afraid to get stuck in, whether dressing up as Dumbledore for big weekend (more of that later) or recently enduring the NHS ice bucket challenge. 'You may as well just join in and buy yourself a nerf gun,' he muses. Quite.

Entrance: 'Nearly' non-selective, welcoming all-comers at nursery and pre-prep. 'Subtle' testing and previous reports used to guide later entry decisions. Covid has meant temporary reduction in overseas students, including usually a dozen or so Spanish boarders, attracted in the main by the school's Roman Catholic ethos.

Exit: No pattern to leavers' destinations, which span 20 different schools in the last few years. Hereford Cathedral most popular, followed by Chetham's School of Music, Eton, Radley, Concord. Cheltenham College, Clifton College, Malvern, Uppingham and Christ Church Brecon have also featured. Twelve scholarships in 2021.

Our view: Even a cursory glance at Moor Park's social media tells you everything you need to know.

Barely a photo taken inside, it's all about the outdoor space: 85 acres of glorious, windswept, rolling countryside. And that's not because the main building disappoints. The sweeping driveway snakes its way through a deer park to a rather handsome redbrick Queen Anne house with a stack of original features (leather wallpaper anyone?) and spectacular views. Turn 360 degrees and play spot the real world. Main school comprises a wood-panelled dining hall, boarding accommodation and chapel, a high-ceilinged, elegant ex-ballroom which certainly affords the required serene calm for, rather unusually, mid-morning assemblies. Although the school follows the teaching of the Roman Catholic church, with compulsory fortnightly mass, they believe that 'faith is personal' and the chapel provides pupils with a 'moment of reflection, whatever their belief'.

The real magic happens out back, within a courtyard of multicoloured, single-storey wooden huts, each displaying its own individual subject interest. Granted, this teaching space is not nearly as polished as the main house, but no corridors means everyone gets a breath of fresh air between lessons. Parents tell us 'it's rougher round the edges in terms of facilities than some schools, but has a lovely feeling.'

Since arriving, head has instigated a whirlwind of repurposing. Library, junior boarding, Tick Tock and pre-prep all relocated. The latter two are now integrated within a well thought out early years unit, enabling seamless transitions from one year group to the next and with ready access to an outdoor learning garden with boxes, tyres, mud and hosepipes for messy play and acres of green space. Pre-prep can bolt straight out at break to fast pedal their bikes over the rolling greenery. Music, drama and dance (under new management) are now sited in a refurbished umbrella performing arts block. A research centre, to allow greater access to technology across all subjects, is in development and 'the horrid bits', where the music department used to be, mothballed. Disappointingly, the Tree House, a triumph of eco-friendliness, which used to house junior boarding, is currently out of use. Mr Minogue would not be drawn on its fate: 'I'd have to kill you if I told you what I was doing with that.'

Class sizes are small, around 12 as an average. The traditional system is overlaid at year 6 with even smaller mixed year tutor groups of around eight pupils who remain with the same tutor for their last three years to encourage real 'bonding'. Tutors rapidly become the first port of call for children and parents alike. It's a long old day, with clubs finishing at 6.15, but parents report that the vast majority of prep is done at school. Compulsory Saturday mornings for year 6 and up. Otherwise years 3-5 (as well as the wider local community) can sign up for Saturday Smash, a veritable smorgasbord of activities ranging from bushcraft to show songs, sewing, bike maintenance, orienteering and everything in between.

Boarding seems like a right old romp. Homely dorms in the eaves and spooky cellars for hide and seek provide the perfect spots for all types of mischief

Sport timetabled daily, with fixtures and clubs on top. Teams 'punch well above our weight on the circuit'. A teams are selective, B and beyond mixed ability. 'Everybody is in a team.' There's a deliberate culture of inclusivity. 'We find an avenue' for those who are less keen. Admirable, assuming you want to be included. Year 6 encouraged to develop leadership skills by taking on coaching roles. 'Sport is about learning about yourself and working with others,' states the head. 'It's really opened their eyes,' reflects the head of sport. Sports hall functional, but corrugated metal walls give it the look and feel of a temporary agricultural building. Recent pool renovations now allow all-year use, although parents tell us it's still 'character-building'; 'freezing in winter, boiling in summer'. All-weather cricket pitch explains the plethora of cricket fixtures in equal measure for girls and boys. Golf nets and a nine-hole golf course in summer. Under-utilised squash court 'used a bit, not massively'.

Over half of pupils take speech and drama despite the additional cost – 'It's in the culture.' New head of performing arts is a real ball of fire, with hefty ambitions to take performance outdoors – 'I want Proms in the Park, Midsummer Night's Dream with fairy lights…' In the meantime check out the Facebook video of a highly accomplished cellist playing Bach to a shed full of cows. Reception upwards take advantage of specialist teaching in art, science, IT and DT, with pre-prep just as likely as anyone to wield drills, hammers, saws and hot glue guns. Serious year 8 artists treated like grown-ups, with dedicated space to create in the scholars' loft. Future rock stars and DJs also catered for by music tech suite and recording studio.

SEN headed up by full-time head of learning support with a lengthy experience, particularly with dyslexia. Needs are diagnosed via maths and literacy assessment on entry or through teacher referral. School more than able to meet the needs of those with dyspraxia, discalculia and ASD, as well as having taught pupils with more specific conditions such as PDA in the past. Accommodations are 'pupil centred' and may include additional individual support (paid for), use of technology in lessons and differentiated or supported prep.

Parents are a hotchpotch of old farming families, local business owners and home counties refugees, many first time buyers and 'not at all pretentious'. 'There's always a congregation of us having a natter in front of the log fire in the entrance hall,' they tell us. All are enchanted by the wholesome, rustic aspects of school life, waxing lyrical about their children climbing trees and coming home with pockets full of stones and leaves. This is a school with its own mud run, where conker fights are de rigeur. There's den-building and pond-dipping and you can learn to shoot an air rifle. Pupils can apply for their own small allotments to grow fruit and vegetables. Everyone gets involved in the autumn when it comes to feeding apples into the press and creating some rather delicious juice. Techno-heads (as well as some health and safety purists) may struggle. No electronic prep systems and not a sniff of a mobile phone. Owning one is more of a year 8 exit rite of passage and parents 'reluctant to be the one to start it' before then.

Boarding: Boarding seems like a right old romp. Homely dorms in the eaves and spooky cellars for hide and seek provide the perfect spots for all types of mischief. 'It's not boarding, it's home.' So there's home-cooking at the weekend (don't forget the washing up!) and the morning alarm call is an over-enthusiastic sproodle called Fudge. Full, weekly and flexi boarding is available at sensible nightly rates from year 3, although the reality of demand makes it more like year 5 and above. Head says, 'We don't push boarding, it happens naturally.' However, with most families local, numbers of full/weekly boarders usually only creep into the mid-teens and Covid has pushed this well down into the single digits. Flexi seems popular with the year 5s and up, particularly on Fridays and after sports clubs.

Themed termly big weekends are the highlights of the school calendar and no-one is half-hearted about dressing up. Wild west weekend with bucking bronco, Harry Potter night complete with live owls, camo weekend with rations and sleeping under canvas, live human Hungry Hippos (far too complicated to explain) and Fright Night, a (slightly disturbing) Halloween night walk with replica spooky graves and steaming cauldrons; 'We scare the bejesus out of them!' Parents like that it 'breaks down the barriers' to future full boarding.

Money matters: Scholarships up to 30 per cent of fees available for year 3-7 entry. Means-tested bursaries available according to need and funds in the coffers.

The last word: The Moor Park ethos is perhaps reminiscent of a time when childhood was simpler and, for many parents, the bubble of 'pleasing innocence' is all part of its appeal. A traditional country prep that maintains strong family values and a culture of kindness, while also adding some innovative teaching into the mix. No wonder they turn out more than their fair share of scholars.

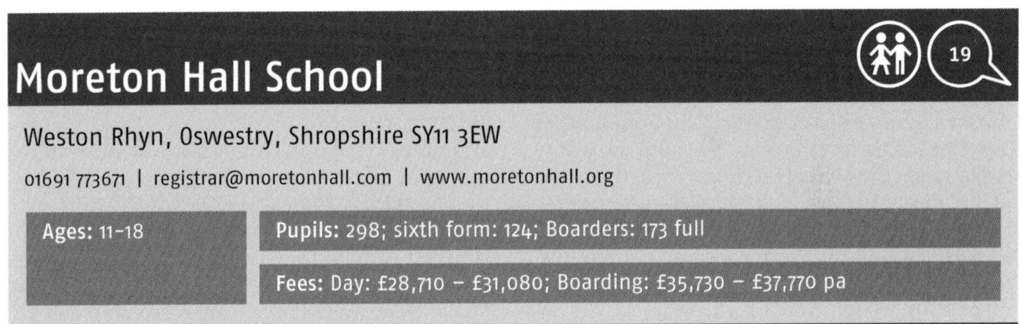

Moreton Hall School

19

Weston Rhyn, Oswestry, Shropshire SY11 3EW

01691 773671 | registrar@moretonhall.com | www.moretonhall.org

Ages: 11–18

Pupils: 298; sixth form: 124; Boarders: 173 full

Fees: Day: £28,710 – £31,080; Boarding: £35,730 – £37,770 pa

Principal: Since 2019, George Budd, previously deputy head at Godolphin, Salisbury. A geographer (Durham University), his background is almost exclusively at independent girls' schools, having also worked at Lady Eleanor Holles for three years – first as head of geography and subsequently assistant head – and Sir William Perkins's School as head of sixth form for six years.

As of September 2021, Moreton's offering for boys has extended from the prep into the senior school where they can now stay until 13. Mr Budd believes that allowing boys to stay until year 9 saves them 'drifting' for two years (and let's face it, is a more attractive offering to parents). After age 13 he is adamant about the benefits of girls only education, full of statistics about take-up for maths and science. He also says the presence of boys beyond year 9 would change the homely culture of the school – 'At the moment they rock up to breakfast in PJs. That would change.' Parents who have chosen a girls only education for their daughters hear the reassurance, but can be forgiven for suspiciously watching for signs of age 13 becoming the thin end of the wedge.

After a year consulting with parents, staff, Old Moretonians (OMs) and pupils, Mr Budd published a comprehensive document setting out the school's values, vision and commitments. This contained a refreshing number of specific targets in key areas such as teaching and learning, pastoral and estates. 'I'm about concrete steps, not fancy words.' Short-term plans such as a curriculum review, consideration of the Saturday provision, refurbishment of boarding accommodation and the roll-out of a whole school ICT strategy have already been completed. Longer-term targets include continuing to increase uptake of EPQ, increasing the range of nationalities of pupils and redevelopment of the prep, maths and art buildings.

The Rylands Diploma provides girls with a wide range of life skills including budgeting, household and car maintenance, drafting a CV and preparing for interviews

Unlike the prep, there are no plans to increase senior school numbers ('and lose personal relationships'). Instead Mr Budd seeks to build the school's role within the wider community and focus on getting all facilities up to the standard of the newer ones. The aim is to create a 'comfy and pleasant' environment, replicating home rather than the tough-it-out boarding school mentality of the past. 'These days parents care about the quality of mattresses,' he remarks. Quite right.

Married to Nicky, previously director of sport at Lady Eleanor Holles. After years of competitive mountain biking, he has calmed it down: 'I got too old, the job got too important.'

Head of prep: Since 2020 is John Bond, previously deputy head of Hatherop Prep. An ex-housemaster, he is well placed to build boarding take-up and grow pupil numbers to around 100, with current numbers already up by 10 per cent year on year.

Entrance: Gently selective. Admissions policy allows for older prep applicants to sit tests, but parents refer merely to a taster day. Seamless entry from prep into the senior school with entrance exams at years 7 and 9 for external candidates only. Candidates for sixth form take papers in two of their chosen A level subjects.

Exit: In recent years over half of year 6 boys have decamped from the prep to Oswestry at age 11, but with future exits now at year 8 and a new prep head, time will tell. Few girls leave post-GCSE (below 10 per year), most stay the course and head for university, with Leeds, UCL, York, Birmingham, Exeter and Manchester recently popular. One to Oxbridge and three medics in 2021. Two overseas in 2021 – Chulabhorn Royal Academy, Thailand and Glion, Switzerland. Big increase in gap years due to Covid.

Latest results: In 2021, 70 per cent 9-7 at GCSE; 70 per cent A*/A (88 per cent A*-B). In 2019 (the last year in which exams took place), 75 per cent 9-7 at GCSE; 41 per cent A*/A at A level (70 per cent A*-B).

Teaching and learning: They don't half cram it in. Senior school has an extended teaching day with lessons until 5pm, as well as on Saturday mornings. 'Parents take it for granted that we will deliver academically.' Pupils are setted from year 7 in maths, English, humanities and science. Option blocks for GSCE and A level are created around individuals in order to allow 'esoteric' choices. The school will 'find a way' to teach any modern language, even for a single child. Boys in years 7 and 8 study the broad curriculum already offered to girls, alongside individual support to reach year 9 destination schools.

Average class size is 12 in prep and unsurprisingly girls tend to outnumber boys. Current year 5 has achieved equality, but year 6 is all girls. Parents of boys seem unconcerned: 'We knew what we signed up for.' Senior school classes average 12-15, falling to around six by A Level. Parents comment that pupils are 'always stretched but never put under pressure'.

The phrase 'educating the whole child' gets bandied around but Moreton is a gold standard example of how to get it right. Added value is prized above exam league tables and academic enrichment is central. A range of societies contributes to a culture of extracurricular learning more akin to CPD and the world beyond either school or undergraduate studies. The Stables lectures and Jenner, Lady Barbirolli and Bronwen societies offer weekly talks, masterclasses and events in the fields of medicine, music and general intellectual curiosity delivered by significant academics and professionals (as well as introductions that often lead to work experience). Study of spoken English is compulsory at various points in

Oundle School

the academic journey. 'Directors Table' meets six times a year with guests from the world of business and the Moreton Connect initiative provides contacts for girls among parents and OMs. Leiths School of Food and Wine is offered to lower sixth.

'We provide education for life, not just how to pass physics,' states head. With that in mind, the school's Rylands Diploma, a year-long Saturday morning course, is offered to year 12. It provides girls with a wide range of life skills in areas including budgeting and managing bills, essential household and car maintenance, driving theory, cookery, drafting a CV and preparing for interviews.

Learning support and SEN: Learning support is driven by two full-time members of staff, one each for prep and seniors. Provision for dyslexia, autism, ADHD, visual, hearing and physical disabilities and epilepsy. With learning support factored into the fees, it's not just those with specific learning issues that feel the benefit, but anyone that needs that little bit more help at any point during their Moreton journey. Boarding houses have some adapted rooms with wet room and emergency pull cord.

The arts and extracurricular: Currently it's all about drama. Specifically the still-in-the-wrapper, brand new Holroyd Community Theatre with 180 seats and the latest lighting and sound systems. Lessons are already being taught on stage and we observed some superb performances of an excerpt from a challenging play tackling eating disorders. Recent Moreton productions of Chicago, The Addams Family and Aladdin have been up to West End quality, say proud parents.

Art, photography, textiles and history of art are available as separate A levels, the latter enjoying a renaissance under the auspices of an enthusiastic teacher. New DT suite and renovated music department both opened in September 2021. Choir is compulsory and there are chamber and show choirs for the more dedicated. North Shropshire Senior Orchestra is a school-based community project that welcomes local musicians to play alongside pupils every Monday evening.

Unique to the school is the serious CV opportunity offered by Moreton Enterprises. Year 12 manage, stock, staff and market dedicated, open-plan retail premises at the heart of the school site. After a rigorous application process, successful candidates are appointed to business director roles. Beaming with pride, they showed us a tuck counter displaying crisps, sweets no parent would approve of and, of course, obligatory Pot Noodles. A second area sells stationery, pharmacy essentials and jewellery, and a bustling café offers snacks, drinks and smoothies (we fancied the Classic Berry) to customers relaxing on large, bright orange sofas. 'We try to buy from local, female suppliers,' the directors explain. This is no insignificant operation, with a turnover last year of £30,000, sure to increase in the near future with business expanding into ice-cream sales in the new theatre.

Houses have separate accommodation for different academic years, so 'scaffolding can be gradually taken away' and facilities can reflect the age range

Those still with time on their hands can participate in a wide-ranging extracurricular programme including journalism, frisbee golf and touch rugby, among many others.

Sport: Renowned for success in lacrosse ('a religion'), with girls regularly representing England and Wales at junior and senior level. U14s were recent national champions and the senior team ranked in the top eight in the country when we visited. Other core sports – hockey, netball and tennis – are played at an equally high level with regular competition at county and national level. Sports staff tend to be recruited from coaching backgrounds, many with experience coaching and/or playing at national level.

In addition, pupils can try their hands at squash (back from the eighties), cricket, fencing, rowing and swimming. Small numbers of boys in prep and now year 7 make filling rugby and football teams trickier. Instead a range of sports are offered including five-a-side football, hockey and golf. Numbers of boys' fixtures don't suffer though, equalling those of the girls. Indoor pool, 3.7m deep, is great for diving and there's a fully stocked gym. The 5km cross-country running trail marked out in the grounds is known as the 'trim trail'; director of sport grimaces, explaining that girls named it and sadly it caught on.

School has recently launched its new ACE (Achieve, Compete, Excel) performance hub focusing on hockey, lacrosse, tennis and, from late 2121, fencing, to provide coaching, support and programmes for elite athletes. Development camps are also offered for those who are less elite but keen to improve.

Boarding: Around half of pupils are boarders in year 7, rising to 75 per cent during GCSE years and by the sixth form nearly everyone boards. Many day pupils board a few times per week, paying a B&B rate. Flexi boarders get their own beds if staying more than four nights per week for the older age groups, although it's more like one night in the junior house. Booking in for flexi is informal with pupils often just turning up in the morning with a boarding bag – quite unusual for senior boarding.

Houses operate on a horizontal system, with separate accommodation for different academic years. That way 'scaffolding can be gradually taken away' and facilities can reflect the age range. It's all impressively well thought out. Stables welcomes younger senior girls in rooms of up to six, the majority in bunks. There's a wellbeing area, four guinea pigs and a poodle inexplicably named Nonie-Potato. By year 9 the bunks are fewer, the pink gone and after-school time less structured. More cerebral activities – like making pop bottle rockets or floating cardboard canoes on the canal – are cleverly snuck in, under the guise of fun. An upside down map of the world on one wall caught our eye. By this age even the house decor sought to challenge young minds, it was explained. By year 10 single and double rooms come with house responsibilities such as wake up and common room duties.

Sixth form accommodation is ensuite. All do their own laundry by year 11. Mitchell House has been renovated to meet the future additional demand for boys' boarding that accompanies extending to years 7 and 8, although in its first year it currently only houses a small handful of boarders.

With long and active school days, even those that live nearby choose to board. 'It's a damning review of home, but a great review of Moreton,' sighed one parent. Many go home at weekends but those that stay can expect Saturday night activities including mocktails, nail technicians, karaoke, paint by numbers, smoothie bars, ice-cream and waffles. Sundays are for activities such as laser tag or trips to trampoline parks, Alton Towers, food festivals, the beach at Barmouth, shopping in Chester or Shrewsbury or just going for a walk.

Ethos and heritage: Founded in 1913 by Ellen Lloyd-Williams, a feminist visionary in the field of girls' education who began by home schooling her 11 children (of which nine were daughters). From these humble beginnings the school grew like topsy with newer buildings being added as required surrounding the original 16th century house. As a result, the 100-acre site is a study in architecture through the ages. A particularly enthusiastic, experimental triangular period culminated in the building of the 'toblerone', now the distinctive home of the prep. More recent construction has included two (rectangular) sixth form boarding houses, a science centre and the showpiece Holroyd Community Theatre, as well as renovation of the library.

Moreton is no insular private school bubble. There's a strong focus on community. 'We have a duty to share our facilities,' says Mr Budd. The new theatre has been built with this in mind, to be a space for visiting companies to entertain local crowds and for use by local groups. Moreton also provides weekly science lab space, teaching in top set maths and shares facilities for CCF with a nearby state school.

School inspires an unusual level of loyalty from Old Moretonians. Reunions are well attended and OMs never pass up the opportunity to return, over 15 of them sharing their pearls of wisdom in last year's sixth form Bridging the Gap programme, focusing on life skills after the scaffolding of school has gone. Famous alumnae include the actress Sheila Reid, the first female editor-in-chief of The Economist, Zanny Minton-Beddoes, and Dame Linda Dobbs, the first non-white person to be appointed as a High Court judge.

Pastoral care, inclusivity and discipline: Parents and staff alike remark on the 'family' feel of the school, one even referring to her daughter's housemistress as 'her mum at school'. School performances are regularly attended by grounds and kitchen staff.

There's a strong focus on community. The new theatre has been built as a space for visiting companies to entertain local crowds and for use by local groups

Pupils have tutor time twice a week in a group as well as a one-on-one. Director of wellbeing role was reintroduced in January, working closely with health centre and local GP. Programmes are targeted at parents as well as pupils, with advice including how to have difficult conversations and how to grow a teenager. School doesn't shy away from thorny issues eg relating to Everyone's Invited, which head assured us are covered in PHSE and assemblies.

Cornflower Farm (currently more smallholding than farm) opened in 2020 as a pastoral retreat, complete with sheep, geese, ducks and peacocks. The chickens (Lady Mary, Lady Edith and Lady Sybil) often have to be removed from the maths block.

Parents rave about the school's talent for seeking out the best in each child. Mr Budd describes a 'culture of compulsory fun'; when everyone has a go, mental barriers to entry are quickly broken down. 'Positive peer pressure to do new things builds the ability to cope with the unexpected.'

There are very few rules. There's no detention and no red zone. In their place is a 'focus on what matters, not expending energy on pushing back against ridiculous barriers'. No-one bats an eyelid if your hair is down, your shirt is out or if you wear nail polish. So what if some are a bit scruffy? Parents prefer children to express themselves and report them flourishing in this freedom, treated as young adults. You can be 'unapologetically yourself' explains head of senior school. With few rules comes less of a sense of hierarchy, genuine mutual respect and the ability for staff and pupils to work collaboratively: 'there's no them and us'. Girls having coffee and a chat with teachers at break is normal. 'People believe in you,' say sixth formers. International students tell us they have 'become brave'. 'Anything is possible at this school,' they say.

Pupils and parents: School attracts families from Wales, Cheshire, South Shropshire, Staffordshire, with increasing interest from Liverpool, Manchester and London. Some international pupils, mostly from China. Good local contingent. Parents say that socially it's 'a broad church', 'not full of Range Rovers'.

Money matters: Eagle eyes will note the relatively small difference between senior day and boarding fees, but this reflects the similarity between the day and boarding offer – day pupils are welcome at any time and until well after 9pm without booking in or extra charge. Very few extras turn up on the bill and commendably that includes learning support: 'We wouldn't dream of charging for the Accelerated Oxbridge Programme, so why would we charge for SEN?' asks Mr Budd. 'We're more British Airways than Ryan Air,' he adds, 'to create the feeling that you're at home.' Certainly not cheap, but parents say that in the end, 'it's good value for money'.

Scholarships are generous, up to 20 per cent of fees available from year 7. Academic scholarships awarded on entrance exam performance. Sport, music, drama and art awarded on basis of portfolio, audition or interview. Means tested bursaries can cover entire fees (although capped at 50 per cent for prep) if potential is spotted.

The last word: Not for the half-hearted. Parents describe it as a place for children who 'throw themselves into something' rather than those who want to go home at 3pm. The principal likens it to a start-up company, full of 'fizz and energy', instilling a drive to problem-solving and an inventiveness to try things. Pupils leave equipped, not only with solid academics, a jam-packed CV and a network of contacts, but more importantly an inner confidence and strong sense of self. One thing's for sure, we certainly wouldn't want to be up against anyone from Moreton at interview.

The National Mathematics and Science College

20

No 2 The Oaks, Westwood Way, Coventry CV4 8JB

0247 5092950 | admissions@natmatsci.ac.uk | www.natmatsci.ac.uk

Ages: 15-19

Pupils: 58; Boarders: 57

Fees: Day £12,600; Boarding: £39,900 pa

Principal: Since September 2020, Andy Kemp BSc MSc EdD MBA (40s). Headhunted for the role while head of Stephen Perse Foundation Senior School, although the fact that (a) he had never even heard of the college and (b) Stephen Perse was something of a family affair (his wife, Ruth, is a maths teacher there and their two daughters both attend the school) meant he took some persuading. 'But, as with the students, once I understood the concept of the college I found it impossible to resist.' The plan was for the family to move from Cambridge but since Covid put a spanner in the works he's currently resigned himself to a long commute (audiobooks help – currently Colin Dexter's Inspector Morse series) and some overnight stays nearby.

Not so much chose a teaching career as stumbled upon it. Growing up in Surrey, he had 'absolutely no idea what I wanted to do' and wound up picking medicine, then maths and philosophy before finally settling on pure maths ('what I should have chosen in the first place') at Warwick. Dabbled with the idea of ordination, worked in a bookshop for a year, then taught in an evening college as a stopgap where it turned out he had quite a knack in the classroom. So back he trotted to Warwick for his PGCE and latterly part-time to complete his master's and doctorate in maths education. No wonder he sees the college, which is perched on the edge of Warwick University, as 'something of a homecoming'. He also holds an MBA from UCL.

His 18 years in teaching spans across Warwick School, Taunton School and Wells Cathedral Senior School before Stephen Perse – 'means I've been able to take the best from each,' he says. 'Not that I've brought in anything other than subtle changes to the college so far – mostly dull procedural stuff like recruiting a head of curriculum and integrating boarding so it doesn't feel like an add-on.' We think (and parents agree) that he undersells himself as his positive energy sets the tone, his communication keeps parents well informed (no mean feat when they're dotted around the world) and his proactive leadership keeps everyone on their toes in this ever more stimulating environment. 'Supportive', 'always available' and 'friendly', say students.

Entrance: One of the most selective sixth form colleges in the country. We're talking students for whom 8s and 9s at I/GCSE comes naturally (or would do, as nearly all come from overseas) in the subjects they want to study. Three to four applicants for every place, all of whom sit the college's own assessments in maths and English, plus attend an interview to explore interests and aspirations (expect some maths problems to be thrown in too – 'usually the student's favourite bit!' laughs the principal).

Most apply to the two-year A level programme, though some (eight, the year we visited) are advised to join some or all of the one-year pre-A level programme – generally those whose English is weaker or who are a bit rusty in one of the sciences (eg they've decided they want to go into engineering but haven't studied physics for a while). Some students (usually around 10 a year) opt for the Medical Pathway Programme which enhances the core A levels with eg outside speakers (recently a live kidney donor to talk about the patient's experience), additional learning and debates. 'Have you thought about volunteering?' asks one of the questions on the MedSoc noticeboard, and 'Where's your evidence of wider reading?'

Exit: No prizes for guessing the type of degrees most students go on to. Yup, it's STEM, STEM and more STEM, eg mechanical engineering, computing, natural sciences, aerospace engineering – although, to be fair, some do read subjects such as law, PPE, criminology and economics and management. Usually around a quarter of students to Oxbridge (five in 2021), and a further quarter to Imperial and UCL. Others to Warwick, Bristol, Manchester, Leeds and Liverpool. The international cohort means overseas universities are also popular, increasingly in north America, with students having recently gone off to eg UCLA and Penn State University. No medics in 2021, though hopes are high for future years following the launch of the Medical Pathway Programme in 2019.

These classrooms are home to some serious brainboxes. We came across one student who had given up his free period to solve university level physics problems 'for fun'

Latest results: In 2021, 93 per cent A*/A at A level. In 2019 (the last year when exams took place), 61 per cent A*/A at A level.

Teaching and learning: These classrooms are home to some serious brainboxes who are itching to maximise their potential at every turn. Such is their hunger to challenge themselves that the line between lesson time and spare time is among the most blurred we've seen. We came across one student who had given up his free period to solve university level physics problems 'for fun', while a recent maths modelling competition saw more students champing at the bit to give up 14 hours of their weekend than were even allowed to enter. In fact, the college claims to be the highest performing school in the country per capita when it comes to national and international Olympiads and competitions, which (unusually) form part of the curriculum. For the last three years, they've had at least one student make the final team to represent the UK in the international Olympiads and students have achieved countless gold medals and awards in the various maths and science competitions.

This is an unashamedly specialist STEM sixth form college offering A levels in maths, further maths, biology, chemistry, physics, computer science and economics – of which most students take maths and further maths plus two others (though some focus on three). Significantly, further maths is treated as a full A level – 'To do it in the minimum time, as many schools do, takes all the fun out of it, so we give them time to indulge and space to do interesting maths around the edge.'

Like all sixth form colleges, it sees itself as a bridge between traditional schooling and university, with a focus on seminar-style learning and practicals – in chemistry alone, the students complete over 200 practicals across the two-year course. 'The aim here is to ensure they experience what it is like to be to be a scientist, not just learn about what other scientists have done.' You can imagine the disappointment of lockdown, 'but the staff were very good about continuing demos online,' said a student who added, 'In fact, they were very good generally across the pandemic, making sure we still had a full timetable and pastoral backup.' In a biology class we sat in on, the teacher gave all the students coronavirus, dengue fever and other viruses (not literally of course) and challenged them to turn the images into origami, an innovative way to get them thinking about structures and how they work. Even in maths, surely the most theoretical of subjects, teachers stretch students beyond traditional methods of learning. And with the EPQ, which all students start, around half get so carried away with the practical aspect of their chosen project that they decide to focus on that rather than writing it up – 'We leave it up to them as the main thing is to enjoy the learning,' the head of EPQ told us.

In a biology class, the teacher gave all the students coronavirus, dengue fever and other viruses (not literally of course) and challenged them to turn the images into origami

'The truth is we're all a bit geeky and the opportunity to work with exceptionally bright kids stretching the curriculum is just glorious,' said the principal on behalf of the 12 members of teaching staff who take no persuading to go above and beyond – most recently hosting webinars on eg the chemistry of love and on how the Covid vaccine works in granular detail. 'The calibre of teachers is impressive and they all make it clear that no question is too silly – it's a learning environment after all,' said one student, while another told us, 'You're told at the beginning that you'll never be bored in lessons here and it's true.'

Class sizes are an average of eight and a maximum of 12. The day is split into six hourly lessons following 8.20am registration, though the college is currently exploring whether a later start might be better suited to the circadian rhythms of teenagers. 'There's a lot of testing – at least once a week, but we don't mind as it's helpful,' said a student. 'But there could be more focus on careers advice,' reckoned a few parents.

Learning support and SEN: Mild SEN catered for, though only one formal diagnosis when we visited. All support so far has been in class. 'Classes are small so teachers flex teaching accordingly, although we would organise one-to-one support if required,' says principal. A SENCo oversees all support via regular meetings and support plans where necessary. Many students, particularly those on the autistic spectrum, are undiagnosed (often due to the stigma that remains in some countries, thinks principal) and they have access to a small group providing informal support.

EAL is more common than not here due to the majority coming from overseas. These students are tested on arrival and placed in small classes based on ability where they follow Cambridge English (KEY, PET, B2 First, CAE) and IELTS courses depending on the year group. Students who need further support attend extra one-to-one lessons to develop both academic and informal language. If a student gains their IELTS certificate early, they attend advanced lessons to hone their interview skills and develop critical thinking skills about global events.

The arts and extracurricular: Given the college's name, you could be forgiven for thinking drama wouldn't be high on the agenda. But you'd be wrong. Every Saturday morning, students are expected to drag themselves out of bed at 10am (the unpopular bit) to attend a drama programme at the Belgrade Theatre in Coventry (or onsite during Covid) for compulsory drama lessons leading up to a production in the summer term (the popular bit). 'It's good for our confidence and public speaking, as well as bringing us together as a group,' said a student.

The Steinway grand piano in reception suggests music isn't sidelined either – students told us that this, as well as the guitars (and soon to be electronic drums) in the common room, are regularly played for pleasure (including by self-formed bands) and a bunch of peripatetic teachers come in for instrumental lessons. The college choir attracts decent numbers and performs a range of modern and classical pieces at events across the year.

The only art is via art club and house art, of which we saw evidence on a small gallery wall. Other house competitions include cookery, talent shows and coding – just before our visit the house competition was to write some code in Python to calculate as many digits of Pi as possible in 60 seconds, with the winning house getting a lemon meringue pie baked by the head of maths!

Not for these students the jeans and hoodie look of most sixth form colleges – they are suited and booted to look their Sunday best

Where extracurricular really comes into its own is via the societies programme – again, on curriculum (two lessons a week). These bright young things can't resist these opportunities, ranging from the targeted and practical such as PATSoc (preparation for the Physics Assessment Test), MedSoc, ChemSoc, NatureSoc or MathsSoc to the more esoteric, such as PhiloSoc, CodeSoc, PySoc and TechSoc (which looks at programming and robotics). There's also JournoSoc who write the college magazine (The Coventry Comet), MUN and debating, while more social activities include ChessSoc, ArtSoc and GameSoc. One student we met had set up a crocheting and knitting society, which had made 40 hats for premature babies in a local hospital. Trips range from the curricular (university lectures and workshops, science fairs, Bletchley Park, etc) to cultural (including Oxford, Stratford-upon-Avon and London) and sport (eg ski trips).

Sport: 'I came here for the sport,' aren't words you'll hear uttered here – even the principal uses the word 'afterthought'. But despite the college's small size and unapologetically academic bent, it does offer free access to the local sports centre with gym, pool, courts and exercise classes, all just a three-minute (possibly nearer five for those who use it the least) walk away. Warwick University's climbing wall, one of the best in Europe, is also on the doorstep – made good use of by the college's climbing society. There's American football, ultimate frisbee, basketball and football if enough interest can be drummed up – these also get played in the one-and-a-half hours per week that's given over to sport (all self-managed, not taught). The inter-house sports competitions go down well too, with table tennis the most keenly fought.

Boarding: Almost everyone boards or (for under 16s) lives with local homestay families – 42 were in the halls of residence when we visited and 14 lived with families, with two students learning online due to Covid. Boarding is full-time only, so no mass exodus at the weekends although students do occasionally have the odd weekend away with all the relevant permissions. Those who stay have the option to get involved in activities such as go-karting, Alton Towers and escape rooms. During weekdays, there's the (not universally popular, it has to be said) two-hour study time from 7-9pm following dinner, after which it's 'quiet time'. 'The boarding staff are excellent,' a parent told us – 'the students are very well cared for in a warm and friendly atmosphere.'

In September 2022, the college will open its own purpose-built boarding house immediately behind the teaching block, allowing them to increase the number of boarders to 140. Until then, they share one of the private halls of residence used by the University of Warwick, handily located just to the side of the college, taking up three floors of rooms (all single, all ensuite), each with a communal kitchen space shared between seven or eight rooms. Modern, clean and almost hotel like (bar the odd fridge etiquette notice and tell-tale jars of chocolate spread and white loaves by the toasters), we would have happily laid our heads here for the night (and believe us, we don't say that about too many student digs). The rooftop terrace even has an interior private dining room you can hire out for when family come to visit, while the downstairs communal areas have stunning breakout areas including gaming and pool tables.

No need to fear the thought of drunken undergraduates either as most of the other residents are PhD students and in any case there's little or no mixing with them.

Ethos and heritage: In 2011, the college's founders, Dr Martin Stephen (former head of MGS, St Paul's and The Perse) and Geoffrey Robinson (former MP for Coventry), decided there was a need for a specialist STEM college. Their idea was to prepare the world's best students for reading maths, science, medicine and other STEM disciplines at top universities. Following several years of planning, the college opened its doors in 2016 to around 20 students. Numbers are now in the 50s (with a 60:40 gender split of boys to girls and 50:50 among teaching staff), with the longer-term aim to reach around 150.

Our drive to the college took us right through Warwick University – not a bad way to get the scholarly juices flowing ready for a visit to this most academic of hubs. The college is located just where you head out of the university campus and into a business park. Once a vast open-plan office for local government ombudsmen, it has been cleverly repurposed with a mixture of glass (to give the feeling of space) and partitioned walls, that can easily be removed or added to flex to changing student numbers and needs. The result is a contemporary space befitting these most modern of students who will no doubt be shaping our tomorrows. Think black Barcelona chairs, corridors of wall-to-wall shiny white lockers ('300 of the things – we only need half that!' laughs the principal) and minimalist classrooms downstairs, with more practical spaces for the sciences upstairs. Getting from A to B can be time consuming – in a good way – thanks to the whiteboards of regularly updated maths problems that students race to be the first to solve, plus the walk-through library where you'll never hear, 'Shhhh… don't talk' but are likely to hear, 'Oh, what are you reading?' (there's a separate space for quiet study). The biggest facilities challenge is the lack of canteen, though the new boarding premises will solve this problem – until then, the large common room doubles up.

There's a cerebral, professional and mature vibe throughout. Not for these students the jeans and hoodie look of most sixth form colleges – instead, they are suited and booted to look their Sunday best; ditto for the staff. Smart and sharp, right to the core.

Pastoral care, inclusivity and discipline: Parents enthuse about a distinct family feel, undoubtedly helped by the small size – this is a place where everybody knows everybody. Student wellbeing is a priority, with small tutor groups that meet regularly, and there's a visiting counsellor. Unusually for a college, there's a compulsory PSHE programme delivered by specialists – students were tackling the timely issue of consent when we visited. With such a self-motivated bunch, disciplinary issues are practically non-existent, occasional lateness or oversleeping are the biggest behavioural issues they have to contend with. Student council suggest tweaks mainly related to sport and food, the latter having improved dramatically in recent weeks as our deconstructed chicken pie testified. No cliques to speak of, say students.

Pupils and parents: Truly a rainbow of nations, with students coming from all over the world – usually around a quarter from China, a quarter from Russia and the rest from eg America, Belarus, Iran, South Korea, Latvia, Malaysia, Malta, Thailand, Uganda, Ukraine, Uzbekistan and Vietnam, though this list changes year on year. Just one student from the UK when we visited, though the college would like to see more. Most are self-confessed nerds, relieved to have found kindred spirits; the ones we met were reserved, uber polite and highly ambitious. In most cases, it's they who discovered the college, with their parents – usually middle-class and highly aspirational for their children – having had minimal input. Pre-Covid, even parents' evenings were with the students only, though the college is now inviting parents to join by video.

Money matters: Day fees average for the area; boarding fees at the more expensive end, reflected in the quality of boarding accommodation. All fees inclusive of EAL provision where required. Around a quarter of students are on some sort of academic scholarship – these cover anything from a nominal sum to up to 50 per cent of fees and, in some means-tested cases, 100 per cent.

The last word: An exciting community where bright and like-minded students have a whale of a time challenging both themselves and each other and are privy to some of the best STEM-centred teaching around. A college, yes, but somehow it's so much more, with this meeting and stretching of brilliant minds almost certainly sowing the seeds of some of tomorrow's greatest scientific and mathematical innovations. 'Psychologically, my son immediately felt comfortable in this environment – it's as if it was made for him,' said one mother.

Oakham School
21
Chapel Close, Market Place, Oakham, Rutland LE15 6DT
01572 758758 | admissions@oakham.rutland.sch.uk | www.oakham.rutland.sch.uk
Ages: 10-18
Pupils: 1,040 sixth form: 376; Boarders: 516 full/flexi
Fees: Day £18,450 – £22,830; Boarding £22,185 – £37,800pa

Headmaster: Since 2019, Henry Price, previously head of Wellington School in Somerset. Eton and Oxford (classics). A career teacher, first post at Sydney Grammar, Australia, next Sherborne, then Rugby for 13 years where – in addition to being head of classics and a housemaster – he was involved in all manner of extracurricular activities. Acknowledges the difficulties, as a new head, of joining during the pandemic. 'I miss the live chats with the children – there are no pizza evenings in the head's house, no casual encounters with parents at matches either,' he told us on a Zoom during lockdown. Nevertheless, he is making an impression on parents and we found him a breath of fresh air, coming across as personable, quick witted and in control. We noted his attire too – dressed in jacket, open necked shirt and no tie, perhaps in recognition that for pupils, uniform is not de rigueur for online learners. 'Excellent online teaching was organised in record time for the first lockdown,' we heard. Disparages labels but believes Oakham's strength is in what it offers for the 'good all-rounder' at examination stage (A levels, IB and BTEC) and in music, art, drama and sport. 'As a classicist I am convinced that keeping the curriculum as broad as possible, for as long as possible, helps demonstrate the connectedness of knowledge,' he told us. With a 50:50 split of boarders and day pupils he rebuts the idea that Oakham isn't a 'proper' boarding school. 'Three hundred in chapel on a Sunday morning feels like a boarding school,' he told us, and he is proud of the school's status as a pioneer of co-ed schooling (this is the 50th anniversary year). Believes the important message to get across to pupils is, 'Success doesn't happen by accident. If you want to do well, you have to work.' Thinks there is no reason for pupils to be shy of privilege, 'but they should be aware of their good fortune and resolve to give back to society in some way.' Is delighted to be continuing to teach his subject (Greek at A level) – 'it keeps to the heart of the fact that I am a teacher. I think of myself as a schoolmaster, a housemaster and headmaster.' Married to Mary – they have four young children. He tries to keep a level of fitness going, practises yoga and has at least two books on the go, one for self-improvement and a novel for pleasure, currently The Thursday Murder Club Mystery, but Sebastian Faulks and William Boyd are the authors he keeps returning to. Out of term they escape to their house on Anglesey where his wife's family have their roots.

Entrance: At age 10 and 11 from over 30 different preps and primary schools – assessments in maths, English and verbal reasoning. For entry at 13+, a pre-test interview takes place in year 7, usually with a senior housemistress or the head of middle school (online assessment during the pandemic) with places offered subject to a CE mark of 55 or above, or success in school's own papers in English, maths, French and science. Around 55 new pupils enter the sixth form each year; they should be on target for a minimum of seven 6s at GCSE including the subjects they wish to study, plus satisfactory personal and academic references from previous school. All candidates at the three entry points are interviewed.

Exit: Around 12 per cent leave after GCSEs. Around 60 per cent of sixth form leavers to Russell Group universities, others abroad (most recently to Northeastern, Maastricht, Milan, Colorado State, Pueblo, Bolzano, IE University Madrid, EHL Swiss Hospitality School). School employs a Yale fellow who oversees preparation of candidates for US universities. Four to Oxbridge in 2021; other popular destinations are Edinburgh, Loughborough, Nottingham, Oxford Brookes, York, Bristol, Leeds, Manchester and UCL. A good clutch each year to specialist music, art and drama colleges. Oakham has a reputation (several parents spoke of it) for the excellent guidance offered for higher education, apprenticeships and careers. Seven medics in 2021.

Even during the pandemic, they managed to stage a play entitled Decky Does a Bronco to a socially distanced audience

Latest results: In 2021, 66 per cent 9-7 at I/GCSE; 59 per cent A*/A at A level (85 per cent A*-B). Average point score of 35 at IB. In 2019 (the last year when exams took place), 52 per cent 9-7 at I/GCSE; 38 per cent A*/A at A level (64 per cent A*-B).

Teaching and learning: IGCSEs in core subjects: the triple and double science award is offered with French, Latin, Greek, Spanish and German as the language options. Around a third of sixth formers take the IB diploma and results are impressive. Geography is popular at A level, followed by maths, business studies and economics; psychology recently added as an available subject. Two subjects – business and sports science – are available as BTECs, as well as A levels. Also runs the IB middle years programme for 11-13 year olds. 'It encourages pupils to become creative, critical and reflective thinkers.' Online lessons during lockdowns although, 'We have slightly changed lesson times to give everyone a breather from the screen and lunchtimes have been extended.' Parents praise the speed with which 'everything was organised online – lots of structure was put in place with all sorts of virtual events to keep pupils motivated.' School recently gained accreditation to become a World IB MYP School, following three years of embedding the programme across years 7 and 8. The senior academic mentor is responsible for overseeing the intellectual stretching for those with academic awards or who have their sights set on Oxbridge. The scholars' society is 'elitist but not exclusive', says school, and members are drawn from beyond the group of scholars – sometimes talent-spotted by house parents. After all, the school has established pathways to extend and develop sporting, musical and artistic talents. Chosen pupils attend a seminar programme designed to play to particular specialisms and nurture 'genuine intellectual curiosity'.

Over half the pupils board but the lessons on Saturday morning, plus matches and other activities in the afternoon, means day pupils are unlikely to feel they miss out

The Smallbone library (named after a former head) is impressive. The foyer doubles as an exhibition space and is full of pupils' artwork; it's also used for parents meetings. (Parent consultations are all online during the pandemic and many prefer it that way – 'No time wasted queueing and no one overruns their schedule,' said a parent who hopes this continues in the future.) Upstairs, though, it is absolutely silent. Certainly no talking, no whispering and definitely no headphones. 'Up here pupils can hear themselves think,' the librarian told us (very, very quietly).

Learning support and SEN: The learning support department occupies new top floor premises – quiet, calm spaces with lots of technology. Staff have chosen some wonderful artwork for the walls, all by pupils. 'Mild' SEN – mainly dyslexia but also dyscalculia and dyspraxia – catered for via small group teaching, individual lessons (extra charge) or in-class support. Lots of study, organisation and revision support, all described by parents as 'brilliant'.

The arts and extracurricular: Drama and music are big news with countless opportunities to perform at all levels. The aim is to maximise participation as well as foster individual talents – at whole school plays, hymn practice or small in-house showcases to build the confidence of first timers. Over 300 pupils sing in school choirs and the chamber choir has, in the recent past, reached the finals of Songs of Praise School Choir of the Year and is invited each year to perform in the Brandenburg Choral Festival. We were lucky enough to join an audience of townspeople and pupils at one of the weekly lunchtime concerts in All Saints Church. Young and old sat rapt in the pews, listening to virtuoso trumpet and oboe soloists give spellbinding performances. When asked, 'Why Oakham?' a prospective parent sitting nearby simply said, 'It's the music.' Drama is taught right across the school and usually six plays are performed each year. There is a proper theatre all kitted out to provide pupils with the opportunity not only to act, but to learn lighting, stage direction, costume, make up and front of house skills. Even during the pandemic, when pupils were in school, they managed to stage a play entitled 'Decky Does a Bronco' to a socially distanced audience. There are several acting alumni including Miles Jupp. Impressive numbers of top marks for art and DT at GCSE. Specialist teachers in all disciplines including sculpture and textiles, visiting artists run workshops. The courtyard of four art studios was formerly the town prison and the new exhibition space was a workhouse – Oakham can truthfully say that its art takes no prisoners. Wonderful sculpture studio where pupils can create in clay and mixed media on a large scale and even learn stone carving. Not huge numbers taking these subjects at Pre-U/A level but the results are excellent. Two Oakhamians achieved the feat of the highest D1 grade in their Pre-U (higher than A* at A level). Pupils regularly go on to top art schools and to study architecture and fashion design. Exploring Learning camp for younger Oakhamians is a swashbuckling, Treasure Island-themed, problem-solving adventure in the countryside.

Sport: The emphasis these days is on health and fitness as much as competition. Huge choice of over 30 sports, from sailing on nearby Rutland Water to polo (water and four-legged variety) and, yes, all take part, whether by competing or supporting. Outstanding facilities include 40 acres of grass pitches, two floodlit all-weather pitches, multipurpose sports hall, squash and fives courts. The cricket square hosts county matches as well as school fixtures. There are regularly over 100 pupils playing in the national finals of lots of different sports and the school will create 'pathways to foster individual talents, whatever they are'. Oakham's recent sporting honours are evenly spread between boys' and girls' teams with the U14 and U19 netball teams reaching the national finals and the U15 rugby team reaching the NatWest cup semi-finals.

Boarding: 'Transitional' boarding is offered to lower school pupils (10-13 year olds), enabling families to choose when they want to board between two and five nights a week. Full and flexi boarding options are also available. Over half the pupils board but the lessons on Saturday morning, plus matches and other activities in the afternoon, means day pupils are unlikely to feel they miss out. Quite a few local day pupils turn up for the Sunday goings on too. Also helps that there are four lower school houses that combine day and boarding pupils in addition to the separate boarding house. Hodges is away from the main campus where younger children can enjoy their own space. Boys' and girls' middle school (age 13-17) boarding houses are on either side of a large playing field known as 'Donkey' (Doncaster Close). There are two houses (boys and girls) for flexi boarders and four for full boarders. All upper sixth (known at Oakham as 'seventh form') pupils are based in two houses in Chapel Close, next to the marketplace.

Though rooms are fairly standard issue – cabin beds with desks underneath, two or three to a room in the lower years, individual study bedrooms on the ground floor for the lower sixth – there is a constant programme of decoration and updating. Common areas are large and well maintained with the usual exhausted soft furnishings, big wooden bowls of apples ('We keep trying,' smiled the housemaster, indulgently resigned to choosing fruit on the basis of what makes the minimum mess if used as a missile), pool and table tennis tables. Year group integration fostered by lots of competitions and activities and several parents mentioned the benefits to the pupils of mixing between the year groups and the 'family' atmosphere created. During periods of online teaching in the pandemic, 'House roll call happened every morning, my daughter really appreciated that – and a newsletter each weekend.'

Youngest boarders do prep in the house library supervised by a member of staff or prefect until they're ready to work independently. Sensible rules about screens of all kinds, Wifi turned off at 10pm; youngest must hand in everything before bed. The term's programme of matches, activities, exam dates, UCAS deadlines and the like is up in an A3 frame near the entrance and makes exhausting reading. 'We like to do a lot,' said the housemaster, adding, 'This isn't babysitting, we put our heart and soul into boarding at Oakham.'

Food is praised by parents and children alike. It's all prepared in-house and everyone eats together in the Barraclough. The homemade bread and soups, carvery nights and Sunday brunch came in for special praise.

Ethos and heritage: Drive into the charming eponymous town (there's a butcher, baker and by the looks of things no shortage of artisan candle makers), past the Whipper-In hotel (Oakham is home to the Cottesmore, one of England's oldest hunts) and in the corner of the cobbled marketplace you will see Oakham School announced in fine wrought iron. Oakham and its near neighbour Uppingham were both set up as free grammar schools by Archdeacon Robert Johnston in 1584 to teach Latin, Greek and Hebrew to the sons of their respective towns. The two schools' fortunes and sizes waxed and waned over the next 300 years – as late as the end of the 19th century the original one room schoolhouse was still Oakham's only teaching premises. The main site is a horseshoe of teaching and boarding accommodation and if there is a lack of fine or grand architecture then it is more than amply compensated for by the bright green fingers of a first-rate grounds team. If there were Good Schools Guide awards for best-kept school grounds then Oakham would certainly be on the podium. School is very proud of the courtyard garden with its grass-free lawn designed by near-neighbour Bunny Guinness. It's overlooked by the biology labs and no doubt the 30 varieties of native plants that make up the lawn provide a useful study in biodiversity. Fair bit of Monopoly-style buying up of town sites – latest is a former pub which is soon to be reborn as a performing arts centre (plans 'moving forward'); the town's old police station is now a new medical and pastoral centre. Town and gown weave seamlessly in and out – one of the first lessons new pupils receive is about road safety, although we imagine that motorists are held up by pupils crossing, more often than the reverse. Our sixth form guides observed the school's road safety rules to the letter, despite absence of any traffic, we're pleased to report.

Big wooden bowls of apples: 'We keep trying,' smiled the housemaster, resigned to choosing fruit on the basis of what makes the minimum mess if used as a missile

Sensible uniform of black crested blazers, white shirts, ties (boys only) and below the knee black and white kilts for the girls. All seems to be worn as intended: smartly and un-customised. Seventh formers sport the dreaded business dress – although apparently it's not dreaded at Oakham. 'We really look forward to wearing it,' our sixth form guide told us. Former pupils include Stuart Broad, Tom Fell, Josh Cobb (cricket); Alex Goode, Tom Croft, Matt Smith, Lewis Moody (rugby); Crista Cullen (Olympic bronze, hockey, 2012, who opened the new hockey Astro); Matthew Macfadyen, Greg Hicks, Richard Hope, Lydia

Rose Bewley (actors); Miles Jupp (actor/presenter); Thomas Hescott, Katie Mitchell OBE (directors); Phoebe Gormley, Sarah Curran (fashion/business).

Pastoral care, inclusivity and discipline: Pastoral care was singled out for its high quality and 'generous scope' in most recent inspection report and we couldn't find anyone who disagreed. The parents we spoke to commented how observant teachers were – quick to spot and then get to the bottom of changes in mood or attitude. Like most things at Oakham the pastoral system is commendably well organised, and implemented with genuine interest and concern, not a whiff of weary lip-service to a box-ticking set of 'guidelines'. The head of pastoral care told us how important it was that she and her fellow tutors teach: 'It keeps things real,' she observed. Tutor groups are small and pupils keep the same tutor throughout their time in each section of the school. Boarding house matrons are all trained in youth mental health care and are 'eyes and ears', and girls often pass on concerns they may have about boys (who can find it harder to talk). Add to this a 'house family' and buddy system and every child should know plenty of adults or fellow pupils to whom they can turn if necessary. All pupils do a body and mind course that stresses the interdependence of mental and physical wellbeing. Respect, for oneself and others, plus very clear boundaries, govern relationships between pupils.

Pupils and parents: 'You get all walks of life here,' a parent told us. According to the school, the Oakham demographic is solid middle class, 'definitely not socially elite'. Pupils we met officially were clean cut and refreshingly uncynical (they always are) but those we saw from a distance didn't appear to have revolutionary tendencies either. Oakham probably isn't the place for determined bohemians or incipient Bolsheviks, but we've no doubt that the school would welcome them with a smile and find them plenty to do. Around 15 per cent from abroad – mostly Europe.

If there were Good Schools Guide awards for best-kept school grounds then Oakham would certainly be on the podium

Money matters: Comparatively good value, especially the boarding. Even more so if you consider that parents of day pupils are not charged for evening meals if their children have to stay late at school for activities. Wide variety of scholarships at 11+, 13+ and sixth form. Means-tested bursaries also offered, applications considered on an individual basis. Ten per cent discount for Forces families. Certain reductions are in place for both boarding and day fees during school closures due to the pandemic.

The last word: 'The Oakham of today started when we went fully co-ed in 1971,' we were told and it's true that though the school is proud of its origins, four centuries of history are not its defining feature. This is a clear-eyed, energetic, forward-thinking school, aptly summed up by its motto, 'Et quasi cursores vitai lampada tradunt' ('And, like runners, they pass on the torch of life').

Oundle School

22

Great Hall, New Street, Peterborough, Northamptonshire PE8 4GH

01832 277125 | admissions@oundleschool.org.uk | www.oundleschool.org.uk

Ages: 11–19

Pupils: 1,110; sixth form: 380; Boarders: 840 full

Fees: Day £19,155 – £25,185; Boarding £29,880 – £39,315 pa

Head: Since 2015, Sarah Kerr-Dineen MA (50s), previously warden of Forest School in London, is the first female head of Oundle. Seeing her name inscribed on the board outside the school's entrance hall, coming after 450 years' worth of (doubtless splendid) male heads, certainly gives one pause for thought. Mrs Kerr-Dineen was brought up in rural Sussex and educated entirely in the state sector. Both her parents were teachers and she describes herself as a bookish child:

'I read whatever was put in front of me.' After studying English at Cambridge, she went on to Oxford to begin research into the literary reception of the Elgin marbles for a DPhil. Marriage and children pressed pause on her studies (and we got the impression it definitely still is 'pause') and instead she took up a post at the Open University where she taught literature and was a tutor counsellor – despite having told her teacher parents she was never going to go into the family business. This was followed by part-time teaching at Kelly College, where she worked alongside her husband, a music teacher, and then it was back to Oxford where she spent two years at Oxford High and 13 years just down the road at St Edward's, teaching English, heading up a new girls' boarding house and finally becoming director of studies.

'I am basically a teacher,' says Mrs Kerr-Dineen; 'I will always teach.' And she does, as part of Oundle's recently introduced Trivium course for third formers (year 9s). 'We do the grammar, rhetoric, logic of cryptic crosswords, it's great fun.' So that's year 9 sorted out, but how does she get to know the rest of the 1,100 plus pupils? By going to as many events as possible, looking at photographs and 'working very hard to try and remember names'. The practice is paying off – several parents mentioned how impressed they'd been at her recall. Entertains the lower sixth to supper in her sublime 17th century house, Cobthorne, and eats with pupils in their boarding houses.

Mrs Kerr-Dineen, and other members of staff we spoke to, are keen to dispel the myth that Oundle is exclusively full of confident, high-achieving 'alpha' children and that it has a somewhat hardline attitude to boarding. While we saw little evidence to support the former, there probably was some truth in the latter; cue moves to 'breathe more flexibility' into the system. From 2018 another exeat has been added to the long first half of the Lent term for all pupils: 'It's a dark corner of the year and a change of scene is necessary,' says the head. 'But,' she continues, 'apart from exeats, when we are in session, we are all here.' And if a child is tired, ill or just needs a break? There are no hard and fast rules, it's always about the individual and a 'conversation with the housemaster or mistress'.

Mrs Kerr-Dineen possesses both the breadth of experience and the cultural and intellectual heft that such a demanding and high-profile role requires, but without the excess of ego that could accompany it. Parents concur, while conceding that her appointment initially set off a 'bit of chuntering' among the 'more traditional types'. 'Her parent talks are excellent, she has a clear vision and has made good appointments.'

One of the head's first actions was to set up an anonymous telephone questionnaire for parents and she has, apparently, applied herself 'forensically' to the responses. 'She absolutely understands the importance of the individual in such a large school. There were one or two blurry lines when it came to pastoral care and she addressed these straight away.' One parent thought that in the past it might have been possible for a pupil to pass through Oundle 'unnoticed', but that this 'definitely wouldn't happen now'.

The Patrick Engineering Centre, part of a newly completed STEM campus, made us feel we'd walked out of a school and into a high-spec, hightech light engineering company

One change noted by several parents is perhaps atmospheric, rather than material: 'We don't seem to hear so much about suspensions and expulsions now – not that there were loads before. There just seems to be a different mood when it comes to discipline.' 'School is listening more – to pupils and parents.' And, last but not least, 'It's terrific to have a female head, not to mention women in the school's other significant positions. They're great role models.'

Entrance: Most join from prep schools: Witham Hall, Beeston Hall, Orwell Park, Old Buckenham Hall and Belhaven are the principal feeders. Modest but growing number from preps in the south-east eg The Dragon, Summer Fields and Ludgrove. Parents are advised to plan ahead – entrance at 11+ and 13+ is very competitive. Trusty registrar makes it his business to ensure only those who will succeed are entered. Not many sixth form places going spare so bar is high. Minimum for entry is three As and three Bs at GCSE (or numerical equivalents), but successful external applicants will typically have all A*s and As.

Exit: Very few pupils leave post-GCSE. University destinations are the usual Russell Group suspects – Edinburgh, Durham, Newcastle, Bristol, Exeter and Manchester among the most popular. Mixed views on Oxbridge preparation; 'fantastic' say some, one or two thought it could be 'a bit' more proactive; 14 places in 2021, and 12 medics. Increasing numbers to US universities. History, modern languages and engineering are the most popular degree choices.

Latest results: In 2021, 87 per cent 9-7 at GCSE; 68 per cent A*/A at A level (91 per cent A*-B). In 2019 (the last year when exams took place), 59 per cent 9-7 at GCSE; 48 per cent A*/A at A level (79 per cent A*-B).

Teaching and learning: A big school means a broadish intake at years 7 and 9, hence there's room for Cs and Ds, even the odd E, among the many As at GCSE and A level. Nor has school adopted the habit of kicking out GCSE underperformers. Most favoured A level subjects are maths, chemistry, history, biology, physics, English lit and geography – a healthy mix. And, hurrah, modern foreign languages are up there too, with great results and as many opting for French A level as economics, psychology and religious studies. Spanish and Latin aren't far behind. Music and drama are popular options at I/GCSE, but only a handful choose to continue with them to A level – although both are keenly pursued as extracurricular activities.

Oundle has a great tradition of choral singing. Apparently, the thing is to ensure that Oundle's rendition of Jerusalem is louder than Uppingham's at matches

Oundle has a proud engineering heritage and, from what we saw, is determined to ensure the subject has an equally bright future. We are accustomed to the arms race of facilities in independent schools so it takes something very special to render us almost lost for words – but Oundle's Patrick Engineering Centre (design, engineering and technology), part of a newly completed STEM campus, did just that. We felt we'd walked out of a school and into a high-spec, high-tech light engineering company. Not only, we were told, does it have the largest footprint of any design and technology department in any school in the country, the equipment is so specialised there are probably businesses, and definitely universities (Imperial College London and Swansea University are partners), green-eyed with envy. Whatever next? We would not be surprised to hear that plans were underway for Oundle's own version of the large hadron collider.

Our notes became more and more phonetic as the head of design, engineering and technology proudly showed us one piece of kit after another (if you're interested a full list is on the school's website). 'We're the only school in the country that can 3D print in any material – elastomers, rigid plastics, clear resins, carbon fibre and titanium – pupils can even design their own materials.' He showed us a small model of himself: 'I was scanned and then printed in 3D!' Model racing vehicles made by Oundle's year 9 won first, second and third place, best engineered car and fastest vehicle at the regional finals of F1 in schools.

'It's not all about pressing buttons,' we were told. Pupils in the lower years start by learning 'artisan techniques' such as welding and use of traditional lathes – there's even a forge. The fact that the whole set up feels nothing like a school is deliberate, it's an environment in which pupils are 'challenged to develop their own creative problem-solving skills'. Around a quarter take DT for GCSE and half of those progress to study it at A level.

Science facilities are equally impressive and well equipped, if somewhat more recognisably 'school' than the Patrick Engineering Centre. We dropped in on a lower sixth class occupied with an extension work practical – making their own analgesics. 'They're putting into context what they've learnt on paper,' the teacher told us. EPQ students can set up and run their own experiments in dedicated project rooms.

STEM may be the school's showcase area, but those subjects which require little more than book and pen are taught to an equally high standard. The modern languages department is housed in the Adamson Centre, one of the older buildings. Seven languages including Russian, Arabic and Chinese, are offered as two or three-year courses up to GCSE level and all bar Arabic can be taken at A level. 'We're bucking the trend of language decline at A level,' the head of department told us, 'it's all down to inspirational teaching – what happens in the classroom is what makes pupils choose a language.' Extension opportunities for sixth formers include the school's Quadrivium (Quad) course. Like the third year Trivium course, Quad features rhetoric and public debate and challenges pupils to read widely and think laterally.

Learning support and SEN: The pace is fast but support is there for those who need it – whether via academic voluntaries, weekly drop-in sessions for pupils who want one-to-one help with any aspect of their work, or from the educational support department. The department has six specialist staff who support pupils with (mild to moderate) SEND and EAL requirements. All pupils are screened for learning difficulties on arrival. Parents tell us that pupils are stretched and challenged, rather than pushed, 'they really want them to do well'. Nevertheless, Oundle probably isn't going to be first choice for a child who really struggles with organisation or needs significant support.

The arts and extracurricular: Standing in beautifully tended gardens is the Yarrow Gallery, built in memory of Eric Yarrow, a former pupil who was killed at Ypres in 1915. It was originally a science and art museum but is now the school's exhibition space for both pupils' work and that of visiting artists. When we visited the gallery was exhibiting A level exam work of astonishing maturity and skill: intricate paper cuts, pen and ink drawings, light box work, collages and a surprising amount of sculpture – beautifully detailed portrait busts and some very lifelike iguanas basking on rocks. A level art and Pre-U art history are offered; emphasis is on fine art (drawing, painting, sculpture). No separate textiles or photography A levels but these can be pursued as part of the art A level.

Oundle has a great tradition of choral singing and everyone gets to participate, whether in one of the school's four choirs or at weekly congregational practice. Apparently, the thing is to ensure that Oundle's rendition of Jerusalem is louder than Uppingham's at matches. There are multiple orchestras, ensembles and chamber groups and any number of performance opportunities, from popular weekly lunchtime concerts in the town to playing at CCF ceremonies. School has not one, but four, organs and what started out as a small festival dedicated to that instrument has grown into the annual Oundle International Festival – a celebration of music, film and theatre organised by the Oundle Music Trust and enjoyed by the whole town. Compared to other areas the music department did look a tiny bit tired, but fear not, it is, we were told, next on the list for enhancement.

School plays are programmed alongside performances from national touring companies at the Stahl Theatre, converted from a former chapel in the town. The theatre has its own director, technical team and support staff who work with pupils to give them experience in all aspects of putting on plays in a professional setting. House plays are entirely run by pupils; houseparents are not involved at all – 'That's very Oundle,' said a parent.

Nearly half the pupils participate in CCF (army, Royal Navy and RAF). It's compulsory for all pupils in the fourth form (year 10) and many continue with it afterwards. For those who don't want to do drill on a Wednesday afternoon there's the community action programme, so successful and popular that the organisers have had to look considerably beyond Oundle – as far as Kettering, Corby and Peterborough – for worthy causes. Pupils work in special needs schools, supervise riding and rowing and help with primary school sports coaching and homework clubs. They can take part in environmental enterprises, work in local museums or even get involved in renovation projects at the Nene Valley Railway. We had a welcome sit down in the community action office – staff are genuinely proud of the difference pupils can make in the local community and the way in which they develop through their voluntary work.

On Tuesday and Thursday afternoons it's Vols time, with pupils choosing between reading, music commitments, academic surgeries and activities and societies. There are nearly 50 options including debating, climbing, design engineering and technology, or taking a turn running OSCAR, the school's radio station that broadcasts from its own studio in the music department. One pupil decided to make use of the facilities in the Patrick Engineering Centre to restore his family's 1940s bread van, a real labour of love.

Sport: Forget the STEM campus – that was last year, now it's all about the Sports MasterPlan. The existing facilities looked pretty good to us, but the swimming pool, athletics track and car park have since been flattened to make way for a new pool, sports centre and 'hospitality suite' overlooking the cricket pitch – opens autumn 2020. This will also provide a much-needed whole school venue – none of the existing buildings is large enough.

'We're the only school in the country that can 3D print in any material – elastomers, rigid plastics, clear resins, carbon fibre and titanium – pupils can even design their own materials. I myself was scanned and then printed in 3D!'

Director of sport wants to build on Oundle's undoubted sporting strengths in rugby, cricket, hockey, swimming and netball, develop rowing, and focus on other activities such as dance and cycling that may appeal to the ball shy. School has four floodlit Astros, masses of pitches, two boathouses and an indoor and outdoor shooting range. Girls' cricket, football and rugby are growing fast with competitive teams fielded in each sport. The focus is not only on competitive sport, but also on encouraging pupils to develop a life-long interest in physical wellbeing and challenging traditional gender stereotyping in sport.

Boarding: Oundle stands firm against the prevailing trend to dilute school boarding to a homeopathic version of its original self. There are no flexi, part-time or weekly options, it's either boarding or day. The resulting consensus makes for a very stable, cohesive community and all the boarders we spoke to – not just our 'official' guides – were genuinely positive and insightful about the choice they and their families had made. There are eight boys' houses and five girls' houses plus Laxton, a house for the 180 or so very local day pupils and Berrystead, a junior mixed boarding house, for the 40 boarders in years 7 and 8. Day pupils in years 7 and 8 now enter a mixed junior day house adjacent to Berrystead. This move is designed to allow greater specialist provision for the youngest pupils, graduating their transition to the senior school and maximising opportunities for friendships between day and boarding pupils.

There are no flexi, part-time or weekly options, it's either boarding or day. The resulting consensus makes for a very stable, cohesive community

Like practically everything we saw at Oundle the houses, which are spread across the town, are spacious, well-resourced and very efficiently run. The head said that Oundle works because the house system subdivides it effectively into mini schools, and we saw this in action as we enjoyed a delicious lunch in Sanderson, one of the girls' houses. All meals are taken in house, giving staff frequent opportunities to check how pupils' days are going, pick up on any changes in mood or follow up quickly on anything that may have happened earlier. Each house has its own chef whose competencies are by no means exempt from the fierce inter-house competitive spirit. 'We lost our French chef – he went to another house. He was so good at puddings,' one of our lunch companions sighed. We felt it was our solemn duty to test the new chef's pudding skills and enjoyed every last morsel of scrumptious banoffee pie – not part of the standard French repertoire. 'Pupils are expected to eat what's on the menu', but they meet with the house chef every fortnight to help plan meals. Food in the boys' houses is, apparently, 'very different'.

Saturday is a full school day with lessons in the morning and sport in the afternoon until 5.30pm; Sunday is 'more relaxed', breakfast is optional (and can be eaten in pyjamas), although chapel isn't. Chapel services (Sunday plus two in the week) are on a rota because it's not large enough to hold the whole school. We asked boarders what happens for the rest of the Sunday: 'catching up with work' was one option, but going into a coffee shop in town for a 'full cooked breakfast, wearing chapel clothes' sounded like a better bet. Parents and grandparents can also visit for the day and will often scoop up friends whose parents live abroad and take them out for lunch too. International families like the fact there are no exeats and appreciate that a night away from school could be arranged if they happen to be in the country – on a case by case basis.

Rooms we saw were spacious and comfortable; accommodation varies between individual houses but usually it's small dorms of two or three in lower years and single rooms or bedsits for sixth formers. In Sanderson the head of house has her own bed sitting room, complete with stag's head on the wall. Of course each house is different, but that difference comes from its occupants as much as a predetermined identity. It's traditional for pupils to join the same house as a parent who attended, but apart from that the advice is to try and ignore 'reputations', consult the website and then visit a few before deciding.

Ethos and heritage: Oundle's earliest origins have been traced to the 15th century when it was a school serving the town's 29 guild houses. Officially it dates from 1556 when wealthy Oundle merchant, Lord Mayor of London and Master of the Worshipful Company of Grocers, Sir William Laxton, left some of his London properties to the Grocers' Company to endow his former school. Oundle's fortunes waxed and waned and waned again – beset both by poor choice of headmasters and wider troubles such as the civil war and the Great Fire of London (the latter destroyed many of the Grocers' properties, including those bequeathed by Laxton). The 19th century wasn't much better, with more sub-par headmasters and an outbreak of typhoid threatening the school's future until in 1892 the Grocers appointed a complete outsider, Frederick Sanderson, as head. Sanderson was not only a scholarship boy from a poor family, for his time he was also an educational radical, believing that science, engineering and modern languages were as important as the classics. Despite initial resistance, his ideas about offering boys a wider education proved popular, not just at Oundle but throughout the public school system, and numbers increased. During the first world war Oundle deployed its scientific and engineering facilities as workshops, producing horseshoes and metal parts for shells and torpedoes – the tradition of 'workshop weeks' actually continued until the 1990s. Oundle went coeducational in 1990 and is now the third largest boarding school in the country.

The market town of Oundle and its eponymous school (or is that the other way round?) combine to make a large campus that is both public and private. The school's centre is a cluster of mainly late Victorian buildings (cloisters, great hall, chapel) and boarding houses, playing fields and teaching departments fan out from there. Townspeople enjoy the school's gardens, make use of its sports and leisure facilities and attend events and exhibitions; pupils and staff must dominate every aspect of the town in term time and are no doubt much missed by local businesses during the holidays. Pupils are on show as they move between houses and lessons – uniform (girls distinguished by their beloved long culottes) is worn by all, but some kind of unofficial consensus means bags are carried by none, so new pupils must learn quickly to negotiate some busy roads while balancing a pile of folders and books. A five-minute period of grace has now been introduced to allow for travel time between lessons.

Old Oundelians (OOs) include writers Al Alvarez (poet), David Edgar (playwright) and Roderick Gordon (children's novelist), Bruce Dickinson (singer with Iron Maiden – do Google why he was expelled), Arthur Marshall, Sir Alan Budd, Sir Peter Scott and Professor Richard Dawkins, plus any number of engineers, industrialists, soldiers and public servants.

Pastoral care, inclusivity and discipline: All of the above came in for unsolicited praise from parents. 'The houses are really well run, they're just the right size and the unit works brilliantly.' Tutors are pupils' and parents' main point of contact and the system was described to us as 'robust, in a good way'. That confidence notwithstanding, several told us that things can be tough at first for the youngest boarders, more so if they haven't come from a boarding prep, 'The size of the school is a bit daunting at first, but they soon find their group and community.' Day pupils are really well integrated and every effort is made to 'eliminate the difference'. Laxton, the day house, even has its own PTA (not usually found in boarding schools) and parents organise socials, secondhand uniform sales and raise funds for travel bursaries.

Head was keen to talk about the importance of wellbeing and mental health, praising the structures that were already in place when she joined: 'It's something we all talk about a lot, everyone who works at the school has a role to play. In addition to house parents, tutors and prefects who are all alert to potential problems, we also have a dedicated suite of rooms where pupils can make an appointment or call in and talk safely and confidentially to a trained, independent listener.'

While many agree that the additional exeat was long overdue, we found little demand for additional exeats from older pupils, and definitely none from the parents we spoke to: 'It's much better than in one weekend and out the next, that can be unsettling,' and 'It's the best thing in the world, especially in the lower sixth. No parties – you're free to focus on work – my daughter loves it.' (We didn't get the daughter in question's take on this.)

Uniform (girls distinguished by their long culottes) is worn by all, but a kind of unofficial consensus means bags are carried by none, so new pupils must learn to negotiate some busy roads while balancing a pile of folders and books

We heard plenty of comments to the effect that Oundle is 'not a hand holding school' and the same applies to pupil relationships: hand holding or other PDA is a very serious disciplinary matter. A mother observed: 'It's not fast – boys and girls have pretty healthy relationships as friends, those girls don't take any nonsense.' School sets high standards and expects pupils to learn quickly, take responsibility and 'self regulate'. 'It's the implied contract of the place,' said another parent.

Pupils and parents: Consensus is that school is 'pretty good at picking the right pupils – and parents'. Pupils come from all over the country, about 20 per cent from abroad (full boarding makes it popular with expats). 'It's definitely not London-centric,' said one parent; another thought that while some families were wealthy, it wasn't a 'glossy' place; 'Lots of pupils have bursaries, but no one knows (or cares) who they are,' they added. That was our impression too, we didn't see any pupils taking liberties with uniform, hair or make up. Even the sixth form girls we met hadn't fallen out of love with their culottes. 'We heard the new head might get rid of them,' confided one, 'but it was just a rumour.' Phew. No mutterings about fundraising for high profile building projects either: 'They think very carefully about how they spend money – it's needs driven.' Governing body publishes a very readable annual review with key facts, figures (including income and expenditure) and 'objectives'. Top marks for transparency.

Money matters: Boarding and day fees in line with similar schools. Wide and widening range of bursaries – around 30 per cent of pupils receive some fee remission, with the average bursary award just over 70 per cent of fees. No fee remission is attached to a scholarships as Oundle is keen to stress the integrity of their honorary capacity. All scholarships can be underpinned by bursary assistance.

The last word: 'Flying high', 'On top of its game', 'There's a real buzz.' Oundle has always been one of the UK's top-performing co-ed boarding schools, but parents sense a new energy about the place. We too were bowled over by this dynamic, innovative, forward-thinking school. Oundle challenges itself, as well as its pupils, to be prepared intellectually, personally and spiritually, for whatever the future holds.

Packwood Haugh School
23
Ruyton XI Towns, Shrewsbury, Shropshire SY4 1HX
01939 260217 | admissions@packwood-haugh.co.uk | www.packwood-haugh.co.uk
Ages: 4-13
Pupils: 208; Boarders: 60 full, 60 flexi (from age 7)
Fees: Day £9,318 – £19,398; Boarding £24,795- £27,969 pa

Headmaster: Since 2019, Rob Fox BSc, PGCE (1997) taking up his first headship after returning from six years in Hong Kong as head of pastoral care and part of the team setting up Harrow International School. On paper his wife Kate is head of admissions, but this seems to be a wildly elastic role which involved the swift procurement of multiple summer play costumes on the day of our visit. Parents remark that they got 'more than just a new head' out of the deal. Their three children all now attend Shrewsbury, the youngest glimpsing two years at Packwood before his departure.

Within weeks of joining, Mr Fox was smiling all over the local press, heartily shaking hands (how retro) with the head of Shrewsbury, confirming that Packwood was joining the Shrewsbury school family, which also includes three international schools based in the Far East. The move formalises an already strong relationship, with over a third of pupils currently exiting in that direction. Mr Fox assures us that the link with Shrewsbury won't compromise independent advice on prospective schools and that there is 'no aim for growth' in the numbers joining. He explains that not only will Packwood benefit from greater investment, joined up governance and marketing, but also shared facilities, teaching staff and interaction with seniors. Parents are positive, reporting planned taster sessions in Greek, use of the music department and sports hall, before Covid spoiled everyone's fun.

Contracts signed with Shrewsbury, Mr Fox moved on to coaching and developing staff, creating a faculty structure and rejigging the school day. Extending lessons to 45 minutes gives, he says, 'more time to get stuck in' and, far more importantly, increases the length of lunch play.

Pupils appreciate the fact that he joins in, whether it be refereeing sports tournaments or leading firelighting activities: 'He's not so health and safety,' they grin conspiratorially. They describe him as approachable, understanding ('he sees two sides of things') and someone who 'won't go ranting'. Before even starting he endeared himself to parents by flying over from Hong Kong for a meet and greet. Subsequent parent points have been gained from his visibility in the car park for drop off every day during Covid.

Entrance: Non-selective with no entrance assessment, just a taster day and review of school reports. Additional meeting with head of learning support if there are known issues. Language testing for overseas applicants.

Exit: A third to Shrewsbury, with a handful each year to Malvern, Sedburgh, Eton and Cheltenham Ladies'. Approximately one in three gain onward academic scholarships.

Our view: You'll need a sat nav to find it. Just about as far into the middle of nowhere as you can get in Shropshire and tucked away at the top of an unlikely looking lane in the curiously named village of Ruyton-XI-Towns (a village, so not even one town, never mind eleven). Parents like the fact that 'there's no sloping off to the shop'.

Because there is no shop. Main school, an attractive Victorian country house, sits atop 65 acres of rolling greenery, disguised on approach by the tall hedging of a delightful formal garden that screams Shakespearean comedy. An enchanted tree (okay so we made the enchanted bit up, but you'll know it when you see it) surrounded by a circular bench is the perfect starting point for hide and seek, a magical centrepiece for the outdoor Christmas concert and a photographer's dream for school marketing. Girls wear kilts and despite the best efforts of Mr and Mrs Fox, boys still wear grey corduroy trousers. According to parents, who voted overwhelmingly to keep the said trews, they 'wash well and take a lot of hammering'.

With plenty of choice for girls-only schools in the region, Packwood is unsurprisingly boy heavy (about two-thirds). Class numbers are rigidly capped at 18, with a preference for fewer. Small numbers means there's no need for teachers to raise their voices to be heard, and shared soldering irons in the DT suite. English Speaking Board exams are compulsory at years 2, 4 and 6 ('really rewarding' say parents). Maths setted from year 3, with three academic streams from year 6.

Younger children are separately accommodated in Acorns pre-prep. Younger years enjoy specialist lessons in music, languages, PE, computers, forest school (complete with yurt and pond) and swimming. A dedicated natural adventure climbing area includes an outside kitchen, water play and football goal. The Acorns bank savings scheme encourages years 1 and 2 savers to bring in coins in a purse, to be rewarded with the whole pot at the end of the year.

There's pottery everywhere in the art room, which has two wheels and a kiln. The buzz was about the annual whole school art competition, theme 'Here Comes the Summer'; it's a serious affair, with a gallery for parents and chance for sixes points (we'll explain later). Abstract is encouraged: 'Some get caught up in the paint and can't help themselves,' explains the head of art as we both puzzle over which way up one entry should go. Surprisingly not many recent ongoing art scholars, although many do art as part of an all-rounder scholarship. DT suite is chock-full of machines we had never heard of. We nodded casually and knowledgeably while being presented with gerbil plastic cutters, scroll saws, CMC machines and 3D printers. Transcending both art and DT is the infamous Christmas hat competition, which generates intricately designed (although rather uncomfortable-looking) headgear to be paraded at the Christmas feast.

Games every day, with PE and after-school sports on top. There's a floodlit Astro, six-hole golf course and now, at the recent request of the children, a mountain bike course. Parents are impressed by the respect given by coaches to sports captains who genuinely discuss tactics and advise on how to host visiting teams. Older swimmers, who currently bus out to Shrewsbury, bemoan the size of the indoor pool, much more suitable for teaching the younger years. Commendably, year 7 do external sports leadership courses and year 8 learn about disability sports using a dedicated set of school wheelchairs.

Physical activity doesn't finish when the lesson does though. The newly extended lunch break means there's now time to pad up to face a few cricket balls, swing a golf club, grab your racquet and head to the tennis court (locally known as 'the bombsite'), play outdoor ping pong, whizz about on scooters, skateboards and ripsticks, hotfoot it to the treehouse, clamber over the 'space net' or run down to the spinney to climb a few trees.

The head of drama is also a specialist in dance so don't think you're going to get a sit down here either. There's ample space in the 280-seat theatre for self-expression. In an improvisation lesson we observed, eager hands flew up, waving to gain maximum attention, when Cap'n Silvertongue (aka the teacher) asked for volunteers to crew an imagery pirate ship. 'Three, two, one! Blast!' she shouted, and they all reeled from the impact of the explosion. Recent school productions include Dream On, a take on A Midsummer Night's Dream, Bugsy Malone with real splatter guns and the staff panto, last year Harry Potter Saves Christmas. Children are encouraged to get involved in sound and lighting, translating into recent technical drama scholarships.

Difficult to know whether it was a compliment or insult that the head's son chose to board even though he could see his own bedroom window from the boys' house

Around 75 per cent of children take additional music lessons. 'We cater for any instrument; French horns, oboes, you name it,' the head of music assures us. 'Apart from maybe bagpipes,' she caveats. Performance opportunities aplenty at termly music concerts (outdoors in the formal garden in the summer), as well more intimate stages provided for those with upcoming exams. There are junior and chamber choirs, junior and senior orchestras, as well as ensembles geared to the level of the child, with music impressively written by the teacher.

New from September 2020 is the Packwood Award, a Mr Fox initiative designed to 'join the dots between forest school and DofE' (very popular with parents). Activities include lighting fires, den-building and 'smoke me a kipper' with cooking on Trangias. Year 6 took part in Model United Nations for the first time this year. The annual Packwood French poetry speaking competition has 'snowballed', now involving 40 independent and state schools across 20 countries, after the head of French reached out to his online contacts through Twitter and Facebook. A rebrand is now required as it now includes Spanish, German, Welsh, Italian and English as a foreign language as well as French.

Learning support is managed by the deputy head (Junior). The school recognises that it is not specialist, but is comfortable dealing with children with dyslexia, dyspraxia (not motor) and ADHD. Parents report children dropping a language to do LS if required.

What we would call houses, they call sixes. Confusingly, there are only four of them, each with an unnecessarily long double-barrelled name. Competition between sixes comes into play for sports day, house matches and singing

No surprise that Mr Fox, a previous pastoral head, has upped the game in this area. New 'walk and talk' chats ensure that care is 'more proactive than reactive'. Parents report that there are 'no flies' on matron (glad to hear it!), ever present around school and rocking the fluorescent look on the rugby pitches. Expectations of behaviour are described in the Packwood Way, which sets out desired positive principles including respect, honesty and forgiveness. The associated Packwood Code spells out the detail, including a lengthy paragraph avoiding any loopholes in the strict no-devices-at school policy. Intriguingly (and highly specifically) the list of serious offences includes 'piercing yourself or someone else at school'. Pupils were keen to explain that there were also plenty of opportunities for reward, often resulting in the head dipping into his secret stash of gummy strawberries and fizzy snakes. A missed opportunity not to mention this in the Code, we thought.

What we would call houses, they call sixes. Confusingly, there are only four of them, each with an unnecessarily long double-barrelled name. Competition between sixes comes into play for sports day, house matches, singing competitions and annual extracurricular day, most recently a democracy day with children creating their ideal country with national anthem and sports. Acorns pre-prep children have multicoloured sixes bird boxes in the foyer filled with tokens for good behaviour.

Boarding: Bucking the downward trend in prep school boarding numbers, Packwood is thriving, with 60 full borders and three-quarters of all pupils regularly flexi boarding at least once per week. Some internationals (mainly from Far East, Spain and France) have been temporarily lost due to Covid. Difficult to know whether compliment or insult that the head's own son chose to board even though he could see his own bedroom window from the boys' house. 'Boarders are at the forefront of everything we do in the school,' remarks Mr Fox. 'We've captured the market in this area,' he goes on, explaining that boarding has become the natural progression beyond year 5. House parents actively push boarding and a new boarding award almost shamelessly seeks to convert occasional to full boarders.

No complaints about the food: 'You get the biggest slices of pizza,' say the kids. There are activities every Sunday, recently including bell-ringing, a tour of Anfield stadium, zorbing, fishing (surprisingly so popular that you'll need to sign up quick), drum workshop and bubble football, as well as the more puzzlingly titled 'random night'.

Military parents are particularly complimentary about the support they receive; summer uniforms are sourced (and name tagged), hems are adjusted and videos of fixtures sent, all without specific request.

Money matters: Scholarships up to 20 per cent available for academic, sport, art/DT, music and all-rounders. Bursaries available on a means-tested basis.

The last word: Look up in the entrance hall and the observant will notice names of ex-headmasters inscribed in gold. Under their traditionalist watchful eyes Packwood retains its long-established focus on boarding and balance between academic and the outdoors. Mr Fox brings a modern interpretation that reinforces the existing culture of fun, discovery and development, and a gleam in his eye that suggests that he's only just got going. 'I forgive them that I have lost my child to boarding school,' sighs one very satisfied parent.

Ratcliffe College

Fosse Way, Ratcliffe-on-the-Wreake, Leicester, Leicestershire LE7 4SG

01509 817000 | registrar@ratcliffecollege.com | www.ratcliffecollege.com

Ages: 3-18

Pupils: 866; sixth form: 140; Boarders: 100 full

Fees: Day: £11,281-17,345; Boarding: £22,234 – £33,142 pa

Head: Since 2017, Jon Reddin (40s). Sports science and recreational management at Loughborough. Very interested in sport physiology and science. Started doing lots of coaching: 'This is where my love of teaching began.' Stayed at Loughborough for PGCE. Taught geography and PE. Spent a couple of years teaching in the private sector before sport called again. Worked for the RFU with the U19 rugby squad whilst studying for his masters in sports science. Missed teaching (and the pay and prospects). 'I realised I could teach, play my own sport and do some sport science on a part-time basis – I could have my cake and eat it.' Has always worked in the private sector. Came to Ratcliffe via Kimbolton Licensed Victuallers and Brentwood School, as deputy head.

A devout Catholic whose faith is very important to him. 'I was educated through the Catholic route and Ratcliffe ticked all the boxes.' Chose the pastoral path rather than academic for career progression; 'It's what I'm good at.' Liked by parents: 'such a nice bloke'. Described as grounded and hardworking with a high profile around the school. Joins the children every morning at boarders' breakfast. Parents find him approachable and all say he knows their children. 'It could have been hard for him as deputy to take on the headship, but he managed it very smoothly.' According to the pupils he is much stricter than the previous head; not a criticism, an observation; and parents like this: 'He's firm and clear. The children know the rules and there's no messing around.'

A tall, imposing man with strong opinions. Doesn't appear to suffer fools and knows his stuff. Happy to chat, once he thaws out. Bit of a natty dresser, note the jazzy socks that don't match the tie. Two daughters at the school, and wife teaching French.

Prep head: Father Christopher Cann (Oxbridge), loved by every parent. 'They are very different, Father Christopher is much quieter and more reserved, but knows children well.' His third headship. Converted to Catholicism five years ago. Office is by entrance to prep so all parents see him. 'He knows all the parents as well as the pupils.' All parents said how much he cares about the children and how approachable he is. Softly spoken and gentle.

Entrance: Catholics and those with siblings given first dibs. Large intake into year 5, pupils assessed academically. Entry to senior school not automatic, but very rare indeed for pupil not to make it; and if this is the case parents are well aware. Exam for internal pupils mainly for setting purposes. Normally 100 per cent of year 6 move to senior school, and make up most of year 7. Integration for new year 7s can be tricky for some. 'My daughter went into a class of 11 where she was one of three new children, one of whom was a boy. It took her a while to settle, but she got there, was well supported, and is now very happy.' Parents of current prep pupils talk about 'the easy transition', hence the rise in numbers in year 5. Both schools virtually full. About 25 join the sixth form; six grade 6s or above at GCSE including English and maths are required. Many from other local independents, some from local academies; the school has a talent scholarship which attracts these pupils.

Exit: Some 20 per cent leave after year 11, usually to other independents or vocational colleges locally. Many pupils start at the age of 3 and leave at 18. Virtually every sixth form leaver goes to university, many to Russell Group. Durham, Keele, St Andrews, Nottingham and Edinburgh all popular. One to Oxbridge and one medic in 2021, plus one overseas (Hong Kong to study architecture). Apprenticeships are not being embraced as yet. Head sitting back to see outcome of new government schemes.

Latest results: In 2021, 48 per cent 9-7 at GCSE; 58 per cent A*/A at A level (82 per cent A*-B). In 2019 (the last year when exams took place), 47 per cent 9-7 at GCSE; 33 per cent A*/A (63 per cent A*-B).

Rugby School

Teaching and learning: All parents throughout both schools spoke of 'great academic support, enthusiastic teachers (in the main) who are easy to contact'. 'They are bringing the best out of my child.' Academic progress closely monitored and help quickly offered if needed. 'They very quickly worked my child out, and how best to support them academically.' Pupils happy to approach staff for help. Prep pupils taught by teacher up to year 5. In year 6 many subjects taught in main school, by senior staff, to help with transition. 'The school celebrates pupils doing well, and their peers do too.' Interesting that the odd parent thought some departments unfairly got more recognition, and funding, than others, but 'they are good at finding the children's talents.' Languages from reception; everyone takes one at GCSE, not many two. Teaches Latin, French, German and Spanish to A level. Happy to do one-to-one teaching to meet demand.

We got the impression that once the day pupils have left, boarders feel the school is theirs, with access to the large grounds, sports and art facilities

Children friendly and welcoming, and happily involved in lessons. Interesting that many of the prep school staff are young men; good to see. Informal setting in prep, formal in senior school. Parents with older pupils very positive about UCAS help: 'It's a strength of the school, and teachers are so supportive on results' days, whether it's good news or not.'

Class sizes 18 in prep and no more than 22 in senior, much lower in sixth form; what many parents chose the school for. School has a partnership with Leicester City Football Club where a number of young Thai men attend the school in the mornings, learning English, and train at the club in the afternoons.

Learning support and SEN: Around 90 with SEN needs, some 60 of whom have learning support. Parents spoke of very supportive staff who help with study skills and keep in close touch. EAL pupils, mostly boarders from overseas, well catered for.

The arts and extracurricular: Music and drama popular across both schools. Lots and lots of bands, orchestras, choirs; you name it, they've got it. Plenty of school productions, whole school and year groups and hotly contested house competitions. All children expected to join at least two extracurricular groups a week, one at lunchtime and one after school.

DofE to gold, CCF available. Lots of school trips, sporting and curricular, including a prep residential, which our guides were very much looking forward to. Some parents felt there should be more local trips.

Sport: As expected with the head's background, sports play an important part in life at Ratcliffe, with facilities to match. Large grounds with plenty of pitches. New fitness suite and sports hall under construction. Team sports play an important part with, according to some parents, individual sports such as running being less high profile. 'Primary, everyone gets a chance to represent the school; senior, it's all about winning,' is the view of some parents, despite there being B and C teams. Others appreciated that effort is recognised as well as attainment. 'Sport in the prep school is fantastic. They used to be more focused on the boys, but this is no longer the case.' Girls' cricket new this summer in the prep, though no plans as yet in the senior school. Some parents felt the quick turnover of specialist coaching staff in the senior school did not help with continuity. They appreciated the skill-set offered but felt that, at times, staff did not know their child very well. All parents agreed there was opportunity for everyone who was prepared to make an effort. Lots of after-school and lunchtime practice sessions; and lots of choice on offer, including basketball, fencing and gymnastics. Swimming pool on site.

Boarding: Boarding available from year 7. About two-thirds boys, due to the accommodation available, and virtually full. They keep a few spare beds for flexi boarding. Around half each English and international (including expats); about a third are full-time boarders. Prep and common rooms shared between sexes, accommodation (separate) upstairs in the main school. 'It's home,' said our guide, whom we enjoyed tea and cake with.

Plenty of space on offer with a small kitchen, larger common room and roomy bedrooms. Younger pupils share, up to three in a room, double for years 9-11; sixth formers have their own rooms. Supervised prep for younger years, older pupils allowed much more independence. Mass every Sunday and night prayers twice a week. Baking very popular with boarders – we can attest to its excellence; science block opened up so they have access to the kitchen. We got the impression that once the day pupils have left, boarders feel the school is theirs. Access to the large grounds, sports and art facilities. They never feel trapped, despite the school being rural, as staff always happy to give them a lift in the minibus.

Lots of trust between staff and boarders; staff happy for boarders to stay with day pupils if parental permission granted. Plenty of trips and outings, ranging from trips to the local supermarket to shopping in London and Alton Towers, all included in the fees. School keen to show international boarders 'British culture'. We got the impression of a tight-knit unit with strong friendships forged. Parents we spoke to talked of boarding for the older years 'being a stepping stone for uni'. 'There are nice staff and a great atmosphere.' Flexi boarding much appreciated by local parents.

Ethos and heritage: Ratcliffe College sits on the ancient Roman Fosse Way. The first school we've visited with its own junction off a dual carriageway. But don't let that deter you. The college sits in over 200 acres of grounds, and the sixth form has its own car park. The attractive Victorian gothic building that was once a seminary dominates the skyline, with the south terrace proving popular for sitting outside. A tranquil atmosphere, with wood-panelled rooms, stone floors and mullioned windows showing the building's past. The school was founded in 1847 by the Blessed Antonio Rosmini. The buildings, based round a quad, have been tastefully added to over the years and are based around a quad. A large 1960s chapel rather dominates. But this is the heart of the school where mass is held daily, quiet reflection welcomed and where the whole school meets. Note the memorial to fallen soldiers from WWI and II.

A tranquil atmosphere, with wood-panelled rooms, stone floors and mullioned windows. The school was founded in 1847 by the Blessed Antonio Rosmini

Originally a boys' boarding school, girls were introduced to the sixth form in 1977 and it became fully co-ed in 1984. The prep school opened in 2001, and moved into a new building in 2014. It offers, as expected, all mod cons. Mirroring the main building, built around a quad, it flows well. Children encouraged to be children here; note the muddy 'tractor suits', wellies and trainers donned at lunchtime so they can have fun on the school field; 'no-one minds if we get dirty then,' said our guides. Excellent.

Sixth form has its own premises, named after the founder, including large supervised free period area and small café where they can get light refreshments. 'We get a lot of work,' said our guide, 'so happy for free periods to be monitored.' A bar on the ground floor, where popular fortnightly bar nights are held, also houses pool tables. Alcohol is served occasionally, very strongly policed.

The school is unashamedly Catholic, with crosses and statues dotted around the premises. Over 30 per cent of staff are Catholic. But its doors are open to everyone whatever their creed; they pride themselves on their diversity. Parents buy into the atmosphere and the ethos, whatever their background, and fully embrace it. This is a caring, kindly school where pupils are encouraged to find their inner peace. Service and sacrifice are a common thread, as is the strong sense of community.

Pastoral care, inclusivity and discipline: Every parent spoke about excellent pastoral care reflecting the ethos of the school, and many said that this ethos quickly spread to the children. 'They care about each other and want their peers to do well.' There's a resident chaplain whom pupils can turn to, as well as trained counsellors, and year 13s who have trained as student listeners. The school nurse also offers succour. Each year group has its own common room which encourages inter-form mixing, and the different years mingle too. DofE candidates help prep school pupils with reading. Parents speak of 'kind and thoughtful' teachers and peers. Most felt their child is well supported and, if the form teacher is proving ineffective, know they can bypass them to get to a head of year easily. 'Their mental health awareness has improved hugely over the years. They teach the children resilience, which is excellent.' Unkind behaviour does exist; school usually sorts this quickly and pupils often handle this themselves. Parents and pupils happy with discipline and problems appear to be nipped in the bud quickly.

Pupils and parents: Around a quarter of parents are Catholics, the remainder from all denominations, or none. But all are buying into the Catholic ethos of the school. Quite a diverse mix of professionals, entrepreneurs, business owners and farming families. Parents appreciate flexi boarding and breakfast club to help accommodate long working hours. Many children are second generation at the school. Many families live in villages in the A46 corridor, generally within 10 miles. The Ratcliffe idyll could be viewed as rather insular, but pupils seem to be capable, and aware of what is out there.

Money matters: Scholarships available – academic, sport and arts – up to 50 per cent of fees. Bursaries also available.

The last word: The large, isolated site with its strong campus feel could be insular for boarders, but staff ensure they can get out and about. The Catholic ethos is embraced by parents and pupils, many of whom spend all their school years here.

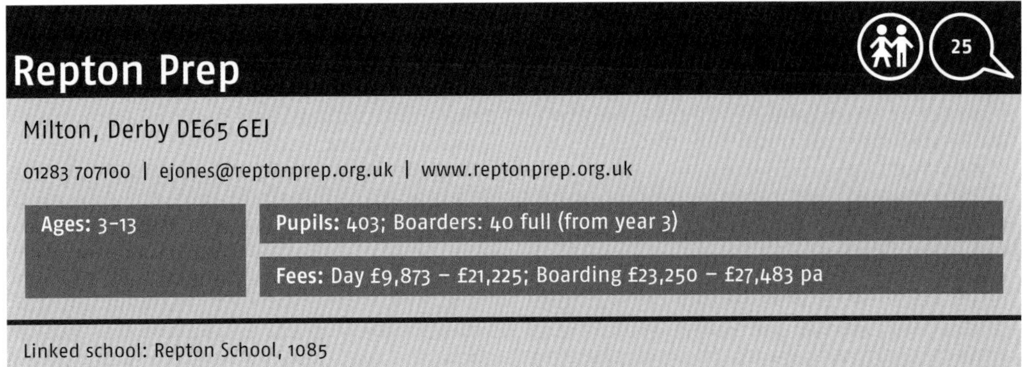

Repton Prep

Milton, Derby DE65 6EJ

01283 707100 | ejones@reptonprep.org.uk | www.reptonprep.org.uk

Ages: 3–13

Pupils: 403; Boarders: 40 full (from year 3)

Fees: Day £9,873 – £21,225; Boarding £23,250 – £27,483 pa

Linked school: Repton School, 1085

Headmaster: Since September 2021, Mark Brotherton BEd FCCT NPQH. Has been director of education for Independent Association of Prep Schools (IAPS) since 2015, representing them on the Independent Schools Exam Board (ISEB) education committee. Is also a board director of the Independent Schools Council (ISC) and board director for the Independent Schools Teacher Induction panel (ISTIp). Recently awarded a fellowship of the Chartered College of Teaching.

To be replaced in September 2022 by Victoria Savage, currently head of Sarum Hall School, London. Previously deputy head and acting head at Newland House School, London, and before that director of music at Dragon School, Oxford. Educated at Edinburgh University and the Royal Academy of Music. Engaged to Chris Harding, a professional musician. A keen runner, having completed four marathons and over 13 half-marathons, she is also big on walking – including a recent 65km walk with four other women to raise £10,000 for Cystic Fibrosis. Other interests include cooking and skiing, and she is a governor at North London Collegiate School.

Entrance: This is essentially non-selective, although those who wish to enter from year 3 onwards will be given introductory papers to assess their abilities in English, maths and reasoning. The expectation and the reality is that children will progress to year 8, ultimately following either scholarship or Common Entrance systems of study. The learning enhancement department numbers four and works both in and out of the classroom, providing individualised and small-group guidance for those in need of assistance, especially in literacy and numeracy. There are up to 20 overseas students (all of whom have been assessed) and this international spread is encouragingly wide, students coming from Japan and Russia, Hong Kong, Spain and China. There is an EAL department to assist in their transition.

Exit: Being Repton's preparatory school, it is hardly a surprise that around 90 per cent of year 8 students advance to the senior school. Other popular schools, from a wide selection, include Uppingham, Denstone College, Rugby, Eton, Harrow, Shrewsbury and Oundle.

Our view: Shakespeare had it that 'all that glisters is not gold'. Repton Prep's website is amongst the best we have seen; dazzling with high-quality photographs and text, a selection of enticing videos (one of which reminded us of an opening sequence to the Great British Bake-Off) and more menus than one would find in a chain of restaurants. Like many, it claims to be 'the leading prep school in the Midlands' (a phrase increasingly reminiscent of the 'best beer' Heineken advert) but does it live up to its promise?

Certainly, it makes a stunning start as, at the end of a long, well-tended, rhododendron-fringed drive, the Georgian hall comes into view, resembling part of a wing at Blenheim Palace. As we drew up, a gardener (hard to credit in early November) was cutting one of the perfect grass rectangles. Everything is immaculate. Sweeping steps herald the entrance to the front hall where sofas and log fires deepen the style. Home-made biscuits are served with coffee.

Throughout the school the facilities are impressive. Many join the pre-prep where play areas, consisting of a wooden adventure trail and a green area with tunnels and mounds that looks like something out of Tellytubby land, introduce the new building. The great majority of Repton Prep's infrastructure is presented with similar polish.

The quad development, along with the adjacent Thomas Davies building, features rooms of a scope and flair that would in no way be out of place in a senior school, and, indeed, would be superior to many. Tremulous pupils, however, might not be too encouraged by the sign on the door of the history room which instructs entrants to 'abandon hope'.

The library will inspire, as will the theatre and the sports hall. The triple highlights, though, are the Charles Jennings music school (named after Handel's librettist) and the exceptional art studio and DT centre. We especially liked the pencil portraits in the former, while the latter is the pit-stop for four electric racing cars. These compete on circuits such as Goodwood and Rockingham, the school holding the course record at Aintree, on the track – adjacent to the Grand National fences – that used to host the British Grand Prix.

It is a truism that the most important factors in a school's success are the students and the staff, but the buildings and the beauty of the grounds at Repton Prep all help to set the tone. Taste for the best of both the ancient and the modern is all-embracing.

Brand new dining room. The food is fantastic, as evidenced by our spectacular Thai curry (head chef was recently shortlisted in the LACA School Chef of the Year awards).

One Russian mother had scoured England for a school that would be flexible enough to allow her daughter to develop her high-class ice-skating

At lunch, we talked with some girls from year 3 whose 'best things about the school' were flapjacks on Wednesdays and 'golden time' – 'where we can do drawing'. On the same table was a year 8 boy, hopeful of a place next year at Eton, who was of the outlandish opinion that Repton Prep was 'the most rounded school in England'. We challenged him to detail his knowledge of all schools from Durham to Cornwall. He smiled, and without a touch of Trump-like arrogance, coolly explained that he could not imagine a better school, 'for all that it has done for me'.

And it is clearly not just because it prepares the way for students to enter some of the best senior schools. The extracurricular holy trinity of sport, music and drama sparkles. Girls play hockey, netball and cricket, boys football, hockey and cricket. A multiplicity of teams exists for sportists at every level and the school celebrates the Repton Prep Football League which runs alongside the pattern of school fixtures. This year Barcelona (still without Messi) were the winners. There is sailing on the lake, athletics, fencing (a year 6 girl has recently won the IAPS national épée title), swimming, triathlon and even an equestrian team.

Music fills many pages in the yearbook – The Preptonian – detailing the calendar of concerts, both in and out of school, and the excellence of orchestras, ensembles and choirs. The chamber choir sings at Remembrance Sunday at the National Arboretum in front of 5,000 people. This year's senior dramatic production was Twelfth Night. There are class plays too, and visits from the Young Film Academy and the Young Shakespeare Theatre Company. LAMDA recently introduced.

Given this whirligig of opportunity, parents gush about the school's brand of education. One Russian mother, for example, who had met the head in Moscow, had scoured England for a school that would be flexible enough to allow her daughter to develop her high-class ice-skating. According to her, 'everything is superb'. Another reported that her family's transfer from Yorkshire had gone well because of 'the excellent academic experience and also the experience of life that Repton Prep gives'. A third said that 'staff cannot be faulted. They take them way beyond the curriculum.' When asked about the lead up to year 8 examinations, the view was that 'they are very good at managing the pressure and making the hard decisions regarding Common Entrance and scholarship selection.' Parents kept well informed by the school's weekly newsletter, text alerts working smoothly if triggered by late cancellations. We were left with the words... 'Children have such fun. They're tired and they love it.'

Excellent provision during the pandemic, with school having been awarded the Business Remote Learning Award for online teaching during that time.

Alumni include Georgie Twigg – a GB hockey gold medallist at Rio, the actor Tom Chambers, and England U21 footballer, Will Hughes.

Boarding: Full, weekly and flexible boarding options are available and around 40 students are in on weekends, cared for by the dozen members of staff who live on site. The girls' house, Nightingale, has a cottage-style feel to it and could have been decorated and furnished by a joint design team from Laura Ashley and Cath Kidston. There are two boys' boarding houses, Francis and Burdett. Francis's rooms take their names from their original function: hence there is the Gun Room and the Wine Cellar, the Still Room and the Butler's Pantry. As in Nightingale, the rooms are spacious and elegant.

Money matters: A range of scholarships and awards are available – for academic prowess at 7+ and for prowess and promise in music, sport and drama at 11+.

The last word: And so, does Repton Prep, founded in 1945, live up to its marketing promises after its first 70+ years? If it is affordable – fees might be too much of a stretch for many – our visit confirmed that the shimmering straplines are justified. It is, perhaps, an indication of the school's standing that, in the county of Derby's recently produced edition of Monopoly, Repton Prep, has been awarded a green square: rather appropriately, given its heritage, Regent Street. As all Monopolists know, the third green property is Bond Street, where jewelled gold glitters. There is plenty more to be discovered at Repton Prep.

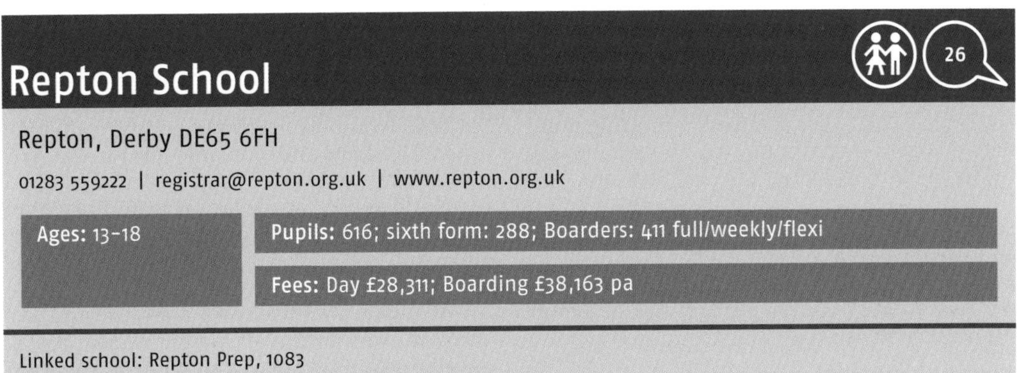

Repton School

26

Repton, Derby DE65 6FH

01283 559222 | registrar@repton.org.uk | www.repton.org.uk

Ages: 13–18

Pupils: 616; sixth form: 288; Boarders: 411 full/weekly/flexi

Fees: Day £28,311; Boarding £38,163 pa

Linked school: Repton Prep, 1083

Head: Since 2019, Mark Semmence, previously head of Mount Kelly. An economist with degrees from Durham (BA and MBA), London (PGCE) and Warwick (MA). Played cricket for England Schools U19 and Durham University; a member of MCC Youth Cricket Committee. In fact, it was a cricket match that 'changed my life'. Having been all geared up for law school he found himself unexpectedly pulled aside in his cricket whites and asked on the spot if he'd like to join the Argentinian Cricket Association – a dream come true. 'But what will you do when you get back before starting law school?' came a voice from behind. 'You could always come and help out with the cricket at Ludgrove!' Which is exactly what he did, staying for another term, then another, until law became a distant memory. Left for a stint in international sports marketing (and still can't resist a catchy phrase, telling us for example that Repton is 'grounded, rounded and unbounded in aspiration') before doing his PGCE. Thence to Rugby, where he longed to become housemaster but wound up bagging the even more sought-after role of assistant head, before moving to Mount Kelly for five years. Perhaps, having grown up in Hurstpierpoint College, it was always to be – 'education is in the blood,' he agrees.

His oak-panelled study is so orderly that we mistook it for a meeting room. The irony amused him as he'd recently made his predecessor's study – which incorporates the original 1400s tower – just that. 'I moved because there were just too many doors to get through to reach it.' 'That figures,' reckoned a student, 'he's very present – a big change for us.' They told us he's 'interested' and 'very open to criticism', though he doesn't teach. Softly spoken, but don't let that fool you – this is a dynamo of a man who has wasted no time in sharpening and refining and he is leaving no stone unturned. Includes creation of an all-through school (main local feeder has now become Repton Prep), an injection of new blood in the teaching staff, using data more effectively for tracking and monitoring, a boost to university support and more one-to-ones to help pupils make the right subject choices. Big push on widening curriculum, with sixth formers now able to access courses on eg introduction to economics, personal finance, geopolitics and public speaking 'which doesn't come naturally to most people but is such an important skill'. Has also recruited a new wellbeing manager and promises a much, much greater focus on swimming (remember, he came from Mount Kelly). 'Very much the businessman', 'great at communications', 'refreshingly honest, especially in Covid', say parents.

Still finds time to play cricket, among other sports, with other interests including art and architecture, travel, food and business. Married to Alison, who helps out at the prep and teaches in a local primary school. They have two young daughters, both at the prep.

Entrance: Increasingly competitive, so plan ahead. Common Entrance pass of around 50 (or international equivalent) required. Around half join from Repton's nearby prep, others from an increasingly wide range of preps including S. Anselm's, Malsis, Orwell Park, as well as internationally. Around 50 join at sixth form, when applicants need a minimum five GCSEs at 6+ (7+s for chosen A level subjects).

Exit: Nobody left post GCSEs in 2021 – not untypical. Over 70 per cent to Russell Group universities. Exeter, Durham and Bristol popular. Five to Oxbridge in 2021 plus one medic. Growing numbers overseas including to top US universities – nine in 2021, including Yale and Stanford.

Latest results: In 2021, 72 per cent 9-7 at I/GCSE; 64 per cent A*/A at A level (90 per cent A*-B). In 2019 (the last year when exams took place), 67 per cent 9-7 at I/GCSE; 35 per cent A*/A at A level (63 per cent A*-B).

Teaching and learning: Repton sits comfortably among the top co-ed boarding schools for academic achievement and shines particularly brightly in terms of value added. But now, more than ever, teachers are kept on their toes and are heavily praised for being 'happy to go over anything that's not understood in class – they are very open to kids that maybe don't get it the first time round.' Inspiring too – 'My eldest hated history at prep but came out of sixth form with an A at A level.'

Science facilities stand out thanks to impressive Science Priory with labs, seminar rooms, reptile room and university-style lecture theatre, plus an observatory on the roof

Science facilities stand out thanks to impressive glass-fronted Science Priory with labs, seminar rooms, reptile room and a much-loved university-style (better than some universities, actually) lecture theatre with 3D projector (imagine animated images of a human kidney inches from your eyes). Plus, there's an observatory on the roof – great for those dark Derbyshire skies. But does the teaching match up? 'Oh yes,' say students, who also pull out history as a top department. Maths, until recently, considered a weak spot 'but now brilliant thanks to three new amazing teachers,' according to a student. We watched one in awe as he made trigonometry sound fun.

All are streamed on arrival then set in almost every subject – 'with plenty of movement,' we were assured. Spanish, German and French from year 9, with at least one taken at GCSE. Latin optional, again from year 9. Of the 10 or 11 GCSEs that pupils take, English and maths results top the bill, but only just. Among the most popular A levels (of which most students take three) are economics and English. Numbers have fallen in Latin and Greek, but school will run the tiniest of classes, as we saw for ourselves with a German A level class featuring just one. BTec in sport recently introduced. EPQ has 50 per cent take-up but head (who was instrumental in creating the original business and economics EPQ at Rugby) is pushing for a full house. 'It's wonderful for them to have in-depth knowledge on something other people don't – great for university and job interviews and you can carry it through your whole life.'

All pupils have their own Win10 device with access to every note made in every lesson, as well as being used for targeted pastoral care. The director of digital development is one of the original six Microsoft Fellows, and there are six more Microsoft Innovative Educator Experts on the staff. Did the school no harm at all during Covid when it bagged the Education Business Award for outstanding remote learning provision, though some students would like computing to feature as a standalone subject.

Learning support and SEN: A small but mighty department run by a popular SENCo who tests all students on arrival. 'I have twice-weekly sessions – they've made all the difference,' said a student. 'I don't even have the words for the SENCo – not only has she organised support in groups and one-to-ones but she has put herself between him and his teachers so they understand exactly what he needs,' a parent told us. 'Came into school on a Sunday once so they could walk together because she'd heard he was unhappy,' we also heard.

The arts and extracurricular: Great excitement in the drama department when we visited – the costumes for Frankenstein had just arrived. The rails of West End-worthy getups would be enough to bring out the thespian in anyone – including, it seems, a girl whose melodramatic shrieks instinctively gave us cause for concern until we clocked that she was performing a monologue in character. The 1930s Hollywood swashbuckler Basil Rathbone first trod the boards at Repton and one imagines he'd be mighty impressed by the professional-standard facilities enjoyed by students today – including a black box studio and spectacular 315-seat theatre largely run by students backstage but with professionals such as choreographers brought in when required. 'The results are spectacular,' exclaimed a parent. LAMDA, and especially public speaking, taken seriously – we watched students practising impromptu speeches for grade 8.

The 1930s Hollywood swashbuckler Basil Rathbone first trod the boards at Repton and one imagines he'd be mighty impressed by the facilities enjoyed by students today

Next stop, textiles – a veritable feast of fabrics metamorphosed into all manner of attire. All students do at least a term of textiles and there are drop-in classes for those who want to do an 'off timetable' GCSE. The biannual fashion show is a big deal and completely sixth-form run, from choosing the models (other students), making the outfits, marketing, music, sound, lighting and social media. The theatre is extended to include a catwalk and it plays to 500 people over two nights, raising money for, as our tour guide put it, 'people who can't afford their own clothes'. Around the other side is the village gallery (former shop) where students' and visiting artists' work is displayed for passers-by.

A short walk away the art department is affectionately known as the 11th house due to the sheer amount of time students spend here (well-loved leather sofas help). Ambitious in scope, students produce everything from ceiling paintings to surrealist films – one recently made tea for 15 hours as live performance art. 'Where are the pencils?' asked a year 9 tentatively when paper was handed out for a drawing task, but the teacher had more imaginative means in mind and by the end of the lesson they'd done everything from wiping their faces on it to wiping the floor. Both A and AS level art are popular and almost all candidates get A* or A – ditto for photography and textiles. In DT we observed year 10s fastidiously making metal tea light holders and a teacher patiently explaining the intricacies of a twist drill. 'Shame these subjects are only on a carousel in year 9, though,' felt one parent – 'means you can wind up with very little of each.'

Music on par with sport, according to pupils, and that's saying something at Repton. Whether music is your everything or you just like belting hymns in chapel there's plenty of scope. 'Not just top choirs but junior choirs and house music all approached with similar gusto,' confirmed a parent. Spacious department boasts recording studio (electric guitars at full throttle during our visit, and students have performed for Radio 4), 22 practice rooms, classrooms (where we lingered in a lively GCSE music discussion) and a performance space with new Steinway – 'the jewel in the crown' (though the chapel's Harrison & Harrison organ ain't half bad either). 'But it's hard to commit to music and sport,' cautioned one student – 'if you pick orchestra over hockey practice or vice versa you upset the other department.'

Clubs include everything from chess to the very popular debating. Pick a subject and put a 'soc' in it and you've probably named one of the school societies. 'Some are secret and you have to be invited,' whispered a wide-eyed pupil. For outdoors pursuits, CCF (army or RAF) has a distinguished history at Repton and DofE is popular; school also has its own outward bound options.

Sport: Not a rugby school – the oval ball finds itself in the unaccustomed category of a minority sport here. Hockey and football are where it's at, with cricket, swimming and tennis hot on their heels. 'Sport was the reason we chose the school,' said parent after parent, who also appreciate that elite is both 'normal and nurtured'. 'My daughter plays U16 for England and that's not unusual here.' For hockey alone there are two floodlit water-based Astros, a sand-based Astro and indoor pitches – plus eye-in-the-sky for nuanced analysis. No fewer than twelve football pitches and Repton girls are currently national champions in every year group while boys have gone on to play professionally for Watford, Derby County and Sheffield Albion. Cricket pitches in enviable nick and it was lovely to see the courts being used (as are many of the facilities here) by villagers. Swimming teacher coached the Australian Olympic swimming team and underwater cameras soon to be fitted in line with head's aim to boost performance in this sport. Eton fives popular – courts recently refurbished. Niche options include golf, fencing and badminton. Strength and conditioning commended by students, including dedicated gym space – 'great for post-injury,' said one. Weekly online gym classes and oodles of fitness videos during lockdowns. But with no floodlit pitches the winter timetable comes in for an unpopular rejig. 'It's hard sitting in an English lesson at 6pm on a Friday.' 'Not enough attention on athletics,' was another niggle.

Boarding: 'Proper' boarding only (no flexi or weekly) with 70 per cent boarders. Parents recommend reading each of the 10 house profiles on the website, plus the Twitter feeds, then narrowing it down to visiting at least three – and that goes for day pupils too, who all belong to one. Sound advice, though many wind up choosing on word of mouth, dynasty links (one current student is fifth generation), and their child's interests – 'for example, Mitre is known for being sporty whereas Abbey is more mixed,' said a student. Ten in total, spread across the campus and village – the six boys' ones are based in the heritage houses; the four girls' houses are newer, purpose built and with smaller rooms. House loyalty is strong 'but we're always in and out of others for socialising'. 'Of course!' smiled our tour guides when we enquired about student relationships, but school strictly only allows one mixed common room per house.

Rooms well personalised, some tidier than others – 'only rule is that cleaners can see the floor,' said a student

Homely dorms mainly two to a room for younger years (though sometimes three or four); sixth formers get individual study bedrooms. A rolling refurb programme means nowhere should wait too long for a lick of paint though don't expect five star – the carpets are well worn, some of the furniture is quite dated and one boy told us he couldn't stand up in his shower. Rooms well personalised, some tidier than others – 'only rule is that cleaners can see the floor,' said a student. Masses of praise heaped on houseparents (as well as their families and pets), along with the live-in matrons and resident tutors.

Unusually these days, all meals are formal and taken in house – 'the best bit of boarding,' reckon pupils, who love mixing with other year groups on their tables. Means staff can keep an eye on every individual and how their day is going too. Teachers rotate which houses they eat in and it was evident from our unforced conversations over fish and chips and treacle pudding (yum) with the delightful boys in School House that they're well accustomed to entertaining whoever lands at their table.

On Saturdays it's morning lessons and afternoon sports, with themed evening socials in Grubber (sixth formers in JCR), while on Sundays it's chapel, then catching up with work or signing up to Slops (Sunday leisure options) – anything from go-karting to Alton Towers to shopping in Derby, a good job as students warn that 'being in a small village does have its downsides'. Two flexible privilege weekends to head home per term plus fixed exeat weekends. Boarders can also go out for Sunday lunch with parents, returning by 9pm.

Ethos and heritage: Founded on the site of a 12th century Augustinian priory by bequest of Sir John Port in 1557. In exchange for their education, pupils were obliged to pray for the Port family's souls – arguably a less painful form of recompense than the school fees forked out by today's parents. The next 300 years saw acrimonious legal disputes, fluctuating pupil numbers and a general decline that was not reversed until the middle of the 19th century. Fragments of the original priory buildings remain, notably parts of the arch that marks the entrance to the school and a tower that was incorporated into the building. Girls admitted from the 1970s, fully co-ed by 1991. Now something of an empire, with seven international schools spanning the Middle East, Egypt, Malaysia and China and further plans for Bulgaria, Kazakhstan and more in Egypt.

So intertwined are the school and village that it's not always easy to separate them. Even that ancient arch isn't as prominent as you might think – we drove straight past it. School owns 100 of the local houses for staff and the Spar shop must see a dramatic fall in its profits during the holidays. A few grumbles among students that the pub is out of bounds, 'but sixth formers are allowed some wine,' said a pupil. Grounds pristine – lawn lines were being perfected when we visited, framing the picturesque (more quaint than grandiose) buildings. The library, chapel and head's house would win the beauty contest.

Many eminent military, sporty and clerical types among former pupils, as well as MPs both red and blue. Includes Roald Dahl and Jeremy Clarkson (neither of whom recall their time with affection), poet James Fenton, comedian Graeme Garden, novelist and screenwriter Christopher Isherwood, artist Anthony Gross and recent field hockey Olympic medallists Georgie Twigg and Ellie Watton.

Pastoral care, inclusivity and discipline: The smallish size (whole school can fit in the chapel), caring staff and friendly vibe are among clinchers for families when picking the school. For many, it was a 'gut feeling' and they 'knew straightaway it was right'. House is everything and this (especially the meals being taken in house) also wins many over. 'Everything from the care that is taken of each child in house to the house music, drama etc means they really feel part of a family,' said one parent. The joined-up approach is valued – if a student has eg a music exam, all relevant staff are informed. 'They're understanding about commitments too – I have a match in Germany this weekend and they don't mind and said they'll help me catch up with the work.' Lots of awards, though one parent felt 'the same old kids, mainly the very bright ones, wind up with loads while mine never gets anything.'

Skin fades (for boys), hair down (for girls) and shoddily worn uniform (for either) are no-nos and could land you an early morning call (getting yourself to head's office in uniform ultra-early) or detention. Drink and drugs? 'It happens but they act swiftly and openly, never brushing it under the carpet,' said a parent. But don't expect the usual zero tolerance speech – 'What even is that? There are always grey areas, there is always context and we deal with things on a case by case basis,' says head. Everyone's Invited taken seriously, say both school and students, with one of the school governors having been responsible for rooting out misogyny in senior police – 'If anyone's on it, she is.' LGBTQ+ societies and lots of discussion around Black Lives Matter. Bullying generally nipped in the bud.

Pupils and parents: Once very much a local boarding school with majority of families from Midlands, Cheshire, Yorkshire, Lincolnshire and Lancashire but reach now stretches way further as many parents consider it 'a more traditional and academic Millfield'. More SME owners than landed gentry and increasingly lawyers and bankers from the south-east. Seventeen per cent international contingent, again more widely dispersed than in the past when Hong Kong and China dominated. Parents love the formalities, heritage and traditions of Repton but say, 'It's not posh.' Parents of day pupils often buy or rent houses in or very near Repton village itself. Students are full of life – they have to be to cope with the daily 9pm finish and seven-day week; they converse easily with strangers, the younger ones inevitably more shy.

Money matters: Range of scholarships and exhibitions – some titular only, some worth up to 20 per cent off fees. Fees broadly in line with similar schools.

The last word: Repton has long been a safe bet academically but equally it is not a school to stand still, with new leadership tweaking and brushing up from all angles, perhaps especially in sport. A (relatively) more grounded offering than some of its flashier competitors, and a great fit for the all-rounder.

Rugby School

27

Lawrence Sheriff Street, Rugby, Warwickshire CV22 5EH

01788 556216 | enquiries@rugbyschool.net | www.rugbyschool.co.uk

Ages: 13–18

Pupils: 868; sixth form: 405; Boarders: 672 full

Fees: Day £24,126; Boarding £38,454 pa

Executive Head Master: Since 2020, Peter Green MA PGCE (50s), educated at St Joseph's College in Dumfries and studied geography at Edinburgh. Has been headmaster here since 2014 but the growth of the Rugby empire group both at home and abroad precipitated his elevation to executive and the appointment of Gareth Parker-Jones as head (see below). The 'sort of' job share means Mr Green can be hands on with Rugby's international avatars which at the time of our visit numbered Thailand, Mexico and most unusually Japan, plus others that 'are coming but we can't say anything about those yet'. We'll get the oft heard 'two heads are better than one' remark out of the way, but on a practical level there's a lot of truth in it. Short of cloning, Mr Green can't be in Japan (11 trips so far and counting) and cheering on the second XI. Not that he doesn't try, in fact from what pupils told us we'd say he manages to be as, if not more, present than the average large boarding school head. 'We see him round school loads and his speeches are so good.' Described to us as a 'strong character with lots of ideas,' and by an infallible source (local taxi driver) as, 'a very nice chap'. Some parents said that they didn't have much to do with either head but all felt confident in leadership and that their children were known. One observed that 'the heads are largely irrelevant when teachers, tutors and house parents are so good,' which we suppose is a compliment.

Rugby's international incarnations are not the subject of this review, but they are clearly a big part of Mr Green's executive role and indicative of the school's ambitious, outward looking ethos ('taking international schools to a different level' no less). The ink is hardly dry on the Rugby Japan agreement, it's a partnership with a Japanese university with the modest aim of 'transforming Japanese education'. Plans are for a school ('a British school in Japan, not an international school') near Tokyo, plus an 'enrichment campus' on the island of Hokkaido. That's a lot of acreage in a country where land is at a premium, so who's footing the bill? Is it a franchise? we asked. 'It's not a badge above the door franchise. It is a heavily managed franchise, we have absolute rights to pull our name. The project in Japan is being developed by the Clarence Education group and funded by property developers.'

Negotiating in Japan, governors' meetings via Zoom with Rugby Thailand – the 'heavy' management of Rugby's international schools is a huge responsibility and more than enough on its own, but Mr Green is just as engaged with developing Rugby UK England. He describes a 'restless desire for excellence' which has resulted in some 'deep dives into specific areas', asking parents to grade the school from one to ten on various fronts. We slightly lost track of the actual process, but apparently the 'Net Promoter' score was 74, which is 'excellent'.

Head: Since 2020, Gareth Parker-Jones MA and PGCE (Oxon), prior to this he was deputy head (academic) here. Educated at Queen Elizabeth's Hospital School in Bristol where he was a boarder and head boy; thence to Pembroke College, Oxford where he read history. His grandfather was a teacher but Mr P-J had no leanings in that direction until a gap year job in a school in Australia 'set me on the path'. Has taught at Harrow, University College School and Sevenoaks where he was head of history and fell in love with the IB, 'It was so enjoyable to teach; the range, the pace was exciting. Pupils could develop a greater breadth of background knowledge.' Just the right person then to launch the IB at Rugby. 'It takes some planning', he said, with what we thought was probably characteristic understatement.

Says he was attracted to Rugby partly by its 'exceptional' bursary provision. Working with the Arnold Foundation and its various charitable partnerships the school currently offers places to up to 40 pupils a year who have a 'need' for boarding and aims to grow this number. The support doesn't just stop at the end of term, it continues for pupils (and also parents) when they are at home too.

House staff also key to admissions process, one pupil told us that 'you have to get into the house, as well as the school'

A calm, confident demeanour, his role as 'operational' head is (among many, many other things) to be present: 'I don't travel'. Parents confirm this and seem to understand the arrangement. He's there every morning with the head boy and girl to greet pupils as they go into chapel. Still teaches history to F block (year 9), 'I really enjoy it and it gives me a bit of credibility with pupils.' His wife Amanda works at the University of Buckingham and they have two children.

Entrance: No more 11+ admissions. Local children can sit exams in year 6 for deferred entry in year 9. Others sit aptitude pre-test and interview in year 7. CE pass mark is 55 per cent but average is higher. Boys and girls come from more than 300 feeder schools across the country, including Dragon, Packwood Haugh, St Anselm's and nearby Bilton Grange (now part of the Rugby School Group).

House staff also key to admissions process, one pupil told us that 'you have to get into the house, as well as the school.' House master told us, 'We want to pick people who will complement each other, there's no house type.' Parents are advised to visit up to three houses before stating a preference.

Keen competition for sixth form places when around 40 new pupils (mostly girls, but some boys) join. UK candidates need at least three 7s and three 6s at GCSE. They sit sixth form entrance exams and have a house interview. Potential scholars are invited back at a later date for interviews.

Exit: Some leave after GCSEs – entry to sixth form not automatic and a few pupils don't make the grades. Around 94 per cent to Russell Group universities most years with Durham, Newcastle, UCL, Bristol and Edinburgh being popular choices. Three to Oxbridge in 2021, plus four medics. Interest in US universities is growing. Pupils wishing to pursue alternative routes such as graduate apprenticeship schemes are also well supported.

Latest results: In 2021, 91 per cent 9-7 at GCSE; 83 per cent A*/A at A level (95 per cent A*-B). In 2019 (the last year when exams took place), 77 per cent 9-7 at GCSE; 64 per cent A*/A at A level.

Teaching and learning: GCSEs, A levels (29 subjects, including PE), EPQ – which was developed at Rugby – and now the IB which has attracted 30 takers in its inaugural year. Both heads referred to an upward push on the academic front and pupils and parents we spoke to all mentioned, approvingly, that they were aware of increased rigour. Indeed, the school defines its three Rs as restlessness, reflection and rigour. We waded through results from the last decade (excluding pandemic years) and saw a reassuringly gradual upward trend, especially at A level, the latter probably helped by very selective intake of 40 or so extra pupils to sixth form. Maths, economics and sciences are top choices and the strongest performers at A level; history and English lit also do very well. School is quite prepared to hoof out underperformers at GCSE, 'a bit of a wake-up call' said one parent, 'keeps them on their toes to know that getting into the sixth form isn't automatic.' Russell Group universities are the destination of nearly all leavers; number of Oxbridge places goes up and down – generally between 5 and 10. One parent observed, carefully, that they felt the school's size and ethos got the very best out of bright children who might be demoralised at some 'more austere', famously cerebral schools.

Small classes and close academic monitoring mean pupils' progress is meticulously tracked and there's little chance of anyone slipping under the radar if they're struggling (or coasting) in a particular subject. Pupils set their own target grades and teachers 'hold them to account.' Parents said they knew the school would give their children exactly the right amount of help, push (or friendly encouragement) as necessary. Tutors were singled out for praise, 'We get regular personal emails about our son's academic progress from his tutor. Staff really seem to know him – his strengths and weaknesses, how he's performing and whether he's slacking for any reason.' No particular concerns re setting: 'You have to trust the teachers.' Interesting perspective from one pupil on a side benefit of boarding, 'When you see others [in your house] are working hard it sets an example and you want to do the same.' Impressive programme of visiting speakers, recently Poet Laureate Simon Armitage plus eminent academics and business people.

We sat in on an IB history class about Pitt and income tax via Hogarth's political cartoons. No textbooks or ring binders lugged into lessons, source materials on electronic whiteboard and laptops – keeping eyes off the latter and on the former is the 21st century teacher's challenge. School is 'largely paperless' especially since pandemic but fortunately this doesn't apply to the excellent library, the Temple Reading Room. Lesson was a lively mix of quick-fire group work, research and questions but perhaps too early in the academic year for all in the class (of nine) to feel at ease entering into debate.

Full marks from parents and a deserved sense of pride from staff on Rugby's response to the pandemic. Two days into the first lockdown everything was up and running virtually, not just lessons but sport, music and even house singing. Chapel too, with the chaplain broadcasting from an empty building – very moving apparently. 'Everyone joined in with the hymns from all over the world – even parents and grandparents.'

Learning support and SEN: Learning development department of five supports pupils in small groups or individually. Head says that there is now much more integration between learning development and other academic departments. 'Mild to moderate' dyslexia, dyscalculia etc catered for plus study skills, organisation etc. 'They pick up problems very quickly,' a parent told us, 'the ethos is robust but also very accommodating.'

Full marks from parents on Rugby's response to the pandemic. Two days into the first lockdown everything was up and running, not just lessons but even house singing

The department works closely with teaching and house staff to support pupils with additional needs including specific learning difficulties and pupils for whom English is an additional language. Pupils taking learning development lessons follow a structured programme that is adapted to meet individual needs and considerable emphasis is placed on building confidence and improving self-esteem. Pupils with additional needs who do not have lessons are supported by dedicated learning development liaison teachers attached to each boarding house. As one of our pupils reflected recently, 'It's not just English...it helps with everything.'

The arts and extracurricular: One professional standard theatre, three studio performance spaces and a dance studio staffed by professional actors and dancers. LAMDA offered up to diploma level. Myriad opportunities to tread the boards – whole school productions plus house and year group plays. Around 10 or so take A level theatre studies so no solo performances necessary. Very high standard of music – concerts mentioned by several parents as another of Rugby's highlights. Around 500 individual lessons a week which either means very nearly all pupils take them or some are doing two or three each. As elsewhere A level music is a minority choice, but results are good. Twenty or so music scholarships awarded every year and lots of musical outreach work in local schools.

In September 2022 school is launching a junior chorister programme at Bilton Grange which will give up to 40 boys and girls a cathedral standard choral and musical education but without the weekend obligations. The choristers will have daily morning rehearsals and sing at four Rugby chapel services a week. The director of music writes that the choristers will 'need to have stamina as well as talent.' At a time when music is unfortunately being sidelined in many schools Rugby is bucking the trend – a wonderfully optimistic and brave initiative.

Large number do art and design at GCSE and A level, gaining excellent results; not many opt for specialities such as fashion and textiles or photography.

Just talking to the school's supercharged female director of sport was enough to make us feel like a little lie down. Sport is Rugby's biggest department

As much going on off the sports field as on; a long day and 90-minute lunch break allows plenty of time for co-curricular, defined by school as: creativity, action and service (CAS) and there are more than 200 options. Community action, known as 'Rugby 360', is described as integral, not an 'add on' is approached with customary energy as pupils go out to volunteer in care homes, primary schools, boys' clubs and with activities such as Riding for the Disabled. CCF (Army, RAF and Royal Marines) and DofE also pursued with typical Rugby rigour.

Sport: Brace yourself! Just talking to the school's super-charged female director of sport was enough to make us feel like a little lie down. It's timetabled activity all the way, including sixth form, plus cocurricular, a huge fixture list and whole school events. Sport is Rugby's biggest department and academic teachers must participate too, whether it's coaching, refereeing or taking the register, 'No notes from mum', joked (sort of) the director. Quite a big ask we suggested to a group of staff, but this met with a stern rebuff and reminder of school's mantra, 'Whole person, whole point'. Nor was lockdown an excuse to be off games, pupils were expected to carry on with recorded coaching and other activity sessions, tracked via Strada and marked by staff. 'During the second lockdown nothing was pre-recorded, pupils joined live, virtual group activities of their choice so that we [staff] could see how they were interacting and to keep motivation and the social aspect.' School traditions such as the Barby (5k) and Crick (10k) cross country runs didn't fall by the wayside either, 'We had pupils running at the same time, all over the world.'

Top notch facilities, some open for public use, include 13 rugby pitches – 12 plus the famous one – 33 tennis courts, a 25m swimming pool and two polo fields. Recent acquisition of nearby Bilton Grange prep school has added a golf course to the mix. Twenty-five sports activities on offer, with equal opportunities for boys and girls, 'We don't see gender anymore', the director of sport boldly claimed, 'Girls' cricket is through the roof, we're building girls' rugby and boys and girls train together for hockey and strength and conditioning.' Three levels of ability and interest: participation, competition and excellence are defined to support fitness and enjoyment, team playing and A team standard respectively. Saturday fixtures can see as many as 15 hockey and 13 rugby teams playing against rivals Oakham, Uppingham, Oundle and Bromsgrove as well as local leagues. Boys' and girls' teams play nearby state schools in football, netball and hockey. No such thing as 'minor' sports at Rugby, we were told, but non-core options include Rugby fives, badminton, fencing, golf and squash and rackets (described to us as 'massive squash'). Expectations are clear: all pupils must represent the school or house in a sports team and they must also turn up and show support at 'one sporting event a year.' Very close to perfect, but not quite: 'The riding is too basic, an eventing team would be great,' one parent told us.

Is the sporting bar at Rugby set just a notch higher than elsewhere? We thought so. Perhaps it's inevitable when an international sport bears your name. We saw the very field where it all began in 1823, each historic blade of grass seemingly being attended to by a team of grounds people. 'Some visitors actually kneel down and kiss it', we were told (not by way of invitation).

Boarding: Proper full boarding, no flexi/weekly. Eleven boarding and two co-ed day houses (one boys, one girls, next to each other), all run on the same lines. Those we saw were kitted out to an impressively high spec – new beds and desks, specially designed and made for the school and without any handles 'handles always get knocked off'. Head of house told us how much he appreciated the new beds, at over 6 foot he can now sleep comfortably! All houses have or will have ground floor rooms adapted for disabled pupils. During refurbishment pupils decanted to a newly completed house, all bedrooms ensuite, which was also used for quarantine during Covid. Around 50-60 in each house, pupils are split into 'families', a mix of year groups which becomes a 'house within a house.' All meals eaten in house – no central dining (see below). House parents plus pets, deputies, tutors, matron and other resident/associated staff (around 25) create a welcoming, family atmosphere and a very strong pastoral network. Common areas are comfortable and well provisioned with colourful noticeboards and lots of photos on walls. Younger years share – up to five in a dorm, most sixth formers have larger, single ensuite rooms. Small kitchens for toast, drinks etc and heating up pizzas, 'some boys get more creative and cook steaks.'

Day pupils (around a quarter) have study rooms in their houses – with activities going on until 9 or 10 at night they need a base to rest, eat and do homework. Do boarders go out to socialise with day pupils we asked? Seems it's the other way round and day pupils come in to do their socialising at school. 'There isn't a divide between day and boarding, no one sees any difference.' Could be a good thing that the attractions of Rugby town itself appear relatively modest (even though so many appear on schools 'out of bounds' list); Pizza Express and Costa seemed to be the highlights.

At one boys' house we visited we admired spectacular hanging baskets – Rugby grounds staff certainly deserve a special mention. The 1930s décor, especially the dining room – wooden benches, fireplace, parquet floor, high windows – had all been taken out and put back exactly as before during a recent upgrade. No shabby corners, all clean, well lit (600 windows apparently) and as un-institutional as possible. Spacious terrace outside with sofas and the latest boarding must-have, a fire pit. Laundry room full of huge washers and driers and rails of beautifully ironed shirts, but we couldn't help feeling sorry for the woman we met whose job it was to press 50 or so shirts a day on one rather ancient looking ironing board.

Weekend house activities include the usual film nights, etc plus go-karting and trips to adventure parks. Plenty of opportunities apart from lessons for meeting pupils from other houses – Saturday socials in Old Big School are a highlight – 'not every week, but there's a DJ at the end.' Sundays are for drama and choir rehearsals, sports practice and maybe a bit of down time. Interhouse competition is intense – everything from house singing (pupils were gearing up for this at the time of our visit with huge excitement) to an annual pushcart race.

Ethos and heritage: Rugby was founded in 1567 as a free boys' grammar school with money bequeathed for the purpose by Lawrence Sheriff, grocer to Elizabeth 1. It came to prominence in the mid-19th century as one of the nine schools named in the 1868 Public Schools Act, for the educational reforms of Dr Arnold, headmaster between 1828 and 1842, and as a result of Thomas Hughes' semi-autobiographical book, Tom Brown's School Days, published in 1857. Despite Elizabethan origins and the Georgian architecture of School House and the central quadrangle, Rugby presents a solid, red brick Victorian Gothic revival edifice to the town, many of whose prosperous 19th century villas now form part of its estate.

We couldn't help feeling sorry for the woman we met whose job it was to press 50 or so shirts a day on one rather ancient-looking ironing board

It's a widely spread site and pupils and staff travel back and forth across public and private roads to reach houses and classrooms, 'walking fast is one of the things here,' our guides confirmed. We saw plenty of ramps into buildings and school says it can accommodate pupils with mobility problems. Some boarding houses have specially adapted ground floor rooms.

Some Rugby vocab for new pupils to learn and 'lots of acronyms,' but nothing too daunting. Uniform is sensibly low-key, blue tweedy blazers for all, pleated skirts for girls (currently no option for girls to wear trousers but school says this is 'under review'). School rules on appearance, behaviour, drugs, alcohol, relationships etc are clearly explained and firm – pupils must sign them annually.

Rugby's marketing material is, perhaps, a little on the sententious side, though endless repetition of the 'Whole person, whole point' mantra has certainly been successful in making it stick. We heard it from heads, teachers (perhaps not so surprising) but also parents. While alluding to the school's holistic ethos, the words also evoke a robust, no-nonsense approach, in keeping with both its location (Rugby describes itself, with a certain performative modesty, as 'a town school in the Midlands') and its most famous headmaster Dr Thomas Arnold's brand of 'muscular' Christianity.

'You are in Thomas Arnold's actual study; those are his bookshelves' we were told. We were thrilled and Mr Green seems still to get a kick out of overseeing operations from the same room as his famous predecessor. Mr P-J is based opposite in what was Mrs Arnold's sitting room – larger and overlooking the garden. Heavily graffitied ancient desk lids and beautiful stained glass windows in Upper Bench give an idea of what the school was like for pupils in Arnold's time, but his legacy is about much more, his words from the 19th century: 'courage to question', 'contest, not conform', still echo with renewed relevance.

Pastoral care, inclusivity and discipline: High praise for all aspects of school's pastoral care. 'Absolutely brilliant, proactive and responsive,' said a parent. 'There are so many different people you can speak to in your house or outside', 'Someone's there to help, whatever the problem,' pupils told us. Posters and notices about sources of support prominently displayed throughout. Levée (as Rugby's prefects are known) also have a pastoral role.

Pupils told us about the school's response to the murder of Sarah Everard. There was a vigil in the chapel and girls were invited to leave anonymous written testimonies about hostile experiences they had been through (requests for help not shared) which were then read, at a different time, by the boys. It seemed to have made a deep and lasting impression on all concerned.

Rugby's marketing material is, perhaps, a little on the sententious side, though endless repetition of the 'Whole person, whole point' mantra has certainly made it stick

Mr Parker-Jones described revelations on the Everyone's Invited website as a 'difficult moment' and added 'it's societal, things happen during the holidays and when pupils are not in school.' He says that with pupil input they have now redesigned the sixth form PHSE programme, 'There's a real sense of ownership, pupils know we are always open to their views.' The Black Lives Matter movement has also been a 'catalyst for curriculum change,' Rugby is part of the 'Schools of Empire' research project and has made its archives available to Oxford and Warwick universities. Pupils' views and opinions are genuinely welcomed – Mr P-J commended their 'refreshing activism.' In 2020 school set up an equity, diversity and inclusion Levée (prefect) team of five senior pupils who work with staff and fellow pupils to promote those values in the school.

Discipline is 'firm but fair' and expectations on everything from alcohol to relationships are clearly communicated. Consistent policies across houses on use of mobile technology – F Block (first years) are issued with burner phones which can be used for calls and texts only and must be handed in before bed. Aim is to 'drip feed' increased freedoms as responsibility is demonstrated. Same for parents too, 'Sometimes we also have to remind parents to respect our mobile phone policy,' said a housemaster.

'Restlessness' is one of Rugby's self-defined three Rs and could perhaps apply to the effects of the school's non-stop activities as much as intellectual curiosity. Parents told us, 'School life is very full on and the pace can come as a shock at first, even for children who have arrived from prep school.' Another said, 'A child has to have stamina to thrive, they also need to be confident enough to say enough is enough when they're tired.' We felt sure that house parents and other staff would notice and act swiftly if a pupil was seen to be flagging.

No central dining, pupils eat in their houses but menu is the same for all and supplied by an external provider. We always ask about school food, it's a topic that all pupils have an opinion on and it's very, very important – never more so than at a boarding school. We usually get a fairly predictable list of favourite and less favourite meals so we weren't prepared for the widespread dissatisfaction voiced by pupils (and some parents) about Rugby's catering. Breakfast seemed to escape criticism but not lunch or supper. It's not the kitchen staff, pupils were at pains to point out, 'they're brilliant', 'it's the quality of what's provided'. We had lunch in one of the boys' houses: the cottage pie was edible, but when it came to pudding our dining companions warned us: 'don't.' Mr Green said he was 'aware' of the issue. Thank goodness then for 'Stodge', a tuck shop located next to a statue of 'Thomas Arnold, I think'. We heard that moves from on high to make the fare here less stodge and more veg were met with universal outrage and pizzas and flatbreads prevail – for now. Unsurprisingly, local Deliveroo does a roaring trade, bringing in supplies of Chinese food, burgers, pizzas etc.

Pupils and parents: Pupils struck us as less glossy and more grounded than might be expected – no particular Rugby 'look' or type. Parents endorse this: 'We really like the fact it's diverse – international pupils and pupils from all parts the UK,

Heavily graffitied ancient desk lids and beautiful stained-glass windows give an idea of what the school was like in Arnold's time

it's not London heavy.' 'Our daughter has friends from different cultural and social backgrounds.' 'It's a great benefit to go to a school where not everybody is like you.' Around 100 trained 'parent ambassadors' welcome others to events and are another point of contact for families when new to the school. School runs programme of lectures and seminars for parents – external speakers deal with topics such as internet safety, health and wellbeing and teenagers.

Among pupils there's a noticeably strong sense of community and appreciation of the value of lifelong friendships forged here. Somewhat patchy knowledge of school's history on the part of our tour guides was rather endearing. On being shown 'King's Oak', a tree near the chapel, we were told it commemorated 'some monarch' and apparently the stern chaps in portraits 'could be headmasters,' but love for and loyalty to their school came through loud and clear and that's what matters. Delicious list of ORs (Old Rugbeians), bevvies of bishops and brigadiers (as ever) are outnumbered by politicians and many, many cricketers. We've picked a few choice names: A N Wilson, Wyndham Lewis, Neville Chamberlain, Charles Dodgson (Lewis Carroll), Rupert Brooke, Anthony Horowitz, Arthur Ransome and Sir Salman Rushdie – no doubt soon to be joined by equally successful women.

Money matters: Approximately 41 per cent of pupils receive some form of fee assistance and at any one time up to 40 Arnold Foundation pupils attend on fully funded bursary places. Scholarships (fee concession of five per cent) abound, academic, sport, music, art, DT, drama and computing and can be augmented by means tested bursaries of up to 100 per cent. For those who pay the full whack, whether boarding or day, it's a huge financial commitment – if not quite up to the £40k plus a year charged elsewhere (yet).

The last word: A thriving, confident school; open-minded, innovative and with a strong sense of purpose and genuine commitment to social responsibility. Rugby honours its past and celebrates its traditions but keeps its face to the future. So much more than a famous name (or game).

S. Anselm's School

Stanedge Road, Bakewell, Derbyshire DE45 1DP

01629 812734 | headmaster@anselms.co.uk | www.sanselms.co.uk

Ages: 3-16

Pupils: 210; Boarders: 2 full, 60 weekly/flexi

Fees: Day £11,340 – £21,435; Boarding £26,100 pa

Headteacher: Since January 2020, Frank Thompson. Previously head at Stoke College. Other posts include deputy head at Mount St Mary's, head at Kilgraston and director of admissions at Ampleforth College.

Entrance: Most pupils join the non-selective nursery or pre-prep; prep school entry subject to an interview with the head and report from their previous school. New entrants to the college have an assessment and interview with the head and head of college. When one recent recruit instinctively opened the door for us, the deputy mused that students soon slot into the S. Anselm's way of life.

Exit: School is to end provision for students aged 14-16. Year 11 students will complete their GCSE courses as planned, to graduate in summer 2022, but they will be the last cohort to do so. Exit destinations at 13 include Eton, Harrow, Winchester, Shrewsbury, Oundle and Repton.

Latest results: In 2021, 73 per cent 9-7 at GCSE.

Teaching and learning: Setting off a high-altitude balloon and tracking it from the comfort of a classroom is nothing new, but this is the kind of school that literally goes the extra mile, or hundred. S. Anselmians think nothing of jumping in a minibus and driving four hours to Norfolk on an epic balloon chase while tracking the progress on laptops. Project based learning was introduced in collaboration with a Danish school and Harvard University several years ago and staff are now starting to see it embed. Software is up to date, think 3D printers, trials of VR, and their Lego Innovation Studio which showcases 3D inspired chess sets. When Griselda, a forest monster, terrorised the local woodland, pupils were so engrossed in using adjectives that they wanted to work through the dinner bell.

Projects have ranged from the prerequisite Roman V's Celt battle (two-day stopover and an actual catapult: no cardboard boxes here); giant plastic turtles, an ethical nod to the modern-day plastic problem; Tudor houses set on fire to allow pupils to experience the Great Fire of London (some cried); lessons in surgery with an actual pig's lung and a digestive system made out of Lego. The list is endless… anything goes in the name of learning. We tried to ignore the proudly displayed newspaper reports lacking in the fundamentals, with spelling mistakes in headlines, and pupils grappling with knives in cooking without basic chopping techniques. On the plus side pupils were self-reflective, one reasoning that she needed to take more risks in her work, another learning collaboration as part of a group.

S. Anselm's boarders are busy making the most of their time; with so much to fit in we are not even sure the TVs in the common rooms are used

Maths students were genuinely enthusiastic about their double lesson last thing on a Friday. Parents remark that it is 'a truly wonderful school' and that 'My boys look forward to going every morning and come home full of stories of what they have done that day.'

Learning support and SEN: The school is more than happy to accept children with special needs. This is backed up by a strong learning support department with dedicated spaces, three specialist teachers including speech, language and communication therapists and dyslexia experts, one-to-ones, group work and EAL support, as well as plentiful resources for specific needs such as specialised laptops. Additional charge for learning support lessons.

The arts and extracurricular: Music is strong, boasting 15 peripatetic teachers and 15 ensembles: everything from rock bands to modern music and chapel choirs. The proof of the pudding is in the listening – mesmerising sounds of music flood through open windows, showcasing the ability and dedication of pupils. The Hargreaves Hall auditorium offers a great performing space for all ages, with modern repertoires ranging from Fight Club monologues to full on productions of Around the World in 80 Days and Fantastic Mr Fox.

Art rooms are a hive of activity and include a ceramics studio plus specialist teacher, with textiles offered as a separate subject. When we visited, a local exhibition of art produced by the prep included handcrafted toys, product launches, metaphorical poems sewn and draped on a mannequin's skirt, the cabinet of curiosities containing ceramic fantasy creatures and even a bird's skull which the pre-prep discovered and donated. The whole exhibition – a work of art in itself.

After-school activities cover every taste. The rule is, if there isn't an activity with your name on, then there soon will be. Not a space is left unused here, with the gardens being the next big project – pupils have already started crafting grand designs.

Sport: No shying away from competition here: it's embraced at all levels, with the key being inclusion. Children are divided into A, B and C teams with the As naturally playing more fixtures. 'We wipe the floor with other schools, despite our small size,' say PE staff. Pupils compete nationally in swimming and netball and have had an unbeaten season in rugby. The large range of sports from shooting to steeplechase, cricket for both girls and boys to the usual netball, hockey and tennis mean that players achieve at all levels including regional and county. Parents said the Astroturf pitch was 'a real bonus and all the children (and mums) are enjoying the hockey tuition' with families being invited in for weekly coaching. Smallish swimming pool.

Boarding: 'We have a pillow fight every Wednesday morning, so they can get it out of their system,' boasts the housemaster. Under his charming aegis, the pupils gush boarding accolades with superlatives galore. A few years 6-8 boarders are international pupils; in some cases, families have moved nearby so they can send siblings as day pupils.

One parent told us they live only four miles away, yet their son has chosen to board. Who can blame him when weekend activities range from watching live ice hockey matches and paintballing to water parks? Lots of staff are on site: no one wants to miss out on the fun. Older pupils earn the privilege to wander down to Bakewell and spend a pound. 'It's a wonder what they come back with,' chuckles the housemaster.

We have a pillow fight every Wednesday morning, so they can get it out of their system,' boasts the housemaster. Under his charming aegis, the pupils gush boarding accolades with superlatives galore

Junior dorms have been spruced up with bright, but slightly garish and stereotypical wallpaper: flowers in the girls' dorm, and a world map in the boys'. We did wonder why the girls only got daisies. Senior dorms are slightly worn looking, if not dull, and could do with a lick of paint. Bathroom facilities are modern and clean. None of which matters, really, because S. Anselm's boarders are too busy making the most of their time, with prep, music, supper, sports, swimming and the Lego Innovation Studio to fit in; we are not even sure the TVs in the common rooms are used.

Ethos and heritage: The successful pre-prep and prep school expanded to open the college in 2015 but the last college students will leave in 2022. Locality – in the awe-inspiring Peak District – is massively important: 'It's everything about us and shapes us as a school.' Simple things like using Derbyshire oatcakes in their pancake day races, and studying iconic Derbytonians. Since most children live in the locality, it is easy for the school to integrate naturally into local life and create a sense of community. Local state schools are invited periodically for sporting events, computer programming and science workshops.

There is so much going on here that it's not a case of ticking boxes, but more what boxes can we come up with next to tick off. Staff are positively buzzing with enthusiasm.

Pastoral care, inclusivity and discipline: There is the S. Anselm's way based on common sense, sensible skirt lengths, no make-up, ensuring children remain children. We listened to the excited chattering of pupils and sampled Friday's fish in the cosy, sociable dining hall. Pupils went out of their way to help visitors and took delight in clearing away our things. Parents are confident their offspring are eating well, remarking, 'The boys tell me how good the school lunches are and my eldest loves the full English on a Saturday morning.' Staff are not afraid to address any issues head on – whether it's lesson time or not – with one teacher taking a pupil aside for a heart-to-heart when we were there.

Pupils are, on the whole, dressed smartly. The house system, based on four national heroes – Pitt, Churchill, Nelson and Wellington – is used at every opportunity to provide competition amongst pupils and staff of all ages, with the latter exchanging friendly banter about a recent quiz night.

Pupils and parents: Pre-prep pupils showed great honesty with their opinions: 'It's too easy, I did fractions last year, and I have to do them again this year.' Another, exasperated, 'We have to work until 5pm.' They don't. Pre-prep finishes at 3.20pm, with after-school clubs available. We found pupils enthusiastic and on task in class, barely glancing up. They were polite, courteous and relaxed. The Guide was not immune to the inevitable plethora of prepped answers by the older students, but found genuineness when probing. 'Good sport, no pressure.' 'Lots of opportunities and mix of everything.' 'Feels like a family' and 'really family-friendly environment'.

Staff use online learning journals in early years and reception to record pupils' progress for parents. While all agree it provides great communication, it ironically leaves staff with little to say on parents' evenings. Some can also get carried away with recording, as one teacher openly admitted she had conducted 38 observations on one child in nine weeks because 'they were achieving so many amazing things' and she just wanted to 'capture them for the parents'.

Lots on offer for parents, from quiz and curry nights to pet shows and the weekly Sunday supper where families can enjoy a delicious roast with all the trimmings.

Money matters: Academic, music, art and sports scholarships at 7+. Some means-tested bursaries.

The last word: S. Anselm's tries to keep it real, true to the motto: Esse Quam Videri – to be, rather than to seem to be. The school embraces its Derbyshire roots, preparing students for modern life with traditional values. Individuality is key, and pupils leave with their characters intact, nurtured rather than remodelled. A juxtaposition of old and new, with a dash of good nature, humour and honesty that just seems to work.

St David's College

29

Gloddaeth Hall, Llandudno, Conwy LL30 1RD

01492 875974 | admissions@stdavidscollege.co.uk | www.stdavidscollege.co.uk

Ages: 9–19

Pupils: 240 (boys 159, girls: 81); sixth form: 65; Boarders: 100 full

Fees: Day £12,270 – £19,455; Boarding £25,350 – £36,315 pa

Headmaster: Since 2017, Andrew Russell BSc (early 50s). Studied economics and accounting at Southampton University but after a brief flirtation with accountancy, wanting to enjoy a more outdoor, wholesome life, he arrived at St David's 28 years ago and has stayed ever since. During that time has had roles which include head of maths, head of careers, housemaster, assistant head and deputy head. His wife Kate's father was a housemaster here and their three children attend the school. 'Andy and his family are St David's to the core,' a member of staff told us.

St David's has a long pedigree of highly successful home-grown heads and as we got to know the school we could understand why. Mr Russell was initially drawn here because it was a place where he could combine his love of teaching with his sporting and outdoor enthusiasms. He once ran cross-country for Wales; now he walks the dog a few times a day and plays five-a-side football with the sixth form boys. He says that what drives him is people and as we watched him talking to parents, staff and children and heard him reflect on his time as a housemaster, we could see that this is true. He knows everyone and never forgets an old student. He is warm, relaxed, extrovert and comes across as well balanced and positive. Kate teaches English and is very involved in school life.

Mr Russell is totally committed to the boarding ethos and life of the school. He has invested in an expansion to the girls' boarding house, 17 extra beds in single and twin rooms, and aims to increase boarding numbers. He believes the faith foundations of the school are still its beating heart and, supporting the chaplain's focus on spirituality rather than doctrine, he emphasises that the spirit is one of the three pillars of the school, along with the body and the mind. He would like to make the most of the (albeit limited) expansion possibilities of the site and wants everyone to shout from the rooftops about all the wonderful things that go on at the school. Above all, he remains utterly committed to what he believes is the core purpose of his school: to ensure there are no barriers to learning and children are allowed the freedom to flourish.

Entrance: Not academically selective, places are offered following an interview with the head and information gathered from present school reports and, where appropriate, other educational professionals. The school has relationships with other independent schools who have occasional students for whom orthodox education isn't working.

Exit: Career advice is expert, personalised and well honed – it's a strength of the school. Many sixth formers go on to university, others have gained places on apprenticeship schemes. We hear that companies who have once had a St David's student, come back to the school for more. As well as traditional academic degrees at redbrick universities, what stands out is the range of applied degree courses the students go on to – automotive design, architecture, product design, even cybersecurity and ethical hacking – one we hadn't come across before. Oxford Brookes, Lancaster, John Moores, Manchester, Belfast and Cardiff recently popular.

Latest results: In 2021, 35 per cent 9-7 at GCSE; 51 per cent A*/A at A level. For BTec, 51 per cent distinctions. In 2019 (the last year when exams took place), 19 per cent 9-7 at GCSE; seven per cent A*/A at A level. For BTec, 42 per cent distinctions.

Teaching and learning: As the head acknowledges, many pupils at St David's, though by no means all, do have barriers to learning. 'External exam results aren't why parents choose St David's College,' a parent told us. That may be true, but they will always be a factor in any decision about a school. In fact, the headline results are consistently sound. For a school that specialises in teaching dyslexic pupils, the GCSE English results are a real achievement.

In the sixth form, traditional academic A levels are offered along with BTecs in performing arts, production arts, music, outdoor education or PE options in the sports qualification, business studies and three levels of computer aided design qualifications. Art and design, including engineering, is one of the school's consistent strengths.

Students are encouraged to enter national and international competitions in areas where they excel – a group of sixth formers had just completed a global maths competition. The whole tenet is that each child is different and although many schools will say this, at St David's there is a genuine flexibility – a successful attempt to make each child's education work for them not for the convenience of the school.

Everything drives towards enabling pupils to become independent learners. In many cases, though difficulties will not disappear, the children learn strategies to work around them and enjoy successful careers and fulfilling lives. Children often arrive having not enjoyed their educational experience to date, many have not 'fitted' into the rigid box of other academic institutions. 'My form teacher in year 7 told me I would never get any GCSEs,' a sixth former now applying to universities told us. 'At St David's,' a parent commented, 'children don't even realise they are being taught' and can finally relax into learning. Some teachers bring their dogs into lessons and a therapy dog is part of creating a learning atmosphere that is stress free.

In the sixth form there's lots of emphasis on preparing for real jobs and the atmosphere in the DT and art workshops was more like the workplace than a school

The school is at the forefront of dyslexia teaching but the St David's approach is more than just being about dyslexia or dyspraxia, ADD or autism; it is about finding the best way of teaching that will help every individual. Class sizes are small, which helps of course, and there is smaller group and individual support.

In the sixth form there's lots of emphasis on preparing for real jobs and the atmosphere in the DT and art workshops was more like the workplace than a school. An oak-framed garage has been rebuilt for automobile technology. Kit cars are built, old cars and motorbikes restored and souped up! The vocational courses such as product design and computer aided design allow some students to go straight into industry, working in for eg graphic design and film animation. Projects relate to live issues. One girl has designed a prosthetic limb for a child, linked with a manufacturing business and it is now being produced. In three of the last four years, St David's students have been in the top three for the global BTec Business and Enterprise Award. Students' DT projects are also regularly among the top 30 chosen by the Welsh Board for showing most innovation at A level. In CAD, one boy who redesigned the aerobar for endurance cycling worked in collaboration with Swansea University to see the project through from design to manufacture.

These achievements show just how much St David's offers dyslexic children. But children without dyslexia who are visual learners, or like to learn by doing, or are creative thinkers, can also gain more in terms of challenges than in a traditional school environment. The individualised approach and number of specialist staff available explains why students and parents to whom we spoke, not all of whom were dealing with dyslexic issues, were unanimous in commending the stretch and intellectual excitement offered.

Learning support and SEN: Alongside mainstream teaching in small classes, St David's College has the highly regarded Cadogan Centre, a learning support centre specialising in helping pupils with dyslexia and additional learning needs. The centre features a wide range of assisted learning technology as well as 20 individual support teachers for any pupils who need them. The department has considerable expertise across a range of specialisms and staff are constantly developing their skills with the aim of supporting pupils to achieve their best using the latest teaching techniques.

Staff work with children who are able and talented as well as children who, when they arrive, have hardly gained anything from their previous formal education. More importantly, all staff, not just SEN support staff, are trained in how to work with the learning needs of every single child and are expected to use multi-sensory approaches in their lessons: 'This is such an energising place to work, we are all encouraged to think outside the box when it comes to getting the very best for each child.' Every child and member of staff has a device that includes speech and text recognition. Familiarity with computer aided learning meant the school was able to swing into lockdown remote provision with ease.

The arts and extracurricular: Plenty of music, lots of singing and jazz in particular, drama productions every term. But the absolute standout at St David's is outdoor education, not surprising given its location looking out onto the peaks of Snowdonia and within easy reach of the glorious north Wales coast. All pupils up to year 10 have a whole day every fortnight to make the most of all the area offers and the programme culminates in an overseas expedition at the end of year 10. There is climbing, sailing, kayaking, caving, cross-country runs, camp cooking, navigation, mine exploration and even 4x4 off-road driving. If your child can't bear fresh air, St David's probably won't make your shortlist of schools.

Outdoor education is part of the draw of the school for staff as well students. Teachers know the confidence-building value of outdoor challenges for everyone and particularly those who struggle with conventional learning. DofE is huge and in addition to highly qualified instructors the school has masses of professional equipment to support the extensive range of outdoor opportunities. Pupils too can gain qualifications in outdoor leadership. These regional pursuits grow into regular international outdoor education opportunities, for example kayaking in Norway. St David's also has strong connection with Uganda and a group of pupils visits every year to support a school there.

The school recently won national recognition with an Independent Schools Association award for extracurricular provision.

Sport: A plethora of sports, both team and individual – the school does well in terms of regional success and national representation. There are St David's students in national Wales golf, cross-country, table tennis and swimming teams and in team GB for sailing, fell running, kickboxing and climbing. Staff members too were in national teams for rugby, rounders and fell running.

Boarding: Around a third of pupils board. Some boarding houses are in the old buildings with large airy rooms – recent refurbished. In newer purpose-built accommodation there are two or three-bed dorms for younger children; sixth formers mainly have their own rooms. Judging from house noticeboards, plenty goes on in the evenings and at weekends, trips organised away from school as well as the chance to experience even more outdoor adventures. However, if your child wants a taste of city life they are going to have to travel some distance for that particular buzz. Llandudno is no London or Manchester – which is of course its appeal for some. While overseas students are resident at weekends, boarders who live closer tend to go home for at least some. The boarding staff we met were incredibly positive about the lifestyle and share this enthusiasm with pupils.

Ethos and heritage: The school incorporates a Tudor hall (Grade 1 listed), the Victorian expansion, modern buildings from when the school moved in in the 1960s as well as the new boarding facilities mentioned above. There are further building plans afoot. At the heart of the school is Gloddaeth Hall, part of the original country house, with its panelling and minstrels' gallery. One of the boys' boarding houses is located in this original manor house.

There is an unusual atmosphere in the school, a potent mix of gentleness, kindness, energy and high-octane enthusiasm. It is an atmosphere the founder of the school, John Mayor, would recognise and relish. He set the school up in 1965 to offer hope to the children he had seen throughout his teaching career who struggled in mainstream schools, losing confidence with every failed exam. He was driven by strong Christian principles but while the present leadership stress the faith basis of the school and recognise how it contributes to the close-knit life of the community, they do so without Mayor's rather fervent missionary zeal.

With under 300 pupils, everyone knows everyone else and the school encourages the family atmosphere by ensuring older pupils interact with younger ones in lots of ways

We enjoyed a long assembly that in many ways encapsulated the ethos of St David's. The whole community was involved, including the most junior members and local parents who sang. It took place in one of the old parts of the school, the old barn in fact, with a lovely beamed roof and a certain charm, but not smart in any way (although there was highly effective amplification and IT). There was nothing particularly polished about the performances or the question and answer session a member of staff led with a group of seniors who had been to Africa during the summer, but there was an authenticity and sense of a real community that was beguiling.

On the day of our visit, sheets of rain swept across the wild landscape. The school has a number of separate buildings so everyone is used to getting a bit wet as they splash from class to class, but nobody seems bothered.

Pastoral care, inclusivity and discipline: The approach to pupil welfare is so holistic it seems artificial to separate pastoral from everything else in the school. With under 300 pupils everyone knows everyone else and the school encourages the family atmosphere by ensuring older pupils interact with younger ones in lots of ways – both academically through, for example, paired reading and also socially in the houses and in

St Hugh's School (Woodhall Spa)

extracurricular activities. 'I love knowing everyone,' a younger child told us.

Some of the children arrive having been bullied, staff told us. Those scars don't heal quickly and we came across children who were needing much loving care. This was recognised not just by the staff but also by the other children. 'We all look out for each other,' an older girl told us. 'I can tell the new ones that I was really miserable and lonely too before I came here but now I can get involved in everything and have loads of friends.'

The school is mindful of the difficulties for overseas parents and has a senior member of staff with special responsibilities for working on smooth, helpful communication with them. In addition to the regular newsletter and updates, she has set up a WhatsApp group for them. Parents appreciate the school's efforts here.

The school is at the forefront of dyslexia teaching but the approach is about more than just dyslexia or dyspraxia, ADD or autism; it is about finding the best way of teaching to help every individual. Class sizes are small and there is smaller group and individual support. All staff are trained to work with pupils' learning needs

The school has its own caterers and, like other school employees, many have been part of the school community for a long time – 30 years plus is not uncommon. The kitchen staff know the children and are quick to pick up if someone is not eating enough or overeating. The head chef, whose experience includes a number of the posher Welsh hotels, devises menus in collaboration with pupils.

Behaviour management is very much on an individual basis with every effort made to talk through actions that are unhelpful to others or the community. That said, there are clear sanctions for alcohol and drug use and the school does do random drugs tests.

Pupils and parents: Boys outnumber girls though at the lower end of the school the balance is more or less 50/50 so things may become more equal as time goes on. The girls we met were determined and gritty. Staff say girls tend to find it easier to work out ways to overcome dyslexia problems than boys do. The girls are outdoor enthusiasts – though more inclined to don walking boots than riding boots and certainly not worried that they are a hundred miles away from the nearest Harvey Nichols.

The sixth formers we met would have been very impressive in any context and given the challenges some of them have overcome we thought they were exceptional young people. As well as overall enthusiasm for the school, one message came across from everyone – 'It is okay to ask for help.' A past pupil to whom we spoke described going to university and being astonished that other students were reluctant to ever ask tutors anything, being almost frightened to articulate a problem. The result of the St David's training means that when the students move on, they know how to make progress through accessing support when they need it.

A pupil told us, 'I want to get out of bed every morning now so I can get to school early.' Parents told us that they and their children felt comfortable and at ease in an environment that was not all about showing off academic accolades. Everyone seems to be accepted as part of the school family; 'I don't have to try to be someone else at St David's,' one boy said to us.

We met parents who have moved from other parts of the country to be able to send their children to St David's as day pupils. One parent movingly told us, 'Our child had been broken by the state system. St David's has put him back together again.'

Money matters: Fees are mid-range for a boarding school. Weekly individual or small group SEN tuition is charged in addition. Discounts of 10 per cent for siblings, children of clergy, services personnel and former pupils. There is a small number of scholarships and bursaries and some pupils come with local authority support.

The last word: This is a school that parents still seem to stumble upon and those that are lucky enough to do so are often both thrilled and relieved. St David's manages to combine many of the attractive features of independent education – highly motivated pupils, outstanding staff, an exceptional outdoor education programme, fabulous site, historic buildings – with quite exceptional learning support. Glossy and socially sophisticated it is not, but its holistic expertise deserves to be much more widely known. Founder John Mayor said that his school should be a place where every child would have the 'freedom to flourish'; it continues to be that place today.

St Hugh's School (Woodhall Spa)

Cromwell Avenue, Woodhall Spa, Lincolnshire LN10 6TQ

01526 352169 | office@st-hughs.lincs.sch.uk | www.st-hughs.lincs.sch.uk

Ages: 2-13

Pupils: 163; Boarders: 40 weekly/flexi (from year 3)

Fees: Day £9,510 – £15,990; Boarding £20,085 pa

Headmaster: Since 2019, Jeremy Wyld, formerly deputy head at Holmewood House School in Kent. French degree from Leicester plus a PGCE in modern languages; he taught French and sport at The Judd, then was boarding housemaster and French teacher at Sevenoaks before joining Holmewood in 2013. He has moved to Woodhall Spa with his wife Niki and family.

Entrance: Majority of the children rise through the ranks of the school's nursery and pre-prep with some recruitment in years 3 and 4. Prospective pupils spend a day at the school for assessment. Six minibuses bring children from wider areas.

Exit: Leavers to Oakham, Repton, Uppingham, Greshams and Lincoln Minster in 2021.

Our view: Located in the attractive, former Victorian spa resort of Woodhall Spa, in the midst of what was RAF heartland, St Hugh's is based in a leafy avenue of traditional, Edwardian villas. Founded by the Forbes family in 1925 as a boys' boarding school, loyalty to the school has been strong and successive generations of often farming families continue to be educated here. A charitable trust since 1962 and coeducational since 1981.

Whilst first impressions are of a modest establishment, once through the door the extent of the buildings and facilities becomes immediately apparent and the newly acquired playing field now allows the grounds to be described as extensive for a school of this size. New Astroturf; this addition to the functional yet well maintained sports hall and swimming pool provides sporting facility gold, particularly for the hockey players. An adventure playground and nature pond – increasing use of the natural environment, staff undertaking forest school training, part of a green school kitemark. Boarding facilities in the upper echelons of the main school house, well away from classrooms.

Nursery and pre-prep classrooms flow through a building across the playground from the older children. Bright, well resourced and full of colourful displays. Corridors adorned with interesting displays and children's work provide a sense of pride and commitment from staff. Good specialist facilities for science, music, art and DT with whiteboards in each classroom, a dedicated ICT suite and wireless connectivity throughout the school.

Scholarship success particularly in sports, music and arts, and the school plans to strengthen further the number of academic and all-rounder awards. In the early years foundation stage, the new department head has developed investigational skills in maths. Specialist French starts in nursery, increasing across subjects so that by year 5 all teaching is by specialists, with German and Latin introduced and setting for mathematics and science. Classes are grouped according to ability from year 5 with an average of 14 in a class. Whilst teaching broadly follows the national curriculum, there is a weekly session for senior pupils to enhance independent learning. Ten per cent SEN, mainly dyslexia and dyspraxia though several children with EHC plans. Personalised learning plans, good coordinated strategies between SENCo and teachers, with one-on-one support where required. Rated excellent for academic achievement and personal development in recent ISI report.

Parents tell us that they 'love the wonderful family atmosphere' and that the children 'mix throughout the year groups and are very supportive and encouraging of each other'

Sport rules the roost. Focus on traditional team sports and swimming, and everyone encouraged to play in a team. Good fixture list mainly against local independents but outlying location involves lengthy travelling times. It really is 'sport for all' – no one is left out. Hosts an annual netball tournament using boarding accommodation for teams from far afield.

Music flourishes with three-quarters of pupils from year 3 playing an instrument. Plenty of performance opportunities with termly concerts and musicals, and public recitals for the two choirs; two orchestras with seniors scaling symphonic heights; string and wind ensembles. Joint production with drama each year – recently the Wizard of Oz and Bugsy Malone – though plays, sketches and nativities, as well as assembly presentations, give lots of scope for budding luvvies. Elocution competitions too.

Expressive arts thrive in well equipped, dedicated rooms with specialist art, pottery and design technology workshops and weekly scholarship classes. Textiles and cookery are included throughout the curriculum.

St Hugh's pupils get out and about on numerous curriculum enriching visits and outings. Years 5 and 7 have residential French trips and year 8 has a week's outdoor pursuits experience. Biennial hockey and rugby tours to Dublin and South Africa.

Positive reinforcement is key to rewards and sanctions, with gold points accumulating for the benefit of the pupil and their house. Not just academic achievement: effort, good behaviour and citizenship are all equally recognised. We were wowed by the Wow board displaying individual exceptional achievements. When needed, clearly defined sanctions escalate through report cards to detentions. Parents feel very well informed about their children's progress through teacher emails and regular reports.

Pupils and staff are polite, friendly and welcoming; evidence of real rapport between teachers and pupils, anecdotal comments tinged with humour and respect; no doubt that every child is known well here. Citizenship prized – and awards presented at weekly assemblies. St Hugh's Award for actions above and beyond – recently presented to one of the house captains who went home for a night to bake a cake to cheer up a young house member who had sustained a complicated broken femur on the rugby pitch. Strong house structure (named for three previous heads) with sporting, general knowledge and arts competitions and fundraising activities. Peer mentors in years 7 and 8; worry boxes discretely placed for confidential concerns. Everyone (children, teachers and parents) agrees that the food is 'fantastic', with plenty of choice.

Parents tell us that they 'love the wonderful family atmosphere' and that the children 'mix throughout the year groups and are very supportive and encouraging of each other'. One parent told us, 'I have seen older year groups, unprompted, clapping and encouraging the little ones as they walk through the dining hall to go to perform in a play, which gave them such a boost.'

Boarding: Attuned to changing needs (and a declining number of Forces children), the metamorphosis of boarding has seen children deciding to board occasionally. The place is absolutely spotless throughout.

The last word: St Hugh's turns out well rounded children who are polite and self confident. Happy children – and parents.

Shrewsbury School

The Schools, Shrewsbury, Shropshire SY3 7BA

01743 280552 | admissions@shrewsbury.org.uk | www.shrewsbury.org.uk

Ages: 13–18

Pupils: 819; sixth form: 381; Boarders: 619 full

Fees: Day £26,415 – £27,840; Boarding £38,505 – £41,520 pa

Headmaster: Since 2018, Leo Winkley, previously head of St Peter's School, York. Read theology at Lady Margaret Hall, Oxford. Taught at Ardingly College and Cheltenham Ladies' College as head of religious studies; has also been managing head at Bedales. Married to Jules, a palliative care doctor; they have three children, two at the school.

He was born into a teaching family and in fact for two years he and his father (who was head of Uppingham) were HMC heads at the same time – 'it was lovely.' Grew up as a staff child at Cranleigh School in Surrey, staying on as a boarder with his brother when his father was appointed second master of Winchester College.

A strong advocate of boarding (he has chaired the Boarding Schools' Association), he observes that, 'You have to be authentic at boarding school, because no one can stay in a role 24/7. Pupils and staff have to be themselves.' A typically thoughtful take, more humane than the usual 'boarding is character building' line that we often hear.

From what parents tell us it seems that he has brought light and air to the school; they describe him as, 'friendly, genuine, absolutely dedicated.' Pupils are no less delighted, 'He's lovely and so passionate about the school,' 'He's very positive, that sets the tone.' It is telling that he has moved his office, which used to be 'tucked away,' into the Pentagon – a many windowed ground floor room.

Says he 'loves chapel and the school's strong Christian ethos,' but is also interested in 'different faith pathways and open-minded about meaning and purpose.' Big questions that are no doubt explored in his theology and philosophy lessons with the third years.

Shrewsbury has two schools in Bangkok and one in Hong Kong. That sounds relatively manageable compared to the much larger international portfolios of near rivals Rugby and Malvern. 'All the income from these schools goes towards bursaries.' Bursaries and widening access are Mr W's particular preoccupations and while this is true for most independent school heads, we felt a strong moral conviction driving genuine and purposeful ambition in this area.

He has balanced the numbers of male and female teachers in line with the school now being fully co-ed and has made some interesting appointments including a head of adventure and a head of futures. The former gets pupils out in the Shropshire countryside, hiking and exploring as an 'antidote to these risk averse times.' The latter also leads a kind of exploring but the role is encouraging pupils to think more widely about higher education choices and careers, introducing them to options they may never have considered. It's a dynamic, personal take on careers advice, not to mention a canny way of cementing alumni involvement. At the other end of the school, year 9 pupils follow the new 'origin' curriculum, named after Old Salopian Charles Darwin's On the Origin of Species. Darwin is a fortuitous poster boy for Shrewsbury. Pale and male he may be, but like his statue (erected in 2000 but looks older) his reputation for intellectual daring, bravery and scholarship still stands.

Mr W describes his reading as 'omnivorous,' everything from the poetry of Auden and Larkin to books on art, design and leadership. His hobbies are running, walking and 'painting watercolours, sketching landscapes.' One of his watercolours was made into a Christmas card and sold to raise money for local foodbanks. He and his wife head to a cottage on the north York moors when their demanding jobs allow. And if he hadn't followed in the family tradition and become a teacher? 'I'd have been a writer, or maybe a footballer. Actually, cricket journalist, that's a perfect job.'

Charles Darwin is a fortuitous poster boy for Shrewsbury. Pale and male he may be, but like his statue, his reputation for intellectual daring, bravery and scholarship still stands

In our many years visiting schools we have rarely encountered a head so absolutely in their element as Leo Winkley seems to be at Shrewsbury. He is neither eccentric nor a maverick and his background is textbook headmaster. Nothing at all to frighten the traditionalists, and yet he is different. Establishment but with a refreshing streak of anti-establishment informality, just like his school. The Salopian ethos he describes is one of 'engagement, intellectual curiosity and dissent, mischief, responsibility to others and serious fun.' We'll borrow that last one to describe Mr W. We met him several times during the day of our visit and he was either smiling, looking on proudly or deep in conversation with pupils – often more than one at the same time. As everyone we spoke to agreed, he's the perfect fit.

Entrance: Fairly broad church, looks for potential. At 13+ from 60+ different schools, largest number from Packwood Haugh and Prestfelde. Entry mainly via CE (55 per cent required) or academic scholarship (held in the May before entry). School's own tests in English and maths for those at non-CE schools. A few join in the fourth form (year 10) if things have not worked out elsewhere but must be able to 'hit the ground running'.

Some 30 boys and 30 girls join for sixth form – a number from local state schools. School looks for able candidates who will also contribute to school life – sport, music academic, drama. Assessment weekend in Nov prior to entry – candidates can choose three or four subjects in which to be assessed, plus a reference from current school, interview, and personal statement.

Exit: About 27 per cent take a year out – Shrewsbury International School in Bangkok useful source of employment for gappies; travel scholarships available for interesting and challenging gap years. Nearly all to university, mainly

Russell Group – Exeter, UCL and Durham are most popular, followed by Newcastle, Oxford Brookes, Bristol, Edinburgh, Cardiff, Loughborough, Warwick, University of the Arts, Manchester, Birmingham, King's and Imperial. Seven to Oxbridge and 15 medics in 2021, five overseas (to USA, Canada and the Netherlands). Anyone who does not achieve at least five 6s at GCSE will be asked to leave – parents get plenty of warning if this is likely and it doesn't happen very often.

Latest results: In 2021, 76 per cent 9-7 at GCSE; 66 per cent A*/A at A level/Pre-U (87 per cent A*-B). In 2019 (the last year when exams took place), 64 per cent 9-7 at GCSE; 44 per cent A*/A at A level/ Pre-U (72 per cent A*/B).

Teaching and learning: GCSE options as expected plus computing, astronomy, classical civilisation and triple science, which most pupils do, though a small number will be entered for dual award. More takers for Spanish than French and Chinese wins out over German. Majority of results are at 9-7 with a particularly strong showing in maths, sciences, English literature and history, but lower grades are represented too – Bs and Cs (grades 5-4) are by no means unheard of. At A level and Pre-U maths is the most popular choice, followed by sciences, English, history, business, economics. History of art, computer science, classical civilisation, Latin, ancient Greek and PE are also on the menu but attract relatively few takers – as elsewhere.

The cool-sounding John Peel Music Society is run by an English teacher who introduces pupils to different musical genres, 'like thrash metal', which they then discuss

Year 9 follow the 'origin' curriculum, a non-examined programme which has been developed to 'inspire a love of learning' and gives pupils in their first year of senior school something, 'refreshing and exciting' to do after the grind of preparing for entrance exams. 'The whole curriculum has tangible links and follows big enquiry-based topics. The course also focuses on skills such as research, data analysis, communication and presentation.' It's all part of the school's 'Floreat' model of whole person education. Head has no plans to introduce the IB, 'It was created to give the education a great British school provides.' Rousing, not to say controversial words there Mr W (we hope they're not listening at Rugby!).

We spent a very interesting time hearing about this and the sixth form 'Futures' activities from their respective programme directors and were only slightly distracted by the presence in the room of Charles Darwin's actual notebook (complete with doodles), in a glass case. We're sure he would approve of the curriculum he inspired.

Covid gains include 'massive upskilling' in use of technology and upgrading of systems – Shrewsbury is a Microsoft school (somehow we thought it more of an Apple kind of place). Online learning, though school's provision generally hailed as excellent, takes a toll and this was addressed by a technology free teaching and learning week held once everybody was back in person. The aim was to focus on communication, collaboration, talking and presentation skills in the classroom, 'It was absolutely vital post-Covid and we may repeat it in the future.'

Every pupil has an academic tutor and progress is closely tracked. Online parents' evenings have proved surprisingly popular and parents appreciate being able to email individual subject teachers, 'They are very responsive.'

The 'Futures' faculty at Shrewsbury (school has faculties, not departments) connects sixth formers with a diverse network of Old Salopians who share skills and knowledge and advise about working in a wide range of fields. And it's not just for pupils. 'We have found that parents are increasingly anxious about their children's higher education and career choices. We want to educate them about the many different options out there.' This entails a greater push on non-traditional pathways like degree apprenticeships and perhaps encouragement to look at success in terms other than Oxbridge. It also introduces things such as the liberal arts degrees offered by US universities, growing in popularity with Shrewsbury's talented rowers, footballers and other pupils who are snapped up by leading institutions over the pond. The school offers tuition for SATs (American university entrance exams) and is a registered SAT centre.

The most recent addition to complete the triumvirate of Shrewsbury's academic leaders is a head of 'academic innovation' whose job it is to promote 'creativity and risk taking'. It's about innovation in teaching and learning – using creativity and research-based teaching. Apparently, 'It's not about gadgets, it's about teachers – they are the ultimate tools.' Ahem. Some of the eduspeak put us in mind of BBC satire W1A – maybe we'd breathed in a bit of that Salopian mischief the head is so keen on. We hear a lot of this kind of thing at schools and while we applaud the aims, we wonder whether theorising to the point of obscurity can lead to great teaching and learning. We think some of Shrewsbury's eclectic traditions such as termly 'Field Days' when everyone goes off campus to follow interests – from farmers' markets to art galleries to mountaineering – and prize competitions such as 'Spells' (when pupils extemporise on a short passage of literature), already do the job but without the fanfare. Most of the parents we spoke to were only vaguely aware of these initiatives, one observed that the school's culture of healthy dissent could be trusted to knock the corners off anything too high falutin.

'Bee keepers are as celebrated as first XI players here,' says head. No doubt, but it will be a while before Shrewsbury is as well known for apiary as it is for cricket and rowing

The Moser library is open from 8.30am- 9pm seven days a week and a splendid home to 40,000 books as well as classes, clubs and society meetings. Big emphasis on reading for pleasure but also developing research skills beyond Googling. The original 1916 building was remodelled in 2017 and now displays its founder Edward Moser's collection of watercolours as well as some of the very rare books from the school's archives. There's the Chained Library too, with its jaw-dropping collection of priceless books and artefacts, including Cromwell's death mask, Newton's Principia (bought by the school on first publication in 1687) and Charles Darwin's letters and notebooks.

Learning support and SEN: About 130 pupils with SEND – mainly mild dyslexia. One full- and five part-time members of staff provide support. EAL offered but pupils must be able to follow the curriculum. Pupils are assessed on arrival and those with SEND are given an individual learning plan and receive individual or small group tuition outside the teaching timetable. 'There's no one size fits all, we can accommodate all those who have met the entrance criteria.

The arts and extracurricular: First stop on our tour was the stunning Barnes Theatre, venue for ten shows a year, house plays, A level and EPQ drama projects and more besides. It's named after a former pupil who was CEO of Astra Zeneca and opened in 2020 with a roaring production of Fame and a blast of glitter cannons, 'It was the first thing we did after Covid.' Downstairs there are spacious backstage areas and workshops for set building. The large, light foyer is a versatile open-plan design, large enough to host exhibitions and receptions. Upstairs are music and dance studios – dance is big here (it's one of the sports options) with 20 classes running each week in ballet, tap and jazz. Facilities are shared with the local community – we saw children from a local primary school enjoying a dance session. Drama is a popular GCSE option and around 10 or so a year take theatre studies A level. Music A level attracts notably good numbers, occasionally tipping into double figures, and very creditable results. Regular flow of leavers head for music college, drama school or take up university choral or organ scholarships.

The music department is housed in the Maidment Building with its distinctive acoustic roof shaped like an upturned boat. Music is 'absolutely fantastic', we were told by more than one parent. There are many talented singers and musicians at the school but it's not all about being a virtuoso. All pupils have one free trial lesson on an instrument of their choice when they join with the aim of getting as many as possible participating in music at some level. On the day of our visit the school was gearing up (and we did spy costumes) for the house singing competition which was to be live-streamed to parents with a Eurovision-style commentary. Every pupil, whether or not singing is their thing, takes part and it's a highlight of the autumn term. Chapel choir sings at all school services and is a regular at Cathedral evensongs. What the school refers to as a 'homegrown' musical is devised and performed every two years and then taken to the Edinburgh Festival. Online concerts kept everyone practising and performing during lockdown. Symphonic Sundays is a project that brings together musicians from the school and local area to play together as an orchestra and work towards a concert performance.

Clubs, societies and extracurricular activities are an appropriate mix of trad and quirky, ranging from CCF (all four services, 'RAF go gliding on Long Mynd') to the cool-sounding John Peel Music Society run by an English teacher who introduces pupils to different musical genres, 'like thrash metal' which they then discuss.

Sport: 'Bee keepers are as celebrated as first XI players here' says the head. In the next breath he told us that Shrewsbury's girls' cricket team were national champions and that the school had 'invented' cross country running. No doubt all these things are true, but it will be a while before Shrewsbury is as well known for apiary as it is for cricket and rowing. Parity of sports provision for boys and girls is progressing fast with rowing, cricket, football, running and fives now co-ed and the long list of sporting Old Salopians who have gone on to represent their country is no longer exclusively male.

The Royal Shrewsbury School Hunt, known as 'hunt', is the UK's oldest running club and was founded in the early 19th century. Cross country running is still a big thing here with annual whole school events such as 'The Tucks', a three-and-a-half mile race, and a weekly one-and-a-half mile dash around the campus known as the 'Benjy' (after a former headmaster). School also has a claim to being in at the start of football – Salopians were involved in drawing up the first rules, the oldest set of which are held in the Moser Library.

The boat house, just a dash down a rough track from the main school site, is an evocative shrine to the Royal Shrewsbury School Boat Club's illustrious history as well as a formidable powerhouse containing all the technology and equipment demanded by today's elite rowers. We were shown the RP3 (row perfect) which simulates a real boat and the tank with static boats set up for sculling. Performance is tracked direct from boats via telemetry reports, 'it's all quite science-y,' said a pupil. Walls are covered in generations of crew photos and colourful, intricate charts recording boats' performance in 'bumps', or school competitions over the years. The school has so far clocked up 14 Henley Royal Regatta wins and individual rowers have gone on to national and international success, but there's plenty of competition and events for those who want to row at a less intense level. Boarding means 'there's no fight between rowing and rugby or rowing and orchestra, there's time for both,' we were told, although did we detect just a fractional eyebrow raise at this claim?

House loyalty is such that whichever house a pupil belongs to will be the best in their eyes, so the choice probably won't matter

Unusually (but v on brand for Shrewsbury), pupils are encouraged to pursue whichever sport or activity that suits them best right from the word go. Core sports include hockey, football, rugby, lacrosse, cricket but there are plenty of other options, 'You can do polo, we train just down the road, or go hiking, cycling or orienteering on the outdoor programme.' Participation, fitness and enjoyment are key and there's high quality coaching for all levels of ability. The most talented have every opportunity to excel – the school's cricket centre has produced ten professional players in the last decade – but not at the expense of the rest, 'they get the balance right,' said a parent.

Boarding: It could appear that girls do a bit better than boys on the boarding front, just because the girls' houses are newer and purpose built, but then again boys are based (on the other side of the campus) in rather grand Edwardian and in most cases, listed buildings. Renovation works have meant some boys decamping into other houses, 'not ideal', said a parent. No such thing as sporty or musical houses pupils assured us. Parents advise visiting a few and choosing on the basis of the staff, 'It's such an important relationship, you need to gel.' House loyalty is such that whichever house a pupil belongs to will be the best in their eyes, so it probably won't matter. Outdoor furniture and fire pits, currently de rigueur, seem to have been allocated to all.

The girls' house we saw was really impressive, partly down to the light, modern building, comfortable rooms and ample communal space, but mostly because of the dedicated and fun staff and genuinely happy girls we met while we were there. Nice touches like photo displays, a big jigsaw left out for everyone to complete, 'Things I'm thankful for' whiteboard and small breakout areas – a great idea. All upper sixth pupils have single rooms, lower sixth 'rotate' between double and single rooms. Small kitchen for making snacks, toast and 'lots of noodles.' Day girls number between 10 and 15 in houses of 70+, have rooms with desk, bookcase and wardrobe, or 'floordrobe' as the house mistress commented wryly on opening the door. We rather like to see a bit of teenage mess – shows pupils feel at home.

Boys' houses seem more traditional – probably because they are – visiting one was really the only time we were reminded that this was once a boys' school. What Ridgemount (the boys' house we saw) lacked in open plan space, colourful walls and motivational posters was more than made up for by a fantastic view over the river to the Wrekin, leather sofas and a basement gym (another Covid gain). A cupboard which once housed the pay phone has been converted into 'a smelly boot room.' Access to those mobile devices which made the pay phone obsolete is sensibly managed according to age and individual behaviour, 'We encourage boys to use their time wisely.' Ironically, several parents told us they had to ask house staff to give their sons a nudge to get in touch with the folks back home – maybe a Sunday night call from the payphone was a more reliable arrangement. Plenty of social activities with girls' houses – pizza, tennis, quizzes and films. There are two separate day boy houses but day girls are part of boarding houses, 'it was logical to put them in boarding houses for integration' and we heard no

Restrictions on pupils' personal technology are also appreciated: 'Getting them to hand in phones at 9pm would be beyond us'

real concern about the mix of day and boarding peers. Being a day pupil in such a full-on boarding school only makes sense if you live pretty close by.

Ethos and heritage: Shrewsbury School was founded by Edward VI in 1552 as a free grammar school for the boys of Shrewsbury and in 1868 was designated as one of England's seven public schools along with the likes of Harrow, Eton and Winchester. Girls were first admitted to the sixth form in 2008 and school became fully co-educational in 2014. In the nineteenth century the school relocated to a more spacious site on the other side of the River Severn with views over a park to its eponymous (but differently pronounced) town. The early history of the school makes for entertaining reading with accounts of disputes over staffing, involvement in the Civil War and a mass walk out by pupils protesting about food.

Main school is late 18th century, chapel is Victorian gothic and other buildings are a mix of later styles, several more recent ones designed by Old Salopian architects. Chapel services every Sunday for all but one boarding house in turn and once a week according to year group.

Around a hundred sixth formers apply to become postors (praepostors, or prefects), and a third are successful. And if the privilege of sporting a fancy waistcoat isn't reward enough for the office another perk is a bike – handy for getting to lessons on what is quite a large campus.

'If we are doing something, how can we share' is the Shrewsbury approach. Community action, widening access and charity fundraising are fixtures in most schools but here they are front and centre, much more than window dressing or Duke of Edinburgh award and personal statement tick boxes. Recent achievements include £80k raised by a whole school 30km walk over Long Mynd, pupil-led Christmas fairs netting up to £5k, ongoing support for the local foodbank (pupil volunteers and donations). Inter-house competition for charity fundraising ups the ante and everyone gets involved. School supports local and global charities including an orphanage and hospital in Malawi. And then there's The Shewsy Youth and Community Club (Shrewsbury House Youth Club) in Everton, which was set up in 1903 by a master from the school and remains a key focus for fundraising and personal involvement. The Shewsy provides after school activities, football, pool, a tuck shop, trips to Blackpool or Scotland and other support to young people in what is still a deprived area of Liverpool. Lower sixth pupils go there for a three-day stay every year and the school hosts reciprocal visits and shared residential trips. We met one pupil who had attended The Shewsy and was now at Shrewsbury on a football scholarship with plans for university in the USA. He said he had been worried about leaving home and fitting into boarding school life, but his mother had encouraged him to take the chance and he hadn't looked back.

Pastoral care, inclusivity and discipline: Pupils told us that the school's PHSE programme was 'very good' and they had lots of different people they could go to with any worries, 'and friends too.' When asked about the Everyone's Invited website several said they had 'heard of it' but we got the impression it wasn't high on their agenda. School has responded with the 'Respect Project', a holistic approach to equity, diversity and inclusion involving pupils, staff and parents, it's 'framed positively, we're asking what positive behaviour should be as well as looking at negatives.' Pupils are encouraged to speak out, indeed the head says he would welcome greater politicisation, more challenge, 'but respectfully.'

Heartfelt praise from international families for the way house parents and other staff keep them updated on their children's activities and welfare, particularly during the pandemic, 'Covid protocols have been so clear and well managed, it's meant peace of mind even though we're far away.' Likewise if pupils have friendship problems or anxieties of any kind, 'The house master or matron will phone us straight away if they have any concerns.' School also works hard to get parents involved in whole school activities such as charity fundraising, 'It's not just about making donations, we can take part in things like sponsored walks from where we are. We don't feel left out.'

Sensible rules with the emphasis on learning to self-regulate. A parent confided, 'Staff are so experienced, they've seen it all. It's the right environment for teenagers because they are kept so busy, not just during the week but at weekends too, there's no time to be idle.' Restrictions on pupils' personal technology are also appreciated, 'Getting them to hand in phones at 9pm would be beyond us.'

Everyone eats in Kingsland Hall, the rather cavernous canteen remembered (not entirely fondly) by Old Salopians who left 30 plus years ago. We're sure it's vastly improved since then – the pupil art on the walls was very impressive and food quality or quantity wasn't raised as a serious grievance among those we spoke to. 'It's okay most of the time and you can order takeaway on a Saturday night.' Getting everybody through and fed is quite an undertaking, so much so that one enterprising sixth former developed an app to monitor queues and speed things up as his EPQ project. 'Grot' (the school shop), is good for snacks. Sixth formers have the privilege of eating breakfast in their houses.

Sixth form centre, known as 'Quod', is run by a pupil committee. During the week this serves as a café and on Saturday night only it transforms into a bar (with a limit of two beers or one glass of wine). Upper sixth are allowed into town, lower sixth given the same privilege once they are deemed trustworthy.

Pupils and parents: Still plenty of loyalty with generations of the same families' sons (and now daughters) attending. Roughly 20 per cent international ('it varies'), majority of the rest live within two hours of Shrewsbury. Not a significant destination for London families – yet. Pupils we met were delightfully unselfconscious, a real mix of personalities but all polite and eager to tell us about their school, houses and teachers. Parents like the fact that their children 'don't grow up too fast' here, 'They're charmingly unsophisticated,' said one. We're not sure that's entirely true, certainly of the sixth formers, many of whom were quite as glossy as their counterparts in schools closer to the M25. Still more boys than girls, especially below the sixth form, but the school feels unquestionably co-ed, quite an achievement in a relatively short space of time.

Old Salopians pop up all over the place. Predictably lots of churchmen, scholars, diplomats and soldiers; footballers, rowers and many, many cricketers, including Warwickshire's Issy Wong. Co-founders of Private Eye Richard Ingrams, Willie Rushton and Paul Foot; artists Christopher Nevinson and Kyffin Williams; warrior poet Sir Philip Sidney; novelist Nevil Shute; Sir Michael Palin; chef and Instagram star, Tom Straker; TV presenter Nick Hancock and former MP and deputy prime minister, Michael Heseltine. Oh, and Charles Darwin of course.

Money matters: Range of Foundation awards and scholarships worth up to 50 per cent can be topped up with a bursary – testing, interviews and consultation with prep schools (and some primary schools) for talented children who can't afford fees. Academic, sports, all-rounder, drama, music, DT and arts awards offered. Sixth form Margaret Cassidy Sports Scholarship worth up to full fees for talented footballer, cricketer or oarsman, and Alex Wilson day boy scholarship also worth up to full fees, for academic and sporting excellence (we assume girls not eligible for these).

Huge drive to increase financial support, head's ambition is to see more than eight pupils per year group and over 40 pupils across the school on 'transformative bursaries' by 2030 – so that you can walk into any classroom and know that there is at least one pupil in there on a transformative bursary.

The last word: One of England's great schools. Establishment through and through but at the same time fresh, unstuffy and just a bit maverick. Does the business academically and offers so much more along the way. Big-hearted, light-hearted, creative and disruptive, Shrewsbury is a school full of spirit and optimism. Serious? Of course. Fun? Definitely.

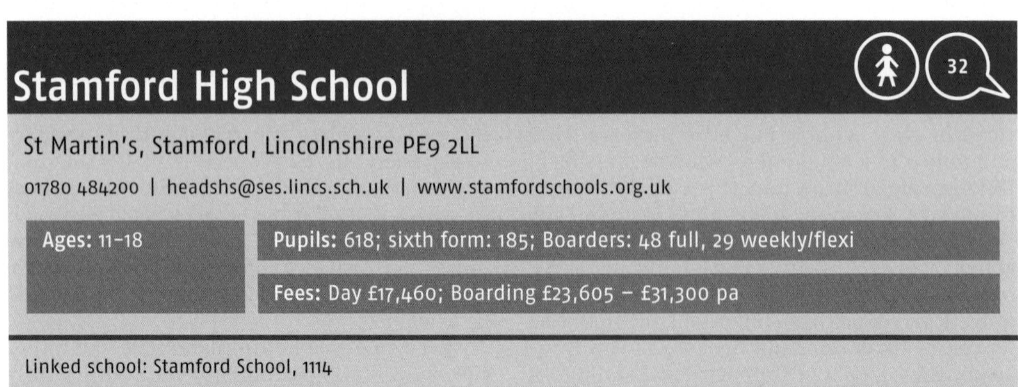

Stamford High School

32

St Martin's, Stamford, Lincolnshire PE9 2LL

01780 484200 | headshs@ses.lincs.sch.uk | www.stamfordschools.org.uk

Ages: 11–18

Pupils: 618; sixth form: 185; Boarders: 48 full, 29 weekly/flexi

Fees: Day £17,460; Boarding £23,605 – £31,300 pa

Linked school: Stamford School, 1114

Head: Since 2015, Mrs Vicky Buckman (50s). The daughter and sister of heads, she grew up in the schoolhouse of a large urban grammar school in Cheshire which she later attended. Never planned to follow in their footsteps, but in her final year at Leeds University (BSc agricultural and animal sciences) she decided teaching was for her. Her first post was at Christ's Hospital in West Sussex where, at the age of 25, she became the youngest ever housemistress. 'It was a way of life and was great fun,' she says. 'I get how girls work. I got used to championing them.' In 2006 she moved to become deputy head of City of London Freemen's School. Has always worked in the independent sector.

Comes across as friendly, approachable and positive. One of her first jobs was to move her office 'from the back of beyond' to the ground floor so she could see what was going on. Teaches biology to year 8. 'I think it's important everyone sees the head teaching and writing reports,' she says. 'And it keeps my hand in.'

When Mrs Buckman started she asked pupils to give her time to get to grips with the role and explained that, initially, they might not see that much of her. The girls say she's now out and about – eating with them in the dining hall, attending concerts and supporting sports teams on the touchline. Clearly wants to be visible. Every Wednesday from 8 to 8.30am she has Open Door when girls can go to her office and talk to her about anything on their mind. They seem to like this.

A trained ISI inspector, she is also a keen musician, gardener and swimmer and a qualified open-water scuba diver. She believes in responsible risk-taking, something that particularly resonates with girls, she says. Married to Stephen, a vicar; they have a son and daughter, both in their 20s, and a family cat called Borodin 'who is large, fluffy and ginger,' she says.

Entrance: Automatic entry from the junior school at 11. Entrance exam for outsiders and those after a scholarship.

Sixth form entrants (internal and external) schould have at least five GCSEs at grade 6.

Exit: Around 10 per cent leave after GCSEs. Nearly all sixth formers into higher education, many to Russell Group universities. Newcastle, Bristol, Leeds, Nottingham Trent, Durham, Loughborough, York, UWE and Northumbria all popular. Sprinkling to Oxbridge though none in 2021. Two medics in 2021. A few to apprenticeships.

Latest results: In 2021, 66 per cent 9-7 at GCSE; 58 per cent A*/A at A level (84 per cent A*-B). In 2019 (the last year when exams took place), 56 per cent 9-7; 24 per cent A*/A at A level (52 per cent A*-B).

Teaching and learning: The head believes if girls work hard, listen to advice and take advantage of all the opportunities, anything is possible. 'I want them to be the best they can,' she says. It is certainly no academic pressure cooker. There is pressure and competition but girls we spoke to said this comes from each other rather than teachers. As one year 11 pupil said, 'The school pushes us to work hard but teachers also encourage us to take a step back before launching ourselves completely into revision. A lot of the pressure comes from ourselves because we want to do well. Our teachers are so passionate about their subjects and that rubs off on us so that we become passionate too.'

One pupil went as far as saying, 'They inspire me. I thought I wanted to become a lawyer but I'm now thinking of becoming a teacher.'

SES uses the diamond model which involves girls and boys being taught together in the junior school, separately in their senior schools then together again in sixth form

There's mutual respect here and you get the impression that although expectations are high the school has a friendly, caring environment where girls can ask for help and support if they need it. Class sizes around 20 with no more than 14 pupils for A level subjects. Teaching staff ratio of women to men is 50:50. The head's senior leadership team comprises mostly women.

Stamford High School forms part of Stamford Endowed Schools (SES,) which also includes Stamford Nursery and Junior Schools and Stamford School (boys). SES uses the diamond model which involves girls and boys being taught together in the junior school, separately in their senior schools then together again in the sixth form.

The girls seem to like this approach. As one younger pupil pointed out, 'It's nice having boys close by but good you don't have to see them all the time.' And a sixth former added, 'It's been the perfect mix for me. Having just girls around in senior school allowed me to grow up freely. In the sixth form it's felt like starting a new school and I've enjoyed mixing with the boys.'

The head believes more and more schools will follow Stamford's example: 'We became a diamond school in 2000 but we will always be true to the founding principle that we are a single-sex school with a mixed sixth form. Girls thrive in lessons here in a way that they don't in a co-ed school. They ask questions, they are supportive of each other. Classes are more productive and teachers are teaching in one style to meet the needs of girls. Inevitably, in a co-ed school you tend to teach to the boys rather than the girls. The model works well because it offers the best of both worlds.'

Automatic entry from the junior school. Everyone else sits an entrance exam (non-verbal reasoning, maths and English). This means the ability range is quite broad. Most take 10 GCSEs including three sciences and a language. Rich choice of languages on offer: French or Spanish in year 7 then can add German or Russian in year 8. The brightest currently take French a year early then complete a short course in Spanish, although this is under review.

The five GCSEs at grade 6 boundary for progressing to the sixth form doesn't seem to be set in stone, according to some parents. We checked with the head who says each case is treated individually and there is flexibility. 'Ultimately we want our girls to achieve something for their efforts over two years,' she says. 'For some, a coursework approach may be better.'

Some 26 subjects offered at A level plus BTecs in sports science and business. Most study three A levels. Most popular and strongest performing subjects, with girls as well as boys, are biology, chemistry and maths.

Plans afoot for a pre-A level course (subject to interest) for 15-16-year-old international students – intended for those who may be too young to join year 12, and/or have a lower level of English.

Learning support and SEN: The school currently has no statemented pupils but has a watching brief on 195 girls who are on a learning needs list. These are pupils who have a below average score on a test that measures skills such as verbal reasoning, working speed and memory, mostly pupils with dyslexia. All teachers are aware of those pupils on the list and make adjustments in the classroom to meet learning needs. Extra lessons also available for those with English as an alternative language. No charge for special support although a nominal fee is added if a pupil gets extra help over lunchtime.

The arts and extracurricular: Some 176 music lessons every week with plenty of concerts (string and band), choirs and ensembles. Dance productions too. A state-of-the-art performing arts centre at Stamford School is the venue for large-scale productions, such as Grease, Les Misérables, and Hairspray. The High School has its own hall which has recently been refurbished with a portable stage and retractable seating so it can seat 600. More than 280 pupils take speech and drama and many are prepared for the LAMDA exams.

Regular visits to art galleries and exhibitions and recent overseas trips to Italy and Paris. No Saturday morning school but more than 80 voluntary activities offered such as bridge, golf and driving lessons for 16-year-olds. Thriving CCF – this year's new recruits in the army section numbered 12 boys and 31 girls. Around 40 gold DofE awards each year. Girls encouraged to volunteer and get involved in the local community through charity work.

Sport: Plenty of sport on offer including hockey, netball, cross-country, gymnastics, tennis, athletics, badminton and sailing (at nearby Rutland Water) with success at county, regional and national level. The U14 hockey team are currently county champions. We counted some 18 hockey teams and 24 netball teams so there seems lots of opportunity to have a go whatever your level, particularly lower down the school. For hockey, some age groups field three or four teams and at U12 there are five. Girls in the top teams are expected to commit to several training sessions a week and a match at the weekend, not unusual in the independent sector. As one parent pointed out, 'If you are sporty, a lot is expected of you.'

The girls we spoke to loved boarding. One said if she didn't board she wouldn't do her prep – compulsory every night in the school library

Fantastic facilities available – a £6.1m SES sports centre (up for redevelopment) complete with all mod cons including fitness suite and 25m indoor pool. These are a 20-minute walk away at the boys' school – not ideal, but part and parcel of being a town centre school. Swimming available at the junior school's pool. Stamford High School does have its own onsite sports hall, which has recently been updated to house a fitness suite.

Boarding: This is a day school with about 10 per cent boarders. Around a quarter of these are from overseas and the school is actively recruiting with recent trips to mainland China, Russia, Ukraine, Thailand, the US and Nigeria. The rest are mostly local girls with parents in the Forces; Lincolnshire is home to several airbases.

Three boarding houses. We looked at Welland (11 to 16 years) – just around the corner from the school's main site and a 10-minute walk into town. It has a homely feel with two big TV rooms complete with large sofas and beanbags. Four or five students to a dorm with sixth formers sharing two to a room. Pupils also get the use of a fully fitted kitchen where they can make toast, bake cakes and even do their own laundry if they want to. There is a lovely large garden at the back. This is also home to two rabbits, which the girls help to look after.

Girls seem to enjoy a fair amount of freedom here. They are allowed to walk into town from year 7 at different times provided they are with another pupil. The houseparent is keen to encourage independence: girls can attend sleepovers or parties at the weekend with day girls provided parents give permission. The girls we spoke to loved boarding. One said if she didn't board she wouldn't do her prep – compulsory every night in the school library.

Boarders can opt for a three, four, five or seven night package. Around 22 girls stay on a Friday evening with 16 or fewer on site on a Saturday. A new service, aimed at busy London families, offers accompanied travel to and from King's Cross on Friday evenings and Monday mornings.

Ethos and heritage: Beautiful mellow limestone buildings, quirky narrow passages and stunning riverside views. What's not to like about Stamford? The SES schools sit at the heart of this picture postcard town with its 600 listed buildings (the TV adaptation of Middlemarch was filmed here). Stamford High School was founded in 1877 as part of the legacy left the schools in the Browne's Hospital Trust. It still occupies its original site on the south side of the River Welland.

The school entrance is not very obvious. We were so busy gazing up at the town's beautiful architecture that we missed it. But then we spotted a group of pupils who were obviously from SHS. The uniform is distinctive – navy blazer, long pleated below-the-knee navy skirt, white open shirt and black shoes (no heels). It sounds old fashioned but we liked it and, more importantly, the girls we saw love it. If they do have a gripe it's to do with tying their hair back, a rule the new head introduced. Parents support the head on this one, we believe.

Once inside, the atmosphere is calm and orderly. Girls move about the corridors with a sense of purpose. No rushing around or shouting. On the walls hang pictures and short profiles of inspiring alumnae including Sarah Outen, the first woman to row solo across the Indian Ocean, and international Emmy award-winning actress Lucy Cohu.

Girls are friendly and come across as confident, cheerful and relaxed around their teachers. The ones we spoke to were certainly not snooty. A couple of spirited sixth formers were keen to take us on a tour, pointing out the newly refurbished dining hall and home economics centre recently opened by former Bake Off judge Mary Berry.

They then showed us the new ideal classrooms, an initiative being rolled out as part of the head's drive to use the latest ideas and approaches in class. Interconnecting desks are covered in interactive whiteboards enabling pupils to write on their desks, save information and use digital technology to share it with the rest of the class.

Pastoral care, inclusivity and discipline: All girls have a form tutor who is a main point of contact for both pupils and parents. One pupil said, 'Everyone is so friendly and the teachers are so nice. If you have a problem you can go to anyone.' And a parent added, 'Pastoral care is very good. I contacted the school about an eating issue and the school was fantastic.'

On the walls hang pictures and short profiles of inspiring alumnae including Sarah Outen, the first woman to row solo across the Indian Ocean

Strict rules around the use of mobile phones. Years 7 to 9 must keep them in their lockers during the school day. Boarders have to hand in all devices 15 minutes before they go to bed. Some girls have tried to get round this by having several devices but the houseparent is one step ahead of them. Main sanction is being gated.

Pupils and parents: Mostly local families from a large catchment area and from all walks of life, thanks to range of bursaries available, with lots of military families who like a modern boarding option. For day girls an extensive network of bus routes from as far afield as Newark in the north to Peterborough in the south.

Some parents looked at the grammar school option but chose SES because they like the diamond model – particularly those with sons and daughters. One parent with a daughter in year 11 and a son at Stamford School said she loved the feel of the place when she looked round. 'It has a warmth about it. My daughter was very unhappy at her junior school. It was as though I had lost her, then when she started at Stamford High School I got her back. When my son and daughter come home after the first day of term they are so excited they can't stop talking. The schools are like one big happy family.'

One parent who had two daughters at the school said it suited both girls despite them having different strengths. 'My oldest is into science while my younger daughter is more into the arts and drama. But there are opportunities for both. The school is good all round.'

Another acknowledged her daughters had been very happy and had formed incredibly strong friendships. All said that given their time again they would still choose Stamford High School.

Money matters: Bursaries means-tested and up to full fees, scholarships worth between £500-£1,000 pa. Academic, music and sports scholarships available at 11+ and art, drama and all-rounder scholarships added at 13+. Similar number in the sixth form.

The last word: Traditional atmosphere but with modern teaching methods turning out spirited, well-rounded, confident girls keen to get out there and test themselves. Former pupil Flight Lt Kirsty Moore, the first woman pilot in the Red Arrows, says, 'I arrived a shy 11-year old and seven years later I felt ready to step out into the world and make it my own.' We think plenty more will feel inspired to do the same.

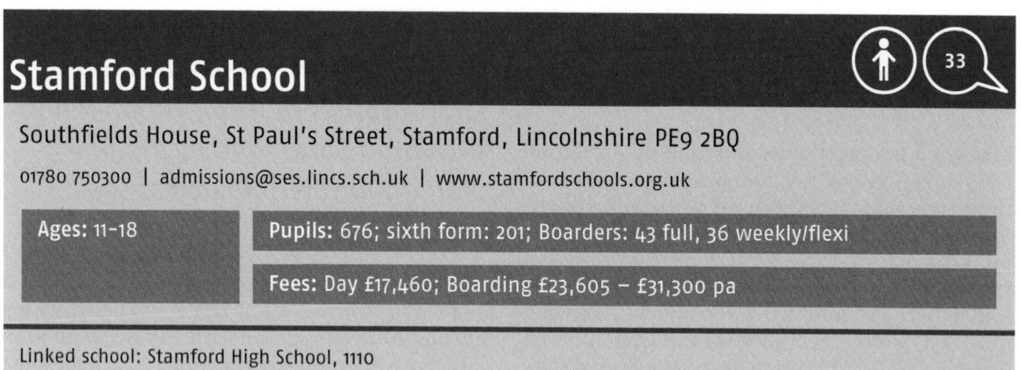

Stamford School

33

Southfields House, St Paul's Street, Stamford, Lincolnshire PE9 2BQ

01780 750300 | admissions@ses.lincs.sch.uk | www.stamfordschools.org.uk

Ages: 11-18

Pupils: 676; sixth form: 201; Boarders: 43 full, 36 weekly/flexi

Fees: Day £17,460; Boarding £23,605 – £31,300 pa

Linked school: Stamford High School, 1110

Head: Since 2016, Nick Gallop. A social and political sciences graduate from Durham, with an MSc in educational leadership and management; joined Stamford from the senior leadership team at Portsmouth Grammar School. He had been head of department at Wellington College after stints at Loughborough Grammar School and St Mary's, Walsall, so widely experienced. He knows what a good school looks like and has seen how to manage change successfully.

The Stamford Endowed Schools diamond structure (co-ed junior school, single sex teaching from 11-16 then co-ed in sixth form) means Mr Gallop works closely with the two other heads and chief exec, Will Phelan, who was the popular former head of Stamford School. The boys say he is very open and friendly, 'not at all stuffy', and has really tried to get to know them. He is enjoying the contrasts with the south and finds the community welcoming, open and modest. One of his tasks has been to reflect to the school just how first-rate it is. The boys are getting the best education they could get anywhere, he tells us.

Mr Gallop is is lively and very articulate and boys and staff tell us he is a very good listener. He has the reputation for being reliable and trustworthy as well as flexible enough to respond to new challenges. Parents enjoy talking to him at social events and appreciate his Twitter feed and use of social media. He is busy making sure everyone understands the heritage of liberal educational thinking. He has encouraged a broadening of the year 7 and 8 curriculum, introducing The Challenge, a programme designed to embed cross-curricular skills.

He articulates the values the school holds dear, defining what it means to be a good man in today's world. He wants the boys to be clear that kindness, respect and discipline are values that underpin everything at the school. He holds creativity to be a key 21st-century skill, for the technologically savvy as well as for the artist and entrepreneur, and is ensuring that the boys absorb all these elements through the opportunities Stamford offers. 'He is a forward looking head,' one parent told us.

He is a strong advocate, as you would expect, of the diamond model. It allows boys, at an age when they could drift, to organise events and take on formal caring roles such as mentoring, which in co-ed schools he has seen dominated by girls. Sport is a personal passion and he believes in the values of cooperation and belonging that team sports can bring. He is married to a teacher, has two daughters in the junior school and has been known to play the ukulele in a school rock concert.

Leaving in July 2022 to take up a new post as headmaster of Brighton College International, Bangkok.

Entrance: Main entrance at year 7, with papers including English and maths, and GL assessment reasoning tests for ability as well as attainment. 'It is only a snapshot,' says the head. The school tries to look deeper into the profile of each applicant, weighing up their all-round skills and the characteristics of determination and aspiration. About 40 per cent of boys come from the junior school, the rest from a mix of state and independent local schools.

For automatic entry into sixth form (year 12), at least five GCSE passes at grade 6 or better, including in the subjects to be studied at A level. Some 20 or 30 join from outside and they usually integrate quickly and well, a testament to the friendly atmosphere.

Although the school is oversubscribed and increasingly so, the raw score is not the only criterion – which is good news for boys who don't perform at their best in exams but would flourish in the Stamford environment. The school is interested in the aspirations of the family and whether they will buy into Stamford School values.

Exit: Some 20 per cent leave after GCSEs. About 90 per cent of sixth form leavers to university – all over the country and to read a wide range of subjects. Newcastle, Bristol, Leeds, Nottingham Trent, Durham, Loughborough, York, UWE and Northumbria recently popular. Occasional few to Oxbridge, but none in the last couple of years. Two medics in 2021. Increasing interest is being shown in apprenticeship schemes and other high-quality technical training options.

Latest results: In 2021, 62 per cent 9-7 at GCSE; 58 per cent A*/A at A level (84 per cent A*-B). In 2019 (the last year when exams took place), 39 per cent 9-7 at GCSE; 24 per cent A*/A at A level (52 per cent A*-B).

Teaching and learning: Given a fairly broad academic ability range on entry, results are good. EPQ results strong, as are BTec sport level 3, though numbers here are small at the moment. They have also introduced a BTec in business studies. There is considerable flexibility around finding the right exam course for a particular cohort of boys – 'just because we have always done that one' won't wash here. French, German, Spanish and Russian are all available, as well as Latin, and get excellent results.

There is a serious focus on the intellectual hinterland around the curriculum. Developing intellectual curiosity as well as aspiration is important. Boys have set up a school blog to voice ideas on a range of academic matters. In the sixth form, an enrichment module extends the core three A level curriculum to include, for example, options of EPQ work, Microsoft accredited courses, sports leadership, an extra AS or even survival cooking. The 1532 Club offers serious academic enrichment outside the classroom. There are debates, talks by staff, boys, old boys and visitors aimed at introducing topics not necessarily in the curriculum. It can be used as another way of sharing the fascinating EPQ projects and adding to the preparation for university.

There is a real thirst to draw on the intellectual world beyond school. A group of sixth formers had just arrived back from a cutting edge science conference in Texas

Every other Thursday afternoon, the whole school is off timetable. We happened to visit on a Thursday and enjoyed the amazing buzz. Year 7 were building a mechanical car and programming it for the climax of the afternoon, a race. Years 10 and 11 were asking questions in the middle school debating finals and year 9 were completely absorbed in a complicated trade game. It was a complete delight to observe these learning opportunities way outside of any exam curriculum.

There is a real thirst to draw on the intellectual world beyond school too. A group of sixth formers had just arrived back from a cutting edge science conference in Texas that had generated huge enthusiasm.

Everyone told us maths and sciences are strong and popular. The labs have all recently been refurbished, with space for practicals and for theoretical learning. There is a telescope and astronomy area. Some classrooms have walls are all covered in whiteboards and the tables to be written on.

Boys, particularly those who have experience of other schools, comment on how excellent the teaching is and how teachers are 'always there for you'.

Plans afoot to introduce a one-year pre-A level course (subject to interest) for 15-16-year-old international students – intended for those who may be too young to join year 12, and/or have a lower level of English.

Learning support and SEN: Learning support is taken very seriously. Most learning support assistants work within classes and this has had a very positive impact on progress. The school is constantly reviewing data to determine when to set and who will succeed best where. There is some one-to-one learning support available, normally focusing on study skills. One EAL specialist. A parent with two mildly dyslexic sons spoke appreciatively of how the school kept her very well informed of just what interventions and progress were going on.

There are occasional Saturday morning sessions as GCSEs loom. Teachers are happy to be emailed with an academic problem and respond very quickly.

The arts and extracurricular: The head is rightly proud of the large numbers of boys who sing in the various choirs; over 100 year 7 and 8s make up a non-auditioned junior choir. There are lots of ensembles to cater for different levels and tastes including rock bands. We watched a rehearsal where musicians from the boys' and girls' schools played side by side with a Royal Marines band to prepare for a joint town concert that evening. If it allowed the band leader to extol a music career in the Marines (no tuition fees, a degree, getting paid for playing your instrument), who can blame him?

All years 7 and 8 take performing arts subjects and there is a very healthy take-up of drama and theatre studies at A level and GCSE. Drama is very popular and the staff – who teach across the boys' and girls' schools – are 'fantastic', according to parents and boys. SES remains one of the largest independent examination centres for LAMDA, with around half getting distinction. Joint productions with the girls' school; rehearsals for Hairspray were in full swing when we visited. There is a big musical every three years and a number of smaller productions in between. House drama competitions ensure everyone is involved, even if not the next RSC star. There is a large performing arts centre with a theatre seating about 350 as well as smaller performance spaces.

There is a thriving joint CCF (of three sections) with a contingent of about 350 cadets – one of the oldest and largest in the UK. DofE, also joint, is taken seriously here, along with debating, astronomy club, robotics, dissection club, bush craft, chess – and on the list goes. The boys say there is no pressure to do things but they are clearly in tune with the school's message that there is something that everyone can feel passionate about. Parents like the fact that a boy doesn't have to be the best rugby player to be respected. 'They can have as quirky interests as they like,' one parent told us, 'and the others will just be very interested in them too.'

Community service features strongly. Boys help at a home for the elderly, reading and writing with visually impaired people. The staff believe it is this sort of exposure to the needs of the wider society that informs the boys' future careers just as much as their A level results.

Politics in the widest sense is a priority for the head. He encourages the boys to learn about and discuss current affairs and they are well informed and interested.

Sport: Masses of sport goes on with the aim to encourage a lifelong commitment to physicality, so there are options alongside the major sports, and the fitness suite is well used. 'It really is not just a rugby school,' parents were keen to assure us, with fresh opportunities such as water polo. At the elite end, some boys are in national development squads and the teams do well in highly competitive fixture programmes. 'But if you have a pair of boots and want to play, you will be put in a team – the D, E and F teams have lots of matches too,' we were told by both parents and staff. Once a year the whole school community takes part in the Burghley Run, a cross-country in the glorious nearby Burghley House grounds. A bonding experience, we are told, whether you love it or loathe it. The facilities, based on the Kettering Road, are up for redevelopment and expansion – including a second full-size hockey pitch and new pavilion.

Boarding: The boarding side of the school is relatively small and this creates, the boys say, a very close-knit community, though one that is thoroughly integrated with the rest of the school. Resident tutors and housemasters also teach, so there is always help at hand with homework. There are overseas boarders from a range of countries, but flexi-boarding – often taken advantage of by London families – is increasingly popular. Facilities are just right for boys and have recently been upgraded. We were particularly impressed by the very attractive large house kitchen where the boys all congregate after prep. There are billiards, snooker, computers, ping pong, lots of sport on Saturdays and trips to adventure parks, bowling, ice-skating, but also space to just be, for the boy who wants none of those things.

Overseas boarders from a range of countries, but flexi-boarding – often taken advantage of by London families – is increasingly popular

There are occasions when all the boarders across the SES schools get together. The Christmas formal meal for the seniors is one and Chinese New Year another. The boys are keen that these opportunities should increase and like the idea of building a whole school boarding identity.

Ethos and heritage: Stamford, the town, must be one of the most charming urban environments in the country, with its gracious Georgian principal streets and the river flowing through. The main school site is amazingly spacious and open considering that it is in the centre of the town. Other buildings are close by. This aids the sense that Stamford School is at the heart of Stamford itself, and the link is very important to everyone there. Some of the buildings date back to the original foundation in 1532, including a lovely chapel, and there are also modern buildings – some less attractive but serviceable, others pleasing. The boys like the fact they can stroll out into the town or do the 10-minute walk to the girls' school for some sixth form lessons.

The school also keeps close ties with old boys, quite a number of whom send their own children here. Old boys visit to share their career experiences and there's an overseas network that can be tapped into. Midnight mass on Christmas Eve in the school chapel attracts back old boys as well as staff, present pupils and a choir of 50. Old boys drop in whenever they are back in Stamford and there were a few helping with the Hairspray production.

The diamond structure is very popular. Sixth form boys said they all felt the benefits of the joint sixth form with the girls' school and increasing activities together. 'It gets a bit more serious in the sixth form, with the girls joining us,' some said, though a few told us 'they do talk a lot'. Younger boys said they would like more integration with the girls and with the juniors, but certainly don't want to have them there all the time.

The diamond structure is very popular. 'It gets a bit more serious in the sixth form, with the girls joining us,' some said, though a few told us, 'they do talk a lot'

There is a purposeful but relaxed atmosphere round the school. Parents say it is an environment where boys are respected for working hard and being clever. The boys we met were completely charming – open, modest, well grounded.

Pastoral care, inclusivity and discipline: The behaviour around school was excellent without being regimented. Boys say that most discipline issues are sorted out at an individual level with teachers spending time in one-to-one meetings. There are the usual grades of detentions, suspension and exit, but not much gets to the serious level. Boys can lose their scholarships if they don't pull their weight academically.

The assemblies in the old chapel take place in the middle of the day and boys say these are a welcome break in their busy day for quiet reflection on a broadly Christian theme. There are informal staff mentors when needed and overall we sensed a concerned, caring staff. Boys and parents clearly feel relationships are very positive.

The PSHE programme underpins the pastoral ethos. Boys felt it was relevant and forward looking, covering topics such as feminism and anorexia, as well as well-trodden internet safety topics.

Pupils and parents: It is usual in these reports to say how smart everyone looked. Well, the boys didn't, particularly – what they did look like was normal adolescent boys, which backs up the school's view that it is interested in individuals not production lines. Much more important than the odd shirt untucked was the obvious friendliness and openness of the boys. Parents comment on the healthy social mix in the school, though a few, who remember when the school could offer a lot of assisted places paid for by the local authority, are conscious that there are more well-heeled families than there used to be. Many parents are from business backgrounds, with quite a few working in London.

An extensive network of school buses brings children in from the surrounding areas – the farming villages but also Peterborough, Grantham, Newark, which widens the social mix. We talked to a number of parents who are both working to pay the fees.

Money matters: This is a value for money school. Fees are very moderate for the independent sector in this part of the world, particularly on the boarding side. Scholarships and bursaries are available. About a fifth of all families receive some bursary support

The last word: There are big hitters in the area and Stamford is well able to hold its own. Those much more expensive schools probably win out on the uniformity of excellent buildings and state-of-the-art facilities, but Stamford is determined to keep the school as accessible to as many as possible while not compromising the things that really matter in a boy's education. Parents were very aware of the richness of the opportunities and all saw the school as producing grounded individuals who can function in the real world. It is a gem of a school.

Uppingham School

High Street West, Uppingham, Rutland LE15 9QE

01572 822216 | admissions@uppingham.co.uk | www.uppingham.co.uk

Ages: 13–18

Pupils: 832; sixth form: 370; Boarders: 796 full

Fees: Day £24,450; Boarding £39,412 pa

Headmaster: Since 2016, Dr Richard Maloney MA (theology at St Andrews), PGCE (Cantab), (40s), previously the head of St Bede's Senior school. High flying career began in West Yorkshire, then head of RS at Chigwell, later head of sixth form. In 2006 he was appointed deputy head of Sutton Valence (simultaneously completing his PhD) and three years later became head of St Bede's. Charming, energetic, and lightning quick on the draw, he is clear about his priorities being 'to focus on intellectualism and the curriculum innovation that prepare pupils for the future'. Parents impressed by speed with which he has got down to the task of making necessary changes to staffing and see it as a sign of confidence: 'He seems unafraid of potential resistance to change and gets on with it.' They also comment that he is 'very good at delegating, especially to pupils; he lets them run with their own ideas.'

Not an arm's length head, he continues to have direct contact with pupils both through his own teaching commitment (A level philosophy) and lunchtime encounters with pupils in the houses. Believes fervently in the power of education and has challenged what he called the old, 'meat and two veg' style of teaching. Has managed to appoint staff to key positions ('every resignation is an opportunity') and is well on the way to his aim of 'an outward looking, diverse school, that pupils leave, wanting to know other people'. Chooses staff who 'love their subject and want to teach it. The pedagogic instinct must be there.' Not at all fixated on Oxbridge and Russell Group universities, though these are still the destination for most leavers: 'There are so many more opportunities opening up for the future; the whole educational scene is becoming far more international.' He feels 'very at ease here' and loves the sense of community, 'demonstrated each morning when the whole school gathers in the chapel and we raise the roof singing'.

Married to Tracey, who runs an educational consultancy, and they have two children, both at the school. How does he relax? 'Rarely during term. Life is full on, including at the weekends, but I spend the holidays in France and that's another pace altogether.' (Reading and wine were mentioned.) Plays rugby, cricket and football and claims to 'play several instruments, badly'. A gifted, happy head.

Entrance: Merging with Maidwell Hall in September 2022, so watch this space for more news on entrance. But for now, process starts about three years before date of entry. The system is easy to navigate with plenty of advice and information offered at each stage. Most join at 13+ but a significant number join at 16+, often from all-girls schools.

There is pre-testing at 11 (year 7) with a paper in English and an online reasoning test together with an interview and references from current school. Conditional places are offered at this stage. A further test in year 8, when pupils sit Common Entrance (55 per cent average pass mark) or the school's own exam, consisting of maths and English with a further interview.

At sixth form level, there is a six GCSE at grade 6 minimum requirement for everyone but very few existing pupils don't make the cut. For those coming from elsewhere there are scholarship and non-scholarship exams, plus two interviews – a house and an academic one.

Exit: Apart from a very few post-GCSE leavers, the great majority leave at 18 for university. Some to Oxbridge each year (eight in 2021) with the majority going to the likes of Durham, Exeter, Edinburgh, Newcastle, UCL, KCL and Bristol. Over 10 to study overseas in 2021, including Cornell and NYU. A handful study drama and art but more common subjects include history, law, international relations and – for 20 per cent – sciences. Degree apprenticeships are now very much included in the range of possibilities and careers advice is wide ranging, though UCAS applications receive the attention they need. House as well as subject staff are involved in the process.

Latest results: In 2021, 85 per cent 9-7 at GCSE; 85 per cent A*/A at A levels/Pre-U (97 per cent A*-B). In 2019 (the last year when exams took place), 69 per cent 9-7 at GCSE; 45 per cent A*/A at A levels/ Pre-U (73 per cent A*-B).

Teaching and learning: Consistently high levels of achievement at GCSE and A level are more a consequence of the broad education and excellent teaching on offer than overt grade chasing. Emphasis is on offering a balanced approach: 'Exams matter, but so does enjoying learning for its own sake, as that is what stays with us through life.' Parents approve, one mentioning that 'we wanted to avoid the relentless pressure of the London and Cambridge day schools,' while another said, 'Being happy matters, you learn better as well.' Touché.

Neither sciences nor arts predominate, there is strength right across the curriculum and pupils are encouraged to select contrasting A levels from both sides of the so-called divide (easy, there are 29 subjects to choose from). Setting for maths, sciences and languages. Pupils learn three modern languages (French, German and Spanish) during their first year and then make a selection; all take at least one language through to GCSE unless English is an additional language in which case the time is used for extra support instead. At A level the 'core' subjects remain popular but Latin, philosophy and music have plenty of takers. Art and design have outstanding facilities (Leonardo building) and pupils regularly go on to study at various august institutions. Similarly for drama. 'We really can do maths, Latin and art if we want,' we were told and where four A levels are taken, one at least will be in a contrasting subject.

EPQ study is timetabled for all lower sixth. Sixth formers appreciate being allowed 'to organise our week for ourselves. We aren't pigeon-holed and it gives us the chance to learn ways of working independently.' The school library is staffed and open until 9pm: 'I love working there after supper. It is quiet and I find it easier to concentrate.' The average class size is 17 before GCSE and around 10 for A levels.

Learning support and SEN: There is support for those with the mild learning difficulties found in a selective school, or who have difficulties with English (extra charge).

The arts and extracurricular: All-round artistic endeavour is encouraged throughout the school. Several major productions staged each year and 'you don't have to be the next Olivia Colman to have a part'. There are opportunities to learn stage management as well as to act and pupils say, 'It's a really good way to get to know people when you are new.' Some highly talented pupils do move on to drama schools and there is an atmosphere of support from their friends, 'who all come and watch us', rather than bitter rivalry.

The musical education on offer is deservedly renowned. With a department of over 40 staff, many professionally successful in their own right, there is provision for an incredible range of abilities on every imaginable instrument, as well as top notch teachers for piano and organ. Pupils study right up to diploma level and many go on to full-time careers in music. There is a plethora of choirs, all levels catered for, orchestras, ensembles, quartets, you name it, it is all going on. Lots of opportunity for performers to gain confidence with informal recitals as well as the big occasions. All tactfully handled: 'They have the sense not to stick a beginner next to someone at diploma stage.' Visiting musicians hold masterclasses and the selective choirs and orchestras have a programme of tours at home and abroad. Everyone speaks with fondness of the school's congregational singing in chapel led by the choirs: 'We all love it, it's a great start to the day. I think I will miss it more than anything when I leave.' Spectacular buildings for teaching, performing and practising. Music technology, recording studios and a radio station encourage those not following more classical traditions. The school's Battle of the Bands showcases talent and is extremely popular.

Everyone speaks with fondness of the congregational singing in chapel led by the choirs: 'I think I will miss it more than anything when I leave'

Art and design, taught in the Leonardo building, is also popular, with several pupils each year going on to study full-time at a variety of institutions. Everyone benefits from the chance to learn from gifted staff, even those who feel that they have few artistic skills. 'We believe in building up a pupil's confidence to give things a go, not putting them off trying.'

All can do CCF and DofE until sixth form when there are other possibilities for community service. Pupils organise drama workshops, sports coaching, musical recitals and masterclasses, including Latin, for local schools, visit elderly people or take part in various overseas aid projects. 'Our pupils know they are fortunate and learning to give something back is part of what we are about as a community.'

Sport: As the timetabled week includes three sessions of sport for everyone, Saturday matches plus the continual walking to and fro between lessons and houses, it's not surprising that pupils are super fit. Playing fields, courts and sport and fitness centres are of outstanding quality and a recently built pavilion incorporates stunning space for entertaining spectators during matches and 'for pilates and yoga which we can choose in the sixth form instead of team games'. Most continue to enjoy team sports, if only at house level: 'I am not the most sporty but I still enjoy house netball.' The first three years play all the usual team sports, plus fives and cricket (boys and girls). The large number of teams in all categories give plenty of chance for match play and 'sport is definitely not just for the super athletes,' we were told.

Boarding: Full boarding for all but a handful of pupils (mainly either very local and/or staff offspring) so weekends include the traditional aspects of Saturday morning school followed by matches, Sunday chapel and a roast lunch. The introduction of exeat weekends, three per year, is a recent innovation and welcomed on all sides: 'They live life at full tilt, weekends included, so the home break means they have a chance to not do much and recharge,' said one mother, and pupils agree. Boarding houses are scattered throughout the town, six for girls, including two specifically for pupils joining in the sixth form, and nine for boys. Around 60 in a house, vertically grouped, allowing bonds to be extended between different ages and leadership for those at the top end. Everyone spoke of the strong friendships forged and the benefits of learning to get along with 'whoever you happen to find yourself with'. Skills for life, and parents are very aware of it: 'We chose the school because we wanted proper boarding, not somewhere that empties on Saturday afternoons.' House parents live on the premises, together with two matrons and some resident tutors. All staff eat lunch in houses on a rotational basis so pupils have contact with staff they don't necessarily know already. Meals are relatively formal, pupils sitting at a designated table, passing the water jug and waiting for people to finish. Sunday breakfast is later and 'we have it in our pyjamas'.

Houses are a mixture of the substantial, rather grand older buildings, complete with original sweeping staircases, and modern, purpose-built houses. Parents can look round several and the school makes the decision about which house pupils are placed in, taking into account parents' views. Siblings can choose whether to join older brothers or sisters in the same house. The houseparent is responsible on a day-to-day basis for their pupils and their happiness. Parents have free access and houses produce blogs and regular items on other social media to keep parents up to date with various house happenings. Pupils all have a study – teeny weeny cell-sized spaces but they are just for them and they are allowed to decorate walls with family photographs or posters and keep their tuck box and treasures there. Bedrooms are mostly for three or four sharing, with own rooms (many en suite) in the sixth form. Houseparents decide who sleeps where and beds and rooms are regularly swapped about to help prevent 'dorm' issues arising. 'They grumble about moving sometimes,' said one houseparent, 'but they understand the reason behind it.'

Ethos and heritage: An Elizabethan foundation, school and town have been happily integrated for over 400 years. Set in rolling countryside, close to Rutland Water, Uppingham benefits from being a country school but one that is incredibly easy to get to from all parts of the country. The eponymous town is small and charming, complete with marketplace, a few independent shops and various hostelries.

Everyone spoke of the strong friendships forged by boarding and the benefits of learning to get along with 'whoever you happen to find yourself with'

The school has grown and extensive building programmes in the past twenty years have transformed the spaces it occupies. 'We love the different sorts of buildings, nothing looks the same,' say pupils and it is true. Ancient archways, cobbled courtyards and mullioned windows happily mix with the new builds, many of exceptional design in their own right, notably the science and music buildings and the Leonardo Centre. Pupils move constantly about the town, and the expression 'campus' is never used by staff or pupils, who say, 'We are all mixed up together, we are part of the town.' Chapel is at the heart of the school and an extension (very 60s design) enables the whole school to be together at the start of the day, 'singing our heads off; it is the best start to the day,' we were told by pupils.

Being a full boarding school means 'total immersion during term time,' say parents, pupils and staff. Idle moments are rare, even at weekends, as pupils rush from playing fields to houses to play rehearsals, music or other activity, usually in the company of others. Parents comment, 'They are kept really busy, in the company of

friends, which is perfect. We are talking about teenagers!'

Alumni include novelist Mark Haddon (The Curious Incident of the Dog in the Night-Time), Rick Stein, Stephen Fry, Boris Karloff and Ralph Freeman, the civil engineer who designed the Humber suspension bridge (and whose father designed the Sydney Harbour bridge).

Pastoral care, inclusivity and discipline: Praise is heaped on the school's care for pupils: 'You cannot beat it,' said a parent. 'We are kept in the picture, communication is brilliant.' 'We are a family school, brothers and sisters are welcomed at matches and events. My sister was invited to join in with the choir once when she was visiting. There is a carefully structured programme for new pupils (year 9) with assigned mentors in houses. 'The house bond is so important. It really is a home from home while they are there', say parents. 'Matrons, especially in the boys' houses, are very maternal. They invite the boys in for hot chocolate, give them attention and time when they need it.' Close friendships are forged. 'The peer group is all important,' one mother commented. 'You make all these choices and worry about which school is best but with good friends there is every chance they will be fine.' Subject staff know the pupils really well: 'It is the great benefit of boarding, you know the teachers away from the classroom.' Toddler-sized boots and coats in the cloakroom act as a reminder that houses are homes for staff families as well as pupils.

Being a full boarding school means 'total immersion during term time'. Idle moments are rare as pupils rush from playing fields to houses to play rehearsals or other activities

A local GP runs a daily surgery in the medical centre and a variety of specialists, psychologists and counsellors are available for pupils when needed. House staff are aware that pupils sometimes just 'feel a bit low and need a listening ear and we can provide that'. Older pupils also undertake training in listening skills and there is widespread acceptance of the need for openness and honesty about feelings. A sad event in the recent past 'really showed the school at its best; things were handled so sensitively and help of all sorts was on offer,' said one mother. Boarding life does encourage self-confidence and independence but the days of expecting pupils to grin and bear it are long gone. 'We try to deal with issues as they arise and before things get serious,' said a housemaster, and an older pupil said, 'We all know someone to turn to if we get stuck.' We heard several mentions by pupils of 'feeling trusted; sometimes we get it wrong but we learn from it.'

The Life Skills programme covers the usual topics of concern to this age group and self-help techniques are taught for dealing with exam stress and friendship difficulties: 'They know they are dealing with teenagers,' said a parent. There are clear rules and sanctions on bullying, smoking, drugs and alcohol, the shorthand version being three strikes and you are out, but 'We do take circumstances into account.' Bottles of spirits are taken more seriously than a few cans of beer. Smoking is 'pretty minimal, though you never get rid of it completely. Over 18s are allowed to use the school bar or visit a local pub once in a while and parents approve: 'They've got to be ready for life when they leave.'

Pupils and parents: The school's good road and rail connections mean pupils come from all over the country, including Scotland, with the registrar claiming, 'Edinburgh is just four hours away.' Majority however hail from the home counties, Suffolk and prosperous areas of the Midlands and Yorkshire. 'We were looking for a school within two hours that suited all three children, one keen on drama and running, one on textiles and one who played the bagpipes!' Around 20 per cent are from overseas and a great variety of nationalities are represented, which parents like. They also rate the welcome given 'to the whole family. It's as if we have all joined the school,' said a mother, and an older pupil mentioned how much her parents enjoyed visiting the school and Uppingham itself: 'It will be so sad for them when I leave!' Most parents are from the professional and business classes, some are established boarding families, but there are plenty of first time buyers in the mix. Parents comment, 'We wanted a school away from the London pressure cooker,' and 'The school is quite low-key, not a pushy place.' The pupils themselves have a confident attractive manner, very articulate, but down to earth: 'We know we are lucky to be here, we just want to make the most of it.' Several times we heard the comments, 'We want to give something back' or 'The school encourages us to think of being part of a bigger community'. The ethos of service really seems to be taken seriously. Parents feel the school prepares the pupils well for the world they will be going to live in. 'They turn out humble, really nice people who know how to join in and get on with others.'

Parents also rate the welcome given 'to the whole family. It's as if we have all joined the school,' said a mother

Money matters: Scholarships are given at 13+ and 16+ in science, music, art, design and technology, sports, drama and the Thring award for an all-rounder. Scholarships are modest, around five per cent of fees, but bursarial support is available to make the necessary top-up, if necessary up to 100 per cent of fees. The school is committed to broadening access and the size of bursary offered is dependent on the financial and other pertinent circumstances of the applicant. Bursarial awards are made on the basis of funds available, with those in receipt of a scholarship at the front of the queue for help. There is a drive to increase the endowment and make more awards possible.

The last word: Offers an intellectually rigorous and adaptable education with outstandingly good provision for music, art and drama. Though rural, Uppingham is not isolated and pupils benefit from the excellent relations the school and town enjoy. Surroundings are idyllic, opportunities to learn, discover, and create abound and five years will pass in a flash if you dive in and enjoy all that's on offer. Pupils are modest, aware of their good fortune and are well prepared to move on to the next stage in their lives.

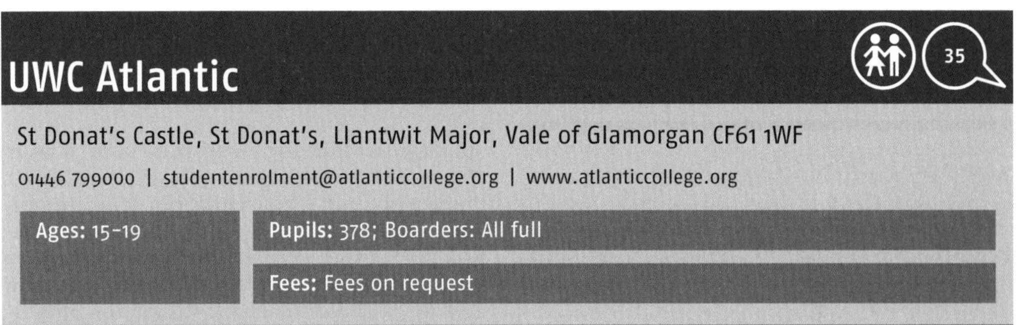

UWC Atlantic

35

St Donat's Castle, St Donat's, Llantwit Major, Vale of Glamorgan CF61 1WF

01446 799000 | studentenrolment@atlanticcollege.org | www.atlanticcollege.org

Ages: 15–19

Pupils: 378; Boarders: All full

Fees: Fees on request

Principal: Since September 2021, Naheed Bardai (30s). Born and raised in Canada, he was previously head of upper school at Upper Canada College in Toronto. Prior to that, he spent 10 years (the final three as senior school principal) at the Aga Khan Academy in Mombasa, Kenya, an educational organisation with values so similar to UWC they could almost be cousins. As befits the role, his global experiences don't stop there – he spent a year travelling in Thailand and Asia after doing a business degree at Western University, Ontario, followed by a stint in Sydney as a management consultant. Then it was back to Toronto as head of marketing for a business start-up before doing a BEd at the University of British Columbia: 'I realised education is the baseline of everything, that it is education that ultimately shapes lives.' The ink must have still been wet from his final assignment when he seamlessly moved into his master's in comparative education. 'As a great mentor told me during my BEd, the magnitude on your shoulders that's involved in working in education requires more than a PGCE equivalent.'

There's excitement in the Atlantic air around this appointment – a sense that this is the man who will give back the power to the student committees, improve communications and take mental health more seriously, to name a few. We found him eloquent, erudite and persuasive, especially when he gets going on peace and sustainability, which sit at the core of UWC's values. 'There can be absolutely nothing more noble to work towards,' he smiled, adding ('not too loftily, I hope') that he sees his role as the 'moral compass of the community'. Superlatives aplenty from students, who describe him 'incredible' and 'inspirational'. Parents like his 'informal approach', 'youthfulness' and 'engagement with students'. 'He's slightly reserved but kind and empathetic – just what the school needs,' mused one.

He arrived under the shroud of Covid which, feel some parents, the school has been 'ridiculously over-the-top about,' with rules around bubbles, isolation periods and use of masks 'far stricter and longer-lasting than government guidelines' – perhaps not the best managed either, with one mother telling how her child was left without food for 24 hours when in isolation.

Lives smack, bang in the middle of the sprawling site with his partner and their two young children – 'You see them about, they're so sweet,' said a student. Enjoys music, being outdoors (especially hiking), time with family and 'a nice dinner party' – the ultimate conversationalist, no doubt. Orientalism by Edward Said is his current bedside read.

Entrance: Brace yourself – the labyrinth admissions process requires Odysseus-levels of persistence and admin headaches as you've never known them. All comes from the fact that (a) the world is its catchment area (90 nationalities currently) and (b) most students apply for UWC not an individual college (meaning they could be sent to any one of the 18 colleges globally). One parent felt it's also because 'the demands of a UWC education are so huge that the application process aims to sift out those who won't handle it – no bad thing in my view.' Highly competitive too, with seven to eight applications per place and just 20 available for UK nationals.

Not for the faint of heart. An exceptionally demanding curriculum covering emotional, intellectual and practical terrain that many adults would find hard going

Two main pathways. By far the most popular (used by 90 per cent) is via one of the 150+ UWC national committees made up of alumni (students and staff) volunteers. After an initial burst of form filling, essay writing, reference collecting and interviews, shortlisted participants are invited to one-to-three days of observed activities in their home country. No specific GCSE (or equivalent) requirements – 'that would be missing the point of UWC which is about attracting motivated students who are passionate about making a difference in the world' – but let's just say academic competency won't go amiss given the rigours of the IB diploma. Applicants are expected to provide evidence of worthy pursuits – one recent successful applicant had helped to fundraise for new kitchen equipment in the poorest part of their community, while another worked on a solar powered device to charge a mobile phone. Final decision communicated around February, when you also find out if you qualify for support with fees and whether it is in fact UWC Atlantic you're heading off to or another of their global colleges altogether. Those that only have eyes for Atlantic are better off applying via the second route of the global selection programme – done through the UWC international website and marginally less complicated but you'll have to get past front-of house (a feat in itself) and pay full whack fees, no ifs no buts.

Exit: US universities snap up 40 per cent of students (offering $30m worth of scholarships most years), with US admissions tutors zooming in early like dealers at a jumble sale before the doors open to the general punters. Recent destinations include Harvard, Cambridge, Brown, MIT, Yale, Princeton, UCL, Sherbrooke and Cornell. Thirty per cent head off to UK universities, mainly Russell Group (three to Oxbridge in 2021), then it's up to 10 per cent or so to Netherlands and Canada and the rest dotted across the globe. Around 20 students a year take a gap year or go off to complete national service. Courses many and various. Around 70 per cent end up in humanitarian-linked careers, though more are starting to lean towards the sciences.

Latest results: School won't publish results.

Teaching and learning: Not for the faint of heart. The academic component of the IB – no picnic at the best of times – is squeezed into five mornings a week (8am-1pm) while afternoons are given over to compulsory co-curricular activities on Tuesday, Wednesday and Thursday afternoons and community building time (committees) on Monday and Friday afternoons. Each of these afternoons (much of it self-taught – 'You could go a whole afternoon without seeing a staff member in some cases,' said one student) focuses on the redemptive powers of active, selfless participation that add to the IB's magnificent seven and tick off its creativity, activity and service component en route. Students may focus on the great outdoors (eg by learning marine search and rescue skills), social justice (eg working at a refugee centre in Cardiff or in local hospitals or primary schools), global matters (eg organising peace events) or sustainability (eg working out ways to shrink the college's carbon footprint) – among others. All feeds back into the morning lessons alongside students' direct (and diverse) life experiences.

This is education the immersive way, real world, practical applications dovetailing with the academics. 'Besides making it more stimulating, it makes it more real,' felt a student. One spoke of the 'incredible opportunity of having the input of a Syrian refugee when learning about that part of the world'; another was in awe that she'd been able to invite refugees on campus for a week – 'that's got to be unique for a sixth form'. Most recently, the so-called changemaker curriculum aims to take this interdisciplinary aspect one step further still by bringing about actual change to society. A recent example included students measuring wave patterns in the Bristol Channel and sharing data with coastal authorities with a view to harnessing wave energy in the longer term.

Teachers are as won over by the UWC philosophy as the students, with few moving back to conventional posts. Students love this about them and say this, plus first-name terms and mutual respect, quickly builds rapport. Parents praise teachers for 'going the extra mile', particularly in the run up to IB exams, when one-to-ones often become the norm. Humanities teaching gets the biggest thumbs-up from students and while languages doesn't exactly get thumbs down some feel 'it could be better'. No shortage of breadth, though, with nine options and a further 21, including Khmer, Mongolian and Welsh, as self-taught subjects.

In short, an exceptionally demanding curriculum covering emotional, intellectual and practical terrain that many adults would find hard going. It's certainly not for those with league-leaping performance as sole aspiration. In fact, college lips are firmly sealed on IB results – principal claims it's because success is measured by the effect the students have on the world, though parents find it frustrating – 'It's part of the whole picture you need to consider when applying – why hide it?' We're with the parents on this one too.

Learning support and SEN: English is a second language for vast majority of students, though very few need EAL support since a good grasp of English is a prerequisite for entry. SEN screening during the recruitment process means learning needs (mostly mild dyslexia, autism and ADHD) are picked up early, with both classroom support and one-to-ones available at no extra cost. Campus is surprisingly wheelchair accessible given that it's mainly a castle.

The arts and extracurricular: Derring-do comes with the territory and there's very little these students will say no to trying, whether that's consorting with top scientists and politicians at a climate change summit or learning how to build a boat. All comes down to founder Kurt Hahn's belief that fallibility is an essential part of the learning process – the acquisition of skills in graceful failure, explained a student, are as important as trappings of success.

Of all the extracurricular on offer (though it's so core to the UWC principles that it feels odd to even call it that), outdoor pursuits are most popular – mainly split into aquatic activities such as kayaking, surfing and lifeboat training etc and land-based pursuits such as mountain walking, navigation, emergency first aid and climbing (Brecon Beacons are just a few miles inland). Debating is a favourite here too, with the three to four student-led conferences among the calendar highlights of the year. Pitched and voted on the previous academic year, most recent topics were Fem Com (feminism), Challenges in the Indian Subcontinent and Queer Issues and Challenges.

While physical activity is compulsory, organised sport isn't and what happens and whether it happens at all is largely down to students

As for music, drama and art, it's all available but not compulsory and mostly comes down to supply and demand. So no college orchestra or large-scale performances but there was – because of the current cohort's interest – a string quartet and an a capella group when we visited. Certainly, there's no shortage of tuition or facilities, with peripatetic music teachers available on request and a very whizzy recording studio. Ditto for drama – that is, you can expect good facilities including an atmospheric theatre, but performances (usually a couple a year) tend to be student led. Art studio disappointingly empty on the day we visited but we were assured everything from photography to ceramics to multi-media is available and regularly features as part of large-scale projects eg a recent pop-up museum on police brutality.

Sport: While physical activity is compulsory, organised sport isn't and what happens and whether it happens at all is largely down to students. There is no head of sport and no pitches groaning with glory-seeking team endeavours. 'Not an obvious choice for top athletes or anyone who wants a very structured sports programme,' confirmed a student. But basketball, football, rugby and swimming are up for grabs if is the interest is there and gym nuts will be suitably impressed with the iron-pumping facilities. There's a decent sports hall too and the pool – with backdrop of castle grounds one way and sea the other – knocks the socks off many spa pool settings.

Boarding: Inner core of steel probably helps, given policy of full boarding only and picking roommates for differences, the more apparently irreconcilable the better. Israelis share dorms with Palestinians; future royalty (quite a few recently) with refugees. The busy schedule, well-liked houseparents and trained boarding mentors all help keep homesickness at bay – though one parent worried that the latter can be emotionally draining for the mentors themselves.

Former students are to be found in some of the most powerful organisations and administrations in the world, from the Chinese and US governments to top banks

Eight boarding houses – six old and two new, dotted round the campus – are home to just under 50 students each, usually girls on top floors and boys on the bottom. Facilities are simple but spacious, with areas to hang out, work and cook in – plus to do laundry (students do their own). Dorms – with four students apiece – a mixture of tidy, messy and really messy. Some single showers, others communal – yikes.

Evenings are as jam packed as the daytimes, with countless student councils chewing the fat, finding solutions or running events. The week we visited, the sustainability council had been working out how to reduce the amount of parcels ordered online (to save on both delivery and packaging), the peace council was debating the current situation in Afghanistan and the wellbeing council had been discussing how student mental health could be improved. On Friday nights, there's 'soc' (a weekly disco with 'light teacher presence') and 'hideout' (for those who prefer the idea of a quiet board game or table tennis). Weekends are freer, we heard – time to crash, we imagine, although in non-Covid times there's also the tempting opportunity to head off to the local pub.

Ethos and heritage: In the 1960s, while hippies might have given peace a chance by putting flowers in gun barrels, educationalist Kurt Hahn's solution to unify a world riven by the Cold War and ward off what he saw as the physical and moral decline of the young was to found a school (two, if you count Gordonstoun which he set up in the 1930s), many more if you count schools in the international organisation he started (Round Square). The aim was to create a harmonious blend of nations and cultures, pairing opposites of every sort, oppressors and oppressed, poor and rich, who by living and studying together would develop shared outlook and common purpose (though it wasn't until 1967 that they got round to admitting girls). The college remains a one-off in the UK and was the first of what is now an 18-strong United World Colleges international movement. Its niche status and relatively low profile (even among heads, let alone the public) is, however, in inverse proportion to behind the scenes clout. Former students are to be found in some of the most powerful organisations and political administrations in the world, from the Chinese and US governments to top banks; an under the radar alternative to conventional old boys' (and girls') networks.

There aren't too many schools we visit that are based in an 800-year-old castle by the sea and, yes, it's as striking as it sounds apart from the tatty reception hut (front of house gloss is clearly not part of the UWC ethos). Drive under the barrier, though, and you get what you came for: ancient arches, heavy oak doorways and cobbled pathways – all with the backdrop of the mighty ocean. No wonder it's as popular with production companies and wedding planners as students.

In addition to as many corkscrewing staircases as you can shake a medieval flail at, castle interior features terrific library and grand dining hall (although food is a longstanding complaint – 'annoying as you want to know, as a parent, that they are eating well,' said one who said she wasn't alone in 'sending nutritional supplements to help'). Humanities lessons compete with hard-to-improve vistas through arrow slits to wooded hills beyond, while art, music and drama are located in the converted stables. Other subjects are taught in 1970s teaching blocks – science and maths in crumbliest and flakiest – 'science equipment is very outdated,' said one student; we concur.

Lack of uniform results in jeans and hoodies for most and this – together with the campus layout and first-name terms with teachers – gives a university vibe. American style two-term structure follows the beat of the IB drum.

Pastoral care, inclusivity and discipline: Mollycoddling parents, be warned – students are treated as adults, with 'authentic responsibility' an oft repeated phrase. Nobody wakes them up or cracks the whip if they don't turn up to lessons or activities. That's not to say that attendance isn't taken seriously – and the college does give talks on good sleep habits and even the odd nudge where necessary – but it all comes back to the Hahn philosophy of adolescents learning by seeing the results of their own actions. While big issues go to the wire, there are minimal rules elsewhere, nous and good sense taken as read. Seems, for the most part, to do the trick. 'But a few students can't hack it and leave quite early on – and you do get the odd ones excluded for drugs,' confided a student.

A tutor system, house mentor, two full-time counsellors, nursing staff and access to doctors keep things ticking over pastorally and medically though there is a strong feeling among students and parents that they could do more for serious mental health concerns – 'When you consider some of the backgrounds these students have come from, the pastoral care should be more, not less, robust than your typical British boarding school, yet the answer seems to be just to send students home who can't manage mentally,' said one parent.

High level of student involvement in nuts and bolts of college operations, with open book policy on everything from finances to rebuilding ensuring that student voice isn't merely heard but a force to be reckoned with. Ranges from spontaneous orations in assembly on whatever issues take their fancy to meetings dedicated to indignation over any perceived high-handedness.

Huge anti-racism focus, with students engaging in deep exploration of root causes and thought-provoking campaigns via multiple mediums; big LGBT movement too. Feminism, Me Too, Everyone's Invited – all these are debated, presented on and solutions are sought.

Pupils and parents: Ethnically, 40 per cent European, 30 per cent Asian, 10 per cent North American, 10 per cent South American and 10 per cent African. Socio-economically, encompasses a spectrum far wider than most of us ever experience. Two-thirds female. Not a shrinking violet among them, though this opinionated bunch aren't in-your-face either. Effortlessly idealistic and candid, they are among the most self-assured and impressive bunch of students we've ever met. Greta Thunberg, eat your heart out. 'Forget it if your child isn't intrinsically motivated, academically sound and a multitasker – or they'll go nuts!' cautioned one parent. Not the place for the materialistic either – the (just under half of) families that pay full whack will even sometimes fund not only their own child but others' too. Philanthropy is a way of life among alumni, many of whom donate generously, as well as coming back to give lectures, help with committees and careers guidance and muck in with things like sorting out the gardens and redecorating rooms. Many of the great and the good from kings and queens to CEOs of multi-billion-pound corporations also support the UWC cause vocally and financially, endorsements from everyone from Nelson Mandela to Queen Noor of Jordan having long set the tone.

Money matters: Admissions process supported by large fundraising and development department working overtime to bring in the dosh – raises £3m in philanthropy a year. Means you don't have to splash the cash to stand a chance, with a whopping 30 per cent of students on fully funded places (a potential godsend with annual fees of £37,500 per year); overall, 51 per cent of students on some sort of financial support from 15 per cent upwards. All very impressive, but we do think that they could invest just a little into paying someone to answer the phone more than they do.

The last word: Isolated this college may be, but its perspective is anything but. Among the most – if not the most – outward-looking school we've come across, it offers a unique, transformative education with a mind-boggling diversity of students and breadth of enrichment. Once a glorious experiment – and still surprisingly unknown – it provides an education as remarkable and full-on as the gutsy, impassioned students it attracts. But it won't suit most and there's plenty of room for improvement, though perhaps not for long under bold new leadership.

Warwick School

36

Myton Road, Warwick CV34 6PP

01926 776400 | admissions@warwickschool.org | www.warwickschool.org

Ages: 7–18

Pupils: 1137; sixth form: 283; Boarders: 56 full

Fees: Day £12,282 – £14,337; Boarding £32,256 – £34,575 pa

Head Master: Since June 2020, James Barker, an Old Warwickian and philosophy graduate who began his teaching career at Banbury School before returning to his alma mater for the first time in 2004. He was upper master (head of sixth form) at Abingdon and the assistant head co-curricular at the Royal Grammar School in Worcester before re-joining Warwick as deputy head in 2015, moving to senior deputy head in 2018.

As teacher and former pupil Mr Barker has had a 30-year association with Warwick and his commitment to the school and its pupils is immediately apparent. His academic specialisms are theology and philosophy and he is a firm believer that schools should inspire intellectual curiosity and equip pupils to think critically and independently. The school's curriculum places an increasing influence on these skills alongside an ongoing drive for excellence in teaching and learning.

Having led and managed co-curricular activities in his previous posts, this aspect of Warwick's provision is one in which he takes a particular interest. He has even gone so far as to sign himself up for the school's music scheme which requires every pupil to learn an instrument during year 7. He has also played a key role in developing the voluntary service pathway that forms part of every pupil's experience, 'so boys leave Warwick School as well-rounded young men who can play a positive role in the world'.

Mr Barker represented his university on the rugby field while studying in Cardiff, and still has a firm interest in sport.

Junior head: Since 2016, Andrew Hymer (50s), formerly head at Wolverhampton Grammar Junior School which he helped to set up. Before that he was deputy head at King's Hawford School, Worcester and had also taught at RGS Worcester. He has introduced a structured outdoor education programme and gets stuck in there himself – literally. On a recent potholing expedition, there are reports of a very wet and muddy Mr Hymer.

One of those heads who rolls his sleeves up and can be found making tea at parents' evenings and out in the car park at crunch times, his personal interest is hugely valued by the boys and their parents. Parents feel his comments on the boys' reports show he understands their sons and his head's commendations for good work are keenly sought. Teaches history to year 5, in part so he can be an advocate for the boys with the senior school when the time comes. He sends a photo to parents of him giving the boy the commendation certificate – the sort of personal touch that adds all round value. Warm, children focused newsletters draw parents into the community.

His leadership specialism is assessment and he has instigated new ways of monitoring progress through tracking. Formerly a keen cricketer, both playing and coaching, these days he tends to be a keen spectator of all sports. This is nicely balanced with his interest in art – he describes himself as a modest collector and the school art rooms and high standard of displays are testament to someone with an eye for the visual. His wife is a GP and they have two grown up sons.

Entrance: Boys moving from Warwick prep to the junior school are assessed internally and almost all move on to senior school. External candidates sit tests in English, maths, reading and short story writing. The head meets with any year 5 parents individually where there is a query about suitability for senior school. The main senior school intake is at 11+ with some additional places at 13+. The exams consist of English, maths, ability and science and a modern foreign language for 13+. There is also a short interview.

Boarding houses are in the historic part of the school and some rooms have views over the Avon to Warwick Castle. Communal areas are brightly painted and attractively decorated

At sixth form, the minimum requirement is 51 points from the best eight GCSEs. There is also an interview with the head of sixth form and a deputy head.

Exit: Nearly all boys go through to the sixth form and thence to a range of universities, 90 per cent Russell Group. Nottingham, Exeter, UCL, Bath and Durham all popular. Sciences and medicine are popular as is computer sciences. Five to Oxbridge in 2021, plus seven medics. School is starting to encourage the boys to look at the top end apprenticeships eg Aston Martin, Barclays, IBM, Jaguar Land Rover, PWC, Shell, Warwickshire County Council and Police.

Latest results: In 2021, 84 per cent 9-7 at GCSE; 80 per cent A*/A at A level (95 per cent A*-B). In 2019 (the last year exams took place), 66 per cent 9-7 at GCSE; 48 per cent A*/A (75 per cent A*-B).

Teaching and learning: Chemistry and maths consistently top performers along with computer science, DT, economics, art and Latin.

Although fairly traditional, the curriculum is evolving to provide greater depth and breadth. In the senior school ICT has been separated into coding and functional skills. The year 7 language offer allows the boys to choose two languages and is now focused on linguistics and the value of learning a language rather than just naming family members and asking the way to the shops. There is work going on to encourage boys to reflect more on their own learning and on the links between subjects. All boys start Latin in year 7 and ancient Greek is taught as an option from year 9 to A level. There is some flexibility in this to suit individual needs, particularly for those with English as a second language or dyslexia. Recent curriculum developments in the senior school have included critical thinking for year 7, independent projects in year 9, a year 10 philosophy course and from 2020 the entire year 12 cohort will work on EPQs. The whole aim, driven by Dr Smith, is to reinvigorate academic curiosity and scholarship.

Staff themselves are heavily involved in research projects. There are teaching and learning groups and coaching conversations which are both part of the staff performance management and work with the boys. Consensus is that this is raising the profile of pedagogy in an exciting way.

The junior school introduces specialist teaching in year 5 and doesn't set boys, though there are intervention groups for those who require support in a particular area. School is pressing ahead with all aspects of technology to improve teaching and learning, keeping a watching brief on AI and forging ahead with VR sets to bring the wonders of the natural world alive, among other things. Five science lessons a week ensure boys have a very sound early foundation in STEM.

Class sizes of between 20 and 24 are a bit bigger than in some independent schools, but this is mitigated by the high quality of resources. There are strategically deployed teaching assistants and both junior and senior staff say that quality of teaching and ethos are more important for progress than class size.

Learning support and SEN: The academic support department is highly commended by parents. One mother of a dyslexic boy praised the willingness of the school to be flexible – her son doesn't do a foreign language, using the time for support lessons in English and maths instead. There were comments that boys had to make some effort to access support – they needed to do more than just sit there and wait for it to happen to them.

The arts and extracurricular: Parents say that the school offers everything a boarding school can in terms of opportunities for co-curricular pursuits. Music is huge. It starts in the junior school with small group strings lessons for all, a 150 strong choir, big band, rock bands, jazz groups, hand bell ringers, quartets and larger orchestral groups. All boys are given an orchestral instrumental to learn when they join the senior school with the most able having musicianship lessons. Everyone is involved in a performance at the end of year 7. Parents and staff say that going to concerts never feels like a chore, the standard is invariably high.

The Warwick Hall can accommodate the whole school and is a concert and drama venue of professional specifications, indeed professional touring groups hire it regularly. It includes an exhibition space where as well as senior students' work, local primary schools have been invited to exhibit. A separate venue, Bridge House Theatre, seats 250. From year 6 boys start taking responsibility for all the backstage technical stagecraft supported by a professional backstage theatre team.

An arts festival is held every couple of years. A project from the last one resulted in a striking installation of wicker sea monster devouring a boat, now on display outdoors

School is particularly keen to get as many boys involved as possible in the arts and an arts festival is held every couple of years. A project from the last one resulted in a striking installation of a wicker kraken devouring a boat which has joined the series of powerful outdoor sculptures on display around the 50 acre site.

Within the huge range of co-curricular opportunities there are some that reflect the technological focus of the West Midlands, for example buggy building and young engineers in the junior school, electronics and robotics for seniors. The school hopes to further develop academic societies to promote wider research skills and give opportunities for boys to present topics to each other that are way beyond the school curriculum.

Sport: All sport is on site and the facilities are impressive, some are used by the local community and there are plans to expand involvement in this area. School has a very strong sporting reputation, particularly for rugby, but is keen to shine the light on recent triumphs in other sports such as junior squash, county hockey, cricket, swimming and water polo. The aim is to get boys to try out lots, with an emphasis on having a go, doing your best and learning from each other. In the junior school, triumphalism at matches is not encouraged. Parents are asked not to whoop from the sidelines and there are no knee slides when goals are scored. Lots of teams are sent out every week and much effort is put into finding opposing D teams to play at all age levels.

Boarding: Although boarding is available from year 9 it's essentially a sixth form affair with around 60 boarders, mostly from Hong Kong and China. In some ways this is surprising as schools often tell us that overseas families prefer schools with a majority of UK boarders. Warwick's experience goes to show that parents are quite happy for their children to live in a reassuringly familiar culture so long as the academic offer is delivering. International boarders mix well with the home pupils in lessons and are paired with an English 'buddy' when they arrive. Full boarding of this kind does mean that the boarding houses are bustling at weekends – there is no grand exodus to homes within travelling distance.

Boarding houses are in the historic part of the school and some rooms have views over the Avon to Warwick Castle. Communal areas are brightly painted and attractively decorated with huge photos. House staff arrange plenty of low-key weekend leisure activities.

Ethos and heritage: Warwick is one of the oldest surviving schools in the world, believed to have been founded by Aethelflaed, Queen of Mercia, in 914. The Victorian building on this site was constructed in the 1870s and speaks of the ambition and confidence of those years when secondary education for more than just a highly privileged few was starting to be taken seriously by the good and the great. The spacious and thoughtfully designed campus is nearly finished after work to bring all the Foundation schools together on the one site. Details of the Foundation's ancient history (such as a statue of Aethelflaed), sit alongside the contemporary new builds. Visually the schools convey what is important to a lot of parents – a sense of successful tradition combined with forward-facing vision.

In the junior school, triumphalism at matches is not encouraged. Parents are asked not to whoop from the sidelines and there are no knee slides when goals are scored

Staff understand parents are busy people and try very hard to make communications simple and clear. Both schools receive very positive press from parents who say that they are quick to respond via email or face to face, as appropriate. Close relations between senior and junior schools are clearly effective but at the same time both maintain their individual atmospheres. Parents say the contrast is important so that the boys feel they really have moved on when they go to the senior school at 11.

The senior school is large (nearly 1,000 pupils) and some feel this is not the school for a boy who would struggle academically or lacks confidence. One parent said 'the average boy might feel he was failing'. However, the general feeling is that the size is an advantage in terms of opportunities and also that it caters for a diverse range of boys. School is making determined efforts to mitigate the potential anonymity of being in a large institution.

Everyone went out of their way to tell us that the school's reputation for being posh wasn't fair. This may be so, but to us it seemed a bit less diverse than similar schools in Coventry and Birmingham.

Eclectic list of old boys includes several rugby internationals, a couple of MPs, Iain Pears the novelist, Marc Elliott (East Enders), Christian Horner (Red Bull motor racing), theatre critic Michael Billington and, from the ranks of the departed, the poet John Masefield.

Pastoral care, inclusivity and discipline: The junior school has a warm but disciplined atmosphere and this is where the social ethos of the schools starts to be embedded. Staff model positive behaviour and virtues such as humility and considerate manners are articulated for the boys so that they learn the language to express good behaviour. Match teas are still sit down events where you are expected to talk nicely to the opposition. Gentleness and kindness are recognised through consideration certificates.

Boys who don't want to spend their break times in high octane communal activities can chill out (not literally) in an 'igloo'. A card system has been introduced for misdemeanors with a rather gentler nomenclature than the former 'strikes'. Juniors may get a yellow card for talking when the teacher talks and the boys assure me that most of the boys and their parents take these very seriously. There are red cards and you can get suspended for eg racist comments or deliberate acts of vandalism.

In the senior school the house structure has been reinstigated. The pastoral concerns tracking system allows for early intervention where any problems, often quite small, are picked up.

Considerable effort goes into ensuring a smooth transition between year 6 and year 7, both for those already in the school and those who are arriving from elsewhere. As well as pre-Autumn visits there is a bonding trip after the first few weeks that seems very popular. There are two form tutors to each form in year 7 so the boys will all feel they are known as individuals quickly. The school is considering more mixed age tutor groups to enhance the community feel.

Grass roots pastoral care happens effectively at form tutor level and time for tutors to spend with their group has been extended in the senior school to allow for relationships to be strengthened and for form tutors to pick up the small changes that can be significant. PSHE supports pastoral development with sessions on mindfulness

Boys who don't want to spend their break times in high octane communal activities can chill out (not literally) in an 'igloo'

and self worth. There are two school counsellors plus teaching assistants in classes where there are boys with special concerns such as high anxiety. Teachers have received useful pastoral training particularly round autism. The school does not shy away from difficult gender issues and uses its single sex status to allow the boys to explore subjects such as consent and pornography.

In the senior school, yellow cards can be given for eg chewing gum or using your phone when you shouldn't. Parents think the school has done the best it can when there are serious discipline issue. There were a few grumbles about card happy teachers and inconsistency generally in punishments from the boys, but no more than we usually hear about when visiting senior schools.

The head of sixth form likens his role to that of a boarding house master. The pastoral work goes on through relaxed conversations and leading by example. What he and other pastoral leaders are aiming for is that each boy will feel that there is someone who is genuinely interested in them and their wellbeing. Parents report that he has got this absolutely right.

Pupils and parents: This a school where pupils are quite likely to be the children and grandchildren of alumni. Staff assured us that there is a range of parental backgrounds from landed gentry to those who need full bursary support, though the cars dropping off boys suggested rather more towards the top end of the spectrum. Nearby Jaguar Land Rover is a big employer (and source of some of those cars!) as are local large hospitals and universities. Some parents commute to London.

Parents told us that one of the lovely aspects of the school was how charming their sons' school friends were so we were looking forward to chatting with the pupils. As it turned out the boys we met, while perfectly well mannered, were rather reticent and trying to get anything beyond platitudes out of them was like pulling teeth. Apparently their teachers were 'great', the school was 'great', the head was 'great', oh and 'nice' as well. Either we didn't ask the right questions or else we didn't get to meet the right boys!

Money matters: Fees towards the top end for Midlands day schools. The school is fortunate in benefiting from a number of ancient charities, some specifically aimed at boys living in the town of Warwick. Scholarships are offered in music and academics but not for sport. About a quarter of boys in the school receive some financial assistance.

The last word: The Warwick Foundation feels it has its version of the diamond model right: boys and girls together up to year 3 then separated for lessons. It will be interesting to see how this develops in coming years now the girls' High School has moved onto the site and there is a new joint sixth form centre. This school is a Midlands institution that manages to be dynamic and forward facing without losing sight of its historic past. The fact that it perhaps lacks the edginess of the nearby big city schools is part of the attraction for many families.

Winchester House School

37

44 High Street, Brackley, Northamptonshire NN13 7AZ

01280 702483 | registrar@winchester-house.org | www.winchester-house.org

Ages: 3–13

Pupils: 300; Boarders: 30 weekly; 50 flexi (from year 3)

Fees: Day £10,905 – £19,230; Boarding £24,330 pa

Head: Since January 2022, Antonia Lee, previously head of prep at St Helen's School. She has taught in all boys, all girls and co-ed schools across all age groups and has successfully prepared pupils for scholarships to eg Magdalen College School and Cheltenham Ladies College, as well as for Oxbridge entry. She has also been a GCSE geography examiner. She is a governor at The Iffley

Academy and currently serves on her district committee for IAPS, having been the association's inaugural sustainability subject advisor. Educated at Eastbourne College, she studied geography at St Hugh's College, Oxford alongside rowing for the college 1st VIII and serving as vice president of the Oxford University Rag committee before doing her teacher training at Homerton College, Cambridge. She has a son and daughter, both at university, and is a keen sports fan (particularly cricket, rugby, tennis and athletics), amateur artist, theatregoer, rambler and skier.

Entrance: Non-selective into pre-prep with automatic entry to prep. All assessed prior to entry into year 3 and above to identify learning needs. Pupils mainly local (within 10 miles) supported by a minibus network bringing pupils in from further afield. The busiest bus service brings pupils in from Chipping Norton.

The main building so characterful it even moonlights as a wedding venue in the holidays

Post pandemic, the school is noticing – like many others – increasing numbers of families fleeing London. Strong old school, rather than aspirational, bias. Lots of former pupils in parent cohort. Some year groups oversubscribed.

Exit: Almost everyone stays through year 8, with co-ed boarding schools the usual next step. The school prides itself on sending its pupils to a broad range of destinations. Though the numbers going to each aren't shared on the website, Stowe is consistently the most popular (the school is just down the road from Stowe and is now a member of the Stowe Group, with Stowe and Swanbourne House School), with Radley, Rugby, Uppingham, Oundle, Bloxham and Tudor Hall popular choices after that. Odd ones go to Millfield, Abingdon, Headington, Eton, St Edwards and Winchester.

Our view: Based in and around a former hunting lodge, approached directly from the charming high street, with grand wrought iron gates guarding an 18-acre, Tardis-like campus. It must definitely wow escaping Londoners, the main building so characterful it even moonlights as a wedding venue in the holidays. Founded in 1875 in coastal Sussex, the school moved here in 1918 to be safer from possible attacks.

Delightful pre-prep setting (across a small road) with large, bright classrooms, every possible millimetre of space adorned with creative offerings and the ceilings festooned with bunting and mobiles. Seamless transition for the youngest from on-site nursery, housed in a light and spacious extension. Years 3 and 4 housed in own building, with much evidence of the 'creative curriculum' followed on display.

A newer innovation from a previous head of English has been the introduction of 'kinetic letters' in reception, a multi-sensory method of preparing children's whole bodies for writing. The sight of children doing the plank and lying down to write may be unusual but one mother could not believe the difference in handwriting between her sons who'd been through the programme and her two sons who had not – 'It's very clever, almost like a gym class, but it's been phenomenal for them.'

'Proper computer science' is taught as part of the curriculum, and pupils have twice won Rugby's annual digital scholarship – involving coding, web design etc.If parents were slightly underwhelmed with the online teaching provision during the first lockdown, the school nailed it second time around with full live lessons, and marvellous co-curricular ideas including a virtual pet show, contest to build the longest marble run (with brilliant ensuing Twitter posts), and guest speakers from around the world. 'We were really keen first time round that children weren't in front of screens all day but also able to get out in that amazing weather,' says school. 'But in fact parents said, "Actually, we need to work," and we are proud of how we reacted to their input.' Any family with three of more children was offered the loan of a Chromebook, and pupils were required to wear uniform while studying at home – 'There were moans initially, but actually it's allowed children to differentiate between school and leisure time,' explains school.

Also useful in lockdown was the school's increased focus on wellbeing (partly in response to increasing exam pressures in year 6) which has been supported by a restructured senior management team and new heads of year who encourage children (and parents) to have more open discussions. House at Home workshops are run to help parents support their children emotionally and academically, and these continued through lockdown.

That the school has a higher proportion of SEN pupils than average may be down to the learning development department's thorough screening. School claims it's much better at identifying learning needs and putting in plans. 'It's a real strength,' says head. Dedicated SENCo and seven LD staff 'aim for as little withdrawal from the classroom as possible', although those with greatest need are withdrawn from Latin to receive extra support. In counterpoint, high achievers work with the head of HLP (higher learning potential), some of them those children we've all met who are very gifted academically but find emotions harder, and may need attention in both areas. 'They have designated sessions with our head of HLP – it's very bespoke to each child but has been a massive improvement on just giving them extra work in the classroom.'

Many secondary schools would envy the enormous sports hall and full-sized Astroturf. A lovely outdoor pool and cricket nets sit among the manicured lawns of the walled garden with the main playing fields across the road (though the pool is unheated so sadly for summer use only). Each year group has its own play area – some with super modern equipment and all with new, rainbow striped 'buddy benches'. The real magic of Winchester House, however, is in its enchanting and unique features – a secret garden tucked through a tiny archway, where year 8s are allowed to 'hang out' and lower years tend allotments and sit around camp fires; a beautifully panelled dining room where lunch is served family-style by teaching staff; tongue-in-cheek rules on the walls of the girls' boarding house (our favourites: no whining, laugh a lot and break the rules... sometimes) and a creative collection of vibrant works of art by visiting artists and pupils.

Fully co-ed, with a charming cohort of pupils who mix easily together and come across as children enjoying being just that – no ties, lots of untucked shirts and not a hiked up skirt or gelled quiff in sight.

The innovative 'creative curriculum' followed in the lower part of the school is well established and revered by staff and pupils alike – head speaks passionately about its execution: staff burying artefacts to be found by children with metal detectors (Romans) and children arriving at school to find snowy footsteps leading to their classrooms, which were draped in fur throws (Frozen Worlds).

Pupils in year 3 and above are each assigned a tutor, who keeps a beady eye on their pastoral and academic wellbeing, stepping in to help them handle heavy workloads around exam time or making sure they keep up their sporting commitments when academics threaten to take over. The school day is quite long (8.30 to 5pm from year 3 with an optional breakfast club and after school prep, tea and activities til 6.30pm), but parents say 'it does balance out', with prep done and dusted by the time a child goes home. Science a strength, with all three sciences taught separately by specialist teaching staff through 'as much practical work as we can manage,' according to the physics teacher. French from reception by native speakers (they only talk to children in French), Latin from year 6 and Greek from year 7. Setting from year 3 in maths and English, when pupils start to move between teachers, leading to entirely specialist teaching from year 5.

Parents told us that when concerns were recently raised about class sizes increasing in one year group, the school responded swiftly, hiring a new teacher and adding a new form. Another change has been ending academic teaching on a Saturday. 'Children – and staff – are really busy during the week and we were really concerned about fatigue,' says school, which claims it's had a very positive effect on wellbeing. The parents we spoke to felt the move fitted with modern trends. To smooth the transition, some inter-house matches are still held on Saturdays (so working parents may spectate) and a Mastery Morning enrichment event is organised one Saturday each term, with pupils required to sign up for at least two a year. Topics may range from CE revision techniques to a talk from a BAFTA-winning documentary maker, and this weekend provision is no doubt part of the reason the school's fees are a little higher than some competitors in the area.

Performance is one of the key aspects of the school, and you don't have to be brilliant; school sees it as part of confidence building, according to parents

Another innovation is ILT – Independent Learning Time – during the day for year 7s and 8s, in which top-up or catch-up clinics are offered, children may drop in with any concerns, and scholarship preparation is done, rather than having a scholarship stream. 'It has revolutionised how we up-skill pupils to become more independent learners,' says school.

A school alive with the sound of music, particularly singing, with parents describing the termly concerts in glowing terms. A massive 80 per cent or so learn an instrument, with choirs (both auditioned and otherwise, and choir tours), bands and ensembles aplenty for musicians of all levels. Performance is one of the key aspects of the school, and you don't have to be brilliant as school sees it as part of confidence building, according to parents. Specialist taught drama on the curriculum to year 8 and around 60 per cent take up LAMDA. Strong art department (complete with a kiln, 3D printer etc) focuses on much more than just drawing, with visiting artists offering masterclasses on disciplines from woodcarving to animation.

In 2021 Winchester House became a member of the new Stowe Group (see above), a three-school alliance facilitating shared expertise, resources and cost efficiencies. Stowe is also investing substantially in infrastructure plans, and Winchester House pupils may also make greater use of Stowe's facilities. The scheme gives more families incentives to send their children on to Stowe, 'though we are certainly not Stowe's prep school,' adds the school.

Hockey is especially big here but everyone will represent the school in something, and there is a great variety, including an equestrian team run by horse-mad mums

On the sporting front WH are again high achievers because 'We invest heavily in good quality coaching and do sport every day except Thursday.' Hockey is especially big here – and in the Midlands generally – but everyone will represent the school in something, and there is a great variety, including an equestrian team (run largely off-site by horse-mad mums).

Many leading prep schools run internal programmes or awards schemes alongside CE and here it is the much enjoyed Learn to Lead programme. Initially designed to help pupils develop resilience, take risks and manage failure with a sense of humour through expeditions and on-site activities, it has lately expanded to incorporate more charity and community work – consider the school's dementia choir, started in 2019, which sings to and with local care home residents, even doing so remotely through lockdown. 'Parents know their children are privileged but want to keep them grounded too,' says school.

Some 46 clubs run each week, and many, such as squash, chess, gymnastics, laser shooting and debating are included in fees, with others like skiing (at Milton Keynes) and golf charged as extra.

Daily minibus services bring children to school from locations including Chipping Norton, Bloxham and South Newington.

Boarding: Pupils can board from year 3, and some do, in one of two single sex boarding houses – boys upstairs in the main school building, girls in a purpose built block. Unsurprisingly, the girls' house with its cosy dorms (sleeping up to 10) has a homelier feel than the boys', although both are comfortable, with plenty of spaces for down time. School says boarding 'really takes off' in years 7 and 8, with an 'all or nothing' approach for the oldest pupils who are required to board all week rather than occasionally, as is allowed lower down the school – 'so it's not hot-bedding, it's a community'. Boarders have their own schedule of after-school activities, and are full of praise for the food.

Money matters: Means tested bursaries of up to 100 per cent are available from year 3, with five per cent of the pupil body currently receiving one.

The last word: Winchester House excels on many fronts. From enterprising teaching systems to sport, learning support and beyond, parents are effusive in their praise, and particularly value the happy environment and friendships between pupils. Small wonder almost no one leaves before year 8. As one parent puts it, 'It says it all, how excited the children are to go back...'

Witham Hall Preparatory School

38

Witham-on-the-Hill, Bourne, Lincolnshire PE10 0JJ

01778 590222 | admissions@withamhall.com | www.withamhall.com

Ages: 4–13

Pupils: 254; Boarders: 105 weekly/flexi (from 8 years)

Fees: Day £10,545 – £17,775; Boarding £23,985 pa

Headmaster: Since September 2020, William (Will) Austen, formerly deputy head at Ludgrove School. Read chemistry at St Andrews. From a farming family 'obsessed with horses', he started training racehorses after graduating. This didn't last long and he applied for a job at Summer

Fields. 'I don't think they had many sporty scientists applying for the job so I got it.' Spent nine years there teaching science and coaching rugby, cricket and soccer teams. Became a housemaster before rising to assistant deputy head. Married to Jossie, his 'greatest asset', whom he met at university. Jossie was registrar and head of development at Ludgrove and formerly housemistress at Summer Fields. They very much come as a team, Will might be the star of the show but Jossie very much his leading lady.

They had never heard of Witham when he applied for the job. 'Why on earth not?' he says. 'It more than holds its own against some of the best in the country. I'm a country bumpkin at heart so wanted to get out of the M4 corridor and back to my rural roots. We wanted our two sons to be brought up at a quieter pace of life where children stay children for longer. Witham offers this.' The couple were completely blown away by the beauty of the school, its surroundings, facilities and the area and still can't quite believe their luck that they are here. But both are very aware that Witham has been hiding its light under a bushel and needs to be 'out there'. 'Witham should be considered along with the best prep schools in the country,' says Will. 'We have excellent facilities and offer a good all-round education. I am determined its profile will be raised.'

A tricky time to start during a pandemic but parents are slowly getting to know him. 'He's been very visible when we were picking up and dropping off.' He knows all the pupils and teaches prep children PHE; getting to know parents slowly and using remote Team sessions to do so. 'Remote learning has taught us a lot and remote parents evenings were very successful; something we might continue to do this way.'

Entrance: The school is oversubscribed all the way through but don't hesitate to approach them. To guarantee a place in reception it's wise to register before child is 2. First come, first served in this respect. Non-selective in the pre-prep but don't be complacent. Every child is interviewed – as are the parents. A taster day is offered before a place is guaranteed and parents looked at closely too. Reception children come from local nurseries; more join throughout the pre-prep – most from local primary schools. Many children registered to come in year 4, and many more turned away as no places. Children tested for entry from year 3. Again, every child interviewed along with parents. Children come from a wide area, many travelling up to an hour, further afield once boarding starts in year 4. Traditionally a country school for 'old money', local landed families and gentry. This is no longer the case with many more professional parents – often both working – and a larger London contingent now joining the fray, albeit many of these with connections to the area. Many second generation pupils, the odd third. The blend seems to work with all parents talking about how 'sociable and friendly' the school is.

Exit: Just one or two pupils depart at age 11 for the local grammar school or to follow siblings, but majority stay on. Around 70 per cent of leavers go as boarders to Oakham, Oundle, Uppingham, Rugby, Stamford High, Shrewsbury, Millfield and Wycombe Abbey. Head keen to encourage parents to look further afield if appropriate. Fourteen scholarships in 2021.

Our view: The school is just over 60 years old, having started in 1959 with six children. A fantastic setting, fabulous limestone mansion set in beautiful grounds in a pretty Lincolnshire village. It couldn't be more quintessentially English. Over the years new buildings have been built and old ones adapted so that the original house is now home to the boarders, oak-panelled dining room and admin staff. Teaching is in two separate buildings within the grounds.

'The staff eat with the children at lunchtime and attention is given to good table manners and behaviour, which I think is excellent'

The school day is long: all pupils from year 4 stay until 5.15pm with supervised prep sessions (the pre-prep day ends at 3.30pm, but clubs and activities carry on till 5pm). Supper is then served with most pupils staying for one of the many after-school club or sports practices and picked up at 7pm. Parents like this, as 'we don't have to sit and do the dreaded homework after school.' Many parents commute to London and this is why flexi-boarding is so popular. Saturday morning school for all from year 4, followed by matches. 'If you choose Witham you have to commit to the school and buy into the lifestyle,' said one parent. 'School has to come first, but it's worth it,' was another comment. 'Saturday morning schooling isn't ideal for country families that want to shoot or hunt,' says one parent, 'but we've bought into it and know what is expected of us from the start. I suppose it's a price we have to pay and we are happy to.'

Academically, parents are happy with progress, 'particularly now they have sorted out the maths department'. Pupils graded for ability further up the school; head introducing it in year

5 now, which is a year earlier, and in more subjects: English, maths, sciences and Latin. 'I want to make sure that the bright children are given more opportunity so we have done some tweaking.' Gifted and talented programme introduced and two-year scholarship pathway now up and running. All parents spoke about how easy it is to get in touch with a teacher. Regular reports on progress.

The dreaded home schooling during Covid has 'been as successful as it could be,' said one parent, 'but anyone who says it works is lying. It's hard and is not successful but Witham are doing the best job they can; certainly better than the school my children were at before. And they've improved teaching quality through the second closure with much more interaction between teachers and pupils with lessons on Teams so the children can see each other. They even manage PE lessons.' Another parent said, 'They are cracking on with teaching and despite a few early IT teething problems it's working well. But it does mean that one parent has to be with the children all the time; but that would be true of any school and Witham are doing a good job.'

Even children living in the village board, usually at the pupil's behest: 'It's fun.' Many board on the same night as a friend or because they have a club

All children tested for dyslexia in year 2. Nineteen pupils with SEN, some offered one-to-one support, others one-to-two. And this has carried on during home schooling with extra lessons offered before the school day starts. All parents said their teacher knew their child well and stepped in to suggest extra help if it was felt to be needed. Many commented on the discipline. 'They don't stand any nonsense.' Good. Sound advice offered about future schooling, appreciated by the parents.

This is a sporty school with lots of it, but not just rugby, hockey and netball. Girls now play cricket. Yoga for reception and fly fishing on the school lake as well as a nine-hole golf course. Chance to play in a team for all whatever the ability which means all parents are involved with Saturday matches and get to enjoy the social side of school. No swimming pool as yet but head has it on his radar. He's keen to bring more emphasis to other sides of school too. Very impressive art work on display in the converted stables that are now the art rooms. Special room given over to the scholarship students – we can see why so many win art scholarships. Music and drama also a strong part of the school with enthusiastic teaching. Most of the children learn an instrument. Head keen to introduce CDT to the curriculum with planning already in for a new building.

Pastoral care excellent according to all parents. 'Any niggles and problems are sorted out quickly and efficiently.' Very much a caring place, with staff well aware of any mental health problems that can develop. Counselling offered if needed with counsellor visiting weekly. One mother talked about the emphasis given to good manners. 'The staff eat with the children at lunchtime and attention is given to good table manners and behaviour, which I think is excellent.' Many staff and their families live on site, or within the village, adding to the family atmosphere. 'They turn out nicely behaved and well-mannered children.'

Very much a community feel and most parents chose the school because of this. 'We fell in love with the place as soon as we walked through the door.' 'It's a delightful place; my children are so happy here.' The children are cheerful and chatty. Working hard, but seemingly not under great pressure.

Boarding: Large, airy, freshly decorated dorms in the main house each sleep up to 10. Pupils are encouraged to decorate dorms with a competition for the best one. Friendly boarding staff and matrons. Wednesday nights are the quietest because of match fixtures so those not involved have 'family nights' with the houseparents, joining them for pizza. Mobile phones are not allowed in the boarding house and definitely no social media. Girls' and boys' sections have comfy lounges where pupils enjoy hot chocolate, cake and 'downtime'. Trips feature bowling and such like and pupils have the run of the grounds during the summer.

Around 28 are weekly boarders but the vast majority are flexi-boarders, varying from one night a week to five. Flexi-boarding must be a logistical nightmare, but it works. Some 125 of the 167 pupils in the prep department board over the course of the year. Even children living in the village board, usually at the pupil's behest: 'It's fun.' Friday night is the most popular. Many board on the same night as a friend or because they have a club and this means some bed-hopping and lots of sheet changing, but all handled well to fit in with parents. Boarders staying two or more nights keep the same bed. Interesting to note that boarding parents did not seem to be aware of any Covid regulations. There are obviously some in place with regards to 'bubbles' but parents not concerned and trust the school to handle everything.

No outbreaks so far that anyone is aware of; hope that's not tempting fate.

Money matters: Means-tested bursaries but no scholarships.

The last word: Witham offers a tremendous start to a child's education. Pupils are taught to focus, strive and 'do the best you can'. But it's not just books and learning, they are encouraged to try new things, spend lots of time outside and are taught the importance of courteous, thoughtful behaviour. Perfectly set up for the future, with parents queuing to get this start for their children. Hidden gems are all very well, but the new head is keen for Witham to take its chance to shine. We are sure he will succeed.

Wrekin College

Sutherland Road, Wellington, Telford, Shropshire TF1 3BH

01952 265603 | admissions@wrekincollege.com | www.wrekincollege.com

Ages: 11–18

Pupils: 511; sixth form: 150; Boarders: 58 full, 35 weekly/flexi

Fees: Day £15,690 – £18,960; Boarding £29,430 – £34,440 pa

Head: Since 2016, Tim Firth, BA English Literature, Sheffield University, PGCE Oxford University. Previously deputy head and then acting head at Hurstpierpoint College, West Sussex; came to the school after Wrekin's unfortunate run of heads (three in quick succession). Nothing Lady Bracknell-ish about losing all these heads, just a quirk of fate. And possibly one that has benefited Wrekin since it resulted in the arrival of Mr Firth, who is, according to parents, a 'great fit', a 'dynamo who is very energising' and brings 'solid leadership'. Parents like him; children like him. They say he is approachable and chatty and after the first few weeks of him arriving, 'everyone relaxed'. Being the warm, funny, open sort of chap that he is, we imagine that he will be very adept at taking people with him on what he plans will be an 'enlightened evolution' of the school. We hope everyone's ready: his development plan, outlining numerous aims including targets for value added to pupil grades and a reformed appraisal system for teaching staff, suggests the evolution will be pacy.

In the past parents may have selected Wrekin for its happy vibe and reputation for pastoral care, rather than its academics. Mr Firth has set about addressing this. A big change has been to introduce Challenge Grade Review cards; parents tell us that they finally know where their child stands academically. Clear targets are given to each pupil based on his or her ability, regarding where pupils could be if they successfully carried out measurable tasks. They are given clearly defined 'stretch' work to enable them to meet these challenge grades (head describes the process as a coaching manual) and teachers are able to see which pupils might need a bit of extra support (one on one, for example). Having recruited new heads of lower and middle school to work alongside the tutor system, he says there is now a whole team around each child academically. Greater coordination. Greater tracking. The head says they want to harness the excellent pastoral care that allows frank but supportive conversations about academic achievements

While raising the school's academic profile is a clear goal, head is also acutely aware that young people are entering a competitive job market and their employability needs to be equally strong. To that end a new business school opened in 2016, which focuses not just on CV and interview preparation, but also offers a wide programme of career talks on practical topics like 'what an office is like' and industry-focused subjects, such as engineering. Pupils are introduced to apprenticeship schemes and discover what could work best for them as individuals post school. The centre's curriculum is designed to include pupils of all ages. While Mr Firth has far too much humility (and realism) to claim these aims are unique, the dedicated nature of the centre perhaps is. He describes it as a 'standalone temple to employability' – not a phrase you hear very often. It's certainly shaping up into a significant USP and is especially popular with those parents who are in business and want their children to be better prepared for the world of work.

Mr Firth recognises that the straight A student, who may have been a bit spoon-fed along the way, does not always make the most agile, creative, resourceful presence in the workplace. The centre is dedicated to resolving that conundrum. His ambition is for Wrekin students to be more stalagmite, less snowflake. He refers in passing to the high number of golds in the Duke of Edinburgh awards clocked up by Wrekin students, testament to their sturdy, resourceful characters.

Above all, Mr Firth is keen for Wrekin to continue to be an inclusive environment, one which reflects a broad spectrum of children. Or as one impressed parent put it, quoting the head's words in his first communication with them, 'no one under the radar, no one on the bench'. That phrase went down like manna with parents. He says he relishes the diverse intake because it reflects the real world and this mix 'breeds thoughtful teachers'.

Mr Firth is a keen sportsman, particularly interested in cricket (he was a cricket blue), loves reading, particularly poetry, and Bob Dylan (he has 60 albums). He and his wife, Jane, have three children.

Entrance: Around half come from the on-site prep, Old Hall. Rest from local primaries and preps including Packwood Haugh and Prestfelde. All candidates sit 11+ exam, papers in maths, English and non-verbal reasoning, but bar is not set too high for entry. Entry at 13 + by Wrekin entrance exam.

Exit: Nearly all sixth form leavers head for university and the spread is typically broad for both subjects and locations. Parents praised the UCAS support. Most choose northern, Midlands or Welsh universities: Leicester Bangor, Cardiff, Keele, Leeds, Manchester, Hull, Sheffield, York. Economics, engineering, business management and sports courses (sport science, sport and health education) seem popular. Not many takers for arts degrees, just a few for English lit and languages. Often a few to Oxbridge; ditto for medics (two in 2021).

Latest results: In 2021, 42 per cent 9-7 at GCSE; 45 per cent A*/A at A level (73 per cent A*-B). In 2019 (the last year when exams took place), 30 per cent 9-7 at GCSE; 23 per cent A*/A at A level (50 per cent A*-B).

Teaching and learning: Wrekin offers a broad curriculum to suit its diverse intake, including BTecs and A levels in subjects like accounting and psychology. Languages are fairly healthy: 52 per cent of students take one or more languages at GCSE; 12 per cent continue to A level. School is very supportive of apprenticeships and does not automatically assume that university is the right path for everyone. Classes are small: typically no more than 20 for the younger pupils and 8-15 at A level.

Most of the A*s at A level were in maths and further maths with a sprinkling across languages.

Wrekin is a Christian foundation and worship – four times per week – is very much part of the makeup. Services are also a chance for pupils to perfect their public speaking

Tutoring system means each pupil has personalised academic support. Pupils' academic progress is closely monitored with twice-weekly meetings. The mix of pupils means teaching, as Mr Firth explains, is all inclusive but differentiated, depending on stage and ability (this might manifest itself in slightly different homework).

The Franklin Society is in place to challenge the most academically gifted pupils. It is aimed at developing logic, science and the arts (game theory, science projects, study of the classics, architecture). After a rebranding, there are now timetabled weekly lessons. Pupils are chosen from second form upwards based on their performance in non-verbal reasoning and/or exams (pooling all the academic data). About 10 out of 60 students in a year get the nod.

There are also the usual subject-related extension activities, mind-expanding lectures and academic challenges in national and inter-house competitions. Parents say head has added polish to the teaching and upped ambition in pupils (although one parent wondered if staff might be a bit stretched, mastering of a lot of roles).

Learning support and SEN: Good learning support team for mild to moderate difficulties. A learning profile is drawn up for all pupils, identifying strengths/areas for development, as well as strategies to help teachers. All have agreed termly targets. Progress is measured against these targets and reassessed each term. Support also available on a temporary or permanent basis for pupils experiencing difficulty with a particular area of the curriculum. No extra cost.

The arts and extracurricular: House system provides a healthy platform for competitiveness, team playing and support. Parents say it results in every child wanting to participate in a range of activities and have a go; it 'puts fire in their bellies', as one parent said.

Very vibrant art department with an annual exhibition and trips to back it up, like a recent Photoshop workshop with a local artist. Around 200 pupils have music lessons every week and there is the usual array of orchestras, bands of all types (rock and jazz) and choirs. A regular programme of school soirées ('soirées at six') recitals and concerts means heaps of opportunities to perform for all, including house singing competitions and house concerts. Also, Wrekin Musician of the Year competition, concerts off-site at eg Shrewsbury Abbey and overseas tours. Recent very ambitious production planning of Carmina Burana involved 200 singers. Music is a clear strength of the school, with a new music school opening in 2020. At least one whole school play per year and lots of house productions, from Macbeth to Shadowlands. House drama competitions allow senior students to manage younger ones.

Around 130 pupils each year are involved in CCF. DofE popular – remember that healthy stash of gold awards. Lots of trips, including annual house camping; cultural visits to Hampton Court, Tate Modern, design and business trip to Jaguar Land Rover.

Sport: All the usual sport is on offer (vast grounds, lots of playing fields): netball, rugby, football, rounders, cricket, cross-country, tennis, athletics. Also fives and fencing. Large sports halls, gym and tip top swimming pool. Very good to see the girls have a strong six-a-side football team. Netball teams seem to excel, frequently ending up county champions. Second Astro recently added, plus new dance studio.

Boarding: One girls' boarding house and two boys'. Rooms are fine, not huge – pretty standard boarding fare. Younger years share four or five to a dorm, older students have their own study bedrooms, some with ensuites. Communal facilities are okay, some have had a refurb so are a tad smarter. All houses have common rooms with decent sofas, cushions, relaxed vibe, kitchens (fridge, toaster, microwave) and games rooms (pool tables). Boys can visit the girls' common rooms for a short time after prep; one girl called their common room a 'social hub'.

All well supervised, houseparents on hand along with matron and prefects, who have a duty roster. Phones are allowed but wireless turned off at 10.30pm. Day pupils don't go into the boarding areas but common rooms for day students, within the houses, are open to boarders so there is a fair bit of downtime mingling. On site medical centre staffed throughout the day and a nurse is always on call overnight.

Lots of trips into nearby Shrewsbury, Ironbridge, Chester, Birmingham and London. Also, there are a great many clubs on a Saturday morning from squash to jewellery making, horse riding, archery, rowing, maths.

Ethos and heritage: Founded in 1880 by Sir John Bayley on a large and lush site above Wellington, a market town in Shropshire, Wrekin is a combination of old and new buildings (no eyesores), on a large campus with plenty of green space. It became co-ed in the 70s and in 2006 merged with the Old Hall School, which moved onto the same site.

Cheerful studiousness might best capture the atmosphere, students going about their business with a smile. Classrooms have an old-style charm, some with the smell of refurbs, like the chemistry labs. In the corridors displays don't jump out at you, but it all feels very friendly and 'community-led' with all the information and updates pupils need.

Inevitably, lots of hoofing required to cover distance between boarding houses and buildings – our legs could tell we had walked a fair distance by the end of our visit.

Pastoral care, inclusivity and discipline: By all accounts, a massive strength of the school. As one parent said, every day their son 'had gone to school with a smile on his face and come home with a smile on his face'. Others spoke of a happy and secure environment where children are social, look people in the eye and are making the best of who they are.

House system provides a healthy platform for competitiveness, team playing and support. Parents say it means every child wants to have a go; it 'puts fire in their bellies'

While every school says there is a caring environment, the students we saw and spoke to – who really did smile and make eye contact without knowing who we were – looked cheery. We also noted the impeccable manners – door opening, standing aside. They didn't seem formulaic, just natural consideration, true courtesy.

A very inclusive environment; most parents seemed to think the house system was instrumental here – the spectrum of inter-house competitions (a house play, a house singing competition etc) all offering a sense of identity. The children relish being part of a group, not wanting to let the group down. First and second form (years 7-8) are all in Lancaster house, which parents said was an excellent stepping stone and a good way of introducing them to the whole school. From the third year, they join one of three boys' or two girls' houses. Parents say pupils all look after each other and being part of the house is viewed as an honour.

Experienced counsellor on site and all the usual assemblies on pastoral matters. Pupils can train as mentors, identified by a distinct badge to encourage others to approach them. Every new pupil is issued with a school handbook and it is genuinely useful, packed full of all the information necessary (mobile phone use, security, map, routines, who does what on the staff).

Wrekin is a Christian foundation and worship – four times per week – is very much part of the makeup. Services are also an opportunity for pupils to perfect their public speaking – prefects often give 'thought for the day' talks on topics such as 'determination to achieve goals'.

Our House is a week's compulsory boarding for sixth formers who have to cook and clean for themselves – good preparation for university

Pupils and parents: Pupils are friendly, social, polite and without a whiff of arrogance or entitlement. As the head says, Wrekin's broad mix ensures its leavers are rounded and prepared for the world beyond school.

Parent demographic is similarly broad; many have business backgrounds (this is a part of the country where manufacturing still thrives); others are professions or from the farming and county set. Head welcomes parents' support – and their high expectations. Those we spoke to said home-school communication is good and they appreciate the open-door policy. Head has also started discussion forums where parents can contribute ideas and give feedback about the school.

Money matters: Boarding and day fees are somewhat lower than similar schools further south. In a nod to today's economic climate, interest-free monthly payment plans are offered, as well as a reduction loyalty scheme for those who attend its associated Old Hall prep.

The last word: A wonderfully nurturing and inclusive school which is on the up academically but also offers something rare: the chance for pupils, in this tough old world, to hone their employability factor.

Northern England, Scotland and Northern Ireland

Cheshire
Cumbria
Durham
East Riding of Yorkshire
Greater Manchester
Lancashire
Merseyside
North Yorkshire
Northumberland
South Yorkshire
Tyne and Wear
West Yorkshire
SCOTLAND
NORTHERN IRELAND

1 TYNE AND WEAR
2 NORTH YORKSHIRE
3 LANCASHIRE
4 EAST RIDING OF YORKSHIRE
5 WEST YORKSHIRE
6 GREATER MANCHESTER
7 MERSEYSIDE
SCOTLAND
Elgin
Inverness
Aberdeen
Montrose
Dundee
Perth
St. Andrews
Edinburgh
Glasgow
Ayr
NORTHUMBERLAND
Newcastle Upon Tyne
Carlisle
Hartlepool
CUMBRIA
COUNTY DURHAM
Darlington
Thirsk
Harrogate
York
Stonyhurst
Blackpool
Leeds
Blackburn
Southport
Bolton
Oldham
SOUTH YORKSHIRE
Liverpool
Sheffield
Warrington
CHESHIRE
DERBYSHIRE
Chester
WALES
Derby
Nottingham
STAFFORDSHIRE
Leicester
Londonderry
NORTHERN IRELAND
Belfast
Dublin
20 40 60 Miles

NORTHERN ENGLAND, SCOTLAND AND NORTHERN IRELAND

Ardvreck School

Gwydyr Road, Crieff, Perthshire PH7 4EX

01764 653112 | admissions@ardvreckschool.co.uk | www.ardvreckschool.co.uk

Ages: 3–13

Pupils: 135; Boarders: 70 (from age 7)

Fees: Day £17,070; Boarding £25,650 pa

Head: Since 2018, Ali Kinge, previously deputy head and English teacher (she still teaches – we saw her in action, helping older pupils with their CVs and personal statements). Has been at the school for almost two decades, moving from Malvern Girls' College in Worcestershire. BA in Spanish and French from Nottingham, where she met her husband Stephen, followed by an MEd at the same university. Housemistress and modern languages teacher at Moreton Hall, followed by a period teaching in Peru. Initially moving to picturesque Perthshire to accompany her husband who came up to be deputy head at Glenalmond College, she started off as a part-time music teacher, and within weeks was head of English and then Latin. She joked with us, 'I've pretty much done every job in the school. It was a natural progression to become head.' Her husband, changing his depute post for head of department, now lives with her on site.

The school's first headmistress, you can't help but be inspired by her tenacity and joie de vivre, achieving a British Citizen Award for her charity fundraising, including the Etape Royal 100-mile cycle race, the Great Kindrochit Quadrathlon (swimming, fell running, kayaking and cycling) and the London Marathon. Despite being involved in a tragic cycling accident in 2013, with a prognosis of potential paraplegia, she was determined to get back to full health and told us, 'I wasn't prepared to accept that and 10 months later I ran the London marathon.' She has three sons, a year apart in age, but is now an empty nester (except for the 135 pupils).

Entrance: Children come from all over UK, although predominantly Scotland, with the majority from Perthshire and surrounding area. Most children arrive between the ages of 8 and 10. Informal testing and chat with form teacher to consider suitability.

Exit: The majority to independent schools in Scotland and England. Ampleforth, Eton, Fettes, Gordonstoun, Harrow, Kilgraston, King's Canterbury, Malvern, Marlborough, Merchiston, Milton Abbey, Oundle, Queen Margaret's York, Radley, Robert Gordon, Rugby, Sedbergh, Sherborne, Shrewsbury, St Mary's Ascot, St Mary's Calne, Stowe, Strathallan, Uppingham and Winchester and, of course, a sizeable proportion to nearby Glenalmond College, which historically had a close relationship to the school.

Our view: On first impression, it would be easy to assume that this school has leapt straight from the pages of an Enid Blyton novel (we loved a Malory Towers tale as much as the next child), but don't be fooled... While these are among the politest schoolchildren we've ever encountered (it's not often that we are stopped by a tiny person to enquire how we are and if we are enjoying our tour), these kids are made of strong stuff. Resilience was a word we heard many times and our observation was if they didn't have it when they started, they'd certainly have it by the time they left. Grey and drizzly on the morning of our visit, we saw a gaggle of pupils dressed in waterproofs bounding up the hill, dripping wet and with flushed faces but broad smiles. As they say, 'There's no such thing as bad weather – only the wrong clothes.' And with 42 acres of woodland as their playground and verdant hills and mountains as a backdrop to school life, it's a philosophy they clearly embrace. Parents we spoke to really treasured this: 'Such a beautiful place, they take advantage of it in a way that other schools in the area don't.' 'It's almost like a summer camp every day.'

Prepare to be impressed – a recent outing (including the headmistress) involved bagging six Munros in a day, where the pipe band played at the top of Ben Nevis

Outdoor education begins at nursery in the charming nursery located in a former bungalow, where all teachers are trained in Forest School principles. We were greeted by a bubbly nursery teacher in pigtails and with the enthusiasm of a Blue Peter presenter. 'Sorry, we can't chat, we are all going on a mud slide,' she said, before heading off into the woods.

Mrs Kinge can often be heard saying, 'Classrooms don't need walls,' and this spirit of adventure is core to being an Ardvreckian, whether it be studying erosion in the local river, bushcraft in the 'dams and dens' area, or an Adventure Friday where a different class goes out each week for a day of excitement. At the helm of all this action is the geography teacher (qualified in masses of outdoor activities) and the affectionately known Biscuit (derived from his real name, Rich T), who seems to have a 'little bit of magic' in encouraging even the more hesitant children to participate. 'I don't know how they do it, but they give the children the confidence and self-belief to give it a go,' said a parent. Prepare to be impressed – a recent outing (including the headmistress) involved bagging six Munros in a day, where the pipe band played at the top of Ben Nevis. The next day, all were up early for canoeing and camping under the stars in yurts and tepees. A parent confided in us that this can require a period for children to adjust, saying, 'Children have to build up a lot of stamina. They are bushwhacked but happy and get strong as a result.' Opening access to the state school sector, they have launched the Scottish Adventure School, providing residential activity weeks.

What one parent described as 'a bit of a bumpy phase' (there were some parental concerns about staffing a few years ago) seems now to be deemed past history, thanks to new leadership. Indoor lessons are delivered in the main Victorian house (established in 1883) as well as a series of satellite buildings. Classrooms are fairly traditional but teaching styles modern and interactive. We saw an energetic English teacher conduct eager pupils into song about vertebrates, with all enthusiastically stamping their feet. Small class sizes that are split when numbers go over 16. Lessons also run on a Saturday for children aged 8–13. With so many activities, the Saturdays buy a little extra time, and tend to be outdoors and topic based. When studying WWII, they visited the local sweet shop with a ration book. A parent reported, 'Our neighbours would quite often say, "Oh, Saturday school, poor you", to which our kids responded, "Saturday morning school – yay!" They love and thrive on it.' All pupils have Chromebooks and have coding classes, but otherwise careful about exposure to too much technology, with no phones during school hours. Parents praised its excellent communication, with one parent saying, 'We all have the teachers' phone numbers – quite a special thing to be able to do, particularly over lockdown.'

Support for learning and wellbeing highly rated. Pupils with additional needs around 25-30 per cent, the national average, and conditions often identified more quickly because of small class sizes. 'Within 15 minutes they picked up on it... and put things in place before we had to ask. We are so thankful we found that space for him,' a parent told us.

Mini kings and queens reside in the turrets above the school. While not swish, the dorms are homely and comfortable, beds are adorned with soft toys and fairy lights

Punches above its weight in sport for a small school with a wide array of teams in hockey, rugby, cross-country and cricket. Small, heated and covered pool. Swimming lessons are part of the curriculum. Small but delightful, light-filled art department with vaulted ceiling, with decorations of the Lion King hanging from the walls. A dummy wall had been put up to hang more pictures though it was bare on our visit. Hopefully, it is now bedecked with pupils' artwork. All children play at least one instrument and have weekly instrumental lessons and practice sessions (more for boarders). Colour-coded reward system to encourage practising, with a coveted blue sticker for outstanding achievement and a mention in assembly.

Boarding: Mini kings and queens reside in the turrets above the school. While not swish, the dorms are homely, cosy and comfortable, with beds adorned with soft toys and fairy lights. Phones are permitted for half an hour every second night for communications; otherwise calls to home can be made from the office or surgery. Full and flexi boarding available. Around 90 per cent of boarders are from the UK, with the rest international. Some landed gentry families and farmers, but increasingly double-income hardworking professionals.

The last word: The headmistress, while she may be biased, describes Ardrveck as 'the school every parent wished they had attended themselves'. It's hard to disagree.

Ashville College

Green Lane, Harrogate HG2 9JP

01423 566358 | admissions@ashville.co.uk | www.ashville.co.uk

Ages: 2-18

Pupils: 750; sixth form: 107; Boarders: 92 full, 4 weekly/flexi (from age 8)

Fees: Day £9,480 – 16,755; Boarding £19,650 – £32,715 pa

Head: Since September 2021, Rhiannon Wilkinson, the college's 11th head and first female one. Modern history degree from Oxford. Has taught in and led schools in the UK, Hong Kong and Brunei, most recently as founding head of Whittle School in Shenzhen.

Entrance: At 2+ by informal assessment; at reception by 'ready for school' assessment. Prep applicants come for a taster day, part of which includes English and maths tests, plus reports and references from their current school. External year 7 entry by maths and English, verbal, numerical and non-verbal tests plus reference. Prep school pupils only take entrance tests if they are trying for a scholarship; many join in year 4 in preparation for a seamless transition to the senior school.

Around 20 join sixth form each year, with entrance based on predicted GCSE grades (five GCSE passes for entry, with 6+ required in subjects to be studied) and references.

Exit: Around 70 per cent of year 11 moves up to the sixth form, with the rest moving to state schools or college courses. Virtually all leavers to university, some 50 per cent to Russell Group. Durham, Edinburgh, King's College London, Leeds, Newcastle and Warwick among recent destinations. Fewer Oxbridge entrants than might be expected. Good numbers overseas – recently to University of London Institute in Paris (international politics), Istituto Marangoni (fashion design foundation) and University of Queensland (exercise and sports sciences).

Latest results: In 2021, 56 per cent 9-7 at GCSE; 64 per cent A*/A at A level (82 per cent A*-B). In 2019 (the last year when exams took place), 52 per cent 9-7 at GCSE; 34 per cent A*/A at A level (54 per cent A*-B).

Teaching and learning: Pupils do well at Ashville. Prep and pre-prep are positive and purposeful learning environments with a great buzz. Impressive written work on display, which is commented on by the school's most recent ISI report. With specialist teaching in languages from the senior school teachers, pupils study Spanish from reception upwards and French and Spanish from years 3 to 6. Even the youngest we spoke to was confident and comfortable to have a go in French. There is also a Mandarin club available from reception onwards with a waiting list. The senior school specialists also teach IT, with every prep pupil having touch-typing lessons.

As a result of school commissioning an independent report, as well as seeking parent views, there is now stronger monitoring of teaching and learning. The timetable has been changed to make sure the students have more time for English and maths and less time wasted moving between lessons. Parents we spoke to were pleased with the changes, though some would like more emphasis on business and commerce earlier on. Students said the online homework package works well, although they bemoaned the fact that it leaves them with no hiding places in terms of getting their work done.

Very good value added. Certainly in the sixth form the stronger focus on academic rigour is already showing good results and the sixth formers we spoke to were at great pains to tell us that they had been working harder and achieving more since the school began its big academic push.

Ashville has over 150 American students with families who work locally. Its US and international studies department, run by a former US high school principal, offers a variety of different academic pathways combining aspects of both US and English curricula, but all can lead to the award of an American High School Diploma. There is even a Fourth of July graduation ceremony.

Learning support and SEN: Special needs support has been reviewed and restructured. The team of four specialist teachers and two TAs supports, in particular, students with dyslexia and autism, one-on-one, in small groups and in class. It also runs lunchtime and after-school homework clubs.

The arts and extracurricular: Art is exceptional, with the head of art (himself a practising artist with some very strong work on display) obviously providing an inspirational role model. The work wasn't all about painting, with some lovely sculptures and architectural models that would not have looked out of place in a London gallery. Regular senior and junior drama productions such as Blood Brothers and an interesting Matilda Mash Up. There are inter-house music and drama competitions and regular external performances such as the annual carol concert in Ripon Cathedral. At the Friday celebration assembly, where the school band played students out to Proclaimers music, the atmosphere was warm, enthusiastic and inspirational, students obviously proud of their school and of their own and others' achievements. A parent praised the 'fantastic' work to promote good communication through speech and drama but thought that 'this is so important that it should be within the basic curriculum and not an add on'. The new head of drama should address this.

'Be the best version of yourself' is Ashville's mantra, repeated wherever you go. Many parents quoted this and felt it allowed their children to develop as individuals

Alongside these extracurricular options, there are some 120 activities with clubs including verse speaking, ballet and tap from the prep upwards. The mantra of the deputy head with the enrichment remit is 'it's all about the children', and the range on offer is truly staggering. Unusually and refreshingly, talented musicians can also join in sport fully, with staff going the extra mile and involving themselves in extraordinary organisation to make this happen. Clubs, trips and fixtures are very rarely cancelled or rearranged and parents really like that. This also means that take up for enrichment options doesn't drop off as students get older, with sixth formers leading many of the activities. The soft skills really are important here. One parent commented that 'what we are paying for is roundedness'.

Involvement in community and environmental issues includes a student-led scheme recycling crisp packets for the whole of Harrogate. The school has also won national recognition for its determination to support local traders, buying its books from the local independent bookshop and launching a loyalty card giving discounts at local businesses for students, staff and parents. Student voice is heard on matters as varied as boarding and food.

Sport: The school has a very strong sporting tradition with all the usual teams and fixtures, the head bringing his enthusiasm and expertise in basketball to add an extra dimension and meet the needs of both the UK and international students. The sports centre is open to the public and includes not only a lovely sports hall but also a 30-metre pool, a 3G Astroturf, two squash courts, a climbing wall, dance studio and a full multi-gym, with 15 tennis courts completing the picture. Students throughout the school were very enthusiastic about the facilities and opportunities, with prep school pupils saying this was one of the big reasons for coming to Ashville, though senior pupils were quick to point out that you don't have to be a great sportsperson in order to succeed here.

Boarding: Boarding is in four houses, two senior boys', one senior girls' and Greenholme for prep students from 7 upwards. Boarding staff are warm, caring and long-serving members of the Ashville community. Interestingly, the majority come from the PE department – useful for encouraging extracurricular participation – though recently a broader range has been recruited. That said, the atmosphere in boarding is very much home from home. Bright, modern and spacious rooms for the girls with somewhat more dated accommodation for senior boys, due to be refurbished in the near future. Warm, comfortably furnished sitting rooms, all with decent kitchen areas, though boarders eat meals in the school dining room. Plenty of boys seen cooking and many choose to do some of their own washing. Matron even gives ironing lessons.

The boarding houses are set slightly apart from the main school buildings, which gives a feeling of going home. There are plenty of school staff living on site and lots of nice touches like indoor bike racks, boot rooms, pianos and pool tables throughout. The boarders were a bright and friendly group who spoke very highly of the staff, the teaching and, of course, the food. They said the staff genuinely care for them, and clearly enjoyed being at Ashville. Some students have boarded from the age of 7 and all see a route through the Ashville system into the senior school and sixth form as a natural rite of passage. The usual moans about temperamental IT systems and firewalls which make study difficult, particularly for the sixth form, but overall this looks to be a very positive boarding experience. Lots of nationalities represented, primarily Chinese and Spanish alongside British. Nearly three-quarters of boarders are from overseas, and the school has won the TES award for the quality of its weekend enrichment programme for boarders.

Ethos and heritage: 'Be the best version of yourself' is Ashville's mantra, repeated wherever you go. Many of the parents we interviewed quoted this and felt it allowed their children to develop as individuals and not be stereotyped. Founded by the Methodist Church in 1877, the school has a very strong commitment to principles of Methodism and the values of working together, mutual support and community. There is a quiet humility here coming from staff and students which downplays the great work the school is doing in producing some well-rounded and well-educated young people. A lot of time is spent nurturing the Old Ashvillians Association and the history of the school is clearly important.

The atmosphere around the school is buzzy and busy. Students and staff work together in a respectful but fairly informal way. Movement around the school is calm and there is a workmanlike atmosphere in classrooms. Lunchtime is a little frenetic as the dining room is currently a little small for the number of students, however there are plans underway to rectify this. The range of food in the dining room is healthy and delicious. The school values its support staff as much as the teaching staff and was keen that they should meet the Guide alongside the teachers. The site is meticulously well maintained, the DT area is the tidiest we have ever seen and the mission to show all areas of the school as part of a continuous whole is clearly being achieved.

Pastoral care, inclusivity and discipline: With able form tutors and heads of year, strong house events and teaching staff leading boarding, Ashville's reputation for pastoral care is excellent, according to the ISI, and, more importantly, to the parents, staff, students and governors we spoke to. Knowing the children and supporting them in their journey from pre-school through to prep, senior school and sixth form is an important part of the school's philosophy. Staff spoke about supporting and encouraging diffident sixth formers to take on leadership roles and to speak in assemblies, allowing them to gain confidence in a safe environment.

The 24-hour medical centre is for boarders and day pupils. There's a well-established prefect system: Red Ties are heads of school with a role keeping good discipline, and Green Ties keep an eye on new year 7s, including running trips for them. The older students showed great confidence that their authority is respected by the younger ones. A parent commented that some other schools 'focus so heavily on the academics that the care of the child is lost. Ashville probably does need to push academics more, but not at the expense of the great pastoral care.'

The boarders were a bright and friendly group who spoke very highly of the staff, the teaching and, of course, the food

We asked students how well the large number from different cultures fit in, and they seemed surprised that this might be an issue. They felt that a struggling student would be supported by both staff and fellow students. One student said, 'This isn't a mean school. There's so much to do that it would be very hard to feel left out.'

Pupils and parents: One very happy parent of two students who have now moved on to Russell Group universities said, 'Academically they could not have done better, and oh boy, did they have fun.'

Boarding parents were very pleased with the school. One, initially critical of some of the accommodation (upgrade planned), recognised that there is a genuine family atmosphere and care for students which other schools struggle to live up to. Her advice was to look once at Ashville, look at other schools and then look again at Ashville. 'The school will take average pupils who might be overlooked in other schools and give them that extra push and confidence to help them succeed.' 'Take advantage of the opportunity for a boarding trial, my kids loved it.'

Another day parent has had five very different students through Ashville. 'The first two were moved reluctantly from other schools but quickly found their feet and began to thrive. The others all had different needs and I can't praise the school highly enough for their flexibility in allowing my children to adapt their courses to meet their needs.' 'If you start in year 7 the head of year is amazing for settling kids in; the transition is such a big thing and she makes it as easy as possible!'

'The school has done a fantastic job for my daughter. Her previous school was more academic in theory but here she is pushed to improve her handwriting (she's left-handed) and basic maths, and getting these basics right has helped her improve academically. It's a dream come true: she's grown in confidence. My son was quickly recognised as having some special needs and support was put in place. The speech and drama has improved their confidence.'

'The Methodist moral code and values aren't pushed at you but you can see them through everything the school does. The pastoral care is fantastic.'

Money matters: Academic, music, sports, art and drama scholarships, awarded on entry into year 7, year 10 and sixth form and reviewed at key stages. Means-tested bursaries of up to 100 per cent of fees, either in conjunction with scholarships or on a stand-alone basis. Additional discounts are awarded to the children of Methodist ministers and Forces parents.

The last word: This is a great school. The common sense of purpose that runs from the head and governors down to the youngest child in Acorns is very strong. Results for children are already good and are noticeably improving. The family atmosphere, strong sense of community, values-driven curriculum, superb extracurricular activities and warm, caring boarding environment make for a well-rounded package. The campus is delightful and the sporting facilities second to none. Well worth a serious look.

Aysgarth School

Newton-le-Willows, Bedale, North Yorkshire DL8 1TF

01677 450240 | enquiries@aysgarthschool.co.uk | www.aysgarthschool.com

Ages: Boys 3-13; girls 3-7

Pupils: 201; Boarders: 84 full, 45 weekly/flexi (from age 8)

Fees: Day £8,715 – £21,420 pa; Boarding £27,060 pa

Headmaster: Since 2015, Rob Morse BEd (40s). Previously head of Perrott Hill, Somerset for seven years. A Cornishman and graduate of de Montfort University where he studied geography and physical education, Mr Morse taught geography and games at Bedford before moving on to Mount House and then S. Anselm's where he was deputy head and housemaster. Arriving at Aysgarth is very much like arriving at a warm and welcoming country home; 'Happy boys learn better,' he says. 'We prepare them for what they will face in a changing world, academics are important but we also want boys who make good eye contact, shake hands, understand service and what you can do for people. We prepare them to go on to the best schools in the country.' His energy, commitment and principled leadership to this ethos is writ large throughout the school, and helped towards the recent ISI exemplary judgement. School is straightforward and unpretentious with a warmth and sense of energy and purpose. Mr Morse is also keen that that school should allow the boys to be children that little bit longer with time to play and enjoy themselves. So, conkers and pillow fights are still allowed (all properly risk assessed, of course).

Mr Morse and his wife Lottie, also a teacher at Aysgarth, come very much as a team, leading the first form house and thus getting to know the boys very well as soon as they arrive at school. Parents agree: 'He knows all the boys inside out and that feeds down to the teachers.' The couple have a son, currently at Harrow, who is a former pupil and along with their daughter and two black Labradors they confidently set the 'home first' scene that is central to the Aysgarth philosophy.

Entrance: Some join from pre-prep and there is the opportunity for pupils to join prep at any stage. Non-selective, no entrance test, but be prepared for a two to three hour tour including an interview. Willingness to get involved and take advantage of the very large number of opportunities on offer here is important. There is a very good SEN department but limited one-to-one provision. Although school is also clear that it probably wouldn't be the right place for a pupil with significant mobility issues they have an excellent track record with visually impaired boys.

Exit: Aims high for all its pupils. From a mixed ability intake, boys move on to many of the major independent schools in the UK including Harrow, Eton, Uppingham, Shrewsbury, Sedbergh and Stowe – it's one of the main reasons parents choose Aysgarth. Good sprinkling of academic, art, drama, music and sports scholarships.

Our view: Founded in 1877 by the Reverend Clement T Hales, the school was initially based in near Aysgarth Falls before moving to the current purpose-built site complete with tower and fives court in 1890. Hales chose the oak tree as the school crest and the motto Ex quercu non ex salice (Of oak, not of willow).

School proudly and sensibly adapts its learning cycle to suit the boys' needs and rhythms, getting the balance of work, exercise, food and play right. A long day keeps the boys busy but also allows them to mix academic study with games and the huge number of other extracurricular opportunities on offer. The timetable is adapted to make the most of daylight hours in summer and winter, ensuring there is ample time for sports. Two reading periods during the day allow out-of-lesson space for the music tuition that is available to all boys and taken up by the vast majority. The academic curriculum is standard fare with French and Latin on offer (from form 2 onwards) and good provision to help boys who come later to catch up in these subjects; ancient Greek also available. We saw some very strong written work where creativity was clearly in evidence, as was excellent progress in mathematics.

Boarding provision is amongst the best we have seen. Dormitories with between four and eight beds were bright, warm and with fantastic views towards the North York Moors

Subject-based specialist teaching begins at the start of prep school with good facilities for science and design technology, an excellent art area, and a large, well-equipped theatre. Classrooms are light and beautifully presented and a class size of twelve or so is the norm. In the top two years all boys are issued with Chromebooks and about 40 per cent of work is completed using IT. Parents we spoke to praised the teaching: 'My son came home excited about the periodic table, they make the boring stuff fun.' Another commented that she 'only had to raise something once and I had feedback within 24 hours'. One summed things up as 'turbo-charged learning with fun'.

Sport (with new director of sport from Bromsgrove Prep) is as strong as you would expect. The new sports hall (opened by alumnus Sir Matthew Pinsent) is excellent with indoor cricket nets used all year round, three badminton courts and indoor tennis court. The swimming pool is superb (water polo is a regular feature) and there are ample playing fields (rugby and football), an Astro for football and tennis as well as cricket pitches maintained to a professional standard. Sports trips go all over including to Oxford, Edinburgh and Rosslyn Park. Cross-country, gymnastics, free running and golf are just a few of the other sports options.

Head is clear that this isn't just a school for sporty boys and there is no place for a testosterone-driven culture. 'If there is a poetry competition [the boys] all want to be in it, they aren't pigeonholed into stereotypical behaviour by the presence of girls.' The place is alive with boys practising music and there's strong competition for a place in the choir ('the boys are as excited about getting into choir as they are about getting into the rugby team'). Fifteen per cent of boys take bagpipe lessons instructed by a Newcastle pipe band major. Lots of opportunity to perform at home in the beautiful Arts and Crafts chapel (with tremendous pipe organ), or away in venues as diverse as Ripon Cathedral, Chatsworth and the cathedrals of northern France. The artwork we saw demonstrated real skill and maturity.

The boys we chatted with over lunch could not speak highly enough of their school, or the food: 'Superb! How do they do it for so many of us, and the catering staff are all so kind to us.' Thoughtful and eloquent, they sang the praises not just of the sports offer but of all the activities, especially the drama and their forthcoming production of Private Peaceful. They were articulate about the problems of settling in to boarding school and issues of homesickness, but full of praise for not only the houseparents (including the head and his wife) but also the school nurse and the counsellor. We heard that pastoral care extends to parents as well as boys: 'They are very switched on pastorally, I was very wobbly when my first son went but had regular contact with the head's wife which was extremely reassuring.'

Aysgarth certainly seems to walk the talk when it comes to mental health – counselling sessions are provided for all boys coming up for Common Entrance and both boys and parents said they could not be better prepared for moving on to senior school. 'Everybody is treated the same but allowed to be different.' 'It's good how you work really hard in the classroom and then you get your reward, there are no lessons after Common Entrance.'

We found Aysgarth boys to be gentlemen in every sense. Unfailingly polite, they meet everyone with a smile and a friendly handshake; they seem to care for each other too. One boy approached us 'just to say hello'. Wherever we went the head was greeted warmly and clearly knew a great deal about his charges. That the 'school is family first' came through time and again.

Uniform is smart but sensible – comfortable pullovers and ties. Blazers are worn for formal occasions such as school trips and chapel (every day including Sunday). The school's strong Christian ethos is one which the head is keen to continue, as witnessed by his own faith and leadership of worship.

New sports hall (opened by alumnus Sir Matthew Pinsent) is excellent with indoor cricket nets used all year round

Buildings are mostly purpose-built Victorian and while inevitably some bits are better than others, everything is maintained to a high standard, as are facilities and grounds. There is a country house feel about the place and the Bedale hunt is a regular visitor. Pre-prep takes boys and girls and is based in Oak House, a short walk from the main school. It has excellent facilities, a forest school and committed staff.

Apart from the odd niggle about communication we found parents to be very supportive. A lot of families live locally but choose either full or regular (part week) boarding. Many boys' fathers had also been educated here but those we spoke to said that the school was by no means a foregone conclusion and that they had tested others to check Aysgarth was the best for their sons. As the only all-boys prep school in the north of England parents said that they valued the opportunity it gave their sons to get involved in activities in a non-gender-stereotyped way and excel at them where they might not have done in a coeducational context. The size of the choir and the high number of boys involved in music and drama are evidence of this.

Parents described Aysgarth to us as a 'proper' prep school in the way that it prepares its pupils for the rigours of senior school and they also approve of school's emphasis on developing good manners as a preparation for life. Another parent told us that the school 'excels at crafting an individual path for each boy, making it constructive, spotting when there is turbulence in a boy's life and helping them through it'.

Boarding: Boarding provision is amongst the best we have seen. All accommodation is in the main school building but with clear delineation between the three age-related houses. Dormitories with between four and eight beds were bright, warm and with fantastic views towards the North York Moors. Bathrooms are modern and well equipped and there are common rooms for each year group.

Money matters: Means-tested bursaries (up to 100 per cent) and a few scholarships of between five and 25 per cent are available. Siblings and Forces discounts available.

The last word: We left Aysgarth having found very little to criticise. This is a great school, with a warm, caring but rigorous approach and a clear track record of preparing boys well for some of the best schools in the UK.

Barnard Castle School

Newgate, Barnard Castle, County Durham DL12 8UN

01833 696030 | admissions@barneyschool.org.uk | www.barnardcastleschool.org.uk

Ages: 11–18

Pupils: 718; sixth form: 162; Boarders: 170 full, 51 flexi

Fees: Day £14,628; Boarding £26,424 pa

Headmaster: Since 2017 Tony Jackson BA (late 30s), the youngest HMC head nationally at the time of his appointment. Joined the school as second master in 2016, having previously taught history at Radley and been a housemaster for five years.

Ex-Bradford Grammar, he studied politics and history of the Middle East at Durham followed by two years' banking in Sydney and a stint of professional rugby in Spain before returning to the UK to work with Barclays. Following in his career teacher father's footsteps, he completed a PGCE at Oxford.

With ex-rugby player stature, Mr Jackson is warm, engaging, articulate and passionate about the school and teaching; sees headship 'as a vocation not a job' and looks for that commitment from his staff. A new breed for HMC headship, education as a second career after banking, can see why the governors snapped him up with just a year's experience in the school as deputy. Totally identifies with the school's ethos, and he's gone down a storm with parents, with one aptly describing him as a 'huge personality who fills me with confidence every time I engage with him. He is Barney.'

An inclusive leader, from the outset he got the school community to consider and articulate the school's purpose in the 21st century. Whilst raising academic standards, he also wants Barney pupils to 'light up the room', believing that examination results 'open the door but what you do once you've stepped over the threshold is more important'. A focus has been the top 10 skills needed to be successful at work.

Ambitious plans for its future: intends to build upon the school's reputation for academic success plus sport, music and drama, as well as developing existing opportunities for pupils to learn skills for life through public speaking, social skills, leadership and CCF programmes. Has appointed a new head of sixth form, head of junior boarding and pastoral deputy head and created a strong senior management team. Big 'people person' – believes that whatever your role in school you should feel valued and respected. One of his early priorities was providing a new common room for staff with work spaces and social seating, which has been much appreciated.

School's values are community, endeavour, integrity, compassion, duty and enjoyment, enshrined as the Barney Way. They run through the school like Brighton rock

Is well aware of the challenges northern boarding schools face maintaining pupil numbers, but Barney has a stable school roll and early indications are encouraging for some small growth next year. Tuned to the changes in the independent school market and intent on the need to communicate the message that Barney 'is a viable alternative in a changing society'. He says its strength is that 'there is a real sense of belonging and every pupil can leave here feeling they were part of something special and with bonds that will last a lifetime. I visit many schools and I know it's those things that make Barney different.'

Gained a rugby blue at Twickenham. He is married to Dawn, a geography teacher at a Durham school, and has three young children. They live on campus but enjoy their bolthole on Northumberland coast in the holidays.

Entrance: From independents Aysgarth, Mowden Hall, Terrington Hall and Cundall Manor; state schools in Richmond, Bedale and Darlington. Good school transport links and recruitment area extending even as far as the Lake District.

All interviewed – by Skype if overseas. Maths and English tests at 11+ and computer adaptive baseline test as well at 12+. At 16+ entrance test with some subject-specific tasks plus personal statement. Offers subject to GCSE results.

Exit: Most go on to university, predominantly northern. York most popular, then Northumbria, Durham and Leeds Beckett. Occasional few to Oxbridge or to study medicine, but none in 2021. Courses range from law to agriculture to sport and exercise science to politics with international relations.

Latest results: In 2021, 44 per cent 9-7 at GCSE; 42 per cent A*/A at A level. In 2019 (the last year when exams took place), 25 per cent 9-7 at GCSE; 28 per cent A*/A at A level (46 per cent A*-B).

Teaching and learning: Not a big hitter in the league tables but solid and consistent results over the last three years at A level. Head a big fan of the EPQ for the depth of independent study undertaken and pupils are encouraged to take it on. Independent study lesson introduced in year 7 increases incrementally to four sessions per week in GCSE years, pupils gaining experience in effective research – good training for EPQ.

Twenty-plus A levels on offer including Latin, classics, French, German and Spanish, in classes of between four and 16. Newly introduced vocational qualifications in sport, media and technical IT. Personal tutor provides academic and pastoral advice with experienced UCAS adviser and careers coordinator on site; lecture programme covers a wide range of careers and the skills needed for success at work. With a whole range of enrichment activities including performing arts, CCF and DofE, not to mention black tie lectern club formal speaking dinners and leadership posts as heads of house or monitors, this is a full multifaceted preparation for life beyond Barney.

GCSE results sound. All take nine to 10, including English literature and language; more than half take three separate sciences; most do a modern language and top maths set take IGCSE early. Year 10s take Microsoft Office Specialist award. Broad curriculum includes computer science, design technology and classics – top set learns Latin from year 8. Set by ability from year 7 in English, mathematics, French and humanities. Years 7 and 8 have a week off-timetable working on a multidisciplinary project – in 2018, design your own school.

Very positive feedback on pupil/teacher relations from parents: 'The staff work incredibly hard and genuinely have the best interests of their pupils at heart.' More than 30 staff have been in school more than 10 years and class size averages 14-16, depending on subject. Careers advice starts in earnest from year 10 with aptitude testing and introduction to careers specialists.

Learning support and SEN: A wide range of abilities and capabilities. Currently more than 60 pupils receive learning support – charged in half-termly blocks. Support focuses on English and maths, but also helps with specific topics, always working closely with class teachers. These lessons are normally one-to-one, with occasional group activities; learning support teachers may go into some classes to do group work. Some pupils' intervention may focus on one aspect of learning and last for half a term; others may require an ongoing, longer-term programme. School organises testing for dyslexia, dyspraxia and Asperger's and has close links with external specialists and psychologists. Parents kept well informed on their child's progress and how they can provide support at home.

Over 40 EAL pupils – dedicated EAL teacher, five lessons per week in years 7-11, one or two for sixth formers to support university entry certificates etc. Pupils can sit IGCSE ESL, IELTS, FCE.

The arts and extracurricular: Art popular and good take-up at GCSE and A level. Resourced well with opportunities to explore a wide variety of genres, including pottery and photography in class and in weekly activities programme. Three exhibitions a year and work proudly on display around the school. DT timetabled for years 7-9 and an option at GCSE and A level. Light, glass-fronted workshops well equipped for budding engineers and designers; Arkwright scholars here too.

Music House motto is 'making music happen' and Barney is certainly alive with the sound of music. Classrooms, practice rooms and a performing space enable the nearly 200 pupils having voice/instrument tuition to make themselves heard. Chapel choir and two others; groups, ensembles and orchestras; led by music scholars, plenty of performance opportunities with in-house lunchtime recitals and concerts, plus two full productions a year. Outreach too in local churches and stunning locations like neighbouring Bowes Museum; music tour to Ypres in the WWI centenary year. School hosts regional heat of Rotary Club's young musician of the year with some success for its pupils.

With OBs starring on stage and screen there's a tradition of drama here: a drama studio for small-scale productions and Big Hall for the big performances, with professional lighting and sound operated by pupils and retractable, tiered seating for 200. An annual senior play and musical together with house competition ensure both spaces are put to good use.

Mind, body and soul activity programme, compulsory until year 9, runs three times a week from 4.00-5.00pm with over 30 activities on a carousel system, pupils changing activities every five weeks. Great pride in flourishing CCF, both army and RAF, complete with shooting range and 110 years of history; DofE silver and gold too. Plenty of trips to the wide world outside Teesside – both nationally and internationally, with cultural, sporting and community/adventure in Africa.

Sixth form privileges – breakfast in the house and a laundry to do your own washing. Housemistress has introduced an appreciation box for kind words and deeds

Sixth-form-led charity committee raises over £10,000 annually for chosen charities; most recently My Name's Doddie Foundation launched by former international rugby union player diagnosed with motor neurone disease; latterly Smile for a Child, which helps disabled children enjoy sport.

Sport: Barney is renowned for its sporting strength and has some OB rugby legends. All pupils have five timetabled games lessons a week, and practices and sports clubs form part of the activity programme between 4pm and 5pm daily. Matches most Saturday afternoons with over 75 per cent of pupils representing the school; inter-house competitions galore. Whole school runs the Barney Bash qualifiers, a prequel for hardy harriers to shine in the annual Barnard Run. Extensive pitches, courts and sports hall. Small, rather dated indoor swimming pool, although it was a first for a British boarding school in 1896. Competition swimming at local sports centre, the other side of town. Professional coaching in less mainstream sports too: fencing, rock climbing, kayaking, for example; basketball matches, squash, rifle shooting and fitness training are among weekly activities.

Boarding: The junior boarding house is home to some 28 pupils aged 8-13 from the prep and senior school. It is staffed by senior and prep school teachers and a couple of recent OBs as 'gappies'. At the end of the school day a welcome awaits in the kitchen with its large table to gather around – a nice touch. There's a lounge with a TV that's rarely used (no time), a fox-themed snug with games and toys, a Lego room used for bed-time stories and a small library complete with a bank of mobile phone chargers. A sticker chart recording kind words and deeds builds to a reward of extra mobile phone use. Outside are banks of lockers and a cycle/scooter rack complete with helmets. The medical centre is now banished to a Portakabin adjacent to the house.

Built in château style, the school opened in 1882 and sits in an attractive campus of 50 acres

Comfortable three and four-bed rooms, some bunks, with quality furniture and adequate storage, sometimes ensuite. Personal touches encouraged; termly room changes, best friends discouraged from sharing as 'too much of a good thing'. Meals, apart from Sunday morning breakfast, in the school dining room; tuck allowed Saturday night only. A number join local sports clubs, Scouts and Guides but year 7s and 8s only allowed into town unescorted on Saturday afternoons.

Boys' houses Northumberland and York sit side by side in the upper echelons of the main school, with nearly 80 14-18-year-olds living cheek by jowl. Each house has a separate identity and traditions and provides responsibility posts for older boys. The Friends and Rivals Cup is part of the collection of house silverware on display and fiercely contested by the two houses annually.

Very warm and cosy, thanks to newly installed biomass boiler, year 9 and 10 boys are in good sized, modern two or three-bedded rooms, all with wash-basins; year 11 and up in single studies. Amazingly there wasn't a clod of mud in sight and the school is working on getting a laundry facility in place for personal use. The matron is the only female member of the house team, though as strong female role models, academic tutors go some way to redress this imbalance. Junior and senior common rooms, including the largest cinema screen for miles around. Girls allowed over three evenings a week and it's a happening place for dinners, movie nights and other social gatherings.

More than 40 girl boarders in Longfield. Double rooms for younger girls and single studies for sixth formers. Sixth form privileges – kitchen breakfast in the house and an in-house laundry to do your own washing. Recently appointed new housemistress has introduced an appreciation box for kind words and deeds.

Houses accessible to boarders all day – no excuse for forgotten books. Music school and sports facilities open for boarders to use on Thursday and Friday evenings. Ninety per cent of boarders remain at weekends, a third at exeats. Lots of in-house events such as team building, quizzes and movie nights; many involved in sports fixtures after Saturday morning school and there are trips to watch northern teams play or half-termly retail therapy in Gateshead, Leeds or York. Sundays see DofE or CCF activities as well as organised excursions to theme parks, adventure attractions and activities like go-karting, paint-balling, bowling, trampolining, ice-skating and cinema.

Ethos and heritage: Barnard Castle was founded thanks to the combined efforts of Victorian visionaries who were determined to improve education in the north east of England. It opened in 1882 as North Eastern County School and moved to its permanent location in Barnard Castle in 1886. The chapel, an integral part of the school, opened in 1912 with chairs and desks made by boys in the school joiner's shop from donated timber. Since the 1920s the school has honoured its 151 WWI dead (from 740 ex-pupils and staff who marched to death or glory) with oak panels on the chapel walls, and a special memorial website chronicling their lives was commissioned in 2018.

The prep school was founded in 1914 in adjacent Westwick Lodge and in 1924 school's name changed to Barnard Castle School. Girls joined the sixth form in 1982, boarders living in accommodation in the town until their boarding house was completed in 1987. Five years later the prep school became coeducational.

Built in château style by the same contractor as next-door Bowes Museum, the school sits in an attractive campus of 50 acres. The subject areas are organised in a series of teaching blocks – some built in the 1960s/70s, sadly out of keeping with the older buildings. The jewel in the crown is certainly the Kenneth King sixth form centre opened in 2016. Its contemporary corporate feel is a great backdrop for its business-suited sixth formers to get a first taste of life beyond Barney – and a money spinner for external conference hirings in the long holidays. The new physics/ICT building also provides an up-to-date facility well fitted out with hardware.

The school's values, which have remained unchanged throughout its history, are community, endeavour, integrity, compassion, duty and enjoyment, and are enshrined as the Barney Way. They run through the school like Brighton rock, underpin the philosophy of learning and codes of behaviour and this collegiality remains for life. There is a flourishing Old Barnardians network of over 5,000 members who not only support recent leavers at university and taking first career steps but turn up for school events.

Famous OBs are the rugby-playing Underwood brothers and Rob Andrews, actor Kevin Whately (Inspector Morse and Lewis) and Bentley Beetham, explorer and member of the 1924 Everest expedition.

Pastoral care, inclusivity and discipline: House system intrinsic to the Barney Way. Five day and three boarding houses, where pupils go to register, meet at break and lunchtimes and for house meetings and after-school sessions. Myriad house competitions range from the Barney Bash to cake decorating, public speaking and art. The year group tutors are the first port of call for pupils and parents and the houseparents have an open door.

Rules and escalating sanctions seen by pupils as clear and fair. Zero tolerance of drugs – two pupils expelled in recent years, though this was an isolated incident. Peer support provided by sixth formers trained to listen to any issues with the underlying message, 'respect is always deserved, and you are never alone'.

Pupils well turned out in practical, washable navy blazers and grey skirts or trousers, distinguished by house ties. Sixth formers smartly attired in business dress in keeping with their corporate sixth form building. Nutritious meals enjoyed by all we spoke to, served in the dining room in the oldest part of the school.

Pupils and parents: Diverse backgrounds. Parents including wealthy landowners, business people and a declining but significant number of service personnel. Two-thirds are day pupils and there are nine bus routes, mostly up to 20 miles, but including an 'express' service down the A1 from Thirsk.

Predominantly British, Barney pupils are known for being unpretentious, well grounded, modest, and pretty well behaved and friendly. One of our tour guides was an England schools' hockey player but it only came to light when we spotted a news article about him on a house noticeboard. Fewer than 50 international pupils – no nationality dominates, but a good proportion German and Spanish, who come for a year and then stay for longer; small numbers of Hong Kong Chinese, assorted Europeans, Chileans, Mexicans and Indians.

Parents' group Barney Friends supports school events and raises money through social activities, ranging the cake stalls at sports days to wine tasting evenings. Funds raised, including those from the secondhand uniform shop, are shared between charitable causes and school projects.

Money matters: Scholarships and discounts for Forces and Foreign Office families all 10 per cent. Some means-tested bursaries. Discounts for siblings.

The last word: Regeneration is taking place at Barney, embracing traditional values whilst ensuring pupils have the life skills required for success in their brave new 21st-century world. Driven by the energy, commitment and enthusiasm of the newish head and his team and welcomed by the school community as a whole, it's resonating with a wider new audience too. One to watch.

Belhaven Hill School

Belhaven Road, Dunbar, East Lothian EH42 1NN

01368 862785 | headmaster@belhavenhill.com | www.belhavenhill.com

Ages: 7–13

Pupils: 107; Boarders: 65 full (from age 8)

Fees: Day £11,250 – £20,610; Boarding £26,925 pa

Head: Since July 2020, Olly Langton, formerly housemaster at Radley College. Mr Langton was educated at Radley College and has a history degree from Edinburgh, after which he started his teaching career at Ludgrove. Has coached rugby and cricket to U14s, directs plays and organises charity events. He is a keen sportsman, having played cricket at school and university and has also qualified as an instructor for able-bodied and disabled skiers. Married to Rosie, with whom he has three young children. Rosie has taught at St Edward's Oxford, St Paul's boys' in London and at Radley, and is also a freelance graphic designer.

Entrance: No formal test but register as soon as possible. Children spend a taster day (and sometimes a night) the year before they come. Here they attend lessons and take part in sport and activities.

Exit: To the big hitters north and south of the border – Ampleforth, Fettes, Glenalmond, Marlborough, Rugby and Sedbergh most popular. Oundle, Eton, Radley, Harrow, Tudor Hall, Glenalmond and Uppingham also often feature.

Our view: Originally a boys' boarding prep school, it went co-ed in 1995 and thereafter welcomed day pupils. The heart of the school is a mid 18th-century country house with various add-ons out the back. The location, at the edge of the town of Dunbar, close to an 18-hole golf course and the beach, is peachy. Pretty house with delightful grounds. This editor would happily relocate there.

Eight classrooms all tightly grouped around a pond at the rear of the main house. Light, bright rooms and very easy to nip between classrooms. Class sizes 'generally 12-ish'. One computer room plus individual iPads available for pupils. Setting from age 9 – in maths, English, science and languages. Latin and Greek both on offer. No separate scholarship stream: potential scholars have extended learning and additional tuition. Big push on computing in recent years.

Learning support in a new centralised location, with team of four learning support teachers. One-to-one teaching, small groups – whatever is needed. Children can pop into The Hub during quiet reading time (every day after lunch) for a catch-up on any subject. If a child has particular difficulties school 'wouldn't say no' to parents employing additional support but would try to find other solutions first to prevent the child 'standing out or feeling different'.

Drama and dance very popular. Plays for all, nativity for the younger ones. Public speaking encouraged through the annual competition: every pupil has to speak on a topic of their choice for four minutes. Inspirational art that is clearly celebrated and displayed around the school. Woodwork/DT room where tasks involve creativity and problem-solving with a healthy dollop of fun. It's not all about curriculum learning – 'we don't just want to be a sausage factory'. On the day of our visit, fabulous ramshackle boat creations all lined up ready for an America's Cup moment on the school swimming pool.

Sport for all. Two cricket pitches, tennis courts (grass court in the summer), Astroturfs and swimming pool, open for the summer term and first half of autumn term. Swimming lessons once a week and pool often used by the boarders for muckabouts at the weekend. Annual school swimming gala in summer term. Boys play rugby, hockey and cricket while the girls' main sports are netball, hockey and rounders. Lots of sporting success but also an ethos that sport is for all and everyone gets a shot at representing the school. Tennis, golf, skiing, athletics and football also on offer. Functional sports hall, which doubles as theatre for school plays. Lots of extracurricular activities from taekwondo to croquet, fly-tying and horse riding. Piping very strong; lots of music lessons and choir.

Rather than causing merry chaos, both the dogs and the children seem to be happy and calm in each other's company

All of the 7-year-olds and most of 8-year-olds are day pupils. The majority of older pupils board. School operates a bi-weekly boarding programme, finishing every other weekend on a Friday at 1pm. Buses operate on these weekends – to Perth, Stonehaven and Thornhill (Dumfries) – to help parents who live further afield. Pupils return either on the Sunday night or first thing on Monday morning.

Day pupils from form 4 upwards are expected to attend school every other Saturday from 8.30am to 4.30pm for lessons and games matches.

Walled garden is well kept but not manicured and children can plant up garden plots of their own. The plots are blank canvases – from vegetables to pond digging to tractor tyres, some major earthworks, anything goes. These mini gardens aren't show pieces for visitors but are for the children to have the freedom to guddle about and have fun in. Fierce competition for the annual garden trophy.

Time to mention the animals... Let's kick off with the dogs. Lots of them. Some teachers bring their dogs into their classrooms, where they can be petted between lessons and sit quietly once the lesson begins. There are 11 'school dogs' at the moment. Rather than causing merry chaos, both the dogs and the children seem to be happy and calm in each other's company. Two guinea pigs too – Honeycomb and White Fang.

Still perceived as Scotland's school for toffs and grandees, although head tells us that now 30 per cent of parents are first-time buyers. Some children of former pupils, some from south of the border – often with Scottish connections. However, the base has widened out somewhat with many more families from East Lothian and the borders. Lots of social parents and good friendships. Numbers had taken a dip but are now on the up again. No plans to change to weekly/flexi boarding. Head says, 'We see ourselves as the pre-eminent full boarding school in Scotland.'

Boarding: For the boarders, Sunday kicks off with a chapel service taken by the headmaster or visiting preachers. Headmaster has introduced new fun-packed activities on Sundays for boarders – bubble football being a particular favourite. Head has done much to improve communications with parents through fortnightly newsletter, Facebook and Instagram. Manners are important and any bullying is kept firmly under control – 'educating the children and talking about it is key'.

Boys' dorms in the main building, recently refurbed, with new bathroom and kitchen. Light and bright rooms, dull tartan curtains. Older boys have new snazzy desk/bed combos – very smart and popular. Girls accommodated in a fab new building separate from the main house. Super cosy, homely dorms, very prettily decorated. Big pinboards, floral curtains. Circular common room (Rosie room), plasma telly and piles of beanbags. Boarders aren't allowed phones but can phone home from their dorms. iPod shuffles allowed for music. We hear that the 'matrons are lovely' and the 'pastoral care fantastic'.

Children tell us that food is good ('great match teas') and there's plenty of it, although a couple of junior gourmets reported that the breakfast sausages were 'way more tasty than the ones at supper time'.

The last word: We saw so many well mannered, happy children on our visit, and time and time again we hear that parents are 'delighted with the school'. This is a traditional prep school in a beautiful setting with an all-round approach to education that is hard to fault.

Bootham School

51 Bootham, York, North Yorkshire YO30 7BU

01904 623261 | admissions@boothamschool.com | www.boothamschool.com

Ages: 3–19

Pupils: 613; sixth form: 141; Boarders: 63 full, 17 weekly/flexi (from age 11)

Fees: Day £7,290 – £18,900; Boarding £20,250 – £34,410 pa

Head: Since 2016, Chris Jeffery BA PGCE (50s). Educated at Bristol Grammar School, history at York University, PGCE at Exeter University. Taught history and head of house at Bristol Grammar (eight years); head of middle school and deputy head at The Perse, Cambridge (eight years), head of The Grange School, Cheshire (11 years). Currently teaches personal, health and social education here; has taught history, English and RE.

Very committed to pupil wellbeing (founding chair of Headmasters' and Mistresses' Conference wellbeing working group), genuinely cares as much about pupils' happiness at school and in their future lives as their academic prowess and greatly values the school's primary focus on relationships and Quaker ideals (wearing a white as well as a red poppy when we visited – plus a very jolly multicoloured tie). Good sense of humour, modest and approachable: pupils address him – and all staff – by his first name and have, he says happily, no inhibitions about visiting him to express criticisms on school matters. 'Inspirational and very child-focused,' said a parent. 'Quickly knows every child, and their parents, by their first name.'

Married to Carol, a nurse; two adult sons and a daughter at Bootham sixth form. Enjoys song writing and performing, all sports (supports a number of 'spectacularly underachieving teams', as he puts it), 'Spotify addict', walking, travel and attending church.

Junior School head: since 2013, Helen Todd BA MEd (late 30s). Attended All Hallows RC High, Macclesfield, then English at Warwick University. Taught English at Durston House, head of English Aysgarth School, deputy head Edge Grove. Appointed vice chair of Independent Association of Prep Schools for 2018. Does various teaching at Bootham. Married to David, IT manager at Cundall Manor School; boy at Aysgarth, daughter at Bootham. Enjoys amateur dramatics, walking, travel.

Dynamic and 'ambitious for the school'. Has broadened curriculum to cover cultural studies and focus more on skills, to prepare children for 21st century future. Revels in learning opportunities through freedom from Sats constraints. Straightforward, businesslike, flexible, approachable, supportive and 'very present', say parents.

Entrance: Junior school: non selective. Taster day – a normal day in school, with future classmates, to allow child and teacher to get to know each other and ensure school is a good fit, plus meeting with head and report from current school. Year 5/6 entry has English and maths test included.

Eleven plus: initial 30-minute interview with the headmaster before enrolment about what the child enjoys most/least at school and leisure activities; reference from head of current school (child needs to be at least at national average level for reading, writing and maths). Optional taster Saturday morning in autumn term before entry. Assessment day in January: science and art activities, challenges, brief maths and English comprehension tests.

At 12+,13+ and 14+: all do maths and English papers; years 9 and 10 also do French/German/Spanish paper; short interview with head or deputy head.

Sixth form entry: minimum of seven GCSEs at 4 or above (or six GCSEs, of which three must be at 6 or higher), including maths and English, and requirements of chosen A level subjects (20-25 join).

Exit: Almost all junior school pupils progress to the senior school. Up to a third leave post-16 for more vocational courses at local sixth form colleges. Several to top universities (three to Oxbridge in 2021) to study a broad range of subjects, including art and music. LSE, Central St Martins, Imperial, Durham, Bath, Royal Vet College, Bristol, Warwick, Queen's Belfast, Leeds College of Art, Royal Academy of Music, UCL, St Andrews, Nottingham, Newcastle, Manchester and King's College London all popular. One overseas in 2021 – to Le High University, USA.

Latest results: In 2021, 68 per cent 9-7 at GCSE; 98 per cent 9-4 in both English and maths. At A level, 60 per cent A*/A at A level (83 per cent A*-B). In 2019 (the last year when exams took place), 46 per cent 9-7 at GCSE; 41 per cent A*/A at A level (64 per cent A*-B).

Teaching and learning: Steady A level results. Standard choice including classics, Latin, EPQ; strong modern langs, maths, physics, chemistry, psychology, art. Good gender balance for maths and science uptake. Average sets of 11.

GCSE achievement generally strong – including Latin – with no gender difference. After-school astronomy in historic observatory, with use of original William Cooke telescope – one of the first schools to have its own observatory in 1850s; open to state school students, too. DT product design the only technology. Sets of 15-20.

Year 7 curriculum includes thinking skills, classics, health and the environment. Latin, German and Spanish (in addition to French) added in year 8. Maths and French sets from year 8; classes of around 18. Creative approaches, eg building a model medieval castle competition.

Inclusive gifted and talented policy: students undertake ambitious and imaginative projects, eg building eco car to race in Greenpower Challenge; creating astronomy GCSE textbook; displaying dreams of refugee children from different parts of the world on a large dreamcatcher. Much involvement in York independent–state schools enrichment partnership. Success in national competitions – MFL debating, chemistry, maths.

Head cares as much about pupils' happiness at school and in their future lives as their academic prowess and greatly values the school's Quaker ideals

Juniors: enlightened curriculum – core skills plus cross-curricular topics, creative and flexible approaches with practical tasks, eg building flood-proof house, cooking with war-time rations. Different European language studied each year from years 2-4, including cultural studies; Latin and Mandarin for years 5 and 6. Thinking skills taught through Philosophy4Children. ICT skills developed through topic work and dedicated lessons. Plenty for the very bright and talented, eg challenge and enrich workshops, also open to state schools. Big focus on outdoor learning and trips – specialist outdoor education and forest school trained teacher for outdoor skills, from whittling to firelighting. Classes of 15-20 higher up, can be as small as 10 or 12 lower down.

Learning support and SEN: Well-qualified SENCo; mainly wide range of mild to moderate learning difficulties but would consider more challenging pupils to see if school could meet their needs. Reading test for all at start of each year to identify literacy support needs; initial dyslexia screening within department on referral (free), charge for full exam access arrangements assessment. Years 7-11 small support groups. EAL individual and small group support; older students prepared for IELTS (no extra charge).

Junior children monitored for additional needs such as dyslexia as they progress (high praise from parent about support for this; another spoke of child's emotional needs being 'subtly and gently addressed') – very capable SENCo, who works closely with senior school SENCo, says she can tell by years 3 or 4 if a child needs a more appropriate school and will help family to find it and child to settle in. Younger children have in-class support, mainly small groups outside the classroom for the older ones; families helped to pre-teach topics. EAL support – many children from overseas. Very engaging resident therapy dog, but we were less taken by the (caged) snake in the foyer.

The arts and extracurricular: Very attractive arts centre with colourful, large, collaborative cranes mobile and studio-sized concert hall/lecture theatre. Free weekly lunchtime programme of arts performances and lectures in Georgian recital room open to public. Quantities of very high level and varied music – more than 20 different ensembles, over 60 per cent learn instrument (scholarships to top music colleges), has hosted York guitar festival. Recent drama productions include Shakespeare, The Wind in the Willows, Peter Pan. No cultural opportunities wasted – poems posted on loo doors by head of English.

Excellent art in various media displayed throughout school, including several collaborative pieces. Artist in residence; all art teachers practise and exhibit. Outstanding DT department produces unusual number of Arkwright scholars and successful engineers, male and female – much work to promote engineering careers. 3D printer (used to make a Dalek), laser, three CAD/CAM machines; professional-looking finished artefacts. Links with the real world, eg designing Antarctic research station task set by engineering consultancy. Good percentage of girls do DT at GCSE and A level.

Quaker values and ethos are central. Relationships and mutual respect, come first; co-operation, peaceful approaches to conflict, individuality and equality are all fostered

One hour of timetabled leisure activities every week day – choice of up to 80, including bell-ringing, candle making, mini drone flying, world shaper action group. Community service very big, via DofE and the Bootham Challenge: awards at four levels for the development of soft skills through extracurricular activities. Sustainability taken very seriously – very high standards in new buildings; environmental action group successfully conducted switch-off-fortnight to cut use of gas and electricity; eco schools' Green Flag award.

Thoroughgoing careers programme; year 10s do work experience.

York's cultural and gastronomic advantages exploited; visits to four continents; exchanges with Quaker school in Washington.

Juniors: varied extracurricular. Thriving music and drama – much active contact with York Theatre Royal, annual musical. Interesting art in different media, very well equipped ICT and food tech rooms – we enjoyed observing a boy, in a fetching apron, critically sampling his hot savoury dish. Senior school DT department provides woodwork, mechanics and computer-aided design opportunities. Good choice of extracurricular clubs; residentials for all, including a very popular night in a tent at school for reception.

Sport: Abundant sports facilities, including climbing wall. Wide choice of standard (success at regional level) and additional sports. Recent international fencer, Olympic swimmer and cyclist, national orienteering competitors, plus academy footballers. Tours to California and Spain. Varied PE in juniors too.

Boarding: The girls' house consists of three elegant Georgian houses, with shared flats for sixth formers as preparation for university; comfortable common room, kitchen, cheerful bedrooms. Similar modernised Georgian houses for the boys: the single room we saw looked very cramped, but the shared ones are more spacious; two basement common rooms with games consoles, drum kit, pool table and mega TV screen, plus challenging outdoor climbing frame. Additional sixth form boys' house. Full, weekly and flexi-boarding. House staff supported by recently graduated university students. Saturday morning school followed by good programme of weekend activities and treats, eg late Sunday morning brunch. Happy boarders, apart from the odd grumble about things taking a while to get repaired.

Ethos and heritage: Situated in the centre of York on a nine-acre estate. Gracious Georgian frontages and interiors with skilfully harmonised modern additions. The main building, the original house, has a warm, homely atmosphere – attractive dining room with wooden furniture and red and cream curtains; the original library has been supplemented with a modern mezzanine floor and is lavishly supplied with reference and fiction books.

Founded 1823 by the Society of Friends for boys, fully co-ed by 1983. Only a minority of Quakers now, but Quaker values and ethos are central and make it distinctive. Relationships, based on mutual respect, come first; co-operation, peaceful approaches to conflict, individuality and equality are all fostered – staff and students are currently working on a new chapter of expectations that applies to both groups; school council pupils interview teaching candidates. The goal is to produce young people who are 'happy in their own skins, confident without being arrogant' (head), who assume they will find purpose and contentment in life through contributing to the community and wider world – many go on to work in the voluntary sector – rather than just pursuing materialism and competition: people who recognise and develop 'that of God' in themselves and others. Facilities widely shared with state schools and the community.

The pupils we met were impressively thoughtful and mature, articulate, open, relaxed. They spoke warmly about their teachers. 'They care about you and your development'

The morning Meeting – a short period of silent reflection – is valued by the pupils: 'When I was in year 7 I thought it was boring, but now I appreciate it' (year 9 boy); 'It gives you time to think about what you want, or not think at all'; 'It's a good time to relax, not be busy'.

Fab choice of high-quality food made in house: hot and cold, carnivore and veggie – we can understand why many parents are keen to take up the open invitation to have lunch as a family on Saturdays (no charge), after the optional Meeting, and term it the 'best restaurant in York'.

More relaxed (and cheaper) uniform than most – years 7-9: polo shirt, hoodie, black trousers/tartan skirt; years 10-11: smart casual; sixth: free choice so long as appropriate for school.

Junior school acquired 2002 – purpose built, intimate size. Extensive grounds with playing fields (shared with senior school), courts and thoughtfully equipped playgrounds – we particularly liked the covered picnic tables with built-in games boards and the outdoor oven. Yurt for quiet time in breaks, peace garden, plus amphitheatre for small-scale performances. Attractive spacious classrooms with colourful displays; delightful early years/before and after-school area (wraparound care 7.30am-6pm).

Quaker values displayed on the walls and developed, for example, through encouragement to be active citizens – awareness of politics, school council, charity fundraising, singing carols to old people. We liked the 'disposition boxes', containing tokens for displays of independence, resilience, being collaborative, creative, reflective and adventurous – not competitive, other than aiming to improve on the previous term or year, though plenty of matches and house competitions on offer as well. Strong sense of community, being mutually supportive; individual achievements seen as the result of group effort. Children take the initiative, eg bid for funds raised by (very active) PTA, then choose and order equipment; interview teaching candidates; year 6s plan and lead their residential.

Parental praise for chef, who cares about the children as individuals and provides a great diversity of high-quality food. They also like the staff eating with the children, encouraging them to eat correctly, and the amount of time the year 5-6s spend at the senior school, which helps them to adjust easily when they move up. 'The school is very good at developing confidence and self worth and sees the children in a holistic way – they want to know about any outside school difficulties as well and are very helpful with them.'

A deeply impressive number of very distinguished ex-pupils dating back to the 19th century. Scholars – 17 fellows of the Royal Society; mathematician Lewis Fry Richardson ('father of fractals'); historian AJP Taylor; child psychiatrist Michael Rutter. Politicians, eg anti Corn Law leader John Bright and Olympic athlete and Nobel Peace Prize winner Philip Noel-Baker. A tradition of social reform exemplified by members of the Rowntree family and actor and disabled champion Brian Rix. More recently: Olivia Garfield, CEO of Severn Trent Water (one of 2013 Fortune Magazine's top 10 high flyers under 40), Elizabeth Waterman (in list of top 50 women in engineering), Emily Sutton, artist and illustrator, Benjamin Leftwich, singer-songwriter.

Pastoral care, inclusivity and discipline: Wellbeing a particular focus. Pupils talked appreciatively of readily accessible health centre services: 'You can go there whenever you want, even if you're in a lesson.' Access to a counsellor. Programme of external speakers on mental wellbeing much appreciated – a parent of three boys of different ages reported, 'The material has been new and interesting; they understand things from a young person's perspective.' Sixth formers provide peer listening scheme.

Punishment seen as opportunity for offender to learn more about the reasons for their behaviour and its effects on others. Education in downsides of mobile use – restricted for younger boarders at night; older students only allowed them in relaxation time.

Pupils and parents: Day pupils mainly from York and the surrounding area, up to a 25-mile radius. Senior pupils from the junior school, prep schools, state primaries. Boarders from the UK plus over

20 other countries. Parents from a range of backgrounds – business, professionals, public service, academics; ethnically mixed. 'Our parents want their children to become good people, have purposeful, meaningful lives,' says head; they value the Quaker ethos and educational values. Parents we spoke to in general delighted with the school – just the odd comment about occasional failures of communication.

The pupils we met were impressively thoughtful and mature, articulate, open, relaxed. They spoke warmly about their teachers. 'They care about you and your development as a person… They want to know how you are and feel.' Space given to discussion of politics (in lessons and morning Meetings) and the practice of it – eg the recent mock election (Labour won – just) and EU referendum (Remain won 70:30). They also appreciate the priority given to relationships, the non-authoritarian and relatively relaxed atmosphere, with freedom to speak your mind in lessons, friendliness and sense of community.

Money matters: Means-tested bursaries awarded according to need and academic performance in 11+ and 13+ exams. Music scholarships of up to 50 per cent of fees based on tests and audition plus performance in entrance assessment. Bursaries for children from Quaker families from age 3. Means-tested scholarship/bursary for candidates from state-maintained schools who gain a minimum of eight grades 7+ at GCSE.

The last word: Strikingly friendly and calm atmosphere, with priority genuinely given to the development of emotional intelligence, as the way to future happiness, and respect for individual differences, rather than on academic and other kinds of achievement. Not that results don't matter – parents say they bring out the best in children in all ways and that talents are cultivated to the highest level.

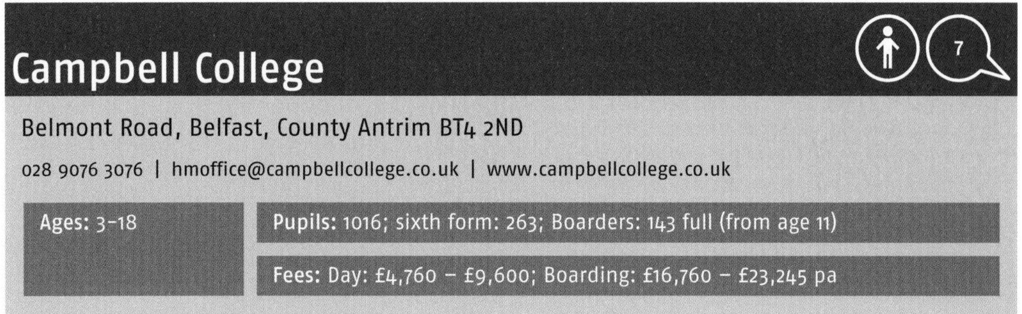

Campbell College

7

Belmont Road, Belfast, County Antrim BT4 2ND

028 9076 3076 | hmoffice@campbellcollege.co.uk | www.campbellcollege.co.uk

Ages: 3–18

Pupils: 1016; sixth form: 263; Boarders: 143 full (from age 11)

Fees: Day: £4,760 – £9,600; Boarding: £16,760 – £23,245 pa

Headmaster: Since 2012 Robert M Robinson MBE BSc MEd PQH (NI). Married to Sharon; they live in a house in the grounds and have two grown up children. He grew up in Belfast and went to Methody (Methodist College) and read chemistry at Queen's, where he also took a master's in education. He had planned to go into the church and says he 'fell into teaching'. His first job was at Glastry High School where he 'learnt to bring out the best in each pupil and how good teaching could transform lives'. He taught chemistry at Regent House before moving to Rainey Endowed School, where he spent 10 years as headmaster – he transformed the school and was awarded an MBE for services to education – he collaborated with other schools in the town and shared best practice which broke down barriers – 'It was a very exciting time,' he says.

Softly spoken but passionate about the school, he says, 'You can feel the 120 years of history in every corner of the place'; 'I would not have moved for any other position.' He says that joining a boarding school was a leap of faith as he expected it to be grim dorms and iron bedsteads; he was pleasantly surprised and would now like to grow the boarding. 'The ethos here is simple and complex,' he says, 'to encourage every boy to be the best he can, be as this will breed confidence and success.' 'Boys will jump as high as the bar is set.' 'Our aim is the development of character and leaderships skills, and we want boys to believe they can truly make a difference to society.' He believes that single-sex education suits boys as 'They tend to showboat for the girls, and here they don't have to worry about perceptions and can feel comfortable about getting involved with the choir or the arts.' He is approachable and easy to talk to, and is a regular on the touchline at matches and at school pick-up time. He sends signed birthday cards to every boy in the school, 'a lovely touch,' said a mother, 'and makes the school feel like a huge family'. Ever modest, he says, 'I fear I am one-dimensional, as

Ardvreck School

my great pleasures are reading, playing the guitar, walking and running and the church.'

Three of the five families living on site are called Robinson, in fact it is almost a requirement for working here, and causes some wonderful confusion with emails.

Entrance: Entry to the junior school at 3+ or 4+. Most boys join the senior school at 11+ or 16+, but will take applicants at any time if space available. Eleven plus entrance is via the Northern Ireland CEA and GL assessment (similar to the English 11+ and with similar problems with over-tutoring). Language test for non-native English speakers – their English must be good enough for them to be able to access lessons. A minimum of six GCSEs at grade 5 or above including English and maths plus a specified number of points required to join the sixth form – both from within the school and external candidates. Sometimes it is suggested that a boy might take a different path.

Exit: Nearly all junior school boys move up to the senior school. Around a third leave after GCSES; about half of sixth form leavers go to Russell Group universities. Cardiff, Coventry, Glasgow, Newcastle, Queen's University Belfast, Stirling and Ulster all popular. Boys study a wide range of subjects including biomedical sciences, business and media studies, art and design and computer science – STEM subjects are increasingly popular. Three medics in 2021, and one student off overseas (to ETH Zürich to study engineering).

Latest results: In 2021, 39 9-7 at GCSE; 46 per cent A*/A at A level (72 per cent A*-B). In 2019 (the last year when exams took place), no results released for GCSE but in 2018, 76 per cent 9-7. In 2019, 28 per cent A*/A at A level.

Teaching and learning: Only 70 per cent of pupils joining at 11+ are academically selected, which puts these results into context. Offers 26 subjects at GCSE and 27 at A level, and curriculum tweaked each year according to demand. Good range of hard academic subjects including politics offered at A level as well as media studies, leisure studies, PE and BTECs in hospitality and sport. The most popular and successful A levels are maths, history, physics, chemistry and business studies.

As well as the usual subjects, computing and ICT, business studies, hospitality & catering, motor vehicle studies, leisure & tourism and Chinese offered at GCSE. Most take individual sciences but dual award offered and a handful take the single award. All taught in quite old-fashioned labs – a new science block is on the headmaster's wish list.

Numerous academic competitions and trips: physicists visit CERN and technology students often take part in Sentinus Young Innovators finals at Ulster University. Business studies students visit the BMW factory in Munich and there is a history trip to the battlefields and war graves of northern France.

Rugby is king here and the top rugby players are heroes. The school has won the Ulster Schools Cup 23 times and boys have represented Ulster and Ireland

Some subjects shared with Strathearn Girls' School – girls come over for drama and boys go to Strathearn for media studies. German is shared between the two schools with good results, thanks to an inspirational teacher. All boys study home economics for the first two years, with particular emphasis on healthy eating.

The headmaster says that 'every boy has the right to be pushed academically' and there is subject streaming from year 8 (English year 7). GCSE class sizes about 18, dropping to 14 in sixth form and as low as three for some subjects like further maths.

Very low turnover among the staff, which gives stability and a sense of belonging. Says the head, 'Once you teach at Campbell it gets into your bones.' Still a good age range and balance of male and female staff, with almost half being female. 'Teachers know their stuff and go the extra mile for us,' said a pupil.

Warm, light-filled library with a full-time librarian as well as pupil librarians, well equipped with computers and printers, a popular space for studying. Busy careers department with three staff. 'Boys need to see the context of what work can do and need to meet people in the work place,' says the headmaster. Old Campbellians are keen to give back to the school and come to give talks about the world of work via the Leaders in Society programme, eg what it is actually like to be a young barrister. They also help with personal statements, interview technique and how boys should present themselves. Boys expected to do three days of work experience in year 13 (English year 12) – old boys very helpful and school has a good network of contacts.

Learning support and SEN: Fairly large SEN department with a SENCo and a team of assistants who can liaise with external agencies if necessary. Most are identified by screening and careful observation by staff or self-referral. Pupils taught in mainstream classes with extra help as required in one-to-one sessions or small groups. Those needing any extra help are given an IEP, the SEN department works closely with teaching and pastoral staff and parents are kept up to date. Those with literacy difficulties can choose not to take both English GCSEs. About 28 statemented children in the school, with conditions ranging from autism and hearing difficulties to wheelchair users – managed discreetly so boys can join in as much as possible and take part in some sports.

EAL team of three – about 70 pupils need some form of assistance; department offers pastoral as well as language support and international students see the head of EAL as their first point of contact. Pupils can take a GCSE in their own language and the department will prepare pupils for the IELTS exams.

The arts and extracurricular: Head of music reinvigorating the department – about 120 learn an instrument and performance is part of the new remit. There is a large choir, chamber choir, orchestra, jazz band and string quartet. Active drama department, with 120-seat theatre and drama studio – girls from Strathearn come over to join in and the two schools collaborate on large-scale musicals.

Well-equipped technology department which offers CAD and a laser cutter, and impressive art and ceramics displayed around the school; we were particularly struck by a red chalk drawing of a boy's grandfather. Not that many take art and design at GCSE, but those who do get very good results with vast majority top grades.

Wide range of after-school activities every day. Campbell College has one of the largest combined CCFs in the UK with over 300 members – all voluntary and includes a pipe band. The army is by far the most popular but many attracted to the RAF as a way of getting a pilot's licence. Members of the CCF can take a BTEC in public service.

About 85 boys involved with DofE with 12-15 each year getting gold. One sixth former has contested and won Youth Parliament elections and represents East Belfast in the MYP. About 40 do Young Enterprise each year with recent projects including selfie sticks and software for keeping track of your phone.

Sport: 'Sporting prowess is part of the fabric of the school,' says the prospectus. Rugby and hockey the main sports but school also fields three football teams. Badminton, basketball and table tennis popular with the international students. Rugby is king here and the top rugby players are heroes. The school has won the Ulster Schools Cup 23 times and boys have represented Ulster and Ireland. Matches played all over Northern Ireland as well as south of the border and in Britain, and there is a rugby tour to South Africa, Canada or Australia every three years. 'You don't have to be brilliant, though, and boys have a lot of fun at the lower levels and it is even okay not to play at all,' said one less sporty boy. Athletics and cricket the main summer sports, with two cricket teams per year group.

At weekends boys can take a taxi into Belfast and go to the cinema or karting or a rugby match – boys organise and staff facilitate

Eleven rugby pitches, including the hallowed first XV Fox's Field overlooked by Stormont. Two synthetic pitches for hockey, a 25-metre pool, a fitness suite, two sports halls and a running track; boys can play golf at the local Shandon golf club. The school has its own rifle range and has a good record of success at Bisley – although some of the younger boys complain that they don't get a chance to shoot. The school will support boys who want to take part in outside activities; for example, one keen showjumper put together a school team to take part in local competitions.

Boarding: 'The ethos of boarding runs through the whole school' and many staff and their families live on site all year round. Numbers have grown recently and there are now nearly 150 boarders from all over the world: Northern Ireland, including some expats, rest of UK and Europe, especially Spanish, and what the headmaster calls the far-away pupils – about 40 from Hong Kong and China and usually a handful from the Cayman Islands and the UAE, who come for the rugby.

They live in School House. The original dorms were for 50 boys each but now junior boys (aged 11-13) share small rooms of up to five and all senior boys from year 11 (English year 10) have their own study bedrooms. Upper sixth have a separate house with ensuite bathrooms, which also accommodates up to 16 girl boarders from Strathearn School (separated by locked, alarmed doors). The conversion of the original Victorian building has posed a few challenges but all the rooms we saw were light and airy and extremely tidy. Dedicated head of boarding (another Mr Robinson) and a team of staff look after the boys and the girls have their very own Miss Honey to take care of them.

Some local boys go home for the weekend but usually 90-100 in on Saturday nights. Sports and activities for all on Saturday mornings and most day boys come in. Sundays are quieter but weekend activities are consistently being reviewed. Boys can take a taxi into Belfast and go to the cinema or karting or a rugby match – boys organise and staff facilitate. Plenty organised during the week and boys have access to the fitness suite every evening and to the swimming pool on Thursdays and can play squash or take part in house football, badminton and basketball competitions. 'Sport is a good way to socialise and get to know people,' said an international boarder. House cookery is popular and boys are allowed to go to Tesco on Monday nights and cook their own supper. Library for junior prep as well as a games room, sitting areas and a television and Xbox rooms – 'although we hardly ever watch television,' said one boarder.

Ethos and heritage: Founded in 1894 with a bequest from Henry Campbell, a philanthropist who had made his fortune in the linen trade and wanted to give something back to society, the school is set on a 100-acre wooded site in East Belfast. The main building is a monument to imperialism with an imposing, red-brick façade complete with clock tower, and radiates high Victorian ideals. Inside it is all wooden panelling and displays of silverware with an open fire in the entrance lobby. The galleried central hall with a stained-glass rose window is at the heart of the school and is used for plays, concerts, assemblies and chapel services. The school is very conscious of its history and traditions – pictures of the fallen from both world wars line the walls, but it is not a backward looking place and respect and tolerance are part of its fabric. CS Lewis attended the school for a short time, and it is rumoured that the gas lamp in the drive is the inspiration for the one in the Narnia books.

Old Campbellians come back to the school and give talks about the world of work via the Leaders in Society programme, eg what it is actually like to be a young barrister

Boys are smartly turned out and wear black badged blazers and black trousers with a white shirt and house tie. Whole-school charity strategy driven by the boys – all vote for the school's charity of the year and raise about £6,000 a year. They run large and small events – pumpkin carving at the local hospice, a touch rugby family festival, Christmas market, a jingle bell run which brings in the local community.

Kindergarten and junior school for boys aged 3-11 in the grounds is quite separate from the senior school, but shares some of the facilities, including the swimming pool and sports pitches, and boys come up to the main dining hall for lunch. A very well-designed multipurpose space with an opening roof and classrooms leading off. Has its own ICT suite, library, Astro and sports hall. Lots of outdoor learning, including a mud kitchen, and boys can build dens in the woods.

Produces confident, friendly boys who are able to stand up and do a presentation by the age of 7. They are made aware of the world of work from an early age, and doctors and dentists visit the school to talk about their work, to help make learning real. Boy-friendly approach to reading and writing with male authors coming in to give talks, and artwork is linked to topics. Boys from the senior school act as mentors and positive role models, and are trained to help with reading sessions – this works both ways as also looks good on a UCAS form.

Wraparound care is available from 8am until 6pm to help working parents and those with sons in the senior school.

Distinguished list of old boys with a good representation from the army including a VC and an air chief marshall, rugby players, numerous MPs, film makers, judges, media people and journalists as well as Tim Martin, founder and chairman of Wetherspoons and actor David Caves of Silent Witness fame.

Pastoral care, inclusivity and discipline: Six houses for day boys and one for boarders, with healthy competition between them in the form of debating, assemblies and sports day. Each has a housemaster and all boys have a personal tutor attached to the house, who is also the first point of contact for parents. Boys can take risks and learn that it is okay to get things wrong. The ones we spoke to were very happy with single-sex education: 'It means we can focus on our studies and get good grades and play lots of sport.' 'It is a lovely environment to learn in,' said a parent, 'where boys can be boys but are treated as young adults, and are encouraged to do everything to their full potential.'

Everyone eats lunch in the enormous dining hall, though despite the good and plentiful food – even the bread is baked on site – some prefer to bring in a packed lunch.

The school has a robust set of policies to deal with any misdemeanours – immediate suspension if a boy seriously breaches the school's code of conduct, which can lead to permanent exclusion, but issues dealt with on a case-by-case basis. Bullying is not tolerated and the house system means tutors know boys well and can nip it in the bud.

A counsellor comes in one day a week, and several members of staff are also trained as counsellors – parents and staff can refer pupils or boys can self-refer. Quick to pick up problems and get in touch with parents if they are concerned. A close eye kept on time management to make sure boys don't take on too much, especially in sixth form.

Pupils and parents: Some parents very affluent and others struggle to send their children here, but all want to give their sons the very best education and are supportive of the school. About 40 per cent of boarders are foreign nationals, mainly from Europe and the Far East – the headmaster goes on marketing trips to Hong Kong. Some of the Europeans only come for a year and can take a pared-down GCSE course.

There is no PTA but a parents' forum helps them feel involved in their sons' lives. Three progress cards and one report per year plus ongoing communication makes parents feel part of the community, and a parent Campbellian gives parents a voice and acts as a way of raising concerns. Old boys are extremely loyal to their school and the Old Campbellian Society has over 5,000 members spanning four generations. They support scholarships and international exchange visits and there are a number of get-togethers throughout the year including dances and dinners and the Boxing Day rugby fixture.

Produces well-rounded boys 'of management quality' who are ready for life after school.

Money matters: The school is a Voluntary B grammar school, which means that fees for senior day tuition for EU passport holders are under £3,000 pa (over £8,000 pa for non-EU). All tuition, teachers' salaries etc are paid for by the state but the school has to pay for the upkeep of the buildings. The senior boarding fee for EU citizens including tuition is over £15,000, over £20,000 for non-EU citizens. Academic scholarships for up to 50 per cent of fees and the school offers bursaries of up to 100 per cent of fees based on academic performance for boys on free school meals.

The last word: A highly successful school with a strong sense of history, where academic achievement and excellence on the rugby pitch are highly rated – but still a tolerant and inclusive community with strong pastoral care.

Cargilfield School

45 Gamekeeper's Road, Edinburgh EH4 6HU

0131 3362207 | registrar@cargilfield.com | www.cargilfield.com

Ages: 3–13

Pupils: 276; Boarders: 53 weekly/flexi

Fees: Day £10,890 – £17,250; Boarding £40 per night – £21,150 pa

Headmaster: Since 2014, Rob Taylor. English degree from Durham and PGCE from Cambridge. Previously the registrar at Harrow School, he also has experience of running Ashdown Prep in Sussex and has taught at Wellington College, where he was also a housemaster.

A very popular head. 'He knows each child off to a T. Very approachable and brilliant at energising everybody.' He and his wife Sarah decided to return to her Scottish roots with their three children, partly because of the more balanced pace of life and partly because 'Cargilfield is so highly regarded by the big schools down south.'

Entrance: Every child is assessed to some degree, even at nursery level, although it is 'age appropriate'. It's not selective, apparently, but more to check that they school can support their needs. But if you're keen to get your little darling in as quick as possible, be aware, there are waiting lists for quite a few of the year groups.

Exit: There is a joint staff effort to make links with senior schools across the UK, and the success of their pupils in recent years means that they are firmly on the radar of many of the big hitters down south. Head says, 'The irony is that Cargilfield is better known down south than in Edinburgh.' Fettes and Glenalmond the most popular destinations but others to Eton, Oundle, Uppingham, Harrow, Winchester and Winchester. Scholarships in sport, art, academic, all rounder and music in 2021, plus an art exhibition.

Our view: Under the guidance of Rob Taylor and his wife, Cargilfield is 'buzzing', according to some parents. Within the last three years Cargundians have won a King's Scholarship to Eton, the top scholarships at Wycombe Abbey and Rugby, two Winchester elections, a Harrow music scholarship and scooped the top scholarship to Fettes for two years running.

Does that sound a little academically heated? Less than you'd think, apparently. 'Our child is definitely mid-range. Not struggling particularly, but not super bright, but they really seem to bring out the best in him,' said one parent.

Head says at the top end of the school they try to keep streaming to a minimum for the two Common Entrance classes so that nobody feels they have been downgraded in any way. Then in form 8 they have a scholarship class for those who are really 'pushing ahead academically'.

'We think it's important that we don't define academic ability too early, so that those who are struggling don't get downhearted. We stream them from form 7, although maths is in sets from form 4.' He adds, 'A good number of families are coming to us from down south because they want to escape that pressure-cooker of achievement. We want to provide a balance.'

And if your child is in need of learning support, there are three part-time staff plus the head of the junior school on hand to help out. But one parent we spoke to felt they needed to strengthen their approach by upskilling all of the staff to a greater degree, although once a problem was diagnosed they were very good at dealing with it.

One of the most contentious features of academic life at Cargilfield is the No Prep rule. Yes, quite an unusual decision for a prep school, you'd think, but they're adamant it's for the best. The parents we spoke to loved it, on the whole: 'The days are long enough without prep'; 'We still have to practise cello and learn vocab'; although a couple of parents felt it meant they had no idea what their children were up to until parents' evening and were worried about their ability for independent study later on. Rob Taylor says they're addressing this with the form 8s by introducing periods of independent revision, and learning support has developed a programme to help progress this further.

And if the children haven't got their nose in a book, there is certainly a huge range of clubs and activities to keep them busy; everything from skiing to fly tying. But as one parent told us, 'There is so much on offer you have to make sure they don't burn themselves out. It was actually a teacher who told me that!' New outdoor learning centre popular too.

Now over the years Cargilfield has won the reputation of being a bit of a sporting behemoth, in Scottish terms at least (although, with more pupils than anyone else, that might be considered a given). But does that mean that your non-sporty child will struggle to get into any teams? 'In the past, definitely,' said one parent, 'but I notice an effort to improve that.' Certainly, a change since our last visit, we were very cheered to see that the girls' sporting achievements are as much centre stage as the boys'.

The school does run some full year group boarding weekends, which bring together each year for a big bonding session. One parent we spoke to said, 'I don't see what's wrong with a bit of boredom. They should learn how to entertain themselves too'

One child we spoke to said, 'I'm definitely not sporty and in my last school there was the "cool" gang who were in all the top teams, but it really doesn't matter here. You just have a go and nobody makes fun of you!' 'I came from a state school so I had no idea how to play a lot of the sports, but they spent time giving me extra coaching and now I'm in the rugby firsts and going to Sedbergh.'

We were also pleased to hear that there is a big increase in the sheer volume of games being played (two new Astroturf pitches ensure there's enough space all year round). This, we're told, is part of a serious attempt to get every child to pull on a Cargilfield jersey at least once a term.

There is also a 50-minute break in the day, four times a week, for activities and clubs. And this doesn't have to be sport; the children, they say, are just as likely to play chess, go to coding club or run around the big treehouse system built in the grounds. The staff also put on outdoor pursuits such as mountain biking, kayaking or climbing twice a week for anyone not keen on team sports.

Musically, Cargilfield seems to be very much on song with four music scholarships last year. They say it is very unusual for a child not to do some form of music. Boundless enthusiasm all round; choir, pipe band, wind group, orchestra. 'We try to get them playing in a group as soon as possible so that they get that sense of belonging. It must be a socially advantageous thing.' Lessons on just about everything you can think of, except a full drum kit, apparently.

Art abounds, with some ambitious and impressive projects and an art club to help pupils build up their portfolios. Bigger emphasis is being put on finding emerging talent further down the school. And for those who remember with joy those prep school plays, every year group from nursery upwards takes to the stage at least once a year. One parent we spoke to, however, thought the drama could definitely be stronger.

Pre-prep seems to be bursting at the seams and is now rather hard to get in to. Set in a delightful, newly refurbished colonnaded building across a courtyard from the main school, it's a bustling place run by the highly respected Emma Buchanan. She describes it as very much 'active' and 'discovery' learning. Lots of running outside, trying new things, although as they've just completed a big review of how maths is taught in the pre-prep, we're assuming the three Rs are firmly on the agenda too. Reading is Jolly Phonics and Oxford Reading Tree and they can all read by form 4. If you're a working parent there is a useful after-school club to six o' clock.

PHSE plays a very important part, says Rob Taylor. 'All the teaching staff have noticed how much more pressure the children are under and mental health is on the agenda from pre-prep.'

Rob Taylor and his team have also instigated biannual staff meetings when every child is discussed in detail, in an effort to make sure the 'quiet ones in the middle get just as much attention as the others'. As for parents, staff say they operate an open door policy and work hard to build good relationships. As one parent said, 'If you have a niggle about something you can mention it to Sarah (Taylor) and she's totally on it. She's always there in the background offering support and a lovely smile.'

Boarding: Most prep school boarding houses are cosy, homely affairs these days, but that said Cargilfield does provide its young charges with some very nice accommodation (new since 2021). Is it populated by a big proportion of boarders? Mmm... There are only 13 weekly boarders in the upper school and the rest are flexi-boarders, which means they stay over one or two nights a week or over a boarding weekend. During the summer term this means they can have as many as 50 pupils staying overnight, but for the hard-core weekly boarders it must be tough during the winter months watching your classmates go home to mummy.

The boys' house now has a young male master in charge, which has been a 'huge success', they say. With big dormitories for the boys, dorm cricket is a very regular event. For the girls, it's smaller, pinker rooms and cosy chats on the sofa with matron of an evening.

Cargilfield prides itself on its fortnightly boarding weekends with a dizzying array of activities laid on for the children. But again, you won't find the weekly boarders staying on for this; this really is more of an exciting babysitting service for the day pupils. The school does run some full year group boarding weekends, which bring together each year for a big bonding session. One parent we spoke to said, 'I don't see what's wrong with a bit of boredom. They should learn how to entertain themselves too.'

The last word: 'Very happy with it. Very nurturing, cosy school. I like the ethos and the values.' 'I really feel when we pick our two up that the teachers know what kind of day our children have had and if there are any problems.' Parents here are a very happy bunch.

Casterton, Sedbergh Preparatory School

9

Kirkby Lonsdale, via Carnforth, Lancashire LA6 2SG

01524 279200 | emma.goligher@sedberghprep.org | www.sedberghschool.org/prep

Ages: 6m–13

Pupils: 185; Boarders: 35 full, 48 weekly/flexi

Fees: Day £8,859 – £17,337; Boarding £21,534 – £25,692 pa

Linked school: Sedbergh School, 1265

Headmaster: Since 2017 Will Newman. BA(Ed) from Exeter, MA (from University of Victoria, Canada, he won a Commonwealth Scholarship for postgraduate study there), previously deputy head of Taunton Prep. He breezes in to meet us in sports kit, all warmth and affability, apologising for being in mufti (the children are marking the Women's World Cup in Paris by wearing red, white or blue). Clearly loves the school, the Sedbergh ethos (more of that later) and is – it turns out – very appreciative of the parental welcome and support he has received since arriving (which is not something you always hear, at least not with authenticity). Parents say he makes you feel welcome, that he joins in with the children (even on very long runs): 'We like him a lot.'

Since arriving he has set in motion a number of curriculum changes: STEM is being given greater emphasis, computer science has been added and the DTE (Design, Technology and Engineering) offering revved up so pupils are more like 'young engineers than cookie cutters'. (So no lessons where 16 lookalike bird feeders are churned out.) The music and drama departments have also been combined into 'performing arts' to allow for greater collaboration and participation; every child from pre-school to year 8 has the opportunity to perform in an annual school production.

The lazy cliché that Sedbergh is all about sport is even more slothful than ever – the arts are just as keenly pursued. Both, Mr Newman emphasises, feed into character. True, pupils still play mainstream team sport nearly every day but Mr Newman has dropped one session per week and broadened the options to tennis, athletics, badminton, more swimming.

Mr Newman loves the outdoors – mountain biking and surfing being top the list. In quieter moments, he continues to teach himself to play the guitar (badly, he says). Married to Liz – also a teacher (not currently working) and well known to all the parents. They have a son who has just started at the senior school and a daughter at the prep.

Entrance: Non-selective – entry by taster day. Previous school reports requested. Assessments for scholarships or where there might be a high level of SEND support required. Assessments for 11+ scholarship take place in October.

Exit: Almost all to Sedbergh senior school (60 per cent of these received a scholarship award for year 9 entry in 2021).

Our view: Around 13 to a class. Broad curriculum which becomes more specialist as the children get older – maths, English, science, art, PSHE, games, humanities, French, Latin (in years 7 and 8) and classics, RE, computer science and DTE. The latter merits a special mention not just for the technology (PCs with 3D modelling software and five highfalutin 3D printers), but for the engineering-style approach. Year 6 were making some rather magnificent cranes to a sophisticated and tight brief. Year 8, litter pickers. In robotics pupils were creating and coding Sumo Robots for a battle and there was drag-racing opening up aerodynamics and friction. The teacher (who used to teach the subject at GCSE and A level) is taking it to new heights. Parents seemed happy with the academic side of things, one saying, 'they seem to bring it alive for the kids'. Small class sizes, another commented, meant you 'can't hide'.

Art, in a beautiful large light space, looked dazzling and the children seemed both interested and proud of the 'artist of the month' accolade for pupils. 'You can do your own thing too,' a pupil said, meaning facilities were open for individuals to work on projects or pieces. There are light, bright science labs for the three sciences, a theatre and well-stocked ICT rooms.

Head defines being a Sedberghian as 'superb resilience'. He feels the school produces children who are down to earth and confident without being overbearing

At three points throughout the year all pupils, apart from reception, are assessed in reading, spelling, maths and writing levels. Reception pupils are assessed throughout the year against the early learning goals and complete a test at the end of the year. Any difficulties picked up are discussed in the twice-weekly staff meetings and referrals to SEN teachers are made if necessary. The head cited a few recent examples of mild learning differences being detected at school by teachers (one of which we had never heard of) so the school seems alert to this. Homework is around 45 minutes a night and the school is introducing a pick 'n' mix of various activities so pupils can do more if they wish, tackle difficult areas or reinforce ones that need more practice.

There is a rich extracurricular offering with lots of performance opportunities. School plays across years, recently a bold production of The Lion King, and children are encouraged or coaxed into public speaking. In year 8 pupils are all expected to speak in chapel and events like poetry competitions promote it further. Parents say it is a supportive environment. LAMDA is on offer too.

Lots of music: house music competitions, half-termly concerts, musical workshops and choir tours. At the time we visited there was a wonderful masterclass given by a classical pianist, providing children with one-to-one tuition in front of the class. Everyone got their moment in the spotlight. Other masterclasses have included saxophone, violin and vocals with an opera singer. The variety of everything on offer is clearly a selling point for parents who seemed most wowed by the musical concerts where the children got up the courage to play in front of a large audience.

While Sedbergh is not all about sport, the trophies and gongs on display are testament to a proud heritage that is still going strong today. Boys play rugby, rugby sevens, hockey, cross country, fives, swimming, cricket, tennis and athletics. Girls get stuck into netball, hockey, tennis, rounders and athletics. The school has stables and there are riders of all abilities with lessons open to all. Pupils can have structured, weekly riding lessons or attend stable management sessions. Head says the sport philosophy is not to win at all costs but instead to take risks. 'The Epic', a school tradition, is a run done by years 7 and 8. It is a microcosm of the school community and ethos, according to the head – camaraderie and cheering on (and probably some hard muddy slog).

There is a range of activities on offer that includes fives, clay pigeon shooting and kayaking. Parents say there are opportunities to do all sorts and try different things

The form tutor is first port of call for pastoral matters – each child has a prep diary into which teachers note down successes (and presumably difficulties) both in the classroom and around school. Year 7s apply for positions of responsibility and service of which there are many, from librarian to reading buddy. It's all taken very seriously and children are interviewed by a member of staff and recognised in assembly for their achievement. No mobile phones during the day – they are returned at night for journeys home or given to boarders for an hour to make calls. No social apps which have a 13+ restriction are allowed. This has had 'universal support from parents,' head says.

Head says there is a great sense of belonging and refers to the 'brown' (the colour of the uniform) which runs through every pupil. He defines being a Sedberghian as 'superb resilience'. He feels the school produces children who are tough, down to earth, part of a team, confident without being overbearing. He reels this off with aplomb but having visited the senior school not so long ago and seen how the location – not just the surrounding hills but the remoteness from high street glitz – feeds into character, there really is something in it. It's hard not to have that appreciation for nature, adventure and a can-do attitude when children are exposed to the great outdoors 24/7. Or as one pupil put it to us: 'You definitely build up your personality.' She was shy when she arrived, she said, and while she found it hard to pin down the components that helped her blossom (there was no trace of shyness talking to us) she settled on: 'The hockey really helped.'

We felt, though, that despite all the talk about resilience, this is also very much a nurturing prep. The atmosphere was one of great warmth and friendliness which envelops you the moment you walk into the cosy lamp-lit hallway. Warmth emanates from all the staff too. So when the head said children who might not like sport – and there are plenty apparently – would still really enjoy the school, we were inclined to believe him. Parents of day children say they come back happy which is a 'massive thing'. Another parent, whose child had some specific issues, felt the school fully understood what was involved, made allowances and everything worked well.

A fantastic lecture programme also runs, on subjects from Macbeth to the ascent of Everest. Pianos scattered about are a reminder that this is a school about arts as much as sport, though they were considerably outnumbered by framed shirts of famous sportspeople – the legacy of generous old boys and girls.

Communications solid, though one parent commented that they were not necessarily great when it came to last-minute changes. Another said any small issue raised gets dealt with quickly and that teachers are 'very hands on'.

The 200-year-old school is in a village in the stunning Lune valley and has the same secluded feel as the senior school with which it merged in 2013. There are numerous places in the school grounds where the sight of the rolling hills takes your breath away. Children get to hang out in play areas, on climbing frames and in stables, surrounded by all that gorgeous green. It really does have an Enid Blyton feel, an impression deepened when the children pointed out the hens and goats to us. You can apply for an animal badge to help with the livestock and walk the goat, they said proudly.

Lovely canteen, healthy food; table manners important, children told us. The library, with its invitingly squishy sofas and bean bags struck just the right note too. Corridors seemed vibrant with posters and the classrooms of the younger children were especially stimulating with great displays of work

Parents seem a friendly, down-to-earth lot, mostly local families but some from as far as Carlisle or North Yorkshire who take advantage of the flexi-boarding.

Boarding: Around 60 to 70 full or weekly boarders, with additional flexi-boarders each night (school also now has a tri boarding option whereby children stay over for a specified three nights per week, with same room each time). Separate girls' and boys' boarding houses and there is a range of activities on offer that includes fives, clay pigeon shooting and kayaking. Parents say there are opportunities to do all sorts, 'even if your child is not that into it'.

The boys' boarding house has cheery common rooms (one with pet hamsters) and kitchen. All very jolly and surprisingly tidy. The rooms also astonishingly tidy, though we were assured not for our benefit: two to three per room, desks and sink. Similar set up with the girls: likewise, clean, tidy and very cosy – with smart bright kitchen, lovely common room, a handy juke box in one corner.

We spoke to a couple of articulate, mature and well-mannered pupils about the inevitable homesickness you feel on arrival, especially if you are an international boarder. They talked about everyone doing things together, not being left on your own and throwing yourself into activities 'so your mind is off your parents'. They loved boarding now. One parent said her child had difficulty sharing with a noisy room-mate – a quiet word was all it took to sort it swiftly.

Between 10 and 15 per cent are international boarders from a range of nationalities: Spain, France and China are the most common.

The last word: This is a warm and friendly prep where children are encouraged to reach their academic potential, explore a vast array of interests and enjoy the magnificent great outdoors which surrounds them.

Dollar Academy

Dollar, Clackmannanshire FK14 7DU

01259 742511 | rector@dollaracademy.org.uk | www.dollaracademy.org.uk

Ages: 5-18

Pupils: 1,311; sixth form: 302; Boarders: 90 full, 5 weekly (from age 9)

Fees: Day £10,899 – £14,571; Boarding £28,197 – £33,723 pa

Rector: Since 2019, Ian Munro BSc PGCE MA (30s). Flood of media attention when first appointed as youngest-ever head (aged just 34) in the independent sector when at Kelvinside in Glasgow. But his time there was short-lived – 'The opportunity to lead Dollar was too great to pass over. It's a top Scottish school.'

Born in Aberdeen, he was state school educated at Hazlehead before moving over to the independent sector to George Heriot's School in S3. Degree in zoology, followed by a PGCE biology, both from Edinburgh. Never resting on his laurels and with a passion for learning, gained a master's from Cambridge in educational leadership and school improvement, and recently completed leadership distance learning course with Harvard. Formerly a teacher at Heriot's (head of year and biology) and deputy head at Shiplake College. Most inspired, however, by his time at Gordonstoun (head of biology).

Grounded, likeable and efficient (he responded to our emails both quickly and personally – not always the case with heads). Gorgeous office too, among the nicest we've seen – think Hotel du Vin, with inky dark blue cupboards and chic lighting.

Future plans are to enhance the curriculum through engagements with businesses and unis – all hush-hush at the moment, but watch this space (and it should be worth the wait, judging by innovative programmes he's put in place at previous schools). He did let us in on one partnership with Cambridge that has led to school hosting a sustainability conference, with schools invited from around the world to discuss how the education system can evolve and to ensure kids are better equipped to deal with the climate crisis.

Lives in Dollar with wife Catherine, a history teacher at an independent school, and their cocker spaniel, Charles Darwin. No children. Loves the outdoors, sailing, walking, climbing, rugby – anything sporty. Doing more cycling since he moved from Glasgow and is often spotted on his bike in the surrounding Ochil Hills.

Deputy rector (from August 2020), Simon Burbury BA PGCE MA. Been at Dollar Academy since January 2015. Was 'singled out for praise on recent inspection,' says school. Degree in music performance from the Royal Conservatoire of Scotland; master's in music from Lancaster; teaching qualification from Homerton College, Cambridge. Previously director of music at schools in Egypt and Singapore and director of music at Gordonstoun. Wealth of experience in pupil wellbeing and child protection. Contributes to the music department whenever he can and is a sub-lieutenant and dinghy sailing instructor for the CCF Royal Navy section. Set up the annual trip to Romania to help disadvantaged and disabled children at Little John's House.

Entrance: Pupils mainly join at 5 (P1), 10 (J1) or 12 (form 1), although entries are welcome for other year groups, subject to availability. Entry from P3 to form 2 is by selective entrance exam. Entry to all other years via interview. Can be oversubscribed for entry at fifth and sixth forms, but each case is individually considered based on grades, previous school reports and good references. Prep and junior pupils automatically move up to senior school. School says, 'When you're in, you are in.' Open day in September, but parents and prospective pupils are welcome to visit at any point of the year. Current waiting list for certain year groups.

Exit: Dollar has the reputation of having the highest percentage of graduates of any town in the country and leavers from this school certainly have high aspirations. Most off to the free Scottish universities – top three destinations are Edinburgh, Glasgow and Aberdeen. Outside Scotland, Loughborough, Liverpool and Durham are popular. Trickle to Oxbridge most years (one in 2021); ditto overseas (Prague, Czech Republic, and Stanford, USA in 2021). Four medics in 2021. Law and engineering also popular. Heaps of support, so if don't get first choice, they will call around other unis. Support available after pupils have left school. No booting out for lower achievers. Support can be offered to underperforming pupils by 'little bit of school, little bit of something else, like college,' according to the rector, who says they can build a bespoke programme for them.

Latest results: In 2021 at National 5, 98 per cent grades A-C; at Higher 89 per cent A-B; and at Advanced Higher, 89 per cent A-B.

Teaching and learning: 'A grades the highest of any school I've ever led,' says rector. Most pupils consequently gain their first choice of university.

The Sunday Times Scottish independent secondary school of the year in 2018, offering the Scottish curriculum and widest choice of Highers in the country. No columns for subject choices; based around student choices. Sciences popular as are economics, engineering and history and modern studies. Ditto modern languages, with German and French getting more take-up than Spanish – all three taught from junior school, plus some Mandarin, Russian, Italian. Latin, Greek and classical studies also available. Philosophy and music technology among less traditional offerings.

A stone's throw from the school on the beautiful campus, the small homely boarding houses (two for girls and one for up boys) are cosy

Class sizes 15-20, with high numbers of teachers; smaller in senior school, especially at Advanced Higher. Staffing very stable, with new appointments usually down to retirements or promotions. To avoid stagnation, a robust professional learning programme includes lectures and workshops in leadership, practitioner enquiry and support for learning (SfL). Three males to four females in senior management.

Careers advisor and UCAS advisors on hand to help with uni applications. Online career profiling from early on and every pupil meets a member of senior management to discuss careers and aspirations from form 2. Careers convention for all year groups with over 70 professions represented. Series of lectures including jobs and careers of the future, eg in sustainability. Edinburgh Uni in to talk about the admissions process.

'Learning is tailor-made to your child and their learning style,' thought parent.

Learning support and SEN: SEN support a significant strength. The SfL team work closely with year heads and guidance staff to ensure a smooth transition between major stages. Small group work and some one-to-one extractions. EAL provision at no extra charge. SfL newsletter for parents, termly.

The arts and extracurricular: Pipe Band have been world champions for six out of eight previous years. 'Pupils board from the US just because they want to be part of the pipe band,' says rector. Huge Xmas concerts and performances in Usher Hall, Edinburgh and the Concert Hall in Perth. Oodles of concerts in school, from tinies to top-notch orchestras. Auditions for the chamber choir, but the mixed voice choir open to everyone. Huge posters of concerts over the years: chamber choir in Prague, Usher Hall, Christmas concert, Footloose. School musicals and plays aplenty, and sixth years write and direct their own play. Yearly fashion and art shows. Huge art studio that mimics uni experience for sixth years. Every success is celebrated at assemblies – most recently, the quiz team who became the Scottish champions.

Over 80 co-curricular clubs. All the usuals, plus beekeeping, ultimate frisbee (winning the university cup), sea angling in Arbroath and the mapping club, where pupils – supported by teachers – explore cartography's role in informing humanitarian aid work. Having mapped different areas in Africa, they share the information with humanitarian organisations. Impressive stuff. CCF is huge, voluntary and consistently win national competitions. DofE biggest in the country. Sixth years run the charities committee, organising events such as the bi-annual sponsored walk, which recently raised over £68,000.

Trips abroad are carbon offset by plans to plant a forest (literally), as well as trees on campus. Trips include Costa Rica (biology), France (skiing), China (business), Romania (every summer, to help children with profound special needs). Local trips include P1s to Loch Leven and annual J2 team-building trip to Benmore. CCF out to Canada on cadet scholarships.

Sport: Notable national and international successes. Rugby and hockey teams often in national finals, with the girls' hockey first XI often winning the Scottish League and the Scottish Cup, and the boys' rugby first XV consistently in the top four winning teams. Some of the senior boys go off on day release to Glasgow Warriors. The first XI cricket team are U15 and U18 Scottish Schools Champions and recently got a write-up in Wisden, the cricket magazine. The shooting team have been Scottish champions at Bisley for over 20 years. But what about pupils that are less sporty? 'The focus is on taking part – almost everyone plays rugby or hockey and teams are for every ability and are all coached in the same way,' assured the school; parents concur. Dollar has recently launched a golf academy in collaboration with Gleneagles.

Boarding: Around 90 boarders in total – half from UK, half international (US, Asia, Germany, Spain, Russia). 'We continue to board for all the right reasons, and to increase diversity in the local population,' says rector. Highly regarded, offering an authentic Scottish experience, represented by the ever-increasing demand for boarding places.

A stone's throw from the school on the beautiful campus, the small homely boarding houses (two for 41 girls and one for up to 49 boys) are cosy, with lots of places to hang out and study, including the music room with piano and drums, small BBQ area with wooden tables and common room with table tennis and pool. Extremely well-organised, shoes go in boxes as soon as they enter the house and laundry is to be brought down in trays.

Evening meals are served in the dining hall, which is just off the school grounds – could be a dreary walk in inclement Scottish weather. Supper is served in the boarding houses later in the evening – burgers, wraps, homemade pizzas etc, which some parents feel could be better (especially less fried food), but which senior houseparent says go down a storm – 'No celery or carrots here in the boys' house!' The cooks were making home-made sausage rolls on our tour and Mac, the houseparents' dog who accompanied us, was more than a little interested.

We found everywhere as shiny as a new pin – exceptionally clean and tidy. One parent impressed 'by how clean and organised the boarding houses are, yet they don't feel institutional or overly regimented.' The houseparents are teachers and say, 'We are approachable at any time.' A parent agreed, saying, 'A definite strength of the boarding experience is that the houseparents are warmly attentive while also being just hands-off enough to allow the kids' independence and resourcefulness to develop.'

Pipe Band have been world champions for six out of eight previous years. 'Pupils board from the US just because they want to be part of the pipe band,' says rector

House tutors are on hand during the week. Up to second year, homework done in the main living areas downstairs (not in bedrooms) so no study space in rooms. Older kids have desks in rooms, but doors stay open so staff can check regularly that they are studying. Odd ensuite room but generally bath/shower rooms are shared between two to three bedrooms. Good relationships are formed with day pupils so it is common to stay with a local family at the weekend (permissions sought), but at exam time most stay in. Almost all are full boarders with a few weekly. School says, 'Not really space for flexi-boarders, some tried it for a few days and then stayed. If there's space we could look at it, but we're already full for next year.'

Programme of activities and trips includes go-karting, fishing, mountain-biking and book group. Plus some shared (between houses) social events such as karaoke, movie and pizza nights, the formal boarders' ceilidh at Christmas and intellectual talks on Sunday evenings (optional).

The annual team-building event sounds super fun and has seen all 90 on giant inflatables.

WiFi is off by 11pm, but a bit 'patchy', according to one parent, 'which can cause temporary communication issues' (could be more of a regional coverage issue than a school-specific shortcoming, though, she added). Allowed phones in rooms from third year, before that need to hand them in at bedtime.

Ethos and heritage: Founded in 1818, this is the oldest coeducational day and boarding school in the world. No denying the wow factor as you drive through the entrance and are struck by the fine Doric façade and grand neoclassical design of the Playfair building, comparable to the swishest of Edinburgh's schools. It's the setting that really steals the show, however – a stunning 70-acre campus surrounded by the beautiful Ochil Hills. Newer additions include the award-winning Westwater building for languages and economics.

Historically, has been considered a relatively low-budget school, avoided by the super-rich and with boarders typically sons of farmers or of Scottish servicemen. But seemed pretty posh to our eye, especially given that you are met by a huge signed photo of the Queen and Prince Philip (vintage 1994) in the reception area. Any intimidations are eased, however, by the extremely cheery receptionist and just as smiley rector.

'Would be a good fit for students who are serious about developing themselves,' reckoned parent – and 'to a child who can appreciate nature and the outdoors'

Lots of super-smart blazered misters and madams wandering the grounds. A quiet buzz of learning, with no rowdiness at all at breaks or lunchtimes. Even in prep (which is very bright and colourful, every inch of space covered), you could have heard a pin drop at story time.

Traditional ethos of working hard, getting involved and being kind (before it became a hashtag). 'Would be a good fit for students who are serious about developing themselves,' reckoned parent – and 'to a child who can appreciate nature and the outdoors'. New website built and streamlined on the back of feedback and testing from parents.

Extensive list of notable former pupils, eg Sir James Dewar, inventor of the vacuum flask; Sir David Gill, astronomer; Sir William Snadden, politician; Rt Hon Lord Keen of Elie PC QC, politician; Alan Johnston, BBC journalist; George Henry Paulin, sculptor; Caroline Flanigan, former president of the Law Society of Scotland. Also various members of the Ethopian imperial family; James McArthur of Milton, chief of Clan Arthur; John Barclay, rugby player; Jennifer McIntosh, Olympian rifle shooter; Tom Kitchin, Michelin-starred chef.

Pastoral care, inclusivity and discipline: Multi-layered pastoral care includes form tutors, heads of year, assistant heads of year, senior staff group, school councillors and medical centre team. Pupils and parents can reach out to whoever most comfortable with, 'even if it's the dinner lady,' according to rector. In prep/junior school, first port of call tends to be class teacher; in senior school, it's head of year; and for boarders, the houseparents. No exclusions since current rector joined. A parent told us concerns are 'dealt with there and then'. 'The pastoral care is truly excellent – we have had peace of mind despite having our child so far away,' concurred a boarding parent.

All pupils do self-supporting wellbeing exercises and if teachers have any pupil concerns, they fill in 'yellows' – these online forms are sent to the pastoral team so they can keep their finger on the pulse and address the problem, eg if someone is finding a subject difficult, which is making them unhappy. Team of mental health ambassadors made up of form six pupils, and peer mentoring from senior pupils who lead lessons on representing each other's rights. Gooseberry Planet, an online programme to keep children safe online, has been rolled out across the school.

Assemblies three time a week in the senior school with hymns and bible readings. The prep and junior schools have joint assembly once a week. A Christian ethos with all singing.

Pupils and parents: Diverse group of middle-class families from overseas and UK. Large numbers from the local community – especially popular with the town of Dollar itself, with some 400 day pupils from here. Impressive number of buses from within a 30-mile radius of the school. Late buses run each day for those at after-school activities. Lively social scene for both parents and pupils. 'Dollar has a community that really gets behind the school,' said a parent. Rector says parents 'work hard and make real sacrifices to send their kids to the school'.

Money matters: Means-tested academic bursaries for form 1 entry, plus ESU, Forces and boarding bursaries (usually means-tested, with tuition not covered). Fees very reasonable.

The last word: Up there with the best, offering an authentic Scottish boarding experience, as well as catering for local kids. Set in a beautiful tranquil setting, it's a school with a solid, traditional ethos and top academic results.

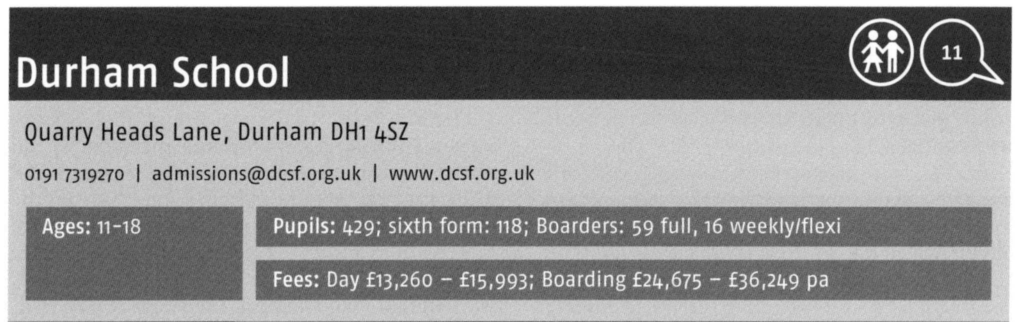

Durham School
11
Quarry Heads Lane, Durham DH1 4SZ
0191 7319270 | admissions@dcsf.org.uk | www.dcsf.org.uk
Ages: 11–18
Pupils: 429; sixth form: 118; Boarders: 59 full, 16 weekly/flexi
Fees: Day £13,260 – £15,993; Boarding £24,675 – £36,249 pa

Headmaster: Since 2014, Kieran McLaughlin, previously deputy head (academic) at Rugby School. He studied natural sciences at Cambridge, specialising in physics and theoretical physics. Has been head of science and technology at Sevenoaks and head of physics at City of London Girls. He attended selective boys' school St Edward's College in Liverpool, having won an assisted place. In the past, he was the bass player in an obscure Liverpudlian rock band, as well as pursuing the ancient martial art of jiu-jitsu to black belt level. Married with three children.

After the successful merger of Durham School and The Chorister School to form the Durham Cathedral Schools Foundation in 2021, Mr McLaughlin feels the schools are in an exciting period of growth. This is evident after a record number of enquiries in 2021. Durham is a city where education does matter and word of mouth really counts. One parent we spoke to told us that they had researched in depth seven schools before selecting Durham School.

Mr McLaughlin has an easy manner and collegiate management style; teaches physics to year 12. Very strong vote of confidence from parents, with one summing up their views thus: 'He is an asset to the school and clearly has a firm grasp on the challenges within education and the strategic development needed to stay ahead and maintain standards of excellence.'

Entrance: Children joining the senior school at year 7 sit 11+ entrance examinations in English, mathematics, verbal and non-verbal reasoning. Those joining in year 9 sit entrance examinations in English and mathematics.

Sixth form candidates must satisfy minimum entrance criteria of five GCSEs at grade 6 (or equivalent) and English language and mathematics at grade 4. Pupils who join in other years or part way through the year will normally be required to sit an entrance test appropriate to their age. International pupils need a minimum academic IELTS score of 5.5 in mathematics and English.

Exit: A very small number (seven in 2021) leave at the end of year 11 for vocational courses or jobs and a few at the end of year 12. Newcastle, Imperial, Loughborough and Durham all popular universities. A few to Oxbridge (three in 2021). Wide range of subjects: civil and chemical engineering popular choices as well, as business, biomedical sciences and psychology, plus a few medics (seven in 2021) and lawyers. One off to Geigenbauschule Brienz, Switzerland in 2021 to study violin-making.

Latest results: In 2021, 55 per cent 9-7 at GCSE; 62 per cent A*/A at A level (83 per cent A*-B). In 2019 (the last year when exams took place), 40 per cent 9-7 at GCSE; 33 per cent A*/A at A level (61 per cent A*-B).

Teaching and learning: A level results probably why school is working to develop academic aspects of the sixth form ('more rigour', a study centre, supervised study time, more intellectual societies). Wide choice of subjects includes economics, politics, psychology, philosophy and ethics, government and politics, classical civilisation, photography, theatre and business studies. EPQ now available together with an enrichment programme which includes a lecture series and five societies, supervised by staff but run by students: academic, politic, heretics, Tristram (scientists) and medsoc (would-be medics). Very good support with university applications and Oxbridge/elite university preparation.

Separate sciences or dual award and a modern language compulsory at GCSE. Option choice includes Latin, classical civilisation, ethics and drama, music, PE, DT graphic products and Greek, off timetable. German or Spanish added to French in year 9 (can also do Latin) and language awareness days, with themed meals. Most recent inspection praised pupil-staff relationships, teaching and use of monitoring, but commented on some marking inconsistency, which school is addressing.

The majority of boarders are from overseas (plus Forces children) – most from Hong Kong, mainland China and Europe – and room allocations mix nationalities

Classrooms tend to be traditional, with just one computer plus projector (only a few interactive whiteboards), some darkish, but also some new ones and some modern ICT facilities with a stock of iPads. 'Bring your own device' has been introduced. Wifi connectivity has improved and there's a VLE.

Thorough-going gifted and talented policy – systematic identification and monitoring, early maths GCSE, fourth A level and extra, challenging activities.

Learning support and SEN: Strong learning support department – well qualified, flexible, sensitive; can cope with most needs apart from severe behavioural problems. The spread-out nature of the campus could be a problem for anyone with major physical disabilities. Screens all new entrants for dyslexia and ESL, if from overseas (extra charge for ESL – full-time specialist – and learning support sessions); trains other staff.

The arts and extracurricular: Very accomplished choral singing – TV appearances, radio broadcasts, including Radio 4's Sunday Worship and a number of CDs. All Steinway school so plenty of pianists. Orchestras, jazz band, rock group; performance opportunities abound with concerts at the Sage, Gateshead and Durham Cathedral, plus foreign tours.

Plenty of opportunity to showcase their dramatic talents in a variety of genres and settings – big musicals like Les Misérables in Durham's Gala Theatre or plays like The Great Gatsby in the school's own performance space, the Luce. Also more informal performances take place in the school's modern studio theatre.

Inter-house competition is rife with the show-stopping annual music competition (staged alternate years in the Sage and the Chapel) top of the bill. Sporting and drama events are staged throughout the year with much-coveted trophies for the winners.

Wide choice of activities from creative writing to computer programming, peer support to the languages film club. DofE and CCF (all three sections). School participates in BBC School Report (writing news bulletins and reports) and the lively and entertaining school newspaper, The Durham Eye, printed in house, has reached the finals of a national schools media competition. Careers education now expanding using network of Old Dunelmians.

Lots of fundraising for charity and foreign trips – staff and pupils seem to have bags of energy and enterprise; Chinese exchange visit to Chengdu; World Challenge to Borneo, Africa, Ecuador, Vietnam or India, cricket tour to Antigua, hockey tour to Portugal, rowing camps in Belgium and Norway, winter walking in Scotland, ski trip to the Alps – plenty of opportunities to do good and see the world.

Sport: Astroturf, functional swimming pool, sports hall, playing fields, very good rowing facilities and access to top flight coaching. Individuals and teams successful at regional, county and national levels with rugby first XV reaching the Natwest Trophy semi-finals and the hockey teams getting to the National Schools regional finals recently.

One of the oldest rowing clubs in the country (dates from 1847) – the whole 1970 crew represented GB and has current international stars. Water polo taking off in a big way, ski team reached finals of English Schools' Championships, a GB fencer; also cross-country, golf, squash, boxing, rifle shooting, windsurfing and climbing. All pupils participate in 4.5 hours of sport and physical activity per week, still partly compulsory in the sixth form. Girls have more chance of being in teams through being in a minority.

Boarding: With boarding all is possible – full, weekly and part-time. Four of the five houses include day and boarding pupils – three for boys and one for girls. The majority of boarders are from overseas (plus Forces children) – most from Hong Kong, mainland China and Europe – and room allocations mix nationalities. Each house, located along a street outside the main campus, has studies (shared or single), common rooms, kitchen and leisure facilities, and they have had some refurbishment. The boarding provision was graded good in the last inspection – a relaxed atmosphere, flexible eating arrangements on Sundays, plenty of activities. Good range of food (we can recommend the home-made veg soup), but boarders we met wanted a more substantial meal later in the evening, after their sports training.

Ethos and heritage: One of oldest schools in the country – goes back to Cardinal Langley's re-founding of Durham Cathedral in 1414; at the end of the last century became more or less independent of the dean and chapter. Originally situated on Palace Green, next to the cathedral; moved to present site on other side of River Wear in 1844; only five minutes' walk from city centre.

The entrance to the school provides an attractive glimpse of the site – though there is no time to enjoy it if arriving at break times. Hordes of pupils stream across the car park on the way to their houses, seemingly oblivious to any car navigating its way to the tightly packed parking bays.

Once stationary, just enjoy the view; mellow sandstone buildings flank grassy lawns leading to the hill that ascends to the chapel. The 98 steps all commemorate old boys who died in the two world wars. On Remembrance Day the whole school lines the stairs at twilight, holding candles, while a wreath is laid on the memorial plaque, which must be very moving. Stunning view of viaduct, cathedral and school from the top. The 1926 traditional chapel has pews etched with the names of all leavers.

Further up is the Astroturf and beyond, up again, are rugby pitches. You need to be pretty fit just to get to them, let alone train and play. The sports hall and sixth form centre can be found in this vicinity after passing the quirky classics building.

There is a real feel of a traditional rural boarding school, with lovely views of sports fields and gardens containing many mature trees. Although the majority of the pupils don't board (day ends at 6pm), each has a house where they have common rooms and their own space to retreat to before and after school and during breaks in the day. Registration is held here each morning with the houseparent and there are strong bonds between fellow house members.

Girls were introduced into the sixth form in 1985 and Durham became fully coeducational in 1998. Girls feel that there has been a move in recent years to fully integrate them in what is now a true coeducational setting. They are outnumbered two to one by the boys, but feel 'very comfortable with the balance', having single-sex houses.

There is a strong sense of community and leadership opportunities with house captains and monitors (prefects) who are now selected through written application and interview.

Chapel plays a central role in school life with three assemblies a week. There are also strong links to the cathedral with services and concerts held there. Various school councils and pupils told us that they feel their voices are heard. A parent told us that 'the school finds where the individual can develop and works with it'. Not only discovering academic, sporting or musical latent talent but 'developing confident individuals with great self belief'. Parents like the house system, providing 'ever greater maturity and acceptance of responsibility' to pupils – and the competition too: 'They all get very involved.'

Pastoral care, inclusivity and discipline: Pastoral care centred on form tutor and house staff, plus chaplain – rated outstanding by inspection, which glowed about relationships in general and moral and social development. Bullying not seen as a problem – pupils we met felt should it occur, it would be dealt with quickly and effectively (school would exclude if necessary), anti-cyber-bullying policy devised by staff and pupils. There is a clear escalation of staff to speak to about any problems, academic or pastoral. Pupils we met told us that they knew who they were and would be happy to talk to a number.

Very accomplished choral singing – TV appearances, radio broadcasts, including Radio 4's Sunday Worship and a number of CDs. All Steinway school so plenty of pianists

Senior prefects and school and house monitors support younger pupils – 'It's a very caring environment: the house system works very well'. A sixth former who joined in year 12 from a state school spoke of how quickly he had been integrated into friendship groups that 'conducted themselves so differently' from his previous school.

New children have an acquaintance day in the summer term before entry, an induction day just before term starts and a 'buddy' in their house when they arrive. Prep school pupils will also have used the senior school facilities regularly and visited for a day in year 5.

Pupils and parents: At 11, most from the prep school, the rest from state primaries; at 13 and 16 from a range of state and independent schools. Many of day and weekly boarding pupils from within or close to Durham, others from as far as Sunderland, Newcastle, North Yorkshire and the Borders. A range of ethnic and financial backgrounds but mostly professional or self-employed.

Plenty of contact with generally satisfied parents – weekly e-letter, website, academic diaries, meetings, a parents' forum. Forthcoming, well-mannered, confident pupils. Proud of their school and appreciative of what they have gained; one boy told us, 'I often wonder what person I would be now if I hadn't been at Durham'. Certainly, new sixth formers joining from local secondaries are bowled over by the collegiality, welcome and attitude to learning.

Money matters: Various academic, music, drama, art and sports awards, at 11+ and 13+, Burkitt and Peter Lee scholarships at 16+. Sibling, Forces and clergy discounts. About 150 pupils have means-tested assistance and 105 non-means-tested admissions scholarships of a maximum of £1,000.

The last word: A sense of community and history binds the pupils together, underpinned by the strong house system for day and boarding pupils alike. The school produces well-rounded, confident young people, who have opportunities to develop a wide range of talents to a high level in a supportive, peaceful and very attractive environment.

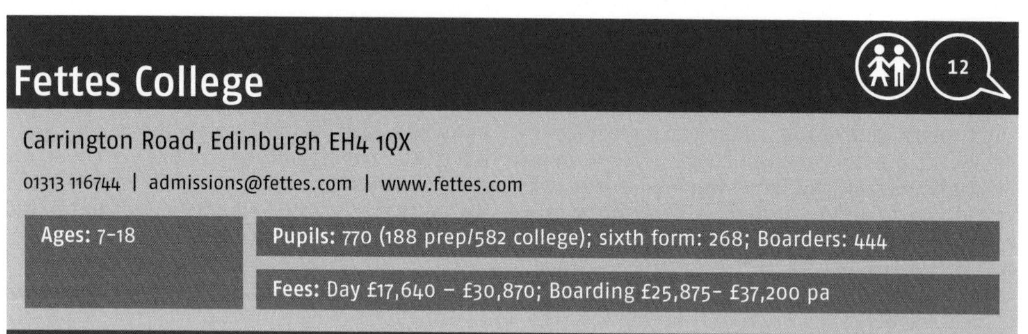

Fettes College

12

Carrington Road, Edinburgh EH4 1QX

01313 116744 | admissions@fettes.com | www.fettes.com

Ages: 7-18

Pupils: 770 (188 prep/582 college); sixth form: 268; Boarders: 444

Fees: Day £17,640 – £30,870; Boarding £25,875- £37,200 pa

Head: Since 2019, Helen Harrison, the first female head in the school's 150-year history. Previously deputy head for over 12 years and before that geography teacher at the school since 1996. She took over after previous head Geoffrey Stanford left after only two years, following discussions with the school's board of governors on its 'future strategic focus'. Geography degree from Jesus College Cambridge (for which she also rowed), then taught EFL in Portugal post-degree before taking up her first teaching post at Clifton College, where she was the first female assistant in a boys' house and acting head of department.

While the spouses of male heads often join them in a supporting role, we rarely hear of it the other way round – so hurrah for husband Rob taking a 'full and active role' supporting his wife at Fettes, where he also teaches English and was previously a housemaster. Family (and dogs) still take centre stage in her spare time, as well as making the most of the great Scottish outdoors.

Entrance: To prep by assessment test and interview held annually. Entry points in every year group of the prep school.

CE or school's own exam to senior school at 13+, limited availability for entry at 14+ via school's own entrance exams and then approx 30 students a year join the sixth form after GCSE elsewhere, currently much sought after as pupils pile in from other, mainly Scottish, schools (one in six chance of admissions and competition very stiff). Only boarding places offered at 14+ and 16+ entrance. All assessments include face-to-face interviews or Skype interviews for those sitting exams abroad.

Exit: Virtually all juniors to senior school (automatic entry). Hardly any (sometimes none) leave post-GCSE. Most to university – Bath, Bristol, Cambridge, Durham, Edinburgh, Exeter, Glasgow, Imperial, Newcastle, St Andrews etc to study eg engineering, English, maths or law. Usually some to Oxbridge, and several overseas.

Latest results: In 2021, 81 per cent 9-7 at GCSE; 71 per cent A*/A (81 per cent A*-B). IB average point score of 39. In 2019 (the last year when exams took place), 71 per cent 9-7 at GCSE; 56 per cent A*/A (83 per cent A*-B). IB average point score 38.

Teaching and learning: Prep school like a mini campus complete with chicken coop and veg garden (to tie in with science, of course). Latin early, masses of artwork on the walls, science labs in the corridors, plenty of laptop computers. 'We decide when they can use them.'

Only school in Scotland top-rated across the board for leadership, care and wellbeing; inspectors described the school as having 'a culture of kindness'. This writer was certainly very well looked after; lemon and ginger tea appeared in minutes to soothe a persistent cough and cold. Close to 50/50 split between boys and girls; completely co-ed and no lingering feeling of its history as a boys' school. Good staff-pupil ratio – average of 15 pupils per class in prep school, max 19; 20 max in senior school.

No SQA exams: like many of the big Edinburgh players, prefers the English system. 'Following the English curriculum is an attraction for many parents.' Added the IB in 2006. Pupils can choose whether they want to specialise, and do A levels, or take the broader IB syllabus. Over 40 per cent doing IB, a number of them home-grown, with excellent results. Value added impressive across the board.

Three sciences on offer throughout, plus trad French, German and Spanish, as well as Mandarin (available for beginners as well as for native speakers) and Latin (optional). No particular bias – physics, chemistry, biology and geography outstanding at GCSE, maths and English almost equally strong; results in all disciplines equally impressive at A level. Broad curriculum, with at least one modern language studied at GCSE. Strong classics and Mandarin departments.

The stunning old library has seven different spaces including a study centre with computing suite and university-type resources. Hot chocolate is served at break time to encourage pupils in and poetry recitals take place in the evenings. The prep school has its own cosy little library with reading logs; reading time is built into the weekly curriculum.

Learning support and SEN: For foreign pupils EAL is on hand (although the college requires an excellent level of English: pupils who don't have good working knowledge of the language are encouraged to do an English language course before they arrive).

Teachers in bases at dedicated times for academic support when needed.

The arts and extracurricular: Wide range of opportunities: some 25+ sports and 90+ extracurricular activities. More unusual prep school clubs include circus skills and parkour.

Rich music tradition with loads of bands, orchestras, choirs, string quartet etc etc, two popular concerts in spring and autumn plus carol service, all in aid of charity. Keen drama with imaginative productions, recently Arabian Nights, Equus and Beauty and the Beast (in the prep school, with over 100 pupils involved); pupils often perform at the Edinburgh Fringe.

Variety of whole-school events: ceilidhs, Burns Night suppers, black tie dinners. Everyone – including staff and parents – joins in the annual 5k, 10k or half marathon, some from the rowing club electing to travel by water instead. Every house chooses a charity they wish to support for this event and average totals raised hit £20,000.

Only school in Scotland top-rated across the board for leadership, care and wellbeing; inspectors described the school as having 'a culture of kindness'

CCF, community service, DofE etc. Masses of outings, everywhere, for everything: prep trip to Rome (included in the fees), choir to France, ski trips.

Sport: Usual suspects for traditional team games: hockey and athletics for both sexes; rugby and cricket for boys, and lacrosse and tennis for girls. Needle matches with Glenalmond and Merchiston on the rugby field and Strathallan in hockey. Big sports centre and swimming pool providing a wide range of other sports. Huge playing fields with water-based Astro and athletics track. Recent rugby and cricket triumphs (including Watsonian cricket club young player of the year).

Boarding: About 75 per cent of pupils board. Two prep and eight senior school houses, all single sex, for day and boarding pupils, with tutors attached. Each staff member is attached to a boarding house, whether as tutor, sports coach or teacher, creating a sense of community. 'They get to know the teachers in a completely different way.'

Newish posh co-ed boarding house – Craigleith, very modern – for the upper sixth. The pair of curved blocks form two identical wings, one for boys and one for girls, with carefully controlled access from a central space. Individual rooms, allowing them to focus for their exams, and the onsite tutor specialises in UCAS progress. Provides a transition between the disciplines of school and uni, with pupils being able to cook snacks and some meals if they want to. They have cookery lessons and take responsibility for their own washing, ironing and cleaning their rooms (with matron offering ironing lessons when needed).

Ethos and heritage: William Fettes (later Sir William), the son of an Edinburgh grocer, made his fortune during the Napoleonic Wars when 'he became Scotland's leading contractor for provisions for the army'; his only son died in 1815, and William in 1836. While he had originally intended to found a hospital, he later 'decided to create a school for orphans and the needy'. After prudent investment, the trustees decided that with £166,000 in the kitty, there were enough funds to acquire land, build and endow a school: Fettes opened in 1870 with 50 boys.

Purpose-built, designed by architect David Bryce, it's hard not be impressed by the vast Grimms' fairy tale of a building, complete with turrets, acres of wood panelling and shiny black floors. One of the admin staff reassured us as we entered: 'Don't feel intimidated.'

Various Victorian edifices are scattered about the school's wonderful 90-acre grounds, bang in the middle of Edinburgh. The collection of new and converted buildings that house the prep department are much bigger than they look from the outside. The newest Fettes addition is the impressive Spens building, opened by Nobel Prize winning author and economist Sir Angus Deaton (and Old Fettesian) in 2015. A combination of new-build and refurbishment, it is home to the modern languages, mathematics, geography, economics departments, plus a music school with music practice pods and huge light-filled art school that extends into the roof void.

Variety of whole-school events: ceilidhs, Burns Night suppers, black tie dinners. Everyone – including staff and parents – joins in the annual 5k, 10k or half marathon

Pupils meet every morning for assembly and congregational singing in the beautiful chapel. 'The house hymns are more like anthems.' Non-denom Sunday service.

Caring ethos and traditional values. Pupils stood up as we entered the room. Hard work ethic; pupils are expected to give their very best. The former famous trad boys' school is now genuinely co-ed.

Old Fettesians include John de Chastelaine, Ian McLeod, James Bond, Lord Woolf,Tony Blair, Sir Angus Deaton and composer Lorne Balfe.

Pastoral care, inclusivity and discipline: Everyone can visit their tutor to discuss how they are doing... 'Not just academically, a confidante. Peers, prefects, head of house, matron, tutor, medical centre staff, chaplain. Always someone you can trust.' Tells us it is the only school in Scotland to be rated excellent by the Care Inspectorate across all areas for several years.

Three-tier system on the discipline side: housemaster, deputy head, head; rustication/formal warning and suspension or expulsion. Zero tolerance policy on drugs; this resulted in a well-reported expulsion a few years ago. Anyone who has watched Trainspotting will know Edinburgh has a long-standing drugs problem, in common with most big cities, causing a headache for schools. The older pupils are young adults and have the freedom to go to the city centre within curfew times. Young adults make mistakes and you can't help but feel that the press enjoy ramping it up because it's an expensive independent school.

Very clear house-visiting rules – no overt demonstrations of affection; bonking equals out (as an 18-year-old A-grade pupil found out after relations with another youth on a school excursion). They do lose the occasional pupil for all these misdemeanours, ditto bullying. Strong anti-bullying ethos.

House loyalty is strong; there are house 'attainment' and 'effort' awards. 'Effort is what you do with what you've got. To have the right attitude of hard work.' School meals should be impressive and they were when we visited: a myriad healthy options, colourful salads and fresh fish. You'd be hard pushed not to find something you like.

Very attractive uniform – most noticeable are the boys' burgundy striped blazers and the girls' tartan skirts.

Pupils and parents: The flavour has changed from home-grown Scots to more international: some 60 per cent from Scotland, 15 per cent from the rest of the UK, 15 per cent British expats and 10 per cent foreign nationals (from over 40 countries – North America to Hong Kong). Very strong Old Fettesian stream, plus loads of first-time buyers, intellectuals etc etc. Good vibrant mix.

Money matters: Well-endowed with scholarships including academic, music, sports, all-rounder, piping, art, up to 10 per cent of fees. Also means-tested bursaries: 'The level of these awards depend upon parents' financial means and can cover up to the full value of the fees.' Over 70 students are already in receipt of large-scale bursaries (covering 80–100 per cent of the fees). Due to a very large anonymous donation, school has launched the Fettes KickStart campaign, which will see two pupils per year join the prep school for their entire schooling up to 18. School is working with six local primary schools on this project to identify eligible pupils. Special (Todd) bursaries for Old

Cargilfield School

Fettesians, 12.5 per cent discount for Forces (not so many of these around).

The last word: Still lives up to its reputation and is undoubtedly the strongest school in Edinburgh. With an ethos for hard work, there is every opportunity for pupils to excel academically, on the sporting field, creatively and culturally. Exciting cosmopolitan mix of pupils in an exciting city.

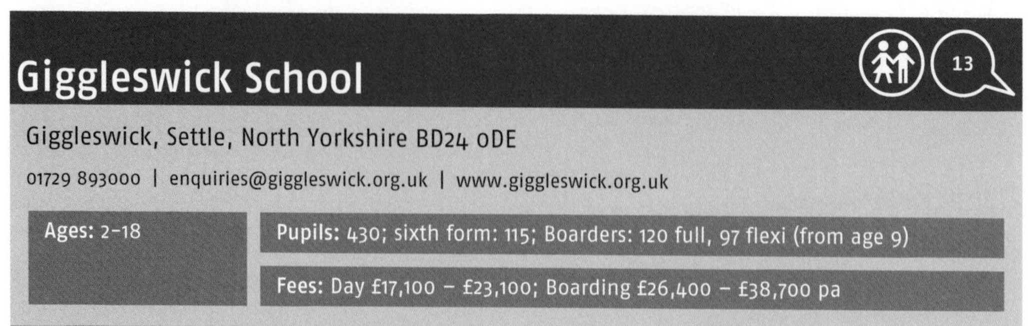

Giggleswick School

Giggleswick, Settle, North Yorkshire BD24 0DE

01729 893000 | enquiries@giggleswick.org.uk | www.giggleswick.org.uk

Ages: 2-18

Pupils: 430; sixth form: 115; Boarders: 120 full, 97 flexi (from age 9)

Fees: Day £17,100 – £23,100; Boarding £26,400 – £38,700 pa

Headmaster: Since January 2021, Sam Hart, who has a degree in engineering from Edinburgh. Previously at Winchester College where he was a housemaster, head of the CCF and formerly head of sport, as well as being a physics teacher. Had a successful career in the Army Air Corps where he flew Lynx helicopters and was awarded the NATO Meritorious Service Medal for outstanding leadership. Sam is married to Lucy and has two young children.

Head of junior school: since 2015, James Mundell LLB, PGCE (University of Wales), who has been at the school, in various roles, since 2004. On taking the reins, he implemented a number of academic changes, including moving maths and English to the morning when young minds are fresh. Lesson time was lengthened to one hour and two languages introduced so pupils are better prepared for year 7. Aware that young children are more predisposed to anxiety in modern times, he also ramped up the wellbeing programmes. Friendly, chatty, down to earth, he still does games lessons with the children; at the time we met him, he had just accompanied them on the three peaks challenge: 'I like to stay in touch with the grass roots.'

Entrance: Entry to the junior is not selective but the school needs to feel it can support the needs of any potential pupil.

All go through to the senior school and make up 50 per cent of its intake. An increasing number join from state schools.

At age 11 by Giggleswick entrance exam, at age 13 normally CE together with interview and previous school's report. Entrance into sixth form is by a minimum of five GCSEs at grade 6; around 35 new sixth form entrants per year.

Exit: Small fall-out after GCSEs – often under 10 per cent. Pupils leave the sixth form to study a vast range of subjects from ancient history to events management to real estate and midwifery at mostly northern universities, though a few down south. Exeter, London, York, Bath and Bristol all popular. Sometimes a few to Oxbridge, though none in 2021. Two vets in 2021, plus two overseas (Moscow and Stuttgart).

Latest results: In 2021, 50 per cent 9-7 at GCSE; 69 per cent A*/A at A level (85 per cent A*-B). In 2019 (the last year when exams took place), 43 per cent 9-7 at GCSE; 32 per cent A*/A at A level (63 per cent A*-B).

Teaching and learning: In the junior school, alongside English and maths, a wide curriculum includes science, history, art, design (they make fabulous things like abstract clocks), music (all learn the violin in KS1) and languages (German and French). Class sizes are 18 max but usually smaller (school has around 80 pupils). Generally equal between the genders, though this varies.

Maths and English done in ability groups (though they do not sit in these groups). Sometimes, children move up to a different year group (or down). The latter sounds dispiriting to a young mind, but a parent whose child was in a spelling group two years behind said the child was now 'positioned to succeed' in weak areas. Academic progress tracked via cognitive assessments but the whole picture is viewed.

Lots of cross-curricular themes, and much learning, school says, is child-led; if little Elliot brings in a fossil, it initiates discussion. Parents say teaching 'is creative and adapted to the child'. A lovely addition is 'philosophy for children', exploring muddy questions like 'what's fair?' (if only we knew the answer to that one). Wellies are a must; lots of nature walks, dens and outdoor storytelling chairs. Outdoors is integral; if they are studying rock types, they go find them. New forest school includes outdoor kitchen, reading chair and tepee.

Parents who had moved their children to Giggleswick felt they had taken giant strides forward, from handwriting, which was flourishing, to confidence, which was soaring. One parent said Giggleswick had changed her child's 'thinking about learning'.

Year 7 in the senior school maintains breadth; three sciences and four languages on offer, French, Spanish, German and Latin (16 pupils out of 52 took a language A level; 49 out of 63 took at least one language GCSE in 2018). Small class sizes and academic clinics available for a booster. One parent said, 'They change things quickly if approaches are not working.'

The girls' boarding house we saw was lovely; the common room stuffed with sofas inviting chat, opening on to a terrace; a small field beyond with a volleyball net

According to another parent, the academic side had 'really stepped up' under the previous head; there had been a turnover of staff 'in a good way' (though some departments needed more teachers). Much parental praise for the 'brilliant' new reporting system. 'Everybody knows where they're at,' parent said.

And so they do. Pupils normally take nine or 10 GCSEs from a wide array of options. Science particularly strong; typically over 90 per cent of candidates in physics and over 80 per cent in biology and chemistry achieve A*/A grades. Broad selection of subjects offered at A level including classics.

All students study EPQ; school likes the independent and critical thinking involved. BTECs on offer in business and sport and gather a very fine crop of results.

Learning support and SEN: Mild learning differences like dyslexia seem well catered for; the previous current learning support coordinator is now assistant head.

The arts and extracurricular: For schools in a glorious rural setting, participation in extracurricular is key (loafing in Starbucks is not an option). Children are simply encouraged to have a go here. 'They take a child out of their comfort zone but there is lots of encouragement and togetherness. No one is singled out,' a parent said. This same parent had watched a strapping rugby player pupil approach a bespectacled boy to congratulate him for finishing a cross-country race. 'It's that sort of school,' she said. Another parent felt 'quieter children flourish at Gigg; it brings them out of themselves.'

Junior trips are plentiful, to places like Jorvik Viking Centre or Hornby Castle. A good array of clubs from gardening to computers, outdoor adventure to construction. Residential experience further up the school; den-making in Wales in year 5 (they build fires and toast marshmallows). In year 6, a week in the Lake District, kayaking and sailing. An annual drama production in which years 3-6 take part, recently Wind in the Willows, and parents speak enthusiastically about performance opportunities.

The Richard Whiteley (an alumnus) theatre seats over 200 and the mob-like popularity of it – the drama director terms it 'the emotional hub' of the school – is notable. (The theatre is also a venue for touring players which adds gravitas.) Serious school productions run alternately with big-scale musicals like Sweeney Todd. Pretty much everyone – parents, pupils, teachers – bestow great praise on these glistening productions. Shakespeare in Schools also runs annually which means students limber up to bringing natural cadence to Shakespearean verse in a big theatre setting, like nearby Leeds. Wonderful stuff.

Debating is also popular with the weekly All Talk discussing topics like 'I have the right to be offended'. Although the school culture is one of tolerance, open discussion is encouraged. It was fantastic to hear a pupil say, 'I attribute 90 per cent of my successes to my involvement in debating.'

Music is very strong with bands, orchestras and choirs – one parent described it as 'stupendous'. The school's chamber choir Schola Cantorum gets to sing in Durham Cathedral, St Paul's, even Westminster Abbey. But there are also rock groups, an annual rock concert and a Young Musician of the Year.

Clubs are wide ranging from astronomy to ceramics to student media. Duke of Edinburgh results in a nice stash of gold – and the whole year group does CCF. There is a fair amount of travel with language exchange programmes in Germany and Spain and national trips, to places such as Westminster.

A charming quirk is the school's 30-year history of manning the scoreboard at the Open at Royal Birkdale golf club.

Sport: In the junior school, heaps of sport is on offer– cricket, football, rugby, netball, rounders, hockey. After-school activities include badminton, squash, tennis and golf. Lots of competitive fixtures and tours. Lots of outdoor pursuits too, including the Ribble Ramble and the Rawthey Run.

At senior school, the same sports are played, at every level (not just the A team sporting stars). Lots of inter-school fixtures and overseas tours to places like South Africa. Outdoor pursuits are notable, whether it's Scarrig, the annual hill race or having a go on the school's mountain bike track. Pupils get opportunities to test these skills still further: winter training on the Isle of Skye, anyone? Bring it on.

Boarding: Overall, 40 per cent of boarders are flexi; 80 per cent live within three hours. Around 15 per cent are from overseas, many Forces children. Others just come for a year – from Spain, Germany, China – but may choose to stay on. A mix of around 17 nationalities exists at any one time; the school stresses it works hard at integrating and keeps the proportion of internationals below 20 per cent. Day pupils can also be around till 9pm.

Catteral is the boarding house for years 5-8, though most boarders are from year 7 upwards. Catteral common room is delightful, with amazing views. A vast room downstairs for games like Catteral's Got Talent, although the school encourages children to play outside in the fields beyond the house. When we visited, a new kitchen was being created 'where they can mess about and do cooking,' the experienced housemother said. One parent felt Catteral provides 'an extra security blanket for children'. Another said the few problems her child had experienced boarding were nipped in the bud immediately and the follow-up was 'superb'. Rooms are fine; six to a room in bunks (wardrobes, drawers, some with sink). Baths and showers clean and cheery. The sharing configurations don't change; the housemother feels 'children have to learn to get along'. The rooms of the youngest children are close to the housemother with own loos (no roaming about). Buzzers on every floor. Lots of trips, from Pizza Express to the Lake District.

Six houses for years 9s upwards: Carr and Style for girls, Morrison, Nowell, Paley and Shute for boys. An almost equal balance of boys and girls.

The girls' boarding house we saw was lovely; the common room stuffed with sofas inviting chat, opening on to a terrace; a small field beyond with a volleyball net. The rooms are fairly standard but, as usual, festooned with fairylights and cushions. Girls share in twos in years 10 and 11; lovely views, two desks and sink. At this age, room configurations change termly to 'develop mutual respect, cooperation, tolerance,' housemother says. A close eye is kept on potential friendship problems and, if identified, 'I might have a quiet word with them while walking the dog or ask the older girls to look at it,' she says. One parent told us it was immediately spotted when her daughter was 'not as close' to her friends at one point. Height and weight subtly taken at the start of term; staff are vigilant at meal times. In years 9 and 10 phones handed in at bedtime.

For schools in a glorious rural setting, participation in extracurricular is key (loafing in Starbucks is not an option). Children are encouraged to have a go, 'They take a child out of their comfort zone but there is lots of encouragement and togetherness

When we visited, the school's boarding accommodation which was undergoing a swanky transformation (to the tune of several million smackers). Nowell is the first boarding house to be revamped. We saw the 'show rooms' – a slick, university-style pod, light and bright with white units, vivid yellow chairs. A modern common room; stylish, grown up with boho touches, like pics in gilt frames. It's all going to be rather luxe.

It's fair to say the boys' accommodation pre-revamp is distinctly average. Usual fare of beds, wardrobes, desks... half-eaten bowls of cereal, grubby sports kit lying about. A large games room and kitchen. One of the houses has a wonderful kitchen mural painted by two pupils before they left the school. (A mark of how much they loved it. And how much, perhaps, they recognised that it needed a cheery facelift.)

Heaps of age-related activities happen, from pizza-making nights to croquet to paintballing.

Ethos and heritage: School was founded 500 years ago, moving to its present location in 1869. A 200-acre site, landscaped school gardens framed by magnificent Yorkshire Dales. Jaw-dropping beauty.

The purpose-built junior school, which opened in 2007, is bursting with ideas; no wall space for more. The library's huge picture window frames the hills. Wonderful art space, age-appropriate science lab. Loads of courts, playing fields and pitches.

Beautiful old buildings define the senior school, along with a splendid chapel perched on a hill. Walking into the reception is an upbeat experience, not just the cheeriness but the hush of the library directly to the right; enticing magazines, from Prospect to Business Review.

Lots of corridor and classroom displays. Nothing too arresting but all stimulating. The art department, also a gallery space, has great views and a resident ceramic artist. The student union, all leather sofas and a tiny bar, is nicely preparatory for the next stage of life.

Pastoral care, inclusivity and discipline: In the junior school, the form teacher handles the pastoral side, but there are worry boxes, buddies and a calm club. As one parent put it, metaphorically speaking 'the school gives you a hug'. Lots of responsibility as they get older: house captains, playground buddies etc. Many enthusiastic endorsements from parents: 'a loving and caring school,' one said. All asserted there is no exclusion, no sidelining: 'Even if you are not good at sports, they cheer you on.'

In the senior school, flying in the face of the current trend, phones are allowed. The head girl said this was 'under consideration' (implying pupils really do have a voice here) 'but autonomy is important to people'. School also says any restrictions should be student-led. All sensible grown-up stuff which will appeal to parents who want their children to make sound decisions themselves, rather than be steered into them. One parent felt pupils were removed from social media and 'don't seem to bother much with their phones'. The same seems to apply to alcohol. Students of the legal age are allowed two small units of wine at the 'student union bar'. A member of staff confidently stated, 'And because of that, we don't have an alcohol problem.'

There is a health centre with access to a school counsellor. Regular chapel services and chaplain provide another pastoral layer. Chapel, a pupil said, is 'a time for appreciation of philosophy and gives meaning'. Just so. Inclusivity here, respect for all faiths and nationalities, really does seem to carry some substance.

All pupils belong to the house system and are assigned a tutor. Information-sharing sessions are run on topics like university entrance.

The size of the school means, as one parent put it, 'When life's difficulties arise, everyone knows. It's the Giggleswick bubble.' This, we imagine, might sometimes feel a tad claustrophobic, but the head is clearly seeking to make the school more outward looking.

Pupils and parents: Parents blend of two-income professionals, farmers and entrepreneurs. 'Genuinely supportive,' junior head says.

Pupils come from Ilkley, Bowland, Clitheroe, Harrogate, some from Blackpool or as far north as Kendal. Minibuses collect pupils from a clutch of these destinations.

Money matters: Each year there are approximately 20 to 25 scholarship awards available across three year groups – year 7, year 9 and lower sixth. These include academic, all-rounder, music and sport scholarships.

The last word: A happy, supportive, inclusive school in a wonderful setting where good academic results are on the up and the extracurricular enrichment genuinely caters for every child. A school where joyous participation, without pressure or expectation, is very much the ethos.

Glenalmond College

14

Glenalmond, Perth PH1 3RY

01738 842000 | registrar@glenalmondcollege.co.uk | www.glenalmondcollege.co.uk

Ages: 12–18

Pupils: 350; sixth form: 144; Boarders: 255

Fees: Day £15,300 – £23,400; Boarding: £24,600 – £38,100 pa

Warden: Since April 2020, Dr Michael Alderson, most recently deputy head at Durham School. Read modern languages at Durham where he also took a master's in historical narratives and a doctorate (subject: church history of the Reformation). PGCE from Homerton College,

Cambridge. Married to Emma; enjoys running, skiing and walking.

Entrance: Common Entrance is on the wane, apparently, with fewer coming in from the prep route, so the school also tests independently for maths and English. There is no waiting list so entry is fairly straightforward at the moment if you wave a cheque book, but with the new buzz around the place this may well change.

Exit: Around a quarter leave after GCSEs, most returning to home countries, notably Germany. Around 40 per cent to Russell Group. UCL, Glasgow School of Art, Durham, Edinburgh, St Andrews, Bristol and Exeter have all featured recently. Courses range from architecture and archaeology to biomedical. Two medics and one student to Oxbridge in 2021.

Latest results: In 2021, 89 per cent 9-7 at GCSE; At A level, 61 per cent A*/A (83 per cent A*-B). In 2019 (the last year when exams took place), 49 per cent 9-7 at GCSE; 30 per cent A*/A at A level (59 per cent A*-B).

Teaching and learning: One of the biggest changes recently has been 'improving academic rigour and ambition'. This has been achieved by introducing the Learning Project – a big name for a radical restructuring of the way the children and the teachers are monitored and taught.

The idea is that 'no-one is alone and that everyone is supported'. Teachers now routinely observe each other's lessons to spread good practice and help eliminate the bad and are coached and supported if improvements are needed. Meanwhile, the pupils' academic and social movements are now closely tracked, with regular meetings between house teachers, academic teachers and senior staff to evaluate progress and pastoral needs. Prep is now being monitored for all but upper sixth (one parent told us their child was thrilled by this development as they were actually getting work done). In addition, there are tutorials to help pupils develop core skills for learning including essay planning, revision strategies, mind-mapping, time management, literacy and numeracy foundation skills.

A housemaster says they are all discussing pupils and their welfare far more than they used to. Sharing best practice is common and all the house staff have meet every week to discuss pupils and their progress. Senior management aren't being left on the shelf either. They're being trained to manage their departments in a more effective and supportive way.

So a huge upskilling all round, but is it working? Apparently! Education Scotland is recommending they spread this good practice asap. Meanwhile, parents we spoke to felt that both the children and the teaching standards are beginning to reap the benefits. '[My son] actually looks forward to his supervised study... incredible.'

Ambitious plans to make more of what is a truly fabulous outdoor location include the possibility of fishing on the river Almond, which flows through the grounds

Glenalmond will never be an academic hothouse, but would like us to judge them on how much the pupils improve on their journey through the school.

Subjects on offer cover the usual spectrum from politics to history of art (26 subjects on offer at A level) and are now being supplemented by Mandarin and computer science at GCSE and computer science at A level. Now offers 13 subjects at Higher level; 64 per cent A grades in 2018.

The staff ratio is particularly good at 1:7 and class sizes rarely exceed 16. The bottom sets may have as few as six or seven pupils. They recruited heavily for new staff recently (there was a lot of stagnation to deal with in our view) and the results are new faces with enthusiasm and drive. Another school head has commented that there seems to be a real buzz about the school and they are attracting some real talent to their ranks.

Learning support and SEN: A significant proportion of the school is involved with the learning support department at some level. This ranges from extra time in exams all the way through to a reader and a scribe. There is a policy of free screening for all pupils who enter the school in second, third or fourth form. Thereafter there are charges for eg additional assessments and individual support sessions. More support offered via break and lunchtime prep club.

The arts and extracurricular: There are ambitious plans to make more of what is a truly fabulous outdoor location which include the possibility of fishing on the river Almond, which flows through the school. DofE enthusiastically pursued, as are clay pigeon shooting, tennis, whitewater rafting, skiing. The activity programme is booted up further at the weekend, and at Cairnies, the newly created junior boys' house (second and third form), there are compulsory activities so that they are kept busy.

Expressive arts have always been somewhat understated at Glenalmond, but things are improving and dance has been introduced at GCSE. With the old warden's house now being repatriated as an admin hub, there is also a permanent display area for any artistic endeavour, while neatly putting it in front of any prospective parents.

Sport: There has been a complete restructuring of the sports department so that it functions coeducationally, ie boys' and girls' games are given equal billing (rather than the rugger buggers hogging the limelight). Touch rugby has also been introduced for girls. In fact the school now has heads for hockey, lacrosse and rugby and hopefully soon tennis, golf and cricket. 'One of the best things about Glenalmond is the great support the parents give to sport.'

Parity has also been brought for the firsts lacrosse team, who now share the former firsts rugby pitch, Neish's, as it's known. This has been revamped and a new stand has been built (this time facing the right way, ie towards the beautiful hills). The sporting facilities also include a first-class swimming pool and now an Olympic-standard water-based hockey pitch, which has already hosted some international players, plus a new Astro and a new indoor golf hub with simulation screens.

Boarding: Girls are being given a bigger slice of the pie and are being 'promoted' to the Quad. This is the Oxbridge-style area at the heart of the school, traditionally the site of three boys' houses. Now one of them, Goodacres, has been made over to girls. Neighbouring boys' house Patchell's is the Testosterone Towers of the school, housing a lot of the rugby boys in long dorms in something akin to horse boxes. They seem to love it, though. Another house, Cairnies, formerly for fifth form girls, has been turned into a junior house for second and third form boys – increasing in numbers apparently due to more pupils arriving from destinations other than traditional prep schools.

All of the staff live on site, so the pupils get to see them in their civvies and leading a normal life. Relationships tend to be stronger because currently this 'really is a full boarding school', but be warned if your child doesn't fit in, there is very little escape. However, weekly and flexi boarding introduced from 2019.

Ethos and heritage: 'How many schools have a front and back avenue, Mum?' Well, probably more than we realise, but it does emphasise the sheer grandeur of the place both in architectural and scenic terms. Going down the drive on a warm summer's day (they do happen, apparently) or a crisp winter one with snow on the hills can be an uplifting experience. The school was founded by the former prime minister William Gladstone to keep young men free 'from the sins of the city', and to a certain extent that still happens. Sadly, after years of dodgy mobile phone reception, the pupils can call out with ease, but there is still a feeling of beautiful isolation which helps keep the worst offenders out of trouble, and if your child is sociable and likes the outdoors, they will probably form friendships to last a lifetime. Be prepared to blink when you see the school uniform. The boys are traditional in grey flannels and blazers, with tweed jackets for upper sixth. But the girls, well the girls have navy floor-length skirts. 'Victorian parlour maids' was one description, but according to the school the girls are adamant they won't have it any other way. Reports say they enjoy wearing their pyjamas and wellies underneath in bad weather, so who could blame them? And school believes it helps with evening out those body image crises that so many other schools have to deal with.

Pastoral care, inclusivity and discipline: The school has appointed a deputy head of pastoral care who oversees the eight housemasters/mistresses and there is far more exchanging of information so that nobody slips through the net. House staff and teachers meet weekly to discuss pupils, especially any there are concerns about.

Navy floor-length skirts described as like 'Victorian parlour maids,' but according to the school the girls won't have it any other way

Discipline appears to have improved since the arrival of the current warden. Drugs have never really been an issue at the school, but alcohol could be. This, parents say, has definitely been tightened up, although the occasional lapse still occurs.

Pupils and parents: A high 70 per cent are UK boarders. The school has traditionally been the 'county' choice, or 'tweed central', as some have dubbed it, so many from surrounding Perthshire, Angus, Fife and Aberdeenshire, and the other 30 per cent are international with Germany leading the table. You are less likely to get hard-working lawyer or property developer parents and more likely to see well-heeled farmers and castle dwellers.

Money matters: They stress they don't buy in talent, so no 100 per cent scholarships for the rugby gorillas, but they do support four pupils every year on a bursary basis of 90 to 100 per cent. This isn't based purely on academic potential, but if there is a child who would clearly benefit from the boarding experience then they will try to help. The total remission pot is £2 million a year of which the lion's share goes to bursaries. Scholarships (available in art, drama, music – including pipes and drums – golf, sport and all-round talent) get the usual 10 per cent reduction. Most applicants will try for both.

The last word: Get in fast, Glenalmond is on the up and up. If they can continue to combine academic rigour and making use of their spectacular setting then Glenalmond is set for a cracking future over the next few years.

Gordonstoun

Elgin, Moray IV30 5RF

01343 837837 | admissions@gordonstoun.org.uk | www.gordonstoun.org.uk

Ages: 7–18

Pupils: 535; sixth form: 173; Boarders: 375 full

Fees: Day £12,300 – £31,080 Boarding £27,150 – £42,750 pa

Principal: Since April 2017 Lisa Kerr BA (music, York), a former governor at the school with a long career in business, mostly as a strategy and PR consultant. Married to John (Royal Marines officer) with three children at the school.

Appointed simultaneously to the new post of headmaster was Titus Edge BA (history, Newcastle). An old pupil of Gordonstoun or OG, Titus is married to Marina (another OG) and also has three children at the school. Joined Gordonstoun in 2013 as the deputy head. Previously head of history at Dulwich College.

Head of junior school: since November 2021 (but interim head since August), Cath Lyall. A graduate of Glasgow University, she has taught at state and independent schools including Applegrove Primary and Glasgow Academy over a 20-year career that has also seen her involved in sports coaching and drama direction, as well as support for learning. Lives on site with her husband Andrew; both their children attend the school.

Entrance: Interview with head plus report and references from current school. Maths, English and verbal reasoning tests for potential scholars entering year 9. For sixth form entry, five grade 4+s at GCSE, two of which should be English and maths.

Exit: Up to 10 per cent leave after GCSEs. Majority head off to English universities – Edinburgh, Manchester, Exeter, UCL, Royal Holloway London, KCL, Cardiff, Goldsmiths, Nottingham and Newcastle – to study a wide range of subjects including economics, mechanical engineering, psychology, geography, maths, PPE and war studies. Others to eg St Andrews and Glasgow. Sometimes a few to Oxbridge though none in 2021. Six medics in 2021, plus six to study overseas at European Business School, Varna, Monaco, IE Madrid, TAI Madrid and Georgia Tech.

Latest results: In 2021, 41 per cent 9-7 at GCSE; 37 per cent A*/A at A level. In 2019 (the last year when exams took place), 33 per cent 9-7 at GCSE; 26 per cent A*/A at A level (49 per cent A*-B).

Teaching and learning: Fair to say that Gordonstoun has never been known as an academic hothouse and recent results bear that out. Most students choose three subjects at A level, but the school offers the EPQ or an additional A level, such as further maths. A Level courses include everything from art, biology and business studies to photography and theatre studies. They also offer the vocational BTEC qualifications in physical education and A level applied business studies.

Pupils typically study nine GCSE subjects, with options including dance and drama.

So they're not firing them out by the dozen from the classroom straight into the quads of Cambridge or Oxford. But then that isn't what Gordonstoun is about. They would argue that as a school which is largely non-selective and which takes a much less 'traditional' approach to education, they do remarkably well with the overwhelming majority of students meeting or exceeding their baseline predictions.

All of the parents we spoke to were more than happy with the academic offering. 'I'm expecting a really good set of A levels. The small classes and excellent teaching support has been great for my son.' 'My son came from a school down south. He's a different boy without the pressure. In fact his work is improving simply because he's happy.'

The school says, 'We're going through a curriculum review right now. We want to broaden our offering and vocational BTEC qualifications are part of that, along with looking at collaborations with colleges. Thirty years ago it wasn't so much of a problem if you left school without some kind of recognised qualification. Now you need that "golden ticket" to get you to the next stage.'

Most recently, the school launched the Gordonstoun Diploma, which records students' achievements across their years at school – students are awarded a distinction, merit or pass (or not achieved) according to their commitment and approach in the four areas of academic learning; outdoor learning; arts, culture and sport; and citizenship and service.

The junior school, Aberlour, Is one of the cosiest little preps we've ever visited. Very small classes, lots of smiling faces. 'The majority of the children move on to the senior school. Our children rarely do Common Entrance these days, but if necessary we can prepare them,' says school.

Outdoor learning increasingly a focus.

Learning support and SEN: 'The learning support department has been outstanding for my child.' With three full-time members of staff (plus two in the junior school), the learning support team offers both one-to-one and group help in and outside of class. In addition, any student, regardless of need, can access the school's post-lesson curricular support programme. They also offer enhanced support for the 'most able' students, including a scholars' programme of seminars, debates, dialogue society and Model UN.

The arts and extracurricular: Thanks to Kurt Hahn and his belief in the taking responsibility for helping others, service, as it's called, is integral to the Gordonstoun ethos. Every pupil must pick one of nine services: fire brigade, coastguard, lifeguard, tech crew, first aid, community service, conservation, outdoor leadership or sports service. After training they provide support in the school and the local community. 'This teaches them the value of helping others and gives them valuable life skills,' says school.

Wow drama, wow dance, wow music. Wonderful facilities and a thriving creative environment. Three major drama productions a year with a series of minor ones dotted in between. Pupils regularly leave for drama school here in the UK or in the States. There's a sprung-floored dance studio. The music department is thriving – every child in the junior school learns an instrument and most continue to learn in senior school too.

The art department has a teacher from virtually every discipline, fine art to photography.

Sport: Well, where to start, that's the real question. We've all heard schools talking about the importance of physical exercise on the young mind, but Gordonstoun really does walk the walk. In fact, thanks to its founder, the inspirational Jewish educationalist Kurt Hahn, it invented the walk. Having been released from prison in Nazi Germany, Hahn was encouraged to set up Gordonstoun as an example of his educational theory. In his case this included plenty of outdoor pursuits, cold showers and runs. We're assured there hasn't been an intentional cold shower at Gordonstoun for many a year, but that passion for activity still runs like a golden thread through everything they do.

Describes itself as one of the last true boarding schools in the UK. A third of the pupil body is international (carefully mixed so no one country dominates)

On offer are all the traditional school sports – rugby, cricket, hockey – along with horse riding, skiing, mountain biking, snowboarding, karate, aerobics. They also have Scotland's only five-hole golf course, but the area abounds with plenty of full fat courses. This is Scotland, after all. They have recently completed a magnificent new sports centre with an indoor climbing wall, a fully equipped strength and conditioning room and a floodlit hockey Astroturf, a 400m running track, an indoor swimming pool, squash courts and a.22 rifle range.

All sounds pretty amazing, but be aware this school is not about the culture of the sports jock. There is no worshipping of the first XV. And their sheer distance from the majority of the private school sporting circuit means they don't regularly play the schools who do. 'We play a lot of local teams in Elgin and other places. We much prefer that to spending hours on a coach. We do play other independent schools but it's good to mix it up.'

Outdoor pursuits are huge and every single student gets involved. Sailing, skiing, hillwalking, climbing. The school owns an 80-foot sail training vessel, Ocean Spirit, which makes annual trips to destinations such as the Arctic. Sailing is taught in the same kind of cutters as those used by Prince Philip when he was at Gordonstoun. Why? Because they have a crew of eight and teamwork is integral. All pupils are trained in expedition skills and try everything from backpacking and canoeing to exploration. And of course the school offers a full DofE programme – they did invent it after all, naming it after their most famous alumnus.

It was vaguely comic to watch a group of pupils in full firefighting gear ferociously hosing down a hedge, but there is serious intent. As part of the school's fully trained fire service, these pupils are called out to real blazes across the local countryside.

Boarding: Gordonstoun describes itself as one of the last true boarding schools in the UK. Its relatively remote location plays a part, along with the fact that a third of the school is international (carefully mixed so no one nationality dominates). There are four boys' houses, three girls' and one small boys' sixth form house. They're run by a live-in houseparent with a deputy and a matron for back up. The house we saw was modern, clean, and surprisingly homely and the housemaster young enough to relate to his young charges. And, perhaps more surprising in this day and age of flexi-boarding, the junior school has a healthy percentage of full-time boarders. Junior boarders have their own home, Aberlour House.

In 2019, Altyre House was opened – a larger boarding house for sixth form boys.

Ethos and heritage: 'Plus est en vous' – 'There is more in you'. Yes, we know. We don't usually start a description about a school by dusting off its long-forgotten motto. But let us tell you a story. You may have heard of the miraculous rescue of a group of 12 boys from a series of caves in Thailand. It's an amazing tale of bravery and fortitude and one of the unsung heroes of that episode was OG Connor Roe. When Connor returned to Gordonstoun to tell of his experiences, he made it clear that the one thing that kept him going through the fear and the challenging conditions was the school motto, 'There is more in you'.

Now you might think that's a bit cheesy, but really that kind of sums Gordonstoun up. If you push all the royal razzmatazz to the side – Prince Phillip was an OG as was Prince Charles (albeit unhappily – maybe they hadn't switched on the hot water at that point), Prince Andrew and Prince Edward too. Forget about the sons of rock stars and Hollywood actors (David Bowie and Sean Connery) and look at what Gordonstoun is about: there is a real ring of truth about the place. As the head says, 'One headmaster said to me at a conference, "The thing about Gordonstoun is you don't really have to sit chewing your pen trying to think of what makes your school unique".'

Thanks to Kurt Hahn they were the originators of the 'holistic' education. He believed that the challenge of outdoor activities, internationalism and service to others were as important as academic pursuits in creating a happy, rounded person.

Kurt Hahn believed that the challenge of outdoor activities, internationalism and service to others were equally as important to young people as academic pursuits

'I've seen the stress leave my child's face ever since he started here.' 'Somebody told me my son was "humble" the other day. I was so proud. That's the thing about Gordonstoun, they produce pupils who are as happy talking to a prince as to the cleaner.'

Pastoral care, inclusivity and discipline: As well as the houseparents, there are tutors and 'every member of staff is trained to look after the children'. There is a secure online system to keep track of every child and share necessary information. Recently appointed head of pastoral care is a school inspector, so she ought to know her stuff. 'The pastoral set-up is the best I've seen. Well planned, supportive and built around the child.'

Pupils and parents: Pupils arrive from all directions, from Scunthorpe to Singapore. The royal link still pulls them in from abroad, but on the home front there is a mix of Hahn idealists, first-time adopters who find it a less 'threatening' public school environment than some, and trad public school families.

Money matters: More than 30 per cent of students receive some sort of bursary. School constantly searching for non-fee ways of funding education. Scholarships give 10 per cent discount.

The last word: Gordonstoun doesn't have to try to be different – it just is. It's the original holistic education, using outdoor challenges and service to others to build confidence and improve academic performance. If straight As are all that matter to you and your child then you might want to look elsewhere. But if you want an escape from the academic sausage factory and the chance to think out of the box, sign up now.

Harrogate Ladies' College

16

Clarence Drive, Harrogate, North Yorkshire HG1 2QG

01423 537045 | admissions@hlc.org.uk | www.hlc.org.uk

Ages: 11–18

Pupils: 305; sixth form: 90; Boarders: 125 full

Fees: Day £17,520; Boarding £33,000 – £41,355 pa

Principal: Since 2013, Sylvia Brett BA MA (50s). Exudes a calm and engaging sense of purpose and confidence. Read theology at Durham, followed by masters in philosophy and religion at University of London. Lay chaplain and head of RS at Caldicott followed by head of lower school, RS teacher and year 7 housemistress at Downe House, before being appointed as sole deputy at Roedean. She knows her school, has a clear ethos of inclusivity and a determination that HLC will stick to its guns by insisting that an all-round balanced education is as important as academic outcomes. 'Those who want an academic hothouse will be disappointed, but those who want a school where the progress of every child in every sphere, academic, sporting, artistic and being a decent human being is important will find a home at HLC.' If the school isn't right for a particular child, she 'will say so.' She is proud of the strong family feel of the school.

Parents like the genuine personal knowledge and interest she has in pupils. 'Mrs Brett is calm and statesmanlike which gives you a real sense of order and certainty,' one added. The school has an unashamedly traditional curriculum but it is driven by the values of inclusivity and celebration of individuality espoused by the principal (and all the staff we spoke to). The girls know that they have a voice.

Her approach to Covid was determined, compassionate and pragmatic, we heard. With online learning immediately established as the new normal she was also quick to recognise the need for 'no Zoom' days, and in winter longer lunch breaks so girls had time to get outside and exercise in daylight. This mirrors her wider commitment to mental health and wellbeing for all.

Married to Justin, a classics teacher, and has one daughter in the sixth form. When time permits her interests include music (singing and piano), art, swimming, family and friends.

Entrance: Main entry points are 11, 13 and 16 but school flexible. For year 7 (upper three) entry, taster day in autumn term, school entrance test (maths, English, VR) and interview with the principal together with reports from previous school. Highfield is the linked co-ed prep school – about half the girls from here carry on to HLC, with the rest taking advantage of the very strong state provision in the area.

Sixth form entry is on a case by case basis but minimum of five 5s at GCSEs plus an assessment in English and maths. International pupils (who make up around half of the 90-strong sixth form) sit the school's own English and maths tests under independently supervised conditions and are then interviewed by the principal. EAL support available but the school will say no it they feel that poorer English would be a barrier to the student being successful here. There are academic, music, drama, art, textiles and sporting scholarship programmes.

Exit: Usually 20 per cent leave after GCSEs because of the appeal of very strong state sixth form provision in the area. Well over 90 per cent of sixth formers leave for a wide selection of universities, the majority to Russell Group. No Oxbridge students in the last few years but UCL, King's College London, Bristol, Durham, Edinburgh, Exeter, Glasgow, Keele, Lancaster, Leeds, Manchester, Sheffield, Warwick and York have all featured recently. One medic in 2021, and four overseas to Amsterdam, Osaka, Debrechen and the Chinese University of Hong Kong. Wide range of courses: economics and business feature strongly but includes international relations and politics, 3D design and architecture, medicine, PPE, engineering, mathematics and law.

Latest results: In 2021, 62 per cent 9-7 at GCSE; 69 per cent A*/A at A level (83 per cent A*-B). In 2019 (the last year when exams took place), 55 per cent 9-7 at GCSE; 24 per cent A*/A at A level (61 per cent A*-B).

Teaching and learning: Results place the school comfortably as the highest performing in the Harrogate area for both GCSE and A level. Traditional curriculum offer but with an ever stronger focus on cross-curricular links and developing independent learning skills to follow on from the curriculum developments already under way at Highfield. Interestingly, this work is being led by input from sixth form students as well as staff.

Sciences are a strength, lots of good (if a bit dated) labs and the option for double or triple science at GCSE. On the day we visited there was a mock CSI investigation taking place with students in hazmat suits undertaking analysis of crime scene samples – lots of fun with a learning purpose. Good range of subjects on offer and the majority of pupils we spoke to were able to get the choices they wanted (school builds the GCSE and A level curriculum around students' choices wherever possible, which they appreciate). All students take Latin, French and German from year 7 (upper three) with the option to introduce Spanish by year 8 (lower four). Study of a modern language is preferred at GCSE but not compulsory. GCSE top set maths do further maths as standard and further maths is an option at A level. In the sixth form the EPQ has 30 per cent take up.

Boarding houses are late Victorian villas a short walk from the main campus. All very comfortable and decorated with a real sense of flair and design. Possibly the warmest boarding atmosphere we have yet come across

A strong tracking and monitoring system kicks off with testing for all from the off, followed by 'learning conversations' with teachers to help make sure every girl is on track and gets support if needed. Huge praise among girls for subject clinics. A parent commented these clinics 'really helped my daughter, who started GCSEs halfway through year 10 (lower fifth), to catch up very easily.' Pupils said they could email any teacher at any time if they have a problem. Quite heavy on homework but with adjustments made if necessary. Immediately after school there is 90 minutes of prep for the boarders with day girls also welcome to join. There is a real sense throughout the school that learning really is a two-way process 'done with' rather than 'done to'. In a world where so many schools are obsessed with the use of targets and data as a means of improving performance the HLC approach seems both much more civilised, sensible and to really involve the girls in their own learning journey.

Maximum class size of 24, with many much smaller. It was clear from all we spoke to that the girls are very well known by their teachers. Classrooms are a mixture of old and new but all are well maintained. There is a super library, the corridors are red carpet throughout.

Careers education taken seriously. A new careers programme launched in 2019 under the title of 'Inspire – preparing today for tomorrow's workplace'. Activities throughout the year for all pupils including weekly careers talks, careers fairs and a work experience programme for year 11.

Learning support and SEN: Around 10 per cent SEN, mainly dyslexia, ADHD, dyscalculia and dyspraxia. Specialist trained SENCo leads a small additional needs team and seems to just 'get' what learning support is about, according to parents. The school uses primary data and its own screening to identify any specific needs. In class teacher support is free, and parents also commented on the support for dyslexia in boarders' prep. There is a scale of charges for a more individual programmes including communication and interaction skills, emotional and mental health, and sensory and physical support. Although the school would accommodate physical disabilities, the age and layout of the buildings could be a limiting factor. Overseas students encouraged to sit exams in their native language; EAL tuition available.

The arts and extracurricular: Music is the life blood of the school. Dedicated music house accommodates ensembles galore from samba to string and four choirs; majority of girls learn an instrument or two. Musicians regularly take prizes at the Harrogate Festival. The chapel choir is a real strength with tours in both the UK and overseas including singing in Barcelona's Sagrada Familia, Prague and Venice. Recent success includes a second in the Barnado's national championships.

School has a drama studio and assembly hall with retractable seating. A level theatre studies on offer and the girls spoke with great pride about their peers who had moved on to prestigious dramas schools. Many girls take LAMDA (honours and distinctions the norm). The Wizard of Oz, The Crucible and Oliver! are among recent productions. Art, photography and textiles are all on offer at A level with a superb art studio and photography room. Good facilities and the results of talented artists on show around the school. Although the school has a fully functioning DT area, this isn't currently offered at exam level, to the disappointment of some of the girls.

An extensive extracurricular menu includes over 20 clubs, ranging from Apprentice to Babel Fish, Eco Leaders, Dumbledore's Army and two fascinating (if a little scary sounding) English extension clubs, the Order of Athena and the Sisterhood of Freedom Writers. Plenty for the science sort with 'Ingeneurs', Chemistry Olympiad and Maths Club. Strong DofE and masses of charity and community work. School runs own business programme, Duchy Enterprise, which is an enterprise opportunity for all pupils from year 10 through to year 13. Pupils work in teams to create a business venture and sell their products for charity. Trips are extensive, including music and sports tours, classics, battlefields and Normandy D-Day landing trips as well as French, German and Spanish exchanges and cultural visits. Plus a popular ski trip.

Sport: Sport is a major part of school life with lacrosse at the heart of the school's sporting success. Current U18s Scottish Schools lacrosse champions and there is also good representation at county and regional level. Good range of other competitive team sports with recent successes in tennis, netball and rounders, athletics and cross-country.

Good facilities include plenty of tennis and badminton courts, multi-gym, newly re-developed 25-metre pool (with spa vibe) and a sports hall which doubles up as a venue for social events, speech day etc. There is no all-weather pitch yet, though, and some girls commented that a greater focus on hockey and netball would be welcomed. Girls in year 11 (upper five) and above can opt to go horse riding at a local riding school or to David Lloyd leisure centre during their timetabled games lessons.

Boarding: The four boarding houses offer a real sense of home from home. Housed in late Victorian villas they are a short walk from the main campus with a definite sense of going home. Think shabby chic meets country house with plenty of cosy sitting rooms, comfy settees, games equipment and so forth. Meals are all taken in the school dining rooms but each house has a well-equipped kitchen where girls can also prepare their own food and share house dinners. Laundry is all done but there is the option for girls to do their own if they want. Rooms are comfortable, doubles triples and a few singles and fours. No ensuite bathrooms and while not the most modern we have seen the houses are very comfortable, decorated with a real sense of flair and design. Possibly the warmest boarding atmosphere we have come across.

Two resident housemistresses in each house (some with dogs) provide what one parent described as 'outstanding care not just in normal times but particularly in the pandemic. I've never felt more part of the school than during the pandemic, the communication has been first class and even though the girls couldn't get home for so long I knew they were safe and cared for as well as I could.' The boarding staff certainly go the extra mile here and parents described the head of boarding as 'absolutely incredible, she's super approachable and the girls are her number one priority'.

The principal and girls spoke separately, clearly and without any sense of political correctness about the support that was given to, for instance, LGBTQ pupils

Upper sixth only in Tower with room for 40 and a much greater sense of independence and preparation for university life. Parents and students also like the fact that the town location allows the girls to have a degree of (carefully monitored) independence as they get older.

Weekly and flexi boarding are on offer, as is the option to have breakfast and dinner at the college. Full boarding offers weekends full of trips and activities, off and on site, with over 90 boarders remaining in school most weekends. Day students are able to join their boarding friends on these trips and we saw no sense of a division between day and boarding here. As part of bringing day and boarding pupils together, day pupils receive one night free boarding per term and breakfast and dinner is also included in the standard day fees

Ethos and heritage: HLC was founded in 1893 before moving to its purpose-built home on the current site within walking distance of the busy town centre. The comfortable, not overly grand, Victorian buildings combine with modern additions such as the sports hall and swimming pool on a leafy site with immaculate grounds. There is a beautiful chapel (home to the chapel choirs) with services three times a week. While these are broadly Christian in ethos they are led by staff and students and reflect the multicultural nature of the pupils. The separate sixth form centre in main school gives girls their own (shared) studies as well as a study centre, kitchens, AV room and its own stylish coffee shop.

Uniform is blazer and tartan skirt for the main school and a smart business suit for the sixth form. Food has seen a marked improvement in the choice and quality of meals available in the recently refurbished dining room, we heard. The food we ate was first class, and did we mention the cake? Staff and girls dine together in main dining room, self-service with occasional formal dining. All meals here for boarders during the week except when they cook their own house meals.

Separate sixth form centre in main school gives girls their own (shared) studies as well as a study centre, kitchens, AV room and a rather stylish coffee shop

Strong OG network, including Cokie van der Velde, 2015 Barclays Woman of the Year; Julie Mulligan, chair of the Police Advisory Board for England and Wales; Juliet Bremner, TV news reporter; Laura Winwood, former president of the Oxford Union; Phillipa Martin, producer of contemporary music festivals at the Sydney Opera House and Polly Lane, legal advisor on national security to the Home Office. There's a vibrant community for alumni with strong engagement with the school. As well as reunions (virtual during the pandemic) there's a business network group for alumni to support each other and current pupils.

Pastoral care, inclusivity and discipline: Committed to supporting mental health and wellbeing. Indeed, the attractive and calming Wellness Centre does much more than support medical needs. With a therapist and classes in mindfulness and Pilates, there is a real sense of looking after the whole person. Undoubtedly a happy school, with a real sense of girls being able to be themselves which translates into a well behaved and polite community where individuality and difference are clearly respected. The principal and girls spoke separately, clearly and without any sense of political correctness about the support that was given to, for instance, LGBTQ pupils. Girls were clear that any (rare) bullying was dealt with in a calm and compassionate way, the emphasis being on resolution and developing the skills to manage relationships

Pupils and parents: Lots of girls from the Harrogate area; day girls also come from other parts of West and North Yorkshire. About 30 per cent are boarders, with around 24 nationalities represented although Hong Kong and South East Asia predominate. Covid meant that many were unable to go home for many months and there appeared to be strong links established with their UK-based peers during this time.

Money matters: A range of scholarships worth five per cent of day fees. Fee reductions of 15 per cent for UK armed forces, ten per cent for offspring of former pupils and five per cent for siblings. Means-tested bursaries up to 110 per cent of day fees to include transport, uniform, books etc.

The last word: A focused, warm, lively and independent-minded school. Its emphasis is on girls' individuality and a genuine commitment to making them partners in the learning process. This produces articulate, well-rounded young women clearly ready to take their place in the world. It offers a very good range of opportunities for the sporty, musical and arty on top of a rigorous academic education. The setting couldn't be more conducive to helping it achieve all of this.

Kilgraston School

RC 17

Bridge of Earn, Perthshire PH2 9BQ

01738 812257 | admissions@kilgraston.com | www.kilgraston.com

Ages: 5–18

Pupils: 259; sixth form: 60; Boarders: 26 full/flexi

Fees: Day £12,240 – £20,805; Boarding £27,150 – £35,535 pa

Headmistress: Since 2015, Dorothy MacGinty. Must be the only head we've met who left teaching to become a make-up artist, although she returned to her original vocation just a couple of years later. Having started out in the state sector at the Catholic faith school, St Aidan's in Wishaw, just outside Glasgow, her make-up work took her to the bright lights of London where she stayed teaching in various locations as both a teacher of PE and biology. Next up was an 11-year post at

Cranbrook as head of department and boarding housemistress, after which she was deputy head at Aldenham before taking on her first headship at St Francis' College. A formidable woman in twinset and pearls, she is poised, articulate and completely dedicated to the girls' all-round success and welfare. 'Such a wonderful, hands-on headmistress. I felt impressed by her style of leadership and how she was involved. She knew all the children by first name, and she had just started,' said one parent.

Unafraid to speak her mind, she is quoted in TES (2014) when leaving St Francis' College as partly doing so due to her dismay to changes in the English system, measuring success by exams, in favour of Scotland's broader Curriculum for Excellence. Seven years later she stands by the same principle: 'People skills are more valuable than straight As.' She uses her daughter (who works in advertising and marketing) as an example, nodding to her portrait hanging on her office wall (painted by a former pupil). 'The biggest advantage of a girls' school is the confidence they gain, they can be comfortable in their own skins,' she says.

'Surviving Covid has been my biggest achievement,' she told us, and she took particularly pride in the upskilling of her staff who all got new laptops to enable continued online teaching. 'By God, the teachers tried to make it interesting,' said a parent. Rewarded for their efforts, Kilgraston was shortlisted in the Independent Schools of the Year's award in 2021 in the response to Covid category.

Married to Frank, they have three children, and she enjoys playing golf, swimming, theatre, art galleries and spending time with family.

Entrance: No entrance exam but head meets every girl and her parents to make sure that they're offering the right style of education. Then a report and reference from the previous school.

Exit: Half of sixth formers head off to Russell Group. Most to Scottish universities especially St Andrews, Edinburgh and Glasgow. Small number to England unis. STEM subjects most popular. Occasional Oxbridge. One medic in 2021.

Latest results: In 2021, 99 per cent A-C at National 5; 95 per cent A-B at Higher, and 100 per cent A-B at Advanced Higher. In 2019 (the last year when exams took place), 96 per cent A-C at National 5; 79 per cent A-B at Higher.

Teaching and learning: 'Best results in over 10 years,' says head (though this is true for many schools in 2021). 'Hugely accessible teachers. Teaching staff have been incredibly good, really do know them,' a parent told us. Subjects typical of the Scottish system, plus environmental science at National level, and psychology at Higher. One parent was a bit disappointed about subject choices: 'It's a small school so limited number of subjects for Higher and Advanced Higher.' She continued: 'On the other hand, they move heaven and earth to let the girls do what they want to do, adjusting the timetable to suit.'

For boarders the typical weekend consists of sport (matches) every Saturday morning, followed by a city trip each or other activities led by the boarding staff

Sciences are the most popular subject choices, double the national average, followed by languages and English. Impressively one of the girls on our tour told us she was heading off to study aeronautical engineering at Glasgow. A parent told us, 'A big push for STEM – girl power, emancipation and all that!' The science department has its own separate snazzy centre, a new(ish) build from 2014. Utilised by the junior school too, which also runs the extracurricular science club here.

French and Spanish both on offer, with all choosing a minimum of one language to Nat 5 and 65 per cent at Higher when Latin is also available. German got dropped recently – sadly, we are seeing this more often as the subject seems to have fallen from grace among pupils. A few parental grumbles about this, but the head of languages, a native French-speaker, told us that she aspires for a dedicated language lab and to introduce Italian to the curriculum (watch this space). 'The girls' accents are phenomenal,' says a parent. Long-standing exchange programme through the Sacred Heart network, but this is on pause for the moment.

In a Nat 5 English class, the bubbly teacher in pink, with fairy lights adorning her desk, embraces interactive teaching and initiates Of Mice and Men bingo. With the winner set to win the coveted prize of a packet of Percy Pig sweets, you could hear a pin drop. Meanwhile in Nat 4 maths (an option for those struggling at Nat 5 level), we saw lots of individual, personal support by the head of department (rated highly by parents) to a group of four girls. 'She is absolutely brilliant – honestly think they would never have done as well at another school,' said a parent. Maths surgeries also run on Tuesdays and Thursdays for after-school support. Small class sizes of 10 to 15 average for English and maths.

Juniors have specialist teachers in art, music, science, modern languages and sport.

The head clearly wants to change the mindset of girls, finding inspiration in the book The Skills: How to Win at Work by Mishal Husain. 'We want to instil greater ambition in the girls, to think of themselves as entrepreneurs.' As recent winners in the regional final of the Young Enterprise Programme, these girls are not resting on their laurels. Their Women in Business initiative also sees a series of successful businesswomen come in to share their experiences.

Learning support and SEN: The only school in Scotland (and only one of six in the UK) with CReSTeD status. All have an education plan and they meet with parents and share progress every six weeks. 'It is very much part of the ethos of school,' the head told us. Around one-third of pupils on SEN register, above the national average, and follow a bespoke timetable. Support for learning head is a full-time primary specialist, part-time senior specialist for English, part-time maths and science specialist and a dyslexia specialist.

We drew a breath when entering the art department, with its stunning corniced ceiling, Doric columns and circular balustrade, with views onto school life below

A parent told us of her child, 'It has been a joy to see her come out of her shell. She blew the teachers out of the water with her progress.' She continued, 'There's no stigma in the department. If a kid misses English, they'll do English at learning support. They don't miss out.'

The arts and extracurricular: We drew a breath when entering the art department, with its stunning corniced ceiling, Doric columns and circular balustrade, with views to school life below. The department was bustling with Nat 5 students working on their inspirational photos and other busy sewing bees in the textiles room, who were creating colourful head-and-shoulder pieces. A piece of wearable art inspired by Covid also caught our eye. A level art has been recently dropped in favour of the Scottish Advanced Higher.

Music for everyone, with a clear ambition for every girl to play two instruments. Everyone in junior school is in junior choir, who were the proud winners at a recent Performing Perth Arts Festival. With no live performances at the school due to restrictions, we watched one of the magical annual pre-Covid Christmas concerts at Perth Concert Hall. Determined not to drop the Christmas concert baton during the pandemic, the head of music worked his socks off to put on a digital performance in the school car park as a drive-through for parents and pupils, in three separate sittings. Instrumental and vocal lessons, plus ensembles, orchestras and choirs for all ages and stages, and a jazz group and trad music clubs for fiddle, pipes and drums.

Drama up to Advanced Higher, and a senior drama club, junior musicals club and LAMDA lessons (at an extra charge). Annual show this year is a digital production of The Little Mermaid by the junior school. On our tour, one of the guides was accosted into the recording studio to bravely record her rendition of Kiss the Girl to add audio to the visuals. The senior school is putting on A Midsummer Night's Dream.

Pupils not stuck for choice with masses of extracurricular activities, with more unusual offerings including a botanical society, the moral and ethical society and an opera appreciation club.

Sport: The dream of many a horse-loving little girl, this is Scotland's only school that has an equestrian centre, hosting the Scottish championships for dressage, showjumping and cross-country. They currently house around 20 horses and have space for girls to bring their own. Riding lessons are charged separately.

'Who Doesn't Love PE?' they post on their Twitter feed. Lazy teenagers be warned, there's no rest for the wicked here. But with over 50 activities a week, there should be something for even the most reluctant. 'So many things you can do – good all-round, that's the draw,' said a parent.

With three Astro pitches, a 25m pool and acres of land, girls can compete in inter-house hockey, tennis, netball and athletics. Hockey is a big deal, with some participating in the premiership of the Scottish Hockey ladies' leagues.

PE from National level to Advanced Higher, with options ranging from zumba to yoga, Scottish country dancing and skiing. Clubs for oodles of sports including climbing, dinghy sailing, ballet (some free, some with an extra charge).

Boarding: 'Boarding mistress took great care of them. The school provided everything they needed – a home away from home,' a parent told us. Numbers, however, have been hit by the pandemic and travel restrictions – currently around 50 boarders, plus another 10/15 flexis. 'Normally more international boarders would make up numbers,' says head – indeed they normally hail from Germany, Spain, Mexico, France, Monaco,

Nigeria, Turkey, Sweden, Thailand, China, Hong Kong and more, with a limit of no more than five from one country to encourage English speaking. Offers full-time, weekly and flexi-boarding, with flexi becoming more popular, but majority there on a Saturday night. A parent told us of her daughter, 'She had a fantastic time in boarding and made excellent friends, so much so that when she came home [to her mother country], she came with two other students from Kilgraston.'

Parents love the family feel of the school and praise the sense of self and self-esteem that the girls have – 'a balanced approach to being female,' said one

Typical weekend consists of sport (matches) every Saturday morning, followed by a city trip each weekend or smaller activities led by the boarding staff. Chapel on a Sunday and homework in the evening and some chill-out time. During the week, girls are kept busy in the evenings with extracurricular activities and riding. Facetime/Zoom calls home weekly. No mobiles in school policy, but boarders are given phones in evening if need to phone home and they are allowed them at weekends.

Junior boarders (all girls) aged 8–12 have shared dorms, with dividers to give them their own space, from age 8. The majority are senior boarders, aged 13 and above, all of whom have their own rooms with shared bathrooms (though there are lots of them). Sixth formers are in Barat or Swinton and have their own kitchen and common room.

Ethos and heritage: Founded in 1930, Kilgraston is set in idyllic countryside in Perthshire and makes the most of all its benefits through its wide programme of activities. The stunning Palladian-style mansion, with its sweeping stairway and stunning upper entrance hall, may give an impression of grandeur but there's no evidence of any Scarlett O'Haras here. 'We're not soft and fluffy,' says head. Indeed, the pupils we met were quietly confident and self-assured without the overt outspokenness we sometimes see. Hearty though – the upper 6s recently embraced dawn swimming in the sea at St Andrews – and not a wetsuit in sight! Parents love the family feel of the school and praise the sense of self and self-esteem that the girls have – 'a balanced approach to being female,' said one. 'They feel nurtured and are secure in who they are.'

The junior school now educates a few boys although we felt they looked a little out of place. However, a parent reassured us that her son 'gets on with everybody. Such amazing grounds, they play football at lunch and swing from the trees.' Head says, 'Kilgraston senior school and sixth form will remain as girls-only but recruitment into the co-ed junior school is strong and an ongoing priority.' The junior school is situated in a brilliantly converted stable block with a glazed central atrium for assemblies, homework clubs and socials with Merchiston boys. Embracing Forest School principles, younger pupils make the most of the acres of surrounding land.

Part of 200-strong network of Sacred Heart schools and colleges, this is a Catholic school with its own large chapel. But pupils of all or no faiths are also embraced – in fact, a pupil told us, 'The majority are not Catholic. We think about community rather than religion.' But as a faith school, naturally myriad charitable endeavours. The latest fundraising event saw the whole school line-dancing to Cotton-Eyed Joe on the lawn.

Pastoral care, inclusivity and discipline: You may be surprised to hear that BFGs roam the corridors of Kilgraston. Alas, there are no big, friendly giants, but instead 'big, friendly girls', in the form of upper 6s (all child-protection trained) who provide a buddy system and act as a big sister to the younger children. Formal pastoral care support is provided through form tutors and year heads, with boarders receiving extra support from the boarding mistress. Tutor meetings every Tuesday and a counsellor is also available. But it's the house system that forms the real heart of the pastoral provision, with house meetings or year group meetings every Friday morning. 'My children live and breathe Kilgraston, the houses are a major thing for them and very proud to be a part of them,' said a parent. Parents also applaud the school for pulling out all the stops during the pandemic, including ensuring the final year was still special for the uppers 6s. 'My U6 still managed to have a great time. Her sixth-year teacher was like a surrogate social partner.' Interaction with the opposite sex through socials with the boys at Merchiston – though they get their pick of the girls from St George's too.

Regular PHSE sessions and social studies in the sixth form covers age relevant hot topics such as Everyone's Invited, drug awareness and how to handle unwanted attention out of school. Another big school concern is the sexualisation of women in social media (the head recently featured in The Spectator on this topic). Hence, girls' phones must be kept in lockers during the day. Some of the girls are youth ambassadors for the Rape and Sexual Abuse Centre in Perth and Kinross.

No-nonsense approach to bullying. Try to nip it in the bud early. A parent confided in us saying, 'It was picked up immediately and they had an open discussion about other words that could have been used. Delighted to hear it was dealt with calmly and without shame.' Head's mantra is, 'That's not the Kilgraston way.'

Pupils and parents: High praise from parents for communications between home and school, with all tutors phoning girls individually during lockdown. Teachers and the head are 'responsive to any concerns,' added a parent, although one felt there could have been more information about the decision to go co-ed in junior school (head says, 'parents were informed by letter before the boys were introduced'). No PTA but there is a boarding committee. Overall, parents are a mixed cohort from different backgrounds – 'not all farmers,' joked one parent; 'diverse, I never felt out of place,' reported another.

Money matters: Up to 10 academic, art and music scholarships. Also riding, tennis and sporting scholarships. Almost a quarter receive assistance by bursaries.

The last word: Girls' boarding school (with a few boys in junior school) adhering to the Scottish education system, as well as the only Scottish school with CReSTeD status and its own equestrian centre. A non-pressurised environment dedicated to promoting the advancement of women, particularly in STEM and science, they turn out confident, self-assured young women with good results, achieved in a relaxed, sporty, happy and not overtly religious atmosphere.

Lathallan School

18

Brotherton Castle, Johnshaven, Angus DD10 0HN

01561 362220 | admissions@lathallan.org.uk | www.lathallan.org.uk

Ages: 6m–18

Pupils: 193; Boarders: 8 full, 11 weekly (from age 10)

Fees: Day £8,256 – £20,643; Boarding £25,590 – £28,299 pa

Headmaster: Since 2009, Richard Toley BA MPhil PGCE. He joined Lathallan in 2006 as director of co-curriculum from nearby High School of Dundee. Degree from St David's Lampeter, MPhil from St Andrews and PGCE from Strathclyde. He and his wife live on-site, with their young now in the junior and senior schools. A historian, charming and relaxed, Mr Toley teaches classical studies and history in the senior school. He also leads learning on the school farm and this regular interaction with pupils gives him a greater working knowledge of their individual needs. Four alpacas have recently joined the farm where pupils learn in a hands-on way about animal care, conservation and sustainability.

Mr Toley runs the school with senior school head, Duncan Lyall BSc PGCE, an Edinburgh lad, and Pamela Hossick, head of the junior school since 2020. Mr Lyall, who read mechanical engineering at Edinburgh, is married with young children and joined Lathallan from Peebles High, having previously taught in both the borders and Aberdeen. As well as running the senior school he is head of mathematics. Mrs Hossick completed her MA in Music at the University of Aberdeen and PGCE at the Northern College of Education. Mrs Hossick's husband also works at Lathallan as head of music and their two children are Old Lathallians.

Entrance: Lathallan nursery: from six weeks, 80 tinies registered but no more than 49 at any one time. Entrance to junior school seamless from nursery test-ette for problems and 'nearly all go' (95 per cent). Juniors are checked 'carefully' and if problems obvious, they get a 'proper test'.

Entry to senior school at any time to any year group if places available, many come via junior school. Otherwise form 5 (P7: 11, 12-year-olds). Taster day. Informal tests in English, maths and verbal reasoning, but not a selective school. Numbers up from prep school, 10/12 a year. Currently full first three years of senior school (and nursery and pre-junior school, ie ages 5 and 6).

Exit: Tiny trickle leaves for trad independents age 13, occasional departure age 8, otherwise the odd relocation. Some 75 per cent of leavers from the tiny sixth form to university, mostly Scottish, especially Edinburgh, Aberdeen, Heriot-Watt, Strathclyde and Edinburgh Napier. Some to Plymouth and Exeter. Mechanical engineering, aeronautical engineering and veterinary science recently popular course choices. Four medics in 2021.

Latest results: In 2021, 92 per cent A-C at National 5; 88 per cent A-B at Higher; 92 per cent A-B at Advanced Higher.

Teaching and learning: Scottish curriculum: 17+ subject options at all levels. Non-selective and for some a C or a D may be a real achievement. Variety pack of languages on offer – Mandarin (number of native speakers in school) plus French (from P1) and Spanish (S1) (native speakers). Not a lot of take-up in the former, though occasional outstanding results at all levels. Pupils study both French and Spanish throughout S2 before opting for one or t'other for Nat 5s. Latin from age 11 (classical studies at Higher and Advanced Higher), crash course in Italian (ab initio) – offered at Higher level, but no take-up – plus the usual suspects: maths, English, three sciences, history, geography (pleasing and popular), business and classical studies, art, PE and drama, and managing environmental resources (MER).

Class sizes around 13 (max 16), pupils streamed for maths and English; both taught in refurbed classrooms in the castle, interactive whiteboards all over. IT impressive – Dell computers plus Apple Macs in senior school. iPads for all seems to be the current flavour of the month (last time we did a round-up it was the 'virtual learning experience') but only for those in the dyslexia stream at Lathallan. We were told that Mr Toley 'was not convinced' by rolling 'em out across the board.

Science centre has three dedicated labs plus one for environmental study and junior science lab. Plus accessible loos, shower and pupil-inspired 'treehouse' (to enhance outdoor learning experiences).

Staff whom we have met are young, enthusiastic and fun. Peris pulled in for the more esoteric subjects (or instruments). No apparent problem in attracting staff, particularly in the current financial climate, when property prices have in some quarters reached basement level. The Aberdeen catchment area was pricey.

Learning support and SEN: All assessed for dyslexia et al on arrival. Two dedicated learning support staff, one-to-one, clusters, or co-teaching, throughout school. Costs the same as a piano lesson. Back-up for the bored and the brightest.

The arts and extracurricular: Music everywhere – bagpipe boxes all over the porch and hall, both girls and boys in pipe bands much in demand for charities and have entertained Princess Anne of late, played in the Angus show, the Glamis gathering, the Scottish Parliament etc. Pipes and drums played at the battlefields in Belgium during the Great War memorial year and compete in the Royal Pipe Band competitions with success. Scottish country dancing no longer has parental input; marvellous photographs in the porch of a junior Scottish country dancing lesson – note the kilt loops and the ecstasy on the faces of the young. Strong drama: head of music previously with Aberdeen Youth Theatre; no orchestra per se (yet) but wind and ceilidh bands.

Both girls and boys in pipe bands are much in demand for charities and have entertained Princess Anne of late, played in the Angus show, the Scottish Parliament etc

First two years of senior school spend six days in the mountains, mountain rescue, navigation (shades of Round Square). Skiing, both at home and abroad, for all. Huge emphasis on outdoor education, resilience, and leadership training. Newish 80-metre zip wire in the wood (100-foot drop). Scary. Six pupils and guides did an unsupported exploratory expedition to eastern Greenland.

Sport: Mr Toley has introduced a formal school-wide traditional PE programme, which 'through age-appropriate indoor exercises aims to improve co-ordination and mental agility both in and outside the academic classroom' 'We realise the importance of exercise.' 'We want our pupils to be well-rounded by participating in PE/sports and outdoor ed.'

Thrashing all-comers in under-16 rugby 7s, new games pavilion (board member head of SRU). All 7-year-olds and older play sport daily, tennis courts double up for netball (Astroturf), 10 acres of playing field overlooking the North Sea and own beach (bracing), plus refurbished gym. Lots of jolly rugby trips and netball tours. Sea at the bottom of the garden, but no sea sports – too rough. Impressive games area adjacent to junior/baby school. Astro, tennis, you name it; plus dedicated gym (though hall in main school building equally adaptable).

Head of outdoor education is Munro-potty, 'probably climbed them all three times,' says Mr Toley. DofE timetabled and huge numbers – school claims 'highest percentage of participation in the DofE scheme in all of the country [Scotland]'.

Boarding: Influx of foreign boarders since full boarding reopened: 30 boarders housed in separate wings of the castle (previously staff quarters), co-ed boarding tidily arranged, mainly from Thailand, China, Spain, Nigeria, Russia. Scottish Guardian Overseas Association oversees them (and individual guardians have to pick up the flack if their charges are sent 'home', ie gated). Some locals, bed and breakfasting available. ESOL on hand to help with language glitches.

Ethos and heritage: Founded in the imposing Victorian Brotherton Castle (1867) in the early 1930s. Originally trad boys' boarding prep school, set in 62 acres of woodland which catered for 'the folk over the hill'; now a thriving nursery (handful of real babes being pushed out in three prams when we visited; good North Sea air) through to Advanced Highers co-ed offering full, weekly or flexi-boarding (from age 10).

First two years of senior school spend six days in the mountains, mountain rescue, navigation (shades of Round Square). Skiing, both at home and abroad, for all. Huge emphasis on outdoor education, resilience, and leadership training

Regular exchange programmes with 'smallish' schools in Canada, Switzerland and Australia; the latter were enjoying their six weeks in Angus during a previous visit. More than 25 clubs; 'we rotate them,' says Mr Toley.

William Bruce houselets (which predate the castle) guard corners of the long-abandoned formal garden which makes a splendid play area. Library and resource centre in main building with classrooms and nursery in bright converted stable block with massive additions (and home to new science build, see above). Some lessons in temporary classrooms. Irritating steps both too shallow and too wide link the two sites. Nursery/junior wing surrounded by play/games areas, stunning nursery playground. Collection of toddler-sized loos and mini basins: one wonders how they cope at home.

Newly refurbed common room for senior school pupils. School uniform provided in house, with jolly fleecy waterproof jackets which staff wear too. Staff all have to take the minibus test.

Pastoral care, inclusivity and discipline: School small enough for every child to be known (cherished is a word that comes to mind if it didn't sound so soppy), strong anti-bullying policy. Occasional gatings for wickedness, no child yet asked to leave. School is 'bespoke, focused'.

Pupils and parents: Increasing number of first-time buyers. FPs supportive, strong parental input, parents will drive many miles out of their way to drop off their tinies in the nursery. Return buses for older children from Stonehaven, Edzell and Aberdeen with coaches from Brechin, Forfar and Montrose.

Aberdeen business community plus local farmers, commuters, usually from within 90-minute radius (which takes you to Dundee). Rob Wainwright an old boy (and does the odd spot of coaching), ditto Ian Lang (Lord Lang of Monkton).

Niche school, perfect for the occasional non-performing refugee from bigger trad schools: Fettes, Merchiston, Robert Gordons. Children thrive in the smaller environment. 'We care.' (Those parents to whom we spoke fell into the latter category. Their relief was palpable.)

Money matters: Money matters 'under control', up to 100 per cent bursaries (and extra help if necessary); huge raft: academic, sports, rugby 7s, netball, music and pipes and drums. Sibling discount. Secondhand clothes shop. Will keep child if parents fall on hard times with the usual caveat of being up front about the problem.

Lathallan nursery in partnership with Aberdeen County Council (discounts). Hours roughly 7.30am to 6pm but check fee structure, deeply expensive if child not collected by designated time (emergency cover and charged by the quarter hour). This is a 50-week nursery with two weeks off for Christmas.

The last word: We have visited Lathallan over the past 20 odd years and met no fewer than six headmasters. Two (or was it three?) heads ago, the brave decision was made to expand, on a year-by-year basis, to become a fully fledged school, with Highers and Advanced Highers and all. We thought they were nuts, but we were wrong. Very wrong. Lathallan is a remarkable success story which keeps on growing.

Lomond School

10 Stafford Street, Helensburgh, Argyll and Bute G84 9JX

01436 672476 | admissions@lomondschool.com | www.lomondschool.com

Ages: 3-18

Pupils: 341; sixth form: 38; Boarders: 38 full, 10 weekly

Fees: Day £9,200 – £13,065; Boarding £22,550 – £30,250 pa

Principal: Since 2014, Johanna Urquhart, who grew up in Loch Lomond. Previously deputy head (academic) at George Watson's College and Breadalbane Academy. She has a degree in maths and statistics, and a master's in education, specialising in leadership and management. Previous roles as maths teacher, head of maths and deputy head in the state and independent sector on Scotland's east coast – she says working in Helensburgh 'feels like coming home'.

She visited Lomond before applying for principal's post and 'fell in love with the school'. Her own two children attend. We found her friendly and with a businesslike approach; pupils describe her as 'fair', 'efficient', but 'not afraid to give a telling-off if misbehaving'.

No capital development is planned but her focus is on developing the school's philosophy and values (we were given a compact booklet to explain them). A flow chart outlines the guiding principles of internationalism, environmentalism, adventure, leadership, lifelong learning, service, 'focusing on the individual' from nursery to S6.

Passionate about adventure and outdoor learning, so much so she appointed a head of adventure and service (playing to the school's strengths in terms of location). Married to local businessman, and a lover of outdoor pursuits: skiing, sailing, water-skiing and travelling.

Entrance: Non-selective with open presentation policy. Don't pull weaker links if not going to succeed. Entrance assessment for potential pupils to measure level of support or challenge they may need. Waiting list for T1/T2.

Nursery from age 3 and no entry requirements. Priority goes to those with siblings already at the school. Intake generally from local primaries or people moving to the area. Vast majority move from junior to senior school.

Exit: Majority go to Scottish universities: Edinburgh, Glasgow and Glasgow School of Art all popular. Others to eg UCL. Small numbers do apprenticeships, or move on to college or the workplace. STEM subjects and economics currently popular. Sometimes a few to Oxbridge or going into medicine, though none in 2021. One overseas in 2021 – to Sorbonne, Paris.

Latest results: In 2021, 98 per cent A-C at National 5; 90 per cent A-B at Higher; 91 per cent A-B at Advanced Higher. In 2019 (the last year when exams took place), 75 per cent A-B at National 5; 51 per cent A-B at Highers; and 73 per cent A-B at Advanced Highers.

Teaching and learning: The first school in Scotland to offer two IB programmes for pupils in S5 and S6. The IB diploma programme and IB careers-related programme now run alongside a new HNC in business and the school's current model of SQA Highers and Advanced Highers. Flexibility indeed.

Mix of international boarders as well as some from the Western Isles and military families from the nearby naval base

A few per cent behind Glasgow's big, top-performing independent schools in Highers results, but this is a non-selective school with an open presentation policy and strong academic results nonetheless.

Max class size 20ish, under 20 in junior school and smaller class sizes once subjects have been chosen. French is taught from nursery and is required from J5 to S2. Spanish is a core subject from S1/S2, replacing German as lots of pupils were requesting it. Vast majority take a language to Nat 5 level, with small numbers to Higher and Advanced Higher. Principal says school strong in the sciences with STEM subjects popular at

Loretto School

Higher and AH. Broad range of subjects with business management and graphic communications on the curriculum, but unusually modern studies (the study of politics, sociology and international relations) not available until Higher as a one-year course. Economics available at Higher.

School has head of careers and future destinations with a programme of careers education as well as individual advice and support for pupils to guide through UCAS, college or work applications.

Learning support and SEN: SEN department in junior and senior school, with head of support for learning offering in-class support and extraction where needed. Number of international students, so EAL support is on hand. Low turnover of staff with some serving as long as 40 years. Refreshingly, 75 per cent of senior management are female.

The arts and extracurricular: Musical productions, driven forward by the head of music, have recently included a senior school production of Guys and Dolls. Two-thirds of the junior school learn a musical instrument and there is an assortment of music clubs: jazz band, sax ensemble, traditional music, orchestras. Small proportion take music to exam level. 'Straight As for those that do at Nat 5 and Higher level.' Drama taught from junior school with a subject specialist. 'Helps develop wider skills, communication and confidence,' and goes up to AH. Eleven pupils did Higher drama in 2018.

Clubs are free if run in-house (vast majority). Cost to parents for skiing and a contribution towards maintenance of sailing boats. Wraparound care in the junior school until 6pm.

The outdoors theme continues with art, featuring sailing and the natural environment, displayed around the school. Local landscapes by S4s feature in the principal's office. Higher photography on the curriculum (taught by the art and the physics depts).

DofE very popular. Giving back to the community has seen S6s working on the regeneration of hermitage park and volunteering at the local hospice Robin House. Academics are not left out with the philosopher's café and a film and video production club for the creatives.

Sport: Brace yourself… don't expect pupils to be humming and hawing to decide between hockey or rugby here. We loved the focus on embracing a sense of adventure (how exciting for young kids and young adults): sailing, skiing, climbing and orienteering are all part of the curriculum.

Significant variety of sports for a small school and plenty of success stories too. Some students play on the Scotland netball team, a cricket internationalist, two S5s in GB sailing squad, the list goes on… Other outdoor pursuits include water-skiing, wakeboarding and keelboat sailing.

Playing fields and huge indoors sports hall with climbing wall a short trip down the road in the school minibus. Shared with local community, it also has a dance studio and gym and caters for basketball, badminton, netball and cricket. Archery another option.

Boarding: Modern, purpose-built boarding school, opened in 2002. The principal describes Lomond as 'unique' in Scotland, as it's largely a day school with boarding. Between 40 and 60 boarders, most full-time, with a small number of flexi-boarders from age 10 up, but the majority staying over at the weekend. Mix of international boarders as well as some from the Western Isles and military families from the nearby naval base. We heard through the grapevine, however, that cuts in school fees funding for naval base families has affected numbers at the school.

Day school friends are welcome to go round and hang out with boarders. The boarding house is just a few minutes' walk away, so boarders can go home, get changed and go back to the school to join in with extracurricular activities. Senior school boarders have more freedom

They've gone to great lengths to make boarding house as homely as possible; kids chose the design and colour scheme of common areas. Dining room with themed menus and nights (Spanish when we visited). Nice big communal areas with computers, pool and table tennis, and outdoor basketball courts at the back. It was empty on our visit as all the boarders were in school, but we did see a cosy (and tidy!) boys' four-bed dorm, home to international students, with clean shared bathrooms in the hall. S4-S6s have their own space on the upper floors with twin and single rooms and ensuite shower rooms. Girls' and boys' rooms are on separate floors with state-of-the-art security system using biometric readers. Tutors on each floor are there to support and supervise.

Day school friends are welcome to go round and hang out with boarders. The boarding house is just a few minutes' walk away, so boarders can go home, get changed and go back to the school to join in with extracurricular activities. Senior school boarders are given more freedom and are able travel into Glasgow, for example.

All have iPads to Facetime and keep in touch with families, but no phones in corridors during the school day. Office space is available if anyone is missing family or they are on a different time zone. Free time to use phones in the evening, if they don't have an after-school club. Younger ones' phones are taken away before bedtime.

Ethos and heritage: On the northern edge of the seaside town of Helensburgh, the present school is an amalgam of Larchfield Academy for Boys, founded in 1845, and St Bride's girls' school, founded in 1895. The schools combined in 1977 and a partial rebuild followed. It is a curious combination of modern and traditional.

'Friendly and welcoming school' with a 'homely atmosphere' and good local reputation. Strong links with the naval base and an international boarding community mean it's a multicultural environment, not usually the case in rural Scotland

The senior school looks deceptively modern from the front and the light-filled entrance is corporate-like, even the carpet branded with a Lomond blue colour scheme. The rear of the school harks back to the past: the turn-of-the century St Bride's Hall plays home to school musicals, opening its doors to the local community. Nursery and junior school children (up to J5) are taught in the beautiful listed building Clarendon, which is loved by the parents we spoke to, one saying, 'I have two happy children who skip into school each day, feel valued and are growing in confidence.' Nursery was gorgeous, with wood panelling and a nook with fireplace in the arch. Lots of good old-fashioned fun in the playground where children were climbing, running and scoring goals.

Celebrated its 40th anniversary in 2017 and exciting events took place throughout the year, like black-tie dinners in Hong Kong, London and Leipzig, as well as a black-tie ball in Helensburgh in June as a culmination of the celebrations.

'Friendly and welcoming school' with a 'homely atmosphere'; students describe themselves 'as trying our hardest, being determined and courageous'. Strong links with the naval base and an international boarding community mean it's a multicultural environment, which is not usually the case in rural Scotland. Good local reputation, though a café worker we spoke to said she felt distanced from the school as most people in local area couldn't afford it. Helensburgh, however, is for the most part an affluent area, so many day school kids will be local.

Impressive former pupils include Charlotte Dobson (Olympic sailor) and television inventor John Logie Baird; WH Auden and Cecil Day Lewis briefly taught at the school.

Pastoral care, inclusivity and discipline: A pastoral care team and depute are in charge of looking after the boarders. School year heads and form teachers are there to lend an ear to parents and pupils. No problems with discipline, but they impose sanctions when needed. Parents can get in touch with teachers or the pastoral team at any time. Three houses have competitions throughout the year, which most of the youngsters get involved in.

S6 pupils can sign out, but the rest are on site for school meals. Catering service has won awards for healthy eating, though we didn't see dining area at lunchtime.

Reports every six weeks and annual written reports as well as weekly newsletter. School FB page is used more than Twitter.

Buses from Killearn, Drymen, Balloch and around the peninsula (paid for by parents). Good local transport links; train is a 10-minute walk from the school.

Pupils and parents: Middle-class parents that are hands-on and organise events throughout the year: the Halloween party, Boden shopping evening, Christmas fair. Mix of local professionals and international military families, as well as the support services and medical professionals connected to the naval base. All pupils wear the smart uniform with blue blazers, with the girls in kilts.

Money matters: Food is included in the cost for boarders. Day pupils pay for uniform, lunch, sports kit and transport on top of school fees. Means-tested bursaries available from five to 100 per cent. Range of scholarships also available.

The last word: Seaside independent day school (nursery to senior) with boarding. Non-selective and multicultural with strong academic results and brilliant opportunities for outdoor adventure. Popular with naval families based at nearby Faslane as well as local families.

Longridge Towers School

Berwick-upon-Tweed, Northumberland TD15 2XQ

01289 307584 | enquiries@lts.org.uk | www.lts.org.uk

Ages: 3–18

Pupils: 326; sixth form: 42; Boarders: 4 full, 7 weekly (from age 11)

Fees: Day £10,050 – £14,250; Boarding £21,000 – £29,400 pa

Headmaster: Since 2016, Jonathan Lee MA PGCE ACA (40s), previously housemaster and maths teacher at Uppingham. Psychology degree from St Andrews and a first career in corporate finance, qualifying as an accountant. His finance skills stand him in good stead with a small school housed in beautiful but expensive-to-maintain premises. Few endowment funds means total dependence on current income. Numbers have been growing, allowing recent investment in teaching, technology and buildings, whilst managing to keep fees inclusive and affordable.

Believes in interaction between the younger and older pupils, prizes good etiquette and behaviour and encourages pupil collaboration. He says that 'the school has a big heart' and is an open door to a broad and diverse range of pupils; a quarter of pupils have additional learning support.

In first two years of tenure he has brought in 'incremental and subtle changes'. Parents believe that he has the right focus, 'has the children's interest and learning at the forefront'. Not one to sit behind closed doors, he is an upbeat and affable presence around school talking to pupils.

Current Scottish fives doubles champion, charity runner, a bit of climbing and, closer to home, gardening. Lives nearby off campus with his family, ex-nurse wife training to be a midwife and their five children, two of whom are pupils at the school.

Entrance: A taster day (or two) with assessment for all, followed by an interview with the head and a character reference from previous school, but will take anyone capable of benefiting from what's on offer. Entry at 16+ by papers in A level subjects, dependent on six grade 4s at GCSE or four National 5s at C, with 5s at GCSE in A level subjects.

Since Longridge pupils come from Scotland and England with different systems involving changes of school at 7, 11, 12, 14 and even different age cut-off points (September for England but March for Scotland), they need careful induction and class sizes are unpredictable.

Exit: Those who stay to upper sixth go mostly to university, about 40 per cent to Russell Group. Wide variety of courses: agricultural management, theatre, art, business and engineering. Popular destinations include York, Newcastle, Warwick, Bristol, Dundee, Leeds, Nottingham and Strathclyde. Four medics in 2021.

Latest results: In 2021, 50 per cent 9-7 at GCSE; 32 per cent A*/A at A level (60 per cent A*-B). In 2021 (the last year when exams took place), 32 per cent 9-7 at GCSE; 32 per cent A*/A at A level (52 per cent A*B).

Teaching and learning: Dusting of A*/As across most subjects at A level and a consistently solid pass rate but also quite a smattering of C/Ds. Good choice of subjects include sports science, computer science and psychology; EPQ for those up to it. Inevitably small groups – will put on a mainstream subject for one pupil in sixth form, French a current example.

At GCSE, good sprinkling in biology and maths and a few in English literature. Wide range of GCSE subjects with flexible timetabling based on the needs of each particular year group so that 95 per cent get to take what they want – almost everyone takes drama.

Strong languages: French is started at age 3, German and Spanish added at 11 on a carousel of the three; pupils choose two from 13. Italian and Latin available as extracurricular (up to GCSE); junior department Spanish and Latin offered off-timetable. With pupil numbers in the 30s per year group there is streaming of teaching groups in core subjects in the senior school.

In the junior department there is a broad and creative curriculum, whilst focus on core subjects, key skills woven into themes and topics, such as 'evolution and inheritance' in year 6, 'may the force be with you' in year 5 and 'dinosaurs' and 'ourselves' in EYFS. 'Learning is fun here,' say the children. Increasing specialist teaching as children move up through the school. Well-equipped designated science classroom used from year 3 upwards. Homework (extended projects and learning logs) set over two weeks, in higher years time given shortens in preparation for senior school.

Regular feedback to pupils and parents on their progress – effort grades given every three weeks and progress grades every six weeks. Two interim reports and one detailed report sent each year. Teachers show real passion, quickly picking up learning style of each pupil due to the small teaching groups. Teacher-led activities have timetabled slots outside teaching time; classroom-related topics spill over into the programme and, whilst optional, children are expected to take part, and they do.

Learning support and SEN: Successful track record with children across the whole ability spectrum has seen a rise in numbers over the last few years. Currently over 80 pupils receive additional support, tailored to individual need and delivered by a dedicated team, through a mixture of tailored timetabling and/or small support groups. Appropriate personal education plans keep teachers aware of needs and are reviewed at regular intervals. Key skills for all at KS3 and year 10s can choose study skills instead of one GCSE option. English help for the small number of EAL pupils and efforts to provide extra stimulus for the very bright.

The arts and extracurricular: Lots of choir, orchestra, jazz groups etc and nearly a third of the school has individual tuition, but little take-up of academic music beyond GCSE. Informal lunchtime concerts much enjoyed by all. Special centre for peripatetic music in a pretty gothic house in the grounds.

The grand façade of this Victorian mansion is dominated by the elaborate portico added to shelter the Prince of Wales's carriage (it's not documented whether he ever visited)

Drama in the round in quirky theatre converted from former convent chapel, with jazzy lighting. Drama on timetable, as well as enthusiastically contested in annual house competition. Each spring the school production is performed in Berwick's Maltings Theatre – recent production Our Day Out. Senior pupils tackle weightier stuff too, such as Euripides' Medea. Tinies in the junior department present the nativity each Christmas and KS2 have a summer production in the school theatre, most recently Peter Pan. Nearly a third of the school takes LAMDA examinations.

Art has an airy space at the top of the building and there are splendid examples of pupils' work around the school. Fine arts studied at A level but photography and textiles along with big pictures, murals and bio-art (fusion of art and biology) on offer in the co-curriculum programme.

The co-curriculum programme extends all through the school from year 3 to sixth form – 4.00pm to 4.45pm daily (buses run at 4.50pm). An alphabet of activities from archery to zoolology – supervised study is provided as an option too.

Lots of opportunity to travel: German exchange, cultural trips to France and Spain, sport tours, ski trips etc. Biennial expedition trip for sixth form combining adventure, community service and relaxation – 2019 destination Central America. DofE bronze and gold for seniors – very popular – and Adventure Service challenge for juniors. Annual junior residentials as eco-explorers to places such as Grinton Lodge or outdoor pursuiters at Boggle Hole. Lots of out of school experiences as all junior teachers are MIDAS-qualified minibus drivers.

Sport: For a small school, punches well above its weight across a wealth of disciplines. Fields teams in traditional sports; some national rugby players and county hockey players. Badminton has gone from strength to strength with a number of county champions. Regional and national schools' representation in athletics, equestrianism, mountain biking, netball, squash, dressage and cycling. Longridge pupils now also hold British vaulting, swimming and Scottish tetrathlon medals.

Nearly three hours of sport a week plus enrichment programme. Spacious sports hall (takes a marquee inside for prize days and dances) and at last has an Astroturf; minibuses take swimmers to Eyemouth pool. Grounds lend themselves to hosting local cross-country etc.

Boarding: With just 20 or so boarders, about half of them full, and a dedicated non-teaching housemaster in charge (ably assisted by four non-teaching boarding staff), it's a very different boarding experience here; more 'an extended family', said one girl boarder. Certainly the easy camaraderie and gentle joshing between those we met and with their housemaster felt just like that.

Accommodation is on two upper floors of the mansion school building, boys above and girls below. Spacious, mostly two-bedded rooms, a few with ensuite showers, adequate storage, decoration up to scratch though many walls obscured with posters and personal paraphernalia. After prep and up to 8.30pm, everyone congregates in the pleasant and well-planned girls' common room with spotless kitchenette, counter seating and generous supplies of fresh fruit, hot and cold drinks. A games room with a striking, pupil-composed mural is an alternative attraction, as well as the school's art and sports facilities – the television only features in winter.

Weekend activities can include occasional boarders – some marooned from Holy Island homes by the tides – and day pupil friends. Saturdays start with a leisurely brunch then an afternoon trip into Berwick with occasional cinema, theatre or speedway visits in the evening. Sunday for more adventurous outings such as paintballing, go-karting or tenpin bowling. Transport is organised for those wishing to attend local church services.

Communication and support for parents is excellent. House staff will attend parents' evenings on behalf of those who cannot get there and provide a detailed follow-up email.

Ethos and heritage: The grand façade of this remarkable Victorian Tudor mansion, built in the 1870s, is dominated by the elaborate portico added to shelter the Prince of Wales's carriage (though it's not documented whether he ever arrived to use it). Built for Sir Hubert Jerningham, a Liberal MP, on the estate inherited by his wife Annie Liddell, it was designed to impress – and it's not lost its touch.

Set in 80 acres of parkland, it was Sir Hubert's home until his death in 1922 when it became a hotel. In 1951, an Ursuline convent school for girls, St Mary's, moved here from nearby Berwick and was restructured in 1983 to found co-educational Longridge Towers School.

Whilst in a fantastic rural setting with imaginative use of the castellated grand areas, the school also has the problem, and expense, of making stone staircases, high ceilings and a warren of corridors work for 21st-century education. The modern language classrooms are well below stairs, in basement rooms originally intended for food preparation. Upstairs, wide corridors with hammer-beam ceilings are lined with lockers, and a breathtaking stone arch leads to the original library. A clever makeover has provided a mezzanine gallery giving working space. Timetabled library lessons and focus on reading ensure this is a well-used space with an ambitious programme of visiting authors etc too.

Four adequately equipped science laboratories, all functioning but some rather antiquated. Interactive whiteboards in some classrooms, two computing/ICT suites as well as laptops and chrome books for mobile use. 'Service wings' house rather drab dining rooms and kitchens on the ground floor – a choice of hot and cold dishes, with not too many complaints.

All obviously well used and well cared for, but lots of echoey passages and stairwells improved by pupil artwork, showing signs of the tight purse strings that have been necessary for some years. Everything clean and mainly litter free and not unnaturally tidy.

The junior department is housed in two buildings in the shadow of the grand mansion. Named after benefactors, Stobo houses years 3 to 6 in a compact one-storey, well cared-for building. A central hall for daily gatherings, merit assemblies on Fridays, displaying an eclectic mix of the pupils' work, evidence of the breadth of curriculum here. Classrooms light and roomy – an environment stimulated by the wealth of displayed children's work and relevant topic information.

Manages extremely well with the disadvantages of scale, and a magnificent but costly stately pile to maintain, to provide breadth of subjects and opportunities

Across a rather drab and unexciting junior playground, early years to year 2 are accommodated in humbler but fully refurbished single-storey quarters, named Jerningham. Rather like Aladdin's cave: opening the door reveals a wealth of colour, imaginative sensory material and even recorded birdsong. Quiet room for numeracy and literacy, ability not age driven; theme-based curriculum led by children, planning and executing a teddy bear rescue from the adjacent wood a recent favourite. A pleasant, fenced outdoor area for younger pupils with weather play equipment that gets enthusiastic use.

Pastoral care, inclusivity and discipline: Pastoral care is a real strength of the school. Pupils talk about it 'being open and welcoming', the size encouraging friendships across the years – especially valuable in such a small and variable boarding situation, their excellent relationships with their teachers – all endorsed by their parents and recognised in the latest ISI inspection.

Sixth formers do not feel their small population is detrimental to their university preparation. Most have a post of responsibility as a prefect, head of house or leading some of the enrichment activities in the junior school. They are instrumental in the organisation of house charity events, the Christmas ball, annual leavers' dinner and school council. Plenty of house competition all the way through the school.

Three house system encourages vertical integration in senior school; tutor groups aligned to individual houses. The tutor is the prime contact for parents; tailored academic mentoring introduced from year 9. Sixth form mixed into three tutor groups with an academic tutor who mentors one or two students. Pupils respect and value the system and the genuine interest of staff, so problems are picked up quickly and children tend to monitor and report issues like bullying before they become serious. Qualified full-time nurse works closely with the pastoral and boarding teams, liaising with outside agencies on mental health issues. This link is being strengthened further by involvement of other members of the pastoral team underpinned by extensive PSHE curriculum.

The junior department has five core values – honesty, endeavour, achievement, responsibility and togetherness – that underpin the code of conduct and behaviour. At the start of the school year each class draws up its own class rules. Led by head of junior department, weekly 'time to talk' sessions, part of the philosophy for children programme, ignite debate.

Popular junior school council discusses school matters and charities to support in their fundraising. An annual whole-school off-timetable day has themed activities and allows time for reflection on such issues as rights and responsibilities or, most recently, an environmental day.

Pupils and parents: A fleet of minibuses covering 14 routes bring pupils coming from a scattered area which includes not only Berwick-upon-Tweed and the surrounding border country in both England and Scotland, but also the Holy Island (Lindisfarne) population, whose children need to board on days when the tide cuts off their journey to or from school.

So boarding at Longridge is more flexi than most and the population fluctuates. A few boarders from abroad, mainly Spain for a year, Middle East or Hong Kong, otherwise a largely British intake.

Everyone looks quite smart in blue blazers, white shirts, grey trousers and knee-length straight skirts with prominent kick pleats in blue, white and grey tartan. Very tinies wear navy sweatshirts and joggers, though uniform not compulsory.

Parents run an active programme of events and raise significant amounts for equipment etc – contributed £20,000 to the long-awaited Astroturf. Governors take an active interest in the school and the local worthies, whose families give the names to houses, support it with visits and interest.

Money matters: Not a rich school but awards available for academic (up to 50 per cent), sporting (up to 10 per cent) or musical (free tuition) excellence. Means-tested governors' bursary scheme subject to the usual assessment and interview admissions procedure. Pupils from Holy Island are sponsored by the local authority, which would otherwise be unable to provide adequate hostel accommodation.

The last word: Pupils of all abilities flourish in this warm, supportive and enabling small school community. Manages extremely well with the disadvantages of scale, and a magnificent but costly stately pile to maintain, to provide the breadth of subjects and opportunities so that pupils do not lose out. Parents say their children leave as well-rounded individuals who know their strengths and weaknesses and have confidence in their abilities. A great alternative for the people of the borders and north Northumberland to have on their doorstep.

Loretto School

21

1-7 Linkfield Road, Musselburgh, East Lothian EH21 7RE

01316 534444 | admissions@loretto.com | www.loretto.com

Ages: 3-18

Pupils: 516 (150 junior school; 366 senior school); sixth form: 146; Boarders: 96 full, 88 flexi (from age 11)

Fees: Day £8,499 – £24,300; Boarding £19,800 – £35,700 pa

Headmaster: Since 2014, Dr Graham Hawley BSc PhD PGCE. Previously six years as headmaster of Kelly College in Devon. First class honours degree from Durham University (natural sciences). A keen sportsman, he represented Middlesex U18s at cricket. Before his teaching career his scientific research expeditions took him all over the world. He's a thinker but without an ego – clever, articulate and happy in his own skin. Parents report that 'he is very approachable and astute' and greets all the children each morning. Married to Rachel (rave reviews from parents, 'she's terrific – bright, friendly and observant') with two teenage young.

Pupils tell us that on his appointment as headmaster he worked at the coalface, at all hours of the day (and night), alongside the teachers, cleaners, groundskeepers and the catering teams to establish exactly how the school ticked. Smart move, as it also earned him a great deal of respect from his pupils.

Head of junior school: since 2018, Andrew Dickenson, previously head of junior school at Kelvinside Academy. MA (50s); studied modern history at St Andrews. Started teaching career in London in early 1990s, then the Edinburgh Academy Junior School (deputy head). Passionate about promoting digital learning across the school as well as outdoor learning. Married with two grown-up daughters.

Entrance: Entrance to new pre-school (3-5 year olds) by 'informal interview'. Junior school admissions by taster day with assessment tests. Years 8-11, English, maths and verbal reasoning tests, plus interview. Sixth form admissions also depend on GCSE grades.

Exit: Nearly all the Nippers move up to the senior school at the age of 12 and most stay right through to the end of sixth form. Sixth form leavers to a broad selection of universities including Bath, Bristol, Durham, Exeter, Edinburgh, Glasgow, Heriot Watt, Leeds, Liverpool, Newcastle and Southampton. Usually a few to Oxbridge (two in 2021) and medics (one in 2021). Two overseas in 2021 – to Bucharest and Florida State.

Latest results: In 2021, 57 per cent 9-7 at GCSEs; 61 per cent A*/A at A level (80 per cent A*-B). In 2019 (the last year when exams took place), 45 per cent 9-7 at GCSE; 23 per cent A*/A at A level (52 per cent A*-B).

Teaching and learning: Senior school follows the English education system of GCSEs and A levels. Results have stepped up recently despite still being a 'broadly unselective school'.

Music, drama and PE can be taken at A level and GCSE. Psychology A level a recent introduction. Boy/girl ratio fairly even across all subjects possibly helped by new female head of science. Economics, business and accounting popular A level choices, and economics can also be taken at GCSE. History and politics department also thriving with excellent record of public examination success. Main modern languages are French and Spanish.

Interactive whiteboards and networked computers throughout. Various societies for brainboxes and those keen to learn more – Reimann Society for those mathematically gifted. Mavor Society – lectures given by the sixth formers on any topic that interests them – an opportunity to extend an academic passion. Excellent visiting speakers each week (recently Olympians Heather Stanning and Steve Cram); pupils spoke about the lectures with real enthusiasm.

The Golf Academy, established in 2002, is Loretto's USP and is top in Europe, attracting young golfers from around the world

Open classroom policy at lunchtime for staff. Senior pupils tell us that there's always someone available to help them with their studies and that the teachers are very approachable. Interview practice for sixth formers and individual support with UCAS personal statements.

Junior school teachers get excellent feedback from the children and parents. 'Nothing is too much effort and if there's a problem or a child needing help they will always sort it out.' One young pupil told us that she liked her maths lessons as it was the first time any teacher 'had made maths fun' for her.

International English Language Testing System (IELTS) available for international pupils who need it.

Learning support and SEN: Learning support available throughout junior and senior schools – one learning support teacher plus two assistants. In sixth form support is timetabled on a needs basis.

The arts and extracurricular: Chapel choirs, training choirs, jazz bands, rock bands, chamber ensembles… new groups spring up depending on who wants to play or sing. The junior school choir have been runners-up in the BBC Songs of Praise School Choir of the Year competition. The choirs tour regularly in the UK and abroad (Limousin in June – can we all go?) and have made a number of CD recordings. Junior school parents commented that both instrumental and choral music are 'tremendous and taken seriously' and that seen as 'cool'; 'all the children want to be in the choir, no coaxing is required'.

However, we hear of slight wobbles in the senior school music department, with parents reporting that the department staff are in 'a state of flux' at the moment, that 'the situation needs sorting out' and that 'music isn't as strong as it used to be or as strong as in the junior school, which is disappointing as it was fantastic'.

Other excitements include the conversion of the old exam hall into a dance studio. Highland, hip hop, ballet and a range of other styles for all ages and growing in popularity (still more with the girls than the boys – Footloose the Musical is coming soon). Highland dancers often accompany the tip-top pipe band to major events. Pipe band has performed with Sir Paul McCartney (twice) and entertained the Pope on his visit to Edinburgh.

Drama workshops include puppetry and stage fighting (small child heaven). Substantial productions in both junior and senior schools. When we visited the junior school was warming up for the end of term production of Treasure Island. Greasepaint, bloomers and enthusiastic cutlass wielding in evidence – happy children.

Art department (senior school) has multiple studios and a dark room – pupils can also work with clay, stone and wood. A level students (at present all girls but we are told more boys next year) have their own studio with an art college atmosphere. An abundance of talent evident in the department, but not much on display.

Many of the full-time boarders stay with local school friends at weekends but apparently 'staying in' is popular too, with lots of activities and social events

The art room in the junior school is a thing of wonder and clearly run with dollops of passion, skill and imagination. Fantastic creations of every shape and form and much of it displayed around the school. Impressive and outstanding. The junior school uses many of the senior school facilities such as the main theatre, the chapel and the eyeball-searing blue Astroturf ('the smurf turf').

Loretto Radio launched in 2009. Children can learn about technical operation, presentation and production skills. Radio presenter from Forth 1 (FM radio station for Edinburgh & East of Scotland) trains small groups of pupils.

Borealis Society for sixth formers offers the opportunity to go on major trekking/academic expeditions to northern areas. Recently the destination was Iceland for five weeks under canvas to climb five of the highest mountains in the country and study birds and Arctic flora. Serious stuff and a major undertaking. CCF compulsory in fourth form, voluntary later (good take-up). Focus on adventure. Army and navy only.

Sport: Sport is a big deal, with pupils in regional and national teams from rugby to judo. Sport traditional: rugby for boys, lacrosse for girls (specialist coach from the US, and girls represent Scotland at U17 and U19), hockey, tennis and cricket (though boys' cricket teams only) for both. Lots of teams so everyone is included, not just the sporting legends. This inclusion is a double-edged sword with some parents thinking it's a huge positive that all children have the experience of playing in a team. One junior school parent commented, 'They don't always put their best teams forward and this is a shame as the teams could be more successful than they are.' However, junior school children mentioned 'sport' as their 'favourite' part of school life and the parents say that 'the children are very proud of their sporting teams and their success'.

And so, to golf. The Golf Academy, established in 2002, is Loretto's USP and is top in Europe, attracting young golfers from around the world. To the east of the school lie the golf courses which provide the fairway for the Academy – Craigielaw and Archerfield; state of the art practice facilities on campus. The Golf Academy indoor centre includes a studio with video analysis and Trackman.

Golf is offered to everyone and is part of PE curriculum for the junior school. In their final two years at the school, the 'senior squad' can choose to play golf as their sole sport. Success rate is high with eight national titles recently. Summer residential golf camps ensure that the school is earning its keep over the holidays while at the same time showcasing its facilities to potential new pupils. Golf scholarships are available and carry a fee reduction of up to 10 per cent.

Boarding: Boarding now in the senior school only – full, weekly or flexi (very popular). There's no 'hot-bedding', so even the flexiest of boarders has their own bed.

Sixth form boarders can leave the school grounds at weekends for cinema, shopping, concerts etc. Many of the full-time boarders stay with local school friends at weekends but apparently 'staying in' is popular too, with lots of activities and social events organised within the school. This is a 'proper' boarding school (70 per cent of senior school board) but one that takes advantage of its proximity to a major city.

There are six single-sex boarding houses, all different in character and with their own distinctive layouts and common areas, plus one co-ed day house. Four boarding houses are for 12 to

16-year-olds, with up to six beds in a room, two for sixth formers, with twin and single rooms and mixed common rooms for socialising.

Ethos and heritage: Founded in 1827, this is Scotland's oldest boarding school. Fully co-ed since 1995. Located in Musselburgh, a small coastal town on the outskirts of Edinburgh. Proximity to the bright lights of Edinburgh works in its favour – pupils can take full advantage of the art galleries, drama and music as well as the opportunities for sport and leisure.

Parents say that it is small enough to include everyone but large enough to let children go the distance and achieve their potential

Senior school buildings predominantly painted in the traditional East Lothian yellow ochre, while the attractive stone-built Pinkie House (sixth form boys' boarding house plus headmaster's house) overlooks a pretty walled garden (good party venue, according to our young guides, used for weddings in the holidays). Campus is quite spread out and somewhat disjointed (lots of walking) with the junior school (known as The Nippers), nursery and some playing fields north of the River Esk (footbridge crossing). Junior school feels separate from the senior school, due to the geographical layout rather than any difference in ethos. Nippers mostly use senior school facilities for matches and special occasions.

Excellent Communication and Resource Centre situated at the heart of the campus incorporates the library and sixth form centre. Popular with students during the day when there's no time to return to their houses to work – encourages independence and a university ambience for the older students.

Elegant and unusual chapel (Tardis-like – appears small/intimate but seats a lot of bottoms), good sized theatre (240 seats), shooting range and squash courts.

Red blazers for all, no ties, kilts on Sundays. Flat shoes – strictly no heels.

We heard time and time again from pupils and parents about the friendliness of the school. That there was 'no pupil hierarchy' and that 'the pupils mix well between the year groups'. The overwhelming feedback that we got from parents is that their children are 'incredibly happy and confident' at the school and many parents felt that this was as important as academic results.

Pastoral care, inclusivity and discipline: Houseparents and live-in house tutors look after boarders. Sixth form tutors also help with academic targets. Pastoral care reinforced by weekly PSHE lessons, including seminars and tutorials.

Parents report that the pastoral care is exceptional. Ladder for punishments but each misdemeanour treated on a case-by-case basis. Gatings and letters to parents for smoking. Automatic expulsion for supplying drugs, but 'experimenting' leads to suspension and then on to a drugs testing programme. Suspension for alcohol and then a final warning before you're out. Escalating series of sanctions for bullying and cyber-bullying.

Pupils and parents: Twenty per cent international pupils (some expats) from 21 countries, highest proportion from Germany. Large numbers of OLs' sons, daughters and grandchildren, but also a good many first-time buyers. Not particularly a Scottish grandee or Sloane Ranger school, although there'll be a smattering. We hear that 'parents are very friendly' and 'quite a diverse mix' and that 'it's easy to make a network of friends'. Old Lorettonians include Lord Lamont, Andrew Marr and Alistair Darling.

The Golf Academy now attracts pupils from further afield than ever before. Parents are supportive of this, even the non-golfers, saying, 'It has resulted in broadening the mix of pupils which can only be a good thing.'

Good bus service to just about everywhere: East Lothian, central Edinburgh and even down to the borders.

Money matters: Scholarships (10 per cent of fees) from year 9 for general academic, music, art, golf, sport, drama and piping. Some means-tested bursaries of up to 105 per cent of fees, the extra five per cent to cover transport, uniform etc, reviewed annually. Fifteen per cent remission for children from Forces families; sibling discounts available.

The last word: A famous Scottish public school that's warm, friendly and has a rounded approach to education. Parents all said that it is small enough to include everyone but big enough to let children go the distance and achieve their potential, a school where the individual matters. Not a hothouse, although strong academic results are important (one parent commented that Loretto is 'as academic as you want it to be'). Ethos is to educate the whole person 'in mind, body and spirit'. Headmaster tells us that it is a school 'to prepare pupils for the rest of their lives'. Loretto sells itself on being a 'small school with a big heart and big ambitions' and fulfils the brief – and more.

The Mary Erskine School

Ravelston, Edinburgh EH4 3NT

0131 347 5700 | admissions@esms.org.uk | www.esms.org.uk

Ages: 12-18

Pupils: 760; sixth form: 252 (co-ed sixth form with Stewart's Melville College); Boarders: 30 full

Fees: Day £13,038; Boarding £25,509 – £26,163 pa

Linked school: Stewart's Melville College, 1268

Principal: Since August 2018, Linda Moule, who runs the twin senior schools (Stewart's Melville College and The Mary Erskine School – or ESMS) with two heads and the head of the co-ed junior school. She spends part of the week in each school (separate campuses) with offices in both. After graduating in theology from Manchester University, she has held positions in the teaching profession in Bristol, Stockport, Manchester and was deputy head of Holy Trinity College, Bromley, before becoming vice-principal of New Hall School, Chelmsford in 2004. She was appointed head of Mary Erskine School in 2009, and became vice-principal of the ESMS in 2016. Mrs Moule is married with two sons, both of whom have attended Stewart's Melville College.

Head: since August 2018, Kirsty Nicholson, who has taught geography at both Stewart's Melville College and The Mary Erskine School, was a very successful head of house at Mary Erskine and, through her role on the management team in charge of S1 and of admissions for the whole school, has very much been its public face in recent years.

Entrance: At age 11, 12, 13, fifth year and sixth form. Automatic entrance from junior school. A broadly non-selective school. Children are assessed (English, maths, verbal reasoning) before entrance. Numbers are up. The waiting lists remain first come, first served and there are no plans to cherry-pick the more able pupils. The school was adamant about this.

Exit: Minimal leakage pre-Highers with most going on to university. Majority to Scottish Universities – St Andrews, Glasgow and Glasgow School of Art popular. South of the border, Bristol, Durham, UCL and LSE. SATs (for American colleges) not a problem – two to US in 2021, to Harvard and Princeton. Thirteen medics in 2021.

Latest results: In 2021, 86 per cent A-B at Advanced Higher; 91 per cent A-B at Higher; 97 per cent A-C at National 5. In 2019 (the last year when exams took place), 56 per cent A at Advanced Higher.

Teaching and learning: ESMS follows the 'diamond' model of education. The boys and girls are educated together at the junior school, separately in the senior school from 12-17 and back to a co-ed set up in their final year. The principal and her heads of school are all strong advocates of this system: 'we can tailor the teaching for boys and girls'; 'boys and girls learn differently'. The pupils 'look forward to sixth form and don't lose contact with each other as they go through'. Class sizes of around 20-22 for first two years – S1 and S2 – reducing in size to 20 or fewer for S3-S5 and then between 12 and 15 for the final year (sixth form). Parents of boys and girls see it as a 'better learning environment' and pupils say that 'the separation doesn't affect the friendships between the boys and girls'. Many of the sixth formers say, 'We have the same group of friends, boys and girls, as we did in the junior school; we don't lose touch.'

Pupils study for eight National 5 exams in S3 and S4. English, mathematics, a science and a modern language are compulsory at this stage. In their penultimate year (S5), they study for five Higher exams, while in their final year they study for Advanced Highers in twinned classes with Stewart's Melville College. Girls can now take economics at National 5 and then progress to Higher and Advanced Higher.

Many pupils do three Advanced Highers (some do more) with considerable success. For these exams pupils have to undertake a dissertation and, in some cases, a scientific investigation which teaches them the skills of independent study that will be necessary at university. Recent results are strong. French, German, Latin and Spanish all on offer to Advanced Higher. The principal tells us 'there is a strong work ethic here'. This was echoed by parents – 'It's a school that produces conscientious children.'

Firefly Learning, an online virtual learning platform, has recently been implemented throughout the school. This allows teachers and students to publish and access information from anywhere with an internet connection. Parents, staff and girls appreciate the effective system to keep track of homework, study tasks, school events and individuals' progress in learning. Pupils do not bring in their own laptops but can sign out and use a school laptop (kept in school library) whenever they need to. However, pupils are still encouraged and expected to use books for their academic research as well as online resources ('both are important skills').

We hear from parents that drama is 'quite extraordinary'. It is part of the curriculum for younger pupils and can be taken up to Higher and Advanced Higher

Pupils tell us that if there is anything academic that they need help with there are drop-in centres every lunchtime where a teacher is available to help them – in all subjects. Strong links with the Merchant Company, whose members offer all final year pupils mock interview practice. Big, bright custom-built common room for sixth formers and study areas available.

Learning support and SEN: Strong learning support both in and out of the classroom. We hear reports of 'great classroom assistants'.

The arts and extracurricular: Outstanding drama – 'sport and the performing arts are equally strong here'. We hear from parents that drama is 'quite extraordinary'. It is part of the curriculum for younger pupils and can be taken up to Higher and Advanced Higher. The Tom Fleming Centre for Performing Arts, at the Stewart's Melville site, can seat audiences of up to 580. It's a renovated Victorian assembly hall – an impressive venue with comprehensive production, sound and lighting facilities. Drama is for all, with plays and performances throughout the year for all age groups with regular performances at the Edinburgh Festival. Masses of orchestras and choirs at all age groups (22 bands, orchestras, ensembles and choirs running). Annual house music and house rock competitions, both keenly fought with performances described by one parent as 'bloody amazing'. Choir performs annually at the Royal Edinburgh Military Tattoo. More than 200 girls have instrumental music lessons and there are 45 visiting music teachers. Pipe band thriving.

A staggering variety of clubs and societies on offer to all. It's all here – from video editing to curling and everything in between. These take place at lunchtime and after school. Many of the clubs are sporting – squash, football, netball – but there's certainly something for everyone in the line-up.

Voluntary CCF very popular with over 300 pupils involved. Strong RAF section – over 100. Even split between boys and girls. ESMS are the biggest provider of DofE in Scotland with over 70 pupils awarded gold recently.

Splendid art – and up-to-date displays around the school, wondrous paintings from this year's art exams already up and framed on the walls. Schools often display fabulous art that we then discover has been hanging there for years. Here the boys and girls can see their creations being valued while they are still at school, when it matters most.

Design and manufacture is available as a Higher and Advanced Higher. Exceptional displays of the girls' product design projects line the corridors.

Sport: As you would expect for the largest (joint) independent school in Europe, sport is massive. Great achievements in hockey with the first XI team winning the Scottish Schools' Cup. There are successes across the more minor sports as well with national accolades in athletics, badminton, dance, curling and swimming. Dance is popular and available at Higher level. Basketball has also become very popular. For those not so enamoured with team sports, there are plentiful options, including cycling, golf, climbing and cross-country. The school offers 30 extracurricular sports clubs.

Boarding: Only a tiny percentage of pupils board; this is still predominantly a day school. Erskine House accommodates up to 29 boarders, most of whom are full-time. Occasional flexi-boarding if space allows. The house isn't purpose built and it feels more like a large family house. The bedroom sizes vary and accommodate between one and three girls. Sixth formers may have their own room depending on numbers. The house is well furnished and very well equipped.

At weekends the boarders have planned activities such as surfing, cinema trips etc but they may also go into the city centre if they wish. The Sunday morning service in the local church remains compulsory to all boarders. They are free to use the school sports centres (pool and fitness suite) in the evening and over weekends.

Boarders come from Scotland, south of the border and also abroad, often with family connections to the school (offspring of FPs), expats. Predominantly UK citizens rather than foreign nationals.

Ethos and heritage: Mary Erskine was founded in 1694, as the Merchant Maiden Hospital, and moved to its present site in Ravelston in 1966, changing its name to The Mary Erskine School and amalgamating with the boys' school (Stewart's Melville College) in 1972. The majority of the buildings are from the 1960s (designed by William Kininmonth in 1964). White and cube-like (could be mistaken for a hospital), but light and spacious inside. These buildings surround the pretty, but somewhat overwhelmed, Ravelston House, built in 1800 by Alexander Keith in the late Adam manner.

At weekends boarders (most of whom are full time) have organised activities such as surfing, cinema trips etc but they may also go into the city centre if they wish. They can also use the school sports centres (pool and fitness suite) in the evening and over weekends

The attractive grounds here are much more expansive than those at Stewart's Melville (and there's more car parking space too). This means that the girls play nearly all of their sport on site and don't need to be bussed out to other playing fields.

Senior pupils share the site with the nursery pupils and the lower half of the ESMS junior school. Final year pupils who are back in the co-ed set-up with Stewart's Melville are bussed to classes between the two school campuses (they're situated about a mile apart). Mind-boggling timetabling but, according to both pupils and staff alike, it runs like clockwork.

Coaches from Dunfermline, Bathgate, Eskbank and Haddington as well as around Edinburgh.

Pastoral care, inclusivity and discipline: The school runs a tutorial system for the first year with groups of 20 girls led by their form tutor, after which the school is divided into six houses. Each has a head of house and an assistant head who together look after the girls as they move through school. These houses are common to both Stewart's Melville and Mary Erskine, so the various inter-house competitions have mixed teams. Weekly inter-house challenges range from maths quizzes to basketball matches. Sixth formers are divided into small tutor groups with a personal tutor, under the umbrella of the director of sixth form.

Excellent anti-bullying policy. 'Cyber bullying in school-aged children now more of a threat than normal bullying' and they have a full programme to educate the pupils and make them aware of the pitfalls. We hear from parents that 'any bullying shenanigans or friendship issues are handled very well and quickly', that there is 'fantastic pastoral care' and pupils are made to feel 'safe, valued and that they belong'. Sophisticated PSE programme throughout the school.

'Zero tolerance' and expulsion if pupils found in possession of, or dealing in, drugs of any kind. Booze and smoking normally end in suspension – principal says 'unacceptable but not an issue in school'.

Pupils and parents: A real mixture of parents. Many first-time buyers and children of FPs (former pupils). Parents report 'a broad cross-section of families', mostly from central Edinburgh and suburbs. Not really a toff school, although there will be a smattering. Taking over a third of Edinburgh's independent secondary pupils, it is less elitist than some of its neighbours. Children living far out can spend the night when doing evening activities (as long as there's room). Alumni include Tom Fleming, actor and broadcaster.

Money matters: Bursaries – up to 100 per cent – and scholarships throughout. Those doing well in the entrance exam are invited to sit a scholarship exam. Music scholarships (together with free music tuition) are also available.

The last word: This is a big school with big ambitions. With terrific success stories on every front, not just academically, it is a formidable operation. Not every child will thrive as a small fish in such a big pond, and such a large operation may leave the nonconformist with less room to manoeuvre. However, its sheer size has tremendous benefits – parents report 'the school pulls in great staff' and provides pupils with 'incredible opportunities'. Well-mannered, ambitious children leave the school with self-confidence and 'a strong work ethic'. Parents across the board say they 'can't fault it'. An outstanding school with impressive results.

Merchiston Castle School

294 Colinton Road, Edinburgh EH13 0PU

01313 122201 | admissions@merchiston.co.uk | www.merchiston.co.uk

Ages: 7-18

Pupils: 471; sixth form: 138; Boarders: 237 full/flexi

Fees: Day £15,330 – £26,040; Boarding £22,080 – £35,880 pa

Headmaster: Since August 2018, Jonathan Anderson, previously senior deputy head at Worksop College. Geography degree from Queen's Belfast; joined Christ's Hospital as a geography teacher and was promoted to assistant housemaster and housemaster. After nearly 14 years, he moved to Worksop. He is married with two young daughters.

Entrance: Entry into junior school by assessment using computer-based InCAS software – measuring reading, general maths and mental arithmetic. Online screening assessment also required, plus interview. Automatic entry to the senior school from the junior school (around 40 pupils per year).

Senior school entry at 13+ from preparatory schools via Common Entrance, or by mathematics, English and science exams, plus interview.

Sixth form entrance depends on GCSE or National 5 performance, or entrance exams, plus interview.

Exit: Six per cent left after GCSEs in 2021 – significantly less than the previous year. Scottish universities are popular, notably Glasgow and Aberdeen. Durham, Exeter, Imperial, Newcastle, Sheffield, UCL and Warwick also feature. Two to Oxbridge in 2021, and three medics. Lots overseas in 2021 – Northwestern University, Illinois; Kutztown University, Pennsylvania; University of Alabama, Salford; Providence College, Rhode Island; Tufts University, Massachusetts; University of Rochester, NY – all to study liberal arts. Plus one student to Sirindorn International Institute of Technology, Thammasat University, Thailand to study computer engineering.

Latest results: In 2021, 72 per cent 9-7 at GCSE; 71 per cent A*/A at A level (92 per cent A*-B). In 2019 (the last year when exams took place), 57 per cent 9-7 at GCSE; 73 per cent A*-B at A level.

Teaching and learning: Junior school pupils start at J4 (primary 4, age 7/8) and stay in the junior school until they finish year 8 (S1, age 12). The tinies (age 7-9) are taught in the Pringle Centre classrooms and move up to take lessons in the main school aged 10. Set from age 11 and follow three individual sciences from age 12. At 13 they move seamlessly up to the senior school without taking an entrance exam. Languages taught from the start, specialist teachers for maths, science and the arts. Pupils in the junior school also have access to a bank of iPads in the Pringle Centre.

School continues to follow the mainly English system. A few do sit a combination of A levels and Scottish Highers. Tiny numbers doing Advanced Highers and a small number Highers. All boys must do two separate sciences at GCSE and many go on to study science at A level. Maths still the most popular subject at A level. Sciences and English are also strong. No plans to change to IB; head says, 'We looked at IB twice but it wouldn't suit us and wouldn't work for the majority of our boys.'

The science labs are well kitted out with full multimedia facilities and video microscopes – they are also equipped to do a certain amount of genetics work. Much to the delight of most of the boys there is also a menagerie of animals including a boa constrictor, a chameleon and a tarantula. Recent developments include Mount Olympus, a suite of classrooms for geography, classics and economics which also includes the popular Masterchef kitchen. This was launched in 2011 with the aim of preparing leavers for life after school. Each boy in his final year has six sessions to learn basic cookery skills. For the ambitious there is the annual, hotly fought and popular Masterchef competition where the boys can showcase their skills.

Parents report that the teaching staff in general are 'top drawer' and 'go out of their way to help the boys'.

Learning support and SEN: School supports boys with a range of needs – dys-stream, Asperger's, ADHD. Broadly non-selective, but boys 'must be able to access the curriculum'. Pupils' support needs are assessed before admission and progress is monitored on an ongoing basis. Pupils are taught either individually or in small groups in timetabled classes in the learning support department. Support is there for actual diagnosable problems but also for getting some boys up to speed. Good feedback about this department – 'it's all dealt with' and 'good communication with the parents'.

The arts and extracurricular: Strong DT department, subject available at A level. Super art, painting displayed in the department and around the school. Music for all. Two-thirds of the boys play a musical instrument. Chapel choir, choral society (over 120 pupils), jazz band, ceilidh band. Fantastic junior and senior pipe bands. Plus many other formal and informal music groups. Many of the weekday school assemblies include music performances. Parents report that the boys 'sing and dance with great enthusiasm' and 'they don't think it's uncool to be in the choir'.

Modern and well furnished, all rooms are ensuite and more akin to a new-build hotel than a traditional boarding house

Flourishing CCF with rifle range built into school wall. Sister school – St George's School for Girls – has recently joined as a cadet company and the schools train together at Merchiston during the summer term.

Drama in partnership with St George's. At least two main productions each year, with a biennial musical, for all year groups. Merchiston Juniors also have their own musical in alternate years.

Sport: Merchiston has long been associated with a tradition of sporting excellence, in particular on the rugby pitch. Sport is played along traditional lines with rugby in the autumn and spring terms and cricket and athletics in the summer. The school is currently represented at national and international level in many sports, including athletics, cricket, rugby and target shooting.

Make no mistake, rugby is still big here – 66 Merchistonians have played at full international level. Parents say, 'Hockey and football are becoming more popular but rugby is still the main sport.' However, with six senior and 12 junior teams, there are opportunities at all levels and everyone is given a chance to represent the school. Boys are enormously proud of their rugby heritage. We hear that at weekends boys don't necessarily rush home when their rugby matches are finished – many choose to stay on the touchline to support their first team. Team tours, including overseas.

Sports facilities are good with a rifle range, golf nets, putting green, fives, tennis (three all-weather floodlit courts) and squash courts, an indoor swimming pool and sports hall. The boys are encouraged to be involved in sport outside the 'core sports' during the school week. Senior boys often help coach the younger children – works well, clearly popular with the younger ones and the coaches. School is embarking on the biggest sporting development for a generation which will include a new sports centre, 25m pool and a 3G synthetic pitch for football and rugby.

The school established a tennis academy in 2007 with 13 players and it has now grown to around twice that size. These players pursue a bespoke academic timetable and an individual tennis programme. Students join the academy by invitation, after passing an assessment.

The golf academy (in association with Kings Acre Golf Club) likewise provides an environment where young golfers can maximise their potential. The academy takes part in junior and senior tournaments throughout Scotland and the UK with plenty of success stories, and there's help with applying for golf scholarships in the US.

Boarding: Traditionally a boarding school; 65 per cent of the boys are boarders and this rises to 80 per cent in sixth form. Junior school offers what they call 'step-up' boarding (flexi), reviewed termly – subject to beds being available. Pringle House (juniors) can sleep a maximum of 46 boys. Lovely cosy house, enclosed in its own secret garden. Homely dorms, spacious kitchen and comfy dayroom, supervised by the head of juniors, resident tutors, a housemother and a team of prefects chosen from upper sixth formers.

In the senior school the boys are divided 'horizontally' rather than 'vertically', so all in each year group are in the same house. Four houses: those for the first three years have a combination of shared and single rooms; when the boys reach lower sixth they move into the impressive Laidlaw House. Boarders are split between Laidlaw North and South, with Evans House accommodating the day pupils. Laidlaw is pretty super-duper. Modern and well furnished, all rooms are ensuite and more akin to a new-build hotel than a traditional boarding house – lucky boys. No wonder boarding numbers increase in sixth form. Six kitchens, in-house laundry, gym and stunning views of Edinburgh.

No step-up boarding in the senior school. A day boy may sleep over for up to three nights per week but beyond this he has to pay the full boarding fee, if beds are available.

Sixth form prefects are billeted to a house for the year to act as mentors. Parents report that the boys 'look up to the prefects mentoring them' and they are their 'role models'. The boys have a different housemaster each year and have to learn to build a new relationship with a senior person, which is 'an important lesson and skill to have,' say parents.

For boarders and day boys alike, Saturday is a normal school day. Lessons in the morning and sports fixtures after lunch. Entertainment in the evening – pizza/DVD evening, cinema or theatre trip, or an evening with a sister school – disco or ceilidh. Sundays have either a whole school service (boarders and day boys) or a morning or evening service for boarders only. Often there are Sunday trips for the boarders – into Edinburgh city centre, bowling, swimming, go-karting, hill-walking. Boys may go out and visit friends or family by arrangement with their housemaster.

This is a 'proper' boarding school, not one composed of flexi-boarders who empty out every weekend. Lots of weekend activities. Each house has telephones for pupils to use and set rules about mobiles. Computer available in Pringle for Skyping.

Ethos and heritage: School was founded in 1828 by Charles Chalmers. Moved to Merchiston Castle, an early 15th-century tower, in 1833. In 1930 moved three miles down the road to the current greenfield site at Colinton, four miles from the centre of Edinburgh. Present day buildings date from this time, though the original Colinton House now houses the science department.

Beautiful mature trees and exceptional views – lovely setting. Compact campus, buildings all quite close together – easy for boys to get from A to B quickly

Buildings set within 100 acres of park-like playing fields. Beautiful mature trees and exceptional views – lovely setting. Compact campus, buildings all quite close together – easy for boys to get from A to B quickly. Nothing flashy but everything well kept and in good heart. Juniors in Pringle House are cosily tucked away in the south west corner of the school grounds but still have easy access to and use of entire campus.

Sick bay with visiting sports physiotherapist and own ultrasound machine. Dining hall with servery and buffet service. Boys quick to praise the food: 'It's good and there's always enough.' First-floor Memorial Hall doubles as chapel and dance hall. An impressive space with balconies all round and a stage at the front, it can seat the whole school – lots of tartan. Big on Scottish reeling. Girls are regularly bussed in from sister schools – St George's (Edinburgh) and Kilgraston (Perthshire) – for reel parties and socials. Girls can visit at weekends and join the boys in the sixth form club.

Uniform of blue blazers, white shirt, tie. Dark, grown-up suits for sixth formers (popular with the boys – badge of honour). Kilts and green jackets for outings/special occasions.

Impressive website – information on just about everything. Full disclosure on academic results – by year and subject. A great window into the school.

Pastoral care, inclusivity and discipline: The feedback that we got from both boys and parents about the matrons and the nurses was second to none – 'top notch', 'fantastic', 'they're lovely', 'totally on it'. The boarders reported that they keep in touch with their previous house matrons as they move up the school.

The horizontal house system works well for controlling potential bullying. Good PSHE programme. Each house has a wellbeing prefect in whom other pupils are encouraged to confide.

Smoking dealt with on a case by case basis. Punishments: detention or clean-up task. Smoking within school buildings results in suspension. The school tries to educate pupils about the risks in consuming alcohol, which is dealt with on a case by case basis. Drugs: instant expulsion for supplying. Expulsion also for drug use except in 'exceptional cases', where a 'supportive regime' may be offered. However this option is 'unlikely to be applied when drugs are used on school premises'.

Pupils and parents: Parents strongly middle class. Many have family connections to the school – former pupils. Plenty of first-time buyers as well. Lots from Edinburgh but also boarders from further afield, Perthshire, borders, Stirlingshire – many from Scottish prep schools. A few from south of the border. Around five per cent expats, 22 per cent from overseas – from 22 countries, particularly Hong Kong and Germany. The boys we met were all open, friendly, confident, well-mannered and proud of their school. Manners matter here.

Money matters: Academic scholarships at 13+, 14+ and sixth form – school's own examinations. All-rounder scholarships, music, sport, art & design. No money off fees – awarded for the honour alone. Parents may apply for means-tested assistance (up to 100 per cent of the fees). Reductions in fees for siblings attending 'sister' schools (St George's School for Girls, Edinburgh; Kilgraston School, Perth and Queen Margaret's School, York).

The last word: The only boys-only boarding school left in Scotland. Traditional, warm and personal school – small enough for everyone to know everyone. Blessed with lovely grounds, with the bonus of having Edinburgh on the doorstep and well placed to attract good staff. Rugby is still very much a religion here but don't underestimate the rest. They're no slouches off the pitch either.

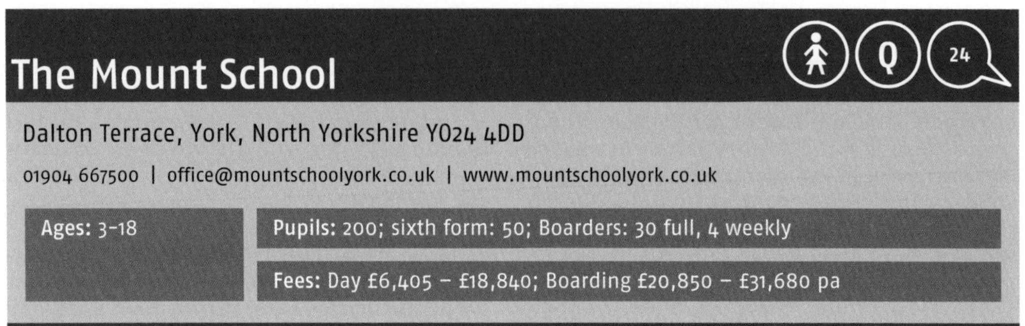

The Mount School
Dalton Terrace, York, North Yorkshire YO24 4DD
01904 667500 | office@mountschoolyork.co.uk | www.mountschoolyork.co.uk
Ages: 3-18
Pupils: 200; sixth form: 50; Boarders: 30 full, 4 weekly
Fees: Day £6,405 – £18,840; Boarding £20,850 – £31,680 pa
Q
24

Principal: Since January 2022, David Griffiths, previously head at Wycombe Abbey School in Changzhou, China, which more than tripled in size under his leadership to almost 1,400 pupils. This was largely thanks to him widening opportunities, from building cars and learning about manufacturing processes through to EPQ projects and studying geopolitics through the major arctic boreal expeditions that he leads.

Head of junior school: since 2012, Rachel Capper BEd. Studied music at Bretton Hall College, University of Leeds. Taught in the state sector in Wales and north London, with positions of responsibility in English, SEN, music and IT, then class teacher at junior school here. Teaches music in the early years and supports junior school English and maths teaching. Pleasant, low-key personality; enjoys walking, theatre, dance and musical performances. Sees her main foci as overseeing effective introduction of iPads and the computing curriculum, raising academic standards (eg through more use of tracking processes) and developing transition to senior school programme and the role of performing arts.

Entrance: Pre school (3-4 years): informal assessment at taster day. Junior school: informal assessment of personal, social and academic development at taster day. Year 7-10 external candidates: English and maths papers, plus interview by principal. Sixth form: minimum six GCSE subjects at grade 6 or above, including A level subjects; 7 for science and maths, plus interview by principal. Girls come from local state and independent schools.

Exit: Almost all from junior to senior school – no exam, unless trying for academic scholarship. Girls have won academic, performing arts and sports scholarships to the senior school and music and academic ones to eg Wycombe Abbey and St Paul's Girls.

Around a quarter leave after GCSEs for co-ed state schools or post-16 colleges, eg York or Askham Bryan. The rest depart post A level to a wide range of universities, including good percentage to Russell Group. Bristol, Durham, LSE, Manchester and Edinburgh all popular. Occasional Oxbridge place, plus some to prestigious international destinations. Wide range of subjects including medicine, English, psychology, geography, finance and zoology.

Latest results: In 2021, 81 per cent 9-7 at GCSE; 67 per cent A*/A at A level (87 per cent A*-B). In 2019 (the last year of exams), 25 per cent A*/A at A level (60 per cent A*-B).

Teaching and learning: At A level, very good art and design and DT, good science and maths – two Ogden Trust physics award winners. Wide choice of subjects, including Latin, classical civilisation, three modern languages, graphic communication, EPQ – will run subjects for just two, even one on occasion, though such small groups, whilst enjoying an exceptional amount of teacher attention, also have disadvantages; average size four to eight.

At GCSE, particularly strong English, history, Spanish, Chinese, PE, geography and DT. Average class size 12 (max 20); approximately half of staff well established; eight men. Parents very happy with teaching, regard paid to individual needs and the way confidence is developed; girls find lessons interesting and are very appreciative of how much support and encouragement they receive.

Junior school: no Sats or secondary school entry preparation, which frees teachers to be creative – some separate subject approach higher up, but mostly skills based, cross-curricular topics. The Mount is an international PeaceJam Foundation school of excellence, the first school in the UK to introduce into the classroom the juniors' programme, focused on the lives and work of Nobel Peace Laureates and activities enhancing conflict resolution skills and character development.

Specialist teaching of French, music, dance, gym, sport and swimming from reception, plus German from year 3. New equality and careers programme for year 6. Independent thinking encouraged. iPads in all classrooms – two digital leaders per year group; ongoing e-safety programme. Forest school for outdoor learning, such as building shelters or habitats for creatures, whittling sticks and lighting fires, takes place in nearby garden and woodland area.

Low numbers in some years mean mixed age classes years 1-4 (13 children in total), with separate years 5 and 6, though they have some lessons together where it is felt to be educationally beneficial. Exceptionally spacious, light classrooms and recent life science room – older girls also enjoy use of senior school labs.

Pleasant, good size, recently refurbished, shared bedrooms (mostly two to four beds). Varied trips and activities programme which girls help to plan and run

Pre-school (2-4 years): two huge, light rooms (tiny reception class, nursery currently bigger). Specialist French and music teaching; forest school. Individual online learning records; each child has key worker for their welfare and development who stays with them throughout their time at the school.

Learning support and SEN: Warm, very committed, full-time SENCo, qualified in dyslexia and literacy, works closely with parents and subject teachers, assisted by two teaching assistants in the junior school. Mostly dyslexia, but has covered autism, ADD, mild hearing and visual impairment, developmental coordination difficulty. Girls allowed to play to their strengths in GCSE choices, eg DT, PE. School would be difficult for those with serious physical disabilities, owing to the nature of the building; those with severe behavioural difficulties 'probably wouldn't be very well suited'. Fees for additional individual and group support going beyond one hour. Individual and small group EAL support from specialist.

The arts and extracurricular: Plenty of music learning and performing, including in York Minster – standard has risen noticeably latterly, say parents, though 'not up to elite standards' (school's small size will have a bearing here). Enterprising drama productions – History Boys (or Girls?), The House of Bernarda Alba – plus musicals; much theatre going, a recent RADA entrant and lots of distinctions in LAMDA exams. Drama offered at GCSE and A level.

High-quality, individual art in various media – kiln in ceramics room and artist in residence established in interestingly designed top floor studio; we were struck by the year 7 masks and ceramic owls. Also some very inventive DT work – textiles, art and design and, unusually for a girls' school, resistant materials at GCSE, though no food tech. Particularly good take-up for DT at A level – two girls recently successful in a national engineering competition. Biennial arts festival.

Wide range of extracurricular activities, including the Prince's Trust, robotics, Amnesty International (very big), much community service within the school and in the wider community; outdoor pursuits residentials from year 2 upwards. Careers programme from year 9; all year 11s do two weeks of work experience. Sixth formers have programme of lectures, workshops and presentations (Specials) covering careers and university applications, plus first aid, budgeting and wider issues, such as ethical matters.

Juniors: thriving music, dance, speech and drama exams and drama productions, eg The Wizard of Oz, The Lion King, Joseph and the Amazing Technicolor Dreamcoat. Plenty of art in a variety of media – has access to the senior school art department. Good choice of clubs, from coding to cricket, cooking to creative writing. Much use made of York's cultural opportunities and beyond. Older children do junior award scheme for schools which recognises achievement in extracurricular activities. All ages represented on school and eco councils.

Sport: Success in swimming and netball competitions, with individual county and international stars at netball, cross-country, biathlon and hockey. Inclusive approach to teams and fun focus to encourage girls to enjoy sport and fitness activities as adults, eg dance skill games. Tag rugby sports club on offer.

Juniors: wide range of sports, including fencing; successful in city-wide events, especially netball and swimming.

Boarding: Full, weekly, or flexi. Only one boarding house now – two previously – with seniors on top floor sharing some of their facilities with the juniors, not always a happy arrangement. Pleasant, good size, recently refurbished, shared bedrooms (mostly two to four beds). Well-resourced relaxation rooms; varied trips and activities programme which girls help to plan and run. Approximately 70 per cent Asian (no cap on number of Chinese girls) with only about one fifth English, so non-Chinese speakers can feel left out. Staff accompanying international trips meet parents to discuss girls' progress.

Ethos and heritage: Founded in 1785 by Esther and William Tuke to provide an education for the daughters of Quakers – fees were 14 guineas a year, for 'instruction, board and washing'. Moved in 1856 to its current site, 16 acres of gardens and playing fields in the heart of York. The gracious original building, School House, dominates the architecturally mixed campus, giving a pleasing sense of the past.

Another central Quaker value, peace, is seen in the PeaceJam Global Thinking programme – focused on inspiring young people to make positive change

Exceptionally spacious classrooms throughout – the English room has large bay windows looking out onto lawns. Attractive, traditional library with wooden bookcases and window seats where girls can read. All sixth formers have their own study, usually shared with one or two others, in the modern sixth form centre, and a well-equipped common room – but girls in the years below would also like their own relaxation/study space.

Some of junior school building has a tired look (school says refurbishment programme in place). Very good choice of high-quality, stylishly presented food – more like eating in a restaurant than a school canteen.

Strikingly calm and harmonious atmosphere – a small, friendly, welcoming school where everyone knows each other and friendships cross years. Girls are encouraged to be independent thinkers and to have a strong sense of social responsibility, within the school community and beyond (the school shares its facilities with a large number of outside groups).

The Quaker ethos is central, even if only a small percentage of actual Quakers amongst staff and pupils, with focus on tolerance of individual differences, spiritual awareness, reflection, empathy, care for others, sustainability and equality (excellent rating for personal development – as well academic and other achievements – in very recent Independent Schools Inspectorate report). All attend morning Meetings. We liked the shout-out board in the sixth form common room, on which appreciative comments about people are posted.

Another central Quaker value, peace, is seen in the PeaceJam Global Thinking programme – at this level focused on inspiring young people to make positive change in their local school and city communities as well as abroad, and enabling them to talk to people in power. Democracy realised through various school councils and committees (food, eco, charity, boarding). Six sixth formers share college leadership responsibilities equally.

Year 6 children take responsibility for the junior Meetings (just two-minute silences), act as playground leaders looking after younger pupils, captain sports teams and direct their own end-of-year assembly. Quaker values are linked to learning and form part of the reward system – a Golden Ticket can be won for social as well as academic skills. Wraparound care available from 3 years: 7.30am-6pm.

Notable old girls: actresses Dame Judi Dench and Mary Ure, author sisters Dame Margaret Drabble and Dame Antonia Byatt, journalist Hilary Wainwright, astrophysicist Dame Jocelyn Bell Burnell.

Pastoral care, inclusivity and discipline: Usual structure of tutor groups and heads of upper school and sixth form, plus boarding house staff and full-time school nurse ('fantastic' – parent); older girls act as peer mentors to younger ones. Access to counsellor and boarders can speak to an independent listener – 'The school is very committed to the girls' wellbeing,' said a parent. Friendship issues sorted swiftly and effectively – 'Teachers know the girls very well… there are plenty of people to talk to about any anxieties… a caring attitude across the community.'

Effort made to reduce exam stress by 'do the best you can' message and years 7-9 are given comments rather than marks for their work. Mobile use banned in school hours, except for emergencies; plenty of online dangers education.

Pupils and parents: Mainly from York and the surrounding areas, plus boarders from various countries, predominantly China, Hong Kong and Thailand. Girls we met were open, confident, happy with the single-sex environment – only the odd grumble, mostly about minor things.

Socially diverse families. Parents able to express views at termly forum and pleased – in most cases – by teachers' quick response to their concerns (however, this writer has experienced exceptional difficulties in obtaining responses from the school).

Juniors: parents have educational workshops to bring them up to speed with learning methods. The children we met, very smart in dark blue tartan skirts, blue cardies and white blouses, presented as open, confident, articulate and kind – they appreciate the amount of attention they receive from teachers, their 'exciting', 'challenging' lessons and the friendly atmosphere.

Money matters: Day fees reduced in 2018, so lower than local independent schools. Year 7: academic, music, performing arts and sport scholarships with fees remission; year 9: academic, drama, music and sport; sixth: academic, drama, music and art. Bursaries (15 per cent have these) up to a maximum of 50 per cent of fees, and for year 12 state school entrants with seven or more 9-7 GCSE grades.

The last word: A happy, nurturing and peaceful school with high academic standards.

Mowden Hall School
25
Newton, Stocksfield, Northumberland NE43 7TP
01661 842147 | info@mowdenhall.co.uk | www.mowdenhall.co.uk
Ages: 3-13
Pupils: 193; Boarders: 110 full/flexi
Fees: Day £12,480 – £18,480; Boarding £25,335 pa

Head: Since July 2020, Kate Martin, formerly deputy head. Came to Mowden Hall in 2011 after teaching in schools including Oundle, Ampleforth and two day schools in Newcastle.

Entrance: Prospective parents visit most days. Be careful with open days – we spoke to one family who visited on one with no intention of enrolling their children but 'were so overwhelmed with the fun and happy atmosphere and the setting that we made a decision on the spot'. Wide ability range – non-selective, but then again 'not just anyone': maintaining the school's ethos and dynamic is important, so if it really wouldn't work for a new a child alongside existing pupils then the head is prepared to say so. Informal assessment, usually during a taster day spent in school, plus interview with head. Vast majority of pre-prep transfer to prep. Pupils local or from prep schools all over the north of England and southern Scotland – Northumberland, Yorkshire, Cumbria, Dumfries and Galloway, Scottish borders. Small number of overseas boarders (mainly Spanish), and although some teachers are TEFL trained, applicants must have a 'reasonable command of English' to be offered a place.

Exit: Barnard Castle, Oundle, Ampleforth, Sedbergh, Stowe and Uppingham most popular in 2021. Shrewsbury, Fettes, Rugby, Eton, Newcastle High, Radley, Queen Margaret's and RGS Newcastle have also featured in recent years, plus a good few others. Around 40 per cent awarded scholarships recently. Few, if any, leave at 11.

Our view: Mowden Hall School was founded in Darlington by Mr Frank Marchbank in 1935. The school was evacuated to Fallbarrow, Windermere, at the start of the war, before acquiring its present impressive site at Newton Hall, near Newcastle-upon-Tyne, in 1945. Originally a traditional, boys-only, boarding prep, Mowden Hall welcomed girls in 1982, and opened a pre-prep department in 1993. Much work was done in the school's early years at Newton to convert the former home of the Joicey family, built in 1835 by the distinguished northern architect John Dobson, into a fully functioning prep school. Now part of the Cothill Trust, a group of seven mainly prep schools spread around the UK.

Splendid setting, on a 50-acre site with fine views. You can get a mobile signal here, but it's irrelevant, at least as far as the children are concerned. No mobiles, iPods or electronic devices allowed other than Kindles for bedtime reading. Boarding pupils communicate with home via the old-fashioned means of weekly letters, email/Facetime/Skype (access after supper) or use of the two payphones. No complaints from pupils and parents are both delighted and relieved.

There's a croquet lawn that (unusually) really is used by the children, alongside impressive sports fields, tennis courts and terrific new all-weather pitches

The dormitories, dining room, common rooms, library and head's house are all in the main building, with an adjoining classroom block and IT rooms. The original stable yard was converted in 1992 to house additional classrooms, science labs and a gloriously colourful art room. The pre-prep building was designed specifically and built adjacent to the school in 1993. The nursery, in a brand new wing, was officially opened in 2014 and shares a number of hard and soft play areas with the pre-prep, allowing learning inside and out. Other additions include a swimming pool, used year-round by everyone, plus sports hall and theatre.

All facilities and resources are shared by children throughout the school, right from nursery. A couple of temporary classrooms add valuable teaching space for the older children but their days are numbered and (hopefully) soon to be replaced by something both more permanent and more attractive. No lack of rigour – essential if they are to maintain or even improve on current CE success; expectations are high and the children respond accordingly. Plenty of teaching from subject specialists. Smartboards are gradually being replaced by Clevertouch interactive boards, linked to the use of iPads as teaching tools.

Prep children are set for English and mathematics for years 4 and 5, streamed from year 6. The top class studies Greek and a number sit scholarships (good track record). Maximum class size 17: 'any bigger than that would contradict our ethos,' says the school. French for all from nursery; Latin from year 5. Good and imaginative teaching at all levels. Pre-prep classrooms especially attractive, prep could do better on classroom displays. 'Our teachers make learning exciting,' said one pupil to a chorus of nodding heads. SENCo with specialist dyslexia qualification provides support throughout the school; one-to-one support is available (charged) if required.

Focus on CE kicks off in year 7 after the unique experience of 'entente cordiale', a term spent at Château de Sauveterre near Toulouse, immersed in French and the French way of life. Away from home and their mother-tongue, this is where the children find their inner coping mechanisms, and most describe it as a major highlight of their time at Mowden. Many understand little during their first 10 days at Sauveterre but then quickly develop a real sense of empowerment as they become fluent in the language – 'confidence is a valuable commodity,' say the staff. The children enter a number of competitions – writing, art and the like – both locally and nationally. They are allocated to one of four houses, named after illustrious northerners, with plenty of healthy inter-house rivalry.

It's not all work. In addition to the wide sporting programme, the nurturing is clear. Staff-pupil relationships are good with high levels of trust and support, seen as a real boon by parents. Music is strong, with choirs, bands, orchestras and plenty of individual music on offer. Art and drama are popular, the school is a centre for LAMDA and public speaking is big: even if it's announcing the hymn numbers for assembly, everyone finds their voice. That, and the ability to look people in the eye when speaking, are valuable tools for a generation usually more used to looking down at screens. These are well-mannered children with more of a sense of responsibility than entitlement. Links with a Kenyan school and also a local school for children with disabilities keeps it real.

There's a croquet lawn that (unusually) really is used by the children, alongside impressive sports fields, tennis courts and cricket nets. Hidden from sight just off the main driveway are terrific new all-weather pitches, a major recent investment and transformational in that they allow year-round matches, even this far north. There's an hour of games every day. Trad team sports are popular – rugby, football, hockey and netball with rounders, tennis and cricket during the summer and swimming and gymnastics year round. Away from the school site the children also enjoy a range of other activities including fishing, paddle-boarding and horse-riding.

Bags of enthusiasm from sports staff and gap students, a number of whom live on site. This 50-acre site also encompasses a large woodland which provides a muddy but exciting landscape for den-building competitions and a BMX trail. Manicured lawns host an annual garden fête, barbecue and leavers' matches, and a beautifully kept rose garden provides all the floristry for speech day and is also a cherished location for the delivery of Common Entrance exam results

The Mount School

(weather permitting). New sports kit has proved enormously popular with all – gone are the heavy rugby shirts and old-fashioned kit, recently replaced by quick-drying, body-wicking fabrics and hoodies, appreciated by both pupils and parents. Interestingly, old kit, along with old uniforms and desks, has been shipped out to a partner school in Kenya, for whom the children raise money on a regular basis.

Smiling, bright-eyed year 6 pupils shared their joy of a recent camping trip to 'some random place in the countryside' where the wind was howling, the rain was relentless and they had an 'amazing time', sustained by the school's (allegedly) famous camping stew and doughnuts. Lunches are cooked in-house and very popular; old-fashioned dining room with trestle tables, conversation is encouraged and children clear the tables afterwards. For these busy and active children food is clearly important and they describe the food on offer in school as 'incredible', favourites being fish and chip Fridays, including an offer of smoked salmon and mackerel for more refined tastes, and mint lamb kebabs and fajitas for midweek suppers. There is, of course, also a salad bar.

Weekends are busy, plenty of staff on hand and no time to be bored. Boarding is especially popular on a Wednesday as there's no prep and it is also tuck night

It's a rural school so no surprise to see corduroy trousers, kilts, checked shirts and tweeds as part of the school uniform, mostly green and navy – it's attractive and they like it. A rare heatwave allows shirt sleeve order and ties are removed after supper. You'll notice the wellies in the school porch as you arrive. They are out in all but the very worst of the winter weather. Scooters, go-carts, bikes and ripsticks are hugely popular. Sensibly, the pre-preps wear waterproof boilersuits, enabling them to make the most of the school's wonderful outdoor environment without ruining expensive school uniform. There's even a woodland classroom where the children drag logs across the soggy ground to build dens, bake bread on campfires and experience the enjoyment of whittling. There's a wide range of extracurricular activities– all the usual suspects plus badminton, computer coding, ballet, nature detectives, golf, Airfix model-making, tapestry, Japanese, jewellery-making, magic tricks, cookery and cross-country running.

The next step is a big one and the school has close links with a wide range of day schools (independent and state) and boarding schools across the UK. Choices helped by regular reporting through prep years; effort and attainment grades every three weeks; ranking every quarter; full written report each term. Pupils de-stress after CE with a diverse and challenging three-week leavers' programme. During our visit they had been tasked with rehearsing and producing a play in the school theatre – in three days from beginning to end.

The parent profile is diverse, reflecting the local demographic. There's a daily complimentary bus picking up from Jesmond and Gosforth for busy parents wishing to avoid the sluggish early morning commute from Newcastle. No school transport on offer at the end of the school day but there's plenty of sensible lift-sharing going on. It's a staggered finish with a wide range of afterschool activities for day pupils as well as boarders; day pupils tend to do everything – except sleep – at school, though even that's a popular option on Friday nights.

Boarding: Just over half board. Some only live a short walk away but such is the pull (from the children, not the school) to stay overnight that parents are drawn into the boarding bubble. About half are full boarders, the rest flexi. Separate accommodation for girls and boys in dorms with four or six beds. Rooms are spacious and colourful and children personalise their own space. Super live-in housemistress with bags of experience is running the show with the support of the head and matrons. Weekends are busy and fairly structured, plenty of staff on hand and no time to be bored. Boarding is especially popular on a Wednesday night as there's no prep and it is also tuck night. Speaking of prep, it's one hour of supervised homework most nights (usually two subjects) for the older children, Latin prep is apparently 'challenging' – schola obdurate, clearly.

The last word: Good traditional prep school with lots going on, exuding energy from the top down. Concentrates on developing confident, well-rounded individuals whilst still aiming for those highly competitive top scholarships. A number of parents say the school has 'surpassed their expectations, engaging and developing all the children and bringing out the best in them – an excellent equilibrium of sport and scholastics'. Were it in a different neck of the woods, geographically speaking, it would be bursting at the seams, but its boarding prowess may eventually encourage a few from overflowing southern schools to venture north. And why not? You'd struggle to find better.

Queen Ethelburga's College

Thorpe Underwood Hall, Ouseburn, York, North Yorkshire YO26 9SS

01423 333300 | admissions@qe.org | www.qe.org

Ages: 3m – 18

Pupils: 1,192; sixth form: 423; Boarders: 868 full/flexi

Fees: Day £8,412 – £18,507; Boarding £33,642 – £42,036; International Boarding £41,550 – £52,368 pa

Acting Principal: Since 2021, Dan Machin. Joined QE in 2005, latterly head of College, then vice-principal. Studied management at Hull followed by a PGCE in economics and business at Warwick and started his career in comprehensives in Wakefield after a stint in the retail sector. Quiet and unassuming, he is a QE man to the core who has seen the school evolve dramatically in the last 17 years, including coping with some significant challenging situations (now resolved) as well as the resulting negative publicity. Still teaches and leads from the front, in keeping with school's motto 'to be the best I can with the gifts that I have'. QE has more than doubled in size in recent years with 868 boarding places and just shy of 1,200 pupils across the four different schools. Principal comments, 'Being a large school allows us the freedom to provide a very flexible curriculum.' They have certainly achieved that for senior students at least with parallel vocational and academic offers. He speaks with pride about the opportunity they provide to help every student achieve their potential in the right area for them.

We asked about some of the controversial practices around the use of CCTV and scholarships criticised by both ISI and this guide in the past and felt reassured that the right changes had been implemented. He says, 'We aren't the school with the horses that some think any more.' The school was judged excellent by ISI in 2019 and everything we saw suggested that QE has successfully moved on from its historic difficulties. The principal is very clear they are committed to supporting all students to have a voice regardless of ethnicity, gender, etc. 'The school has engaged in methodical and thorough reviews of all aspects of its provision to be as strong and transparent on all aspects of inclusion and safeguarding as possible.' Our conversations with pupils suggested that this isn't just lip-service. We met several sixth form scholarship students who said that those from ethnic minority backgrounds felt significantly more included at QE than they had in their previous schools. Not afraid to exclude a student who crosses the boundaries, the principal is also clear that each case will be dealt with on its own its merits. His methodical approach is shown in his comment that 'when something needs addressing we review the situation thoroughly and make sure we deal with it fairly and effectively'.

With a keen interest in cars, motor racing and football, he isn't the typical independent school leader and is all the more refreshing for it. Having studied in both independent and state education, and worked both in and out of the sector, his favourite part of the role is working with students, whether it's the prefects to implement change, teaching GCSE and A Level students, or working with the teaching and learning team.

Entrance: Without question a very selective school. College is as selective as any grammar school and more so than the majority of sixth forms. All pupils from year 4 have to sit a CAT 4 ability test and undertake an interview. School reports are assessed for those currently at QE and a headteacher's report is requested from those coming from other schools. International students take a series of English assessments which are done in person with the school's agent in their home country.

School repeats CAT 4 tests in year 9 to assess which GCSE route students should follow, the top 40 per cent are offered the College (academic) or the Faculty (vocational and academic); the remainder are offered the Faculty route. Some of those offered College will opt for Faculty; there is probably less flexibility for those offered Faculty to try College.

At the end of year 11 roughly 75 per cent of College continue into the sixth form, for which the minimum requirement is GCSE grade 7 in any subject to be taken at A level. Faculty asks for GCSE grade 6 or equivalent for A level subjects and grade 5 for BTECs. There is flexibility for College students to move to Faculty at 16 and Faculty students do take A levels alongside their BTECs. It's a system which parents and students need to understand fully if planning to be at QE for the long haul, however our view is that it provides excellent opportunities for pupils to specialise appropriately and to excel. Students love the two different options and in 2021 57 per cent of year 9 moved on to Faculty for year 10. One parent said of the two pathways, 'I wish the whole country was going this way and following the child's interests.'

Exit: In total 91 per cent go on to university, just over half to Russell Group. Somewhat more College leavers go on to higher education but this is appropriate given the courses being studied by Faculty, some of which give direct entry into employment or further education. Nevertheless, a third of Faculty students went on to Russell Group universities in 2021 proving that vocational courses are welcomed there. Seven to Oxbridge in 2021.

Latest results: In 2021, College 85 per cent and Faculty 47 per cent GCSE grades 9-7. In the sixth form, College 85 per cent A*/A at A level; Faculty 77 per cent A*/A at A level and 94 per cent Distinction* to Merit in BTECs. Even given the selection that takes place, these are very strong results. Independent data shows that QE pupils performed significantly above expectations at A level in every year between 2012 and 2020.

Teaching and learning: QE is divided into four distinct areas, each with its own head. Chapter House (three months to year 5) is the nursery and prep element of QE. Head since 2010 is Karen Kilkenny, a maths and technology graduate (Hull). Another well-established senior leader, she exudes drive and enthusiasm for the role even after 11 years in post. Chapter House has its own newly refurbished base adjacent to the main areas of QE. Divided into kindergarten, nursery and reception, pre-prep and prep (specialist rooms upstairs getting pupils ready for senior school), each area is spacious and well equipped with plenty of room to play and learn. In addition to a lovely play space linked to a forest school area there's a baby sleep room and early years dining space. The mantra here is the four Cs: curiosity, creativity, collaboration and community. We saw some impressive examples of active learning such as the reception movement for learning class focusing on grip (ready for writing) and jumping to land on two feet linked to learning of numbers. Parents enthused about this work to develop fine motor skills. A year 2 group were writing about castles and showed some very good work. Year 4 were in the science lab doing 'icky modelling' which gave a pretty revolting but very practical understanding of how the human digestive system works. Chapter House has its own design technology room for food, textiles and crafts, good cross-curricular links with for instance history making Anglo-Saxon flatbreads. Spanish from reception onwards and Mandarin introduced from year 1. Pastoral care seems strong including peer mentors from the sixth form and there's a real sense of family. Around a third of Chapter House pupils board (from year 3).

Faculty has its own study centre for students, with a team of mentors for additional help, especially those who have a very high commitment to playing sports

Carved from the prep and senior schools in 2011, King's Magna (years 6-9) is led by Steven Turner, at QE since 2011 and originally deputy head of Faculty. An economic studies graduate, he has an obvious passion for educating young people in business, enterprise and financial awareness. He is proud that many of the pupils will make an active choice for Faculty for their GCSEs, testament to the inclusive educational philosophy we saw throughout QE. Year 6 have the same teacher for English maths and science and then specialists for everything else, getting a real head start on secondary education. Setting in maths from year 7, broad banding in science and mixed ability teaching for other subjects. A careers convention in year 8 allows pupils to begin to opt for subjects in year 9. Here they have to take a core of English, maths, science, PE and personal development plus four options including a language and a humanities subject and two others. Essentially this is an early start to GCSE style content and learning. There's a term each of French, Spanish and German in year 6, after which they choose one language to take in years 7-9. Optional second language (including Mandarin) has to be done as part of the three hours of curriculum enrichment. No classics. King's Magna shares some facilities with College, which again suggests that year 9 is much more of a GCSE preparation year. A lovely calm atmosphere in lessons, pupils engaged with their work and using IT. Class sizes are small, rarely more than 22 and some with fewer. Classrooms for year 6 were much smaller than we saw elsewhere at QE but well presented.

The College (years 10-13) is where pupils follow a conventional GCSE and A level route. Head since 2016 is Kevin Oldershaw, who joined QE in 2005 as head of geography. Degree in geography and previous experience teaching in a state school in Sussex and a field study centre. One son educated at QE from year 9 and now studying law.

College has its own teaching spaces, good modern science facilities, other specialist areas shared with Faculty. Entry to College GCSE courses is selective. Almost all do 11 subjects including English literature and language, maths and further maths, three separate sciences and four options from a completely free choice, so there's no insisting on a language or humanities subject. They usually do two options and maths in year 10 (but only if they are predicted at least a grade 7) and two in year 11. Choice of French, Spanish and German at GCSE (no classics). Drama, economics, geography, statistics, photography and psychology also on offer so a much wider choice than in many schools. Setting in English, maths and science. At A level College still offers four AS qualifications in year 12 and three in year 13. Now abandoned by most schools in favour of a two-year A level, QE justifies continuing with AS levels believing them to be the best preparation for exams and predictor of final outcomes for university entrance. Maths is the most popular A level subject with 90 per cent take-up in year 12. Only around a quarter take the EPQ, which surprised us given the high academic ability of the College students although the remainder will take other super-curricular options.

The Faculty (years 10-13) is where pupils combine GCSE and A level with BTEC vocational qualifications. Head since 2018 is Erica Papaglimis. She trained as a PE teacher at De Montfort University, Bedford and after three years in the state system joined QE as head of year 10 in 2008. Her brief was to 'up the game' of the Faculty, and looking at the numbers and outcomes of Faculty students this has been achieved. Warm and approachable, she is obviously driven by a real commitment to the ethos of vocational education and the independence of Faculty from the rest of QE. The Faculty mission is built around the concept of team QE with the strapline 'Pride, ambition, responsibility'. The students who showed us round definitely displayed this with confidence but without the sense of entitlement we sometimes see.

Faculty is housed in the enormous Genesis building completed in 2009 where we also saw the sports hall and swimming pool plus a top-floor boarding house. School is proud of the broad curriculum it is able to offer here. Mostly GCSEs for years 10 and 11, some like design technology and media can only be taken by Faculty students, plus BTECs in music and enterprise. Photography and drama also available. We spotted a well-equipped food technology room but this subject does not appear to be on offer other than as an activity. Class sizes are generally on the small side (maximum 24), facilities are excellent and students are well motivated. Alongside good teaching this ensures some very strong results. Students we spoke to said, 'The teachers are always there for us, they are always prepared to go the extra mile.'

Post-16 there is a real mix on offer: some do pure A levels and some combine these with BTECs. Same A level options as College plus a very impressive range of ten different BTECs. Maximum class size of 16 at this level. If they all run each year it gives a fantastic opportunity for students to specialise. Those we spoke to, some of whom had chosen to move from College after GCSEs, couldn't praise the opportunities they had highly enough. One said, 'It has a reputation as the sporty school, but academics comes first.' BTEC students move on to play full-time sports for the likes of Durham county cricket and Castleford Tigers, to sports scholarships in the US and to drama schools. Faculty has its own study centre for students, with a team of mentors for additional help, especially those who have a very high commitment to playing sports.

All areas of the school were praised for providing lessons during lockdown on Teams but also for the constant communication with pupils and separately with parents.

Learning support and SEN: Two SEN teachers and four teaching assistants work closely with the pastoral team. Relatively newly appointed head of learning development brings lots of experience and good practice from the state sector and shows the level of commitment the school gives to high-quality SEN provision as well as supporting students across the school. Pupils are assessed on application and school caters for cognition and learning difficulties, some physical disabilities and autistic spectrum disorder. An occupational therapist offers intervention for handwriting, fine motor skills and dyslexia. Parents of pupils with SEN were full of praise for the support given especially the way staff help to build confidence.

The arts and extracurricular: Exceptional facilities include a full-scale theatre (which would be the envy of many small towns), used for professional lets as well as school shows. Three productions a year and all are inclusive so as many as possible can be involved. Four drama studios (plus dance studio) accommodate the five different performing arts courses on offer. Music is equally well provided for with practice rooms and bands galore, 150 peripatetic lessons a week and a recording studio. Art and design aren't neglected with lovely art rooms, darkroom, textiles (head of creative arts comes from a fashion design background) and ceramics – we saw some great student work on display.

The co-curricular programme here is enormous. The Queen's and King's academies offer a host of sporting and other activities including

CCF, DofE, volunteering opportunities, charitable fundraising, visits in the UK and overseas such as a cattle farm in Australia and a conservation trip to Thailand. There really is something for everyone from holiday camps to public speaking and even the 'dog reading' scheme where younger children read aloud to the CEO's dog, allowing them to read without too much intervention (other than the odd woof).

Sport: Sports are the heartbeat of QE with facilities that would be the envy of many university campuses. All the usual options but on a massive scale with 34 acres of floodlit pitches and six all-weather pitches. Indoor provision is no less impressive: a 25-metre pool (including hot tubs), aqua treadmills and ice tanks for sports recovery (we declined the invitation to try them) as well as sauna and steam rooms. A spinning room, skate park and climbing wall, martial arts room and fencing studio plus a full-size boxing gym complete the picture – have we missed anything – surely some squash courts somewhere? Professional sports coaches on the staff as well as physio and massage therapists. Lots of fixtures and staff say good opportunities for children of all abilities to play, although we did notice that some clubs and activities are by invitation only. Younger pupils said they would like sports to be less gender determined with requests for girls' rugby and boys' netball.

Boarding: A good three-quarters of QE students board in 12 houses. Juniors have their own house away from the older students. Nice family atmosphere with a common room and cinema area. They have lots of adult support plus sixth form mentors. One overseas boarder told us just a few weeks after arriving that she had been very homesick but that she had been offered lots of care and attention which had made things much easier for her.

The senior houses are based around a 'village green', all well equipped; several have been refurbished to a high standard in the last couple of years. Houses, named after the Harry Potter actors, are vertical from years 7 to 10, creating a family feeling. No single rooms but everything is ensuite. School is moving away from TVs in rooms (quite an unusual feature in any case) to encourage boarders into the very nice common areas. Year 11 and sixth form are based in six houses in the same building surrounding a huge atrium with common rooms on galleries, a central dining area and a 26-foot-high transformer bumblebee. Year 11 rooms are triples, spectacularly well-equipped studios with PlayStation and kitchenette including a washer/dryer, dishwasher, coffee machine and cooking facilities. Far better than they will get at university.

Houseparents, matrons and other residential staff are assisted by a sophisticated app that enables them to ensure boarders' safety. Students say boarding is amazing, they love the facilities, although some felt that those in the boys' houses lacked the extras such as microwaves that the girls have. Two students independently told us that 'boarding is my second home'. During the pandemic several were unable to travel home and commented that 'the staff lived with us throughout it all and did their best to make sure we were okay'.

No single rooms but everything is ensuite. No longer TVs in rooms (quite an unusual feature in any case) in order to encourage boarders into the very nice common areas

From year 11 onwards there is freedom to go into York or Harrogate with careful systems in place to ensure safe return. The nature and size of the site mean that it is self contained and there would be very little reason to go off site other than to spread your wings. Unusually there is no curfew on phones after year 10, a privilege we have not encountered in many other boarding schools.

Ethos and heritage: School was originally founded in Harrogate in the 1900s by the Woodard Trust. In 1991 it was bought by the Martin family and re-located to their family home at Thorpe Underwood. Since then it has grown significantly, with massive investment in facilities. Although based around an old manor house, complete with stuffed tigers in the entrance hall which may not be to everyone's taste, this is essentially a new school. CEO Amy Martin is very much hands-on with a firm grasp of educational ethos as well as the economics of running this multi-million pound business. She lives on site and takes a very active role in the day-to-day life of the school (see dog reading, above). While the school undoubtedly nods in the direction of a typical high-performing independent school it is in a different mould altogether. Refreshingly, the majority of staff we met had not come through the independent sector in either their own education or their careers. The curriculum has lots of traditional elements but in addition there is an extensive vocational offer that many similar schools would shy away from, but which really does meet pupils' needs.

Pastoral care, inclusivity and discipline: As well as heads and assistant heads of year there's a mental health specialist and all staff have at least level one mental health awareness training. Medical centre and a pastoral hub where young people can go for support when necessary all linked with boarding pastoral care. There are extra evening sessions for academic support for those who need it and day pupils can access this via Teams. We pressed students on how it felt if you are a bit different at QE. They said that when bullying happened it was dealt with fairly and everyone felt there was someone they could go to if necessary. Younger pupils said that there was a bit of a divide between day pupils and boarders but this clearly disappears in later years as the number of boarders outweighs day pupils. One said, 'It is a second family, I've made friends here I know I will have for life.' Girls didn't feel they were treated any differently from boys. We saw instances of normal misbehaviour in lessons being proactively dealt with by staff. Uniform is extremely smart and obviously worn with pride, however skirts are compulsory for girls – something that sits uneasily with an inclusive agenda and many girls would like to see change here (which we understand may be on the way). Pupils said the schools deal with LGBTQ and transitioning students well.

Parents cannot speak highly enough about the pastoral care. Several commented that their quiet child had become a confident and outgoing young adult at QE. Most praised the excellent communication: 'The communication trail continues from teacher to teacher through the school, it really feels like a partnership.' In general parents like the emphasis placed on hard work and examination success although one or two felt things could sometimes get a little too pressured.

Pupils and parents: Day pupils come from a roughly 40-mile radius, many via an extensive bus network. Lots of Forces children, both day and boarding. Boarders make up around 75 per cent of the school, 20 per cent are international (around a quarter from China). Pupils are polite, well behaved and very industrious. They know that 'if you are at QE you have to knuckle down, there's lots to do especially in sport but we know that academics comes first.' Parents seem delighted with the school – they love the good results, facilities and opportunities but it is the pastoral care that came in for the very highest praise.

Money matters: Fees are amongst the highest we have seen, topping £40K a year for UK boarding students and £50K for overseas. There are some scholarships and families with financial support from the armed forces will find it much more affordable. That being said, with this level and quality of facilities you are certainly getting what you pay for and day parents in particular feel the fees are comparable to the competition in Leeds, York and Harrogate.

The last word: You cannot help but be impressed by the sheer ambition of QE with its two equally well provisioned senior school pathways – testament to the strong belief that success looks different for different pupils. Facilities are spectacular, staff committed and clearly able, students delightful. There is a strong focus on hard work and determination to succeed which may not be for everyone, but if you can afford it and you make the grade academically then the opportunities here are tremendous.

Queen Margaret's School For Girls
27
Escrick Park, Escrick, York, North Yorkshire YO19 6EU
01904 727600 | admissions@queenmargarets.com | www.queenmargarets.com
Ages: 11–18
Pupils: 215; sixth form: 75; Boarders: 107 full, 88 weekly/flexi
Fees: Day £20,070; Boarding £29,910 – £34,680 pa

Head: Since 2019, Susan Baillie, previously pastoral director at Newcastle Royal Grammar. Started her career at Barnard Castle School, has been head of history and politics at selective day and boarding schools, and was second deputy head at Kimbolton. Enjoys walking, running and cooking: feels her greatest victory has been winning the local village cheese scone competition. Married to a Yorkshireman with a young daughter plus a cockapoo called Monty, an elderly cat called Polly and six hens.

Entrance: Own assessments at 11, 12 and 13; mathematics, English, dyslexia screening and observation of group working in two classroom activities. Additional intake into sixth form: two 7s and three 6s at GCSE, at least a 5 in maths and English and a minimum of a 6 in the subjects proposed for study at A level. Interviews for all admissions. Taster days for new boarders prior to admission with buddies for first years and guardian angels for third years, most popular boarding entry point.

Exit: Post-16, up to a third of girls become restless and move to co-ed, local sixth form colleges or boarding schools like Uppingham and Oundle, usually 'for a valid reason not a worrying reason,' says school. A number go and look elsewhere before deciding to stay put. Virtually all sixth formers to higher education nationwide – the majority to Russell Group universities. Durham, Edinburgh, Exeter, Warwick, London Universities and Oxford Brookes all popular. Courses cover a wide spectrum and include engineering, business and finance, languages, law and 'ologies'. Heartening to see numbers going on to prestigious art colleges, eg Central St Martins. One overseas in 2021 – to Istituto Europeo di Design, Milan, to study interior design. Sprinkling to Oxbridge and a few medics in some years though not in 2021.

Latest results: In 2021, 67 per cent 9-7 at GCSE; 77 per cent A*/A (95 per cent A*-B). In 2019 (the last year when exams took place), 58 per cent 9-7 at GCSE; 42 per cent A*/A (71 per cent A*-B).

Teaching and learning: Excellent academic results almost taken as read by parents and success matters despite entry not being particularly selective. Overall A level performance consistently good and improving. Mathematics, biology, economics, English, chemistry, languages and the arts popular and no weaknesses; psychology a new addition. Mathematics, sciences, humanities and art all tend to have an excellent proportion of top grades at GCSE.

At A level, choice of 31 subjects; the girls mostly take three, plus an enrichment activity under the umbrella of the QM diploma, which covers excellence inside and outside the classroom, independent thought, learning and research, emotional maturity, and community and school activity and participation

At GCSE, 23 subjects offered – timetables are built around each girl's choices, generally including one MFL. French, Latin and a choice of either Spanish or Mandarin are on the timetable for the first two years. German an option in the third year; all are on offer at GCSE and A level.

Class sizes around 10-12, maximum 16, and we saw evidence of interactive teaching and engaged pupils across a number of subjects, notably a history lesson considering WWI propaganda posters.

IT embedded in the curriculum but not given high profile, though plenty of computers and WiFi site wide. Surprisingly no overt computing or programming clubs, though the head of physics is a Raspberry Pi educator and led the QM-SkyPi project, which culminated in a high-altitude balloon launch for Margaret the knitted teddy bear.

Learning support and SEN: Around 90 girls receive some sort of SEN support, mainly mild difficulties and dyslexia (all pupils have a screening test as an entry requirement). Two teachers work closely with academic colleagues to provide classroom and prep support where needed, some one-on-one where girls have slightly reduced timetables. Around 50 girls have individualised programmes for EAL taught by suitably qualified specialist teacher; small group and individual sessions according to need.

The arts and extracurricular: About a third of girls have individual instrument lessons with plenty of ensembles to showcase their talents, from wind to rock band, orchestra to songwriters' collective. Year 7 and 8 choir compulsory, training for the senior chamber choir, together with close harmony pop-up group covering popular repertoire. Weekly informal concerts, summer and Christmas concerts, annual musical production.

Younger girls envious of the privilege of pain au chocolat delivered to sixth form houses for breakfast – all very civilised. Dining hall has a cappuccino machine

Fabulous drama facilities for aspiring luvvies. Two productions a year, one in collaboration with the music department – recently an open-air Midsummer Night's Dream (a brave decision in Yorkshire) and a musical version of the edgy and gritty Bad Girls. Recently shortlisted in Performing Arts School of the Year category by Independent School Parent magazine.

Not overwhelmingly arty school but plenty of choice across the genres, textiles and photography as well – though no electronics, product design or resistant materials. A handful of girls go on to the top performing art and fashion colleges each year. Home economics for all through to small uptake at A level with Leiths food and wine certificate part of sixth form enrichment. Inter-house Masterchef competition hotly contested and first year tea party a high spot on the calendar.

The extensive range of extracurricular activities offers something for everyone and extends to clay pigeon shooting, driving remote-control cars and climbing walls. A breadth of activities ranges from science and mathematics Olympiads to dance and music qualifications, DofE gold to Queen Margaret's Princes Trust, Model United Nations to Amnesty International.

Sport: Sport for all here with games keenly contested at house level and a full inter-school fixtures list. Stunning facilities – floodlit all-weather pitch, two swimming pools (one indoor, one outdoor), sports hall, tennis/netball courts, dance studio, new sixth form cardio suite, fitness trail etc – hard to find something that's not on offer. Riding popular (private riding school on campus); some girls bring ponies, school keeps a number.

Traditional team sports, winter lacrosse, hockey and netball and summer tennis, athletics and cricket. Links with local sporting clubs and training offer opportunities for talented sportswomen, scholars receive weekly sports conditioning session with a personal trainer. School supports and encourages girls whose sporting prowess involves competition at regional, national or international level. Sports tours – recently to Sri Lanka.

Boarding: Horizontal boarding structure: girls live with their year group all the way through. Really liked by both girls and parents. 'Enables great camaraderie and the foundations of lifelong friendships,' observed one pleased parent. For 11-year-olds Red House is a welcoming home from home with a Cath Kidston inspired kitchen for tea, toast and conversations around the Aga. For the next three years girls are in houses at the top of school buildings whilst year Vs (15 to 16-year-olds) move out into the grounds to purpose-built boarding house, Winnie's (named after old girl, journalist and writer Winifred Holtby). Lower sixth are in the heart of the school in Cloisters and enjoy the privilege of sitting and walking on the quad lawn. 'Modern loft-style living' twin rooms with individual study areas enable girls to be well organised for busy lives.

The jewels in the boarding crown are the upper sixth cottages: 'something to look forward to,' the girls say. Reminiscent of the Emmerdale set, stepping back in time, the line of cottages all have large kitchens, 'great for entertaining', communal sitting rooms, individual study rooms. Cottage life has the feel of a college campus though head girl has the first pick of houses. Breakfast and snack preparation, responsibility for all their laundry, non-uniform dress code all contribute to the girls' transition to post-school independent living.

Has recently introduced flexi-boarding and day girls, a quarter of pupils, all have allocated beds and can stay for a nightly charge. House activity nights for all on Fridays; a programme of weekend trips and visits and shared café and social spaces encourage girls of different ages to mix. Community weekends four times a term require girls to stay in school but at other times about 70 per cent remain. Greater freedoms for sixth form which they are careful not to abuse – cars allowed, York at free times on Wednesdays and Saturdays, supervised Cellars bar open on campus on Saturday nights – alcohol allowed with parental permission.

Jewels in the boarding crown are the upper sixth cottages: 'something to look forward to,' girls say. The cottages all have large kitchens, 'great for entertaining'

Parents commented that their daughters feel hugely supported by house staff who 'adapt their life around ours'.

Ethos and heritage: Founded in 1901 as a Woodard school in Scarborough; moved to Escrick Hall, a John Carr built Georgian country house in 70 well kept acres in 1949. Independent from Woodard since 1986, a large yet compact and cohesive campus with a number of Victorian additions, clever conversions, complementary new-build with award-winning centenary theatre, chapel and indoor swimming pool. A throwback to earlier times, a cluster of timber cabin classrooms add a quirky touch.

Circular dining hall (once an indoor lunging school) serves all meals to award-winning standard, with school rarities such as a cappuccino machine and balsamic vinegar; younger girls envious of the privilege of pain au chocolat delivered to sixth form houses for breakfast – all very civilised.

Girls are expected and encouraged to think big here, challenged to break out of their comfort zone and aim high. Focus now on providing each girl with the confidence, strengths, maturity and values for an unknown future. 'A greenhouse not a hothouse,' says school. Confident, articulate, reflective girls show great loyalty to their school and say, 'We know we're in a bubble but we know what we're in for.' Many house activities, communal social areas, buddying, mentoring and guardian angel schemes, not to mention the size of the school, make this a very supportive and close-knit community.

Whilst 20 per cent of boarders are from overseas, this is not an international school. Girls find that where there are wide cultural differences this can preclude close friendships: 'We're friendly but not all best friends,' say sixth formers. Parents comment on the overseas pupils 'whose priorities are different and they are not so interested in sport or drama' – they would not like to see this number grow. Cultural festivals are celebrated communally in house.

Good exposure for girls to global and topical issues through debating, extracurricular organisations and mock elections such as Brexit hustings and vote. Parents aware that this is a privileged life and take responsibility for widening their daughters' experiences, though would like to see the girls do more in the community.

Uniform is an attractive tartan and charcoal – no skirt lengths above the knee: a first for us. Own clothes worn after tea – don't provide anything that you wouldn't want boil-washed. Relaxed smart casual dress code rather than uniform for sixth form.

OMs include Winifred Holtby (author), Ann Jellicoe (playwright), Sarah Connolly (opera singer), Dame Justice Eleanor King (High Court judge).

Pastoral care, inclusivity and discipline: Parents cannot speak highly enough of the pastoral care: as one put it, 'Compassion and kindness run through the veins of this school.' Together with house staff each girl has a personal tutor (of varied quality, say parents) who meets boarding staff daily with any concerns to SLT weekly. Sixth formers have a personal mentor who acts as a guide.

Girls and parents feel the rules are very clear. Zero tolerance for smoking, unsupervised repeat offenders, but girls and staff were quick to point out that behaviour is not a problem here with no full exclusions in the last two years. An army of sixth form posts of responsibility: head girl with three deputies, prefects covering the gamut of school life and six house captains.

Evolving from meditation groups, mindfulness is a recent introduction to PSHE lessons (and at lunchtime for a group of staff). The head has introduced a 10-session course on mindfulness-based stress reduction and cognitive therapy delivered by a trained practitioner.

Pupils and parents: A real sense of collegiality across the campus, lots of smiling faces. Girls aim high in every arena – whatever their talent; higher education is a foregone conclusion.

Parents mainly upper and middle class: landowners, farmers, professionals. Boarders some 20 per cent from overseas – span tens of nations and four continents; head using Spanish and South American networks to widen further. Many from Scotland, Cumbria, East Anglia and of course Yorkshire. Essentially the main catchment is the east coast train line – head keen to open the eyes of London prep schools to God's own county, unexplored territory for many; however, shrinking numbers over the past five years.

Money matters: Scholarships at 11,13 and sixth form; academic, art, choral, dance, drama, music and sport scholarships. Means-tested bursaries. Sibling remission of five per cent, maximum 15 per cent for three or more sisters in school.

The last word: A supporting and enabling atmosphere where girls thrive and their talents are developed, whether they are academic, sporting or arts based. All rave about the pastoral care and the breadth of opportunity on offer. Girls prepared go to on to post-school life with their eyes open. As a number of parents told us, it seems 'they've got the balance right'.

Queen Mary's School

28

Baldersby Park, Topcliffe, Thirsk, North Yorkshire YO7 3BZ

01845 575000 | admissions@queenmarys.org | www.queenmarys.org

Ages: Girls 3–16, boys 3–7

Pupils: 221; **Boarders:** 10 full, 15 weekly, 55 flexi (from age 7)

Fees: Day £9,030 – £20,115; Boarding £22,365- £27,465 pa

Head: Since 2015, Carole Cameron BA MA (education) PGCE NPQH FRGS ('ancient but young at heart'). Geography degree from Reading; also studied at Nottingham and the Open University. Various roles in state schools plus abroad, including the Cayman Islands; head of Highfield Prep,

Harrogate; deputy head Queen Margaret's, York. Teaches PSHE and some English. Two adult daughters, educated in the Caribbean and at Queen Margaret's. Interests include travel, choral music and walking.

She took over in difficult circumstances involving a premature departure, and an interim year under the aegis of a previous much-loved head who returned from retirement, so has had to make her mark with care and flexibility. Her conventional suit, shoes and pearl necklace and courteous, unassuming manner accompany a steely commitment to raising standards of teaching, which she 'won't compromise on', being 'prepared to take tough decisions'. This is being accomplished through a major focus on staff training (the school has joined the Yorkshire Schools Teaching Alliance), close monitoring of teachers and departments, new, much approved appointments and significant development of digital technology. Parents appreciate the (very necessary) improvements made: 'She's doing incredible things for the school... a very effective operator... She's slowly and subtly taking the school forward, not forgetting its traditions and past' – though we encountered the odd regret for the loss of some of the earlier, less health and safety-conscious ways.

She identifies with the spiritual values of the Woodard Foundation (having attended a Woodard school herself, she points out). Keen to know exactly what is going on all the time, she loves working in a small, intimate school where she can know all the girls very well individually – she greets them every morning and has her own tutor group that changes each year. Popular with parents, who see her as very dedicated, accessible and responsive to fair criticism: 'She doesn't make excuses, deals with it and gets back to you with a solution'. She doesn't stand on her dignity, taking part in the whole-school Christmas run warm up wearing a complete Santa costume and in the Easter egg hunt dressed as an Easter bunny – so indeed 'young at heart'.

Entrance: Into junior school by taster day, with more visits for girls joining at a later point and a 'good neighbour' to help them settle in. Assessment tests in English, maths and non-verbal reasoning at 11, 12 and 13, with report from previous school.

Exit: Boys leave at the end of year 2, mostly for Aysgarth or Stokesley. Almost all girls transfer to senior school at the end of year 6; a few to Ripon Grammar. At 16 to Sedbergh, Durham, Barnard Castle, Repton, Ampleforth, Uppingham, Stonyhurst, St Peter's York, Queen Margaret's York, Ripon Grammar. Sixth form destinations include Shrewsbury School, Fettes College, Sedbergh School. One to Oxbridge in 2021, with a choral scholarship.

Latest results: In 2021, 63 per cent 9-7 at GCSE. In 2019 (the last year when exams took place), 39 per cent 9-7 at GCSE.

Teaching and learning: Despite its small size, offers a wide choice including German, Spanish and French (almost all take a modern foreign language GCSE), Latin, classical civilisation, physical education and further maths. Some tiny sets of one to three – which the girls like, because of the amount of individual attention afforded, though we wondered how drama could work with only two girls; average size: 12 (bigger classes lower down). AS critical thinking too.

We were amused to see in the (very well designed and comprehensive) planners that weekly awards can be obtained for making people laugh and 'being a good egg'

Maths being developed to increase challenge and match traditionally high English standards – all of top set to do further maths in future; more focus on STEM career opportunities. Regional success in literature quiz and maths challenges. Developing use of interactive, online approaches to enable more personalised learning (IT in the curriculum from nursery to year 8), plus integration of junior and senior curriculum, together with more outdoor learning, so content more child-led and motivating (eg year 8 garden plots link with science course). Saturday morning school controversial, as not all parents and older girls feel it is worth coming in if it just amounts to two academic lessons and the eucharist service, but it does create extra time for the wider curriculum.

Six-weekly pupil profiles, with detailed extracurricular comments, discussed with girls in tutor group time and sent to parents, part of very thoroughgoing monitoring and tracking of girls' progress and involvement in learning overseen by excellent, extremely dedicated director of studies.

Girls say lessons are interesting and enjoyable and teachers immensely helpful and understanding; they appreciate the generous access to individual extra support. Close trusting relationships based on 'mutual respect', according to a year 10 girl. Stable staff – average age 45 – who come across as friendly, jolly and happy in their work; parents find them very accessible – quick responses to emails. Gifted and talented enrichment for scholars open to all – cultural trips, conferences, lectures, subject days out, weekly Queen Mary's society ('some amazing speakers').

Junior school has separate coeducational nursery and pre-prep departments for 3 to 7-year-olds. No Sats tests but systematic assessment and monitoring. Specialist teaching in science (own lab), French (from year 1), IT, food technology, art, music, drama and sport; success in national competitions and challenges. Classes can be very small – average 10, max 16; mainly girls. Attractive, bright, well-equipped classrooms with very good displays. Parents pleased with progress achieved and amount of differentiation in tasks set.

Learning support and SEN: Very well qualified and supported SENCo: children with varying special needs accepted, including dyslexia, dyscalculia, emotional/behavioural, a range of autism spectrum disorders plus sensory and physical impairment, so long as the school concludes these can be met. Personal support plans with bespoke timetables if needed and guidance for teachers; individual and small group support, in and out of the classroom (no extra cost); liaison with school counsellor, visiting clinical psychologist and other outside agencies, as well as parents – very flexible approach; students progress very well. High praise from a parent of four dyslexic daughters: 'They have all been treated normally, not made to feel they have great problems... They love going to learning support – there's no stigma.' Another gave more qualified praise, having struggled before her daughter's official diagnosis to get her very individual needs met, but said once diagnosed the school could not have done more to help her. EAL support for occasional short stay pupils from France and Spain.

The arts and extracurricular: Exceptionally high level music – a finalist in the BBC chorister of the year competition: 'fabulous music department... has helped me develop a lot' – with plenty of internal and external performance opportunities and a more inclusive approach being introduced; rock band as well as Fauré Requiem and annual carol concert in Ripon Cathedral. Music block, converted from old coach house, looks due for makeover and extension.

Drama productions include Annie and My Fair Lady; plentiful top grades for speech and drama exams; lots of theatre visits. Accomplished art in different media; food tech and art and design GCSEs, but no provision for resistant materials in the curriculum.

Wide range of clubs includes pheasant plucking (yes – really) and archery; much DofE; all year 8s do young leaders award. Energetic fundraising for international and local charities, eg whole school run over challenging obstacle course and house fashion show competition organised by year 10 girls.

The equestrian centre is a relaxing world apart. Boarders and day girls can bring their own horses and riders have been successful in local and national competitions

For juniors, energetic music – year 4 orchestra (all learn violin or cello), junior brass, super strings and recorder groups, two junior choirs and a junior orchestra (but a remarkably mature young critic we met observed that having instrument lessons in core subjects was a disadvantage academically – and that 30 minutes for lunch, including queueing, was too rushed). Performances in Ripon Cathedral.

Termly drama productions – My Fair Lady, Cinderella Rockerfella, Dream On (based on A Midsummer Night's Dream); year 5s perform a French play. Many speech and drama – and music – exams distinctions and merits. Good choice of clubs; outdoor education residentials plus trip to France.

Sport: Particularly strong sport, especially riding. The equestrian centre, at the end of the delightful Rhododendron Walk running beside a ha-ha, stream and wild flowers, is a relaxing world apart: horses (boarders and day girls can bring their own) peer over stall gates and the manager's dogs run around; improvements are cannily funded through sponsorship. Won recent national schools showjumping championship, beating 48 other teams. Strong netball, tennis, rounders and athletics at regional level; very testing climbing wall up a high archway. Only a small indoor pool, but outdoor swimming, canoeing and kayaking in the River Swale, which runs through the grounds. A parent we spoke to liked the way girls get 'pushed to do things a bit out of their comfort zone' in a kind way, by being encouraged and reassured. Newest facilities include new floodlit Astro and pavilion.

Juniors have strong netball, football, swimming, tennis, cross-country, trampolining (particularly high-level coaching) and gymnastics at local/county level; sports not stereotyped in years where boys present.

Boarding: Full, weekly and flexi; junior, senior and year 11 areas (weekly or flexi boarding possible from year 3). Light, pleasantly furnished rooms, with two to seven bunk or cabin beds, some with lovely views of lawns and woods, but walls could do with refreshing (school says this is in hand).

Friendly, family atmosphere – older girls mentor and support younger ones. Generously staffed – 'They're lovely... it's like talking to your parents when you get home from school... always there if you are homesick or need to talk about home problems... [The two gap year girls are] like an auntie or older sister' (boarders); 'It's a home from home – they're happy as Larry' (parent). Lots of weekend activities and trips, eg Christmas shopping in Edinburgh. We were amused to see in the (very well designed and comprehensive) planners that weekly awards can be obtained for making people laugh and 'being a good egg'.

Ethos and heritage: Founded by the Woodard Corporation in 1925 at Duncombe Park; moved to Baldersby Park, near Thirsk, North Yorkshire, in 1985, as a 3–16 years school. The gracious main building is almost 300 years old, with a grand hall encompassing an impressive central staircase presided over by huge portraits of Queen Mary and George V, borrowed from the Queen's collection, no less. Elegant reception rooms now used as the very fortunate head's office, smallish library and English classroom. Lovely, peaceful, 40-acre grounds, with lawns, two ha-has, views of grazing sheep, cobbled courtyards and clocktower.

Underpinned by Anglican values – most take religious education GCSE. Warm, family feeling through small sizes. Seniors pair with juniors for Easter egg hunt, when girls seek camouflaged teachers wielding water pistols (enabling sweet revenge on classroom chatterers), and charity Santa run. Dog friendly – teachers often bring in own dogs, though a junior child observed they could be distracting during tests.

Girls very smart in red tartan skirts, blue shirts and short, light-green jackets with brown collars resembling hacking jackets, and, according to the ones we met, happy with the single-sex environment – 'There's less social pressure – you can be yourself... it's okay to work hard.' 'It allows them to grow up in their own time... they're free to explore who they are' (parent); 'There's a real celebration of all kinds of diversity and achievements, not just academic ones' – a mother whose daughter enjoyed the tag rugby, football and street dance. 'A moral compass is seamlessly set... the girls are very caring and open... they don't moan – they just get on with it,' said another.

All year 11s have a position of responsibility; top posts – complete with academic gowns – require written application, interview and vote by whole school and staff. Strong careers provision includes information about apprenticeships.

Good choice of food (we particularly admired the wide-ranging, very attractively presented salad bar), but some grumbles about the hot food – and the low standard of cutlery washing. Accessible and flexible cooks – catering manager answerable to school council.

Notable old girls: actresses Katie Gibson, Adi Calvert, Hebe Beardsall, Oscar-winning director Serena Armitage, businesswoman Amanda Staveley, artist Tanya Still.

Pastoral care, inclusivity and discipline: Very thoughtful and aware approach to mental health and wellbeing – team includes counsellor, clinical psychologist, independent listener, chaplain and school nurse, and planners contain extensive contact details for internal and external support. However, a couple of parents we spoke to suggested the sex education given could involve scenarios that were 'a bit more realistic' and less 'naïve', with more about 'healthy relationships outside marriage'. Sensible, constructive approach to discipline.

Pupils and parents: From a wide range of local state and independent schools, from North Yorkshire, York and into Teeside; mostly professional, military and business white British families. Confident, open, enthusiastic, thoughtful, articulate and appreciative girls.

Parents told us they like the way their daughters are 'pushed to do things out of their comfort zone' that in a kind way, by being encouraged and reassured

High-level communication with parents, eg very clear, detailed, holistic guidance re expectations and how best to help children, careful preparation for residentials. Termly Saturday morning sessions on various topics.

Money matters: Purely honorary academic, art, music and sport scholarships at 11, 12 and 13 entitling participation in enhanced programme: written exam plus interview with head including questions on current events; looking for sharp, wide-ranging thinkers. Means-tested bursaries and sibling, MoD and CofE remissions.

The last word: Mixture of Palladian architecture, bone china tea service and secluded rural environment with hard-working, aspirational, outdoorsy girls who 'enjoy their food' (head) and are not made to feel 'academic results are everything' (parent). Developing very systematic, modern approach to education that is producing high achievement, along with time made for emotional wellbeing, extracurricular activities and fun. We wondered if such a protected early life might leave girls unprepared for the more rigorous challenges of the outside world, but more than one parent maintained that most emerge with inner confidence and an empowering, secure sense of who they are, so that only a few fail to thrive in their sixth forms.

Rockport School

29

15 Rockport Road, Craigavad, Holywood, County Down BT18 0DD

028 9042 8372 | info@rockportschool.com | www.rockportschool.com

Ages: 3-18

Pupils: 225; sixth form: 30; Boarders: 35 full, 5 weekly (from age 12)

Fees: Day £8,520 – £18,435; Boarding £20,910 – £229,970 pa

Headmaster: Since 2012, George Vance LLB BEd PQHNI (50s). He joined the school in 2007 as deputy head. His teacher training was at Stanmillis University College, part of Queen's University Belfast, and he read law at the University of Ulster. His first teaching post was at Regent House School, where he would spend 25 years, 22 of them as head of DT. His two great ambitions when he became headmaster were for Rockport to join the Round Square group of schools and to open a sixth form, both now achieved. As a student teacher he read an article by Kurt Hahn which made a lasting impression, and one of the reasons he joined Rockport was because he felt it was a 'Round Square school in waiting'.

'He lives and breathes the school, is approachable and welcoming and is just right for the school,' said a father. 'Kids warm to him as a person but also respect him as the headmaster, and no parent or child would hesitate to knock on his door.' He wears a gown for official events, can be spotted bicycling round the grounds, and The Belfast Telegraph likened him to Mr Chips, but he will put his shoulder to anything – 'He can be super smart,' said a pupil, 'but will also round up the chickens when they escape.'

A qualified mountain leader, he is passionate about the Mourne Mountains and takes every child over the age of 8 hillwalking. He loves the outdoors and has been involved with the DofE for over 30 years. He keeps his hand in by teaching DT as cover. He lives on site with his wife, Susan, a special needs teacher at a local school, and they have three grown-up children.

Entrance: Not hugely selective. Most children from the prep school move on to the senior school and there is a big intake from local state schools at 11.

Exit: School will prepare children for the transfer test to the grammars at 11+ as well as Common Entrance to independent schools in Britain. About a quarter leave after GCSEs for larger schools with a wider choice of A levels – Gordonstoun and Glenalmond are popular choices – but increasing numbers choosing to stay for the sixth form. Recently students have gone off to study accountancy at Queen's University Belfast, law at Liverpool, drama at Ulster and business at Harper Adams.

Latest results: In 2021, 33 per cent 9-7 at GCSE; 61 per cent A*/A at A level. In 2019 (the last year when exams took place), 21 per cent 9-7 at GCSE; 35 per cent A*-B at A level.

Teaching and learning: Not really selective and will accept all children who can access the curriculum. The environment is much more nurturing and supportive than at local grammars, and the breadth of ability means they can welcome whole families. It is not unusual for children to leave for the grammars and then come back. 'The children are not pushed but gently supported,' said one mother, but another felt that perhaps they could be stretched a bit more. Impressive GCSE results in terms of value added with most pupils outperforming their predicted outcomes by at least two grades. The small year groups mean that the statistics are less meaningful than in a larger school. The sixth form opened in 2015 with the second cohort (nine pupils) sitting A levels in 2019. Eighteen subjects offered at GCSE; options include media and business studies, Arabic and learning for life and work. Can accommodate a range of abilities within one class and the average size is 12, but there are sometimes as few as five in a GCSE class and three in an A level class. The choice of A levels at the moment is very much pupil driven and includes the popular moving image arts, sports studies, ICT, art and geography.

The headmaster had to have difficult conversations with some members of staff a few years ago and now has a dynamic team of teachers who are happy to go on courses and update their skills.

CAT tests for all pupils annually, and most improve on predicted grades – the school likes to call it the Rockport effect. Teaches separate sciences from year 8 in newly refurbished labs and uses the grounds and the beach as outdoor classrooms (as well as a bespoke forest classroom). Home economics (which can include child development) from year 8 is popular with boys and girls at GCSE. Well-equipped ICT suite – there are over 90 computers throughout the school.

Lower sixth required to do a week's work experience – parents are very supportive and often offer work shadowing.

Learning support and SEN: SEN is housed in the cottage in the grounds with two full-time dyslexia specialists and part-time specialists in maths and dyspraxia, who all work closely with the teaching and boarding staff. Seven statemented children in the school, two with classroom assistants. Very supportive and inclusive and the school has a record of success with school refusers from elsewhere. EAL support teacher comes in once a week – usually one-to-one teaching but depends on the need. Will even take a child with no English.

The arts and extracurricular: About 20 per cent learn an instrument, some up to grade 8, or take singing lessons. 'Singing is massive,' said a pupil, and there are two choirs run as clubs as well as a string quartet and a woodwind group – the school is not big enough for an orchestra. Pupils sing at Holywood music festival and everyone takes part in the summer concert, which is preceded by canapes and fizz on the lawn.

Art particularly strong, with A level art being the most popular subject – the visual arts programme is mentored by an artist and the children exhibit their work at the Belfast museum; 'we love it when the artists come in,' said a pupil. We were particularly struck by the beautiful stained-glass windows in the art department.

Energetic drama department with something going on most terms. Senior and junior drama societies and GCSE plays – very inclusive and we 'pick children who would not necessarily volunteer'. Also have the opportunity to get involved with stage management, and lighting is linked in with ICT.

There are often exchanges with other Round Square schools; two pupils attended the global conference in Singapore

Range of after-school clubs, many based outdoors, such as the fly fishing and angling clubs, orienteering and hillwalking clubs; most gain silver DofE and 12-15 take part in the Young Enterprise scheme – projects have included commissioning, branding, marketing and selling granite candlesticks, paperweights and pampered pet pouches. Outings include a visit to a potato crisp factory and a print workshop, theatre trips and a physics trip to Queen's University, Belfast.

Sport: Pupils have to take part in some sort of sport until they are 14, with rugby, hockey, football and netball being the main team sports. The school is probably too small to win any of the big rugby tournaments, but boys play with great enthusiasm and two are in the Ulster development squad. 'The Astro is our new baby,' said a pupil, 'and we can now host tennis and hockey matches.' The school also hosts a netball tournament and barbecue for 600 children, and the junior team recently won the Northern Ireland tournament – everyone is put forward for trials and 'they push us beyond our boundaries,' said a pupil.

Children are encouraged to try new things like kayaking from Rockport's own beach and sailing from Ballyholme Yacht Club. The latter is offered from the age of 3, culminating in the annual Rockport Regatta – the school has produced four international sailors, half the Irish team and a Commonwealth Games team member who was in the pre-Olympic squad for Tokyo. They have also set up the Rockport Golf Academy and everyone plays golf once a week from the age of 3. There are five affordable courses within a few minutes' drive and school keen to spot talent and bring it on through development and elite squads – the junior girls' team are Ulster and Irish champions and a boy has recently won the Junior Irish Open. 1970s sports hall also used for exams, tests and speech day, with swimming at the local leisure centre. Rockport runs its own Wimbledon tournament – all involved, no-one is left out and finals are held on the front lawn followed by a barbecue. Everything is a family affair and usually involves drinks and food for parents.

Boarding: Offers full, weekly and flexi boarding and can accommodate the occasional casual boarder, but doesn't have much space. Some 40 boarders from the age of 12, with about 20 in at weekends. No Saturday school but outings like swimming and ice skating are arranged and 'we try to make it as much like home as possible,' says the matron. Lots of investment in boarding areas and a cosy family feel – boys in single or double rooms, younger girls in small dorms and older girls have their own rooms. Comfortable sitting room with tartan sofas and a television and boarders can make toast and bring in food. Reward night on Thursdays – maybe go-karting, movie night or trampolining. Boarders have structured evenings with a supervised second prep with staff on hand to help; sixth formers are given more independence. International boarders often come for just a term and have a week of outings in the summer when everyone else is doing exams.

Ethos and heritage: The school was founded in 1906 by Geoffrey Bing with the aim of 'preparing boys for the Public Schools and the Royal Naval College, Dartmouth'. It was built as a private house in the 19th century and is set in 25 acres on the shores of Belfast Lough on Northern Ireland's gold coast. It is the only fully independent school in Northern Ireland, has no church involvement and there are no clergy on the board of governors – unique in Northern Ireland. The school is not secular but has a light-touch Christian ethos and has a long relationship with the parish church where the Remembrance Day and carol services are held, but mostly plays down religion and welcomes families from all faiths and none.

Head loves the outdoors and is a qualified mountain leader. He is passionate about the Mourne Mountains and takes every child over the age of 8 hillwalking

The sixth formers are delighted with their social and study area in a chalet in the grounds overlooking the lough. As the school is so small everyone has to mix between years and join in. Academic achievement is only part of the picture and there is a strong sense of community, but it's not highly competitive – there are cups for everything but winning is not the be all and end all.

Attractive school uniform; the main school pupils wear a green kilt or grey trousers and green jumpers with blazers for best. There has been much consultation about the uniform for the sixth form and they have settled for grey trousers or a Black Watch skirt and navy blue jumpers.

The school became a global member of the Round Square in 2016 and the education at Rockport is underpinned by Kurt Hann's six IDEALS of internationalism, democracy, environment, adventure, leadership and service, which fit well with its ethos. There are often exchanges with other Round Square schools, two pupils recently attended the global conference in Singapore and four sixth formers represented the school at the Cape Town conference. There are elections for everything and a strong culture of service. The junior choir sings in old people's homes at Christmas and sixth formers volunteer in charity shops and at the Camphill Community for those with severe learning difficulties, and all get involved in the annual sponsored walk. Pupils are taught to think about what they can do for others and offer a helping hand. 'Never give up, rise to the challenge, do what you enjoy and treat everyone equally wherever they come from.' 'They don't tell kids what they can't do but what they can,' said a parent.

Pastoral care, inclusivity and discipline: Children can talk to anyone and everyone if they are struggling, school contacts parents immediately if there is a problem and a full staff briefing every morning keeps everyone in the loop. 'Everyone knows each other and there are no invisible children at Rockport,' said a parent. Children also have access to an external counsellor.

The usual social media issues, but zero tolerance of bullying: 'It is nipped in the bud and we all look out for each other,' said a pupil. The school has a team of student anti-bullying ambassadors who attend a training session to become peer mentors, with particular focus on social media. There has not been a drugs issue in living memory.

The school hosts the Amazing Brains programme to help students cope with the stress of revision and exams. Two houses, Green House and White House, which compete against each other in the founders' day cross country-race, swimming gala and declamations.

All meals made from scratch and the food is 'the best – even better than my mum's,' said a pupil (not necessarily what a mother wants to hear).

Pupils and parents: Almost half are from local postcodes but a good train line means some from as far as 40 miles away – the local station is only a short walk. Combination of old money, professionals and self-made entrepreneurs with about a third receiving some financial assistance with the fees. Most children are from Northern Ireland but a growing international community in Belfast means that it is often the school of choice for expats. There is a large American contingent and the school now hosts a Thanksgiving dinner. Parents very engaged and generous with their time and money and the parents' association is involved with the planning of the numerous social gatherings and fundraising events such as the camping weekends and the quiz night, and is very welcoming to new parents. A parent described the children as 'well rounded and confident, will stand up for themselves and speak out and are willing to swim against the shoal'. They have a strong sense of right and wrong and are very understanding of those who are not doing well.

Former pupils include rugby star, Paddy Wallace; the rock band, Snow Patrol; former Lord Mayor of London, Sir Peter Gadsden; and the leader of the House of Lords, Natalie Evans. The school promotes free thinking, says the headmaster, and has produced a number of MPs and life peers representing the full range of political opinion.

Parents kept informed via regular progress reports and regular meetings and the headmaster's witty and informative Friday newsletter.

Money matters: One-third have some financial assistance including five to 10 per cent on full bursaries. Academic, music and golf scholarships worth up to 20 per cent of fees, which can be topped up to 100 per cent with a with a bursary.

The last word: A charming, gentle, small school on the shores of Belfast Lough which feels like one big family, where 'there is top-down happiness from the headmaster and staff to the children and everyone seems to be smiling'.

Rossall School

Broadway, Fleetwood, Lancashire FY7 8JW

01253 774201 | admissions@rossall.org.uk | www.rossall.org.uk

Ages: 11-18

Pupils: 760; sixth form: 234; Boarders: 240 full, 53 weekly/flexi

Fees: Day £8,865 – £14,430; Boarding £15,095 – £41,175 pa

Head: Since 2018, Jeremy Quartermain, previously deputy head (academic) at Brentwood School. History degree from Cambridge and MPhil in medieval history from Trinity College Dublin, where he also tutored undergrads. Taught English overseas for a while then did a PGCE at the University of East Anglia. Was a history and classics teacher at Gresham, where he was later promoted to head of sixth form. He is also a freelance tutor for the Holocaust Educational Trust.

Parents describe him as 'charismatic' and 'an excellent communicator' with 'a passion for high quality education'. His drive to move Rossall on underpins everything he says and he has clearly excelled at bringing staff and parents with him on his journey too – their buy-in is evident. He told us his vision is the product of his own personal experiences and belief in caring for children as much as his intellectual beliefs. Also a keen musician, he is dedicated to ensuring that Rossall's long-standing reputation for sports is balanced with an equally strong commitment to the arts and especially music. The staff room has seen major changes since he arrived including new deputy head, head of the junior school and directors of teaching and learning and sixth form. One staff member told us, 'We came here because we wanted to work with Jeremy – children are at the heart of everything he believes in and does.' The head told us,'I am confident we have a common room of staff with the highest aspirations which has helped lead the surge in results.'

Married to Fiona, who hails from County Galway. She is head of learning support at Rossall and has taught at both primary and secondary level. They have three young daughters all at the school.

Entrance: Entrance tests in English, maths and non-verbal reasoning. Interview with head for all

Rossall School

applicants, who also have to produce a handwritten personal statement of no more than two sides of A4. Rare for the school to say no, though – only really happens if they can't meet the pupil's needs. School is biggest it ever has been – a good job perhaps as its excellent provision of online learning during Covid lockdowns has led to a significant increase in applications from other local schools. Higher numbers (including of high achieving students) are coming in at sixth form too, which head puts down to the school's improving academic results. Five 5s at GCSE needed at this point, with some subjects requiring a 6 or 7.

International applicants are assessed for English via an online interview – the ones we spoke to had excellent command of English and the school is clear it will not encourage students to start courses where they will struggle to succeed. Those going into years 7 to 10 are put into mainstream classes with EAL support; year 11s are put in a pre-sixth form stream to prepare for A level or IB.

Exit: Around a third leave after GCSEs. Most sixth form pupils go on to university, over 60 per cent to Russell Group or other top 20 universities. Destinations include Imperial, King's College London, Bristol, Warwick, Leeds, Manchester and Durham. Four medics in 2021, and two heading off to US universities in full scholarships. Sometimes a few to Oxbridge, though none in 2021.

Latest results: In 2021, 55 per cent 9-7 at GCSE; 61 per cent A*/A at A level (83 per cent A*-B). Average IB score 35. In 2019 (the last year when exams took place), 47 per cent 9-7 at GCSE.

Teaching and learning: Results reflect the broad intake but are on the up. Parents appreciate the recent changes made to the curriculum especially the greater focus on pupils' academic attainment. Maths, sciences, English, technology and art do particularly well. Drama is a key part of curriculum. Languages are important, with the opportunity to learn two out of French, German and Spanish from year 7 and all three offered at GCSE, IB and A level. Classics has been re-introduced, Latin is available at A level and a handful study ancient Greek. Students told us the absence of computing limits their choices at GCSE and A level – school says it's on the case. School has a resident astronomer and its own observatory which allows for the study of astronomy, including at GCSE. Roughly a third of sixth formers (mostly international) do the IB. BTEC in sport now available. Class sizes of 18-20 (occasionally 22) in years 7-11 and 18 in sixth form, though parents feel the increasing popularity of the school is putting pressure on this.

Inclusion is the mantra on everyone's lips. Both staff and parents we spoke to feel the school is about much more than academia and that it doesn't focus resources and attention on high flyers at the expense of those in the middle or who are struggling. One mum was impressed that her children were not just 'being taught to conform'. Parents say sets are constantly under review and that tracking of students' performance has also improved, with sensible targets given. 'We just didn't know how well the kids were doing in the past, but that's all changed under the new head,' said one. Students – especially senior ones – also recognise that the school has changed and feel well supported to achieve a good balance between hard work and extracurricular. Staff are keen to support students to become independent learners and marking is now focused on constructive feedback not just simple correction – parents approve.

There is something for everyone at Rossall, with seemingly endless extracurricular opportunities, especially for arty and musical children and outdoorsy types

This is one of the most international schools in the UK. Students come from 42 different countries, and around 60 per cent of students sitting GCSE, A level and IB exams have EAL. For those whose English isn't fluent (or near fluent), there's an intensive EAL support stream – it's not separate as such, just about ensuring students get all the top-up help they need, with some students only receiving EAL support for a term or two. International students joining in year 11 are invited on the Pre Sixth Form programme, within which there are two streams adapted to the level of English support required; these students prepare for a selection of IGCSE qualifications in a mix of main school and tailored lessons to prepare them for entry to sixth form. Parents love the internationalism and several commented that their children had maintained friendships with international pupils long after they had returned to their home country.

Parents were impressed by the way school immediately moved learning online during the first lockdown and felt that learning had not suffered significantly during Covid restrictions. iPads for all helped, they told us. As a result, the school was a finalist for two BIBA awards in 2021 – best Covid Response in Business and Education Establishment of the Year.

Learning support and SEN: High-quality SEN support headed up by head's wife, who comes in for high praise from parents particularly for her knowledge of students' individual needs. Dyslexia, ADHD and ASD all catered for. In-class support and curriculum adjustments can be made. TAs and one-to-ones available at an extra cost. The school is honest with parents if it can't support a child. Therapeutic support for emotional health and wellbeing is provided through the school farm. We noticed the complete lack of stigma attached to additional needs here, which leads to students often coming to ask for support proactively. Sixth form students also give support as part of their community service.

The arts and extracurricular: There is something for everyone at Rossall, with seemingly endless extracurricular opportunities, especially for arty and musical children and outdoorsy types. More unusual examples include film making, cryptography, psychology, jazz band, knitting, Warhammer and astrophysics – and this is just the tip of the iceberg. DofE and CCF are both popular. There is also a literary society, which meets regularly to discuss poetry, books and culture.

A new performing arts centre was completed in 2018 and the new director of music is a former West End director with a master's in choral conducting. There is a strong choral tradition, closely bound in with the life of the historic chapel. Students play different types of music in various performances and concerts throughout the year – one we spoke to had performed in Berlin, Paris and Westminster Abbey. They can learn instruments at school with visiting tutors for an extra fee. When we visited, 12 new Steinway pianos were due to arrive, including a concert grand, making it an All-Steinway School with tuition available for those with a particular talent. The first such student was recruited when we were there – she had beaten 120 entrants in a Rossall international piano competition.

Students and staff speak enthusiastically about the dramatic opportunities here and the chance to act in productions or be in involved in stage and costume design is open to all ages. The school puts on two plays a year in one of two well-equipped performance spaces. The drama department also has links with a local theatre school and casting agency, which has enabled some pupils to appear in national radio and television productions. The displays in the art department are exceptional. Keen artists are allowed to use the well-stocked workshops and studios every day after school. Each year in the Lent term Rossall devotes a week solely to art, music and drama and parents told us that even the highest performing sports players are never discouraged from getting involved in the school play or any other creative endeavour.

Sport: This is a very sporty school for both girls and boys. Ian Botham sent his son Liam here and many alumni have gone on to play rugby, hockey or cricket professionally. Several current students are playing football at club and national level. More than a dozen pupils, male and female, currently play hockey for Lancashire. There are countless sports options beyond the more obvious team games: pupils can also play basketball, squash or badminton, or lift weights, climb, dance or shoot, and there are golf and football academies. The football academy recruits boys and girls from both home and abroad and is linked to Fleetwood Town football club. Four girls currently play for Manchester City and Manchester United. The academy director has recently been recruited to manage the England under-16 team. The golf academy is ranked number one for senior golf by the Independent Schools' Golf Association. It boasts an indoor golf centre with putting range, golf nets and a simulator to allow students to improve their shots – despite encouragement, we didn't try it out.

No hint of social snobbery, we simply saw young people having a lovely time. Great encouragement to be who you are and pupils are encouraged to find their niche

Facilities are among the best we've seen; almost all sports offered are catered for on site. Includes an extensive range of top-quality pitches, playing fields, squash courts and the like. There's a 25-metre indoor swimming pool and in 2019 a new £4m sports centre was opened. Six badminton courts, an indoor sprint track and indoor long and high jump pits also feature.

Rossall sport is steeped in tradition. Ross hockey is a unique game, a hockey-rugby hybrid played only on the school's private beach. School regularly competes in rugby fives tournaments at prestigious public schools as well as hosting its own national Rossall Fives tournament each October.

Boarding: Pupils can board for weekdays only or the whole time. If day pupils want to temporary board, which they often do, then they stay in spare beds within their own house. Temporary boarding allows day pupils to stay at the school for a night or longer for pretty much any reason.

They typically temporary board on a Friday night if they have to be at school early the next morning for a match or on a Saturday night if they want to tag along on the boarding house's Sunday outing. Some also choose to flexi-board, a more regular option, the same night each week with supervised prep, extracurricular activities and tea provided as part of the package.

Although there are no Saturday classes, this is a busy day for sports practice and fixtures. On Sundays boarders can, at no extra cost, go on an outing to eg bowling, crazy golf, Alton Towers, Manchester Christmas markets. Just under 25 per cent of boarders are international and these will be met at and delivered back to Manchester Airport by a representative of the school at the start and end of term. Pupils also have the option to stay in school during the holidays for a fee.

The boarding houses, including the junior house for 7 to 13-year-olds, are homely and more cosy than typical university halls of residence. Any pupil can use them to relax and socialise during lunchtimes. Some are more up to date than others but the school has used Covid to begin an extensive round of refurbishing the houses on a five-year cycle. Rooms are mostly singles, and are spacious and comfortable. Common rooms, kitchens and other social spaces are plentiful. Consequently there's lots of scope for different age groups and both local and international pupils to mix. Each pupil has a desk in their room and the freedom to put up pictures and customise their living space. Each house has a pair of live-in houseparents who are either teachers or support staff. The ones we met were warm and affectionate, their love of the job reflected in the way the children spoke about them. 'They look out for you and you can talk to them about anything.'

Ethos and heritage: Founded in 1844 by St Vincent Beechey as a sister school to Marlborough College, which had been founded the previous year. It was the first school in the UK to have CCF, which received the Queen's colours in 2010. The campus is expansive and grassy, the buildings redbrick, grand and turreted; beyond them stretches a thin strip of pale yellow beach before the misty sea. The school says it's the only one with its own private beach, gifted by Queen Victoria. Even on a grey day, it is picturesque and peaceful. The newer areas of the school are the most impressive, with some of the older teaching spaces a little tired but watch this space as there are ambitious plans in place.

The fact that it's a boarding school, and a very international one, is integral to Rossall life. There is a seamless integration between day and boarding, UK and international students. Even if they're not staying for a sleepover, this is a school where older pupils in particular just don't want to go home. They can stay late for prep (with teachers on hand to help) and have their tea at school. For day pupils who stay late there are prep clinics with one-to-one support, plus the option to stay for tea.

Almost all sports offered are catered for on site. Facilities are among the best we've seen and include extensive top-quality pitches

Big on tradition. Every year during Christmas dinner in the imposing, oak-panelled dining hall, the pupils sing The Twelve Days of Christmas, each house taking a different verse. No-one tells them to do it, the pupils explain, 'it just sort of happens, spontaneously'. It gets quite competitive, each house singing more boisterously than the last. One pupil said this sums up what's special about Rossall. We found no hint of social snobbery, we simply saw young people having a lovely time. There is great encouragement to be who you are and everyone we spoke to said that any student could find their niche here.

Alumni include Booker-Prize-winning novelist JG Farrell; Father Thomas RD Byles, the Catholic priest who refused to leave the Titanic so that he could help other passengers; eminent figures in the world of sport, music and industry; and a few bastions of the Establishment: a governor of a couple of colonies; a private secretary to Queen Victoria; and the magnificently named Sir Walton Clopton Wingfield, who patented the game of lawn tennis.

Pastoral care, inclusivity and discipline: Several parents identified the quality of pastoral care as the single thing they most appreciated about Rossall. One parent was full of praise for the care and individual attention shown during a recent family bereavement, not just to the pupil but also to the rest of the family. Mental health and wellbeing are prioritised, with a staff member dedicated to these areas. 'I don't know how our child would have managed without her during Covid,' said a parent.

Religion is part of school life – there's a Church of England school chaplain and the whole school attends chapel every Friday. The chapel is a beautiful building, for which students feel a great deal of affection. Students said the religious aspect is inclusive, not just of other religions but atheism too. One student was deeply moved when describing his experiences of singing in the chapel in both the school choirs.

Discipline is firm, with serious breaches of rules dealt with case-by-case. Pupils we spoke to couldn't think of any instances of bullying and spoke with real conviction about how caring an environment this is; parents told us any bullying is dealt with appropriately. Everyone feels the school is accepting of difference, perhaps not least because of the international diversity.

Pupils and parents: Quite a few parents are alumni of Rossall. Lots of state-educated too. Some pupils get help with fees from grandparents or from the school's own means-tested bursary scheme. Three-quarters of families are from the UK, the rest international – further up the school, more than 60 per cent are international. Pupils are grounded, polite and universally positive about the school. Well presented too – uniform, blazers and tie for all, kilts for girls, all impeccable. We saw no arrogance and a remarkable sense from all of them that the school is a family. One day pupil since the age of three had chosen to board for the sixth form – 'I've grown up here, it's been so much more than developing my academic ability, I'm really nearly ready for the world,' she told us. Another international student said, 'No-one feels more Rossallian than anyone else. It welcomes you in.' We met students who hadn't been home for many months during the pandemic when the school stayed open for boarding. They were full of praise for the teaching and boarding staff and the fact that no infections passed on within school. All commented on how all the school had supported them.

Money matters: The school has been in very good financial health for a number of years. About 25 per cent of pupils in the senior school receive significant means-tested bursaries (a 50 per cent reduction of fees or more, with 100 per cent bursaries for local sixth form students). There are also scholarships available for high performers in sport, music, drama or academia.

The last word: A warm, welcoming and happy school that embraces the diversity of its community in an unselfconscious and genuine way. The buildings are grand and imposing from afar but once inside you can't help but be bowled over by the enthusiasm, purposefulness and inclusivity.

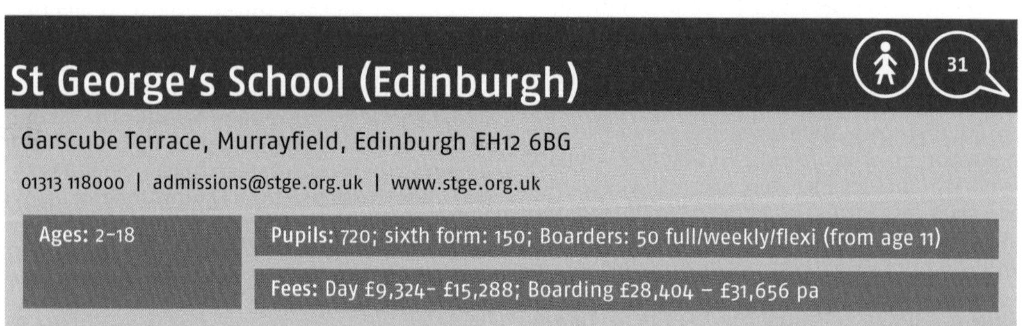

St George's School (Edinburgh)
31
Garscube Terrace, Murrayfield, Edinburgh EH12 6BG
01313 118000 | admissions@stge.org.uk | www.stge.org.uk
Ages: 2-18
Pupils: 720; sixth form: 150; Boarders: 50 full/weekly/flexi (from age 11)
Fees: Day £9,324- £15,288; Boarding £28,404 – £31,656 pa

Head: Since January 2017, Alex Hems. Previously deputy head of Wycombe Abbey. English degree from Oxford, then an English teacher; has also been head of sixth form at North London Collegiate, head of senior school at St Paul's Girls and deputy head at Francis Holland.

Her main areas of focus so far have been reviewing both the curriculum in the lower school (10–13-year-olds) and the GCSE exam process (15–16-year-olds), with classroom time extended in English and maths to ensure good habits are established early. Changes include P6s and S1s now having double periods of specialist science teaching, and language carousel from P7.

'Mrs Hems is approachable and professional, a leader,' said a parent. She is married to William and they have two daughters at the school. William is a research chemist and teacher. Reads 'a huge amount', loves walking in the countryside and some sport, 'if I have the time'. Quietly spoken and down-to-earth, she is like many working mums in constantly trying to balance between work and family time – 'I'm always juggling,' she laughs.

Leaving in July 2022.

Entrance: Entry via nursery or interview aged 4 or 5. Plenty of clever clogs, going by exam results, but they consider all girls able to keep up with the pace of academic life. Entry by assessment, school report and interview. Entry to sixth form is by entrance assessments and a school report; external pupils by interview and previous school report. These sixth form places are in high demand.

Exit: Almost all juniors move up to the senior school with few leaving after GCSEs/National 5s; otherwise a gap year, uni, or higher education of all sorts. Scots law popular, as are the sciences, medicine (three medics and a dentist in 2020), engineering and business management. Around 60 per cent opt for free Scottish universities. Rest to universities in England and around the globe. St Andrews, Edinburgh, Glasgow, Durham, Newcastle and Aberdeen all popular recently. Around 90 per cent get into their first choice of uni or college. One to Oxbridge in 2021, plus five medics.

Latest results: In 2021, 61 per cent 9-7 at GCSE; 89 per cent A/B for Highers; 99 per cent A/B for Advanced Highers. In 2019 (the last year when exams took place), 50 per cent 9-7 at GCSE; 82 per cent A/B for Highers; 89 per cent A/B for Advanced Highers.

Teaching and learning: School describes itself as 'the best of British' – a girls-only school that offers both the English and Scottish system, depending on what best fits the bill for the individual pupil. The reasoning, they say, is that 'unis value Highers and Advanced Highers' but English GCSEs are more substantial – 'You have to work harder and they distinguish excellence. Content is greater and they work over two years to develop these skills and have a good overlap with Highers. They really get to know the subject.' Small numbers still do Nat 5.

Super-duper results. The HPQ (Higher Project Qualification) also proves popular – an independent research project in lower 6, studied alongside GCSEs. This enables pupils to extend themselves in a cross-curricular project and to learn project management skills. Head calls it a 'special opportunity to do something different and good prep for Higher and Advanced Higher'.

One-to-one interviews to discuss GCSE subjects with the girls. Most take eight subjects, leading to nine, but some take seven. Curriculum is designed around pupil choices with column structure designed to reflect that. All girls take at least one science, one language and one social science – 'It is often said that no two girls take the same subjects in upper 6 due to the bespoke nature of our provision.' Art A Level more popular than the Scottish Higher: 'Prepares them better for university,' says head. Around a third of girls go into STEM subjects.

P7s (which they call 'remove') have a secondary experience, moving from the primary classroom to specialist teachers, and experience the language carousel from P7. Mandarin, French, Spanish and German all the way through. Serious language teaching from P5. All choose one language at exam level. At Higher, about a third take a language. Can accommodate a variety of languages, eg Russian and Mandarin.

Staff tend to stay, with longest-serving member of staff having taught there 37 years. But also young teachers with creative ideas. Senior management team has three men among six women.

Edinburgh's only all-girls school with a tradition of excellence and an international take on things. Suited to a wide range of abilities, though most are high achievers

Work experience is co-ordinated by the head of careers who has lots of contacts on the St G's network (an online network of current and former pupils). Career education starts in junior school; lower school has World of Work day; upper school has weekly lunchtime sessions where pupils can talk about what they want to do.

Learning support and SEN: Strong EAL department and much-praised learning support. 'No sense of stigma,' said a pupil, while one parent couldn't rate the school highly enough for her dyslexic child – 'a very shy pupil that has gone on to achieve great things'. Support, added the parent, was 'tailored to meet my child's individual needs' and 'my child is treated in a holistic way with a person-centred approach.'

The arts and extracurricular: Junior (including nursery), lower and upper schools each have their own music facilities, with the (recently upgraded) Robertson Music Centre, a 200-seat auditorium with its own recording studio at the centre of things. Hosts oodles of individual music lessons and performances from 22 ensembles (brass, strings and wind), as well as orchestras, and jazz, ceilidh and concert bands. Just a trickle at exam level, but at A grade.

Vibrant art department, with art offered at both A Level and Higher (more do A Level than Higher – either fine art or textiles). Drama to Advanced Higher, though numbers small. Lots of participation in schools shows – recently Mary Poppins (junior and lower school), Ibsen's A Doll's House (upper) and creative shows directed by sixth formers, who often join forces with Merchiston Castle boys.

CCF runs jointly with Merchiston, with its summer camp for U4–U6s. Outreach outdoor education from P5. Tons of after-school clubs including the popular Model UN club. Trips too reflect the school's international outlook, ranging from local experiences such as an Edinburgh museum to NASA and foreign exchange programmes (from age 12) in Canada, Hong Kong, Australia, New Zealand and South Africa. 'They have many formal and informal gatherings and fantastic opportunities to take part in the exchange programme, ski trips, cultural trips and global support projects,' said a parent. 'Also being in the heart of Edinburgh means they have a whole city on their doorstep – a huge advantage for rural girls like ours.'

All of S2 do DofE bronze, with around 30 doing silver and only a few less than that doing gold. Youth Philanthropy Initiative popular in S3.

Sport: School's inclusive approach to PE is based on 'come along and we'll believe in you', though one pupil had a bit of a grumble, feeling that sport should be encouraged to 'help those more who excel'. School explains that it is 'not an elitist sporting school – unlike some others in the local area – but with good success'. Marvellous facilities – the sports hall with its viewing area over the squash courts, lacrosse and all-weather pitches for hockey and tennis. Everyone gets a chance to play all sports and local sports clubs use the facilities, such as Grange Junior Hockey. Wide variety of sports and not just the usual suspects for girls – includes lacrosse, judo, athletics, cricket and fencing. All free except for sailing (a coach-ride away), judo and fencing.

Boarding: Houldsworth House comprises a couple of converted Edwardian villas with views of Edinburgh Castle. Full, flexi, termly, weekly and occasional boarding. Houses around 50 girls aged 11-18 years old. Attracts those from the Scottish islands, London market, international students and British families. Around half the boarders are from the UK, rest from overseas. Array of nationalities but higher numbers from Hong Kong and mainland China than most. No closed weekends and over half will be there on a Saturday night. Full boarders can stay with day girls for the weekend, providing permission is sought from both sets of parents. Head tries 'to make it feel as much like a home experience as we possibly can', though this is the mantra of pretty much all boarding schools. After-school care in boarding house. Very flexible and girls can board during exams if they choose or if transport is compromised, for example when the Forth Bridge closed. Sixth formers have struck it lucky with their own bungalow, which resembles uni halls of residence, with each girl having her own room – though they do have to do their own laundry to prepare them for the future. After-school club for younger boarders and oodles of cultural and recreational outings at the weekend for all. Security code entry to all buildings. A parent told us, 'The Boarding House offers a safe, caring and supportive environment with flexibility.'

Ethos and heritage: Founded in 1888 by a sparky bunch of female Victorian campaigners, headed by Dame Sarah Mair, leading the way for the admission of women to Scottish universities and raising educational standards for school-age girls. Moved to its current location in leafy Ravelston and Murrayfield in 1914. Set in 15 acres of landscaped grounds, with a beautiful colonial neo-Georgian 1914 complex, created by the Scottish architect AF Balfour-Paul, juxtaposed against more modern additions – swish extension for junior school complete with dance studio and a dedicated nursery area with its cantilevered first floor. School is divided into three departments based on age and stage – junior, which encompasses the nursery, plus lower and upper schools.

Edinburgh's only all-girls school with a tradition of excellence and an international take on things. Suited to a wide range of abilities, though most are high achievers. Small school that operates around knowing everyone and establishing a family community. Suits families who don't want their daughters to compete with or be distracted by boys. There's something in that – the girls stood out from most we meet on our tours. Respectful and well-mannered, yet they expressed their feelings with gusto, giving unfiltered and honest opinions. They made this editor laugh with their teenage grumbles about the food or that sport could be better. However, felt like they could be successful women of the future, unafraid to express their opinions (and this is definitely not always the case on our school visits).

Casual navy and red uniform for the junior school. Uppers with tartan skirts and maroon blazers, but no ties. One pupil quipped, 'Everything is laid back here.' Sixth formers wear clothes of their own choice within a dress code. Given the relaxed uniform, quite strict rules around make-up and unnatural coloured hair (both big no-nos).

Charities committee with representatives drawn from each year group to organise wide-ranging charity work, such as Kids Love Clothes, which sees the school piled high with laundered and specially wrapped parcels of clothing to help those in need. The nursery visits care homes and lots of cake and candy stalls, raffles etc.

The St George's Foundation is an online network of former and present friends and colleagues. The latest news and updates are posted as well as careers advice, networking events and socialising. Head says, 'The network prepares girls for their future and offers ongoing support, and to keep in touch with other professionals.' She adds that it 'offers internships and helps them get up and running by drawing on a resource of old St G's girls, who keep in touch for life'.

Attracts those from the Scottish islands, London, international students and British families. Around half the boarders are from the UK, rest from overseas. No closed weekends and over half will be there on a Saturday night. Sixth formers have their own bungalow

As one parent put it, 'Our overall impression of St G's is that it produces strongly academic, empowered and aspirational young women.' We concur. School magazine, aptly named Independent Women (watch out Beyoncé) and monthly e-newsletter to parents, which includes the head's blog, school news and events, and advice, such as making subject choices. One parent felt communications could be stronger.

More than a few outstanding women who were notable former pupils: Alice Thompson (novelist), Annie 'Spitfire' Penrose (Britain's most famous fighter plane was named after her), Candia McWilliam (author and Booker Prize judge), Cordelia Fine (academic psychologist), Emily Dudgeon (athlete), Felicity Hammond (opera singer), Margaret Houldsworth (British campaigner for women's education and a philanthropist), Kathleen Scott (sculptor, pupil of Rodin), Kay Adams (television presenter), Marie Stopes (author, palaeobotanist, academic, eugenicist, campaigner for women's rights, and pioneer in the field of birth control), Phyllis Bone (20th-century Scottish sculptor), Sheila Burnford (author).

Pastoral care, inclusivity and discipline: Team of heads of year are on hand for lower and upper school who track the personal, social and academic development of students. They are supported by a team of tutors who meet weekly to discuss any concerns. Their goal is that every student is known well by at least one member of staff and for the girls to feel that they are supported and always have someone to turn to. The apron strings are loosened for senior pupils to prepare them for life beyond school. Parents say it works, with one reporting that 'the school is happy to deal with problems directly' and is 'led by a strong management team, where any issues seem to be well investigated and sensible, fair measures put in place'. No exclusions.

Reports for each year group each term, as well as parents' evenings and form tutor meetings. Six school houses. Food prepared by school chef, with all staff eating with the girls. We had a memorable meal with staff, accompanied by fresh strawberries and lashings of cream – however, one of the girls thought that their food wasn't always as nice as it is in the boarding house. P1s sit with teachers and are served; everyone else is buffet style.

Pupils and parents: Typical St G's girls may come across as gregarious high-achievers but they do accommodate a range of pupils. 'My daughter is the polar opposite of that, shy and introverted who would hide in class, and has grown and developed into a strong, caring, independent woman,' a parent told us. 'Both my daughters are quite different and were encouraged to follow their individual paths,' said another.

Parents are not all Edinburgh bourgeoisie. 'The school would suit a wide variety of families – I would say St George's has a very diverse parent group and isn't a one model fits all – they offer flexibility, a broad curriculum and opportunities that suit many families,' says a parent. Mostly a local bunch with a mix of international boarders.

Free shuttle bus runs rom Haymarket, otherwise (vastly subsidised) buses operate from Colinton, East Lothian, Portobello, Inverkeithling, Southside and West Lothian. Surveys are sent out to parents so they can meet their needs.

Money matters: Tuition fees are inclusive of textbooks, stationery, junior school day trips and personal accident premiums. Extras are kept to a minimum but extra is charged for individual music lessons, after-school and holiday clubs, English as a second language, external examination fees and some activities where an external instructor is hired. For three or more sisters, the third sister will receive one-third off tuition fees. Discount scheme for those with brothers at Merchiston. Third child discount does not apply for nursery. Limited number of means-tested bursaries, for up to 100 per cent of school fees, awarded on the basis of financial need. Has maintained its charitable status since 2013.

The last word: Widely regarded as the best girls' school in Scotland, and the only all-through girls' school in Edinburgh (except for boys in nursery) with an international outlook. Produces gregarious, academic, independent women, and focuses on finding their strengths as individuals.

St Leonards School

South Street, St Andrews, Fife KY16 9QJ

01334 472126 | contact@stleonards-fife.org | www.stleonards-fife.org

Ages: 5-18

Pupils: 565; sixth form: 150; Boarders: 131 full, 7 weekly/flexi

Fees: Day £9,840 – £15,939; Boarding £24,342 – £37,920 pa

Headmaster: Since September 2021, Simon Brian, previously deputy head at Charterhouse in Surrey and before that deputy head at Cheltenham College. Grew up in England and Hong Kong and educated at Ripon Grammar School in North Yorkshire. Studied French and German at Edinburgh. Taught in France and Austria before qualifying as a teacher at the IoE, London, after which he rose through the ranks at Dulwich then Highgate School. Married to Veronique, who is from Rouen, France; they have three sons and share a passion for languages and travel.

Entrance: At any time, including mid-term. Accepts CE, but usually own (written) entrance assessment (English and maths) or scholarship exam. Seamless transition from juniors to seniors. Six GCSEs or equivalent for sixth with 7s and 6s in subjects to be studied at higher level in the IB. 'We usually pick up 15/20 at sixth form entry' for IB. School prefers to meet with international applicants but, if pushed, will Skype.

Exit: 'Minimum' drop-out at transition from juniors to seniors and some (around a quarter) depart post-GCSE (only accept good English speakers to sixth form). Around 90 per cent to universities – mostly Scottish. Edinburgh and Glasgow most popular recently. Often good numbers overseas. One to Oxbridge in 2021. Occasional medics but none in 2021.

Latest results: In 2021, 60 per cent 9-7 at I/GCSE; average IB score 35 points. In 2019 (the last year when exams took place), 45 per cent 9-7 at I/GCSE.

Teaching and learning: School prides itself on 'high quality education right from the preparatory school through to the senior school'. Sixth form focuses on the IB (school is one of just two in the UK to actively offer all four IB programmes: the PYP, the MYP, the CP and the DP). New IB subjects include business management, computer science, psychology and sports science. Sixth formers help out in junior school as part of the charitable leg of the IB (CAS) with up to 50 hours' assistance reading, 'riting, 'rithmetic sort of thing. Also offers BTECs in business and sport combined with IB courses for those who need a more vocational option.

Most pupils take GCSEs/IGCSEs in the normal way; however, now teaches the IB primary years and middle years programmes. A one-year pre-IB course ticks all the boxes for those joining school age 15 (often refugees from state systems) as well as international students who sit fewer IGCSEs/GCSEs, and, if needed, get up to speed in English (about a fifth of non-native English speakers need some EAL help, and must pass a written proficiency test – ESOL). St Andrews Uni fields a raft of international speakers; St Leonards boasts help in 'a wide range of native languages in all year groups'... 'be aware that some of this tuition may be subject to an additional charge', 'dependent on number of students and language'.

School says, 'The IB is probably the least tinkered about with qualification in the world – its basic philosophy of keeping a breadth of subjects going into the sixth form but also studying three to a level comparable to Advanced Higher or A level has remained.' 'Native language' for IB may be English, Russian, German, French, Mandarin (currently on offer) or whatever, while Latin qualifies as a foreign language, as well as French, Spanish, German, Italian (ab initio). UCAS gives points for individual subjects studied under the IB system which means that non-linguists/mathematicians, previously disadvantaged in the overall IB grading, now get full credit for their strong subjects.

Most study two or three languages, with all doing French from year 1 and Spanish and/or German/Latin from 10/11. Max class size 20, smaller for practical or specialist subjects.

School appoints a St Leonards associate researcher or two, often a PhD student at St Andrews, to liaise with pupils and point them at the joys of research – or, as we said previously, 'helping them to develop an appreciation and knowledge of research'. Quite. Senior pupils have access to the university library and regularly attend lectures. (Lots of profs' children and consequently no dearth of academic governors or visiting speakers.)

Learning support and SEN: Dyslexia/dyspraxia support – 'no statemented pupils accepted' – mostly provided for 'a small proportion of pupils' in mainstream teaching, but a good programme of withdrawal, group sessions and one-to-one if necessary (stunning, said one thrilled parent – 'saved our lives') at extra cost. School tests if they reckon extra help needed; specialist staff of four straddle both senior and junior schools.

The arts and extracurricular: Outstanding art department, attracting pupils outside normal lessons as well as curricular – huge range of alternative media, darkrooms, textiles etc. Head of art was hanging fiendish model birds from the ceiling during our visit – complete with two elderly black Labs – preparatory to the next biannual art show – open to the public. Artists in residence. Regularly in the ribbons for local photography prize – the Kodak Cup.

Music strong in fabulously designed centre. St Leonards Junior School pupils sang in front of the cameras at the televised St Andrews royal wedding breakfast celebrations. Rash of bands/orchestras, 'choir for every day of the week', ambitious singing programmes. Pipe band; we were treated to a brilliant rendition by an 11-year-old, who warned us that his favourite piece was 14 minutes long. We heard about four (though it seemed to take him longer to find his pipes).

Rugby, lacrosse, hockey against Glenalmond, Strath and Dundee High. The hallowed main school site (birth of lacrosse in the UK) now boasts rugby matches et al

Drama on the up; school performs twice a year in the revamped nearby Byre Theatre in St Andrews (popular with both school and public); students must study history of theatre as well as pounding boards. Drama types take shows to Ed Festival and go on mega drama-fest to Broadway every other year. Trips (one per subject per year) planned on a two-year cycle. DofE of course. Youth Enterprise with goodies often sold in aid of local school-adopted fav charity TICCL.

Sport: Proper matches for chaps as well as chapesses. Think Edinburgh schools, Robert Gordon's... Full range of sporting options – rugby, lacrosse, hockey against Glenalmond, Strath and Dundee High: the hallowed main school site (birth of lacrosse in the UK) now boasts rugby matches et al (roll over, Dame Louisa). Girls' sports still strong, with usual mass of international lax players. Practice matches held on beach if games pitches frozen. Great all-weather pitch, with just the medieval school wall separating it from the beach. Currently fundraising for new sports hall development.

Loads of individual sports and international coaches – needle chaps' tennis match in progress during our canter: judo, trampoline, skiing, badminton, swimming – university uses pool for water polo; snowboarding and surfing; rock-climbing as well as expeditions to the Alps. Annual skiing trips both at home and abroad; sailing now thoroughly embraced, ditto windsurfing and all 'local water sports activities' – and about time too. Local (and not-so-local) racehorse trainers use beach for exercise, as does the Scots Guards polo team, now based at Leuchars, and St Andrews uni polo team. It being St Andrews, golf reigns supreme with about a third of the school playing; all lucky boarders can and do become youth members of the St Andrews Links Trust (as residents in St Andrews) so they can play the Old Course.

Nearby well-equipped BHS riding centre (moderately expensive, but not over the top) with a hot horse shower (wow!) offers a variety of options, from bringing your own nag to renting one of theirs. 'Weekly lessons available for keen able riders.'

Boarding: Weekly and termly boarding from year 7: emphasis is on day. Fairly harum-scarum boarding houses, passages littered with rather grand bookcases and rows of servants' bells – relics of a former age. Day pupils in the sixth form included in house system with 'day rooms' in boarding houses. Couple of small dorms, mostly single rooms, usual teenage tip sort of thing, but they were in the midst of revising. Stunning shower (and this was in a house about to be done up!). A £4 million refurb of all three boarding houses started recently – first two revamped ones opened recently (design brief: country house style): 'Aspects of the interior patterns have been created using a sketch by a current student (and art scholar) – a Bishopshall Toile has been created of signature St Leonards scenes, and appears on all the curtains as well as cushions in the boarding house.' Ollerenshaw boys' boarding house now has ample kitchen space which 'has enabled the boys to prepare special meals together and host dinner parties for fellow boarders and day pupils'.

No Saturday lessons. We were concerned at possible lack of organised activities for boarders at weekend, but were assured, several times, 'that they were too busy with their various IB projects'. Various jaunts to Edinburgh and Dundee were mooted but we are still a tad concerned. Head adds, 'Boarders generally are taken up with sport on Saturdays, there is a boarders' outing every Sunday, beach kite buggies on West Sands, go-karting, bubble football, etc etc.'

Ethos and heritage: Founded by dons and wives of St Andrews profs for their daughters in 1877 in what was once a medieval priory, backing on to the sea wall, the sprawling hotch-potch collection of impressive-looking granite has neither form nor symmetry.

Once Scotland's girls' academic (boarding) school of choice, St Leonards has weathered the storm caused by so-called brother schools opening their doors to the fairer sex to counteract (their) falling numbers. Breakthrough came when junior school absorbed local co-ed prep, New Park, in 2005: chunk of New Park Educational Trust kicked in. Boys and girls work their way up the school in true co-ed fashion: now roughly 50/50. Adopted the IB in 2006 and head is an enthusiast: 'better to have scientists who can write essays'; it's also popular with international pupils.

Bracing sea air and bone-chilling easterly gales. Tracksuits are essential for games. Golf, riding, the beach and trips to surrounding countryside are great draws

Curious combo of gracious living – elegant house drawing rooms reminiscent of Country Life plus lawned courts nestling among old stone building in dreaming spires style – combined with faintly scruffy corridors, classrooms, common rooms. The external fabric is in need of serious help (sea breezes are hell on paintwork): some windows and sills are flaking, though much has been done within the neglected exteriors. An ongoing rolling programme of upgrading (£3 million is a sum regularly bandied about).

St Leonards inhabits a notoriously windswept corner of Fife, on the sea, bracing air, bone-chilling easterly gales, tracksuits popular for games. Nay, essential. Golf, riding and the beach all great draws, as well as trips up town and forays to the surrounding countryside. Castle and cathedral a couple of minutes away. Mega library and selection of Maryana in Queen Mary's House (oddly flanked by a boys' loo). Library much in use by those in sixth form, but available to all. Mary Queen of Scots and King Charles II reputed to have stayed at Queen Mary's Library when it was a private house, but not, of course, at the same time.

Splendid menu posted online: lunch we had was sumptuous and imaginative. All food sourced 'locally' (ie within 100 miles). International students can and do cook their own dishes. Veggie option, naturally, and fresh fruit available whenever. Central dining room recently given an internal overhaul: outside still pretty rank.

Comprehensive buses for day pupils: Dundee, Kirkcaldy, Auchtermuchty, Perth, the East Neuk, and presumably special pick-up at Leuchars following deployment of Scots Guards. Juniors can be dropped off early (8am) and collected late (5.30pm). This represents a reduced school day but incorporates time for activities, which has 'settled down well and parents appreciate it'. Otherwise return journey leaves 5.40pm.

Sixth formers wear suits (or a fair approximation thereof) during the working day. Boys rather tidier than some we have seen at that age; girls less so: sixth formers adopt a theme (or two) in black – quite short shorts and thick tights apparently okay (skool says they were quite short skirts, not shorts). Machine-washable blazers and blue tartan kilts for girls, grey breeks for chaps are senior/junior school uniform with blue woolly pullies. Ah but we hanker for the cloaks of yesteryear. Secondhand shop run by the 'bullish' parents' association which also organises family fun tennis etc.

School is proud of its Scottish heritage and tradition – Burns Day celebrated, though Scottish country dancing is apparently only taught in the junior school.

Famous seniors include Betty Harvey Anderson, Dame Kathleen Ollerenshaw (previous president of St Leonards), past head Mary James, Gillian Glover of the Scotsman (who didn't last the course), Stella Tennant (ditto), Baroness Byford and Anji Hunter.

Pastoral care, inclusivity and discipline: School rules feature punctuality, security and civilised behaviour; the student handbook has a rash of rules, most of which are sheer common sense: L-drivers may not drive other pupils and the like. But members of the sixth form have privileges – can visit some (some definitely out of bounds) local pubs if aged 18 and over and are generally expected to behave like grown-ups. No smoking, no under-age drinking and absolute zero tolerance of drugs. Parents like the drugs policy – random drugs testing and testing on suspicion, out for pushing, forfeit right to remain in school for using – depends on individual and other factors and for how long, and pupils may be allowed back under fairly arduous conditions. No chaplain but team of local ministers who regularly preach. Plenty of fundraising for good causes.

Pupils and parents: Boarding now from age 11, with a small number of UK boarders but most from abroad, particularly at sixth form level, when incomers swell the ranks to follow the IB course – a boon. Those pupils whom we met (either IB or newbies) were a more sophisticated bunch – particularly the former – than we would normally expect in a school which is so geographically challenged – with sea on three sides.

Eclectic mix of international and first-time buyers: Fifers see school as a viable option. Think butcher, baker, candlestick maker, farmer, landed estate owner and very senior CEOs. Parents, both past and present, are very positive about the place.

St Leonards has a strong old girls' network and many at the school are offspring or grand offspring of Seniors. Some concern previously from Seniors about school's new direction though others welcomed its new impetus.

Money matters: A means-tested assisted places scheme in operation from year 5; open to application from existing parents in financial difficulties; sibling discount. Raft of scholarships, though only of nominal monetary value, and usually only lasting a couple of years – ranging from academic through music, drama and sport – golf scholarships very popular (as you might imagine).

The last word: A school that runs seamlessly from age 5 to 18, with the IB niche giving it an academic edge with an international flavour.

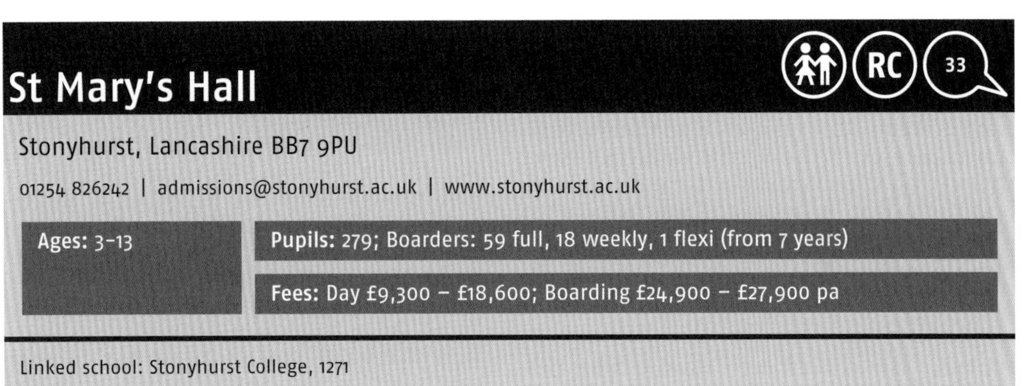

St Mary's Hall

Stonyhurst, Lancashire BB7 9PU

01254 826242 | admissions@stonyhurst.ac.uk | www.stonyhurst.ac.uk

Ages: 3-13

Pupils: 279; Boarders: 59 full, 18 weekly, 1 flexi (from 7 years)

Fees: Day £9,300 – £18,600; Boarding £24,900 – £27,900 pa

Linked school: Stonyhurst College, 1271

Headmaster: Since 2014, Ian Murphy (Durham BA, PGCE), previously head at All Hallows, Somerset. Charismatic and open; his vision of education is about formation: helping to 'form' young people to be their best selves and excel. This view and vocabulary are, in part, born of the spiritual values underpinning the school. Its motto, Quant Je Puis – roughly translated, strive to be the best you can – is the heartbeat of school daily life because unlike many a concocted mission statement, this is no hollow refrain: it rests upon an impressive 400-year heritage.

Yet heritage is only part of the story, as Ian Murphy is a force for energising change in the here and now. Viewing academic excellence as a 'given' for SMH, he has focused on reinvigorating the arts and sport. He has also been busy instigating enhancements to the fabric of the school, moving the music department from stuffy attics to a swanky ground floor wing with cutting edge technology. A tennis dome was also recently added (opened by Tim Henman) and an idyllic garden created for younger children to understand life cycles. Very Mr McGregor and utterly charming.

On top of this, he has revitalised the curriculum, integrating the Stonyhurst crown jewels (its jaw-dropping private collection of 70,000 artefacts, including the First Folio of Shakespeare) into lessons as teaching tools to nurture intellectual spark. Parents say he has brought great energy and has had a 'massive impact' academically.

Acutely aware the school needs to be tuned into the modern world, head's innovatory zeal is a continuum; currently he is assessing the benefits of Saturday morning school. Innovation, he suggests, complements the school's spiritual values and refers to the Jesuits centuries ago being pragmatically alert to the need to evolve. The school's literature reinforces its Jesuit heritage a fair bit, making it clear worship is part of the school's make-up. So if you desire your child to have a

Catholic upbringing this is marvellous, and those parents we spoke to certainly emphasised the immense personal importance of this to them. But what about other faiths?

The head is sensitised to Catholic schools sometimes struggling with their message in this area. So let's be clear, this school is accessible to all, supportive of all and utterly inclusive. If you are not Catholic then, yes, accepting worship as part of pupil life and unfamiliar lingo – references to Our Lady, to saints – is part of the experience. But do not, whatever you do, let these get in the way of embracing this school's wonderful ethos. The spiritual values the school holds are about forming wise, eloquent, generous young people. An uplifting aspiration which cuts across humanity, no matter which jack in a box of faith you spring from.

Inevitably, leading the school dominates term time (his wife also teaches there), but holidays are spent with their teenage children sharing their mutual love for sport and music. Personal reflection comes walking the dogs in the breathtaking Ribble Valley.

Leaving in September 2022. To be replaced by Fr Christopher Cann, currently head of Ratcliffe College Prep in Leicestershire and previously head of Leicester Prep and Denstone College Prep. MA in French from St Andrews and in theology from the Oxford. A former Anglican priest who was received into the Catholic church in 2011, he is now a priest of the Ordinariate of Our Lady of Walsingham. Married to Honor, a GP, he has six children and two grandchildren.

Entrance: Admission is via a meeting with the head and staff; pupils are invited for a day. Those transferring from another school provide school reports and reference. Students who speak little English are welcomed. Those entering in year 7 sit an 11+ exam.

Exit: Virtually full cohort transfers to Stonyhurst for year 9. (A few overseas boarders return home.) There is an exam at the end of year 8 but this is not related to the right to transfer (just preparation for senior school). School says it is not pressured, includes revision guidance; the results are important to the 'handover' process.

Our view: Although day pupils greatly dominate, this is a boarding school in outlook: most day pupils stay for prep until 7pm. All mix in 'playrooms' – year groups – though they are also members of 'lines', which are akin to houses in that they encompass all age ranges and meet for sporting and special interest interline competitions.

Ages 3-7 attend Hodder House, a delightful building, packed with colour. The focus is on social development, literacy, numeracy, art, PE, swimming and French. There is outdoors teaching, exploring woodland and insects. Children have access to iPads. The whole school comes together for assemblies, easing the transition to the main building.

Some super clubs, like Big Thinkers (philosophy, neurology) and astronomy club. Parents said children were encouraged in whatever area they showed interest

Within SMH, pupils' academic progress is rigorously measured by assessments, diagnostic tools to ensure all are on track and to identify those excelling and those who need extra help. A detailed picture of each child is built up, including pastoral wellbeing. Parents spoke of the school working on little weaknesses with the children, who didn't feel pressured, didn't notice 'tests'. Average class size is 15-18.

The national curriculum, enriched by the International Primary Curriculum, integrates cross-curricular themes, providing an opportunity to utilise the extraordinary Stonyhurst collection: studying the Tudors means touching Anne Boleyn's prayer book or Thomas More's hat. Wow. Evolution lessons, viewing dinosaur poo (oh yes). Artefacts enliven learning as pupils are asked what it tells them about the human story. And it's not just the artefacts either; Lord of the Rings must have extra sparkle knowing Tolkien wrote in the guest rooms. Not to mention that Oliver Cromwell, the cheeky wee scamp, slept on a school table before the battle of Preston. The grounds are used for activities from fossil hunting to looking at natural landforms.

Every class has an interactive whiteboard. Older pupils have timetabled access to a well-equipped IT suite. Internet safety is impressed from the start; portable laptops are used across the school to help pupils develop discerning research skills.

Currently 20 per cent of pupils receive learning support. School develops individual plans, ranging from one-to-one to group interventions to in-class support. Staff receive specialist training in areas like dyslexia. One parent whose child had been in a 'not very academic' box at his previous school said he blossomed academically after transferring to SMH. Another slightly dyslexic pupil had benefited enormously from teachers picking up she needed a worksheet next to her, rather than looking at a whiteboard; she is now 'flying academically'. High performers receive extension work.

Years 7 and 8, whilst still living and learning in SMH, are taught mainstream academic subjects by Stonyhurst teachers, some in college classrooms.

The director of music has expanded opportunities considerably: orchestras, choirs, big bands, the ukulele Odd Bod band. Some 75 per cent of pupils have music tuition and there are lots of concerts. While we visited, the interline music competition had unleashed pupil enthusiasm to the tune of 270 auditions.

There is a cracking theatre and each year group performs a show: Grease, The Jungle Book, Bugsy Malone. Some older pupils prefer the technical side. Public speaking is encouraged; a Question Time style Brexit debate was one event (a trip to the Supreme Court in London the day before saw them meeting Dominic Grieve MP QC). Parents waxed lyrical about the confidence-imbuing aspects of all this. One talked about her previously shy daughter flourishing to become head girl.

The sports facilities are tremendous; tennis dome, huge sports hall, netball courts, athletics field, cricket pitch, rugby fields, use of Stonyhurst's Astroturf pitch, heated pool and nine hole golf course. Other activities include fencing and horse riding. Parents enthused about increased sporting fixtures since Ian Murphy's arrival; one parent was astonished that her previously unsporty daughter was keen to join a netball summer school.

Frequent educational trips but the annual trip to the Somme stands out. Each pupil is given a photo of a SMH pupil who died in the Somme and asked to research their life. Parents say they 'adopt that person' and are immensely moved on finding their grave. Visits from charities, like the Society for the Blind, also widen the perspective beyond me me me.

Some super clubs, like Big Thinkers (philosophy, neurology) and astronomy club. Parents said children were encouraged in whatever area they showed interest.

Head feels all pupils benefit from the familial pastoral set-up in place for boarders. While in their playroom, a pupil can wander over to a teacher and mention a worry. One teacher said informality in the dining room meant staff could pick up eating problems; it might seem relaxed but vigilance prevails. Weekly staff pastoral meetings mean any worries are logged and monitored. Each child's pastoral log stays with them their entire time at SMH and Stonyhurst

Mobile phones not allowed during the day. Boarders have phones for 45 minutes a night. Certain day pupils are permitted them to travel on school transport but they are signed in and out. Day pupils join boarders in mass each week in the theatre (the magnificent chapel can't host the whole school).

Parents spoke of excellent communication. One parent of a boarder praised staff who nursed her son after he broke his hand in a sports match and her daughter when she hit puberty: 'This level of support for teenage girls is vital.' Parents said the tiniest query is sorted the same day.

This ancient school is set in magnificent grounds amidst beautiful scenery. The vibe within the school is a little two-tonal: corridors which have been Ian Murphy'ed are light, bright, covered in large photos of pupils in action which, he says, 'tell the story of the school'. They do, and it feels uplifting. Other corridors, lined with traditional annual school photos, seem an echo of the past; as one parent politely put it, 'shabby chic'.

The playrooms for each year group however – the social and pastoral planks of the school – are full of inspiring pictures, quotes, games tables. They are terrific and age-appropriate, each room having its own distinct identity.

Director of music has expanded opportunities considerably: orchestras, choirs, the ukulele Odd Bod band

Parents are a blend of entrepreneurs, professionals and old money. No competitive inquiries, 'Why isn't Jimmy reading Tolstoy now he's 8?' but empathy with the school's ethos and respect for its heritage. Certainly the parents we spoke to placed great emphasis on their children acquiring a broader view of the world, an awareness of the plight of others less fortunate. (Life beyond 'selfies'.)

Boarding: The 59 boarders are there seven days per week, sleeping in galleries of up to six. The boys' gallery seemed a little functional (though with breathtaking views of lush green hills), the girls' cosier with cushions and photos. One parent wished for more storage space. Lovely gender-specific sitting rooms; a joint playroom and kitchen. Staffing levels are 1:7. One of the houseparent couple, a former pupil, exudes enthusiasm and writes an effusive weekly newsletter (about pupils watching Man United play, a trip to Blackpool Tower, snooker games, watching a movie).

The last word: In one of the playrooms, there is a fabulous poster of St Ignatius saying: 'Go forth and set the world on fire.' These children are being emboldened, their intellect and sensibilities refined, to do just that.

St Mary's Music School

Coates Hall, 25 Grosvenor Crescent, Edinburgh EH12 5EL

0131 538 7766 | admissions@st-marys-music-school.co.uk | www.stmarysmusicschool.co.uk

Ages: 9-19

Pupils: 62; sixth form: 13; Boarders: 23 full

Fees: Fees before aided place: Day £27,075 – £30,274; Boarding £38,358 – £41,557 pa

Headteacher: Since 2013, Dr Kenneth Taylor BSc PhD PGCE PG Dip (50s). Scholarship to Dulwich College, read chemistry at Edinburgh University and spent three years as a research chemist before moving into teaching. Came to St Mary's from Biggar High where he was depute head, having progressed though a couple of schools in the local authority sector.

A keen sportsman (hill-running a passion) he also plays the piano, violin and viola although stresses his musical skills are pedestrian compared to his pupils. Lives in Edinburgh with his family and regularly cycles to school (across Edinburgh). Delightful and outgoing, he enjoys encouraging the youngsters in all manner of disciplines and has a deprecating sense of humour. One parent told us, 'He's outstanding. He takes the children running and encourages them to get outside which is no mean feat considering the kind of kids they are and how their whole world revolves around their music.' We got the impression he cares passionately.

Entrance: Free advisory auditions available year round with applicants encouraged to apply for this initially to assess potential before applying for full auditions. Full auditions in either discipline (chorister or instrumentalist) each term. Places may be available halfway through year though most join at the start of the academic year. If successful, a two-day stay is required for final mutual assessment. 'This was perfect for our boy. He'd never been away from home and it was a chance for him to find out what boarding would be like.'

Advisory auditions held online for the time being, formal auditions at school unless distance prevents.

Exit: All choristers traditionally leave at the end of S2, although some may come back as instrumentalists; the remainder usually leave after Advanced Highers to some form of tertiary education. Sixth form extension year means pupils who joined further up the school can stay until 19. 'Our daughter is staying on because her piano teacher is so incredible – better than many professors at the conservatoires,' said one. Majority to music college or conservatoire or to study music at university, but this is by no means set in stone. Oxbridge features frequently – one in 2021. Pupils are encouraged to choose the best pathway, with previous leavers having studied maths, physics, geology and similar subjects at university. Regular career talks from FPs and professional musicians, opportunities to work with Scottish Chamber Orchestra and professional performance opportunities prepare for next stage. (Option to apply for three-year sixth form programme – which includes sixth form extension year – particularly suited to those wishing to develop musical skills further before applying to conservatoire). Most recent leavers to eg Royal College of Music, University of Edinburgh and Royal Birmingham Conservatoire.

Latest results: In 2021, 93 per cent A-B at National 5; 97 per cent A-B at Higher; 96 per cent A-B at Advanced Higher. In 2019 (the last year when exams took place), 79 per cent A*/A at National 5; 68 per A*/A at Higher and 71 per cent A*/A at Advanced Higher.

Teaching and learning: Complicated. In the junior school, pupils from P5/7 often form a composite class, where they follow standard subjects with IT tabled throughout. Splendid triple classroom with interactive telly – iPads being introduced. Delicious old-fashioned desks – alas without the Bakelite inkwells. Tiny classes (as you might expect with annual intake of only 10). German and French from early. Latin mandatory S1/2 – and available at both Advanced Higher and SQA.

From P5-S6 school moves seamlessly through to Nat 5s to Highers and Advanced Highers. Highers are successfully crammed into three and a half hours a week rather than the usual five or so. Much smaller classes means the education is 'really personalised and pupils can't hide,' one parent told us. Impressive results across the board. School really too small to supply individual subject results. Maths (strong), English, Advanced Higher music and Higher English at S5. Currently Cambridge Pre-U for music in S6 – harmony, counterpoint, composition – with seven distinctions and three merits in 2020. One small gripe, however – 'Because school is so small, more unusual subjects like philosophy or photography are not available.'

The junior school is composed of choristers and instrumentalists, more of the former (both boys and girls – the latter introduced in 1976, though young instrumentalists since 1972). Choristers, both boys and girls, leave school at the end of S2, some may re-audition and return as instrumentalists.

Learning support and SEN: Arrangements in place for pupils who need extra support. Those with personal statements have one-to-one sessions, otherwise withdrawn from class and IEPs. Dyslexia and dysgraphia the main culprits. This said, the school is so intimate there is a 'good general understanding' among staff of how each child is faring and what support they need.

The arts and extracurricular: Small art room more or less adjacent to head's office, stuffed with tables and artwork on shelves. Both flat and 3D stuff on display.

All pupils, both junior and senior, spend roughly 50 per cent of their time doing some form of music, be it practice or individual lessons: we came across a variety pack. 'Coaching sessions with an accompanist gets them used to it,' says Dr Taylor and we found one young piano-accompanied flautist sharing her lesson not only with a splendid Steinway, but also with a somewhat overpowering organ.

Hideously complicated timetable, but sung evensong most evenings at 5.30pm for choristers in the cathedral and regular rehearsals either in Song School or cathedral itself (latter has 'soft' acoustics – 'ideal for singing but not practical for orchestral practice').

Music, of course, is what the school is all about, with all genres catered for from classical to jazz and traditional. Regular concerts at venues all over Edinburgh, with informal weekly concerts by pupils and staff in the former chapel. School itself has nowhere big enough for both orchestra and audience – former chapel too long and thin, dining room too low and cramped.

Any and every instrument played and taught mostly by a strong group of peripatetic and part-time teachers. 'We're really proud of our teaching staff – many of them are professional musicians themselves and we have no problem attracting the best,' says Dr Taylor. School handy for Haymarket (and Glasgow) – they try to arrange a full day's teaching for visiting (musical) peris; odd orchestral player, 12 full-time staff.

Director of music takes instrumentalists to concerts (28 last year) and usually manages to get reduced rate. Regular masterclasses from a whole range of international musicians, including an annual one by Nigel Murray – school sources suitable spaces for numbers (130 violinists and their teachers last time). The school can extend invitations to young musicians from around Scotland and frequently does.

Occasional foray into performing at the Edinburgh International Festival (sung services and concerts at St Mary's Cathedral). Regular large-scale concerts, plus pupils do their own thing, performing both a Schubert string quintet and 'a specially commissioned piece', along with jazz in Dumfries and Galloway. Friday evening concerts and strong input on the charity front.

Highly acclaimed and popular Saturday morning classes for up to a 150 youngsters aged 4-13. Kodály and Dalcroze techniques used, covering a whole range of musical areas and instruments from violin to clarsach and choral to theory. 'These classes are an enjoyable introduction to music,' says head.

'We're really proud of our teaching staff – many of them are professional musicians themselves and we have no problem attracting the best,' says head

If you really want to get a taste of what St Mary's is about, try their free Zoom Tunes every Friday afternoon. It's open to all P3 to P4s (Oh, we're coming over all Julie Andrews just at the thought of it!)

They have 'absolutely aced' online teaching, say parents. 'We had zoom lessons up and running before virtually anyone else. We're blessed with small classes and committed pupils who love their music,' explains the head.

Sport: Catch-all all-weather surface area (school rather grandly calls it a sports court) serves its purpose. No gym (so mandatory one hour PE per week must be achieved by other means). Boarders are members of Drumsheugh baths, a stout half-mile distant, and the school running club.

Boarding: Two floors of accommodation for boarders in Coates Hall; mainly twins with a few singles, all ensuite. Free time mostly spent practising.

'The pastoral care in the boarding houses is amazing – the houseparents really care,' said one parent. Another told us, 'During lockdown we were worried that they were being too strict with the kids preventing them from leaving the school except for exercise, but they were absolutely right.'

Ethos and heritage: Tucked away in an enchanting corner off Grosvenor Crescent some 300 metres from the cathedral, St Mary's was founded in 1880 as song (choir) school for the (Episcopal) Cathedral Church of St Mary the Virgin (funded by heiress sisters Barbara and Mary Walker and built to a design by George Gilbert Scott in 1879). Based in Old Coates Hall and the Song School, the latter still used for daily practice (magical Phoebe Traquair murals) within the cathedral precinct until 1995, St Mary's (name changed 1971) bought Coates Hall, which had closed in 1994. Neophyte Anglican priests had rather fallen off the radar; the 18th-century Old Coates Hall (part of the original bequest) is now the Edinburgh Theological Institute, providing accommodation, teaching and meeting rooms for both ordained and Anglican seminarians, albeit on a smaller scale.

One parent told us, 'We have travelled around the world and we have never encountered a school with such respect from the teachers towards the children'

Coates Hall, built in 'baronial' style by David Bryce in 1850, and bought by the Edinburgh Theological College in 1891, when Sydney Mitchell (better known for banks and psychiatric hospitals) added the splendid Gothic chapel to the right of the main door – now used for regular weekly concerts by pupils and staff and featuring a brand new Steinway Model D piano. Bryce also designed the gatehouse. Extensive-ish grounds (for the middle of Edinburgh) filled with trees, a greenhouse and raised beds for the eco club, badly parked cars (as ever in danger of small children with balls), and a couple of ugly modern teaching blocks. Plus the inevitable catch-all 'sports surface'.

Considering the expense of maintaining a highly complicated Victorian roof, the building is in remarkably good (if complex) heart, though we weep at the carving of rooms into offices. Head's study is in a former garage.

The main building is rabbit-warreny in the extreme, with staircases going off in random directions – five steps here sort of thing – leading to a hotchpotch of bedrooms (seminarians had great views), now almost all ensuite, twins and singles (school is let in hols to boost funds – which is why one of the practice rooms boasts a basin). Wiggly IKEA mirrors grouped in pairs throughout, and myriads of photographs – often with tinies overwhelmed by the size of their instrument.

Stop press! All this could be set to change, however. There are plans afoot to move the school into the old Royal High School building on Calton Hill. If this exciting development gets the go-ahead it will mean much more space including more practice rooms, bigger rehearsal spaces and a purpose-built concert hall. As Dr Taylor says, 'It will allow the school to play a much more visible and accessible part in the musical culture of Edinburgh and Scotland as a whole. The concert hall will allow us to invite the public into the school to experience both the wonderful talents of our children and our regular roster of visiting world class musicians. We will also be able to expand our community-based programmes exponentially.'

Pastoral care, inclusivity and discipline: All choristers are day pupils. No reported disciplinary hiccups; pupils are more likely to be found discussing some obscure German 15th-century composer than indulging in verbal point scoring. During our visit (break time) four really quite small people came out to the playground, one fell and was immediately surrounded (not sure about tears) by her own peer group and some elder children who were close by, who picked her up and escorted her back inside. Now that is what we like to see in a school.

One parent told us, 'We have travelled around the world and we have never encountered a school with such respect from the teachers towards the children. Naturally the children respond in kind. It's magical.' Wow, we say.

Pupils and parents: Pupils come from all over and a wide social background too. Musical talent is the common denominator. No obvious social grouping. Terrific parental support. Youngsters from abroad need local guardians.

Money matters: Oodles of bursaries but you need a UK passport to be eligible. Cathedral will cover 30 per cent of chorister fees. Scottish government contributes a chunk (aided places) and music school doles out bursaries – rigorously – with financial background of applicants tooth-combed.

Fair to say that no musical prodigy from any background would be left wanting. Dr Taylor says, 'Parents make an affordable contribution.'

The last word: From a small fishing town on the west coast of Scotland to practising every day on a Steinway – that's one pupil's story. It's a fantastic journey and if your child has a prodigious musical talent, you couldn't do much better than St Mary's. And if the school gets the go-ahead to move into bigger premises, the future for the school itself couldn't strike a better note!

St Mary's School (Melrose)

35

Abbey Park, High Street, Melrose TD6 9LN

01896 822517 | office@stmarysmelrose.org.uk | www.stmarysmelrose.org.uk

Ages: 2–13

Pupils: 159; Boarders: 43 flexi (from age 7)

Fees: Day £14,319 – £17,169; Boarding + £600 – £2,400 pa

Headmaster: Since 2010, Liam Harvey BEd (early 50s), himself a proud old boy of St Mary's. Following eight years working in the senior state sector on Merseyside and in North Yorkshire, he took the opportunity to move back to his roots in the Borders as housemaster at Belhaven School before returning to St Mary's as head. Having grown up in nearby Coldstream (father a local GP and mother a midwife) he progressed from being a day boy at St Mary's to full boarding at George Watson's followed by a degree in physical education and English at Liverpool John Moores. He has a clear understanding of and commitment to the local community, a very modern approach to boarding and a determination to maintain a strong academic curriculum and extracurricular programme. As a parent said, 'He's given us solidity and consistency.' This has helped the school to revive the previously flagging fortunes of the boarding houses, re-opening a previously closed house and at the same time ensuring that pupils are supported to move on to some of the best schools in Scotland and beyond. Married to Marnie who runs the website, works at the school in learning support and is also a houseparent. They have two daughters who also attended St Mary's before moving on to senior schools. Universal praise for the head from staff, parents and governors for the way he has moved the school forward. And he has ambitious plans for further improvements which were clearly underway during our visit. One member of staff commented, 'When I was growing up in Melrose there was no real link between the school and the town; that has all changed now, we really feel a central part of the community.'

Entrance: No entrance test. Pupils and parents are invited to tour school with head and then pupil will spend a day in school so that everyone is happy that it will be a good match. On the visit day pupils are tested to assess whether or not they have any additional needs. That being said a lot of pupils progress seamlessly into pre-prep and then prep from the school's kindergarten. Recruitment is mixed ability, very much from the Borders region, fair number of parents who are past pupils and others trying the independent sector for the first time. School is proud of its strong record of support for students with additional learning needs and is clear that potential barriers to learning such as dyslexia are there to be overcome. Head proudly asserts that the school has had a strong success rate with students of all different abilities. The scholarship boards are evidence of many students who arrived 'just coping' but who have been nurtured to success. All teaching takes place on the ground floor so wheelchair access would not be a problem, although it might be in the boys' boarding house. School runs morning buses from outlying areas but evening transport is parents' responsibility.

Exit: Historically pupils have moved on to one of the Scottish senior schools which follow the GCSE and A level pathways (Fettes, Merchiston and Glenalmond). In recent years school has also sent pupils on to Loretto, Oundle, Ampleforth, Strathallan, Eton, Sedbergh, Kilgraston and St George's School for Girls. The reinstatement of the Borders railway line means that the Edinburgh day schools are now easily accessed. Ten scholarships in 2021.

Our view: Strong traditional curriculum emphasises preparation for Common Entrance. French and Spanish from pre-prep onwards, classics in pre-prep becomes ancient Greek from form 7 and Latin from form 4. Sciences taught by specialists from form 3 onwards in a well-equipped lab. School has recently started teaching environmental science to all middle and senior school pupils via a combination of classroom study of environmental issues with a practical approach to conserving the local environment. Has won a number of awards for this and leads the community in projects such as planning a mile of oaks to commemorate the end of World War I. Proudly single use plastic free and has championed this work in other schools across Europe. On the day we visited an ITV film crew was looking at school's lead work on plastic-free Melrose and River Clean Initiatives. Staff say that projects such as this help to broaden the horizons of pupils beyond the parochialism of the Borders, prepare them for senior school and teach them to be 'thoroughly decent citizens, contributing to the world around them in a school that is at the heart of its community'.

Two-thirds board between one and five nights a week. Pupils say it 'helps us get ready for senior school without having to feel we are away from mum and dad for too long'

Music and drama came in for the highest praise. With two staff working from kindergarten and up through the school over two-thirds of pupils learn at least one instrument – bagpipes definitely on offer, as you would expect. Two school shows a year make sure that every child has the chance to perform – a parent commented, 'What they do so well is confidence, there's not a child who doesn't get up on that stage and do their thing.' There are junior and senior choirs open to all and incredibly for a school of 150 there is a 25-strong orchestra. In 2019 six pupils took part in the Scottish National Youth Choir. Several music and drama senior school scholarships in recent years. Art is also well catered for with specialist facilities and obvious high standards evidenced by being four-time winners of the Edinburgh Fringe poster competition.

Sport, especially rugby, features large. Situated immediately next to Melrose RFC ground, the school benefits from use of their Astro and one member of staff is a semi-professional rugby player. On the day we visited the whole school enthusiastically turned out to watch the visiting Scotland rugby team training in biting cold February winds. One of the few complaints we heard was from girls who wanted more opportunities to play rugby and other more traditionally male sports. Hockey is flourishing and one of the girls has played cricket for Scotland.

School takes academic success seriously. Unusually (and possibly unpopularly) there's no May half term, this is to allow for a strong focus on Common Entrance up to exam time. Once exams are out of the way it leaves time to take advantage of the better weather and the whole school is involved in activities including camping trips and outdoor pursuits.

Pupils have sessions from a qualified counselling psychologist to help them manage the pressure of exams. Support from the excellent learning support department is designed to be unobtrusive and available to as many pupils as need it. Department is proud of its record with students who 'arrived with little self-belief and then flew at senior school getting A*s at A level'. Individual support is available in the middle school but there is then a strong emphasis on reintegration back into mainstream classes. Head is clear that academic prowess should not define success and the presence of a national dyslexia champion on the staff underlines this. Parents also praised the Accelerated Reader programme for the encouragement it gives to pupils (especially boys) to improve their reading. There is good access to IT including iPads.

There are two kindergarten classes (Kindi) of twelve, split by age. Scottish Curriculum for Excellence is followed combined with some aspects of Montessori. Excellent outdoor space. Pre-prep (again two classes of twelve) is currently the poor relation in terms of accommodation, however on our visit we saw the nearly completed new pre-prep which was due to open by Easter 2020. There are strong links between Kindi, pre-prep and the main school which ensure that nearly all pupils who start at age 2 move through the school seamlessly.

Buildings are light, airy, mostly purpose-built in the last twenty years with specialist art, music, drama and science spaces as well as a small library. There are good playing fields and tennis courts but no sports hall (as yet, the head has exciting plans to work with the community on an indoor sports facility) or specialist design technology space.

The atmosphere is purposeful but happy and relatively laid back. Children here look happy and relaxed but have a sense of purpose. The pupils say the staff are 'genuinely nice to hang around with' and 'I can speak to anyone about anything'. They were also keen to emphasise the friendships between pupils in different years, no age-related cliques here. They were adamant that they saw no real bullying and that most issues were dealt with through a 'conversation'. Parents like the use of circle time to help pupils learn how to treat different people and to manage conflict situations. This echoed the comments of staff who seem to be keen to involve pupils in decision making. A parent commented on the power of 'mum, child and teacher sitting down together to sort things out when there are problems'. Pupils appreciated the range of activities and trips open to them (dodgeball, gadget club, debating society, art trips to Edinburgh, history to Bannockburn and Edinburgh Castle) and the commitment of staff to sports, drama and music. They said, 'Learning here is fun.' Parents like the frequent communication from school and value the invitation into assemblies to hear visiting speakers, including senior school heads.

Boarding: Boarding is genuinely very flexible indeed. Head believes that parents need the option to arrange for their children to board as and when rather than be straitjacketed. Parents approve: 'They allow you to play around with boarding which is really helpful.' No full boarding, it's essentially weekly with just the occasional Saturday night (eg for the termly black tie dinner dance). About two-thirds of pupils board between one and five nights a week. Pupils agreed that 'this helps us get ready for senior school without having to feel we are away from mum and dad for too long'. As a result the pupils say there are no real issues of homesickness and 'pretty much everyone tries it at some point'. Boarding facilities are comfortable, the girls' house is in new accommodation while the boys share School House with the head and his family. Rooms are for between three and six pupils and both houses are warm and homely with good social spaces. There are lots of activities and the pupils are regularly consulted on the food offer. Boarding staff are knowledgeable and forward thinking with an infectious enthusiasm for their work that should reassure even the most anxious of parents.

The last word: St Mary's ticks a lot of boxes: sensibly managed academic challenge, committed staff prepared to go the extra mile, lots of accessible extracurricular activities (and they don't cost the earth here either), lovely, warm and very flexible boarding and opportunities to broaden young minds well beyond the Borders.

St Peter's 8-13

36

Queen Anne's Road, York, North Yorkshire YO30 7WA

01904 527416 | enquiries8-13@stpetersyork.org.uk | www.stpetersyork.org.uk/st_peters_8_13

Ages: 8-13

Pupils: 403 (30 choristers); Boarders: 7 full, 7 flexi (from age 11)

Fees: Day £13,380 – £16,260; Boarding £24,540 – £29,400 pa

Linked school: St Peter's School, York, 1261

Master: Since 2005, Andy Falconer MBA BA (late 40s). Read education and professional studies at University of Lancaster, MBA at University of Leicester. Previously head of geography and outdoor education at Terrington Hall Prep; same plus IT at Craigclowan Prep; deputy head at Chafyn Grove Prep – always also teaching sport. Covers lessons here. Has been chair of Independent Association of Prep Schools (IAPS) and on boards of Independent Schools Council and Independent Schools Inspectorate. Co-opted member of University of York St John's People Committee.

Wife is school nurse; three daughters, all at St Peter's. Interests: running marathons and ultra marathons – aiming to run all the Olympic city marathons – and photography (films matches with drone to provide analysis material).

Very pleasant and approachable, financially savvy, believes in paying attention to small as well as big details (sharp eye for litter and stray items of uniform), very happy in his job. Parents say: 'He has a reassuring strength… a quiet and self-assured leader who knows the children very well – he sits with them at lunchtime to have a chat and makes a point of congratulating any child whose work is displayed on the merit table.' 'Very visible: his door is always open (literally), for children and parents, unless he's in a meeting.'

'Fair, committed, hard-working and hands on... definitely there to support the children.'

Entrance: All St Peter's 2-8 pupils move up; also up to six year 4 places, 10 year 6, 20 year 7. Family tour with head plus assessment day: computer-based maths, mental maths, reading, spelling and reasoning plus creative writing and team challenges – designed to show how children think rather than what they have covered; average or above ability expected.

Exit: Almost all to St Peter's 13-18, with a clutch of music and academic scholarships, and just the odd pupil going to eg Eton, Sedbergh, Oundle, Queen Margaret's.

Our view: Situated in 47 acres beside the River Ouse, in the heart of York. Founded 1876; in 1901 became St Peter's prep; went co-ed 1987. Housed in what was previously a larger school, so the very well-resourced classrooms are plentiful and generously proportioned. Attractively furnished, extensive library.

Saturday morning school, but 'You soon get used to it, and it gives you time to do your own things' (parent). No Sats nor Common Entrance tests, which is a great liberation. Almost all progress to St Peter's: they do take the entrance exam, but only to supply information about where they are academically, so no pressure. First two years have mix of topic-based and separate subject-based learning (specialist teachers for the latter), then specialist subjects approach takes over. Teachers ('very skilled... very committed, supportive and invested in the children... thorough marking' – parents) follow children's curiosity; children see lessons as fun as well as educational – 'Inspirational!' enthused one, aged 10.

Years 4-6 have French, German and Spanish, with focus on speaking confidently and learning about culture, continuing with two in years 7-8, along with separate sciences. Classics added in year 6, Latin from year 7 – lively, engaging approaches. Philosophy for years 4-5 encourages challenging thought. Setting only in maths, from year 4. Sensible amounts of homework and valued session on how to help children revise for parents. Average of 20 per class in years 4-5, 22 in years 7-8. Three-fifths female teachers to two-fifths male; good mix of long-standing and new staff.

Quantities of computers and all sorts of allied clubs, but children also develop practical life skills such as cookery, bushcraft and first aid in ongoing, off-timetable life skills programme. Opportunities for gifted and talented, eg national competitions, masterclasses.

Takes growth mindset theory very seriously – children are encouraged to see trying hard, learning from mistakes and taking risks as more valuable than coming top, to develop an 'I can't do it yet' attitude. Also focuses on eight learning habits – collaboration, creativity, curiosity, embracing challenge, empathy, flexible thinking, initiative, perseverance – taught through all subjects.

Parents told us that teachers are 'very skilled... very committed, supportive and invested in the children... thorough marking' and that they follow children's curiosity

Well qualified and resourced learning support department – small group or individual support (no extra charge), works with class and subject teachers plus parents. Has had children with mild/moderate learning difficulties, autistic spectrum, ADHD – 'children who can manage being part of a predominantly above-average cohort'. Some of the site would be hard to access for children with severe physical difficulties, but the school would try to accommodate where feasible.

Sport across the ability range is colossal – 1,000 fixtures played one year; much success at regional and national levels; shortlisted for independent school of the year sports award. Very inclusive approach, despite being one of the top preps for sport in the country: happy to play less strong children in the A team against a much smaller school, whole-year tours to south west England, Italy (rugby), Barcelona (netball). All the trad sports, plus rowing. Employs eight recent sports graduates to coach while trying out teaching as a career.

Music also huge – nearly three-quarters learn an instrument; wide range of musical ensembles, including rock and jazz bands, guitar group, choirs, with plenty of performances; years 4 and 5 have three class lessons of music a week, including a chance to learn a variety of instruments. York Minster choristers are now educated at St Peter's 8-13.

Impressive art, especially the ceramic work – we particularly liked the display of ceramic poppies made by all in the school; well-presented paintings in glass frames throughout. Much drama – unusually, children handle the technical aspects of their Shakespeare Schools Festival entry as well as acting – and speech and drama clubs.

Over 50 clubs, such as ornithology and Mandarin; charity committee; school council; several children help run the library ('The librarian is fantastic – will get any books needed,' praised a parent). Year 8s do a high-powered enterprise project and organise a gala evening in their last term – all have a position of responsibility. Things ecological taken very seriously: food grown for use in school meals; flowers, bushes and trees planted; worked with local willow artist to create a willow tunnel and woven deer statues; library garden made into a biodiverse haven with bird and insect boxes, storytelling chair and reading circle made of 12 solid oak cubes. 'They have lots of fun outside the curriculum,' said a parent, citing the It's a Knockout competition day as a highlight of the school year.

All staff have a mentor group of 10-12 children of mixed years, staying with them as they move through the school (siblings join too), so they get to know them very well. Support from whole school chaplain, own lay chaplain and senior school pupils, and access to private counsellor arranged if needed. Vertical houses appreciated by parents – 'It feels like a boarding school for day children... the older ones mentor the younger ones, who mentor the ones younger than them.' 'The pastoral care routes are very clear... teachers are always immediately available if there's a problem... everything is taken seriously even if it's a small matter.'

Children eat lunch in house groups with house staff – good choice of food, hot, cold and veggie, with themed days, eg street food, different national dishes. Citizenship programme and much focus on key values of friendship, trust, wisdom, compassion, endurance, humility and hope. However, one parent we spoke to saw the school as having a 'robust culture', so less suitable for the more sensitive child.

Children very engaged in all the classes we saw; the ones we talked to were happy, secure, very busy and enthusiastic about the school. Most from York or outlying primaries, covering a very large area as far as Harrogate, Thirsk, Malton, Bramham, Selby, Stamford Bridge, Doncaster. Mostly professional and business parents, mainly white British plus some ethnic minority and several Europeans. They value the seamless, well-prepared transitions through the three schools and the common campus.

Boarding: Junior boarding house for years 7-8, full boarding from year 7, weekly or part-time. We were struck by the homely atmosphere: the common room is more like a living room, with comfy sofas and armchairs, flowers, fruit bowl and tasteful pictures. Well-equipped games room and pleasantly furnished dorms.

Money matters: Means-tested bursaries of up to full fees from year 7. York Minster chorister fees are same as regular tuition fees with a subsidy of 60 per cent from York Minster (with additional means-tested funding available).

The last word: A school that approaches education – in the widest sense – in a very thoughtful and enlightened way.

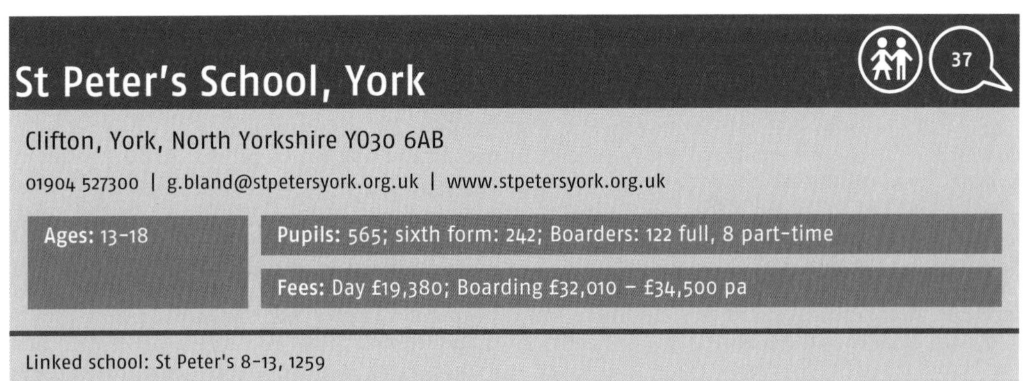

St Peter's School, York

37

Clifton, York, North Yorkshire YO30 6AB

01904 527300 | g.bland@stpetersyork.org.uk | www.stpetersyork.org.uk

Ages: 13-18

Pupils: 565; sixth form: 242; Boarders: 122 full, 8 part-time

Fees: Day £19,380; Boarding £32,010 – £34,500 pa

Linked school: St Peter's 8-13, 1259

Head Master: Since 2019, Jeremy Walker MA, previously head of King's School Rochester. MA (Oxon) (40s). Educated at Sherborne School and read theology at Oxford before taking an MA in educational leadership and management at the Institute of Education, University of London. Started his career at Bishop Stopford School, a state secondary in Kettering, and became head of department after a year. Then moved to Ardingly, where he was head of religious studies and of theory of knowledge, and housemaster, before becoming head of sixth form and senior manager at Berkhamsted School, Hertfordshire. He is married to Harriet, and their two children have joined the school.

Entrance: Automatic entry from St Peter's 2-8 to St Peter's 8-13 (St Peter's junior school) and then from St Peter's 8-13 to St Peter's 13-18. Seventy per cent follow this route, rest by CE and school's own entrance test at any age including 13 or 16 (minimum six GCSE grade 6 passes). Assessment and filtering does take place in prep and pre-prep to weed out those who won't cope with the demands of St Peter's, but it is rare. Generally entry to St Peter's 8-13 requires a child to have a reading age at least a year ahead of chronological age (sympathetic to siblings). Will take pupils who pass exam at any time provided a place is available. Other main feeder schools: Terrington Hall, Cundall Manor and Aysgarth, some state schools also.

Exit: Around 10-15 per cent leave at the end of year 11. At uni, subjects range from economics and fine art to engineering and broadcast journalism. Five to Oxbridge in 2021 (though UCL and Imperial often favoured by high flyers). St Andrews and Exeter both popular. Many take gap years. Five medics in 2021.

Latest results: In 2021, 75 per cent 7-9 at I/GCSE; 71 per cent A*/A at A level/Pre-U (91 per cent A*-B). In 2019 (the last year when exams took place), 69 per cent 9-7 at I/GCSE. At A level/Pre-U, 59 per cent A*/A (85 per cent A*-B).

Teaching and learning: Consistent achiever, sets the bar high in a robust local market. Strong work ethos with plenty of stretch and challenge; normal to try hard but fine-tuning from the top is pushing to 'broaden the pupil experience', ie accumulation of exam certificates is great but balance is also important.

Takes the academic rigour for granted; bright pupils will always do well, but hard workers also do well here, hence the very positive value-added. Believes good results are down to having really good teachers as well as selective but not highly selective intake; no weak subject areas; staff know what is expected and are multitalented and self-driven. Learn Something New is a St Peter's initiative that persuades staff to share interests and learn from each other with a range of activities across the school(s) encouraging staff to try out and learn new skills – 'learning teachers teach better' is the strapline.

Class size averages 18 in the middle school (maximum 24) and 12 in the sixth form. The occasional D or E grade creeps in at GCSE. IGCSEs in maths, science and languages.

Gifted and talented programme in place but doesn't target top 10 per cent. 'All the children here are bright; it would be wrong to concentrate on a handful.' Olympiads and similar challenges stretch those with real talent. Global Perspectives an additional course for sixth form with Horizons introduced for middle school. Does not allow students to take any GCSE early and moving towards more challenging IGCSEs.

St Peter's was founded in 627 AD by Paulinus, first Archbishop of York, and is one of the world's oldest schools; 'only two older,' we are told

Careers advice and support flagged up by parents as something to be worked on and improved, especially important for boarders whose parents are not around to have those all-important conversations. They are getting pupils into good and great universities, but what next? Both pupils and parents feel they would like more guidance and direction as life beyond university becomes tougher and more competitive. The school has responded swiftly by bringing in a second careers adviser and opening up careers events, visits, conferences plus 'exploration week' for the lower sixth – 'life after St Peter's' is a drum they will keep on banging.

Learning support and SEN: Some support for the handful with mild dyslexia – must be bright and able to cope. Part-time dyslexia specialist. Approximately 10 per cent have an ed psych report; five per cent qualify for extra time in exams. Third modern language replaced by extra English and study skills for some.

The arts and extracurricular: Very good art facilities, including super gallery. Art department appears in the Guinness Book of Records for a remarkable 100 per cent A*/A grade pass rate achieved four years running, though recent years have seen lower grades creep in – 'We were pleased, it took the pressure off, allowed the pupils to experiment, be more creative rather than formulaic,' said one art master. Many learn a musical instrument or two, 300 individual lessons each week with professional specialist music staff, 160-strong choir and plenty of opportunities to perform; director of music described as 'inspirational'. Each boarding house has a practice room with piano. The school became the choir school for York Minster in September 2020. Over 100 pupils involved with Community Action projects and all participate in charity fundraising.

DofE and CCF flourishing. Plenty of trips including expeditions to Morocco, sports tours

St Peter's 8–13

to New Zealand and South Africa, language holidays and music tours to the USA, Prague, Italy.

Sport: A surprising amount of outdoor space; you'd never guess it is so close to the city. Nearest to the school is the hallowed ground of the first XV rugby pitch, but there are plenty of others beyond. Sport is compulsory for all. Facilities include two sports centres, one with super climbing wall, multi-surface pitch, fitness centre, indoor swimming pool, extensive well-kept playing fields, boathouse and tennis and squash courts. Rugby popular and strong, rowing crews regularly pick up national honours and awards, boast 20 international rowers in the last eight years. Hockey, rowing and netball are the most popular girls' sports but tennis, athletics, squash, swimming and usual suspects on offer for all. Generally put best coaches with best teams but playing opportunities for all via B teams and house competitions. Competitiveness and fair play are a prominent feature of the school and success is universally applauded at weekly assembly.

Boarding: Around a quarter of pupils board, of whom 30 per cent are from overseas. Most are full boarders but a few stay on a flexi/weekly basis. Six day and four boarding houses, the latter well equipped with a selection of common rooms, games rooms and a kitchen for snacks (all eat in school dining hall). Pupils and staff strike a good balance between amity and mutual respect. Houses are headed by husband and wife teams and supported by resident and non-resident assistants. Good pastoral care, 'just wonderful,' say parents. They describe houseparents as 'something out of the ordinary', creating boarding houses that are 'home from home' with all the care and support that may be needed and equally 'a kick up the jacksy as required'. Staff vigilant – invariably have one or two they're watching for eating problems etc.

Ethos and heritage: The school was founded in 627 AD by Paulinus, first Archbishop of York, and is one of the world's oldest schools; 'only two older,' we are told. In 1844 it was established on its present, impressive, green, Grade II listed site in Clifton, with 47 acres, river access and all within walking distance of York Minster, the city centre and station.

Beyond the imposing main building, others are a mix of ancient and modern. Some classrooms and corridors are a bit tatty round the edges; we get the sense that it's not a priority – it's a workhorse, not a show pony. Good range of facilities, with all angles covered, though pupils tell us they are pestering the head for a new sports hall; 'It could be so much better.' It's one of the head boy's pet projects, though not on the agenda (yet) – might have to settle for a new boathouse instead. Pupils rave about the new swimming pool, opened by Olympic diver Tom Daley. Other recent additions include four bright biology labs, a sixth form microbiology lab, chemistry lab and design and technology room with CadCam technology; new maths and languages building under construction. Three computer rooms are complemented by clusters of computers throughout the school and houses – virtual learning environment with Wifi throughout the campus.

Six day and four boarding houses, the latter well equipped with a selection of common rooms, games rooms and a kitchen for snacks (all eat in school dining hall)

Old Peterites include Guy Fawkes, Alcuin (eighth-century scholar), Greg Wise, John Barry, Laurence Eusden (poet laureate), Harry Gration (journalist, TV presenter), C Northcote Parkinson (inventor of Parkinson's Law) and Clare Wise (previous director of the British Film Commission).

Pastoral care, inclusivity and discipline: Advice, help and support may be sought from tutors, house staff, resident health centre staff or the school chaplain. Pupils tell us that the unforgivables are drugs and bullying; if caught smoking it's three strikes and you're out.

Pupils are allowed to visit town twice a week (more in older years) and for younger ones a timetable of supervised events is on offer. All eat in the modern dining hall. Menus offer a wide choice with mixture of typical school meal fare, continental options, salad bar, sandwiches, fruit and healthy eating options. Pupils say food is 'great', with 'boy-sized portions'; Sunday brunch is legendary.

Pupil voice has grown and developed through a pupil symposium. Head's question time is chaired by the head boy or girl – 'direct-government-type stuff' – raising all kinds of ideas and questions from the downright silly to the well-considered and serious.

Middle school uniform uninspiring, disliked, yet (bizarrely) defended, by pupils – when push comes to shove there's nothing more conservative or radically opposed to change than your average 15-year-old: brown blazer, grey trousers for boys, and brown checked skirt for girls. Apparently the current line is 'brown is good'. Sixth form (boys and girls) wear dark business suits.

Strong Christian ethos; pupils meet thrice weekly for collective act of worship in school chapel – the chaplain has 'livened things up a bit,' pupils tell us with a grin; assemblies at other times.

Pupils and parents: Day pupils mainly from North Yorkshire, Harrogate, Leeds conurbation, York, and surrounding villages. Majority of boarders live within an hour's drive but others from wide area in the UK. Parents in business and the professions, a popular choice for Forces families, minority from overseas – 'it's a world view we need to develop'. Mix of Hong Kong, China, Russia, one or two others – about 25 per cent overall.

'Parents,' says school, 'are interested – but not helicopters'; ambitious and driven; quite a few first-time buyers here but also dynasties with names all over the honours boards.

Money matters: Not a rich school but has increased bursary funding considerably over the past few years. Means-tested bursaries available at 11, 13 and at sixth form regardless of previous school. Qualification criteria for bursaries on a sliding scale from 10 to 100 per cent based on need, and typically if household income is less than £45,000. Honorary (ie no dosh) subject scholarships are awarded; music awards, including fee remission, available for tuition and instruments.

The last word: Very much the big brother of the 2-18 triumvirate of St Peter's schools, encompassing St Peter's 2-8 and St Peter's 8-13 ('continuity, but difference' is the mantra here) and you get the impression that this is where it all becomes rather serious. If it were a car, we'd probably describe it as a Volvo, albeit a top of the range high performance 4WD version with sporty extras such as a ski rack and maybe a tow bar. It can accommodate the whole family and you can't doubt the quality, reliability and solidity of the product it delivers, pretty much unfailingly, in all areas.

Sedbergh School

Malim Lodge, Sedbergh, Cumbria LA10 5HG

01539 620535 | enquiries@sedberghschool.org | www.sedberghschool.org

Ages: 13–18

Pupils: 569; sixth form: 249; Boarders: 559 full

Fees: Day £26,443 – £26,559; Boarding £35,898 – £36,075 pa

Linked school: Casterton, Sedbergh Preparatory School, 1168

Head master: Since 2018, Dan Harrison, who has been here for 25 years and was previously second master. He read natural sciences at Cambridge, where he also completed his PGCE.

Previous head Andrew Fleck is now principal, in overall charge of the senior and prep schools.

Entrance: The school is modestly selective. Most admissions via Common Entrance or school's own exam but the bar is not set too high, so the intake tends to be a broad mix. Admissions policies are changing so see the school website for the latest details. Pupils joining at a later stage in the school take maths and English exams. Sixth form entry depends on GCSE results.

Exit: Around 15 per cent leave after GCSEs. A third to Russell Group universities with the odd trickle to Oxbridge (though none in 2021), some applying post-A levels. It's fair to say there is latitude here for improvement, which may well come via initiatives like the 9 Star programme. A real blend and variety of destinations and subjects; the more traditional like art history, law, chemistry, classics and maths sit alongside the professional vocational ones such as engineering and medicine (two medics in 2021). There is also a sprawl of more modern courses: sport science, international business management, fashion design, broadcast journalism. Northumbria, Durham, Newcastle, Loughborough and Oxford Brookes all popular.

Latest results: In 2021, 59 per cent 9-7 at GCSE; 50 per cent A*/A at A level (72 per cent A*-B). In 2019 (the last year when exams took place), 40 per cent 9-7 at GCSE; 22 per cent A*/A (44 per cent A*-B).

Teaching and learning: School cites geology as a strength (the geology classroom, crammed with a huge collection of rocks, with desks sloping upwards like a university lecture room, is incredible). Maths results are also particularly good.

School responds to its broad intake by setting pupils from year 9 by ability. A tutor monitors progress, liaising with subject teachers. Added value is measured for every level of ability (though those stats weren't available to us). There is a broad curriculum; year 9 take up French, and German or Spanish is on offer (though very few take languages at A level). More offbeat options are available at GCSE, like jewellery design. There are alternative options in sixth form beyond A level – a BTEC in agriculture in conjunction with Newton Rigg College in Penrith.

A 2017 inspection report states 'assured and inspiring teachers with high expectations and expertise in their subject successfully encourage most pupils... to achieve their potential and fulfil their ambitions'. Where pupils would benefit from extra lessons, they are arranged. Everything is on tap, this being a full boarding community.

ICT used for eg organising notes or recording class discussions. There are also what are described as 'pioneering academic opportunities', like the 100-hour revision challenge for years 11, 12 and 13 over the Easter holidays (as in, 21 days' hol, five hours a day etc).

Results are good overall (bearing in mind the very broad spread of intake) and on the up for the last few years. Particular strengths are English, English literature, maths, biology, chemistry, physics and geography.

Learning support and SEN: Some 120 pupils have learning difficulties; most of the extra support is around dyslexia or dyspraxia and is often one-to-one. Learning support works across both ends of the spectrum, though, including the 9 Star programme for year 9s, aiming to develop their logical and critical thinking. One parent, whose son was on the programme, felt he was flying academically. Another parent felt the academic side of things was generally 'on the rise'.

The arts and extracurricular: Sedbergh has a national reputation for sports prowess but this is only part of the story (the old perception that this is a school for rugby players is past its sell by date). Frankly, it was a joy hearing the rugby-playing sixth former, who had set his sights on Cambridge, wax lyrical about the music department and refer with awe and respect to a recent school production of A Christmas Carol as 'very professional – dead arty and stuff'.

Performing is dominant, with high numbers taking LAMDA. School plays attract great interest; a recent production of Les Misérables had a cast of 78 and inspired pupils to debate the concept of redemption – whilst in Cabaret, the moral dilemmas and the lack of courage were chewed over. Pupils spoke to us casually about regular debating competitions, about having to prepare a topic quickly and thinking on their feet. They didn't seem fazed.

Founded 1525 by Roger Lupton, a provost of Eton, the school nestles amidst the fells in the beautiful old town of Sedbergh. It has a huge campus

Musical opportunities run the spectrum: choral, orchestra, swing band (a big jazz and swing night had the pupils entertaining 150 guests). Everyone participates at some level; there is a house singing competition, for example. Professional musicians give concerts but there are also scholars' concerts and small informal musical soirées. The choristers get to sing in vast spaces like Durham Cathedral and recently went on tour around Italy. One pupil made it into the national youth choir. It's all on tap, again; you can pitch up at the music school before or after lessons and have a practice.

Unless they have the head's permission, all join the school contingent of the CCF where they can experience scuba diving, gliding, piloting. However, the pupils we spoke to had done voluntary work instead – helping in local schools – and seemed to have got a great deal of satisfaction out of it. Pupils are also prepared for the finer things in life: events to practice etiquette, confidence-builders for social settings (balls). This is all reinforced by the fact that staff and pupils have three civilised meals a day together in each house.

Loads of trips, some to incredibly exotic climes, such as an ecology trip to Madagascar. Some fantastic clubs for those with big academic appetites (there is also an inter-house academic challenge): Polyglots (languages), the Invisible society (science), classics soc, Rogers society (economics).

Sport: Each house fields teams for the inter-house competitions and the school itself continues to have a reputation for excellence. Pupils clearly love the Saturday sports matches where the whole school turns out to support. A vast array of activities: lacrosse, athletics, horse riding (Sedbergh has an equestrian team), but also orienteering, fishing, kayaking, mountain biking, fell running, badminton, sailing, shooting, squash, tennis. The facilities match all this and have just got a whole lot better with a new sports centre. Expert sports coaching is also available, often with video analysis. Staff are aware of the relationship between sport and good mental and physical health and note the increase in requests for early morning coaching around exam times. Parents enthused about the freedom Sedbergh offers; that (subject to H&S) children get to experience activities like river bathing, mud sliding and wild camping (usually off menu in a lot of red-tape schools). The expression 'it toughens them up' was used a lot by parents. (Here, a note of caution; the school's 'joining in' ethos might mean those more apprehensive by nature may not be so well suited.)

The pupils we spoke to effervesced about the school's 125-year-old Wilson run (a 10-mile cross-country fell race for 16+ pupils, described by the Guardian newspaper as 'hell in the fells'), about the camaraderie it engendered, the 'supporting each other through' it, the rapturous applause at the finishing line. It's all very reminiscent of the Brownlee brothers' spirit, because this is a run which requires grit and a can-do attitude which pretty much sums up what Sedbergh is all about. Its multiplicity of extracurricular activities nurture resilience and teamwork (qualities which most of the working world is crying out for right now).

Boarding: There are nine houses (six boys, three girls), each with its own style and character to foster a sense of belonging: its own library, common rooms, computer suite, dining room. Each with a houseparent, resident matrons and associated house tutors. We visited the newest girls' house, a delightful building, all white-washed stone walls, individual rooms with bow windows and fireplaces (each room for year 10s upwards has a desk – year 9s do prep together, supervised by prefects). The house communal rooms have lovely furniture (piano, chandeliers), a super dining area, veranda, bright cushions and clean kitchen areas. A big TV is tuned into the news to top up their current affairs knowledge.

Around five to a room in the lower years, two or three higher up, with sixth formers on their own. Room mates change every term, and the houseparent uses their good judgement to make the final decision (with the best will in the world, problems bubble up and, as one pupil muttered, term times can feel intense). One of the housemistresses we met was a tour de force of warmth and intellect; she knew who would be sitting next to whom at lunch, what vegetables they liked and where each of them were at any time. She exuded quiet competence, iron grasp of detail and seemed to possess mountains of energy.

Houseparents feed any worries – eg homesickness – back to parents. One mother spoke of visiting her sons' boarding house for the first time, seeing a row of black wellies outside the door and being struck by how homely it all was. Discipline, she felt, was good, as the boys respected the housemaster.

Pupils are allowed to use their phones outside lesson and prep times but not at night.

Ethos and heritage: Founded 1525 by Roger Lupton, a provost of Eton, the school nestles amidst the fells in the beautiful old town of Sedbergh. It has a huge campus with gorgeous old stone buildings. Lots of fresh air inhaled whilst walking from building to building. The school corridors, lined with traditional photos, have an old world charm about them. Nothing too edgy – the biology lab had geraniums on all the windowsills when we visited. Great exhibition space for art, nice DT workshops, decent labs and IT equipment. The library is out on its own in a beautiful old building. New sports hall built into the hill overlooking the playing fields with an arched sedum roof. Views of hills to make the heart sing.

We visited the newest girls' house, a delightful building, all white-washed stone walls, rooms with bow windows and fireplaces

Girls joined in 2001 and now make up around 40 per cent of students. Sedbergh merged with Casterton School in 2013. The Sedbergh juniors moved to the merged junior school on the Casterton site (known as Casterton, Sedbergh Preparatory School), whilst the Casterton seniors moved to the merged senior school, named Sedbergh School, on this site.

Pastoral care, inclusivity and discipline: School regularly seeks pupils' views in discussion groups, runs anonymous surveys and takes safeguarding extremely seriously. Any hint of bullying is tackled immediately. The school is open to all faiths and has Sunday services. The chaplain is an extra layer in the pastoral system. There is a health centre with a doctor, nurses and physio.

Older pupils are allowed to wander into town. The pupils have many socials on campus, though: Caribbean evenings, fancy dress parties, sketch shows. Minor disciplinary issues (being late for lessons) mean you will get endorsements, and too many of those means you may not attend socials. One parent, whose son had been sent home due to a teenage misdemeanour, praised the calm way with which it had been dealt and said how easy it had been to reintegrate on his return.

Pupils and parents: In addition to Sedbergh's prep school, Casterton, pupils come from prep schools usually within a three-hour radius: Scotland, Newcastle, York, Lancashire and Derbyshire. The net has started to be cast out wider, pulling in some pupils from the home counties. Around 60 per cent boys, and 20 per cent from overseas (there is specific information for Chinese students on the admissions page of the website).

Parents are described as enthusiastic, keen to work with the school to solve any problems. There are parent invites to garden parties and dinners and everyone congregates for tea in the local hostelry, The Dalesman, after sports matches.

Parents praised the excellent communication (although one expressed disappointment that a week-long trip to Cambridge had been called off without explanation and not rearranged). Generally, though, it was felt updates were frequent and staff very accessible.

Money matters: A number of scholarships available across academic, music, art, DT, drama, sport or even for being an all-rounder. There are also means-tested bursaries.

The last word: The caring enfold of this beautiful school gives young adults an opportunity to find their passions, draw on inner resources and reach their academic and personal potential. If you want your child to have an outdoorsy experience and be imbued with the robust spirit of a self-starter, this is the place. Couch potatoes or teenagers with a partiality for clubbing probably shouldn't apply.

Stewart's Melville College

39

Queensferry Road, Edinburgh EH4 3EZ

0131 311 1000 | admissions@esms.org.uk | www.esms.org.uk

Ages: 12–18

Pupils: 785; sixth form: 252 (co-ed sixth form with The Mary Erskine School); Boarders: 30 full

Fees: Day £13,038; Boarding £25,509 – £26,163 pa

Linked school: The Mary Erskine School, 1212

Head: Since September 2021, Anthony Simpson, previously at Giggleswick school, first as a teacher in his early career then – after a period of teaching in a range of inner-city academies – as deputy head and with responsibility for child protection, safeguarding and welfare issues. He joked about returning to the school where he first started his career: 'I've done everything you shouldn't do, but always done what has felt right.' That includes moving to Scotland, with the support of his wife, a proper Yorkshire girl 'who only wanted to move north'. He has two daughters, both of whom attend the ESMS family of schools, and a black labrador named Tessa. 'A perfect move for his family,' he says. A keen triathlete, he has represented Great Britain in both European and world championships.

Principal: since August 2018, Linda Moule. Previously vice-principal of ESMS since 2016 and head of The Mary Erskine School since 2009. She runs the twin senior schools (Stewart's Melville College and The Mary Erskine School) with two heads and the head of the co-ed junior school, spending part of the week in each school (separate campuses) with offices in both. Degree in theology from Manchester and has held teaching positions in Bristol, Stockport and Manchester. Has also been deputy head of Holy Trinity College, Bromley, before becoming vice principal of New Hall School, Chelmsford in 2004. Married with two sons, both of whom have attended Stewart's Melville College.

Entrance: At age 11, 12, 13, fifth year and sixth form. Selective but automatic entrance from junior school. Children are assessed (English, maths, verbal reasoning) before entrance. Numbers are up.

Exit: Minimal leakage pre-Highers with most going on to university. Some 55 per cent to Scottish universities, the rest to English, Irish, European or American universities. SATs (for American colleges) not a problem. In 2021, students went off to Harvard and Princeton. Back in the UK, St Andrews, Glasgow, Bristol, Durham, UCL, Glasgow School of Art and LSE all popular. In 2021, 13 medics. Usually a few to Oxbridge.

Latest results: In 2021, 94 per cent A-C at National 5; 92 per cent A-B at Higher; 87 per cent A-B at Advanced Higher. In 2019 (the last year exams took place), 60 per cent of Advanced Highers awarded A and 64 per cent of Highers awarded A.

Teaching and learning: ESMS follows the diamond model of education. So the boys and girls are educated together at the junior school, separately in the senior school from 12–17, and back to a co-ed set-up in S6. All based on the school's principle that 'boys and girls learn differently'. 'It didn't mean that much to me initially but seeing how they teach the boys and engage them, I now believe them,' said one parent. In contrast to the girls' school (which has a more formal approach to teaching, according to some parents), a parent told us, 'In the boys' school, the teachers seem to engage with them on a more conversational level, with discussion and debates. The boys enjoy the banter with their teachers, especially in sixth year.' Indeed, we were lucky enough to observe this on our tour in a superb S3 Latin lesson – embracing the latest technology, the boys were using their personal devices interactively in the lesson (though they were put away for noun revision). Relaxed, chatty atmosphere and pupils very much at ease. But it was the physics lesson that stole the show. The young dynamic teacher has his own YouTube channel, Answer Me with Mr B, and we were treated to a lesson on 'Physic is true, ya,' where he performed on the ukulele to the tune of 'Hallelujah', finished off with a round of applause from the class of boys. An exemplar of modern teaching that keeps boys engaged and interested.

In general, teaching staff are rated highly by parents and pupils for their subject knowledge and passion for teaching. As one parent put it, 'I've not come across the teacher who is doing it just to pay their mortgage.' Another reported, 'They know how to educate boys and really like boys. Incredibly positive about being male.'

Class sizes of around 20-22 for first two years, reducing in size to 20 or fewer for S3-S5 and then 12-15 for S6. Following the Scottish curriculum, all pupils study for eight National 5 exams in S3 and S4. English, maths, a science and a modern language are compulsory at this stage. In S5, they study for five Higher exams (they must do Higher English) while in their final year they study for Advanced Highers (usually three) in twinned classes with Mary Erskine. French, German, Latin and Spanish all on offer from S1 to Advanced Higher.

We caught the extracurricular concert band in full swing, performing a foot-stomping rendition of the spaghetti western classic, Moment for Morricone

Firefly Learning is their online virtual learning platform, used to keep track of homework, study tasks, school events and individuals' progress in learning, and proved invaluable as a teaching hub during the lockdowns during the pandemic. Keen to embrace the best of technology, all pupils are provided with their own learning devices.

Learning support and SEN: Strong learning support both in and out of the classroom. Numbers are below the national average because it's a selective school. Natural transition into the senior school. A small number will take National 4s instead of National 5s and drop a language for learning support, depending on the child's individual needs. No dedicated hub, but 'SfL has been extremely helpful and supportive,' one parent told us.

The arts and extracurricular: Outstanding arts provision and incredible breadth of extracurricular. A parent reported, 'It's an exciting week when choosing extracurricular activities, and makes for good dinner-time chat. Can't imagine them doing mountain biking, pottery and singing in the Edinburgh Tattoo elsewhere.' Staggering variety of clubs and societies on offer to all – from Warhammer to music tech and board games, all with specialist teachers. A parent told us, 'At least once a month the mountain biking club goes down to Glentress. The teachers take all the clubs and get really involved, forming really good bonds with the kids.' CCF is very popular with over 300 pupils involved – particularly strong RAF, with over 100. Biggest provider of DofE in Scotland with large numbers completing gold.

Masses of orchestras, bands and choirs at all age groups. We caught the extracurricular concert band in full swing, performing a foot-stomping rendition of the spaghetti western classic, Moment for Morricone. Pupils describe the annual house music and house rock competitions as 'such fun'. By all accounts the choir performing annually at the Royal Edinburgh Military Tattoo is something really special (and our tour guide told us not just for tourists). More than 200 boys have instrumental music lessons and there are 45 visiting music teachers.

Drama is part of the curriculum for younger pupils and can be taken up to Higher and Advanced Higher. The Tom Fleming Centre for Performing Arts, a renovated Victorian assembly hall with a series of beautiful arched windows, can seat audiences of up to 580 and offers full production, sound and lighting facilities. We also visited the stunning, newly acquired Dean Church on our tour, where we saw the thriving pipe band – another breathtaking performance venue, with its original pipe organ, that is starting to welcome parents back to school concerts and choir recitals. Drama for all, with plays and performances throughout the year for all age groups during normal times and with past performances at the Edinburgh Festival. Productions in 2021 include the Little Shop of Horrors and We Will Rock You.

Parents speak highly of the art department, with pupils' artwork proudly displayed on the walls.

Sport: Sport is a big deal here, with successes in local, national and international arenas. Biggest amongst the boys is undoubtedly rugby, with a whopping 27 teams, and not only for the most talented. A parent told us, 'My son is not a first team player, but it doesn't matter. He's still enthusiastic and there's a real team spirit there.' Masses of FPs that have made it in the sporting world have framed pictures in the Sporting Honours Wall in the large sports centre to inspire current pupils. On our tour we caught a glimpse of a charity football match being actively supported as well as extracurricular activities in table tennis (popular with the younger students) and seriously dedicated indoor rowers. The main sports of rugby or hockey and cricket or athletics are compulsory for the younger pupils, but the choice widens further up the school so there is something for everyone – as well as swimming (there's a 25m pool on site), cricket, badminton, cross country and many more. The pitches at the front of the school are used mostly for PE lessons, but for training and matches the boys are bussed to the pitches at Inverleith.

Boarding: Predominately a day school that offers a small boarding option, mostly attractive to older pupils (over half are S5s/S6s). Housing up to 32 boarders, Dean Park House has the feel of a grand house with stunning original features combined with luxurious modern amenities – think contemporary kitchen, common rooms with a touch-table computer and an electric piano. This is the swishest boarding accommodation we've seen. Boarders follow a normal timetable the same as day pupils. Boarders in S4 and under have to hand in their devices in the evening and Wifi is switched off at bedtime. Sleeps up to 11 girls and 21 boys in small dorms as well as four single rooms and one double.

For younger pupils, planned weekend activities involve trips to the cinema, paintballing, visiting local beaches or a treasure hunt around Edinburgh

Flexibility is a selling point for the older pupils, who tend to occupy themselves at the weekend, hanging out or staying over with friends. For younger pupils, planned weekend activities involve trips to the cinema, paintballing, local beaches or a treasure hunt around Edinburgh. Handily located on site, boys only have a few minutes' walk into their classes each morning. Flexi-boarding if space is available. Boarders are a mix of Scottish, UK and international pupils.

Bit of a grumble from one parent about the food, but otherwise high praise, particularly for the boarding housemaster. 'He is excellent,' we heard from a parent, 'as are all the staff – their kindness and warmth of personality make all the difference. He is also a pleasure to work with as a parent and he instantly provides confidence.'

Ethos and heritage: Stewart's Melville campus is based around the magnificent Daniel Stewart's Hospital. Designed by David Rhind, it was opened in 1855 by the Merchant Company of Edinburgh. When Daniel Stewart (whose wealth came from India) died in 1814, he left a sum of money and instructions that, once it had reached £40,000, it should be used to create a hospital for needy boys within the city. The hospital was transformed into Daniel Stewart's College in 1870. In 1972 the school merged with Melville College. The David Rhind main building is large and Victorian Gothic in design. Think fairytale pile, now surrounded by some necessary modern additions. Games pitches to the front, mostly used for PE and by the junior school, and car parks front and rear, chock full at the time of our visit.

Senior pupils share the site with upper junior school of ESMS. Sixth formers, who are back in the co-ed set-up with Mary Erskine, are bussed to classes between the two campuses, about a mile apart. A very large, traditional school with the best of modern teaching methods, parents told us that good academic outcomes is the expectation. One parent reported, 'It's quite no-nonsense but in a good way.' Another said, 'Wouldn't suit a very bohemian family who don't believe in rules.'

Pastoral care, inclusivity and discipline: School is divided into six houses, which they stay in from S1–S6. Each has a head of house and an assistant head. These houses are common to Stewart's Melville and Mary Erskine, so the various inter-house competitions have mixed teams. From S1–S2 pupils have dedicated tutors and sixth formers are divided into small tutor groups with a personal sixth form tutor.

Working towards the LGBT gold charter – the head was wearing a Pride badge. He told us, 'We accept pupils for who they are,' and said they can choose which pronoun the school should use, can adjust the uniform to suit and move to Mary Erskine if they prefer. School acknowledged they were listed on Everyone's invited but are unaware of the circumstances. Toxic behaviours and gender violence are discussed in PHSE, but they have also subscribed with the Scottish government's initiative, Equally Safe at School, to bring greater focus to the issue. With 15–20 per cent of pupils from BAME backgrounds and a pupil-led equality and diversity committee, they recently undertook a large survey to celebrate different religions, festivals and celebrations to ensure that all pupils see themselves represented around the school.

Pupils and parents: Pupils seem ambitious but modest and well-mannered. As for parents, we spoke to a real mixture, from those with a pupil receiving bursary support to first-time buyers, children of FPs (former pupils) and families living in the local neighbourhood. Attracting over a third of Edinburgh's independent secondary pupils, it is less elitist than some of its neighbours. Coaches from Dunfermline, Bathgate, Eskbank and Haddington as well as around Edinburgh. Few grumbles that a later bus doesn't run, meaning some kids miss out on extracurricular activities, depending on where they live. But children living far away can spend the night when doing evening activities (as long as there's room).

Money matters: Bursaries of up to 100 per cent, as well as scholarships throughout. Those doing well in the entrance exam are invited to sit a scholarship exam. Music scholarships (together with free music tuition) are also available.

The last word: Undoubtedly a big school, but its sheer size provides tremendous benefits. Parents praise the staff as being very knowledgeable and dedicated to their subjects and as having a focus on academic rigour. Immense array of extracurricular activities and sporting successes too. An impressive school with terrific results.

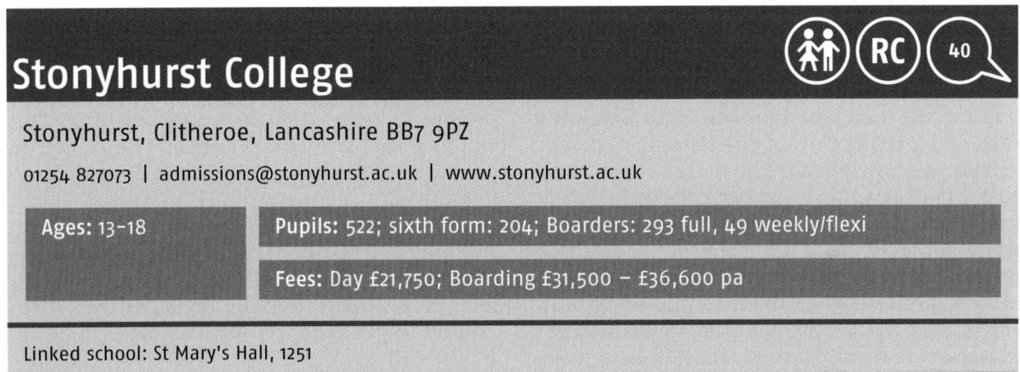

Stonyhurst College

Stonyhurst, Clitheroe, Lancashire BB7 9PZ

01254 827073 | admissions@stonyhurst.ac.uk | www.stonyhurst.ac.uk

Ages: 13–18

Pupils: 522; sixth form: 204; Boarders: 293 full, 49 weekly/flexi

Fees: Day £21,750; Boarding £31,500 – £36,600 pa

Linked school: St Mary's Hall, 1251

Headmaster: Since 2016, John Browne, BA (Bristol, music), LLB, MBA (40s), previously head of St Aloysius' College, Glasgow. Says it was a blend of accident and design that led him to teaching: as organ scholar at Westminster Cathedral, he 'fell' into the choir school by accident, later diverting to law and then an MBA because 'teachers need to think strategically too'. Taught by Jesuits at St Ignatius College, it was the Jesuit chaplain of Westminster Cathedral Choir School who first asked John, 'When are you going to be a teacher?' This was not to be for another two years as he completed his LLB, but as the City beckoned so did music, and instead he took up his first post as assistant director of music at The Latymer School, returning to the Westminster Cathedral Choir

School as the youngest headmaster (then aged 32). From there to Ampleforth as deputy head, then to Glasgow and now Stonyhurst.

Strategic thinking very much in evidence both internally – he has made changes to Stonyhurst's leadership infrastructure – and globally: Stonyhurst is in the process of opening a school in Malaysia. He has appointed five new assistant heads to be responsible for pulling pastoral and academic together in each year group (and who follow pupils through the school), so each pupil is viewed holistically. One parent (a big fan) told us that when he started, head asked a retired Independent Schools' Inspector to review Stonyhurst afresh and held open consultations with staff and parents. An MBA style approach, perhaps, and one senses that continuous improvements will be a defining characteristic of his leadership. Stays on the pulse of the school by meeting five students per week for lunch, which he describes as his 'five-a-day'. They 'help him see what needs to be different'.

Head refers to the writers who have passed through (Conan Doyle was a pupil, Tolkien was a resident and the poet Gerard Manley Hopkins taught here)

He is a big believer in punctuating school life with unforgettable moments (for him, it was going to the Royal Albert Hall to perform every year). He feels the opportunities Stonyhurst offers, trips to the Vatican for example, are crucial. They light the spark. 'If you find a child's passion, the rest falls into place.' This fits neatly with the overall ethos of the school, its motto, 'Quant je puis' (What is the most I can achieve with what I have?) is a dominant backbeat. 'What can I do to change the world?' is what the head wants his students to ask themselves. The spiritual thinking which underpins this philosophy is clear, but he is keen to stress that while worship is part of the school's makeup (60 per cent of pupils are from Catholic families), as a Jesuit school it is very much outward looking.

There was no better testament to his effectiveness than the two boys who were selected at random to show us part of the school. (The selection was so random, in fact, that with the desperate air of an adolescent Just William, one of the boys was furtively and desperately trying to smarten himself up, tucking in his slightly bedraggled shirt as we went along.) 'The head sorts everything out,' one said, with a knowing nod to the evening academic clinics, designed to help students with work problems. 'Oh, they've always been there,' the other pointed out. 'Yes, but they actually work now, they're good, they're longer,' his friend asserted. The pair exuded colossal pride in the school, able to reel off its heritage with enthusiasm you just can't fake.

The head's recreation is walking his dogs in the Ribble valley and spending time with his wife (Marie, a company director) and son. We left him on the day of our visit pondering which object he should take from the vast Stonyhurst collection of treasures to illustrate a talk he was due to give that evening. He 'loves objects which tell a story'. He refers to the writers who have passed through (Conan Doyle was a boy here, Tolkien a resident whilst his son was an English master, the poet Gerard Manley Hopkins taught here). Apparently Tolkien's middle earth was meant to be close to the River Hodder. He wants to bring everything all together, connect the past and present.

Entrance: One third of students come from school's prep, St Mary's Hall. Entrance exam plus reports and reference for candidates at 11+, 13+ and 16+. Overseas students are assessed for English level to check that they will be able to tackle the subjects with ease.

Exit: Leavers go on to study a broad spread of subjects at universities all over the UK – half to Russell Group. Bristol, Manchester, Loughborough and Sheffield currently popular. Some to European universities. Usually a few medics (three in 2021) and sometimes a few to Oxbridge. Business management is the most popular course.

Latest results: In 2021, 65 per cent 9-7 at GCSE; 55 per cent A*/A at A level (81 per cent A*-B). In 2021, average IB score 37. In 2019 (the last year when exams took place), 44 per cent 9-7 at GCSE; 26 per cent A*/A at A level (57 per cent A*-B). Average IB score 35.

Teaching and learning: Broad curriculum allows students to follow their interests. Psychology A level recently introduced. Languages are strong; around 75 per cent take two languages at GCSE, 14 per cent at A level. The IB is predominantly taken by international students, but popularity is steadily increasing. Fairly mixed ability intake (school accepts all siblings) makes results all the more impressive. Small class sizes, 20 max.

The head is enthusiastic about how IB educates the whole person. The IB's CAS components – where students design their own projects around the creativity, activity and 'service to others' modules – are now applied to the whole school. School is also rolling out the IB careers programme.

Academically, each child is tracked and results analysed for patterns. If they are a bit below their target, why? The whole person is looked at, all knowledge, both academic and pastoral, pooled to provide answers (back to those new assistant head roles). Parents say some of the teachers are truly inspirational.

Steady stream of big canvas events, like a fashion show with African couture, a literary festival (biennial) and all the usual balls. Trips include South Africa and China

If pupils feel they need to brush up on an aspect of the curriculum, the evening subject drop-in clinics do the trick. Or as the head puts it, if the target grades are down, then a clinic 'becomes a priority'. Back to the motto again – all that I can: the benchmark is set high for all students and they are encouraged to aspire.

A unique aspect of teaching at the school is its integration with the Stonyhurst collections (started in 1609). Artefacts from these extraordinary collections are deployed to bring the curriculum to life. We actually got to touch Shakespeare's First Folio and saw Mary Queen of Scots' book of hours. History lessons must be much enlivened by articles such as Sir Thomas More's hats and the Gunpowder Plot vestments. Art lessons can draw on original works by Turner and Rubens. These and other remarkable items are currently being curated into a small museum ('The story of the collections and English Catholicism'). The school's heritage is very much part of the learning experience in the here and now; even the observatory in the grounds is put to full use and ties up with head's desire to bring together past and present.

Learning support and SEN: For those needing extra help, there's learning support in the form of bespoke programmes, including use of mentors and educational psychologists.

The arts and extracurricular: Art is nurtured here; there is an artist in residence and head would like to extend similar hospitality to a poet. Music runs the gamut with big choirs, big bands, orchestras, ensembles. There are headmaster's concerts as well as weekly performances. Dance is on offer in all its genres – street, tap, modern, zumba – with some nicely ambitious productions to showcase those skills (Moulin Rouge and Wicked). The Stonyhurst dancers recently got to spend time with the Birmingham Royal Ballet (doubtless one of those unforgettable experiences so valued by the head).

There is a good drama space with professional sound and lighting and a chain of performances, from the ubiquitous Les Mis to Fiddler on the Roof and Hedda Gabler. A wonderful Much Ado, condensed into 45 minutes, was performed in a modern style with a Christmas morning setting. Students pitch in from backstage too, with lighting and costumes.

Clubs include politics, philosophy, robotics, astronomy, economics. Impressive range of speakers, recently Professor Robert Winston, historian Lord Hennessy, plus academics and politicians (we imagine Jacob Rees Mogg was thought-provoking at the very least). CCF compulsory for the first two years and most continue thereafter. DofE strong.

Steady stream of big canvas events, like a fashion show with African couture, a literary festival (biennial) and all the usual balls. Trips include South Africa, China and closer to home: museums (Louvre!), Houses of Parliament and top universities. Interline (house) competitions in everything from tennis, maths, croquet to poetry reading.

Sport: Impressive array of sports facilities: tennis dome, squash courts, golf course, shooting range, swimming pool, heaps of sports pitches. Dazzling successes in boys' and girls' sport (rugby team won the Lancashire Cup and the girls had just returned from a netball tour to Dubai).

Boarding: Most of the boarders are full time so lots of cinema trips and outings to York and Manchester. Boarding houses are called playrooms. Each pupil has a tutor (and an online pastoral log) who meets them in small groups every week. The new assistant heads preside over this process to ensure everything is joined up.

Boarders start off sharing five to a room; single rooms for older pupils. Rooms are fairly trad, many have magnificent views over the grounds. 'Every morning it looks different,' one pupil said. Boys' and girls' rooms differ only in that the girls have made theirs cosier. Showers and loos not palatial but in good order.

Girls' boarding area has rooms clustered around a central glass office with staff on duty – very reassuring, we thought. Sitting room looked comfortable and there was a well-equipped, homely kitchen with washing machines. Day pupils also have a desk in the boarding areas.

Ethos and heritage: Founded in 1593 in France, the school moved to its present site in the beautiful Ribble valley in 1794. The building and its grounds, with their formal waterways, have a stately grandeur that certainly inspired former pupil, Sir Arthur Conan Doyle – the description of Baskerville Hall is based on Stonyhurst.

The library in main use has a very grown-up feeling, but the other ancient historical libraries are something else. The fact that students have seminars in these rooms must set the tone for high achievement. Wonderful college chapel, St Peter's, lends a Brideshead grandeur.

Multi-million pound restoration developments are the norm here. Like any great estate, its treasures need to be maintained and extensive projects are ongoing to give its ailing beauties, such as the canals and the baroque gardens, some TLC.

There can be no radical modernisation in a listed building and it is all the better for it. True, the school's 'slightly worn in places' interior vibe prevails – indeed, approach it with the wrong mindset and certain corridors might seem a little gloomy. Nevertheless, classrooms are cheery, there are decent science labs, dance and drama studios, and don't forget all those incredible sports facilities.

The spiritual runs through the school, mass is celebrated every week and each playroom goes on an annual retreat. Yet although many parents say the school lives the Jesuit ethos, some felt its Catholic values should be celebrated more

Plenty of wall displays, not dominant or dazzling but interesting; we commented on some pictures of famous scientists to a couple of pupils. Shame so few women scientists, we thought, looking at all the men displayed. 'What's the name of the woman who was part of the team who discovered DNA? She should be up there,' we say, racking our addled brains for her name. 'Oh, you mean Rosalind Franklin,' came the reply, barely missing a beat. (Yep, we think to ourselves, impressed, that's the one.)

Pastoral care, inclusivity and discipline: The playrooms at break times certainly seem friendly places, a mad throng of chat. Parents enthused about the seamless blend of day and boarding and liked a recent initiative to invite day pupils to spend three nights in the school for free.

Onsite health centre. Lots of school talks and workshops for students on walking tall, building resilience and looking at the nuances of behaviour; how you can subtly exclude someone and the impact that can have. Head of pastoral/boarding said the girls will flag up concerns about others and it's a very supportive environment. The real aim is to give students the skills to deal with issues themselves. Mild concerns were expressed in this area by one or two parents who suggested perhaps students needed 'a bit extra' pastorally; others thought the same for the academic side of things (some pupils need extra cosseting, some need pushing).

The spiritual runs through the school, mass is celebrated each week and each playroom goes on an annual retreat. Yet although many parents say the school lives the Jesuit ethos, some felt its Catholic values should be celebrated more and 'shouted about'. We imagine it's a delicate balance for the school between inclusivity and celebration.

Pupils and parents: Pupils mainly come from the north of England and London (families looking for something less pushy). Good mix of international boarders; recent increase in European pupils who come for the IB.

Overseas parents are emailed frequently, relaying what their children are going to be studying and details of their performance. Parents in the UK described the comms as superb, saying you heard back from a teacher within a couple of hours of emailing. The chain of connection goes on well beyond leaving Stonyhurst; many parents are themselves former pupils. The head sees all ex-pupils as ambassadors for the school.

The pupils we spoke to seemed a down-to-earth and diverse bunch. The head refers to the first hockey team, 'the cool kids', lobbying him to help with the refugee crisis. He was keen to impress the importance of the real commitment on them (helping is not a whim). The end result was the head of the Jesuit refugee service came to give a talk and the village is now looking to host a Syrian refugee family.

Money matters: Boarding fees in line with similar schools. Scholarships (music, sport, academic and all-rounder) and means-tested bursaries up to value of £3 million annually.

The last word: An outward-looking and inclusive Catholic boarding school where students are encouraged to become their best selves, give back to the world and aspire to great heights academically.

Strathallan School

Forgandenny, Perth, Perthshire PH2 9EG

01738 812546 | admissions@strathallan.co.uk | www.strathallan.co.uk

Ages: 7–18

Pupils: 553; sixth form: 187; Boarders: 305 full

Fees: Day £15,474 – £24,474; Boarding £25,140 – £36,036 pa

Headmaster: Since 2017, Mark Lauder, who by his own admission is anything but a 'patrician' public school head. After a Scottish state school education, marred by the teachers' strikes of the early 1980s, he showed his mettle by earning an MA in English Literature and history at Aberdeen. He then went to win a graduate scholarship for research to Oxford and two half blues in rowing.

Clearly made of strong stuff, and we found him to be an eloquent and charming communicator with a strong vision for the future of the school. Previously head of Ashville College, he has also been deputy head and head of boarding at Felsted School, Essex, head of history and then housemaster at St Edward's School, Oxford, and before that head of history and master in charge of rowing at Shiplake College, Henley-on-Thames, coaching rugby and rowing throughout. So lots of experience and he certainly seems ready to use his widespread contacts to bring Strathallan into the limelight.

He is married to peripatetic saxophone and piano teacher, Caroline, with two teenage sons.

Head of Strathallan Prep: is is Mrs Emma Lalani.

Entrance: Entrance to the Junior House is at age 9, 10, 11 or 12 by school report and assessments, or scholarship held on entrance day in early spring. Senior entrance is at 13+, via open scholarship examination (late February/early March), Common Entrance (June) or/and school report. Sixth form entry is either via the sixth form scholarship examination (November) or on the basis of a satisfactory school report and/or GCSE/National 5 results. All pupils are screened for learning difficulties on entry and IEPs plus ed psychs rolled in if necessary. Excellent route map for parents unfamiliar with public school entry procedures.

Exit: To a range of universities – 60 per cent Scottish, nearly all the rest English. Sometimes a couple to Oxbridge, though none recently. One to study medicine in 2021. Forces popular.

Latest results: In 2021, 60 per cent 9-7 at GCSE; 65 per cent 9-4 in both maths and English. At A level, 83 per cent A*/A at A level (84 per cent A*-B). At Higher, 65 per cent A-B. In 2019 (the last year when exams took place), 33 per cent 9-7 at GCSE; 47 per cent A*/A at A level (79 per cent A*-B).

Teaching and learning: The school describes results to date as 'good for a broad ability school but can still do better'. But that, says Mr Lauder, with great gusto and a swirl of his kilt, is where great changes are afoot.

'We have so many pupils competing in sport at a very high level, we need to adapt our approach to better balance their contact with teachers and sharpen up our overall academic performance.' According to their figures, from the junior school right up to fifth form, 100 per cent of pupils represented the school in team sport. In sixth form it was 88 per cent. Ten per cent of the school competed at national or international level. Very, very impressive, but we can see where this might lead to pressure on academics.

We were a bit bowled over by the tartan carpet in the boys' house that we toured. Houses have regular supply of milk, bread and fruit

'We're reviewing lots of different ways of improving quality teaching time. Teachers are being split into working parties to help "staff engagement" and everyone is being encouraged to look at ways of sharpening up their teaching time and working harder on ensuring that core subjects are given more emphasis.'

Head says the school has a better than average staff-to-pupil ratio and they should be able to use that advantage to 'blend the curriculum' around the child rather than the other way around.

As for the curriculum itself, you could say the school plays the system in a way. Everyone sits GCSEs, but after that the school offers both English A levels and rather controversially Scottish Highers over two years (it's normally a one-year course). Some would argue this makes the A level results look better as less academic pupils can take the Higher route, but Mark Lauder staunchly defends this. He says 75 per cent follow the A level route but the 25 per cent who choose Highers do so for a variety of reasons. Yes, some may be less academic, but others don't want to lose breadth of subject choice or they want to study medicine in Scotland (Strath is one of the very few schools to offer Higher human biology, which suits medical applications) or they are just incredibly busy and doing Highers over two years is an achievable option.

'The captain of rugby, for example, was called up to play for Scotland U20s. It was a fabulous opportunity, but if he weren't doing Highers over two years he would have really struggled with his academic work.'

As for the subjects on offer, they're a pretty regular selection, although Mr Lauder says social sciences and the arts are being beefed up with new A levels in psychology, theatre studies and PE, and GCSEs in drama and RE. They are also changing the third form curriculum to introduce music and drama and increasing the contact time for English, maths and Latin.

Piping is very, very strong. Rather like the Queen, the head has his own piper. Three pipe bands play all over the UK and abroad (Barbados, USA, Italy and France)

Interesting take on GCSE science: rather than just doing either triple or all single sciences, they have come up with an additional third pathway, foundation single science. This, they claim, is again all about offering flexible options.

One practice which got our attention is the fifth form 'post trial exam' interview. This is an individual interview with the head, the houseparent and the deputy head of academics. The idea is to discuss with each child how they felt the exams went and to map out what they should be doing next to get the best results in the real exams. This is followed by a second interview with the UCAS and careers adviser. We thought it sounded terrifying, but parents said it was handled incredibly well. 'We think this really raised the bar for our son. It made him sit up and take notice and he really felt they were paying attention to him.' 'Mark's really shaken things up in the best possible way. He's making it clear that only giving your best is good enough.'

Some pragmatic steps and a lot of positive thinking, but will he really manage to make headway? Well, he certainly seems to have got off on the right foot with some of the parents. 'I'm really excited about him and what he's doing with the school.' 'He's the right kind of person; enthusiastic and passionate.' 'He and his wife are really good for the school. From what we hear the kids are responding really well to them.'

Scottish Highers recently introduced, and this is the first Scottish school to join the Pre-Senior Baccalaureate. We also like the sound of the new rewilding initiative, which aims to improve the biodiversity on campus and provide an ongoing subject for zoological and entomological study; also includes new nature walks, with maps and interactive interpretation boards.

Learning support and SEN: Learning support is free and seems fairly well covered. All pupils are screened on entry and ed psychs are brought in where necessary. It has its own small area within the school and support is delivered in a variety of ways: one-to-one, small groups, after-school clinics in various disciplines. There are two full-time trained staff, plus ancillaries, and they cover the entire age range. The school says they can cope with mild Asperger's/autism. Teachers have now been provided with briefings on issues such as dyslexia and the focus has been on helping departments adapt approaches and materials to pupils' different needs. Programmes have also been introduced to help pupils who have English as a second language. Focus is now on taking more learning support and more EAL into the classrooms so academic time is not lost. Most classrooms are on the ground floor and one building has a lift.

The arts and extracurricular: The art provision is rather impressive. The art school is over three floors with marvellous light and some inspired work. We were pleased to see a group of relaxed and engaged students with their sleeves rolled up during their lunch hour, more than happy to talk to us about their work.

Musically, the school hits the top notes too. Piping is very, very strong. Rather like the Queen, the head has his own piper. They currently have three bands who play all over the UK and abroad (Barbados, USA, Italy and France). Loads of drama: small theatre, new dance and drama studio. Pupil media team is bringing the school mag into the digital age.

Plenty of charity work under way across the school. They have a strong link with Kenya and send pupils out every year with a supply of clothes and provisions. Lots of DofE and community service, plus popular CCF.

Sport: Head is adamant when it comes to upholding the reputation of their all-conquering rugby squad: 'We are NOT buying rugby pupils.' He claims that if you take a snapshot, 11 of the 15 will generally have joined Strath at third form or earlier. We're not arguing. We imagine those big rugger buggers can put up a fair fight. That said, there have been frequent mutterings around the Scottish school circuit about Strath's alleged practice of bringing in 'ringers'. But the parents we spoke to are right behind the school: 'The bad reputation is nonsense; there are a lot of sour grapes out there.'

We were agog when the head greeted us at the front door of the main school in full kilt. But we had arrived on Wednesday when everyone goes to chapel and the kilt is mandatory. If you think that marks Strathallan out as stuffy, you'd be completely wrong

What we can say with confidence is that sport at this school is incredible. And we mean incredible. We were treated to what we can only describe as the 'wall of glory': a dazzling photographic display of all the pupils currently representing the school at national and international level. There are county, national, international, Commonwealth and Olympic presences across the board and at all ages: including rugby, footie, tennis, hockey, skiing, netball, swimming, shooting (clay and small bore), fencing, golf (own course), sailing. They have coaches who have themselves played at county, national and/or international level in most sports. The facilities we saw were wonderful. They now have a huge gym hall that allows full hockey games etc to be played in foul weather.

Boarding: No prizes for architecture at Strathallan. There you are sweeping up the beautiful drive with that wonderful backdrop of hills then it's 'I'm sorry? I didn't realise there was a Travelodge so near, oh in fact, there's another one. And another one. And...' You get the general drift. That said, none of the pupils we spoke to was complaining. Girls have their own study bedrooms for their last five years at the school, boys for four. Fairly functional but lovely views. Lots of kitchens and common room areas on each floor. We were a bit bowled over by the tartan carpet in the boys' house that we toured. Disabled loos and lifts are available to all floors. Houses have regular supply of milk, bread and fruit.

No exeats. Chapel every other Sunday (as well as Wednesdays) with a 'very funny and engaging' chaplain. On the other Sundays, it's a lie in and brunch.

Day pupils allocated to one of the houses; daily buses to and from Perth, Kinross, Auchterarder, Stirling, Crieff and Dundee. About a third or more come daily, with many younger day children converting to boarding on going to senior school age 13. Boarding increases as you go through the school. If you are in a play etc you can stay over and not be charged. Buses leave the school grounds at 7.30pm.

Ethos and heritage: We were agog when the head greeted us at the front door of the main school in full kilt. But we had arrived on Wednesday when everyone goes to chapel and the kilt is mandatory. If you think that marks Strathallan out as stuffy, you'd be completely wrong. Founded in 1913 by Harry Riley, the school is set in a breathtaking 153 carefully manicured acres, with everything you could imagine including a canoe slalom and a loch stocked with trout for the angling club. Wow! The buildings, as we've mentioned, are rather utilitarian, but the pupils we spoke to didn't care and why should they? It does what it says on the tin.

Nearly the first building you come to as you come up the drive is the junior house, Riley. This boasts a lovely atrium and a library, music practice rooms etc. Younger boarders and day children also have a dedicated sports and play area. Think of the junior house, Riley as a middle school (from age 9), with the children moving into the senior school at 13. Virtually everyone in Riley moves up to Strathallan without having to sit Common Entrance. The whole school eats in the bright and airy dining room. The pupils we spoke to thought the food was very good.

So what is it about Strathallan that's different? Well, that's an interesting question. If you talk to children from other public schools around Scotland, they'll roll their eyes and say Strathallians are a pretty clannish bunch. 'They don't mix with other schools and keep themselves to themselves.' So what do the current crop of Strathallians think?

'We're not as snobby as the other schools.' 'We're there for each other. We're really close, really loyal.' 'I think we mix. No idea where that came from.'

Pastoral care, inclusivity and discipline: Seven houses in senior school, four for boys and three for girls. Houseparents live on site with two staff on duty in each house every night. Academic tutor attached to each pupil and tutorial team in every house. Tutors often use the time available for informal chats.

Staff 'aware that things happen' and talk of 'zero tolerance' on drugs but rural setting means incidents involving drugs and alcohol are not very frequent. Instead, says the head, fitness suite is packed at 9 every night. (Strath is a sporting behemoth, after all.)

School works hard on bullying awareness with lots of briefings – expectations, ownership, relationships, 'be reasonable'. Punishment system for misdemeanours called 'fatigues' (colloquial name for disciplinary). This involves jobs around the buildings and grounds, of which obviously there's no shortage.

Another of head's initiatives is 'Monday drop-in'. This is when anyone in the school can pop into his office for a chat. Nothing is off limits, apparently, and he's done everything from bereavement counselling to advising on the best way to look after your shoes. He's even had the odd pupil who just wanted to see what his office looked like.

On a more formal basis, the sixth form have regular discussion groups (15 at a time) with the head, where they cover topics such as Brexit, American politics etc. 'Mr Lauder is so easy to talk to.'

Pupils and parents: Some 20 per cent of the pupils are from overseas, eg Spain, Russia, Africa, China, Eastern Europe, Hong Kong and Germany; a further 18 per cent are expats. The school is an easy one-hour drive from Edinburgh and Glasgow. New short stay international programme.

We would say this is not a school for toffs; probably more regional Scottish accents than other similar schools. Parents tend to be farmers or successful businessmen and women.

Money matters: School says they're financially strong. Junior scholarships, open scholarships and sixth form scholarships available plus academic, all-rounder, sport, music, design technology, piping and art scholarships. Strong track record with prestigious Arkwright Scholarships for aspiring engineers.

Parents can apply for means-tested help with fees via bursaries. Sibling discount, Forces and Old Strathallian discounts available.

The last word: Fiercely proud and competitive, Strathallan hits a lot of high notes, especially with sport, art and music. Amazing setting and some awesome facilities. Not known for mixing well with other schools, but then maybe they're too busy and happy to bother.

Terra Nova School

42

Jodrell Bank, Holmes Chapel, Crewe, Cheshire CW4 8BT

01477 571251 | admissions@tnschool.co.uk | www.tnschool.co.uk

Ages: 2-13

Pupils: 305; Boarders: 20 full, 32 flexi

Fees: Day £11,178 – £15,510; Boarding £18,450 – £20,988 pa

Head: Since September 2021, Paul Campbell, previously executive head of three schools (two primaries; one senior) in East London, which all stepped up from troubled histories to outstanding schools under his leadership. His 20 years' experience as a teacher kicked off overseas with spells in Ghana, the Ukraine and Borneo, after which he progressed to head of Primrose Hill Primary and then Monteagle School in Dagenham, which also faced considerable difficulties when he took on the role.

Entrance: Pupils from junior prep onwards are invited for a taster day and do an English and maths assessment. Broad intake; not 'selective' in the strict sense. School interviews prospective pupils to gauge whether a child is curious about the world and has an interest in learning. School likes to talk to parents too to see if they too are keen to support their child. Children 'who are just interested in one thing' might not fit well, says school.

Exit: Most pupils stay on until 13 with a few leaving for local day schools at 11. As the school niftily puts it, it doesn't sit within 'the Cheshire bubble' and TN parents like to look beyond the local 'usual suspect' senior schools to consider Sedbergh, Shrewsbury, Repton or, in the case of around one student per year, Eton. Parents, says the school, often arrive dead set on a local senior day school for their child, only to do a volte face mid-way through and start looking at boarding schools elsewhere in the country. Other popular destinations are Millfield, Uppingham, Rugby and Wrekin. Pupils also go on to local independent day schools, including The Grange (at 13), Manchester Grammar and Stockport Grammar.

Our view: Terra Nova is unique in Cheshire, being the only day and boarding 13+ prep (this kind of flexibility may be commonplace in other parts of the country but not round here). Pupils can enter at 2.5 years and teaching is differentiated all the way through. The pre-school is a wonderful learning environment – a farm area, mud kitchen, the works. In the junior prep (ages 5-9) English and maths are core (school has increased time devoted to those across the board; there is setting from year 3 in maths) all alongside specialist teaching in French, music, art, design and technology. In the crucial reception year, children read three times per week with teachers. At the time of our visit, children were counting in 2s, 5s, 10s using pine cones and thinking about 'where they would fly if they were a butterfly'. Half-termly cross-curricular themes are child-led so if a topic is not engaging them, 'we shift to something which does,' the teacher says emphatically. French is taught from the pre-school upwards; taster term of German, Spanish and Latin in years 5 and 6. Large grounds and a forest area mean the younger children spend a lot of time outside, risk-taking within a safe environment, wellies and waterproofs always on hand. It's a 'very outdoorsy' school, one member of staff said.

In senior prep (ages 9-13) the teaching becomes more specialist across all subjects, including science (on which there is a big emphasis) and computer science which includes lots of coding and robotics. Humanities is split into geography, history and RE with lots of cross-curricular links. English literature study also becomes more sophisticated; we looked in on a lesson where war poetry was being nicely critiqued. Senior art looked incredible and DT was very high tech with a 3D printer, scanner and laser cutter and a super-enthused female teacher, wanting children to be 'educated with skills for jobs that don't yet exist'.

One parent said recent academic improvements were both welcome and needed. Another spoke glowingly of the 'positive changes'. Teachers are diverse blend of genders and ages – 'driven and motivated,' the school told us. Teachers stressed all teaching is child-led: one teacher was a big fan of an informal 'rate my lesson' approach. Brave.

Terra Nova is unique in Cheshire, being the only day and boarding 13+ prep (this kind of flexibility may be commonplace in other parts of the country, but not round here)

Termly assessments track progress and identify children who need additional support. SEN seems catered for very well; school says it is used to picking up mild cases and nipping underlying issues 'in the bud early'. Help usually comes in the form of booster lessons, at most two half-hours per week. Not really, we think, the place for anything other than mild learning difficulties.

The impressively packed curriculum and extracurricular – as well as the vast spectrum of options across the arts, IT, performance and sport – are possible partly because of the long school day. For senior prep, the day finishes at 5pm after an hour's prep has been completed, after which there might be clubs. This is a boarding school rhythm (the school has now expanded to full boarding in fact) and very much about encouraging children to explore. Clubs change termly and could include anything from croquet to debating to fashion designing to shooting. On average, pupils end up doing around ten hours per week extracurricular and parents are in awe of the 'sheer variety of opportunity'.

The school is especially strong on sport, with a swag bag of trophies to prove it. All the mainstream sports and activities are on offer (an outdoor pool too) plus dance, riding, golf, sailing – and more. Girls' teams for football and cricket also – no major successes as yet but there is a growing appetite for competitive fixtures across the county. Not a school where children are forced into one major sport, there's plenty of choice, but sport is a cornerstone here and if your child wouldn't enjoy 10 hours a week, this might not be the school for them.

Lots of music and a recital each term, three large choirs and many music competitions or local festivals, like Alderley Edge or Bowden. Drama is popular, LAMDA available and many productions; years 5 and 6 recently put on The Amazing Adventures of Super Stan (the pics looked very professional).

Heaps of trips from the Grosvenor Museum to Norton Priory. Also overnighter adventure trips in later years and abroad in senior prep years to France or Switzerland. Plus competitions to stretch, like Young Mathematician Award or Prep School Art Competition – school currently first in the Lego League for robotics.

One parent said that when she encountered a few difficulties with her child, she found the teachers both engaged and effective in sorting a collective strategy: 'There is genuine all-round care', suggesting the pastoral side works well. They also enthuse about the 'achievement' assemblies. Children are encouraged to get on their feet to explain what they have been doing – 'We want them confident without being over-confident.' There is a school council, house system and lots of positions of responsibility.

There is a very clear structure of sanctions should misbehaviour kick in. We were told all about the yellow stamps: a certain number and parents are called in. Generally one stamp and a supportive chat around the behaviour seemed to work.

We chatted to one of the two girls in year 8 who said it was difficult at first, especially when her other female friend was doing different activities. She felt she had a good rapport with the boys, though, and this certainly seemed the case in class. For sport, they joined the year 7 girls. School says there is now a good balance but it would probably be wise to check this at the time of your visit.

There is what can only be described as a sizeable beach (modestly called a 'sandpit') with a large pirate boat at the centre. Seaside day in activity week featured an ice cream van and fish and chips

Founded in 1897, Terra Nova has a history of mobility; established in Melton Mowbray, moving to Southport in 1901 then to its current site in 1939. Today, it has the look and feel of a grand Cheshire stately home with attractive courtyards around which outbuildings are clustered (all classrooms). It's all very country estate and covers around 35 acres. The generous grounds accommodate a shooting range, Astroturf, tennis courts, and outdoor swimming pool for the summer months. There's also a performing arts centre (no theatre as yet) and a good library.

The pre-school deserves a special mention, housed in a delightful separate part of the grounds with its own goat, hens and guinea pigs. As well as the usual play area and mud kitchens, there is also what can only be described as a sizeable beach (modestly called a 'sandpit') with a large pirate boat at the centre. The children must love it. The seaside day in activity week featured an ice cream van, fish and chips and paddling pools to complete the picture. Reception is also in a separate area so the transition is easy for the children from pre-school; a beautiful outbuilding, grounds with outdoor classrooms dotted about, the forest behind it. All very bucolic.

Parents are a mix of Cheshire old money and entrepreneurs (known locally as 'Cheshire's Silicon Valley'). Ambitions for their children may veer between wanting an uber-academic senior day school in Manchester to full boarding in Cumbria.

Comms are good – newsletter, a parents' app and half-termly talks to parents on various topics. Three termly reports per year. Parents say it's easy to chat to form teachers or go higher. They describe it like a family but say 'you can be involved as much or as little as you want'.

Boarding: Full boarding became available from September 2019 with a new head of boarding. Head wants school to be a balanced and blended community; boarders are buddied up with another boarder to help them learn the ropes. There is one house for all boarders, separated by different levels and alarmed doors. It is very much a family feel. Rooming is based on age with year 7/8 rooms, year 5/6 rooms and year 3/4 rooms. Phone and device use is monitored and is dependent on age. Boys' rooms are large and cheery, around four or five beds in each, great views mostly. Girls' rooms are, as usual, cosy. Couple of comfy common rooms in bright colours – a cheery environment. Lots of activities on offer like acting classes, table tennis or dodgeball. Parents said their children who were occasional boarders loved it. One parent whose child was a little reluctant to taste boarding was impressed by the way the staff sat everyone sat down to sort out a solution so that her child was at ease.

Money matters: Day fees known for being higher than other local independent schools. Bursaries on the increase though.

The last word: A rarity in Cheshire – a happy school where exploration and academic achievement is nurtured and which gives parents very broad options regarding the next crucial step for their child's senior education.

Terrington Hall School

Terrington, York, North Yorkshire YO60 6PR

01653 648227 | admissions@terringtonhall.com | www.terringtonhall.com

Ages: 3–13

Pupils: 180; **Boarders:** 170 flexi

Fees: Day £9,030 – £15,540 pa; Flexi boarding from £25 per night

Head: Since September 2020, Simon Kibler BA (Leicester) (40s). Twinkly eyed, warm and with a zest for life. Clearly feels very at home in North Yorkshire after many years down south – loves the fact that people are 'very straight in Yorkshire, as there's no point hiding things'. Formerly deputy head at Dover College, he has been working in independent education for his whole career in both prep and senior schools and says 'boarding is in my blood'. He and his wife Kate have previously been houseparents at Abbotsholme School in Derbyshire and Milton Abbey School in Dorset, where he was also assistant head. They have four children, with the two youngest girls at Terrington.

On duty at 7.15am, knows every pupil's name and meets and greets them and their parents at the door every morning, alongside his two deputies (academic and pastoral) and bursar. His delight in seeing the family's black labrador joining in with playground frolics was infectious, although the dachshund had gone on strike as it was raining. Having two resident canines to play with is evidently popular with pupils of all ages.

During our visit he served lunch to pupils and sat down to eat it with them; they clearly felt relaxed chatting with him. Parents commented that he is 'very nice', 'very personable' and a 'good communicator'. But this is still a school where children leap up from their desks as soon as he enters the classroom.

A keen sportsman and former director of sport at Abbotsholme, it was his experience as a ski instructor while at university (Eddie 'The Eagle' Edwards taught him how to ski), that made him realise his vocation was in teaching. His eureka moment came while teaching a blind 70-year-old man how to ski on a dry slope in east Sussex – 'I had a moment of knowing that I wanted to teach.' Teaching is also in the blood – his father become a teacher after a career in science.

Mad about cricket, he was a volunteer junior girls' Kent county cricket coach and has big plans for introducing girls' cricket and becoming a North Yorkshire hub for the girls' sport. That said, he thinks 'too much focus' has previously been made on competitive sport, and it's now time to 'focus on other areas'. Also keen to improve provision for performing arts, believing that all pupils would benefit from more opportunities of speaking in public (he wants all pupils to have taken part in LAMDA exams before leaving in year 8). With new plans also afoot for their own chickens and vegetable plot, it seems that his vision of 'developing the bubble of a perfect childhood experience' is well on course.

Entrance: Most join in the nursery or reception aged 3+ or 4+ and move into pre-prep, with another main intake in year 3. Pupils can be accepted into all year groups up to year 8 depending on spaces being available. The first step for parents is to visit the school and meet the headmaster, after which a taster day is encouraged for children to find out if they are suited to the school. There are no formal entrance tests, but staff will assess children informally during taster days.

Exit: Most go on to senior schools within the local area, including St Peter's, Sedbergh, Ampleforth, Giggleswick, Bootham, Pocklington and Scarborough College, with The Mount and Queen Margaret's being popular girls-only choices. Scholarships to eg Durham, Sedbergh, The Mount and Ampleforth. A small number head further afield as full boarders, with Uppingham, Repton and Shrewsbury being preferred destinations outside of north east.

Our view: It's hard not to be impressed with the approach to the school, with the journey to the village from the A64 taking you past the tree-lined avenues and spectacular follies of the Castle Howard estate. Travelling by obelisks and mighty oaks with leaves aflame in their autumn splendour, we felt as if we were entering an Austen novel, and indeed would have felt very much at home arriving in a horse-drawn carriage. But while the beautiful stone building – originally built in the 1800s as a rectory and with pillars at the entrance – is grand and imposing, once inside it feels homely, with fires roaring in both the entrance hall and the head's office on the day we visited.

The whole of the prep building could do with a lick of paint, but the decorators are booked in, we were assured. The head was certainly convincing when he talked about being keen for the children to have a nice environment and look after things. The nursery and pre-prep classrooms are bright and colourful with a separate playground with fun play equipment. Meanwhile, prep classrooms are mostly in a separate modern brick building and the playground area has recently been improved by benches, an all-weather ping pong table and plant pots to brighten it up. The library is well stocked and popular and a chill-out area for older pupils is due to be redecorated with pictures and sofas.

There are a number of elite sport pathways established for hockey, cricket, rugby, football, athletics and rounders, with extra fitness and technical sports sessions for those who excel in sport

In the classrooms, we observed fun, interactive lessons and the teachers clearly know their pupils' strengths and weaknesses. 'It's been fantastic for my girls and I couldn't fault it,' one parent told us. The atmosphere on the day of our visit was buzzy, with pupils practising instruments at one end of the corridor, and a class enthusiastically reading through their parts for a production of Charlie and the Chocolate Factory at the other. Pupils are confident, friendly and polite.

We certainly heard no complaints about the teachers, with parents commenting that they are 'fantastic practitioners' who are 'incredibly committed' and 'throw themselves into school life'. Particular praise was given to the academic deputy head, who is also head of maths, who has 'taught my daughter to love maths' and is a 'miracle worker', according to some parents.

For SEN, there is a full-time head of learning support who does intervention work within the classroom as well as small-group work for those who need it from pre-prep to year 8. Within the first three weeks of joining school, all pupils are baseline tested and receive a 'settling in' report. Any concerns are flagged up and a learning support plan is then put in place to help struggling pupils to improve. Parents find this 'very reassuring' without putting any stigma on pupils who need more academic support than their peers.

There have been some grumbles from parents of older pupils that they haven't been stretched enough in the past, something which the new head is keen to address and 'galvanise the year 7 and 8 curriculum'. His plans include additional lessons on leadership, peer mentoring and community service, as well as an 'adventure award programme'. Another new plan is to create a technology centre where older children can learn hands-on mechanical skills by renovating a classic Land Rover Defender. Year 8 boys we spoke to couldn't get enough of this idea – parents concurred, saying they felt this year group had outgrown prep school and were becoming a bit 'switched off'.

Generally, though, parents are extremely supportive of the school, although a common grumble was that previously communications could be 'haphazard' and that there were 'too many letters and emails'. This has recently been streamlined to an online calendar updated every fortnight, with requirements set out for what is needed by each year group on a daily basis. There are also parent reps for each year group who have a termly meeting with the head. He says this is important as he 'would rather know about the problem and deal with it' than having parents moaning to each other.

Mental health and wellbeing are taken seriously, with a pastoral welfare committee meeting every week to chat through any concerns. Bullying is nipped in the bud, with pupils telling us that they feel confident to stand up to anyone who is being mean and know when they need to tell a teacher. Mobile phones are not allowed on school premises.

Sport facilities are excellent, including a large indoor sports hall, cricket and rugby pitches, and a large Astro pitch for hockey. The outdoor sports fields have stunning views over Ryedale, which would be enjoyable in the summer while watching the cricket with a glass of Pimm's. The netball courts need resurfacing, and the small swimming pool is functional rather than luxurious, but improvements are in the pipeline.

While virtually all pupils get to represent the school in some capacity during their time at Terrington Hall, the school is very competitive and enjoys a win. There are a number of elite sport pathways established for hockey, cricket, rugby, football, athletics and rounders, with extra fitness and technical sports sessions for those who excel in sport. There is a strong pedigree of representative honours, several pupils currently representing Yorkshire at cricket and hockey. A number of alumni have gone on to international honours in rugby and cricket at U19, U18 and U21 level for England and Scotland.

Seventy-five per cent of pupils have music lessons, and plans have been approved for the construction of a new music hub which will be built in the centre of the school grounds. Currently music provision is in a standalone building next to the sports fields, and performances are held in the sports hall. The new hub will ensure there is a proper performing arts space for both pupils and parents to enjoy.

The food is popular, with the mid-morning snack of homemade soup and bread a firm favourite; even the cauliflower soup is well liked (that must be a first). We enjoyed tasty lasagne and sticky toffee pudding on our visit, with pupils telling us that the chef (who recently moved up to Yorkshire after running an Italian restaurant in Shoreditch) is happy to accept their feedback and adapt menus if there's something they really don't like. There's a standalone food committee to make sure that the chef is kept on track.

As well as flexi boarding, full wraparound care is provided, with the school open from 7.30am to 8pm. Children can have breakfast and stay for tea and prep before going home.

Boarding: While the décor downstairs in the main building is a bit tired, the boarding dorms upstairs are bright and airy with high ceilings and beautiful views across the Howardian Hills. Dorms are packed with cheery bunkbeds and festooned with fairy lights – very tidy too, we noticed, which is no mean feat considering that some pupils starting boarding from year 3. The boarding housemistress, who has been at the school for 15 years, says that tidying up is an expected part of school life.

Many pupils opt for flexi boarding, with a handful of weekly boarders. The head is a huge fan of boarding life and is keen to encourage full boarders from further afield in the UK and Europe. He believes that boarding is beneficial for children to become fully immersed in school life – 'The advantages of boarding are in developing independence, resilience and building a strong community.'

During our visit, we spoke to lots of children who were very excited about their upcoming Halloween sleepover, and there are regular themed supper nights and movie nights.

Money matters: Scholarships are available for sport, music and academic excellence, as well as means-tested financial bursaries. Fee discounts are available for siblings, as well as armed forces and clergy families.

The last word: A friendly, unpretentious school where pupils come from a range of backgrounds. Has a real family feel where children can truly be children and where they become happy, successful and ready for the challenges of their chosen senior school.

Windermere School

Browhead, Patterdale Road, Windermere, Cumbria LA23 1NW

01539 446164 | admissions@windermereschool.co.uk | www.windermereschool.co.uk

Ages: 11–18

Pupils: 226; sixth form: 60; Boarders: 67 full, 9 weekly

Fees: Day £16,860 – £19,050; Boarding £28,110 – £33,315 pa

Headmaster: Since January 2022, Tom Hill. Educated at QEGS, Blackburn and then Hutton Grammar School, Preston before studying English and sports science at Loughborough, PGCE at Hull and an MA in educational leadership and management at Warwick. Previously head of the senior school at Brighton College Al Ain, Abu Dhabi since 2018, and before that senior deputy head at Bedford Girls' School and head of sixth form at Lincoln Minster School. He is active in sports, holding coaching qualifications in rugby, athletics, football, hockey and basketball. He also plays piano and acoustic guitar.

Tom is married to Shema, an experienced design technology and physics teacher, and they have three teenage children.

Entrance: Nearly all juniors move up to the senior school, making up the majority of the 11+ entry. The school likes to look for 'potential' rather than performance and 'well-rounded students with a genuine interest in education in the broadest sense of the word,' say staff. Candidates for entry (below 16+) sit papers in English, mathematics and non-verbal reasoning. Year 12 places conditional on a minimum of five GCSEs at grade C or above.

Exit: Around 10-20 per cent leave after GCSEs. Most sixth form leavers continue in higher education, some via gap years. St Andrews, Cardiff, Exeter, Edinburgh, King's College London and Manchester all popular destinations and usually a few overseas. Sometimes odd ones to Oxbridge though none in the last couple of years.

Latest results: In 2021, 53 per cent 9-7 at GCSE; average score of 36 for IB. In 2019 (the last year when exams took place), 45 per cent 9-7 at GCSE; average score of 34 points for IB.

Teaching and learning: Windermere pupils might not be dancing right at the top of the league tables but they appear hard-working and happy. Due in part to the broad intake, the results at GCSE, whilst undoubtedly solid, can't compete with bigger, more selective schools so it focuses on its considerable international appeal. Crucially, however, it is the highest performing independent school in Cumbria post-16, not least because there is no A level on offer here; it's the rigour of IB or a small choice of BTECs, and that's it. Exams and the choice of exams are a natural sieving process and the school's choice of the IB route means the game is raised considerably in sixth form. Now accredited to teach the IB career-related programme alongside the diploma. With small classes (around 12), teaching is up close and personal, there's nowhere to hide, and pupil-teacher relationships appear warm and relaxed. Personal academic tutors guide and, if necessary, hand-hold, helping students in their choice of subjects and mentoring them along the way. Parents tell us 'there are many inspirational teachers here', with a number of them prepared to offer extra tutorials on request at lunchtime or after school.

French, German, Italian and Spanish are all taught in this language-rich environment, with Latin and Greek being offered off-timetable as extras, classes running every Thursday evening. Outside of class, eager young linguists who keep their ears open can experience over 20 languages being spoken around school. Students are given the opportunity to participate in worldwide exchanges by spending up to a term in another Round Square school. There are also annual language trips to France and Spain and Germany.

Learning support and SEN: Full-time head of learning support, dyslexia specialist and two part-time assistants; it's a strong department. Parents are charged for the support according to whether it's in-class or on an individual basis.

The arts and extracurricular: Art takes place in the old stables; super natural light and plenty of Apple Macs for those with a penchant for design and design technology, and kilns for keen potters; it's an appropriately messy yet inspirational space. Drama is popular; it's a small school so very inclusive, and everyone who wants to take part can do, whether centre stage or behind the scenes.

Word of mouth is the biggest factor in attracting parents, both locally and from overseas. There are a few expat Forces parents who love the leadership challenges here

Lots of individual tuition in music, and the Holst Room, a space designed for its acoustics, is a valuable teaching and performance space. It's not the strongest subject here, according to parents, so a particularly musical child may not be able to shine, but there is undoubtedly a 'have a go' attitude to the subject, as with everything else.

The school supports community projects in South Africa; each year students help out with resources and provide physical help to a project with Tiger Kloof School – in fact just mentioning the name of the school brings a warm smile and glow of pride to the faces of the older students, who view it as an extension of their school life at Windermere.

A highly rated international summer school is proving increasingly popular and has effectively added a fourth term to the school year.

Sport: Built on a slope; the site brings its own challenges and there aren't acres of pitches here; the biggest area of flat ground is the lake, so that's where most activities take place. Better suited to small team sports, and there are probably more expeditions than fixtures, but they do have an Astroturf and a sports hall for year-round play.

Whilst they can't compete with the big boys at team sports, they take it seriously and offer the full range of usual school sports and others besides, including equestrianism, sailing and kayaking. Hodge Howe, the school's own watersports centre and the only school centre in the country to hold RYA British Youth Sailing Recognised Club status, has two boathouses, a private beach and a pavilion with a classroom (also available for wedding receptions...) and a fleet of sailing boats and kayaks. Other outdoor activities include camping trips, fell walking, ghyll scrambling, orienteering, caving and climbing, so if you are the adventurous type and not joined at the hip to your hair straighteners or worried by a patchy mobile phone signal, there's plenty here for you. All students in years 7, 8 and 9 complete the Windermere Adventure Award. They also spend one morning a fortnight outside school doing anything from mountain biking to conservation and environmental work.

Boarding: Despite the national park location, it's only 90 minutes to either Manchester or Liverpool airports (outside London considered a safer option by some nervous parents), three hours to London by train and the school has a fleet of shuttle buses catering for students' many and varied travel needs.

Word of mouth is the biggest factor in attracting parents, both locally and overseas. There are a few expat Forces parents who love the leadership challenges here, and whilst more than half of the students are from within the UK, the rest represent around 24 different countries far and wide, including China, Germany, Hong Kong, Lithuania, Poland, Romania, Ukraine, Spain and Russia.

Customary dorms in single-sex houses on site for boarders aged 8-16 (only a handful of junior boarders); there are a few single rooms but not many choose them, most preferring to share. Plenty of messy individualisation of space with One Direction posters, soft toys and family photos. Each house has a staff house 'family', comfortable shared common rooms with views across the lake for socialising, karaoke and TV watching, and well-equipped kitchens for snacking. In the girls' house at least, baking seems popular with Mary Berry cake recipes much in evidence. Food cooked in-house, good quality and plentiful, just as well with all that fresh air.

Well-behaved sixth formers earn the right to have more space and freedom in self-contained flats in a coeducational house on site – still supervised, of course, but a step along the road to preparation for life beyond school. A sixth form bar allows (with parental permission) two drinks with dinner on a Saturday night; younger pupils love the occasional takeaway, shared with friends in the boarding house. If that sounds a little tame, there's not much else you can get up to here (a definite plus for many parents), but cinema visits and occasional weekend trips to the Trafford Centre in Manchester or Alton Towers keep restless adolescents happy. They are also very busy after school, so much so that a parent of a day boy told us they relocated to be on the school's doorstep simply because their son was 'reluctant to go home after school – way too much going on'.

Ethos and heritage: On this site since 1924 and co-ed since 1999, there is a good mix of boys and girls here. Extensive additional building took place in the '70s and '80s, but the national park setting places real limitations on new building – essentially it's all about how the place looks from the lake. Some attractive newer and recently refurbed buildings are scattered around the grounds of the Victorian mansion of the original Browhead estate, some boarding facilities, others classrooms and labs. Highlights are the Jenkins Centre for music, performing arts, languages and a superb dining room and Crampton Hall – a spacious auditorium for theatrical and musical productions.

Built on a slope; the site brings its own challenges and there aren't acres of pitches; the biggest area of flat ground is the lake, so that's where most activities take place

Round Square is a worldwide association of schools that is all about the whole person – the Kurt Hahn view that says students can only understand life by experiencing it in exciting and challenging ways. Opportunities for travel and exchanges to other Round Square schools bring extra opportunities, and they welcome international students who wish to experience British culture whilst bringing with them their own perspective and world view. There is a real sense that, although surrounded by mountains here, their hearts and heads go way beyond the valley and into the wider world beyond. The core of the IB diploma programme encompasses many of the Round Square principles, making the curriculum ideal here. Daily reflection is an important start to the day and something valued hugely by the students themselves. 'It lifts you up,' they tell us; 'you're in school, lessons haven't started yet but you're saying hello to everyone'; 'it's a nice place to be' and it is often, apparently, like a mini TED talk to start your day, food for thought and a valued and laudable touchstone. Outside speakers are welcomed as regular visitors and students also attend conferences and exchanges worldwide.

Notable former pupils include dressage Olympian Emma Hindle and internationally respected soprano Claire Booth.

Pastoral care, inclusivity and discipline: Many parents are attracted by the fact that the school isn't especially selective – telling us they didn't want their offspring to be a 'public school product' but rather they 'wanted their individuality to be valued'. They appreciate the weekly online newsletter and feel that they 'could walk into the school at any time if they had any concerns at all'. Also of great value to parents is the way in which 'teachers respond very promptly to even the smallest queries… pastoral care is excellent,' they say. Overseas parents enjoy a 'close relationship' with the staff and love the fact that their offspring often enjoy tea or dinner with the head and his wife.

Staff do, of course, keep a careful watching brief, but essentially Windermere pupils are encouraged to be self-disciplined. Problems are rare, as older and younger students jog along happily in the knowledge that they want for nothing (except perhaps a Starbucks) in this sprawling, healthy and supportive environment. Strong views from the sixth formers themselves on smoking – 'Why would you?' It seems there's a degree of self-policing going on.

Students appear comfortable and relaxed but with an uncommon sense of responsibility too; they recently 'simply couldn't stand back and do nothing' following the recent earthquakes in Nepal, and within hours were actively fundraising within the local community in support of the victims. Charity fundraising such as this, alongside work in a soup kitchen and orphanage, affords them a 'very different reality', say parents – 'one which puts their very privileged life into sharp focus'.

Pupils and parents: Any passing traffic is likely to be either hikers or tourists, so recruitment is a challenge, though undoubtedly helped in the overseas market by the Beatrix Potter and Peter Rabbit connection. It's a lifestyle choice living here in the Lake District, and some parents have huge commutes to city offices, whilst others are simply escaping the city altogether. Fewer landed gentry than in days of old, more hard-working hotel and restaurant owners or young semi-retired professionals who have made their money in the City and moved here for a breath of fresh air.

High on the list of attractions for many is the extensive programme of adventurous outdoor activities – something the pupils coming through from the school's own prep department have already enjoyed in abundance. It seems to result not only in hardy pupils but also in a can-do attitude, parents buying in to the opportunities for growth and independence in a safe environment. The words 'warmth' and 'friendliness' are oft repeated by parents when talking about the staff; they are aware that this is more typical of a small school and for them, it's a valid and valuable trade-off for bigger and better facilities.

Money matters: Non means-tested scholarships are available in performing arts, visual arts, general academic subjects and sport. There are some means-tested bursaries available.

The last word: A glorious backdrop in which to learn and grow, and the school makes full use of it. On a sunny day you can see for miles. On other days you can't see your hand in front of your face. The weather can change in an instant, but no one allows that fact to get in the way of an existence where hard work, good friends, rosy cheeks and fresh air in your lungs are all part of the package.

State boarding schools

SCOTLAND
14
Edinburgh
Glasgow
NORTHERN IRELAND
Belfast
22
21
Dublin
Newcastle Upon Tyne
12
Keswick
6
19
Ripon
13
Bradford
Leeds
Kingston Upon Hull
Liverpool
Sheffield
ENGLAND
Stoke-on-trent
Nottingham
9
15
Leicester
25
Norwich
Birmingham
Coventry
Cambridge
4
10
23
3
WALES
20
Colchester
Oxford
1
17
8
London
Cardiff
11
5
Warminster
2
16
24
18
Southampton
Brighton
7
Exeter
20
40
60
Miles

STATE

Beechen Cliff School

1

Alexandra Park, Kipling Avenue, Bath, Somerset BA2 4RE

01225 480466 | headteacher@beechencliff.org.uk | www.beechencliff.org.uk

Ages: 11–18

Pupils: 1,318; sixth form: 439; Boarders: 32

Fees: Day free; Boarding: £11,300 pa.

Headteacher: Since September 2021, Tim Markall (40s). Home grown, having joined the school as a maths teacher fresh from his PGCE (Bath) back in 2005, since when he's risen through the ranks as head of maths, assistant head and finally deputy head before taking the helm. A local boy, he grew up in Nailsea, near Bristol, where he attended Bristol Grammar before studying maths and statistics at the University of Bath. Caught teaching bug while tennis coaching as part of his degree: 'I realised just how much I enjoy working with younger people.' Sadly no time for teaching these days, 'but I'm hoping to fit some in further down the line,' he told us, and what he loses in classroom time he gains in developing the school's outdoors education, more of which later.

'Big shoes to fill' is the consensus from parents, but most are already won over by his 'caring attitude', 'down to earth approachability' and 'clear vision, with a clear path for the school'. He had just recovered from Covid when we met him (via Zoom) so probably the only path he wanted to be on was towards his bed – all the more impressive, we thought, that he remained on point and impassioned throughout.

Lives nearby with his wife and two children, one at primary school and the other at secondary school. Still enjoys tennis and is involved in his local church. Loves the outdoors, especially walking and hiking.

Entrance: Around 300 apply for 162 day places in year 7. Priority given to looked-after boys, followed by siblings, staff children and then 12 sporting aptitude places. Eighty per cent of remaining places to those living within Bath City boundary, divided between those living north and south of the River Avon (split reviewed annually). Boys come from nearly 30 different primary schools – and the odd prep. Boys and girls joining the co-ed sixth form need at least five 6s at GCSE with 6s in the subjects to be studied (or related subjects) – a minimum of 50 join at this stage, sometimes as many as 100.

Up to seven boarding places available in year 7, with three to four available per year after that (you can apply in any year group but around half the boarders are sixth formers). Similar criteria to day places but principally a 'significant degree of boarding need' with priority to Forces children (though only one or two Forces families currently). Some boarders are tied in with sporting programmes (eg Southampton FC or Bath Uni's specialist sports training) and a couple of places are kept for moments of crisis. All now hail from the UK – the international cohort having dwindled away post Brexit and since Covid.

Exit: Around a third leave after GCSEs – some to local colleges for more vocational courses, others to schools with less academic sixth forms. Some 80-90 per cent of sixth formers to universities all over the country, 40 per cent to Russell Group. Three to Oxford in 2021, and five medics. Cardiff, Bath, Durham, Exeter, Manchester, Leeds and Loughborough all popular. Maths and sciences courses get the biggest numbers.

Latest results: In 2021, 48 per cent 9-7 at GCSE; 92 per cent 9-4 in both maths and English. At A level, 49 per cent A*/A (73 per cent A*-B). In 2019 (the last year when exams took place), 33 per cent 9-7 at GCSE and 83 per cent 9-4 in both maths and English. At A level in 2019, 27 per cent A*/A (52 per cent A*-B).

Teaching and learning: Although non-selective, the school reflects the population of Bath and tends to get more able boys (and, in sixth form, girls). A work ethic seems to be pretty well automatically assumed. Cognitive ability tests in year 7 give a good basis for value-added measurement, followed by plenty of monitoring throughout. 'They cater well for my children's different academic abilities and very much keep us in the loop,' said a parent, though another felt, 'They could be more proactive in saying, "This is what your son is doing, this is what we need him to be doing and this is when we need him to be doing it by" – more clarity, in other words, when it comes to academic targets.' Plenty of homework but there's a chance to do it supervised after school three days a week, sometimes made compulsory for those who need help getting organised. Class sizes are commonly about 28, stretching to 32 for the top maths sets and dropping much lower for minority exam subjects and for bottom sets (there's setting in English and maths from year 7 and in sciences from GCSE). French from year 7, with German, Spanish or Italian added in year 8.

Three different pathways at GCSE. Around 70 per cent take the academic EBacc route, consisting of nine GCSEs (10 for the third of students who take separate sciences or even 11 if they take further maths too). The rest are split between a more flexible, vocational route (eg Level 2 sports science instead of PE GCSE; Level 2 art and design or interactive media instead of art GCSE) and a bespoke curriculum for a small number with SEN (taking fewer subjects overall). Geography and sciences do particularly well.

The competitive sixth form gets a few into Oxbridge and medicine every year. 'Truly an academic sixth form now!' one parent commented. Twenty-seven subjects offered at A level, no drama, textiles or classical languages. Four or five groups in some subjects with sciences, history and geography most popular but prepared to put on minority subjects for very small groups, eg two for German and Italian. Most take three plus core maths, an AS language or EPQ (around 30 to 40 students per year do the latter).

Boarders get one of the best views in Bath from the terrace which opens from their spacious common/dining room and is used for outside dining in the summer

'Covid forced the school to try new things digitally and they've become much more open to technology such as Google Classroom, and all the better for it,' said a parent. Nobody we spoke to felt their child had got left behind in terms of learning during the pandemic which, says the school, is why they were able to prioritise all the things the students had missed when they came back – science practicals, extracurricular and an in-person pastoral programme among them.

Learning support and SEN: Full-time SENCo plus teaching assistants (equivalent of seven full-time), necessary in a school that takes some EHCP pupils – 17 when we visited. All students with SEN have a comprehensive support plan, which is passed on to every class teacher. Some have additional sessions – usually in ones or twos – for numeracy and literacy, the whole way through if required. These sessions can take the place of MFL if a student really struggles with languages. 'My son is expected to do one language in lower school when he'd rather do none but if he still finds it as challenging next year, I think we'll ask to stop and I'm pretty sure they'll be fine about it. I applaud that as it's good to give it a go but I know they're also realistic about expectations,' a parent told us.

The arts and extracurricular: Sport and outdoors education rule but music gets enough interest to run at both GCSE and A level (two A levels in fact – straight music and music technology). Big, well-used music centre brims with exciting equipment and there are plenty of alumni at music college. All the usual choirs, orchestras and ensembles, all of which perform in concerts, carol concerts etc; there had just been a piano recital involving 30 students when we reviewed the school. Drama is outsourced to Bath Theatre School, which offers students the opportunity to do drama club and whole-school performances, eg Little Shop of Horrors, although most of the performers come from lower school. No LAMDA and no GCSE or A level drama. Art, on the other hand, runs two GCSE classes every year, with both art and photography available at A level, as well as more vocational options. The department is split across an unreconstructed collection of buildings, but is none the worse for it. Outstanding photography equipment and a light-filled studio plus full printing workshop. Some very fine work in all media is on display.

Challenge is a key buzzword, with many of these youngsters champing at the bit to get outdoors – CCF, DofE, Ten Tors, Three Peaks, the Centurion walk and a cross-Devon bike ride all attract big numbers and likely even bigger still if the current head has anything to do with it. Other clubs and activities abound, allowing young Warhammer and Lego enthusiasts, for instance, to retain their small boy passions, while societies range from MedSoc to Christian Union to French film club. Sporty clubs are particularly popular, notably rugby and cricket, but the likes of Dungeons and Dragons and Scrabble also bring in the punters. 'The sheer amount of clubs is one of the things that drew us to the school – there are so many extracurricular opportunities,' extoled a parent.

All year 7 boys get to stay in a remote and primitive Welsh cottage, which teaches them to value such luxuries as running and hot water and electric light, as well as focus on team building. All the usual foreign trips with some financial help if needed.

Sport: Illustrious sports record, as one would expect from a school which offers places to rugby players in the ACE scheme in conjunction with Bath Rugby. Both sixth form admission standards and year 7 entry criteria adjusted for outstanding players. The enormous sports honours board in the entrance says it all, starting with Roger Bannister and including rugby players Freddie Burns and John Hall, football manager Paul Tisdale and Olympic gold medal sprinter Jason Gardner and skeleton bob champion Amy Williams (GB's only gold medallist in the 2010 Winter Olympics). 'If you have a rugby child, this place is absolutely amazing – they get the right coaches and guidance and they just love it,' said a parent.

As well as the staples of rugby, football, tennis, cricket and hockey, rowing and other minority sports all get a look in. Meanwhile for sixth form girls, there's netball and some hockey – as well as rugby (Ailis Egan of Ireland Ladies is an old girl). This is one of the few state schools offering a full sporting programme on Saturday, and with school's philosophy that everyone should have a go, you can count on masses of opportunities for less skilled enthusiasts. 'There is an elite element which is incredibly talented, but at the same time the less sporty are very much included,' said a parent. 'And if a child really doesn't like sport, they just opt for the outdoor challenges or a minority activity like clay pigeon shooting.' Beautifully kept pitches plus Astros. Super sports hall with exterior climbing wall at one end, funded through parental gift aid. School also uses 50m pool and other facilities at nearby Bath University.

Boarding: A small part of the school, with just 30-ish boarders. Results in a family feel, with sixth formers (who make up the majority) doing a grand job of looking out for younger ones. But don't expect a live-in housemaster or mistress with young kids and family dog to be running the place as in some boarding schools – four members of staff take it in turn to cover this role. Good, clean, spacious rooms, all ensuite – some singles, some twins. 'Functional, not swish – just as it should be,' said one parent. They get one of the best views in Bath from the terrace which opens from their spacious common/dining room and is used for outside dining in the summer.

Parents told us there are sensible rules around gaming, phone usage etc and there are plenty of organised activities, especially sports-related, but also local trips and paintballing for the majority (but not vast majority) who stay at weekends. 'They're kept nice and busy and they're very much encouraged to use the communal spaces rather than hide away in their rooms,' said one parent, though another felt there could be more

The atmosphere is friendly but definitely traditional with tidy hair, smartly tied ties, natty striped shirts and smart black blazers

things such as barbecues in the summer – 'I was quite shocked they don't do more in that sense.' We heard plenty of praise for the focus on independence – 'The boys all do their own washing, which is wonderful,' said a mum. Pastoral care is a strong point, we also heard – 'Nobody is left in any doubt that they're cared for and who they can talk to if they have any concerns.' Head regularly joins the boarders for tea – a nice touch, we thought. 'I always enjoy it, they're a great bunch,' he told us.

Ethos and heritage: Superb site is akin to an independent school minus the plush reception areas and plus the odd dilapidated corner and shabby classroom. Bath stone softens the distinguished 1930s main buildings and the panoramic views and lush greenness do the rest. Originally the Bath City School, founded in the Guildhall in 1896, it moved to Beechen Cliff in 1932 as the City of Bath Boys' School. Its present name dates from the 1970s when the City of Bath school amalgamated with Oldfield Boys' School, a local secondary modern, to form a comprehensive school. A huge campaign saved it from being axed in the 1990s. A founder member of Bath Educational Trust, set up in 2009, a collaboration between 10 local secondary schools, both universities in Bath and City of Bath College.

Steadily improving facilities to match the academic and sporting prowess of its pupils. The atmosphere is friendly but definitely traditional with tidy hair, smartly tied ties, natty striped shirts and smart black blazers (good secondhand shop run by PTA). Sixth form girls wear office attire. Discipline, courtesy, academic confidence and pride in the school are encouraged by the high standards and the gentle courtesy with which staff and pupils treat each other. Lots of past pupils on the staff vouch for how highly they value the school. Old boys/girls (Old Sulians) and former members of staff come in to teach extra sessions – for love. The dining room is pleasant and practical with pleasingly solid furniture and a calm friendly feel. 'And the food is great, even my very fussy kids approve!' said a parent.

Old Sulians include Arnold Ridley (Private Godfrey in Dad's Army), Andrew Lincoln (Drop the Dead Donkey, This Life, Love Actually), Curt Smith (Tears for Fears), Sir Richard Roberts (Nobel

Prize winning biochemist – mechanism of gene-splicing – and generous benefactor), Dan Rivers (ITN News correspondent) and the ex-head of MI6, Sir John Sawers.

Pastoral care, inclusivity and discipline: Mental health and wellbeing have been taken particularly seriously since Covid – 'We were aware of a lot of anxiety among some students during isolation,' says head. A full-time school counsellor is available, including via self-referral, and 60 members of staff are now trained in a solutions-focused approach to pastoral conversations. 'If you're not okay, that's okay – that's a key message to students,' says school. Four houses (which include sixth formers) form the bedrock of the pastoral system – named after the (four white male) literary figures which gave their names to the roads in this residential area of Bath, known as Poets' Corner. Mixed age house assemblies meet twice a week, providing a way to integrate older and younger pupils. Head of sixth form pastoral care gives more specialist help to sixth formers, who 'massively trust' the staff and regard them as 'expert godparents'. One parent commented that the staff all work amazingly hard, taking on anything they think will benefit pupils.

The head told us that equal opportunities take precedence in everything from school trips (ensuring inclusion of disadvantaged students) to increasing discussions around respect and tolerance (including around Everyone's Invited, Black History Month, British Values, Show Racism the Red Card etc). 'What's right? What does respect really mean? How can you feel confident to challenge what you see? These are the kinds of conversations we are having more and more,' says head. Certainly the school must be on its toes since a 'prejudicial' video shared on social media in 2020 appeared to show a student being subjected to racist taunts by another pupil, which followed a very serious racist incident involving pupils in 2018.

Strong reward culture for achievements (exemplified by the school's apparently limitless supply of Mars bars handed out to boys who have 'gone the extra mile') is balanced by traditional sanctions for both academic and social misdemeanours. Uniform breaches, turning up late, slacking on homework and forgetting equipment for lessons land you in detention after school or worse on a Saturday – or supervised after-school homework sessions. Usually around 25 temporary exclusions per year and one or two permanent ones. 'The formal approach to discipline wouldn't suit all kids,' reckoned one parent.

Pupils and parents: Bath's middle class aspiring parents obviously love Beechen Cliff. Fierce criticism from Ofsted a few years back was not borne out by parental surveys and sparked public expressions of support for the school, both from parents and current pupils. Its wide entry from a strictly drawn and very local catchment, including some much less affluent areas, is also appreciated. Supportive PTA runs a gift aid scheme, providing extra equipment of the sort that the independent sector takes for granted – rugby balls, for example. A few grumbles about school comms.

The last word: An exceptional, thriving school with a heritage feel. Great on the academics but not an exam machine, with a focus on sport, clubs and the great outdoors comparable to many schools in the independent sector. The fact that children from all walks of life can get a slice of the cake is, understandably, a huge source of pride for both the school and its parents and pupils.

Brymore Academy

Cannington, Bridgwater, Somerset TA5 2NB

01278 652369 | office@brymoreacademy.co.uk | www.brymoreacademy.co.uk

Ages: 11–17

Pupils: 335; Boarders: 40 full, 98 weekly

Fees: Day free; Boarding £11,175 – £12,120 pa

Head: Since 2011, Mark Thomas (early 50s). Originally from Cornwall, he came to Brymore from Courtfields School, Wellington, where he had been deputy and acting head. Previously deputy head at Brittons Academy in Rainham, his early teaching career was mainly in London after studying geography at Kingston and a PGCE at Liverpool.

Married to a PE teacher, their young son is delighted that his dad works in a castle (the main house has turrets) and drives tractors. A geography and PE teacher, his main sport has always been athletics and he loves to run. Down to earth and approachable, parents have 'nothing but praise'. With his zero-tolerance approach to bullying, he is 'very firm but fair', we were told; 'it's obvious he cares deeply about the boys and wants them all to thrive.'

In the ten years he has been here Mr Thomas has taken Brymore from strength to strength, developing the site, increasing numbers (now oversubscribed) and creating a unique school that fills a gap for many parents. For boys who thrive on practical learning as well as those who struggle academically, Brymore is a good find. 'But we have become a victim of our own success,' he explained. Demand for places is high and although SEN numbers have grown, he insists that Brymore is fundamentally a mainstream school, providing support and opportunities to boys of all abilities.

Moreover, he appreciates the role that Brymore plays in the local farming community: creating a skilled workforce that is used to hard work and responsibility. He would love to help more boys, he told us, but he is not willing to increase numbers; its small size is one of the reasons it works so well. Understandably, this makes the entrance interviews even harder for him. He says he can spot a boy who would benefit from Brymore straight away, but due to high demand he can't always offer a place. 'This is heartbreaking,' he told us, but he is determined to keep Brymore just so.

Entrance: Boarders are assessed on 'suitability for boarding'. Outboarders (day pupils) are accepted on the usual Somerset criteria and straight line distance from school. Due to growing demand the furthest distance has dropped from 20 miles to less than five miles in recent years. Year 7 intake is made up of 40 outboarders and 30 boarders.

Visits plus taster nights and fun bonding activities mean that boys settle quickly. Year 7s are allocated four buddies to help them navigate each area of school life: boarding, sports, academia and farming.

Exit: All leave after GCSEs and around a third go on to study for A levels at sixth form college or independent schools (often with scholarships). Others head off to agriculture colleges like Hartpury or take up apprenticeships in farming, horticulture, agricultural engineering or motor vehicles.

Around six or seven former pupils go on to university each year. A good number join the armed forces or work within local government, the medical profession or vet sciences; others end up running their own businesses.

Latest results: School has not published results for the last few years.

Teaching and learning: Brymore is a mainstream school with a USP – boys can learn practical and technical farming and horticultural skills alongside the national curriculum. This unique learning environment gives boys the opportunity to get hands-on – driving tractors from 13, milking (in a state-of-the-art milking parlour recently opened by rugby hero Phil Vickery), feeding cattle, calving and lambing, growing vegetables and maintaining the grounds. Understandably, Brymore is popular with aspiring farmers, but the broad curriculum offers a good balance of academia, sports and some arts too.

Horticulture and agriculture are compulsory for first three years but not at GCSE. There is however a consistently high take-up in practical land-based subjects each year, including a BTEC in agriculture and City & Guilds Technical Awards in horticulture or land-based studies. Other popular options include engineering studies (NCFE, level 2), PE (BTEC) and geography (GCSE). Design technology is compulsory at GCSE. Sciences are usually combined but can be taken separately if interest is high. Students can choose to follow an academic pathway that includes computer science and non-practical subjects. As a small school it can sometimes be difficult to accommodate every wish.

Brymore is a mainstream school with a USP – boys can learn practical and technical farming and horticultural skills alongside the national curriculum

For English and maths, boys are split into three sets based on ability. Class sizes are 25 in the two higher sets and 20 in the lower. With additional qualified in-class SEN assistants in the latter, the pupil teacher ratio rises to 6:1, providing those that need it with valuable extra support.

Reading progress is tracked up to year 9 and boys are expected to log at least 20 minutes of reading every day. Motivation is an effective reward system including a readers' hall of fame. Our guides proudly pointed out their latest achievements and rewards. Progress scores are high and among the highest in Somerset. In 2019, 49 per cent got 9-4 in maths and English at GCSE.

Boys are challenged appropriately and encouraged to do extra work in small groups. Parents say that their sons gain confidence here and become motivated and determined. 'Teachers are really encouraging. [My son] has moved up sets since starting, he now believes in himself, ' explained one. 'They follow the head's approach with discipline and recognition of good work,' added another.

No French or other modern languages taught, but Latin has been introduced in years 7 and 8. This may come as surprise to some, but Latin has being making a comeback in state schools in recent years. It can support literacy by teaching children how languages (English and others) are structured, as well as understanding grammar and the roots of vocabulary. Not only does this help with English language development but it also builds a good foundation for future modern language learning. For Brymore boys, its relevance in the horticultural world has been welcomed and results have exceeded expectations: 'The boys love it,' enthused the head.

Much of what Brymore offers is certainly special, if not unique, but the core curriculum is the same as other state schools. It caters for a full range of ability (including SEN), as well as challenge for the most able. All the boys are encouraged to aim high and there are plenty of trips and enrichment activities to boost curiosity and enhance subject knowledge.

Brymore 'deals with the mixed abilities very well' and academically able boys also thrive. Parents of two very different boys explained how Brymore has suited both well. One is particularly sporty and working his way towards a career in farming; the other is more studious and is going on to study aeronautical engineering.

Learning support and SEN: Provides support for dyslexia, dyscalculia and ASD. In fact, almost half of boys have additional needs and around 14 per cent have ECHPs. Some facilities have been adapted for pupils with visual and hearing impairments. One parent explained: 'Our son has a few learning issues and Brymore just seems to fit him and how he learns. His grades have improved considerably and he actually really enjoys going to school now.' Another added, '[My son] has always struggled academically. Practically, though, he thrives. It's definitely his strong point; he loves making things and taking things apart. He loves being out on the farm and is really useful! Brymore has provided opportunities you just don't find in a "normal" mainstream school.' The reason that Brymore can provide additional and individual support is in part due to its small size; boys feel they can ask for help. One explained how he was struggling with maths but after a chat with his teacher he started one-to-one weekly tutorials after school.

The arts and extracurricular: Central to everything is agricultural and horticultural practice and theory. In addition to the school day lessons, every boy takes his turn in working on the farm, boarding for seven days in order to be up at 6am come rain or shine. Alongside the farm are greenhouses, polytunnels and an impressive walled garden where boys can request their own allotment. If they look after it well, they can expand their empire. One boy grew 48 tomato plants last season and sold them to his dad to use in his restaurants. This entrepreneurial spirit is positively encouraged at Brymore and boys regularly sell their produce at open days and local events.

Parents are 'blown away from the word go'. 'Diligentia et labore' is the motto: labour with diligence. Manners, respect and hard work are a way of life here

Brymore's metal and wood workshops, including smithy and foundry, teach practical, transferable professional skills. We saw a year 10 metal class making bottle openers and a year 7 group mastering saw skills in woodwork. Extracurricular activities include blacksmithing, silversmithing and coppersmithing.

Music and drama are taught up to year 9. There is a choir and an annual school production, which is 'good fun', but performing arts are definitely not centre stage at Brymore. Art is offered in every year.

Sport: A sporty school, the main school house is surrounded by rugby fields and the MUGA (multi-usage games area). Chad's Run, so called because it takes place on Chad's Hill, is an almost two-mile cross-country run every day after school. A Brymore tradition for over 32 years, the boys take it seriously. It's up to them when and how many times they run, but the goal is to beat your personal best. Lists of running times are displayed throughout the school and competition is rife. However, boys were keen to point out that it doesn't matter how good you are – points are rewarded for just finishing. We were struck by how accepting the boys are of each other. 'Everybody's good at different stuff,' shrugged one lad.

Rugby is the main sport. Team players train seriously – weekly circuits, weights and Chad runs. But fear not if rugby is not your thing as the sports department, led by the resident PE teacher of nearly four decades, has a whole load of activities on offer. 'There's something for everyone,' say parents – 'You don't necessarily have to be sporty, but you do need to embrace it all and give things a go.' Importantly, nobody is left out – 'He ended up representing the school in athletics at events, never going far but he enjoyed being involved… For a child who doesn't always find sport easy, these opportunities mean the world.'

An outdoor heated swimming pool is well used in the summer with the highlight being an end of year gala. Boys love that it's kept open after Chad's Run in the summer months. Another favourite with boys is the well-worn BMX track, built by past pupils.

Boarding: For many parents, boarding was not their first choice and some admitted being more than a little apprehensive. None have looked back – 'In the summer it's hard to persuade them to come home!' chuckled one.

Three boarding houses, 50 boys in each. Two were built in 2010, one for year 7s and the other for full-time boarders. School House is in the original main school building and houses weekly and flexi boarders. A rolling refurbishment project ensures all rooms are routinely spruced up with boys voting on carpet patterns and décor.

Dorms sleep four, except in the main house, where it's up to six. Boys are asked who they would like to share with, then rooms are allocated accordingly. Dorms were clean and, for teenage boys, surprisingly tidy – although we did spy a rather excessive pile of clothes on one desk – obviously scooped up from the floor in a rush. Rooms are spacious and light with homely touches – fake grass mats for year 7s to play toy tractors was particularly lovely to see.

Common rooms have pool tables, games consoles, a kitchen, and plenty of sofas for movie nights. All tech is handed in at night. Any boys that don't (or give in dummy devices) get a ban. Houseparents 'run a very tight ship but are very caring and protective'. Boys admitted they were homesick at first but they soon settled, thriving on the routine, making good friends. One boy confided: 'It makes me appreciate home more.'

Plenty of evening and weekend activities on offer including mackerel fishing, paintballing, rugby matches and manhunts in the woods. Some choose to flexi board just so they 'can benefit from the full Brymore experience'.

Ethos and heritage: Brymore was established in 1951 by Somerset County Council at a cost of £6,000 as a Secondary Technical School of Agriculture on an impressive 60-acre farm on the edge of Cannington, between the Quantocks and the Bristol Channel. A contemporary, understated sign guides visitors through a tree-lined drive leading to the original 13th-century house, once owned by Cromwell's financier John Pym. The modern reception in this historic building sets the scene: traditional but forward-thinking.

Plenty of evening and weekend activities on offer. Some choose to flexi board just so they 'can benefit from the full Brymore experience'

Parents are 'blown away from the word go'. 'I remember thinking how polite and well-mannered the boys were; I loved the "old school" feel with the boys holding doors open.' 'Diligentia et labore' is the motto: labour with diligence. Manners, respect and hard work are a way of life here.

Buildings are dotted around the site, all within easy strolling distance. It's all fairly accessible but unsurprisingly muddy and bumpy in places. Most classrooms are in the main teaching block, built in 2010, but others, including maths, are in cabins. A bright and airy dining hall was built in 2015, but easily the most impressive addition to the site is the £500k farm building opened in 2019.

'A private school feel but without the fees,' we heard, although we felt it seemed less formal or rigid than many private schools. The atmosphere was light and the boys seemed able to be themselves. With just 330 pupils, everybody gets to know each other either in the boarding houses, on the runs or on the farm working as a team. There is a real sense of camaraderie here. 'Brymore oozes a family feeling of security with boys looking out for each other (in my son's opinion),' one parent told us.

The boys feel that it is their school. If something isn't working, staff will create a pupil panel and a teacher panel to discuss and resolve issues together. A good example of this is when pupils and teachers voted to end school on Saturdays. The general consensus (perhaps not surprisingly) was that they already worked long, hard weeks and needed an extra day of rest.

Past pupils visit frequently and are still part of school life. One teaches blacksmithing at Brymore alongside his own small business, another is head of boarding and a former head boy is now head of agriculture. Others include agriculture minister MEP Neil Parish, Mark Irish, England U21 rugby player and Alex Wright, British race walking champion.

Pastoral care, inclusivity and discipline: 'At a time when boys are perhaps at their most challenging and in danger of making many wrong decisions, Brymore offers the support and structure to help them become conscientious, diligent and hardworking,' one mother reflected. Year 8s are given garden duties, year 9s do a week of farming duties and older boys can step up to become head of duties (HOD). After a thorough interview process and selection, HODs help younger boys with milking and duties on the farm.

Housemasters and tutors meet pupils weekly. Vertical tutor groups mean the oldest mentor the year 7s and get to know all age groups. Day boys or 'outboarders' and boarders mix well, as do year groups in boarding houses.

'Boys love the routine; know what's expected of them... Rules and boundaries are clear,' reported parents. Discipline is firm but fair. Level 1 equates to a verbal warning, level 2 detention and level 3 isolation for the day. Apparently this is enough to put off even the worst potential offenders. 'Bullying is not tolerated; it happens of course, but is dealt with instantly,' parents confirmed.

Boys are encouraged to aim high and are rewarded for achievements, whether that be winning, finishing or making a good effort. 'Every child shines no matter what they're good at,' say parents. As well as an end of year prizegiving, effort and attainment in all subjects are rewarded at the end of each term. Parents are impressed how well the boys respond to this. One told us, 'His confidence in himself has come on in leaps and bounds, he's put himself up to do readings in church, he put himself forward for cross-country, he's shown prospective parents around the school and he is a school counsellor. If someone had told me he'd be doing any of that a year ago I wouldn't have believed them.'

Lots of grumbles (from parents) about the food, mainly inadequate portion sizes. Apparently boarders take extra food to school each week. When questioned, boys said it was 'a bit healthy' but had improved.

Pupils and parents: Parents are farmers, business owners, health and education professionals – a diverse, friendly and hard-working bunch. Most live within a two-hour commute in Devon, Cornwall, Somerset, Gloucestershire. A few further afield with the occasional overseas student. Popular with the local farming community.

Excellent communication between school and home – 'The door is always open,' say parents. MyEd app is popular to keep track of things and parents love the postcards home and the weekly planners that are 'great to go through together as a family on Sundays'.

Boys are unpretentious, upbeat, happy and polite. Not only are they proud of their school and happy to be there, but they feel lucky to be there. To see their commitment in action, go along to one of Brymore's open days. These are no ordinary open days – with around 4.5k punters to look after, boys take on jobs of all sorts from car parking attendant to catering to tours and demonstrations.

Well known in the local area, Brymore boys are often seen at agricultural events proudly showing their animals or helping out. They are very much part of the farming community and during the floods in recent years boys have eagerly helped farmers clearing the land and caring for animals.

Money matters: Fees only for boarding, not tuition. All day boys have to board and pay for the weeks they are on farm duties. Educational grants may be available from home LAs.

The last word: We need more schools like Brymore. This is a school that understands that the academic route is not for everybody and has created a practical and hands-on learning environment that is simply outstanding. By helping boys find their strengths and giving them support in areas of need, they gain the confidence to take on the impressive range of opportunities that Brymore offers – and they thrive.

Burford School

3

Cheltenham Road, Burford, Oxfordshire OX18 4PL

01993 823303 | head.4040@burford.oxon.sch.uk | www.burford.oxon.sch.uk

Ages: 11–18

Pupils: 1,475; sixth form: 250; Boarders: 88 full

Fees: No day fees; Boarding £11,250 pa

Headteacher: Since 2021, Mr Matthew Albrighton MA (Cantab) PGCE FRSA (40s). No stranger to the region, he was born in Northamptonshire and attended Warwick Grammar School before reading geography at Cambridge and training as a teacher. First post was at King Edward VI

Birmingham, followed by a return to his alma mater before taking over as head of geography and IB co-ordinator at Wellington College, then deputy head at St Edward's Oxford.

Describes this as 'a very special school – we sit in a niche space, 450 years old this year, so it's got that real heritage, that cultural heritage'. As for moving from the independent sector, 'there are some nuances round resources, but in the end it's still young people – there will be times when they get it right and times when they get it wrong,' he mused, 'I'm interested in education in the wider level – as headteachers we have a role to keep questioning what we are doing.' Our conversation touched on the long academic standing of the school and then to its rural setting – 'the most delightful village in any county,' he says. 'What I want to do is harness that rural setting – the connection with the landscape is genuine here.'

Married to a history and EAL teacher, with two school-age children, he continues to teach geography at KS3. Parents haven't all met him yet but one commented, 'He comes with a good reputation and is not remotely stressed about chatting with the parents.' Another felt the high standards came 'from the top down'.

Entrance: Non-selective. Oxfordshire County Council entry procedure, taking from nine partnered primary schools, with an effective catchment area beyond of about four miles. Entry for boarding places is wider – applicants with a British passport considered from UK and beyond including Falkland Islands, Africa and Middle East, with 15-20 per cent Forces families. Joiners to the sixth form need six GCSEs (four at grade 5 and two at grade 6).

Exit: Approximately half leave after GCSE for local FE colleges – Abingdon and Witney, City of Oxford or Cirencester Colleges popular. 'Academically ambitious – geared for university in the main,' said a parent of the sixth formers. Good numbers to Russell Group. One to Oxbridge, and one medic in 2021. Alternatives include apprenticeships and vocational courses.

Latest results: In 2021, 35 per cent 9-7 at GCSE; 81 per cent 9-4 in both maths and English. At A level, 36 per cent A*/A (60 per cent A*-B). In 2019 (the last year when exams took place), 25 per cent 9-7 at GCSE; 70 per cent 9-4 in both English and maths. At A level, 21 per cent at A*/A (50 per cent A*-B).

Teaching and learning: Any school that celebrates its 450th birthday can't be short of savoir-faire, and Burford regularly turns out steady academic results from an interesting and broad curriculum. Year 7s are split into tutor groups to cover a solid range of subjects, as well as Spanish and a choice of German or French. Class sizes average 26 (20 for practicals), with some setting from year 8. Younger years have their days filled with a blend of creative and academic courses, including some unusual additions, eg business and enterprise, drama and photography. Year 9 students benefit from a head-start in double or triple science, while other GCSE options (trad subjects plus some less familiar ones such as PE, business and further maths) from year 10, alongside more coursework-based subjects like travel and tourism, child development (BTECs) and OCR Cambridge National award in sport. The vast majority of KS5 have their sights set on university, so academic subjects are popular, with additional options in economics, business, media and psychology, among others. An EPQ or AS is encouraged.

In The Acre, students learn about crops and vegetable production, alongside the local wildlife. 'We are the natural home for a rural skills programme,' the head tells us

Parents we spoke to commented on the improved results – 'My son became very academically motivated,' said one, with praise for the catch-up sessions and lunchtime clubs. 'Academically focused' was another's verdict, while a dad said, 'I can't stress enough the impact (of the school) in terms of confidence, in terms of her school work, she's expanded in maths and science.'

Parents were satisfied with the Covid online learning. 'They adjusted and adapted really quickly – we were able to contact various teachers and they made themselves available,' said one.

Learning support and SEN: Average numbers of children with learning support in the Learning Zone, with some one-to-one after school or lunchtime and some TAs in class or for exams. One mum felt that SEN support was not full or timely enough for children with milder needs – 'I feel I've had to chase and request things rather than they being forthcoming.' Therapies available through partnership with NHS services.

The arts and extracurricular: Timetabled art, photography and ceramics 'circus' for years 7 to 9, which develops a strong interest; good uptake in the exam years when art and photography can be studied as independent A levels. Displays in the school hall and in a divinely cluttered art block were bold and ambitious. We saw students quietly composing drawings from images they had observed at the Pitt Rivers Museum. The photography teacher was marking some stunning studio compositions for A level, a few developed with traditional methods in the school's darkroom. Two kilns and wheels allow for budding potters to get messy. A parent commented, 'The art is diverse. It wasn't just about drawing or painting it was a bit of everything. Burford has given her that confidence to look at art in a wider perspective.'

Burford is a music hub, providing tuition not only for its own students but for primary schools in west Oxford as part of the Institute of Music. The venture is supported by St Anne's College in Oxford and produces regular orchestras, bands and ensembles – the main music event of the year uses the Sheldonian, Oxford.

The school stages a West End musical – shows have included Beauty and the Beast and Les Mis. The boarding house has five pianos, and staff organise individual music practice and lessons at weekends, as well as informal gatherings round the common room piano.

The Burford School farm, responsible for training generations of local farming families, closed in the 1980s but a renewed interest in the language of conservation and agriculture has prompted the school to create a smaller plot, The Acre, opened by David Cameron in 2015. Here the students learn about crops and vegetable production, alongside the local wildlife. 'We are the natural home for a rural skills programme,' the head tells us, 'and we are re-engaging with the environment through Cotswold National Landscape and FarmEd.'

All life is here in organised lunchtime activities, from knitting club to rock school. One boy, who had previous experience of independent schools, said, 'There are as many sports – mountain biking, skiing – it has still got loads of facilities.' After-school clubs in drama and sports take advantage of late buses three times a week and an active riding club meets at a local stables and competes in the National Schools Equestrian Association competitions. Inspired trips take advantage of the labs and museums of Oxford as well as field trips to the Windrush valley, which bring the curriculum to life. All levels of DofE are open to students from year 9. Year 7 get to know each other in a residential shortly after joining, and other years enjoy, among other things, a water sports trip to Spain and an annual alpine ski trip.

Sport: With over 40 acres of land and a long heritage, Burford is a formidable competitor in the local leagues. Cricket on the home square, in front of a picturesque thatched pavilion, is particularly strong, frequently earning the school a place in the Cricketer Top 100 schools. There are exchange matches with Argentinian and Australian schools in rugby, hockey, netball and cricket (photos and cups proudly displayed in the hall), over 300 inter-schools and inter-house fixtures, as well as a massively cool sports tour every three years to Australia and New Zealand. Individual and specialist games (eg squash, Eton fives, badminton) complete the picture of a subject taken seriously both as part of the curriculum and at club level. One mother of three sporty children was delighted that the dedicated boarding staff taxied her children to local rugby clubs in Stowe and Chipping Norton in the evenings – 'the flexibility has been incredible' – as well as to A&E in Oxford after a particularly robust tackle.

Boarding: As one of only 34 state boarding schools in the country, Burford provides full-time boarding places for 100 UK passport holders at a fraction of the cost of independent boarding schools. Lenthall House, the 450-year-old schoolhouse in the heart of Burford's medieval town (with newer 17th-century additions), is now exclusively for boarders. Students hot-foot it up the steep high street to and from 'Top School', dodging tourists and shoppers.

We snooped on a bunting-strewn dorm for three girls. 'Our room is the social room – we play music, put on our LED lights and chill out,' one told us

Clustered in a quad round an inner courtyard are a collection of dorms, common rooms and a refectory. Boarders sleep in small single-sex dorms (between two and seven beds) with their own year group, as well as having the use of a kitchen to make toast and hot chocolate and a common room with games consoles, ping-pong and foosball tables. We snooped on a bunting-strewn dorm for three girls. 'Our room is the social room – we play music, put on our LED lights and chill out,' one told us. There's a homespun cinema room, as well as a tiny gym for evening activities. The overall impression is not opulent but comfortable and treasured. Outside the playground is used for knockabout volleyball or rugby passes or toasting marshmallows at a fire pit, and there's an allotment, tended by the green-fingered boarders of gardening club.

Students eat breakfast, tea and dinner together, rolling up to breakfast at the cafeteria-style counter in their PJs, or inviting a friend from the local community to a fresh-cooked meal (the day we visited there was chicken stroganoff or spag bol). A supervised prep session takes place every weekday evening in a communal classroom, and weekends are filled with activities and community service, from paintballing and crazy golf to CCF. The house is pretty full at weekends – 'There were a few times when she should have been home, but she chose to stay,' said one dad.

We met children from Forces families who had previous experience of a range of schools and rated Burford higher for the privacy of its self-contained boarding house. 'I prefer it without the day pupils – the boarding is more relaxed,' said one. Another added, 'I'm a lot less in my room. I go and look round the house and see if there's something going on.' The relaxed vibe is subtly engineered by an energetic team of house staff, equipped with smart technology. 'We're not over-protective', said the head of boarding. 'We know where every kid is at any one moment.' Parents praised the attention to detail – 'It's like my daughter's second home, [she] treats them as if they are hers; when she was unwell, she brought her a picture of her horse and her favourite teddy.' About homesickness, one mum commented, 'The boarding staff were so patient, they let him read in the middle of the night – by Easter he was fine.'

'I love the discipline in the boarding house,' said a parent, with the head of boarding telling us, 'I do have traditional standards, manners, holding doors open etc. But if they make a mistake, it's more about educating them.'

Ethos and heritage: Founded by local merchant Simon Wysdom in 1571 as a grammar school for the sons of Burford's tradesmen, the school is still conscious of its rich history and displays a copy of its original charter in the reception hall. Now a co-ed comp and located in an extensive site off the busy Oxford–Cheltenham A40, the school combines tradition with serviceability. One longstanding parent, whose older children have now graduated to university, described her first impression: 'It was quite Grange Hill at the time.' Spread out across 12 buildings from the main two-storey frontage – where we found reception and hall – the site straggles to include an impressive new English and drama block in the barn-conversion style, some charmless single-storey 1970s classrooms, as well as converted farm cottages in local colours. Grass pitches (plus an Astro), avenues of trees and a view of the golf course evoke its pastoral heritage.

Exams were in progress in the hall as we toured but a similar industrious quiet emanated from the other classrooms. We saw a silent biology class, labelling anatomy, front facing with traditional tables, teacher at the board. The music cohort were more chatty, composing their tunes with software on Apple desktops and keyboards. Elsewhere we had glimpses of a sports hall – 'Could do with a good paint,' reckoned one parent. A self-contained sixth form block contains a common room with worktables as well as a library and IT suite. Covid had forced some lessons outdoors, where covered corridors and picnic tables were used as classrooms; a canteen with newly built canopy served open-air lunches in a former parking space, or what the head hoped would become 'the green heart of the school'.

Smart uniform. 'Every single child's top button is done up, every single girl has a normal length skirt,' one proud parent declared, and it's true!

Smart uniform of navy crested blazer, shirt and tie, with trousers or skirt. 'Every single child's top button is done up, every single girl has a normal length skirt,' one proud parent declared, and it's true! Sixth formers wear own clothes, within parameters (picture guidance on the walls advises against ripped jeans, collarless shirts and piercings).

Pastoral care, inclusivity and discipline: There are tutors for academic support, a school parliament for day-to-day issues and the school has formal arrangements with independent listeners, as well as a counsellor for mental-health support. 'You'll always get student anxieties,' said a teacher, 'but they are more open in an informal discussion, especially the girls.' Parents praised the pastoral care: 'I lost my way and it was a teacher that pulled me away from the dark side,' said one dad about his own schooldays, but he had no such fears for his daughter at Burford – 'They have a positive plan and they care.'

A robust pastoral structure of rewards such as house point competitions or Dorm of the Week is counterbalanced by sanctions which might lead to 'community service' such as digging the garden or a 6.30am wake-up call. Formal measures such as suspensions and exclusions are rare, we heard. 'The kids have impeccable manners,' said a parent; 'It has the sense of a grammar school about it,' voiced another.

Pupils and parents: Parents, we heard, are 'all quite different', including many 'working parents too busy to go to matches'. Day pupils' families are drawn from the local Cotswold villages, while boarders' parents live far and wide. 'Some are very wealthy but there are lots of parents who are not in that position,' said one. One parent who had lived in Africa had chosen the school 'largely because of the cosmopolitan, international flavour'. Parents say they are not aware of any division between boarding and day students – 'Some of my children's friends have a different cultural bent to them – they've liked that,' said one, and boarders who take part in local clubs form friendships in the community too. Although Covid has made meeting up in person more difficult, there were a lot of online meetings. 'We met up in the summer with other parents before the girls even started at the school,' said one mum. An active PTA supports all music and drama productions and raises money for extras. Mixed views on comms. 'I like the way they are not constantly bombarding us with information,' said one mum, while another wished for more – 'Communication hasn't been as good,' she said. All are unanimous in their praise for the office staff and general response to email and phone enquiries – 'brilliant, friendly, welcoming and go out of their way'. Students are articulate and sensible. 'Reasonably balanced', we also heard.

Money matters: LA-funded education, with boarding at £11,250 pa. 'Very reasonable,' said parents.

The last word: Like the green pastures of the Cotswold landscape, Burford School has withstood the ravages of time, providing a bedrock academic education and an ever-evolving creative experience. Both day and boarding pupils are kept busy and motivated, at work and play. The paint may have faded a bit over the years, but the standards haven't.

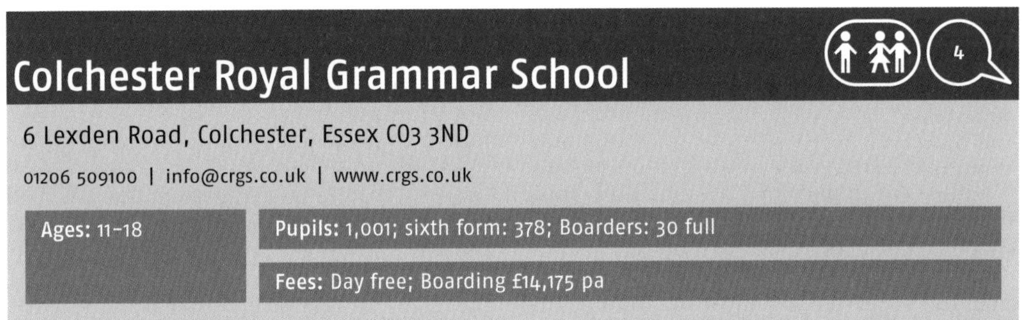

Colchester Royal Grammar School
4
6 Lexden Road, Colchester, Essex CO3 3ND
01206 509100 | info@crgs.co.uk | www.crgs.co.uk
Ages: 11–18
Pupils: 1,001; sixth form: 378; Boarders: 30 full
Fees: Day free; Boarding £14,175 pa

Headmaster: Since 2015, John Russell BSc MA ARCS, previously deputy head of Cranbrook. Grew up in the village of Goring on the west side of Reading, where he attended the local comp then Henley College before studying physics at Imperial. Narrowed down his career options to a toss-up between medical physics and teaching – chose the latter 'because I loved being in the classroom'. First job in a Loughton comprehensive before becoming head of physics at Ilford County High.

A natural diplomat, he is unintimidating and hands-on, squeezing in GCSE or A level teaching, sometimes even both – 'it depends where the boss wants me,' he smiles. His weekly drop-in session is appreciated by parents, and staff say he is highly supportive and consultative. Pupils approve of his mutual respect – no standing up when he walks in the classroom etc. 'He's not like a headmaster – he's one of the team and the students love him for it,' a parent told us.

Enrichment is a keyword. 'We are recognised for our huge academic success but the reality is the school is run through enrichment – everything from for modern languages to Fun Fridays, which we've just re-introduced.' Latter involves a focus on mental health in sixth form – could involve a parent lending a reindeer at Christmas, playing dodgeball or doing karaoke, 'which I recently performed in, very badly'.

Parents say he steered the ship well during Covid. Pretty much every lesson went live on Teams on the first day of the first lockdown – 'the problem I had was not keeping everyone on track academically, but slowing down the pace because it's actually easier to get through more work in online lessons,' he says. 'More importantly, on the pastoral side, we made sure everyone had a laptop and invited any student not engaging online back into school. And when all the students came back to school, we focused on the social side of things' (which – judging from the number of year 11s who joined their tutorials even when they'd normally have left school – shows how much it had been missed).

Must be lots of lab talk at home – his wife Michelle is a chemistry teacher. They have three children, two who went through the sixth form in recent years. Describes himself as an 'enthusiastic sportsman if not a very accomplished one', with football and racket sports topping the bill. Music also a big part of his life.

Entrance: Highly competitive September 11+ exam, made up of English (including verbal reasoning) and maths papers. Around 450 apply, with 128 places available and awarded in rank order, of which 12 are set as priority places for pupil premium. No catchment, so pupils don't have to live in Essex (many don't).

Co-ed sixth form – 'our flagship' – even more popular, with around 500 applying for the 80-odd external places (around a third are girls). These applicants, along with pupils already at the school, need 38 points in their top five GCSEs and grade 7s in the subjects to be studied. 'But because places are awarded in rank order, in reality they'll need a lot of 9-8s,' says the head.

Boarding in sixth form only – candidates must meet the academic requirements first and foremost, then it's down to boarding need (too far to travel or eg mental health) and for overseas boarders a British passport or relevant visa. About half the boarders come from the UK, the rest from abroad, with 50 per cent of those from Hong Kong and others from all over including a growing number of expats from Dubai.

Exit: Over 90 per cent stay on for sixth form – 'The five or so boys who leave usually do so because we aren't offering the courses they want,' says head. Vast majority to university, three-quarters to Russell Group. The Telegraph ranks CRGS as the top performing grammar in the country for Oxbridge – 21 went in 2021. Imperial and Bath also feature regularly. Most popular courses include medicine (11 in 2021), economics, maths, sciences, engineering and classics. Small numbers overseas – including to Berkeley and Columbia in 2021. School supports students heading off to music conservatories and to do degree apprenticeships – most recently to Dyson, 'which is a really impressive apprenticeship so I'm hoping we get more students on to this,' says head.

Latest results: In 2021, 87 per cent 9-7 at GCSE; 83 per cent A*/A at A level (96 per cent A*-B). In 2019 (the last year when exams took place), 83 per cent 9-7 at GCSE; 69 per cent A*/A at A level (91 per cent A*-B).

Teaching and learning: Academic standards are right at the top end for the state sector, with the school having long enjoyed the number one spot in the government league tables. No wonder it has something of a reputation as a hothouse, though parents roll their eyes at the suggestion. 'It's not an exam factory – they go well beyond the curriculum with competitions, debating, clubs and societies and they really encourage non-academic pursuits,' said one. In any case, you couldn't hold this lot back if you tried, with self-study very popular – one girl recently chose to do nine A levels 'and I still saw her with a normal literature book in her hand,' says head. But nine? 'If the school doesn't teach an A level a student desperately wants to do, we try to provide one lecture a week if the student agrees to self-teach the rest – the sky's the limit,' explains head, citing government and politics and Mandarin as recent examples.

Class sizes 32 in year 7 and 8, 25 in years 9-11 and 20 in years 12 and 13. There's not much call for setting with this narrow range of ability, though there's some in French and maths from year 9 purely for the pace – 'Set 4 pupils will still be expected to achieve 9-8 at GCSE.' Language provision stands out – French and Latin in year 7, with a choice of German or Greek added in year 8. Good take-up for languages at GCSE (when French is compulsory) and, bucking the national trend, at A level (when French is common, with smaller numbers doing Spanish or Greek). Most pupils, as you'd expect, take triple science but there's usually one class doing the double award – 'not because they're weaker but because they want to do triple languages or creative choices like art and music,' says head. Majority takes 10 or 11 GCSEs, though some – especially those doing Spanish, extra maths or astronomy – do up to 13.

Academic standards are right at the top end for the state sector, with the school having long enjoyed the number one spot in the government league tables

At A level, it's four for most though some do more – often AS politics off the back of the weekly politics lectures to which all sixth formers are invited (and usually attend, in their droves). Further maths also attracts big numbers. No weak spots, but best results in humanities, maths, sciences, DT and economics. Compulsory enrichment for all sixth formers, with EPQ taken by a quarter and Young Enterprise also popular. We were privy to one of a series of children's books that students had created to celebrate the different continents, having been responsible for the concept, words, design and publishing – it would

Because boarding is sixth form only, boarders are afforded plenty of independence and have guidelines rather than rules

not have looked out of place in Waterstones. We also heard of a generational project that got younger ones spending time with old folk and making books of their memories.

Teachers are praised for their commitment to keeping every student intellectually stretched and on track to meet their targets. They provide extra support and revision clubs as necessary, as well as being available out-of-hours via email. 'There's lots of talk about where you should be at and how to achieve it,' said a student. Then there's the sheer quality of teaching. 'They keep it imaginative, fresh and innovative at all times.' 'They're not afraid to throw the textbooks aside.' Not a single inattentive expression spotted during our visit. Parents say it's made clear that it's ok to fail – that's how you learn – and that teaching is relevant, always brought back to how it fits in the real world. 'It's more than about getting these youngsters to pass exams – it's about where this learning is going to take them in life.'

Learning support and SEN: Mainly ASD and a few dyslexic. 'With our son, they have taken a difficult autistic boy and grown him into a wonderful young man – coping with his complexities and outbursts in their stride and celebrating every minor success. The staff should be getting an OBE in my opinion,' one parent told us. Some students have physical disabilities, including visual impairments. Lots of EAL students but few need anything more than a bit of support on the side, which school is happy to cater for.

The arts and extracurricular: Head calls music 'the soul of the school,' and parents say it is just that. Located in its own converted three-storey house, there are plenty of practice and performance spaces, with 200 learning an instrument (many are donated by old boys) and there's live music in every assembly, along with the usual orchestra, ensembles and choirs. Up to 90 attend the annual music tours, with opportunities to eg perform in the squares of Barcelona. 'Our son is musical, but I didn't know what to expect with this school because it's better known for the academia, but the opportunities for learning and performing have massively impressed us,' said one parent.

Beauty and the Beast rehearsals were in full swing during our last review – a welcome return to the annual school musicals post-Covid. Unusually these focus on year 7s and sixth form, though other years are allowed to dip in. Drama is only offered as extracurricular but nevertheless popular, and it crops up in other subjects too – a classics play was being prepared when we visited, and there's a French play every year, which is open to the public.

Spacious and light art block where average work sits side-by-side the obvious greats – hurrah to that. 'If I'm honest, art is not my son's strongest subject, but he still wanted to do it for GCSE and he's been encouraged at every turn – the school understands that the benefits of art aren't just for those who are brilliant at it,' remarked a parent. Around 20 do art GCSE art; ditto for A level – the benefit of a large sixth form. During lockdown, one student set up a virtual walk-through art gallery wit the aim of publicising local artists but it was so popular that she wound up with artists from overseas too. DT rooms also spacious, and clearly well-used and loved.

Debating is huge, with lots of wins in public speaking competitions including on the international stage. 'You should see them in action!' said a parent. CRGS are also current national champions of the French spelling bee. Masses of academic societies, many student led – 'gets them used to on the spot question and answer sessions and really prepares them for the future,' says head. And even with our unstoppable note taking, we couldn't keep up with the long list of competitions. Clubs feature sports and music, plus everything from BBC Young Reporters' Club to Swedish club and even a colouring club. Trips range from cultural days out in London to a year 7s bonding trip to the cinema, as well as eg classics trip to Italy and sports tours all over. Plenty of charity work, including an award-winning mental health charity, Time to Talk, which was set up by students themselves.

Sport: Cricket and rugby rule, with regular fixtures against state and independent schools and some representation at national level. Increasing focus on athletics – one semi-professional sixth former trains for an afternoon a week; head says he 'always tries to support such students' and 'won't be restrictive in terms of time off,' citing another student who is in a national fencing team. Significant improvement in sixth form girls' sport in recent years, with netball and rugby top of the pops. But it's not all about the top players, parents assured us – 'sport here is inclusive.' Extensive playing fields (including cricket pitches with trad pavilion and scoring board that students love sitting in) five minutes' walk away, while school has its own tarmacked area and heated outdoor pool on site – the latter also used by the local community. More niche opportunities include sailing and weight-training.

Boarding: Full boarding only although the odd few go home at weekends. Two co-ed boarding houses for sixth formers, both with a combo of two-beds (for year 12s) and singles (for year 13s). Not the smartest or tidiest we've seen but perfectly adequate and all have benefited from a recent rolling refurb programme. There are cooking facilities and a communal area in each house and a good staff to student ratio, with head of boarding living in one house plus three sets of boarding parents and a boarding assistant and boarding graduate (the latter is part of a new rolling programme whereby sports teaching graduates come from North Bucks Uni on a placement).

Head calls music 'the soul of the school,' and parents say it is just that. There's live music in every assembly, along with the usual orchestra, ensembles and choirs

Because boarding is sixth form only, boarders are afforded plenty of independence and have guidelines rather than rules. Plenty of freedom to go into town, albeit with a strict signing in and out system. 'Some go into London too, as well as to stay with local friends, although we need permission from their parents for that,' the housemaster told us. Big focus on induction including weekends away at an activity centre 30 miles away and there are regular trips out ranging from cycling to cinema though for the most part, they seem content to hang around the school where they get use of sports and music facilities. On weekdays, free time until dinner at 6pm, then it's study time from 7-9pm and lights out at 10.30pm (11pm on weekends).

Ethos and heritage: Directly descended from a Colchester town school that existed in 1206 and granted royal charters by Henry VIII in 1539 and Elizabeth I in 1584. Set in an affluent residential area of Colchester, the main buildings date back to the late 19th century. These are home to some classic grammar school classrooms, with big windows overlooking the shiny floored corridors, plus a very traditional, well-stocked library, complete with oil paintings of old headmasters on the wall, and additional silent room at the side. Newer additions – which include blocks for science and engineering, computing and art and renovated music and drama facilities – fit well with the attractive old school buildings. Wonderful to see sixth form engineering students hard at work on imaginative projects (top secret, we were warned when we busily scribbled down the details – but all proper real world stuff that could potentially change lives). The sixth form centre is home to a lively common room, with a large, all-school, cashless refectory to the side. Lovely, well-tended site of a standard unusual in a state school, featuring quiet and private sitting areas for students – in full use when we visited.

Uniform includes a vivid purple blazer, and for sixth formers, it's smart dress. Loud, old-fashioned bell system that's a bit of a bone-shaker until you get used to it. Food good, with newish catering manager who used to own his own restaurant – now also with second food outlet, The Pod, for grab-n-go options.

Old boys include Telegraph columnist Giles Smith, economics commentator Tim Congdon, costume designer and double Oscar winner Jim Acheson, founder of Freeserve, John Pluthero and former BBC education correspondent Mike Baker. 'Our alumni are very supportive,' says the head. 'If we have a big project on the go, they always try to help and they are very keen to support anyone who is in a financially vulnerable position – those who would otherwise miss out on an opportunity. They are also supportive when it comes to careers, helping sixth formers move on, offering internships, interview advice and networking.'

Pastoral care, inclusivity and discipline: Not much by way of misbehaviour – most students are highly motivated self-starters with little time for disruption, although there are about five fixed term exclusions and a few permanent ones most years for those who do mess up. Support, respect, generosity and compassion are the core values which students are constantly reminded of. Robust pastoral system includes new post of wellbeing manager. There's also a buddy scheme, part-time school counsellor and an emphasis on transition to make sure year 7s and new year 12s settle in well. The Tootoot app provides an anonymous way for students to raise concerns, with the opportunity for students to be put in touch with a mentor. A fair amount of stress, particularly around exam time but parents say teachers are on it: 'My son had a wobble due to the pressures of work and the school dealt with it very compassionately, gathering together the relevant teachers to support him and keep us informed.' School is all ears when it comes to student voice – when CRGS was mentioned on the Everyone's Invited website, students were the first port of call for the school so it could find out their views on the issues. School also works hard to tackle any racism – recently the African Caribbean Society agreed there isn't any but said there is sometimes a lack of understanding of culture which school says it's currently addressing.

Pupils and parents: Years 7-11 mainly from Colchester and surrounding area but students travel up to an hour each way each day, including from Ipswich and even east London. Students come from a complete mix of families, both ethnically (including international, especially in the sixth form boarders contingent) and in terms of wealth and class. All feel grateful. Active PA (called CRGSA).

Money matters: Tuition free; boarding costs.

The last word: One of the country's top selective boys' state schools, rivalling many independents. Stands out for enrichment and lacks the hard edges that schools of this calibre can have. Any academically able and hard-working boy (and sixth form girl) should thrive here.

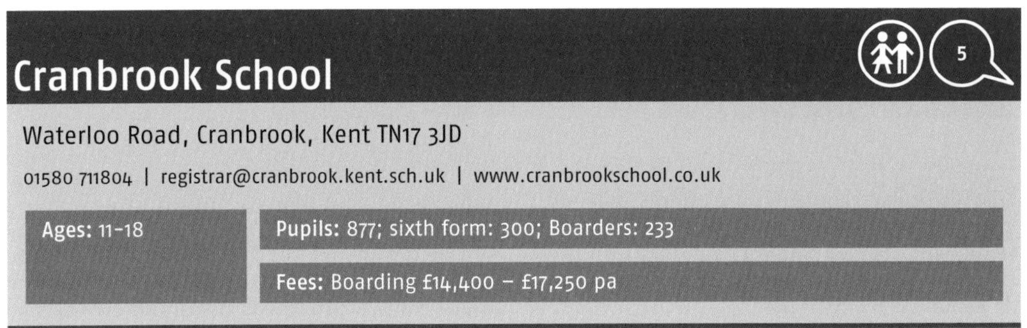

Cranbrook School

Waterloo Road, Cranbrook, Kent TN17 3JD

01580 711804 | registrar@cranbrook.kent.sch.uk | www.cranbrookschool.co.uk

Ages: 11-18

Pupils: 877; sixth form: 300; Boarders: 233

Fees: Boarding £14,400 – £17,250 pa

Headmaster: Since January 2021, Will Chuter, previously deputy head and head of classics at Gresham's School in Norfolk and before that at Uppingham. He was educated at Cranbrook and studied ancient history at Durham before starting his teaching career in Italy, then spent a number of years working in educational publishing.

Entrance: Selective, catering for the top 20-25 per cent ability range and always oversubscribed. Entrance at 11+ is via the Kent Test and is run by Kent County Council with papers in English, maths, verbal and non-verbal reasoning with about 240 applicants for 60 places. Tight catchment area which is strictly enforced keeps house prices high in the surrounding villages.

Total of 52 boarding and 38 day places offered in year 9. School runs its own 13+ CAT tests plus papers in maths and English with tests in the November before entry. Boarders sit the same tests and also have an interview. A handful of boarders and about 16 day pupils join the sixth form and it is rare for spaces to become available in other years.

Exit: Around 20 per cent leave after GCSEs. Most on to university – mainly Russell Group and mostly to academic courses with Nottingham, Cardiff, Bristol and Exeter recently popular. The occasional pupil to US universities. One to Oxbridge in 2021, and one vet – numbers often bigger. The school is raising awareness of degree apprenticeships for those who don't want to go to university. Very few leave after GCSEs and hardly any have to leave because they don't make the grades.

Latest results: In 2021, 67 per cent 9-7 at GCSE; 57 per cent A*/A at A level (82 per cent A*-B). In 2019 (the last year when exams took place), 48 per cent 9-7 at GCSE; 71 per cent A*-B at A level.

Teaching and learning: Fifteen subjects offered at GCSE including art and design, drama and food preparation and nutrition. Good science results – most students take three separate sciences but the dual award is also offered. Offers French, Spanish and Latin with trips to Rome and Pompeii and Roman sites in the UK. Pupils are encouraged to take a practical or creative subject to complement their academic GCSEs and the school says it wants pupils to be 'well rounded with their feet on the ground'. Consistent praise from parents for maths and science teaching throughout the school. School keen to keep the classics flag flying. All pupils take Latin in years 7 and 8 and although numbers taking GCSE are fairly small, the results are strong. Chinese GCSE offered to native speakers outside the timetable. Years 7-9 learn computing including programming and coding but it is not offered as a GCSE. Technology GCSE was lost to funding cuts. Most achieve the EBacc at the end of year 11 (GCSEs in English language, literature, maths, a science plus history or geography and a foreign language).

At A level, 18 subjects offered including drama, economics, psychology and government and politics. Most popular with both boys and girls are maths, history, economics, and the sciences with very few taking modern languages. There is a dedicated co-ordinator for the EPQ and about 25 students a year take part, with very few dropping out.

Class sizes are about 30 in lower years, reducing to 25-30 in GCSE years and 15-20 in sixth form, depending on subjects. Academic expectations are high and teaching is increasingly collaborative in the sixth form where students are expected to be self-reliant and to find things out for themselves. Teachers are a good mix of age and experience – keen, new young staff and experienced older ones who know how to get the best out of the pupils.

Plenty of advice available from the careers programme but students are not spoon fed and are expected to go looking for it. A weekly bulletin provides information about university courses, lectures, taster days and apprenticeships and the charity CXK offers careers advice and runs careers fairs. Oxbridge candidates are offered help with interview practice and preparation for entrance exams and former students give talks on their experiences in the workplace. All are expected to do some work experience after GCSEs which is well organised and overseen by the careers department who have a good network of contacts.

School has its own observatory and pupils can join the astronomy club and take an astronomy GCSE off timetable

The school has its own observatory and pupils can join the astronomy club and can take an astronomy GCSE off timetable. 'This is a wonderful facility,' says a parent, 'and it is a pity that the school does not make more of it.'

Learning support and SEN: Strong education support department with a SENCo and three staff who are quick to pick up potential problems, says a parent. About 30 students need help mainly for dyslexia; a few have behavioural issues and a handful are on an EHCP. School wants to support the widest possible range of students but they must be able to keep up with the curriculum. Very able students are stretched with some differentiation in lessons as well as activities and visits. Some overseas boarders need EAL which is done through SEN.

The arts and extracurricular: About 300 students take part in the DofE – mainly year 9s taking bronze but 5-10 achieve gold each year – the school is a licensed centre. CCF offered in the army and air force – popular with year 9 but small numbers keep going throughout, with pupils given the opportunity to learn to fly and take part in military exercises. Some lucky year 10s were able to spend six weeks in Canada with the army division – 'a life changing experience,' says a parent.

Performing arts centre with drama and dance studios and plenty of practice space. Thriving music scene which is part of the curriculum in the lower years – music GCSE has been lost in the funding cuts but still possible ex-curriculum. About 120 students learn an instrument or sing – with 20 peripatetic teachers coming into the school. Range of ensembles and musical groups including a jazz band, choir and chamber choir, sax group, string quartet, rock group as well as a full orchestra, with opportunities to play in concerts and recitals as well as school and house assemblies and the Battle of the Bands and the renowned house singing competition.

The Queen's Hall Theatre is home to the drama department and is also used for outside performances. One big school drama production each year as well as the junior drama club annual play and performance evenings by GCSE and A level students and the annual DanSing when everyone has a chance to get involved. 'I was blown away by the talent,' said a father. Students can also get involved behind the scenes with sound, lighting and stage management and also work with external performances. Around 30-40 students take GCSE drama but smaller numbers go on to take it for A level.

Art increasingly popular, with 50 or so taking GCSE and about 14 for A level. One or two to art school most years and the recent launch of the autumn charity art show has given the department a higher profile.

Wide range of after-school clubs in which students are expected but not made to take part – they are regularly reminded about the benefits for their UCAS form and CV. New students are given a presentation of what is on offer and clubs include current affairs and politics, chess, robotics and cookery as well as a range of dance clubs and musical theatre. Vibrant debating club – a recent student won the national historical association debating competition and junior debating is run by sixth form students. The school is also very supportive of students who want to start their own clubs.

Some parents regret that some activities have been lost or curtailed owing to funding cuts but another said, 'You have to remember that this is a state school and the opportunities are pretty amazing.'

Range of trips every year including the battlefields tour, diving in Egypt, a skiing trip, an expedition to Nepal and an international sports tour every other year, most recently to South

Dallam School

Africa. The school also has an exchange partnership with a school in Kerala, south India – students spend two weeks staying with families in India and then invite the students back to Cranbrook: 'It is a mind-broadening and enriching experience for those lucky enough to take part,' says a parent.

Sport: The school has a proud sporting tradition and sport is compulsory throughout, including for sixth formers, with the opportunities far exceeding most state schools. Ditto for facilities, which include a sports hall, dance studio, gym, weights room, cardio suite, outdoor pool, netball and tennis courts, squash courts and 50 acres of playing fields, as well as an athletics track and an Astro. Busy sports programme with inter-house competitions and Saturday matches against state and independent schools and close links have been formed with local clubs. The school will often field a C and D team as well as the As and Bs if the demand is there and many get involved in county and national cup competitions. Strong rugby and cricket tradition and girls have recently taken up cricket. Hockey also strong and Cranbrook were finalists in girls' schools national hockey championships in 2019.

Boarding: Boarding from year 9 with about 240 boarders throughout the school. Education is free and parents only have to pay the boarding fees. Many boarders are from just outside the very tight catchment area and others from London and abroad. All students have to be EU or British passport holders. Popular with Spanish and French as well as those from Hong Kong and Bermuda who hold British passports.

Six boarding houses (four for boys and two for girls) in a variety of architectural styles dotted around the town with 40-45 boarders per house. Most houses have a vertical structure but all year 9 boy boarders spend their first year in School Lodge before moving to other houses. Year 9s and some year 10s share rooms but almost all have their own rooms from year 11 upwards.

Boarders share the same school life as their day counterparts until the end of the school day. Like the day houses, all have a personal tutor and senior students act as mentors to help younger students. All meals eaten in the central dining room but each house has a kitchen for preparing snacks, baking cakes etc. Each house also has a common room and computer room and sixth form have their own kitchen and common room. Local students can go home after school on Fridays and outings and shopping trips are organised for those staying in. Boarders allowed to use some facilities after school and the weights room and cardio gym are supervised in the evenings. Joint house barbecues arranged and students can visit each other's houses as long as they remain downstairs. The girls' house we visited was immaculate and the laundry system has been turned into an art form.

The girls' boarding house we visited was immaculate and the laundry system has been turned into an art form

Ethos and heritage: The school was founded in 1518 by John Blubery and in 1574 Queen Elizabeth I granted the school its royal charter, still displayed in the library, and the school began its life as the 'Free Grammar school of Queen Elizabeth in Cranbrook'. Located in School House, a fine Georgian mansion, the school has 70 acres of buildings, gardens and playing fields close to the centre of Cranbrook. Although non-denominational, it has close links with the parish church and the vicar of Cranbrook is an ex officio governor of the school.

One of the few state boarding schools in the country, it is interwoven with the town and the local church is used for special events. Some parents mourn the gradual erosion of traditions as the school has grown and money is tight but 'the boarders anchor the school and give it the atmosphere of an independent school,' says another. 'It has one foot in tradition with the structure of the boarding houses but is also forward thinking with an open and friendly culture – it is academically selective but not elitist.'

There are six day houses including a junior house for years 7 and 8 and all went co-ed in 2019 – 'a great improvement and reflects real life,' says a parent. They are run along similar lines to the boarding houses and each house has a tutor for every year group and house captains play a major part in the running of the house. Tutor groups of 15-20 in day houses and 10-15 in boarding houses and most teachers are involved in house tutoring. All houses, both day and boarding, have their own distinct personality and sense of identity and inter-house competitions, quizzes and the annual house shout are keenly contested.

The old sports centre has been transformed into the sixth form centre and gives A level students a space of their own with distinct areas for work and socialising and 'makes the sixth form something to aspire to,' says a parent.

All have to wear uniform until year 11, regulation suits for the boys and the distinctive long grey skirts and maroon jumpers for the girls.

Sixth formers are expected to dress as if they were going to an interview.

Notable alumnae include co-founder of the Eden Project, Tim Smit; comedian, Harry Hill; astronaut, Dr Piers Sellers; English rugby player, Ruaridh McConnochie; author, Louise Dean; and artist and stage designer, Es Devlin.

Pastoral care, inclusivity and discipline: Rigorous attention to pastoral care and mental health issues. The school has engaged the services of the mental health charity Place2B (partly funded by the PA) which offers one-to-one and group counselling. It is woven into the pastoral system and large numbers of staff are trained in mental health first aid – 'The school offers an integrated safety net from the form teacher upwards,' says school. Since mobile phones were banned during the day (after consultation with parents), cyber bullying has 'dropped off a cliff', according to school. Phones are allowed in some lessons and in the sixth form centre but otherwise have to be locked away.

Expectations are high and day-to-day behavioural management is dealt with through the house system. Most students are well behaved and miscreants are dealt with firmly in an educational way. School favours internal sanctions like detention but will exclude repeat offenders if necessary.

Consistent praise for the quality and variety of food which is paid for via a thumbprint – very few bring in a packed lunch.

Pupils and parents: A large number of parents are local business people or commuters and on the whole feel a lucky bunch. They are supportive and involved, with a very active PA which organises the usual social events like Burns Night and summer ball.

The school turns out 'confident, curious, employable and well-rounded school leavers' and suits most children. One parent said, 'We have three children, one arty, one sporty and one academic and it caters from them all – we moved house to get into the catchment area and don't regret it.' However, students need to be hardworking, self-motivated and mature to get the best out of their time here and sometimes those who have been overcoached for the entry tests struggle with so much independence.

The first port of call for parents is their child's tutor. All are given a talk on how to support their children and how to spot mental health issues but it is up to them find out what is going on in school via the parent portal and sometimes it can be a bit 'hit and miss', says one.

Cranbrook asks parents for support, which is willingly given – both financial and with extracurricular support and with match teas and other events. There is a suggested monthly donation which is confidential and not pushed and parental contributions have helped fund the sixth form centre and pay for some top-quality sports coaches.

Money matters: The school offers nine academic scholarships for external and internal candidates entering year 9. There is a small financial reward and inclusion in the high achievers gifted and talented programme. Also offers two music scholarships to cover the cost of a year's music or singing.

The last word: A state school which offers boarding and has the feel and atmosphere of an independent school with its house system and wide range of sports and after-school activities which suits confident, curious students who think for themselves.

Dallam School

6

Milnthorpe, Cumbria LA7 7DD

015395 65165 | enquiries@dallamschool.co.uk | www.dallamschool.co.uk

Ages: 11–19

Pupils: 1,082; sixth form: 200; Boarders: 53

Fees: Day free; Boarding £12,160 – £13,550 pa

Executive headteacher: Since January 2021, Rachael Williams (40s). First headship. Previously acting head of North West Community Campus in Dumfries, part of a 15-year stint of teaching in various Scottish state schools which followed a similar but shorter spell in state schools throughout England. Also has experience of international schools as her teaching career kicked off in

Kuwait, plus brief taster of the independent sector back in the UK teaching at JAGS.

With an astrophysics degree (Cardiff), she could have been a rocket scientist but chose teaching instead. Still gets her fix of igniting sparks and lighting fires, she insists, declaring that 'there's absolutely nothing better than teaching the next generation – I loved it since I first stepped into the classroom.' She had just stepped out of the classroom, in fact, when we met her ('borrowing' classes from teachers is still a favourite aspect of the job, she says). PGCE from Warwick and MEd from Sterling.

Spent her childhood 'moving around a lot', which didn't surprise us one iota since there's something decidedly global and outward looking about this self-possessed, eloquent woman. Was attracted to Dallam, she says, by 'the inner blend of traditional with forward and outward thinking innovation, along with all the outdoor education and community centred package' (and no, she wasn't reading from a script). 'She's fab,' is the general consensus among parents. 'Very involved and consultative,' said one – 'she's got some great new ideas but isn't ramming them down people's throats, instead really taking time to listen.'

Enjoys walking, reading ('especially a good sci-fi') and getting out and about with friends and family, particularly in her beloved cities of Edinburgh and Glasgow.

Entrance: Over 40 feeder schools, some large, some tiny rural schools, from near and far. No appeals as yet – all who want a place have one, though latest jam-packed open day suggests that could change. Unselective for all year 7 day pupils who apply via the local authority. For sixth form entry, applicants need at least five 4s at GCSE (or foreign equivalent) including English and maths.

Boarders join throughout. All meet head of boarding and assistant head to check 'suitability for boarding'. Around two-thirds from overseas, mainly ex-pat families in Nigeria and Hong Kong, with others from everywhere from Oman to Cyprus – all must hold a UK passport. Inevitable falling-off of European students post-Brexit though school has cleverly responded with its new Dallam Experience students (currently six) who come from mainly France, Spain and Germany for up to six months for 'the cultural experience' (some students are currently petitioning the UK government to allow them to remain) – they join in any year group except exam years. Remainder of boarders from right across the UK. Forces families get a boarding discount although there aren't any at the moment.

Exit: Around 40 per cent stay on post 16; rest to college to study more vocational courses such as hairdressing or construction or to start apprenticeships. Majority of sixth form leavers into higher education, around a third to Russell Group. King's College London, Warwick, Durham, Leeds, York and Edinburgh all popular. Several overseas, most recently to Leiden, Tilburg, Groningen, Cattolica (Milan), Erasmus (Rotterdam), Northern Colorado and Medical School Berlin.

Latest results: In 2021, 27 per cent 9-7 at GCSE; 79 per cent 9-4 in both maths and English. At A level, 38 per cent A*/A at A level (54 per cent A*-B). In 2019 (the last year when exams took place), seven per cent 9-7 at GCSE; 72 per cent 9-4 in both maths and English. At A level in 2019, 21 per cent A*/A (52 per cent A*-B).

Teaching and learning: 'Learning for all, learning for life' is school's mantra and despite the broad intake, results sit comfortably alongside selective schools in the area, beating national averages. School puts it down to 'absolute dedication by teachers to support pupils'; students agree they are 'friendly and supportive'. The constant flow of newbies training to teach here under the Dallam Teaching Alliance umbrella means school is never short on fresh energy, enthusiasm and talent, nicely complemented by those longer in the tooth – although one parent told us, 'There was a bit of a high turnover before this head arrived.'

School was quick to embrace online learning during Covid, with parents praising the high level of feedback – 'far better than any of my friends' schools in the area'

Good primary liaison helps with a smooth transition, important with so many feeder schools. No setting in years 7 and 8; streaming from year 9 with added setting in English and maths from year 10. Homework proportional – the older they are, the more they get, though never silly amounts. French and Spanish taught throughout, with super-keen linguists able to access other languages upon request. Class sizes are around 30, apart from sixth form, where they are smaller.

Students typically take nine GCSEs. A third take triple science. A language is encouraged but not compulsory. No particularly strong subjects on results day – pretty even across the board, though parents pull out maths and RE as particularly well taught. In sixth form, there's a choice of A levels (mainly traditional, though criminology and sociology get the biggest numbers) and BTECs (eg travel and tourism) – and you can mix and match. Some subjects are available in both camps, eg business, computing and PE. Most do three in total and around a third do an EPQ.

School was quick to embrace online learning during Covid, with parents praising the high level of feedback – 'far better than any of my friends' schools in the area,' said one. Teaching areas are well equipped and unusually tidy, as are corridors and shared spaces. There are seven science labs and impressive teaching suites for design technology and food tech.

Learning support and SEN: A SENCo is supported by a small team of TAs to provide support in the classroom as well as in booster groups or one-to-ones where required. The school is proud of its inclusive ethos and there is no stigma. EHCPs in all year groups, with the likes of OTs and SaLTs brought in where necessary. School's approach to independent learning, teamwork and activity helps – didactic teaching methods aren't welcome here.

The arts and extracurricular: Back when Adventure Learning School status was a thing, Dallam was first in the UK to bag it. That trademark may be long gone but the school's legacy is to continue taking full advantage of its proximity to both the Lake District and Yorkshire Dales national parks, with students and staff regularly participating in canoeing, hiking, camping and other assorted adventurous pursuits. Year 7 students have a residential experience at Borrowdale and year 8 at Ennerdale, and the principles of outdoor challenge are embedded across the whole curriculum. Typically this will involve different subject departments working together with students on extended studies, often of an investigatory nature, proving learning need not be entirely classroom-based. Everyone was upset by how much this outdoor education provision suffered during Covid.

There's a real buzz around music, with around half of the students learning an instrument with peripatetic teachers available across the usual range of instruments, plus various choirs and two bands, including a swing band, and a strong ensemble. Performances (including virtually during lockdown) happen 'whenever and wherever we can make them happen'. Christmas celebrations include a visit to the village church for nine lessons and carols. 'It's a really lovely department with wonderful concerts,' said a parent.

'The drama teachers are brilliant with the kids and appear to be able to engage even the shy ones – my child is naturally introverted but came home full of it about a monologue she'd done the other day,' reported a parent. No productions during Covid but the annual whole-school performance gets great reviews and includes plenty of backstage opportunities for those less keen on being in the limelight. Students told us that, as with music, drama is great for integration of different year groups – something they really value. Very popular at GCSE and A level. No LAMDA.

A particular source of pride is the international aspect of the school which boarding allows for, with around two-thirds of boarders from overseas

High-quality artwork on display throughout school – a real variety is evident, everything from portraiture to still life and from wild and wacky ceramics to expressive sculptures. 'The stuff they bring home is of a very high standard – same with DT – but most importantly they get them to enjoy it,' remarked a parent.

Clubs range from all the usual sport and music options right through to the more niche equestrian to crochet. There's a drama studio, separate dance studio and theatre, but a bigger auditorium is next on the wish list – 'a space we can all gather,' says head.

Sport: A sporty culture but school doesn't claim to beat all-comers, perhaps because they don't major in any one sport, favouring a wider range to suit all. That said, some of the students currently excel in fell running and triathlons and we met a lovely netball player currently playing at national level – clearly no lack of inspiration or aspiration. The BTEC outdoor programme sees students paddling rivers, surfing waves, capsizing canoes and mountain walking, clearly fearless in all weathers. School is good at sharing its Swallows and Amazons culture too, offering twilight sessions for local primary pupils and holiday sports camps. Great all-year-round facilities include two great sports halls at the Milnthorpe site, plus fitness suite and Astroturf and multiple pitches nearby – all used by local community, dance groups and local football teams. Add to that a further sports hall at Heversham (home to the boarders) alongside all-weather tennis courts.

Boarding: A particular source of pride is the international aspect of the school which boarding allows for, with around two-thirds of boarders from overseas. 'Some of the most interesting people I've met here are from other countries,' said one student. 'Cumbria is a very white mono-ethnic area and boarding brings diversity,' added a parent. At one time there were 20+ different nationalities – Brexit put a stop to that but hats off to the school for coming up with the Dallam Experience programme that means European students can come, if only for six months.

Boarders' home-from-home is the former Heversham Grammar School in the tiny upmarket village of Heversham. It's not far from school but far enough and different enough to feel like home. If you are up in time, you take the minibus shuttle into school each day and back late afternoon or evening; if you're a late riser you'll have to walk and make your excuses when you get there. Parts of the building are Hogwarts-ish: the charmingly named Big School is a communal space within the former school hall, with high ceilings, impressive fireplaces and honours boards of former pupils on display. A plethora of outbuildings and green play space house a music studio, all-weather floodlit tennis courts, sports hall and a wet store housing climbing ropes, wetsuits and kayaks. There is also a fives court.

Staff are much admired – buckets of warmth and care and very much on their game, with the head herself staying over three nights a week. All younger boarders get a buddy and boarders are encouraged to take up offers to go to local students' houses for tea and invite them back too.

Tons of outside recreational space, with the mountains of the Lake District visible in all directions – heaven. A very long way from a Starbucks...

Younger boarders are in rooms of two, three or four – not masses of space, but it's their space and that's important; sixth formers get individual ensuite rooms. All in decent nick, but not the smartest. Girls outnumber boys in the boarding stakes, but only slightly, and for peace of mind there is fobbed and timed security into all the main buildings and also between boys' and girls' dorms. Food – all cooked on site – is popular, with national and international preferences catered for, and staff keep busy with relentless laundry, all very motherly rather than matronly – there's real warmth and pride in looking after their charges here.

Weekends are packed full with lots of extra sport plus weekend shopping trips, overnight camping in tepees, paintballing, waterfall and mountain hiking, cinema outings, ice-skating, visits to the theatre and opera, attending pro football and rugby matches, raft-building as well as seasonal activities such as carol singing and bonfire night.

Ethos and heritage: The original school was founded in 1613 by Edward Wilson, whose descendants still live locally and continue to work with the school. Back then it was located a mile or so away in the former Heversham Grammar School, now home to the boarders and Dallam community education. These days, main school is on the site of the former Milnthorpe secondary in an attractive, multi-purpose, low-level, well-maintained and very green and spread-out teaching site. Ideal during Covid – none of the cramming into corridors that other schools had to endure, almost certainly contributing to keeping cases low. Tons of outside recreational space, with the mountains of the Lake District visible in all directions – heaven. All set on the edge of the large and pleasant village of Milnthorpe and a very long way from a Starbucks which – rather wonderfully – the students don't seem to mind in the least. Students told us they feel safe, have 'a good level of independence' and there is praise too for the calm yet purposeful atmosphere, opportunities for community involvement, public speaking and charity events – in fact if you don't take them up, 'you'd be missing out,' say parents.

Students were elated when school catering returned after Covid – the bacon buns, if you arrive for breakfast, are 'legendary', we heard. Uniform is smart with a trad blazer badge and lapel badges indicating awards and honours; shirts and ties for all. Sixth formers expected to be smart so no jeans, T-shirts or hoodies, though some feel there's possibly too much wriggle room, especially for girls.

Notable former pupils include Times cartoonist Peter Brooke, opera singer Emma Stannard and BBC journalist and presenter Rob Broomby.

Pastoral care, inclusivity and discipline: 'We're pretty well-behaved here, it's because we're rural kids,' said one sixth former, summing up the general view, though head reckons it's also down to good rapport among students and staff, high expectations, visible staff keeping a watchful eye and students themselves role modelling good behaviour – 'all combines to make it normal to be respectful,' she says. Still, these youngsters are growing up and some inevitably make mistakes, for which discipline generally takes a restorative slant – 'more mentoring and coaching than punitive,' reckoned a parent. Indeed, temporary exclusions kept to less than one per cent of students and no permanent exclusions in recent times. But school doesn't let standards slip, with punctuality currently being clamped down on, and low-level disruption and uniform are also taken seriously – we spotted students quickly tucking their shirts in when they saw us approaching.

School works hard on communicating core values of respect, with a recent emphasis on providing information, support and advice around issues coming out of Everyone's Invited and Black Lives Matter. 'We spend a lot of time listening to our students and students groups are there to support one another, as well as receive support from us,' says head. Pupils like the responsibility they are given, especially in the older years. Sixth form prefects have walkie-talkies giving them direct access to staff if they feel the need to bring in the heavies whilst on duty and amusingly, even in this digital age when all carry a mobile phone, these remain the envy of younger prefects.

Communication is good, report parents – 'Most staff return calls swiftly, parents are taken seriously, our concerns addressed and we are kept informed of outcome,' said one.

Pupils and parents: Families come from as far as Lancaster, Kendal, Morecambe, Grange and beyond – all serviced by a good school bus system. Boarding families come from across the UK and beyond. Parents are a real mix – everything from university types (Lancaster), teachers (many who teach here) and headteachers through to businessfolk and farmers, among others. All are attracted by a school that feels rural yet doesn't suffer the restraints of small rural secondaries elsewhere in the area. It may be sited in a large village but strong numbers means there are no problems in generating sports teams, maintaining a healthy sixth form and being able to offer good facilities, making it the envy of others. Students are a likeable bunch, at ease with themselves and their surroundings but with no lack of aspiration and ambition.

Money matters: Fees for boarding but not for tuition.

The last word: Highlights include the academic rigour, focus on outdoor pursuits in a stunning setting, the genuinely happy vibe and – unusual for a state school – the boarding.

Exeter Mathematics School

7

Rougemont House, Exeter, Devon EX4 3PU

01392 429020 | admissions@exeterms.ac.uk | www.exetermathematicsschool.ac.uk

Ages: 16–18

Pupils: 134; **Boarders:** 37

Fees: Weekly boarding up to £10,410 pa

Headteacher: Since 2014, Kerry Burnham, founding headteacher. West Country through and through, educated at Plymstock School and Exeter university, BSc in maths and education. Accredited advanced skills teacher. From 1998 maths teacher and gifted & talented coordinator at Torquay Boys' Grammar. Not imbued in the least with a sense of manifest destiny and had never considered going for a headship until the Exeter Mathematics School (EMS) job came up. It's the maths that got her blowing the moths off her CV; she just can't get enough of it. Like any maths teacher anywhere she is perfectly certain that hers is the most important subject of them all.

A big step up, starting a new school from scratch. She's at ease with the responsibilities and conspicuously good at people. Warm, cordial, intuitive, fun to be with. No side to her at all; indeed, her candour may be her most refreshing and appealing attribute. Has presided over, inter alia, an Ofsted inspection just two and a bit years postlaunch. It rated EMS outstanding across the board. So: Ms Burnham makes things happen. What's more, she pays heed to students and parents. One parent told us, 'She takes our suggestions seriously and if they're any good acts on them.'

Married with children, Ms Burnham has fond if distant memories of biking, badminton, modern jive and walking on Dartmoor. All have been more or less sidelined by her workload. But, now that her school has developed beyond baby steps, she is beginning to win back lost recreational territory.

Entrance: At year 12 only – none at year 13. Maths and science GCSEs at grade 8-9 plus six others at 5 and above, a 6 at Eng lang preferred. Some intelligent flexibility. References, interview and school's own entry exam in maths. Head spelt out paramount criterion: 'We want no dutiful learners here: you must love maths and be prepared to be challenged.'

Exit: Almost all to universities everywhere to study STEM subjects overwhelmingly. A few to degree apprenticeships and accounting. Eight to Oxbridge in 2021; others off to Warwick, Exeter, Southampton, UCL, Birmingham, Cardiff, Leeds, Bath, Loughborough, Heriot-Watt, Swansea, Portsmouth, Bristol, University of the West of England and Nottingham Trent.

Latest results: In 2021, 77 per cent A*/A grades at A level (91 per cent A*-B). In 2019 (the last year when exams took place), 69 per cent A*/A at A level (91 per cent A*-B).

Teaching and learning: As you may suppose, the curriculum goes way beyond A levels – in the head's words, 'We're not thinking about exams, we're thinking about maths.' What you must be in no two minds about is that the diet is basically maths enriched with more maths. So everyone does A level maths and further maths plus either physics or computer science. If you don't want to do one of the latter two, you can choose a fourth option over at the Exeter (tertiary) College campus 10 mins walk away. But EMS is not a school for Renaissance students, it's a specialist school: it's for students and teachers who can't get enough of pursuing and assigning value to that tantalising shapeshifter they call x. Adding the option of philosophy to the A level mix could arguably work rather well for pure mathematicians, but there are no plans to do so.

The curriculum goes way beyond A levels – in the head's words, 'We're not thinking about exams, we're thinking about maths.' The diet is maths enriched with more maths

On top of A levels you take your Exeter Mathematics Certificate, a unique qualification co-designed with Exeter University's maths department. The idea is to pique curiosity, inspire self-directed study and encourage you to play to your particular mathematical strengths and – head's words – 'personal passions'. Lots of stress on problem solving. In the first year, a variety of activities including working on a task set by one of the school's industry partners, which include ATASS Sports, QuinetiQ, the Met Office, the Hydrographic Office, Apple and Dyson. In the second year you undertake your own research project and present your findings on a poster and in a formal presentation to your fellow students (scary, obvs) and members of the public (scarier still). Students are mentored by maths undergrads from the university and work with peers across the south west. They enjoy fortnightly Inspire lectures, an academia sans frontières programme designed to join up all knowledge about everything. The guiding idea is to enable you to segue effortlessly into your chosen university. The aptness of the process is self-evident.

So, a hothouse-cum-sweatshop characterised by fiendish pressure and fevered stress, then? Quite the contrary. First impressions are that EMS closely resembles, in tone and structure, one of those progressive schools. Or Google. The ambience is notably relaxed-seeming. And collaborative. Mutually supportive. Convivial. A student told us, 'No one's trying to prove they're better than anyone else.' There's a very popular ping-pong table. We encountered a group of students playing cards... until we realised that what they were actually doing was maths. We didn't encounter a single serried rank in any of the classrooms and the observable status gap between teachers and students is close to zero. But make no mistake, there's masses of maths going on – in the head's words, 'There are no dutiful learners here.' And given that much of a mathematician's work is at the level of the subconscious, everything we saw came across as wholly appropriate. A student told us that 'the focus is on enjoying maths, not being driven'. Another said, 'There's a good level of intensity – keeps you focused, not stressed.' Other quotes from students: 'The big emphasis here is on formulating and researching a problem'; 'The teaching is amazing'; and 'Such a shame it's only two years'. A teacher told us, 'I feel lucky to teach here; you can cherish every student.' The head told us, 'We tell them it's okay to be wrong, you learn so much from your mistakes. It's all right to say "I don't know".' A parent said, 'The school teaches in such a way that subjects are relatable to the real world, and the level of enthusiasm in the teaching is transmitted from teachers to the students.'

As EMS establishes itself, competition for places is hotting up and (head's words), 'We are taking additional care with the selection process to ensure the students that will most benefit attend.' Expect exam results to improve in line with this. In 2020 they harvested their fifth crop of results. Very high value-added. Not surprising that a student told us, 'I feel a long way from where I was. I'm ready now for university.' Students rate the guidance they get in this respect. We spoke to a former student who'd had

The idea of specialist maths schools is new to the UK. They make sense inasmuch as mathematicians constitute a distinct clan

a last-minute change of heart about the university she'd chosen. Much praise for the guidance she got and the invitation to come into school in her 'lost' year and keep maths-fit.

Learning support and SEN: More than 25 per cent have a learning difficulty and/or disability, a significant minority on the autistic spectrum, the remainder the customary range, eg dyslexia. The school is fully geared to this. For students on the spectrum EMS's size is an important factor in the socialisation process. With only 60-odd students per year group, you 'soon get to know everyone and it's easy to make friends'. Whole-school approach to learning support includes specialists, one of whom observed, 'Outstanding teaching is the best way of helping those with special needs.'

The arts and extracurricular: You'd think the small number of students here would restrict the scope for extracurricular activities, but in this context EMS students join up with their fellows at Exeter College, which supports a wide enough range to engage almost 6,000 students. In short, there's heaps to choose from. Do EMS students tend to get stuck in their mathsy bubble and not get out enough? Well, there's a strong and insistent requirement to commit to recreation and there's also respect for those who, whether by disposition or because of undeveloped social skills, find it hard to do so. Insistence is firm but gentle, yet some parents aren't quite yet altogether happy with the school's extracurricular provision. It's a work in progress. Worth pointing out that one parent told us her daughter, who has autism and is physically disabled, was perfectly comfortable doing an AS level up at the college.

Sport: Lots use the gym. Important to sign up for courses and activities before all the places are gone. A parent told us, 'The option is there and the school encourage students to take advantage of it, but ultimately it comes down to the student.'

Boarding: Supervised accommodation for those who live more than an hour away – around 30 of them. Families in financial need can access a bursary to cover the cost. Some live in flats on the campus – ensuite bedroom and living room, six per flat, grouped by age. Two staff members on duty overnight. Boarders do a food and hygiene qualification, cook for each other (supported by staff) and are coached in keeping clean and tidy and living with others. A tutor told us, 'It's a great way to learn life skills.' Agreed. No access during the day. Popping into town for an alcoholic drink in the evening flatly, utterly and remorselessly banned. Always.

Ethos and heritage: EMS occupies Rougemont House in the heart of Exeter next door to the castle – a pretty enough spot and a great location. No grounds to speak of. Sort of Tuscan-style building of negligible architectural value protected by a flattering Grade II listing. Regrettable. Has a rambling quality which imparts something of an MC Escher vibe. Perhaps. Point is, it serves.

The idea of specialist maths schools is new to the UK. They make sense inasmuch as mathematicians constitute a distinct clan (just as ballet dancers, musicians and performing artists do and, say, geographers on the whole don't). STEM subjects (science, technology, engineering and maths) are trending big-time right now and ex-prime minister May wanted a maths school in every town in Britain to enable the country to 'stand tall in the world after Brexit'. It won't happen because a number of universities have mulled it over and for various reasons (terror of accusations of elitism, mostly) said no. Politics and local feasibility apart, the business case is entirely sound. EMS is sponsored by the University of Exeter. This relationship makes for a fast track and ensures students already have a foot in university before they leave school. The school's co-sponsor, Exeter College, complements what EMS can offer in terms of fourth-choice A levels and what they call enrichment. So EMS is deficient in nothing. Critics of specialist maths schools claim that their existence will open a gulf between good and poor standards in maths education and deprive non-elite mathematicians of great teaching, but in fact the reverse is the truth: EMS works with teachers throughout the south west to improve maths education for all – eg year 10 residentials, enhancement courses, maths student community.

The social climate is relaxed, with an egalitarian flavour. It's easily possible that some prospective parents looking round could find themselves stifling a harrumph and coming to the conclusion that it's all a bit free and easy and unstructured. Let's address that. We visited on a warm spring day when most of the male teachers were wearing shorts. Students are schooled not to address their teachers as Sir or Miss but by their first names. So yes, informal. But according to serving parents and students there's plenty of respect for teachers: respect based on esteem. Yes, there's rigour. Teachers here don't sweat the small stuff but, in the words of a parent, 'they come down hard on what really matters'. We are in no doubt about that. The ethos here is college, not school so, in the words of a parent, 'The school rightly expects students to be proactive and engaged in order to maximise their potential.'

Clan values mean that students here really enjoy being around, and sparking off, each other. For some this is the first time at school that they have discovered fellow spirits. They flourish in an environment where, a parent told us, 'everyone can be themselves'.

Pastoral care, inclusivity and discipline: Pastoral care is shared among teachers and a specialist team who spoke to us with full-strength seriousness and much fervour about their role and its importance, because 'these students spend a long time outside their comfort zone'. We heard about an autistic student who had outstripped predictions and developed a capability for independent living. The philosophy is that when a student has a problem it is acknowledged as being of equal perceived gravity by staff. Nothing is ever trivialised. Given the complexity of needs presented by some students, pastoral care here has to be the best it can. We are in no doubt that it is. The highly personal approach is of course aided by the school's small size. Everyone knows everyone so there's no slipping under the radar. A former student told us, 'When I needed them they really were there for me.' A parent told us, 'I've been impressed with how well the teachers seem to know my son, and how encouraging they are, with specific advice for improvements. They are happy to talk to parents about any concerns or questions at any time.'

Pupils and parents: Catchment area is Devon, Dorset, Somerset and Cornwall. Currently, most from Exeter and environs, but furthest flung student from Penzance. Open to students at independent schools, keen that they are not disproportionately favoured but by no means anti either. Prospective students from schools with a sixth form likely to come in for persuasion to stay on. We spoke to a head who had 'lost' a brilliant mathematician to EMS. He said bravely, 'We would have loved him to have stayed but it's important that the right student finds the right course.' Only natural he was wistful because a star student is a feather in the cap.

Mission to recruit students from low income homes and currently 20 per cent are. Proportion of female students has increased from a fifth to a third, below the school's current target of 40 per cent, the national average for female learners taking maths A level. However, well above the national average for girls doing physics and further maths. Year groups 64 strong and no plans to expand. Currently, four out of 120 transgender.

Money matters: EMS enjoys £350,000 a year on top of its statutory funding to enable the school to deliver its outreach programme. Additional funding to support, and give accommodation bursaries to, students from lower income families.

The last word: A birds-of-a-feather school which owes its existence to the theory that elite maths ability is best turbocharged in a specialist environment, but never to the exclusion of other educational and cultural experiences. EMS is a young school now hitting its stride. Students are well looked after and, far from dematerialising into a mathsy parallel reality, are closely in touch with all the day to day stuff that animates young people everywhere. Great teaching a given. Attention to life skills especially impressive.

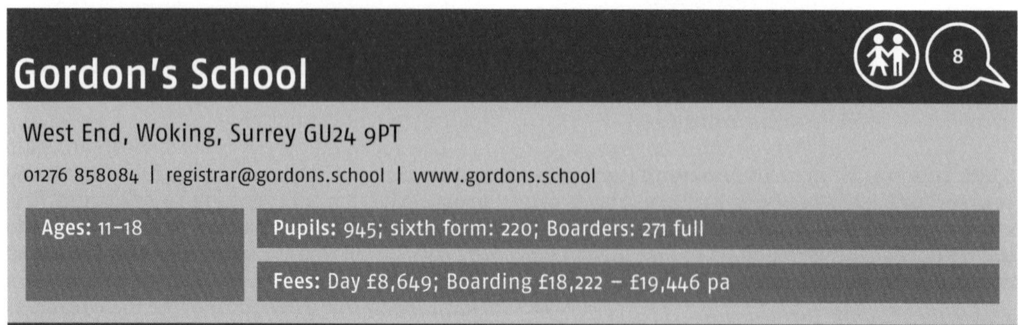

Gordon's School

8

West End, Woking, Surrey GU24 9PT

01276 858084 | registrar@gordons.school | www.gordons.school

Ages: 11–18

Pupils: 945; sixth form: 220; Boarders: 271 full

Fees: Day £8,649; Boarding £18,222 – £19,446 pa

Head teacher: Since 2010, Andrew Moss BA MEd NPQH (50s). Started teaching in 1992 and has worked in a variety of boarding and day schools, including most recently a headship in a Cognita independent school. Before that he was a deputy head in Hampshire, and deputy director of studies and housemaster at Wymondham College (also a state boarding school).

He's 'businesslike' and 'no-nonsense', say parents. While insisting he is 'approachable' and 'responsive', one summed up, 'I wouldn't want to mess with him' while another voiced, 'He's straight talking and demands a high level of commitment from both the students and families – that is not for everyone so don't even think about coming here unless you're prepared to go all in.' One recalled an information evening about the sixth form, in which his message was, 'If you don't want to work, don't come here – it's that simple.' Students say he's 'interested', 'visible' and 'knows us by name'. Known for his signature stern, tough chapel talks; one student said, 'He is assertive and authoritative, but he's also friendly.' We found him old-school when it comes to manners and rules, but modern in his outlook – pretty much the perfect combo for this military influenced school.

An academically rigorous curriculum. It is an all-ability school, for which students are not selected via entrance exams, yet its results are top notch

Despite his strong ideas, he is big on using staff and parents as a sounding board ('you can't build capacity all by yourself') and takes feedback seriously, with one student telling how they recently 'blocked a change that the school wanted to make around the structure of prep time – it did not suit us and he heard us.' Regularly meets with parents at everything from tea and cake afternoons (before exeats) to information evenings. Keeps a finger on the pulse by standing in for teachers when he can.

Has two children of his own (both attended the school) and is a keen skier in his spare time.

Entrance: Tough. There are typically 400 applications for the 116 year 7 places on offer (of whom around 32 board) and around half of these are generally swallowed up by siblings. Non-selective, so no entrance exams. Full or weekly boarder places prioritised by 'need to board'. This usually means children from Forces families from the UK and overseas.

For admission as a 'day boarder' think purely of location. Catchment varies but typically you'll need to live no further than 1km from the school. Needless to say, school is popular among local estate agents. A small number of places allocated each year to children with statements of special educational needs.

Between 30 and 40 additional places available for the sixth form, where the entry requirement for both existing and new pupils is a minimum of five 5s at GCSE (including English and maths) plus, in some cases, grade criteria for individual subjects.

Exit: Around 30 per cent leave after GCSEs, most wanting a wider breadth of courses. Most sixth formers on to university; over half to Russell Group. One Cambridge place in 2021, plus nine medics. Popular universities include Exeter, Nottingham, Southampton, Liverpool, Birmingham and just about every course you can think of, with STEM on the up and economics, law, computer studies and business and management popular choices. In 2021, three students took up golf scholarships in American universities, with a further four studying at overseas universities. There were six apprenticeships in 2021.

Latest results: In 2021, 37 per cent 9-7 at GCSE; 94 per cent 9-4 in both maths and English. At A level, 58 per cent A*/A (84 per cent A*-B). In 2019 (the last year when exams took place), 42 per cent 9-7 GCSE; 67 per cent 9-4 in both maths and English. At A level, 38 per cent A*/A (73 per cent A*-B).

Teaching and learning: Among the very best state offerings in the country, with an academically rigorous curriculum. It is an all-ability school, for which students are not selected via entrance exams, yet its results are top notch. Value added is also a stand-out point, with the school in the top one per cent for progress from GCSE to A levels.

Head believes in putting progress under the spotlight. 'Attainment will take care of itself if progress is prioritised, so tracking is our number one thing.' Nobody slips through the net here, say students. 'If someone isn't keeping up, there are lots of interventions to help get them up to scratch,' said one. While the school has always had a real push on effort and working hard, they are now even more forensic about ensuring everyone is reaching their potential and the students (who even get ranked in their year on effort) literally refer to their efforts in decimal points. Students also get target and working grades, and every half term they receive significant feedback on what they need to do next. 'You can't be brilliant at everything but the beauty about effort is that you can control it,' says head. Message is clearly getting through, with one student telling us, 'It's not all about As and A*s here; it's about doing your very best, whatever grade that might mean.'

Teachers 'really care', say students. We were told a story of one 'who'd been a bit of a rogue' walking into his maths exam: 'He said to his maths teacher, "I'm going to get a B for you." The teacher told him to get the B for himself, but the student was insistent. "No, miss, this will be for you." That pretty much sums this school up.' Parents praise the 'strong and disciplined' teaching team and their 'high expectations for students'. Lessons are fairly formal – nearly all desks were facing forwards in the classrooms we visited and behaviour was impeccable in all but one classroom where a boy threw his pen at a classmate then looked very sheepish when he spotted us.

Everyone is set for English, maths and science (six sets per year group) and also for languages in years 7 and 8 – a language is compulsory at GCSE; either German, French or Spanish.

They plough through the work here, books filled at a pace, and there are plenty of practice papers and timed tests to make sure everyone is well prepared for GCSE. 'It can be daunting at the time, but when it comes to the exams, you're so well prepared,' said one student. 'The new linear exams suit us,' says head.

Sixth formers take mainly traditional A levels ('those with gravitas, the ones that open doors') although there are now three BTECs available in sport, ICT and business. Parents like it that sixth formers are more likely to work during their 'study periods' (they are not called free periods here!). Around a third do EPQ.

In 2018 the school announced its partnership with Harlequins and now runs the RFU-endorsed DiSE (diploma in sporting excellence) programme for talented 16 to 18-year-old rugby players wishing to pursue a career in the game.

Learning support and SEN: Lowish requirements for additional support; 16 students have help for EAL and 25 have EHCPs, led by full-time SENCo and delivered in small groups and individually. 'We don't have a big learning support department,' admits head and parents told us they 'haven't been great around SEN in the past' but insist that is no longer the case. 'They've helped my son through his problems with English because they know his success in that subject will impact on all his subjects,' said one.

The arts and extracurricular: Everyone here burns the candle at both ends and that's just how they like it – 'We all know busy people achieve more,' explains head. After what would be the end of the school day at most state schools, the compulsory extended day here begins with 'period 7' – anything from sport to cooking, bagpipe lessons, golf, equestrian team training or ICT coding. After that, it's tea and then prep.

All year 10 students do DofE every year, including a striking number of golds. And all three forces are represented in Gordon's combined cadet force – quite a feat to manage a naval unit in landlocked Surrey.

Every student learns to march and takes part in every one of the eight parades and chapel services held each year

Great tradition of hard-fought inter-house competition gets everyone involved, regardless of ability (boys' rugby is a highlight of the year), not just in sport but also in art, music and drama, with specialist facilities for all. Music very big here, with a junior boys' choir the newest kid on the block, joining the orchestra, choirs (including male teachers' choir) and concert band, as well as the pipes and drums band which, together with marching practice, is a major focus on the school. LAMDA has grown in recent years and there are junior and senior productions every year too, plus drama ambassadors who direct, stage and light their own smaller productions. Earlier this year, Arts Council England awarded the school an Artsmark silver award. Student-led initiatives more generally are on the up, with a growing number of societies such as eco society and global social leader programme, as well as the Sudan Society (Gordon's is the only European school ever to have gone to Khartoum). Runs a Model United Nations programme and is the only state school to host its own MUN conference. There are two annual art exhibitions, with improving take-up for art at both GCSE and A level, following a dip in numbers.

Sport: Masses of sport on offer, with good facilities on site – more than 40 acres of playing fields, and all the usual football, rugby and hockey pitches, to the less usual (for a state school) shooting range, Astroturf, BMX track and rowing centre. Gordon's teams are happy to take on the toughest opponents and often play independent schools. The first football team has twice reached the semi-finals of the English Schools FA Cup in recent years. The partnership with Harlequins has resulted in rugby players at the school representing the west London club and progressing on to England squads. But it's not just about the elite, with all students encouraged to participate and there's an impressive engagement rate for older girls (who often drop out of sports at other schools).

Boarding: Although two-thirds of its pupils live at home, the school is structured as a boarding school. Day pupils, known as 'day boarders', are organised in the same way as the wholly residential boarders and share an extended school day. So everyone is in a house, with houseparents, and follows the same programme, including after-school clubs, supper and supervised homework until 7.30pm (or 6.45pm for some of the younger ones), and everyone attends Saturday morning school. To cover this parents of day boarders are charged a fee of £7,000+ a year.

There are six day houses and four residential houses, plus a co-ed house for year 7s. Boys and girls are allowed freely in each other's houses, but no boy is allowed upstairs in the girls' boarding houses and vice versa. Common rooms are spacious yet cosy – like genuinely lived-in homes – and are kitted out with the likes of pool and table tennis tables. All sixth formers have study rooms, even in the day houses – around two to four desks in each room, with some particularly swanky new ones. All understandably more relaxed than other parts of the school, there is nothing sterile or pristine about these boarding houses. Ofsted's inspection of boarding facilities pronounced them 'outstanding' in every respect. Boarders say 'it's home from home'.

Ethos and heritage: Ceremony and discipline are in the DNA of Gordon's, which was founded in 1885, at the behest of Queen Victoria, as a national memorial to General Gordon who was killed at Khartoum. The reigning monarch has been the school's patron ever since and every teaching block is named after a country (s)he visited.

Every student learns to march and takes part in every one of the eight parades and chapel services held each year, accompanied by the pipes and drums marching band. There is marching practice every Friday, and once a year students go to London and literally stop the traffic when they march down Whitehall past the Cenotaph, ending up at the bronze statue of General Gordon on the Embankment. Although right up the street of the keen musicians in the band, it can be rather a chore for some of the others. 'It's not exactly my favourite thing, but it's just part of school life so you get on with it and actually you become more fond of it as you get older,' said one student. 'Well, it's no bad thing for students to do things well that they don't necessarily want to do – it's a good lesson for life,' retorts the head, adding that it gives 'a great edge' and 'story for interview' when applying to uni. Definitely part and parcel of what makes this school different, it is also seen to encourage camaraderie and is part of the discipline that feeds into the classrooms.

Day to day, things are rather less regimented, but all very orderly – head describes atmosphere as 'purposeful calm'. The school is built around a large quadrangle, where the students hang out during break and lunch if they are not in their houses. Alongside the original Victorian buildings are some less pretty 1960s additions, and (much better) 21st-century facilities, including the new science block, sixth form centre and (most recently) sports hub, maths centre and business and IT centre (with new performing arts centre currently under construction). Classrooms are large, light and spacious, in both the older and newer buildings, and well resourced. Stunning chapel, built in 1894, which houses numerous school treasures, including a book which lists the names of all the Gordon's boys killed in the two world wars. Pupils are never for a moment in any doubt about their school's heritage.

Pastoral care, inclusivity and discipline: Houses form the backbone of this school and the fact that they are physical houses helps create a genuine village culture. Very close companionship among students, including across year groups – 'houses are like a brotherhood,' one student told us. Every residential boarding house has two houseparents, a day matron, two residential tutors and a graduate assistant tutor, 'so we are spoilt for choice about having someone to talk to as you'll always get on really well with at least one of them, probably more,' said one student. Plenty of peer mentoring. Counsellor available, to which students can and do self-refer. Full mental health agenda, including guest speakers and mental health ambassadors, and the school is about to start benchmarking for happiness and wellbeing.

Ofsted's inspection of boarding facilities pronounced them 'outstanding' in every respect. Boarders say 'it's home from home'

There's not much allowance for anyone stepping out of line at this highly disciplined school, but for those obedient souls happy to stay within the set boundaries there are plenty of rewards and responsibilities on offer. Pupils quickly pick up on what's expected of them and are generally hardworking and appreciative of what's on offer. Simple good manners are prioritised and it shows. Similarly picky about uniform. If a girl's skirt is deemed too short (and we didn't see any) she will be given a week's grace to get a new one. Sex, drugs and rock and roll? 'It's a residential school, so I can't say it doesn't happen but instances are very, very low,' says head.

School admits they 'are not without bullying incidents, but what we don't have are repeat incidents', which they put down to the (you guessed it) house system, plus anti-bullying ambassadors. Very clear sanctions system with the first offence a verbal warning, followed by a bad comment on the online platform, which can be assed by their parents – usually that's enough, but if not, it's a detention which is seen as a very big deal here. Around seven or eight temporary exclusions a year – 'it would be lower if we did not choose to have such a high bar'; permanent exclusions very rare.

Pupils and parents: Although it's a state school, most parents have money, certainly parents of boarders who have to cover the boarding fees. Parents of day boarders must be able to afford the £7000+ day boarding fees and will be in a certain socio-economic demographic to live in the catchment; of necessity they must live practically next door and some move house to get this education for their children. Aside from these locals, parents are a huge mix of professional, diplomatic and Forces. Weekly boarders typically live within an hour's drive, full boarders come from all over the UK, with about 15 per cent from overseas (expats).

We found students friendly, polite, happy and very proud of their school; all regular young people, not quiet and cowed by the rules and regulations, but confident and ambitious types who seem to thrive in the order of everything.

Money matters: The education is free, but parents pay for the boarding and parents of day students must pay for the after-school activities, house staff, Saturday school and meals. Around 10 per cent of places funded by means-tested bursaries and there are 12 sixth form scholarships in sports and creative arts.

The last word: A very different state offering – more like a private school without the price tag and elitism. Committed to traditional values, high standards, good discipline – doesn't share its 'semper fidelis' motto with the US marine corps for nothing. Those happy with the 'heads down and work' ethos are rewarded with an all-round, top-notch education, pastoral care par excellence and enviable opportunities for sport. Suits focused, self-directed types and is definitely not a soft option.

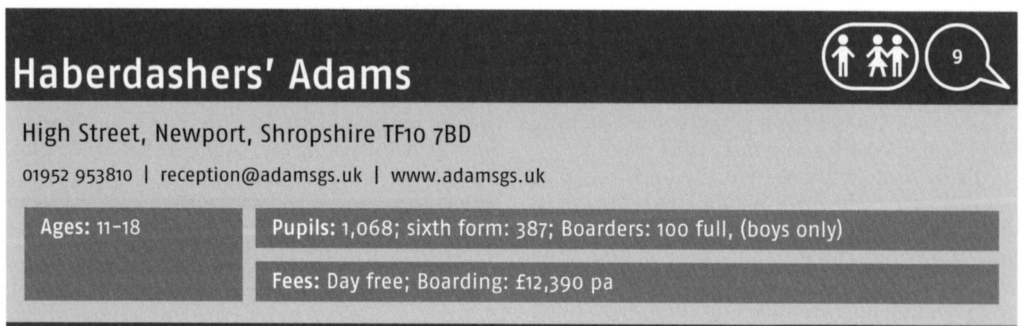

Haberdashers' Adams

High Street, Newport, Shropshire TF10 7BD

01952 953810 | reception@adamsgs.uk | www.adamsgs.uk

Ages: 11–18

Pupils: 1,068; sixth form: 387; Boarders: 100 full, (boys only)

Fees: Day free; Boarding: £12,390 pa

Headmaster: Since 2015, Gary Hickey BA (music, Manchester Metropolitan) MA in education (Birmingham) and Fellow of the Royal Society of Arts. Previously deputy head at Ercall Wood Technology College in Wellington, became deputy head at Haberdashers' Adams in 2009, head in 2015. Since then, he has set about transforming the outlook and ethos of this boys' state grammar (also offers boys' boarding and open to day girls at sixth form) with great vigour and a clear social focus.

Ten years ago, he tells us, Adams was perceived as a closed shop to locals. One parent described it as 'the Willy Wonka' factory, iron gates firmly shut. 'Elitist and inward looking' is how he himself sums up the ghost of Adams' past, a school turning out hearty medics with a penchant for rugby. A lingering perception he has set about dismantling. For starters, he has strengthened school's links with the diverse community it serves, actively seeking to attract as broad a base of pupils as possible. He has taken on a specific head of outreach who spends a lot of time in local primary schools. Mentoring is offered and pupils on free school meals have priority entrance, as do local pupils. He has also done his best (he concedes this is a WIP) to make its entrance exam tutor-proof. Open events see parents, whose children are in local state primaries, flooding in. Oiling the wheels for social mobility in this way, it's no wonder he was invited to 10 Downing Street to discuss the role grammars might play in society.

Another key change has been a greater emphasis on the arts. Mr Hickey alludes to the 46 after-school clubs on offer; you put opportunity on the table, he says, and then it is up to every pupil to take advantage. As a serious professional musician himself, who also directs plays and films (as you do), he feels the arts are crucial in creating well-rounded personalities. So if the Adams pupil of today likes rugby (and plenty do), it will be rugby plus Chekhov.

Senior boys board at Beaumaris, a modern building but a wonder to behold. The kitchen is a replica of an American diner with a juke box and all the 1950s trimmings

We imagine all these changes have caused a ruffled feather or two among the hearty Old Novaportans who thought things were just fine the way they were, so it's only right to stress that these changes are not in any way about eroding Adams' enriched 400-year heritage. On the contrary, Mr Hickey is, in fact, incredibly proud of the school's heritage, so much so that in 2018 the school's name was changed to Haberdashers' Adams (which – surprise, surprise – also proved a tad controversial with a certain segment of parents). It is a change that reinforces the school's links with its founder, Alderman William Adams, a haberdasher. The backing and support from the Habs' brand, he says, runs through the school like a stick of rock. It is part of the Haberdashers' Adams Federation Trust, which also includes Haberdashers' Abraham Darby.

Married to Rhian, a teacher, they have three children. A quietly spoken innovator, he is mightily high-profile as well as being something of a polymath; invited to give lectures at international 'Inspiring Leaders' conference, garnering a special commendation in the National Teaching Awards and gaining a fellowship from Cambridge University. In his beautiful wood-panelled office, there is a notice on the wall: 'Follow your heart but take your brain with you.' This sums up both the man and the reinvigorated spirit of the school over which he presides.

Entrance: Priority is given to those on a pupil premium. The school has introduced an 'attendance area' (catchment area) which was extended in September 2020 to include large parts of Telford and Wrekin; boys who pass the entrance test and attend one of the primary schools in these areas have priority over those from other schools.

Hugely over-subscribed, with 1,000 sitting the exam for a 100 places. From September 2021, 30 additional year 7 places. One of those state grammars where parents might be tempted to fake ID or pretend a distant cousin is really a younger brother to get a place. Beware. Stringent scrutiny is applied. No one makes it through the Adams ID-detector, even with a cunning plan and a fake moustache.

The entrance exam, according to a pupil, has a science/maths bias and Mr Hickey agrees with this but says the test is being reviewed to make it more creative.

External candidates, including girls, may enter at sixth form (application form and reference from previous school). Five GCSEs at grade 7 required and at least a grade 7 in their chosen A level subject.

Exit: Nearly 30 per cent leave after GCSEs. In 2021, four to Oxbridge and 16 medics. Leavers go to universities all over the UK. Cardiff, Birmingham, Manchester, York and Liverpool popular. A smattering go on to study arts and humanities, but most opt for science or business: biology, biochemistry, engineering courses, economics, maths.

Latest results: In 2021, 70 per cent 9-7 at GCSE; 53 per cent A*/A at A level (78 per cent A*-B). In 2019 (the last year exams took place), 61 per cent 9-7 at GCSE; 53 per cent A*/A at A level.

Teaching and learning: Mr Hickey believes in breadth of curriculum; an overview of the results, however, suggests that while results in GCSE English language/ literature and modern languages are strong, the school still really excels in maths and the three sciences, with GCSEs and A levels boasting a swag bag full of A*s (and 8s and 9s) across those subjects year on year. That said, the humanities do pretty well too.

The sixth form pupil who showed us round was a poster for the well-rounded Adams student; studying double maths and physics at A level, he had a place at a top university to read music. Music A level had not been on offer but a few pupils had been keen to take it and so hey presto, it was sorted. This is not necessarily the norm, however; one parent mentioned her son had not been able to take the (fairly standard) combo of arts subjects he wanted. Yet things are transitioning, the curriculum is being broadened, geology is a recent addition as an A level and drama GCSE is next in line. All pupils have to take two languages from year 7. At present, 98 per cent of pupils take one language at GCSE but only around three per cent go on to study a language at A level. All pupils sit EPQ in sixth form.

One parent grumbled a little about the recent emphasis on languages, his son not having a flair for them, but he was impressed by the support plan offered in the form of booster lessons and mentoring. Performance is tracked carefully at Adams and monitored every six weeks. Every pupil sits down with a mentor-tutor twice a year to discuss progress. Parents say the school works on small weaknesses and although class size is around 30, the teachers are tuned in to nuance. They describe the teaching as outstanding across the board.

Performance is tracked carefully and monitored every six weeks. Every pupil sits down with a mentor-tutor twice a year to discuss progress

One parent queried the value-added to Adams pupils, suggesting a tough entrance exam meant only the academic cream got through and so the crop of stellar results was not surprising. Conversely, another parent said her son failed to get in at 11, got in at 13 as a boarder, didn't necessarily fit the academic mould but had been catapulted into straight As. Go figure.

Learning support and SEN: Growing emphasis on helping pupils with barriers to learning. Mr Hickey is keen on this. One-to-one is available and there is every effort to identify issues at an early stage. The school uses information from previous schools, listens to the concerns of pupils and parents, and undertakes its own observations and assessments.

The arts and extracurricular: Every school says they are about the well-rounded child but here this is no empty cliché. Yes, the school excels at science and maths but parents say the drive is about cross-fertilising interests, getting students to find other passions.

Alongside the usual character-building DofE and CCF, there is an astounding array of clubs: astronomy, debating, creative writing, raspberry pi robot building, engineering, sculpting, taiko drumming. Clubs start up if pupils want it, Mr Hickey says, referring to bridge club with its handful of members.

Lots of trips; recently Washington, charity trips to Africa and sport tours to South Africa, not to mention a music tour of Australia. Likewise, heaps of competitions, such as the Royal Society of Chemistry's Schools Analyst Competition, Young Enterprise, Maths Feast... it goes on. Mr Hickey has also kickstarted a rich array of speakers on world affairs, topics like 'What's the difference between a refugee and a migrant?' – all presented like university lectures.

The house system means lots of competitions, small to large scale. Parents enthused about the house music, where participation levels were very high and the full spectrum of opportunity available, including choirs, swing bands, saxophone group, and guitar groups.

A greater emphasis on drama now within the school. One or two school productions happen per year, most recently Anything Goes and Jekyll and Hyde.

Responsibility in the final year comes in fairly traditional form – team captains, house captains and head boy and head girl. Lots of opportunity to experiment, too: the lower sixth developed an AGS radio station.

Sport: Sport figures highly – playing fields are down the road – boys can choose from rugby, hockey, football, cricket, athletics, badminton and cross-country. A swimming pool (now with roof) is an added bonus. Sixth form girls have hockey, netball, rounders and athletics. Athletics and cross-country are strong, as is the recently introduced dance option.

Boarding: The school is one of nine state boarding grammars in the country. There are around 100 boarders, of whom 25 per cent are international students. Boarders can go home at weekends but some choose not to, to take advantage of trips to Alton Towers, treasure hunts or archery competitions. There are themed events, such as the circus when magicians and jugglers came. A wilderness weekend saw them camping out and skinning rabbits. Two houses, Longford Hall for years 7 to 10 and Beaumaris for years 11 to 13.

Diving down an off-track road and seeing a Georgian mansion at the end (Longford Hall) seemed more Mr Darcy than state grammar. Overlooking vast playing fields, it took our breath away. It has a welcoming entrance (likewise the house master was warm and cheery) very decent rooms, charming sash windows, many with great views. Boys are bussed in and out each day (five-minute journey). Dorms house three to five boys, bunk beds until years 9 and 10. The configuration of pupils tends to stay the same but boys can request a move if they feel the dynamic isn't working. Lovely TV room which, with its long billowy curtains and high ceiling, reinforced the stately home air. Mobile phones are allowed till 9pm. In the spring/ summer evenings, the boys play outside on the vast playing fields after school, with a chance to let off steam, then tea and prep. Parents very happy with the communication and the way in which school deals with any issues. One mother said she felt listened to and spoke glowingly of how the school had eased her child's initial homesickness.

Senior boys board a couple of minutes away from the school, and while Beaumaris is a modern building, it is also a wonder to behold. Chairs, beanbags, cushions in vibrant jewel colours, a huge graffiti mural on entering saying 'senior'. The kitchen – hold the dogs – is a replica of an American diner with all the Juke Box 1950 trimmings, great attention to detail. The housemother exuded warmth and a realistic understanding of what makes teenage boys tick. (Put it this way, those boys know not to leave mess in the kitchen and understand how to use a washing machine.) Rooms are single, double or triple, all ensuite and very roomy. Great games room and every effort made to integrate the new arrivals. Paintballing is a typical ice-breaker. Lots of theme nights, sushi nights, Halloween party (even a Valentines' night – clearly just a crafty excuse for a jolly but the boys looked mortified when it was mentioned).

Mentoring system in place and everything seemed super organised. Older pupils can go out into Newport which, boasting agricultural university Harper Adams, has a student feel.

Ethos and heritage: The school was founded in 1656 by Alderman William Adams. Within, it has a traditional vibe, corridor displays were varied, some departments opting for huge glossy photos, others for more modest subject-related poster displays. It is a mishmash of the new (eg 2021 teaching block, 2013 sixth form centre) and the historical. Some, but not all, areas laden with charm. The main library, where the school was started originally, is dripping with heritage, vast black and white photos of previous heads on the back wall.

A general sense of focused industriousness as we walked about. Lots of quiet study places for students

Science labs are nice and dapper, music department newly minted. Performance spaces adequate. A general sense of focused industriousness as we walked about. Lots of quiet study places for students. It's a team-driven school, the huge poster showing all the staff is in alphabetical, not hierarchical, order and in a nice quirky touch has mug shots of the school dogs.

Ex Dragon's Den Judge Nick Jenkins is an old boy, so too the former leader of the labour party, Jeremy Corbyn. The latter, not being a fan of selective education nor his schooldays, was invited by Mr Hickey to see the many changes to the school. The invite was never taken up but the story made it onto national TV news. Mr Hickey says pupils especially love listening to old boy Radzi Chinyanganya (ex-Blue Peter and Winter Olympics presenter) talk about his time at school.

Pastoral care, inclusivity and discipline: Pastoral care is centred round the house system – five houses in total. Parents said this fostered a great sense of belonging and was a buffer zone between the leadership team and the pupils. The pupil showing us round was a tad more low key about it, saying that like anything else the blend of people in your house was a matter of chance.

One parent, whose son took a while to settle into the school, spoke enthusiastically of the 'bespoke pastoral programme' the school had assembled, structuring it around extracurricular activities. His son went from not wanting to go to school to absolutely loving every day. It wasn't so much the immediate success of the plan, the parent told us, more the fact that they all worked together and would have carried on working together until a good solution had been forged. Alongside all this, there is a respecting and valuing diversity programme. Or, as Mr Hickey niftily puts it, 'challenging the rugby ethos'.

Disciplinary matters or a perceived whiff of bullying are dealt with quickly. One parent told how her son had been sent home after a misdemeanour for an afternoon of cooling off and had been dealt with brilliantly.

In the sixth form the ratio of boys to girls is roughly 2:1. This would not suit every girl and in the past – perhaps when the school had a different vibe – some girls apparently found it was not for them. It is worth re-emphasising that Mr Hickey is laying down a very different sort of culture within the school now. One parent told us their daughter loved it, felt the teaching was better than her previous (very good) all-girls school and her confidence had grown enormously, so much that she was now able to do public performances in music where previously she had felt inhibited.

Pupils and parents: Social mix is broadening and 60 per cent of pupils, the head estimates, have two working parents. Mr Hickey's initiatives have only been going since 2015 so it will take a little while for parents to feel there is a true cross-section of society but it is getting there. All parents enthused about how much their sons loved it, some children making the voyage from initial uncertainty to a life-defining loyalty by GSCE stage.

The boys we spoke to – across all years at school – seemed down to earth, friendly, enthusiastic and without arrogance.

Money matters: Boarding is a fraction of the cost of the independent sector and the accommodation great.

The last word: A wonderful state grammar with stellar academic standards and a multitude of enrichment activities on offer to create real depth of character. Boarding is incredible for the price.

Hockerill Anglo-European College

10

Dunmow Road, Bishop's Stortford, Hertfordshire CM23 5HX

01279 658451 | admin@hockerill.com | www.hockerill.com

Ages: 11–18

Pupils: 857; sixth form: 244; Boarders: 167 full, 225 weekly/flexi

Fees: Day: free; Boarding £7,767 – £18,042 pa

Principal: Since September 2020, David Woods, previously campus and secondary principal at the International School of Geneva. Before that, head of senior school at Tanglin Trust School in Singapore, which followed positions as assistant principal, head of sixth form and teacher roles in various English state schools. BSc in geography from Liverpool; MSc in rural resources and environmental policy from the University of London. Was a boarder himself, having attended Wymondham College, a state boarding school in Norfolk. Married with two children, currently at UK universities. Enjoys all sport, notably cycling, table tennis and skiing.

Entrance: Over 1,000 applications from over 60 primary schools for 120 places in year 7. Hertfordshire residents are allowed four choices at year 7, and you can use two of these to apply for both a day and boarding place. Places are allocated on the basis of siblings, language and music aptitude tests, children of staff and distance. For boarders, priority is given to Forces and diplomatic personnel plus boarding need. Those looking to board are interviewed – away from their parents – to assess how well they would adapt to life away from home. Boarders pay for board and lodgings but not tuition. About half of the 130 places in year 12 are reserved for boarders.

Exit: Around 40 per cent leave post GCSEs, some because they prefer A levels, some because they don't meet the entrance criteria and some because they fancy moving to a sixth form college or other local school. Post IB, over 90 per cent get first choice of university, with around three-quarters to Russell Group universities including 10 to Oxbridge in 2021, plus six medics. UCL is the most popular university, with others going to Exeter, Durham, Edinburgh, Bristol, Nottingham and Warwick, among others. Quite a few overseas. Wide range of courses including maths, military history, biological sciences, molecular bioengineering, social anthropology, music, international business management, psychology, law, economics, French, Spanish, Japanese, geography and international relations. 'We get lots of help to apply for universities, both here and overseas,' said one student.

Latest results: In 2021, 55 per cent 9-7 at GCSE: 95 per cent 9-4 in both maths and English. Average point score for IB was 37. In 2019 (the last year when exams took place), 53 per cent 9-7 at GCSE. Average point score for IB was 36.

Teaching and learning: One of the most successful comprehensives in the country. Also one of the top non-selective state schools post-16, with excellent IB scores.

Part of the DNA of the school is to bookend GCSEs with the IB, with an IB middle years programme that means all pupils continue with a language, arts and technology. Class sizes average around 24, dropping to 18 at sixth form. Setting in English and maths from year 7 and science from year 9. Students expect to (and largely do) work hard and study hard, with Saturday morning school compulsory and plenty of prep (two hours a night by year 10). But this isn't just a school for the academically gifted; it has a wide mix of ability. 'You're not pressurised to get good grades, but you are expected to do your best,' said one student. Another, who has now left to study A levels at an independent school, said, 'Unlike my current school, which is all about teaching you how to get top marks, learning exam techniques, and basically being an alpha student, Hockerill's ethos is that education should be much broader, and I love that I left with so much more than a bunch of qualifications.'

Unusual curriculum model. Even in the gilded private sector, you'll be hard pushed to find a school where years 8, 9 and 10 are taught geography and history in either French or German – a programme with 80 per cent participation and which really sets the pace for this truly international school, where languages are genuinely embedded in the curriculum. Seven languages as separate subjects also currently on offer, including Japanese and Mandarin, with less than a handful of students doing fewer than two languages.

Truth be told, nothing here is taught in siloes, with students expected to link humanities with languages, languages with art etc. Teachers are particularly praised for making subjects exciting and offering careers support in their topic area. 'There's a real passion among teachers about preparing us for both university and life beyond university,' said one student.

Learning support and SEN: The college had 15 children with a statement of SEN when we visited, including one wheelchair user, extreme dyslexia and Asperger's, all of whom are dealt with by the SEN co-ordinator, both in and outside the classroom. 'The transition in year 7 was faultless, with the school knowing all about our daughter and her needs before she'd even started,' said one parent, who added, 'The reviews are excellent, the head of SEN is accessible and there's a great emphasis on any extra help being made to be enjoyable.' Meanwhile, the EAL co-ordinator helps the international students who need assistance with language and settling into a different way of teaching. 'We keep abreast of teaching styles in the countries these students come from,' explains school.

The arts and extracurricular: The IB requires a mood of involvement and pupils here lap this up, with over 70 popular clubs, including fencing, public speaking, knitting and dance. 'Younger students really get stuck in, trying new things out before they find where their interests lie,' said one student.

Music, drama and art part of the curriculum until year 10, with plenty of individual musical instrument lessons, including the organ (the director of music is an organ scholar). Regular performances from the popular orchestras and choirs, with a good balance of classical and modern, of which one parent said: 'You always go away with goosebumps because they're just so good.' There's a rotating pattern for drama performances – one year, there's a whole-school production; the next, there's a dance show; and the next there's an art-based competition. Art and DT boast good facilities and interlinked rooms.

Given the global theme of the school, it will come as no surprise that there are some impressive international trips, including to India and Uganda, as well as language exchanges in years 8, 9, 10 and 12, whilst in-school pastimes include Amnesty International and Model United Nations.

Sport: Sport is strong, with girls playing mainly hockey, netball, rounders and athletics, whilst boys are largely drawn to rugby, cricket and football. Fixtures against both state and private schools, and there's some exceptional individual talent too, with national champions in golf and karate, among others. New sports hall will soon supplement the pitches and courts.

Boarding: Alongside full and weekly boarding, there's a flexi boarding option from 7.15am till post-prep 9pm with a requirement to stay 7-10 nights per year. 'You do everything the boarders do, except actually sleep here,' explained one student.

Even in the private sector, you'll be hard pushed to find a school where years 8, 9 and 10 are taught geography and history in either French or German

Six single-sex boarding houses for different age groups, where teachers also have flats, all bright, well-maintained and welcoming, with all pupils having a study bedroom, sharing until year 12, then winning their own private space in their final year. Downstairs reception rooms in Thames boast polished floors, leather Chesterfields, beautiful fireplaces and large windows, whilst the other more modern boarding houses include comfortable and homely reception rooms.

All boarders are cared for in relaxed manner by houseparents, some with own family. Supervised prep sessions for all boarders, as well as plenty of opportunities for clubs and organised activities, events and trips. In fact, boarders enjoy the vibrant lifestyle so much that many choose to hang around even on exeat weekends. School prides itself on constantly evolving its boarding offering according to student feedback, and there are several forums (eg entertainment committee and food committee). Pastoral care praised. 'My eldest was horrendously homesick for a very long time, and the school was brilliant,' said one parent. 'They make sure there's a real sense of community among the boarders,' said another.

Ethos and heritage: Compact and leafy site close to Bishop's Stortford town centre with an attractive mix of Arts and Crafts, 1930s and contemporary buildings, and new science labs in the offing. The school's calendar is similar to a conventional independent boarding school, with longer holidays to allow boarders to return home for two weeks at October half term, three weeks at Christmas and nine weeks in the summer. Pupils make good use of the extra time – 'It allowed me to go to China,' said one. Classrooms are quiet, teachers politely addressed. Very strong community feel, with everyone getting involved. 'Not just a place to be – a place where you grow up,' said one remarkably mature young man. Strong sense of mutual respect between teachers and pupils: 'Teachers give a lot. We want the knowledge and the teachers help us to learn'.

Pastoral care, inclusivity and discipline: A traditional but non-denominational school, where teachers are called Sir or Ma'am and everyone has sensible haircuts and wears uniform (blue in the lower school, black and white in the sixth form). Not excessive on school rules, though, with more of an emphasis on expectations of politeness, kindness and punctuality. 'If you set the right tone, you avoid major issues,' says school, with low level prep-related detentions about as harsh as it has to get on the discipline front. Attendance problems and defiance non-existent, which students attribute to being well aware there are 10 applications for every place. 'There's an ethos that we are fortunate, and with that comes responsibility,' explained one. Incidents of bullying extremely rare, with incidents of unkindness dealt with quickly. Pastoral care is praised.

Pupils and parents: Some 40 per cent of boarders (who are required to hold an EU passport) come from overseas, with significant numbers from eg Spain, Germany, Italy and France. Twenty-four nationalities altogether. Weekly boarders generally from 1.5 hours travelling radius. Pupils are articulate, mature, friendly and confident, appearing genuinely to enjoy interaction with adults. Hockerill Parents and Friends Association, which includes both current and former parents, is an active fundraising and social community responsible for changes such as refurbishment of the library and chapel, and which runs staff bids in the summer term which have resulted in eg 3D printers and a camera for sixth form.

Money matters: Boarding fees far cheaper than a conventional independent boarding school, starting with a flexi boarding option at £7,000+.

The last word: 'There is no such thing as a typical Hockerill student,' the head girl wrote in a speech she was about to deliver when we visited, and you really do feel variety is the spice of life at this extremely well-run school, where students are encouraged to gain a genuinely holistic education, but with enough opportunity to follow real passions. For students who are willing to knuckle down (and this doesn't necessarily mean they have to be highly academic), this is an exciting and dynamic place to learn and grow up, knocking the socks off many fee-paying schools.

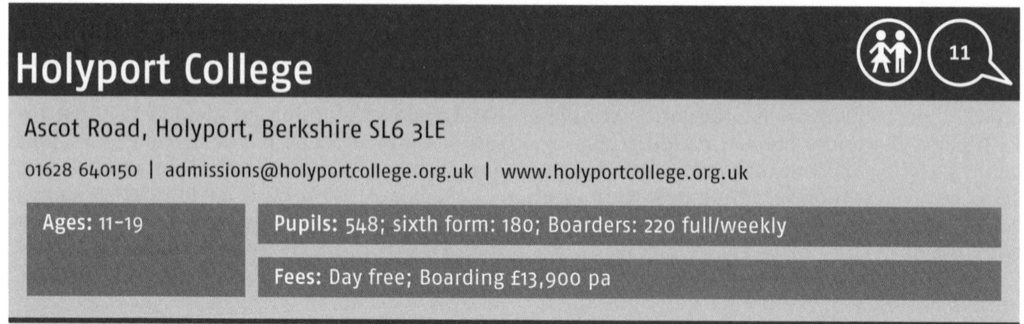

Holyport College

11

Ascot Road, Holyport, Berkshire SL6 3LE

01628 640150 | admissions@holyportcollege.org.uk | www.holyportcollege.org.uk

Ages: 11–19

Pupils: 548; sixth form: 180; Boarders: 220 full/weekly

Fees: Day free; Boarding £13,900 pa

Head: Since 2019, Ben McCarey BA (York) PGCE (Oxford). Has been involved with Holyport College since its foundation, starting as deputy headmaster in 2014 followed by two years as acting head. Coming from a family of teachers (he grew up in a boarding house and even his grandparents were teachers), there was only one solution – to swear blind never to go into teaching himself. But as many headteachers have learned, when teaching is in the blood it has a way of luring you in – in his case, a direct result of an argument with his mother in which she reminded him she was still paying his way as a graduate. 'I lied that I'd applied for teacher training so then of course I had to!' All came out in the wash though, as 'the moment I set foot in a classroom, I loved it.' Started at the Bicester School, where he got short shrift from a colleague when he disclosed his plans move into the independent sector – 'You're an idiot!' he told him. 'Just imagine what these kids could do if they'd had your chances.' Stayed for six years, latterly as head of English, before moving to Ark Evelyn Grace Academy as assistant head prior to Holyport.

Came as a bit of a shock to hear that modernising the school is top of his inbox – it isn't even a decade old! 'We were set up as an uber traditional state school but that doesn't represent our students,' he explains. 'So I'm trying to modernise practices and policies – revamping uniform, upgrading houses so they're not named after dead white men. We got two upper sixths on payroll once they'd left to spend five weeks researching and writing an anti-racism curriculum. That sort of thing.'

The 'first boarding free school'. May not look like a private school, but in many ways runs like one: scholars' programme with talks and events to stretch the cleverest

Lives on site with wife Becky, who works in HR, and their two young children Millie and Felix, three cats and Dolly the spaniel who, while not officially a school dog, can often be found with students in the quad. Cooking, long walks and 'ferrying my kids around' takes up any spare time.

Entrance: Oversubscribed, though places are less like gold dust since school decided to get all day pupils in at year 7 (it used to be split between years 7 and 9). Receives around 260 applications from 50+ schools (state and independent) for 52 day places and 18 boarding places in year 7; another 18 boarding places become available in year 9. Academically non-selective but the parade of priorities includes the usuals – looked-after or adopted children, those with a special medical need, siblings – but also children of the school's founders (none left of school age, luckily for locals!), children receiving pupil premium (up to 20 per cent of intake) and children of staff. Only then does proximity come into play though if you live in Holyport, you now have a reasonably good chance as catchment has shrunk from 1.8 miles to 0.2 miles.

Boarding places require an interview to establish 'suitability to board'. Then priority is given to boarding 'need', with Forces families at the top of the pack. Around 50 per cent of boarders live within a five to 10-mile radius, the rest further out including west London.

Around 50-60 come in at sixth form, making up half the cohort. Minimum requirement is an average of 6s across your best eight GCSEs and minimum of 7s in the subjects to be studied.

Exit: Around half stays on for sixth form. Some don't make the cut, others choose to move elsewhere to pursue less traditionally academic subjects or vocational courses. All but around two per cent of sixth formers go to university, 60 per cent to Russell Group. Exeter, Kings College London, Nottingham and Cardiff all popular. STEM courses and economics (and related courses) get good take-up although overall there's a broad eclectic mix. Four to Oxbridge in 2021, plus five medics and one overseas.

Latest results: In 2021, 51 per cent 9-7 at GCSE; 92 per cent 9-4 in both English and maths. At A level, 52 per cent A*/A (79 per cent A*-B). In 2019 (the last year when exams took place), 31 per cent 9-7 at GCSE; 80 per cent 9-4 in both English and maths. At A level (first year of results for the school), 19 per cent A*/A (44 per cent A*-B).

Teaching and learning: Purposeful. Prefers to offer a traditional, fairly narrow, EBacc-centred, academic curriculum rather than to faff about on frippery. No IB, Pre-Us, IGCSEs or BTECs. Single sciences, but no business studies or DT. STEM subjects are big: half of sixth form uptake is for maths or sciences subjects. Also offers economics, politics, PE, computing and art at A level. Languages do well – French, Spanish and Latin for all from year 7, with at least one language compulsory at GCSE, with growing numbers taking two. Setting on the up – in science from year 7 (but only when school have had a chance to do their own assessments), maths from year 8 and English from year 10. Most take three A levels plus something else – either EPQ, core maths, another A level or gold DofE. Sixth formers also supervise afternoon prep sessions.

At first glance, classrooms can appear stuffy and overly ordered but scratch below the surface and the vibe is calm, happy and surprisingly relaxed. School refuses to subscribe to a particular pedagogy – 'We encourage the teachers' individual teaching methods and passions, which means a very varied style.' All are accessible to students, including outside the classroom, eg during evening duties with the boarders and via staff rooms when not teaching – especially so

Haberdashers' Adams

for older students. These staff members are carefully chosen, many from independent schools or state boarding. 'They listen to, act on and are very open with parents,' said a mum. 'I cannot express enough how impressed I am by them.'

School kept things ticking over online throughout Covid but is more proud of staying fully open in the second lockdown including for boarders and with every teacher (illness and shielding permitting) in school. So-called 'super curriculum' also still ran – the scholars' lectures, plus redesigned UCAS programme for all which involves 20 sessions over two years (and although no longer online now, school still records and streams them as parents enjoyed having access to them during the pandemic).

Learning support and SEN: Pupils we spoke to praised the SEND provision, which is based in the curriculum support department. The team is made up of non-teaching specialists with visiting specialists in dyslexia, speech and language etc. They work with teachers to ensure differentiated support in the classroom but there are no one-to-ones available except for those with EHCPs. School is brutally honest about who it can't take – basically, anyone who can't cope with the compulsory 5pm finish, Saturdays, the rigorous academic curriculum and full extracurricular programme – 'For some kids, even a normal school is too much, and we expect even more than that,' explains head.

The arts and extracurricular: The extended day – 8.30am to 5pm for all pupils, boarding and day – is the school's secret sauce. The long afternoon (and the whole afternoon on Wednesdays) allows time for a phenomenal co-curricular programme with offerings ranging from mindful colouring to real tennis, Young Enterprise to ballet. 'And it's a bonus for working parents too,' a mum reminded us. Tons of societies including MedSoc, FemSoc, LGBTQ+, Harry Potter Club (run by sixth formers, along with Kahoot Club and Countries of the World Club, among others). Older pupils may take part in some Eton societies. Pupils get outside more than ever – and not just for sports – with all year 7s now promised at least an hour a week donning wellies to weed, garden and work the land (watch this space for the possible addition of livestock, though head says he can't promise). Evenings can be busy, and not just for boarders – pupils can attend talks by visiting speakers either at Holyport or Eton on Tuesday, Wednesday and Thursday evenings. DofE thrives – 70 per cent of year 9s do bronze, and silver and gold are also available. Boys and girls can do CCF from year 9 at Eton – these pupils love nothing more than rolling around in ditches and shooting each other.

There are three choirs. Pupils get the opportunity to sing at Windsor Castle and at Holyport's Christmas carol concert held at Eton

Some 40 per cent learn a musical instrument and school is more than happy to find new instruments – this recently happened when a pupil wanted to learn the harp, and now others are being encouraged to take it up. There are three choirs, with 60 per cent of pupils voluntarily attending the junior one. Pupils get the opportunity to sing at Windsor Castle and at Holyport's Christmas carol concert held at Eton, plus there's a school orchestra and various ensembles. School is keen not to overpromise on the musical front, however, and recently had to drop music A level as the head of music was shielding during Covid. 'I was a 12-year-old chorister for whom music was everything, so I know how important it is to be honest and say, yes, we do a lot of music but we are not Eton standard,' says head. As with music, drama is on curriculum from years 7-9, with clubs for all key stages. Annual junior and senior productions include a musical which is performed in Maidenhead Town Hall. Art popular – so much so that they had to throw in an extra A level art class last year. Focus is on portraiture and increasingly graphic design, but very much within the context of fine art. Well resourced too – 'My head of art is always wanting to go shopping and I support that,' says head.

Sport: Games and sport rule, and no excuses. Games and PE three or four times a week in the younger years (less after year 9). Main sports for girls: netball, hockey, tennis and athletics. For boys: football, rugby, cricket and athletics. Loads of other sports too. There can't be many other schools – state or private – where every child learns to play Eton fives (soon to have their own facility) and it does a PE module of rowing too. 'When we first set up the school, Eton didn't push anything, but they did ask if the children might perhaps learn to play Eton fives,' says school. Regular Saturday morning matches against independent schools (day pupils come in for these), some held at Eton; Wednesday matches against state schools. LVS and Marist College are arch-rivals. 'We get very good at losing in the younger years and learn how to lose well; further up, pupils get these chances to win and win very well,' says head.

Boarding: Feels like a boarding school, not – like many schools – a day school with boarders. So how do they ensure the day pupils and boarders don't feel like separate entities? Simple – day pupils are treated like boarders (staying late, doing most of the same activities etc) and boarders are treated like day pupils (eating lunch with them, not being allowed back to dorms in the day etc). Also helps that all pupils are assigned to a house – girl day pupils join a boys' boarding house; boy day pupils join boarding girls.

Feels like a boarding school. Day pupils are treated like boarders (staying late, doing most of the same activities) and all pupils are assigned to a house

Almost equal numbers of boy and girl boarders (half from a five to 10-mile radius, the rest from further afield including an international contingent) are housed directly above the classrooms in a school version of 'living over the shop'. Certainly unique: day pupils walk through the boarders' common rooms to reach their study area on the floor above. The biggest dormitories house five; sixth formers room in pairs. Fourteen staff, plus their families, live on campus. No mistresses here: female heads of houses are referred to as 'housemasters'. Boarders can arrange to spend a school night at home each week, eg to attend to take part in a local activity or sports team. Also allowed to go home on Saturdays after their sports obligations (if any). About half are in school all weekend when there are all the usual activities – bowling, cinema, baking, crafts etc. 'Many are first-time boarders – keeping them busy is key to keeping homesickness at bay,' says school. Happy boarders need well-established routines, then you need to break those routines to stop things being boring, is the school's ethos.

Ethos and heritage: The 'first boarding free school' opened in 2014, with much ado and a visit from the Queen, Prince Phillip and Theresa May (the school's in her constituency). Set snugly on Ascot Road in affluent rural Berkshire ('If you want a mix, it's easier to get less-advantaged families to come to a school in an affluent area than to get well-off children to attend school in a poor area,' explains school).

A compact school – it began with 68 day pupils and 55 boarders in years 7-10, and enrolled its first lower sixth year group in 2017. Lowish numbers make many things possible (discipline, personal touch, small class sizes) but create some limitations (range of sixth form subjects). Also small physically, with minor irritations (parking, shortage of music practice rooms). In the running for our coveted 'most hidden school office' award – reception is tucked behind the main school (took us nine minutes to find, had to employ satnav, step-counter and phone-a-friend). This beating heart of the school, the SNW, is named for Sir Nicholas Winton who rescued 699 children, most of them Jewish, from Czechoslovakia on the eve of WW2. Sir Nicholas attended the school's opening (at the age of 105) and pupils strive to carry on his altruistic example through community service and links with a school in Gambia. New-build school quad is functional but dreary – not for long, though, with an orchard being planned. We were there on a stuffy winter day: a bit of ventilation in some of the classrooms would work wonders.

May not look like a private school, but in many ways runs like one: scholars' programme with talks and events to stretch the clever clogs. Lord Adonis handed out awards at prize-giving. The pupils are proud of the school's relationship with Eton and there's no chip on shoulder weirdness about it. Indeed the relationship seems to work both ways, with Eton and Holyport learning from each other.

A sense of fun prevails. In fact, head has all but ditched the original school motto of 'high aspiration, traditional values' – 'Nobody has ever been able to describe the latter as anything other than dead white men, so I'm keen to work with more liberal values, values that prioritise happiness.' The academics and hard work aren't always fun, he points out – so you have to inject that fun with eg pancake races every Shrove Tuesday, nations' day with food stalls and flag parades every November, the blasting out of a 150-strong playlist into the quad during Black History Month etc.

Pastoral care, inclusivity and discipline: At the heart of the pastoral ethos is pupils being encouraged to understand each other. 'You never know what someone's going through or why they're behaving a certain way, so the only option is to respond with kindness – that's our one, overriding message,' says head. Parents agree it is a kind school, also praising the welfare team for being flexible – and they can bring in eg drama and art therapists, plus a counsellor. Diversity and inclusion are high on the agenda and it was refreshing to see year 7 boys discuss with pride how they belong to the LGBTQ+ society. Curriculum recently overhauled with anti-racism microscope and there is now a whole portion given over to gender called 'Beyond Equality' that covers everything from Everyone's Invited to the glass ceiling.

Not too much by way of behavioural issues, though school is realistic. 'Zero tolerance' isn't a phrase you'll hear, even when it comes to drugs and alcohol, for example – head believes it's wrong and immoral when you consider the national statistics of young children who experiment. 'The one-strike-and-you're-out rule can be catastrophic for young people's lives,' he says, instead encouraging more honest communication so that when these youngsters leave for university, the wheels don't fall off spectacularly. A combination of talks and honest debates around dangers (and searching where necessary) seems – for the most part – to do the trick.

Pupils and parents: Feel lucky to be here. The requirement to be at school until 5pm of an evening filters out most slackers and compulsory sports scares off the rest. Aspires to being a carefully orchestrated melting pot of abilities, ethnicities and social backgrounds, and comes darn close. The school has the highest percentage of looked-after and adopted children in Windsor and Maidenhead LA and over 12 per cent of pupils are on free school meals (roughly the national average). That said, more children come from Privet Lane than Benefits Street. Children's behaviour that we witnessed was impressive. 'It's an academic school,' a parent told us, 'but what I like most is that they're expected to say please and thank you, to tuck in their shirt, to clean their shoes, to show respect.'

The last word: A school with the modest aim of transforming lives. Much has been invested in this school – not just money but reputations. So far, so excellent, especially STEM.

Keswick School

12

Vicarage Hill, Keswick, Cumbria CA12 5QB

01768 772605 | admin@keswick.cumbria.sch.uk | www.keswick.cumbria.sch.uk

Ages: 11–18

Pupils: 1,351; sixth form: 292; Boarders: 44 full

Fees: Day free; Boarding £12,225 pa

Headmaster: Since 2012, Simon Jackson (early 40s), a biologist who was previously deputy head. With impressive academic credentials, MA (Oxon) and MEd, FRSA, he is proud to be only the eighth head since the school was refounded in 1898 as one of the country's first truly coeducational schools. Married with two young children, who are both eagerly anticipating joining Keswick as pupils themselves, he is an energetic, bright and charismatic head teacher who is clearly well respected both in the school and the wider community. Academy status has brought with it the freedoms for the school to grow in a controlled way while retaining its unique characteristics, commitment to education in its widest sense and the confidence not to kowtow to the latest government edict if it is not deemed to be in the best interests of the pupils.

He has an enormous respect for both his students and staff, a rigorous, intelligent and pragmatic approach to education and an obvious pride in the school he leads. He is still very active in the classroom and sees this as an essential element of his leadership despite the other demands on his time. As well as leading a growth in pupil numbers at Keswick, he now heads up a multi-academy trust which incorporates a local primary school, allowing for additional important work on transition at age 11. A committed enthusiast for outdoor and adventurous learning (pretty much essential given the stunning location of the school and the uninterrupted views of Lakeland peaks from just about every classroom), he is committed to ensuring that all pupils have the opportunity to benefit from all that their location offers.

Entrance: The school is consistently oversubscribed and manages a number of appeals every year. In recent years the number of students commuting from out of catchment has significantly increased and the school is now comfortably at seven forms of entry (non-selective).

Unusually, offers sixth form scholarships in science (the Steven Luckman Bursary) and EPQ (the Gilbert Smithson Adair Bursary). Sixth form entry by a minimum combination of grades 5 and 4 in English and maths plus the individual A level subject requirements – at least 6s for sciences and maths.

Exit: Around a third leave post GCSEs. Some 80 per cent of sixth formers to university, mostly in the north, with increasing numbers following the college and apprenticeship routes, others heading into agriculture and tourism. Edinburgh, Durham, Newcastle, Manchester, Liverpool, York, Leeds and Warwick all popular. Sixth formers were confident about the school's support for Oxbridge, medical and veterinary applications. Three to Oxbridge in 2021, and four medics.

Latest results: In 2021, 35 per cent 9-7 at GCSE; 89 per cent 9-4 in both maths and English. At A level, 38 per cent A*/A (66 per cent A*-B). In 2019 (the last year when exams took place), 54 per cent 9-5 in both maths and English. At A level, 34 per cent A*/A (61 per cent A*-B).

Teaching and learning: Student results at both GCSE and A level are amongst the best non-selective results in the country, with strong value added. The school is proudly comprehensive and inclusive but pupil outcomes would rival those of many selective schools. With students having just slightly above average ability on entry, the school is working hard to ensure every child does as well as they possibly can. It was notable all staff, from the head downwards, were clear that they were not just interested in the high flyers. One teacher commented, 'Two Es at A level is just as much of an achievement as three A*s, if the student has worked hard and met their potential.' The staff were also very proud that students who might not have gained the entry criteria for other sixth forms were succeeding at Keswick.

The students are very proud of the success of the girls' rugby teams. As one young woman put it, 'Girls throw people to the ground as well, you know!'

At GCSE pupils take English x 2 and maths plus, for the great majority, three separate sciences. The school has strong links with the Lake District National Park and the Energy Coast and is keen to give students real-life opportunities to practise their science. Particularly high numbers, including many girls, take physics A level. The school was keen to point out that it has a very strong complement of teaching staff in all subjects including specialists in all the sciences and maths, a rarity these days.

Everyone takes take an additional three GCSEs, but with plenty of other opportunities for those with the keenness and aptitude, such as astronomy and Latin (in 2018, 60 per cent 9-7s amongst the year 9s that took Latin GCSE). Everyone learns French or German, most both, and are strongly encouraged to take at least one to GCSE. French and German exchanges; the latter, with Königslutter, is now in its 54th year and some families have had three generations participate. An international language centre was due to open on campus in 2019. The school has an unashamedly academic curriculum, with a few vocational options, BTECs in business and digital applications.

The sixth form is a strength of the school, with students travelling long distances for what they see as 'the best education in the area'. 'Nowhere else seemed to have as good academic standards'; 'the school has the edge and it is very professional'. On our tour we witnessed lively and energised classes where debate was clearly the norm.

Staffing is very stable, as is often the case in similar schools. However there is a regular input of new staff and the head is clear that it is not a 'semi-retirement' option for keen walkers and climbers. There is a strong commitment to staff development: Keswick leads a Teaching School Alliance and has links with various universities, ensuring that staff are knowledgeable and well engaged with educational development.

Learning support and SEN: Staff who were also parents were keen to point out that the school has strong and supportive provision for students with special needs that 'allows them to fly'. There is strong provision for students with moderate learning difficulties including autism and the school has good disability access.

The arts and extracurricular: Art is clearly a strength. From the entrance onwards there were some lovely pieces of work displayed including sculpture, stained glass, painting and, on the English corridor, some fantastic poetry. The students spoke with great enthusiasm about the annual school productions and we observed a very positive drama lesson.

Music is celebrated throughout with various choirs, ensembles, orchestras and bands, and a professional recording studio. Students participate in the Young Musician of the Year competition with notable national success. Concerts every term, including in the Theatre by the Lake in Keswick.

The head girl was recently chosen as the Citizenship Society's student barrister of the year. The students have just launched their own student-driven online publication Vocalise. The Lego League teams successfully presented

The majority of students join from small village schools and the feel of an extended family is strong. Students clearly like being there

their hydraulics project, raising awareness of plastic waste and coming 10th in a national competition. As the head says, 'It's about getting everyone together, creating a collective community through sport, music, drama, business and enterprise.' Students regularly take part in the UK Youth Parliament.

Sport: Sports and games take centre stage with a great number of students. Considerable sporting successes include national representation in sports as diverse as rugby, fell running, skiing, martial arts and karting. The students are very proud of the success of the girls' rugby teams. As one young woman put it, 'Girls throw people to the ground as well, you know!' A strong tradition of rowing (on Derwentwater): the club has 50+ rowers and recently won a Sport England grant to purchase a new carbon fibre quad boat. The school boasts its own dry ski slope as well as the usual complement of playing fields, sports hall, all-weather pitch and tennis courts.

Boarding: Boarding received a recent outstanding judgement from Ofsted and it was clear from speaking to the boarders that their experience is a very positive one. One boarding house for all 54 boarders from years 7-13. Matron lives in and provides a strong and stable support for students with the help of a team of houseparents. The accommodation is clean, tidy and modern and provides a good sense of home from home. There is a large, comfortable common room with matron's flat just across the corridor. The students spoke highly of the wide range of activities they are involved in from the CCF to sporting activities, trips and visits. Relationships between different age groups appeared strong and the sixth form valued their independent living week when they do everything for themselves, including cooking and cleaning, in preparation for life after home. Both day and boarding students commented that there was no perceptible divide between the two groups.

Ethos and heritage: A central part of its local and wider community. Originally two schools, it came together on one stunning site in 1980, looking forward to Derwentwater, Cat Bells and Causey Pike and back to Skiddaw. The buildings are an eclectic mix of the original school, 1950s and 60s extensions and a more recent build. All are refurbished and well maintained and the school is bright, modern and with a stylishness that the students say encourages them to take a pride in their learning as well as look after their space. Well-equipped drama and music spaces as well as a beautiful art suite are certainly great assets.

The majority of students join the school from small village schools and the feel of an extended family is strong. Primary children regularly come for sporting activities and curriculum days. During lessons the corridors are quiet and purposeful while classrooms seem to buzz with a generally healthy learning noise. The school is clear that while a quiet classroom can sometimes be important students should be actively engaged in their learning through practical work and discussion. Students clearly like being at school. Many live in remote parts and meet friends largely at school, mixing comfortably across the age ranges.

Pastoral care, inclusivity and discipline: This is a school that prides itself on being smart. A traditional badged blazer, tie and shirts firmly tucked in are the standard. Maroon jumpers with the school crest and motto, Levavi Oculos, are the rule for the sixth form. High standards are expected and maintained. Phones are out of site, jewellery is not allowed and hair is well kept and in natural colours. The students are proud of their uniform.

Many students join Keswick sixth form from other schools and commented that there was a warmth and inclusivity here that helped them not just to settle in well but allowed them to be their own person. The students made some very genuine and moving comments (which were borne out by the staff) that the school places a high value on inclusion and the celebration of diversity. The sixth form are clearly proud of their prefect status and feel empowered (mostly) to exercise a role of authority over younger students. They were highly complementary about not just the classroom teaching but also the additional support available.

During our visit we saw nothing other than good behaviour and courtesy, both in lessons and around school. The students take great pride in being self-managing and the prefect system is clearly strongly embedded in school culture. As it is relatively unusual to find students so confident in managing their peers, we checked and this does seem to be the case, with younger students reflecting a genuine aspiration to follow the role models and become prefects themselves. The school says that it has its fair share of students with troubled backgrounds and works hard to support these to behave well. Incidents of exclusion are very rare but the head is clear that this is necessary at times. One parent, who had moved her children from elsewhere, spoke of the positive impact this had on their education and social development.

The school is clearly well attuned to the growing demand for support for mental health and wellbeing and is proactive in meeting this need. Unusually, there is a nurse on site. Staff and students agree that generally there is very little bullying. SEN students have a safe place to go at break and lunch times and support with socialisation. There is a transgender support group.

Pupils and parents: This really is a comprehensive school. Prospective Oxbridge students comfortably rub shoulders with those with SEN, and those from affluent backgrounds with pupil premium students. Trips and visits to other parts of the country and overseas are a regular feature. The presence of 50+ boarders from all over the world helps to ensure that this is a cosmopolitan community. One parent commented, 'My kids have blossomed since they came here. The boarding house helps brings a diversity of friendships from all over the world.'

The last word: This is an outstanding local school with a strong international dimension. It believes equally in inclusion, aspiration and excellence. Despite its rurality there are plenty of options for parents in the local area from other good schools and the independent sector. Students and parents are clear that Keswick offers the best of all worlds. This is a school where it is still cool to succeed. It has very high aspirations for its young people and it is certainly meeting them.

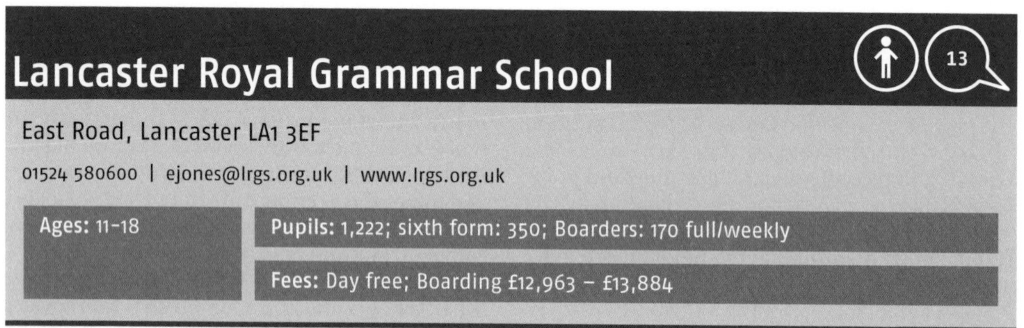

Lancaster Royal Grammar School

13

East Road, Lancaster LA1 3EF

01524 580600 | ejones@lrgs.org.uk | www.lrgs.org.uk

Ages: 11–18

Pupils: 1,222; sixth form: 350; Boarders: 170 full/weekly

Fees: Day free; Boarding £12,963 – £13,884

Headmaster: Since 2012, Dr Christopher Pyle MA (Cantab) PhD (Cantab) NPQH. Previously deputy head at The Perse School, Cambridge and before that head of geography there (explains his particular interest in glaciers, hydrology and climate change). Briefly a manager at Anglian Water before taking up teaching. Former churchwarden and PCC member of a large Anglican church. A keen runner, he has participated in the Devizes to Westminster charity canoe race and is a fan of the Lakeland fells. Has relished the chance to return to his roots in the north, attracted to LRGS as 'the nearest thing to an independent school'. Says LRGS is 'virtually unique in the state sector – selective and ambitious, day and boarding, a broad academic curriculum (from computing to ancient Greek) and prizing extracurricular opportunity and excellence for every pupil.'

Head continues to impress parents with his 'excellent skills of communication' and a 'sensible but firm' leadership style, which they say has 'brought certainty in uncertain times to all the constituents that make up the school'. Widely praised too for modernising the school by masterminding the introduction of girls into the sixth form and making the school a more diverse place to learn.

LRGS did 'a terrific job' during the pandemic, according to parents. Lessons were via Teams and engagement was closely monitored to avoid any loss of focus, particularly for those in important exam years. 'My son is in year 11 and I really do think his education has continued to be first rate,' said a parent, while another praised the teaching staff for awarding the usual commendations; a third approved the use of stick as well as carrot – 'Our son was both praised and encouraged, and occasionally quite rightly admonished, to ensure he kept up during a crucial examination year.'

Married to Sally, with three sons – two at the school.

Entrance: Usually around 400 boys apply for the 174 places in year 7 made up of local day pupils, regional day pupils and boarders. Assessments in English, maths and verbal reasoning. Local day pupils given preference; about 40 places go to those further afield. Boarders considered separately but all 'must be of an aptitude and ability suited to an academic curriculum' and must be UK subjects or have a UK passport and a UK guardian.

For co-ed sixth form, minimum of six grade 6s at GCSE, including grade 5 or above in English and maths (grade 7 maths for those taking maths A level). Same requirements for both internal and external candidates, all of whom must submit a personal statement and attend an interview, at which they are asked to explain 'why we should give you a place here'. Number of external sixth form applicants on the up thanks to growing interest from independent schools. Girls have been admitted as sixth form day pupils since September 2019 and as sixth form boarders since September 2020.

Exit: Up to 10 per cent leave after GCSE for other schools, colleges or apprentice schemes. Vast majority of sixth formers secure places at top universities, eg Newcastle, Manchester, Leeds, UCL, Bristol and Loughborough. In 2021, 10 to Oxbridge and 18 medics.

Latest results: In 2021, 70 per cent 9-7 at GCSE; 62 per cent A*/A grades at A level (83 per cent A*-B). In 2019 (the last year when exams took place), 63 per cent 9-7 at GCSE; 54 per cent A*/A grades at A level.

Teaching and learning: Traditional grammar school ethos alive and well here – spirit of healthy competition, aiming high and working hard. The result is that the school is a regular in the list of the county's top 100 schools and near the top of the regional table at GCSE. Particularly strong value added (always impressive for academically selective schools – the challenge is finding room to improve on such high-calibre entrants).

Traditional grammar school ethos alive and well here – spirit of healthy competition, aiming high and working hard. Near the top of the regional table at GCSE

Maths and sciences (all taught separately throughout) particularly outstanding, but there is also a pleasing breadth to the rest of the curriculum, which includes a strong classics offering, twilight Mandarin lessons and compulsory GCSE technology. Teaching is 'first class in all areas,' approves a parent and this high-performing atmosphere 'drives every child to become the best that they can possibly be'.

Average of 30 boys in a class. Setting in maths, English and French. Ten GCSEs the norm. with choices in languages and technology. A third of sixth formers (boys and girls) take four A levels from the choice of over 20 subjects – maths and sciences are most popular. A quarter choose to add on EPQ (well regarded by university admissions teams). School says it strives to appoint 'schoolmasters' (of any gender), rather than simply teachers.

Accelerated Reader programme, supported by English department and librarian, for boys in years 7 and 8 who collect points per book read and see their results published in a league table. Pupils may bring their own mobile devices.

Learning support and SEN: Very able pupils are a speciality here and LRGS's learning support staff know how to inspire them to ever greater heights. The school's SENCo (who has a postgrad diploma in SEN) is also experienced in working with pupils with literacy difficulties, as well as those on the autistic spectrum, while other members of the learning support team have particular SEN specialisms. Boys with dual-exceptionality are well catered for, and all pupils with high SEN are allocated a key worker to liaise with parents. SEN training is made available to teachers and TAs, who are also positively encouraged to consult the learning support team for practical advice and help with classroom implementation of strategies.

The arts and extracurricular: 'One size does not fit everyone,' says head. This is a place where there are opportunities for all interests. Around 20 per cent of pupils learn a musical instrument, with ensembles to suit every taste, from blues to philharmonic – and a range of well-attended choirs. Annual music and drama production staged in city theatre, often in conjunction with Lancaster sister school; recently Kiss Me Kate and Les Misérables. All pupils are invited to get involved whether that be in acting, singing or backstage roles. The English and drama department put on a Strolling with Shakespeare production to a delighted audience of parents and the wider school community moving around various locations around the school site.

Impressive art and design work is reflected in the GCSE and A level results. The art room sits on the top site with breathtaking views across the historic city of Lancaster and Morecambe Bay towards the Lakeland fells. Students host exhibitions of their work and have raised money for charity by selling their works. At A level, around 10 students a year take fine art or photography.

Alongside the usual round of clubs for sports, the performing arts, debating, CCF and DofE, there is an eclectic range of extracurricular activities, many humorously titled (Texas Hold'em Society and Bad Boyz Bakin, to name but two), often (you guessed it) student initiated and led.

Volunteering and fundraising are big here – wide participation in projects close to home as well as around the world through school's outreach gifted and talented programme, InspirUS. In sixth form the Praesis ut Prosis Award and the Erasmus programme help bring a global perspective.

Sport: Team games are traditional with a full programme of Saturday fixtures. Rugby and cricket taken seriously (giving the independent schools a run for their money) with frequent tours to the UAE, South Africa, Hong Kong, Australia, Japan and the 'Windies'. Individual sports and minority interests – orienteering, hockey, kayaking and handball – are gradually gaining ground. With the Lake District on the doorstep, plenty of scope for hearty outdoor pursuits, including rowing on the Lune (which has smoothed the waters for some successful pairs at Henley). Much encouragement to join in.

Boarding: Boarding is a rarity in state schools but very much part of the identity, with around 10-12 per cent of years 7 to 9 boarding, increasing to 20 per cent in year 10. Many are 'first generation' boarders, often from the Lakeland valleys; a third are international from a dozen or so countries.

There are half, half weekly and full boarders, though fees are the same for all and weekly boarders may stay at weekends to work around sports fixtures and the like. With the Ashton Memorial as a backdrop, the junior boys' years 7 to 9 boarding house has bunk-bedded dorms, comfortable sitting rooms and a homely kitchen for after-school tea and toast. School House and Ashton House are for years 9 to 13 boarders, and each has its own character: School House is a well designed, conference centre-style building adjoining a Victorian villa, with ensuite single studies, relaxed sitting rooms and a modern kitchen, while Ashton House is more traditional, with bigger rooms of up to four beds, recreational spaces and kitchen facilities. Both houses exude family atmosphere (with gardens, tree planting and chickens) and boarders speak warmly of them. All houses have communal study areas as well as desks in dorms or bedrooms. Lots of organised activities at weekends, but boarders also have a fair amount of freedom to explore the small city of Lancaster.

Ethos and heritage: An ancient foundation, founded in 1235 and endowed in 1472. Moved to its current location in 1852 when Queen Victoria

Both houses exude family atmosphere (with gardens, tree planting and chickens) and boarders speak warmly of them

donated £100 – the 'Royal' of the title – and the school still receives the same amount (sadly not index-linked) annually from the Duchy. Could be mistaken for an independent school, if a lack of lavish funding weren't so evident in some areas. Skirting either side of hilly East Road around a busy intersection (pupils cross two roads confidently between lessons), the school's extensive, fragmented site is characterised by buildings spanning the centuries, from Gothic to modern on the outside. A little scruffy round the edges whereas inside, attention is being paid to the parts that matter – spaces for teaching and learning, and an ambitious plan of sprucing up has already begun with the science labs and sixth form centre (students had a say in the design concept).

Old boys include Nobel prizewinner Sir Peter Ratclife; Prof T Hugh Pennington, microbiologist; Lord Cecil Parkinson; Kevin Roberts CNZM, CEO Worldwide Saatchi and Saatchi; Jason Queally, Olympic cycling champion; Scott Durant, Olympic rower; Tom Sutcliffe, journalist; Lord Ashton James Williamson; and 19th-century naturalist, Sir Richard Owen.

Pastoral care, inclusivity and discipline: A strong pastoral system for day as well as boarding pupils, managed by staff who are described by parents as 'dedicated and sensible' and who 'have pupils' needs at heart'. Thriving mentor scheme encourages senior boys and girls to spend time with junior boys with similar interests. Prefects have weekly tutor time with year 7s, helping with pastoral and organisational issues. Pupils respond well to the no-nonsense approach of the staff and there is a mutual respect and an expectation that everyone in the school community will behave according to their own innate high standards. Very little misbehaviour. Parents applaud the school's efforts to embrace diversity 'in all manners' and also to 'bring the school into the 21st century with the introduction of girls and girl boarders in the sixth form'.

Pupils and parents: School's population reflects its small town environment, with a mix of people from all walks. 'We have some quirky characters and they are all valued,' says head. Considered locally as 'the school on the hill', although this is not a middle-class enclave or a 'school for the over-privileged', as one parent put it. Parents say their children view their school with 'pride, mixed with humility and a sense of belonging'. Its regional standing is certainly cause for admiration. 'LRGS is an awesome place to be,' said one boy, reflecting the popular view. Once a pupil, you never leave – you simply become an Old Lancastrian and continue to contribute, eg by attending dinners, sports fixtures or giving talks and advice. Some interview current students, providing valuable experience for university or employment.

The last word: A vibrant, selective grammar school with a big regional reputation. Unashamedly academic but takes all-round education seriously and delivers a wealth of opportunities.

Oban High School

14

Soroba Road, Oban, Argyll PA34 4JB

01631 564231 | enquiriesobanhigh@argyll-bute.sch.uk | www.obanhigh.argyll-bute.sch.uk

Ages: 11–18

Pupils: 977; sixth form: 99; Boarders: 78

Fees: Hostel accommodation provided for pupils from the islands. No boarding fee.

Head teacher: Since 2008, Peter Bain MA MSc PGCE. Since 2019, executive head of both Oban High School and Tiree High School. Left school (Musselburgh Grammar) at 16 'because the lure of civil service pay was better than staying on'. Five years later, he supported himself through a history degree then a master's in historical research at Edinburgh University after his parents died suddenly. Following a three-year stint in retail – which saw him rise to regional manager and head of customer relations across Scotland for Texas Homecare – he felt the calling of education and did a PGCE at Jordanhill College in Glasgow. Reached the top job within just 11 years, his journey having included teaching in six different schools and leaving a depute headship at Eyemouth High School in Berwickshire to become head at Oban.

Within six years of joining, he had formulated a business plan to build a new £36m building to bring it into the 21st century. And well over a decade on, wow, you should see this place. 'A school isn't so different from any other business,' he insists – 'it may not operate on profit and loss in quite the same way but even that's important, especially at Oban where we have such a broad curriculum that we have to find money to bring in outside tutors.' He runs the school with four deputes and (Covid times aside) finds time to teach history. 'A real driver of the school,' said a parent, with others describing him as 'very forward thinking', 'inspirational' and 'highly involved in the wider community'.

Married to Theresa, local college manager, with two children, both at university and following in his footsteps in one way or another – one at Glasgow studying history, the other at Edinburgh studying to be a PE teacher. Though the mere mention of spare time prompts a burst of laughter, he does find time for family, including watching football with his son, visiting restaurants with his daughter and going for dog walks with his wife.

Entrance: Catchment is vast, with pupils coming in from 19 partnership primary schools spanning up to an hour in all directions. In two of those primary schools the first language is Gaelic. Although the school is very popular, all who want a place currently get one – 'We built the school deliberately big enough.' A fairly transient community so there is some coming and going throughout the year groups. Around eight per cent are boarders – most live on the islands but some in far flung spots of the mainland.

Exit: Virtually all to official Scottish definition of a 'positive destination' which means they went to university, college or straight to a job. Forty per cent to university, usually in Scotland. Glasgow and Edinburgh currently most popular, followed by University of Highlands and Islands. Wide range of courses from international relations to history to business. 'We do a lot of work making sure they get into the right university – Edinburgh is good on law and medicine, for example, while

Robert Gordon stands out for business.' Forty per cent straight into employment, but usually after staying for sixth year. Some 16 per cent to FE colleges in Oban or Glasgow. Occasional students to Oxbridge (three in 2021) or going into medicine. 'Careers advice could be introduced earlier on,' reckoned a parent.

Latest results: In 2021 at National 5, 82 per cent grades A-C; at Higher, 64 per cent A-B; and at Advanced Higher 64 per cent A-B.

Teaching and learning: This is the broadest curriculum in Scotland, offering over 100 courses. On a recent royal appointment, Princess Anne asked to extend her visit so she could get round the whole thing. Everything on offer from Nat 5s to Highers to IB, and tons of vocational offerings ranging from beekeeping to forestry. 'We provide the necessary qualifications and experiences for any youngster to gain entry to any course in any Scottish university or for any career pathway of their choosing,' says school.

That's quite the undertaking, but parents say the school delivers. One, who has had several children go through the school, said, 'It used to be a very staid curriculum and they were only interested in results but that's completely changed. It's a modern and diverse curriculum now with huge breadth and a young team of forward thinking, creative teachers who keep things interactive.' If you have a vision of secondary education as a linear, largely shared academic experience with national exams strategically placed along the way, think again. Oban High, school probably more than any other secondary school we have visited, has fully embraced the idea of the Curriculum of Excellence and shaping an education to each individual child.

Outdoor learning is a focus – everything from beekeeping (with own bee shed) to agriculture to animal handling, most of it taking place on school's own land

Our tour began not in the latest science labs but in the rather luxurious cosmetology suite, where some pupils were administering facials and massages to each other. Further along the corridor were well-appointed hairdressing salons and then we arrived at the spacious building and construction areas. Sorry, are we still in a school? Doesn't this kind of provision impinge on the territory of the local college? 'We have an excellent relationship with our local college, in part because their manager is my wife!' says the head. 'They send us the tutors for cosmetology, construction, marine engineering, rural skills and childcare. We do a mixture of awards and qualifications which go from SVQ level 4 to 7. Our aim is not just to deliver academic results but to give each child the benefit of wider experiences.'

Another interesting departure is the school's partnerships with over 100 local businesses – from vets to picture framers to golf clubs (for groundsmen opportunities) and from local hospitals (for physiotherapy) to primary schools (for teaching). Still can't find anything you fancy? Chances are they'll tailor something for you, eg they recently set up a partnership with the Scottish Association of Marine Science. Before any child is sent out on a work placement they will be required to achieve a customer service award to improve their chances of making a good impression. A particularly interesting recent partnership is with the private historic trust Dunollie Castle where the school has set up a classroom on site for a whole host of activities from history research to suitable work placements.

'Education should not just be for the top 30 per cent who can get a Higher,' says head, but that's not to say the school doesn't cater for the more trad routes too. Every year around 10 pupils sit the Scottish Baccalaureate, which offers four subject areas at AH level including social sciences, languages, expressive arts and science and an interdisciplinary project designed to expand independent thinking. 'But regardless of the route, it's the added value courses that are getting more of our pupils, academic or otherwise, into positive destinations than ever before,' he believes. For example, in S5 and S6, over 250 children are doing an SVQ level 5/6 leadership award. This includes personal development, Scottish studies, Scots language awards, religious belief and values.

The school is also now delivering foundation apprenticeships in engineering, construction, business and IT, and children and young people. It has even created its own special awards in recognition of the children for whom 'going down the street on their own and buying a bun' is an achievement. Outdoor learning is a focus – everything from beekeeping (with own bee shed) to agriculture to animal handling, most of it taking place on school's own land where an area is dedicated to growing crops and rearing animals including chickens and sheep. 'An average of five students a year head off to agricultural college,' says head.

No last-minute scrambles to prepare for lockdowns as Oban already had a suite of Google applications in place before Covid hit. Any child without a device was given one and the school bought 4G dongles for those with weak connectivity, as well as setting up parent support sessions online. Not a school to work in siloes – for example, the design, manufacture, construction and use of the bee hut was all tasked to pupils as part of their education in the relevant departments.

Learning support and SEN: The school has a special unit to cater for children with complex needs (as well as dealing with milder needs) so those that might normally opt for a special school don't have to. Some have two members of staff all to themselves, with 39 staff running the unit overall, making it the largest learning unit in Scotland. Facilities include a physiotherapy room and low and high sensory rooms. Autism is a strength. Although the school's wealth of outdoor is available for all students, it has been found to particularly benefit those with SEND and is therefore developed accordingly – includes access to canoeing in the loch, sailing, hiking, biking and bushcraft. The John Muir Award is popular among SEND students – and in recognition of the benefit of animals for some of these students, the school has a partnership with Riding for the Disabled as well as utilising dog therapy for those who are anxious about coming to school.

The arts and extracurricular: Inspirational School of Traditional Music, as it is known, is based in shiny soundproofed piping building and run by one of the top pipers in the world. The school pipe band is a very big deal, having been world champions twice in the last 12 years. 'My boys love it – the band is heavily involved in the community and even if you're not in the band there's huge pride around it,' said a parent. Apart from the piping, school has a nationally ranked accordion teacher and offers coaching in the fiddle (Scottish violin), clarsach (Gaelic harp), piping, whistle and flute, piano, guitar, accordion, drums and voice. Pupils perform everywhere from New York to Ireland, from Inverness to the local M&S. Notable numbers head off to the Royal Conservatoire of Scotland – rumour has it that the conservatoire's annual visiting workshops are as much a talent spotting opportunity as anything else.

Drama less important than music, according to parents, but it's all relative at Oban and performing arts is clearly a well loved department. Not only do they teach stage and sound production but they have a specific workshop where they build their own sets for the drama studios. The stage, which is neatly concealed in the assembly area, has the same kind of kit available as a London theatre; there is an entire lighting rig concealed in the ceiling.

New art teacher is an internationally recognised practitioner, supported by a practising artist and head of department. Ceramics important, thanks to own kiln. No digital art, but photography popular.

Hostel accommodation is homely, with plenty of communal space. Students arrive on a Sunday evening, heading back on the boats after school on Friday, only staying weekends in bad weather

Over 50 different clubs from the record club, which is all about the music, to the debating society. Dance, archery, skiing, basketball and hockey are all on the agenda, plus John Muir and DofE.

Sport: Shinty (hockey without rules, to the unacquainted) is on the up and up – about half the school plays it. Special mention must also go to the School of Rugby and their technologically edgy artificial pitches. Apparently the superior performance of the school's rugby squad brought the Scottish Rugby Union to their door and they are now supported with top-notch coaching and mentoring. Football is as big as rugby, as we saw for ourselves while strolling around the grounds. And athletics badminton, hockey, table tennis, netball, skiing, gymnastics and strength and conditioning are also on offer. The SVQ sport coaching is a big thing and they have developed an agreement with the local primaries that their children can go and try out their coaching skills on the younger pupils so that they gain 'more valuable experience'.

Boarding: Covering the education requirements of islands such as Colonsay, Coll, Mull, Lismore, Iona, Kerrera, Shuna and Easdale as well as the remote Bridge of Orchy, the local authority has no option but to offer hostel accommodation, which is located a five/10-minute walk away. Accommodation is homely, with plenty of communal space. 'My elder son had to share his room in the first year, which he didn't like, but he has his own room now and is much happier, whereas my younger son much prefers sharing – main thing is there are opportunities for both,' said a parent. Currently there are around 50 children staying with a hostel manager, an assistant manager and about eight houseparents. 'They look out for the pupils well although if they needed a cuddle I'm not sure they'd be the best people,' said a parent. All arrive on a Sunday evening, heading back on the boats after school on

Friday, only staying weekends in bad weather. Plenty of activities on offer – football, cinema, games nights, with time for study also factored in. 'There is loads available – if anything, they don't have enough hours to fit it all in.' Parents particularly appreciate the skills of independent learning that boarders are taught, although there are some grumbles around food – 'It's just not that nice, although I'm not sure how much of that is to do with guidelines about having to reduce salt, fat etc.'

Ethos and heritage: The first school in Oban was founded in 1862, although Oban High School as a formal institution didn't come into existence until 1890. Has always been on the current site, with five different extensions added over the years until 2018 when the school had a £36m new building. 'Designed by teachers for teachers,' says head. And it is a wonderful building: bright, imposing and quite rightly proud of itself. The classrooms are clean, spacious and well equipped. There are amazing beauty and hairdressing salons, building and construction areas, wonderful dance studios, fully soundproofed music block and impressive sporting facilities such as a gym and the latest artificial pitches. The central hall transforms into a fully equipped theatre (but why can't they accommodate all of the school in one single space? Just asking!).

Every year, the day after the famous Argyllshire gathering (highland games), Oban High School girds its loins and takes over the field of action ready for battle. In a spectacular march worthy of Braveheart, the school band pipes each clan (or house) down to the field behind its own pennant and the battle commences. Tossing the caber and the hammer, sword and highland dancing, piping competitions and huge tugs of war. 'From Easter to summer the kids are trained to throw the caber, hammer etc. It's a huge event for the school and the town as a whole and it just makes us so proud to be there competing and proud to be Scottish.' Uplifting and upbeat and, well, unified – and that is probably how we would describe Oban High School. It is a very together school.

A quick Google search of the school reveals that uniform can be a bone of contention, with some parents (though it quickly became apparent to us that it's a small, very vocal minority) currently blasting the uniform rules, in particular claiming girls are 'treated more harshly'. But school makes no apology for its strict uniform requirements and insists it is affordable and that there is no gender inequality.

Pastoral care, inclusivity and discipline: School operates on fairly traditional clan (house) system. Every clan has a depute head teacher in charge, who is responsible for the academic and pastoral care of each child (along with a full-time principal teacher of guidance). Each clan also has a full-time family liaison officer whose support extends to anything from filling in forms to helping families deal with teenage angst (head says this is unique in Scottish schools). All clan provision is available in school, at home (where practical) and at the four outreach centres which are placed across the school's catchment area and allow pupils and parents to receive academic or pastoral support nearer to home. One is based in a college, one in primary school, two in community centres. Parents say it's a 'caring' school, with one telling us her daughter was referred to the school nurse when their family hit a wobble – 'I think that's what kept her balanced, she was able to talk about anything that was worrying her.' Teachers are described as 'approachable' and 'well thought of'. One parent told us how her daughter 'got a dodgy boyfriend and one of her teachers saw a wee change in that she wasn't doing so well at school and took her aside to say, "Be careful, you've got potential and don't want to spoil things." It was all it took to get her back on track.' There is a free all-year-round breakfast club and the school offers study support from Monday to Thursday in the evenings and during the Easter holidays before exams.

School of Traditional Music is run by one of the top pipers in the world. The school pipe band have been world champions twice in the last 12 years

School doors shut at 9am sharp and all latecomers are interviewed. If kids arrive without a uniform they are given one. For repeated patterns of misbehaviour parents are invited in promptly and 'we work together to make sure the pupil behaves'. Everyone's Invited not on the school's radar, but school did tell us issues like peer-on-peer harassment and abuse are covered in PHSE.

Pupils and parents: Everything from very rich with their own helicopters to real rural poverty. Boarders arrive on a ferry on a weekly basis, while around 10 are flown in. Many take the train to school and even greater numbers are bussed in. Parents range from farmers, architects, fishermen, shop workers and doctors to lots of people working from home via computer. Comms could be better, say parents – 'My son is in an exam year and I've got no idea if he's where he should be,' said one (school says there are monthly tracking reports for each child and the head writes to parents – and makes a video version – every two weeks).

The last word: We struggle to describe this as a school: more a complete educational experience. Inspiring leadership has meant they tackle a huge and complex catchment area with commitment and dedication. Some parents feel they may stretch themselves too far in their efforts to offer everything to everybody, but our impression is that they have a very good sense of the area and its requirements.

Old Swinford Hospital

15

Heath Lane, Stourbridge, West Midlands DY8 1QX

01384 817300 | admissions@oshsch.com | www.oshsch.com

Ages: 11–18

Pupils: 612; sixth form: 219 (134 boys, 85 girls); Boarders: 200 full and weekly, 190 flexi

Fees: Day free; Boarding £12,136, Flexi boarding £6,168 pa

Headmaster: Since 2014, Paul Kilbride (40s), previously deputy head at Bethany School, Kent. Has taught in just about every type of school – state and independent, day and boarding, selective and non-selective, single sex and mixed. Good grounding for this hybrid school. His own education was at a British Army school in Germany from where he went on to Magdalen College, Oxford to read modern history. Career options (he felt) were limited to police ('I was too short sighted'), army ('I didn't like the rigid structure and hierarchy') and teaching ('I liked the idea of public service and the autonomy'). So teaching it was. Tremendously popular. Pupils say he's the staff member they see the most of, his energy, engagement and informality clearly putting them (and us) immediately at ease. 'It's crazy, but he knows every single student's name and even some of their relatives,' lauded one boy. Parents equally smitten – we heard how he's pushed up academic standards and aspirations, shines when it comes to preparing pupils for university and the world of work (pupils regularly made references to both during our visit) and that his engagement with all aspects of school life is legendary. 'He knows the pulse of the school – his eyes are everywhere and nothing gets missed,' said one. We met him in the Hogwarts-esque Oak Room, his 'for best' office where founder Tom Foley's sombre face stared down at us (well, an oil painting anyway). Was 'amazing' during lockdown, we heard, with military precision when it came to planning ahead and adapting online learning to pupil needs – 'How he's still standing, I don't know.' Fond of educational jargon – take a glossary.

Lives on site with wife Emma, another Magdalen alumnus, and their three sons who attend local schools 'because they didn't want to be at a school where Dad was headmaster – quite understandable,' he laughs. If you ask him about spare time and hobbies, prepare for a blank look. 'This is a 24/7 job which has morphed into a lifestyle so I do the job and go to bed, just hoping I don't get a call from one of the boarding houses!' But then he remembered running – 'Ah yes, running. That's where I get my headspace. A bit like Forrest Gump.'

Entrance: Complicated. Most join in year 7, around a third each of full boarders, flexi boarders and day pupils (a small minority get a bespoke option, known as tailored boarding). Day pupils arrive in time for registration and finish after lessons. Flexi boarders can arrive for breakfast and leave after prep but are required to stay over at least three or four nights a term. Remaining boarders are split into termly (a third) and weekly (two-thirds – they go home on Fridays after prep). Application deadlines different for each. For day pupils, there is no entry testing, with the majority coming from three local CofE feeder schools. Other day pupils can come from anywhere, with the usual criteria of looked-after children and EHCPs first, then it's down to distance from school. For flexi boarders, entry is selective, with a computer-based academic test taken in year 6 (around six pupils per year get in on sport or music rather than academic aptitude). Flexi boarders are also assessed for suitability for boarding via an interview and school reference. Weekly and termly boarders don't do the test but are assessed for boarding suitability via interview.

Since September 2021, the school has admitted a greater number of pupils (part of a five-year expansion programme, though remaining small by state school standards). At the same time it became co-ed throughout, with 80 boys and 60 girls in the first co-ed 11+ cohort. Day and flexi boarding places into year 7 are highly sought after – it is regarded as the best state day school in the area. Worth noting that not all co-curricular activities are available to day pupils, which is why families are keen on the flexi boarding option. A few join in year 9 and even fewer in years 8 and 10, but only as weekly or termly boarders (there's now a waiting list in year 9).

Sixth form entry criteria for existing pupils and newcomers (usually around 60) are six 5s at GCSE, including maths and English (or agreed equivalent for overseas candidates). For some A levels, eg maths and science, pupils need 7s in those subjects.

Exit: A quarter leave at the end of year 11, usually to sixth form colleges to do triple BTECs, plus a few apprenticeships. Most sixth formers to university, with Nottingham the current favourite; others to Aston, Birmingham, Cardiff, Durham, Exeter, Liverpool, Loughborough, Portsmouth, Queen Mary London, Royal Holloway, Sheffield, Swansea, Warwick and York. Sometimes a few to Oxbridge, though none in 2020. Two medics in 2020. Quite a few get prestigious apprenticeships – most recently KPMG and HS2.

Latest results: In 2020, 39 per cent 9-7 at GCSE; 94 per cent 9-4 in both maths and English. At A level, 21 per cent A*/A at A level (43 per cent A*-B). In 2019 (the last year when exams took place), 30 per cent 9-7 at GCSE; 88 per cent 9-4 in both maths and English. At A level, 25 per cent A*/A at A level (44 per cent A*-B).

Teaching and learning: Results have been on an upward trajectory ever since the current head joined. 'Previous heads were all about the sport but this one has brought in academic rigour, measurement and accountability, he's done a great job,' said a parent. The addition of girls in lower years means co-ed teaching is now the norm except for science, which will be taught separately in years 7-9 'on the back of research that shows girls can get switched off in science when they pick up unhelpful stereotypes'.

Setting in maths and English from year 7, and in science from year 9. French or Mandarin chosen from year 7; languages not compulsory at GCSE. Most take nine GCSEs, around half do triple science. Maths and sciences do very well. Popular non-core options include economics, PE and business studies. At sixth form, three A levels are the norm, plus EPQ which all start and half complete. Some take a BTEC in sport in place of an A level and vocational qualifications are offered in business and ICT. Psychology, maths, sciences and sport all popular. Maths, art and geography get impressive results. A few parents feel the science teaching could be stronger throughout, especially physics.

For a school in the middle of a Midlands town, there's a heck of a lot of green space – a joy to see year 7s learning circus skills on one of the fields when we visited

Standardised assessments in years 7, 9 and 12 for baseline tracking. Lots of extra help available, and actively encouraged especially in the lead-up to exams. 'One of my children isn't massively academic and I worried he was in danger of being lost in the middle – but that hasn't happened, while our more intellectual child gets plenty of stretch,' said a parent. It's not often that pupils we meet have such an in-depth understanding of the specialist areas of interest of staff right down to genetics and metaphysics but our tour guides seemed to know them all – 'really impacts on their teaching, it's great,' reckoned one.

Learning support and SEN: SENCo oversees four learning support assistants, the latter mainly support those with EHCPs (six when we visited). The team is known for its compassion and humour. One-to-one sessions for non-EHCP pupils with SEN (mostly dyslexia and dyspraxia, of which there are just above average numbers) are rare as most academic support is provided through differentiation in class. Must do the trick as value added for those needing learning support is high. A good site for physical disabilities – 'They put everything in place that he needed, he's never had a down day,' said parent of a pupil who uses a wheelchair.

The arts and extracurricular: Tangible irritation among the whole school community that music was essentially mothballed during Covid. In normal times it is the beating heart of the school. Very inclusive, very skilled staff, we heard. A quarter of pupils have instrumental lessons and there are 20 ensembles (most recently trombone – 'my instrument, so I'm thrilled!' said head) and bands, plus three choirs and a school orchestra, all of which perform in the school and in outside venues, including tours. Caters for eclectic and multicultural tastes – we happened upon a year 8 class ramping up their keyboard skills with Brazilian music, and all year 7s perform African pieces for an annual concert.

No timetabled drama, but the English department runs a club putting on productions such as Jesus Christ Superstar, Joseph and Oliver! Head hopes the addition of girls in the lower years may generate demand for drama GCSE.

Art gets good numbers at GCSE and A level and is available as a two-hour daily club for boarders. Several students go on to foundation courses at art college. Plenty of different media to try, with eg dark room and printing press. Visiting artists are a regular feature, and textiles is popular. We'd have liked to see more displays but enjoyed getting first glance of year 8's freshly glazed ceramic bird feeders showing a range of abilities, and we enjoyed chatting to sixth form girls about their A level work – 'We're allowed to really experiment,' said one.

For day pupils in years 7 to 9, clubs are mainly confined to music and sport and if they represent the school they are expected to attend the relevant club eg rugby team or orchestra. CCF (which has grown massively) and DofE available from year 9. STEM club popular for all. Boarders are expected to commit to at least three clubs a week from a long list including fencing, boxing and street dance – nobody needs persuading. Opportunities for voluntary work in the local community for older pupils. Participation is carefully monitored by pastoral staff to ensure everyone is as involved as possible in the broader life of the school. Senior pupils have the opportunity to coach junior teams and run clubs.

Sport: Rugby is king, according to pupils and parents, though head says he's 'never been convinced we're a rugby school'. Either way, the school is well able to hold its own against the large independent schools, with a former England player running a values-driven rugby coaching programme of humility and hard work. 'I had no interest in rugby when I came in year 7 but loved it a term later!' said one pupil. Other main sports for boys are cricket and football. Basketball increasingly popular. For girls, it's netball, cricket and rounders. Athletics for all in the summer – some local competition success. Not a sports fan? One of our tour guides wasn't and assured us 'it's fine, it really doesn't matter'. 'And there's always the stuff like climbing, badminton and fencing,' shrugged another. Great excitement all round for the annual staff vs student football match followed by a BBQ.

Boarding: The school is strongly committed to boarding. In fact, the last head did away with day pupils altogether, though current head (who brought them back) says he's 'never sure why'. The school is acutely aware of what a jump boarding can be, particularly for younger boys, so they may start off staying one night a week, then increase it to two and three and then all week at their own pace. 'At the beginning of year 7, I used to get quite homesick but loved it by the end of the year,' one pupil told us.

The extracurricular offering comes into its own with boarding since everything takes place on site. On Saturdays, mornings are given over to sport and there's free time in the afternoons; on Sundays, there's a carousel of trips to eg Alton Towers, Go Ape, Old Trafford. The sports hall and music school are open in the evenings and at weekends. 'They spend a lot of time outside in the evenings – you see them playing tag on the fields, it's wonderful,' said a parent.

Boarders are expected to commit to at least three clubs a week from a long list including fencing, boxing and street dance – nobody needs persuading

There are six houses altogether, with dorms of varying sizes. Year 7 boys get their own house, as do the girls, with the remaining four home to a mix of boys from years 8 to 13, with the older ones getting first dibs on the double and single rooms. All airy, light, clean and tidy-ish with standard issue blue bedding and bedroom furniture. Not a trace of personality to be seen anywhere in the rooms we visited (tends to be the case with boys' boarding). Graduated access to mobile phones, depending on age – 'If it was up to me, they'd have them never!' laughed a housemistress.

Ethos and heritage: One of those sprawling campuses that you wonder how on earth the youngsters get to know their way around so quickly – and yet they do ('in about three days,' reckoned one). Founded over 350 years ago, the school is a mixture of highly atmospheric historic buildings dating back to its foundation and more modern additions. With the notable exception of the newly acquired (from Birmingham Metropolitan University) Swinford Court – a modern, glass-fronted, three-storey block of classrooms, spacious sixth form area, second gym and sports hall – the school is not, as one parent put it, 'quite as polished as upper echelon schools', but it's all there. And for a school in the middle of a Midlands town, there's a heck of a lot of green space (a joy to see year 7s learning circus skills on one of the fields when we visited – an end of term treat), with even more fields off site. 'Look how well the grass is kept,' said our tour guide, clearly proud of his surroundings (poor chap was mortified when we almost immediately stumbled across a stranded plastic bottle – the only litter we saw all day, though).

The school is strongly committed to boarding. Saturday mornings are given over to sport and there's free time in the afternoons; on Sundays, there's a carousel of trips – Alton Towers, Go Ape, Old Trafford

Everyone appreciates the strong sense of community and we heard no complaints about the school going co-ed throughout – far from it. 'There's a lot of integration between the year groups,' said a pupil, and we noticed a good rapport between staff and pupils too. Overall, there's a dynamic, structured feel about all aspects of school life. We thought the food was excellent (our scotch egg wouldn't have been out of place in a fancy deli) but some pupils felt it's a bit 'samey' – 'You know what to expect every day,' said one. Pupils are suited and booted right up to the end of sixth form, but nobody seems to mind – 'It's good because we'll be prepared for the world of business,' said one (they'll be in for a nice surprise if they wind up working in a media or tech firm).

Pastoral care, inclusivity and discipline: 'Nurturing, caring and strict, but not overly so,' summed up a parent. The wide range of backgrounds and needs of the pupils make it essential that the pastoral care here is effective, and it is. Some boys are on carefully monitored welfare plans but all benefit from the considerable experience of the pastoral teams. Mental health is paramount, especially since Covid. Peer mentoring and counselling are both available, and there's an online facility run by a cyber charity that offers confidential advice for sixth formers. The advent of girls in the younger years has brought conversations about 'how we treat each other' to the top of the agenda, says head – 'including how it's easy to make mistakes with the best of intentions'. We were surprised to find some blank looks we got when we mentioned the Everyone's Invited website – 'What's that?' said more than one pupil (we're still trying to decide whether that's a good or bad thing). School keeps a beady eye on what it calls micro-aggression to ensure it doesn't turn to bullying.

'Where they are more rebellious, they tame it and those on the quieter side are pulled out – the ultimate aim is to send them out into the wider world to make a good contribution and be good citizens,' said a parent. Another, whose son went through a phase of 'getting into lots of trouble', said she thought at one point they might need a plan B for A levels – 'but the school helped him turn a corner and he wound up deputy head boy!' Pupils told us expectations are clear and that sloppy uniform, disruption in class and late homework are among the biggest no-no's. The warning system is widely used and detentions are common. Suspensions are 'rare and just', say pupils, and the head has only ever excluded pupils for illegal drugs – the last time in 2019. Head intervenes if he hears of unregulated pop-up or house parties and works closely with parents where necessary.

Pupils and parents: The school's ethnic and social diversity was the main draw for several parents we spoke to. State boarding schools are a hybrid between state and independent sector (tuition is free for all but there is a charge for boarding) and this means that you get everything from children who are sponsored to board by a charity because of home circumstances right through to the exceptionally wealthy. Fee-payers appreciate the comparatively low cost – 'Because you only pay for the boarding and not the tuition, it winds up costing the same as a day place in an independent school,' said one. Most families are dual income and live within 90 minutes of the school, though some come from further afield. Round about 10 per cent of boarders are from overseas, mainly from Hong Kong, Middle East and North America (and historically the EU, though 'Brexit has put a stop to that,' says head). It's also a popular choice for Forces families. Good comms between home and school, say parents. Pupils don't fit a mould – we met shy ones, outspoken ones, witty ones and serious ones, but they all shared good manners.

Money matters: If you are considering boarding, OSH represents amazing value for money and is well worth a visit. Tuition is free and parents just pay for the boarding side.

The last word: A school that lives up to its local reputation as the best in the area, with an exceptionally popular head. The boarding element brings a sense of community and – unusually for a boarding school – reflects modern Britain in its social and ethnic diversity. Along with the ever improving academics, a fabulous extracurricular offering and spacious site, it's no wonder parents increasingly choose it over traditional independent Midlands boarding schools. Not for those who yearn for something more academically or socially exclusive.

Peter Symonds College

Owens Road, Winchester, Hampshire SO22 6RX

01962 857500 | psc@psc.ac.uk | www.psc.ac.uk

Ages: 16–18

Pupils: 4,393; Boarders: 66 full

Fees: Day free; Boarding £15,600 – £16,800 pa

Principal: Since 2018, Sarah Russell BA (history, Reading), previously deputy principal and then principal of Alton College. Lengthy experience in sixth form education and sits on several policy groups.

Entrance: Base entry is five 4s at GCSE including English and maths, but most have considerably more than this. Some subjects – including sciences, maths and languages – have additional entry requirements. No defined catchment area; instead, the college works closely with 19 partner schools in the area whose students get first dibs, provided they meet the academic criteria. Any spare places (and there always are some) go to students from additional state schools, and around 14 per cent come from independent schools. Students can restart and do something different if subject choices really aren't working out.

Exit: Some leave after year 12 to go to other sixth form colleges, agricultural college or vocational college. Ninety per cent to university, 40 per cent to Russell Group. In 2021, 56 to Oxbridge, making the college one of the top five Oxbridge feeder schools, in the illustrious company of Eton, Westminster and Hills Road Sixth Form College in Cambridge. Masses of medics too – 68 in 2021. Universities in the south and south west are longstanding favourites, notably Bristol, Bath and Southampton. STEM courses popular. As with other sixth form colleges, students here are more likely to get first class and upper second degrees. Plenty of gap years. Some go on to apprenticeships and directly into employment.

Latest results: In 2021, 41 per cent A*/A at A level (68 per cent A*-B). In 2019 (the last year when exams took place), 36 per cent A*/A at A level (63 per cent A*-B).

Teaching and learning: Often chosen for its academic reputation, results here are excellent. 'Head and shoulders' above other options, said a student. All the more impressive when you consider that the college is non-selective – magic ingredient is value added, up one grade across three A levels. 'Education is most important here,' a student told us as she described wearily how in some schools everything is important – 'here: education,' she said simply.

Setting is so last decade, with college firmly of the philosophy (which is well evidenced) that working with motivated, succeeding and more able students pulls everyone else up the ladder. Classes of 16-20 students are therefore completely mixed ability, backed up with three types of workshop for every course – support workshops for the struggling (attendance might be obligatory); extension workshops to push the able; and structured workshops for exam revision.

Students value the independent learning style here, which makes for smoother transition to university

College has no trouble recruiting top-notch staff – they apply in their droves though are only taken on if they can prove a willingness to innovate and take on new ideas. 'It's not just about delivering content but seeing teaching as a craft.' All are expected to work their socks off in every lesson and workshop to pull up those at the bottom end and stretch those at the top. Some, such as those working in computer science, have industry experience.

Broad selection of A levels includes the less traditional environmental science and 3D design.

BTECs on the up, now including media, ICT, business, performing arts, music performance, digital music, sport, health and safety care, among others. Students take three or, if they're doing further maths, four. A small cohort is doing the T level in education and childcare – the college was one of the first wave providers of this new qualification which is equivalent to three A levels/BTECs. Students report some subject gender divide – more girls take sociology, English, classics and law; more boys take economics and computer science. But STEM subjects are well balanced, especially maths which is massive here, with up to 1,300 students across the two years taking it. Psychology also popular. Significant growth in those doing criminology – 450 study this A level across the two year groups, not bad considering it was only introduced three years ago. Students said they would like more information before they start on subjects such as this which are not offered at secondary school – ditto with methods of teaching; 'can go in and love or hate,' said one, but they do have a taster day when they can try out subjects and get a course overview.

No setting. College firmly of the philosophy (well evidenced) that working with motivated, succeeding and more able students pulls everyone else up the ladder

About 20 per cent do the EPQ – 'Ah, love it,' said one student. 'If you have a burning passion…' 'Nice to escape the "write this argument" restriction of A level,' said another, while another told us she'd just got a 'reduced offer from university because of it'.

Students value the independent learning style here, which makes for smoother transition to university – there's not the coercion you get at school, they say. 'Because you choose the subject, failing is only your own fault. So pull yourself up – and people do.' It's a different vibe to school, one explained: 'It's cool to do well.' In this supportive student body, 'uppers help lowers,' said a student, or teachers will help out. Study support is very good, said a parent – 'Grand at helping you study independently… if you seek it out.' It's not a place for those who need hand-holding, parents agree.

Careers advice on tap for those unsure what lies ahead – careers week and careers fair well attended. Great preparation for competitive university entrance too – includes interview practice, and there's a dedicated Oxbridge tutor.

Not the quickest to respond to the first lockdown during Covid, but teachers more than made up for it. 'It was not trouble free, but one very good thing was the attendance – it was higher than it's ever been!' says college. Some whole-college events have continued online, which students love – every cloud, and all that.

Learning support and SEN: College talks about learning differences, not difficulties – 'We are the ones that need to adjust to them not vice-versa. We work hard to find creative ways to do that.' Can be on micro level, eg changing fonts to be dyslexic friendly, giving directions on a page in a different colour or saying assignments out loud. For more significant needs, one-to-ones and other assistance available, eg the physio room with plinth means that student in wheelchairs can come and take a rest; the frame allows another student to work in a standing position. Many students with no diagnosed need pop in and out to eg develop independent study skills or because they need a booster in literacy skills. College doesn't count how many students have formally diagnosed SEN but told us 20-25 per cent of have access arrangements for exams, which provides a clue. All sounds an SEN utopia, although it's worth bearing in mind the onus is on the student to seek help. One parent told us her mildly dyslexic son gets extra time in exams, but that's it. The help is there if he asks for it, thinks the parent, but her son is 'slightly embarrassed and lazy…'.

The arts and extracurricular: All students have to do at least one timetabled enrichment activity from a lovely long list that includes dance team challenge, debating society, Symonds News, film clubs, Medsoc and LAMDA. First aid is popular as students get a qualification out of it. In addition, the college supports many activities that are set up by students, eg PSC Homeless Initiative works with the local Winchester night shelter to support local vulnerable people. DofE popular, and the level 2 sports leader students work with local specialist schools to support children with additional needs.

Vibrant music department mainly attracts students who are either studying a music-related course or who get one of the 12 coveted places on the college's Hampshire Specialist Music Course – the cream of music provision. Successful applicants get one and half hours of individual tuition a week, as well as opportunities to form chamber groups and orchestras. Many of those doing music A level also have instrument tuition and these students also often take part in the large number of very high quality concerts including in the local community. Budding pianists will be pleased to hear the college is currently trying to bag a number of Steinways.

Full, term-time boarding only, with most families taking up the opportunity because they live too far to travel in

Relatively small numbers do drama, performing arts and dance A level, but the college will run them even for small numbers. Good breadth of art A levels – fine art, textiles, photography and sculpture. Sun pours through the slanting glass roof of the art block, which has doors that open out onto grass; a nice space to work in, though no designated spaces for individual students, so work can't be left out.

Sport: Sport is not always a forte of sixth form colleges, but this could not be further from the truth here as Peter Symonds is the national leading sixth form for games. If you excel at sport the chances are you will quickly be in a team – but only one team in your favourite sport as competition is huge. In fact, it can be quite a shock for those who were the big shot on the school rugby field to arrive here, compete against 500 others and not even make the fourth team. The college regularly wins national college competitions and participation for playing recreationally is also strong – including among girls who are often the first to drop a sporting pursuit around the age of 16 or 17. Lots of breadth, with all the usuals of football, rugby, netball and hockey on offer, and there are teams for swimming, tennis, squash and badminton. Volleyball, basketball and go-karting also feature, with others coming and going in response to demand. One parent told us her kids opted to take up lacrosse – a new sport to most, so an assurance of a place on the team.

Boarding: Full, term-time boarding only, with most families taking up the opportunity because they live too far to travel in – anything from 30 or 40 miles away to right across the UK. A smattering of internationals too. This includes the Falkland Islands, for which Peter Symonds is the sixth form, though numbers are small – around 10 in each year group. Others from all over the place – there are even three students from Tristan de Cunha, the remotest islands on the planet. Many boarders come from Forces families.

The two boarding houses are School House (smaller and older) and Falkland Lodge (distinguished by its ensuite twin rooms and a feeling of Premier Inn). Both are run by houseparents and have a common room, study room and kitchen, where students help themselves to breakfast. If students have a preference, the houseparent tries to accommodate that. 'There are close communities in both, particularly the smaller house,' reported one student, though don't expect any mollycoddling. It's a 'boarding facility, not a boarding school,' the head of boarding told us firmly. 'Not like the packed schedule for boarders at Winchester College, and students should not have these expectations,' said a parent, although boarders are taken out for a team building day at the beginning of the year, and have various themed dinners. But you 'don't have to go out, don't have to go to dinner,' said a student who'd experienced independent school boarding, with evident relief.

Students here are treated as young adults. They can come and go as they please to the gym and sports hall after school hours and they don't have to sign out to leave campus – they just need to be back by the generous curfew times of 10.20pm during the week, 11.00pm on Friday and Saturday for lowers, 11.30pm for uppers. But nor is it a free-for-all, with compulsory quiet study time from 6.30-8.30pm, and an emphasis on safeguarding. There's a care plan for each child and students can be expected to be dragged out of bed if they've got a 9am lesson. There are rotas for kitchen duty (only the odd prompt necessary, say houseparents) and students do their own laundry.

Ethos and heritage: The college sits in an expanse of daisied green, a mixture of the old grammar buildings and modern additions, the swish and the less so. The atmosphere is relaxed, though purposeful and confident – 'a stepping stone from school to university, freer and more open than school,' according to the college. One parent told us her daughter opted to leave private education for Peter Symonds – she liked the informality, and 'being in control of her own destiny'.

No shortage of facilities or, for that matter, technology – 'austerity is not an issue here,' said a student. Notable library resources too – they will get hold of any book or journal that a student needs. The last time we visited, the biggest problem was finding space to study – but the Hopkins Study Centre has helped and there are always lists of free classrooms. Food is good, if a little pricey (though college keeps an eye on this), and lots nip to Tesco for a meal deal.

Pastoral care, inclusivity and discipline: The Hub is the pastoral focal point, although students told us they also turn to tutors and teachers for support. The Hub was a response to the tsunami of low-level mental health problems, such as anxiety and low mood – and that was pre-Covid, so you can imagine the need for it now. One parent said it was 'a lifesaver for my daughter'; a student said they are 'cool about everything'. Staffed by two full-time mental health specialists and a team of five counsellors, they do everything from providing classes on mindfulness and wellbeing to regular one-to-ones. They are also planning a comeback for the in-college therapy dog service.

There's a nurse and sexual health clinic – 'very discreet,' say students. Free condoms (six a week) and chlamydia tests available from student services, and the college can send students to a pharmacy for free emergency contraception. Students here don't feel the need to titter embarrassedly about sexual health.

We wondered how shy introverts might fare at this huge college. One student compared its vastness with the size of a small town but added that there are communities of people within the vastness, which usually come down to subject passions. 'With such diversity of subjects, you can find someone whose views and interests are like yours. No one goes through without making a friend.' Bullying not a problem, say students – 'rare,' agrees college, 'something students have left at school.' Parents are largely not involved, but would be contacted early with any concerns, whether pastoral or academic.

As at university, there's a student union, which 'is prominent and has a strong voice,' said the elected members, who meet with SMT. We also liked the sound of SPOCs (student perception of course) discussions (with no tutor present) at the end of each course – gives qualitive feedback to subjects heads so they can constantly evolve. The college recently appointed five equality and diversity officers to audit provision – 'We're working on the curriculum first to reflect on all areas,' says college.

College works hard at drugs education, and second chances are possible here. But students may be suspended (around 20-30 a year) if not attending, not doing work, or behaviour is distracting others from learning – and a few are asked to leave. Behaviour outside college is not ignored if it brings the college into disrepute, eg smoking outside the gates.

Pupils and parents: Students mainly from Winchester, Basingstoke and Southampton, though stretches 15-10 miles in most directions up to Andover, over to Salisbury, down to Portsmouth and eastwards to Petersfield. Marginally more ethnically diverse than when we last reviewed the college but still largely reflective of the white, middle-class make-up of the area. Most use public transport which can be poor and make students late; for those driving in, parking can be challenging.

Communication home is via email and the parent portal shows details of homework, progress, effort and attendance. Regular progress reviews too. Parents' evening slots are initially allocated to students about whom there is a concern, then others invited to snap up the rest on a first-come-first-served basis – less than ideal, according to some parents we spoke to who said they 'would like more parents' evenings, or a detailed report'; 'can go through the whole thing with seeing anyone…'.

The last word: For independent learners with good work habits, high aspirations and a love of academics, this could be educational nirvana – a kind of halfway house between school and university, with excellent teaching across the board. And even if youngsters are not all these things, there's a good chance most will get swept along with the crowd, though some may struggle.

Reading School

17

Erleigh Road, Reading, Berkshire RG1 5LW

0118 901 5600 | admissions@reading-school.co.uk | www.reading-school.co.uk

Ages: 11–18

Pupils: 1,105; sixth form: 357; Boarders: 81 weekly

Fees: Day free; Boarding £12,660 pa

Head: Since 2012, Ashley Robson BA NPQH MBA, previously deputy head since 2005. History degree from Newcastle University. First jobs at Princes Risborough School and Royal Grammar School, High Wycombe before becoming head of history, head of house and assistant headteacher at Aylesbury Grammar School. Still teaches history.

'Building good men' is his catchphrase, repeated by every parent we spoke to – message clearly resonating that this is 'not just an academic school but also one where we develop character'. A big thinker, and a worthy one too – must be the first head we've interviewed who didn't respond to our questions about Covid by ploughing straight into the usual diatribe about seamlessly moving online (though they did that too), instead explaining with pride and in great detail what the school did for the community, notably organising onsite cabins for NHS staff at the Royal Berkshire Hospital opposite to stay in during the height of lockdown. School was also the site for charity box collection and distribution, while behind the scenes he got students writing cards to vulnerable OBs. School organised drops of food and resources to students from disadvantaged backgrounds, and so the list goes on.

For intellectually inquisitive, bright and highly motivated boys, this school is likely to feel a very natural fit. Maths a strength; huge breadth in languages

A big hit with staff (surely the only state school head to provide access to a personal trainer as an employee perk?) and pupils (who describe him as 'really friendly and funny' and 'the ideal headmaster because you know he really cares about us'). Parents also keen: 'Well respected.' 'Makes a concerted effort to be available.' 'I put some comments on a comment board the other day and he literally jumped on them.' 'A strong asset of the school.' He is ably supported by a charismatic deputy head.

Lives an hour's drive away in Bucks with his wife, with whom he has three grown-up children. Loves football and travel.

Entrance: Highly competitive 11+ exam – the school's own – comprising papers in English, maths and (a new addition) creative writing ('we want more creativity in our students'). Familiarisation sheet on the school website but no practice papers available, to help stop over-tutoring (although they do it anyway of course – 'Those with the "we will get our son in" approach have been known to start as young as 8,' said one parent). Over 800 sit the test for the 138 year 7 day boy places and a similar ratio for the 12 boarding spaces – you can only apply for one or the other. Priority given to applicants from disadvantaged backgrounds – at 10 per cent, school now has more than twice the national average for grammar schools ('probably the thing I'm most proud of,' says head).

To stay on into sixth form (or join as a newcomer) boys need the equivalent of at least 56 (54 for disadvantaged backgrounds) points across eight GCSEs, and at least a 7 in the subjects chosen. Around 150 apply for the 40 or so additional places.

Exit: Only loses around five per cent post GCSEs – 'usually to a sixth form college nearer where they live, say Basingstoke or Henley, or they don't make the grades,' says head. At 18, almost all to university, 70 per cent to Russell Group, with Imperial, Bristol, UCL, Warwick, Birmingham, Bath and Exeter currently popular. In 2021, 21 to Oxbridge. Very strong numbers to read economics-based subjects, with second most popular course engineering, followed by medicine (32 medics in 2021). Also prevalent, but in smaller numbers, are history, English, classics, maths and music.

Latest results: In 2021, 96 per cent 9-7 at GCSE; 84 per cent A*/A at A level (96 per cent A*-B). In 2019 (the last year when exams took place), 91 per cent 9-7 at GCSE; 68 per cent A*/A at A level (88 per cent A*-B).

Teaching and learning: For intellectually inquisitive, naturally bright and highly motivated boys, this school is likely to feel a very natural fit. Maths a strength, set from year 8. 'My son is in top set where they already go above and beyond the GCSE syllabus and this year they've taken the brightest ones to the next level still.' Up to 30 boys in top sets, 12 in bottom. STEM highly valued and imaginatively taught. Huge breadth in languages, with German, French, Spanish and Latin all taught in year 7; Latin and two of the others selected in year 8; and at least one taken at GCSE (Latin, Spanish and German most popular). Mandarin also available and offered as a GCSE.

All take 10 GCSEs, plus HPQ (pre-cursor to EPQ) in a subject that's been dropped. In sixth form, boys take three or four A levels. Maths, physics, chemistry and, again, economics (also available at GCSE) all popular. Latin and classical civilisation too. Around 15 a year take EPQ and all do enrichment of some kind or other, eg mentoring of younger students, primary schools coaching, entering national subject competitions. Well-regarded Inspire lecture series – 'provides an opportunity to learn about the achievements of former students and parents, and to have those role models is really important for these young men,' said a parent.

'Every teacher here goes the extra mile,' a pupil told us, 'not just in the classroom but in terms of extra help including subject drop-in clinics and one-to-ones if you need them.' Rapport between teachers and boys good-humoured and mutually respectful. 'They like making learning fun,' reckoned one pupil. Parents like how they instil independence from the off – 'right down to getting them to pack their bags the night before in year 7.'

Copious clubs and societies. Chess and public speaking taken particularly seriously – one student recently came third in the world in impromptu speaking

'Fewer live lessons and less imaginative task setting than I'd have liked,' said a parent about Covid, but majority said quite the opposite: 'The school was amazing, they switched to online learning immediately and the boys knew they could contact the tutors any time.' 'Excellent transition into year 7, even during Covid.'

Learning support and SEN: SENCo and her small team support boys mainly with ASD and dyslexia outside the classroom, as well as working closely with student support team and individual teachers to join the dots. 'The SENCo is not backward in coming forward and really champions the boys, recognising that some staff get their needs and some don't,' one parent told us, adding, 'She is very collaborative with parents too, even letting me run a session with staff to explain what my son's condition is like to live with.'

The arts and extracurricular: 'The academics are so strong that I was worried this might be at the expense of extracurricular but that couldn't be further from the truth,' said a parent, and she wasn't the only one. School day recently rejigged to allow for new Electives programme, which involves years 7-11 spending one period a day (except Fridays) doing one of 12 activities covering service, sport, character development, STEM, language practice, academic enrichment etc. 'It's one of the best things to come out of Covid,' says head, 'because I know we wouldn't have thought it possible before.' Copious clubs and societies too, many student-led. Chess and public speaking taken particularly seriously – one student recently came third in the world in impromptu speaking. 'I love that my son comes home not just talking about the academics but tells me he's been doing things like tinkering with a car,' said a parent.

Lots of drama. What they lack in facilities they gain in staff – the industry experience of the head of department would be the envy of many full-time actors, and he is currently writing a play to celebrate the school's 900-year anniversary. Big productions now co-ed with nearish girls' school, Queen Anne's. Focused productions also feature widely – performed outside in all weathers during Covid. Good links with the London theatre scene. 'I don't know anyone who doesn't like drama here – it's not even like a lesson, but a way to express yourself and let off steam,' said a pupil.

Music suffered during Covid but new director of music is busy getting orchestra, ensembles, choirs etc back up and running, and two students had just gone off to Oxford to study music when we last reviewed the school. 'You go along to performances thinking it might be quite lame but actually the bands are really cool and the classical music just incredible – there is some phenomenal talent,' said a parent. Much anticipated house music competition – 'Even if you're not mega into music, like me, it's a great night – we all love it,' said a pupil.

Increasing opportunities in art, with fine art, history of art and photography all available as A levels from 2022. Staff are artists in their own right. Creativity favoured over house style, with recent projects having explored the impact of AI in criminal justice and the increasing pressure on young men to meet beauty standards. Some students have gone on to study eg architecture, graphics, illustration and animation. Not all parents sang the praises of the department, however.

Trips aplenty, all helped by school's partnerships with schools in eg Tasmania, China and Denmark. School is particularly proud of its Kenyan links, where it has set up a centre for leading and character within a school for children from a local orphanage – some boys get to travel out there. Sports tours and language exchanges all over. Financial support available for those who would otherwise miss out.

Sport: For parents who see this school as an alternative to a high-performing independent school (many do), sport is a reality check. No acres of green fields, rows of pristine tennis courts or whizzy sports hall. But watch this space as school has plans for a 4G pitch and sports centre, and it has to be said that the existing sports field is a sight to behold when skies are blue and boys are out in their cricket whites (as they were when we visited). In any case, boys don't have far to travel (400m) to use the pitches just the other side of the hospital opposite. We heard no complaints when it comes to teaching, with a newly appointed head of sport and PE described as 'inspirational'. Football and cricket both strong, rugby less so

Holyport College

although the school does have a partnership with Rams Rugby Club. Boys are national champions for KS3 badminton, and lacrosse and athletics are both increasingly successful. 'My son is really into sport and has certainly not been disappointed, especially when it comes to badminton,' said one parent. More niche sports range from table tennis to canoeing, and the ultimate frisbee team does so well that they have their own kit.

Boarding: 'Could easily feel like an add-on as there are only 12 boarding places per year group, but really doesn't,' said parent. Much is made of the family feel, which parents appreciate. Particular praise for the boarding staff, who are described as 'phenomenal'. 'That's one of the things we've been most impressed with – they're great mentors.' 'Boarding is a family decision, impacting on everyone within the family and the housemaster really gets that.' 'Brilliant at communicating.' And because housemasters have young families, there are often young children about too: 'My first sight when I open my eyes in the morning is usually of the housemaster's daughter waving at me,' laughed one boy.

Rooms scored for tidiness daily and the weekly winner gets an extra £5 on their refectory card – judging from the pristine rooms we saw, it clearly works

Weekly boarding only, so majority head home Friday night, returning Sunday night or Monday morning, 'although a few stay on Friday night if they've got a fixture the next day.' Two boarding houses (some friendly rivalry between them) accommodate a maximum of six boys each per year group. Décor no-frills and, as one parent put it, 'quite antiquated', but all agree it's comfortable, with boys touchingly proud of the space spread among the eight common rooms (complete with pool tables, table football and TVs – 'particularly great fun when we all get together to watch a game'), as well as kitchens, music practice rooms and study spaces. Singles up to three-bed dorms – space and privacy increase as boys get older. Rooms scored for tidiness daily and the weekly winner gets an extra £5 on their refectory card – judging from the pristine rooms we saw, it clearly works.

Sociability factor considered a major plus point and a source of some envy among the day boys. 'Our daughter has asked to go to boarding school because she sees how much fun her brothers have!' Certainly plenty going on after school – clubs from 4pm (at least three on offer per evening), dinner at 5.30pm then study time from 6.30 to 8pm, with some flexibility for sixth formers. Much anticipated biannual boarding trips in summer and winter include the likes of theme park and West End theatre.

Ethos and heritage: Founded as part of Reading Abbey in 1125, the school is estimated to be the 10th oldest school in England (some argue there may have been a school running in Reading prior to this) and the 20th oldest in the world. Moved to current site in 1870 and now consists of an attractive red-brick Grade II listed building with two wings, framed by a beautifully manicured field. Expect all the usual grammar school features – parquet flooring, green tiles on the corridor walls, windows into the classrooms etc – while newer additions include science block (a joy to watch boys excitedly making benzoic acid), Page building (art, computer science, maths and IT), John Kendrick building (library plus more classrooms), the music school (far end of the field) and South House (one of the boarding houses – the other, East Wing, is attached to the main block). 'There's nothing we want for when it comes facilities,' said a pupil. All results in a leafy green, university-like campus, complete with scholarly yet relaxed vibe. Some pupils feel boys can get 'a bit competitive', hankering for more of a team spirit, but others disagree.

Uniform is plain grey suit with house ties. Food good – now with bigger portion sizes ('Thank God,' said a parent) – although one parent felt they could do with healthier, less carb-ridden choices, especially at breakfast for boarders (school disagrees).

Old boys include Christopher Renshaw (theatre director), Damian Green (former Secretary of State for Work and Pensions), Ross Brawn (Formula 1), William Laud (Archbishop) and Joe Eyre (actor, writer and theatre director).

Pastoral care, inclusivity and discipline: Recent push on sense of belonging, alongside that building of good character that the head is so keen on – neatly summed up as the Reading Way, explaining the RW you see on the school sports kit. 'It's great because what you don't want to wind up with is a bunch of brilliant mathematicians who can't have a conversation or have no mates,' said a parent.

Understands that young people sometimes get things wrong – tiered detention system hardly used and often as little as one fixed-term exclusion per term and no permanent exclusions for several years. 'When boys mess up here, it's usually just a silly mistake – and the school wants us to learn from it, rather than warn us that severe punishments are waiting around every corner, which would just make us disenfranchised with school life,' one boy explained. Non-negotiables include respect and the school doesn't shy away from discussing issues like misogyny and sexist banter (especially off the back of Everyone's Invited) although works hard to frame things positively – 'We need to get these boys on board by talking about positive masculinity, not to lose them by going on about toxic masculinity,' says head. Some impressive activities showcased on Twitter around Black History Month.

Staff wellbeing seen as critical. 'If staff are happy and healthy, they pass that on to the students,' says head. The first school we've talked to that told us it's menopause friendly; also gives free flu jabs, plus the personal training. Recognises that mental health has been a particular issue for some since Covid and that anxiety can be an issue especially at exam time – support available via teachers, heads of house (which exist instead of heads of year) and a counsellor. PSHE classes described by boys as 'insightful'. Bullying rare.

Comms leave a lot to be desired, say some parents. 'I wonder if there were complaints that there weren't enough as we have been bombarded – too much and from all directions. Even the WhatsApp groups explode with what's happening on a daily basis, which is quite annoying. I really feel they need someone to streamline it,' said one parent.

Pupils and parents: Around half of pupils are Asian British, the other half white British or from elsewhere in Europe. Socio-economically diverse. Day pupils travel up to around 15 miles – majority from Reading and Wokingham. 'Most boys travel in by bus or train and the journey is under an hour,' says head. Boarders' families tend to live in the M4 corridor within a couple of hours' drive, though school is considering branching out internationally, eg Hong Kong. Parents a pretty vocal lot. Active PA.

The last word: One of the leading state schools in the country academically but that's only part of the picture, with personal development taken every bit as seriously. 'They are not churning out academic robots but really well rounded young men,' said a parent. A school that gives erudite boys wings to fly.

Richard Huish College

18

South Road, Taunton, Somerset TA1 3DZ

01823 320 800 | enquiries@richuish.ac.uk | www.huish.ac.uk

Ages: 16–18

Pupils: 1,985; **Boarders:** 47 full, 7 weekly/flexi

Fees: Boarding £11,000 pa (EU or UK); £18,300 pa (international)

Principal: Since September 2020, Emma Fielding, previously deputy principal for two years. Before that, assistant principal at Exeter College, following a stint as head of school at Varndean College. Read contemporary history at Sussex, where she also gained an MA in Russian and East European studies.

Entrance: Requires five GCSEs at grade 4 or above including maths and English language. Offers a 12-month GCSE resit programme – around 60-65 students are currently on this.

Prospective students can join taster sessions and days. Students can choose a combination of A levels and BTECs and there is a two-week period at the beginning of term when changes can be made. Good parent feedback on this. 'Starting at college is always daunting, however RHC made it a controllable process, offering flexibility, points of contact for concerns with a sensible amount of time allowed for it. Plus I feel it was the start of a process where students took responsibility for their future and started to stand on their own feet by seeking answers to any concerns.'

Exit: Around 75 per cent go on to university, with a third gaining Russell Group places. The most consistently popular subjects are psychology and law, with nursing, sport, history and English always in the top 10. Usually double figures heading off to Oxbridge; ditto for medicine. Odd ones overseas.

Latest results: In 2021, 36 per cent A*/A at A level (65 per cent A*-B). In 2019 (the last year when exams took place), 23 per cent A*/A at A level (52 per cent A*-B).

Teaching and learning: One of the best sixth form colleges in England, in the top 10 for A level results for the last eight years. Consistently good results at BTEC too. RHC is a Beacon college designated 'outstanding' by Ofsted.

Over 35 subjects offered at A level. As well as traditional subjects, options include archaeology, critical thinking, environmental studies, early modern history, law and philosophy. Plus BTECs in applied science, business, media, health and social care, popular music, music production, public services, sport and digital, IT and computing. Applied science extended diploma (equivalent to three A levels) and drama and theatre extended certificate also now available. Most popular courses are psychology, biology and maths. Best value-added results are in science and maths. Statistics recently revealed by the A Level Performance System (ALPS) show that Huish ranks in the top 100 out of 1,164 for the value it adds to students. Value added is measured by comparing students' predicted achievement based on their GCSE results with their actual achievement at A level.

This is a college for the students. The website makes this clear: student case studies and videos, student quotes and stories; it is aimed at students, not parents

Students follow a study programme of three core A Levels, an extended diploma, or a combination of A levels and subsidiary diploma. Any combination is possible.

Learning support and SEN: As long as students achieve the grades for entry, all are accepted. Fully wheelchair accessible. If needed, specialist one-to-one study support, specialist equipment and software, support during exams and links to external specialists can be provided. One student with sensory integration dysfunction commented, 'All my exam scribes have been excellent.' Another with visual impairment said, 'I am thoroughly enjoying it, all the subjects have been able to adapt resources and I feel that I am keeping pace with the class.'

The arts and extracurricular: Along with sport, music is hugely popular. There are concerts and gigs including performances from the choirs, orchestra, jazz bands, big bands and ensembles. To date there are 35 pop bands, and they all do gigs. Teachers regularly set up tours in local pubs and venues; this is a big hit with the budding musicians, their friends, and of course the parents and teachers. Annually the college hires a venue for two nights to showcase their greatest hits. RHC even has links with the organisers of the John Peel stage at Glastonbury, giving bands the chance to perform, and media students the chance to work with the BBC crew. The standards here are very high, and just this year two guitarists were accepted at the Royal Northern College of Music – a highly competitive university where only musicians who have passed grade 8 music exams are considered. Another success story is the student who wrote and conducted his own rock opera featuring a full orchestra, choir and soloists.

The drama department puts on three big productions a year. When we were there, we saw Sweeney Todd in rehearsal in both the dance and drama studios. There must have been at least 50 students involved in just that one part.

The art department is split into three large studios. Wide range of creative media including painting, drawing (weekly life-drawing classes), mixed media, installation, print making, 3D, textile arts and contextual studies. Plus facilities for dyeing and constructed textiles, a dedicated print room, a large-scale printing press, a studio and a dark room. For Apple Mac enthusiasts, top software is available in the media and film studies departments. Recently students have produced a film called Hitting the Road, aimed at giving bikers practical advice to stay safe. Somerset Road Safety has commissioned it.

Enrichment activities take place during the school day as most students are restricted by bus timetables. For this reason, the college day finishes at 4.35pm. Subject enrichment activities include politics, debating and public speaking. There's Active Huish for sports, a wide range of musical activities, the DofE, BELA, and drama and dance productions. Plus trips – volunteering in Sri Lanka, trips to Iceland, skiing and snowboarding in France and archaeology trips to Rome.

Sport: Sport is huge here. Participation is nearly double the national average of other colleges, and many compete at a national level in a whole range of sports. Academies for cricket, tennis, football, golf and recently rugby union. One student recently chose to come to the college solely because of the excellent reputation of the cricket academy, even though it meant a daily three-hour commute. Hockey men's and women's first teams

No regular bins on campus: after rigorous campaigning, they have all been replaced by more eco-friendly recycling bins

are reigning South West League Champions. There are regular fixtures for first, second and third teams for most sports so all abilities can get involved. And the Active Huish scheme, part of enrichment activities, encourages students to take part less competitively in sports like ultimate frisbee and dodgeball.

New two-storey state-of-the-art sports hall, including a full-size multi-sports arena, a viewing gallery, changing rooms, a gym and a classroom, next to the sports fields. Most sports activities take place on campus, but some facilities are used at Taunton Vale Sports Club, the Wyvern Sports Club and Kings College.

Boarding: Oak House, a 53-bed boarding house, opened in 2017 to house international students (who have the alternative of staying with local families), plus some flexi boarding for home students.

Ethos and heritage: Originally founded as a grammar school for boys in the 18th century as the result of an endowment by Richard Huish (died 1615). It became a sixth form college in 1993 and since then has grown from 660 full-time students to nearly 2,000. It has expanded again to include Huish Business School for adults (adult students make up less than five per cent of the college's full-time equivalent students), International Huish, and even a driving school.

The 20-acre campus, in the south of Taunton, is predominantly sports fields. The college itself is alleged to be on the site of an old arboretum and each building has been named after a tree. Most buildings are new and have been designed with the same footprint. Each department has its own study centre, which is more informal than the learning centre (library); students can work in groups or chat while working. Learning resource centre is at the heart of the campus. There are two silent zones, PCs, and a careers area with two staff on hand. Over the last few years, there has been an impressive programme of improvement and new building. The Juniper building with its state-of-the-art editing suites, is a purpose-built centre for a range of media studies. The newish Cedar building accommodates a range of teaching in 10 classrooms, and all laboratory facilities have been upgraded. The new Maple building houses an art studio and graphic design Mac suites as well as state-of-the-art computing and computer science teaching rooms. Most recently, the Aspen music centre opened to include two recording studios, two soundproof live rooms for recording, a Mac suite, editing/production suite, plus classrooms and practice rooms. Finally, there is the new two-storey café, complete with Costa restaurant.

RHC has long been Wifi enabled. A remote desktop service is available as well as a free laptop loan system. Simply scan the lockers with an ID card, take a laptop, return when finished. No printers on campus; all have been replaced by multi-function devices: more convenient, greener and cheaper. Students can log on to any device and print their work. No regular bins on campus either: after rigorous campaigning by the environmental group, they have all been replaced by more eco-friendly recycling bins.

Former pupils include science fiction writer and inventor Arthur C Clarke, a former pupil of Huish's Grammar School; Andrew Castle, former British number one tennis player and television presenter; William Gibson, professor of history; Rebecca Huxtable, former co-presenter on Radio 1; Keith Parsons, cricketer; and Andy Robinson, former head coach of the England national rugby union team.

Pastoral care, inclusivity and discipline: There are three clear and simple expectations of students at Huish: be on time, do the work given (if you can't, ask for help), and be nice. No strict policies or statutory rules – one of the differences between a sixth form college and a school. One family told us, 'We did consider other colleges, but chose Richard Huish mainly due to the respect the teachers gave the young people and how they treated them as adults.' They went on to say, 'At this stage parents obviously need to be involved/kept in touch but I found that trusting [my son] and his teachers to work together as a team resolved most issues.'

Students have their own tutor and all tutorials are one-to-one. There are group tutorials initially when the term starts, but these are the exception. Tutors assess students individually and set out plans based on individual needs. For example, a tutor may decide to see one pupil weekly and another less frequently. Students are encouraged to speak to their tutors and ask questions whenever needed. They are also made aware, through tutorials and signposting throughout the college, of the help and counselling on offer.

Parents praised 'the support and caring nature of the staff at the college'. One parent whose child had had some difficulties said the 'tutor is amazing and has been a real rock for our [child] through a very difficult time, going over and above to [help].' Another family told us that when their child had to extend their studies due to unforeseen medical issues, the college was more than accommodating and supportive. The college provides 'fantastic out of lesson support,' they said.

Pupils and parents: This is a college for the students. The website makes this clear: student case studies and videos, student quotes and stories; it is aimed at students, not parents. Of course parents are involved, but it is obvious they are not the main customer. Parents are happy with this approach. 'Communication has been fantastic and staff are very approachable,' said one. Another confirmed, saying, 'Newsletters kept coming, informing us of the college's activities, and termly reports were very informative, covering the areas which parents like to know: attendance and level of work quality. Contact details were available if we needed to contact the college and when we used them we had prompt, honest responses.'

The students we saw looked presentable and happy. Green hair after Halloween is standard. There's bound to be a real mix of people here due to high volumes, and individuality is encouraged. The college isn't producing clones as some schools tend to do; they are encouraging the students to develop with confidence, and providing them with the best tools and environment to do so. One parent explained, 'He had loads of potential, but was headstrong. We hoped RHC would channel all that enthusiasm in a positive way and help him to mature and fulfil his potential; they did exactly that. I feel this was achieved by working with him almost as mentors, not teachers, and by treating him as an adult. I think if he had stayed at a school sixth form he would still have felt like a schoolboy, not a young adult.' Another parent gave a similar view, 'He has benefited more than he would at a school sixth form. We can see he has become more independent and self-driven and studies hard to a high standard, which has all been encouraged by the college.' Students come from all over Somerset, and some from as far as Devon and Dorset.

Money matters: RHC can help with travel costs, and college discretionary bursaries are available. Eligibility depends on household income or benefits received. There is also a Care to Learn scheme to help young parents, and a 19+ means-tested bursary. The Heathcoat Trust Bursary is for students from the partner schools of Uffculme, Cullompton and Tiverton High Schools who apply to university; it is worth £3,000 over three years.

The last word: The results are impressive year on year. The facilities are enough to make any teenager (or young adult) want to learn. The opportunities are endless due to economies of scale. College life here is far more exciting than at many a school sixth form, and the adult approach to learning is a positive step towards university and work. Some parents may find it hard to take that leap of faith, but from everything we saw and heard, we think it's worth it.

Ripon Grammar School

19

Clotherholme Road, Ripon, North Yorkshire HG4 2DG

01765 602647 | admin@ripongrammar.co.uk | www.ripongrammar.co.uk

Ages: 11–18

Pupils: 928; sixth form: 365; Boarders: 94 full/weekly

Fees: Day free; Boarding £11,719 – £13,601 pa

Headmaster: Since 2017, Jonathan Webb MA, previously deputy head at Durham School for five years. Educated at Batley Grammar School and has a history degree from Cambridge. Taught history at Pocklington School (where he was director of teaching and learning and head of history), the Manchester Grammar School and Giggleswick.

Last time we met this razor-sharp, amiable head he was busy upping the ante on sports and the arts, as well as developing young people as leaders. With the strong academics already a given, he felt it was this more holistic ethos where input was most needed. Having now (and parents concur) achieved that, his current areas of focus include improving post-Covid social interactions ('social life has frayed so we need to get students back on track'), the school estate (so far a new and improved front of school, including head's office no longer hidden away) and extending boarding to include 10 more places (now 110 total).

'I really like the head because he's real, not unknowable,' said a parent, with others telling us he's 'not intimidating but has an air of authority' and 'knows the pupils'. One told her how son was 'delighted when he got a head's award'. Another was pleased that 'he is very keen on parent/teacher school engagement, which impressed me because not all schools are, especially at secondary level.' Quite.

He is proud that the school continues to work well with the local authority (North Yorkshire) and resists academisation. This is a community school which is happy with its current size and, at present, has no ambition to grow significantly.

He and his wife Helen live near Ripon and they have two sons. In his spare time he enjoys cricket, walking and gardening.

Entrance: Heavily oversubscribed at 11+, with around 260 (360 in the year we last reviewed them) applications for 117 places. Selection is by local authority verbal and non-verbal reasoning tests; school takes top 28 per cent of cohort, which is wider than in other selective areas. Pupils mainly come from local primaries (all of which the head has visited) and a smattering from prep schools, about 50 schools in total. Another 13 places at 13+.

Demand for boarding places (14 in year 7 and an additional four at year 9 and about 16 at year 12) is growing, from North Yorkshire, the rest of the UK and beyond, especially post-GCSE, with lots of interest in girls' boarding. Boarders have to demonstrate suitability to board – requires a form for year 7 entry, and an interview thereafter.

The sixth form has around 100 external applicants for some 45 places – applicants need six 6s at GCSE but the vast majority comfortably exceed this, achieving mainly 9-7s.

Exit: At least 85 per cent stay on for the sixth form. Over 60 per cent to Russell Group universities, with a strong Oxbridge record (five in 2021); ditto for medics (nine in 2021). The most popular destinations are Newcastle, Durham, Edinburgh, Birmingham, Warwick, Nottingham, Sheffield, Bangor, Manchester, Liverpool, Leeds, York, Exeter, Cardiff, Sheffield, Bristol, Hull, UCL, LSE and Surrey. Four overseas in 2021 – two full scholarships to Princeton and Grand Canyon and one to Malta and Belarus. Excellent careers advice has led to leading apprenticeships for those considering alternatives to university.

Latest results: In 2021, 72 per cent 9-7 at GCSE; 60 per cent A*/A at A level (81 per cent A*-B). In 2019 (the last year when exams took place), 61 per cent 9-7 at GCSE; 48 per cent A*/A at A level (76 per cent A*-B).

Teaching and learning: Exam results are consistently very good, 'but it's not push, push, push,' insisted a parent. 'I wouldn't like it if there was too much pressure and there isn't,' agreed another. Teaching described as 'exemplary' – 'They are able to bring quite dry subjects to life.' Teachers also known for being supportive – 'They are happy to give up lunchtimes or after school for one-to-ones,' we heard. Good on value added, including for those (few) students in the middle ability – school is in the top two per cent nationally for this measure. Disadvantaged students (again only a few) progress at least as well as others.

There is an air of purposefulness – a quiet hum from classrooms and sensible movement between lessons. Students wear their leadership and rewards badges with obvious pride

Setting in maths from year 8. French taught from year 7, with choice of German or Spanish added in year 8 and at least one taken at GCSE (French most popular, followed by Spanish, then German). The curriculum is ambitious even for a selective school with everyone taking between 10 and 12 GCSEs including further maths for the top two sets. Most students get their first choice of subjects, which include astronomy, classical civilisation and most recently PE, with Latin and ancient Greek offered off timetable. History and geography are the most popular non-core subjects, with results particularly dazzling in maths and chemistry.

STEM subjects are extremely strong at A level too – roughly equal numbers of girls and boys take chemistry and maths, while in physics the proportion of girls taking the subject continues to grow. Results in art are exceptional. Politics recently added as an A level option. Most take three in total (a few do four especially if they're doing further maths), as well as a compulsory enrichment programme called Plus One which includes EPQ, IT and study skills, volunteering, leadership and community engagement (anything from reading with SEN students to gardening to working in local care homes). Enrichment by no means confined to sixth form, with off-timetable cross-curricular themed challenge days for years 7-9 providing opportunities for leadership, teamwork and problem-solving, working with external advisers. This lays the groundwork for later success in Young Enterprise and Prince's Trust competitions, and there is well-regarded work experience in year 10s and 12.

School admits it took a while to find its feet in the first lockdown – hardly unusual – eventually deciding on a blend of 50 per cent live lessons and 50 per cent set work, along with regular tutor groups. 'Considerably better than other local state schools,' reckoned a parent.

Learning support and SEN: Very good SEN support includes provision for visual and hearing impairment alongside a range of needs including ASD. The learning resource manager works with the SENCo on intervention strategies. Paired reading with sixth formers during assembly time is set up for those identified by online literacy assessments. The sixth form students told us they value the skills this helps them to develop as well as the help it provides. The school is well equipped for students with physical disabilities and sensitive timetabling ensures all are able to access specialist facilities when needed. Two of three EHCPs at any one time.

The arts and extracurricular: There are some phenomenally talented students when it comes to music. 'Some of the kids from Hong Kong are extraordinary on the piano,' we heard. But the music department – which is headed by a newish multi-instrumentalist – isn't only interested in the brightest stars, with one parent telling us, 'One thing our son isn't into is singing but they encouraged him to sing in a concert.' Indeed, choral music is a specialism, with four choirs having just sung Abide with Me at the Remembrance service on the day of our last review. There is live music in every Friday assembly and everyone loves the annual house music competition. Great facilities for teaching, practice and recording, while boards list an array of musical opportunities from junior strings and guitar to the chamber orchestra and five choirs which perform regularly in Ripon Cathedral and further afield, including foreign tours. They have recorded a CD of Christmas music. Several students have gone on to win choral and music scholarships at prestigious universities including the first girl to win Durham University's cathedral choral scholarship. More than 100 students have instrumental lessons in school and all year 7s do grade 1 music theory.

Drama sadly not on curriculum, but productions range from a whole-school musical every other year – they squeezed Little Shop of Horrors in before lockdown – to separate junior and senior productions. As with music, the house drama is a big deal. The hall doubles up as the dining room and is relatively small for a school of this size but there is a drama studio in the sixth form centre.

Art results do extremely well and a tour of the school reveals some thought-provoking work not only in the department itself, but in the head's office and throughout the school corridors. Students have exhibited and sold work in local galleries and a number have won prestigious awards such as the Royal Society of British Artists Young Artist award.

STEM subjects are extremely strong at A level too – roughly equal numbers of girls and boys take chemistry and maths

With over 90 different clubs and activities on offer, ranging from the Greenpower electric car and Pageturner book club to philosophy, there's something for even the most reluctant to get involved in. With the strong emphasis on developing leadership, students are encouraged to take the initiative to set up and run activities and clubs which include politics, history and feminist societies. Eco society has recently taken off – pupils recently planted 250 trees and successfully applied for a large grant to plant hedgerows. Debating a bit of a missed opportunity, we felt. The annual charity week is run by the sixth form and encompasses a range of fundraising activities for the school's chosen charities such as the local hospice. Plus, there's DofE (bronze and gold), biennial World Challenge, trips to Iceland, Sorrento, Sri Lanka and India, the Normandy battlefields, Berlin, Auschwitz, Edinburgh and the annual French exchange, as well as the more local curriculum enriching visits.

Sport: 'One of the reasons we chose the school,' said a parent (not the only one). Rugby dominates for boys, hockey for girls – school does well in both, including against independent schools, having recently played Ampleforth and Durham School, among others. Area and regional successes not unusual. Some individual successes too, recently in cross-country. Cricket, football and lacrosse also popular, and there are mixed hockey, badminton, rock climbing, dance and swimming in the impressive 25m indoor swimming pool. PE and games get a lot of airtime here – an impressive three hours on timetable up to sixth form. Onsite facilities are excellent, including an Astro, five badminton court sports hall with climbing wall paid for by a fundraising campaign, available for local use too. Everyone raves about the new 3G pitch and there's also a drained, levelled and seeded first XV rugby pitch, as well as six all-weather tennis courts.

Boarding: 'If you don't live in catchment, boarding is the only option,' summed up a parent – one of many who wanted to bag a place no matter what. Not that the pupils need persuading – 'He absolutely loves it and can't get back there quick enough; sometimes we have to take him back on a Sunday night to give him extra time,' said a parent who – like the majority – use weekly boarding. Number of termly boarders is increasing and now constitutes a quarter of the smallish boarding community. No flexi – 'being a grammar, that could be open to abuse,' says head.

Boarders come from mainly from North Yorkshire and beyond (increasingly into Leeds), with a small minority from India, Africa, Caribbean, Nigeria and Hong Kong – all need a UK passport. Numbers recently increased to 110 boarding places (55 for boys; 55 for girls), split across two houses. School House for boys in the main school building has rooms of two to four for years 7 -11 and single rooms for the sixth form, all with shared bathrooms. It's bright and well maintained with plenty of social spaces although as a Victorian building it is prone to being draughty and needs TLC in places. The boys eat in the school dining room. The girls, in the much newer and purpose-built Johnson House, have their own new catering facilities and garden, in four-bed rooms plus singles for the sixth form. They too share bathrooms, which are bright and modern with good levels of privacy.

Boarders have a personal tutor and are in mixed-age tutor groups. As majority of boarding staff are teachers, 'boarders are very well known as individuals'

Boarders have a personal tutor and are in mixed-age tutor groups. As majority of boarding staff are teachers, 'boarders are very well known as individuals'. 'The boarding staff are so warm and caring – we've been bowled over by the whole experience,' said one parent. The boarders are well integrated too – not seen as outsiders – although those who join the sixth form tend to find their friendship groups within the boarders. Days are well structured, with plenty of activities – everything from craft based to sport. 'We need more day trips at the weekends, though,' admits school – watch this space. One parent also felt they need to be more upfront about what students are expected to do for themselves – 'It came as a shock to us that sixth formers don't get any of their laundry done and we would have prepared for that although to be fair they have taken time to teach him.'

Ethos and heritage: The school has a very long history; there has been a grammar school in Ripon since Anglo-Saxon times. Originally housed in the city centre under a foundation granted by Queen Mary in 1555, RGS moved to its present green and pleasant 23-acre site in 1874 – the land was a gift from the marquis of Ripon. The original Victorian buildings were added to over the years, not always sympathetically. More recent builds, including the sports hall, sixth form centre, mathematics and engineering block, music facilities, observatory, girls' boarding house and a humanities and modern languages block bring more gravitas to the school façade.

There is an air of purposefulness – a quiet hum from classrooms and sensible movement between lessons. Uniform is smart throughout and is also worn by sixth formers (with different tie) but they don't seem to mind. Students wear their leadership and rewards badges with obvious pride. Food could be better, but could be a lot worse too. Houses compete in sport, rock climbing, debating, MasterChef, University Challenge, drama and music.

Former pupils include fashion designer Bruce Oldfield, rugby international Peter Squires, William Hague MP, David Curry MP, Guardian editor Katharine Viner, TV presenter Richard Hammond and Olympic gold medallist diver Jack Laugher.

Pastoral care, inclusivity and discipline: The pastoral support officer has recently gone full time and the school has appointed a counsellor for three days a week who also supports teachers in relevant techniques. Teams of form tutors ably support heads of schools. Pupils speak of good relations with staff and they look after each other too; newcomers are 'buddied' with existing pupils to ease integration. One student who had moved from a local comprehensive at 13 spoke extremely positively about his integration – 'It's cool to be geeky here, people are really pleased for you when you achieve well.' The students we met were keen to explain how supportive the staff were of their development, their mental health and careers rather than simply pushing them through examinations. School says it's on particularly high mental health alert since lockdown, with more targeted provision than perhaps it had in the past, as well as ensuring pupils know where to go for help. 'We want to avoid presentation overload, although of course presentations are important too.'

As with many schools where it's cool to be clever, disruption to lessons is rare. Poor behaviour in other aspects is also uncommon and, at worst, usually sorted by after-school detention, though the odd fixed-term exclusion is necessary for eg social media misdemeanours. 'Very good on online training for parents – what to look out for, how to monitor your child's online activity etc,' said a parent. Strong protestations from both girls and boys on question of true equality and diversity: 'not an issue here,' they say, while issues of peer-on-peer harassment and abuse are explored in PHSE.

Sixth formers have significant leadership responsibilities in publicity, community relations and pastoral care as well as the usual head boy and head girl. They are trained to be peer listeners with younger students and they themselves feel well supported in their transition into the sixth form and on to university.

One parent (initially sceptical that RGS could do more than provide good results) was clear that the school's historic reputation as simply an examination machine was far from the reality: the holistic approach is at the core of the school. Another, with five boys of varying abilities and enthusiasm, felt all had been catered for and known as individuals and had consequently flourished. A third valued the clear structure that boarding gave to her daughter as well as the good communication, development of personal skills and very strong integration for new students.

Pupils and parents: A local school – most day pupils come from Ripon and its outlying villages. Even many of the boarders are from only just outside the catchment area although numbers from further afield are on the rise. Wide range of parental backgrounds and wealth (or lack of it) though only a handful are eligible for free school meals. Parents feel well informed on their child's progress with regular reports three times a year and an annual parents' evening. School comms are praised by parents and there is a supportive PTA.

Pupils are warm, friendly, courteous, articulate, confident and insightful, with a real pride in their school. Lots of heads up, eye contact and smiles as you walk around. This is a can do, will do school – pupils talk of friendly rivalry, pushing each to achieve.

Money matters: Yorkshire's only state boarding school, it is free for day pupils. There is a charge for boarding, but this is still about a third the price of independent alternatives.

The last word: A high-achieving school that is not overly pressurised and where learning and life skills opportunities are increasingly valued. Blending tradition, academic rigour and high expectations with innovation, up-to-date technology and opportunities for development, it is no wonder that parents have complete confidence in the school getting the best out of their child. Very community driven too.

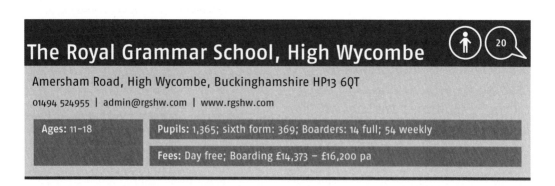

The Royal Grammar School, High Wycombe

20

Amersham Road, High Wycombe, Buckinghamshire HP13 6QT

01494 524955 | admin@rgshw.com | www.rgshw.com

Ages: 11–18

Pupils: 1,365; sixth form: 369; Boarders: 14 full; 54 weekly

Fees: Day free; Boarding £14,373 – £16,200 pa

Headmaster: Since 2015, Philip Wayne, previously head of Chesham Grammar. He studied at Manchester University and the Royal Northern College of Music. Following a number of years as a freelance organist, pianist, conductor and lecturer, he qualified as a teacher and held several leadership posts in the Midlands. He moved to Buckinghamshire in 2004 as deputy head of John Hampden Grammar and became head of Chesham Grammar School in 2007.

Pragmatic and plain-spoken, he's widely considered to be exactly the breath of fresh air the school needed. 'He had his work cut out as the school had been resting on its laurels, but he's risen to the challenge, bringing renewed energy and direction,' said a parent, while others report that 'he's very much in touch with the pupils' and 'has his finger firmly on the pulse'. Pupils describe him as 'approachable' and 'inspirational' and like that he turns up to so many events and sports fixtures; he also runs student conferences and sees every boy on his 12th birthday. Has humility (quicker to praise the boys and staff than himself) and while all heads speak about their school with pride, his loyalty seems particularly heartfelt: 'I didn't enjoy my own secondary schooling,' he admits. 'In fact it was only when I got to university, I realised what a phenomenal education everyone else had had. But if I'd come to a secondary school like this, with its academic and sporting focus, I'd have absolutely loved it.' Big on the independent school mindset, but devoted to the state sector.

Lives in a nearby Buckinghamshire village with his wife and teenage twins (son at the school). Passionate musician and loves watching sport, family life and cooking.

Entrance: Places highly sought after, with selection subject to success at the (new, more rigorous) 11+ exam and Buckinghamshire criteria, including the ever-moveable feast of catchment. School has its own testing process after 11+, with a waiting list of around 80. Little movement out of the school these days, but they do expand in years 8, 10 and for the sixth form. Around 40 places for the latter, about 10 in the boarding house, with around 60 applications – you need eight Bs or above (Or numerical equivalent) and As in certain subjects to be studied at A level.

Worth considering boarding at 11 if a day place looks unlikely and candidate has a high 11+ score. Forces families and boys in care are prioritised and these are mixed with some overseas pupils (although they must have a British/EU passport) and locals keen for the boarding experience.

Think twice if you have to tutor your son to death to get him in. 'It's not a school for scraping by,' say pupils.

Exit: Over 90 per cent stay on to sixth form. Majority straight into top universities – Durham, Exeter, Birmingham, Leeds are popular, as are music colleges. Between 15 and 20 into Oxbridge most years. Good university advisory provision in place, with specialist support for those hoping for entry to international universities. 'I've got three tutors helping me with my Cambridge application and I can't believe how much time they're giving up,' one pupil told us.

Latest results: School is not publishing 2021 results. In 2019, 71 per cent 9-7 at GCSE; 48 per cent A*/A at A level (73 per cent A*-B).

Teaching and learning: Consistently delivers a good showing in national league tables for academics and although hasn't quite caught up with the area's top performing grammar for GCSE results, they are only a whisker behind at A level. Value added on the up. Currently phasing out IGCSEs, 'which have not been compatible with league tables.'

Good university advisory provision. 'I've got three tutors helping me with my Cambridge application and I can't believe how much time they're giving up,' one pupil told us

Majority take 10 GCSEs, with modern languages, history and geography among the most popular and top performing subjects. Wide-ranging but traditional curriculum, including computing (stunning results), classical civilisation and Latin, with school making no apology for not offering the likes of economics and business studies. 'We offer a good solid curriculum that doesn't close doors unwittingly to the best universities,' says head. A language (French, German or Spanish) is compulsory and there is large take up of all three at both GCSE and A level, with Mandarin, Italian and Japanese available 'on tap.' Music thriving, with a one-year course for those that don't want it to take up an option space.

All boys expected to start with four A levels – 'partly for breadth, partly to minimise impact of unwise choices,' but school is open to boys dropping one if it all gets too much. Sciences (physics Pre-U and A level), maths, further maths and economics all popular and do very well. Classics, Latin and modern languages also strong. Good take up of EPQ.

Six classes of 32 in each year group, with setting in maths, English and languages from year 9, when boys are taught in groups of around 25 for most subjects. In years 7-9, boys are offered a carousel of music, art, drama, cookery (not food tech – boys made pizzas rather than design them), DT, computing in smaller groups. School 'goes in heavy with homework from the word go', according to parents, with at least three 30-minute pieces per night (all set online), but boys seem to take this in their stride – as they do the rigorous tests they take in every topic. 'School is excellent at monitoring progressing and acting on it,' said one parent. No coasting here. Boys use a range of technologies including iPads and the VLE is well-used.

Teachers' passion for their subjects is evident as you walk round the school; noticeable lack of bellowing, with positive staff/pupil relationships – 'you really feel they want the best for you,' said one boy. Some pupils would like email contact, 'but most teachers make themselves available at lunchtimes – they definitely go the extra mile,' said one. That said, a few boys with heavy extracurricular programmes (eg rugby takes up three lunchtimes a week) said they find it harder to track down extra teacher support. Some parents alluded to a few substandard teachers 'and you do wonder why they are still there, but on the whole, the teaching is phenomenal.' Some parents told us they tutor their boys outside school, but school insists this isn't necessary. Lots of practicals in science – 'I haven't had a chemistry lesson without a practical this term,' one year 9 boy told us. Good staff retention; CDP exceptional; and most teachers visit other schools 'to get new ideas'; and in keeping with the independent school ethos, they are encouraged to get involved in sport and/or school trips.

Learning support and SEN: SEN at the milder end, with strong learning support department, which helps boys in and outside the classroom. 'It's all very discreet,' says the head – 'No waving inclusion banners here – we just get on with offering what help is needed.' School is also adapted for wheelchair use – 'also handy for the grandmas who want to come to the concerts,' says school.

The arts and extracurricular: Thursday afternoon activities (TAA) allow boys to choose from a vast array of sporting or academic enrichment activities ranging from Japanese or Mandarin to social services. This is in addition to after-school activities and indulges boys' passions for more marginal activities like climbing (the school boasts an impressive 40ft climbing wall in main sports hall) and astronomy or endeavours like the Caterham Project which sees year 13s building a car from scratch. D of E and CCF also extremely popular from year 10, with 200 boys taking part in the latter. Boys enthuse about extracurricular at every given opportunity, listing everything from Model UN and debating to Dr Who club and RGS Has Talent. 'Not expected, but encouraged – and, really, you'd be mad not to,' said one pupil.

Music 'really, really strong', according to parents, with the charismatic director of music running a large number of ensembles including symphony orchestra, massed choir, wind, string and jazz bands, close harmony group. Biannual shows such as Les Mis and My Fair Lady (which has got two million hits on YouTube), both in conjunction with local girls' school. Most orchestral instrument lessons on offer (around a quarter of boys learn one or more instrument), plus singing, guitar, piano and organ, with top professionals including BBC big band leader and West End singer forming part of the peripatetic team. Plenty of opportunities to get involved for non-performers too, with the school's stage lighting and sound team proving hugely popular.

Art improving, thanks to new leadership, with students creating everything from fine art to 3D work and decent take-up at GCSE, plus collaboration with Wycombe Museum.

Rugby, rugby and more rugby: over 400 boys regularly involved and playing top independent schools, as well as local fixtures. 'It's important to have a USP,' believes head

Trips, tours and exchanges galore. World Challenge scheme starts in year 7 then branches out globally higher up the school, with destinations in recent years including China, Vietnam and Belize.

Sport: Rugby, rugby and more rugby, with over 400 boys regularly involved and playing top independent schools, as well as local fixtures. 'It's important to have a USP,' believes head. But this is by no means a rugger-bugger school, with 14 other competitive sports, and many more non-competitive ones, on offer. Hockey has taken off considerably since the installation of a new floodlit, all-weather pitch; cricket involves regular fixtures, with boys playing in prestigious festivals; rowing (they use facilities in Marlow) is popular, with around 50 boys performing well in regattas; plus Eton fives, squash, tennis (burgeoning), table tennis, karate all offered. Some pupils and parents grumble other sports don't get the same quality fixtures or kudos as the rugby teams, and boys in these other sports should certainly not expect the same hero-worship in the playground. That said, there are sighs of relief from some non-rugby parents as it's a 'major commitment' with training five times a week and fixtures most weekends in season. 'Still no football and that won't change,' says head (to the inevitable disappointment of some boys). And if you're not sporty? 'That's ok-ish,' was the response from parents and pupils.

Boarding: Boarding offers great value for money, with full boarding costing less than most day school fees. Some 70 boarders (full boarding only from year 10, with the odd exception in year 9 – weekly up until then) reside in the bright, modern boarding house (1999), located in the heart of the school campus. Boarders say 'it's very relaxed and homely' and the boarding house has an upbeat vibe, partly dictated by the energetic and approachable head of boarding. 'If you miss home, they are onto it immediately,' one boy told us. Each academic subject has a pupil champion that younger boys can approach if they need guidance with any part of their studies and the pupil food and boarding council electorate voices collective opinions about how the boarding house is run.

Younger boys are housed in spacious four-man dorms, decorated with personal effects to varying degrees. Years 12 and 13 are in cabin-like single rooms with en-suite shower rooms and the communal areas are peppered with boy toys like pool tables, table tennis and air hockey tables and flat screen TVs. No wonder most years are oversubscribed.

Boys return to the boarding house after school to get the blood sugar levels back up with a snack then participate in organised group activities on two or three afternoons a week. All meals are taken in the boarders' own canteen ('better food than in the main school', agree pupils) and prep takes place after supper from 7.30 to 9pm ('either doing supervised prep in the computer room, great for keeping on track, or doing prep in our room'), while the sixth-formers can manage their own study time.

The majority goes home at weekends, with around 20 – mainly international pupils – staying. The schedule at the weekend is 'pretty relaxed' and boys are allowed into town in groups of two or three. Half-termly big trips – paintballing, go-carting and Thorpe Park are annual highlights. Note you can't convert a boarding place to a day place until the end of year 11; and you must have a valid British or EU passport to be eligible for a boarding place.

Ethos and heritage: Founded in the 12th century and given a royal charter in 1562. Centred around an attractive red-brick Queen Anne style building, although someone in the 1960s thought it was a good idea (it wasn't) to obscure this from view with a new block that, as one pupil puts it, 'is unfortunate to look at, especially from the street, but with good practical space inside.' An interesting mix of ancient (the oldest classrooms recently had their 100th birthdays) and modern, including a bright, modern canteen, cookery suite and fitness suite with panoramic views of the beautifully kept sports fields. Outside, there's plenty of pitches and the fives courts have been refurbished; there's a new all-weather pitch; and the sports hall has a swimming pool with retractable roof which, despite its 40-year vintage, still knocks spots off many we've seen. Large airy library with plenty of space for quiet study and there are plans to build a new sixth form centre. Size of the vast music block gives away the school's collective passion for music, which includes a music technology centre. 'Not exactly your most up-to-date, modern school in terms of facilities – and some of it looks really tired,' said one parent (and boys say 'some of the toilets are disgusting'), but there is a rolling programme of refurbishment.

Overall vibe of the school is traditional, with a modern twist and 'the roundedness of public school,' as one parent puts it. The majority join from state primaries, however. A true camaraderie between year groups is immediately visible in the playground and boarding house and we found boys polite, fun and confident. 'Perhaps not as embracing of issues like gender fluidity and being gay as other schools, though,' said one parent; and one pupil told us, 'The fact that so many pupils excel here can feel like a double-edged sword – it can mean it's hard to get recognition when you do really well at something.'

Boarders say 'it's very relaxed and homely' and the boarding house has an upbeat vibe, partly dictated by the energetic and approachable head of boarding

A plethora of high profile alumni from the sporting, political and showbiz worlds England rugby players Matt Dawson, Nick Beal and Tom Rees; GB hockey captain and Olympian Jonathan Wyatt; professional golfer Luke Donald and, representing the artsy crowd, pop stars Howard Jones and the late Ian Dury and comedian Jimmy Carr. Many are very supportive of the school and visit.

Pastoral care, inclusivity and discipline: A positive culture of praise and heads of year meet weekly to make sure no pupil is missed if they're wilting under the pressure. Boys we spoke to were aware of mental health risk areas from self-harm to eating disorders, with mindfulness classes available (also to staff), plus chaplain and three part-time counsellors. Good induction routines for year 7s, followed by mentoring systems. Surprisingly new house system. Full care for boarders from matron, housemasters and tutors.

Generally a well-behaved bunch – largely complying with the zero-tolerance policy on drugs, drinking and smoking; those that don't are hauled before the head and face exclusion, as they are for insolence, fisticuffs and bullying (around 20 temporary exclusions in the last two years; less than a handful of permanent). New sanctions system, which includes a detailed list of unacceptable behaviours and their consequences, was surprisingly well received by pupils. 'It's now completely consistent whereas before some teachers were much stricter than others,' one explained. Parents informed even when pupils get a first warning, three of which mean a detention. Strict on uniform. 'Some older boys throw their weight around a bit, but the school does clamp down on bullying,' one pupil told us.

Pupils and parents: Boys come from leafy south Bucks villages and a range of suburbia on the way to High Wycombe. Fewer come from the town itself, but school has outreach programmes to address this. Ethnic mix changing rapidly and school is now about 30 per cent non-Caucasian (higher in lower years), reflecting the local community. Parents of boarders lean towards the middle classes, often professional dual income families, and internationals. About half a dozen girls join for specific lessons (Greek, classics) in year 13. Parents report excellent communications with school, but one unimpressed that 'you have to choose six teachers to see on parents' evening – at other schools, you get to see every teacher.'

Money matters: Proactive approach to state grants through the Condition Improvement Fund have enabled capital projects to take place. PA active and successful in fundraising. Parents are generous in their support of the 'annual fund' and the various 'friends of' groups (rugby, hockey, rowing, cricket and music). Old boys also generous donors.

The last word: Don't believe the hype pitching The Royal Grammar School as a hotbed of rugger boys. Yes, they play rugby to an exceptionally high level, but there are 14 other competitive sports, as well as outstanding music, drama and academics all wrapped up in a supportive, friendly package. Parents at other local grammars might consider it 'a bit God and country,' but the traditional values that have the school competing ably with its independent and state maintained neighbours – and thrashing many top public schools on the sports field – mean boys (and their parents) benefit from a private school ethos without the hefty price tag.

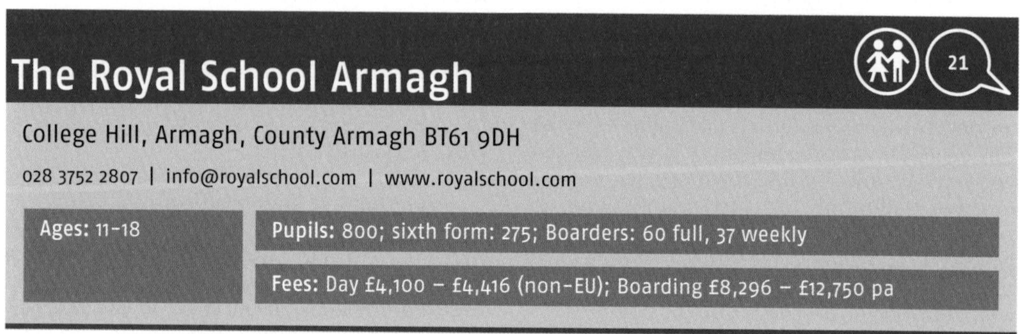

The Royal School Armagh
21
College Hill, Armagh, County Armagh BT61 9DH
028 3752 2807 | info@royalschool.com | www.royalschool.com
Ages: 11-18
Pupils: 800; sixth form: 275; Boarders: 60 full, 37 weekly
Fees: Day £4,100 – £4,416 (non-EU); Boarding £8,296 – £12,750 pa

Head: Since 2018, Graham Montgomery. Previously principal of Cookstown High School, a position he'd have gladly have remained in for years were it not for this role – which he considers the ultimate coup – coming up. Growing up just 10 miles away, he has long been in awe of the 'ethos, atmosphere, history and rapport between staff and students' which he experienced briefly for himself when he did some practice teaching as part of his PGCE (from Queen's Belfast, where he also has a degree in politics and modern history). When a job came up in the English department two decades ago, he wasted no time in getting his wife (now head of English) to go for it and they also sent their son here and later their daughter. Now it's his turn and he's tickled pink. Parents (a discerning lot) and pupils feel they're in safe hands and we can see why – there's something almost doctorly about his compassionate, competent and exacting manner.

'A love of my subject' drew him into teaching – 'I was completely inspired by my history teacher at secondary school and knew within days that I wanted to follow in his footsteps.' Joined Friends' School Lisburn as a resident boarding master and taught history as well as government and politics, becoming head of year and latterly head of sixth form and senior teacher with pastoral responsibilities. In 2012 he was appointed vice-principal pastoral and acting principal at Cookstown High School, becoming principal a year later. No longer teaches but if a spreadsheet is boring him to death, it's still a classroom he heads off to in order to re-energise and he's involved in pupil focus groups and meets senior prefects. Lives on site, with current affairs, church activities and watching school sport taking up any spare time.

Entrance: At 11+, 100 places up for grabs. At least 85 are snapped up by day pupils who are selected via Common Entrance Assessment (similar to the English 11+). They come from the school's own prep school (around six or seven a year) and 33 feeder primary schools across county Armagh. Oversubscribed, with around 1.5 applicants for every place.

For the 15 boarding places, applicants are interviewed and may be required to sit tests in maths and English. References also sought from current school. The process is purposefully holistic and includes probing questions, both academic and to ensure a genuine need to board, eg geographical or family situation. For students whose first language isn't English, there is a minimum requirement of IELTS level 4 or equivalent.

Sixth form applicants (including existing pupils) need 10 points at GCSE with at least 6s in subjects to be studied at A level.

Exit: About five per cent leave after GCSEs. Queen's University, Belfast (Russell Group) and the University of Ulster are inevitably popular, but increasingly to England (especially Exeter) and some to Scotland and Wales. Very broad range of subjects studied with law, engineering, education and medical related courses currently topping the bill. Three or four to art college most years and about one every other year to Oxbridge (one in 2021). Eight medics in 2021, plus three overseas – Lynn (USA), ESSEC Paris, and Amsterdam. Excellent careers guidance infused in the curriculum, with a quarter doing work experience, for which school can help with placements.

Latest results: In 2021, 79 per cent 9-7 at GCSE; 47 per cent A*/A at A level (77 per cent A*-B). In 2019 (the last year when exams took place), 71 per cent 9-7 at GCSE; 38 per cent A*/A at A level (71 per cent A*-B).

Teaching and learning: 'Good qualifications will get you the interview and good character will get you the job' is school's mantra and pupils are constantly reminded they go hand in hand. Patience is also a strong point, with teachers often taking significant chunks of time out to help a pupil who is slower at reaching a level of understanding than his or her classmates.

Everyone CAT tested on arrival at 11+ to understand current ability and potential for development, and teaching is based on the personalised learning programme. All students have their own online pupil dashboard, which includes their minimum attainment line and targets are set accordingly. Grades are issued every six weeks so problems can be spotted quickly and the gifted and talented can be stretched. The aim is 'to work smarter not harder', and pupils are taught how to learn and how to be organised. If someone is underachieving the school looks at the full picture including the home situation – perhaps they have nowhere to do their homework or don't know how to revise; they need parents to be on board. All are issued with a revision booklet including tips on diet and hydration.

Grades are issued every six weeks so problems can be spotted quickly and the gifted and talented can be stretched. The aim is 'to work smarter not harder'

Four classes of 25 per year – no setting ('ability is already narrow') with the possible exception of a slightly differentiated class of pupils who don't take a language at GCSE so they can concentrate on English or maths. French from year 8 (which is the English year 7), Spanish added in year 9 (which is the English year 8).

Offers 25 subjects at GCSE including business studies, sports studies, psychology, home economics, agriculture and music. ICT and technology both popular, as are history and geography. Pupils take anywhere between eight and 12, occasionally even 13. About 40 per cent take triple science. Language no longer compulsory. Foreign nationals can sit a GCSE in their native language, eg Cantonese, Irish, Finnish, Polish.

Three sixth form pathways available, dependent on number of GCSE points gained – three or four A levels, ditto for BTECs or a combination of both. Offers 25 A levels and will run any subject even for a handful of pupils (often happens with Spanish, French and music, for example). Vocational subjects like construction and health and social care are available alongside more traditional subjects. BTEC courses recently introduced in agriculture, engineering, travel and tourism.

Learning support and SEN: Head of SEN is supported by a team of classroom assistants including experts in dyslexia and ASD. Support mainly in the classroom via differentiated learning, breaking down barriers to learning, embedding coping mechanisms and extra support, eg preparing individual revision notes on spider diagrams or mind maps. 'We are not overly big on learning styles as it can create false tram tracks but we do pay attention to the child's particular disposition, for example if they learn more visually.' Teachers are well briefed on the child's ILP and work to specific targets. One-to-ones available (and suggested) if needed, as is input from outside agencies. Statemented children across most year groups, some of whom need their own classroom assistant. School works hard to get those with SEN into appropriate courses and jobs beyond school. A handful of pupils, all boarders, need EAL support and are progressed through IELTS – they are usually taken out of prep in the evenings.

The arts and extracurricular: All staff are involved in clubs and societies, with every pupil encouraged to do at least one a week (no problem there – school admits to struggling to fit them all in). Everything from chess to modern dance and from Scripture Union to debating (school does very well in the latter). The CCF was founded in 1916 and about 100 pupils take part in either the army or air force – the air force offers the opportunity to gain a pilot's licence. DofE massively popular, with 200 pupils engaged in bronze, silver or gold at any one time (40-50 complete gold every year).

Singing rules in the music department – this lot love nothing more than warming up their vocal cords for eg inter-school choral competitions. Huge take up for the range of choirs. Ensembles popular, along with school orchestra. About 20 per cent of pupils learn a musical instrument but school says this is misleading as many more do so outside school. The two musical highlights of the year are the carol service and the spring concert held in Armagh cathedral. 'They are top-notch events,' said a parent, 'and lift the hairs on the back of your neck.'

'Boarding improves the atmosphere of the school and gives it more of a family feel,' said a parent. Matrons take care of everything pastoral and housemasters and mistresses sort out the practical side

Another calendar highlight is the large school musical that takes place every other year – young thespians play to a packed house for four nights on the trot, and pupils can take part behind the scenes as well in technical lighting, costumes etc. Drama also offered through the junior drama club and as an A level – many join the school at sixth form specifically because they want to get involved in the drama, sport or charity (or all three!).

Art housed in two light, bright rooms and there is particular emphasis on drawing but also increasingly on ceramics, textiles, photography and multimedia. Rare is the year when at least some pupils aren't invited to exhibit their GCSE or A level work at Ulster Museum in Belfast, and some three or four head off to art college each year. Self-expression favoured over formulaic pieces – 'Often parents are drawn to a certain piece on display and I'm at a loss to explain what it means!' smiles head.

Numerous trips including business studies to New York, geographers to Iceland, skiing to Italy, languages trips to France and Spain and a CCF trip to Canada or Kwa Zulu Natal.

Sport: One compulsory two-hour sports session a week with the rest extracurricular. Two-term rugby and hockey school and 'rugby is almost a religion,' said a pupil, although another insisted that 'you don't feel excluded if it is not your thing'. Pupils regularly reminded not to pigeonhole themselves – means strapping rugby players are happy to eg sing in the choir – nobody feels it has to be one or t'other. Inclusive, with four senior rugby teams playing most Saturdays; ditto for hockey – 'It's about breadth.' An old boy has returned as rugby development officer. The girls have their own rugby team and sometimes they play for Ulster – so just to be fair the sixth form boys have formed a hockey team. The school also fields a team for golf and showjumping and rowing is offered at Portadown Rowing Club. The school has a gym and sports hall and fitness suite as well as tennis and squash courts, rugby pitches and two all-weather hockey pitches, with swimming at the local leisure centre.

Boarding: Boarding is always oversubscribed – they could fill it twice over though they always leave space for the occasional ad hoc boarder in an emergency. About half hail from Northern Ireland, the rest from overseas – Hong Kong represents biggest group although most are from the Republic of Ireland, Germany, Spain, Italy etc. 'Boarding improves the atmosphere of the whole school and gives it more of a family feel,' said a parent.

One girls', one boys' and a sixth form boarding house – all have family feel and all have benefited from a £2 million refurbishment, with pupils accommodated in small, light rooms of mostly two to four beds (no larger dorms since Covid), and most of the older pupils have their own study bedrooms. All houses have common rooms with a television, Xbox and a games room and boarders have their own cinema. Breakfast, lunch and supper served in main school, and each house has its own kitchen for preparing snacks.

School now owns four houses in the Georgian mall adjacent to the school which have been refurbished and converted into the sixth form house with a flat for the housemaster. Boys and girls share homely and comfortable communal living areas but are separated by alarmed doors at night. Sixth formers are not allowed back to their house during the day and have to swipe in and out so staff know if someone is having an unscheduled lie in.

Younger pupils' prep carefully monitored, with teachers on hand – handy if they get stuck. Matrons take care of everything pastoral and there are housemasters and mistresses in residence who sort out the practical side of things, including ferrying them around, eg to boys' and girls' brigade (both popular). 'Boarding should not be an end to involvement in the community,' says head. As such, boarders often go to stay with friends at weekends – a measure of how well they mix with day pupils, particularly through the house system and sport. No Saturday school but matches and CCF on Saturday mornings. About half stays at weekends (mainly the international cohort), for which there are weekly activities such as escape rooms, paddle boarding and shopping trips to Belfast and Dublin. There is a boarding parents' group.

Ethos and heritage: One of five Planation Schools founded in 1608 by James I to educate the sons of Scottish and English merchants and farmers who had been sent to settle in Ulster after the Irish earls fled in 1607. The school moved to its current 27-acre site in 1774. It is now a voluntary grammar school and became co-ed when it amalgamated with the Armagh Girls' High School in 1986. It is officially Reformed Christian but welcomes all faiths and none. The original school is an imposing limestone building with enormous windows and wide corridors, with an elegant boardroom and an ancient library displaying the school's honours boards, and with computers discreetly hidden behind a glass screen. There is an impressive quad where you can no longer park your carriage but which is now used for barbecues, and the crunchy gravel is a deterrent to illicit flits between the boys' and girls' boarding houses. New sixth form facility underway. There is a strong sense of history and tradition – Armagh has been the ecclesiastical capital of Ireland since the fifth century and has a Protestant and a Catholic cathedral, and an unbroken line of archbishops have been chairmen of the board of governors for the past 400 years. There is a small prep school on site which opened in 1940.

This is a worthy school, which raises £10-15,000 per year for charitable causes. Sixth form committee decides what to support and then how to do it – most recently shoebox appeals during Covid, with more innovative examples including the colour run where everyone threw powder paint at each other. Pupils go carol singing in old people's homes and the hospital. The Royal is involved with two schools in Uganda but the pinnacle is the ASHA Project in a slum in New Delhi, where a group of sixth formers spend a fortnight every other year working alongside the community. The (heavily subsidised) triennial rugby tour to the southern hemisphere always involves a charitable element.

There is an impressive quad which is used for barbecues, and the crunchy gravel is a deterrent to illicit flits between the boys' and girls' boarding houses

Smart uniform comprises blue blazer and grey skirt or trousers, including for sixth formers, with crimson (woe betide you if you call in purple, as we did) honours blazers for particular achievements in sports, debating or music.

Well-known alumni include Irish rugby international and British and Irish Lion, Tommy Bowe; British foreign secretary, Viscount Castlereagh; politician, Lord Reg Empey; Oxford maths professor, John Lennox; Cambridge professor of ophthalmology, Keith Martin; as well as numerous senior naval and military figures.

Pastoral care, inclusivity and discipline: Carol Dweck's growth mindset is the framework here, encouraging students to view challenges and setbacks as a tool for learning. The pastoral team meets regularly and all pupils have a weekly meeting with their tutors, while heads of year run monthly focus groups. Pupils know they have a lot of people to watch out of them and there's an independent counsellor and school partnership with Thrive Academy, a local organisation focusing on self-esteem and mental health. Parents and pupils say you are immediately made to feel part of the family and 'everyone is accessible and you can have a chat with anyone at any time'. In lockdown, school made a big effort to keep in touch with parents, especially those of more vulnerable children, and has since appointed mental health ambassador pupils (who are trained to identify issues), as well as promoting mental health messages in assemblies. Effective peer tutoring programme involves sixth form tutors being trained each September to help younger pupils with maths and English, as well as acting as confidants. Leads to increased confidence for both sides and improved organisational skills for the tutors. The four houses (named after previous archbishops of Armagh) encourage students to mix vertically and compete in sports, debating and photography and in the annual inter-house talent show, which often brings hidden talents to the fore. 'It's great for those who don't make the school teams,' said a parent.

A largely well-behaved lot, with any discipline problems tending to be low level and uniform related – but even these rules have relaxed since Covid, and school is adamant that although appearance matters relationships with staff should not be damaged by small things. If a student is caught wearing eg jewellery, they will more likely be called aside and given a gentle reminder than humiliated publicly or sent to detention. One or two suspensions a year is the norm – but rarely, if ever, a first response – and there have been no expulsions in 20 years. 'There are some cyber niggles but on the whole the kids get on well,' and everyone knows everyone across the year groups. 'The school has a good handle on things and any issues are dealt with effectively,' said a parent.

The school responded quickly and decisively to a mention on the Everyone's Invited website, offering to meet with the young woman in question and they have since implemented a big drive on respect.

Pupils and parents: Parents are a broad church, cutting right across the social spectrum – some rural, others urban and sophisticated; some wealthy, others struggling to make ends meet. Some Ulster expats want their children to have what they had and so send them back as boarders, and some 12 per cent of the total school population and 30 per cent of boarders are non-British. Those hailing from Northern Ireland span a 40-mile radius – impressive given that the area is served by excellent schools. All are very supportive of the school and told us they are made to feel part of their children's education and 'you can ring at any time and the school knows who you are'. Pupils generally quietly confident and modest. 'The school turns out well-mannered considerate children who hold doors open and stand back – very natural and not forced,' said a parent. Old Armachians speak of being 'Royal loyal' and have regular get-togethers as well as an annual dinner. Most stay in Northern Ireland but those who move away usually come back in later life.

Money matters: Tuition is free for residents of Northern Ireland. The boarding fee is much lower than anywhere in England or Scotland – too cheap, say some parents (of day children). The annual fee for day pupils who pass the 11+ is a paltry £400 – pays for insurance, extracurricular and capital works.

The last word: A compassionate and caring school where the 'holistic approach runs through the school like a stick of rock' and where the development of character is equally as important as academic achievement.

The Royal School Dungannon

22

2 Ranfurly Road, Dungannon, County Tyrone BT71 6EG

028 8772 2710 | info@rsd.dungannon.ni.sch.uk | www.royaldungannon.com

Ages: 11–18

Pupils: 662; sixth form: 154; Boarders: 52 full

Fees: Day: £9,300 (non-EU); Boarding: £8,400 – £21,000 pa

Headmaster: Since 2009 Dr David Burnett BA PhD NPQH (50s). Educated at Lurgan College grammar school in County Armagh and read history and politics at Queen's University, Belfast where he also took a PhD. He joined King Edward VI Grammar School in Chelmsford via the licensed teacher scheme and gained QTS (qualified teacher status) via on the job training. He became head of history and politics in 1998, moved on to Westcliff High School for boys in 2006 and spent three years as deputy headmaster before taking on the headship at Dungannon. He is married to Nicola and they have two daughters and a son. He hadn't really planned to come back to Northern Ireland but family reasons pushed him in that direction and he was offered the headship at here.

He no longer has much time for teaching, but occasionally teaches history to some senior years to keep his hand in. He has a passionate interest in sport, especially Ulster rugby, and used to be a keen player, but now confines his sporting talents to golf and tennis. Loves history and historical fiction and always has a book on the go, and says he has a bit of a weakness for computer strategy games. He says the school is about the personal development of young people and he is happy to try new and different approaches. He feels that holistic education is part of the DNA of the school and 'although exams matter and children must be pushed to do as well as they can, they will only succeed if the foundations are right... Achievement comes through effort and hard work – the best geologist is the one who has seen the most rocks.' 'He is highly visible around the school and approachable and is well regarded, but can be quite reserved,' said a parent. He wants parents to be as involved as possible and was instrumental in setting up the PTA.

Entrance: From 20-30 local primary schools – primaries very supportive of grammar schools and lots of past pupils work in local primary schools. Entry via the Common Entrance Assessment with exams in English and maths. The tests are in the November before entry and parents can choose a school once they have the results. Sixth form entry only if there are spaces and all must achieve at least six GCSEs at 6 or above to join or move into the sixth form.

Entry for international boarders is via the school's own tests in English and maths plus an interview and report from the current school.

Exit: Around 25 per cent leave after GCSEs. Over 90 per cent go on to higher education. Just over half stay in Northern Ireland and go to Queen's University, Belfast or Ulster University. Others to Dublin (Trinity College and UCD, also with moderate fees). Some 40 per cent go to university in Scotland, England or Wales with the occasional pupil going to Oxbridge. The most popular subjects are engineering, food and nutrition, medicine, dentistry, business/economics, teaching and the allied health professions. About two per year go to art school and about three go into nursing. Seven medics in 2021. Two pupils began degree apprenticeships. Not many take a gap year – some take part in the Dilworth scholarship and spend a year in New Zealand. Good links with local businesses for those who don't want to go to university; four pupils began higher level apprenticeships in 2021.

Latest results: In 2021, 64 per cent 9-7 at GCSE; 59 per cent A*/A at A level (84 per cent A*-B). In 2019 (the last year when exams took place), 45 per cent 9-7 at GCSE; 34 per cent A*/A (65 per cent A*-B).

Teaching and learning: 'Pupils are encouraged to do their best but are not pushed too hard,' said a parent. Twenty-one subjects offered at A level including music and food technology. Psychology, drama, politics and media taught at St Patrick's Academy, the local Catholic grammar and partnership school. Further maths only offered to AS level. French and Spanish offered at GCSE and A level and Hong Kong Chinese can take Cantonese GCSE, but no lessons offered and have to do the work in their own time. Science, dual award or individual subjects, is taught in well-equipped modern labs. It's popular with the girls and all the physics teachers are female. Now offers health & social care A level plus life & health science. Both boys and girls choose home economics and an old boy is a pastry chef at the Ritz. Science, maths and home economics the most popular A levels, followed by history and geography, with not many takers for modern languages. Many take maths GCSE a year early and further maths GCSE in year 12 (English year 11).

Science, dual award or individual subjects, is taught in well-equipped modern labs. It's popular with the girls and all the physics teachers are female. Both boys and girls choose home economics and an old boy is a pastry chef at the Ritz

Pupils are put into four mixed-ability classes of 25 on arrival with setting in English and maths from year 10 (English year 9). Some 18-20 per class in GCSE years drops to 10-15 at A level – and this is a state school.

Well-equipped careers library, and children are taught employability skills from the first year; subject careers boards are dotted around the school. Lots of help with UCAS forms and pupils are allocated a personal careers adviser. All upper sixth take part in an interview day and former pupils who are at university come back and talk. All lower sixth have to do some work shadowing – they are supposed to find work on their own but school can help if necessary.

Good balance of well-qualified teachers including a small number of beginner teachers and a handful in their 50s – there have been considerable changes in the last 10 years and the school now has a young and approachable team. 'The teachers want the kids to do well and they are easy to talk to – they will always ring back if there is a problem,' said a parent.

Learning support and SEN: Full time SENCo with a team of six or seven classroom assistants. The school is wheelchair friendly and there is a handful of children with autistic spectrum disorders, but the biggest groups are dyslexics and dyspraxics who usually only need modest adjustments in class – all are given an IEP. Three EAL teachers, with lessons after school most evenings.

The arts and extracurricular: 'Music is the constant heartbeat of the school,' says the headmaster. Around 200 pupils a week involved with some sort of music: junior and senior choirs, which are open to all, chamber choir, chamber orchestra, pipe band, string band – something for everyone and the music block has a computer suite for pupils to make their own compositions. The carol service and spring concert are the highlights of the musical year and there is something musical going on most lunchtimes.

About eight full and weekly boarding places in each year group. Boarders sometimes only come for a term or a year, and originate from all over the world

Thriving drama department and the school is 'well known for putting on a good show,' said a parent. Annual play for the senior school which alternates between a musical and a more serious drama, and the lower years put on their own productions.

Busy art department – drawing and painting are particular strengths. Impressive textiles and paintings are displayed in cabinets around the school and there is an annual joint arts exhibition with St Patrick's Academy.

Range of lunchtime and after-school clubs including the popular Scripture Union, and public speaking and debating societies as well as Young Enterprise and computer games design. About 20 per year achieve gold DofE and have joint expeditions with St Patrick's Academy. Annual sports tours to Scotland and Europe and rugby and hockey tours to New Zealand or South Africa every five years. History and RE trip to Rome, art and French trips to Paris and PE and Spanish trips to Barcelona.

Sport: Strong emphasis on sport, especially boys' rugby. Girls play hockey, as well as recently introduced tag rugby and football. All play cricket and a range of minor sports are offered. Good onsite facilities including rugby pitches and a floodlit all-weather hockey pitch, a shooting range, two sports halls and a fitness suite which they share with the wider community. Swimming at the Dungannon leisure centre. The school has been Northern Ireland orienteering champions in recent years and shooting is popular with both girls and boys – the school usually has reps in the Northern Ireland teams. Hockey and rugby training three times a week with matches on Saturday mornings, but often find it hard to compete with the bigger schools in the area. Sports at lunchtime and after school and sixth form have to take some sort of exercise twice a week– the Hong Kong girls tend to prefer keep fit and zumba.

Boarding: About eight full and weekly boarding places in each year group. Boarders sometimes only come for a term or a year, and originate from all over the world including Irish Republic, Ukraine, Nigeria, Russia and Spain. The largest contingent is from Hong Kong – many are the relatives of former pupils who came to Dungannon in the 1970s. On the whole they integrate well and make local friends, 'although the Hong Kong Chinese can stick together,' said a parent. Usually over 40 in at weekends and staff put on an activities programme, maybe baking or a trip to a shopping centre or Belfast, and children are allowed to walk into the town and go to the cinema or swimming. 'Staff are very dedicated and try to make it feel like home,' said a parent. Boarding accommodation light and airy with small dorms for the younger children and double rooms for sixth formers, together with common rooms and kitchen areas for making hot drinks and snacks. Boarders not allowed back into their rooms during the day.

Ethos and heritage: One of five Planation Schools founded in 1608 by James I to educate the sons of Scottish and English merchants and farmers who had been sent to settle in Ulster after the Irish earls had been driven out in 1607. Originally set up in Mountjoy near Lough Neagh in 1614, it moved to Dungannon town later in the century. It was founded as a boys' school but amalgamated with Dungannon High School for girls in 1986 when large parts of the campus were rebuilt and it is now a co-ed voluntary grammar. The school is set in 50 acres and the main building, built in 1789, is known as the Old Grey Mother owing to its grey cement cladding. A mix of architectural styles ranging from the Georgian buildings to the Victorian cloister, which was originally used for

Ripon Grammar School

PE and assemblies, as well as 20th-century additions. Twenty-eight new classrooms, science labs and a sixth form centre were added in 2003. All surrounded by neat lawns and flowerbeds. The entrance hall is all blond wood and pastel colours with silverware and sporting photos lining the walls and passages. The Marshall Library, which is well equipped with computers and a computerised library system, was originally the 19th-century gym. It was redesigned in the 1980s and is lined with portraits and photos of worthies of the school.

The school fosters a sense of public service and is determined to involve students in the wider community. It has strong links with local sports clubs, churches and businesses and shares its facilities – primary school children come in for sports, science and creativity days. The charities committee decides how to raise and spend money – one recent popular initiative was to sell roses on Valentine's Day, and they always take part in the Christmas shoe box appeal. Sixth formers help out as classroom assistants at a local special school and other years help with sport at local primaries and go carol singing in old people's homes. The school is also involved with the Fields of Life charity, which has set up the Bethel Royal School in Uganda; a group of sixth formers visit each year and the Ugandan children have been on a return visit to Dungannon. They raise about £5,000 a year for the school.

Children 'quietly confident and believe in themselves and have great manners,' said a parent; 'they always say hello and hold the door open.' 'They are proud to be part of the school and tend to be ambitious and want to make something of themselves,' said another

James Dilworth, a former pupil, left money in his will to found Dilworth School in New Zealand in 1906, and there are still close ties with gap year exchanges between the schools.

Four houses named after well-known people connected with the school. Inter-house sport and debating competitions provide leadership opportunities for senior pupils and enable children to get to know other year groups.

Well-known alumni include: open golf champion, Darren Clarke; Irish rugby captain, Paddy Johns; director general of the probation service, Eithne Birt (nee Wallis); pioneering orthopaedic surgeon, Derek McMinn; and MP and life peer, Lord Maginnis of Drumglass.

Pastoral care, inclusivity and discipline: Broadly Christian ethos provides a moral compass, but school is interdenominational and welcomes all faiths and none. Strong focus on pastoral care with boards outside all the classrooms and children know who to turn to. 'Everyone feels valued and part of the family,' said a parent. Zero tolerance on drugs, although head says that there has not been an incident while he has been in post. Occasional issues with alcohol – 'once in a blue moon,' says the headmaster. There is one 'formal' per year but no alcohol is allowed – a hip flask was once found in the bathroom but that is about as bad as it gets. Dungannon is popular with the Hong Kong families because it is socially conservative and safe.

School very hot on anti-bullying and holds an anti-bullying week. 'The school is on top of cyber issues,' said a mother and parents can attend talks on cyber bullying and are given tips on how to keep children safe online. The pastoral team consists of a pastoral head, the head of year group and form tutors; upper sixth pupils are buddied with first years and a counsellor comes in one day a week – most problems are fairly minor. Pupils generally not hugely worldly wise or sophisticated compared with children in England, and are happy to wear their smart brown blazer edged with magenta into the sixth form – the school has a strict uniform policy.

Food good with plenty of choice by online payment and card which also enables staff to monitor what children eat. Some bring in packed lunches.

Pupils and parents: Parents mostly local and often know each other in the wider community – many attended the school themselves. Former pupils have a strong affinity with the school and are keen to give something back, and in many families several generations have attended the school.

Children 'quietly confident and believe in themselves and have great manners,' said a parent; 'they always say hello and hold the door open.' 'They are proud to be part of the school and tend to be ambitious and want to make something of themselves,' said another.

Parents say they can get as involved as they want to, are kept well informed by the data secretary and are invited to the school for regular information evenings, on topics such as how to help their children with revision techniques. Active parents' association organises social and fundraising events – they arrange quizzes and shopping trips for parents, host a welcome evening for first year pupils and have recently raised funds to buy soundboards for the stage and extra equipment for the science labs, and also help raise money for foreign trips.

Money matters: Tuition is free for those within Northern Ireland and EU/Ireland and boarders only have to pay the boarding fee. Fees for those from further afield much lower than in England and Scotland.

The last word: A charming, small, rural grammar school with a tight-knit community where everyone knows everyone. The children achieve good results but do not feel pressurised and the school experiences few of the problems common in street-savvy city schools.

St George's School (Harpenden)

Sun Lane, Harpenden, Hertfordshire AL5 4EY

01582 765477 | admin@stgeorges.herts.sch.uk | www.stgeorges.herts.sch.uk

Ages: 11-18

Pupils: 1,380; sixth form: 400; Boarders: 113 full

Fees: Day free; Boarding £13,890 pa

Headmistress: Since 2017, Helen Barton BA PGCSE MEd (50s). Previously deputy head since 2008 and assistant head since 2005. Following a degree in geography (University of Wales), she trained as an accountant before seeing the light and taking a PGCE (Institute of Education). Taught geography at Stopsley High School, Luton then Marriotts School, Stevenage ('difficult but rewarding') before moving into the independent sector at what is now Bedford Girls' School. No longer teaches – 'it's a very busy school and it's hard, as a head, to have consistency in the classroom' – but does break and lunch duties and nobody could say she's remote.

Affable, pragmatic and straight talking, with a clear sense of ownership of the school ('my staff', 'my pupils', 'my classroom dynamics' etc). Parents – a discerning bunch – describe her as 'a marmite head'. 'I really like her, she's down to earth and knows what she wants for the school, but you know very well where you stand with her which some people don't like,' said one; another told us, 'I was put off by the "don't you feel smug living so close to the school?" speech she gives new parents.'

Lives locally and enjoys reading and travelling – she had just downloaded eight new books (from one on how to get rid of bureaucracy right through to 'a good thriller') for her half term holiday in Mauritius (though not all holidays are so exotic – she loves travelling in Britain too). Likes walking and has recently started running.

Entrance: The most oversubscribed of Harpenden's three secondary schools, with around three applicants for every one of the 170 year 7 places. Non-selective academically, with priority given to families who have regularly attended church for at least two years (minister's letter required) and then the child's siblings. Tie-breaking decisions for these church members always comes down to distance – fluctuating anywhere between 800m and, in the year before we visited, 1.4km. Bottom line: forget it if you're not living within the town. Genuine devoutness not put to the test – local parents can cynically choose to pray rather than pay as long as they think ahead and accept that their child will have to attend chapel at school on at least three Sundays a term. A handful each year from local prep schools.

The 120 boarding places (10 available in year 7) are not oversubscribed – 113 were taken up in the year we last reviewed the school. Applicants must hold British passport or have the right to a British education and are interviewed by head and director of boarding to assess suitability. Reference also required from their previous school. 'Need' also comes into play – for example children with both parents working or in the Forces (not many military families recently, though), with occasional children switching from day to boarding to save time on the daily commute. Applications encouraged as early as possible in the year before entry although interviews have been known to go on right through to April.

Exit: Up to 80 per cent stay on into sixth form – leavers generally move to colleges or other schools with different courses. Vast majority to university, more than two-thirds to Russell Group. Loughborough,

Exeter and Leeds currently popular. In 2021, five to Oxbridge, two medics and one off to study in the US. Over a third into STEM-related courses, just under a third into the likes of humanities and law and the rest split between finance and business and the arts, performing arts and languages.

Latest results: In 2021, 51 per cent 9-7 at GCSE; 94 per cent 9-4 in both maths and English. At A level, 50 per cent A*/A at A level (73 per cent A*-B). In 2019 (the last year when exams took place), 54 per cent 9-7 at GCSE; 92 per cent 9-4 in both maths and English. At A level in 2019, 40 per cent A*/A (65 per cent A*-B).

Teaching and learning: As a non-selective school regularly delivering high results, parents can bank on St George's when it comes to value-added. Teaching is interactive and creative, with a good range of styles to keep students on their toes. 'One of my strengths is the interaction between students and teachers,' says head. 'My staff dynamic means they are willing to go off on tangents if something comes up in discussion,' she adds. Maths, 'without reservation', is the jewel in St George's crown and the most popular A level choice for boys and girls – 'It's phenomenal to see how much they enjoy it.' Art also outstanding, with school boasting the highest percentage of top grades in the county at both GCSE and A level.

Maths, 'without reservation', is the jewel in St George's crown and the most popular A level choice for boys and girls – 'It's phenomenal to see how much they enjoy it'

French from year 7 and German added in year 8, with both (plus Spanish) available at GCSE and A level (though German and Spanish A levels only through the consortium). Setting in maths has been replaced with mixed-ability classes for vast majority, with a small top class for the gifted and talented and ditto for those needing extra support at the bottom end – 'What we are trying to get away from is people ranking themselves in numbered sets which can be really unhealthy – we're all about the potential,' says head. In English, setting has been ditched altogether 'because everyone brings something to the discussion'.

Ten GCSEs are the norm, with compulsory RE among them leading, unusually, to a full class at A level. Parents appreciate flexible approach to timetabling at GCSE. Most take three A levels, with a whole raft of enrichment add-ons available including EPQ (usually completed by 30-40 students), science Olympiads and maths challenges.

'The school is amazing at instilling independent learning and building confidence in the classroom right from the start,' said one parent, though another felt that 'it can feel overwhelming if you don't fit the mould.' All agree tutoring is rife. 'Okay but not fantastic' is the general consensus on how the school dealt with Covid – 'There was a strong sense in Harpenden that they were a bit behind the curve during lockdowns,' said one, with some additional grumbles that 'music and drama seemed to stop altogether'. Some parents would like to get more than one report a year.

Learning support and SEN: A full time SENCo and seven teaching assistants provide a blended approach to learning support involving differentiation in every classroom through to ad hoc sessions for students in eg English or maths or a programme of one-to-ones for dyslexia. Not a school to say, 'Right you've got this, so you need this' – more a case of support waxing and waning towards need over the whole educational journey. Broad-ish range of learning needs, some coming in with diagnoses, others getting them while at the school. Usually around seven or eight EHCPs.

The arts and extracurricular: Possibly the best art department of any school for miles around – 'the pride of the school,' say students. Every inch of the art corridor walls and ceilings festooned with breathtakingly creative and technically exemplary work also spilling over to cover most walls throughout school. Outstanding paintings, drawings, sculptures and installations – no two the same – assault the senses. Creative facilities also superb, with three huge DT labs – again with some wonderfully turned work on display – and two huge art rooms provide yet more exhibition space for students' superb creative endeavours. Textiles, photography, sculpture and graphic design all on offer.

House music had just taken place in St Albans Abbey (sometimes it's other venues) when we last reviewed the school – a whopping 400 students had taken part. All the usual choirs, orchestras, ensembles and bands attract students from across the age groups, with some extremely talented musicians, although school takes an inclusive attitude overall. Around 320 students have instrumental or singing lessons with Musicale (located onsite).

Three drama productions per year – upper school in November, house drama (open to all year groups) in February and lower school in June. Recent examples include Godspell and Cinderella for older ones and Reduced Works of Shakespeare and Tales of the Arabian Nights for the youngsters. Winners of the house drama attend the

We are assured that the sparse decorations in the younger boys' dorms and common room are purely by choice ('It's not cool to have posters up,' explained one of our guides)

National Youth Drama Festival in Welwyn Garden City. Lots of backstage opportunities.

Great on clubs, which range from sewing to gardening and chess to DofE (30-40 students start gold every year, albeit with some finishing it in their first year of university) – great for boarders and day pupils alike. Annual summer activities week packs in both day and residential trips, as well as activities (some self-generated) within school. All the usual school trips to eg Iceland, Florence, Berlin and Brittany.

Sport: 'Feels like a private school when it comes to sport – in fact, we are the only non-private school to turn up to some fixtures,' said one parent. For lacrosse – the main girls' sport here – St George's is the only state-maintained school in the south of England to even play it. For boys, rugby is a huge strength (Owen Farrell, George Ford, Jack Singleton and Maro Itoje all came here) and although not officially affiliated with Saracens, there are strong informal connections. Cricket does well, and as with rugby, A-C teams are put out most weeks in all year groups. A few parents feel the sport is a bit gendered – 'I would say they need to open their minds to girls playing cricket and rugby and it's a shame there's no football,' said one. But for every parent that feels the school is elitist ('They're not really that interested unless you're in the A team') there's another insisting, 'You are just as relevant whatever team you're in and that's a strength of the school.' Netball, rounders, basketball, tennis, athletics and, to a limited extent, dance also available – and, in sixth form (sports participation is compulsory to year 13), table tennis, badminton and trampolining. Decent sports centre includes gym and weights room. One parent praised the friendship side of sport – 'It's a big social thing for my child – she loves that about the sport here.'

Boarding: Boarding is a huge source of pride – 'It's a lovely addition to the school that's very special. Our kids get to mix with a really international cohort and that's a great experience,' lauded one parent. We're not talking big numbers (maximum capacity 120, with anything between five and 15 each of boys and girls in any given year group), but they are very well integrated with friendships flourishing between day and boarding pupils and visits to day pupils' homes encouraged. Far from feeling like a minority group, boarders take pride in their status to the point of having requested their own, slightly different, tie.

Girls up to year 12 are housed in the old school building – safely tucked away up what seems like 15 flights of stairs – in dorms which sleep anything from two to six: 'We tailor it according to intake from year to year and girls' individual needs.' Boys up to year 12 are in a stand-alone block with a less cosy, more practical feel – though we are assured that the sparse decorations in dorms and common room are purely by choice ('It's not cool to have posters up,' said one of our guides). Co-ed sixth form house has single rooms and ensuite bathrooms with weekly enrichment activities specifically aimed at preparing them for university, eg study skills and cooking on a budget. All houses have tons of communal space – massive common rooms furnished with plenty of squashy sofas and other nooks and crannies around the house with beanbags, armchairs and computers for boys and girls to congregate outside of school hours. Well-equipped kitchen areas too so they can make themselves snacks – and there are baskets of goodies out to keep them going after school.

Boys and girls are allowed to visit each other but only in common rooms – although apparently romantic liaisons are incredibly rare: 'There is a strong sibling-like feel amongst the boarders,' say pupils. The terms 'flexi' and 'weekly' are not used and, although some boarders go home more frequently than others, all pay the same fees (less by some stretch than most private day schools) and have the same status. Around half stay for weekends (more boys than girls), with all meals apart from weekend breakfasts taken in the main school dining room. Pupils from year 9 allowed into Harpenden with permission in twos and many attend classes such as yoga or dance in the village. Students grumble that school is too strict about them leaving the premises – parents breathe secret sighs of relief.

Boarding houses have friendly family feel, helped by much-loved director of boarding living on site. Usual activities at weekends – Thorpe Park, cinema trips, shopping etc. Boarders also have their own formal dinner or ball each term, organised by senior pupils. Younger pupils have a fixed programme of after-school activities including boarding skills – learning how cook, do their laundry, make jam etc. One parent told us how she 'just knew my son wouldn't want to go on the paintballing activity so I asked them to try gently encouraging him but definitely not forcing him and the next thing I knew my son phoned me really excited about going. They knew just what to say to him – they get him totally.' Communications home come in for high praise – helped by boarders being allowed phones (until bedtime).

There's been a recent shift from more traditional sanctions towards restorative justice when boarders mess up – 'It's about understanding what you've done and learning from it rather than a punishment for punishment's sake,' says head.

Ethos and heritage: More like a private school than some private schools we know – and certainly wins the prize for smartest comprehensive school uniform with its green Harris tweed blazers for the boys and pleated kilts for the girls. Situated a stone's throw from Harpenden High Street, school was founded in 1907 by the Rev Cecil Grant as a non-denominational Christian foundation with its own chaplain and weekly Sunday chapel service, which occasionally hosts up to 400 members of the school community and their families. One of the longest established fully coeducational boarding schools in England, and retains many of its historic traditions, with pupils taking great pride in their house competitions, formality of chapel, speech days and all the different ties awarded.

Certainly wins the prize for smartest comprehensive school uniform with its green Harris tweed blazers for the boys and pleated kilts for the girls

Original Victorian Gothic-style building still provides the heart of the school, with various additions and extensions which run the full gauntlet from occasionally gleaming (sports hall, language block) to 1960s flat-roofed monstrosities. Last time we visited most of it looked downright shabby but school is now down to its last prefab and the ongoing TLC across the site is paying off. All hangs together with a feel of purposefulness and functionality. Sixth form common room and study areas not exactly swish but with 400 youngsters in and out every day they get heavy use and nobody seems to mind.

Alumni include philosopher and political theorist Michael Oakeshott, classicist and writer Rex Warner, actress Laura Haddock and one-time captain of the England Lacrosse team Laura Merrifield.

Pastoral care, inclusivity and discipline: 'The house system is the anchor for everything,' said a parent, who described each of the four houses as 'a school within a school that really fosters as sense of belonging by wrapping its arms around you'. Each house has a head and assistant head, plus pastoral assistant. Student services department supports children with mental health needs – includes qualified counsellor. Issues such as consent and racism are discussed openly as part of eg assemblies and PHSE and, refreshingly, transgender is a complete non-issue among these students who take difference in their stride.

Parents like that it's a 'strict' school where 'students know right from wrong and behave well or else'. 'They are particularly hot on manners, time management, respect and responsibility,' said one. 'If you're even a couple of minutes late or your shirt isn't tucked in, you'll know about it – a behaviour point, no question.' One parent told us of a couple of boys getting into a fight 'and the whole year was brought in – there's no way they tolerate that kind of thing.' A handful of suspensions per term but no permanent exclusions for a good few years. Occasionally pupils 'don't work out' on the boarding side, we heard, but in the main everyone agrees that traditional values and caring ethos makes school tick. Pupils rewarded for demonstrating school's core values of courtesy, integrity, manners and discipline.

Pupils and parents: Middle-class? You bet – this is affluent Harpenden. Boarders mainly from further afield, with around 55 per cent of these from overseas, with no one country dominating – Hong Kong, Middle East, Nigeria and much of Europe feature currently. A highly involved and vocal parent body turns out in droves for matches, concerts and shows and the Sunday service in chapel is very well attended. Comms could be improved, we heard: 'Nothing is centralised so you have to go to each department, can be such a headache,' said one parent. 'Sometimes it feels like parents are the enemy,' voiced another.

Money matters: No bursaries offered. Buildings are owned by the school's foundation, which has to find 10 per cent of the cost of all capital projects and ongoing building maintenance from very limited funds. 'There is a lot of do-it-yourself work here'; school enlists the assistance of its active parents' association for fundraising support throughout the year.

The last word: Riding high as one of the top non-selective state schools in the country, St George's combines a Christian community with top-notch results. Coupled with its heritage feel and traditions, Hogwarts-esque main building, herringbone blazers and lacrosse, you could be forgiven for mistaking it for an independent school.

Steyning Grammar School

Shooting Field, Steyning, West Sussex BN44 3RX

01903 814555 | sgsboarding@sgs.uk.net | www.sgs.uk.net

Ages: 11-18

Pupils: 2,287; sixth form: 395; Boarders: 127 full

Fees: Day free; Boarding £10,215 – £12,495 pa

Associate headteacher: Since 2019, Nat Nicol. Joined the school in 2012 as an assistant head (leading on CPD) and was promoted to deputy head in 2015. Read English literature and drama at Roehampton before doing her PGCE at Sussex, where she also did her MEd. Kicked off her teaching career at Worthing High School in 1999, moving to Peacehaven Community School, where she was head of English and drama for 10 years.

Co-headteacher since 2019, Noel Kennedy. Joined the school in 2018 as deputy headteacher and before that was assistant principal for curriculum, behaviour and safeguarding at Harris Academy Bermondsey. Read geography at Queen's University Belfast and did his teacher training at Liverpool Hope, after which he started teaching in Liverpool and then Surrey.

From Easter 2022, they will be replaced by Adam Whitehead, currently founding head at Bohunt School, Worthing, and before that deputy head at The Weald School, Billinghurst. He has also previously worked at St Paul's in Burgess Hill and Oathall Community College in Haywards Heath as part of his 25 years in teaching.

Entrance: Strong relationships with local primary schools. Catchment is some 200 square kilometres encompassing Henfield to Storrington. The local authority handles the year 7 and year 9 intakes. Only boarding is selective – online application and Zoom/Skype interviews for prospective boarders. School aims for 50 per cent of each sex in every year group. The sixth form is amongst the largest in the south east of England. Admission is usually a grade 6 or above in the subjects of choice.

Exit: Up to half leave after GCSEs. After the year 13 leavers' celebration, they get into limos and head off to a club in Worthing, thrilled there is no room on site for something more low key. Seventy per cent head off to higher education. Exeter, Leeds, Bournemouth, Portsmouth and Sussex popular destinations. Sprinkling to Oxbridge most years; ditto for medics.

Latest results: In 2021, 38 per cent 9-7 at GCSE; 84 per cent 9-4 in both English and maths. At A level, 41 per cent A*/A (69 per cent A*-B). In 2019 (the last year when exams took place), 24 per cent 9-7 at GCSE; 70 per cent 9-4 in both English and maths. At A level, 41 per cent A*/A (69 per cent A*-B).

Teaching and learning: Reflections on learning are intrinsic to the school success – whether that is implicit in weekly year group 'collective worships' (hall only holds 350) or explicit in the title of the school's communication sheets. The size of the school means that over 50 A levels and just as many GCSEs are on offer. Class sizes normally 24 with up to 16 at A level.

Years 7 and 8 are in the Towers and Rock Road campuses, where their atmospheric classrooms have parquet floors and a maze of doorways leading to subject-based areas. Learning is far from low tech, though; there are banks of computers and we saw a fizzy drink can that had been rigged to record sound. At the other end of the tech spectrum, a class loved building the rock cycle using plasticine. The library was buzzy with authors visiting and pupil volunteers. However, by the time they have made their GCSE choices pupils are panting to get the open corridors and swell of new students in the Shooting Fields site. The latter is dominated by the huge and successful A level specialist sixth form, which feels more like a college but with the pastoral support of a school – a real draw for the third of students who join in year 9.

Tutorials are one-to-one and a curriculum reform means pupils now do fewer topics but more richly. Project-based learning is electric here; the pupils love it and the opportunities it provides to anchor their academic subjects in the practical and take the experience back into the classroom: a trip to the European Organisation for Nuclear Research in Cern; Kimmeridge for biology and geology; the Globe Theatre; Oviedo for Spanish.

The learning resource centre is not just about books – a remote access system means students can log on at home and avoid emailing documents back and forth. The mezzanine level is the sixth form domain and students congregate here even in break time, a sure sign of their commitment to learning – they also gather in the canteen and a learning zone behind that.

Engaging teachers make for the most popular A level subjects, maths, politics and chemistry at present – science labs have loads of space for practicals, which might have 16 in each class compared to 20 in extended subjects. During the GCSE years the pupils become responsible for booking their parents' appointments and act as their guides on the parents' evening itself – family feedback is that this independence works well.

Learning support and SEN: The Cuthman Centre is a separate building that acts as a haven for the more vulnerable students (category 3 SEN), eight at present with specific learning difficulties; they have roll-call or more casual tea and toast there when needed, and there are NHS nurses, a counselling programme funding by pupil premium and enabled by GP referrals. In-class SEN support with learning support mentors is targeted and the impact evaluated: it ranges from laptops in exams for those with illegible writing to an SEN passport created with parent and carers. The gifted and talented are supported outside lesson time with book clubs and an Oxbridge programme.

The arts and extracurricular: The music department is thriving with ticketed performances each season and some 20 A level students, but would love more space (who wouldn't). Logic is used for composition on Macs, there are opportunities for mixing with the use of the live room. Plenty of individual practitioners, eg a boy playing the violin, guitar, piano; a ukulele and keyboard in a shared room in the boarding house.

The pupils are really joyful about the different cultural traditions that they get to experience, from jollof rice on Nigerian Independence Day to Chinese New Year

Art and technology is exhibited throughout the halls of the school – and the drama hall is open to the public. The whole school competition is Steyning's Got Talent – some kids think it is profoundly uncool, others use it as a springboard to more public performances across the county. Full school performances such as The Wedding Singer might involve 300 people in the six-night production – set, backstage, make-up as well as performers.

The 50th school anniversary trip to the Norfolk Broads had just passed when we visited. Jailbreak is another riot of a challenge where the whole of year 13 is locked up and has to escape from the science department windows, source vehicles, collect permits and get to Horsham for their recapture. This, and other initiatives such as Macmillan coffee mornings, Pink Day, Comic and Sport Relief, all add up to raising around £15,000 each year for charity.

For prospective medics and vets there are established links with Brighton University and timetabled prep. There are opportunities for students to become equalities, digital or eco-commissioners, do DofE and Young Enterprise, as well as lunchtime enrichment activities and independent learning working across year groups.

Sport: Competitive sports are netball, rugby, football, rounders and cricket, with fixtures against both independent and state schools across the county – and the Marylebone Cricket Club. The site itself has two rugby and one football pitch; sixth formers have free access to the town leisure centre adjoining the school – they can use facilities such as the pool, squash courts and dance studio (external reputation for good boys' dance). They also love the chaos of the sixth form sports day with its wheelbarrow races and Fairy Liquid slide. The equestrian team (pupil-owned horses) trains at Hickstead. If PE is not a GCSE choice, then pupils have non-competitive sport a couple of times a week.

Boarding: On the State Boarding Schools Association committee and in the second tier of state boarding in terms of numbers. Judged outstanding by Ofsted. The boarders take enormous joy in their international mix, while grounding themselves by earning money on shifts in the canteen and volunteering.

Four boarding houses, two adapted and two purpose built, all with live-in houseparents. The pupils share rooms in the younger years, and are really joyful about the different cultural traditions that they get to experience, from jollof rice on Nigerian Independence Day to Chinese New Year; they promote their differences yet all order takeaways together. In the most modern house the year 13 pupils have a wet-room shower/toilet ensuite; they prop their doors open to their shared corridors and apparently are very responsive when told to turn their music down – 10.30pm curfew in the week and 11pm at weekends. The (mostly) boys watch the Premier League on their laptops; they have an ironing board and a kettle in their shared kitchen; when fending for themselves they eat toasties and pizza since health and safety dictates there is no proper oven. The houseparents lend their kitchen when a bake-a-thon is organised for charity.

The girls have photos as well as their names up on their doors – the images are taken by a photography student, whose work also features on the achievement board; this is the most obvious sign of a real sense of supportive celebration of peers. One girls' common room is huge and more homely, with desks for quiet study places too, since this is a realistic experience away from home, with scheduled time for work, although laundry returned to your cubby within a day would be unusual at home…

Independence is highly valued here, and pupils often ask teachers for help on what suits them best in terms of learning. The staff are committed and respond swiftly

Facebook photos posted (eg rocket club with powder paint ejected from a parachute) and well-dones handed out by the houseparents for being tidy and general good, with prizes drawn at the end of term – once it was a helicopter ride! There is chance to pitch to a 'houseparents' Dragons' Den' for a new piece of equipment, whether a freezer or a pool table. As elsewhere, technology is used to facilitate rather than trumpeted for its own sake: Skype interviews for prospective boarders; applications scanned and emailed in; Wifi or ethernet with hotspots means that Skyping home via an iPad is easy; WhatsApp is used to tackle awkward time differences.

Ethos and heritage: Founded in 1614, turned co-ed in 1953 and now spread over two sites in the small Sussex towns of Storrington and Steyning with architectural styles ranging from chocolate box Elizabethan black and white, through classic 50s secondary modern school architecture, to the super-functional and crisp boarding house, not yet a decade old. Sixth form is moving to a new site imminently. Character-based learning is at the centre of the curriculum – teaching, assessing and reporting home on learning characteristics like grit, growth mindset, curiosity and zest.

The 'Steyning family' is made up of children who are encouraged to take risks so that they are not afraid of failure, and staff who are set on preparing the next generation to take over – 'the sooner the better!' says the school. The ethos of the school is printed large on boards in both sites, and the children are resilient and well supported through exam and everyday academic pressures. The infrastructure for boarding, with the 125 teaching staff and 150 support staff, helps to produce excellent outcomes for disadvantaged students in particular. The staff tenure is traditionally long (30 years is not that unusual), since it is a big school with plenty of space to develop and enough room for children to escape a parent/teacher's shadow.

Far from an inner city urban intake, but everyone is aware of where they stand in the wider society – boarders from the Caribbean come across occasional piercings and extensive LGBT support, the local village kids taste cultures from Barbados to Spain, and parents say, 'It opens up everyone's minds.'

Busy, big and teeming with children at break time – especially in wet weather, when they head to the gym, eat lunch in the classrooms or the school canteen. No hall large enough for a whole-school gathering, but the split site means that the pupils have a real sense of progression and responsibility, from getting a key to their own locker in year 7 to wearing their own clothes in the sixth form, and using the canteen as a study space as well as one to eat in.

Independence is highly valued here, and pupils often ask teachers for help on what suits them best in terms of learning as an individual. The staff are committed and respond swiftly and with initiative; the 400-year heritage adds gravitas when looking for aspirational connections. Ofsted, the State Boarding School Association and CofE status are all three seen as important benchmarks, but by no means the most important measure of the school's success.

Steyning joined the Bohunt Education Trust (BET) in December 2020 – a family of eight secondary schools in Liphook, Portsmouth, Worthing, Petersfield, Steyning, Wokingham, Basingstoke and Horsham. BET also provides school improvement support to City Academy Norwich.

Pastoral care, inclusivity and discipline: Both school and year councils provide feedback on issues such as uniform, the colour of leavers' hoodies, the learning resource centre, internet access to YouTube research etc. Prospective head boys and girls write a letter of application, then the school participates in an online survey, meaning year 13s get some input even though they are leaving – then they must pitch with a speech to the whole of the boarding cohort.

Horizontal pastoral system through year head and form tutor; the tutors have 12 students each and the learning mentors 10. Their aim is to personalise the school – whether that is via checking in at the Cuthman Centre and munching a piece of toast or through Pizza and Paragraphs for English Support. Growing confidence is vital, and the classes of 24 are a practical maximum to enable that.

More casually, there is supported (by the heads of year) revision in the dual-purpose school canteen – peer mentors enable paired reading and might meet for breakfast in Boltons (one of the boarding houses).

No truancy, no smoking on site and no drinking. If a kid impacts the learning in a classroom then they are removed from that classroom. The student could end up in the Cuthman Centre, then a follow-up and reintegration. The range and policy of sanctions is reportedly reassuring for kids who have been beating at the boundaries at other schools: 'It's different here, you know what to expect.' The documentation and communication of the next steps are vital for everyone involved. Academic, social or emotional barriers are identified and everyone gets analysing, understanding and working together – parents and grandparents included – with reflection and using principles of restorative justice. School says, 'We see the best of the students' behaviour at school…'

Pupils and parents: Local, rural and coastal catchment area encompasses a huge range of parental employment – multinational companies, small business owners, teachers; families will relocate and buy within the area to ensure they can get access to such a good state secondary education. A state boarding school can be a niche choice for many students – from Northern Ireland, Antigua, Denmark, to name just three.

Pupils arrange their own social lives, which is part of the independence that the school aims to build, and since so many walk, ride or bus into the school there is very little chance to of casual school gate friendships between parents.

Money matters: No fees for tuition, just for boarding; discounts available for up to three siblings.

The last word: A grammar school by name only, non-selective with a huge sixth form and all the curriculum choices that size enables. Diversity of boarding provision enables the broadening of everyone's minds – from Sussex villagers to Caribbean islanders.

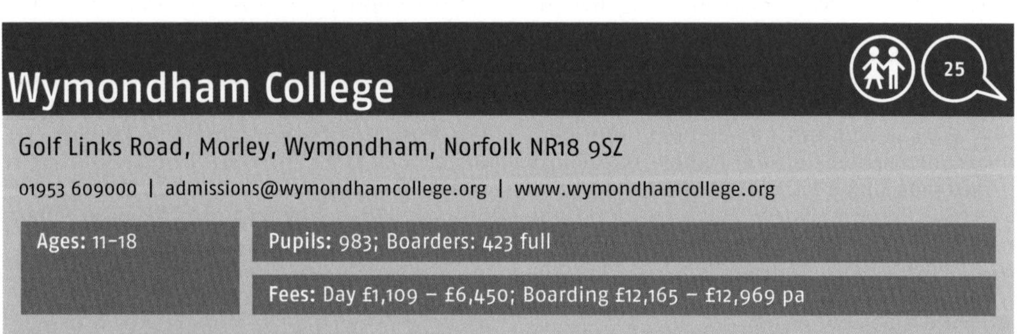

Wymondham College
25
Golf Links Road, Morley, Wymondham, Norfolk NR18 9SZ
01953 609000 | admissions@wymondhamcollege.org | www.wymondhamcollege.org
Ages: 11-18
Pupils: 983; Boarders: 423 full
Fees: Day £1,109 – £6,450; Boarding £12,165 – £12,969 pa

Headteacher: Since 2017, Dan Browning, a history graduate from Anglia Ruskin with postgrad qualifications from Cambridge, UEA, and the Institute of Education. Previous posts have included executive principal of St John's & King Richard School for British Forces children in Cyprus and vice principal of Tendring Technology College. He still teaches history, and lives on the college campus with his wife Sarah, two daughters and their golden retriever, Mabel.

Entrance: The recently opened prep school (on the same site) currently accepts day pupils into reception, year 1 and year 5 with boarders admitted to years 5 and 6. But the main intake is at 11+, with some places also available at 13 (boarding only) and again in the sixth form. Day and boarding places are split roughly 50:50. Day places to the college are very oversubscribed and awarded according to the LEA criteria of (in order of priority) looked-after children, SEN, siblings, distance from the school and those in year 6 of the prep school. Once other categories have been dealt with, the distance from the school can be as little as 0.6 miles, though commonly up to four miles. Check carefully – despite the name, the town of Wymondham itself is not in the catchment for day places. Up to eight day and eight boarding places are offered each year for those with musical aptitude. Competition for such places is fierce.

All potential boarders are interviewed to check that pupils are prepared for all that boarding entails (a hard call in a 10-minute chat). Places are less competitive, but still oversubscribed. It is perhaps worth adding that although you can apply for both day and boarding places, you must list them in order of preference, and if allocated a boarding place you cannot make a crafty switch to day later on. The number of places in each category is fixed.

Most remain for the sixth form, assuming they meet baseline attainment of an average of 5.5 across pupil's eight best GCSEs and a minimum of 4 in English and maths (also note that certain A levels have course-specific requirements). Not a high bar, but as numbers applying from outside significantly exceed places available, admission is effectively dependent on rank order of results at GCSE for those applying from elsewhere.

Exit: Around 20 per cent leave after GCSEs. Majority of sixth formers – some 90 per cent – move on to higher education. Wide range of degree subjects studied though a definite bias towards the sciences, maths, computing and business. Three to Oxbridge in 2021, plus nine medics. UEA, Durham, Leeds, Lincoln, Nottingham, York and Bath currently popular. The resident Lincoln Fellow in the sixth form is an Oxbridge graduate with a brief to dispel myths about the application process and help pupils with UCAS generally.

Latest results: In 2021, 42 per cent 9-7 at GCSE; 48 per cent A*/A at A level (75 per cent A*-B). In 2019 (the last year when exams took place), 29 per cent 9-7 at GCSE; 83 per cent of pupils got 9-4 in both English and maths. At A level, 32 per cent A*/A (61 per cent A*-B).

Teaching and learning: Though strictly speaking non-selective, the varied intake (50 per cent boarding) plus provision of music and sports places – and a perception in the area that 'it's for bright children' – means pupils appreciate their good fortune in being there and are motivated to work hard. Parents are a strong support and the school's results reflect all round achievement. Modern languages (French and Spanish) are compulsory including at GCSE. Ditto for RS (taken by the resident chaplain) – interesting for a non-faith school.

Sixth form definitely academic – despite a relatively low bar, most do well. Maths is taken by over half the cohort; sciences also have a high take-up. Head feels this may reflect current anxieties about the need to take degrees that help lead to good jobs, but 'we are holding the line that subjects should also be studied for their own sake'.

School has a well-established system for identifying the very bright early on, with an Aim High programme in place for these students. They spend an extra two periods a week, plus own time, comprising a research project and an extra course chosen from space science, Russian, Latin, literature and ideas and government and politics. The presence of postgraduate fellows in the sixth form and some also resident in the houses help pupils learn good work habits – we saw a light-hearted revision session in action during GCSE study leave – and give sixth formers insider guidance with UCAS and Oxbridge entrance. A programme of visiting speakers and workshops are led by local university staff, notably from UEA and Cambridge.

Flexi or part boarding is not on offer and swapping from boarding to day is impossible, so a decision to board, taken at aged 10, has to be considered carefully

Learning support and SEN: As the school is regarded as 'being for bright children', there are relatively few pupils, around 12 per cent, requiring learning support, and these are milder cases of dyslexia/dyspraxia/dyscalculia, with only a small number of EHCPs. Well resourced and a positive attitude about extra support. There are also breakfast and catch-up clubs run by individual departments for those needing an extra boost. All new pupils do a standardised CAT test on entry to the school. There is also a structured programme for teaching EAL.

The arts and extracurricular: Music important. The annual Mair cup is an opportunity for all pupils to perform in a competition between houses and is extremely popular. Around 160 have individual instrumental lessons and there are choirs and excellent jazz and concert bands that perform at events locally – including the Royal Norfolk Show. A string group is also well established.

Flourishing art and textiles, which are taught in the Tech block, a light and airy building designed around a central atrium with good provision for display of finished efforts. Good take-up at GCSE and A level and significant numbers go on to study at degree level.

Keen involvement in DofE, and CCF also offered.

Sport: If sporty, there is plenty on offer. Usual team games – rugby included, and an extensive match schedule for the most competent though fewer games for those lower down the rankings. Games are compulsory up to sixth form, when they become optional. Pupils themselves run the five-a-side football league that operates at lunchtimes. Good facilities including swimming pool, gigantic sports hall which doubles for assemblies/concerts, Astroturf, pitches and courts galore.

Boarding: There are seven boarding houses – five for the main school, one for sixth form and one for prep. Drearily functional, though homelike enough upstairs in the dormitories. Houses are all mixed, though girls and boys have separate floors for sleeping, and day pupils as well as boarders return to houses at break and lunchtimes. Plenty of staff, matrons and resident fellows around, and pupils are cheerful and well behaved.

A few struggle with homesickness at the beginning. Flexi or part boarding is not on offer and swapping from boarding to day is impossible, so a decision to board, taken at aged 10, has to be considered carefully. 'It's not for everyone and this is why we interview all potential boarders,' we were told. Those joining in year 9 generally have fewer problems settling. The houses provide something of a refuge at break and lunchtimes when most return to base, although 'It is annoying if your friends are in another house,' said one pupil. House staff around at all key times, and matrons remain on the premises at night. The majority go home at weekends but plenty remain and outings/activities are planned throughout the term. Exeats once each side of half term.

There is lots of 'promenade' time out in fresh air between lessons, which seems to contribute to the calm and disciplined atmosphere

Day+ and day++ arrangements replace the old day boarding for relatively modest fees and are a popular option (they include meals and various after-school activities). Sixth formers who opt for day++ have their own room for studying.

Ethos and heritage: Founded in 1951, the brainchild of Sir Lincoln Ralphs, then chief education officer for Norfolk. It is the largest state boarding school in the country. The site is a former US military hospital and, despite the utilitarian nature of the buildings, it is very peaceful and in the middle of nowhere (Wymondham itself is several miles off). Some of the newer buildings – modern languages, for example – are interesting and well designed, but the most interesting of all is the single remaining Nissen hut, now listed and used, rather effectively, as the chapel. The college has a Christian ethos, but this is non-denominational and the school welcomes pupils from a diverse range of cultures and backgrounds. There is great pride in the school's history and traditions, with a memorial garden and key anniversaries celebrated regularly. Striking new sixth form centre, set around a courtyard, with boarding facilities in individual rooms with ensuite bathrooms, a refectory, working and computer areas.

Traditional uniform (including ties for girls) compulsory up to year 11, but it is the cheap and cheerful sort – no Harris tweed or boaters. Office dress for sixth formers. Pupils don't mind the slightly bleak boarding houses: 'You get used to it so quickly, and anyway, we like the people,' we were told by one pupil, with nods and agreement from others. The old system of year 7s being kept in their own separate house has been discontinued and everyone is mixed up from the start. Saturday morning school for all (though not sixth form) accepted readily enough – holidays slightly longer than usual in state schools to compensate. One of the virtues of the site is that there is lots of 'promenade' time out in fresh air between lessons, and this seems to contribute to the calm and disciplined atmosphere of the school.

Pastoral care, inclusivity and discipline: House-based tutor groups with tutors overseeing academic and extracurricular activities from years 7 to 11. Emphasis is on good relationships, with pride, positivity and passion the three watchwords. 'Work hard, be kind' is the phrase coined and we heard it quoted by year 11s quite cheerfully, if slightly tongue-in-cheek. The presence of resident fellows in the houses helps with friendship and other difficulties and in addition to house staff, the school also has two counsellors and a chaplain, so there is a network of support. Looking out for younger pupils is encouraged and there is very little evidence of bad behaviour or bullying, though school is ever alert and anti-bullying strategies are in place. The parent liaison office helps to smooth communications between home and school, especially for parents of boarders.

Pupils and parents: Day pupils come from Norfolk and boarders from further afield thanks, in part, to the improvements to the A11. School now provides transport for sixth formers from areas without public transport. A quarter are from overseas, plus those with parents working abroad. Fewer Forces families than formerly; the majority of parents are professional or managerial. 'It's an unpretentious place, not for show-offs, and we like that,' said a parent, and that is the common view. Quite a few have chosen the school because it is a state-funded one and without the perceptions of privilege that independent boarding schools may possess. Pupils regard themselves as fortunate and appear straightforward and hard working.

Money matters: Tuition is free; fees are payable for boarding provision only and compare favourably with the cost of a local day independent schools. Up to three full scholarships are offered each year for students with exceptional academic, musical or sporting potential and competition is fierce – up to 50 pupils apply.

The last word: Has a well deserved reputation locally, and increasingly nationally as a leading state boarding school. It is a bargain for parents who want a boarding education for their children, but without the associations of privilege or having to fork out fortunes in school fees. It is a big school and hard-working, socially outgoing types do best.

You may also like to read....

The Good Schools Guide London North
We have plundered the knowledge and experience of our North London based writers and advisers to provide not just the opinionated and unbiased school reviews for which The Good Schools Guide is renowned, but also fascinating pen portraits of the capital's diverse areas. An invaluable guide for any family considering education in the capital.

The Good Schools Guide London South
Packed with local South London knowledge, candid reviews and parent comments, not to mention a full run-down of how the English education system works.

The Good Schools Guide online subscription
Read all our reviews plus exam data, catchment maps, university entrance information, and advice on choosing a school, tutors, SEN, talented children and much more.

The Good Schools Guide International online subscription
The one-stop educational shop for ex-pats, it reviews the best schools round the globe, plus insider knowledge on life overseas.

All available via: www.goodschoolsguide.co.uk/shop-online

Boarding schools index

List of advertisers

Advertisers (Website) **Page**

Advertisers (Website) .... Page

House Ads ....

Notes

Notes

Notes

Notes